RACEHORSES
OF 1996

Price £67.00

A TIMEFORM PUBLICATION

AGE, WEIGHT & DISTANCE TABLE

Timeform's scale of weight-for-age for the flat

Dist	Age	Jan 1-16	17-31	Feb 1-16	17-28	Mar 1-16	17-31	Apr 1-16	17-30	May 1-16	17-31	June 1-16	17-30
5f	4	10-0	10-0	10-0	10-0	10-0	10-0	10-0	10-0	10-0	10-0	10-0	10-0
	3	9—5	9—5	9—6	9—7	9—7	9—8	9—8	9—9	9—9	9—10	9—10	9—11
	2						8—0	8—1	8—3	8—4	8—5	8—6	8—7
6f	4	10-0	10-0	10-0	10-0	10-0	10-0	10-0	10-0	10-0	10-0	10-0	10-0
	3	9—2	9—3	9—4	9—5	9—5	9—6	9—7	9—7	9—8	9—8	9—9	9—9
	2									8—0	8—2	8—3	8—4
7f	4	9-13	9-13	10-0	10-0	10-0	10-0	10-0	10-0	10-0	10-0	10-0	10-0
	3	9—0	9—1	9—2	9—3	9—4	9—4	9—5	9—6	9—6	9—7	9—8	9—8
	2											7—13	8—1
1m	4	9-13	9-13	9-13	9-13	10-0	10-0	10-0	10-0	10-0	10-0	10-0	10-0
	3	8—12	8-13	9—0	9—1	9—2	9—2	9—3	9—4	9—5	9—5	9—6	9—7
	2												
9f	4	9-12	9-12	9-12	9-13	9-13	9-13	9-13	10-0	10-0	10-0	10-0	10-0
	3	8—10	8-11	8—12	8-13	9—0	9—1	9—2	9—2	9—3	9—4	9—5	9—5
	2												
1¼m	4	9-11	9-12	9-12	9-12	9-13	9-13	9-13	9-13	9-13	10-0	10-0	10-0
	3	8—8	8—9	8—10	8-11	8—12	8-13	9—0	9—1	9—2	9—2	9—3	9—4
	2												
11f	4	9-10	9-11	9-11	9-12	9-12	9-12	9-13	9-13	9-13	9-13	9-13	10-0
	3	8—6	8—7	8—8	8—9	8—10	8-11	8—12	8-13	9—0	9—1	9—2	9—2
1½m	4	9-10	9-10	9-10	9-11	9-11	9-12	9-12	9-12	9-13	9-13	9-13	9-13
	3	8—4	8—5	8—6	8—7	8—8	8—9	8—10	8-11	8—12	8-13	9—0	9—1
13f	4	9—9	9—9	9-10	9-10	9-11	9-11	9-11	9-12	9-12	9-12	9-13	9-13
	3	8—2	8—3	8—4	8—5	8—7	8—8	8—9	8-10	8-11	8-12	8-13	9—0
1¾m	4	9—8	9—8	9—9	9—9	9-10	9-10	9-11	9-11	9-11	9-12	9-12	9-13
	3	8—0	8—2	8—3	8—4	8—5	8—6	8—7	8—8	8—9	8-10	8-11	8-12
15f	4	9—7	9—8	9—8	9—9	9—9	9-10	9-10	9-11	9-11	9-11	9-12	9-12
	3	7—13	8—0	8—1	8—2	8—4	8—5	8—6	8—7	8—8	8—9	8-10	8-11
2m	4	9—6	9—7	9—7	9—8	9—9	9—9	9-10	9-10	9-11	9-11	9-11	9-12
	3	7—11	7-12	7—13	8—1	8—2	8—3	8—4	8—5	8—6	8—7	8—8	8—9
2¼m	4	9—5	9—5	9—6	9—7	9—7	9—8	9—9	9—9	9-10	9-10	9-10	9-11
	3	7—8	7—9	7—11	7-12	7—13	8—0	8—2	8—3	8—4	8—5	8—6	8—7
2½m	4	9—3	9—4	9—5	9—6	9—6	9—7	9—7	9—8	9—9	9—9	9-10	9-10
	3	7—5	7—7	7—8	7—9	7—11	7-12	7—13	8—1	8—2	8—3	8—4	8—5

For 5-y-o's and older, use 10-0 in all cases
Race distances in the above tables are shown only at 1 furlong intervals.
For races over odd distances, the nearest distance shown in the table should be used:
thus for races of 1m to 1m 109 yards, use the table weights for 1m;
for 1m 110 yards to 1m 219 yards use the 9f table

AGE, WEIGHT & DISTANCE TABLE

Timeform's scale of weight-for-age for the flat

Dist	Age	July 1-16	July 17-31	Aug 1-16	Aug 17-31	Sept 1-16	Sept 17-30	Oct 1-16	Oct 17-31	Nov 1-16	Nov 17-30	Dec 1-16	Dec 17-31
5f	4	10–0	10–0	10–0	10–0	10–0	10–0	10–0	10–0	10–0	10–0	10–0	10–0
	3	9–11	9–12	9–12	9–12	9–13	9–13	9–13	9–13	10–0	10–0	10–0	10–0
	2	8—8	8—9	8–10	8–11	8–12	8–13	9—0	9—1	9—2	9—2	9—3	9—4
6f	4	10–0	10–0	10–0	10–0	10–0	10–0	10–0	10–0	10–0	10–0	10–0	10–0
	3	9–10	9–10	9–11	9–11	9–12	9–12	9–12	9–13	9–13	9–13	9–13	10–0
	2	8—5	8—6	8—7	8—8	8—9	8–10	8–11	8–12	8–13	9—0	9—1	9—2
7f	4	10–0	10–0	10–0	10–0	10–0	10–0	10–0	10–0	10–0	10–0	10–0	10–0
	3	9—9	9—9	9–10	9–10	9–11	9–11	9–11	9–12	9–12	9–12	9–13	9–13
	2	8—2	8—3	8—4	8—5	8—6	8—7	8—9	8–10	8–11	8–12	8–13	9—0
1m	4	10–0	10–0	10–0	10–0	10–0	10–0	10–0	10–0	10–0	10–0	10–0	10–0
	3	9—7	9—8	9—8	9—9	9—9	9–10	9–10	9–11	9–11	9–12	9–12	9–12
	2			8—2	8—3	8—4	8—5	8—6	8—7	8—8	8—9	8–10	8–11
9f	4	10–0	10–0	10–0	10–0	10–0	10–0	10–0	10–0	10–0	10–0	10–0	10–0
	3	9—6	9—7	9—7	9—8	9—8	9—9	9—9	9–10	9–10	9–11	9–11	9–12
	2					8-1	8—3	8—4	8—5	8—6	8—7	8—8	8—9
1¼m	4	10–0	10–0	10–0	10–0	10–0	10–0	10–0	10–0	10–0	10–0	10–0	10–0
	3	9—5	9—5	9—6	9—7	9—7	9—8	9—8	9—9	9—9	9–10	9–10	9–11
	2							8-1	8—2	8—4	8—5	8—6	8—7
11f	4	10–0	10–0	10–0	10–0	10–0	10–0	10–0	10–0	10–0	10–0	10–0	10–0
	3	9—3	9—4	9—5	9—5	9—6	9—7	9—7	9—8	9—8	9—9	9—9	9–10
1½m	4	10–0	10–0	10–0	10–0	10–0	10–0	10–0	10–0	10–0	10–0	10–0	10–0
	3	9—2	9—2	9—3	9—4	9—5	9—5	9—6	9—7	9—7	9—8	9—9	9—9
13f	4	9–13	9–13	10–0	10–0	10–0	10–0	10–0	10–0	10–0	10–0	10–0	10–0
	3	9—0	9—1	9—2	9—3	9—4	9—4	9—5	9—6	9—6	9—7	9—8	9—8
1¾m	4	9–13	9–13	9–13	10–0	10–0	10–0	10–0	10–0	10–0	10–0	10–0	10–0
	3	8–13	9—0	9—1	9—2	9—3	9—3	9—4	9—5	9—5	9—6	9—7	9—7
15f	4	9–12	9–13	9–13	9–13	9–13	10–0	10–0	10–0	10–0	10–0	10–0	10–0
	3	8–12	8–13	9—0	9—1	9—1	9—2	9—3	9—4	9—4	9—5	9—6	9—6
2m	4	9–12	9–12	9–13	9–13	9–13	9–13	10–0	10–0	10–0	10–0	10–0	10–0
	3	8–10	8–11	8–12	8–13	9—0	9—1	9—2	9—3	9—3	9—4	9—5	9—5
2¼m	4	9–11	9–12	9–12	9–12	9–13	9–13	9–13	9–13	10–0	10–0	10–0	10–0
	3	8—8	8—9	8–10	8–11	8–12	8–13	9—0	9—1	9—2	9—2	9—3	9—4
2½m	4	9–10	9–11	9–11	9–12	9–12	9–12	9–13	9–13	9–13	9–13	10–0	10–0
	3	8—6	8—7	8—8	8—9	8–10	8–11	8–12	8–13	9—0	9—1	9—2	9—3

For 5-y-o's and older, use 10-0 in all cases
Race distances in the above tables are shown only at 1 furlong intervals.
For races over odd distances, the nearest distance shown in the table should be used:
thus for races of 1m to 1m 109 yards, use the table weights for 1m;
for 1m 110 yards to 1m 219 yards use the 9f table

Years of Timeform

Timeform has a long history of innovative race sponsorship. In 1961 Timeform created and sponsored the most valuable two-year-old race ever run in Great Britain (now the Racing Post Trophy) and in 1971 organised then Britain's richest one-day meeting, Timeform Charity Day. Now, in 1997, Timeform has its largest ever sponsorship programme in celebration of fifty years in racing.

Cheltenham Saturday January 25th
The '50 Years of Timeform' Novices' Chase

Stratford Monday March 10th
Timeform Day at Stratford

Bath Monday May 19th
Timeform Day at Bath

Newcastle Wednesday June 4th
Four Timeform-sponsored races

York Saturday June 14th
The 27th Timeform Charity Day

Doncaster Sunday June 29th
The '50 Years of Timeform' Handicap

Beverley Tuesday July 29th
Timeform Ladies Race

Sandown Thursday August 14th
Timeform Day at Sandown

Pontefract Tuesday September 2nd
Timeform Day at Pontefract

Ayr Thursday September 18th
Timeform Harry Rosebery Trophy

Chepstow Saturday October 4th
Timeform Free Handicap Hurdle

Cheltenham Monday October 28th
The '50 Years of Timeform' Handicap Chase

Ascot Saturday November 22nd
The '50 Years of Timeform' Juvenile Hurdle

CONTENTS

Compiled and produced by

G. Greetham, B.A., (Director), J. D. Newton, B.A. (Editor-in-Chief), R. J. C. Austen, B.A. (Editor), E. K. Wilkinson (Editor), D. Cleary, B.A., S. N. Copeland, J. Ingles, B.A., G. M. Johnstone, W. Muncaster, G. J. North, B.Sc., R. O'Brien B.A., O. C. Pennant Jones, B.A., S. D. Rowlands, B.A., P. E. Turner, S. L. Walker, C. S. Williams and C. Wright, B.A.

© **Portway Press Limited 1997**   ISBN 0 900599 91 X

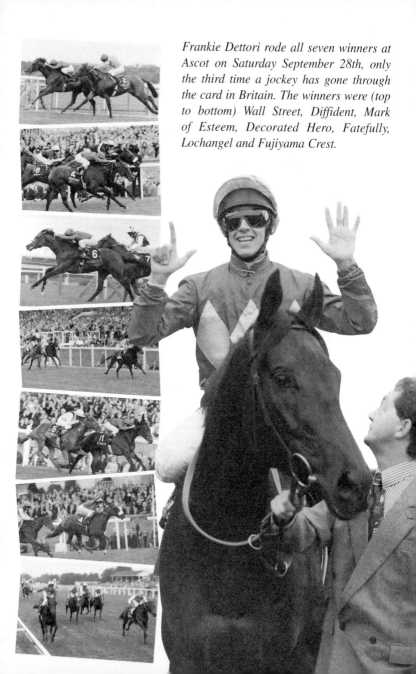

Frankie Dettori rode all seven winners at Ascot on Saturday September 28th, only the third time a jockey has gone through the card in Britain. The winners were (top to bottom) Wall Street, Diffident, Mark of Esteem, Decorated Hero, Fatefully, Lochangel and Fujiyama Crest.

Racehorses of 1996

Introduction

'Come back Lester, all is forgiven.' The message pinned to one bookmaker's board at Ascot provided a wry footnote to the most abiding memory of the flat-racing year. The Saturday of Ascot's Festival of Racing in September was a truly astounding afternoon's racing, the momentousness of Frankie Dettori's seven-out-of-seven transcending the normal boundaries of the sport. The tension, excitement and scenes of jubilation were incredible as Dettori rode his fifth, then his sixth and, finally, that amazing seventh on Fujiyama Crest, amid unprecedented exchanges in the betting ring. Dettori's 'Magnificent Seven' cost the bookmakers a fortune but did racing a power of good by capturing front-page headlines and priceless TV news coverage such as the sport gets once in a blue moon. Whatever else he achieves in his burgeoning career, Dettori's feat at Ascot ensures him a place alongside racing legends like Fred Archer, Gordon Richards and Lester Piggott. Dettori already shares one distinction with Archer and Richards in that they are the only three jockeys to have ridden two hundred winners in a British flat season more than once. Dettori, who passed the two-hundred mark in 1994 and 1995, saw his chances of a third successive jockeys' championship disappear when he broke his elbow in a parade-ring fall at Newbury in June. From August onwards, however, Dettori was seldom out of the headlines as he chalked up victory after victory in the top races. Bahamian Bounty and Halling started the Dettori revival in the Prix Morny and the Juddmonte International, and five other Group 1's followed in Europe before Singspiel crowned Dettori's truly memorable year in the Japan Cup in November. One of the Group 1 victories in between came from **Mark of Esteem** in the Queen Elizabeth II Stakes on 'Dettori Day'. His essay deals in detail with the events on the track and in the betting ring, as well as tracing Mark of Esteem's rise in the autumn to the top of the miling tree. The colt had begun the year with a hard-fought victory in the Two Thousand Guineas in which Dettori's riding of Mark of Esteem got him into trouble with officialdom on two counts: he received an eight-day ban for improper use of the whip (there was a similar sting in the tail after his St

'Are you Frankie Dettori? Can I have your autograph?'

*'Spontaneous displays of emotion . . . are on the increase'—
Frankie Dettori dismounts from Mark of Esteem after the Guineas,
Olivier Peslier opts for arm-waving near the finish of the Arc*

Leger win on Shantou) and he was also fined £500 for performing a flying dismount while Mark of Esteem was still on the racecourse. The happy-go-lucky Dettori treated the Ascot crowd to the dismount twice, after Mark of Esteem and after Fujiyama Crest, though the Ascot stewards had asked him not to jump off 'for safety reasons'. Dettori's command performance at Ascot, however, would hardly have been complete without what has become his big-occasion trademark.

*Pat Eddery and Bosra Sham
after the One Thousand Guineas*

Spontaneous displays of emotion by successful jockeys aren't popular with some sections of the racing public but they are on the increase, particularly among some of the leading young jockeys. Olivier Peslier, Dettori's counterpart in France, celebrated his Prix de l'Arc victory on the impressive **Helissio** with an extravagant display of arm-waving which he explained as imitating a helicopter (the name of Helissio's dam translates as rotor blade in French). Such antics have no place in the repertoire of Pat Eddery, however, who was champion jockey in Britain for the eleventh time. Eddery matched Dettori's two British classic victories on the fillies **Bosra Sham** and **Lady Carla**, one journalist unkindly reporting after Bosra Sham had filled the only gap in her rider's classic record that Eddery 'greeted

'Is this a dagger I see before me?'—
Henry Cecil and Sheikh Mohammed lighten the Champion Stakes presentation

the applauding Newmarket crowd after an historic One Thousand Guineas win like he'd just caught the whiff of a bad smell.' Lester Piggott's post-race demeanour was always similarly undemonstrative, leading him to be described once as having 'a face like a well-kept grave.' It takes all sorts! Dettori and Eddery, incidentally, were among twenty-one jockeys who fell foul of the Haydock stewards for refusing to ride in the Sycamore Nursery at Haydock on October 16th. Their protest, over the safety of the track, forced the meeting to be abandoned. An inquiry by the Jockey Club stewards was still pending at the time of writing!

Eddery's partnership with Bosra Sham, who finished a clear second to Mark of Esteem in the Queen Elizabeth II Stakes, also produced a memorable victory in the Dubai Champion Stakes at Newmarket in October. That victory seemed to give Henry Cecil a very strong chance of lifting another trainers' championship after an epic duel with Godolphin's trainer Saeed bin Suroor, a rivalry given an additional edge following the much-publicised split the previous autumn between Cecil and Sheikh Mohammed who set up the elite Godolphin operation. The post-race scenes after the Champion Stakes provided the season with a sporting moment to remember as Sheikh Mohammed enlivened the presentation ceremony by jokingly turning the trainer's prize of an ornamental dagger on himself. The story of Godolphin's triumph in the trainers' championship is also covered in the essay on the Racing Post Trophy winner **Medaaly** who is one of the Godolphin's main classic hopes for 1997 when its operation is being expanded further. Two unbeaten colts **Bahhare** and **Revoque** head the winter ante-post market on

9

the Two Thousand Guineas, the former due to be ridden by veteran Willie Carson whose up-and-down season (including victories on **Matiya** in the Irish One Thousand and **Ta Rib** in the French equivalent) ended in September when a kick from a two-year-old filly in the paddock at Newbury put him in intensive care for a week. Another rider whose year was blighted by a life-threatening injury was Walter Swinburn who completed his comeback when winning the Breeders' Cup Turf on the Prix de l'Arc runner-up **Pilsudski** who beat **Singspiel, Swain** and St Leger winner **Shantou** as the Europeans filled the first four places. Pilsudski, Singspiel and Shantou all contributed significantly to record earnings by British-trained horses on foreign soil, the details of which appear in the essay on Singspiel who himself surpassed the previous earnings record for a horse trained in Britain when winning the Japan Cup. The world earnings record is held by the redoubtable American champion **Cigar** whose victory in the inaugural Dubai World Cup—in which the Americans enjoyed a 1, 2, 3—took his unbeaten run to fourteen, later extended to sixteen, equalling the record sequences of two of the best post-war champions Citation and Ribot.

The Derby winner **Shaamit** followed in the footsteps of the previous year's winner Lammtarra by taking the race on his first start as a three-year-old. He failed to win again, though he did come a very good third to the top-class four-year-old **Pentire** in the King George VI and Queen Elizabeth Diamond Stakes. Shaamit will be at the National Stud in 1997 while Lammtarra has followed a number of other recent Derby winners to Japan. The scale of the exodus of stallions to Japan is discussed in the essay on Pentire who was also bought by Japanese interests during the year. Pentire's previous owner Mollers Racing also had the high-class miler **First Island** who stays in training. Pentire wasn't quite the best older horse trained in Europe in 1996. That honour belonged, marginally, to the splendid five-year-old **Halling** who again completed the Coral-Eclipse —Juddmonte International double. Among the three-year-old middle-distance performers following in the wake of Helissio, only the runaway Irish Derby winner **Zagreb** put up a performance on a par with those of Shaamit, while the best of the rest were much of a muchness. Part of the essay on **Dushyantor**, runner-up in the Derby and the St Leger, is devoted to the controversy surrounding that hardy perennial, the Jockey Club's whip guidelines.

The nine-times Irish champion Mick Kinane got off 20/1-shot Zagreb (trained by his main stable) to ride one of the British challengers at the Curragh **Dr Massini** who had been favourite for the Epsom Derby before suffering lameness. Kinane may have missed a victory in the only Irish classic he has not won, but he had another fine year at the big meetings in Britain. He was the top jockey for the third year in a row at Royal Ascot where his five winners included **Classic Cliche**, the first British classic winner to go on to success in the Gold Cup for nearly half a century. The Gold Cup runner-up **Double Trigger**, who had landed the stayers' triple crown in 1995, returned from a lengthy absence after Royal Ascot to win the Doncaster Cup, but his brother **Double Eclipse** missed most of the season through injury after promising much with two good victories in the spring, the second of them over the leading French Cup horse **Nononito** who finished third at Royal Ascot and went on to win the Prix du Cadran.

Record crowds flocked to Royal Ascot—Yeast is pictured winning the Hunt Cup

Kinane's other winners at Royal Ascot included **Oscar Schindler** in the Hardwicke Stakes and **Charnwood Forest** in the Queen Anne Stakes, but he came in for some criticism after Poule d'Essai des Poulains winner **Ashkalani** went down in a very close finish with the doughty **Bijou d'Inde** who gained ample compensation for a narrow defeat behind Mark of Esteem and **Even Top** in the English Guineas. Royal Ascot's King's Stand Stakes also produced a close finish, **Pivotal** and **Mind Games** fighting it out on opposite sides of the track. The performances established them as the best sprinters around at the time, but they soon had to take a back seat to the July Cup winner **Anabaa**, the first horse trained in France for many years to head the list of the season's top sprinters in Europe. The two-year-old races at Royal Ascot were only average, one of the most promising performances coming from **Dazzle** who landed some good bets when winning the Windsor Castle Stakes on her debut. After her next win, in the Cherry Hinton, she became a hot favourite for the 1997 One Thousand Guineas but fell from grace on her last two starts and went into the winter no better than fifth choice in the betting behind the Cecil-trained pair **Sleepytime** and **Reams of Verse** and the first two in the Cheveley Park **Pas de Reponse** and **Moonlight Paradise**.

Royal Ascot was, as usual, a magnificent example of the spectacle and entertainment racing can offer. The crowds were up by eleven per cent on the previous year and the attendance of 232,360 was a record for the four days. Ascot's figures for their other fixtures were equally impressive, racecourse director Douglas Erskine-Crum attributing the success to a combination of 'specific marketing of fixtures, improved facilities and luck with the weather.' Overall, however, the British Horseracing Board's 'turnstile-friendly' fixture list, with its spread of evening and Sunday meetings, appears to have made little impact on racecourse attendances, which rose only fractionally in total to 4,739,888 in 1996 and produced the second-lowest average crowd figure for eleven years, 4,224. The Sunday racing initiative suffered a set-back when average attendances fell by over

11

a quarter from 1995. The courses making general progress were mostly those staging the best racing—Goodwood and York were others that stood out—which should serve as a timely reminder to the race planners. Notwithstanding the impact that good racecourse management can have on attendances, it is a truism that the racing public enjoy seeing good horses. It is largely the quality of the racing that generates the excitement among racing regulars for Royal Ascot and the other major festivals such as those at Goodwood and York. The sense of tradition and occasion associated with these fixtures also helps to make them a shop window for racing.

Unfortunately, the supply of good horses is finite and the image of the sport at the grass roots is different from that presented by the showpiece meetings. The facilities at some courses leave plenty to be desired, with inferior toilets, over-priced and under-staffed bars, and high admission prices being among the most-voiced complaints. There is major criticism too of the quality of entertainment offered at many of the low-grade meetings. Many of the changes in race programmes in recent years have rightly come under fire for 'pandering to mediocrity' and there is a fairly general feeling that there is too much racing at the height of the flat season (there's arguably a need for *more* in the autumn). In a recent rather surprising change of policy, the Racehorse Owners' Association has adopted a similar view, arguing that with prize money 'scarce'—more cuts have been made in minimum prize money levels for 1997—the resources need to be divided up among a smaller number of races. The ROA favours a ten per cent cut but the British Horseracing Board, evidently unmoved by all the arguments, has actually announced a record 1,177 fixtures for 1997. A slight shortening of the summer evening racing season, with racing on four nights each week instead of five (none on Thursday), has been complemented by a restoration of some afternoon meetings to 'fill criteria gaps'.

The advent of the National Lottery—which is now staging a second draw in midweek—has been blamed widely for the decline in betting on horseracing, though betting shops (which have fallen below 9,000 for the first time) were disappearing, admittedly at a less alarming rate, before the effects of the lottery began to be felt. Hills and Ladbrokes both announced in the spring a slump in profits on betting for 1995, while Ladbrokes reported in mid-year that betting turnover on horseracing had fallen in its shops by four per cent, at the same time as there had been an increase in turnover on betting on other sports. Significantly, both Hills and Ladbrokes have launched spread-betting operations, while, along with most other bookmakers, introducing fruit machines and offering competition to the lottery with their own Lucky Choice and 49's numbers games. Horseracing now accounts for just over seventy per cent of off-course betting with bookmakers, compared to over seventy-five per cent at the start of the 'nineties. Greyhounds account for about twenty per cent but the growth area is in sports betting, now taking seven per cent. The major bookmakers recovered well in the first part of 1996, announcing increases in profits despite a further drop in turnover on betting on horses. For racing the message is clear: it must, as a matter of priority, increase its appeal to those who bet (Timeform's suggestions can be found in the introductions to the last two editions of *Racehorses*). Owners, racegoers, off-course punters and sponsors are said to be the four groups that the BHB tries to satisfy when planning the racing programme, but off-course punters, who bring a massive contribution through the levy (which makes up half of racing's prize-money) often seem to get short shrift.

The 'great mediocre racing debate' over the past couple of years, and the response by the BHB to the widespread criticism of the dullness of so many of its race programmes, has generated enough hot air to have taken Richard Branson's balloon twice round the world. David Oldrey, the BHB's race planning director, has remained obdurate throughout, writing in one of his many letters to the racing papers that 'in my view there is not too much wrong with racing here that a major cut in the level of tax, and consequent increase in betting's contribution to the sport on which it depends, will not remedy.' Racing's declining share of the betting market is made all the more worrying by the BHB's apparent refusal to address the criticisms made by racing's most important customers. Perhaps the failure of the latest Budget submissions will shake Mr Oldrey and some of his colleagues out of their complacency. The racing authorities and the bookmakers did not see eye to eye on how any further cut in betting duty might be distributed. The bookmakers pressed for a reduction in betting duty of 1¼%, which they promised to make up to a 1½p cut in total deductions for betting-shop punters (currently at 9p in the pound). The BHB's submission was for a 1¾% cut, with 1% going to punters and the rest directly to the levy, an argument for a division that had been unsuccessful the previous year. In the event, the Chancellor, presenting his last Budget before the General Election, considered that neither 'racing' nor 'betting' had provided so strong a case as twelve months earlier when he had announced a 1% cut, all of it passed on to punters. Racing had also benefited from deregulation (Sunday racing, evening opening for betting shops, fruit machines, etc) and from the VAT registration scheme for owners (said to be worth up to £20m a year on running costs alone). In short, racing had had quite enough help already. The BHB's submission was plainly and simply greedy, providing further evidence of its attitude towards off-course punters. Pleading a case for a direct transfer to 'racing' (in effect to owners) of a reduction in the tax on punters takes some brass neck. Off-course punters make their contribution to racing through the levy and perhaps if the BHB had paid more attention to punters' needs they wouldn't now be betting in increasing numbers on alternative attractions. There seems to be little prospect of racing winning its present case for more tax concessions, whatever the political persuasion of a future Chancellor, and the BHB clearly needs to go back to the drawing board. Any submissions to future Chancellors would also do well to bear in mind that while punters are taxed on their hobby, many racehorse owners no longer are.

The bar chart illustrates the declining share of betting on horseracing with off-course bookmakers.

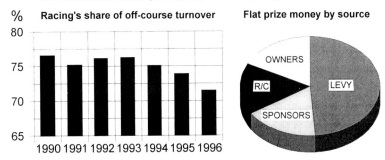

Racing's share of off-course turnover — % (80, 75, 70, 65) — 1990 1991 1992 1993 1994 1995 1996

Flat prize money by source — OWNERS, LEVY, SPONSORS, R/C

Lord Hartington (right) retired as chairman of the British Horseracing Board and was succeeded by Lord Wakeham

The first chairman of the BHB Lord Hartington retired in early-June with thanks and praise ringing in his ears for his part in smoothing the transfer of power from the Jockey Club and setting the new administration on its way. The new chairman Lord Wakeham has had a rougher ride as criticism of the BHB has mounted. A number of prominent owners announced they would be cutting back, among them Peter Savill, elected to the Racehorse Owners Association council in July and one of the BHB's most vociferous critics. Savill described owning horses as 'a financial bloodbath'. Another owner Andrew Reid labelled the BHB 'essentially the Jockey Club in disguise' while Wafic Said, owner of Bosra Sham and Lady Carla, joined the chorus when (speaking through his racing manager at the Gimcrack dinner in December) he said the BHB was 'like the wheat that was sown on shallow ground. It sprang up vigorously and then withered away, returning to the traditional bureaucracy.' Apart from Lord Hartington, racing's list of retirements also included Guy Harwood, who had six successive top-four placings in the trainers' championship in the 'eighties, and Tom Jones, trainer of St Leger winners Athens Wood and Touching Wood and the legendary jumper Tingle Creek.

As usual, all the horses highlighted in this introduction are among those dealt with in essays in the main body of the book. The essays now appear in an increased type size to make for better readability. Another improvement in **Racehorses** this year is the extended coverage of overseas racing. The Timeform 'Top Horses Abroad' section now includes a review of the racing year in Ireland, on mainland Europe and in North America, as well as extensive lists of Timeform ratings.

February 1997

14

TIMEFORM CHAMPIONS OF 1996

HORSE OF THE YEAR
BEST THREE-YEAR-OLD COLT · BEST MILER
RATED AT 137

MARK OF ESTEEM

BEST TWO-YEAR-OLD FILLIES
RATED AT 116
DAZZLE
RED CAMELLIA

BEST TWO-YEAR-OLD COLTS
RATED AT 122p
BAHHARE
REVOQUE

BEST THREE-YEAR-OLD FILLY
RATED AT 132
BOSRA SHAM

BEST OLDER MALE
RATED AT 133
HALLING

BEST OLDER FEMALE
RATED AT 125
TIMARIDA

BEST SPRINTER
RATED AT 130
ANABAA

BEST MIDDLE-DISTANCE HORSE
RATED AT 136
HELISSIO

BEST STAYING PERFORMANCES
RATED AT 124
CLASSIC CLICHE*
OSCAR SCHINDLER*
SHANTOU
* Achieved higher rating at middle distances

BEST PERFORMANCES IN
HANDICAPS IN BRITAIN

Sprint Distances
COASTAL BLUFF
ran to 117
Won Ayr Gold Cup

7–9 Furlongs
FIRST ISLAND
ran to 120
Won Hambleton Rated Stakes
at York

Middle Distances
ELA-ARISTOKRATI
ran to 117
Won Racing Channel Handicap
at Epsom

Staying Distances
CORRADINI
ran to 112
Won Sitwell Arms Mallard
Handicap at Doncaster

BEST PERFORMANCE ON
ALL-WEATHER IN BRITAIN

DECORATED HERO
ran to 112
2nd in Bass Wulfrun Stakes
at Wolverhampton

BEST HORSE IN NORTH
AMERICA
RATED AT 138
CIGAR

15

THE TIMEFORM 'TOP HUNDRED'

Here are listed the 'Top 100' two-year-olds, three-year-olds and older horses in the annual.

Two Year Olds

122p	Bahhare
122p	Revoque
116	Bahamian Bounty
116	Majorien
116	Red Camellia
116	Varxi
116	Zamindar
116d	Dazzle
115	Deadly Dudley
115	Easycall
115	Muchea
114	In Command
114	Medaaly
113p	Musical Pursuit
113p	Pas de Reponse
113p	Poteen
113p	Putra
113p	Shaka
113+	Indian Rocket
112p	Daylami
112p	Fantastic Fellow
112p	Mantovani
112p	Mousse Glacee
112+	Hello
112	Air Express
112	Benny The Dip
112	Sahm
111p	Moonlight Paradise
110p	Musheer
110p	Shell Ginger
110+	Desert King
110	Desert Story
110	Ryafan
110	Sheer Reason
110	Yashmak
109	Abou Zouz
109	Brave Act
109	Deep Finesse
109	Elegant Warning
109	Equal Rights
109	Falkenham
109	Hurricane State
108P	Sleepytime
108p	Grapeshot
108p	Joyeuse Entree
108p	Kahal
108p	King Sound
108p	Reams of Verse
108p	Voyagers Quest
108+	Besiege
108	Compton Place

108	Golden Oriental
108	Nombre Premier
108	Ocean Ridge
107p	Monza
107+	Bianca Nera
107+	The West
107	New Frontier
107	Referendum
107	Verglas
107?	Carmine Lake
106p	Entrepreneur
106	Fine Fellow
106	Proud Native
106	Tomba
105p	Indiscreet
105	Check The Band
105	Khassah
105	Shigeru Summit
104p	Johan Cruyff
104	Grand Lad
104	Papua
104	Tipsy Creek
103p	Happy Valentine
103p	Hidden Meadow
103p	Strawberry Roan
103	Great Ovation
103	Royal Amaretto
103	Seebe
102p	High Roller
102p	Panama City
102	Azra
102	Dance Parade
102	Ivan Luis
102	Musical Dancer
102	Raphane
102	Starborough
102	Wind Cheetah
101p	Intikhab
101	Andreyev
101	Arethusa
101	Barnum Sands
101	Boojum
101	Magical Times
101	Mount Kamet
100p	Golden Aventura
100p	Sarayir
100p	Za-Im
100+	Daylight In Dubai
100+	Demolition Man
100	Dame Laura
100	Falak
100	Gretel

100	Nigrasine
100	Sandstone

Three Year Olds

137	Mark of Esteem
136	Helissio
132	Bosra Sham
128	Ashkalani
127	Bijou d'Inde
127	Even Top
127	Shaamit
127	Zagreb
125	Lavirco
125	Spinning World
124	Pivotal
124	Shantou
123	Alhaarth
123	Darazari
123	Dushyantor
123	Kistena
123	Lucayan Prince
122	Grape Tree Road
122	Lady Carla
122	Shake The Yoke
121p	Last Second
121	Glory of Dancer
121	River Bay
120	Annaba
120	Pro Trader
120	Radevore
120	Sorbie Tower
120	Tarator
119p	Busy Flight
119	Dance Design
119	La Blue
119	Luna Wells
119	Mons
119	Wurftaube
118	Ali-Royal
118	Blue Duster
118	Wall Street
117	Baroud d'Honneur
117	Beauchamp King
117	Centre Stalls
117	Danehill Dancer
117	Grey Risk
117	Key Change
117	Le Destin
117	Loup Solitaire
117	Mystic Knight
117	Polaris Flight
117	Predappio

16

117	Ragmar	130	Anabaa
117	Rainbow Blues	129	Pilsudski
117	Samraan	128	Classic Cliche
116	Android	127	First Island
116	Atraf	127	Oscar Schindler
116	Bad Bertrich Again	127	Singspiel
116	Le Triton	126	Key of Luck
116	Matiya	125	Charnwood Forest
116	Night Petticoat	125	Swain
116	Passion For Life	125	Timarida
116	Royal Court	125	Valanour
116	Russian Revival	124	Germany
116	Santillana	124	Iktamal
116	Sil Sila	124	Luso
116	Tagula	124	Strategic Choice
116	Ta Rib	124	Vetheuil
115	Amfortas	123	Double Trigger
115	Blackwater	123	Laroche
115	Dr Massini	123	Posidonas
115	Duke of Flite	123	Running Flame
115	Farasan	123	Soviet Line
115	Jack Jennings	122	Bishop of Cashel
115	Kharizmi	122	Diffident
115	Maroussie	122	Double Eclipse
115	My Emma	122	Flemensfirth
115	Raiyoun	122	Gabr
115	Snake Snap	122	Spectrum
115	St Mawes	121	Definite Article
115	Wandering Star	121	Eveningperformance
115	Zafzala	121	Mind Games
114	Accento	121	Nononito
114	Cayman Kai	121	Sunshack
114	Chief Contender	121	Tamayaz
114	Desert Boy	120	Annus Mirabilis
114	Heron Island	120	Bin Rosie
114	Missile	120	Gunboat Diplomacy
114	Miss Tahiti	120	Montjoy
114	Mongol Warrior	120	Protektor
114	Papering	120	Riyadian
114	Sensation	120§	Moonax
114	Shamadara	119	Artan
114	Storm Trooper	119	Decorated Hero
114	Surako	119	Hollywood Dream
113p	Sasuru	119	Kassani
113	Acharne	119	Needle Gun
113	Altamura	119	Phantom Gold
113	Arbatax	119	Poliglote
113	Don Micheletto	119	Shaanxi
113	Gothenberg	118	Bequeath
113	Kahir Almaydan	118	Bulington
113	Khalisa	118	Burooj
113	Lidanna	118	Court of Honour
113	Time Allowed	118	Hever Golf Rose
		118	Idris
Older Horses		118	Lucky Di
138	Cigar	118	Oxalagu
133	Halling	118	Red Roses Story
132	Pentire	118	Restructure

118	Sacrament
117p	Coastal Bluff
117	Always Earnest
117	A Magicman
117	Carling
117	Diamond Mix
117	Donna Viola
117	Ela-Aristokrati
117	Heart Lake
117	Housamix
117	Miesque's Son
117	Salmon Ladder
116+	Celeric
116	Camp David
116	Helen of Spain
116	Manzoni
116	Midnight Legend
116	Mistle Cat
116	Nec Plus Ultra
116	Overbury
116	Percutant
116	Slicious
116	Tot Ou Tard
116	Wizard King
115	Always Aloof
115	Astrac
115	Catch The Blues
115	Concepcion
115	Cool Jazz
115	Dance Treat
115	Devil River Peek
115	Galtee
115	Ger's Royale
115	Grey Shot
115	Kutta
115	Sanmartino
115	Sinyar
115	Smart Alec
115	Song of Tara
115	Spout
115	Valley of Gold

1996 STATISTICS

The following tables show the leading owners, trainers, jockeys, sires of winners and horses on the flat in Britain during 1996 (Jan 1–Dec 31). The prize-money statistics, compiled by *Timeform*, relate to win-money and to first-three prize money. Win money has traditionally been used to decide the trainers' championship, though in 1994 the BHB and the National Trainers' Federation established a championship decided by total prize-money as determined by the *Racing Post*. The jockeys' championship has traditionally been decided by the number of winners.

OWNERS (1,2,3 earnings)	Horses	Indiv'l Wnrs	Races Won	Runs	%	Stakes
1 Godolphin	39	23	38	121	31.4	1,824,735
2 Sheikh Mohammed	161	70	89	508	17.5	1,349,635
3 Mr Hamdan Al Maktoum	204	79	104	685	15.1	1,104,551
4 Mr K. Abdulla	93	57	82	337	24.3	1,046,485
5 Mr Wafic Said	16	11	17	63	26.9	771,541
6 Maktoum Al Maktoum	85	29	45	307	14.6	755,089
7 Mollers Racing	7	2	5	24	20.8	600,869
8 Mr Khalifa Dasmal	2	1	1	8	12.5	575,200
9 Cheveley Park Stud	50	18	26	186	13.9	435,013
10 HRH Prince Fahd Salman	48	26	34	174	19.5	356,107
11 Mr R. E. Sangster	61	24	30	223	13.4	306,251
12 Mr J. S. Morrison	6	2	2	19	10.5	246,804

OWNERS (by win-money)	Horses	Indiv'l Wnrs	Races Won	Runs	%	Stakes
1 Godolphin	39	23	38	121	31.4	1,375,341
2 Sheikh Mohammed	161	70	89	508	17.5	971,792
3 Mr Hamdan Al Maktoum	204	79	104	685	15.1	705,719
4 Mr Wafic Said	16	11	17	63	26.9	646,404
5 Maktoum Al Maktoum	85	29	45	307	14.6	584,950
6 Mr K. Abdulla	93	57	82	337	24.3	578,821
7 Mr Khalifa Dasmal	2	1	1	8	12.5	523,100
8 Mollers Racing	7	2	5	24	20.8	473,273
9 Cheveley Park Stud	50	18	26	186	13.9	320,483
10 HRH Prince Fahd Salman	48	26	34	174	19.5	264,477
11 Mr R. E. Sangster	61	24	30	223	13.4	182,587
12 Sheikh Ahmed Al Maktoum	51	24	32	175	18.2	156,064

TRAINERS (1,2,3 earnings)	Horses	Indiv'l Wnrs	Races Won	Runs	%	Stakes
1 Saeed bin Suroor	49	30	48	158	30.3	1,932,235
2 H. R. A. Cecil	116	75	113	396	28.5	1,890,991
3 J. H. M. Gosden	140	56	75	460	16.3	1,063,547
4 M. Johnston	145	72	116	817	14.1	1,050,012
5 M. R. Stoute	133	54	73	438	16.6	1,039,254
6 R. Hannon	201	79	109	1080	10.0	933,833
7 J. L. Dunlop	142	58	88	596	14.7	915,220
8 P. F. I. Cole	115	54	74	430	17.2	868,716
9 G. Wragg	48	16	28	178	15.7	850,891

10	W. J. Haggas	34	17	28	153	18.3	847,572
11	B. W. Hills.............................	118	61	84	528	15.9	793,442
12	D. R. Loder	88	44	58	268	21.6	712,726

			Indiv'l	Races			Stakes
TRAINERS (by win-money)		Horses	Wnrs	Won	Runs	%	
1	Saeed bin Suroor.................	49	30	48	158	30.3	1,451,009
2	H. R. A. Cecil	116	75	113	396	28.5	1,282,824
3	W. J. Haggas	34	17	28	153	18.3	735,994
4	J. H. M. Gosden	140	56	75	460	16.3	716,920
5	M. R. Stoute	133	54	73	438	16.6	684,868
6	M. Johnston	145	72	116	817	14.1	679,587
7	R. Hannon	201	79	109	1080	10.0	643,694
8	J. L. Dunlop	142	58	88	596	14.7	621,921
9	G. Wragg	48	16	28	178	15.7	608,585
10	B. W. Hills............................	118	61	84	528	15.9	592,254
11	P. F. I. Cole.........................	115	54	74	430	17.2	584,353
12	D. R. Loder	88	44	58	268	21.6	486,849

TRAINERS		Indiv'l	Races					
(with 100+ winners)		Horses	Wnrs	Won	2nd	3rd	Runs	%
1	M. Johnston	145	72	116	117	105	817	14.1
2	H. R. A. Cecil........	116	75	113	62	56	396	28.5
3	R. Hannon...............	201	79	109	114	98	1080	10.0
4	J. Berry	101	54	101	88	86	738	13.6

						Total	
JOCKEYS (by winners)		1st	2nd	3rd	Unpl	Mts	%
1	Pat Eddery	186	137	97	463	883	21.0
2	T. Quinn	149	117	124	493	883	16.8
3	K. Fallon	136	140	137	494	907	14.9
4	J. Weaver	129	123	96	483	831	15.5
5	L. Dettori............................	123	74	60	311	568	21.6
6	K. Darley.............................	113	120	104	530	867	13.0
7	J. Reid	113	102	101	495	811	13.9
8	S. Sanders............................	97	91	88	667	943	10.2
9	R. Cochrane..........................	86	83	71	388	628	13.7
10	J. Fortune.............................	83	78	114	511	786	10.5
11	W. Ryan...............................	81	55	46	313	495	16.3
12	M. Hills	80	53	67	351	551	14.5

		Races			Stakes
JOCKEYS (1,2,3 earnings of £1m+)		Won	Rides	%	£
1	Pat Eddery	186	883	21.0	2,590,178
2	L. Dettori	123	568	21.6	2,445,435
3	M. Hills...	80	551	14.5	1,977,468
4	T. Quinn..	149	883	16.8	1,391,883
5	J. Reid...	113	811	13.9	1,346,774
6	M. J. Kinane	29	166	17.4	1,194,724
7	J. Weaver	129	831	15.5	1,110,626
8	K. Fallon	136	907	14.9	1,046,726
9	K. Darley	113	867	13.0	1,029,460

JOCKEYS (by win-money)	Races Won	Rides	%	Stakes £
1 L. Dettori	123	568	21.6	1,931,345
2 Pat Eddery	186	883	21.0	1,686,115
3 M. Hills	80	551	14.5	1,558,967
4 T. Quinn	149	883	16.8	972,811
5 J. Reid	113	811	13.9	853,477
6 M. J. Kinane	29	166	17.4	784,549
7 K. Fallon	136	907	14.9	691,378
8 J. Weaver	129	831	15.5	680,037
9 K. Darley	113	867	13.0	653,850
10 W. Ryan	81	495	16.3	562,400
11 R. Hills	71	475	14.9	532,205
12 R. Cochrane	86	627	13.7	528,209

SIRES OF WINNERS (by win-money)	Horses	Indiv'l Wnrs	Races Won	Stakes £
1 Mtoto (by Busted)	39	19	27	713,699
2 Caerleon (by Nijinsky)	50	22	38	615,880
3 Darshaan (by Shirley Heights)	28	12	17	504,453
4 Salse (by Topsider)	63	23	36	492,850
5 Sadler's Wells (by Northern Dancer)	88	33	45	473,889
6 Diesis (by Sharpen Up)	41	20	28	472,532
7 Cadeaux Genereux (by Young Generation)	58	27	43	415,414
8 Woodman (by Mr Prospector)	33	13	18	393,144
9 Be My Guest (by Northern Dancer)	36	14	20	372,253
10 Warning (by Known Fact)	64	29	37	353,930
11 Green Desert (by Danzig)	90	33	47	336,605
12 Alleged (by Hoist The Flag)	20	9	14	319,523

SIRES OF WINNERS (1,2,3 earnings of £500,000+)	Races Won	Runs	%	Stakes £
1 Sadler's Wells (by Northern Dancer)	45	304	14.8	975,124
2 Mtoto (by Busted)	27	205	13.1	822,993
3 Salse (by Topsider)	36	277	12.9	691,058
4 Diesis (by Sharpen Up)	28	185	15.1	683,117
5 Caerleon (by Nijinsky)	38	196	19.3	678,205
6 Warning (by Known Fact)	37	311	11.8	603,118
7 Cadeaux Genereux (by Young Generation)	43	341	12.6	597,733
8 Darshaan (by Shirley Heights)	17	127	13.3	555,580
9 Green Desert (by Danzig)	47	373	12.6	538,062
10 Woodman (by Mr Prospector)	18	124	14.5	508,568

LEADING HORSES (1,2,3 earnings)	Races Won	Runs	%	Stakes £
1 Shaamit 3 b.c Mtoto – Shomoose	1	2	50.0	575,200
2 Halling 5 ch.h Diesis – Dance Machine	2	3	66.6	377,582
3 Bosra Sham 3 ch.f Woodman – Korveya	3	4	75.0	369,030
4 Mark of Esteem 3 b.c Darshaan – Homage	3	4	75.0	356,452
5 Dushyantor 3 b.c Sadler's Wells – Slightly	2	5	40.0	340,447
6 Pentire 4 b.c Be My Guest – Gull Nook	1	2	50.0	320,950
7 Shantou 3 b.c Alleged – Shaima	3	8	37.5	299,134
8 Classic Cliche 4 b.c Salse – Pato	2	3	66.6	280,954

EXPLANATORY NOTES

'Racehorses of 1996' deals individually, in alphabetical sequence, with every horse that ran on the flat in Britain in 1996 (including on the all-weather tracks), plus a number of foreign-trained horses that did not race here. For each of these horses is given (1) its age, colour and sex, (2) its breeding, and, where this information has not been given in a previous Racehorses Annual, a family outline (3) a form summary giving details of all its performances during the last two seasons, together, where applicable, with the horse's rating in 1995, which appears at the start of the form summary, (4) a rating of its merit in 1996 (which appears in the margin), (5) a Timeform commentary on its racing or general characteristics as a racehorse, with some suggestions, perhaps, regarding its prospects for 1997, and (6) the name of the trainer in whose charge it was on the last occasion it ran. For each two-year-old the foaling date is also given.

The book is published with a twofold purpose. Firstly, it is intended to have permanent value as a review of the exploits and achievements of the more notable of the flat-racing thoroughbreds in 1996. Thus, while the commentaries upon the vast majority of the horses are, of necessity, in note form, the best horses are more critically examined, and the essays upon them are illustrated by half-tone portraits and photographs of some of the races in which they ran. Secondly, the book is designed to help the punter to analyse races, and the notes which follow contain instructions for using the data. The attention of foreign buyers of British bloodstock, and others who are concerned with Timeform Ratings as a measure of absolute racing class in terms of a standard scale, is particularly drawn to the section headed 'The Level of the Ratings'.

TIMEFORM RATINGS

The Timeform Rating of a horse is simply the merit of the horse expressed in pounds and is arrived at by careful examination of its running against other horses using a scale of weight for distance beaten which ranges from 3 lb a length at five furlongs and 2 lb a length at a mile and a quarter to 1 lb at two miles. Timeform maintains a 'running' handicap of all horses in training throughout the season.

THE LEVEL OF THE RATINGS

At the close of each season all the horses that have raced are re-handicapped from scratch, and each horse's rating is revised. It is also necessary to adjust the general level of the handicap, so that all the ratings are kept at the same standard level from year to year. This explains why, in this book, the ratings are, in general, different from those in the final issue of the 1996 Timeform Black Book.

RATINGS AND WEIGHT-FOR-AGE

The reader has, in the ratings in this book, a universal handicap embracing all the horses in training it is possible to weigh up, ranging from tip-top classic performers, with ratings from 130 to 145, down to the meanest selling platers, rated around the 20 mark. All the ratings are at weight-for-age, so that equal ratings mean horses of equal merit: perhaps

21

it would be clearer if we said that the universal rating handicap is really not a single handicap, but four handicaps side by side: one for two-year-olds, one for three-year-olds, one for four-year-olds and one for older horses. Thus, a three-year-old rated, for argument's sake, at 117 is deemed to be identical in point of 'merit' with a four-year-old also rated at 117: but for them to have equal chances in, say, a mile race in May, the three-year-old would need to be receiving 9 lb from the four-year-old, which is the weight difference specified by the Age, Weight and Distance Tables on pages 2 and 3.

USING THE RATINGS

In using Timeform Ratings with a view to discovering which horses in any race have the best chances at the weights, we have two distinct cases, according to whether the horses taking part are of the same age or of different ages. Here is the procedure in each case:-

A. Horses of the Same Age

If the horses all carry the same weight there are no adjustments to be made, and the horses with the highest ratings have the best chances. If the horses carry different weights, jot down their ratings, and to the rating of each horse add one point for every pound the horse is set to carry less than 10 st, or subtract one point for every pound it has to carry more than 10 st. When the ratings have been adjusted in this way the highest resultant figure indicates the horse with the best chance at the weights.

Example (any distance: any week of the season)

2 Good Girl (9-6)	....	Rating 119	....	add 8	....	127
2 Paulinus (9-4)	....	Rating 113	....	add 10	....	123
2 Abilene (8-11)	....	Rating 107	....	add 17	....	124
2 Bob's Joy (8-7)	....	Rating 108	....	add 21	....	129
2 Time Warp (8-2)	....	Rating 100	....	add 26	....	126
2 Eagle Eye (7-7)	....	Rating 92	....	add 35	....	127

Bob's Joy (129) has the best chance; Good Girl (127) and Eagle Eye (127) are the next best

B. Horses of Different Ages

Take no notice of the weight any horse receives from any other. Instead, consult the Age, Weight and Distance Tables on pages 2 and 3. Treat each horse separately, and compare the weight it has to carry with the weight prescribed for it in the tables, according to the age of the horse, the distance of the race and the month of the year. Then, add one point to the rating for each pound the horse has to carry less than the weight given in the tables: or, subtract one point from the rating for every pound it has to carry more than the weight prescribed by the tables. The highest resultant figure indicates the horse most favoured by the weights.

Example (1½ miles on June 30th)

(Table Weights: 5-y-o 10-0; 4-y-o 9-13; 3-y-o 9-1)

6 Nimitz (10-2)	....	Rating 115	....	subtract 2	....	113
4 Red Devil (9-9)	....	Rating 114	....	add 4	....	118
6 Sweet Cindy (9-5)	....	Rating 115	....	add 9	....	124

22

3 Jailhouse (9-2)	....	Rating 120	....	subtract 1	....	119
4 Haakon (8-11)	....	Rating 101	....	add 16	....	117
3 Fine Strike (8-7)	....	Rating 108	....	add 8	....	116

Sweet Cindy (124) has the best chance at the weights,
with 5 lb in hand of Jailhouse

TURF AND ALL-WEATHER RATINGS

When a horse has raced on turf and on all-weather and its form on one is significantly different from the other, the two ratings are given, the all-weather set out below the turf preceded by 'a'.

Thus with FREE FOR ALL 47
a55

the top figure, 47, is the rating to be used in turf races, and the one below, a55, is for use in all-weather races. Where there is only one rating, that is to be used for both turf and all-weather.

NOTE ON RIDERS' ALLOWANCES

For the purposes of rating calculations it is assumed that the allowance a rider is able to claim is nullified by his or her inexperience. The adjustments to the ratings *should therefore be calculated on the weight allotted by the handicapper, or determined by the conditions of the race.* No extra 7lb should be added to the rating when a rider claims 7lb. This is the general routine procedure; but of course, after the usual adjustments have been made the quality of jockeyship is still an important factor to be considered when deciding between horses with similar chances.

WEIGHING UP A RACE

The ratings tell you which horses in a particular race are most favoured by the weights; but complete analysis demands that the racing character of each horse, as set out in the commentary upon it, is also studied carefully to see if there is any reason why the horse might be expected not to run up to its rating. It counts for little that a horse is thrown in at the weights if it has no pretensions whatever to staying the distance, or is unable to act on the prevailing going.

These two matters, suitability of distance and going, are no doubt the most important points to be considered. But there are others. For example, the ability of a horse to accommodate itself to the conformation of the track. Then there is the matter of temperament and behaviour: nobody would be in a hurry to take a short price about a horse with whom it is always an even chance whether it will give its running.

A few minutes spent checking up on these matters in the commentaries upon the horses concerned will sometimes put a very different complexion on a race from that which is put upon it by the ratings alone. We repeat, therefore, that the correct way to use Timeform, or this annual volume, in the analysis of individual races is, first to use the ratings to discover which horses are most favoured by the weights, and second, to check through the comments on the horse to discover what factors other than weight might also affect the outcome of the race.

THE FORM SUMMARIES

The form summary enclosed in the brackets shows for each individual horse the distance, the state of the going and where the horse finished in each of its races on the flat during the last two seasons. Performances are in chronological sequence, the earliest being given first.

The distance of each race is given in furlongs, fractional distances being expressed in the decimal notation to the nearest tenth of a furlong. Races on an all-weather surface are prefixed by letter 'a'.

The going is symbolised as follows: h=hard or very firm; f=firm (turf) or fast (all-weather); m=on the firm side of good; g=good (turf) or standard (all-weather); d=good to soft, dead; s=soft, sticky or holding (turf) or slow (all-weather); v=heavy, very heavy or very holding.

Placings are indicated, up to sixth place, by the use of superior figures, an asterisk being used to denote a win.

Thus [1995 81: 10s* 12f^3 1996 11.7g a11g^2 Sep 7] signifies that the horse was rated 81 in 1995, when winning over 10 furlongs on soft going first time out and finishing third over twelve furlongs on firm going next time out. In 1996 he finished unplaced, not in the first six, over 11.7 furlongs on good going, and then second over eleven furlongs on standard going on an all-weather track. The date of his last run was September 7.

Included in the pedigree details are the highest Timeform Annual ratings during their racing careers of the sires, dams and sires of dams of all horses, where the information is available.

Where sale prices are given F denotes the price in guineas sold as a foal, Y the price in guineas sold as a yearling. The prefix IR denotes Irish guineas.

THE RATING SYMBOLS

The following symbols, attached to the ratings, are to be interpreted as stated:-

p   likely to improve.

P   capable of *much* better form.

+   the horse may be better than we have rated it.

d   the horse appears to have deteriorated, and might no longer be capable of running to the rating given.

§   unreliable (for temperamental or other reasons).

§§   so temperamentally unsatisfactory as to be not worth a rating.

?   the horse's rating is suspect. If used without a rating the symbol implies that the horse can't be assessed with confidence, or, if used in the in-season Timeform publications, that the horse is out of form.

RACEHORSES OF 1996

Horse	Commentary	Rating

A-AASEM 3 ch.c. Polish Precedent (USA) 131 – Janbiya (IRE) 89 (Kris 135) [1995 76: 6m 6g⁶ 7m⁴ 1996 10.5d⁵ 8f⁴ 10g² 10m 10.5d Sep 28] strong, close-coupled colt: fair maiden handicapper: well below form last 2 starts then sold 21,000 gns Newmarket Autumn Sales: stays 1¼m: acts on firm ground, pulled too hard last try on dead: sent to Dubai. *H. Thomson Jones* — **76**

ABACAXI (IRE) 2 b.c. (May 17) Alzao (USA) 117 – Judicial (USA) (Law Society (USA) 130) [1996 6m 6f 6m 7g Aug 14] IR 38,000Y: smallish, close-coupled colt: second foal: brother to 3-y-o 9.4f winner Law Dancer: dam, won from 11f to 1¾m in Ireland, out of close relation of Green Dancer: showed modest form in Newbury maiden on debut: didn't progress, soundly beaten in claimer on final start: bred to stay at least 1m: headstrong: sold 3,800 gns Newmarket September Sales and sent to Czech Republic. *R. Charlton* — **61 d**

ABAJANY 2 b.c. (May 19) Akarad (FR) 130 – Miss Ivory Coast (USA) (Sir Ivor 135) [1996 10g⁵ Oct 24] 5,000Y: second foal: dam French 9f winner: unable to quicken when over 3½ lengths fifth of 8 finishers to Indifferent Guy in steadily-run median auction maiden at Nottingham: may do better. *M. R. Channon* — **57**

ABALENE 7 b.g. Forzando 122 – Riva Renald 57 (Try My Best (USA) 130) [1995 43: 12m 12g 12m* 13f⁶ 15m³ 1996 12m⁵ 12m* Jul 5] small, workmanlike gelding: poor maiden handicapper: again won at Beverley (amateurs) in July: should have stayed beyond 13.6f: acted on fibresand and good to firm ground: blinkered (respectable effort) final 6-y-o start: dead. *T. W. Donnelly* — **43**

ABEYR 3 ch.f. Unfuwain (USA) 131 – Haboobti (Habitat 134) [1995 NR 1996 8.2m* 7g* 8.1m⁵ 7g⁴ 8m² 8d⁵ Oct 11] 25,000Y: useful-looking filly: fourth foal: dam poor daughter of sister to high-class miler Noalcoholic: useful performer: won maiden at Nottingham and minor event at Leicester in the spring: best efforts next start and when neck second of 18 to Fatefully in listed rated stakes at Ascot: stayed 8.2f: went well on top-of-the-ground: sweating last 2 starts, also very edgy final one: stud. *M. A. Jarvis* — **106**

ABIR 3 ch.f. Soviet Star (USA) 128 – Nafhaat (USA) 91 (Roberto (USA) 131) [1995 68p: 7m² 1996 8m⁶ 8d 7m² 7m² Aug 15] sturdy filly: best effort when second in handicap at Yarmouth (made most) final start: probably best at around 7f: hung right penultimate start: keen sort: visits Hamas. *H. Thomson Jones* — **73**

ABLE CHOICE (IRE) 6 b.g. Taufan (USA) 119 – Great Land (USA) (Friend's Choice (USA)) [1995 49, a80: a10g a12g² 9.7d 11.9m 10g³ 8m 8m⁵ a7g* 10d 11.5s a10g 1996 a10g a10g² 9.9d a9.4g a10s Nov 19] good-topped gelding: fair handicapper on the all-weather: stays 1½m: blinkered (out of form) final 4-y-o start: inconsistent. *R. W. Armstrong* — **a78**

ABLE SHERIFF 4 gr.g. Doulab (USA) 115 – Rich Lass (Broxted 120) [1995 48: 5g⁶ 5g³ 6g 5m 5m² 5m⁵ 5f 5.1d⁶ 6g 5g⁶ 1996 5g² 5g 5g 5f* 5f 5m³ 5m⁵ 5m² 5g³ 6f⁴ 5f² 5.1d 5m* 5m⁶ 5g 5m⁴ Oct 23] close-coupled gelding: has a round action: modest handicapper: won at Thirsk in June and Ayr in September: has form at 6f, raced almost exclusively at 5f when improved performer in 1996: acts on good to firm and soft ground: usually blinkered nowadays: none too consistent. *M. W. Easterby* — **65**

ABOU ZOUZ (USA) 2 b.c. (Feb 13) Miswaki (USA) 124 – Bold Jessie (Never So Bold 135) [1996 5m* 6d² 6m* 7m⁴ Oct 1] — **109**

'At six he had won, at six and a half he was half empty and at seven he had gone. It will be back to sprinting.' Trainer David Loder was reporting the jockey's comments after Abou Zouz had finished only fourth when a warm favourite for the Tattersalls Houghton Sales Conditions Stakes at Newmarket in October. At 350,000 guineas, Abou Zouz was the most expensive purchase among the twenty-three sales graduates taking part, and was one of only three

25

Scottish Equitable Gimcrack Stakes, York—from left to right, Abou Zouz, Compton Place and The West

sent off at shorter than 10/1 in a field in which, typically for these valuable restricted events, there was a wide range of ability on show. Less typically for a field of such size it was a falsely-run race, and to some further from the action than Abou Zouz's jockey Dettori—ourselves included—the horse did not perform like an obvious non-stayer. He was undeniably well below his best, held up behind the pace and caught flat-footed two furlongs out, and, after briefly looking a danger when squeezing through on the rails just inside the final furlong, he went down by two necks and a head behind Papua, Mukaddar and Granny's Pet.

Abou Zouz had been seen to much better advantage over six furlongs in the Gimcrack Stakes at York in August, his first outing for three months. He had been the first of his stable's youngsters to see the racecourse, having started off in a maiden at Newmarket on Two Thousand Guineas day and, like fortyfive per cent of the stable's two-year-olds the previous season and thirty-three per cent in the latest, had started with a win. Afterwards Loder told the Press that he was the best two-year-old colt he had trained so far, but a defeat when odds on for a minor event at Kempton three weeks later led to plans for Royal Ascot being abandoned and, with connections at a loss to explain the below-par effort, he was rested until York. Abou Zouz looked to have done well during his break and started third favourite in the nine-runner Gimcrack behind the Goodwood maiden winner The West and Richmond Stakes winner Easycall. The remainder of the field consisted of the Woodcote winner and Richmond fourth Proud Native, his stable-companion the rank outsider Select Choice, dual winner Compton Place and a trio of northern-trained colts, Nigrasine, Hula Prince and For Your Eyes Only, all seeking a third win. When the race drew to its climax, Abou Zouz, who had travelled smoothly behind the pace set by Compton Place, found plenty under pressure, wore down the leader to beat him half a length with The West, who had run green and drifted left, one and a quarter lengths behind in third. The first three finished clear of Easycall who had possibly been at a disadvantage towards the far side with the runners coming down the centre of the track.

		Miswaki (USA) (ch 1978)	Mr Prospector (b 1970)	Raise A Native
				Gold Digger
Abou Zouz (USA) (b.c. Feb 13, 1994)			Hopespringseternal (ch 1971)	Buckpasser
				Rose Bower
		Bold Jessie (b 1988)	Never So Bold (b 1980)	Bold Lad
				Never Never Land
			Jubilee Song (b 1976)	Song
				Sylvanecte

Abou Zouz's sire Miswaki has had comparatively few runners trained in Britain and his only pattern winner here before Abou Zouz was the Jersey Stakes winner Midyan. Most of Miswaki's best performers have raced in

France (where he won the Prix de la Salamandre) and North America (the minor Charles Hatton Stakes at three) and he has sired good-class winners over a variety of trips despite having had stamina limitations himself. Among them are the Arc winner Urban Sea, Breeders' Cup Classic winner Black Tie Affair, the high-class and versatile Italian horse Misil, and the latest Prix de l'Abbaye winner Kistena. Speed dominates the bottom half of Abou Zouz's pedigree. His dam Bold Jessie succeeded where he failed in winning a valuable sales race, in her case the six-furlong Tattersalls Breeders Stakes at the Curragh. That proved to be Bold Jessie's only win in a six-race career during which she obviously had problems (she refused to go to the start on one occasion) and she was retired after beating one home when 100/1 for Kooyonga's Irish One Thousand Guineas. Nonetheless, she won more prize-money in that one victory than her dam's very speedy offspring Prince Sabo and Millyant managed between them in longer and more prestigious careers. Abou Zouz is Bold Jessie's second foal after a filly by Sovereign Dancer called Yorkrun Express who was sent to Brazil. Her next foal, a colt by Dixieland Band, will probably be seen here in due course as he was a 110,000-dollar purchase by Shadwell Stud at Keeneland in 1996. Bold Jessie's dam, another five-furlong winner, is a sister to the useful seven-furlong and one-mile performer Band On The Run and the Nell Gwyn Stakes runner-up Shark Song; the next dam Sylvanecte had more stamina and won over a mile and a quarter.

Abou Zouz, who, incidentally, first went through the sales ring as a foal, fetching 145,000 dollars, had made up into a well-made, imposing colt by the autumn and was easily the paddock pick at Newmarket (though he did swish his tail throughout the preliminaries). He has shown his best form at six furlongs and will almost certainly prove best as a sprinter. *D. R. Loder*

ABOVE THE CUT (USA)   4 ch.c. Topsider (USA) – Placer Queen (Habitat 134) [1995 –: 7.9m⁴ 8m 1996 8.1g 8m⁴ 10m 8f Jul 24] close-coupled, good-bodied colt: has a quick action: generally disappointing since 2 yrs: should stay beyond 7f: raced only on a sound surface: blinkered since second 4-y-o start: has been mulish and blanketed for stalls entry: joined C. P. Morlock. *P. W. Harris*   –

A BREEZE   2 br.c. (Feb 14) Precocious 126 – Wasimah 84 (Caerleon (USA) 132) [1996 6m⁶ 6m 5g⁴ 5m* 6m⁶ 6s Oct 26] compact, attractive colt: half-brother to 3-y-o Cadeau Elegant (by Cadeaux Genereux): dam 2-y-o 5f winner from sprinting family: progressive form first 4 starts, readily winning maiden at Pontefract in August: creditable sixth in nursery at Newmarket on penultimate start: stays 6f: ran too freely in visor on soft ground final one. *D. Morris*   75

ABSOLUTE CHARLIE   2 ch.c. (May 3) Prince Daniel (USA) – Absolutely Blue 42 (Absalom 128) [1996 7g Jul 24] leggy, short-backed colt: third reported foal: dam poor maiden: 100/1, tailed off in seller at Catterick. *D. W. Barker*   –

ABSOLUTE LIBERTY (USA)   2 ch.c. (May 21) Gold Alert (USA) – Mutter-fly (USA) (Muttering (USA)) [1996 6f⁴ 7.6d 7.9g Oct 9] sparely-made colt: first known foal: dam thrice-raced half-sister to smart performer at around 1m Mistle Cat: sire (by Mr Prospector) very useful stakes winner at 8.5f and 1¼m: probably only a fair maiden (contested steadily-run races last 2 starts): not bred to be suited by beyond 1m. *S. P. C. Woods*   62 ?

ABSOLUTELY ABSTONE   2 gr.f. (Apr 30) Petong 126 – Odilese 82 (Mummy's Pet 125) [1996 5g⁴ 5g³ 5m⁴ May 7] 3,400Y: leggy, angular filly: sister to 5f winner Tutu Sixtysix and half-sister to 3-y-o 6f (at 2 yrs) and 7f winner Oriole (by Mazilier): dam 6f winner: poor form in maiden auctions and a seller (visored). *P. D. Evans*   44

ABSOLUTELY FAYRE   5 ch.g. Absalom 128 – June Fayre (Sagaro 133) [1995 68: 7.6m 10m⁵ 12f a10g 1996 a14.8g Jan 3] fair performer: stays 10.8f: acts on good to firm ground and soft, no form on all-weather: joined V. Soane: gelded. *R. Akehurst*   –

ABSOLUTELYSTUNNING   3 br.f. Aragon 118 – Dramatic Mood (Jalmood (USA) 126) [1995 –p: 6m 5g 1996 10.2g 10m⁶ 10m* 10g 8.2m 10g² 10m 11.4m⁶ 10.3g² 12g a10g⁴ a10g* a10g Dec 20] sparely-made filly: modest handicapper: won   63 at Nottingham in May and at Lingfield (apprentice minor event) in December: will probably stay 1½m. *Mrs Barbara Waring*

ABSOLUTE MAGIC 6 b.g. Doulab (USA) 115 – Trickster 92 (Major Portion 85 129) [1995 82: 7m 7g² 7m 7m 1996 7.6d⁵ 8m 6d⁵ 7g* 8.1s* a8.5g⁵ Nov 16] sturdy gelding: usually impresses in appearance: poor mover: fairly useful handicapper: lightly raced since 4 yrs, reportedly suffering from foot problems: clearly best efforts at 6 yrs when winning at Yarmouth and Musselburgh in the autumn: stays 8.1f: possibly suited by give when on turf nowadays, and acts on heavy and fibresand. *W. J. Haggas*

ABSOLUTE RULER (IRE) 5 ch.g. Absalom 128 – Princess Biddy 86 (Sun 42 Prince 128) [1995 65d: 6.5s³ 7g 6f 6g 7.8f⁵ a10g⁶ a9.4g a10g 1996 a8g⁵ a16g 8g⁵ a– 8.1g³ 10d 8m² 10m³ 10m 9.2f 10d 8.2g⁴ a11g Nov 18] lengthy gelding: only poor maiden nowadays: stays 8.2f: acts on firm and soft ground: blinkered/visored: inconsistent. *J. L. Harris*

ABSOLUTE UTOPIA (USA) 3 b.g. Mr Prospector (USA) – Magic Gleam 69 (USA) 122 (Danzig (USA)) [1995 NR 1996 8.2d⁵ 8g⁶ 10.2g 8g⁶ 10m⁵ 8.5m⁴ 9m 8s Nov 9] quite good-topped gelding: has been hobdayed and had soft palate operation: second foal: brother to fair 1m winner Touch A Million: dam, winner of Child Stakes, stayed 1m: fair maiden: sold out of E. Dunlop's stable 1,700 gns Newmarket July Sales after fourth outing: stays 8.5f, may get 1¼m: acts on good to firm ground: inconsistent. *N. E. Berry*

ABSTONE AGAIN (IRE) 2 b.g. (Apr 12) Roi Danzig (USA) – Empress Wu 62 43 (High Line 125) [1996 5d⁵ a5g⁴ a6g⁵ 6g⁴ 5f 5s⁴ Jul 4] 3,000Y: lengthy gelding: good mover: third foal: half-brother to 3-y-o 1¼m winner Kernof (by Rambo Dancer): dam ran twice: poor sprint plater: well beaten on soft ground: visored/blinkered on 4 occasions. *P. D. Evans*

ABSTONE QUEEN 2 b.f. (Mar 8) Presidium 124 – Heavenly Queen (Scottish 66 Reel 123) [1996 a5g³ 5m³ a6g³ a7g³ 7m³ a7g³ 7g² a6g³ 6g* 6m³ 7g* 6f⁴ 6m* 6g⁵ a48 6m⁴ 7m⁴ a7g⁴ 6d³ 6m 7g* 7g 6m⁵ Oct 29] 2,500Y: leggy filly: first foal: dam little form: fair performer: won sellers at Yarmouth and Catterick in August and non-selling nurseries at Redcar in August and Catterick in October: best form at 7f: acts on good to firm ground, had form on fibresand early in year: blinkered or visored nowadays: sometimes on toes (ran poorly when very stirred up once): often mounted on track: ran poorly both starts at Hamilton: very tough. *P. D. Evans*

ABTAAL 6 b.h. Green Desert (USA) 127 – Stufida (Bustino 136) [1995 a7g* a8g⁶ 52 a7g² a8g² a7g⁴ a8g 1996 a7g⁵ a7g a6g 7f 10.8f 10m 11.6g⁵ 10d⁵ 10g Sep 3] a– good-bodied horse: won 4-runner handicap at Nad Al Sheba in January, 1995, for E. Charpy before sold 22,000 gns Newmarket July Sales: modest form at best in 1996: stays 11.6f, best form at up to 1m: acts on the sand and soft going: inconsistent. *R. J. Hodges*

ACADEMY STAR 2 b.f. (Apr 30) Royal Academy (USA) 130 – Startino 111 65 p (Bustino 136) [1996 7d Oct 2] sixth living foal: closely related to fairly useful winner at around 1¼m Stoney Valley (by Caerleon) and half-sister to 4-y-o Advance East (by Polish Precendent) and a winner in Germany by Be My Guest: dam 1m and 1½m winner also third in Park Hill: 14/1, probably needed race when around 6 lengths seventh of 19, improving 2f out then fading, to Entice in maiden at Salisbury: bred to stay at least 1m: will improve. *J. R. Fanshawe*

ACCENTO 3 b.c. Midyan (USA) 124 – Daleside Ladybird 66 (Tolomeo 127) 114 [1995 5s* 6m⁴ 7g³ 8s⁶ 1996 7.5g³ 8s² 9m² 8g² 8g 8g* 8d² Oct 13] second foal: half-brother to 4-y-o Hong Kong Dollar (by Superpower): dam sprinter: won maiden at Cologne then kept smart company at 2 yrs: improved in 1996: demoted after passing post first in listed race at Dusseldorf in April on first outing: clear of remainder when 1¼ lengths second of 14 to Lavirco in Mehl-Mulhens-Rennen at Cologne in May next time: back to form when winning Group 2 event at Cologne in September by a neck from A Magicman: stays 1m, respectable effort at 9f: acts on soft ground: blinkered (ran poorly) fifth 3-y-o start. *R. Suerland, Germany*

ACCESS ADVENTURER (IRE) 5 b.g. Al Hareb (USA) 123 – Olwyn 109 78 d (Relko 136) [1995 78: 10m³ 11.9m 10m* 10m⁴ 10m* 10m 19m6 a10g⁴ a10g³ a8g⁶ 10m² 10.1m³ 10f 8m 12g 8m 10f⁵ Oct 15] big, close-coupled gelding: fair performer at best: stays 1¼m: acts on equitrack and good to firm ground: blinkered (no form)

penultimate 5-y-o start: has won when sweating: often front runner: inconsistent.
R. Boss

ACCESS SUN   9 b.g. Pharly (FR) 130 – Princesse du Seine (FR) (Val de Loir   40
133) [1995 42: 15.4g 17.2m 17.2m³ 17.2f² 1996 16m⁴ 17.2m⁵ Jun 29] leggy gelding:
unimpressive mover: poor handicapper: stays 17.2f: acts on firm ground: races
prominently. *J. S. King*

ACCONDY (IRE)   4 gr.c. Sadler's Wells (USA) 132 – As You Desire Me 112   79
(Kalamoun 129) [1995 NR 1996 7.5f³ 12.3m⁶ 8m³ Jul 5] 105,000Y: tall, strong colt:
closely related to 2 winners by Be My Guest, including untrustworthy but useful
Intimate Guest (up to 1m), and half-brother to several winners, including once useful
Great Heights (stayed 13.3f, by Shirley Heights): dam winning miler in France: third
in maidens at Beverley (coltish) and Warwick (well backed, drifted right and faded
final 1f) in midsummer: may prove best short of 1m. *C. E. Brittain*

ACCOUNTANCY JEWEL (IRE)   3 b.f. Pennine Walk 120 – Polyester Girl   –
(Ridan (USA)) [1995 71p: 7d a7g* 1996 a8g⁵ a8g⁴ Feb 27] fair form second 2-y-o
start: well beaten at 3 yrs: should stay 1m: acts on equitrack. *K. McAuliffe*

ACCOUNTANCY LEADER (IRE)   2 b.f. (Apr 22) Anita's Prince 126 –   41 +
Diewitt (IRE) (Dara Monarch 128) [1996 5.2s 6g 5m³ Jul 18] IR 1,100Y: angular
filly: first foal: dam unraced half-sister to Moyglare Stud Stakes winner Daness:
keeping-on third in seller at Leicester in July on final start: pulled hard over 6f:
showed ability on soft ground on debut: sent to Sweden. *B. Palling*

ACERBUS DULCIS   5 ch.g. Hadeer 118 – Current Pattie (USA) 102 (Little   –
Current (USA)) [1995 NR 1996 a16g a11g Dec 3] of little account. *M. C. Chapman*

ACHARNE   3 ch.c. Pharly (FR) 130 – Sibley 84 (Northfields (USA)) [1995 90:   113
7m³ 7g⁵ 7m⁴ 7.1d² 8d⁶ 1996 8s* 8d⁵ 11.5f⁶ 12m 12f² 10g² 10.5m 10s³ 8m Nov 10]
well-made colt: has a quick action: smart performer: won minor event at Doncaster
in March: placed in Prix Eugene Adam at Saint-Cloud (length behind disqualified
Desert Boy) and Prix du Prince d'Orange at Longchamp (3½ lengths behind Baroud
d'Honneur) 2 of last 4 starts: stays 1½m: acts on firm ground and soft: tends to hang
left: good type for listed/Group 3 races in Europe in 1997. *C. E. Brittain*

A CHEF TOO FAR   3 b.c. Be My Chief (USA) 122 – Epithet 105 (Mill Reef   77
(USA) 141) [1995 NR 1996 6.9f⁵ 7m⁴ 7.3s* 12m 8g 8d Oct 12] 10,500Y: leggy,
close-coupled colt: half-brother to several winners, including fairly useful Kiltimony
(5f in Ireland, by Sharpo) and Sugar Plum Fairy (best around 1¼m, by Sadler's
Wells): dam, 5f and 6f winner who stayed 1½m, half-sister to smart (up to 7f)
Columnist and now grandam of Shaamit: fair form in maidens, easily making all at
Newbury in May: down the field in competitive handicaps: bred to stay at least 1m
but is a keen sort: acts on soft ground, probably on firm: has had tongue tied down.
R. Rowe

ACHILLES HEEL   5 br.g. Superlative 118 – Ela-Yianni-Mou 73 (Anfield 117)   60
[1995 54d: a7g⁶ a10g² a10g³ 12g* 12m 12g⁶ 13g 13.9g⁶ 10g 14.9m⁵ 12m⁵ 10m 12d
12.1g³ 12.1g⁴ 12m⁵ 11.9m⁴ 1996 10.9d 12d 11.9f⁵ 12m² 11.9m* 20f 14.6g 13.3f⁴
12m⁴ Aug 7] smallish gelding: modest handicapper: won at York (apprentices) in
June: better at 1½m than shorter, not disgraced at 2½m: best efforts on a sound
surface: blinkered (ran poorly) third 5-y-o start: has worn near-side pricker: sometimes looks lazy: inconsistent. *C. N. Allen*

ACONORACE   4 b.g. Midyan (USA) 124 – Saint Cynthia (Welsh Saint 126)   –
[1995 –: 9.9m⁶ 10.1g 10g⁴ 1996 a8g 10g Sep 3] sturdy, close-coupled gelding: no
worthwhile form. *R. A. Fahey*

ACQUITTAL (IRE)   4 b.g. Danehill (USA) 126 – Perfect Alibi (Law Society   48
(USA) 130) [1995 61: a8.5g⁴ 8.3v² 9.7m³ 10m⁶ 11.1m* 11.6m³ 14m⁶ 10m⁴ 12.1m³
12m 1996 a16g a14.8g⁵ 10m 10m 8f⁴ 8.1m 8.3m 8m 10f² Sep 28] only poor form for
new stables (J. Mackie first 2 starts only) in 1996: stays 1½m: acts on any ground:
usually blinkered/visored nowadays: inconsistent. *A. Streeter*

ACROW LINE   11 b.g. Capricorn Line 111 – Miss Acrow (Comedy Star (USA)   –
121) [1995 –, a37: a14.8g³ 16.2m a16.2g* a16g² 1996 a16g 16.1f a12g Nov 25]
stocky gelding: no encouragement on flat in 1996: thorough stayer: acts on fibresand,
good to firm ground and heavy: still a fair hurdler. *D. Burchell*

ACTION JACKSON 4 ch.g. Hadeer 118 – Water Woo (USA) 102 (Tom Rolfe) 58
[1995 66, a–: 7g⁵ 8m² 8m² 10m⁶ 9.7f⁴ a9.4g 7f a8g⁵ a8g⁵ 1996 8m 8.3g⁴ 8g² a–
10m* 12m 10d⁴ 10g* 10.1m 10f Oct 15] close-coupled, angular gelding: modest
performer: consistent in claimers and sellers (narrow winner at Nottingham and,
gamely, Pontefract) in 1996: stays 1¼m: acts on firm and dead going: tried with
tongue tied down. *B. J. McMath*

ACTION REPLAY 3 ch.g. Fearless Action (USA) 116 – Pentland Beauty 49 –
(Remainder Man 126§) [1995 NR 1996 11.8m a14.8g Nov 30] tall, angular gelding:
has a round action: fourth reported foal: dam, maiden, stayed 1m: soundly beaten in
maiden and claimer 6 months apart. *R. Hollinshead*

ADALOALDO (USA) 4 ch.g. Arctic Tern (USA) 126 – Alicia's Lady (USA) (Al –
Nasr (FR) 126) [1995 57: 12s 12g 12f³ 11f a10g⁵ 1996 a12g* a12g a11g² a11g a12g⁴ a56
a11g* 12d 12.3g a12g⁴ 8g 8m a11g Jun 14] leggy, close-coupled gelding: modest
handicapper: won at Southwell in January (apprentices) and March: stayed 1½m:
acted on firm ground and fibresand: visored (well beaten) twice: inconsistent: dead.
J. Parkes

ADAMTON 4 b.g. Domynsky 110 – Berwyn (Sharpo 132) [1995 –: 5d a8.5g⁴ 75 p
a8.5g 1996 a6g⁶ 6f 10.1m* a10s* a11g² a10g* Dec 31] lightly-raced gelding: shaped
with conspicuous promise on reappearance and jockey claimed he was hanging on
officially good to firm ground next time: off course over 4½ months and progressed
very well from October onwards: made all in handicaps at Newmarket and Lingfield
(twice), best effort when merely kept up to his work to hold on last time: stays 11f:
acts on good to firm ground and all-weather surfaces: has swished tail, but is game:
capable of better still. *Mrs J. Cecil*

ADELAIDE (IRE) 3 b.f. Alzao (USA) 117 – Al Joharah 103 (Mill Reef (USA) –
141) [1995 NR 1996 10m 10m Jun 21] second known foal: dam won twice at around
1m in France: considerably-handled eighth in maidens at Newmarket, eyecatching
effort last time: should stay further than 1¼m: sent to Saudi Arabia. *L. M. Cumani*

ADILOV 4 b.g. Soviet Star (USA) 128 – Volida 105 (Posse (USA) 130) [1995 67?: 56 d
a8.5g⁵ 8f⁴ 10m 1996 8.3m³ 8.1d 7g a8g 10m 8m 11.5m 8m a10g a16g⁵ a13g⁴ Dec
31] rangy gelding: modest maiden: only start for R. Phillips, claimed £3,000 on
reappearance: failed by long way to repeat the form, next 5 starts for K. Cunningham-
Brown: stays 1m: acts on firm going. *J. J. Bridger*

ADLER (IRE) 3 b.g. Warning 136 – Orangerie (FR) (Gay Mecene (USA) 128) –
[1995 –p: a8.5g⁵ 1996 a7g a7g Jan 26] well beaten, in sellers (blinkered last time) in
1996. *M. J. Camacho*

ADMIRALS FLAME (IRE) 5 b.g. Doulab (USA) 115 – Fan The Flame 69 84
(Grundy 137) [1995 79, a–: a7g a10g⁶ a8g 8g 8m⁴ 7m 10g⁶ 8.3m* 8f⁵ 8f* 8m 8m³ a–
8g 8f² 1996 8m 8s² 8g⁴ 8m⁴ 8m³ 8.3d* 8g 8d Oct 12] leggy gelding: fairly useful
handicapper: consistent (except on reappearance) before narrowly winning rated
stakes at Windsor in August under strong ride: stays 8.3f well: acts on firm ground,
very best form on a soft surface: sweating (ran poorly) eleventh 4-y-o start: wears
bandages. *C. F. Wall*

ADMIRALS REALM 7 gr.g. Another Realm 118 – Bedeni 100 (Parthia 132) –
[1995 –: 5g 6m 1996 6m 5m 5d May 22] lengthy gelding: no form since modest at 5
yrs. *A. G. Newcombe*

ADMIRALS SECRET (USA) 7 ch.g. Secreto (USA) 128 – Noble Mistress 64
(USA) (Vaguely Noble 140) [1995 71: a12g⁵ 12g* 12g* 12.3f² 11.6g⁵ 11.6m²
13.8m* 15.9m⁶ 14.4m 12g⁵ 12m 1996 13.8s³ 14.1s 12d⁴ 12g 11.8m 11.5f⁴ 12m⁵ Jul
19] good-quartered gelding: carries condition: has a round action: fair handicapper:
generally disappointing in 1996: stays 1¾m: acts on any turf going and on equitrack:
normally held up: inconsistent. *C. F. Wall*

ADMIRAL'S WELL (IRE) 6 b.h. Sadler's Wells (USA) 132 – Exotic Bride 107
(USA) (Blushing Groom (FR) 131) [1995 107: 16.2m⁶ 20m³ 16f⁵ 16m* 18g⁴ 20s⁵
1996 16.4d⁴ 22.2f* 16f 18m⁴ 16m Oct 5] good-bodied horse: usually looks very well:
has a round action: useful performer: won Queen Alexandra Stakes at Royal Ascot
by 2½ lengths from Speed To Lead: reported to have gurgled in Goodwood Cup:
6 lengths fourth of 6 to Double Trigger in Doncaster Cup: ran as if something
badly amiss final start: stays very well: acts on firm ground and soft: held up/tracks

leaders: genuine: sold 53,000 gns Newmarket Autumn Sales, reportedly to join G. Mikhalides, but sent to Saudi Arabia. *R. Akehurst*

ADMONISH 2 b.f. (Feb 28) Warning 136 – Ashdown (Pharly (FR) 130) [1996 6m⁵ 6f² Jul 21] fourth reported foal: half-sister to 3-y-o 5f (including at 2 yrs) and 6f winner Standown (by Reprimand): dam thrice-raced granddaughter of Irish 1000 Guineas winner Favoletta: 2 lengths second of 3 behind Zugudi in maiden at Yarmouth in July: reported by trainer to have been injured afterwards: bred to stay 1m. *M. A. Jarvis*   57

ADONISIS 4 b.c. Emarati (USA) 74 – Kind Lady 56 (Kind of Hush 118) [1995 –: 9m³ 1996 12s Oct 26] smallish, sturdy, rather dipped-backed colt: off course nearly 16 months, behind in claimer at Newbury. *D. R. C. Elsworth*   –

ADVANCE EAST 4 b.g. Polish Precedent (USA) 131 – Startino 111 (Bustino 136) [1995 74: 10g⁶ 10.3m² 12g² 12g² 11.9s 1996 12g 14m⁴ 14.1m 11.9m⁶ 12f 11.9m 10f⁴ 10.3m⁴ 10m³ 8g³ 9m⁶ 10.1m⁵ Oct 23] big, good-topped gelding: unimpressive mover: still a maiden: only modest in 1996, and left Mrs J. Ramsden after tenth start: stays 1½m but not 1¾m: acts on firm ground: has been equipped with tongue grip: held up: won novice hurdle Nov 6: has found little. *M. Dods*   61

ADVANCE REPRO 2 b.f. (Feb 11) Risk Me (FR) 127 – Sunday Sport Gem 42 (Lomond (USA) 128) [1996 6d 5f 5f* a5g² a6g* a7g a6g⁶ Dec 31] 1,400Y: first foal: dam, ran only at 2 yrs when placed over 6f, out of half-sister to Irish Oaks winner Olwyn: modest performer: won sellers in Folkestone in June and Wolverhampton (readily) in July: no form afterwards, off course nearly 5 months before final start: should stay 7f, raced freely when tried: acts on firm ground and fibresand: blinkered last 5 starts: retained 2,000 gns Newmarket Autumn Sales. *J. Akehurst*   56 a61

AEGEAN SOUND 2 b.f. (Mar 2) Distant Relative 128 – Imperatrice (USA) (Kings Lake (USA) 133) [1996 6m⁵ 5.1f² 6g* 6d³ 6m² 6s a6g Nov 12] 2,400Y: fifth foal: half-sister to 3-y-o 7f (at 2 yrs) and 1m winner Sound Check (by Formidable): dam ran once in France: made all in 3-runner median auction maiden at Epsom in July: good efforts in nurseries next 2 starts: some way below form last 2 outings: will be suited by further than 6f: acts on good to firm and dead ground, probably on firm. *R. Hannon*   71

AERLEON JANE 3 ch.f. Caerleon (USA) 132 – An Empress (USA) (Affirmed (USA)) [1995 85p: 7m² 1996 8d⁵ 6.9m* 9m⁴ 7.1d* 8m 7g⁴ Oct 10] sturdy filly: 89

Queen Alexandra Stakes, Royal Ascot—
favourite-backers end the meeting on a winning note thanks to Admiral's Well

fairly useful handicapper: won at Folkestone (maiden) and Sandown in the spring: effective at 7f and probably at 9f: acts on good to firm ground and dead, yet to race on extremes: sent to USA. *J. H. M. Gosden*

AERLEON PETE (IRE) 2 b.c. (May 24) Caerleon (USA) 132 – Bristle 96 (Thatch (USA) 136) [1996 7m 7f³ Oct 15] 44,000Y: quite attractive colt: half-brother to 3-y-o Premier Generation (by Cadeaux Genereux) and several winners here and abroad, including 6f (at 2 yrs) to 1m winner Big Leap (by Auction Ring) and fairly useful 6-y-o 7f performer Rakis (by Alzao): dam Irish 2-y-o 8.5f winner: made promising debut: finished well under hand riding when 2½ lengths third of 10 to Attitude in maiden at Leicester later in month: will stay 1¼m: will do better. *M. R. Stoute* **79 p**

AEROKING (USA) 5 b.g. Lear Fan (USA) 130 – Blue Grass Baby (USA) (Icecapade (USA)) [1995 82: 8.1m 10g⁴ 8f⁴ 10m 9g⁵ 10d 9d⁶ 8m² 1996 8s 9m 8g³ 8f⁶ 9f 9.9f⁴ 10f 8f Sep 27] lengthy, good-topped gelding: fair creditably only at Newmarket on third start, and retained by stable 600 gns Newmarket Autumn Sales: stays 1¼m: acts on firm ground, possibly not a soft surface: sometimes takes strong hold: has worn net muzzle: inconsistent. *G. Harwood* **80 d**

AETHRA (USA) 3 ch.f. Trempolino (USA) 135 – All For Hope (USA) (Sensitive Prince (USA)) [1995 89p: 8f² 1996 10.5d⁵ 10m 8f² Jun 25] tall, leggy filly: failed to confirm debut promise: should be fully effective over at least 1¼m, though takes a strong hold: blinkered (ran poorly) second 3-y-o start. *Lady Herries* **76**

AFICIONADO (IRE) 2 b.g. (Mar 5) Marju (IRE) 127 – Haneena 118 (Habitat 134) [1996 6g³ 6m³ 5f 6m 6m⁶ 7m⁵ 8g* a8.5g⁴ Nov 11] IR 16,000Y: work-manlike gelding: fluent mover: half-brother to several winners, including 1992 2-y-o 7f winner Antester (by Soviet Star) and smart French miler North Haneena (by Far North): dam sprinter, later raced in USA: looked to be going wrong way then won 21-runner seller at Newmarket in November: stays 8.5f: acts on good to firm ground and fibresand: blinkered twice. *R. F. Johnson Houghton* **73 d**

AFISIAK 3 b.f. Efisio 120 – Maestrette 77 (Manado 130) [1995 60: 5g⁵ 5g² a5g* 1996 6d⁴ 6.1d 6.1m Apr 30] tall, unfurnished filly: off course 11 months and long way below 2-y-o form in the spring. *A. B. Mulholland* **–**

AFON ALWEN 3 ch.f. Henbit (USA) 130 – Brenig 68 (Horage 124) [1995 NR 1996 a9.4g³ 10f* 10m³ 10f Oct 15] angular filly: third foal: dam lightly-raced maiden: modest form: won slowly-run maiden at Brighton in September, holding on well despite wandering: stiff task final start: stays 1¼m: acts on firm ground: tends to carry head high: front runner. *S. C. Williams* **61**

AFRICAN-PARD (IRE) 4 b.g. Don't Forget Me 127 – Petite Realm 95 (Realm 129) [1995 70: 7.1m⁶ 8m² 8.1g³ 8m⁶ 8.1m³ 7.1d⁴ 7.1g⁶ 1996 10.8f a9.4g³ 8m⁵ 8.3g 7.1m³ 7.1m² 7g⁵ 8m a9.4g a7s Dec 19] good-topped, attractive gelding: fair maiden handicapper: stays 9.4f: acts on good to firm and soft ground and fibresand: blinkered/visored fifth to penultimate 4-y-o starts: sometimes rather too keen. *D. Haydn Jones* **66 a59**

AFRICAN SUN (IRE) 3 b.g. Mtoto 134 – Nuit d'Ete (USA) 90 (Super Concorde (USA) 128) [1995 –: a7g 7g 1996 9m a8.5g⁵ 12m 10m⁴ 10m⁵ Jun 28] angular gelding: little worthwhile form: sold (B. Hanbury to M. C. Chapman) 2,400 gns Newmarket July Sales. *B. Hanbury* **–**

AFTER HOURS 2 b.f. (Mar 28) Polar Falcon (USA) 126 – Tarasova (USA) (Green Forest (USA) 134) [1996 7.1s Oct 22] 3,200Y: third foal: half-sister to fairly useful 3-y-o 5f and 6f winner Galine (by Most Welcome) and 4-y-o 7f and 1m winner Wild Palm (by Darshaan): dam twice-raced half-sister to top-class French middle-distance colt Le Marmot: 50/1, slowly away and never a threat in late-season maiden at Chepstow. *D. J. S. ffrench Davis* **–**

AGAINST THE CLOCK 4 b.g. Puissance 110 – Sara Sprint (Formidable (USA) 125) [1995 7v³ 7s 10m⁵ 9g 8g² 9f 7.5g³ 8m 1996 a16g Feb 13] 10,000F: 7,000Y: ex-Irish gelding: second foal: dam Italian 6f and 7f winner: modest maiden (rated 59) at 3 yrs for N. McGrath: tailed off only start here: stays 1¼m: acts on good to firm and heavy ground: disappointing hurdler, sold 1,200 gns (October) and 580 gns (December, to P. Bowen) at Ascot Sales. *J. W. Mullins* **–**

AGAIN TOGETHER 3 b.f. Then Again 126 – Starawak 68 (Star Appeal 133) 59
[1995 58: 7m 7g² 7m 7m³ 7g² 6m 1996 a7g² a6g⁶ 7g 8f⁴ 11.5f⁴ 12m² 10f⁵ Jul 17]
rather leggy filly: modest maiden handicapper: stays 1½m: acts on firm ground and
all-weather: sent to South Korea. *G. L. Moore*

AGDISTIS 3 b.f. Petoski 135 – Kannbaniya (Mouktar 129) [1995 NR 1996 9f 68
10m² 10m² 11.8g 11.4m Sep 17] first foal: dam winning 2½m hurdler: fair maiden:
ran poorly last 2 starts: stays 1¼m: won over hurdles in October: has joined Mrs.
D. Haine. *H. Thomson Jones*

AGENT 3 ch.g. Anshan 119 – Maria Cappuccini 70 (Siberian Express (USA) 125) 62
[1995 70+: 6.1d 6g⁵ a6g² 1996 a7g² a8g³ a6g³ 8f⁴ 6d 6.1d⁶ 7m 8.2s² a8.5g² a8.5g³ a70
Dec 28] leggy gelding: fair maiden handicapper on all-weather: stays 8.5f: acts on
fibresand and on soft ground: occasionally unruly at start: none too consistent.
J. L. Eyre

AGENT MULDER 2 b.g. (Apr 25) Kylian (USA) – Precious Caroline (IRE) 60 –
(The Noble Player (USA) 126) [1996 7d Oct 2] first reported foal: dam 1¼m winner:
sire (by Sadler's Wells) unraced son of middle-distance winning half-sister to Storm
Bird: 50/1, never dangerous in 18-runner maiden at Salisbury. *P. D. Cundell*

AGE OF REALITY (USA) 3 b.f. Alleged (USA) 138 – Isticanna (USA) 96 57
(Far North (CAN) 120) [1995 63p: 8m⁶ 7g 1996 11d 7m⁶ 10m² 10m 12g6 10.2g
Aug 26] big, strong filly: modest maiden handicapper: sold 7,000 gns Newmarket
September Sales: may prove suited by test of stamina: acts on good to firm ground:
blinkered (below form) final start. *H. Candy*

AGGIES DREAM 5 ch.g. Librate 91 – Achnahuaigh 79 (Known Fact (USA) –
135) [1995 NR 1996 a7g a10g⁶ Feb 20] leggy gelding: of little account. *J. M. Bradley*

AGNELLA (IRE) 3 b.f. Polish Patriot (USA) 128 – Annaberta (GER) (Alpen- 79 d
konig (GER)) [1995 84: 5m⁴ 6g* 7.3m 7g³ 1996 6g³ 8.1m 8.1m 8.1s 6g Nov 2]
good-topped filly: fair performer: reportedly operated on for chips in knees after final
2-y-o start: well beaten after 3-y-o reappearance: should stay 1m. *G. A. Butler*

AGOER 4 ch.f. Hadeer 118 – Abuzz 101 (Absalom 128) [1995 58: 7m² 6m² 7g⁴ –
7m⁵ 7m⁵ 8g 7s 7f* a7g a7g 1996 a10g a8g⁶ a8g Feb 12] modest handicapper: well
below form in 1996: should stay 1m: acts on good to firm going, well beaten on soft
(once) and the all-weather: sold 9,000 gns Newmarket December Sales, covered by
Mystiko. *C. E. Brittain*

AGONY AUNT 2 b.f. (Mar 7) Formidable (USA) 125 – Loch Clair (IRE) 53 75
(Lomond (USA) 128) [1996 7.1d⁴ 8.2g 8g⁵ Oct 25] robust filly: has scope: first foal:
dam, thrice-raced maiden half-sister to smart middle-distance filly Wind In Her Hair,
granddaughter of Highclere: fair form in maidens when slow-starting fourth to River
Usk at Haydock and fifth to Calypso Grant at Doncaster: poor effort in between:
seems likely to stay well. *Mrs J. Cecil*

AGWA 7 b.g. Local Suitor (USA) 128 – Meissarah (USA) (Silver Hawk (USA) 73 d
123) [1995 81: 6m 6m⁶ 5m³ 5g² 6m 6f⁶ 6m 6g 5s 5m a6g 1996 a6g⁶ a7g a8g 6f* 6f 6g
6m 5f⁶ a7g a7g Nov 15] small, sturdy gelding: only fair form when making all in
claimer at Brighton in April: well below even that form otherwise in 1996: stays 7f:
acts on firm ground (probably on soft) and on equitrack: usually races prominently:
broke blood vessel third 7-y-o start: inconsistent. *R. J. O'Sullivan*

AHJAY 6 br.g. Tina's Pet 121 – City Link Rose (Lochnager 132) [1995 60: 6g² 6m –
7g* 7g⁴ 8m³ 7g 7g⁵ 7d⁶ 7f 7f*dis 1996 6g 6m⁶ 7m 6s 7g 7f⁶ 8g 7m Sep 18] strong,
workmanlike gelding: well beaten in 1996, leaving T. J. Naughton after seventh start:
stays 1m: acts on any ground: inconsistent. *G. L. Moore*

AILESBURY HILL (USA) 3 ch.f. Woodman (USA) 126 – Golden Oriole 68
(USA) (Northern Dancer) [1995 77: 6f⁴ 7f² 8.1m² 8g 8.2d² 8g 1996 10g 12d 10m³
12g 10m⁵ 10.3m Sep 11] good-quartered, attractive filly: good walker: unimpressive
mover: fair maiden: rated on form at 1¼m, best efforts (at 2 yrs) over 1m: acts on
firm and dead ground: has been bandaged behind: made running last 2 starts:
inconsistent: sent to USA. *P. W. Chapple-Hyam*

AILLEACHT (USA) 4 b. or br.f. Chief's Crown (USA) – Poster Beauty (USA) 111
(Codex (USA)) [1995 7v 6m⁶* 8g 5g² 6m² 6g³ 5m² 6m* 7f 6g⁴ 5g* 7d 1996 5m²
5g² 5f 6m⁶ 5m* 5m 6g 6d* 5m² 5d 6s⁵ Oct 19] $50,000Y: quite attractive filly: fourth
foal: half-sister to minor winners in North America by Turkoman, Dahar (sprinter)

and Sunshine Forever: dam, placed twice from 6 starts, half-sister to dam of Dayjur: smart performer: narrowly won maiden at Naas and 2 handicaps at Leopardstown at 3 yrs: twice short-headed before winning from small fields in listed races at Tipperary in July by 1½ lengths from Sunset Reigns and (after found to be clinically abnormal eighth start) at Leopardstown in August by short head from Ger's Royale: ½-length second to Eveningpardsperformance (who was not at her best) in Flying Five at Leopardstown in September: behind in King's Stand Stakes fourth start: stays 6f: acts on good to firm ground and soft: races prominently: game. *J. S. Bolger, Ireland*

AIM FOR STARDOM   4 b.c. Polish Precedent (USA) 131 – Aim For The Top   62
(USA) 111 (Irish River (FR) 131) [1995 NR 1996 10s 8d⁴ 10g Apr 27] only 1,700 gns 3-y-o: lengthy colt: third reported foal: half-brother to useful pair Dancing Prize (11.5f listed third) and Dance To The Top (1993 2-y-o 7f winner), both by Sadler's Wells: dam 6f (at 2 yrs) to 8.5f winner, from good family: fourth of 14 in claimer at Warwick in April, only form: has tongue tied down. *M. J. Ahern*

AIM SEVEN   2 b.c. (Mar 31) Pursuit of Love 124 – Figini 74 (Glint of Gold 128)   74
[1996 6m 6f² 7.1m⁵ 5f⁴ 6m³ Oct 4] 26,000Y: good sort: has scope: sixth foal: half-brother to 3-y-o 6f (at 2 yrs) and 1m winner Mimosa (by Midyan), 8.2f winner Killy (by Dominion) and a winner in Germany: dam lightly-raced half-sister to high-class middle-distance colt Electric: fair form in maidens and a minor event: found 5f too sharp, raced too freely at 7f (should stay): has swished tail: sold 15,500 gns Newmarket Autumn Sales. *R. Hannon*

AIRBORNE HARRIS (IRE)   3 ch.g. Persian Heights 129 – Excuse Slip (USA)   68
(Damascus (USA)) [1995 NR 1996 7.1g⁵ a8g Dec 11] IR 2,000Y, 10,000 2-y-o: half-brother to 2 winners, including Assert Star (12.5f in Ireland by Assert): dam, placed in US, daughter of good juvenile filly Cut Class: 25/1 and in need of race, staying-on fifth of 10 in maiden at Haydock under 7-lb claimer on return: retained 600 gns Doncaster October Sales: last in claimer at Lingfield on return. *A. Bailey*

AIR COMMAND (BAR)   6 br.g. Concorde Hero (USA) 101 – Hubbardair 60   – §
(Town And Country 124) [1995 49§, a–§: a8g 9.7g 12.5g⁵ 10m⁶ 8g⁴ 10.5d³ 12f⁴ 12s 12g⁶ a12g 1996 a16g 8g 10.5d 11.5f 14m Jul 13] no longer of account. *C. T. Nash*

AIR COMMODORE (IRE)   5 b.g. Elegant Air 119 – Belle Enfant 87 (Beldale   90
Flutter (USA) 130) [1995 101: 8.1m² 8m 8m 8f* 8.1m⁶ 1996 7.6d 7m 8m³ Sep 21] strong, lengthy gelding: reportedly suffered recurrence of off-fore injury in July 1995 when with P. Cole: off course nearly 14 months before return: failed to reach peak form, well backed when third of 16 (taking long time to find full stride) in £17,800 event at Newbury: stays 1m well, and bred to stay 1¼m: acts on firm and soft ground: blinkered (well below form at Epsom) once as 3-y-o: bandaged at 5 yrs: held up/tracks leaders nowadays. *D. W. P. Arbuthnot*

AIR EXPRESS (IRE)   2 b.c. (Apr 26) Salse (USA) 128 – Ibtisamm (USA) 71   112
(Caucasus (USA) 127) [1996 6m² 6g³ 7m⁴ 7.1g³ 6m* 8g⁶ 7g³ Oct 18] well-made colt: eighth foal: half-brother to 4 winners, including 4-y-o 8.3f winner Rubbiyati (by Cadeaux Genereux) and useful 1¼m to 11.9f winner Aljazzaf (by Mtoto): dam 1m winner: smart performer: in frame in July Stakes at Newmarket, Lanson Champagne Stakes at Goodwood and Solario Stakes at Sandown second to fourth starts and in Dewhurst Stakes (best effort, beaten a head and a neck by In Command and Musical Pursuit) at Newmarket on final outing: made all in minor event at Yarmouth in September, beating Grand Lad readily by 1½ lengths: effective at 6f, ran well when sixth to Benny The Dip in Royal Lodge at 1m: has raced only on a sound surface. *C. E. Brittain*

AIR OF DISTINCTION (IRE)   2 br.f. (Apr 20) Distinctly North (USA) 115 –   96
Kaysama (FR) (Kenmare (FR) 125) [1996 7g⁴ 6d* 6.3g* 7g Sep 8] 7,000 F, IR 40,000Y: ninth foal: sister to useful 3-y-o Rabican (up to 7f) and half-sister to 4 winners, notably Kayfa (rated 106, 1m to 1¼m, by Shernazar): dam, winning French sprinter, half-sister to 3 listed winners, out of a useful French sprinter: useful Irish filly: won maiden at Leopardstown then 4-runner Anglesey Stakes at the Curragh (by 1½ lengths from Sharemono) in August: third race in a fortnight and well below best in Moyglare Stud Stakes at the Curragh, tracking pace on inside but quickly beaten 2f out: stays 6.3f. *A. P. O'Brien, Ireland*

AIR OF MYSTERY   4 ch.f. Ballad Rock 122 – Keep Looking (USA) (Mr Pros-   –
pector (USA)) [1995 –: 8.1d a7g 1996 a8g a8g Feb 23] of no account. *N. E. Berry*

AIR QUEST 3 b.c. Rainbow Quest (USA) 134 – Aryenne (FR) 125 (Green 95 +
Dancer (USA) 132) [1995 NR 1996 11d* 12.3g^5 May 7] tall colt: has a markedly
round action: eighth foal: brother to Quest For Fame and very useful stayer Silver
Rainbow and half-brother to 2 middle-distance winners, notably smart Yenda (by
Dancing Brave): dam, from fine family, won Criterium des Pouliches and Poule
d'Essai des Pouliches: won maiden at Newbury in April by 5 lengths: favourite and
looking very well, looked ill-at-ease on track when only fifth of 6 in Chester Vase 18
days later: said by trainer to have returned very sore: should be very well suited by
1½m+: reported in July as having been put away until 1997. *R. Charlton*

AIR WING 3 ch.c. Risk Me (FR) 127 – Greenstead Lass (Double-U-Jay 120) –
[1995 83p: 5m^3 5g* 1996 6.1g 6m 5m 5g 6g 8g 9g Nov 1] strong colt: unimpressive
mover: well beaten in 1996: tried visored. *M. H. Tompkins*

AJAAD ALJAREE (IRE) 3 b.c. Sadler's Wells (USA) 132 – Impudent Miss –
105 (Persian Bold 123) [1995 NR 1996 10m Apr 16] 105,000Y: smallish, stocky,
angular colt: half-brother to several winners, including Good Reference (up to 1m,
by Reference Point): dam, Irish 2-y-o 5f winner, half-sister to very smart sprinter
Sayyaf: 16/1, very burly and green and moved poorly to post, always in rear in
maiden at Newmarket: remains in training. *A. C. Stewart*

AJAYIB (USA) 2 b.f. (Apr 13) Riverman (USA) 131 – Maplejinsky (USA) 73
(Nijinsky (CAN) 138) [1996 7g^2 7m^2 8.1g* Aug 26] fourth foal: half-sister to
high-class American 1m/1¼m performer Sky Beauty (by Blushing Groom): dam US
Grade 1 winner at 9f and 1¼m, closely related to Dayjur: made all at good pace and
just held on from Nile Valley in maiden at Chepstow: will stay 1¼m: may do better.
J. L. Dunlop

AJDAR 5 b.g. Slip Anchor 136 – Loucoum (FR) 93 (Iron Duke (FR) 122) [1995 –: 52
a12g^6 1996 a11g* a13g^2 a11g^5 11.9f^2 15.4f^4 12.3g^4 12m 12m 10.1g^5 11.6m^6 Jul 22] a55
angular gelding: modest handicapper: often runs in amateurs races, winner at Southwell in January: finds 1¼m a bare minimum, and stays 15.4f: acts on firm ground and
the all-weather: visored (well beaten) only 4-y-o start: has joined O. Brennan. *Miss
Gay Kelleway*

AJKUIT (IRE) 3 b.g. Persian Heights 129 – Hazar (IRE) 75 (Thatching 131) –
[1995 –: 6.9g 1996 10g 8g a8g Dec 13] no worthwhile form. *J. J. Sheehan*

AJNAD (IRE) 2 b.c. (Apr 23) Efisio 120 – Lotte Lenta (Gorytus (USA) 132) –
[1996 6g Aug 25] IR 58,000Y: third foal: dam unraced: 25/1, fourteenth of 19 in
median auction maiden at Goodwood. *C. J. Benstead*

AKALIM 3 b.g. Petong 126 – Tiszta Sharok 81 (Song 132) [1995 83: 6.1m^6 6m^5 –
6m* 6g 6g^6 6.1m* 1996 6m 6m^6 6f 5m Jul 6] good-topped gelding: has a quick
action: poor efforts after encouraging reappearance: sold (D. Morley to L. Cottrell)
10,000 gns Doncaster August Sales and gelded: stays 6f. *D. Morley*

AKHLA (USA) 3 ch.f. Nashwan (USA) 135 – Beautiful River (USA) (Irish River 84
(FR) 131) [1995 NR 1996 10d^4 10m* Jun 8] $100,000Y: good-topped, plain filly:
has scope: fourth foal: half-sister to winning sprinters in USA by Storm Bird and
Soviet Star: dam, minor winner at around 1m, is half-sister to Grade 1 9f winner
Beautiful Melody: 25/1, promising fourth of 16 to Shantou in maiden at Sandown
before winning maiden at Newmarket in June: looked sure to progress: stud.
H. R. A. Cecil

AKIL (IRE) 4 b.c. Cyrano de Bergerac 120 – Nonnita 71 (Welsh Saint 126) [1995 99
94: 7.1g^3 8.5m* 7.3m 8.1m* 8d* 7d 7.9m^2 9d 1996 8d 8.1g 8m^5 8m 7m 7m 7.3m^2
7g* Aug 24] close-coupled colt: useful handicapper: fluent mover: career-best effort
to win rated stakes at Goodwood in August, setting less than a true pace: stays 1m
(not beaten by trip at 9f): acts on good to firm and dead ground: blinkered
(unfavourably drawn) sixth 4-y-o start: not so consistent as at 3 yrs: sent to Dubai.
R. W. Armstrong

AKIYMANN (USA) 6 b.g. El Gran Senor (USA) 136 – Akila (FR) (Top Ville 54
129) [1995 NR 1996 16m^2 11.9d^5 9.7m Jul 15] useful-looking gelding: half-brother
to several middle-distance winners in France: dam unraced daughter of Licata, dam
also of Acamas, Akiyda and Akarad: has run in claimers on flat, soon off bit in rear
and staying on late first 2 starts: needs further than 9.7f (stays 2m): fair but ungenuine
hurdler. *M. C. Pipe*

AKOLA ANGEL 4 ch.f. Indian Ridge 123 – Heavenly Note 82 (Chief Singer – 131) [1995 –: 7.1m 6m a10g 1996 a11g Jan 5] no form on flat. *C. R. Egerton*

ALABANG 5 ch.g. Valiyar 129 – Seleter (Hotfoot 126) [1995 51+: 10.3m³ 8.5d 77 7f⁵ 1996 7m 9m* 9.2g² 10m⁴ 10.1m* 10.3m⁴ 10f² 10m* 11f⁵ Aug 9] plain, quite good-topped gelding: fair handicapper: won at Redcar in May, Newcastle in June and Nottingham (strongly-run minor event, cruising through over 2f out) in July: stays 1¼m: acts on firm ground, seldom raced on a soft surface: sometimes slowly away: easy winner of both novice hurdles late in year. *M. J. Camacho*

AL ABRAQ (IRE) 3 b.c. Reprimand 122 – Dazzling Maid (IRE) 64 (Tate Gallery 92 (USA) 117) [1995 89p: 7.1m* 7d⁶ 1996 8.1g⁶ 8f 8m⁴ 10m Aug 2] attractive, good-bodied colt: fairly useful handicapper: looked in outstanding condition last 2 starts, improved form at Newmarket but behind (over 1¼m) in £34,000 event at Goodwood: best at up to 1m: acts on firm and dead ground. *J. W. Hills*

ALAFLAK (IRE) 5 b.h. Caerleon (USA) 132 – Safe Haven (Blakeney 126) 84 [1995 a9g 1996 10.9m 8f⁶ 10.2g² 10.2m* 10m⁵ 11.9m 12m Sep 7] good-bodied horse: fairly useful handicapper: accomplished little in 3 races in Dubai in 1995/6: won at Chepstow in July: tongue tied, pulled up final start: sold only 2,000 gns Newmarket Autumn Sales: should stay 1½m (beaten too far out to blame trip when tried): probably acts on firm and dead going: lacks a turn of foot. *Major W. R. Hern*

ALAJYAL (IRE) 3 ch.f. Kris 135 – Yaqut (USA) 77 (Northern Dancer) [1995 NR 1996 7d 7d 8f 10m 8f Aug 5] well-made filly: fifth foal: half-sister to 3 winners, notably useful Estimraar (10.2f to 1¼m, by Bustino): dam 2-y-o 7f winner from family of Alydar: no worthwhile form: has looked headstrong: visits Green Desert. *P. T. Walwyn*

ALAKHLUKI 3 b.f. Aragon 118 – Hawaiian Bloom (USA) 87 (Hawaii) [1995 44 57p: 6d⁶ 7.1s 6m⁵ 1996 5d 5.1g 7g⁴ 8g a10g Nov 14] workmanlike filly: maiden: failed by long way to repeat 2-y-o form: finished lame final start. *G. Lewis*

ALAMBAR (IRE) 3 b.c. Fairy King (USA) – Lightino (Bustino 136) [1995 71: 78 7d 7g² 7g² 1996 9.9m⁶ 8d² 8.5m* 9m² 8.2f⁴ 10.1m³ 12g⁵ 10.5s Oct 5] tall, good-topped colt: has a quick action: unimpressive walker: fair handicapper: made all in maiden at Beverley in June: sold 15,500 gns Newmarket Autumn Sales: effective at 1m to 1¼m (not 1½m): acts on firm and dead ground, possibly not soft: sometimes a front runner: consistent. *P. T. Walwyn*

ALAMEIN (USA) 3 ch.g. Roi Danzig (USA) – Pollination 100 (Pentotal) [1995 87 77: 6m 7m³ 6m³ 6m⁴ 1996 6m³ 7g* 7f* 8f⁶ 7.1m³ Jul 5] workmanlike gelding: fairly useful performer: won maiden at Catterick and minor event at Thirsk, then good efforts in handicaps at Royal Ascot (Britannia) and Sandown, all within 5 weeks: stays 1m: acts on firm ground, unraced on a soft surface: blinkered since second 3-y-o start: tends to carry head slightly high: consistent. *W. J. Haggas*

ALANA'S BALLAD (IRE) 3 b.f. Be My Native (USA) 122 – Radalgo (Ballad – Rock 122) [1995 NR 1996 10.5d 10.8g May 25] IR 1,000Y: leggy filly: fourth foal: dam tailed off only outing: no promise. *B. P. J. Baugh*

ALARABY (IRE) 4 b.f. Caerleon (USA) 132 – Circo 77 (High Top 131) [1995 – 77: 10.5m 10g⁴ 10.2h⁵ 14m* 12m³ 14d⁶ 14m² 1996 14.1g Apr 22] smallish, lengthy filly: tailed off only start for new stable: should stay 2m: acts on good to firm ground. *Martyn Wane*

ALARICO (FR) 3 ch.g. Kadrou (FR) 126 – Calabria (FR) (Vitiges (FR) 132) – [1995 NR 1996 10g 10s Oct 24] 30,000 francs F: 120,000 francs Y: strong gelding: sixth foal: half-brother to 2 winners in France, including prolific middle-distance performer Calagueto (by Galetto): dam French 6f winner: well beaten in maidens at Nottingham (unruly in stalls, slowly away) and Newbury 15 days later. *I. P. Williams*

ALASKA 3 b.f. Polar Falcon (USA) 126 – Priceless Bond (USA) 75 (Blushing 68 d Groom (FR) 131) [1995 8g⁵ 1996 8s 9d⁵ 11m 9m 7d² 7m 9m a8.5g 8m Oct 7] light-bodied ex-Irish filly: second foal: dam, 9f winner at 2 yrs, stayed 1¼m, half-sister to high-class middle-distance colt Majesty's Prince: fair maiden: left P. Doyle after seventh 3-y-o outing: well beaten last 4 starts: seems to stay 11f: blinkered (not on all-weather) since fifth 3-y-o start: inconsistent: sent to South Korea. *M. G. Meagher*

AL AVA CONSONANT   2 b.f. (Mar 28) Reprimand 122 – Dragonist 82 (Drag-   63 ?
onara Palace (USA) 115) [1996 5m⁶ 5m³ 6m 7g 8g Sep 25] 4,000Y: tall, unfurnished
filly: sister to a modest maiden and half-sister to useful sprinter Come On Chase
Me (by Sharpo) and middle-distance winners by Ardross and Homing: dam winning
sprinter: staying-on third in maiden at Beverley in July, easily best effort: bred to
sprint: not easy to assess. *J. D. Bethell*

AL AZHAR   2 b.c. (Feb 9) Alzao (USA) 117 – Upend 120 (Main Reef 126) [1996   92 P
7m² 8.1g* 8m* Sep 12] 100,000Y: well-made colt: fourth foal: half-brother to useful
middle-distance performer Shortfall (by Last Tycoon): dam, 1¼m and 1½m winner,
half-sister to dam of Royal Gait: easy winner from Panama City of Chepstow maiden
in August: followed up in valuable 17-runner nursery at Doncaster (ridden out after
looking likely to win well) in September: will stay at least 1¼m: capable of much
better form and looks a smart colt in the making. *I. A. Balding*

ALBAHA (USA)   3 br.g. Woodman (USA) 126 – Linda's Magic (USA) 114 (Far   81
North (CAN) 120) [1995 81: 6g³ 7g⁶ 7m⁴ 1996 9g 7m⁵ 7g 6d² 6m 6f³ 10m⁴ 8.5m
10m 12g a12g* Dec 27] big, robust gelding: fairly useful handicapper at his best:
left R. Armstrong after eighth start: very easy winner of maiden at Southwell in
December: stays 1½m: acts on good to firm and dead ground, and on fibresand:
blinkered fourth (only good effort in them) to sixth 3-y-o starts: usually races
prominently: inconsistent. *J. E. Banks*

ALBERT THE BEAR   3 b.g. Puissance 110 – Florentynna Bay 61 (Aragon 118)   80
[1995 75: 5.1g 5m 5m⁵ a6g 5f* 5.7h* 6m* 6.1m⁴ 6m² 6d 1996 6g 5.7m² 7m* 7f²
7m⁵ 7d³ Aug 30] tall, leggy, useful-looking gelding: easy mover: fairly useful
handicapper: won at Chester (goes well there) in June: stays 7f: acts on hard and dead
ground, showed nothing on fibresand: consistent. *J. Berry*

AL BLU (IRE)   2 br.c. (Apr 22) Exit To Nowhere (USA) 122 – Kiri 85 (Kris 135)   75
[1996 6g⁶ 7d Oct 2] approx. 25,000Y: seventh foal: half-brother to 2 winners in USA,
notably smart horse Kiri's Clown (by Foolish Pleasure), Grade 1 1½m winner
in 1995: dam 8.5f winner in USA out of half-sister to very good broodmare
Miss Manon: staying-on seventh of 18 in maiden at Salisbury final start: dead.
L. M. Cumani

ALCALALI (USA)   2 ch.f. (Mar 26) Septieme Ciel (USA) 123 – Princess Verna   94 p
(USA) (Al Hattab (USA)) [1996 10s Nov 2] $18,000Y: half-sister to several minor
winners in USA: dam lightly-raced maiden: 283/10, 8¼ lengths seventh of 10 to
Shaka in Criterium de Saint-Cloud on debut:clearly good enough to win a race.
P. A. Kelleway

ALDANEH   4 ch.f. Indian Ridge 123 – Maiyaasah 75 (Kris 135) [1995 77: 7m*   –
8m 7.6m² 7g⁴ 8.3m* 8.1d 8f⁴ 1996 8m 10.3g 10m Jun 27] lengthy filly: fair
performer: well below form in 1996: stays 8.3f: acts on firm ground: inconsistent.
R. Hannon

ALDEVONIE   4 b.f. Green Desert (USA) 127 – Kintail 76 (Kris 135) [1995 75p: 66
8.1g² 1996 8f May 6] off course nearly a year, failed to repeat debut form in maiden at
Warwick, prominent long way: will stay 1¼m: sold 6,400 gns Newmarket December
Sales. *H. R. A. Cecil*

ALESSANDRA   3 ch.f. Generous (IRE) 139 – Kiss 88 (Habitat 134) [1995 81:   101
6g² 7m⁵ 7.1d² 1996 10g² 11.4g⁴ 12.1g* 12m 12.5g⁴ 12g⁶ Sep 29] good-topped filly:
useful performer: made all in maiden at Chepstow in June: improved form when 2
lengths fourth of 10 to Vadsa Honor in listed race at Deauville: should be suited by
further than 12.5f: acts on good to firm and dead ground. *B. W. Hills*

ALESSIA   4 b.f. Caerleon (USA) 132 – Kiss 88 (Habitat 134) [1995 91: 10m⁵ 10m⁴   –
12d 8s 1996 7.1d 8.5m 8.1s Oct 22] robust filly: fairly useful as 3-y-o: well beaten
for new stable in 1996: stays 1¼m: acts on good to firm ground and dead: blinkered
second 4-y-o start. *W. R. Muir*

ALEZAL   2 b.c. (Feb 21) Anshan 119 – Dance On The Stage (Dancing Brave   81 p
(USA) 140) [1996 7m² Oct 23] 5,200Y: first foal: dam unraced daughter of smart
1¼m performer Gesedeh, half-sister to Ardross and Larrocha: 25/1, slow-starting
¾-length second of 11, clear, to Sekari in maiden at Yarmouth, travelling smoothly
then running on strongly: will stay 1¼m: sure to improve, and should win a race.
W. Jarvis

ALFAHAAL (IRE) 3 b.c. Green Desert (USA) 127 – Fair of The Furze 112 – (Ela-Mana-Mou 132) [1995 62+: 7.1d 7d 1996 7g May 4] robust, well-bred colt: modest maiden: never dangerous after stumbling start at Thirsk only 3-y-o start: cost 280,000 gns as a yearling but sold (H. Thomson Jones to R. F. Johnson Houghton) 6,400 gns Newmarket July Sales. *H. Thomson Jones*

ALFAHAD 3 b.c. Doyoun 124 – Moogie 103 (Young Generation 129) [1995 NR – 1996 10.5d 9m Jun 21] 4,200Y, 8,400 2-y-o: fourth foal: closely related to fair 1994 2-y-o 6f winner Mood Swings (by Shirley Heights): dam 2-y-o 6f winner suited by 9f at 3 yrs: behind in maidens: joined Dr. J. D. Scargill. *Miss Gay Kelleway*

ALFAYZA 3 b.f. Danehill (USA) 126 – Dahlawise (IRE) 76 (Caerleon (USA) 51 132) [1995 63: 5g⁶ 5g⁶ 5f⁵ 5m⁴ 5g² 7h* 7.1m⁴ 8g 1996 8m a7g 10m 8f⁶ 8g 6.9f⁶ 8.2d⁴ a33 10.4g 10.1m² 12g a10g³ Nov 14] close-coupled filly: modest handicapper: should prove effective at 1½m: acts on hard ground: inconsistent: sold 5,700 gns Newmarket December Sales. *J. D. Bethell*

ALFREDO ALFREDO (USA) 4 b.g. Miswaki (USA) 124 – Alleged Queen 71 p (USA) (Alleged (USA) 138) [1995 NR 1996 8m⁴ 7m⁶ 10d⁵ Aug 10] $52,000F, $42,000Y: first foal: dam unraced: twice caught the eye under tender handling in maidens at Warwick in July: 11/8 favourite, rather disappointing on dead ground at Ayr in August: subsequently gelded: should stay at least 1m: looked worth another chance: stays in training. *J. L. Dunlop*

AL HAAL (USA) 7 b.g. Northern Baby (CAN) 127 – Kit's Double (USA) – (Spring Double) [1995 NR 1996 a12g a13g⁵ Dec 31] fair maiden (rated 68) at 3 yrs for P. Walwyn: winning hurdler since, but no worthwhile form on return to flat. *R. J. O'Sullivan*

ALHAARTH (IRE) 3 b.c. Unfuwain (USA) 131 – Irish Valley (USA) (Irish 123 River (FR) 131) [1995 126p: 7g* 7f* 7.1m* 7g* 7m* 1996 8m² 8m⁴ 12m⁵ 12m 8m³ 8g³ 8d* Oct 6]

The five straight wins of 1995 were followed by six straight defeats —Alhaarth's three-year-old season was not quite what had been predicted. At the start of April, he was 6/4 favourite for the Two Thousand Guineas and 3/1 favourite for the Derby. His drubbing of Danehill Dancer in the Dewhurst (the last of four pattern wins, in the course of which he had faced just thirteen opponents) was better form than anything achieved by his fellow two-year-olds, and he looked set for better still. When the wraps came off, however, it turned out that Alhaarth had not improved by even a pound more than normal weight for age. At least, he did not show that he had on the racecourse, but reports of his laziness were rife and tactical changes later in the year seemed to centre on efforts to wake him up. Things did not, however, go nearly so badly as with the only serious contender for Alhaarth's two-year-old crown, Royal Applause. He failed to come close to his juvenile form. Alhaarth, contrastingly, performed to a consistently high level, but others improved past him. Some shot by.

For much of the season, those who clung to Alhaarth as the top horse of his generation could still muster some hope, or excuses. First off, the Craven Stakes had been run at a muddling pace and Alhaarth was beaten by only a neck by Beauchamp King, after pulling hard. In the Guineas, for which he started favourite at 2/1, Alhaarth came in fourth overall but best of those who raced on apparently softer ground up the centre. The chief hope for him, though, was that he needed middle distances—his sire, after all, had not even attempted less than

Prix du Rond-Point, Longchamp—it is October before Alhaarth wins as a three-year-old; he is followed in by Shaanxi and Bin Rosie

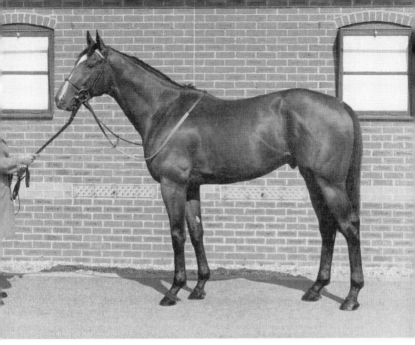

Hamdan Al Maktoum's "Alhaarth"

		Northern Dancer (b 1961)	Nearctic Natalma
	Unfuwain (USA) (b 1985)		
		Height of Fashion (b 1979)	Bustino Highclere
Alhaarth (IRE) (b.c. 1993)			
		Irish River (ch 1976)	Riverman Irish Star
	Irish Valley (USA) (ch 1982)		
		Green Valley (br 1967)	Val de Loir Sly Pola

one and a half miles as a three-year-old. The outcome of the Derby, however, did not differ much from that of the Guineas; this time Alhaarth was sent off a 15/2 co-fourth favourite and, staying on in fifth, it wasn't the trip that beat him. A new theory, that he hadn't been putting it all in, gained some credence when it was announced that he would wear blinkers in the Irish Derby, one paper reporting that they had recently galvanised him into beating gallops companion Lower Egypt by twenty lengths, compared to one length just before the Derby. Alhaarth's performance at the Curragh was indeed transformed but, unfortunately, this time it was his turn to be beaten almost out of sight: hard to settle, he made headway on the turn but was a spent force two and a half furlongs out. After that, it was back to the drawing board and back to a mile. Third with the blinkers on in the Sussex Stakes was followed by third again without them, but with new forcing tactics, in the Celebration Mile. These tactical permutations were completed—front-running, with the blinkers back on—in the Prix du Rond-Point at Longchamp on Arc day. Speedily away from his inside stall, Alhaarth was never headed. Shaanxi made a creditable bid to peg him back, but the eight other runners in this Group 2 race hardly mattered.

The issue of Alhaarth's stamina provoked lengthy debate at the end of his two-year-old season and is not a lot clearer now. On pedigree, sire Unfuwain is set against dam Irish Valley (a half-sister to Green Dancer) whose disappointing racing career ended over six and a half furlongs. To repeat, Alhaarth shaped as if he stayed a mile and a half in the Derby. That is clearly much too far when the blinkers are fitted though, and, thanks to the Rond-Point, Alhaarth's best three-year-old form (by some 4 lb) is at a mile. It is also on dead ground, but his efforts as a two-year-old suggest that that at least is misleading. A mile and a quarter may yet enter calculations because the good news is that, after wintering in Dubai, Alhaarth is due to race again as a four-year-old. He will be the first top-rated two-year-old to do so since the 1988 Dewhurst dead-heater Scenic. A strong, well-made colt, Alhaarth is a good mover with a powerful action. *Major W. R. Hern*

ALHAWA (USA)   3 ch.c. Mt Livermore (USA) – Petrava (NZ) (Imposing (AUS))   83 [1995 76p: 7g* 1996 7.6m* 10d 8f 10m⁶ 8m 8.1g 8d Oct 12] unfurnished colt: fairly useful performer: gamely won minor event at Lingfield in May: creditable efforts in 3 competitive handicaps afterwards: sold 24,000 gns Newmarket Autumn Sales: stays 1¼m: possibly needs a sound surface: blinkered (below form, dead ground) final start. *C. J. Benstead*

AL HELAL   4 b.c. In The Wings 128 – Rosia Bay 102 (High Top 131) [1995 NR   59 d 1996 10g 12g³ 16d 12g 16g 9g⁴ 9g⁴ a12g⁶ Oct 5] inconsistent maiden: ran once in Britain at 2 yrs: trained until after seventh 4-y-o start by A. Mullins in Ireland: little form last 5 starts: tried blinkered, no improvement. *J. R. Jenkins*

ALICIA (IRE)   3 b. or br.f. Darshaan 133 – Tribal Rite 95 (Be My Native (USA)   73 122) [1995 –p: 7g 1996 10m 10m⁴ 11.9d² 14m⁵ 11.5d 10.3g³ 11f Nov 5] leggy filly: fair maiden handicapper: should stay beyond 1½m: acts on dead ground, probably on good to firm: sometimes wanders/hangs under pressure: inconsistent: sold 40,000 gns Newmarket December Sales. *J. L. Dunlop*

ALICIA LEA (IRE)   4 b.f. Cyrano de Bergerac 120 – Sasha Lea (Cawston's   – Clown 113) [1995 NR 1996 a7g Nov 15] half-sister to a winning selling hurdler: dam never ran: soon behind in claimer at Lingfield. *A. Moore*

ALIFANDANGO (IRE)   2 b.f. (Mar 14) Alzao (USA) 117 – Fandangerina   – p (USA) (Grey Dawn II 132) [1996 8m Oct 17] 28,000F, 70,000Y: useful-looking filly: sister to 4-y-o Alzoomo, closely related to 2 winners, including useful 1987 2-y-o 6f and 7f winner Western Gun (by Lypheor), and half-brother to 2 winners, including useful 7f (at 2 yrs) to 12.2f winner Ocean Air (by Elegant Air): dam won at up to 1m in USA: 20/1 and green, never-dangerous eighth of 17 to Royal Crusade in maiden at Newmarket: will improve. *A. C. Stewart*

A LIKELY TALE (USA)   3 b.c. Alleged (USA) 138 – Thatsallshewrote (USA)   81 (Graustark) [1995 78p: 8d⁴ 1996 11.8s³ Mar 28] tall, sparely-made colt: has a round action: third of 5 in maiden at Leicester. *M. Bell*

ALIKHLAS   2 b. or br.f. (Mar 9) Lahib (USA) 129 – Mathaayl (USA) 79 (Shadeed   81 (USA) 135) [1996 6m² 6m Sep 7] tall, lengthy, rather unfurnished filly: has scope: first foal: dam, 6f and 1¼m winner, half-sister to useful 1988 2-y-o 6f winner Muhbubh: 2 lengths second of 5 to Well Warned in maiden at Haydock in August: something may have been amiss only subsequent start (favourite): bred to stay 1m: joined R. Hern. *H. Thomson Jones*

ALIMERJAM   2 b.f. (Feb 20) Thowra (FR) – Sicilian Vespers 44 (Mummy's   – Game 120) [1996 5g 5s⁴ 6g⁵ 6m 6g 8f⁶ a8g⁶ a10g Nov 26] well-grown, good-topped filly: third live foal: sister to 4-y-o 1¾m winner Bellara: dam won 7f seller: little worthwhile form. *J. White*

ALI-ROYAL (IRE)   3 b.c. Royal Academy (USA) 130 – Alidiva 105 (Chief   118 Singer 131) [1995 87p: 7g⁴ 7g* 1996 8m³ 7g* 7m⁵ 8m 7m² 8f² 8d* 8g* Nov 2] rather leggy colt: smart performer: won listed race at Newmarket in May by 8 lengths from Rabican, minor event at Bath in September by 12 lengths from Nijo and steadily-run listed race back at Newmarket in November (never far away, quickening on well over

King Charles II Stakes, Newmarket—an eight-length winner in Ali-Royal

1f out) by 1¼ lengths from Nijo: effective at 7f and 1m: acts on firm and dead ground: a little out of depth in Sussex Stakes fourth start, otherwise most consistent: stays in training. *H. R. A. Cecil*

ALISADARA 2 b.f. (Apr 11) Nomination 125 – Nishara (Nishapour (FR) 125) [1996 a5g⁴ 6g⁴ 6d⁴ 6m 7m 6g⁵ 6m⁶ 5m⁶ 7d Aug 10] 500Y: sparely-made filly: first foal: dam poor half-sister to Irish 2000 Guineas winner Dara Monarch: poor maiden on balance of form: stays 6f: best run on a soft surface: blinkered (no improvement) penultimate start. *N. Bycroft* —

ALIS PRINCESS 3 ch.f. Sayf El Arab (USA) 127 – Princess Zeddera (English Prince 129) [1995 –: 7.5m 1996 8m Jun 17] off course nearly 10 months, soundly beaten in seller. *M. P. Bielby* —

ALISURA 3 br.f. Lead On Time (USA) 123 – Iosifa 108 (Top Ville 129) [1995 –p: 7.1s 1996 10m⁵ 11.5g⁵ 12f³ 16m 14d a12g Dec 20] smallish, lengthy, sparely-made filly: modest maiden: better at around 1½m than shorter and should stay further: acts on firm ground, no worthwhile form on a soft surface or all-weather: sold out of J. Fanshawe's stable 3,700 gns Newmarket Autumn Sales after penultimate start. *D. T. Thom* 65

ALJAZ 6 b.g. Al Nasr (FR) 126 – Santa Linda (USA) (Sir Ivor 135) [1995 64d: a7g⁴ a7g³ a7g a6g³ a7g⁶ a6g³ a6g 6v* 7m a7g 7.1d a6g⁶ a6g a6g 1996 5s a6g⁴ a5g* a6g⁵ 5.1g a6g a5g² a5g⁵ Dec 28] modest handicapper: won at Wolverhampton in August: stays 7f: acts on fibresand and on heavy ground: blinkered (no improvement) final 5-y-o start: inconsistent. *Miss Gay Kelleway* 52

ALKARINE 4 gr.g. Alias Smith (USA) – Colly Cone 52 (Celtic Cone 116) [1995 NR 1996 a14g Mar 1] fourth foal: dam middle-distance stayer: no promise over hurdles or (visored) in claimer: sold 2,000 gns Ascot July Sales. *M. P. Bielby* —

ALKATEB 4 ch.g. Rock City 120 – Corley Moor 97 (Habitat 134) [1995 98: 9f* 10.2m³ 8.1m* 10g² 10m⁴ 10g⁵ 1996 10d³ Oct 12] big, workmanlike gelding: unimpressive mover: useful performer: injured again when creditable third of 8 to Proper Blue in rated stakes at Ascot on belated return, hanging right under pressure: stays 1¼m well: acts on firm and dead ground. *Miss Gay Kelleway* 98

ALL APOLOGIES (IRE) 4 b.g. Common Grounds 118 – Living Rough (Wolverlife 115) [1995 10g 7d 1996 a7g a7g⁵ a7g* a7g a6g a5g a7g a7g⁶ Jun 8] ex-Irish gelding: fourth foal: dam Irish 7f winner: 33/1 and claimer ridden, worthwhile form only when winning 6-runner maiden at Wolverhampton in February by 5 lengths, making all: sold 1,500 gns Doncaster October Sales. *R. Hollinshead* 66 d

ALLEGRO 2 b.c. (Mar 9) Night Shift (USA) – Merry Rous 66 (Rousillon (USA) 133) [1996 6f² 6g Sep 29] 45,000Y: third foal: half-brother to 3-y-o 5f (at 2 yrs) and 59 +

7.5f winner Clincher Club (by Polish Patriot) and 1994 2-y-o 5f winner Bruton Stream (by Taufan): dam, 2-y-o 6f winner, half-sister to smart sprinter Tina's Pet: set strong pace when second in maiden at Brighton in August: only seventh of 8 in similar event at Hamilton following month: bred to stay 1m: sent to UAE. *D. R. Loder*

ALLEZ CYRANO (IRE)   5 b.g. Alzao (USA) 117 – Miss Bergerac (Bold Lad   71 (IRE) 133) [1995 –: 8m 8f 7.3m 10m 7g 1996 a7g* a7g⁴ a16g⁶ 8d² 6.9f 7d May 6] leggy gelding: seems fair at best nowadays: won claimer at Wolverhampton in February, making virtually all: sold 2,000 gns Newmarket Autumn Sales: stays 1m: acts on firm and dead ground and on fibresand: inconsistent. *M. Bell*

ALLEZ PABLO   6 b.g. Crisp 87 – Countess Mariga (Amboise 113) [1995 NR 1996 8.1d 10f 9.7g⁶ 14m 14d Oct 2] small, leggy gelding: no worthwhile form: blinkered on debut. *R. Rowe*

ALLIED ACADEMY   2 ch.c. (Feb 13) Royal Academy (USA) 130 – Tsungani   67 p 64 (Cure The Blues (USA)) [1996 8g⁶ 6m⁶ Oct 4] short-backed colt: fourth foal: half-brother to 5-y-o 8.5f to 15.4f winner Ayunli (by Chief Singer): dam, 2-y-o 6f winner, is half-sister to useful 1983 2-y-o 6f winner Keep Tapping: never-dangerous sixth of 12 to Bint Albaadiya at Lingfield on second start, better effort: should stay beyond 6f. *S. C. Williams*

ALL IN GOOD TIME   3 b.g. Shadeed (USA) 135 – Good Thinking (USA) – (Raja Baba (USA)) [1995 –: 7g 1996 a8g 9.2d 12.1m 14.1m Jul 29] rather leggy, angular gelding: no form, and possibly ungenuine: sold 1,300 gns Doncaster September Sales. *C. W. Thornton*

ALL IN LEATHER   2 b.f. (Feb 1) Saddlers' Hall (IRE) 126 – Ivana (IRE) 82   76 (Taufan (USA) 119) [1996 6g³ 7.6m³ 7f³ Oct 14] first foal: dam, placed over 7f/ 1m, seemed irresolute: progressive form when third in maidens, keeping on ¾ length behind Vanishing Trick at Leicester last time out: will stay 1¼m. *W. J. Haggas*

ALLINSON'S MATE (IRE)   8 b.g. Fayruz 116 – Piney Pass (Persian Bold 123)   70 [1995 79, a71: a8g a7g⁴ a7g⁶ a7g⁵ a7g³ 6.9m* 8m⁵ 7m⁵ 7g 7g* 7f⁴ 7m* 7m² 7h³ 7.6m³ 7g 7g 7g 1996 a6g⁶ a7g⁴ a7g a7g⁵ 7s⁵ 7.5m 8g 7g 7.1g 7g⁴ 7g⁴ 7m⁶ 7m 8.1g⁴ 7.1g* 7.1m³ 7m⁶ 7m 7m⁴ 8g⁴ 7g⁶ 7g* 7g⁵ a8g³ a7g Nov 29] small, robust gelding: carries penalty: unimpressive mover: fair handicapper: generally not so good as at 7yrs, but won at Musselburgh in July and at Catterick (fifteenth success, ridden by 7-lb claimer, clearly best 8-y-o effort) in October: effective at 7f to 8.5f: acts on firm ground, dead and all-weather: sometimes blinkered/visored: usually held up: tough: retained 3,000 gns Doncaster November Sales. *T. D. Barron*

ALL IS FAIR   2 b.f. (Feb 25) Selkirk (USA) 129 – Allegra 73 (Niniski (USA)   79 p 125) [1996 6m³ 6f* 7g Sep 6] big, good-topped filly: has plenty of scope: third foal: half-sister to Irish 3-y-o Ludden Chief (by Be My Chief): dam, 1½m winner, half-sister to Irish Oaks third Arrikala and Last Second: readily won maiden at Hamilton in August: raced freely but still did well when seventh to One So Wonderful in minor event at Kempton final start: bred to stay 1¼m: will probably do better. *Sir Mark Prescott*

ALLMOSA   7 b.m. Alleging (USA) 120 – Wimosa 92 (Mossborough 126) [1995   – –: 10g 17.2m⁵ 14.1g⁴ 1996 16s 16d 16.1f 16.1m Aug 26] leggy, close-coupled mare: no form since fair 5-y-o: stays 2½m: acts on any going. *T. J. Naughton*

ALL ON   5 ch.m. Dunbeath (USA) 127 – Fresh Line 60 (High Line 125) [1995 46:   37 a12g⁵ a12g* a12g⁶ 14.1m 9.9d² 9.9m³ a12g⁵ a12g 10.9g 10g 1996 16.2m⁵ a12g²   a59 a12g* 12g³ a14g Dec 3] workmanlike mare: modest handicapper: improved to win at Wolverhampton in October by 10 lengths: effective at 1½m and shapes as if stays 2m: acts on dead ground, best form on fibresand. *J. Hetherton*

ALL STAND   3 ch.f. Dominion 123 – Now In Session (USA) (Diesis 133) [1995   58 NR 1996 7d 7m⁵ 7f 10m Oct 24] 2,400Y: angular filly: third reported foal: half-sister to a 1¼m winner in Holland by Warrshan: dam unraced: modest maiden: should stay beyond 7f. *Major D. N. Chappell*

ALLSTARS DANCER   3 b.f. Primo Dominie 121 – Danzig Harbour (USA)   35 (Private Account (USA)) [1995 –: a7g a8g 1996 a7g⁵ a6g⁴ 7.6m 6m 5g Sep 7] poor sprint maiden. *T. J. Naughton*

ALLSTARS EXPRESS 3 b.c. Rambo Dancer (CAN) 107 – Aligote (Nebbiolo 70
125) [1995 NR 1996 7g a8g³ 8g³ 10f* 9f³ 10g⁵ 10f² 10.8f* 11.5f⁴ 10f³ 8f⁴ 8.5g⁶
11.5m⁴ a12g⁵ a12g³ a10g² Nov 7] 3,500F: seventh reported foal: half-brother to 2
winners, including fairly useful From The Wood (6f at 2 yrs, to 1m, in Ireland, by Tap
On Wood): dam Irish 7f and 1¼m winner: fair handicapper: won at Lingfield and
Warwick in midsummer: stays 1½m: acts on firm going and equitrack: consistent on
form, but tends to wander under pressure, and has found little: sold 18,000 gns
Doncaster November Sales. *T. J. Naughton*

ALLSTARS ROCKET 3 b.c. Puissance 110 – Sally Delight (Homing 130) 61
[1995 NR 1996 6f 8.3m 10.2f 8.5g⁴ 8.3m* 10g 7f⁵ a8.5g² 9g³ a7g Nov 11] 2,800F:
second foal: dam little sign of ability: modest handicapper: won maiden event at
Hamilton in August, carrying head rather high: best effort at 9f: acts on fibresand, has
raced only on a sound surface on turf. *T. J. Naughton*

ALL THE JOYS 5 b. or br.m. Adbass (USA) 102 – Joytime (John de Coombe 47
122) [1995 47: 7f 10m⁶ 8g⁶ 9.7g 12f² 11.9f² 14d* 15.9d 12g³ 12m⁶ 1996 a12g⁴ a16g⁵ a40
15.4f 9m⁵ 12.3m 12g* Jul 10] rather leggy mare: poor handicapper: back to form to
win at Folkestone final start: stays 1¾m: acts on firm and dead ground: seems suited
by being held up in strongly-run race: sold, covered by Anshan, 2,500 gns Newmarket December Sales. *C. A. Cyzer*

ALLTIME DANCER (IRE) 4 b.g. Waajib 121 – Dance On Lady (Grundy 137) –
[1995 64: 7g 5m⁵ 7g 6g 8m 10m 10g* 9.9m 12m⁴ 8.1g² 8m* 1996 10.2f Sep 12]
robust gelding: impresses in appearance: useful hurdler: modest on flat, always
behind only 4-y-o start: stays 1¼m: has raced only on a sound surface on flat:
blinkered last 3 starts at 3 yrs. *O. Sherwood*

ALLWIGHT THEN (IRE) 5 gr.g. Dancing Dissident (USA) 119 – Abergwrle 69 d
(Absalom 128) [1995 76: 5g 5m² 5m 5m⁴ 5m³ 5m 5f 5.1m 1996 a5g 5g 5.3f² a–
5.1g 5m⁵ 5.1m 5m 5.1d 6m⁴ 6d⁵ a6g 6m Oct 28] neat, good-quartered gelding: has a
quick action: fair handicapper at best: trained first 7 starts at 5 yrs by R. Peacock, on
eighth by T. Caldwell: stays 6f: acts on firm ground: blinkered (no improvement)
twice at 4 yrs: used to be a front runner, held up for current stable: inconsistent.
D. J. S. Cosgrove

ALLYANA (IRE) 4 b.f. Thatching 131 – Miss Loving 89 (Northfields (USA)) –
[1995 73: 6m³ 6g² 6m³ 6g² 5d* 5g⁴ 5m 5f⁴ 1996 6m 5m May 10] quite attractive filly:
fair handicapper: considerably handled on reappearance, well beaten (in blinkers)
11 days later: stays 6f: acts on firm and dead going: covered by Efisio *R. Hannon*

ALMAPA 4 ch.g. Absalom 128 – More Fun (Malicious) [1995 60d: 5.1m⁵ 7g* 8f 51
7g 7f 8h⁵ 1996 6.9s⁶ 8f 7m 5m³ 7d² 8f 7f⁵ 8.1f⁵ 6.9g⁶ Jul 3] workmanlike gelding:
modest handicapper: should stay 1m: acts on good to firm and soft going: won over
hurdles in October: inconsistent. *R. J. Hodges*

ALMASI (IRE) 4 b.f. Petorius 117 – Best Niece 84 (Vaigly Great 127) [1995 63d: 72
6f 6m 6m⁵ 7m 9.7s 7f 8.2m 1996 7s 6.1g 6.1m* 6g² 6g* 6g³ 6d⁴ 6m² 6m 6d³ 6m
7m Oct 5] sparely-made filly: fair handicapper: won at Nottingham in April and
Doncaster in June: best form at 6f: acts on good to firm and soft ground: sometimes
slowly away, and usually comes from behind: better, and more consistent, at 4 yrs
than 3 yrs. *C. F. Wall*

AL MASROOR (USA) 2 b.c. (Mar 27) Red Ransom (USA) – Gaye's Delight 65 p
(USA) (Imperial Falcon (CAN)) [1996 7.1m 7m 6.1m⁵ Sep 16] $100,000Y: well-
made colt: has a round action: first foal: dam sprint winner at 2 yrs, half-sister to
Grade 3-placed winning sprinter Gallant Step: progressive form in maidens without
ever looking fully fit: should stay 7f: almost certainly capable of better. *J. W. Payne*

ALMATY (IRE) 3 b.c. Dancing Dissident (USA) 119 – Almaaseh (IRE) 63 110
(Dancing Brave (USA) 140) [1995 110: 6g⁵ 5g* 5g* 5m* 5f² 5d⁶ 1996 5g⁴ 5f³ 5m Jul
30] leggy, workmanlike colt: smart performer: little over a length fourth of 6 to Anzio
in Ballyogan Stakes at Leopardstown then 4 lengths third of 17 to Pivotal, keeping
on gamely, in King's Stand Stakes at Royal Ascot: visored, tended to hang in King
George Stakes at Goodwood and reportedly lame behind: speedy, but should stay 6f:
acts on firm going: has worn tongue strap: joined J. Gosden. *C. Collins, Ireland*

ALMI AD (USA) 2 b.f. (Feb 25) Silver Hawk (USA) 123 – Mashaarif (USA) (Mr 78
Prospector (USA)) [1996 8.1s² 8g⁴ Oct 25] leggy, unfurnished filly: fluent mover:

third foal: half-sister to 3-y-o Tashjir (by Slew O'Gold): dam unraced daughter of Larida, dam also of Magic of Life and half-sister to Miss Oceana: second to Noble Dane at Haydock then fourth to Calypso Grant at Doncaster in October, both maidens: may not stay much beyond 1m: sweating and edgy second start. *D. Morley*

ALMOND ROCK 4 b.g. Soviet Star (USA) 128 – Banket 120 (Glint of Gold 101 128) [1995 88p: 8m 8m³ 8g* 8f² 8g³ 8d* 1996 8.1g² 8m² 8d* 10g⁵ 9m Oct 5] strong, lengthy gelding: shows a rather round action: useful handicapper: just got up to win the Ripon Rowels in August, tending to hang: 7¼ lengths fifth of 11 in Group 2 event won by Artan at Frankfurt: down the field in Cambridgeshire: stays 1¼m: acts on firm ground and dead: usually held up. *J. R. Fanshawe*

AL MUALLIM (USA) 2 b.c. (Apr 19) Theatrical 128 – Gerri N Jo Go (USA) 79 p (Top Command (USA)) [1996 6m⁴ 6g* Oct 18] $80,000Y: fifth foal: half-brother to a winner in USA by Gulch: dam 6f/7f stakes winner, sister to Grade 1 9f winner Five Star Flight: won maiden at Catterick by ¾ length from Erosion, ridden to lead inside last: will stay further than 6f: slowly away on debut: will improve again. *J. W. Payne*

ALMUHIMM (USA) 4 ch.g. Diesis 133 – Abeesh (USA) 77 (Nijinsky (CAN) 92 138) [1995 76: 8.3m⁴ 10.1m⁵ 10d³ 1996 7m³ 7m² 6d⁵ 7m* 7m* 7m⁴ 8m 7m 7g⁶ 7m Sep 28] big, rangy gelding: fairly useful handicapper: won at Newmarket and Newcastle in June: met trouble in running in prestigious events at Newmarket (unlucky loser) and Goodwood next 2 starts: below best afterwards: best at 7f/1m: best form on top-of-the-ground: keen sort, but often slowly away and usually held up: sold 46,000 gns Doncaster November Sales: reportedly joined T. D. Barron. *E. A. L. Dunlop*

ALMUHTARAM 4 b.g. Rambo Dancer (CAN) 107 – Mrs Mainwaring (FR) 64 72 (Home Guard (USA) 129) [1995 71: a7g⁴ a8.5g* 7.1m 7m 8.2m⁶ 11.4d 7g 8d⁴ 9f* a80 10f⁴ 9m a10g* 1996 a9.4g⁴ a10g² a10g² a10g⁵ 12g⁴ 10f⁴ 10g 12.1m⁴ 11f* 10m⁴ 11.6g 11f² 11m³ 12g⁴ᵈⁱˢ 12g² a12g² Oct 28] strong, good-bodied gelding: good mover: fair handicapper: won at Redcar in July: left Miss G. Kelleway after fourteenth start: career-best effort when short headed at Lingfield final start: stays 1½m: acts on firm ground and the all-weather: usually blinkered nowadays: has been bandaged: normally held up. *G. Lewis*

ALMUSHTARAK (IRE) 3 b.c. Fairy King (USA) – Exciting (Mill Reef (USA) 108 141) [1995 85: 5f⁶ 6m 6g* 6g 1996 7m* 7m³ 7m⁴ 7.6f* 7m Jul 27] good-quartered colt: useful performer: won handicap at Kempton in June: best form when 2¼ lengths fourth of 16 to Lucayan Prince in Jersey Stakes at Royal Ascot and when winning listed rated stakes at Lingfield (by short head from Double Blue) in July: reportedly lost a shoe in Beeswing Stakes at Newcastle final start: likely to prove best at up to 1m: acts on firm ground, yet to race on a soft surface: bandaged behind at 3 yrs: suited by waiting tactics: has joined Dr. J. D. Scargill. *Miss Gay Kelleway*

AL NUFOOTH (IRE) 4 b.g. Green Desert (USA) 127 – Reine Maid (USA) (Mr – Prospector (USA)) [1995 88: 6m 6m⁶ 1996 6d May 22] big, rangy gelding: has a long stride: only fairly useful form in spring at 3 yrs: stiff task, in need of race and well beaten only start in 1996: sold only 900 gns Newmarket Autumn Sales: bred to stay beyond 6f: acts on good to firm ground: possibly temperamental. *Major W. R. Hern*

ALPHABET 2 b.f. (Mar 16) Saddlers' Hall (IRE) 126 – A-To-Z (IRE) 101 80 + (Ahonoora 122) [1996 7g² 8.1m² 8.2g Oct 9] 40,000Y: first foal: dam won Nell Gwyn: placed in minor event won by Oh So Wonderful at Kempton and maiden won by Fiji at Sandown on first 2 starts: disappointing final outing: likely to prove best short of 1m: wears bandages behind. *M. R. Stoute*

ALPHETON PRINCE 3 b.g. Prince of Cill Dara – Batsam Lady (Battle Hymn – 103) [1995 –: a5g⁶ a6g a8.5g⁶ 1996 a8g a6g 8.2d⁵ 9.9g May 11] small gelding: bad mover: poor maiden plater: stays 8.2f: inconsistent. *J. L. Harris*

ALPINE HIDEAWAY (IRE) 3 b.c. Tirol 127 – Arbour (USA) 76 (Graustark) 80 [1995 70: 7.1g 6m 1996 7.1g² 6.9f² 7.6g 6m² 7m 6d³ 7m² 6m⁵ 8m⁶ 7f* 7g Nov 2] useful-looking colt: has a short, round action: fair performer: not at best last 4 starts, though won apprentice maiden at Leicester in October by 5 lengths: should stay at least 1m: acts on firm ground, probably on dead: blinkered (finished last) final 3-y-o start: hung right under pressure second 3-y-o start: has been bandaged. *B. Hanbury*

ALPINE JOKER 3 b.g. Tirol 127 – Whitstar 93 (Whitstead 125) [1995 –p: 7.1g 55 7.1s 6m⁶ 1996 8.1g³ 8m⁵ 8.3s² 9.2s³ May 9] lengthy gelding: modest maiden: should prove suited by further than 8.3f: acts on good to firm and soft ground: joined P. J. Hobbs. *Mrs J. R. Ramsden*

ALPINE MUSIC (IRE) 2 b.g. (Feb 23) Tirol 127 – Holy Devotion (Com- – manche Run 133) [1996 7.1f 5.7d Sep 30] IR 12,000Y: second foal: half-brother to 3-y-o 6f (at 2 yrs) and 7f winner Honorable Estate (by High Estate): dam stayed 1½m in Ireland: soundly beaten in maidens. *J. M. Bradley*

ALPINE PANTHER (IRE) 3 b.c. Tirol 127 – Kentucky Wildcat 64 (Be My 65 Guest (USA) 126) [1995 NR 1996 7s⁶ 7g 6.9m 10m³ 9g³ May 22] IR 50,000Y: tall, useful-looking colt: fourth foal: half-brother to British 5f and 6f winners Two Moves In Front (later up to 1m in France, by Ballad Rock) and Randonneur (as 2-y-o, later at 1¼m in Belgium, by Red Sunset): dam, maiden, stayed 2m: fair maiden: barely stays 1¼m: acts on good to firm ground. *W. Jarvis*

ALPINE STORM (IRE) 4 b.f. Al Hareb (USA) 123 – Alpine Dance (USA) 62§ – (Apalachee (USA) 137) [1995 37, a26: 8m 12.5g⁵ a8.5g 10.8m 14.1m³ 10d 10g⁵ 9m a28 a10g⁶ a12g³ 1996 a13g⁴ a12g³ a12g⁴ a16g⁴ Feb 15] poor maiden handicapper: stays 13f: acts on the all-weather: tried blinkered, no improvement. *M. D. I. Usher*

ALPINE TIME (IRE) 2 b.f. (Apr 5) Tirol 127 – Millie Musique (Miller's Mate 80 116) [1996 5m* 6g² 6m* 6m⁴ Jun 19] 25,000Y: leggy, quite attractive filly: good mover: second foal: dam once-raced daughter of top-class French filly Luth Enchantee: won median auction maiden at Beverley and minor event (workmanlike) at Pontefract in May/June: never going well at Ripon in June on final start: will stay 1m. *D. R. Loder*

ALPINE TWIST (USA) 3 b.f. Seattle Dancer (USA) 119 – Polar Bird 111 89 (Thatching 131) [1995 68p: 7g⁵ 1996 5d* 6m 7.1d² May 27] strong, compact filly: won maiden at Warwick in April: improved form, setting false pace, when second of 7 in handicap at Sandown: stays 7.1f: acts on good to soft ground, disappointing on good to firm: sent to Australia. *P. W. Chapple-Hyam*

ALRAYYIH (USA) 3 b. or br.c. Mr Prospector (USA) – Cheval Volant (USA) 71 (Kris S (USA)) [1995 NR 1996 8m⁵ 8f³ 7m⁴ 7g Sep 6] tall colt: fluent mover: second foal: brother to useful 1995 3-y-o 1m winner Amanah: dam won from 5.5f to 8.5f in USA, twice in Grade 1 events: fair maiden: will be suited by further than 1m: sweating and edgy (well below form) final start: has had tongue tied: sent to Dubai. *J. H. M. Gosden*

ALREEH (IRE) 3 b.f. Priolo (USA) 127 – Fleeting (USA) (Lear Fan (USA) 130) 76 [1995 66: 7m 6.1d 7g⁵ 1996 8.2m⁶ 8g³ 10m* 10.1f³ 10m² 9.9m* Jul 5] good-topped filly: has a round action: fair handicapper: won at Redcar (maiden) in May and Beverley in July: best form at around 1¼m: acts on firm ground, ran poorly only start on a soft surface: blinkered (ran respectably) final 2-y-o start: sent to UAE. *J. H. M. Gosden*

AL REET (IRE) 5 b.m. Alzao (USA) 117 – Reet Petite (Thatching 131) [1995 – 6m 7d⁵ 6.5s* 7g 8.5d³ 6g⁴ 6m² 6d* 7d² 1996 8s 6g 7m 8.5m 8.1d 7g Nov 2] angular mare: second foal: half-sister to German 5f (at 2 yrs) and 7f winner Raja Hitam (by Persian Bold): dam fairly useful sprinter: rated 92 at 4 yrs in Ireland for J. Burns, winning maiden at Sligo and handicap at the Curragh before excellent second of 16 in listed race at Leopardstown: sold 10,000 gns Newmarket December (1995) Sales: seventh of 24 in Lincoln at Doncaster on reappearance but well held afterwards: probably stays 8.5f, best effort at 7f: probably acts on good to firm and soft ground, best efforts on dead: blinkered (ran poorly) sixth 4-y-o start. *M. D. Hammond*

ALSAHAH (IRE) 3 b.f. Unfuwain (USA) 131 – Princess Sucree (USA) (Roberto – (USA) 131) [1995 NR 1996 12m⁶ Aug 10] good-topped, quite attractive filly: reportedly cracked off-hind joint at 2 yrs: seventh foal: sister to 1½m winner Muntafi and closely related to 3 winners, including smart middle-distance performer Burooj (by Danzig): dam, placed over 6f and 8.5f at 4 yrs in USA, half-sister to Kentucky Derby winner Cannonade: 16/1, burly and green, 10½ lengths sixth of 8 to Fine Detail in maiden at Newmarket, never able to challenge: sold 68,000 gns Newmarket December Sales. *D. Morley*

ALSAHIB (USA) 3 b.g. Slew O' Gold (USA) – Khwlah (USA) 99 (Best Turn 73 (USA)) [1995 74p: 7f⁴ 1996 8m 10.5d⁵ 10m⁴ 10.5v 8d² 8g Nov 2] big, robust gelding: fair maiden at best: sold out of H. Thomson Jones' stable 9,000 gns

Newmarket July Sales after third start: probably stays 10.5f: fair form on firm ground on debut, easily best efforts at 3 yrs on dead: tongue tied (edgy, ran well despite slow start) final 3-y-o outing. *W. R. Muir*

AL'S ALIBI 3 b.c. Alzao (USA) 117 – Lady Kris (IRE) (Kris 135) [1995 73: 5m⁶ 7d³ 7g 6.9g² 6.9m⁵ 1996 10.3s⁶ 10g⁵ 12d* 12.3g 12d⁵ May 18] smallish, sturdy colt: has pronounced knee action: fairly useful handicapper: won at Newbury in April: badly hampered next start, probably had too much use made of him last time: better at 1½m than shorter, and will stay further: effective on good to firm ground at 2 yrs, best effort on dead. *W. R. Muir* — 82

AL SHAATI (FR) 6 b.m. Lead On Time (USA) 123 – With You All (Free Round (USA)) [1995 –, a46: a6g a5g⁶ a6g 1996 a6g a8g a6g 7g 5.1f⁴ a6g a7g Dec 11] leggy mare: poor handicapper: effective at 5f and stays 1m: acts on firm ground, soft and equitrack: tried blinkered, well beaten. *R. J. O'Sullivan* — 37

AL SHADEEDAH (USA) 3 br.f. Nureyev (USA) 131 – Copperama (AUS) (Comeram (FR) 127) [1995 74+: 6f⁵ 6g 7f³ 1996 7.3d⁶ 8f* 8m 10.1m⁴ Sep 18] tall filly: good mover: fairly useful handicapper: won at Warwick in June: best form at 10.1f: acted on firm going: took keen hold: stud. *L. M. Cumani* — 86

AL SHAFA 3 b.c. Midyan (USA) 124 – Thundercloud 70 (Electric 126) [1995 84: 6g³ 6f² 6m² 6f* 7.3d 7g* 7.3d 1996 9g 8m* 8m⁴ 8.1d 9m* 10g² 12m 10.4m 10m Sep 26] quite attractive colt: useful handicapper: won at Ripon in April and Sandown in June: best effort when unlucky length second of 13 to Freedom Flame in £20,900 race at Newmarket in July: ran as if something amiss next start, disappointing afterwards: sold 30,000 gns Newmarket Autumn Sales: shapes as if will stay beyond 1¼m: acts on firm ground, unsuited by a soft surface. *J. L. Dunlop* — 99

ALTAMURA (USA) 3 b.f. El Gran Senor (USA) 136 – Narwala 120 (Darshaan 133) [1995 82: 8g³ 8.2m² 1996 10.1g³ 10m* 10g* 10.1m⁴ 12g* 12d⁵ 10.5s⁶ 10v Nov 30] unfurnished filly: progressed into smart performer: successful in maiden at Ripon and listed races at Salisbury in August and at Ascot (by 2 lengths from Time Allowed, travelling well, quickening 2f out and running on strongly) in September: shade disappointing on a softer surface afterwards: better suited by 1½m than shorter: acted on good to firm ground: tended to get on toes: flashed tail: retired. *J. H. M. Gosden* — 113

ALTERMEERA 8 br.g. Noalto 120 – Mac's Melody (Wollow 132) [1995 NR 1996 14.1g Apr 22] looked ungenuine in 1993, rated 45 when winner of 1 of 2 starts in 1994: well beaten only start in 1996: stays 1½m: acts on good to firm and soft ground: blinkered/visored nowadays. *Mrs Barbara Waring* — –

ALUMISIYAH (USA) 2 b. or br.f. (Apr 7) Danzig (USA) – Mathkurh (USA) 97 (Riverman (USA) 131) [1996 5.3f* 6f³ Sep 5] second foal: half-sister to 3-y-o Mutamanni (by Caerleon): dam sprinting half-sister to useful 1988 2-y-o 6f winner Muhbubh: won maiden at Brighton in August: creditable third of 7 to Dancing Drop in minor event at Salisbury following month, left with plenty to do when steady pace quickened: will stay 7f: sent to Dubai: will improve again. *H. Thomson Jones* — 80 p

ALVILDE 2 b.f. (May 2) Alzao (USA) 117 – Volida 105 (Posse (USA) 130) [1996 5m⁵ 6.1m⁶ 5g⁵ Oct 19] small, quite attractive filly: fluent mover: seventh foal: half-sister to winners in Italy by Darshaan and Unfuwain: dam, half-sister to Supreme Leader from family of Pebbles, won over 5f at 2 yrs and later appeared suited by 1m: fair form: did best of those drawn on unfavoured side at Catterick final start: bred to stay 1m: has had tongue tied down: sold to join D. Cosgrove 4,200 gns Newmarket Autumn Sales. *J. R. Fanshawe* — 70

ALWARQA 3 b.f. Old Vic 136 – Ostora (USA) 83 (Blushing Groom (FR) 131) [1995 –p: 7.1s 1996 8.2d 12m⁶ 11.6m⁵ 17.2g² 14.1f* 14.1f⁴ 12f³ 12m a12g⁶ 17.5m 17.1m* 18g Oct 21] sturdy filly: carries condition: has a long stride: fair handicapper: won at Yarmouth in June: sold out of R. Armstrong's stable 8,500 gns Newmarket July Sales after sixth start: showed little for D. Nicholls next 4 outings: best effort to win at Pontefract in October: stays 17.1f: acts on firm going. *M. D. Hammond* — 69

ALWAYS ALIGHT 2 ch.g. (Apr 5) Never So Bold 135 – Fire Sprite 83 (Mummy's Game 120) [1996 5.1m 7g a6g 6.9d 6g³ 6v³ Nov 11] 5,200Y: quite good-topped gelding: fourth foal: half-brother to 3-y-o Trible Pet (by Petong) and ungenuine 1994 2-y-o 5f winner Six For Luck (by Handsome Sailor): dam 2-y-o 5f — 60

Harvest Stakes, Ascot—a second listed win for Altamura

winner: poor maiden: third in median auction events late in year: stays 6f: acts well on heavy ground: blinkered last 3 starts. *K. R. Burke*

ALWAYS ALOOF (USA) 5 b.h. Alleged (USA) 138 – Miranda (USA) 109 (Forli (ARG)) [1995 107: 16m* 18.7m 20m 16.1m⁵ 15.9m³ 15.5g² 1996 16.2m³ 15.5d³ 20m⁴ 15.9m² 15.5m* 20d⁶ Oct 5] tall horse: smart performer, better than ever in 1996: comfortably held behind Double Trigger in Sagaro Stakes at Ascot, Double Eclipse in Prix Vicomtesse Vigier at Longchamp and Classic Cliche in Gold Cup at Royal Ascot first 3 starts: 2 lengths second to Celeric in listed race at York before change of tactics and made most to win 6-runner Prix Gladiateur at Longchamp in September by ¾ length from Kassani: possibly best at around 2m: acts on good to firm and heavy ground: held up prior to penultimate 5-y-o start: consistent. *M. R. Stoute* 115

ALWAYS EARNEST (USA) 8 b.g. Alleged (USA) 138 – Nettie Cometti (USA) (Giacometti 130) [1995 120: 15s⁵ 15.5s* 15.5v³ 20s* 1996 15m 15.5d⁵ 20d³ 15.5d⁵ 15s² 14v² Nov 30] angular gelding: smart French performer: niggled along in rear early on in 2½m Prix du Cadran at Longchamp (race he won in 1995), running on to 117

Prix Gladiateur, Longchamp—
a change of tactics sees the 1995 runner-up Always Aloof go one better

finish 3½ lengths third of 10 to Nononito: no similar form in 1996: needs a thorough test of stamina nowadays: acts on heavy going: has worn blinkers since final 5-y-o start: lazy sort, quite often hangs right and is not an easy ride. *Mme M. Bollack-Badel, France*

ALWAYS GRACE 4 b.f. Never So Bold 135 – Musical Sally (USA) (The Minstrel (CAN) 135) [1995 65, a56: a7g⁴ a6g² 6f* 5m 6m a7g 1996 a6g⁶ a6g⁵ 6.1g⁵ 6m 6f 6g* 7f³ 6m 6m* 6f⁵ 7m⁶ 7f Sep 5] strong filly: shows knee action: modest handicapper: came from behind to win at Brighton in May and July: stays 7f: acts on all-weather surfaces and firm ground, well beaten on heavy: inconsistent. *Miss Gay Kelleway*   64 a54

ALWAYS HAPPY 3 ch.f. Sharrood (USA) 124 – Convivial 81 (Nordance (USA)) [1995 73: 7g⁴ 8m⁴ 1996 10g⁶ 8.5g 10.8f⁶ 8m* Jun 21] unfurnished filly: has a fluent, round action: fair performer: dropped in class, first 3-y-o form to win claimer at Newmarket (claimed £10,000) in June: should stay 1¼m: has raced only on a sound surface: winning hurdler for M. Pipe: joined Miss G. Kelleway. *J. R. Fanshawe*   73

ALWAYS LOYAL (USA) 2 b. or br.f. (Apr 9) Zilzal (USA) 137 – Balbonella (FR) 120 (Gay Mecene (USA) 128) [1996 7.5s* Nov 2] third foal: half-sister to top-class French 4-y-o sprinter Anabaa (by Danzig), also successful at up to 1m, and high-class 5-y-o 1m and 1¼m winner in Dubai/USA Key of Luck (by Chief's Crown), 5f and 6f winner in France at 2 yrs: won 8-runner minor event at Saint-Cloud in November by 1½ lengths from Gracie Lady: an interesting prospect. *Mme C. Head, France*   98 p

ALWAYS ON MY MIND 2 b.f. (Apr 9) Distant Relative 128 – Fleur Rouge 71 (Pharly (FR) 130) [1996 6m⁴ Sep 7] fifth living foal: half-sister to 3-y-o 7f winner Roushan (by Anshan), fair 7f/1m performer Red Valerian (by Robellino) and fair middle-distance stayer Addicted To Love (by Touching Wood): dam 2-y-o 6f winner: 50/1, disputed lead long way when fourth to Calypso Lady in maiden at Kempton: will improve. *P. J. Makin*   75 p

ALYPORTENT 2 b.c. (Apr 25) Warning 136 – Alilisa (USA) (Alydar (USA)) [1996 6g 7g Oct 30] angular, unfurnished colt: first foal: dam 12.8f winner in Ireland: midfield in late-season maidens at Newmarket and Yarmouth: slowly away on debut: will probably do better. *W. J. Haggas*   – p

ALZABELLA (IRE) 3 b.f. Alzao (USA) 117 – Believer 112 (Blakeney 126) [1995 NR 1996 10.5g³ 10d* 10s⁵ 12m⁴ 12m⁴ 13.5g⁴ 14.6m⁶ Sep 11] IR 13,000Y: seventh foal: half-sister to fairly useful 1989 2-y-o 5f winner Please Believe Me (by Try My Best): dam won Princess Royal Stakes: useful form: won maiden at Milan in April: best efforts when 8½ lengths fourth of 10 to Tulipa in Ribblesdale Stakes at Royal Ascot and 6¼ lengths fourth of 5 to Shemozzle in listed race at Newmarket: better at 1½m than shorter (out of depth but ran poorly all the same in 14.6f Park Hill Stakes): goes well on good to firm ground, winner on dead, well beaten on soft: sold 35,000 gns Newmarket December Sales. *J. W. Hills*   98

ALZANTI 3 b.c. Alzao (USA) 117 – Mumtaz Flyer (USA) (Al Hattab (USA)) [1995 88: 7g⁶ 7f* 7g* 7d³ 8m² 1996 10m³ May 2] well-made colt: fairly useful form: stiff task, held up when 9¾ lengths last of 3 in steadily-run minor event at Salisbury only start in 1996: sold only 2,000 gns Newmarket Autumn Sales: should stay 1¼m: acts on firm and dead ground: made running/raced prominently at 2 yrs. *P. F. I. Cole*   –

ALZEUS (IRE) 3 b.c. Alzao (USA) 117 – Rentina 67 (Adonijah 126) [1995 NR 1996 8m² 10d* 10d³ 8.5f 12f² 12s 10d 11f⁵ Oct 18] 34,000F, IR 32,000Y: small, attractive colt: first living foal: dam, placed at up to 1¾m, half-sister to very smart middle-distance filly Upend and to the dam of Royal Gait: won maiden at Newbury in May for C. Horgan in good style: placed in Grade 3 event at Belmont (beaten 9 lengths) and allowance race at Saratoga (beaten a nose) for new trainer: stays 1½m: acts on firm and dead ground. *N. Zito, USA*   98

ALZOOMO (IRE) 4 b.g. Alzao (USA) 117 – Fandangerina (USA) (Grey Dawn II 132) [1995 68: 10m 11.8m 8.2d³ 8m a12g³ 1996 a12g² a11g³ a12g⁴ a11g⁴ Mar 9] robust gelding: fair maiden handicapper: should stay 1¾m: acts on dead ground and fibresand: fair winning hurdler. *J. A. Glover*   68

ALZOTIC (IRE) 3 b.g. Alzao (USA) 117 – Exotic Bride (USA) (Blushing Groom (FR) 131) [1995 53+, a71: 8.2d 7d⁶ 7d 8f a8g² a8g⁴ 1996 7d 10.3m 10g 12s⁶   –

Prix de la Foret, Longchamp—
German-trained A Magicman will just hang on from Miesque's Son (right)

14.1m 15.8g Sep 21] smallish, sturdy gelding: no form for new stable in 1996: bred to stay middle distances: best on fibresand: visored (made running) last 2 starts: flashed tail last time. *J. Norton*

AMADOUR (IRE) 3 b.c. Contract Law (USA) 108 – Truly Flattering (Hard 71 Fought 125) [1995 –: 8g 8d² 9f² 10g³ 11.4m⁵ 11.9g* 11.9g Oct 10] workmanlike colt: fair form: narrowly won maiden handicap at Brighton in October, short of room before just getting up: will stay beyond 1½m. *P. Mitchell*

A MAGICMAN (FR) 4 br.c. The Wonder (FR) 129 – Ayanapa (FR) (Pharly (FR) 117 130) [1995 110: 8.5s 8g³ 11s⁶ 12m 8m* 8d* 8g* 1996 8g³ 8g⁵ 8s⁴ 7g* 8g 6.5d⁶ 6g³ 8g² 7d* Oct 20] smart German-trained colt: won 6-runner Prix de la Porte Maillot at Longchamp in June by 2 lengths from Bashaayeash and, after good placed efforts at Baden-Baden and Cologne, 11-runner Prix de la Foret at Longchamp in October by head from Miesque's Son: best form at up to 1m, though should stay further: acts on good to firm ground and soft. *H. Steguweit, Germany*

AMAHSAN (IRE) 4 ch.g. Nashamaa 113 – Singing Filly (Relkino 131) [1995 8g – 8m⁵ 7s³ 6.5m* 8g⁶ 6d 1996 a7g 7s 6g 5.1g Apr 22] ex-Irish gelding: first reported foal: dam French 1m and 11f winner: fairly useful performer (rated 81) at 3 yrs for P. J. Flynn, winning handicap at Sligo in August: well beaten in 1996: stays 1m: acts on good to firm and soft ground. *C. D. Broad*

AMANITA 3 ch.f. Lead On Time (USA) 123 – Amana River (USA) 77 (Raise A – Cup (USA)) [1995 72: 5m⁶ 6m* 7m 6g³ 7d⁴ 1996 6g 6g May 22] fair juvenile in 1995: no form in 1996: stays 7f: acts on good to firm and dead ground: tends to sweat and get edgy: sent to UAE. *J. W. Watts*

AMANIY (USA) 3 b.f. Dayjur (USA) 137 – Muhbubh (USA) 108 (Blushing – Groom (FR) 131) [1995 96: 5g³ 5.1m* 6.1g² 6f* 6g³ 5s³ 1996 6m⁶ 6m 6m Sep 11] strong, good-topped filly: half-sister to much-improved 4-y-o Kayrawan, Grade 2 7f winner in USA in 1996: useful juvenile in 1995, no worthwhile form in 1996: better form at 6f than 5f: well below form on soft ground: visits Indian Ridge. *H. Thomson Jones*

AMARELLA (IRE) 2 ch.f. (Mar 14) Soviet Lad (USA) 94 – Eight Mile Rock 76 67 ? (Dominion 123) [1996 6g 7m 7g⁴ Aug 24] 4,800Y: small filly: poor mover: fifth foal: half-sister to 1m (at 2 yrs) and 10.2f winner World Express (by Jareer) and useful French 9f and 1½m winner Macruby (by High Estate): dam 7f winner: possibly flattered when always-prominent fourth to Fleet River in steadily-run maiden at Goodwood final start: will stay 1m. *M. J. Haynes*

AMARYLLIS (IRE) 2 b.f. (May 20) Sadler's Wells (USA) 132 – Heartbreak 71 p (USA) (Stage Door Johnny) [1996 7m⁴ 7d³ a7g* Nov 16] closely related to smart

French/US 1m/9f winner (probably stayed 1½m) Corrazona (by El Gran Senor) and half-sister to 2 winners in USA by Slew O'Gold, including Breeders' Cup Classic third Thirty Six Red: dam won at up to 9f in USA: made all in weak maiden at Wolverhampton in November: will stay at least 1m: remains capable of better: sent to France. *J. H. M. Gosden*

AMAZE 7 b.g. Natroun (FR) 128 – Entrancing 95 (Posse (USA) 130) [1995 NR – 1996 11.9d May 6] rated 88 at best in 1994: offered little on return to flat: stays 1¼m: needs give in the ground (acts on heavy): blinkered (well beaten) once as 4-y-o: often bandaged: edgy sort: fair winning hurdler, though sometimes finds little. *Lady Herries*

AMAZING BAY 3 b.f. Mazilier (USA) 107 – Petriece 64 (Mummy's Pet 125) 100 [1995 98: 6g* 6m* 6g5 5m4 5.2m* 5d5 1996 6g 5f 5.1m2 5m 5g2 5d 5m2 5.2m3 5g Sep 29] angular, lightly-made filly: unimpressive mover: useful performer: generally ran with credit in 1996, beaten head by Anzio in listed race at Doncaster seventh start: has won at 6f, raced only at around 5f since 3-y-o reappearance: acts on good to firm going, possibly unsuited by a soft surface: held up: sold 100,000 gns Newmarket December Sales. *I. A. Balding*

AMAZING GRACE (IRE) 3 b.f. Polish Patriot (USA) 128 – Sepideh (Habitat – 134) [1995 NR 1996 7m May 3] 7,200F: angular filly: half-sister to minor winners in Ireland (5f, by Law Society) and Italy (6f, by Be My Guest): dam, unraced, closely related to Sigy: 50/1, moved badly to post and tailed off throughout in maiden at Newmarket. *S. C. Williams*

AMAZON PRINCESS 3 b.f. Inca Chief (USA) – Forest Nymph (Native Bazaar – 122) [1995 NR 1996 10s Oct 24] sparely-made filly: third foal: dam never ran: showed nothing in maiden at Newbury: sold 600 gns Ascot December Sales. *J. Ffitch-Heyes*

AMBASSADORI (USA) 3 b.c. Lear Fan (USA) 130 – Czar's Bride (USA) 78 64 (Northern Dancer) [1995 NR 1996 10m4 10.1g6 10m 10m 13.9g 11.4m 7m 7m a10g* Nov 14] $8,700Y, resold $25,000Y: sturdy, close-coupled colt: good mover: ninth reported foal: half-brother to several winners, notably smart 4-y-o Inzar (up to 7f, by Warning): dam middle-distance maiden out of half-sister to Fanfreluche and Barachois: fair handicapper: well beaten for 5 starts: before winning at Lingfield (dictated steady pace, quickened clear) in November: best form at 1¼m: acts on good to firm ground and equitrack. *C. E. Brittain*

AMBASSADOR (USA) 3 b.c. Hansel (USA) – Taba (ARG) (Table Play) [1995 96 NR 1996 7s5 10m4 10.3g6 10m* 10.3g* 12m 13.9m Aug 21] $250,000F: good-topped, attractive colt: has scope: unimpressive mover with knee action: twelfth foal: half-brother to numerous winners in USA, a couple of them useful performers, and another, Turkoman (by Alydar), champion older horse in 1986: dam champion 2-y-o filly in Argentina: useful performer: won maiden at Pontefract and £10,500 handicap at Doncaster in June: close up long way and not discredited in very strongly-run Ebor Handicap at York final start: will eventually prove suited by further than around 1¼m: acts on good to firm ground (gave impression ill-at-ease running downhill at Goodwood sixth start though): may progress further: sent to UAE. *B. W. Hills*

AMBER FORT 3 gr.g. Indian Ridge 123 – Lammastide 93 (Martinmas 128) 82 [1995 72: 7g6 7m 8.2d 6g2 5m a6g3 1996 5g5 7m5 6m 8.5m4 7f5 a7g* 8m 7m2 7m2 7g3 7s* 7g6 Nov 2] tall, close-coupled gelding: fairly useful handicapper: won at Lingfield (claimer, claimed out of P. Cole's stable £11,000) in June and at Newbury (apprentices) in October: stays 7f: acts on firm and soft ground and on equitrack: usually blinkered/visored: usually races prominently: used to look a difficult ride, but has done little wrong of late. *D. R. C. Elsworth*

AMBER RING 3 ch.f. Belmez (USA) 131 – Ring of Pearl (Auction Ring (USA) – 123) [1995 NR 1996 10g 8m 10m 11.6m 10.8m 17.2f Jul 24] 14,000F, 8,800Y: smallish, sturdy filly: sixth foal: half-sister to 4 winners (fair form at best) including Manabar (1m, by Reprimand): dam ran 3 times at 2 yrs: no worthwhile form, for M. Channon first 3 starts. *Miss K. M. George*

AMBIDEXTROUS (IRE) 4 b.c. Shareef Dancer (USA) 135 – Amber Fizz 57 (USA) (Effervescing (USA)) [1995 59: 10.2m 10.3m 10m3 12m 7m a8.5g 1996 a12g5 10d5 12.3g5 10g 12.1g5 11.1f* 11.1f* 11.1g2 11.1g3 11.1m3 10m 11.1m3 11.9m4 12.1f4 12.1m4 10f Sep 10] good-bodied colt: modest handicapper: won twice at Musselburgh in June: stays at least 12.1f: acts on firm and dead ground: tried visored, no improvement: held up: won selling hurdle in December. *E. J. Alston*

AMEER ALFAYAAFI (IRE)   3 b.g. Mujtahid (USA) 118 – Sharp Circle (IRE)   55
83 (Sure Blade (USA) 130) [1995 –p: 7.1g 1996 7g 8d 7f 7.1m⁶ 7f⁵ 8g 10f⁶ 9.7d Oct 21] small, sturdy gelding: carries condition: modest maiden handicapper: seems to stay 1¼m: acts on firm ground: blinkered (forced strong pace, well beaten) final 3-y-o start. *R. Akehurst*

AMELANCHIER   3 ch.f. Cigar 68 – Frost In Summer (Busted 134) [1995 –: 7g   62
1996 9m 8g⁶ 7.1m⁶ 7.1m Jul 11] stocky filly: best effort in maidens on second 3-y-o start: tailed off final outing: bred to be suited by further than 1m. *G. B. Balding*

AMELIAJILL   3 ch.f. Aragon 118 – Crackerjill 37 (Sparkler 130) [1995 NR 1996   47
5d 5m 6g 6m⁶ 6.1m 6m 6m⁴ 6m Aug 22] sparely-made filly: sister to useful sprinter Arabellajill and half-sister to fair 7f winner Petonellajill (by Petong): dam stayed 1m: trained first 3 starts by J. O'Shea: poor maiden handicapper: sold 600 gns Newmarket Autumn Sales: may well prove suited by further than 6f: inconsistent. *R. Hannon*

AMERCIUS   4 ch.g. Old Vic 136 – Elarrih (USA) (Sharpen Up 127) [1995 48:   –
a8.5g⁴ 10.3g 14.1g³ 12.5m⁵ 14.1g 14.1m 1996 14.1g 14.1m Apr 30] sparely-made gelding: poor maiden: well beaten for new stable in 1996: probably a stayer: blinkered twice at 3 yrs (only form) and second 4-y-o start. *J. L. Harris*

AMERICAN WHISPER   2 b.c. (Mar 8) Dixieland Band (USA) – Only A Rumour 115 (Ela-Mana-Mou 132) [1996 7g³ 7.1f⁶ Sep 12] 7,000Y: leggy, unfurnished   76
colt: has quick action: fifth foal: half-brother to 4 winners in France and USA, including French 1¼m winner Only Wood (by Woodman): dam French 1¼m to 12.5f winner: close third behind Gonzaga in Salisbury maiden in August: disappointing in Chepstow maiden following month: will stay at least 1¼m. *P. W. Harris*

AMFORTAS (IRE)   3 b.c. Caerleon (USA) 132 – High Spirited 80 (Shirley   115
Heights 130) [1995 NR 1996 8m 10g 10d 12f* 12m Jun 30] 80,000Y: unfurnished colt: second foal: half-brother to fairly useful 1995 3-y-o 10.4f winner Motakabber (by Sadler's Wells): dam, 1¾m and 2m winner, sister to High Hawk, the dam of In The Wings: 66/1 and in fine shape, vastly improved when winning 7-runner King Edward VII Stakes at Royal Ascot by ½ length from Desert Boy, dictating pace,

King Edward VII Stakes, Royal Ascot—a fine way to get off the mark for 66/1-shot Amfortas (left); Desert Boy (centre) and Shantou cannot reel him in

Mr B. H. Voak's "Amfortas"

seeming to idle then running on splendidly: last in Irish Derby at the Curragh 9 days later, reportedly returning jarred up: sure to stay beyond 1½m: acts on firm ground, ran poorly on dead: reportedly to race on in 1997. *C. E. Brittain*

AMIARGE 6 b.g. Reference Point 139 – Scotia Rose (Tap On Wood 130) [1995 51?: 14.6g 13f² 14g 16m* 17.1m³ 16m 16d² 14s² 13.9g⁴ 1996 12.4d⁵ 14g⁴ 16.5g⁵ 14.6g 16m⁵ 16g⁶ 16.4g 15.9g² 17.9g* 18g a16g Nov 18] small, leggy gelding: modest handicapper: won at Nottingham in October: stays 17.9f: acts on firm and soft going: tried visored/blinkered, no improvement: often soon off bridle: none too consistent. *M. Brittain*   53

AMICO 2 b.c. (Feb 15) Efisio 120 – Stormswept (USA) 74 (Storm Bird (CAN) 134) [1996 6g 7.1v a6g⁵ Nov 18] leggy colt: has a round action: first foal: dam, 2-y-o 5.1f winner, closely related to Colonel Collins: staying-on fifth in maiden at Southwell final start: refused to enter stalls Dec 19. *C. W. Thornton*   52

AMID ALBADU (USA) 2 b.c. (Jan 14) Sheikh Albadou 128 – Dream Play (USA) (Blushing Groom (FR) 131) [1996 6g² 6m² 7d* 7f* Oct 15] IR 90,000Y: quite good-topped colt: has a round action: ninth foal: half-brother to 4 winners, including 3-y-o 1½m winner Ragsak Jameel (by Northern Baby) and smart Party Cited (1m to 1¼m, by Alleged): dam won at up to 9f in USA: fairly useful form: made heavy weather of winning maiden at Chester in August: made most and responded well when beating Arabian a short head in minor event at Leicester 6 weeks later: will stay 1m: acts on good to firm and dead ground: looked tricky ride second and third starts but did nothing wrong last time. *J. L. Dunlop*   89

AMID THE STARS 2 b.f. (Feb 10) Midyan (USA) 124 – Celebrity 101 (Troy 137) [1996 7g⁴ 7m Jul 19] 15,500Y: fourth foal: sister to Irish NH Flat race winner   61

Entertainment and half-sister to fairly useful 5-y-o 9.7f to 2m winner Stompin (by Alzao): dam 10.2f winner suited by 1½m: slow-starting third to Ryafan in maiden at Doncaster in June: soundly beaten at Newmarket 3 weeks later. *R. Boss*

A MILLION WATTS 5 b.g. Belfort (FR) 89 – Peters Pet Girl (Norwick (USA) – 125) [1995 –, a73: a8g² a10g⁵ a8g* a8.5g² 10m a8g² 9.7m 1996 a8g Dec 11] fair handicapper: trained at 4 yrs by Lady Herries: off course over 18 months, always behind in claimer at Lingfield: stays 1¼m: acts on firm and soft ground and the all-weather: blinkered (finished last) final 2-y-o start. *G. M. McCourt*

AMINGTON LASS 3 ch.f. Cree Song 99 – Millfields House 70 (Record Token 70 128) [1995 47+: 5g 5d⁵ 1996 7.9g⁶ 5.2m⁴ a5g* Dec 28] leggy, workmanlike filly: fair form: off course 3½ months, won handicap at Wolverhampton in December, getting up well inside final 1f: best form at 5f, should prove as effective back over further. *P. D. Evans*

AMLAH (USA) 4 gr.g. Storm Bird (CAN) 134 – Old Mother Hubbard (USA) 61 (Al Hattab (USA)) [1995 6s² 10d 8g 9g² 7g⁵ 11f³ 10g⁵ 8m³ 1996 10.1m⁵ 12.1m Jun 30] $270,000Y: eighth foal: half-brother to 5 winners in USA, notably a listed stakes winner by Our Michael best at around 1m: dam minor winner in USA at 6f and 7f: fair maiden (rated 73) in Ireland before sold out of K. Prendergast's stable 15,500 gns Newmarket July (1995) Sales: below form in 1996: stays 11f: acts on good to firm and soft ground: blinkered (below form) twice at 3 yrs: fair hurdler: gelded. *P. J. Hobbs*

AMNESIA (IRE) 5 b.m. Don't Forget Me 127 – Amboselli 73 (Raga Navarro – (ITY) 119) [1995 41?: 8.1g⁶ 10g⁶ 9.2f⁴ 9.2f³ 15.1f 1996 8.3s 8.1g⁶ 9.2g 11.1f 11.1f Jun 24] lengthy mare: no worthwhile form in 1996: best effort at around 1m: acts on firm ground: no improvement in blinkers/visor. *Mrs S. C. Bradburne*

AMNESTY BAY 4 b.f. Thatching 131 – Sanctuary Cove (Habitat 134) [1995 – 63d: 8m 7g 8g* 8.2f⁶ a8g 1996 6.1g 7m 10d 8.1g 10.2m Jun 15] light-framed filly: poor at best nowadays: should stay beyond 1m: visored last 2 starts. *M. D. I. Usher*

AMOEBA (IRE) 3 b.f. Distinctly North (USA) 115 – Lady Ingrid (Taufan (USA) 51 119) [1995 66d: 6g² 5g² a6g⁶ 6g 5s³ a6g⁶ 1996 a6g* a6g⁵ a7g⁶ 6g⁵ 5.9f² 7f 5.9f⁴ Jun 26] workmanlike filly: only modest nowadays: won claimer at Southwell in April: sold 4,000 gns Doncaster September Sales: suited by 6f: acts on fibresand and firm ground: inconsistent. *J. Berry*

AMRAK AJEEB (IRE) 4 b.c. Danehill (USA) 126 – Noble Dust (USA) (Dust 112 Commander (USA)) [1995 91: 7.1m² 8m⁵ 7g* 8m 8g⁴ 10.5m* 10m² 10m² 10d 9g 10m⁵ 9d 1996 7m 10m 8m⁶ 8s* 9.8g² 8m 8m⁵ 10.4m 10.4m* 8.9g 8g* 10g⁶ Oct 30] leggy, good-topped colt: tends to take eye in appearance: useful handicapper on most form: led inside final 1f to win at Newbury (back to form) in May, York (rated stakes) in August and Ascot (£29,700 event) in September: by 10 lb career-best effort at Ascot, set plenty to do, weaving through, then strong burst to beat Hal's Pal by 1¼ lengths: effective at 1m to 10.5f: acts on good to firm and soft ground: has run well when sweating: has been taken early to post: takes good hold, and is usually held up: runs the odd bad race. *B. Hanbury*

AMRON 9 b.g. Bold Owl 101 – Sweet Minuet (Setay 105) [1995 90d: 6g 6m 6m⁶ 67 6m 6f 5.6m 6g 6g 1996 7g 6g⁶ 6m 6d² 6d 6m 6m 5d³ 6m 6m 6s⁵ 5m³ 6m 6m² Oct 23] sparely-made gelding: no longer the force of old, only modest handicapper most starts in 1996: stays 6f: acts on firm and soft ground (won on heavy at 2 yrs): usually held up. *J. Berry*

Mail On Sunday Mile Final (Handicap), Ascot—
a storming late run from Amrak Ajeeb accounts for 24 others led in by Hal's Pal

AMUSING ASIDE (IRE)   3 ch.f. In The Wings 128 – Most Amusing (Blushing   63
Groom (FR) 131) [1995 NR 1996 10g⁶ 12m⁵ 10m⁴ 10.5g 10.3m a8.5g⁴ Sep 7]
workmanlike filly: second foal: closely related to modest 8.5f winner Lorelei Lee (by
Old Vic): dam unraced half-sister to Saratoga Six and Dunbeath: modest maiden:
disappointing since third start: probably stays 1½m: has been bandaged: sent to UAE.
J. W. Watts

AMY   2 b.f. (Apr 13) Timeless Times (USA) 99 – Rion River (IRE) (Taufan (USA)   –
119) [1996 5.1g⁶ 5m⁵ 5g 5f 7d a5g Aug 16] small, lengthy filly: second foal:
half-sister to 3-y-o Gagajulu (by Al Hareb), successful at around 5f at 2 yrs: dam
Irish 1¼m winner: no form: blinkered in seller final outing. *C. Smith*

AMYAS (IRE)   2 b.c. (Apr 26) Waajib 121 – Art Duo 86 (Artaius (USA) 129)   85
[1996 6g⁵ 7m⁶ 6g* 6g* 6m Oct 17] IR 8,000F, 33,000Y: sturdy colt: third foal: dam
fourth in listed event at 2 yrs but failed to train on: won maiden at Catterick in
September: held up well off strong pace, then led on bit 1f out when winning nursery
at York following month by 2 lengths: bandaged near-hind, never able to get into
contention in nursery at Newmarket final start: bred to stay 7f: stirred up and swished
tail to post final start. *B. W. Hills*

AMY LEIGH (IRE)   3 b.f. Imperial Frontier (USA) 112 – Hollyberry (IRE)   62 d
(Runnett 125) [1995 78: a5g* 5m 5g³ 6.1m⁴ 5.1m³ 5g² 5f² 5m 1996 5d⁵ 5g 5d 5.1f
5.1g 5.1g 6m a5g⁶ a5g⁴ a7s a5g⁶ Dec 28] small, sturdy filly: only modest at best
in 1996: raced mainly at 5f: acts on firm ground and fibresand: tried blinkered, no
improvement: inconsistent. *Capt. J. Wilson*

AMYLOU   3 b.f. Dunbeath (USA) 127 – La Chiquita 84 (African Sky 124) [1995   –
NR 1996 5g² Jul 5] second foal: dam 1m winner in Ireland, later best over 5f here:
achieved little in weak seller at Hamilton: refused to enter stalls week later. *R. Allan*

ANABAA (USA)   4 b.c. Danzig (USA) – Balbonella (FR) 120 (Gay Mecene   130
(USA) 128) [1995 6d² 8d* 6m* 7s⁴ 7m⁶ 6d³ 1996 5.5g* 5.5g* 5g* 5d* 6m*
6.5d* 5d² Oct 6]
　　To the layman, the veterinary term 'wobbler' does not sound like a
terribly serious condition, now does it? Unlike, say, 'strangles.' Here, however,
is the definition of 'wobbler' given in *Black's Veterinary Dictionary*: 'The
name given to a horse which shows the following symptoms: a slight swaying
action of the hindquarters, or stumbling, with worsening of the condition until,
after 6 to 9 months, he cannot trot without rolling from side to side and falling.
The cause is unknown, but possibly a spinal cord injury gives rise to these
symptoms—seen in yearlings and two-year-olds; occasionally three-year-
olds'. 'They very rarely come back', reflected trainer Criquette Head in the
summer. But she had charge of one who did: Anabaa was affected by a spinal
injury and written off by vets as a two-year-old. How close he came to being
put down may or may not have been exaggerated, but the condition was serious
enough for his owner Sheikh Maktoum Al Maktoum to give this son of Danzig
out of a Group 1 winner away for nothing to trainer's father Alec Head who
hoped that the colt might recover sufficiently to be a teaser. Now Anabaa will
be allowed to go the whole hog himself. He returned to training in May 1995
and was offered back to Sheikh Maktoum before embarking on a racing career
for the Head family that took him to the status of Europe's undisputed
champion sprinter. The four-year-old Anabaa realised the loftiest ambitions
suggested by his pedigree and by far exceeded the most optimistic prognosis
that had been given during his illness.
　　Anabaa's three-year-old season must have been the cause of no little
satisfaction, boasting useful form to win a minor event at Maisons-Laffitte and
a handicap at Chantilly from six starts, but it was not until 1996 that he really
came into his own. Six races fell to Anabaa on the trot, and all of them in style:
listed events at Evry in March and April saw him clear by four lengths and
five lengths respectively; the step up in class for the Prix de Saint-Georges at
Longchamp in May resulted in an even longer winning margin, six lengths over
Bouche Bee; and in the Prix du Gros-Chene at Deauville in May, Freddie Head
never had to lift his whip in guiding Anabaa to a two-length success over Easy

Darley July Cup, Newmarket—Anabaa makes nearly all to see off Lucayan Prince

Option. The only criticism that might be levelled at Anabaa was that he had scared off the opposition; he started odds on in all four of those races and faced a total of just eighteen opponents.

A more hostile reception awaited Anabaa in the July Cup at Newmarket. Eight years had elapsed since Soviet Star took this Group 1 prize, twenty-one years since Lianga was the penultimate French horse to do so. Those to have failed since Soviet Star were Golden Opinion (second) in 1989; Lycius (second), Polar Falcon (fourth) and Exit To Nowhere (sixth) in 1991; Zieten (third) in 1993; and Dolphin Street (second) in 1994. Of the nine British-trained horses to take on the latest French challenge, only Iktamal had not won a pattern race—and he was about to put that right very shortly. Pivotal headed the betting after his reappearance win in the King's Stand Stakes, with Anabaa second favourite at 11/4. It was Anabaa who was a neck in front after half a furlong and one and three quarter lengths in front at the line. In between time, Hever Golf Rose and Gothenberg tried to match him early on, and Mind Games and Pivotal attempted to do so at the two-furlong marker, but Lucayan Prince was the only conceivable threat going into the final furlong and in the last hundred yards he had been well and truly beaten off as well. Anabaa strode clear.

Anabaa's remaining two races, both Group 1, were the Prix Maurice de Gheest at Deauville and the Prix de l'Abbaye de Longchamp. At Deauville, Anabaa won even more easily than at Newmarket, but this time did so after

Prix Maurice de Gheest, Deauville—waiting tactics account for Miesque's Son (far side) and Danehill Dancer in Anabaa's sixth win on the trot

being held up, cruising through to lead one furlong out and going on to beat the never-dangerous Miesque's Son by a length and a half. So to Longchamp. At this stage, there could be no grounds for confusion when racing folk were heard to sing the praises of a horse called Anabaa—few could have suggested that the champion sprinter would be upstaged on Arc weekend not only by the three-year-old filly Annaba, who bolted up in the Prix de Royallieu, but also by one of his own stable-companions in the Abbaye. Anabaa was sent off at odds on for the sixth time in six races in France as a four-year-old but looked poor value from the off, a little slowly away and then outpaced in the early stages. The danger, however, was even further back; Anabaa worked his way to the front over a furlong out only to have the three-year-old filly Kistena follow him through and beat him by a neck. Both these Head runners were later found to have a chip in the left knee, which in Anabaa's case hastened his departure for the Haras de Quesnay where he will be standing at a fee of 100,000 francs. The Breeder's Cup Mile had been an option before the injury but, because of his back problems, Mme Head had already expressed strong reservations about sending him round a turn. Let's hope his back will now stand up to the demands of life in the breeding shed. He is reportedly also to stand in New South Wales.

		Northern Dancer (b 1961)	Nearctic Natalma
	Danzig (USA) (b 1977)		
		Pas de Nom (b or br 1968)	Admiral's Voyage Petitioner
Anabaa (USA) (b.c. 1992)			
		Gay Mecene (b 1975)	Vaguely Noble Gay Missile
	Balbonella (FR) (b or br 1984)		
		Bamieres (br 1978)	Riverman Bergamesque

Mme A. Head's "Anabaa"

Mme Head was frequently asked to compare Anabaa with the last French Abbaye winner Sigy, whom she trained to win the race in 1978. Her answer was that Anabaa did not have Sigy's speed, and, on form, his six-furlong figure in the July Cup is indeed his best. His first three-year-old win was over a mile. A most imposing colt, big and good-topped, Anabaa did not race on extremes of going in the latest season. He is the fourth son of Danzig to win the July Cup—following Green Desert (1986), Polish Patriot (1991) and Hamas (1993)—and the second son of Balbonella to leave a striking impression in 1996: Balbonella's only previous foal, Key of Luck (by Chief's Crown), won the Dubai Duty Free race in March by twenty lengths. Key of Luck is an erstwhile stable-companion of Anabaa's and showed useful form to win the Prix d'Arenberg and Criterium d'Evry in 1993. Balbonella was another to race for the Head stable, but her Group 1 win in the Robert Papin had come on the last of four unbeaten starts for provincial trainer Francis Rohaut. Her debut had been at Mont-de-Marsan. A reported five million francs took her to Mme Head's, for whom she showed high-class form as a three-year-old, winning over seven furlongs and finishing runner-up in the Maurice de Gheest, before she won another four races (including the eight-and-a-half-furlong Grade 3 Dahlia Handicap) as a four-year-old in the United States. Her dam Bamieres also began her career in the French Provinces, but ended it there as well, achieving very little. She is a daughter of Bergamesque who won twice on the Paris tracks, at around eleven furlongs. The task of continuing Balbonella's good record as a broodmare lies with a 1994 filly by Zilzal and a 1995 filly by Seattle Slew. The former, called Always Loyal, made an excellent start when winning over seven and a half furlongs in the colours of Maktoum Al Maktoum and in the care of Mme Head at Saint-Cloud in November. *Mme C. Head, France*

ANAK-KU 3 ch.g. Efisio 120 – City Link Lass 92 (Double Jump 131) [1995 NR 73 1996 a8g⁶ a8g² a10g³ 8.5m⁵ 7m² 7f³ 8.1g* 10f² Aug 5] 7,000Y: leggy gelding: half-brother to several winners, easily best being useful John Rose (up to 9f, by Tina's Pet): dam 2-y-o 6f and 7f winner: won maiden at Musselburgh in July: stays 1¼m: acts on equitrack and firm ground: blinkered/visored since sixth 3-y-o start: gelded. *Miss Gay Kelleway*

ANALOGUE (IRE) 4 b.g. Reference Point 139 – Dancing Shadow 117 (Dan- – cer's Image (USA)) [1995 62: 10m⁴ a12g a12g 1996 a12g 15.4m Apr 16] strong, sturdy gelding: no form since 3-y-o reappearance: tried visored/blinkered, no improvement: joined R. J. Eckley. *P. Mitchell*

ANASTINA 4 ch.f. Thatching 131 – Nikitina 106 (Nijinsky (CAN) 138) [1995 –: 80 8d 10g 1996 a7g* a8g² 8s* 8d 8m 7.3m 8m 7s Oct 24] lengthy, good-topped filly: has been freeze-fired on forelegs: fairly useful handicapper: won at Southwell (maiden) in February and at Leicester (by 7 lengths) in March: off course 4½ months after fifth start: made all on unfavoured far side at Newbury (apprentices) final start, eased close home when clearly held by those on stand side: stays 1m: acts on fibresand and on good to firm and soft ground: tends to race close up nowadays. *N. A. Graham*

ANATOMIC 2 b.f. (Mar 29) Deerhound (USA) 64 – Bouncing Slew (USA) – (Seattle Slew (USA)) [1996 5s 5m⁵ Jun 21] 1,000Y: second foal: dam twice-raced half-sister to Rousillon: sire, 7f to 9f winner, closely related to Wolfhound: saddle slipped on debut in March: tailed off in seller 3 months later. *M. R. Channon*

ANAXAGORAS 6 b.g. Mtoto 134 – I'll Try 71 (Try My Best (USA) 130) [1995 – NR 1996 10.1m a6g a8g⁶ a8g Nov 22] no form since fairly useful 2-y-o. *S. Gollings*

ANCHOR CLEVER 4 b.c. Slip Anchor 136 – Mountain Bluebird (USA) 79 98 (Clever Trick (USA)) [1995 106: 12f⁴ 10m² 12m 14m* 16.2m 15g³ 14.6d⁶ 14s 1996 15.9m⁵ 18g³ 12f Sep 13] strong, lengthy colt: useful performer at best: off course nearly 11 months and sweating, respectable fifth of 7 to Celeric in listed race at York: well behind form afterwards: should prove better at 2m than shorter: acts on any going: not easiest of rides: needs treating with caution: sent to France. *P. A. Kelleway*

ANCHORENA 4 b.f. Slip Anchor 136 – Canna (Caerleon (USA) 132) [1995 77?: 62 11.4m² 12s⁵ 14.1m⁵ 1996 a12g a12g⁶ a16g a11g a11g 9.9d² 10g⁵ 9.9m⁴ 12g* a11g² a48

57

12m 14.1f 12f³ a14g a12g⁴ Jul 27] tall, angular filly: modest form: stayed on well to win claimer at Thirsk (claimed out of J. A. Harris' stable £7,000) in May: well below form last 5 starts: won over hurdles for Miss V. Williams, now with D. W. Barker: should stay beyond 1½m: acts on good to firm and fibresand: tried visored, no improvement: flashed tail and carried head high sixth 4-y-o start, tended to hang next time: not one to trust implicitly. *Mrs A. Swinbank*

ANCHOR VENTURE 3 b.g. Slip Anchor 136 – Ski Michaela (USA) (Devil's Bag (USA)) [1995 50+: 8g³ 7.9g 1996 12m⁴ 12.3g⁵ 12f⁵ a16g⁴ 14.1f³ 14g Jul 5] rangy gelding: modest maiden: pulled hard final start: subsequently gelded: should stay further than 1½m: acts on firm ground: inconsistent. *S. P. C. Woods* — 61

ANCIENT QUEST 3 b.g. Rainbow Quest (USA) 134 – Racquette 120 (Ballymore 123) [1995 NR 1996 10.3g 12g² 13.1d² 12m⁶ Jun 14] tall, workmanlike, rather leggy gelding: ninth reported foal: half-brother to several winners, including smart French 1m to 1¼m performer Splendid Moment (by Storm Bird) and smart 1986 French 2-y-o 1m winner Grand Chelem (by Be My Guest): dam, third in Irish Oaks, is half-sister to Irish 1000 Guineas winner Arctique Royale: fair maiden: will stay 1¾m: acts on dead ground, ran poorly (seeming to falter over 1f out) on good to firm: gelded. *N. A. Callaghan* — 78

ANDREYEV (IRE) 2 ch.c. (Apr 28) Presidium 124 – Missish (Mummy's Pet 125) [1996 6f⁴ 5m* 6.1d* 6m⁴ 6m 7d* 7.3s⁶ Oct 24] 24,000Y: tall, close-coupled colt: fourth foal: brother to 3 winners at up to 7f, including 3-y-o Centurion, 5f winner at 2 yrs, and 6f/7f winner Petomi: dam unraced: useful form: won minor event at Windsor in June and Chester in August: useful efforts in Mill Reef Stakes at Newbury and Middle Park Stakes at Newmarket before beating Dacoit 3½ lengths in useful conditions event at Ascot in October: disappointing in Horris Hill Stakes at Newbury final outing: stays 7f well: acts on good to firm and dead ground: looked extremely well last 3 starts. *R. Hannon* — 101

ANDROID (USA) 3 b. or br.c. Riverman (USA) 131 – Action Francaise (USA) 108 (Nureyev (USA) 131) [1995 NR 1996 8m⁶ 8d* 8g* 10m³ 10d² 10s² Sep 22] third foal: dam 7f and Group 3 1m winner in France, daughter of outstanding Allez France: smart French colt: won minor event in May and 6-runner Prix de la Jonchere in June (beat Manninamix a length), both at Longchamp: 2 lengths third of 10 to Grape Tree Road in Grand Prix de Paris at Longchamp, short-head second of 9 to Sasuru in Prix Guillaume d'Ornano at Deauville and 1½ lengths second of 5 to Baroud d'Honneur in Prix du Prince d'Orange at Longchamp: stays 1¼m: acts on good to firm and soft ground: consistent. *A. Fabre, France* — 116

ANDSOME BOY 3 ch.g. Out of Hand 84 – My Home 61 (Homing 130) [1995 –: a6g 6.1d⁶ 6f 1996 6m 8.3m⁶ 8.1d 8g 7.1g⁵ 8.2m Jun 24] neat gelding: poor maiden: stays 8.3f: acts on good to firm ground: inconsistent. *C. R. Barwell* — 42

ANDY COIN 5 ch.m. Andy Rew 103 – Legal Coin (Official) [1995 NR 1996 8m 10.8m 10g Sep 3] first foal: dam of little account: of no account. *W. M. Brisbourne* — –

ANETTA 2 ch.f. (Apr 26) Aragon 118 – Pronetta (USA) (Mr Prospector (USA)) [1996 6g 7f Nov 5] 5,200Y: leggy, unfurnished filly: half-sister to fairly useful 3-y-o 5f (at 2 yrs) and 6f winner Mallia (by Statoblest) and several winners in North America: dam won at up to 7f in USA: bandaged behind, down the field in late-season maidens at Pontefract. *Miss S. E. Hall* — –

ANGAAR (IRE) 3 b.c. Fairy King (USA) – Decadence (Vaigly Great 127) [1995 77P: 5s* 1996 5m* 6.1g⁵ 6m⁶ 5m⁶ 7g* 7m² 7d⁴ Aug 24] sturdy, angular colt: generally progressive handicapper: got up closing stages when winning at Thirsk (minor event) in April and at Leicester (by a short head after ducking right close home) in July: best form at 7f, should prove fully effective granted good test at 6f: acts on good to firm and soft ground: has run well when sweating: may well prove best with exaggerated waiting tactics: consistent: sent to UAE. *A. C. Stewart* — 88 +

ANGEL CHIMES 3 ch.f. Most Welcome 131 – Bell Toll 87 (High Line 125) [1995 77: 7m 7m² 5d* 7d 8f³ 7m² 1996 7m* May 3] smallish, workmanlike filly: has a markedly round action: won handicap at Newmarket in May, staying on strongly to get up close home: should stay beyond 1m: acts on firm and dead ground: comes from behind: carried head high (ran well) final 2-y-o start. *J. E. Banks* — 77

ANGEL FACE (USA) 3 b.f. Zilzal (USA) 137 – Touching Love 109 (Touching Wood (USA) 127) [1995 –: 7m 1996 7.6m⁴ 7f 6.1m a10g* a8g² a9.4g² a10g* a10g — 75

Dec 31] rather leggy filly: trained by B. Preece first 3 starts as 3-y-o: much improved for present stable, winner of seller and amateurs handicap at Lingfield late on: effective at 1m to 1¼m: acts on all-weather surfaces: often unruly in preliminaries. *P. D. Evans*

ANGLESEY SEA VIEW 7 gr.m. Seymour Hicks (FR) 125 – Lexham View 72   62
(Abwah 118) [1995 66: 16.1g* 22.2m⁴ 1996 16.2g⁶ 14.9d 18.7g 16g⁴ 14d⁴ 20f 15.9m 16.5m⁴ 16g⁵ 15.9d⁵ 16g⁵ 15.1s² a16g Dec 11] leggy, angular mare: modest handicapper: should stay further than 2m: acts on good to firm and soft ground, tailed off on equitrack: blinkered (ran well) twelfth 7-y-o start: won maiden hurdle in November. *A. Bailey*

ANGUS-G 4 br.g. Chief Singer 131 – Horton Line 89 (High Line 125) [1995 67p: 89
8.2d⁴ 8m⁵ 1996 8g⁵ 8m³ 10m 10f³ 10f* 10m* 10m² 10.3m² 9m³ Oct 5] big, useful-looking gelding: generally progressive handicapper: narrow winner twice at Newmarket in the summer: better form in big fields afterwards, third of 38 to Clifton Fox in Cambridgeshire: shapes as if will be well suited by further than 1¼m: shaped well on dead ground on debut, but has raced almost exclusively on top-of-the-ground. *Mrs M. Reveley*

ANGUS MCCOATUP (IRE) 3 ch.c. Mac's Imp (USA) 116 – In For More   51
(Don 128) [1995 65: 5f⁵ 5g 6g 6g⁵ a7g⁴ a7g² a7g⁵ 1996 7s 6m⁵ 7.1d 6.1m 7g⁵ a8.5g⁴   a60
7.6m⁶ a7g⁵ 8m a8.5g² a8.5g³ 7f³ a8.5g Oct 19] strong, lengthy colt: carries condition: modest maiden handicapper: sold (B. McMahon to M. Hammond) only 1,600 gns Doncaster October Sales: may prove best at up to 8.5f: acts on fibresand and firm ground, well below form both starts on a soft surface: tried blinkered, no improvement: takes keen hold. *B. A. McMahon*

ANIMATION 3 ch.f. Superlative 118 – What A Looker (USA) (Raise A Native)   –
[1995 –: 6m⁶ 6m 1996 8g a9.4g 8.5m 11.9f⁵ Aug 7] sparely-made filly: no worthwhile form: retained 2,000 gns Newmarket Autumn Sales. *K. McAuliffe*

ANISTOP 4 b.c. Nomination 125 – Pounelta 91 (Tachypous 128) [1995 48, a59:   50
7f 8.3m 10m⁶ 8g² 8m 8.5s a8g* 1996 a10g⁵ a12g² a12g⁵ a12g² 12d a12g² 10m³ a12g   a59
11.1g May 20] sparely-made colt: modest handicapper: left R. Akehurst after fourth 4-y-o start: ran poorly last 2 starts: stays 1½m: best on the all-weather, acts on firm ground, probably on soft: often soon off bridle. *J. L. Eyre*

ANITA'S CONTESSA (IRE) 4 b.f. Anita's Prince 126 – Take More (GER)   56
(Frontal 122) [1995 61, a68: 7d⁶ 6m 6g⁶ a6g⁵ a6g 7.1g 6.9g* a6g⁴ a7g a6g⁵ 1996 6m   a60
6f a6g³ a6g 7f a6g⁶ a6g⁵ a6g² a7g⁵ a7g⁵ Dec 28] leggy, sparely-made filly: modest handicapper: effective at 6f and 7f: acts on good to firm and dead ground and fibresand: usually races prominently: inconsistent. *B. Palling*

ANJOU 4 b.g. Saumarez 132 – Bourbon Topsy 108 (Ile de Bourbon (USA) 133)   –
[1995 72: a7g⁴ a10g³ 12s⁵ 12m* 11.8f 12m a12g⁶ a16g* 1996 a16.2g⁴ a16g⁵ Feb 24] rangy gelding: fair handicapper: no form in 1996: probably better suited by 2m than 1½m: acts on good to firm ground and equitrack: none too consistent. *J. Pearce*

ANNABA (IRE) 3 ch.f. In The Wings 128 – Anna Matrushka (Mill Reef   120
(USA) 141) [1995 75p: 8d³ 1996 10m* 10m³ 11.9m⁵ 10.1m⁵ 12.5d* 12d*
Oct 20]

After the high promise of her third place in the Nassau Stakes had twice gone unfulfilled, Annaba came good at Longchamp in October, winning the Prix de Royallieu and the Prix du Conseil de Paris in the space of a fortnight with an authority that entitles her to be regarded among the best of her age and sex at a mile and a half.

Annaba did not come to hand in time for the Oaks; the Nassau Stakes was only her second race of the season, only her third in all. It represented a big step up from the Windsor maiden which she had won back in June, but she was in the firing line from three furlongs out and finished less than three lengths behind the winner Last Second. By comparison, defeats on similar ground behind Eva Luna in the Galtres Stakes at York and Flame Valley in a listed event at Yarmouth were disappointing to say the least: each time she raced keenly in the lead then weakened into fifth, giving the impression she might not stay so well as her breeding suggested she would. Annaba's trainer commented

Prix de Royallieu, Longchamp—the other Annaba makes her name

after the Royallieu that he thought she beat herself at the stalls at York and Yarmouth, and was thankful for the presence of a pacemaker at Longchamp —the Aga Khan's Haramayda, acting on behalf of the eventual third Zafzala. Annaba's jockey Dettori got a lead from Haramayda until half a mile out, where he decided to press on. His mount responded very strongly and was well on top from halfway up the straight; she passed the post four lengths clear of Whitewater Affair who just held on for second.

The Royallieu is confined to fillies and mares. Annaba's six opponents in the Prix du Conseil de Paris were all colts. They were headed by the good-class French four-year-old Poliglote, winner of the Grand Prix d'Evry and third of nine to Helissio in the Grand Prix de Saint-Cloud earlier in the season. Annaba improved further to beat him by two lengths. The contest went much like the Royallieu for her. After Poliglote had forced the pace as he often does, Annaba, having sat on his tail from the start, kicked on in the straight. Poliglote fought back, the only one to make a race of it, but the winner just needed to be pushed out with hands and heels.

Annaba (IRE) (ch.f. 1993)	In The Wings (b 1986)	Sadler's Wells (b 1981)	Northern Dancer / Fairy Bridge
		High Hawk (b 1980)	Shirley Heights / Sunbittern
	Anna Matrushka (ch 1984)	Mill Reef (b 1968)	Never Bend / Milan Mill
		Anna Paola (ch 1978)	Prince Ippi / Antwerpen

Annaba's form is already superior to that of the dam's best previous runner Anna of Saxony (by Ela-Mana-Mou). That filly was placed in the Park Hill Stakes and the Princess Royal Stakes at three, then she improved at four to win the Park Hill and come second in the St Simon Stakes. Annaba is to be kept in training, too, with prospects of improvement of her own and prospects of staying as far as her half-sister did (a mile and three quarters) provided she

Prix du Conseil de Paris, Longchamp— she has to work rather harder to beat the four-year-old colt Poliglote

doesn't run so freely as at York and Yarmouth. Clearly, having a lead was important at Longchamp. The softish ground prevailing on both occasions might also have been important to her—she certainly acted well on it—though her Nassau form on good to firm leaves some room for doubt. The workmanlike Annaba is the fifth foal and fourth winner out of her unraced dam. The family is a good German one—the second dam Anna Paola won the Preis der Diana and her daughter Anno Luce came third in the event in 1996—but it has become well-established in Britain. Several of Anna Paola's foals have raced here, notably the middle-distance performers Atlaal and Anna Petrovna, the latter now the dam of Annus Mirabilis. *J. H. M. Gosden*

ANNA SOLEIL (IRE) 3 b.g. Red Sunset 120 – Flying Anna (Roan Rocket 128) 72
[1995 NR 1996 11.1g² 12d³ Apr 26] 20,000Y: half-brother to several winners (fair form at best), most at middle distances: dam Irish 5f winner: fair form placed in maidens at Musselburgh and Carlisle in April: should stay further than 1½m: looks one paced: joined O. Sherwood. *M. R. Channon*

ANNECY (USA) 3 b.f. Mr Prospector (USA) – Lake Country (CAN) (Caucasus 77
(USA) 127) [1995 73p: 8m³ 1996 10g 10.5d³ 12m 10.1m⁵ 11.9g⁵ 14.1g Oct 24] medium-sized, good-topped filly: fair maiden: stays 10.5f: acts on dead ground and good to firm: sold 140,000 gns Newmarket December Sales. *H. R. A. Cecil*

ANNO LUCE 3 ch.f. Old Vic 136 – Anna Paola (GER) (Prince Ippi (GER)) [1995 105
8d* 8v 1996 10.5g* 11v² 11v³ 11s² 12g² 12m* 14d Sep 29] eighth foal: half-sister to 3 winners at around 1¼m+, notably the dam of 4-y-o Annus Mirabilis, and also to dam of Anna of Saxony (rated 111, would have stayed 2m) and 3-y-o Annaba: dam leading German filly at 2 and 3 yrs, winner of Preis der Diana: useful German filly: won maiden at Gelsenkirchen at 2 yrs and minor event at Mulheim in April: placed in 2 listed races, Preis der Diana (beaten 7½ lengths) at Mulheim in May, and Group 3 event at Hamburg (beaten 1½ lengths) and listed race at Krefeld (beaten 1¾ lengths) in the summer: won 13-runner Group 1 event at Hanover in September by 2½ lengths from The Blade: tailed off in German St Leger at Dortmund: stays 1½m: acts on good to firm and heavy ground: blinkered since second 3-y-o start: consistent: joined J. Gosden. *U. Ostmann, Germany*

ANN'S MUSIC 3 b.f. Clantime 101 – An-Go-Look (Don't Look 107) [1995 –: 5g –
6h 7.5m 7.5d 1996 a6g Nov 18] no form. *J. M. Jefferson*

ANN'S PEARL (IRE) 5 br.m. Cyrano de Bergerac 120 – Pariscene 86 (Dragon- 72 d
ara Palace (USA) 115) [1995 80: 5m 5.2m 5.1m* 5g 5.7m 5.1m² 5m⁶ 5g 5d 5s 1996 5.1f³ 5m 5.7m 5.7m⁶ Jun 29] fairly useful handicapper: well beaten after respectable 5-y-o reappearance: best at 5f: acts on firm and dead going, below form on equitrack: blinkered (tailed off) final 5-y-o start: inconsistent. *J. W. Hills*

ANNUS MIRABILIS (FR) 4 b.c. Warning 136 – Anna Petrovna (FR) 90 120
(Wassl 125) [1995 120: 10.4g² 9g² 8m⁵ 12m³ 10.4m³ 10.9g* 1996 a8s⁴ 10d³ 12f² 12g³ 12m⁵ 10d* 9f* Oct 5]
In early-October, on one of the busiest and most important weekends of the racing year, news came through from Japan of another win there for the Godolphin team, one that offered some consolation for the subsequent reverses suffered by Classic Cliche and Easy Option at Longchamp. Annus Mirabilis, so often the bridesmaid in Europe, had accounted for eleven locals in the Mainichi Okan in Tokyo on the first occasion the Group 2 event had been open to international competition. Ridden by the then Japan-based Darryll Holland, he had picked up a purse not much short of £400,000 by a margin of one and a half lengths with a performance that seems to equate to his best over here. Annus Mirabilis at his consistent best has not been good enough to win in Europe, though he came close in the Irish Derby, the Dante Stakes and the Prix Jean Prat as a three-year-old, and was placed in the latest season in the Tattersalls Gold Cup, the Hardwicke Stakes and the Princess of Wales's Stakes prior to tackling the King George VI and Queen Elizabeth Diamond Stakes. In that last race he seemed to run as a pacemaker for Classic Cliche, setting a strong pace to the home turn, visored for the first time and 33/1. Just when it

Godolphin's "Annus Mirabilis"

seemed that a horse with the ability to run Oscar Schindler to half a length in the Hardwicke might complete another year still short of a pattern-race win, connections lined up a good opportunity in the £19,300 Group 3 Winter Hill Stakes at Windsor in August which he seized readily, by three quarters of a length and the same from Salmon Ladder and Storm Trooper. Next came that adroit piece of placing in the Far East.

	Warning	Known Fact	In Reality
	(b 1985)	(b 1977)	Tamerett
Annus Mirabilis (FR)		Slightly Dangerous	Roberto
(b.c. 1992)		(b 1979)	Where You Lead
	Anna Petrovna (FR)	Wassl	Mill Reef
	(b 1987)	(b 1980)	Hayloft
		Anna Paola	Prince Ippi
		(ch 1978)	Antwerpen

Annus Mirabilis' family made further news in the autumn through the exploits in France of the greatly-improved three-year-old middle-distance filly Annaba, whose dam is by Mill Reef out of Annus Mirabilis' grandam, the German Oaks winner Anna Paola. Less newsworthy, but interesting in context, is that Annus Mirabilis' half-sister Sophia Antipolis (by Nordico) showed winning form at five furlongs and seven furlongs as a two-year-old in Italy in 1996. Annus Mirabilis remains in training, requiring further careful placement, in all probability, if his winning streak is to continue. A tall colt, he is effective at nine furlongs to a mile and a half and on any type of ground on turf, but finds sand against him judged on one run in testing conditions in Dubai. He is usually held up and has shown a tendency to come off a true line under pressure (though when Dettori took him to race against the far rail at Windsor he kept on very strongly, getting on top well inside the final furlong). He was visored again there and again at Tokyo. *Saeed bin Suroor*

ANOKATO 2 b.g. (Apr 1) Tina's Pet 121 – High Velocity 53 (Frimley Park 109) 66 [1996 6g⁶ 5.7m³ 5.2g⁴ 5.7m³ 6d⁶ 5m 5f³ 5m* 5m³ Oct 3] leggy gelding: has a round action: fourth foal: brother to 3-y-o 5.1f winner Mindrace: dam 5f performer: modest form: won rating-related maiden at Folkestone in September: creditable third behind Meliksah in Newmarket nursery on final outing: stays 6f: acts on firm ground: seems best in blinkers. *K. T. Ivory*

ANONYM (IRE) 4 b.g. Nashamaa 113 – Bonny Bertha (Capistrano 120) [1995 67 71: 8m³ 8f 10m 9f³ 10f⁴ 7f* 8g* 7m³ 7m⁵ 7d 1996 6s 6g 7m 8g 8g⁴ 8f⁵ 7m 7s⁴ 7.1m* 7g⁶ 8f³ 8f⁶ 8s 8g⁴ 8m⁴ 7f³ 8.2g⁵ 8g⁵ a7g⁶ a7g Dec 28] leggy, lengthy gelding: has a quick action: fair handicapper: won claimer at Musselburgh in July: best at 7f/1m: acts on firm going, below best on soft surface and on only run on all-weather: blinkered since fourteenth 4-y-o start: often ridden by 7-lb claimer J. Bramhill: often edgy: sometimes looks reluctant. *D. Nicholls*

ANORAK (USA) 6 b.g. Storm Bird (CAN) 134 – Someway Somehow (USA) 46 (What Luck (USA)) [1995 46: a8g a11g a11g⁶ a9.4g⁵ 12m² 11.1m³ 10.9g² 12m⁴ 1996 10f⁵ 12s 12m Aug 6] leggy gelding: has a round action: poor performer: no form after reappearance: stays 1½m: unsuited by soft ground, probably acts on any other, including all-weather: normally visored nowadays: sometimes hangs left and finds little. *G. M. Moore*

ANOTHER BATCHWORTH 4 b.f. Beveled (USA) – Batchworth Dancer 67 72 (Ballacashtal (CAN)) [1995 63: 7g 6m 5.3f⁵ 5.3f² 7m² 6d 5.3g a5g² a6g* a5g a6g³ a6g 1996 6m² 5f² 6g 5g 5.3m² 5m 5.3m³ a6g 5.1m² 5.1g* 5m* 5.1g² a5g² a5g³ a5g⁶ Dec 5] lengthy filly: fair handicapper: won at Nottingham and Redcar (minor event) in October: effective at 5f (best form) and 6f: acts on firm and soft ground and the all-weather: blinkered since ninth 4-y-o start: sometimes early to post: front runner. *E. A. Wheeler*

ANOTHER EPISODE (IRE) 7 b.g. Drumalis 125 – Pasadena Lady (Captain – James 123) [1995 –: a5g⁶ a5g⁶ 5m⁵ 196m 5g 5g 5m 5g 5f 6m Jul 12] leggy, lengthy gelding: sold out of J. Berry's stable 4,000 gns Doncaster March Sales before reappearance: no form since fair 5-y-o. *Miss L. A. Perratt*

ANOTHER FIDDLE (IRE) 6 b.g. Waajib 121 – Elmar 87 (Lord Gayle (USA) – 124) [1995 69: 8g 8m 8m⁶ 8m⁵ 8f⁵ 8f⁶ 8f² 8g² 9.7s² 1996 9.7m⁴ a10g Nov 26] fair handicapper: shaped as if retaining ability only start for S. Dow: showed little (all-weather debut) 4½ months later: shapes as if stays 9.7f: acts on firm and soft going: sometimes carries head awkwardly: has been bandaged behind: none too consistent. *B. A. Pearce*

ANOTHER NIGHT (IRE) 2 ch.c. (Apr 30) Waajib 121 – Little Me (Connaught 77 130) [1996 7g² 7f² 7m³ Sep 11] IR 20,000Y: leggy colt: fourth foal: half-brother to 3-y-o Natatarl (by Roi Danzig), 6f (at 2 yrs) and 1½m winner Last Laugh (by Last Tycoon) and Irish 1½m winner Blue Diana (by Bluebird): dam Irish middle-distance winner: placed in maidens: below form at Epsom final start: will be suited by further than 7f: takes long time to find stride. *R. Hannon*

ANOTHER NIGHTMARE (IRE) 4 b.f. Treasure Kay 114 – Carange (Known 59 Fact (USA) 135) [1995 –: a6g 5m 5g 5g⁵ 5m 5f 5f⁶ 5m 5m 1996 6d 5d 5m 5g⁴ 5f 7.1g 5d⁴ 6m⁵ 5m² 7g³ 7g 6f* 7g⁶ 5m⁵ 6s* 6f² 6.1m⁴ 6m⁶ 6d 6d 6m 6m 8.1s a6g Nov 18] leggy, sparely-made filly: with T. Dyer first 4 starts in 1996: modest handicapper: won apprentice races at Hamilton (hung markedly right) and Ripon in August: suited by 6f: acts on firm and soft ground: none too consistent. *R. M. McKellar*

ANOTHERONE TO NOTE 5 ch.g. Beveled (USA) – Dame Nellie 84 (Dom 42 inion 123) [1995 51d: a6g³ a6g a6g³ a8g 6m 6f a6g⁶ a5g a7g⁵ 6g 8f⁴ a7g a7g⁵ 1996 a8g³ a8g a7g a11g⁴ a12g⁵ Feb 19] poor maiden handicapper: probably best at 1m: acts on the all-weather and on firm ground, well beaten on soft: no improvement in visor/blinkers: pulls hard: inconsistent. *N. P. Littmoden*

ANOTHER PICEA 3 b.g. Picea 99 – Atoka 97 (March Past 124) [1995 –: 5m 6m 8.2m 1996 10s⁵ Jul 4] well beaten. *N. Tinkler*

ANOTHER QUARTER (IRE) 3 b.f. Distinctly North (USA) 115 – Numidia 47 (Sallust 134) [1995 57: 7g 8.2m⁵ 1996 8.2m 8g⁶ 10.2g³ a8.5g⁴ 10m² 9.7g⁴ 10.1f² a61 a12g* 12m* 15.8g a14g⁶ Dec 3] sturdy filly: modest form: easy winner (making all) of sellers at Southwell and Pontefract (sold out of S. Woods's stable 6,100 gns) in the summer: stays 1½m: acts on firm ground, best form on fibresand: effective blinkered (was fourth to seventh 3-y-o starts) or not: sometimes bandaged. *M. C. Chapman*

ANOTHER TIME 4 ch.g. Clantime 101 – Another Move 69 (Farm Walk 111) 84 [1995 79p: 6g⁵ 8m⁵ 8m⁶ 8g* 8g 8d* 8g² 10f* 1996 10s 10m² 10.8g⁶ 10m* 10g⁵ 10m* 10v 10.2f³ 9m⁴ 10s⁵ Oct 24] neat gelding: has a quick action: fairly useful handicapper: won at Ripon (minor event) and Lingfield in summer: best efforts last 3 starts, including when fourth of 38 in the Cambridgeshire at Newmarket: best at up to 1¼m: acts on firm and soft ground, not on heavy: usually held up. *S. P. C. Woods*

ANSAL BOY 4 b.c. Robellino (USA) 127 – Son Et Lumiere (Rainbow Quest – (USA) 134) [1995 7v² 6s³ 6.5v² 7.8f* 8s 7m⁵ 8g⁵ 7m 7d 1996 a7g a8g⁶ a8g a7g 7s Apr 29] 14,000Y: ex-Irish colt: first foal: dam poor daughter of very useful miler Soprano: fair handicapper (rated 72) at 3 yrs for T. Lacy, below form after winning at Dundalk: well beaten in 1996, trained first 4 starts by Miss G. Kelleway: stays 1m: acts on any going: no improvement in blinkers. *Michael Cunningham, Ireland*

ANSELLMAN 6 gr.g. Absalom 128 – Grace Poole (Sallust 134) [1995 78: 6g 5g⁵ 89 6d⁶ 5.1m² 5m³ 6m 5m* 5.1h² 5m³ 6g 5g 5m⁵ 1996 5s 5g 5.1g* 5.1f⁶ 6d 5.1f* 6.1m² 6m³ᵈⁱˢ 6g 5.6m 5d⁵ 5s² 5g 5g⁵ a5g³ Nov 22] sturdy gelding: carries condition: has a round action: fairly useful handicapper: won at Bath in April and at Chepstow in July: ran well in competitive races in the autumn: effective at 5f and 6f: acts on any ground, including fibresand: effective blinkered/visored or not. *J. Berry*

ANSWERS-TO-THOMAS 3 b.g. Komaite (USA) – Launde Abbey 75 51 (Absalom 128) [1995 62: 5g⁶ 5f² 5d⁴ 6d 5m 6m⁵ 1996 6g³ 5.9f 5.9f Jun 26] lengthy gelding: has a round action: modest maiden: shaped as if retaining his ability only on reappearance: should stay 6f: acts on firm and dead ground. *J. M. Jefferson*

ANTARCTIC STORM 3 b.g. Emarati (USA) 74 – Katie Scarlett 70 (Lochnager 62 132) [1995 72?: 6m 7g 1996 8.2d 6.9f 8.3m* 8m 7m Oct 29] strong, close-coupled gelding: looked to have gone very much the wrong way temperamentally, but then won handicap at Windsor in June: sold out of E. Dunlop's stable 10,500 gns Newmarket July Sales: off course 4 months, well held on return: stays 8.3f: acts on good to firm ground. *R. A. Fahey*

ANTARES 2 b.c. (Mar 5) Governor General 116 – Eucharis 41 (Tickled Pink 114) 54 [1996 5g 5g 5g³ 5m 5f 5f² 5f 6m a5g Aug 16] 6,200Y, 16,000 2-y-o: strong colt: fifth foal: brother to 3-y-o 5f winner Chalice and a winner in Norway and half-brother to winning sprinter Barbara's Cutie (by Tina's Pet): dam, maiden, stayed 1m: modest maiden: well beaten in sellers last 2 starts: best form at 5f: acts on firm ground: blinkered (showed little) fifth start. *N. Tinkler*

ANTARTICTERN (USA) 6 b.g. Arctic Tern (USA) 126 – False Image (USA) – 79 (Danzig) [1995 48: 12m⁵ 11f⁵ 9m³ 10m² 10.1f⁶ 12g 10g² 8.9g 14.1m 1996 a12g⁴ 12d 10g 11m Oct 29] good-bodied gelding: ungenuine hurdler: poor on flat: no form after reappearance: stays 1¼m: acts on firm and soft ground: tried blinkered/visored, no improvement. *G. R. Oldroyd*

ANTHELIA 3 b.f. Distant Relative 128 – Confection (Formidable (USA) 125) 100 [1995 100p: 5m* 6g* 6f³ 1996 8g 8m² 8m³ 10m³ 10.1g⁵ Oct 30] lengthy, quite attractive filly: useful form: around ½-length third of 10 to Sardonic in listed race at Newbury fourth start, staying on well: off course 4½ months afterwards: stays 1¼m well, may be unsuited by return to 1m at 4 yrs: has raced only on a sound surface, acts on firm: sold 55,000 gns Newmarket December Sales. *G. Wragg*

ANTIGUAN JANE 3 b.f. Shirley Heights 130 – Dabbiana (CAN) (Fappiano 71 (USA)) [1995 56p: 7m a7g³ 1996 10g Apr 26] good-topped filly: has scope: has a quick action: 66/1 and burly, best form when ninth of 14 in maiden at Sandown, losing prominent place early in straight then keeping on steadily: will be suited by middle distances: tail flasher. *R. W. Armstrong*

ANTONIA BIN (IRE)   3 gr.f. Sadler's Wells (USA) 132 – Lady Capulet (USA)   50
116 (Sir Ivor 135) [1995 NR 1996 11.5g 12m³ Jul 15] IR 50,000Y: sister to 3 winners,
including smart El Prado (up to 1m at 2 yrs in Ireland), and half-sister to high-class
Entitled (stayed 1½m, by Mill Reef): dam won Irish 1000 Guineas: third of 6 in
maiden at Folkestone: sent to Australia. *M. Bell*

ANTONIA'S CHOICE   2 ch.f. (Feb 22) Music Boy 124 – Mainly Sunset (Red   73
Sunset 120) [1996 5g³ 5.1g* May 9] 26,000Y: strong, lengthy filly: has scope: keen
walker: fluent mover: fourth foal: sister to Irish 5f and 6f winner Musical Sunset and
half-sister to 3-y-o 6f winner Madrina (by Waajib) and 1994 2-y-o 5f winner Daily
Starshine (by Petorius): dam once-raced half-sister to useful sprinters Tod and Great
Chaddington: improved significantly when winning maiden at Chester in May by 3
lengths from Swift Refusal, making all: not seen out again: looked speedy. *J. Berry*

ANTONIAS MELODY   3 b.f. Rambo Dancer (CAN) 107 – Ayodessa 78   86 d
(Lochnager 132) [1995 69: 5m 5m² 6m⁶ 6.1d* 6d 5m³ 5m⁵ 1996 6g⁶ 6g* 7.3d 6m²
6m 6v 6g 7m a5g a8.5s Dec 19] good-topped, workmanlike filly: disappointing
handicapper: won at Ripon in April: virtually no form after much improved effort
fourth start: stays 6f: acts on good to firm and dead ground: tried blinkered, no
improvement: usually apprentice ridden: races prominently. *S. R. Bowring*

ANY COLOUR   3 b.f. Anshan 119 – Council Rock 74 (General Assembly (USA))   –
[1995 –: 6g⁶ 7m⁶ 1996 8g a7g 8g May 23] compact filly: no worthwhile form: sent to
Austria. *M. J. Camacho*

ANYTIME BABY   4 b.f. Bairn (USA) 126 – Cindys Gold 69 (Sonnen Gold 121)   –
[1995 46, a53: a8g a8g 7m 7f 5d⁴ 5d a5g* a6g a5g⁴ a5g⁴ 1996 a5g a6g Jan 30] lengthy
filly: modest sprint handicapper: soundly beaten in 1996: acts on equitrack and dead
ground: comes from behind: covered by Absolom. *P. T. Dalton*

ANZIO (IRE)   5 b.g. Hatim (USA) 121 – Highdrive (Ballymore 123) [1995 79:   112
a8g 8g 6m³ 6f 6g⁴ 5g* 5f³ 6f⁶ a5g² 6m⁴ 6f 5m* 5m² 5m⁴ 6g 6d* 7g 6.1s⁴ 6f⁴ a7g* a7g   a77 +
1996 a6g a7g a6g* 6s* 6g 5.2d* 5.1g* 5g* 6f 5m* 5m³ 6s⁴ a7g Dec 7] quite attractive
gelding: has a round action: won claimer at Lingfield (claimed out of B. Pearce's
stable £6,000) in February: dramatically improved, and now a smart performer: won
handicap at Doncaster and rated stakes at Newbury and Chester in the spring,
Ballyogan Stakes at Leopardstown (by a short head from Ailleacht) in June and listed
race at Doncaster (after near 3-month absence, by head from Amazing Bay,
swooping to lead close home) in September: effective at around 5f (best form) and
stays 7f: acts on firm and soft ground and on equitrack (ran poorly at Wolverhampton

Doncaster Bloodstock Sales Scarbrough Stakes, Doncaster—
the last of six wins in an amazing season
as blinkered Anzio squeezes through to beat Amazing Bay

final start): best in blinkers: usually held up these days: game: a credit to his trainer. *Miss Gay Kelleway*

APACHE LEN (USA)   3 br.c. Rahy (USA) 115 – Shining Skin (USA) 78 (Fappiano (USA)) [1995 76: 7m⁶ 7f² 7f² 1996 8m 7.1d⁴ 8g⁶ 11.4g 10g 9g² 10.2f 10m³ 8d 10.3g Oct 25] tall, rather leggy colt: fair maiden handicapper: sold 14,000 gns Newmarket Autumn Sales: stays 1¼m: acts on firm and dead ground: blinkered/visored since sixth 3-y-o start: hung right on eighth 3-y-o: inconsistent. *R. Hannon*   76

APACHE RAIDER   4 br.g. Dancing Brave (USA) 140 – Calandra (USA) 114 (Sir Ivor 135) [1995 NR 1996 14d Jun 7] 4,100F: heavy-topped, workmanlike gelding: half-brother to 3 winners, including Reef Lark (1¾m, by Mill Reef) and useful Golden Temple (1m in Ireland, by Golden Fleece): dam Irish 1m and 1¼m winner and fourth in Irish Oaks: 20/1 and backward, showed nothing in maiden at Haydock. *F. Murphy*   –

APACHE STAR   2 b.f. (Apr 18) Arazi (USA) 135 – Wild Pavane (Dancing Brave (USA) 140) [1996 7f² 7d* Oct 28] second foal: half-sister to 3-y-o 1¼m winner Stately Dancer (by Be My Guest): dam (unraced) out of half-sister to On The House: won maiden at Lingfield in October by 1¾ lengths from Sweeten Up, pair 4 lengths clear: will be suited by further than 7f: will improve again. *G. Wragg*   80 p

APARTMENTS ABROAD   3 b.f. Prince Sabo 123 – La Graciosa (Comedy Star (USA) 121) [1995 54, a62: 5d 6g 6f 5g⁵ 5m⁴ 6m⁵ 5g³ 5.3d 7f³ 7m⁴ a8g* 1996 a8g⁴ a8g a10g⁴ a8g⁶ a8g³ 8.1g⁵ 8g 7.1m⁵ 7.5m⁶ 8.1m 6g 6.9d⁶ a12g Oct 28] leggy filly: poor performer: sold 4,000 gns Newmarket Autumn Sales: stays 1m: acts on firm and dead ground and the all-weather: tried visored/blinkered, no improvement: headstrong and wayward: inconsistent. *K. McAuliffe*   43 a46

APICELLA   3 ch.c. Pharly (FR) 130 – Sixslip (USA) 94 (Diesis 133) [1995 60p: 6.9s⁵ 1996 10m 10m Apr 29] unfurnished colt: modest maiden: sold 2,300 gns Newmarket Autumn Sales: sent to Spain. *J. Pearce*   –

APICULATE (IRE)   2 b.c. (May 11) Exactly Sharp (USA) 121 – Reine de Chypre (FR) (Habitat 134) [1996 5s⁵ 5g⁶ 5g⁵ 7f 7.1g² 7.1m⁴ 7g⁶ 8g⁶ 7.5m 7m Oct 2] 800Y, resold 500Y: close-coupled colt: half-brother to 1m and 8.3f winner Solid (by Glenstal) and several winners abroad: dam French 6f and 7f winner: had favoured rail when appearing to show only worthwhile form in Musselburgh seller on fifth start: stays 7f: blinkered third outing. *W. T. Kemp*   –

APOLLONO   4 b.g. Cyrano de Bergerac 120 – Daima (Dominion 123) [1995 86: 7g³ 7.1m 7m² 8f* 8.1m² 8.5m* 8d 8m 8m 1996 7f² 7.6g 8.5m 10.1f² 10m⁵ 10m⁵ 12m⁶ 10f⁵ 10.4g⁵ 8.2g a10g Dec 30] angular gelding: fair handicapper: below best after August, and sold (J. Fanshawe to R. Lee) 9,000 gns Newmarket Autumn Sales after penultimate start: stays 1¼m (not beaten because of trip at 1½m): acts on any going: blinkered/visored once each, below form: usually held up. *R. Lee*   79

APOLLO RED   7 ch.g. Dominion 123 – Woolpack (Golden Fleece (USA) 133) [1995 50, a58: a6g⁵ a6g³ a7g⁶ a6g a7g a7g³ 6m² 7f 6f 7m a7g³ a7g a7g² 1996 a6g a8g³ a6g⁴ a7g³ a6g 6f³ 5.3f* 7f* 7g a7g a7g* a7g* Dec 11] smallish, sturdy gelding: fair handicapper: won at Brighton and Lingfield (sweating, ladies race) in the spring and twice at Lingfield (claimer first occasion) late on: effective at 5f to 7f: acts on equitrack, firm and dead ground: blinkered (below best) once at 5 yrs: effective visored (not tried since early 1995) or not: best when able to dominate. *A. Moore*   63 a69

APPEAL AGAIN (IRE)   3 br.g. Mujtahid (USA) 118 – Diva Encore 74 (Star Appeal 133) [1995 –p: 6g 7f 6m 1996 8.5d 8g 9.9m⁴ 12m⁶ Apr 29] leggy gelding: poor maiden plater: stays 1¼m: has carried head high: tends to pull hard: one to treat with caution: joined D. Burchell. *Mrs J. R. Ramsden*   43

APPEARANCE MONEY (IRE)   5 b.m. Dancing Dissident (USA) 119 – Fussy Budget (Wolver Hollow 126) [1995 NR 1996 9.9m a14g Nov 22] IR 2,000Y: half-sister to several winners including fairly useful stayer Artful Dodger (by Akarad): dam second over 9f at 2 yrs in Ireland: modest maiden (rated 53) at 3 yrs for B. Kelly in Ireland: tailed off on return: stays 9f. *F. Murphy*   –

APPLAUD (USA)   3 ch.f. Rahy (USA) 115 – Band (USA) (Northern Dancer) [1995 105p: 5g* 5f² 6g* 1996 7m² Oct 28] small, sturdy filly: first run since winning Cherry Hinton, not right in coat, grinding teeth, and 2 handlers, ½-length second of 4   84 +

to Mashmoum in minor event at Leicester, quickening from front halfway and running on gamely: no longer easy to assess. *D. R. Loder*

APPLE BRANDY (USA)　2 ch.f. (Feb 27) Cox's Ridge (USA) – Channel Three – (USA) (Tri Jet (USA)) [1996 7g Nov 2] $70,000Y: second foal: dam Grade 2 7f winner: 33/1, slowly away when last of 23 in maiden at Newmarket. *G. Lewis*

APPREHENSION　2 b.c. (Feb 16) In The Wings 128 – First Kiss 84 (Kris 135)　95 p [1996 7.1f* Sep 7] close-coupled, quite attractive colt: fourth living foal: half-brother to 3 winners, including smart 6f (at 2 yrs) to 1m winner Kissing Cousin (by Danehill) and fairly useful stayer Shahi (by Shahrastani): dam 1¼m winner, half-sister to smart 1m winner Miller's Mate out of daughter of top-class middle-distance filly Pistol Packer: odds on, won maiden at Haydock in September by 5 lengths from Social Pillar, going clear inside last: will stay at least 1¼m: sure to improve. *D. R. Loder*

APRIL IN PARIS　2 b.f. (Apr 2) Inca Chief (USA) – Plectrum 58 (Adonijah 126) – [1996 5.1m 6g Jul 29] first reported foal: dam middle-distance maiden out of half-sister to Band and Zimbalon: no form in median auction maiden or seller. *C. James*

APRIL JACKSON　2 b.f. (Apr 23) Petong 126 – Raintree Venture (Good Times – (ITY)) [1996 6.1m⁵ 6m 6.1m Jul 6] 5,500F, IR 4,400Y, 5,400 2-y-o: workmanlike filly: has a round action: sixth foal: half-sister to 1½m winner in Italy by Celestial Storm: dam poor daughter of half-sister to smart dam of Oaks winner Polygamy: well beaten in maidens. *P. T. Dalton*

APRIL'S JOY　3 b.f. Mazilier (USA) 107 – Ziobia 78 (Tribal Chief 125) [1995 56:　56 d 5m³ 5m² 5g⁴ a6g⁵ 5g⁴ a5g⁴ 5.1m³ 5m³ 5h* 5g² 5g 1996 5s⁴ a6g 5m 6f 6g Jul 24] small, light-framed filly: modest performer: no form after reappearance: best form at 5f: acts on hard and soft ground: visored final 3-y-o start. *J. Norton*

APRIL THE EIGHTH　3 b.c. Statoblest 120 – Miami Melody (Miami Springs　95 121) [1995 95+: 5.2m³ 5f 5m* 6f* 6m⁶ 1996 8d⁵ 6d² 6m 7g⁴ 6m 6g 8m⁴ 8.5m³ 7.9g³ Oct 9] tall, angular good-topped colt: good mover: useful handicapper, in frame 4 times in rated stakes: stays 8.5f: acts on firm and dead going: blinkered (raced too freely) sixth 3-y-o start: tends to race prominently: sent to USA. *B. W. Hills*

AQUADO　7 b.g. Green Desert (USA) 127 – Meliora 73 (Crowned Prince (USA)　61 § 128) [1995 54: a7g⁵ a6g a6g a7g* a8g² a8g³ a7g* a8g a8g* a7g⁴ 7g² 7m⁵ 5g* 7g 6.9m⁶ a7g³ 6m 1996 a7g⁵ a8g⁴ a7g a6g a8g 6g⁶ 7g 5g* 6g² 6m⁵ 6.1m 5m⁵ 5m⁵ 7f² 6g 6f Sep 7] good-topped gelding: modest performer: won minor event at Carlisle in May: refused to race final start: effective at 5f, and stays 1m: acts on firm and dead ground and on fibresand: tried visored, blinkered at 7 yrs: tends to hang and usually wears a brush pricker near side: not one to rely on. *S. R. Bowring*

AQUA STAR (IRE)　3 br.g. Village Star (FR) 131 – First Water (FR) (Margouillat – (FR) 133) [1995 NR 1996 10m 12g Jun 12] 11,500Y: sturdy gelding: fourth reported living foal: half-sister to French winners Invite d'Honneur (up to 12.5f, by Be My Guest) and Priviligiee (1¼m, by Highest Honor): dam, useful French 2-y-o 7f winner, stayed 1½m: showed little in maidens: sold (J. Dunlop to A. Dunn) 1,100 gns Ascot July Sales. *J. L. Dunlop*

AQUATIC QUEEN　2 b.f. (Apr 17) Rudimentary (USA) 118 – Aquarula 88 – (Dominion 123) [1996 7f 8g a6g⁶ Dec 5] lengthy, angular filly: half-sister to 1992 2-y-o 5f winner Nicky Mygirl (by Chief Singer) and winning middle-distance performer To Be Fair (by Adonijah): dam 2-y-o 5f and 6f winner: no worthwhile form in maidens. *R. J. Weaver*

AQUAVITA　2 b. or gr.f. (Apr 9) Kalaglow 132 – Aigua Blava (USA) (Solford – (USA) 127) [1996 8m Sep 19] first reported foal: dam, tailed off only start, out of half-sister to Canadian Grade 1 13f (turf) winner Great Neck: 50/1, slowly away and always behind in 15-runner maiden at Yarmouth. *C. A. Cyzer*

ARABIAN　2 ch.c. (Mar 26) Arazi (USA) 135 – Bustara 92 (Busted 134) [1996 7f²　83 p Oct 15] sixth foal: half-brother to smart 8-y-o middle-distance horse Young Buster (by Teenoso): dam, 2-y-o 6f winner who stayed 10.2f, half-sister to Ela Romara: 10/1, short-head second of 5 to Amid Albadu in steadily-run minor event at Leicester, held up then finishing strongly: sure to improve, and should win a race. *M. R. Stoute*

ARABIAN DESIGN　4 b.g. Shareef Dancer (USA) 135 – Classic Design (Busted – 134) [1995 NR 1996 8.5f⁶ 12.3m 8m Sep 20] 5,000Y: good-quartered gelding:

second foal: closely related to very speedy 5-y-o Eveningperformance (by Night Shift): dam unraced half-sister to Tirol: yet to beat a rival: sold (G.M. Moore to J. Ringer) 1,100 gns Newmarket Autumn Sales. *G. M. Moore*

ARABIAN FLIGHT 4 ch.c. Sayf El Arab (USA) 127 – Smooth Flight 78 (Sand-   – hurst Prince 128) [1995 –: 8.3m 6m 8.3m 1996 a9.4g 9.2s May 2] of no account. *T. T. Clement*

ARABIAN HEIGHTS 3 ch.g. Persian Heights 129 – Arabian Rose (USA)   51 (Lyphard (USA) 132) [1995 –: 6m 1996 6s a6g⁴ 7.1g 8m³ 10m 10.3g* 12s 12m⁴ 12m 10m 10.5m⁵ Aug 16] lengthy gelding: modest handicapper: won at Doncaster (amateurs) in June: sold (Mrs J. Ramsden to J. Mackie) 6,800 gns Doncaster September Sales: should stay beyond 10.5f: possibly unsuited by soft ground: headstrong: inconsistent. *Mrs J. R. Ramsden*

ARABIAN STORY 3 gr.c. Sharrood (USA) 124 – Once Upon A Time 77   104 (Teenoso (USA) 135) [1995 78p: 7f* 1996 8g² 11.6g* 12m⁶ 12g* 11.9g* 12g 12m² Oct 17] tall, angular colt: shows knee action: useful handicapper: won at Windsor (minor event) in July, at Epsom (quite valuable amateurs event, by 11 lengths) in August and at York (rated stakes, cruised to front 3f out, eased inside last) in September: stays 1½m well: acts on firm ground, yet to race on a soft surface: wears bandages: game: may progress again at 4 yrs. *Lord Huntingdon*

ARABOYBILL 5 b.g. Aragon 118 – Floral 82 (Floribunda 136) [1995 65d: 8m   55 d 10.8f 9.7f³ 9.7g* 12m 10m⁶ 10m⁶ 10f² 10m 10d 10g 8f 1996 a8g⁵ a9.4g a12g⁶ a7g⁴ a10g⁴ 10f² 10f⁵ 10.2g⁶ 10m 10.8f a11g⁵ a12g Nov 11] workmanlike gelding: only modest at best nowadays: left R. Simpson after ninth 5-y-o outing: stays 1¼m: acts on fibresand and firm ground, appeared to run very well on heavy final 2-y-o outing: blinkered since fourth 4-y-o start: inconsistent and not one to trust. *J. Neville*

ARABRIDE 4 ch.f. Unfuwain (USA) 131 – Model Bride (USA) (Blushing Groom   107 (FR) 131) [1995 104: 8m⁵ 8m² 8f* 8g⁴ 8g* 8g⁶ 1996 8.1m⁴ 8g⁴ Sep 8] lengthy filly: useful performer: not seen out until August for new stable: showed plenty of zest when 3¼ lengths fourth of 11 to Wandering Star in listed race at Sandown: well below that form in Group 3 race at the Curragh only 8 days later: should stay beyond 8.1f: yet to race on a soft surface. *Lord Huntingdon*

ARAK (USA) 8 b.g. Clever Trick (USA) – Twilight Flight (USA) (Quack (USA))   – [1995 NR 1996 10.1m 8m a8.5g Oct 19] rated 82 for M. Johnston in 1994, badly injured final start: no form on return. *G. C. Bravery*

ARAMON 6 b.g. Aragon 118 – Princess Mona 56 (Prince Regent (FR) 129) [1995   – –: 11.5m 18.2m 1996 12m⁵ Aug 20] modest hurdler: no worthwhile form on flat. *M. J. Haynes*

ARANTXA 2 b.f. (May 18) Sharpo 132 – Amalancher (USA) 85 (Alleged (USA)   72 p 138) [1996 6s 6v* Nov 11] rather leggy filly: unimpressive mover: eighth foal: half-sister to several winners, including useful Irish middle-distance performer Damancher (by Damister) and fairly useful 6f and 8.5f winner Ysatirous (by Ahonoora): dam French 2-y-o 1m winner: won late-season median auction maiden at Folkestone: will stay further than 6f: acts on heavy ground: probably capable of further improvement. *M. Bell*

ARAPI (IRE) 2 b.f. (Jan 27) Arazi (USA) 135 – Princess Pati 124 (Top Ville 129)   89 [1996 7d⁵ 7.1s³ 6m* a6g² a7g⁵ Dec 14] angular, workmanlike filly: eighth foal: half-sister to several winners, including 3-y-o 10.2f and 10.4f winner Pasternak (by Soviet Star) and smart middle-distance stayer Parthian Springs (by Sadler's Wells): dam won Irish Oaks: fair form: successful late in year in maiden at Leicester and nursery at Southwell but disappointed final outing: effective at 6f, bred to stay beyond 1m: acts on good to firm ground and fibresand. *Sir Mark Prescott*

ARASONG 4 b.f. Aragon 118 – Songstead 92 (Song 132) [1995 72d: 6m² 6m 6g   – 5m 5f⁴ 5.2m* 6f³ 5m⁵ 6m a5g 6.1d 6g⁵ 1996 5g 5g a5g Sep 9] modest handicapper: not seen until August, below form: stays 6f: acts on firm ground. *E. Weymes*

ARAVINDA (IRE) 3 b.f. Superpower 113 – Surmise (USA) 75 (Alleged (USA)   – 138) [1995 NR 1996 10.1g 10g Jul 15] third foal: half-sister to a winning sprinter in Italy by Be My Guest: dam 7f winner: no promise. *Lady Herries*

ARBATAX (IRE) 3 b. or br.c. Mtoto 134 – Caprarola (FR) 113 (Bellypha 130)   113 [1995 9d⁶ 9d² 10g⁵ 1996 12g* 11f² 12g* 12m 10d 12m⁵ Sep 15] IR 19,000F:

close-coupled, rather unfurnished colt: second foal: closely related to French 10.5f and 11f winner Antioco (by Shernazar): dam, winner of Prix Cleopatre, stayed 10.5f: smart French colt: won minor event at Saint-Cloud and Prix Hocquart (beat Dark Nile 1½ lengths) at Longchamp, both in the spring: off course 2½ months (reportedly running a temperature and coughing) before apparently good effort (giving 5 lb to rest of field) when around 2½ lengths seventh of 9 to Sasuru in Prix Guillaume d'Ornano at Deauville: looking really well and tongue tied, 6½ lengths fifth of 10 to Helissio in Prix Niel at Longchamp, held up in rear fighting for his head then staying on unable to land a blow: stays 1½m: possibly won 11f: acts on firm and dead ground: carried head awkwardly fourth 3-y-o start. *P. Bary, France*

ARCADY 3 b.f. Slip Anchor 136 – Elysian 94 (Northfields (USA)) [1995 63: 6m 7g 7m³ a7g⁶ 1996 10.2g³ 10d⁵ 12g 11.5f² 14m⁵ 11.7f³ 11.9f³ 16s 13.1m* a14.8g² a12g² 15.8g³ a12g a14.8g* Nov 25] leggy filly: fair handicapper: won at Bath (maiden event) in September and at Wolverhampton (gamely, by short head) in November, making all: stays 15.8f: acts on firm ground and fibresand, poor efforts on a soft surface: sold 7,800 gns Newmarket December Sales. *P. T. Walwyn*   67 a64

ARCATURA 4 b.g. Beveled (USA) – Bar Gold 80 (Lucky Brief 128) [1995 67, a60: 8g 8g 8m⁵ 8g 8d³ a8.5g⁴ a9.4g⁵ 1996 a9.4g 10g⁵ 8g⁶ 10m³ 11.6d⁴ 10.8m 12m 8m² a10g⁴ a10g* Dec 30] modest performer: won seller at Lingfield in December: stays 1¼m: acts on good to firm and dead ground: blinkered (below form) third 4-y-o start: inconsistent. *C. James*   54

ARC BRIGHT (IRE) 6 b.h. Trempolino (USA) 135 – Brillante (FR) 118 (Green Dancer (USA) 132) [1995 50, a65: a16g² a16g* a16g³ a16g² a16g³ a14.8g a16g² 16.2m 14.1g³ 21.6f 14.1f* 14.9g 14.1m⁵ 14.1m* 14.1m³ 14.1f⁴ 17.2f² 16m⁵ 17.2h* 15.9m³ 1996 16m 17.1m Oct 7] leggy, workmanlike horse: fair handicapper: off course over a year, no form in 1996: stays 17.2f: probably acts on any going: not blinkered since 1994: usually races prominently: very tough and genuine at 4 yrs/ 5 yrs. *R. Hollinshead*   –

ARCH ANGEL (IRE) 3 ch.f. Archway (IRE) 115 – Saintly Guest (What A Guest 119) [1995 55: 6m⁶ 6g* 7f² a7g* 7f⁴ 6m⁶ 8g a8g a7g⁵ a7g 1996 a8g² a8g² a8g a8g² a11g⁵ a8g⁵ a8g a8.5g 6.9d Oct 21] light-framed, plated-backed filly: modest performer: first past post in seller at Southwell (disqualified after hanging) in January: below form after fourth start, leaving D. Ffrench Davis after sixth: stays 1m: acts on firm ground and fibresand: no improvement in visor: sometimes slowly away. *G. F. H. Charles-Jones*   55 d

ARCHELLO (IRE) 2 b.f. (Apr 24) Archway (IRE) 115 – Golden Room (African Sky 124) [1996 5m² 6f³ Sep 28] IR 1,300Y: tall filly: fifth foal: dam Irish sprint maiden: similar form in maidens behind Jhazi at Beverley and dead-heaters St Lucinda and Thahabyah at Redcar: stays 6f: may do better. *G. R. Oldroyd*   69

ARCH ENEMY (IRE) 3 gr.c. Archway (IRE) 115 – Rosserk (Roan Rocket 128) [1995 NR 1996 6m⁶ 5g 6m 8.3m Aug 3] good-bodied colt: half-brother to 2 winners, including fairly useful 6-y-o Pine Ridge Lad (up to 9.4f, best on all-weather, by Taufan): dam, lightly-raced Irish maiden, sister to very speedy dam of Ballad Rock: modest maiden: best effort on debut: sold out of M. Channon's stable 1,600 gns Ascot July Sales after third start. *Miss K. M. George*   55

ARC LAMP 10 b.g. Caerleon (USA) 132 – Dazzling Light 116 (Silly Season 127) [1995 53, a47: a6g⁵ a6g a6g⁶ a6g a5g 6.1m a6g⁵ a6g 7f⁵ 5f² 6f* 6m* 6m⁴ 6g 1996 a6g a6g⁵ 6.1g 5g 7m 7g May 25] workmanlike, angular gelding: modest handicapper: soundly beaten in 1996: stays 7f: acts on firm ground and fibresand: blinkered (below form) once at 5 yrs: often bandaged near-hind. *J. A. Glover*   –

ARCO COLORA 2 b.f. (Feb 8) Rainbow Quest (USA) 134 – Bella Colora 119 (Bellypha 130) [1996 7g⁵ Oct 25] smallish, leggy filly: half-sister to several winners, including high-class 1¼m performer Stagecraft (by Sadler's Wells) and smart 1m winner Hyabella (by Shirley Heights): dam 6f and 1¼m winner, half-sister to Colorspin (dam of Opera House): 7/2, one-paced fifth of 12 to Sophomore in maiden at Doncaster: showed a short, quick action: will stay at least 1¼m: should improve. *M. R. Stoute*   64 p

ARC OF THE DIVER (IRE) 3 ch.g. Archway (IRE) 115 – Inner Pearl (Gulf Pearl 117) [1995 60d: 5g⁵ 5f⁵ 6m⁶ 8g² 7d 1996 7m 8.1m² 11.1m⁵ 11.9m⁵ 13.8g² 11.1d³ 12m² 13.6m a11g² 15.1s⁴ a16g⁵ Nov 18] leggy gelding: modest maiden   58

handicapper: stays 15f: acts on good to firm and soft ground, and on fibresand: blinkered (except once, when ran creditably) since second 3-y-o start. *J. Berry*

ARCTIC FANCY (USA)   3 ch.g. Arctic Tern (USA) 126 – Fit And Fancy (USA)   85
(Vaguely Noble 140) [1995 79p: 8.2d 9g² 10m³ 1996 12g³ 14d² 14d* 12m 13.3f²
14m 13.9g Sep 4] big, good-topped gelding: fairly useful handicapper: won maiden
at Haydock in June, despite veering right: below form last 2 starts: will be suited by
test of stamina: acts on firm and dead ground: tends to carry head high. *P. W. Harris*

ARCTIC THUNDER (USA)   5 b.g. Far North (CAN) 120 – Flying Cloud   93
(USA) (Roberto (USA) 131) [1995 99: 12m⁶ 11.9m* 10.4g³ 13.9m² 11.9d⁶ 13.3d²
1996 13.3d⁵ 12m⁶ 14m³ Jun 27] leggy, workmanlike gelding: shows knee action:
useful handicapper: failed to recapture best form in 1996: stays 1¾m: acts on good to
firm and dead ground: usually bandaged: has run well when sweating: sometimes has
tongue tied down. *Lady Herries*

ARCTIID (USA)   3 b. or br.c. Silver Hawk (USA) 123 – Arctic Eclipse (USA)   93 p
(Northern Dancer) [1995 61p: 6m⁴ 1996 10d⁴ 10g* 10.3g² 10.4m³ Jul 13] big,
good-topped colt: carries condition: 5/4 on, very easy winner of 17-runner maiden at
Ripon in May: creditable third of 17 to Wilcuma in Magnet Cup at York, running
wide into straight and staying on well: front runner: looked capable of better still,
particularly over further than 10.4f: remains in training. *J. H. M. Gosden*

ARCUS (IRE)   3 ch.g. Archway (IRE) 115 – Precision Chop (Hard Fought 125)   70 d
[1995 7d 1996 6d 7s 7v⁶ 5m⁴ 5d³ 5d⁶ 8d⁶ a7g a8g a7s Dec 19] ex-Irish gelding: fair
maiden at best: sold out of T. Stack's stable 6,500 gns Newmarket Autumn Sales
after seventh start: seems effective from 5f to 7f: probably acts on any going: tried
blinkered, below form. *W. R. Muir*

ARDENT   2 b.c. (Mar 13) Aragon 118 – Forest of Arden (Tap On Wood 130) [1996   –
6s Oct 24] 17,500Y: well-made colt: sixth foal: closely related to useful 4-y-o 6f (at 2
yrs) to 7.3f winner Forest Cat (by Petorius) and half-brother to 2 winners, including
1¼m to 1½m winner Annacurragh (by Shardari): dam Irish 7f winner out of
half-sister to Sarah Siddons: 40/1, in need of race and green, missed break and always
well behind on unfavoured far side in maiden at Newbury. *C. J. Benstead*

ARDILAN (IRE)   3 b.c. Kings Lake (USA) 133 – Akelei (Orofino (GER) 125)   106
[1995 7g* 7m⁴ 8s² 8s 1996 8d⁴ 10g* 10.3g³ 11g⁶ 10g 10g⁶ Oct 3] German colt:
second foal: dam, 7f and 1m listed winner in Germany, from useful family: won
maiden at Cologne and good second in quite valuable event at Dusseldorf at 2 yrs:
won Group 3 event at Frankfurt in April by 1½ lengths from Mongol Warrior: ran
well when about 6½ lengths sixth of 14 to Oxalagu in similar event at Hoppegarten
last time: stays 11f. *H. Howart, Germany*

ARECIBO (FR)   4 ch.g. Cricket Ball (USA) – Anahita (FR) (Gay Mecene (USA)   –
128) [1995 –: 6g 8.3m 7g 1996 a11g a8g⁵ a8g a8g⁴ a8g 9.9d a14g⁶ 10g 8.5m May 10]
of little account. *J. Parkes*

AREED AL OLA (USA)   3 b.c. Chief's Crown (USA) – Ballerina Princess   –
(USA) (Mr Prospector (USA)) [1995 NR 1996 8m Apr 17] IR 115,000Y: deep-
girthed colt: third foal: half-brother to smart 4-y-o Salmon Ladder (suited by 1½m,
by Bering): dam, placed, out of smart stakes winner at up to 1¼m Aladancer,
half-sister to good stayer Duke of Marmalade: 16/1, very much in need of race and
green, tailed off in newcomers event at Newmarket: sent to UAE. *A. C. Stewart*

AREISH (IRE)   3 b.f. Keen 116 – Cool Combination 76 (Indian King (USA) 128)   44 ?
[1995 NR 1996 8m a7g 11.6g⁶ 10f⁵ a7g⁶ a10g Dec 11] fourth foal: half-sister to 3
winners, including modest sprinters Mixed Mood (by Jalmood) and Indian Dreamer
(by Midyan): dam, 2-y-o 6f winner, out of staying half-sister to 3 speedy fillies: poor
maiden: may prove best up to 1m: blinkered last 2 starts, apparently best effort on
first occasion. *J. Ffitch-Heyes*

AREN'T WE LUCKY (IRE)   3 b.c. Project Manager 111 – Keshia (Buckskin   –
(FR) 133) [1995 NR 1996 10.5d 11.9m* 12g⁴ 11.9m 15.8g Sep 21] second foal: dam
Irish 9f to 1½m winner: no worthwhile form. *J. J. O'Neill*

ARETHUSA   2 ch.f. (Feb 16) Primo Dominie 121 – Downeaster Alexa (USA)   101
(Red Ryder (USA)) [1996 5m* 5.2g² 5m 6m² 6m* 6m⁵ Oct 1] 16,000F, 15,500Y: big,
leggy, quite good-topped filly: has scope: first foal: dam Irish 2-y-o 5f winner out of
Moyglare Stud Stakes winner Phils Fancy: useful form: successful twice at Kempton,

beating Maserati Monk by a neck in listed race at Kempton on penultimate outing: beaten a neck by Bianca Nera in Lowther Stakes at York on fourth outing: never-dangerous fifth behind Pas de Reponse in Cheveley Park Stakes at Newmarket on final start: stays 6f: raced only on a sound surface: bandaged in front last 2 outings: held up. *R. Hannon*

ARGYLE CAVALIER (IRE)   6 b.g. Simply Great (FR) 122 – Fete Champetre   –
80 (Welsh Pageant 132) [1995 67, a75: a16g* a14.8g* a12g² a16g² 18g 16m 16m* 18.7m⁵ 16m² 16m³ 13f² 20m 1996 16.2m 15.9g Sep 25] leggy, angular gelding: good walker: fair handicapper: off course over 13 months, no worthwhile form for new stable: stays 2½m: acts on any going, best on all-weather. *B. J. Meehan*

AR HYD Y KNOS   2 b.f. (Jan 16) Alzao (USA) 117 – Top Table 65 (Shirley   – p
Heights 130) [1996 6g 6m Sep 7] neat filly: first foal: dam maiden who stayed 1½m, out of sister to 1000 Guineas winner On The House: always midfield in maidens at Salisbury and Kempton: will be suited by 1m+: likely to do better. *R. Charlton*

ARIAN SPIRIT (IRE)   5 b.m. High Estate 127 – Astral Way (Hotfoot 126) [1995   56
42: a16g* a16g⁵ 12.3d⁴ 14.1f⁶ 13f⁴ 16m² 15.1f⁵ 15.1m³ 16.2g² 15.1f* 17.1m⁴   a–
16.2m² 16m³ 17.5g 17.1m* 18f⁶ 1996 a16g 16.1s* 16.2m² 21.6m⁵ 16m* 14.1m⁴ 16.5m² 15d* 16d³ 18g⁶ 15.1s a14.8g Nov 25] small, workmanlike mare: modest handicapper: won at Newcastle in March, Redcar (twice, wandering under pressure on second occasion) in May and Ayr (amateurs) in August: stays 2¼m: acts on good to firm and soft ground and on equitrack: blinkered (ran poorly) once at 3 yrs: occasional front runner: tail swisher: consistent. *J. L. Eyre*

ARIETTA'S WAY (IRE)   3 b.f. Darshaan 133 – Captive Island 116 (Northfields   71
(USA)) [1995 NR 1996 10g 10m⁵ 11.8m⁵ 14.1f⁵ Jun 21] 37,000Y: leggy filly: sister to useful 11f winner Rubhahunish and half-sister to smart 4-y-o middle-distance stayer Court of Honour (by Law Society) and a 10f to 11f winner in France by Raise A Cup: dam French 6f and 1m winner: fair maiden: should stay beyond 11.8f: bandaged near-hind first 2 starts. *R. Charlton*

ARISAIG (IRE)   2 ch.g. (Apr 21) Ela-Mana-Mou 132 – Glasson Lady (GER) 108   –
(Priamos (GER) 123) [1996 7.9g 8s Nov 9] IR 15,000Y: brother to 3-y-o 1¼m winner Male-Ana-Mou and half-brother to 2 winners, including 1¼m winner Glassblower (by Shareef Dancer): dam useful Irish 7f winner: behind in maidens at York and Doncaster. *P. Calver*

ARKTIKOS (IRE)   3 b.c. Sadler's Wells (USA) 132 – Arctic Heroine (USA)   70
(Arctic Tern (USA) 126) [1995 NR 1996 10g 12m⁴ 10.3g⁶ 14.1m 14.1f³ 12m 11.5m* 11.5d⁵ 14m Sep 19] strong, heavy-bodied colt: third foal: brother to 12.3f winner Jabaroot and half-brother to 1m and 1½m winner Mezaan (by Royal Academy): dam twice-raced half-sister to very useful middle-distance filly Ghaiya out of half-sister to dam of Nonoalco: fair handicapper: won at Lingfield in August, setting steady pace and just holding on: below form afterwards: stays 1¾m: acts on firm ground: visored since seventh 3-y-o start: inconsistent: sent to UAE. *J. H. M. Gosden*

ARLINGTON LADY   3 b.f. Prince Sabo 123 – Flitcham 57 (Elegant Air 119)   –
[1995 65d: 6g⁶ 6m* 5m² 6f⁶ 6m² 6m 6m³ 7.6m 7m 1996 a6g³ a7g⁶ a6g⁶ 6m 8m   a40
6.9g Jul 3] tall filly: modest performer on turf, no form in 1996: poor at best on the all-weather, well beaten after reappearance: sold 1,600 gns Newmarket July Sales: probably stays 7.6f: yet to race on a soft surface: tried blinkered: wears bandages behind: sent to Macau. *N. A. Callaghan*

ARNHEM   3 b.c. Damister (USA) 123 – Baltic Leap (USA) (Northern Dancer)   97
[1995 NR 1996 10.3s² 10g³ 10.3g⁴ 12g* 16.2m 14.8m³ 14f³ Aug 1] tall, lengthy, quite attractive colt: fifth foal: half-brother to 2 lesser winners abroad by Hadeer: dam ran 6 times in North America: useful form: won maiden at Newmarket in May: best effort when third in listed race at Newmarket (outpaced over 3f out then plugging on, 10¼ lengths behind Persian Punch) in July: stays 14.8f: acts on firm ground, probably on soft. *C. E. Brittain*

AROUND FORE ALLISS   2 b.g. (Jan 25) Reprimand 122 – Artistic Licence   69
(High Top 131) [1996 7f⁵ 6m⁵ 6m a8g² Dec 20] 11,000F, 9,800Y, 12,500 2-y-o: a66
fifth foal: dam, stayed 1¼m, out of half-sister to Circus Plume: fair maiden: should stay beyond 1m: acts on equitrack and firm ground. *T. G. Mills*

ARRIVING   2 br.f. (Feb 17) Most Welcome 131 – Affirmation 75 (Tina's Pet 121)   67 p
[1996 7g⁴ Aug 12] second foal: dam 5f (at 2 yrs) and 1¼m winner: running-on fourth

of 13, slowly away, to Crown of Light in median auction maiden at Leicester: will be suited by further than 7f: likely to do better. *J. W. Hills*

ARRUHAN (IRE) 2 b.f. (Apr 20) Mujtahid (USA) 118 – Wakayi 87 (Persian 78 + Bold) [1996 5m* 6m³ 6f⁴ Sep 5] fourth foal: half-sister to headstrong 3-y-o Ashik (by Marju) and 6f winner Fata (by Machiavellian): dam, 2-y-o 5f winner, half-sister to smart sprinter Reesh: came from well behind when winning maiden at Salisbury in June: reared stalls then raced too freely next time out: held up in steadily-run race and always too much to do final start: bred to be a sprinter: may be capable of better. *P. T. Walwyn*

ARTAN (IRE) 4 br.c. Be My Native (USA) 122 – Cambridge Lodge 65 (Tower 119 Walk 130) [1995 7.5g* 8g² 10g* 12m⁵ 12g² 12g* 10d⁶ 1996 11d⁴ 11d³ 8g⁴ 10d⁶ 10m* 10g* 10g⁴ 10g* Oct 30] smart German colt: third foal: half-brother to a fair winning hurdler by Lafontaine: dam, 6f winner, out of half-sister to Val d'Erica (rated 119, Oaks d'Italia): won listed race at Dusseldorf, minor event at Hoppegarten and (after fifth in German Derby) Norwegian Derby at 3 yrs: successful in 1996 in Group 3 at Baden-Baden in August by 4 lengths from Devil River Peek, Group 2 at Frankfurt (settled contest with turn of foot early in straight then held Sir Warren by a length) in September and Group 3 at Marseilles (gave 4 lb and beat Bulington ¾ length) in October: stays 1½m, at least as effective at 1¼m: possibly suited by a sound surface: has turn of foot: consistent, and generally progressive. *M. Rolke, Germany*

ARTERXERXES 3 b.g. Anshan 119 – Hanglands (Bustino 136) [1995 63p: 7m⁶ 83 1996 7g⁵ 6.9f* 8.3m⁵ 7f² 7m² 7f² 7m³ 7m Sep 12] lengthy, quite attractive gelding: fairly useful handicapper: won maiden at Folkestone in April: possibly best at up to 7f: acts on firm ground: front runner: genuine and consistent. *M. J. Heaton-Ellis*

ARTFUL DANE (IRE) 4 b.c. Danehill (USA) 126 – Art Age (Artaius (USA) 76 129) [1995 81?: 8m² 10g 8f³ 8.3m* 7.6m 8d 7s⁶ 1996 8.2d 7g⁴ a8.5g 8.1m 8.2m 8m* 8.1m 8f 8g 8m* 8d⁵ 8g³ 8g⁶ Nov 2] strong, good-quartered colt: good walker: fair handicapper: won at Bath in August and Newbury (£17,800 event) in September: stays 8.3f: acts on firm and dead going: visored (has run consistently well) since tenth 4-y-o start: takes strong hold: inconsistent without headgear in 1996. *M. J. Heaton-Ellis*

ARTHUR'S SEAT 2 b.c. (Apr 29) Salse (USA) 128 – Abbey Strand (USA) 78 – (Shadeed (USA) 135) [1996 6g Aug 14] good-bodied colt: first foal: dam, 1m winner, half-sister to smart 6f to 10.5f winner Church Parade and smart middle-distance stayer Castle Rising: 12/1 and in need of race, last of 14 in maiden at Salisbury: moved fluently to post: bred to need further than 6f. *Lord Huntingdon*

ARTIC BAY 4 b.g. Arctic Lord 114 – Galley Bay 55 (Welsh Saint 126) [1995 NR 71 1996 12.1d⁵ 11.6m 9m⁶ 12m* 11.6d⁶ 12g⁴ 12m⁵ 11.5m* 12d Oct 11] first foal: dam 1¾m winner, later fair hurdler: fair handicapper: won amateurs events at Salisbury (coming from off very strong pace) in July and, returning to form, at Lingfield (minor event), in October: sold 38,000 gns Newmarket Autumn Sales: will stay beyond 1½m: acts on good to firm ground, possibly not on dead. *Mrs P. N. Dutfield*

ARTIC COURIER 5 gr.g. Siberian Express (USA) 125 – La Reine de France 87 (Queen's Hussar 124) [1995 82: 12g² 12m⁶ 12m² 14m 12f² 12.3f* 11.8g² 11.9f³ 12m² 12g⁴ 12d 12s⁶ 12m 1996 12g⁵ 14.9d 12m* 12m⁴ 12g* 11.8g⁴ 12m² 12g⁵ 12m³ 12g² 12g Oct 11] good-topped gelding: fairly useful handicapper: won at Kempton (awarded race) in May and Epsom in July: retained by trainer 12,000 gns Newmarket Autumn Sales: best at up to 1¾m: acts on firm and soft ground: tried blinkered (including first 2 starts at 5 yrs), best without: sometimes wanders under pressure: normally held up: consistent. *D. J. S. Cosgrove*

ART TATUM 5 b.g. Tate Gallery (USA) 117 – Rose Chanelle (Welsh Pageant – 132) [1995 50: 11.8d 12m⁶ 10m⁵ 1996 a8.5g Apr 13] disappointing handicapper: last for new stable only 5-y-o start: suited by 1½m+: acts on heavy ground: well beaten in blinkers: sometimes soon off bridle: sent to Belgium. *G. M. McCourt*

ARZANI (USA) 5 ch.h. Shahrastani (USA) 135 – Vie En Rose (USA) (Blushing 59 Groom (FR) 131) [1995 74d: 8.3m³ 8m 10m⁵ 8m⁶ 10d⁶ 1996 6.9g 8.2g 10g a10g* a10g* a10s a10g a10g⁶ Dec 20] plain horse: fair handicapper at best: soundly beaten in 1996 before winning twice at Lingfield (amateurs first occasion) in November: stays 1¼m: acts on good to firm ground and equitrack: inconsistent. *D. J. S. Cosgrove*

ASAS 2 b.c. (Feb 1) Nashwan (USA) 135 – Oumaldaaya (USA) 111 (Nureyev 95 (USA) 131) [1996 8m* 8g Oct 26] tall, rangy colt, a shade unfurnished: has plenty of scope: first foal: dam, 7f (at 2 yrs) and 1¼m (including Italian Group 2) winner, half-sister to Derby winner Erhaab: 14/1, always prominent when winning maiden at Newmarket in good style by 2½ lengths from Jaunty Jack: close up 5f when well-beaten last of 9 in Racing Post Trophy (supplemented at cost of £15,000) at Doncaster later in month: will stay 1¼m at least: looked promising on debut. *Saeed bin Suroor*

AS FRIENDLY 2 b.c. (Mar 14) Arazi (USA) 135 – Zawaahy (USA) 89 (El Gran 64 Senor (USA) 136) [1996 7m a8.5g³ Sep 21] first foal: dam 1m winner, closely related to Golden Fleece: made running when third to Mystic Quest in maiden at Wolverhampton: may be a stayer: sent to UAE. *M. R. Stoute*

ASHANTI DANCER (IRE) 3 b.f. Dancing Dissident (USA) 119 – 66 Shanntabariya (IRE) (Shernazar 131) [1995 71: 7d⁶ 8g² 1996 7g 8g⁶ 7m⁶ 7g⁴ 7g⁴ 7m Oct 4] leggy filly: fair maiden handicapper: ran no sort of race final start and sold 3,400 gns Newmarket Autumn Sales: may stay further than 1m: sent to Holland. *M. J. Haynes*

ASHBY HILL (IRE) 5 ch.m. Executive Perk 120 – Petite Deb (Cure The Blues 74 (USA) 136) [1995 9d 10m⁵ 11.9g 12m 1996 12f* 10g⁵ 12.1d 9.7m* 8.1m⁴ 10g 10m³ 10m³ 10g* 10m⁶ 8g* 8d* 8g Nov 2] compact ex-Irish mare: first foal: dam maiden stayer in Ireland: trained in Ireland to end of 4-y-o season: fair handicapper: won at Folkestone in April and June, Salisbury in August, Goodwood (awarded race) in September and Salisbury in October: has won at 1½m, but best form at 1m to 1¼m: probably acts on any going: held up and suited by good pace. *R. Rowe*

ASHDREN 9 b.g. Lochnager 132 – Stellaris (Star Appeal 133) [1995 56: 7.5m 7g⁶ 7m⁵ 6m 7.5m⁶ 7f⁴ 7g 8d⁵ 7g 1996 a7g⁵ a8g⁶ Mar 1] modest performer: well beaten in 1996: stays 1m: probably acts on any going: occasionally visored/blinkered, no improvement: swishes tail. *A. Harrison*

ASHGORE 6 b.g. Efisio 120 – Fair Atlanta 73 (Tachypous 128) [1995 77: a7g* 88 d 7g 6g a6g 1996 a7g* a7g a7g² a7g³ a7g² a7g² 7.5m⁴ a8g³ 6m 7m a8.5g Nov 16] good-topped gelding: fairly useful performer: has reportedly had leg problems: made all in handicap at Wolverhampton in January: between 7 lb and 15 lb below that level when placed 6 times in next 3 months: left M. Johnston after eighth 6-y-o start: off course 5½ months, well below form on return: effective at 6f to 7.5f: probably acts on any going on turf (best efforts on top-of-the-ground) and goes well on the all-weather: usually races prominently: game. *J. L. Eyre*

ASHIK (IRE) 3 b.g. Marju (IRE) 127 – Wakayi 87 (Persian Bold 123) [1995 –: 6.1d 5.7m 1996 7.1g 5d 5d Jul 5] robust gelding: tailed off for new stable in 1996: sold 825 gns Ascot August Sales: tried blinkered, no improvement: headstrong, and one to steer clear of. *L. J. Barratt*

ASHJAR (USA) 3 b.c. Kris 135 – Jathibiyah (USA) 89 (Nureyev (USA) 131) 88 [1995 81: 7m² 7d⁴ 7g⁴ 7g* 1996 8d⁴ 7m* 7m⁵ 7f⁵ 7m³ 7m⁶ Aug 26] big, lengthy colt: has a round action: fairly useful handicapper: made all at Lingfield in May: sold only 7,000 gns Newmarket Autumn Sales: takes keen hold, and unlikely to stay much beyond 7f: acts on good to firm ground, below form on a soft surface: sweating and free to post (below form) on 3-y-o reappearance. *H. Thomson Jones*

ASHKALANI (IRE) 3 ch.c. Soviet Star (USA) 128 – Ashtarka (Dalsaan 128 125) [1995 111p: 8m* 8g* 1996 8m* 8g* 8f² 8m* 8m⁵ Sep 28]

    At the same time as they made a fairly low-key return to the British racing scene, on the other side of the Channel the Aga Khan's horses enjoyed their best season for some while, keeping him in contention for leading owner virtually throughout and eventually giving him his ninth title, narrowly from Sheikh Mohammed. Standard-bearer for the Aga Khan's eighty-strong team in training with Alain Royer-Dupre at Chantilly was the three-year-old Ashkalani, a colt who in the course of compiling a hundred-per-cent record in France attracted a huge fan-club there, most of whose members seemingly came to regard him as the best miler in Europe before a comprehensive defeat in the Queen Elizabeth II Stakes at Ascot in September—his second defeat at Ascot,

Dubai Poule d'Essai des Poulains, Longchamp—
Ashkalani gives Gerald Mosse cause to celebrate;
Spinning World and Cash Asmussen finish fast for second

following a narrow one in the St James's Palace Stakes—made such sentiments difficult still to own.

Ashkalani contributed three wins, all of them gained at Longchamp, to the team's 1996 total. He made his reappearance in the Prix de Fontainebleau in April, when for the last time in his career he was not sent off favourite. The race attracted a small, select field on trial for the classics, headed by the Grand Criterium winner Loup Solitaire, and the outcome seemed likely to have a strong bearing on the Dubai Poule d'Essai des Poulains three weeks away. Ashkalani pressed his claims by beating Eternity Range and Spinning World decisively, with Loup Solitaire fifth. The second and third had also shown good form at two; Ashkalani at that age had won the Prix Thomas Bryon on the second of two starts. Ashkalani was sent off at 5/4-on in a ten-runner Poulains. His main rivals among the outnumbered home-trained contingent seemed to be Eternity Range and Spinning World again, while the overseas challenge consisted of the Two Thousand Guineas sixth Danehill Dancer, the Free Handicap winner Cayman Kai, Don Micheletto, Gothenberg, and those placed behind Danehill Dancer in the Greenham Stakes, Kahir Almaydan and Tagula. Thanks to Gothenberg's efforts the race was run at a good pace and, in our view, won by the best horse on the day although some considered the strong-finishing second Spinning World very unlucky, as he had met trouble in improving from the rear on the rails. Ashkalani himself had to wait for room to get to the outside in the straight. He hit the front around a hundred metres from home and then held Spinning World comfortably by three quarters of a length, with Tagula, Cayman Kai and Kahir Almaydan bang on the premises as well. Ashkalani was the Aga Khan's first Poulains winner since Nishapour in 1978; already in France he was being associated with the more famous one of 1977—hailed as 'the new Blushing Groom', no less.

Ashkalani's reputation preceded him to Royal Ascot where he started a heavily-backed 13/8 favourite to beat the Two Thousand Guineas winner Mark of Esteem and the Irish Two Thousand Guineas winner Spinning World in the St James's Palace Stakes. He did that all right and from early in the straight until the last fifty yards seemed likely to extend his successful run at the expense of Bijou d'Inde; but having comfortably gone around a length up at the furlong pole he couldn't resist the latter's renewed effort, losing out virtually on the line. Ashkalani's trainer blamed Michael Kinane for committing too soon and allowing the horse to lose concentration in front. Kinane in defence mentioned

Emirates Prix du Moulin de Longchamp—
Ashkalani finishes in front of Spinning World for the fourth time in 1996

that he was not the colt's usual partner, just standing in (for the first time) for suspended stable-jockey Gerald Mosse and had received inadequate instructions. The outcome would still have been close, and might have gone the same way, had Kinane waited longer.

Ashkalani by-passed Deauville en-route to yet another meeting with Spinning World, by now the Marois winner, in the Prix du Moulin de Longchamp in September. Confidence in Ashkalani's ability to dispose of the all-French opposition was extraordinarily high—he started at 5/4-on again—and was proved well and truly justified. On this occasion he sat on Spinning World's tail and beat him for speed, taking the score between them to four-nil. The race attracted five of the Marois field, including the second, Vetheuil, and the third, Shaanxi, plus the Coronation Stakes winner Shake The Yoke and another good filly, Carling. Ashkalani settled in fourth place behind the pacemaker Metaphor, Carling and Spinning World, and as the field began to come together halfway up the straight he produced a fine burst of acceleration to pass Spinning World on the outside. The outcome was never in doubt afterwards. Spinning World kept on for second place, a length and a half down, just hanging on from the strong-finishing Shake The Yoke.

Ashkalani seemed to be improving race by race. Improving or not, he was undeniably the best French miler, and his presence lent credence to the billing of the Queen Elizabeth II Stakes as the milers' championship of Europe. In the event, 9/4 favourite, he failed to make much of an impact after showing a short, scratchy action and pulling hard to post. When asked to improve from the rear in the straight he edged right and was well outpointed by Mark of Esteem and Bosra Sham, in coming fifth of seven looking much the same horse as First Island and Charnwood Forest. In early-October news came from France that Ashkalani would not meet his engagement in the Breeders' Cup. He was recovering well from the pinched nerve in his back 'suffered at Ascot' and a decision on his future would be made shortly. The upshot was that he has been retired to the Irish National Stud and will stand in 1997 at a fee of IR £12,500, October 1st terms. His owner/breeder has retained a significant shareholding and, naturally, will be supporting him strongly.

If ever a horse was bred to win a Poulains, Ashkalani was. His sire Soviet Star won the race in 1987, and three of the Aga Khan's home-bred winners besides Ashkalani have family links—the second dam Asharaz is a half-sister to Zeddaan, winner in 1968 and sire of the 1973 winner Kalamoun

H. H. Aga Khan's "Ashkalani"

Ashkalani (IRE) (ch.c. 1993)	Soviet Star (USA) (b 1984)	Nureyev (b 1977)	Northern Dancer Special
		Veruschka (b 1967)	Venture VII Marie d'Anjou
	Ashtarka (gr 1987)	Dalsaan (b 1977)	Habitat Dumka
		Asharaz (gr 1967)	Sicambre Vareta

as well as of Nishapour. Furthermore, Ashkalani's dam, whose second foal and first runner he is, won over a mile in France as a three-year-old. Unlike Zeddaan, Asharaz had a staying sire and the pick of her offspring was a stayer, the Prix du Cadran winner Shafaraz.

The lengthy, good-bodied Ashkalani spent all his racing life at a mile, looking thoroughly in his element at the distance. He also spent it on a sound surface, handling firm ground well. He had, as no doubt Spinning World's jockey would be among the first to testify, an excellent turn of foot. We make him consistent too, and have him a lot less below form in the Queen Elizabeth II Stakes than the 'turfistes' back home evidently did. *A. de Royer-Dupre, France*

ASHKERNAZY (IRE)   5 ch.m. Salt Dome (USA) – Eskaroon (Artaius (USA)   50
129) [1995 48, a54: 5.1m⁶ 5g⁴ 5.7m 5m 5.1m⁴ a5g*ᵈⁱˢ 5.1m² 5m⁵ 1996 5.7g a5g 5m*
5f 5.1f² 5m a5g⁶ Dec 13] sparely-made mare: modest handicapper: won at Windsor
(apprentices) in August: stays 6f: acts on fibresand and firm ground, unraced on soft
surface: visored/blinkered last 4 starts at 3 yrs: races prominently. *N. E. Berry*

76

ASHOVER 6 gr.g. Petong 126 – Shiny Kay 65 (Star Appeal 133) [1995 64, a73: 51
a11g* a12g* a11g² 12g⁴ 12.3f* 12f³ 12m⁵ 12m* 12f³ 12f³ 12.3m 10.4g 12d* 11.9m³ a73
1996 a11g* a12g⁴ 12.3g 12.3s 12g⁵ 12g 10.9m 12.1d 12m³ 11.9g⁶ 12d Oct 21]
compact gelding: fair handicapper at best: won at Southwell in January: off course
4½ months after third start and failed to regain his form: should stay beyond 1½m:
acts on firm and soft ground, best on all-weather: blinkered (raced too freely) once as
4-y-o: sometimes tongue tied: often apprentice ridden: effective ridden up with pace
or held up. T. D. Barron

ASHTINA 11 b.g. Tina's Pet 121 – Mrewa (Runnymede 123) [1995 94d: 5.2m –
5.1m* 5f 5m 5.1m⁴ 5m 5g 5m 5m 5d 5s 5m 5m 5m a6g a5g⁴ 1996 5g 5.1g 6f 5g
5m 5m Jun 7] leggy, good-topped gelding: fairly useful in his prime: no form in 1996.
B. A. Pearce

AS-IS 2 b.g. (Apr 7) Lomond (USA) 128 – Capriati (USA) 83 (Diesis 133) [1996 55
7m⁵ 7.1d 6m⁶ Oct 23] 5,200Y: sturdy gelding: shows knee action: second foal: dam
placed at up to 1¼m here and won twice at up to 9f in USA: modest form in maidens:
better suited by 7f than 6f, bred to stay further. M. Johnston

ASKERN 5 gr.g. Sharrood (USA) 124 – Silk Stocking 109 (Pardao 120) [1995 74: 79
10g* 9.2f* 10f² 11.1f³ 10.5m* 13.9m 13.1g 12m 12m 1996 10g 10m³ 10.9d 13g²
10.2m³ 10.2f³ 11.7f² 11.1m* 11.1m* 11.1m* 11.9m 12m 10m⁶ 11.1d² 12g 10g 10f* Nov 5]
tall, good-topped gelding: has a round action: fair handicapper: won at Hamilton
(twice in space of 6 days, best efforts) in August and at Redcar in November:
probably stays 1¾m: acts on firm and dead ground: blinkered (out of form) final
3-y-o start: tends to hang when in front: inconsistent. D. Haydn Jones

ASKING FOR KINGS (IRE) 3 b.g. Thatching 131 – Lady Donna 92 (Dom- 73 d
inion 123) [1995 62: 6m 6m⁴ 6m² 7s⁵ 6m 1996 8.5s 10v⁴ 10v³ 10s 12s 9g 8.2m 10s²
10s⁴ May 29] angular gelding: modest maiden: failed to repeat form shown at Cagnes
early on: stays 1¼m: acts on heavy going. S. Dow

ASPECTO LAD (IRE) 2 ch.g. (Feb 18) Imp Society (USA) – Thatcherite (Final 43
Straw 127) [1996 5m a6g 6g a8g³ a8g Dec 11] 25,000Y: sturdy gelding: fifth foal:
half-brother to useful 3-y-o 5f/7f performer Unconditional Love (by Polish Patriot)
and modest 1¼m and 11f winner Bajan (by Taufan): dam unraced half-sister to
Kampala: poor maiden: stays 1m: looks difficult ride. M. Johnston

ASSESSOR (IRE) 7 b.h. Niniski (USA) 125 – Dingle Bay (Petingo 135) [1995 112
113: 16g² 15.5f⁵ 14.5d* 1996 14.1g² 15.5d⁴ 16.4d² 20m 15g⁵ 18m⁶ Sep 12]
useful-looking horse: fluent mover: very smart stayer as 4-y-o, but comfortably best
effort in 1996 when second in Henry II Stakes at Sandown (rec 4 lb, 7 lengths behind
Double Trigger) in May, third start: did not beat a rival afterwards: stayed long
distances: best on a soft surface: usually wore bandages: held up: bought for around
1,327,000 francs and retired to stand at La Roche-sur-Yon. R. Hannon

ASSIGNMENT 10 b.g. Known Fact (USA) 135 – Sanctuary (Welsh Pageant 132) 41 d
[1995 56d: a6g⁴ a6g⁴ a6g 8m 9.7m⁵ 7m a6g⁴ a6g a7g 1996 a6g⁴ a6g a7g⁶ a6g 6f 5m
7f 6m Jun 28] strong, deep-girthed gelding: very much on the downgrade. J. E. Long

ASSUME (USA) 2 br.c. (Apr 14) Known Fact (USA) 135 – Free Spirit (USA) 80 +
(Avatar (USA)) [1996 6g² 5f² Jul 17] $65,000Y: useful-looking colt: brother to a
winner in USA and half-brother to several other winners there, one placed in Grade 3
events at 8.5f and 1¼m: dam won at up to 9f in USA: second to Magic Blue in median
auction maiden at Leicester in June and ready winner Seebe in maiden at Sandown in
July: will prove suited by further than 5f. J. W. Hills

ASSUMPTA 2 b.f. (Apr 17) Superpower 113 – Russell Creek 80 (Sandy Creek 62 +
123) [1996 a5g⁶ a5g* Aug 16] third reported foal: half-sister to a winner in Denmark
by Valiyar: dam 1m winner: won seller at Southwell in August from Just Loui: will
stay 6f: sent to Sweden. C. B. B. Booth

ASTERITA 4 b.f. Rainbow Quest (USA) 134 – Northshiel 85 (Northfields (USA)) 103
[1995 103: 10m⁵ 11.5f* 12m⁵ 12g⁶ 14.6m 12d² 14g² 1996 13.9f⁵ 11.8g⁶ 11.9g 16m²
12d⁶ 12s Oct 26] leggy filly: useful performer on her day: well below form first 3
starts in 1996 and left R. Hannon: off course nearly 3 months, good efforts in
steadily-run rated stakes at Goodwood and in Princess Royal Stakes (paddock pick,
off bit and in rear 5f out, staying on very strongly) at Ascot: wintry in appearance,

tailed off in St Simon Stakes at Newbury: stays 2m: acts on firm and dead ground, possibly not soft: sold 53,000 gns Newmarket December Sales. *D. R. Loder*

ASTERIX   8 ch.g. Prince Sabo 123 – Gentle Gael 97 (Celtic Ash) [1995 53: 6.1g³   47
5.9m⁶ 6g 7m² 7.1m² 7g 6.1m³ 6.1m² 8.1m* 9.2m⁶ 7.1m² 7f 6f 6f⁵ 1996 6f 6.1g 8f 8g
8g 7f³ 7.1g 6.1m⁵ 8.1m* 8.1f² 8.3g 7m 7.1m 9.9m⁴ Jul 30] smallish, lengthy gelding:
unimpressive mover: poor handicapper: won at Chepstow (ladies) in June: below
form last 4 starts: effective at 6f to 1m: acts on any going: visored or blinkered: good
mount for inexperienced rider. *J. M. Bradley*

ASTON MANOR (IRE)   4 b.g. Cyrano de Bergerac 120 – Mamie's Joy (Prince   54
Tenderfoot (USA) 126) [1995 59: 6s a6g² a6g² 1996 a6g⁵ a5g Jan 11] modest maiden
handicapper: respectable effort in 1996 only on first start: should stay 7f: acts on
all-weather. *R. Hannon*

ASTOR PLACE (IRE)   3 b.c. Sadler's Wells (USA) 132 – Broadway Joan   111
(USA) (Bold Arian (USA)) [1995 106p: 7g⁴ 7g* 8m⁵ 1996 10.4f³ 12m 12f* 12.5g³
9f Dec 1] rangy, attractive colt: fluent mover: reportedly had wind operation during
the winter: smart performer: beaten about 4 lengths when staying-on seventh of 15 to
Ragmar in Prix du Jockey-Club at Chantilly, having looked uneasy round turn: same
form when winning falsely-run minor event at Ascot (flat-footed on home turn,
responding gamely to get up on post despite changing legs and edging right, from
Acharne) and when 3¼ lengths third of 6 to Darazari in Prix Maurice de Nieuil
at Maisons-Laffitte: behind in Hollywood Derby: stays 1½m: acts on firm ground,
yet to race on a soft surface: tends to get on toes: held up: remains in USA.
P. W. Chapple-Hyam

ASTRAC (IRE)   5 b.g. Nordico (USA) – Shirleen (Daring Display (USA) 129)   115
[1995 96: 6m⁵ 6f* 6m 6g 7g⁶ 6d³ 1996 7m⁶ 6m 6f 7.1d⁵ 6m 5g⁶ 6g⁴ 6.1s* 6s* 6s*
Nov 22] sturdy gelding: impresses in appearance: smart performer: left R. Akehurst
after fifth start: much improved efforts for new yard, winning minor event at
Nottingham in October and listed races at Doncaster (got up under very strong
driving to beat Diffident a short head) and Evry (gave 8 lb, beat Linoise a length)
in November: stays 7f, very best form at 6f: has won on firm ground and fibresand
but probably suited by soft: effective from front or held up: a credit to his trainer.
Miss Gay Kelleway

ASTRAL INVADER (IRE)   4 ch.g. Astronef 116 – Numidia (Sallust 134) [1995   54
68d: 6m⁵ 8m 7.6m³ 7g 6g 6m 5.1f⁴ 5.7h³ 5.7h⁶ 6g 6.1d⁶ 7s 7.1d 1996 6g 5d³ 6g⁵
6m 5.1f³ 6m 5.1m² 5.7f⁵ 7f³ 7.6m⁴ 8f 7.1f a7g Dec 28] leggy gelding: seems only
modest nowadays: stays 7.6f: acts on any going: no improvement in visor: inconsistent. *M. S. Saunders*

ASTRAL'S CHANCE   3 ch.g. Risk Me (FR) 127 – Astral Suite 82 (On Your   –
Mark 125) [1995 59: 5m⁴ a5g⁵ 1996 6.1m 5d 5g 5.1g a5g⁴ 7g Aug 21] small gelding:
well beaten since spring at 2 yrs, including in blinkers. *K. R. Burke*

ASTRAL WEEKS (IRE)   5 ch.g. Astronef 116 – Doon Belle (Ardoon 124)   66
[1995 –: 8m 7g 8m 8m 8.3m 10d 8m 1996 10.1s* 11.1d² 12.1d³ 12.4d 12.1d
Sep 30] rangy gelding: poor mover: fair form at best for new stable: unimpressive in
appearance, won steadily-run race at Newcastle in March, leading post: below form
after next start: stays 11.1f: acts on good to firm ground and soft: blinkered (out of
form) final 4-y-o start. *L. Lungo*

ASTRA MARTIN   3 ch.f. Doc Marten 104 – Bertrade 75 (Homeboy 114) [1995   –
–: 6g 6.1d 6f 1996 9.7f 12m May 2] no form: visored in 1996. *P. G. Murphy*

ASTROJOY (IRE)   4 ch.f. Astronef 116 – Pharjoy (FR) 85 (Pharly (FR) 130)   –
[1995 50d: 8.1m 6g² 6m 8h⁶ 10d 8m a7g a7g a6g a7g 1996 a12g Jan 5] disappointing
maiden: tried blinkered. *S. G. Knight*

ASTROLABE   4 b.g. Rainbow Quest (USA) 134 – Sextant 98 (Star Appeal 133)   –
[1995 81: 10.3g³ 12f 12.3m* 14g³ 14.9m² 14m³ 20f 1996 14.9d 14.1g 16m Jun 24]
leggy, close-coupled gelding: fairly useful handicapper at 3 yrs: tailed off for new
stable in 1996: stays 14.9f: acts on good to firm ground: blinkered/visored (except on
reappearance) since third 3-y-o start. *J. M. Bradley*

ATH CHEANNAITHE (FR)   4 ch.g. Persian Heights 129 – Pencarreg 87   –
(Caerleon (USA) 132) [1995 9g 9f⁴ 6g³ 6g 9f* 13g⁵ 12m 9f² 9m* 8.5m² 8g 8m
1996 8.3m May 20] fair form (rated 69) in Ireland at 3 yrs, winning 2 handicaps at

Dundalk: sold out of N. Meade's stable 20,000 gns Newmarket Autumn (1995) Sales: blinkered, tailed off in claimer on return: stays 9f: acts on firm going: best without blinkers: won novice hurdle in October. *J. Neville*

ATHENIAN ALLIANCE 7 ch.m. Ayyabaan 91 – Springaliance (Reliance II – 137) [1995 NR 1996 10m 10m 5.7m Aug 8] first foal: dam won selling hurdle: of little account. *J. M. Bradley*

ATHENRY 3 gr.c. Siberian Express (USA) 125 – Heresheis 69 (Free State 125) 107 [1995 87p: 8d⁵ 10m⁵ 1996 12.4g* 13.9m* 16.2m² 14.8m² Jul 11] tall, leggy colt: has a long, round action: won maiden at Newcastle and minor event at York in the spring: length second of 14 to Gordi in Queen's Vase at Royal Ascot then 1½ lengths second of 6 to Persian Punch in listed race at Newmarket: dyed-in-the-wool stayer and will prove best at 2m+: acts on good to firm ground: thoroughly genuine: looked capable of better but tore a tendon sheath in August. *J. Pearce*

ATHERTON GREEN (IRE) 6 ch.g. Shy Groom (USA) – Primacara 58 54 (Rusticaro (FR) 124) [1995 –: a11g⁵ a12g⁶ 10f 1996 14.1m³ 16.2m³ 16.2m 16m Sep 16] small gelding: modest handicapper nowadays: stays 16.2f: acts on good to firm and soft ground: inconsistent. *J. A. Glover*

ATHINAR 4 b.f. Tina's Pet 121 – Highland Rossie 67 (Pablond 93) [1995 40: a7g⁵ – a8g³ 1996 a8g 8.3m May 13] of little account. *C. P. Wildman*

ATIENZA (USA) 3 ch.f. Chief's Crown (USA) – Hattab Voladora (USA) 56 (Dewan (USA)) [1995 65: 8g 8.2m³ 1996 7m 12.3g 12g⁵ 13.8s³ 12.1g² a14g⁶ 16m⁵ 11.9g 17.9g Oct 9] sparely-made filly: modest maiden handicapper: stays at least 2m: acts on good to firm ground: inconsistent. *S. C. Williams*

ATLANTIC DESIRE (IRE) 2 b.f. (May 6) Ela-Mana-Mou 132 – Bold Miss 86 (Bold Lad (IRE) 133) [1996 7f 8.5m* 10f² 10g⁵ Nov 2] IR 20,000Y: workmanlike filly: sixth foal: sister to fairly useful 1993 2-y-o 7f winner Lomas and middle-distance stayer Mystery Lad and half-sister to Irish 1¾m winner Tellyrand (by Cut Above): dam unraced: made all in maiden at Epsom in September: fairly useful efforts afterwards, around 3 lengths fifth of 10 to Silver Patriarch in listed race at Newmarket on final start: will be suited by 1½m+: front runner. *M. Johnston*

ATLANTIC MIST 3 ch.g. Elmaamul (USA) 125 – Overdue Reaction (Be My 64 Guest (USA) 126) [1995 54: 7g³ 7g 7f 8d 1996 12s⁴ 14.1g²ᵈⁱˢ 12d⁶ 11.6m* 11.4d* 10.2g³ 11.6g 14m⁶ 11.6m² 11.9m 11.4m Sep 17] close-coupled gelding: modest handicapper: won at Windsor and Sandown in May: below form last 2 starts: needs further than 1¼m and stays 1¾m: acts on good to firm ground and dead: has worn crossed noseband: headstrong: inconsistent. *B. R. Millman*

ATLANTIC STORM 3 b.g. Dowsing (USA) 124 – Tatouma (USA) 79 (The 73 Minstrel (CAN) 135) [1995 NR 1996 7g 7f² 6g² 7.6m⁵ Aug 17] well-made gelding: third foal: half-brother to 1994 2-y-o 7f winner Trimming (by Thatching): dam, 2-y-o 5f and 6f winner, from family of Law Society and Legal Bid: fair maiden: gave trouble at stalls second intended start: subsequently visored, found nothing and finished distressed final start: sold 6,500 gns Newmarket Autumn Sales: stays 7f: has raced only on a sound surface: made running last 3 outings: one to treat with caution: sent to Germany. *J. H. M. Gosden*

AT LIBERTY (IRE) 4 b.c. Danehill (USA) 126 – Music of The Night (USA) 89 (Blushing Groom (FR) 131) [1995 96: 7g 9m² 10m² 10g* 10.1m⁴ 12m⁴ 12f a12g 1996 10g 12m 10m⁶ 12m 12m³ 11.9g 13.3f 8m* 11.9m 10m⁵ 12g 12m⁶ 12s Oct 26] sturdy, neat colt: has a quick action: just a fairly useful handicapper in 1996: third of 20 in Bessborough Stakes at Royal Ascot: won poor claimer at Goodwood in August: sold 14,000 gns Newmarket Autumn Sales: stays 1½m: acts on soft ground and good to firm: none too consistent. *R. Hannon*

ATNAB (USA) 2 b. or br.f. (Apr 27) Riverman (USA) 131 – Magic Slipper 97 62 (Habitat 134) [1996 6m 7.1s Oct 22] seventh foal: half-sister to 3-y-o Azwah (by Danzig) and 3 winners at up to 7.1f, including useful 1994 2-y-o Muhab (by Lyphard): dam, 1¼m and 11.5f winner, half-sister to Fairy Footsteps and Light Cavalry: eighth in maidens at Lingfield and Chepstow (eased) in autumn: may do better. *P. T. Walwyn*

ATOMIC SHELL (CAN) 3 ch.c. Geiger Counter (USA) – In Your Sights – p (USA) (Green Dancer (USA) 132) [1995 NR 1996 8.3m Aug 3] $18,000Y: first foal:

dam unplaced: 40/1 and green, eyecatching effort in maiden at Windsor, seeming to have plenty of running in him when switched over 1f out, never dangerous and not knocked about: seemed sure to do better. *C. F. Wall*

ATRAF   3 b.c. Clantime 101 – Flitteriss Park 62§ (Beldale Flutter (USA) 130)   116
[1995 89+: 6g⁴ 5m² 5m* 5m² 5m³ 6m³ 6g⁶ 6f 1996 6d* 6m² 6g² 6m* 6m* 7m 6d² 6g 6g Oct 19]

'Not one to trust' is just about the last phrase we would use to describe Flitteriss Park nowadays. Rated 62§ at three years in 1987 and 41§ at four, she has a rather more impressive record as a broodmare. The one-win-from-nineteen-starts strike rate as a racehorse has been succeeded by four winners from four runners. And that is not the half of it, for whereas Flitteriss Park's greatest triumph as a runner came in a 0-75 handicap at Redcar, those of her offspring have been in the Richmond Stakes with Son Pardo, the Great St Wilfrid Handicap with Whittle Woods Girl, the Wokingham with Emerging Market and the Cork And Orrery Stakes thanks to Atraf. Son Pardo and Emerging Market are in the top handful of runners by their respective sires Petong and Emarati (also the sire of Whittle Woods Girl) and Atraf is the best by his sire, the non-thoroughbred Clantime.

Atraf's and Emerging Market's wins over the six-furlong course at Royal Ascot came within twenty-four hours of each other. At that stage, Atraf had been in the frame in six of his eight runs at two years and in the first two in all five as a three-year-old. His only disappointing effort had come on firm ground in the Redcar Two-Year-Old Trophy, and there had been three previous wins, in a maiden at Newcastle in 1995, a minor event at Leicester in April and the £22,125 Coral Sprint Handicap at Newmarket off a mark of 104 nineteen days before his appearance at Royal Ascot. The Cork And Orrery was a wide-open affair, with its usual sizeable field of mixed talent. They split into two groups. On the far side, Irish filly Catch The Blues was the only one that mattered in the final furlong, while up the rails on the stand side it was 12/1-shot Atraf who mastered Watch Me in the last seventy yards, with market leaders Woodborough and Iktamal just behind them. Atraf's winning margin was a length, over Catch The Blues. Atraf ran four times after Royal Ascot. Second to Carranita in a listed race at Newmarket in August was even better than the Cork And Orrery form, but the three other races were nothing like it. He had an excuse—trouble in running—when trying seven furlongs for the first time in the Beeswing at Newcastle, and a possible excuse—he reportedly slipped up on arrival at the start—in the Prix de Seine-Et-Oise at Maisons-Laffitte, but, as far as we know, thirteenth of fifteen in a listed event at

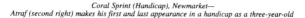

Coral Sprint (Handicap), Newmarket—
Atraf (second right) makes his first and last appearance in a handicap as a three-year-old

Cork And Orrery Stakes, Royal Ascot—Atraf moves into the lead on the stand side and overall

Newmarket on his final start just has to go down as a poor effort. Judged on his career as a whole, good runs should heavily outweigh the poor in 1997 when he returns from wintering in Dubai.

Atraf (b.c. 1993)	Clantime (ch 1981)	Music Boy (ch 1973)	Jukebox
			Veronique
		Penny Pincher (b 1970)	Constable
			Midnight Dollar
	Flitteriss Park (b 1984)	Beldale Flutter (b 1978)	Accipiter
			Flitter Flutter
		Geopelia (b 1974)	Raffingora
			Little Bird

Mr and Mrs Watson have just six broodmares, but, amazingly, they notched up a hat-trick at the 1996 Royal meeting as, in addition to Atraf and Emerging Market, they were also breeders of the Royal Hunt Cup winner Yeast. All three are related, having Little Bird as their great grandam. Little Bird herself was a fairly useful five-furlong winner at two years but tailed off on her only start at three. She was bought for the Watsons by Tim Molony for 4,500 guineas as a six-year-old when carrying Atraf's grandam Geopelia. Geopelia put together a string of useful efforts over five furlongs at two years. Half-sister Gundi showed even less ability than Flitteriss Park but Gundi's daughter Orient (the dam of Yeast) was very speedy—she holds the five-furlong course record at Ascot—and Geopelia's daughters Lady of Hearts and Snipe Hall were respectively the winners of a Group 3 sprint in South Africa and runner-up in the Queen Mary. Geopelia and Flitteriss Park apparently liked to race away from the rest, but the smallish, well-made colt Atraf looks a straightforward ride. He was a rare Doncaster purchase on behalf of Sheikh Hamdan, making 32,000 guineas as a yearling, 10,000 more than the second highest-priced yearling by Clantime that year and 26,000 more than his median. A tough and genuine five-furlong handicapper who was best as a six-year-old, Clantime was another to be bred by the Watsons. The task of extending Flitteriss Park's brilliant stud record still further rests with the 1996 two-year-old Swift Sovereign (by Petong, and in training with John Gosden), a 1996 filly by First Trump and the foal due in 1997 by Owington. *D. Morley*

ATTALOS 3 ch.c. Cadeaux Genereux 131 – Messaria 68§ (Ile de Bourbon (USA) 133) [1995 NR 1996 10g 10m⁴ Jun 14] big, long-backed colt: fourth foal: half-brother to fairly useful trio Main Offender (should stay 1½m, by Be My Chief), Backgammon (stayed 1¾m, by Midyan) and Big Sky (stayed 7f, by Never So Bold): dam, ungenuine maiden who stayed 1¼m, out of 1000 Guineas second Tolmi: beaten at least 11 lengths in maidens at Ripon and (making most but already beaten when hampered) Sandown: sent to France. *H. R. A. Cecil* –

ATTARIKH (IRE) 3 b.g. Mujtahid (USA) 118 – Silly Tune (IRE) (Coquelin (USA) 121) [1995 –p: 6m 1996 7d⁵ 8f⁴ 10m⁶ 8.1m³ Jul 6] has been hobdayed: fair maiden handicapper: sold (J. Gosden to Mrs A. L. M. King) 6,200 gns Newmarket July (1996) Sales, and gelded: stays 8.1f (carried head awkwardly at 1¼m): acts on firm going, probably on dead: visored (good effort) final start. *J. H. M. Gosden* 74

AT THE SAVOY (IRE) 5 gr.g. Exhibitioner 111 – Hat And Gloves (Wolver Hollow 126) [1995 46, a64: a7g a7g² a8g⁵ a7g² a7g² a6g⁴ a8g* a7g⁵ a6g³ a6g³ 7.1g⁴ 34 a62 a6g* a6g^6 7g^5 7m a7g^3 7.1m^2 8.1f^2 7.6m 7m^2 7m 8m^6 a7g^2 7m a6g a6g^3 a8g 1996 a7g^5 a7g^2 a7g a6g^5 a7g^2 a6g^2 a6g a7g^4 6.9d^3 a6g a6g^6 10m Jun 19] compact gelding: sold out of T. D. Barron's stable 2,700 gns Doncaster March Sales after eighth start: modest all-weather performer, poor on turf: effective at 6f to 1m: acts on any going, including all-weather: effective blinkered/visored or not: inconsistent. *Mrs L. Stubbs*

ATTITRE (FR)   2 b.f. (Apr 11) Mtoto 134 – Aquaglow 84 (Caerleon (USA) 132)   88 [1996 8m 8.2m* 7m^5 10g^4 Nov 2] 2,000F, IR 13,500Y: sturdy, good-bodied filly: fourth foal: half-sister to useful 3-y-o 6f and (at 2 yrs) 7f winner Please Suzanne (by Cadeaux Genereux) and a winning sprinter in Italy by Kalaglow: dam 7f and 1m winner: fairly useful form: behind in May Hill Stakes on debut: made all in maiden at Nottingham later in September: over 1½ lengths fourth of 10 to Silver Patriarch in listed race at Newmarket on final start: may well stay further than 1¼m: refused to enter stalls on one occasion. *C. E. Brittain*

ATTITUDE   2 b.g. (Feb 27) Priolo (USA) 127 – Parfum d'Automne (FR) (Sharpen   83 p Up 127) [1996 7.1m 7f* Oct 15] second foal: dam no worthwhile form: won October maiden at Leicester by 2 lengths from River's Source: will stay 1m: should progress again. *H. Candy*

ATTRIBUTE   2 b.f. (Jan 20) Warning 136 – Victoriana (USA) (Storm Bird (CAN)   69 134) [1996 6m^4 5m 7f 7m^2 7g Oct 2] third foal: half-sister to 3-y-o Victorian Style (by Nashwan), winner at around 1m, and 4-y-o 2m winner Sea Victor (by Slip Anchor): dam, French 5f winner, closely related to Grand Criterium second Masterclass from family of Try My Best and El Gran Senor: fair form: best effort fourth start: poor run at Brighton final outing: will stay beyond 7f: sold to R. Guest 12,500 gns Newmarket December Sales. *R. Charlton*

AUCHINLECK JUDGE   3 b.g. Precious Metal 106 – Pharly Rose (Pharly (FR)   – 130) [1995 NR 1996 a8g Nov 22] first foal: dam never ran: 33/1, tailed off in Southwell claimer: joined J. L. Harris. *R. M. McKellar*

AUCKLAND CASTLE   5 b.g. Chilibang 120 – Palace Tor (Dominion 123)   – [1995 NR 1996 a12g a8g Feb 23] poor maiden: dead. *S. R. Bowring*

AUCTION HALL   2 b.f. (Mar 26) Saddlers' Hall (IRE) 126 – Single Bid 68   59 (Auction Ring (USA) 123) [1996 6m 7g^5 5m^5 10m^5 7.9g^6 Oct 10] lengthy, robust filly: seventh foal: half-sister to several winners, including useful sprinter Bid For Blue (by Primo Dominie) and 1m and 1¼m performer Bid For Elegance (by Nordance): dam ran only at sprint distances: modest maiden: needs further than 5f, stays 1¼m: sold 22,000 gns Doncaster October Sales, to race in Scandinavia. *M. Bell*

AUDE LA BELLE (FR)   8 ch.m. Ela-Mana-Mou 132 – Arjona (GER) (Caracol   47 d (FR)) [1995 NR 1996 9.7s 16g 15.4m 12g 15.9m^5 16.2m 17.2m^4 15.4g Sep 27] small, light-framed mare: had foal in 1995 and covered by Robellino in 1996: as a racehorse very much on the downgrade. *S. G. Knight*

AUDENCIA (IRE)   2 b.f. (Apr 4) Arazi (USA) 135 – Celtic Assembly (USA) 95   50 p (Secretariat (USA)) [1996 5g^4 Sep 2] half-sister to 3-y-o 1m winner Keltoi (by Soviet Star) and several other winners, notably very smart French 6f/7f performer Cherokee Rose (by Dancing Brave): dam 10.6f winner, out of top 1975 Irish 2-y-o filly Welsh Garden: slow-starting fourth to Solfegietto in maiden at Hamilton: sold 70,000 gns Newmarket December Sales: will stay beyond 5f. *M. Johnston*

AUDREY GRACE   5 b.m. Infantry 122 – Fair Nic (Romancero 100) [1995 51:   49 8m 8m^2 9.7m 7m a8.5g^5 8g 8g^3 1996 7m^5 8m^5 7g^3 8m 8f^5 Sep 5] lengthy mare: poor maiden handicapper: should stay beyond 1m: acts on good to firm and dead ground: visored (no improvement) last 3 starts at 4 yrs: inconsistent. *Miss Gay Kelleway*

AUGUSTAN   5 b.g. Shareef Dancer (USA) 135 – Krishnagar (Kris 135) [1995 68:   57 9.9m^3 10m a12g^5 12m 9.9m^2 10g 10g^3 12d 12g^5 11.9m* 10f^2 12m^5 10.3m^5 10.5m^2 12m^3 10m 11.9m 13.9g a11g 1996 10g 10.8g^5 10.1m^5 12m^5 11.9m^3 10m^3 14.6g^6 11m^2 11f^6 10f^4 12.1m* 12m^5 10g 10f Nov 5] good-topped gelding: has a markedly round action: just a modest handicapper nowadays: won at Chepstow (amateurs) in July: stays 12.1f: acts on firm and soft going: no improvement in visor: usually held up: consistent at 5 yrs. *S. Gollings*

AUNT DAPHNE   2 b.f. (Apr 14) Damister (USA) 123 – Forbearance 77 (Bairn   – (USA) 126) [1996 7.1s Oct 22] first foal: dam 1m winner at 2 yrs, also won over hurdles: never dangerous in maiden at Chepstow in October. *B. A. McMahon*

AUNTY JANE   3 b.f. Distant Relative 128 – Aloha Jane (USA) 57 (Hawaii) [1995   92
NR 1996 7d² 7g* 8.5m 8g*ᵈⁱˢ 7g 8g⁶ Aug 8] tall, good-topped filly: has scope: has a
quick action: third foal: half-sister to fairly useful Asian Jane (stayed at least 8.5f, by
Persian Bold): dam twice-raced 2m winner: fairly useful form: made all in maiden at
Chester in May and got up near finish (disqualified for interference) at Doncaster in
June: has twice run as if something amiss: stays 1m. *B. W. Hills*

AURELIAN   2 ch.g. (Apr 22) Ron's Victory (USA) 129 – Rive-Jumelle (IRE) 78   59
(M Double M (USA)) [1996 6m 7f³ 6g⁴ 8f Nov 5] sparely-made gelding: first foal:
dam 1¼m winner: staying-on third in median auction maiden at Brighton in July: off
course 3 months before final (well beaten) start: needs further than 6f. *M. Bell*

AUTOBABBLE (IRE)   3 b.g. Glenstal (USA) 118 – Almalat (Darshaan 133)   49
[1995 68: 5g2 5m5 6m a7g² a7g a8g⁴ 1996 a10g 12s⁵ a10g⁵ 10f 9f 11.9g⁴ 12d 12.3g⁴
Oct 26] useful-looking gelding: modest maiden as juvenile: below form in 1996,
leaving R. Hannon after fourth start: should stay middle distances: acts on equitrack:
tried blinkered, no improvement. *S. A. Kirk, Ireland*

AUTOFYR   3 br.f. Autobird (FR) 71 – Fyrish 60 (Mr Fluorocarbon 126) [1995 –:   –
6f⁴ 7.1g 7f 8f 1996 6d a7g 8.3s May 2] smallish filly: no form. *J. S. Wainwright*

AUTUMN AFFAIR   4 b.f. Lugana Beach 116 – Miss Chalk 60 (Dominion 123)   –
[1995 100: 7.3m³ 8m 7g⁶ 8d 8s² 7m⁶ 1996 8s 8.1g 9s 10m⁴ 8m 7.9m Aug 22] leggy
filly: useful performer at 3 yrs: well behind in maiden at Brighton on good to firm
ground and soft: blinkered (raced too freely) third 4-y-o start. *C. E. Brittain*

AUTUMN COVER   4 gr.g. Nomination 125 – Respray 64 (Rusticaro (FR) 124)   78
[1995 54d: 7g 8m 7f⁶ 7.1m 8m 8m³ 8d 8s 8g 9m 12m 1996 a8g³ 8f* 8f* 8m⁴ 8.1m*
8.5m 10m² 8m* 8d 9g* 8g⁴ 9m a7g a10g Dec 11] strong, lengthy gelding: generally
progressive handicapper on turf: won twice at Brighton in April: left R. Flower's
stable after fourth start: won at Sandown in June, and at Goodwood in July and
(£14,700 race) September: effective at 1m and 1¼m: acts on firm ground, well beaten
on dead at 4 yrs: no improvement in blinkers: often bandaged in front: often makes
the running: runs the odd bad race, but has proved game in a finish. *P. R. Hedger*

AUTUMN (FR)   3 ch.f. Rainbow Quest (USA) 134 – River Nomad 99 (Gorytus   –
(USA) 132) [1995 55+: 7f 8f⁴ 8.2d 1996 a8.5g a10g Feb 10] signs of ability at 2 yrs:
stiff tasks, tailed off for new stable in 1996: should stay beyond 1m. *C. Murray*

AVANT HUIT   4 ch.f. Clantime 101 – Apres Huit 66 (Day Is Done 115) [1995 55:   –
a5g³ a5g² 5.1g 1996 a5g a6g a5g 5m a6g a6g a5g a5g Dec 28] seemed no longer of
much account in 1996. *Mrs N. Macauley*

AVANTI BLUE   2 b.c. (May 2) Emarati (USA) 74 – Dominion Blue 66 (Dominion   –
123) [1996 7.1f 7f Oct 15] 12,000Y: fifth live foal: half-brother to a winner in
Belgium by Runnett: dam 1¼m winner: down the field in autumn maidens: looked
rather temperamental (veered left) final start. *K. McAuliffe*

AVENUE FOCH (IRE)   7 gr.g. Saint Estephe (FR) 123 – Marie d'Irlande (FR)   –
(Kalamoun 129) [1995 –: a9.4g 1996 a9.4g⁶ a16.2g Jan 17] no worthwhile form.
F. Murphy

AVERTI (IRE)   5 b.h. Warning 136 – Imperial Jade 105 (Lochnager 132) [1995   104
97: 5m 6f² 7m 5m⁴ 7g 1996 6f⁴ 6d* 6f 5.2m⁶ 6m 6g 6s⁵ 6s Nov 9] robust, attractive
horse: useful performer: upset in stalls and withdrawn from Wokingham, but career-
best effort to win minor event at Haydock 2 weeks later: respectable efforts 4 of 6
starts afterwards, but ran as if something amiss final one: effective at 5f to 7f, very
best form over 6f: acts on firm and dead ground, probably on soft *W. R. Muir*

AVINALARF   2 ch.f. (Mar 27) Fools Holme (USA) – Pure Formality 84 (For-   60
zando 122) [1996 7m* 7f⁵ 6m² 7f Sep 3] tall, lengthy, angular filly: first foal: dam
2-y-o 6f winner, granddaughter of Irish Oaks winner Celina, family of Sayyedati:
won claimer at Salisbury in June: stays 7f: races keenly: tail flasher. *W. G. M. Turner*

AWAAMIR   3 b.f. Green Desert (USA) 127 – Kadwah (USA) 80 (Mr Prospector   102
(USA)) [1995 85p: 7f³ 7m* 1996 8m* 8.1m 8d⁴ 9d³ Oct 24] tall, lengthy filly: useful
performer: won handicap at Pontefract in August: best form in frame in listed races
at Ascot (sweating and very edgy, made most) and Longchamp last 2 starts: stayed
9f: acted on good to firm ground, better form on dead: bandaged all round first 2
starts at 3 yrs: visits Silver Hawk. *J. H. M. Gosden*

AWAFEH 3 b.g. Green Desert (USA) 127 – Three Piece (Jaazeiro (USA) 127) 49
[1995 51: 6m⁵ 7.1m 5g 6g 8f 5s 1996 a6g² a8g² a8g a8g⁵ a7g a7g Aug 17] poor
maiden handicapper: stays 1m: acts on fibresand and equitrack: no form in blinkers/
visor: takes keen hold: inconsistent. *S. Mellor*

AWASH 2 b.c. (Mar 27) Reprimand 122 – Wave Dancer 76 (Dance In Time – p
(CAN)) [1996 7d Nov 8] tall, rangy, unfurnished colt: sixth foal: half-brother to
German 1m winner Wavelet (by Sharrood) and French 9f winner Toby Henry (by
Jalmood): dam 11.7f winner, is sister to smart middle-distance horse Sailor's Dance
and half-sister to Gold Cup winner Longboat: never-dangerous thirteenth of 20 in
maiden at Doncaster in November: will probably do better. *B. W. Hills*

AWASHA (IRE) 4 b.f. Fairy King (USA) – Foliage (Thatching 131) [1995 57: 68
7m⁵ a7g⁵ a8g³ a7g³ 1996 a6g² a6g³ a6g³ a5g² a5g* 5g* 5g⁵ 5g⁴ May 25] smallish
filly: fair handicapper: won at Lingfield (maiden) in February and at Thirsk in May:
effective at 5f (best form) and ran creditably over 1m: blinkered (ran creditably)
once: looked possibly capable of better: has joined G. Lewis. *Miss Gay Kelleway*

AWESOME POWER 10 b.g. Vision (USA) – Majestic Nurse 80 (On Your Mark –
125) [1995 52d, a69d: a10g² a10g³ a10g² a10g a10g 10.8m⁵ 10m a10g 10m⁶ 10m a55
a10g a10g² 1996 a10g⁶ a10g a12g² a10g* 10m 10m a10g³ a10g² a12g a10g*
a10g⁵ Nov 26] strong gelding: seems only modest nowadays: won seller in March
and minor event in November, both at Lingfield: stays 1¼m, and seemingly 1½m:
best on equitrack: tried blinkered earlier in career. *J. W. Hills*

AWESOME VENTURE 6 b.g. Formidable (USA) 125 – Pine Ridge 80 (High 55
Top 131) [1995 55, a–: 7g 8f 7m⁴ 7m 8g 7g 6g² 6m⁶ 7f² 5.2m⁴ 6m 6m³ 6m 6m⁶ 7g 6g a83
a6g 7m 7f⁴ 1996 a7g² a6g² a6g⁴ a6g² a7g a6g⁴ a6g² a7g² a6g² a7g² a6g³ 7s⁴ a8g*
a6g³ 8m a8g* 7m a7g³ a7g* 7.5m³ 7.5f⁵ 7m⁵ 8g⁴ 7f² 7g² 8m⁶ 7m⁵ 7f 7m 6m 8f²
9m Oct 8] big gelding: fairly useful handicapper on the all-weather: won 3 races at
Southwell (including 2 claimers) in April/May: only modest on turf: effective at 6f to
1m: acts on firm and soft ground, best on fibresand: effective visored (not tried since
1995): blinkered (well beaten) twice: normally held up: tough. *M. C. Chapman*

AWESTRUCK 6 b.g. Primo Dominie 121 – Magic Kingdom 76 (Kings Lake –
(USA) 133) [1995 –, a50d: a11g a12g³ a12g* a11g a12g* a12g⁶ a12g a16.2g⁴ a12g⁴
a12g⁴ 14.1g⁵ a14.8g a12g² a14.8g³ 10.5m⁵ 11.8m a12g² a12g a12g a12g⁶ a14.8g
a16g⁶ 1996 a14.8g Aug 31] modest performer: well beaten only start in 1996:
probably stays 1¾m: acts on fibresand and on firm and dead ground, well beaten on
soft: effective blinkered/visored or not: none too consistent. *B. Preece*

AXEMAN (IRE) 4 b.g. Reprimand 122 – Minnie Tudor (Tudor Melody 129) –
[1995 86: 7m⁵ 8.1m 7f⁴ 7g 7.3d 7g⁵ 1996 7g 7g⁴ 8f 7.9g Sep 4] leggy, good-topped
gelding: disappointing since third 3-y-o start: stays 7f: best form on a sound surface:
blinkered final 3-y-o start: joined Miss J. Bower. *D. Nicholls*

AXFORD (USA) 3 ch.c. Woodman (USA) 126 – Timely 104 (Kings Lake (USA) 85
133) [1995 95: 7g² 8m² 8d⁶ 1996 10g² 10m² 8m³ 7.9m 8.5m³ 8m³ Oct 7] rather
unfurnished colt: fairly useful maiden, placed 7 times: sold 16,000 gns Newmarket
Autumn Sales: will prove best at up to 1¼m: acts on good to firm ground: takes good
hold: usually races prominently: sent to USA. *P. W. Chapple-Hyam*

AYBEEGIRL 2 b.f. (Feb 24) Mazilier (USA) 107 – So It Goes 73 (Free State 66 ?
125) [1996 5m² 5d 6f⁵ 5.1m³ 5f⁴ 5.1m* 5g 5.3f⁶ 6.1m² 7g⁴ 6m Oct 17] 10,000Y:
close-coupled, quite attractive filly: third reported foal: sister to 1993 2-y-o 5f winner
Eleuthera and half-sister to 1½m winner Ttyfran (by Petong): dam, 2-y-o 6f winner,
is half-sister to smart Italian 5f to 1m winner Melbury Lad: won maiden at Chester in
July, best form: stays 7f: acts on good to firm ground: best form visored. *Mrs J. Cecil*

AYDIGO 3 b.g. Aydimour – Briglen (Swing Easy (USA) 126) [1995 NR 1996 33
13.8g 10g 11.8f 16.4v³ a16g Dec 11] third reported foal: dam of no account: worthwhile form only when 9¾ lengths third of 11 in claiming handicap at Folkestone.
J. Pearce

AYE READY 3 ch.g. Music Boy 124 – Cindy's Princess (Electric 126) [1995 –: –
6g 1996 6s a6g 5s⁴ 5g 5g⁶ 7.1f 7s 7m 6m Aug 3] workmanlike gelding: little sign of
ability: tried blinkered and visored. *Miss L. A. Perratt*

AYUNLI 5 b.m. Chief Singer 131 – Tsungani 64 (Cure The Blues (USA)) [1995 81
71: 10g 10m a8.5g* a8.5g a8.5g a9.4g* a9.4g² a9.4g⁶ 10g⁴ 12.1g* 11.9m* 12m 12m*

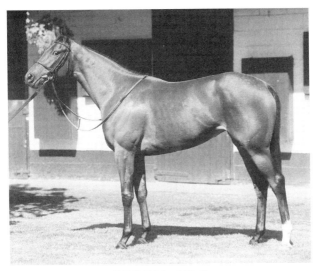

Mr D. H. W. Dobson's "Azra"

1996 a9.4g 12m 12g⁵ 11.9m 12g* 14.4g² 12.1m* 15.4g* 12.1d* 11.5m³ 15s 14v Nov 30] tall, leggy mare: fluent mover: fairly useful handicapper: won at Pontefract (apprentice minor event) and (all within 8 days) Musselburgh, Folkestone (by 6 lengths) and Hamilton in September: effective at 1½m, stayed at least 15.4f: acted on good to firm and dead ground (impossible tasks last 2 starts), and on fibresand: visits Royal Academy. *S. C. Williams*

AZRA (IRE)   2 b.f. Danehill (USA) 126 – Easy To Please 102 (What A Guest 119)   102 [1996 5s⁴ 5s* 6g* 7g* 6m* 6g⁶ 6.3g⁴ 7g³ 7g³ 7g⁴ Oct 5] second foal: half-sister to fair Irish 1995 2-y-o 5f winner Capellino (by Imperial Frontier): dam won Queen Alexandra Stakes, also successful over 1m at 2 yrs in Ireland: useful Irish filly: successful at Leopardstown in maiden in April, listed race in June then conditions event and 6-runner listed race (beat Check The Band a short head) in July: best efforts afterwards when creditable third at the Curragh to Bianca Nera in Moyglare Stud Stakes and Desert King in National Stakes: will stay 1m+: acts on good to firm and soft ground: blinkered last 3 starts. *J. S. Bolger, Ireland*

AZIZZI   4 ch.g. Indian Ridge 123 – Princess Silca Key 61 (Grundy 137) [1995   100 NR 1996 7m* 7.6f² Jun 1] 70,000Y: third foal: half-brother to fairly useful sprinter Silca-Cisa (by Hallgate): dam, lightly-raced 7f winner, out of half-sister to very speedy 1980 2-y-o Labista: 33/1 and carrying plenty of condition, won 13-runner maiden at Kempton on debut, quickening in good style 2f out: 5 lengths second of 7 to Green Perfume in minor event at Lingfield just over month later: likely to prove best at up to 1m. *C. R. Egerton*

AZTEC FLYER (USA)   3 b.g. Alwasmi (USA) 115 – Jetta J (USA) (Super   56 Concorde (USA) 128) [1995 63?: 7m 7m 6g³ 7.9g⁵ 7d 8f 8f 1996 14.1m³ 15m⁴ 16.1m Oct 2] tall, narrow gelding: seems a modest handicapper at best: probably stays 1¾m. *Mrs M. Reveley*

AZTEC TRAVELLER   2 b.g. (Apr 13) Timeless Times (USA) 99 – Chief   65 d Dancer 49 (Chief Singer 131) [1996 5g* 5.1g⁵ 6d² 5f* 6m⁵ 5m⁶ 7m 6m⁵ a8g Nov

15] 8,200Y: workmanlike gelding: easy mover: first foal: dam maiden: won maiden auction at Haydock in April and claimer at Beverley (left J. Berry's stable £9,000) in June: lost form badly after: stays 6f: acts on firm and dead ground: blinkered (no improvement) penultimate outing: failed to handle home bend at Chester on second start: sent to Sweden. *G. L. Moore*

AZWAH (USA) 3 b.f. Danzig (USA) – Magic Slipper 97 (Habitat 134) [1995 65: 65 6m 1996 7.1d⁴ 7.1m⁴ 6m 6d 6d⁴ Oct 21] strong filly: fair maiden at best: stays 7.1f: acts on good to firm and dead ground, yet to race on extremes: sold 43,000 gns Newmarket December Sales. *P. T. Walwyn*

B

BAAHETH (USA) 2 ch.c. (Mar 10) Seeking The Gold (USA) – Star Glimmer 78 ? (USA) (General Assembly (USA)) [1996 7d⁵ 8m a8.5g Dec 14] $100,000F, $200,000Y: small colt: first foal: dam thrice-raced half-sister to Breeders' Cup Juvenile Fillies winner Pleasant Stage: form only when running-on fifth in maiden at Newmarket on debut: sold out of R. Armstrong's stable 13,000 gns Newmarket Autumn Sales after second start. *S. C. Williams*

BAASM 3 br.g. Polar Falcon (USA) 126 – Sariah 87 (Kris 135) [1995 NR 1996 8g⁶ – May 31] first foal: dam 7f winner who stayed 9f: 33/1, dropped away as though in need of race in maiden at Bath: sold (Major W. R. Hern to J. Norton) 3,400 gns Newmarket July Sales: some promise in novice hurdle Nov 7. *Major W. R. Hern*

BABA AU RHUM (IRE) 4 b.g. Baba Karam 117 – Spring About (Hard Fought 63 125) [1995 NR 1996 15g 9g 8.1f 8g⁶ 8d 8.2g⁴ 8m³ Oct 28] ex-French gelding: third foal: dam unraced: modest form here: stays 8.2f: acts on good to firm ground, possibly on dead. *I. P. Williams*

BABE (IRE) 2 b.f. (Mar 16) Treasure Kay 114 – Nujoom (USA) 61 (Halo (USA)) – [1996 7m⁶ 7g 7g Oct 30] IR 6,000Y: first foal: dam ran 3 times: well beaten in maidens. *M. H. Tompkins*

BABINDA 3 b.c. Old Vic 136 – Babita 107 (Habitat 134) [1995 92p: 6g³ 7m* 1996 100 10.3g⁴ 12m 12m⁴ 11.6d⁵ Aug 24] tall, angular colt: good mover: useful performer: easily best efforts when fourth in listed race at Chester and well-contested minor event at Newbury: stays 1½m: acts on good to firm ground, possibly not on a soft surface: joined C. Clement in USA. *C. E. Brittain*

BABSY BABE 3 b.f. Polish Patriot (USA) 128 – Welcome Break (Wollow 132) 94 [1995 88: 5m* 5g² 6f 1996 6m⁴ 5m⁴ 6m⁵ 6m⁶ 6d* 6m 6m Oct 4] tall, quite good-topped filly: not a good walker: fairly useful handicapper: lost all chance with very slow start fourth 3-y-o outing: won at Haydock in July: should stay 7f: acts on good to firm and dead ground: has flashed tail under pressure. *J. J. Quinn*

BABY JANE 2 b.f. (Mar 27) Old Vic 136 – Sutosky 78 (Great Nephew 126) 63 p [1996 6m⁴ 7g⁵ 8.1g⁵ Aug 26] fourth foal: half-sister to 3-y-o 1¼m and 1½m winner Montecristo (by Warning) and 4-y-o 7f winner Dancing Sioux (by Nabeel Dancer): dam suited by 1m to 1¼m: modest form in maidens: will be suited by middle distances. *R. Guest*

BABYSHOOZ 3 b.f. Efisio 120 – Payvashooz 78 (Ballacashtal (CAN)) [1995 –: – 5m 5g 6m 1996 6d 6m Jun 18] small, compact filly: no worthwhile form and possibly ungenuine. *M. Brittain*

BACHELORS PAD 2 b.c. (Feb 21) Pursuit of Love 124 – Note Book 94 94 (Mummy's Pet 125) [1996 6m² 6m* 7m⁵ Oct 4] rather leggy, useful-looking colt: fifth foal: half-brother to 3 winners, including 3-y-o Line Dancer (by Shareef Dancer), 6.1f winner at 2 yrs and 1994 2-y-o 5f and 6.5f winner The Jotter (by Night Shift), both useful: dam, 6f winner, half-sister to smart miler Long Row out of Irish 1000 Guineas winner Front Row: useful form: won maiden at Goodwood in September by 3½ lengths: good effort when around 5 lengths fifth of 8 to Grapeshot in listed race at Newmarket (scratched to post) following month, ridden along some way out and never a factor: stays 7f. *W. Jarvis*

BACK BY DAWN 3 b.g. Risk Me (FR) 127 – Moonlight Princess 49 (Alias –
Smith (USA)) [1995 54: 5m 5g⁴ 6m 6m⁵ 7f⁶ 1996 12m 10m 10g 10.8f⁶ 10s Oct 24]
leggy, close-coupled gelding: unimpressive mover: modest maiden: no worthwhile
form at 3 yrs: sold 2,000 gns Newmarket Autumn Sales: sometimes bandaged
behind: sometimes flashed tail and carried head high at 2 yrs. *D. R. C. Elsworth*

BACKDROP (IRE) 3 b.c. Scenic 128 – Knapping (Busted 134) [1995 74p: 7.1s⁴ 107
1996 10g* 12.3g* 12m² 16.2m⁵ 16.1m⁶ Jun 29] leggy, useful-looking colt: has a
quick action: useful performer: won falsely-run median auction maiden at Pontefract
(ran in snatches) in April and handicap at Chester (awarded race) in May: 1¾ lengths
second of 15 to Bahamian Knight in Derby Italiano at Rome, running on while
hanging left: shade below that form when 2¼ lengths fifth of 14 to Gordi in Queen's
Vase at Royal Ascot and about 4 lengths sixth of 13 to Celeric in Northumberland
Plate at Newcastle: best form at 1½m, though stays 16.2f: acts on good to firm
ground: soon off bridle and is a hard ride: may be worth a try in blinkers/visor: carries
head high: sent to Australia. *P. W. Chapple-Hyam*

BACKGAMMON 5 b.g. Midyan (USA) 124 – Messaria 68§ (Ile de Bourbon 97
(USA) 133) [1995 84: 12m⁶ 1996 12m³ 14s² 12m* Jun 7] strong gelding: better than
ever when winning £21,200 rated stakes at Epsom in June, just getting up: stayed
1¾m: acted on firm and soft ground: visored (ran well) final 3-y-o start: wore
dropped noseband at 5 yrs: died after fire at stable. *J. A. B. Old*

BACKHANDER (IRE) 4 b.g. Cadeaux Genereux 131 – Chevrefeuille 87 (Ile de 56 d
Bourbon (USA) 133) [1995 56: 7g 7.3m 7.1g 6g a7g⁶ 8m² a12g³ 1996 a8g a6g² 7.1g²
7m⁴ a6g⁵ 8.2m 7g² 6f⁴ 8.1g⁴ 6.9f 6m⁶ 7m⁴ 9f 6f Aug 19] sturdy gelding: modest
maiden handicapper: effective at 6f to 1m: acts on firm ground and on fibresand:
blinkered (no improvement) last 2 starts: has hung under pressure: inconsistent:
joined R. Phillips. *Martyn Wane*

BACK IN THE USSR (IRE) 2 ch.g. (May 25) Soviet Lad (USA) 94 – Bilander 53 ?
78 (High Line 125) [1996 6g⁴ 5f⁴ 7.1g³ 6m Aug 10] IR 4,000Y: fourth foal: brother
to 3-y-o 1m (at 2 yrs) and 1½m winner White Sea and half-brother to useful sprinter
Humbert's Landing (by Cyrano de Bergerac): dam, stayed 1½m, from staying
family: modest form: below best in sellers last 2 starts, completely failing to handle
home bend at Musselburgh on first occasion: should stay beyond 6f: races keenly.
M. Johnston

BACKVIEW 4 ch.g. Backchat (USA) 98 – Book Review (Balidar 133) [1995 65, –
a68: 12.5m 10.2m 10.2f³ 8m⁴ 12.5g² 14m⁶ a12g* 11.6m 12s 12.1s a10g 1996 a14.8g a77
a16.2g⁵ a12g³ a12g* a12g a14.8g* a12g³ 14.9d⁵ a14.8g³ 12.3m⁴ 14.9m a14g a12g
Dec 7] short-backed gelding: fair handicapper: first past post at Southwell in
February and at Wolverhampton in March and (demoted to third) April: long way
below form last 4 starts: stays 14.8f: acts on fibresand and firm going: blinkered (well
beaten) on 4-y-o reappearance. *B. J. Llewellyn*

BACKWOODS 3 ch.g. In The Wings 128 – Kates Cabin 96 (Habitat 134) [1995 70
–: 6m 1996 7.1g 10g 12.3g 11.8d 11.8g⁴ a12g⁵ a14.8g* 14s 15.8g* 16g* 14.1s a63
a14.8g⁴ a12g Nov 30] sturdy gelding: fair handicapper: won at Wolverhampton in
August and at Catterick and Nottingham in October: well beaten afterwards: suited
by test of stamina: acts on fibresand, no form on a soft surface. *W. M. Brisbourne*

BADAWI (FR) 6 ch.g. Script Ohio (USA) – Beautiful Bedouin (USA) (His –
Majesty (USA)) [1995 NR 1996 a14.8g³ a16g* a16g Feb 16] modest handicapper: a49
made most to win at Southwell in January by 11 lengths: clearly something amiss
next time: stays 2m well: acts on the all-weather and firm ground, yet to race on a soft
surface: tried blinkered/visored. *N. M. Babbage*

BAD BERTRICH AGAIN (IRE) 3 b.c. Dowsing (USA) 124 – Ajuga (USA) 116
102 (The Minstrel (CAN) 135) [1995 5s³ 5m 8g⁴ 7d* 1996 10g⁴ 11s 12v 10m 12g*
12s⁵ 12f Oct 5] fourth foal: half-brother to Ajanta (rated 74, 8.2f winner at 2 yrs, later
Czech winner, by Rousillon): dam, 6f and 7f winner, out of Cairn Rouge (rated
1¼m, rated 127): German colt: won quite valuable event at Gelsenkirchen at 2 yrs:
improved considerably to win Group 2 event at Hoppegarten in August by 1¾
lengths from below-form Lavirco: below form in Lawrence Realization but ran well
in Turf Classic (7 lengths behind Diplomatic Jet), also at Belmont, last 2 starts: stays
1½m: acts on firm and dead ground, possibly not on very soft. *A. Lowe, Germany*

BADGER BAY (IRE) 3 b.f. Salt Dome (USA) – Legit (IRE) (Runnett 125) 64 §
[1995 67: 5m² 5g² 5m 5g² 5g 6m² 1996 a6g⁴ a7g² a7g⁴ a6g⁶ 6m 6m 8f³ 7g 8f² a54 §
7m⁶ 7.6m⁴ Aug 17] leggy filly: modest maiden handicapper: stays 1m: acts on
firm ground and equitrack: visored (hung badly left) final 3-y-o start: unreliable.
C. A. Dwyer

BADIUS (IRE) 3 b.f. Sadler's Wells (USA) 132 – Bay Shade (USA) 90 (Sharpen –
Up 127) [1995 NR 1996 10.5d May 6] 180,000Y: fourth foal: half-sister
to useful Abury (should have stayed beyond 1½m, by Law Society) and a winning
sprinter in Norway by Green Desert: dam 2-y-o 7f winner who later won 1m listed
race in Italy: 8/1, blanketed and upset in stalls, tailed off in maiden at Haydock: sold
70,000 gns Newmarket December Sales. *J. H. M. Gosden*

BADLESMERE (USA) 2 b.c. (Mar 13) Geiger Counter (USA) – Arising (USA) 87 p
72 (Secreto (USA) 128) [1996 8s² Oct 26] $40,000Y: tall colt: has scope: first foal:
dam, placed at up to 1m here before winning at up to 9f in USA, is out of half-sister
to Valdez, top class at around 1¼m: sire, minor sprint winner, well-bred son of Mr
Prospector: 2 lengths second of 7 to Tempting Prospect in minor event at Newbury,
pushed along from 3f out, looking green, then staying on: sure to improve, and should
win a race. *P. F. I. Cole*

BAD NEWS 4 ch.f. Pharly (FR) 130 – Phylae (Habitat 134) [1995 53?: 7g 7m 44
9.9m 10m 10m a10g 7g⁴ 8f 1996 a8g⁶ 8d³ 10.8f 8.2m³ 8m 8m 10.8m 8.3m a8g a9.4g a–
Nov 11] close-coupled filly: poor maiden: has had 4 trainers since start of 1995: may
prove best at around 1m: blinkered (pulled hard, tailed off) third 3-y-o start: often
wears crossed noseband: has had tongue tied down: inconsistent. *J. M. Bradley*

BAG AND A BIT 3 b.f. Distant Relative 128 – Vaigrant Wind 75 (Vaigly Great 51
127) [1995 NR 1996 5.1d 5.1g 5m⁵ 7f* 8m⁶ 7g² 6f³ Jul 17] small filly: third foal:
sister to fairly useful 4-y-o sprinter Tart And A Half: dam 2-y-o 6f winner: modest
form at best: won claimer at Warwick in June: sold (B. Meehan to N. Babbage) 1,800
gns Doncaster September Sales: best efforts at 7f: acts on firm ground: hung left sixth
3-y-o start. *B. J. Meehan*

BAGBY BOY 4 b.g. Puissance 110 – Miss Milton (Young Christopher 119) [1995 –
–: 10d 12s 14g 1996 9m 9f⁶ 7.6m Aug 4] tall, non-thoroughbred gelding: no sign of
ability. *P. R. Hedger*

BAG OF TRICKS (IRE) 6 br.g. Chief Singer 131 – Bag Lady 86 (Be My Guest 55
(USA) 126) [1995 57, a64: a10g⁶ a12g² a10g³ a12g³ a12g⁶ a12g* 12m² 11.9f 12g a57
10m³ 12f² 12m 12f³ 12m⁶ 1996 a12g⁴ a12g⁶ a12g³ 11.9f* 11.9f 12d 11.9g³ 11.6m Jun
10] strong gelding: modest handicapper: won claimer at Brighton in April, leading 5f
out: suited by middle distances: best form on a sound surface (looked none too keen
on dead) or equitrack: takes strong hold. *S. Dow*

BAGSHOT 5 b.h. Rousillon (USA) 133 – Czar's Bride (USA) 78 (Northern 68 §
Dancer) [1995 84: 8g⁶ 8m 7.3g⁴ 8f 8.1f³ 7.3d⁶ a8g³ a8g³ 1996 8s 7f⁵ 8.3m⁴ 8.1d⁶ a61 §
a10g² a7g⁵ a10g² Dec 30] good-topped horse: disappointing in 1996: sold out of R.
Hannon's stable 3,000 gns Newmarket Autumn Sales after fourth start: seems to stay
1¼m: acts on firm ground, dead and all-weather: carries head high: normally held up:
looks ungenuine nowadays. *G. L. Moore*

BAHAMIAN BOUNTY 2 ch.c. (Feb 10) Cadeaux Genereux 131 – Clarentia 116
111 (Ballad Rock 122) [1996 6m² 5.2f* 6g* 6m* 7g⁴ Oct 18]
What can you get for a million pounds nowadays? Just over half a Luna
Wells and eighty-five per cent of a yearling colt by Woodman out of Danse
Royale, but it was widely reported that the price was right for Bahamian Bounty
when Sheikh Maktoum Al Maktoum concluded negotiations with Lucayan
Stud Ltd on the eve of the Middle Park Stakes. After the Middle Park, he would
doubtless have had to pay a bit more. Punters had taken the hint and backed
Bahamian Bounty down to 7/4 favourite and these two gambles were landed
in somewhat suspenseful circumstances. Bahamian Bounty was a worthy
favourite to follow up an 11/1-on triumph in a maiden at Yarmouth and his
infinitely more meritorious short-neck win over Zamindar and Pas de Reponse
in the Prix Morny Piaget at Deauville, but he faced some interesting opponents.
Eleven runners for the Middle Park had been bettered only once (in Cajun's

Prix Morny Piaget, Deauville—Bahamian Bounty (left) deprives Zamindar

year, 1981) since Djebel beat nineteen rivals in November 1939, and, in addition to Bahamian Bounty, five of them had already won a pattern race and another three had made the frame in one. The chief dangers to the favourite turned out to be the German Group 2 winner Muchea, Champagne Stakes second In Command and National Stakes fourth Fantastic Fellow and, in a strongly-run race, all four appeared on the scene late in the day. In Bahamian Bounty and Muchea's case it was after waiting for a gap, Bahamian Bounty pulling double going down into the Dip then being pushed through on the stand rails by Frankie Dettori and lengthening in good style, getting up close home. The million-pound purchase had looked suitably unconcerned in the preliminaries and relaxed through the race, boosting enthusiasm for his bid to register a hat-trick of Group 1 victories over a furlong further in the Dewhurst Stakes fifteen days later. Starting co-favourite, though, Bahamian Bounty could not reproduce his Middle Park form and finished fourth of eight, about a length and a half behind In Command; he was checked slightly in the Dip, but did not leave the impression that a perfectly clear passage would have made much difference. He will probably turn out to be a sprinter.

		Young Generation	Balidar
Bahamian Bounty (ch.c. Feb 10, 1994)	Cadeaux Genereux (ch 1985)	(b 1976)	Brig O'Doon
		Smarten Up (ch 1975)	Sharpen Up
			L'Anguissola
	Clarentia (ch 1984)	Ballad Rock (ch 1974)	Bold Lad
			True Rocket
		Laharden (b 1979)	Mount Hagen
			Sinella

The belief that Bahamian Bounty did not stay in the Dewhurst is strengthened by a look at his pedigree. Cadeaux Genereux was champion

Middle Park Stakes, Newmarket—£1 million well spent?;
Bahamian Bounty (right) provides a swift return in the close finish with Muchea (left)

sprinter and is an influence for speed, and there is a predominance of speed on the dam's side as well, as is evident from Clarentia's racing record. She had twenty-five races, but only one over so far as six furlongs. Trained by Mark Usher, it was a stop-start career, busy and at her best as a two-year-old when she won twice and was third in the Cornwallis Stakes; unraced as a three-year-old; twice-raced (winning once then breaking a blood vessel) at Cagnes-Sur-Mer in February as a four-year-old; and having a second full season only at five years when she was a fairly useful handicapper and won twice. Her dam Laharden was unraced and her dam Sinella had just three starts as a two-year-old, winning one of them, but this is a family of huge achievement as Sinella is a daughter of Djerella, the unraced filly given away by Phil Bull, who became famous as the dam of Stilvi. When Zamindar met Bahamian Bounty, however, it was a case of Zafonic's brother clashing with the half-brother to fairly useful two-year-old sprinter Forentia (by Formidable) and two maidens. Clarentia was sold in December 1994 for 13,500 guineas to go to Italy, and ten months later the yearling Bahamian Bounty was picked up for 45,000. If he is to enhance his value even further, it will be in the top sprints. A rather leggy, quite good-topped colt with scope, Bahamian Bounty is not the best of walkers but an easy, fluent mover in his faster paces. He won on firm ground at Yarmouth (which proved little) and good to firm in the Middle Park. Bahamian Bounty is wintering in Dubai. *D. R. Loder*

BAHAMIAN KNIGHT (CAN)   3 b. or br.c. Ascot Knight (CAN) 130 –   110 Muskoka Command (USA) (Top Command (USA)) [1995 95: 5m^2 6g^2 6m* 6m^3 1996 8m^2 10m^2 10.4m 12m* 12m 10f Aug 25] quite attractive colt: smart performer: won 15-runner Derby Italiano at Rome in May by 1¾ lengths from Backdrop, leading 2f out and running on well: not at all discredited in Gordon Stakes at Goodwood and Secretariat Stakes at Arlington last 2 starts: stays 1½m: has raced only on a sound surface: visored (no improvement) final European start: joined N. Drysdale. *D. R. Loder*

BAHAMIAN SUNSHINE (USA)   5 ch.h. Sunshine Forever (USA) – Pride of   96 Darby (USA) (Danzig (USA)) [1995 105: 12.5v^3 12d^2 12.5d^5 14g^2 13.9m* 12d 1996 14.4m^2 16.4d^5 22.2f^4 13.9m^4 18g^4 Sep 3] tall, lengthy horse: useful performer, not so

Derby Italiano, Rome—a one-two for the British raiders thanks to Bahamian Knight and Backdrop

good as at 4 yrs: left D. Loder after penultimate start: stays extreme distances: acts on firm and heavy going: no longer consistent. *R. Akehurst*

BAHER (USA) 7 b.g. Damister (USA) 123 – Allatum (USA) 81 (Alleged (USA) 28 138) [1995 NR 1996 a16g² a16g⁴ a14g³ a16g⁴ a16g⁵ a14g Dec 3] off course 2½ years, bad form on return: effective in blinkers. *Mrs A. Swinbank*

BAHHARE (USA) 2 b.c. (Apr 24) Woodman (USA) 126 – Wasnah (USA) 122 p 96 (Nijinsky (CAN) 138) [1996 7g* 7m* 7f* Sep 13]
First things first. It's as well to clear up the pronunciation—'Ba-har-ree', three syllables—as this is a name (arabic for sailor) that looks sure to be on everyone's lips come Guineas time. A sizeable home reputation preceded Bahhare to the racecourse and he started a hot favourite for the maiden that opens the Newmarket July meeting. The race had been won the previous year by the same owner's Alhaarth in a close finish with Mark of Esteem. Bahhare's performance fulfilled expectations. Racing alone in the centre of the course, he stretched clear in good style inside the final furlong after looking green when first pushed along two furlongs out. Bahhare won by three and a half lengths, from the second favourite Equal Rights, the first five home being newcomers in a field that overall, on looks at any rate, was less inspiring than in 1995, though the second, fifth, seventh and eighth won next time. The general 16/1 quote about Bahhare for the 1997 Two Thousand Guineas became a general 12/1 quote after he had landed odds of 3/1-on in a minor event over the same course three and a half weeks later, looking even more a colt destined to go on to very much better things. He slaughtered three opponents, two of whom had contested pattern events at the July meeting, settling the issue in a matter of strides when given the office going into the Dip and winning easing down by six lengths.
With the eleventh-hour withdrawal of Revoque because of the firm ground, Bahhare again faced only three opponents in the Laurent-Perrier Champagne Stakes at Doncaster in September, a race in which Alhaarth had met only two the previous year. Bahhare's rivals—In Command, Musheer and Reliquary—all appeared to be held in high regard, though, like Bahhare, they were being tested in a pattern race for the first time. The result was another resounding victory for Bahhare who forged clear under pressure, after being patiently ridden, to beat In Command by three and a half lengths. Bahhare, who was a shade reluctant at the stalls, swished his tail several times as Carson rode him out but there was no sign of any slackening in his finishing effort. It was difficult, at the time, to be sure what the form was worth—the pace was strong (the two-year-old course record was broken) yet the time-value of the winner's performance was not exceptional. In Command's subsequent performances, especially his victory in a substandard Dewhurst, did it no harm though. Bahhare himself wasn't seen out again, his owner Sheikh Hamdan having been adamant after Bahhare's first two races that he should have just one more run. 'Bahhare is still a little immature behind the saddle and his second thigh is not fully developed yet,' he had said. The view was shared by Bahhare's trainer—'still immature and not really fully furnished'—and by jockey Willie Carson.

Laurent-Perrier Champagne Stakes, Doncaster—four well-touted colts and a clear-cut winner in Bahhare

Describing Bahhare as 'just a frame of a horse,' Carson pointed out that he was a different type of two-year-old from Alhaarth. 'Alhaarth was a complete horse at the end of his two-year-old days, but this one is still a bit of a baby. The frame is there but he needs time to develop it.' Bahhare's owner announced he was setting up his own Godolphin-style operation in Dubai at the end of the season and it was widely expected that Bahhare would be among the two-year-olds sent there over the winter, especially as Alhaarth's anti-climactic three-year-old campaign was thought to have influenced Sheikh Hamdan to follow the 'Dubai experiment'. Despite newspaper reports to the contrary, however, Bahhare was wintered in Britain, after being flown out to Dubai for five days in late-autumn for a thorough veterinary check-up.

		Woodman (USA) (ch 1983)	Mr Prospector (b 1970)	Raise A Native Gold Digger
Bahhare (USA) (b.c. Apr 24, 1994)			Playmate (ch 1975)	Buckpasser Intriguing
		Wasnah (USA) (b 1987)	Nijinsky (b 1967)	Northern Dancer Flaming Page
			Highest Trump (b 1972)	Bold Bidder Dear April

The rather unfurnished, rangy, attractive Bahhare, who is by Bosra Sham's sire Woodman, should train on into a candidate for top honours as a three-year-old. His half-brother Bahri (by Riverman), a better-developed individual than Bahhare at the same stage of his career, stepped up considerably on his two-year-old efforts—his only victory in four starts came in a minor event at Nottingham—and went on to win the St James's Palace Stakes and the

Hamdan Al Maktoum's "Bahhare"

Queen Elizabeth II Stakes after finishing third in the Guineas. Bahhare is the
third foal of the Nijinsky mare Wasnah, a maiden who showed more stamina
than speed; her second foal the filly Istiglal (by Diesis) has yet to reach the
racecourse. Wasnah would almost certainly have stayed a mile and a half, her
performances including a staying-on second in the Pretty Polly Stakes over a
mile and a quarter at Newmarket. Bahhare's grandam Highest Trump won the
Queen Mary Stakes at two and was placed the next year in the Irish One
Thousand Guineas and the Coronation Stakes. At stud she has produced three
pattern or graded winners: the Northern Dancer colts Dance Bid and Northern
Plain both won the Group 3 Tetrarch Stakes and stayed middle distances, while
Winglet won the Grade 2 Princess Stakes over eight and a half furlongs in the
States. The average winning distance of Woodman's progeny aged three and
above is around nine furlongs and he himself, a winner over a mile at two,
wasn't bred to get further. Woodman's most notable winner over a mile and a
half is the Belmont Stakes winner Hansel; Bosra Sham's top-class full brother
Hector Protector finished fourth in the Derby after his stamina ran out in the
last furlong or so. It's reasonable to draw the conclusion, judged on pedigree,
that Bahhare's best prospects of classic success will come in the Two Thousand
Guineas, though it would be unwise to rule him out of the Derby on grounds of
stamina just yet. He was still a racehorse in the making as a two-year-old and
there is still much to learn about his racing character. He could be anything.
Bahhare, a fluent mover, acts on firm ground and didn't encounter ground
softer than good in any of his three races though it's worth bearing in mind that
a good proportion of his sire's progeny tend to go well with give in the ground.
J. L. Dunlop

BAHRAIN QUEEN (IRE)   8 ch.m. Caerleon (USA) 132 – Bahrain Vee (CAN)   –
(Blushing Groom (FR) 131) [1995 –: 16.2m⁵ 1996 17.2m Jun 29] no worthwhile
form on flat: modest winning hurdler. *C. Smith*

BAILEYS FIRST (IRE)   3 b.f. Alzao (USA) 117 – Maiden Concert (Condorcet   72
(FR)) [1995 74: 6f³ 6m³ 7d³ 6m 1996 6m² 7.5m 9.9m³ 10m⁶ 10.5g 7g⁴ 6m⁴ 6f
6d 8m Aug 22] smallish, good-quartered filly: fair maiden handicapper: best form
at 7f to 1¼m: acts on firm and dead ground: blinkered (over 6f) eighth 3-y-o start:
inconsistent: sold 16,000 gns Newmarket December Sales. *M. Johnston*

BAILEYS IMP (IRE)   2 ch.g. (Feb 24) Imp Society (USA) – Best Academy   57
(USA) (Roberto (USA) 131) [1996 5f 5.1m⁶ 6m Sep 26] IR 15,000Y: strong,
workmanlike gelding: carries condition: first foal: dam Irish 8.5f winner: modest
form: best effort second start: off course 3 months afterwards: should stay 6f: sold
1,300 gns Doncaster September Sales: sent to Denmark. *M. Johnston*

BAILEYS SUNSET (IRE)   4 b.g. Red Sunset 120 – Stradey Lynn 57 (Derrylin   62
115) [1995 72d: a5g* a5g⁶ a5g² a6g² a6g² 6s⁴ 5m* 5.1g⁴ 5g⁵ 5g 5m³ 5m⁵ 5m³ 5f³ 5g*
5f⁶ 6f* 6f⁶ 6f³ 6g⁵ 6d 5g 5f 1996 a5g 6f² 5.1g* 5.1g 5.7g³ 5g May 31] neat gelding:
only modest form for new stable in 1996: won claimer at Nottingham in April:
stayed 6f: acted on hard going and equitrack: blinkered (below form) once at 3 yrs:
collapsed and died final start. *J. M. Bradley*

BAILIEBOROUGH BOY (IRE)   2 ch.g. (Apr 17) Shalford (IRE) 124§ – Sal-   61
ique (Sallust 134) [1996 5m³ 5m³ 6g a6g⁴ Dec 27] IR 9,000F, IR 9,500Y: quite
attractive gelding: closely related to useful Irish 3-y-o Tirol Hope (by Tirol), 6f and
7f winner at 2 yrs, and half-brother to several winners, easily best of them useful 6f
and 7f winner Simply Henry (by Simply Great): dam second over 7f in Ireland: third
in maiden auctions at Doncaster and Redcar in May: off course nearly 4 months, failed by long way to repeat form: should prove suited by further than 5f. *T. D. Barron*

BAILIWICK   3 b.g. Dominion 123 – Lady Barkley (Habitat 134) [1995 46: 6m   –
6.1m 6m 7.6m 8g⁵ 8m 1996 a8g* a7g³ a8.5g³ a8.5g² 11.6m 11.8d a12g Jun 20]   a54
workmanlike gelding: modest handicapper: won at Southwell (seller) in January:
stays 8.5f: acts on fibresand: blinkered at 3 yrs: races prominently. *N. A. Graham*

BAIRN ATHOLL   3 ch.f. Bairn (USA) 126 – Noble Mistress 80 (Lord Gayle   –
(USA) 124) [1995 NR 1996 6m 6.9d Oct 21] sturdy filly: half-sister to a poor
winning sprinter by Daring March: dam 2-y-o 6f winner: showed a glimmer of ability
in claimer (moved poorly to post) and seller. *R. J. Hodges*

BAIZE 3 ch.f. Efisio 120 – Bayonne 72 (Bay Express 132) [1995 94: 5g* 5m*   95
5m³ 6m⁵ 6f⁴ 1996 6m 6m² 8f⁴ 8f⁵ 8.5f⁴ Sep 15] workmanlike filly: unimpressive
mover: useful performer: good second in minor event at Kempton final start for
F. Johnson Houghton in Britain: probably stays 8.5f has raced only on a sound
surface. *Kathy Walsh, USA*

BAJAN FRONTIER (IRE) 4 ch.f. Imperial Frontier (USA) 112 – Sajanjal   –
(Dance In Time (CAN)) [1995 41, a54: 5m 5g⁵ 5d³ 6f 5m a5g a5g* 1996 a5g a5g 5g
5g a5g a5g a5g a6g Aug 9] compact filly: modest handicapper: no form in 1996: sold
1,500 gns Doncaster September Sales: best form at 5f: acts on fibresand and on good
to firm and dead ground: tried visored: one to treat with caution: sent to South Korea.
F. H. Lee

BAJAN (IRE) 5 b.g. Taufan (USA) 119 – Thatcherite (Final Straw 127) [1995 66:   –
10g⁵ 10m* 12f 10.1m* 1996 10m 12d Oct 11] lengthy, good-bodied gelding: fair
handicapper: off course nearly 14 months, no form on return: should stay 1½m: acts
on good to firm ground: visored last 5 starts (winner first occasion, failed to repeat
form) at 3 yrs: inconsistent. *Lady Herries*

BAJAN ROSE 4 b.f. Dashing Blade 117 – Supreme Rose 95 (Frimley Park 109)   89
[1995 78: 6m 6m 6m⁶ 6m 6m² 5.2m⁵ 6g² 6g 5d 5g⁵ 6d⁵ 6.1s* 1996 6g 6s² 5.1m* 5m⁴
6.1m 5.2m³ 5m 6m 6m² 6g³ 6s³ 6f Nov 5] leggy filly: fairly useful handicapper: won
at Chester in June: best efforts when in frame afterwards: stays 6f: acts on firm and
soft ground: effective from front or held up. *M. Blanshard*

BAKED ALASKA 2 b.f. (Mar 4) Green Desert (USA) 127 – Snowing (USA)   90 p
(Icecapade (USA)) [1996 6g* Oct 18] angular, good-topped filly: third foal: half-
sister to 3-y-o On The Piste (by Shirley Heights): dam, won 4 races in USA,
half-sister to smart sprinter Two Punch (by Danzig): 33/1, burly and green, won
22-runner maiden at Newmarket running on strongly by a length from Miss Sancerre:
will stay 7f: will improve. *A. C. Stewart*

BAKER 3 b.g. Cigar 68 – Bread 'n Honey 51 (Goldhills Pride 105) [1995 52?: 6m   –
6m 5g³ 6m 7.3d 1996 a7g 8.2d 7f 11.6m Jun 10] angular gelding: no form in 1996:
sold 600 gns Ascot July Sales. *J. Akehurst*

BAKERS DAUGHTER 4 ch.f. Bairn (USA) 126 – Tawnais 80 (Artaius (USA)   57
129) [1995 51, a57: a8g* a10g² a8.5g⁴ a8.5g 8g* a10g³ 8m a10g a12g a10g³ 1996   a61
a8g² a8g a8g³ a8g³ a8g 8.1m³ 8m³ 8.3g³ 10g* a10g* 10m⁵ 10.2f 10d⁵ a10g³ a10g
Dec 30] sparely-made filly: modest handicapper: won at Windsor and Lingfield in
the summer when consistent: stays 1¼m: acts on good to firm ground and the
all-weather: blinkered (ran well) sixth 4-y-o start. *J. R. Arnold*

BAKERS' GATE (USA) 4 b. or br.c. Danzig (USA) – Alydaress (USA) 124   77
(Alydar (USA)) [1995 79p: 8m² 8g³ 1996 8g 10m⁵ 10.3m Jul 13] robust colt:
has a quick action: fair maiden at his best: off course nearly a year and failed to
progress as had been anticipated: sold 10,000 gns Newmarket Autumn Sales: should
stay 1¼m: visored (ran badly) final start: carried head awkwardly second 4-y-o start.
J. H. M. Gosden

BAKHETA 4 b.f. Persian Bold 123 – Vielle 123 (Ribero 126) [1995 46: 12m 8.3m   68
12s 10d 9m⁴ a10g a8g 1996 10g³ 10d* 10m* 10m³ 10m* 10.5g⁵ Jul 6] robust filly:
fair handicapper: back with original yard and won at Sandown, Windsor (dead-heat)
and Newbury in May/June: best form at 1¼m, but should stay further: acts on good
to firm and dead ground: often front runner: sold 16,000 gns Newmarket December
Sales. *Miss Gay Kelleway*

BALALAIKA 3 b.f. Sadler's Wells (USA) 132 – Bella Colora 119 (Bellypha 130)   106
[1995 NR 1996 9m* 10m⁵ 12m² 11.9m 10.1m² 12g⁵ 10g⁴ Nov 1] 510,000Y: strong,
rangy, attractive filly with scope: has a powerful, round action: sister to 2 winners,
notably high-class Stagecraft (best at 1¼m), and half-sister to smart 1m winner
Hyabella (by Shirley Heights): dam, 6f and 1¼m winner, half-sister to Irish Oaks
winner Colorspin (dam of Opera House, by Sadler's Wells): won maiden at Kempton
in June: contested listed events afterwards, showing useful form on 4 occasions, best
effort 2 lengths second to Shemozzle at Newmarket third start: has raced
only on good to firm and good ground: stays in training. *L. M. Cumani*

BALANCE OF POWER 4 b.g. Ballacashtal (CAN) – Moreton's Martha   76
(Derrylin 115) [1995 72: 7g⁴ 7m⁶ 6m⁵ 7.1g⁵ 6f⁵ 6m 7d⁶ 6g³ 1996 6f 6d 7m 7f³ 7g* 7g

8m* 7f² 8.5m⁶ 8d 8.2g Oct 24] useful-looking gelding: fair handicapper on his day: won at Epsom and Brighton (stayed on well) in the summer: below form after next start: best form over 7f, should prove better at 1m in due course: acts on firm ground, not on a soft surface: tried blinkered, no improvement: has run well when sweating: inconsistent. *R. Akehurst*

BALASARA (IRE)   6 ch.g. Don't Forget Me 127 – Tameen (FR) (Pharly (FR)   – § 130) [1995 79§: 8m² 8m² 9m² 9d² 9m³ 8d² a10g 1996 8m May 1] stocky gelding: fair maiden handicapper: stays 11.7f: acts on good to firm ground and dead, well beaten on equitrack: usually blinkered: pulls hard, carries head high and has flashed tail: reluctant to race on only 6-y-o start: one to avoid. *R. J. O'Sullivan*

BALATA BAY   5 ch.g. Chief Singer 131 – Lets Fall In Love (USA) (Northern   – Baby (CAN) 127) [1995 NR 1996 9.2s 8.5g May 11] lengthy gelding: rated 63 at best at 3 yrs (stayed 1m) for R. Hannon: soundly beaten on return. *J. J. Birkett*

BAL HARBOUR   5 b.h. Shirley Heights 130 – Balabina (USA) 110 (Nijinsky   113 (CAN) 138) [1995 110: 12f³ 12g⁴ 12m⁴ 11.6m² 12g² 10m* 1996 10.1m* 10m* 10f⁴ 10d² 12f⁵ 10m⁵ Sep 25] good-bodied horse: good walker and fluent mover: has had his problems, but is a smart performer: comfortably made all in fairly valuable minor event at Epsom and listed race at Kempton (3 ran, beat Jural 2½ lengths) in June: in frame in listed race at Newbury (shade edgy) and Prix Gontaut-Biron at Deauville (length behind Carling) next 2 starts: shade disappointing last 2 starts: effective at 1¼m and stays 1½m: acts on firm ground and dead ground: stays in training. *H. R. A. Cecil*

BALINSKY (IRE)   3 b.f. Skyliner 117 – Ballinacurra (King's Troop 118) [1995   55 NR 1996 7s 7f³ 7g 7f⁴ a8.5g⁴ a7g³ a8s⁵ a8.5g⁶ Dec 28] IR 4,800Y: angular filly: sister to 2 winners, notably smart sprinter Blyton Lad, and half-sister to a winner abroad: dam ran once: modest maiden: stays 7f: acts on firm ground and equitrack. *J. Berry*

BALIOS (IRE)   3 b.g. Be My Guest (USA) 126 – Clifden Bottoms (Wolver   57 Hollow 126) [1995 56p: 8.2m a8.5g² 1996 a11g* a11g³ 14.1g 12m⁶ 12.1g⁴ a14.8g²   a70 12f³ Jul 22] tall, lengthy gelding: fair form on all-weather: made virtually all in maiden at Southwell in February, flashing tail under pressure: modest on turf: claimed by W. G. M. Turner £6,000 final start: seems to stay 14.8f: acts on fibresand and firm ground: has looked uncooperative and may benefit from blinkers or visor. *M. Johnston*

BALI PARADISE (USA)   2 b.g. (Feb 5) Red Ransom (USA) – Dream Creek   95 (USA) (The Minstrel (CAN) 135) [1996 5d⁵ 6d³ 7g⁶ 7.3m* 7.3s⁵ Oct 24] $100,000Y: tall, sturdy gelding: has scope: fifth foal: half-brother to a winner in North America (by Turkoman) and US 3-y-o Majestic Dream (by Majestic Light), minor stakes winner at 2 yrs: dam won at up to 9f in USA: awarded maiden at Haydock in May: given good front-running ride when winning nursery at Newbury in September: sweating, edgy and free to post, well-beaten fifth of 8 to Desert Story in Horris Hill Stakes (unseated rider on way down) at Newbury on final start: bred to stay 1m: acts on good to firm and dead ground. *P. F. I. Cole*

BALI-PET   2 b.c. (Apr 2) Tina's Pet 121 – Baligay 84 (Balidar 133) [1996 a7g⁶   ? a7g² 7f⁵ a7g 10f a8.5g² a8g* a7g² Dec 7] first foal: dam effective from 5f to 7f: a57 modest form: won seller at Southwell in November: stays 8.5f: form only on fibresand: blinkered since fifth start. *W. G. M. Turner*

BALI TENDER   5 ch.g. Balidar 133 – Highest Tender 56 (Prince Tenderfoot   – (USA) 126) [1995 36: 8.5d 7.5m 12.3f⁵ a8g 6m⁴ 6f⁵ 7m 5g⁶ 1996 10.3d 12.1g Apr 4] strong gelding: poor maiden handicapper: probably stays 12.3f: acts on firm and dead ground: has joined T. Wharton. *M. W. Easterby*

BALLADOOLE BAJAN   2 b.f. (May 2) Efisio 120 – Rectitude 99 (Runnymede   75 123) [1996 5f³ 5m² 5g* 6m* 6.1s³ Oct 31] 6,800Y: strong, neat filly: half-sister to several winners, including 3-y-o 11.1f winner Divine (by Dowsing), useful 1985 2-y-o 7f winner Normanby Lass (by Bustino) and fairly useful stayer Farmer's Pet (by Sharrood): dam winner at up to 8.5f: won median auction maiden at Thirsk in August and nursery at Epsom (despite looking ill at ease on track) in September: will stay beyond 6f: acts on soft and good to firm ground: retained by trainer 17,000 gns Doncaster November Sales. *M. Johnston*

BALLAD RULER   10 ch.g. Ballad Rock 122 – Jessamy Hall 77 (Crowned Prince   – (USA) 128) [1995 –: a14g 17.2m 14.1m 1996 a13g a13g Feb 10] of little account. *P. A. Pritchard*

BALLADUR (USA) 3 b.c. Nureyev (USA) 131 – Ballinderry 112 (Irish River 86 (FR) 131) [1995 83+: 7g³ 7f⁴ 1996 8m* 10g Jul 10] rather unfurnished colt: narrowly won maiden at Newcastle in June, always well there and staying on: tailed off in £20,900 handicap at Newmarket, carrying head awkwardly and finding little when headed 2f out: sold (H. Cecil to Mrs J. Pitman) 15,000 gns Newmarket Autumn Sales: bred to stay further than 1m but looked less than tractable last time: one to have some reservations about. *H. R. A. Cecil*

BALLARD LADY (IRE) 4 ch.f. Ballad Rock 122 – First Blush (Ela-Mana-Mou 49 132) [1995 49: 7.5m 8m 10m 8.1d* 7g 8g⁵ 12m² 10.5m 10.4g⁶ 15g 10g⁶ 1996 8s³ 8g⁵ 8.3s a8g 8m⁴ 8m⁴ 7g 7.1d* 7.6m⁴ 6d* 7g⁵ 6.1m 6m⁵ 6m⁴ 7g a6g³ Nov 18] big, good-topped filly: shows traces of stringhalt: shows a round action: poor handicapper: won at Haydock (apprentices, idled) in July and Ayr (soon pushed along, led near finish) in August: stays 1½m, clearly as effective at 6f/7f: acts on good to firm and (best form) dead ground, also on fibresand: visored (stiff task) final 2-y-o start: inconsistent. *J. S. Wainwright*

BALLERINA'S DREAM 2 b.f. (Apr 22) Suave Dancer (USA) 136 – Our – p Reverie (USA) (J O Tobin (USA) 130) [1996 6f Oct 8] 4,000Y: sparely-made filly: fifth foal: half-sister to useful 1¼m and 1½m winner Peter Quince and 1¾m winner Our Kris (both by Kris): dam, stakes winner at up to 11f, half-sister to Sharrood: slowly away and never on terms in maiden auction at Warwick: likely to do better over much further than 6f. *Martyn Meade*

BALLET DE COUR 3 b.g. Thowra (FR) – Chaleureuse (Final Straw 127) [1995 – NR 1996 10m 12g⁵ 13.8g⁴ Jul 24] 1,500F: third foal: half-brother to Amorem (by Liboi), poor maiden here winner at 9f in 1995 in Holland: dam ran once: well beaten in maiden events. *C. W. C. Elsey*

BALLET HIGH (IRE) 3 b.c. Sadler's Wells (USA) 132 – Marie d'Argonne 73 (FR) 104 (Jefferson 129) [1995 NR 1996 12m³ 10m⁴ 11.5m² 13.4g³ Sep 25] 150,000Y: tall, sparely-made colt: fifth foal: closely related to 2 winners, notably high-class Polar Falcon (stayed 1m, by Nureyev), and half-brother to 4-y-o 1m winner Mokuti (by Green Desert): dam won at up to 1¼m in France/USA: fair maiden: stays at least 1½m: yet to race on a soft surface: looks one-paced. *I. A. Balding*

BALL GOWN 6 b.m. Jalmood (USA) 126 – Relatively Smart 76 (Great Nephew 98 126) [1995 88, a–: 10m² 12g* 12f⁶ 12m³ 10m*dis 10m⁴ 10m³ 10d² 9g² 10v 8m 1996 a– 10m* 10.4f⁶ 10f 10g 10m⁵ 10m⁴ 10m⁴ 10d* 11.1m⁶ Sep 7] small, leggy mare: useful handicapper: won rated stakes at Newmarket in May and August: probably needs good test at 9f nowadays, and stays 1½m: acts on good to firm ground (possibly not firm) and dead (won a seller on soft, seemed unsuited by heavy): no form in 3 races on all-weather: usually held up: sometimes bandaged behind: has worn crossed noseband: tough and genuine. *D. T. Thom*

BALLPOINT 3 ch.c. Indian Ridge 123 – Ballaquine 56 (Martinmas 128) [1995 77 62: 6d 7g 7g⁴ 1996 7m 8.1m² 10g 8g³ 8g⁴ 10.1g* 8.9g⁴ 11.5m² 11f Nov 5] small colt: poor mover: fair performer: won claimer at Epsom (led 1f out) in August: left R. Hannon after eighth start: stays 1½m: acts on good to firm ground. *G. M. Moore*

BALLYDINERO (IRE) 2 b.c. (Feb 8) Ballacashtal (CAN) – Nutwood Emma 43 (Henbit (USA) 130) [1996 5m 5.9g 5.9f⁴ 7.1g⁵ 7m 7g 10f⁵ a8.5g Nov 2] IR 4,300F, IR 2,000Y: third reported foal: half-brother to 3-y-o Fiddles Delight (by Colmore Row) and winning sprinter Little Hooligan (by Rabdan): dam (poor maiden) possibly temperamental: poor maiden: stays 1¼m: has raced only on a sound surface on turf (well beaten on fibresand). *Capt. J. Wilson*

BALLYKISSANGEL 3 ro.g. Hadeer 118 – April Wind 91 (Windjammer – (USA)) [1995 –: 6f 7.1d 6m 1996 a6g⁶ 8g 6m 8.3m 7g 12.1g a8g Dec 27] tall gelding: no worthwhile form. *N. Bycroft*

BALLYMAC GIRL 8 gr.m. Niniski (USA) 125 – Alruccaba 83 (Crystal Palace – (FR) 132) [1995 63: 18g 16.2m⁴ 15.4g² 14.1g a16g 16g⁵ 18.2g⁵ 14s* 16.1g³ 15.1s a14.8g* a14g a14.8g* a12g⁵ 1996 a14.8g a16.2g³ Jan 17] modest handicapper: raced more prominently than usual in January, and below form: stays well: acts on good to firm and soft ground and fibresand: covered by Alzao. *J. M. Bradley*

BALLYMOTE 2 b.g. (Apr 10) Chilibang 120 – Be My Honey (Bustino 136) 74 [1996 5d 5.1m⁴ 5m² 5f* 5f⁵ 6g 5m* Sep 23] 1,900F, IR 6,000Y: lengthy gelding:

third foal: half-brother to 4-y-o NH Flat race winner Rock On Honey (by Rock City): dam unraced close relative of high-class middle-distance horse Bedtime: won maiden auction at Redcar in July and nursery (4 ran) at Musselburgh in September: bred to stay beyond 5f (stiff task when tried) but races keenly: acts on firm ground. *J. Berry*

BALLYNAKELLY 4 ch.g. Deploy 131 – Musical Charm (USA) 78 (The   90
Minstrel (CAN) 135) [1995 73: 8m 8.3g 8m 12.1d a12g* a13g* 1996 a12g* 14.6g*
14f* 14m* 14m* 13.3m* 18g⁶ Oct 19] strong, lengthy gelding: won at Lingfield in
January before off course 6½ months: won at Doncaster, Lingfield and Sandown
(twice) in the summer: ran a tremendous race when dead-heating with Kutta in Tote
Bookmakers Autumn Cup at Newbury in September, very game to hold on after
looking sure to be beaten: unusually held up (plenty to do) before staying on well for
sixth of 26 to Inchcailloch in the Cesarewitch: stays 2¼m, and effective over shorter:
acts on equitrack and good to firm ground: races prominently: thoroughly game and
genuine: sold 70,000 gns Newmarket Autumn Sales, to Saudi Arabia. *R. Akehurst*

BALLYRAG (USA) 5 ch.g. Silver Hawk (USA) 123 – Dancing Rags (USA)   –
(Nijinsky (CAN) 138) [1995 NR 1996 a11g⁴ a12g⁵ a12g³ a9.4g 10.3d Mar 21] tall
gelding: second foal: half-brother to a winner in USA by Private Account: dam,
winner in USA, from very good family: fairly useful 1m winner in France as 3 yrs for
A. Fabre: nothing like so good here: dead. *R. A. Fahey*

BALLYSOKERRY (IRE) 5 b.g. Hatim (USA) 121 – Wonder Woman (Horage   –
124) [1995 –: 12g 10.4m 1996 10g 7.5f 8.2m a5g Jul 6] robust gelding: of little
account: tried blinkered. *J. Parkes*

BALLY SOUZA (IRE) 2 b.f. (May 9) Alzao (USA) 117 – Cheese Soup (USA)   70
(Spectacular Bid (USA)) [1996 6.1m 7g³ 7m⁵ Oct 17] IR 24,000Y: smallish,
close-coupled filly: sixth reported foal: half-sister to 1995 2-y-o 5f winner Shafir (by
Shaadi), useful 1m winner A La Carte (by Caerleon) and a winner in North America
by Chief's Crown: dam unraced: stayed on strongly when third to Beryllium in
steadily-run maiden at Chester in September: will be suited by 1m+. *M. Johnston*

BALMORAL PRINCESS 3 b.f. Thethingaboutitis (USA) 106 – Fair Balmoral   –
(Hasty Word 84) [1995 –: a7g 1996 a9.4g a12g a14.8g a12g Jul 15] no form on flat:
tried blinkered: poor winning hurdler. *J. H. Peacock*

BALOUSTAR (USA) 3 b.f. Green Forest (USA) 134 – Ballerina Star (USA)   61
(Forli (ARG)) [1995 –: 7g³ 6.1m 1996 7m 8m May 16] lengthy, unfurnished filly:
66/1, keeping-on 9¼ lengths ninth of 16 in maiden at Newmarket on reappearance,
only form: should stay beyond 7f. *S. P. C. Woods*

BALPARE 3 ch.f. Charmer 123 – Balinese 86 (Balidar 133) [1995 60, a55: 6m³   50
7m a7g 6m* 5.3f⁴ 7.3m 6m 8h³ 7g 8g⁵ 8m 8m⁴ a6g a8g³ 1996 a6g 8m⁶ 6f 7f³
8.3g⁶ 8m 8.3m⁴ 8m* 8m⁴ Aug 10] good-topped filly: modest handicapper: won at
Yarmouth (seller, despite being hampered) in August: stays 1m: acts on hard ground
and equitrack: sent to Saudi Arabia. *N. A. Callaghan*

BALTIC DREAM (USA) 3 b.f. Danzig Connection (USA) – Ascot Princess   –
(USA) (Vanlandingham (USA)) [1995 77: 7g* 7.6m³ 7d 1996 8.1g 11.6g 10.1m Aug
15] tall, lengthy filly: has lost her way completely: sold 20,000 gns Newmarket
December Sales. *K. R. Burke*

BANDIT GIRL 3 b.f. Robellino (USA) 127 – Manx Millenium 66 (Habitat 134)   70
[1995 –: 6s 1996 7.3s³ 7m 7m* 8.3m⁶ 7g⁶ 8g* 8m³ Aug 19] lengthy, good-topped
filly: unimpressive mover: gradually progressive handicapper: won at Salisbury
(maiden) and Leicester in the summer, leading close home: stays 1m: acts on good to
firm ground: sold 46,000 gns Newmarket December Sales. *I. A. Balding*

BAND ON THE RUN 9 ch.h. Song 132 – Sylvanecte (FR) 70 (Silver Shark 129)   98 d
[1995 98: 7m 7m 7.1m⁶ 7m 7.3g³ 8.1g³ 7.1m* 8.1f⁵ 7.1d³ 8d* 7d 8m a9.4g 1996 8d⁶
8d⁶ 7.1d³ 7.9m⁶ 8.1d² 7.1d⁴ 7.1d² 8m⁵ 7.3m 7.6d 8m 8g Oct 19] good-topped horse:
carries condition: poor mover: useful handicapper: as good as at 8 yrs only on 3
successive in-the-frame finishes at Haydock: no form last 4 starts: effective at 7f to
1m: winner on good to firm ground in 1995, best efforts since on dead: has won in
blinkers, but below form last 6 attempts in them. *B. A. McMahon*

BANDORE (IRE) 2 ch.c. (Mar 27) Salse (USA) 128 – Key Tothe Minstrel   81 p
(USA) 108 (The Minstrel (CAN) 135) [1996 7.1m⁵ 7.6m* 7m Oct 1] 28,000F,

84,000Y: good-topped colt: has scope: has a quick action: half-brother to several winners, including 1m winner Go On Smile (by Diesis) and Irish 8.5f winner Best Academy (by Roberto): dam 2-y-o 6f winner and fourth in Fillies' Mile, is out of unraced half-sister to top-class animals Fort Marcy and Key To The Mint: first run for over 3 months, made all in maiden at Lingfield in September: beaten about 10 lengths in valuable sales race at Newmarket on final start: will probably stay 1¼m: likely to do better. *D. R. Loder*

BANG IN TROUBLE (IRE)   5 b.g. Glenstal (USA) 118 – Vaguely Deesse   61
(USA) (Vaguely Noble 140) [1995 56: 17.5g⁵ 14s 16m 15.1s⁵ 1996 14s² Oct 5]
close-coupled gelding: good walker: modest maiden handicapper on flat: beaten a
neck at Haydock on belated return: a stayer: acts on good to firm ground, best efforts
on soft: tried once (at 2 yrs, ran poorly) on fibresand: held up. *J. J. O'Neill*

BANGLES   6 ch.m. Chilibang 120 – Vague Lass 85 (Vaigly Great 127) [1995 73:   70
5.1h² 5m 5m* 5.1d³ 5g 6g 5m 1996 6g 5.2m 5.1f⁴ 5.1m³ 5.2m³ 5m* Aug 19]
workmanlike mare: good mover: fair handicapper: steadily back to form and won at
Leicester (led 1½f out) in August: effective at 5f and 6f: acts on hard and dead
ground, yet to race on soft: visored (well beaten) final 4-y-o start: usually races
prominently: covered by Beveled. *Lord Huntingdon*

BANKERS ORDER   2 b.c. (May 8) Prince Sabo 123 – Bad Payer 72 (Tanfirion   –
110) [1996 6d Jun 7] good-quartered colt: fourth reported live foal: half-brother to
winning sprinters Penny Hasset (by Lochnager) and Pocket Edition (at 2 yrs in 1994,
by Domynsky): dam 2-y-o 5f winner: backward, tailed off in maiden at Haydock
(moved poorly down) in June on only start. *T. D. Easterby*

BANNERET (USA)   3 b.c. Imperial Falcon (CAN) – Dashing Partner 71   62
(Formidable (USA) 125) [1995 NR 1996 8d 8g⁴ May 20] $11,000Y: good-bodied
colt: fourth foal: half-brother to 2 minor winners in USA: dam, 2-y-o 6f winner,
half-sister to smart miler Alert: soon pushed along before staying on late in maidens
at Newbury (40/1 and burly) and Bath: may do better. *Lord Huntingdon*

BANZHAF (USA)   3 ch.c. Rare Performer (USA) – Hang On For Effer (USA)   74
(Effervescing (USA)) [1995 75: 6g⁶ a7g* a6g⁴ 1996 a7g* a8g* a8g⁴ 6m 6f⁵ 7g 7m²   a82
7f³ 7m⁶ Aug 2] big, good-topped colt: fairly useful handicapper on the all-weather,
successful twice at Lingfield in January: fair on turf, best effort when second in
£18,400 contest at Epsom: effective at 6f to 1m: acts on firm ground (yet to race on a
soft surface) and on equitrack: often early to post: joined T. Powell. *G. L. Moore*

BAPSFORD   2 b.c. (Mar 1) Shalford (IRE) 124§ – Bap's Miracle (Track Spare   61 d
125) [1996 5g⁶ 5f 5.1m⁴ 6g⁵ 6g⁵ 7m 6.9v Nov 11] 10,500F, 12,000Y: neat colt: half-
brother to several winners, including 1987 2-y-o 5f and 6f winner Master of The
Roll (by Stanford) and useful 7f winner Zeb (by Cyrano de Bergerac): dam unraced
half-sister to Queen Anne Stakes winner Baptism: modest maiden: twice unplaced in
sellers: stays 6f: visored twice (good effort first occasion). *G. L. Moore*

BARACHOIS LAD   2 b.g. (Apr 20) Nomination 125 – Barachois Princess (USA)   43
62 (Barachois (CAN)) [1996 7.1m⁶ 6m 7g⁶ 5m a8.5g* Nov 2] second foal:
half-brother to 3-y-o 8.5f winner Nicola's Princess (by Handsome Sailor): dam
stayed 1¼m: 33/1, won selling nursery at Wolverhampton in November: stays 8.5f:
form only on all-weather (soundly beaten in sellers on turf): blinkered fourth start:
sold 5,800 gns Doncaster November Sales. *J. J. O'Neill*

BARANOV (IRE)   3 b.g. Mulhollande (USA) 107 – Silojoka 95 (Home Guard   64
(USA) 129) [1995 NR 1996 a8g⁵ a7g² a7g⁵ a7g² a7g⁵ 6.9m 7f 10.8m* 9.7m³ 10.8f⁴
12.1s Oct 22] IR 4,600Y, IR 3,600Y, 17,000 2-y-o: half-brother to winners The Bould
Vic (up to 1¾m in Ireland, by Bold Arrangement) and Yamrah (up to 11.5f, by
Milford): dam sprinting daughter of half-sister to very smart Golden Horus: modest
form at best: won maiden handicap at Warwick in July: stays 10.8f (off course 3
months before travelling well long way over 12.1f on soft ground): acts on firm
ground and equitrack: keen sort. *D. J. G. Murray Smith*

BARAQUETA   4 b.c. Sayf El Arab (USA) 127 – Coqueta 53 (Coquelin (USA)   –
121) [1995 NR 1996 10.1d⁶ 10g⁵ 12f³ 10g 12g 9.9g 8g Sep 7] small colt: first foal:
dam, probably stayed 1½m on flat, won over hurdles: no worthwhile form. *J. L. Eyre*

BARATO   5 ch.g. Efisio 120 – Tentraco Lady 65 (Gay Fandango (USA) 132) [1995   72
76: 6g 6m² 5g 6g* 6m⁴ 6m² 6m⁴ 6.1m⁴ 5m³ 5m 6g 6g³ 6s 6d 6f 1996 5s³ 6g 6.1g³

5.9d 5.9m² 6.1m³ 6d⁶ 5m* 6m 5.9f² 6m 7g 6m 6g³ 6d³ 6f* 6m⁵ 6f Nov 5] sturdy gelding: fair handicapper: won at Pontefract (minor event) in June and at Redcar (apprentices, second run in as many days) in September: effective at 5f to 7f: acts on firm and soft going: effective visored or not: bandaged near hind of late: usually held up: sometimes carries head high: consistent. *Mrs J. R. Ramsden*

BARBA PAPA (IRE)   2 b.c. (Apr 3) Mujadil (USA) 119 – Baby's Smile 68 ? (Shirley Heights 130) [1996 8s² Nov 10] 26,000F: seventh foal: half-brother to several winners here and abroad, including 1m (at 2 yrs) and 1½m winner Smiles Ahead (by Primo Dominie): dam suited by good test of stamina: runner-up in minor event at Milan in November: will probably stay middle distances. *L. M. Cumani*

BARBARA'S JEWEL   4 b.g. Rakaposhi King 119 – Aston Lass 66 (Headin' Up) – [1995 NR 1996 8s 8m⁶ 10d Aug 10] no worthwhile form. *A. Bailey*

BARBAROJA   5 ch.g. Efisio 120 – Bias 108 (Royal Prerogative 119) [1995 –: 80 10.4g⁶ 8g⁵ 1996 8s³ 10g 10.3g 8.1d 8s² Nov 2] good-topped ex-English gelding: unimpressive mover: fairly useful form: third of 24 to Stone Ridge in the Lincoln at Doncaster on reappearance, easily best of 4 outings in 1996 for J. FitzGerald: second in apprentice race at Saint-Cloud in November: stays 1¼m: acts on soft ground: tried blinkered. *E. Chevalier du Fau, France*

BARBASON   4 ch.g. Polish Precedent (USA) 131 – Barada (USA) (Damascus – (USA)) [1995 –: 8d 10g 1996 a10g³ a7g* a7g a7g⁵ 6m 10g⁵ a8g³ a8g⁴ a8g⁴ a7g³ Dec a61 20] compact gelding: won weak maiden at Lingfield in February: refound form late on: stays 1m: acts on equitrack. *A. Moore*

BARBRALLEN   4 b.f. Rambo Dancer (CAN) 107 – Barrie Baby 86 (Import 127) 38 [1995 38: 8m 8.5m 10m 7m⁵ 7g a7g 1996 8.3m 6.9m⁵ 8.2d 7.1m a6g a8g Nov 18] workmanlike filly: poor maiden handicapper: headstrong, withdrawn at start at Brighton in August, jockey reporting her unsafe round bends: stays 7f: acts on good to firm ground: inconsistent. *Mrs L. C. Jewell*

BARDIA   6 b.m. Jalmood (USA) 126 – Bauhinia 70 (Sagaro 133) [1995 38: a12g 32 10.9m³ 12.4g 10g² 10m 10f⁴ 10m³ 11f² 10m 10m³ 11.1g⁶ 11f⁴ 10f 1996 8m 10g 10m⁵ 10f⁶ 11f a12g 11f 12m⁴ Aug 18] small, lengthy mare: poor handicapper: stays 1½m: acts on dead going and firm: held up: inconsistent. *Don Enrico Incisa*

BARDON HILL BOY (IRE)   4 br.g. Be My Native (USA) 122 – Star With A 96 Glimer (Montekin 125) [1995 80: a10g* a10g⁵ 12.3m⁶ a9.4g* 10m⁴ 10.1m a9.4g³ 11.9m⁵ 10m² 10.3d⁴ 9.2g 1996 a8g⁴ a10g³ a10g⁶ 10.2f* 12s² 12f² 11.9m⁶ 12.4m² 16.1g 10m* 10d⁴ 10.1m 10m Sep 21] leggy, lengthy gelding: useful handicapper: won at Bath in May and Newmarket in August: below form afterwards, as if all were not right last time: effective at 1¼m to 1½m, doesn't stay 2m: acts on the all-weather, firm and soft ground. *B. Hanbury*

BAREEQ   2 b.c. (May 8) Nashwan (USA) 135 – Urjwan (USA) 98 (Seattle Slew 87 (USA)) [1996 7m* 7g 8.1f⁵ Sep 7] medium-sized, quite attractive colt: fifth living foal: half-brother to 3-y-o 13.9f and 18.2f winner Jiyush (by Generous) and fairly useful 10.3f winner (seemed to stay 2¼m) Dawlah (by Shirley Heights): dam, 1m winner from 2 starts, out of Kentucky Oaks winner White Star Line: favourite, made all in maiden (beat Al Azhar) at Kempton in August: tailed-off last in minor events at Kempton and Haydock (blinkered) afterwards: stays 7f: went too freely final start: sold 10,000 gns Newmarket Autumn Sales: sent to USA. *H. Thomson Jones*

BARFORD SOVEREIGN   4 b.f. Unfuwain (USA) 131 – Barford Lady 93 72 (Stanford 121§) [1995 72: 8m⁶ 9.9m² 10m³ 12m³ 11.5m³ 1996 16.4g⁴ 16d⁵ 12m⁶ Jun 21] lengthy filly: has a light action: winning hurdler: fair maiden handicapper: stays well: acts on good to firm and dead going: has run well when sweating: consistent. *J. R. Fanshawe*

BARGASH   4 ch.g. Sharpo 132 – Anchor Inn 48 (Be My Guest (USA) 126) [1995 69 d 71: 7g² a7g⁶ 6m 6m⁴ 6m* 6.1m 6f² 7m 6m 7m 5.1d⁵ 6g 1996 7g* 6.1g³ 7.1g 7m⁵ a45 7g⁴ 7g⁵ 6d 7s 6d a7g⁶ a7g³ Dec 11] sturdy gelding: fair handicapper on turf at best, poor on all-weather: won seller at Catterick in March: well below form last 3 turf starts: stays 7f: acts on firm and soft ground and on equitrack: tried blinkered/visored, no improvement: none too consistent. *P. D. Evans*

BARIK (IRE)   6 b.g. Be My Guest (USA) 126 – Smoo 84 (Kris 135) [1995 58: – a6g³ a6g² a8g² a10g³ a7g* a5g³ 7g 6d a6g 1996 8.1g 8m Oct 23] small, sturdy gelding: soundly beaten both starts in 1996, sold out of Mrs A. Swinbank's stable 550 gns Doncaster July Sales in between: stays 1m: acts on soft going and the sand. *B. Mactaggart*

BARITONE 2 b.c. (Mar 11) Midyan (USA) 124 – Zinzi (Song 132) [1996 6g³ 6m³ 70 6g³ 6s Oct 26] 40,000Y: close-coupled colt: fifth foal: brother to a winner in Hong Kong and half-brother to 3-y-o Primo Lad and 2 winners (all by Primo Dominie), including useful sprinter Sarcita: dam Irish 5f winner at 4 yrs: fair form when third in maidens: off course 3 months afterwards, very stiff task on return: likely to be suited by further than 6f: acts on good to firm ground: ran in snatches third start. *J. W. Watts*

BARK'N'BITE 4 b.g. Reprimand 122 – Tree Mallow 71 (Malicious) [1995 54: 12m³ 14.6m⁶ 14.1m 13f³ 12.1m* 12m* 13f⁴ 14.1m 15g⁵ 1996 12.1d 17.9g⁵ 18g Oct 21] workmanlike gelding: has a long stride: modest handicapper: twice ran as if something amiss in 1996: should be suited by test of stamina: acts on good to firm ground and soft. *Mrs M. Reveley*

BARNBURGH BOY 2 ch.c. (Mar 19) Shalford (IRE) 124§ – Tuxford Hideaway 70 p 102 (Cawston's Clown 113) [1996 5m⁵ 5d⁵ 6g⁶ 5f⁴ 6m⁴ Aug 25] 38,000Y: sixth foal: half-brother to several winners, including 1995 2-y-o 5f winner Branston Jewel (by Prince Sabo) and very smart 6f/7f performer Branston Abby (by Risk Me): dam sprinter: fair form: best effort final start when well-backed favourite: stays 6f, likely to prove as effective at 5f: takes keen hold: remains capable of better. *T. D. Barron*

BARNUM SANDS 2 b.c. (Feb 24) Green Desert (USA) 127 – Circus Plume 124 101 (High Top 131) [1996 7m⁴ 7.6d* 8.1m* 8d² 8g² Nov 1] quite attractive colt: sixth foal: half-brother to several winners, including 3-y-o Scarlet Plume (by Warning), useful 1m winner at 2 yrs, and middle-distance performer Circus Colours (by Rainbow Quest): dam, 7f winner at 2 yrs, won Oaks: useful colt: won maiden at Lingfield in August and 3-runner minor event (from Cinema Paradiso) at Sandown in September: caught on post last 2 starts by High Roller in listed race at Ascot and River Usk in 4-runner minor event (gave one swish of tail) at Newmarket: will stay middle distances: has won on good to firm but best efforts with give. *J. L. Dunlop*

BARNWOOD CRACKERS 2 ch.g. (Feb 25) Be My Chief (USA) 122 – 58 Tartique Twist (USA) 78 (Arctic Tern (USA) 126) [1996 6m 6f* 7f* 8d⁶ 7.1m⁶ a8g Dec 11] sturdy gelding: third foal: half-brother to fair 16.2f winner Tabdeel (by Waarshan): dam 1¾m and 2m winner out of half-sister to dam of good French performers Salpinx and L'Emigrant: modest form: hung left when short-head winner of seller at Yarmouth in June and claimer at Brighton (final outing for N.Callaghan, claimed £7,000) in July: will be suited by middle distances: acts on firm and dead ground: fractious type, not an easy ride. *Miss Gay Kelleway*

BARONESS BLIXEN 3 b.f. Cyrano de Bergerac 120 – Provocation 66 (Kings – Lake (USA) 133) [1995 56?: 5m² 5g 6s 6g 1996 6f⁶ Jul 17] well beaten since debut: sent to South Korea. *D. J. G. Murray Smith*

BARONESS GOLD 3 ch.f. Ron's Victory (USA) 129 – Baroness Gymcrak 53§ – (Pharly (FR) 130) [1995 –: 6f 7f⁵ 6m 1996 8g May 29] leggy filly: of little account. *T. D. Easterby*

BARON HRABOVSKY 3 ch.g. Prince Sabo 123 – Joli's Girl 79 (Mansingh 56 (USA) 120) [1995 –: 6.9g 8f 1996 8m 10m⁵ a12g 8m⁵ 11.8f Oct 15] unfurnished gelding: modest maiden: sold (P. Cole to G. Thorner) 10,500 gns Newmarket Autumn Sales: best efforts at 1m: blinkered (no form on fibresand) fourth 3-y-o start: inconsistent. *P. F. I. Cole*

BAROSSA VALLEY (IRE) 5 b.g. Alzao (USA) 117 – Night of Wind 101 84 (Tumble Wind (USA)) [1995 77: 5.1m⁴ 6g 5.2f⁴ 5f 6m 1996 a7g² a8g³ a8g² a10g* a10g* Dec 30] fairly useful performer: sold out of P. Chapple-Hyam's stable 4,000 gns Newmarket Autumn Sales before reappearance: back to very best late on, winning claimer (by 12 lengths) and handicap (soon clear, held on well), both at Lingfield: stays 1¼m well: acts on firm ground and equitrack: effective in blinkers, not tried in 1996: front runner of late. *P. Butler*

BAROUD D'HONNEUR (FR) 3 gr.c. Highest Honor (FR) 124 – Petite Soeur 117 (USA) (Lyphard (USA) 132) [1995 8g 8g* 8d* 1996 8g* 8d⁵ 9m⁵ 8g* 8s* 9.5d* 10s* Sep 22] fourth foal: half-brother to 3 minor winners in France, by Slip Anchor (1¼m), Baillamont (up to 1m) and Top Ville (up to 13f): dam, placed in France, daughter of Sigy (sprinter, rated 132): smart French colt: successful in 5 minor events (once at Evry, otherwise in Provinces) and a listed race in the Provinces before landing 5-runner Prix du Prince d'Orange at Longchamp in September by 1½ lengths from Android: stays 1¼m: acts on soft ground: may yet improve further. *J. F. Bernard, France*

BARRACK YARD 3 b.c. Forzando 122 – Abbotswood (Ahonoora 122) [1995 NR 1996 7m 8.3m a8g* 8.3g⁵ a7g* Jul 27] 17,500F: lengthy, well-made colt: third foal: half-brother to poor 1½m winner Mr Abbot (by Midyan) and a winner in Malaysia: dam maiden: won maiden and handicap at Southwell in the summer: effective at 7f/1m: comfortably best form on fibresand, but we expect him to prove as good on turf: should do better still. *A. C. Stewart* 62 p

BARRANAK (IRE) 4 b.g. Cyrano de Bergerac 120 – Saulonika 94 (Saulingo 122) [1995 58?: 8.1g 5g⁵ 6.1d a6g 1996 6m 5m³ 5m 6m 10g 6m³ 5m 5m⁴ 5g* 5d⁴ 5m 5f⁶ Sep 23] compact, deep-bodied gelding: modest handicapper: won at Ripon (maiden, made all) in August: stays 6f: acts on good to firm and dead ground, yet to race on anything softer: blinkered (ran poorly) fourth 4-y-o start. *G. M. McCourt* 64

BARREL OF HOPE 4 b.g. Distant Relative 128 – Musianica 92 (Music Boy 124) [1995 79, a–: 8m² 7m³ 8m 8g⁵ a6g 7.5g 7.1g 7d* 8.2m⁴ a7g 1996 a8g³ a8g⁶ 8s 7g² 6m* 7g³ 6m 6m 7m 6v⁴ 7g 7s a7g³ a9.4g* a8g³ Dec 27] sturdy gelding: fair handicapper: won at Pontefract in April and at Wolverhampton in December: effective at 6f, and stays 9.4f: acts on good to firm and heavy ground and on fibresand: nearly always blinkered nowadays: often makes running: inconsistent at 4 yrs: gelded. *J. L. Eyre* 82 a73

BARRESBO 2 br.c. (Mar 15) Barrys Gamble 102 – Bo' Babbity 75 (Strong Gale 116) [1996 5.9f 6m⁶ 6g⁴ 6m 7g a6g⁵ a6g a5g Dec 3] strong, lengthy colt: has a quick action: fourth live foal: half-brother to useful 5-y-o sprinter Blue Iris and a winner in Jersey (both by Petong): dam, 2-y-o 5f winner, half-sister to high-class sprinter Anita's Prince: modest maiden: stays 6f: blinkered (ran poorly) final start. *C. W. Fairhurst* 55 a?

BARRIER KING (USA) 2 b.c. (Mar 15) Sovereign Dancer (USA) – Coastal Jewel (IRE) (Kris 135) [1996 6m² 6.1g² 7m 5f* Jun 29] 30,000Y: good-topped colt: first foal: dam unraced daughter of useful Irish 2-y-o 5f winner Rising Tide: made all in maiden at Lingfield in June on final start: took strong hold in Chesham Stakes (wore net muzzle to post) at Ascot third outing: bred to stay 7f: races keenly: sent to Hong Kong. *P. F. I. Cole* 83

BARTOK (IRE) 5 b.h. Fairy King (USA) – Euromill (Shirley Heights 130) [1995 8s 8m³ 8d⁶ 9g* 8d⁶ 10g* 8m⁶ 1996 a10g a10g² 8.5f⁴ 8.5f² 8.5f 6.5f³ 8f⁴ 5.5f⁶ Nov 15] useful horse: second foal: dam, Irish middle-distance stayer, out of Irish and Yorkshire Oaks-placed Green Lucia, a half-sister to Old Vic: trained in 1993 (won maiden and listed race) by C. Collins in Ireland, then in 1994 and 1995 (won listed race at 3 yrs, 2 minor events at 4 yrs) by A. Renzoni in Italy, and rated 106 at best: sold 58,000 gns Newmarket December (1995) Sales: well beaten in listed race at St Moritz (on snow) then second of 6 in minor event at Lingfield (for P. Kelleway) in Europe in 1996: claimed $62,500 out of W. Shoemaker's stable penultimate start: stays 1¼m: probably acts on any going: blinkered final start. *M. Polanco, USA* 94

BASHFUL BRAVE 5 ch.g. Indian Ridge 123 – Shy Dolly 74 (Cajun 120) [1995 76: 5m* 5m² 5m* 5f⁶ 5f* 5m* 5m² 5.2m 5.3f² 5m 5d 1996 6f* 6m 6m⁵ 6f³ 5m 5m⁵ 5g 6d a7g a5g⁶ a5g⁶ a5g Dec 13] smallish gelding: fair handicapper on turf: won at Brighton in April: finished lame next time: left J. Payne after seventh 5-y-o start: long way below form afterwards: stays 6f: acts on firm ground, possibly unsuited by a soft surface: blinkered (well beaten) seventh 5-y-o start: usually races prominently: inconsistent. *B. P. J. Baugh* 76 d

BASHTHEBOARDS 3 b.g. Dancing Dissident (USA) 119 – Vilanika (FR) 81 (Top Ville 129) [1995 –p: 7.1s 7m 1996 7.1d 10.1g a8g 8.3g Sep 29] leggy gelding: temperamentally unsatisfactory. *J. J. Quinn* –

BASIC IMPULSE 2 b.c. (May 28) Rudimentary (USA) 118 – Double Finesse 97 (Double Jump 131) [1996 7m Oct 23] 17,000Y: closely related to 3-y-o Crimson Rosella (by Polar Falcon) and half-brother to several winners, including smart 6f to 1m winner Larionov (by Balidar) and high-class sprinter Mr Brooks (by Blazing Saddles): dam won at up to 1m: prominent 5f in maiden at Yarmouth. *C. Murray* –

BASMAN (IRE) 2 b.c. (Feb 23) Persian Heights 129 – Gepares (IRE) (Mashhor 51 p Dancer (USA)) [1996 8.2g Oct 24] IR 2,500F, IR 4,500Y: first foal: dam unraced half-sister to Prix de Diane winner Sil Sila: never-dangerous ninth of 15 in maiden at Nottingham: probably capable of better. *B. Smart*

BASOOD (USA) 3 b.f. Woodman (USA) 126 – Basoof (USA) 83 (Believe It 60 (USA)) [1995 60: 6f³ 7g 8m 1996 6.9s² 9.7f⁵ 10.2g⁴ 8m a8.5g 11.9g⁴ 12g³ a11g⁶ a12s* a13g² a13g Dec 13] leggy filly: modest handicapper: sold out of E. Dunlop's stable 13,500 gns Newmarket July Sales after third start: won at Lingfield in November: found less than expected next start, and reported by jockey to have been reluctant to race when crowded last time: stays 13f: acts on firm and soft ground, best all-weather form on equitrack: tried visored/blinkered, no improvement: has put head in air and hung fire: not an easy ride. *S. P. C. Woods*

BATALEUR 3 b.g. Midyan (USA) 124 – Tinkerbird 76 (Music Boy 124) [1995 63 NR 1996 6f 5m³ 5g 6g* 7g Oct 25] first live foal: dam winning sprinter: clearly best effort to win 18-runner apprentice handicap at Hamilton in September by short head, drifting right across track from unfavoured far side and leading 2f out: stays 6f, poorly drawn at 7f: acts on dead ground. *Miss J. Bower*

BATHE IN LIGHT (USA) 2 ch.f. (Apr 20) Sunshine Forever (USA) – Ice 66 p House 89 (Northfields (USA)) [1996 6m⁶ 7.1m Sep 18] IR 25,000Y: fifth foal: closely related to 1993 2-y-o 1m winner Silver Hut (by Silver Hawk) and French 1m winner Icy Knight (by Lear Fan) and half-sister to a French 1m winner by Java Gold: dam 2-y-o 1m winner, is sister to smart middle-distance winner Open Day out of smart sister to Reform: modest form in maidens at Newbury (backward) in June and Sandown (travelled comfortably behind Sleepytime, not knocked about) in September: will stay 1m: remains capable of better. *Lord Huntingdon*

BATHILDE (IRE) 3 ch.f. Generous (IRE) 139 – Bex (USA) 116 (Explodent 102 (USA)) [1995 72p: 7m⁵ 1996 10.4m* 12m⁵ 10.2m³ 11.9m⁴ 12m⁴ Sep 7] small, leggy filly: fluent mover: useful performer: green, won very strongly-run minor event at York in May, soon off bit and plenty to do, strong run to lead inside last: fourth in listed race at York (behind Eva Luna, best effort) and minor event at Kempton last 2 starts: better suited by 1½m than shorter: has raced only on good to firm ground. *M. R. Stoute*

BATH KNIGHT 3 b.g. Full Extent (USA) 113 – Mybella Ann (Anfield 117) – [1995 44+, a65?: 5.3m⁴ 5g³ 5.3f² 5g³ 5g 5.1f 5.3f 7.1m 8m² a7g⁵ a10g a8.5g² a8g a65 d 1996 a10g³ a10g² a10g² a10g⁴ a8.5g 11.9f² 9f⁶ a10g 8m a8.5g Sep 7] strong, lengthy gelding: fair maiden: best form (in January) on the all-weather: stays 1¼m: visored (well beaten) fifth 2-y-o outing: usually races prominently: inconsistent. *D. J. S. ffrench Davis*

BATOUTOFTHEBLUE 3 br.g. Batshoof 122 – Action Belle (Auction Ring 65 (USA) 123) [1995 –: 7.1d 7m 1996 8s⁴ 10g⁵ 12g⁴ 11.9m³ 12.3m⁴ 12m a14g* a14.8g* a70 14.1m⁵ Oct 17] big, strong gelding: poor walker: fair handicapper: won strongly-run race at Southwell and minor event at Wolverhampton (did not look like winning for much of race, powered clear final 1f, by 5 lengths), both in September: will be well suited by 2m: goes well on fibresand: seemed unsuited by good to firm ground final start, though had previously shown form on it: not easiest of rides. *W. W. Haigh*

BATSMAN 2 b.c. (May 26) Batshoof 122 – Lady Bequick 81 (Sharpen Up 127) 66 p [1996 5m² 5m Sep 6] 14,000Y, 17,000 2-y-o: quite good-topped colt: half-brother to numerous winners, including smart 6f (at 2 yrs) and 1m winner Cloud of Dust (by Aragon) and useful 4-y-o 5f performer Crowded Avenue (by Sizzling Melody): dam 2-y-o 5f winner: staying-on second in maiden at Folkestone on debut: never-dangerous seventh in similar event at Haydock following month: remains capable of better. *W. J. Musson*

BATTERY BOY 4 b.g. K-Battery 108 – Bonny's Pet 55 (Mummy's Pet 125) – [1995 –: 12.4g⁵ 10f 10.5d 8f 15.1g⁵ 1996 a12g 10m 10.5d 8f Jun 22] useful-looking gelding: no worthwhile form since 2 yrs: blinkered nowadays. *C. W. C. Elsey*

BATTLE COLOURS (IRE) 7 b.g. Petorius 117 – Streamertail 81 (Shirley – Heights 130) [1995 64d: a8g² a8g⁴ a7g² a7g⁴ a8g² a7g² 8d⁵ a8g 8.9m 8g 8m² 8.3f³ 6.9h² 8m⁵ 7d 7g 8.2m 1996 a7g 8g a8g⁴ 8.3s 8g 8m a8g 6.9f 8m⁵ 7f⁶ 8.5f 8s Aug 27] smallish gelding: on the downgrade. *Don Enrico Incisa*

BATTLE GROUND (IRE) 2 b.g. (Apr 2) Common Grounds 118 – Last 59 d
Gunboat 50 (Dominion 123) [1996 5m⁶ 6g³ a6g 6m⁶ 5f 7m³ 6d⁵ 6.9v a7g⁴ Nov 15] a47
23,000Y: eighth foal: brother to fair 7f winner Final Frontier and 1993 Irish 2-y-o 1m
winner La Berta and half-brother to 3 winners, including Group 3 Italian 11f winner
Bateau Rouge (by Red Sunset): dam, middle-distance maiden, is half-sister to
Oaks-placed Suni and Media Luna: modest maiden: probably needs at least 7f: acts
on good to firm ground, well beaten on a soft surface: blinkered (not disgraced) final
start: inconsistent. *N. A. Callaghan*

BATTLESHIP BRUCE 4 b.g. Mazilier (USA) 107 – Quick Profit 78 67
(Formidable (USA) 125) [1995 67, a76: a8g* a8g² a8.5g⁴ 10m 8m 8m 10g⁴ 11.4d a–
8d 9.7g² 9m⁵ 1996 6.9s⁴ 8.2d² 10g 10s³ 10.2g⁶ 10m⁶ a8g Dec 11] sturdy gelding:
unimpressive mover: fair handicapper: left N. Callaghan after fourth 4-y-o start, Miss
Gay Kelleway after sixth: should stay beyond 1¼m: acts on soft ground (probably on
good to firm) and on equitrack (well beaten twice on fibresand): blinkered (below
form) fourth 4-y-o start: usually bandaged behind. *T. Casey*

BATTLE SPARK (USA) 3 b.g. Gold Seam (USA) 124 – Flick Your Bick (USA) 75
(Bicker (USA)) [1995 NR 1996 8d 7g⁴ 10d⁵ 8.1d³ 8m³ 9m⁴ a9.4g Jul 6] $25,000F,
13,500Y: tall, angular gelding: has a round action: half-brother to several winners in
USA, including Le L'Argent (by What A Pleasure), runner-up in Grade 1 events at
1m/9f: dam won 8 races in USA: fair maiden: seems to stay 1¼m: acts on good to
firm ground and dead, tailed off on fibresand. *C. A. Cyzer*

BAUBIGNY (USA) 2 b.c. (Feb 23) Shadeed (USA) 135 – Pearl Essence (USA) 76 ?
54 (Conquistador Cielo (USA)) [1996 8m 8d 8s⁵ Oct 26] 72,000Y: tall, rangy
colt: has plenty of scope: first foal: dam 13.6f winner, sister to smart 7f and 1m
winner Zelphi out of Argentinian Oaks winner Frau Daruma: about 10 lengths
fifth of 7 to Tempting Prospect in minor event at Newbury on final outing, losing
touch with principals last 2f, apparently easily best effort: will be suited by 1¼m+.
M. R. Channon

BAXWORTHY LORD 5 b.g. Arctic Lord 114 – Sugar Pea (Bold As Brass 95) –
[1995 NR 1996 8.1d⁶ May 27] second foal: dam never ran: well beaten over jumps
and in maiden at Chepstow. *C. L. Popham*

BAY BOB (IRE) 7 b.h. Bob Back (USA) 124 – Princess Peppy (Pitskelly 122) –
[1995 NR 1996 a10g Jan 18] of little account. *T. Casey*

BAYDAH 3 b.f. Green Desert (USA) 127 – Al Theraab (USA) 81 (Roberto (USA) –
131) [1995 NR 1996 7m Jun 13] good-quartered filly: first foal: dam, 1m winner
better at 1½m, from family of Sunshine Forever: burly, late headway after slow start
in maiden at Newbury: moved short to post: sold 11,000 gns Newmarket December
Sales. *A. C. Stewart*

BAYFORD THRUST 2 ro.g. (May 7) Timeless Times (USA) 99 – Gem of Gold 83
52 (Jellaby 124) [1996 5d² 5g* 5g* 5m² 6g⁵ 6m Oct 17] 6,000Y: fifth foal:
half-brother to fair sprinters Gi La High (3-y-o, by Rich Charlie) and Captain Carat
(5-y-o, by Handsome Sailor): dam sprinter: won maiden auction at Musselburgh and
minor event at Doncaster in May/June: stiff task in Redcar Two-Year-Old Trophy on
final outing: best form at 5f: acts on good to firm ground, probably on dead: has been
bandaged. *J. Berry*

BAYIN (USA) 7 b.g. Caro 133 – Regatela (USA) (Dr Fager) [1995 79: 6m 6g 7m 79
6g* 6g 6m³ 6m 5.1m 6g² 6m³ 6m⁵ 6m 1996 6m 6d 6d⁴ 6g² 6m³ 6m² 6f* 6m⁴ 6m 6.1d
6m 5f³ 6g 5g 6m 6m* Oct 28] tall, lengthy gelding: usually impresses in appearance:
has a round action: fair handicapper: won at Newbury in July and Leicester in
October: best at 6f/7f: acts on firm and soft ground: blinkered (raced too freely) once
as 4-y-o: often bandaged in front: sometimes slowly away, and usually set plenty to
do: seems to need 2 or 3 runs at start of season, otherwise consistent. *M. D. I. Usher*

BAYRAK (USA) 6 b.g. Bering 136 – Phydilla (FR) 126 (Lyphard (USA) 132) 74 d
[1995 79: 11.8d 12g* 12g⁴ 12g⁵ 12.1g* 12g² 12m⁴ 20m 12s 12m 1996 11.8g² 13s
12.1g* 12g³ 11.6m³ 12.3m 11.6g³ 11.4g 11.8m⁴ 12.1m a14g⁴ a14.8g 12v Nov 11]
compact, good-bodied gelding: only a modest performer most starts in 1996:
comfortably made all in claimer at Musselburgh in May: left M. Ryan after twelfth
start: stays 1¾m, but found 2½m beyond him: acts on good to firm ground and
fibresand, well beaten on soft/heavy on flat: front runner: inconsistent at 6 yrs: sold

(G.L. Moore to P. Kelleway) 6,000 gns Doncaster November Sales, after final outing. *G. L. Moore*

BEACON HILL LADY 3 b.f. Golden Lahab (USA) – Homing Hill (Homing – 130) [1995 NR 1996 8g 10m a7g Aug 16] leggy filly: fifth foal: half-sister to a bumpers winner by Ra Nova: dam bumpers winner: no promise. *B. Ellison*

BEACONSCOT 2 b.f. (Apr 6) Sheikh Albadou 128 – Model Village 101 (Habitat 69 134) [1996 6f³ 6.9m⁴ Aug 20] third foal: dam 7f and 1m winner: in frame in maidens at Brighton and Folkestone: stays 7f: sent to UAE. *D. R. Loder*

BEACONTREE 3 ch.g. Lycius (USA) 124 – Beaconaire (USA) (Vaguely Noble 74 140) [1995 –p: 8.1s 1996 10.1d³ 9g⁵ 10s³ 10g 10.8g⁶ 10.8g 9g⁵ Nov 3] best effort in maidens when third of 6 at Newcastle, carrying head awkwardly and flashing tail when ridden: tame effort next time, and subsequently gelded: sold out of M. Johnston's stable 11,500 gns Newmarket July Sales: raced in Belgium and France subsequently: stays 10.1f: seems to act on soft ground. *Mme M. Heese, France*

BEANO SCRIPT 3 b.g. Prince Sabo 123 – Souadah (USA) (General Holme 73 (USA) 128) [1995 NR 1996 8m 7f³ 8m Oct 7] 13,000Y: strong, lengthy gelding: third foal: half-brother to 5-y-o Make The Break (by Dominion), winner from 5f (at 2 yrs) to 7f: dam unraced: backed at long odds, third of 9 in maiden at Redcar in September: not at all knocked about final outing: stays 7f, far from certain to get much further: upset in stalls and withdrawn second intended start: joined J. Hanson. *Miss S. E. Hall*

BEAR HUG 3 b.g. Polar Falcon (USA) 126 – Tender Loving Care 105 (Final 72 p Straw 127) [1995 NR 1996 8.3g⁴ Jul 8] sixth foal: half-brother to 1990 2-y-o 7f winner Noble Destiny (by Dancing Brave): dam, 2-y-o 7f winner, half-sister to useful juveniles Satinette and Silk Pyjamas: fourth of 17 in maiden at Windsor, chasing leaders, not knocked about once outpaced: seemed sure to improve. *Lady Herries*

BEAR TO DANCE 3 b.f. Rambo Dancer (CAN) 107 – Pooh Wee 71 (Music Boy – 124) [1995 46: 5m 7m⁵ 7d 6f 1996 a7g⁴ a10g 7f May 9] leggy filly: poor maiden: soundly beaten in 1996, as if something amiss penultimate start: blinkered (out of form) final 3-y-o start. *John Berry*

BEAS RIVER (IRE) 3 b.g. Classic Music (USA) – Simple Annie (Simply Great – (FR) 122) [1995 77: 7.6d⁵ 7d⁶ 6g 6g* 6f³ 1996 7s 7m Apr 16] workmanlike gelding: fair juvenile in 1995: below form in 1996: headstrong, and is a sprinter: acts on firm going: sent to Hong Kong. *W. R. Muir*

BEA'S RUBY (IRE) 2 b.f. (May 24) Fairy King (USA) – Beautiful Secret (USA) 77 + (Secreto (USA) 128) [1996 6m⁴ 7.1v³ 6m² Oct 28] 15,000Y: leggy, rather un-furnished filly: third foal: half-sister to 3-y-o 1m and 1¼m winner Distinct Beauty (by Pancho Villa) and a winner in USA by Mining: dam unraced: in frame in maidens: stays 7f: probably acts on any going. *A. Bailey*

BEAT OF DRUMS 5 b.h. Warning 136 – Nyoka (USA) (Raja Baba (USA)) 114 [1995 114: 8m⁴ 7m* 7m² 5f⁵ 6g² 7m* 6.5m 6g* 6g* 6g* 6d³ 1996 6m³ 6d* 6g⁶ 6m 6d* 7d⁶ 6s² Nov 17] smart Italian horse: won Group 3 event at Rome in May by 3 lengths from Macanal and minor event at Rome in September: creditable neck second of 10 to Golden Oriental in Premio Umbria at Rome: stayed 8.8f, but at least as effective at 6f: acted on good to firm ground and heavy: stud. *G. Botti, Italy*

Craven Stakes, Newmarket—Beauchamp King is the first to beat Alhaarth

BEAU BRUNO 3 b.g. Thatching 131 – Lady Lorelei 105 (Derring-Do 131) [1995   76
NR 1996 8m² 8.3m 8d 7m³ a7g³ 6m⁶ Aug 9] leggy, workmanlike gelding: closely
related to smart Gussy Marlowe (around 1¼m, by Final Straw) and half-brother to
fair Athene Noctua (up to 10.5f, by Aragon): dam 5f to 1m winner: fair maiden
handicapper: best form at 7f: acts on fibresand and good to firm ground. *M. Bell*

BEAUCHAMP JADE 4 gr.f. Kalaglow 132 – Beauchamp Buzz 85 (High Top   105
131) [1995 82: 12g⁴ 12.1m³ 11.8g² 11.8f² 12m 1996 10g⁴ 12m* 12g* 12m⁴ 11.8g*
13.9m² 14.6m³ 12g⁶ Sep 29] lengthy filly: fluent mover: progressed steadily into a
useful handicapper: won at Newmarket and Doncaster in May and at Leicester in
July: placed in the Ebor at York (not best of runs then finished strongly behind
Clerkenwell) and Park Hill Stakes at Doncaster (6¾ lengths behind Eva Luna) next 2
starts: better at around 1¾m than shorter: raced almost exclusively on a sound
surface, and acts on firm: has given trouble at stalls: held up: consistent. *H. Candy*

BEAUCHAMP JAZZ 4 ch.c. Nishapour (FR) 125 – Afariya (FR) (Silver Shark   97
129) [1995 99: 8d 8m* 10m⁵ 8m² 8.1m⁴ 8f 8s² 1996 8s⁶ 9m 8.1d 8m 8.1g 8m⁵ 7.9m
8m Sep 14] tall, leggy colt: useful handicapper: seventh of 31 in Hunt Cup at Royal
Ascot: failed to repeat the form: sold 36,000 gns Newmarket Autumn Sales to
continue career with Mike Machowsky in California: stays 1m well: acts on firm and
soft ground: visored (raced freely, well beaten) final 4-y-o start: takes keen hold.
J. L. Dunlop

BEAUCHAMP KATE 3 b.f. Petoski 135 – Beauchamp Buzz 85 (High Top 131)   –
[1995 61p: 6g⁶ 6d 6g 1996 6m 8g 6g 6m⁴ 8g⁵ 8m Aug 26] sturdy filly: disappointing
maiden handicapper in 1996: needs further than 1m: blinkered (looked none too
keen) third 3-y-o start. *H. Candy*

BEAUCHAMP KING 3 gr.c. Nishapour (FR) 125 – Afariya (FR) (Silver Shark   117
129) [1995 114p: 7f³ 7m* 8.1d* 8v* 8m* 1996 8m* 8m⁵ 8d⁵ 8f⁴ 10g 8g Aug 24]

Mr E. Penser's "Beauchamp King"

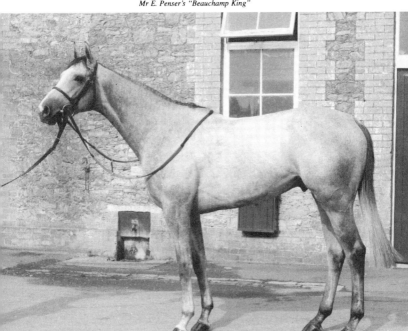

angular colt: has a rather round action: smart performer: won Racing Post Trophy at Doncaster at 2 yrs: won steadily-run Craven Stakes at Newmarket (by neck from Alhaarth) in April: respectable efforts in respective 2000 Guineas at Newmarket and (3½ lengths third of 10 to Spinning World) at the Curragh: ran well when about 2½ lengths fourth of 9 to Bijou d'Inde in St James's Palace Stakes at Royal Ascot: finished last on final 2 starts, Eclipse Stakes at Sandown and Celebration Mile at Goodwood: should stay 1¼m: acts on any ground: sometimes keen/edgy in preliminaries: often wears American halter: held up: stays in training. *J. L. Dunlop*

BEAUCHAMP KNIGHT 3 ch.g. Chilibang 120 – Beauchamp Cactus 86 (Niniski (USA) 125) [1995 NR 1996 8m 8g 10m Jul 18] big, deep-girthed gelding: second foal: dam suited by good test of stamina: shaped quite well on debut, but failed to confirm the promise. *H. Candy*   67 ?

BEAUCHAMP LION 2 ch.c. (May 19) Be My Chief (USA) 122 – Beauchamp Cactus 86 (Niniski (USA) 125) [1996 7m 8.2m 8f Oct 15] leggy, useful-looking colt: third foal: half-brother to 3-y-o Beauchamp Knight (by Chilibang): dam suited by good test of stamina, half-sister to smart middle-distance performer Beauchamp Hero: carrying plenty of condition, well held in maidens: has been bandaged: a middle-distance stayer in the making. *J. L. Dunlop*   – p

BEAUCHIEF 4 br.g. Kind of Hush 118 – Firdale Rosie 78 (Town Crier 119) [1995 –: 8.5m 10f 8m 1996 a12g⁶ a8g Mar 18] no worthwhile form: tried blinkered. *R. F. Marvin*   –

BEAUMAN 6 b.g. Rainbow Quest (USA) 134 – Gliding 94 (Tudor Melody 129) [1995 66: 12m 11.9m⁵ 10g 10.5d 10.5m⁵ 8.1d⁶ 10d 10d a8g² 1996 a9.4g² a8g⁴ a11g³ a11g⁶ a12s⁵ Dec 19] fair handicapper: stays 1½m: acts on good to firm ground and fibresand, used to go particularly well on soft: effective in blinkers (not tried for long time): visored (ran badly) once in 1995: has worn bandages behind: none too consistent. *P. D. Evans*   66

BEAU MATELOT 4 ch.g. Handsome Sailor 125 – Bellanoora 60 (Ahonoora 122) [1995 60: a8g a11g² a12g³ 12.3d³ a12g⁶ 10f⁴ 10m⁵ 9f⁵ 9.9m⁵ 1996 10m Apr 29] leggy, angular gelding: modest maiden handicapper: below form for new stable only start in 1996: stays 12.3f: acts on fibresand and firm and dead ground. *Miss M. K. Milligan*   –

BEAUMONT (IRE) 6 br.g. Be My Native (USA) 122 – Say Yes (Junius (USA) 124) [1995 63: 9m 10.5g 10f⁴ 10.1g⁵ 10f a8g⁴ a11g* 1996 a11g⁶ a12g* a12g² 10.8f² 12f² 12m⁵ 13.9g³ 15.9g* 13.9g* 14.6g⁴ Oct 25] compact gelding: usually impresses in appearance: fair handicapper: won at Wolverhampton in January, Chester in September and York (best effort, leading 2f out and quickening away most impressively) in October: stays 15.9f well: acts on fibresand and any turf ground: blinkered (took good hold, below form) third 5-y-o start: normally held up: consistent. *J. E. Banks*   75

BEAU ROBERTO 2 b.g. (Mar 18) Robellino (USA) 127 – Night Jar 102 (Night Shift (USA)) [1996 7.5m³ 7m 7.1f⁶ 8m Sep 20] 25,000Y: strong, good-bodied gelding: first foal: dam 5f to 7f winner: modest form in maidens and a nursery: gelded after final start: *M. Johnston*   51

BEAUTIFUL BALLAD (IRE) 3 b.f. Ballad Rock 122 – Delightful Time (Manado 130) [1995 84: 5m⁴ 5g* 5d² 5m³ 6g 6g³ 6g³ 6f⁵ 1996 6g May 6] sparely-made, quite attractive filly: fairly useful performer: below form for new yard in 1996: stays 6f: seems suited by an easy surface: usually bandaged behind: covered by Lure. *A. C. Stewart*   –

BEAUTY TO PETRIOLO (IRE) 3 b.f. Scenic 128 – Overspent 85 (Busted 134) [1995 7g⁵ 7.5g* 8g⁴ 7m³ 9g³ 1996 7.5d³ 8.5s* 8g² 8g* 8g* 10d⁴ 8m 10g⁴ 10d Sep 29] IR 4,000F: tall filly: half-sister to several winners, including German miler Gallery (by Tate Gallery), and maiden Out of Funds (rated 87, stayed 1¾m, by Ela-Mana-Mou): dam won over 6f on only start: useful Italian filly: successful in 2 minor events at Naples and a listed race at Rome before winning 14-runner Premio Regina Elena at Rome in April by a neck from Sagar Pride: not disgraced in Prix Saint-Alary at Longchamp and Prix de Sandringham at Chantilly but below form in listed race and Group 2 event back at Rome: probably stays 1¼m: probably acts on good to firm and soft ground. *L. Camici, Italy*   103

BEAU VENTURE (USA) 8 ch.h. Explodent (USA) – Old Westbury (USA) 75
(Francis S) [1995 82: 5g 5m⁶ 5g 5f* 5m⁴ 5f² 5f³ 5m 5g 5g 5m 5m 1996 5g⁶ 5m a–
5g 5.7m* 5f⁴ 5m² 5m⁶ 5.1m 5.2m 5.1d 5m 5.1g 6m² a6g a6g Dec 20] leggy, quite
good-topped horse: unimpressive mover: fair handicapper, not so good as at 7 yrs:
left F. Lee after third 8-y-o start: won at Bath in June: below form after seventh start:
stays 6f: acts on firm and dead ground, well below form on the all-weather: blinkered
twice, not since 1993: used to be held up, raced prominently in 1996: below form
when sweating and edgy. *B. Palling*

BEAVER BROOK 6 gr.g. Bairn (USA) 126 – Lucky Song 91 (Lucky Wednesday –
124) [1995 NR 1996 8f May 6] modest maiden at 2 yrs for R. Hannon before sent to
Switzerland: ran 9 times there 1993-1995 and placed twice, including over 9f in
1994: well beaten in Warwick maiden on return. *R. Ingram*

BECHSTEIN 3 ch.c. Rainbow Quest (USA) 134 – Anegada 79 (Welsh Pageant 82
132) [1995 NR 1996 8d⁶ 10d² 11.8m 11.9m 11.9v⁴ 14.1g⁵ Oct 24] 205,000Y: tall,
good-topped colt: half-brother to several winners, including very smart John French
(at up to 1½m, by Relko) and smart Flamingo Pond (at up to 1¼m, by Sadler's
Wells): dam showed ability at 2 yrs: fairly useful maiden: should prove suited by
further than 11.9f: acts on heavy going, went in snatches both starts on top-of-
the-ground: blinkered last 2 starts: sent to Sweden. *J. L. Dunlop*

BECKY BOO 6 b.m. White Mill 76 – Aber Cothi (Dominion 123) [1995 21: –
10.8m⁴ 13.1f² 1996 a12g Apr 1] poor plater: stays 13.1f. *D. Burchell*

BEDAZZLE 5 b.g. Formidable (USA) 125 – Wasimah 84 (Caerleon (USA) 132) 41
[1995 38: 7.1d³ a7g⁶ 7m⁴ 8.3f³ 8.2m⁵ 7m⁴ 7.1g² 1996 8.1g* 7.1g⁶ 7d 8.1g 8m² 8m⁶
7.5m² 8m 8.1m⁶ 8.2d Aug 25] small gelding: poor handicapper: well backed, won at
Musselburgh (seller) in April: stays 8.3f: acts on firm and dead ground: blinkered
(well beaten) third 5-y-o start: effective from front or held up. *M. Brittain*

BEDOUIN HONDA 2 b. or br.c. (May 19) Mtoto 134 – Bedouin Veil (USA) –
(Shareef Dancer (USA) 135) [1996 7.1m Jul 24] IR 26,000Y: third live foal:
half-brother to 1995 2-y-o 6f winner Eastern Paradise (by Mujtahid) and 1¼m
winner Sariyaa (by Persian Bold): dam French 9f winner, daughter of Ma Biche:
never a threat in Sandown maiden: reluctant stalls. *C. E. Brittain*

BEE DEE BEST (IRE) 5 b.g. Try My Best (USA) 130 – Eloquent Charm (USA) 37
(Private Account (USA)) [1995 37: 8f 6f⁵ 7g 8.3m⁵ 8h⁵ 1996 6m³ Jun 3] leggy
gelding: poor maiden handicapper: probably stays 11f: acts on firm going. *J. P. Smith*

BEE HEALTH BOY 3 b.g. Superpower 113 – Rekindle 70 (Relkino 131) [1995 72
67: 5m 5g⁶ 5g⁵ 5m² 7h⁶ 6m 6m⁶ 5g³ 5g 6s* 5d⁴ 7m 1996 a6g 6g 6s* 6f⁵ 6m* 5g²
6d* 6m 6m 5s Nov 8] lengthy, good-topped gelding: fair handicapper: won at
Catterick, Doncaster and Newmarket in the summer: stays 6f: acts on good to firm
and soft ground: effective blinkered or not: successful when sweating: usually races
prominently. *M. W. Easterby*

BEENY 3 b.g. Lugana Beach 116 – Child Star (Precocious 126) [1995 64+: 5m –
5.7h⁶ 6m⁴ 5.1m⁴ a5g* a6g a5g³ a5g 1996 a6g⁵ 6.1g 5.1g 5.3f 6m Jun 28] modest a53
performer: well below form in 1996: unlikely to stay beyond 6f: acts on good to
firm ground and equitrack (always struggling on fibresand): visored last 2 starts:
inconsistent. *A. P. Jarvis*

BEGGER'S OPERA 4 ch.g. North Briton 67 – Operelle 44 (Music Boy 124) –
[1995 –: 8f a10g a8g 1996 10g 7m 10m 8m 12m 9.7f 12g 10.3g Oct 26] compact
gelding: of little account. *Pat Mitchell*

BEGORRAT (IRE) 2 ch.g. (Mar 10) Ballad Rock 122 – Hada Rani (Jaazeiro 77
(USA) 127) [1996 6m⁴ 7g Oct 2] IR 4,300F, 6,400Y: rangy, angular gelding: has
scope: closely related to a winner in Belgium by Bold Lad, half-brother to a German
1½m winner by Salt Dome: dam, ran twice, daughter of sister to smart Irish
middle-distance performer Klairvimy: nearest finish when fourth of 24 to Speedball
in maiden at Newbury in September: well beaten at Brighton next time: should stay
beyond 6f. *B. J. Meehan*

BEGUINE (USA) 2 br.f. (May 3) Green Dancer (USA) 132 – La Papagena 77 p
(Habitat 134) [1996 7g Nov 2] sixth live foal: half-sister to 4-y-o Zygo (by Diesis),
high-class 1m/1¼m performer Grand Lodge (by Chief's Crown), also successful in
Dewhurst Stakes, and 11.5f winner Rose Noble (by Vaguely Noble): dam unraced

daughter of very smart 5f to 1m winner Magic Flute: 14/1, around 4½ lengths seventh of 23, keeping on, to Palisade in maiden at Newmarket: will stay 1¼m: will improve. *W. Jarvis*

BEHAVIOUR 4 b.c. Warning 136 – Berry's Dream 101 (Darshaan 133) [1995 96: 8f* 7.9m* 8f 7.9m³ 7m³ 1996 10g 8m² 7.9m 8.5m² 7.9g³ 10m* 10d⁵ 10.9m³ 9g Oct 18] sturdy, compact colt: has a quick action: useful performer: 1¼ lengths second of 8 to Blomberg in Diomed Stakes at Epsom in June: won falsely-run rated stakes at Ascot in July: effective at around 1m and stays 10.9f: acts on firm going, shaped well at 2 yrs and stiff task at 4 yrs on dead: held up and has turn of foot: has gone early to post. *Mrs J. Cecil*   106

BELACQUA (USA) 3 gr.f. Northern Flagship (USA) 96 – Wake The Town (FR) (Kalamoun 129) [1995 NR 1996 a8g⁶ a7g a11g a12g⁴ 10d⁴ a7g 14.1m 12f a9.4g 11.1m⁵ 8f 14.1m⁶ a12g Aug 9] small filly: sixth reported foal: dam unraced half-sister to Nishapour: bad maiden selling handicapper: stays 11.1f: blinkered since fourth 3-y-o start: thoroughly inconsistent: sent to South Korea. *D. W. Chapman*   30

BELBAY STAR 3 b.f. Belfort (FR) 89 – Gavea (African Sky 124) [1995 NR 1996 7m⁴ 9m⁶ 7f 7g 7g 7g a6g⁶ Dec 5] fourth reported foal: dam twice-raced half-sister to very smart 1m to 1¼m performer Cataldi: poor and inconsistent maiden. *J. L. Eyre*   53 d

BELDRAY PARK (IRE) 3 b. or br.c. Superpower 113 – Ride Bold (USA) (J O Tobin (USA) 130) [1995 58: 5f⁴ 6m 6g⁶ 5f⁴ 1996 6s* 6d⁶ 6m 6s 7m Sep 10] angular colt: won maiden at Folkestone in March, leading final 1f: failed by long way to repeat the form in 4 handicaps: stays 6f: acts on soft ground. *Mrs A. L. M. King*   72 d

BELFRY GREEN (IRE) 6 ro.g. Doulab (USA) 115 – Checkers (Habat 127) [1995 99: 7m³ 7m 7m 7m⁵ 6f 8g 7.3d 7d 1996 8m* Jun 7] lengthy gelding: unimpressive mover: useful handicapper: as at 5 yrs went well first time out, winning at Goodwood in June, getting up near finish under hands and heels: suited by 7f/1m: acts on good to firm and dead ground: held up (takes good hold) and has turn of foot: genuine. *C. A. Horgan*   99

BELGRAVIA 2 b.c. (Mar 31) Rainbow Quest (USA) 134 – Affection Affirmed (USA) (Affirmed (USA)) [1996 6f* 7m³ 7.1g⁴ 7m Jul 31] leggy, close-coupled colt: fluent mover: fifth foal: half-brother to 3-y-o Sweet Times (by Riverman), unreliable 7f/1m performer River Deep (by Riverman), smart on his day, and useful middle-distance performer Dreamer (by Zilzal), 5f and 1m winner at 2 yrs in 1994: dam, 1m to 9f winner, half-sister to dam of Zoman (by Affirmed): won maiden at York in May: third to Shamikh in Chesham Stakes at Ascot: disappointing afterwards: bred to stay middle distances: blinkered final outing: raced in snatches and wandered first 2 starts, and not an easy ride. *P. F. I. Cole*   88

BELIEVE ME 3 b.c. Beveled (USA) – Pink Mex (Tickled Pink 114) [1995 97: 6f* 7f⁵ 7m⁴ 7d⁵ 7g* 8d³ 8m* 1996 8g 9m 8.1d³ 10.1m⁴ 8f 10g 10m 7m⁵ 7g Aug 24] strong, good sort: fairly useful handicapper: below best after fourth start, campaigned in smart company: awkward leaving stalls and pulled up (jockey believed horse had injured back) last time: stayed 1¼m: acted on firm and dead ground: dead. *R. Hannon*   97

BELINDA BLUE 4 b.f. Belfort (FR) 89 – Carrula (Palm Track 122) [1995 –: 8g 6m⁶ 1996 5g 5g² 6.1m a5g² 5f⁴ a6g⁵ a5g⁶ a6g 5g a6g⁶ Dec 3] big, lengthy filly: modest maiden handicapper at best: stays 6f: acts on firm ground and on fibresand: tried visored, no improvement: often slowly away: inconsistent. *R. A. Fahey*   50 d a55 d

BELLACARDIA 3 b.f. Law Society (USA) 130 – Clarista (USA) 67 (Riva Ridge (USA)) [1995 49: 6m⁶ 8.1s 1996 6m 7g a8.5g 8.3g 7.9g a8.5g a7g⁶ Nov 7] leggy filly: shaped well on reappearance but failed to confirm that promise: left G. Lewis after sixth outing: should stay at least 1m. *A. Moore*   –

BELLA COOLA 4 b.f. Northern State (USA) 91 – Trigamy 112 (Tribal Chief 125) [1995 50: 6m 7g 6g⁴ 7m 7m 1996 5g 7g 6.1m 8m a8.5g⁶ a6g 6m² Aug 3] lengthy filly: poor maiden handicapper: headstrong sprinter: inconsistent. *Martyn Meade*   31

BELLA DANIELLA 2 br.f. (May 16) Prince Daniel (USA) – Danse d'Esprit 54 (Lidhame 109) [1996 7m 7.9g Sep 4] 1,000Y: small, leggy, sparely-made filly: second foal: sister to 3-y-o Noir Esprit: dam 2-y-o 7f winner: behind in maiden auctions. *T. T. Clement*   –

BELLAF 2 gr.g. (Feb 8) Belfort (FR) 89 – Gavea (African Sky 124) [1996 5d 5m⁶ 6g² 7m⁶ 6m⁶ 5f 7m⁶ Jul 29] 800F, IR 7,200Y: plain, rather leggy gelding: brother to   46

3-y-o Belbay Star: dam twice-raced half-sister to very smart 1m to 1¼m winner Cataldi: second in seller at Catterick in June: best form at 6f: twice blinkered, racing freely on first occasion. *M. W. Easterby*

BELLAPHENTO 3 b.f. Lyphento (USA) 108 – Nautical Belle 59 (Kind of Hush – 118) [1995 –: 7m 1996 10m 11.9f⁵ a10g⁵ a16g Dec 5] tall, workmanlike filly: no sign of ability. *J. Ringer*

BELLARA 4 b.f. Thowra (FR) – Sicilian Vespers 44 (Mummy's Game 120) [1995 55: a10g⁶ 9.9m⁴ 12g⁴ 14.1m* 16d 17.2m 16.1g⁶ 1996 14.1s* 14m* 16.1m⁵ 17.2d Sep 30] small filly: fair handicapper: won at Nottingham (by 9 lengths) and Salisbury (soon pushed along, rallying well) in the spring: off course nearly 4 months afterwards and below form: should stay beyond 1¾m: acts on good to firm ground and soft. *N. M. Babbage* 65

BELLA SEDONA 4 ch.f. Belmez (USA) 131 – My Surprise (Welsh Pageant 132) [1995 56: 9m⁶ 7.5d 7m⁵ a9.4g 1996 11.8d⁴ 14.1g a16g³ 14.9g³ a12g Oct 5] lengthy, sturdy filly: modest maiden handicapper: barely stays 2m (and that in slowly-run race): yet to race on extremes of going. *Lady Herries* 59

BELLAS GATE BOY 4 b.g. Doulab (USA) 115 – Celestial Air 96 (Rheingold 137) [1995 66: 9m 8m 10m 8g² 10g⁶ 8f 1996 9.7s² a8.5g 9m 10.1g 8m 7m 10f 10.9m⁴ Sep 19] leggy gelding: modest maiden handicapper: failed by long way to reproduce reappearance form: stays 10.9f: acts on soft ground and good to firm: blinkered (stiff task) third 3-y-o start: usually races prominently. *J. Pearce* 65 d

BELLA'S LEGACY 3 b.f. Thowra (FR) – Miss Lawsuit (Neltino 97) [1995 –: 6d 1996 6m 7d 7f 6m 6g 6g³ 7g⁴ 6m Aug 22] sparely-made filly: poor maiden: should stay beyond 6f: inconsistent. *R. J. Hodges* 48

BELLATEENA 4 b.f. Nomination 125 – Bella Travaille 82 (Workboy 123) [1995 57: a10g a8g 7m 11.6m 10f* 10.1m³ 10m⁵ 10d 8.2m* a10g² 1996 8m 10m 10g 8.3g 10g 12g a10g³ a10g Dec 20] sturdy, good-bodied filly: only a poor handicapper nowadays: soundly beaten in 1996 except penultimate start: stays 1¼m well: acts on firm ground and equitrack, tailed off only start on a soft surface: tried visored, no improvement. *H. J. Collingridge* 44

BELLATOR 3 b.g. Simply Great (FR) 122 – Jupiter's Message (Jupiter Island 126) [1995 61: 6d⁵ 6m⁵ 7f 8m 10d⁶ 1996 9g² 12.3g⁴ 14d* 14d⁶ 11.9v³ 12.1s³ Oct 22] compact, workmanlike gelding: has a roundish action: fair handicapper: won at Haydock in May: well suited by test of stamina: acts on heavy ground: never on bridle and hung (at Chester) second 3-y-o start: highly promising juvenile hurdler, wide-margin winner of both starts in the autumn, but suffered stress fracture of near-fore ankle. *G. B. Balding* 80

BELLE BIJOU 2 ch.f. (May 12) Midyan (USA) 124 – Pushkar (Northfields (USA)) [1996 8s Nov 9] 8,800Y: leggy filly: half-sister to several winners here and abroad, notably high-class 3-y-o 1m and 1¼m performer Bijou d'Inde (by Cadeaux Genereux), 7f and 1m winner at 2 yrs: dam unraced: eighth of 14 to Moon River in median auction maiden at Doncaster: likely to do better. *M. Johnston* – p

BELLE DANCER 2 b.f. (Mar 16) Rambo Dancer (CAN) 107 – Warning Bell 88 (Bustino 136) [1996 5g a5g a8g Dec 3] leggy filly: has scope: sister to 3-y-o Lady Isabell and half-sister to 1994 2-y-o 5f winner Warning Shot (by Dowsing) and fairly useful 1¼m performer Virtual Reality (by Diamond Shoal): dam, 1¼m winner, daughter of half-sister to top 1981 2-y-o filly Circus Ring: no form. *T. Wall* –

BELLE'S BOY 3 b.g. Nalchik (USA) – Ty-With-Belle 67 (Pamroy 99) [1995 59: 10g a8g a8.5g* 1996 a10g a11g 10d² 12.5g* 12m a14g a16g Aug 29] angular gelding: fair performer: won weak claimer at Warwick in April: well beaten afterwards: stays 12.5f: acts on all-weather and dead ground: front runner. *B. Palling* 64 a–

BELLE VUE 2 b.f. (Feb 10) Petong 126 – Bellyphax (Bellypha 130) [1996 5m⁴ a6g* May 27] 16,000Y: sturdy filly: first living foal: dam unraced half-sister to very smart sprinter Forzando: made all in maiden at Southwell in May, winning by 5 lengths: stays 6f: looked sure to improve again. *Sir Mark Prescott* 78

BELLO CARATTERE 3 b.c. Caerleon (USA) 132 – Hyabella 111 (Shirley Heights 130) [1995 NR 1996 8g 8d 8m Sep 20] compact, attractive colt: has a round action: first foal: dam, 1m winner, half-sister to high-class 1¼m performer –

Stagecraft, out of half-sister to Irish Oaks winner Colorspin: never figured in maidens at Newbury and Newmarket. *Lord Huntingdon*

BELLROI (IRE) 5 b.g. Roi Danzig (USA) – Balela (African Sky 124) [1995 NR 1996 18m⁴ 17.1m* 16d Aug 25] modest handicapper: won (first time) at Pontefract in August: stays 2¼m: acts on good to firm ground, well beaten on dead: visored (below form) final 2-y-o start: won 2 handicap hurdles in September. *M. H. Tompkins* | 49

BELLS OF HOLLAND 3 b.f. Belmez (USA) 131 – Annie Albright (USA) (Verbatim (USA)) [1995 60: 7f⁵ 7m² 6m³ 5g 6g² a8g⁶ 1996 a7g² a6g⁵ a8g³ a7g⁵ a7g⁴ Feb 21] modest maiden handicapper: failed to repeat form of reappearance: stays 7f: acts on equitrack, poor efforts on fibresand: visored (raced too freely) penultimate 3-y-o start: rather headstrong, and often taken down early: one to have reservations about. *W. R. Muir* | 58 d

BELMARITA (IRE) 3 ch.f. Belmez (USA) 131 – Congress Lady 93 (General Assembly (USA)) [1995 –p: 7f 7m 1996 14m³ 14.4g⁴ 14g³ 13.8g² 12m² 12m⁴ 13.9g 14m² 14g⁵ Oct 18] good-bodied filly: fluent mover: fair maiden handicapper: will stay beyond 1¾m: has raced only on a sound surface: lacks turn of foot: consistent: joined G. Hubbard. *M. H. Tompkins* | 76

BELMONTEE 2 b.c. (Mar 26) Belmez (USA) 131 – Annie Albright (USA) (Verbatim (USA)) [1996 7g Jun 29] 17,000Y: robust, close-coupled colt: fifth foal: brother to 3-y-o Bells of Holland and half-brother to useful sprinter Shamanic (by Fairy King): dam, Irish sprint maiden, half-sister to smart 6f and 7f winner Crystal Gazing: 10/1 when well-beaten eighth of 10 behind Benny The Dip in maiden at Newmarket: seemed likely to improve: sent to France. *H. R. A. Cecil* | –

BELOW THE RED LINE 3 gr.g. Reprimand 122 – Good Try 92 (Good Bond 122) [1995 –: 7g 1996 a8g 8g a6g 7d Aug 23] small, stocky gelding: of no account: sold 500 gns Doncaster November Sales. *Mrs N. Macauley* | –

BEL PROMISE (IRE) 7 ch.m. Soughaan (USA) 111 – Linbel (Linacre 133) [1995 NR 1996 a12g⁶ Feb 22] half-sister to numerous winners, including Ardoony (5f to 1m, by Ardoon) and smart hurdler Neblin (by Nebbiolo): dam Irish 9f winner: little form over jumps or in a Lingfield claimer. *P. R. Webber* | –

BELZAO 3 b.c. Alzao (USA) 117 – Belle Enfant 87 (Beldale Flutter (USA) 130) [1995 86: 6g³ 5.2g³ 5.7h⁴ 1996 7m⁵ 11.7m⁴ 7m 7.1s⁵ 8.2s⁴ a7g⁵ Nov 7] sturdy colt: has been hobdayed: disappointing maiden handicapper: left M. Channon after third 3-y-o start: stays 8.2f: best efforts on an easy surface. *D. R. C. Elsworth* | 63

BEMONT PARK (ITY) 5 br.m. Love The Groom (USA) 123 – Boscher Queen (IRE) (Ela-Mana-Mou 132) [1995 10g 10d⁵ 8g³ 8m² 10g* 8g* 10s 10m⁶ 8m 9g² 8.5g⁵ 8g* 9g* 8m 10d* 1996 8d* 9g² 8g⁴ 10g⁵ 8g* 8m* 8g² 10g⁵ 8s² 10d 8s² 9g* 8m 11.3s⁶ Dec 26] first known foal: dam, won 5 races at around 1m in Italy, is sister to Premio Regina Elena second Fire of Star: useful Italian mare: has had productive career between 7f and 1¼m, generally in handicaps and listed races, winning listed event at Rome (for second year running) in May: won Group 3 event at Milan in June by 1¼ lengths from Lara: good effort when short-neck second of 9 to Lara in Group 3 event at Milan then won restricted race at Rome: stays 1¼m, at least as effective over 1m: acts on good to firm and soft ground. *R. Brogi, Italy* | 104

BE MY BIRD 3 b.f. Be My Chief (USA) 122 – Million Heiress (Auction Ring (USA) 123) [1995 65d: 6m 6m⁵ 7m³ 6.9g⁵ 7g 8g 10d 8g a8.5g³ 1996 a8g⁵ a8g⁵ a8g⁴ a8g⁶ a11g Feb 16] poor maiden nowadays: left B. Meehan's stable after second 3-y-o start: should stay middle distances: acts on good to firm and the all-weather: tried blinkered, no improvement: covered by Timeless Times. *W. J. Musson* | 46

BENATOM (USA) 3 gr.g. Hawkster (USA) – Dance Til Two (USA) (Sovereign Dancer (USA)) [1995 82p: 7m 10m² 1996 12m* 12.3g⁵ 14d⁴ 16.2m 16.1g* 14f* 15.9m⁶ 14g Oct 18] well-made gelding: has a short, quick action: progressed into a useful handicapper: won at Thirsk (maiden) in April, at Newmarket in July and at Goodwood in August: well held last 2 starts: stays 16.2f, as good at 1¾m: acts on firm ground, good effort at the time on dead: effective from front or held up: game: gelded. *H. R. A. Cecil* | 102

BEN'A'VACHEI BOY 3 gr.g. Rock City 120 – Vacherin (USA) (Green Dancer (USA) 132) [1995 58: 5m⁴ 5g 5m 6m² 6d 1996 a6g a8g⁴ a8g⁵ Mar 23] modest maiden: stays 1m: acts on good to firm ground and fibresand: well beaten both starts | 57

on equitrack: blinkered (ran well only on first occasion) 3 times: inconsistent: sold 3,000 gns Doncaster March Sales: sent to Sweden. *J. D. Bethell*

BEN BOWDEN 3 br.g. Sharrood (USA) 124 – Elegant Rose 72 (Noalto 120) 63 d [1995 62: 7f 7.6d 8g 1996 8g⁵ 11.6m 8.3m 15.4g⁵ 14m Sep 19] leggy gelding: modest form: well beaten after reappearance: unlikely to stay much beyond 1m: refused to enter stalls (for second time) third intended 3-y-o outing: won juvenile hurdle in August: has joined S. Woodman. *M. Blanshard*

BEND WAVY (IRE) 4 ch.c. Kefaah (USA) 124 – Prosodie (FR) (Relko 136) 88 [1995 78: 8g³ 8f⁴ 1996 8.3m² 10m³ 8.5m* 8m Aug 1] good-topped colt: fairly useful handicapper: readily won at Beverley in July, leading over 1f out: sold (L. Cumani to T. Caldwell) only 13,000 gns Newmarket Autumn Sales: will prove best at up to 1¼m: acts on good to firm ground, yet to race on a soft surface: consistent. *L. M. Cumani*

BENEFICIAL 6 b.h. Top Ville 129 – Youthful (FR) (Green Dancer (USA) 132) – [1995 9f 9f 10f⁶ a8f 1996 10s⁵ 9g Oct 18] small, quite attractive horse: carries condition: fluent mover: rated 117 at 4 yrs: ran in USA in 1995 with little success: long way below his best in Group 3 event at Maisons-Laffitte then listed race at Newmarket on return: stays 1½m: acts on firm and soft ground: held up and tends to idle in front: pulled too hard second 4-y-o start: game and genuine. *G. Wragg*

BENFLEET 5 ch.g. Dominion 123 – Penultimate (Final Straw 127) [1995 89: 76 a12g* a12g* a12g 10d* 10m³ 11.8m 10.3m⁶ 10m² 12f³ 12m⁴ 10m 12g² 12f 12g⁵ a79 16.2d² 16.2s⁵ 12m⁴ a10g² 1996 a12g⁵ a16g³ 12m 8g 12m⁶ 12m 15.9m 14m⁴ 14m 13.9m 13.9g 16.2d³ 16s⁴ Oct 24] small, lengthy gelding: just a fair handicapper in 1996: sold 17,000 gns Newmarket Autumn Sales and gelded: stays 16.2f: acts on firm and dead ground (probably on soft) and on equitrack (yet to show his best in 3 tries on fibresand): often early to post: held up of late, and seems best in strongly-run race: formerly tough and consistent, seemed inconsistent in 1996. *R. W. Armstrong*

BEN GUNN 4 b.g. Faustus (USA) 118 – Pirate Maid (Auction Ring (USA) 123) 60 [1995 76: 7f 6g 6m* 7f³ 1996 7g 6g 7s 7g 8s a7g³ a7g a10g² Dec 20] good-bodied gelding: only modest at best in 1996: stays 1¼m: acts on firm ground and dead (probably on both all-weather surfaces), well beaten on heavy. *P. T. Walwyn*

BENJAMINS LAW 5 b. or br.g. Mtoto 134 – Absaloute Service 96 (Absalom 49 128) [1995 62: 10f³ 10.3m 10g³ 10g 10m⁶ 14g 10f⁴ a7g a9.4g* a10g³ a7g² a9.4g* a70 1996 a9.4g⁵ a8g² a8g* a8g⁴ a12g⁴ 8g⁶ 8f⁴ 12m 9f⁵ 8m⁴ 10f Jul 20] rangy, workman-like gelding: fair handicapper: won at Southwell in January: stays 1½m: best form on fibresand (only poor on turf or equitrack): usually tracks leaders. *J. A. Pickering*

BENJARONG 4 ch.f. Sharpo 132 – Rose And The Ring (Welsh Pageant 132) – [1995 41: a8g⁵ a7g⁵ 8.1d 6s 8.3g⁴ 7m 7.1m 7m a7g 8g⁵ 8.3g* 7d⁴ 7.1s⁵ 8m a8g 1996 a10g 8.1g Apr 4] poor performer: well beaten in 1996: stays 8.3f: acts on good to firm ground, soft and fibresand: has joined W. G. M. Turner. *R. M. McKellar*

BENNING (USA) 3 b.f. Manila (USA) – Belle Pensee (USA) (Ribot 142) [1995 68 NR 1996 10g³ 14.1g Oct 24] closely related to 2 winners by Lyphard, notably smart Beccari (up to 1¼m in France), and half-sister to several winners, including high-class 1983 French 2-y-o Treizieme (by The Minstrel) and Gold Cup runner-up Eastern Mystic (by Elocutionist): dam, French 1¼m winner, half-sister to Junius and Gentle Thoughts: promising keeping-on 5 lengths third of 10 to Torremolinos in maiden at Nottingham: well below that form there (made most to 3f out) 15 days later: may be suited by return to shorter than 14.1f: sold 130,000 gns Newmarket December Sales. *J. H. M. Gosden*

BENNY THE DIP (USA) 2 b. or br.c. (Mar 25) Silver Hawk (USA) 123 – 112 Rascal Rascal (USA) (Ack Ack (USA)) [1996 7.1m² 7g* 7m* 8g* 8g³ Oct 26]
'Never kick a man when he's down . . . he might get up again.' If you're not a regular reader of *The Sporting Life* you may have missed an article by its chief reporter David Ashforth in early-June headlined 'How good is Gosden?' You'd have been hard put, on the other hand, to miss the storm that broke over Ashforth's head as a result of the article, particularly after trainer John Gosden ended an eight-year wait for his first British classic winner when Shantou won the St Leger. Drawing on material published in the *Timeform Statistical Review*,

Ashforth had pointed out that 'no trainer can match the 170-plus inmates of Stanley House Stables for quality in depth.' Between 1993 and 1995 Gosden had trained seventy-six horses rated 100+, Henry Cecil coming next with fifty-eight. In the light of such 'enormous strength in quantity and quality', Ashforth described Gosden's record in the most prestigious races as 'surprisingly thin . . . comparing very unfavourably with that of Andre Fabre, Sheikh Mohammed's other major European trainer.' Whilst acknowledging that the emergence of the Godolphin operation, which deprived Gosden of the likes of Halling, Red Bishop and Darnay, might have had an effect, Ashforth's article came over as a scathing attack on Gosden's ability as a trainer, one which had admirers leaping to the trainer's defence. For a long time in the latest season, Gosden looked like having, in his own words, 'my worst season ever'. By the start of Royal Ascot the stable had saddled only seventeen winners, 'muscle enzyme problems' with the string and set-backs to some of the best prospects, including Lord of Men, Sacho and Santillana, being among the reasons. Notwithstanding the slow start, Gosden ended the year in third place in the trainers' table in Britain, behind bin Suroor and Cecil, the highlights of a successful autumn also including three pattern winners at Longchamp's two-day Arc meeting. David Ashforth, a witty and well-informed writer with an unimpeachable reputation for fairness and objectivity, also ended the year on a high note, taking the Derby Award as racing journalist of the year.

The Gosden stable's four winners at the St Leger meeting included the promising two-year-olds Benny The Dip and Cape Cross, both of whom are in the ante-post lists for the Two Thousand Guineas. Cape Cross, owned by Sheikh Mohammed, looked a very useful colt in the making when winning a maiden on Doncaster's Friday programme but wasn't seen out again. Benny The Dip, owned and bred by an American patron of the stable, Landon Knight, went on to make his mark in pattern company after winning the Queen's Own Yorkshire Dragoons Stakes, a useful conditions event, on the opening day. Benny The Dip was already a winner by the time the St Leger meeting came round—he'd been off the course for over two months with a sore back after winning a Newmarket maiden on his second start—and he showed he was going the right way with a workmanlike victory over another previous winner, Desert Story. The pair met again at the end of the month in the Gtech-sponsored Royal Lodge Stakes at Ascot. The race is one of the traditional autumn targets for classic aspirants—Mister Baileys was the last winner to go on to classic success—and Benny The Dip won in a style that suggested he'd at least have a say in the destination of the spring trials. A lazy type, he won with more in hand than his three-quarter-length winning margin, leading a furlong and a half out and running on again when strongly pressed inside the final furlong, pricking his ears and giving the odd swish of his tail. Desert Story was runner-up again, with the Cecil-trained Besiege, winner of his two previous races, and Equal

Gtech Royal Lodge Stakes, Ascot—Benny The Dip (left) comes again to rob Desert Story

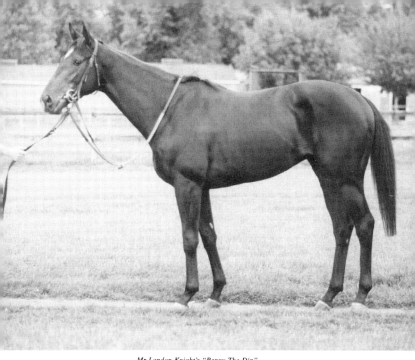

Mr Landon Knight's "Benny The Dip"

Rights, successful in the Futurity Stakes at the Curragh, third and fourth. It was reported afterwards that Benny The Dip would be put away for the year but connections had a change of heart and he made his last appearance in the Racing Post Trophy at Doncaster in October. Opposed again by Besiege and the Royal Lodge fifth Medaaly, among others, Benny The Dip started a well-backed favourite but he couldn't complete the big-race double. In finishing third to Medaaly and the promising Poteen, Benny The Dip probably wasn't far below his Royal Lodge form (fourth-placed Besiege finished three quarters of a length closer to Benny The Dip than he had at Ascot). Benny The Dip was doing his best work at the end of a strongly-run mile and will stay at least a mile and a quarter as a three-year-old, when he should continue to do well.

Benny The Dip (USA) (b. or br.c. Mar 25, 1994)	Silver Hawk (USA) (b 1979)	Roberto (b 1969)	Hail To Reason Bramalea
		Gris Vitesse (gr 1966)	Amerigo Matchiche II
	Rascal Rascal (USA) (b or br 1981)	Ack Ack (b 1966)	Battle Joined Fast Turn
		Savage Bunny (b or br 1974)	Never Bend Tudor Jet

The good-bodied, attractive Benny The Dip, who is not the best of walkers, and spoiled his appearance at Ascot by sweating, is a half-brother to the same owner's 1992 Horris Hill Stakes winner Beggarman Thief (by Arctic

Tern). Their dam Rascal Rascal—Benny The Dip takes his name from a character in Damon Runyon's stories—was acquired by Mr Knight at the Spendthrift Farm dispersal in 1986 and he has sent most of her offspring since then to be trained by Gosden. Rascal Rascal died after foaling a filly by Brocco in the latest season. A winner at up to nine furlongs, Rascal Rascal was by American Horse of The Year in 1971, Ack Ack, a speedy individual who had enough stamina to win top races at a mile and a quarter, and whose European runners mostly stay a mile and a quarter. The second dam Savage Bunny gained all four of her wins at sprint distances. A number of Rascal Rascal's offspring have failed to stay as far as could reasonably be anticipated from their pedigree. Beggarman Thief's sire Arctic Tern was an influence for stamina but the sometimes-excitable Beggarman Thief was never raced beyond a mile during his time with Gosden. The same applied to the fair performers Alpha Rascal (by Alphabatim), a two-year-old mile winner, and Key Suspect (by Alleged), successful over an extended seven furlongs as a three-year-old. Benny The Dip's sire Silver Hawk, placed in the Derby at Epsom and the Curragh, has turned out to be a reasonable influence for stamina at stud. Benny The Dip has done all his racing so far on a sound surface. *J. H. M. Gosden*

BEN'S RIDGE 2 b.c. (Mar 27) Indian Ridge 123 – Fen Princess (IRE) 72 (Trojan Fen 118) [1996 5m 5d³ 6g³ 7m³ a6g⁴ 7.5f⁴ᵈⁱˢ a7g* 8g² 8m 7.1m* 8.3g⁴ a8.5g a8.5g⁶ Nov 25] 14,000Y: close-coupled colt: first foal: dam 15f winner at 4 yrs: fair performer: successful in nurseries at Wolverhampton and Musselburgh in August: below form last 2 starts: suited by 7f/1m: acts on firm and dead ground and on fibresand. *P. C. Haslam*   78 a71

BENTICO 7 b.g. Nordico (USA) – Bentinck Hotel 74 (Red God 128§) [1995 74: a9.4g⁴ a9.4g⁴ a9.4g³ a9.4g⁴ a8g* a9.4g* a9.4g⁶ a10g 10m 8m⁴ 8g 8.2m⁶ 10.1f⁶ a8.5g² a8.5g³ a7g² a8.5g² a7g* 7g² 8g 8g* 8.2m⁶ a8g³ a7g⁵ a8g a7g⁶ 1996 a8g² a8g³ a9.4g a8g⁶ 8m 8m 10f⁶ a8.5g* a9.4g⁶ 8m⁵ 7.6m⁵ a8.5g² 9g 8m⁵ a9.4g³ 8.5m⁶ 8f³ a7g² 8f² 7g a8.5g³ a8g² a9.4g⁵ a9.4g Dec 28] lengthy, well-made gelding: carries condition: poor mover: fair handicapper on the all-weather: won at Wolverhampton in June: ran as though something amiss final start: modest form nowadays on turf: effective at 7f to 1¼m: best turf form on a sound surface: effective blinkered/visored or not: sometimes bandaged: tough. *Mrs N. Macauley*   58 a80

BENTNOSE 2 b.c. (Feb 28) Saddlers' Hall (IRE) 126 – Blonde Prospect (USA) – (Mr Prospector (USA)) [1996 8m a8.5g Dec 14] third foal: half-brother to 8.2f winner White Palace (by Shirley Heights) and a winner in Spain by Polish Navy: dam, lightly raced in USA, from family of Ajdal, Formidable and Arazi: well beaten in maidens at Goodwood (for Lady Herries) and Wolverhampton 2½ months later. *D. Morris*

BENT RAIWAND (USA) 3 b.f. Cadeaux Genereux 131 – Raiwand 106 (Tap On Wood 130) [1995 NR 1996 8d 6m⁴ 8f 5m 6m 6m a6g a6g⁵ Nov 18] well-made filly: has a round action: fourth foal: half-sister to a winner in Denmark: dam probably stayed 1½m: disappointing maiden: sold out of B. Hanbury's stable 2,400 gns Newmarket July Sales after third start. *Don Enrico Incisa*   67 d

BENZOE (IRE) 6 b.g. Taufan (USA) 119 – Saintly Guest (What A Guest 119) [1995 86: 6m 6f 6m* 5g 5m² 5m 5m⁶ 6m² 6m⁴ 6g 6g 5m 6g 6g 7m 6g* 6m² 5m 6f³ 6m³ 6f² 6f* 6m 6m 6v 6g 7m Oct 29] tall gelding: has a round action: fairly useful handicapper: reportedly broke blood vessels in the past: best in middle of season and won at Thirsk in May (for second year running) and August: stays 6f: acts on any ground: effective blinkered or not, disappointing in visor seventh 5-y-o start: sometimes jinks themselves at stalls, and often slowly away. *Mrs J. R. Ramsden*   86

BEQUEATH 4 ch.c. Rainbow Quest (USA) 134 – Balabina (USA) 110 (Nijinsky (CAN) 138) [1995 89p: 10g³ 10g² 1996 12f* 12g* 12g⁵ Jul 9] rather unfurnished colt, out of a sister to Quiet Fling and Peacetime: off course 11 months, won 3-runner maiden at Beverley in good style: beat 3 smart performers in listed race at Newmarket 17 days later in June in deeply impressive fashion, eased close home to beat Commoner 4 lengths: moved short to post under restraint for Princess of Wales's Stakes at Newmarket, under strong pressure 3f out and unable to quicken, beaten over 8 lengths behind Posidonas: stays 1½m: acts on firm ground, yet to race on   118

Heath Court Hotel Fred Archer Stakes, Newmarket—the unfulfilled promise of Bequeath

soft surface: looked to have a bright future after second 4-y-o start: stays in training. *H. R. A. Cecil*

BERENICE 3 b.f. Groom Dancer (USA) 128 – Belle Arrivee 87 (Bustino 136) 100 [1995 NR 1996 10g³ 11.4g⁶ 11.9d³ 10m³ 10.3g² 10m* 12m⁵ 10.1m² 10m 10.3d Nov 8] angular, quite attractive filly: fluent mover: foal: half-sister to 1995 3-y-o 7f winner Kafani Al Widd (by Royal Academy): dam, 1¼m winner, closely related to Mtoto: useful performer: won maiden at Pontefract (swishing tail) in July comfortably: best effort when 3½ lengths equal-second of 9 to Flame Valley in listed event at Yarmouth in September: likely to prove as good at 1½m as 1¼m: acts on good to firm ground, possibly not dead. *G. Wragg*

BERGE (IRE) 5 b.h. Most Welcome 131 – Miss Blitz 83 (Formidable (USA) 125) – [1995 68, a77: a7g*dis 6g* 7g a7g* 7f³ a6g³ a6g* 1996 a7g* a7g² a7g* a6g³ a5g* a81 6.1g a7g* a7g* Aug 16] lengthy, workmanlike horse: reportedly difficult to keep sound: has had knee surgery: fairly useful performer: won claimers at Southwell in January and February, handicap at Lingfield in March and (after 3-month break) claimers at Wolverhampton and Southwell in the summer: best at up to 7f: goes well on the all-weather (first past post 6 of last 7 starts at Southwell), best turf form on good ground: effective blinkered (usually is) or not: held up: genuine and consistent. *W. A. O'Gorman*

BERKELEY BOUNDER (USA) 4 b.g. Diesis 133 – Top Socialite (USA) 117 – (Topsider (USA)) [1995 73: 6.9g⁶ 8m³ 10.3m⁵ 10f² 12m² 11.7h³ 12g² 11.8g* 14.6m 1996 10.5m⁶ 12.3s Aug 31] lengthy gelding: has a round action: fair handicapper: showed nothing in 1996: stays 1½m: acts on firm ground. *Mrs M. Reveley*

BERLIN BLUE 3 b.g. Belmez (USA) 131 – Blue Brocade 91 (Reform 132) 84 [1995 NR 1996 10g 8.1d⁶ 8m⁵ 12.3m* 15m* 13.9m Aug 20] robust gelding: sixth foal: half-brother to 2 winners, notably useful 4-y-o stayer Orchestra Stall (by Old Vic): dam 10.6f winner: fairly useful handicapper: won at Ripon and Ayr (rated stakes, idled) in July: well below form final start: stays at least 15f: acts on good to firm ground. *J. W. Watts*

BERNARD SEVEN (IRE) 4 b.g. Taufan (USA) 119 – Madame Nureyev (USA) 85 d (Nureyev (USA) 131) [1995 90d: 8d³ 8m² 7.6m* 8m* 8m 10m⁴ 10d 7g a7g a8g⁵ 1996 a9.4g* a10g a9.4g a12g a10g 10m 8.5m 8f² 8.1m 8m 8.1d 8.5m 10.3g² Oct 26] neat gelding: just a fairly useful handicapper at best: won at Wolverhampton in January, making most: sold (C. Brittain to M. Dods) 4,500 gns Newmarket Autumn Sales: stays 9.4f: acts on firm and soft ground and on fibresand: visored at 3 yrs, blinkered nowadays: races prominently: most inconsistent. *C. E. Brittain*

BERT 2 b.c. (Mar 9) Mujtahid (USA) 118 – Keswa 94 (Kings Lake (USA) 133) – [1996 6d⁵ 6.1d 8m 8m Oct 23] 13,000Y: third foal: dam 1m (at 2 yrs) and 1½m winner out of half-sister to Celestial Storm: well beaten in varied events: visored second start: swerved stalls first 2 outings: sold 3,000 gns Newmarket Autumn Sales: sent to Spain. *P. T. Walwyn*

BERYLLIUM 2 b.g. (Apr 15) Tragic Role (USA) – Flower Princess (Slip Anchor 86 136) [1996 7g 7g 7.1f³ 7g* 7g³ 8g Oct 21] sparely-made, leggy gelding: first reported foal: dam unraced daughter of Fillies' Mile winner Nepula: set steady gallop when winning maiden at Chester in September: probably flattered when third behind Great Ovation in steadily-run minor event at York next time: well beaten in listed race on

115

Tote Sunday Special Handicap, Ascot—
Better Offer provides a big win for Guy Harwood in his final season as a trainer

final outing: likely to stay 1¼m: acts on firm and good to soft ground: sold 21,000 gns Newmarket Autumn Sales. *R. Hannon*

BE SATISFIED 3 ch.g. Chilibang 120 – Gentalyn (Henbit (USA) 130) [1995 55: a8g a7g⁴ a6g⁵ 1996 a8g² a8g⁵ 6.9m a10g a6g a8g Dec 26] modest maiden: well beaten after 3-y-o reappearance: stays 1m: acts on equitrack. *A. Moore* — 55 d

BESCABY (IRE) 5 ch.g. Dominion Royale 112 – Elegant Act (USA) (Shecky Greene (USA)) [1995 NR 1996 a12g⁴ a12g⁵ a12g Feb 9] third foal: dam won 5 races in USA: no form: sold 900 gns (July), 1,250 gns (August) Ascot Sales. *J. A. Harris* —

BESIEGE 2 b.c. (Jan 25) Rainbow Quest (USA) 134 – Armeria (USA) 79 (Northern Dancer) [1996 8.5g* 8.1f* 8g³ 8g⁴ Oct 26] tall, close-coupled, quite good-topped colt: has plenty of scope: has a fluent action: third living foal: brother to useful 3-y-o 1¼m winner Quota and top-class 1992 2-y-o 1m winner Armiger, also winner of Chester Vase and second in St Leger: dam, suited by 1¼m, half-sister to Park Hill winner I Want To Be, from good family: won maiden at Beverley in August and minor event at Haydock (by a head from Sandstone) in September: 2 lengths third of 8 to Benny The Dip in Royal Lodge Stakes at Ascot and 3 lengths fourth of 9 to Medaaly in Racing Post Trophy (having led 2½f out and kept on well) at Doncaster last 2 starts: will be suited by middle distances: yet to race on a soft surface: may be capable of better. *H. R. A. Cecil* — 108 +

BESTELINA 2 b.f. (Apr 23) Puissance 110 – Brittle Grove 79 (Bustino 136) [1996 6.1m⁶ 7g a7g⁴ a7g⁶ Dec 7] 3,600Y, 5,800 2-y-o: sixth foal: half-sister to 3 winners abroad, including German listed sprint winner Green's Maud Earl (by Night Shift): dam ran twice over 6f at 2 yrs: no worthwhile form. *D. J. S. Cosgrove* —

BEST KEPT SECRET 5 b.g. Petong 126 – Glenfield Portion 86 (Mummy's Pet 125) [1995 64: a6g³ 5.1g² 6f 7m² 6g³ 7.1m⁵ 5.9f³ 6m⁵ 7f³ 5h⁵ 6g³ a7g⁶ 8.1d⁶ 7m 1996 a6g⁴ a7g⁶ a7g⁶ a8g a5g⁵ a6g³ 7.1g⁵ 6d² 5s² 5m 7g⁵ 8f 5.9f³ 6d³ 7.6m 7f 6f 7f⁶ 7m² 8f a7g Nov 29] neat gelding: has a quick action: modest performer: trained until after penultimate start by P. D. Evans: stays 7f: probably acts on any going: often blinkered/visored: tends to hang and carry head awkwardly: none too keen: inconsistent. *L. J. Barratt* — 56 §

BEST OF ALL (IRE) 4 b.f. Try My Best (USA) 130 – Skisette (Malinowski (USA) 123) [1995 77: 6m 6g 8.1s* 1996 8s 8d 7m³ 10d 7m 7.1d⁴ 8.3m³ 7g⁵ a8g 8d 7.1s 7g⁵ 7m² 8.1s a7g² a8g* a9.4g Dec 7] rather leggy filly: fair handicapper: won claimer at Southwell in November: stays 8.3f: acts on good to firm and soft ground and on fibresand: effective blinkered or not: none too consistent. *J. Berry* — 70

BEST OF BOLD 4 ch.g. Never So Bold 135 – I'll Try 71 (Try My Best (USA) 130) [1995 70d: 8m⁴ 8f⁵ 8g⁴ 6m 7d⁶ 7g 8g a7g 1996 a7g⁵ 8.3g* 8g* 7g* Aug 30] fair maiden at best in Britain, sold out of N. Graham's stable 2,200 gns Newmarket July Sales: won 3 minor races in Germany afterwards: stays 1m: acts on good to firm ground: tried blinkered. *C. von der Recke, Germany* — 70

BESWEETOME 3 b.f. Mtoto 134 – Actraphane (Shareef Dancer (USA) 135) [1995 NR 1996 7d Apr 4] 12,000Y: strong, lengthy filly: has scope: has been freeze fired: first foal: dam won at 11.8f in France: looking well but very green, tailed off —

116

in maiden at Leicester: quite a nice sort who looked type to do better, but sold (J. Gosden to J. Pearce) 6,400 gns Newmarket July Sales. *J. H. M. Gosden*

BE TRUE 2 b.g. (May 3) Robellino (USA) 127 – Natchez Trace 52 (Commanche 54 Run 133) [1996 5f 7f 6m⁶ 6f³ 7f Sep 3] 1,900Y, 9,000 2-y-o: first foal: dam poor maiden who should have been well suited by further than 1m, half-sister to smart French 7f to 1½m performer Lighted Glory and smart middle-distance stayer Torus: modest form: best efforts at 6f but should stay 1¼m. *A. Moore*

BETTER OFFER (IRE) 4 b.g. Waajib 121 – Camden's Gift (Camden Town 110 125) [1995 102: 12m⁵ 10m³ᵈⁱˢ 10m* 10m² 12m* 11.9d² 12d² 11.9g² 1996 10m 14s⁵ 12m* 12m³ 13.9m 12g* 18g 12s Nov 9] tall gelding: useful handicapper: won at Ascot in July and (career-best effort in Tote Sunday Special Handicap, weaving through in straight to beat Sheer Danzig 1¼ lengths) September: suited by good test at 1½m and stays 13.9f, seemed not to stay 2¼m in Cesarewitch: acts on soft ground and good to firm: fully effective when sweating: carries head high and has wandered under pressure: held up. *G. Harwood*

BETTYNOUCHE 2 b.f. (May 14) Midyan (USA) 124 – Colourful (FR) 97 (Gay 69 + Mecene (USA) 128) [1996 5d* 6m³ 5m⁵ 7d⁴ 7d⁴ 6d 8d 8d Oct 21] approx 250,000 francs Y: smallish, leggy filly: half-sister to several winners here and abroad, including fair middle-distance performer Bookcase (by Siberian Express): dam French 2-y-o 5f winner out of high-class French staying 2-y-o First Bloom: won maiden at Warwick in April: left R. Hannon's stable after third start: fourth at Dieppe, only time in frame in claimers in France: stays 7f. *H. Honore, France*

BEVELED CRYSTAL 2 ro.f. (Mar 19) Beveled (USA) – Countess Mariga – (Amboise 113) [1996 6m Sep 7] sparely-made filly: sixth live foal to a thoroughbred stallion: dam never ran: never a factor in maiden at Kempton. *C. James*

BEVELED MILL 2 b.f. (Jun 3) Beveled (USA) – Lonely Shore (Blakeney 126) – [1996 8g a8g⁶ a8g Dec 3] fifth foal: sister to a winner in Italy at up to 1m: dam 13.5f winner in Italy: no form. *P. D. Evans*

BE WARNED 5 b.g. Warning 136 – Sagar 74 (Habitat 134) [1995 85: 7m 6m 6g⁶ 72 d 6m³ 8g 8m 6m 6g* 7d 7g 6d² a7g* a7g⁴ 1996 7d 7m 7.3s³ 6d 6m 6m⁴ 6g 6m⁵ 7m 6d 6f Nov 5] good-topped gelding: unimpressive mover: fairly useful handicapper: sold out of N. Callaghan's yard 6,200 gns Newmarket Autumn Sales after tenth start: ideally suited by 6f/7f: acts on good to firm and soft ground and on fibresand: best 4-y-o form in blinkers, they made no difference in 1996: held up. *M. Dods*

BEWITCHING LADY 2 ch.f. (Apr 12) Primo Dominie 121 – Spirit of India 60 (Indian King (USA) 128) [1996 5.2f 6m³ 6g⁶ 6m 7.3s Oct 26] 12,000F, IR 19,000Y: strong, lengthy filly: second live foal: half-sister to 3-y-o Polar Spirit (by Polar Falcon), 1m seller winner at 2 yrs: dam unraced: third to Hawait in maiden at Lingfield in August, only form: bred to be a sprinter: sold 52,000 gns Newmarket December Sales. *D. W. P. Arbuthnot*

BEWITCHING (USA) 3 ch.f. Imp Society (USA) – Mrs Magnum (USA) 104 (Northjet 136) [1995 87?: 5m³ 5.1m⁴ 6f* 7m⁴ 6f 1996 7m* 7m³ 7.6f³ 7m 7m⁶ Aug 15] leggy, lengthy filly: has scope: useful form: won minor event at Leicester in June, drifting markedly right under pressure: good third to Lucayan Prince in Jersey Stakes at Royal Ascot and to Almushtarak in listed rated stakes at Lingfield: well below form (spread a plate first occasion) last 2 starts: stays 7.6f, should get 1m: has raced only on top-of-the-ground: edgy sort, usually early to post. *J. A. R. Toller*

BEX HILL 4 ch.f. Grey Desire 115 – Pour Moi 73 (Bay Express 132) [1995 –: – a8.5g⁶ a7g a6g a7g a6g 1996 a8g a8.5g a7g⁵ a7g Jan 24] of little account. *D. Haydn Jones*

BEYOND CALCULATION (USA) 2 ch.c. (Feb 19) Geiger Counter (USA) – 79 Placer Queen (Habitat 134) [1996 6m⁴ Jul 27] seventh foal: half-brother to 4-y-o Above The Cut (by Topsider), 7f winner at 2 yrs, 1m winner Agnes Fleming (by Al Nasr) and 1989 2-y-o 6f winner Invisible Halo (by Halo): dam ran 3 times here before winning at up to 1¼m in Canada: sire only minor sprint winner but well-bred son of Mr Prospector: 15/2, over 5½ lengths fourth of 9, slowly away, to Revoque in maiden at Ascot: green and nervy beforehand, not knocked about in race: looked sure to improve. *P. W. Harris*

BEYOND DOUBT 4 ch.f. Belmez (USA) 131 – Highbrow 112§ (Shirley Heights 87
130) [1995 82p: 10m* 12f* 1996 8s 10m 12m² 14.6m⁵ 12m⁴ 12g Oct 11] quite
attractive filly: reportedly suffered slight stress fracture on near-hind after final 3-y-o
start: fairly useful performer: better at 1½m than shorter (impossible task at 14.6f):
acts on firm going, shaped well on dead only 2-y-o start, mid-division in the Lincoln
on soft. *Lord Huntingdon*

BEYOND OUR REACH 8 br.g. Reach 122 – Over Beyond 78 (Bold Lad (IRE) 43
133) [1995 NR 1996 8.1g⁶ 10m 13.1f Jul 8] fair staying hurdler: fairly useful in his
prime on flat, only poor nowadays: probably stays 13f. *R. J. Hodges*

BIANCA CAPPELLO (IRE) 3 b.f. Glenstal (USA) 118 – Idara 109 (Top Ville –
129) [1995 –: 7m 7.6d 7d 1996 8m 8m 9.7g a8.5g a10g Dec 13] big filly: half-sister
to Idris: no worthwhile form: tried blinkered. *P. S. Felgate*

BIANCA NERA 2 b.f. (Apr 11) Salse (USA) 128 – Birch Creek (Carwhite 107 +
127) [1996 5f* 6m* 7g* 8d⁴ Oct 6]
    Bianca Nera's learning curve was a steep one. In early-August she was
still unraced; by early-September she had won the Lowther Stakes and the
Moyglare Stud Stakes, two of the top races for two-year-old fillies. Just a week
after making a winning debut in a five-furlong maiden at Beverley, she was
pitched into better company in the Lowther Stakes at York and gave a
determined display against fillies already experienced in pattern races. Always
prominent, she was one of four in line across the track over a furlong out with
the favourite, the Princess Margaret winner Seebe, and the Queen Mary third
Moonshine Girl challenging on one side and outsider Arethusa on the other.
After being headed briefly, Bianca Nera reasserted to hold Arethusa by a neck
with Seebe and the Molecomb winner Carmine Lake in close attendance, a
length and a half covering the first four home.
    Bianca Nera was involved in another tight finish on her next outing, in
the Moyglare Stud Stakes at the Curragh in September, though it would have
been a different story had she got a clear run. She started second favourite to the
Newbury listed race winner Crystal Crossing there and was followed in the
betting by Star Profile, fifth in the Heinz 57 Phoenix Stakes, and the third
British-trained filly Ryafan, who had won a Doncaster maiden on her only start.
Bianca Nera did not race so prominently on this occasion and had to be
switched twice, first over two furlongs out and again when looking for room
between the leaders Ryafan and Azra, but once clear she quickened well to run
out the winner by half a length from Ryafan with less than a length covering the
next three home.
    There was more trouble in store for Bianca Nera on her final start in the
Prix Marcel Boussac at Longchamp where she was just beginning to go in her
coat. Drawn towards the inner, she was soon hemmed in against the rail and had

Stakis Casinos Lowther Stakes, York—
Beverley one week, a Group 2 prize the next, as Bianca Nera shades Arethusa

to be snatched up on the turn. She then failed to get the best of runs in the straight before staying on for fourth, beaten about four lengths by Ryafan. Bianca Nera had achieved much in a short time, and is better than the bare form at the Curragh and Longchamp would suggest. All the same, it has to be said that the standard of the three pattern races contested was average at best.

Bianca Nera (b.f. Apr 11, 1994)	Salse (USA) (b 1985)	Topsider (b 1974)	Northern Dancer
			Drumtop
		Carnival Princess (ch 1974)	Prince John
			Carnival Queen
	Birch Creek (gr 1982)	Carwhite (gr 1974)	Caro
			White Paper
		Deed (b 1970)	Derring-Do
			Aurorabella

Bianca Nera is her sire Salse's second Moyglare Stud Stakes winner in four years following Lemon Souffle in 1993. Bred by the Stowell Hill Stud, Bianca Nera is the fourth winner and much the best performer of her dam Birch Creek's seven foals to date. An earlier mating with Salse resulted in My Mariam who won a six-furlong maiden at Newmarket on her debut but has proved disappointing since. Birch Creek's earlier winners were Final Deed (by Final Straw) who won over seven furlongs at two and a mile and a quarter at three, and Crackling (by Electric), a nine-furlong and mile-and-a-half winner who stayed two miles. A maiden from six starts when she was trained in France, Birch Creek scraped some black type by finishing third in Turin's Premio Royal Mares, a Group 3 mile event. Her dam Deed produced seven winners, best of them the useful sprinter Great Deeds and Busaco, a smart gelding who won over seven furlongs at two (when he was second in the Horris Hill Stakes) and a mile and a quarter, including in Goodwood's Extel Handicap, at three. Deed, who ran only at two years when she won at five furlongs, was out of Aurorabella, a one-paced sister to the Goodwood Cup winner Double Bore and half-sister to the dam of the Two Thousand Guineas winner Only For Life.

The good-bodied Bianca Nera, a quick-actioned filly, was bought for just 23,000 guineas as a yearling at the December Sales; she has already won more than six times that amount. Bianca Nera was stepped up in trip for each of her starts, racing on a progressively easier surface each time, and while she did well to win over five furlongs on her debut she gave a staying performance at Longchamp and seems certain to get further than a mile. She will need to show plenty of improvement to figure in the classics and her Group 1 penalty will make life difficult in lesser company. *D. R. Loder*

Moyglare Stud Stakes, the Curragh—
the gap looks plenty big enough now as Bianca Nera (centre) gains her third win in 24 days

BIANCA'S SON (BEL) 6 ch.h. Bacalao (USA) – Bianca Girl (McIndoe 97) –
[1995 NR 1996 11.8f 10.3g a12g Nov 7] big, plain, lengthy Belgian-bred horse: had
8 races in Belgium, winning a handicap at Sterrebeek and placed twice (over 7f), not
seen since mid-1994: no form here. *J. M. Plasschaert, Belgium*

BIBA (IRE) 2 ch.f. (Mar 26) Superlative 118 – Fahrenheit 69 (Mount Hagen (FR) –
127) [1996 a6g 6g 6m Sep 18] half-sister to several winners, including smart 3-y-o
sprinter Farhana (by Fayruz), 6f winner at 2 yrs, and fairly useful sprinter Alasib (by
Siberian Express): dam ran twice at 3 yrs, placed at around 7f and 1m: well beaten in
maidens. *R. Boss*

BICTON PARK 2 b.c. (Mar 2) Distant Relative 128 – Merton Mill 68 (Dominion 61 +
123) [1996 6m 7.1d 7m⁴ 6d Nov 8] workmanlike colt: first reported foal: dam stayed
2¼m: modest form on balance (probably flattered third outing): bred to stay at least
1m: blinkered (best efforts) last 2 starts. *D. Morley*

BIFF-EM (IRE) 2 ch.c. (Feb 7) Durgam (USA) – Flash The Gold (Ahonoora 68
122) [1996 5d 6d³ 5g* Jun 3] IR 2,100F, 4,000Y: second reported foal: dam, placed
over 5f in Ireland at 2 yrs, probably stayed 7f: progressive form: won median auction
maiden at Hamilton in June: stays 6f: sold 9,200 gns Doncaster October Sales:
looked capable of better. *Miss L. A. Perratt*

BIG BANG 2 b.c. (Mar 7) Superlative 118 – Good Time Girl 65 (Good Times 56
(ITY)) [1996 8.1g⁶ 8.1s Oct 22] 2,000F, 5,200Y: sixth foal: half-brother to 4-y-o 7f
and 7.5f winner Move With Edes (by Tragic Role): dam 2-y-o 5f and 6f seller winner:
well beaten in maidens: trained by M. McCormack on debut. *M. Blanshard*

BIG BEN 2 ch.c. (Feb 15) Timeless Times (USA) 99 – Belltina 41 (Belfort (FR) 87
89) [1996 6g 5m* 5f* 5m⁴ 5s³ 6d⁵ 5v⁵ Oct 6] 5,600Y, 7,400 2-y-o: small, leggy colt:
second foal: brother to 3-y-o Ticka Ticka Timing, 6f seller winner at 2 yrs: dam,
plater, stayed 7f: fairly useful form: made most when winning maiden at Sandown in
July and minor event at Lingfield in August: fourth of 5 to Janib in listed race at York
next start, best subsequent effort: probably best at 5f: acts on firm ground, below
form all starts on soft/heavy: sold 10,500 gns Newmarket Autumn Sales. *R. Hannon*

BIGWIG (IRE) 3 ch.c. Thatching 131 – Sabaah (USA) 65 (Nureyev (USA) 131) –
[1995 NR 1996 8.3m 10m a12g a16g Dec 5] IR 37,000Y: first foal: dam, lightly-
raced maiden, closely related to Maroof: no sign of ability. *A. Moore*

BIJOU D'INDE 3 ch.c. Cadeaux Genereux 131 – Pushkar (Northfields 127
(USA)) [1995 106p: 6m² 6f² 7m* 8m* 8d⁵ 1996 8m³ 8d⁴ 8f* 10g² 10.4m³ 8m⁶
Sep 28]

For a period of seven weeks in the summer, Bijou d'Inde could be
regarded as the top three-year-old trained in Britain. He had beaten the English,
Irish and French Two Thousand Guineas winners in the St James's Palace
Stakes and then taken himself to the head of the middle-distance crop as well
when going down by a neck to top-class five-year-old Halling in the Eclipse.
Some said that Bijou d'Inde was the best three-year-old in Europe, suspecting
Zagreb's runaway triumph in the Irish Derby was too good to be true. More
importantly, Mark of Esteem, Helissio and Bosra Sham had yet to show their
true colours. When they did—beginning with Mark of Esteem in the Celebration Mile in late-August—Bijou d'Inde was left treading water, but while
unable to end the season rated the very best of his generation, he made a
powerful impression with those game performances at Royal Ascot and
Sandown.

In the St James's Palace, Bijou d'Inde just would not be denied. The
intention had probably been to make as much of the running as possible, but
100/1-shot World Premier had the lead for the first two furlongs and, making
the apparently decisive move, heavily-backed favourite Ashkalani had it
almost throughout the last two. The two other Guineas winners, Mark of
Esteem and Spinning World, were unable to muster a challenge from early in
the straight, but Ashkalani looked worth every penny that had been wagered on
him to extend his unbeaten record. Bijou d'Inde duly went around a length
down to him at the furlong pole and it was a losing battle right up until the last
fifty yards when Bijou d'Inde's resolution matched Jason Weaver's every call

to see the positions switched again virtually on the line. Ashkalani's trainer blamed Michael Kinane for going too soon and allowing his mount the time to lose concentration in front. If that means that Bijou d'Inde showed the greater mettle, well, who could argue with the result. Eighteen days later, Bijou d'Inde was the one to lose out narrowly, but his reputation was enhanced—in finishing runner-up in the Eclipse, the horses he split were Halling and Pentire. Bijou d'Inde had been sent off at 12/1 against Britain's two top older horses and four others. Trying a mile and a quarter for the first time and bidding to be the first three-year-old St James's Palace and Eclipse winner for sixty years, he tracked the all-the-way leader before launching a typically determined, neck-out challenge over the last two furlongs.

When the season ended, however, Halling had beaten Bijou d'Inde twice and so had Mark of Esteem. Bijou d'Inde's two races after the Eclipse were respectable efforts but not up to his best; he was about four and a quarter lengths further behind Halling when third in the International at York and then sixth of seven in the first-rate set of milers led home by Mark of Esteem in the Queen Elizabeth II Stakes at Ascot. The encounter with Mark of Esteem that onlookers will surely remember best, however, took place nearly five months earlier in an epic race for the Two Thousand Guineas. The Godolphin colt had taken their measure over a furlong out but Even Top and Bijou d'Inde were bearing down strongly on him again at the death in that short head-head finish. On *Timeform* ratings, Bijou d'Inde had improved over the winter by only a pound less than the winner. On the strength of that performance, Mark Johnston's charge was made second favourite for the Irish Two Thousand but, for the only time in 1996, he was well below form. A lost shoe had interrupted his preparation, but the soft surface was probably at least as much to blame. As Royal Ascot demonstrated less than a month later, a sound surface suits Bijou d'Inde well. Sand should be on the agenda for him in 1997 because he has been

St James's Palace Stakes, Royal Ascot—Bijou d'Inde's courage deprives Ashkalani (noseband)

entered in the Dubai World Cup. His Guineas performance was, of course, a fine advert for a Yorkshire winter, such a fine advert that he will be spending Christmas 1996 in Dubai, as part of his preparation for the big race and so that his trainer can learn at first hand how beneficial it is for a horse to winter in a warm climate. A big, leggy, quite good-topped colt, Bijou d'Inde is high class at a mile and a mile and a quarter.

Bijou d'Inde (ch.c. 1993)	Cadeaux Genereux (ch 1985)	Young Generation (b 1976)	Balidar Brig O'Doon
		Smarten Up (ch 1975)	Sharpen Up L'Anguissola
	Pushkar (b 1980)	Northfields (ch 1968)	Northern Dancer Little Hut
		Chippings (b 1972)	Busted Chip

Writing in his column in *The Sporting Life* in July, Johnston reflected on why he splashed out 20,000 guineas for Bijou d'Inde as a yearling and gave an insight into his methods when selecting at the sales: 'I have a principle that I will never buy a horse that I did not select from the catalogue before going to the sale regardless of how good it looks . . . As to his (Bijou d'Inde's) conformation, I don't remember too much about it. I had only written one word on the page—beside the name Cadeaux Genereux I had written "Typical".' He pointed out, as we had in *Racehorses of 1995*, that Cadeaux Genereux was in a different class to the sires of Pushkar's eight previous foals, and yet she still had a good winner-to-runner ratio and two of her winners, Eradicate (by Tender King) and Hebridean (by Norwick), had been well above average. Johnston had also, by the way, bought Pushkar's 1996 two-year-old Belle Bijou, a filly by Midyan who has been well beaten on her one race so far. Pushkar was not covered in 1994 and died after producing a Magic Ring filly in 1996. Two of

Mr J. S. Morrison's "Bijou d'Inde"

her less distinguished offspring came out of the woodwork to be sold in July, the talentless six-year-old Kirkadian (by Norwick) for 15,000 guineas and the unraced five-year-old About Face (by Midyan) for 25,000. *M. Johnston*

BILKO   2 gr.c. (Feb 6) Risk Me (FR) 127 – Princess Tara 85 (Prince Sabo 123)   88 +
[1996 5d* 5m² May 1] 22,000Y: first foal: dam 6f (at 2 yrs) and 1m winner, half-sister to high-class French sprinter Kind Music: won maiden at Lingfield in April: caught post by Smokey Pete in minor event at Ascot in May on final start: looked speedy. *G. Lewis*

BILLADDIE   3 b.g. Touch of Grey 90 – Young Lady (Young Generation 129)   60
[1995 55p: 8d 7m 6m⁶ 1996 a8g* a10g³ a8g⁴ Feb 15] modest performer: narrowly won minor event at Lingfield in January: respectable efforts there afterwards: probably stays 1¼m: acts on equitrack. *R. Boss*

BILL MOON   10 ch.g. Nicholas Bill 125 – Lunar Queen 96 (Queen's Hussar 124)   –
[1995 28: 8g 7.1m 7m⁶ 6f 1996 8f Sep 27] leggy gelding: poor handicapper: no promise on belated return: stays 1m: acts on firm, dead ground and equitrack, not very soft. *D. T. Thom*

BILLYBACK   6 b.g. Absalom 128 – Petit Secret 64 (Petingo 135) [1995 –: 9.7m   –
1996 a12g Apr 24] of little account nowadays. *P. R. Webber*

BILLY BUSHWACKER   5 b.g. Most Welcome 131 – Secret Valentine 71   97
(Wollow 132) [1995 96: 8m* 7m⁶ 8m⁴ 10m 7.9m 9g 8m⁴ 1996 8s 10.3m² 10m² 9.2g²
10.4m 10m⁶ 10m 10.4m 10.3m³ 9m Oct 5] rather leggy, workmanlike gelding: useful handicapper: kept good company in 1996 and generally ran well: stays 1¼m: acts on good to firm and dead ground: occasionally blinkered, at least as good without: carried head high second 5-y-o start: held up. *Mrs M. Reveley*

BILLYCAN (IRE)   2 b.c. (Apr 25) Mac's Imp (USA) 116 – Sassalin (Sassafras   –
(FR) 135) [1996 6m 6d⁶ a7g 7g 6m Aug 19] 2,100Y: close-coupled colt: unimpressive mover: half-brother to 3 winners, including 1987 2-y-o 7f winner Lincroft Boy (by Crofter): dam won over 7.5f at 2 yrs in Ireland: well beaten in sellers: visored third start. *B. P. J. Baugh*

BILOELA   6 ch.m. Nicholas Bill 125 – Maple Syrup 89 (Charlottown 127) [1995   64
NR 1996 9.9m 12.4d² May 6] lengthy, good-bodied mare: rated 67 at 3 yrs: third run on flat since, second of 8 at Newcastle last time: stays 12.4f: acts on good to firm and soft going. *J. G. FitzGerald*

BINLABOON (IRE)   5 b. or br.h. Polish Precedent (USA) 131 – Aldhabyih 86   –
(General Assembly (USA)) [1995 –: a12g⁶ a9.4g a7g 11.5g 1996 8m Jun 5] poor winning hurdler: little sign of ability on flat: tried blinkered. *K. G. Wingrove*

BIN ROSIE   4 b.g. Distant Relative 128 – Come On Rosi 77 (Valiyar 129)   120
[1995 113: 7m³ 7.6m² 8g* 8m⁵ 8m² 7.3m³ 7g² 8g* 8m³ 8g 1996 7g⁴ 7g³ 8m²
8g* 7.3m* 8m² 8d³ Oct 6]
        Bin Rosie has several traits that we don't like to see in a racehorse, and rather more that we do. Above all he has class, and shows it on a regular basis. He needed his first two runs to hit form in the latest season, but was a reliable enough proposition after that, winning one listed race and one pattern race, finishing runner-up in two pattern events and third in another. He was placed in six of his seven starts in 1996, fourth in the other. Winning, though, is what has sometimes looked problematical, dramatically so on occasions as a three-year-old when Bin Rosie's habitual tendency to carry his head high was sometimes accompanied by one to down tools after hitting the front. On consecutive appearances in the autumn that year he twice moved stylishly into the lead two furlongs out in listed races at Newmarket, going on to a two-length victory on the first occasion and going down tamely to be third one month later. That is history. Bin Rosie seems to have eliminated a few of those quirks from his repertoire and connections have settled on a way to get the best out of him—you would seldom find Bin Rosie taken into the lead as early as the two-furlong marker nowadays
        An exception, apparently, was the six-runner listed race at Maisons-Laffitte in July in which, the *Paris-Turf* tells us, the early pace was 'ridiculously

slow' and Bin Rosie 'accelerated brutally' entering the straight. He went on to justify even-money favouritism by two and a half lengths from the five-year-old mare La Fra Angelico. The opposition was a good deal stronger in the Hungerford Stakes at Newbury and the Park Stakes at Doncaster on his next two starts, and so was the early pace. This made the waiting tactics a lot easier and got the best out of Bin Rosie. That was not enough to cope with Bishop of Cashel at Doncaster, but at Newbury, after the take-no-prisoners efforts of Green Perfume and Mistle Cat, Bin Rosie was unleashed entering the final furlong and won his first pattern race by a length and three quarters. That should not be the last pattern success because, although to some extent Bin Rosie needs things to go his way, there should be plenty more opportunities —he was gelded before he made his racecourse debut.

		Habitat	Sir Gaylord
	Distant Relative	(b 1966)	Little Hut
	(b 1986)	Royal Sister II	Claude
Bin Rosie		(b 1977)	Ribasha
(b.g. 1992)		Valiyar	Red God
	Come On Rosi	(b 1979)	Val Divine
	(b 1987)	Victory Kingdom	Viceregal
		(b 1975)	Happy Victory

Bin Rosie's sire Distant Relative won six pattern races, including the Hungerford. He also used to carry the Wafic Said colours and come with a late rattle, but did so in a very different fashion, after usually getting behind and needing vigorous pushing form his jockey in the early stages. He has been standing at £3,500 for the last two seasons. Bin Rosie is the best of his first crop and My Branch the best of his second. He has quite a few useful performers as well and one of those is Come On Rosi's second foal Shanghai Girl, another head-in-air character who must surely have her idiosyncrasies judged on her record in handicaps after finding dramatic improvement to breeze in over five furlongs at Doncaster in October. The two-year-old Generous Libra (by Generous) was third of six in the Houghton Stakes at Newmarket on his only run so far. Come On Rosi herself was not so good as any of her first three foals, winning one minor event (easily her best effort at three years) from five starts over six furlongs. A granddaughter of the Canadian Oaks winner Happy Victory and a half-sister to The Deep's dam Duende, Come On Rosi was purchased by Wafic Said's Addison Racing for 19,500 guineas at the end of her three-year-old season. They tried to sell Bin Rosie, but apparently never did so although the sales returns show him being knocked down for 21,000 guineas as a foal and IR 35,000 guineas as a yearling. They must be glad to have kept him. A smallish, angular gelding, Bin Rosie is effective at seven furlongs to a mile, acts on good to firm ground and ran respectably (on dead ground in the 1996 Prix du Rond-Point) on his only start on a soft surface. He went without headgear on his first three starts, was visored for his next three and blinkered on all since. *D. R. Loder*

BINT ALBAADIYA (USA) 2 ch.f. (Feb 4) Woodman (USA) 126 – Pixie Erin 110 (Golden Fleece (USA) 133) [1996 6m* Oct 4] IR 50,000Y: half-sister to 1¼m winner Ericolin (by Ahonoora): dam, 7f to 1¼m winner, half-sister to smart middle-distance colt Skaramanga and Star Pastures: weak in market when winning maiden at Lingfield by head from Shifting Time: will stay at least 1m: should improve. *M. R. Stoute* **77 p**

BINTANG TIMOR (USA) 2 ch.c. (Feb 1) Mt Livermore (USA) – Frisky Kitten 77 (USA) (Isopach (USA)) [1996 6d² 7g⁴ Oct 19] $180,000Y: medium-sized, stocky colt: singularly unimpressive mover: fourth foal: half-brother to minor winners in USA by Proper Reality and Afleet: dam minor stakes winner at up to 9f: in frame in maiden at Ascot (behind Dances With Dreams) and Houghton Stakes at Newmarket (never dangerous behind Crimson Tide) in autumn: bred to stay 1m: wore dropped noseband both starts. *P. F. I. Cole*

BINT BALADEE 2 b.f. (Apr 28) Nashwan (USA) 135 – Sahara Baladee (USA) 94 d 79 (Shadeed (USA) 135) [1996 7d² 8m⁴ 7.3s⁶ 7d³ Nov 8] rather leggy, unfurnished filly: good mover: third foal: half-sister to useful 3-y-o 1¼m winner Shanaladee (by Darshaan) and a winner in Sweden by Alzao: dam (maiden) would have stayed beyond 1m: useful form in frame behind Reams of Verse in maiden at Newmarket and May Hill Stakes at Doncaster first 2 starts: failed to progress, turning it in final outing: bred to stay 1¼m: blinkered last 2 starts: hung first 2 outings, carried head high third: ungenuine, and one to treat with caution. *Saeed bin Suroor*

BINT ROSIE   2 b.f. (May 31) Exit To Nowhere (USA) 122 – Butterfly Rose   –
(USA) (Iron Ruler (USA)) [1996 7d Oct 28] 4,000Y: seventh foal: half-sister to 4 winners, including French 6f to 1m winner Sound Tap (by Warning): dam champion filly in Norway at 2 and 3 yrs: never-dangerous seventh in maiden at Lingfield: very awkward at stalls. *M. J. Fetherston-Godley*

BINT SALSABIL (USA)   3 ch.f. Nashwan (USA) 135 – Salsabil 130 (Sadler's   110
Wells (USA) 132) [1995 104p: 6f* 7m* 8g 7m* 1996 7m² 8m 12m 10m* 10g² 12m 10m⁴ Oct 5] strong, lengthy filly: good mover: capable of smart form: short-headed by Thrilling Day in Nell Gwyn Stakes at Newmarket: edgy, ran as if something amiss (reportedly had heart problem) in the Oaks at Epsom: awarded minor event at Newmarket (after finishing neck behind Poppy Carew) but demoted in Prix de la Nonette at Deauville (finished first, neck ahead of Bint Shadayid), both in August: stayed 1¼m: acted on firm ground: sometimes sweated (did so badly before below form in Prix Vermeille): didn't always find much off the bit: visits Mr Prospector. *J. L. Dunlop*

BINT SHADAYID (USA)   3 gr.f. Nashwan (USA) 135 – Shadayid (USA) 122   109
(Shadeed (USA) 135) [1995 105p: 6g* 7m* 8d² 1996 8m³ 8d 10g³ 10.1m⁶ Sep 17] angular, unfurnished filly: fine mover: looked in fine shape after a winter in Dubai and ran very well when about 1½ lengths third to Bosra Sham in 1000 Guineas at Newmarket, held up and staying on: reportedly returned clinically abnormal after Irish 1000 Guineas: neck second to Bint Salsabil in Prix de la Nonette at Deauville in

Hamdan Al Maktoum's "Bint Salsabil"

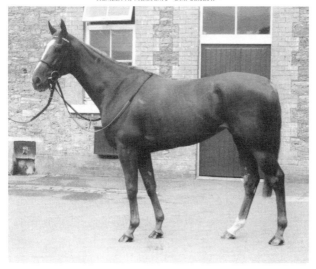

August, but pair demoted for hampering Luna Wells 1f out: disappointing final start, racing bit too freely and edging left under pressure: stayed at least 1¼m: acted on good to firm and dead ground: visits Indian Ridge. *Saeed bin Suroor*

BIRCHWOOD SUN   6 b.g. Bluebird (USA) 125 – Shapely Test (USA) (Elocu-   –
tionist (USA)) [1995 69: 6v³ 6s 5.9m⁵ 7g³ 6.9f⁵ 7m⁶ 6f* 6m 5.9f* 6f 6m⁵ 7m² 6f³ 6f⁵ 6m³ 6g⁶ 7d* 7.1d 6m 1996 7.5d 7g 6g 6s 5.9m 6.9g 6g Jun 3] compact gelding: poor mover: fair handicapper: disappointing in 1996, and pulled up lame final start: stays 7f: acts on any going: best in blinkers: often gets behind. *M. Dods*

BIREQUEST   5 ch.g. Rainbow Quest (USA) 134 – Artic Mistral (CAN) (Briartic   –
(CAN)) [1995 –, a77: a10g* a10g* a10g² a10g⁴ a10g 10.8d 8.3m 1996 10.1m Oct 23] big, workmanlike gelding: fair handicapper: in need of race, always in rear for new stable on belated return to flat: stays 1¼m: easily best efforts on equitrack: front runner. *D. Moffatt*

BIRTHDAY BOY (IRE)   4 b.g. Scenic 128 – Thank You Note 73 (What A Guest   48
119) [1995 69d: 10m 11.6m⁶ 11.6m 10g 10f² 11.5m² 10f⁵ 11.6m 10.1m⁵ 11.5g 10d³ 1996 12m⁴ 16.2f 12m⁶ Aug 16] rangy, good-topped gelding: fair maiden handicapper at best on flat: well below form for new stable after reappearance: stays 11.6f (took keen hold, finished last over 2m): acts on firm ground: tried visored/blinkered, no improvement: joined Miss J. Bower. *J. R. Jenkins*

BISCAY   3 b.f. Unfuwain (USA) 131 – Bay Bay 101 (Bay Express 132) [1995 NR   67 p
1996 7m³ a6g⁴ a9.4g⁴ 8m 7.1d⁶ Sep 28] sturdy, quite attractive filly: fluent mover: third foal: closely related to fairly useful 1993 2-y-o Baskerville (sprinter, by Night Shift) and half-sister to 4-y-o Great Bear (fairly useful 2-y-o sprinter, modest at 1m later, by Dominion): dam 7.6f winner: fair maiden handicapper: may well prove best short of 1m (races freely), and possibly on a sound surface: probably capable of better. *R. Charlton*

BISHOP OF CASHEL   4 b.c. Warning 136 – Ballet Classique (USA) 84   122
(Sadler's Wells (USA) 132) [1995 114: 7g 8d² 8g² 8g* 8d⁴ 1996 8.1g 8m² 8g² 8m* 8d⁴ 7m² Oct 17]

Here was one bishop in 1996 who retired to take up other duties with his reputation untarnished. Bishop of Cashel's third season, like his second, was

Britain's Fastest Railway Park Stakes, Doncaster—
a smooth success for Bishop of Cashel (blaze) over Bin Rosie

crowned by victory in the Park Stakes at Doncaster. Sponsored by Kiveton in 1995, the 1996 edition was called the Britain's Fastest Railway Park Stakes. That Bishop of Cashel was a long way ahead of the British Rail Sprinter class had been clear very early in his career, indeed he won a pattern race in all three seasons, but the latest Park Stakes, along with the Celebration Mile nearly three weeks earlier, represented a significant improvement. One and a half furlongs out in the Celebration at Goodwood, it was not possible to tell who was going the better, Bishop of Cashel or Mark of Esteem. The issue was fairly speedily resolved in Mark of Esteem's favour, but there was no disgrace to Bishop of Cashel in that; beaten three and a half lengths, he came in three quarters of a length in front of third-placed Alhaarth. Restructure, Distant Oasis and Gothenberg all finished further behind that day but took on Bishop of Cashel again in the Park Stakes at the St Leger meeting, as did Nijo who'd been runner-up to him twelve months earlier. More of a threat in the eight-runner field was the Hungerford Stakes winner Bin Rosie, but Bishop of Cashel again loomed up on the bridle, and this time never looked like being headed; Bin Rosie was beaten three quarters of a length, Restructure another length and a quarter. Despite being the form choice, Bishop of Cashel had been preferred to in the betting by both Restructure and Distant Oasis, the reason probably being that the ground at Doncaster was good to firm and Bishop of Cashel was thought to need give, a theory supported by his never having raced on top-of-the-ground in his first two seasons and by his improved showing on good at Goodwood. Strange to relate then that on the two other occasions that he encountered an easy surface in 1996, Bishop of Cashel was below form. The second of these was when favourite for the Prix du Rond-Point at Longchamp

Cheveley Park Stud's "Bishop of Cashel"

in October. While still below his best, finishing second to Charnwood Forest in the Challenge Stakes back on good to firm eleven days later was a better note on which to usher Bishop of Cashel into retirement.

Bishop of Cashel (b.c. 1992)			
	Warning (b 1985)	Known Fact (b 1977)	In Reality
			Tamerett
		Slightly Dangerous (b 1979)	Roberto
			Where You Lead
	Ballet Classique (USA) (b 1987)	Sadler's Wells (b 1981)	Northern Dancer
			Fairy Bridge
		Estaciones (b 1975)	Sonny Fleet
			Estacion

A good-bodied colt, Bishop of Cashel was probably effective at seven furlongs and a mile, and acted on good to firm and heavy going. He will be standing at the Cheveley Park Stud for £4,500. Half-brother Fletcher (by Salse) was a fairly useful five-furlong two-year-old winner in the latest season but looked temperamental and has already been gelded. It took a bid of 105,000 guineas from Reg Akehurst to secure another half-brother, by Royal Academy, at the 1996 Houghton Yearling Sales, and a brother to Bishop of Cashel was born in 1996. Their dam Ballet Classique was a fairly useful mile-and-a-half winner and a half-sister to two useful sorts in the middle-distance filly New Coins and stayer Kublai. Grandam Estaciones and great grandam Estacion both won in the United Stakes, the latter thirteen times after four earlier successes in Argentina. *J. R. Fanshawe*

BISHOPS COURT   2 ch.g. (Feb 24) Clantime 101 – Indigo 86 (Primo Dominie   81 p 121) [1996 5m³ 5g* Sep 29] lengthy, good-quartered gelding: has plenty of scope: second foal: brother to 4-y-o 5f winner Surprise Mission: dam 2-y-o 5f winner: won median auction maiden at Hamilton in September in good style: sure to improve further, and make a useful sprinter. *Mrs J. R. Ramsden*

BISQUET-DE-BOUCHE   2 ch.f. (Feb 16) Most Welcome 131 – Larive 80   – (Blakeney 126) [1996 7.1s 8s Nov 9] 2,500Y: half-sister to 3 winners, including 7f and 1m winner Mister Blake (by Damister) and 15.4f winner Limosa (by Jalmood): dam 1½m winner who stayed 2m: well beaten in maidens at Chepstow and Doncaster: bred to stay well. *R. Dickin*

BITCH   4 ch.f. Risk Me (FR) 127 – Lightning Legend 71 (Lord Gayle (USA) 124)   – [1995 39: 7m 10m 8m⁶ 8.2m 6.9f³ 8m⁵ 1996 a12g a8g a6g⁵ 5m Apr 18] shallow-girthed, narrow filly: poor performer: no form for new stable in 1996: stays 1m: acts on good to firm ground and fibresand: tried blinkered. *G. P. Kelly*

BITES   3 b.f. Risk Me (FR) 127 – Sundaysport Splash (Lord Gayle (USA) 124)   – [1995 46: 5d⁶ 5m³ a5g² a5g⁵ 6g² 6g 6m³ 6s 6f 1996 a8g a8.5g a11g Jul 22] plater: well beaten for new stable in 1996: stays 6f: no form on a soft surface. *T. T. Bill*

BITE THE BULLET   5 ch.g. Ballacashtal (CAN) – Longgoe 70 (Lorenzaccio   – 130) [1995 –: a11g 7g 7.1m a12g 1996 8f 17.2f⁶ Jul 8] leggy gelding: of little account. *A. J. Chamberlain*

BIT OF BOTHER (IRE)   3 b.g. Millfontaine 114 – Mother White (Jukebox 120)   69 [1995 58: 5g⁴ 5g² 5f² 1996 a7g a6g⁴ a6g² a6g² a8g* a8g* a8.5g³ a9.4g² 8.2g a8g² a8g⁵ May 9] fair performer: won handicap and claimer at Southwell in February: claimed out of T. D. Barron's stable £8,000 penultimate start: stays 9.4f: acts on firm ground, best form on fibresand: usually waited with. *Miss S. J. Wilton*

BIT ON THE SIDE (IRE)   7 b.m. Vision (USA) – Mistress (USA) (Damascus   86 (USA)) [1995 82: 12g 12m 12m⁵ 13.3g³ 13.3g⁴ 12g* 12d⁶ 12s 12m 1996 10.8d* 12s 12g 10s⁴ Oct 24] leggy, lengthy mare: fairly useful handicapper: won at Warwick in April: sold 17,000 gns Newmarket Autumn Sales: effective at 1¼m and stays 1¾m: has form on good to firm ground but seems suited by some give and acts on soft: sometimes sweats and gets on toes. *N. E. Berry*

BITTER MOON   5 b.m. Rambling River 111 – Elitist 72 (Keren 100) [1995 NR   – 1996 16m Jun 11] fifth foal: dam promised to stay 1¼m: no promise under NH rules and fell fatally on flat debut. *N. Chamberlain*

BLAAZIING JOE (IRE)   5 b.g. Alzao (USA) 117 – Beijing (USA) 89 (Northjet   –
136) [1995 NR 1996 16m⁶ 16s Oct 24] strong, lengthy gelding: rated 99 at 3 yrs: sold
out of P. Cole's stable only 4,200 gns Newmarket July (1995) Sales: no promise on
belated return: dead. *D. L. Williams*

BLACK AND AMBER   4 ch.f. Weldnaas (USA) 112 – Palimony (Com-   45
munication 119) [1995 NR 1996 a8g⁶ a8.5g a6g³ 6.1g Apr 8] half-sister to fair 5f
winner Double Gift (by Cragador): dam never ran: form only when keeping-on third
of 9 in weak maiden at Wolverhampton: will stay beyond 6f. *P. R. Webber*

BLACK AND BLUES   10 b.g. Music Boy 124 – Blackeye (Busted 134) [1995   23
NR 1996 9.2m 8.1m 11.1m² 10.9m Sep 19] workmanlike gelding: very lightly raced
in points 1991-1994: bad form at best on return to flat: stays 11.1f. *J. S. Goldie*

BLACK BOY (IRE)   7 br.g. Auction Ring (USA) 123 – Relic Spirit (Relic) [1995   41
34: a7g a5g a6g⁶ 5m 5.2g⁵ 5f 1996 a6g⁴ a6g May 9] poor maiden handicapper: best
at up to 7f: acts on fibresand, seems to need a sound surface on turf: usually blinkered
or visored: inconsistent. *R. F. Marvin*

BLACKPATCH HILL   7 br.g. Efisio 120 – Myrtlegrove (Scottish Rifle 127)   –
[1995 NR 1996 16g 12g⁶ 11.9v 11.9g 12g 10f a14g Nov 22] lengthy, good-bodied
gelding: has a poor, round action: rated 92 in 1994 for J. Dunlop: fair hurdler for new
stable: seems no longer of much account on flat. *N. Tinkler*

BLACKWATER (USA)   3 b.c. Irish River (FR) 131 – Fruhlingstag (FR) 112   115
(Orsini 124) [1995 NR 1996 8m* 8d* 9m³ 10m⁵ 8d 7d Oct 20] big, strong colt:
brother to French 1¼m winner Bergenia (later good winner in Scandinavia), closely
related to 2 winners by Riverman and half-brother to 2 winners: dam second in
Poule d'Essai des Pouliches: smart French performer: won newcomers event at
Longchamp in April and 6-runner listed race at Deauville (by ¾ length from Star-
maniac) in May: 2½ lengths third of 6 to Le Triton in Prix Jean Prat at Chantilly
(decidedly edgy, raced sluggishly early on) then best form when around 2½ lengths
sixth of 10 (promoted) to Grape Tree Road in Grand Prix de Paris at Longchamp: off
course 3½ months, below best in pattern events at Longchamp (gave deal of trouble
at stalls first occasion) afterwards: stays 1¼m: acts on good to firm ground (best
form) and dead: has reportedly been sold. *M. Zilber, France*

BLAIN   5 gr.g. Roaring Riva 103 – Miss Colenca (Petong 126) [1995 NR 1996   –
11.1g May 20] no longer of much account. *B. S. Rothwell*

BLAKENMOR   3 b.g. No Evil 98 – Kinz (Great Nephew 126) [1995 –: 6m 1996   –
8.1f Sep 12] soundly beaten in sellers. *J. Neville*

BLANCHLAND   7 gr.g. Bellypha 130 – Premier Rose 117 (Sharp Edge 123)   39
[1995 –: 9.7m 8g 9m 10m 10.1m⁵ 1996 12m⁵ 14.9m⁴ 14.9m Jul 13] tall, lengthy
gelding: won maiden hurdle in May: seemed only poor for new stable on return to
flat: stays 14.9f: blinkered (hung badly right) once: inconsistent. *P. C. Ritchens*

BLANE WATER (USA)   2 b.f. (Feb 20) Lomond (USA) 128 – Triode (USA)   93
105 (Sharpen Up 127) [1996 6m* 7m⁶ 6m⁴ 7.3s Oct 26] 28,000Y: smallish, quite
attractive filly: fluent mover: third foal: closely related to 3-y-o Threesome (by
Seattle Dancer) and a winner in Germany by Storm Bird: dam 1m winner from the
family of smart middle-distance filly Trillionaire: won maiden at Kempton in
September by 4 lengths: stayed on well when beaten 1½ lengths or so in falsely-run
valuable sales contest at Newmarket and Redcar Two-Year-Old Trophy (sweating,
fourth behind Proud Native): ran poorly in listed race at Newbury final outing: best
form at 6f, should stay 1m: possibly unsuited by soft ground. *J. R. Fanshawe*

BLASTED   4 ch.g. Statoblest 120 – Apprila (Bustino 136) [1995 61: 8.5m³ 7g 7f⁵   –
7g 8f* 7.1m⁶ 8f² 6g 7m a7g⁶ 1996 a10g⁵ a8g a13g Feb 3] modest performer: well
below form for new stable in 1996: stays 8.5f: acts on firm and soft ground: modest
maiden hurdler. *G. Thorner*

BLATANT OUTBURST   6 b.g. War Hero 116 – Miss Metro 65 (Upper Case   81 d
(USA)) [1995 NR 1996 8.2m⁴ 11.5g⁴ 9f² 10g² 10.1m⁶ 10.6d 8g⁴ 8m⁴ 8g Oct 29] rangy
gelding: third foal: dam (should have stayed 1¼m) won over hurdles: modest form in
NH Flat races, winning once: poor novice hurdler: fairly useful maiden on first 3
starts, respectable efforts at best afterwards: sold (G. Bravery to Miss S. Wilton)
9,000 gns Newmarket Autumn Sales: should prove suited by further than 9f: acts on
firm ground: one paced. *G. C. Bravery*

BLAZE AWAY (USA) 5 b.h. Polish Navy (USA) – Battle Drum (USA) (Alydar 80 (USA)) [1995 86: 16m³ 14m* 16m⁵ 16m⁴ 13.9m⁵ 16.1m 16.2g³ 16m* 16g⁶ 17.2m 18m 16.5m⁶ 1996 18s³ 18.7g 16.5g⁶ 14m⁴ 16g⁵ 17.2d 18g Oct 19] tall horse: fair handicapper: stayed 2¼m: acted on soft going and good to firm: blinkered (took keen hold, well beaten) sixth 4-y-o start: effective from front or held up: fairly useful winning hurdler: dead. *I. A. Balding*

BLAZE OF OAK (USA) 5 ch.g. Green Forest (USA) 134 – Magic Robe (USA) 53 (Grey Dawn II 132) [1995 69: 10.1m² 10m⁴ 10m⁵ 8.9g² 8.5d 8.2d² 7d 1996 10.8d 10.2f 10.1m³ 8f 10.8f Oct 8] tall gelding: just a modest maiden for new stable: effective at 1m and 1¼m: acts on firm and good to soft ground: takes keen hold: carries head high: inconsistent. *J. M. Bradley*

BLAZE OF SONG 4 ch.c. Jester 119 – Intellect (Frimley Park 109) [1995 85: 82 d 7.5m² 8m⁵ 10.3m* 8g* 8.1g* 8m 1996 8.1g 8d² 8m 10m 8.1m⁶ 8.1d⁶ 8m 8.1d 9m 8g a10g⁶ Nov 14] good-bodied colt: just a fair handicapper in 1996 after second start: effective at 1m, and stays 10.3f: acts on good to firm and heavy ground: blinkered/ visored (no improvement) seventh to tenth 4-y-o starts: inconsistent. *R. Hannon*

BLAZING CASTLE 2 gr.g. (May 21) Vague Shot 108 – Castle Cary 69 (Castle 73 Keep 121) [1996 5d³ a6g⁴ 5m* 5g 5.3f² 5.7m Aug 13] smallish, leggy gelding: first foal: dam sprinter: made all in maiden at Beverley in July: suited by top-of-the-ground: claimer ridden last 4 outings: sometimes wanders. *W. G. M. Turner*

BLAZING IMP (USA) 3 ch.g. Imp Society (USA) – Marital (USA) (Marine – Patrol (USA)) [1995 NR 1996 7m⁵ 8m 6g³ 6m Aug 10] fourth foal: dam won twice from 3 sprints in USA: signs of ability, but no worthwhile form. *W. S. Cunningham*

BLAZON OF TROY 7 b.g. Trojan Fen 118 – Mullet 75 (Star Appeal 133) [1995 53 NR 1996 14d⁵ 14.1m³ 14.6g⁵ 14.8m⁶ Jul 20] good-bodied gelding: fair hurdler, better than ever in 1995/6: modest handicapper (not so good as at 4 yrs) on return to flat: should be suited by test of stamina nowadays. *T. Thomson Jones*

BLENHEIM TERRACE 3 b.g. Rambo Dancer (CAN) 107 – Boulevard Girl 80 69 (Nicholas Bill 125) [1995 49: a7g³ a7g 6m 7.9g 1996 12m 10m⁴ 10m⁴ 11.1g* 14.1m² 12m² 11.8g² 12.1m² 13.9g Oct 12] sturdy gelding: fair performer: won minor event at Musselburgh in July: better form when second next 4 starts: stays 1¾m: has raced only on a sound surface on turf: has tended to idle in front and will prove ideally suited by waiting tactics. *C. B. B. Booth*

BLESSED SPIRIT 3 ch.f. Statoblest 120 – Kukri (Kris 135) [1995 65: 6m 7m 84 1996 6s² 6f³ 6m⁴ 7g² 7s⁶ 8.3m² 8m* 8.1g² 8.1m⁵ 8m⁴ Oct 7] unfurnished filly: fairly useful handicapper: won at Doncaster in July, short of room then quickening well: better at around 1m than shorter: modest form on firm and soft going early on, progressed on a sound surface late on: held up: consistent. *C. F. Wall*

BLESSINGINDISGUISE 3 b.g. Kala Shikari 125 – Blowing Bubbles 72 84 d (Native Admiral (USA)) [1995 84: 5m 5g* 5g² 5d² 5f 1996 6g 6g⁴ 6m 6d⁴ 6m 5m 7.1d 6g⁵ 7g Oct 25] strong, good-topped gelding: fair handicapper: failed by long way to repeat form of second 3-y-o start: stays 6f: best form so far on an easy surface: blinkered (stiff task) final 2-y-o start: inconsistent. *M. W. Easterby*

BLOCKADE (USA) 7 b.g. Imperial Falcon (CAN) – Stolen Date (USA) (Sadair) 64 [1995 73: 8d 7m* 8.1g 8g 9f* 8m* 8m⁴ 8f⁴ 7m² 8f* 8.9g⁴ 1996 7g 8m³ 8m³ 8g* 8m 7f* Jul 25] leggy, close-coupled gelding: tubed: modest performer nowadays: won claimers at Yarmouth and Brighton in July: probably stays 1¼m, but not raced beyond 9f since 1992: acts on firm and dead going: sometimes sweats: usually a front runner. *M. Bell*

BLOMBERG (IRE) 4 b.c. Indian Ridge 123 – Daniella Drive (USA) (Shelter 109 Half (USA)) [1995 100: 7g* 8m² 7.9m 7m² 1996 7m⁵ 8m 8.1d* 8m⁴ 8m 8m⁴ 8m 8g 9g⁴ a9.4g Dec 7] smallish, sturdy colt: useful performer: won rated stakes at Sandown in May and Vodafone Diomed Stakes at Epsom (by 1¼ lengths from Behaviour, leading 2f out and staying on well) in June: stiff tasks, ran well when fourth in Group 3 contest at the Curragh (just over 4 lengths behind Idris) in August and listed race at Newmarket (staying on, 5½ lengths behind Tarawa) in October: stays 9f: acts on firm and dead ground (behind in listed race on fibresand): tended to have tongue tied down on latter starts: best waited with. *J. R. Fanshawe*

BLONDANE 3 b.g. Danehill (USA) 126 – Whos The Blonde (Cure The Blues — (USA)) [1995 NR 1996 a8g a8.5g a8g a6g Dec 3] 2,200Y, 5,100 2-y-o: first living foal: dam, winner at 7f in Ireland, out of sister to speedy pair Bitty Girl and Hot Spark: no worthwhile form. *S. R. Bowring*

BLONDE ROCK 2 ch.f. (Apr 15) Rock City 120 – Golden Scissors 76 43 + (Kalaglow 132) [1996 6g⁵ 6f⁴ 7m² Jun 11] leggy, lengthy filly: third foal: half-sister to 4-y-o 5f to 7f winner Scissor Ridge (by Indian Ridge): dam stayed 2m on flat, 3m over hurdles: poor form: second in seller at Redcar (mulish at start) last time, pulling very hard early on: stays 7f: has raced only on a sound surface. *M. R. Channon*

BLOOD ORANGE 2 ch.c. (Jan 26) Ron's Victory (USA) 129 – Little Bittern — (USA) 73 (Riva Ridge (USA)) [1996 6g 6g⁵ Nov 1] 12,500Y: half-brother to 4-y-o Club Elite (by Salse) and a winner in Germany by Glint of Gold: dam, maiden, should have stayed 2m on flat: poor form in maidens 2½ months apart. *G. G. Margarson*

BLOOMING AMAZING 2 b.g. (Apr 11) Mazilier (USA) 107 – Cornflower 71 Blue (Tyrnavos 129) [1996 7g² 7m⁶ 7.9g 6g Oct 9] 5,200Y, 9,000 2-y-o: tall, close-coupled gelding: third foal: half-sister to useful lightly-raced sprinter Tuxford Hideaway (dam of Branston Abby): second in maiden auction at Thirsk in August, best effort: stays 7f: raced freely final start. *J. L. Eyre*

BLOOMSY BABE 2 b.f. (Mar 17) Batshoof 122 – Mia Fillia 65 (Formidable — (USA) 125) [1996 6m 5.9f⁵ 6.1m 7g⁵ Aug 16] 2,200F, IR 4,400Y: second foal: dam (maiden) suited by 1¼m: no form, including in a seller: bolted before being withdrawn final intended outing *J. J. Quinn*

BLOSSOM DEARIE 3 b.f. Landyap (USA) 112 – Jose Collins 91 (Singing 56 d Bede 122) [1995 –: 7m 1996 6m⁴ 8g 6m 6m Jun 27] good-topped filly: failed to confirm promise of reappearance. *R. G. Frost*

BLOSSOMVILLE 3 gr.f. Petong 126 – Ruthenia (IRE) (Taufan (USA) 119) — [1995 NR 1996 7f 8f 10m⁶ 10f a8.5g Sep 7] second foal: dam unraced sister to smart 7f/1m performer Pasticcio: no worthwhile form. *M. A. Jarvis*

BLOW DRY (IRE) 6 b.g. Glenstal (USA) 118 – Haco 104 (Tribal Chief 125) 44 [1995 61: 6s⁴ 6g 6.9f³ 7g 8.3f⁶ 7.1m⁵ 6m* 6g 7d* 6g 8g⁶ 7g 7m 1996 6.1g 6s⁶ 5.9m 8g a7g 7.1g⁵ 7m 6d Sep 30] good-topped gelding: only poor form in 1996: probably stays 1m: acts on good to firm ground, very best efforts on an easy surface: well beaten on fibresand: visored (below form) final 4-y-o start: inconsistent. *Martyn Wane*

BLOWING AWAY (IRE) 2 b. or br.f. (May 5) Last Tycoon 131 – Taken By — Force (Persian Bold 123) [1996 7g Oct 25] leggy filly: eighth foal: half-sister to 3-y-o He's My Love (by Be My Guest) and 3 winners, including fair 7f (at 2 yrs) to 1½m winner Hunter Valley (by Valiyar): dam Irish middle-distance winner: well beaten in maiden at Doncaster. *M. H. Tompkins*

BLOWN-OVER 2 ch.f. (Feb 10) Ron's Victory (USA) 129 – Woodwind (FR) 41 + 103 (Whistling Wind 123) [1996 6f⁶ 6g 8.3d⁶ 6g⁵ Oct 29] half-sister to numerous

Vodafone Diomed Stakes, Epsom—a most successful step up in class for Blomberg

winners, including very smart sprinter Piccolo (by Warning) and smart miler Tahilla (by Moorestyle): dam 6f winner: poor form: blinkered final start: probably a sprinter: sold 9,500 gns Newmarket December Sales. *A. C. Stewart*

BLUE AND ROYAL (IRE)   4 b.g. Bluebird (USA) 125 – Cat Girl (USA) (Grey Dawn II 132) [1995 65d: 10g⁶ 12m 12f³ 12m 12d 1996 a12g⁶ 17.9g Oct 9] well beaten for new stable: stays 1½m: tried blinkered, no improvement. *V. Soane*   –

BLUEBELL MISS   2 b.f. (May 4) High Kicker (USA) – Mio Mementa 61 (Streak 119) [1996 6d 6d* 6d 6g 7m Oct 28] 1,800Y: leggy, unfurnished filly: seventh foal: half-sister to 3 winners, including smart 7f/1m performer Just Three (by Tina's Pet) and 1¾m seller winner Chantelys (by Ballacashtal): dam sprint maiden: 25/1-winner of maiden at Leicester in May: off course 2½ months afterwards and no form in nurseries on return: stays 6f. *M. J. Ryan*   72 d

BLUEBERRY FIELDS   3 gr.f. Shernazar 131 – Be Easy 110 (Be Friendly 130) [1995 –: 6m 1996 a8g⁴ a10g² 11.6m 10m Jun 3] leggy, quite good-topped filly: modest maiden handicapper: sold 6,800 gns Newmarket Autumn Sales: probably stays 11.6f. *C. F. Wall*   –
a57

BLUE BOMBER   5 b.g. Tina's Pet 121 – Warm Wind 84 (Tumble Wind (USA)) [1995 81: 8m 8g⁵ 7f⁶ 6m 7f* 1996 7g 7g³ 6m 6m 6d* 7g* 6f* 7g Aug 16] close-coupled gelding: not so good as at 4 yrs, though more successful as dropped in class after fourth start: won seller and claimer (claimed out of T. D. Barron's stable £4,000) at Catterick and seller (sold out of G. M. Moore's stable 4,600 gns) at Newcastle in the summer: stays 7f: acts on firm and dead going, tailed off on heavy. *V. Thompson*   75 d

BLUE DOMAIN   5 b.g. Dominion 123 – Blue Rag 70 (Ragusa 137) [1995 –: 7d 1996 a6g Dec 3] sturdy gelding: one-time modest performer, on the downgrade. *R. Craggs*   –

BLUE DUSTER (USA)   3 b.f. Danzig (USA) – Blue Note (FR) 122 (Habitat 134) [1995 116p: 5m* 5m* 6g* 6d* 1996 7f* 6.5d⁵ 6f² Sep 7]   118

If twelve months earlier supporters of Blue Duster had been told that she would keep her unbeaten record until mid-August, they would probably have been delighted. She had won four races as a two-year-old, three of them pattern races, including the Cheveley Park, and was vying for favouritism in the One Thousand Guineas. The meeting with Bosra Sham was eagerly anticipated, one of the talking points of the winter. Like so many of these 'mouth-watering clashes,' however, this one dried up. The foot-sore Bosra Sham only made the field at the eleventh hour, and getting to the course on Guineas day proved beyond Blue Duster. She had managed it for a workout after racing at the Craven meeting, but disappointed onlookers by not being taken above half speed ('the ground was too firm'). That was, nevertheless, sufficient to reveal the recurrence of a back muscle problem that had affected her intermittently as a two-year-old, and four days later it was confirmed that Blue Duster would be scratched from the Guineas.

Blue Duster and Bosra Sham both had to miss Royal Ascot (Blue Duster jetting out to Dubai to aid her recovery) but, alas, this was the last occasion in which the plans for these two three-year-olds in any way converged. When Blue Duster finally did reappear (on July 21st) it was in a £5,000 conditions race at Yarmouth. The manner in which she landed the odds from the useful Unconditional Love was pleasing enough, the form of what she achieved a lot less impressive, and it was the latter which looked the more realistic three weeks later when Blue Duster was beaten about seven and a half lengths into fifth of nine in the Prix Maurice de Gheest at Deauville. Bosra Sham, of course, eventually emerged from her injury-shaped campaign with an awful lot more, but Blue Duster's was by no means a write-off. Not to the form student anyway, because although Blue Duster failed to win her one remaining start, she demonstrated at last that she had improved from two to three. The proof came in the Haydock Park Sprint Cup in which Blue Duster, a 9/1 chance, tracked the leaders against the rails, went on approaching the final furlong but lost out to Iktamal close home and was beaten a length.

Blue Duster (USA) (b.f. 1993)	Danzig (USA) (b 1977)	Northern Dancer (b 1961)	Nearctic Natalma
		Pas de Nom (b or br 1968)	Admiral's Voyage Petitioner
	Blue Note (FR) (b 1985)	Habitat (b 1966)	Sir Gaylord Little Hut
		Balsamique (b 1973)	Tourangeau Bruyere

That she was returned to sprint distances obviously diminishes confidence in Blue Duster's ability to get a mile. *Racehorses of 1995* was guardedly optimistic about her prospects at the trip and she was apparently a possible for the seven-furlong Premio Chiusura in November when it was announced that she would be sent to Dubai and return under the Godolphin banner in 1997. So Blue Duster may yet make that clash with Bosra Sham. A compact filly and a good walker, she acts on firm and good to soft going. There is no need to go into the intricacies of her pedigree again beyond a reminder that she is a sister to the Middle Park and Challenge Stakes winner Zieten (now at the Irish National Stud) and a daughter of the Maurice de Gheest winner Blue Note. Blue Note's next foal is the unraced two-year-old Blue Lustre (by Nureyev) who was also in training with David Loder. *D. R. Loder*

BLUE FLYER (IRE)   3 b.g. Bluebird (USA) 125 – Born To Fly (IRE) 57 (Last   78
Tycoon 131) [1995 67: 6d 6s⁶ a6g³ a7g a8g³ 1996 a10g⁶ a8g² a8g* a8g* a8g² 6m⁵   a84
7m 7f* 8m 7.1m⁵ 7.6m³ 8d a7g a8g⁴ a7g Dec 20] workmanlike gelding: has a quick action: fairly useful performer: won maiden and minor event at Lingfield in February and handicap at Salisbury in August: suited by 7f/1m: best efforts on equitrack/firm ground, showed nothing on soft ground second 2-y-o start: probably effective blinkered or not: usually races prominently: none too consistent. *R. Ingram*

BLUE GOBLIN (USA)   2 gr.c. (Apr 22) Trempolino (USA) 135 – Blue Daisy   88
(USA) 108 (Shahrastani (USA) 135) [1996 6g² 7d³ 7.1f² 7d⁴ 7g⁵ Oct 26] workmanlike colt: first foal: dam 7f/1m winner, including in Ireland at 2 yrs, from good Canadian family: fairly useful maiden: will stay middle distances: acts on firm and dead ground: often on toes: consistent. *L. M. Cumani*

BLUE GRIT   10 b.g. Thatching 131 – Northern Wisdom (Northfields (USA))   56 d
[1995 56: 7.1g⁵ 6f 8g³ 6g 6m a6g⁶ 6m³ 6m⁴ 1996 7.1g 6g³ 6m⁶ 7d 7m⁴ 6m⁴ 7.1g 8m 7f Aug 9] good-topped gelding: modest performer: below form last 3 starts: won at 9f in 1991, best recent form over 6f/7f: acts on firm and soft ground: effective in visor/blinkers or not: has won when sweating: none too consistent. *M. Dods*

BLUE HOPPER   2 b.f. (May 12) Rock Hopper 124 – Kimble Blue 56 (Blue   58
Refrain 121) [1996 7m³ 7g² 7g Aug 12] 2,200Y, 5,700 2-y-o: workmanlike filly: sixth foal: half-sister to 3-y-o sprint maiden Good To Talk (by Weldnaas): dam 2-y-o 5f winner: placed in maiden auctions first 2 starts: tailed off final outing: likely to stay at least 1m. *M. R. Channon*

BLUE IMPERIAL (FR)   2 gr.c. (May 9) Bluebird (USA) 125 – Real Gold 113   –
(Yankee Gold 115) [1996 7d 7f Oct 15] 110,000 francs F, 44,000Y: fifth foal: half-brother to 3 winners in France, including 1m/9f winner Midi Et Demi (by Mouktar) and 1¼m/1½m winner C'Est Moi (by Akarad): dam Irish 2-y-o 7f winner, third in 1¼m Criterium de Saint-Cloud: towards rear in autumn maidens: likely to stay middle distances. *J. W. Hills*

BLUE IRIS   3 b.f. Petong 126 – Bo' Babbity 75 (Strong Gale 116) [1995 104p:5g*   105
5.2g* 6f* 1996 5m 5m³ 5m⁴ 6g 5m* 5m⁴ 5m² 5d⁵ Oct 27] lengthy filly: unimpressive mover: useful performer: bounced back to best to win 20-runner £12,000 handicap at York in August: in frame in listed races at Doncaster and Newmarket (collared near finish after hanging right) then creditable fifth of 9 to Don't Worry Me in Prix du Petit Couvert at Longchamp: effective at 5f and 6f: acts on firm and dead ground: usually races prominently. *M. A. Jarvis*

BLUE JUMBO (IRE)   3 b.f. Bluebird (USA) 125 – Finalist 78 (Star Appeal 133)   –
[1995 NR 1996 7d 6m 8m Sep 20] 3,900Y: tall, lengthy filly: third foal: half-sister to winners Cubist (7f seller, by Tate Gallery) and Tryst (up to 8.5f, by Thatching): dam twice-raced daughter of Galtres winner Deadly Serious and half-sister to smart Irish

middle-distance colt Runyon: behind in maidens: likely to be suited by further than 1m. *W. J. Musson*

BLUE LAMP (USA) 2 ch.f. (Mar 24) Shadeed (USA) 135 – Matter of Time 68 (Habitat 134) [1996 6g Jul 10] $8,000Y resold 23,000Y: rather unfurnished filly: fifth foal: half-sister to winners in USA (by Fast Play) and Brazil (by Danzatore): dam 6f winner at 2 yrs in Ireland, later successful in USA: in need of run, seventh of 17 to Imroz in maiden at Newmarket: reportedly injured afterwards: looked likely to improve. *M. A. Jarvis*

BLUE LUGANA 4 b.g. Lugana Beach 116 – Two Friendly 54 (Be Friendly 130) – [1995 41: 6g 6g 5f⁶ 5f² 5g⁶ 6f 1996 a6g a6g⁴ a6g 5g 7d 6m⁶ 5f⁶ 6g 5d⁵ 5m 5g 6s Aug 31] big gelding: poor maiden handicapper: well beaten in 1996: tried blinkered. *N. Bycroft*

BLUE MOVIE 2 ch.c. (Jan 29) Bluebird (USA) 125 – Zoom Lens (IRE) 65 71 d (Caerleon (USA) 132) [1996 5s* 5m⁴ 6d⁴ 5g 6m 7.9g⁶ 7.3s Oct 26] 17,000Y: sturdy, lengthy colt: good walker: first foal: dam (maiden) should have been suited by further than 1½m: won maiden at Newcastle in May: disappointing in nurseries last 4 starts: stays 6f: acts on good to firm and soft ground: blinkered final outing: sold 4,000 gns Newmarket Autumn Sales: sent to Italy. *M. Bell*

BLUE RIDGE 2 ch.c. (Apr 2) Indian Ridge 123 – Souadah (USA) (General 95 Holme (USA) 128) [1996 6m 5f* 6m⁶ 6g⁵ 5d Oct 12] 68,000Y: leggy, unfurnished colt: fluent mover: fourth foal: half-brother to 3-y-o Beano Script (by Prince Sabo) and 5f (at 2 yrs) to 7f winner Make The Break (by Dominion): dam unraced daughter of speedy Bitty Girl, dam also of smart Irish performer Beaudelaire and sister to Hot Spark: 4-length winner of Sandown maiden in June: ran in pattern races afterwards, best efforts when sixth of 7 to Easycall in Richmond Stakes and last of 5 to Bahamian Bounty in Prix Morny: stays 6f: acts on firm ground, possibly unsuited by soft. *R. Hannon*

BLUE RIVER (IRE) 2 ch.c. (Mar 29) River Falls 113 – Royal Resident 86 88 + (Prince Regent (FR) 129) [1996 7.1g⁵ 7.1m⁴ 7m* 8d* 8g⁵ 8d⁵ Oct 12] IR 12,500F, 15,000Y: strong, rangy colt: progressed well physically: half-brother to Italian 3-y-o 7f winner Debra Zebit (by Fayruz) and several winners in Ireland, including 7.9f to 11f winner Persian Envoy (by Persian Bold): dam stayed very well: successful in maiden and nursery in summer: tailed-off last of 5 in listed races at Goodwood and Ascot (came back with runny nose according to trainer) last 2 starts: likely to stay beyond 1m: acts on good to firm and dead ground. *T. G. Mills*

BLUES QUEEN 2 b.f. (Apr 11) Lahib (USA) 129 – Queens Welcome 60 85 + (Northfields (USA)) [1996 5.2f³ 5.1m⁴ 5.1m² 6.5m⁵ 6m* 7m 6m 7.3s Oct 26] 13,000Y: quite attractive filly: seventh foal: half-sister to fairly useful 3-y-o 7f (at 2 yrs) to 1¼m winner Quality (by Rock City) and 7f winner Susanna's Secret (by Superlative): dam, ran only at 2 yrs, is half-sister to high-class 1973 sprinter The Blues: fairly useful form: won nursery in good style at Ayr in September: may have been flattered (never a factor) when seventh of 25 to Proud Native in Redcar Two-Year-Old Trophy in October on penultimate start: should stay 7f: acts on good to firm ground, probably outclassed on soft: taken last and quietly to post sixth outing. *M. R. Channon*

BLUE SUEDE HOOFS 3 br.g. Nomination 125 – Massive Powder (Caerleon 61 (USA) 132) [1995 73: 7g 6m 6f² 1996 6m 6m⁴ 6m 5.1g⁶ 6f² 7f 5f Sep 17] strong, lengthy gelding: fair maiden: sold 1,300 gns Newmarket Autumn Sales: stays 6f: has raced only on a sound surface: tried blinkered, no improvement: sometimes looks none too keen: inconsistent: sent to Italy. *B. J. Meehan*

BLUEYGREEN 2 b.f. (Apr 22) Green Desert (USA) 127 – Bluebook (USA) 120 67 (Secretariat (USA)) [1996 6m 7g Nov 2] fourth foal: half-sister to Irish 3-y-o Nakayama Express (by Warning) and useful 1m and 1¼m winner Salt Lake (by Mtoto): dam, winner at up to 7.3f, is daughter of Pushy: modest form in late-season maidens at Newmarket: raced freely final start: should stay 7f. *P. W. Chapple-Hyam*

BLUE ZULU (IRE) 4 gr.f. Don't Forget Me 127 – Aldern Stream 102 (Godswalk 87 (USA) 130) [1995 94: 8m* 10m 8f³ 8m⁴ 8.3m³ 1996 8m 10m 8.1g 7.6f⁵ 9m³ 8.5m Sep 24] tall, lengthy filly: fairly useful handicapper, not quite so good as at 3 yrs: effective at 1m, and stays 1¼m: acts on firm ground: none too consistent. *J. R. Fanshawe*

BLUNTSWOOD HALL   3 b.g. Governor General 116 – Miss Sarajane 74 –
(Skyliner 117) [1995 NR 1996 a7g a8g⁵ a9.4g a12g Jul 15] first foal: dam effective at
1m to 1¼m: well beaten. *R. Hollinshead*

BLURRED (IRE)   3 ch.g. Al Hareb (USA) 123 – I'll Take Paris (USA) (Vaguely   85 p
Noble 140) [1995 NR 1996 10g³ 9.9m³ 8d⁶ 12.3m⁶ 10.3m² 10m 10f³ 10.3g* 11f⁴
Nov 5] IR 2,600F, 5,800Y: heavy-topped gelding: brother to poor 1995 3-y-o 14.8f
winner Fools of Pride and half-brother to winners abroad by Lyphard's Wish and
Youth: dam French 2-y-o 1m winner: fairly useful handicapper: first past post at
Doncaster and Redcar (best form, bumped way out inside last, demoted) in the
autumn: should stay 1½m, but best efforts at shorter: acts on firm ground, raced on
unfavoured part of track on dead: well below form for amateur: capable of better yet.
M. H. Tompkins

BLUSH   2 b.f. (May 9) Gildoran 123 – Rather Warm 103 (Tribal Chief 125) [1996   50 p
10f³ Oct 14] half-sister to several winners, including 1991 2-y-o 6f winner Prince
Emilio (by Prince Sabo) and middle-distance performer Woodurather (by Touching
Wood): dam won at up to 7.6f at 2 yrs: nearly slipped up on home turn then stayed
on well when third in seller at Leicester in October: will stay long distances: will
improve. *M. C. Pipe*

BLUSHING DESERT   2 b.f. (Feb 16) Green Desert (USA) 127 – Blushing   – p
Storm (USA) 102 (Blushing Groom (FR) 131) [1996 6d⁵ Oct 11] rather leggy, quite
good-topped filly: first foal: dam (maiden) third in Ribblesdale and Lancashire Oaks,
would have stayed further than 1½m: very green, hampered stalls when fifth of 7 to
Dances With Dreams in maiden at Ascot: will improve. *R. Hannon*

BLUSHING FLAME (USA)   5 b.h. Blushing Groom (FR) 131 – Nearctic   109
Flame 111 (Sadler's Wells (USA) 132) [1995 108: 10m² 12m² 12m 13.9m 12g 12m*
12m* 1996 12d⁶ 11.8g⁴ 14m* 14m Sep 21] deep-bodied, lengthy horse: impresses in
appearance: had a splayed action: generally progressive throughout his career,
peaking to win 10-runner Budweiser Guinness Curragh Cup in June by 4 lengths
from Fill The Bill, allowed uncontested lead and running on splendidly: stiffish task,
headed approaching straight and faded gradually in Irish St Leger there nearly 3
months later: stayed 1¾m well: acted on good to firm ground, below form on heavy:
to stand at Kirtlington Stud, Oxfordshire at £2,000 (Oct 1). *M. R. Stoute*

BLUSHING GRENADIER (IRE)   4 ch.g. Salt Dome (USA) – La Duse 66   55
(Junius (USA) 124) [1995 55: 6.1g 6m 6m⁴ 7g⁴ 6g* 7f 8g³ 6m⁴ 6d⁴ 6.1d 7s⁵ 7g⁴ 7d
1996 8d 6f 6m⁶ 6g* 7m 7m 7g 7.1f 6d a7s² Dec 19] poor maiden: modest
handicapper: enterprisingly ridden to win at Windsor in July: disappointing afterwards until final start: effective at 6f, and stays 1m: acts on good to firm and soft
ground, and fibresand: usually blinkered/visored, not last time: sweating and upset in
stalls sixth 4-y-o start. *M. J. Fetherston-Godley*

BLYTON STAR (IRE)   8 b.g. Horage 124 – Saintly Angel 87 (So Blessed 130)   –
[1995 NR 1996 a6g a6g a7g⁶ a6g Mar 6] poor maiden: stays 7f: acts on firm ground
and on fibresand: blinkered (pulled hard) once in 1993. *Miss J. F. Craze*

BOATER   2 b.c. (Mar 12) Batshoof 122 – Velvet Beret (IRE) (Dominion 123)   74
[1996 7f 6.1s a7s³ Nov 19] medium-sized, unfurnished colt: first foal: dam unraced
half-sister to smart 7f/1m performer Luzum: much improved form in minor event at
Lingfield in November final start: will stay 1m: may do better still. *D. Morley*

BOBALUNA   3 b.c. Inca Chief (USA) – Davemma 81 (Tachypous 128) [1995 NR   –
1996 a5g a6g a8.5g May 25] fifth foal: half-brother to modest 2-y-o winners by

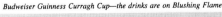

Budweiser Guinness Curragh Cup—the drinks are on Blushing Flame

Noalto (at 7f) and Ballacashtal (at 8.1f): dam, disappointing maiden, stayed 1½m: no sign of ability. *R. F. Marvin*

BOBANLYN (IRE) 4 b.f. Dance of Life (USA) – Sheer Innocence (Shirley 68 Heights 130) [1995 60: 8m 9m 8f⁴ 10.1m 8.3m 10.1g⁵ 10g* 9f 10.3m⁵ 8f⁶ 10f 1996 9.9m 9.9m 9.2s 10m² 12m² 11.9m² 12.1g* 11.1g* 12.1m* Jul 8] sparely-made, angular filly: in the best form since 2-y-o days when ending her career with 3 wins in a week at Musselburgh in July, by 5 lengths under 10-4 last time: stayed 1½m: acted on firm and soft ground: in foal to Deploy. *J. S. Wainwright*

BOBBITT 2 b.f. (Apr 20) Reprimand 122 – Pleasuring 68 (Good Times (ITY)) – [1996 7.1m 7f 7d Oct 28] 13,000F, 25,000Y: quite attractive filly: first foal: dam, maiden who stayed 6f, out of half-sister to very smart 2-y-o Splashing (dam of Bassenthwaite): midfield at best in auction maidens: not bred to stay further than 7f: may do better. *W. Jarvis*

BOBBY BLUE (IRE) 5 gr.g. Bob Back (USA) 124 – Yuma (USA) (Caro 133) – [1995 NR 1996 a12g a16g a16g⁶ a16g⁶ 10f⁶ Jun 25] small gelding: of little account nowadays: left Ronald Thompson after fourth 5-y-o start. *T. Hind*

BOBBY'S DREAM 4 b.f. Reference Point 139 – Kiralyi (FR) (Kings Lake 42 (USA) 133) [1995 50: 11.6m 11.8g⁶ 14.1g² 16m⁶ 15.8g² 17.1m⁵ 12m 1996 a12g a16g 14.1s 15.8g³ 16m 16m 12m 18g⁵ 14.1g² 16.4v⁶ Nov 11] small, sturdy filly: poor mover: only poor maiden handicapper in 1996: thorough stayer: acts on good to firm ground, seems unsuited by heavy. *M. H. Tompkins*

BOB'S PLOY 4 b.g. Deploy 131 – Santa Magdalena (Hard Fought 125) [1995 94: 78 9m 10.2m² 10m* 10.1m⁶ 12m² 12f 11g 12d 1996 12m 12m 12m 10m 10m 14m³ 15.9g⁶ 16.2d⁶ 12g 14.1s Oct 31] good-topped gelding: well below 1995 form for new stable in 1996: stays 1¾m: acts on good to firm and soft going: usually held up: has become inconsistent. *M. H. Tompkins*

BOB THE BROKER (IRE) 2 b.c. (Mar 28) Bob Back (USA) 124 – Java Jive 88 63 (Hotfoot 126) [1996 5s 5d² 6d* 7m Jun 20] 3,000F: close-coupled colt: half-brother to 1½m winner Miss Foxtrot (by Bustino): dam best at sprint distances: won maiden at the Curragh in May by 4½ lengths: well-beaten eighth of 12 in Chesham Stakes at Ascot on only subsequent outing: likely to stay 1m: acts on good to soft ground. *P. J. Flynn, Ireland*

BOFFY (IRE) 3 ch.c. Mac's Imp (USA) 116 – No Dowry (Shy Groom (USA)) – [1995 66: a5g³ 5g⁵ 5.1g⁴ 5.1m⁴ a5g² 5m³ 5m⁵ 5m* 6g* 5g a5g⁶ 6f 1996 a6g⁴ a5g* a75 d a6g² a5g* a5g² a5g⁵ 6.1d 5d 6d 6.1m a6g a6g⁶ 5m⁵ 5m a6g 6m a6g a6g a6s a5g² Dec 28] quite attractive colt: fair performer: won sellers at Wolverhampton and Southwell early on: long way below best after sixth 3-y-o start, ran to 55 in handicap at Wolverhampton final one: best form at 5f: acts on fibresand, best form on turf on a sound surface: blinkered last 2 starts: normally held up. *B. P. J. Baugh*

BOGART 5 gr.g. Belfort (FR) 89 – Larnem 43 (Meldrum 112) [1995 59: a7g⁴ a7g³ – 7.5m 5.9m 7m² 7m³ 8f 7.1m 7m³ 7f³ a7g⁴ 7m 8.1s a7g² a7g⁵ 1996 a8g a8g 7g a7s Dec 19] tall, angular gelding: modest handicapper: well beaten in 1996: stays 7f: acts on equitrack and on firm ground, possibly not on soft: visored (not well drawn) final 5-y-o start. *C. W. Fairhurst*

BOLD ACRE 6 ch.g. Never So Bold 135 – Nicola Wynn 83 (Nicholas Bill 125) – [1995 –: a9.4g 10f a12g 1996 a11g⁵ Jan 22] no form on flat since 1994: fair hurdler: has joined J. M. Bradley. *D. Burchell*

BOLD AFRICAN 2 b.g. (Feb 8) Emarati (USA) 74 – White African (Carwhite 79 127) [1996 5g⁵ 5g⁴ 5.1g 5m³ 5m² 5.1m² 5f² 5f² 5.7m³ 5m 5m* 5f* 5.3f³ 5m* 5s² 5.3f⁴ 5m Sep 19] 1,750F, 3,800Y: good-quartered gelding: has a roundish action: third foal: brother to 3-y-o White Emir, 5f winner at 2 yrs: dam unraced: fairly useful form: successful in claimer at Musselburgh in July and nurseries at Thirsk and Haydock in August: good second to For Old Times Sake in £6,200 event at Ripon on third-last outing: probably best at 5f: acts on any going: best form in blinkers/visor: has had tongue tied down: races prominently: tough. *P. D. Evans*

BOLD AMUSEMENT 6 ch.g. Never So Bold 135 – Hysterical 68 (High Top 74 131) [1995 84: 8.9m 10.4m 8.5m* 8f⁵ 8m⁵ 10.3d 8.5d 7m 1996 a8g 8d 9m² 9.2g⁵ 10m⁶ 8.3m² 8.3f 9m 12g⁵ Oct 26] strong gelding: fair handicapper: stays 1½m: acts on good to firm and soft ground, possibly not on firm: seems effective blinkered or not: reportedly suffered irregular heartbeat second 6-y-o start. *W. S. Cunningham*

BOLD ANGEL   9 b.g. Lochnager 132 – Lobela 77 (Lorenzaccio 130) [1995 73:   49
7g⁵ 6m 7m⁵ 7m³ 7m* a7g⁵ 7.6m² 7.1d 8g² 8g 8.2m⁵ 1996 7g³ 8.3m³ 8.2g⁵ 8m Oct
28] strong, close-coupled gelding: carries condition: has been fired: has a round
action: only poor for new stable in 1996: probably stays 1m: acts on any going:
blinkered once at 3 yrs: usually held up. *K. A. Morgan*

BOLD ARISTOCRAT (IRE)   5 b.g. Bold Arrangement 127 – Wyn Mipet   –
(Welsh Saint 126) [1995 36, a53: a6g a6g³ a6g³ a7g 7d 8g a7g⁴ a6g* a6g³ a6g⁵ 7m   a63
6g⁵ 6d⁵ a7g⁶ a8g a6g a6g 1996 a6g a6g a6g* a6g⁶ a6g⁵ a6g³ a6g* a6g a6g⁵ 5.9d
a6g a5g⁴ a6g² a6g a6g³ a6g² a6g² a6s a6g² Dec 27] quite attractive gelding: modest
performer on the all-weather: won claimer and selling handicap at Southwell early
on: should stay 7f: acts on firm and dead ground and on fibresand: has worn pricker
near side: usually held up: tends to carry head high. *R. Hollinshead*

BOLD BRIEF   2 b.g. (Apr 22) Tina's Pet 121 – Immodest Miss 73 (Daring   65
Display (USA) 129) [1996 5m 5d⁶ 5m⁵ 5m* 6g⁶ 5g⁵ 6g Aug 16] 2,600F, 3,900Y:
leggy, close-coupled gelding: has a round action: closely related to fairly useful 5f (at
2 yrs) and 7f winner Itsagame (by Mummy's Game) and half-brother to useful 1985
2-y-o 5f and 6f winner Prince Pecadillo (by Dragonara Palace) and a winner abroad:
dam won 1¼m seller: ready winner of maiden auction at Ayr in June: struggled
afterwards, stiff task in nursery (carried head high) final outing: should stay 6f: acts
on good to firm ground. *Denys Smith*

BOLD BUSTER   3 b.g. Bustino 136 – Truly Bold 76 (Bold Lad (IRE) 133) [1995   – p
NR 1996 10s Oct 24] 24,000Y: third foal: good-topped gelding: half-brother to sprint
winners Dead Calm (by Another Realm) and Hever Golf Star (by Efisio): dam ran
twice at 2 yrs: 20/1 and burly, remote eighth in maiden at Newbury: should do better.
I. A. Balding

BOLD CATCH (USA)   2 ch.c. (Jan 28) Diesis 133 – Social Wish (USA)   85 +
(Lyphard's Wish (FR) 124) [1996 5m⁵ 5m⁵ 5.1m* 6f⁴ 6d³ Aug 24] small colt: has a
round action: second foal: half-brother to a winner in USA: dam unraced half-sister
to very smart 1¼m winner Two Timing out of half-sister to champion US filly Chris
Evert: won maiden at Nottingham in June: very good third in nursery at Newmarket:
subsequently sold 27,000 gns Newmarket Autumn Sales: stays 6f: acts on good to
firm and dead ground: best form held up: sent to USA. *R. Charlton*

BOLD CLASSIC (IRE)   3 b.c. Persian Bold 123 – Bay Street 117 (Grundy 137)   83
[1995 7g⁴ 7.5g⁵ 1996 10f 12.1d⁴ 14.1f² 14.1f* 14.1f* 17.2m² 16.1m 17.2d⁶ Sep 30] tall,
ex-German colt: half-brother to numerous winners, including very useful Bex
(middle distances, by Explodent): dam 7f and 8.5f winner: ran in 2 German maidens
at 2 yrs: fairly useful form here: won handicap at Yarmouth in July: ran poorly last 2
outings: sold (J. Dunlop to C. Grant) 25,000 gns Newmarket Autumn Sales: looks a
thorough stayer: acts on firm ground: visored final 3-y-o start. *J. L. Dunlop*

BOLD DEMAND   2 b.c. (Feb 7) Rainbow Quest (USA) 134 – Dafrah (USA) 78   72 p
(Danzig (USA)) [1996 8d⁴ Nov 8] big, lengthy colt: has scope: second foal:
closely related to Irish 3-y-o Dafwan (by Nashwan): dam 1m winner out of smart
winner at up to 11f Capo di Monte, the family of Nashwan and Unfuwain: odds on
though green and on toes, around 7 lengths fourth of 6 to Catienus in minor event at
Doncaster, off bridle 2f out, not knocked about when held: likely to improve.
Saeed bin Suroor

BOLD EFFORT (FR)   4 b.g. Bold Arrangement 127 – Malham Tarn (Riverman   92 +
(USA) 131) [1995 101: a7g² a6g* a5g³ a6g* a6g 6m 6m* 7f³ 6g² 6m* 6m 6g 5.6m²
6g 5d 6g⁵ 6d 1996 7m 6f 6f 7.1d⁶ 6f 6m 8d* 5g³ 5.6m 6s* 5g 6d a6g* Dec 20]
good-quartered, dipped-backed gelding: poor mover: only fairly useful form in 1996:
disappointing in first half of year: sent to France and won minor event at
Clairefontaine in August and valuable handicap at Maisons-Laffitte in September:
returned to win handicap at Lingfield in December: effective at 5f, and stays 1m: acts
on good to firm and soft ground and the all-weather: effective blinkered/visored or
not: often makes running/races prominently. *K. O. Cunningham-Brown*

BOLD ELECT   8 b.g. Electric 126 – Famous Band (USA) (Banderilla (USA))   54
[1995 –: 9.9m 12.3f⁴ 1996 a14.8g 16.2m 17.1g 13s 12m³ 12.3m² 14.1f* 15.1g* Jul
1] sturdy, lengthy gelding: carries condition: modest handicapper: back to form for

new stable: won at Redcar in June and at Musselburgh in July: effective at 1½m and stays 2m: acts on any going: usually held up. *E. J. Alston*

BOLD ENGAGEMENT 2 b.f. (Apr 13) Never So Bold 135 – Diamond House – (Habitat 134) [1996 7m Oct 8] 700F, 1,600Y: sixth foal: sister to 3-y-o Bright Diamond and 1m winner Bold Jewel and half-sister to 7.6f (at 2 yrs) and 1½m winner Kimberley Boy (by Mtoto): dam sister to useful filly Life At The Top (stayed 1¼m): in rear in claimer at Redcar. *M. Dods*

BOLD ENOUGH 3 ch.f. Bold Arrangement 127 – Sweet Enough 79 (Caerleon 55 (USA) 132) [1995 63+: 6f 6m 5.7h⁴ 6d³ 7d* 7s⁶ a7g 1996 7f 8g⁴ 8g³ 8f⁵ 8m 7g⁶ 10g 10.1m³ Oct 23] smallish, good-topped filly: modest handicapper: sold 8,000 gns Newmarket Autumn Sales: stays 10.1f: acts on good to firm ground, may be unsuited by very soft/fibresand. *B. W. Hills*

BOLDER STILL 3 ch.g. Never So Bold 135 – Glenfinlass (Lomond (USA) 128) – [1995 NR 1996 10g 7m⁶ Aug 15] compact gelding: second foal: dam out of very useful 7f and 10.5f winner Glowing With Pride: still in need of race, signs of ability in 7f maiden at Salisbury, left behind from 3f out. *R. T. Phillips*

BOLD FRONTIER 4 gr.g. Chief Singer 131 – Mumtaz Flyer (USA) (Al Hattab (USA)) [1995 58, a75: a6g² a7g⁴ a6g⁴ 5g⁴ᵈⁱˢ a6g² a5g* 1996 a6g Dec 20] fair handicapper: off course 20 months, signs of retaining some ability at Lingfield on belated return: effective at 5f to 7f: acts on fibresand, probably on equitrack: effective blinkered/visored or not: has worn bandages. *K. T. Ivory*

BOLD FUTURE (IRE) 3 b.g. Treasure Kay 114 – Mother Courage 67 (Busted – 134) [1995 –: 6m 7g 6g 1996 8g 10g Aug 17] tall, lengthy gelding: no form: tried blinkered: dead. *J. W. Watts*

BOLD GAYLE 2 ch.f. (Feb 24) Never So Bold 135 – Storm Gayle (IRE) (Sadler's 49 p Wells (USA) 132) [1996 5g⁵ 5m Sep 18] first foal: dam, showed signs of ability, daughter of sprinting half-sister to smart sprinter Ubedizzy and Middle Park winner Cajun: signs of ability, late headway, in maidens at Hamilton (slowly away) and Beverley: bred to be a sprinter: sure to do better. *Mrs J. R. Ramsden*

BOLD HABIT 11 ch.g. Homing 130 – Our Mother 95 (Bold Lad (IRE) 133) 44 [1995 67, a57: a8g² a8g³ 8m a8g 8d* a10g⁵ 1996 7f 8g 8m 6.9m a9.4g a8g 6.9g⁶ 8.2g a10g⁵ a11g⁴ Dec 27] sturdy, strong-quartered gelding: carries condition: very much on the downgrade: stays 8.5f: acts on any going except very soft: blinkered/visored once each, and below form: held up. *J. Pearce*

BOLD JOKER 5 b.g. Jester 119 – Bold Difference 66 (Bold Owl 101) [1995 –: 10m 13.8f⁶ 11f 1996 a8g⁶ 10m 14.1f 15.1m a14g Nov 22] lightly-made gelding: no sign of ability. *G. R. Oldroyd*

BOLD MOTION 2 b.f. (May 18) Anshan 119 – Fast Motion 86 (Midsummer Night II 117) [1996 7g 7f³ a6g 10f Oct 14] 3,000F: unfurnished filly: half-sister to several winners here and abroad, notably high-class middle-distance colt Raami (by Be My Guest): dam 2-y-o 6f winner: poor form in sellers: should stay 1¼m. *C. Murray*

BOLD ORIENTAL (IRE) 2 b.c. (Apr 17) Tirol 127 – Miss Java 78 (Persian 79 Bold 123) [1996 6s 6d² 6f³ 6m 7f⁴ 6g⁶ 5.3f² 8m 8m* Sep 26] 30,000F, IR 70,000Y: useful-looking colt, rather leggy: third foal: half-brother to 1994 2-y-o 5f winner Noosa (by Petorius): dam, 1m winner who stayed 11.5f, out of half-sister to good 2-y-o's Welsh Harmony and Sovereign Crest: fairly useful form: won nursery at Goodwood in September: likely to stay 1¼m: acts on good to firm and dead ground: blinkered (below form) sixth start. *N. A. Callaghan*

BOLD PATRIOT (IRE) 3 b.c. Polish Patriot (USA) 128 – Don't Be Cruel 79 (Persian Bold 123) [1995 60: 6m 7d 1996 6.9m⁵ 8d* 8g⁶ Jun 8] useful-looking colt: fair performer: improved to win minor event at Ayr in May, making all: ran poorly in handicap at Doncaster: sold (J. Hills to Bob Jones) only 3,200 gns Newmarket September Sales: will stay beyond 1m: acts on dead ground. *J. W. Hills*

BOLD PURSUIT (IRE) 7 b.g. Thatching 131 – Pursue 78 (Auction Ring (USA) 54 123) [1995 –: a14g³ 1996 a12g⁶ a12g⁵ a12g⁶ 12d* 12.3g⁴ a12g Apr 29] tall, lengthy gelding: modest form in 1996, winning seller at Beverley: stayed 1½m: acted on good to firm and dead ground and on fibresand: held up: often soon off bridle: tried blinkered: pulled up lame final start: dead. *J. G. FitzGerald*

BOLD RESOLUTION (IRE)   8 b.g. Shardari 134 – Valmarine (FR) (Val de   75
Loir 133) [1995 NR 1996 14m² Jun 15] rated 80 on his day at 6 yrs: keeping-on
second of 8 in steadily-run handicap at Sandown on first run for 21 months: suited by
a test of stamina: acts on good to firm and soft ground: usually held up. *C. A. Cyzer*

BOLD REVIVAL   4 b.f. Never So Bold 135 – Convivial 81 (Nordance (USA))   –
[1995 56d: 7.5m⁶ 6f² 6m 6.1d 1996 7d Apr 4] good-topped filly: poor maiden plater:
dead. *Mrs P. Sly*

BOLD RISK   2 b.c. (Mar 8) Midyan (USA) 124 – Madam Bold (Never So Bold   66
135) [1996 5g³ 5d⁵ Jun 8] leggy colt: third foal: half-brother to 3-y-o Willie Miles (by
Dancing Dissident) and 1994 2-y-o 5f winner Rigsby (by Fools Holme): dam
(unraced) from family of Sigy and Sonoma: third in maiden at Newcastle in May: not
seen out after June: looked sure to improve over sprint distances: sold 3,800 gns
Newmarket Autumn Sales. *J. Berry*

BOLD SAINT (IRE)   2 b.c. (Apr 19) Persian Bold 123 – St Clair Star (Sallust   61 ?
134) [1996 7f⁶ 8g Sep 7] IR 26,000F, IR 30,000Y: seventh foal: closely related to
1991 Irish 2-y-o 6f winner Echo Rock (by Ballad Rock) and half-brother to 3
winners, including 7f and 1m winner Clairification (by Shernazar): dam, winner in
Canada, is half-sister to Superlative: never a threat in maidens at Salisbury and
Thirsk: not bred to stay much beyond 1m. *P. W. Harris*

BOLD SPRING (IRE)   2 b.c. (Feb 28) Never So Bold 135 – Oasis (Valiyar 129)   77
[1996 6s 6.1g⁴ 6.1m³ 5.7m⁶ 6g² 7d 6.1s a7g² a6g³ Dec 13] tall, good-topped colt: has
scope: second foal: half-brother to 3-y-o 7f winner White Settler (by Polish Patriot):
dam winner twice over hurdles, half-sister to smart 1995 2-y-o Magic Ring: fair
form: stays 7f: best form on a sound surface on turf, acts on equitrack: visored (raced
too freely) sixth outing. *R. Hannon*

BOLD STREET (IRE)   6 ch.g. Shy Groom (USA) – Ferry Lane (Dom Racine   68
(FR) 121) [1995 72: a7g a6g³ 6.1m 6g 5g 6g 6s a6g⁵ a6g³ a6g 1996 6d² 5g⁴ 6d
a6g⁶ a6g a6g² 7.1s a7g⁴ a7g⁴ Nov 15] workmanlike gelding: fair handicapper:
should stay 7f: acts on all-weather surfaces and soft going: usually blinkered/visored:
inconsistent at 6 yrs. *A. Bailey*

BOLD TIME MONKEY   5 ch.m. Bold Owl 101 – Play For Time (Comedy Star   –
(USA) 121) [1995 NR 1996 a6g a9.4g 6f 6m a7g Jun 8] sparely-made mare: rated 58
at 2 yrs for Jack Berry: well beaten in 1996. *M. Tate*

BOLD TINA (IRE)   2 b.f. (Mar 20) Persian Bold 123 – Tinas Image (He Loves   68
Me 120) [1996 5.1m² 5f³ 5.1m³ 6m⁵ 7f Oct 14] leggy, close-coupled filly: sixth foal:
half-sister to several winners, including useful 6f to 1m performer Indian Fly (by
Indian Ridge) and 1m/8.3f winner Tony's Mist (by Digamist): dam showed little
ability: modest form: will probably prove best at 5f: raced only on top-of-the-ground:
takes a keen hold. *R. Hannon*

BOLD TOP   4 ch.g. Bold Owl 101 – Whirlygigger 69 (Taufan (USA) 119) [1995   43
45: 12m 14.1m 10m³ 9f 9.9m² 10m² 10m 10.4g 10.4m 1996 12d³ 12.3g 16.2m 14.1m
12f³ 12f 10m² 9.9g 10g³ 10m⁵ 12m 10.1m a11g Nov 18] close-coupled gelding: poor
maiden handicapper: best at up to 1½m: acts on firm ground and dead, ran poorly on
fibresand: effective in blinkers/visor or not: inconsistent. *B. S. Rothwell*

BOLD WELCOME   2 ch.g. (Feb 10) Most Welcome 131 – Song's Best (Never   66
So Bold 135) [1996 5.1d⁵ 5.1m² 5g⁴ Jun 15] 35,000Y: tall, rather leggy gelding: third
foal: half-brother to useful 4-y-o sprinter Lennox Lewis (by Superpower): dam
unraced half-sister to Reesh: in frame in median auction maidens in the Midlands:
not seen out after June: will be suited by further than 5f: early to post all starts.
J. Wharton

BOLD WORDS (CAN)   2 ch.c. (Mar 1) Bold Ruckus (USA) – Trillium Woods   90 p
(USA) (Briartic (CAN)) [1996 7g 7m 8d* 8g* 10g Nov 2] $110,000Y: strong,
lengthy colt: second foal: dam, won at up to 9f in USA, closely related to smart
Grade 1 9f/1¼m winner Exchange: found his form in the autumn, winning maiden at
Salisbury and nursery at Newmarket: seemed not to stay 1¼m (travelled well then
unable to sustain effort) when seventh of 10 to Silver Patriarch in steadily-run
listed race at Newmarket on final start: likely to make useful colt at around 1m.
E. A. L. Dunlop

BOLERO BOY 2 b.c. (Apr 18) Rambo Dancer (CAN) 107 – Barrie Baby 86 97 (Import 127) [1996 5g⁵ 5m³ᵈⁱˢ 5g² 5g* 5f⁴ 6m³ 7m⁴ 8m 6m² 7g² Oct 10] 6,000Y: strong, workmanlike colt: has scope: has a quick action: fifth foal: brother to 4-y-o Barballen: dam, 7f to 9f winner, stayed 1¼m: useful form: won maiden at Newcastle in May: showed plenty of improvement afterwards, best effort when second to Blues Queen in nursery at Ayr on penultimate start: best form at 6f/7f: raced only on a sound surface: sold 42,000 gns Newmarket Autumn Sales. *M. W. Easterby*

BOLIVAR (IRE) 4 b.g. Kahyasi 130 – Shuss (USA) (Princely Native (USA)) 77 [1995 12m⁴ 12f³ 11g⁵ 10m⁶ 14g⁶ 12g 12.5g* 1996 12m 14d 16m⁴ 16.2f* 16.2m* 14.8d⁵ Aug 23] well-made ex-Irish gelding: carries condition: fourth reported foal: half-brother to minor sprint winner in USA by Smart Style: dam minor US winner: fair handicapper: trained at 3 yrs by J. Oxx, winning maiden at Thurles: won handicaps at Ascot in June and July: a stayer: acts on firm ground (acts in the mud over hurdles): goes well in blinkers: genuine. *R. Akehurst*

BOLLERO (IRE) 2 b.f. (May 12) Topanoora 118 – Charo (Mariacci (FR) 133) 61 [1996 5s² a5g³ 5g² 6g* 6m 6g⁴ 6g 6m Sep 14] IR 5,000Y: tall filly: has scope: half-sister to 1987 2-y-o 6f winner Superbest (by Try My Best), 5f (at 2 yrs) to 10.3f winner Bescaby Boy (by Red Sunset) and a winner abroad: dam, Irish 1½m winner, is out of sister to high-class sprinter On Your Mark: won maiden auction at Hamilton in June: stiff tasks afterwards: will be well suited by 7f+: acts on soft ground. *J. Berry*

BOLLIN DOROTHY 3 b.f. Rambo Dancer (CAN) 107 – Bollin Harriet 60 (Lochnager 132) [1995 73: 6d² 5f³ 5m² 1996 8g 6g 7s* 7m 6m⁵ 6d 6f⁶ 7.1s⁵ Oct 5] strong filly: modest performer: won maiden at Catterick in July, making most: stays 7f: acts on firm and soft ground: inconsistent. *T. D. Easterby*

BOLLIN FRANK 4 b.c. Rambo Dancer (CAN) 107 – Bollin Emily 82 75 (Lochnager 132) [1995 62: 7.1g⁴ 6m⁶ 8m⁴ 6g⁵ 7f³ 6g 8.1m* 7.5g⁶ 8m 7.9g³ 8.1g 8.1s² 1996 8m⁵ 8m² 8.5g² 8.1d* 8.1d* 10f⁵ 7.9g 9g³ 8d² 8m 8g Oct 19] good-topped colt: good walker: fair handicapper: won at Haydock in May and June: best at up to 9f: probably acts on any ground, goes particularly well with some give: blinkered (bit below form) once at 3 yrs: sometimes hangs: often a front runner: game and genuine. *T. D. Easterby*

BOLLIN HARRY 4 b.c. Domynsky 110 – Bollin Harriet (Lochnager 132) [1995 82 70: 6g* 6g⁴ 5g* 5g⁵ 6f⁴ 6m² 5m⁶ 5g 7.1g⁵ 6s 1996 5s² 5g⁵ 6.1g* 6m² 6m 6m* 6g⁵ 5m 6m 6m 6v 5g Oct 19] robust, full-quartered colt: impresses in appearance: fairly useful handicapper: won at Nottingham (despite all but unseating rider when stumbling leaving stalls) in April and Pontefract in June: probably stays 7f: acts on good to firm and soft ground: races prominently. *T. D. Easterby*

BOLLIN JACOB 3 b.c. Efisio 120 – Bollin Emily 82 (Lochnager 132) [1995 NR 62 1996 8g 7d⁴ 7g 8g 8g³ 8.1d⁶ 10m Jun 17] strong, close-coupled colt: poor mover: fifth foal: half-brother to 4-y-o 1m winner Bollin Frank (by Rambo Dancer): dam sprinter: modest maiden handicapper: didn't get run of race last 2 starts: stays 1m: acts on dead ground. *T. D. Easterby*

BOLLIN JOANNE 3 b.f. Damister (USA) 123 – Bollin Zola 90 (Alzao (USA) 100 117) [1995 75: 5g² 1996 6g² 7g⁴ 6m² 7.9m² 7.1d³ 6g* 6m* 6g⁵ 6m 6g* Oct 12] strong, close-coupled filly: useful handicapper: won at Catterick (maiden) in July, Ripon in August and at York (23-runner £17,600 contest, improved effort, beat Double Splendour by 2 lengths, travelling strongly just off pace and asserting 1f out) in October: has form at up to 1m, but best as a sprinter: acts on good to firm and dead ground: bandaged since fifth 3-y-o start. *T. D. Easterby*

BOLLIN TERRY 2 b.c. (Mar 9) Terimon 124 – Bollin Zola 90 (Alzao (USA) 58 p 117) [1996 7m 6g⁵ 8.1m⁵ Sep 6] quite good-topped colt: fourth foal: half-brother to 3-y-o 6f winner Bollin Joanne (by Damister): dam 5f (at 2 yrs) and 7.6f winner: progressive form: considerably handicapped when still on burly side final outing: not certain to stay much beyond 1m: capable of better. *T. D. Easterby*

BOLSHOI (IRE) 4 br.g. Royal Academy (USA) 130 – Mainly Dry (The 103 Brianstan 128) [1995 74: 5m* 6.1g 6.1m² 5m⁴ 6g 6m 1996 6s 6m⁴ 5m* 5g² 6m² 6f⁵ 5g⁴ 5m* 5m 5m* 6m⁴ 6g⁴ 5.6m⁵ 6m 5g* 5d⁴ 5g Oct 19] tall, lengthy gelding: made into a useful handicapper: won at Doncaster (claimer) in May, Beverley and Ascot (rated stakes) in July and at Ascot (another rated stakes after 4 good efforts in defeat in some of the top handicaps) in September: effective at 5f and 6f: acts on good to firm and dead ground: usually blinkered: often held up: ridden by Emma O'Gorman for last 3 successes: tough and consistent. *J. Berry*

BOMBAY SAPPHIRE 3 b.f. Be My Chief (USA) 122 – Ginny Binny 113 – (Ahonoora 122) [1995 NR 1996 7d 7g 7m⁶ Jun 6] well-made filly: fourth foal: sister to fairly useful 1995 3-y-o 1m and 9.2f winner My Gina: dam won in Italy: well beaten in maidens. *R. Hannon*

BONANZA PEAK (USA) 3 b.c. Houston (USA) – Bunnicula (USA) (Shadeed – (USA) 135) [1995 NR 1996 10.4g⁶ 10s Oct 24] $50,000Y: sturdy compact colt: second reported foal: half-brother to French 1¼m to 11f winner Fenicula (by Bering): dam unraced half-sister to smart sprinter Gwydion: bit backward, 11¼ lengths sixth of 10 in maiden at York, running on steadily, never dangerous: showed little on soft ground 2 weeks later. *Mrs J. Cecil*

BONARELLI (IRE) 3 b.c. Dancing Dissident (USA) 119 – Sovereign Dona 117 99 (Sovereign Path 125) [1995 100p: 7m² 7m* 8.1m* 8g* 1996 9m 10.3g⁵ 8m 8.2d² 8f Sep 13] sturdy, attractive colt: fluent mover: useful performer: seems to stay 10.3f: acts on good to firm and dead ground: visored (raced freely) second 3-y-o start: leary (well beaten) final start: sometimes sweats: sent to UAE. *M. R. Stoute*

BON GUEST (IRE) 2 ch.c. (Mar 23) Kefaah (USA) 124 – Uninvited Guest 57 64 ? (Be My Guest (USA) 126) [1996 5m 6m 7f Oct 15] IR 600F, IR 2,600Y: fifth reported foal: dam placed at up to 7f in Ireland: modest form: apparently easily best effort second outing: likely to stay at least 1m. *T. J. Naughton*

BON LUCK (IRE) 4 ch.g. Waajib 121 – Elle Va Bon (Tanfirion 110) [1995 72: 75 7g 7.1g² 7f⁴ 1996 7s⁵ 8.1m² 8.5m² 8.1d⁴ 8m⁴ Sep 21] fair handicapper: sold (J. Fanshawe to J. A. Bennett) 8,000 gns Newmarket Autumn Sales: stays 8.5f: acts on any going: blinkered last 2 starts at 2 yrs: consistent. *J. R. Fanshawe*

BONNE ETOILE 4 b.f. Diesis 133 – Bonne Ile 115 (Ile de Bourbon (USA) 133) – [1995 94p: 8d² 8f* 8f* 10.1g* 1996 10m Jul 27] tall, rather lightly-made filly: progressive form in 1995: just in need of race after 11-month absence, last of 11 in rated stakes at Ascot, improving home turn then fading and eased: better at 1¼m than 1m (dam seemed to stay 1¾m): acts on firm and dead ground: flashes tail and carries head awkwardly. *D. R. Loder*

BONNE VILLE 2 gr.f. (Apr 29) Good Times (ITY) – Ville Air 85 (Town Crier 58 119) [1996 8.1m 10.2d⁵ a8.5g* a8.5g a8g² Nov 29] 1,800Y: fifth foal: sister to middle-distance maiden Air Time and half-sister to 3-y-o 5f (at 2 yrs) and 1½m winner The Butterwick Kid (by Interrex): dam 2-y-o 6f winner on only start: won seller at Wolverhampton in October: will stay at least 1¼m: acts on fibresand. *B. Palling*

BONNIE LASSIE 2 gr.f. (Feb 23) Efisio 120 – Normanby Lass 100 (Bustino 69 136) [1996 5g⁵ 6m³ 7g³ a8g* Nov 4] leggy filly: sixth foal: half-sister to fair a74 middle-distance stayer Keep Your Distance (by Elegant Air): dam 2-y-o 7f winner: won median auction maiden at Southwell in November by 10 lengths: will prob-ably stay 1¼m: acts well on fibresand: didn't handle home bend well at Catterick. *C. W. Thornton*

BONNY MELODY 5 b.m. Sizzling Melody 117 – Bonny Quiver 67 (Gorytus 49 (USA) 132) [1995 52d, a42d: a7g a8.5g⁶ 6s 6m 6.1m 6f⁶ a5g* 5m⁴ 5.1g 5m a6g a5g* a– a5g 5m⁶ 5.1m 6g 5g a5g⁶ a6g 1996 a5g 5s³ Mar 25] smallish mare: has a quick action: modest handicapper: effective at 5f to 7f: acts on any going, including fibresand: blinkered/visored (below form) once each: usually waited with, and suited by strongly-run race: none too consistent: covered by Cosmonaut. *P. D. Evans*

BON SECRET (IRE) 4 b.g. Classic Secret (USA) 91 – Bon Retour (Sallust 134) – [1995 –, a71: a5g* a5g³ a6g³ a5g⁴ a5g* a5g⁶ a6g² a6g² a6g* a6g⁵ a8g² a8g 7.1d a7g a71 1996 a7g a8g* a10g³ a10g³ Dec 30] fair all-weather handicapper: back to best to win claimer at Lingfield in December by 5 lengths: effective at 5f to 1m: has form on firm ground and fibresand, but seems best on equitrack: effective from front or held up. *T. J. Naughton*

BONSIEL 2 b.f. (May 10) Skyliner 117 – Shawiniga 58 (Lyphard's Wish (FR) 43 124) [1996 a5g a7g² a6g⁶ 6m Aug 10] 900Y: second reported foal: dam won in France at 2 yrs and from 5f to 8.5f here as 4-y-o: second in seller at Southwell in

July: showed nothing on turf: stays 7f: sold 1,600 gns Doncaster September Sales. *J. G. FitzGerald*

BOOGIE BOPPER (IRE)   7 b.g. Taufan (USA) 119 – Mey 78 (Canisbay 120)   – §
[1995 NR 1996 a16.2g a16g Aug 10] sold out of M. Pipe's stable 900 gns Ascot June Sales: seemed of little account on return. *B. A. Pearce*

BOOJUM   2 b.f. (Apr 30) Mujtahid (USA) 118 – Haboobti (Habitat 134) [1996   101
6.1m* 7m² 7g⁴ 7m 7.3s* 6.5d⁶ Nov 9] 27,000Y: lengthy filly: has a quick action: fifth foal: half-sister to useful 3-y-o 7f and 8.2f winner Abeyr (by Unfuwain): dam lightly-raced daughter of sister to high-class miler Noalcoholic: useful form: successful in maiden (dead-heated) at Nottingham in June and listed Radley Stakes (led close home after leaders had gone too fast) at Newbury in October: ran very well when sixth to Deadly Dudley in Criterium des Deux Ans at Evry on final outing: will stay 1m: acts on good to firm ground, goes well on soft. *B. W. Hills*

BOOST   4 b.g. Superpower 113 – Sirene Bleu Marine (USA) (Secreto (USA) 128)   –
[1995 46: 6g 7m⁵ 7m⁴ 7m2 7f³ 8g 7f⁶ 7m 7m⁶ 1996 a10g⁶ a7g⁵ a7g⁵ 6m 10m 8m⁶
Aug 8] sturdy gelding: poor maiden: well below form for new stable in 1996: should stay 1m: acts on firm ground: tried visored/blinkered, no improvement. *Mrs N. Macauley*

BOOZEROO   3 ch.g. Never So Bold 135 – Show Home 90 (Music Boy 124)   –
[1995 NR 1996 8d Mar 21] 11,500Y: angular gelding: fourth live foal: half-brother to fairly useful winners Musica (5.3f, by Primo Dominie) and Scottish Castle (7f, by Scottish Reel): dam 2-y-o 5f winner probably stayed 6f: tailed off in maiden at Doncaster. *M. R. Channon*

BORN A LADY   3 ch.f. Komaite (USA) – Lucky Candy 61 (Lucky Wednesday   53
124) [1995 70: a5g* 6f⁶ 5g² 5g⁴ 6f³ 5g⁵ 5f³ 6.1m⁴ 1996 a5g⁴ a5g⁶ a6g³ 6.1g 6.1m a5g
5g 8f 8m 8.2m³ 8m³ 8.5m⁵ 8f³ 8f⁴ a6g 10d 8.5m 10f⁴ Sep 23] useful-looking filly: has a round action: only modest at best in 1996: left N. Littmoden's stable after second start: stays 1m: acts on firm ground and fibresand: often blinkered/visored: sometimes reluctant at stalls: went in snatches final 3-y-o start: usually races prominently. *S. R. Bowring*

BORN ON THE WILD   3 b.f. Golden Lahab (USA) – First Born 43 (Be My   –
Native (USA) 122) [1995 NR 1996 6g 7g Sep 21] first foal: dam maiden: well beaten in maidens. *S. E. Kettlewell*

BOSRA SHAM (USA)   3 ch.f. Woodman (USA) 126 – Korveya (USA) 116   132
(Riverman (USA) 131) [1995 115p: 6m* 8d* 1996 7.3d* 8m* 8m2 10g*
Oct 19]

'And the nominations are . . .' There are so many awards ceremonies nowadays that it can't be long before one of those recipients 'who is unable to be present tonight' makes his or her 'live' acceptance speech from the venue of a different awards ceremony, rather than from the dressing room of a West End theatre or the side of a swimming pool in California. Yet, even as more award ceremonies spring up, there are still some who continue to invest them with a significance out of all proportion to that which they deserve. The Labour Party's campaign headquarters, for example, was discovered encouraging its members to flood Radio 4's *Today* programme with nominations for Tony Blair as Personality of the Year. Senior managers at the BBC decided to close nominations as soon as the 'rigging' was discovered, before Mr Blair had received enough support to make the final short-list of six, and then made adjustments to take into account irregularities in the voting for John Major (who was nonetheless still the winner!). Members of the BBC themselves came under suspicion when Hills suspended betting on the BBC Sports Personality of the Year after betting activity and a tip-off from a mystery caller strongly suggested that the result had leaked out. Such incidents can only serve to make a cynical public even more apathetic about awards, and the star-studded ceremonies that so often go with them. One award in racing that has stood the test of time better than most is the original 'official' Horse of the Year award established by the Racecourse Association in 1965 and taken over by the Racegoers Club in 1978. It goes to the horse which, in the opinion of a voting

Pertemps One Thousand Guineas Stakes, Newmarket—
Bosra Sham is not on top form, but still finishes clear of Matiya and Bint Shadayid (left)

panel of twenty or so leading racing journalists, has 'contributed most to the interest, excitement and pleasure of racing during the year.' Bosra Sham was the latest winner, receiving eleven of the twenty votes, the others going to Pilsudski (four), Mark of Esteem (three) and Singspiel (two). Bosra Sham is the third filly to take the award in the past five years, following User Friendly in 1992 and Lochsong in 1993. Fillies have quite a good record, with Park Top, Dahlia (twice), Pawneese, Habibti and Pebbles among the earlier winners.

Given that horses which have not run in Britain during the year are ineligible (Helissio and Cigar, for example, didn't qualify) it still came as something of a surprise that Bosra Sham ran out such an emphatic winner. Mark of Esteem, who received Timeform's vote in the poll, had a similar record to Bosra Sham. Both were classic winners who went on to establish themselves as exceptional performers by beating the best of the older horses. Mark of Esteem beat Bosra Sham the only time they met, when the pair were first and second in the Queen Elizabeth II Stakes at Ascot. The pair certainly contributed greatly to the 'interest, excitement and pleasure of racing during the year', including playing major parts in the protracted battle between their respective stables to secure the trainers' championship.

Henry Cecil had seldom needed a boost more than the one provided by Bosra Sham's impressive victory over Bint Shadayid and Matiya in the Fillies' Mile at Ascot as a two-year-old. He was smarting from public criticism by Sheikh Mohammed only twenty-four hours before, following the Sheikh's decision to remove his horses, including Mark of Esteem, from Warren Place. Bosra Sham, described by Cecil as 'the best two-year-old filly I have had since Oh So Sharp' assumed the mantle of the Warren Place flagship in the latest season and was seldom out of the news. Cecil reported she had done well through the winter and was scarcely able to conceal his excitement when talking to journalists after a sparkling gallop by Bosra Sham just over a week before the Dubai Duty Free Fred Darling Stakes at Newbury in April. Starting at 9/2 on, Bosra Sham had to stretch only over the final furlong to record an impressive six-length victory, the 66/1-shot Keepers Dawn being the only serious challenger in a field of nine over the last two furlongs. The return to a mile in the Pertemps One Thousand Guineas seemed sure to suit Bosra Sham and with doubts growing about the participation of Cheveley Park winner Blue Duster and French challenger A Votre Sante, Bosra Sham, described by jockey Pat Eddery as 'brilliant . . . a proper champion' after the Fred Darling, was as short as 7/4 on for Newmarket afterwards. Ten days before the Guineas, however, Bosra Sham sustained a bruised near-fore foot which continued to cause concern right up to the day of the race. She had suffered a similar problem at two, missing the May Hill Stakes, and was rated only 'fifty-fifty' to line up two days before the Guineas when Cecil reported she was lame. 'Our farrier re-did her foot, re-shod her and built it up and by lunchtime she was sound,' reported Cecil. 'She won't run unless I think she can give one hundred per cent, but there's only one British classic for her as she's a miler and won't get a mile and a half.' Bosra Sham eased to 11/10 on and she kept her unbeaten record by a hard-fought length and a half from Matiya, with Bint Shadayid a head away third followed by Cheveley Park runner-up My Branch (in the second colours of Bosra Sham's owner) who was unlucky not to be placed after being short of room. Judged on the Fillies' Mile, in which Bosra Sham beat Bint Shadayid by three and a half lengths and Matiya by seven, there wasn't much room to doubt that Bosra Sham wasn't at her best on Guineas day. She edged left under the whip inside the final furlong, almost certainly feeling the weakness in her near-fore on the firmish ground, though the Newmarket stewards didn't see it that way, adjudging Eddery, who kept his whip in his right hand, guilty of careless riding and suspending him for two days. Bosra Sham's victory gave Eddery a long-awaited triumph in the one British classic that had eluded him and he went on to enjoy another splendid season, taking his total of British classic victories to thirteen with Lady Carla in the Oaks and also moving into third place, behind Sir Gordon Richards and Lester Piggott, in the all-time list of winning jockeys on the flat in Britain. With a charismatic figure like Dettori around it was all too easy to overlook such outstanding achievements. Eddery's victory in the jockeys' championship put him level on eleven titles with Piggott. Bosra Sham's Guineas victory also enabled her trainer to equal Dick Hern's tally of sixteen British classic winners, to which he added further when Lady Carla won the Oaks. Cecil confessed to feeling 'weak and tearful' at the tremendous reception he received as he made his way into the winner's enclosure to greet Bosra Sham. Here was a clear demonstration of the public's sympathy for Cecil in the face of the previous autumn's tribulations, something which continued to be felt as the battle with Godolphin's Saeed bin Suroor for the trainers' championship gathered momentum in the second half of the season.

Bosra Sham's continuing training troubles—she returned 'very sore and bleeding' after the Guineas—kept her off the course until the end of September. She missed successive engagements in the Coronation Stakes—the stable drew a blank at Royal Ascot for the first time in over twenty years—the Sussex Stakes at Goodwood and the Juddmonte International at York. After a gallop at Doncaster on St Leger day, she returned in the Queen Elizabeth II Stakes at Ascot which looked set to decide the milers' championship of Europe, six of the seven runners having won Group 1 events during the year. Bosra Sham confirmed herself much better than her Guineas form, leading early in the straight and, though going down by a length and a quarter to Mark of Esteem, drawing four lengths clear of third-placed First Island, with Charnwood Forest, Ashkalani, Bijou d'Inde and Soviet Line further behind in a race that lived up to its billing in no uncertain manner. Next stop for Bosra Sham was the Dubai Champion Stakes, back at Newmarket in October, when she ran into another Godolphin star, the dual Coral-Eclipse and Juddmonte International winner Halling. With Cecil now trailing by around £50,000 in the trainers' table, he and those working with Bosra Sham at Warren Place had to endure another anxious build-up as the filly suffered a recurrence of tenderness and bruising to her troublesome foot. Halling, unbeaten on turf for two seasons, started even-money favourite, Bosra Sham at 9/4 and the high-class Irish filly Timarida at 15/2, with 14/1 bar in a field of six. Bosra Sham's trainer informed readers of his column in *The Sporting Life* that 'the Queen Elizabeth II Stakes . . . has certainly done her a great deal of good and she seems to have come on quite a bit if her homework is anything to go by.' Bosra Sham impressed in appearance, though she had gone in her coat, and put up another top-class performance to beat Halling by two and a half lengths, held up in steadily-run affair before being sent to the front with a little less than two furlongs to go and outspeeding Halling, drifting left in the closing stages. Timarida came third, just ahead of the Two Thousand Guineas runner-up Even Top with fifth-placed First Island beaten a little over half as far again by Bosra Sham as he had been

Dubai Champion Stakes, Newmarket—a really good field is left trailing by Bosra Sham at her best

at Ascot. The Newmarket winner's enclosure was host to more tumultuous scenes as Bosra Sham and, more particularly her trainer, who received three cheers, met another Cheltenham Festival-style reception. To his credit, Sheikh Mohammed, whose family sponsored the race, was first with congratulations on a victory that looked at the time as if it might well decide the trainers' championship (in fact the Godolphin operation regained the lead with victory in the last Group 1 of the season, the Racing Post Trophy). In a sporting moment to be remembered, Sheikh Mohammed took the edge off a potentially awkward situation by jokingly shying away, hand covering his heart, as he presented the trainer's prize, an ornamental Arabian dagger. Cecil joined in the play-acting by also shrinking back in mock horror. Godolphin will be increasing its strength in the next season but will not have Mark of Esteem or Halling, both of whom have been retired. Cecil, however, will have Bosra Sham, a filly who has turned out every bit as brilliant as her trainer always insisted—if anything, by our reckoning, a shade better than Oh So Sharp. If all remains well with her—the damaged outside wall of her foot should grow back over the winter—she is sure to have a big say in the destination of the major all-aged championship races at a mile and a mile and a quarter.

The rangy, attractive Bosra Sham is a rarity in more ways than one. At 530,000 guineas, the sum she made at the Houghton Sales, Bosra Sham was the highest-priced yearling sold in Britain and Ireland in 1994. The record of highly-priced yearlings generally illustrates the adage that the only way to make a small fortune out of owning racehorses is to start with a large one. The top-priced yearling of 1984, the Shergar colt Authaal, who still remains Europe's record-priced yearling at IR 3,100,000 guineas, won the Irish St Leger for Sheikh Mohammed, while another long-standing holder of the record, Sayajirao, whose 28,000-guinea purchase represented an enormous sum in 1945, won two classics, the St Leger and the Irish Derby before becoming a notable stallion. But the failures have far outnumbered the successes, the three holders of the record immediately before Authaal, for example, Trojan Prince, Convention and Hero Worship, all seven-figure purchases in 1983, turning out to be poor racehorses. Of the nine individual sale-toppers in Europe in the years between Authaal and Bosra Sham, only Richard of York and Song of Tara went on to achieve notable successes while the 2,400,000-guinea purchase Classic Music, a brother to Sadler's Wells, was among three who never even saw a racecourse. The benevolence of Bosra Sham's owner Wafic Said, a Saudi financier and construction magnate, has not, incidentally, been welcomed in some areas of British life as it has in racing and in the autumn the dons of Oxford University's congregation voted against the vice-chancellor's proposal to allocate a playing field for a business school to be built with a £20 million donation offered by Mr Said. By the time Bosra Sham passed through the sale-ring, her dam Korveya had already bred two winners of the Poule d'Essai des Poulains, Bosra Sham's full brother Hector Protector and Shanghai (by Procida). Bosra Sham's One Thousand Guineas success puts her dam in exalted company alongside such as Set Free (dam of Juliette Marny, Julio Mariner and Scintillate) and Irish Bird (dam of Bikala, Assert and Eurobird) who also

145

Mr Wafic Said's "Bosra Sham"

		⌠Mr Prospector	⌠Raise A Native
	⌠Woodman (USA)	⎨ (b 1970)	⎨Gold Digger
	⎟ (ch 1983)	⎩Playmate	⎩Buckpasser
Bosra Sham (USA)	⎨	(ch 1975)	⎩Intriguing
(ch.f. 1993)	⎟	⌠Riverman	⌠Never Bend
	⎩Korveya (USA)	⎨ (b 1969)	⎨River Lady
	(ch 1982)	⎩Konafa	⎩Damascus
		(b 1973)	⎩Royal Statute

produced three individual classic winners. All three of Korveya's famous winners, which have come from her first six foals of racing age, have been sired by sons of Mr Prospector. Korveya visited Mr Prospector himself in 1995 and 1996, the first of those matings producing a colt. Perhaps there will be more classic winners to come. Extensive details of Bosra Sham's pedigree were provided in *Racehorses of 1995*. Her dam was a smart racemare at up to nine furlongs and her grandam Konafa, also dam of the high-class sprinter Proskona, was second in the One Thousand Guineas. Konafa was a half-sister, among others, to the Yorkshire Oaks winner Awaasif, the grandam of Lammtarra who was out of Awaasif's 1989 Oaks winner Snow Bride. Three British classic winners—a One Thousand Guineas, a Derby and an Oaks—to add to the French, is some haul in an eight-year-period. *H. R. A. Cecil*

BOSTON ROCK (IRE) 4 ch.g. Ballad Rock 122 – Miss Boston (FR) (River River (FR) 117) [1995 –: 7.1m 1996 8g⁶ 8.5m 8s 9m² 10m⁶ Jun 27] big, strong gelding: fair maiden handicapper: may prove best at distances short of 1¼m: acts on good to firm ground, below form only start on soft. *P. W. Harris*   62

BOSTON TEA PARTY 3 b.f. Rambo Dancer (CAN) 107 – Tea-Pot 77 (Ragstone 128) [1995 40?: 6m 7.1m 6m³ 7g 6g a7g 1996 10f⁶ 12m a16g⁵ 11.9f a10g Dec 20] leggy filly: poor maiden plater: stays 2m. *A. Moore*   42 ?

BOUCHE BEE (USA) 4 b.f. Naevus (USA) – Miss Henderson Co (USA) (Silver Hawk (USA) 123) [1995 95: 7m 6g² 6m² 7g* 7m* 7g* 7f⁵ 7.9m⁵ 1996 5g² 6m 8g⁴   106

8g³ 6.5f 8.5f² 8f² Dec 4] lengthy ex-French filly: poor mover: useful performer, improved for new stable: no match for Anabaa in Prix de Saint-Georges at Longchamp: mid-division in Cork And Orrery Stakes at Royal Ascot: best efforts when just over a length fourth of 8 to Grey Risk in Prix Messidor and when 3¼ lengths third of 6 to Bin Rosie in listed race, both at Maisons-Laffitte: left J. Hammond and finished second in 2 allowance races at Hollywood Park: stays 8.5f: acts on firm going, unraced on a soft surface: sometimes bandaged behind. *W. Greenman, USA*

BOUNDARY BIRD (IRE)   3 b.g. Tirol 127 – Warning Sound (Red Alert 127)   –
[1995 56: 5f⁴ 6m a7g³ 8g 7d⁵ a8g 1996 8.3d 8g⁶ a7g a9.4g 8f⁶ 7d 15.1m⁶ Sep 23] big, leggy gelding: little sign of ability in 1996 and one to avoid: sold 1,100 gns Doncaster September Sales. *M. Johnston*

BOUNDARY EXPRESS   4 b.g. Sylvan Express 117 – Addison's Jubilee 73   –
(Sparkler 130) [1995 64: a9.4g² a8g⁶ a11g⁵ 11.1g⁴ 8m⁴ 12m⁴ 8.3g² 10m 9.2f⁵ a9.4g 12m* 14.1m³ 11.9g* 15g² 14s⁶ 14m⁴ 1996 14.1m May 10] workmanlike gelding: modest handicapper: tailed off only start in 1996: should stay 2m: acts on fibresand and good to firm ground, probably on soft: seems unsuited by blinkers/visor. *E. J. Alston*

BOURBONIST (FR)   3 b.g. Soviet Star (USA) 128 – Bourbon Topsy 108 (Ile de   63 p
Bourbon (USA) 133) [1995 NR 1996 8m Jun 5] third foal: half-brother to fair 1½m and 2m winner Anjou (by Saumarez): dam, middle-distance stayer, half-sister to top-class middle-distance performer Most Welcome out of smart half-sister to Teenoso: 20/1, tenth of 13 in steadily-run maiden at Yarmouth, already one paced when hampered 1f out: seemed likely to do better, particularly over further than 1m. *L. M. Cumani*

BOURDONNER   4 b.g. Pharly (FR) 130 – Buzzbomb 98 (Bustino 136) [1995   –
10s⁵ 12m 8g 13g² 14m³ 12m³ 14m* 13g⁵ 1996 a14.8g⁶ 16.2m Jul 16] IR 13,000Y: ex-Irish gelding: third foal: dam middle-distance performer: rated 58 at 3 yrs (won maiden at Tralee) for M. O'Toole: soundly beaten on flat in 1996: sold out of W. Jenks's stable 2,200 gns Doncaster March Sales after first start, twisted a shoe and found to be lame on second outing: stays 1¾m: acts on good to firm ground: modest winning hurdler: retained 3,200 gns Doncaster October Sales. *M. D. Hammond*

BOUT   2 br.f. (Feb 4) Batshoof 122 – Reyah 83 (Young Generation 129) [1996 7m   65
8.1d⁶ Sep 28] good-bodied filly: half-sister to several winners, including useful 7f (at 2 yrs) and 1m winner Abs (by Nureyev) and 1991 2-y-o 5f winner Isdar (by Known Fact): dam 6f and 8.2f winner: never a serious factor in maidens at Lingfield and Haydock: sold to join R. McKellar 4,500 gns Newmarket Autumn Sales. *J. H. M. Gosden*

BOUTON D'OR   3 b.f. Mazilier (USA) 107 – Cow Pastures (Homing 130) [1995   53 d
53: 5m 5g 6g a5g⁵ a6g a5g² 1996 a5g³ a5g³ a5g² a5g⁶ 5d 5m 5f a5g⁴ a5g⁴ Jul 26] lengthy filly: modest maiden: no worthwhile form since third 3-y-o start: sold 1,350 gns Newmarket September Sales: best at 5f: acts on equitrack, has shown little on turf/fibresand. *P. Howling*

BOWCLIFFE   5 b.g. Petoski 135 – Gwiffina 87 (Welsh Saint 126) [1995 58:   51
10.5d 9.7f⁵ 14m⁴ 14g⁶ 1996 12.3d 10.9d 8.1g* 8.1f 8.1m 10.4g 7g 8.1s Nov 7] good-topped gelding: modest handicapper: won at Musselburgh in May: well held otherwise in 1996: effective at 1m, seems to stay 1¾m: acts on good to firm and dead ground, below form on extremes: tried blinkered/visored: inconsistent. *Mrs A. M. Naughton*

BOWCLIFFE COURT (IRE)   4 b.g. Slip Anchor 136 – Res Nova (USA)   75
(Blushing Groom (FR) 131) [1995 68: 10m 12m³ 12d* 12m⁴ 15g 14g² 14m⁶ 1996 14.1g⁵ 13.9m 15.8g² 16.4g² 16m 16s⁶ 15.9g⁴ 16s* 16.5s³ Nov 9] close-coupled gelding: unimpressive mover: fair handicapper: hung left and looked none too hearty on start before winning at Newbury in October: sold out of B. Hills's stable 19,000 gns Newmarket Autumn Sales before final one: stays 16.5f: best efforts with give in the ground and acts on soft: sometimes hangs fire under pressure, did nothing wrong last 2 starts: won maiden hurdle in December. *R. Akehurst*

BOWCLIFFE GRANGE (IRE)   4 b.g. Dominion Royale 112 – Cala-Vadella   56
110 (Mummy's Pet 125) [1995 23: a8.5g 6.9f 8m 6m 5g³ 1996 a6g a6g⁶ 5.9d 5s⁶ 6m² a6g⁶ 5f* 5f³ 5f* 5f³ 5d 5g* 5m* 5m³ 5m a5g⁵ 5.3m⁶ Aug 28] good-topped gelding: modest handicapper: made all at Beverley, Lingfield, Windsor and Doncaster in the

summer, twice in apprentice contests: below form last 3 starts: suited by sharp 5f: acts on firm ground: blinkered (except once) since ninth 4-y-o start: enthusiastic front runner with blistering early speed. *D. W. Chapman*

BOWDEN ROSE   4 ch.f. Dashing Blade 117 – Elegant Rose 72 (Noalto 120)   98
[1995 90: 6.1g 8g 7g 7m⁴ 6f* 6m* 6g* 6m² 6m⁶ 5m⁶ 5.7h³ 5.3g* 5s 6d 6f³ 1996 5.2d 6m 6d⁴ 5m² 6m 5m⁴ 5.1f² 5m⁶ 6m⁵ 5g* 5d² 6g 5.2m 5g 5g 5g Oct 26] angular, shallow-girthed filly: fairly useful performer: won minor event at Salisbury in August: effective at 5f and 6f: acts on firm and dead ground (missed break badly on soft): blinkered since third 3-y-o start: often a front runner, but sometimes slowly away and is also effective held up: often edgy: somewhat wayward (and was mulish in preliminaries fifth 4-y-o start) but has won for apprentice. *M. Blanshard*

BOWLAND PARK   5 b.m. Nicholas Bill 125 – Macusla (Lighter 111) [1995 NR   –
1996 a12g 12g 10.2g 8f 12f⁵ Jul 6] second foal: dam fair 2m hurdler: poor form in 3 NH Flat races: no worthwhile form on flat. *E. J. Alston*

BOWLED OVER   3 b.g. Batshoof 122 – Swift Linnet (Wolver Hollow 126)   86
[1995 67p: 6s³ 1996 8.2d² 10m 10.3g³ 12.1d³ 11.9m* 12m³ 15d⁵ 13.9m 10.3d 10.3m⁴ 13.3m 10.4g Oct 9] angular, workmanlike gelding: has a fluent, round action: fairly useful performer: won maiden at York in June: below that form after next start: probably better over 1½m than shorter, seemed not to stay (wandered under pressure) 15f: acts on good to firm and dead ground: visored (took strong hold, tailed off) eighth 3-y-o start: one to treat with some caution. *C. A. Cyzer*

BOWLERS BOY   3 ch.g. Risk Me (FR) 127 – Snow Wonder (Music Boy 124)   78
[1995 –p: 6f 6m 1996 5m³ 6g 6d⁵ 6g 5m² a5g³ 6m* 6d 6g² 5m* 6g Oct 12] workmanlike gelding: fair handicapper: won at Pontefract (minor event) in July and (improved effort, coming from last to first) September: stays 6f: acts on good to firm ground: sometimes carries head high. *J. J. Quinn*

BOY BLAKENEY   3 b.g. Blakeney 126 – Sarah Bear (Mansingh (USA) 120)   –
[1995 7f⁵ 8f 8.3d 1996 8m 10m⁴ 10m a12g⁴ 12.4m⁴ Aug 7] small ex-Belgian gelding: third reported foal: half-brother to 4-y-o 1½m seller winner North Bear (by North Briton): dam winner in Belgium: well held on Continent in 1995: no worthwhile form here: blinkered final 3-y-o start. *Mrs S. J. Smith*

BOYFRIEND   6 b.g. Rolfe (USA) 77 – Lady Sweetapples (Super Song 73) [1995   –
NR 1996 a10g⁵ Jan 30] rated 52 in 1994: well beaten in maiden at Lingfield on return: modest hurdler: joined Mrs J. Pitman. *D. R. C. Elsworth*

BRAES'O'SHIELDHILL   3 ch.f. Music Maestro 119 – Dalchroy (Hotfoot 126)   –
[1995 –: 5d⁶ 5g a6g⁴ a6g 1996 7d a8.5g Dec 28] leggy filly: no worthwhile form. *A. Bailey*

BRAFFERTON BELLA   4 ch.f. Sylvan Express 117 – Janie-O 62 (Hittite Glory   –
125) [1995 NR 1996 a7g a11g Feb 10] little sign of ability. *J. M. Jefferson*

BRAILLE (IRE)   5 br.g. Vision (USA) – Winning Feature (Red Alert 127) [1995   77
77: 8g 6d 10f⁴ 10.3m⁴ 11.1g 10g 10m⁵ 14f 11.9m* 10f* 10.3m* 10m³ 10.3d² 10d² 11.9g³ 10.5s⁴ 1996 11.9d² 12.3g May 9] lengthy gelding: fair handicapper: game effort at Haydock: below form at Chester only 3 days later: stayed 1½m: acted on any going: visored (well beaten) twice: dead. *M. G. Meagher*

BRAMBLE BEAR   2 b.f. (May 25) Beveled (USA) – Supreme Rose 95 (Frimley   71 d
Park 109) [1996 5f⁵ 5m 5.1m³ 5.1f* 5m 5g 5m⁶ Oct 3] leggy, unfurnished filly: fourth foal: half-sister to useful 3-y-o sprinter Rambling Bear (by Sharrood) and fairly useful sprinter Bajan Rose (by Dashing Blade): dam sprinter: progressive form first 4 starts, winning 5-runner median auction maiden at Bath in July: poor efforts in nurseries after: raced only at 5f on top-of-the-ground. *M. Blanshard*

BRAMBLES WAY   7 ch.g. Clantime 101 – Streets Ahead 67 (Ovid 95) [1995 NR   55
1996 7s 6.9d 6.9m³ 8g² 6.9g⁴ 8m 8f 9.2f⁵ 10f* 10.1m⁵ 10f a11g Dec 3] strong, lengthy gelding: modest handicapper: left W. Barker after sixth start: won (first time) seller at Redcar in September: may well be suited by further than 1¼m: acts on firm and dead ground, well held (in blinkers) on fibresand: often visored, effective without: progressive (and potentially useful) winning hurdler. *Mrs M. Reveley*

BRAND NEW DANCE   2 b.g. (May 17) Gildoran 123 – Starawak 68 (Star   68 p
Appeal 133) [1996 8s⁵ Nov 9] half-brother to 3-y-o Again Together and fairly useful 4-y-o 7f and 1m winner Fame Again (both by Then Again) and useful middle-distance stayer Army of Stars (by Posse): dam, 1½m winner, half-sister to

Spring In Deepsea, smart winner at up to 9f: staying-on fifth of 16 to Polar Flight in median auction maiden at Doncaster in November: will stay well: will improve. *D. W. P. Arbuthnot*

BRANDON COURT (IRE)   5 b.g. Law Society (USA) 130 – Dance Date (IRE)   79
(Sadler's Wells (USA) 132) [1995 NR 1996 11.4g^5 14.8m^5 Jul 20] rated 90 in 1994: showed he retains most of his ability, fifth at Sandown and Newmarket in July: stays 1¾m: acts on any going: effective from front or held up: consistent. *I. A. Balding*

BRANDON JACK   2 ch.c. (Jan 28) Cadeaux Genereux 131 – Waitingformargaret   81
78 (Kris 135) [1996 6.1m^3 7f^3 6.1d* 7g* 7g^3 Sep 25] 11,000Y: lengthy colt: third foal: half-brother to 3-y-o Tarry (by Salse), 7f winner at 2 yrs, and 6f (at 2 yrs) and 7f winner Linger (by Sharrood): dam, 2-y-o 5f winner, out of useful sprinter Princess Seal: fairly useful form: successful in maiden auction at Nottingham in August and nursery at Goodwood in September: will be suited by further than 7f: acts well on dead ground, wandered around (at Brighton) on firm. *I. A. Balding*

BRANDON MAGIC   3 ch.c. Primo Dominie 121 – Silk Stocking 109 (Pardao   97
120) [1995 99: 6m^3 6g^2 6g* 6d* 7s* 7.3d^3 1996 7m^5 8s^5 8.5m 8f 8.1g^5 8m 10m^2 11.9g^5 10m 10m Oct 4] good-topped, lengthy colt: useful handicapper: stays 11.9f: acts on soft ground, probably on firm: blinkered (refused to settle) penultimate 3-y-o start. *I. A. Balding*

BRANDON PRINCE (IRE)   8 b.g. Shernazar 131 – Chanson de Paris (USA)   64 §
(The Minstrel (CAN) 135) [1995 70: 18g 14.9d 16m 21.6f* 17.2m 1996 14.9d^4 21.6m 17.2f May 11] close-coupled gelding: impresses in appearance: modest handicapper, on the downgrade: stays extreme distances: acts on soft and firm ground: seems effective blinkered or not: usually held up: has run well when sweating: inconsistent and cannot be relied upon nowadays. *I. A. Balding*

BRANDONVILLE   3 b.c. Never So Bold 135 – Enduring (Sadler's Wells (USA)   –
132) [1995 72: 6d^6 6g^4 6.9g^4 1996 6m^5 8d 8g 7m^5 7g^4 9f Aug 9] big, leggy colt: fair maiden: long way below form in 1996 for new stable: should stay 1m. *N. Tinkler*

BRANSTON ABBY (IRE)   7 ch.m. Risk Me (FR) 127 – Tuxford Hideaway 102   110
(Cawston's Clown 113) [1995 118: 5m^3 6m 7m^4 6m^2 6g^3 6d^6 6g^2 7.1g^5 6f 6m* 6m^4

Mr J. David Abell's "Branston Abby"

7m*dis 6.5g2 7g* 6.5m5 6g* 6d2 7g* 6g 6d3 7d5 7m 6m2 6d2 7f 1996 6m 7g3 6m5 7f4 6f2 6d 6m* 7.1d2 6m 6m6 7g* 6g4 6f 7m3 6.5d* 7g4 7m 6m 6.5s* 6g 6s* 7d3 6s Nov 22] tall, lengthy, sparely-made mare: smart performer: won 24 races, a post-war record for a British-trained mare: successful in 1996 in listed race at Newmarket in June, minor event at Yarmouth (soon off bridle) in July and listed races at Munich in August and (beat Macanal a head) October and at Cologne (beat My Cadeaux a neck) in October: 2¼ lengths third of 12 to Macanal in Group 3 event at Milan in November: effective at 6f and 7f: acted on any ground: highly-strung and often mounted on track (sometimes early to post): held up, and ideally suited by strongly-run race: tough: to be covered by Mark of Esteem. *M. Johnston*

BRANSTON DANNI 3 b.f. Ron's Victory (USA) 129 – Softly Spoken 87 — 64 d (Mummy's Pet 125) [1995 73: 5.1m2 5m5 5f* 5m 5m6 6m2 6.5m 6g2 1996 6f 6m 5g5 6g 6.1m 6m 5g Oct 19] close-coupled filly: fair handicapper at best: little form at 3 yrs except for third start: sold 2,700 gns Newmarket Autumn Sales: stays 6f: winner on firm going at 2 yrs: sent to Spain. *Mrs J. R. Ramsden*

BRANSTON JEWEL (IRE) 3 ch.f. Prince Sabo 123 – Tuxford Hideaway 102 — — (Cawston's Clown 113) [1995 95: 5m5 5g* 5.5g2 1996 5m Jul 27] lengthy, sparely-made filly: fairly useful as juvenile: suffered cannon-bone injury (requiring screws) final 2-y-o start: looking very fit and well backed, last of 15 in handicap at Newcastle only start in 1996: raced only at around 5f: tends to edge left: reportedly has been retired. *M. Johnston*

BRANSTON KRISTY 4 b.f. Hallgate 127 – Bare Spectacle (Welsh Pageant — 39 132) [1995 41: a6g a6g5 a5g3 a5g 1996 a5g a6g6 a8g a7g6 a8g5 a6g4 a7g 6f 6.9m 6m 5f3 5f 5m Jul 16] sparely-made filly: poor maiden sprint handicapper: acts on firm ground (yet to race on soft) and the all-weather: visored/blinkered at 4 yrs: inconsistent. *C. Smith*

BRASS TACKS 4 br.f. Prince Sabo 123 – Brassy Nell 72 (Dunbeath (USA) 127) — 42 [1995 62: 7f6 6g3 6g 8m3 7f* a7g 8f5 1996 9.7m 7f4 Jul 25] angular filly: only a poor performer for new stable: stays 1m: acts on firm ground, ran poorly on soft and on fibresand: blinkered final 4-y-o start: sent to Saudi Arabia. *R. T. Phillips*

BRAVE ACT 2 b.c. (Apr 24) Persian Bold 123 – Circus Act (Shirley Heights 130) — 109 [1996 7s* 7m* 7m2 7.1g* Aug 30] 31,000Y: close-coupled, good-topped colt: has plenty of scope: fourth foal: half-brother to 3-y-o 1¼m winner Circus Star (by Soviet Star) and useful middle-distance stayer Jellaby Askhir (by Salse): dam unraced daughter of Circus Ring: very useful youngster: beat Musheer by 4 lengths in Ayr maiden in July: progressed with every run after, winning minor event at Redcar in July and Solario Stakes at Sandown (made all, beat Falkenham a short head) in August: will be well suited by 1m+: acts on good to firm and soft ground: game: joined R. McAnally in USA. *Sir Mark Prescott*

BRAVE EDGE 5 b.g. Beveled (USA) – Daring Ditty (Daring March 116) [1995 — 108 102: 5.2m2 5m* 5g* 5f4 6f3 6m 5m 5d3 1996 5.2d5 6m5 5m2 5m* 5m6 6f 5m 5m 6m 5d4 5m3 5m4 5s2 Oct 13] good-topped gelding: useful performer, better than ever: won strongly-run listed race at Kempton (by 1¾ lengths from Double Quick) in June: 1¼ lengths second of 7 to Leap For Joy in Group 3 event at Milan in October: effective at 5f and 6f: acts on firm and soft ground: usually held up. *R. Hannon*

BRAVE ENVOY 2 b.g. (Apr 7) High Estate 127 – Restless Anna (Thatching 131) — — [1996 7d Oct 2] 8,000F, 8,000Y: second foal: dam thrice-raced half-sister to fairly useful sprinter Catherines Well: raced freely then not knocked about in maiden at Salisbury in October: subsequently gelded: may do better. *M. J. Heaton-Ellis*

BRAVEHEART (IRE) 2 br.g. (Feb 28) Mujadil (USA) 119 – Salonniere (FR) — 79 + 88 (Bikala 134) [1996 5g4 5g* 5m2 5.1g3 5g4 6.1d3 6m5 Sep 19] 12,500Y: lengthy gelding: third foal: half-brother to fairly useful 1¼m winner Kissair (by Most Welcome), also winner of Triumph Hurdle, and 1994 2-y-o 6f seller winner Red River Rose (by Red Sunset): dam 10.4f winner who stayed 1½m: won median auction maiden at Thirsk in May: apparently beat subsequent effort when third to Andreyev in minor event at Chester (following 3-month break, could be rated 86) in August: bred to stay beyond 6f: acts on good to firm and dead ground. *M. R. Channon*

BRAVE KRIS (IRE) 2 b.f. (Feb 10) Kris 135 – Famosa (Dancing Brave (USA) — 82 140) [1996 7f 8.2g2 8g3 Oct 25] 31,000F, 340,000 francs Y: well-made filly: second foal: half-sister to 3-y-o 7f to 1m winner Divina Luna (by Dowsing): dam, French

1½m winner, half-sister to Lowther winner Kingscote, dam of very smart colt Rainbow Corner: fairly useful form when placed in maidens at Nottingham and Doncaster (behind Calypso Grant) last 2 starts: bred to stay beyond 1m: takes good hold: had 2 handlers in paddock final outing: should win a race. *L. M. Cumani*

BRAVE MONTGOMERIE　2 ch.c. (Feb 10) Most Welcome 131 – Just Precious 77 (Ela-Mana-Mou 132) [1996 6m² 7s³ 7m* Sep 19] 10,500F, 15,000Y: third reported foal: half-brother to 2-y-o sprint winners Just Baileys (by Midyan) and Just Buy Baileys (by Formidable): dam 7.5f and 1m winner: progressive form in maiden events at Ayr: off course 2½ months before winning in September: will be well suited by 1m+: likely to continue improving. *Miss L. A. Perratt* 　77 p

BRAVE PATRIARCH (IRE)　5 gr.g. Alzao (USA) 117 – Early Rising (USA) (Grey Dawn II 132) [1995 –: 8g 8m 1996 9.9m 11.8g⁵ 14g⁶ May 17] good-topped gelding: seems just a fair handicapper nowadays: joined N. Henderson and won novice hurdle in August: sold only 2,600 gns Newmarket Autumn Sales: stays 1½m: acts on dead ground, below form (once each) on firm and soft. *J. L. Dunlop* 　68

BRAVE SPY　5 b.g. Law Society (USA) 130 – Contralto 100 (Busted 134) [1995 62: a10g⁵ a10g³ a11g³ a16g³ 16g⁴ a14.8g* a16g³ a14.8g 1996 a12g⁵ a14.8g 11.8d a12g³ a16g a16g a13g Dec 13] strong, lengthy gelding: unimpressive mover: no worthwhile form in 1996. *C. A. Cyzer* 　–

BRAVO STAR (USA)　11 b.g. The Minstrel (CAN) 135 – Stellarette (CAN) (Tentam (USA)) [1995 NR 1996 18f 13.1f Jul 8] of little account. *Paddy Farrell* 　–

BRAWLING SPRINGS　2 b.g. (Apr 21) Belfort (FR) 89 – Oyster Gray 61 (Tanfirion 110) [1996 5m⁶ 5m⁵ 5f Jun 12] 2,800F, IR 10,500Y: leggy, close-coupled gelding: brother to fairly useful sprinter Magic Pearl: dam maiden best at up to 6f: well beaten in varied events. *M. W. Easterby* 　–

BRAYDON FOREST　4 b.g. Presidium 124 – Sleekit 78 (Blakeney 126) [1995 65: 10g 10m⁶ 10m⁵ 8.3g³ 9m² 10m³ 10g 10d⁵ 8d 1996 11.8d 11.6m 11.6g⁵ 10m 11.6d² Aug 12] good-topped gelding: just a modest maiden handicapper at best in 1996: stays 11.6f: acts on good to firm and dead ground: no improvement in blinkers or visor: inconsistent. *C. J. Drewe* 　51

BRAZILIA　2 b.f. (Mar 10) Forzando 122 – Dominio (IRE) 99 (Dominion 123) [1996 5.1f⁴ 6f² 6m² a6g³ 7g⁵ a5g Nov 7] second foal: dam suited by 5f: modest maiden: will prove best at up to 7f: well beaten on equitrack final start: sold 4,800 gns Newmarket December Sales. *P. T. Walwyn* 　63 a55

BREAK THE RULES　4 b.g. Dominion 123 – Surf Bird (Shareef Dancer (USA) 135) [1995 80: 7g⁴ 8f² 9.2f³ 8m* 8d 1996 9.2d⁴ 10m 8g³ 10m² 11.1g² 12.3m* 10v⁴ 12g 12.1d⁴ 10.5v² 12g³ 10.3g* Oct 26] strong gelding: keen walker: fair performer: won minor event at Chester in July and weak claimer at Doncaster (comfortably, claimed to join M. Pipe £15,000) in October: stays 12.3f: acts on any going: carries head high under pressure, tends to hang and may prove best with strong handling. *Mrs M. Reveley* 　76

BRECON　3 b. or br.c. High Estate 127 – No Can Tell (USA) (Clev Er Tell (USA)) [1995 70: 6.1m⁴ 7m³ 6m⁴ 7m⁵ 7.3d⁶ 6.9m³ 1996 a8g a8.5g⁴ Dec 28] fair form at 2 yrs for P. Cole: well beaten on belated return: should be suited by 1m+. *W. R. Muir* 　–

BRECONGILL LAD　4 b.g. Clantime 101 – Chikala 81 (Pitskelly 122) [1995 81: 6g 6m³ 6m 7m³ 6g* 6m³ 5m* 6g⁴ 7m 1996 6s 6g 6m 5m 6m 6d 6m⁵ 5f* 5m² 6m 5g⁶ 5g⁴ 5s Nov 8] tall, leggy gelding: fair handicapper: won at Beverley in August: effective at 5f to 7f: acts on firm ground, seemingly not on a soft surface: used to be blinkered, not since sixth 4-y-o start: tends to hang and carries head high: has raced prominently of late. *Miss S. E. Hall* 　73

BREEZED WELL　10 b.g. Wolverlife 115 – Precious Baby (African Sky 124) [1995 42: 10g 7f 8g⁵ 7.5m³ 10f a8g 8d 11.5s⁶ 1996 a8g a7g 10g⁵ 7f 8g 7.1g² 7.5f³ 12m 8f⁴ 11.5m Oct 4] smallish, sparely-made gelding: poor mover: poor handicapper who usually contests amateurs/ladies events: stays 11.5f: acts on any going: blinkered (below form) once at 3 yrs. *B. R. Cambidge* 　40

BREFFNI (IRE)　2 b.f. (Mar 12) Mac's Imp (USA) 116 – Bon Retour (Sallust 134) [1996 6g 5.2f³ 6g² 6f² a5g⁴ 6.1m 6f⁵ Sep 23] sparely-made filly: fourth foal: half-sister to 5f and 6f winner Bon Secret (by Classic Secret): dam Irish 2-y-o 1m 　47

winner but no form afterwards: modest plater: stays 6f: yet to race on a soft surface: trained first 5 outings by C. Allen. *R. Dickin*

BRENTABILITY (IRE) 3 b.g. Dancing Dissident (USA) 119 – Stanerra's Song — (USA) (Seattle Song (USA) 130) [1995 NR 1996 10g 8d 7m 10m a12g⁵ 13.1m Sep 9] 16,000Y: big, sturdy gelding: has scope: easy mover: second foal: dam unraced daughter of high-class Irish mare Stanerra, best at 1¼m/1½m: no worthwhile form, though was gambled on fourth start. *G. Lewis*

BRESIL (USA) 7 ch.g. Bering 136 – Clever Bidder (USA) (Bold Bidder) [1995   35
37, a–: 10g 8g 12g 10m 12m 13.1f* 14g⁴ 14.1m 14.1m³ 14s a14g a13g 1996 14.1s⁴   a–
a12g 12d 12m 12f⁵ 14.1f² 13.1f⁵ 14.1f⁵ 14m⁴ 14.1m 14d Oct 2] lengthy gelding: unimpressive mover: poor handicapper nowadays: stays 1¾m: acts on firm and soft going, no form on the all-weather: visored (well beaten) seventh 7-y-o start: inconsistent. *K. R. Burke*

BREYDON 3 ch.g. Be My Guest (USA) 126 – Palmella (USA) 89 (Grundy 137)   50
[1995 NR 1996 8.2d 8.2s 10g 12m⁶ 13g³ a14g² 12m³ 11.1m² Aug 29] 5,800F, 9,200Y: angular, plain gelding: closely related to a winner by Northfields and half-brother to several winners, including fair sprinters Furiella (by Formidable) and Final Ace (by Sharpo): dam, 1¼m winner who stayed 1½m, half-sister to Teenoso and Topsy: poor maiden handicapper: probably stays 1¾m: best form on a sound surface: joined P. Monteith. *M. H. Tompkins*

BRICK COURT (IRE) 4 ch.f. Bluebird (USA) 125 – Palmyra (GER) (Arratos — (FR)) [1995 –: 12m 10.4m 10d a12g 1996 14.1s 12d a16g⁶ 13.1f 14m Oct 4] rather leggy filly: no worthwhile form: tried blinkered. *R. F. Johnson Houghton*

BRIDE'S REPRISAL 2 b.f. (May 6) Dunbeath (USA) 127 – Matching Lines 72   87
(Thatching 131) [1996 5f* 5f 5g² 5g* 6m³ 6m³ 5.2m⁵ 6f⁶ Sep 5] tall filly: third foal: half-sister to 1994 2-y-o 5.1f winner Oneineverycolour (by Midyan): dam a sprinter: fairly useful form: won median auction maiden at Carlisle in June and nursery at Musselburgh (second run in 3 days) in July: stays 6f: raced only on a sound surface: held up: bit slipped through mouth when hanging badly sixth outing. *M. R. Channon*

BRIDLINGTON BAY 3 b.g. Roscoe Blake 120 – City Sound 63 (On Your Mark — 125) [1995 –: a8.5g 1996 a8g a8g 11.1d Sep 30] no worthwhile form. *J. L. Eyre*

BRIEF GLIMPSE (IRE) 4 b. or br.f. Taufan (USA) 119 – Mini Look (FR) (In   102
Fijar (USA) 121) [1995 108: 8.5m³ 8m 7f* 7.3m 8g 7d 1996 8d 6m⁶ 8g 7m 7m 7m Sep 26] tall, leggy, close-coupled filly: good mover: useful performer: well below form in 1996 except when 6½ lengths seventh of 9 to Sensation in Group 2 event at Newmarket third start: will prove best at up to around 1m: acts on firm ground: blinkered (finished last) fifth 4-y-o outing: sold 38,000 gns Newmarket December Sales. *Major D. N. Chappell*

BRIGANOONE 3 b.g. Cyrano de Bergerac 120 – Zareeta (Free State 125) [1995   —
44, a52: 5m a6g⁴ a6g 5m 7g 8f a5g 1996 a6g³ a7g* a7g⁵ a9.4g³ 6.1d 6s 7.5g May 11]   a53
sturdy gelding: modest handicapper: won at Wolverhampton in January: should prove effective over 1m+: acts on good to firm ground, best form on fibresand: tried blinkered, no improvement. *S. R. Bowring*

BRIGGS TURN 2 b.g. (Apr 28) Rudimentary (USA) 118 – Turnabout (Tyrnavos — 129) [1996 7d Nov 8] big, lengthy gelding: fifth foal: dam unraced: very on toes, well beaten in maiden at Doncaster in November: rather mulish exiting onto track. *W. Jarvis*

BRIGHSTONE 3 ch.c. Cadeaux Genereux 131 – High Fountain 102 (High Line — 125) [1995 95p: 7f* 8m* 1996 10g 8d 7g⁶ Jul 4] strong, sturdy colt: has a quick action: well beaten in 1996, beginning in Sandown Classic Trial: sold (H. Cecil to D. Elsworth) 2,000 gns Newmarket Autumn Sales: should stay 1¼m: possibly unsuited by a soft surface: one to treat with caution. *H. R. A. Cecil*

BRIGHT DESERT 3 b.c. Green Desert (USA) 127 – Smarten Up 119 (Sharpen — Up 127) [1995 NR 1996 8.5m 10d Aug 10] 45,000Y: strong colt: half-brother to several winners, including top-class sprinter Cadeaux Genereux (by Young Generation) and useful middle-distance stayer Brightner (by Sparkler): dam sprinter: towards rear in maidens at Beverley and (after sold out of E. Dunlop's stable 3,500 gns Newmarket July Sales) Ayr 3½ months later. *R. M. McKellar*

BRIGHT DIAMOND   3 b.f. Never So Bold 135 – Diamond House (Habitat 134)   52
[1995 58: 6.1m 6d 7m⁴ 7.3d 1996 8.2g 8g 6m⁵ 7m 7f 8f 7f⁴ 6m⁶ Oct 23] modest
maiden handicapper: decidedly flattered penultimate start: stays 7f: acts on firm and
dead ground: blinkered (well beaten) sixth 3-y-o start: inconsistent: sold 1,600 gns
Newmarket December Sales. *J. R. Arnold*

BRIGHT ECLIPSE (USA)   3 br.g. Sunny's Halo (CAN) – Miss Lantana (USA)   57
(Danzig Connection (USA)) [1995 –p: 7.9m 1996 a10g³ 10g 8m⁴ 8g² a8g⁴ 8.1g³
8.3g⁵ Jul 5] strong gelding: has a quick action: modest maiden: stays 1m: acts on
good to firm ground and equitrack, yet to race on a soft surface: blinkered (found
little) final 3-y-o start: tends to carry head awkwardly: has joined Miss K. Whitehouse. *J. W. Hills*

BRIGHTER BYFAAH (IRE)   3 ch.g. Kefaah (USA) 124 – Bright Landing 78   47
(Sun Prince 128) [1995 –: 10m a10g⁶ 1996 11.1g⁶ 12m 14.1m⁶ 14.1m* a16g Nov 12]
well-made gelding: poor form: won bad selling handicap at Nottingham in July: stays
2m: acts on good to firm ground and equitrack: blinkered (took fierce hold) third
3-y-o start. *N. A. Graham*

BRIGHT GOLD   2 ch.g. (Apr 6) Clantime 101 – Miss Brightside 41 (Crofthall   53
110) [1996 6m 5m⁶ 6d Nov 8] sturdy gelding: first foal: dam (maiden) effective from
5f to 7f: poor form in sprint maidens. *A. Smith*

BRIGHTON ROAD (IRE)   3 b. or br.g. Pennine Walk 120 – Share The Vision   79 d
(Vision (USA)) [1995 7g 7m 7g⁴ 7s* 7d² 9d 1996 8d 7.1d² 8.1m 8m 9g⁵ 8.1g 7.1s
8.2s Oct 31] IR 1,500F: IR 2,600Y: lengthy ex-Irish gelding: fourth foal: half-brother
to a winner in Norway by Exhibitioner: dam never ran: trained by T. Regan at 2 yrs,
winning nursery at Gowran Park: easily best effort here when second of 11 at
Sandown in May: should stay 1m: possibly needs a soft surface: one to treat with
caution. *G. B. Balding*

BRIGHT PARAGON (IRE)   7 b. or br.g. Treasure Kay 114 – Shining Bright   –
(USA) (Bold Bidder) [1995 48d, a–: 5d 5m⁵ 5.3m 6f 6g 6d⁴ a8g 1996 5g a5g⁶
Dec 31] workmanlike gelding: poor handicapper: left M. Chapman after 7-y-o
reappearance: stays 7f: acts on any going: tried visored, no improvement. *K. T. Ivory*

BRIGHT PET   3 ch.f. Anshan 119 – Morica 88 (Moorestyle 137) [1995 NR 1996   –
8g 8m 8g 11.1m 10m 12.4m⁵ Aug 7] smallish filly: fifth foal: half-sister to 2 winners,
including fair Espla (at up to 7f, by Sure Blade): dam, 2-y-o 6f winner, stayed 1¼m:
half-sister to Aragon out of half-sister to Song: seems of no account. *Mrs S. J. Smith*

BRIGHT WATER   3 b.c. Caerleon (USA) 132 – Shining Water 111 (Kalaglow   110
132) [1995 95p: 8f* 1996 11d⁴ 10m* 10g Nov 1] well-made, attractive colt, the
brother of talented colt had choked, almost collapsed and had failed to
handle softish going on reappearance: off course 6 months (had suffered from a
pricked and infected hoof in interim), much-improved form to win smart conditions
event at Newmarket in October by 2½ lengths from Desert Shot, leading 2f out, green
and edging right into Dip then staying on strongly: quickly beaten 3f out in listed race
there 15 days later, and possibly found race coming too soon: will prove suited by
1½m: flashed tail under pressure first 2 starts at 3 yrs: stays in training. *H. R. A. Cecil*

BRILLIANT RED   3 b.c. Royal Academy (USA) 130 – Red Comes Up (USA)   94
(Blushing Groom (FR) 131) [1995 93: 6g³ 6g² 7m* 8.1d³ 7.3d⁵ 1996 7.3f⁶ 8m⁵ 10m
Aug 16] tall, lengthy colt: has a long stride: useful form: stiff task, back to form in
handicap at Newbury last time, racing freely early on, no impression straight: sold
(P. Cole to P. Hedger) 24,000 gns Newmarket Autumn Sales: seems to stay 1¼m: acts
on good to firm and good to soft ground. *P. F. I. Cole*

BRIN-LODGE (IRE)   3 b.f. Doubletour (USA) – Nordico's Dream (Nordico   –
(USA)) [1995 NR 1996 a7g 8g a6g 5m a5g 5m Sep 18] leggy filly: first foal: dam
lightly-raced Irish maiden: no worthwhile form. *K. S. Bridgwater*

BRISAS   9 ch.g. Vaigly Great 127 – Legal Sound 85 (Legal Eagle 126) [1995 45:   45
a5g a6g⁴ a6g* a6g⁶ a6g⁴ a6g⁶ a6g 6g 5.9f³ 5f⁶ 5.9f³ 6m³ 5f⁴ 5m⁴ 5h³ 6g a6g⁵
5g 6g Jul 24] strong-quartered gelding: bad mover nowadays: poor sprint handicapper: acts on fibresand and hard ground, possibly unsuited by heavy: effective
blinkered/visored or not: sometimes looks none too keen. *C. W. Fairhurst*

BRISKA (IRE)   2 b.f. (Apr 14) River Falls 113 – Calash (Indian King (USA) 128)   69
[1996 6m⁵ 6g³ 7f* 7m⁶ 7m Oct 1] IR 13,500Y: lengthy, quite attractive filly: fourth

reported foal: half-sister to 3-y-o 5f and 6f winner Little Noggins (by Salt Dome), and 5.7f to 7f winner Master Millfield (by Prince Rupert): dam half-sister to smart 1983 2-y-o 7f winner Knoxville: won maiden auction at Warwick in June: well held in nurseries after: stays 7f: sold 9,000 gns Newmarket Autumn Sales. *R. Hannon*

BROADGATE FLYER (IRE) 2 b.g. (Feb 27) Silver Kite (USA) 111 – Fabulous Pet (Somethingfabulous (USA)) [1996 6m⁶ 7m⁵ 6g 7g³ a6s⁴ Dec 19] IR 10,000Y: rather unfurnished gelding: third foal: half-brother to Irish 7f winner Something Super (by Superpower) and 4-y-o (stays 1½m) Something Speedy (by Sayf El Arab), 8.5f winner at 2 yrs: dam modest Irish 1½m winner, is half-sister to smart sprinter Orojoya and very smart American colt Bywayofchicago: modest maiden: sold out of W. Jarvis' stable 1,700 gns Newmarket Autumn Sales after fourth start: will stay at least 1m: acts on good to firm ground, well below best on fibresand. *Mrs L. Stubbs* — 60 a?

BROAD RIVER (USA) 2 b.c. (May 4) Broad Brush (USA) – Monture Creek (USA) (Stop The Music (USA)) [1996 6g Sep 5] $160,000Y: rather leggy, angular colt: fifth foal: half-brother to 2 winners in USA, one placed at 9f in Grade 2 event: dam thrice-raced half-sister to smart American sprinter Beveled: sire Grade 1 1¼m winner: lost touch with leaders from halfway in York maiden in September: moved short to post: will do better. *E. A. L. Dunlop* — – p

BROADSTAIRS BEAUTY (IRE) 6 ch.g. Dominion Royale 112 – Holy Water (Monseigneur (USA) 127) [1995 77, a85: 5g² 5m² 5m* 5g* 6m 5g⁵ 6g 5g 6d a6g a5g* 1996 5s⁵ 5g 5g Jul 9] workmanlike gelding: has a quick action: fairly useful handicapper: creditable effort on reappearance, but subsequently left S. R. Bowring and well below best: effective at 5f (best form) to 7f: acts on good to firm and heavy ground and on fibresand: best in blinkers or visor when sprinting, hasn't worn either over further: bandaged: front runner: joined D. Shaw. *P. Howling* — 73 a–

BROCKVILLE BAIRN 3 b.g. Tina's Pet 121 – Snow Chief 90 (Tribal Chief 125) [1995 42: 5m 5g 6m a5g 6m a6g 1996 a7g⁴ Feb 23] poor sprint maiden: acts on fibresand. *Mrs A. Swinbank* — –

BROCTUNE BAY 7 b.g. Midyan (USA) 124 – Sweet Colleen 42 (Connaught 130) [1995 –: 14g 1996 13.9g⁴ Oct 12] big, workmanlike gelding: maiden handicapper, rated 67 at 5 yrs: fairly useful winning hurdler: shaped well, never nearer, at York on belated return: stays 13.6f: acts on good to firm ground: sold only 1,900 gns Doncaster November Sales. *Mrs M. Reveley* — 53 +

BROCTUNE GOLD 5 b.g. Superpower 113 – Golden Sunlight (Ile de Bourbon (USA) 133) [1995 67d: 7g* 6f* 7g 7f 5.9h³ 8g 1996 7d² 7g* 7m 7.1f* 7s⁵ 8.1m* 10m 8.5f* 8m⁵ 8m³ 8.1s² Nov 7] leggy, workmanlike gelding: easy mover: fair performer: held his form better in 1996 than previous 2 seasons: won at Thirsk (seller) in May, Musselburgh in June (claimer) and July (handicap) and Beverley (claimer, set steady pace) in August: effective at 6f to 8.5f: acts on firm and soft ground: sometimes has tongue tied down: forces pace. *Mrs M. Reveley* — 73

BROCTUNE LINE 2 ch.c. (Apr 29) Safawan 118 – Ra Ra (Lord Gayle (USA) 124) [1996 5.9f 7m⁵ 7d 7f 6s⁶ 8f a7g⁴ Nov 29] 4,100Y: close-coupled colt: sixth foal: half-brother to 4 winners, including 1994 2-y-o 7f winner Suile Mor (by Satin Wood) and fair 6f winner Efra (by Efisio): dam unraced: poor form: likely to stay middle distances: acts on good to firm ground and fibresand. *Mrs M. Reveley* — 43

BRODESSA 10 gr.g. Scallywag 127 – Jeanne du Barry 74 (Dubassoff (USA)) [1995 62: a16g² a14.8g⁴ 16m* 14.1f* 15.1m² 14.1f 16.2m* 14.1m* 15.1g² 17.1m 1996 16m² 16m* 14.1m² 16.2f* Aug 15] big, workmanlike gelding: modest performer: won claimer at Nottingham in June: looked none too keen next start, but did nothing wrong when winning seller at Beverley in August: stays 16.2f: acts on firm and dead ground and fibresand: effective held up or from front: suitable mount for amateur: won claiming hurdle in September. *Mrs M. Reveley* — 62

BROGANS BRUSH 3 ch.c. Jendali (USA) 111 – Sweet 'n' Sharp 71 (Sharpo 132) [1995 –: 5m⁵ a5g⁴ 6g⁶ 7m a7g 5m 7.1s 1996 9.2d 13.8g⁴ 15.1f 13.8g Sep 21] poor plater: visored twice at 2 yrs. *J. S. Haldane* — –

BROMFYLDE FAYEMAID (IRE) 4 b.f. Treasure Kay 114 – Fayes Ben (Don 128) [1995 NR 1996 8.3m 5m⁶ Jun 5] second foal: half-sister to modest 6-y-o 1m — –

winner Phase One (by Horage): dam poor Irish maiden: no sign of ability: tried blinkered. *J. R. Jenkins*

BRONHALLOW 3 b.g. Belmez (USA) 131 – Grey Twig 68 (Godswalk (USA) 130) [1995 –: 8d 1996 10g 8g 10d 14m 11.6g 10m Aug 7] good-bodied gelding: no form. *Mrs Barbara Waring* –

BRONZE MAQUETTE (IRE) 6 b.m. Ahonoora 122 – Working Model 99 (Ile de Bourbon (USA) 133) [1995 –: 9.7m 1996 11.9f 11.7g³ 10m⁵ 10m 12g⁴ 11.5f 12m⁵ 9.7g⁶ Jul 3] long-backed mare: good walker: poor handicapper: stays 1½m: acts on good to firm and dead going, probably not on soft: blinkered (below form) once as 3-y-o: inconsistent. *T. Hind* 39

BRONZE RUNNER 12 gr.g. Gunner B 126 – Petingalyn (Petingo 135) [1995 44, a–: 10m⁶ 10m 10m* 11.5m* 9.7m 11.6m³ 11.6m⁴ 10.8f² a10g⁶ 12d 1996 10m 10m 10m⁶ 13.1f 10.8m 11.6m 12m 10m 10m Sep 18] leggy gelding: very bad mover: capable of only poor form nowadays: effective at 1¼m to 1½m: acts on any going: has been visored, wears blinkers nowadays: inconsistent. *E. A. Wheeler* 34 a–

BROOKHEAD LADY 5 b.m. Petong 126 – Lewista (Mandrake Major 122) [1995 62, a49: a6g⁵ a6g⁴ 6m* 6f 5.9f 5.9f⁶ 6m³ a6g² 6f³ a7g⁴ 5.9h* 6g² 6.1d 6g a7g 1996 a6g³ a6g² a6g a6g⁶ 6g⁴ 5.9f⁶ 5.9f⁵ a7g a5g⁶ 6f 6m⁵ 6m 6m 6d Sep 30] leggy, angular mare: modest handicapper: left P. D. Evans after penultimate start: stays 7f: acts on hard and dead ground and on fibresand: inconsistent. *T. Wall* 49 d a56 d

BROOM ISLE 8 b.m. Damister (USA) 123 – Vynz Girl 82 (Tower Walk 130) [1995 46+, a68: a14.8g* a12g² 13g³ 1996 a12g a14g⁶ a11g⁵ a16.2g Jul 26] well below best in 1996, pulled up final start: stays 2m: best efforts on fibresand: acts on firm ground, seems unsuited by a soft surface. *D. Burchell* – a45

BROTHER ROY 3 b.c. Prince Sabo 123 – Classic Heights (Shirley Heights 130) [1995 60: 6m⁵ 1996 10m⁵ 8m⁵ 8.2g 9g 12v Nov 11] off course 16 months after debut and no worthwhile form on return. *T. G. Mills* –

BROUGHTONS CHAMP 4 b.g. Dowsing (USA) 124 – Knees Up (USA) (Dancing Champ (USA)) [1995 –p: 8f 1996 a10g Nov 26] no show in claimer and seller: withdrawn after bolting to post on intended reappearance. *W. J. Musson* –

BROUGHTONS ERROR 2 ch.c. (May 26) Most Welcome 131 – Eloquent Charm (USA) (Private Account (USA)) [1996 5g⁵ 7g 6g⁴ 6d 6m 7g* a8g⁴ Nov 15] 2,500Y: workmanlike colt: half-brother to some moderate animals: dam poor maiden out of winning sister to Ribblesdale winner Nanticious: won nursery at Doncaster in October: should stay 1¼m at least: best turf form on good ground, respectable effort on equitrack. *W. J. Musson* 67

BROUGHTONS FORMULA 6 b.g. Night Shift (USA) – Forward Rally 84 (Formidable (USA) 125) [1995 57, a66: 11.8d 12g 14m⁶ 11.8g³ 11.4g³ 11.4m⁴ 14g 11.6m² 12f* 14m* 14m⁴ 14.4m⁶ 14g 12m a13g⁴ a13g* a13g* 1996 a13g 12m 12m 11.6m 12d 16.4g 16m* 15.8g³ 16.1f³ 13.6m* 16g a16g⁶ a16g² a13g² Dec 31] compact, good-bodied gelding: poor mover: modest handicapper (has won several apprentice events): well out of form until winning (in big fields) at Nottingham and Redcar (well ridden) in the autumn: stays 2m: acts on firm and dead ground and best form on the all-weather: normally blinkered nowadays: quirky, and often gets well behind. *W. J. Musson* 51 a56

BROUGHTON'S PORT 6 b.g. Reesh 117 – Tawnais 80 (Artaius (USA) 129) [1995 –: 8g 8m 8f 1996 a8g a8g Jan 22] no worthwhile form since mid-1994: sold 750 gns Ascot November Sales. *W. J. Musson* –

BROUGHTON'S PRIDE (IRE) 5 b.m. Superpower 113 – French Quarter (Ile de Bourbon (USA) 133) [1995 55: a12g 9.9m 10g² 9.2g² 10.3m 10g 9.9m² 10d⁴ 8d³ 8g³ 10f 1996 9.9m 8.2m* 8f 8f 8g 8.9g⁵ 7g³ 8.1s² Nov 7] rangy mare: modest handicapper: left J. Glover after second 5-y-o start: won at Nottingham (apprentice maiden, narrowly) in May: pulled up (reportedly broke blood vessel) next time but good efforts last 3 starts: effective at 7f to 1¼m: acts on good to firm ground and soft: visored (well beaten) first 4-y-o start. *J. L. Eyre* 56

BROUGHTONS RELISH 3 b.f. Nomination 125 – Mosso 81 (Ercolano (USA) 118) [1995 NR 1996 a8g a8g Dec 26] 2,700F: 3,000Y: half-sister to 2 winners, including Mossy Rose (up to 1m, by King of Spain): dam 2-y-o 5.8f and 6f winner: showed nil in claimer and maiden. *W. J. Musson* –

BROUGHTONS TURMOIL 7 b.g. Petorius 117 – Rustic Stile (Rusticaro (FR) 81
124) [1995 68, a60: a8g* a8g⁵ a8g* a8g 8m 7f² 8.3m⁶ 7m* 7f⁵ a8.5g 7.1m* 7.3d⁴ 7g² a–
7g⁴ 1996 8s 8m⁶ 7m³ 7m³ 7m⁴ 7g³ 7.6m³ 7g* 8m 8g 7m² 7g⁶ 7g⁵ Nov 2]
workmanlike gelding: fairly useful handicapper: won at Kempton in August: stays
1m, should prove effective at 6f: acts on firm and dead ground and the all-weather:
sometimes bandaged off-fore: has run creditably when sweating: held up: consistent.
W. J. Musson

BROWBEAT 2 ch.c. (Mar 9) Diesis 133 – Gentle Persuasion 95 (Bustino 136) –
[1996 7m Aug 17] rather unfurnished colt: sixth foal: brother to a modest maiden and
half-brother to 3-y-o 1¼m winner Punkah (by Lear Fan) and 2 winners, notably smart
5f to 7f winner Sharp Prod (by Sharpo): dam 2-y-o 6f winner, later suited by 1m: last
of 17 in maiden at Newbury: sold 1,000 gns Newmarket Autumn Sales. *R. Charlton*

BROWN EYED GIRL 4 ch.f. Sharpo 132 – Ella Mon Amour 65 (Ela- 43
Mana-Mou 132) [1995 70d: 7g² 7g⁵ 8.3m 9m² a8.5g 8.1d 1996 a9.4g 9.7s 10.8g 10g⁶
11.7g 10d 10.8m 10g 15.4g Sep 27] compact filly: has a quick action: only poor form
in 1996: sold out of B. Meehan's stable 1,400 gns Newmarket July Sales after sixth
start: no promise afterwards: stays 9f: well below form on a soft surface/all-weather:
tried blinkered, no improvement: inconsistent. *B. J. McMath*

BROWNIE'S PROMISE 3 b.g. Grey Desire 115 – Telegraph Callgirl 67 –
(Northern Tempest (USA) 120) [1995 NR 1996 7.5f 8m 5.9f 10f 10g 10f 10.4g Oct
10] unfurnished gelding: second foal: dam 7f and 1m winner: of no account: sold
1,050 gns Doncaster Sales. *M. Brittain*

BRUTAL FANTASY (IRE) 2 b.g. (Apr 20) Distinctly North (USA) 115 – Flash 64
Donna (USA) 70 (Well Decorated (USA)) [1996 5g* 5f² 6g² 6g³ 6m 5g Oct 18]
9,400Y: good-quartered gelding: seventh foal: brother to 3-y-o Zuno Princess and
half-brother to fairly useful 5f (at 2 yrs) to 9f winner Second Chance (by Digamist)
and a winner in Scandinavia (at up to 2m 5f) by Cyrano de Bergerac: dam best at 2
yrs: trained by N. Tinkler first 2 starts, winning seller at Musselburgh in May: placed
in non-selling nurseries afterwards: stays 6f: raced only on a sound surface: has been
bandaged behind. *J. L. Eyre*

BRUZ 5 b.g. Risk Me (FR) 127 – My Croft (Crofter (USA) 124) [1995 –: 5m 1996 29
13m⁴ 13g⁶ Jun 3] lengthy gelding: bad performer: tried visored, no improvement.
P. Monteith

BRYAN ROBSON (USA) 5 b.g. Topsider (USA) – Queen's Visit (Top Com- –
mand (USA)) [1995 69d: 6m⁵ 6m 6m 5m 5.1m 1996 6g 6m 5m 6m Jun 15]
smallish, sturdy gelding: fair handicapper: below form in 1996: should stay 7f: acts
on good to firm and dead ground: visored (out of form) once: inconsistent: joined
J. W. Mullins. *G. B. Balding*

BRYANSTON SQUARE (IRE) 3 b.g. Taufan (USA) 119 – Noble Treasure –
(USA) (Vaguely Noble 140) [1995 NR 1996 8.3g 10s Oct 24] 20,000F, 21,000Y:
strong gelding: has a rounded action: half-brother to middle-distance winners by
Shareef Dancer, Lyphard and Sadler's Wells, and to an Italian 7f winner by Shareef
Dancer: dam unraced half-sister to 10 winners, including dams of Glint of Gold,
Diamond Shoal and Media Starguest: well beaten in claimer and (burly after 3-month
absence) maiden: sold 1,100 gns Doncaster November Sales. *C. R. Egerton*

BRYNKIR 2 b.c. (May 5) Batshoof 122 – Felinwen (White Mill 76) [1996 8d⁶ 61
8.1s 8g Oct 29] 5,000Y: second foal: dam unraced daughter of half-sister to dam of
Primo Dominie: modest form in maidens: should stay beyond 1m. *D. J. G. Murray
Smith*

BUBBLE WINGS (FR) 4 b.f. In The Wings 128 – Bubble Prospector (USA) 77
(Miswaki (USA) 124) [1995 71p: a7g* 1996 a8.5g⁵ 7f² 8g* 8.2m⁵ 8g* 8f³ 8.1f³ 10m²
10.1m² Oct 23] workmanlike filly: unimpressive mover: generally progressive
handicapper: won at Brighton in May and Pontefract in July, leading inside final 1f:
best efforts last 2 starts: should stay beyond 10.1f: acts on firm ground (yet to race on
a soft surface) and equitrack. *S. P. C. Woods*

BUBBLY 2 b.c. (May 5) Rudimentary (USA) 118 – Champagne Season (USA) 54 74 p
(Vaguely Noble 140) [1996 7m⁵ Aug 7] 32,000Y: second foal: half-brother to 3-y-o
Champagne Prince (by Prince Sabo), 7f and 7.5f winner at 2 yrs: dam ran twice at 2

yrs: one-paced fifth of 12 to Bareeq in maiden at Kempton in August: will stay at least 1m: should improve. *J. L. Dunlop*

BUCKLEY BOYS   5 gr.m. Grey Desire 115 – Strip Fast 71 (Virginia Boy 106)   – [1995 51, a45: a8.5g 7m 11.5g² 10.1g 10.8g a11g² a12g 1996 a12g a11g Apr 9] compact mare: modest maiden: disappointing in 1996: stays 1½m: acts on good to firm and soft ground and on fibresand: tried blinkered, no improvement: joined Mrs L. Williamson. *A. Bailey*

BUDBY   3 ch.f. Rock City 120 – Lustrous 73 (Golden Act (USA)) [1995 64P: 6g   72 1996 6g³ 8g³ 10m³ 8.3g² 8.5g* 8m⁴ 8.1f² Sep 7] sturdy, attractive filly: fair form: won maiden handicap at Epsom (finishing strongly to lead close home) in July: stays 1¼m: has raced only on a sound surface, and acts on firm: consistent. *A. C. Stewart*

BUDDING ANNIE   3 b.f. Lord Bud 121 – Gold Paper (FR) (Rheingold 137)   – [1995 –: 6m⁵ 7.6d 1996 8f 10f⁶ 10m 10.8m 11.8g Oct 29] lengthy filly: still a maiden: well beaten after second 3-y-o start: stays 1¼m: sold 700 gns Ascot December Sales. *J. R. Bosley*

BUDDING PROSPECT   2 b.f. (Mar 27) Rudimentary (USA) 118 – City Link   – Rose (Lochnager 132) [1996 5m Jun 10] 4,600Y: workmanlike filly: sixth foal: half-sister to winning sprinters City Link Pet (by Tina's Pet) and Bodari (by Prince Sabo) and 7f winner Ahjay (by Tina's Pet): dam showed signs of ability on last out of 3 starts: backward and green, behind in Pontefract maiden auction in June. *W. J. Haggas*

BUDDY'S FRIEND (IRE)   8 ch.h. Jester 119 – Hasta (Skymaster 126) [1995   – 56, a69: a8g⁶ a8g³ a8.5g* a8g² a8g⁴ a8g⁶ 9g 7.5g⁴ 8.1m 8m 1996 8d a8g 10m 8m 8m⁶ 8m⁶ Jul 5] workmanlike horse: poor mover: fair handicapper at best: no worthwhile form in 1996: stays 1¼m: acts on the all-weather, probably on any turf ground: usually held up. *R. J. R. Williams*

BUD'S BET (IRE)   8 b.g. Reasonable (FR) 119 – Pearl Creek (Gulf Pearl 117)   – [1995 29, a42: a14g⁴ a16.2g 15.8g⁵ 1996 14.1f Jul 6] compact gelding: probably no longer of much account. *Miss J. F. Craze*

BUILT FOR COMFORT (IRE)   4 b.f. Nordico (USA) – Dewan's Niece   – (USA) (Dewan (USA)) [1995 64: 8g⁵ 10f² 8m 9.7g 1996 a11g a8g Feb 19] still a maiden: tailed-off last for new stable in 1996, visored last time. *N. M. Babbage*

BULINGTON (FR)   4 b.c. Sicyos (USA) 126 – Barbra (FR) (Le Fabuleux 133)   118 [1995 10.5g⁶ 10.5g* 11.5g* 11.8g* 12g² 12d 12g³ 11.5g⁴ 9.5g³ 11.5d⁴ 11g² 10g² 10d⁵ 1996 11g² 10m* 10g* 10m² 10g* 10d⁵ 10.6d* 12g³ 10g² 10v² Nov 16] seventeenth foal: half-brother to numerous winners, and closely related to Beaune (gave impression would have been well suited by 1½m, rated 121, by Lyphard) later the dam of Bering (stayed 1½m well, rated 136): dam, useful at up to 1¾m, sister to Bourbon (rated 129, Prix Royal-Oak) and half-sister to Beaugency (rated 130, Gran Premio di Milano): very smart French colt: won 4 minor events and placed in Group 3 event at 3 yrs: improved in 1996: won listed races at Longchamp in April and June then (after head second of 9 to Dance Treat in La Coupe at Saint-Cloud) Grand Prix de Vichy (beat Diamond Mix 1½ lengths) in July and listed race in the Provinces (by 10 lengths) in September: stays 1½m: acts on good to firm and heavy ground: tough, and consistent. *H. Pantall, France*

BULLFINCH   3 ch.c. Anshan 119 – Lambay 88 (Lorenzaccio 130) [1995 92:   90 7.1m* 7d⁶ 7g² 8m³ 1996 8g 8.1g⁵ 7.9f 8.1d 8f Jun 18] leggy colt: has a fluent action: fairly useful handicapper: caught the eye when tenth of 31 to North Song in Britannia Stakes at Royal Ascot last time, finishing well having been last 2f out: sold (P. Walwyn to R. Phillips) 17,000 gns Newmarket Autumn Sales: stays 1m: may be unsuited by a soft surface. *P. T. Walwyn*

BULLPEN BELLE   3 b.f. Relief Pitcher 120 – Hopeful Waters 66 (Forlorn River   – 124) [1995 64: 7.1s 8.2m² a8g⁵ 1996 10g 10.3m⁶ 7f 8.1m⁶ Jun 30] good-bodied filly: still a maiden: well held on flat in 1996: sold (P. Walwyn to R. Thompson) 550 gns Doncaster November Sales. *P. T. Walwyn*

BULSARA   4 b.g. Dowsing (USA) 124 – Taiga 69 (Northfields (USA)) [1995 59:   65 7g a6g 10m* 10m 10m³ 9f* 9f⁵ 8d 9f 1996 8m⁶ 8.1f⁴ 8f³ 10f* 10.1m* 10.1f⁴ 9g 9.2g⁵ 9m Oct 8] strong gelding: fair handicapper: won at Redcar and Newcastle in July: below form last 4 starts: stays 1¼m: acts on firm and dead ground. *C. W. Fairhurst*

Computer Timeform Nursery Handicap, Pontefract—Burlington House is on his own

BUMBLEFOOT (IRE) 3 b.f. Cyrano de Bergerac 120 – La Vosgienne   53
(Ashmore (FR) 125) [1995 61d: 6f⁴ a7g* 7.6m³ a8.5g² 8m a8g⁶ a8g⁵ 1996 a8g⁴ a8g²
a8g⁴ a8g⁵ a8.5g² a11g³ a8g Mar 9] modest form: left M. Johnston after sixth start:
stays 8.5f: acts on fibresand. *J. A. Harris*

BUNTY BAGSHAW 3 b.f. Arctic Lord 114 – Sarah Carter 57 (Reesh 117) [1995
NR 1996 8.3d 8.1f Sep 12] first reported foal: dam, 2-y-o 5f seller winner,
out of half-sister to high-class Gold Rod: showed nothing in maiden and seller.
J. L. Spearing

BUNTY BOO 7 b.m. Noalto 120 – Klairove 74 (Averof 123) [1995 110: 6g 5m 6d   94
6g⁶ 5m* 6g 6m⁶ 5m* 5d 6d 5f* 1996 5.1m⁵ 5m 5g⁴ Aug 14] leggy mare: smart
performer: well below best in 1996: effective at 5f (best form) and 6f: acts on firm
and soft ground: usually races prominently: covered by Salse. *R. Hannon*

BURBERRY QUEST 2 gr.f. (Apr 9) Thornberry (USA) 110 – Flying Joker   –
(Kalaglow 132) [1996 5s a5g May 2] 500Y: first foal: dam twice-raced granddaughter of very smart Joking Apart: sire (by Diesis) best at 1m: well beaten in
maiden auctions early in year. *B. R. Millman*

BURJ 3 b.g. Aragon 118 – Aspark (Sparkler 130) [1995 58?: 5m 6m 6g 6m 6.1s   –
1996 a6g a9.4g Apr 13] no form since second 2-y-o outing: tried blinkered, no
improvement. *N. A. Graham*

BURKES MANOR 2 b.g. (Apr 8) Presidium 124 – Miss Nelski 84 (Most Secret   79
119) [1996 5m³ 5f* 5m³ 6g⁴ 5f⁴ 6d⁴ 6g² 6m³ 6g³ a6g* Oct 19] 8,000Y: small,   a84
sturdy gelding: half-brother to 3 winners by Welsh Captain, including 3-y-o Welsh
Mountain, 5f winner at 2 yrs, and fairly useful sprinter Ski Captain: dam 5f winner
who stayed 7f: fairly useful performer: won maiden at Redcar in June and claimer at
Wolverhampton in October: stays 6f: acts on firm ground, good to soft and fibresand:
sent to Sweden. *T. D. Barron*

BURLESQUE 2 b.c. (Feb 9) Old Vic 136 – Late Matinee 84 (Red Sunset 120)   60 +
[1996 7d⁶ 8g Sep 7] fourth foal: dam 2-y-o 6f winner: considerably-handled sixth to
The Fly in median auction maiden at Ayr in August: little show only subsequent start:
should stay beyond 7f. *J. D. Bethell*

BURLINGTON HOUSE (USA) 2 br.c. (Jan 29) Housebuster (USA) – Queluz   84
(USA) 59 (Saratoga Six (USA)) [1996 5g³ 5.1g⁵ a6g* 6m⁵ 7m⁵ 5g* 7g⁴ 6m³ 6m⁵ Oct
17] $57,000F, $37,000Y, $47,000 2-y-o: small, quite good-topped colt: second foal:
dam, out of middle-distance winning daughter of Oaks winner Monade, placed over
7f from 3 starts here at 2 yrs and later successful at up to 9f in USA: sire top sprinter
in USA and stayed 1m well: fairly useful form: made most to win maiden at
Wolverhampton in May and nursery at Pontefract in September: creditable efforts
last 2 starts: stays 7f, best form at 6f: yet to race on a soft surface: races keenly: sold
30,000 gns Newmarket Autumn Sales. *P. F. I. Cole*

BURNING COST 6 br.m. Lochnager 132 – Sophie Avenue (Guillaume Tell   –
(USA) 121) [1995 NR 1996 a14g a14g a14.8g Dec 14] no longer of any account.
R. E. Peacock

BURNING FLAME 3 b.f. Robellino (USA) 127 – No Islands (Lomond (USA)   42
128) [1995 NR 1996 7d 7m 8g 9.7g 12m⁴ a16g 10m 11.9g 9g⁶ a10s Nov 19]
3,000Y: first foal: dam once-raced daughter of sister to Park Hill winner Quay Line:
poor maiden handicapper: probably stays 1½m: tried blinkered, better without:
inconsistent. *R. M. Flower*

BURNING TRUTH (USA)   2 ch.c. (Feb 8) Known Fact (USA) 135 – Galega   57 p
(Sure Blade (USA) 130) [1996 7d Oct 2] first foal: dam French 9f winner out of close
relative of Quiet Fling and Peacetime: midfield throughout in maiden at Salisbury in
October: should stay at least 1m: likely to do better. *R. Charlton*

BURNING (USA)   4 b.c. Bering 136 – Larnica (Alydar (USA)) [1995 103:
10m* 12g³ 12m⁶ 12f⁴ 13.9m 12d 10v 12m 1996 10g 12m 12m 10m 12m 9d⁵ Aug 25]
big, rangy colt: useful handicapper at 3 yrs: well below form in 1996: best efforts
at 1½m: acts on firm ground, seemingly not on a soft surface: tried blinkered, no
improvement: held up. *G. Harwood*

BURNT OFFERING   3 b.c. Old Vic 136 – Burnt Amber (Balidar 133) [1995 75:   79
7.1d 8g⁴ 1996 a12g³ a10g* 10.3d 12.3m³ 12g⁴ 12d⁴ 10.1m⁵ 10g Jul 10] close-
coupled colt: fair handicapper: won bad maiden at Lingfield in February: should stay
beyond 1½m: won on equitrack, best form on good/dead ground, probably acts on
good to firm. *C. E. Brittain*

BURNT SIENNA (IRE)   4 b.f. Don't Forget Me 127 – Ribot Ann (Kampala 120)   –
[1995 54: 10m 7f 7g 8m 8.2m 9.7g 11.6m 8.3m⁶ 8.3m* 7.6m³ 8f³ a10g⁶ 1996 a8g
a8g 8.3m 8.3m 10m 10.2m 8m 7f Jul 25] sparely-made filly: poor performer: no
worthwhile form in 1996: stays 8.3f: acts on firm going: tried visored, no
improvement: poor winning hurdler: changed hands 2,300 gns Ascot November
Sales: sent to South Korea. *J. S. Moore*

BURNTWOOD MELODY   5 gr.g. Merdon Melody 98 – Marwick (Roan   –
Rocket 128) [1995 –: 16.2m 1996 a12g⁶ Jan 8] seems of little account. *J. A. Harris*

BUROOJ   6 br.h. Danzig (USA) – Princess Sucree (USA) (Roberto (USA) 131)   118
[1995 111: 10m* 10m³ 10.1f* 10f² 12m* 13.3m⁴ 11.1g* 12d³ 10m³ 1996 12m² May
3] big, good-topped horse: had a quick action: smart performer: better than ever
when neck second of 9 to Riyadian in Jockey Club Stakes at Newmarket in May,
meeting some trouble in running but squeezing through to challenge inside final 1f:
stayed 13.3f: acted on firm and dead ground: often got on toes and sweated up in
preliminaries: held up: game: sprained a tendon in June and has been retired.
D. Morley

BURROUGH HILL LASS   6 b.m. Northern State (USA) 91 – Hawthorne Vale   –
(Richboy 117) [1995 NR 1996 a12g Jan 8] no worthwhile form: tried visored.
Mrs N. Macauley

BURSUL LADY   3 b.f. Be My Chief (USA) 122 – Neverdown 50 (Never So Bold   –
135) [1995 –: 7m⁵ 1996 10m 11.6d⁶ a16g Nov 12] of no account. *Miss B. Sanders*

BURUNDI (IRE)   2 b.c. (Apr 23) Danehill (USA) 126 – Sofala 103 (Home Guard   76
(USA) 129) [1996 8m 7f² Oct 8] 56,000Y: tall, rather angular colt: ninth foal:
half-brother to 3-y-o Smooth Asset (by Fairy King) and several winners, including
useful stayer Bourbon Boy (by Ile de Bourbon) and useful 6f and 7f winner North
Queen (by Northfields): dam won at up to 8.5f: second in maiden at Warwick in
October on final start: should stay 1m: may do better. *P. W. Chapple-Hyam*

BUSHEHR (IRE)   4 b.c. Persian Bold 123 – Shejrah (USA) (Northjet 136) [1995   –
68: 8.3m³ 8m³ 10g* 10m⁴ 12.1m² 13.8m³ 11.8m² 15.8g 1996 a14.8g a16g Feb 5]
fair performer at 3 yrs: tailed off all 3 flat outings for new connections: should
stay beyond 1½m: has raced only on a sound surface on turf: tried blinkered, no
improvement. *S. Coathup*

BUSY FLIGHT   3 b.c. Pharly (FR) 130 – Bustling Nelly 94 (Bustino 136)   119 p
[1995 100p: 8g 8d² 7.3d² 1996 10g⁶ 12m 12.3d* 12f² 12m* Oct 4]
   While age may be finally catching up with five-time Jockey Club Cup
winner Further Flight, the future looks bright for his much younger close
relation, stablemate 'Busy' whom we already rate 1 lb higher than Further
Flight at his best. Busy Flight's trainer reportedly regards him as Prix de l'Arc
material and intends starting him off as a four-year-old in the John Porter Stakes
or some similar race.
   Busy Flight was trained for the Derby after showing useful form in the
autumn as a two-year-old—he'd finished a close second to Tumbleweed Ridge
in the Horris Hill Stakes on his final start—but cut no ice at Epsom or in the
preceding Sandown Classic Trial. At both Sandown and Epsom overkeenness

O. & K. Troy Stakes, Doncaster—a horse on his way up; Busy Flight holds off Kalabo and Minds Music

spoiled whatever chance he had, and he caused a lot of trouble in the Derby as he dropped back coming down the hill. Winning a maiden became the next objective. He achieved it first go, in an above-average contest at Ripon in late-August, leading throughout and coasting in by six lengths from the odds-on Multicoloured. Further evidence that Busy Flight hadn't been greatly overrated was soon forthcoming, when he again made all in the O. & K. Troy Stakes at Doncaster; he showed admirable resolution to account for a field of useful or better animals, winning by a length and a half from Kalabo. With the future in mind Busy Flight wasn't asked to carry on much longer as a three-year-old, and although he looked an ideal candidate for the St Simon Stakes when winning the Racing Post Godolphin Stakes at Newmarket in early-October next time out, his season ended there. Up against Key To My Heart, Sharaf Kabeer and Heron Island, Busy Flight started 11/8 favourite for the Godolphin and won convincingly by four lengths from an in-form Key To My Heart, making the running and stretching out very well under pressure from the Dip. From a family with a justified reputation for producing late-developers, he can improve even on this, and the proposed step up from listed races is a logical progression.

		⎧ Lyphard	⎧ Northern Dancer
	⎧ Pharly (FR)	⎨ (b 1969)	⎩ Goofed
	⎪ (ch 1974)	⎩ Comely	⎧ Boran
Busy Flight	⎨	(ch 1966)	⎩ Princesse Comnene
(b.c. 1993)	⎪	⎧ Bustino	⎧ Busted
	⎪ Bustling Nelly	⎨ (b 1971)	⎩ Ship Yard
	⎩ (gr 1981)	⎩ Flying Nelly	⎧ Nelcius
		(gr 1970)	⎩ Flying By

The relationship between Busy Flight and Further Flight is as close as this—both are by Pharly, while Busy Flight's dam, the quite useful middle-distance mare Bustling Nelly, is a daughter of Further Flight's dam, the 1974 Cambridgeshire winner Flying Nelly. On breeding, Busy Flight will stay further than a mile and a half, and although his style of racing is different from Further Flight's, in that he is a front-runner who still occasionally takes a keen hold, there is little doubt about it. Workmanlike, with a free, round action, Busy Flight acts on firm going and on good to soft; he has yet to race on soft. Already it is evident that he shares with Further Flight an enthusiasm for the game. He is sure to win more races. *B. W. Hills*

BUTTERWICK BELLE (IRE)   3 b.f. Distinctly North (USA) 115 – Forest –
Berries (IRE) (Thatching 131) [1995 64: 5m² 5m³ 6g⁴ 1996 7g 7m⁵ 6g 6d a6g 8m 8m
Oct 28] sparely-made filly: modest as a juvenile: showed little in 1996: should stay
beyond 6f: wears bandages: sold 3,800 gns Newmarket December Sales. *R. A. Fahey*

BUT WHY   2 ch.g. (Mar 11) Then Again 126 – Pleasure Island 57 (Dalsaan 125)   74
[1996 5m⁵ 5.1m⁵ 6g* 6g³ 7g* 8g⁴ 7g Aug 30] 7,500F: leggy, good-topped gelding:
half-brother to a winner in Austria by Petorius: dam 7.5f winner: won seller at
Leicester in May (final start for C. Murray) and 6-runner claimer at Vichy in July:
stays 1m. *G. E. Mikhalides, France*

BUZZARDS HALL   6 ch.m. Buzzards Bay 128§ – Nikoola Eve 69 (Roscoe –
Blake 120) [1995 NR 1996 a12g a12g Jan 15] no worthwhile form. *M. C. Chapman*

BUZZBY   2 b.c. (Feb 23) Buzzards Bay 128§ – Capricious Lady (IRE) (Capricorn   80
Line 111) [1996 5.2s⁵ 5f 7g* 7.5g* 8m 8s 10d³ 8d⁶ 10v⁴ Nov 30] small colt: first foal:
dam in frame in NH Flat races: won seller at Newmarket in July (final outing for
A. Foster) and claimer at Deauville in August: stays 1¼m: acts on any ground: has
worn bandages. *G. E. Mikhalides, France*

BUZZBY BABE   2 b.f. (Mar 19) Presidium 124 – Aposse Ad Esse (Record Run –
127) [1996 6m a7g Dec 11] second reported foal: dam unraced: well beaten in
maidens. *A. G. Foster*

BY THE BAY   4 b.f. Shareef Dancer (USA) 135 – Beryl's Jewel 86 (Siliconn 121)   53
[1995 64d: 7m⁴ 7m 7g³ 7m³ 7g³ 7m 8g 7s a10g⁴ a7g⁶ a7g⁶ 1996 a8g⁵ a8g⁴ 9m⁴ a12g   a37
a10s⁵ Nov 19] rather leggy filly: modest maiden: left C. C. Elsey's stable and off
course 7 months after second 4-y-o start: stays 9f: acts on good to firm ground, well
beaten on soft: has run well when sweating. *S. Dow*

C

CABALLUS (USA)   3 b.g. Danzig Connection (USA) – Rutledge Place (USA)   75
(Caro 133) [1995 NR 1996 12m³ 11.4m² 12m⁴ 16m Aug 16] $62,000Y: big, lengthy
gelding: fifth foal: half-brother to 4 winners, including very useful 6f (at 2 yrs) and 7f
winner Firm Pledge (by Affirmed), later Grade 3 winner in USA: dam unraced
half-sister to good French sprinter Gem Diamond: fair maiden: finished last final 2
starts: sold (Lord Huntingdon to Mrs J. Pitman) 5,000 gns Newmarket Autumn Sales
and gelded: stays 1½m: takes good hold (got loose and bolted second intended start)
and is a front runner: not one to trust implicitly. *Lord Huntingdon*

CABARET (IRE)   3 b.f. Sadler's Wells (USA) 132 – Chamonis (USA) 101   103
(Affirmed (USA)) [1995 NR 1996 9g* 10m⁴ 11.9g 10.1m⁵ 8m 10.8s² 10v⁴ Nov 30]
IR 28,000Y: big, rangy filly with plenty of scope: fifth foal: sister to winners
Theatreworld (up to 2m in Ireland, smart hurdler) and Zermatt (up to 1¼m) and
half-sister to useful 7f winner Danish Heights (by Danehill): dam, 6f and 7f winner,
is half-sister to dam of 2 high-class American performers: useful performer: won
maiden at Ripon in May: highly tried afterwards: best efforts when about ½-length
fifth of 11 (off bridle 4f out, finishing very strongly) to Hagwah in listed rated stakes
at Newcastle and neck second of 10 to Mistra in listed event at Le Croise-Laroche:
should prove well suited by further than 10.8f: acts on good to firm and soft ground.
P. W. Chapple-Hyam

CABCHARGE BLUE   4 b.f. Midyan (USA) 124 – Mashobra 75 (Vision (USA))   57 d
[1995 67d: 8d 6m 8.3g 7m a8g a6g a7g 1996 a12g⁴ a12g a8g* a7g a8g⁴ a8g⁴
a8.5g⁶ a7g Apr 1] fairly useful performer as 2-y-o: disappointing since: won weak
handicap at Southwell in January: below form last 3 starts: best form at up to 1m: acts
on fibresand, best turf efforts on a soft surface: tends to hang, and is a tricky ride.
T. J. Naughton

CAB

CABCHARGE GEMINI 2 b.c. (Apr 18) High Kicker (USA) – Miss Noname – 102 (High Top 131) [1996 6m Aug 4] half-brother to fairly useful 1985 2-y-o 6f winner Karmo (by Thatch), an Irish NH Flat race winner by Glenstal and several winners abroad: dam best at up to 1¼m: tailed off in maiden at Lingfield. *G. G. Margarson*

CACHARRO 5 b.g. Aragon 118 – Jalopy 71 (Jalmood (USA) 126) [1995 NR – 1996 7.1g 5g 5.9f Jun 13] rated 72 at best at 3 yrs: well beaten in 1996. *Miss Z. A. Green*

CACHET NOIR (USA) 3 b.c. Theatrical 128 – Irish Wisdom (USA) (Turkoman 109 (USA)) [1995 8m² 1996 10g* 10.5m² 10.5g⁵ 14g* 15d³ Jul 6] $100,000Y: first foal: dam minor sprint winner: narrowly won minor event at Longchamp in April and steadily-run Prix du Lys at Saint-Cloud (beat Stage Pass ¾ length) in June: 13 lengths third of 5 to Tarator in Prix Hubert de Chaudenay at Longchamp last time: stays 1¾m, at least in steadily-run race: acts on good to firm ground: blinkered (last in Prix Lupin) third 3-y-o start. *P. Bary, France*

CADBURY CASTLE 2 b.f. (May 10) Midyan (USA) 124 – Orange Hill 75 56 (High Top 131) [1996 8g⁴ 8d Oct 2] small filly: sixth foal: half-sister to useful 3-y-o 7f (at 2 yrs) to 10.3f winner Jackson Hill (by Priolo) and 2 winners by Rainbow Quest, including 6-y-o middle-distance stayer Old Provence: dam, won Cesarewitch, half-sister to top Canadian filly Carotene: backward, fourth to Home Alone in maiden at Goodwood on debut: tailed off only subsequent start: bred to stay middle distances. *M. Blanshard*

CADDY'S FIRST 4 b.g. Petong 126 – Love Scene (Carwhite 127) [1995 46, a62: – a8g⁶ 7g³ a6g⁵ a7g³ 7g 6g a7g* a7g² 7m⁴ a9.4g 1996 8.3d 8.2d a7g⁶ a8g Nov 26] leggy, quite good-topped gelding: modest handicapper: never a threat in 1996: best form at 7f: acts on good to firm ground and fibresand, well below form on a soft surface: below form blinkered and visored. *S. Mellor*

CADEAU ELEGANT 3 ch.f. Cadeaux Genereux 131 – Wasimah 84 (Caerleon 64 p (USA) 132) [1995 NR 1996 6m 6f 6m⁵ Jul 19] 22,000Y: lengthy filly: second foal: dam 2-y-o 5f winner from sprinting family: caught the eye when 4¼ lengths fifth of 6 to Navigate in maiden at Newmarket last time, travelling strongly with leaders then not given anything like hard time final 1f: looks a sprinter: pulls hard: looked capable of better. *N. A. Callaghan*

CADEAUX CHER 2 ch.g. (Apr 3) Cadeaux Genereux 131 – Home Truth 98 78 + (Known Fact (USA) 135) [1996 5g 5.1m² 5f² 5m⁴ Sep 27] 22,000Y: lengthy gelding: unimpressive mover: third foal: dam 7f and 1m winner: second in maidens then off course 3½ months before finishing very good fourth of 8 in nursery at Folkestone: will probably be better suited by further than 5f: hung left when runner-up, badly so on first occasion: possibly capable of better. *B. W. Hills*

CADEAUX TRYST 4 b.c. Cadeaux Genereux 131 – Trystero (Shareef Dancer 106 (USA) 135) [1995 107: 8m 7m² 7g* 7m 7g² 7d⁶ 10m⁴ 1996 8d⁵ 8d³ 8m² 8m⁶ 8m⁴ 8m* 8d⁴ Oct 10] robust colt: shows knee action: useful handicapper: 1½ lengths second to Idris in listed race at Leopardstown in May: won valuable event at Velie-fendi in Turkey in September in close finish: creditable fourth of 6 to Decorated Hero in listed race at Longchamp final start: very best form at 7f/1m, far from discredited at 1¼m: acts on good to firm ground and dead: usually bandaged: normally held up: consistent. *E. A. L. Dunlop*

CA'D'ORO 3 ch.g. Cadeaux Genereux 131 – Palace Street (USA) 103 (Secreto 60 (USA) 128) [1995 63: 5m⁶ 6m 1996 5d 6m 7g⁵ 6g 8m* 8m⁶ 8g 7m⁴ 7m⁴ 7s³ Oct 24] small, rather leggy gelding: modest handicapper: narrowly won maiden event at Bath in August: stays 1m: acts on good to firm and soft ground: consistent. *G. B. Balding*

CAERFILLY DANCER 2 ch.f. (Mar 1) Caerleon (USA) 132 – Darnelle 83 89 (Shirley Heights 130) [1996 6m* 6m 7m⁴ Oct 5] 15,000Y, 46,000 2-y-o: neat filly: has a quick, unimpressive action: fourth foal: half-sister to 3-y-o 7f winner Consort (by Groom Dancer) and a winner abroad (including at 1½m) by Unfuwain: dam, 7.6f (at 2 yrs) and 9f winner, half-sister to Oaks and Irish Oaks second Bourbon Girl: won maiden at Ascot in August: better subsequent effort when over 5 lengths fourth of 7 to Sarayir in listed race at Newmarket in October: bred to stay at least 1¼m: slowly away second start. *R. Akehurst*

CAHERASS COURT (IRE) 5 b.m. Taufan (USA) 119 – Grass Court (Thatch – (USA) 136) [1995 –: a6g a6g a6g a6g a8.5g a7g a6g a7g 1996 a6g a6g a7g a8.5g Jul 11] no form since 1994. *B. Preece*

CAIRN DHU 2 ch.g. (May 15) Presidium 124 – My Precious Daisy (Sharpo 132) 53 [1996 6m⁵ 5f⁵ 6m 6d⁴ Sep 27] 11,000Y: robust gelding: has scope: fifth foal: half-brother to 4-y-o 5f performer Swan At Whalley (by Statoblest): dam Irish sprinter: modest form in maidens and nurseries: stays 6f: reluctant stalls on debut. *Mrs J. R. Ramsden*

CAJUN SUNSET (IRE) 2 b.g. (Apr 6) Red Sunset 120 – Carcajou (High Top 56 131) [1996 7m 7s 7g 7g³ 7g⁵ 8g³ 8f⁴ 8.3d* Sep 30] IR 19,000Y: rather leggy gelding: easy mover: brother to 3-y-o Hollywood Sunset and 3 winners, including smart 1m to 11f winner Sunset Boulevard, and half-brother to several winners here and abroad: dam lightly-raced daughter of smart stayer Wolverene: modest form: won nursery at Hamilton in September: will stay at least 1¼m: acts on firm ground but better form with some give: sometimes hangs, and isn't an easy ride: sold 6,000 gns Newmarket Autumn Sales. *T. D. Easterby*

CALA-HOLME (IRE) 2 b.f. (Jan 18) Fools Holme (USA) – Calaloo Sioux – (USA) 100 (Our Native (USA)) [1996 5m 7m⁶ 6m Jun 18] IR 3,600Y: fifth reported living foal: half-sister to useful Irish 1m winner Master Tribe (by Master Willie), Irish 4-y-o 1¼m and 1½m winner Double Colour (by Doyoun) and a winner in Norway: dam 7.6f winner out of half-sister to 3 speedy fillies: no form in median auction maiden and sellers: sold 500 gns Doncaster August Sales. *T. D. Easterby*

CALAMANDER (IRE) 2 b.f. (Apr 21) Alzao (USA) 117 – Local Custom (IRE) 55 (Be My Native (USA) 122) [1996 5.7g 6.9g⁴ 5.1m⁶ 7f Sep 3] IR 19,000Y: first foal: dam, Irish maiden, half-sister to Middle Park Stakes winner Balla Cove: modest form: should stay at least 1m: raced only on a sound surface. *P. F. I. Cole*

CALANDRELLA 3 b.f. Sizzling Melody 117 – Maravilla 73 (Mandrake Major 46 122) [1995 NR 1996 8.3g 8.3m 7m 6m⁵ 6.1m 8d Sep 30] 6,000Y: sixth foal: sister to 1991 2-y-o 5f winner Sultry Singer and half-sister to several winners, including Summer Villa (1m, by Nomination): dam maiden who stayed 1m: form only when fifth of 18 in claiming handicap at Salisbury: probably a sprinter. *G. B. Balding*

CALCANDO 4 b.f. Teenoso (USA) 135 – Musical Princess 66 (Cavo Doro 124) – [1995 –: 12m 11.9d 1996 12.1m⁴ 16.5g 13.1m 16.1m⁶ 17.2m Aug 28] sturdy filly: no worthwhile form. *E. Weymes*

CALCHOU 2 gr.f. (Apr 19) Barrys Gamble 102 – Ping Pong 65 (Petong 126) ? [1996 5g a5g³ 5g⁵ a5g* 5g⁶ a5g Dec 3] first living foal: dam 2-y-o 6f winner: made a65 all in median auction maiden at Southwell in June: failed to repeat the form: speedy: acts on fibresand. *C. W. Fairhurst*

CALDER KING 5 ch.g. Rakaposhi King 119 – Name The Game 66 (Fair Season 68 120) [1995 61, a66: a8g 10m 8m 8.5m³ 8g 8m 8g³ 10f⁶ a7g² 9f a9.4g⁴ a9.4g⁵ 8g 8.1g² a75 8g⁵ a7g² 8.1s a9.4g³ a11g³ 1996 a11g² a11g² a11g² a8g² a12g³ 10.3d 11.1d* 12.1d⁴ 10m 11.1s* 8.3s 10g⁵ 12f⁴ 12g² 12.3m⁶ 10.4g³ 10.9m² 11.9d 10.4g 10g 10f⁴ Nov 5] stocky, lengthy gelding: fair handicapper: none too consistent on turf in 1996, but won at Hamilton in April and May (amateurs): effective at 1m, unlikely to stay beyond 1½m: acts on firm ground, soft and goes well on fibresand: usually visored/blinkered nowadays: held up: has hung, and sometimes wears near-side pricker. *J. L. Eyre*

CALENDULA 3 b.f. Be My Guest (USA) 126 – Sesame 117 (Derrylin 115) [1995 62 NR 1996 12m 10s⁵ 11.5m⁵ 10.5s 12g Nov 1] sturdy, lengthy filly: unimpressive mover: first foal: dam, middle-distance stayer, is half-sister to smart stayer Celeric: modest maiden: will stay beyond 11.5f: acts on firm and soft ground. *D. Morley*

CALGARY GIRL 4 ch.f. Weld 122 – Calgary 63 (Run The Gantlet (USA)) – [1995 –: 10d a8g⁶ a8g 1996 a13g Jan 13] no form on flat. *P. C. Ritchens*

CALLALOO 3 b.g. Mtoto 134 – Catawba 98 (Mill Reef (USA) 141) [1995 70: 7m³ 8g⁶ 7g 1996 10m a9.4g Dec 7] fair form at best: well beaten in 1996: sold out of Mrs J. Cecil's stable 2,200 gns Newmarket Autumn Sales after reappearance: should prove a stayer. *R. Harris*

CALLING JAMAICA 4 b.f. Elmaamul (USA) 125 – Tolstoya (Northfields – (USA)) [1995 –: 12.5m 1996 a11g Feb 10] rated 59 in 1994 for P. Cole: no form afterwards: broke leg on hurdling debut: dead. *M. C. Pipe*

CALL ME 3 b.f. Most Welcome 131 – Stylish Sister 66 (Great Nephew 126) [1995 75 NR 1996 a7g* 5g⁶ a7g² 9g* 10.1m⁶ 10g³ 10f³ 9.2m* 9m³ Aug 7] 1,000Y: strong, lengthy filly: has a scratchy action: third reported foal: dam once-raced half-sister to Cesarewitch winner Sir Michael and very speedy 1974 2-y-o Fats Waller: fair performer: won maiden at Southwell in April, minor event at Newcastle in May and 4-runner handicap at Hamilton in August: sold 24,000 gns Newmarket Autumn Sales: stays 1¼m, may well get further: acts on fibresand, raced only on sound surface on turf: genuine and consistent: sent to USA. *C. W. Thornton*

CALL ME ALBI (IRE) 5 ch.g. Glenstal (USA) 118 – Albeni 84 (Great Nephew 42 126) [1995 49: a13g a16g³ a16g⁴ a16g² 11.9m 17.2f 11.6m² 12f² 14d a16g⁴ 1996 a16g⁴ a16g³ a16g⁵ Feb 29] poor handicapper: stays 2m: acts on equitrack and firm ground, possibly not on dead: effective blinkered/visored or not: chasing with Mrs L. Richards. *G. L. Moore*

CALL ME FLASH 4 ch.g. Presidium 124 – Relkisha 58 (Relkino 131) [1995 –: – 10m 8m·a8g³ 19m a8g a12g Mar 9] no form on flat since debut. *Mrs P. Sly*

CALL ME I'M BLUE (IRE) 6 b.g. Reasonable (FR) 119 – Bluebutton 65 57 (Blue Cashmere 129) [1995 91: 6g 5m 5g⁶ 6m 5g⁶ 5m 5.6m⁴ 5d⁴ 5s 5m 6f 1996 7g 5m 5g 7m 6g 6m 5.1m³ a6g Aug 16] robust, lengthy gelding: useful handicapper (rated 107 in 1993) at best: well below form in 1996, pulled up as though something amiss fourth start: stayed 5.6f: acted on firm and dead going: well beaten only try in blinkers: tended to edge left: dead. *N. Tinkler*

CALL MY GUEST (IRE) 6 b.g. Be My Guest (USA) 126 – Overcall (Bustino 136) [1995 NR 1996 a16.2g⁵ 16.4g 17.2f 16.1f Jun 10] close-coupled gelding: fair handicapper at 3 yrs in Ireland: well beaten on return to flat: stays at least 1½m: acts on heavy ground: tried blinkered at 2 yrs: fairly useful hurdler. *R. E. Peacock*

CALLONESCY (IRE) 4 b.g. Royal Academy (USA) 130 – Take Your Mark – (USA) (Round Table) [1995 57: a7g a9.4g² a10g 10g a7g⁶ 1996 a10g⁵ a13g⁴ a10g³ a16g a12g a10s Nov 19] modest maiden at best at 3 yrs for C. Brittain: sold cheaply, and no worthwhile form (tried blinkered) on return. *D. C. O'Brien*

CALL TOPHORSE 4 b.g. Today And Tomorrow 78 – Sum Star 67 (Comedy 50 Star (USA) 121) [1995 –: a7g⁴ a8g 10.8m 19m a6g⁴ a7g a8g* a8g Mar 29] modest performer: best effort to win selling handicap at Lingfield in February: reportedly swallowed tongue there final start: stays 1m: acts on all-weather: blinkered last 2 starts. *C. Murray*

CALL TO THE BAR (IRE) 7 b.g. Kafu 120 – Papun (USA) (Mount Hagen 55 (FR) 127) [1995 66d: 5m 6f³ 5m 5m 5m 6g 1996 5g 5d⁵ 5g⁴ 5g² 5f⁶ 5.9f Jun 26] leggy, sparely-made gelding: seemed only modest in 1996: stayed 6f: easily best form on a sound surface: below form when blinkered (bolted) and visored: burst blood vessel and died final start. *M. Dods*

CALYPSO GRANT (IRE) 2 b.f. (Apr 11) Danehill (USA) 126 – Why So 91 p Silent (Mill Reef (USA) 141) [1996 7f² 7g² 8g* Oct 25] compact filly: fourth foal: sister to useful 4-y-o 7f (at 2 yrs) to 1½m winner Poppy Carew and half-sister to 3-y-o Pennyfair (by Fairy King): dam unraced daughter of Pretty Polly Stakes and Lancashire Oaks winner Sing Softly: fairly useful form when running on really strongly to win maiden at Doncaster by 1¾ lengths from Summer Dance: will stay 1¼m: possibly suited by strongly-run race: will improve further. *P. W. Harris*

CALYPSO LADY (IRE) 2 ch.f. (May 10) Priolo (USA) 127 – Taking Steps 100 88 (Gay Fandango (USA) 132) [1996 6m* 7m³ Sep 20] IR 15,000Y, 20,000 2-y-o: rather unfurnished filly: fifth foal: half-sister to 4 winners, including 3-y-o 7f winner (stays 1½m) Slip Jig (by Marju) and useful German middle-distance performer Last Step (by Last Tycoon): dam Irish 9f winner (also third in Irish 1000 Guineas) who probably stayed 11f: 50/1-winner of maiden at Kempton in September: staying-on 3 lengths third of 9 to Etoile in minor event at Newbury later in month: will stay 1¼m: may do better. *R. Hannon*

CAMBRIDGE BALL (IRE) 2 b.f. (Mar 21) Royal Academy (USA) 130 – Boat 64 Race (USA) (Seattle Slew (USA)) [1996 6m² 7g⁴ 6.1d² 5f⁵ 6g⁵ Oct 21] 7,500 2-y-o: leggy filly: fifth foal: half-sister to useful Irish 4-y-o 6f and 7f winner America's Cup (by Fairy King) and a winner in Hong Kong by Bluebird: dam short-headed over 1m on first of 2 starts in Ireland, is half-sister to Grade 2 11f winner Sword Dance from an excellent family: modest maiden: needs further than 5f, should stay 1m: acts on firm ground and dead. *M. Johnston*

CAMDEN'S RANSOM (USA) 9 b.g. Hostage (USA) – Camden Court (USA) – (Inverness Drive (USA)) [1995 –, a61: a10g² a10g⁵ a11g a11g* a11g⁴ a10g* a10g a11g⁴ 10m 10d a10g a10g⁴ 1996 9g a10g Sep 10] good-bodied gelding: modest handicapper: well beaten on belated return: suited by strongly-run race at 1m to 11f: acts on good to firm ground, soft and all-weather surfaces: has won for apprentice: normally held up. *H. G. Rowsell*

CAMERON EDGE 3 ch.f. Komaite (USA) – Rapid Action 64 (Gunner B 126) – [1995 NR 1996 8m 10m 12.4m⁶ 8g 7g Oct 25] third living foal: dam best at around 1m: well beaten: has been heavily bandaged in front. *A. B. Mulholland*

CAMIONNEUR (IRE) 3 b.g. Cyrano de Bergerac 120 – Fact of Time (Known 53 Fact (USA) 135) [1995 57: 5m⁴ 6m 5f⁴ 5m⁴ 5g⁵ 6f⁴ 7.9g 6g 5m² 6f⁵ 5m⁴ 1996 6g 7.5g⁴ 6m 7.5m 7.5f⁶ 5.9f⁴ 6g⁴ 6s⁴ 6m³ 5m² 6m* 5m³ 6m⁴ 5g 6s 5.1m⁴ 5m 6f⁶ 6m⁴ Oct 23] workmanlike gelding: modest handicapper: won maiden event at Ripon in July, meeting trouble and getting up final stride: effective at 5f, and stays 7.5f: acts on firm and soft ground: effective blinkered (usually is) or not: pulls hard: tends to carry head awkwardly: consistent. *T. D. Easterby*

CAMPASPE 4 b.f. Dominion 123 – Lady River (FR) (Sir Gaylord) [1995 –: a8.5g 60 a8g⁴ a7g 6f 1996 12m* 14.1g³ 14.1m 12m² 12g² 12.3m² a12g⁵ 12.1m³ 12m* 13.6m⁶ a– Oct 17] leggy filly: modest handicapper: won at Beverley in May, unlucky at Doncaster in July on fourth start, then won back at Beverley (much improved form in strongly-run race, by 9 lengths) in September: probably stays 13.6f: yet to race on a soft surface, no form on fibresand: suited by a truly-run race. *J. G. FitzGerald*

CAMP DAVID (GER) 6 b.h. Surumu (GER) – Capitolina (FR) (Empery (USA) 116 128) [1995 16g* 16v⁵ 16m* 15m* 14g* 1996 16g* 16g* 15m* 16g* 20d⁴ Oct 5] smart German stayer: second foal: half-brother to German 6f (at 2 yrs) to 1¼m winner Classic Cara (by Nikos), listed placed: dam French 8.3f (at 2 yrs) to 1¼m winner: unbeaten in Germany in 1996, taking listed race at Mulheim in May for second year in succession, Oleander-Rennen at Baden-Baden (beat First Hello 2 lengths) in June and listed races at Dusseldorf in July and Baden-Baden in August: ran well when 4½ lengths fourth of 10 to Nononito in Prix du Cadran at Longchamp, hampered and squeezed onto rail towards end of back straight, keeping on unable to quicken in straight: stays 2½m: acts on good to firm and dead ground, seemingly not on soft or heavy: consistent. *A. Wohler, Germany*

CAMP FOLLOWER 3 b.c. Warrshan (USA) 117 – House Maid 95 (Habitat 89 134) [1995 ?: 6g* 1996 10g² 11.8g³ 14m⁴ Jun 27] neat colt: good mover: fairly useful form: failed to reproduce reappearance (Rome) form in Britain: sold 11,000 gns Newmarket Autumn Sales. *J. L. Dunlop*

CAMPHAR 3 ch.f. Pharly (FR) 130 – Camomilla (Targowice (USA) 130) [1995 – NR 1996 7d May 22] half-sister to 1986 Irish 2-y-o 7f and 1m winner High Taidgh (by High Line) and 3 winners abroad: dam never ran: 50/1, showed nil in maiden at Salisbury. *R. M. Flower*

CAMPORESE (IRE) 3 b.f. Sadler's Wells (USA) 132 – Campestral (USA) 97 111 (Alleged (USA) 138) [1995 NR 1996 10.5d* 12m⁴ 13.5g² 12.5d⁶ Oct 5] rather leggy filly: shows traces of stringhalt: has rather a round action: first foal: dam, winner at 7f at 2 yrs who stayed 11.5f as 3-y-o, out of very useful daughter of Cheveley Park winner Sookera: smart performer: won maiden at Haydock in May by 9 lengths, making all: 10 lengths fourth of 10 to Lady Carla in the Oaks at Epsom, jostled back to rear on turn before running on well: best effort when short-neck second of 6 to Helen of Spain in Prix de Pomone at Deauville in August, making most: respectable sixth of 13 to Annaba in Prix de Royallieu at Longchamp in October: stays 13.5f: yet to race on extremes of going. *P. W. Chapple-Hyam*

CANADIAN FANTASY 2 b.g. (Jan 28) Lear Fan (USA) 130 – Florinda (CAN) 76 (Vice Regent (CAN)) [1996 6.1m³ 6m² 6m² 6m⁴ 7m² 10m³ Oct 7] 16,500Y: strong, lengthy gelding: unimpressive mover: second foal: dam unraced half-sister to Irish Derby runner-up Insan: fair form in maidens: stays 1¼m: raced only on top-of-the-ground: blinkered final start: flashes tail: has gone early to post. *M. Johnston*

CANADIAN JIVE   3 b.f. Dominion 123 – Ural Dancer (Corvaro (USA) 124) – [1995 NR 1996 10m Jun 3] third foal: dam French 9f and 11f winner: 50/1, tailed off in maiden at Windsor: withdrawn (burst out of stalls) Oct 24. *D. W. P. Arbuthnot*

CANARY BLUE (IRE)   5 b.m. Bluebird (USA) 125 – Norfolk Bonnet (Morston – (FR) 125) [1995 –: a14.8g a12g 1996 15.8g 17.2m Aug 28] workmanlike mare: rated 59 in 1994: no form on flat since: stays 1¼m: blinkered (below form) twice: has joined P. W. Hiatt. *P. R. Webber*

CANARY FALCON   5 ch.g. Polish Precedent (USA) 131 – Pumpona (USA)   52 (Sharpen Up 127) [1995 60, a66: a10g⁵ a10g⁵ a7g* a7g⁴ 8m⁶ 7m³ 12m 8.1g⁵ 6d   a64 7d 7m⁴ a7g a9.4g² a9.4g 1996 a11g a10g a8g³ a10g a8g⁶ 9.7s 7.5m 11.5f⁶ 10g⁵ 11m⁶ a12g* Dec 28] compact gelding: good mover: modest handicapper: left John Berry after sixth 5-y-o start: blinkered first time, made all at Wolverhampton in December, winning by 10 lengths: stays 1½m: acts on good to firm ground and the all-weather: tried visored, no improvement: modest winning hurdler: none too consistent. *R. J. O'Sullivan*

CAN CAN CHARLIE   6 gr.g. Vaigly Great 127 – Norton Princess 76 (Wolver – Hollow 126) [1995 –, a66: a12g³ a10g² a12g⁵ a9.4g* a9.4g 9.7s⁶ 1996 a10g a10g⁵ a12g Dec 20] fair handicapper: below form on belated return: stays 1¼m: acts on good to firm ground, soft and all-weather surfaces: blinkered (no improvement) final 4-y-o start: held up: none too consistent: fair hurdler. *J. Pearce*

CAN CAN LADY   2 ch.f. (Mar 10) Anshan 119 – Agama (USA) 44 (Nureyev   71 (USA) 131) [1996 5.9f⁴ 5.9f* 6m⁴ 6m 6.5m 8m* 8m⁵ Sep 26] 3,400Y: tall, leggy, unfurnished filly: first foal: dam showed poor form in 2 starts here at 2 yrs, then won over 13.5f in France as 3-y-o: fair form: won maiden auction at Carlisle in July and nursery at Yarmouth in September: will probably stay 1¼m: acts on firm ground: races up with pace. *M. Johnston*

CANDLE LIGHT (IRE)   2 b.f. (Feb 22) Petorius 117 – Alberjas (IRE) (Sure – Blade (USA) 130) [1996 5.1g a5g⁵ a7g⁶ Aug 17] IR 2,000Y: first foal: dam once-raced half-sister to smart middle-distance winner Street Line out of smart sprinter Street Light: no form in maiden auctions and a seller. *A. P. Jarvis*

CANDLE SMILE (USA)   4 b.c. Pleasant Colony (USA) – Silent Turn (USA)   99 (Silent Cal (USA)) [1995 93: 11m⁴ 13.9m³ 1996 10m⁵ 10.1d² 12.1m² 13.1d* 20f³ 18.7m⁴ 14.6m² 16m* 18g Oct 19] very big, leggy colt: shows knee action: useful handicapper: won at Ayr (maiden event) in May and Goodwood (rated stakes, uncontested lead, set steady pace and drew clear from over 1f out) in September: sweating, edgy, early to post, pulled hard and ran as if something amiss in Cesarewitch last time: fully effective at 14.6f, and (third in Ascot Stakes) stays 2½m: acts on firm and dead ground, yet to race on soft: appears to need strong handling: suited by front-running tactics: genuine. *M. R. Stoute*

CANDLE SMOKE (USA)   3 b. or br.g. Woodman (USA) 126 – Light The   75 Lights (FR) 123 (Shirley Heights 130) [1995 –: 8m⁵ 1996 12m 12m* 16.5m³ 16.2f⁵ 16.4m* 16.4g² 16g⁴ Sep 14] rangy, good sort: has plenty of scope: fair handicapper: successful at Folkestone in July (maiden) and August (running in snatches), both apprentice events: good efforts at Sandown (short-headed) and Goodwood (pulled hard in crossed noseband but kept on well) under 7-lb claimer afterwards: sold only 4,000 gns Newmarket Autumn Sales: will stay further than 16.5f: acts on good to firm ground. *G. Harwood*

CANDRIKA   3 b.f. High Estate 127 – Chevisaunce 75 (Fabulous Dancer (USA)   72 124) [1995 72?: 7m² 1996 10.3g 12g⁶ 12m 11g³ Sep 8] leggy filly: fair maiden at best: seemingly best effort when 7½ lengths third of 6 to Grey Way in minor event at Milan in September: probably stays 11f. *L. M. Cumani*

CANDY'S DELIGHT   3 b.f. Dunbeath (USA) 127 – Simply Candy (IRE) 42 – (Simply Great (FR) 122) [1995 –: 7.5m⁶ 7.5d⁶ 8.3g 6f 1996 10f⁶ 10m 8g Oct 29] no worthwhile form. *Mrs S. J. Smith*

CANE THEM   3 ch.c. Risk Me (FR) 127 – She's A Sport (Jalmood (USA) 126) – [1995 NR 1996 6.9m 6g 6m⁶ Aug 20] 8,000F: first foal: dam (unraced) out of very useful 1971 Irish 2-y-o 5f winner Celtic Twilight: well beaten. *T. J. Naughton*

CANNIZARO (IRE)   4 b.f. Gallic League 119 – Paradise Regained 41 (North – Stoke 130) [1995 58d: a8g* 10g 7m 10g⁵ 1996 a8g a9.4g Mar 6] no worthwhile form since 3-y-o reappearance: sold 1,500 gns Doncaster March Sales: covered by Alhijaz. *R. J. R. Williams*

CANON CAN (USA)   3 ch.g. Green Dancer (USA) 132 – Lady Argyle (USA)   104
(Don B (USA)) [1995 76: 9m² 8g⁵ 10g 1996 10m³ 12m⁴ 16.1m* 18g* 18g³ Oct 19]
tall, good-topped gelding: has scope: fluent mover: useful performer: won handicap
at Newmarket in August (off bit 3f out but led in Dip and stayed on very strongly)
and Phil Bull Trophy at Pontefract in September (beating Kristal's Paradise), both in
small fields: gone in coat, below form (ran to 95) when ½-length third of 26 to
Inchcailloch in Cesarewitch, but far from discredited, always handy, having long
battle before nosing ahead in Dip, just run out of it: very much a stayer: acts on good
to firm ground, yet to race on a soft surface: thoroughly genuine: sure to win more
races. *H. R. A. Cecil*

CANOVAS HEART   7 b.g. Balidar 133 – Worthy Venture 76 (Northfields   81
(USA)) [1995 64, a59: 5d* 5m⁴ 5.1m² 5g⁴ a5g* a5g² 7d⁴ 5g⁵ 1996 5g* 6g³ 5s⁵ 5m*   a–
5m* 5m 5m 5g⁶ 5.2m* Sep 17] neat gelding: has quick action: fairly useful handicapper, had a fine year: won at Warwick (unbeaten in 3 starts there) on reappearance,
at Folkestone in May, York (competitive contest) in June and Yarmouth in September: effective at 5f and 6f, probably at 7f: acts on good to firm and soft ground and on
fibresand: usually races prominently: genuine and consistent. *Bob Jones*

CAN SHE CAN CAN   4 b.f. Sulaafah (USA) 119 – Dominance (Dominion 123)   –
[1995 49: 11.1f⁶ 11.1m⁴ 12.1f² 14.1m² 16m 16.2m³ 14.1m 16.2m³ 15.8g* 1996 a16g
a16g 12d⁵ 12.3g 16.2g 14.1g⁶ 16m 17.2m Jun 29] workmanlike filly: poor handicapper: no worthwhile form in 1996: stays 2m: acts on firm ground: blinkered (out of
form) final 4-y-o start. *C. Smith*

CANTE CHICO   4 b.c. Reference Point 139 – Flamenco Wave (USA) 103   61
(Desert Wine (USA)) [1995 68: 10g 10g⁶ 10f³ 14.6m 1996 12f* 11.9m 9.9m⁵ 10m
Aug 31] sturdy colt: modest performer in 1996: ridden by 7-lb claimer, didn't need to
show best to win steadily-run claimer at Beverley in June: stays 1½m: has raced only
on a sound surface: none too consistent. *O. Brennan*

CANTON RON   2 ch.c. (Mar 24) Ron's Victory (USA) 129 – Briery Fille 81   53
(Sayyaf 121) [1996 8.2m a6g⁵ 6g² a7g Nov 18] big, lengthy colt: has plenty of scope:
first reported foal: dam, 5f (at 2 yrs) to 1¼m winner, stayed 1½m: modest form in
median auction maidens second and third starts: not certain to stay beyond 6f.
C. A. Dwyer

CANTON VENTURE   4 ch.g. Arctic Tern (USA) 126 – Ski Michaela (USA)   80
(Devil's Bag (USA)) [1995 63, a69: 9g 10m⁴ 12m a12g* 11.8g⁵ a14.8g a12g* 12m
a12g 1996 a12g² a11g* 12m* 12.5f* 12m* 12.3m² 12.4m* 12.1m⁶ 11.9f* 11.5f³
11.9f* 11.9m² 12g 12m⁶ Sep 13] lengthy, angular gelding: fair handicapper: well
placed and had a tremendous season: won at Southwell (apprentices), Folkestone
(minor event), Warwick, Thirsk, Newcastle and twice at Brighton, all between May
and August: should stay further than 12.5f: goes well on top-of-the-ground and acts
on fibresand: blinkered (ran badly) once as 3-y-o: front runner/races prominently:
winning hurdler: tough and genuine. *S. P. C. Woods*

CANTSAYNOWT   2 b.f. (Feb 28) Rambo Dancer (CAN) 107 – Petiller 37   48 d
(Monsanto (FR) 121) [1996 5m³ a5g 6f² 6g 5f⁴ 7s⁶ 5m⁶ 5g⁶ 6f 6d 5m 7m 5s a5g
Nov 16] 3,100Y: sparely-made filly: fifth foal: sister to 5f winner Ramborette and
half-sister to 2 winners by Nicholas Bill, including 1993 2-y-o 7f winner Just Bill:
dam poor sprint maiden here, won in Belgium at 4 yrs: poor form placed in claimer
and seller (final start for R. Fahey) early on: of little account afterwards: stays 6f:
blinkered final start. *R. M. McKellar*

CANYON CREEK (IRE)   3 b.c. Mr Prospector (USA) – River Memories   87 p
(USA) 123 (Riverman (USA) 131) [1996 NR 1996 8m* Oct 7] leggy, quite attractive
colt: third foal: dam, high-class French middle-distance performer, out of half-sister
to Celestial Storm: well-backed favourite, impressive winner of 14-runner maiden at
Pontefract, back on bit over 1f out and beating Yukon Hope by 2 lengths: a useful
performer in the making, sure to win more races. *J. H. M. Gosden*

CAPE CROSS (IRE)   2 b.c. (Mar 13) Green Desert (USA) 127 – Park Appeal   88 p
122 (Ahonoora 122) [1996 7d⁴ 8f* Oct 7] strong, angular colt: carries condition:
has a lethargic disposition: fifth foal: half-brother to 3 winners, including 7f winner
Pastorale (by Nureyev) and useful French 1½m winner Lord of Appeal (by Sadler's

Wells): dam, won Cheveley Park and successful over 8.5f at 4 yrs in USA, half-sister to Desirable and Alydaress: won maiden at Doncaster in September by 1¼ lengths from Shaya, quickening to lead 1f out: bandaged behind both starts: not certain to stay beyond 1m: very useful colt in the making. *J. H. M. Gosden*

CAPE MERINO 5 ch.m. Clantime 101 – Laena 72 (Roman Warrior 132) [1995 NR 1996 5.1g* Apr 30] leggy, lengthy, rather plain mare: useful performer: missed 1995 due to a virus: reportedly suffered career-ending injury in well-contested minor event at Bath in April, clear at halfway and holding Wavian by 3½ lengths despite drifting right: effective at 5f and 6f: acts on any going. *Major D. N. Chappell* — 103

CAPE PIGEON (USA) 11 ch.g. Storm Bird (CAN) 134 – Someway Somehow (USA) (What Luck (USA)) [1995 65: 8.3m4 8.3m* 8.3m4 8.3g* 1996 8d 8.3m* 8.3m5 8.3g2 8.3g* 8.3d3 9g4 8.1f3 Sep 12] big, strong gelding: carries plenty of condition: fair performer: has won a race or 2 in each of last 6 seasons, in 1996 landing claimers at Windsor in May and July: stays 8.3f: acts on any going: usually blinkered or visored: made the running 3 of last 4 starts. *L. G. Cottrell* — 70

CAPILANO PRINCESS 3 b.f. Tragic Role (USA) – Lady Capilano 87 (Nebiolo 125) [1995 75, a60: 5s4 a6g3 a6g6 a7g4 7.1s3 7m* 1996 8m 7.3d* 8g2 8f 8m6 8.1g Aug 30] angular, workmanlike filly: fair handicapper: first past post at Newbury in May (leading over 1f out and wandering) and Doncaster (demoted to second for interference that took place before home turn) in June: stays 1m: acts on any ground on turf, only modest form on fibresand. *D. Haydn Jones* — 79 a–

CAP JULUCA (IRE) 4 b.c. Mtoto 134 – Tabyan (USA) 68 (Topsider (USA)) [1995 117p: 8g5 8.3m* 8g* 10m* 7.9m* 9g* 1996 10f Jun 18] good-bodied colt: fluent mover: ended 1995 with tremendously impressive win under top weight in Cambridgeshire at Newmarket, making all: endured a couple of set-backs in spring: in need of race in Prince of Wales's Stakes at Royal Ascot, helping force very strong pace before dropping away quickly in closing stages: stays 1¼m: has raced only on a sound surface: reported in September to have suffered another set-back. *R. Charlton* — –

CAPSTONE 3 b.f. Shirley Heights 130 – Doumayna 79 (Kouban (FR)) [1995 –p: 7f 8f 1996 10g 12.5f May 6] leggy filly: well held in maidens and (blinkered) in handicap: sold 8,800 gns Newmarket July Sales: should be suited by good test of stamina: bandaged behind. *W. Jarvis* — –

CAPTAIN CARAT 5 gr.g. Handsome Sailor 125 – Gem of Gold 52 (Jellaby 124) [1995 69: 6g 6d 6.1g 6m 6m* 6m 6d 6m 6m2 6.1m6 6f3 6m2 6m4 5g4 6g6 5g 5d 6m 1996 5s4 5g4 5g* 6m 6m6 5g* 6d5 6m 6m6 5f2 6g6 5m4 5m3 6.1m5 5m3 5f 5m 6g6 5m2 5m 5g a5g4 Dec 28] tall gelding: fair handicapper: won at Pontefract (apprentices) in April and Newcastle in May: sold out of Mrs J. Ramsden's stable only 4,200 gns Newmarket Autumn Sales after penultimate start: ran quite well on return: effective at 5f and 6f: acts on any turf ground and on fibresand: has run well when sweating: best held up, and suited by strongly-run race: usually bandaged near-fore: has won (and given trouble in stalls) when apprentice ridden: tough and consistent. *D. Nicholls* — 70

CAPTAIN CARPARTS 2 b.c. (May 18) Hubbly Bubbly (USA) – Choir (High Top 131) [1996 8.5g 7.1v Oct 6] leggy colt: ninth foal: brother to 3-y-o Whitley Grange Boy and 4-y-o 7f and 8.5f winner Cashmere Lady and half-brother to several winners, including fairly useful 7f to 1½m performer Celestial Choir (by Celestial Storm): dam behind in 4 races: signs of ability though behind in maidens: may do better. *J. L. Eyre* — – p

CAPTAIN COLLINS (IRE) 2 gr.c. (Feb 24) El Gran Senor (USA) 136 – Kanmary (FR) 117 (Kenmare (FR) 125) [1996 7g2 8s3 Oct 26] lengthy, angular colt: brother to Colonel Collins, placed in Derby and 2000 Guineas, and 1996 Breeders' Cup Sprint winner (also successful at up to 1m) Lit de Justice and closely related to 1991 2-y-o sprint winner Stormswept (by Storm Bird): dam stayed 9f: beaten a head by Falak in minor event at Kempton on debut: went like best horse for a long way when 6 lengths third of 7 to Tempting Prospect in minor event run on very soft ground at Newbury (unimpressive to post) on only subsequent start: will improve, and is sure to win a race or two. *P. W. Chapple-Hyam* — 99 p

CAPTAIN FLINT 2 b. or br.g. (May 19) Bedford (USA) 109 – Sun Yat Chen (Chou Chin Chow 99) [1996 5s5 7m 10f a7g a8g Nov 29] 650Y: first reported foal: dam winning Irish pointer: no worthwhile form. *A. Smith* — –

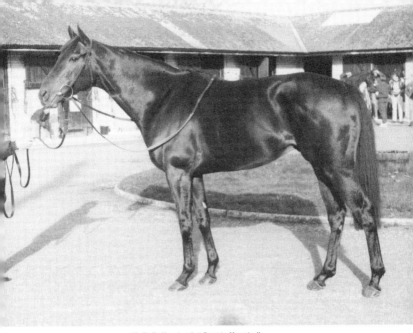

Mr D. R. Hunnisett's "Captain Horatius"

CAPTAIN HORATIUS (IRE) 7 b.h. Taufan (USA) 119 – One Last Glimpse   114
73 (Relko 136) [1995 114: 10m* 12m² 10g² 10m² 10.9g² 10d 1996 10g³ 10d⁵ 10s*
10m⁴ 10.5m³ Aug 10] tall, close-coupled horse: unimpressive mover: smart and
thoroughly likeable campaigner who has earned over £350,000 and has never been
rated lower than 112 in 6 seasons: best efforts in 1996 when winning listed race at
Goodwood in May by 2½ lengths from Wijara and when 6¾ lengths third of 8 (kept
on strongly late on after taking time to get going) to Tamayaz in Group 3 contest at
Haydock in August: suited by middle distances: acts on good to firm and heavy
ground: held up for turn of foot: tough and genuine: stays in training. *J. L. Dunlop*

CAPTAIN MARMALADE 7 ch.g. Myjinski (USA) – Lady Seville 64 (Orange   –
Bay 131) [1995 47, a54: a13g⁵ a10g⁴ a10g² a10g⁴ a10g³ a10g² a10g⁴ a8g⁵ a10g 8.2g²   a48
9.7g⁵ 10g* 9g a8.5g² 8g 9m a8.5g⁴ 10.1m 8m⁵ a10g 9.7s⁵ a9.4g⁶ a10g 1996 a16g²
a16g a13g⁴ a16g⁶ 10.3d a16g* 15.4m a12g⁶ a16g May 13] workmanlike gelding:
modest handicapper: won claimer at Lingfield in March: reportedly finished lame on
2 of 3 starts afterwards: stays 2m: acts on good to firm going, soft and all-weather
surfaces: probably effective visored or not: often contests ladies/amateur events: held
up and sometimes gets well behind. *D. T. Thom*

CAPTAIN PICARD 2 b.c. (Mar 23) Today And Tomorrow 78 – Nimble Dancer   –
(Northern Wizard 100) [1996 a5g 6m May 29] 3,000Y: eighth reported foal: dam
unraced: well beaten in maiden auctions early in year. *D. C. O'Brien*

CAPTAIN'S DAY 4 ch.g. Ballacashtal (CAN) – Seymour Ann (Krayyan 117)   70 d
[1995 82: 9d 8.1m 7f 8m² 7m³ 7.1m³ 8f⁵ 8.1m 7.6d⁵ 7g 1996 10.8d 7s 8f⁶ 8m a8g
8.2m 9f 8.1f⁵ 8m Sep 25] sparely-made gelding: poor mover: lost his form, and sold
only 1,200 gns Newmarket Autumn Sales: should stay further than 1m: acts on firm
and soft ground: tended to hang when ridden third 4-y-o start. *T. G. Mills*

CAPTAIN'S GUEST (IRE)   6 b.g. Be My Guest (USA) 126 – Watership (USA)   –
(Foolish Pleasure (USA)) [1995 NR 1996 11.6d⁶ 16m⁵ 18g Oct 19] tall gelding: rated
100 in 1994, winner of Cesarewitch: tailed off on belated return: stays 2¼m: acts on
firm and dead ground. *G. Harwood*

CAPTAIN TANDY (IRE)   7 ch.g. Boyne Valley 107 – Its All A Dream (Le   –
Moss 135) [1995 NR 1996 8g a8g Nov 18] sturdy gelding: winning jumper: one to
treat with caution on flat. *C. Smith*

CAPTAIN WILLIAM (IRE)   2 b.c. (Mar 1) Shernazar 131 – Our Galadrial   90
(Salmon Leap (USA) 131) [1996 7.1m⁶ 7d² 7m² Aug 23] 6,600F, 25,000Y: sturdy,
useful-looking colt: third foal: half-brother to 4-y-o 12.1f winner Westminster (by
Nashamaa): dam unraced daughter of useful performer at up to 7f Brightelmstone:
1¼ lengths second of 6 to Widar in listed race at Baden-Baden in August on final
start: will stay 1½m: sure to win a race. *I. A. Balding*

CAPTIVE SONG (IRE)   4 b.c. Danehill (USA) 126 – Tony Award (USA)   –
(Kirtling 129) [1995 NR 1996 10s Mar 28] sturdy colt: first foal: dam, minor sprint
winner at 4 yrs in USA, half-sister to dam of Breeders' Cup Classic winner Skywalker: burly and green, tailed off in maiden at Leicester. *P. W. Harris*

CAPTURE THE MOMENT   3 b.f. Keen 116 – Shaieef (IRE) 66 (Shareef   –
Dancer (USA) 135) [1995 7¹: 5m⁴ 5m² 5g² 5g* 5f 6m⁴ 6m³ 7m⁶ 7m a6g 1996 8d⁶
10.3m 8g 5g 6g 8m⁵ 6m 7g⁵ Jul 3] plain, sparely-made filly: fair form at best:
disappointing in 1996: sold 2,400 gns Newmarket July Sales: stays 6f: acts on good
to firm ground: tried blinkered, no improvement: sent to Bahrain. *R. J. R. Williams*

CARATI   2 b.f. (Mar 16) Selkirk (USA) 129 – Clytie (USA) 73 (El Gran Senor   86
(USA) 136) [1996 6f⁴ 6.1m* 6f² 6m Oct 1] 8,000Y: tall, leggy filly: easy mover
with a long stride: first foal: dam twice-raced granddaughter of outstanding racemare
Shuvee: fairly useful form: won maiden auction at Nottingham in June: last of 8 in
Cheveley Park Stakes at Newmarket last time: will be well suited by further than 6f:
raced only on top-of-the-ground. *R. Boss*

CARBURTON   3 b.c. Rock City 120 – Arminda (Blakeney 126) [1995 91p: 6.1d³   86
7.1s* 7m* 1996 8d³ 8.1g 8g a7g Dec 7] well-made colt: looked sure to make into a
useful 3-y-o: third in Newbury rated stakes on reappearance: ran poorly at Sandown
(trainer reportedly felt horse was wrong) second start, in April: mid-division in
£22,900 event at Newmarket (fading final 2f) in November: should be suited by 1m+:
acts on good to firm and soft ground, soundly beaten on fibresand: reportedly to be
aimed at the Cambridgeshire in 1997. *J. A. Glover*

CARE AND COMFORT   4 ch.f. Most Welcome 131 – Whipp's Cross 93 (Kris   –
135) [1995 64d: 6d⁶ 6.9g 8g 8g⁴ 9.7m 8d⁶ 8m* 7f⁴ a8.5g 8m 8.2m 9m 1996 7.1g 10g
7d 7m 9.2f Aug 19] modest performer at best: disappointing in 1996: sold out of
N. Tinkler's stable 1,600 gns Doncaster July Sales after fourth start: stays 1m: acts on
good to firm ground, tailed off on all-weather: visored (saddle slipped) tenth 3-y-o
start. *G. M. Moore*

CAREFUL (IRE)   3 gr.f. Distinctly North (USA) 115 – Caring (Crowned Prince   –
(USA) 128) [1995 59+: 5m 6m 7g 6g⁴ 7s⁴ 6.1s 1996 a8g 6.1m 7.1m 8f 16.1m
Oct 2] tall, lengthy filly: has a quick action: disappointing in 1996: sold 6,000 gns
Newmarket Autumn Sales: should be suited by further than 6f: seems unsuited by
soft ground. *B. W. Hills*

CARIAD CYMRU   2 b. or br.g. (Mar 15) Welsh Captain 113 – Daddy's Darling   52
52 (Mummy's Pet 125) [1996 5.1f⁵ May 11] 900Y: first foal: dam 1¼m and 1½m
winner: fifth in maiden auction at Bath in May on only run. *R. Akehurst*

CARIBBEAN DANCER   3 b.f. Shareef Dancer (USA) 135 – Deposit 73   71
(Thatch (USA) 136) [1995 60: 7g 8.2m⁴ 1996 8.5m⁵ 8g* 10m⁵ Jun 4] small, angular
filly: fair form: won maiden (getting up near finish) at Thirsk in May, despite starting
slowly and handling bend none too well: stays 1¼m: acts on good to firm ground, yet
to race on a soft surface. *M. R. Stoute*

CARIBBEAN QUEST   3 b.f. Rainbow Quest (USA) 134 – Jammaayil (IRE) 80   90
(Lomond (USA) 128) [1995 85p: 8m* 8d 1996 10m⁶ 10g Aug 14] smallish, unfurnished filly: fluent mover: fairly useful performer: about 6 lengths sixth of
10 to Sardonic in listed race at Newbury on reappearance: sweating and edgy,
tailed off in similar event at Salisbury 2 months later: should stay 1½m: bandaged

(except near-hind) on 3-y-o reappearance: sold 54,000 gns Newmarket December Sales. *B. Hanbury*

CARIBBEAN STAR 2 b.f. (Mar 13) Soviet Star (USA) 128 – Whos The Blonde 72 (Cure The Blues (USA)) [1996 6d³ 6m⁴ 7g² 7.1v⁶ Oct 6] good-topped filly: second foal: half-sister to 3-y-o Blondane (by Danehill): dam Irish 7f winner out of sister to Bitty Girl and Hot Spark: fair form in maidens: will probably stay 1m: acts on good to firm ground, not discredited on heavy. *M. R. Stoute*

CARIBBEE BEACH (IRE) 2 ch.f. (Mar 4) Magical Strike (USA) 114 – – Madam John 105 (Ballad Rock 122) [1996 5.3f⁶ Apr 22] IR 1,350F, IR 4,000Y: fifth reported foal: half-sister to Irish 3-y-o 7f winner Sir Big John (by Martin John): dam Irish 2-y-o 7f winner, suited by 1m: tailed off in maiden auction at Brighton in April: retained by trainer 600 gns Newmarket September Sales. *C. A. Dwyer*

CARICATURE (IRE) 3 b.g. Cyrano de Bergerac 120 – That's Easy (Swing 84 Easy (USA) 126) [1995 84: 5.2m² 5.3f³ 6g⁴ 5m² 5m⁶ 6m³ 6m* 1996 8d 8.1g 7f³ 7m 7m 7.3m 8.1g⁵ 7m⁴ 7m⁵ 6g 6.1s² Oct 22] sturdy gelding: fluent mover: fairly useful handicapper: sold 15,000 gns Newmarket Autumn Sales: effective at 6f, and stays 1m: acts on firm and soft ground: effective blinkered/visored or not: sometimes looks none too keen: none too consistent. *G. Lewis*

CARLING (FR) 4 b.f. Garde Royale 120 – Corraleja (FR) (Carvin 127) [1995 117 119: 8d³ 8d² 10.5m* 8g 12d* 12d 12f 1996 10f² 10.5m 12m 10d* 8m⁵ 10s² 10g³ Oct 27] leggy French filly: won Prix de Diane and Prix Vermeille at 3 yrs: 1½ lengths second to Valanour in Prix d'Harcourt at Longchamp in April: won 10-runner Prix Gontaut-Biron at Deauville in August by a length from Bal Harbour: again ran well when 3¾ lengths fifth of 9 to Ashkalani in Prix du Moulin de Longchamp, just respectably when 1½ lengths second of 8 to Running Flame in La Coupe de Maisons-Laffitte then 1¾ lengths third of 8 to Wandering Star in Grade 2 event at Woodbine: stays 1½m: acts on firm ground and soft: genuine. *Mme Pat Barbe, France*

CARLITO BRIGANTE 4 b.g. Robellino (USA) 127 – Norpella 95 (Northfields 85 (USA)) [1995 72: 7.1m 8.5m 7.1m⁴ 8m 8g⁴ 10m³ 10m⁵ 10.3f* 9h* 11.9m 10.3d 8.1g 10.5s 8.9g² 1996 10.3d 9.9m² 10g* 10.3m³ 10.1m⁴ 8.9m² 10f⁴ 10.3g 10.4m⁴ Jul 13] good-bodied gelding: fairly useful handicapper: won at Pontefract in April: ran very well when staying-on under 3 lengths fourth of 17 to Wilcuma in £58,200 Magnet Cup at York: should stay further than 10.4f: acts on hard ground, below form on a soft surface: sometimes early to post and has given trouble at start: held up: suited by a sound pace and strong handling: has joined P. R. Webber. *Mrs J. R. Ramsden*

CARLTON EXPRESS (IRE) 6 b.g. Persian Heights 129 – Snow Finch 100 44 (Storm Bird (CAN) 134) [1995 NR 1996 9.9d 10g² 10.3m⁵ 8m⁵ 12g³ 10f Jun 21] lengthy, good-bodied gelding: poor handicapper: as in 1994, pulled up lame final start: stays 1½m: acts on firm ground and equitrack: visored (finished last) once at 3 yrs. *J. L. Eyre*

CARLTON (IRE) 2 ch.c. (Apr 17) Thatching 131 – Hooray Lady 92 (Ahonoora – 122) [1996 6m⁶ 6m 5v Nov 11] 20,000F, 38,000Y: sturdy, good-bodied colt: third foal: dam won 5 times at around 1m and seemed to stay 1½m: little worthwhile form: off course nearly 4 months after debut. *G. Lewis*

CARLYS QUEST 2 ch.c. (Mar 18) Primo Dominie 121 – Tuppy (USA) (Sharpen 60 ? Up 127) [1996 a7g 7f⁴ a8.5g 8f Oct 8] 6,500Y, 16,000 2-y-o: third foal: half-brother to a winner in Italy by Old Vic: dam once-raced daughter of half-sister to Pebbles: modest form in maidens first 3 starts: pulled up in nursery final outing: stays 7f: has been bandaged. *J. Neville*

CARMARTHEN BAY 3 ch.c. Prionsaa 76 – Pattie's Grey 71 (Valiyar 129) 68 [1995 63, a83: 6m 8.1s 6.1m³ a6g* 19m a6g a7g² a8g* a8.5g⁵ 7.6m 7.1m⁵ 8.1g 7g⁴ a86 7m² 8g Oct 22] neat colt: fairly useful handicapper on all-weather, winner at Lingfield in February: fair on turf: stays 1m: acts on good to firm ground and equitrack: inconsistent. *G. L. Moore*

CARMENOURA (IRE) 4 ch.f. Carmelite House (USA) 118 – Flower Petals – (Busted 134) [1995 12m 11.9f 12m 1996 a8g 12.1d 12g 12.1m⁶ 9f 8.3m Aug 14] ex-Irish filly: half-sister to useful Irish 7f to 1¼m performer Ballykelt Prince (by Thatching): dam, Irish 1¼m winner, is sister to smart middle-distance performer Bog Road: trained at 3 yrs by T. Lacy: no form: visored final 4-y-o start. *E. J. Alston*

Jockey Club of Kenya Molecomb Stakes, Goodwood—
Carmine Lake (No. 5) pips Connemara, with Deep Finesse third

CARMINE LAKE (IRE)   2 ch.f. (Feb 9) Royal Academy (USA) 130 – Castilian   107 ?
Queen (USA) 82 (Diesis 133) [1996 5m* 5.1g³ 5m* 6m⁴ 5d⁵ Oct 6] IR 25,000Y:
lengthy, unfurnished filly: first foal: dam, 2-y-o 6f winner, daughter of Breeders' Cup
Mile winner Royal Heroine: useful form: successful in maiden at Newmarket in
April and Jockey Club of Kenya Molecomb Stakes (beat Connemara a neck) at
Goodwood in August: ran well when around 1½ lengths fourth of 9 to Bianca Nera in
Lowther Stakes at York in August and again (though never a threat) when 4 lengths
fifth of 10 to Kistena in Prix de l' Abbaye de Longchamp in October: stays 6f: acts on
good to firm and dead ground: has been awkward at stalls. *P. W. Chapple-Hyam*

CARMOSA (USA)   3 ch.f. Blushing John (USA) 120 – Bobbinette (Whitstead   53
125) [1995 65, a55: 6g⁶ 7.1s a7g⁴ a6g³ 1996 7s 7.1g⁵ 8.1g² 7g³ 8.1f 12f Aug 2]
lengthy filly: modest maiden handicapper: stays 8.1f: possibly unsuited by soft
ground: sold 2,000 gns Newmarket December Sales. *D. Nicholls*

CARNIVAL OF LIGHT   4 b.f. Squill (USA) 122 – June Fayre (Sagaro 133)   ?
[1996 5.1g a6g Dec 5] no sign of ability at 2 yrs for J. Balding: won twice over sprint
distances in Czech Republic at 3 yrs and once in summer: showed little on return to
Britain: difficult to assess. *J. S. Moore*

CAROL AGAIN   4 b.f. Kind of Hush 118 – Lady Carol 42 (Lord Gayle (USA)   –
124) [1995 40d: 5g⁵ 6m 7m 5g 7f 1996 a8g² a11g² a11g⁴ a8g a8g² a12g³ a8g⁵ a11g*   a48
a12g* a12g a11g⁵ a11g 8m 12.1s a11g a11g² Dec 27] close-coupled, angular filly:
poor handicapper: easy winner of maiden event and apprentice race at Southwell in
April: ran poorly afterwards until respectable effort final start: stays 1½m well: acts
on fibresand. *N. Bycroft*

CAROL'S DREAM (USA)   4 ch.c. Risen Star (USA) – Merle Halton (USA)   75
(Rattle Dancer) [1995 75: 7.1m³ 8.3m⁵ 9.9m 10f² 10m² 11.5m² 8m⁴ 1996 a10g* a7g
Nov 7] had soft palate operation after final 3-y-o start: fair handicapper: made most
when easy winner of maiden at Lingfield in March: off course 5 months afterwards:
probably stays 11.5f: acts on firm ground and equitrack. *J. W. Hills*

CARRANITA (IRE)   6 br.m. Anita's Prince 126 – Take More (GER) (Frontal   111
122) [1995 106: 7.1g⁴ 7.1g² 7.3g⁴ 7g 6g* 6d 6d 6m* 1996 5d* 6m* 6m⁴ 7f² 7.1d³
6m⁴ 6g* 7m 6d* 6m 6g 6s⁴ 6s⁴ Nov 22] leggy, angular mare: has a markedly round
action: smart performer: better than ever in 1996: won weak listed race at Beverley
in March, minor event at Thirsk in April and listed races at York (beat Daring Destiny
4 lengths) in July and Newmarket (beat Atraf a length) in August: stays 7.1f: useful
form on good to firm ground, very best efforts at 6 yrs with some give: tough and
game. *B. Palling*

172

CARREAMIA 3 b.f. Weldnaas (USA) 112 – Carribean Tyme 85 (Tyrnavos 129) 62
[1995 NR 1996 6m⁵ a8.5g³ a8.5g Nov 11] fourth foal: dam 2-y-o 6f winner: not seen
out until October, showing modest form in maidens first 2 starts. *J. L. Eyre*

CARROLLS MARC (IRE) 8 b.g. Horage 124 – Rare Find (Rarity 129) [1995 53
51: a16.2g³ a14.8g⁴ a14.8g⁵ a12g 1996 a12g* a12g* a13g² a12g⁵ a12g⁶ a12g Dec
20] modest performer: won selling handicap and minor event at Lingfield in January:
effective at 1½m, and stays 2m: acts on good to firm (possibly not firm) ground, dead
and the all-weather: held up. *C. Murray*

CARTOUCHE 2 gr.g. (Feb 17) Terimon 124 – Emblazon 91 (Wolver Hollow 66 p
126) [1996 7m 7f⁵ 7m Aug 26] 7,800Y: half-brother to 3-y-o Embroidered (by
Charmer) and several winners here and abroad, including 6f and 1m winner Taranga
(by Music Boy) and 1989 2-y-o 6f winner Walkern Witch (by Dunbeath): dam,
winner at up to 1½m, daughter of good staying 2-y-o Slip Stitch: modest form in
auction maiden events: will be well suited by 1m+: not entirely at ease on track at
Brighton second start: will do better. *Sir Mark Prescott*

CARWYN'S CHOICE 3 b.f. Then Again 126 – Over My Head (Bay Express – §
132) [1995 –: 7.1d 6g 7g 10g a5g 1996 a7g 8f 7.6m 11.9f a10s Nov 19] tall, lengthy
filly: more sign of temperament than ability, refusing to race once. *P. C. Clarke*

CASHAPLENTY 3 ch.g. Ballacashtal (CAN) – Storm of Plenty (Billion (USA) –
120) [1995 NR 1996 a12g⁵ a8.5g Nov 11] third foal: dam winning hurdler: well
beaten in maidens at Wolverhampton in April and November. *N. P. Littmoden*

CASHMERE LADY 4 b.f. Hubbly Bubbly (USA) – Choir (High Top 131) [1995 77
75p: 7g² 8m³ a8.5g* a7g* 1996 a7g² a8g⁵ a8.5g* 8m⁴ 7m⁴ a8.5g² 8.3g⁵ 8m² 8g³ a91
8.3m⁴ 8d⁴ 7m⁵ 8.9g Oct 12] fairly useful handicapper on the all-weather, winner at
Wolverhampton in March: fair on turf: should stay beyond 8.5f: acts on fibresand and
good to firm ground, respectable effort on dead: consistent. *J. L. Eyre*

CASINO CHIP 3 br.c. Daring March 116 – Important Guest 53 (Be My Guest –
(USA) 126) [1995 –: 7g a6g 1996 a8g 8m 5m Aug 19] no promise in varied company:
tried blinkered. *T. T. Clement*

CASPIAN BELUGA 8 b. or br.g. Persian Bold 123 – Miss Thames 105 (Tower –
Walk 130) [1995 NR 1996 a12g a12g Jan 20] fair front-running handicapper in 1994:
tailed off on return: suited by middle distances: acts on any ground: modest jumper,
lame and not seen again after winning novice chase Jun 29. *S. G. Knight*

CASPIAN MORN 2 b.f. (Mar 5) Lugana Beach 116 – Parijoun (Manado 130) 63 d
[1996 6m³ 6f* 6g 7g 7f 6m⁴ Oct 4] well-made filly: has a quick action: half-sister to
3-y-o Insideout (by Macmillion) and 7f winner Caspian Gold (by Clantime): dam of
little account: won median auction maiden at Lingfield in August: below form after:
stays 6f: raced only on a sound surface: visored final start. *A. P. Jarvis*

CASSIMERE 4 ch.f. Clantime 101 – Poshteen 86 (Royal Smoke 113) [1995 –: 55
6.1d⁵ 6m⁶ 1996 6m⁵ 5d⁵ 5f 7g Aug 1] workmanlike filly: modest maiden handicapper: below form after reappearance: stays 6f: acts on good to firm and dead ground.
Major D. N. Chappell

CASTAN (IRE) 3 b.g. Persian Bold 123 – Erzsi 80 (Caerleon (USA) 132) [1995 77
69: 5m⁴ 5m² 6.1m 6m³ 6d 6.9m 1996 6.9f⁶ 10g⁴ 8.1d⁴ 7f* 7m³ 7.5m³ 8.2g* 7g Oct

Portland Place Properties Hopeful Stakes, Newmarket—
Carranita (right) runs on strongly to beat Atraf (striped cap)

19] quite attractive gelding: fair handicapper: steadily progressive in 1996, winning at Brighton in June and Nottingham (first run for over 2½ months, smoothly) in October: sold 16,000 gns Newmarket Autumn Sales: stays 8.2f: acts on firm ground, probably on dead: has run well when sweating and edgy: to USA. *J. L. Dunlop*

CASTEL ROSSELO 6 br.h. Rousillon (USA) 133 – On The House (FR) 125 60 (Be My Guest (USA) 126) [1995 88, a91: a7g² 8g 7m⁴ 8m³ 7g³ 8g a6g a8g 1996 a9.4g 8s 9.2d⁵ 7m 8g 7.6m⁶ 6d 8.2m 6g Jul 3] smallish, sparely-made horse: usually impresses in appearance: only modest at best in 1996: stays 1m well: acts on good to firm and soft ground and on fibresand: tried blinkered, no improvement: joined I. Campbell. *R. Harris*

CASTLE ASHBY JACK 2 gr.c. (May 19) Chilibang 120 – Carly-B (IRE) 42 67 (Commanche Run 133) [1996 a5g² 5m³ 5m 5.1m³ 5f³ 6m 5.2f² Jul 23] strong, lengthy colt: second foal: dam, plater, stayed 1¾m: modest maiden: best at 5f: acts on firm ground: best form in blinkers, below best visored last 2 outings: sometimes wanders: sold 2,800 gns Newmarket Autumn Sales. *P. Howling*

CASTLE GOVERNOR 3 b.g. Governor General 116 – Sorcha (IRE) (Sher- 53 nazar 131) [1995 45: a6g 5d⁶ 7f 1996 a6g⁴ a6g* a7g⁵ a6g a6g⁶ Feb 14] modest performer: claimer ridden, won handicap at Lingfield in January: sold 3,000 gns Doncaster March Sales and won over 7f in Denmark in April: acts on firm and dead ground and the all-weather: inconsistent. *P. C. Haslam*

CASTLE HOUSE 2 b.c. (Jan 3) Risk Me (FR) 127 – Moonlight Princess 49 67 d (Alias Smith (USA)) [1996 5.1d² 5.3f* 5m⁴ 6d 6m⁵ 5.7m 6d 5.3f 5.3g⁵ a5g⁴ Oct 5] 3,500Y: angular colt: fifth foal: brother to 3-y-o Back By Dawn and 2 winners, including middle-distance stayer Lunar Risk: dam 10.8f seller winner: won maiden auction at Brighton in April: deteriorated badly after fourth outing: probably stays 6f: acts on firm and dead ground: tried visored, ran too freely in blinkers: sold 4,500 gns Newmarket Autumn Sales. *J. Akehurst*

CASTLEREA LAD 7 b.h. Efisio 120 – Halo 51 (Godswalk (USA) 130) [1995 83 d 91: 6g* 6d 6m⁶ 6f* 6m⁵ 6m* 6g⁵ 6f⁶ 6m 5f⁶ 6m 6m 1996 6s⁴ 6g⁵ 6m⁵ 6m 6m 6d 6m 6m³ 6m 6g 6f 6m 6f⁴ 6m 5f⁵ 6f⁵ 6g⁶ 6m 6m 6f a6g a6g⁴ a6g a7g Dec 20] good-topped horse: on the downgrade after the spring: stays 7f: very best form on a sound surface: tried visored (well beaten): usually held up. *R. Hollinshead*

CASTLES BURNING (USA) 2 b. or br.g. (Jan 25) Minshaanshu Amad (USA) 56 91§ – Major Overhaul (Known Fact (USA) 135) [1996 6g⁴ 6m 7g 8.1g 7.6m⁴ 8m a73 7m³ 6d² 8f³ a10g² a7g³ Dec 11] 4,400F: sturdy, compact gelding: seventh foal: half-brother to several winners in USA, including a minor stakes-winning sprinter at 2 yrs by Procida: dam unraced half-sister to Irish 1000 Guineas third So Fine: modest form on turf, fair form on all-weather: stays 1¼m: acts on firm and dead ground, best form on equitrack. *C. A. Cyzer*

CASTLE SECRET 10 b.g. Castle Keep 121 – Baffle 87 (Petingo 135) [1995 57: 59 a16.2g⁶ a16g² a12g a16g 1996 a16g² 17.2m² 18f² Jul 2] quite attractive gelding: fairly useful hurdler: modest handicapper on flat: thorough stayer: acts on any going, except possibly soft: blinkered (ran well) and hooded earlier in career. *D. Burchell*

CASTLETOWN COUNT 4 b.g. Then Again 126 – Pepeke 78 (Mummy's Pet 49 125) [1995 –: 10f 8m 10m 10.5d 12m 12m 1996 10g² 12f⁴ Jun 6] tall gelding: poor performer: stays 1¼m, seemingly not 1½m. *K. W. Hogg, Isle of Man*

CASUAL COTTAGE (IRE) 2 b.f. (Apr 28) Thatching 131 – Non Casual 75 49 (Nonoalco (USA) 131) [1996 5g³ 5g⁶ 5m⁶ 5g⁴ Jul 22] IR 8,000Y: half-sister to 1m winners Commanding General (by General Assembly) and Bahama Mama (in Ireland, by Ela-Mana-Mou): dam 2-y-o 5f winner: poor form in maiden auctions and a nursery: visored last 2 starts: has been bandaged: sold 3,200 gns Newmarket Autumn Sales. *C. Murray*

CASUAL WATER (IRE) 5 b.g. Simply Great (FR) 122 – Top Nurse (High Top 73 131) [1995 79+: 11.6m⁵ 12g* 12.1m* 14.9m* 14m² 12m² 11.9g* 12m³ 1996 11.9m 12m⁵ 12m 11.9g⁶ 14.8m⁴ 12m* 12g³ Aug 26] lengthy, angular gelding: poor mover: fair handicapper: won at Goodwood in August, leading post: effective at 1½m and stays 14.9f: acts on firm and dead ground: visored/blinkered last 4 starts at 3 yrs: usually held up, and suited by strongly-run race. *A. G. Newcombe*

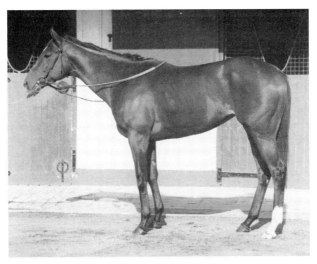

Mrs H. M. Keaveney's "Catch The Blues"

CATCHABLE   2 b.c. (Feb 2) Pursuit of Love 124 – Catawba 98 (Mill Reef (USA)   83 p
141) [1996 8m⁶ 8m² Oct 17] good-topped, attractive colt: fluent mover: fifth foal:
half-brother to 3-y-o Callaloo (by Mtoto) and middle-distance winners Isle of Pines
(by Kris) and useful Licorne (by Sadler's Wells): dam, 1¼m winner who stayed
1½m, daughter of Ribblesdale winner Catalpa: fairly useful form in Newmarket
maidens won by Asas and Royal Crusade late in year: will stay middle distances:
likely to do better, and win a race. *H. R. A. Cecil*

CATCH THE BLUES (IRE)   4 b.f. Bluebird (USA) 125 – Dear Lorraine (FR)   115
(Nonoalco (USA) 131) [1995 7s* 7g⁵ 9g⁶ 7m² 7g³ 6d⁶ 7g⁶ 7d³ 1996 5s⁶ 6g³ 6d² 6m²
5m* 6g⁵ 5m⁵ 6f³ 5m³ Sep 14] tall, lengthy filly: half-sister to 3 winners, none better
than herself: dam French 1¼m winner: won maiden at the Curragh at 3 yrs: improved
into smart performer at 4 yrs: second to Lidanna in Greenlands Stakes at the Curragh
and to Atraf in Cork and Orrery Stakes at Royal Ascot before winning valuable
handicap at the Curragh in July: 2½ lengths fifth of 8 to Pivotal in Nunthorpe Stakes
at York (badly outpaced much of way, stayed on strongly) then 2¼ lengths third of 11
to Iktamal in Haydock Park Sprint Cup: outpaced much of way in Flying Five at
Leopardstown last time but only ¾ length behind Eveningperformance at the line:
best at up to 7f: acts on firm and soft ground: effective blinkered/visored or not, and
has worn headgear since fourth 4-y-o start. *A. P. O'Brien, Ireland*

CATCH THE LIGHTS   3 b.f. Deploy 131 – Dream Chaser 92 (Record Token   86
128) [1995 81p: 6d⁶ a8g* 1996 7m 7m 8m⁴ 8.1m* 8m* 7.1m* 9m 8m 7f⁴ 8m 8g 8g
Nov 2] lengthy, angular filly: fairly useful handicapper: won at Chepstow, Salisbury
and Sandown in July: effective at 7f and 1m: acts on equitrack and firm ground: held
up: joined Miss C. Johnsey. *R. Hannon*

CATECHISM (USA)   2 b. or br.f. (Apr 8) St Jovite (USA) 135 – Sunday Best   81
(USA) (Halo (USA)) [1996 6.1f² 6m² 6m* 6.5m 7m Oct 1] \$12,500F, \$45,000Y:
leggy, quite good-topped filly: third foal: dam maiden half-sister to a minor 1m

stakes winner: won maiden at Newbury in August: took strong hold final start: bred to stay at least 7f: sent to USA. *J. H. M. Gosden*

CATHEDRAL (IRE) 2 b.g. (Mar 6) Prince Sabo 123 – Choire Mhor 100 83 (Dominion 123) [1996 5.2s³ May 29] 13,500Y: lengthy, workmanlike gelding: sixth foal: half-brother to 1994 2-y-o 8.5f winner Legitimate (by Last Tycoon) and 11f winner Themeda (by Sure Blade): dam (ran only at 2 yrs) 6f-winning granddaughter of smart 6f and 1¼m winner Sleat, grandam of Reprimand and Wiorno: burly, close third to Raven Master in maiden at Newbury in May: subsequently gelded: looked sure to improve. *B. J. Meehan*

CATHERINE'S CHOICE 3 ch.g. Primo Dominie 121 – Bambolona 108 64 (Bustino 136) [1995 –: a8.5g⁵ 1996 a8.5g 8d⁴ 8m⁶ 8.3m a8g* 8d a8g³ 8.1g 10.3g a73 Oct 25] workmanlike gelding: fair performer on all-weather, winner of minor event at Southwell in July: well below form last 4 starts on turf: sold (J. Bethell to M. Hammond) 8,400 gns Newmarket Autumn Sales: should stay further than 1m: acts on good to firm and dead ground and fibresand. *J. D. Bethell*

CATHIES FLOWER 2 b.f. (Feb 8) Rock Hopper 124 – Deflowered (Red God – 128§) [1996 8d⁶ Nov 8] 3,100Y: leggy, plain filly: half-sister to 7f seller winner Tamana Dancer (by Gay Fandango) and several winners abroad: dam twice-raced half-sister to smart 6f to 1½m winner Duke of Normandy: refused to enter stalls for seller at Nottingham in October: tailed off in minor event at Doncaster following month. *J. A. Harris*

CATIENUS (USA) 2 b. or br.c. (May 16) Storm Cat (USA) – Diamond City 93 (USA) 104 (Mr Prospector (USA)) [1996 7g⁵ 7m³ 7.1v* 8d* Nov 8] strong, close-coupled colt: has a round action: first foal: dam 7f to 1¼m winner, later successful in USA and placed in Grade 3 9f event: made all in maiden at Haydock in October, winning by 8 lengths: responded gamely when following up by head from Sunbeam Dance in minor event at Doncaster: will stay 1¼m: acts well on heavy ground: strong-running type. *M. R. Stoute*

CATRIA (IRE) 2 br.f. (May 7) Caerleon (USA) 132 – Embla 121 (Dominion 123) 76 [1996 6m⁶ 6m 7.1s² 7f⁶ a6g⁶ Nov 22] seventh foal: sister to 7f winner Ghost Tree, closely related to 3-y-o 1¼m winner Enriched (by Generous) and half-sister to 2 winners abroad by Shareef Dancer, including French 9f winner Nordic Myth: dam 6f (Cheveley Park Stakes) and 1m winner: second in maiden at Chepstow in October, easily best effort: should stay 1m: acts well on soft ground (well beaten on very firm), respectable effort on fibresand: last and quietly to post fourth start. *J. H. M. Gosden*

CATS BOTTOM 4 ch.f. Primo Dominie 121 – Purple Fan (Dalsaan 125) [1995 59 73d: 6m⁴ 5m⁴ 6m⁶ 6g 6g⁴ 7m² 7m 7m⁵ 10m⁴ 7m⁶ 6d 1996 6f 7g 8m⁴ 7m⁶ 8m 10.2m 8f 7m 8m² 8f² 8m⁵ a7s⁶ a8g* Dec 27] angular filly: unimpressive mover: just a modest handicapper nowadays: won at Southwell in December: stays 1m: acts on firm and dead ground, and on fibresand: blinkered at 3 yrs: sometimes slowly away. *A. G. Newcombe*

CATUMBELLA (USA) 3 ch.f. Diesis 133 – Benguela (USA) 76 (Little Current 73 (USA)) [1995 69p: 8m³ 1996 8g³ 8m² 8s⁵ a8s² Nov 19] lengthy filly: unimpressive mover: fair maiden: has raced only at 1m: acts on good to firm and soft ground, respectable effort on equitrack: sent to USA. *J. H. M. Gosden*

CATWALK 2 b.f. (Feb 2) Shirley Heights 130 – Moogie 103 (Young Generation 92 129) [1996 7m⁶ 7m* 8m 8d⁴ Oct 12] 26,000Y: leggy, quite good-topped filly with a quick action: fifth foal: sister to 1994 2-y-o 6f winner Mood Swings and a fair staying maiden and closely related to 3-y-o Alfahad (by Doyoun): dam 2-y-o 6f winner, suited by 9f at 3 yrs: fairly useful form: 20/1-winner of Sweet Solera Stakes at Newmarket in August, outbattling Fernanda by a head: well beaten after in May Hill Stakes at Doncaster and listed event at Ascot: should stay 1¼m: acts on good to firm going: tail swisher. *W. J. Haggas*

CATWALK GIRL 3 b.f. Skyliner 117 – Pokey's Pet 56 (Uncle Pokey 116) [1995 – 53: 5m⁵ 6g² 7m³ 7f² 7m* a7g 1996 7g⁶ 6m 7.5m 7g Jul 25] workmanlike filly: has a round action: well beaten for new stable in 1996: stays 7f: soundly beaten on fibresand: often visored/blinkered: joined T. D. Easterby. *Miss J. F. Craze*

CAUDA EQUINA 2 gr.g. (Jan 28) Statoblest 120 – Sea Fret 96 (Habat 127) 74 [1996 5g³ 5g 6g Aug 25] 8,800F, 30,000Y: good-topped, attractive gelding: unimpressive mover: half-brother to several winners here and abroad, including 3-y-o Flying Squaw (by Be My Chief), useful 5f and 6f winner at 2 yrs, and Irish 2m winner Top Wave (by High Top): dam, 2-y-o 6f winner, out of smart Fluke, a half-sister to Buoy and Bireme: burly and very green, promising third to Deadly Dudley in maiden at Goodwood on debut: rather disappointing afterwards, off course 3 months before final start: may prove best at 5f. *M. R. Channon*

CAUSLEY   11 br.g. Swing Easy (USA) 126 – Four Lawns 77 (Forlorn River 124) [1995 –: 10.8f 8.1d 7d 8f 1996 a8.5g 8m 14m 8m Jul 27] good-topped, workmanlike gelding: a splendid performer up to end of 9-y-o season, but no sign of retaining ability. *D. M. Hyde*   –

CAUTION   2 b.f. (Mar 31) Warning 136 – Fairy Flax (IRE) 97 (Dancing Brave (USA) 140) [1996 5s² 5m³ 6m* Sep 19] 7,000Y: small filly: second foal: half-sister to 3-y-o 1¼m winner Fairywings (by Kris): dam, 6f winner, half-sister to smart miler Hoy out of close relative of smart 1¼m colt Elegant Air: won maiden auction at Ayr on final start, much improved effort: will progress again over 7f+. *Mrs J. R. Ramsden*   78 p

CAVERS YANGOUS   5 b.g. Daring March 116 – Rapid Lady 63 (Rapid River 127) [1995 76: 6v⁶ 6.9m³ 6g* a6g² 6.9f² 6m² 6m 6g⁶ 7.6m 7g 1996 7g⁴ 7g³ 6m 7m³ 6g 7m 6f³ a6g 6m⁶ 7m a6g Nov 4] sturdy gelding: good walker: fair handicapper: below form after fourth start at 5 yrs: stays 7f: acts on firm and soft ground and on fibresand: blinkered/visored since third 5-y-o start: inconsistent. *M. Johnston*   68

CAVIAR AND CANDY   2 b.f. (Apr 23) Soviet Star (USA) 128 – Blue Brocade 91 (Reform 132) [1996 5s³ 5g⁴ 5.1d³ 5m⁶ a5g 6g³ 6m³ 6f² 5m⁴ 6g2 Jul 4] £,200Y: quite good-topped filly: seventh foal: half-sister to 3-y-o 12.3f and 15f winner Berlin Blue (by Belmez), useful 4-y-o 2m winner Orchestra Stall (by Old Vic) and 1993 2-y-o 7f winner Oubeck Blue (by Chief Singer): dam 10.6f winner: poor maiden: sold 5,000 gns Newmarket July Sales after final start: bred to stay much further than 6f: seems to act on any going. *D. J. S. Cosgrove*   47

CAVIAR ROYALE (IRE)   2 ch.c. (Mar 26) Royal Academy (USA) 130 – Petite Liquerelle (IRE) (Shernazar 131) [1996 5m² 5m* 6m³ 5f⁵ 6m² 6d² Aug 12] IR 20,000Y: strong, lengthy colt: fluent mover: third foal: half-brother to Irish 3-y-o 11f winner Dancing Bluebell (by Bluebird) and 1994 Irish 2-y-o 1m winner Federico (by Waajib): dam unraced granddaughter of Irish Oaks and Poule d'Essai des Pouliches winner Corejada: easy winner of maiden at Lingfield in May: best efforts last 2 starts when second in nursery at Goodwood and minor event at Windsor: sold 62,000 gns Newmarket Autumn Sales: will be suited by further over 6f: very coltish third start. *R. Hannon*   94

CAVINA   6 b.m. Ardross 134 – Royal Yacht (USA) 65 (Riverman (USA) 131) [1995 –, a64: 16.2m⁶ 14.9g a16g* 14d 19m a16g Dec 26] modest performer: fit from hurdling, well beaten only run on flat in 1996: stays 2m: acts on equitrack. *N. A. Graham*   –

CAYMAN KAI (IRE)   3 ch.c. Imperial Frontier (USA) 112 – Safiya (USA) (Riverman (USA) 131) [1995 109: 5g* 5d² 5f³ 5m² 5m⁴ 5m² 5d* 6f² 1996 7m* 8g⁴ 8f⁵ 8m Jul 31] sturdy, good-quartered attractive colt: smart performer: won Free Handicap at Newmarket in April by 1¾ lengths from Projection, quickening well in Dip: best efforts when 2 lengths fourth of 10 to Ashkalani in Poule d'Essai des Poulains at Longchamp and about 3¾ lengths fifth of 9 to Bijou d'Inde in St James's Palace Stakes at Royal Ascot: not clear run in Sussex Stakes at Goodwood final outing: stays 1m: acts on firm ground and dead: held up. *R. Hannon*   114

CD SUPER TARGETING (IRE)   3 ch.f. Polish Patriot (USA) 128 – Hazy Bird (Ballymore 123) [1995 47+: 5.2m⁶ 1996 7d 7m 10s² 10.2g* 9m⁵ 8.3g⁶ Sep 29] workmanlike filly: modest form: won maiden at Bath in May: off course over 3½ months, well below form in claimer last time: sold 3,500 gns Newmarket Autumn Sales: much better suited by around 1¼m than shorter: acts on soft ground, not on good to firm: front runner. *M. R. Channon*   62

CEANOTHUS (IRE)   2 ch.f. (Apr 2) Bluebird (USA) 125 – Golden Bloom (Main Reef 126) [1996 7f 8g Oct 25] leggy, sparely-made filly: fourth living foal: half-sister to fairly useful 3-y-o 6f (at 2 yrs) to 8.2f winner Golden Pond (by Don't Forget Me) and Irish 9f/1¼m winner Mayfield Prince (by Thatching): dam unraced daughter of half-sister to Connaught: down the field in maidens at Salisbury (slowly away) and Doncaster: probably capable of better. *J. H. M. Gosden*   – p

177

CEBWOB 3 br.f. Rock City 120 – Island Ruler 79 (Ile de Bourbon (USA) 133)   60
[1995 85: 7m³ 7d* 7f³ 1996 8g a7g 7m⁴ 10m² 11.1m³ Aug 29] small, sparely-made
filly: only modest form in claimers in 1996: sold 9,000 gns Newmarket Autumn
Sales: stays 1¼m: best effort on firm ground, winner on dead at 2 yrs: has been
bandaged behind. *P. F. I. Cole*

CEDAR DANCER 4 b.f. Rambo Dancer (CAN) 107 – Nonasalome (Absalom   45 d
128) [1995 46: 6m³ 6.1g 6f 8.2m 5.1m 6f² 8.1m⁵ 6g⁶ 6f 1996 7d⁴ 6f⁴ 5.1g 6f 8g a11g
6m⁶ 8.3g 8m² 8m Sep 9] workmanlike filly: poor mover: poor performer: sold 1,350
gns Ascot November Sales: stays 1m: acts on firm and dead ground and fibresand:
inconsistent. *R. J. Hodges*

CEDAR GIRL 4 b.f. Then Again 126 – Classic Times 82 (Dominion 123) [1995   44
44: 7f⁴ 5.7f 6m 6g⁴ 6m 6f 1996 a5g⁵ a6g 5m 5g a7g³ 7.1m 7m Aug 6] poor
handicapper: left Mrs N. Macauley after second start to return to 3-y-o trainer: stays
7f: acts on firm ground and all-weather (poor efforts on soft): races prominently:
covered by Cosmonaut. *R. J. Hodges*

CEDEZ LE PASSAGE (FR) 5 br.h. Warning 136 – Microcosme 100 (Golden   73
Fleece (USA) 133) [1995 95: a12g² 12g 10m⁵ 10d⁴ 12d 10.1f⁵ 12m 10.4m 8g 10g⁴   a80
10m 10d³ 9.8m 10d⁶ 1996 8s 10g 12m 8m 10g 10d⁵ 10d a10s⁵ a9.4g* a9.4g⁶
a10g³ a9.4g⁴ Dec 28] leggy, close-coupled horse: mostly well below best for new
stable in 1996 but won claimer at Wolverhampton in November: stays 1½m: acts on
firm ground, dead and fibresand: sometimes blinkered, including last 6 starts at 5 yrs.
K. O. Cunningham-Brown

CEE-JAY-AY 9 gr.g. Free State 125 – Raffinrula 75 (Raffingora 130) [1995 69§,   59
a56§: a7g⁶ 8g 10.8d 8g⁶ 8m³ 7.6m 8g 7g⁶ 8m⁴ 8m⁴ 7.6m⁵ a8.5g⁵ 7.6m⁴ 8f³ 7.6m 8d
8g⁴ 8.1g 7.1d² 8m 1996 a7g 7.5d⁶ 10.8g 8m 8.5m 8g⁵ 6.9g⁵ 10.3m⁵ 8f 8f² 7.6m³ 8m
6.9f* 7.5f² 7.5g⁶ 6.9m⁴ 8.5m 8f³ 9m³ 8m⁴ 8m² Oct 29] smallish, workmanlike
gelding: usually looks well: only modest handicapper at best nowadays: went 48
races without success before winning minor event at Carlisle in August: raced mainly
at up to 1m, but seems to stay 1¼m: acts on any going: blinkered (below form) once
at 4 yrs: usually slowly away and sometimes badly so. *J. Berry*

CEE-N-K (IRE) 2 b.c. (May 9) Thatching 131 – Valois (Lyphard (USA) 132)   65 +
[1996 6g 6m⁴ a6g² a6g⁶ a6g² a8g* Dec 11] 16,000F, 12,500 2-y-o: half-brother to   a77
fairly useful 7f winner Shannon Cottage (by Shecky Greene), 1985 2-y-o 7f winner
Shannon Vale (by Irish River) and French 10.5f winner Actualite (by Polish
Precedent): dam half-sister to High Top and the dam of Old Vic: fair form: won
nursery at Lingfield in December, making most: better at 1m than shorter: acts on
all-weather. *M. Johnston*

CEILIDH STAR (IRE) 3 b.f. Soviet Star (USA) 128 – Highland Ball 73 (Bold   72
Lad (IRE) 133) [1995 63+: 7m 7d 8g⁵ 1996 12m³ 12m² 12m³ 12.4f² 11m* 11.9m³
11.4m 14m⁵ 11.8g³ a12s⁵ Nov 19] rangy, unfurnished filly: has quick action: fair
form: won minor event at Redcar in August, rallying: below form afterwards: should
prove suited by further than 1½m: acts on firm going: usually held up: blinkered
(except one) since fifth 3-y-o starts: sold 13,000 gns Newmarket December Sales.
B. W. Hills

CEIRSEACH (IRE) 3 br.f. Don't Forget Me 127 – Beparoejojo (Lord Gayle   100
(USA) 124) [1995 94: 6g⁵ 7m* 8m⁴ 7g 7d³ 8d³ 7g⁶ 9d² 1996 8s² 10s⁴ 9f² 12m² 12m
10m⁶ 12m³ 14g⁶ 12d³ 12m⁴ 9.6g* 8g Oct 13] smallish, workmanlike filly: useful
performer: in frame in 4 listed races, 2 minor events and a handicap in Ireland before
winning minor event at Gowran Park in September: stiff task, well beaten in
Ribblesdale Stakes fifth start: stays 1½m: acts on firm and soft ground: effective
blinkered or not. *J. S. Bolger, Ireland*

CELANDINE 3 b.f. Warning 136 – Silly Bold (Rousillon (USA) 133) [1995 80:   –
6g³ 6m³ 5.7m* 6f⁴ 1996 a6g⁶ a5g⁶ 5g 6m Jun 10] leggy filly: has a quick action:
disappointing for new stable in 1996: stays 6f. *J. L. Eyre*

CELEBRANT 2 b.f. (Apr 29) Saddlers' Hall (IRE) 126 – Cathedra (So Blessed   66
130) [1996 6.1m² 6m⁴ 6d⁵ Aug 24] 8,000Y: workmanlike filly: half-sister to several
winners abroad, including useful 1988 Irish 2-y-o 6f and 7f winner Tantum Ergo (by
Tanfirion): dam poor daughter of Park Hill winner Collyria: showed form in maiden
auction at Nottingham on debut: below that form after: bred to stay beyond 6f: sold
to join A. Hide 9,500 gns Newmarket Autumn Sales. *R. Hannon*

CELEBRATION CAKE (IRE)   4 b.g. Mister Majestic 122 – My Louise 54   81
(Manado 130) [1995 63: 6g 8g* 7g³ 8f³ 8g³ 8m⁶ 7g 10.5s 1996 8.1m 8.3m² 8.3m* 8d²
8.1m* 7.9g 8m⁵ 7m* 9.2g Sep 29] workmanlike gelding: fairly useful handicapper:
reportedly operated on for a wind problem, and not seen until July: improved form
on return: won at Hamilton and Haydock in August and at Ayr in September: stays
8.3f: acts on firm going (possibly on dead), below form on soft: visored (below form)
once as 3-y-o. *Miss L. A. Perratt*

CELERIC   4 b.g. Mtoto 134 – Hot Spice (Hotfoot 126) [1995 100p: 12.5f*   116 +
14.1m* 12m 13.3g* 16m² 13.9g* 14g³ 1996 12m⁶ 13.9m* 13.9m² 16.1m*
13.9m* 15.9m* 18m² 16m* Oct 5]
'He's a suspicious horse, and that's just the sort of thing to catch his
eye', commented trainer David Morley after his Celeric had apparently taken
too much interest in a TV camera car when short-headed at York in June. It will
be very surprising if anyone connected with the horse is ruing that defeat and
harbouring dark thoughts about Channel 4 Racing now. As far as the punter is
concerned, suspicious he may have been, but Celeric was the last horse to be
suspicious of. He won five out of seven starts after a ring-rusty reappearance,
and after that on-the-nod disappointment at York the only horse to beat him was
Double Trigger. The improvement of 16 lb or so that he found in 1996 has taken
him from useful handicapper to a leading 1997 Cup race candidate.
The races that Celeric won on the way were a £7,375 handicap at York,
the £57,350 'Newcastle Brown Ale' Northumberland Plate at Newcastle, the
£11,451 Foster's Silver Cup Rated Stakes at York, the listed Lonsdale Stakes at
York and the Jockey Club Cup at Newmarket. Apart from winning a healthy
amount of beer money himself, Celeric must also have paid for a few rounds
—he was backed down to favourite five times in 1996, to co-favourite on a
sixth and second favourite on his two remaining appearances. The style of his
victories might have led to a stiff drink or two as well because his challenge was
delayed until the last minute, tactics fine-tuned by that aforementioned defeat at
York when he had gone on two furlongs out. In the Northumberland Plate,
Celeric was pushed along the length of the straight and cut through a mass of
horses to take Snow Princess a hundred yards from home. For his other major
triumph, in the Jockey Club Cup, Celeric was on the bridle and poised on the
heels of the leaders, but still contrived to alarm his supporters by idling once in

'Newcastle Brown Ale' Northumberland Plate, Newcastle—
Celeric lands a gamble by three quarters of a length from Snow Princess

Jockey Club Cup, Newmarket—Celeric is pressed closely by Sanmartino (rails)

front; he had a head to spare over Sanmartino at the post. The Jockey Club Cup was Celeric's second venture into pattern races, having been runner-up to Double Trigger in the Doncaster Cup over three weeks earlier. Beaten two lengths in receipt of 7 lb, Celeric is well held by Double Trigger on the book, but there will be those backing him to turn the tables in 1997. Some will do so because the waiting tactics looked to be rather overdone at Doncaster, but, more importantly, there is the good chance that Celeric will be an improved horse again with another year under his belt. 'He's still immature physically and mentally' said his trainer in the autumn when deciding not to let Celeric carry a tempting weight for the biggest beer-money prize going, the Foster's Melbourne Cup. It was reported that City Index had been negotiating to underwrite the trip to Australia, but not for any of the other European challengers. It is not difficult to see why they should want so much to have their name associated with Celeric.

		Busted	Crepello
	Mtoto	(b 1963)	Sans Le Sou
Celeric	(b 1983)	Amazer	Mincio
(b.g. 1992)		(b 1967)	Alzara
	Hot Spice	Hotfoot	Firestreak
	(b 1978)	(br 1966)	Pitter Patter
		Persian Market	Taj Dewan
		(br 1972)	Londonderry Air

A tall, close-coupled gelding, Celeric is a good walker and shows a quick action. Two and a half miles will pose no problems for him come Gold Cup day but a soft surface might—he has encountered it only once before, when showing promise as a two-year-old, and clearly goes well on top-of-the-ground. There is a theme to the sons and daughters of broodmare Hot Spice: she had six foals to reach racing age prior to Celeric, the winners Turmeric (by Alias Smith), Sesame (by Derrylin) and Zucchini (by Absalom) followed by the maidens Camomile (by Bay Express), Horseradish (by Chief Singer) and Myrrh (by Salse). Easily the best of them was Sesame, a smart mile-and-a-half performer who was considered suited by extreme waiting tactics for most of her career but then made virtually all to gain her one pattern victory, in the Blandford Stakes as a five-year-old. Hot Spice accomplished next to nothing on the racecourse, but her dam Persian Market was a useful individual, awarded the eight-and-a-half-furlong Princess Elizabeth Stakes (then a Group 3 race) at Epsom on the demotion of Juliette Marny. David Morley trained Hot Spice at a time when he would have been best known for his exploits as a trainer of jumpers. He has never sent out as many winners in a flat season (thirty in 1988 is his best score) as he did over jumps, but the last few years have seen his highest-profile successes since Calaba won the 1975 Cumberland Lodge Stakes in his second season with a licence. Fard took the 1994 Middle Park, Fahal was fourth in the 1995 Derby and Atraf's Cork And Orrery was added to Celeric's big-race wins in 1996. Now fifty-seven, Morley had forty horses listed in the 1996 *Horses In Training,* twenty-four of which were owned by Sheikh Hamdan. *D. Morley*

CELESTIAL CHOIR 6 b.m. Celestial Storm (USA) 132 – Choir (High Top 94 131) [1995 88, a80: a9.4g⁴ 8g 9.9m 8g⁴ 8m⁴ 7m 7g³ 8.1g 8.5m 7g⁴ 9f 8m³ 8m* 8m² 8d⁴ 8g 9g⁵ 8m 8m a8.5g² a8g 1996 a10g* a12g* a9.4g⁴ a12g⁴ 8s⁵ 8g² 8g 10g 11.9m² 10.3g³ 12.3m² 10.3m* 11.9m* 10.3m 10m³ 12s Nov 9] angular mare: fairly useful handicapper, better than ever: won at Lingfield and Southwell (minor event) in January, at Doncaster in July and York (£17,300 event, leading over 1f out to beat Sheer Danzig 1¼ lengths) in August: finds 7f a bare minimum, and stays 12.3f: acts on good to firm and dead ground (possibly not very soft) and the all-weather: blinkered twice (no improvement) earlier in career: has run well when sweating: usually held up: tough and consistent. *J. L. Eyre*

CELESTIAL DOLLAR 5 b.g. Celestial Storm (USA) 132 – Pennies To Pounds – 80 (Ile de Bourbon (USA) 133) [1995 –: 11.7f⁵ 8.1g 10m 10.2m a12g 1996 12.1m 8m Aug 13] tall gelding: no worthwhile form. *O. O'Neill*

CELESTIAL FIRE 4 gr.g. Celestial Storm (USA) 132 – Fiery Gal (CAN) – (Explodent (USA)) [1995 –: 12m 10g 1996 11.6g⁴ Jul 15] no worthwhile form on flat. *J. White*

CELESTIAL KEY (USA) 6 br.g. Star de Naskra (USA) – Casa Key (USA) 106 (Cormorant (USA)) [1995 106: 6m 6m⁵ 7m* 7g⁴ 8.1g* 7m* 7g 7.6m 8f 7m³ 7.9m 7m⁶ 8d⁶ 7d 9g 8m* a9.4g 1996 8.9g⁵ 7g⁴ 9m³ 7m 7g² 8.1s⁶ 7g³ 8g⁴ a9.4g Dec 7] close-coupled, good-topped gelding: impresses in appearance: has a quick action: useful handicapper: not seen until September, best efforts when ½-length second of 7 to Verzen in rated stakes at York and 3¾ lengths fourth of 8 to Ali-Royal in steadily-run listed race at Newmarket: effective at 7f to 9f: acts on good to firm and dead ground and on fibresand: blinkered (soundly beaten) once as 4-y-o. *M. Johnston*

CELIA'S RAINBOW 3 gr.f. Belfort (FR) 89 – Mrs Skinner 53 (Electric 126) – [1995 NR 1996 8g 9g⁶ May 19] leggy, sparely-made filly: first foal: dam, plater, stayed 1m: well behind in maidens. *M. P. Bielby*

CELTIC LADY 5 b.m. Kabour 80 – Lady Gilly (Remainder Man 126§) [1995 – NR 1996 7.1d a7g Jun 8] first foal: dam unraced: no sign of ability: tried blinkered: covered by Cosmonaut. *Mrs N. Macauley*

CELTIC LILLEY 6 ch.m. Celtic Cone 116 – Pal Alley (Pals Passage 115) [1995 – NR 1996 a16g Jun 6] 775 4-y-o: half-sister to a winning Irish jumper by Rymer: dam lightly raced: poor novice hurdler for R. Hoad: no promise on flat debut: has joined J. Ffitch-Heyes. *P. Mooney*

CENSOR 3 b.g. Kris 135 – Mixed Applause (USA) 101 (Nijinsky (CAN) 138) 92 [1995 84p: 8m 8.2m* 1996 8.1g⁵ 9s⁶ 8m³ 8m⁵ Aug 3] big, lengthy gelding: fairly useful handicapper: best effort when fifth of 9 to Hammerstein in £14,000 conditions event at Goodwood final start: sold (H. Cecil to D. Nicholls) 30,000 gns Newmarket Autumn Sales, and gelded: effective at 1m, bred to stay further: acts on good to firm going: races prominently. *H. R. A. Cecil*

CENTRE STALLS (IRE) 3 b.c. In The Wings 128 – Lora's Guest 99 (Be My 117 Guest (USA) 126) [1995 89: 7d* 7.3d 1996 8g² 9m 8.1m* 8g* 8d 8g Nov 2] good-bodied colt: short to post when tailed off (reportedly jarred up) second 3-y-o start: ran on strongly to lead final 1f when winning both minor event at Sandown and listed race at Kempton (by 9 lb best effort, beat Wizard King 1¾ lengths) on return: smart at around 1m, and should stay further:

yet to race on extremes of going: pulled hard (behind steady pace) final 3-y-o start. *R. F. Johnson Houghton*

CERBERA   7 b.g. Caruso 112 – Sealed Contract 76 (Runnymede 123) [1995 –:   –
a6g 1996 a6g⁴ a5g⁵ a6g a6g Mar 30] no worthwhile form: tried blinkered. *J. P. Smith*

CERDAN (USA)   3 ch.c. Zilzal (USA) 137 – Vie En Rose (USA) (Blushing   82
Groom (FR) 131) [1995 74p: 6m³ 1996 7.3s⁵ 7m² 7f³ 10m⁴ 9f Dec 6] rather leggy, attractive colt: good walker: fairly useful maiden handicapper: left M. Stoute after penultimate start: best effort (though pulled hard) at 1¼m: acts on firm ground, apparently not on soft. *D. Hofmans, USA*

CERISE (IRE)   3 b.f. Red Sunset 120 – Noble Nancy (Royal And Regal (USA))   53 d
[1995 49: 6m⁶ 7f⁴ 6m 7g⁴ 7.5d 7.9m 8f⁴ 1996 8.2g² 8m 8g 8f⁶ 8.2f⁴ 10f 7m 8.3g a8.5g⁶ Nov 2] workmanlike filly: modest maiden handicapper: disappointing after reappearance: sold 2,400 gns Ascot November Sales: stays 1m: acts on firm ground, no form on dead: normally blinkered: sent to South Korea. *C. W. C. Elsey*

CERTAIN MAGIC   2 ch.c. (Feb 25) Faustus (USA) 118 – Dependable (For-   64
midable (USA) 125) [1996 6g⁵ 6s* 7.3m⁶ Sep 20] 6,200Y: strong, lengthy colt: second foal: dam unraced daughter of half-sister to Chilibang: won median auction maiden at Ripon in August: never a factor in nursery final start: should stay beyond 6f. *W. R. Muir*

CERTAIN WAY (IRE)   6 ch.g. Sure Blade (USA) 130 – Ruffling Point (Gorytus   –
(USA) 132) [1995 –, a66: a8g² a7g⁴ a8g a9.4g a8.5g a7g* a8g a9.4g⁶ a7g* 1996 a8.5g⁵ Jan 10] fair handicapper: never going well only start in 1996: subsequently gelded: stays 9.4f: acts on fibresand: usually visored at 2 yrs: blinkered (tailed off) third 4-y-o start. *N. P. Littmoden*

CEZANNE   7 b.h. Ajdal (USA) 130 – Reprocolor 114 (Jimmy Reppin 131) [1995   111
NR 1996 a8g⁴ a9.9s² a10g² 10d⁶ 10f⁵ 11.1m⁴ Sep 7] tall, lengthy horse: rated 121 at 5 yrs, but only smart nowadays: off course nearly 3 months, close fourth of 7 to Sacrament in September Stakes at Kempton, tracking leaders and staying on well: may prove better at 1½m than 1¼m these days: acts on firm ground, dead and on sand: held up. *Saeed bin Suroor*

CHABROL (CAN)   3 b.c. El Gran Senor (USA) 136 – Off The Record (USA)   82 d
(Chas Conerly (USA)) [1995 NR 1996 8m⁶ 10.3g⁵ 9s⁴ 10m 10.1m* 9g 10.1m 10.3g 9g Nov 1] $60,000Y: tall, leggy colt: first foal: dam, winner at around 6f in USA, half-sister to Canadian Grade 1 winner Proper Evidence: sold out of H. Cecil's stable 1,300 gns Ascot July Sales after third start: well-backed winner of claimer (set steady pace, subsequently left R. Harris' stable) at Yarmouth in August: stays 1¼m: tongue tied of late. *T. T. Clement*

CHADLEIGH LANE (USA)   4 ch.g. Imp Society (USA) – Beauty Hour (USA)   –
(Bold Hour) [1995 –, a68d: a7g⁵ a7g⁵ a7g² a7g* 12.3m 8g⁶ a8.5g a7g a7g a9.4g 1996   a69
a7g⁶ a8g* a7g* a8g⁴ a7g³ a7g⁴ a8.5g* a7g⁵ a8.5g³ a8g⁵ a9.4g⁴ a8g a9.4g² a8g* Nov 22] quite attractive gelding: fair performer: successful in apprentice claimer and handicap at Southwell and seller at Wolverhampton early on, then in claimer at Southwell in November: stays 9.4f: acts on good to firm and soft ground, goes well on fibresand: seems effective visored or not. *R. Hollinshead*

CHADWELL HALL   5 b.h. Kala Shikari 125 – Cherrywood Blessin (Good   73
Times (ITY)) [1995 64, a69: a6g⁴ a6g* a6g² a6g⁴ a6g² a5g² a5g* 5m⁵ a5g² a5g²   a84
a5g⁵ a6g² 5.1d* 5d³ 5m² 5f 1996 a5g² a5g⁴ a5g* a5g² a5g 5g² 5g* 5.1m⁵ 6m⁴ 5m* 6m 5m 5.2m⁶ 5.1d 5m 5m⁶ 5.1g³ 5g⁶ 5s² a5g a6g* a6s² Dec 19] plain horse: has a round action: fairly useful handicapper: won at Wolverhampton in January, Ripon (apprentices) in April, Warwick in July and Southwell (claimer) in November: effective at 5f and 6f: goes well on fibresand and acts on good to firm and dead ground: usually blinkered: often claimer ridden: usually bandaged off-hind: usually has tongue tied down: races prominently and with plenty of enthusiasm: rare below-par effort when sweating: splendidly tough, game and consistent. *S. R. Bowring*

CHAIN REACTION (IRE)   2 b.f. (Apr 11) Fayruz 116 – Timiya (High Top   63
131) [1996 6g³ 5g³ 5m⁵ 6m* 7m Sep 17] IR 3,000Y: angular filly: second living foal: sister to a winner abroad: dam unraced: modest form: won median auction maiden at Brighton in August: stays 6f: raced freely final start. *M. A. Jarvis*

CHAIRMANS CHOICE 6 ch.g. Executive Man 119 – Revida Girl 63 (Habat 127) [1995 58+, a82: 8.2g⁴ 8f⁵ 10m³ 8g⁶ 8m² 7g³ 8m* 8f³ 7.9g* 7g a9.4g* a8g² 1996 a9.4g 8m³ 8s⁴ 7f* 7m³ 8m Jul 30] leggy gelding: has a screw in his knee: fairly useful handicapper on the all-weather (though well beaten only start in 1996), fair on turf: won at Brighton (apprentices) in June, making virtually all: effective at 7f, and stays 9.4f: acts on firm ground (below form on soft) and on fibresand: edgy sort: moved poorly to post (well below form) final 6-y-o start. *A. P. Jarvis* 65 a–

CHAIRMANS DAUGHTER 2 b.f. (Feb 17) Unfuwain (USA) 131 – Ville Sainte (FR) (Saint Estephe (FR) 123) [1996 6f⁴ 7g 6.9m 8f* 10m² 8f 8f Nov 5] tall filly: has round action: second reported foal: dam French 1¼m winner out of half-sister to To-Agori-Mou: blinkered only time, won selling nursery at Leicester (left P. Cole's stable) in September: very much a stayer: acts on firm going: visored final start. *J. Pearce* 60

CHAI-YO 6 b.h. Rakaposhi King 119 – Ballysax Lass (Main Reef 126) [1995 NR 1996 8.1s Oct 22] first foal: dam lightly-raced at 2 yrs in Ireland: 66/1 and ridden by 7-lb claimer, signs of ability in minor event at Chepstow on flat debut, staying on late: progressive winning hurdler. *J. A. B. Old* – p

CHAKALAK 8 b.g. Damister (USA) 123 – Wig And Gown (Mandamus 120) [1995 51: 16m 14.1m 13.9g 16.4g⁵ 17.2m² 16.2f⁵ 16.2g* 16.5f³ 16.4m 15.4m³ 17.2m³ 16m⁶ 1996 15.4m 21.6m² 16.2g⁵ a16g* 16.4m³ 17.2m³ a13g* 14.9m⁵ 16.5m Aug 1] strong, compact gelding: has reportedly had leg trouble: poor mover: only modest handicapper on turf nowadays, fair on the all-weather: first runs on all-weather for nearly 5 years when winning selling events at Lingfield in May and June: effective at 13f, and stays very well: needs a sound surface on turf, acts on all-weather: often takes plenty of driving. *S. Dow* 51 a68

CHAKRA 2 gr.g. (Mar 30) Mystiko (USA) 124 – Maracuja (USA) (Riverman (USA) 131) [1996 6s May 22] good-topped, well-grown gelding: third foal: half-brother to German 3-y-o Massada (by Most Welcome), useful 7f and 1m winner at 2 yrs: dam, French 2-y-o 1m winner, out of half-sister to graded stakes winner and excellent broodmare Lassie Dear: burly, tailed off in maiden at Goodwood. *S. Dow* –

CHALAMONT (IRE) 3 ch.f. Kris 135 – Durtal 121 (Lyphard (USA) 132) [1995 88: 6m⁴ 7.5d⁴ 6.1d² 6f* 6.1d* 1996 6g May 17] good-quartered, unfurnished filly: good mover: fairly useful juvenile in 1995: raced too freely when well beaten in minor event at Newbury only 3-y-o start: takes keen hold and looks a sprinter: acts on firm and dead ground. *P. W. Chapple-Hyam* –

CHALCUCHIMA 3 gr.g. Reprimand 122 – Ica (Great Nephew 126) [1995 65, a54: 7d⁶ 7g⁶ a8.5g⁵ 1996 11.4m 14d Sep 28] big, workmanlike gelding: has scope: has a fluent, round action: easily best effort on debut: no promise in 1996, though not bred to stay 11f+: sold (R. Charlton to N. Hawke) 4,000 gns Newmarket Autumn Sales. *R. Charlton* –

CHALICE 3 b.f. Governor General 116 – Eucharis 41 (Tickled Pink 114) [1995 69: 6.1d 6.1d 5s² 5d⁵ 1996 6m⁶ a6g⁴ a5g 5g* 5m 5m⁴ 5g 5m 5m Oct 3] unfurnished filly: fair handicapper: won maiden at Doncaster in May: should prove effective at 6f: acts on good to firm and soft ground, below form on fibresand: often apprentice ridden: sold 1,500 gns Doncaster November Sales. *J. Balding* 69

CHALK DUST (USA) 3 b.f. Unbridled – Charmie Carmie (USA) (Lyphard (USA) 132) [1995 80p: 7.1s⁶ 7m² 1996 8.3g⁵ 7f² 6m Aug 10] leggy filly: has scope: fair maiden: better at 7f than shorter and should stay 1m: sold 54,000 gns Newmarket December Sales. *P. F. I. Cole* 73

CHALKY DANCER 4 br.g. Adbass (USA) 102 – Tiny Feet (Music Maestro 119) [1995 47: 10m 11.5m 9m⁴ 8g² 7.5m² 7.1g⁴ 7f a10g 1996 a8g 7f 8m⁵ 8m² 8f a10g a8g a7g Dec 28] sturdy gelding: poor mover: poor maiden handicapper: stays 1m: acts on firm ground, no form on the all-weather: tried blinkered, no improvement. *H. J. Collingridge* 38 a–

CHALLENGER (IRE) 3 b.g. Nordico (USA) – Sweet Miyabi (JPN) (Royal Ski (USA)) [1995 NR 1996 7g 8g 9f⁵ 10g Jul 8] fourth reported foal: dam unraced: no worthwhile form: trained by T. J. Naughton first 2 starts: flashed tail when hit with whip third start. *J. J. Sheehan* –

CHALUZ 2 b.c. (Apr 21) Night Shift (USA) – Laluche (USA) 100 (Alleged (USA) 54 p
138) [1996 5m⁶ 6m 8g a8.5g² Nov 25] small, well-made colt: type to carry condition:
fluent mover: sixth foal: half-brother to useful 3-y-o 1½m winner Lallans (by Old
Vic), smart middle-distance stayer Landowner and 1¾m winner Lala Musa (both by
Kris): dam, from excellent family, won from 6f to 1m at 2 yrs: first form when
second in nursery at Wolverhampton in November: likely to stay middle distances:
acts on fibresand: sold (M. Johnston to K. Burke) 5,400 gns Ascot December Sales.
M. Johnston

CHAMPAGNE GRANDY 6 ch.m. Vaigly Great 127 – Monstrosa 70 (Mon- 84
santo (FR) 121) [1995 84: 6g 6m⁶ 6m 6g 7g* 6m* 6.1m 7m 6g 7.3d* 8.1g 6g 6.1s 6f
1996 6.5g 7d* 7f 7.1d 7m 6f 7.6m³ 7f⁵ 6m 7d 7m 7m³ 8g Sep 29] leggy, close-
coupled mare: has a quick action: fairly useful handicapper: won at Lingfield in
April: only a few creditable efforts afterwards: stays 7.6f: acts on good to firm
ground, very best efforts on a soft surface: ran poorly on fibresand. *M. R. Channon*

CHAMPAGNE N DREAMS 4 b.f. Rambo Dancer (CAN) 107 – Pink Sen- 47
sation 69 (Sagaro 133) [1995 57: 7g 8.1g* 8g³ 7g⁵ 7.1f⁴ 9.9g 10m⁴ 10g 10.5s 1996
9m⁶ 8m⁶ 8m³ 8m 8.1m 12f³ 12.3g Aug 17] sturdy filly: only a poor handicapper in
1996: effective at 1m to 1½m: acts on firm ground, below form only run on a soft
surface: blinkered (below form, raced freely) fifth 4-y-o start: sweating (below form)
second 4-y-o start. *D. Nicholls*

CHAMPAGNE ON ICE 2 b.f. (Apr 16) Efisio 120 – Nip In The Air (USA) 114 46
(Northern Dancer) [1996 5g 5.1g 6.1m 6.1m² 6m⁴ 7f 6s Oct 5] 2,400F, 7,500Y:
small filly: closely related to a winner in Germany by Formidable and half-sister to
numerous winners here and abroad, including useful Irish 6f (at 2 yrs) and 1¼m
winner Little Bighorn (by Blakeney): dam stayed 1¼m: poor form in sellers 2 of last
4 starts: stays 6f: soundly beaten on soft ground. *P. D. Evans*

CHAMPAGNE PRINCE 3 b.c. Prince Sabo 123 – Champagne Season (USA) 92
54 (Vaguely Noble 140) [1995 89: 6g² 7m* 7m⁴ 7.5m* 7m* 7.3d⁴ 1996 8m⁵ 7m⁵
10m 10.3d³ 10.1m⁴ 9m 10s Oct 24] smallish colt: has a roundish action: fairly useful
handicapper: best efforts in 1996 when in frame at Chester and Epsom: stays 10.3f:
acts on good to firm ground and dead, below form on soft: sometimes takes keen
hold. *P. W. Harris*

CHAMPAGNE TOAST 2 ch.c. (Mar 15) Mazilier (USA) 107 – Saraswati 55 66
(Mansingh (USA) 120) [1996 5g 6g 6g³ 8m 7m Oct 17] 22,000Y: rather leggy,
unfurnished colt: first foal: dam ran only at 2 yrs , closely related to Norfolk Stakes
winner Petillante: third in median auction maiden at Kempton in August, easily best
effort: ran in seller final start: stays 6f: raced only on a sound surface: sold 7,500 gns
Newmarket Autumn Sales: sent to Italy. *R. Hannon*

CHAMPAGNE WARRIOR (IRE) 3 b.f. Waajib 121 – Late Swallow (My 48
Swallow 134) [1995 –: 6m⁶ 7m 7m 1996 10g⁶ 12m² 12m³ a12g⁴ 12s² 12.1m⁵ 13.8g⁴
Sep 21] good-bodied filly: poor maiden handicapper: well suited by at least 1½m:
acts on good to firm and soft ground: blinkered (below form) final 3-y-o start.
M. J. Camacho

CHANCANCOOK 3 ch.f. Hubbly Bubbly (USA) – Majuba Road (Scottish Rifle –
127) [1995 NR 1996 13.8g⁵ 11.8f a14g a11g Dec 27] second reported foal: dam
winning jumper: not much promise. *J. L. Eyre*

CHANCEY FELLA 5 ch.g. Sylvan Express 117 – Musical Piece 91 (Song 132) –
[1995 57: 8g 8.3m 8f⁴ 7m⁵ 8m 7g 1996 a10g Jan 4] modest handicapper: well below
form only 5-y-o start: stays 8.2f well: acts on firm ground, probably on dead: usually
blinkered/visored: has looked a hard ride: won twice over hurdles in the summer.
K. T. Ivory

CHANGED TO BAILEYS (IRE) 2 b.g. (Apr 1) Distinctly North (USA) 115 – 58
Blue Czarina (Sandhurst Prince 128) [1996 5d 5m⁵ 5g³ 5g³ 5m⁵ Oct 3] 16,000Y:
leggy, useful-looking gelding: has scope: fourth foal: dam unraced half-sister
to smart Italian sprinter Ginny Binny: modest form: may prove suited by fast
conditions/sharp 5f: ran well in blinkers final start. *J. Berry*

CHANSON D'AMOUR (IRE) 2 b.f. (Mar 17) High Estate 127 – Wind of –
Change (FR) (Sicyos (USA) 126) [1996 5g⁴ 5m⁵ 5g⁶ 7.1m 7m 8.1m 8.3d Sep 30]
IR 4,600F, 6,800Y: second foal: dam French maiden: half-sister to useful Irish 6f

and 1¼m winner Little Bighorn: poor form, including in a seller: visored final start. *Miss L. A. Perratt*

CHANT D'ALOUETTE 3 b.f. Buzzards Bay 128§ – Singing Lark (Sir Lark 101) [1995 NR 1996 8.3g 14m⁶ Aug 4] first reported foal: dam never ran: showed nil. *R. J. Hodges* –

CHANTRY BEATH 5 ch.g. Dunbeath (USA) 127 – Sallametti (USA) 69 (Giacometti 130) [1995 57: 11.9m 14.1m⁶ 13f³ 12.3f 14f⁴ 14m⁵ 13.9g 12.1g* 12.1g 12m⁶ 1996 a12g⁴ a12g 12g 12.3m 12g 12.1m⁶ 15.1s Nov 7] sturdy, lengthy gelding: only poor at best in 1996: stays 1¾m: acts on any ground: sold (C. Thornton to P. Murphy) 7,200 gns Doncaster November Sales. *C. W. Thornton* 49 d

CHARCOL 3 b.f. Nicholas Bill 125 – Dutch Princess 70 (Royalty 130) [1995 NR 1996 10m Aug 19] ninth foal: sister to useful stayer Double Dutch: dam staying maiden: no promise on debut. *J. E. Banks* –

CHARISSE DANCER 3 b.f. Dancing Dissident (USA) 119 – Cadisa 82 (Top Ville 129) [1995 –: 7f 1996 m⁶ 5g³ 7m³ 8.3d⁴ 10f⁴ 8m Sep 19] sparely-made filly: modest maiden handicappper: stays 8.3f, seemed to find 1¼m (even in less than truly-run race) stretching her stamina: acts on firm and dead ground. *C. F. Wall* 52

CHARLIE BIGTIME 6 b.g. Norwick (USA) 125 – Sea Aura 89 (Roi Soleil 125) [1995 51: a11g⁶ a12g⁴ a16g⁶ a12g⁴ a12g* a14.8g⁴ a12g³ a12g 10g⁵ 12m² 12g a12g³ 11.8m* a9.4g³ a12g⁴ 1996 a12g³ a14.8g⁵ 12.1d a12g³ 14g a12g 12m 12m⁶ a12g³ a12g 11.9m⁴ 11.9f⁵ a14.8g⁴ 14s⁶ a12g a12g Dec 14] sturdy gelding: unimpressive mover: poor handicapper: left R. Harris after penultimate start: probably stays 2m: acts on good to firm ground and fibresand, tailed off 4 of 5 starts (respectable effort last time) on a soft surface: used to be effective visored/blinkered or not: sometimes bandaged: inconsistent. *I. Campbell* 52 d

CHARLIE CHANG (IRE) 3 b.g. Don't Forget Me 127 – East River (FR) (Arctic Tern (USA) 126) [1995 82p: 7m a8g* 1996 7m⁴ 7.9f⁴ 8s⁵ 8g 7.1m⁶ 8.2m² 7m⁶ 10.5m⁴ 8m 8.2g Oct 24] close-coupled, good-topped gelding: has a quick action: fair handicapper: sold 11,000 gns Newmarket Autumn Sales: likely to prove best at up to around 1m: acts on firm going and on equitrack, seemingly unsuited by soft: blinkered (raced too freely) fourth 3-y-o start: inconsistent. *R. Hannon* 73

CHARLIE SILLETT 4 ch.g. Handsome Sailor 125 – Bystrouska (Gorytus (USA) 132) [1995 87p: 6m³ 6d⁶ 6s* 6d 7m* 1996 7m 6d⁶ 7m⁶ 6v 7g 6.1s* 7g Nov 2] tall gelding: fairly useful handicapper: gelded in mid-summer: having second outing in 4 days, best effort to win 20-runner race at Chepstow in October, getting up near finish having had plenty to do from unfavourable draw: stays 7f: acts on good to firm and soft ground: bandaged: usually early to post. *B. W. Hills* 89

CHARLOTTE CORDAY 3 b.f. Kris 135 – Dancing Rocks 118 (Green Dancer (USA) 132) [1995 63p: 6f⁵ 1996 7m³ 7g² 8g* 10g⁴ Jul 10] angular filly: fairly useful form: won steadily-run maiden at Salisbury in June: good fourth of 13 to Freedom Flame in £20,900 handicap at Newmarket month later: stays 1¼m. *G. Wragg* 86

CHARLTON IMP (USA) 3 b.f. Imp Society – Percentage (USA) (Vaguely Noble 140) [1995 –: 6.1d⁶ 1996 7d⁶ 8d 6m 6.1d 8.3m⁵ 10m 8.1f* 8.3m 8m* 8.2d² 7f⁶ 8m Sep 25] workmanlike filly: modest performer: won sellers at Chepstow in July and Bath in August: best form at around 1m: acts on firm and dead ground. *R. J. Hodges* 59

CHARLTON SPRING (IRE) 2 ch.f. (Apr 5) Masterclass (USA) 116 – Relankina (IRE) (Broken Hearted 124) [1996 5m² 5.1m 6m⁶ 6g² 6d* 7m 6g Sep 3] IR 4,100Y, 7,000 2-y-o: leggy, sparely-made filly: first foal: dam unraced half-sister to smart sprinter Perion: runner-up in sellers before winning non-selling nursery at Windsor in August: best form at 6f: acts on good to firm ground, best form on a soft surface. *R. J. Hodges* 70

CHARM DANCER 4 b.f. Rambo Dancer (CAN) 107 – Skelton 70 (Derrylin 115) [1995 55: 9.9m* 10g⁶ 11.5f³ 10.1m³ 8g⁵ 8g 1996 a10g⁵ a8g³ a8g⁵ Feb 24] modest form: stays 11.5f: acts on the all-weather, yet to race on a soft surface. *M. C. Pipe* 53

CHARMED AGAIN 3 b.f. Midyan (USA) 124 – Charming 83 (Glenstal (USA) 118) [1995 NR 1996 10.8m Aug 26] 4,800F, 2,900Y: first foal: dam 7f winner who stayed 1m: 25/1, tailed off in seller. *M. S. Saunders* –

CHARMED LIFE 7 b.g. Legend of France (USA) 124 – Tanagrea (Blakeney 126) [1995 –: 12m⁵ 16d 16.1g 14.1m 16.4m 1996 16.1s a14g Apr 9] no longer of much account. *Mrs A. L. M. King* —

CHARMING ADMIRAL (IRE) 3 b.g. Shareef Dancer (USA) 135 – Lilac Charm 87 (Bustino 136) [1995 –: 8.2m 1996 10g 12m⁵ 11.6m 13.1m³ 14d² 14d² a9.9g 10.9g² Dec 13] close-coupled, workmanlike gelding: fair handicapper, trained first 6 outings in 1996 by C. Wall: stays 1¾m: acts on dead ground, probably on good to firm, yet to race on extremes: tended to wander under pressure fifth 3-y-o start. *Ali Mohsen Khair Al Dine, UAE* 71

CHARMING BRIDE 3 b.f. Charmer 123 – Loredana 64 (Grange Melody) [1995 56: 6m² 6m⁴ 1996 a7g* 6g 7f 7m⁵ 6g³ 7g 7f a7s a7g Nov 22] modest handicapper: landed odds in 4-runner maiden at Lingfield in February: should stay further than 7f: acts on equitrack: blinkered (well beaten) last 2 starts: inconsistent. *S. C. Williams* 56

CHARM THE STARS 2 ch.f. (Feb 10) Roi Danzig (USA) – Deloraine 73 (Pharly (FR) 130) [1996 6g 7g Jul 24] 13,500Y: angular, quite good-topped filly: third foal: half-sister to 1993 2-y-o 6f seller winner Two D's (by Dunbeath) who became very temperamental: dam lightly-raced half-sister to Breeders' Cup Turf winner Northern Spur and smart stayers Kneller and Great Marquess, also the family of Salsabil: down the field in maidens at Newmarket and Leicester (auction event): may do better over further. *M. H. Tompkins* —

CHARNWOOD FOREST (IRE) 4 b. or br.c. Warning 136 – Dance of Leaves (Sadler's Wells (USA) 132) [1995 116p: 7m* 8m² 7.9m* 1996 8d² 8f* 8m² 8d⁴ 8m⁴ 7m* 8g Oct 26] 125

Unlikely though it seems in hindsight, for a good part of the latest season it looked as if Godolphin's best hope for champion miler might not lie with Mark of Esteem. They will have known otherwise of course, and everyone knew the true score after Mark of Esteem's brilliant wins in the autumn, but before that as much attention had been paid to the year-older Charnwood Forest. Which of the two seemed the more likely champion on the Tuesday at Royal Ascot? In the Queen Anne Stakes, Charnwood Forest put four lengths between himself and runner-up Restructure; two races later, Mark of Esteem came within half a length of finishing last of nine. Charnwood Forest had started 11/10-on favourite, without a pattern race penalty for his promising but frustrating three-year-old campaign with Henry Cecil, and only a neck away

Queen Anne Stakes, Royal Ascot—Charnwood Forest forges clear of Restructure and the grey Mistle Cat

from earning one for his Group 1 reappearance clash with Soviet Line in the Lockinge at Newbury. The manner in which he loomed up to challenge over two furlongs out at Royal Ascot, and then forged clear inside the last, demonstrated that an extra 5 lb on his back would have made no difference to the Queen Anne finishing order.

But Charnwood Forest never did acquire the right to that Group 1 penalty. He started even money to do so in the Sussex Stakes at Goodwood, outpaced by First Island in the final furlong and beaten a length, and a short price again when coupled in the betting for the Prix Jacques le Marois at Deauville, running respectably in fourth. How expectations for him had declined is illustrated by his 14/1 starting price in the Queen Elizabeth II Stakes at Ascot in September on his next start; judged on his now well-established form, Charnwood Forest ran as well as could have been expected in finishing five and three quarter lengths behind Mark of Esteem. He was only a neck and a nose behind him in the Breeders' Cup Mile, neither colt however ending his career in a blaze or even spark of glory, but between Ascot and Woodbine an opportunity was found for Charnwood Forest to register a last victory in Europe. It took a drop back to Group 2 company, but he won in good style, justifying favouritism by two lengths in a sprint with Bishop of Cashel from the two-furlong marker in the Challenge Stakes at Newmarket.

Before that win, Charnwood Forest's sale had been agreed to the Rathbarry Stud in Ireland. That makes three noteworthy sons of Warning—Charnwood Forest, Bishop of Cashel and Piccolo—who will be at stud in Europe in 1997, but Warning himself will not be here. The news broke in September that, after six seasons covering in Britain, Warning had been sold to Japan for what was thought to be eight million dollars, similar, apparently, to the amount paid for Pentire whose essay gives more details on the scale of the current stallion exodus to Japan. All the indications are that Warning will be missed. The 1987 champion two-year-old, 1988 champion miler and 1989 Queen Anne winner, was not initially visited by a star-spangled batch of mares, and his starting fee of £15,000 had fallen to £8,000 in 1993. That, however, was the same year that Warning's first crop hit the racecourse and hit it running, making him the top first-season sire in terms of both races won and money won. Charnwood Forest, from his second crop, is the closest Warning has come so far to siring a top-class horse, but he has had several knocking on the door and was in the top ten stallions judged on his progeny's median ratings as two-year-olds, three-year-olds and overall in Britain 1993-1995. Northern Dancer does not feature in Warning's pedigree, something that would have made him increasingly attractive to breeders in an age in which 188 (68%) of the 277 yearlings in the latest Houghton Yearling Sales catalogue featured Northern Dancer in their

Challenge Stakes, Newmarket—another Group 2 race for Charnwood Forest; Bishop of Cashel (right) is second

three-generation pedigree. That number would have been increased by at least 10% in a four-generation analysis. Mr Prospector, incidentally, featured in 15% of the total. Charnwood Forest has Northern Dancer in his pedigree via the dam's sire Sadler's Wells. That dam, Dance of Leaves, failed to see the racecourse. Disappointments are rare enough in Sadler's Wells's producing record, but they are almost unheard of in that of grandam Fall Aspen, whose amazing achievements are detailed most recently in this Annual in the essay on Charnwood Forest's two-year-old half-brother Medaaly (by Highest Honor). Suffice to say here that Charnwood Forest could not come from a better family on the dam's side.

Charnwood Forest (IRE) (b. or br.c. 1992)	Warning (b 1985)	Known Fact (b 1977)	In Reality
			Tamerett
		Slightly Dangerous (b 1979)	Roberto
			Where You Lead
	Dance of Leaves (b 1987)	Sadler's Wells (b 1981)	Northern Dancer
			Fairy Bridge
		Fall Aspen (ch 1976)	Pretense
			Change Water

Charnwood Forest is also a strikingly handsome colt in appearance —rangy and good-bodied—and was a genuine and consistent racehorse. We are confident that he would have stayed a mile and a quarter but, although the stable stated that they were keen to try him at the trip when he appeared in the five-day entries for the Eclipse, it was never put to the test with Halling in the same division. The drop to seven furlongs at Newmarket in October probably had more to do with securing the trainers' championship than new theories about Charnwood Forest's distance requirements, but he looked as good on that day as he had been at a mile. Second in the Lockinge was a good effort on dead going, but he was apparently considered best on top-of-the-ground. He wore a tongue strap in 1996, and sometimes got a little on edge. *Saeed bin Suroor*

Godolphin's "Charnwood Forest"

CHARNWOOD JACK (USA) 3 ch.c. Sanglamore (USA) 126 – Hyroglyph – (USA) (Northern Dancer) [1995 NR 1996 8m 10g 10m Jun 4] $13,000Y: strong, close-coupled, deep-girthed colt: half-brother to several winners, including fair Sure Sign (1¼m, by Sure Blade): dam lightly-raced close relative of very smart 1¼m performer Upper Nile and top-class filly at up to 1¼m De La Rose: no worthwhile form, though showed signs of ability first 2 starts: joined I. Campbell. *R. Harris*

CHARNWOOD MEG (IRE) 3 ch.f. Scenic 128 – Cathryn's Song (Prince – Tenderfoot (USA) 126) [1995 NR 1996 a9.4g Aug 9] IR 5,100F, IR 10,000Y, 8,800 2-y-o: half-sister to several winners, including 1¼m performer Katy's Lad (by Camden Town) and leading 1995/6 novice hurdler Indefence (by Conquering Hero): dam never ran: 50/1, always behind in maiden at Wolverhampton: sold 1,200 gns Newmarket Autumn Sales. *R. Harris*

C-HARRY (IRE) 2 ch.c. (Mar 16) Imperial Frontier (USA) 112 – Desert Gale 61 (Taufan (USA) 119) [1996 5s⁴ 5g³ 5.1d 5d² a5g³ a6g* 5m² 5d* 6.1s a6g² a7g² a67 a7s⁴ Dec 19] IR 4,500F, IR 2,500Y: workmanlike colt: unimpressive mover: third foal: dam Irish 1½m winner: modest performer: won sellers at Wolverhampton and Haydock in spring: off course 5 months after eighth start, good second in nurseries at Southwell on return: stays 7f: acts on good to firm and dead ground and fibresand: probably effective visored or not. *R. Hollinshead*

CHARTER 5 b.g. Reference Point 139 – Winter Queen 60 (Welsh Pageant 132) – [1995 NR 1996 14.1g⁴ 11.7f² 10d 10m Aug 2] sturdy gelding: sixth living foal: brother to 4-y-o Tibetan (unsatisfactory on flat, but promising hurdler), closely related to smart 1m to 1¼m winner Main Objective (by Main Reef) and half-brother to smart stayer Safety In Numbers (by Slip Anchor): dam Irish 4-y-o 13f winner: fair NH Flat race winner: well held all starts on flat proper, but signs of some ability: joined T. J. Naughton and gelded. *Major D. N. Chappell*

CHARTERHOUSE XPRES 3 b.g. Clantime 101 – Uptown Girl 65 (Caruso – 112) [1995 72, a69: 5m⁵ 5m a6g³ a6g² a6g⁴ 6d 7d a5g³ 5d* a5g³ a5g³ 1996 a5g* Jan a69 2] fair performer: won claimer at Lingfield in January: races keenly (has gone too fast on more than one occasion) and best at sprint distances: acts on fibresand and equitrack, best turf form on an easy surface: visored/blinkered since seventh 2-y-o start: has been gelded: sent to Macau. *M. McCormack*

CHASETOWN FLYER (USA) 2 b.c. (Mar 9) Thorn Dance (USA) 107 – 49 Thought Provoker (USA) (Exceller (USA) 129) [1996 5.9g 5.1m 6g⁶ a6g⁶ a8g³ a7g a7g² Dec 27] $6,000F, 4,000Y: workmanlike colt: closely related to a minor stakes winner in USA at 1m by Dixieland Band and half-brother to 2 winners in USA: dam unraced daughter of Cheveley Park winner Gentle Thoughts: poor maiden plater: stays 1m: acts on fibresand. *R. Hollinshead*

CHASTLETON 4 b.f. Presidium 124 – Double Stitch 74 (Wolver Hollow 126) – [1995 43d: a10g⁴ a8g² a8g³ a9.4g* 8.3s⁵ 8.3g⁵ 10m 10f 8.5m³ 10f⁴ 10m 10.2h⁵ 8.3m 8h 10d 8.3g⁶ 1996 a9.4g Mar 6] poor performer: well beaten only 4-y-o start: stays 1¼m: acts on the all-weather and on firm and dead ground, ran poorly (hanging left) on soft: covered by Whittingham. *M. R. Channon*

CHATEAUHERAULT (IRE) 2 b.g. (Mar 30) Contract Law (USA) 108 – 50 Secret Hideaway (USA) (Key To The Mint (USA)) [1996 6m 7m 6m 10m⁴ Sep 24] 38,000Y: tall, leggy gelding: fifth foal: half-brother to Italian 3-y-o 6f (at 2 yrs) to 9f winner Golden Cristina (by Classic Secret) and fairly useful 5f (at 2 yrs) and 7f winner Muchtarak (by Try My Best): dam unraced: poor form: easily best effort final start: seems suited by a test of stamina. *P. C. Haslam*

CHATHAM ISLAND 8 ch.g. Jupiter Island 126 – Floreal 68 (Formidable 77 (USA) 125) [1995 73, a91: a9.4g² a12g² 12m⁴ 10m 12g* 11.8g⁶ 12.3m 11.4m⁴ 12m⁴ a– 1996 a12g⁶ 12g 11.8g 12f² 12m² 12g³ 11.5f² 12m 14.1m* Aug 8] rangy gelding: impresses in appearance: good walker: best form on all-weather, well beaten only try in 1996: fair handicapper on turf: gradually back to form then held it well, winning at Yarmouth in August: stays 14.1f: acts on firm going, yet to show his form on a soft surface: effective from front or held up: game: consistent at 8 yrs. *C. E. Brittain*

CHAUVELIN (IRE) 3 ch.c. Durgam (USA) – Kaliala (FR) (Pharly (FR) 130) 55 [1995 57p: 8.1s a10g⁴ 1996 a8.5g* a8.5g⁴ Mar 30] blind in right eye: dropped into a seller and won at Wolverhampton in February: effective at 8.5f, and should stay beyond 1¼m. *M. Johnston*

John T. L. Jones jnr/Mrs John Magnier's "Check The Band"

CHECKPOINT CHARLIE 11 b.g. Artaius (USA) 129 – Clouded Issue – (Manado 130) [1995 NR 1996 12g⁶ 11.9g May 30] no longer of much account. *J. M. P. Eustace*

CHECK THE BAND (USA) 2 gr.c. Dixieland Band (USA) – Check Bid (USA) 105 (Grey Dawn II 132) [1996 5s⁴ 5d* 6m² 6g⁵ 6m² 6g 6g³ 5g* 6g* 5d² Oct 12] $77,000F, IR 38,000Y: strong, lengthy colt: third foal: dam maiden: useful form: won minor event at the Curragh in April and minor event at Navan and listed race (by 1½ lengths from Fairy Song) at the Curragh in October: good second to Easycall in Cornwallis Stakes at Ascot final start: bred to stay beyond 6f but has plenty of speed: acts on good to firm ground and dead: twice blinkered, running well first occasion. *A. P. O'Brien, Ireland*

CHEEK TO CHEEK 2 b.f. (Feb 3) Shavian 125 – Intoxication 73 (Great – Nephew 126) [1996 7g Aug 24] 2,200F, 9,500Y: angular, workmanlike filly: sixth foal: half-sister to 14.6f winner Innerglow (by Kalaglow) and a winner in Spain and France (at 9f) by Never So Bold: dam stayed 1½m, daughter of Princess Royal winner Shebeen: bit backward, tailed off in maiden at Goodwood. *C. A. Cyzer*

CHEEKY CHAPPY 5 b.g. Sayf El Arab (USA) 127 – Guilty Guest (USA) 59 78 (Be My Guest (USA) 126) [1995 40+, a49: a5g³ a6g⁵ a6g⁴ a6g⁵ 5g 6m a5g 6.1m⁶ a63 a5g² a5g⁶ 5g² a5g⁵ 5f 5m⁴ 5f⁵ 5h² 5m* 5m⁶ a5g* a5g* a5g³ 1996 a5g* a5g² a5g⁵ a5g a5g⁶ a5g² a5g 5g⁶ 5s⁵ 5m* a5g 5g³ 6.1m* 6g³ 6g² 6g* 5m* 5m⁵ 6m³ 6g* 6f³ 6.1m* 6g⁴ 6f³ 6d a6g 6m a6g 5m 6f 5m a6g³ a6g 6m a6g* a6g⁵ a5g⁴ a5g a6g⁵ a7g a5g⁴ a6g³ a7s a5g a5g Dec 31] lengthy gelding: carries condition: poor mover: improved into a fair handicapper: won at Wolverhampton in January, Hamilton (apprentices) in May, Nottingham in June and at Yarmouth, Folkestone, Catterick and Nottingham in July: mostly below peak from mid-August, but still won at Wolverhampton in November: effective at 5f and 6f: acts on hard ground and all-weather surfaces, possibly unsuited by heavy going: nearly always blinkered: usually races prominently: successful for claimer: very tough. *D. W. Chapman*

CHEERFUL ASPECT (IRE) 3 b.g. Cadeaux Genereux 131 – Strike Home 82 81
(Be My Guest (USA) 126) [1995 77: 7g⁶ 8g³ 8d⁵ 8m⁴ 1996 8g* 10.2g⁴ 12f⁴ 10f⁶
13.1s⁵ 10v³ 10m Oct 1] big, workmanlike gelding: has a round action: fairly useful
form: won minor event at Pontefract in April, soon off bridle: stays 1½m: acts on any
going: sometimes flashes tail: joined T. Forster. *E. A. L. Dunlop*

CHEERFUL GROOM (IRE) 5 ch.g. Shy Groom (USA) – Carange (Known 48
Fact (USA) 135) [1995 41: a6g³ a6g² a6g³ a6g a7g⁴ a6g 6.9m 6d a5g a6g⁶ a6g a7g² a41
6d 7d 7m 1996 a6g a8g a7g² a6g⁶ a8g a7g⁵ 7m* 6.9g 7.5m Jul 5] sturdy gelding: poor
handicapper nowadays: won at Doncaster in May: should stay 1m: acts on fibresand
(mostly below form in 1996) and any turf going: visored (out of form) once as 3-y-o:
sometimes has tongue tied: wears crossed noseband: joined D. Shaw. *S. R. Bowring*

CHELWOOD 4 b.f. Kala Shikari 125 – Cherrywood Blessin (Good Times (ITY))
[1995 NR 1996 5g 6d⁵ 5m 5g 7.1m Sep 23] robust filly: poor mover: third foal:
sister to fairly useful 5-y-o Chadwell Hall and half-sister to modest 6-y-o My Cherrywell (by Kirchner), both tough sprinters: dam never ran: well beaten, including in
blinkers. *L. R. Lloyd-James*

CHEMCAST 3 ch.g. Chilibang 120 – Golden October 62 (Young Generation 68
129) [1995 68, a59: 5.1m⁵ a6g⁵ 5.1g³ 5m 5.7h² a5g² 5m* 5m* 5d 5g⁶ a6g a5g 1996 a72
a6g a5g* a5g* 5d 5f⁴ 5.1m⁵ 5f* 5s⁴ 5m 5m⁶ 5m⁴ 5m³ 5m 5s a5g* a5g⁴ Dec 5]
lengthy gelding: fair handicapper: won at Lingfield in January (twice within 3 days,
fortunate to be awarded claimer on second occasion) and at Musselburgh in June: left
D. Nicholls after thirteenth start: won at Lingfield in November: speedy, and easily
best efforts at 5f: acts on the all-weather and on firm ground (soundly beaten on a soft
surface): blinkered last 7 outings for former trainer: races prominently. *J. L. Eyre*

CHEROKEE FLIGHT 2 b.g. (Jan 23) Green Desert (USA) 127 – Totham 84 65
(Shernazar 131) [1996 5m⁴ 5m⁴ 5.1m* 7m 6m 6d⁵ Sep 27] 48,000Y: strong, robust
gelding: has plenty of scope: second foal: dam, 1½m winner, granddaughter of Full
Dress II: fair form: won maiden at Nottingham in July: bred to be suited by further
than 5f: acts on good to firm ground: raced too freely when visored final start: sold to
join S. Mellor 10,500 gns Newmarket Autumn Sales. *Mrs J. R. Ramsden*

CHERRY BLOSSOM (IRE) 2 br.f. (Mar 26) Primo Dominie 121 – Varnish 85 84
(Final Straw 121) [1996 5.2d* 5m⁴ May 20] IR 14,000Y: leggy, rather unfurnished
filly: second foal: half-sister to 3-y-o Shine (by Sharrood): dam 2-y-o 7f winner: won
median auction maiden at Newbury in April by 3½ lengths: long odds on, last of 4 in
minor event at Windsor following month, eased when beaten, and not seen out again:
looked speedy on debut. *R. Hannon*

CHERRY GARDEN (IRE) 3 b.g. Treasure Kay 114 – Door To Door (USA) 51
(Nureyev (USA) 131) [1995 61, a57: 6m⁴ 6m a7g³ 7.6m² 8g 1996 a8g⁴ a7g³ 11.6m
7f⁴ 8.2m⁶ 8.5g⁴ 9.7g 10.1g³ a10g³ Sep 10] modest maiden: stays at least 1¼m: acts
on firm ground and fibresand: blinkered (ran poorly) final start: inconsistent.
T. J. Naughton

CHERRY MUNA 3 ch.f. Say Primula 107 – Muna (Thatch (USA) 136) [1995 –
NR 1996 10.5d 8m 16m Jun 11] unfurnished filly: half-sister to fairly useful 1985
2-y-o 5f winner Shelhoub (by Music Boy) and 5f winner Pampered Dream (by Kafu):
dam never ran: no sign of ability: visored (looked reluctant) last time. *C. W. Fairhurst*

CHESTEINE 3 ch.f. Soviet Lad (USA) 94 – Makalu 79 (Godswalk (USA) 130) –
[1995 NR 1996 8.3m 7.1m 8.3d 10f⁵ 10.8f a12g Nov 7] 2,500Y: fourth foal:
half-sister to fairly useful sprint handicapper Mr Bergerac (by Cyrano de Bergerac):
dam stayed 1¼m: no worthwhile form. *P. J. Makin*

CHESTERS QUEST 4 ch.g. Domynsky 110 – Chess Mistress (USA) 59 (Run –
The Gantlet (USA)) [1995 NR 1996 10m 12f⁶ Aug 14] plain gelding: first reported
foal: dam, French 1½m winner, half-sister to US Grade 3 1¼m winner Rugged
Bugger: tailed off. *R. Hollinshead*

CHEVALIER (USA) 4 b.c. Danzig (USA) – Royal Touch 121 (Tap On Wood 74
130) [1995 82: 8.2m² 10.1m² 1996 a11g² a12g⁶ 10.8d a9.4g³ a9.4g a12g⁴ a12g⁴
a11g⁴ a12g³ a11g a9.4g a11g Dec 3] lengthy colt: fair maiden handicapper: barely
stayed 1½m: visored (no improvement) twice at 4 yrs: dead. *I. Campbell*

CHEVAL ROC 2 ch.c. (Feb 18) Keen 116 – Gentle Gain 58 (Final Straw 127) 67
[1996 6m 6m 7d a8g Nov 15] 6,400Y, 10,000 2-y-o: close-coupled colt: third foal:
dam maiden, should have been suited by further than 7f: modest form in maidens:
showed little last 2 starts: should stay 1m. *R. Hannon*

CHEVELEY DANCER (USA) 8 b.g. Northern Baby (CAN) 127 – Alwah 34
(USA) (Damascus (USA)) [1995 42: 9.7d^4 9.7g 10g 10g 11.6m 1996 a12g 10g^4 12d
12m^4 10g 12m^4 12.1m 10f^2 Aug 7] big, lengthy gelding: winning plater over hurdles:
poor maiden handicapper on flat: stays 1½m: acts on good to firm ground: tried
visored: pulls hard: inconsistent: joined G. L. Moore. *T. J. Naughton*

CHEWIT 4 gr.g. Beveled (USA) – Sylvan Song (Song 132) [1995 81, a84: a6g^2 88 +
a7g^2 a6g* 6m^2 7f^5 5.3f^5 5s a6g^3 a5g^4 1996 a6g* a6g* 6g 6f^6 6f^5 5m^4 5m 7m* 7.6m* a99
7m a7g^3 Dec 7] leggy gelding: useful handicapper on all-weather, winner in January
and February: only fairly useful on balance of turf form: won twice at Lingfield
(second occasion a minor event) in September: effective at 5f to 7.6f: acts on firm
ground, goes very well on equitrack: visored (below form, setting pace) seventh
4-y-o start: usually ridden by Candy Morris. *A. Moore*

CHEYENNE SPIRIT 4 ch.f. Indian Ridge 123 – Bazaar Promise 58 (Native 107
Bazaar 122) [1995 107: 6m* 5m 7f^2 6g^6 6m* 6m 6m* 7f^2 6m* 6m^3 6m* 6g^2 1996 6m
6m^4 6f^2 Jun 12] lengthy, quite attractive filly: useful performer: creditable efforts on
form when fourth to Branston Abby in listed race at Newmarket (flashed tail and
wandered under pressure) then when second of 3 to comfortable winner Warning Star
in minor event at Yarmouth (visored): effective at 6f and 7f: acts on firm ground,
not at best on soft: races prominently: sold 40,000 gns Newmarket December Sales.
B. Hanbury

CHEZ CATALAN 5 b.h. Niniski (USA) 125 – Miss Saint-Cloud 102 (Nonoalco –
(USA) 131) [1995 53: 14.1m 14s 15.8g^3 16.2g 16.1f^2 15.4m^2 a16g^3 1996 a12g a13g
16.4m^5 15.4g a12g Dec 20] modest handicapper: showed little in 1996: stays
16.1f: acts on firm ground and equitrack, twice well beaten on soft: best in blinkers.
R. Akehurst

CHICKAMAUGA (USA) 2 gr. or ro.f. (Mar 8) Wild Again (USA) – Gray And –
Red (USA) (Wolf Power (SAF)) [1996 7d Oct 2] first known foal: dam won at up
to 7f in USA: not knocked about in rear in maiden at Salisbury: may do better.
I. A. Balding

CHICKAWICKA (IRE) 5 b.h. Dance of Life (USA) – Shabby Doll 69 (North- 90
fields (USA)) [1995 90: 8g 8g 7.6m 9m 8m 7f^2 7g* 6m^5 7m 7d 6.1s 1996 7g^4 8g^3
7.6g^4 7.1m 8m 7g* 7m^2 7d^5 7m 7g^5 8.1s^5 a7g Dec 7] lengthy horse: fairly useful
handicapper: won at Epsom in July: effective at 6f to 1m: acts on firm and soft
ground, well beaten first start on fibresand: effective blinkered/visored or not:
usually a front runner: won novice hurdle in November. *B. Palling*

CHIEF BURUNDI (USA) 4 b.g. Alleged (USA) 138 – Lantana Lady (CAN) 106
(Vice Regent (CAN)) [1995 NR 1996 8g* 8.1d^3 10g 10m 8g^5 Sep 6] tall gelding:
promising at 2 yrs, but gelded and changed hands only 8,000 gns Newmarket
Autumn 1995 Sales: won maiden at Thirsk and third to Blomberg in rated stakes at
Sandown in May: sweating, not entirely discredited in listed race at Kempton final
start: should stay at least 1¼m (behind in very valuable handicaps when tried): acts
on dead ground: forced pace (found little) fourth 4-y-o start: sold 40,000 gns Newmarket Autumn Sales to USA. *L. M. Cumani*

CHIEF CONTENDER (IRE) 3 b.c. Sadler's Wells (USA) 132 – Minnie Hauk 114
(USA) 100 (Sir Ivor 135) [1995 NR 1996 12m 12m* 12m* 12m 12s* 12m^2 15g^3
15d^3 12s Oct 26] $385,000Y: tall, lengthy colt: has a short action: brother to fair 1¼m
winner Tafrah, closely related to smart Aviance (at 6f to 1m, by Northfields) later
dam of Chimes of Freedom, and half-brother to winners in USA by Kings Lake and
Chief's Crown: dam, winner at 7f and 1m, is sister to Malinowski and Gielgud, and
half-sister to the dam of El Gran Senor: smart performer: won maiden and 3-runner
minor event at Salisbury in May and listed race in July: placed in Gordon
Stakes (head behind St Mawes) at Goodwood, Prix Kergorlay (1¾ lengths behind
Kassani) at Deauville and Prix de Lutece (length behind Tarator, setting good pace
and battling on well) at Longchamp: stays at least 15f: acts on good to firm and soft
ground: carried head awkwardly first 2 starts: effective from front or held up: most
consistent until final start. *P. W. Chapple-Hyam*

CHIEF ISLAND 2 b.f. (Feb 16) Be My Chief (USA) 122 – Clare Island 108 62 p
(Connaught 130) [1996 7m Jul 13] 7,800F: half-sister to 3-y-o Carina Clare (by Slip
Anchor) and several winners, including useful stayer Clare Heights (by Shirley
Heights) and fairly useful 1½m winner Island Lake (by Kalaglow): dam, winner over
7f and 8.5f, is half-sister to very smart 1½m horse Caliban: never a threat in July
maiden at Salisbury: likely to do better over middle distances. *W. G. M. Turner*

CHIEF MOUSE 3 b.g. Be My Chief (USA) 122 – Top Mouse (High Top 131) 68
[1995 61: 8d 8.2m 1996 a8.5g* 10g 12.5f⁶ May 6] sturdy gelding: good mover: won
maiden at Wolverhampton in March: below form afterwards: stays 8.5f, should get
further: visored (well below form) final 3-y-o start: fair hurdler for Miss H. Knight,
winner in November. *R. Charlton*

CHIEF PREDATOR (USA) 2 ch.c. (Apr 6) Chief's Crown (USA) – Tsavorite ?
(USA) (Halo (USA)) [1996 7.1f 7d 7d a8g³ a8g² Dec 11] $32,000Y: close-coupled a68
colt: sixth foal: half-brother to 3 minor winners in USA: dam ran 6 times in USA: fair
maiden: will be suited by at least 1¼m: acts on equitrack. *R. Hannon*

CHIEF'S LADY 4 b.f. Reprimand 122 – Pussy Foot 83 (Red Sunset 120) [1995 39
55d: 5g⁶ 5m⁶ 5.3f⁵ 6f⁶ 7m² 6d 7s 7f 7f 1996 a7g a7g a6g⁴ a6g 6f 6f⁴ 6m 6m⁴ 8m 8m
8f 8.3m Aug 3] smallish filly: poor at best in 1996: stays 7f, possibly not 1m: acts on
firm ground and equitrack, well beaten on soft surface. *J. M. Bradley*

CHIEF'S SONG 6 b.g. Chief Singer 131 – Tizzy 79 (Formidable (USA) 125) –
[1995 58: 16m 16.4m 14m 14d⁴ 14g 1996 16g 12d Aug 25] tall gelding: useful
winning hurdler: still a maiden handicapper on flat: tailed off both starts in 1996:
should stay beyond 1¾m: acts on heavy ground: visored (finished last) 6-y-o reappearance. *S. Dow*

CHIEFTAIN'S CROWN (USA) 5 ch.g. Chief's Crown (USA) – Simple Taste 42
(USA) 93 (Sharpen Up 127) [1995 –: 8.3m 8.3m 1996 10m 10.1f* 10f² 9.7g Jul 3]

Mrs John Magnier's "Chief Contender"

strong, good-bodied gelding: poor handicapper: won at Yarmouth (apprentices) in June: stays 10.1f: acts on firm going: possibly best in blinkers: has joined T. Hind. *Miss K. M. George*

CHIK'S SECRET   3 ch.f. Nalchik (USA) – Lana's Secret 79 (Most Secret 119) [1995 –, a50: a5g² 6.1m⁴ 7f 7m 10d 1996 12g a11g⁴ a12g⁶ 11.8g⁶ a16g Nov 18] lengthy filly: maiden plater: stays 11f: acts on fibresand: inconsistent. *B. Palling*   – a49

CHILDREN'S CHOICE (IRE)   5 b.m. Taufan (USA) 119 – Alice Brackloon (USA) (Melyno 130) [1995 63: 10.3g* 12m² 12g 10.9m 12f⁵ a12g 8.2m 12m 1996 a12g 12m⁵ 14.1m* 14.1d² 13.9g 12m⁴ 14s³ 16.1f⁵ 13.8g⁶ 14.1s Oct 31] leggy, workmanlike mare: modest handicapper: won at Yarmouth (ladies) in August: probably stays 16.1f: acts on firm ground and soft, well beaten on all-weather: blinkered (ran creditably) sixth 5-y-o start: usually races prominently. *C. N. Allen*   60

CHILIBANG BANG   3 b.f. Chilibang 120 – Quenlyn (Welsh Pageant 132) [1995 61: 5s* 5f² 5m² 5m 5f² a5g* a6g* 6g a7g² 1996 a7g⁵ a7g* a6g⁵ a7g* a6g² a7g 6s⁴ 7g a7g a8.5s Dec 19] angular filly: fair performer on all-weather: won handicap in January and seller in February, both at Southwell: well below form last 5 starts: stays 7f: best form on soft ground or fibresand: visored (poorly drawn) fourth 2-y-o start: successful for claimer. *J. Berry*   – a68 d

CHILI BOUCHIER (USA)   2 br.f. (Feb 23) Stop The Music (USA) – Low Approach (Artaius (USA) 129) [1996 6m⁵ Sep 28] 12,000Y: tall filly: fourth foal: half-sister to useful Irish 1m (at 2 yrs) and 2m winner Regal Access (by Lear Fan) and 1992 2-y-o 7f winner Known Approach (by Known Fact): dam, placed 3 times in USA, half-sister to Irish 1000 Guineas winner More So: backward, well-beaten last of 5, slowly away, in Blue Seal Stakes at Ascot. *D. Marks*   –

CHILI CONCERTO   2 ro.f. (Mar 15) Chilibang 120 – Whirling Words 75 (Sparkler 130) [1996 5m² 5g* Jul 29] third reported living foal: dam 7.5f to 8.3f winner out of half-sister to smart sprinter Sound Barrier: had favoured rail when winning maiden at Windsor in July by 3½ lengths: not seen out again: will stay 6f: may improve again. *P. J. Makin*   76

CHILI HEIGHTS   6 gr.g. Chilibang 120 – Highest Tender 56 (Prince Tenderfoot (USA) 126) [1995 62: 6m 7g 7g⁵ 7m⁶ 7g² 6m⁵ 7.1m 7.3d 8d⁶ 7.1d⁴ 7d³ 1996 7f⁶ 6m 8f 7s 7g Nov 2] strong, compact gelding: modest handicapper: well held in 1996: sold (G. Balding to K. Bishop) 1,900 gns Ascot November Sales: acts on good to firm and soft going: usually wears visor: gets behind. *G. B. Balding*   –

CHILI-WAH-WAH   5 ch.g. Chilibang 120 – Abalone (Abwah 118) [1995 NR 1996 11.5m 10.1m 13.4g Sep 25] 4,600 2-y-o: half-brother to 4 winners, all at up to 9f: dam unraced: poor form in NH Flat races: of no account on flat. *C. A. Smith*   –

CHILLAM   3 ch.g. Chilibang 120 – Tissue Paper 95 (Touch Paper 113) [1995 –, a60: 5m a5g⁴ a5g³ 5f 1996 a6g a6g⁶ a6g a5g⁵ 5s 5.1g Apr 22] well beaten in 1996, including in blinkers: sold 500 gns Doncaster August Sales. *J. P. Leigh*   –

CHILLED WINE   2 gr.f. (Feb 5) Chilibang 120 – Persian Joy 45 (Persian Bold 123) [1996 5s⁵ a5g⁶ 5.1g³ 5m⁴ 5m a5g 5m May 21] strong, lengthy filly: third foal: half-sister to 3-y-o Sea of Blue (by Superlative): dam (maiden) stayed 1¼m: poor sprint plater. *N. Bycroft*   43

CHILLI BOOM   2 gr.f. (Apr 13) Chilibang 120 – Silent Sun 90 (Blakeney 126) [1996 5g 6f 6g 7g Oct 2] half-sister to 3-y-o Fro (by Salse), fairly useful 5.7f to 1m winner Silent Expression (by Siberian Express) and 1989 2-y-o 6f to 1m winner Closed Shop (by Auction Ring): dam won over 1¼m here and 1m in France: soundly beaten in maidens and nursery. *T. J. Naughton*   –

CHILLING   2 gr.f. (May 15) Chilibang 120 – Appealing 49 (Star Appeal 133) [1996 5.7g² 6.1m⁶ 5m 5.7m a6g a6g⁵ a6g³ Nov 30] 1,000F: fifth foal: half-sister to 1990 2-y-o 6f seller winner Second Star (by Final Straw) and 2 winners abroad: dam 4-y-o 1¼m winner: second in maiden at Bath in June on debut: no comparable form, including in sellers: stays 6f. *P. G. Murphy*   60 d a40

CHILLINGTON   3 gr.g. Chilibang 120 – Saskia's Pride (Giacometti 130) [1995 –: 7.1s 1996 12.5g⁶ a12g a12g 11.8d May 28] of no account. *W. M. Brisbourne*   –

CHILLY LAD   5 ch.g. High Kicker (USA) – Miss Poll Flinders (Swing Easy (USA) 126) [1995 –: 10g 1996 9.9d³ 10g 8.3s⁵ 12d 10d⁶ a11g⁶ a11g 10m 11.5m a10g 12s a10g⁵ a11g Dec 3] tall gelding: has badly scarred near-fore: modest handicapper: 55 d stays 1½m: acts on fibresand and heavy ground, below form on firm: usually blinkered/visored: reportedly bled from nose eighth 5-y-o start: most inconsistent at 5 yrs: has joined R. Juckes. *M. J. Ryan*

CHILLY LOOKS 3 b.f. Siberian Express (USA) 125 – Exceptional Beauty 94 – (Sallust 134) [1995 38+: 6g 7m 7f³ 7.5m⁵ 6s 1996 7d 7g⁶ 8m 7s⁶ 8.2f⁶ Jul 20] tall, leggy filly: no promise in 1996. *D. W. Barker*

CHIMANIMANI 5 b.g. Petong 126 – La Primavera (Northfields (USA)) [1995 – –: 14.9d 14m 11.9m⁴ 12.3m 14m 12m³ 11.1f⁵ 1996 12m 12f⁶ Aug 3] workmanlike, sparely-made gelding: no longer of much account. *N. Tinkler*

CHINA CASTLE 3 b.g. Sayf El Arab (USA) 127 – Honey Plum 57 (Kind of 56 Hush 118) [1995 51, a62: 5g 7m⁶ a7g* 7.1m⁶ 7g a6g a7g 1996 a7g* a10g* a8.5g* a76 a10g⁴ a8g⁴ a11g* a12g³ 10.3d a9.4g 8m a8.5g³ 12.1f³ a9.4g a9.4g a12g⁴ a9.4g⁴ Dec 7] good-topped gelding: only modest on turf: fair handicapper on the all-weather: won at Southwell (twice), Lingfield and Wolverhampton in January/February: inconsistent in second half of 1996: effective at 8.5f and stays 1½m well: soon comes off bridle, and well ridden by J. Fortune. *P. C. Haslam*

CHINA GIRL (IRE) 2 b.f. (Apr 30) Danehill (USA) 126 – Chamonis (USA) 91 101 (Affirmed (USA)) [1996 5m* 6m 5f* Aug 22] well-made, attractive filly: has a quick action: sixth foal: sister to useful 7f winner Danish Heights and half-sister to 3 winners by Sadler's Wells, including 3-y-o Cabaret (at 9f) and 4-y-o Theatreworld (1¼m to 2m and smart hurdler in Ireland): dam, 6f and 7f winner, is half-sister to dam of 2 high-class American performers: useful form: won maiden at Newcastle in June and minor event at Salisbury (by 3 lengths from Dancethenightaway) in August: eased-up last in Princess Margaret Stakes at Ascot in between: speedy: acts on firm ground: should win more races. *P. W. Chapple-Hyam*

CHINA HAND (IRE) 4 ch.g. Salt Dome (USA) – China Blue (Ahonoora 122) 39 [1995 44: 5g 5d⁴ 5m⁵ 5f⁶ 5g⁴ 5d 1996 5g 5g 5g⁵ 5f 6g 5s² 5m⁴ 5g² 5m 5m 5g⁵ Sep 7] sparely-made gelding: good mover: poor maiden handicapper: sold 800 gns Doncaster October Sales: raced mainly at 5f: acts on firm and dead ground: tried blinkered, no improvement. *Martyn Wane*

CHINA RED (USA) 2 br.c. Red Ransom (USA) – Akamare (FR) (Akarad (FR) 86 130) [1996 6m⁴ 6m² 7g⁴ Sep 4] $45,000Y: quite well-made colt: first foal: dam French 1¼m winner, later successful in North America: fairly useful form in maidens, fourth to Fantastic Fellow at York last time: will stay 1¼m: capable of winning a race. *J. W. Hills*

CHINENSIS (IRE) 3 ch.c. Lycius (USA) 124 – Chinese Justice (USA) (Diesis 86 133) [1995 NR 1996 8d⁵ 8.2s 7.1d³ 8f² 10m⁵ 8m* 8f* 8m 8f* Aug 18] well-made colt: has a round action: third foal: half-brother to 1993 2-y-o 5f winner Desert Lore (by Green Desert): dam Irish 2-y-o 6f winner: fairly useful handicapper: made all at Ripon and Redcar (minor event, easing down) in July and Brighton (improved effort, all out) in August: may prove best at 1m/9f: acts on firm and dead going: seems best with forcing tactics: sent to Dubai. *L. M. Cumani*

CHINGACHGOOK 2 b.g. (Mar 5) Superlative 118 – Petomania 34 (Petong 61 126) [1996 6.1m⁴ 6m 7d 5.3f⁵ 6m⁵ Sep 24] 11,000Y: useful-looking gelding: second foal: brother to winning Italian sprinter Petline: dam sprint maiden: modest form: last and steadily to post then tried to break out of stalls final intended start: stays 6f: acts on firm ground. *P. W. Harris*

CHIPALATA 3 b.g. Derrylin 115 – Kirsheda 73 (Busted 134) [1995 NR 1996 8.2d – 9.9m 9.9g 16.2f Aug 15] workmanlike gelding: second foal: dam staying maiden on flat, winner over hurdles: no real promise. *T. W. Donnelly*

CHIPET 2 b.f. (Apr 15) Tina's Pet 121 – Chinese Princess (Sunny Way 120) [1996 – 8.2g Oct 9] 3,000Y: half-sister to several winners here and abroad, including 7f winner Cunning Plan (by Belfort): dam unraced: well beaten in seller: sold 4,500 gns Newmarket Autumn Sales: sent to Holland. *A. P. Jones*

CHIRICO (USA) 3 b.c. Danzig (USA) – Colour Chart (USA) 122 (Mr 79 p Prospector (USA)) [1995 NR 1996 7m 8.1d⁴ 8.3m 7.1m⁵ 7m* Oct 8] robust sort: unimpressive mover: first foal: dam won from 1m (at 2 yrs) to 1¼m in France and is daughter of champion Canadian filly Rainbow Connection: first run for nearly 3 months, much improved form to win 20-runner handicap at Redcar in October: best form at 7f, but will ultimately prove at least as effective over 1m+: acts on good to firm ground: capable of better still: sent to UAE. *J. H. M. Gosden*

CHIVALRIC (IRE) 2 b.c. (Mar 5) Arazi (USA) 135 – Air Distingue (USA) 120 83 (Sir Ivor 135) [1996 7m² 8m⁵ Oct 1] medium-sized, angular colt: has a quick, fluent action: eighth foal: closely related to 1¼m winner Lodestar (by Rainbow Quest) and half-brother to several winners, notably Poule d'Essai des Poulains winner Vettori (by Machiavellian): dam 6f to 8.5f winner and third in Prix de Diane: running-on second to Harry Wolton in maiden at Yarmouth on debut: fifth to Asas in similar event at Newmarket following month: not certain to stay beyond 1m. *D. R. Loder*

CHLOELLA 4 b.f. Shaadi (USA) 126 – Echoing 93 (Formidable (USA) 125) 27 [1995 34: a6g a6g⁵ 5g 7.1g 1996 a6g a6g a6g⁴ a6g a6g⁵ Apr 1] bad sprint maiden. *C. B. B. Booth*

CHLOE NICOLE (USA) 2 b.f. (Feb 9) Personal Flag (USA) – Balakhna (FR) 67 (Tyrant (USA)) [1996 5.2f⁴ Jul 19] $19,000F, 260,000 francs Y: rangy, unfurnished filly: has scope: sister to French 1¼m/11f Gattopardo and half-sister to 3 winners abroad, including smart French 1987 2-y-o 5f and 5.5f winner Balawaki (by Miswaki): dam, French 5f to 1m winner, half-sister to dam of Zieten and Blue Duster: sire (by Private Account) good class at middle distances: odds on, never really threatened when fourth of 5 to Song of Skye in maiden at Newbury in July: bred to stay middle distances: looked sure to improve. *P. F. I. Cole*

CHLOE'S MARK 2 b.f. (Feb 8) Crowning Honors (CAN) – Junuh 80 (Jalmood – (USA) 126) [1996 5g⁶ 5f⁶ 7.1g⁵ Jul 2] first reported foal: dam 2-y-o 7f winner: soundly beaten in claimer and sellers. *R. M. McKellar*

CHLOEZYMP (IRE) 2 b.f. (Mar 27) Mac's Imp (USA) 116 – Genzyme Gene – 38 (Riboboy (USA) 124) [1996 a5g a5g May 13] 2,900Y, 3,000 2-y-o: half-sister to several winners here and abroad, including 3-y-o Veshca Lady (by Contract Law), 5f and 7f winner at 2 yrs: dam, plater, stayed 1¼m: well beaten in sellers: blinkered final start. *J. Balding*

CHOCOLATE ICE 3 b.g. Shareef Dancer (USA) 135 – Creake 80 (Derring-Do 70 d 131) [1995 NR 1996 8.2s 10g³ 12g³ 14m⁵ 12.3m 12.3m³ 16f⁴ 11.9f⁴ a16g⁵ 10.1g⁴ 13.1m 11.5m⁴ 12g a16g Dec 11] 16,500Y: smallish, sturdy gelding: half-brother to several winners, including Creake's Pet (6f in Ireland, by Mummy's Pet) and fairly useful Kiyonaga (1¾m, by Kalaglow): dam 1½m winner (from 3 starts) out of half-sister to Blakeney and Morston: showed fair form early in 1996 but is a disappointing maiden: sold out of C. Cyzer's stable 3,500 gns Newmarket Autumn Sales after penultimate start: stays 2m: acts on firm going: blinkered (ran poorly) eleventh 3-y-o start. *R. J. O'Sullivan*

CHOPIN (IRE) 2 b.g. (Mar 27) Classic Music (USA) – La Toulzanie (FR) 54 ? (Sanctus II 132) [1996 5.1d⁵ 5.3f⁴ 7f 6.9m 5g 8f Sep 10] 5,200F, 5,200Y: unfurnished gelding: closely related to 1¼m winner Tabardar (by The Minstrel) and half-brother to 3-y-o Notaire (by Law Society), useful 1m to 1¼m winner Tamourad (by Blushing Groom) and a winner in Scandinavia by Riverman: dam winner (including listed race) at around 1½m in France: modest form: off course 3½ months and being beaten after second start: bred to stay 1¼m: blinkered final 2 starts. *R. F. Johnson Houghton*

CHORUS SONG (USA) 2 b.f. (Mar 30) Alleged (USA) 138 – Performing Arts 70 104 (The Minstrel (CAN) 135) [1996 6m⁵ 7m² 7.1d 7.3s Oct 26] quite good-topped filly: second foal: half-sister to smart 3-y-o Woodborough (by Woodman), 6f and 6.3f winner at 2 yrs: dam, 2-y-o 5f and 6f winner third in Irish 1000 Guineas, sister to good miler The Noble Player: fair form: best efforts on good to firm ground: has been bandaged near-hind. *P. W. Chapple-Hyam*

CHRIS'S LAD 5 b.g. Thowra (FR) – Stockline (Capricorn Line 111) [1995 –: 69 14f⁴ 1996 16.1f⁶ 20f a16.2g⁴ 14g* a16g² 16d² 16.4g* 18g Oct 19] close-coupled a55 gelding: fair handicapper: won at Salisbury and Sandown (nosed ahead near line) in August: should stay 2½m: has won on good to firm going, better form on fibresand or with give in the ground (acts on soft): blinkered since fourth 5-y-o start: tends to run in snatches: effective from front or held up. *B. J. Meehan*

CHRISTIAN FLIGHT (IRE) 7 b.m. Fayruz 116 – Opening Flight (Falcon 41 131) [1995 48: a8g a6g³ a6g³ a7g⁴ a6g⁴ a6g⁴ a6g a6g 6.1m* 5f³ 1996 6.1m 6g⁵ 5m

5m a6g 5.1m⁶ 7m a5g Sep 9] workmanlike mare: poor handicapper: acts on firm ground and fibresand: tried visored and blinkered. *S. Gollings*

CHRISTIAN WARRIOR   7 gr.g. Primo Dominie 121 – Rashah 67 (Blakeney – 126) [1995 –: 7g 6g 7.1m 7g⁶ 6.1m a8.5g 6f 8h 1996 a6g 10.2g Aug 26] no longer of much account. *R. E. Peacock*

CHRISTMAS KISS   4 b.f. Taufan (USA) 119 – Ancestry (Persepolis (FR) 127)   82 [1995 82: 7g⁴ 7d 6m* 7m⁴ 7g³ 5f* 6g⁶ 6g 1996 7d 7m 7f³ 8.5m 6m Jun 28] rangy filly: fairly useful performer: ran to form at 4 yrs only when third of 6 to Isla del Rey in listed race at Lingfield in May: effective at 5f to 7f: acts on firm ground, probably on dead: blinkered since third 4-y-o start. *R. Hannon*

CHRISTMAS ROSE   2 gr.f. (Mar 11) Absalom 128 – Shall We Run (GB) 59   – (Hotfoot 126) [1996 7g 5.1m Sep 9] 11,000Y: first foal: dam placed over 5f at 2 yrs, sister to useful 1¼m performer Fire Top and half-sister to very smart but unreliable sprinter Dead Certain (by Absalom): behind in auction maidens. *H. Thomson Jones*

CHUCKLESTONE   13 b.g. Chukaroo 103 – Czar's Diamond 66 (Queen's Hus-   38 sar 124) [1995 –: 14m 17.2f 17.2h⁴ 16.4m 16.1f⁶ a16g 1996 17.2m 17.2f⁴ 17.2m* 16d Aug 25] sturdy gelding: veteran staying handicapper: 8 times a winner at Bath, most recently in steadily-run race in August: suited by a sound surface: visored (tailed off) earlier in career: game. *J. S. King*

CHYNNA   2 b.f. (Apr 26) Golden Heights 82 – What A Present (Pharly (FR) 130)   58 [1996 6g³ a6g⁶ a8g Dec 20] second reported foal: half-sister to fairly useful 1994   a? 2-y-o 6f and 7f winner Prussian Flag (by Infantry): dam unraced granddaughter of Scarcely Blessed: remote third in maiden at Yarmouth in July: well held on all-weather over 5 months later. *M. H. Tompkins*

CICERONE   6 br.g. Tina's Pet 121 – Emma Royale 69 (Royal And Regal (USA))   59 [1995 48, a51: a8g a8g⁴ a8g² a7g⁶ a8g⁶ a9.4g 8f³ 8f* a9.4g⁶ a8g⁶ 1996 a8g⁶ 8.2d⁵ 7d*   a– 8g* May 19] leggy, angular gelding: poor mover: modest handicapper: won sellers at Leicester in April (second run in 3 days) and Ripon (well drawn and visored first time, made all) in May: stays 1m: acts on firm and soft ground and on fibresand: below best when blinkered. *J. L. Harris*

CIGAR (USA)   6 b.h. Palace Music (USA) 129 – Solar Slew (USA) (Seattle   – Slew (USA)) [1995 a8.5f* a9f* a10f* a9f* a9.5f* a9f* a10f* a9f* a10f* a10s*   a138 1996 a9f* a10g* a9f* a9f* a10f² a9f* a10f² a10f³ Oct 26]
The result of the inaugural running of the richly-endowed Dubai World Cup in the Arabian Gulf in March made it even harder to understand why American racing—in contrast to its more internationally-minded European cousin—has remained so insular for so long. The one-two-three by Cigar, Soul of The Matter and L'Carriere proved conclusively that horses trained in North America are capable of making a major impact outside their own borders. Let's hope their domination of the first Dubai World Cup, over a mile and a quarter on a sand-based surface at Nad Al Sheba, will result in leading American horses also being sent to challenge for the major turf races at the likes of Ascot and Longchamp.
All three of the American-trained challengers for the Dubai World Cup were specialist dirt horses. Cigar had won the previous autumn's Breeders' Cup Classic from L'Carriere with Soul of The Matter fourth and Europe's big hope Halling well beaten. Halling was also in the Dubai World Cup line-up, along with another top-class European performer Pentire. With general doubts about how the American horses would perform away from home (medication permitted in the States was banned in Dubai), the top Europeans were expected to give a very good account of themselves. Cigar himself, who had won all his ten starts in 1995, eight of them in Grade 1 company, had had an interrupted preparation. After winning his first race of the year at Gulfstream Park in February, which extended his run of victories to thirteen, Cigar developed a hoof abscess which caused him to miss an intended engagement in the Santa Anita Handicap before travelling to Dubai. Reports leading up to the race recorded that he had missed eleven days training and quoted his trainer as saying 'If we can win, it's great. If not, it's not the end of the world.' After

keeping up with a very strong pace from the start, racing wide, Cigar moved easily to the front just under half a mile from home, only to be very strongly challenged soon afterwards by the much more patiently-ridden Soul of The Matter. Indeed, Soul of The Matter looked the likely winner when showing in front a furlong out, before Cigar battled back tenaciously to regain the lead a hundred yards out for a half-length victory. L'Carriere finished eight lengths further back, just ahead of Pentire. The Dubai World Cup was off to a memorable start!

'A good horse should be able to act on any ground' is one of the silliest cliches in racing. Few horses possess the ability to give their best whatever the underfoot conditions. The differences can be particularly marked when a horse switches from turf to dirt, or vice versa. Halling, for example, never proved in top-class competition that he was capable of reproducing his turf form on dirt or sand, though he did win four times at Nad Al Sheba, including crushing a small field in his final preparatory race for the Dubai World Cup. Cigar, on the other hand, didn't begin to look a racehorse of much note until his connections switched him from grass (on which he had eleven of his first thirteen races) late in his four-year-old campaign. Cigar was transformed on dirt, winning his last two races that year, the second of them the Grade 1 NYRA Mile Handicap by seven lengths. His ten successive victories as a five-year-old, when he was Horse of the Year in America, and his first two wins at six left him firmly established as the nearest thing racing had to a world champion and needing two more wins to equal the benchmark for an unbeaten sequence by a modern-day champion on the flat in North America or Europe. Italian-trained Ribot was unbeaten in a sixteen-race career, which included the King George VI and Queen Elizabeth Stakes and successive victories in the Prix de l'Arc de Triomphe on his only appearances outside Italy. Like Ribot, Citation was one of the great post-war champions, winner of the US Triple Crown in 1948 when he was successful in nineteen of his twenty races, including his last fifteen (after missing a season with tendon trouble, he won on his reappearance in 1950). Citation, incidentally, earned an entry in the very first Timeform annual *Racehorses of 1948* which summed him up as 'undoubtedly an exceptional horse, probably the best ever to race in the USA'. After adding the Massachusetts Handicap at Suffolk Downs in June, Cigar lined up for his record-equalling attempt in the appropriately-named Citation Challenge, a race specially staged at Arlington in July. Cigar successfully conceded 12 lb to very smart performers Dramatic Gold and Eltish, despite again being forced to race wide; he drew away in the straight to secure his place in racing history, winning by three and a half lengths, equalling, incidentally, the average winning margin during his sixteen-race sequence. Cigar's run came to an end when Dare And Go beat him in the Pacific Classic at Del Mar where we thought that lying too close to a strong early pace contributed to his defeat. Cigar had a hard race in the Pacific Classic and, after winning the Woodward Stakes, he went down in photo-finishes to Skip Away in the Jockey Club Gold Cup and to Alphabet Soup and Louis Quatorze in the Breeders' Cup Classic. Both races might have gone his way if circumstances had been slightly different but, even if he had won, his efforts would have represented form some way below his best. Cigar had clearly passed his peak—prompting one American journalist to tell his readers that these defeats proved that Cigar 'was only human'. Though his career ended in something of an anti-climax for his legion of fans, Cigar undoubtedly deserves to be regarded as the best horse to race in the States since Spectacular Bid. There was a consensus, however, more measurable once Cigar was defeated, that there were fewer good horses around than in the golden era between Secretariat in 1973 and Spectacular Bid in 1980. Andy Beyer of the *Washington Post* summed it up before the Breeders' Cup Classic: 'I don't view Cigar as a super horse, rather as a really admirable, gutsy competitor who has been an over-achiever. We have two years of evidence about him and he has never run the speed figures of the great horses like Spectacular Bid or Seattle Slew. Cigar was very fortunate to come along at a time and in a lot of races

Dubai World Cup, Nad Al Sheba—Cigar's record comes under threat from Soul of The Matter (No. 4)

when there have been no real top horses to knock him off.' Cigar's trainer Bill Mott put a different slant on the horse's achievements: 'I don't see how you can leave out Cigar when you are talking about great horses. It's true he didn't win a Kentucky Derby, a Preakness or a Belmont . . . maybe if he had, that would have enhanced his reputation . . . Cigar has had to fight for every bit of recognition he has had and all I know is that, during his streak, Cigar beat every

Arlington Citation Challenge (Invitational)—Cigar (Jerry Bailey) equals Citation's sixteen

horse that was led over to him.' Perhaps Mott, who deserves great credit for the way Cigar was handled, might have added, 'If you run them often enough they get beaten.' It is testament enough to Cigar's place in racing history that millions followed his progress as world-wide interest mounted in his quest for the record. It was a fine advertisement for the glamour and excitement of racing.

Cigar (USA) (b.h. 1990)	Palace Music (USA) (ch 1981)	The Minstrel (ch 1974)	Northern Dancer Fleur
		Come My Prince (ro 1972)	Prince John Come Hither Look
	Solar Slew (USA) (b or br 1982)	Seattle Slew (b or br 1974)	Bold Reasoning My Charmer
		Gold Sun (ch 1974)	Solazo Jungle Queen

Cigar, who takes his name from an aircraft checkpoint in the Gulf of Mexico, was bred by his owner Allen Paulson, formerly best known, in Europe at least, as the owner of Arazi in whom Sheikh Mohammed bought a half share after a spectacular victory in the Breeders' Cup Juvenile. Cigar's first trainer Alex Hassinger, who had him as a two- and three-year-old, described him as 'a big, gawky horse with structure but no mass.' When we saw him before the Pacific Classic we thought him a lengthy and attractive individual. Cigar's sire Palace Music, winner of the 1984 Champion Stakes, went on to make a name for himself after being transferred to the United States where he became a top performer on grass, second to Last Tycoon in the Breeders' Cup Mile as a five-year-old. He has had a varied career at stud, alternating between the States and New Zealand in his early years, then standing for a time in Australia before finally ending up at the Yushun Stallion Station in Japan. Cigar's female line is Argentinian, his dam Solar Slew, who was placed several times, being a daughter of the multiple winner Gold Sun, whose victories included one in one of Argentina's top sprints, the Gran Premio Internacional Ciudad de Buenos Aires. One of Solar Slew's other foals, a filly by Raised Socially, became a leading three-year-old in Puerto Rico, the country where Camarero set the world record of fifty-six consecutive wins between 1953 and 1955. The game and genuine Cigar stayed a mile and a quarter and showed easily his best form on dirt. His owner turned down a reported 30 million-dollar offer from Japan and will stand Cigar at the Ashford Stud in Kentucky. *W. Mott, USA*

CIM BOM BOM (IRE)   4 b.c. Dowsing (USA) 124 – Nekhbet 74 (Artaius   74
(USA) 129) [1995 93: 6m 8.1m⁴ 7.1m³ 8.1g 1996 8d 7.1d 8.3m⁶ 8.1d⁵ 8m 7g³ 6g*   a96
6m³ 6f⁵ 6m³ 6d a6g* a7g* Dec 7] strong, heavy-bodied colt: carries condition: injured (reportedly has screws in near-fore) final start in 1995: fair handicapper on turf on return: won at Pontefract in July: useful on all-weather, winning twice at Wolverhampton (£13,900 event on second occasion) late on: best recent efforts short of 1m: acts on firm and dead ground, goes well on fibresand: visored since sixth 4-y-o start: usually ridden by 7-lb claimer G. Faulkner: front runner. *M. Bell*

CIMMERIAN   2 ch.f. (Apr 18) Aragon 118 – Relatively Easy 70 (Relkino 131)   50
[1996 6.1m 6f⁵ 6g 7m Oct 28] 4,000Y: leggy filly: third foal: sister to 2-y-o 5f and 1m winner (stayed 1½m) Beats Working and half-sister to 2m winner Uplift (by Bustino): dam middle-distance stayer who also won over jumps: poor form in maidens and nursery: joined M. Johnston: raced under an incorrect pedigree (Risk Me – Dark Kristal). *Mrs J. R. Ramsden*

CINDY KATE (IRE)   3 br.f. Sayf El Arab (USA) 127 – Marton Maid 74 (Silly   49
Season 127) [1995 NR 1996 a6g a6g³ 6s⁵ 6m Jun 10] sister to 2 modest winning sprinters, and half-sister to fair Mr Devious (winner at up to 1½m, by Superpower): dam, inconsistent maiden, is half-sister to good-class sprinter Haveroid: poor maiden: trained first 2 starts by C. C. Elsey: probably a sprinter. *W. R. Muir*

CINEMA PARADISO   2 b.c. (Mar 30) Polar Falcon (USA) 126 – Epure   83
(Bellypha 130) [1996 6f* 8.1m² 10g Nov 2] IR 32,000Y: tall, leggy colt: eighth foal: half-brother to 3-y-o Needwood Epic (by Midyan), useful stayer Pashto (by Persian Bold) and several winners abroad: dam, 11.5f winner in France, is closely related to high-class 1m and 11f winner Al Nasr: fairly useful form: won maiden at Newbury in

July: second to Barnum Sands in 3-runner minor event at Sandown in September, better subsequent effort: should stay beyond 1m: headstrong last 2 starts. *P. F. I. Cole*

CINNAMON STICK (IRE) 3 ch.g. Don't Forget Me 127 – Gothic Lady (Godswalk (USA) 130) [1995 –: 5m⁵ a6g 6g⁴ 1996 6.1d 9.9g⁶ a11g 8.2m Jun 24] close-coupled gelding: poor plater: seems to stay 1¼m. *P. S. Felgate* –

CIRACUSA (IRE) 4 b.g. Kahyasi 130 – Miranisa (Habitat 134) [1995 –p: 11.8g 14.1m³ 1996 a16g⁴ 14.1g² 14.1m³ 12.3m³ 11.8m Jul 18] neat gelding: fair staying maiden handicapper: acted on good to firm ground, tailed off on fibresand: dead. *J. Mackie* 67

CIRCLED (USA) 3 gr.f. Cozzene (USA) – Hold The Hula (USA) (Hawaii) [1995 83: 7d 7.1d* 8s⁵ 1996 14g⁵ 10m 14.6g⁵ Oct 25] tall filly: well held in 1996: should stay further than 7f, but not bred to stay 1¾m: sold 8,000 gns Newmarket December Sales. *B. W. Hills* –

CIRCLE OF MAGIC 2 gr.f. (Apr 13) Midyan (USA) 124 – Miss Witch 59 (High Line 125) [1996 5.1m 6m⁵ 6d 6.1m 8g a7g Nov 25] 9,000Y: unfurnished filly: first foal: dam middle-distance maiden sister to very smart French 7.5f to 10.5f winner Metal Precieux: modest form: should stay 1m: has given trouble stalls. *P. J. Makin* 53

CIRCUS STAR 3 b.g. Soviet Star (USA) 128 – Circus Act (Shirley Heights 130) [1995 65P: 7g 6m⁵ 6m 1996 10f* 11.9d Sep 27] tall, good-topped gelding: well supported, won maiden at Nottingham in July on final start for Sir Mark Prescott: caught the eye under considerate handling final start: stays at least 1¼m: promising juvenile hurdler: remains capable of better. *D. Nicholson* 76 p

CIRO'S PEARL (IRE) 2 b.f. (Mar 29) Petorius 117 – Cut It Fine (USA) (Big Spruce (USA)) [1996 6.1m⁵ 7g² 6g Aug 31] IR 2,500F, IR 4,000Y: sixth reported foal: half-sister to 3-y-o 1m (at 2 yrs) to 1¼m winner Deadline Time (by Fayruz) and two 2-y-o winners, including Specific (7f, by King of Spain): dam stayer: fair form when second in median auction maiden at Leicester in August: down the field in Tattersalls Breeders Stakes at the Curragh later in month: likely to be suited by 1m+. *M. H. Tompkins* 76

CISERANO (IRE) 3 ch.f. Mujtahid (USA) 118 – Blue Persian 112 (Majority Blue 126) [1995 69: 6g² 6m³ 6m⁴ 7g⁴ 1996 6.9s 8.3d⁴ 6f² 7m⁶ 6s⁶ 5.1g* 6.1m 6m 5m⁴ 5.9f⁵ 5m 6m² 7.1g⁵ 6g⁵ Aug 1] sturdy, lengthy filly: modest sprinter: won claimer at Bath in May: acted on firm ground: often a weak finisher: dead. *M. R. Channon* 64

CITY GAMBLER 2 b.f. (Mar 20) Rock City 120 – Sun Street 73 (Ile de Bourbon (USA) 133) [1996 6m³ 6m⁴ 7m 8f² Oct 8] 1,900F, 6,600Y: rangy, unfurnished filly: fourth foal: half-sister to 6-y-o thorough stayer Upper Mount Clair (by Ela-Mana-Mou) and a winner in Slovakia by Sharrood: dam out-and-out stayer: improved effort when second in nursery at Warwick final start: will probably stay 1½m: raced only on top-of-the-ground: flashed tail on debut. *G. C. Bravery* 71

CITY HALL (IRE) 2 gr.c. (Apr 29) Generous (IRE) 139 – City Fortress (Troy 137) [1996 8m 8g⁵ Oct 29] big, leggy, angular colt: fifth foal: half-brother to smart 3-y-o middle-distance performer Desert Boy (by Green Desert), 6f winner at 2 yrs, 1m winner Avignon (by Machiavellian) and high-class French/US performer at 1m/1¼m Fastness (by Rousillon): dam French 1¼m and 12.5f winner: better effort in late-season maidens when nearest-at-finish fifth to Musalsal at Leicester: awkward at stalls on debut: will be well suited by middle distances: has joined M. Stoute: will do better. *P. W. Chapple-Hyam* 66 p

CIVIL LIBERTY 3 b.c. Warning 136 – Libertine 114 (Hello Gorgeous (USA) 128) [1995 87p: 7f⁶ 7m² 1996 7g² 7g² 8f 8.3m* 10m⁴ 7g 8.5m⁴ Sep 24] big, well-made colt: has plenty of scope: fairly useful performer: made all in maiden at Windsor in August: good fourth in steadily-run rated stakes at Epsom (carried head high under strong pressure) final start: at least as effective at around 1m as 1¼m: has raced only on a sound surface. *G. Lewis* 93

CLAIRE'S DANCER (IRE) 3 b.g. Classic Music (USA) – Midnight Patrol (Ashmore (FR) 125) [1995 NR 1996 8m 10g* 10.8f⁵ 10m 11.5d⁶ 11.4m 11.9g Oct 10] IR 15,000F, 13,000Y: fifth foal: closely related to Punta Baluarte (7.5f winner here at 2 yrs, up to 15f in Italy, by Viking) and half-brother to Viceroy Jester (winner up to 1½m, by Jester): dam placed over 1¼m in Ireland: won 4-runner apprentice 65 d maiden at Lingfield in May: well held afterwards, no form last 3 starts: should stay further than 1¼m. *Andrew Turnell*

CLAIRESWAN (IRE) 4 ch.g. Rhoman Rule (USA) – Choclate Baby (Kashiwa – 115) [1995 65: a8g⁵ a8.5g⁵ a8g⁴ 10.5d⁴ 12.3f⁶ 13f* a16.2g* 15m* 14.1m² a16g* 15g 1996 11.9g 18g Oct 19] workmanlike gelding: fair handicapper: burly, hampered and fell on belated return: well beaten in Cesarewitch 9 days later: stays 16.2f: acts on firm ground and the all-weather: best with forcing tactics: won maiden hurdle in the autumn. *M. H. Tompkins*

CLAN BEN (IRE) 4 ch.c. Bluebird (USA) 125 – Trina's Girl (Nonoalco (USA) 101 131) [1995 101: 8.3m² 8m* 8g* 9d² 8.1s⁴ 8m⁵ 1996 8d 8m² 7.9m³ 10m⁵ 10.4m⁵ 10.1m² 10m 9m 8.1s* Oct 22] sturdy, lengthy colt: impresses in appearance: good mover: useful handicapper: best efforts in 1996 when placed in £21,300 event at Kempton, and rated stakes at York (listed) and Epsom: won minor event at Chepstow (taking while to pick up, led final 1f) in October: stays 10.4f: acts on good to firm and soft ground: blinkered last 2 starts: stays in training. *H. R. A. Cecil*

CLANCASSIE 3 b.f. Clantime 101 – Casbar Lady 79 (Native Bazaar 122) [1995 – NR 1996 6g 7m 6f Jul 17] 1,200Y: half-sister to 3 winning sprinters, none better than fair: dam 5f winner: soundly beaten. *E. J. Alston*

CLAN CHIEF 3 b.g. Clantime 101 – Mrs Meyrick 42 (Owen Dudley 121) [1995 87 p 64: 5g³ 5m³ 5m² 5.1g² 5.1m⁴ 1996 5m⁵ 5f² 5.2m² 5m* 5m* 5m* 5m² 6m* Sep 14] sparely-made gelding: fairly useful handicapper: got better with every start in 1996, winning twice each at Sandown and Goodwood between July and September: gamely made all in 21-runner £15,000 contest at Goodwood last time: stays 6f: raced only on a sound surface: usually bandaged behind: has won when sweating: genuine and consistent: capable of better still. *J. R. Arnold*

CLANCY'S EXPRESS 5 b.g. Faustus (USA) 118 – Pink Pumpkin 52 (Tickled – Pink 114) [1995 34: a10g 6m 8.3m 10m 12g 10m⁶ 8.1m 1996 9m Apr 29] sturdy gelding: poor maiden: set strong pace 6f then weakened rapidly on only start for new stable: probably stays 1¼m: best efforts on an easy surface: blinkered twice in 1993. *J. C. Fox*

CLAQUE 4 ch.c. Kris 135 – Mixed Applause (USA) 101 (Nijinsky (CAN) 138) – [1995 63: 12m⁶ 14.1f a12g a16g 1996 a12g a10g a13g* a16g⁴ a13g* a11g* a12g a70 d 10.3d 9.9d 10g 13s a12g* a12g² 15d⁶ a14.8g a14g a12g a14g a14g a13g⁴ a12s⁶ Dec 19] angular, useful-looking colt: good mover: has reportedly had back problems: no form on turf in 1996: fair handicapper on all-weather: won at Lingfield (twice, in amateurs race second occasion) and Southwell in February and at Wolverhampton in June: little form after next start: stays 13f: acts on all-weather and good to firm ground: blinkered since third 4-y-o start: made most for last 2 wins. *D. W. Chapman*

CLARA BLISS (IRE) 2 b.f. (May 16) Fayruz 116 – Kinosium (Relkino 131) 70 [1996 5.2d⁶ 5g⁶ 6f* 5.2f 5.3f³ 5f* 6m⁴ 5m 5g⁵ Oct 18] IR 5,000Y: strong, compact filly: seventh foal: sister to 1992 5f winner Iron Merchant (later successful at up to 1m in Sweden) and a winner in Italy and half-sister to a winner in Italy by Stalker: dam maiden with best run at 9.4f: fair performer: won seller at Thirsk in June and claimer at Sandown in September: stays 6f, may prove best at 5f: acts on firm ground: races keenly: sold 6,200 gns Newmarket Autumn Sales: sent to Sweden. *B. J. Meehan*

CLASH OF SWORDS 3 b.c. Shaadi (USA) 126 – Swept Away 106 (Kris 135) 58 § [1995 NR 1996 10g 10m 10.1g 10m 12.3m⁵ 12.3m⁶ 15.8g² 17.2m⁶ 15.8g Sep 21] good-bodied colt: fifth foal: dam French 9f and 1¼m winner out of smart French miler Costly Wave: modest staying maiden handicapper: looked far from resolute last 3 starts: one to treat with caution. *P. Calver*

CLASS DISTINCTION (IRE) 2 ch.c. (Mar 27) Masterclass (USA) 116 – 71 + Brook's Dilemma 80 (Known Fact (USA) 135) [1996 5g 5f² 5m* 7m³ 5.2f 6m 6g Oct 9] IR 5,400F, IR 4,000Y: useful-looking colt: good mover: sixth foal: half-brother to 3-y-o Magic Solution (by Magical Wonder), 4-y-o 5f winner Royal Dome (by Salt Dome) and 1m winner Kay's Dilemma (by Ya Zaman): dam, 6f winner, is half-sister to very useful 1987 2-y-o Obeah: made most to win maiden auction at Pontefract in June: stiff tasks last 3 outings: may prove best at 6f: sweating final start. *R. Hannon*

CLASSIC AFFAIR (USA) 3 ch.f. Trempolino (USA) 135 – Coupole (USA) 71 66 (Vaguely Noble 140) [1995 59: 6s⁵ 7f 1996 9m⁶ 9.7m 10m a8g a11g³ 12g⁵ 16m* a54

16m⁶ 16.1m⁴ a14.g⁵ 16m 16g a14.8g⁶ Nov 16] neat filly: fair handicapper: best effort
to win strongly-run race at Nottingham in August: suited by test of stamina: acts on
good to firm ground: sold 11,500 gns Newmarket December Sales. *R. Harris*

CLASSIC BALLET (FR)   3 b.f. Fabulous Dancer (USA) 124 – Tyranesque   68
(USA) (Key To The Mint (USA)) [1995 75: 8.1d⁴ 7d 8.1s² 1996 9g⁴ 10g³ 11.6m³
11.8d⁴ 8f* 10.1f⁴ 8m⁶ 10.1m 8.5g 8.2g a12g⁴ Nov 16] sturdy filly: fair handicapper:
not so good as at 2 yrs: trained until after third 3-y-o start by S. Williams: won at
Yarmouth in June: well below form last 5 starts: effective at 1m and stays 11.8f: acts
on firm and soft ground: has joined I. Campbell. *R. Harris*

CLASSIC BEAUTY (IRE)   3 b.f. Fairy King (USA) – Working Model 99 (Ile   65
de Bourbon (USA) 133) [1995 63p: 6m⁴ 7f⁴ 1996 a10g³ a8.5g⁴ a9.4g⁴ 7m² 7g⁶ 7f³
a9.4g 7m 11.1m* 12m⁶ 8g⁵ 7g Nov 2] sturdy filly: modest handicapper: won weak
maiden event at Hamilton in August, hanging fire when initially brought to challenge: long way below form afterwards: should stay 1½m: acts on firm ground and
equitrack: finds little under pressure: none too reliable: sold 13,000 gns Newmarket
December Sales. *R. Harris*

CLASSIC CLICHE (IRE)   4 b.c. Salse (USA) 128 – Pato 90 (High Top 131)   128
[1995 120: 10.4g* 12g⁴ 12f² 12m⁵ 14.6d* 1996 13.9f* 20m* 12m² 12d Oct 6]
   The terms 'St Leger type' and 'Gold Cup type' aren't, perhaps, quite so
belittling as they were a few years ago. There may still be a long way to go
before the staying races recapture anything approaching their former glory, but
things are certainly looking up. For the first time since Ocean Swell in 1945,
one of the previous season's classic winners went on to win the Gold Cup at
Royal Ascot. The race produced one of the blockbusters of the season, St Leger
winner Classic Cliche challenging the domination of long-distance champion
Double Trigger who had landed the stayers' triple crown of Gold Cup, Goodwood Cup and Doncaster Cup in 1995. Double Trigger, third in the 1994 St
Leger, had beaten the 1994 St Leger winner Moonax by five lengths in that
Gold Cup, leading from pillar to post. Double Trigger's run-up to the latest
Royal meeting showed him at least as good as ever when repeating his victories
of the previous year in the Sagaro Stakes at Ascot and the Henry II Stakes at
Sandown, slamming his rivals in the last-named. He pulled off a shoe on the
gallops the week before Royal Ascot, damaging part of a foot, but seemed
likely to take plenty of beating on the day. Classic Cliche took the Yorkshire
Cup route to the Gold Cup as Moonax had done the year before when Double
Trigger, unsuited by the step back to a mile and three quarters, had finished a
staying-on fourth in the York race. Double Trigger didn't contest the Yorkshire

East Coast Yorkshire Cup, York—Classic Cliche is too good for Strategic Choice and Court of Honour

Cup this time and Classic Cliche won by a length and a half from the previous season's Irish St Leger winner Strategic Choice. The Gold Cup trip of two and a half miles was unknown territory for Classic Cliche for whom, on pedigree, stamina doubts had justifiably been raised before he tackled even the St Leger. Connections said after the Yorkshire Cup that they were 'hopeful' he would get the Gold Cup trip because 'he's so relaxed and has a lot of class.' It was stressed, however, that the Gold Cup would be a 'one-off' and that, whatever the outcome, Classic Cliche would revert to shorter distances afterwards, probably going for the top middle-distance races.

With Dettori on the side-lines, Mick Kinane took the ride on Classic Cliche in the Gold Cup and was oozing confidence a long way from home. 'Double Trigger had his ears pricked and was idling in front,' Kinane said afterwards. 'He was clearly not going as fast as Jason wanted in Swinley Bottom which suited me.' Kinane moved Classic Cliche on to the heels of Double Trigger coming off the home turn and the writing was on the wall. For a moment it seemed as if Classic Cliche would win as his rider pleased, but Double Trigger kept on pulling out more before Classic Cliche finally drew ahead inside the final furlong for a length and a half victory. French challenger Nononito came third, three lengths behind Double Trigger, with Always Aloof fourth and Latahaab, grossly flattered to finish so close in a race not run at an end-to-end gallop, fifth. Double Trigger's jockey was blamed by some for not setting a testing enough gallop, added to which the horse lost his off-fore shoe during the race. Alas, the argument about what might have been will have to wait another year—both horses remain in training with the Gold Cup again on the agenda—for there was little likelihood of their meeting again during the latest season. It was back to a mile and a half for Classic Cliche who next took on Pentire and the Derby winner Shaamit in the King George VI and Queen Elizabeth Diamond Stakes at Ascot in July. The Godolphin team did their best to set up the race for Classic Cliche, asking Annus Mirabilis, a good horse in his own right, to set a blistering gallop. Classic Cliche stuck to his task in admirable style once Annus Mirabilis had done his job, and kept on well to hold off Shaamit though he had no answer to Pentire's spectacular last-to-first run. Classic Cliche's attempt to go one better in the Prix de l'Arc de Triomphe in October was hindered by training troubles. He missed intended preparatory races in the Geoffrey Freer Stakes at Newbury, the September Stakes at Kempton and the Prix Foy at Longchamp and seemed doubtful for the Arc after failing to please connections in his work a week before the big race. In the event he ran as if something was amiss, quickly beaten in the straight, causing plans to send him for the Melbourne Cup (for which he had been allotted top weight) to be shelved.

Godolphin's "Classic Cliche"

Classic Cliche (IRE) (b.c. 1992)	Salse (USA) (b 1985)	Topsider (b 1974)	Northern Dancer
			Drumtop
		Carnival Princess (ch 1974)	Prince John
			Carnival Queen
	Pato (b 1982)	High Top (br 1974)	Derring-Do
			Camenae
		Patosky (b 1969)	Skymaster
			Los Patos

That the good-topped, attractive Classic Cliche should turn out to be essentially a stayer must have been a surprise to those who regard racehorse breeding as a science. The bare facts of his pedigree are that his sire Salse, whose sire and dam were both best at sprint distances, made his name chiefly over seven furlongs, while his dam Pato, a sister to the very smart sprinter Crews Hill, showed nothing at a mile and a half and seemed suited by a mile and a quarter. Salse, however, has turned out to be represented by any number of progeny who stay much better than he did, and there is stamina further back on both sides of Classic Cliche's pedigree, his great grandam Los Patos being a winner at two miles. Pato's 1993 foal, My Emma (by Marju), won the Prix Vermeille. Classic Cliche, who can be very reluctant at the stalls, is as genuine as they come once racing. He is effective in a strongly-run race at a mile and a half and stays two and a half. He has yet to race on soft going. *Saeed bin Suroor*

CLASSIC COLLEEN (IRE)   3 b.f. Sadler's Wells (USA) 132 – Nawara 75   79
(Welsh Pageant 132) [1995 NR 1996 12d⁴ 14m² 12.3m³ 11.9g 14.1f² 16.2f Aug 14]
IR 130,000Y: big, workmanlike filly: poor mover: half-sister to several winners,
notably good miler Alhijaz (by Midyan): dam 10.2f winner: trained on debut by S.
Williams: fair maiden: stays 14.1f (weakened quickly well over 2f out over 2m): acts
on firm going: hung badly left on debut and tends to carry head rather high: joined
I. Campbell. *R. Harris*

CLASSIC COLOURS (USA)   3 ch.g. Blushing John (USA) 120 – All Agleam   68 §
(USA) (Gleaming (USA)) [1995 –: 7.1d⁵ 8f 1996 8.2d⁴ 9.9m² 10.3m² 10d⁵ 10m³
10g 11m⁴ a8g Sep 9] unfurnished gelding: fair maiden handicapper: trained by
S. Williams until after third 3-y-o start: poor efforts last 3 starts and looked to be
shirking issue last 2 occasions: subsequently gelded: stays 10.3f: very best form on
good to firm ground: blinkered (reluctant to race) final 3-y-o start: carries head high,
and one to treat with caution: joined I. Campbell. *R. Harris*

CLASSIC DAISY   3 b.f. Prince Sabo 123 – Bloom of Youth (IRE) (Last Tycoon   –
131) [1995 45, a39: 6m 7m³ 7.1f³ 7f 6g⁶ 7.1s a6g a8g 1996 2.2m 8.2m
a11g Dec 27] no worthwhile form for new stable: usually blinkered/visored at 2 yrs.
R. C. Spicer

CLASSIC DAME (FR)   3 gr.f. Highest Honor (FR) 124 – Reem El Fala (FR)   72
(Fabulous Dancer (USA) 124) [1995 NR 1996 7f⁶ 9m³ 11.5m³ 10.5v Oct 6] 30,000Y:
leggy filly: first foal: dam French 7.6f and 11f winner: fair maiden: shapes as if stays
11.5f: acts on good to firm ground, finished last on heavy. *R. Harris*

CLASSIC DEFENCE (IRE)   3 b.c. Cyrano de Bergerac 120 – My Alanna   75
(Dalsaan 125) [1995 58: 7.1m 7.5d 6d 1996 8.1g* 8m 8g³ 10m* 10.2f² 9f 9g Aug 24]
fair handicapper: won at Musselburgh (maiden) in April and at Goodwood (made all,
staying on despite tending to wander) in June: retained by trainer 23,000 gns Newmarket Autumn Sales: stays 10.2f: acts on firm ground: won over hurdles in October.
J. W. Hills

CLASSIC DELIGHT (USA)   3 b.f. Green Forest (USA) 134 – Weather Girl   –
(USA) (One For All (USA)) [1995 55: 6.1m a7g⁴ 7.5d⁵ 7s 1996 a7g a8g 10m a10g
Sep 10] lengthy filly: soundly beaten in 1996: joined I. Campbell. *R. Harris*

CLASSIC EAGLE   3 b.c. Unfuwain (USA) 131 – La Lutine 95 (My Swallow   88
134) [1995 89p: 8.1s* 1996 8m 12.3g⁶ 12m 12m 7.1g⁶ 14.1f⁴ 14.6g Oct 25] close-
coupled, workmanlike colt: fairly useful on balance of form: trained until after
second 3-y-o start by S. Williams: 200/1, flattered (never a factor, coming from rear)
when 9½ lengths eleventh of 20 in the Derby at Epsom next outing: well beaten last 3
starts: stays 1½m: won on only start on soft ground: joined I. Campbell. *R. Harris*

CLASSIC FIND (USA)   3 br.c. Lear Fan (USA) 130 – Reve de Reine (USA) 97   94
(Lyphard (USA) 132) [1995 NR 1996 10g 10m* 12m³ Jun 6] 60,000Y: good-
bodied colt: brother to fairly useful 1m winner Rose de Thai and half-brother to 2
other winners in France, notably very useful Roi de Rome (up to 9.2f, by Time For A
Change): dam French 8.5f to 9.2f winner out of Poule d'Essai des Pouliches and
Grand Prix de Saint-Cloud winner Riverqueen: final start for S. Williams, won
maiden at Redcar in May: improved good deal when third of 7 in handicap at
Goodwood, switched under 2f out and running on: better at 1½m than 1¼m: wore
bandages first 2 starts: joined I. Campbell. *R. Harris*

CLASSIC FLYER (IRE)   3 b.f. Alzao (USA) 117 – Sea Harrier (Grundy 137)   78
[1995 80: 6m⁵ 7m* 7m⁵ 7d 1996 10m⁵ 12g² a9.4g⁶ 10.3m⁶ 10.5s Oct 5] good-topped   a82
filly: fluent mover: fairly useful maiden at best: left S. Williams after second 3-y-o
start: stays 1½m: seemed all at sea on soft ground: none too consistent: joined
I. Campbell. *R. Harris*

CLASSIC FORM (IRE)   3 b.f. Alzao (USA) 117 – Formulate 119 (Reform 132)   58
[1995 NR 1996 7f² 10g⁴ Oct 9] IR 50,000Y: sturdy filly: half-sister to several
winners, including smart Game Plan (1¼m, by Darshaan): dam top staying 2-y-o
filly of 1978, but ran only twice afterwards: in frame in maidens at Thirsk (moved
badly, eventually staying on) and Nottingham (unable to land a blow) 2½ months
later: joined I. Campbell. *R. Harris*

CLASSIC LADY   2 ch.f. (Feb 6) Ron's Victory (USA) 129 – Lady St Lawrence   –
(USA) 65 (Bering 136) [1996 a6g⁵ a6g⁶ Jun 8] 1,400Y: first foal: dam 1½m winner

out of good winner (at up to 11f) Lady Norcliffe: tailed off in Wolverhampton sellers: sold 500 gns Doncaster September Sales. *R. Hollinshead*

CLASSIC LEADER   3 b.c. Thatching 131 – Tenderetta (Tender King 123) [1995   76
74: 6m² 1996 6.9m⁶ 8m² 8d³ 8m⁵ 8m³ Jun 20] 55,000Y: good-bodied colt: has scope: first foal: dam won at 6f and 7.9f as 2-y-o in Ireland: fair maiden: trained until after second 3-y-o start by S. Williams: stays 1m: acts on good to firm and dead ground: carries head high: blinkered last 2 outings: looks a hard ride: consistent: joined I. Campbell. *R. Harris*

CLASSIC LINE   2 b.f. (Mar 17) Last Tycoon 131 – Classic Beam (Cut Above   – p
130) [1996 6.1f 6m 7f Sep 5] leggy, useful-looking filly: fifth foal: half-sister to German 7f and 7.7f winner Coronati (by Bluebird): dam, in frame in Irish 2m maiden and NH Flat races, from family of Salsabil, Marju (by Last Tycoon) and Kneller: signs of ability in maidens: may require long distances. *J. L. Dunlop*

CLASSIC LOOK (IRE)   3 b. or br.f. Classic Music (USA) – Mini Look (FR) (In   58
Fijar (USA) 121) [1995 –p: 6m 1996 7d⁶ 10m 8m 7.1f⁵ 8.1m Sep 18] leggy, angular filly: half-sister to smart 5f (at 2 yrs) to 7f winner Brief Glimpse (by Taufan): modest maiden handicapper: should stay 1m: inconsistent. *Major D. N. Chappell*

CLASSIC LOVER (IRE)   3 b.f. Taufan (USA) 119 – Sound Pet (Runnett 125)   68 d
[1995 71: 6g² 8.2d⁴ 9g³ 8f⁶ 1996 10.3s⁴ 11.1d 12.3m⁵ 8g 10f⁶ 8m⁴ Aug 22] workmanlike filly: failed to repeat form of reappearance: stays 10.3f: sold 2,000 gns Newmarket Autumn Sales: sent to South Korea. *R. Harris*

CLASSIC MYSTERY (IRE)   2 ch.g. (Feb 14) Classic Secret (USA) 91 –   60
Mystery Bid (Auction Ring (USA) 123) [1996 5.2d 6m 6.1m⁴ a7g 7.3m Aug 17] IR 9,000Y: lengthy gelding: fluent mover: fourth foal: brother to 1½m winner Secret Service and half-brother to 3-y-o 1m and 1¼m winner Contract Bridge (by Contract Law): dam Irish maiden, stayed 1½m: modest form: should stay at least 7f: blinkered (raced freely) final start. *B. J. Meehan*

CLASSIC PARISIAN (IRE)   3 b.f. Persian Bold 123 – Gay France (FR) 91   79
(Sir Gaylord) [1995 NR 1996 10.5d³ 10m 10m² 10.2f³ 12m⁶ 10s² 12g³ 11.9v Oct 6] 34,000Y: plain filly: half-sister to several winners, including very useful Lucayan Princess (7f at 2 yrs, by High Line) and useful Canaska Dancer (6f at 2 yrs, by Green Desert): dam 2-y-o 6f winner: fairly useful maiden: trained debut by S. Williams: left impression stamina may be stretched by testing conditions at 1½m: acts on good to firm (probably on firm) and soft ground. *R. Harris*

CLASSIC PARK   2 b.f. (Apr 13) Robellino (USA) 127 – Wanton 106 (Kris 135)   94
[1996 5s* 5d³ 6g² 5m⁶ 5m⁴ 6g² 6g 6m Oct 17] 30,000Y: smallish, good-quartered filly: sixth foal: half-sister to 4 winners, including 3-y-o Rumpipumpy (by Shirley Heights), 8.5f winner in USA at 2 yrs, and 4-y-o 5f (at 2 yrs) and 9f (in UAE) winner Magongo (by Be My Chief): dam sprinter best at 2 yrs: won maiden at the Curragh in April: kept useful company after, including twice in Britain, best effort when head second of 6 to Desert Ease in listed race at the Curragh on sixth outing: stays 6f: acts on good to firm and soft ground: blinkered (below form) fifth start. *A. P. O'Brien, Ireland*

CLASSIC PARTYGOER   2 ch.g. (Apr 10) Prince Sabo 123 – Star Arrangement   54 d
(Star Appeal 133) [1996 5s⁵ 5g⁵ 5g 5m 7m 7g⁶ 7.5m 6s Oct 5] 5,500F: close-coupled gelding: fourth foal: half-brother to a sprint winner in Holland by Never So Bold: dam poor maiden half-sister to smart performer at up to 1¼m Bold Arrangement: modest maiden: didn't progress after debut: probably stays 7f: acts on soft ground: blinkered twice: sold 1,350 gns Doncaster October Sales. *M. W. Easterby*

CLASSIC PET (IRE)   4 b.f. Petorius 117 – Checkers (Habat 127) [1995 49: 6m   –
5m 8g 8.3m 6g 6.1m 6f 5m* 5.1d 1996 a6g⁶ a6g 6m 5f 6m 6m⁵ 5f 5g 8.3d 6.9m 6m Aug 22] compact filly: modest sprint handicapper: disappointing in 1996: sold 2,000 gns Ascot October Sales: tried visored. *C. A. Horgan*

CLASSIC RIBBON (IRE)   3 b.f. Persian Bold 123 – House Tie (Be Friendly   63 p
130) [1995 NR 1996 7g⁵ Sep 21] IR 55,000Y: closely related to Spanish 1995 3-y-o 9.5f and 10.5f winner Acecho (by Ballad Rock) and half-sister to several winners, including fairly useful sprinter Bag O'Rhythm (by Be My Guest) and Academic (French, up to 1¼m, by Mill Reef), as well as dam of Alderbrook: dam Irish 1m winner out of high-class 2-y-o Mesopotamia: 33/1, around 7 lengths fifth of 13 to

Tote Ebor, York—Clerkenwell hangs on from Beauchamp Jade and Corradini

Don Bosio in maiden at Catterick, soon pushed along, nearest at finish: will stay at least 1m: joined I. Campbell. *R. Harris*

CLASSIC ROMANCE   3 b.f. Cadeaux Genereux 131 – What A Pity 97 (Blakeney 126) [1995 79: 7.1s* 8.1d³ 1996 8m 11.5f⁵ 10.2f² 10m 8.3d 12g a9.4g⁶ a14g⁵ Nov 22] fair handicapper: easily best effort in 1996 when second of 6 at Chepstow: should stay beyond 10.2f: acts on firm and soft ground: inconsistent: sold 15,500 gns Newmarket December Sales. *R. Harris*   74 d

CLASSIC ROYALE (USA)   3 b.f. Chief's Crown (USA) – Cuidado (USA) (Damascus (USA)) [1995 NR 1996 7m 8.1m 8m a7g⁶ a11g 8m Sep 19] $62,000F, 50,000Y: strong, deep-girthed filly: second foal: dam, winner at 2m in USA, half-sister to Rockfel winner At Risk: trained by S. Williams on debut: no worthwhile form: sold 1,800 gns Newmarket Autumn Sales. *R. Harris*   –

CLASSIC SERVICES   2 br.g. (May 24) Totem (USA) 118 – Loving Doll 72 (Godswalk (USA) 130) [1996 5d⁶ 5m 5m 7m a5g Jul 11] 2,300Y: unfurnished gelding: half-brother to 6f to 9f winner Nobby Barnes (by Nordance) and 1¼m winner Ash Amour (by Hotfoot): dam stayed 7f and would have been suited by further: behind in sellers and a claimer: blinkered twice. *B. Palling*   –

CLASSIC VICTORY   3 b.g. Puissance 110 – Seattle Mama (USA) (Seattle Song (USA) 130) [1995 72?: 5m 6d 7.1m 6f* 6m⁴ 6m 6d 1996 a6g a7g a6g 8.3d² a7g a8.5g 8g 8m Jun 8] tall, quite attractive gelding: form in 1996 only when beaten a head in seller at Hamilton in April: barely stays 8.3f: acts on firm and dead ground, no form on fibresand: blinkered and hooded of late: needs treating with caution: joined I. Campbell. *R. Harris*   58 a–

CLASSIC WARRIOR   3 b.g. Sharpo 132 – Petty Purse 115 (Petingo 135) [1995 NR 1996 6m 7g 7m Sep 10] 55,000Y: heavy-topped gelding: half-brother to several winners, including fairly useful Cajun Cadet (up to 1m, by Cadeaux Genereux) and fair Nijmegen (1¾m, by Nijinsky): dam 5f to 7f winner out of smart sprinter Parsimony, a half-sister to Mummy's Pet: yet to beat a horse in maidens: joined I. Campbell. *R. Harris*   –

CLASSY CHIEF   3 b.g. Be My Chief (USA) 122 – Jalopy 71 (Jalmood (USA) 126) [1995 78: 8g 7f³ 8m² 1996 8.1g 8.3m⁵ 7f³ 10m 10m⁶ 11.5d 8g 8.2g² 7g 7g Oct 25] big, good-bodied gelding: fair maiden at best: virtually refused to race fourth 3-y-o start: joined J. White: probably stays 1¼m: acts on firm going: most inconsistent and not one to trust. *R. Boss*   72 §

CLEAR THE AIR   2 ch.f. (Mar 24) Salse (USA) 128 – Belle Enfant 87 (Beldale Flutter (USA) 130) [1996 7m 8.1g 8f³ Sep 10] 21,000Y: tall, leggy, lightly-made   58

filly: has a quick action: fifth foal: half-sister to 3-y-o Belzao (by Alzao), 4-y-o 1m winner Spanish Steps (by Danehill) and useful 1m winner Air Commodore (by Elegant Air): dam, 1½m winner, half-sister to Dewhurst winner Dashing Blade: well beaten in maidens: apparently modest form when remote third of five at Leicester final start: bred to stay beyond 1m. *P. F. I. Cole*

CLEDESCHAMPS 7 b.m. Doc Marten 104 – Cape Farewell (Record Run 127) [1995 37: a7g 6s² 5.9m a7g a7g 1996 7d a7g Jun 20] smallish, lengthy mare: probably no longer of much account. *M. W. Ellerby*   –

CLEMENTE 3 b. or br.c. Robellino (USA) 127 – Gravad Lax 82 (Home Guard (USA) 129) [1995 70: 7.1d 7d⁴ 8.1s³ 1996 9g³ 10m² 11.6m⁴ 11.4d 12.1s Oct 22] good-bodied colt: fair maiden handicapper: best efforts on first 2 starts at 3 yrs: should be suited by 1½m+: acts on good to firm and dead ground: blinkered (well beaten) fourth 3-y-o start: sold 5,500 gns Newmarket December Sales. *R. Hannon*   78

CLERKENWELL (USA) 3 b.c. Sadler's Wells (USA) 132 – Forlene 108 (Forli (ARG)) [1995 75p: 8g⁴ 1996 10g² 12m³ 12m² 16.2m 14g* 13.9m* 15d Oct 5] sturdy, attractive colt: good mover: useful performer: easy winner of maiden at Sandown in July: apprentice ridden at overweight, easily best form to win 21-runner Tote Ebor Handicap at York in August, never far away despite very strong early pace, quickening clear over 2f out then holding Beauchamp Jade by ¾ length: missed the St Leger because of sore heel: well below form in Prix de Lutece at Longchamp, travelling well into straight then quickly beaten: best at around 1¾m (stamina seemed stretched, and carried head high, in Queen's Vase): acts on good to firm ground, possibly not on a soft surface: looks type to do well at 4 yrs. *M. R. Stoute*   108 +

CLEVER CLICHE 3 b.c. Danehill (USA) 126 – Beacon Hill 81 (Bustino 136) [1995 NR 1996 8.2s* 10m⁴ 10f Jun 18] 78,000Y: lengthy, good-bodied, attractive colt: impresses in appearance: fifth living foal: closely related to 1¼m to 2m winner High Summer (by Green Desert) and half-brother to 2 winning stayers: : dam, sister to high-class middle-distance filly Height of Fashion (later the dam of Nashwan and Unfuwain), was placed over 1¼m from 3 starts: made up a lot of ground to win maiden at Nottingham in April: best form when fourth of 5 to Mick's Love in listed race at Newmarket (reportedly pulled a muscle) in May, hanging right and flashing tail under pressure: soon beaten in straight in Prince of Wales's Stakes at Royal Ascot last time: will probably prove better at 1½m than shorter: went to UAE, though reportedly to go to Hong Kong. *H. R. A. Cecil*   100

CLIBURNEL NEWS (IRE) 6 b.m. Horage 124 – Dublin Millennium (Dalsaan 125) [1995 61, a48: a13g² a14.8g³ a13g³ a12g⁴ a12g³ a13g⁴ 11.8d* 11.8m 13g⁵ 11.8m* 14.1m⁴ 14.1m⁴ 10g 13.8f² 1996 11.8d² 10g⁶ 14.1m⁵ 12m⁵ 11.8d⁶ 11.8m⁶ 14.1m⁶ Jun 19] sparely-made mare: modest handicapper: rather disappointing last 3 starts: stays 15f: acts on the all-weather and any turf going: usually held up: rejoined A. Forbes: inconsistent. *A. Streeter*   61 a–

CLIFTON FOX 4 b.g. Deploy 131 – Loveskate (USA) 78 (Overskate (CAN)) [1995 84: 10.3g 8.5m* 10.5m³ 7.9g 8m* 10.5g⁵ 8g⁵ 8d 8m⁴ 8m 1996 10d 8g³ 9.2s* 8.5m² 8.5m⁴ 10m⁶ 10m³ 10m³ 10.3m³* 9m* 10g³ 12s* Nov 9] close-coupled gelding: improved steadily throughout 1996 and is now verging on a smart handicapper: won at Hamilton in May then £15,700 race at Doncaster, Tote Cambridgeshire (ran on very strongly to draw clear up the hill, beating Missile 2½ lengths) at Newmarket and   109

Tote Cambridgeshire Handicap, Newmarket—
Clifton Fox gives his stable yet another win in the race; Missile and Angus-G come next

Tote Credit November Handicap, Doncaster—
as the sun begins to set on the season, Clifton Fox pulls back Kutta (right)

(after good third to Proper Blue in listed race at Newmarket) Tote Credit November Handicap at Doncaster (finishing strongly to catch Kutta on post) in the autumn: stays 1½m: acts on good to firm and soft going: sometimes hangs badly, and has carried head rather awkwardly: genuine and consistent: sold privately and has joined J.J. O'Neill. *J. A. Glover*

CLIFTON GAME 6 b.g. Mummy's Game 120 – Brave Maiden 63 (Three Legs 50 128) [1995 –, a51: a12g² 11.8d 1996 11.5m* 16.4g⁴ Aug 30] tall gelding: lightly raced: claimer ridden for new stable on first start for over 16 months when winning maiden handicap at Yarmouth by 7 lengths: stays 1½m, not 16.4f: acts on good to firm ground and fibresand: novice chaser. *M. R. Channon*

CLINCHER CLUB 3 b.f. Polish Patriot (USA) 128 – Merry Rous 66 (Rousillon 53 (USA) 133) [1995 77: 5g 5m 5m* 6m³ 6d² 6g 6m 6.1m 1996 5f 5m 7.5m* a8.5g⁴ 6.9f² 7m⁴ Aug 10] smallish filly: only modest form in 1996, winning claimer at Beverley in July: failed to repeat it: sold 8,400 gns Doncaster August Sales: stays 7.5f: acts on good to firm ground, best 2-y-o form on dead: below form on fibresand: takes good hold: inconsistent. *M. Johnston*

CLONAVON GIRL (IRE) 2 b.f. (Feb 14) Be My Guest (USA) 126 – Welcome 44 Addition (Habitat 134) [1996 5g 5d 6g⁶ 7f³ 7.5m² a7g⁵ 7.5f 8f Sep 10] IR 2,300Y resold 2,400Y: compact filly: fourth reported foal: dam unraced half-sister to Invited Guest (by Be My Guest): poor plater: stays 7.5f: ran badly on fibresand: sold 4,500 gns Doncaster October Sales. *M. J. Camacho*

CLOSE RELATIVE (IRE) 2 b.c. (Mar 22) Distant Relative 128 – Jamaican 89 Punch (IRE) (Shareef Dancer (USA) 135) [1996 6m² 6.1m* 6g⁴ 6m 6.1d² Aug 31] smallish, quite attractive colt: has a quick action: second foal: half-brother to 3-y-o 1½m winner Oversman (by Keen): dam ran twice: won maiden at Nottingham in June: in frame after in July Stakes at Newmarket (fourth to Rich Ground) and minor event at Chester (sweating and edgy, second to Andreyev): will be suited by further than 6f: sold 66,000 gns Newmarket Autumn Sales: sent to USA. *R. Charlton*

CLOUDS HILL (FR) 3 b.c. Sarhoob (USA) 124 – Dana Dana (FR) (Pharly (FR) 70 130) [1995 84p: 8g⁵ 7d³ 1996 10g 9m⁵ 12d 11.5m⁴ Jul 12] tall, quite good-topped colt: disappointing maiden: ran if something amiss last 2 starts. *R. Hannon*

CLOVER GIRL 5 bl.m. Spin of A Coin 88 – Byerley Rose (Rolfe (USA) 77) – [1995 NR 1996 a12g 15.8m⁶ Aug 6] second foal: dam unraced: tailed off in sellers: visored second start: poor winning hurdler. *B. Ellison*

CLUB ELITE 4 b.f. Salse (USA) 128 – Little Bittern (USA) 73 (Riva Ridge 26 (USA)) [1995 27, a34: 8.2m a8g⁶ a8.5g⁴ a8g 8f⁵ 10.8m a14.8g² 14d⁵ 14.1m⁴ 16.2m⁵ 1996 a16g⁶ 17.2m 14.1f⁴ 14.1f⁶ 15.8m⁵ Aug 6] workmanlike, angular filly: bad maiden: stays 14.8f: acts on firm ground and fibresand: tried visored/blinkered, no improvement. *M. F. Barraclough*

CLUED UP 3 b.f. Beveled (USA) – Scharade 74 (Lombard (GER) 126) [1995 –: 57 7.5g a7g⁴ 7g 1996 10.8m a12g⁶ 7m⁵ 10m* 8.1m⁵ 10d⁶ 11.5m³ 10g 10.8f Oct 8] tall, workmanlike filly: modest performer: won claimer at Redcar in August: stays 11.5f: acts on good to firm ground: probably effective blinkered/visored or not: inconsistent. *P. D. Evans*

CLYTHA HILL LAD 5 b.g. Domitor (USA) 98 – Quae Supra 79 (On Your Mark 34 125) [1995 NR 1996 a8g a8g⁵ 8g 10m 8m 10.8m⁵ Jul 13] big, lengthy gelding: poor maiden. *J. M. Bradley*

COACHELLA 3 b.f. Warning 136 – Cockatoo Island 99 (High Top 131) [1995 80 NR 1996 a7g* a7g* 8g 7m 10g⁶ 10m Aug 3] strong, workmanlike filly: fourth foal: half-sister to 1¾m winner and Champion Hurdler Collier Bay (by Green Desert): dam 1½m to 14.8f winner: won maiden at Wolverhampton in January and claimer at Lingfield (claimed out of Sir Mark Prescott's stable £12,000) in February: pulled up lame final start: shaped as though she stayed 1¼m: dead. *M. J. Ryan*

COALISLAND 6 br.g. Kind of Hush 118 – Hit The Line 71 (Saulingo 122) [1995 – 34d: a10g a10g⁵ a10g a7g 5m 7m 6m 6g 9m 14m 11.6m 11.9f⁴ 1996 6m 5f Sep 17] good-bodied gelding: seemed of little account in 1996. *R. Ingram*

COAL TO DIAMONDS 2 b.f. (Mar 25) Merdon Melody 98 – Dubitable 59 – (Formidable (USA) 125) [1996 6g³ 7m 8.2g Oct 9] first foal: dam maiden (stayed 11.7f) daughter of very smart 1m/1¼m performer Duboff: no form: trained by R. Harris on debut. *G. F. Johnson Houghton*

COASTAL BLUFF 4 gr.g. Standaan (FR) 118 – Combattente (Reform 132) 117 p [1995 97p: 5d 5.1g* 5m⁵ 6g⁴ 6m² 5d³ 5s* 1996 6f 5g* 6m* 6m* Sep 21]
The paltry sum of 1,150 guineas was enough to purchase Coastal Bluff at the Newmarket December Sales in 1992, 2,700 at the Doncaster Lincoln Handicap Sales in 1993—and the first of those sales failed to go through. Pity the man who rejected him. More is spent on hunters with anonymous pedigrees and names such as Tommy or Toby that bring up the rear in many of the lesser Doncaster catalogues. Coastal Bluff probably has the size to carry some gentleman to hounds, but he would not be the ideal conveyance. We see him rather as a leading candidate for 1997 champion sprinter. That is a bold ambition for a horse that has yet to line up in a pattern or listed race, let alone win one, but Coastal Bluff has fulfilled nearly every expectation so far and we are not about to desert him now.
Starting 1996 on a BHB mark of 88, it took only four outings for Coastal Bluff to prove himself effectively too good for handicaps. His reappearance in the Wokingham on firm ground at Royal Ascot, however, did not see any advance. Punters had expected one and backed him from 33/1 to

Vodac Stewards' Cup, Goodwood—Coastal Bluff slams a strong field

favourite in the ante-post lists, but, returning to the scene of his eye-catching win from stall twenty-two the previous October, Coastal Bluff was unable to repeat the feat with a draw two places higher; he finished thirteenth, not given a hard race once beaten. The Weatherbys computer responsibile for the draw was the only thing that came close to getting him beaten afterwards. At York three weeks later, the pacesetters were drawn low to middle and Coastal Bluff was in stall twenty-two of twenty-two. With plenty of ground to make up at halfway, he tacked across to the far side and got to the front inside the final furlong, holding off Tedburrow by a head. The computer also completed its random selection in eye-catching style on Coastal Bluff's two remaining starts in 1996. Only Lochsong had won racing up the stand side in the previous dozen runnings of the Stewards' Cup at Goodwood. Coastal Bluff avoided that problem when he was allotted stall twenty-nine of thirty, but no-one who has seen this race can possibly believe that the numbers made any difference to his winning or losing—he won and won with total authority. Pushed into the lead two furlongs out, Coastal Bluff was a couple of lengths clear almost immediately and breezed in over the last fifty yards, passing the post three lengths ahead of the other 10/1 favourite, Double Bounce. Seven weeks later, Coastal Bluff had gone up 13 lb in the weights and was seeking to be the first top-weight to win the Ayr Gold Cup since Roman Warrior in 1975. The betting public had few doubts that he could do it—no question of sharing favouritism this time, Coastal Bluff was 3/1 at the off. As at Goodwood, he had the draw on his side; three of the previous four winners had been drawn twenty-seven or higher; and Coastal Bluff had number twenty-eight of twenty-nine—and, again as at Goodwood, he was firmly in charge over the last two furlongs. Mr Bergerac got the closest to him, a length and a half.

That superb weight-carrying display convinced us of what we already strongly suspected, that Coastal Bluff will win pattern races. The last horse to win the Stewards' Cup and Ayr Gold Cup was Lochsong, and she went on to win eight of them, and be our top-rated sprinter for the next two seasons. Will Coastal Bluff emulate her? Well, he looked to be improving at a similar rate in 1996, and ended the season rated 6 lb higher than she had been at the same stage. That, of course, shows only that it can be done. A drop to five furlongs for the first time in her career played a big part in Lochsong's improvement, but we doubt whether five or six will make much difference to Coastal Bluff. Some give in the ground *might*—because his trainer has frequently said that he needs it, yet the going was good to firm at both Goodwood and Ayr. His view may be explained by Coastal Bluff's apparently one-time suspect legs. 'I had to be here to put his bandages on', said Barron at Goodwood, and Coastal Bluff was heavily bandaged behind in the latest season, 'more heavily than the Invisible Man' according to Alastair Down. Physically, we think that Coastal Bluff should emerge a better horse again as a five-year-old. A tall, quite good-topped gelding, he has thrived so far and has the scope to strengthen even further. Iktamal and Eveningperformance are the pick of the established sprinters left to face him in 1997.

		Zeddaan	Grey Sovereign
	Standaan (FR)	(gr 1965)	Vareta
	(gr 1976)	Castania	Orsini
Coastal Bluff		(b 1969)	Chios
(gr.g. 1992)		Reform	Pall Mall
	Combattente	(b 1964)	Country House
	(b 1978)	Tenzone	Aggressor
		(b 1966)	Tina II

David Barron bought Coastal Bluff in the first place only to accompany a home-bred colt he 'thought the world of' but who turned out to be 'useless'. Coastal Bluff's breeding and birth also contained more than the usual element of chance because his dam used to conceive twins every year and the vet had to abort one of the foals. A filly was lost in this way when Coastal Bluff was in the womb. The dam Combattente never produced to a registered stallion again and

is now dead. She was bought for a reported IR 2,200 guineas at Goffs in 1987 and subsequently produced two other living foals, an unraced colt by Scorpio and Combatglow (by Kalaglow) who won once at a mile and a quarter on the Continent. Three of her four previous foals had run in Italy, Royal Contest (by Lord Avie) winning three times from five and a half furlongs to nine furlongs and being represented herself in 1996 by the Italian listed winner Counterplot. Combattente and her dam Tenzone also ran in Italy, Combattente winning once over seven furlongs at three years and being placed on numerous occasions, and Tenzone winning three times at a mile. The unraced third dam Tina II also produced the smart Guillotina (ancestress of such as One Way Street and Ever Genial) and Tenzone threw the Gran Steeplechase di Milano winner Duel. Coastal Bluff is the best European offspring of the smart sprinter Standaan, possibly the best overall but we would not like to make hard-and-fast judgments about his Australasian progeny headed by the 1986 New Zealand Two Thousand Guineas winner Steely Dan. Standaan was sent back to stand in Ireland in 1988 and died in 1993. After his five-year-old season, we wrote that 'Time and again he showed in the highest class that nothing was capable of living with him over three furlongs.' That exceptional early pace stretched far enough for him to justify favouritism in the Stewards' Cup as a three-year-old but won him only one pattern race, the Palace House Stakes. Expect Coastal Bluff to do a good deal better. *T. D. Barron*

COAST ALONG (IRE) 4 b.g. Satco (FR) 112 – Golden Flats 79 (Sonnen Gold 121) [1995 39: 10m 13.8g⁴ 16m 12m³ 13f⁵ 1996 a12g⁶ a12g Jun 22] poor performer: well beaten for new stable only start on flat in 1996: stays 1¾m: acts on good to firm ground: blinkered (ran poorly) once as 2-y-o: sometimes slowly away, and often gets behind: won handicap hurdle in July. *P. J. Bevan* –

COASTGUARDS HERO 3 ch.g. Chilibang 120 – Aldwick Colonnade 62 (Kind of Hush 118) [1995 –: 6.1m⁵ 6m 1996 a6g³ a6g* a6g⁵ a7g⁵ a6g⁵ 7m⁴ 5.1g 7m² 8m² 8.5g⁵ Jul 3] lengthy gelding: modest performer: won maiden at Southwell in February: headstrong, and will prove best at up to 1m: acts on fibresand and good to firm ground. *M. D. I. Usher* 57

COCKNEY LAD (IRE) 7 ch.g. Camden Town 125 – Big Bugs Bomb (Skymaster 126) [1995 8s⁴ 12g* 1996 8s⁵ 12g* 12m 12.3m 12m³ 12g⁶ 16s⁵ Oct 19] sparely-made Irish gelding: brother to smart and thoroughly genuine 1¼m Irish mare Cockney Lass: dam won over 6f, 1m and over hurdles: useful hurdler: fairly useful handicapper: first past post twice from 3 starts at 5 yrs, then won at Leopardstown in April, 1995 and in May, 1996: behind in Bessborough Stakes at Royal Ascot: creditable third at Galway in August: stays 1½m well: acts on good to firm ground, probably on soft. *N. Meade, Ireland* 90

COCOLOBA (IRE) 2 b.f. (Apr 30) Distinctly North (USA) 115 – Born To Fly (IRE) 57 (Last Tycoon 131) [1996 5.1m Jun 10] IR 2,600F, 5,000Y: neat filly: second foal: half-sister to fairly useful 3-y-o 7f and 1m winner Blue Flyer (by Bluebird): dam suited by 6f: behind throughout in maiden at Nottingham in June. *P. D. Evans* –

COCOON (IRE) 3 b.f. Cyrano de Bergerac 120 – Arena 86 (Sallust 134) [1995 51+: 5g 5m⁴ 6g 1996 a8g a8g a6g⁵ a8g 8.2m 11f⁵ Sep 27] rather leggy filly: poor –

maiden: no form in 1996: sold 2,000 gns Doncaster October Sales: sent to South Korea. *C. W. Thornton*

CODE 2 b.g. (May 7) Mystiko (USA) 124 – Farewell Letter (USA) (Arts And – Letters) [1996 6g⁵ Jul 29] half-brother to several winners, including smart stayer Parting Moment (by The Minstrel): dam very smart over middle distances: well beaten in seller in June: dead. *B. J. Meehan*

CODE RED 3 b.c. Warning 136 – For Action (USA) 83 (Assert 134) [1995 NR 66 1996 10g 10m⁶ 10.2g⁵ 12.5f³ 13.1m⁵ 14.1f⁵ 16.4g a14.8g³ a14g⁴ a14g³ a16g Dec 26] leggy, unfurnished colt: first known foal: dam suited by thorough test of stamina: disappointing maiden: stays 14.8f: sold out of J. Hills's stable 1,800 gns Newmarket Autumn Sales after seventh start: visored (tailed off) final one. *W. R. Muir*

COEUR FRANCAIS (FR) 4 b.g. Hero's Honor (USA) – Marie d'Anjou (FR) – (Free Round (USA)) [1995 64: 8d⁶ 8s 1996 a7g a10g Jul 27] no form: sold (W. Musson to N. Waggott) 1,100 gns Newmarket September Sales. *W. J. Musson*

COH SHO NO 3 b.f. Old Vic 136 – Castle Peak 90 (Darshaan 133) [1995 NR 57 1996 9m⁵ 12.1g 10m 11.9g a13g³ a16g⁴ a16g³ a13g Dec 31] first foal: dam, 1½m winner, half-sister to smart French stayer Sought Out out of smart filly (stayed 10.5f) Edinburgh: trained until after third start by I. Balding: modest maiden: stays 2m: acts on good to firm ground (yet to race on a soft surface) and equitrack. *S. Dow*

COINTOSSER (IRE) 3 b.f. Nordico (USA) – Sure Flyer (IRE) (Sure Blade 66 (USA) 130) [1995 NR 1996 a7g³ 6.9m² 8m² 7g* 8.2f* 8g* 8.1m⁴ 8m³ 8.1f* Sep 12] IR 7,800Y: leggy filly: has screws in near-fore knee and has fractured a hind leg: first foal: dam, Irish maiden, placed at 5f and 7f at 2 yrs: fair performer: awarded seller at Yarmouth then won claimer at Nottingham and seller at Leicester (sold out of S. Woods's stable 7,500 gns), all in July: good efforts in frame in handicaps before winning seller at Chepstow in September: effective at 7f and stays at least 8.2f: acts on firm ground, yet to race on a soft surface: sometimes hangs under pressure: won first 3 starts over hurdles, joining R. Frost before third: most consistent. *M. C. Pipe*

COIS NA FARRAIGE (IRE) 3 b.c. Nashamaa 113 – Persian Sparkler (Persian 87 Bold 123) [1995 7m 7.8m³ 1996 6d 7v 9m⁶ 12m² 12m* 12f⁵ 12g² 12m² 14g⁶ 13.1m 11.9v Oct 6] tall, leggy ex-Irish colt: fifth foal: half-brother to a winning Irish sprinter by Nordico: dam Irish 1¼m winner: fairly useful handicapper for J. Bolger, winning at Roscommon in May: off course nearly 3 months and backward, well beaten both starts in Britain: stays 1½m: acts on firm ground. *Miss L. A. Perratt*

COLD LAZARUS 2 br.g. (May 9) Warning 136 – Indian Pink (USA) (Seattle – p Slew (USA)) [1996 7f Oct 8] 7,000Y: leggy, quite attractive gelding: fourth foal: half-brother to 1½m winner Lady Tjonger (by Sharrood): dam, placed in Holland, from same family as Oaks winner Intrepidity and smart sprinter Acushla: backward, signs of ability in steadily-run maiden at Warwick in October. *R. T. Phillips*

COLD STEEL 2 b.c. (Feb 21) Warrshan (USA) 117 – Rengaine (FR) (Music Boy 65 124) [1996 7f⁵ Oct 15] 21,000Y: fifth foal: half-brother to smart 5f (at 2 yrs) to 1m winner Holly Golightly (by Robellino) and a winner abroad: dam French 8.5f and 11f winner: fifth to Attitude in maiden at Leicester in October: will probably stay 1¼m: sold 7,000 gns Newmarket Autumn Sales. *W. Jarvis*

COLEBROOK LEADER 4 b.g. Governor General 116 – Sharp Reality – (Dreams To Reality (USA) 113) [1995 NR 1996 a8.5g 7g Oct 25] first foal: dam, unraced, half-sister to useful 7f and 7.6f winner Sharpalto: tailed off. *J. R. Bosley*

COLEBROOK WILLIE 3 br.g. Dowsing (USA) 124 – A Little Hot (Petong – 126) [1995 NR 1996 8.3m 9f 10.8m 7g Sep 14] first reported foal: dam sprint maiden: no form: tried visored. *J. R. Bosley*

COLERIDGE 8 gr.g. Bellypha 130 – Quay Line 117 (High Line 125) [1995 53: 57 § 16.4m 17.2m⁶ 14.9g² 16.1g⁶ 16.4m 16g⁶ a16.2g 15.4m⁵ 16.1g* 16m³ 16.5m a16g³ a61 § a16g² a16g* a16g⁶ 1996 a16g² a16g² a16g² a16g² 18s 17.2f* 16.4m 20f 14.9m³ 16f³ 20m 16.1f 16g⁶ a16g² a16g² a16g⁶ Dec 11] tall, leggy gelding: unimpressive mover: modest handicapper: won at Bath in May: thorough stayer: acts on all-weather, best turf form on sound surface: best in visor/blinkers: tends to go in snatches: very slowly away/reluctant to race on 2 occasions: needs treating with caution. *J. J. Sheehan*

COLINS CHOICE 2 ch.f. (Mar 25) Risk Me (FR) 127 – Give Me A Day (Lucky 59 Wednesday 124) [1996 a5g⁵ a5g a6g³ a7g² a7g³ Nov 25] 2,300Y: fourth foal: sister to 3-y-o Daily Risk and a winner at up to 11f in Italy: dam plater: modest form: off course nearly 6 months after second start: best form at 7f, likely to stay further: acts on fibresand. *J. L. Spearing*

COLLEGE DON 5 gr.g. Kalaglow 132 – Westerlake (Blakeney 126) [1995 73: 12g⁴ 11.8g⁴ 14.1m* 14.6g⁴ 14.6m⁴ 14.8m* 16.1m* 1996 16.2f Aug 14] fair handicapper: pulled up on belated reappearance: seems suited by test of stamina: acts on firm and soft ground. *M. P. Bielby* —

COLLEGE NIGHT (IRE) 4 b.f. Night Shift (USA) – Gertrude Lawrence (Ballymore 123) [1995 50: 9.9m³ 12g⁶ 10m 10.1m⁵ 7m 12m⁶ 12d 11.9d 14.1m³ 12m 12m⁶ 1996 9.9d 8f² 8f² 7f³ 8g⁴ 8f 8m 7g⁵ 8m 8d⁵ Sep 30] angular filly: poor mover: modest maiden handicapper: best efforts at around 7f to 1m: acts on firm and dead ground: visored (below form) eighth 4-y-o start: often forces pace. *C. A. Dwyer* 54

COLLEGE PRINCESS 2 b.f. (Mar 2) Anshan 119 – Tinkers Fairy (Myjinski (USA)) [1996 6f 5d a5g Nov 12] unfurnished filly: first foal: dam ran twice: well beaten. *C. A. Dwyer* —

COLOMBIA (IRE) 2 ch.f. (Apr 18) Mujtahid (USA) 118 – Camarat 69 (Ahonoora 122) [1996 6d* 6m² 6g³ 7g⁴ Aug 26] 34,000Y: medium-sized, workman-like filly: second foal: half-sister to a 6f winner in Austria by Polish Patriot: dam, 9f winner, half-sister to Park Hill winner Trampship out of half-sister to Prix Vermeille winner Paulista: won maiden at Haydock in July: no improvement after: better form at 6f than 7f: looked none too keen in visor third outing: sent to Saudi Arabia. *M. R. Stoute* 71

COLONEL'S PRIDE 2 ch.c. (Feb 7) Superpower 113 – Yankeedoodledancer (Mashhor Dancer (USA)) [1996 5m 5m 5m² 5.1m⁶ Jul 26] good-topped colt: second foal: half-brother to 3-y-o Poppy My Love (by Clantime): dam of little account: modest form: should stay 6f: moved poorly to post then withdrawn lame from nursery in October. *R. M. Whitaker* 59

COLORFUL AMBITION 6 b.g. Slip Anchor 136 – Reprocolor 114 (Jimmy Reppin 131) [1995 76: 10.3m 9g* 9m* 10.5g² 10.3f⁵ 10.3d 1996 a9.4g 12g 12g 10f Sep 27] lengthy gelding: unimpressive walker: no form in 1996, very slowly away on penultimate start and refused to leave stalls final one: stays 1½m: acts on dead ground and good to firm: not one to trust. *Mrs A. Swinbank* – §

COLOSSE 4 b.f. Reprimand 122 – French Cutie (USA) (Vaguely Noble 140) [1995 58, a–: a7g 8m² 10f 8m² 8.2m³ 12.1g² 12m a12g⁶ a12g⁵ a10g 1996 a8g a12g* a12g³ a12g* 13d 12m⁵ 12g a12g a12s² a12g Dec 28] useful-looking filly: has a round action: modest handicapper: won at Lingfield in February and March: should stay beyond 1½m: acts on good to firm ground (possibly not on dead) and all-weather: blinkered (over inadequate trip) on 4-y-o reappearance: visored last 2 starts: normally held up. *J. L. Eyre* 55

COLOUR COUNSELLOR 3 gr.g. Touch of Grey 90 – Bourton Downs 74 (Philip of Spain 126) [1995 46, a51: a5g³ a6g⁵ 7m⁶ a7g a7g⁵ a6g 7.1m⁵ 8.1m³ a8.5g⁶ 10d 1996 a8g a10g 10m 11.9g* 14.1f 12f 15.4g⁴ 11.9f⁵ 11.9f⁵ 10f 11.9f* 12m Sep 20] poor handicapper: won sellers at Brighton in May and (apprentices) September: better at around 1½m than shorter: acts on firm ground and on fibresand: often visored/blinkered, has won without: often front runner: most inconsistent. *R. M. Flower* 47

COLOUR KEY (USA) 2 b.g. (Apr 16) Red Ransom (USA) – Trend (USA) (Ray's Word (USA)) [1996 7.6d Aug 29] $11,000Y, 23,000 2-y-o: second foal: dam won 8 times at up to 9f in USA from 4 to 7 yrs: green and not given hard time when eighth of 9 in maiden at Lingfield won by Barnum Sands: will improve. *D. R. C. Elsworth* 60 p

COLSTON-C 4 gr.g. Belfort (FR) 89 – Grand Occasion 63 (Great Nephew 126) [1995 73, a54: a8g a6g 5.1m⁵ 5.1m⁵ 5g⁴ 7.1m² 8m³ 8m* 5.1f² 5m² 5.7h* 5.7h 7g a6g³ a5g a7g 1996 a7g 5.7m 6.1m⁶ 5.1m 5.1f 5m 5g 6m a6g³ a5g Dec 31] angular, close-coupled gelding: only modest at best in 1996: trained by C. J. Hill on first, then R. Baker second to fourth 4-y-o starts: trainer fined and jockey suspended under non-triers rule on sixth: effective at 5f to 1m: goes well on top-of-the-ground, and acts on equitrack: visored (below form) once as 3-y-o: usually a front runner. *P. D. Evans* — a54

COLT D'OR 4 ch.g. Beldale Lark 105 – Nijinsgayle (FR) (Nice Havrais (USA) – 124) [1995 –: 6.9m 10m 12.5g⁶ 1996 11.7f⁵ Jul 24] no form: dead. *J. White*

COLWAY BRIDGE 3 b.g. Colway Radial 57 – Bell Bridge Girl (Coded Scrap – 90) [1995 55: 5m⁴ 5f⁶ a8g 1996 11f Sep 27] sturdy gelding: soundly beaten since debut: sold 2,900 gns Doncaster October Sales. *Mrs M. Reveley*

COLWAY RAKE 5 b.g. Salse (USA) 128 – Barely Hot (Bold Lad (IRE) 133) 71 [1995 76: 6d 5g³ 6g* 6g² 6f 5m⁶ 6m² 6d 6g² 6g 1996 5g 6m 5g⁴ 6d 6m⁶ 6d⁶ 6m⁶ Jul 21] strong, deep-bodied gelding: fair handicapper: stays 6f: acts on firesand and on good to firm and soft ground: effective blinkered (was at 5 yrs)/visored or not: inconsistent. *J. W. Watts*

COMANCHE COMPANION 6 b.m. Commanche Run 133 – Constant 73 d Companion 84 (Pas de Seul 133) [1995 88, a–: 7g 8.3g 7.1m² 8.5m 8f² 8m⁵ a8g 7.1d* a– 8d³ 7g* 8m 1996 8s a8g⁶ 7g 8.1g 8m 8m 8.3d 8d 7g² 7g Oct 30] plain, close-coupled mare: has a quick action: just a fair handicapper at best in 1996: effective at 7f to 9f: probably acts on any turf going, modest form at best on the all-weather: has won for apprentice and when sweating. *T. J. Naughton*

COME DANCING 2 b.f. (Apr 5) Suave Dancer (USA) 136 – Cominna (Dom- 48 + inion 123) [1996 6g⁶ 6m⁵ a5g Nov 12] 17,000Y: third foal: half-sister to irresolute 3-y-o 2m winner Go With The Wind and 4-y-o Prima Cominna (6f winner at 2 yrs), both by Unfuwain: dam unraced sister to Primo Dominie: modest form: probably needs further than 5f: races keenly: slowly away on debut. *M. Johnston*

COMEDIE ARRETE (FR) 4 b.f. Old Vic 136 – Seattle Siren (USA) 101 – (Seattle Slew (USA)) [1995 11g² 10s³ 15g 12g 1996 8m a16g 11.5g a11g a12g³ a14g Aug 16] ex-French filly: sixth living foal: half-sister to 4 winners, including Distant Beat (up to 1¾m, by Touching Wood): dam, 6f winner at 2 yrs, half-sister to very smart middle-distance winner Pole Position: fair form on first 2 of 4 starts at 3 yrs for Mme M. Bollack-Badel but sold only 1,100 gns Newmarket December Sales: well beaten in 1996: stays 11f: tried blinkered, no improvement. *M. C. Chapman*

COMEDY RIVER 9 br.g. Comedy Star (USA) 121 – Hopeful Waters 66 52 (Forlorn River 124) [1995 NR 1996 a10g 9m 8.5m³ 10m⁴ 9.2g⁶ 10m² a10g* 10.8f* 11.5m a10s³ Nov 19] leggy, rather sparely-made gelding: modest performer: off course nearly 3 months before winning selling handicap at Lingfield and claimer at Warwick in the autumn (hampered in melee on home turn at 11.5f): acts on firm ground (unproven on soft surface) and equitrack. *N. E. Berry*

COME ON IN 3 b.g. Most Welcome 131 – Lominda (IRE) 80 (Lomond (USA) – 128) [1995 –: 7g 10g 1996 14.1g Oct 24] no form. *R. Dickin*

COMEONUP 5 b.g. Most Welcome 131 – Scarlet Veil 75 (Tyrnavos 129) [1995 64: 7g 8m 8.3g* 7.1d 1996 6d 8.2g 8.2g a9.4g a9.4g Nov 25] sturdy gelding: looked of little account in 1996. *J. M. Bradley*

COME TOGETHER 2 b.f. (Jan 31) Mtoto 134 – Pfalz 101 (Pharly (FR) 130) – [1996 5f 7.1v⁵ 6m Oct 28] 10,000Y: small, sturdy filly: second foal: half-sister to 3-y-o False Alarm (by Warning): dam, seemed to stay 1¼m, from family of Bassenthwaite, Hadeer and Braashee: never a threat in maidens: bred to be suited by 1m+. *D. W. P. Arbuthnot*

COME TOO MAMMA'S 2 ch.f. (Mar 9) La Grange Music 111 – Purchased By 53 Phone (IRE) 48 (Wolverlife 115) [1996 a5g³ a5g² a5g* 5d⁴ a6g⁴ 5m³ a5g³ a5g* 5g⁶ a5g⁵ a6g Nov 14] 2,200Y: leggy filly: first foal: dam won 3 times over 5f from 5 starts at 2 yrs: successful in sellers at Southwell in May and Wolverhampton in July: stays 6f: acts on firesand and good to firm ground, probably on equitrack: consistent. *J. Berry*

COMIC FANTASY (AUS) 3 b.f. Rory's Jester (AUS) – Enchanted Dream (NZ) 77 d (Danzatore (CAN) 120) [1995 87: 6g⁴ 5m⁶ 5.1h* 5f³ 5.1m² 5g² 5g³ 5m 1996 5m⁶ 5.1m⁴ 5m³ 7s⁵ 6f⁴ 6f 5m⁴ 5g⁴ 5g 6d 8g 5m 5m⁴ 7g Oct 25] lengthy filly: fluent mover: fair form at best in 1996: left Martyn Wane after eleventh outing: best at 5f: acts on hard ground: very best form in blinkers: inconsistent. *J. L. Eyre*

COMIC OPERA (IRE) 2 b.f. (Feb 12) Royal Academy (USA) 130 – Miss – p Toshiba (USA) 113 (Sir Ivor 135) [1996 7.1s Oct 22] half-sister to several winners here and abroad, including useful 1½m winner (second in Park Hill) Guilty Secret (by Kris) and fairly useful 1¼m winner Ikebana (by Sadler's Wells): dam won from

7f to 1½m: soundly beaten, slowly away, in maiden at Chepstow: should do better. *P. W. Chapple-Hyam*

COMIC'S FUTURE (USA) 3 b.c. Carnivalay (USA) – Destiny's Hour (USA) – (Fit To Fight (USA)) [1995 NR 1996 12.4g⁴ 10d May 18] 42,000Y: big, strong, lengthy colt: second foal: dam, unraced, from good family: backward, showed nil in maidens: sold 3,000 gns Newmarket July Sales. *P. W. Chapple-Hyam*

COMMANCHERO 9 gr.g. Telsmoss 91 – Count On Me 77 (No Mercy 126) – [1995 NR 1996 a13g Feb 1] rated 40 in 1994: tailed off on return: stays 17.2f. *R. J. Hodges*

COMMANDER GLEN (IRE) 4 b.g. Glenstal (USA) 118 – Une Parisienne 66 (FR) (Bolkonski 134) [1995 61: 10.2f 10m 12.5g 8f⁶ 5.9f* 7m³ 8m 6f² 7m 7m⁵ 8h* 8.5s 12g 1996 7s 7.1g 8.5m² 7.1g 6.9g* 8m² 8f⁵ 8.2m 10g² 10g⁶ 9.2m⁶ 8m 10m 10.9m Sep 19] smallish, sturdy gelding: modest handicapper: won at Carlisle in May: left Mrs J. R. Ramsden after penultimate start: stays 1¼m: acts on firm going: tried blinkered/visored: held up: often looks none too keen: modest winning hurdler. *M. D. Hammond*

COMMANDER JONES (IRE) 2 b.g. (Apr 27) Common Grounds 118 – Play 84 A Golden Disc (Ashmore (FR) 125) [1996 5f⁵ 5.1m³ 5.7f 5m⁴ 6m* 7g⁵ 6m* a6g⁵ Oct a? 19] IR 11,000Y, 20,000 2-y-o: leggy, lengthy gelding: half-brother to Irish 9f winner Golden Success (by Doulab) and several winners in Italy: dam won over hurdles: fair form: won claimers at Haydock in September and Lingfield in October: likely to stay at least 7f: acts on good to firm ground, well below form on fibresand: very stirred up in blinkers fourth start (subsequently gelded): sent to Sweden. *B. J. Meehan*

COMMIN' UP 3 b.f. Primo Dominie 121 – Ridalia 56 (Ridan (USA)) [1995 67: 70 d 6.1d 6g 6.9g³ 1996 7.3d² 7m 8f⁵ 8.3m 9g a8s⁶ a10g Dec 13] lengthy filly: has a quick action: disappointing maiden handicapper: probably stays 1m: probably acts on firm and dead going. *J. W. Hills*

COMMITTAL (IRE) 3 b.c. Lycius (USA) 124 – Just Cause (Law Society 97 (USA) 130) [1995 106: 7.1m³ 8d² 7.9g* 8m⁶ 1996 8m 8.1m⁶ 9s 8g Nov 2] strong, well-made colt: has a round action: easily best effort in 1996 when sixth of 8 in minor contest at Sandown in August: stiff tasks on that form when well held in good handicaps afterwards: stays 1m: strong-running type: sent to UAE. *J. H. M. Gosden*

COMMON DIVINE (IRE) 3 b.f. Common Grounds 118 – Day Dress (Ashmore (FR) 125) [1995 –: a6g⁶ 1996 a5g a6g⁴ 8f Jul 26] angular filly: no worthwhile form. *C. Murray*

COMMONER (USA) 4 b.c. Far North (CAN) 120 – Searching Around (USA) 110 (Round Table) [1995 112: 10m² 11.5f⁵ 12g 10m* 12m² 11.1g² 12g⁶ 12f⁶ 1996 12d⁵ 12m⁵ 10d⁶ 12g² 9f² 11f 12f⁴ 10f⁴ Nov 27] attractive colt: smart performer: creditable 4 lengths second of 4 to Bequeath in listed race at Newmarket in June (fourth outing and final one for R.Hannon): 6 lengths fourth of 8 to Dernier Empereur in Grade 2 event at Santa Anita in November penultimate start: stays 1½m: acts on firm ground, and seems unsuited by a soft surface: effective held up or from front. *J. Noseda, USA*

COMMON ROCK (IRE) 2 b.f. (Apr 13) Common Grounds 118 – Quatre 44 Femme 76 (Petorius 117) [1996 6m a7g* a7g Aug 9] IR 5,000Y, 7,000 2-y-o: first foal: dam 6f winner, closely related to very useful sprinter Sharp N'Early: won bad seller at Southwell in July: stays 7f: visored last 2 starts, tailed off last time. *J. Norton*

COMPACT DISC (IRE) 2 b.f. (Mar 14) Royal Academy (USA) 130 – Sharp 48 Circle (IRE) 83 (Sure Blade (USA)) [1996 5m⁵ 5.1m 6s⁵ 5m³ 5g 8f a7g* a8g⁴ a8g Dec 3] 8,500Y: smallish, angular filly: second foal: half-sister to 3-y-o Ameer Alfayaafi (by Mujtahid): dam, 1m winner better at 11.5f, half-sister to very smart sprinter Greenland Park and Coventry Stakes winner Red Sunset: modest form: won seller at Southwell in November: stays 7f: acts on fibresand, best turf form (debut) on good to firm: takes keen hold: inconsistent. *M. Johnston*

COMPASS POINTER 3 gr.c. Mazilier (USA) 107 – Woodleys (Tyrnavos 129) 67 [1995 –: 7g 7.9m 8m 1996 10g 11.6m⁴ 11.8d² 13.3m 11.6g 11.8g 14m² 14d 13.9g 14.1s⁴ 12v² a14g* a16g Dec 11] rather leggy, close-coupled colt: fair handicapper: won at Southwell in November: stays 14.1f well: acts on good to firm and heavy ground and on fibresand: has had tongue tied: inconsistent. *J. M. P. Eustace*

COMPATIBILITY (IRE)   2 b.c. (Mar 20) Common Grounds 118 – Nikki's   – Groom (Shy Groom (USA)) [1996 6m Jul 11] IR 19,000F, IR 40,000Y: second reported foal: half-brother to German 12.5f winner Dr Albano (by Ballad Rock): dam Irish maiden, fourth over 1¼m: backward, eighth of 13 to Grapeshot in maiden at Newmarket in July: looked sure to improve. *J. H. M. Gosden*

COMPTON PLACE   2 ch.c. (Apr 20) Indian Ridge 123 – Nosey 96 (Nebbiolo   108 125) [1996 5.1m* 5m² 6g* 6m² 5m² Sep 14] IR 92,000Y: leggy, useful-looking colt: sixth foal: half-brother to useful 3-y-o Quakers Field (by Anshan), 6f and 7f winner at 2 yrs, and 5f winner Lloc (by Absalom): dam Irish 2-y-o 5f and 6f winner: very useful form: won minor events at Bath in June and Salisbury in August: second other starts, very good efforts when beaten ½ length by Abou Zouz in Gimcrack Stakes at York and 1½ lengths by Easycall in Flying Childers Stakes at Doncaster: probably better suited by 6f than 5f: raced only on a sound surface: races keenly. *J. A. R. Toller*

COMTEC'S LEGEND   6 ch.m. Legend of France (USA) 124 – Comtec   34 Princess 73 (Gulf Pearl 117) [1995 –, a45: a11g⁶ a12g* a12g⁵ a12g³ a11g⁵ 12m 12m   a43 a12g a12g* 1996 a11g³ a12g⁶ a12g³ a14.8g² a12g⁵ 12.3g* a12g 16.2g May 11] small mare: poor handicapper: won selling event at Ripon in April, leading near line: stays 14.6f: acts on good to firm and dead ground (possibly unsuited by very soft) and the all-weather: sometimes hangs left: often bandaged near-fore: inconsistent. *J. F. Bottomley*

CONCEPCION (GER)   6 b.h. Acatenango (GER) 127 – Comprida (GER)   115 (Windwurf (GER)) [1995 115: 11v⁴ 12s⁴ 11s⁶ 11m 12g³ 12s 10d* 10d* 1996 11s* 10g⁴ 10d⁴ 10m³ 11d 12f³ 11g² 12g² 12s Oct 13] smart German performer: won listed race at Cologne in March: creditable 2 lengths fourth of 9 to Hollywood Dream in Group 1 event at Rome in May and length second of 13 to Grecian Dart in listed race at Bordeaux penultimate start: stays 1½m: acts on heavy ground, not discredited on firm. *H. Jentzsch, Germany*

CONCER UN   4 ch.g. Lord Bud 121 – Drudwen (Sayf El Arab (USA) 127) [1995   100 82: a7g a7g⁴ a8.5g³ 8.3v* 8f² 9.2g² 8.1g³ 7m³ 7g³ 7m⁴ 7.5g² 8h* 8m* 8m² 8.5m² 8g* 8d 1996 8m 8m* 8m* 8.1g* 8m 7.9m* 7d* 8m 8g Oct 19] smallish, lengthy gelding: useful handicapper: in tremendous form in the summer, winning at Bath (twice), Sandown, York (Bradford & Bingley Rated Stakes, beat North Song a length) and Chester: effective at 7f, and stays 9.2f: acts on any going: splendidly tough, game and genuine. *S. C. Williams*

CONDITION RED   3 b.f. Sayf El Arab (USA) 127 – Forever Mary 81 (Red Alert   – 127) [1995 NR 1996 8f⁵ a8.5g Dec 28] 7,000Y: half-sister to 2 winners, including fair Blue Topaze (up to 1m, by Fast Topaze): dam sprint maiden here later successful in USA: 100/1, tailed off in useful minor event and modest maiden. *M. S. Saunders*

CONDOR RIDGE   3 b.g. Inca Chief (USA) – Second Flower 50 (Indian Ruler   47 (USA) 104) [1995 –: 6s 6d 1996 7g 9.7f a8g 8m³ a7g 7g Jul 3] leggy gelding: a– third in Goodwood claimer, only worthwhile form: tried blinkered: best left alone. *B. J. Meehan*

CONFRONTER   7 ch.g. Bluebird (USA) 125 – Grace Darling (USA) (Vaguely   84 d Noble 140) [1995 84: 8d* 8s² 8g² 8s⁴ 8m* 8m³ 8m 8m² 8m² 8m³ 7m 8f² 8g* 8g* 7.9m⁴ 1996 8s 8v⁴ 8v⁴ 7.5v² 8s⁵ 8.1g 7.6m⁴ 8.5m 8m⁴ 8f³ 8m⁶ 8d 8m 8g 8.2g Oct 9] tall gelding: fair handicapper at best: best efforts at 7f/1m: acts on any turf going and on equitrack: has run well in blinkers/visor, not tried since 5 yrs: effective held up or from front. *S. Dow*

Bradford & Bingley Rated Stakes (Handicap), York—front row (left to right),
Concer Un, Tregaron, Moments of Fortune and North Song, with strong-finishing Nagnagnag just behind

CONGO MAN 3 b.c. Rainbow Quest (USA) 134 – African Dance (USA) (El 86 p
Gran Senor (USA) 136) [1995 NR 1996 12f⁵ 10m* Sep 18] second foal: dam Irish
maiden out of very useful Irish 9f and 1¼m winner and Irish Oaks second Fleur
Royale, a well-related broodmare: won 5-runner maiden at Sandown in September,
off bridle over 4f out but responding well from 2f out and leading inside last: will
ultimately prove better at 1½m than shorter: will improve again. *M. R. Stoute*

CONIC HILL (IRE) 5 ch.g. Lomond (USA) 128 – Krisalya 98 (Kris 135) [1995 51
–: 10.8m 8m 1996 a12g⁶ a12g 10m 10m⁶ 10.1m 9f² 9.7g 10f 10m Aug 2] lengthy,
quite attractive gelding: only modest at best in 1996: no form last 3 starts: stays 1¼m:
acts on firm going (used to on dead): formerly effective blinkered (not tried at 5 yrs)
or not. *J. Pearce*

CONNEMARA (IRE) 2 b.f. (Jan 16) Mujadil (USA) 119 – Beechwood (USA) 99 +
(Blushing Groom (FR) 131) [1996 5g* 5.1g* 5m⁴ 6g 5m² Aug 2] lengthy filly: has
scope: sixth foal: half-sister to 3-y-o 7f winner Ned's Contessa (by Persian Heights)
and 1993 2-y-o 7f winner Imposing Groom (by Posen): dam French 10.8f winner:
useful form: won median auction maiden at Warwick and £7,400 event at Chester in
spring: in frame after behind Dance Parade in Queen Mary Stakes at Ascot and
Carmine Lake in Molecomb Stakes at Goodwood: edgy then set off much too quickly
when last of 9 in Cherry Hinton Stakes at Newmarket on fourth outing: speedy, and
best form at 5f: raced only on a sound surface. *C. A. Dwyer*

CONON FALLS (IRE) 2 b.c. (May 13) Sadler's Wells (USA) 132 – Cocotte 111 86 p
(Troy 137) [1996 7m 8.1g³ Aug 30] close-coupled, good-topped colt: seventh foal:
half-brother to top-class middle-distance colt Pilsudski (by Polish Precedent) and 2
other winners, including fairly useful 7f and 1m winner Glowing Ardour (by
Dancing Brave): dam 1¼m winner: 5 lengths third of 6 to ready winner Medaaly in
minor event at Sandown in August, final and better effort: will be suited by middle
distances: sure to improve, and win a race. *J. H. M. Gosden*

CONQUISTAJADE (USA) 3 b. or br.f. Conquistador Cielo (USA) – Uncut –
Jade (CAN) (Vice Regent (CAN)) [1995 54: 6m⁴ 7m a8.5g³ 1996 a8.5g a10g⁶ a8g
a8g a8g 12s Mar 27] tall, close-coupled filly: no form since debut: tried blinkered.
S. P. C. Woods

CONSIDERABLE CHARM 4 ch.f. Charmer 123 – Leap In Time (Dance In –
Time (CAN)) [1995 51: a7g⁴ a7g² a7g⁴ 8m a7g 1996 a7g a7g⁶ 8.3m 10f a13g Dec
13] no worthwhile form in 1996: left Lord Huntingdon's stable after (pulled hard in
visor) 4-y-o reappearance. *A. Moore*

CONSORDINO 3 b.f. Alzao (USA) 117 – Consolation 95 (Troy 137) [1995 88: 90
7m 6m⁵ 7m⁴ 7g* 7d² 8m⁶ 1996 7m 7.1d⁶ 8f 9.2g* 10.5s Oct 5] stocky filly: carries
condition: off course 3 months, easily best effort at 3 yrs when winning handicap at
Hamilton in September, making virtually all and staying on strongly: should be well
suited by further than 9.2f: acts on dead ground: sent to UAE. *L. M. Cumani*

CONSORT 3 b.c. Groom Dancer (USA) 128 – Darnelle 83 (Shirley Heights 130) 91
[1995 NR 1996 6.9m² 7m* 8.1g³ 7m⁵ 7m 8d⁴ Oct 12] smallish, good-topped colt: has
a quick action: third foal: half-brother to 4-y-o 6f Yugoslavian winner Halongbay
(by Unfuwain): dam, 7.6f (at 2 yrs) and 9f winner, half-sister to Oaks and Irish Oaks
second Bourbon Girl: fairly useful form: off course 4 months, won maiden at
Salisbury in August: good fourth of 24 in handicap at Ascot final start: better form at
1m than 7f: acts on good to firm and dead ground: on toes penultimate 3-y-o start,
shade edgy final one: has reportedly been sold. *G. Harwood*

CONSPICUOUS (IRE) 6 b.g. Alzao (USA) 117 – Mystery Lady (USA) 88
(Vaguely Noble 140) [1995 82: a9.4g⁵ a8g⁶ 10m² 9f² 10m* 10m² 9g* 8s² 8m 1996
10.3g 10d 10.1m⁴ 10f³ 8m⁴ 8m 9d* 9g 9m Oct 5] close-coupled gelding: has a quick
action: fairly useful handicapper: best effort to win minor event at Goodwood in
August: effective at 1m when conditions are testing, and stays 10.1f: acts on the
all-weather and on any turf ground: visored (ran poorly) sixth 6-y-o start: takes good
hold and is waited with. *L. G. Cottrell*

CONSPIRACY 2 b.f. (Mar 7) Rudimentary (USA) 118 – Roussalka 123 (Habitat 98 p
134) [1996 6d² 5f* 5m³ 5.1g² 5m* Sep 19] medium-sized, sparely-made filly, with a
sharp action: closely related to high-class sprinter Gayane (by Green Desert) and half-
sister to several winners, including smart 7f performer Shahid (by Green Desert) and
smart 1m and 1¼m performer Ristna (by Kris): dam won 7 races at up to 1¼m, and is

Timeform Harry Rosebery Trophy, Ayr—Conspiracy shows a clean pair of heels to eventual fourth Joza

sister to Our Home and half-sister to Oh So Sharp, same family as St Leger winner Shantou: progressive form: won maiden at Sandown in June and Timeform Harry Rosebery Trophy (in good style by 3 lengths from Superior Premium) at Ayr in September: should be as effective at 6f as 5f: acts on good to firm ground, probably creditable effort on dead on debut: will improve further. *J. L. Dunlop*

CONTENTMENT (IRE) 2 b.c. (Apr 5) Fairy King (USA) – Quality of Life 69 + (Auction Ring (USA) 123) [1996 6g 6m 6g² Sep 21] 26,000Y: fourth foal: half-brother to St Leger winner Bob's Return (by Bob Back): dam Irish 2-y-o 6f winner: modest form in maidens: should stay further than 6f: may do better. *J. W. Hills*

CONTRACT BRIDGE (IRE) 3 b.f. Contract Law (USA) 108 – Mystery Bid 51 (Auction Ring (USA) 123) [1995 57d: 5g 5f³ 6m² 7g⁶ 7.1s a7g 1996 a11g⁴ 8m⁶ 8g* 10m 11.1g³ 8.5m⁶ 8m⁵ 9.9f⁴ 10d* 12.1g⁵ Sep 29] smallish filly: unimpressive mover: modest handicapper: won at Carlisle in May and Ripon in August: stays 12.1f: acts on firm and dead ground: ridden by 7-lb claimer last 2 starts: consistent: sold (C. Thornton to P. Murphy) 5,000 gns Doncaster November Sales. *C. W. Thornton*

CONTRAFIRE (IRE) 4 b.g. Contract Law (USA) 108 – Fiery Song (Ballad 76 Rock 122) [1995 75: a8.5g* a8.5g³ a10g* 10.3g² 12.3d² 12.3m⁶ 10g 10.5m³ 11.5m* 11.9g² 10.9g² 11f⁴ 1996 10.8g⁴ 12m⁴ 10m⁴ 10.1m² 12g* 12f⁴ 12g⁵ Aug 26] angular gelding: poor mover: fair handicapper: made all at Catterick in July: below form afterwards: won over hurdles for Mrs A. Swinbank in October: likely to get further than 12.3f: acts on firm and dead going and the all-weather. *W. Jarvis*

CONTRARIE 3 b.f. Floose 99 – Chanita (Averof 123) [1995 –: a8g a7g a8g 1996 37 11.8d a12g 11.5m 12.1s⁴ 16.4v⁴ Nov 11] poor maiden: should stay 1¾m. *M. J. Ryan*

CONTRAVENE (IRE) 2 b.f. (Apr 15) Contract Law (USA) 108 – Vieux Carre 54 (Pas de Seul 133) [1996 5s⁴ a5g² 5m* 5m³ 6m³ a6g⁴ 6m⁵ 6f* 5m⁵ 6m² a7g* 7g⁵ 6m a64 Oct 29] 3,200Y: leggy, close-coupled filly: fourth foal: sister to 3-y-o John's Law: dam poor maiden, sometimes appeared reluctant: won seller at Beverley in April, claimer at Hamilton in August and selling nursery at Wolverhampton in September: stays 7f: acts on firm ground and fibresand: sometimes front runner. *J. Berry*

CONTROL FREAK 2 b.f. (Mar 22) Inca Chief (USA) – Forest Nymph (Native – Bazaar 122) [1996 6.9m 8.2m 8.2g⁵ Oct 9] fourth foal: dam unraced: well beaten in maidens and a seller. *A. G. Foster*

CONVENT GUEST (IRE) 3 ch.f. Be My Guest (USA) 126 – Point of View – (FR) (Sharpman (FR) 124) [1995 NR 1996 a5g⁶ a7g⁶ Jan 26] third foal: dam once-raced half-sister to dams of Lypharita (won Prix de Diane) and Belmez: well held in claimer and seller: covered by Fraam. *M. R. Channon*

220

CONWY 3 ch.f. Rock City 120 – Degannwy 52 (Caerleon (USA) 132) [1995 –p: –
7g 1996 10d a9.4g⁴ a12g Dec 14] smallish, workmanlike filly: has a round action: no
form: trained until after reappearance by N. Graham. *S. C. Williams*

COOCHIE 7 b.m. King of Spain 121 – York Street (USA) (Diamond Shoal 130) –
[1995 NR 1996 17.2m⁶ 13.1f Jul 8] of no account. *R. J. Baker*

COOL CAPER 3 b.c. Inca Chief (USA) – Rekindled Flame (IRE) (Kings Lake 42
(USA) 133) [1995 53?: a5g⁴ a6g 1996 7d³ a8g Apr 29] small, lengthy filly: bad
maiden plater: should stay 1m, stiff task when tried: visored (never a factor after
4-month break) second 2-y-o start. *A. G. Foster*

COOL EDGE (IRE) 5 ch.g. Nashamaa 113 – Mochara (Last Fandango 125) 112
[1995 84: 6.1g⁵ 5g* 5m⁴ 5m⁴ 6d² 6g³ 7g² 7.1d² 8g² 7g³ 7.9m⁵ 8m 1996 8s* 8d² 7.1d*
8.1d⁴ 7.3m* 7g³ 7g² 8g⁶ Nov 2] rangy gelding: smart handicapper, greatly improved:
won at Doncaster in March, listed rated stakes at Haydock in May and rated stakes at
Newbury (by 1½ lengths from Akil) in August: placed in rated stakes at Goodwood
(not getting run of race) and 5-runner Concorde Stakes at Tipperary (1½ lengths
behind Wizard King) next 2 starts: effective at 7f to 8.1f: probably acts on any going:
visored (ran well) twice at 4 yrs: often early to post: keen sort, usually waited with in
touch: consistent. *M. H. Tompkins*

COOL FIRE 3 b.c. Colmore Row 111 – Into The Fire 74 (Dominion 123) [1995 76
59: 6m⁵ 7f 1996 a8g* 8g² 8m 10m a9.4g a9.4g⁵ 8m 8g a10s Nov 19] leggy, a78
useful-looking colt: unimpressive mover: reportedly fractured cannon bone at 2 yrs:
fair form: won maiden at Lingfield in March: probably stays 1¼m: best efforts on
all-weather or good ground: blinkered (no form) penultimate 3-y-o start: sometimes
carries head awkwardly: inconsistent and needs treating with caution. *S. P. C. Woods*

COOL GREY 2 gr.f. (Apr 30) Absalom 128 – Crisp Air (Elegant Air 119) [1996 49
8.1m a7g⁶ a7g³ a7g⁴ Dec 7] 3,100Y: workmanlike filly: second foal: dam unraced:
always prominent when in frame in sellers at Southwell and Wolverhampton: should
stay 1m. *J. J. O'Neill*

Henry B. H. Chan's "Cool Edge"

COOL JAZZ 5 b.h. Lead On Time (USA) 123 – Amber Fizz (USA) (Effervescing 115 (USA)) [1995 116: 6g 7m² 7m⁶ 7.1g³ 6g³ 6m* 7m 5.6m³ 6g⁵ 6d* 5d 7m 7f 1996 6s³ 6m⁵ 5m* 5g 6m 6m 5m⁴ 5m 6f 6m Sep 28] strong, lengthy, good-topped horse: impresses in appearance: has a long stride: smart performer: won Dubai Racing Club Palace House Stakes at Newmarket in May by ¾ length from Lucky Lionel, racing against favoured stand rail and coming from well off strong pace: best efforts afterwards when fourth in King George Stakes at Goodwood and seventh in Nunthorpe Stakes at York: well beaten last 2 starts: effective at 5f to 7f: acted on good to firm and dead ground, had won on soft: blinkered/visored (below form) once each: took keen hold: reportedly had foot problems: often hung and looked a difficult ride: fetched only 16,000 gns at Newmarket Autumn Sales: reportedly to stand at Louella Stud, N. Yorks at £1,000 (Oct 1). *C. E. Brittain*

COOLOWEN FLASH (IRE) 5 gr.m. Standaan (FR) 118 – Little Cynthia 76 41 (Wolver Hollow 126) [1995 5s 5g⁵ 5s⁴ 5g² 5m* 5g³ 5m⁶ 5m³ 5m⁵ 1996 5g 5g⁶ 5m 7.5g 5.1m⁵ 5g Sep 29] leggy, angular ex-Irish mare: half-sister to 4 winners, none better than fair: dam stayer: modest and consistent handicapper (rated 57) in Ireland at 4 yrs, winner at Bellewstown for J. Walsh: poor at best in 1996: suited by 5f: acts on good to firm and soft ground. *J. L. Eyre*

COPPERBEECH (IRE) 2 ch.f. (Mar 26) Common Grounds 118 – Caimanite 68 62 (Tap On Wood 130) [1996 5.2d² 6d⁶ 5m⁶ 6.1s Oct 22] IR 15,000Y resold 42,000Y: leggy, unfurnished filly: shows knee action: fourth foal: half-sister to 1m winner (including at 2 yrs) Blair Castle (by Waajib): dam, maiden placed at 6f and 7f, half-sister to dam of smart 7f winner Mahogany: modest form: best effort on debut in April: off course nearly 5 months after second start: should stay beyond 5f: soundly beaten on soft ground final outing. *P. W. Chapple-Hyam*

COPPER BRIGHT 3 b.g. Mon Tresor 113 – Arabian Nymph 49 (Sayf El Arab 67 (USA) 127) [1995 –: 5.1m⁴ 6m 5m 6m 6m⁴ 6g⁵ 7.1g 1996 a5g⁴ a7g⁴ a5g² a5g⁵ a5g⁵ a6g* a6g* a6g⁶ a5g⁴ Mar 18] fair performer: won sellers at Lingfield and Wolverhampton (bought in 5,200 gns) in February: well beaten afterwards: sold 4,400 gns Doncaster March Sales: stays 6f: acts on the all-weather, has raced only on a sound surface on turf: usually visored/blinkered nowadays. *P. C. Haslam*

COPPER SHELL 2 ch.g. (Apr 5) Beveled (USA) – Luly My Love (Hello – Gorgeous (USA) 128) [1996 7.1m Jul 24] fourth reported foal: brother to French middle-distance winner Beloved Love: dam unraced half-sister to useful stayer Stavordale and very smart French middle-distance performer Alfred's Choice: slowly away and never a threat in Sandown maiden in July on only start. *A. P. Jones*

CORAL ISLAND 2 b.g. (Mar 29) Charmer 123 – Misowni (Niniski (USA) 125) – [1996 6s 8.3d⁴ 7.9g Oct 9] 8,000Y: well-made gelding: fifth foal: half-brother to 4-y-o 7f and 1m winner Jalmaid (by Jalmood): dam unraced half-sister to Bustomi: poor form in varied auction maiden events. *J. G. FitzGerald*

CORAL SPRINGS (USA) 2 b. or br.f. (Feb 15) Minshaanshu Amad (USA) 91§ – – Distinctiveness (USA) (Distinctive (USA)) [1996 7m 5m Jul 22] sister to smart 1990 2-y-o 5f winner and Middle Park runner-up Distinctly North, closely related to a winner in Mexico by Be My Guest and half-sister to several winners: dam half-sister to American Derby winner Determined King: poor form in median auction maidens: sent to Australia. *P. W. Chapple-Hyam*

CORAL STRAND 2 ch.f. (May 16) Indian Ridge 123 – Sea Venture (FR) 98 69 ? (Diatome 132) [1996 6m 7m⁴ 7m⁴ Oct 29] compact filly: half-sister to numerous winners, including smart middle-distance performer Sailor's Mate (by Shirley Heights) and useful 1980 French 2-y-o 6f winner Grecian Sea (by Homeric), latter dam of Yorkshire Oaks winner Hellenic: dam, from family of Reform, won over 6f at 2 yrs and placed over 1m: staying-on fourth in steadily-run minor event at Ayr on second start, best effort: tailed off final outing: likely to stay at least 1m. *J. W. Watts*

CORETTA (IRE) 2 b.f. (Feb 11) Caerleon (USA) 132 – Free At Last 115 (Shirley 78 p Heights 130) [1996 7g³ Nov 2] first reported foal: dam, 7f winner here at 2 yrs and fourth in 1000 Guineas (later stakes winner at up to 1½m in USA), half-sister to Barathea: slow-starting third of 23, keeping on, to Palisade in maiden at Newmarket: sure to win races over middle distances. *L. M. Cumani*

CORINCHILI 2 ch.f. (Mar 25) Chilibang 120 – Corinthia (USA) (Empery (USA) 55 128) [1996 5s⁵ Mar 28] sturdy filly: sixth foal: half-sister to 1989 2-y-o 6f winner

Dubai Racing Club Palace House Stakes, Newmarket—
Cool Jazz (right) and Lucky Lionel (second left) finish strongest;
the others are Westcourt Magic and Ya Malak (noseband)

Rambadale (by Vaigly Great) and 7f winner Barlogan (by Dunbeath): dam, lightly raced in France, is half-sister to smart miler Nino Bibbia: gambled-on fifth, making most, in median auction maiden at Leicester in March on only start. *G. G. Margarson*

CORINTHIAN (IRE)   2 b.c. (Mar 30) Lycius (USA) 124 – Royal Recreation   75 +
(USA) (His Majesty (USA)) [1996 8d⁴ 8.1s Oct 22] IR 35,000Y: second foal: half-brother to 3-y-o 1½m winner Royal Diversion (by Marju): dam Irish maiden, stayed 2m: fourth in maiden at Salisbury on debut: below that form only subsequent start: bred to stay 1¼m: sent to USA. *R. Hannon*

CORKY'S GIRL   4 b.f. Today And Tomorrow 78 – Rectory Maid 74 (Tina's Pet   –
121) [1995 –: a7g 1996 8.1g⁵ 8.3m⁴ Aug 21] no sign of ability. *R. M. McKellar*

CORNCRAKE (IRE)   2 b.f. (Feb 21) Nordico (USA) – Lemon Balm (High Top   51
131) [1996 5.1m⁵ 5.3f³ 5m⁵ 6d 7d³ a6g⁴ 8.2g³ Oct 9] 6,500Y: strong, sturdy filly: third foal: sister to 4-y-o Quintus Decimus, 7f winner at 2 yrs: dam ran twice on flat then showed a little ability over hurdles: placed in sellers: stays 1m: sold 3,200 gns Newmarket Autumn Sales: sent to Sweden. *B. J. Meehan*

CORNET   10 b.g. Coquelin (USA) 121 – Corny Story 75 (Oats 126) [1995 NR   –
1996 15.1s Nov 7] fairly useful but moody chaser: probably no longer of account on flat. *Denys Smith*

CORNICHE QUEST (IRE)   3 b.f. Salt Dome (USA) – Angel Divine   61
(Ahonoora 122) [1995 63d: 5g³ 5.1m 6g² 6m³ 6m² 5.7h³ 6m⁵ 5g⁴ 6g⁴ 7g⁵ 6g⁵ 5f³
5s⁴ 1996 8g* 8m⁵ 7f 6m³ 7g*ᵈⁱˢ 6m⁶ 7g 7g 7d³ 7d⁴ 7f⁴ 6m* 7m 6.9d* a8g Nov 4]
leggy filly: modest performer: well placed to be first past post in maiden at Brighton in May, seller at Yarmouth (disqualified for interference soon after start) in July, handicap at Yarmouth in September and seller at Folkestone (carried head awkwardly and drifted left) in October: effective at 6f to 1m: acts on firm ground (looked ill at ease on hard) and dead, soundly beaten on fibresand. *M. R. Channon*

CORNISH SNOW (USA)   3 br.c. Storm Cat (USA) – Pleasantly Free (USA)   96
(Pleasant Colony (USA)) [1995 70p: 6s⁴ 1996 a7g* a7g* 7g⁵ Jul 4] lightly-raced colt: landed the odds in maiden and handicap (barely came off bridle) at Lingfield in February: tailed off in useful minor event at Yarmouth in July: stays 7f: acts on equitrack: to UAE. *D. R. Loder*

CORONA GOLD   6 b.g. Chilibang 120 – Miss Alkie 58 (Noalcoholic (FR) 128)   –
[1995 46: 8m⁶ a7g³ a8g a7g⁵ a7g* 7.1m³ a8g 7d 1996 8.1m a7g 7m 8g 7.5g Aug 24]
sturdy gelding: seemed of little account in 1996. *J. G. FitzGerald*

CORPORAL NYM (USA)   3 gr.g. Cozzene (USA) – Fiji Fan (USA) (Danzig   69
(USA)) [1995 85p: 6g⁴ 6m³ 8m³ 1996 7m 8m⁶ 6v Oct 6] good-bodied gelding: good mover: fairly useful as a juvenile: subsequently gelded: off course 10 months and below best on return: sold (P. Cole to J. Poulton) 3,400 gns Newmarket Autumn Sales. *P. F. I. Cole*

CORRADINI 4 b.c. Rainbow Quest (USA) 134 – Cruising Height 112 (Shirley 112
Heights 130) [1995 92: 11m 11.9m* 13.9m2 1996 16d3 18.7g3 16.5g4 13.9m* 14.6g*
13.9m3 14.6m* 16g Nov 1] good-topped colt: unimpressive mover: smart performer:
third in Chester Cup in May but looked reluctant next time: progressed very well next
4 starts, winning rated stakes at York, minor event at Doncaster and (after good third
in the Ebor) strongly-run £10,300 event at Doncaster (soon niggled along in rear, led
1f out), all between June and September: ran badly final start: a stayer: acts on good
to firm ground: sometimes flashes tail: consistent: stays in training. *H. R. A. Cecil*

CORRINA CORRINA 3 b.f. Risk Me (FR) 127 – Dona Krista 84 (King of –
Spain 121) [1995 NR 1996 6m May 5] 26,000Y: third foal: sister to useful sprinter
Risky: dam 2-y-o 6f winner, best run at 7f: speed only to halfway in maiden at
Salisbury. *R. Hannon*

CORSINI 2 b.f. (Mar 7) Machiavellian (USA) 123 – Dangora (USA) 98 (Sove- 88 p
reign Dancer (USA)) [1996 7m* 6m2 Sep 28] leggy, lightly-made filly: second foal:
half-sister to French 3-y-o Delegate (by Polish Precedent), 6f winner at 2 yrs: dam,
lightly-raced 2-y-o 6f winner, closely related to smart miler Zaizafon, herself dam of
Zafonic: won maiden at Lingfield in September: keeping-on ¾-length second of 5 to
Lochangel in Blue Seal Stakes at Ascot later in month: likely to be suited by at least
7f: will probably improve again. *H. R. A. Cecil*

CORTES 3 ch.f. Roi Danzig (USA) – Jumra (Thatch (USA) 136) [1995 NR 1996 –
10m Jun 3] 8,000Y: fourth foal: half-sister to 1990 2-y-o 1m seller winner Sharp
Glow (by Reach): dam never ran: 50/1, in rear in maiden at Windsor. *B. Gubby*

COSCOROBA (IRE) 2 ch.f. (Feb 23) Shalford (IRE) 124§ – Tameeza (USA) 47
(Shahrastani (USA) 135) [1996 6m3 Jul 27] IR 1,800Y: first foal: dam well beaten
only start in Ireland: burly, third in seller at Newcastle in July. *J. Berry*

COSMIC PRINCE (IRE) 2 b.c. (Mar 22) Teenoso (USA) 135 – Windmill 85 p
Princess 55 (Gorytus (USA) 132) [1996 7m6 7f3 7g* Oct 2] tall, useful-looking colt:
has scope: second foal: half-brother to 4-y-o Shahrani (by Lear Fan): dam, maiden
placed at 1m and 11f, out of half-sister to Blakeney and Morston: made most when
winning maiden at Brighton in October: races keenly but will stay middle distances:
could well improve again. *M. A. Jarvis*

COTTAGE PRINCE (IRE) 3 b.g. Classic Secret (USA) 91 – Susan's Blues 42
(Cure The Blues (USA)) [1995 –: 5m 7g a8.5g 1996 8m 11.1m 8.5m 8m3 9.9g5
11.1g3 Sep 2] good-bodied gelding: poor maiden handicapper: stays 11.1f: acts on
good to firm ground: winning hurdler. *J. J. Quinn*

COUCHANT (IRE) 5 b.g. Petoski 135 – Be Easy 110 (Be Friendly 130) [1995 –
66: 12s3 1996 10m 14.9g May 25] fair maiden: always behind in 1996: stays 1½m:
acts on good to firm and soft ground: has looked ungenuine over hurdles. *J. White*

COUNT BASIE 3 b.g. Batshoof 122 – Quiet Harbour (Mill Reef (USA) 141) 87
[1995 NR 1996 10m2 10d3 10m* 12m 11.9g Jul 12] 27,000F,IR 30,000Y: medium-
sized, deep-girthed gelding: fluent mover: half-brother to several winners, notably
quite useful Jazz Ballet (middle distances, by Jaazeiro): dam lightly-raced half-sister
to Coronation Cup winner Quiet Fling: fairly useful form: won maiden at Windsor in
June, leading 3f out: should stay further than 1¼m (almost fell first occasion, tended
to hang last time): best form on good to firm ground: joined L. Eyre and gelded.
H. R. A. Cecil

COUNTESS OF CADIZ (USA) 3 b.f. Badger Land (USA) – Cokebutton (Be –
My Guest (USA) 126) [1995 NR 1996 10m 10g 10m Jul 29] fifth foal: half-sister to
3 winners, including fair Wajih (around 1¼m, by Woodman): dam unraced: tailed off
in maidens: joined Miss J. Craze. *T. Kersey*

COUNTLESS TIMES 2 ch.c. (Jan 31) Timeless Times (USA) 99 – Arroganza 55
62 (Crofthall 110) [1996 5g 5g 6m 5m6 a7g a6g3 a5g2 Dec 31] 18,000Y: neat colt:
third foal: half-brother to 5f winners Eluned May and (3-y-o) Johayro, both by
Clantime: dam 2-y-o 5f winner: modest maiden at best: best form at sprint distances:
acts on equitrack: flashed tail and hung fourth start: slowly away (ran well) final one.
W. R. Muir

COUNT OF FLANDERS (IRE) 6 b.g. Green Desert (USA) 127 – Marie de –
Flandre (FR) 109 (Crystal Palace (FR) 132) [1995 NR 1996 8.9g Sep 4] lengthy

gelding: fairly useful at 3 yrs over 1¼m: visored, always well behind in claimer at York on return: won selling hurdle in October. *K. A. Morgan*

COUNT ROBERTO (USA) 2 ch.c. (Apr 5) El Gran Senor (USA) 136 – Numeral (USA) (Alleged (USA) 138) [1996 7m⁴ 7d³ 6m⁶ 6m* Oct 7] angular colt: fourth foal: brother to 3-y-o Foreign Judgement and a minor winner in USA: dam, minor winner in USA, half-sister to Grade 2 winners Luminaire and Wistful: started off in listed race at Newbury: won nursery at Pontefract on final outing by 3½ lengths: bred to be suited by further than 6f: sold 30,000 gns Newmarket Autumn Sales. *P. W. Chapple-Hyam*   84

COUNTRY LOVER 5 ch.g. Thatching 131 – Fair Country 89 (Town And Country 124) [1995 81: 8g 10m 10m⁵ 8.9m 10.4m 10f 8m 8d² 8m⁵ 8m 1996 8s⁵ 8v 7.5v 8s⁵ 8s 8m 10m⁴ 10s* 12m 9f 10d⁵ 12d² 12s² Oct 26] strong gelding: fair handicapper: won weak claimer at Goodwood in May: stays 1½m: acts on firm and soft going: probably effective visored (usually was in 1996) or not: joined M Pipe. *Lord Huntingdon*   77

COUNTRY THATCH 3 b.g. Thatching 131 – Alencon (Northfields (USA)) [1995 56p: 6d 5s 1996 6g 7m 7g 8.1m Sep 18] neat gelding: modest maiden handicapper: disappointing in 1996: should prove suited by further than 7f. *C. A. Horgan*   –

COUNT TONY 2 ch.g. (Apr 7) Keen 116 – Turtle Dove (Gyr (USA) 131) [1996 a7g⁴ 8g 8m Sep 19] half-brother to numerous winners, including 3-y-o 1½m winner Jump The Lights (by Siberian Express) and useful middle-distance stayer Path of Peace (by Warpath): dam ran once: modest form: may do better over middle distances. *S. P. C. Woods*   59

COURAGEOUS DANCER (IRE) 4 b.f. Cadeaux Genereux 131 – Hafwah (Gorytus (USA) 132) [1995 94: 7m³ 8.2m³ 6g* 7m* 7g⁵ 7m⁴ 6m⁵ 7g 8d² 8s⁴ 1996 7g³ 7s 8.1d⁵ 6.1m 7.9g⁶ 10.1m² 8.3d⁶ 8g² 8.1d 7g Oct 19] strong, lengthy filly: only a fair handicapper in 1996: stays 1¼m: winner on good to firm ground but best form on a soft surface: has had tongue tied. *B. Hanbury*   79

COURAGEOUS KNIGHT 7 gr.g. Midyan (USA) 124 – Little Mercy 90 (No Mercy 126) [1995 NR 1996 7.1m Jul 25] rated 60 for J. M. Bradley on reappearance at 5 yrs: well beaten only outing in 1996: stays 10.2f: best efforts on a sound surface: modest hurdler. *P. Hayward*   –

COURBARIL 4 b.g. Warrshan (USA) 117 – Free On Board 73 (Free State 125) [1995 65: 8.5d⁶ 10s⁵ 10s* 10s 10.3g⁶ 12m² 12.5f⁴ 11.6m⁵ 12m³ 14m 11.9f* 11.6m³ 12g 12g⁶ 1996 a12g⁴ a12g 11.9f³ 15.4f² 17.2f³ 16d 11.5f 12m 11.9f² 11.6d² Aug 12] neat gelding: modest performer on flat: refused to race (under inexperienced amateur) eighth start: claimed £8,000 after winning over hurdles in September and won for M. Pipe 4 times in October: stays 17.2f when conditions aren't testing: acts on equitrack and on any turf going: visored (ran well) ninth 4-y-o start: temperamental. *S. Dow*   61 §

COUREUR 7 b.g. Ajdal (USA) 130 – Nihad 76 (Alleged (USA) 138) [1995 71: 8g² 8.5d* 10f³ 8.5m³ 8.9g 10f 1996 10.3d 8g 8.5g* 8s² 8.5m³ 8m Sep 20] big, close-coupled gelding: had a round action: fair handicapper: won at Beverley in May: won 2 novice hurdles in the summer but reportedly finished lame in October: effective at 1m to 1¼m: acts on any going: dead. *M. D. Hammond*   73

COURSE FISHING 5 ch.g. Squill (USA) 122 – Migoletty 59 (Oats 126) [1995 47: 10m⁴ a8.5g 12.5g 10.8m 10.8m* 12m⁵ 10m⁵ 10m² 10.2m* 10m 10.4m 1996 8f⁶ 10g 10f 12.3m* 12.3g⁵ 10.2g⁴ 14s 13.6m Oct 17] leggy, short-backed gelding: poor mover: poor handicapper: won strongly-run race at Ripon in August, leading inside final 1f: stays 12.3f: acts on firm and dead ground, possibly not on soft: takes good hold. *B. A. McMahon*   49

COURT EXPRESS 2 b.c. (May 4) Then Again 126 – Moon Risk 62 (Risk Me (FR) 127) [1996 7.1f⁵ 7g 6m⁵ Oct 23] leggy, unfurnished colt: second foal: half-brother to 3-y-o Cawdor Lady (by Clantime): dam twice-raced half-sister to smart sprinter Jonacris: modest form in maidens: best effort final start: bred to stay 1m: gelded: may do better. *T. J. Etherington*   60

COURT HOUSE 2 b.c. (Feb 12) Reprimand 122 – Chalet Girl (Double Form 130) [1996 a5g a6g⁵ 5g 7m⁶ Aug 26] 5,400F, 4,200Y: leggy, sparely-made colt: eighth foal: closely related to a winner abroad by Runnett and half-brother to 2   59 others: dam unraced: modest form: stays 7f: sweating last 2 starts: difficult stalls final outing: has flashed tail. *B. A. McMahon*

COURTING DANGER 3 b.g. Tina's Pet 121 – Court Town 60 (Camden Town 125) [1995 57+: 6d 6d⁴ 1996 8d³ 7m May 3] workmanlike gelding: fair maiden: tailed off as though something amiss final start: stays 1m: acts on dead ground. *D. R. Gandolfo* — 67

COURTING NEWMARKET 8 b.g. Final Straw 127 – Warm Wind 84 (Tumble Wind (USA)) [1995 43: a7g a7g 7m 7g 7.1m 9m⁶ 8.1m² 8.3m 1996 8d 6f⁶ 7f 7m Jul 10] leggy, good-topped gelding: unimpressive mover: only poor at best nowadays: should stay 1m: acts on firm and dead ground, and the all-weather: tried blinkered, not for long time: inconsistent: joined Miss K. George. *N. M. Babbage* — 41

COURT JESTER 5 gr.g. Petong 126 – First Experience 58 (Le Johnstan 123) [1995 NR 1996 a10g 16m Sep 16] seems no longer of much account. *M. J. Ryan* — –

COURT OF HONOUR (IRE) 4 b.c. Law Society (USA) 130 – Captive Island 116 (Northfields (USA)) [1995 118: 12.3m² 12m² 12f⁵ 12m 12d³ 15s² 12d* 1996 13.9f³ 16.4d³ 14d² 16m 12g Nov 16] strong, rangy colt: smart performer: placed behind Classic Cliche in Yorkshire Cup (beaten 3½ lengths) and Double Trigger in Henry II Stakes at Sandown in the spring then behind Moonax in minor event at Haydock in September: well beaten in Melbourne Cup at Flemington, under 4 lengths eighth of 11 in Group 2 race at Sandown, both in Australia: shapes as if will prove suited by a thorough test of stamina: acts on firm and dead ground, probably on soft: has joined P. Hayes in Australia. *P. W. Chapple-Hyam* — 118

COURTSHIP 2 b.c. (Apr 28) Groom Dancer (USA) 128 – Dance Quest (FR) 117 (Green Dancer (USA) 132) [1996 7m² 7m* Oct 23] rangy, attractive colt: has scope: good walker: seventh living foal: brother to very smart 6f to 1m performer Pursuit of Love and half-brother to 3-y-o 7f winner Divine Quest, smart French sprinter Divine Danse and a winner in Singapore (all by Kris): dam French sprinter: odds-on winner of slowly-run maiden at Yarmouth in October: will stay 1m: almost certainly capable of further improvement. *H. R. A. Cecil* — 88 p

COVEN MOON 6 ch.m. Crofthall 110 – Mayspark 50 (Stanford 121§) [1995 39: a8g² a8g⁶ a8g 10.8m a9.4g 10m* a10g⁶ 1996 8.2m⁵ 9.7g 8g⁵ 8f Jul 17] leggy mare: poor performer: effective at 1m and 1¼m: acts on good to firm and soft ground and the all-weather: visored nowadays: inconsistent. *D. Morris* — 30

COVERED GIRL (IRE) 3 b.f. Thatching 131 – Tootle (Main Reef 126) [1995 NR 1996 7d 7g 7m a8g 8d Sep 30] IR 24,000Y: strong, compact filly: fourth foal: half-sister to 2 winners, notably fairly useful Suaad (7f at 2 yrs, by Fools Holme): dam (sprint winner in France) daughter of Prix Saint-Alary winner Tootens: modest maiden: well beaten after second start: sold 800 gns Newmarket December Sales. *B. W. Hills* — 58

COWBOY DREAMS (IRE) 3 b.g. Nashamaa 113 – Shahrazad (Young Emperor 133) [1995 –: 6m⁵ 6m 7.1d 1996 8m 6.9m⁴ 8.3g⁶ Jul 5] rather leggy, angular gelding: signs of just a little ability: visored (finished last) final 3-y-o start. *M. H. Tompkins* — –

COWRIE 2 b.f. (Jan 19) Efisio 120 – Bawbee 91§ (Dunbeath (USA) 127) [1996 5m* 6f⁵ 6m⁴ 6m Oct 5] small, good-bodied filly: second foal: closely related to 1994 2-y-o 6f winner Chattel (by Forzando): dam, ungenuine, stayed 1½m and from staying family: won maiden at Leicester in June: appeared to run very well when never-dangerous fourth to Air Express in Yarmouth minor event on penultimate start: bred to stay beyond 6f: gave trouble at stalls on debut and when withdrawn from Queen Mary Stakes: sold 11,000 gns Newmarket Autumn Sales: sent to Norway. *R. F. Johnson Houghton* — 86 ?

COWTHAREE 2 ch.f. (May 4) Arazi (USA) 135 – Hawait Al Barr 100 (Green Desert (USA) 127) [1996 6.9m³ Aug 20] first foal: dam best at 2m, from the family of Crowned Prince and Majestic Prince: made running when third in maiden at Folkestone: should improve. *M. R. Stoute* — 70 p

COYOTE BLUFF (IRE) 3 gr.g. Fayruz 116 – Ikala (Lashkari 128) [1995 74: 5d⁵ 7g a6g³ 1996 9g³ 7.5m* Apr 25] leggy, useful-looking gelding: second foal: half-brother to Italian 4-y-o 1m winner Runaway Wel (by Fayruz): dam fourth in Irish 2½m bumpers: fairly useful performer: won rated stakes at Beverley in April, — 83 leading 2f out and battling on well: stays 9f: acts on good to firm and dead ground, below form on fibresand: game: has been gelded: sent to Hong Kong. *P. W. Chapple-Hyam*

CRABBIE'S PRIDE   3 ch.g. Red Sunset 120 – Free Rein (Sagaro 133) [1995 NR 1996 7.1g[4] 10.3g 10.5d[6] 9m[6] 10.3d a8.5g 14d Sep 28] 6,200F, 11,500 2-y-o: plain gelding: brother to 6 winners (fairly useful at best) including fair Ice Magic (1¼m): dam unraced from family of Troy: fair maiden: left A. Bailey after fourth start: no form afterwards: stays 10.5f: hung badly left on debut. *M. G. Meagher*   69 d

CRAIGIE BOY   6 b.g. Crofthall 110 – Lady Carol 42 (Lord Gayle (USA) 124) [1995 65d: 5g 6g[3] 7m 5g 6f[6] 6m 6m 6d 6g 6d[3] 6g[2] 5d[6] 5m 6m 1996 7.5d 5g 6d[6] 6s* 5s[3] 7g 6g[2] 6g[6] 6m 6d[6] 6s 5g[5] 6d 6m a7g[6] a7g a6g[2] Dec 27] leggy gelding: just a modest handicapper nowadays: well drawn, won at Hamilton (fourth course success, no wins elsewhere) in May: stays 6f well: probably acts on any going (poor form on fibresand), though best recent form on a soft surface: usually blinkered/visored nowadays: tends to wander: inconsistent. *N. Bycroft*   58 d a44

CRAIGIEVAR   2 b.c. (Mar 1) Mujadil (USA) 119 – Sweet Home (Home Guard (USA) 129) [1996 6m[4] 6f* 6.1s* Oct 31] 9,800F, 8,500Y, 14,500 2-y-o: leggy, unfurnished colt: has a quick action: seventh foal: half-brother to 3 winners abroad, including French 1m winner Warshanor (by Warrshan): dam 6f winner in USA from the family of Irish 1000 Guineas winner Miralla: progressive form: won maiden auction at Warwick in October: useful performance when winning nursery at Nottingham later in month by 5 lengths, travelling strongly throughout: will stay 7f: acts on any going: will improve further. *J. R. Fanshawe*   94 p

CRAIGMORE MAGIC (USA)   3 br.g. Simply Majestic (USA) – Some Rehearsal (USA) (Halo (USA)) [1995 –: a6g[6] 7m[5] a7g 7.1g[6] 1996 6.9m[3] 8g a8g 8m[5] 9.9g 12g Oct 18] sturdy gelding: has a round action: poor maiden: should stay further than 1m (ran poorly when tried): tried blinkered, no improvement. *Miss M. K. Milligan*   41

CRAIGNAIRN   3 b.g. Merdon Melody 98 – Bri-Ette 53 (Brittany) [1995 76: 5f[3] 6f[3] 7g[6] 6h[6] 7.1m[5] 6g[2] 6m[2] 1996 7s 6m 5.9f* 7s 6m[4] 6f 6g[4] 6d 7g a6g Dec 27] angular gelding: only modest at best in 1996: made all in maiden at Carlisle in June: left Jack Berry after eighth 3-y-o start: tailed off on return: stays 6f: best efforts on top-of-the-ground: blinkered (except once) since third 3-y-o start: most inconsistent. *J. L. Eyre*   64 d

CRAMBELLA (IRE)   4 b.f. Red Sunset 120 – Simbella (Simbir 130) [1995 NR 1996 8m 12f[4] 12m[3] 12.1m[4] Sep 23] sixth foal: half-sister to Irish 1m winner Class Apart (by Martinmas) and sister to a winning hurdler: dam Irish 1½m winner: bad maiden: stays 1½m. *G. P. Kelly*   30

CRANDON BOULEVARD   3 b.c. Niniski (USA) 125 – Last Clear Chance (USA) (Alleged (USA) 138) [1995 NR 1996 10.2g 12m[2] 14m[4] Aug 22] small colt: closely related to fairly useful Bridal Train (stayed 9f, by Gorytus) and half-brother to 2 winners, including fair Diskette (up to 1½m, by Local Suitor): dam ran once: progressive maiden: may do better over further than 1¾m: joined Mrs J. Pitman. *Lord Huntingdon*   69

CRAVEN COTTAGE   3 b.g. Inca Chief (USA) – Seymour Ann (Krayyan 117) [1995 56: 6m 7.6d 1996 8g 7f 7f 6f[5] 6g 10f[3] Aug 18] leggy gelding: well beaten in 1996: should stay beyond 6f: visored (well beaten) fourth 3-y-o start: tends to sweat. *C. James*   –

CRAVEN HILL (IRE)   2 gr.g. (Mar 1) Pursuit of Love 124 – Crodelle (IRE) (Formidable (USA) 125) [1996 7m Oct 3] 10,000Y: leggy, unfurnished gelding: first foal: dam French 9.5f winner: slow-starting eleventh of 16 in maiden at Newmarket: awkward stalls, swishing tail constantly: probably capable of better. *N. A. Graham*   – p

CRAZY CHIEF   3 b.c. Indian Ridge 123 – Bizarre Lady (Dalsaan 125) [1995 80: 7.6d[2] 7d[2] 6d[3] 1996 7g[5] 6.9m[3] 8m[4] 8.3m* 8.1d[2] 8.3m[4] 10m[2] 10.3d Aug 30] lengthy, useful-looking colt: fairly useful handicapper: won maiden at Windsor in May: disappointing effort only at Chester final start: stays 1¼m: acts on good to firm and dead ground, takes keen hold, and races prominently: consistent. *P. F. I. Cole*   85

CREDIT CONTROLLER (IRE)   7 b.g. Dromod Hill – Fotopan (Polyfoto 124) [1995 –: 14s 1996 a8.5g 14m[5] Aug 22] fourth foal: dam winning hurdler: no promise on flat. *J. Ffitch-Heyes*   –

CREDITE RISQUE   3 b.f. Risk Me (FR) 127 – Lompoa (Lomond (USA) – 128) [1995 42: 5g 5.1m 5m⁵ 1996 6.1d Apr 12] leggy filly: poor juvenile for M. McCormack: stiff task, well held only start in 1996. *J. R. Fanshawe*

CREEKING   3 b.f. Persian Bold 123 – Miller's Creek (USA) 62 (Star de Naskra   53 (USA)) [1995 59p: a6g² 1996 a8g⁴ a7g² a8g² a8g⁴ 8.1f⁵ 8f² 8.1g⁶ 10f⁴ 7f² 7.1m⁴ 8m   a65 Sep 19] modest maiden: effective at 7f, and stays 1¼m: acts on equitrack (best form) and firm ground: blinkered (no improvement) twice at 3 yrs: front runner: consistent. *Sir Mark Prescott*

CRESTED KNIGHT (IRE)   4 gr.g. Night Shift (USA) – Casual (USA) (Caro   58 133) [1995 69: 10.3g 10.8m⁴ 8f² 7.1g 8s 9.7g 1996 8f 12m⁴ 14g 12m⁴ 14m 13.1m 8m* Sep 25] leggy, good-topped gelding: just a modest handicapper nowadays: won claiming handicap at Goodwood in September, leading under 3f out and staying on: similar form in 1996 at 1m and 1½m, may prove suited by the shorter trip: acts on firm ground, shaped well on soft: has worn net muzzle: inconsistent. *C. A. Horgan*

CREST WING (USA)   3 b.c. Storm Bird (CAN) 134 – Purify (USA) (Fappiano   – (USA)) [1995 NR 1996 10d 8g 10g⁴ Jul 20] tall colt: fourth foal: half-brother to 3 minor winners, including French middle-distance stayer Sanzio (by Greinton): dam minor winner at around 1m: tailed off in maidens: sold (P. Chapple-Hyam to T. McGovern) 5,000 gns Newmarket Autumn Sales: gelded. *P. W. Chapple-Hyam*

CRETAN GIFT   5 ch.g. Cadeaux Genereux 131 – Caro's Niece (USA) 86 (Caro   82 133) [1995 62, a78: a6g² a6g* a6g 6m a6g⁴ 6.1d² a6g* a6g* 6f⁵ 7m a7g a6g² 1996   a94 a7g⁴ a6g³ a6g⁴ a7g² a7g² 6.1g² 7m a5g* a6g⁶ 6m² 6.1m a7g² 6m² a6g* 6g⁴ 6m⁶ 6m³ 7.6m⁶ 6m⁶ 6.1d⁴ 5.1d 6f⁵ 5.1m* 6m* 6g 5g 6f* a7g⁵ Dec 7] lengthy gelding: had a very good season and is a fairly useful handicapper: won at Wolverhampton in April (claimer) and June, at Nottingham and Ayr (Silver Cup, held Thwaab by a short head despite drifting left) in September, and at Redcar (25-runner contest, by a short head) in November: effective at 5f to 7f: acts on firm and dead ground and on fibresand:

Ladbroke (Ayr) Silver Cup (Handicap)—a blanket finish; the first five are Cretan Gift, Thwaab (No. 22), La Petite Fusee (No. 3), Wardara (No. 19) and Denbrae (No. 17)

usually blinkered/visored, ran well only 5-y-o outing when without: wears crossed/dropped noseband: very tough. *N. P. Littmoden*

CRIMSON ROSELLA 3 b. or br.f. Polar Falcon (USA) 126 – Double Finesse 97 (Double Jump 131) [1995 –p: 7f⁶ 1996 6.9m 7m⁶ 7f⁶ 10f 12m³ 14.1f a12g Aug 9] leggy, attractive filly: fluent mover: seems just a modest maiden at best: tailed off last 2 starts: probably stays 1½m: inconsistent. *W. J. Haggas* — 54

CRIMSON TIDE (IRE) 2 b.c. (Mar 27) Sadler's Wells (USA) 132 – Sharata (IRE) (Darshaan 133) [1996 7d² 7g* Oct 19] leggy, quite attractive colt: fluent mover: third foal: half-brother to useful Irish 4-y-o 9f to 1¾m winner Sharatan (by Kahyasi): dam unraced half-sister to Shahrastani: won Houghton Stakes at Newmarket in October running on well by a length from Danetime: will stay middle distances: probably a very useful prospect. *J. W. Hills* — 95 p

CRINOLETTE (IRE) 2 b.f. (May 7) Sadler's Wells (USA) 132 – Organza 105 (High Top 131) [1996 8.2g Oct 24] 240,000Y: third foal: half-sister to Irish 3-y-o 1½m winner Dansk (by Danehill) and very smart Irish 6f/7f performer Desert Style (by Green Desert): dam, 1¼m winner, half-sister to Brocade, dam of Barathea (by Sadler's Wells): very slowly away in maiden at Nottingham: almost certainly capable of better. *J. H. M. Gosden* — – p

CRISSEM (IRE) 3 b.f. Thatching 131 – Deer Emily (Alzao (USA) 117) [1995 70: 6m⁵ 5f³ 5f* 7d 1996 5d Apr 24] workmanlike filly: has scope: fair form as a juvenile: tailed off only 3-y-o start: will probably stay 1m. *R. Hollinshead* — –

CROAGH PATRICK (IRE) 4 b.g. Faustus (USA) 118 – Pink Pumpkin 52 (Tickled Pink 114) [1995 NR 1996 7m 7m 8.3m 7s a7s Dec 19] second foal: dam sprinter: behind all starts. *J. C. Fox* — –

CROESO CYNNES 3 ch.f. Most Welcome 131 – Miss Taleca (Pharly (FR) 130) [1995 70d: 5.1m 6g* 6m⁶ 6f⁵ 6.1d 6d 6.1s 1996 6g⁴ 6m² 5f⁴ 6g* 6m² 6m⁴ 5m* 6d⁴ 6m Sep 6] compact filly: fair handicapper: won at Windsor and Kempton in the summer: successful at 6f, best form at 5f: acts on dead going, very best form on a sound surface: visored (below form) final 2-y-o outing: takes keen hold, and usually races prominently. *B. Palling* — 70

CROFTERS CEILIDH 4 ch.f. Scottish Reel 123 – Highland Rowena 59 (Royben 125) [1995 –: 5f⁴ 6g 5m 1996 5m 5.1f⁴ 5g 5m 5.2m 5.1d 5.2m⁴ 5.1g* 5s³ 5g⁶ 5g Oct 26] leggy filly: fairly useful on balance of form, flattered by fourth of 9 to Struggler in minor event at Newbury (could be rated 98) on seventh 4-y-o outing: — 90

Owen Brown Houghton Conditions Stakes, Newmarket—useful youngsters Crimson Tide (right) and Danetime

won strongly-run race at Chester in September: ideally suited by 5f on a sound surface: blinkered/visored since sixth 4-y-o start. *B. A. McMahon*

CROFT POOL 5 b.g. Crofthall 110 – Blackpool Belle 70 (The Brianstan 128) 111 [1995 99, a86: a6g* a6g² a6g⁵ a6g³ 6m² 5g⁵ 6m² 6g² 6m 6m 6.1m² 6f² 6m 6g 5g* a– 5m*ᵈⁱˢ 5m* 6m⁴ a6g 1996 5m 5m³ 5m² 5m³ 5m³ 6m 5f* 5m⁵ 5g³ 5m* 5d² 6s Nov 9] sturdy, quite attractive gelding: impresses in appearance: smart performer, better than ever in 1996: won minor event at Leicester and listed race at Newmarket (got up near finish to beat Blue Iris ¾ length) in the autumn: placed in King George Stakes at Goodwood fifth start and Prix du Petit Couvert at Longchamp penultimate one: effective at 5f (best form) and 6f: acts on firm and dead ground (rare poor effort on soft) and successful on the all-weather: visored (below form) once: tends to idle: tough and consistent. *J. A. Glover*

CROMABOO CROWN 5 b.m. Crowning Honors (CAN) – La Belle Epoque – (Tachypous 128) [1995 NR 1996 a12g⁶ Jul 27] fourth foal: dam ran once: tailed off in seller. *P. J. Bevan*

CROSBY NOD 2 b.g. (Mar 31) Shalford (IRE) 124§ – Kirkby Belle 44 (Bay – Express 132) [1996 6s 6m 6d Nov 8] 5,800Y: strong, sturdy gelding: has scope: first foal: dam poor maiden, stayed 7f: well beaten in varied events: very burly first 2 starts. *E. Weymes*

CROSSILLION 8 b.g. Rousillon (USA) 133 – Croda Rossa (ITY) (Grey 84 Sovereign 128§) [1995 NR 1996 7.6g May 9] lengthy gelding: carries condition: easy mover: rated 88 in 1994: seventh of 18 at Chester on only run since, not unduly knocked about once held: effective at 1m to 1¼m: acts on firm ground, dead and equitrack: effective held up or making the running. *G. Wragg*

CROSS OF VALOUR 3 b.g. Never So Bold 135 – X-Data 93 (On Your Mark 79 125) [1995 NR 1996 7m 6f* 6f² 7m 6m 6m² 7.3m a6s Dec 19] 3,600F, 7,200Y: smallish, sturdy gelding: half-brother to several winners, notably fairly useful sprinter Dry Point (by Sharpo): dam winning sprinter: fair form: won maiden at Folkestone in June: sold out of J. Toller's stable 7,500 gns Newmarket Autumn Sales after penultimate start: stays 6f (pulled hard over 7.3f): raced only on top-of-the-ground on turf, tailed off on fibresand: inconsistent. *P. Howling*

CROSS TALK (IRE) 4 b.g. Darshaan 133 – Liaison (USA) (Blushing Groom 70 (FR) 131) [1995 70: 8d 12f 8m⁶ 11.1f² 13.4m² 13.8g* 10.5s 11.8g 11.8f⁵ 1996 a12g a62 a16g a12g⁵ a12g⁴ a11g a11g⁵ a16g⁴ 13.8s* 12d a12g⁴ a16g⁶ 14.1g⁴ 12g⁵ 12s 12g a14.8g 12g² 14.1g* a14g⁴ a12g⁶ Dec 20] close-coupled gelding: poor mover: fair handicapper on turf: won at Catterick in March, best effort: sold out of R. Hollinshead's stable 5,000 gns Doncaster August Sales after fifteenth start, then trained by N. Tinkler until after penultimate one: won weak claimer at Yarmouth in October: probably stays 2m: acts on firm ground, soft and all-weather: sometimes hangs. *R. M. Stronge*

CROSS THE BORDER 3 b.g. Statoblest 120 – Brave Advance (USA) 98 (Bold 96 d Laddie (USA)) [1995 89: 6g 5m² 5m* 5f² 5g³ 6g³ 1996 5g² 5d⁵ 5s 5f 5m 6v 5g 5s Nov 8] strong, attractive gelding: looking in need of race, best effort when second of 9 in rated stakes at Sandown on reappearance, soon disputing lead and battling on

JRA Nakayama Rous Stakes, Newmarket—Croft Pool beats Blue Iris and Anzio (rails)

well: disappointing afterwards, showing virtually no form: left R. Hannon after fourth start: easily best form at 5f: acts on firm ground. *D. Nicholls*

CROWDED AVENUE   4 b.g. Sizzling Melody 117 – Lady Bequick 81 (Sharpen   105
Up 127) [1995 101p: 6m 5.1f⁶ 5g* 5m* 5m² 5m* 5m² 5m* 5m* 5g 1996 5.1g 5m³
5f³ 5m 5m⁵ 5m 5m* 5g Sep 29] compact gelding: useful performer: 3 lengths fifth to
Rambling Bear in King George Stakes at Goodwood: won rated stakes at Sandown
in August, travelling smoothly and asserting inside final 1f: raced mainly at 5f: acts
on firm ground: held up, and has a good turn of foot: sometimes wears tongue strap:
tends to be on toes: sometimes sweats. *P. J. Makin*

CROWN AND CUSHION   3 b.g. High Adventure 82 – Soulieana 58 (Manado   –
130) [1995 NR 1996 a8.5g a9.4g 10.8f 10f Jul 20] third reported foal: dam maiden
raced only at 2 yrs: no sign of ability on flat: 100/1-winner of juvenile hurdle in
November: joined T. R. Greathead. *K. S. Bridgwater*

CROWN COURT (USA)   3 b.c. Chief's Crown (USA) – Bold Courtesan (USA)   91 p
(Bold Bidder) [1995 NR 1996 8m⁶ 10d⁶ 8.5f³ 8g* 10m³ 9m Oct 5] $80,000Y:
big, heavy-topped colt: unimpressive mover with a round action: half-brother to
useful 7f/1m performer Diesan (by Diesis) and a winner in France: dam, showed a
little ability at 2 yrs in France, sister to high-class French sprinter Parioli: generally
progressive form: easy winner of handicap at Newmarket in July: again in
tremendous shape, best effort when third of 14 to Fahim in £34,000 handicap at
Goodwood: has shown his form at 1¼m but may well prove ideally suited by slightly
shorter: acts on good to firm ground, did not look entirely at ease on firm: normally
bandaged: has plenty of physical scope, and should make a better four-year-old.
L. M. Cumani

CROWNING TINO   4 b.f. Crowning Honors (CAN) – Tino Reppin 46 (Neltino   –
97) [1995 –: 8.2d 8m 7g a7g 1996 a7g a12g a7g 6.1m 7m May 27] sparely-made
filly: seems of no account. *Mrs N. Macauley*

CROWN OF LIGHT   2 b.f. (Feb 2) Mtoto 134 – Russian Countess (USA) 104   77 p
(Nureyev (USA) 131) [1996 7g* Aug 12] fourth foal: half-sister to Irish 3-y-o 6f
winner Cossack Count (by Nashwan), useful 7f and 8.5f winner Romanzof (by Kris)
and a winner in Belgium by Reference Point: dam won at 1m at 2 yrs in France: won
median auction maiden at Leicester in August on only start by head from Ciro's
Pearl: will be suited by 1m+: sure to improve. *M. R. Stoute*

CRUMPTON HILL (IRE)   4 b.g. Thatching 131 – Senane 86 (Vitiges (FR)   94
132) [1995 88: 8m* 8.1g³ 8g 8d 9g 8m 1996 8m³ 8m³ 7m* 7m³ Aug 10] workman-

Ladbroke Bunbury Cup (Handicap), Newmarket—Crumpton Hill just prevails from Rabican and Mullitover

like gelding: fairly useful handicapper: ran in competitive events in 1996: third at Kempton and Royal Ascot: won 16-runner Ladbroke Bunbury Cup at Newmarket in July, finding trouble-free run in rough race and getting up inside final 1f to beat Rabican ½ length: good third of 14 in New Zealand Handicap there (bumped halfway, quickened and every chance final 1f) following month: effective at 7f to 9f: acts on good to firm going, probably on dead: has a high head carriage: has run well when sweating: takes keen hold, and usually held up. *N. A. Graham*

CRUZ SANTA 3 b.f. Lord Bud 121 – Linpac Mapleleaf 69 (Dominion 123) [1995 NR 1996 7s² 7f⁶ 5g 6g 7g Sep 21] 900Y: fourth reported foal: half-sister to fairly useful 5-y-o 5f and 6f winner Palo Blanco (by Precocious): dam 11.5f winner at 5 yrs: modest maiden: should stay 1m: best effort on soft ground. *T. D. Barron*   53

CRY BABY 3 b.g. Bairn (USA) 126 – Estonia (Kings Lake (USA) 133) [1995 51: 7g⁶ a7g 7f 8.3g⁶ 8f 1996 10.8g⁶ 12m 10.8g* 10m⁵ 12.1g³ 10.1f⁵ Jul 21] leggy gelding: poor performer: won weak claimer at Warwick in May: sold (N. Tinkler to A. Whillans) 2,500 gns Doncaster August Sales and gelded: probably stays 1½m: blinkered since third 3-y-o start. *N. Tinkler*   40

CRYHAVOC 2 b.c. (Feb 26) Polar Falcon (USA) 126 – Sarabah (IRE) 83 (Ela-Mana-Mou 132) [1996 5.7f 6f⁴ 5g³ 6m* 6m* Oct 17] 30,000Y: sturdy, quite attractive colt: first foal: dam 1¼m winner: progressive form: won maiden at Epsom in September and nursery at Newmarket in October: will probably stay 1m: acts on top-of-the-ground: open to further improvement. *J. R. Arnold*   90 p

CRYSTAL CROSSING (IRE) 2 b.f. (Mar 3) Royal Academy (USA) 130 – Never So Fair 65 (Never So Bold 135) [1996 6m² 6f* 7g⁶ Sep 8] lengthy, unfurnished filly: has a quick action: third foal: half-sister to 3-y-o 1¼m winner Lady Banks (by Alzao): dam thrice-raced close relative of smart 5f performer Amaranda and half-sister to very smart (at up to 1m) Favoridge: useful form: won listed race at Newbury in July readily by 2 lengths from Omaha City: short of room for much of straight when 2½ lengths sixth of 10 to Bianca Nera in Moyglare Stud Stakes at the Curragh on final start: stays 7f: may do better. *P. W. Chapple-Hyam*   99

CRYSTAL FALLS (IRE) 3 b.r. Alzao (USA) 117 – Honourable Sheba (USA) (Roberto (USA) 131) [1995 82: 7.5g⁶ 6m² 6m² 7g³ 8g 7.1s² 8m* 1996 7g Apr 8] fair performer: some promise in handicap at Newcastle only 3-y-o start: will stay beyond 1m: acts on good to firm and soft ground. *J. J. O'Neill*   –

CRYSTAL FAST (USA) 3 b.g. Fast Play (USA) – Crystal Cave (USA) (Nearctic) [1995 –: a8g 1996 a8.5g⁵ a8g⁵ a8g² 10.3s 8.2d a12g⁶ 9.9g⁵ 8m 7.5m 8m Aug 2] big, workmanlike gelding: modest maiden on all-weather: poor on turf: stays 1¼m: blinkered (stiff task, made most) final 3-y-o start: inconsistent. *P. A. Kelleway*   40 a57

CRYSTAL GOLD 2 ch.c. (Apr 6) Arazi (USA) 135 – Crystal Land (Kris 135) [1996 7f 7g Oct 30] strong, useful-looking colt: third foal: half-brother to 1¼m winner King's Crown (by Lead On Time): dam lightly-raced daughter of Greenland Park, dam also of Fitnah: signs of ability in autumn maidens: coltish on debut: capable of better. *M. R. Stoute*   66 p

CRYSTAL HEARTED 2 b.c. (Apr 25) Broken Hearted 124 – Crystal Fountain (Great Nephew 126) [1996 7.1m⁴ 7f* Oct 8] 8,600Y: tall, leggy colt: half-brother to several winners, including 1993 2-y-o 6.9f winner Summer Hail (by Thatching) and useful stayer High Fountain (by High Line): dam once-raced half-sister to Royal Palace (also the family of Broken Hearted): won maiden at Warwick in October by 1¾ lengths (value 5) from Burundi: will stay 1¼m: will improve again. *H. Candy*   85 p

CRYSTAL HEIGHTS (FR) 8 ch.g. Crystal Glitters (USA) 127 – Fahrenheit 69 (Mount Hagen (FR) 127) [1995 71: a6g* a6g⁴ a6g² a6g³ a7g⁴ a6g² 7m⁶ 6f⁴ 6f⁵ 6m⁴ 7m 6.9g² 7f* a7g⁴ 7m² 8.5s 7g* a7g² a7g 7g* a7g⁵ a7g* 7f⁶ 7f 7f 7g³ 7m 7f* 6f* 6f* 6g Aug 24] big, strong, lengthy gelding: fair handicapper: won at Lingfield in February and 3 times at Brighton (hasn't won elsewhere on turf) in the summer: stays 7f: acts on firm ground and all-weather surfaces, possibly not on soft: tried blinkered/visored at 4 yrs, no improvement: often bandaged: often slowly away. *R. J. O'Sullivan*   73

CRYSTAL HILLS (IRE) 2 b.c. (Feb 20) Darshaan 133 – Lustre (USA) 90 (Halo (USA)) [1996 8d Oct 2] fifth foal: closely related to smart 4-y-o middle-distance filly Valley of Gold (by Shirley Heights): dam, 2-y-o 6f winner who stayed   – p

9f, is half-sister to smart middle-distance filly Whitehaven and daughter of Kentucky Oaks winner White Star Line: needed experience when never dangerous in maiden at Salisbury: should do better. *J. H. M. Gosden*

CRYSTAL LOOP 4 b.f. Dowsing (USA) 124 – Gipping 72 (Vision (USA)) [1995 69, a77: a6g* a6g⁵ a6g² a7g* a5g⁴ a6g* 5g 6m 6.1m 5g² 6g² 5.1g 6m⁴ 6m² 5.1m* 6m⁵ 5f 5f 5m* 5.1d 5g 5g a6g a6g 1996 a5g Jan 24] fair handicapper: broke leg at Wolverhampton on reappearance: stayed 7f: acted on all-weather surfaces and good to firm ground: raced prominently: dead. *A. Bailey* —

CRYSTAL WARRIOR 3 b.f. Warrshan (USA) 117 – Crystal's Solo (USA) (Crystal Water (USA)) [1995 55p: 7.1s⁵ 1996 8d 10g⁴ 10m 10m 11.1m a9.4g Nov 11] workmanlike filly: modest maiden: failed to reproduce form of second 3-y-o start: should stay further than 1¼m: reluctant at stalls third 3-y-o outing. *D. Nicholls* 62 d

CUANGO (IRE) 5 b. or br.h. Mtoto 134 – Barinia (Corvaro (USA) 124) [1995 78d: 14.1g³ 14m³ 13.9g³ 14g⁵ 14g⁴ 16.2f 14.6g⁵ 14m³ 14.8m⁴ 14f⁶ 13.9g 15.9d 14s 12.1d³ 14.6m³ 14.1m* 15.1s a14.8g² a16g⁵ 1996 a13g* a16g³ a12g* a12g⁵ a12g² 12g⁶ 11.8d 14.1s³ 14.1g⁴ 14.1m* 13.3s⁵ 14d⁵ 14.1m⁴ Jun 19] close-coupled horse: fair handicapper, formerly unreliable: won at Lingfield in January (amateurs) and February and at Nottingham in April: sold only 2,200 gns Newmarket Autumn Sales: stays 2m: acts on the all-weather and on soft and good to firm ground: normally held up: sent to Saudi Arabia. *R. Hollinshead* 63 a76

CUBAN NIGHTS (USA) 4 b.g. Our Native (USA) – Havana Moon (USA) (Cox's Ridge (USA)) [1995 60d: 8g 6m 8m 6f 8.5g 8f³ 9m² 10m 10m⁴ 12s⁶ 9.7g 1996 a11g⁶ a9.4g² a12g* a12g⁵ a12g* a12g⁵ 10.5d 14f⁵ Jul 13] sturdy ex-Irish gelding: modest handicapper: won at Wolverhampton in March and at Southwell in May: failed to reproduce that form back on turf: stays 1½m: acts on firm ground and fibresand: blinkered last 4 starts in Ireland: modest winning hurdler. *B. J. Llewellyn* — a70

CUBAN REEF 4 b.f. Dowsing (USA) 124 – Cox's Pippin (USA) (Cox's Ridge (USA)) [1995 52: a10g a8g a12g 7m³ 7m* 7g 7f³ 8.2m² 1996 8m 8g 8m³ 8.3m 8.3g 8.2m² 8.1m⁵ 8.3d⁵ 10.4g⁴ 10m* 8.9g 10.1m Oct 23] modest handicapper: won at Sandown (apprentices) in September by short head, last into straight: retained by trainer 14,000 gns Newmarket Autumn Sales: stays 10.4f: acts on firm ground, below form on the all-weather: has run well when sweating: reared leaving stalls fifth 4-y-o start. *W. J. Musson* 52

CUFF LINK (IRE) 6 ch.g. Caerleon (USA) 132 – Corinth Canal 77 (Troy 137) [1995 107: 14.4m* 16.4m⁶ 22.2m* 16f 15.9m² 18g⁵ 16g⁵ 1996 13.3d May 18] angular gelding: useful performer, twice winner of Queen Alexandra Stakes: tailed off in listed race at Newbury only 6-y-o start: stays 22.2f: acts on firm ground and dead. *Major W. R. Hern* —

CUGINA 2 b.f. (Mar 16) Distant Relative 128 – Indubitable 87 (Sharpo 132) [1996 6m 7d⁶ 7.1s Oct 22] sturdy filly: second foal: half-sister to 3-y-o Reiterate (by Then Again): dam stayed 1¾m: stayed on never dangerous in maidens last 2 starts: upset in stalls on debut: will be suited by 1m+. *G. B. Balding* 68

CULRAIN 5 b.g. Hadeer 118 – La Vie En Primrose 104 (Henbit (USA) 130) [1995 –: a12g⁵ 1996 a14.8g a12g May 2] looks of little account on flat nowadays: poor winning hurdler. *T. H. Caldwell* —

CULTURAL ICON (USA) 4 b.g. Kris S (USA) – Sea Prospector (USA) (Mr Prospector (USA)) [1995 10g 1996 a10g⁵ a12g a11g 7g Sep 14] $46,000Y: ex-Irish gelding: tenth foal: half-brother to 3 minor winners in USA: dam well-bred 6f winner: tailed off in listed race for D. Weld before sold 8,000 gns Newmarket Autumn (1995) Sales: no promise on return. *P. Mitchell* —

CUMBRIAN MAESTRO 3 b.g. Puissance 110 – Flicker Toa Flame (USA) 85 (Empery (USA) 128) [1995 67: 6d 6m⁵ 6m³ 6m⁴ 6m⁴ 8m 8g³ 7d³ 6m 1996 8.5d 8d 8m 11m⁵ 14d 9.9f* 10d² 10.4g⁶ 10.9m Sep 19] tall gelding: modest handicapper: disappointing in 1996 until winning at Beverley in August: should stay 11f: acts on firm and dead ground: probably effective blinkered or not: seems best racing up with pace. *T. D. Easterby* 61

CUMBRIAN QUEST 2 b.g. (Mar 20) Be My Chief (USA) 122 – Tinkerbird 76 (Music Boy 124) [1996 5d⁶ 6m Jun 28] 7,800Y: second foal: half-brother to 3-y-o 6f winner Bataleur (by Midyan): dam sprinter: no form: dead. *T. D. Easterby* —

CUMBRIAN RHAPSODY 6 ch.m. Sharrood (USA) 124 – Bustellina 81 60 §
(Busted 134) [1995 62§: 16.1g⁵ 14g⁶ 12.4m³ 11.9m⁴ 17.5g³ 11.9g 14s 1996 12.3m³
Aug 5] leggy, lengthy mare: has a round action: only a modest handicapper since 4
yrs: at least as effective at 1½m as 15f: acts on any going: none too consistent: sold
1,600 gns Newmarket December Sales. *T. D. Easterby*

CUPLA FOCAIL 3 b.f. Inca Chief (USA) – Lizzie Bee (Kind of Hush 118) [1995 –
–: a5g 6m⁶ 6m a6g 1996 a10g⁶ Jan 6] little sign of ability. *W. R. Muir*

CURRENT LEADER 3 b.g. Primo Dominie 121 – Trelissick (Electric 126) –
[1995 67: 5.2m 5m 7f 7f² 7g³ 7.5d 1996 8g 10m 8m⁶ 8.3g 7f⁶ Aug 7] seemed of little
account at 3 yrs: sold 1,700 gns (out of R. Hannon's stable after fourth start) in July,
500 gns in December, at Ascot Sales. *Miss K. M. George*

CURRENT SPEECH (IRE) 5 b.g. Thatching 131 – Lady Aladdin (Persian 74
Bold 123) [1995 71+: 8m 8g 8g 10d³ 10.5s 1996 10g⁵ 10m⁶ May 27] tall, close-
coupled gelding: fair handicapper: sold only 950 gns Doncaster August Sales:
will probably stay 1½m: acts on good to firm and soft ground: blinkered at 5 yrs.
T. D. Easterby

CURTELACE 6 ch.g. Nishapour (FR) 125 – Khandjar 77 (Kris 135) [1995 60§: 59 §
12m⁵ 10m⁴ 10d 10d⁴ 9f² 10g² 10f⁵ 1996 12g 10g² 10m⁵ 10f⁶ 8.9m 8.1f⁴ Jun 24] big,
plain gelding: modest handicapper: sold (Mrs M. Reveley to S. Campion) only 950
gns Doncaster August Sales: should prove at least as effective at 1½m as 1¼m: acts
on firm ground, probably on dead: blinkered (no improvement) twice: carries head
high and hangs: finds little and is not one to trust. *Mrs M. Reveley*

CURZON STREET 2 b.f. (Mar 3) Night Shift (USA) – Pine Ridge 80 (High Top 64
131) [1996 6m² 6m 7m 6g⁵ Sep 29] robust filly: ninth foal: sister to high-class 1m
to 1½m filly In The Groove and half-sister to several winners: dam 1½m winner:
running-on second in Lingfield maiden on debut: didn't progress: should stay at least
1m. *M. R. Stoute*

CUTTHROAT KID (IRE) 6 b.g. Last Tycoon 131 – Get Ahead 58 (Silly 67
Season 127) [1995 66: 12g 13v² 16f⁵ 13.1g⁵ 12.1g 1996 11.1d⁵ 13d 13s³ a16g³ 15.8s²
16f⁴ 15d 13.1g³ Aug 21] sturdy gelding: has a round action: fair handicapper:
ran poorly last 2 starts: stays 2m: acts on any going: normally visored or blinkered.
Mrs M. Reveley

CYBERTECHNOLOGY 2 b.c. (Mar 17) Environment Friend 128 – Verchinina 85
99 (Star Appeal 133) [1996 7g 7.9g* 7m² Oct 29] workmanlike colt: half-brother to
several winners, including middle distance performers General Haven and Golden
Hadeer (both by Hadeer): dam 1m winner: won steadily-run median auction maiden
at York in October, rallying gamely: ran well over shorter trip good first start: will be
suited by middle distances: raced only on a sound surface. *B. W. Hills*

CYCLONE (IRE) 5 b.g. Treasure Kay 114 – Pallachine (FR) (Lichine (USA) –
117) [1995 NR 1996 8d⁶ 11.9f Apr 22] of no account. *B. R. Millman*

CYMBALO 5 ch.g. Sharpo 132 – Cynomis 82 (Shergar 140) [1995 –: 10g 9.2f⁶ –
10.9g 1996 6d Apr 11] no sign of ability. *Miss L. A. Perratt*

CYPRESS AVENUE (IRE) 4 b.g. Law Society (USA) 130 – Flying Diva 100 –
(Chief Singer 131) [1995 95: 11m⁵ 12m³ 13.9m² 14.1f⁴ 14.6m³ 14.8g⁵ 14g⁵ 1996 16g
16d 16.4g 14g⁶ 17.2f⁴ 20m 16d Aug 25] big, strong gelding: looked of little account
in 1996: sold (R. Hannon to Mrs V. Ward) 6,000 gns Newmarket September Sales:
should stay 2m: acts on good to firm ground: no improvement in blinkers: not one to
trust. *R. Hannon*

CYRANO'S LAD (IRE) 7 b. or br.g. Cyrano de Bergerac 120 – Patiala (Crocket 104
130) [1995 96: 8.3m³ 6f² 7.6g* 7m³ 8f 7m 7g 6g² 7g* 7m³ 6d 1996 6m⁶ 7g⁴ 5m⁶ 6m*
6.1m* 6m 6m⁴ 6m⁴ 6g² 5.6m 6g⁶ 6g Oct 19] tall, good-topped gelding: unimpressive
mover: useful handicapper: made all in rated stakes at York and Chester in June: best
at up to 7f: acts on firm ground, well beaten on dead: front runner/races prominently:
game. *C. A. Dwyer*

CYRILLIC 3 ch.f. Rock City 120 – Lariston Gale 81 (Pas de Seul 133) [1995 73: 88
5m² 5m 6m* 6f³ 6m⁵ 7g 1996 8g⁶ 7m Apr 16] lengthy, sparely-made filly: improved
form when 4¾ lengths sixth of 13 to Sea Spray in falsely-run listed race at Kempton,
held up and staying on: well beaten in Nell Gwyn Stakes at Newmarket 10 days later:

stays 1m: has raced only on a sound surface: sold 4,000 gns Newmarket December Sales. *P. A. Kelleway*

CZARNA (IRE)   5 b.g. Polish Precedent (USA) 131 – Noble Dust (USA) (Dust Commander (USA)) [1995 90: 8g⁵ 7m 7m⁴ 8.1m² 8m 7g 6g 10m⁴ 1996 8d 7g² 7m³ 8m 7.1d⁴ 7m 10m 10.1m⁴ 9g 10.4g 7g a8g a9.4g Dec 7] big, good-topped gelding: impresses in appearance: fairly useful handicapper: failed to repeat the form of his placed efforts at Newmarket and Newbury early in season: stays 1m, possibly 1¼m: acts on good to firm going, below form on a soft surface and fibresand in 1996: usually races prominently. *C. E. Brittain*   84 d

D

DAANIERA (IRE)   6 gr.g. Standaan (FR) 118 – Right Cash (Right Tack 131) [1995 –, a57?: a5g⁵ a6g a5g a5g a5g⁶ a5g⁵ a5g a5g⁶ 1996 a5g a5g⁴ a5g a5g a5g⁶ a5g a5g⁴ a5g⁵ a5g⁴ Dec 31] poor handicapper: effective at 5f to 7f: acts on the all-weather and on any turf going: often blinkered/visored: inconsistent. *P. Howling*   –
a45 d

DAAWE (USA)   5 b.h. Danzig (USA) – Capo di Monte 118 (Final Straw 127) [1995 –: 8g⁶ 8.9m 7m 7m 8.1s 1996 a7g⁶ a8g⁵ a6g* a7g² a6g a6g a6g* a6g 6.1g² 6m* 6g⁴ a5g* 6m* 6m 6f⁵ 6d⁴ 6g 5m³ 5d 5g 6g³ 6f³ 5s Nov 8] robust, good-bodied horse: fairly useful handicapper: won 3 times at Southwell and once each at Doncaster and York by mid-June: effective at 5f to 7f: acts on fibresand and on firm and dead ground: visored most starts at 5 yrs, not (and including 2 best efforts) last 3 starts: races prominently: game. *Mrs V. A. Aconley*   80

DACHA (IRE)   4 b.c. Soviet Star (USA) 128 – Shadywood 96 (Habitat 134) [1995 83p: 11.8f⁴ 1996 10m² 12g* 11.9m⁴ 11.9f* 12g³ Sep 29] tall, good sort: won maiden at Pontefract in July and rated stakes at Haydock (ridden to lead under 2f out then idling and edging left) in September: been form, and best of those up with pace throughout, when 2¼ lengths third of 20 to Better Offer in £44,700 handicap at Ascot, keeping on bravely: will prove best at 1½m+: acts on good to firm ground (showed promise on dead): hung right only 3-y-o start and carried head awkwardly second 4-y-o outing: joined Miss M. Rowland: generally progressive. *H. R. A. Cecil*   103

DACOIT (USA)   2 b.c. (Feb 24) Red Ransom (USA) – Krishka (CAN) (Drone) [1996 7d* 7d² Oct 12] $110,000F: medium-sized, good-topped colt: half-brother to numerous minor winners in USA: dam 2-y-o sprint winner in North America out of Canadian champion 3-y-o filly Northern Queen: won maiden at Salisbury in October by ½ length from Crimson Tide (flashed tail when hit once with whip): rallying second to Andreyev in useful conditions event at Ascot later in month: will stay at least 1m: will improve again. *M. R. Stoute*   92 p

DAFFODIL EXPRESS (IRE)   3 b.f. Skyliner 117 – Miss Henry 78 (Blue Cashmere 129) [1995 44: 6m 5g⁴ 6.9s 6g 1996 6g 6m⁴ 7m 6m 5m a7g a6g Nov 18] tall,   48 d

Michael Sobell Silver Tankard Handicap, York—
right to left, Daawe, Cretan Gift, Chadwell Hall and Mister Westsound

workmanlike filly: poor maiden handicapper: likely to prove best short of 7f: visored (finished last) final 3-y-o start: inconsistent. *M. J. Ryan*

DAHIYAH (USA) 5 b.g. Ogygian (USA) – Sticky Prospect (USA) (Mr Prospector (USA)) [1995 64: a7g a8g⁴ 6m⁵ 6f* 6f 6m⁶ 6m⁶ 6f² 6g 1996 a6g a7g² a6g* a6g³ a5g⁶ 6f⁵ a6g 7f³ 6m* 5.1m 6f³ a7g 7g Oct 25] rangy gelding: fair handicapper: won at Lingfield in January and Goodwood (24-runner seller) in June: sold out of G. L. Moore's stable 6,500 gns Newmarket July Sales and below form afterwards: will prove best at up to 7f: acts on firm ground and equitrack: usually visored: races prominently: joined B. Smart. *D. L. Williams*   67 a62

DAILY RISK 3 ch.g. Risk Me (FR) 127 – Give Me A Day (Lucky Wednesday 124) [1995 68: 5m⁵ 5g⁶ 6m 7g⁵ 7g² 7.3d⁴ 1996 8s⁶ 10v 8s 8.2g⁵ 8g 7f⁴ 7m*ᵈⁱˢ 7d a8g Jun 15] smallish gelding: fair maiden: first past post (disqualified for causing interference soon after start) in claimer at Salisbury in May, making all: sold out of S. Dow's stable 3,500 gns Ascot June Sales after penultimate start: stays 1m: acts on good to firm and soft ground, ran poorly on equitrack: inconsistent. *D. W. Chapman*   68

DAILY SPORT GIRL 7 b.m. Risk Me (FR) 127 – Net Call 108 (Song 132) [1995 40: 12.5g² 11.1g⁴ 1996 12.1d⁵ 11.8m² 13g³ a12g Jun 22] lengthy mare: unimpressive mover: poor handicapper: will probably prove suited by further than 13f: acts on good to firm ground and fibresand: tried blinkered earlier in career. *B. J. Llewellyn*   43

DAINTREE (IRE) 2 b.f. (May 2) Tirol 127 – Aunty Eileen (Ahonoora 122) [1996 7m 6m⁵ 5v⁵ Nov 11] IR 3,000Y resold 11,000Y: fifth living foal: half-sister to 4 winners here and abroad, including 3-y-o Astuti (by Waajib), 6f winner at 2 yrs, and 5f winner Moving Image (by Nordico): dam unraced half-sister to smart sprinter Lugana Beach: modest form in maidens and a minor event: stays 7f. *H. J. Collingridge*   66

DAIRA 3 br.f. Daring March 116 – Ile de Reine 64 (Ile de Bourbon (USA) 133) [1995 57: a7g⁵ 8.3g³ 7m⁵ 1996 12d 9.9m² 12g* 12.3m 12f² 10.3d² 10m² 10m⁵ 10.4g 10m⁶ Oct 29] tall, leggy filly: fair handicapper: won maiden at Catterick in May: will eventually prove best at 1½m+: acts on firm and dead ground. *J. D. Bethell*   72

DAISY BATES (IRE) 3 b.f. Danehill (USA) 126 – Martha Stevens (USA) 102 (Super Concorde (USA) 128) [1995 NR 1996 6g⁴ 6m a7g³ a6g a6g Dec 5] quite attractive filly: fourth foal: half-sister to modest 11f winner Hester Stanhope (by Lomond): dam Nell Gwyn winner out of CCA Oaks winner Magazine: modest maiden at best: saddle slipped second start: stays 7f: bolted to post and withdrawn second unraced start. *P. W. Harris*   60

DAJRAAN (IRE) 7 b.h. Shirley Heights 130 – Sugarbird 82 (Star Appeal 133) [1995 NR 1996 22.2f Jun 21] rangy horse: smart performer for A. Fabre in 1992, winner of Group 2 Prix Hubert de Chaudenay at Longchamp, and only bit below that form at his best in 1993: successful in UAE in 1994: modest winning form over hurdles: tailed off in Queen Alexandra Stakes at Royal Ascot on return to flat: stays 15.5f. *N. A. Twiston-Davies*   –

DALLY BOY 4 b.g. Efisio 120 – Gay Hostess (FR) (Direct Flight) [1995 43: 10m a11g 12m 8f a9.4g⁴ a11g 1996 16.1s Mar 26] fair winning hurdler (stays 3m): poor maiden handicapper on flat: seems to stay 11f: acts on fibresand, and on good to firm and soft ground over hurdles. *T. D. Easterby*   43

DALMENY DANCER 2 b.c. (Apr 14) Batshoof 122 – Greek Goddess 82 (Young Generation 129) [1996 5m⁴ 5.1g² 6g* 6m⁶ 7m⁵ 7.1g² 7f⁵ 6g² 6g⁵ 8m 6m 6s⁶ Oct 26] 15,500Y: strong, smallish colt: fourth foal: brother to 3-y-o Myrtle, 7.5f winner at 2 yrs, and half-brother to 1993 2-y-o 6f winner Grecian Garden (by Sharrood): dam should have stayed beyond 6f: made all in median auction maiden at Brighton in May: best efforts when fifth to Shamikh in Chesham Stakes at Ascot and second after in minor events at Sandown and Salisbury: stays 7f: below form on soft ground: keen in blinkers penultimate outing: sold 10,000 gns Newmarket Autumn Sales. *B. J. Meehan*   83

DALWHINNIE 3 b.f. Persian Bold 123 – Land Line (High Line 125) [1995 –: 8m 1996 10d⁶ 10m 13.3m³ 12g a11g 14d 12.1s⁶ 12g² 12v Nov 11] quite attractive filly: poor mover: fair maiden handicapper: stays 13.3f: acts on good to firm and dead ground, tailed off on heavy. *J. W. Hills*   67

DAMANKA (IRE) 2 b.f. (Mar 3) Slip Anchor 136 – Doumayna 79 (Kouban – (FR)) [1996 8g 7g Nov 2] 22,000F, 18,000Y: workmanlike filly: eighth foal: sister to fairly useful 1½m winner Foil Stone and half-sister to useful middle-distance stayer Bondstone (by Miller's Mate): dam, 2m winner, is half-sister to Darshaan (by Shirley Heights) and Darara: burly and green, well beaten in maidens at Doncaster (ran very wide home turn) and Newmarket in autumn. *M. Bell*

DAMARITA 5 ch.m. Starry Night (USA) – Sirenivo (USA) 113 (Sir Ivor 135) 32 [1995 –: 11.9d 1996 11.7g⁵ 12g 9.7m³ Aug 16] bad maiden handicapper: will be suited by further than 11.7f. *Lady Herries*

DAME LAURA (IRE) 2 b.f. (Apr 10) Royal Academy (USA) 130 – Aunty (FR) 100 114 (Riverman (USA) 131) [1996 5m² 5m* 5m² 5m² 6g 8m² Sep 12] 13,000Y: leggy filly: eighth foal: half-sister to 3-y-o Majdak Jereeb (by Alzao) and 2 winners by Sadler's Wells, notably useful 1988 Irish 2-y-o 5f and 6f winner Kyra: dam French 1¼m winner, is half-sister to Ebor winner Crazy out of smart French middle-distance winner Aunt Zara: won maiden auction at Newmarket in May: runner-up on 3 occasions after, beaten length by Dance Parade in Queen Mary Stakes at Ascot on fourth start and 2 lengths by Reams of Verse in May Hill Stakes at Doncaster on last: will probably stay beyond 1m: acts on good to firm ground: has joined H. Morrison. *P. F. I. Cole*

DANAMICH (IRE) 3 b.g. Fayruz 116 – Galapagos 71 (Pitskelly 122) [1995 –: – 6m 1996 6s Mar 23] strong, lengthy gelding: behind in maidens. *J. Berry*

DANA POINT (IRE) 4 br.g. Phardante (FR) 123 – Wallpark Princess (Balidar 66 133) [1995 65p: 8m* 1996 10.1s⁶ 8.2d⁴ 10g 10m⁴ 10.9d⁶ 12g* Oct 19] stocky gelding: fair performer: off course 5½ months, won apprentice claimer at Catterick in October (claimed £4,000), making most: stays 1½m: seems to need a sound surface: won novice hurdle for Mrs S. Smith in December. *T. D. Barron*

DANCE A DREAM 4 b.f. Sadler's Wells (USA) 132 – Exclusive Order (USA) 107 120 (Exclusive Native (USA)) [1995 115: 11.4m* 12m² 12m⁴ 11.9m⁶ 1996 13.4g⁵ 12f⁶ 12g³ Jun 29] sturdy, lengthy filly: carries condition: second in Oaks at 3 yrs: only useful form in 1996, behind Oscar Schindler in Ormonde Stakes at Chester (headed 3f out) and Hardwicke Stakes at Royal Ascot (unable to land a blow), then behind Bequeath in listed race at Newmarket (beaten 5 lengths): should have been suited by further than 1½m: unraced on a soft surface: sent to USA. *M. R. Stoute*

DANCE DESIGN (IRE) 3 b.f. Sadler's Wells (USA) 132 – Elegance In 119 Design 105 (Habitat 134) [1995 107: 7s* 7m* 7g⁴ 8d⁴ 1996 8d² 8m³ 10m* 12m* 10g² Sep 14]

If the home side was weakened by the absence of Zagreb from the Irish Champion Stakes at Leopardstown in September it hardly showed, the first two places in the race being filled by those notably reliable and progressive Irish-trained fillies Timarida and Dance Design. The latter could not match the older filly's turn of foot and was beaten a length and a half, but did very well to keep the four colts at bay, albeit in a contest where things went her way. Handed the lead, she quickened the steady pace on the home turn and kept on strongly afterwards.

Dance Design was the pick of the Irish three-year-old fillies and showed it time after time, beginning in the Airlie/Coolmore Irish One Thousand Guineas at the Curragh in May on her reappearance, in which she finished three lengths second of twelve, keeping on, to Matiya. She went one better in her next classic, the Kildangan Stud Irish Oaks at the same track in July. Before that she had two other races, much the more demanding the Coronation Stakes at Royal Ascot where she came up against the first two in the Pouliches, Ta Rib and Shake The Yoke. The way Ta Rib had been ridden at Longchamp it would not have been a surprise had she made the running in the Coronation Stakes, but it was Dance Design who dictated the pace and, briefly, looked likely to hold on a furlong out. Ultimately though, Shake The Yoke wore Dance Design down and Last Second was produced late to snatch the runner-up spot in a cracking finish, a neck and half a length covering the three of them. On this form Dance Design had a clear edge on her six rivals in the Independent Newspapers Pretty

Polly Stakes at the Curragh on the step up from a mile to a mile and a quarter in preparation for the Irish Oaks, and she was little troubled to land her first pattern event by a length and a half from Zafzala, having allowed Hagwah to set the pace this time.

The Irish Oaks cut up badly, largely as a result of the presence of runaway Epsom winner Lady Carla who started at 2/1-on in the field of six. Dance Design started second favourite at 9/2 ahead of the Prix de Malleret winner Shamadara (6/1), the Ribblesdale Stakes second Key Change (8/1), the Cheshire Oaks winner Tout A Coup (14/1) and the Irish maiden French Ballerina (100/1). There was some doubt on breeding about her getting the longer trip but very little on the way she'd been finishing her races, particularly the latest. Lady Carla made the running but never looked like breaking away. The others kept close order until well into the straight, Dance Design being held up in fourth or fifth with Key Change running second and Shamadara third. Lady Carla began to throw out distress signals around two furlongs from home, challenged by Key Change and Shamadara, with Dance Design improving on the outside. Key Change managed to get past Lady Carla under driving but couldn't quicken like Shamadara or Dance Design who had the race between them from around a furlong out. The battle went to Dance Design in the last stride by a short head, both fillies responding generously to strong pressure. Two lengths behind, Key Change easily kept the below-par Lady Carla out of third spot. Dance Design was trainer Dermot Weld's second Irish Oaks winner, following Blue Wind in 1981. Two weeks earlier in the Irish Derby stable-companion Zagreb had ended the trainer's long wait, with some near misses, for the full set of Irish classics.

Dance Design was bred by, and carries the colours of, one of the stable's leading patrons, Moyglare Stud Farms, whose owner Walter Haefner purchased

Kildangan Stud Irish Oaks, the Curragh—
hard-ridden Dance Design gets up from Shamadara, Key Change (hidden) and Lady Carla

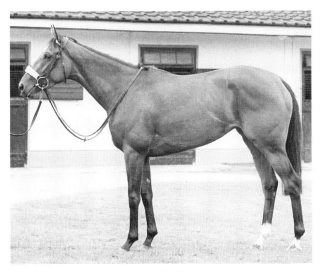

Moyglare Stud Farms Ltd's "Dance Design"

the grandam Areola shortly before she won the Phoenix Stakes on her final start as a two-year-old in 1970. Areola was very speedy at that age, and her only defeat in three previous starts had been at the hands of Cawston's Pride in the Queen Mary Stakes at Royal Ascot. She proved a judicious purchase, for although unplaced in her only race as a three-year-old she went on to produce numerous winners, notably the high-class seven-furlong and one-mile filly Chalon, her sister Elegance In Design and the smart one-mile-to-mile-and-a-quarter colt Executive Perk. Dance Design's dam Elegance In Design finished four lengths fifth of thirteen to Ensconce in the Irish One Thousand Guineas for the Moyglare/Weld combination. She was put back to sprinting afterwards, looking particularly effective at six furlongs. Dance Design has been the high spot of her producing career so far. Her only previous foal Orchestral Designs (by Fappiano) soon became disappointing, and unfortunately a younger sister to Dance Design has died; there is a colt by Darshaan following on.

Dance Design (IRE) (b.f. 1993)	Sadler's Wells (USA) (b 1981)	Northern Dancer (b 1961)	Nearctic
			Natalma
		Fairy Bridge (b 1975)	Bold Reason
			Special
	Elegance In Design (ch 1986)	Habitat (b 1966)	Sir Gaylord
			Little Hut
		Areola (ch 1968)	Kythnos
			Alive Alivo

Given Elegance In Design's racing record and pedigree there was bound to be a doubt about Dance Design's stamina. However, Sadler's Wells came up trumps again. The sturdy Dance Design is effective at a mile to a mile and a half. She has shown smart form on good to firm to good to soft ground and would almost certainly be able to reproduce it on soft—she made a winning two-year-old debut in a Galway maiden delayed half an hour by a spectacular electrical storm accompanied by monsoon-like rain. As we have seen, she is amenable to being held up or ridden in front, and is altogether a tough, genuine and likeable filly. *D. K. Weld, Ireland*

DANCE D'ORE (SWE) 4 b.c. Ore 116 – La Grande Danseuse (USA) 79 (North 98
Pole (CAN)) [1995 a11.5g² a11.5g* a12g* a12g² a12g* a12g a13.3g* 14d⁴ 14s²
a12g² 1996 a11.5g² a12g a12g² 22.2f⁵ 13g² 12.9g* Jul 22] angular Swedish colt:
fairly useful performer: first past post on 5 occasions in 1995, demoted to fourth after
winning Norwegian St Leger by 6 lengths on last occasion before beaten a head in
Swedish St Leger at Taby: just under 8 lengths fifth of 10 to Admiral's Well in Queen
Alexandra Stakes at Royal Ascot, staying on and never nearer: won listed race at
Taby in July narrowly from Dulford Lad: stays extreme distances: probably acts on
any going. *L. Reuterskjold, Sweden*

DANCE KING 4 b.g. Rambo Dancer (CAN) 107 – Northern Venture 80 (St 70
Alphage 119) [1995 70, a64: a7g³ a8g 8m² 8m² 10g³ 8m* 8m² a9.4g 8.5d 10g
1996 a7g⁵ a10g 10.8g 8m⁴ 11.4m* 8m 12m⁵ 12.3m⁴ 10m⁵ Aug 2] neat gelding: fair
handicapper: won handicap at Sandown in June, leading over 1f out: stays 11.4f: acts
on any going on turf and on equitrack: blinkered (ran creditably) second 3-y-o start:
usually races prominently: joined T. T. Clement: inconsistent. *R. Harris*

DANCE MELODY 2 b.f. (Feb 25) Rambo Dancer (CAN) 107 – Cateryne –
(Ballymoss 136) [1996 6m 6m⁶ 8.1m 7f⁶ a8.5g Nov 11] rather leggy filly: half-sister
to 3 modest winners at up to 8.2f, including 1982 2-y-o 6f winner Hot Potato (by
Class Distinction): dam ran once: well beaten, including in a seller. *G. R. Oldroyd*

DANCE MODEL 3 b.f. Unfuwain (USA) 131 – Bourgeonette 81 (Mummy's Pet –
125) [1995 NR 1996 10m 10m 9m 15.4g 17.9g a14.8g Nov 25] 2,000Y: unfurnished
filly: has a round action: half-sister to several winners, including useful Wantage
Park (up to 7f, by Pas de Seul) and fairly useful The Where Withal (up to 2m, by
Glint of Gold): dam 1m and 1¼m winner: no form. *J. J. Sheehan*

DANCE MOTION 4 b.g. Damister (USA) 123 – Tantalizing Song (CAN) (The –
Minstrel (CAN) 135) [1995 –: 10m 1996 a11g Mar 18] sturdy gelding: has seemed of
little account since 2 yrs. *A. B. Mulholland*

DANCE OF JOY 4 b.f. Shareef Dancer (USA) 135 – Lady Habitat (Habitat 134) 48 d
[1995 –: 8.2g 10.3m 10g 10f⁵ 1996 a8.5g 8g* 8m 9.9m 8m 8.1g 10m 8m³ a10g⁶
Dec 31] strong, lengthy filly: only poor at best nowadays: won apprentice selling
handicap at Newcastle in April: should stay further than 1m: has raced only on a
sound surface on turf, well beaten on fibresand: inconsistent. *J. M. Carr*

DANCE ON A CLOUD (USA) 3 b.f. Capote (USA) – Sharp Dance (USA) –
(Dancing Czar (USA)) [1995 76p: 7.1g⁶ 7f* 1996 10m⁶ 9m 10m Jun 14] lengthy,
good-topped filly: has a quick action: fair performer: faced stiffish tasks in handicaps
in 1996, tailed off final start: probably stays 9f. *M. R. Stoute*

DANCE ON SIXPENCE 8 b.g. Lidhame 109 – Burning Ambition (Troy 137) –
[1995 –: a8.5g 8m 1996 a8.5g a12g Jan 31] no longer of account. *J. H. Peacock*

DANCE PARADE (USA) 2 ch.f. (Mar 8) Gone West (USA) – River Jig (USA) 102
98 (Irish River (FR) 131) [1996 5m* 5m* 5m* 8d Oct 6] good-topped, rather leggy
filly: good mover: fifth foal: sister to useful 1m winner Western Reel: dam 9f (at 2
yrs) and 1½m winner in Italy: useful form: won maiden at York, minor event at
Beverley and Queen Mary Stakes (by a length from stable-companion Dame Laura,
staying on in good fashion) at Royal Ascot: had a bacterial problem afterwards, down
the field in Prix Marcel Boussac at Longchamp (raced freely) on only subsequent
start: should stay 1m: acts on good to firm ground. *P. F. I. Cole*

DANCER MITRAL 3 b.c. Shareef Dancer (USA) 135 – Almitra (Targowice 107
(USA) 130) [1995 6m* 7g* 7.5f⁴ 7.5g* 8g³ 8g 1996 7g* 7.5g³ 8d³ 8d* 12m⁵ 11g*
12s 10m 10v* Nov 27] IR 18,000Y: eighth reported foal: best of siblings was sprinter
Bay Hero (rated 99, by Bay Express): dam, Irish 9f winner, is half-sister to dam of
Las Meninas (won 1000 Guineas, rated 115) out of Donna Cressida (stayed 1¼m,
rated 116): useful Italian colt: won 3 races at 2 yrs, including in listed company:
successful in the spring in minor event and Premio Parioli (by short neck from

Dankeston), both at Rome: creditable fifth in Derby Italiano: off course 3 months, won listed race in September, also at Rome: below form afterwards: effective at 1m to 1½m: acts on good to firm and soft ground: seems effective blinkered (was in Parioli) or not. *L. Brogi, Italy*

DANCE SEQUENCE (USA)   3 ch.f. Mr Prospector (USA) – Dancing Tribute   104
(USA) 115 (Nureyev (USA) 131) [1995 105: 5m² 5m² 6g² 6m* 6d⁴ 1996 8m⁶ 6m 7g⁶ 7m² 6m² 7m³ Sep 12] close-coupled, rather unfurnished filly: tends not to impress in appearance: fluent mover: useful performer: creditable sixth in 1000 Guineas on reappearance, but very best efforts in 1996 when 3 lengths second of 9 to Iktamal in Beeswing Stakes at Newcastle and 2½ lengths third of 7 to My Branch (pushed along vigorously at halfway, stayed on steadily) in listed race at Doncaster: stays 1m: best efforts on good to firm ground: edgy sort. *M. R. Stoute*

DANCE SO SUITE   4 b.g. Shareef Dancer (USA) 135 – Three Piece (Jaazeiro   94
(USA) 127) [1995 84, a61: 11.6m* 12m² 11.5m³ 14g⁵ 10.5s* 12.1s⁵ a10g³ 1996 12g*   a–
12m* 12m 10m⁶ 10.4m³ 12g⁴ 12g³ 12s⁶ Nov 9] close-coupled gelding: fairly useful handicapper: won at Newbury in May and at Epsom (apprentices) in June: generally ran creditably in competitive events afterwards: stays 1½m, seemingly not 1¾m: acts on good to firm and soft ground and (modest form) on equitrack: wears a dropped noseband. *P. F. I. Cole*

DANCE STAR   3 b.f. Damister (USA) 123 – Glen Dancer 102 (Furry Glen 121)   72
[1995 75p: 7g 8.2m* 1996 10.3m 10.5d⁴ Sep 28] leggy, workmanlike filly: not seen out until September, better effort when fourth of 9 in handicap at Haydock: should stay further than 10.5f: yet to race on extremes of going. *M. A. Jarvis*

DANCES WITH DREAMS   2 b.f. (Mar 29) Be My Chief (USA) 122 – Oh So   98 p
Well (IRE) (Sadler's Wells (USA) 132) [1996 6d* 8s² Nov 18] good-topped filly: has scope: second foal: dam unraced daughter of Soba: quickened well when winning maiden at Ascot in October: much better effort when beaten 1½ lengths by Yxenery in listed race at Evry in November: bred to stay beyond 1m: raced only on a soft surface: probably capable of further improvement. *P. W. Chapple-Hyam*

DANCES WITH HOOVES   4 b.c. Dancing Dissident (USA) 119 – Princesse   82
Legere (USA) (Alleged (USA) 138) [1995 75: 8d³ 8g 1996 8s³ 7.5m² 8s Nov 9] tall, leggy colt: fairly useful performer, still lightly raced: shaped promisingly twice in the spring, but off course 7 months and well held on return: will stay beyond 1m: acts on good to firm and soft going. *D. J. S. ffrench Davis*

Queen Mary Stakes, Royal Ascot—
Dance Parade wins from Dame Laura (extreme left) and Moonshine Girl (second left)

DANCETHENIGHTAWAY 2 gr.f. (Mar 13) Efisio 120 – Dancing Diana 82   82
(Raga Navarro (ITY) 119) [1996 5.1f³ 5.1m* 5f² 6g² 5.2m⁴ Sep 21] leggy filly: fifth
foal: half-sister to several winners, including 3-y-o 7f winner Silver Harrow (by
Belmez) and 7f and 1m winner Prince Rodney (by Don't Forget Me): dam 5f (at 2
yrs) to 1m winner: won maiden at Bath in August: second after in minor event at
Salisbury and nursery at Kempton: stays 6f: raced only on a sound surface: active
sort: carried head high final start. *B. J. Meehan*

DANCE TREAT (USA) 4 ch.f. Nureyev (USA) 131 – Office Wife (USA) (Sec-   115
retariat (USA)) [1995 84: 8.1m 10.8g* 12s² 10.5v³ 12g* 1996 12d⁴ᵈⁱˢ 12f 10g³ 11s⁶
10g⁶ 10m* 10g⁴ 10d⁶ 12.5d⁴ 10.5s* 10.5s² Nov 18] leggy ex-English trained filly:
vastly improved: useful form at best in 1996 until winning La Coupe at Saint-Cloud
in June by a head from Bulington: back to that form when winning 14-runner Prix de
Flore at Saint-Cloud by 2½ lengths from Dapprima and when 2½ lengths second of
11 to Maroussie in Prix Fille de l'Air at Evry in November: stays 12.5f: acts on good
to firm and heavy ground: blinkered since eighth 4-y-o start. *D. Sepulchre, France*

DANCING CAVALIER 3 b.g. Nalchik (USA) – Miss Admington 71 (Double   72 §
Jump 131) [1995 –: a8.5g 7.1s 7m a7g a8g a7g⁶ 1996 a8g³ a8g* a11g* a11g² a11g²
a12g⁴ 10.3d³ 12s³ a11g² 14.1g² 14.1m⁶ 14d³ 11.8g³ 16m⁴ Sep 24] quite attractive
gelding: fair handicapper: won at Southwell in January and February: below form
last 4 starts, looking reluctant (subsequently gelded) after second of them: stays
1¾m: acts on soft ground (possibly not good to firm) and fibresand: often gets well
behind, and may benefit from blinkers/visor: not one to trust. *R. Hollinshead*

DANCING DEBUT 3 b.f. Polar Falcon (USA) 126 – Exclusive Virtue (USA) 94   83
(Shadeed (USA) 135) [1995 58p: 8.2m⁴ 1996 10m² 10s² Oct 24] angular filly: fairly
useful form when second in maidens at Newmarket (badly hampered 2f out or would
have gone close) and Newbury 4½ months later: stays 1¼m well: acts on good to
firm and soft ground. *J. H. M. Gosden*

DANCING DESTINY 4 b.f. Dancing Brave (USA) 140 – Tender Loving Care   48
105 (Final Straw 127) [1995 70d: 10g 10.8g² 11f² 9.9m 8g 10f 11f a8g 1996 12.3m
10.1g 11f² 10.1g⁶ Aug 1] quite attractive filly: only a poor maiden in 1996: gambled
on when second in handicap at Redcar: stays 11f: acts on firm and dead ground.
R. Bastiman

DANCING DROP 2 b.f. (May 6) Green Desert (USA) 127 – Moon Drop 103   92
(Dominion 123) [1996 5g² 5m 5m³ 6g* 7m³ 6f* 7m³ Oct 5] small, sturdy filly: fifth
foal: half-sister to 3 winners, including 3-y-o Wisam (by Shaadi), useful 5f winner at
2 yrs, and useful 5f (at 2 yrs) and 7f winner Moon King (by Cadeaux Genereux): dam
sprinter: won maiden at Windsor in July and steadily-run minor event at Salisbury in
September: third in listed races at Sandown (¾ length behind Vax Star) on third start
and at Newmarket on fifth and final (around 4 lengths behind Sarayir) outings: stays
7f: acts on firm ground. *R. Hannon*

DANCING HEART 4 b.g. Thowra (FR) – Miss Lawsuit (Neltino 97) [1995 72,   72
a76: 7f⁴ 7g* 7m 7f⁴ 7f² 6g 7s³ a6g⁶ 6.1s a8g⁴ a7g* a6g a8g³ a7g 1996 7f 6g⁶ 6.9m⁶
a7g⁴ 6m² 6m⁵ 6m 7m 7.1m⁴ 8f a7g² Oct 28] stocky gelding: fair handicapper: sold
5,000 gns Newmarket Autumn Sales: stays 7f, faded over 1m: acts on any going, including equitrack: effective blinkered or not: usually races prominently: inconsistent:
sent to Italy. *B. J. Meehan*

DANCING IMAGE 3 ch.g. Salse (USA) 128 – Reflection 111 (Mill Reef (USA)   85
141) [1995 71: 6g³ 7m⁶ 7d⁵ 1996 8m² 8g³ 8g* 8m* 7.1m² 7m² Aug 2] compact,
attractive gelding: good mover: progressive handicapper: won at Kempton and
Ripon in June: 3 lengths second of 18 to Green Barries in £21,700 event at Goodwood final start: stays 1m: acts on good to firm ground, bit below best on a soft
surface: pulls hard: ideally suited by waiting tactics in truly-run race. *I. A. Balding*

DANCING JACK 3 ch.c. Clantime 101 – Sun Follower (Relkino 131) [1995 56:   58 d
5g 5m³ 5d⁵ 5m⁶ 5m⁴ 5g⁵ 5g⁶ a5g⁴ a6g a5g* a6g³ a6g³ 1996 a5g² a5g⁴ a5g² a6g⁵ a6g²
6f⁴ 5m 6g 5m 6f⁶ 5m a6g a10g a5g a5g Dec 31] workmanlike colt: modest performer:
below form last 9 starts: effective at 5f and 6f: acts on equitrack and firm ground:
usually races prominently. *J. J. Bridger*

DANCING JAZZTIME 5 b.m. Clantime 101 – Dance In Spain 50 (King of   –
Spain 121) [1995 –: 5d a6g 1996 7.5f 6d 6m 5g Aug 23] of no account. *J. S. Wainwright*

DANCING LAWYER 5 b.g. Thowra (FR) – Miss Lawsuit (Neltino 97) [1995 – 75, a80: a7g 6m⁵ 7f³ 7m⁴ 7f⁴ 7m⁶ 8f⁴ 8f³ 7.1m² 7.1d⁴ a8g* a8g 1996 a10g⁶ a8g* a8g a87 d 8f 7f 5.7m⁶ 6m a6g 8.5m a7g a7g a8g Nov 26] sturdy gelding: carries condition: fairly useful handicapper: won at Lingfield (claimer) in January: failed by long way to repeat that form: took heavy fall fifth start: effective at 7f, probably at 1¼m: acts on firm and dead ground and on equitrack: takes keen hold. *B. J. Meehan*

DANCING MAN 3 ch.g. Executive Man 119 – Lyne Dancer (Be My Native – (USA) 122) [1995 –: 5g 6s 7m 1996 6m 6s May 23] big, good-topped gelding: no promise. *Mrs M. E. Long*

DANCING MYSTERY 2 b.g. (May 1) Beveled (USA) – Batchworth Dancer 67 – (Ballacashtal (CAN)) [1996 5d 6g⁴ Oct 29] third reported foal: brother to winning 4-y-o sprinter Another Batchworth: dam won at up to 7f: poor form in median auction maidens. *E. A. Wheeler*

DANCING QUEEN (IRE) 2 b.f. (Apr 21) Sadler's Wells (USA) 132 – Bay 69 + Shade (USA) 90 (Sharpen Up 127) [1996 6m⁴ 7m³ Aug 10] 130,000Y: strong, good-topped filly: fifth foal: sister to 3-y-o Badius and half-sister to Cheshire Oaks winner Abury (by Law Society) and a winner in Norway by Green Desert: dam 2-y-o 7f winner, later won listed 1m event in Italy: fair form: would probably have won maiden at Redcar in August on final start but for hanging badly left: will stay middle distances. *M. Bell*

DANCING RAINBOW 3 b.f. Rambo Dancer (CAN) 107 – Heemee 81 (On – Your Mark 125) [1995 61: 5m* 5g 5m⁴ 5g⁶ 6m 1996 a5g 7.5m 5f 5g Jul 1] compact filly: looked of no account in 1996. *M. J. Camacho*

DANCING SIOUX 4 b.g. Nabeel Dancer (USA) 120 – Sutosky 78 (Great Nep- 66 d hew 126) [1995 61: 8g 6m⁴ 6f a7g 5m⁴ 6f² 5d² 5g 5.1d 8f⁵ a7g³ a9.4g⁶ a7g⁶ a7g 1996 a80 d a7g* a7g* a7g 7.1g⁵ a7g³ 7g a8.5g a7g 7g a7g⁴ a7g 7g a6g Nov 4] angular gelding: fair handicapper: won at Southwell (by 10 lengths) and Lingfield (apprentices) in February: trained until after sixth start by R. Guest: below form afterwards: stays 7f: acts on any turf going, usually goes well on the all-weather (though not at Wolver-hampton): tried blinkered, no improvement. *D. Nicholls*

DANCING STAR (IRE) 2 b.f. (May 9) Waajib 121 – Havana Blade (USA) 46 d (Blade (USA)) [1996 a5g⁴ 5.1g² 5m⁵ a5g⁵ a5g a6g 5g⁴ a5g³ a6g⁶ 6m 6g² 5d⁶ 6.1m 6f a5g a8.5g 8f Nov 5] 1,800Y: small filly: fourth foal: half-sister to 3-y-o 13.8f seller winner Havana Heights (by Persian Heights): dam, won from 7f to 8.5f in France, half-sister to Grade 1 US 2-y-o winner Tiltalating: poor plater: stays 6f: acts on fibresand, best turf efforts on good ground: effective visored or not/blinkered once. *P. D. Evans*

DANDE FLYER 3 b. or br.c. Clantime 101 – Lyndseylee 96 (Swing Easy (USA) 77 126) [1995 77: 5.1m⁵ 5.1m⁴ 5g⁶ 5.1f³ 5.3f² 5.3f⁴ 5m² 5d⁵ 5.3d 5g* 5.2f* 5m* 5m³ 1996 5.1g 5.1g⁵ 5g³ 5.7m³ 5f⁴ 5m⁴ 5m⁵ 5g Aug 12] neat colt: fair handicapper: best at 5f: acts well on top-of-the-ground: blinkered (poorly drawn) final 3-y-o start: best efforts ridden with restraint: sometimes used to be slowly away: usually band-aged in front: sometimes hangs left: sometimes finds little. *D. W. P. Arbuthnot*

DANDY REGENT 2 b.g. (Feb 25) Green Desert (USA) 127 – Tahilla 112 – (Moorestyle 137) [1996 6m Sep 13] 22,000Y: angular, quite attractive gelding: fifth foal: half-brother to fair winning sprinter Pluck and 7f winner Self Reliance (both by Never So Bold): dam, suited to 1m, half-sister to Piccolo: slowly away and always behind in maiden at Goodwood: moved badly to post. *C. A. Cyzer*

DANEGOLD (IRE) 4 b.g. Danehill (USA) 126 – Cistus 123 (Sun Prince 128) 81 § [1995 86, a58+: 10.3g³ a10g³ a10g⁵ 8m* 8.1m 8g² 8g² 8m* 8.5m² 10m* 8m 10.1m⁴ a– § 10f 10d 8.1d* 10d 8d 10d 1996 10.1m 8m⁶ 10.5g² 10m⁵ 9f 10.2f 8m⁵ 10.5d³ 8d 8g 10s Oct 24] sturdy gelding: fair handicapper: sold 9,000 gns Newmarket Autumn Sales: effective at 1m, and stays 10.5f: acts on good to firm and soft ground: below form on the all-weather: visored since third 3-y-o start: reluctant to race sixth 4-y-o outing: inconsistent and not one to trust: winning hurdler. *M. R. Channon*

DANEHILL DANCER (IRE) 3 b.c. Danehill (USA) 126 – Mira Adonde 117 (USA) (Sharpen Up 127) [1995 117: 6g* 6m* 7f* 7m² 1996 7d* 8m⁶ 8g 6m⁵ 6.5d³ 6f Sep 7] big, strong, lengthy colt: carries condition: smart performer: won Green-ham Stakes at Newbury in April by 1½ lengths from Kahir Almaydan: below form in

2000 Guineas at Newmarket and Poule d'Essai des Poulains at Longchamp: much better efforts, behind Anabaa, when staying-on fifth of 10 in July Cup at Newmarket and about 1¾ lengths third of 9 in Prix Maurice de Gheest at Deauville: effective at 6f, and should stay 1m: acts on good to firm ground (struggling by halfway in Haydock Park Sprint on firm) and dead: held up. *N. A. Callaghan*

DANEHILL PRINCE 2 b.g. (Feb 26) Danehill (USA) 126 – Santarem (USA) 71 (El Gran Senor (USA) 136) [1996 7m 7f³ 5f² Sep 18] 3,600Y: first foal: dam thrice-raced staying maiden half-sister to smart stayer Al Maheb: placed in seller at Brighton (final start for M. Channon, visored) and claimer at Sandown: dead. *G. L. Moore*   **69**

DANEHILL PRINCESS (IRE) 2 b.f. (Apr 19) Danehill (USA) 126 – Top Glad (USA) (I'm Glad (ARG)) [1996 5g⁴ 5.1g³ 6.1m⁴ 6m⁴ 6m² 5.9f² 6d³ 7m⁵ 6m² 7m³ 7g⁵ 6.1m⁵ 6f⁴ 6m a7g a7g³ Dec 28] IR 11,000Y: stocky filly: second foal: half-sister to 3-y-o Love Bird (by Bluebird): dam won at up to 9f at 2 yrs in USA: modest maiden: stays 7f: acts on firm and dead ground, poor form on all-weather: effective visored or not: sometimes starts slowly, and has also run in snatches. *R. Hollinshead*   **62** / **a50**

DANETIME (IRE) 2 b.c. (Mar 27) Danehill (USA) 126 – Allegheny River (USA) (Lear Fan (USA) 130) [1996 5m⁴ 6m* 7g² Oct 19] IR 13,000F, IR 36,000Y: quite attractive colt: has a quick action: third foal: half-brother to Irish 3-y-o Tirano (by Tirol), 6.5f winner at 2 yrs: dam Irish 7f winner: won maiden at Newcastle in October: length second of 6 to Crimson Tide in Houghton Stakes at Newmarket later in month: stays 7f: likely to keep improving. *N. A. Callaghan*   **96 p**

DANICO 3 ch.g. Most Welcome 131 – Spica (USA) 76§ (Diesis 133) [1995 59: 7m⁴ 7m⁶ 1996 a8g⁶ 8.1g⁴ 9.9m³ 8.3s² 8.3s* 8g a8.5g² 8m 7f 8.2m a11g⁴ Jul 1] leggy gelding: modest performer: having second race in 24 hours when winning maiden at Hamilton in May: well beaten last 4 starts: sold 2,100 gns Newmarket July Sales: effective at 1m to 1¼m: acts on soft ground and fibresand: sent to Holland. *S. C. Williams*   **57**

DANIEL DERONDA 2 b.c. (Mar 6) Danehill (USA) 126 – Kilvarnet 78 (Furry Glen 121) [1996 7.1v² Oct 6] 36,000Y: good-topped colt: fifth foal: half-brother to 3 winners, including 7f (at 2 yrs) to 1¼m winner Ferdia (by Petorius) and 1¼m winner McGillycuddy Reeks (by Kefaah): dam 5f (at 2 yrs) and 7.6f winner: staying-on second in maiden at Haydock in October: will stay beyond 1m: should improve. *P. W. Harris*   **70 p**

DANISH AYR 2 b.f. (Apr 11) Danehill (USA) 126 – Cumbrian Melody 83 (Petong 126) [1996 6g 5m⁶ Jul 25] 13,000Y: good-bodied filly: fourth foal: half-sister to German 3-y-o 6f winner Woodfighter (by Ballad Rock) and 5-y-o 7f winner Titanium Honda (by Doulab): dam 2-y-o 5f and 6f winner: modest form in maiden events in the summer: may do better. *M. R. Channon*   **49 +**

DANISH CIRCUS (IRE) 3 b.c. Danehill (USA) 126 – Circus Maid (IRE) (High Top 131) [1995 74: 7.1d⁵ 7g³ 7f³ 1996 8.3m⁴ Jun 24] small colt: fair maiden here: won over 1m and 9f in Denmark: acts on firm and dead ground. *M. J. Heaton-Ellis*   **75**

DANISH RHAPSODY (IRE) 3 b.g. Danehill (USA) 126 – Ardmelody (Law Society (USA) 130) [1995 NR 1996 8g 10s² Oct 24] IR 21,000F, IR 34,000Y: good-topped gelding: third foal: half-brother to Irish 2-y-o 6f to USA Grade 2 1½m winner Memories (by Don't Forget Me): dam unraced from family of Ardross: changed hands 1,300 gns Newmarket September Sales after debut: off course 5 months, ½-length second of 16, clear, in maiden at Newbury, leading from halfway until over 1f out and keeping on strongly: better suited by 1¼m than shorter: acts on soft ground: sure to win a race. *Lady Herries*   **81**

DANJING (IRE) 4 b.g. Danehill (USA) 126 – Beijing (USA) 89 (Northjet 136) [1995 89: 10g* 14m⁵ 12f 10m 12m⁴ 10.1m³ 13.3d 12g* 12m⁶ 1996 16.4g³ 18.7m² 16.1m 18g Oct 19] well-made gelding: useful juvenile hurdler before sold out of S. Sherwood's stable 28,000 gns Ascot June Sales: fairly useful handicapper on flat: best effort when strong-finishing second of 9 in £15,200 event at Chester: suited by test of stamina: acts on good to firm ground and soft: blinkered last 2 starts in 1995: has become most unreliable over hurdles. *M. C. Pipe*   **94**

DANKA 2 gr.g. (Feb 16) Petong 126 – Angel Drummer 59 (Dance In Time (CAN)) [1996 6m 7g⁶ 7.6d 7f⁴ Sep 27] 11,000Y: good-bodied gelding: fifth foal: half-brother   **61**

to 1993 2-y-o 6f winner Wandering Angel (by Sharrood): dam, 2-y-o 7f winner, later successful over hurdles: modest form in maidens and nursery: may stay 1m: visored final start. *P. T. Walwyn*

DANKESTON (USA)   3 b.c. Elmaamul (USA) 125 – Last Request 92 (Dancer's   107 Image (USA)) [1995 96: 5s² 5.1m* 7m³ 7m² 7m* 7m³ 7m* 6f 8g⁶ 1996 8g⁵ 8d² 8g³ 10f⁴ 10m* 11.9m⁶ Aug 20] leggy, workmanlike colt: useful form: in frame in Premio Parioli (short-neck second of 14 to Dancer Mitral) at Rome, Prix de la Jonchere (2½ lengths behind Android) at Longchamp and Prince of Wales's Stakes (6 lengths behind First Island) at Royal Ascot: won Group 3 event at Frankfurt (beat Sir Warren a nose in a blanket finish) in July: should stay 1½m (refused to settle in Great Voltigeur when tried): acts on firm ground and soft: visored fourth 2-y-o to first 3-y-o starts: game and genuine. *M. Bell*

DANLORA   3 b.f. Shareef Dancer (USA) 135 – Loreef (Main Reef 126) [1995 NR   74 d 1996 6m⁵ 7.1d 7g² 8f⁵ 9g Nov 1] sturdy, lengthy filly: fifth foal: half-sister to fair 6f (at 2 yrs) to 1¼m winner North Reef (by Danehill) and to a winner in Japan: dam, maiden who stayed 1½m, half-sister to On The House: fair maiden: failed to repeat debut effort: stays 1m, bred to stay further: ran badly on dead ground. *W. Jarvis*

DANNISTAR   4 br.f. Puissance 110 – Loadplan Lass 63 (Nicholas Bill 125) [1995   47 57: a8.5g⁵ a8.5g² a9.4g* a9.4g⁶ 1996 a8.5g a12g⁴ 10.8m² a12g 10f Sep 28] form in 1996 only when second of 15 in seller at Warwick (after 3-month break) in August, leading 2f out to line: stays 10.8f: acts on fibresand. *P. D. Evans*

DANTEAN   4 b.g. Warning 136 – Danthonia (USA) 80 (Northern Dancer) [1995   32 –: 9m 14g 10g 1996 a8g³ a8g a8g 8f 6f⁵ 6m 7.1m 7f⁴ Aug 7] tall gelding: poor maiden handicapper: stays 7f: has raced only on a sound surface on turf: tried blinkered, no improvement: inconsistent. *R. J. O'Sullivan*

DANTESQUE (IRE)   3 b.c. Danehill (USA) 126 – I Want My Say (USA) (Tilt   69 p Up (USA)) [1995 NR 1996 8.3m⁵ 8d⁵ Aug 24] 115,000Y: lengthy, attractive colt: fourth living foal: dam, ran once in France, out of Poule d'Essai des Pouliches winner Rajput Princess: still in need of race, fifth of 12 in maiden at Newmarket, held up, edging left 2f out then staying on under hands and heels: will be suited by further than 1m: seemed likely to improve again. *G. Wragg*

DARATOWN   3 b.g. Tragic Role (USA) – Darakah 78 (Doulab (USA) 115) [1995   – NR 1996 a8.5g a8.5g⁶ a8s Nov 19] first foal: dam suited by 7f/1m: well beaten. *P. D. Evans*

DARAYDAN (IRE)   4 b.g. Kahyasi 130 – Delsy (FR) (Abdos 134) [1995 107:   107 12g* 12g* 12g³ 12m 16d⁴ 12m⁴ 16m* 1996 12s² 16.2m⁴ 18.7g² 16g 16.1m 16f⁴ Aug 1] close-coupled gelding: useful performer: fourth of 7 to Double Trigger in Sagaro Stakes at Ascot and 6 lengths second of 18 to Merit (under 9-10) in Chester Cup in May: long way below form next 2 starts, back to best when 6 lengths fourth of 7 to Grey Shot in Goodwood Cup final one: stays 18.7f: acts on firm ground and soft: blinkered (below form) 3 times: twice coltish, and has been gelded: has run well when sweating: joined M. Pipe, and won over hurdles in December. *Lady Herries*

DARAZARI (IRE)   3 b.c. Sadler's Wells (USA) 132 – Darara 129 (Top Ville 129)   123 [1995 NR 1996 10g² 12d⁴ 12g* 12.5g* 12m² 12d Oct 6] strong, well-made colt: sixth

Prix Maurice de Nieuil, Maisons-Laffitte—
progressive Darazari strides away from Leeds and Astor Place (rails)

foal: closely related to Dardjini (rated 99, winner at 1m at 2 yrs to 1½m, by Nijinsky) and half-brother to 3 winners, including Dariyoun (rated 115, stayed 2½m, in France, by Shahrastani): dam, won Prix Vermeille, half-sister to Darshaan (rated 133) and Dalara (rated 114): very smart performer: won minor event at Chantilly in June and 6-runner Prix Maurice de Nieuil at Maisons-Laffitte (by 2½ lengths from Leeds) in July: ran very well when length second of 10 to Helissio in Prix Niel at Longchamp, held up, not clear run early in straight then staying on strongly: disappointing in Prix de l'Arc de Triomphe at Longchamp 3 weeks later: stays 12.5f: yet to race on extremes of ground: reportedly wintered in Dubai. *A. de Royer Dupre, France*

DARB ALOLA (USA)   2 b.c. (Apr 18) Nureyev (USA) 131 – Kristana 96 (Kris   96
135) [1996 5.2s² 5m⁶ 5d² Oct 28] $100,000Y: good-quartered, attractive colt: sixth foal: closely related to 2 winners in USA by Storm Bird and half-brother to 2 winners, including 1989 Prix Robert Papin winner Ozone Friendly (by Green Forest): dam, 1¼m winner, is daughter of half-sister to St Leger winner Athens Wood: useful maiden: slow-starting sixth (2 handlers in paddock, free to post) to Tipsy Creek in Norfolk Stakes at Ascot on second start: off course over 4 months afterwards, short-head second of 9 to Jennelle in minor event at Lingfield on return: will stay 6f: sure to win a race or two. *M. R. Stoute*

DARBY FLYER   3 ch.c. Dominion Royale 112 – Shining Wood 65 (Touching   –
Wood (USA) 127) [1995 49: 6d a6g³ 1996 a5g⁶ a6g Jan 23] poor maiden: below form in January: should stay at least 7f. *W. R. Muir*

DARCEY BUSSELL   4 b.f. Green Desert (USA) 127 – Docklands 91 (On Your   66
Mark 125) [1995 59: 8.1g 7f 8m⁴ 7.1s 8f² 7f⁴ 1996 7m 7g* 8.2m⁴ 8m* 8m* 7f⁴ Jun 25] shallow-girthed filly: reportedly in foal to Efisio: fair performer: in good form in June, winning minor event at Catterick and handicaps at Thirsk and Ripon (apprentices, career-best effort) Newmarket: should have stayed further than 1m: acted on firm ground: sold 34,000 gns Newmarket December Sales. *B. W. Hills*

DAREROCK   3 b.g. Daring March 116 – Marock Morley 59 (Most Secret 119)   –
[1995 –: 5m 5f⁵ 5m⁶ 5g 7f 1996 6s 8.3d⁶ Apr 3] robust gelding: no form. *M. Dods*

DARGO   2 b.c. (May 10) Formidable (USA) 125 – Mountain Memory 109 (High   74 p
Top 131) [1996 7m² 7d⁵ Aug 10] 32,000Y: fourth foal: half-brother to 3 winners, including 7f winner Nawaasi (by Green Desert) and 13.6f to 2m winner Mystic Memory (by Ela-Mana-Mou): dam, 6f (at 2 yrs) and 8.2f winner suited to 1¼m, is sister to Derby Italiano winner My Top: staying-on second in median auction maiden at Newcastle: better form when front-running fifth to The Fly in similar event at Ayr 12 days later: will stay 1m: likely to do better. *M. Johnston*

DARIKA LAD   8 gr.g. Belfort (FR) 89 – Lindrake's Pride (Mandrake Major 122)   – §
[1995 NR 1996 a11g a8g Jan 26] of no account: sold 1,050 gns Doncaster March Sales. *A. Harrison*

DARING DESTINY   5 b.m. Daring March 116 – Raunchy Rita (Brigadier   113
Gerard 144) [1995 104: 6g⁵ 5.5s² 7f* 6m² 6m 7f⁶ 6m 6g 1996 6s 5.2d³ 7.1d⁶ 6m* 6g² 6f 6g* 6g* 6m 7m Oct 17] big, strong, workmanlike mare: has a round action: smart performer: won minor event at Newmarket in June: career-best efforts when winning Phoenix Sprint Stakes at Leopardstown (by head from Farhana) and Jacobs Goldene Peitsche at Baden-Baden (beat Hever Golf Rose a short head), both in August: below form last 2 starts: has won at 7f, but best as a sprinter: acts on firm and soft ground, below form on heavy: effective blinkered/visored (was most of 1996) or not: has run well when sweating and edgy. *K. R. Burke*

DARING FLIGHT (USA)   2 b.c. (Apr 15) Danzig (USA) – Life At The Top 107   80
(Habitat 134) [1996 5m⁴ 6g⁴ 5.7d 6m Oct 17] small colt: has a round action: third foal: dam 6f and 7f winner at 2 yrs, stayed 1¼m: close up throughout when fourth to Tycoon Todd in maiden at York in September, easily best effort: rider reportedly felt something amiss final outing: stays 6f: showed little on dead ground. *Lord Huntingdon*

DARING RYDE   5 b.g. Daring March 116 – Mini Myra 49 (Homing 130) [1995   45
45: 7g 8.2m⁶ 8g* 8.2m⁵ 8.1m 8m 10m 8.1d³ 8.2m 1996 8g 10d 8m⁶ 7.1m⁶ 8.1m 8.2g Oct 24] tall gelding: poor performer: should stay beyond 1m: acts on good to firm ground: inconsistent. *J. P. Smith*

DARING VENTURE   3 b.f. Dowsing (USA) 124 – Berberana 68 (Never So   –
Bold 135) [1995 –: 6m 1996 8.2d 6f⁵ 6.1m 6g Jul 8] leggy, sparely-made filly: no worthwhile form: sold 700 gns Ascot October Sales. *T. J. Naughton*

DARK DEED (USA)   3 ch.f. Known Fact (USA) 135 – Sin Lucha (USA) (North-   85
fields (USA)) [1995 81: 6m³ 6m² 6g² 1996 5m³ 6m* 6g 6m Aug 2] small, sturdy
filly: poor mover: fairly useful performer: comfortably best effort in 1996 to win
strongly-run maiden at Pontefract in June, staying on gamely to lead inside final 1f:
will stay at least 7f: has raced only on a sound surface: sold 9,500 gns Newmarket
December Sales. *B. W. Hills*

DARK GREEN (USA)   2 ch.c. (Jan 25) Green Dancer (USA) 132 – Ardisia   89
(USA) 87 (Affirmed (USA)) [1996 7.1g³ 8m³ Oct 1] angular, useful-looking colt:
has a fluent, quick action: first foal: dam, won 3 times at around 1¼m, daughter of
Musidora winner Princess of Man: fairly useful form when third in maidens won by
Gretel at Sandown and Asas at Newmarket 3 months later: will be well suited by
middle distances: sure to win a race. *P. F. I. Cole*

DARK MENACE   4 br.g. Beveled (USA) – Sweet And Sure (Known Fact (USA)   51
135) [1995 71d: 6m³ 6g⁶ 6f 6g 5.3f³ 7f³ 5.7h 6d 1996 6m 6m 6f* 6m⁶ 6m 7m a7g a6g⁵
a7g² Dec 11] workmanlike gelding: only modest at best in 1996: won poor maiden
handicap at Brighton in July: should stay 7f: acts on firm ground and equitrack, ran
poorly on heavy final 2-y-o start: probably effective blinkered or not: inconsistent.
E. A. Wheeler

DARK MILE (USA)   2 b.f. (Apr 9) Woodman (USA) 126 – Fateful (USA) 90   86 p
(Topsider (USA)) [1996 5m² Aug 19] second foal: half-sister to smart 3-y-o 7f and
1m winner Fatefully (by Private Account): dam 6f (at 2 yrs) and 7f winner: slow-
starting second to Joza in maiden at Windsor, headstrong to halfway but still running
on strongly: will stay 6f: will improve. *J. H. M. Gosden*

DARK SHOT (IRE)   4 b.g. Rock City 120 – Jeanne Avril 99 (Music Boy 124)   62
[1995 65: a8.5g⁵ a7g* a5g³ a6g⁵ a6g* 6.1g² a6g⁵ a5g a6g 1996 5.9f⁵ a7g a6g⁴ 8g 7m
Sep 17] compact gelding: fluent mover: modest performer at best: left R. Fahey after
second start: sold 2,000 gns Doncaster September Sales: effective at 6f and 7f: acts
on the all-weather and dead ground: no improvement in blinkers/visor: inconsistent.
N. Tinkler

DARK SOUND (IRE)   3 b.g. Darshaan 133 – Second Guess (Ela-Mana-Mou   –
132) [1995 NR 1996 12g May 4] IR 7,200Y: first reported living foal: dam Irish 1¼m
winner: showed nil in maiden. *A. B. Mulholland*

DARK TRUFFLE   3 br.f. Deploy 131 – River Dove (USA) 86 (Riverman (USA)   69 d
131) [1995 59: 6m 1996 8.3m³ 8.1m 10d 10.3g 12g Nov 1] strong, sturdy filly: failed
by long way to repeat form of third in Windsor maiden on reappearance: should be
suited by further than 8.3f: blinkered (pulled hard) final 3-y-o start: joined T. George.
Mrs J. Cecil

DARK WATERS (IRE)   3 b.c. Darshaan 133 – Grecian Sea (FR) (Homeric 133)   –
[1995 82p: 7m 8.2d² 1996 10m Aug 19] robust, attractive colt with scope: weak in
market, never placed to challenge nor knocked about in maiden at Windsor on
belated return: will prove well suited by middle distances: sold 18,000 gns Newmarket Autumn Sales. *M. R. Stoute*

DARLING CLOVER   4 ch.f. Minster Son 130 – Lady Clementine 68 (He Loves   79
Me 120) [1995 62: a11g⁴ a12g⁴ a12g² 11.6m* 11.8g 11.6m 10m⁵ 10.1m² 10m³ 1996
9.9m* 9.9g² 10g 9.9m* 9.9f* 9.9f² 8.9g* 10.1m⁶ 9.2g⁶ 8.9g 8m⁶ 8s Nov 9] leggy
filly: has a quick action: fair handicapper: won at Beverley 3 times (in a ladies race
second occasion) and at York once (claimed out of D. Morley's stable £14,000)
between April and September: well below form last 4 starts: best form at 9f/1¼m but
has won at up to 11.6f: acts on fibresand and firm ground: held up: game. *R. Bastiman*

DARLING FLAME (USA)   3 b.f. Capote (USA) – My Darling One (USA)   101
(Exclusive Native (USA)) [1995 101: 6g² 6f* 6g² 6m 1996 7m⁶ 8d 8m 7m* 7d Oct
21] tall, lengthy, unfurnished filly: useful form: creditable sixth of 11 to Thrilling
Day in Nell Gwyn Stakes at Newmarket on reappearance: easily won steadily-run
minor event at Redcar in October, cruising through on bridle to lead near finish: stays
1m: seems to need a sound surface: joined J. Noseda in USA. *J. H. M. Gosden*

DARNAWAY   2 b.c. (Mar 14) Green Desert (USA) 127 – Reuval 102 (Sharpen Up   82 p
127) [1996 7g⁴ Oct 30] eighth foal: brother to smart 7f/1m performer Ardkinglass
and half-brother to 3-y-o 1¼m winner Kinlochewe (by Old Vic) and useful 1¼m
winners Jura (by Rousillon) and Pitcroy (by Unfuwain): dam suited by 1m: not

knocked about when fourth to Happy Valentine in maiden at Yarmouth: will stay 1m: will improve. *H. R. A. Cecil*

DARTER (IRE) 4 b.c. Darshaan 133 – Mamouna (USA) 113 (Vaguely Noble 140) [1995 72: 12.3m^3 13.4d^6 11.9d^5 11.8f^3 1996 16.4g* Apr 26] good-topped colt: did well physically: useful juvenile hurdler: looking very well, improved form for new stable when impressive 5-length winner of handicap at Sandown: suited by test of stamina: below form on a soft surface: looked sure to win more races, but reportedly injured a tendon. *R. Akehurst* **82**

DARYABAD (IRE) 4 b.c. Thatching 131 – Dayanata (Shirley Heights 130) [1995 7g* 8g 7f^3 8d^4 8g* 1996 9s 8.1d 10.1m 7m 8g 7m^5 7m* 7.1m 8g a8.5g Nov 16] big, strong ex-Irish colt: second foal: half-brother to Irish 1¾m winner Dayadan (by Shernazar): dam unraced sister to Darshaan: useful when trained at 2 and 3 yrs by J. Oxx, winning 3 races: only fair form in Britain: easily best effort in 1996 to win handicap at Redcar in August, leading 2f out: stays 1m: acts on firm and soft ground: probably effective blinkered or not. *T. J. Naughton* **81**

DASHING BLUE 3 ch.g. Dashing Blade 117 – Blubella 86 (Balidar 133) [1995 96p: 6m^2 5g^4 5m^2 6m* 6d^4 6m* 1996 5g* 6d^3 6m 6g^6 5m^4 6m 5m^3 5m^2 Aug 31] big, good-bodied gelding: useful handicapper: won rated stakes at Sandown (impressively) in April: good efforts at York and Sandown (another rated stakes, ¾-length second of 13 to Crowded Avenue, making most) last 2 starts: subsequently gelded: effective at 5f and 6f: best efforts on a sound surface: not the easiest of rides, but has run well for apprentice: may benefit from blinkers. *I. A. Balding* **103**

DASHING DANCER (IRE) 5 ch.g. Conquering Hero (USA) 116 – Santa Maria (GER) (Literat) [1995 65: 6g^5 6f^4 6g^2 5m^4 6f^3 6m 6m^2 6m^5 6d 6f^2 1996 6.1g 6f^2 6f 6m^5 6m^6 6g^4 a8.5g Sep 21] strong, compact gelding: modest maiden: sold out of R. Akehurst's stable 1,850 gns Ascot August Sales after sixth start: stays 6f: acts on firm and soft ground: sometimes early to post: has joined A. Forbes. *B. P. J. Baugh* **58**

DASHING INVADER (USA) 3 ch.g. Pirate Army (USA) 118 – Cherie's Hope (USA) (Flying Paster (USA)) [1995 –: 8d 8.2m 1996 10g 11.6m 11.8d 12g 14.9m 12m^4 12m^3 14.1d Aug 25] heavy-topped gelding: poor maiden handicapper: stays 1½m: acts on good to firm and dead ground. *P. W. Harris* **48**

DASHING ROCKSVILLE 2 b.f. (Mar 10) Rock City 120 – Dash (Connaught 130) [1996 6d^5 5.9g* 5.1m^5 7m^4 7g^3 7m* 7g 7g Aug 26] 2,300Y: well-made filly: has scope: fifth foal: half-sister to 4-y-o 1m and 11f winner Eden Dancer (by Shareef Dancer): dam poor maiden who stayed 1½m: modest form: won maiden auction at Carlisle in May and claimer at Thirsk in August: ran badly last 2 outings: stays 7f: acts on good to firm ground: sold 10,000 gns Newmarket December Sales. *M. R. Channon* **57**

DASUL 2 ch.f. (Apr 6) Risk Me (FR) 127 – Bocas Rose 106 (Jalmood (USA) 126) [1996 6m May 29] 6,800Y: third foal: sister to 4-y-o Moody, 6f winner at 2 yrs, and a winner in Norway: dam sprinter: faltered halfway in maiden auction at Folkestone in May, coming back well beaten: not seen out again. *G. Lewis* **–**

DATO STAR (IRE) 5 br.g. Accordion – Newgate Fairy (Flair Path 122) [1995 95p: 16.2m^5 12m^4 13.4d^2 12m 12m^2 1996 14.1g^3 12s^4 Nov 9] rangy gelding: good mover: smart hurdler: best efforts on flat when in frame in last 2 runnings of November Handicap at Doncaster, rallying 2½ lengths fourth of 22 to Clifton Fox last time: effective at 1½m and will stay beyond 1¾m: acts on good to firm ground and soft: remains well capable of winning races on flat. *J. M. Jefferson* **97**

DATUM (USA) 3 br.g. Dayjur (USA) 137 – My Ballerina (USA) 94 (Sir Ivor 135) [1995 NR 1996 6m Jun 4] small, stocky gelding: first living foal: dam 1¼m and 1½m winner: burly and green, well beaten in maiden at Pontefract: sold (M. Bell to G. Enright) 750 gns Newmarket July Sales. *M. Bell* **–**

DAUNT 4 b.g. Darshaan 133 – Minute Waltz (Sadler's Wells (USA) 132) [1995 90p: 8d* 1996 8d 10.3g 9f* 10m^3 11.9m^5 12m^2 12g 10d^5 Oct 12] rangy gelding: useful handicapper: dead-heated at Newbury in July, joined on line: best form at Doncaster (held up, looked sure to win when cruising through to challenge 2f out, beaten ¾ length by Spillo) in September: sold (J. Gosden to F. Jordan) 100,000 gns Newmarket Autumn Sales: barely stays 1½m: acts on firm and dead going: some- **100**

times taken alone to post: tended to hang left final 4-y-o start: usually front runner. *J. H. M. Gosden*

DAUNTING DESTINY (BEL)   3 b.c. Formidable (USA) 125 – Heavy Land   85
(FR) (Recitation (USA) 124) [1995 77: 6m 7g 7f² 6m 6.9g⁴ 7f² 8f* 1996 10m⁴ 10.2g⁶ 10m² 10g 10m* 10.5m* Aug 9] quite good-topped colt: unimpressive mover: fairly useful handicapper: improved form to win at Ascot and Haydock: would have stayed further than 10.5f: acted on firm ground: dead. *R. Hannon*

DAUNTING TIMES   2 b.f. (Apr 19) Timeless Times (USA) 99 – Dauntless   –
Flight (Golden Mallard 103) [1996 7f Sep 27] fifth reported foal: sister to 3-y-o Time To Fly and half-sister to 6f winner Dauntless Fort (by Belfort): dam unraced: soundly beaten in median auction maiden at Redcar. *B. W. Murray*

DAUNTLESS FORT   5 gr.m. Belfort (FR) 89 – Dauntless Flight (Golden Mal-   –
lard 103) [1995 38, a–: a6g a7g 7g a7g a8g 6m⁵ 5g 6f 1996 a6g a6g a5g Jul 27] looked of little account in 1996. *Mrs V. A. Aconley*

DAUPHIN (IRE)   3 b. or br.g. Astronef 116 – Va Toujours 109 (Alzao (USA) 117)   48
[1995 –p: 7.1m 6f 1996 a6g⁶ a7g⁵ 10.8g 10m 8m 10g 12m 12m² 11.9m* 12m 11.9g 9g⁴ Nov 1] workmanlike gelding: has a round action: poor handicapper: won at Haydock (amateurs) in September by 5 lengths: stays 1½m: acts on good to firm ground: flashes tail: inconsistent. *W. J. Musson*

DAVID JAMES' GIRL   4 b.f. Faustus (USA) 118 – Eagle's Quest 62 (Legal   –
Eagle 126) [1995 65d: a7g a6g² a7g a7g* a7g⁴ a8.5g⁶ 7.6m² 6.9f² a8.5g 7m a7g a6g   a57
a6g⁵ a7g³ 1996 a8g⁴ a8g⁵ a7g⁵ a8g* a8.5g³ a8g³ a8.5g a8.5g a9.4g² a9.4g⁴ a9.4g⁶ a7g³ a7g* a8g a7g³ 7.6m a8g⁶ 7d a12g⁵ Sep 7] leggy filly: modest performer nowadays: won sellers at Southwell in March and (apprentices handicap) June: below form last 6 starts: stays 9.4f: acts on good to firm and soft ground and on fibresand: best held up in strongly-run race. *A. Bailey*

DAVIDS REVENGE   2 b.c. (Feb 26) Reprimand 122 – Tribal Lady 80 (Absalom   70 p
128) [1996 6s Oct 24] 12,000F, 10,000Y: big, useful-looking colt: shows keen action: second foal: dam 2-y-o 5f and 6f winner who stayed 7f: slow-starting seventh of 23 to Za-Im in maiden at Newbury: bred to stay 7f: has plenty of scope, and is sure to do better. *Major D. N. Chappell*

DAVIS ROCK   2 ch.f. (Mar 18) Rock City 120 – Sunny Davis (USA) 71 (Alydar   69
(USA)) [1996 a7g² 5m² a7g² a6g* a8g⁵ a5g⁶ a7s Dec 19] second foal: half-sister to 3-y-o Warming Trends (by Warning), 6f and 7f winner at 2 yrs: dam, 2-y-o 7f winner, out of sister to Larida (dam of Magic of Life) and half-sister to Miss Oceana: won maiden at Wolverhampton in October: sold out of Sir Mark Prescott's stable 11,000 gns Newmarket Autumn Sales afterwards, and bit below best last 3 starts: stays 7f: acts on fibresand and good to firm ground. *W. R. Muir*

DAVOSKI   2 b. or gr.c. (Mar 29) Niniski (USA) 125 – Pamela Peach 81 (Habitat   77
134) [1996 7m³ 8m⁶ Oct 17] quite good-topped colt: third foal: half-brother to fairly useful 3-y-o Marl (by Lycius), 5.2f winner at 2 yrs, and Italian 1¼m winner Arcidiavolo (by Night Shift): dam maiden here (effective at 6f/7f) who later won in USA: slow-starting third of 5 to stable-companion State Fair in listed race at Newbury in August: hampered start when never-dangerous sixth in Newmarket maiden 2 months later: will be suited by middle distances. *B. W. Hills*

DAWADAR (USA)   9 b.g. Exceller (USA) 129 – Damana (FR) (Crystal Palace   –
(FR) 132) [1995 NR 1996 13.9g 18g Oct 21] angular gelding: fairly useful staying handicap hurdler in 1994/5: once fairly useful on flat: showed nil in 1996. *J. S. Goldie*

DAWALIB (USA)   6 ch.g. Danzig Connection (USA) – Centavos (USA) (Scout   65
Leader (USA)) [1995 71, a75: a7g⁵ a6g³ a6g⁴ a7g³ a7g³ 7g* 6m² 7.6m* 8.1g² 7g² 7f²   a–
7g⁶ 7m* 6d 6g 1996 7d 6.9f 7m 7.6g 7s² 7.3s³ 7m 6m 7f⁴ 7m⁵ 6m 8f⁶ 7.1f² 7m 8d Oct 2] good-topped gelding: poor mover: fair handicapper: effective at 6f to 1m: acts on firm and soft going and on fibresand: effective visored, but not tried for long time: inconsistent. *D. Haydn Jones*

DAWAM ALLAIL   2 b.g. (Mar 5) Night Shift (USA) – Veronica (Persian Bold   71
123) [1996 7g⁶ 7f³ 7f⁴ 6m⁵ Sep 26] 50,000Y: sturdy gelding: second foal: closely related to 1993 2-y-o 1m winner Truckhaven Secret (by Secreto): dam placed several times in Ireland and won at around 1m in USA: fair form in maidens: stays 7f: raced only on a sound surface. *M. A. Jarvis*

Mr P. D. Savill's "Daylight In Dubai"

DAWAWIN (USA) 3 b.f. Dixieland Band (USA) – Stalwart Moment (USA) 74 + (Stalwart (USA)) [1995 81p: 7m³ 1996 7d 8.2m* 8d Oct 11] leggy, quite attractive filly: unimpressive mover: off course nearly 6 months, won maiden at Nottingham in September: stayed 8.2f: acted on good to firm ground, twice well beaten on dead: visits Elmaamul. *E. A. L. Dunlop*

DAWNA 3 b.f. Polish Precedent (USA) 131 – Welsh Daylight (Welsh Pageant 132) 106 [1995 NR 1996 8.2m² 8g² 8m* 8f* 8g⁴ 7m Jul 30] strong, lengthy, good-topped filly: half-sister to several winners, including very useful French middle-distance performer Ordinance (by Henbit): dam won twice at 1¼m in Ireland: useful performer: won maiden at Yarmouth and listed rated stakes at Ascot (by ¾ length from Miss Riviera, quickening well), both in June: best effort when 3½ lengths fourth of 9 to Sensation in Falmouth Stakes at Newmarket: better at 1m than 7f, and would have stayed further: acted on firm ground: stud. *H. R. A. Cecil*

DAWN FLIGHT 7 b.g. Precocious 126 – Sea Kestrel 82 (Sea Hawk II 131) [1995 – –: 15.4m 1996 11.6g Jul 1] strong gelding: modest maiden handicapper on flat: well below form since 5 yrs: well below form in blinkers/visor: modest winning hurdler, stays 3m: sold 625 gns Ascot November Sales. *J. R. Jenkins*

DAWN SUMMIT 2 ch.c. (Jan 21) Salse (USA) 128 – Bereeka (Main Reef 126) – [1996 7d 6m Sep 26] heavy-topped colt: fifth foal: dam unraced half-sister to Wollow: behind in maidens: bred to stay at least 1m. *B. Hanbury*

DAYDREAM ISLAND 3 ch.f. Never So Bold 135 – La Belle Vie 73 (Indian – King (USA) 128) [1995 –: 6.1d 7.1s 1996 8g 6.1m 5.1m Jul 18] no form. *R. J. Baker*

DAYLAMI (IRE) 2 gr.c. (Apr 20) Doyoun 124 – Daltawa (IRE) (Miswaki (USA) 112 p 124) [1996 8d* 8g* 10s² Nov 2] first foal: dam French 1¼m (at 2 yrs) and 10.5f winner, second in Prix Penelope: won 9-runner newcomers event at Longchamp in September and 6-runner listed race at Evry (by 2 lengths from Bartex) in October: ¾-length second of 10 to Shaka in Criterium de Saint-Cloud, leading over 1f out to inside last: will stay 1½m: acts on soft going: looks a good prospect. *A. de Royer-Dupre, France*

DAYLIGHT DREAMS   2 b.f. (Apr 9) Indian Ridge 123 – Singing Nelly 56   77
(Pharly (FR) 130) [1996 5g* 6m 6d 6.5m Sep 11] 11,000Y: workmanlike filly: second foal: half-sister to 3-y-o In Tune (by Prince Sabo): dam, lightly-raced maiden, closely related to Further Flight: won maiden auction at Ripon in April: out of depth in Lowther Stakes at York and listed race at Ripon next 2 starts then tailed off in nursery at Doncaster: will stay beyond 6f. *C. A. Cyzer*

DAYLIGHT IN DUBAI (USA)   2 ch.c. (Apr 4) Twilight Agenda (USA) 126 –   100 +
Lady Godolphin (USA) (Son Ange (USA)) [1996 5.2d* 5g³ 6f² 6m* 7g 8g⁶ Oct 26] $100,000F, $130,000Y: tall, useful-looking colt: has plenty of scope: fluent mover: half-brother to several winners, notably smart 1994 2-y-o Sri Pekan (up to 7f, by Red Ransom): dam won at up to 7f in USA: sire (by Devil's Bag) useful 7f/1m winner in Ireland, later Grade 1 9f winner in USA and second in Breeders' Cup Classic: won maiden at Newbury in April and P V Doyle Railway Stakes (by ½ length from Check The Band) at the Curragh in June: kept smart company on other starts, second in Coventry Stakes at Ascot on third outing and running well though unplaced in National Stakes at the Curragh and Racing Post Trophy at Doncaster in autumn: may well stay 1¼m: acts on firm ground and dead: sent to USA. *P. W. Chapple-Hyam*

DAYRELLA   2 ch.f. (May 27) Beveled (USA) – Divissima 62 (Music Boy 124)   –
[1996 6m 6.1m 5m 6m Oct 17] 1,200F: lengthy, unfurnished filly: sixth foal: half-sister to 1992 2-y-o 6f winner Nut Bush (by Aragon): dam 6f winner, half-sister to smart 1978 2-y-o sprinter Eyelet: behind in maidens and a nursery. *W. R. Muir*

DAYTONA BEACH (IRE)   6 ch.g. Bluebird (USA) 125 – Water Spirit (USA)   –
(Riverman (USA) 131) [1995 66: a8g² a8g* 9g* 8m 9.7m³ a9.4g² 8.3m⁵ a8.5g² 8m⁴ 10.3m² 7.6m 7.1m 1996 8.2g Oct 9] fair handicapper: in need of race only start in 1996: stays 9.7f: acts on firm ground and fibresand: tried visored/blinkered at 3 yrs, no improvement: broke down badly over hurdles Oct 22. *D. J. S. ffrench Davis*

DAYVILLE (USA)   2 b.f. (Jan 19) Dayjur (USA) 137 – Chain Fern (USA)   79
(Blushing Groom (FR) 131) [1996 5.1m³ 6.9g³ a6g* 6d² Sep 27] leggy, lengthy filly: fourth foal: half-sister to 4-y-o Tarian (by Lyphard) and fairly useful 1m winner (stayed 11.4f) Woodwardia (by El Gran Senor): dam unraced sister to Al Bahathri: fair form: won maiden at Wolverhampton in July by 6 lengths: creditable second in nursery final start: best form at 6f: wears bandages: sold 30,000 gns Newmarket December Sales. *R. Charlton*

DAZZLE   2 b. or br.f. (Mar 28) Gone West (USA) – Belle Et Deluree (USA)   116 d
(The Minstrel (CAN) 135) [1996 5f* 6g* 6m⁴ 7g² Oct 18]

Two defeats at Newmarket in the autumn took the shine off Dazzle's highly promising performances in the summer. Her first two victories were impressive enough to make her favourite for the One Thousand Guineas, but those reverses must have left connections merely hoping that she was still a Guineas filly.

Dazzle was clearly highly regarded from the very start, so much so she made her debut at Royal Ascot in the Windsor Castle Stakes. The only debutant in a field of ten which included seven winners, Dazzle was green and on her toes in the paddock, accompanied by two handlers—as she was to be for all her starts—but created a favourable impression overall in the preliminaries, and showing a fluent, round action. Despite her lack of experience, she started a well-backed favourite. Dazzle overcame a jink at the start from her wide draw and was well on top at the finish to beat Vax Star two and a half lengths after leading inside the last.

The Ascot form received a boost when the runner-up in a listed race at Sandown four days before Dazzle reappeared in the Hillsdown Cherry Hinton Stakes but Dazzle soon provided further evidence of her own ability with a highly impressive win at Newmarket, a performance which still rates as the joint-best put up by a two-year-old filly all season, along with that of Red Camellia at Goodwood. She faced eight opponents in the Cherry Hinton, three of whom—Dame Laura (second), Connemara (fourth) and Lycility (tenth)—

had contested the Queen Mary Stakes at Royal Ascot, and another two —Khassah and Well Warned—who had fought out the finish of a maiden at Ascot. Eye Shadow, third in a listed race over the Cherry Hinton course and distance, Rich In Love, the winner of a Ripon minor event, and Ocean Ridge, who had made a successful debut in a Newbury maiden, made up the field. Initially held up, Dazzle moved through to chase the pace at halfway before quickening clear from two furlongs out, putting five lengths between herself and Ocean Ridge by the line, with three and a half lengths and four back to Well Warned and Eye Shadow. The fillies who had competed in the Queen Mary filled the last three places. The timefigure—0.72 fast, impressive for a two-year-old filly—provided further proof that this was a smart performance, and her jockey Fallon was particularly taken: ' The acceleration she has off a fast pace is unbelievable . . . I've never ridden a horse with such a turn of foot. She puts her head down and races just like at Ascot, I couldn't pull her up.' Dazzle was immediately made 7/1 favourite for the One Thousand Guineas.

Dazzle was rested for three months before her main target, the Cheveley Park, as her trainer was keen not to give her too many races on firm ground. No filly had emerged in the interim seriously to challenge Dazzle's place at the head of the Guineas market. Indeed, her position looked stronger than in July, with the Cherry Hinton runner-up Ocean Ridge winning the Prix Robert Papin next time out. By Cheveley Park time Dazzle's odds for the Guineas had contracted to 7/2. More immediately Dazzle looked to have an excellent chance in the Cheveley Park itself and she started at 9/4 on with only Godolphin's recent acquisition Moonlight Paradise and the French filly Pas de Reponse also at shorter than 10/1 in the eight-runner field. Ocean Ridge reopposed, best fancied of the outsiders. Fallon gave Dazzle what, if things had gone to plan, would have been called a confident ride. Settled in last place off the steady pace set by Ocean Ridge, Dazzle was outpaced as the tempo quickened at the top of the hill, and while only a couple of lengths down on the eventual winner Pas de Reponse and upsides Moonlight Paradise who ran on for second, Dazzle became unbalanced in the Dip and was unable to find any further acceleration, beaten a total of two and a half lengths in fourth as Ocean Ridge held on for third. The headlines in the trade papers left no doubt as to where they thought the blame for Dazzle's defeat lay, *The Sporting Life* leading with 'Fallon fails to dazzle', while *Racing Post* made reference to the filly who deposed Dazzle as Guineas favourite: 'Sleepytime beckons for under-fire Fallon.' The jockey defended himself by saying 'If she had been the same horse which won the Cherry Hinton she would have won . . . I did not have the same horse under me.' Had Dazzle run anywhere near her best and been beaten a fast-finishing head or neck the criticisms would have carried more weight, but as it was she was some 10 lb below the form she had shown on the July course.

Windsor Castle Stakes, Royal Ascot—Dazzle makes a winning debut

Hillsdown Cherry Hinton Stakes, Newmarket—Dazzle again, by five lengths from Ocean Ridge

Dazzle was given the chance to redeem herself in the Rockfel Stakes at Newmarket seventeen days later, partnered by Swinburn whose serious fall early in the year in Hong Kong had made him unavailable for Dazzle's races in the summer. Dazzle's participation was in some doubt with firm ground threatening, but, gone in her coat, she was only second favourite to the Cheveley Park runner-up Moonlight Paradise. There were no excuses to be made for Dazzle on this occasion. She had every chance two out but was again unable to quicken with Moonlight Paradise up the hill and went down by two and a half lengths in second place, slightly more than she finished behind Moonlight Paradise in the Cheveley Park but showing a similar level of form.

Gone West, best known in Europe for his Two Thousand Guineas winner Zafonic, had an excellent season with his two-year-olds which included the Queen Mary winner Dance Parade, the Gimcrack third The West and Zafonic's brother Zamindar, who was placed in the Prix Morny and, like The West, the Salamandre. Two-year-olds accounted for the majority of Gone West's runners in Britain and Ireland in the latest season, ten out of fourteen of whom had won by the end of the turf campaign. Gone West's older representatives were headed by the high-class mile-and-a-quarter colt Tamayaz and the Breeders' Cup Mile winner Da Hoss.

		Gone West (USA) (b 1984)	Mr Prospector (b 1970)	Raise A Native
Dazzle				Gold Digger
(b. or br.f.			Secrettame (ch 1978)	Secretariat
Mar 28, 1994)				Tamerett
		Belle Et Deluree (USA) (b 1985)	The Minstrel (ch 1974)	Northern Dancer
				Fleur
			Sophisticated Girl (b 1980)	Stop The Music
				Close Control

Dazzle, Tamayaz, Zafonic and Zamindar, and the smart sprinter Western Approach are all out of mares by The Minstrel. Dazzle is the fifth foal out of Belle Et Deluree and her fourth to win, following minor winners Musical Prospect (by Tank's Prospect) in Eastern Europe, Paula Sue's Prince (by Cozzene) in the United States and Jinx Joke (by Miswaki) in Italy. The Cheveley Park Stud has the dam's yearling filly from the first crop of Gone West's brother Lion Cavern. Belle Et Deluree was tried in top-class company as a two-year-old but was found wanting, finishing ninth in the Prix Marcel Boussac. She had won over a mile prior to that however and was successful for a second time at Longchamp as a three-year-old over a mile and a quarter. Belle Et Deluree ran once in the United States before being sold for 140,000 dollars at the Keeneland November Sale as a four-year-old. A close relative, Dancing Tribute, was also trained by Stoute and in 1988 headed the One Thousand Guineas ante-post market once during her two-year-old career before being beaten at odds on for the Cheveley Park. Dancing Tribute's own daughter Dance Sequence also contested the Cheveley Park for the stable, finishing fourth in 1995 having been narrowly beaten in the Cherry Hinton, and finished sixth in the Guineas. Belle Et Deluree's and Dancing Tribute's dam Sophisticated Girl was best at around a mile, showing very smart form at two when second in the Oak Leaf Stakes, and was the second foal of the minor two-year-old winner Close Control to be placed in Grade 1 company at two after the Matron Stakes runner-up Fair Advantage.

Dazzle is a good-bodied, quite attractive filly. She has the scope to train on as a three-year-old, and if she manages to recapture her Cherry Hinton form she will obviously be well up to winning another good race. But whether she will recapture it must be open to doubt at this stage. Dazzle has shown plenty of speed but the way she kept on in the Rockfel Stakes suggests she should stay the Guineas trip. She has won on firm going and has yet to encounter a soft surface. *M. R. Stoute*

DAZZLE ME 4 ch.f. Kalaglow 132 – Defy Me 75 (Bustino 136) [1995 –: 7g 7m – 7.1m 1996 5.1m Sep 16] sparely-made filly: no form: tried blinkered. *A. G. Newcombe*

DAZZLING 3 b.f. Rambo Dancer (CAN) 107 – Azaiyma 58 (Corvaro (USA) 74 d 124) [1995 NR 1996 8m⁴ 10m⁴ a9.4g⁵ a12g Aug 17] second foal: dam placed at up to 1½m: well beaten after debut: should prove suited by further than 1m. *D. C. O'Brien*

DAZZLING STAR 3 gr.f. Thatching 131 – Dazzlingly Radiant 81 (Try My Best 43 (USA) 130) [1995 50p: 6g 6g 1996 7d⁵ 8.2d³ 6.1g⁵ 5.1g⁶ Apr 30] quite good-topped filly: poor maiden: sold twice, second occasion for 4,500 gns Newmarket Autumn Sales: stays 8.2f: blinkered (no improvement) final 3-y-o start: sometimes looks none too hearty. *R. Hannon*

DAZZLING STONE 2 b.g. (Feb 20) Mujtahid (USA) 118 – Lady In Green 76 p (Shareef Dancer (USA) 135) [1996 6f² Aug 19] third foal: brother to a 1996 winner in USA and half-brother to 1994 2-y-o 6f winner Green Seed (by Lead On Time): dam unraced: finished well when second in maiden at Hamilton in August: sold to join Lady Herries 14,000 gns Newmarket Autumn Sales and gelded: should improve. *M. R. Stoute*

D-DAY-SMOKE 2 ch.c. (Jun 7) Cigar 68 – Little Pockthorpe (Morston (FR) 125) – [1996 a5g⁵ Apr 2] second reported foal: dam ran twice: well beaten in April seller. *N. P. Littmoden*

DEAD AIM (IRE) 2 b.g. (Feb 13) Sadler's Wells (USA) 132 – Dead Certain 78 p 123§ (Absalom 128) [1996 7g⁶ 7f⁶ 6s⁶ Oct 24] 180,000Y: strong, lengthy gelding: has scope: third foal: brother to useful Irish 3-y-o 7f and 1¼m winner Hamad: dam sprinter, became temperamental: never dangerous in maidens, catching eye when strong-finishing sixth behind Za-Im at Newbury on final start: likely to be suited by at least 7f: sort to do well in handicaps. *I. A. Balding*

DEADLINE TIME (IRE) 3 b.c. Fayruz 116 – Cut It Fine (USA) (Big Spruce 88 (USA)) [1995 77: 5m³ 6.1m⁵ 6m 6g⁵ 7s³ 8g* 7.3d³ 1996 10.3d² 12s² 12.3g 10d* 11.4d⁶ 10m² a9.4g* 8.1g 10.3m Sep 11] angular colt: has a round action: fairly useful handicapper: won at Salisbury (minor event) in May and at Wolverhampton (not hard ridden) in July: moved badly to post and virtually pulled up (reportedly lame) final start: effective at 9.4f to 1½m: acts on good to firm and soft ground and fibresand: visored twice (ran well) at 2 yrs and once (raced too freely) at 3 yrs. *Mrs M. Reveley*

DEADLY DUDLEY (IRE) 2 gr.c. (Apr 13) Great Commotion (USA) 123 – 115 Renzola (Dragonara Palace (USA) 115) [1996 5g* 5g* 6f³ 6g 6.5d* Nov 9]

Owner Edward St George seems to have come up with a promising method of naming horses who run in his Lucayan Stud colours. First Lucky Lionel, named after his chauffeur, and then Deadly Dudley, named after his butler. Both horses were smart two-year-olds, the latter returning from a four-month break to win the Group 2 Criterium des Deux Ans at Evry in November. Deadly Dudley went into that race as the outsider of the four-strong British challenge in a field of eight, but showed improved form to beat the French-trained favourite Sheer Reason and the Prix Eclipse winner Hurricane State by three quarters of a length and one and a half lengths, finishing strongly on his first outing on a soft surface. Deadly Dudley had looked highly promising in winning his first two races back in May, a four-runner maiden at Goodwood and the listed Winalot National Stakes at Sandown, the latter in fine

Criterium des Deux Ans, Evry—
British raiders Deadly Dudley (No. 2) and Hurricane State (No. 3) come first and third,
split by the favourite Sheer Reason (rails)

style by four lengths from Roman Imp. He seemed to lose his way after that and was a rather disappointing favourite in both the Coventry Stakes at Royal Ascot, where he reportedly got jarred up on the fast ground in finishing third of fifteen to Verglas, and the July Stakes at Newmarket, where his saddle slipped when leaving the stalls and as at Ascot he took a strong hold. Commenting on the decision to rest him after Newmarket, the trainer said: 'Deadly Dudley went a little bit over the top on me, so I decided to put him to one side and let him tell me when he was back.' The colt must have been showing plenty again in the autumn to have been persevered with in good company.

Deadly Dudley (IRE) (gr.c. Apr 13, 1994)	Great Commotion (USA) (b 1986)	Nureyev (b 1977)	Northern Dancer Special
		Alathea (b 1975)	Lorenzaccio Vive La Reine
	Renzola (gr 1983)	Dragonara Palace (gr 1971)	Young Emperor Ruby's Princess
		Bright Brook (ch 1974)	Deep Diver Caronbrook

Deadly Dudley's successes provided a much-needed boost for his sire Great Commotion, the 1989 Irish Two Thousand Guineas runner-up who went on to become a smart sprinter. Great Commotion's stud career has so far been plagued by fertility problems, so much so that he was offered free to approved mares during the 1995 breeding season having attracted just ten bookings the previous year. Deadly Dudley, who is from Great Commotion's second crop and cost 22,000 guineas as a yearling, is by far the sire's best representative to date. He is also the best offspring of Renzola, an unraced half-sister to the dam of the good middle-distance winner Millkom. Renzola had produced three winners prior to sixth foal Deadly Dudley, the best of these being the Hannon-trained Miss Nosey Parker, a useful sprinter by Cyrano de Bergerac whose four victories included the listed Harry Rosebery Challenge Trophy at Ayr in 1991. Another Cyrano de Bergerac half-sister to Deadly Dudley was bought on Hannon's behalf for 15,500 guineas at the 1996 Newmarket October Yearling Sales, while a half-brother by Paris House fetched 32,000 guineas as a foal nearly two months later. The dam's side has been a rich source for two-year-old talent, but it does not inspire too much confidence in Deadly Dudley's prospects of making up into a better three-year-old. However, the fact is that Deadly Dudley showed easily his best form on the last of his five outings. In appearance he was leggy and unfurnished as a two-year-old.

It is reported that the seven-furlong Greenham Stakes at Newbury is the next target for Deadly Dudley. Although he looked headstrong in Britain, he stayed the six and a half furlongs well at Evry. He is not bred to stay much further and sprinting may be where his long-term future lies. Meanwhile his owner has reportedly already decided that he will one day have a horse called Rambling Rose, in honour of his Portuguese cook. *R. Hannon*

DEANO'S BEENO   4 b.g. Far North (CAN) 120 – Sans Dot 92 (Busted 134)   80
[1995 85: 12m³ 12.3m² 11.9m 11.9g⁵ 10.3d 8.5s⁴ 1996 10g⁶ 10.8g 12f³ 12f³ 14.9f³ 16.4g 14m² 16.1m 14.6m⁶ 13.1m 14.1m³ 14.6g² Oct 25] rangy gelding: good mover: fairly useful handicapper in 1996: somewhat disappointing: sold (M. Johnston to M. Pipe) 24,000 gns Newmarket Autumn Sales: one paced, and should be suited by test of stamina: acts on firm ground, seemed to act on dead at 2 yrs: often front runner: won novice hurdle in December. *M. Johnston*

DEARDAW   4 b.f. Tina's Pet 121 – Faw (Absalom 128) [1995 42d: a6g 5.1m³ 6m   39
5m 5g 1996 6m 5m 6m 5m 5.7m 6m 6m 5.1f² 5f 5.1m⁴ 5g a5g 5.1m 5m Sep 25]
workmanlike filly: poor maiden: left M. Usher after tenth start: best form at 5f: acts on firm going: tried visored, no improvement: usually races prominently: inconsistent. *Miss L. C. Siddall*

DEAR DRUE   2 b.f. (Apr 16) Jupiter Island 126 – Top And Tail (USA) 81 (Tilt   –
Up (USA)) [1996 8g a8g Nov 14] angular filly: fourth reported foal: half-sister to ungenuine winning sprinter So Superb (by Superlative): dam sprinting half-sister to smart French middle-distance stayer Petit Montmorency: showed nil in maidens. *C. E. Brittain*

DEAR LIFE (USA)   3 b.f. Lear Fan (USA) 130 – Charming Life (NZ) (Sir   100
Tristram 115) [1995 NR 1996 10g² 10.5d 10m⁶ 11.5f* 11.5m² 12f* 12g 11.9g³ 12m* 12m* 12m⁴ Oct 17] leggy filly: first foal: dam, 7f winner in Australia, sister to Grade 1 winner in Australia: progressed well into a useful handicapper: won at Lingfield (running wide on turn) and Carlisle in the summer, and at Epsom and Newmarket (chased strong pace, led under 3f out, kept on) in the autumn: will probably stay beyond 1½m: acts on firm going: flashed tail (ran creditably) fifth 3-y-o start: sweating and on toes (respectable effort) final 3-y-o start: goes well for Martin Dwyer: consistent. *Mrs J. Cecil*

DEAUVILLE DANCER (IRE)   4 ch.g. Al Hareb (USA) 123 – Bru Ri (FR) (Sir   – §
Gaylord) [1995 –§: 10f⁵ 9m 10m 1996 11.1m⁶ 16g 10.1m Oct 23] one to leave alone: has joined M. Heaton-Ellis. *D. Nicholls*

DEBONAIR   2 b.f. (Feb 5) Batshoof 122 – Celestial Air 96 (Rheingold 137) [1996   50 +
6m⁶ 7m⁴ 6m 7m Oct 17] 8,000F, 8,500Y: half-sister to 3 winners, including fairly useful Deer Hunt (by Hadeer), best at 9f/1¼m, and 1½m winner Bellton (by Bellypha): dam 1½m winner: signs of ability in varied races, including a seller: bred to stay middle distances: carried head high second start: sold 1,800 gns Newmarket Autumn Sales: sent to Sweden. *G. Lewis*

DEBUTANTE DAYS   4 ch.f. Dominion 123 – Doogali 93 (Doon 124) [1995   70
72p: 10m 10m³ 10m² 10m* 10g⁵ 10.5d⁴ 1996 10.2m⁴ 11.9v⁶ 10s 14.1s 16.5s Nov 9]
strong, lengthy filly: fair handicapper: stays 1¾m: acts on good to firm and soft ground: sometimes hangs under pressure: very slowly away (and well below form) final 4-y-o outing. *C. R. Egerton*

DECISION MAKER (IRE)   3 b.g. Taufan (USA) 119 – Vain Deb 66 (Gay   78 d
Fandango (USA) 132) [1995 80: 6g 7f⁴ 7f 8g² 8d² 1996 8.2d⁴ 8d⁵ 10d⁵ 10m⁶ 10.2f
Jul 8] good-bodied gelding: has a round action: fair performer: disappointing after reappearance at 3 yrs: gelded after final outing: sold (R. Hannon to K. Burke) 4,500 gns Newmarket Autumn Sales: stays 8.2f: acts on dead ground: blinkered/visored last 2 starts at 3 yrs, no improvement. *R. Hannon*

DECORATED HERO 4 b.g. Warning 136 – Bequeath (USA) (Lyphard 119
(USA) 132) [1995 110: 7f* 8m* 7.9m³ 7.3m² 7d² 9g 8.1s² 1996 7g³ 8.1g 8m*
7m* 8d* 8d* 8v² a9.4g² Dec 7]

The figures 141 next to Decorated Hero's name on the Doncaster race
card were not his form figures; they were there to draw attention to the number
of days he'd been off the track. A lengthy absence is less of a cause for concern
with one of John Gosden's than most other trainers', but this one had run as if
something had gone amiss on his last start, in the Sandown Mile back in April;
and on top of that he seemed to be facing a fairly searching comeback in a rated
stakes handicap. In fact, Decorated Hero returned as good as ever. It transpired
that for at least some of the time away he'd been fulfilling a role as lead horse
for the good two-year-old Benny The Dip. Decorated Hero travelled sweetly
for much of the race and produced a good turn of foot to get up on the line from
Hi Nod after being slightly hampered.

Decorated Hero went on to share further in the glorious autumn enjoyed
by stable and stable-jockey who earlier that afternoon had won the St Leger. He
showed substantial improvement next time out and kept in sparkling form right
into December. From Doncaster he was sent on to Ascot for the £50,100 Tote
Festival Handicap, a race he'd come second in in 1995. Not only did he go one
better in winning an ultra-competitive affair by three and a half lengths from
Kayvee, under top weight he put up one of the handicap performances of the
season, one to rival First Island's at York. He was also the fourth of Dettori's
winners on that memorable Saturday, clearest-cut of the seven. From now on
handicaps were out for Decorated Hero. He was given an extended run in better
company which resulted in victories in listed events at Longchamp (by six
lengths) and Evry, and second places in the Group 3 Prix Perth at Saint-Cloud
and the listed Bass Wulfrun Stakes at Wolverhampton. The best he came up
against in France was the smart three-year-old River Bay, a much improved colt
who started favourite for a well-contested Prix Perth and beat him a length and
a half, finishing the stronger over a very testing mile. Given the well-aired
doubts about Decorated Hero's effectiveness beyond a mile, and seeing that he
was making his debut on sand, it was slightly surprising to see him sent off
favourite for the all-weather showpiece over nine furlongs and seventy-nine
yards at Wolverhampton. It was a compliment to his form, nevertheless. He ran
very well but those seventy-nine yards just found him out. After he'd quickened
past Royal Philosopher into the lead inside the last furlong, looking all over a
winner, he began to tie up and give hope to the riders of Royal Philosopher,
Prince of Andros and Punishment, and the previous year's winner Prince of
Andros caught him on the line in a rousing finish.

Decorated Hero's dam Bequeath was a nine-furlong maiden winner
in the French Provinces for Sheikh Mohammed. She is well bred, being by
Lyphard out of a stakes-placed winner in the USA, and has proved a bargain at
20,000 guineas, the sum she made at the 1990 December Sales carrying her
first foal. That foal was Beneficiary (by Jalmood), winner of six races at up to
seven furlongs. Decorated Hero came next, followed by his sister Give Warning who won as a two-year-old in Germany, Santa Rosa (by Lahib), in training

*Tote Festival Handicap, Ascot—Decorated Hero gives weight all round;
the grey Kayvee battles on for second, with Russian Music (rails) in third*

Herbert Allen's "Decorated Hero"

Decorated Hero (b.g. 1992)	Warning (b 1985)	Known Fact (b 1977)	In Reality
			Tamerett
		Slightly Dangerous (b 1979)	Roberto
			Where You Lead
	Bequeath (USA) (b 1986)	Lyphard (b 1969)	Northern Dancer
			Goofed
		Bequa (gr 1976)	Never Bend
			Hula Girl

in the latest season with John Dunlop, and then a colt by Lahib sold to Shadwell Estates for 65,000 guineas at the latest Houghton Sales and now with Gosden. Decorated Hero is the dam's only foal of racing age not to have been seen out as a two-year-old. When he did appear at three he'd been freeze fired in front and gelded. As they say, he still hasn't many miles on the clock, and there is no reason to suppose he won't do well again in 1997 in listed and pattern company at up to a mile, perhaps even at up to nine furlongs on his performance at Wolverhampton. On the small side, with a quick action, he almost certainly acts on any going. He possesses a good turn of foot. *J. H. M. Gosden*

DEE-LADY 4 b.f. Deploy 131 – Bermuda Lily 78 (Dunbeath (USA) 127) [1995 93d: 8g⁴ 9.9m² 8g⁶ 10g⁵ 8m⁵ 8f⁵ 7g 10g 8m⁴ 8g⁴ a10g⁵ a8g⁴ 1996 10s⁵ 8m 10m⁵ 8.1d 11.9g 8.1s³ 8g a9.4g Dec 14] small, sturdy filly: only fair at best in 1996: stays 1¼m: probably acts on any going (shaped well on heavy) on turf, well below form on equitrack: often bandaged: inconsistent. *W. G. M. Turner*   76 a–

DEE PEE TEE CEE (IRE) 2 b.g. (May 10) Tidaro (USA) – Silver Glimpse 108 (Petingo 135) [1996 7m* 6f⁶ 6g⁶ 7.9g⁵ 8m⁵ 8f 8g⁶ 8f⁶ Nov 5] IR 2,000F: tall gelding: has a round action: half-brother to several winners here and abroad, including 1¼m   57

258

and 11.7f winner Hintlesham Harry (by Pas de Seul): dam 7f winner at 2 yrs in France: sire (by Chieftan) 1½m to 15.5f winner and also hurdles winner in France: won seller at Redcar in June despite wandering: never really a factor in nurseries after: probably requires thorough test of stamina. *M. W. Easterby*

DEEP FINESSE 2 b.c. (Feb 12) Reprimand 122 – Babycham Sparkle 80 (So 109 Blessed 130) [1996 5g* 5m³ 5.5m* 5d* 5m³ 5m³ 6m⁵ 5d Oct 12] IR 22,000Y: sturdy, strong-quartered, sprint type: half-brother to 3-y-o Merrily (by Sharrood) and 3 winning sprinters, including Champagne Girl (by Robellino), 5f winner at 2 yrs in 1993: dam, 2-y-o 5f and 6f winner, half-sister to smart French middle-distance colt El Famoso: useful sprinting youngster, successful in median auction maiden at Warwick, listed race at Evry and Prix du Bois at Longchamp early in season: held his form well after, third in Molecomb Stakes at Goodwood and Flying Childers Stakes at Doncaster and fifth in Middle Park Stakes (2½ lengths behind Bahamian Bounty) at Newmarket, until running poorly in Cornwallis Stakes at Ascot on final outing: stays 6f: acts on good to firm and dead ground: sweating and edgy at Ascot. *M. A. Jarvis*

DEEPLY VALE (IRE) 5 b.g. Pennine Walk 120 – Late Evening (USA) (River- 69 man (USA) 131) [1995 69: 7m 6f 7m 6g⁶ 7f 7d 7g³ a6g² a6g² a7g³ a7g 1996 a7g³ a76 a6g⁴ a7g⁴ a6g* a7g 6m* a7g* a6g⁵ a7g Dec 20] strong, lengthy gelding: fair handicapper: won at Wolverhampton (amateurs) in March, at Folkestone (apprentices) in April and at Lingfield (claimer, claimed out of G. Moore's stable £5,500) in November: effective at 6f and 7f: acts on the all-weather and on good to firm and soft ground: occasionally gets upset in stalls, has been withdrawn: consistent. *E. A. Wheeler*

DEEP WATER (USA) 2 b.c. (Jan 18) Diesis 133 – Water Course (USA) (Irish 82 p River (FR) 131) [1996 8f³ Oct 15] 78,000Y: second foal: dam (unraced) from family of Star of Gdansk and Mt Livermore: favourite, wandered around when third to Our People in maiden at Leicester: bred to stay 1¼m: will improve. *P. F. I. Cole*

DEERLY 3 b.f. Hadeer 118 – Grafitti Gal (USA) (Pronto) [1995 66: 6g* 6g³ 6m⁵ 50 6m⁴ 7g³ 6m³ 6m 6.1m 1996 6.1m 7g⁵ a6g⁶ 7f 6d 6g 7.1f 6.1m Sep 16] quite attractive filly: only poor at best in 1996: left D. Morris after third start: probably stays 7f: acts on good to firm ground. *C. A. Smith*

DEEVEE 7 b.h. Hallgate 127 – Lady Woodpecker 61 (Tap On Wood 130) [1995 69 d 80: 8m* 8m 8g² 8f⁶ 8g² 8.1m 8d 1996 8m 8m⁶ 8.5m 8g 8.3d 8d 8m Oct 17] close-coupled horse: carries condition: poor mover: seemed on the downgrade in 1996: best at around 1m: acts on firm and dead ground, no form on soft: tends to hang: usually slowly away, and held up: inconsistent. *C. J. Benstead*

DEFINED DANCER (USA) 3 ch.f. Nabeel Dancer (USA) 120 – Meissarah 91 (USA) (Silver Hawk (USA) 123) [1995 91: 5.1m* 5.2m² 6m* 6g³ 1996 7f⁴ 7m 6m⁴ 6m³ Oct 4] quite attractive filly: fairly useful performer: should be at least as effective at 7f as 6f: has raced only on a sound surface: game: sold 10,000 gns Doncaster November Sales. *M. R. Stoute*

DEFINITE ARTICLE 4 b.c. Indian Ridge 123 – Summer Fashion 84 Moore- 121 (style 137) [1995 121: 10g* 12m² 10g⁴ 10m⁴ 1996 10d* 10d* 10g⁵ 12m⁴ 12f⁶ Oct 5] lengthy colt: good walker: very smart performer: won listed event in April and 8-

Tattersalls Gold Cup, the Curragh—Definite Article holds on from Timarida, with Annus Mirabilis third

runner Tattersalls Gold Cup (looked really well, gamely held Timarida by a length) in May, both at the Curragh: bit below his best when fifth of 7 to Halling in Coral Eclipse Stakes at Sandown (one of first off bridle), 3¾ lengths fourth of 7 to Pilsudski in Grosser Preis von Baden and sixth of 10 to Diplomatic Jet in Turf Classic at Belmont: stayed 1½m: did not race on extremes of going: blinkered (ran well) final start at 3 yrs, visored in Eclipse: usually held up in touch: to stand at Morristown Lattin Stud, Co Kildare, at IR 6,500 gns. *D. K. Weld, Ireland*

DEGREE   3 b.f. Warning 136 – Krill (Kris 135) [1995 81p: 7.5d² 1996 8m³ 10g²   73
10g Aug 12] fair maiden: looks decidedly short of pace and should be suited by further than 1¼m: didn't stride out at all well on good to firm ground: sold 11,500 gns Newmarket December Sales. *H. R. A. Cecil*

DELIGHT OF DAWN   4 b.f. Never So Bold 135 – Vogos Angel 54 (Song 132)   67
[1995 74: 6m 7f⁶ 8m 1.1m 7g² 7f⁶ 7m⁵ 7m* 7g* 7m* 7m⁴ 6g 6d³ 6m² 7m⁴ 7m⁵
1996 7f 6m 8.3m* 10m 8.1f⁶ 7m⁶ 7.1m⁵ 8f⁴ 8m⁴ 10m 7g 10m 8g Oct 29] angular filly: fair handicapper: won claimer at Windsor (under 7-lb apprentice, claimed out of K. Ivory's stable £10,000) in May: stays 1m: acts on firm ground and dead: tends to hang: usually bandaged: often slowly away, and held up. *R. M. Stronge*

DELILAH (IRE)   2 b.f. (Apr 23) Bluebird (USA) 125 – Courtesane (USA)   75 p
(Majestic Light (USA)) [1996 7.1d³ Sep 28] 72,000Y: tall, quite good-looking filly: has scope: fourth reported foal: half-sister to French 1¼m winner Mesoraca (by Assert) and a winner in USA by Vigors: dam placed twice in USA: very green, third to River Usk in steadily-run maiden at Haydock, finishing well having taken long time to realise what was required: will be suited by 1m+: sure to do better. *M. R. Stoute*

DELLA CASA (IRE)   3 ch.f. Royal Academy (USA) 130 – Diamond Spring   –
(USA) (Vaguely Noble 140) [1995 58p: 7m⁵ 7.1g 7f 1996 10f⁶ 12m Aug 3] angular, unfurnished filly: modest maiden: failed to progress as anticipated in face of stiff tasks in 1996: should be well suited by middle distances: sent to Saudi Arabia. *J. L. Dunlop*

DELMOUR   5 b.g. Seymour Hicks (FR) 125 – Delbounty (Bounteous 125) [1995   –
–: a9.4g 10m 8g 7.1m⁶ 7.6m 7m 8.1m 1996 8f May 6] no form: joined C. Popham. *W. M. Brisbourne*

DELPHINE   3 b. or br.f. Formidable (USA) 125 – Archaic 65 (Relic) [1995 NR   72
1996 6m³ 6m⁶ 7m² 6f³ Jun 22] 10,000Y: sparely-made filly: half-sister to several winners, including very smart sprinter Schweppeshire Lad (by Decoy Boy): dam maiden: fair maiden: well below form final start: stays 7f: has raced only on top-of-the-ground. *M. Bell*

DELROB   5 b.m. Reprimand 122 – Stoneydale 83 (Tickled Pink 114) [1995 52,   –
a62: a5g³ a5g⁵ a6g a5g⁴ a5g³ a7g³ a7g⁵ 5.1m* 5f³ 5m a5g a6g 1996 a6g a5g⁵ a5g 5g   a57
6m a5g⁴ a5g⁵ a6g a5g³ a5g³ a6g* a5g² 5g a6g* a6g a6g⁴ a6g⁶ a7g Nov 30] sparely-made mare: modest handicapper: won at Wolverhampton in June and Southwell in August: best form at up to 6f: acts on firm ground and dead: well on fibresand: blinkered/visored since ninth 5-y-o start: often apprentice ridden. *D. Haydn Jones*

DELTA SOLEIL (USA)   4 b.c. Riverman (USA) 131 – Sunny Roberta (USA)   94
(Robellino (USA) 127) [1995 96p: 7.9g* 10.1g 7g⁴ 8m³ 1996 8s⁵ 7m 7g⁴ 7g 8g Nov 2] good-bodied colt: usually looks well: fairly useful handicapper: some encouraging efforts in 1996, but off course 5 months after fourth of 10 (having cruised into lead 2f out) at Doncaster in May: off course 5 months afterwards: will prove effective at 6f, and stays 1m when conditions are not testing: acts on good to firm ground, shaped well on soft: taken last and quietly to post second and third 4-y-o starts. *P. W. Harris*

DEMOISELLE   4 b.f. Midyan (USA) 124 – Little Mercy 90 (No Mercy 126)   –
[1995 NR 1996 a7g Aug 16] well beaten both starts, nearly 2 years apart: sold 800 gns Doncaster November Sales. *C. W. Thornton*

DEMOLITION MAN   2 br.c. (Mar 7) Primo Dominie 121 – Town Lady 93   100 +
(Town Crier 119) [1996 5g⁴ 6d* 6m² 7m² 8m² 8f³ 8f⁵ Nov 30] 11,000Y: well-grown, leggy colt: half-brother to several winners here and abroad, including 1¼m and 1½m winner The Freshes (by Good Times): dam 2-y-o 5f winner: won maiden auction at Haydock in July: second in competitive nurseries at Newmarket, York and Newcastle: subsequently left J. W. Watts: ran well when under 3 lengths fifth to Hello in

Grade 3 event at Hollywood Park in November: stays 1m: acts on firm and dead ground. *W. Shoemaker, USA*

DENBRAE (IRE)   4 b.g. Sure Blade (USA) 130 – Fencing (Viking (USA)) [1995   75
73: a6g* 6.1g* 6m² 6m⁴ 6.1m⁶ 7g a6g 7.1d⁵ 1996 7s⁴ 6g 6m³ 6f³ 6d⁴ 6m² 6m⁴ 6m⁴
6.1m* 6m 6f 6m⁵ 6m Oct 28] lengthy gelding: fair handicapper: won at Chepstow
(led near finish) in June: good effort afterwards only when close keeping-on fifth of
28 in Silver Cup at Ayr in September: raced mainly at 6f, should prove at least as
effective at 7f: acts on fibresand and on firm and dead ground: often soon off bridle:
normally consistent. *D. J. G. Murray Smith*

DENOMINATION (USA)   4 br.g. Danzig Connection (USA) – Christchurch   61
(FR) 88 (So Blessed 130) [1995 NR 1996 a10g 10.8g² 10g 10m 8.1d³ 10.8m Jul 5]
stocky gelding: modest handicapper: sold out of I. Balding's stable 7,600 gns Ascot
June Sales after penultimate start: should stay beyond 10.8f: blinkered (took keen
hold) fourth 4-y-o outing: has worn tongue strap: modest winning hurdler. *M. C. Pipe*

DENSBEN   12 b.g. Silly Prices 110 – Eliza de Rich 57 (Spanish Gold 101) [1995   59
59: 6v 6g 5.9m 5.9f⁵ 7g 6m⁵ 6.1m² 6f³ 6m 7f 6m⁶ 6m⁴ 7m 6g* 6g* 7g 6d 5f⁵ 6m
1996 6d 5.9d 5.9m 6g⁵ 6m⁵ 6m⁶ 6m³ 6.9f 6m² 7m⁴ 6m⁶ 6d* 8m Oct 17] smallish,
sparely-made gelding: modest handicapper nowadays: won claimer at Haydock
(repeat success) in September: suited by 6f/7f: acts on any going: below form when
blinkered/visored: sometimes starts slowly, and is held up: tough. *Denys Smith*

DENTON LAD   2 b.c. (Apr 21) Prince Sabo 123 – Dahlawise (IRE) 76 (Caerleon   61
(USA) 132) [1996 5m⁶ 6m 6g 7g Oct 19] 18,500Y: rather unfurnished colt:
second foal: half-brother to 3-y-o Alfayza (by Danehill), 7f winner at 2 yrs: dam,
2-y-o 6f winner, should have stayed 1¼m: modest form in maidens and nurseries:
stays 6f: takes a keen hold. *J. W. Watts*

DEPICTION   3 b.g. Hadeer 118 – Depict 84 (Derring-Do 131) [1995 NR 1996 7s³   70
a6g³ 7g⁵ 6s 6f³ Jun 28] 6,000Y: half-brother to several winners, including fairly
useful sprinter Careless Whisper (by Homing): dam, 6f and 7f winner, sister to 2000
Guineas third Dominion: fair maiden: well held last 2 starts: sold 3,800 gns
Newmarket July Sales: stays 7f well. *R. Guest*

DEPRECIATE   3 ch.c. Beveled (USA) – Shiny Penny 70 (Glint of Gold 128)   84
[1995 84: 6g* 6.1g* 6m⁴ 1996 6m⁴ 6m Jun 1] leggy colt: fairly useful handicapper:
ran creditably (especially since badly hampered on reappearance) in good events in
1996: stays 6f: has raced only on a sound surface. *C. James*

DE QUEST   4 b.c. Rainbow Quest (USA) 134 – De Stael (USA) 93 (Nijinsky   114
(CAN) 138) [1995 120p: 12v² 12d² 10.5g² 12.5g* 12s* 12m 1996 12m⁴ 12m⁵ 12m⁶
Jun 30] close-coupled colt: smart French performer: very much on toes, just over 5
lengths third of 4 to Swain in slowly-run Coronation Cup at Epsom, taking keen
hold in rear, looking completely unable to respond when pace quickened: below best,
beaten 9 lengths, in Grand Prix de Saint-Cloud final start: likely to stay beyond 12.5f:
acts on good to firm ground and soft: stays in training. *A. Fabre, France*

DEREK'S BO   3 b.f. Rambo Dancer (CAN) 107 – Mother Hubbard (Mummy's   –
Pet 125) [1995 –: 5m a5g 6m⁵ 5.1m⁶ 7g 7.1s 1996 a7g Jan 5] no form. *N. Bycroft*

DERI SUE   3 b.f. Relief Pitcher 120 – Royal Rabble 65 (Rabdan 129) [1995 NR   –
1996 a8.5g Nov 2] second foal: dam, winning plater, stayed 1¼m: showed nil on
belated debut. *B. J. Llewellyn*

DERRYBELLE   5 ch.m. Derrylin 115 – Pokey's Belle (Uncle Pokey 116) [1995   –
NR 1996 12s 14.1g Oct 30] plain mare: first foal: dam well beaten over hurdles: well
held in claimers. *D. L. Williams*

DESERT BEAUTY (IRE)   2 b.f. (Feb 4) Green Desert (USA) 127 – Hellenic   76 p
125 (Darshaan 133) [1996 7g Sep 6] good-topped filly: has scope: second foal:
half-sister to smart 4-y-o 1¼m and 13.3f winner Election Day (by Sadler's Wells):
dam won Yorkshire Oaks and second in St Leger: burly, keeping-on eighth to One So
Wonderful in minor event at Kempton: wasn't knocked about, and is sure to do better
over 1m+. *M. R. Stoute*

DESERT BOY (IRE)   3 gr.c. Green Desert (USA) 127 – City Fortress (Troy 137)   114
[1995 100p: 6m* 6d⁵ 1996 7m⁶ 10.3g² 12f² 10g³ 12m 14.6m Sep 14] good-bodied
colt: fluent mover: smart performer: best efforts when ½-length second of 7 (under
very strong pressure good way out) to Amfortas in King Edward VII Stakes at Royal

Ascot and when demoted after beating Radevore ½ length in 7-runner Prix Eugene Adam at Saint-Cloud in July: stays 1½m, tailed off in St Leger: acts on firm ground, tailed off (when sweating) on dead: sold to Hong Kong. *P. W. Chapple-Hyam*

DESERT CALM (IRE) 7 br.g. Glow (USA) – Lancette (Double Jump 131) 58 d [1995 8s 10d⁵ 8s 8g 10f 10g 9.5g² 10m 9m² 8g 10g 10m⁴ 1996 7.5d 15.4m 7m³ 8s 8f⁶ 9m 8m⁵ 8.3g⁴ 10m⁶ 8f⁵ 7.1f Sep 12] tall gelding: half-brother to several winners, notably smart performers Darcy's Thatcher (best up to 1m, by Thatching) and Rasa Penang (also best up to around 1m, by Gay Fandango): dam, half-sister to Gimcrack winner Golden Horus, placed at up to 1½m in France: fairly useful performer at his best in Ireland (winner of 4 races) but only occasional fair form in 1995 for K. Prendergast: only modest at best in Britain in 1996: stays 9.5f: acts on firm and soft ground: normally blinkered: tends to get behind: sold 2,000 gns Newmarket Autumn Sales. *Mrs P. N. Dutfield*

DESERT CAT (IRE) 3 b.c. Green Desert (USA) 127 – Mahabba (USA) 74 – (Elocutionist (USA)) [1995 78: 7g⁵ 7.1s³ 8f⁴ 1996 7.6g 8g Jun 12] big, strong, rangy colt: carries condition: disappointing maiden: sold (H. Thomson Jones to M. Wane) 1,000 gns Newmarket Autumn Sales. *H. Thomson Jones*

DESERT CHALLENGER (IRE) 6 b.g. Sadler's Wells (USA) 132 – Verily – (Known Fact (USA) 135) [1995 NR 1996 12d Oct 11] disappointing maiden: blinkered final 4-y-o outing. *J. R. Jenkins*

DESERT DUNES 3 b.g. Unfuwain (USA) 131 – Palm Springs (Top Ville 129) 77 [1995 NR 1996 10g 12m⁴ 14m⁴ 14m⁵ 16.1m Oct 2] lengthy gelding: has a quick action: second foal: half-brother to 10.2f and 11.7f winner Endowment (by Cadeaux Genereux): dam unraced half-sister to pattern winners Pushy, Jupiter Island and Precocious out of Mrs Moss: fair maiden handicapper: stays 1¾m, worth another try at 2m: raced only on a sound surface: gelded. *N. A. Graham*

DESERT FIGHTER 5 b.g. Green Desert (USA) 127 – Jungle Rose 90 (Shirley 72 Heights 130) [1995 –: 10m 1996 13.8s 12g 10.3m 10f³ Sep 27] good-topped gelding: fair but untrustworthy hurdler: fair form on flat nowadays: should stay 1¾m: acts on firm ground. *Mrs M. Reveley*

DESERT FORCE (IRE) 7 b.g. Lomond (USA) 128 – St Padina 91 (St Paddy – 133) [1995 –: a16g a14g 1996 12d⁴ 16.2m 21.6m Apr 29] sturdy gelding: poor performer: probably stays 2m: acts on good to firm and dead ground: no improvement in blinkers: joined A. Streeter: winning hurdler. *G. Fierro*

DESERT FROLIC (IRE) 3 b.f. Persian Bold 123 – Try To Catch Me (USA) 94 (Shareef Dancer (USA) 135) [1995 62p: 7g 7.1s⁴ 1996 8.5f⁴ 11f* 12f* 13.1s* 12f* 12.3m* 11.8g² 13.9m 13.4d⁵ Aug 31] leggy filly: useful handicapper: won at Redcar (maiden), Carlisle (twice), Ayr and Chester within 3 weeks in midsummer: below form last 2 starts, at York (set too strong a pace in Ebor) and Chester: stays 13f well: acts on firm and soft ground: front runner. *M. Johnston*

DESERT GREEN (FR) 7 b.g. Green Desert (USA) 127 – Green Leaf (USA) 97 102 (Alydar (USA)) [1995 101: 7m 8m* 8.1m⁵ 8f³ 8f³ 7m⁵ 8d 8m² a9.4g 1996 8.1g⁴ 8m* 8.1d 8m 8m 7.9m 9s Oct 26] rangy, attractive gelding: impresses in appearance: useful handicapper: won Jubilee Handicap at Kempton in May for second year running: failed by some way to repeat that form in good company: stays 1m well: acts on firm ground, well beaten on soft and on fibresand: has run well when sweating: formerly looked highly strung, and goes well under tender handling: normally held up: pulled up lame second start over hurdles in December. *R. Hannon*

DESERT HARVEST 4 b.g. Green Desert (USA) 127 – Mill On The Floss 117 58 § (Mill Reef (USA) 141) [1995 76§: 8g⁶ 7.3m⁵ 7g 7m⁶ 1996 12m 8.3m⁴ a8.5g⁵ Jun 22] good-topped gelding: only modest at best in 1996: claimed out of G. McCourt's stable £4,000 second 4-y-o start: unlikely to stay 1½m: blinkered (refused to enter stalls) once: temperamental and one to treat with caution. *J. Cullinan*

DESERT HORIZON 2 b.c. (Feb 16) Danehill (USA) 126 – Sand Grouse (USA) 91 p (Arctic Tern (USA) 126) [1996 8m⁴ 8.2s* Oct 31] good-topped colt: has had shins freeze fired: fourth foal: brother to useful 3-y-o 7f winner Sandhill and a winner abroad and half-brother to a winner in Hungary by Persian Heights: dam French 1¼m winner: rallied well when winning Nottingham maiden in October by ½ length from

Jaunty Jack: will be suited by 1¼m+: acts on soft ground: type to go on to better things. *J. H. M. Gosden*

DESERT INVADER (IRE)   5 br.g. Lead On Time (USA) 123 – Aljood 111   57
(Kris 135) [1995 57, a69: a7g⁵ a8g⁶ a8g* a8g a7g³ 6d 7g 5m 6m a6g 6g⁴ 8m a6g*   a78
a6g⁶ 6g a7g⁴ a8.5g a6g³ a7g³ 1996 a8.5g a7g⁴ a6g⁴ a7g* a6g³ a6g² a6g² 7m 6s³ 8.3s
a7g² a8.5g 6m⁵ a6g⁴ a9.4g⁵ a7g² a8.5g a7g⁴ a9.4g⁶ a6g⁵ 6d² 7g a7g a6g² a7g⁴ a6g²
a7g³ Dec 28] strong, lengthy gelding: good mover: fair handicapper on the
all-weather, modest on turf: won amateurs race at Southwell in February: best at up
to 1m: acts on good to firm and soft ground and the all-weather: tried blinkered, no
improvement: not an easy ride: tough. *D. W. Chapman*

DESERT KING (IRE)   2 b.c. (Mar 31) Danehill (USA) 126 – Sabaah (USA)   110 +
65 (Nureyev (USA) 131) [1996 7g² 7m² 8d* 7g* 7g⁶ Oct 18]
The National Stakes at the Curragh was sponsored by the Aga Khan's
Studs in 1996, as the first part of a three-year sponsorship deal. As a result the
winner's prize-money rose to more than £116,000, and the race became the
most valuable event for two-year-olds in the British Isles. The Aga Khan has
been instrumental in getting more radical changes to the race in future—'I
would like to see it run over a mile rather than seven furlongs and pushed back
in the Calendar.' The Turf Club has complied with both requests. Traditionally
run towards the end of September, the National Stakes provided a good step-
ping-stone to the Dewhurst—Vincent O'Brien used it on many occasions. The
race will become another Group 1 mile event in the European two-year-old
calendar in October, a month which already has the Racing Post Trophy, the
Grand Criterium and Italy's Gran Criterium, not to mention the Dewhurst itself.
Before the latest National Stakes, Desert King had finished second in
a maiden at Leopardstown and a listed race at the Curragh—both over seven
furlongs—and had got off the mark in a one-mile maiden at Tralee later in
August. That left him with plenty of improvement to find at the Curragh if he
was to trouble the likes of 6/4 favourite Sahm, the disqualified runner-up in
the Lanson Champagne Vintage Stakes, the Coventry one-two Verglas and
Daylight In Dubai, and the filly Azra who had finished third in the Moyglare
Stud Stakes over course and distance earlier in September. Desert King was an
11/1-chance along with his stable-companion Johan Cruyff who had won his
only start; only the once-raced maiden Stonehaven started at longer odds in

Aga Khan's Studs National Stakes, the Curragh—in the clear at last,
Desert King (striped cap) catches up with Referendum (dark cap) and Azra (blinkers)

the field of ten. In a steadily-run race, Desert King and Walter Swinburn—deputising for the suspended Christy Roche—had an eventful journey. They were still last over two furlongs out, and with a furlong to run still had more in front of them than behind. Desert King was done no favours by his stable-companion as Swinburn looked for room inside the last but a narrow gap appeared between Azra and Fantastic Fellow, and Desert King quickened through to collar the front-running Referendum near the line, his winning margin a neck. Two and a half lengths covered the first seven home.

If anything, Desert King shaped as though seven furlongs was on the short side for him in the Dewhurst a month later, when a well-backed third favourite. One of the first off the bit over two out, he was an outpaced last running into the Dip but stayed on very strongly to finish just over two lengths down on In Command in sixth place, running close to his Curragh form.

		Danzig	Northern Dancer
	Danehill (USA)	(b 1977)	Pas de Nom
	(b 1986)	Razyana	His Majesty
Desert King (IRE)		(b 1981)	Spring Adieu
(b.c. Mar 31, 1994)		Nureyev	Northern Dancer
	Sabaah (USA)	(b 1977)	Special
	(ch 1988)	Dish Dash	Bustino
		(b 1979)	Loose Cover

Desert King gave trainer Aidan O'Brien his first Group 1 success; he was the second son of Danehill to win the National Stakes in Michael Tabor's colours in two years, following Danehill Dancer. Those valuable wins helped to make Danehill the leading sire of two-year-olds in Britain and Ireland in 1995 and 1996. Desert King is bred along similar lines to the shock 1994 Queen

Mr M. Tabor's "Desert King"

Elizabeth II Stakes winner Maroof; he is by a son of Maroof's sire out of a daughter of his dam. Sabaah was a modest maiden who ran four times at around seven furlongs and a mile. Her full brother Sayaarr won over an extended twelve furlongs in the French Provinces. After her brief career on the track, Sabaah was sold at successive Newmarket December Sales, fetching 13,000 guineas on the first occasion and 30,000 guineas when in foal to Thatching a year later. The colt she was carrying, Bigwig, has shown nothing in three starts. More will be expected of her third offspring, her yearling by Indian Ridge bought by Shadwell for IR 330,000 guineas at the Goffs October Sales. Sabaah also has a filly foal by Catrail. Maroof is much the best of Sabaah's siblings—he came close to winning the National Stakes incidentally, sustaining a fractured off-fore cannon bone when beaten half a length by Fatherland—but from a total of six winners Dish Dash has also produced a couple of useful two-year-old seven-furlong winners in Arrasas and Mawwal. The Ribblesdale winner Dish Dash was the best of seven winners out of the useful miler Loose Cover.

A 175,000-guinea purchase as a yearling at the Goffs October Sales, Desert King is a sturdy, good-quartered colt (in that respect he is typical of his sire's stock) with a powerful, round action. He will be suited by a move up to a mile or more as a three-year-old, but will need to show plenty of improvement to figure in any of the Guineas. He usually wears a tongue strap. *A. P. O'Brien, Ireland*

DESERT LORE 5 b.g. Green Desert (USA) 127 – Chinese Justice (USA) (Diesis 44 133) [1995 NR 1996 a8g⁴ a7g⁴ 7.1g Apr 15] rated 70 at best in 1994: only poor form on return, leaving Mrs J. Ramsden after second start: stays 1m: acts on good to firm ground, probably on heavy: joined R. McKellar. *D. A. Nolan*

DESERT LYNX (IRE) 3 b.f. Green Desert (USA) 127 – Sweeping 104 (Indian 74 King (USA) 128) [1995 65: 6.1d⁵ 7d 6f 1996 6d* 6g 6s³ 6m⁶ 8g³ 8m 7.1d³ 7.1s³ 8f 10.3g Oct 25] small, plain filly: fair handicapper: won at Newcastle in May: stays 1m (never a threat over 10.3f): best efforts with give in the ground: inconsistent. *T. R. Watson*

DESERT MAN 5 b.g. Green Desert (USA) 127 – Grayfoot 87 (Grundy 137) – [1995 NR 1996 a7g⁶ a7g a12g a8g⁵ a7g Mar 18] 38,000Y, 1,200 2-y-o, 7,000 3-y-o: fifth foal: half-brother to an 11f winner in Sweden by Commanche Run: dam, maiden half-sister to Irish Oaks winner Swiftfoot, was possibly temperamental: no worthwhile form: sold 580 gns Doncaster October Sales. *R. D. E. Woodhouse*

DESERT POWER 7 b.g. Green Desert (USA) 127 – Rivers Maid 83 (Rarity 129) – [1995 67: 10.3m 10g 12.1g⁴ 10f 10.2m* 8g 9.9m³ a9.4g 1996 a12g Jan 31] fair handicapper: tailed off only 7-y-o start: stays 11.7f: acts on firm and heavy ground. *D. Burchell*

DESERT PRESIDENT 5 ch.g. Polish Precedent (USA) 131 – Majestic Kahala – (USA) (Majestic Prince (USA)) [1995 36: a16g⁴ a12g⁵ a16.2g 1996 a16g⁵ a16g⁵ Jun 6] probably no longer of much account. *P. Mooney*

DESERT SCOUT 3 b.g. Picea 99 – Queens Pearl (Queen's Hussar 124) [1995 §§ NR 1996 8.3m 12m 7.6m⁶ 8.1f 10f Sep 23] seventh reported foal: half-brother to winning sprinters Queen's Tickle and Albert Henry (both by Tickled Pink): dam of little account: ungenuine maiden: sold 500 gns Doncaster October Sales: one to leave alone. *K. McAuliffe*

DESERT SERENADE (USA) 3 b.f. Green Desert (USA) 127 – Sanctuary – (Welsh Pageant 132) [1995 NR 1996 6g 7.1d Aug 23] sister to top-class sprinter Sheikh Albadou and half-sister to 2 winners at up to 7f and to 5-y-o middle-distance stayer Durham (by Caerleon) and useful stayer Captain Jack (by Salse): dam unraced half-sister to Little Wolf: still travelling quite well when clipping winner's heels under 2f out in maiden at Salisbury on debut: again bandaged, showed little second start. *E. A. L. Dunlop*

DESERT SHOT 6 b.g. Green Desert (USA) 127 – Out of Shot 116§ (Shirley 109 Heights 130) [1995 116: 9m* 10m⁵ 10g 10m* 11.1g⁶ 1996 9m⁶ 10f 10m³ 10m³ 12f⁴ 10.9m² 10m² Oct 17] close-coupled gelding: quite often sweating and unimpressive in appearance: has a fluent action: useful performer: consistent but not quite at his best in 1996: stays 1½m: acts on dead going, very best form on a sound surface: visored twice, racing creditably: very free to post (well below form) fourth 6-y-o start: held up and well suited by strongly-run race: sent to Dubai. *M. R. Stoute*

DESERT SKIMMER (USA) 3 ch.f. Shadeed (USA) 135 – Massorah (FR) 108 44 (Habitat 134) [1995 NR 1996 7d 7m 6g 6m 5g a6g Dec 5] 68,000Y: well-made filly: has a quick action: sixth foal: half-sister to 4 winners, including Mashoura (1m in France, by Shareef Dancer): dam French sprinter: poor, inconsistent maiden: stays 6f: sold 8,800 gns Newmarket December Sales. *M. Bell*

DESERT SPRING 4 b.c. Green Desert (USA) 127 – Little Loch Broom 60 – (Reform 132) [1995 69: 10m⁵ 9m 1996 11.9d⁶ 10m 10m⁶ Jun 10] tall colt: poor mover: maiden: off course nearly a year, long way below form in 1996: should stay beyond 1¼m. *P. W. Harris*

DESERT STORY (IRE) 2 b.c. (Apr 27) Green Desert (USA) 127 – Aliysa 110 126 (Darshaan 133) [1996 6d* 7m² 8g² 7.3s* Oct 24]

The ghost of the 'Aliysa affair' was well and truly laid in 1996, the Aga Khan having horses trained in Britain for the first time since his dispute with the authorities over disqualification of his 1989 Oaks 'winner', and getting off the mark with Mandilak at Yarmouth in October, one of the batch of two-year-olds sent to Luca Cumani. Aliysa's trainer Michael Stoute will be sent horses again in 1997. Aliysa herself is now dead. She died from an injury to her spine in 1994, by which time she had been sold to Maktoum Al Maktoum. But she had been productive in her short spell at stud and was well represented by her offspring in the latest season, notably by her final one Desert Story. The well-made, quite attractive Desert Story made a winning debut in a five-runner maiden at Newmarket in August. The Queen's Own Yorkshire Dragoons Condition Stakes over an extra furlong at Doncaster was a tougher test but he showed plenty of improvement in the five-runner contest, having every chance from halfway until the final furlong where Benny The Dip proved the stronger by one and a half lengths. Stepped up to a mile for the Gtech Royal Lodge Stakes at Ascot later in September, Desert Story met Benny The Dip again and found further improvement, running on once clear in the straight and halving the distance which separated them at Doncaster, though Benny The Dip, who tended to run lazily in front, again held Desert Story quite decisively.

Desert Story was spared a third meeting, missing the Racing Post Trophy in favour of a drop in grade and distance to contest the Vodafone Horris Hill Stakes at Newbury at the end of October. Desert Story's form was much better than any of his seven rivals' and he started the 6/4 favourite. Showboat and Hidden Meadow, maiden winners at Leicester and York respectively, were next in the betting, followed by the recent Hyperion Stakes winner Andreyev and Royal Amaretto, another graduating from a maiden win. Ridden by his fourth different jockey in as many starts, Desert Story was going well behind

Vodafone Horris Hill Stakes, Newbury—
Desert Story has to be hard ridden to account for Royal Amaretto (rails) and Hidden Meadow

Hidden Meadow as that horse came to challenge Royal Amaretto under two out but, once on terms, Desert Story made hard work of mastering the leaders inside the last, finally managing to get up by three quarters of a length from Royal Amaretto with Hidden Meadow a head away third. Desert Story did not reproduce his Ascot form here and gave the impression that he will be ideally suited by a return to further.

Desert Story (IRE) (b.c. Apr 27, 1994)	Green Desert (USA) (b 1983)	Danzig (b 1977)	Northern Dancer Pas de Nom
		Foreign Courier (b 1979)	Sir Ivor Courtly Dee
	Aliysa (b 1986)	Darshaan (br 1981)	Shirley Heights Delsy
		Alannya (b 1972)	Relko Nucciolina

All four of Aliysa's foals are now winners. The first, Alaiyda (by Shah-rastani), won for the Aga Khan over a mile and a quarter in Ireland. Four-year-old Munaadee (by Green Dancer), now with Bob Jones, won an eleven-furlong maiden at Southwell on his only outing in the latest season while the three-year-old All For Show (by Mr Prospector) has won twice over a mile for Criquette Head. It was not until November 1990, nearly eighteen months after the event, that Aliysa's defeat of Snow Bride in the Oaks was finally declared void after a routine test revealed traces of camphor in her system. That left Aliysa as officially the winner of a nine-furlong maiden at Wolverhampton and the Oaks Trial at Lingfield. After Epsom she was second to Alydaress in the Irish Oaks and tenth in a rough Prix de l'Arc de Triomphe, running a little below her best both times. Aliysa is survived by her dam Alannya, one of the senior members of the Aga Khan's band of broodmares, who has now produced fifteen foals, seven of whom are winners, including the Park Hill third Altiyna, and Aleema, dam of the Prix du Jockey-Club runner-up Altayan. Alannya won twice over a mile in France where she was also placed in Group 3 company over an extended mile and a quarter. The next dam Nucciolina also won in France and her descendants include grandsons Nishapour (winner of the Poule d'Essai des Poulains) and Nassipour (winner of the Rothmans' International) and great-granddaughter Last Second (successful in the latest Nassau and Sun Chariot Stakes).

Since the 1989 winner Tirol went on to win the Two Thousand Guineas, the victories of Lion Cavern in the Greenham Stakes and Painter's Row in the Craven Stakes are the only successes recorded by Horris Hill winners as three-year-olds. Desert Story will no doubt contest one of the Guineas trials, but it will take a much improved performance to make him anything other than an outsider in the Guineas itself. Although by Green Desert, Desert Story should stay further than a mile—stamina was his dam's strong suit and she would have stayed the St Leger trip had she been given the chance. Desert Story acts on good to firm and soft ground. *M. R. Stoute*

DESERT TIGER 3 br.f. Green Desert (USA) 127 – Desert Bride (USA) (Key To –
The Kingdom (USA)) [1995 90p: 5m³ 5g* 5m² 6m* 6.5m² 1996 5m 6m Jun 20] smallish, lengthy filly: fairly useful (though highly strung) as a juvenile: no form in 1996: stays 6.5f: sent to Australia. *M. Johnston*

DESERT TRACK 2 b.c. (Apr 11) Green Desert (USA) 127 – Mill Path (Mill 76 p
Reef (USA) 141) [1996 7f⁵ Sep 10] angular, useful-looking colt, shade unfurnished: fifth foal: half-brother to useful 6f (at 2 yrs) and 7.1f winner Queen's View (by Lomond) and Irish 9f winner Alexanders Way (by Persian Heights): dam once-raced half-sister to Irish Oaks winner Give Thanks, an excellent family: took strong hold when fifth to Sunbeam Dance in maiden at Leicester: wore bandages behind: will stay 1m: sure to improve. *J. H. M. Gosden*

DESERT WARRIOR (IRE) 2 b.c. (Mar 11) Fairy King (USA) – Highland Girl –
(USA) (Sir Ivor 135) [1996 6m Sep 26] 14,000F: brother to Italian 3-y-o 5f winner Maruru and half-brother to fairly useful 4-y-o sprinter Fantasy Racing (by Tirol) and 3 winners in France, including listed 1989 2-y-o 6f winner Cut My Heart (by General

Assembly): dam twice-raced sister to Princess Ivor, smart winner at up to 9f in USA: very slowly away and always behind in maiden at Goodwood: subsequently joined Dr J. D. Scargill. *Miss Gay Kelleway*

DESERT WATER (IRE)   4 b.g. Green Desert (USA) 127 – Ozone Friendly   – (USA) 107 (Green Forest (USA) 134) [1995 47: 6d 7g 7m a7g a8g³ a8g a7g⁵ 1996 a6g a6g a7g⁵ a6g⁵ 5g Jul 15] poor maiden: left J. Bridger's stable after fourth 4-y-o outing: stays 7f: tried blinkered/visored, no improvement. *T. M. Jones*

DESERT ZONE (USA)   7 ch.g. Affirmed (USA) – Deloram (CAN) (Lord   57 Durham (CAN)) [1995 57: 8f⁵ 8.5m⁵ 8m 8g⁶ 1996 a7g 10.8m⁶ 8g 10.1m 8m⁵ 8m*   a69 a8g* 8.1s³ a8g² a8g³ a9.4g* Dec 7] rangy gelding: has had problems: fair handicapper: won at Leicester (apprentice claimer), Southwell and Wolverhampton (by 8 lengths) late on in 1996: stays 1¼m: acts on good to firm ground, soft and fibresand: sweating (well beaten) third 7-y-o start. *J. A. Harris*

DESIGNER LINES   3 ch.g. Beveled (USA) – Parrot Fashion 86 (Pieces of Eight   75 128) [1995 NR 1996 6m⁶ 6g 7.6m* 8m Sep 7] rather leggy, close-coupled gelding: half-brother to several poor animals: dam best at 1¼m: 25/1, easily best effort to win maiden at Lingfield in August, leading near line: should stay 1m (stiff task when tried): visored last 2 starts. *C. James*

DESPINA   2 ch.f. (Mar 13) Waajib 121 – Staiconme (USA) (Pancho Villa (USA))   – [1996 6m Sep 21] 5,400F, 27,000Y: big filly: second foal: half-sister to 3-y-o Fantasy Fair (by Salt Dome): dam poor Irish maiden daughter of high-class winner at up to 1m Equanimity: never a factor in Speedball's maiden at Newbury: may do better. *H. Candy*

DETACHMENT (USA)   3 b.g. Night Shift (USA) – Mumble Peg (General   72 Assembly (USA)) [1995 89: 7.1g² 7f² 7g³ 1996 7.1d⁵ 6m⁵ 6d 8f⁴ Oct 8] close-coupled gelding: only fair at best in 1996: sold 8,000 gns Newmarket Autumn Sales and gelded: stays 1m: acts on firm ground: tried blinkered and visored, no improvement. *P. W. Chapple-Hyam*

DE-VEERS CURRIE (IRE)   4 b.f. Glenstal (USA) 118 – Regent Star (Prince   59 d Regent (FR) 129) [1995 –: 10f⁴ 1996 6.9d⁵ 10d* 12g a12g 11.1d a7g Nov 22] tall filly: worthwhile form only when winning falsely-run maiden claimer at Ayr in May on final start for R. Fisher, getting up close home: sold out of M. Todhunter's stable 3,000 gns Doncaster October Sales after fifth start: stays 1¼m: acts on dead ground. *D. Moffatt*

DEVIL RIVER PEEK (USA)   4 b.c. Silver Hawk (USA) 123 – Black Tulip   115 (FR) (Fabulous Dancer (USA) 124) [1995 7.5g 8g⁶ 9s³ 8m⁵ 8m 8g² 8s* 8.5v² 8d² 1996 8g² 8s³ 9m* 8g² 10d⁵ 10m² 8g³ Sep 21] $15,000Y: first foal: half-brother to 3-y-o Ribblesdale winner Tulipa (by Alleged): dam won 7 races at 1¼m to 1½m in France and second in 2 Grade 2 events in USA: smart German colt: won maiden at Cologne, minor event at Dusseldorf and quite valuable event at Hoppegarten as a 2-y-o and quite valuable event at Baden-Baden at 3 yrs: successful in 1996 in 10-runner Grosser Preis der Dortmunder Wirtschaft in June by 2 lengths from Accento: good efforts when placed in 3 pattern events afterwards: stays 1¼m: acts on good to firm ground and heavy: consistent. *B. Schutz, Germany*

DEVILRY   6 b.g. Faustus (USA) 118 – Ancestry (Persepolis (FR) 127) [1995 –:   – 12.1s⁴ 1996 12m Sep 18] probably no longer of account on flat: ungenuine jumper, winner of novice chase in October. *R. Craggs*

DEVIL'S DANCE (FR)   3 b.g. Mujtahid (USA) 118 – Dance of Leaves (Sadler's   – Wells (USA) 132) [1995 NR 1996 8.2s 8m 10g⁴ 11.8g Aug 12] well-made gelding: second foal: half-brother to high-class 4-y-o 7f and 1m winner Charnwood Forest (by Warning): dam unraced: headstrong, and well beaten: sent to UAE. *M. R. Stoute*

DEVON PEASANT   4 b.f. Deploy 131 – Serration (Kris 135) [1995 74: 10g⁶   – 10m 10g² 10d² 10m 10g⁶ Apr 27] stocky filly: fair maiden: in need of race only 4-y-o start: will stay beyond 1¼m. *L. G. Cottrell*

DEWHURST HOUSE   3 ch.f. Emarati (USA) 74 – Spring In Rome (USA) (Forli   61 (ARG)) [1995 NR 1996 6g³ 5m⁶ 6m Oct 8] 1,050F: small, sparely-made filly: half-sister to numerous winners, including useful Cherry Hill (stayed 1½m, by Shirley Heights): dam once-raced granddaughter of champion American filly Cicada: failed by long way to repeat debut form: sent to South Korea. *W. W. Haigh*

268

DHES-C 3 b.f. Lochnager 132 – Keep Cool (FR) 42 (Northern Treat (USA)) [1995 55 d
–: a8.5g 1996 a6g⁶ a5g⁴ a6g³ a7g⁵ a6g³ a5g³ a6g* a8.5g⁶ a6g a5g a6g 7g⁵ a6g a6s
Dec 19] tall, workmanlike filly: modest handicapper: won seller at Wolverhampton
(led near finish) in March: well below form afterwards: effective at 5f and should
stay 7f. *R. Hollinshead*

DHULIKHEL 3 b.f. Reprimand 122 – Travel Storm 77 (Lord Gayle (USA) 124) 59
[1995 54, a43: a6g⁵ a5g⁵ 7f⁴ a6g³ 7f* 7g 7g a7g 9g 1996 10.8g* 10.2g⁵ 11.6m a8g 10.2f⁶ a45
8f³ a10g² 12m Sep 25] angular filly: fair handicapper: won at Warwick in April: only
poor form at end of career: stayed 10.8f: acted on firm ground and equitrack: dead.
D. Marks

DIA GEORGY 5 b.h. Reesh 117 – Carpadia (Icecapade (USA)) [1995 49, a58: –
6.9d 8m 8m⁶ 7g a10g² a8.5g* a9.4g* a8.5g 9.7g³ 10g a9.4g⁴ a10g² a9.4g a8g
a10g a10g⁵ 1996 a12g⁴ a8g a8g⁴ a10g a10g⁶ a7s Nov 19] modest handicapper: no
form for new stables (Mrs N. Macauley first 4 starts) in 1996: probably stays 1½m:
acts on any going, including all-weather: tried blinkered, no improvement: tail
swisher. *C. A. Dwyer*

DIAMOND BANGLE 4 b.f. Chilibang 120 – My Diamond Ring 65 (Sparkling –
Boy 110) [1995 –: a6g a8g a5g⁶ 1996 a6g a6g a6g 6.1g 5d⁶ 6.9m May 29] no
worthwhile form: trained until after fourth 4-y-o start by C. C. Elsey. *W. R. Muir*

DIAMOND BEACH 3 b.c. Lugana Beach 116 – Cannon Boy (USA) (Canonero 74 §
II (USA)) [1995 78: 6m 6d⁵ 7d² 6f 1996 7m³ 8f² 7f⁵ 7.6m² 7.1m⁴ 8m⁵ 8g Oct 29] tall,
quite attractive colt: good mover: looked none too keen after
second start: sold (B. Hills to G. M. Moore) 13,000 gns Newmarket Autumn Sales:
stays 1m: effective on dead ground and on firm: not one to trust. *B. W. Hills*

DIAMOND CROWN (IRE) 5 ch.g. Kris 135 – State Treasure (USA) (Secre- 50
tariat (USA)) [1995 50: 10f 11.1g 10m² 10g³ 10m 11.1m⁶ 12m* 12h² 18m³ 12.1g
10.8g 13.8f⁴ 1996 10m³ 12m 14.1f 11.1g⁴ 10m³ 10m⁵ 12g 6.9f³ 10f⁵ 10m³ 10f⁴ 8m*
8m 8.1s⁶ Nov 7] leggy gelding: unimpressive walker: modest performer at best:
won claiming handicap at Newcastle in October, slowly away, leading near finish:
effective at 1m to 1½m: acts on firm ground, shaped quite well on soft, tailed off on
fibresand: held up and sometimes set plenty to do. *Martyn Wane*

DIAMOND CUT (FR) 8 b.g. Fast Topaze (USA) 128 – Sasetto (FR) (St Paddy 59
133) [1995 NR 1996 11.9d⁴ 12m Jul 13] rather leggy gelding: fair performer on
flat in 1992: modest form on reappearance: stayed 1½m: fell fatally over hurdles.
M. C. Pipe

DIAMOND DANCE (IRE) 3 b.f. Sadler's Wells (USA) 132 – Diamond Field 65
(USA) 71 (Mr Prospector (USA)) [1995 NR 1996 8.1m⁶ 10.5d⁵ 14.1g Oct 24] leggy
filly: fourth foal: closely related to very useful 6f to 10.9f (in Dubai) winner Storm
Canyon (by Storm Bid) and half-sister to 6f (at 2 yrs) to 9f winner Wafayt (by
Danehill): dam, placed over 5f at 2 yrs from 2 starts, out of sister to top-class
middle-distance filly Drumtop, dam of Topsider: regressive form in maidens: retired.
J. H. M. Gosden

DIAMOND EYRE 2 ch.f. (Feb 5) Then Again 126 – Renira 60 (Relkino 131) 45
[1996 7f⁵ a7g⁵ a7g a7g Nov 22] 1,000Y: seventh foal: half-sister to 1m winner Hotsocks
(by Hotfoot), 1990 2-y-o 5f winner Summer Sands (by Mummy's Game) and 2
winners abroad: dam lightly-raced maiden: poor form: reportedly had blood disorder
final start (not given hard time in seller at Southwell). *J. L. Eyre*

DIAMOND LIL 2 b.f. (Apr 23) Environment Friend 128 – Cataclysmic 78 –
(Ela-Mana-Mou 132) [1996 6m 6m⁶ Jul 15] fifth foal: half-sister to 3-y-o Energy
Man (by Hadeer), 5-y-o 1¾m and 2m winner Wannaplantatree (by Niniski) and a
winner in Holland by Siberian Express: dam 1½m winner: no form in maidens: bred
to require at least 1m. *C. E. Brittain*

DIAMOND MARKET 4 gr.g. Absalom 128 – The Victor Girls (Crofthall 110) –
[1995 50: 8.5d⁶ 8m 8m⁴ a7g² a12g⁴ 9.9m⁵ 8.1s⁶ a8.5g³ a11g a8.5g³ 1996 a8.5g Jun
28] modest performer at best: well beaten on belated return for new stable: stays 8.5f:
acts on fibresand and good to firm ground: inconsistent. *B. R. Cambidge*

DIAMOND MIX (IRE) 4 gr.c. Linamix (FR) 127 – Diamond Seal 93 (Persian 117
Bold 123) [1995 120: 10.5s* 10.5d* 12g⁶ 10m³ 1996 10.5s⁴ 10g⁴ 10.5m⁶ 10g 10m³
10g² 10d 10d³ Oct 15] smallish, close-coupled colt: smart performer: ran creditably

in Prix Exbury at Saint-Cloud and Prix Ganay at Longchamp in the spring, second and third starts: respectable efforts at best afterwards: stays 1¼m: acts on good to firm ground and heavy. *A. Fabre, France*

DIAMONDS ARE 2 b.f. (Apr 22) Touch of Grey 90 – H R Micro 77 (High Award 119) [1996 a6g 7m a6g a7g a8g⁴ a8g Dec 3] third known foal: dam sprinter: seems of little account: blinkered debut, visored fourth start. *D. T. Thom* –

DIASAFINA 3 b.f. Safawan 118 – Diana Dee 74 (Blakeney 126) [1995 –: 7g a7g 1996 a8g a11g⁴ a11g⁵ 14.1m a14.8g⁵ Jun 8] bad maiden: stays 11f: blinkered since third 3-y-o start. *S. C. Williams* 33

DICENTRA 3 b.f. Rambo Dancer (CAN) 107 – Be Noble (Vaguely Noble 140) [1995 –: a6g a8.5g 1996 10g 11.1g⁴ May 20] no worthwhile form. *E. Weymes* –

DICKIE BIRD (IRE) 2 ch.c. (Feb 6) Shalford (IRE) 124§ – Peace In The Woods (Tap On Wood 130) [1996 6g 6f⁶ 7m* 7m⁶ 7g⁶ 7.3m Sep 20] IR 12,000F, 22,000Y: sturdy, compact colt: unimpressive mover: third living foal: dam unraced twin: won maiden at Goodwood in August: creditable efforts in nurseries next 2 starts: stays 7f: raced only on a sound surface: sold 8,000 gns Newmarket Autumn Sales. *R. Hannon* 76

DICK TURPIN (USA) 2 br.c. (May 2) Red Ransom (USA) – Turn To Money (USA) (Turn To Mars (USA)) [1996 7m⁶ Aug 17] $90,000Y: strong, lengthy colt: has scope: third foal: half-brother to a winner in USA by Carnivalay: dam won 7 times at up to 7f in USA from 2 to 4 yrs, including minor stakes: running-on sixth of 17, hampered inside last, to Monza in maiden at Newbury: moved fluently to post: a most likeable type who's sure to improve and win a race or two. *Lord Huntingdon* 71 p

DICTATION (USA) 4 b.g. Dayjur (USA) 137 – Mofida 115 (Right Tack 131) [1995 79: 6m⁴ 6m² 7m³ 6f⁵ 1996 6s 5g 6m 6d 6g 6m 6m a7s Dec 19] good-quartered gelding: only a modest maiden in 1996: likely to prove best at sprint distances: blinkered (no improvement) final start: needs treating with caution. *J. J. O'Neill* 63

DIEBIEDALE 4 b.f. Dominion 123 – Welwyn 92 (Welsh Saint 126) [1995 58: 5g⁵ 5m⁴ 6g² 5m 6.1d 1996 6.1m 5m a5g⁵ 5g 8m² 8d⁶ Sep 30] workmanlike filly: modest maiden handicapper: better at 1m than shorter: acts on good to firm (best effort) and dead ground. *R. Boss* 50

DIECI ANNO (IRE) 3 b.f. Classic Music (USA) – Moira My Girl (Henbit (USA) 130) [1995 6g⁶ 6g 7g 7s⁵ 1996 7s 7v 6g 5m² 5d⁴ 6g 5g⁴ 6m⁴ 5f* 5m a6g a5g a6g a5g Nov 30] IR 5,000Y: ex-Irish filly: fourth foal: half-sister to 3 winners (up to 7f) by Fayruz: dam placed over middle distances in Ireland: fair performer: won 5-runner maiden at Down Royal in July on penultimate outing for S. Treacy: no form in Britain: best form at sprint distances: acts on firm and soft ground: effective blinkered or not: none too consistent. *B. Palling* 72 d

DIEGO 3 b.g. Belmez (USA) 131 – True Queen (USA) 79 (Silver Hawk (USA) 123) [1995 89: 7f⁶ 9m³ 8.1d³ 10g⁴ 1996 a10g* a10g⁵ 10.3d 9.9m 12.3g 10s³ 12g²⁻ 16.2f 12.3m 14m² 14m³ 14m² 11.8f⁴ 16g Oct 24] small, rather leggy gelding: only a fair performer in 1996: successful in maiden at Lingfield in January and claimer at Doncaster in June: ideally suited by 1¾m (pulled hard over 2m): acts on equitrack and firm and dead ground: has spells in and out of form: gelded. *C. E. Brittain* 71

DIET 10 b.g. Starch Reduced 112 – Highland Rossie 67 (Pablond 93) [1995 58: 6v 6g 5m 5g* 5g 6g 5g⁴ 6f⁴ 5f⁵ 5f² 7.1m² 6f² 7.1f* 6m² 6f* 6m⁵ 6f² 6m 5g 6g 6m 8.1s 1996 8.1g⁵ 6d 7.1g* 5s 6.9m² 5m⁴ 7.1g 6g 5.9f 6m 6m 8.1f² 7.1g 7.1m² 6m⁶ Jul 12] sturdy, good-quartered gelding: carries condition: modest performer: rarely races outside Scotland, and successful 8 times at Hamilton: won selling handicap at Musselburgh in April: effective at 5f to 7f: acts on any going: blinkered earlier in career, normally visored nowadays: sometimes hangs under pressure, but suitable mount for inexperienced rider: usually races prominently: none too consistent in 1996. *Miss L. A. Perratt* 58 d

DIFFIDENT (FR) 4 b.c. Nureyev (USA) 131 – Shy Princess (USA) 117 (Irish River (FR) 131) [1995 119: 7m* 8m⁶ 5g² 6g* 6.5g⁴ 1996 a6g² 7m* 6f 7g 6m* 7g* 6s² Nov 9] small, attractive colt: has a smart action: very smart performer: trained at 3 yrs by A. Fabre: beat Heart Lake a nose in Prestige event at Abu Dhabi in February: in rear in Duke of York Stakes and Criterion Stakes next 2 outings: back in good form in the autumn, leading inside final 1f to win both Diadem Stakes at Ascot in September and £8,300 event at Doncaster (by head from Russian Revival) in 122

*Racal Diadem Stakes, Ascot—Dettori and Diffident just hold on
from the fast-finishing Lucayan Prince (blinkers) and Leap For Joy (rails)*

October: tongue tied, very good effort when short-headed by Astrac in listed race at Doncaster last time, leading from 1f out until near finish: probably best at up to 7f (respectable sixth in 2000 Guineas): acts on good to firm and soft ground and on sand: sweating fourth and fifth 4-y-o starts. *Saeed bin Suroor*

DIGITAL OPTION (IRE) 2 b.g. (Feb 8) Alzao (USA) 117 – Elevated (Shirley — Heights 130) [1996 a8.5g 7m Oct 8] 23,000F, 36,000Y: second foal: dam French 1½m and 13.5f winner: no form in maiden and claimer. *P. R. Webber*

DIGPAST (IRE) 6 ch.g. Digamist (USA) 110 – Starlit Way 92 (Pall Mall 132) 59 [1995 –, a73: a7g² a7g⁶ a7g³ a7g* a7g² a7g* a8g³ 8.3m 7f a8g⁵ a8g a7g 1996 a10g² a77 a8g* a8g⁶ a10g⁶ 9.7m 10m 10m⁵ 9m 8.3g⁶ Jul 8] lengthy, workmanlike gelding: fair handicapper: won at Lingfield (amateurs) in February: lightly raced and nowhere near so good on turf: effective at 7f to 1¼m: acts on equitrack and any turf going: blinkered nowadays: often slowly away, and usually held up. *R. J. O'Sullivan*

DIGWANA (IRE) 3 b.g. Digamist (USA) 110 – Siwana (IRE) (Dom Racine (FR) — 121) [1995 –: 5s 5g 6.1g⁶ a7g 1996 a8g⁶ 10d a8g 6f⁶ Jun 28] no worthwhile form. *T. M. Jones*

DIJON 2 ro.g. (Mar 13) Chilibang 120 – Princess Fair (Crowned Prince (USA) — 128) [1996 7g Jul 24] 5,600Y: strong, plain gelding: half-brother to a winner in Hong Kong by Absalom: dam unraced: burly, tailed off in maiden auction. *Bob Jones*

DILAZAR (USA) 3 ch.g. Zilzal (USA) 137 – Dictina (FR) (Dictus (FR) 126) 94 [1995 NR 1996 8m² 8g 8.3m³ 8d² 10.1m 8m* Oct 17] IR 120,000Y: close-coupled, useful-looking gelding: sixth foal: half-brother to 9f winner Legal View (by Riverman), later useful middle-distance performer in Italy, 1½m winner Riz Biz (by El Gran Senor) and a leading performer in Norway by Sharpen Up: dam won Grade 3 9f event: much improved form when impressive winner of handicap at Redcar in October, storming 6 lengths clear inside final 1f: best at around 1m: looked capable of better but sold only 6,000 gns Newmarket Autumn Sales: sent to Saudi Arabia. *J. R. Fanshawe*

DIL DIL 3 b.f. Puissance 110 – My Croft (Crofter (USA) 124) [1995 67: 6m 5m⁶ 47 5g⁴ 5g* 6m 6m⁴ 6.1d⁶ 6d 1996 6g 6.1m 8m 6m 7.1f⁶ 8m 8.2f² 8f⁴ 8.3m² 8f⁶ 6d Sep 30] rather leggy, quite attractive filly: only poor form in 1996: left R. Hannon after third start, sold out of W. Haggas's stable 3,100 gns Newmarket September Sales after penultimate one: resold 900 gns Doncaster October Sales: stays 8.3f: acts on firm and dead ground: inconsistent: sent to South Korea. *Mrs J. R. Ramsden*

DIMAKYA (USA) 3 b.f. Dayjur (USA) 137 – Reloy (USA) 119 (Liloy (FR) 124) 76 [1995 83: 6g² 6f² 6g² 7m² 1996 8.2m⁴ 8g³ 8g³ 10g² 7.5g* Oct 13] quite attractive filly: fluent mover: fair form: trained until after second 3-y-o start by D. Loder: won maiden at Tarbes in October: probably stays 1¼m: acts on firm ground, yet to race on soft surface. *J.-C. Rouget, France*

DIMINUET   3 b.f. Dominion 123 – Primulette 82 (Mummy's Pet 125) [1995 71: 5m 5g² 6m 6f² 6g* 7m 1996 7d Apr 24] leggy filly: capable of fair form: better at 6f than 5f: put back out on debut: broke blood vessel on 3 starts, including 3-y-o reappearance: sold 5,200 gns Newmarket December Sales. *J. W. Watts*

DIMINUTIVE (USA)   3 b.c. Diesis 133 – Graceful Darby (USA) (Darby Creek   86
Road (USA)) [1995 79: 7m⁶ 7f² 7m³ 1996 6.9m⁵ 8s⁶ 8f* 8f 10.3m⁵ 10.2f* 10.1m*
11.4d³ 10.1m⁵ 10m 10s Oct 24] leggy, close-coupled colt: has a round action: fairly useful performer: won maiden at Thirsk and minor events at Bath and Yarmouth in the summer: stays 10.2f: acts on firm and dead ground: has run creditably when sweating and on toes. *J. W. Hills*

DINO'S MISTRAL   3 b.g. Petong 126 – Marquessa d'Howfen 93 (Pitcairn 126)   –
[1995 –: 6f 7.1g 7f 1996 a12g 8.1g⁶ 11f⁴ 12g Oct 18] rather leggy gelding: sign of ability only when fourth in maiden seller at Redcar third 3-y-o start. *F. H. Lee*

DIRAB   3 ch.g. Groom Dancer (USA) 128 – Double Celt 93 (Owen Dudley 121)   81
[1995 67: 7.6d⁶ 8g⁴ 1996 a7g⁵ a8g⁶ a11g* 11.1g 12f 12.3m⁶ 14.1m* 16f³ 16d* 15m Sep 19] sturdy gelding: fairly useful handicapper: won at Southwell in February and at Redcar (landed gamble, under very forceful ride, got up on post) and Thirsk (making all) in the summer: ran as if something amiss last time: better form at 2m than shorter: acts on firm and dead ground and fibresand. *T. D. Barron*

DIRECT DIAL (USA)   4 br.g. Phone Trick (USA) – Jig Jig (USA) (Never Bend)   –
[1995 68: 7g³ 7.1g⁵ 7.1m 1996 a10g 11.5m Aug 22] no form in 1996, leaving J. Toller's stable after reappearance: stays 7f. *Miss Gay Kelleway*

DISALLOWED (IRE)   3 b.f. Distinctly North (USA) 115 – Miss Allowed   72
(USA) (Alleged (USA) 138) [1995 76: 5m⁶ 6.1m³ a7g⁴ 8m² 7.9g² 8g² 8d⁵ 1996
12.4g² 9m a8g 9m³ 10.1g⁵ 9m* 8m⁶ 10d⁶ 8.3d 8.1m 8f³ 8f⁶ Oct 14] useful-looking filly: has a roundish action: fair handicapper: ridden by 7-lb claimer, won maiden event at Ripon in July: largely disappointing afterwards: sold (M. Bell to Miss H. Knight) 16,500 gns Newmarket Autumn Sales: should be suited by middle distances: acts on firm ground, below form on a soft surface: visored last 2 starts, running well first occasion: sometimes finds little: won juvenile hurdle in December: inconsistent. *M. Bell*

DISCO BOY   6 b.g. Green Ruby (USA) 104 – Sweet And Shiny (Siliconn 121)   46
[1995 59: a5g⁶ a6g³ a6g⁶ a6g a6g a5g³ a6g 1996 a6g² a6g³ 5g a5g a7g⁶ a6g 6.1m   a57
a6g² a6g² 6s⁴ 6d⁴ a6g a6g a6g Dec 14] neat gelding: modest sprint handicapper on the all-weather, poor on turf: acts on fibresand and soft ground, probably on good to firm: probably effective blinkered/visored or not: usually races prominently: none too consistent. *P. D. Evans*

DISC OF GOLD (USA)   3 ch.f. Silver Hawk (USA) 123 – Equal Change (USA)   77
(Arts And Letters) [1995 –p: 7f 1996 a12g* 14d⁶ May 24] small, sturdy filly: poor mover: made all to win maiden at Southwell in March by 20 lengths: stiff task in handicap at Haydock nearly 3 months later, best form though left behind from 2f out: probably stayed 1¾m: retired. *M. Johnston*

DISCORSI   4 b.g. Machiavellian (USA) 123 – Bustara 92 (Busted 134) [1995 –:   –
10m 10m⁴ 10m 12.3m 1996 a13g a12g⁵ a16g Feb 13] seems of little account. *Miss Gay Kelleway*

DISMISSED (USA)   3 b.c. Dayjur (USA) 137 – Bemissed (USA) (Nijinsky   99
(CAN) 138) [1995 99+: 6g* 7.1m⁵ 7d³ 10g² 1996 11.5f⁵ 12m 8.5m Jun 7] good-topped colt: useful form in steadily-run Derby Trial at Lingfield (pulled hard) and Derby Italiano at Rome (6¾ lengths seventh of 15 to Bahamian Knight, weakening final 2f and tending to carry head rather high) in May: stays 1½m: acts on firm and dead ground: sent to USA. *P. F. I. Cole*

DISPOL AGENDA   3 b.f. Jendali (USA) 111 – Welsh Fashion (Welsh Saint 126)   –
[1995 NR 1996 12m 9.9m 8g May 19] 1,500Y: lengthy filly: third reported foal: dam unraced: well beaten: sold 520 gns Doncaster August Sales. *G. R. Oldroyd*

DISPOL CONQUEROR (IRE)   3 b.g. Conquering Hero (USA) 116 – Country   37
Niece (Great Nephew 126) [1995 38: 5m 8.5m⁶ 7g 8f 1996 10d 8g 10m 9f⁵ 10.3g 12s

Jul 3] workmanlike gelding: poor maiden handicapper: stays 1¼m: visored (no form) 3 times: gelded: joined P. Calver. *G. R. Oldroyd*

DISPOL DANCER 5 ch.g. Salse (USA) 128 – High Quail (USA) (Blushing Groom (FR) 131) [1995 –: a14g 1996 12m a16g a14g 13.8g Oct 19] tall, lengthy gelding: of little account. *Mrs V. A. Aconley*

DISPOL DIAMOND 3 b.f. Sharpo 132 – Fabulous Rina (FR) (Fabulous Dancer 70 d (USA) 124) [1995 NR 1996 6g 7.1d 7.5m³ 7.5m³ 8m⁴ 8.5m 8f³ 8m 8s⁴ 8g 7g Oct 25] 2,000Y: leggy filly: fifth foal: half-sister to 7f winner Sehailah (by Mtoto): dam, French 1¼m winner, is closely related to smart French middle-distance performer Lys River: disappointing maiden: stays at least 1m: acts on firm ground, probably on soft: inconsistent. *G. R. Oldroyd*

DISPOL DUCHESS 3 b.f. Rock City 120 – Antum 56 (Hittite Glory 125) [1995 41 NR 1996 5m 6.1g 6.1m 7s⁴ 7m 8m 8g Sep 7] 8,000F, 1,900Y: small, leggy filly: half-sister to 3 winners, including Jarmo (1½m in France, by Jalmood): dam showed ability on debut but seemed not to train on: poor maiden plater: left G. Oldroyd after sixth outing: probably stays 1m. *J. L. Eyre*

DISPOL GEM 3 b.f. Rambo Dancer (CAN) 107 – Andbracket (Import 127) 72 d [1995 NR 1996 8g 8g⁵ 8.5m⁴ 8d⁴ 8d 8m³ 9m³ 9m⁵ 10d 8f 9m 8m³ 8s⁴ Nov 9] 2,400Y: lengthy filly: shows a quick action: first foal: dam unraced: fair maiden handicapper at best: stays 9f: acts on firm and soft ground. *G. R. Oldroyd*

DISPUTED 3 b.c. Common Grounds 118 – Family At War (USA) 71 (Explodent 85 (USA)) [1995 6.5m³ 9g 6g⁴ 1996 6m³ 6m* 7d Aug 24] 5,000Y: robust colt: first foal: dam 2-y-o 5f winner: fairly useful form: in frame in minor events at Chantilly and Evry at 2 years for A. Fabre: won maiden at Newmarket (staying on strongly to lead on post) in August, easily best effort in 1996: should be suited by 7f, pulled hard when tried: acts on good to firm ground: often sweats: to UAE. *M. A. Jarvis*

DISSENTOR (IRE) 4 b.g. Dancing Dissident (USA) 119 – Helen's Dynasty 44 (Habitat 134) [1995 44: 7m 6.9m 7m a6g⁵ a7g⁵ 1996 a5g⁶ a6g* a6g⁵ a6g a6g⁶ a6g² a58 a7g² a6g³ 6.1g 6m a6g 6m⁵ 6f⁴ 6m⁶ a5g a7g a6g Dec 3] compact gelding: modest handicapper on the all-weather, poor on turf: won (first time) at Southwell in January: stays 7f: acts on fibresand, below form on equitrack: usually visored/blinkered: none too consistent. *J. A. Glover*

DISSINGTON TIMES 2 ch.g. (Jun 8) Timeless Times (USA) 99 – Zam's Slave – (Zambrano) [1996 5.9g a7g⁶ Jul 22] first foal: dam staying hurdler/chaser: seems of little account: joined W. McKeown. *J. Norton*

DISTANT DYNASTY 6 br.g. Another Realm 118 – Jianna 60 (Godswalk (USA) – 130) [1995 46, a58: a6g² a5g⁴ a5g² a5g² a6g a5g² a5g³ 5d³ 5m² 5.3m⁵ 5g 5m 7m a6g a58 d 7.6m 6f a5g² 1996 a6g a5g² a5g a5g⁶ a5g a5g a5g⁶ a7g 6m a5g a7g a6g a5g Dec 13] lengthy, angular gelding: has a round action: modest handicapper at best: effective at 5f (best recent form) to 7f: acts on good to firm and heavy ground and on all-weather: rather headstrong, and often makes running: inconsistent. *B. A. Pearce*

DISTANT OASIS (USA) 3 b.f. Green Desert (USA) 127 – Just You Wait 111 (Nonoalco (USA) 131) [1995 NR 1996 8m* 8d⁴ 8g⁵ 8m⁴ 10m Oct 5] strong, good sort: eighth foal: closely related to useful middle-distance performer Waiting (by Polish Precedent) and half-sister to 3 winners, including very smart pair Reprimand (miler, by Mummy's Pet) and Wiorno (up to 1½m, by Wassl): dam unraced daughter of very useful 1¼m winner Sleat: won minor event at Ascot (very slowly away) in May: smart form, 5 lengths fourth of 12 to Matiya in Irish 1000 Guineas, 5¾ lengths fifth of 7 to Mark of Esteem in Celebration Mile at Goodwood (after 3-month break) and 2½ lengths fourth of 8 to Bishop of Cashel in Group 3 event at Doncaster: should prove suited by further than 1m (gone in coat when tailed off in Sun Chariot Stakes): yet to race on extremes of going: sent to USA. *H. R. A. Cecil*

DISTANT STORM 3 ch.g. Pharly (FR) 130 – Candle In The Wind 90 (Thatching 40 131) [1995 63?: 7g 7f* 7.3m 7f⁶ 7f 1996 11.9m⁵ 15.8m² Aug 6] robust gelding: only poor form in 1996, better effort in visor (ran on, too much to do) last time: sold (M. Bell to B. Llewellyn) 3,000 gns Newmarket September Sales: seems to stay 15.8f: has raced only on a sound surface: blinkered second to fourth starts at 2 yrs. *M. Bell*

DISTINCT BEAUTY (IRE) 3 ch.f. Pancho Villa (USA) – Beautiful Secret – (USA) (Secreto (USA) 128) [1995 69: 7f⁶ 7m a7g² 1996 a10g* a8g² a10g⁶ 10g⁵ a8g* a71 a10g³ 8f 8.2g Oct 24] workmanlike filly: fair performer on the all-weather, yet to show comparable form on turf: won minor event at Lingfield in January and handicap at Southwell in May: sold 7,500 gns Newmarket Autumn Sales: stays 1¼m: acts on all-weather: seems effective visored/blinkered or not: sent to Saudi Arabia. *W. A. O'Gorman*

DISTINCTIVE DREAM (IRE) 2 b.g. (May 30) Distinctly North (USA) 115 – – Green Side (USA) 37 (Green Dancer (USA) 132) [1996 6g 7.9g 6m 6d Oct 21] IR 3,000Y 5,200 2-y-o: lengthy gelding: second foal: dam, 10.7f winner in France at 3 yrs who showed only poor form here as 4-y-o, half-sister to useful French sprinter West Man: signs of ability on debut but little after: very slowly away on second start: sprint bred. *K. T. Ivory*

DISTINCTLY SWINGIN (IRE) 3 b.f. Distinctly North (USA) 115 – Swoon – Along (Dunphy 124) [1995 60?: 5m³ 5g⁵ 1996 7g 8m 5g⁵ 6m 5g⁴ Jul 22] no form in 1996: sent to South Korea. *Miss L. A. Perratt*

DITTY BOX 2 b.f. (Mar 23) Northern State (USA) 91 – Upholder (Young – Generation 129) [1996 a6g a5g a6s Dec 19] fourth reported foal: dam ran 3 times: soundly beaten in sellers. *M. D. I. Usher*

DIVE MASTER (IRE) 2 ch.c. (Feb 18) Masterclass (USA) 116 – Perle's 57 ? Fashion (Sallust 134) [1996 5m³ 5g⁶ 6g⁶ 7.6m 10g⁶ Oct 24] IR 16,000Y: ninth foal: half-brother to 4-y-o Northern Spruce (by Astronef) and 3 winners, including stayer Cost Effective (by Burslem): dam Irish 9f to 1½m winner: modest maiden: stays 1¼m, at least in steadily-run race: blinkered final start: sold 1,200 gns Newmarket Autumn Sales: sent to Holland. *C. Murray*

DIVIDE AND RULE 2 b.c. (Apr 28) Puissance 110 – Indivisible 56 (Remainder 76 Man 126§) [1996 5g³ 6m⁵ 5m* 5g⁵ 5f 5m³ Aug 16] smallish, leggy, quite attractive colt: second foal: dam stayed 1¼m: won median auction maiden at Ripon in June: ran well in nursery final start: bred to stay beyond 5f: raced only on a sound surface. *R. Hollinshead*

DIVINA LUNA 3 b.f. Dowsing (USA) 124 – Famosa (Dancing Brave (USA) 89 140) [1995 –p: 5g 1996 8g* 7f² 8f³ 7.6m* 7f* 7m* 7d⁴ 8m⁵ Sep 28] sturdy, work-manlike filly: fairly useful performer: won maiden at Bath in May, minor events at Lingfield and Warwick in July and handicap at Kempton in August: effective at 7f, stays 1m well: acts on firm and dead ground: most consistent. *J. W. Hills*

DIVINE 3 b.f. Dowsing (USA) 124 – Rectitude 99 (Runnymede 123) [1995 60p: 69 7d³ 1996 7.1m⁴ 7s³ 10.1g² 11.1g* 12m 10.3g Oct 25] unfurnished filly: fair form: easily landed the odds in maiden at Hamilton in September: well below form afterwards: stays 11.1f: best efforts on good ground: sold 15,000 gns Newmarket December Sales. *A. C. Stewart*

DIVINE MISS-P 3 ch.f. Safawan 118 – Faw (Absalom 128) [1995 NR 1996 5m² 68 6g Apr 23] 1,500F, 2,600Y: workmanlike filly: second foal: dam never ran: running-on second of 10 in maiden at Beverley, easily better effort: should stay 6f: bandaged off hind second start. *A. P. Jarvis*

DIVINE QUEST 3 ch.f. Kris 135 – Dance Quest (FR) 117 (Green Dancer (USA) 81 132) [1995 NR 1996 7d³ 8m⁵ 7f⁴ 8m² 7m* 7m⁴ 7m* 7m Oct 29] lengthy, rather unfurnished filly: unimpressive mover: sixth living foal: sister to smart French sprinter Divine Danse and half-sister to good-class 6f to 1m performer Pursuit of Love (by Groom Dancer): dam French sprinter: fairly useful performer: won handi-cap at Yarmouth in August and minor event at Newcastle in October: seemed at least as effective at 7f as 1m: raced predominantly on good to firm ground, looked ill-at-ease on firm at Brighton: carried head high seventh outing, but did nothing wrong under pressure next time: consistent: stud. *H. R. A. Cecil*

DIXIE EYES BLAZING (USA) 2 ch.f. (Mar 5) Gone West (USA) – Maria- – kova (USA) 84 (The Minstrel (CAN) 135) [1996 a8.5g⁶ Nov 30] half-sister to useful 5f (at 2 yrs) to 1m winner Well Beyond (by Don't Forget Me) and 1½m winner Society Ball (by Law Society): dam, placed at 6f and 1m on only 2 starts, is sister to Zaizafon, the dam of Zafonic (by Gone West): well beaten in maiden at Wolver-hampton. *R. Charlton*

DIXIE JAMBOREE (USA)   2 b. or br.c. (Apr 5) Dixie Brass (USA) – Glim-   64
mering 83 (Troy 137) [1996 7m 7d 8.2m⁶ 7m Oct 4] $18,000F, $85,000Y: close-
coupled, quite good-topped colt: eighth foal: half-brother to modest Irish 13f winner
Glimmering Girl (by Spectacular Bid) and 2 winners abroad: dam, maiden who
seemed to go wrong way at 3 yrs, half-sister to Glint of Gold and Diamond Shoal:
sire (by Dixieland Band) won Grade 1 1m Metropolitan Handicap: modest form in
maidens and a nursery: looks a stayer: sold 8,000 gns Newmarket Autumn Sales.
L. M. Cumani

DIZZY DANCER   2 gr.f. (May 2) Rambo Dancer (CAN) 107 – Fancy Flight (FR)   48
74 (Arctic Tern (USA) 126) [1996 5.1g⁵ 6g⁵ May 19] 6,000Y: tall, rather unfurnished
filly: half-sister to useful 1994 2-y-o 5f and 6f winner Sumoquinn (by Then Again),
1¼m seller winner Barley Cake (by Midyan) and a winner in Sweden by Prince Sabo:
dam 1¼m winner: poor form in spring maidens: bred to stay at least 1m. *A. Bailey*

DIZZY TILLY   2 b.f. (Feb 23) Anshan 119 – Nadema (Artaius (USA) 129) [1996   54 ?
6g⁶ 7f⁴ a7g³ 6m 7m Oct 28] 4,000F, 6,500Y: tall, leggy filly: sixth foal: half-sister to
minor winners in USA by Irish Tower and Green Forest: dam unraced half-sister to
smart and prolific 1984 2-y-o Provideo: poor maiden: stays 7f. *T. J. Naughton*

DJAIS (FR)   7 ch.g. Vacarme (USA) 121 – Dame de Carreau (FR) (Targowice   92
(USA) 130) [1995 –: 14.6m⁵ 12m⁴ 1996 10m³ 13.3d⁶ 22.2f Jun 21] good-topped
ex-French gelding: recaptured some form for new stable when third of 5 to Florid in
minor event at Newmarket: behind both starts afterwards: stays 15f: acts on heavy
and good to firm going: twice bandaged at 7 yrs: fairly useful hurdler. *J. R. Jenkins*

D J CAT   3 b.g. Ballad Rock 122 – Four-Legged Friend 101 (Aragon 118) [1995   –
NR 1996 8.2d 8.2s 10s a8g a10g⁶ Nov 15] 25,000F, 13,000Y: rangy gelding: unimpressive mover: third foal: half-brother to fair 1m and 1¼m winner Herr Trigger
(by Sharrood): dam sprinter: no form. *W. R. Muir*

D'NAAN (IRE)   3 b.g. Royal Academy (USA) 130 – Festive Season (USA)   –
(Lypheor 118) [1995 79: 7g 7.1d³ 7d 8f⁵ a8g* 1996 9.9m 11.6m 10m 10g 10f
10m⁶ 14.1m⁶ Aug 15] well-made gelding: fair at 2 yrs: looked of little account in
1996: sold (W. Haggas to M. Pipe) 10,000 gns Newmarket Autumn Sales: won over
hurdles in December. *W. J. Haggas*

DOCKLANDS CARRIAGE (IRE)   2 b.c. (May 4) Anita's Prince 126 –   67
Zestino (Shack (USA) 118) [1996 5g² 5.1m 5m⁶ 5.9g⁵ 6m* 6g* 6g³ 6f 6m 6g Sep 3]
IR 1,400F, IR 6,000Y, 17,000 2-y-o: workmanlike colt: has a round action: sixth foal:
half-brother to 1995 2-y-o 5f and 6f winner Arvzees (by Magical Wonder) and 11.1f
winner Briggs Lad (by Be My Native): dam unraced half-sister to Oaks winner
Ginevra: won seller at Thirsk and nursery at Pontefract in summer: stays 6f: acts on
good to firm ground: best form blinkered/visored. *N. Tinkler*

DOCKLANDS COURIER   4 b.g. Dominion 123 – High Quail (USA)   48
(Blushing Groom (FR) 131) [1995 54: 7a7g⁴ a10g² a10g⁴ 7.9g⁵ 10m 10g a16g a12g   a52
1996 10m 10.1g⁴ a10g² 11f⁶ a9.4g Aug 31] smallish, robust gelding: modest maiden
handicapper: should be suited by further than 1¼m: acts on equitrack. *B. J. McMath*

DOCKLANDS LIMO   3 b.c. Most Welcome 131 – Bugle Sound 96 (Bustino   78
136) [1995 54p: a8g⁵ 1996 a8g* 10.3d⁴ 10g* 9m⁶ 9m² Jun 6] leggy colt: fair performer: won maiden at Lingfield in February and minor event at Nottingham in April: will
stay beyond 1¼m: acts on good to firm ground and equitrack. *B. J. McMath*

DOCKMASTER   5 b.g. Dominion 123 – Surf Bird (Shareef Dancer (USA) 135)   –
[1995 NR 1996 18g Oct 21] neat gelding: shows plenty of knee action: rated 51 in
1994: no threat on return: stays 1¾m: once a fair hurdler. *Miss M. K. Milligan*

DOC RYAN'S   2 b.c. (May 4) Damister (USA) 123 – Jolimo 92 (Fortissimo 111)   77 ?
[1996 7f 7m⁶ 8.1s² Nov 7] half-brother to several winners, including 3-y-o Jolis
Present (by Prince Sabo), 5f winner at 2 yrs, and fairly useful performer at up to 1½m
Osric (by Radetzky): dam won from 1½m to 2¼m: appeared to show fair form in
slowly-run races at Yarmouth and Musselburgh on last 2 starts: will stay beyond 1m.
M. J. Ryan

DOCTOR BRAVIOUS (IRE)   3 b.g. Priolo (USA) 127 – Sharp Slipper (Sharpo   69
132) [1995 71: 7.1s⁶ 7f³ 1996 a8.5g* 8d⁴ 10.5v 10f Oct 15] rangy, rather unfurnished
colt: fair form: made all in maiden at Wolverhampton in January: burly, respectable
fourth of 15 in handicap at Warwick in April: off nearly 6 months and well beaten on

275

return: stays 8.5f: acts on fibresand, probably on firm and dead ground: visored at 3 yrs. *M. Bell*

DOCTOR GREEN (FR) 3 b.g. Green Desert (USA) 127 – Highbrow 112§ 67 (Shirley Heights 130) [1995 –p: 6m 1996 10g 10g 14.1m⁵ 11.7m² 11f⁴ Jun 21] heavy-bodied gelding: has a long stride: modest maiden: sold (Lord Huntingdon to M. Pipe) 21,000 gns Newmarket July Sales, and gelded: stays 1½m: acts on firm going (yet to race on a soft surface): visored since third 3-y-o start: fair winning hurdler. *Lord Huntingdon*

DOCTOR'S REMEDY 10 br.g. Doc Marten 104 – Champagne Party (Amber – Rama (USA) 133) [1995 34: 10f⁵ 10f⁶ 12m³ 12f⁵ 16.2m⁵ 12h* 14.1m³ 12.4g⁵ 15.8g 1996 12.1d 15.8g Sep 21] sturdy gelding: no longer of account. *Mrs J. Jordan*

DODDINGTON FLYER 4 b.c. Distant Relative 128 – Tino-Ella 73 (Bustino – 136) [1995 66, a59: a8g⁵ 10.3g 14.1g* 12.5m⁶ 14.6m* 14.1m⁴ 14g 12.1s 14.6m³ a54 a16g a16g² 1996 a13g³ Jan 11] fair performer: stays 2m: acts on firm and soft going and on equitrack: tends to be slowly away: often sweats: carries head high and sometimes wanders under pressure. *R. Hollinshead*

DODGY DANCER 6 b.g. Shareef Dancer (USA) 135 – Fluctuate 87 (Sharpen – Up 127) [1995 NR 1996 10g Apr 22] close-coupled, angular gelding: fair middle-distance stayer at 3 yrs: tailed off since: joined Mrs L. Williamson: one to treat with caution. *M. D. I. Usher*

DOLLIVER (USA) 4 b.g. Northern Baby (CAN) 127 – Mabira (Habitat 134) – [1995 55: 11.5m³ 12s 10g 1996 10m 10m 11.7f a12g a9.4g Dec 7] workmanlike gelding: modest maiden: well beaten last 3 starts: should prove suited by middle distances: stiff task, soundly beaten on soft ground. *S. Dow*

DOLLY DOLITTLE 5 ch.m. Infantry 122 – Lost Moment (Hotfoot 126) [1995 – –: a11g⁶ a12g 8f 12g 10f 14.1g* 16.2m 11.5g 1996 8.3m 10m 8g 11.6m Jul 22] stocky mare: no sign of ability. *H. J. Collingridge*

DOMAK AMAAM (IRE) 3 b.c. Dominion 123 – La Courant (USA) (Little 78 Current (USA)) [1995 77p: 7g³ 6m² 1996 a7g² 6m⁴ 6d² 6m⁴ 6m³ a6g⁵ 7g³ Aug 21] a73 small, quite attractive colt: fair maiden at his best: below form last 3 starts: effective at 6f and 7f: acts on good to firm and dead ground and on equitrack: has had tongue tied and been bandaged behind: sent to UAE. *J. H. M. Gosden*

DOMAPPEL 4 b.g. Domynsky 110 – Appelania 63 (Star Appeal 133) [1995 73: 80 10.1g* 10d³ 10d 1996 10.8g⁵ 12m² 12m⁶ 11.9m 12f* 12.5f² 13.9g⁶ 12g Oct 26] lengthy gelding: fairly useful handicapper: gradually back to form and won at Thirsk in June: off course 4 months after next start: well below form on return: suited by around 1½m: acts on firm and dead ground: fairly useful winning hurdler. *Mrs J. Cecil*

DOMBEY 3 b.c. Dominion 123 – Arderelle (FR) 80 (Pharly (FR) 130) [1995 85: 111 7g⁴ 7.1d⁴ 1996 a9.4g* 9g* 10.4m* 10m 10f⁶ 8.5f² Sep 22] lengthy, useful-looking ex-English colt: has a rather round action: useful form: won maiden at Wolverhampton (by 10 lengths), handicap at Kempton and £12,900 handicap at York in the spring: left R. Charlton after next start: much improved in Secretariat Stakes at Arlington in August and Grade 3 handicap at Bay Meadows (beaten a head by Matty G) in September: stays 10.4f: acts on firm going. *D. Vienna, USA*

DOME PATROL 5 gr.g. Dominion 123 – Tranquility Base 112 (Roan Rocket – 128) [1995 –, a48: a8g* a8g⁴ a7g⁵ a8g⁴ a8g⁵ a8g⁴ 1996 a7g⁴ a11g a8.5g³ a10g² Aug a46 10] poor handicapper: stays 1¼m, may prove best at slightly shorter: acts on all-weather surfaces: blinkered (ran creditably) once at 4 yrs. *D. Burchell*

DOMETTES (IRE) 3 ch.f. Archway (IRE) 115 – Superetta 65 (Superlative 118) 63 [1995 65: 6m 6f* 6m² 6m⁵ 7m* 1996 a8g⁶ a8g a8g⁵ 7d⁵ 9.7f⁴ 11.6m⁶ 10m³ 10m² a– 10m² 10m* 10.2g⁵ 11.4m² 12m 12s Oct 26] small, sparely-made filly: modest performer: dictated steady pace to win claimer at Leicester in August: sold 4,200 gns Newmarket Autumn Sales: stays 11.6f: acts on firm going, seemingly not on all-weather. *R. Hannon*

DOMICKSKY 8 b.g. Dominion 123 – Mumruffin 101 (Mummy's Pet 125) [1995 57 69d: 5d 5m³ 5m⁶ 6g 5.1m⁴ 5m⁵ 5m⁶ 6g 5m⁵ 5.1m⁵ 5.2g⁶ 5.1m⁵ 5m⁴ 5f⁴ 5m⁶ 5m 5m³ 5m² 5m 5.1d 5g 5.3g² 5.1d³ 5f⁴ 5.1m⁶ 5m³ 1996 5s⁶ 5g² 5g 5m 5g⁶ 6s 5s⁴ May 3] good-topped gelding: hobdayed: poor mover: spent most of his career as fair sprint handicapper (winning 8 races), but successful over 1m as 3-y-o when rated 93: decidedly on downgrade last 2 seasons: acted on any going: dead. *M. R. Channon*

DOMINANT AIR 2 b.g. (Feb 18) Primo Dominie 121 – Area Girl 76 (Jareer (USA) 115) [1996 5m⁶ 5.7d 6g³ 5.2g* a5g a5g* Dec 3] smallish, strong gelding: first foal: dam 5f winner at 2 yrs: fair form: won nurseries at Yarmouth (made all) and Southwell (led 2f out) late in year: almost certainly a sprinter: acts on fibresand, poor efforts on equitrack and (moved poorly to post) good to firm. *Sir Mark Prescott* 77 +

DOMINELLE 4 b.f. Domynsky 110 – Gymcrak Lovebird 84 (Taufan (USA) 119) [1995 56: 6m 5m 6g⁴ 6m⁵ 5f* 5f* 6m³ 5f³ 5m 5h³ 5f⁶ a5g 1996 5g 5.9m 5g 5g 5f* 5f² 5m³ 5m² 6f⁵ 6f³ 5m 5f² 5m⁴ 6m⁴ 6.1m² 6d 5.1g² Oct 9] small, workmanlike filly: shows knee action: modest handicapper: won at Beverley in June: stays 6f: acts on firm and soft ground: blinkered once as 2-y-o: often sweating and edgy: tends to wander: usually races prominently: flashes tail: consistent. *T. D. Easterby* 59

DOMINO FLYER 3 b.c. Warrshan (USA) 117 – Great Dilemma 77 (Vaigly Great 127) [1995 60d: 5g⁵ 7m 5g² 6m 6m⁴ 1996 a8g⁵ 8.3d³ a7g* 9.2s* a12g⁶ a9.4g a8g⁴ a9.4g a8.5g a8g² a8g* a8g³ Dec 3] modest performer: won maiden handicap at Southwell in April and minor events at Hamilton in May and Southwell in November: stays 9.2f: acts on fibresand and soft ground: hung markedly left seventh 3-y-o start: effective from front or held up. *Mrs A. Swinbank* 65 a71

DOMINO STYLE 2 b.f. (Apr 11) Primo Dominie 121 – Corman-Style 52 (Ahonoora 122) [1996 8g 7m⁴ Oct 23] fourth foal: dam poor maiden: running-on fourth in Newcastle maiden, better effort: not certain to stay beyond 1m. *M. J. Camacho* 54

DOMITIA (USA) 4 ch.f. Arctic Tern (USA) 126 – Fast Trek (FR) (Trepan (FR) 133) [1995 69: 8m⁵ 8.2m² 13.8g² 10g⁴ 10.1m² 8m³ 7m⁴ 10d² 10g* 10.5d 10f² a12g³ 1996 10m 9.9g* 10d² 10d 10.1m 9.9f⁶ 10m 9.9f 10f Nov 5] good-topped filly: fair handicapper: won at Beverley in May: well below form after next start: similar form at 7f to 1¾m but races mainly at around 1¼m nowadays: acts on firm and dead ground: often bandaged: sold 9,000 gns Newmarket December Sales. *M. Bell* 73

DOMOOR 3 b.g. Dominion 123 – Corley Moor 97 (Habitat 134) [1995 57: 5f⁴ 7m 5g 7.5d* 8.3g² a8.5g³ a8g² a8.5g⁵ a7g² a10g² a8g* a10g⁶ a8g² a7g² a7g 8d 7.1g 8f 7d Aug 10] quite attractive gelding: unimpressive mover: modest handicapper on the all-weather: won at Lingfield in February: well beaten on turf: sold 6,200 gns Doncaster August Sales: stays 1¼m: acts on dead ground and the all-weather: sometimes flashes tail: sent to Saudi Arabia. *M. Johnston* – a63

DOM RUINART (IRE) 2 b.c. (May 14) Cyrano de Bergerac 120 – Dazzling Maid (IRE) 64 (Tate Gallery (USA) 117) [1996 6m a6g 5f 6g Oct 9] IR 5,200Y: quite attractive, unfurnished colt: second foal: half-brother to 3-y-o Al Abraq (by Reprimand), 7.1f winner at 2 yrs: dam placed at 5f and 6f at 2 yrs, her only season to race: modest form: soundly beaten on fibresand: sold only 750 gns Newmarket Autumn Sales. *J. W. Hills* 50

DOMULLA 6 br.h. Dominion 123 – Ulla Laing 107 (Mummy's Pet 125) [1995 105: 6g² 6m* 6m⁵ 6f 6m 6d* 1996 6s 6m⁴ 6f Jun 1] sparely-made horse: useful handicapper: easily best effort at 6 yrs when fourth of 11 (plenty to do after bumped leaving stalls) in rated stakes at Newmarket: stays 6f well: acts on good to firm and heavy ground: usually races prominently: often bandaged: normally goes well fresh. *R. Akehurst* 105

DOMUSKY 3 ch.f. Domynsky 110 – Roches Roost (Pauper) [1995 –: 7f 1996 7d 7m 8m a11g⁵ 8m 7.1m⁵ Aug 29] small filly: no worthwhile form: trained by A. Mulholland until after fourth 3-y-o start: tried blinkered. *R. Bastiman* –

DONA FILIPA 3 ch.f. Precocious 126 – Quisissanno 76 (Be My Guest (USA) 126) [1995 –: 7d 6d 7m 1996 7.6m 6m 6f⁶ 6g 7f⁶ 7m⁶ Oct 8] good-topped filly: no worthwhile form. *Miss L. C. Siddall* –

DON BOSIO (USA) 3 b.c. El Gran Senor (USA) 136 – Celtic Loot (USA) (Irish River (FR) 131) [1995 NR 1996 8m 8g⁶ 8g² 8f 7.1m⁵ 8.3d³ 7m³ 7g* 7m* 7m Oct 4] 200,000Y: leggy, useful-looking colt: second foal: dam minor winner at around 1m in USA at 4 yrs: useful performer: won maiden at Catterick (by 6 lengths) and handicap at Goodwood (quickened clear 1f out, best effort) within 5 days in September: sold 41,000 gns Newmarket Autumn Sales: effective at 7f and 1m: acts on good to 97 firm and dead going: visored since seventh 3-y-o start: sweating and edgy (respectable effort, edging right) final 3-y-o start. *M. R. Stoute*

DONE WELL (USA) 4 b.g. Storm Bird (CAN) 134 – Suspicious Toosome – (USA) (Secretariat (USA)) [1995 97d: 7f² 7g 8m 10.9g⁵ 1996 10.9m⁶ Sep 21] big, lengthy gelding: carries plenty of condition: no worthwhile form on flat since 3-y-o reappearance: should stay at least 1m: acts on firm ground, below form on dead: fairly useful hurdler. *P. Monteith*

DONIA (USA) 7 ch.m. Graustark – Katrinka (USA) (Sovereign Dancer (USA)) – [1995 52: a11g⁴ a9.4g* a8g 1996 a8g a12g Jan 25] modest performer: no form in 1996: stays 1½m: acts on firm ground, dead and all-weather surfaces: tried blinkered and visored, no improvement: covered by Mukaddamah. *J. L. Harris*

DONINGTON PARK 3 ch.f. Risk Me (FR) 127 – Small Double (IRE) 55 – (Double Schwartz 128) [1995 38+: 5.1g⁵ a5g² a5g⁵ 1996 6m 6.1m a5g⁶ Jul 12] leggy filly: bad maiden: sold 750 gns Doncaster September Sales: to South Korea. *P. T. Dalton*

DON MICHELETTO 3 b.c. Machiavellian (USA) 123 – Circe's Isle (Be My   113 Guest (USA) 126) [1995 94P: 6d 7g* 1996 8g 10g* 12m⁴ 12m Jun 30] small, attractive colt: has quick action: wintered in Dubai: smart performer: looking in outstanding shape, won listed race at Goodwood in May by ½ length from Prize Giving, awkward round top bend, quickening to lead over 1f out, carrying head high and flashing tail under pressure but finding enough to hold on: best form when 2¼ lengths fourth of 15 to Ragmar in Prix du Jockey-Club at Chantilly in June, off bit early in straight then staying on steadily: well beaten in Irish Derby at the Curragh: stays 1½m, may ultimately prove best at around 1¼m: acts on good to firm ground: held up/tracks pace. *Saeed bin Suroor*

DONNA'S DANCER (IRE) 2 ch.c. (Apr 10) Magical Wonder (USA) 125 – Ice   66 On Fire (Thatching 131) [1996 5g 5m⁴ 6m 5m² 5f² 6m⁵ 5g² Oct 18] IR 5,200Y: tall, lengthy, well-grown colt: third foal: half-brother to a winner in Italy by Entitled: dam unraced: fair performer: best form at 5f: raced only on a sound surface: blinkered last 4 starts. *T. D. Barron*

DONNA VIOLA 4 b.f. Be My Chief (USA) 122 – Countess Olivia 80 (Prince   117 Tenderfoot (USA) 126) [1995 95: 8g³ 9m⁵ 10g² 10m³ 7.6m* 8m⁴ 8.2m* 8m⁴ 8.1d* 8d⁵ 8s³ 1996 8.1g⁶ 9s³ 8.5m* 8m⁴ 8g³ 8g* 9.3d* 10f* Nov 3]

Bargain-basement buy Donna Viola must be well in the running for the 'surprise packet of the season' award. She is a classic example of a four-year-old filly improving in the autumn, in her case improving into a filly of some standing internationally having contested handicaps off a mark of 88 in the spring. Donna Viola was a great credit to her trainer and relatively small stable in all three of her seasons. She represented them for the last time when winning the Yellow Ribbon Stakes at Santa Anita in November; straight afterwards she joined her new owner Gary Tanaka's trainer Ben Cecil (Henry's nephew) in California and is to carry on racing in the USA.

Donna Viola spent much of her racing life in Britain in handicaps, bidding farewell to them with a good fourth place behind Yeast in the Royal Hunt Cup. But she had already shown potential in listed races and had managed to win one, the Vodac Victress Stakes at Epsom, coming from way off the pace in a strongly-run affair to get up from Hagwah. That was a fortnight before the Hunt Cup. After Royal Ascot she was campaigned exclusively in pattern races for fillies and mares. The Falmouth Stakes at Newmarket in July looked an extremely tough event in which to make a pattern debut, and in snatching third behind the odds-on French challenger Sensation and the Pouliches winner Ta Rib she had seemed to excel herself. Increasingly better followed from Donna Viola as she reeled off wins in Ireland, France and the USA—in the Group 3 Trusted Partner Matron Stakes at the Curragh, the Group 2 Sunset & Vine Prix de l'Opera at Longchamp and the Grade 1 Yellow Ribbon. The winning margin was half a length on each occasion: held up, she led late on in fields of six, ten and eight respectively. Donna Viola was value for more in a blanket finish to the Prix de l'Opera, a race in which the Matron Stakes second Hagwah came

278

Sunset & Vine Prix de l'Opera, Longchamp—Donna Viola (stars) squeezes through; then come La Blue, Sangria, Khalisa and Hill Silver

sixth, since she had to weave her way through to catch La Blue. The German-trained La Blue had an excellent third to Timarida in a fairly recent Group 1 race in Germany in her record. Donna Viola herself was due to tackle Timarida in the Yellow Ribbon, but the Irish filly was a late withdrawal because of a high temperature, weakening a race from which the USA's Perfect Arc was also a significant absentee. Another blanket finish ensued, barely three lengths covering Donna Viola and the six Americans, led by the previous year's fifth Real Connection. The home side was made up of four five-year-olds and two four-year-olds. The structure of racing in the USA gives much more encouragement to owners to keep good fillies in training past the age of three than Europe's does. That being so, it makes sense not to bring Donna Viola back to Europe, where she would have few opportunities unless she further improved sufficiently to take on the top colts in Group 1 company; she now has a Grade 1 penalty in the lesser events.

			Chief's Crown		Danzig
Donna Viola (b.f. 1992)	Be My Chief (USA) (b 1987)		(b 1982)		Six Crowns
			Lady Be Mine		Sir Ivor
			(b 1978)		My Advantage
	Countess Olivia (b 1978)		Prince Tenderfoot		Blue Prince
			(b 1967)		La Tendresse
			Coralivia		Le Levanstell
			(b 1970)		Hot Coral

Winning the Yellow Ribbon added the equivalent of £225,000 to Donna Viola's earnings and took them, for the latest season only, to well over £320,000. She fetched a mere 3,200 guineas as a foal at the Newmarket Sales and very little more, IR 4,600 guineas, resubmitted as a yearling at Fairyhouse (having been led out unsold at 7,600 guineas at Newmarket). She was from the first crop of the National Stud stallion Be My Chief, a leading two-year-old in 1989 but a failure on his only subsequent start, and is his leading runner so far. By the time Donna Viola reached the yearling stage her dam was having a limited amount of success as a broodmare: all of her seven previous live foals had managed to show at least a modicum of ability and two, Coral Flutter (by Beldale Flutter) and Juliet Bravo (by Glow), had won. The foal the year after Donna Viola, Golden Olivia (by Petong), is now a minor winner in Italy. The pedigree is not a strong one although the three mares on the bottom line are winners. A family member worth a mention is the smart middle-distance horse Ballyhot, winner of the St Simon Stakes in 1973 and a son of Hot Coral.

However unappealing she might have been as a foal, Donna Viola has grown into a tall, workmanlike filly. She is effective at a mile to a mile and a quarter, apt to be particularly effective in a strongly-run race since she is usually held up and nearly always does her best work in the closing stages. She almost certainly acts on any going (those last three wins came on good, good to soft and firm, while she had matched her previous best when third on soft in a rated stakes at Newbury on her second start in 1996). She is also tough and most reliable, all in all a grand sort who will be difficult to replace in the yard. *C. F. Wall*

DON PEPE 5 br.g. Dowsing (USA) 124 – Unique Treasure (Young Generation 66 129) [1995 73: 7.1g* 7g⁵ 7g* 7f³ 7m⁶ 6m 7g 8.2m 1996 7.1g 7f⁶ 7.1g 6m* 6f² 6m 7m 7m⁵ 7.1g² 7m 6m³ 6d² 5.7m 7m* 7m 6m³ 7g a7g Nov 14] leggy gelding: has a round action: fair handicapper: won apprentice races at Goodwood in June and Yarmouth (awarded race) in September: effective at 6f to 1m: acts on firm and dead ground, ran poorly only start on all-weather: found little eleventh 5-y-o start: none too consistent. *R. Boss*

DON SEBASTIAN 2 b.c. (Apr 8) Indian Ridge 123 – Sunley Stars (Sallust 134) 80 [1996 5m⁶ 6f⁴ 5m⁵ 6.9d² 7s² Nov 9] 11,000Y: rather leggy, close-coupled colt: fourth foal: half-brother to 3-y-o All She Surveys (by Mazilier), 5f winner at 2 yrs: dam poor daughter of sister to Runnett: trained by R. Hannon first 2 starts: did better afterwards, particularly when second in Doncaster nursery on final start: will probably stay 1m: best runs on a soft surface. *W. J. Haggas*

DON'T CARE (IRE) 5 b.m. Nordico (USA) – Eyeliner (USA) (Raise A Native) 93 [1995 5s 7m³ 6g 6g* 5g* 6g 5m⁴ 6m³ 6m⁴ 5m² 7g³ 5m⁶ 5m² 5m* 5g* 6g³ 6d 5m 6d⁴ 1996 6s 6d 5g* 5d* 5g² 6m⁴ 7m⁵ 6.3m² 5m⁵ 5m³ 6g* 6m 6v 6g Oct 12] ex-Irish mare: seventh foal: half-sister to Irish 6-y-o 1¾m winner Glowing Lines (by Glow), also successful over hurdles: dam unraced half-sister to Irish Derby winner Malacate: fairly useful handicapper: won at Leopardstown in May, Naas in June and back at Leopardstown (career-best effort) in August: subsequently left J. Bolger's stable: well held in Britain: effective at 5f and 6f: acts on good to firm and dead ground: usually blinkered: tough and consistent in Ireland. *Miss L. A. Perratt*

DON'T CRY 8 b.m. Dominion 123 – Black Veil 53 (Blakeney 126) [1995 27: – 12.3d 13g⁵ 12m 14.1m⁵ 16m⁵ 18m⁵ 16m³ 15.8g⁴ 15.8m 15.8m⁴ 14.1h² 14.1m² 17.1m 1996 12.3g 13s 14.1g 15.8g⁶ 16m 15.8s 14.1f Jul 17] small, lengthy mare: no longer of account. *Don Enrico Incisa*

DON'T DROP BOMBS (USA) 7 ch.g. Fighting Fit (USA) – Promised Star 48 (USA) (Star de Naskra (USA)) [1995 40, a34: a11g⁵ a12g* a12g⁵ a13g² a8g³ 12g a45 12f⁶ 9m⁵ 9.7f⁴ 8m² 12m³ 10f* 11.5g⁵ 8d a12g a12g 1996 a13g² a16g a12g³ a8g* a13g³ a8g² 10.3d 8g 10.1m⁶ 9.7f² 10.1g* 10g⁴ 8m 12g² 10f* a10g² a12g³ a10g³ Dec 11] angular gelding: poor handicapper: mainly runs in amateurs/ladies events: won at Lingfield in February, Yarmouth in July and Brighton (made all) in September: effective at 1m and stays 13f: acts on firm ground and equitrack: usually visored: mostly ridden by Miss J. Feilden: effective from front or held up: game. *D. T. Thom*

DON'T FOOL ME (IRE) 2 ch.g. (Apr 10) Don't Forget Me 127 – Foolish – Passion (USA) (Secretariat (USA)) [1996 a8.5g 8g Nov 2] 4,000Y, 12,000 2-y-o: half-brother to German 3-y-o Great Passion (by Great Commotion), 6.5f winner at 2 yrs, and 3 winners in USA: dam won at up to 9f in USA, from good American family: slowly away and always behind in maiden and seller. *P. Mooney*

DONT FORGET CURTIS (IRE) 4 b.g. Don't Forget Me 127 – Norse Lady 64 § (Viking (USA)) [1995 79d: a7g² 8d⁵ 9m⁶ 9.9m³ 11.4g 10g² 10f 1996 11.1d⁶ 16.2m 13.6m Oct 17] rangy gelding: only a modest maiden at best for new stable at 4 yrs and no form after reappearance: stays 1¼m: acts on fibresand and good to firm and dead ground: unreliable. *G. M. Moore*

DONTFORGET INSIGHT (IRE) 5 b.g. Don't Forget Me 127 – Starlust 79 64 (Sallust 134) [1995 75: 8m 8m⁶ 7m² 7m⁶ 8.1m⁵ 8m⁵ 8f⁵ 10m⁶ 7g 7.6d⁴ 1996 7g⁵ 6.9m⁴ May 29] lengthy, angular gelding: fair handicapper: trained in 1995 by P. Cole: below form for new stable in 1996: sold 500 gns Ascot June (1996) Sales: appears not to stay 1¼m: acts on firm and dead ground: tried blinkered, no improvement: sometimes takes keen hold. *C. P. E. Brooks*

DON'T FORGET SHOKA (IRE) 2 gr.f. (May 3) Don't Forget Me 127 – 45 d Shoka (FR) 86 (Kaldoun (FR) 122) [1996 5s⁵ 5g⁵ 5.3f⁵ a6g² 6.1d* 7f 7m⁴ 6g³ 6m 7.1m Aug 31] IR 950F, 3,400Y: tall, lengthy filly: second foal: dam 10.6f winner from good German family: won poor seller at Chepstow in May: stays 6f: acts on firm and dead ground: inconsistent. *J. S. Moore*

DON'T GET CAUGHT (IRE) 4 b.f. Danehill (USA) 126 – Be Discreet 65
(Junius (USA) 124) [1995 65: 6.5v 8m⁴ 7g⁴ 7m 6f⁶ 10g⁵ 10m⁵ 7g⁵ a7g³ a6g a7g 1996
a7g⁴ a7g a7g³ a8g⁴ a7g⁴ a7g 8.2d³ 7f* 7.1m² 8.5m² 7m* 8g Oct 13] lengthy filly:
reportedly in foal to Pursuit of Love: fair handicapper: in good form in the autumn,
winning at Leicester and, after being unlucky twice, at Newmarket: best efforts at
around 7f/1m: acts on equitrack, best turf form on a sound surface (acts on firm):
tried visored and blinkered, better form without. *J. L. Harris*

DONT SHOOT FAIRIES 4 ch.c. Vague Shot 108 – Fairy Fans (Petingo 135) 73
[1995 77: a10g³ 10.8m⁶ 9.9m* 10.3m⁶ 9.7m² 12g* 12f 10.5g* 10.3d 11.8g 1996
12m⁵ 12m⁵ 12g 13.3s⁴ 11.4m⁴ Jun 14] neat colt: fair handicapper: stays 1½m: acts on
good to firm ground and soft: blinkered (best effort at the time) third 2-y-o start: goes
well with forcing tactics: game. *C. E. Brittain*

DON'T TELL ANYONE 3 gr.g. Petong 126 – Glenfield Portion 86 (Mummy's 51
Pet 125) [1995 55: 5m³ 5.1m⁴ a6g³ 7.1m⁴ a6g⁵ 6f³ 6m⁴ 5m² a5g* 6.1m a5g 1996 a6g⁵
a5g⁴ a6g⁴ a5g⁶ 5.1g⁶ 5.1g⁵ May 7] small gelding: modest performer: best form at
around 5f: acts on fibresand, has raced only on a sound surface on turf: creditable
effort only try in blinkers: tends to sweat: panicked in stalls and withdrawn Jun 7:
sold only 900 gns Doncaster September Sales: inconsistent at 3 yrs. *P. D. Evans*

DON'T TELL VICKI 3 b.f. Mazilier (USA) 107 – Jans Contessa 68 (Rabdan –
129) [1995 52: 5g³ 5d a5g² a5g⁵ 6m³ 6f* 7d² 6m⁶ 6m² 7f 6m⁵ a6g³ 6s a5g a6g 1996
6m 6m 6m Jul 12] smallish, workmanlike filly: has a round action: modest as a
juvenile: no promise in 1996: best form at 6f: acts on firm and dead ground (badly
drawn on soft), and on all-weather. *J. S. Moore*

DON'T WORRY ME (IRE) 4 b.f. Dancing Dissident (USA) 119 – Diva 113
Encore 74 (Star Appeal 133) [1995 99: 6g³ 5m³ 5f⁵ 5f² 5f 5m* 5m 5m⁶ 5f² 1996 10v
7.5v⁵ 6.5d* 6m* 6g* 5d⁵ 5m³ 6m³ 5g⁴ 6g⁶ 6g² 5d 5d* Oct 27] leggy filly: has a quick
action: smart performer: trained at 3 yrs by F. Lee: won at Argentan and in 2
handicaps at Evry in the spring: placed in Prix de Ris-Orangis at Evry and in Prix de
Seine-et-Oise (2½ lengths second to Kistena) at Maisons-Laffitte: best effort to win
Prix du Petit Couvert (by 2 lengths from Croft Pool) at Longchamp last time: a
sprinter: probably acts on firm and dead ground. *G. Henrot, France*

DON'T WORRY MIKE 2 ch.c. (Mar 22) Forzando 122 – Hat Hill (Roan 52 +
Rocket 128) [1996 7m 6m 8g⁶ 7m⁴ 8g Oct 21] 17,500F, 17,000Y, 9,500 2-y-o: leggy,
workmanlike colt: half-brother to 1987 2-y-o 7f seller winner Nore Hill (by Town
And Country), 7f winner City Rocket (by King of Spain) and a winner abroad by
Aragon: dam ran 4 times: modest form in maidens: stays 1m. *F. H. Lee*

DON VITO 3 ch.g. Generous (IRE) 139 – Dance By Night 84 (Northfields (USA)) 107
[1995 NR 1996 10g* 12f⁶ 10.3m² 12m Jul 30] 350,000Y: smallish, useful-looking
gelding: closely related to smart 1995 3-y-o middle-distance performer Don Cor-
leone (by Caerleon) and half-brother to several winners, including very useful Dana
Springs (up to 1½m, by Aragon) and very smart Danseuse du Soir (up to 1m, by
Thatching): dam 2-y-o 7f winner: won maiden at Pontefract in April, never off bridle:
useful form when 1½ lengths second of 8 to Prince of Andros in well-contested minor
event at Chester, dropped out last and running on strongly in straight: made little
impact in pattern company, wearing net muzzle in Gordon Stakes at Goodwood on
final start: sold 74,000 gns Newmarket Autumn Sales, and gelded: should stay
1½m: has raced only on a sound surface: has tongue tied: headstrong: sent to USA.
R. Charlton

DOODIES POOL (IRE) 6 b.g. Mazaad 106 – Barncogue (Monseigneur (USA) 39
127) [1995 51, a41: a8g a8g⁴ a8g a10g 8.3m 7g 8.3m⁴ 7m a7g⁵ 8.5s 8g⁵ 8.2m a10g
a8g 1996 8.3m 8.1g 10m⁶ 8m 8m 8.1m Jul 24] leggy gelding: poor performer
nowadays: unlikely to stay beyond 1¼m: acts on firm ground and equitrack, below
form on a soft surface: tried visored/blinkered, no improvement: looked reluctant
second 6-y-o outing: inconsistent. *P. Burgoyne*

DORADO BEACH 2 b.f. (May 27) Lugana Beach 116 – Cannon Boy (USA) 46
(Canonero II (USA)) [1996 6m 7f Oct 14] sister to untrustworthy 3-y-o Diamond
Beach and half-sister to several winners, including fairly useful 7-y-o 6f to 1½m
winner Maple Bay (by Bold Arrangement) and 7f winner Tender Moment (by
Caerleon): dam won 9 races in USA, including Grade 3 9f event: in rear in maidens.
B. W. Hills

DOREEN'S DELIGHT 10 ch.h. Bay Express 132 – Elizabeth Howard 68 – (Sharpen Up 127) [1995 –: a12g⁵ 1996 10.3m 11.8d May 27] strong horse: of little account. *H. J. Collingridge*

DORMSTON BOYO 6 b.g. Sula Bula 109 – March At Dawn (Nishapour (FR) 125) [1995 –: a12g a14.8g⁶ 1996 a14g Nov 4] of little account. *T. Wall*

DORMY THREE 6 b.g. Morston (FR) 125 – Dominant 86 (Behistoun 131) 67 [1995 73: 12m⁵ 12g⁴ 12f² 12.1m² 14g⁶ 1996 12m⁶ 12m 10.8g³ 10.8f⁴ 12g 10f⁵ 10.2m⁶ 11.7f⁴ 11.6d³ 12.1g⁵ Aug 26] compact gelding: unimpressive mover: fair handicapper: well below form last 6 outings: should stay beyond 1½m: acts on firm and dead going: tried blinkered in France at 3 yrs, not when successful: has looked unenthusiastic and found little: inconsistent. *R. J. Hodges*

DOSSES DAN (IRE) 4 b.c. Danehill (USA) 126 – Flyaway Bride (USA) 104 – (Blushing Groom (FR) 131) [1995 73d: 7.1m³ 7m³ 7g³ 10f⁵ a8.5g 1996 a8.5g Mar 6] disappointing maiden: should stay at least 1m: acts on good to firm ground: blinkered (tailed off) only 4-y-o start. *B. Preece*

DOTH PROTEST (IRE) 4 br.f. Dancing Dissident (USA) 119 – Star of Victoria – (What A Guest 119) [1995 7g 6g⁶ 1996 6m 6f 7.1m⁶ Jun 30] IR 7,000F: IR 7,000Y: ex-Irish filly: third reported foal: dam unplaced: modest form in maidens at 2 yrs for J. G. Murphy: well beaten in Britain. *Noel T. Chance*

DOTS DEE 7 ch.m. Librate 91 – Dejote 60 (Bay Express 132) [1995 31: 11.1g 33 10m⁵ 10m⁴ 10m⁵ 10m 9.7f* 10.1m³ 9.9m 10f 12m⁵ 11.5g 1996 12.3g³ 11.7g 10m 10.5d 9.7f 13.1f* 12.5f³ 11.6m⁵ 12.1m⁵ 16.2f⁶ 14d⁶ Oct 2] smallish, sparely-made mare: poor handicapper: won seller at Bath in July: stays 13.1f: acts on firm and soft ground: often pulls hard: inconsistent. *J. M. Bradley*

DOUBLE ACTION 2 br.g. (Mar 21) Reprimand 122 – Final Shot 91 (Dalsaan 83 + 125) [1996 5m³ 5d⁴ 5m* 5f³ Jun 6] 19,000Y: well-made gelding: good walker: has a quick action: second foal: half-brother to 3-y-o Miss Waterline (by Rock City), 6f winner at 2 yrs: dam won Ayr Gold Cup: won maiden at Thirsk readily in May: staying-on third to For Your Eyes Only in £7,500 event at Beverley in June on final start: will be suited by further than 5f: hung left second and third starts. *T. D. Easterby*

DOUBLE AGENT 3 ch.g. Niniski (USA) 125 – Rexana (Relko 136) [1995 76: 77 7f³ 7.1m⁵ 9g 1996 14d* 14.1m* 13.3m⁵ 16.2f⁴ 14.1m⁶ 15.8g 16s³ Oct 24] rather leggy gelding: fair handicapper: won at Haydock and Nottingham (3 days later) in June: respectable efforts at best afterwards: sold 14,000 gns Newmarket Autumn Sales: effective at 1¾m but should be at least as well suited by 2m+: acts on firm and dead ground, not discredited on soft. *M. Johnston*

DOUBLE ALLEGED (USA) 2 b. or br.c. (Feb 7) Alleged (USA) 138 – 70 p Danseuse Etoile (USA) 102 (Buckpasser) [1996 7g⁶ Oct 30] 5,500Y: half-brother to several winners here and abroad, including smart French colts at around 1m/1¼m Drapeau Tricolore (by Irish River) and Dampierre (by Lear Fan): dam, sister to top-class North American filly La Prevoyante, won over 1¼m in France and at up to 9f in USA: not-knocked-about sixth to Happy Valentine in maiden at Yarmouth: will be suited by middle distances: will do better. *M. Johnston*

DOUBLE BLUE 7 ch.g. Town And Country 124 – Australia Fair (AUS) 104 d (Without Fear (FR) 128) [1995 112: 6g³ 6m 6m 6m* 5.6m 6d 6m 1996 6m⁴ 6m 6m 7.6f⁴ 6m³ 7m 7.6f² 7f⁴ 7m 6g 6g 6g 6f a6g a8g³ Dec 5] sturdy, workmanlike gelding: impresses in appearance: just a useful performer at best nowadays: short-headed in listed rated stakes at Lingfield in July: failed to repeat that form: stays 7.6f: acts on any going: no improvement in blinkers or visor: inconsistent. *M. Johnston*

DOUBLE BLUFF (IRE) 3 gr.g. Sharrood (USA) 124 – Timely Raise (USA) 95 (Raise A Man (USA)) [1995 87: 7m⁴ 8.1g² 1996 8d⁶ 7f⁴ 8.1d 7.1m⁵ 9f* 10g* 10m 10d³ 10.1m³ 9m Oct 5] leggy, good-topped gelding: has a round action: fairly useful handicapper: won at Lingfield (maiden) in June and at Windsor (rated stakes) in July: sold 64,000 gns Newmarket Autumn Sales: will probably stay beyond 10.1f: acts on firm ground and dead: has run well when sweating and edgy: usually front runner: sent to Saudi Arabia. *I. A. Balding*

DOUBLE BOUNCE 6 b.g. Interrex (CAN) – Double Gift 68 (Cragador 110) 94 [1995 85: 6.1m* 6f² 5m⁴ 6d* 6g⁵ 7g⁶ 6g* 1996 6g 6f³ 6m* 6m² 6m⁶ 6m 7m Sep 28] good-quartered, workmanlike gelding: fairly useful handicapper: third in Wokingham at Royal Ascot: won at Newcastle (reportedly lame afterwards) in June: good second to Coastal Bluff in Stewards' Cup at Goodwood: ran creditably over 7f at 5 yrs, but now has much better form over 6f: acts on firm and dead ground: usually bandaged: successful when sweating: often early to post: normally held up: consistent (had excuses last 2 starts). *P. J. Makin*

DOUBLE CREST (IRE) 2 b.f. (Mar 30) Royal Academy (USA) 130 – Sweet- 69 p
bird (Ela-Mana-Mou 132) [1996 a7g^5 a8.5g^5 Dec 14] IR 5,000Y: fifth reported foal: half-sister to 4-y-o 13f seller winner Trumped (by Last Tycoon) and a winning stayer in Italy by Alzao: dam Irish staying maiden sister to useful 1½m winner Natski, later a good stayer in Australia: fifth in maiden events at Wolverhampton late in year: will be suited by middle distances at least: likely to improve further. *M. Johnston*

DOUBLE DASH (IRE) 3 gr.g. Darshaan 133 – Safka (USA) 104 (Irish River –
(FR) 131) [1995 62: 10m^6 a8g^5 1996 13.1d^4 17.2f^5 16f Jul 18] good-topped gelding: not a good walker: disappointing maiden: sold (M. Johnston to D. Moffatt) 5,200 gns Doncaster August Sales: should be suited by 1¼m+: won 3-finisher juvenile hurdle in October: a hard ride and one to treat with caution. *M. Johnston*

DOUBLE DIAMOND (IRE) 3 b.c. Last Tycoon 131 – State Treasure (USA) 92
(Secretariat (USA)) [1995 92: 5m^4 5g^2 6.1m a7g* 7g* 8m^4 7s^5 7m^2 a7g* a8g^6 a8g^5 1996 a8.5g^4 9g^2 8s* 10.4m^5 8f^5 8g^6 8m a8.5f^2 Dec 15] close-coupled, leggy colt: fairly useful performer: won Swiss equivalent of 2000 Guineas at Zurich in May: good fifth of 31 to North Song in Britannia Handicap at Royal Ascot fifth start: left M. Johnston after penultimate outing: probably stays 10.4f: acts on firm ground (seemingly on soft) and fibresand, probably on equitrack: races up with pace. *Carla Gaines, USA*

DOUBLE ECHO (IRE) 8 br.g. Glow (USA) – Piculet 69 (Morston (FR) 125) 55
[1995 –: 11.8d 12g 1996 12g 12m^6 15.8s^6 14.8m^2 14m 14.1d^6 12g 12m* 10m^5 11.9g a12g Oct 28] sturdy, compact gelding: modest handicapper nowadays: won at Newbury (ladies) in September: probably effective at 1½m to 2m: acts on equitrack, firm and dead ground, mostly below form on soft: below form blinkered and visored: usually held up: none too consistent. *J. D. Bethell*

DOUBLE ECLIPSE (IRE) 4 b.c. Ela-Mana-Mou 132 – Solac (FR) (Gay 122
Lussac (ITY) 116) [1995 115: 12m 16.2m^2 12m 16f^2 15.9m* 16g^3 1996 16.2g* 15m* 15.5d* May 19]

After a dream start to the season for the brothers Double Trigger and Double Eclipse, the eagerly-awaited confrontation in the Gold Cup didn't come off. In Derby week their refreshingly open trainer revealed that Double Eclipse was doubtful for Royal Ascot on account of filling in his off-fore. The horse duly missed the meeting, and with the trouble recurring he missed the rest of the season too.

The two brothers had been deliberately kept apart in the spring. It hadn't always been so. On one famous occasion in 1995 they had dominated the finish of the Goodwood Cup, victory going to the much more experienced Double Trigger who was clearly the better at that time. However, Double Eclipse progressed so well in the spring that we would have been hard pressed to choose between them for the Gold Cup, particularly with the near-certainty of further improvement in the younger horse on his debut over two and a half miles. While Double Trigger re-trod the Sagaro Stakes-Henry II Stakes route, Double Eclipse's Royal Ascot preparation involved two visits to Longchamp following a satisfactory win in a conditions-event pipe-opener at Haydock at Easter. The first trip to France resulted in a two-and-a-half-length win and a new track record in the Prix de Barbeville, the first pattern race of the season for stayers. It was an above-average renewal, but nowhere near so stiff an examination of Gold Cup credentials as the Prix Vicomtesse Vigier. Double Eclipse came through the Vigier with flying colours, gamely making all the running in fairly testing conditions and holding on by three parts of a length from Nononito who finished clear of the five other contestants. The filling in the leg manifested itself six days later. Hopes were entertained for a while of a return to the track in the autumn, but they had been virtually abandoned by the end of August.

Prix Vicomtesse Vigier, Longchamp—Double Eclipse steps back up to Group 2 and beats Nononito

		Pitcairn	Petingo
	Ela-Mana-Mou	(b 1971)	Border Bounty
	(b 1976)	Rose Bertin	High Hat
Double Eclipse (IRE)		(ch 1970)	Wide Awake
(b.c. 1992)		Gay Lussac	Faberge II
	Solac (FR)	(ch 1969)	Green As Grass
	(ch 1977)	Soragna	Orvieto II
		(b 1965)	Savigny

Double Trigger had problems of his own during the season, and at one time looked booked for export to the Middle East, but he and Double Eclipse will be in training again with Mark Johnston in 1997. They may yet meet in a Gold Cup, with any luck. As we've said before, everything about Double Eclipse's breeding and racecourse performances suggests strongly that he'll stay well beyond two miles. He needs to improve a few pounds over the longer trips to match Classic Cliche's best staying form. A tall colt with perhaps some physical improvement still left in him, Double Eclipse is round-actioned but does not seem beholden to the ground. He is effective making the running or held up and is thoroughly genuine. *M. Johnston*

DOUBLE-E-I-B-A 2 br.g. (Apr 5) Reprimand 122 – Doppio 62 (Dublin Taxi) – [1996 7.1m 8m 7m Oct 17] 7,000Y: leggy, lengthy gelding: seventh foal: half-brother to 3 winners, including 3-y-o 6f (at 2 yrs) and 7f winner Thordis (by Mazilier): dam 2-y-o 5f winner: well beaten, including a seller. *C. N. Allen*

DOUBLE EIGHT (IRE) 2 b.f. (Feb 24) Common Grounds 118 – Boldabsa 96 – (Persian Bold 123) [1996 6m 7g a7g Nov 16] IR 45,000Y: fourth foal: sister to Irish 1993 2-y-o 1m winner Oliver Messel and 1994 2-y-o 5f and 6f winner Painted Madam and half-sister to 3-y-o Itkan (by Marju): dam Irish 9f and 1¼m winner: behind in maidens. *B. W. Hills*

DOUBLE ESPRESSO (IRE) 2 b.f. (Mar 11) Taufan (USA) 119 – Kilcoy 78 (USA) (Secreto (USA) 128) [1996 6m 7.9g² a8.5g⁴ 8g* 8f² a8g* a8.5g³ Nov 25] IR 1,500Y, resold IR 4,000Y: leggy filly: second foal: half-brother to 3-y-o True Secret (by Anshan), winner over 9.2f in Germany: dam unraced: fair form: successful in nurseries late in year at Pontefract and Lingfield: will stay 1¼m: acts on firm ground and all-weather. *M. Johnston*

DOUBLE FLIGHT 2 b.f. (Mar 22) Mtoto 134 – Sariah (Kris 135) [1996 7f³ 7d 71 8m* 8g Oct 18] IR 6,000Y: big, angular filly: has plenty of scope: second foal:

half-sister to 3-y-o Baasm (by Polar Falcon): dam 7f winner who stayed 9f: won poor maiden at Ayr in August: never a factor in nursery only subsequent start: will be suited by middle distances: sweating and edgy and gave impression something amiss on second start. *M. Johnston*

DOUBLE GLOW 4 b.f. Presidium 124 – Glow Again 78 (The Brianstan 128) – [1995 –: a5g⁶ a6g⁶ 5g 6.1g 5m 6m a5g 6m 5f⁶ a5g a6g a6g⁶ 1996 a6g a6g a8g⁶ a7g⁵ a7g a6g a6g a6g a5g 5f 5s³ 5m⁴ 5m 5m 5g⁶ a5g 5m⁵ 8g 5g 5g⁶ Sep 2] leggy, angular filly: bad sprinter at best since 2 yrs: tried blinkered and visored: sent to South Korea. *N. Bycroft*

DOUBLE GOLD 2 b.f. (May 7) Statoblest 120 – Adriya 94 (Vayrann 133) [1996 74 6g 7m² 7f* 8m 6.5m Sep 11] 7,000 2-y-o: tall filly: sixth foal: half-sister to 1993 2-y-o 6f seller winner Admiring (by Nomination) and Irish 7f winner Adira (by Ballad Rock): dam 7f and 11.7f winner: made all in maiden auction at Warwick and nursery at Newbury in July/August: stays 7.3f: acts on firm going: races keenly. *B. J. Meehan*

DOUBLE IMPRESSION (IRE) 3 b.f. Mac's Imp (USA) 116 – Thalssa 52 (Rusticaro (FR) 124) [1995 6m 6m 1996 a5g 5.1g⁶ 5f⁵ 5g 5f⁶ 5.3f⁴ Aug 7] IR 1,300Y: tall, angular ex-Irish filly: fourth reported foal: dam unraced: trained at 2 yrs by Neil McGrath: modest maiden at best: sold 1,500 gns Newmarket September Sales: looks a sprinter: acts on firm going. *J. L. Harris*

DOUBLE JEOPARDY 5 b.g. Polish Precedent (USA) 131 – Infamy 123 (Shir- – ley Heights 130) [1995 –: 10m a7g⁶ 1996 a13g a10g⁶ Jan 30] no form on flat since fair 3-y-o: blinkered last time. *J. White*

DOUBLE-J (IRE) 2 b.c. (Apr 28) Fayruz 116 – Farriers Slipper (Prince 82 Tenderfoot (USA) 126) [1996 6s³ 5g⁵ 5f² 6.1m² 5m* 5f² 6m⁶ 6m Oct 17] IR 3,500F, 9,000Y, 10,000 2-y-o: close-coupled colt: dam unraced: fair form: won maiden auction at Beverley in July: possibly flattered slightly when never-dangerous sixth of 7 in listed race at Kempton on penultimate start: stays 6f: acts on firm and soft ground: visored (stiff task, well beaten) final outing: ran wide round bend at Warwick on second. *K. McAuliffe*

DOUBLE LEAF 3 b.c. Sadler's Wells (USA) 132 – Green Leaf (USA) 97 109 (Alydar (USA)) [1995 97p: 7m* 7d² 1996 10g⁴ 10.4m⁵ 12m 11.6d² 14f³ 10.1m² Sep 24] tall, leggy, attractive colt: has plenty of scope: has a fluent, round action: well touted but only useful form: never able to challenge in pattern races first 3 starts in 1996, including when 9¼ lengths tenth of 20 to Shaamit in the Derby at Epsom: second in minor events at Windsor (to Shantou, after near 3-month break) and Epsom (carrying head awkwardly) on 2 of last 3 starts: sold 115,000 gns Newmarket Autumn Sales, reportedly to join E. Walden in USA: stays 1½m, not 1¾m: acts on good to firm and dead ground. *M. R. Stoute*

DOUBLE MARCH 3 b.g. Weldnaas (USA) 112 – Double Gift 68 (Cragador 84 d 110) [1995 NR 1996 7d² 7.1m 8.3g 7s 7g a8g a8.5s⁴ Dec 19] sturdy, workmanlike gelding: third reported foal: half-brother to useful 6-y-o sprinter Double Bounce (by Interrex): dam winning sprinter: beaten a head in maiden at Salisbury in May, leading briefly final 1f: failed by very long way to repeat the form: will prove best at up to 1m. *P. R. Webber*

DOUBLE MATT (IRE) 4 b.g. Double Schwartz 128 – Kasarose (Owen Dudley 74 121) [1995 79: 6m⁴ 6m³ 6g 6m⁴ 6g⁴ 7m³ 6g* 1996 6m⁴ 7f⁵ 7s May 23] strong, workmanlike gelding: fair handicapper: below form after first start in 1996: sold (R. Hannon to Mrs P. Sly) only 1,500 gns Ascot July Sales: stays 7f: acts on good to firm ground. *R. Hannon*

DOUBLE NINER (USA) 3 br.c. Forty Niner (USA) – Sure Locked (USA) – (Lyphard (USA) 132) [1995 NR 1996 10m Jun 21] $42,000Y: fourth foal: closely related to fair Lahoob (miler, by Miswaki) and half-brother to fair Keylock (1¾m winner, by Diesis): dam, listed winner at 1m in France, is half-sister to Sure Blade: 20/1 and green, always behind in 13-runner maiden at Newmarket: sent to USA. *H. R. A. Cecil*

DOUBLE-O 2 b.c. (May 19) Sharpo 132 – Ktolo 80 (Tolomeo 127) [1996 6g 8g ? a6g³ a6g* a7s⁵ Dec 19] leggy, quite attractive colt: second reported foal: dam 1½m a77

285

winner: improved form on fibresand late in year, winning maiden at Wolverhampton in December: stays 6f. *W. Jarvis*

DOUBLE OR BUST 3 ch.f. Presidium 124 – Defy Me 75 (Bustino 136) [1995 42: 5g⁵ 5.1m⁶ 6m a5g⁶ 1996 a5g 5.3f⁶ 5f 6.1m⁵ 6g 5m Sep 25] small, light-framed filly: poor sprint maiden: inconsistent. *A. G. Newcombe*   29

DOUBLE OSCAR (IRE) 3 ch.g. Royal Academy (USA) 130 – Broadway Rosie 101 (Absalom 128) [1995 88?: 6g* 6m³ 6m⁴ 7g 7g⁵ a7g⁴ 1996 6m 6.1m⁴ 7f³ 7.1g² 7.1f³ 6.9f³ 8m 6f⁴ 6d⁶ 7m Oct 8] strong, good-bodied gelding: only fair form at best in 1996: sold out of M. Johnston's stable 1,200 gns Doncaster August Sales after eighth outing: should stay further than 7.1f: acts on firm ground: effective blinkered/visored or not: unreliable. *D. Nicholls*   65 §

DOUBLE-O-SEVEN 3 b.c. Tirol 127 – Anneli Rose 56 (Superlative 118) [1995 NR 1996 a7g* a8g² 8m a7g⁴ a8.5g a11g Jul 22] 4,400Y: tall, lengthy colt: not a good walker: second foal: half-brother to 1994 Middle Park winner Fard (by Reprimand): dam, 6f winner, half-sister to Gallic League: won maiden at Lingfield in January: easily best effort when beaten a neck in minor event there in February: off course over 3 months and poor efforts on return: sold 1,100 gns (August) and 1,000 gns (October) at Doncaster Sales: may well stay further than 1m. *M. Johnston*   83 d

DOUBLE PARK (FR) 2 b.f. (May 15) Lycius (USA) 124 – Just Pretty (USA) (Danzig (USA)) [1996 5g² 5m² 5g² 6g* 7m* 7g 8g³ Sep 13] IR 4,000F: leggy filly: first foal: dam unraced daughter of high-class middle-distance filly Fitnah: useful form: made all in nurseries at Ayr and Goodwood in summer: contested pattern/listed races after, 4 lengths third of 5 to Falkenham in Stardom Stakes at Goodwood on final outing: stays 1m: raced only on a sound surface: game: sent to USA. *M. Johnston*   93

DOUBLE QUICK (IRE) 4 b.f. Superpower 113 – Haraabah (USA) 99 (Topsider (USA)) [1995 107: 5g² 5s 5m* 5m* 5f* 5f² 5m⁵ 5m⁴ 5m² 5d⁶ 5g² 1996 5m 5g 5m² 5m⁵ 5f* 5f 6m 5m 5m⁵ 5m 5.6m 5g 5g 6s Nov 9] strong, good-quartered filly: useful sprinter: won minor event at Sandown in June: well below form last 5 starts: best at 5f: has won on heavy going, best form on a sound surface: visored (out of form) final 4-y-o start: early to post: effective from front or held up. *M. Johnston*   100 d

DOUBLE RUSH (IRE) 4 b.g. Doulab (USA) 115 – Stanza Dancer (Stanford 121§) [1995 53, a61: 6.9d* 8.2g 7m 6.9f⁶ 7m³ 8m 8.5s² a10g* a10g 1996 11.9f 10m 9.7m 9f⁶ a10g 12g 10f* 10f* 10g⁴ a10g* a10s* a10g Dec 31] rangy gelding: fair handicapper: successful twice at Brighton in August, tending to hang on first occasion, and twice at Lingfield (minor event first time) in November: stays 1¼m: acts on firm and soft ground and particularly well on equitrack: blinkered (out of form) fourth 3-y-o start. *T. G. Mills*   56 a70

DOUBLE SPLENDOUR (IRE) 6 b.g. Double Schwartz 128 – Princess Pamela 70 (Dragonara Palace (USA) 115) [1995 74p: 6.1g* 5m³ 6m 6g* 6.1d⁴ 6d* 6m* 6.1g* 6g⁴ 6m⁵ 6d² 6m² 6m* 6m* 6g³ 6m⁴ 6g² Oct 12] leggy, good-topped gelding: impresses in appearance: progressed well into a useful handicapper: won at Nottingham in April and at York in July: good efforts in frame afterwards, at Ayr (Gold Cup, fourth of 28 to Coastal Bluff) and York (raced away from main body of field, did particularly well, 2 lengths second of 23 to Bollin Joanne in £17,600 contest) on last 2 starts: stays 6f: acts on good to firm and soft ground and on equitrack: held up, and has good turn of foot: genuine and consistent. *P. S. Felgate*   101

DOUBLE TRIGGER (IRE) 5 ch.h. Ela-Mana-Mou 132 – Solac (FR) (Gay Lussac (ITY) 116) [1995 122: 16.2m* 13.9g⁴ 16.4m* 20m* 16f* 18g* 20s⁴ 16s 1996 16.2m* 16.4d² 20m² 18m* 20d⁵ Oct 5]   123

The Gold Cup promised a classic confrontation: the bludgeon against the rapier, the relentless stayer against the horse with the middle-distance speed. Double Trigger, one of Britain's most popular racehorses, started at 2/1 on to come out on top against the previous year's St Leger winner Classic Cliche in Royal Ascot's most prestigious race. However, Double Trigger's attempt to land the stayers' triple crown for the second year running ended at the first hurdle as Classic Cliche, patently the faster horse, outpaced him in the closing stages of a race that wasn't run at an end-to-end gallop. The Press and the racing public at large focussed on the performance of Double Trigger's jockey Jason Weaver, renowned as one of the best front-running jockeys in the business. Weaver set out to repeat the previous year's pillar-to-post tactics but Double Trigger wasn't really asked to stretch out fully until in line for home. Corroborating evidence that the race didn't provide the thorough test it is designed for came in the form of the proximity of the fourth and fifth horses, Always Aloof and the prominently-ridden Latahaab, particularly the latter who finished under seven lengths behind the winner, a margin that flattered him a good deal. Did Weaver fail to play to Double Trigger's strength? Double Trigger's trainer didn't blame his jockey, saying 'It's a thankless job making the pace.' Interestingly, Classic Cliche's rider reported afterwards that 'Double Trigger had his ears pricked and was idling in front . . . clearly not going as fast as Jason wanted in Swinley Bottom.' The fact that Double Trigger lost his off-fore shoe, causing damage to his foot that kept him off the course until the Doncaster Cup in September, also may well have contributed to his downfall. He tended to hang away from the rail throughout and his trainer was at pains to point out that 'Double Trigger has very tender feet and would certainly not take kindly to running without any protection to one of them.'

There were no complaints about Weaver's riding of Double Trigger on his first two starts of the season as the combination repeated their victories of the previous year in the Insulpak Sagaro Stakes at Ascot and the Bonusprint Henry II Stakes at Sandown, conceding weight all round on each occasion. Grey Shot set a strong pace in the Sagaro and Double Trigger, typically soon off the bit and hard ridden on the home turn, was made to pull out all the stops to head him well inside the final furlong. Double Trigger made all in the Henry II Stakes, dictating only a fair pace in the early stages and galloping powerfully clear once fully opened out to win in tremendous style by seven lengths from Assessor. Double Trigger looked the one to beat in the top staying races after these two performances, but when Gold Cup defeat ended the possibility of a second triple crown Double Trigger looked destined to continue his racing career in the Middle East. His owners accepted an offer, reportedly from Saudi Arabian Prince Mitaab Abdullah, the owner of Polaris Flight, but with Double Trigger lame after Royal Ascot—'he has half a foot missing, so we cannot put a shoe back on yet,' reported his trainer—the deal fell through when the horse failed a veterinary examination. By the time he returned to action, in the Doncaster Cup, his regular rider was on the side-lines. Weaver previously had a very good disciplinary record but fell victim in the latest season to the Jockey Club's penal new 'totting up' system under which any jockey who passed a

Insulpak Sagaro Stakes, Ascot—two game stayers, Double Trigger and Grey Shot (rails)

East Coast Doncaster Cup—Double Trigger bounces back; he is too strong for Celeric and the rest

total of twelve days' suspensions in the year received a further minimum fourteen-day ban; he received twenty-one days (five of which were suspended to the end of the year) after being reported by the Pontefract stewards for irresponsible riding in August, his second such offence of the year and his fifth in all up to that time, following two others for careless riding and one for improper whip use. It was hard not to feel sympathy for Weaver who hadn't appeared at Portman Square since his apprentice days. Dettori took over on Double Trigger in the East Coast Doncaster Cup and the combination made all to beat Celeric by two lengths, galloping home in typically enthusiastic style and smashing Further Flight's course record time in the process. Weaver was back on Double Trigger in the Prix du Cadran at Longchamp in October when, starting favourite, he finished a below-form fifth to Nononito, never getting to the front after being niggled along a good way out. Trainer and owner were apparently unhappy with Weaver for not making enough use of Double Trigger and his troubles were compounded the next day when he fell foul of the Pontefract stewards again, once more for irresponsible riding, receiving a ban which, under the 'totting up' procedure, triggered the five-day suspended sentence from his previous visit to Portman Square and took his total suspensions for the year to forty-two days.

			Pitcairn	Petingo
		Ela-Mana-Mou	(b 1971)	Border Bounty
		(b 1976)	Rose Bertin	High Hat
Double Trigger (IRE)			(ch 1970)	Wide Awake
(ch.h. 1991)			Gay Lussac	Faberge II
		Solac (FR)	(ch 1969)	Green As Grass
		(ch 1977)	Soragna	Orvieto II
			(b 1965)	Savigny

The tall Double Trigger is by King George VI and Queen Elizabeth Stakes winner Ela-Mana-Mou who reached his peak as a four-year-old and was notably tough and game. He has been an influence for stamina at stud, with St Leger winner Snurge and Irish St Leger winner Eurobird among his other high-class winners. Double Trigger's dam Solac ran four times without success in Italy but has done well at stud, Double Trigger's full brother Double Eclipse, with whom he fought out a memorable finish to the 1995 Goodwood Cup, being another of her numerous winners. Provided they keep clear of illness and injury, the brothers should again prove worthy contenders for the top staying prizes in the next season. Let's hope they both get to post fit and well for the

288

Gold Cup which, especially if Classic Cliche is there to defend his crown, should produce another long-distance championship to savour. Double Trigger, who stays two and a half miles well, probably acts on any going. *M. Johnston*

DOUBLE UP 3 ch.f. Weldnaas (USA) 112 – Bel Esprit (Sagaro 133) [1995 50: 8d 72 8f 1996 10.2g⁶ 10g* 10m 10.2f⁵ 10f² 10g⁶ 10m² 10.4g 10m⁴ Sep 19] neat filly: fair handicapper: won at Lingfield in May: sold 8,800 gns Newmarket Autumn Sales: will be suited by further than 1¼m: acts on firm ground: races prominently: sent to Saudi Arabia. *Lady Herries*

DOUBLY·H (IRE) 2 b.g. (Apr 24) Be My Guest (USA) 126 – Pursue 78 (Auction 51 Ring (USA) 123) [1996 8m 6m 6g 7m⁵ Aug 9] 21,000Y: leggy gelding: sixth foal: half-brother to middle-distance winner Bold Pursuit (by Thatching), useful 1m winner at 2 yrs, and 2 winners in Italy: dam 2-y-o 5f winner, is half-sister to smart miler Alert: visored, only form when fifth in seller at Newmarket (carried head high) on final start: stays 7f: blinkered third outing: has been bandaged behind: sent to Sweden. *M. Bell*

DOUCE MAISON (IRE) 5 b.m. Fools Holme (USA) – Cardomine (Dom – Racine (FR) 121) [1995 60, a66: 10m⁶ a8g² 8m 9m 10f² 9f a8.5g² a9.4g³ 10m² 12m³ 12m⁶ 1996 a16g⁶ Feb 16] modest handicapper: stays 1½m, not 2m: acts on good to firm and dead ground and goes well on fibresand: rather headstrong, and wears crossed noseband. *A. P. Jarvis*

DOUG'S FOLLY 3 ch.f. Handsome Sailor 125 – Stern Lass 79 (Bold Lad (IRE) 47 133) [1995 64?: 5m³ 5g² 5m* 6m 7m 5m⁴ 6.1d 5m 7m 1996 5g 6d⁶ 6d⁴ 8.1d 5.9f³ 7g 5.9f⁶ 6s³ 6m 7m 6m Oct 23] sparely-made filly: just a poor handicapper in 1996: sold 1,600 gns Doncaster October Sales: stays 6f: acts on firm and soft ground: often blinkered: none too consistent: sent to South Korea. *M. W. Easterby*

DOVALY 3 b.g. Lycius (USA) 124 – Sedova (USA) (Nijinsky (CAN) 138) [1995 99 NR 1996 10m* 11.5f⁴ 11.8m⁶ Oct 28] big, strong, lengthy gelding: showed a quick, fluent action on debut: third foal: half-brother to useful 1¼m winner Segovia (by Groom Dancer) and fairly useful 1¼m winner Sue's Artiste (by Damister): dam French middle-distance winner: won maiden at Newmarket and 3 lengths fourth of 6 to Mystic Knight in steadily-run Derby Trial (hanging left) at Lingfield in the spring: off course 5½ months and burly, showed little in minor event at Leicester in October: sold 38,000 gns Newmarket Autumn Sales and gelded. *H. R. A. Cecil*

DOVEBRACE 3 b.g. Dowsing (USA) 124 – Naufrage (Main Reef 126) [1995 96: – 5m* 6g* 6m⁵ 7g³ 6.1m* 6m⁵ 5g⁵ 1996 5g⁵ 7.1d 7m 6g 7g 6d Sep 30] leggy gelding: unimpressive mover: useful performer as a juvenile: faced stiff tasks in 1996, and well beaten last 5 starts: will stay beyond 7f: acts on good to firm ground: blinkered/visored last 2 starts. *A. Bailey*

DOWDENCY 4 b.f. Dowsing (USA) 124 – Tendency 77 (Ballad Rock 122) [1995 – 54, a48: a8g⁵ a6g a6g² a7g* a8.5g⁴ 6s² 7d⁶ a8.5g 6.1g⁵ a7g⁶ 7m² 7g 8f a8g⁵ a9.4g⁴ a9.4g 1996 a8g Dec 5] modest performer: out of depth for new stable on belated reappearance: stays 9.4f: acts on fibresand and soft going: none too consistent. *R. J. Weaver*

DOWN THE YARD 3 b.f. Batshoof 122 – Sequin Lady (Star Appeal 133) [1995 34 48: 5m a5g a6g⁶ 6g³ 6m 5.2f⁴ 6m 6m* 7.5m 7.9g 7g 10d 8f 1996 a6g⁶ a7g³ a7g⁶ a11g a42 a8g a8g³ a7g² 7.5g 13.9m⁵ a8g³ 7g a7g⁵ 8m a6g⁵ a8g Dec 27] workmanlike filly: poor performer: stays 1m: acts on good to firm ground and fibresand: inconsistent. *M. C. Chapman*

DOWRY 2 b.f. (Apr 14) Rudimentary (USA) 118 – Priceless Bond (USA) 75 69 (Blushing Groom (FR) 131) [1996 5g⁴ 5m⁴ 6.1f² 7m⁴ 7f² 7m 6d* 6m⁵ 6m⁵ 6m³ 6m² 6.1s Oct 22] small, unfurnished filly: has a round action: third foal: dam, 9f winner at 2 yrs, stayed 1¼m, half-sister to high-class middle-distance colt Majesty's Prince: fair form: won claimer at Lingfield in August: best form at 7f/stiff 6f: acts on firm ground and dead (soundly beaten on soft): sold 6,500 gns Newmarket Autumn Sales: sent to Saudi Arabia. *R. Hannon*

DOYELLA (IRE) 2 b.f. (Jan 25) Doyoun 124 – Santella Bell (Ballad Rock 122) 71 p [1996 7g Nov 2] IR 38,000Y: second foal: dam Irish 1¼m winner, half-sister to smart 7f to 2m winner Santella Man: 20/1, 7 lengths ninth of 23 to Palisade in maiden at Newmarket: bred to stay 1m: should improve. *D. R. Loder*

DOZEN ROSES 2 b.f. (Apr 19) Rambo Dancer (CAN) 107 – Andbracket (Import 47
127) [1996 5s 5.1g a6g⁵ 5f⁴ 5.3f⁴ 5f³ 6f⁴ 5d² 7f⁵ 6.1m 5.3g a7g Dec 13] 1,400Y:
second foal: dam unraced: modest plater: should stay beyond 5f: acts on firm and
dead ground: blinkered since fifth start: inconsistent. *T. M. Jones*

DRAGONADA (USA) 2 b.f. (May 25) Nureyev (USA) 131 – Don't Sulk (USA) 96 +
115 (Graustark) [1996 6.1m² 7f* 7.3s⁴ Oct 26] angular, quite attractive filly: eighth
foal: sister to 3 winners, including Galtres Stakes winner Professional Girl and US
Grade 2 9f winner Caesour, closely related to a winner in France by Nijinsky and
half-sister to a winner in France by Irish River: dam, winner of 1½m Prix de
Royallieu, is sister to Kentucky Derby and Belmont Stakes second Jim French: made
all in maiden at Warwick in October: ran better than fourth-of-9 suggests in listed
race won by Boojum at Newbury, chasing leader almost to line in very strongly-run
race: will stay 1m: acts on firm and soft ground. *H. R. A. Cecil*

DRAGON GREEN 5 gr.g. Green Desert (USA) 127 – Dunoof 92 (Shirley –
Heights 130) [1995 61: 11.6g a7g⁵ 1996 a7g⁵ a7g a6g a10g⁴ a10g Dec 30] modest
performer: below form in 1996 (left J. White after second start): stays at least 9.5f.
J. Cullinan

DRAGONJOY 3 b.g. Warrshan (USA) 117 – Nazakat 68 (Known Fact (USA) –
135) [1995 –, a58+: 5g 6g 6m 6m 6m 7g 8m a7g* a8g² a8g⁶ 1996 a7g³ a7g* a7g* a67
a8g² 8.3d⁵ a8.5g* a9.4g a8.5g* a8.5g⁵ a7g⁵ a8g a9.4g a7g⁵ a8.5g⁶ a7g 8f a7g³ a6g³
a7g³ a8g a9.4g² a9.4g⁵ a8.5s Dec 19] good-topped gelding: fair performer on the
all-weather: won sellers at Southwell in January and February and claimers at
Wolverhampton in May and (final start for J. Payne, for whom often a front runner)
June: would also have won claimer at Wolverhampton in November but for being
eased: stays 8.5f: acts on fibresand, poor on turf: usually blinkered/visored nowadays: inconsistent for new stable. *N. P. Littmoden*

DRAGON ROSE 4 gr.g. Grey Desire 115 – The Shrew 92 (Relko 136) [1995 –: –
7.1m 7.1g 1996 8.2m a12g Jul 6] no worthwhile form: sold 1,000 gns Doncaster
August Sales. *T. P. Tate*

DRAGON'S BACK (IRE) 3 ch.c. Digamist (USA) 110 – Classic Choice (Patch 71
129) [1995 63p: 6m³ 6m³ 6m 1996 10g³ 10m⁴ 10m 8.1d Sep 27] strong, workmanlike
colt: fair maiden: below form last 2 starts, 3 months apart: stays 1¼m: acts on good
to firm ground: sold 2,800 gns Newmarket Autumn Sales. *Mrs J. Cecil*

DRAMA KING 4 b.g. Tragic Role (USA) – Consistent Queen 55 (Queen's Hus- –
sar 124) [1995 –: a11g 10g 1996 a14g⁴ 12.3m a12g* a14.8g² a14g⁶ a12g a14g a46
a14.8g⁵ Nov 30] sturdy gelding: poor handicapper: won at Wolverhampton (maiden)
in August: disappointing after good effort (tended to hang) next start: stays 14.8f:
acts on fibresand (yet to race on equitrack) but no form on turf: blinkered (except
once) since 2 yrs. *S. R. Bowring*

DRAMATIC ACT 3 gr.f. Tragic Role (USA) – Curious Feeling (Nishapour (FR) 48
125) [1995 72: 8d² 1996 8m 8g⁶ 10m 8m⁴ 12.1s Oct 22] sparely-made, leggy filly:
only poor form at best in 1996: disappointing. *C. R. Barwell*

DRAMATIC MOMENT 3 b.f. Belmez (USA) 131 – Drama School 72 (Young 71
Generation 129) [1995 55p: 7f 8.1m⁶ 1996 9s³ 9.7m² 10m* 10f⁵ 12g Aug 14] leggy,
rather unfurnished filly: has a quick action: fair performer: won maiden handicap at
Salisbury in June: worth another try at further than 1¼m: acts on firm ground.
I. A. Balding

DR CALIGARI (IRE) 4 b.g. My Generation 111 – Mallabee 92 (Pall Mall 132) –
[1995 68d: 7g² 7m⁵ 7g² 7m³ 8g⁵ 8m³ 6.9f³ 8.3f² 8g 8.3g⁴ 8f² 7m⁵ a7g⁴ a8g² a8.5g⁴
1996 a7g a7g Jan 29] modest maiden: no form in 1996: stays 8.3f: acts on firm
ground and fibresand, yet to race on a soft surface: visored/blinkered since thirteenth
3-y-o start. *S. Gollings*

DREAM CARRIER (IRE) 8 b.g. Doulab (USA) 115 – Dream Trader (Auction –
Ring (USA) 123) [1995 –, a73d: a7g² a7g* a7g³ a8g⁴ a7g⁵ a7g⁴ a8.5g⁶ a7g⁶ a52
a7g⁶ a7g⁵ 7d a7g⁵ a7g a7g a7g⁴ 1996 a8.5g a8g³ a8g⁴ a7g⁵ a8g³ 10.3d a8g 8g
May 25] strong, close-coupled gelding: carries condition: has a round action: only
modest at best in 1996: stays 1m: acts on firm ground and the all-weather: tried
blinkered/visored: sometimes starts slowly, and usually held up: none too consistent.
R. E. Peacock

DREAM OF MY LIFE (USA)   3 gr.g. Danzatore (CAN) 120 – Sureya (Shar-   –
pen Up 127) [1995 –: a8.5g 1996 a8.5g 11.8s⁵ 12.5g⁵ Apr 8] leggy gelding: of no
account. *P. G. Murphy*

DREAM OF NURMI   2 ch.g. (Apr 11) Pursuit of Love 124 – Finlandaise (FR)   78 +
(Arctic Tern (USA) 126) [1996 7f⁴ 7.5m² a7g² Aug 17] 38,000Y: rather unfurnished
gelding: ninth foal: half-brother to several winners here and abroad, including smart
German performer at up to 2m Flying Dream (by Most Welcome) and 1991 2-y-o 6f
winner Aedean (by Risk Me): dam French 1m and 9f winner: runner-up in maidens:
may well stay beyond 7.5f: visored final outing. *D. R. Loder*

DREAMS AND SCHEMES (IRE)   3 ch.f. Mujtahid (USA) 118 – Continuite   73
(FR) (Pharly (FR) 130) [1995 5g⁴ 6m³ 7m⁴ 8g³ 8g⁶ 9d 1996 7d⁶ 5s 7m 6g 6f² 6.9f
Aug 5] IR 3,500Y: ex-Irish filly: second foal: half-sister to French 7.5f winner
Cricket Player (by Cricket Ball): dam French 10f winner: fair maiden at best: left G.
Hourigan after fourth 3-y-o start: stayed 1m: acted on good to firm and dead ground:
blinkered (well beaten) once in Ireland: broke leg final start: dead. *R. A. Fahey*

DREAMS END   8 ch.h. Rainbow Quest (USA) 134 – Be Easy 110 (Be Friendly   83
130) [1995 87: 12g⁴ 14m 10.5g 11.9s 12.1d 10m² 12m 1996 11.9m⁴ 10f 10.4m 13.9m
13.9g 11.9g² 8.9g* 12g⁴ 8g⁴ Nov 2] sparely-made, quite attractive horse: fairly useful
handicapper: tried tubed as 7-y-o, but not on flat as 8-y-o: second run in 3 days when
winning 27-runner £10,800 event at York in October: won Grade 2 hurdle in
November: still effective at 1m to 1½m (won over 1¾m in 1993): acts on any going:
sometimes bandaged: sometimes sweats: usually held up: none too consistent over
the years, but did nothing wrong last 4 starts. *P. Bowen*

DR EDGAR   4 b.g. Most Welcome 131 – African Dancer 116 (Nijinsky (CAN)   64
138) [1995 72: 10.3g 10g 12.3m 11.8g⁵ 10m* 10m 10m² 9.7g* 1996 10s 11.8g⁶ 9.9g
9g 8f³ 10m³ 10m⁴ 8.1g⁵ 10.3m 12g³ 11.1m⁵ 12g Aug 16] strong, good-bodied gelding: only a modest handicapper in 1996: seems to stay 1½m: has raced predominantly
on a sound surface: takes a good hold: has wandered under pressure: inconsistent.
M. Dods

DRIFT   2 b.g. (May 6) Slip Anchor 136 – Norgabie 94 (Northfields (USA)) [1996   59 p
6.1m 7f 7g Jul 24] 11,000Y: good-topped gelding: second foal: half-brother to 3-y-o
Nostoi (by Rock City), 6f winner at 2 yrs: dam sprinter: signs of ability in maiden
auctions and a minor event: will be suited by 1m+: almost certainly capable of better.
Sir Mark Prescott

DRIFTHOLME   3 b.f. Safawan 118 – Avahra 108 (Sahib 114) [1995 –: 7g 7.1s   27
8m 1996 a12g³ a12g 11.9g 11.9f Sep 3] compact filly: bad maiden plater: sold 2,400
gns Doncaster September Sales: tried visored. *G. L. Moore*

DRIMARD (IRE)   5 ch.g. Ela-Mana-Mou 132 – Babilla (USA) (Raja Baba   –
(USA)) [1995 25, a41: 11.9m⁵ a16g* 18m 16m a16.2g⁶ a14g a14g* 1996 a14g Dec
3] poor performer: well beaten on belated return: stays 2m: acts on fibresand: tried
visored/blinkered: inconsistent. *K. McAuliffe*

DRIVE ASSURED   2 gr.c. (Mar 2) Mystiko (USA) 124 – Black Ivor (USA) (Sir   77
Ivor 135) [1996 6m⁶ 7m 7.1m⁶ 10.2d³ 8g⁵ Oct 25] 15,000Y, IR 26,000Y: smallish,
strong colt: fifth foal: half-brother to 2 winners in Scandinavia: dam unraced: fair
maiden: had stiff task when well beaten at 10.2f on dead ground (raced only at up to
1m on sound surface otherwise). *C. E. Brittain*

DR MASSINI (IRE)   3 b.c. Sadler's Wells (USA) 132 – Argon Laser 107   115
(Kris 135) [1995 NR 1996 8m* 10.4f* 12m Jun 30]
          The Glasgow Stakes at York's May meeting has emerged as an in-
fluential Derby pointer in recent years, with Commander In Chief capturing it
en route to victory at Epsom in 1993 and Tamure narrowly failing to repeat
the double in 1995. Following a series of inconclusive results in the more
traditional Derby trials, the latest renewal of this conditions event (for three-
year-olds without a pattern race win who have run fewer than four times) worth
£8,390 to the winner once again had an impact on the Derby picture. Its winner
Dr Massini shot to the head of the ante-post betting and more or less remained
there until injury forced him out three days before the big race, when he was as
short as 4/1. As that suggests, he won in good style at York, quickening smartly

Michael Seely Memorial Glasgow Conditions Stakes, York—
Dr Massini wins this Derby trial in good style from King Alex

to beat the highly-regarded King Alex by three and a half lengths and seeing out the extended mile and a quarter well in a truly-run race. This performance came just ten days after Dr Massini's promising debut win over one mile in a maiden at Kempton where he beat fellow newcomer Wall Street by one and a quarter lengths.

Connections sought to make amends for their disappointment at missing Epsom by running Dr Massini in the Irish Derby three weeks later. He started 9/4 second favourite but finished a never-dangerous seventh, running some way below the form he had shown at York. Michael Kinane had been due to ride Dr Massini at Epsom and got off Zagreb to do so at the Curragh. Dr Massini could give him no cause for further soul-searching, however, because he did not run again. He had been lame on his off-fore on the week after York, and on the near-fore in the week before Epsom. It is reported that Dr Massini is to stay in training as a four-year-old, a decision which his stable no doubt hopes will be rewarded in much the same way as it was with Rock Hopper—Michael Stoute's injured ante-post favourite for the 1990 Derby who returned to win six pattern races in the following two seasons.

While Dr Massini will almost certainly prove well suited by a mile and a half, it is worth noting that his dam Argon Laser showed her best form at around a mile. A seven-furlong winner, Argon Laser was a useful performer who finished third to Sonic Lady in the 1986 Child Stakes at Newmarket. Both her runners in Britain prior to Dr Massini have also been successful, the fair seven-furlong winner Ower (by Lomond) and the ill-fated Weigh Anchor (by Slip Anchor) who was second in the 1994 Dante Stakes before finishing in mid-division when fourth favourite for the Derby. Argon Laser is also responsible for two other runners, both winners in Japan by Caerleon, and she is well on the way to matching the number of winners of her dam Lighted Lamp, who ended her stud career with a string of disappointing, temperamental animals but before that had produced several smart performers, including the Irish St Leger runner-up Torus, in a total of ten winners. Argon Laser's next two representatives were foaled in America, a colt by Caerleon and a filly by Deputy Minister.

	Sadler's Wells (USA) (b 1981)	Northern Dancer (b 1961)	Nearctic
			Natalma
Dr Massini (IRE)		Fairy Bridge (b 1975)	Bold Reason
(b.c. 1993)			Special
	Argon Laser (b 1983)	Kris (ch 1976)	Sharpen Up
			Doubly Sure
		Lighted Lamp (b 1967)	Sir Gaylord
			Chandelier

A quite attractive colt who fetched 205,000 Irish guineas as a yearling, Michael Tabor's Dr Massini is an athletic sort with a quick action who has only raced on top-of-the-ground so far. He has been held up in all his races so far. Dr Massini clearly has potential to do better but, by his owner's own admission, is 'injury prone', somewhat ironic perhaps for a horse named after the Nice surgeon who operated on Mrs Tabor's back. *M. R. Stoute*

DRUM BATTLE   4 ch.g. Bold Arrangement 127 – Cannon Boy (USA) (Canon-   –
ero II (USA)) [1995 67: 8f⁴ 10d⁵ 10.5g 1996 a12g Jan 31] fair maiden: tailed off only start for new stable. *W. G. M. Turner*

DRUMGOR PRINCE   2 b.c. (Mar 2) Robellino (USA) 127 – Victoria Mill 59   69
(Free State 125) [1996 7.1v⁵ 8.1s⁶ Oct 22] 7,600F: fourth foal: half-brother to French 3-y-o 1¼m and 12.5f winner Victory Mill (by Ron's Victory): dam suited by 1¼m: never-nearer sixth in late-season maiden at Chestow, better effort: will stay 1¼m. *A. P. Jarvis*

DRUMMER HICKS   7 b. or br.h. Seymour Hicks (FR) 125 – Musical Princess   54
66 (Cavo Doro 124) [1995 54d: 10m 10.9m² 9g 11.1m⁵ 10.1m⁶ a11g⁶ 1996 a11g 10.1s³ 12.1g⁵ 10m⁶ 10.9d³ 10d³ 10.5d* 10.5m⁴ 10.4g 10.1m Oct 23] workmanlike horse: impresses in appearance: has a round action: modest handicapper at best nowadays: won at Haydock (amateurs) in June by 5 lengths: only poor form otherwise in 1996: effective at 1¼m to 1½m: probably acts on any going: usually races prominently. *E. Weymes*

DR WOODSTOCK   2 br.c. (Mar 18) Rock City 120 – Go Tally-Ho 66 (Gorytus   –
(USA) 132) [1996 5.2d Apr 19] 3,200Y: tall, leggy colt: first foal: dam 2-y-o 5f winner, also successful over hurdles: backward, well beaten in maiden at Newbury in April. *Martyn Meade*

DRY POINT   10 ch.g. Sharpo 132 – X-Data 93 (On Your Mark 125) [1995 74: 5.7f   –
6g 6m² 6m 6f* 6g⁵ 6f⁴ 5.7h⁶ 1996 6f 7f 6g 6m Jun 26] strong, workmanlike gelding: has a round action: sprinter, but went with little zest in 1996. *J. A. R. Toller*

DRY SEA   5 b.g. Green Desert (USA) 127 – Prickle 114 (Sharpen Up 127) [1995   –
NR 1996 10.2g May 20] leggy, attractive gelding: modest maiden: well beaten only start for new stable. *R. G. Frost*

DTOTO   4 b.g. Mtoto 134 – Deposit 73 (Thatch (USA) 136) [1995 72: 10m 10m²   –
13.4d⁵ 11.8g 1996 17.2m⁶ 10.2m 12.1m 13.1m Sep 9] good-topped gelding: one-time fair maiden: no form in 1996 for new stable. *R. J. Baker*

DUBAI COLLEGE (IRE)   3 b.c. Old Vic 136 – Murooj (USA) (Diesis 133)   69
[1995 –: 6g 6m⁶ 1996 6.9m⁴ 10.3m⁴ 8g⁴ 7f² 7.1m 6m⁵ a8g 7m Aug 22] small colt: good mover: fair maiden handicapper: below form last 4 starts: sold 3,600 gns Newmarket September Sales: should prove effective beyond 7f: has raced only on a sound surface on turf: showed little on fibresand: sent to Germany. *C. E. Brittain*

DUBLIN INDEMNITY (USA)   7 b.g. Alphabatim (USA) 126 – Sailongal   –
(USA) (Sail On-Sail On) [1995 –: a11g 1996 a8g Jan 5] probably no longer of account on flat. *M. P. Bielby*

DUBLIN RIVER (USA)   3 b.c. Irish River (FR) 131 – Vivre Libre (USA)   –
(Honest Pleasure (USA)) [1995 94: 6m* 7m* 8.1d⁵ 8g² 1996 7.1g⁵ 8f Sep 13]
compact colt: good mover: fairly useful as a juvenile: not seen in 1996 until August,
and well beaten: sold 7,200 gns Newmarket Autumn Sales: should stay 1m: acts on
good to firm ground, possibly not on dead. *H. Thomson Jones*

DUCHESSE DE BERRI (USA)   3 ch.f. Diesis 133 – Berry Berry Good (USA)   71
(Shadeed (USA) 135) [1995 NR 1996 8g³ Jun 11] $97,000F: second foal: dam
(unraced) close relative of Leap Lively, the dam of Forest Flower: third of 12 in
maiden at Salisbury, slowly away, green when pushed along over 2f out, then keeping
on: retired. *J. H. M. Gosden*

DUEL AT DAWN   3 ch.c. Nashwan (USA) 135 – Gayane 125 (Nureyev (USA)   90
131) [1995 NR 1996 7g³ 6m² 6f* 6g⁴ 6m 5m 5g⁴ Sep 29] strong, lengthy, good sort:
fourth foal: dam, 6f and 7f winner, half-sister to Sun Chariot winner Ristna out of
Roussalka, a half-sister to Oh So Sharp: fairly useful performer: won maiden at
Lingfield in June: marginally best effort in rated stakes at Ascot last time, making
most: seems suited by sprint distances: has raced only on a sound surface: bandaged
all round: consistent: sent to UAE. *J. H. M. Gosden*

DUELLO   5 b.g. Sure Blade (USA) 130 – Royal Loft 105 (Homing 130) [1995 64,   79
a67: 8d² a8.5g³ a8g⁵ 8.3m² 8m⁶ 8.3m 10m 7m⁵ 7.1m⁴ 8g 7.1d³ 8.5s* 8d² 8s 8.2m
1996 7s² 8g 8s 7.3s* 7m³ 7.1m³ 8m² 8m⁶ 7.9g⁴ 8g⁴ 7.3m* 7m³ 7g 8g² 8g Nov 2]
leggy gelding: has a round action: fair handicapper, better than ever: won at Newbury
in May and September: stays 8.5f, probably not 1¼m: acts on good to firm ground
and fibresand, goes well on an easy surface: blinkered (respectable effort) once as
3-y-o: tough and consistent. *M. Blanshard*

DUET   3 b.f. Loch Pearl 81 – Double Song (Double Form 130) [1995 NR 1996 5.1g   –
7m 5.1g 5.1f 8g⁴ 7g 6.9d Oct 21] workmanlike filly: first reported foal: dam never
ran: no worthwhile form. *J. S. King*

DUFFERTOES   4 ch.g. High Kicker (USA) – Miss Poll Flinders (Swing Easy   –
(USA) 126) [1995 79: 8d 9m 6m 8m 1996 7s 7m 8d⁶ 7g Jun 11] big, rangy gelding:
fair handicapper at best: no form in 1996: stays 9f: acts on heavy ground and good to
firm: blinkered (pulled up) final 4-y-o start: not one to trust implicitly. *M. J. Ryan*

DUGGAN   9 b.g. Dunbeath (USA) 127 – Silka (ITY) (Lypheor 118) [1995 35, a–:   –
11.9m* 12.1m* 12.1m⁶ 15.1f³ 12m⁶ a16g⁵ a12g⁶ 1996 a13g³ a12g⁵ a14.8g⁶ a13g Feb   a25
1] bad handicapper: stays 15f: acts on firm ground: held up: inconsistent. *P. D. Evans*

DUKE OF FLITE (USA)   3 b.c. Alleged (USA) 138 – Stage Flight (USA) (Lord   115
Durham (USA)) [1995 NR 1996 9m² 12d* 12m⁴ 15m* 12s 15d⁵ 14.5g* 14s* Nov
24] $10,000Y: smart Italian colt: seventh foal: half-brother to 5 winners in USA,
notably 9f graded placed Le Merle Blanc (by Mr Leader): dam, ran only at 2 yrs when
listed winner at up to around 1m, half-sister to Bold Buritana (rated 118, best up to
1¼m): won minor event and quite valuable event at Milan, then St Leger Italiano at
Turin and handicap at Rome: beat Lear White on last 2 starts, by a neck on second
occasion: stays 15f: acts on good to firm and soft ground. *R. Rossini, Italy*

DUKE VALENTINO   4 br.c. Machiavellian (USA) 123 – Aldhabyih 86 (General   61
Assembly (USA)) [1995 69, a81: 6d⁵ 7s² 6d 8m⁶ 10m 8.2d⁶ 8m⁴ 8f⁶ a6g* a8g* a7g   a86
a8g² a7g* 1996 a8g a7g a7g² a8g³ a7g² 8s 7.5m 8g a8g² 8.1d 8.1m² 8.1m³ 7m 7.1f
8.1d⁴ a8.5g* a6g³ Nov 26] strong colt: fairly useful handicapper on the all-weather:
won at Wolverhampton in November: modest on turf: effective at 6f to 1m: acts on
good to firm and soft ground, best on all-weather: often sweats: has had tongue tied
down: inconsistent on turf. *R. Hollinshead*

DULAS BAY   2 b.g. (Apr 19) Selkirk (USA) 129 – Ivory Gull (USA) 80 (Storm   –
Bird (CAN) 134) [1996 7.5m 7.5f 6m Oct 23] 11,000Y: tall, leggy, plain gelding:
fifth foal: half-brother to 11f winner Mister Kite (by Damister) and a winner in US by
Local Suitor: dam, sister to Bluebird, won over 6f at 2 yrs then disappointed at 3:
little form, twice slowly away, in seller and maidens. *M. W. Easterby*

DULCINEA   2 ch.f. (Mar 23) Selkirk (USA) 129 – Ahohoney 118 (Ahonoora 122)   – p
[1996 7m Sep 20] rangy, unfurnished filly: has scope: half-sister to 3 winners in
France including smart 4-y-o 1m winner (stays 1¼m) Amato (by Kendor): dam 6f
and 1m winner here at 2 yrs later 10.5f winner in France: backward, very slowly

away and always behind in late-season minor event at Newbury: looks sort to do better. *I. A. Balding*

DUMMER GOLF TIME 3 ch.c. Clantime 101 – Chablisse 69 (Radetzky 123) [1995 NR 1996 a6g² a6g* 6g⁶ 6g⁴ 6m 6g³ 7.1m⁵ 7g² 7m* 7.1f² 8.1m⁵ 7g Oct 12] 22,000Y: lengthy, workmanlike colt: brother to 5.9f (at 2 yrs) to 1m winner Parfait Amour and half-brother to 7f (at 2 yrs) to 1¼m winner Ooh Ah Cantona (by Crofthall): dam, 1¼m to 1½m winner, half-sister to dam of Branston Abby: fair handicapper: won maiden at Lingfield in February and minor event at Leicester in August: stays 1m: acts on the all-weather, has raced only on a sound surface on turf: visored since sixth outing: has been taken early to post: consistent. *Lord Huntingdon* 70

DUNCOMBE HALL 3 b.g. Salse (USA) 128 – Springs Welcome 86 (Blakeney 126) [1995 –: 5m⁵ 1996 9s 11.8m 10f⁴ 12m⁵ a16g¹ 11.9f³ 16m³ 17.9g Oct 9] small, sturdy gelding: poor maiden handicapper: sold 3,000 gns Newmarket Autumn Sales: stays 2m: acts on firm ground. *C. A. Cyzer* 42

DUNDEL (IRE) 2 gr.f. (Apr 29) Machiavellian (USA) 123 – Dunoof 92 (Shirley Heights 130) [1996 6m⁶ 7m⁶ Aug 1] good-topped, attractive filly: has scope: half-sister to several winners here and abroad, including 1¼m winner Mega Tid and fairly useful 3-y-o 1½m winner Old Irish (both by Old Vic): dam, 2-y-o 7f winner, half-sister to high-class middle-distance stayer High Hawk, herself dam of In The Wings: ran significantly better than finishing positions suggest in maidens at Pontefract and Goodwood (had terrible run behind Quintellina) in summer: will stay 1m: slowly away both starts, roused along to go to post second start: tail flasher: capable of better. *B. W. Hills* 82 p

DUNE RIVER 7 b.g. Green Desert (USA) 127 – River Spey 96 (Mill Reef (USA) 141) [1995 79, a99: a8g* 7m 8.5f 1996 7m Jul 13] big, robust, good-topped gelding: good walker: fair handicapper on turf, useful on the all-weather: unable to dominate and well below form only 7-y-o start: stays 1m: acts on firm ground and the all-weather: races up with pace. *D. R. Loder* –

DUNGEON PRINCESS (IRE) 3 b.f. Danehill (USA) 126 – Taplow (Tap On Wood 130) [1995 56: 6g⁵ 6m 1996 8d 6s² 7.1g⁴ 8.3d⁶ 9.7f³ 8.3s⁴ 9.2s² 8m 8f² 8.1f* 8.1m⁴ 8f 8g 7f 7m Oct 4] robust filly: modest performer: won maiden at Musselburgh in June on final start for M. Channon: below form last 4 starts: stays 9.7f: acts on firm and soft going: has hung badly and is a difficult ride: inconsistent. *C. Murray* 62

DUNMEBRAINS (IRE) 3 ch.f. Rich Charlie 117 – Branch Out (Star Appeal 133) [1995 –: 6m⁶ 1996 8g a6s Dec 19] no form. *J. S. Moore* –

DUNROWAN 3 b.f. Dunbeath (USA) 127 – Sun Lamp 76 (Pall Mall 132) [1995 NR 1996 11.1g³ 11f* 12.1s Nov 7] half-sister to winning sprinters by Good Times and Balidar: dam 7f winner: won weak maiden seller at Redcar in September, finishing strongly to lead well inside final 1f: no comparable form: should be suited by further than 11f. *Mrs M. Reveley* 54

DUNSTON GOLD 2 ch.c. (Apr 26) Risk Me (FR) 127 – Maria Whittaker (Cure The Blues (USA)) [1996 7.1v 7f a8g Nov 4] unfurnished colt: third reported live foal: dam ran 3 times: no form in maidens. *P. J. Bevan* –

DUNSTON KNIGHT 3 ch.c. Proud Knight (USA) – Lucy Johnston's (IRE) (Burslem 123) [1995 NR 1996 11.8f Oct 15] 400Y: first foal: dam of no account: tailed off in claimer. *P. J. Bevan* –

DUNSTON QUEEN 3 ch.f. Proud Knight (USA) – Alto Dancer (Noalto 120) [1995 NR 1996 10.5d Sep 27] 400Y: strong filly: first foal: dam lightly-raced maiden: tailed off in maiden. *P. J. Bevan* –

DUNSTON STAR (IRE) 3 b.c. Poet's Dream (IRE) 95 – Cherry Glory 44 (Final Straw 127) [1995 NR 1996 8m a8.5g Nov 11] IR 1,100Y: third reported foal: dam had form only at 1¼m: tailed off in maidens. *P. J. Bevan* –

DUO MASTER 3 b.g. Primo Dominie 121 – Musical Sally (USA) (The Minstrel (CAN) 135) [1995 78p: 6g 5g³ 1996 8g 8.2m 7s⁵ 8d 10g 6m 7m 7f Oct 15] good-bodied gelding: has reportedly had knee operation: disappointing maiden: tried blinkered: one to avoid. *Mrs M. Reveley* – §

DURALOCK FENCER 3 b.g. General Wade 93 – Madame Laffitte 54 (Welsh Pageant 132) [1995 58: 5g² 6.1m 6m 6g 6m⁵ 7.3d 6.9m 1996 a7g³ a8.5g 10.2g 8.1d a7g 8d Sep 30] leggy gelding: has a round action: modest maiden as a juvenile: no worthwhile form in 1996. *P. G. Murphy*

DURHAM   5 ch.g. Caerleon (USA) 132 – Sanctuary (Welsh Pageant 132) [1995 –: 73
a11g^3 1996 a16g a14g^4 a16g^2 16g a16.2g^3 14m^3 17.2f^5 14.1m* a13g^2 13.1f^2 11.7m^3 12m^4 14m* 12f^2 14.4g* 13.1m* 16.2m 13.9g^3 Oct 12] sparely-made gelding: generally progressive handicapper: won at Nottingham (apprentices) and at Lingfield (seller) in the summer: left R. Simpson after next start: successful at Kempton and Ayr, and best form when third at York (kept on well though carried head to one side), all in the autumn: effective at 1½m and stays well: acts on firm and soft ground and on equitrack: blinkered/visored in 1996. *H. S. Howe*

DURSHAN (USA)   7 ch.g. Shahrastani (USA) 135 – Dukayna 103 (Northfields –
(USA)) [1995 54d: a16g 15.4g^5 12g^3 16m^5 14.1g^3 14.4m^4 12f 1996 16.4g 12m 16d^4 16.2d Oct 11] leggy, workmanlike gelding: bad form at best in 1996: stays 2m: acts on good to firm and soft ground: blinkered (below best) once at 3 yrs. *J. R. Jenkins*

DUSHYANTOR (USA)   3 b.c. Sadler's Wells (USA) 132 – Slightly Dang- 123
erous (USA) 122 (Roberto (USA) 131) [1995 92P: 8.2m* 1996 12m* 10.4m^2 12m^2 12m^4 11.9m* 14.6m^2 12g Oct 26]

Rules are rules and must be abided by. But the Jockey Club's whip rules have been a promotional disaster for racing, doing more harm than good by too often attracting adverse publicity for the sport on occasions that should provide its best advertisements. Two of the classics, the Two Thousand Guineas and the St Leger, produced climactic finishes as thrilling as any seen all season, yet most headlines referred to the punishments handed out to the jockeys involved (Dettori, Weaver and Robinson at Newmarket, Dettori and Pat Eddery at Doncaster). To save readers from further punishment, tight editorial guidelines on 'excessive debate of the whip' are now in force in these annuals, which have been strongly critical of the way the Jockey Club has tackled what started as a relatively-insignificant problem. But it seems inevitable that we shall be forced by events to return to this well-worn topic from time to time. The climax to both the Two Thousand Guineas and the St Leger should have been moments to savour but, under the whip rules in force at the time, the stewards had to 'consider holding an inquiry into any case where the rider has used his whip six times or more'. The Newmarket and Doncaster stewards interpreted what they saw either as excessive or improper use, or a combination of both, and stood down the riders involved. There was no question of any of the horses involved suffering abuse—no weal marks, no reports of the horses not eating up afterwards—and the respective trainers involved all went out of their way to emphasise the well-being of their horses in the days that followed. Yet the implementation of the rules, and the headlines afterwards, can only have given the opposite impression to the public at large. Pat Eddery, suspended for two days after riding Dushyantor into a close second in the St Leger had been just as forceful on the same horse in the Derby finish, in which he also came off second best, yet the Epsom stewards decided Eddery had no case to answer for excessive use of the whip on that occasion after holding an inquiry into his riding; they also exonerated Michael Hills on the winner after enquiring into his use of the whip. Eddery gave everything in the Derby and St Leger finishes, riding at the top of his form, and the two-day ban he received at Doncaster, along with the four-day ban imposed on an inspired Dettori on the winner Shantou, was, frankly, ridiculous.

The Jockey Club announced revisions to the whip rules in December for implementation in February 1997, doing away with the 'six-hit' condition and empowering stewards to hold an inquiry if a rider 'has used his whip in such a way as to cause them concern.' For some reason, this seemed to be welcomed on nearly all sides, though only time will tell whether the confidence of jockeys and trainers is well placed. Presumably, stewards can now 'consider' holding an inquiry if a rider uses his whip only once or twice—the RSPCA clearly believes this to be the intention, welcoming the amended instruction with the statement 'some jockeys could seriously injure a horse hitting it only twice'—while announcements from the Jockey Club gave no impression that the new instructions should be taken by jockeys as indicating a general relaxation of the rules. Indeed, the Jockey Club made it clear that it had not ruled out future consideration of disqualifying horses whose riders are guilty of serious whip abuse. In future, all winners and placed horses, plus a sample of the other runners, will be examined by a vet, and injuring a horse through whip misuse will be 'punished severely'. As with the previous instructions, the success or otherwise of the new guidelines will rely greatly—arguably far too much—on individual interpretation and the use of discretion. What causes 'concern' to one set of stewards may well not do so to another.

The wording remains 'woolly' in some critical areas. What, for example, constitutes 'hitting a horse with excessive frequency'? One of the relevant factors, the guidelines say, is 'whether the number of hits was reasonable and necessary over the distance they were given, taking into account the horse's experience', another is 'the degree of force that was used: the more times a horse has been hit, the stricter will be the view taken over the degree of force which is reasonable.' Furthermore, the extensive guidelines (longer than before) contain the catch-all 'It is emphasised that the use of the whip may be judged to be proper or improper in particular circumstances which have not been included above.' Confused? Anyone who believes that the changes guarantee an end to the sport shooting itself in the foot over the whip issue should read them more carefully. There is absolutely nothing in them—the way we see it—to suggest that the jockeys involved in the finishes of the Two Thousand Guineas and St Leger would necessarily have escaped punishment if the new guidelines had been in force.

Eddery was permitted to ride Dushyantor in the St Leger only because of a concession which allows a suspension to be split to enable jockeys to take part in a Group 1 race. He had picked up a two-day suspension for excessive use of the whip after an almost universally-acclaimed ride on the winner of the Galtres Stakes at York, Eva Luna, who fought back to win narrowly after being headed.

The well-backed Dushyantor, favourite to give his trainer a fifth St Leger victory, looked sure to win after cruising into the lead two furlongs out but couldn't quicken again in the closing stages as Shantou nosed ahead under sustained pressure. There was a neck in it at the line. In the Derby, Dushyantor had Shantou a length and a quarter back in third as the pair filled the minor placings behind Shaamit. Dushyantor also started favourite at Epsom after running a promising trial in the circumstances when second in a muddling race for the Dante Stakes at York. A strongly-run mile and a half looked likely to suit Dushyantor much better—he'd already won over the trip at the Newmarket Guineas meeting on his reappearance—and he made a valiant attempt to emulate his half-brother Commander In Chief, encountering plenty of trouble in running, after being scrubbed along to keep up early on, until staying on best of all to take second near the finish, a length and a quarter behind the winner.

Great Voltigeur Stakes, York—
a first pattern-race win for Dushyantor, gained narrowly from Mons with Royal Court third

Dushyantor had a far from smooth race at Epsom and was disappointing when a well-beaten fourth to Zagreb in the Irish Derby on his next outing. He was seen out once more before the St Leger, gaining a deserved pattern-race victory in the Great Voltigeur Stakes at York, finding extra under another strong ride from Eddery to hold off Mons by half a length. Dushyantor's only race after the St Leger was in the Breeders' Cup Turf in which he came a respectable seventh to Pilsudski, two places behind Shantou.

		Northern Dancer	Nearctic
	Sadler's Wells (USA)	(b 1961)	Natalma
	(b 1981)	Fairy Bridge	Bold Reason
Dushyantor (USA)		(b 1975)	Special
(b.c. 1993)		Roberto	Hail To Reason
	Slightly Dangerous (USA)	(b 1969)	Bramalea
	(b 1979)	Where You Lead	Raise A Native
		(ch 1970)	Noblesse

Dushyantor may be on the small side but he really filled the eye with his well-being before most of his races, particularly so before the Derby. Before the St Leger, however, he constantly swished his tail in the preliminaries. None of the latest classic crop had better credentials for the job, judged on pedigree, than Dushyantor. His sire the outstanding Sadler's Wells has yet to have a Derby winner but his dam Slightly Dangerous, second in the Oaks, is the dam of the 1993 winner Commander In Chief (by Dancing Brave). Slightly Dangerous is also the dam of champion miler Warning (by Known Fact), winner of the Queen Elizabeth II Stakes and the Sussex Stakes, and the top-

Mr K. Abdulla's "Dushyantor"

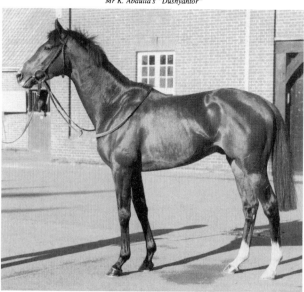

class middle-distance horse Deploy (by Shirley Heights) whose career was ended prematurely by injury after he had finished second in the Irish Derby. Slightly Dangerous has bred eight winners from nine foals to reach the racecourse, the latest of them the Prix Marcel Boussac runner-up Yashmak (by another Northern Dancer stallion, Danzig). Dushyantor's grandam Where You Lead was also second in the Oaks while his great grandam Noblesse was a ten-length winner of the race. Dushyantor may not be the pick of his dam's offspring but he's a very smart performer nonetheless. He is effective at a mile and a half and would probably stay beyond the St Leger trip given the opportunity. He has raced only on a sound surface (being a son of Sadler's Wells, it will be interesting to see him run on a soft surface) and is suited by waiting tactics. *H. R. A. Cecil*

DUSK IN DAYTONA 4 b.f. Beveled (USA) – Mount of Light 61 (Sparkler 130)   51
[1995 64: 7g⁴ 10g a7g² 7f³ a7g⁶ 7f* a7g⁴ a7g a7g³ a7g 1996 a7g a7g⁵ a6g⁶ a6g Feb 15] modest performer: below form in 1996: stays 7.3f: acts on any turf going, and on all-weather surfaces: visored (out of form) final 4-y-o start. *C. James*

DUST DANCER 2 ch.f. (Apr 25) Suave Dancer (USA) 136 – Galaxie Dust   74 p
(USA) 86 (Blushing Groom (FR) 131) [1996 7g⁵ 6m³ Sep 28] close-coupled, unfurnished filly: has a quick action: seventh living foal: half-sister to 3 winners, including useful 7f (including at 2 yrs) and 1¼m winner Bulaxie (by Bustino) and very smart middle-distance performer Zimzalabim (by Damister): dam 2-y-o 6f winner: never-dangerous third of 5 to Lochangel in steadily-run Blue Seal Stakes at Ascot: very slowly away on debut: will stay at least 1m: remains capable of better. *J. L. Dunlop*

DUSTON BOY 2 ch.g. (May 8) Beveled (USA) – Julie's Star (IRE) 45 (Thatching   –
131) [1996 6m 6g a7g Sep 9] workmanlike gelding: second foal: half-brother to 3-y-o 6f (at 2 yrs) and 7f winner King of Peru (by Inca Chief): dam maiden placed at 1m: well beaten in maidens. *J. White*

DUTCH DYANE 3 b.f. Midyan (USA) 124 – Double Dutch 100 (Nicholas Bill   –
125) [1995 NR 1996 a10g a10g Nov 26] 6,400Y: sister to 4-y-o My Dutch Girl: dam stayer: always behind in maiden and seller (never placed to challenge, subject of stewards inquiry) at Lingfield. *G. P. Enright*

DUTOSKY 6 b.m. Doulab (USA) 115 – Butosky 71 (Busted 134) [1995 66, a49:   –
a8g⁴ a10g⁵ 12m 10g² 10m* 9.7g* 10f³ 1996 9.7m 10m 12m Oct 7] strong, compact mare: tends to look well: unimpressive mover: fair handicapper: well beaten in 1996, leaving R. O'Sullivan after reappearance: suited by around 1¼m: acts on any turf ground: blinkered (no improvement) twice at 4 yrs. *John Berry*

DUTY SERGEANT (IRE) 7 b.g. Pennine Walk 120 – Plainsong (FR) (Amen   44
(FR)) [1995 37: 6m a8g⁵ 9.7m 11.9m³ 12m² 1996 12d 11.8d* 12g 12.1m⁵ 10g 13.1g 12d⁵ a14.8g⁴ 14s Oct 5] smallish, sturdy gelding: poor handicapper: game winner at Leicester (apprentices) in May: below form afterwards on turf: stays 1½m: acts on firm ground and dead, probably on fibresand: often used to be blinkered, not since 1994. *P. Mitchell*

DUVEEN (IRE) 6 b.g. Tate Gallery (USA) 117 – Wish You Were Here (USA) 81   61
(Secretariat (USA)) [1995 –: a8g 1996 a12g³ a12g⁵ a11g Feb 2] seems only modest at best nowadays: well beaten last 2 starts: suited by middle distances: used to act on good to firm and dead ground and the all-weather: blinkered (well beaten) final 6-y-o start: used to race up with the pace, held up in 1996. *J. White*

DVORAK (IRE) 5 b.g. Darshaan 133 – Grace Note (FR) 99 (Top Ville 129)   –
[1995 69d: a13g² a12g² 13v³ 12m* 14m⁵ 10f a12g a12g 1996 a16g⁵ a13g a16.2g⁶ a16g 12m 21.6m Apr 29] tall, good-topped gelding: no worthwhile form for present stable: stays 1¾m: acts on good to firm ground and equitrack: blinkered (out of form) final 5-y-o start. *R. Harris*

DWINGELOO (IRE) 3 b.f. Dancing Dissident (USA) 119 – Thank One's Stars   60
(Alzao (USA) 117) [1995 83p: 6d² 5f* 1996 6m 5m⁶ May 29] sturdy, lengthy filly: looked likely to improve from 2 yrs to 3 yrs, but only modest form in handicaps at Kempton (reportedly in season) and Folkestone (weak in market) in the spring: probably a sprinter. *Major D. N. Chappell*

DYANKO   3 b.g. Midyan (USA) 124 – Regain 86 (Relko 136) [1995 49: 6m⁴ 6m   –
1996 7m 8g 11.7m 8.2f 8m 8f a9.4g Dec 28] leggy gelding: poor maiden at best:
should stay middle distances: tried visored, no improvement: has rather unsatisfactory temperament. *M. S. Saunders*

E

EAGER TO PLEASE   2 ch.g. (May 3) Keen 116 – Ackcontent (USA) (Key To   60
Content (USA)) [1996 5.2d 5g⁶ 5.9g a6g* 6f² 6m⁴ a6g³ 6g⁶ a6g* 6m* 7m 6.1s a6g   a67
a5g⁴ a6g³ Dec 31] 10,500Y: unfurnished gelding: fourth known foal: half-brother to
3-y-o 5.3f (at 2 yrs) and 7f winner No Sympathy (by Ron's Victory): dam ran once at
2 yrs in North America: successful in seller at Wolverhampton in June and seller at
Lingfield and claimer at Folkestone in September: stays 6f: acts on all-weather
surfaces (best form) and firm ground (ran poorly on soft): blinkered (poor effort)
eighth outing: tail flasher. *Miss Gay Kelleway*

EAGLE CANYON (IRE)   3 b. or br.g. Persian Bold 123 – Chrism (Baptism   85
119) [1995 72: 7g 7d⁵ 5m⁴ 1996 a10g⁵ 10.3d 9g a8g* 8g² 9g² 10m⁴ 12.3m* 11.4g²
12m⁴ 12m⁴ 11.9g 11.9d 16.2d Oct 11] good-topped gelding: has a round action:
fairly useful handicapper: won at Southwell (claimer) in May and Ripon in June:
well below form last 3 starts: stays 12.3f (quite keen and unlikely to get 2m): acts on
fibresand: yet to race on extremes of going on turf: blinkered (ran poorly) once:
sweating (below form) final 3-y-o start: gelded. *B. Hanbury*

EARLY PEACE (IRE)   4 b.g. Bluebird (USA) 125 – Everything Nice 107   68 d
(Sovereign Path 125) [1995 73: 8g 7g³ 10g⁵ 1996 8.3m 8.1d* 12g 10m 12m 15.4g⁶
17.1m⁶ 13.8g⁵ Oct 19] strong gelding: moved poorly to post but won claimer
(claimed out of R. Hannon's yard £11,000) at Sandown in May, getting up close
home: well below form for new stable: stays 1m: sometimes slowly away: joined
M. Dods: one to treat with caution. *M. J. Polglase*

EARLY WARNING   3 br.f. Warning 136 – Ile de Danse 76 (Ile de Bourbon   –
(USA) 133) [1995 NR 1996 8g 7.1m 7m a10g 10m Sep 7] third reported foal: half-
sister to 5-y-o Sonora (by Blakeney), 10.5f and 11.5f winner in Spain: dam French
10.3f winner at 4 yrs from family of Bonne Ile and Ile de Nisky: no worthwhile form.
C. R. Egerton

EAST BARNS (IRE)   8 gr.g. Godswalk (USA) 130 – Rocket Lass (Touch Paper   37
113) [1995 50, a–: 6g 8.5m 10m* 1996 a8g a11g⁶ a8g a8g⁵ a11g a9.4g 10.3d 7s 8.2d   a–
8g 7m⁵ 8m Oct 23] close-coupled gelding: has a quick action: bad handicapper:
stays 1¼m: acts on firm and soft going and on fibresand: has worn a visor, usually
blinkered: inconsistent. *S. Gollings*

EASTERN EAGLE (IRE)   2 b.c. (Apr 24) Polish Patriot (USA) 128 – Lady's   58 p
Turn (Rymer 121) [1996 6.9d⁵ Oct 21] 3,400F, 11,000Y: seventh foal: half-brother
to a couple of Irish bumper winners by Coquelin: dam ran once: staying-on fifth
in maiden auction at Folkestone late in year: will stay middle distances: should
improve. *J. M. P. Eustace*

EASTERN FIREDRAGON (IRE)   2 b.f. (Apr 23) Shalford (IRE) 124§ –   48
Doobie Do 106 (Derring-Do 131) [1996 5f⁵ 5g⁶ 7g 6s Aug 31] IR 3,800F, 5,400Y:
small filly: half-sister to several winners here and abroad, including 1m winner Do
Run Run (by Commanche Run) and 2m winner Gold Tint (by Glint of Gold): dam
second in Cherry Hinton Stakes: poor form: well beaten last 2 starts: should be suited
by further than 5f: blinkered final outing. *T. D. Easterby*

EASTERN PROPHETS   3 b.g. Emarati (USA) 74 – Four Love (Pas de Seul   93 d
133) [1995 98: 5g⁵ 5m* 5.1f* 6g² 5d* 5m 5.2g 5m² 6g² 5g 5s⁵ 1996 5g⁵ 5.5g³ 5.1g
7m 6m 5f 5m 5g⁵ 5g 5s⁵ Nov 8] good-quartered gelding: only fairly useful form at
best at 3 yrs: creditable third of 6 to Anabaa in listed race at Evry in April: below that
form and inconsistent afterwards: stays 6f: acts on firm and dead ground: sometimes
on toes and sweating. *T. J. Naughton*

EASTLEIGH   7 b.g. Efisio 120 – Blue Jane 81 (Blue Cashmere 129) [1995 –, a58:   –
a8g⁵ a7g⁶ a8g² a8.5g³ a8g⁴ a8g a8g² a8g* a9.4g³ a8.5g³ a8g* a9.4g⁵ a8g⁶ a9.4g a8g⁵   a48
a7g a8g⁴ a8g⁶ 1996 a8g a8.5g⁵ a11g⁵ a8g⁴ a8g⁴ a8g⁴ 7d 8.9g a7g⁴ a10g² a10g⁶ a10g

300

a10g[6] a10g Dec 30] lengthy, workmanlike gelding: poor form on balance in 1996: stays 9.4f: seems best on all-weather surfaces nowadays: tried visored/blinkered, no improvement: inconsistent. *R. Hollinshead*

EAST SHEEN 4 b.f. Salse (USA) 128 – Madam Cody (Hot Spark 126) – [1995 –: 7.6m 7.1m 7f 1996 10m 11.6m 12g Jul 31] close-coupled filly: lightly raced and well beaten since 2-y-o days: sold 800 gns Newmarket September Sales. *C. J. Benstead*

EASYCALL 2 b.c. (Mar 31) Forzando 122 – Up And Going (FR) (Never So 115 Bold 135) [1996 5g* 5m* 6m* 6m⁴ 5m* 6m⁶ 5d* Oct 12]
Easycall capped a fine season by winning the Cornwallis Stakes at Ascot in October; it was his third pattern-race victory of the year and his fifth win all told, one which confirmed him a smart sprinter. Carrying a Group 2 winner's penalty and encountering a soft surface for the first time, Easycall proved easy to back, eventually starting at 11/2 behind joint-favourites Check The Band and the only other pattern winner Deep Finesse. Check The Band was fresh from a couple of wins in Ireland, while Easycall was meeting Deep Finesse for the third time in a month, a length having separated them (in Deep Finesse's favour) in the Middle Park Stakes in their most recent clash. Drawn wide, Easycall led under two furlongs out after a strong pace had been set by Grand Lad, and was driven clear inside the last to beat Check The Band a length and a half which Grand Lad half a length a smart back in third. Deep Finesse ran poorly, beating only one home. The winner's timefigure was a smart 0.72 fast (equivalent to a rating of 118), and 20 lb better than that recorded by Tadeo in winning the handicap over the same course an hour later.
Easycall's first big test had come in the Richmond Stakes at Goodwood in August. He had earned his place in the line-up with convincing wins in a median auction maiden at Leicester and a four-runner conditions event at Newmarket, both over five furlongs. Easycall started second favourite in what looked a substandard renewal of the Richmond to the Curragh Stakes winner Raphane who was also stepping up in trip. Easycall kept his unbeaten record with another clear-cut success, travelling strongly to lead over two furlongs out and quickening three lengths clear of Raphane inside the last. The Gimcrack Stakes at York later in the month brought a temporary halt to Easycall's progress. Held up on the far side of the field, he wasn't ideally positioned when the principals went for home on the stand side and finished fourth behind Abou Zouz. Returned to five furlongs for the Flying Childers at Doncaster in

Richmond Stakes, Goodwood—few problems for Easycall

Polypipe Plc Flying Childers Stakes, Doncaster—
a second Group 2 success for Easycall, from Compton Place (rails) and Deep Finesse (right)

September, Easycall put up a fine performance under his penalty, leading inside the final furlong and staying on strongly to turn the tables on the favourite and Gimcrack runner-up Compton Place, in so doing giving his jockey Michael Tebbutt the first pattern win of his career. Tebbutt kept the ride in Easycall's two remaining races. First of those was the Middle Park, for which Easycall had to be supplemented at a cost of £12,000. Looking in fine shape, he seemed to have every chance of getting at least some of that back over a furlong out, but ultimately he came sixth, just over three lengths behind Bahamian Bounty. The Cornwallis was again something of an afterthought by connections who had originally planned to put Easycall away for the winter after the Middle Park. We did think he looked less well in himself at Ascot but running him paid off handsomely.

		Forzando (b 1981)	Formidable (b 1975)	Forli
				Native Partner
			Princely Maid (b 1967)	King's Troop
Easycall				Moss Maid
(b.c. Mar 31, 1994)		Up And Going (FR) (b 1987)	Never So Bold (b 1980)	Bold Lad
				Never Never Land
			Ergo (b 1976)	Song
				Gold of The Day

Taken individually, neither the record of sire Forzando nor that of Easycall's family is particularly distinguished, but bringing the two together has benefited both on more than one occasion, resulting not only in Easycall but in an earlier Cornwallis winner Up And At 'Em. This pair account for two-thirds of Forzando's pattern winners, his other—also at the minimum trip—being the Ballyogan Stakes winner Great Deeds. Forzando won twelve races in all, including five as a two-year-old, a Group 2 sprint in Italy at three and the Grade 1 Metropolitan Handicap over a mile at Belmont Park at four. On the dam's side, Up And Going had two colts by Cricket Ball before Easycall came along, namely Baskerville and Owen Meany who have both won at up to a mile in France, the latter four times in sprint handicaps in the latest season. Up And Going's next foal, a full sister to Easycall, died but she has a filly foal by the July Cup winner Hamas. The next dam Ergo won once over five furlongs from just three starts as a two-year-old and Up And At 'Em is the best of numerous winners she has produced. Up And At 'Em won the 1992 Cornwallis Stakes for Jimmy Coogan but was not the most consistent of performers; he gained his only subsequent win with Jack Berry as a four-year-old, when beating Lake Coniston a short head in a listed race at Sandown. Easycall's great grandam Gold of The Day was successful in selling company over five furlongs at two and a mile at three. She was a half-sister to the dam of the Two Thousand Guineas winner Mon Fils.

302

Easycall, who was unsold at 9,800 guineas as a yearling, is a good-quartered colt and a good walker. He is clearly a sprinter and has shown his best form at five furlongs. His win at Ascot proved him at least as effective on good to soft ground as on the good to firm he had been racing on most of the summer. A game, genuine and consistent sort, Easycall will be worth his place in the big sprints in 1997, and, with most of the established horses retired, he may well be capable of winning one. *B. J. Meehan*

EASY CHOICE (USA) 4 b.c. Easy Goer (USA) – Monroe (USA) 102 (Sir Ivor 135) [1995 81+: 8g³ 10g⁴ 5g³ 5g⁴ 6.5d⁴ a8g* a8g* a8g* 1996 a9.4g a8g² a10g³ 8.1g 7f 10d 7.6f 10m 8f 12m 10.1m⁴ Sep 24] sturdy colt: fairly useful performer on the all-weather: well beaten on turf in 1996: sold 10,000 gns Newmarket Autumn Sales: stays 1¼m: acts on equitrack (never going well only outing on fibresand), raced only on an easy surface in France: tried blinkered/visored: sent to USA. *P. Mitchell* — a81

EASY DOLLAR 4 ch.g. Gabitat 119 – Burglars Girl 63 (Burglar 128) [1995 109: 7m⁵ 6m³ 8.3m⁴ 8m⁵ 7.3m 6m⁴ 6f² 6m* 7f* 7.3m⁵ 6m³ 8m⁵ 6d 7d 1996 6g² 6m⁴ 7g² 6f 6f³ 6f² 6.5d 6d Aug 23] tall, plain gelding: useful performer: ran at least respectably first 6 starts at 4 yrs, on last of them neck second of 16 to Jayannpee in listed race at Newbury in July, rallying well despite edging left: effective over 6f, and stays 7.3f well: goes well on top-of-the-ground, seemingly not on a soft surface: nearly always visored/blinkered: tends to hang: tough. *B. Gubby* — 108

EASY JET (POL) 4 b.c. Robellino (USA) 127 – Etourdic (USA) (Arctic Tern (USA) 126) [1995 83d: 7.3m² 7.1m² 8m⁶ 8d 8m 1996 7g² 8m² 8m³ 7f³ 8m 8g Oct 19] strong colt: poor mover: fair maiden handicapper: likely to stay beyond 1m: acts on firm ground, ran poorly on dead: visored (well beaten in valuable event) final 4-y-o start. *Lord Huntingdon* — 76

EASY LISTENING (USA) 4 b.g. Easy Goer (USA) – Queen of Song (USA) (His Majesty (USA)) [1995 79p: 10.2f* 1996 10g 10.2f³ 10m² 12m⁶ Jul 27] rangy gelding: off course 10½ months before 4-y-o reappearance: fairly useful handicapper: sold (R. Charlton to N. Hawke) only 11,500 gns Newmarket Autumn Sales: stays 1½m: raced predominantly on top-of-the-ground. *R. Charlton* — 89

EASY NUMBER (USA) 3 ch.f. Easy Goer (USA) – Treizieme (USA) 121 (The Minstrel (CAN) 135) [1995 NR 1996 7.1m Jul 6] $250,000Y: sixth foal: closely related to 2 winners by Alydar and half-sister to a winner by Devil's Bag: dam, French 1m to 1½m filly later successful in USA, half-sister to Gold Cup runner-up Eastern Mystic: weak in betting, tailed off as if something amiss in maiden at Chepstow: sent to USA. *J. H. M. Gosden* — –

EASY OPTION (IRE) 4 ch.f. Prince Sabo 123 – Brazen Faced 84 (Bold And Free 118) [1995 115: 5g⁴ 5.2d* 5d⁴ 1996 a5f³ 5d² 5d⁴ 6g³ 6.1s⁴ Oct 31] lengthy filly: poor walker and unimpressive mover: smart performer: looking really well, best 4-y-o effort when 3 lengths fourth of 10 to Kistena in Prix de l'Abbaye de Longchamp, staying on without posing a threat: below form in listed race at Newmarket and minor event at Nottingham (odds on, off bridle 1½f out, faded) last 2 starts: best at around 5f: goes well on a soft surface, possibly unsuited by sand: tongue tied last 3 starts. *Saeed bin Suroor* — 114

EATON PARK (IRE) 2 ch.c. (Apr 11) Mac's Imp (USA) 116 – Pepilin (Coquelin (USA) 121) [1996 5m² 6g⁴ 6g 7g 6m⁶ Sep 24] 10,000Y: leggy, rather unfurnished colt: fourth foal: half-brother to 3-y-o Peppers (by Bluebird) and a winner in UAE by Thatching: dam Irish 2-y-o 6f winner: modest form on debut: didn't repeat it: probably a sprinter: retained by trainer 7,500 gns Newmarket Autumn Sales. *R. Akehurst* — 62 d

EAU DE COLOGNE 4 b.g. Persian Bold 123 – No More Rosies 74 (Warpath 113) [1995 71: 10m⁵ 9m⁵ 10g* 12m³ 12.3m³ 15g⁴ 13.9g 16d⁴ 15.1s³ 1996 12.1d* 11.8g 13s⁵ 12.3s⁵ 12.1d³ 13.9g Oct 12] good-topped gelding: fair handicapper: won minor event at Hamilton in April: respectable efforts at best afterwards: probably stays 2m: acts on good to firm and dead ground: sold privately 30,000 gns Doncaster November Sales to join Mrs L. Richards. *C. W. Thornton* — 68

EBEN NAAS (USA) 3 b.g. Dayjur (USA) 137 – Regal State (USA) 122 (Affirmed (USA)) [1995 –: a8g 1996 a6g⁵ a7g³ a8g² 7.1g* 8g* 7d 8g 7.1f⁵ Jun 24] — 61

angular gelding: modest handicapper: won at Musselburgh and Leicester (made all) in April: well beaten all 3 starts afterwards: sold only 3,800 gns Newmarket September Sales, and gelded: will prove best at up to 1m: acts on fibresand: blinkered (raced too freely) final 3-y-o start: wears bandages behind: has had tongue tied down: often races prominently. *S. C. Williams*

EBONY BOY 3 bl.g. Sayf El Arab (USA) 127 – Actress 73 (Known Fact (USA) 135) [1995 –, a65: 5s a6g³ a5g² a7g² a7g⁶* 5m 6m a7g⁶ a7g⁴ 1996 a7g⁵ a11g a8.5g⁵ 8.2m a6g a7g⁵ a8g⁴ Dec 3] only poor at best in 1996: stays 7f: best form on fibresand, no form on turf: blinkered (made running, finished last) third 3-y-o start: gelded. *J. Wharton* — a47

EBONY T·A·P·S 3 bl.f. Adbass (USA) 102 – August Seventeenth 55 (Sharpo 132) [1995 –: 7f 7g 1996 8m Jun 26] small filly: has a round action: third foal: dam, maiden, stayed 7f: soundly beaten. *J. S. Moore* —

ECCENTRIC DANCER 3 b.f. Rambo Dancer (CAN) 107 – Lady Eccentric (IRE) (Magical Wonder (USA) 125) [1995 –: 5m⁴ 5m 6f³ 7f 6f 1996 8.2g 6g 7.5g a8.5g³ 10m 8m 8f a9.4g² 7f 8.2s a9.4g a7g Nov 22] lengthy filly: poor maiden: stays 9.4f: acts on fibresand, no worthwhile form on turf: blinkered since sixth 3-y-o start: most inconsistent. *M. P. Bielby* — a47

ECTOMORPH (IRE) 3 ch.f. Sharp Victor (USA) 114 – Hail To You (USA) (Kirtling 129) [1995 NR 1996 10m⁶ Jun 28] workmanlike filly: has a round action: half-sister to 3 winners, including fair Un Parfum de Femme (up to 1½m, by Mill Native): dam minor winner in USA: tailed off in claimer. *J. Pearce* —

EDAN HEIGHTS 4 b.g. Heights of Gold – Edna 92 (Shiny Tenth 120) [1995 78: 7m 8m⁴ 8m⁵ 10m 10g³ 12m² 12s* 14m³ 11.8f² 1996 12g 12m 12m 11.4g* 10m 10m² 10m 10m⁴ 12g 10s* 12s Nov 9] sturdy, plain gelding: fairly useful handicapper: won at Sandown (back to best) in July and Newbury in October: effective at 1¼m and should stay beyond 1½m: acts on firm and soft going: inconsistent. *S. Dow* — 81

EDEN DANCER 4 b.g. Shareef Dancer (USA) 135 – Dash (Connaught 130) [1995 57: 8.1g* 7g 8f⁶ 10f⁵ 11.1f* 9.9m 1996 10.3m 12.3m 12.1m⁵ Sep 23] sturdy gelding: modest performer: no form in 1996: stays 11f: acts on firm and soft ground: fair hurdler: inconsistent. *Mrs M. Reveley* —

EDGAR KIRBY 5 ch.g. Caerleon (USA) 132 – Martha Stevens (USA) 102 (Super Concorde (USA) 128) [1995 –: 8.1m 1996 8m⁴ 7f 8g³ a8g Jun 20] sturdy gelding: modest maiden handicapper: effective at 1m and should stay 1½m: acts on good to firm and dead ground, well below form on fibresand. *P. W. Harris* — 56

EDIPO RE 4 b.c. Slip Anchor 136 – Lady Barrister (Law Society (USA) 130) [1995 NR 1996 14m² 14d⁴ Sep 27] rangy colt: bought 27,000 gns Ascot May (1996) Sales: back to form when second of 5 in minor event at Salisbury on return, staying on late despite carrying head high under pressure: burly and bandaged, very stiff task when tailed off in minor event at Haydock 3 months later: stays 1¾m. *P. J. Hobbs* — 94

ED'S FOLLY (IRE) 3 b.g. Fayruz 116 – Tabriya 61 (Nishapour (FR) 125) [1995 59: 5m 6d 5s³ 5d⁶ 1996 5d 6g 7f³ 7m⁶ 6f Jun 1] good-quartered gelding: modest maiden handicapper: stays 7f: acts on firm and soft going: inconsistent. *S. Dow* — 59

EFAAD (IRE) 5 b.g. Shaadi (USA) 126 – Krismas River (Kris 135) [1995 –: 17.1m 14.1m 1996 a12g⁶ a16g⁶ a16g Jun 6] no form since 2 yrs: visored final 5-y-o start. *J. Norton* —

EFFECTUAL 3 b.g. Efisio 120 – Moharabuiee 60 (Pas de Seul 133) [1995 NR 1996 8m 10m³ 8.1d² 10m⁴ Jun 3] 23,000F, 42,000Y: second foal: half-brother to 1½m to 1¾m winner Risky Rose (by Risk Me): dam, plater, stayed 7f: fair form in maidens: gives impression will prove best at up to 1¼m: yet to race on extremes of going: joined Miss Gay Kelleway. *J. A. R. Toller* — 72

EFFERVESCENCE 2 ch.c. (May 16) Efisio 120 – Petite Elite 47 (Anfield 117) [1996 6m⁶ 5.7f⁴ 5.1m² 5m² 6m⁵ 5m 7d 7g² 7s a7g² a8.5g⁴ a7s² a7g* a7g* Dec 30] 6,200F, 20,000 2-y-o: compact colt: has a short, unimpressive action: third foal: brother to 3-y-o 1m winner Efipetite and half-brother to 1994 2-y-o 5f winner Little Ginger Nut (by Hallgate): dam stayed 7f: improved into a fairly useful performer on the all-weather late in year, winning maiden and nursery at Lingfield: creditable effort at 8.5f but best form at 7f: acts on the all-weather, best turf form on a sound surface: has been bandaged near-hind. *R. Hannon* — 86

EFFICACIOUS (IRE)   3 ch.f. Efisio 120 – Bushti Music 63 (Bustino 136)   49 d
[1995 –, a44: 5m 6f 6f 5g 7.3d a8g⁵ 1996 10.8g⁵ 9.7f² 8.3m 10.1f⁴ 12.5f⁶ 9.7g 10f³
10f⁶ 11.9f² 11.9f a12g a8s⁵ a10g³ a12g a12g⁵ a10g Dec 26] lengthy, plain filly: poor
walker: poor maiden handicapper: sold out of J. Benstead's stable 2,100 gns Ascot
October Sales after tenth start: below form afterwards: stays 1½m: acts on firm
going: inconsistent. *A. Moore*

EFFICACY   5 b.m. Efisio 120 – Lady Killane 62 (Reform 132) [1995 57: a7g a8g   39
a6g⁵ a6g⁴ a5g⁵ a6g* a6g² a6g⁴ a6g* a6g* a6g² a6g⁵ a6g⁶ 1996 a6g⁵ a6g a7g² a7g³   a62
a6g⁴ 6d⁴ 5.1g 6m⁶ 6m a6g² a6g Sep 7] angular mare: bad mover: modest performer
on the all-weather: lightly raced (and poor) on turf: best at up to 7f: acts on fibresand,
below form only outing on equitrack: often apprentice ridden. *A. P. Jarvis*

EFHARISTO   7 b.g. Dominion 123 – Excellent Alibi (USA) (Exceller (USA)   –
129) [1995 a10g⁵ a9g⁴ a8g³ a10g 1996 10g⁵ 9.2s⁵ 12m Jun 19] angular gelding: rated
89 in 1993 for C. Brittain: rather inconsistent in Dubai, sold out of P. Rudkin's stable
26,000 gns Newmarket July (1995) Sales: below best on return: stays 1¼m: used to
act on good to firm ground and dead: effective blinkered/visored or not: won maiden
hurdle in July. *J. White*

EFIPETITE   3 ch.f. Efisio 120 – Petite Elite 47 (Anfield 117) [1995 44: a5g⁵   –
5m 5f⁴ a6g⁴ 6m⁵ 6f 6m a6g³ 7.1g 7d 7m 6f 6f a6g³ a8g 1996 a6g a7g⁴ a8g⁵ a8g³ a6g⁴   a54 d
a8g³ a8g* a7g² a8g³ a8g⁴ a7g³ a7g³ a7g⁴ a8g⁶ a8g⁵ a8g 7s 8f 7d 10g 8m a8g
a8g⁶ Dec 27] close-coupled filly: poor mover: modest performer: won claimer at
Southwell in February: stays 1m: acts on fibresand: tried blinkered, no improvement:
often sweating and edgy: sometimes looks difficult ride: inconsistent. *N. Bycroft*

EFIZIA   6 b.m. Efisio 120 – Millie Grey 52 (Grey Ghost 98) [1995 –: 10d 10.5s⁶   59
10g 10f⁶ 10f 1996 9.9f³ 10m⁵ 10m⁵ Aug 10] sturdy, workmanlike mare: disappointing since 4 yrs: reportedly finished lame final 6-y-o start: probably stays 11f: acts on
any going: usually held up. *G. M. Moore*

EFRA   7 b.g. Efisio 120 – Ra Ra (Lord Gayle (USA) 124) [1995 72: 6g⁶ 6f 6g 6m   72
6g⁵ 1996 6m² 6d⁶ 6d Oct 21] lengthy, good-topped gelding: has a round action: fair
performer: below form in 1995 and 1996 after reappearance: effective at 6f to 7f: acts
on good to firm and heavy ground: blinkered (tailed off) once at 3 yrs: inconsistent.
R. Hannon

EIGHT SHARP (IRE)   4 b.g. Sure Blade (USA) 130 – Octavia Girl 104 (Octavo   –
(USA) 115) [1995 72: 10m² 10.4m 10.1g 1996 12g 7g Apr 8] deep-bodied gelding:
one-time fair performer: well beaten in 1996 for new stable: probably stayed 1¼m:
acted on dead ground, ran respectably (facing stiff tasks) on good to firm: won selling
hurdle in April: dead. *M. D. Hammond*

EIRE LEATH-SCEAL   9 b.g. Legend of France (USA) 124 – Killarney Belle   –
(USA) (Irish Castle (USA)) [1995 63: 16.2m² 16.2g⁶ 1996 11.9m Jun 14] small,
attractive gelding: usually looks well: bad mover: really tough and game handicapper over the years: off course nearly a year, ran as if something badly amiss on
1996 reappearance: effective at 1½m to 2m: acts on firm and dead going, unsuited by
heavy: visored (well beaten) second 6-y-o start: often a front runner. *M. Brittain*

EJEER (IRE)   2 b.g. (Apr 19) Jareer (USA) 115 – Precious Egg (Home Guard   –
(USA) 129) [1996 6g Aug 21] IR 3,000Y: half-brother to 6f winners Easter Glory (by
Dalsaan) and Fox Path (by Godswalk) and a winner in Hong Kong: dam poor half-
sister to Cork and Orrery winner Kearney: slow-starting seventh in median auction
maiden at Kempton in summer: may do better. *M. R. Channon*

EKATERINI PARITSI   2 b.f. (May 22) Timeless Times (USA) 99 – Wych   49
Willow (Hard Fought 125) [1996 5.3f³ 5.1m³ 5s² 6m² a6g² 6f a7g⁵ a7g² a7g a6g³   a52
a5g⁴ Dec 31] 2,100Y: leggy filly: unimpressive mover: first foal: dam unraced:
modest maiden: stays 7f: acts on any going, including all-weather: often blinkered/
visored. *W. G. M. Turner*

ELA AGAPI MOU (USA)   3 b.g. Storm Bird (CAN) 134 – Vaguar (USA)   53
(Vaguely Noble 140) [1995 NR 1996 10.2g 10f 10s⁵ a13g⁶ 10m³ 11.9f² 11.5m a16g
Dec 5] rather leggy gelding: has a round action: first reported foal: dam French 1¼m
winner: modest maiden: left G. Lewis after sixth start: showed little afterwards: stays
1½m: acts on firm ground. *A. Moore*

Racing Channel Handicap, Epsom—
Ela-Aristokrati (light colours) weaves his way through from well back
to collar Tertium (centre) close home

ELA-ARISTOKRATI (IRE)   4 b.c. Danehill (USA) 126 – Dubai Lady 78 (Kris   117
135) [1995 111: 8.1m³ 10.1f* 10.4m² 10.4m⁶ 10m⁵ 1996 10g 10.1m* 10g⁴ 10.5m²
11.1m³ Sep 7] sturdy, quite attractive colt: impresses great deal in appearance: good
mover: smart performer: left M. Stoute after 1996 reappearance: got up close home
in £31,800 handicap at Epsom in June, putting up cracking performance under top
weight: ran creditably in pattern events all 3 outings afterwards, fourth to Halling in
Coral-Eclipse Stakes at Sandown (beaten 7 lengths), second to Tamayaz in Group 3
race at Haydock (beaten 5 lengths) and narrowly-beaten third of 7 (rider dropping
reins 2f out) to Sacrament in September Stakes at Kempton: stays 11f well: acts on
firm going, not disgraced only start on a soft surface: held up last 4 starts: has joined
M. Tompkins. *L. M. Cumani*

ELA MAN HOWA   5 b.g. Mtoto 134 – Top Treat (USA) 101 (Topsider   50
(USA)) [1995 58: 12g² 11.9m⁴ 14g³ 14.1m³ 14g⁴ 14m³ 11.8m⁵ 14.4m* 1996 12.3g
12g⁴ 14.1f 13.1g⁶ 12m 16g⁴ 16.4g⁵ 13.1m⁶ 15.9g Sep 25] rather leggy, lightly-
made gelding: disappointing over hurdles and only poor in 1996 on flat, leaving
N. Tinkler's stable after second start: stays 2m: acts on good to firm and dead ground
and equitrack: blinkered (raced too freely) last 2 starts: effective from front or held
up. *A. Bailey*

ELA-MENT (IRE)   4 b.g. Ela-Mana-Mou 132 – Dorado Llave (USA) (Well   –
Decorated (USA)) [1995 –: 11.5s a8.5g 1996 a12g 11.9f 9m a16g a16g Nov 12] of no
account. *B. A. Pearce*

ELA PATRICIA (IRE)   2 ch.f. (Mar 12) Shalford (IRE) 124§ – Alice Brackloon   –
(USA) (Melyno 130) [1996 6m 7m 8f⁵ Sep 10] IR 6,000F, IR 8,000Y: sturdy, work-
manlike filly: has a quick action: third reported foal: half-sister to 5-y-o 9.7f to
14.1f winner Children's Choice (by Taufan) and winning Irish sprinter Swinford
Swinger (by Salt Dome): dam unraced half-sister to top-class middle-distance colt
Argument: behind in maiden auctions and a maiden: sold 750 gns Ascot October
Sales. *D. J. G. Murray Smith*

ELASHATH (USA)   3 b.c. El Gran Senor (USA) 136 – Gorgeoso (USA)   71
(Damascus (USA)) [1995 –p: 8m 1996 10g 10m⁶ 9f* 10f* 10m⁴ 10m² 10f² Sep
27] strong, lengthy colt: has a round action: fair handicapper: won at Redcar in
June and July: good efforts, narrowly beaten, last 2 starts: should stay 1½m: acts on
firm ground, yet to race on a soft surface: seems rather lazy sort: sent to Dubai.
J. H. M. Gosden

EL ATREVIDO (FR)   6 ch.g. Rainbow Quest (USA) 134 – Majestic Peck (USA)   63
(Majestic Light (USA)) [1995 72: a10g* a10g³ a10g* 10m a8g a10g 1996 a10g³

a12g Feb 22] ex-French gelding: fair performer: respectable effort in claimer at Lingfield on reappearance, much his better 6-y-o effort: stays 1¼m: acts on equitrack: sold only 520 gns Doncaster March Sales. *N. J. H. Walker*

ELA-YIE-MOU (IRE) 3 ch.c. Kris 135 – Green Lucia 116 (Green Dancer 84 (USA) 132) [1995 63p: 8g⁶ 8d 8.2m⁵ 1996 12d 12m³ 14.1m* 14d³ 12m⁴ 14f 14.6g Oct 25] tall, rather unfurnished colt: has a fluent, round action: fairly useful handicapper: won at Nottingham in May: best effort next start, but found little next 2 outings, and subsequently left L. Cumani: ran as if something amiss last time: stays 14.1f: acts on good to firm and dead ground. *S. Dow*

ELBAAHA 2 ch.f. (Apr 3) Arazi (USA) 135 – Gesedeh 117 (Ela-Mana-Mou 132) 78 [1996 6m³ 8.1d² 8.2g³ Oct 9] sixth foal: half-sister to 3-y-o Kulshi Momken (by In the Wings): dam, suited by 1¼m, half-sister to Ardross and Larrocha: fair form placed in maidens: will stay beyond 1m: seems one paced. *M. A. Jarvis*

EL BAILADOR (IRE) 5 b.g. Dance of Life (USA) – Sharp Ego (USA) (Sharpen 68 Up 127) [1995 68: 10m⁵ 10g a8g* a10g⁵ 10m* 10m 12d⁴ 10.5s⁵ 10f² 1996 a12g* a11g⁴ Mar 18] fair handicapper: won minor event at Southwell in February (staying on well), much his better effort in 1996: stays 1½m: acts on good to firm ground, soft and all-weather: blinkered (well beaten) twice at 3 yrs. *J. D. Bethell*

EL BARDADOR (IRE) 3 b.g. Thatching 131 – Osmunda (Mill Reef (USA) 59 141) [1995 NR 1996 8.1d 8.2m 7m 9.9g⁴ a11g 10.1m* 11.9g 11.5m 12s⁴ Nov 11] IR 20,000F, 14,000Y, 26,000 2-y-o: lengthy gelding: half-brother to 3 winners, including fairly useful middle-distance stayer Icecapped (by Caerleon): dam, Irish 1¼m winner, is half-sister to smart middle-distance performers Snow and Icelandic: modest form: dropped to seller and blinkered first time, won at Yarmouth in September: stays 1½m: acts on good to firm and soft ground (well beaten on all-weather debut): blinkered since sixth 3-y-o start: sometimes slowly away: has looked difficult ride: sold (W. Jarvis to R. Hodges) 6,000 gns Doncaster November Sales: not one to rely on. *W. Jarvis*

ELBURG (IRE) 6 b.g. Ela-Mana-Mou 132 – Iosifa 108 (Top Ville 129) – [1995 65: a16g³ a16g⁴ a16g⁴ 18g⁴ 16m⁶ 21.6f*ᵈⁱˢ 1996 a16g⁵ 18s Mar 22] lengthy gelding: modest handicapper: tailed off both starts in 1996 on flat: stays extreme distances: acts on firm ground, dead and on equitrack: visored (tailed off) on 6-y-o reappearance: completed hat-trick over hurdles for T. George in December. *R. P. C. Hoad*

EL DON 4 b.g. High Kicker (USA) – Madam Gerard 50 (Brigadier Gerard 144) – [1995 –: 8m 7g 8.2m⁵ 10d 8m 8.2m a10g 1996 8.2m⁶ 11.8d 10.1m 10.1m a11g Dec 27] very tall, quite good-topped gelding: disappointing maiden on flat: tried blinkered, no improvement: fair winning hurdler. *M. J. Ryan*

ELDORADO (IRE) 2 b.c. (Mar 16) Ela-Mana-Mou 132 – Happy Tidings (Hello 97 p Gorgeous (USA) 128) [1996 10.2d* 10g² Nov 2] IR 5,200F, 10,000Y: fifth reported foal: half-brother to Irish 1½m to 2¼m winner Fleeting Vision (by Vision) and a winner in Spain: dam unraced half-sister to Snurge (by Ela-Mana-Mou): finished very strongly when winning maiden at Bath in September: ¾-length second of 10 to Silver Patriarch in steadily-run listed race at Newmarket 5 weeks later, first to be pushed along, still only fifth inside last but staying on really well: sure to do better again, and make a useful middle-distance stayer at least. *M. Johnston*

ELEANOR MAY 3 b. or br.f. Crofthall 110 – Melaura Belle 94 (Meldrum 112) – [1995 NR 1996 5.1d 5m 7g Jun 1] leggy filly: second reported foal: half-sister to useful hurdler/chaser Major Bell (by Silly Prices): dam sprinter: signs of a little ability but no worthwhile form: sold 8,000 gns Doncaster July Sales. *T. D. Barron*

ELECTION DAY (IRE) 4 b.c. Sadler's Wells (USA) 132 – Hellenic 125 114 (Darshaan 133) [1995 –p: 10m 10g* 13.4g² 13.3d* 12f 12s⁴ Nov 9] sturdy, attractive colt: smart performer: won maiden at Pontefract in April: 1½ lengths second of 7 to Oscar Schindler in Ormonde Stakes at Chester: impressive 4-length winner from Minds Music (pair 9 lengths clear) of 8-runner listed race at Newbury in May, looking better the further he went: reportedly injured near-fore at Royal Ascot next time, and off course 4½ months: well supported and visored, struggling after 2f in listed race at Doncaster on return: not sure to be suited by as short as 1½m, and will stay further than 13.4f: acts on dead ground. *M. R. Stoute*

ELEGANT DANCE 2 ch.f. (Mar 15) Statoblest 120 – Furry Dance (USA) 57 (Nureyev (USA) 131) [1996 7m Aug 1] 4,800Y: rather leggy filly: second foal: dam once-raced close relative of useful middle-distance horse Florid, from the family of Ribblesdale winners Catalpa and Strigida: backward and green, never dangerous in summer maiden at Goodwood: unimpressive to post: may do better. *J. J. Sheehan*

ELEGANTISSIMA 3 b.f. Polish Precedent (USA) 131 – Ela Meem (USA) (Kris – 135) [1995 57p: a8g⁴ 1996 a7g⁵ 7d 6s 7.1g Jun 13] lengthy filly: disappointing in 1996: sold 850 gns Ascot July Sales. *S. Dow*

ELEGANT WARNING (IRE) 2 b.f. (Mar 13) Warning 136 – Dance It (USA) 109 (Believe It (USA)) [1996 6m² 6m³ 6m* 6g* Oct 26] tall, leggy filly: has a quick action: fourth foal: half-sister to 8.3f selling winner Kama Simba (by Lear Fan), 1993 2-y-o 7f winner Rawya (by Woodman) and a winner in USA by Saros: dam winning sprinter in USA: very progressive form: won maiden at Newmarket (by 1½ lengths from Meshhed) and 7-runner listed race at Doncaster (led on bridle over 1f out and quickened clear in good style when beating Open Credit by 5 lengths) in October: bred to stay 1m: has raced only on a sound surface: showed some temperament first 2 starts but did nothing wrong after. *B. W. Hills*

ELFIN QUEEN (IRE) 3 b.f. Fairy King (USA) – West of Eden (Crofter (USA) 50 124) [1995 64d: 5g³ 5f² 5f⁴ 5.2d 1996 a6g⁵ a6g⁶ a5g⁴ a5g⁶ a6g Mar 9] modest maiden: disappointing after reappearance in 1996 for new stable: should stay 6f: acts on equitrack and firm ground: blinkered (tailed off) final 3-y-o start: covered by Dolphin Street. *J. L. Harris*

ELHAFID (USA) 2 ch.c. (Mar 24) Nureyev (USA) 131 – Shy Dame (USA) 66 + (Damascus (USA)) [1996 7m 7m 8m Sep 25] $200,000Y: seventh foal: half-brother to 3 winners in USA, including Cadillac Women (by Carr de Naskra), third in Breeders' Cup Juvenile Fillies: dam unraced: midfield throughout in maidens on southern tracks: not certain to stay much beyond 1m: may do better. *Major W. R. Hern*

ELITE BLISS (IRE) 4 b.f. Tirol 127 – Krismas River (Kris 135) [1995 NR 1996 44 12g³ 10.2g³ 10m⁴ 10.3g 11f 11m⁵ a11g⁴ a14g³ Nov 29] 10,000Y: big, workmanlike filly: fifth foal: half-sister to a winner in Italy: dam Irish 1¼m winner: third of 18 in NH Flat race (pulling hard) in March: poor maiden handicapper: stays 1¾m. *M. J. Camacho*

ELITE FORCE (IRE) 3 b.g. Fairy King (USA) – La Petruschka (Ballad Rock 80 d 122) [1995 82p: 7g⁵ 6d⁴ 1996 8g³ 7d² 7.6g 6m⁶ 7.1m⁶ 8m Oct 17] leggy, lengthy gelding: fairly useful maiden at best: below form after second 3-y-o start: sold only 3,000 gns Newmarket Autumn Sales. *P. W. Chapple-Hyam*

ELITE HOPE (USA) 4 ch.f. Moment of Hope (USA) – Chervil (USA) 71 (Greenough (USA)) [1995 84: 6g 7.1g² 7m⁴ 7m⁶ 7.3d 7m⁵ 1996 8.1g 7.6g 7.1m⁶ 7m 8.3d⁶ 8.1d 8.9g 10m a7g² a6g a7g* a7g a7g* Dec 28] small, sturdy filly: only fair at best in 1996: left C. Egerton after sixth start: won at Wolverhampton in November (by 7 lengths) and December: stays 7.1f: best form on a sound surface, acts on fibresand: blinkered (soundly beaten) sixth 4-y-o start. *N. Tinkler*

ELITE JUSTICE 4 ch.g. Absalom 128 – Persian Express (Persian Bold 123) [1995 65: 7.9g 8m⁴ 8m⁶ 10f³ 10f² 8g⁴ 1996 a11g a11g a11g a11g 9.9f⁶ Jun 6] workmanlike gelding: tailed off for new stables (N. Tinkler first 3 starts) in 1996: has raced only on a sound surface on turf: blinkered (ran poorly) once. *S. Gollings*

ELITE RACING 4 b.f. Risk Me (FR) 127 – Hot Stone (Hotfoot 126) [1995 69d: 41 8f* 9.7g 8d 8m⁴ 8.5m* 8f³ 8.5m² 9m⁵ 8.3m⁶ 8m 8f 1996 7.5m 8.1g* 8m 8m⁴ 10.8m 8.3m 9.2f Aug 19] leggy, quite good-topped filly: poor handicapper nowadays: won seller at Musselburgh in May: well beaten last 3 starts: stays 8.5f: acts on firm ground and soft: tried blinkered, no improvement: found nothing under pressure eighth 3-y-o start: inconsistent. *N. Tinkler*

ELITE REG 7 b.g. Electric 126 – Coppice (Pardao 120) [1995 NR 1996 18f⁵ Jul – 2] poor maiden on flat: tailed off only 7-y-o start: stays 2m: acts on good to firm ground: tried blinkered/visored: fairly useful hurdler/chaser. *M. C. Pipe*

ELIZA 2 ch.f. (Apr 21) Shavian 125 – One Degree 80 (Crooner 119) [1996 7.1s – p Oct 22] seventh foal: half-sister to 1m winner Waldo (by Northern State) and useful

1987 2-y-o 5f winner Pea Green (by Try My Best): dam 6f winner: signs of ability when midfield in late-season maiden at Chepstow: should stay 1m: likely to do better. *Lord Huntingdon*

ELLA LAMEES 2 b.f. (Mar 4) Statoblest 120 – Lamees (USA) (Lomond (USA) – p 128) [1996 6.9d 6d Nov 8] 6,800Y: third foal: half-sister to 3-y-o Lomberto (by Robellino), useful 7f winner at 2 yrs, and 1994 2-y-o 5f and 6f winner Don Alvaro (by Forzando): dam unraced daughter of useful French 1¼m and 10.5f winner Vachti: not well drawn or knocked about in maiden auction at Folkestone and maiden at Doncaster: will probably stay 1m: almost certainly capable of better. *W. J. Musson*

ELL ELL EFF 3 ch.f. Pharly (FR) 130 – Yen (AUS) (Biscay (AUS)) [1995 NR – 1996 10m 10m Jun 28] strong, lengthy filly: half-sister to 2 winners, including modest Savings Bank (1m, by Shernazar): dam ran once in Australia: last in claimers, visored and pulling hard second occasion. *A. Hide*

ELLE MAC 3 b.f. Merdon Melody 98 – Tripolitaine (FR) (Nonoalco (USA) 131) – [1995 –: 5.1m 6m 7d 1996 7f6 10m a7g Nov 29] good-topped filly: of little account. *M. P. Bielby*

ELLENS LAD (IRE) 2 b.c. (May 6) Polish Patriot (USA) 128 – Lady Ellen 67 81 p (Horage 124) [1996 6m 5g 7m 5f3 5m* 6s5 5g* Nov 1] IR 12,000Y: good-quartered colt: third foal: dam, placed over 5f at 2 yrs, half-sister to Indian Ridge: fair form: won nurseries at Folkestone in September and Newmarket (readily) in November: best form at 5f on a sound surface: capable of further improvement. *R. Hannon*

ELLIE ARDENSKY 4 b.f. Slip Anchor 136 – Circus Ring 122 (High Top 131) 100 [1995 96: 9m* 10.8g2 12m4 10f* 10.1g3 10g5 1996 10.1m5 10f2 11.9g 10m 10.1m 12m2 12g Sep 29] useful performer: best efforts when second in valuable handicap at Ascot (behind Salmon Ladder) in June and in minor event at Kempton (behind Poppy Carew) in September: stays 1½m: acts on firm going: on toes and edgy (well below form) final 4-y-o start: none too consistent. *J. R. Fanshawe*

ELLWAY LADY (IRE) 2 br.f. (Mar 6) Be My Native (USA) 122 – Scaravie 58 (IRE) (Drumalis 125) [1996 5m 6f4 6g 8m4 Sep 26] 11,000F: second foal: dam twice-raced half-sister to smart Irish middle-distance colt Arctic Lord, also the family of Ardross: staying-on fourth in nursery at Pontefract on final outing, much improved effort: clearly well suited by a good test of stamina. *I. A. Balding*

ELLY FLEETFOOT (IRE) 4 b.f. Elmaamul (USA) 125 – Fleetwood Fancy 58 (Taufan (USA) 119) [1995 63: 10m 10m 11.8g 11.6g* 11.5f4 a12g a10g 1996 a12g6 a– a12g6 a10g a10g4 12.1d 9.7m 10.2m 11.6g2 11.6m3 11.6g2 11.6m a10g 10m Sep 18] leggy, sparely-made filly: modest performer: left B. Meehan after fourth 4-y-o outing: should stay at least 1½m: acts on good to firm ground: effective blinkered or not: inconsistent. *M. J. Ryan*

ELMI ELMAK (IRE) 3 b.c. Fairy King (USA) – Ascensiontide (Ela-Mana- 95 p Mou 132) [1995 NR 1996 7m2 8m* 8.1m* Aug 10] IR 27,000F, IR 34,000Y: quite attractive colt: closely related to a winner abroad by Glow and half-brother to another by Astronef: dam Irish 1½m winner out of Child Stakes winner Rose Above: won maiden at Ayr in July and rated stakes at Haydock (much better form, travelled smoothly, wore down Intidab to win by short head, pair 6 lengths clear) in August: will stay further than 8.1f: raced only on good to firm ground: sent to Dubai. *L. M. Cumani*

ELNADIM (USA) 2 b. or br.c. (Apr 24) Danzig (USA) – Elle Seule (USA) 122 83 p (Exclusive Native (USA)) [1996 6m4 6g2 Nov 1] big, good-topped colt: has plenty of scope: has a powerful, round action: sixth foal: closely related to fairly useful sprinter Jawlaat (by Dayjur), very smart miler Mehthaaf (by Nureyev) and French 1990 2-y-o 7.5f winner Only Seule (by Lyphard): dam French 1m to 10.3f winner out of outstanding broodmare Fall Aspen: heavily backed though very green and coltish, fourth to impressive Indiscreet in valuable maiden at York in August on debut: pulled hard early when keeping-on second to Kumait in steadily-run maiden at Newmarket 2½ months later: will stay 1m: to winter in Dubai: will do better. *J. L. Dunlop*

EL NIDO 8 ch.g. Adonijah 126 – Seleter (Hotfoot 126) [1995 –, a63: a16g* a14g* a63 13v4 a14g2 a12g2 a16.2g a14g4 1996 a16g3 a14.8g3 a12g4 a14g2 a14g2 Dec 3] modest performer: belatedly back to form in Southwell claimer final start: stays 2m: used to go well with some give in the ground, best form on the all-weather: wears crossed noseband. *M. J. Camacho*

EL OPERA (IRE) 3 b.f. Sadler's Wells (USA) 132 – Ridge The Times (USA) 78 100 (Riva Ridge (USA)) [1995 71p: 7d⁴ 1996 7f* 7m* 8g⁵ 10.1m⁶ 10.2f⁴ Sep 12] robust filly: has scope: useful performer: comfortable winner of maiden at Brighton in June and handicap at Warwick in July, leading inside final 1f both times: better form when fifth of 9 at Deauville and sixth of 11 (tending to hang before staying on well) at Newcastle (handicap), both in listed races, and when last of 4 to Min Alhawa in minor event at Chepstow: stays 10.2f well: acts on firm ground. *P. F. I. Cole*

EL PENITENTE (IRE) 3 b.g. Ela-Mana-Mou 132 – Penny Habit (Habitat 134) 93 [1995 NR 1996 8f* 8m Oct 3] IR 30,000Y: quite attractive gelding: half-brother to 5 winners, notably smart sprinter Fire Dome (by Salt Dome): dam unraced close relative of high-class French miler Delmora, herself dam of good French middle-distance performer Corvaro: favourite, won 18-runner maiden at Warwick in May by 4 lengths: last of 9 in listed race at Newmarket (unimpressive to post) 5 months later: gelded. *D. R. Loder*

ELPIDA (USA) 4 b.g. Trempolino (USA) 135 – All For Hope (USA) (Sensitive 66 Prince (USA)) [1995 68d: 10g 10m a14.8g* 11.5s⁴ a12g⁵ a14g a16g 1996 11.9m 11.6m 10f* 10m 12g Jul 3] compact gelding: easily best efforts since 2 yrs for his 2 wins, coming from behind in strongly-run minor event at Brighton in June: sold 750 gns Newmarket Autumn Sales: stays 14.8f: acts on firm ground and fibresand: has worn severe noseband. *J. Pearce*

ELPIDOS 4 ch.g. Bold Arrangement 127 – Thalassa (IRE) 94 (Appiani II 128) – § [1995 79: 10.3g 12.3d⁵ a12g⁴ 10m³ 9g³ 10.1f² 8g⁴ 9f 8m* 8.1m 8g 8d³ 8m 8m 1996 7.5m 8.5g 8m 6s 8m 12.1d 10.1m Oct 23] workmanlike gelding: fair winning hurdler: well held in 1996 on flat: stays 1¼m: acts on firm and dead ground: tried blinkered 3 times, no improvement: has had tongue tied: inconsistent, and not one to place maximum faith in. *M. D. Hammond*

EL PRESIDENTE 3 b.c. Presidium 124 – Spanish Princess (King of Spain 121) – [1995 NR 1996 10m 10.2f 8.5m 10d 9.7d Oct 21] third foal: half-brother to modest 1m to 1¼m winner Real Madrid (by Dreams To Reality): dam lightly raced on flat and poor over hurdles: no worthwhile form. *G. P. Enright*

ELRAAS (USA) 4 b.g. Gulch (USA) – Full Card (USA) (Damascus – (USA)) [1995 –: 6.9g 1996 8m 7g 5g 5.3m⁶ a6g a5g Dec 28] stocky, close-coupled gelding: no worthwhile form: tried visored: trained until after penultimate start by H. Collingridge. *R. J. O'Sullivan*

ELRAYAHIN 2 ch.f. (Apr 18) Riverman (USA) 131 – Gracious Beauty (USA) 67 76 (Nijinsky (CAN) 138) [1996 7g³ 7m⁴ 8.1d³ 8m³ 8m Sep 26] leggy, angular filly: has a roundish action: second foal: sister to 3-y-o 11.7f winner Labeed: dam, maiden who stayed 1¼m, closely related to Dayjur out of champion American sprinter Gold Beauty: fair form in frame in maidens and a nursery: stays 1m: acts on good to firm and dead ground: blinkered last 2 starts: lacks turn of foot. *Major W. R. Hern*

ELRIYADH (USA) 2 b.g. (Feb 3) Time For A Change (USA) – All My 80 Memories (USA) (Little Current (USA)) [1996 7m² 8.5g³ Aug 24] $100,000Y: angular, unfurnished gelding: ninth foal: half-brother to several winners in USA, including 3-y-o Grade 1 9f winner Memories of Silver (by Silver Hawk): dam won at up to 7f in USA: sire very smart 7f to 9f winner: took keen hold when second to Blue River in Newmarket maiden on debut: only third (raced with tongue hanging out, subsequently gelded) at Beverley on only other start: may stay 1¼m. *P. F. I. Cole*

ELSALEET (USA) 3 b. or br.c. Storm Cat (USA) – Blushing Redhead (USA) 96 p 104 (Blushing Groom (FR) 131) [1995 NR 1996 7m⁶ 7m* May 5] $120,000F: sturdy, good-bodied colt: sixth foal: half-brother to 3 winners, including fairly useful American sprinter Early Sunshine (by Miswaki): dam Irish-trained 7f (at 2 yrs) to 1¼m winner: narrowly won maiden at Newmarket in April, making most: refused to settle in rear when last of 6 in falsely-run minor event there following month: should prove as effective at 5f as 6f: looked capable of better: to UAE. *J. H. M. Gosden*

ELSHABIBA (USA) 3 b. or br.c. Dayjur (USA) 137 – Sweet Roberta (USA) 103 (Roberto (USA) 131) [1995 93p: 6g² 6m* 1996 8g³ Apr 6] big, robust colt: has plenty of scope: improved form when 2 lengths third of 10 to Regiment in falsely-run listed race at Kempton, always close up and disputing lead 2f out: may well prove at least as effective at 7f as 1m: sent to Dubai. *J. L. Dunlop*

ELTON LEDGER (IRE)   7 b.g. Cyrano de Bergerac 120 – Princess of Nashua – (Crowned Prince (USA) 128) [1995 –, a74: a6g⁴ a7g 1996 a6g a6g a6g³ a6g a8g⁴ a77 a6g* a7g* a6g⁴ a7g² a7g⁵ a5g⁴ a5g² a5g* a6g⁴ a7g³ a7g⁶ a5g* a6g² a8g² Nov 22] fair handicapper: won at Southwell in March (twice), June and September: effective at 5f to 7f, 1m stretches his stamina: acts on any going, best recent form on fibresand: often blinkered or visored: consistent at 7 yrs. *Mrs N. Macauley*

ELUSIVE STAR   6 b.m. Ardross 134 – Star Flower (Star Appeal 133) [1995 NR 1996 a8g⁶ Jan 30] third foal: half-sister to a winner in Macau and a winning hurdler: dam poor half-sister to good stayer Duky, out of half-sister to Gold Cup winner Shangamuzo: poor novice hurdler: well beaten in claimer on flat debut. *J. White*

EL VOLADOR   9 br.g. Beldale Flutter (USA) 130 – Pharjoy (FR) 85 (Pharly 55 (FR) 130) [1995 55, a72: 14d 12.1d 12m* a12g⁴ 1996 a12g³ a12g* a12g² a12g* a81 a12g³ 12g 14.1m³ 14.4g Sep 6] sturdy, workmanlike gelding: poor mover: fairly useful handicapper (successful 9 times) on equitrack at Lingfield: won there in January (claimer, claimed out of R. O'Sullivan's stable £5,000) and in March: modest at best on turf nowadays: stays 1¾m: goes very well on equitrack, acts on firm and dead ground and on fibresand: successful for claimer: best held up: genuine. *C. N. Allen*

E-MAIL (IRE)   2 b.c. (Mar 16) High Estate 127 – Water Pixie (IRE) (Dance of 63 Life (USA)) [1996 7g 6s 5v⁴ a6g² Dec 7] IR 9,700F, 16,000Y: smallish, sturdy colt: first foal: dam unraced: modest form: bred to require further than 5f: acts on heavy ground and fibresand. *J. M. P. Eustace*

EMBANKMENT (IRE)   6 b.g. Tate Gallery (USA) 117 – Great Leighs 87 81 d (Vaigly Great 127) [1995 89: 8g 10m⁵ 9m³ 10.1f⁴ 10f 8.1m 8f 9g² 8.5s⁶ 1996 8d 8m 8s 8.3m³ 8.9m 9f 8m 9g³ 8.1f* 7g² 8g 7.1s² 8g Oct 29] close-coupled, good-quartered gelding: just a fair handicapper in 1996: won minor event at Haydock in September: best form at 1m to 1¼m: acts on firm ground and soft: well below form only run on equitrack: usually held up: has joined N. Henderson. *R. Hannon*

EMBER   3 b.f. Nicholas (USA) 111 – Cinderwench 95 (Crooner 119) [1995 NR 62 d 1996 7m 6m 7m⁴ 10m 10d 8f 12g Nov 1] 6,000Y: sixth foal: half-sister to 2 winners by Star Appeal, notably fairly useful Planet Ash (up to 1½m): dam won from 1m to 1½m: modest maiden: sold out of L. Cumani's stable 8,000 gns Newmarket July Sales after fourth outing: no form afterwards: may prove best at around 1m: acts on good to firm ground. *R. T. Phillips*

EMBEZZLER   4 b.g. Emarati (USA) 74 – Double Touch (FR) (Nonoalco (USA) – 131) [1995 54d: 8.2g a6g⁶ 10f⁶ 10m 9.7m⁴ 7g 8.3m 8m⁶ 9.9m⁶ 7.5m 12m 1996 6g Jun 29] disappointing maiden: sold 1,200 gns Newmarket July Sales: stays 1¼m: acts on fibresand and firm ground: tried blinkered, no improvement: one to leave alone. *S. Gollings*

EMBROIDERED   3 br.f. Charmer 123 – Emblazon 91 (Wolver Hollow 126) – [1995 –: a6g a7g 1996 6f 7f 6.9g a10g 7f 8g Oct 2] of no account. *R. M. Flower*

EMBRYONIC (IRE)   4 b.c. Prince Rupert (FR) 121 – Belle Viking (FR) 83 (Riverman (USA) 131) [1995 81: 12.4g* 13g* 13.1g³ 11.9s 1996 14.1g³ 14d² 16g² 14d 16.1m⁴ 15m⁴ 18.7m³ 16.2f² 16.1m² 14.6m 16.2m⁶ 18g Oct 19] leggy colt: fairly useful handicapper: stays well: acts on firm and dead ground: consistent. *R. F. Fisher*

EMEI SHAN   3 br.f. Inca Chief (USA) – Tricata (Electric 126) [1995 –: 5.7m 6m – 7f 8h 6s 1996 7g a6g a8g Nov 22] of little account. *W. G. M. Turner*

EMERGING MARKET   4 b.g. Emarati (USA) 74 – Flitteriss Park 62§ (Beldale 103 Flutter (USA) 130) [1995 94: 7m² 6m* 6g 6m 7m² 7f 7.3m⁶ 7m³ 7g⁴ 8.5s⁵ 7m² 1996 7m⁴ 7m⁴ 7g⁶ 6f* 7m 6m 6m⁶ 7m Oct 4] smallish, lengthy gelding: has a roundish action: useful handicapper: ran as if something amiss third 4-y-o start: 33/1, won 29-runner Wokingham Stakes at Royal Ascot 5 weeks later by ½ length from Prince Babar, quickening to lead 50 yds out: good sixth of 28 to Coastal Bluff in Gold Cup at Ayr penultimate start, best subsequent effort: stays 7f, probably not 8.5f: acts on

*Wokingham Stakes (Handicap), Royal Ascot—the near side have it,
with Emerging Market leading in Prince Babar, Double Bounce and Green Perfume*

firm going, below form only run on a soft surface: finds little in front, and suited by waiting tactics. *J. L. Dunlop*

EMILY-JAYNE   2 b.f. (Apr 1) Absalom 128 – Tearful Reunion (Pas de Seul 133)   43
[1996 5d 7f⁴ 7g Jul 10] 6,500Y: quite good-topped filly: second thoroughbred foal: dam poor maiden: poor form in maiden auction and sellers: will probably stay beyond 7f. *Mrs M. Reveley*

EMILYJILL   2 b.f. (Mar 2) Emarati (USA) 74 – Crackerjill 37 (Sparkler 130)   47
[1996 5d⁵ 5m⁵ 6.1m⁶ 6m² 5f⁴ 6.1m 6m Aug 19] lengthy, angular filly: half-sister to 3-y-o Ameliajill and useful sprinter Arabellajill (both by Aragon) and fair 7f winner Petonellajill (by Petong): dam stayed 1m: modest form, in sellers last 4 starts: trained first 3 runs by J. O'Shea: stays 6f: sold 700 gns Newmarket Autumn Sales. *R. Hannon*

EMILY-MOU (IRE)   4 b.f. Cadeaux Genereux 131 – Sarajill (High Line 125)   74
[1995 75: 8m* 9f² 8.5m² 10g* 9f⁶ 10f* 11.6m² 10m⁴ 10d* 10g⁴ 10.5d 1996 10g 10.8g 8m² 8m 8m⁴ 8g⁵ 8g² 8.3g⁴ Jul 15] leggy, unfurnished filly: fair performer: inconsistent for new stable in 1996: effective at 1m and stays 11.6f: acts on firm and dead ground, ran poorly on soft and fibresand at 2 yrs: usually bandaged: usually a front runner: covered by Deploy. *M. J. Ryan*

EMMAS BREEZE   2 ch.f. (Apr 26) Anshan 119 – Baby Flo 67 (Porto Bello 118)   44
[1996 5.1g⁶ 6g 7f⁵ 5.2f* 5m 6g Aug 1] 1,000Y: ninth foal: half-sister to 5f winner Banham College (by Tower Walk) and 5f (as 2-y-o here) to 1¼m (in France) winner College Wizard (by Neltino): dam sprint plater: won bad seller at Yarmouth in June by 5 lengths: no other form: stays 6f: acts on firm ground: sold 1,800 gns Newmarket Autumn Sales. *C. A. Dwyer*

EMMA'S RISK   2 b.f. (Mar 30) Risk Me (FR) 127 – Lana's Pet 70 (Tina's Pet   44
121) [1996 a5g 6f³ 5g³ a5g a6g Oct 19] 750F, 2,000Y: third reported foal: sister to   a–
3-y-o Hotlips Houlihan, 5f and 7f winner at 2 yrs: dam placed at 5f and 7f at 2 yrs: poor form: should stay beyond 5f: sold out of R. Williams' stable 950 gns Newmarket July Sales after third outing. *R. Harris*

EMNALA (IRE)   4 b.f. Contract Law (USA) 108 – African Light 65§ (Kalaglow   –
132) [1995 –: a12g⁵ 12g 12.5m 12f⁵ 1996 15.4g a12g 16.4v Nov 11] seems no longer of account. *E. A. Wheeler*

EMPERORS WOOD 5 b.g. Then Again 126 – Silver Empress 63 (Octavo – (USA) 115) [1995 NR 1996 a10g 10m 8.3m May 20] angular gelding: third foal: dam, maiden, suited by 7f: soundly beaten in maidens: sold 500 gns Ascot December Sales. *P. Hayward*

EMY COASTING (USA) 3 b.f. El Gran Senor (USA) 136 – Coast Patrol (USA) 78 ? (Cornish Prince) [1995 NR 1996 7d 6m³ 7d 5g² Jun 8] $75,000F: lengthy filly: sixth foal: half-sister to a minor U.S. winner at up to 1m by Groom Dancer: dam useful winner of 11 races in USA at up to 1m: green still, third of 9 in steadily-run minor event at Kempton second start, staying on well having started slowly: no comparable form and sold only 6,500 gns Newmarket Autumn Sales: should stay at least 7f: possibly requires a sound surface. *P. F. I. Cole*

ENAMEL TIGER 3 ch.g. Risk Me (FR) 127 – Dancing Belle 80 (Dance In Time – (CAN)) [1995 –: 6m 1996 7m 7f a7g Jul 27] big, workmanlike gelding: soundly beaten and possibly temperamental: sold 950 gns Doncaster September Sales: sent to Denmark. *K. McAuliffe*

ENAVIUS (IRE) 2 b.c. (Mar 3) Lycius (USA) 124 – Enaya 99 (Caerleon (USA) – 132) [1996 7m 7f Nov 5] IR 20,000Y: first foal: dam 2-y-o 6f winner, later best at 1¼m, half-sister to very smart performer at around 7f/1m Gabr: in rear in late-season maidens: moved poorly to post final start. *M. Bell*

ENCHANTED GUEST (IRE) 3 ch.f. Be My Guest (USA) 126 – Last Blessing 74 73 (Final Straw 127) [1995 NR 1996 7d 6.9m 7g² 6g* 6m⁴ 6m a8.5g Aug 9] angular filly: second foal: half-sister to fair sprint winner Prime Match (by Primo Dominie): dam 7f and 1m winner: fair handicapper: won at Newcastle in May, making all in group of 3 on far side: tailed off last 2 starts and sold (P. Harris to V. Soane) only 3,000 gns Newmarket Autumn Sales: stays 7f: yet to race on extremes of going: moved badly to post on debut, reportedly made noise and lost action next time. *P. W. Harris*

ENCHANTICA 2 ch.f. (Apr 5) Timeless Times (USA) 99 – North Pine (Import 67 d 127) [1996 5g⁴ 5g² 5.1f² 5g³ 5.1m⁴ 5g³ 5m³ 5s³ a5g⁵ a5g² a5g Nov 29] 8,400Y: a48 workmanlike filly: unimpressive mover: half-sister to several winners, including useful (at up to 7f) Echo-Logical (by Belfort) and fairly useful 5f performer Heaven-Liegh-Grey (by Grey Desire): dam poor half-sister to top-class sprinter Lochnager: modest maiden: raced only at around 5f: probably acts on any turf going, not so good on all-weather surfaces: visored (no improvement) ninth start: has carried head high. *J. Berry*

ENCHANTING EVE 2 ch.f. (Feb 20) Risk Me (FR) 127 – Red Sails (Town 61 ? And Country 124) [1996 5d* 5m⁶ 5d 6d⁴ a6g⁴ a6g* 6.1f⁴ a6g a5g⁴ Dec 3] 1,500Y: a67 leggy filly: first foal: dam poor novice hurdler from the family of Bireme and Buoy: successful in maiden auction at Beverley in March and sellers (easily) at Southwell and Wolverhampton in June: stays 6f: well suited by fibresand (yet to race on equitrack), best turf form on dead ground. *C. N. Allen*

ENCORE M'LADY (IRE) 5 b.m. Dancing Dissident (USA) 119 – Diva Encore 62 d 74 (Star Appeal 133) [1995 71: 5.1m 6g 6f 6m 5f⁴ 7g 6g 5m a5g⁴ a6g* 1996 a6g a6g² a74 d a6g 6g 6m* 6g 7.1g* 7m⁵ 7m⁶ 8g 8.5m 8f 7g a7g a7g a7g² a7s⁵ a6g Dec 27] leggy, good-topped mare: only fair handicapper at best nowadays: won at Pontefract in June and Musselburgh (minor event) in July: mostly below form afterwards: stays sharp 7f: acts on fibresand and firm ground, possibly not on a soft surface: occasionally blinkered/visored: ridden more patiently in 1996 than previously: inconsistent. *F. H. Lee*

ENDAXI SAM 3 b.c. St Enodoc – Stos (IRE) (Bluebird (USA) 125) [1995 NR – 1996 8.3g 7f 8.3d 8d Oct 11] small colt: has a round action: first reported foal: dam never ran: of no account. *R. Ingram*

ENDLESS FANTASY 4 b.f. Kalaglow 132 – Headrest (Habitat 134) [1995 36, – a51: a7g⁵ a12g⁴ 10g 11.6m⁵ 10.4f⁵ a16g² a16g⁶ a16g³ a16g 1996 a12g⁶ Jan 25] modest maiden handicapper: unsuited by trip only 4-y-o start: stays 2m: best on all-weather: joined J. Price. *C. A. Cyzer*

ENDOWMENT 4 ch.g. Cadeaux Genereux 131 – Palm Springs (Top Ville 129) – [1995 75: 10.2m* 12g⁶ 10.2h⁶ 11.6m⁴ 11.7h* 1996 a12g 12m 11.9d Sep 27] attractive gelding: fair performer: no form at 4 yrs (trained reappearance only by

313

R. McKellar) for new stables: stays 11.7f: acts on hard ground, well below form only run on soft surface: blinkered fourth 3-y-o to first 4-y-o starts: won maiden hurdle in the autumn: has plenty of ability, but may not always put his best foot forward. *Mrs M. Reveley*

ENERGY MAN 3 b.g. Hadeer 118 – Cataclysmic 78 (Ela-Mana-Mou 132) [1995 66: 7.1m⁴ 8d 7.9m⁶ 1996 10g 8g 7.5m 7m Jul 29] strong gelding: has a short action: modest as a juvenile: no promise for new stable on return. *M. Dods* –

ENGLISH INVADER 5 b.h. Rainbow Quest (USA) 134 – Modica 89 (Persian Bold 123) [1995 96: 14.4m⁵ 11.7m² 11.5g⁴ 13.9m⁴ 1996 14.9d 14s⁶ 11.9g Jul 12] leggy horse: useful performer at best: tailed off in 1996: stays 1¾m: acts on heavy going and good to firm: has won in blinkers, tried only once at 5 yrs: bandaged near-hind/behind at 5 yrs. *R. Akehurst* –

ENLISTED (IRE) 2 b.f. (Apr 16) Sadler's Wells (USA) 132 – Impudent Miss 105 (Persian Bold 123) [1996 a8.5g² Dec 14] 65,000Y: half-sister to several winners, including 7f and 1m winner Good Reference (by Reference Point): dam, Irish 2-y-o 5f winner, half-sister to very smart sprinter Sayyaf: 8/1, beaten a head in 12-runner maiden at Wolverhampton: will improve. *Sir Mark Prescott* 81 p

ENRICHED (IRE) 3 b.f. Generous (IRE) 139 – Embla 121 (Dominion 123) [1995 NR 1996 11d 10m³ 10.4g³ 10s* 11f³ Nov 5] big, good-topped filly: carries condition: sixth foal: closely related to 7f winner Ghost Tree (by Caerleon) and half-sister to French 9f winner (stayed 1½m) Nordic Myth (by Shareef Dancer): dam 6f (Cheveley Park) and 1m winner out of sister to Blue Cashmere: fairly useful performer: won maiden at Newbury in October, leading approaching final 1f: stays 11f: acts on firm and soft ground: consistent: sent to UAE. *J. H. M. Gosden* 82

ENTICE (FR) 2 b.f. (Mar 2) Selkirk (USA) 129 – Loure (USA) 66 (Lyphard (USA) 132) [1996 7m 7d* 8g* Oct 21] lengthy, quite attractive filly: second foal: dam thrice-raced daughter of smart French 10.5f winner Alliance, a half-sister to Blushing Groom: progressive form: won maiden at Salisbury by ½ length from Wasp 93 p

Tote Silver Tankard Stakes, Pontefract—strong-finishing Entice (left) and Symonds Inn

Ranger and listed race at Pontefract (also in October) by a neck from Fahris, running on really strongly both times: will stay 1¼m: has joined Godolphin: will improve further. *B. W. Hills*

ENTREPRENEUR 2 b.c. (Mar 7) Sadler's Wells (USA) 132 – Exclusive Order (USA) 120 (Exclusive Native (USA)) [1996 7m⁴ 7g* 7.6g* Sep 25] 600,000Y: strong, deep-girthed, attractive colt: brother to smart middle-distance performers Dance A Dream (4-y-o) and Sadler's Image and half-brother to several winners here and abroad: dam French 6f to 7f winner who stayed 1m: heavily-backed odds-on chance, won maiden at Kempton in August in good style by 5 lengths from Falak and steadily-run 4-runner minor event at Chester in September readily by 2½ lengths from Kharir: now winter co-favourite for the Derby: will be well suited by middle distances: made a favourable impression all starts (ridden from front at Kempton, held up at Chester) and looks up to holding his own in pattern company. *M. R. Stoute* | 106 p

EN VACANCES (IRE) 4 b.f. Old Vic 136 – Welcome Break (Wollow 132) [1995 79, a66: 8g 10m⁴ 12.1g² 12.1m⁵ 12g a14.8g² a14.8g³ 16d⁴* 15.9d 16d* 1996 18s 14.9d 16s² 16m² 20f 16m* 13.9g 18g² 16g⁶ Nov 1] lengthy, workmanlike filly: fairly useful handicapper: narrowly won at Newbury (goes well there) in August: best effort when neck second of 26 to Inchcailloch in Cesarewitch, staying on bravely to lead inside last, just caught: very much a stayer: acts on good to firm ground and soft (possibly not firm), and on fibresand: not particularly consistent. *A. G. Foster* | 90 a–

EPAULETTE 2 b.f. (Feb 25) Warrshan (USA) 117 – Dame Helene (USA) (Sir Ivor 135) [1996 5d⁵ Apr 3] lengthy filly: first foal: dam, no worthwhile form, half-sister to high-class French middle-distance colt Sarhoob: soundly beaten in early-season median auction maiden at Hamilton: bred to need much further than 5f. *M. R. Channon* | –

EPIC STAND 2 b.g. (Apr 22) Presidium 124 – Surf Bird (Shareef Dancer (USA) 135) [1996 5f⁵ 5.9f⁶ 5m 6g⁶ 7g 8f* Nov 5] 16,000Y: workmanlike gelding: fourth foal: half-brother to 3-y-o Birsay (by Bustino) and 4-y-o 5f (at 2 yrs) to 12.3f winner Break The Rules (by Dominion): dam thrice-raced half-sister to 4 useful animals out of Oaks third Britannia's Rule: gambled-on winner of nursery at Redcar in November: will be well suited by middle distances: best runs on firm ground: usually slowly away: sometimes takes keen hold: has carried head high. *Mrs J. R. Ramsden* | 63

EPONINE 2 ch.f. (Apr 11) Sharpo 132 – Norska 67 (Northfields (USA)) [1996 6d⁵ 6m⁶ 7d⁵ 8.1d³ Sep 28] 6,600Y: well-grown, rather leggy filly: half-sister to 1990 2-y-o 7f winner Neroli (by Nishapour) and 3 winners in Italy: dam staying maiden at 2 yrs, not so good as 3-y-o: progressive form in maidens: likely to stay beyond 1m: acts on dead ground. *M. R. Channon* | 65

EPSILON 2 b.f. (Apr 16) Environment Friend 128 – Girette (USA) (General Assembly (USA)) [1996 6.9m⁶ Aug 20] fifth foal: half-sister to French 5f and 6f winner Gold Heaven (by Tate Gallery) and Italian 7f winner Globo (by Most Welcome): dam French 1¼m winner: never dangerous in maiden at Folkestone: bred to stay beyond 1m: may do better. *C. E. Brittain* | 62

EPWORTH 2 b.f. (Apr 13) Unfuwain (USA) 131 – Positive Attitude 82 (Red Sunset 120) [1996 8g Oct 25] 35,000Y: useful-looking filly: has scope: third living foal: half-sister to 1m seller winner (stayed 1¼m) Guto Nyth Bran (by Bairn): dam suited by 1m: just in need of run and very green when eighth to Calypso Grant in maiden at Doncaster: will do better over middle distances. *A. C. Stewart* | 66 p

EQUAL RIGHTS (IRE) 2 b.c. (Mar 7) Royal Academy (USA) 130 – Lady Liberty (NZ) (Noble Bijou (USA)) [1996 7g² 7m* 7m³ 8g* 8g⁴ Sep 29] tall, quite good-topped colt: had scope: fourth foal: brother to 3-y-o Taking Liberties and half-brother to 2 winners in Australasia, including a graded winner at 2 yrs by Bluebird: dam Australian Grade 1 1¼m winner: successful in maiden at Ayr in July and Futurity Stakes at the Curragh (by 1½ lengths from Recondite, drifting right, pricking ears and idling) in August: in frame in Lanson Champagne Vintage Stakes at Goodwood in between and in Royal Lodge Stakes (stayed on well to finish over 2 lengths fourth to Benny The Dip) at Ascot: looked a stayer: raced only on a sound surface: bought by Godolphin, but died of colic. *P. W. Chapple-Hyam* | 109

EQUERRY 5 b.g. Midyan (USA) 124 – Supreme Kingdom 85 (Take A Reef 127) [1995 77, a63: 7.1d² a8.5g² 7.1g³ 8.3g⁶ 8.5m⁴ 8g³ a9.4g⁴ 8m⁵ 8.5m⁴ a8.5g* 8f* 1996 7m² 8.5m* 8m* a9.4g 7m* 8.1m 7m 8.9g³ 7m 8m* Sep 20] quite attractive | 85 a–

gelding: fairly useful handicapper: won in small fields at Beverley and Newcastle (2 falsely-run races) in the summer: not at very best afterwards, but still won claimer at Ayr in September: effective at 7f, stays 8.5f: acts on firm and good to soft ground (has seemed only modest on all-weather): effective in blinkers at 3 yrs, not tried since. *M. Johnston*

ERIC'S BETT   3 gr.g. Chilibang 120 – Mira Lady (Henbit (USA) 130) [1995 71:   66
5m⁵ 7m⁶ 7.5g⁵ 7m³ 8.1g⁵ 7g 8.3g* 8f⁴ 7m⁵ 1996 9.9g 8g 8f⁶ 8.5m² 8g⁵ 8d Aug 25]
plain gelding: has a roundish action: fair handicapper: should stay beyond 8.5f:
acts on firm ground (well beaten only try on a soft surface): visored twice (no
improvement) at 2 yrs, blinkered twice (best 3-y-o effort on first occasion) in 1996.
F. Murphy

ERLEMO   7 b.g. Mummy's Game 120 – Empress Catherine 73 (Welsh Pageant   35
132) [1995 NR 1996 16m⁵ 16m Aug 7] bad performer: stays 2m: tried blinkered/
visored, no improvement. *W. Clay*

ERLKING (IRE)   6 b.g. Fairy King (USA) – Cape of Storms (Fordham (USA)   44
117) [1995 –: a8g⁶ a9.4g a9.4g a12g 1996 a12g* a13g⁵ Jan 11] one-time fair
performer: poor form to win strongly-run handicap at Lingfield in January, much his
better effort in 1996: should stay beyond 1½m: acts on soft ground, good to firm and
all-weather surfaces: fair hurdler, pulled up lame May 10. *S. Mellor*

EROSION (IRE)   2 b.c. (May 2) Green Desert (USA) 127 – Swept Away 106   78
(Kris 135) [1996 6g⁵ 6g³ 6g² 7g⁴ a7g* a6g⁴ Nov 22] strong, lengthy, angular colt:
sixth foal: closely related to 3-y-o Clash of Swords (by Shaadi): dam, daughter of
smart French miler Costly Wave, won at 9f (Prix Chloe) and 1¼m in France: fair
form: won nursery at Southwell in November: stays 7f: acts on fibresand: sold 7,800
gns Ascot December Sales. *M. Johnston*

ERRANT   4 b.c. Last Tycoon 131 – Wayward Lass (USA) (Hail The Pirates (USA)   56
126) [1995 65: 8g 8f a7g⁴ a8g⁵ 1996 a10g⁴ a10g² a7g a12g⁵ a8g* a10g* a10g⁶ 10m⁶   a66
10d 11.6m 10f³ a10g a8g⁶ a8g³ Dec 13] fair performer on all-weather: won maiden
in February and minor event in March, both at Lingfield: not so good on turf: stays
1¼m: acts on equitrack. *D. J. S. Cosgrove*

ERTLON   6 b.g. Shareef Dancer (USA) 135 – Sharpina (Sharpen Up 127) [1995   83
86, a99: a7g² a8.5g² a7g² a8g³ 8g 7m* 7m 7.3d 7d 7g⁶ 7f⁴ 8m⁵ a9.4g 1996 a8g a7g   a78
7d 7f³ 7m a8g⁵ 7.1m 6.9f³ 7m 7.6m⁴ 7m 7m*ᵈⁱˢ 8g 8m⁵ 7m⁶ a7g⁴ a8g⁵ Dec 13]
close-coupled gelding: just a fair handicapper on balance in 1996: disqualified (after
bursting through final 1f) in 16-runner apprentice contest at Yarmouth in September:
effective at 7f to 8.5f: probably acts on any ground: blinkered (ran creditably) once
as 4-y-o: has been bandaged and had tongue tied down: usually races prominently:
none too consistent for most of 1996. *C. E. Brittain*

ERUPT   3 b.g. Beveled (USA) – Sparklingsovereign 53 (Sparkler 130) [1995   74 d
79: 5m² 6g 5.7f⁴ 5m⁶ 5m⁵ 5g³ 6g 6.1s* 6.1m² 1996 6g⁴ 6f 6v 6m Oct 28] plain,
leggy gelding: fair performer: off course 5 months after (creditable) reappearance,
and soundly beaten: stays 6f: acts on good to firm and soft ground: visored (except
once) since sixth 3-y-o start. *G. B. Balding*

ERZADJAN (IRE)   6 b.g. Kahyasi 130 – Ezana (Ela-Mana-Mou 132) [1995 NR   –
1996 16.4g⁶ Apr 26] useful-looking gelding: third foal: half-brother to useful Irish
1¼m to 1½m winner Ebaziya (by Darshaan): dam, French 11.5f winner, is half-sister
to French Group 3 10.5f winner Demia: won maiden at Wexford, minor event at
Tipperary and handicap at Tralee (rated 93) for J. Oxx at 3 yrs: useful hurdler for
current stable: no danger when sixth of 13 in handicap at Sandown on return to flat,
soon off bit: should stay well. *Mrs M. Reveley*

ESCOBAR (IRE)   3 br.c. Cyrano de Bergerac 120 – Gale Force Seven (Strong   –
Gale 116) [1995 –p: 6m 6g 6m 1996 7d Apr 24] tall colt: no worthwhile form: sold
1,100 gns Doncaster July Sales. *P. Calver*

E SHARP (USA)   2 b.f. (May 1) Diesis 133 – Elvia (USA) (Roberto (USA) 131)   –
[1996 5d⁵ May 25] $120,000Y: sixth foal: half-sister to 3 winners in USA, including
Elkhart (by Gone West), fairly useful 1m winner here at 2 yrs: dam minor winner at 4
yrs in USA, is daughter of Grade 1 9f winner Chain Bracelet: odds on, fifth of 6 in
weak maiden at Haydock in May: not seen out again: joined W. Haggas. *D. R. Loder*

316

ESHTIAAL (USA) 2 b. or br.c. (Apr 21) Riverman (USA) 131 – Lady Cutlass 79
(USA) (Cutlass (USA)) [1996 7d³ 8.2s⁵ Oct 31] tall, rangy, unfurnished colt: has a
quick action: eighth foal: brother to very smart 1m/1¼m performer Lahib and half-
brother to several winners including smart 4-y-o Nwaamis (by Dayjur), 6f winner at
2 yrs: dam, 5f to 7f winner in North America, is half-sister to high-class middle-
distance performer General Holme: very green, carried head awkwardly then
finished strongly under hands and heels when third in Salisbury maiden on debut:
travelled smoothly then found little off bridle, carrying head high, when fifth in
similar event at Nottingham later in month: bred to stay 1m: to winter in Dubai: may
be capable of better. *J. L. Dunlop*

ESKIMO KISS (IRE) 3 b.f. Distinctly North (USA) 115 – Felicitas (Mr 40
Fluorocarbon 126) [1995 –: 6m 6m 5g 7s 7m 1996 10d 12m 11.9g 10.2m³ 10m⁴
10.8m⁶ 10f² 11.9f⁴ 10m 11.5m⁴ 8g⁴ Oct 29] lengthy filly: poor maiden handicapper:
sold (M. Fetherston-Godley to G. Johnson Houghton) 3,200 gns Newmarket Autumn
Sales: effective at 1m, stays 1½m: acts on firm ground: blinkered/visored (except
once) since third 3-y-o start. *M. J. Fetherston-Godley*

ESKIMO NEL (IRE) 5 ch.m. Shy Groom (USA) – North Lady (Northfields 69
(USA)) [1995 34+: 10.3g 1996 9.9d* 10d⁵ 10s* 9.9m² 11.9d* 10g⁶ Oct 29] small
mare: progressed into useful hurdler in 1995/6: has improved with every start on
flat: won handicaps at Beverley, Nottingham and Haydock in the spring: off course 6
months afterwards: stays 11.9f: acts on good to firm and soft ground. *J. L. Spearing*

ESPARTERO (IRE) 4 ch.c. Ballad Rock 122 – Flabella (Ela-Mana-Mou 132) 106
[1995 106: 6g⁴ 5f* 6m⁴ 5m³ 1996 6m³ 5g⁵ 7.1d⁵ 6f 6f⁴ 6m 5f³ 6d⁶ 6.5f⁴ Dec 26]
good-bodied colt: good walker: useful sprinter: good fourth of 16 in listed race at
Newbury in July: went with little zest last 3 starts in Britain: sold out of Sir Mark
Prescott's stable 20,000 gns Newmarket Autumn Sales: stays 6f: acts on firm and
dead ground: visored (out of form) final 4-y-o start: inconsistent. *D. Vienna, USA*

ESPERTO 3 b.g. Risk Me (FR) 127 – Astrid Gilberto 75 (Runnett 125) [1995 57?: 45 +
6m⁶ 5m 7m 1996 10d* Apr 2] good-topped gelding: gelded over winter: didn't have
to be at best to win seller at Nottingham in April, taking fierce hold, awkward round
bend and plenty to do 3f out, then finishing strongly: stays 1¼m: yet to race on
extremes of going: not a straightforward ride. *J. Pearce*

ESQUILINE (USA) 3 ch.f. Gone West (USA) – Ville Eternelle (USA) (Slew O' –
Gold (USA)) [1995 NR 1996 8g 9m 8m⁵ a8.5g a10g Aug 17] $160,000Y: lengthy,
rather unfurnished filly: fluent mover: first foal: dam, 9.5f to 1½m winner in
France, half-sister to Arlington Million winner Mill Native and high-class 1m and 9f
winner French Stress: signs of ability on turf: tailed off on all-weather: sent to UAE.
J. H. M. Gosden

ESSAYEFFSEE 7 b.g. Precocious 126 – Floreal 68 (Formidable (USA) 125) 67
[1995 59: 10m⁵ 9m² 9.2f² 10.1m³ 11.1m³ 9f⁵ 10m* 11m² 10d² 9f⁵ 10f 10f⁵ 1996
10g³ 9.9f* 10m² 10.1m³ 11m⁵ 10f⁴ 10m* 10f⁶ 10f⁴ 9m⁵ 10g 10f Nov 5] strong,
workmanlike gelding: modest handicapper: won at Beverley in June and Pontefract
(amateurs) in August: effective at 9f, and stays 1½m: acts on firm and soft ground:
blinkered all starts at 3 yrs: sometimes bandaged behind: held up: consistent.
Mrs M. Reveley

ESTA MARIA (IRE) 3 b.f. High Estate 127 – Maria Stuarda (Royal And Regal 30
(USA)) [1995 8g³ 1996 a10g⁵ a10g⁶ 12m a12g² a12g² 10f 10f³ 12f⁵ 11d 12.5d* 12d
a13.5g² a13.5g a12g³ Nov 11] 7,800Y: Belgian-trained filly: half-sister to winners in
Italy by Try My Best (7f to 1m) and Salmon Leap (prolific winner from 1m to 11.5f):
dam good winner in Italy, including in Group 2 1m event at 2 yrs: bought out of
H. Cecil's stable 4,200 gns Newmarket September (1995) Sales: ran 3 times in
Britain in 1996 before returning to Belgium: won handicap at Ostend in August: stays
13.5f: acts on firm and good to soft ground, and the all-weather: blinkered since
seventh 3-y-o start. *Paul Smith, Belgium*

ETERNAL HOST (IRE) 2 b.c. (May 31) Be My Guest (USA) 126 – To The –
Limit (Junius (USA) 124) [1996 8s a8.5g a8.5g Dec 14] IR 6,500Y, 13,000 2-y-o:
sturdy colt: brother to a middle-distance winner in Italy and half-brother to another
by Niniski: dam unraced half-sister to dam of Petoski out of sister to Val De Loir and
half-sister to Valoris: well beaten. *R. Hollinshead*

ETERNALLY GRATEFUL   3 b.f. Picea 99 – Carpadia (Icecapade (USA))   –
[1995 –: 6.1d 7g a7g 1996 8f Jun 13] no form. *C. A. Dwyer*

ETHBAAT (USA)   5 b. or br.g. Chief's Crown (USA) – Alchaasibiyeh (USA) 85   75
(Seattle Slew (USA)) [1995 –: a7g⁵ a9g⁶ 7m 8m 1996 8m 8m⁶ a8.5g³ a8.5g* a7g²
a8.5g* a8.5g⁶ a9.4g 10.2f 10m Sep 24] big, rangy gelding: impresses in appearance:
has a free, round action: fair performer nowadays: won 2 claimers at Wolverhampton
in July, second occasion claimed out of W. Muir's stable £10,000: little worthwhile
form in handicaps for new stable: stays 8.5f: acts on fibresand and good to firm
ground: sent to USA. *M. J. Heaton-Ellis*

ETNA   2 b.f. (Feb 21) Salse (USA) 128 – Top Sovereign (High Top 131) [1996 6m⁵   87 p
6m³ Oct 5] quite attractive filly: second living foal: dam unraced daughter of
smart sprinter Sovereign Rose: running-on third of 13 to Elegant Warning in maiden
at Newmarket, better effort: will probably stay 1m: may well improve again.
L. M. Cumani

ETOILE DU NORD   4 b. or br.g. Tragic Role (USA) – Daisy Topper (Top Ville   –
129) [1995 –: 8f 1996 8m 12s a13g a16g Dec 26] sparely-made gelding: soundly
beaten since 2 yrs. *H. J. Collingridge*

ETOILE (FR)   2 gr.f. (Jan 26) Kris 135 – La Luna (USA) (Lyphard (USA) 132)   99 +
[1996 6g 7m³ 7m* 7.3s³ Oct 26] 580,000 francs Y: quite attractive filly: fifth foal:
half-sister to winners in Germany by Slip Anchor and Reference Point: dam, French
9f winner, sister to Bellypha: progressed well: made all in minor event at Newbury in
September: 1¼ lengths third of 9 to Boojum in listed race at same course following
month, setting very strong pace (went too quickly considering conditions) and no
extra close home: races keenly, but will stay 1m: acts on good to firm and soft ground.
P. W. Chapple-Hyam

ETTERBY PARK (USA)   3 b.g. Silver Hawk (USA) 123 – Bonita Francita   79
(CAN) (Devil's Bag (USA)) [1995 –p: 5m 6g⁵ 7f 7d 1996 10g 10m 12f* 12.3m³ 12s*
a12g* a14.8g* 12.3m² 16.2m 11.8m⁶ 12.3s³ 15m* 15.1m² 16.2m 14g³ Oct 18] small,
sturdy gelding: fair handicapper: trained by Mrs J. Ramsden first 2 starts at 3 yrs:
won at Carlisle, Catterick and Wolverhampton (twice) in the summer, and at Ayr in
September: will stay 2m+: acts on firm and soft ground and on fibresand: effective
forcing pace or held up: genuine. *M. Johnston*

EULOGY (FR)   9 b. or br.g. Esprit du Nord (USA) 126 – Louange (Green Dancer   –
(USA) 132) [1995 36: a14g a12g³ 1996 a16g* a16g⁴ a14.8g⁴ a14g* a11g² 16.1s   a68
a16g³ a16g⁴ a11g² Jun 20] good topped gelding: fair performer: won claimers at
Southwell in January and March: stays 2m well: acts on fibresand: tried visored, no
improvement: often apprentice ridden. *K. R. Burke*

EUPHONIC   6 br.g. Elegant Air 119 – Monalda (FR) (Claude) [1995 NR 1996   62
12d⁴ 14.4g³ 16m Sep 16] leggy gelding: rated 71 in 1993: modest handicapper on
return: stays 1¾m (weakened after setting sound gallop over 2m): used to act on firm
going, possibly not on soft: winning hurdler, including in November. *I. A. Balding*

EUPHORIC ILLUSION   5 ch.g. Rainbow Quest (USA) 134 – High And Bright   –
95 (Shirley Heights 130) [1995 NR 1996 16.2g⁵ 8.2m Sep 24] tall, good-topped
gelding: second foal: dam, twice-raced 1¼m winner, closely related to high-class
middle-distance horse Main Reef: in frame in 2 NH Flat races in 1995/6: well beaten
in maidens. *Mrs S. J. Smith*

EUPHYLLIA   4 b.f. Superpower 113 – Anse Chastanet (Cavo Doro 124) [1995   60 d
70, a–: 8m 6m a7g 7g 7m* 7m 7m a8g 1996 7g⁶ 7m⁶ 7d 7f 7m 7f⁴ 7g 7g Nov 2] rather   a–
sparely-made filly: has a round action: only modest form at best in 1996: should stay
1m: acts on firm ground: tried visored, no improvement: inconsistent. *Bob Jones*

EUROBOX BOY   3 ch.g. Savahra Sound 111 – Princess Poquito (Hard Fought   60
125) [1995 69: 6.9s⁴ 7m³ 7g³ 6.9m 1996 a9.4g⁵ 6.9f 8.3m 8g² 8.3m² 8m⁵ 7.1m⁶ 8m*
8g² 8m* 7.9g 7m² 9m Oct 8] just a modest handicapper in 1996: won at Newmarket
(claimer) and Leicester in the summer: should stay beyond 1m: acts on good to firm
ground: effective visored or not. *A. P. Jarvis*

EURO EXPRESS   3 ch.g. Domynsky 110 – Teresa Deevey 50 (Runnett 125)   –
[1995 54: 5d 6m 7.5m 7m⁴ 7m² 7m 7f² 7g 7f 1996 7d 7g 8g Sep 7] smallish, strong,
close-coupled gelding: modest maiden plater: no form in 1996: stays 7f: below best
in blinkers: inconsistent. *T. D. Easterby*

EUROLINK EXCALIBER (USA) 2 b.c. (Feb 17) Red Ransom (USA) – 79
Queen's Warning (USA) (Caveat (USA)) [1996 6m² 7m² 7.5f² 8m 8.5f⁵ Dec 8]
$36,000F, 25,000Y: quite attractive colt: fourth foal: half-brother to minor winners in
USA by Smarten, It's Freezing and Believe It: dam, won twice at up to 7f at 2 yrs in
USA, half-sister to Grade 1 2-y-o 8.5f winner Sir Dancer: fair maiden: left J. Dunlop
after penultimate start: should stay beyond 1m: raced only on top-of-the-ground.
R. Hess, jnr, USA

EUROLINK PROFILE 2 b.f. (Apr 12) Prince Sabo 123 – Taiga 69 (Northfields – p
(USA)) [1996 6m Sep 18] half-sister to several winners here and abroad, including
7f and 1m winner Miss Sharpo (by Sharpo) and fair 4-y-o 9f and 1¼m winner Bulsara
(by Dowsing): dam 1¼m winner (stayed 1½m) out of sister to Park Hill winner
Quay Line: weak 7/2, eased-up eleventh of 12 in Yarmouth maiden, unable to go
with leaders last 2f having been drawn on wide outside: will probably do better.
L. M. Cumani

EUROLINK RASCAL (IRE) 2 b.c. (Mar 15) Lycius (USA) 124 – Villota (Top –
Ville 129) [1996 7m Oct 8] 13,000F: first foal: dam, ran once in Ireland, daughter of
high-class sprinter/miler Vilikaia: soundly beaten in 20-runner claimer at Redcar:
sold 600 gns Newmarket Autumn Sales. *R. Akehurst*

EUROLINK SPARTACUS 2 gr.c. (Feb 21) High Estate 127 – Princess 76
Eurolink (Be My Guest (USA) 126) [1996 6m³ 6m⁵ 6g⁴ 7.3m⁴ 7m* Oct 8] leggy,
unfurnished colt: has a short, round action: first foal: dam no worthwhile form on flat
or over hurdles: fair form: dropped in class, won 20-runner claimer at Redcar in
October (claimed £10,000), running on strongly to lead inside last: will be suited by
further than 7f: to continue career in Sweden. *J. L. Dunlop*

EUROLINK THE REBEL (USA) 4 ch.g. Timeless Native (USA) – Seeing –
Stars (USA) (Unconscious (USA)) [1995 80: 7g⁶ 8m* 8m² 8f 10.3m 10g⁴ 8s
10.3m* 1996 10g 10.3m May 6] lengthy gelding: fairly useful performer: ran poorly
in 1996, reportedly lame after second start: stays 10.3f: acts on good to firm ground,
possibly not on soft: blinkered/visored since final 3-y-o start: joined S. B. Clark.
M. D. Hammond

EUROLINK WINDSONG (IRE) 2 ch.f. (Mar 24) Polish Patriot (USA) 128 – –
Delvecchia (Glint of Gold 128) [1996 6m Jul 30] sturdy filly: first foal: dam German
2-y-o 7f winner: in need of race and very green, eleventh of 15 in maiden at
Goodwood, some late headway: will probably be suited by further than 6f: moved
well to post: sold 3,800 gns Newmarket Autumn Sales. *L. M. Cumani*

EUROPEX 3 bl.g. Dunbeath (USA) 127 – Afrabela 76 (African Sky 124) [1995 –
45: 5m⁶ 6m 5m³ 7h⁴ 1996 7d May 6] workmanlike gelding: poor maiden: soundly
beaten only 3-y-o start: stays 7f. *T. D. Easterby*

EUROQUEST 2 b.g. (Apr 23) Ron's Victory (USA) 129 – Raaya 40 (Be My –
Guest (USA) 126) [1996 6g⁶ Oct 18] 1,000F, 2,100Y: second foal: dam placed twice
at 1m from 3 starts, sister to high-class middle-distance colt Raami: 50/1, always
behind in maiden at Catterick. *D. Nicholls*

EURO SCEPTIC (IRE) 4 ch.g. Classic Secret (USA) 91 – Very Seldom (Rarity 61
129) [1995 49: 10d 7g⁶ 7.5m* 8.1g² 7.5g* 7.5m³ 8f² 7.5g 8f⁶ 7f 8f 1996 8.5m* 8g 9m
8.5m⁴ 9.9f⁴ 10.1m⁴ 8m⁶ 7.5m² 8.5m⁶ 8f² 8g* 7.5f⁴ 7.5g* 7g 8m 8.2g 8.2g Oct 24]
sturdy, close-coupled gelding: poor mover: modest handicapper: won at Beverley
(apprentices) in May and Thirsk (apprentice seller) and Beverley (got up on line for
fourth course win) in August: below form afterwards: stays 1m: acts on firm and dead
ground: normally blinkered, effective without. *T. D. Easterby*

EURO SINGER 4 br.g. Chief Singer 131 – Crystal Gael 79 (Sparkler 130) [1995 –
60: 8.2m 10m² 10g⁶ 10f³ 12f⁵ 14d² 14s⁴ 1996 a13g Nov 26] modest maiden handicapper: won over hurdles in April: no show on all-weather debut: stays 1¾m: acts on
firm and soft ground. *P. R. Webber*

EURO SUPERSTAR (FR) 2 b.g. (Apr 2) Rock City 120 – Douceur (USA) –
(Shadeed (USA) 135) [1996 7.6d 8.1s 7d Oct 28] third foal: half-brother to 4-y-o
1¼m winner It'sthebusiness (by Most Welcome): dam French 9.5f winner, out of
half-sister to Poule d'Essai des Pouliches winner River Lady and high-class middle-
distance performer No Lute: never a factor in maidens: slowly away on debut. *S. Dow*

Stones Bitter Park Hill Stakes, Doncaster—another game display from Eva Luna

EUROTWIST 7 b.g. Viking (USA) – Orange Bowl (General Assembly (USA)) 42
[1995 –: a11g⁶ 11.9m 1996 12.1d* 13d 15.1s Nov 7] small gelding: poor handicapper: won at Hamilton in April: disappointing afterwards: should stay 1¾m: acts
on fibresand, may well need an easy surface on turf: best held up. *S. E. Kettlewell*

EURYNOME (GER) 3 ch.f. Acatenango (GER) 127 – Eidothea (GER) 104
(Teotepec) [1995 NR 1996 10g⁴ 12g* 13d² 15g* 15d Oct 5] eighth foal: sister to 2
winners, notably stayer Epaphos (rated 113), and half-sister to 3 winners (at up to
11f) by Surumu: dam minor winner: won apprentice race at Saint-Cloud in June and
5-runner Prix Berteux at Maisons-Laffitte (led close home to beat Kharizmi a neck)
in July: tailed-off last of 8 to Tarator in Prix de Lutece at Longchamp over 2 months
later: stays 15f: has raced only on good or dead ground. *P. Bary, France*

EVA LUNA (USA) 4 b.f. Alleged (USA) 138 – Media Luna 119§ (Star Appeal 114
133) [1995 66: 11.4m* 11.9m* 14.6m* 16m⁴ 12s³ 12s² Nov 9] tall, quite good-
topped filly: sister to useful French middle-distance stayer Petralona and half-sister
to fair 12.3f and 2m winner Medicosma (by The Minstrel): dam, winner at 1¼m and
second in Oaks, unreliable half-sister to Suni and Honorius: smart performer: won
maiden at Sandown (by 10 lengths) in July, listed race at York (rallying to beat Time
Allowed a head) in August and Stones Bitter Park Hill Stakes at Doncaster (set
good pace, and found plenty for pressure final 3f to beat Time Allowed 1¾ lengths)
in September: placed in St Simon Stakes at Newbury (5¾ lengths behind Salmon
Ladder) and listed race at Doncaster (¾ length behind Medaille Militaire) last 2
starts: should prove better at around 1¾m than 1½m, and should stay 2m (almost
certainly asked to set too strong a pace when tried): acts on good to firm and soft
ground: genuine and consistent: stays in training. *H. R. A. Cecil*

EVAN 'ELP US 4 ch.g. Executive Man 119 – Recent Events (Stanford 121§) 66
[1995 66: 8.3g 7.5g⁵ 8f³ 8.2f⁵ 8.5g a8g⁵ 8.5d⁶ 8m⁴ 7m⁴ a9.4g⁵ 1996 7s² 7m Apr 19]
good-topped, workmanlike gelding: modest handicapper: pulled up last time: stays
1m: acts on firm and soft ground: visored (once) then blinkered since fourth 2-y-o
start. *J. L. Eyre*

EVENING BRIGADIER 5 bl.g. Al Amead 87 – Evening Horizon (Evening –
All) [1995 NR 1996 a9.4g⁶ a7g⁵ 8m Jun 3] smallish, sturdy gelding: seems of little
account. *N. M. Babbage*

EVENING IN PARIS 3 ch.f. Be My Chief (USA) 122 – Photo Call 73 (Chief –
Singer 131) [1995 NR 1996 10.5d a7g⁴ Dec 31] smallish, sturdy filly: first foal: dam,
9f (at 2 yrs) and 11f winner, granddaughter of 1000 Guineas second Photo Flash, a
half-sister to Welsh Pageant: no sign of ability in maidens (trained by J. Hills on
debut). *M. Johnston*

*Flying Five, Leopardstown—a well-deserved first pattern victory for Eveningperformance;
Ailleacht and Catch The Blues try hard to catch her*

EVENINGPERFORMANCE   5 b.m. Night Shift (USA) – Classic Design   121
(Busted 134) [1995 114: 5m 5m² 5g² 5f⁶ 5.1g 5f² 5m* 5d³ 1996 5m⁶ 5f 5m*
5m⁶ 5m² 5m* 5d⁶ Oct 6]
Eveningperformance lost none of that explosive speed as a five-year-
old and in terms of form she touched new heights on her third-last start, caught
only on the line in the Nunthorpe by Pivotal having crucially denied the
favourite Mind Games the lead. She remains in training with good prospects of
winning more races, especially if she can reproduce her York form, which is
fully 7 lb her best. She didn't need to do so to gain a well-deserved first pattern
win, a shade of odds on, in the Flying Five at Leopardstown in September and
she failed to, running respectably nevertheless, when sixth of ten to Kistena in
the Prix de l'Abbaye de Longchamp.
Eveningperformance is speed, speed, and more speed. So seldom is she
led that when it happened in the King George Stakes at Goodwood—and she
failed to make any impression—there was general surprise. She'd started
favourite to improve on her previous year's second to Hever Golf Rose.
However, reportedly she was later found to be coughing. Eveningperformance
blazed the trail in listed or pattern company on all three appearances in the
latest season prior to Goodwood, in the Palace House Stakes at Newmarket
(challenged by Blue Iris), the King's Stand Stakes at Royal Ascot (effectively
becoming a stalking horse for Pivotal on the stand side) and the Sandown Park
Sprint. Her efforts ultimately went unrewarded on the first two occasions but
she managed to last home in front at Sandown. Events at Sandown served to
illustrate the effect the draw can have when racing on the sprint course there.
Six of the twelve runners tacked right across to the far side and secured a
massive advantage. Eveningperformance led her companions in that group a
merry dance until, as she was being eased, Venture Capitalist finished strongly
to run her to half a length.
Eveningperformance began racing as a three-year-old, at six furlongs,
making three successive appearances over the trip; she didn't win, and has been
kept to five furlongs ever since. Six furlongs looked a perfectly reasonable
starting off point on breeding, perhaps even as a preliminary to a step up in
distance rather than down. She was the second foal, first to run, of an unraced
half-sister by Busted to the Guineas winner Tirol and two speedy fillies, Lady
Donna and Relatively Sharp. A younger half-brother to Eveningperformance,

Eveningperformance (b.m. 1991)	Night Shift (USA) (b 1980)	Northern Dancer (b 1961)	Nearctic Natalma
		Ciboulette (b 1961)	Chop Chop Windy Answer
	Classic Design (b 1985)	Busted (b 1963)	Crepello Sans Le Sou
		Alpine Niece (b 1972)	Great Nephew Fragrant Morn

Well Drawn (by Dowsing), has shown promise for the stable over a mile. Eveningperformance is a typical sprinter in appearance, with powerful quarters. Her ground requirements are not entirely clear-cut even at this late stage. That run in the Nunthorpe came on good to firm in a race won in one of the fastest times seen over the course and distance. Connections seemed to think the more testing conditions were against her in the Abbaye, but she had finished a good third of twelve to Hever Golf Rose on almost identical ground (good to soft) in the same race the previous season. She has done nearly all her racing on a sound surface; her one start on soft resulted in an all-the-way victory in fair company at Newbury back in the autumn of 1994. Like many of her type, full of nervous energy, she often gets on edge and sweats. *H. Candy*

EVEN TOP (IRE)   3 br.c. Topanoora 118 – Skevena 57 (Niniski (USA) 125)   127
[1995 110: 6g⁶ 7m* 8.1d² 7g* 8m² 1996 8m² 12m 11.9m⁵ 8.9g* 10g⁴ Oct 19]
    Starting prices of 40/1 and 11/2 indicate that Even Top was expected to finish out with the washing in the Two Thousand Guineas but challenging for victory in the Derby. They proved no guide at all to his performance. It was the Guineas in which Even Top challenged for victory, and he could hardly have challenged more strongly: getting the worst of his three-cornered battle up front at the furlong pole, nothing was running on as well as him at the death and there was a long, tense wait before it was revealed that the short-head winner had been Mark of Esteem. Even Top had finished a head in front of Bijou d'Inde. Why had he started at 40/1? He was making his reappearance, but there was certainly nothing offputting about him in the paddock. Even Top had been impressive enough to look at as a two-year-old and he was even better on Guineas day, clearly having thrived over the winter. There must have been a strong case against him on other grounds, then, and the most persuasive of these was stamina—Even Top would surely have too much of it. A progressive two-year-old campaign, culminating in second placing in the Racing Post Trophy, had shown that he might well have the potential to figure in a classic, but that that classic was much more likely to be a Derby than a Guineas. It seemed obvious from his pedigree, because, although he had already outrun his parentage, it still could not be ignored that his sire had never been tried at less than a mile and a quarter and his dam had gained her sole victory over an extended two miles.
    Even Top's Guineas performance, then, could hardly have contained more promise. In the heat of the moment that afternoon, his trainer reportedly considered an objection to Mark of Esteem on the technicality of Frankie Dettori's premature flying dismount, but having the Derby favourite in his charge must have been a powerful pacifier. The blood pressure probably rose again, however, in the week before Epsom. 'It's Even Top's Turn!' was the front-page headline in the Tuesday's *Racing Post*, but, alas, the turn referred to was his turn to pick up an injury: six days before the race, it was discovered that he had an infection in a cracked near-fore hoof. Even Top did make it to the start, and was sent off second favourite, but the Derby proved a most uncomfortable experience. There will be no need to remind his supporters that this can be a rough race, because Even Top received a right battering and was beaten before the straight. Mark Tompkins has since told us that if it had not been the Derby he would not have thought of running him with the foot injury. For his pains, Even Top was badly struck into behind as well.

It was the Ebor meeting before Even Top was seen out again, the International being passed over for a seemingly easier opportunity in the Great Voltigeur, but he could not get into things having been held up last of six in a steadily-run race. Another try at a mile and a half is on the agenda in 1997—we still do not know whether he stays—but both remaining starts as a three-year-old were at shorter distances. A workmanlike performance at 11/10 on in a listed race at York in September brought victory (over Tamhid and Missile) but finishing about three and three quarter lengths fourth of seven to Bosra Sham in the Champion Stakes was much better form. The Champion also provided the best indicator so far of Even Top's stamina resources as, having set a fair pace and been headed three furlongs out, he was keeping on strongly again at the death. He is well worth another chance at a mile and a half. First engagement in 1997 is scheduled to be the mile-and-a-quarter Dubai World Cup. One cannot say how he will handle the sand in Dubai, and his ground requirements over here are not much clearer as he has never raced on firm or soft ground and did not encounter good to soft as a three-year-old.

			Ahonoora	Lorenzaccio
	Topanoora	(ch 1975)	Helen Nichols
	(b 1987)	Topping Girl	Sea Hawk II
Even Top (IRE)		(br 1972)	Round Eye
(br.c. 1993)		Niniski	Nijinsky
	Skevena	(b 1976)	Virginia Hills
	(b 1983)	Skhiza	Targowice
		(br 1975)	Anticlea

The international search for Even Top's sire Topanoora had a much happier outcome than that for Helissio's dam Helice. The disqualified 1991 Hardwicke winner, Topanoora was exported after covering just eighteen mares

Mr B. Schmidt-Bodner's "Even Top"

in 1994—and brought back again from the Indian state of Haryana early in 1996. He will presumably be a good deal busier in his new role as a Coolmore National Hunt Stallion. There is a jumps racing connection on the other side of Even Top's pedigree as well, because, like such as Alydaress, Elbio, St Jovite and Ragmar, Even Top is a high-class flat performer out of a dam who raced over jumps. His dam Skevena was a modest racehorse who followed up her one victory on the flat (in a handicap at Folkestone as a four-year-old) with three in novice hurdles (one at Newton Abbot, two at Exeter) from ten starts in her one season over the obstacles. IR 7,000 guineas was enough to buy her (in foal to Risk Me) early in 1989, 110,000 guineas when she was presented again for sale in foal to Common Grounds at the latest Newmarket December Sales. Her 1992 filly Kapiti (by The Noble Player) went for 14,000 one day later, having been sent back from Sweden where she registered her first success in the latest season, bringing to a close the hectic round of cashing in which had begun when a sister to Even Top made 11,000 guineas at the Newmarket October Yearling Sales. Even Top should continue to bring in substantial rewards in his own right. He has yet to win a pattern race, but that cannot be long coming and, appearing in another top race as he surely will, it will be no surprise to see him go one better than he did in the Guineas. *M. H. Tompkins*

EVER FRIENDS 4 ch.g. Crever 94 – Cappuccilli 111 (Lorenzaccio 130) [1995 38 –: a7g⁶ a10g a8g 8m a12g⁶ 14.1m⁴ 1996 a12g 11.9f 21.6m 11.9f⁴ 16.2f a12g Sep 7] sparely-made gelding: poor maiden plater: should stay beyond 1½m: yet to race on an easy surface: blinkered (no form) second 4-y-o start: sweating (well beaten) fifth 4-y-o start: sold 600 guineas Newmarket Autumn Sales: sent to Spain. *R. Harris*

EVERGLADES (IRE) 8 b.g. Green Desert (USA) 127 – Glowing With Pride 101 114 (Ile de Bourbon (USA) 133) [1995 105d: 6m² 7.1g³ 6f 7.6m 7f⁴ 7m⁴ 7m⁵ 1996 6m² 6m 7m* 7m 7.3f² 7m Oct 4] sturdy gelding: carries condition and usually takes the eye: useful performer: short-headed Hi Nod in rated stakes at Newbury in June: stays 7.3f: needs a sound surface and acts on firm: usually held up: has run well when sweating: none too consistent nowadays. *R. Charlton*

EVERSET (FR) 8 b.g. Green Desert (USA) 127 – Eversince (USA) (Foolish 58 Pleasure (USA)) [1995 –, a102d: a7g² a7g² a6g* a8g⁵ 1996 a7g a7g³ a8g a7g⁵ a7g⁵ a79 7s a7g³ 8d⁶ 7.1g² 8.1f 7f 6m 7g Oct 30] close-coupled gelding: unimpressive mover: fair form at best on all-weather: only modest on turf in 1996: well below form last 4 starts: effective at 6f and 7f: best form on fibresand, also used to act on equitrack, firm and dead ground: normally blinkered on turf nowadays: inconsistent. *A. Bailey*

EVER SO LYRICAL 6 b.h. Never So Bold 135 – Lyra (Blakeney 126) [1995 – 77d: 8m 8f³ 8s 8.2m 1996 10s 8g 8m 8g 9.7m 8m Jun 10] strong horse: seems very much on the downgrade. *P. W. Harris*

EVEZIO RUFO 4 b.g. Blakeney 126 – Empress Corina 74 (Free State 125) [1995 – 90: 11g a12g 1996 a9.4g 18s 16.2g⁵ 17.1g 18.7g 11.9v 10.3g⁴ 12v Nov 11] neat gelding: no worthwhile form for long time. *N. P. Littmoden*

EVIDENCE IN CHIEF 3 b.f. Be My Chief (USA) 122 – Ominous 91 63 (Dominion 123) [1995 63: 5.2m⁵ 6g⁶ 7g* 7.9g 7.6m 1996 9.7m 10m 12m³ 10m* 12m 12g 12m* 13.6m³ 12d³ Oct 21] quite good-topped filly: fair performer: won claimers at Sandown in July and Newmarket in October: sold 16,000 gns Newmarket Autumn Sales: stays 13.6f: acts on good to firm going, respectable effort only start on a soft surface: visored since fourth 3-y-o start: sent to Saudi Arabia. *D. R. C. Elsworth*

EWAR ARRANGEMENT 2 b.c. (Mar 15) Bold Arrangement 127 – Emily 53 Allan (IRE) (Shirley Heights 130) [1996 6m 7f 5m⁵ 7d a6g⁵ a7s Dec 19] first foal: dam (no worthwhile form) half-sister to smart sprinter Whippet: modest maiden: stays 6f: probably acts on good to firm and fibresand: has been early to post: inconsistent. *C. E. Brittain*

EWAR BOLD 3 b.c. Bold Arrangement 127 – Monaneigue Lady (Julio Mariner 66 d 127) [1995 NR 1996 10g⁵ 11d⁶ 12.1s³ 17.2g⁶ 11.6m⁶ 12g 16m⁶ 10d 10.8f 8g 15d 12s a12g Dec 28] workmanlike colt: third foal: dam well beaten: showed signs of ability in maidens in the spring: left C. Brittain after fifth outing and well beaten afterwards: stays 12.1f: acts on soft ground: tried blinkered, no improvement. *K. O. Cunningham-Brown*

EWAR IMPERIAL 4 b.g. Legend of France (USA) 124 – Monaneigue Lady –
(Julio Mariner 127) [1995 –: 10f⁴ 10m 11.5m⁶ 9.9m 8m 1996 12.5f⁵ a16g Jun 15] no
worthwhile form: blinkered final 4-y-o start: second in maiden hurdle in July, not
seen again. *K. O. Cunningham-Brown*

EWAR SUNRISE 3 ch.f. Shavian 125 – Sunset Reef (Mill Reef (USA) 141) 67
[1995 67: 6d 7g² 7m 1996 7d⁵ 6g 7m³ 6m a7g⁵ 7g² 8.3m 8g 8g³ 8s⁶ 9d* 8s³ 8g⁴ 6s⁵
8v Dec 6] small ex-English filly: fair performer: trained until after fifth 3-y-o start
by C. Brittain and for next 3 outings by K. Cunningham-Brown: won maiden at
Saint-Malo in September: stays 9f: acts on soft ground. *S. Wattel, France*

EXACTLY (IRE) 3 b.f. Taufan (USA) 119 – Not Mistaken (USA) (Mill Reef 73
(USA) 141) [1995 71: a5g⁴ 5m 5g³ 5m 7.9g⁴ 7.5d 10m⁴ 1996 a11g 10.3d⁶ 10g²
14.6m⁵ 12.3g* 12m⁶ 12.3m 12.4f* 12.3g⁴ 13.9g Sep 4] leggy filly: fair handicapper:
dictated pace when winning at Ripon in May and Newcastle (minor event) in August:
stays 12.4f, respectable effort at 13.9f: acts on firm ground. *J. L. Eyre*

EXALTED (IRE) 3 b.g. High Estate 127 – Heavenward (USA) (Conquistador 86
Cielo (USA)) [1995 88: 7m* 7m³ 8m³ 10m⁶ 1996 12d 10m 10.5d² 10.4m⁵ 12.3m⁵
10m³ 10m a9.4g 11.9v 10.3g Oct 25] good-topped, attractive gelding: carries condition: usually races well: has round action: fairly useful handicapper: sold 30,000 gns
Newmarket Autumn Sales: should be at least as effective at 1½m as 1¼m: acts on
good to firm ground and dead, below form on fibresand and heavy going: none too
consistent: joined W. Jenks, and gelded. *Sir Mark Prescott*

EXCELLED (IRE) 7 gr.m. Treasure Kay 114 – Excelling Miss (USA) (Exceller 33
(USA) 129) [1995 40: 8.3g 11.6m⁶ 11.6m² 11.7h* 14.4m 14d a12g 1996 10m Jun 24]
poor performer: stays 1½m: acts on hard ground: tried blinkered, no improvement.
C. J. Drewe

EXCLUSION 7 ch.g. Ballad Rock 122 – Great Exception 84 (Grundy 137) [1995 41
43: a8g⁵ a10g⁶ a11g 12m² 14.1m⁵ 12.1m⁴ 10f³ 12m⁶ 12.1f* 12m 1996 a12g³ a11g
a11g⁶ a11g⁶ 11.1m⁴ Aug 8] strong gelding: poor handicapper: stays 1½m, may get
1¾m: acts on firm and soft going and on fibresand: visored (out of form) once: races
prominently: unreliable jumper. *J. Hetherton*

EXCLUSIVE ASSEMBLY 4 ch.g. Weldnaas (USA) 112 – Pretty Pollyanna –
(General Assembly (USA)) [1995 48, a60: a7g a6g³ a7g* a7g a8.5g⁶ 8.1m 6m³ 7f
a7g² a8g a7g³ a7g⁵ a8g⁵ 1996 a8g a8.5g May 11] modest performer: soundly beaten
in 1996: stays 1m: best form on all-weather surfaces: acts on good to firm ground,
possibly not on soft. *A. P. James*

EXECUTIVE DESIGN 4 b.g. Unfuwain (USA) 131 – Seven Seas (FR) 76 –
(Riverman (USA) 131) [1995 84: 12.3d* 12.5m² 12g⁵ 14m² 14g⁴ 11.9m⁶ 14.1g²
1996 14d 16.5s Nov 9] sturdy gelding: fairly useful handicapper at best: well beaten
both starts (6 months apart) in 1996: stays 1¾m well: acts on good to firm and dead
ground: useful winning (including in November) hurdler. *Mrs M. Reveley*

EXECUTIVE OFFICER 3 b.g. Be My Chief (USA) 122 – Caro's Niece (USA) –
86 (Caro 133) [1995 NR 1996 10m 14m 10s a8g Nov 4] tall gelding: fourth foal:
half-brother to fairly useful winners Carelaman (stayed 1½m, by Ela-Mana-Mou)
and 5-y-o Cretan Gift (sprinter, by Cadeaux Genereux): dam lightly-raced 1m winner
from good family: no form. *R. M. Flower*

EXEMPTION 5 ch.g. Ballad Rock 122 – Great Exception 84 (Grundy 137) [1995 –
73: 11.8d⁶ 12g 12.1g² 10.2m* 10.2m² 10m 12d⁵ 10.5s³ 10d 1996 10g 10m 12g 12m
Sep 18] strong, lengthy gelding: fair handicapper: no worthwhile form in 1996: stays
1½m: acts on firm and soft going: blinkered (out of form) final 5-y-o start. *H. Candy*

EXHIBIT AIR (IRE) 6 b.m. Exhibitioner 111 – Airy Queen (USA) (Sadair) –
[1995 67, a64: 12m⁴ 11.9f² 11.9f³ 12g 11.9g a12g⁵ a16g⁴ a13g² 1996 12m 11.9f⁶
May 9] good-quartered mare: one-time fair handicapper: no worthwhile form in
1996: stays 2m: acts on firm and dead ground and on equitrack (below form on
fibresand): effective visored/blinkered or not: inconsistent. *R. Akehurst*

EXIT TO RIO (CAN) 2 ch.c. (Mar 2) Mining (USA) – Miami Vacation (USA) 88
(Far North (CAN) 120) [1996 5m³ 5d* 6m⁴ 6g⁵ 5m⁴ 6m⁴ 7d⁴ 8m Sep 12] $65,000Y:
strong, good-topped colt: has scope: second foal: dam won 3 times at up to 9f

(including minor stakes) at 2 yrs in USA: won maiden at Carlisle in May: fairly useful form when staying-on fourth in nurseries: sold 42,000 gns Newmarket Autumn Sales: should be suited by further than 7f: visored fourth outing (seemed reluctant early): usually slowly away: sometimes runs in snatches, and not an easy ride: sent to USA. *Mrs J. R. Ramsden*

EXPANSIVE RUNNER (USA) 4 b.c. Explodent (USA) – Scissors (USA) 50 (Blade (USA)) [1995 –: 10.2m⁶ 11.9d 1996 a12g⁴ 13.8g Oct 19] form since debut only when fourth in handicap at Wolverhampton. *P. W. Harris*

EXPECTATION (IRE) 2 b.f. (Apr 25) Night Shift (USA) – Phantom Row 37 59 (Adonijah 126) [1996 6d⁴ 5.2f 5m 6.1s⁵ 5.2g⁶ Oct 30] IR 20,000Y: leggy, good-topped filly: fourth foal: half-sister to 5-y-o 1¼m winner Kentavrus Way (by Thatching): dam lightly-raced half-sister to smart 1987 2-y-o 5f winner Colmore Row: modest maiden: should stay 7f: best efforts on a soft surface. *P. R. Webber*

EXPEDITIOUS WAY (GR) 3 br.c. Wadood (USA) 97 – Maid of Milan 78 – (Home Guard (USA) 129) [1995 a5g² a5g* 1996 a10g a10g⁵ 10g 8g 8m May 16] medium-sized, well-made Greek-bred colt: dam won over 9f and stayed 1½m: won maiden in Greece in spring at 2 yrs: little form in Britain: returned to Greece. *R. Charlton*

EXPENSIVE TASTE 3 b.f. Cadeaux Genereux 131 – Um Lardaff (Mill Reef 91 (USA) 141) [1995 78: 6.9f* 8.1d⁶ 7d⁵ 1996 7m 10m* 10.4m⁴ 10.1m⁴ 10.3d⁴ Aug 30] tall, rather leggy filly: fairly useful handicapper: won at Lingfield in June, doing well to come from rear: unimpressive in coat and failed to repeat that form next 2 starts: looked well and back to best form at Chester (did not look too hearty under pressure, flashing tail): better suited by around 1¼m than shorter: acts on firm and dead going: has a rather high head carriage: sold 31,000 gns Newmarket December Sales. *M. R. Stoute*

EXPLOSIVE POWER 5 br.h. Prince Sabo 123 – Erwarton Seabreeze (Dun- 64 beath (USA) 127) [1995 –, a57: a10g² 1996 a10g* a10g³ a11g³ a9.4g* 9.7s 8f a77 10g 8.2g⁶ 10.1m² a8.5g⁴ a12g⁵ a9.4g Dec 14] workmanlike horse: fair handicapper on all-weather: won at Lingfield in January and Wolverhampton (made all, easily best effort) in March: inconsistent and only modest at best on turf: stays 1¼m: acts on the all-weather: blinkered (below form) sixth 3-y-o start: sometimes troublesome in preliminaries. *G. C. Bravery*

EXPRESS GIFT 7 br.g. Bay Express 132 – Annes Gift (Ballymoss 136) [1995 – 64: 8d 12m³ 14.6m⁶ 1996 8s Nov 9] angular gelding: useful hurdler: just a modest handicapper on the flat nowadays: never dangerous over inadequate trip on belated return: will eventually show himself effective at 1¾m+: acts on good to firm ground and goes well with plenty of give. *Mrs M. Reveley*

EXPRESS GIRL 2 b.f. (May 30) Sylvan Express 117 – Oh My Oh My (Balla- 75 cashtal (CAN)) [1996 5d* 5d* 5m⁵ 5m⁵ 6.5m 5g³ 5d Nov 8] 500Y: fourth live foal: half-sister to 3-y-o 5f and (at 2 yrs) 6f winner Precious Girl (by Precious Metal): dam poor sprint plater: fair performer: made most to win median auction maiden at Hamilton in April and minor event at Ayr in May: best form at 5f on an easy surface: races prominently. *D. Moffatt*

EXPRESS ROUTING 4 b.c. Aragon 118 – San Marguerite 80 (Blakeney 126) – [1995 62p: 5d 7f⁴ 5g⁶ 1996 7.3s 7g⁶ 10m a9.4g 8g Oct 2] compact colt: carries condi-tion: modest maiden: well below form for new stable (left J. Akehurst after fourth start) in 1996: may prove best at around 1m: blinkered (tailed off on all-weather) fourth 4-y-o start. *V. Soane*

EXTRA HOUR (IRE) 3 b.g. Cyrano de Bergerac 120 – Renzola (Dragonara – Palace (USA) 115) [1995 68: 5.2m 6m² 6m³ 5.2d 5.7m⁴ 6m 1996 6f 6f⁴ 7m 6.1m a6g 8.2f a7g⁵ Dec 30] compact gelding: fair maiden as juvenile: well beaten in 1996: stays 6f: acts on good to firm ground: tried blinkered, no improvement. *W. R. Muir*

EXTREMELY FRIENDLY 3 ch.g. Generous (IRE) 139 – Water Woo (USA) – 102 (Tom Rolfe) [1995 60: 7f 6m a8g⁶ 1996 14m Sep 19] modest as a juvenile: sold 1,100 gns Newmarket July (1996) Sales: tailed off for new stable. *Bob Jones*

EYE SHADOW 2 ch.f. (Apr 9) Mujtahid (USA) 118 – Piney River 63 (Pharly 83 (FR) 130) [1996 5f⁵ 5.1m* 6g³ 6g⁴ 6m 7m⁶ 6m⁶ 6f 7g⁶ Oct 18] 8,000F, 2,500Y: sturdy, good-quartered filly: fourth foal: half-sister to 1m winner Gushing (by Formidable): dam maiden, raced only at 6f/7f, out of half-sister to very smart 1973 2-y-o Splashing, dam of Bassenthwaite: won maiden auction at Nottingham in June: good third of 6, making most, to Moonlight Paradise in listed race at Newmarket later same month: mostly outclassed afterwards: sold 15,000 gns Newmarket Autumn Sales: best form at up to 6f: raced only on a sound surface. *B. J. Meehan*

EZEKIEL 5 ch.g. Be My Guest (USA) 126 – Judeah 69 (Great Nephew 126) – [1995 –: a10g 1996 a5g a6g a6g Feb 26] of little account nowadays. *T. T. Clement*

F

FAATEQ 3 b.c. Caerleon (USA) 132 – Treble (USA) 118 (Riverman (USA) 131) 90 [1995 73: 7.1g³ 7.5m³ 8.1s⁴ 1996 9.9m* 12.4g² 10f* 12g⁵ Jul 3] good-bodied colt: good mover: fairly useful handicapper: won at Beverley in April and Redcar (£13,900 contest) in June: well below form final start and sold 17,500 gns Newmarket Autumn Sales: stays 12.4f: acts on firm going: awkward at stalls first 3 starts at 3 yrs: idles in front: clearly something of a character. *J. L. Dunlop*

FABILLION 4 ch.c. Deploy 131 – Kai (Kalamoun 129) [1995 66: a12g⁶ 10.2f⁵ 75 10g 10.8m⁶ 10d 10g 12.1s² 14.1m² 15.1s⁶ 1996 11.8d⁵ 14.1g* 13s⁵ 14g² 14d 15.9m⁶ Jul 13] workmanlike colt: fair handicapper: won strongly-run event at Nottingham in April: should prove suited by test of stamina: acts on good to firm ground and soft. *C. A. Smith*

FABLE 2 ch.f. (Mar 15) Absalom 128 – Fiction 59 (Dominion 123) [1996 7m 7m – Sep 25] 3,600Y: first foal: dam 2-y-o 5f winner out of Galtres Stakes winner Sans Blague: behind in maidens at Lingfield and Goodwood. *J. A. R. Toller*

FABLED LIGHT (IRE) 2 b.c. (Feb 26) Alzao (USA) 117 – Fabled Lifestyle 60 p (Kings Lake (USA) 133) [1996 7f⁶ 7g Oct 30] 21,000F, IR 100,000Y: fourth foal: brother to useful 7.5f and 10.4f winner Old Hickory and half-brother to a winner in Germany at up to 1½m by Law Society: dam, Irish 9f winner, is half-sister to Lyphard's Wish (by Lyphard): better effort in maidens when 7¼ lengths sixth of 10 to Attitude at Leicester: probably capable of improvement. *G. Wragg*

FABULOUS MTOTO 6 b.h. Mtoto 134 – El Fabulous (FR) 111 (Fabulous Dan- 58 cer (USA) 124) [1995 53d: a10g³ a12g* a12g⁵ a9g a9g a10g 12.1d 16m 14.1m a12g⁶ a– 1996 a16g 17.2f⁶ 14.9g⁴ 11.6m* 11.4m² 12m⁴ 10.2f⁴ 12m* 11.6g⁴ 11.9f³ 11.7m 11.5m⁶ 10f a12g Dec 28] strong, rangy horse: modest handicapper: won at Windsor in June and at Pontefract in July: stays 1½m: acts on firm going. *M. S. Saunders*

FACE IT 2 b.f. (Mar 18) Interrex (CAN) – Facetious 88 (Malicious) [1996 5s⁶ 5d³ 43 5d³ a5g⁵ 6m a6g 5s⁵ a6g⁵ Nov 30] 850Y: lengthy filly: half-sister to several winners, a37 including Ryewater Dream (11.7f, by Touching Wood) and 1989 2-y-o Facility Letter (6f, by Superlative): dam disappointing maiden: poor maiden plater: blinkered (no improvement) sixth start: inconsistent: sold 500 gns Ascot December Sales. *W. G. M. Turner*

FACE THE FUTURE 7 ch.g. Ahonoora 122 – Chiltern Red (Red God 128§) 57 [1995 66: 6g 6m⁵ 6g 6g 6g³ 6f⁵ 6m⁵ 6m³ 6g 6g 6d a7g 1996 6g³ 6.1g⁶ 6m⁵ 5g 6m Sep 19] stocky gelding: has a quick action: only a modest handicapper at best in 1996, leaving S. Dow after second start: stays 7f: acts on firm and dead ground, below form on 3 occasions on very soft: blinkered (well beaten) once as 6-y-o: sometimes hangs left: needs treating with caution. *V. Soane*

FAEZ 6 b.g. Mtoto 134 – Ghanimah 98 (Caerleon (USA) 132) [1995 –: a6g⁴ a7g 54 a8g⁵ 7g a7g 1996 a8g³ a8.5g² a8g a6g Mar 6] moderate performer: stayed 8.5f: acted on soft going and fibresand: tried blinkered: broke down final start: dead. *R. Simpson*

FAG END (IRE) 3 b.f. Treasure Kay 114 – Gauloise Bleue (USA) (Lyphard's – Wish (FR) 124) [1995 88: 6m⁵ 6m* 6g³ 7m* 7m² 7m³ 6.5m 7g³ 1996 8s 10s 8.5m Jun 7] leggy filly: unimpressive mover: fairly useful as a juvenile when genuine and consistent: well beaten in pattern/listed company in 1996: should stay 1m: acts on good to firm ground. *M. H. Tompkins*

Volvo Truck Finance Globetrotter Stakes (Handicap), Goodwood—Fahim comes wide and late

FAHAL (USA)   4 b.c. Silver Hawk (USA) 123 – By Land By Sea (USA) (Sauce   107
Boat (USA)) [1995 118: 10m³ 12f⁴ 11.9m³ 10.5f* 10g² 10m⁶ 1996 10s⁴ 10f⁶ 10m⁵
11.6d⁴ Aug 24] strong, rangy colt: unimpressive walker: smart performer at 3 yrs:
only useful at 4 yrs, finding little in listed race at Goodwood, Prince of Wales's Stakes
at Royal Ascot, Group 3 event at Ayr (blinkered) and minor event at Windsor: stays
1½m: acts on firm and dead ground: needs treating with caution: sent to Dubai.
D. Morley

FAHIM   3 b.c. Green Desert (USA) 127 – Mahrah (USA) 89 (Vaguely Noble 140)   110
[1995 74P: 7g 1996 8.5f* 8m* 10m* 10.4m² 10m³ 8h⁵ a10g³ Dec 27] sturdy,
attractive colt: has scope: smart performer: won maiden at Beverley, handicap at
Newmarket and 14-runner £34,000 handicap at Goodwood (by ¾ length from
Murheb, meeting plenty of trouble in running) in the summer: best form when
½-length second of 16 to Amrak Ajeeb in rated stakes at York in August: trained first
5 starts by A. Stewart: better at 1¼m than shorter: raced only on top-of-the-ground in
1996. *K. P. McLaughlin, UAE*

FAHRIS (IRE)   2 ch.c. (Mar 27) Generous (IRE) 139 – Janbiya (IRE) 89 (Kris   97 p
135) [1996 7f* 8g² Oct 21] good-topped colt: has scope: second foal: half-brother to
maiden 3-y-o handicapper A-Aasem (fair at up to 1¼m, by Polish Precedent): dam,
winner at 7f (at 2 yrs) and 1¼m, sister to Irish 2000 Guineas winner Flash of Steel:
5/2, won steadily-run maiden at Salisbury on debut: neck second of 7 to Entice
in listed race at Pontefract around 2 months later: will stay beyond 1m: joined
B. Hanbury: can improve again. *H. Thomson Jones*

FAHS (USA)   4 b. or br.g. Riverman (USA) 131 – Tanwi 101 (Vision (USA)) [1995   73
8v 10s³ 10m³ 12g* 11m 1996 12m⁴ 12.3g³ 13.3s⁶ 10m³ 10m² 10m 10f² 10m 10m
10.3m⁶ 10m³ Sep 21] strong, good sort: impresses in appearance: first foal: dam,
Irish 5f to 1m winner, out of half-sister to dam of Flame of Tara, dam of Salsabil:
ex-Irish performer: trained at 3 yrs by K. Prendergast, winning maiden at Tramore:
fair handicapper here: effective at 1¼m to 1½m: acts on firm and soft ground: tends
to sweat: usually a front runner. *R. Akehurst*

FAILED TO HIT   3 b.g. Warrshan (USA) 117 – Missed Again 84 (High Top 131)   70
[1995 NR 1996 5g² a9.4g⁴ 6m* 10.5s 8m a7g⁶ Dec 28] 37,000Y: strong, good-bodied
colt: first foal: dam, 1¼m winner, daughter of Oaks third, temperamental Out of
Shot: won maiden at Folkestone in August, never going especially well but staying
on to lead near line: no comparable form: sold out of Sir Mark Prescott's stable 7,500
gns Newmarket Autumn Sales before final outing: should be well suited by further
than 6f. *N. P. Littmoden*

FAILTE RO   4 bl.f. Macmillion 110 – Safe Passage (Charlottown 127) [1995 –:   –
10g 8.2m 12m 1996 a8g Feb 19] well beaten since 2 yrs: sold 1,350 gns Doncaster
March Sales. *J. E. Banks*

Hamdan Al Maktoum's "Fahim"

FAIR ATTRACTION 4 ch.g. Charmer 123 – Fairfields 73 (Sharpen Up 127) – [1995 –: 6g 8m 10.1m⁵ 1996 a12g Jan 25] soundly beaten since 2 yrs. *J. A. R. Toller*

FAIRELAINE 4 b.f. Zalazl (USA) 120 – Blue And White (Busted 134) [1995 60: 54 d a8g³ 7d a9.4g 7f² 7.3g 10.2m⁴ 10g 8f⁴ 8.2m³ 8f⁴ 8.3m 10d⁵ 7s² 8g⁴ 1996 a7g⁶ 7f⁵ 8.3m 10m⁶ 8f Sep 5] smallish filly: disappointing maiden handicapper: trained until after 4-y-o reappearance by A. Jarvis: probably stays 10.2f: acts on firm ground, soft and equitrack: visored (below best) eleventh 3-y-o start: inconsistent. *K. C. Bailey*

FAIR ELLA (IRE) 4 ch.f. Simply Great (FR) 122 – Dance Or Burst (Try My – Best (USA) 130) [1995 36: a7g⁴ a10g⁵ a12g 12m⁵ 8f⁶ 1996 a10g Dec 20] poor maiden: well beaten only outing at 4 yrs: stays 1¼m: acts on equitrack: tried blinkered/visored, running well only on first occasion. *G. L. Moore*

FAIREY FIREFLY 5 b.m. Hallgate 127 – Tremellick 87 (Mummy's Pet 125) 64 d [1995 55: a6g a6g² a6g a6g a6g⁵ 1996 6g* 6g a6g a6g Mar 1] modest handicapper: returned to form to win at Southwell in January: failed by long way to repeat it: stays 6f: acts on good to firm and dead ground and on fibresand: covered by Forzando. *M. J. Camacho*

FAIR LADY (BEL) 3 b.f. Bacalao (USA) – Bianca Girl (McIndoe 97) [1995 NR – 1996 7f 10.3g a7g Nov 7] small filly: sister to 6-y-o Bianca's Son, 7f winner in Belgium: dam, well held only start in Britain, multiple winner in Belgium: well beaten. *J. M. Plasschaert, Belgium*

FAIRLY SURE (IRE) 3 b.f. Red Sunset 120 – Mirabiliary (USA) 74 (Crow (FR) 50 134) [1995 46: 6.1m 6m a6g 1996 9f⁴ 8.5m⁴ 8f⁴ 7.6m* 8m⁵ 7m 7m 7g Oct 25] modest handicapper: won at Lingfield (apprentices) in August: failed to repeat the form, twice unfavourably drawn: best form at around 7f/1m: has raced only on top-of-the-ground when on turf. *N. E. Berry*

FAIR RELATION 2 b.f. (Apr 28) Distant Relative 128 – Gold Flair 93 (Tap On – Wood 130) [1996 7g 7f 10f⁶ Oct 14] good-topped filly: fourth foal: half-sister to fair

3-y-o maiden Milton (by Groom Dancer) and 1993 2-y-o 7f winner Duball Remy (by Roi Danzig): dam, maiden who stayed 1½m, sister to very smart middle-distance colt Nisnas: little form, including in selling company: sold 900 gns Doncaster November Sales: sent to Sweden. *P. F. I. Cole*

FAIRY HIGHLANDS (IRE) 3 b.f. Fairy King (USA) – Breyani 101 (Commanche Run 133) [1995 –: 6g 1996 a8.5g² a8g³ a7g 5.9f⁴ 8.1f³ 8.1g² 10m 12g⁴ 11.9m 12g 10.1m Oct 23] sturdy filly: modest maiden: sold out of S. C. Williams' stable 10,000 gns Newmarket July Sales after sixth 3-y-o start: shapes as if stays 1½m: acts on firm ground and fibresand: inconsistent. *J. S. Haldane*
55
a64

FAIRY KNIGHT 4 b.c. Fairy King (USA) – Vestal Flame 45 (Habitat 134) [1995 82: 8m 10g* 10m² 11.4m² 12f 10m⁴ 10m 10d 8.2m 10f* 12m² a12g 1996 10.3d 10.8g⁶ 10m 10.2f 12g 7f 9f⁴ 10g⁴ 12g² 12m 10m⁶ 12d* 10g* 12v⁴ Nov 11] sturdy colt: has a round action: fair handicapper: beat big fields at Ascot (amateurs) and Leicester (weaving through and quickening well) in October: stays 1½m: acts on firm and dead ground, well beaten on fibresand and bit below best on heavy: tried blinkered/visored, no improvement: sometimes bandaged behind: best held up. *R. Hannon*
77

FAIRY PRINCE (IRE) 3 b.g. Fairy King (USA) – Danger Ahead (Mill Reef (USA) 141) [1995 –: 5m 5.1f⁵ 6m 1996 6.1d 5.1g 5.9f³ 5.9f* 5m² 6m⁴ 5.1m⁶ 5.9f² 6m³ Aug 16] sturdy gelding: modest handicapper: won at Carlisle in June, making virtually all: stays 6f: has raced almost exclusively on top-of-the-ground so far: consistent. *Mrs A. L. M. King*
65

FAIRY RING (IRE) 2 b.f. (May 15) Fairy King (USA) – Emmuska (USA) 68 (Roberto (USA) 131) [1996 6m 6g² Sep 29] IR 2,500F, 11,000 2-y-o: half-sister to winners in Spain by Hello Gorgeous and Beldale Flutter: dam, suited by 1½m, is daughter of May Hill and Galtres Stakes winner Tartan Pimpernel: much better effort when second to Yorkie George in maiden at Hamilton, restrained racing keenly in rear then keeping on well: will stay beyond 6f: will improve again. *R. M. Whitaker*
69 p

FAIRY WIND (IRE) 4 b.f. Fairy King (USA) – Decadence (Vaigly Great 127) [1995 95: 5.1g⁵ 6m 5m* 6.1m⁴ 5g* 5m⁵ 6g⁶ 5f⁴ 5m* 6g⁵ 5m⁵ 5m* 1996 5m* 5g⁶ 5m⁶ Jun 1] leggy, lengthy filly: in foal to Arazi: useful handicapper: better than ever to win £16,300 contest at York in May, leading on bit over 2f out, idling near finish: far from disgraced in Temple Stakes at Sandown but somewhat disappointing (5 days later) in listed race at Kempton: best at 5f: has raced mainly on a sound surface: usually bandaged: has run well when sweating. *N. A. Callaghan*
98

FAIRYWINGS 3 b.f. Kris 135 – Fairy Flax (IRE) 97 (Dancing Brave (USA) 140) [1995 61p: 6g 7f⁶ 1996 8g 7m² 9.9m* 10m² 9.9f* 10.1m⁵ 8m 9.9f³ 9.9m³ 9.9f* 8m² 10m³ 9m⁶ 12g Oct 26] workmanlike filly with scope: has fluent, round action: fairly useful handicapper: won at Beverley in May, June (idled) and August: good sixth of 38 in the Cambridgeshire penultimate start: effective at 1m to 1¼m, shaped like a non-stayer over 1½m: has raced predominantly on top-of-the-ground (acts on firm): has run well when sweating: usually held up, and seems ideally suited by strongly-run race. *Mrs J. R. Ramsden*
85

FAITH ALONE 3 b.f. Safawan 118 – Strapless 84 (Bustino 136) [1995 –, a69: 7f⁶ 7m a7g² a7g* 1996 6m 6m* 6f 6g a7g a8g Nov 26] workmanlike filly: fair handicapper: won at Newmarket in June, always well there: no comparable form at 3 yrs: stays 7f: acts on equitrack and on good to firm ground. *C. F. Wall*
67

FAKIH (USA) 4 b.c. Zilzal (USA) 137 – Barakat 93 (Bustino 136) [1995 79p: 7f* 1996 8m⁵ 10g 8g Jul 3] good-topped colt: fair form at best: off course nearly a year, shaped well when fifth of 31 in handicap at Ascot: no form afterwards: best form at up to 1m, should stay further (dam a stayer), though pulled hard at 1¼m: sometimes taken alone to post. *A. C. Stewart*
77

FALAK (USA) 2 b.c. (Feb 2) Diesis 133 – Tafrah (IRE) 71 (Sadler's Wells (USA) 132) [1996 7g² 7m³ Oct 4] well-made colt: has scope: has a powerful, round action: first foal: dam 1¼m winner, closely related to smart 6f to 1m performer Aviance (later the dam of Chimes of Freedom and grandam of Spinning World) from the family of El Gran Senor: useful performer: made virtually all to win minor event at Kempton by a head from Captain Collins: good third to Grapeshot in listed race at Newmarket on final outing: will stay 1m: strong-running type. *Major W. R. Hern*
100

FALCON RIDGE 2 ch.g. (Apr 3) Seven Hearts 98 – Glen Kella Manx 97 –
(Tickled Pink 114) [1996 5v Nov 11] fourth reported foal: half-brother to 1992 2-y-o
6f seller winner Pat Poindestres (by Interrex): dam 5f and 6f winner, stayed 7f: 33/1,
soundly beaten in minor event at Folkestone. *J. C. Fox*

FALCON'S FLAME (USA) 3 b. or br.g. Hawkster (USA) – Staunch Flame 60
(USA) (Bold Forbes (USA)) [1995 NR 1996 a8g⁴ 6s 7d 8.1g⁴ 11m 12m 8.2m 9.9m
8.5m* 7m⁶ 8m² 8.1m² 10.5m 8.5m 8m Oct 7] $48,000Y: good-topped gelding:
second foal: dam U.S. winner at up to 1m: modest handicapper: won at Beverley
(apprentices) in July, hanging left and seeming to idle: well below form last 3 starts:
sold 17,000 gns Doncaster October Sales: should stay beyond 8.5f: acts on good to
firm ground, no form on a soft surface: inconsistent. *Mrs J. R. Ramsden*

FALKENHAM 2 b.c. (May 10) Polar Falcon (USA) 126 – Barsham 94 (Be My 109
Guest (USA) 126) [1996 6s* 7m* 7.1g² 8g* a8.5f⁵ 8f Nov 30] 18,000Y: rather
sparely-made colt: half-brother to 3 winners, including fairly useful 1¼m and 10.3f
winner Jameel Asmar (by Rock City) and 15.4f winner Guestwick (by Blakeney):
dam, 1¼m winner suited by 1½m, from family of Blakeney and Morston: won
maiden at Goodwood in May, auction event at Salisbury in June and (after short-head
second to Brave Act in Solario Stakes at Sandown) listed event at Goodwood in
September: subsequently left P. Cole: 53/1, good fifth of 10 to Boston Harbour in
Breeders' Cup Juvenile at Woodbine penultimate start, better effort in USA: will be
suited by further than 8.5f: acts on good to firm and soft ground and on dirt: tends to
race with head high. *M. G. Harte, USA*

FALLAH 2 b.c. (Apr 6) Salse (USA) 128 – Alpine Sunset (Auction Ring (USA) 77 p
123) [1996 7m Sep 20] 14,000F, IR 110,000Y: good-topped colt: fourth foal:
brother to 5f to 1m winner Alpine Johnny and half-brother to useful 5f to 6f winner
Afif (by Midyan): dam unraced half-sister to Cyrano de Bergerac: fair form in
maiden (backward) and minor event (seventh of 9 to King Sound) at Newbury: will
probably do better. *Major W. R. Hern*

FALLAL (IRE) 4 b.f. Fayruz 116 – Lady Bidder (Auction Ring (USA) 123) –
[1995 47?: 1996 a6g⁵ 8d⁶ 6m a6g⁵ a6g 1996 a6g Jan 6] poor maiden at best: stays 7f: acts on
equitrack: tried blinkered, ran poorly. *K. McAuliffe*

FALLS O'MONESS (IRE) 2 b.f. (Mar 23) River Falls 113 – Sevens Are Wild 62
40 (Petorius 117) [1996 6g² 6m² 7s 6.9m³ 7m² 6g 7.5m Sep 18] IR 6,000Y:
unfurnished filly: third foal: half-sister to 3-y-o Hoh Majestic (by Soviet Lad), 5f
winner at 2 yrs: dam, lightly raced, placed at 1m: modest maiden: stays 7f (raced too
freely and ran wide on turn over 7.5f): possibly unsuited by soft ground: not
discredited in blinkers penultimate start. *K. R. Burke*

FAME AGAIN 4 b.f. Then Again 126 – Starawak 68 (Star Appeal 133) [1995 86: 86 d
10.3g 8.5m 7m 8m² 7g⁵ 7g⁵ 8m² 7.1g* 7g² 8g³ 7d⁴ 1996 8s 8g 8g 7.6g 6m⁴ 7g³ 6m⁶
6m⁵ 6g⁶ 6f² 6m⁴ 7.5f⁵ 7m 7.1f 7m 7.1s 7g 7g 5s⁵ Nov 8] compact, workmanlike filly:
fairly useful handicapper: below form last 9 starts, particularly so on last 7: stays 1m:
acts on firm and soft ground: held up. *Mrs J. R. Ramsden*

FAMILY MAN 3 ch.g. Indian Ridge 123 – Auntie Gladys 49 (Great Nephew 126) 75
[1995 NR 1996 8d⁶ 8.2m⁴ 8m⁴ 10.1m Oct 23] 10,000Y: angular, workmanlike
gelding: first foal: dam placed at up to 2m: fair maiden: stays 8.2f, disappointing in
10.1f handicap: acts on good to firm and dead ground. *J. R. Fanshawe*

FANADIYR (IRE) 4 b.g. Kahyasi 130 – Fair Fight 84 (Fine Blade (USA) 121) –
[1995 12f⁴ 11f 14m 16m⁶ 1996 13d 13.1m⁴ 12.4m⁴ Jun 29] ex-Irish gelding: eighth
foal: half-brother to 4 winners, including middle-distance performers by Top Ville
and Darshaan: dam 2m winner: rated 73? when trained at 3 yrs by J. Oxx: no worthwhile in Britain: probably a stayer. *W. Storey*

FANCY A FORTUNE (IRE) 2 b.c. (Feb 5) Fools Holme (USA) – Fancy's Girl 63 §
(FR) (Nadjar (FR) 128) [1996 6m 7s³ 7m 7d 7f² 7f 8.1m⁴ 10f 8m Oct 23] 4,400F,
14,000Y: third reported foal: dam Irish maiden, stayed 1¼m: modest form at best:
sold 2,400 gns Newmarket Autumn Sales: stays 1m: acts on any going: visored last 2
starts: unreliable. *J. Pearce*

FANCY CLANCY 3 b.f. Clantime 101 – Bold Sophie (Bold Owl 101) [1995 43: 43 d
5m³ 5f³ 5m 5g 5g 7.1s 5s⁵ 1996 5g⁴ 5f⁶ 5m 5g 5m 5g 5m Oct 17] compact filly:
poor sprint maiden: soundly beaten after 3-y-o reappearance: tried in most types of

headgear, no improvement: carries head high, and sometimes hangs: has pulled hard. *Miss L. C. Siddall*

FANCY DESIGN (IRE) 3 b.f. Cyrano de Bergerac 120 – Crimson Robes 48 – (Artaius (USA) 129) [1995 –: 7m⁶ 7m 1996 6m 7m⁵ 7g a8g⁶ a8s⁶ a8g⁵ Dec 26] good-topped filly: no form: sold 5,000 gns Newmarket Autumn Sales: visored last outing. *P. Mitchell*

FANCY HEIGHTS 3 b.f. Shirley Heights 130 – Miss Fancy That (USA) 99 (The 91 Minstrel (CAN) 135) [1995 59p: 7g⁶ 1996 11.8m³ 13.4m² 14m* 13.9m⁴ Aug 20] tall, unfurnished filly: progressive form: won handicap at Haydock (coming from rear to lead final strides) in August: should be suited by further than 1¾m: acts on good to firm ground: sometimes on edge: flashes tail: sent to Germany. *Lady Herries*

FANNY'S CHOICE (IRE) 2 b.f. (Feb 16) Fairy King (USA) – Gaychimes 90 (Steel Heart 128) [1996 5f³ 6g* 5.2f⁵ 5.2m Aug 17] IR 19,000F, 15,000Y: leggy filly: half-sister to 3 winners, including fair 8.5f to 16.4f winner Keen Bid (by Alzao): dam unraced half-sister to Grade 1 1¼m winner Gaily Gaily: won minor event at Windsor in July: good staying-on fifth after slow start in Super Sprint at Newbury later in month: really needs further than 5f. *R. Hannon*

FAN OF VENT-AXIA 2 b.c. (Mar 23) Puissance 110 – Miss Milton (Young 59 Christopher 119) [1996 5s⁴ 5g a5g³ 7f³ 7g⁴ 7f 8m 8g Oct 21] 7,500Y: small, leggy colt: fifth reported foal: half-brother to sprinter Poets Cove (by Bay Express), winner of Molecomb Stakes at 2 yrs: dam lightly raced on flat: modest form, including in sellers: stays 7f: best efforts on an easy surface: blinkered (fair effort) fourth start. *C. N. Allen*

FANTAIL 2 b.c. (Feb 28) Taufan (USA) 119 – Eleganza (IRE) 67 (Kings Lake 71 ? (USA) 133) [1996 7m 8m 8g⁶ Oct 30] 8,600Y: leggy, good-topped colt: first foal: dam maiden, stayed 1½m: apparently best effort when sixth in Yarmouth maiden on final outing, but possibly flattered in steadily-run race: will stay beyond 1m. *M. H. Tompkins*

FANTASTIC FELLOW (USA) 2 b.c. (May 4) Lear Fan (USA) 130 – 112 p Chateaubaby (USA) 62 (Nureyev (USA) 131) [1996 7g⁴ 7g⁴ 6m⁴ Oct 3] $100,000Y: sturdy, well-made colt: has scope: third foal: half-brother to French 3-y-o Chateau La Riviere (by Irish River), 5.5f winner at 2 yrs: dam maiden half-sister to Henbit: won maiden at York by ½ length from Haltarra: fourth in pattern events afterwards, just over 2 lengths behind Desert King in National Stakes at the Curragh (best effort) then just over a length down on Bahamian Bounty in Middle Park Stakes (led briefly over 1f out) at Newmarket: will stay 1m: looks sort to do well at 3 yrs, and can win a pattern race. *C. E. Brittain*

FANTASY FLIGHT 2 b.f. (Mar 15) Forzando 122 – Ryewater Dream 72 – p (Touching Wood (USA) 127) [1996 6g Aug 23] 2,400F, 7,000Y: first foal: dam 11.7f winner: easy to back, not given hard time in maiden at Thirsk: will improve. *Mrs J. R. Ramsden*

FANTASY GIRL (IRE) 2 br.f. (Jan 29) Marju (IRE) 127 – Persian Fantasy 94 – (Persian Bold 123) [1996 7g 7.6m Sep 19] neat filly: first foal: dam 1½m winner who stayed 2m: slowly away and always behind in maidens. *J. L. Dunlop*

FANTASY RACING (IRE) 4 b.f. Tirol 127 – Highland Girl (USA) (Sir Ivor 78 135) [1995 86: 8d 6m⁶ 6m⁵ 7.3g 6m* 5.1m² 6.1g* 7m⁴ 7m⁵ 7f² 5.9f* 6.9f* 7m 6g⁴ 5.7h² 5.1h* 5.7h² 6f* 7m⁵ 5.7h 6g 5g 6m* 6.1s³ 6f⁵ 1996 6s 6g 5m⁶ 7f⁴ 5m⁶ 6m 5m 6g⁶ 6m 6d³ 6g³ 6g⁶ 5.1d⁵ 6f Sep 7] lengthy, slightly hollow-backed filly: covered by Piccolo: just a fair handicapper in 1996: stays 7f: acts on hard and soft ground: effective in visor, not tried since 2 yrs: successful for claimer. *M. R. Channon*

FAR AHEAD 4 b.g. Soviet Star (USA) 128 – Cut Ahead 85 (Kalaglow 132) [1995 87 85: 8.5m³ 8g² 8.2d* 8m² 7f a8.5g⁶ a10g* a12g³ 1996 a11g⁴ a8g 9.9f⁶ 10m³ 11.1g² a72 12.3m³ 12f* 11.9m³ 12g* 13.1m³ 10.4g 12s a12g Dec 7] angular gelding: fairly useful handicapper: won at Thirsk in August and September: lost form after next start: suited by middle distances nowadays: acts on firm and dead ground and the all-weather: usually held up. *J. L. Eyre*

FARASAN (IRE) 3 b.c. Fairy King (USA) – Gracieuse Majeste (FR) (Saint 115 Cyrien (FR) 128) [1995 NR 1996 8m* 10.3g* 10m⁶ 12m⁶ 11.9m⁴ 10g³ Sep 14] 40,000Y: tall, leggy colt: fluent mover, but did not stride out well to post final 3-y-o

Wood Ditton Stakes, Newmarket—three interesting newcomers;
Farasan (far side) short-heads Whitewater Affair, with Shantou in third

start: third foal: half-brother to useful 4-y-o Suranom (by Alzao), 1m (at 3 yrs) to
1½m winner in Italy: dam 2-y-o 6.5f winner in France from good French family:
smart performer: won minor events at Newmarket (newcomers) in April and
Doncaster (by 8 lengths from South Salem) in June: just over 2 lengths fourth
(demoted for interference) to Grape Tree Road in Grand Prix de Paris at Longchamp
before outclassed in 'King George' at Ascot: 3¼ lengths fourth of 6 to Dushyantor in
steadily-run Great Voltigeur Stakes at York before well below form in Group 3 race
(weak in betting, pulled hard first 3f, found little) at Goodwood: stays 1½m: raced
only on good or good to firm ground: stays in training. *H. R. A. Cecil*

FAR ATLANTIC   3 b.f. Phardante (FR) 123 – Atlantic View (Crash Course 128)   –
[1995 NR 1996 11.5m Sep 17] second foal: dam never ran: tailed off in claimer.
C. A. Dwyer

FARAWAY LASS   3 b.f. Distant Relative 128 – Vague Lass 85 (Vaigly Great 127)   80
[1995 63: 7m 6f⁶ 6m⁵ 1996 6.1m⁴ 6.1m* 6g² 6m* 6g³ 6m² 7f² 7.3m 6g* Oct 12]
rangy filly: has scope: fluent mover: fairly useful handicapper: won at Nottingham
(minor event) in May, at Salisbury (in good style) in June and at York (another minor
event) in October: stays 7f: has raced only on a sound surface (acts on firm ground):
consistent. *Lord Huntingdon*

FARAWAY WATERS   3 ch.f. Pharly (FR) 130 – Gleaming Water 81 (Kalaglow   102 d
132) [1995 83: 6m² 6.1m* 8g 7d 1996 10m² 10s 12m 8m⁴ 10.1m Aug 26] sparely-
made filly: has a quick action: useful performer at best: 5 lengths second of 7 to
Pricket in listed race at Newmarket on reappearance: failed to repeat the form,
respectable 17¾ lengths seventh of 11 to Lady Carla in Oaks at Epsom: probably
stays 1½m: acts on good to firm ground, probably on dead (well beaten on soft):
bandaged behind last 3 starts. *D. W. P. Arbuthnot*

FAR DAWN (USA)   3 b.c. Sunshine Forever (USA) – Dawn's Reality (USA) (In   69
Reality) [1995 NR 1996 8m⁶ 8.3m 10g⁵ 9f 10d 11.7m* 12m⁶ 11.9v Oct 6] sturdy
colt: first foal: dam minor US winner (at up to 9f) out of Grade 1 winner Dawn's
Curtsey: fair handicapper: won maiden at Bath in September, keen hold early on but
responding well to edge ahead 2f out: stays 11.7f: acts on good to firm ground: has
worn tongue strap: promising winning juvenile hurdler. *G. Harwood*

FAREWELL MY LOVE (IRE)   2 b.f. (Mar 14) Waajib 121 – So Long Boys   73
(FR) (Beldale Flutter (USA) 130) [1996 5.1m² 5m* 6m⁶ 6g* 6.5m 7d⁶ 6s⁴ Oct 26]
9,200Y: smallish, sturdy filly: third foal: dam, Italian maiden possibly best at up to
6f, half-sister to smart French pair Common Grounds (over 6f/7f at 2 yrs) and Angel
In My Heart (at 1m/1¼m): fair performer: won 3-runner median auction maiden at

333

Musselburgh in July and valuable seller at Goodwood in August: best form at 6f: acts on good to firm and soft ground: bandaged behind, and on toes, fifth start: races prominently. *P. F. I. Cole*

FARFEN 4 ch.g. Vague Shot 108 – Shirlstar Investor (Some Hand 119) [1995 NR 1996 10m Jul 26] first reported foal: dam of little account: always behind in seller. *C. A. Dwyer* –

FARFESTE 3 b.f. Jester 119 – Our Horizon 57 (Skyliner 117) [1995 49: 7g 7m a7g 1996 8.2g 8m 8g 10.1m⁴ 8m 7d 7m Sep 17] smallish filly: showed little in varied company in 1996: visored last 2 starts. *D. Morris* –

FARHANA 3 b.f. Fayruz 116 – Fahrenheit 69 (Mount Hagen (FR) 127) [1995 79p: 6f² 6m* 1996 6.1d* 6m* 6d* 6g² Aug 11] rangy filly: has scope: progressive sprinter: favourite on all her 3-y-o starts: won handicap at Nottingham, and rated stakes at Salisbury and Haydock (listed, quickened clear over 1f out) in May: not seen out again until August when beaten a head by Daring Destiny in Phoenix Sprint Stakes at Leopardstown: will prove best at up to 6f: yet to race on extremes of going: consistent. *W. Jarvis* 109

FARHAN (USA) 2 b.c. (Feb 3) Lear Fan (USA) 130 – Mafatin (IRE) 74 (Sadler's Wells (USA) 132) [1996 6m⁵ 7.1d² 7f² Oct 8] big, lengthy colt: first foal: dam, 1¼m winner, half-sister to 1000 Guineas winner Fairy Footsteps and St Leger winner Light Cavalry: neck second to River Usk in maiden at Haydock in September: odds on, unsuited by steady gallop when below that form in similar event at Warwick following month: will be suited by 1m+: to winter in Dubai. *P. T. Walwyn* 81

FARIDA SECONDA 3 gr.f. Green Ruby (USA) 104 – Faridetta 107 (Good Bond 122) [1995 –: a6g 5s⁶ 1996 5m⁶ 5.1g 6f⁵ 7f 6g Aug 1] leggy filly: poor maiden: stays 6f: acts on firm ground: inconsistent. *J. L. Spearing* 40

FARINGDON FUTURE 2 b.c. (Jan 20) Distant Relative 128 – Lady Dowery (USA) (Manila (USA)) [1996 6m 6g² 6m⁴ 6.1s⁶ Oct 31] 52,000Y: robust, good-bodied colt: has a quick action: first foal: dam French 11f winner, half-sister to Grade 2 2-y-o 9f winner Minister Wife out of Grade 2 8.5f winner Dowery: fair maiden: had excuses in nursery final start: will be suited by further than 6f. *B. W. Hills* 74

FARMOST 3 ch.g. Pharly (FR) 130 – Dancing Meg (USA) 113 (Marshua's Dancer (USA)) [1995 74p: 6.9g a6g a7g² 1996 a6g* 8d⁵ 7.1d* 7g* 6.9m* a7g² 8f* 7.6f² a7g² a9.4g* Aug 31] only fairly useful form at best, and very well campaigned to gain 6 wins and 3 seconds from 10 starts: successful in maiden at Wolverhampton in January, then in handicap at Sandown, minor events at Brighton and Folkestone (amateurs), and in handicaps at Brighton (made all) and Wolverhampton, all within around 3 months between May and August: stays 9.4f: acts on all-weather and on firm and dead going: has run well 3 times after only a couple of days rest: a credit to his trainer: tough and consistent. *Sir Mark Prescott* 81

FARNESE (IRE) 2 b.c. (Feb 14) Alzao (USA) 117 – Flaxen Hair (Thatch (USA) 136) [1996 7m 7f⁵ Nov 5] good-bodied colt: fluent mover: brother to smart miler Mirror Black and half-brother to several winners, including smart 7f (at 2 yrs) to 1¼m winner Sharpitor (by Montelimar): dam unraced: stepped up on debut form (when green and not given hard time or getting best of runs) when around 3½ lengths fifth of 16, clear, to Tayseer in maiden at Redcar, disputing lead then gradually outpaced final 2f: will improve again. *L. M. Cumani* 77 p

FARO FLYER 3 b.c. Shere Khan – Midyanzie (Midyan (USA) 124) [1995 NR 1996 8.1f 10f 6m Oct 8] first foal: dam no worthwhile form: no form: reportedly broke off-fore pastern final start: dead. *K. T. Ivory* –

FARRINGDON HILL 5 b.g. Minster Son 130 – Firgrove 73 (Relkino 131) [1995 77: 11.8m³ 12g 1996 12m⁶ 14m* 14.6g 14m⁵ 14.1m² 12g⁴ 17.2d Sep 30] rangy gelding: good mover: fair handicapper: won at Sandown in June: sold (Major W. Hern to R. Champion) only 5,000 gns Newmarket Autumn Sales: stays 1¾m: acts on firm and soft ground: usually blinkered: hung and looked tricky ride both starts in 1995: front runner at 5 yrs: not one to trust implicitly. *Major W. R. Hern* 80

FASCINATING RHYTHM 2 b.f. (Feb 2) Slip Anchor 136 – Pick of The Pops 109 (High Top 131) [1996 8.2g* Oct 9] 57,000Y: fourth foal: half-sister to useful 3-y-o 1¼m winner Migwar (by Unfuwain): dam 2-y-o 7f winner from very good family: odds on, won steadily-run 13-runner maiden at Nottingham by 1½ lengths 85 p from Brave Kris, rousted along behind leaders early in straight then staying on to lead well over 1f out: will improve, particularly over further than 8.2f. *H. R. A. Cecil*

FASIH   4 b.c. Rock City 120 – Nastassia (FR) (Noble Decree (USA) 127) [1995 82:   –
8.1g 8m⁵ 10m 10d* 1996 9.2d 12d Apr 24] sturdy colt: unimpressive mover: fairly useful at his best: has history of unsoundness, and broke down final 4-y-o start: stays 1¼m: acts on dead ground. *S. E. Kettlewell*

FASIL (IRE)   3 ch.g. Polish Patriot (USA) 128 – Apple Peel 109 (Pall Mall 132)   90
[1995 NR 1996 8d 8g³ 10d⁶ 10m* 10m 12m* 12g Oct 11] 16,000Y: lengthy gelding: has a round action: half-brother to several winners, including very useful Eve's Error (6f to 8.5f, by Be My Guest) and fairly useful Discord (up to 1¾m, by Niniski): dam 1m and 1¼m winner: fairly useful performer: won minor event in June (leading near finish) and handicap in September (hung right), both at Goodwood: sold (J. Benstead to N. Walker) 26,000 gns Newmarket Autumn Sales: suited by 1½m: acts on good to firm ground: gelded. *C. J. Benstead*

FASSAN (IRE)   4 br.g. Contract Law (USA) 108 – Persian Susan (USA) (Her-   –
bager 136) [1995 8s 10m⁶ 12m 11g² 9m⁶ 14g⁵ 12g 1996 12.1d Apr 11] IR 8,000Y, 8,500 3-y-o: ex-Irish gelding: half-brother to 8 winners, notably fairly useful middle-distance stayer Persian Halo (by Sunny's Halo): dam won at up to 9f in USA: unraced at 2 yrs: fair maiden at 3 yrs for D. Hanley: fit from hurding, well beaten only start on flat in 1996: stays 11f, respectable effort at 1¾m. *M. D. Hammond*

FAST FORWARD FRED   5 gr.g. Sharrood (USA) 124 – Sun Street 73 (Ile de   49
Bourbon (USA) 133) [1995 –: 10d 14g 14g 1996 12f² 12m 14.1m 12m⁵ 14m⁵ Aug 15] big, lengthy, workmanlike gelding: shows knee action: modest maiden: failed to repeat form of 5-y-o reappearance: should stay beyond 1½m: acts on firm ground. *L. Montague Hall*

FASTINI GOLD   4 b.g. Weldnaas (USA) 112 – La Carlotta (Ela-Mana-Mou 132)   53 d
[1995 61d: 9m 8.3m 8h² 8f⁵ 8.1d 8m 9.7g a10g⁵ a12g 1996 12f 10.8f 12d 7.3s⁴ a8g 10m 10g⁶ 10g 8.3m 8m 10d 8d Sep 30] leggy, sparely-made gelding: disappointing maiden: should stay 1¼m: acts on hard and soft ground: tried visored, no improvement: difficult ride: inconsistent. *M. D. I. Usher*

FASTNET   2 ch.f. (Apr 10) Forzando 122 – Lambay 88 (Lorenzaccio 130) [1996   –
5f Jun 29] half-sister to several winners, including fairly useful 3-y-o Bullfinch (at up to 1m, by Anshan), useful 1m to 11f performer My Lamb (by Relkino) and useful sprinter Bay Bay (by Bay Express): dam 2-y-o 7f winner: missed break and always behind in maiden at Lingfield: sold 2,200 gns Newmarket Autumn Sales. *R. F. Johnson Houghton*

FAST SPIN   2 b.c. (Mar 9) Formidable (USA) 125 – Topwinder (USA) (Topsider   60
(USA)) [1996 5g⁶ 7m a7g⁴ 7g⁶ a7g* Dec 27] 9,200Y, 6,000 2-y-o: sturdy colt: first foal: dam ran twice in France: poor form at best on turf: easy winner of seller at Southwell late in year after 4 months off: stays 7f: acts on fibresand. *T. D. Barron*

FATAL BARAARI   2 b.c. (Apr 15) Green Desert (USA) 127 – Possessive (Posse   81 p
(USA) 130) [1996 7.1m³ Sep 18] 180,000Y: leggy, good-topped colt: sixth foal: brother to useful 1994 2-y-o 6f winner Desert Courier and half-brother to 3 winners, including 3-y-o 11.5f winner Possessive Artiste and Irish and Italian Oaks winner Possessive Dancer (both by Shareef Dancer): dam (unraced) from good family: unimpressive to post then refused to enter stalls in Kempton minor event: weak 8/1, 5¾ lengths third of 15 to Sleepytime in maiden at Sandown later in September, disputing lead long way: will stay 1m: will improve. *M. R. Stoute*

FATAL SAHRA (IRE)   2 ch.c. (Apr 26) Caerleon (USA) 132 – Ploy 87 (Posse   67 p
(USA) 130) [1996 7m Oct 23] IR 230,000Y: half-brother to smart Italian miler Poliuto (by Last Tycoon) and half-brother to 7-y-o 7f to 2m winner Sir Norman Holt (by Ela-Mana-Mou): dam, maiden who stayed 1½m, half-sister to Sun Princess and Saddlers' Hall: 16/1, around 7 lengths eighth of 11 to Sekari in maiden at Yarmouth, prominent until outpaced over 1f out: will improve. *J. H. M. Gosden*

FATEFULLY (USA)   3 b.f. Private Account (USA) – Fateful (USA) 90 (Topsider   110
(USA)) [1995 NR 1996 7m² 7d 7f⁵ 8m² 8.1m* 8m* 8d* 8g³ Nov 2] rather leggy filly: good mover: first foal: dam 6f (at 2 yrs) and 7f winner: smart performer: progressed with virtually every start: won maiden at Yarmouth in June and handicap at Sandown, listed rated stakes (by neck from Abeyr) at Ascot and listed race (by 1½

335

lengths from Scarlet Plume) at Ascot in the autumn: good third to Ali-Royal in listed race at Newmarket final start: stays 8.1f: yet to race on soft going, acts on any other: tends to wear a tongue strap: tended to hang once in front last 2 wins: consistent: sent to UAE. *Saeed bin Suroor*

FATEHALKHAIR (IRE)   4 ch.g. Kris 135 – Midway Lady (USA) 126 (Alleged (USA) 138) [1995 –: 7.9g⁴ 8d 8m 1996 10g 8.1f a8g² a9.4g⁵ 7m a8g Aug 16] leggy, angular gelding: unimpressive mover: poor maiden: stays 1m well: acts on fibresand: visored (no improvement) second 4-y-o start: inconsistent. *B. Ellison*   – a42

FATHER DAN (IRE)   7 ch.g. Martin John – Sonia John (Main Reef 126) [1995 59, a64: a10g⁵ a10g* a10g 12m⁵ 11.9f⁴ 10g⁴ 11.8g² 11.4g⁴ 11.1f⁶ 11.6m* 12m⁴ 10d⁵ 12s³ a11g* a12g² a11g⁵ 1996 a12g a12g 10m 10m² 11.5m a10g³ a10s³ a10g² a10g* a10g³ Dec 30] plain gelding: poor mover: modest handicapper: gained deserved success at Lingfield in December: stays 1½m: acts on firm and soft ground and the all-weather: visored (well beaten) final 3-y-o outing. *Miss Gay Kelleway*   65

FATHER EDDIE   2 b.g. (Mar 14) Aragon 118 – Lady Philippa (IRE) 77 (Taufan (USA) 119) [1996 5m 6d⁶ 7d Aug 10] 28,000Y: second foal: dam 1m and 1¼m winner: form in maiden auctions only on second start: gelded: should stay beyond 6f. *J. J. O'Neill*   49

FATTASH (USA)   4 ch.g. Tejano (USA) – Green Pompadour (USA) (Green Dancer (USA) 132) [1995 51: 8g 10m 10g⁶ 12.5m³ 15.4g³ 12g 16.4m a13g 1996 a16g 11.6m 17.2m Jun 29] seemed of little account in 1996: left R. Hoad after 4-y-o reappearance. *P. Mooney*   –

FAUGERON   7 ch.g. Niniski (USA) 125 – Miss Longchamp 94 (Northfields (USA)) [1995 63: 12m 16m* 15.1m* 14d* 12m² 13.1f³ 13.9g⁶ 13.9g⁶ 14.1f⁴ 1996 12f⁵ 16m 14d 14.1m* 14m² 16.2f² Aug 15] leggy, sparely-made gelding: fluent mover: modest performer: won seller at Redcar in July: stays 16.2f: acts on firm ground, respectable efforts at best on a soft surface: blinkered (below form) once as 6-y-o. *N. Tinkler*   57

FAUNA (IRE)   2 b.f. (Mar 15) Taufan (USA) 119 – Labwa (USA) (Lyphard (USA) 132) [1996 7m 7g⁴ Oct 18] IR 4,000Y, resold 14,500Y: seventh foal: half-sister to useful 6f winner Baaderah (by Cadeaux Genereux) and a winner in Germany by Thatching: dam unraced: 10/1, improved on debut effort when 3 lengths fourth of 11 to Kadeena in maiden at Catterick, every chance over 1f out: slowly away both starts: may improve further. *N. A. Graham*   65

FAUSTINO   4 b.g. Faustus (USA) 118 – Hot Case 92 (Upper Case (USA)) [1995 53: a7g³ 8g⁶ 10m⁴ 12.5m⁶ 11.6m⁴ 11.9f³ 12f⁴ 11.5g 1996 13.1m Sep 9] fair winning hurdler: modest maiden handicapper on flat: soundly beaten only start in 1996 for new stable: stays 12.5f: acts on fibresand and firm going, possibly not on soft: blinkered last 2 starts at 3 yrs. *P. J. Hobbs*   –

336

FAYIK 2 ch.c. (Feb 15) Arazi (USA) 135 – Elfaslah (IRE) 107 (Green Desert 76 p
(USA) 127) [1996 7m⁵ Oct 23] second foal: half-brother to 3-y-o Mawjud (by
Mujtahid), 7f winner at 2 yrs: dam, winner 3 times at around 1¼m, half-sister to
White Muzzle: 7/2, around 2½ lengths fifth of 9, unable to quicken, to Courtship in
slowly-run maiden at Yarmouth: sent to Dubai: should improve. *H. Thomson Jones*

FAYM (IRE) 2 b.f. (Apr 16) Fayruz 116 – Lorme (Glenstal (USA) 118) [1996 a6s⁵ 65
a6g² Dec 27] IR 5,800F, 8,500Y: third foal: dam French 6f and 14.5f winner also
successful over jumps, half-sister to very smart 1m to 1¼m horse Princes Gate: much
better effort (ran in seller on debut) when staying-on second of 9 in maiden at
Southwell: should stay 7f. *J. Wharton*

FAYRE HOLLY (IRE) 3 b.f. Fayruz 116 – Holly Bird (Runnett 125) [1995 57: –
5.1m³ 5g 6m⁴ 1996 7g a8.5g Jul 11] leggy filly: modest form as juvenile: well beaten
in 1996: may be a sprinter. *M. J. Heaton-Ellis*

FEARLESS CAVALIER 2 b.g. (Apr 27) Bold Arrangement 127 – Gold Belt 60 ?
(IRE) 61 (Bellypha 130) [1996 7m³ 6m⁶ a6g⁴ a7g⁴ 5f⁴ 6m² 6.1m⁶ 6m³ 6d 6s⁴ 6g³ 5s*
Nov 7] 3,000 2-y-o: unfurnished gelding: has a round action: first foal: dam 1m
winner, daughter of useful 7f and 1¼m winner Golden Braid: modest form: just got
up in selling nursery at Musselburgh in November: winner over 5f, needs at least 6f
to show his best form: acts on fibresand, probably on any turf ground. *R. Hollinshead*

FEARLESS SIOUX 2 b.f. (Apr 27) Formidable (USA) 125 – Washita (Valiyar 48
129) [1996 6g⁵ a6g⁴ a10g Nov 26] third foal: half-sister to 3-y-o winning middle-
distance stayer Los Alamos (by Keen) and 1994 2-y-o 7f winner Last Roundup (by
Good Times): dam poor maiden: poor form in maiden events: should be suited by
further than 6f. *C. W. Thornton*

FEARLESS WONDER 5 b.g. Formidable (USA) 125 – Long View 68 (Persian 50 §
Bold 123) [1995 57§: a11g² 12m³ 14.1m a12g 12m⁶ 12f* 13.8m² 12m⁴ 12.4g² 1996
11.9d 14.1m³ 14.1f 15.8m* 12m Aug 18] sturdy, good-bodied gelding: modest
performer: easily made all in seller at Catterick in August: no headgear, ran as if
something amiss 12 days later: sold (Mrs M. Reveley to D. Bassett) only 1,400 gns
Doncaster September Sales: stays 15.8f: acts on firm ground, dead and fibresand:
usually blinkered/visored: has carried head awkwardly, gone in snatches and hung
left: inconsistent. *Mrs M. Reveley*

FEATHER BED (IRE) 2 b.f. (Feb 17) Fools Holme (USA) – Piffle 87 (Shirley 71
Heights 130) [1996 6g⁴ 5f² 7g⁵ 6g a8g* Dec 20] leggy filly: first foal: sister to middle-distance
performer Frenchpark (5f and 1m winner at 2 yrs in Ireland, later smart in USA) and
useful 4-y-o 6f (at 2 yrs) and 1¼m winner Sayeh: dam 1½m winner who stayed well,
sister to useful stayer El Conquistador out of half-sister to Mountain Lodge: ex-Irish
filly: left C. Collins after third start: didn't need to be at best to win maiden at
Lingfield on first start for new yard: bred to stay further than 1m: acts on equitrack,
raced only on a sound surface on turf. *M. A. Jarvis*

FEATHERSTONE LANE 5 b.g. Siberian Express (USA) 125 – Try Gloria 52 d
(Try My Best (USA) 130) [1995 57, a66: 5.9m 5m⁵ 5g a5g³ 5.1g 5f² 5f² 5.2f³ 5m³ a77 d
5f⁶ a5g⁶ 5m 5m 5m 5.1d a6g² a6g 1996 a5g³ a5g³ a5g³ a5g² a5g* a5g² a5g a5g⁵
5g⁶ 5g 5g³ 5g⁴ 5m⁶ 5.2m⁴ 5d⁴ 5g 6f 5.1m 5m⁵ a6g a5g⁶ 6m a5g³ a5g⁴ a5g a5g³ a5g
Dec 28] angular, workmanlike gelding: fair handicapper on the all-weather, modest
on turf: won at Wolverhampton in February: mainly below best in second half of
year: effective at 5f and 6f: acts on firm and dead ground, best on all-weather
surfaces: usually wears visor, but has run well without: normally waited with. *Miss
L. C. Siddall*

FEBRUARY 3 b.f. Full Extent (USA) 113 – Foligno (Crofter (USA) 124) [1995 –
44, a–: a5g⁵ 5g³ 5m³ 5f³ 6.1m⁵ a7g³ a6g⁶ 6m 6f³ 7f 1996 5m 8m⁵ 7f a7g 8.1f 8f Sep
23] neat filly: of little account for new stable: not one to rely on. *A. J. Chamberlain*

FEEL A LINE 2 b.c. (Mar 11) Petong 126 – Cat's Claw (USA) (Sharpen Up 127) 71
[1996 6m 6m⁶ 5.3f² 6m 5g³ 6m 6s Oct 26] 9,200F, 18,000Y: lengthy colt: third foal:
half-brother to 4-y-o winning hurdler Prophets Honour (by Deploy): dam unraced
granddaughter of US Grade 1-placed filly Funny Cat: fair performer: below par last
2 starts: best efforts at 5f: acts on firm ground: blinkered third to fifth starts: slowly
away fifth outing. *B. J. Meehan*

FEELING HOPE 5 ch.m. Hadeer 118 – Bonnie Hope (USA) (Nijinsky (CAN) –
138) [1995 NR 1996 a12g Jan 18] no worthwhile form. *M. S. Saunders*

FEEL LEGEND (IRE) 2 ch.g. (May 1) Priolo (USA) 127 – Salustrina (Sallust   79
134) [1996 5m⁵ 6s² 6m* Jun 10] IR 4,000Y: attractive gelding, shade unfurnished: has scope: seventh foal: brother to useful Irish 3-y-o middle-distance stayer
Priolina and half-brother to 3 winners, including fairly useful middle-distance performer Ringmaster (by Taufan) and 4-y-o 8.3f and 1½m winner Voila Premiere (by
Roi Danzig): dam Irish 7f winner: didn't need to run to best form when winning
12-runner maiden auction at Windsor by 2½ lengths in June: should be well suited by
further than 6f: gelded. *R. Hannon*

FEET ON FIRE 3 b.f. Nomination 125 – Peregrine Falcon (Saulingo 122) [1995   –
NR 1996 5.1g 6g Apr 23] lengthy filly: half-sister to several winners, including
fairly useful Caroles Express (stayed 1m, by Scottish Reel): dam, half-sister to
Bay Express, ran only at 2 yrs: burly, behind in maidens: joined D. Cosgrove.
W. M. Brisbourne

FELLWAH (IRE) 2 b.f. (Feb 20) Sadler's Wells (USA) 132 – Continual (USA)   66 p
(Damascus (USA)) [1996 7.5m⁴ Sep 18] unfurnished filly: closely related to
2000 Guineas winner Shadeed (by Nijinsky) and half-sister to 9f winner Basoof
(by Believe It) and a winner in USA by Drone: dam 6f and 7f winner: 7/1, slow-
starting fourth of 5 in steadily-run maiden at Beverley: will probably improve.
E. A. L. Dunlop

FEMME SAVANTE 4 b.f. Glenstal (USA) 118 – Femme Formidable (Form-   –
idable (USA) 125) [1995 NR 1996 6m 5g 5m 7m Aug 2] small, leggy filly: poor
mover: rated 89p at 2 yrs: well held in 1996: stays 7f: has raced only on a sound
surface. *R. Hannon*

FENCER'S QUEST (IRE) 3 ch.c. Bluebird (USA) 125 – Fighting Run   –
(Runnett 125) [1995 NR 1996 7m Sep 10] 110,000Y: fifth foal: half-brother to 2
winners, including fair Croire (stayed 1m, by Lomond): dam from family of
Braashee, Bassenthwaite and Hadeer: never a threat in maiden at Lingfield: sold
(R. Charlton to Capt. T. Forster) 10,000 gns Newmarket Autumn Sales. *R. Charlton*

FEN TERRIER 4 b.f. Emarati (USA) 74 – Kinz (Great Nephew 126) [1995 58:   –
a11g* 11.8g 10.1g* a12g⁶ a9.4g² a12g² 11.1f⁵ a12g 12s⁴ 1996 a11g Feb 5] modest
handicapper: well beaten only 4-y-o start: stays 1½m: acts on fibresand and soft
ground: sold (W. Haggas to F. Murtagh) 6,500 gns Newmarket July Sales: fair
hurdler, winner in November and December. *W. J. Haggas*

FERGAL (USA) 3 ch.g. Inishpour 88 – Campus (USA) (Minnesota Mac) [1995   –
48: 5f 5g³ 7.1f⁵ 1996 a6g 12s 14.1g 8f 9.9g 11.9m Sep 6] angular gelding: poor
maiden: also trained by Ronald Thompson (first 3 starts) and T. Kersey (fourth start)
in 1996. *Miss J. F. Craze*

FERNANDA 2 b.f. (Mar 3) Be My Chief (USA) 122 – Flaming Rose (USA)   95
(Upper Nile (USA)) [1996 6.1m* 6m* 7.1m 7m² 7d² 7m² 7.3s² Oct 26] 32,000Y:
quite attractive filly: fifth foal: half-sister to 3-y-o 7f winner Mashmoum (by Lycius),
smart 6f (at 2 yrs) and 1m winner Chipaya (by Northern Prospect) and 4-y-o 8.3f
winner Crimson Shower (by Dowsing): dam, half-sister to smart sprinter Gwydion,
showed some ability in USA: won maiden at Nottingham in May and minor event at
York in June: blinkered, useful form when runner-up in pattern and listed races final
4 starts: refused to enter stalls for May Hill Stakes at Doncaster in September and had
rope halter on next outing: stays 7.3f: acts on good to firm and soft ground: usually
edgy, on toes and swishes tail beforehand, and isn't the easiest of rides: sent to race in
France. *J. L. Dunlop*

FERN'S GOVERNOR 4 b.f. Governor General 116 – Sharp Venita 84 (Sharp   65
Edge 123) [1995 45: 7f 7.1g 8.3m 8g 9m 1996 10m 10d 10m⁴ 10m³ 11.6d* 12d 10m²
10m* 10.4g⁶ 12g 10f Nov 5] big, workmanlike filly: fair handicapper: won amateurs
contests at Windsor in August and Nottingham (easily) in September: winner over
11.6f, but best form at 1¼m: acts on good to firm ground and dead: has found little
off bridle, but did nothing wrong most 4-y-o starts. *W. J. Musson*

FERNWAY 3 ch.f. Handsome Sailor 125 – Redgrave Design 77 (Nebbiolo 125)   –
[1995 –: 5g 1996 5m 5m May 10] no sign of ability: sold 700 gns Ascot July Sales.
R. M. Whitaker

FERNY HILL (IRE) 2 b.c. (Mar 21) Danehill (USA) 126 – Miss Allowed   76
(USA) (Alleged (USA) 138) [1996 6m⁴ a8.5g² 7g⁴ Oct 2] 18,000Y, 45,000Y: half-   a66

brother to 3-y-o 9f winner Disallowed (by Distinctly North) and numerous winners here and abroad, including 1986 Irish 2-y-o 6f and 7f winner Best Try (by Try My Best) and 1½m winner Guest Right (by Be My Guest): dam unraced daughter of smart middle-distance filly Miss Toshiba: fair form in frame in maidens: bred to stay beyond 8.5f. *Sir Mark Prescott*

FERVENT FAN (IRE) 3 b.f. Soviet Lad (USA) 94 – Shannon Lady 67 (Monsanto (FR) 121) [1995 65: 6g 6m* 7m 6g 1996 7f 8g 8.2m 7f Jun 25] fair form as a juvenile: behind in 1996: visored (out of form) final 3-y-o start. *M. Bell*

FIABA 8 b.m. Precocious 126 – Historia 71 (Northfields (USA)) [1995 44: a8g³ a8g³ a8g⁴ a8.5g a8g⁵ a9.4g² a9.4g³ 8f² a8.5g⁵ 10m 8.2m⁶ a10g⁶ 8f 8f a6g² a7g⁴ 1996 a8g a8g⁶ a8g a8.5g a8g* 6m a7g⁶ a8g⁶ a8g⁵ Dec 3] poor performer: won handicap at Southwell in July: effective at 6f and has form over as far as 11.4f: acts on the all-weather and firm ground: blinkered (well beaten) once at 5 yrs, visored since fifth 8-y-o start: inconsistent. *Mrs N. Macauley* — 44

FIASCO 3 ch.f. Dunbeath (USA) 127 – Rainbow Trout 76 (Comedy Star (USA) 121) [1995 NR 1996 10.1d⁵ 10.1g 8g 13g⁴ Jul 5] third living foal: dam, maiden, stayed 6f: signs of ability only on final start. *M. J. Camacho*

FIDDLES DELIGHT 3 b.f. Colmore Row 111 – Nutwood Emma (Henbit (USA) 130) [1995 45d: 5m⁴ a5g⁵ 6f⁴ 6f⁴ 5m 5m⁶ 1996 8m Aug 13] little worthwhile form. *M. R. Channon*

FIELD OF VISION (IRE) 6 b.g. Vision (USA) – Bold Meadows 80 (Persian Bold 123) [1995 68: a6g⁵ a9g a5g⁴ a6g⁶ 7g 7f⁶ 7f⁴ 8.1s³ a8g² a7g a7g³ 1996 a7g a9.4g* a9.4g* a10g⁴ a9.4g⁶ a12g a10g⁵ 9.2d* 13s³ 10g⁴ a9.4g² a9.4g 10f³ 12f² 13m³ 10g⁸ Aug 21] neat, quite attractive gelding: has a quick action: fair performer: won 2 handicaps at Wolverhampton in January and claimer at Hamilton (claimed out of M. Johnston's stable £8,000) in April: stays 13f: acts on any turf going and the all-weather: effective in blinkers or not (not tried since 6-y-o reappearance): modest winning novice hurdler: consistent. *Mrs A. Swinbank* — 77

FIELDRIDGE 7 ch.g. Rousillon (USA) 133 – Final Thought (Final Straw 127) [1995 81: 10m⁶ 10g 10f 10.2h² 10m³ 10m* 9g 10.5g 11.9g 1996 10d⁴ 10.1m 10m⁶ 10g 15.9d Aug 30] tall, lengthy gelding: used to suffer from back problems: fair handicapper: below form after second 7-y-o start: stays 11.7f: easily best efforts on a sound surface: fair winning hurdler. *M. P. Muggeridge* — 77 d

FIERY FOOTSTEPS 4 ro.f. Chilibang 120 – Dancing Daughter 79 (Dance In Time (CAN)) [1995 47: a6g⁴ a5g⁵ 5g 5.1m 5.3m⁴ a5g⁵ 5.3f⁶ 6f⁴ 5.2g a6g a7g² a7g 1996 a6g³ a6g a6g⁶ a6g a6g⁵ a5g⁶ a6g 5m 6m 8m a8g Nov 4] lengthy, sparely-made filly: poor maiden handicapper: probably stays 7f: acts on good to firm ground and the all-weather: tried visored/blinkered, no improvement: has hung badly left: inconsistent: sold 500 gns Ascot December Sales. *S. W. Campion* — 47 d

FIFE MAJOR (USA) 2 b.c. (Mar 19) Gone West (USA) – Fife (IRE) 95 (Lomond (USA) 128) [1996 7d Nov 8] good sort, with scope: second foal: half-brother to 3-y-o Witch of Fife (by Lear Fan), 6f and 7f winner at 2 yrs: dam, 1m winner who stayed 1½m, half-sister to smart stayer El Conquistador out of half-sister to Irish St Leger winner Mountain Lodge: 20/1, green and on toes, twelfth of 20 in maiden at Doncaster in November, steadied start, held up on unfavoured side and never a threat, not knocked about: will do better. *B. W. Hills* — – p

FIGHTER SQUADRON 7 ch.g. Primo Dominie 121 – Formidable Dancer 70 (Formidable (USA) 125) [1995 –, a47: a6g⁵ a7g⁵ 8g 6.9g 7.1m 8.1m 1996 a6g⁴ a6g⁶ 7d 7.1g 7m 8.1m 6m³ a6g³ 6f⁵ Aug 3] leggy gelding: bad handicapper: ideally suited by 6f/7f: acts on firm ground, soft and fibresand: usually wears blinkers/visor nowadays: sometimes hangs markedly left: inconsistent. *R. E. Peacock* — 34

FIGHTING TIMES 4 b.g. Good Times (ITY) – Duellist (Town Crier 119) [1995 67: 10m 11.5m² 14.6m⁶ a12g 1996 10g⁴ 10g² 12m⁴ 12s⁵ 12m 12g 10m 10g 13.9g Oct 12] workmanlike gelding: fair maiden handicapper: below form after third 4-y-o start: probably stays 1½m: acts on good to firm ground: held up. *C. A. Smith* — 70 d

FIGLIA 2 b.f. (Feb 21) Sizzling Melody 117 – Fiorini 54 (Formidable (USA) 125) [1996 5f 5m⁵ 6g⁶ 6m 5d² a5g Nov 16] strong, lengthy filly: second foal: dam 6f seller winner: tongue tied, staying-on second of 13 in nursery at Doncaster in November, hanging left: should prove as effective at 6f as 5f: best effort on dead ground: — 62 blinkered (very edgy first occasion) last 4 outings: sold (C. Booth to J. L. Harris) 1,400 gns Doncaster November Sales. *C. B. B. Booth*

FIG TREE BAY   3 b.g. Puissance 110 – Rose Barton (Pas de Seul 133) [1995 NR   –
1996 5g 8.3m 6m 5.1m Aug 7] half-brother to 2 winners by Hadeer (including fair sprint handicapper My Abbey) and one (at up to 1¼m in Germany) by Formidable: dam unraced: no sign of ability. *T. T. Clement*

FIG TREE DRIVE (USA)   2 b.f. (May 9) Miswaki (USA) 124 – Rose O'Riley   94 p
(USA) (Nijinsky (CAN) 138) [1996 6m* Jun 27] $160,000Y: good-topped filly: has scope: sixth foal: sister to a 2-y-o winner in USA and closely related to winners in USA by Mr Prospector and Conquistador Cielo: dam, 1m winner in France at 2 yrs, is sister to Hollywood Derby winner De La Rose and very smart US 1¼m performer Upper Nile: 7/2, won maiden at Newbury by a neck from Crystal Crossing: will stay 1m: looked sure to improve. *P. F. I. Cole*

FIJI   2 b.f. (Apr 14) Rainbow Quest (USA) 134 – Island Jamboree (USA)   92 p
(Explodent (USA)) [1996 8.1m* Sep 17] second foal: dam, won 10 times in USA (also second in Grade 1 9f event at 5 yrs), out of maiden half-sister to Cacoethes and Fabulous Notion: heavily-backed at odds-on, won 7-runner maiden at Sandown by 1¾ lengths from Alphabet, making all, initially at strong pace, running green on home bend then finding plenty when asked late on: will stay middle distances: sure to improve. *H. R. A. Cecil*

FIJON (IRE)   3 b.f. Doyoun 124 – Tasskeen (FR) (Lyphard (USA) 132) [1995 71:   65 d
7.5m³ 8m² 7g⁶ 8m 1996 10.3m³ 10.2g⁵ 11.7m⁵ 10.8f 14.1f⁵ a12g⁶ 14s Oct 5] leggy, sparely-made filly: unimpressive mover: disappointing maiden: left B. Hills after fifth 3-y-o start: blinkered (looked thoroughly ungenuine) third 3-y-o start: looked one to leave alone on flat, but subsequently won juvenile hurdle. *J. Pearce*

FIKRA (USA)   3 b. or br.f. Gulch (USA) – Bolt From The Blue (USA) (Blue   58
Times (USA)) [1995 67: 6m³ 7m⁶ 7g² 7g 1996 9.9m 10.3m⁵ 10f⁴ a12g⁵ 10.1g Aug 1] tall, leggy filly: modest maiden: not so good as at 2 yrs: best form at 7f but probably stays 10.3f: keen sort: inconsistent. *S. P. C. Woods*

FILIAL (IRE)   3 b.c. Danehill (USA) 126 – Sephira (Luthier 126) [1995 NR 1996   84
8.1m³ 10m* 10m 12m 11.8f⁵ a10s⁶ a12g* Dec 5] smallish, quite attractive colt: half-   a95
brother to several winners, including useful Tatsfield (up to 1m, by Habitat) and French filly Ophira (up to 1¼m, by Old Vic): dam, French 1m winner, half-sister to Sigy and Sonoma: fairly useful form: won maiden at Sandown in August after good duel: failed to repeat the form before sold out of G. Harwood's stable 14,000 gns Newmarket Autumn Sales after fifth start: improved to win amateurs handicap at Lingfield in December: stays 1½m: acts on good to firm ground and on equitrack. *B. J. Meehan*

FILLY MIGNONNE (IRE)   3 ch.f. Nashwan (USA) 135 – Christabelle (USA)   –
(Northern Dancer) [1995 NR 1996 10g 10g 14.1g Oct 24] IR 120,000Y: tall, useful-looking filly: unimpressive mover: fifth foal: sister to useful Irish 4-y-o middle-distance performer Alisidora and half-sister to 3 winners, including fairly useful Caladesi (stayed 14.8f, by Slip Anchor): dam half-sister to dams of Warning and Commander In Chief, and Rainbow Quest: behind in maidens. *B. W. Hills*

FILMORE WEST   3 b.c. In The Wings 128 – Sistabelle (Bellypha 130) [1995   89 p
65p: a8.5g³ 1996 10.4g² 10m* Sep 26] smallish, good-topped colt: rated on second of 12 in maiden at York on belated reappearance: won maiden at Goodwood later in September, making all and eased close home: will do better, particularly over further than around 1¼m. *P. F. I. Cole*

FINAL STAB (IRE)   3 b.c. Kris 135 – Premier Rose 117 (Sharp Edge 123) [1995   –
84p: 7g⁶ 7d* 1996 8m⁵ 8m Jul 11] rangy, angular colt: shows knee action: failed to confirm juvenile promise in handicaps: bred to stay 1m+. *P. W. Harris*

FINAL TRIAL (IRE)   2 b.c. (Apr 17) Last Tycoon 131 – Perfect Alibi (Law   64
Society (USA) 130) [1996 7f⁴ 7d Oct 28] IR 160,000Y: second foal: half-brother to 4-y-o 11.1f winner Acquittal (by Danehill): dam (unraced) from good family: modest form in maidens at Leicester and Lingfield: will stay at least 1m. *G. Wragg*

FINARTS BAY   2 b.f. (Mar 18) Aragon 118 – Salinas 65 (Bay Express 132) [1996   59 p
6m Oct 28] leggy, close-coupled filly: fifth foal: dam maiden, stayed 6f: 12/1, 7

lengths seventh of 13 to Arapi in maiden at Leicester, held up and bit green before making some progress 2f out: will probably improve. *Mrs J. Cecil*

FINE DETAIL (IRE)   3 b.f. Shirley Heights 130 – De Stael (USA) 93 (Nijinsky   93
(CAN) 138) [1995 NR 1996 12m* Aug 10] close-coupled filly: sixth foal: half-sister to several winners, including middle-distance trio De Quest, Source of Light (both by Rainbow Quest) and Wandesta (by Nashwan): dam, 2-y-o 6f winner, sister to Peacetime and Quiet Fling: 15/2, won 8-runner maiden at Newmarket by neck from Flamands, travelling strongly to lead over 2f out, going at least 2 lengths clear, then running green (flashing tail and hanging left) and all out at the line: green and quick-actioned to post: blanketed for stalls entry: stud. *R. Charlton*

FINE FELLOW (IRE)   2 b.c. (Jan 29) Bluebird (USA) 125 – Majieda 91   106
(Kashmir II 125) [1996 5g* 5.5m⁴ 7g² 7s² 8s* 10s⁶ Nov 2] IR 25,000F, 320,000 francs Y: half-brother to several winners in France, including Mahshari (1¼m, by Mouktar), placed in Group 3 at 1½m: dam, closely related to smart miler Mannshour, was placed at up to 10.2f but became temperamental: French colt: won newcomers event at Chantilly in May and Prix La Rochette at Longchamp (by neck from Alpha Plus) in September: below best when sixth of 10 to Shaka in Criterium de Saint-Cloud: stays 1m: acts on soft ground. *Mme C. Head, France*

FINESTATETOBEIN   3 ch.f. Northern State (USA) 91 – Haywain 58 (That-   –
ching 131) [1995 NR 1996 7s 12m 12g Oct 19] 400F, 1,000Y: resold 750Y: sixth foal: dam 7f winner: well beaten. *F. Watson*

FINE TIMES   2 b.c. (Mar 2) Timeless Times (USA) 99 – Marfen (Lochnager 132)   68 ?
[1996 5m⁶ 5m⁵ 5.9g⁶ 5.7m⁴ 5f 5s² 5.2g 5g Nov 1] 10,000Y: compact colt: second foal: brother to 3-y-o 5f and (at 2 yrs) 6f winner Ramsey Hope: dam unraced: apparently much improved form when staying-on second of 12 to Queen's Pageant in maiden at Haydock: soundly beaten in 2 nurseries within 3 days afterwards: best form at 5f: seems very well suited by soft ground. *C. W. Fairhurst*

FINISTERRE (IRE)   3 b.g. Salt Dome (USA) – Inisfail (Persian Bold 123)   65
[1995 52: 5m⁶ 5g 5s⁴ 5d 5s a5g 1996 5s 7m⁶ 5s³ 5m³ 5m 6g* 6m 7m² 7m⁴ 6m² 6g⁵   a61
7g⁶ a6g a8.5s² Dec 19] leggy, rather sparely-made gelding: fair handicapper: won at Ripon in May: stays 8.5f: acts on good to firm ground and fibresand, possibly not on soft: blinkered (well held) fourth 2-y-o start: usually held up: consistent. *J. J. O'Neill*

FINJAN   9 b.g. Thatching 131 – Capriconia (Try My Best (USA) 130) [1995 54,   –
a–: 6g 8d⁴ 7m 7m⁴ 8.1g 10f 1996 8d 10d May 27] sturdy gelding: probably no longer of much account. *A. G. Foster*

FINLANA   3 b.f. Alzao (USA) 117 – Insaf (USA) (Raise A Native) [1995 NR 1996   63
10g⁵ 10m⁶ May 16] 25,000F, 50,000Y: leggy, close-coupled filly: third reported foal: dam unraced daughter of Coronation Stakes winner Kesar Queen: showed promise in maidens at Leicester (burly) and Salisbury (never landed a blow) in the spring: sold only 1,300 gns Newmarket December Sales. *M. R. Stoute*

FINSBURY FLYER (IRE)   3 ch.g. Al Hareb (USA) 123 – Jazirah (Main Reef   69
126) [1995 NR 1996 7.1g* 7m⁴ 8.1m³ 10.2f³ Jul 24] IR 6,800F, 7,400Y: third foal: dam unraced: fair performer: narrowly won claimer at Chepstow in June, in rear before running on to lead near line: ran creditably in small fields last 2 starts: seems to stay 10.2f (though set slow gallop when tried): raced only on a sound surface. *R. J. Hodges*

FIONA SHANN (USA)   3 b.f. Phone Trick (USA) – Aminata 98 (Glenstal   55
(USA) 118) [1995 53+: 6g 6d 6m 1996 8.2g⁴ 10f³ 12f⁴ 14.1d 11.9f 7.5g Oct 13] leggy, attractive filly: modest maiden handicapper: probably stays 1½m: acts on firm ground: blinkered (no form) final 3-y-o start: well beaten first start since sold privately out of J. Dunlop's stable. *D. Henderson, France*

FIONN DE COOL (IRE)   5 b.g. Mazaad 106 – Pink Fondant (Northfields   72
(USA)) [1995 78: 6m³ 7m 7g 7.3g² 7m⁴ 8.1m² 8g 8f* 8.1m² 8d 8m⁶ 7m 1996 8m 7m 8m 8m⁴ 8m³ 8.1d⁵ 9g 8d² 8d³ 8g⁴ Oct 29] sturdy gelding: poor mover: fair handicapper: 20 times in frame but only 1 win in last 3 seasons: needs further than 6f, and stays 9f: acts on firm and dead ground. *R. Akehurst*

FIORENZ (USA)   4 ch.f. Chromite (USA) – Christi Dawn (USA) (Grey Dawn II   –
132) [1995 NR 1996 a12g Jan 22] IR 1,000Y: ninth foal: closely related to a winner in USA by Woodman and half-sister to 4 winners, including fairly useful middle-

FIR

distance stayer Art Form (by Little Current): dam never ran: last of 7 in bad maiden: covered by Suave Dancer. *K. McAuliffe*

FIRBUR 3 b.g. Be My Chief (USA) 122 – La Masse (High Top 131) [1995 –: 8.2m 1996 8m 10m 12m⁵ 10m Jul 26] tall gelding: had quick action: fair maiden handicapper: broke leg final start: stayed 1½m: dead. *N. A. Graham* — 75

FIRE DOME (IRE) 4 ch.c. Salt Dome (USA) – Penny Habit (Habitat 134) [1995 104: 6m³ 6m² 7m 6.5m 6m 6g 5s² 5s² 5f⁶ 6m⁵ 1996 6s* 7g⁵ 7.1d² May 24] close-coupled colt: has a quick action: very useful performer: career-best effort to win listed race at Doncaster (by 1¼ lengths from The Puzzler, pair 5 lengths clear) in March: failed to repeat the form, though not disgraced in minor event at Haydock last time: probably stays 7.1f: acts on good to firm ground, goes well on soft: often has tongue tied down: joined K. Ottesen. *R. Hannon* — 112

FIREFIGHTER 7 ch.g. Sharpo 132 – Courtesy Call (Northfields (USA)) [1995 NR 1996 14.1s 14.1m 11.1m* 11.8d May 27] compact gelding: rated 71 at 3 yrs for R. Hollinshead: off course 3 years before return: form only when winning handicap at Hamilton in May, leading 3f out and holding on well: stays 1½m: acts on fibresand and good to firm and soft ground: none too consistent. *B. P. J. Baugh* — 57

FIRE ON ICE (IRE) 4 b.c. Sadler's Wells (USA) 132 – Foolish Lady (USA) (Foolish Pleasure (USA)) [1995 100: 11.4m* 12g³ 12d 1996 10g 10s³ May 29] smallish, strong colt: unimpressive mover: useful performer at best: stiff tasks and below form in 1996: sold (M. Stoute to Mrs D. Haine) only 1,200 gns Newmarket Autumn Sales and seems far from certain to recapture his best. *M. R. Stoute* — 91

FIRLE PHANTASY 3 ch.g. Pharly (FR) 130 – Shamasiya (FR) (Vayrann 133) [1995 72: 7.1d⁶ 7d 1996 8.2m² 8g 8.5m 7m Oct 8] quite good-topped gelding: has scope: has a round action: fair form at best in maidens: tailed-off last (after racing freely) in handicaps after reappearance: bred to stay middle distances: blinkered (out of form) final 3-y-o start: fitted with rope halter for stalls entry. *P. Calver* — 65 d

FIRM CONTRACT (IRE) 4 b.g. Double Schwartz 128 – Glass Goblet (USA) (Storm Bird (CAN) 134) [1995 56p: 6g⁵ 1996 6m 7m Aug 10] modest maiden: no worthwhile form in 1996, set plenty to do and not knocked about (tongue tied, heavily bandaged) second start: bred to be best at up to 1m. *C. N. Allen* — –

FIRST CHANCE (IRE) 2 b.f. (Mar 10) Lahib (USA) 129 – Honagh Lee (Main Reef 126) [1996 6g 6g⁴ Nov 1] IR 10,000Y good-topped filly: has scope: half-sister to 1990 2-y-o 6f winner Mighty Dragon (by Taufan) and winners abroad by Alzao (including at 11f) and Roi Danzig: dam never ran: burly and very green, slowly away and always behind in maiden at Newmarket in October: around 9 lengths fourth of 11 to Kumait in similar event there next time: will be suited by further than 6f: will improve again. *D. R. C. Elsworth* — 56 p

FIRST GALLERY 3 b.f. Charmer 123 – Hound Song 84 (Jukebox 120) [1995 NR 1996 6f a7g a7g⁶ Nov 12] half-sister to 2 winners, including Lochore (1m, by Nordico): dam sprinter: behind in maidens. *R. M. Flower* — –

FIRST GOLD 7 gr.g. Absalom 128 – Cindys Gold 69 (Sonnen Gold 121) [1995 66, a62: 7s⁴ 6.1g⁴ 7g 6m³ 7g⁶ 8g a7g⁶ a8g² a7g⁴ 5m⁵ 7m⁶ 8.9g⁶ 7g* 6.1d 7.1d⁵ a8g a7g⁴ 1996 a8g⁴ a7g* a7g⁴ a8g a7g⁴ a8g³ 7d⁶ 7d⁵ 6.9m* 7m⁵ 8m a8g a8g 7f 8.2g 7g a7g² a8g⁵ Dec 3] lengthy gelding: carries condition: modest performer at best nowadays: won seller at Southwell in January and claimer at Carlisle in May: effective at 6f to 1m: acts on fibresand and on any turf ground: effective blinkered (usually is) or not: best held up, but pulls hard and not an easy ride. *J. Wharton* — 57 d a62 d

FIRST ISLAND (IRE) 4 ch.c. Dominion 123 – Caymana (FR) (Bellypha 130) [1995 8m* 8g* 7m³ 8f² 9d⁴ 10d⁵ 8m² 1996 8d* 9m³ 8.1g⁵ 7.9m* 10f* 8m* 10.4m² 8m³ 10g⁵ 9m* Dec 8] — 127

The response to the decision to throw open the international series at Sha Tin in December to Group 1 winners must have delighted the organizers. Except for the last-minute withdrawals of Iktamal and star attraction Da Hoss there would have been four of them from overseas in each of the three contests, the Hong Kong Vase, the Hong Kong Bowl and the Hong Kong Cup. If the day's programme can be retained in its present form and continue to offer high levels of prize money—there could be as much as £600,000 at stake in the 1997

342

Prince of Wales's Stakes, Royal Ascot—a track record as First Island masters Montjoy and Tamayaz

Cup, for instance—it may well become regarded by owners and trainers as a worthwhile alternative to the Breeders' Cup, and be seen as something for which to set aside a really good horse. There is at present, though, the uncertainty of what will happen to all aspects of life in the territory when mainland China takes over. Da Hoss's defection from the Cup left the Sussex Stakes winner First Island with a clear-cut chance, and he started favourite despite a potentially tricky high draw. The draw did pose First Island problems but he proved well up to the task of coming from last of twelve to win. He was already making ground as they swung into the short straight, and once in line he cut the field down with an impressive burst of speed on the outside, taking a clear lead a furlong from home before holding on a shade comfortably by three quarters of a length and half a length from Australia-based Seascay and New

Sussex Stakes, Goodwood—First Island moves his way smoothly to the front again, this time past Charnwood Forest and Alhaarth (blinkers)

Zealand-based Kingston Bay. All three were Group 1 winners, penalized 5 lb under the new race conditions.

First Island had become a Group 1 winner in July, in the Sussex Stakes at Goodwood. His rise from middle level was one of the success stories of the season. He began the year helping with Pentire's preparation for the Dubai World Cup, while he himself had the more modest objective of the Stones Bitter Doncaster Mile on the opening day of the flat on turf. That achieved, he had a first listed-race victory to his credit. A first pattern-race victory followed on his fourth subsequent start in the Prince of Wales's Stakes at Royal Ascot. Reverses in between in the Earl of Sefton Stakes and the Sandown Mile suggested the Royal Ascot entry might be over-optimistic, but a stylish win from Green Green Desert under top weight in a hot rated stakes at York in May—it turned out to be the best handicap performance of the season—suggested otherwise. The Prince of Wales's Stakes could not have gone better for First Island. Run at a furious gallop and in course-record time, it brought his now-familiar turn of foot bang into play. He came from well back as most of the pacesetters began to wilt, joined issue approaching the final furlong and quickened when given a smack behind the saddle to win by just over a length and the same from the always-prominent Montjoy and the held-up Tamayaz who came clear of the nine other runners.

While Pentire represented the stable in the Eclipse, First Island was kept in reserve for the Sussex Stakes. The latter was the weaker race, probably not so strong a race as usual with the Queen Anne winner Charnwood Forest seeming to stand out on form and even money in a field of ten. First Island's progress had been so impressive that he started second favourite ahead of another very progressive type in Sorbie Tower and the classic filly Matiya, third in the Diane on her latest start. The gallop was again a true one, as always seemed likely with Mistle Cat on hand. Right up First Island's street again, then, even if he was taking a further significant step up in class. He and Charnwood Forest dominated an event in which there were no hard-luck

Hong Kong International Cup, Sha Tin—First Island holds the Australian horse Seascay

Mollers Racing's "First Island"

stories, Alhaarth in third emerging as clear best of the classic generation on the day ahead of Sorbie Tower. For a few strides First Island did appear in danger of being blocked as he was making his way from the rear from three out, but he quickened through an opening at the distance and ran on really strongly, though edging slightly right, to be a length up and well on top at the line.

First Island continued to run well to the end of his long year, the main reason for a failure to add to his victories in three more outings before his trip to the Far East being that connections repeatedly challenged the best. The colt who had begun the year a conservative 21 lb behind Pentire improved again from the Sussex Stakes to finish three lengths second of six to Halling in the Juddmonte International. He couldn't get to grips with the winner, nor could he with the principals in the Queen Elizabeth II Stakes or the Dubai Champion Stakes. He came third of seven to Mark of Esteem at Ascot, beaten just over five lengths, and fifth of six to Bosra Sham, beaten just over six lengths, at Newmarket. The form-book says he reached his peak at York. We shall be able to see whether he has more improvement in him as a five-year-old, for the good news is that he will be in training.

First Island (IRE) (ch.c. 1992)	Dominion (b 1972)	Derring-Do (br 1961)	Darius Sipsey Bridge
		Picture Palace (b 1961)	Princely Gift Palais Glide
	Caymana (FR) (gr or ro 1985)	Bellypha (gr 1976)	Lyphard Belga
		Antrona (gr 1973)	Royal Palace Ileana

As things stand, First Island is a better racehorse than was his sire, the admirable Dominion, now deceased, who finished third in a Two Thousand

Guineas as well as a Queen Elizabeth II Stakes; First Island is also his sire's best offspring. Dominion seemed not to stay beyond a mile and a quarter and is not noted as an influence for stamina. The dam Caymana won races over a mile and a quarter and a mile and a half in France as a three-year-old, the latter a well-contested handicap at Evry. One of her previous two foals, Cayman Native (by Sarhoob), won in the Czech Republic as a two-year-old. The next two dams were very useful racemares, Antrona (fourth in the One Thousand Guineas and the Diane) at up to a mile and a quarter, Ileana at up to a mile.

Trainer Geoff Wragg, commenting on pre-race doubts about the choice of the Sussex Stakes after the Prince of Wales's, said 'First Island has a great turn of foot, but he switches off so well that, not only was I not perturbed about coming back to a mile, but I would not worry about moving up to a mile and a half . . . next year he could even develop into an Arc horse.' The ten furlongs and eighty-five yards of the Juddmonte International is the furthest at which First Island has been tried. He has a sporting chance of getting a mile and a half and we look forward to seeing him have a go. There are plenty of options should he fail. The good-topped First Island, not the best of movers in his slower paces, has yet to tackle soft ground; he acts on firm and dead. His turn of foot and his willingness to settle are indeed great assets, particularly in strongly-run races. He is genuine and very reliable—jockey Michael Hills knows him so well that his tendency to wander off a true line in front is nothing to be concerned about. He is sure to be a force to reckon with again in 1997. *G. Wragg*

FIRST LAW 3 ch.f. Primo Dominie 121 – Barsham 94 (Be My Guest (USA) 126) 57 [1995 NR 1996 7m 6f⁶ 7.1m⁵ 8.5g 8m Aug 13] 13,500Y: half-sister to 4 winners, including Guestwick (15.4f, by Blakeney) and very useful 1996 2-y-o Falkenham (by Polar Falcon): dam, 1¼m winner suited by 1½m, from family of Blakeney and Morston: modest maiden: should be suited by 1m: sold 2,800 gns Newmarket September Sales. *Miss Gay Kelleway*

FIRST MAITE 3 b.g. Komaite (USA) – Marina Plata (Julio Mariner 127) [1995 83 65: 6m a7g 5d* 6m 5d 1996 a6g² a6g⁵ a6g* a6g* a7g⁶ 7s² 5d² 6g 6d⁵ 6m⁴ 7.1d Sep 28] tall, lengthy, angular gelding: has a round action: fairly useful handicapper: won twice at Southwell in February: off for nearly 4 months in mid-season and respectable efforts at best last 4 starts: best at sprint distances: acts on fibresand and soft ground: usually wears blinkers. *S. R. Bowring*

FIRST MAN 2 b.c. (Apr 1) Man Among Men (IRE) – Sharp Thistle 87 (Sharpo – 132) [1996 a7g a8g a6g Dec 7] second reported living foal: half-brother to a winner abroad by Kalaglow: dam 7f winner at 2 yrs, stayed 1½m: no form. *B. J. Llewellyn*

FIRST OPTION 6 ch.g. Primo Dominie 121 – Merrywren (Julio Mariner 127) – [1995 –: 5g 5f 6g 1996 a6g a5g a6g 5g 5f 5m 5.9f⁶ 5f 5m 6g 5m 5m 5g 5.1g Oct 24] close-coupled gelding: tubed: little worthwhile form since 1994. *R. Bastiman*

FIRST PAGE 2 b.f. (Feb 26) Rudimentary (USA) 118 – Miss Paige (AUS) – (Luskin Star (AUS)) [1996 6m 6m 6m Sep 27] neat filly: unimpressive mover: second foal: closely related to 3-y-o 1m winner Miss Pravda (by Soviet Star): dam won over 5½f in Australia: behind in maidens and claimer: sold 600 gns Newmarket Autumn Sales. *W. Jarvis*

FISIOSTAR 3 b.g. Efisio 120 – Sweet Colleen 42 (Connaught 130) [1995 –: 7.5d 39 7f 1996 8g 7.1f⁴ 8.5m 7m⁴ 7m³ 7.1m³ 7.1m Sep 23] workmanlike gelding: poor walker: poor maiden handicapper: stays 7f: acts on good to firm ground: blinkered since second 3-y-o start: inconsistent. *M. Dods*

FISTRAL FLAME 2 ch.f. (Feb 28) Superlative 118 – Northern Empress 80 – (Northfields (USA)) [1996 7m 7g 8d Oct 2] 2,700Y: workmanlike filly: has round action: half-sister to several winners, including fair 3-y-o 7f winner Press On Nicky (by Nicholas) and fairly useful sprinter Press The Bell (by Belfort): dam won 3 times: no form in varied company at Salisbury. *J. S. Moore*

FIT FOR THE JOB (IRE) 2 ch.g. (Feb 21) Mac's Imp (USA) 116 – Jolly Dale ? (IRE) (Huntingdale 132) [1996 a5g⁵ 5m⁴ a5g³ a5g a5g⁶ a5g³ a5g³ a6g* Dec 7] IR a67 5,200F, 3,000Y, 2,500 2-y-o: unfurnished gelding: first foal: dam unraced daughter

346

of half-sister to the dam of Prix Morny winner Tagula: vastly improved form to win maiden at Wolverhampton in December, making all: stays 6f: blinkered (below form) once: joined T. Wall. *W. G. M. Turner*

FITZWILLIAM (USA) 3 b.g. Rahy (USA) 115 – Early Lunch (USA) (Noble 92 Table (USA)) [1995 NR 1996 10m³ 10g* 13.3f⁵ 12m⁴ 12m² Oct 1] $170,000F: tall, lengthy gelding: easy mover: fifth reported foal: half-brother to minor winners in North America by Baldski (2) and Gate Dancer: dam won 7 stakes races, notably Grade 3 Handicap over 1m at 4 yrs: comfortably made all in maiden at Pontefract in July: improved form in strongly-run rated stakes at Newmarket last time, off bit 5f out and staying on: should be suited by further than 1½m: yet to race on a soft surface. *I. A. Balding*

FIVE LIVE 2 b.f. (Feb 11) Pharly (FR) 130 – Manageress 74 (Mandamus 120) 57 [1996 5f⁴ 5g⁵ 5m² Jul 8] 3,600 2-y-o: workmanlike filly: sister to a winner in Denmark and half-sister to 1988 2-y-o 6f seller winner Pacific Wave (by Blushing Scribe) and 7f/1m winner Dealers Delight (by Ballacashtal): dam 6f winner at 2 yrs: modest form in frame in claimer and maiden auction: will be suited by further than 5f. *M. D. Hammond*

FIVE-O-FIFTY 2 b. or br.c. (May 18) Anshan 119 – Wyns Vision (Vision (USA)) 51 [1996 5.1m² 5s 6.1m 5g Oct 18] 3,000F, 2,000Y, 6,000 2-y-o: leggy, sparely-made colt: has a round action: third foal: dam thrice-raced half-sister to smart 5f and 7f winner Glenturret: best efort when short-head second of 4 in claimer at Nottingham: subsequently left Jack Berry: tailed off on soft ground. *J. L. Eyre*

FIZZY BOY (IRE) 3 b.g. Contract Law (USA) 108 – Generation Gap (Young – Generation 129) [1995 NR 1996 10d 11.1g⁵ Sep 2] fourth foal: dam of little account: behind in maidens. *P. Monteith*

FLAG FEN (USA) 5 b. or br.g. Riverman (USA) 131 – Damascus Flag (USA) 63 (Damascus (USA)) [1995 –: a10g⁵ a11g⁵ 8m 8s 12d 1996 9.2d³ 9.9m 10g 9m⁴ 8f 7.3s 8m 6d⁵ 7f⁴ 8f² 7.6m² 8.1m 10m 8.1d Sep 27] useful-looking gelding: seems only modest at best nowadays: sold (Martyn Meade to J. Parkes) 2,300 gns Doncaster October Sales: stays 11f: acts on dead ground and firm: blinkered (below form) eighth 5-y-o outing: sweating (raced freely, below form) penultimate 5-y-o start: often apprentice ridden: inconsistent. *Martyn Meade*

FLAGSHIP 2 ch.f. (Feb 18) Rainbow Quest (USA) 134 – Bireme 127 (Grundy 77 137) [1996 8d² 8.1s⁵ Oct 22] sister to useful 1992 2-y-o 7f winner Yawl and 1989 2-y-o 7f winner (stayed 1¾m) Trireme, and half-sister to several winners: dam won Oaks: head second of 13 to Bold Words in maiden at Salisbury, disputing lead and keeping on well: well-backed favourite, below that form when fifth of 20 in similar event at Chepstow 20 days later: will be suited by middle distances. *Major W. R. Hern*

FLAGSTAFF (USA) 3 b.g. Personal Flag (USA) – Shuffle Up (USA) (Raja 55 Baba (USA)) [1995 –: 7m 6g a7g a7g 1996 a6g⁴ a6g² 6f² 7f² 6f⁵ 7f⁵ 7f a7s a10g Dec a49 30] close-coupled gelding: modest maiden handicapper: sold (out of G. L. Moore's stable) 3,000 gns Newmarket Autumn Sales after seventh start: likely to prove best at up to 7f: acts on fibresand and firm ground: often visored at 3 yrs (best efforts). *K. R. Burke*

FLAHIVE'S FIRST 2 ch.g. (May 13) Interrex (CAN) – Striking Image (IRE) 69 – (Flash of Steel 120) [1996 5f 8.2g Oct 9] 500Y: first foal: dam 11.6f winner, also winning plater over hurdles: soundly beaten in maiden auction and seller. *J. S. Moore*

FLAHUIL 3 b.f. Generous (IRE) 139 – Sipsi Fach 100 (Prince Sabo 123) [1995 – 62: 8m 8.2d⁴ 7g 7m a6g⁶ 1996 a10g⁵ 10d Apr 2] angular filly: modest at best as a juvenile: well beaten in 1996. *R. Hannon*

FLAIR LADY 5 gr.m. Chilibang 120 – Flair Park 66 (Frimley Park 109) [1995 – 51d: 8.5m 8.1g² 8f³ 8g 8.3g² 8.1g⁶ 8m⁵ a7g⁵ a9.4g 1996 a8g 8.3m Aug 3] seems no longer of any account. *W. G. M. Turner*

FLAMANDA 3 b.f. Niniski (USA) 125 – Nemesia 111 (Mill Reef (USA) 141) 67 [1995 NR 1996 10m⁵ 10f⁴ 10.2d Sep 30] leggy filly: has a quick action: second foal: dam, suited by 1½m+, sister to useful 5f and 7f winner Fairy Tern and closely related to smart 1¼m performer Elegant Air: modest form in maidens, running poorly on dead ground: looks a stayer: sold 3,800 gns Newmarket Autumn Sales: sent to Germany. *C. E. Brittain*

FLAMANDS (IRE) 3 b.f. Sadler's Wells (USA) 132 – Fleur Royale 111 (Mill 92 Reef (USA) 141) [1995 –p: 7g 1996 12f² 12m² 12.3d* 14g* 16g⁴ Nov 1] lengthy, good-topped filly with scope: fairly useful performer: won 3-runner maiden at Chester (despite looking unsuited by slowly-run race on tight track) in August then handicap at Newmarket (sweating and gone in coat, led inside final 1f and just pushed out) in October: good fourth to Orchestra Stall in steadily-run listed rated stakes at Newmarket: stays 2m: yet to race on very soft ground, seems to act on any other: tail-swisher. *L. M. Cumani*

FLAMBORO 4 ch.g. Handsome Sailor 125 – Scottish Legend (Legend of France 49 (USA) 124) [1995 49, a–: 7.6m 6g 7f⁴ 7g⁵ a7g 1996 a6g⁵ 7.1g 6.9d² 7d May 6] leggy, a– workmanlike gelding: only poor nowadays: ran as though something amiss final 4-y-o start: stays 7f well: acts on firm ground and dead, well below form on fibresand: inconsistent: sent to Italy. *J. D. Bethell*

FLAME OF HOPE 3 b.f. Marju (IRE) 127 – Tweedling (USA) (Sir Ivor 135) 56 [1995 –: 7d 7m 1996 8.2s 11.6m 11.6m 9f⁴ 8.2f³ 8g Aug 1] sturdy filly: modest maiden handicapper: should stay further than 9f: acts on firm ground: sold Ascot August (2,000 gns) and Newmarket December (800 gns) Sales: sent to Belgium. *J. L. Dunlop*

FLAME VALLEY (USA) 3 b.f. Gulch (USA) – Lightning Fire 105 (Kris 135) 112 [1995 72: 7m⁴ 7m³ 1996 10g⁴ 11.5f² 10m 10m* 10g⁴ 10.1m² 10.1m* 10m³ 10g² 12f Nov 16] tall, leggy filly: has quick action: progressive performer: game effort to win maiden at Windsor in August: generally contested listed/pattern races, decisively winning at Yarmouth (listed race, beating Balalaika and Berenice 3½ lengths) then placed in Sun Chariot Stakes at Newmarket (4½ lengths third to Last Second) and Grade 2 event at Woodbine (1½ lengths second of 8 to Wandering Star) on last 3 starts for M. Stoute: best form at around 1¼m: acts on firm ground, yet to race on a soft surface: consistent. *C. Clement, USA*

FLAMING JUNE (USA) 3 ch.f. Storm Bird (CAN) 134 – Affirmative Fable – (USA) (Affirmed (USA)) [1995 69p: 7f³ 8f⁶ 1996 10.4g 8m Oct 7] leggy filly: fair maiden as juvenile: not seen out until September, and well beaten: stud. *H. R. A. Cecil*

FLAMING MIRACLE (IRE) 6 b.g. Vision (USA) – Red Realm (Realm 129) – [1995 NR 1996 14.1g 21.6m Apr 29] probably no longer of much account on flat: modest but lightly raced over jumps. *G. Barnett*

FLAMING WEST (USA) 2 ch.c. (Feb 2) Gone West (USA) – Flaming Torch 88 92 (Rousillon (USA) 133) [1996 6m² 7g* 7m⁴ Aug 1] smallish, rather unfurnished colt: fluent mover: first foal: dam, 1m winner at 2 yrs in France and Grade 3 11f winner in USA at 4 yrs, out of close relative to Quiet Fling and Peacetime: won 5-runner maiden at York by 2½ lengths from Sturgeon, edging left across runner-up before drawing clear: last and quietly to post, disappointing in minor event at Doncaster following month, finding little and carrying head high: stays 7f: upset in stalls on debut and last outing: sent to USA. *H. R. A. Cecil*

FLAMMA VESTALIS (IRE) 2 b.f. (Apr 29) Waajib 121 – Splendid Chance 51 (Random Shot 116) [1996 5.7f⁶ 6f⁵ Jul 26] rangy, rather unfurnished filly: half-sister to several winners here and abroad, including Italian 3-y-o 7.5f (at 2 yrs) and 1m winner Gooduglybad (by Great Commotion) and smart 1985 2-y-o 5f and 6f winner Luqman (by Runnett): dam, stoutly-bred Irish 1¼m winner, who stayed 1¾m: never reached leaders in maidens at Bath and Thirsk: needs further than 6f: sold 3,000 gns Newmarket December Sales. *J. L. Dunlop*

FLASHFEET 6 b.g. Rousillon (USA) 133 – Miellita 98 (King Emperor (USA)) – [1995 59: a8.5g a9.4g² a8g⁴ a8g³ a7g* a7g³ a8.5g⁵ 8g 1996 a8g⁶ a7g a8.5g⁵ a7g⁶ Jun 14] just a poor performer in 1996: stays 9.4f: acts on heavy going and fibresand: usually held up: sometimes finds little: inconsistent. *K. Bishop*

FLASHING SABRE 4 b.g. Statoblest 120 – Placid Pet 65 (Mummy's Pet 125) – [1995 52, a56: a5g³ 5f 5g 5m⁶ 5f* 5g 5m 5m³ 5m a5g a5g 1996 a6g a6g a5g 7s Oct 24] last on all starts in 1996: left Jack Berry after penultimate one: sold 660 gns Ascot December Sales. *A. J. Chamberlain*

FLASH IN THE PAN (IRE) 3 ch.f. Bluebird (USA) 125 – Tomona (Linacre 49
133) [1995 –: 6m 6m 6.1d 8f 1996 8.3s³ 9.2s⁴ a9.4g⁶ a14.8g⁶ 12d Oct 21] angular
filly: poor maiden: sold out of M. Bell's stable 2,200 gns Newmarket July Sales after
fourth start: should stay further than 9.2f: acts on soft ground. *J. S. Moore*

FLASHMAN 6 b.g. Flash of Steel 120 – Proper Madam 93 (Mummy's Pet 125) 32
[1995 45: a16g* 18g 17.2m³ 16.5g³ 18m* 18.2m² a16.2g² 16.1g 18f 1996 a16g⁶
a16.2g⁴ Apr 13] poor handicapper: stays 2¼m: probably acts on any going: effective
blinkered (not tried since August, 1994) or not: inconsistent. *B. J. Llewellyn*

FLASHY'S SON 8 b. or br.g. Balidar 133 – Flashy Looker 92 (Good Bond 122) 56 d
[1995 71: 6f³ 5g² 6g³ 6m 6m 5f* 6g* 6m⁶ 6m 7g⁵ 7g³ 6g 8f 1996 5g³ 5g⁴ 5.9f⁴ 6m 8g
6.1m 6f 6m Oct 23] sturdy gelding: on the downgrade in 1996: best form on
a sound surface (acts on firm going): tried blinkered, no improvement: often
bandaged, heavily so (when appeared to go lame) last time. *F. Murphy*

FLEETING FOOTSTEPS 4 b.c. Komaite (USA) – Hyperion Palace –
(Dragonara Palace (USA) 115) [1995 NR 1996 7g 6f 8.2m Jun 24] half-brother to a
winning chaser by Van der Linden: dam ran once at 2 yrs: no form. *M. J. Polglase*

FLEET RIVER (USA) 2 b.f. (Jan 27) Riverman (USA) 131 – Nimble Feet 93 p
(USA) 82 (Danzig (USA)) [1996 7g* Aug 24] well-made filly: fifth foal: half-sister
to useful 3-y-o 8.3f winner Yamuna (by Forty Niner), very smart performer at up to
1¼m Eltish (by Cox's Ridge), smart sprinter Forest Gazelle (by Green Forest) and a
1¼m listed winner in France by Majestic Light: dam, 2-y-o 5f winner who stayed 6f,
sister to good US 1994 2-y-o Contredance: 11/8 favourite though green, made all in
7-runner maiden at Goodwood, setting steady pace then quickening clear from 2f
out, beating Caribbean Star by 9 lengths: sure to stay 1m, probably further: likely to
hold her own in better company. *H. R. A. Cecil*

FLEMENSFIRTH (USA) 4 b.c. Alleged (USA) 138 – Etheldreda (USA) 64 122
(Diesis 133) [1995 121: 9m² 10.5d* 12g⁵ 8m⁶ 9.8s* 1996 9.8d* 10m* Nov 10]
    Flemensfirth made the best of even fewer opportunities in the latest
season, winning the Prix Dollar and the Premio Roma on his only starts. When
sent over to Longchamp in October for the Dollar he was ending an absence of
a year and a week from racing, caused in the first place by injury and then by
lack of 'suitable' ground. Flemensfirth had sustained a small fracture of the
near-fore cannon-bone in the course of winning the Dollar from mainly older
horses as a three-year-old; he was ready to run again by Royal Ascot in 1996
but with firm ground prevailing he was put on one side until the autumn. If
fit, he had an excellent chance of a second Dollar, for the eleven-runner
international field seemed no stronger than the previous year and was not
particularly strong for a Group 2 race on an Arc-weekend card. He justified

Prix Dollar, Longchamp—
Flemensfirth returns from his year off with an impressive defeat of Percutant

favouritism impressively by two lengths from market rival, the consistent French five-year-old Percutant, never looking in much danger once he'd quickened into the lead halfway up the straight, having been settled inmidfield in a race run at a very strong gallop. In 1995 he'd made all, giving weight all round as a result of a penalty for winning the Prix Lupin. Flemensfirth was allowed to take his chance on the unseasonable good to firm ground at Rome in November. Even before his leg injury there had been doubts about his effectiveness on such a surface, and he had gained all his victories on dead or softer. But, while he failed to win with the authority expected of a 2/1-on chance, he ran at least as well as he'd ever done to beat German-trained Group 1 winner Hollywood Dream and Needle Gun by a neck and a length in a good battle, having taken over from the front-running Needle Gun around two furlongs out. Afterwards it was announced that Flemensfirth would remain in training and would start off as a five-year-old in the Dubai World Cup or the Prix Ganay. He needs to improve further to stand a chance in the former.

			Hoist The Flag	Tom Rolfe
Flemensfirth (USA) (b.c. 1992)	Alleged (USA) (b 1974)		(b 1968)	Wavy Navy
		Princess Pout	Prince John
		(b 1966)	Determined Lady
	Etheldreda (USA) (ch 1985)	Diesis	Sharpen Up
		(ch 1980)	Doubly Sure
		Royal Bund	Royal Coinage
		(ch 1961)	Nato

These early plans suggest that Flemensfirth's trainer—who was acclaimed for having him spot on for Longchamp—has come to regard his optimum distance as around a mile and a quarter. However, Flemensfirth ran well on his only start to date at a mile and a half in the Prix du Jockey-Club, finishing under three lengths fifth of eleven to Celtic Swing after meeting trouble in a slowly-run race. Given that, and that his sire is Alleged, and that he is amenable to restraint when it's needed, there is a case to be made for having another crack at the longer trip. Further to his breeding—a stayer of some significance emerged from the family in the latest season in the form of the Queen's Vase winner Gordi, who is out of an Alydar half-sister to Flemensfirth's lightly-raced dam Etheldreda. A rangy colt, Flemensfirth acts on soft ground and good to firm. Bred as he is, lightly raced as he is, and trained by whom he is, he may well have more improvement in him than most five-year-olds. Let's hope that he is seen out more often. *J. H. M. Gosden.*

FLETCHER 2 b.g. (Jan 24) Salse (USA) 128 – Ballet Classique (USA) 84 (Sadler's Wells (USA) 132) [1996 5m* 6f 6g⁴ 7f⁴ 6d 8m² 7.9g Oct 10] 62,000Y: good-topped gelding: easy mover: second foal: half-brother to very smart 7f (at 2 yrs) and 1m winner Bishop of Cashel (by Warning): dam 1½m winner, half-sister to Oaks third New Coins and useful stayer Kublai: won maiden at Newmarket in April then seventh of 15 in Coventry Stakes at Ascot: failed to progress, though ran creditably in nursery at Bath on penultimate start: sold 14,000 gns Newmarket Autumn Sales: stays 1m well: acts on firm ground: carries head awkwardly, and looks of dubious temperament (downed tools at halfway fifth outing). *P. F. I. Cole* **85 §**

FLEUVE D'OR (IRE) 2 gr.f. (May 20) Last Tycoon 131 – Aldern Stream 102 (Godswalk (USA) 130) [1996 6f 6.9d a7g⁶ Nov 16] IR 7,000Y: angular, workmanlike filly: half-sister to several winners, including 1991 2-y-o sprinter Showbrook (by Exhibitioner) and 1m/1¼m performer Smarginato (by Simply Great), both smart: dam 5f and 7f winner: little form. *D. Haydn Jones* **–**

FLIGHT MASTER 4 ch.g. Master Willie 129 – Mumtaz Mayfly 64 (Tap On 63 Wood 130) [1995 65: 9.7m⁴ 11.4g³ 12m⁶ 1996 11.4m⁶ 10g 11.7m* 11.9f³ 10.8m³ 14m 14.1g Oct 30] angular gelding: often tubed nowadays: modest handicapper: won seller at Bath on firm ground: stays 1½m: acts on firm ground: inconsistent. *P. J. Makin*

FLINT AND STEEL 3 b.g. Rock City 120 – Brassy Nell 72 (Dunbeath (USA) 58 127) [1995 58p: 7.1m 8d 1996 6m⁴ 8d Oct 2] useful-looking gelding: modest maiden:

looked capable of better after reappearance, but sold out of R. Hannon's stable 4,400 gns Newmarket July Sales: well beaten only subsequent start. *Bob Jones*

FLIRTING AROUND (USA) 2 b.c. (Apr 10) Silver Hawk (USA) 123 – 82 + Dancing Grass (USA) (Northern Dancer) [1996 7d² 8f 8.2s⁴ Oct 31] $275,000Y: sturdy, good sort: has a short, quick action: fourth foal: half-brother to a winner in USA by Believe It: dam, unraced close relative to useful middle-distance performer Song of Sixpence, from the family of Fort Marcy and Key To The Mint: promising second to stable-companion Yalaietanee in maiden at Newmarket on debut: easily better subsequent effort when fourth of 13, again staying on not knocked about, to Desert Horizon in similar event at Nottingham: will be suited by further than 1m: seems suited by an easy surface: capable of winning a race. *M. R. Stoute*

FLIRTY GERTIE 4 ch.f. Prince Sabo 123 – Red Tapsi (Tap On Wood 130) – [1995 69: 5g³ 5m² 6g³ 7g² 8m 1996 a7g* a7g 8m 7g a7g 6.1m Sep 16] big, lengthy a78 d filly: fair performer: won maiden at Southwell in January by 5 lengths: disappointing afterwards and sold 5,500 gns Newmarket Autumn Sales: stays 7f: acts on fibresand: usually races prominently: sent to Saudi Arabia. *R. Boss*

FLOATING DEVON 2 br.g. (Feb 24) Simply Great (FR) 122 – Devon Dancer 58 (GB) 73 (Shareef Dancer (USA) 135) [1996 6m⁴ a7g⁵ a6g 7m⁴ 7.5f⁶ 7.9g Oct 10] 9,500Y: first foal: dam 7f winner at 2 yrs, stayed 1m: modest form: best effort on debut: should be suited by further than 6f. *T. D. Easterby*

FLOATING LINE 8 ch.g. Bairn (USA) 126 – County Line 75 (High Line 125) 79 [1995 76: 10f⁵ 12m⁶ 12m⁵ 10g* 10.5m⁶ 13.9g⁴ 12d⁵ 11.9g² 14g* 13.9g² 14.6m 1996 13.9m 10m⁴ 12f⁴ 15.9m 14.8m³ 12.3m² 13m⁵ 11.9m 15.9d² 13.1m² 14m* 18g⁴ Oct 19] lengthy gelding: has a round action: fair handicapper: took long time to return to form, but winner then good fourth of 26 in Inchcailloch in Cesarewitch at Newmarket in October: stays 2¼m, and effective over much shorter: acts on firm and dead ground: has run well when sweating: usually races prominently. *E. J. Alston*

FLOCHECK (USA) 3 ch.c. Hansel (USA) – Eurobird 118 (Ela-Mana-Mou 132) 97 [1995 67?: 8m 8.2m 1996 10g⁵ 14.6m² 17.2g⁴ 14d² 18.2m² 16.2m 16.2d* Oct 11] leggy, angular colt: generally progressive handicapper: won at Bath in May and at Ascot in October: very much a stayer: acted on good to firm and dead ground: tended to carry head high and go in snatches: suited by forcing tactics: dead. *J. L. Dunlop*

FLOOD'S FANCY 3 b. or gr.f. Rambo Dancer (CAN) 126 – Port Na Blath (On Your Mark 125) [1995 54: 5m 6m 5.1m 6m* 7m 6g a6g⁵ a6g⁵ 1996 a6g a6g a7g⁶ 8.1d 6m Sep 6] tall, lengthy, rather dipped-backed filly: no worthwhile form in 1996, leaving A. Bailey after second start: stays 6f: acts on good to firm ground and fibresand: tried blinkered, no improvement: modest hurdler. *L. J. Barratt*

FLOOD'S FLYER (IRE) 2 ch.f. (Apr 21) Silver Kite (USA) 111 – Al Shany 92 – (Burslem 123) [1996 5m⁶ 5s⁵ 6m⁴ May 18] 3,400Y: first foal: dam effective at 1¼m to 1½m: soundly beaten in varied company, including selling. *N. Tinkler*

FLOOD'S HOT STUFF 2 gr.f. (Feb 22) Chilibang 120 – Tiszta Sharok 81 – (Song 132) [1996 6m 6m⁶ 5g 8g Nov 2] 10,000Y: workmanlike filly: sixth foal: half-sister to several winners, including disappointing 3-y-o Akalim, 6f winner at 2 yrs, and Irish 9f and 1¼m winner Petofi (both by Petong): dam 2-y-o 5f winner: behind in maidens, claimer and seller: joined N. Littmoden. *M. R. Channon*

FLORENTINE DIAMOND (IRE) 2 b.f. (Mar 22) Primo Dominie 121 – Pop-lina (USA) (Roberto (USA) 131) [1996 5.3f⁶ 5.1m 6g 5m Sep 23] 24,000Y: fourth foal: half-sister to winners in Italy (by Damister) and Germany (up to 13f, by Belmez): dam, French 11f winner, half-sister to champion US older horse Vanland-ingham: always behind in maidens: retained by trainer 10,000 gns Newmarket Autumn Sales: needs further than 5f: sent to Saudi Arabia. *Sir Mark Prescott*

FLORENTINO (IRE) 3 b. or br.c. Machiavellian (USA) 123 – Helens Dream- 73 girl 95 (Caerleon (USA) 132) [1995 –: 6d 1996 8d 7g 9.7m* 10.8f³ 10.2f* 11f⁶ Nov 5] tall, close-coupled colt: has scope: generally progressive handicapper: won at Folkestone in May and Bath in July: off course 4 months, just respectable effort on return: better suited by around 1¼m than shorter and should stay 1½m: acts on firm ground. *B. W. Hills*

FLORID (USA) 5 ch.h. The Minstrel (CAN) 135 – Kenanga 105 (Kris 135) [1995 110 108: 10m⁶ 10m* 10m² 10g² 10f⁴ 12f⁶ 1996 10g⁴ 12d⁴ 10m* 11.5m³ 11.8g³ 10m³

10.1g[3] Oct 30] tall, good-topped horse: tends to look very well: good walker: has a fluent action: useful performer: fourth in John Porter Stakes at Newbury before winning minor event at Newmarket in May: good efforts last 3 starts, in listed and conditions events: stays 1½m: acts on firm and soft ground: normally front runner/races prominently: consistent: joined C. Brooks. *H. R. A. Cecil*

FLORISMART 4 b.g. Never So Bold 135 – Spoilt Again 91 (Mummy's Pet 125) – [1995 8.3m[4] 8.1g 10m 8m a8.5g 1996 a12g 10.5d 12.1m 16.2f Aug 15] sparely-made gelding: seems no longer of much account. *B. P. J. Baugh*

FLORRIE'M 3 ch.f. Tina's Pet 121 – Rosie Dickins 59 (Blue Cashmere 129) – [1995 –: 6f 7m 1996 a7g a8g 6m 8.2m 8g 8.5f 7d a6g[5] a7g Nov 29] big, workmanlike filly: little form. *J. A. Harris*

FLO'S CHOICE (IRE) 2 b.f. (Mar 10) Dancing Dissident (USA) 119 – Miss Siddons (Cure The Blues (USA)) [1996 6g 5g[5] 7g 6m 6m a6g Sep 7] 2,200F, 11,000Y: leggy filly: seventh foal: half-sister to several winners, including Irish 1¾m winner Any Minute Now (by Alzao) and 1¼m winner The Feltmaker (by Shernazar): dam twice-raced half-sister to Princess Pati and Seymour Hicks: well beaten in maidens and a seller: has sweated. *J. A. Harris*

FLOTILLA 2 b.g. (Feb 10) Saddlers' Hall (IRE) 126 – Aim For The Top (USA) 71 111 (Irish River (FR) 131) [1996 5m[6] a6g[2] 6.1g 7g[2] a7g 8f Oct 8] good-topped gelding: poor mover: fifth foal: closely related to useful 1993 2-y-o 7f winner Dance To The Top (by Sadler's Wells), later effective at 1¼m, and half-brother to 3-y-o Right To The Top (by Nashwan): dam, 6f (at 2 yrs) to 8.5f winner, from good family: fair form: sold to join S. Mellor 10,500 gns Newmarket Autumn Sales: should stay further than 7f: reportedly finished sore after being reshod when tailed off penultimate outing: gelded. *Sir Mark Prescott*

FLOURISHING WAY 2 b.f. (Jan 12) Sadler's Wells (USA) 132 – Darayna 78 (IRE) (Shernazar 131) [1996 6m 6m[2] 7.5m[2] Sep 18] good-topped, attractive filly: first reported foal: dam Irish 7f and 1m winner out of very smart 6f/7f winner Dafayna, herself half-sister to Doyoun and Dolpour (by Sadler's Wells): very much in need of race on debut: second in maidens won by Calypso Lady at Kempton and Lyrical Bid at Beverley (set steady pace, edged left and caught on line): stays 7.5f. *R. Charlton*

FLOW BACK 4 gr.g. Royal Academy (USA) 130 – Flo Russell (USA) (Round 62 Table) [1995 5v[5] 6s 7g[2] 1996 8f a10g[6] 12m a12g[*] a12g[6] a13g a11g Dec 3] 60,000Y: ex-Irish gelding: closely related to useful Irish 1m winner Crockadore (by Nijinsky) who later stayed 1½m and won in USA, and half-brother to several winners, notably very useful performer Flowing (by El Gran Senor): dam placed in USA: contested 5 maidens for D. Weld, best effort (rated 82) when blinkered final 3-y-o start: sold 11,000 gns Newmarket Autumn 1995 Sales: springer in market, won handicap at Southwell (under 5-lb claimer) in July: stays 1½m: acts on fibresand. *G. P. Enright*

FLOWER HILL LAD (IRE) 2 b.c. (Mar 11) Sizzling Melody 117 – Persian 62 Tapestry 70 (Tap On Wood 130) [1996 6m 7g[4] 7g[6] 7.9g a7s Nov 19] IR 2,500Y: unfurnished colt: fifth foal: half-brother to modest 3-y-o sprinter Need You Badly (by Robellino): dam 1¼m winner: modest maiden: stays 7f: form only on good ground. *D. J. S. Cosgrove*

FLOWING FORTUNE 2 b.c. (Feb 28) Kenmare (FR) 125 – Green Flower 67 p (USA) 56 (Fappiano (USA)) [1996 7g[2] Oct 18] big, rangy colt: first foal: dam thrice-raced sister to 1985 champion US 2-y-o Tasso: 7/2, backward and green, well-held second to Squeak in 3-runner Newmarket Challenge Cup: should improve. *E. A. L. Dunlop*

FLOWING OCEAN 6 ch.h. Forzando 122 – Boswellia 109 (Frankincense 120) – [1995 79: a7g[*] 8g a7g 1996 a8.5g a7g a9.4g a12g a11g Dec 27] good-topped horse: has had knee problems: sold out of Miss G. Kelleway's stable only 680 gns Newmarket July Sales before soundly beaten in 1996: should stay beyond 1m: acts on fibresand, may well require a soft surface on turf. *D. W. Chapman*

FLUIDITY (USA) 8 b.g. Robellino (USA) 127 – Maple River (USA) (Clan- – destine) [1995 NR 1996 8f Jun 5] modest jumper: never a threat on only flat run since 1994: stays 1½m: tried blinkered/visored. *J. G. M. O'Shea*

FLYAWAY BLUES 4 b.g. Bluebird (USA) 125 – Voltigeuse (USA) (Filiberto 52 §
(USA) 123) [1995 60: 7g 10d 12.3m⁴ 13g 6m² 7g² 8m³ 8f³ 8.3f⁴ 8.3f² 7m² 7g 1996
7g 10g 10d³ 7m 16m 8m³ 8.3g 8.5m Sep 18] tall, angular gelding: good walker:
modest and unreliable maiden: seems to stay 1½m: acts on firm and dead ground:
tends to hang: usually blinkered/visored nowadays: carries head high, and not one to
trust: won selling hurdle (put head in air) in December. *Mrs M. Reveley*

FLYAWAY HILL (FR) 2 b.f. (Apr 13) Danehill (USA) 126 – Flyaway Bride 70 p
(USA) 104 (Blushing Groom (FR) 131) [1996 7m⁵ 7d Oct 2] 290,000 francs Y:
half-sister to 1¼m winner Handmaiden (by Shardari) and a winner in Italy by Kris:
dam Irish sprinter, third in Moyglare Stud Stakes: better effort in maidens when
around 5 lengths fifth of 12 to Indihash at Lingfield: showed nothing on dead ground:
will probably do better. *P. W. Harris*

FLY DOWN TO RIO (IRE) 2 ch.f. (Mar 28) Silver Kite (USA) 111 – Brazilian –
Princess 66 (Absalom 128) [1996 6g⁵ 6f 7m 8.1g 7f 7.5m 6s a8.5g Oct 19] 17,500Y:
leggy, unfurnished filly: fourth living foal: half-sister to German 3-y-o Great Liberty
(by Common Grounds), 6f winner at 2 yrs, fair sprinter Soba Guest (by Be My Guest)
and Irish 9f winner Wolfies Rascal (by Northiam): dam, maiden who stayed 1m, is
half-sister to Soba: well beaten, including in sellers: blinkered last 2 starts: sold 1,000
gns Newmarket Autumn Sales: sent to Spain. *D. W. P. Arbuthnot*

FLYFISHER (IRE) 3 b.c. Batshoof 122 – Inveraven 53 (Alias Smith (USA)) 99
[1995 95: 8m⁶ 7.1d⁵ 10.2m² 10g* 1996 11d² 12m 10m³ 14.8m⁶ 10.9m⁵ 8.1s Oct
22] rangy colt: has scope: fluent mover: useful performer: second in minor event at
Newbury and eighth of 15 in Derby Italiano at Rome in the spring: well beaten
afterwards: sold 26,000 gns Newmarket Autumn Sales: stays 1½m: acts on good to
firm and dead ground: has an awkward head carriage: keen sort, and sometimes front
runner: inconsistent: sent to USA. *G. Lewis*

FLY FISHING (USA) 3 ch.c. Miswaki (USA) 124 – Sharp Flick (USA) (Shar- 88
pen Up 127) [1995 74p: 7g 8.2m³ 8.1s³ 1996 8.5d 8g⁵ 10d² 8g* 8d Aug 15] sturdy,
close-coupled colt: left Mrs J. Cecil after disappointing (looked rather headstrong)
on reappearance: sent to France and won claimer at Maisons-Laffitte in July, and
showed fairly useful form over hurdles: stays 1¼m. *F. Doumen, France*

FLY-GIRL 2 ch.f. (Mar 25) Clantime 101 – Lyndseylee 96 (Swing Easy (USA) –
126) [1996 5.1m⁶ 5.1m Jul 26] good-bodied filly: second foal: sister to fair 3-y-o 5f
performer Dande Flyer: dam best at 5f: well beaten in maidens at Chester (slowly
away) and Nottingham (hung badly left). *B. P. J. Baugh*

FLYING COLOURS (IRE) 2 b.f. (Feb 2) Fairy King (USA) – Crazed Rainbow –
(USA) (Graustark) [1996 7d Oct 28] 29,000F, 7,500Y: third foal: closely related to a
winner abroad (including at 1¼m) by Nordico and half-sister to another by Alzao:
dam, ran once in France, is half-sister to King Of Clubs: 33/1, slowly away when last
of 11 in maiden at Lingfield. *C. J. Benstead*

FLYING FLOWERS 3 ch.f. Thatching 131 – Flying Fairy 79 (Bustino 136) –
[1995 70: 6m⁶ 7g 1996 8f 7.1m 8.2m Aug 7] tall, leggy filly: no worthwhile form in
1996: sold 5,000 gns Newmarket Autumn Sales. *R. Hannon*

FLYING GREEN (FR) 3 ch.g. Persian Bold 123 – Flying Sauce 107 (Sauce 95
Boat (USA)) [1995 80: 7m⁴ 7f² 7d 1996 10.2f* 10m 10m Aug 16] leggy, lengthy
gelding: easily best effort when winning maiden at Bath in July, making all:
subsequently sold out of R. Charlton's stable 30,000 gns Newmarket July Sales:
below form afterwards: stays 10.2f well: acts on firm ground: has joined M. Pipe.
N. J. H. Walker

FLYING HAROLD 3 b.c. Gildoran 123 – Anytime Anywhere 77 (Daring March 45
116) [1995 58: 6d 7m 1996 7m 7m⁶ 7.1m 10m⁵ 8g⁵ 8f² 8.3m² 8m 8m Sep 19]
close-coupled colt: poor maiden: stays 1m: acts on firm and dead ground: front
runner: no battler. *M. R. Channon*

FLYING LEGEND (USA) 3 b.c. Alleged (USA) 138 – L'Extravagante (USA) 98 +
(Le Fabuleux 133) [1995 NR 1996 11.8m⁴ 12.3m* 14.8d* 14.6m Sep 14] very tall
colt: still rather weak: has a long, roundish action: fifteenth foal: brother to smart
Irish 1¼m winner Montelimar and half-brother to numerous winners, including
useful middle-distance performer Duc de Berry (by Chief's Crown): dam, winner 3

353

times at up to 1m, is daughter of outstanding Franfreluche: favourite, impressive winner of maiden at Ripon in June and handicap at Newmarket (heavily backed, sweating and on toes, by 5 lengths) in August: well-beaten ninth of 11 in the St Leger at Doncaster: should stay beyond 14.8f: acts on good to firm and dead ground: stays in training and remains a very useful prospect. *H. R. A. Cecil*

FLYING NORTH (IRE) 3 b.g. Distinctly North (USA) 115 – North Kildare 80 (USA) (Northjet 136) [1995 75: 6f² 5.9f* 6m³ 6m 6f 1996 8g³ 8m 8.2f³ 10.3m⁶ 8m⁴ 8g 8m 9.2g² 8g 8g Nov 2] leggy gelding: good mover: fair handicapper: best efforts in 1996 when in frame: stays 9.2f: acts on firm ground, yet to race on a soft surface: has taken keen hold: carries head a bit high. *Mrs M. Reveley*

FLYING PENNANT (IRE) 3 ch.c. Waajib 121 – Flying Beckee (IRE) 60 72 (Godswalk (USA) 130) [1995 59p: 7.1g 1996 8.2s 8d 7m* 7d⁴ 8g² 8m³ 8.3g² 7g 8.2g Oct 24] strong, good-bodied colt: has a quick action: fair handicapper: awarded claimer at Salisbury in May: first runs for over 3 months, always behind last 2 starts: sold (R. Hannon to M. Bradley) 7,500 gns Newmarket Autumn Sales: stays 8.3f: acts on good to firm ground and dead: usually races prominently. *R. Hannon*

FLYING SQUAW 3 b.f. Be My Chief (USA) 122 – Sea Fret 96 (Habat 127) – [1995 102+: 5m* 6m* 6g⁴ 6m² 6m⁴ 6d* 1996 7.3d Apr 19] sturdy filly: useful form as a juvenile: 25/1, well-beaten last of 9 in Fred Darling Stakes at Newbury only 3-y-o start, finishing distressed: bred to stay beyond 6f: acts on good to firm and dead ground: covered by Barathea. *M. R. Channon*

FLYING THATCH (IRE) 2 b.c. (Mar 23) Thatching 131 – More Candy 98 – (Ballad Rock 122) [1996 6g 6s 6d Nov 8] IR 24,000F, 45,000Y: quite attractive colt: seventh foal: half-brother to 4 winners, including smart Irish 3-y-o sprinter Sunset Reigns (by Taufan): dam Irish 6f winner: always behind in maidens: sold 3,800 gns Doncaster November Sales: sent to Denmark. *R. Hannon*

FLY ME HOME 2 ch.c. (Apr 29) Efisio 120 – My Croft 64 (Crofter (USA) 124) – [1996 6g⁶ 6gy² Nov 2] rather unfurnished colt: third foal: half-brother to 3-y-o Dil Dil (by Puissance), 5f winner at 2 yrs: dam 2-y-o 5f winner on only start: little form in median auction maidens nearly 3 months apart: burly, unimpressive to post and slowly away on debut: sent to Sweden. *B. A. McMahon*

FLY TIP (IRE) 3 b.f. Bluebird (USA) 125 – Sharp Deposit (Sharpo 132) [1995 – 79p: 6d* 1996 6g 6g⁴ 7f 6.1s 8g Oct 29] neat filly: failed to fulfil debut promise for new stable. *B. J. Meehan*

FLY TO THE STARS 2 b.c. (Feb 2) Bluebird (USA) 125 – Rise And Fall (Mill 83 p Reef (USA) 141) [1996 6s³ 7f² Nov 5] 125,000Y: tall colt: has scope: has a round action: fourth foal: half-brother to 3 winners abroad, notably smart French middle-distance performer Danseur Landais (by Damister): dam lightly-raced sister to smart colts Paradise Bay (at up to 1½m) and Special Leave out of smart middle-distance sister to Highclere: 4 lengths third of 23 to Za-Im in maiden at Newbury: length second of 16, staying on strongly having edged right when first ridden, to Tayseer in maiden at Redcar following month: will be well suited by 1m+: sure to improve further, and should win a race. *M. Johnston*

FOG CITY 3 b.g. Damister (USA) 123 – Front Line Romance 89 (Caerleon – (USA) 132) [1995 71+, a83p: 7.1m⁴ 7.1d³ a6g* 1996 6.1d 6g Sep 3] smallish gelding: quite promising as a juvenile: well beaten on belated return, giving impression something amiss last time: subsequently gelded: bred to stay beyond 7f: acts on fibresand: sent to Malaysia. *W. Jarvis*

FOIST 4 b.g. Efisio 120 – When The Saints (Bay Express 132) [1995 –: a7g 7.5m 53 + 7g 9.9m 1996 a6g* a6g* a6g* 5.9d⁵ 5g 6m⁵ 7g³ 8.5m³ 8.9g Oct 12] small, good- a65 + topped gelding: fair handicapper on the all-weather: won twice at Southwell and once at Wolverhampton early in 1996: not so good yet on turf, but promises to be so: stays 8.5f: acts on fibresand, probably on good to firm and dead: blinkered (raced too freely) final 4-y-o start: sure to win more races in 1997. *M. W. Easterby*

FOLGORE (USA) 2 ch.f. Irish River (FR) 131 – Florie (FR) (Gay Mecene 83 (USA) 128) [1996 7d* 7.5d² 7.5s* 8s Oct 12] fifth foal: half-sister to smart middle-distance filly Fanjica (by Law Society), 7.5f and 9f winner at 2 yrs, and useful Italian performer at up to 15f Almanor (by Akarad): dam placed at up to 1½m in France:

won maiden in July and minor event in September, both at Milan: towards rear in Group 3 event there final start: likely to be suited by middle distances: has raced only on a soft surface. *J. L. Dunlop*

FOLLOWMEGIRLS　7 b.m. Sparkling Boy 110 – Haddon Anna (Dragonara Palace (USA) 115) [1995 54: 5d 5m⁶ 5f⁴ 5m⁶ 6m 5f⁴ 5f 5m 5m 6.1d 5d* 5m⁵ 1996 5s 5g 5g 5m 5f Jun 24] leggy, lengthy mare: modest sprint handicapper: broke a leg final start: acted on any going: best recent form in blinkers: dead. *Mrs A. L. M. King*　–

FOLLOWTHE ALLSTARS　3 ch.c. Anshan 119 – Angel's Sing (Mansingh (USA) 120) [1995 NR 1996 8.2d 10f⁶ 9m 10.8m 10f 8f² 8m 10m⁴ 8g a12g⁵ Nov 7] tall colt: third foal: dam unraced: beaten a neck in claimer at Brighton in August, coming from off pace then looking none too keen: no comparable form: stays 1m: acts on firm going: blinkered since sixth 3-y-o start. *T. J. Naughton*　56 d

FOLLY FOOT FRED　2 b.g. (Apr 16) Crisp 87 – Wessex Kingdom 68 (Vaigly Great 127) [1996 5.1g* 5m⁴ 6g⁶ 5.1m⁶ 7m⁵ Jul 5] leggy, unfurnished gelding: fourth living foal to thoroughbred stallion: half-brother to 1990 2-y-o 6f winner Majestic Gambler (by Enchantment) and a winning hurdler by Faustus: dam 5f winner: came from well off pace when winning seller at Nottingham in April by a length: similar form afterwards, mostly in face of stiff tasks: stays 7f. *B. R. Millman*　52

FOND EMBRACE　3 b.f. Emarati (USA) 74 – Detente 87 (Dominion 123) [1995 75+: 5m³ 6f³ 5g⁶ 5.2d³ 1996 5.1g* 5d* 5m Sep 11] leggy filly: useful performer: won median auction maiden at Nottingham in April and minor event at Haydock in May: bred to be as effective at 6f and 5f but races keenly: acts on good to firm and dead ground. *H. Candy*　99

FONTCAUDETTE (IRE)　2 b.f. (Apr 30) River Falls 113 – Lune de Miel 80 (Kalamoun 129) [1996 7g⁵ 7f 6m Sep 18] IR 5,200Y, resold 7,500Y: half-sister to 1993 2-y-o 6f winner Salt Corn (by Chilibang), 8.2f winner Nice And Sharp (by Sharpo) and several winners abroad: dam 2-y-o 6f winner: little form in maidens. *J. E. Banks*　–

FONZY　2 b.g. (Feb 28) Phountzi (USA) 104 – Diavalezza (Connaught 130) [1996 a5g* 5m* 6g⁵ 5g³ 5m² 5f* 5g* Jul 2] 800Y: sparely-made gelding: first foal: dam unraced half-sister to Cherry Hinton third Hilly: successful in maiden auction at Southwell (only outing for R. Boss) and claimers at Thirsk and Musselburgh (2, on second occasion after losing several lengths when rearing start): best at 5f: blinkered last 4 starts, setting off too fast first time: stirred up at stalls second and third outings, and reared over in stalls when withdrawn in mid-July. *Mrs L. Stubbs*　64

FOOLISH FLUTTER (IRE)　2 b. or br.f. (Mar 26) Fools Holme (USA) – Thornbeam (Beldale Flutter (USA) 130) [1996 5g 6g 7.5m 7.1m³ 7g 8f 10m 10g⁵ Oct 24] IR 2,600F, IR 1,100Y: leggy filly: half-sister to 3-y-o 1¼m winner Russian Rose (by Soviet Lad), 1993 2-y-o 6f winner Bet A Plan (by Cyrano de Bergerac) and a winner in Belgium: dam never ran: poor plater: visored or blinkered last 5 starts. *G. R. Oldroyd*　–

FOOLS OF PRIDE (IRE)　4 ch.f. Al Hareb (USA) 123 – I'll Take Paris (USA) (Vaguely Noble 140) [1995 39: a8.5g⁶ a9.4g⁴ a8g⁵ a9.4g⁵ a11g³ a11g² a12g⁵ a9.4g⁵ 12m 16m³ 12m⁵ 16.2g⁶ a14.8g* 16.2m² 16.2m⁶ 13.8g 17.1m a14.8g⁴ a16g 1996 a11g a16g⁴ a14.8g⁴ a13g a16g Feb 29] poor performer: no form in 1996: stays 2m: acts on good to firm ground and fibresand. *R. Hollinshead*　–

FOOT BATTALION (IRE)　2 b.c. (Feb 13) Batshoof 122 – Roxy Music (IRE) 63 (Song 132) [1996 5s⁴ 5g* 5.1g² 6m⁶ 6g 5g² 6.1m³ 7m³ 6.1m² 7g⁵ 6m a7g² Dec 14] IR 7,500Y: strong, close-coupled colt: first foal: dam 7f winner at 2 yrs: fairly useful performer: won median auction maiden at Pontefract in April: stays 7f: acts on good to firm ground and fibresand: has sweated. *R. Hollinshead*　85

FOOTHILL (IRE)　3 b.g. Tirol 127 – Threshold (Alleged (USA) 138) [1995 NR 1996 7g 10m May 13] IR 2,600Y: second foal: dam never ran: tailed off in maidens. *R. T. Phillips*　–

FORCING BID　2 b.g. (May 19) Forzando 122 – Cox's Pippin (USA) (Cox's Ridge (USA)) [1996 5g⁴ 6f³ 5d⁶ 7.1s⁵ Nov 7] 10,500Y, 20,000 2-y-o: fourth foal: half-brother to 4-y-o 7f winner Cuban Reef (by Dowsing) and Carreras (by Most Welcome), winner abroad including German listed 1m event: dam unraced grand-　68 daughter of Irish Oaks winner Regal Exception: best effort when 5 lengths third of 15, leading 5f, to Craigievar in maiden auction at Warwick on second start: should stay 7f: best form on firm ground, poor effort on soft. *Sir Mark Prescott*

FORECAST 3 b.g. Formidable (USA) 125 – Princess Matilda 110 (Habitat 134) [1995 –: a5g 1996 a6g a7g 6.1m* 6d a6g 6f⁶ 7g 7d 10g 6m Oct 7] won seller at Nottingham in April: no other worthwhile form: stays 6.1f: tried blinkered/visored, no improvement. *J. Wharton*   61 d a–

FOREIGN JUDGEMENT (USA) 3 b.g. El Gran Senor (USA) 136 – Numeral (USA) (Alleged (USA) 138) [1995 75: 8d⁶ 7m 1996 10m 10g 10m 12s Nov 11] rather unfurnished gelding: has a round action: fair form as a juvenile: showed little for new stable in 1996. *W. J. Musson*   –

FOREIGN RELATION (IRE) 3 b.f. Distant Relative 128 – Nicola Wynn 83 (Nicholas Bill 125) [1995 NR 1996 5g⁴ 6g⁵ 5m² 7m 8f a7g Nov 30] angular filly: third foal: half-sister to 1m winner Bold Acre (by Never So Bold): dam 1½m winner, is half-sister to dam of Brocade, herself dam of Barathea: modest maiden: ran poorly last 3 starts: probably needs further than 5f: sold 5,000 gns Newmarket December Sales. *P. R. Webber*   57

FOREMAN 3 b.g. Timeless Times (USA) 99 – Skiddaw Bird (Bold Owl 101) [1995 57: 5m 5m* 5m⁴ 5g 6m⁶ 5m 6d 6m a5g³ a6g a7g⁴ a6g⁶ 1996 a8g⁴ a7g⁴ a6g⁴ a7g³ a6g* a7g⁴ 7f⁵ 6f⁶ Aug 5] robust gelding: modest performer: won seller at Lingfield in February on penultimate outing for W. O'Gorman: subsequently gelded and well below form: effective at 6f, and stays 1m: acts on good to firm ground and all-weather surfaces: tried blinkered and visored, no improvement. *R. Simpson*   57

FORENTIA 3 b.f. Formidable (USA) 125 – Clarentia 111 (Ballad Rock 122) [1995 89: 5g* 6g² 6m² 6m⁶ 6g⁵ 1996 6m 6m 7.1m 5m 6m³ 6m Oct 4] good-quartered filly: just a fair maiden at best in 1996: stays 6f: has raced only on a sound surface: visored (poorly drawn) fourth 3-y-o start: sometimes sweats: sometimes hangs badly left: sold 32,000 gns Newmarket December Sales. *J. R. Fanshawe*   69

FOREST BOY 3 b.g. Komaite (USA) – Khadine 79 (Astec 128) [1995 65: a6g² 6.1d a6g⁴ 1996 6s 8.3d* 7d⁴ 8.3s* 8d⁶ 10s May 29] sturdy, workmanlike gelding: fair handicapper: won at Hamilton (maiden) and Catterick in April and at Hamilton (wandered but found extra) in May: tailed off final start and sold K. McAuliffe to J. R. Bosley) 14,000 gns Newmarket Autumn Sales: stays 8.3f: acts on fibresand and soft ground: visored/blinkered (except reappearance) since final 2-y-o start: not an easy ride. *K. McAuliffe*   73

FOREST BUCK (USA) 3 ch.c. Green Forest (USA) 134 – Perlee (FR) 122 (Margouillat (FR) 133) [1995 87p: 8g* 1996 10.3f* 9g³ Oct 18] close-coupled, angular colt: found to have chips in a knee after only 2-y-o start: won smart 6-runner minor event at Doncaster in September by 2½ lengths from Storm Trooper, chasing pace, leading under 2f out and running on strongly: short to post, respectable third of 10 to Tarawa in listed race at Newmarket, niggled along some way out then keeping on well: will be suited by return to further than 9f: stays in training. *H. R. A. Cecil*   111

FOREST CAT (IRE) 4 b.f. Petorius 117 – Forest of Arden (Tap On Wood 130) [1995 91: 7.3g* 7.1m* 7g³ 1996 7.1d⁴ 7.1d⁶ 7m² 7m³ 7m⁵ Sep 12] workmanlike filly: useful performer, lightly raced: much improved form in listed events when placed at Goodwood and York (edging slightly left), and when fifth of 7 to My Branch at Doncaster: will stay 1m: goes well on good to firm ground, winner on dead at 2 yrs: consistent. *Mrs J. Cecil*   103

FOREST FANTASY 3 b.f. Rambo Dancer (CAN) 107 – Another Treat 92 (Derring-Do 131) [1995 47: 5g⁴ 5m⁴ 7d 1996 8g⁴ 10m⁶ 11m³ 12.3m 11f³ 9f* 8m² 10s⁴ 10f Sep 27] workmanlike filly: modest handicapper: won apprentice maiden handicap at Redcar in August: has form at 11f but better over shorter: acts on firm going, possibly not on a soft surface. *J. Wharton*   61

FOREST HEIGHTS 3 b.f. Slip Anchor 136 – Forest Blossom (USA) 56 (Green Forest (USA) 134) [1995 NR 1996 10g 11.8m* 11.8g⁴ 11.9m³ Aug 9] 18,000F: well-made filly: powerful mover: third foal: half-sister to 1½m seller winner Flora Belle (by Glint of Gold): dam, winner in Holland, half-sister to Yorkshire Oaks   81 winner Magnificent Star: fairly useful form: won maiden at Leicester in June, making all and staying on strongly: stiff task, best form when around 9 lengths third of 9 in handicap at Haydock final start: better at around 1½m than shorter: ideally suited by forcing tactics. *Mrs J. Cecil*

FOREST ROBIN 3 ch.g. Formidable (USA) 125 – Blush Rambler (IRE) 87 (Blushing Groom (FR) 131) [1995 79: 5m³ 5m⁴ 6g³ 6g⁴ 7g² 7m⁶ 1996 7g 8.1g² 9m³ 8f 10m³ 8.3d⁴ 8m² 10.4g 10s⁶ 11f Nov 5] good-quartered gelding: fairly useful maiden handicapper: sold out of R. F. Johnson Houghton's stable 21,000 gns Newmarket Autumn Sales after penultimate start: stays 9f: acts on good to firm and dead ground: has been bandaged in front: inconsistent: gelded. *Mrs J. R. Ramsden*

FOREST STAR (USA) 7 b.g. Green Forest (USA) 134 – Al Madina (USA) – (Round Table) [1995 –: a13g 1996 a16g a10g 16s Oct 28] seems no longer of much account: trained by R. Akehurst first 2 starts at 7 yrs. *Michael McElhone, Ireland*

FOREVERFREE 3 b.f. Sylvan Express 117 – Lady Homily 51 (Homing 130) – [1995 NR 1996 a6g a5g Sep 9] second foal: dam suited by 7f: tailed off: sold 500 gns Doncaster October Sales. *R. F. Marvin*

FOREVER NOBLE (IRE) 3 b.g. Forzando 122 – Pagan Queen 83 (Vaguely 60 Noble 140) [1995 –: 5m 1996 8f³ 12m 11.6m⁵ 10m⁴ 9.7m⁵ 14d³ 14d 13.8g⁴ 12s⁴ Oct 26] modest maiden: sold (M. Channon to M. Hammond) 8,500 gns Newmarket Autumn Sales: stays 1¾m: acts on firm and soft ground: inconsistent. *M. R. Channon*

FORGETFUL 7 b.m. Don't Forget Me 127 – Peak Squaw (USA) (Icecapade – (USA)) [1995 40: 8s³ 8f a12g 1996 a12g⁶ a13g Feb 10] seems no longer of much account: sold 4,200 gns Doncaster September Sales. *D. Burchell*

FORGET PARIS (IRE) 3 gr.f. Broken Hearted 124 – Miss Deauville (Sove- – reign Path 125) [1995 NR 1996 8g 8g a11g⁶ 10f 10g 8.5f a8g Dec 3] workmanlike filly: half-sister to temperamental 7-y-o King of Normandy (by King of Clubs) and a winner in Italy by Mummy's Pet: dam twice-raced sister to very useful 6f to 1m winner Miss Paris: no worthwhile form: tried visored. *B. S. Rothwell*

FORGET TO REMINDME 2 b.f. (May 30) Forzando 122 – Sandy Looks 69 – (Music Boy 124) [1996 6.9d⁴ Oct 21] 1,400Y: sixth reported foal: dam, winning hurdler who was lightly raced on flat, daughter of Irish 1000 Guineas second Hannah Darling: 33/1, 10¾ lengths fourth of 12 in maiden auction at Folkestone. *J. S. Moore*

FORGIE (IRE) 3 b.g. Don't Forget Me 127 – Damia (Vision (USA)) [1995 –: 6m 68 8.2d 8.2m 1996 10g 12d³ 14.1m* 14d 11.4f⁴ 16.1m² 17.1m² 16.1m² 14.1m Oct 8] lengthy gelding: has a round action: fair handicapper: won at Redcar (maiden) in May: suited by good test of stamina: acts on firm and dead ground: consistent. *P. Calver*

FORGOTTEN DANCER (IRE) 5 ch.g. Don't Forget Me 127 – Dancing – Diana 82 (Raga Navarro (ITY) 119) [1995 –: a6g⁴ a8g⁶ a6g a7g 1996 6m 8f 6.9m⁵ 7f 6m a8g a10g a10g Dec 30] no worthwhile form for long time. *R. Ingram*

FORGOTTEN EMPRESS 4 b.f. Dowsing (USA) 124 – Vynz Girl 82 (Tower – Walk 130) [1995 60+: a8.5g* 10g 1996 a8g a8g 8g 12.4m⁵ 12.1m⁴ Jul 8] leggy filly: no worthwhile form since last win: should stay beyond 8.5f: acts on dead ground and fibresand: probably none too keen: modest hurdler (joined S. Kettlewell), reportedly finished lame in September. *A. Harrison*

FORGOTTEN TIMES (USA) 2 ch.f. (Mar 17) Nabeel Dancer (USA) 120 – 70 d Etoile d'Amore (USA) 81 (The Minstrel (CAN) 135) [1996 6.1m⁶ 7f⁴ a6g⁴ a7g³ Dec 30] unfurnished, good-quartered filly: eighth foal: half-sister to 3 winners, including fairly useful Moonlight Saunter (7f, by Woodman) and Hadaad (up to 8.5f, by Mr Prospector): dam twice-raced 7f winner out of high-class sprinter Gurkha's Band: best effort in maidens when fourth at Leicester, swerving left leaving stalls then running on: sold out of E. Dunlop's stable 2,400 gns Ascot November Sales afterwards: modest form for new stable at Lingfield: stays 7f. *T. M. Jones*

FOR LARA (IRE) 2 ch.f. (Mar 18) Soviet Star (USA) 128 – On The Staff (USA) – p 117 (Master Willie 129) [1996 6d⁶ Aug 24] IR 3,200Y: fifth foal: dam suited by 1¼m: 14/1, around 12 lengths sixth of 19 in Johnny Staccato in maiden auction at Windsor, unfavourably drawn: will improve, particularly over further than 6f. *H. Candy*

FOR

FORLIANDO 3 b.g. Forzando 122 – Lucky Orphan 73 (Derrylin 115) [1995 41: 6m 7.1d 8g⁵ 10g 8.1s 1996 12s a9.4g⁶ 10.8g⁵ 10.2m 8m a16g Aug 29] sturdy, lengthy gelding: of little account. *M. S. Saunders* —

FORMENTIERE 3 gr.f. Sharrood (USA) 124 – Me Spede (Valiyar 129) [1995 NR 1996 10g 8g 7f 8.2m 13.1f 12m⁶ Jul 30] leggy filly: second foal: dam ran twice at 2 yrs: well beaten. *J. M. Bradley* —

FORMIDABLE FLAME 3 ch.g. Formidable (USA) 125 – Madiyla 73 (Darshaan 133) [1995 NR 1996 8d 10g 10d 10.5s 12.1s Oct 22] 14,000F, IR 7,000Y, 18,000 2-y-o: lengthy gelding: second foal: dam, 1½m winner, half-sister to smart Irish 1993 2-y-o Manntari: signs of ability without showing worthwhile form: off course 4 months and not knocked about last 2 starts: may yet do better. *W. J. Musson* – p

FORMIDABLE LASS 5 ch.m. Formidable (USA) 125 – Stock Hill Lass 87 (Air Trooper 115) [1995 –: 8.3m 11.6m 8m 1996 a7g Jan 23] of little account. *L. G. Cottrell* —

FORMIDABLE LIZ 6 ch.m. Formidable (USA) 125 – Areej (Rusticaro (FR) 124) [1995 66, a–: 6g⁶ 6m 6m⁴ 6m* 6m⁴ 6m 6m 8g³ 7g⁵ 1996 6m 5m 6g² 6g⁴ a7g⁴ 6f 6m* 8g 6.1m³ 7g Sep 21] sturdy, lengthy mare: unimpressive mover: fair handicapper: won at Pontefract in August: best form at 6f, but appeared to stay 7f final start: acts on any turf going and on fibresand: usually races prominently: no improvement in blinkers: covered by Clantime. *M. D. Hammond* — 66 a53

FORMIDABLE PARTNER 3 b.c. Formidable (USA) 125 – Brush Away (Ahonoora 122) [1995 70p: 7m⁵ 1996 7m 8.3m 8.3m² 8.1m⁵ 10m³ 10f 11.8m⁴ 10.4g Sep 4] strong, good-bodied gelding: fair maiden handicapper: sold (R. Armstrong to Mrs V. C. Ward) 11,000 gns Newmarket September Sales, and gelded: stays 1¼m: has raced only on top-of-the-ground: probably effective blinkered/visored or not: often pulls hard: went in snatches last time. *R. W. Armstrong* 70

FORMIDABLE SPIRIT 2 ch.g. (Mar 23) Formidable (USA) 125 – Hicklam Millie 49 (Absalom 128) [1996 5m⁶ a6g a7g⁶ Dec 13] 7,000Y, 12,000 2-y-o: third foal: half-brother to 2 Italian winners, including 3-y-o Mister Ego (6.5f to 9f, by Precocious): dam (maiden) stayed 1¼m: well beaten in maidens. *M. J. Heaton-Ellis* —

FOR OLD TIMES SAKE 2 ch.c. (May 9) Efisio 120 – Blue Birds Fly 78 (Rainbow Quest (USA) 134) [1996 5g a5g* 5m* 5.1g* 5f⁵ 5m* 5m⁴ 6m⁵ 5f* 5s* 5m⁵ 6g⁴ 5d Oct 28] 7,000Y: smallish, strong, lengthy colt: unimpressive mover: first foal: dam thrice-raced 1¼m winner: fairly useful form: won seller at Southwell, minor event at Bath, claimer, minor event and nursery at Beverley and £6,200 event at Ripon before September: ran well in minor event at Lingfield final start: best form at 5f: acts on fibresand and any turf ground: tough and reliable. *J. Berry* 93

Timeform Race Card Juvenile Conditions Stakes, Bath—
the third of six wins for For Old Times Sake

FOR THE PRESENT 6 b.g. Then Again 126 – Axe Valley 89 (Royben 125) 89 [1995 82+: 5m 1996 5m 6m 5m 5m 6f* 5g 6m 5m³ 6m 6g 6.1d³ 5.6m⁶ 6m Sep 21] strong, useful-looking gelding: fairly useful handicapper: won at Redcar in June: first home on far side when creditable sixth in the Portland at Doncaster penultimate start: effective at 5f and 6f: acts on firm and dead ground: held up: genuine. *T. D. Barron*

FORTIS PAVIOR (IRE) 6 b.g. Salt Dome (USA) – Heather Lil (Ballymore – 123) [1995 –: a7g 1996 a7g a6g Jan 26] no longer of much account. *C. W. C. Elsey*

FORT KNOX (IRE) 5 b.g. Treasure Kay 114 – Single Viking (Viking (USA)) 60 [1995 54, a56: 8f⁵ 7.6m 8m* 8.1m 7.6m 8m a7g* a10g⁵ a7g³ a7g⁵ 1996 a6g² a6g⁴ a63 a6g² a7g³ a6g a8g* a7g* a8g⁶ 7f² 9m³ 6.9f⁵ 8g 8f² 6f⁵ a7g⁴ 8f² 8m⁵ 8m⁴ 7f a7g⁴ Dec 20] quite attractive gelding: shows knee action: modest handicapper: won amateurs race and minor event at Lingfield in March: stays 9f: acts on all-weather tracks and on firm going, possibly not on soft: effective blinkered (normally is nowadays) or not: edgy sort (and sometimes early to post) who has been successful when sweating: usually held up, and suited by strongly-run race. *R. M. Flower*

FORTUITIOUS (IRE) 3 b.f. Polish Patriot (USA) 128 – Echo Cove (Slip – Anchor 136) [1995 42: 5m⁵ 5g 6.1m 5f³ 5g⁵ 5m⁶ 6f 8.1m⁴ 10d 1996 a7g 10.1f 9.7g Jul 10] sturdy filly: poor performer: well beaten in 1996: stays 1m: tried visored, no improvement: occasionally swishes tail. *J. R. Jenkins*

FORTUNES COURSE (IRE) 7 b.m. Crash Course 128 – Night Rose (Sove- 54 reign Gleam 117) [1995 –: 14.1m 1996 10m 12.1d 18m* 17.9g Oct 9] smallish mare: form at 7 yrs only to win poor maiden handicap at Chepstow in July, making most: out-and-out stayer: fair jumper. *J. S. King*

FORWARD MISS 2 b.f. (Feb 20) Bold Arrangement 127 – Maiden Bidder 66 – (Shack (USA) 118) [1996 6m Oct 4] third foal: dam stayed 7f: 100/1, very slowly away when tailed off in 12-runner maiden at Lingfield. *Mrs L. C. Jewell*

FOR YOUR EYES ONLY 2 b.g. (Feb 14) Pursuit of Love 124 – Rivers 90 Rhapsody 104 (Dominion 123) [1996 5g³ 6g* 5f* 5m 6m⁶ 6m⁶ 6d⁴ 8m 7s Nov 9] 25,000Y: small gelding: first foal: dam sprinter: fairly useful form: successful in maiden at Ripon and £7,500 event (pulled clear close home having been pushed along behind strong pace) at Beverley early in year: well below best last 2 starts: stays 6f: acts on firm ground and good to soft: wears bandages: retained by trainer 15,000 gns Newmarket Autumn Sales, and gelded. *T. D. Easterby*

FORZA FIGLIO 3 b.c. Warning 136 – Wish You Well 78 (Sadler's Wells (USA) 86 132) [1995 NR 1996 8d² 8m⁴ 8g* 10m³ 12.1m⁵ Jul 11] 8,000Y: strong, angular colt: second foal: dam, stoutly-bred staying maiden, half-sister to very smart 1983 3-y-o Creag-An-Sgor: fairly useful performer: overcame trouble to win maiden at Goodwood in May: should stay beyond 1¼m: yet to race on extremes of going: usually bandaged behind. *Miss Gay Kelleway*

FORZAIR 4 b.g. Forzando 122 – Persian Air (Persian Bold 123) [1995 73: 6g² 73 d 7m⁴ 7m⁴ 6m 6g a6g⁶ a7g³ 6m⁵ a6g 8m 8.2m a8g⁵ a12g* a12g⁶ 10.1s⁵ a12g* 12.3g⁵ 12m 12m² 13g⁴ 9.2g⁵ 10m 10m⁶ a9.4g 14s a12g a11g³ a12g³ a14.8g⁴ Dec 14] sturdy gelding: fair performer at best: won bad maiden in January and seller in April (very easily, sold out of S. R. Bowring's stable 8,000 gns), both at Southwell: stays 1½m: acts on good to firm ground and fibresand: effective blinkered or not. *J. J. O'Neill*

FORZARA 3 ch.f. Risk Me (FR) 127 – Valldemosa 81 (Music Boy 124) [1995 –: 54 6m 5s 1996 5g⁶ 5f⁴ a5g 5m 5g* 5.1m Aug 7] rather leggy filly: modest handicapper: won weak maiden event at Musselburgh in July: no comparable form: looks a 5f performer. *J. Berry*

FOUNDRY LANE 5 b.g. Mtoto 134 – Eider 80 (Niniski (USA) 125) [1995 86: 76 + 13.9g² 12m 11.9m⁶ 14f* 13.9m³ 16.1g⁴ 12m⁵ 1996 16.1m 13.9m 13.9g⁶ Sep 4] rangy gelding: usually looks well: has a fluent, round action: fairly useful handicapper: did not have things go his way in 1996: travelled well long way in Northumberland Plate, chased very strong early pace in the Ebor, then swung wide entering straight before staying on strongly (back at York) on his 3 starts: has shown form from 1½m to 2m: acts on any going: well handicapped if able to recapture his 4-y-o form. *Mrs M. Reveley*

FOURDANED (IRE) 3 b.g. Danehill (USA) 126 – Pro Patria 86 (Petingo 135) 81 d
[1995 81p: 7g⁴ 7m⁴ 1996 8g² 8m⁶ 8m⁵ 8d 10.5m Sep 6] small gelding: fairly useful
maiden at best: most disappointing after second 3-y-o start: stays 1m: carries head
awkwardly: does not always impress with attitude. *P. W. Harris*

FOUR LANE FLYER 4 b.f. Sayf El Arab (USA) 127 – Collegian 90 (Stanford –
121§) [1995 –: 7.1m 5g⁶ 7f³ 7.1s 1996 8g 7m 12g 10.2g 8m Jun 11] lengthy filly:
little sign of ability: tried visored. *E. J. Alston*

FOUR OF SPADES 5 ch.g. Faustus (USA) 118 – Fall To Pieces (USA) 101 58
(Forli (ARG)) [1995 62, a75: a6g a6g⁴ a6g² 7.1g a7g² 7m* 7.1m* 7.1m² 7.6m⁶ 7m⁴ a75
a7g⁶ 6m⁶ a6g* a6g² 5g 6s a5g a7g² a6g³ a7g* 1996 a8g² a7g² a7g a8g² 8m⁶
a8g⁴ 8m³ a10g² a7g² a6g³ 8.3m⁴ a8g⁴ 7g² a7g 7m a7g Nov 2] tall, lengthy gelding:
has a quick action: fair handicapper on the all-weather, modest on turf: left P. D.
Evans after fifteenth 5-y-o start: stays 1m, tired closing stages over 1¼m: acts on
good to firm and dead ground, best form on the all-weather: effective blinkered/
visored (usually is) or not: has run well when sweating: normally races prominently:
tough. *R. J. Hodges*

FOUROFUS 7 b.g. Wassl 125 – Que Sera 91 (Music Boy 124) [1995 NR 1996 –
a13g Jan 2] disappointing maiden. *N. B. Thomson*

FOUR WEDDINGS (USA) 3 b.g. Runaway Groom (CAN) – Kitty's Best 50 §
(USA) (Amen (FR)) [1995 56?: a6g 6m⁵ 6m 1996 a10g 12s⁵ 12.5g² 12m* 12m
12.1m³ Jul 11] sturdy gelding: has a round action: modest performer: narrowly won
seller at Pontefract (sold out of M. Bell's stable 6,200 gns) in April: no form
afterwards: stays 12.5f: acts on good to firm and soft ground, little form on all-
weather: visored/blinkered since second 3-y-o start: one to treat with caution: sold
(M. Pipe to Miss K. George) 1,350 gns Ascot December Sales. *M. C. Pipe*

FOX CHAPEL 9 b.g. Formidable (USA) 125 – Hollow Heart 89 (Wolver Hollow 56 §
126) [1995 NR 1996 a14.8g³ a16g³ a14.8g Mar 16] untrustworthy hurdler: modest
handicapper on flat: probably stays 2m: acts on good to firm and soft ground: below
form when visored. *R. T. Juckes*

FOXES TAIL 2 gr.g. (Mar 15) Batshoof 122 – Secret Gill 88 (Most Secret 119) 74
[1996 6d³ 7.1g* 7.5f⁵ 8m 8m* 8g Oct 25] 1,400F, 2,100Y: tall, unfurnished gelding:
has scope: fifth reported foal: half-brother to 1990 2-y-o 6f winner Secret Haze (by
Absalom), later successful in USA, and a winner there by Busted: dam 7f performer
later successful in USA: fair form: won 6-runner maiden auction at Musselburgh in
July (long odds on) and 10-runner nursery at Ayr (held prominent position in
steadily-run race) in September: didn't have run of race and performance best
ignored on final outing: will stay beyond 1m: wears bandages. *Miss S. E. Hall*

FOXFORD LAD 2 b.g. (May 9) Akid (USA) – Spring Rose (Blakeney 126) –
[1996 7m a8g Dec 20] 1,600Y: sixth foal: half-brother to a winner in Holland by
Belfort: dam poor performer from speedy family: soundly beaten in seller and
maiden. *T. M. Jones*

FRAISE DU ROI (IRE) 4 b.f. Roi Danzig (USA) – Stolen Fruit (Bold Lad (IRE) 66
133) [1995 –: a8.5g 1996 a13g a14.8g² Jan 24] visored, first worthwhile form when
beaten a head in seller at Wolverhampton, just losing out after good tussle: stays
14.8f: acts on fibresand. *Lord Huntingdon*

FRAMED (IRE) 6 b.g. Tate Gallery (USA) 117 – Golden Thread (Glint of Gold 51
128) [1995 62: 7f⁵ a6g 1996 7s 8g⁴ 10.8f 8m⁴ Sep 19] lengthy gelding: modest
maiden handicapper: below form in 1996: stays 1m: well beaten on soft going:
sometimes bandaged in front: tends to hang left. *S. C. Williams*

FRANDICKBOB 2 b.g. (Feb 17) Statoblest 120 – Crimson Ring (Persian Bold –
123) [1996 a5g 6g a5g a6s Dec 19] 5,400Y: half-brother to 8.2f winner Fistful
of Bucks (by Lochnager): dam lightly raced: no form: slowly away all starts.
John A. Harris

FRAN GODFREY 3 b.f. Taufan (USA) 119 – One Last Glimpse 73 (Relko 136) –
[1995 70: 6m 7m a8g² 1996 8d 7m 10f Sep 27] leggy, close-coupled filly: easy
mover: fair form on final start at 2 yrs, none in 1996: bred to stay 1¼m: sold 1,000
gns Newmarket December Sales. *P. T. Walwyn*

FRANKIE 2 b.g. (Mar 19) Shalford (IRE) 124§ – Twilight Secret 70 (Vaigly Great –
127) [1996 6d⁶ Aug 24] 13,500Y: good-bodied gelding: first foal: dam 1¼m winner:

12/1 and very burly, lost touch from halfway when well-beaten last of 6 in maiden at Newmarket. *M. H. Tompkins*

FRANKLINSBOY 4 b.g. Clantime 101 – Sky Fighter 43 (Hard Fought 125) – [1995 NR 1996 a9.4g May 11] poor maiden (rated 42) on all-weather at 2 yrs for Capt J. Wilson: tailed off on return. *C. D. Broad*

FRANKLY FRAN 4 b.f. Petorius 117 – Sunita (Owen Dudley 121) [1995 –: 6g – 8d 1996 10s⁴ a11g 10g 12.1d 12s Oct 26] angular filly: no form: sent to South Korea. *D. W. P. Arbuthnot*

FRECKLES KELLY 4 b.f. Shavian 125 – Choke Cherry (Connaught 130) 58 [1995 50: 10.1g 7m⁴ 7.5m² 5f* a5g² 5g 7f 1996 a5g 6g a5g* a5g* Jun 6] unfurnished filly: improved handicapper in 1996: won at Wolverhampton in May and at Southwell in June, making most: clearly best efforts at 5f: acted on fibresand, raced only on a sound surface on turf: dead. *T. D. Easterby*

FREDDIE'S RECALL 3 b.f. Warrshan (USA) 117 – Coir 'a' Ghaill 38 – (Jalmood (USA) 126) [1995 NR 1996 10.2f 10m 11.6d Aug 12] first foal: dam staying maiden: no form. *M. J. Heaton-Ellis*

FREDERICK JAMES 2 b.c. (Feb 17) Efisio 120 – Rare Roberta (USA) 118 – (Roberto (USA) 131) [1996 6g Oct 9] 9,000Y, 50,000 2-y-o: half-brother to several winners, including 1990 2-y-o 5f winner Beynounah (by Shareef Dancer) and fair 1¼m winner Al Raja (by Kings Lake): dam 6f and 1m winner: 16/1, soundly beaten in 8-runner maiden at York: wore bandages. *M. J. Heaton-Ellis*

FREDRIK THE FIERCE (IRE) 2 b.g. (Apr 21) Puissance 110 – Hollia 72 90 (Touch Boy 109) [1996 5d⁴ 5.1g⁴ 5m² 5.1m* 5.2f 5m* 5m⁵ 5m Sep 14] 20,000Y: tall, unfurnished gelding: half-brother to 5f winners Doubleyoubeay (by Beveled) and Local Heroine (by Clantime): dam 2-y-o 5f winner: fairly useful form: successful in maiden at Chester and 10-runner nursery at Goodwood in summer: never threatened in listed race at York in August and Flying Childers Stakes at Doncaster (visored) in September: speedy: acts on good to firm ground. *J. Berry*

FRED'S DELIGHT (IRE) 5 b.g. Law Society (USA) 130 – Madame Nureyev – (USA) (Nureyev (USA) 131) [1995 –: a12g 12m 1996 a8g a8g a7g a7g Jun 6] no worthwhile form since second 3-y-o start: tried blinkered/visored: not one to trust. *Mrs V. A. Aconley*

FREE AS A BIRD 2 b.f. (Jan 20) Robellino (USA) 127 – Special Guest 67 (Be 58 My Guest (USA) 126) [1996 7.1s⁵ 7g Nov 2] sixth foal: closely related to useful 7f winner Cragganmore (by Faustus) and half-sister to 3 winners, including 1992 2-y-o 5f winner Special One (by Aragon): dam 2-y-o 7f winner who stayed 9f: 16/1, around 9 lengths fifth of 16 to Technicolour in maiden at Chepstow, slowly away and not knocked about when clearly held: similar form in maiden at Newmarket following month. *M. R. Channon*

FREEDOM CHANCE (IRE) 2 ch.c. (Feb 19) Lahib (USA) 129 – Gentle – Guest (IRE) (Be My Guest (USA) 126) [1996 7g 7m a8g⁵ Nov 14] IR 26,000Y: good-topped colt: third foal: dam, unraced, from good family: disappointing after showing signs of ability on debut. *J. W. Hills*

FREEDOM FLAME 3 b.f. Darshaan 133 – Fire And Shade (USA) 91 (Shadeed 97 (USA) 135) [1995 79p: 7g² 7f² 1996 10.3g³ 10g* 10g⁴ 10m 9.5g³ 11m⁴ 8.3s² Nov 18] close-coupled, quite attractive ex-English filly: not the best of walkers: fluent mover: useful performer: won £20,900 contest at Newmarket in July on third-last start for M. Johnston: in frame, including in listed races, in French Provinces: should stay further than 1¼m: sold 64,000 gns Newmarket December Sales. *H. Pantall, France*

FREEDOM OF TROY 2 b.g. (May 6) Puissance 110 – Wing of Freedom (Troy – 137) [1996 6m 6g 8.1s Nov 7] fourth foal: half-brother to fair 3-y-o sprinter Montrestar (by Mon Tresor): dam, placed in Ireland, staying maiden: well beaten in maidens. *J. L. Eyre*

FREEDOM RUN 3 b.c. Polish Precedent (USA) 131 – Ausherra (USA) 106 – (Diesis 133) [1995 NR 1996 a8g Jan 11] first foal: dam won Lingfield Oaks Trial: sold out of Sir Mark Prescott's stable 6,000 gns Newmarket Autumn (1995) Sales: tailed off in maiden: sent to Czech Republic. *R. Harris*

Tote Gold Trophy Stakes (Handicap), Goodwood—
Free Guest's son Freequent sees off Time Charter's daughter Time Allowed

FREEQUENT   3 ch.c. Rainbow Quest (USA) 134 – Free Guest 125 (Be My Guest   103
(USA) 126) [1995 7.5d² 1996 7g³ 8.5m* 8d* 10.1m 10g⁶ 12m* 14g⁴ 12s⁴ 12s Nov 9]
good-bodied colt: appeared as 'Frequent' in Racehorses of 1995: useful performer:
won maiden at Beverley and handicap at Leicester (impressively) in the spring and
Tote Gold Trophy at Goodwood (found extra when challenged close home, held
Time Allowed by ¾ length) in July: fourth in listed race at Goodwood (best effort,
3½ lengths behind Sharaf Kabeer) and very valuable event at Milan next 2 starts:
stays 1¾m: acts on good to firm and soft ground: has edged/wandered under
pressure. *L. M. Cumani*

FRENCH GINGER   5 ch.m. Most Welcome 131 – French Plait (Thatching 131)   53 d
[1995 66: 8f⁵ 6g⁵ 8m³ 7.5d⁴ 7f⁴ 8g 7m 1996 a8g² a7g a10g 10.1m 10f Nov 5] lengthy
mare: poor mover: modest maiden: trained first 3 starts at 5 yrs by R. Ingram: tailed
off for new stable: should stay beyond 1m: acts on good to firm and dead ground, and
on equitrack. *W. Storey*

FRENCH GRIT (IRE)   4 b.g. Common Grounds 118 – Charbatte (FR) 93 (In   78
Fijar (USA) 121) [1995 88: 5g⁴ 6m² 6m* 6g³ 6m⁴ 6g⁶ 7m⁵ 7g 6g 5d 7g 6f⁶ 1996 6g⁶
5m² 6m 6m 6m 6m⁴ 5d⁶ 6f³ 6f² 6g² 5g³ 5m 6f⁵ Nov 5] leggy, workmanlike gelding:
fair handicapper: effective at 5f to 7f: acts on firm ground: wears a crossed noseband:
has raced prominently of late: consistent. *M. Dods*

FRENCH IVY (USA)   9 ch.g. Nodouble (USA) – Lierre (USA) (Gummo (USA)   72
117) [1995 71: 17.2m² 17.2m² 16.2f* 16m⁴ 15.9d² 16.2s³ 1996 16.2g 16.1g⁶ 16.2f³
16.2m* 16.2m⁶ 16.1m⁴ 16d* 16g² Sep 14] leggy gelding: fair handicapper: took time
to return to form, then won at Beverley in July and Goodwood in August: stays well:
acts on firm and soft ground: no improvement when visored twice earlier in career:
usually bandaged: held up. *F. Murphy*

FRENCH KISS (IRE)   2 b.g. (Apr 17) Petorius 117 – Cerosia (Pitskelly 122)   –
[1996 a7g⁴ Dec 28] IR 7,500Y: sixth foal: brother to fair 6.9f (at 2 yrs) to 8.3f winner
Segala: dam Irish maiden: favourite, distant fourth of 6 in poor maiden auction at
Wolverhampton. *M. R. Channon*

FRENCH MIST   2 b.f. (Mar 7) Mystiko (USA) 124 – Flambera (FR) (Akarad   69
(FR) 130) [1996 6f 6g 7m⁵ 8.1d⁶ 8.1m⁵ 7m Oct 1] tall, leggy filly: fluent mover:
fourth foal: half-sister to 1995 2-y-o 7f winner Oblomov (by Most Welcome) and
2 winners abroad, notably very smart American performer at up to 9f Jumron
(by Sharpo): dam 1¼m winner: fair maiden: stays 7f: below form on dead ground.
C. E. Brittain

FRESH FRUIT DAILY   4 b.f. Reprimand 122 – Dalmally 89 (Sharpen Up 127)   70
[1995 76: 7m⁵ 10m 7f² 7m² 7g⁴ 8g a7g² 1996 a10g³ a8g⁴ a8g³ 9m⁵ 7g 8.2m 6d³ a7g   a62
a8g Nov 18] tall, angular filly: fair maiden: stays at least 9f: acts on good to firm and
dead ground: carries head awkwardly. *P. A. Kelleway*

362

FRESH LOOK (IRE) 4 b.f. Alzao (USA) 117 – Bag Lady 86 (Be My Guest 46
(USA) 126) [1995 59d: 7g⁶ 12.5g³ 9m 10.8m 10.1m³ 11.5m⁴ 11.5g* 12.1g⁶ 11.9m
12m a12g a12g 1996 12f 10m 10m³ 10f Jul 20] angular filly: only poor form at best
in 1996: stays 12.5f: acts on good to firm ground, yet to race on a soft surface:
blinkered last 2 starts: sold 7,200 gns Newmarket December Sales. *R. C. Spicer*

FRET (USA) 6 b.g. Storm Bird (CAN) 134 – Windy And Mild (USA) (Best Turn –
(USA)) [1995 44: 12g² 14.1f⁵ 11m 1996 a16g Jan 12] poor at best on flat nowadays:
stays 1½m: probably acts on any going: blinkered (tailed off) only 6-y-o start.
J. S. Wainwright

FREZELIERE 3 b.f. Be My Chief (USA) 122 – Anna Karietta 82 (Precocious 89
126) [1995 84: 6g³ 7g³ 7g⁴ 6m³ 7g⁶ 7d 7s² 1996 8f* 10m² 10g³ 10m⁶ 10m 10m⁶
10.4g Oct 9] leggy filly: has a roundish action: fairly useful handicapper: won
maiden at Brighton in April: ran well at Salisbury, Newmarket (£20,800 race) and
Ascot (wandering off bridle) next 3 starts, poorly on last 3: stays 1¼m: acts on any
going: tried blinkered, no improvement: by no means a straightforward ride: sold
27,000 gns Newmarket December Sales. *J. L. Dunlop*

FRIAR STREET (IRE) 6 b.g. Carmelite House (USA) 118 – Madam Slaney 92 –
(Prince Tenderfoot (USA) 126) [1995 51: 9.2g⁶ 13g a8g⁴ a8g⁵ 7.1g* 1996 a7g⁶ Feb
29] looks modest at best nowadays: probably best short of 1m: blinkered (below
form) once as 3-y-o: has joined A. Witcomb. *C. J. Mann*

FRIENDLY BRAVE (USA) 6 b.g. Well Decorated (USA) – Companionship 78
(USA) (Princely Native (USA)) [1995 72, a80: a8g a7g a10g 10d 8m 6m⁶ 7.6m³ 6g² a75
6m 6m² 6g 5g 5.1d 5.1m⁴ 6f a5g* a5g* 1996 a6g⁴ a5g⁴ a6g a5g⁴ 5g 5m* 5.3f³ 5.1g³
5m⁴ 5d² 5m⁵ 5m⁵ 6m* 6m 5f* 5g³ 5m² 5m 5.1m* 5.1g⁵ 6v⁵ 6g 6.1s 5f² a5g⁵ a6g⁶
Nov 26] good-quartered gelding: impresses in appearance: fair handicapper: won at
Folkestone (minor event) in April, at Goodwood and Folkestone in June and at Bath
in August: stays 7f, but raced at sprint distances nowadays: acts on any turf going,
and on the all-weather: has been blinkered/hooded, but not for some time: bandaged
behind of late: sometimes swishes tail and tends to hang left: often claimer ridden:
usually waited with: tough and consistent. *Miss Gay Kelleway*

FRIENDLY DREAMS (IRE) 3 gr.f. Midyan (USA) 124 – Friendly Thoughts –
(USA) (Al Hattab (USA)) [1995 –: 7.5d 1996 12m 10.8g 8g 14.1m 12g⁶ 14.1f 12m
14.1f Jul 20] good-topped filly: seems of little account on flat: won claiming hurdle
in August, but looked none too keen afterwards: sent to South Korea. *P. T. Dalton*

FRIENDLY KNIGHT 6 b.g. Horage 124 – Be A Dancer (Be Friendly 130) –
[1995 –: 12.1v⁶ 1996 13d Apr 11] modest winning hurdler: of little account on flat.
J. S. Haldane

FRO 3 b.f. Salse (USA) 128 – Silent Sun 90 (Blakeney 126) [1995 –: 5.7m⁵ 6m 53
1996 8.2d 12.1d 11.9g 17.9g⁴ᵈⁱˢ 18g⁴ Oct 21] good-topped filly: looks a modest
staying maiden: sold (T. J. Naughton to H. Alexander) 10,000 gns Newmarket
Autumn Sales. *T. J. Naughton*

FROG 3 b.f. Akarad (FR) 130 – Best Girl Friend (Sharrood (USA) 124) [1995 –p: 84
6f⁵ 6m 6f a6g 1996 10f* 11.5m* 10f* 10f* 12f* 12m 10m Sep 26] strong filly: progressed into fairly useful performer: won minor event at Nottingham, and handicaps
at Lingfield, Brighton, Newbury and Thirsk, all within 3 weeks in July: well held in
better company afterwards: suited by around 1½m+: has raced only on top-of-the-
ground on turf: tough. *Sir Mark Prescott*

FRONTIER FLIGHT (USA) 6 b.g. Flying Paster (USA) – Sly Charmer (USA) –
(Valdez (USA)) [1995 NR 1996 a12g 16.5m 16g Aug 12] rangy gelding: has raced in
Jersey: well beaten on return to mainland: bred to stay 1¼m: won novice chase in
December. *Miss L. C. Siddall*

FRONTMAN (IRE) 3 ch.g. Imperial Frontier (USA) 112 – Countess Kildare 64
(Dominion 123) [1995 67p: a5g³ 1996 6s³ 5.1g⁵ a6g² 5d a5g 6g May 29] stocky
gelding: carries condition: poor mover: modest maiden: stays 6f. *T. D. Barron*

FRONT VIEW 2 b.c. (Mar 25) Backchat (USA) 98 – Book Review (Balidar 133) –
[1996 a6g Dec 7] third foal: brother to 4-y-o 1½m and 14.8f winner Backview: dam
of little account: 40/1, tailed off in maiden at Wolverhampton. *B. J. Llewellyn*

FROST KING 2 gr.g. (Feb 28) Northern State (USA) 91 – Celtic Image 51 (Welsh –
Saint 126) [1996 7.1m 7g 8g a8g Dec 20] tall, angular gelding: second reported foal:

dam (maiden) stayed 1½m: signs of ability in maidens first 3 starts: soundly beaten afterwards. *Miss B. Sanders*

FROZEN SEA (USA)   5 ch.h. Diesis 133 – Ocean Ballad 104 (Grundy 137)   67
[1995 69: 10m³ 10m⁵ 12m³ 12m⁴ 1996 14.1m* 14f⁴ 14.1m⁵ Aug 8] strong horse: fair handicapper: won weak minor event at Yarmouth in June, quickening on over 2f out: well below form afterwards: stays 1¾m: yet to race on a soft surface. *G. P. Enright*

FRUITANA (IRE)   2 b.g. (Apr 26) Distinctly North (USA) 115 – Tadjnama   77 +
(USA) (Exceller (USA) 129) [1996 6m⁶ 5g² 5f² 5m³ 5m² 5s 5g a5g* a5g Nov 26]
IR 8,000F, 13,000Y: rather leggy gelding: has a quick action: second foal: dam ran once in Ireland: fair performer: won nursery at Lingfield in November: best at 5f: suited by a sound surface on turf and acts on equitrack (may not prove so effective on fibresand): front runner. *J. Berry*

FRUITFUL LADY   3 b.f. Puissance 110 – Tamango Lady (Shack (USA) 118)   –
[1995 NR 1996 6g Apr 23] leggy filly: second foal: dam Irish maiden: no show in maiden. *B. P. J. Baugh*

FRUITIE O'FLARETY   2 gr.c. (Apr 11) Environment Friend 128 – Dame Mar-   –
got (USA) (Northern Dancer) [1996 8f 8.2s 8s a7s Nov 19] compact colt: half-brother to several winners abroad: dam unraced: little promise except on debut: reared over at stalls and withdrawn on second intended start: blinkered penultimate start. *C. E. Brittain*

FRUIT TOWN (IRE)   7 b.g. Camden Town 125 – Fruitful (Oats 126) [1995 NR   –
1996 8d Oct 11] ex-Irish National Hunt gelding: of little account. *P. Butler*

FRUTINA   3 b.f. Risk Me (FR) 127 – Queen's Piper 99 (Song 132) [1995 NR 1996   40
7m⁴ 6g 7m Sep 17] second foal: sister to 1992 2-y-o 6f seller winner Risk Proof: dam sprinter: failed to repeat form of debut. *C. Murray*

FUJIYAMA CREST (IRE)   4 b.g. Roi Danzig (USA) – Snoozy Time 65 (Cavo   94
Doro 124) [1995 92p: 9.7m* 11.6m* 12.3m⁴ 16.2f 16.4m 15.9m* 14m* 16.2d* 1996
16g³ 18.7g⁵ 16d³ 20f 16.1m 16.2m* Sep 28] tall gelding: has an unimpressive, quick action: fairly useful handicapper: off course 3 months, won quite valuable event at Ascot in September (under 9-10) for second year running, given fine ride by L. Dettori and battling on gamely to hold Northern Fleet a neck: sold 65,000 gns Newmarket Autumn Sales: suited by around 2m: acts on firm and dead ground: effective visored (was last 3 starts) or not: often bandaged behind/near-hind: sometimes wanders closing stages: front runner nowadays: consistent in 1996. *M. R. Stoute*

FULL OF TRICKS   8 ch.g. Mossberry 97 – Duchess of Hayling VII (Damsire   –
Unregistered) [1995 NR 1996 a10g a16g Feb 13] no form on flat. *J. J. Bridger*

FULLOPEP   2 b.g. (Mar 2) Dunbeath (USA) 127 – Suggia (Alzao (USA) 117)   63
[1996 7.1v 6g² 5m Oct 29] IR 2,700F, 9,800 2-y-o: good-topped gelding: has scope:

Gordon Carter Stakes (Handicap), Ascot—
Fujiyama Crest (left) secures the biggest payout in bookmaking history
as the final leg of Frankie Dettori's seven-out-of-seven

third live foal: brother to 3-y-o Too Hasty, 7f winner at 2 yrs: dam lightly raced and well beaten: easily best form in October maiden events when second of 8 to very easy winner Lady Diesis at Catterick: unsuited by drop back to 5f final start: may be capable of better. *Mrs M. Reveley*

FULL QUIVER 11 br.g. Gorytus (USA) 132 – Much Pleasure (Morston (FR) – 125) [1995 45: 16d 14d³ 1996 11.8d 11.6m 14.1m Jun 10] leggy gelding: unimpressive mover: poor handicapper: stays 14.1f: acts on any going: blinkered (below form) once, often visored: sometimes bandaged: wears tongue strap: sometimes finds little: inconsistent. *Mrs Barbara Waring*

FULL THROTTLE 3 br.g. Daring March 116 – Wheatley (Town Crier 119) 73 [1995 NR 1996 10m 12g 10m 10.8m³ 11.5m² 12.1m* 11.1g* 14m³ 11.8g² Oct 29] half-brother to bumpers winner Last Grain (by Remainder Man) and 3 winners abroad: dam half-sister to high-class sprinter Rabdan: generally progressive handicapper: won at Musselburgh and Hamilton (4 days later, dropping back to last 4f out and needing nearly all the trip to get up) in late-summer: should prove best at around 1½m+: raced only on a sound surface so far. *M. H. Tompkins*

FULL TRACEABILITY (IRE) 2 b.f. (Mar 30) Ron's Victory (USA) 129 – 53 Miss Petella (Dunphy 124) [1996 5d² 5g* 5d 5m³ a5g⁵ 6f³ 5f² 6d 6s a6s Dec 19] a44 3,000Y: workmanlike filly: fourth foal: half-sister to 3-y-o 7f (at 2 yrs) to 11.4f winner Traceability (by Puissance): dam half-sister to 1000 Guineas second Meis-El-Reem: modest form: made all in maiden auction at Musselburgh in April: gave impression something amiss last 2 starts for Jack Berry: well beaten only outing for new stable: best form at 5f: acts on firm and dead ground, poor form first of 2 starts on fibresand: visored twice, no improvement. *J. J. O'Neill*

FULLY BOOKED 2 b.f. (Mar 11) Midyan (USA) 124 – Vielle 123 (Ribero 126) – p [1996 5.1m 6g Aug 25] 4,000F: half-sister to several winners here and abroad, including 4-y-o 1¼m winner Bakheta (by Persian Bold) and fairly useful 1½m winner Chevrefeuille (by Ile de Bourbon): dam very smart middle-distance filly, second in Oaks: slowly away and always behind in maiden events at Bath and Goodwood: may well do better. *J. W. Hills*

FUNCHAL WAY 4 b.g. One Man Band 71 – Dusky Nancy 65 (Red Sunset 120) – [1995 NR 1996 7.3f Jul 19] third reported foal: dam won 1m seller: 100/1 and backward, well-beaten last of 7 in minor event at Newbury. *N. M. Babbage*

FUN GALORE (USA) 2 b.c. (Apr 23) Gone West (USA) – Ma Petite Jolie 92 (USA) 80 (Northern Dancer) [1996 6m* 7m* 7m Jul 31] robust, good-quartered colt: has a quick action: eighth foal: half-brother to a winner in USA at up to 1¼m by Private Account: dam 7f winner, half-sister to top-class North American filly Glorious Song and champion 1983 2-y-o Devil's Bag: won 6-runner minor event at Newbury by a head from Wolf Mountain and 2-runner £6,000 event at Newcastle easily by 2 lengths from Samsung Spirit: moved poorly to post before below form in Lanson Champagne Stakes at Goodwood, already struggling when bumped 2f out: will stay 1m: bandaged off-hind at Newcastle. *B. W. Hills*

FUNKY 3 ch.f. Classic Music (USA) – Foreno (Formidable (USA) 125) [1995 48 69p: 7m⁶ 8.2d³ 1996 5m⁴ 8g⁶ 7g 8m² 8m 9g Nov 1] leggy, quite attractive filly: sold out of L. Cumani's stable 6,500 gns Newmarket July Sales before reappearance: only poor form at best in 1996: stays 8.2f: best effort on dead ground. *D. Nicholls*

FUNNY ROSE 6 b.m. Belfort (FR) 89 – Scottish Rose 69 (Warpath 113) [1995 25 28: 12.1d³ 7.1g⁵ 10m 8.1g⁴ 7.1m⁶ 8f⁴ 11.1f* 10.9g³ 1996 9.2d⁶ 7.1g⁶ 11.1g 11.1f⁶ 12.1m 11.1m⁵ 11.1m⁶ 9.2f Aug 19] leggy mare: bad performer: stays 1½m: acts on firm ground and dead: inconsistent. *P. Monteith*

FUNNY WAVE 3 b.f. Lugana Beach 116 – Comedy Lady 46 (Comedy Star 65 (USA) 121) [1995 NR 1996 7m Apr 29] 1,300Y: leggy, angular filly: half-sister to 1987 2-y-o 5f winner Only In Gest (by Aragon): dam won 8.3f seller: 25/1 and bit backward, mid-division in maiden at Kempton, not handling home turn too well: should have improved. *H. Candy*

FURNISH 2 b.f. (Jan 29) Green Desert (USA) 127 – Eternal (Kris 135) [1996 7m³ 87 p 7g³ Sep 29] strong, lengthy filly: has scope: has a quick action: dam once-raced half-sister to Derby winner Quest For Fame out of Poule d'Essai des Pouliches winner Aryenne: looking really well though just in need of race, 3 lengths

'Michelozzo' Conditions Stakes, Nottingham—
the ten-year-old Further Flight and career win number twenty-two

third of 5 to Benny The Dip in minor event at Doncaster on debut: given plenty to do in minor event won by Kahal at Ascot 18 days later: will stay 1m: seems a keen type: remains open to improvement, and should win a race. *B. W. Hills*

FURSAN (USA) 3 b.g. Fred Astaire (USA) – Ancient Art (USA) (Tell (USA)) 77 [1995 65p: 7m 7g 1996 8.2d³ 8m⁴ 10m⁶ 10m⁴ 13.3m² Jun 27] lengthy, attractive gelding: fair maiden: looked unlucky on reappearance: disappointing next 3 starts: sweating, best effort in handicap at Newbury last time, leading briefly over 1f out: sold (N. Graham to N. Twiston-Davies) 26,000 gns Newmarket July Sales and gelded: stays 1½m: yet to race on extremes of going. *N. A. Graham*

FURTHER FLIGHT 10 gr.g. Pharly (FR) 130 – Flying Nelly 107 (Nelcius 133) 107 [1995 115: 16.2m² 16.2m 13.9g⁵ 16.4m⁵ 14.6m* 16f 18g² 16g* 12d 1996 14.1g* 13.4g⁶ 14.6g³ 16m 14.6d³ Nov 8] leggy, angular gelding: has a round action: usually relaxed in preliminaries: a grand old campaigner, but shade below the form of previous seasons: won minor event at Nottingham in April by 1¾ lengths from Assessor: off course 3 months (had training set-back) before failing to land sixth successive Jockey Club Cup penultimate start: stays 2¼m: acts on firm and dead ground, not on soft: wears small bandages: normally held up: game and genuine. *B. W. Hills*

FURTHER FUTURE (IRE) 3 br.g. Doubletour (USA) – Tamara's Reef (Main 59 Reef 126) [1995 –: 5.3d 6g 7m 1996 a12g⁴ a11g a12g* Mar 23] blinkered first time and dropped in class, first worthwhile form when winning selling handicap at Lingfield in March by 11 lengths, leading over 4f out: stays 1½m. *John Berry*

FURTHER OUTLOOK (USA) 2 gr.c. (Apr 17) Zilzal (USA) 137 – Future 96 Bright (USA) (Lyphard's Wish (FR) 124) [1996 7m² 7.5f* 8.1f³ 8.3g* 8s⁴ Oct 20] $160,000Y: rather leggy, useful-looking colt: has round action: fifth foal: half-brother to 2 winners in USA, including graded-placed Cosmic Fire (by Capote): dam minor stakes winner at 1m and placed in Grade 3 9f event: fairly useful form: won maiden at Beverley in August and minor event at Hamilton (by a head) in September: 7 lengths fourth of 10 to Hello in Gran Criterium at Milan in October: stays 1m: acts on firm ground and soft: races prominently: sold (M. Stoute to Mrs A. Perrett) 160,000 gns Newmarket Autumn Sales. *M. R. Stoute*

FUTURE PERFECT 2 b.g. (Mar 4) Efisio 120 – True Ring (High Top 131) 73 p [1996 7.1v* Oct 6] rather dipped-backed, unfurnished gelding: third reported foal: dam, well beaten both starts at 2 yrs, out of 6f-winning half-sister to top 1981 2-y-o filly Circus Ring: 16/1, green and ridden by 5lb claimer, won 11-runner maiden at Haydock by 1¼ lengths from Daniel Deronda, running on strongly to lead just inside final 1f and not hard ridden: will stay 1m: should do better. *M. W. Easterby*

FUTURE PROSPECT (IRE)   2 b.g. (Apr 27) Marju (IRE) 127 – Phazania (Tap   80
On Wood 130) [1996 5d² 5d* 6f 5m⁵ 5s⁶ Aug 31] IR 15,000Y: tall, useful-looking
gelding: has scope: has a round action: fourth foal: half-brother to 1993 Irish 2-y-o 5f
winner Il Caravaggio (by Tate Gallery) and 1994 Irish 2-y-o 6f winner Dick Ching
(by Dance of Life): dam Irish 2-y-o 6f to 1m winner who later stayed 1¼m: won
maiden at Haydock in June: easily best subsequent effort when 6 lengths fifth of 6
to Raphane in Curragh Stakes in July: bred to be suited by further than 5f: acts on
dead ground and good to firm (soon off bridle when well beaten on soft): gelded.
M. Johnston

FUTURE'S TRADER   3 b.g. Alzao (USA) 117 – Awatef (Ela-Mana-Mou 132)   –
[1995 –p: 8.1s⁵ 1996 10g 10m 12m 11.9g Oct 2] good-topped gelding: poor walker
and mover: signs of only a little ability: sold (R. Hannon to M. Hammond) 5,500 gns
Newmarket Autumn Sales, and gelded: should be suited by at least 1½m. *R. Hannon*

FYORS GIFT (IRE)   3 b.f. Cadeaux Genereux 131 – Miss Fyor (USA) (Danzig   67
(USA)) [1995 65?: 5.2g⁴ 5m³ 7.5d 1996 6g⁴ a6g⁴ a5g a5g 5f* Jun 5] quite good-
topped filly: fair performer: best effort to win maiden handicap at Warwick, always
at head of affairs: sold 8,600 gns Newmarket July Sales: stays 6f: acts on firm ground
and fibresand. *B. Hanbury*

G

GABLESEA   2 b.c. (May 14) Beveled (USA) – Me Spede (Valiyar 129) [1996 7m   59
6.1m² 6f 6g Oct 21] 2,100F, 4,000Y: tall, leggy, unfurnished colt: third foal: dam ran
twice at 2 yrs: beaten a length by Shadow Lead in maiden auction at Chepstow in
July: failed to reproduce that form in similar events at Warwick and Pontefract in
October. *B. P. J. Baugh*

GABR   6 b.h. Green Desert (USA) 127 – Ardassine (Ahonoora 122) [1995   122
a7g³ a8g³ 8f⁵ 7f² 8.5f* 7f⁶ 9f² 8.5f* 8s 1996 9m⁴ 8.1g* 8d⁵ 8f 7g* Jun 29]
Globe-trotting Gabr, back in Britain after running in the Emirates and
the USA in 1995, showed himself better than ever in the latest season and
notched up two more pattern wins before splitting his off-fore pastern at
exercise in late-July, an injury from which vets were unable to save him. Gabr
put up probably the best performance of his career on his final outing when
winning the nine-runner Group 3 Van Geest Criterion Stakes over seven
furlongs at Newmarket, conceding weight all round and forging clear up the
hill to beat Inzar by three lengths. Trainer Robert Armstrong cited the horse's
American experience—he won two allowance races there in 1995—as being a

*Sandown Mile—Gabr (noseband) and Soviet Line (left) are separated by a short head,
with Mistle Cat (the grey) and Nwaamis close up as well*

significant factor in the decision to drop Gabr back in trip following poor efforts in the Lockinge Stakes and the Queen Anne Stakes, in both of which he had raced freely up with the pace before dropping away tamely. 'When he raced in America last season he was taught to break very quickly and he has proved difficult to settle back in Britain,' explained Armstrong, who felt the horse settled better dropped back in trip. Nonetheless Gabr's win came as a surprise; he'd been sent off the outsider of the nine runners. Gabr's rare lapses at Newbury and Royal Ascot came after a good start to the season, following a creditable fourth in the Earl of Sefton Stakes at Newmarket in April with victory in a strongly-run renewal of the Group 2 Sandown Mile, where he was all out to hold the late challenge of Soviet Line by a short head.

		Green Desert (USA) (b 1983)	Danzig (b 1977)	Northern Dancer
				Pas de Nom
			Foreign Courier (b 1979)	Sir Ivor
Gabr				Courtly Dee
(b.h. 1990)		Ardassine (ch 1982)	Ahonoora (ch 1975)	Lorenzaccio
				Helen Nichols
			Santa Luciana (bl or br 1973)	Luciano
				Suleika

Although Gabr ended his career back over seven furlongs, he stayed better than most sons of Green Desert and had smart form at up to a mile and a quarter. There is stamina on his dam's side. Ardassine, whose only victory came over a mile and a half at Clonmel, has produced two other winners, Enaya and Kutta, both also trained by Armstrong. Enaya, a filly by Caerleon, won over six furlongs at two and later stayed a mile and a quarter; while the smart Kutta, a colt by Old Vic, won over thirteen furlongs in 1996. The dam has since produced two full sisters to Gabr, the once-raced Intisab and the yearling Wars, and a full brother, the unraced two-year-old Muhawwil. The second dam Santa Luciana, a winner in Germany, was a half-sister to Sayonara, the dam of Slip Anchor and Sandy Island. Santa Luciana's offspring included the useful stayer Subtle Change. The compact and good-quartered Gabr won nine of his twenty-seven starts—including three pattern races and a listed event—and amassed around £185,000 in prize money. *R. W. Armstrong*

GABRIEL'S LADY 5 b.m. Valiyar 129 – Autumn Harvest (Martinmas 128) – [1995 –: 9f 8m⁶ 6g 6f 1996 a10g Feb 27] of no account. *H. G. Rowsell*

GADGE 5 br.g. Nomination 125 – Queenstyle 58 (Moorestyle 137) [1995 73d: 8g³ 59 7s⁶ 8g³ 8m⁵ 8.1g⁵ a8.5g 7g⁶ 8d 9g 8s 7m 1996 8g 8m⁶ 8m 8g⁵ 8.1m 8m 8.1s⁵ a9.4g⁶ a– a12g Dec 14] sturdy, lengthy gelding: tends not to impress in appearance: shows knee action: just a modest handicapper nowadays: sold out of D. Morris's stable 6,500 gns Newmarket July Sales after fifth start: better at 1m than shorter: acts on good to firm ground, goes well on soft: tried blinkered/visored, no improvement: has been bandaged behind: tail swisher. *A. Bailey*

GADROON 2 ch.c. (Mar 25) Cadeaux Genereux 131 – Greensward Blaze 50 – (Sagaro 133) [1996 8m 6d Nov 8] 37,000F, 40,000Y: angular, good-topped colt: half-brother to very smart 5f (at 2 yrs) to 7f winner Prince Ferdinand (by King of Spain) and a winner in Hong Kong by Crofter: dam won 1m seller: in rear in 17-runner maidens at Newmarket and Doncaster (upset in stalls and started slowly). *P. C. Haslam*

GAD YAKOUN 3 ch.g. Cadeaux Genereux 131 – Summer Impressions (USA) 70 65 (Lyphard (USA) 132) [1995 NR 1996 5m³ 6m⁶ 7g⁵ a7g* a6g a7g Dec 28] 700 2-y-o: half-brother to several winners, including fairly useful Walimu (1m to 1½m, by Top Ville): dam, minor winner at 1m at 4 yrs in France, out of Roussalka, a half-sister to Oh So Sharp: fair form: won maiden at Lingfield in November: ran as if something amiss final start: stays 7f: acts on good to firm ground and equitrack. *M. G. Meagher*

GAELIC STORM 2 b.c. (Mar 22) Shavian 125 – Shannon Princess (Connaught 77 130) [1996 5m³ 5s⁴ 5f* 6g⁶ 5g³ Nov 1] 7,000Y: small, sturdy colt: half-brother to several winners, including smart middle-distance stayer Waterfield (by Le Moss) and useful but unreliable stayer Great Crusader (by Deploy), 10.2f winner at 2 yrs: dam

Irish 1m and 1¼m winner: much improved effort when winning 14-runner maiden auction at Sandown in September: ran creditably in nurseries afterwards: stays 6f, bred to be suited by further: slowly away last 2 outings. *M. Johnston*

GAGAJULU 3 b.f. Al Hareb (USA) 123 – Rion River (IRE) (Taufan (USA) 119) 54
[1995 75: 5s² 5m⁶ 5f² 6g⁵ 6g a5g* 5g⁴ 5.1f* 5g* 5.3f* 5m⁴ 5m 5.1m* 6.1d 5m⁶ 5.2f² 5m 1996 a5g a5g⁶ a5g³ a5g⁶ 5d 5g 5.1m⁶ 5m⁵ 5f⁶ 5m 5m 5.1m⁶ 6m Aug 28] close-coupled filly: only modest at best in 1996: stays 6f: acts on fibresand and on any turf going: tried blinkered, no improvement: successful when sweating. *P. D. Evans*

GAIN LINE (USA) 3 b.c. Dayjur (USA) 137 – Safe Play (USA) (Sham (USA)) 64
[1995 NR 1996 8m 9m⁵ May 18] fifth foal: half-brother to 4 winners, notably very smart middle-distance performer Defensive Play (by Fappiano) and useful sprinter Averti (by Known Fact): dam won from 5.5f to 9f in USA, including a Grade 1 event, and is half-sister to Musical Bliss: better effort in maidens in May when fifth of 12 at Lingfield second start, though still green and failing to handle turn well: sold only 2,400 gns Newmarket Autumn Sales. *R. Charlton*

GALACIA (IRE) 4 br.f. Gallic League 119 – Little Wild Duck 78 (Great Heron 42
(USA) 127) [1995 52: 6f³ 1996 6.1m a6g a7g a8g⁵ Nov 22] leggy filly: poor maiden: stays 6f: acts on firm ground and soft. *W. G. M. Turner*

GALAKA 3 b.f. Slip Anchor 136 – Golden Glint (Vitiges (FR) 132) [1995 –p: 8m –
1996 10m 10.4g 14d Sep 28] quite good-topped filly: has scope: has a powerful, roundish action: little worthwhile form in maidens and handicap: found nil final start: should stay at least 1½m. *L. M. Cumani*

GALAPINO 3 b.g. Charmer 123 – Carousella 62 (Rousillon (USA) 133) [1995 86 d
77d: 5m⁴ 6g³ 7g⁴ 7m⁶ 6.1d 6f 7m 6.9m 1996 a8.5g⁴ a10g³ a10g* a9.4g* a8.5g² 10m 11.4d⁵ 9.9f⁵ 8g⁶ 10m 9.9f⁵ 8m⁶ 7.1f 10g⁴ Oct 2] smallish, leggy gelding: fairly useful handicapper at best: made all at Lingfield and Wolverhampton in February: regressive form afterwards: stays 1¼m: acts on good to firm ground and goes well on all-weather: blinkered (well beaten) penultimate 3-y-o start: sometimes sweats: sold only 4,000 gns Newmarket Autumn Sales and gelded. *C. E. Brittain*

GALB ALASAD (IRE) 3 b.c. Royal Academy (USA) 130 – Soleiade (Posse 69 p
(USA) 130) [1995 NR 1996 8.3d⁶ 8d⁴ Aug 24] IR 75,000F, IR 125,000Y: big, lengthy colt: half-brother to winners abroad by Last Tycoon and Sure Blade: dam unraced half-sister to Comtesse de Loir, same family as Miesque: bandaged behind and tongue tied, fourth of 12 in maiden at Newmarket in August, unable to sustain effort up the hill: should stay further than 1m: should improve again: sent to UAE. *J. H. M. Gosden*

GALIBIS (FR) 2 b.c. (Mar 11) Groom Dancer (USA) 128 – Damasquine (USA) 75
(Damascus (USA)) [1996 8m⁵ 8g Oct 29] 310,000 francs Y: leggy, angular colt: half-brother to several winners abroad, including Devon Port (by Fast Topaze), 4.5f and 5f winner in France then successful in Grade 3 1m event at 2 yrs in 1993: dam French 9f winner: 6½ lengths fifth of 17 to Royal Crusade in maiden at Newmarket, close up over 5f: joint favourite, well below that form in similar event at Leicester 12 days later. *P. A. Kelleway*

GALINE 3 b.f. Most Welcome 131 – Tarasova (USA) (Green Forest (USA) 134) 91
[1995 78: 6g⁴ 6g⁶ a5g* 1996 6m* 5g 6m² 6m⁴ 5m* 6g⁵ 5m⁴ 5f² 5m 6m⁵ Oct 4] strong, lengthy filly: fairly useful handicapper: won at Newmarket in April and June: effective at 5f and 6f: acts on fibresand and firm ground, yet to race on a soft surface: has worn rope halter in preliminaries: held up: consistent. *W. A. O'Gorman*

GALLARDINI (IRE) 7 b.g. Nordico (USA) – Sweet (Pitskelly 122) [1995 55: 45
10.3g 10g 11.9m 10m² 9.9m⁴ 1996 10.3d⁴ 9.9d 12g 16g 12m⁶ 11.9m⁶ 10m 10.3g 10m Jul 8] leggy ex-Irish gelding: only a poor handicapper at best in 1996: probably stays 11f: best form in Ireland on soft ground: tried blinkered/visored, no improvement: inconsistent. *B. S. Rothwell*

GALLIC VICTORY (IRE) 5 b.g. Gallic League 119 – Sally St Clair (Sallust 64
134) [1995 70d: 10m 9.5g⁴ 9m 9m 7g a8g⁵ 1996 a10g³ a10g⁶ a10g⁵ a8g Feb 24] fair performer at his best: broke down final start: stayed 1¼m: acted on good to firm ground and on equitrack: blinkered (well beaten) final 2-y-o start: dead. *John Berry*

GALLOPING GUNS (IRE) 4 ch.g. Conquering Hero (USA) 116 – Jillette – (Fine Blade (USA) 121) [1995 7m⁵ 10f 7m⁵ 8g 1996 10g a8g 7d a14.8g⁵ 8m Aug 13] ex-Irish gelding: half-brother to several winners, none better than fair: dam Irish 1½m winner: unraced at 2 yrs: failed to repeat debut (rated 70) form, leaving D. Weld's stable after third 4-y-o start: soundly beaten afterwards: tried blinkered, no improvement. *B. J. Llewellyn*

GALTEE (IRE) 4 b.c. Be My Guest (USA) 126 – Gandria (IRE) (Charlottown 115 127) [1995 10.5v³ 10.5d* 11.8g⁵ 12v⁶ 8.8g* 10s² 11s* 10.5s* 1996 a9g* a10g* 11s² 10.3g⁵ 11.5g* 11.5g² 10.5d* 11s* 10.5g* 12s³ 10g⁵ 10m⁴ 11g³ 12m² 10g² Oct 3] IR 9,500F: tenth foal: related to 8 winners in Germany, notably listed winner Grand Prince (by Prince Regent): dam, Irish 13f winner, half-sister to Irish Oaks winner Gaia: smart German colt: unraced at 2 yrs and won 4 minor contests at 3 yrs: won 6 races in 1996, including listed races at Munich and Strasbourg: ran well when beaten a head by Oxalagu in Group 3 race at Hoppegarten final start: stays 1½m: acts on good to firm and heavy ground, on sand, and has also won on the snow in St Moritz: tough and consistent. *U. Stoltefuss, Germany*

GALWAY BLADE 3 b.g. Faustus (USA) 118 – Slipperose 72 (Persepolis (FR) 61 127) [1995 66?: 8g⁴ 8d 8g⁵ 8f 1996 12m⁵ 11.8d 11.6m 12g Jun 12] tall, close-coupled gelding: modest maiden at best: no worthwhile form after 3-y-o reappearance: stays 1½m: poor effort on firm ground: won novice hurdle for Miss H. Knight. *A. P. Jarvis*

GAME PLOY (POL) 4 b.g. Deploy 131 – Guestimate (FR) (Be My Guest 90 (USA) 126) [1995 76d: 9m³ 13.4m³ 10m 10d 12.1s 1996 10g 10.2g⁴ 10g* 10g* 10.3m* 9f³ 10m 10.2f² 10m* 9m 10s 12s Nov 9] tall gelding: has a round action: improved into a fairly useful handicapper: successful twice at Windsor (minor event first occasion) and once at Chester, all within 2 weeks in July, and in £16,000 contest at Newbury (in good style) in September: below form afterwards: stays 1¼m: probably acts on any going: held up. *D. Haydn Jones*

GANADOR 4 gr.f. Weldnaas (USA) 112 – Shakana 91 (Grundy 137) [1995 49d: 45 5.1g a7g³ 8.3g⁶ 7g² 7.1m a7g 6.9g 1996 a10g³ a10g a12g a10g⁶ a8g⁶ Mar 14] poor maiden: stays 1¼m: acts on good to firm ground and equitrack: inconsistent: covered by Prince of Birds. *B. Smart*

GANGA (IRE) 2 ch.f. (May 21) Generous (IRE) 139 – Congress Lady 93 (Gen- – eral Assembly (USA)) [1996 7d Aug 23] 30,000F: smallish, sturdy filly: eighth foal: half-sister to fair 3-y-o middle-distance stayer Belmarita (by Belmez), Irish 6f to 8.5f winner Sadlers Congress (by Sadler's Wells) and winners in Italy and Scandinavia: dam, 8.5f winner in France, half-sister to Ragusa out of Musidora winner Ela Marita: 33/1 and burly, well-beaten seventh of 8 to Reams of Verse in maiden at Newmarket: bandaged off-hind. *W. Jarvis*

GARLANDHAYES 4 b.f. Adbass (USA) 102 – Not Alone 84 (Pas de Seul 133) – [1995 NR 1996 10f Jun 4] second foal: dam disappointing maiden, best effort only 2-y-o start: tailed off in claimer: joined Miss K. George. *N. M. Babbage*

GARNOCK VALLEY 6 b.g. Dowsing (USA) 124 – Sunley Sinner 93 (Try My 93 Best (USA) 130) [1995 74d: 8g⁴ 7m 6g 6g 7f 1996 6d³ 5g* 5s⁶ 5g* 6d 5m* 6m⁵ 5m a77 6f 6m 7m 6v* 6g 6f a6g³ Nov 16] neat gelding: fairly useful handicapper: won at Musselburgh (minor event) in April and May, at Ayr in June and at Haydock (equalling career-best effort, blinkered first time, by 5 lengths in 22-runner race) in October: failed to repeat the form: stays 6f: acts on any going on turf, not discredited on fibresand: blinkered (except final turf start) since twelfth 6-y-o start: effective from front or held up. *J. Berry*

GAY BREEZE 3 b.g. Dominion 123 – Judy's Dowry 80 (Dragonara Palace – (USA) 115) [1995 NR 1996 5m 7f 8g Oct 29] compact gelding: fourth reported foal: dam 5f (at 2 yrs, best form) and 1m winner: well beaten. *P. S. Felgate*

GEE BEE BOY 2 ch.c. (May 22) Beveled (USA) – Blue And White (Busted 134) – p [1996 6m Sep 21] strong, close-coupled colt: third reported foal: dam little sign of ability: 50/1 and in need of race, soon pushed along when never-dangerous ninth of 24 in Newbury maiden won by Speedball on debut: should improve. *A. P. Jarvis*

GEE BEE DREAM 2 ch.f. (Apr 17) Beveled (USA) – Return To Tara (Homing 68 130) [1996 6m 6m 6g² 6.5m 7m Oct 1] useful-looking filly: has scope: sister to 3 winners, including 4-y-o 6f (at 2 yrs) and 1m winner Sue's Return and fair sprinter

Cranfield Comet: dam well beaten: fair form: ran creditably when seventh of 14 in nursery at Newmarket final outing: stays 7f. *A. P. Jarvis*

GEE GEE TEE 3 ch.c. Superlative 118 – Glorietta (USA) (Shadeed (USA) 135) 43
[1995 –: 7d 6.9s 7g 6.9m 1996 6.9s 8.3m a11g⁴ 10.8m Jul 13] poor maiden: stays 11f: blinkered (tailed off) final 3-y-o start: sold 500 gns Ascot August Sales. *J. Akehurst*

GEMINI DREAM 3 br.g. Green Ruby (USA) 104 – Dream Again 88 (Blue –
Cashmere 129) [1995 NR 1996 8g Oct 2] sixth foal: dam 2-y-o 5f winner: unruly in preliminaries and withdrawn Sep 7: showed nothing on debut. *R. F. Johnson Houghton*

GENERAL ACADEMY (IRE) 3 b.c. Royal Academy (USA) 130 – Hastening 102
(Shirley Heights 130) [1995 9g* 10g² 9g 1996 10.5m⁵ 10g 7m⁶ 10g 7m³ 10g a9.4g Dec 7] big, lengthy, good sort: ex-Italian: fourth foal: half-brother to winners Alacrity (11f, by Alzao) and General Assembly (13.4f, by Pharly): dam, unraced, from family of Kris: won maiden at Rome at 2 yrs when trained by F. Brogi: useful performer: staying-on sixth of 16 to Lucayan Prince in Jersey Stakes at Royal Ascot: reportedly lame in shoulder after next start, and off course nearly 3 months: below form afterwards: really needs further than 7f, and stays 10.5f: acts on good to firm ground, yet to race on a soft surface. *P. A. Kelleway*

GENERAL EQUATION 3 b.g. Governor General 116 – Logarithm (King of 63 d
Spain 121) [1995 –: 5m a5g 5d a5g 1996 a5g³ a5g⁴ a5g* 5s³ 5d a5g a5g a6g a5g a5g⁶ Dec 13] modest performer: won seller at Southwell in March by 6 lengths, making all: no worthwhile form after next start: will prove best at 5f: acts on fibresand and soft ground: usually claimer ridden: races prominently. *J. Balding*

GENERAL GLOW 3 b.g. Presidium 124 – Glow Again 78 (The Brianstan 128) 64
[1995 –: 7g 7g 10m 1996 12s 14.1g 12d⁶ 13.1m 10f* 11.9f* 9.9f³ 10.5m* 10.5m³ 15m³ 11.8f⁶ 11f Nov 5] tall gelding: modest handicapper: trained until after fourth 3-y-o start by N. Bycroft: successful in the summer at Brighton (twice, by 13 lengths on second occasion) and Haydock: below form last 3 starts: stays 1½m: acts on firm ground. *P. D. Evans*

GENERAL HAVEN 3 ch.g. Hadeer 118 – Verchinina 99 (Star Appeal 133) 74
[1995 –: a10g a7g 1996 a6g³ a6g² a6g³ a7g* a6g³ 8.2m⁴ 8d³ a8g⁵ 8m⁵ 8.3g* a10g⁴ 10f⁴ 10g a12g² a13g² Dec 13] quite good-topped gelding: generally progressive handicapper: won at Lingfield (maiden) in March and at Windsor (coming from well off pace to lead inside final 1f) in July: stays 13f: acts on firm ground and all-weather, tried only once (below best) on a soft surface: genuine sort. *T. J. Naughton*

GENERAL HENRY 3 b.g. Belmez (USA) 131 – Western Star 107 (Alcide 136) –
[1995 –: a8g a7g 1996 a8g a10g⁵ Feb 13] no sign of ability. *A. Moore*

GENERAL JIMBO (IRE) 4 b.g. King Luthier 113 – The Saltings (FR) –
(Morston (FR) 125) [1995 8v 7m 12.5f⁴ 14g 9m 7.8f⁵ 12g 1996 a12g Feb 10] IR 11,000Y: ex-Irish gelding: fifth foal: half-brother to 2 winners, notably smart American 6-y-o 1¼m performer Earl of Barking (by Common Grounds): dam twice-raced half-sister to useful sprinter Dare Me, herself dam of good sprinter Fortysecond Street: modest (rated 58 at best) maiden handicapper: trained at 3 yrs by K. Prendergast: sold 3,000 gns Doncaster September (1995) Sales: tailed off only 4-y-o start: stays 12.5f: acts on firm and soft ground: won selling hurdle in April for J. Cullinan. *F. Murphy*

GENERAL MACARTHUR 3 b.c. Alzao (USA) 117 – Royal Climber (Kings 95
Lake (USA) 133) [1995 83: 6g 7f 8.2d 8g 8f² 1996 10g* 12g* 12m⁵ 11.9m³ 11.9g⁴ 13.3m⁵ 14g⁴ Oct 18] compact colt: has a quick action: fairly useful handicapper: won at Nottingham in April and Beverley (minor event) in May: sold 30,000 gns Newmarket Autumn Sales: probably stays 1¾m (though wandered markedly when driven final 3-y-o start): acts on firm ground: also hung right (looking hard ride) third 3-y-o start: consistent sort on form. *J. L. Dunlop*

GENERAL MONASH (USA) 4 b.c. Habitat 134 – Zummerudd (USA) 107 – Zummerudd 104
(Habitat 134) [1995 101: 8d⁶ 6.5g 1996 6m 7.1d² 5d 5.5g* 6g* 6g⁴ 7d 6.5g* 6s⁶ Nov 22] strong, good-quartered colt: useful form: left P. Chapple-Hyam after third start: won 2 minor events in the Provinces in August and one in November: best 4-y-o efforts when 5¼ lengths fourth of 10 to Kistena in Prix de Seine-et-Oise at Maisons-Laffitte in September and just over 3 lengths sixth of 10 to Astrac in listed

event at Evry in November: creditable effort at 1m, but probably best as a sprinter: respectable effort on good to firm ground, raced mainly with give and impressive only start on soft: retired to Ballyhane Stud, co. Carlow, fee IR £2,250 (Oct 1st). *C. Laffon-Parias, France*

GENERAL MONTY 4 b.g. Vague Shot 108 – State Free (Free State 125) [1995 NR 1996 10.3g Oct 26] third foal: dam of little account: fourth in NH Flat race in June: soundly beaten in claimer. *Pat Mitchell*   –

GENERAL MOUKTAR 6 ch.g. Hadeer 118 – Fly The Coop (Kris 135) [1995 74d: 12g 12m 12.3m³ 14s⁴ 14f³ 11.8g 12f⁵ 12d 14.1m 1996 12m² 12m³ 12g 12m³ 11.9f² 12.5f³ 12g⁶ 12g²ᵈⁱˢ 12m² 11.9f² 12.1m 12m 12g Aug 21] compact, good-quartered gelding: has fluent, round action: seems only a modest handicapper these days: probably effective at 1¼m to 1¾m: acts on firm and soft ground: effective blinkered/visored or not: usually held up: tends not to find much under pressure: hurdling with M. Pipe, has looked most unwilling but did nothing wrong when winning 3 times last on. *B. J. Meehan*   62

GENERAL SHIRLEY (IRE) 5 b.g. Shirley Heights 130 – Adjala 89 (North-fields (USA)) [1995 –§: a10g⁵ 8.3m 1996 a8g a8g⁶ a10g⁴ 10g Jul 8] poor handi-capper nowadays: stays 1¼m: tried blinkered/visored, no improvement: sometimes carries head awkwardly: not one to trust implicitly. *P. R. Hedger*   46 §

GENERAL SONG (IRE) 2 b.c. (Mar 9) Fayruz 116 – Daybreaker (Thatching 131) [1996 7.5g* 6m 7.3s Oct 24] IR 11,000F, 27,000Y: strong, close-coupled colt: has scope: sixth foal: half-brother to 4-y-o 7f (at 2 yrs) and 10.5f winner Noble Sprinter (by The Noble Player): dam poor daughter of half-sister to Derby second Cavo Doro: won race for unraced colts at Rome in September: fairly useful form, never dangerous, in Mill Reef Stakes and (sweating) Horris Hill Stakes at Newbury, after: stays 7.5f. *K. McAuliffe*   87

GENERAL'S STAR 2 b.c. (Mar 29) Night Shift (USA) – Colorsnap (Shirley Heights 130) [1996 6d³ a7g⁶ 7f⁶ 8g* 7.9g* 8m 7.9g Oct 10] 42,000Y: small, good-bodied colt: first living foal: dam unraced half-sister to Bella Colora (dam of Stagecraft), Colorspin (dam of Opera House) and Cezanne: successful in nurseries at Ayr and York (had run of race) in August/September: below form in similar events afterwards: suited by 1m: best form on easy surface (hung left on firm ground): jockey reported horse gurgled when well beaten on fibresand second start (wore tongue strap last 3 starts): edgy in visor final outing: sent to UAE. *M. R. Stoute*   77

GENEROSA 3 b.f. Generous (IRE) 139 – Hotel Street (USA) 93 (Alleged (USA) 138) [1995 80p: 7m² 1996 10g⁴ 10m³ 11.9d² 12m² 13.3f³ 14m* 14.6m 16.5s⁶ Nov 9] tall, rather unfurnished filly: shows knee action: fairly useful handicapper: best efforts at Salisbury and Newbury fourth and fifth 3-y-o starts: easy winner of maiden at Salisbury in August: should stay beyond 1¾m: acts on firm ground, respectable efforts on a soft surface: sweating and edgy (worst effort) penultimate 3-y-o start: sold 56,000 gns Newmarket December Sales. *H. Candy*   90

GENEROSUS (FR) 3 ch.c. Generous (IRE) 139 – Minya (USA) (Blushing Groom (FR) 131) [1995 NR 1996 10m³ 10.1d* 10.3g May 25] 1,200,000 francs Y: big, useful-looking colt: fourth foal: half-brother to very useful French 8.5f winner Minydoun (by Kaldoun) and a winner in Japan (by Sadler's Wells): dam, French 1m winner, daughter of Riverqueen: fairly useful form: long odds on, easy winner of maiden at Newcastle in May, making all: folded tamely in minor event at Doncaster 19 days later: will stay further than 10.1f: stays in training. *H. R. A. Cecil*   88

GENEROUS GIFT 2 ch.c. (Feb 27) Generous (IRE) 139 – Barari (USA) (Blushing Groom (FR) 131) [1996 6s 7g 8g² Sep 7] well-made colt: good walker: fourth living foal: half-brother to useful 3-y-o 6f to 7.5f winner Green Barries (by Green Desert) and a winner in Belgium by Jareer: dam unraced half-sister to very smart French 1m/1¼m performer Colour Chart and Canadian champion Rainbows For Life: first race for 2 months and much improved form when ½-length second of 15 to Ivan Luis in maiden at Thirsk, staying on strongly: well-backed favourite for Goodwood maiden on debut: will be suited by at least 1¼m: sure to improve again, and can make a fair handicapper. *E. A. L. Dunlop*   82 p

GENEROUS LIBRA 2 b.c. (Mar 23) Generous (IRE) 139 – Come On Rosi 77 (Valiyar 129) [1996 7g³ Oct 19] rather leggy, unfurnished colt: third foal: half-brother to useful 3-y-o sprinter Shanghai Girl and very smart 4-y-o 7f and 1m winner   87 p

Bin Rosie (both by Distant Relative): dam 6f winner: 13/2, 3½ lengths third of 6 to Crimson Tide in Houghton Stakes at Newmarket, held up, running green after 3f out then staying on: showed a round action: will improve, particularly over further. *D. R. Loder*

GENEROUS PRESENT 3 ch.g. Cadeaux Genereux 131 – Dance Move 60 (Shareef Dancer (USA) 135) [1995 –: 6m 7m 6g 1996 7.1g 8g 10m 8f* 8.3m* 8f³ 8m 8.1m 9.7d⁶ Oct 21] tall gelding: has a round action: modest handicapper: led well inside final 1f when winning at Carlisle in June and Hamilton in July: failed to repeat the form: may prove suited by further than 1m: acts on firm ground. *J. W. Payne*

GENESIS FOUR 6 b.g. Dreams To Reality (USA) 113 – Relma (Relko 136) 45 [1995 37, a46: a7g² a8g* a8g a8g a12g⁴ a11g⁶ a7g² a8g a8g² a9.4g 8m 8m a42 a8g 8m³ 6m 1996 a8g⁴ a8g⁵ a7g⁴ a11g³ a11g² a12g a9.4g⁵ a8g⁶ 6.9d⁴ a9.4g⁶ 12g² 16m³ a13g 14.1f 16m 16.2f³ 12m⁶ Aug 18] neat gelding: unimpressive mover: poor handicapper: sold out of R. Bowring's stable 2,200 gns Doncaster March Sales after eighth 6-y-o start: seems to stay 2m: acts on firm and dead ground and on all-weather: tried blinkered/visored, no improvement: inconsistent. *Mrs L. Stubbs*

GENTILHOMME 3 ch.c. Generous (IRE) 139 – Bold Flawless (USA) 73 (Bold – Bidder) [1995 100p: 6m 7f² 7m³ 10.2m* 10m* 1996 11.9g Sep 5] tall colt: good mover: progressive form at 2 yrs, winner of Zetland Stakes: sweating and edgy, tired last 2f in rated stakes at York on belated return: out-and-out galloper who should be well suited by 1½m+: has raced only on a sound surface: also sweating third 2-y-o start: races intelligently. *P. F. I. Cole*

GENTLE GAMBLER 5 b.m. Risk Me (FR) 127 – Queen's Lake 75 (Kings – Lake (USA) 133) [1995 NR 1996 12g May 17] second foal: sister to Belgian 11f winner Risky Danseuse: dam stayed very well: ran in NH Flat race before sold out of R. Allan's stable 4,000 gns Doncaster March Sales: showed little in claimer on flat debut. *L. R. Lloyd-James*

GENTLE IRONY 4 b.f. Mazilier (USA) 107 – Irenic 64 (Mummy's Pet 125) 65 [1995 60: a7g 9.9m⁴ 9.9m² 10.8g* 13.8g⁶ 10.1g⁵ 10g⁵ 10m³ 10g⁵ 8.5m* 8f⁵ 8.2m* a– 9m⁶ 10.1m² 8g 8g 7g² a8.5g⁶ 8.2m* 8f⁴ a7g⁵ a8.5g 1996 a8g a7g a10g⁶ 8g⁶ 8g 7g* 8f* 7g⁶ 8.3g³ 7f² Jul 16] small filly: reportedly in foal to Puissance: fair handicapper: well beaten first 3 starts at 4 yrs for W. Musson: won at Salisbury and Brighton within a week in June: effective at 7f to 10.8f: acted on fibresand and any turf going: usually blinkered for previous trainers: raced prominently of late: tough: consistent for last stable. *M. J. Ryan*

GENTLEMAN SID 6 b.g. Brotherly (USA) 80 – Eugenes Chance (Flashback – 102) [1995 52: 12m 16.4g 16.1g³ 18.2m* 16.2g⁴ 16.4m* 1996 a16g⁴ 18s 16.4g 17.2f 16.1f 16.2f 18f⁶ 16.2m Jul 26] strong gelding: seems no longer of account. *P. G. Murphy*

GENTLEMAN'S WORD (USA) 2 b. or br.c. (Apr 22) Red Ransom (USA) – 71 Attacat (USA) (Advocator) [1996 6m 7d⁴ 7m 8g⁶ Oct 18] $70,000Y: tall, quite attractive colt: half-brother to several winners in North America, including 9f minor stakes winner Black Jack Cat (by Dewan Keys): dam won at up to 9f in USA: fair form: visored, ran creditably when sixth of 17 to Bold Words in nursery at Newmarket on final outing, though never really figured after coming off bridle at an early stage: stays 1m. *M. R. Stoute*

GENUINE JOHN (IRE) 3 b.g. High Estate 127 – Fiscal Folly (USA) (Foolish 77 Pleasure (USA)) [1995 6g 6g⁵ 5.8m⁶ 6d⁵ 6m 7d 5d⁶ 1996 7s³ 9d⁶ 8d 8d 7m² 6m 5g³ a70 9g³ 7g 9f⁶ 7g⁵ 8g 11.9f² a8g³ a8.5s Dec 19] ex-Irish gelding: half-brother to Irish 1m winner Minstrel's Folly (by The Minstrel) and a winner in USA: dam, winner in USA, half-sister to Be My Guest: fair maiden: sold out of K. Prendergast's stable 7,800 gns Doncaster September Sales after thirteenth start: has similar form from 7f to 1½m: acts on firm and soft ground and on fibresand: tried blinkered, at least as effective without. *J. Parkes*

GENUINE LEADER 4 b.g. Formidable (USA) 125 – Glorietta (USA) (Shadeed – (USA) 135) [1995 9d 9g 8.5g 13g⁶ 10m 1996 a14.8g Jan 10] IR 12,000Y: first foal: dam unraced daughter of speedy Bitty Girl, a sister to Hot Spark: rated 59 when 7.8f claimer winner at Dundalk in 1994: disappointing in 1995, tried blinkered: sold out of K. Prendergast's stable 1,500 gns Doncaster September (1995) Sales: tailed off on reappearance. *P. G. Murphy*

GEOFFREYS GAMBLE 2 gr.c. (Mar 10) Barrys Gamble 102 – Palace Pet – (Dragonara Palace (USA) 115) [1996 5.1m 5f Aug 15] sparely-made twin: half-brother to 1993 2-y-o 5f winner Bettykimvic (by Reesh): dam ran once: did a 180 degree turn after leaving stalls in claimer at Nottingham on debut, taking no part: last of 12 in claimer at Beverley 8 days later. *B. P. J. Baugh*

GEOLLY (IRE) 4 b.g. Formidable (USA) 125 – Four-Legged Friend 101 – (Aragon 118) [1995 –: a8.5g⁶ a7g 1996 a7g⁶ Jan 8] poor maiden: tried blinkered: dead. *Dr J. D. Scargill*

GEORDIE LAD 2 ch.g. (Apr 19) Tina's Pet 121 – Edraianthus 78 (Windjammer – (USA)) [1996 5.1m 5.7m 5f Sep 17] 3,500F, 2,000Y: plain gelding: fourth foal: half-brother to French 3-y-o Esquive (by Safawan), useful 1m winner at 2 yrs, and 1993 2-y-o 6f winner Close To Reality (by Dreams To Reality): dam best form at 6f: behind in maiden and maiden auctions. *J. A. Bennett*

GEORGE BULL 4 b.g. Petoski 135 – Firgrove 73 (Relkino 131) [1995 68+: 68 10m⁶ 10m 10m 13.3f 11.4d³ 11.8g 1996 12m³ 10m⁴ 10m² Sep 16] tall, angular gelding: fair maiden: stays 1½m: probably acts on good to firm and dead ground, ran badly on firm: one paced. *Major W. R. Hern*

GEORGE DILLINGHAM 6 b.g. Top Ville 129 – Premier Rose 117 (Sharp 83 Edge 123) [1995 84: 12g² 11.9m 13.1g⁴ 13.9m³ 16.1m³ 1996 12d⁶ Apr 24] work-manlike gelding: has a round action: fairly useful handicapper: off course nearly 10 months and backward, ran creditably in steadily-run event at Catterick only 6-y-o start, fading inside last: stays 2m: acts on good to firm ground and heavy: visored (well below form) second 5-y-o outing: genuine. *Denys Smith*

GEORGIE BOY (USA) 3 b. or br.g. Zilzal (USA) 137 – Stealthy Lady (USA) – (J O Tobin (USA) 130) [1995 NR 1996 a7g 8d 6m a8g Dec 26] 22,000Y: rather leggy, close-coupled gelding: fifth foal: half-brother to 1m winner Spanish Grandee (by El Gran Senor) and a minor winner in USA: dam unraced daughter of Stumped, dam also of Sonic Lady: well beaten in maidens: bred to stay 1m: left C. Dwyer after third start. *Miss Gay Kelleway*

GEORGINA (IRE) 2 b.f. (Feb 26) Lycius (USA) 124 – Princess Nawaal (USA) 67 p 86 (Seattle Slew (USA)) [1996 7f⁵ Sep 5] fourth living foal: half-sister to fairly useful 3-y-o stayer Hal Hoo Yaroom (by Belmez) and winners in Belgium and (up to middle distances) Sweden: dam 8.5f and 9f winner: 16/1 and green, 11 lengths fifth of 15 to stable-companion Sarayir in steadily-run maiden at Salisbury, dropped out from wide draw then late progress: will stay at least 1m: will do better. *Major W. R. Hern*

GERMANO 3 b.c. Generous (IRE) 139 – Gay Fantastic (Ela-Mana-Mou 132) 103 [1995 89P: 7g 7m* 10m 10.3g⁵ 12f⁴ 12v Jul 7] tall, close-coupled colt: useful form: on toes, creditable 7¾ lengths fourth of 7 to Amfortas in King Edward VII Stakes at Royal Ascot: tailed-off last of 18 in Deutsches Derby at Hamburg: stays 1½m: acts on firm ground, tailed off on heavy: held up: sent to Germany. *G. Wragg*

GERMANY (USA) 5 b.h. Trempolino (USA) 135 – Inca Princess (USA) (Big 124 Spruce (USA)) [1995 123: 11v* 10s* 12s³ 11m² 10g* 12s* 12g⁴ 10m 1996 12g* 11d* 11d² 10d² 12m² Sep 1] good-topped, attractive horse: very smart performer: did not take to stallion duties in the spring: won minor event at Gelsenkirchen (by 22 lengths) in May then Group 2 race at Baden-Baden in June by 2½ lengths from Oxalagu: creditable second to Protektor in Idee Hansa Preis at Hamburg, to Timarida in Grosser Dallmayr Preis-Bayerisches Zuchtrennen at Munich (again beaten 1½ lengths) and to Pilsudski in Grosser Preis von Baden (caught near finish and beaten ¾ length) afterwards: stays 1½m: acts on good to firm ground, did not encounter very soft conditions (which seemed to suit him well earlier in career) in 1996: most consistent at 5 yrs. *B. Schutz, Germany*

GERMIGNAGA (ITY) 3 b.f. Miswaki Tern 120 – Guida Centrale (IRE) 105 (Teenoso (USA) 135) [1995 7g³ 7.5g³ 8v* 8s² 7.5d* 1996 8d* 8g⁵ 10d* 11d* 11g⁴ 12s⁶ 10d⁴ Sep 29] first reported foal: dam, Italian 1m and 1¼m winner at 2 yrs, half-sister to useful German sprinter/miler Siberian Grey: useful Italian filly: won minor events at Rome and Naples at 2 yrs, and at Rome in April: improved form to win listed race and Oaks d'Italia (beat Blu Meltemi a length) at Milan in May: off course 3½ months, good fourth of 6 to Dancer Mitral in listed race at Rome: below form in valuable race at Milan and Premio Lydia Tesio at Rome (7¼ lengths behind

Grey Way) last 2 starts: stays 11f: acts on heavy going, yet to race on top-of-the-ground. *L. Camici, Italy*

GERSEY 2 ch.f. (Apr 1) Generous (IRE) 139 – River Spey 96 (Mill Reef (USA) – p 141) [1996 7d⁶ Aug 23] 140,000Y: well-made filly: seventh foal: half-sister to 3 winners, including smart middle-distance stayer Jahafil (by Rainbow Quest) and useful 7f/1m winner Dune River (by Green Desert): dam 2-y-o 7.3f winner who later stayed middle distances, is out of sister to very smart Joking Apart: 16/1 and bit backward, around 16 lengths sixth of 8 to Reams of Verse in maiden at Newmarket, left behind after 3f out: looked green and nervy beforehand, and was mulish at stalls: should do better. *M. R. Stoute*

GER'S ROYALE (IRE) 5 ch.g. Dominion Royale 112 – Sister Dympna 63 115 (Grundy 137) [1995 6.5v 5g 6m⁶ 6g 6f⁵ 5g* 7m² 6m⁶ 7f* 6g 9d 6d 6d 7d 1996 8s* 9s² 10d⁴ 8d* 8m 8g 6d² 8d 6g* 9g* 6s* 7d Nov 10] half-brother to a winner in Belgium by Burslem: dam should have been suited by 1¾m+: smart Irish gelding: unraced at 2 yrs and successful 3 times next 2 seasons: better than ever in 1996, winning handicaps at Leopardstown and at the Curragh in the spring, then quite valuable handicap then 2 listed races at the Curragh (beat Burden of Proof 2½ lengths last time) in the autumn: well held in Royal Hunt Cup with first-time blinkers: effective at 6f and stays 9f: has won on both extremes of going, but goes particularly well with give in the ground: usually blinkered at 4 yrs, not in 1996: tough. *P. J. Flynn, Ireland*

GET AWAY WITH IT (IRE) 3 b.c. Last Tycoon 131 – Royal Sister II (Claude) 80 [1995 NR 1996 10m 10g² 10m² 12m 11.4g 10g³ 11.8m² Aug 19] lengthy, good sort: has scope: fluent mover: brother to high-class middle-distance performer Ezzoud and half-brother to several winners, including high-class miler Distant Relative (by Habitat): dam, winner at 1¼m at 4 yrs in Ireland and also successful in Italy, from excellent family: generally progressive maiden handicapper: better at 11.8f and shorter: raced only on good or good to firm ground: visored (no improvement) twice at 3 yrs: should win a race: sent to UAE. *M. R. Stoute*

GET THE POINT 2 b.c. (Apr 9) Sadler's Wells (USA) 132 – Tolmi 122 (Great 85 Nephew 126) [1996 7m⁶ 7m 8g⁴ Nov 1] 60,000Y: sturdy colt: tenth foal: half-brother to 4 winners, including useful 3-y-o 1m winner Unreal City (by Rock City) and useful middle-distance performer Double Dagger (by Reference Point): dam 1000 Guineas second out of outstanding broodmare Stilvi: never dangerous in Acomb Stakes at York and valuable sales contest at Newmarket on first 2 outings: over 4 lengths last of 4 behind River Usk in minor event at Newmarket on only other start, wandering final 2f and not knocked about unduly: will stay middle distances. *R. Hollinshead*

GET TOUGH 3 b.c. Petong 126 – Mrs Waddilove 79 (Bustino 136) [1995 58: 6m 63 6g⁶ 6g 8d⁶ 6.9m 1996 6.9s⁴ 8.3d² 8.2m 10m* 10m³ 9.9m⁶ 10g 11.5m⁴ 11.4m Sep 17] leggy colt: modest handicapper: won at Goodwood in June, leading inside final 1f: stays 11.5f, at least in steadily-run race: acts on good to firm ground, creditable effort at the time on soft: joined E. Wheeler. *S. Dow*

GHARIB (USA) 2 b.c. (Mar 31) Dixieland Band (USA) – The Way We Were 80 p (USA) (Avatar (USA)) [1996 7g⁵ Oct 30] $200,000Y: tenth foal: half-brother to several winners in USA, including a minor stakes winner: dam, won 2 minor events in USA, half-sister to Cacoethes and US Grade 1 winner (including at 2 yrs) Fabulous Notion: 4/1, around 10 lengths fifth of 17 to Happy Valentine in maiden at Yarmouth, travelling strongly at fore of far-side group then given easy time once winner (on opposite side of track) began to draw clear: sure to improve, particularly over 1m+. *A. C. Stewart*

GHATAAS 2 b.c. (Apr 21) Sadler's Wells (USA) 132 – Harmless Albatross 115 94 p (Pas de Seul 133) [1996 7.1v² Oct 6] leggy colt: fifth foal: half-brother to 1½m winner Haniya (by Caerleon) and very smart French 6f (at 2 yrs) to 1¼m winner Volochine (by Soviet Star): dam, French miler, out of Ribblesdale second North Forland: weak 8/1-shot, shaped encouragingly when neck second of 11 to Poteen in maiden at Haydock, travelling smoothly much of way and finishing clear of remainder: will stay 1m+: sure to improve and win races. *J. L. Dunlop*

GHAYYUR (USA) 2 ch.f. (Feb 1) Riverman (USA) 131 – New Trends (USA) 73 106 (Lyphard (USA) 132) [1996 6d² 7m⁵ 7.5g² Aug 24] $200,000Y: tall, quite attractive filly, rather unfurnished: second foal: dam 6f winner at 2 yrs (later suited by 1m), sister to very smart 6f to 11f winner Lyphard's Special and half-sister to champion US sprinter My Juliet: heavily-backed odds-on chance though very green, ½-length second of 6 to Colombia in maiden at Haydock: reportedly broke blood vessel final outing: stays 7f. *J. L. Dunlop*

GHOSTLY APPARITION 3 gr.g. Gods Solution 70 – Tawny 81 (Grey Ghost 53 98) [1995 53: 5m3 5m 5m 5m4 6.1m4 a6g a6g2 6s 1996 a5g3 a7g a6g4 a7g a7g a7g Mar 2] modest maiden: well below form last 3 starts: stays 6f: acts on equitrack (below form all 3 tries on fibresand) and good to firm ground. *John R. Upson*

GHUSN 3 b.c. Warning 136 – North Page (FR) 81 (Northfields (USA)) [1995 NR – 1996 10g 10.2g 10m 10m Jun 17] 46,000Y: lengthy colt: half-brother to several winners, notably smart middle-distance horse Linpac West (by Posse): dam placed at up to 10.6f: no worthwhile form: visored (tailed off) final 3-y-o start: sold 2,200 gns Newmarket July Sales. *T. Thomson Jones*

GIANT NIPPER 3 b.f. Nashwan (USA) 135 – Flamingo Pond 110 (Sadler's – Wells (USA) 132) [1995 NR 1996 9m Jun 1] first live foal: dam 1¼m winner: signs of a little ability (made brief move early in straight) in maiden at Kempton: will benefit from greater test of stamina: may do better. *I. A. Balding*

GIBB'S BEACH (IRE) 2 ch.f. (Apr 28) Shalford (IRE) 124§ – Kuwaiti 77 – (Home Guard (USA) 129) [1996 6m 7m6 6m Sep 27] IR, 6,700Y: half-sister to Irish 7f (at 2 yrs) to 1½m winner Santoline (by Connaught) and 2 winners abroad: dam 2-y-o 5f winner: well beaten in varied races, including a claimer. *C. A. Dwyer*

GIDDY 3 b. or br.f. Polar Falcon (USA) 126 – Spin Turn (Homing 130) [1995 –p: 60 d 7g 1996 7m 9m 8.3m 8m4 10f4 8m 8.3m 8d 8m 8g3 a8g* a9.4g a8g Dec 3] close-coupled filly: modest performer at best: claimed £7,000 out of D. Morley's stable fourth 3-y-o start: won handicap at Southwell in November: best form at up to 9f: acts on good to firm ground and fibresand. *J. Hetherton*

GIFTBOX (USA) 4 b.c. Halo (USA) – Arewehavingfunyet (USA) (Sham 60 (USA)) [1995 8g3 12d 10s 1996 a6g6 a7g a7g6 9.2s* 10.9d4 10.1f4 12f3 8.3g* 9.2m a55 a9.4g2 8.3m6 a8g4 12.1d 10f2 10.1m a11g Nov 4] ex-French colt: fourth foal: half-brother to 1992 2-y-o French 1¼m winner Rive (by Riverman) and French 9f to 1¼m winner Have Fun (by Topsider): dam won 5 races at 2 yrs in USA, including Grade 1 event, from 6f to 9f: trained at 3 yrs by Mme C. Head then sold 4,000 gns Newmarket Autumn (1995) Sales: modest performer: won minor events at Hamilton in May and July: sold out of Sir Mark Prescott's stable 17,000 gns Newmarket Autumn Sales after fifteenth start: stays 1¼m: acts on fibresand and firm and soft ground. *N. Bycroft*

GIFT TOKEN 2 b.f. (May 12) Batshoof 122 – Visible Form 99 (Formidable 71 (USA) 125) [1996 7m3 7m 7.1s4 Oct 22] 2,200F, 2,500Y: half-sister to several winners, including 8.2f and 1¼m winner Living Image (by Taufan) and 1989 2-y-o 6f winner Azeb (by Young Generation): dam 6f and 1¼m winner, out of half-sister to very smart stayer Raise You Ten: improved effort when just over 3 lengths fourth of 16 to Technicolour in maiden at Chepstow, keeping on to finish clear and faring best of those drawn high: will stay 1m: acts on soft ground. *Major D. N. Chappell*

GIGGLESWICK GIRL 5 b.m. Full Extent (USA) 113 – Foligno (Crofter 59 (USA) 124) [1995 66, a–: a7g a7g a6g5 8s5 a7g 6.1g2 6g 5.3m4 5f* 5g 6f3 5m* 5g3 5f a– 5m* 5m4 5m6 5.9f3 5.1m3 5g4 5f3 5.1h5 5f 5.1h3 5.1h4 5m4 5.7h2 5g 5d 5f 5.1m 6m 1996 6.1g6 6m5 5.3f4 5d May 22] leggy, sparely-made mare: fair and tough handicapper at 4 yrs, but seen only 4 times in 1996: effective at 5f, and should stay 7f: acts on hard and soft ground and on all-weather surfaces: often slowly away: covered by Fraam. *M. R. Channon*

GI LA HIGH 3 gr.f. Rich Charlie 117 – Gem of Gold 52 (Jellaby 124) [1995 61: 60 a5g3 a5g* a5g2 a5g* 5.1f2 5g5 a6g4 a5g3 a5g* 1996 a5g3 a5g4 a5g* a5g a5g2 5s5 a5g a5g a5g a6g2 Nov 29] compact filly: poor mover: modest handicapper: made all at Wolverhampton in February: best form at 5f: acts on firm ground and the all-weather: no improvement in blinkers/visor: inconsistent: joined M. Meade. *J. Berry*

GILDING THE LILY (IRE) 2 b.f. (Mar 23) High Estate 127 – Millingdale 58 Lillie 119 (Tumble Wind (USA)) [1996 6g2 6g3 8g Sep 7] 3,400F, 9,400Y: half-sister to several winners, including 1991 2-y-o 6f winner El Cortes and 1¼m winner Sao Paulo (both by El Gran Senor): dam, second in Cheveley Park Stakes and Irish 1000

Guineas, won 8.5f stakes on only start in USA: modest form when placed in median auction maiden at Epsom and maiden at Ayr first 2 starts: well beaten in maiden at Thirsk final outing: should stay further than 7f. *M. Johnston*

GILDORAN PALACE 5 ch.g. Gildoran 123 – Hyperion Palace (Dragonara Palace (USA) 115) [1995 NR 1996 a14g Jun 14] half-brother to a winning chaser by Van Der Linden: dam ran once at 2 yrs: showed nil on belated debut. *T. T. Bill* –

GILDORAN SOUND 3 b.f. Gildoran 123 – Sound of Laughter (Hasty Word 84) [1995 –: 7m 1996 12g 11.9d May 24] workmanlike filly: well beaten: covered by Noble Patriarch. *T. D. Easterby* –

GILLING DANCER (IRE) 3 b.g. Dancing Dissident (USA) 119 – Rahwah 73 (Northern Baby (CAN) 127) [1995 58p: 6.1d 6d⁵ 6m⁴ 1996 8.2m 8m 8.1f⁴ 8f 8f* 8f 8.2m⁶ 8m Aug 8] strong, angular gelding: modest handicapper: won at Carlisle in July, leading over 3f out: failed to repeat the form, and gelded: stays 1m: acts on firm ground: blinkered (very slowly away, tailed off) final 3-y-o outing: sold 2,800 gns Doncaster November Sales: temperament under suspicion. *P. Calver* 60

GINAS GIRL 3 gr.f. Risk Me (FR) 127 – Grey Cree 64 (Creetown 123) [1995 –: a5g 1996 a6g⁵ 5m⁶ 7d⁵ 6m 7m Sep 17] lengthy filly: no worthwhile form: left S. R. Bowring after 3-y-o reappearance: has given trouble in preliminaries. *Miss J. Bower* –

GINGER FOX (USA) 3 ch.c. Diesis 133 – Over Your Shoulder (USA) 77 (Graustark) [1995 NR 1996 10d³ 12g⁵ 12f³ 13.4g* 16s⁶ Oct 24] tall, unfurnished colt: half-brother to several winners, including multiple Grade 1-placed (at up to 9f) Harbour Club (by Danzig): dam sister to very smart (at up to 1¼m) Proctor: fairly useful form: sweating, gamely made all to win maiden at Chester in September: sold (H. Cecil to Mrs J. Pitman) 75,000 gns Newmarket Autumn Sales: stays 13.4f, failed to stay 2m on soft ground under forceful ride: acts on firm and dead ground. *H. R. A. Cecil* 88

GINGER HODGERS 3 ch.f. Crofthall 110 – Jarrettelle (All Systems Go 119) [1995 –: 6m 6f⁵ 5f 7g 1996 7d 10m 8g 12f⁶ 12g² 12m⁵ Jul 30] leggy filly: bad maiden plater: sold 1,450 gns Doncaster September Sales: barely stays 1½m: tried visored, no improvement: sent to South Korea. *R. M. Whitaker* 30

GINGER JIM 5 ch.g. Jalmood (USA) 126 – Stratch (FR) 71 (Thatch (USA) 136) [1995 66: a12g³ a10g⁶ a12g³ 10g³ 12g³ 12m³ 14m³ 12m 11.9d⁴ 14.1m⁴ 1996 a12g Feb 20] modest maiden: well beaten in 1996: stays 1¾m: acts on dead ground and good to firm: tried visored, no improvement: fair winning hurdler. *P. R. Hedger* –

GINGER ROGERS 2 ch.f. (Mar 5) Gildoran 123 – Axe Valley 89 (Royben 125) [1996 7.1s 8s a10g Nov 26] lengthy filly: fifth foal: half-sister to fairly useful 6-y-o sprinter For The Present (by Then Again) and 1991 2-y-o 6f winner Shalou (by Forzando): dam sprinter: behind in maidens. *D. W. P. Arbuthnot* –

GINGERSNAP 2 ch.f. (Mar 27) Salse (USA) 128 – Humble Pie 92 (Known Fact (USA) 135) [1996 7g⁶ Nov 2] fifth foal: half-sister to 3 winners, including 3-y-o 7f winner West Humble (by Pharly) and useful 4-y-o sprinter Leap For Joy (by Sharpo): dam 2-y-o 6f winner from sprinting family: 5/1, 4½ lengths sixth of 23 to Palisade in maiden at Newmarket, racing freely until no extra in Dip: likely to prove effective short of 7f: will improve. *H. R. A. Cecil* 75 p

GINKA 5 b.m. Petoski 135 – Pine (Supreme Sovereign 119) [1995 –: a12g⁶ a14.8g⁵ 11.7m 12d 10.8m 1996 10f 12d⁶ 16d³ 14d³ 17.9g⁴ 16s 16.4v² Nov 11] leggy, light-bodied mare: bad staying maiden handicapper: acts on heavy going: tried blinkered/visored, no improvement. *J. W. Mullins* 30

GINNY WOSSERNAME 2 br.f. (Feb 1) Prince Sabo 123 – Leprechaun Lady 57 (Royal Blend 117) [1996 5m⁵ 6g² a6g⁵ 7m* 7g⁴ 6.9m³ 7f⁴ 8f a7g³ a6g⁶ Nov 11] 2,000Y: angular filly: fourth foal: half-brother and half-sister to winner at up to 13.8f Goodbye Millie (by Sayf El Arab): dam stayer: modest performer: won claimer at Warwick in July: stays 7f: acts on firm going, probably on fibresand: effective with or without blinkers: usually races prominently. *W. G. M. Turner* 50 a36

GINZBOURG 2 b.g. (Jun 5) Ferdinand (USA) – Last Request 92 (Dancer's Image (USA)) [1996 7f⁵ 6.9d* Oct 21] 10,500Y: angular gelding: half-brother to several winners, including useful 3-y-o 5f (at 2 yrs) to 1¼m winner Dankeston (by Elmaamul) and 9f and 1¼m winner Wishiah (by Persian Bold): dam 1¼m winner at 2 yrs: backward, encouraging fifth of 10 in maiden at Warwick, staying on from rear: 86 p

4/1, won 12-runner maiden auction at Folkestone 13 days later by neck from Select Choice, taking time to get on top: will be suited by middle distances: will improve again. *J. L. Dunlop*

GIPSY PRINCESS 2 b.f. (May 15) Prince Daniel (USA) – Gypsy's Barn Rat 47 65
(Balliol 125) [1996 5g 5m³ 5g⁴ 6g⁶ 7g³ 7g* 7.9g² 7g² Oct 19] 700Y: fourth foal: dam suited by 7f or 1m: fair form: won nursery at Catterick in September: unseated rider going to post and withdrawn final intended outing: effective ridden aggressively at 7f, will stay beyond 1m: best form on good ground: blinkered fifth and last 2 starts. *M. W. Easterby*

GIRL OF MY DREAMS (IRE) 3 b.f. Marju (IRE) 127 – Stylish Girl (USA) 51
(Star de Naskra (USA)) [1995 NR 1996 5g 7g 7m 7.1m⁶ 8f Oct 14] IR 30,000Y: second foal: dam unraced: poor maiden: should stay further than 7.1f. *M. J. Heaton-Ellis*

GIVE AND TAKE 3 ch.g. Generous (IRE) 139 – Starlet 119 (Teenoso (USA) 60
135) [1995 NR 1996 10d 11.4m³ 12.3d⁵ 11.9g⁵ Oct 2] quite attractive gelding: third foal: half-brother to 2 winners, notably fairly useful 4-y-o Renown (up to 1½m, by Soviet Star): dam best as middle distance 4-y-o: modest maiden: probably a stayer: sold 12,000 gns Newmarket Autumn Sales and gelded. *Lord Huntingdon*

GIVE ME A RING (IRE) 3 b.c. Be My Guest (USA) 126 – Annsfield Lady 89 p
(Red Sunset 120) [1995 66p: 6d 6g⁴ 6m⁵ 1996 8.5d⁶ 8.3g⁴ a8g² 8.5m* 7.9g* 9m*
8m³ 9m Oct 5] useful-looking colt: has scope: generally progressive handicapper: completed summer hat-trick at Beverley, York and Ripon: best form when length third of 18 to Pride of Pendle in £22,000 event at Ayr in September, gamely making most: creditable eleventh of 38 in Cambridgeshire final start: effective at 1m and will stay further than 9f: acts on good to firm ground: carried head very awkwardly on turn only start on all-weather: should go on again at 4 yrs. *C. W. Thornton*

GLACIER 2 b.f. (Jan 27) Polish Precedent (USA) 131 – Graphite (USA) 80 (Mr – p
Prospector (USA)) [1996 7g Nov 2] fifth foal: half-sister to 7f winner Clovis Point (by Kris): dam, 9f winner, out of smart sprinter Stellarette, a half-sister to champion Canadian filly and good broodmare Kamar: 25/1, never a threat in 23-runner maiden at Newmarket won by Palisade: likely to do better. *Lord Huntingdon*

GLADYS ALTHORPE (IRE) 3 b.f. Posen (USA) – Gortadoo (USA) (Sharpen 75
Up 127) [1995 71: 6g⁵ 7m⁴ 6m* 7m 7g 6.1d 6m 7f 1996 6g 8m* 8m⁶ 8m* 8m* 8.1d²
8g 8g Nov 2] leggy filly: fair handicapper: off course nearly 4 months, won at Redcar and Carlisle in August and at Doncaster (£20,000 contest) in September: had two excuses last 2 starts: stays 8.1f: acts on good to firm and dead ground: held up. *J. L. Eyre*

GLEN GARNOCK (IRE) 4 gr.g. Danehill (USA) 126 – Inanna 105 (Persian 52
Bold 123) [1995 NR 1996 8m³ 5g⁶ 7.1m⁵ 8.9g Oct 12] big, lengthy gelding: modest maiden: probably stays 1m: sold (D. Nicholls to R. Juckes) 1,000 gns Doncaster November Sales. *D. Nicholls*

GLEN PARKER (IRE) 3 ch.c. Bluebird (USA) 125 – Trina's Girl (Nonoalco 83
(USA) 131) [1995 79p: 7g² 1996 8g 8.3g⁶ 8m² 8m* Aug 18] sturdy, good-bodied colt: good mover: brother to useful 4-y-o 1m winner Clan Ben: fairly useful performer: best effort when easy 7-length winner of maiden at Pontefract, never far away and leading over 1f out: should stay 1¼m: stays in training. *H. R. A. Cecil*

GLENVALLY 5 gr.m. Belfort (FR) 89 – Hivally (High Line 125) [1995 46: a8g²
a8g a8g* a8g 1996 a8g a8g 8g 12m⁵ 10g 8m 10.3g⁵ 9.9m Jul 6] angular, workman-like mare: carries condition: has a round action: poor handicapper: no worthwhile form on flat in 1996: stays 1½m: acts on dead ground and fibresand: often blinkered/visored: won over hurdles in December. *B. W. Murray*

GLIDE PATH (USA) 7 ch.g. Stalwart (USA) – Jolly Polka (USA) (Nice Dancer –
(CAN)) [1995 99: 12m³ 12m 11.9m 11.9m² 12f 12g* 11.9g 12m 10g 10.2f⁵
12.3m⁶ 12m⁴ 12f⁶ 12m 11.9d Sep 27] close-coupled gelding: carries condition: usually looks well: has a round action: useful handicapper at his best in 1995: generally disappointing in 1996: should stay further than 1½m: probably needs a sound surface: held up: sold (J. Hills to J. Jenkins) 11,000 gns Newmarket December Sales, and gelded. *J. W. Hills*

GLIMMERING HOPE (IRE) 2 b.g. (May 17) Petorius 117 – Angevin 61 –
(English Prince 129) [1996 7g Sep 25] IR 7,000Y: plain, good-topped gelding: half-brother to 2 winners abroad, including smart Italian sprinter Special Power (by

Lyphard's Special): dam placed at 9f: 50/1, showed nothing in maiden at Chester. *Miss J. F. Craze*

GLOBAL DANCER   5 b.g. Night Shift (USA) – Early Call 102 (Kind of Hush   –
118) [1995 75, a71: a10g³ a12g⁴ a10g⁶ a10g⁶ a12g⁵ 9g 12f* 14f² 12g⁶ 12f⁵ 12m²
11.9g⁶ a12g⁶ a16g⁶ 1996 12m 12g 9.7m⁶ 10m³ 11.6d Aug 12] useful-looking
gelding: fair handicapper in 1995: well below form in 1996, making the running all
starts (at too strong a pace on 3 occasions): stays 1¾m: acts on the all-weather and
goes well on firm going: tried blinkered (below form) earlier in career: joined
L. Wells. *S. Dow*

GLOBE RUNNER   3 b.c. Adbass (USA) 102 – Scenic Villa (Top Ville 129)   50
[1995 60: 6g⁵ 6f⁴ 5f⁵ 6m 1996 8g 8m 6g a6g⁶ a6g 5.9f⁶ 10f⁵ 8f* 6.9f 7d⁵ 8.3g⁵
a12s Dec 19] smallish colt: modest performer: won selling handicap at Thirsk in
July: stays 1m: acts on firm ground: blinkered (pulled hard) once: inconsistent.
J. J. O'Neill

GLOBETROTTER (IRE)   2 b.g. (May 16) Polish Patriot (USA) 128 – Summer   64
Dreams (CAN) (Victoria Park) [1996 6s 6m 7.5m³ 6m 7g Oct 19] IR 8,500Y:
good-topped gelding: has scope: half-brother to useful Irish sprinter Park Dream (by
Ahonoora) and several winners abroad, including 1983 Canadian 2-y-o 5.5f stakes
winner Deputy General (by Vice Regent): dam lightly-raced Canadian 2-y-o winner
at around 5f from good family: fair form: will stay beyond 7.5f: best form on
top-of-the-ground. *M. Johnston*

GLORIA IMPERATOR (IRE)   3 b.g. Imperial Frontier (USA) 112 – English   –
Lily (Runnett 125) [1995 NR 1996 5.1g 5m 7g a5g Nov 30] 7,500Y: tall gelding:
second foal: dam never ran: well beaten, seeming headstrong. *A. B. Mulholland*

GLORIANA   4 b.f. Formidable (USA) 125 – Tudor Pilgrim 58 (Welsh Pageant   71
132) [1995 78: 10g² 10.5g 11.5f⁶ 10f² 9d* 10f⁴ 11.5m³ 10.3m 12g³ 12.1d 1996 12m
10m⁵ 9.7m⁶ 10.2g 8.1m* 8m 10.5v⁶ 8.9g Oct 12] rangy, angular filly: fair
handicapper: won at Haydock in August: effective from 1m to 1½m: acts on any
going: visored (below form) final 3-y-o start: has gone well with forcing tactics: won
maiden hurdle in November. *Lady Herries*

GLORIOUS ARAGON   4 b.f. Aragon 118 – Gloria Maremmana (King Emperor   88
(USA)) [1995 86?: 6m⁵ 6m² 5.1g² 5.2g⁴ 5g 1996 5g³ 5.1g⁶ 6m 5d⁶ 5.2m* 5.1d⁶ 5.1g
Sep 25] sturdy filly: fairly useful handicapper: gained first success in strongly-run
contest at Newbury in August: below that form on easier ground at Chester both
subsequent outings: effective at 5f and 6f: seems best on a sound surface: tends to be
on toes: has run well when sweating. *R. F. Johnson Houghton*

GLORIOUS ISLAND   6 ch.g. Jupiter Island 126 – Gloria Maremmana (King   –
Emperor (USA)) [1995 NR 1996 8m Jun 5] modest maiden at 2 yrs: soundly beaten
in selling handicap only start on flat since: sold 1,800 gns Doncaster November
Sales. *Mrs N. Macauley*

GLORY OF DANCER   3 b.c. Shareef Dancer (USA) 135 – Glory of Hera 99   121
(Formidable (USA) 125) [1995 105p: 6d* 8g² 8g² 8g* 1996 10g² 10.4m* 12m⁴
10m² 10.5m⁴ 10f⁴ 10g³ 10g⁶ Oct 19]

Paul Kelleway's placing of horses in big races over the years has earned
him the tag 'Pattern Race Paul'. He saddled his eleventh Derby runner in the
latest season, but, unlike the previous ten, who had gone off at an average
starting price of 229/1, Glory of Dancer went into the race with a realistic
chance, starting the 6/1 third favourite of twenty. For the record, beginning in
1979, those starting prices were 500/1, 100/1, 22/1, 500/1, 500/1, 150/1, 100/1,
150/1, 66/1 and 200/1. In the event Glory of Dancer wasn't quite good enough,
finishing a creditable three and a half lengths fourth, after leading briefly over
two furlongs out, to Shaamit—who, coincidentally, had also outpointed him in
a much-publicised gallop the weekend before the big race. Glory of Dancer had
shown himself to be a very smart three-year-old on both starts prior to Epsom,
finishing a neck second to Santillana in the Sandown Classic Trial (running
really well under a Group 1 penalty) on his reappearance and then winning
the Homeowners Dante Stakes at York. His win at York came in a slowly-run
seven-runner contest, in which he showed a good turn of foot to beat the

Homeowners Dante Stakes, York—
a slowly-run race goes to Glory of Dancer (dark cap) and Olivier Peslier;
the closest challengers are Dushyantor (left) and Jack Jennings

subsequent Derby runner-up Dushyantor by half a length, doing particularly well considering he lost his place momentarily when the tempo quickened. The Dante provided many British racegoers with their first glimpse of the skills of top French jockey Olivier Peslier, who also rode Glory of Dancer well at Epsom on his first ride over the full Derby course.

The consistent Glory of Dancer was campaigned exclusively in pattern races in 1996 and ran well on all eight of his starts, a feat which might well have seemed unlikely when he finished his two-year-old career in the operating theatre. The operation to remove chips from his joints followed a successful campaign in Italy, culminating with victory in the Group 1 Gran Criterium at Milan. The decision to send Glory of Dancer to Kelleway from Fabrio Brogi's yard in Italy came largely as a result of the Newmarket trainer's successes with Pelder, another ex-Italian horse who suffered from leg problems. Commenting on his stable star during the run-up to the Derby, Kelleway explained: 'We've had to be very careful with him. Apparently he had ankle problems before he was operated on during the winter.' Kelleway's small stable can take a good deal of credit from the way Glory of Dancer managed to hold his form so well throughout a long season. Indeed, just two weeks after Epsom he came very close to gaining another Group 1 success, losing out by a short-head to Grape Tree Road in the Grand Prix de Paris at Longchamp. He also ran creditably on his four starts following a short mid-season break, most notably when making the frame in both the Arlington Million (in which he fared best of the European challengers) and the Irish Champion Stakes at Leopardstown. Another crack at the Arlington race was on the cards for 1997, but soon after his final start it was reported that Glory of Dancer had injured a tendon and had been retired.

Glory of Dancer, who cost 13,000 guineas as a yearling, is one of the better recent representatives of the 1983 Irish Derby winner Shareef Dancer. He is bred along similar lines to two of that sire's best middle-distance performers, Rock Hopper and Possessive Dancer, who were also out of grand-

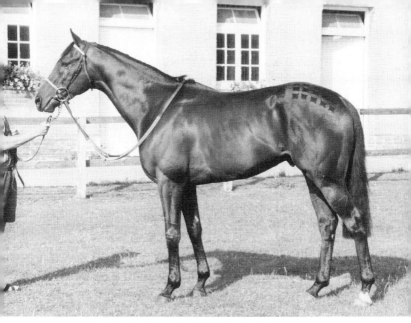

General Horse Advertising SRL's "Glory of Dancer"

Glory of Dancer (b.c. 1993)	Shareef Dancer (USA) (b 1980)	Northern Dancer (b 1961)	Nearctic
			Natalma
		Sweet Alliance (b 1974)	Sir Ivor
			Mrs Peterkin
	Glory of Hera (b 1982)	Formidable (b 1975)	Forli
			Native Partner
		As Blessed (b 1974)	So Blessed
			Asmara

daughters of Forli. Glory of Dancer's dam, the useful Glory of Hera, showed plenty of speed and won twice at five furlongs as a two-year-old, including a listed race at Newbury. A cursory glance at the dam's side of the pedigree suggests more speed than stamina but Glory of Hera's two previous winners on the flat (by Slip Anchor and Shirley Heights) won at around a mile and a half. Glory of Dancer himself was raced mainly at around a mile and a quarter though his Derby effort showed he was effective at a mile and a half. As well as being by far the best of her offspring, Glory of Dancer was also the final foal of his dam, who died after unsuccessful matings in 1993 and 1994. The lengthy, good-topped Glory of Dancer, who didn't always impress in his action, acted on firm and dead ground and was a genuine and most consistent performer. He is standing at the Throckmorton Court Stud, Worcestershire, at £2,500 with the October 1st concession. *P. A. Kelleway*

GLOW FORUM 5 b.m. Kalaglow 132 – Beau's Delight (USA) (Lypheor 118) [1995 43: a12g a16g⁵ 14.1g 12m a16g a13g* 11.9f* 11.8g 12m³ a12g⁵ a13g² 1996 12d* 12m a12g* a12g* 11.5d² a12g* 11.9g⁵ a12g* 12g⁶ a12g Dec 7] leggy, angular mare: much improved handicapper for new stable: fair form on fibresand, winning at Southwell in July and August and at Wolverhampton in September and October: only modest form on turf, winning claiming event at Salisbury in May: stays 1½m: acts on firm and dead ground, goes well on all-weather. *L. Montague Hall*

54
a77

GLOWING JADE 6 b.m. Kalaglow 132 – Precious Jade 72 (Northfields (USA))   75
[1995 75: 7g* 7g⁴ 8m⁶ 8m 8g 7f 1996 8.2d⁶ 8m* 8m 8.2m 7.1m³ 7f² 8m Oct 3] tall,
long-backed mare: fair handicapper: won at Thirsk in April: out of depth final start
(flashed tail much of way): best form at 7f to 9f: acts on firm and dead ground,
probably not on soft: ideally suited by strong pace and waiting tactics. *J. A. Glover*

GLOWING REEDS 3 ch.f. Kalaglow 132 – No Jazz 55 (Jaazeiro (USA) 127)   46
[1995 –: 8m 1996 12m a9.4g a14.8g⁴ 14.1f² 18m a12g 16.4m⁶ Aug 20] leggy, plain   a–
filly: visored first time, worthwhile form only when second of 6 in handicap at
Yarmouth in June: sold 1,365 gns Ascot October Sales: looks a stayer: acts on firm
ground: hung badly on reappearance: also visored last 2 starts. *C. N. Allen*

GO BRITANNIA 3 b.c. Machiavellian (USA) 123 – Chief Celebrity (USA) 85   90
(Chief's Crown (USA)) [1995 NR 1996 8m 7.1m² 8m* 8m⁵ 10m⁵ Aug 10]
185,000Y: first foal: dam, 1½m winner, half-sister to smart stayer At Talaq and Grade
1 8.5f and 9f winner Annoconnor: fairly useful performer: won maiden at Warwick
in July, carrying head rather awkwardly: creditable fifth in handicaps at Newmarket
subsequently: stays 1¼m: has raced only on good to firm going: visored fourth start:
sold 24,000 gns Newmarket Autumn Sales. *D. R. Loder*

GODMERSHAM PARK 4 b.g. Warrshan (USA) 117 – Brown Velvet 68   72
(Mansingh (USA) 120) [1995 73: 7m³ 7g² 7m² 7g² 7m 1996 7g⁶ 7m³ 8d 7g Oct 19]
leggy, lengthy gelding: fair maiden handicapper, lightly raced: not seen until
September, best effort when third of 18 at Lingfield: should stay 1m: acts on good to
firm ground (well beaten on a soft surface): visored final start. *M. J. Heaton-Ellis*

GO FOR GREEN 2 br.f. (Jan 23) Petong 126 – Guest List 85 (Be My Guest   56
(USA) 126) [1996 6.1d 7f³ 7f Oct 14] 12,000Y: leggy filly: fourth foal: half-sister to
1994 2-y-o 7f winner (stays 1¾m) Dangerous Guest (by Deploy), 1m and 8.5f winner
Backstabber (by Flash of Steel) and a winner in Germany by Salse: dam 6f (at 2
yrs) and 7f winner, is half-sister to high-class sprinter/miler Sanedtki: best effort in
maidens when around 9 lengths third of 8 to easy winner Priena in median auction
event at Redcar: slowly away first 2 starts: will probably stay 1m. *Dr J. D. Scargill*

GO FOR SALT (USA) 2 b.f. (Mar 10) Hawkster (USA) – Wall St Girl (USA)   75 p
(Rich Cream (USA)) [1996 7.6d² Aug 29] $25,000F, 15,000Y: second foal: dam,
won 4 times at up to 9f in USA, half-sister to a stakes winner by Silver Hawk: weak
7/1, 1¾ lengths second of 9 to Barnum Sands in maiden at Lingfield, slowly away
then staying on well, finishing clear of third: will do better. *M. R. Stoute*

GO-GO-POWER-RANGER 3 ch.g. Golden Lahab (USA) – Nibelunga   62
(Miami Springs 121) [1995 –: 5g 7f 6.1d 1996 10.1s 11.1g² 12d* 12m² 10.5d 12f
13.8m⁶ 11.8g Aug 12] sparely-made, short-backed gelding: modest handicapper:
won at Carlisle in April: well below form last 4 starts: should stay further than 1½m:
acts on good to firm and dead ground: probably suited by being ridden up with pace:
winning hurdler. *B. Ellison*

GO HEVER GOLF 4 ch.g. Efisio 120 – Sweet Rosina 61 (Sweet Revenge 129)   80
[1995 96, a109: a6g* 6m 6.1m* 7g 6m 5.1m³ a6g 5m 1996 6m 6m 5m 5.1m 6m 5.1g²   a–
4d² 5d 6.1s Oct 22] quite good-topped gelding: poor walker: useful handicapper in
1995: not so good in 1996: sold 13,000 gns Newmarket Autumn Sales: very best
form at 6f: acts on any turf going, goes well on the all-weather: blinkered (ran poorly)
seventh 2-y-o start: usually bandaged behind. *T. J. Naughton*

GOING FOR BROKE 2 b.g. (Feb 8) Simply Great (FR) 122 – Empty Purse   65
(Pennine Walk 120) [1996 5m 6g² a7g 6f² a7g² 8d⁵ 7m² a7s Dec 19] £1,000Y: second   a63
foal: half-brother to a winning 1m plater at 2 yrs: dam unraced: fair form: stays 1m:
acts on firm ground and fibresand, probably on dead: unruly stalls fourth start, reared
stalls and very slowly away sixth. *P. C. Haslam*

GOLBORNE LAD 3 ch.g. Jester 119 – Taskalady 47 (Touching Wood (USA)   –
127) [1995 NR 1996 a6g⁶ a6g 5m Apr 25] 3,200Y: first foal: dam won 11f seller: no
worthwhile form: tried visored. *J. Balding*

GOLD BLADE 7 ch.g. Rousillon (USA) 133 – Sharp Girl (FR) 114 (Sharpman)   72
[1995 51, a66: a11g² a12g* 10.3g 10.5d² 12.3f 11.1f* 9.2m³ 9.9m² 12g³ 12d 1996
a12g² a12g* a13g⁶ 10g* 10.5d² 12.3m⁴ 11.1g³ 10g* 9.2m* 13.1g* 9.9m* 12g* 12m
10.1m a14g a14g⁶ a10g⁵ Dec 11] big, good-topped gelding: poor mover: fair
handicapper, improved on turf in 1996: often contests amateurs races, winning at
Southwell in January, Nottingham in April and completing five-timer at Pontefract,

Hamilton, Ayr, Beverley and Catterick in the summer: stays 13f: acts on any turf ground and used to go particularly well on the all-weather (shaped well final 7-y-o start): sometimes bandaged near-fore: sometimes blinkered earlier in career: held up: usually ridden by Mrs L. Pearce. *J. Pearce*

GOLD CLIPPER   2 b.c. (May 27) High Kicker (USA) – Ship of Gold 78 (Glint of Gold 128) [1996 8g Oct 30] second foal: dam, disappointing maiden, stayed 1½m: 66/1, slowly away and always behind in maiden at Yarmouth. *M. J. Ryan*   –

GOLD DESIRE   6 b.g. Grey Desire 115 – Glory Gold 59 (Hittite Glory 125) [1995 34: a11g 12.1d⁵ 9.2g⁴ 9.2g⁵ 11.1g⁴ 11.1g 12.3f⁴ 10.1f* 10.4g³ 1996 10.1s 12.1g² 12m⁴ 11.1g² 10g⁴ 11.1g⁴ 12m 12.1f⁶ 10m* 11.1m⁵ 11f³ 10.4g* 10m⁵ 11.9g 8.9g 10.1m⁶ Oct 23] sparely-made, plain gelding: has a round action: modest handicapper: won at Newmarket in August and York (apprentices) in September: ideally suited by a strongly-run race at around 1¼m: acts on firm and dead going: visored (ran poorly) once at 3 yrs: held up/tracks leaders. *M. Brittain*   52

GOLD DISC (USA)   3 ch.c. Slew O' Gold (USA) – Singing (USA) 91 (The Minstrel (CAN) 135) [1995 81p: 7g* 1996 8.1g 10m* 12m 10g 10m 10.3d* 10.3m 10m Oct 4] well-made, attractive colt: fairly useful handicapper on his day: won at Pontefract in June and Chester in August, coming from rear: stays 1¼m: sometimes sweats and gets on edge, has been taken last and quietly to post: sometimes a hard puller, but has also come quickly off bridle: inconsistent and not one to trust implicitly: sent to USA. *B. W. Hills*   93

GOLD EDGE   2 ch.f. (Mar 22) Beveled (USA) – Golden October 62 (Young Generation 129) [1996 5s⁵ 5.1m⁶ 5m² 5.3g³ 6d⁶ Oct 21] 3,600Y: sturdy filly: half-sister to fair 3-y-o 5f performer Chemcast (by Chilibang): dam 6f winner: best effort when second of 16 in seller at Ayr: bred to stay beyond 5f. *M. R. Channon*   52

GOLDEN ACE (IRE)   3 ch.c. Archway (IRE) 115 – Gobolino (Don 128) [1995 NR 1996 8d* 7g⁵ May 28] big colt: IR 5,200F, 19,500Y: half-brother to quite useful 1994 Italian 2-y-o Don Fayruz (by Fayruz) and Irish 5-y-o 1m and 1¼m winner Bolino Star (by Stalker): dam won at 7f at 2 yrs in Ireland: 33/1 and burly, led from halfway when winning steadily-run maiden at Newbury in April: easy to back, last of 5 in minor event at Leicester over 5 weeks later. *R. Hannon*   87

GOLDEN ARROW (IRE)   5 ch.g. Glint of Gold 128 – Sheer Luck 72 (Shergar 140) [1995 –: 12m 13.3d 12s 1996 12g³ 16g⁴ 16d⁶ 13.9m² 14d⁴ 20f⁵ 16.2m² 16.1m* 18.2m⁶ Sep 19] workmanlike gelding: fluent mover: fairly useful handicapper: sold out of I. Balding's stable 24,000 gns Ascot June Sales after fifth start: won at Warwick in August: effective at 1½m and probably stays long distances: acts on firm and soft ground: has run creditably for an apprentice: blinkered fifth 5-y-o start: held up, and possibly suited by exaggerated waiting tactics (has looked none too keen). *M. C. Pipe*   85

GOLDEN AVENTURA (IRE)   2 b.c. (Jan 21) Nordance (USA) – Colline Del Po (IRE) (Jaazeiro (USA) 127) [1996 5s* 5.5m⁴ 7g 6m⁴ 8g² 7.5s² 8g² 8s⁶ 8g* 9s* Nov 17] half-brother to 2 winners in Italy by Prince Spruce (including at middle distances) and Mummy's Game: dam ran once: won maiden at Milan early on, then quite valuable event and Group 2 Premio Guido Berardelli (beat Yavlensky 1½ lengths) at Rome in November: likely to stay middle distances: acts well on soft ground: should improve further. *G. Fratini, Italy*   100 p

GOLDEN FACT (USA)   2 b.c. (May 11) Known Fact (USA) 135 – Cosmic Sea Queen (USA) (Determined Cosmic (USA)) [1996 5m² 5.2s⁴ 7f⁴ 7m⁵ 7.3m⁴ 6d Aug 24] $22,000F, $35,000Y: close-coupled colt: seventh foal: half-brother to several minor winners in USA: dam won 11 times at up to middle distances in USA: fair form: stays 7f: hung last 3 starts, and looked most ungenuine, flashing tail, at Newmarket on final outing. *R. Hannon*   75 §

GOLDEN FAWN   3 ch.f. Crowning Honors (CAN) – Hill of Fare (Brigadier Gerard 144) [1995 NR 1996 10g 10.5m² 10f² 11.9g 12g Oct 18] 500F: rather unfurnished filly: half-sister to 6f winner Thorny Bishop (by Belfort) and a winner in Belgium: dam lightly raced: 3½ lengths second of 7 in claimer at Haydock in August, second outing and best effort: sold 4,800 gns Newmarket Autumn Sales: should stay further than 10.5f. *Lady Herries*   60

GOLDEN FILIGREE   4 ch.f. Faustus (USA) 118 – Muarij (Star Appeal 133) [1995 NR 1996 12m 10g a9.4g⁴ May 11] first foal: dam no form: first sign of ability when fourth of 10 in claimer at Wolverhampton final start. *D. T. Thom*   48

GOLDEN GODDESS 2 ch.f. (Feb 28) Formidable (USA) 125 – Tame Duchess – 71 (Saritamer (USA) 130) [1996 6m 7.1s Oct 22] 18,000Y: strong, lengthy filly: has scope: sixth foal: closely related to 7f winner Duke of Dreams and a winner in USA (both by Efisio) and half-brother to a winner abroad by Another Realm: dam maiden, who stayed 1¼m, is half-sister to smart sprinter Son of Shaka: well beaten in maidens: sold privately 1,000 gns Doncaster November Sales: sent to Denmark. *I. A. Balding*

GOLDEN HADEER 5 ch.h. Hadeer 118 – Verchinina 99 (Star Appeal 133) 41 [1995 –: a10g⁶ a12g⁶ 1996 12m⁶ 12.1m⁴ 10m 11.6d 12d a14g³ 12v a14g* a12s³ Dec a50 19] close-coupled horse: poor handicapper: ran mainly in amateurs contests in 1996, winning at Southwell in November: stays 1¾m, should get further: acts on soft ground and fibresand, and probably good to firm: inconsistent. *M. J. Ryan*

GOLDEN HANOOF (USA) 4 ch.f. Slew O' Gold (USA) – Hanoof (USA) 79 77 (Northern Dancer) [1995 8g³ 8g 10m 1996 10.8g⁴ 11g² 8g 12g⁶ a12g⁴ Dec 27] fifth foal: half-sister to useful French 7f and 1m winner Ville d'Amore (by Irish River): dam 11f winner out of Irish Oaks runner-up Little Bonny, a sister to Noelino: fair form: not seen in 1995 after June: in frame in France in 1996 in minor races at Le Croise-Laroche and Fontainebleau: sold out of Mme C. Head's stable 10,500 gns Newmarket July Sales after penultimate start: no promise on British debut: seems to stay 1½m. *Dr J. D. Scargill*

GOLDEN MELODY 2 b.f. (Mar 10) Robellino (USA) 127 – Rose Chanelle – (Welsh Pageant 132) [1996 6.9g 7g⁵ 7.1f 8g Oct 25] seventh foal: closely related to fairly useful stayer Garden District (by Celestial Storm) and half-sister to Italian 3-y-o 1m winner It's Brutal (by Midyan) and 2 winners, including 1993 2-y-o 1m winner Art Tatum (by Tate Gallery): dam unraced granddaughter of Rose Dubarry: always behind in maidens and steadily-run nursery at Doncaster. *R. Hannon*

GOLDEN ORIENTAL (USA) 2 b.c. Glitterman (USA) – Oriental Silk (USA) 108 (Far Out East (USA)) [1996 6m⁴ 6m⁴ 7g⁵ 7g³ 7m⁴ 5m² 7g³ 5g³ 5g* 7.5g² 7g² 8g⁵ 5g* 6g⁵ 6d* 6s⁵ 7.5s 6s* Nov 17] $15,000F, $11,000Y: fifth foal: dam, minor stakes winner in USA at 9f, half-sister to a Grade 3 9f winner: heavily campaigned and broke maiden at Naples only on ninth attempt before winning minor races there and at Rome: stepped up in class and caused a big upset when winning all-aged Group 3 event at Rome in November by neck from Beat of Drums: stays 7.5f, best form as a sprinter: best form on soft ground. *G. Fratini, Italy*

GOLDEN POND (IRE) 3 b.f. Don't Forget Me 127 – Golden Bloom (Main 104 Reef 126) [1995 72: 6.1m⁶ 7f³ 7m 6m 7d⁴ 6m* 7f³ 1996 6s² 6g³ 7m² 7.3d³ 7m² 8.2m* 8f* 8.1g² 8m 8g* 7.5f⁴ Nov 9] tall, leggy filly: improved throughout 1996, and is now a useful performer: won handicap at Nottingham and minor event at Ascot in June: trained until after ninth start by F. J. Houghton: easily best effort when winning listed race at Saint-Cloud in September by short head from Folle Tempete only start for C. Wall: stays 8.3f: acts on firm going: takes good hold: has carried head high/ awkwardly under pressure: front runner final 5 starts in Europe, soon behind on first start in USA: consistent. *M. D. Wolfson, USA*

GOLDEN POUND (USA) 4 b.g. Seeking The Gold (USA) – Coesse Express 89 (USA) (Dewan (USA)) [1995 78: 8.1g 8.3m³ 8m² 10.5g 8f 1996 a8g³ a8.5g² a8g² a7g² 8s⁴ 7d⁴ 6m* 7f⁶ 6d⁶ 6s³ 6m 5m³ 6g* 6f⁵ 6m² 6m³ 6m 6m Sep 21] lengthy, useful-looking gelding: good mover: fairly useful handicapper: won maiden at Thirsk in April and handicap at Epsom in July: has form over as far as 1m, but likely to prove best over 6f or stiff 5f: acts on all-weather surfaces and on good to firm and soft ground: successful in blinkers, at least as effective without: has worn tongue strap, but not of late: has run well when sweating. *Miss Gay Kelleway*

GOLDEN PUNCH (USA) 5 b.g. Seattle Song (USA) 130 – Pagan Winter – (USA) (Pago Pago) [1995 –: a7g 1996 a10g a10g⁴ a16g⁶ a16g⁴ Feb 29] poor maiden staying handicapper: tried blinkered/visored. *C. A. Cyzer*

GOLDEN SILVER 3 b.f. Precious Metal 106 – Severals Princess 44 43 (Formidable (USA) 125) [1995 46: 5g 6m³ 6f⁶ 5g⁶ 5g⁴ 7m 1996 6.1m 6g² Aug 1] narrow filly: has a round action: poor maiden: stays 6f: sweating (below form) final 2-y-o start. *J. S. Moore*

GOLDEN THUNDERBOLT (FR) 3 b.c. Persian Bold 123 – Carmita 79 (Caerleon (USA) 132) [1995 NR 1996 8.3m⁶ 8m⁴ 9m³ 8m² 8m 8.5m⁴ 8g² 7f⁵ Oct 14] neat colt: first foal: dam French listed winner over 1½m: fair maiden: sold 22,000 gns Newmarket Autumn Sales: likely to prove suited by 1¼m+: yet to race on a soft surface. *J. H. M. Gosden*

GOLDEN TOUCH (USA)   4 ch.c. Elmaamul (USA) 125 – Tour d'Argent   67 (USA) (Halo (USA)) [1995 66: 7m 8.2d³ 8m 1996 a8g⁵ a8g a9.4g² a10g³ a8.5g* 9m* 10m* 10.3g⁵ 10d⁵ 8m 10f⁵ 10m⁶ 10m 8m 10g a9.4g² a10s⁵ a9.4g² a8g Dec 27] compact colt: fair handicapper: won at Wolverhampton, Kempton (apprentices) and Newmarket in the spring (trained by N. Callaghan until after eleventh start): re-found form for new stable late in year: stays 10.3f: acts on dead ground, good to firm and all-weather: held up. *D. J. S. Cosgrove*

GOLDEN TYKE (IRE)   3 b.g. Soviet Lad (USA) 94 – Golden Room (African   49 Sky 124) [1995 –: 5m 5f 1996 a6g⁵ a6g⁴ 5s May 2] close-coupled gelding: poor maiden handicapper: tailed off (raced alone on stand side) final start: has raced only at sprint distances. *M. Johnston*

GOLD LANCE (USA)   3 ch.g. Seeking The Gold (USA) – Lucky State (USA)   52 + (State Dinner (USA)) [1995 NR 1996 10d 10m a7g² Dec 31] 1,000,000 francs Y: angular gelding: first foal: dam, French 1m winner, half-sister to Ravinella: sold out of M. Stoute's stable only 4,400 gns Newmarket July Sales after second start, and gelded: second in bad maiden at Lingfield, soon well behind then hanging left and finishing strongly: blinkered final start. *R. J. O'Sullivan*

GOLD LINING (IRE)   3 ch.f. Magical Wonder (USA) 125 – Muntaz (ARG)   – (Search Tradition (USA)) [1995 NR 1996 8.2m 8.3m 10.5d 14d⁵ 12.1m 8m 8.1m 7.1m Sep 23] lengthy filly: third reported foal: dam won 3 races in Spain: no worthwhile form: trained first 3 starts by C. Broad: visored last 2 outings. *E. J. Alston*

GOLDRILL   3 ch.c. Never So Bold 135 – Irish Impulse (USA) 50 (Irish River   – (FR) 131) [1995 –: 6g 1996 5m 6g May 24] workmanlike colt: second foal: dam poor maiden out of smart staying 2-y-o Exclusively Raised: behind in northern maidens. *Miss S. E. Hall*

GOLD SPATS (USA)   3 b.c. Seeking The Gold (USA) – Foot Stone (USA)   87 (Cyane) [1995 NR 1996 8.1g² 8g² 7m* 7.9m 7m Sep 28] $150,000Y: lengthy, attractive colt: fifth foal: half-brother to 6f (at 2 yrs) to 9f (in France) winner Ghalyoon (by Deputy Minister) and a listed stakes winner in USA by Proud Truth: dam minor stakes winner at up to 9f in USA: fairly useful performer: odds on, won maiden at Kempton in June, travelling well to lead over 1f out: below form in 2 valuable events only subsequent starts, checked over 2f out when midfield in £50,100 handicap at Ascot on final one: will stay beyond 1m. *M. R. Stoute*

GOLLACCIA   2 gr.f. (Feb 4) Mystiko (USA) 124 – Millie Grey 52 (Grey Ghost   – 98) [1996 6f⁶ 6m 7m Oct 23] leggy filly: fifth reported foal: half-sister to fair 9f/1¼m performer Efizia (by Efisio): dam, poor on flat, winning hurdler: showed nothing in maidens at Redcar (2) and Newcastle. *G. M. Moore*

GONDO   9 br.g. Mansingh (USA) 120 – Secret Valentine 71 (Wollow 132) [1995   42 50: a5g⁶ a6g a5g 5m 5g⁶ 5g⁶ 5g 5.1g 6m 5m 5f 5.1m 5m³ 6g 6d 8g 5.1d³ 6f 1996 5.9m 5g 5.1m 5d⁵ 5f 5m³ 5m⁶ 5m⁶ 5m 5.1g³ 5g Oct 21] compact gelding: poor mover: modest sprint handicapper at best nowadays: 17 lb out of handicap and flattered when third of 13 in very strongly-run race at Chester penultimate start: probably acts on any turf going, no form for a long time on fibresand: often visored, has form with blinkers (not tried for long time): tends to hang: none too consistent. *E. J. Alston*

GONE FOR A BURTON (IRE)   6 ch.g. Bustino 136 – Crimbourne 83 (Mum-   88 my's Pet 125) [1995 90: 10.8d* 12g² 10.4m⁵ 10.3d 10d 1996 10m 10.4g 10s² 12s Nov 9] workmanlike, rather sparely-made gelding: fairly useful handicapper: not seen out until September in 1996, best effort when second of 21 at Newbury: effective at 1¼m and 1½m: acts on good to firm ground and soft: blinkered final 4-y-o start. *P. J. Makin*

GONE SAVAGE   8 b.g. Nomination 125 – Trwyn Cilan 89 (Import 127) [1995   79 67: 6m⁶ 6m 6g 6f 6m² 5g⁵ 5g⁵ 6m 5m⁴ 6g 6g 6d⁶ 6f 1996 5g⁵ 6m 5d⁴ 5m³ 6m 5g 5f² 5m⁴ 5g* 5m³ 5g² 5m² 5d² 5g* 5m 5s Nov 8] strong, good-bodied gelding: carries condition: fairly useful sprint handicapper: ran consistently well in 1996, winning at Windsor in August and York (23-runner contest) in October: acts on firm and soft ground and on equitrack: blinkered (below form) twice: sometimes bandaged behind. *W. J. Musson*

GONE TO HEAVEN 4 b.g. Aragon 118 – Divine Fling (Imperial Fling (USA) –
116) [1995 NR 1996 6m 5g 5g May 31] good-quartered gelding: rated 71 at 2 yrs for
M. Channon: well held in claimers and seller (well backed) on return: probably a
sprinter: sold 700 gns Doncaster July Sales: blinkered final start. *T. J. Etherington*

GONZAGA (IRE) 2 gr.c. (Apr 2) Pistolet Bleu (IRE) 133 – Gay Spring (FR) 81 p
(Free Round (USA)) [1996 7g* 8s⁴ Oct 26] leggy, angular colt: closely related to 5.5f
(at 2 yrs in France) to 9f (in USA) winner Gravieres (by Saint Estephe) and
half-brother to several winners in France at up to 9f: dam French 6f (at 2 yrs) and 6.5f
winner: backward and very green, won 11-runner maiden at Salisbury in August by
neck from Another Night: similar form when 9½ lengths fourth of 7 to Tempting
Prospect in minor event at Newbury over 2 months later, off bridle soon after halfway
then keeping on strongly when race was all but over: will be suited by further than
1m: sent to race in France. *J. L. Dunlop*

GOODBYE GATEMEN (IRE) 2 gr.c. (Apr 8) Soviet Lad (USA) 94 – Simple –
Love (Simply Great (FR) 122) [1996 5d Oct 21] IR 4,500F, 3,800Y: third reported
foal: dam unraced: 20/1, soon well behind in median auction maiden at Folkestone.
M. J. Heaton-Ellis

GOODBYE MILLIE 6 b. or br.m. Sayf El Arab (USA) 127 – Leprechaun Lady – §
57 (Royal Blend 117) [1995 50, a–: a12g 12.4g 12d² 12.1m* 14.1f 11.1m* 12m⁵
a11g⁶ 12.1g 11.1g³ 12f² 11f³ 1996 12.1g 12.3g 12g⁴ 12.1g⁴ 12m Jun 5] angular mare:
modest performer in 1995: no worthwhile form in 1996, reluctant to race first 2 starts:
one to treat with caution. *J. L. Eyre*

GOOD DAY 2 gr.c. (Mar 17) Petong 126 – Courtesy Call (Northfields (USA)) 56
[1996 6d 6m a7g⁴ 6d⁶ 8g a7g Nov 29] 16,500Y: good-topped colt: has scope: fluent
mover: half-brother to 3 winners, including 6f winner Courioisie (by Thatching) and
8.9f to 12.3f winner Firefighter (by Sharpo): dam thrice-raced half-sister to smart
1976 2-y-o 5f performer Piney Ridge: modest form: well held in nurseries last 3
outings: probably stays 7f. *C. W. Thornton*

GOOD HAND (USA) 10 ch.g. Northjet 136 – Ribonette (USA) (Ribot 142) 79
[1995 79: 16m 16f² 16.1g* 16m 14.6g² 16f⁴ 14f⁵ 16.1g² 17.5g² 13.9g 14.6m⁴ 16.5m⁵
1996 16m* 16.2f 16.5m 15d⁴ 17.5m* 14.1f* 18g Oct 19] close-coupled, sparsely-
made gelding: fair performer: won claimer at Redcar (claimed out of J. W. Watts's
stable £10,000) in June, and handicaps at Ayr and Redcar in September: dyed-in-the-
wool stayer: acts on firm and soft ground: below form when blinkered and visored
earlier in career: sometimes bandaged: held up: often hangs: winning hurdler.
S. E. Kettlewell

GOOD (IRE) 4 b.g. Persian Heights 129 – Tres Bien (Pitskelly 122) [1995 –: 8m –
10g 14.1g 11.4m 8d 12s 1996 10f Sep 10] angular, workmanlike gelding: poor
maiden handicapper: tailed off only start in 1996: tried visored and blinkered.
D. T. Thom

GOOD JUDGE (IRE) 2 b.c. (May 6) Law Society (USA) 130 – Cuirie (Main 49 +
Reef 126) [1996 7.9g 7.5m⁵ 7.9g Oct 12] IR 4,100Y resold 7,600Y, 11,500 2-y-o:
strong, compact colt: fifth foal: half-brother to Irish 11f winner How's It Goin (by
Kefaah): dam unraced: in need of race, never dangerous or knocked about in maiden
auctions at York and Beverley, but showed little (last of 11 after chasing leaders) in
maiden at York on final start. *M. D. Hammond*

GOOD NEWS (IRE) 2 ch.f. (Mar 19) Ajraas (USA) 88 – Blackeye (Busted 134) 61
[1996 5.3f⁵ 5m⁵ 6m Sep 17] IR 1,000F: quite good-topped filly: half-sister to several
winners, including Irish 13f winner Ferragosto (by Nordance): dam unraced half-
sister to Triple First, dam of Oaks-placed Maysoon and Three Tails: easily best effort
in maidens at Windsor second start: still not fully wound up final one: should be
suited by further than 5f. *M. Madgwick*

GOOD SO FA (IRE) 4 b.g. Taufan (USA) 119 – Future Shock (Full Out (USA)) –
[1995 –, a62d: a8g* a8g³ a8g² a10g a10g⁶ 8m a12g a9.4g a10g⁴ 1996 a10g a12g 7.1g
10m 8m 14.1m 9f Jun 22] rather leggy gelding: modest performer on all-weather
early in 1995: has shown nothing for a long time: retained by trainer 500 gns Ascot
July Sales. *C. N. Allen*

GOOD TO TALK 3 b.g. Weldnaas (USA) 112 – Kimble Blue 56 (Blue Refrain 46
121) [1995 48: 5g 5f 5m⁴ 6m⁶ 7g 7g 6s 1996 6g 5f⁴ 5g² 5f 7g 6f 5m² 5g⁴ 5g 5m 5.1g
Oct 24] well-made gelding: poor maiden: best form at 5f on a sound surface: visored/
blinkered 3 of last 5 starts: has had tongue tied: races prominently. *T. D. Easterby*

GOODWOOD LASS (IRE) 2 b.f. (Feb 4) Alzao (USA) 117 – Cutleaf 81 (Kris 71
135) [1996 6s⁶ 7g* 7.3m 8m Sep 26] 15,000Y: smallish, workmanlike filly: first
foal: dam, 10.6f winner, sister to useful middle-distance winners Knifeboard and
Kenanga: needed run on debut: well backed, won 13-runner maiden at Leicester in
July by 2 lengths, making all and running on strongly, giving flash of tail when hit
with whip: failed to progress in nurseries at Newbury and Goodwood (gave
impression something amiss) subsequently: should stay 1m. *J. L. Dunlop*

GOODWOOD ROCKET 3 ch.c. Midyan (USA) 124 – Feather-In-Her-Cap 66
(Primo Dominie 121) [1995 75: 6m³ 6g⁵ 7m⁶ 6m⁵ 7g³ 8d² 1996 9g 8g⁶ 8g 7g Jun 15]
sturdy, lengthy colt: has a quick action: fair performer: well beaten in 3 of 4 races in
1996, sweating and taking keen hold in blinkers final one: sold 12,000 gns
Newmarket July Sales: should be suited by further than 1m: acts on good to firm and
dead ground. *J. L. Dunlop*

GOOL LEE SHAY (USA) 3 b. or br.c. Explodent (USA) – Titled Miss (USA) 55
(Sir Ivor 135) [1995 NR 1996 12m⁶ 10g 8m 8g 10m 8.2m 7m² 8m⁴ 8.3m⁴ 7.5g⁴ 7g
8m Sep 19] £62,000Y, 28,000 2-y-o: workmanlike colt: first foal: dam never ran:
modest maiden handicapper: stays 7.5f: yet to race on a soft surface: visored (well
beaten) penultimate start. *R. M. Whitaker*

GOOSEBERRY PIE 3 b.f. Green Desert (USA) 127 – Supper Time 71 63
(Shantung 132) [1995 NR 1996 10d 9m 8g 8.2m³ 8m⁴ 7f Sep 3] quite attractive filly:
sister to fairly useful 6f to 1m winner Desert Time and half-sister to several winners,
including smart middle-distance stayer Rakaposhi King (by Bustino): dam lightly-
raced 1½m winner: fair maiden handicapper: stays 1m: acts on good to firm ground.
R. Charlton

GOPI 2 b.f. (Feb 27) Marju (IRE) 127 – Chandni (IRE) (Ahonoora 122) [1996 64
5.7g⁴ 5f² 5.2f⁵ 6g³ 5g⁴ Nov 1] leggy, sparely-made filly: first foal: dam (of no
account) out of sister to Kings Lake: modest form: withdrawn on veterinary advice at
stalls in early-August then off course until November, returning with creditable
fourth in nursery at Newmarket: best form at 5f: has been bandaged near-fore.
R. Hannon

GORDI (USA) 3 ch.c. Theatrical 128 – Royal Alydar (USA) (Alydar (USA)) 109
[1995 NR 1996 10s 10d⁴ 10g* 16.2m* 14.6m 14m⁶ Sep 21] tall colt: has scope: has
a long stride: fifth foal: half-brother to 2 winners in USA, including Crary (by Mt
Livermore), second in Grade 1 1m event at 2 yrs: dam, successful in 2 of her 3 starts
in USA at up to 9f, closely related to very smart 1973 US 2-y-o filly Bundler: won
maiden at Leopardstown in May and Queen's Vase at Royal Ascot (forged ahead
inside last to beat Athenry a length): 7/1, well beaten in the St Leger at Doncaster
(edgy) and Irish St Leger at the Curragh (week later, not discredited though never

Queen's Vase, Royal Ascot—six lengths covers the first seven, with Gordi (noseband) on top

Mr Allen E. Paulson's "Gordi"

competitive behind Oscar Schindler): well suited by test of stamina. *D. K. Weld, Ireland*

GORE HILL 2 b.f. (Mar 25) Be My Chief (USA) 122 – Hollow Heart 89 (Wolver – Hollow 126) [1996 7d 7.1s Oct 22] 8,000Y: half-sister to 3 winners, including useful 7f to 8.5f winner Aradu (by Posse): dam 5f winner at 2 yrs: soundly beaten in maidens at Salisbury and Chepstow. *M. Blanshard*

GORETSKI (IRE) 3 b.c. Polish Patriot (USA) 128 – Celestial Path 101 76 (Godswalk (USA) 130) [1995 55: 5d 5m 6f* 6m⁴ 5m⁵ 5g 5m 1996 6d² 6.1d 5d* 5.1g⁴ 5s² 5g² 5.3f² 5m⁶ 6d 5m 5m 5g 5s Nov 8] tall colt: unimpressive mover: fair handicapper: won at Catterick in April: best efforts when close second at Hamilton and Catterick fifth and sixth starts: well below form afterwards, though shaped encouragingly final start: effective at 5f and 6f: successful on firm ground, best efforts on an easy surface: no improvement in blinkers: often ridden by trainer's wife, hasn't won for her: usually races prominently. *N. Tinkler*

GORMIRE 3 ro.f. Superlative 118 – Lady of The Lodge 60 (Absalom 128) [1995 52 NR 1996 5m² 5m 6s⁴ 5g a6g 6d a6g Oct 5] small filly: second foal: half-sister to 1994 2-y-o 5f winner Lady Governor (by Governor General): dam no form after second over 5f on debut: modest maiden: stiff tasks, well below form after third start: probably a sprinter. *J. Hetherton*

GOTHENBERG (IRE) 3 b.c. Polish Patriot (USA) 128 – Be Discreet (Junius 113 (USA) 124) [1995 96: 5g³ 5g* 5g* 6f* 6m 6m⁴ 6f 1996 8g 7m⁴ 7d* 8g 7g³ 8m* 6m 8d 8g⁶ 8m⁵ 8d² 8m⁵ Nov 10] tall, lengthy colt: powerful mover with long stride: smart performer: won Lexus Tetrarch Stakes at the Curragh in April (by 6 lengths from Rainbow Blues) and Sea World International there in June by length from Timarida: in-and-out form afterwards, creditable second to Mistle Cat in Premio Vittorio di Capua at Milan in October: stays 1m: acts on dead and good to firm

Sea World International Stakes, the Curragh—Gothenberg makes all for his biggest success

ground and appeared to act on firm at 2 yrs: edgy type, who often sweats: often front runner nowadays. *M. Johnston*

GO TOO MOOR (IRE)   3 b.g. Posen (USA) – Gulistan (Sharpen Up 127) [1995   62
–: 7f 1996 a10g² Nov 15] twice-raced gelding: tended to carry head high on debut:
off course over a year, staying-on 6 lengths second of 9 in maiden at Lingfield.
G. C. Bravery

GOVERNANCE (IRE)   3 b.f. Imperial Frontier (USA) 112 – La Padma   –
(Sassafras (FR) 135) [1995 NR 1996 6.9m 7m 10.2f a9.4g Aug 31] eighth live foal:
half-sister to several winners at middle distances and to Irish 2m winner Glen of Ealy
(by Glenstal): dam unraced half-sister to Poule d'Essai des Pouliches winner Ukraine
Girl: no promise in maiden events or handicap: visored final start. *K. McAuliffe*

GOVERNOR'S BID   3 b.g. Governor General 116 – Maiden Bidder 66 (Shack   –
(USA) 118) [1995 NR 1996 6f 6.9m⁶ 6f 6.9g 6m 8f⁶ Aug 6] second foal: dam stayed
7f: well beaten in varied company: tried blinkered. *Mrs L. C. Jewell*

GOVERNORS DREAM   3 b.f. Governor General 116 – Friendly Miss (Be   –
Friendly 130) [1995 –: 5m 6s 5m 5.2f⁵ a5g 1996 a5g⁴ a6g Jan 20] robust filly: poor
sprint maiden. *Mrs N. Macauley*

GO WITH THE WIND   3 b.c. Unfuwain (USA) 131 – Cominna (Dominion   69 §
123) [1995 –p: 8g 8d 1996 a7g⁴ 12d⁴ 12g³ 14.1f² 13.1m 12m² 16.2f² 12m⁶ 16.4m
13.1m⁴ 16m* 16.1m⁴ Oct 2] lengthy colt: unimpressive mover: fair handicapper:
won 6-runner race at Nottingham in September: sold (M. Bell to C. Weedon) 9,500
gns Newmarket Autumn Sales: stays 2m: acts on firm ground, probably on dead:
visored (ran creditably) third 3-y-o start, blinkered (ran poorly) fifth one: flashes tail
under pressure: none too resolute and not one to trust. *M. Bell*

GRACEFUL LADY   6 br.m. Bold Arrangement 127 – Northern Lady 95 (The   –
Brianstan 128) [1995 –: 8m⁴ 8f⁶ 5d 1996 a7g Jan 31] strong, compact mare: no
worthwhile form. *E. J. Alston*

GRACEFUL LASS   2 b.f. (Apr 14) Sadler's Wells (USA) 132 – Hi Lass 106   73 p
(Shirley Heights 130) [1996 8.2g⁵ Oct 9] third foal: half-sister to 11f German Oaks
winner Centaine (by Royal Academy): dam, won 2½m Prix Gladiateur, half-sister to
Bonne Ile and Ile de Nisky: 20/1, around 6 lengths fifth of 13 to Fascinating Rhythm
in steadily-run maiden at Nottingham, held up then running on without threatening:
will improve, particularly granted greater test of stamina. *D. R. Loder*

GRACIOUS GRETCLO 3 gr.f. Common Grounds 118 – Gratclo 65 (Belfort – (FR) 89) [1995 54: 5m³ 5m 5.1h⁵ 5g² a7g⁶ a5g⁴ a6g² a7g a5g⁵ 1996 a6g 6.1m 5m a5g a7g Dec 31] leggy filly: modest maiden at 2 yrs: no worthwhile form in 1996, leaving C. J. Hill after reappearance, R. Baker after third start: stays 6f: acts on equitrack (probably on fibresand) and good to firm ground: takes keen hold. *P. D. Evans*

GRANBY BELL 5 b.g. Ballacashtal (CAN) – Betbellof 65 (Averof 123) [1995 55 55: 11.9m 12g 12.1d² 12m 1996 14.1g⁶ 14m⁵ 16s 13.3s* 16m⁶ 18g 14.1s Oct 31] tall, angular gelding: good walker and mover: modest handicapper: won at Newbury in May, leading 4f out, and easily best effort of season: stays 1¾m well: acts on soft ground: tried blinkered at 2 yrs: has won when sweating: none too consistent. *P. Hayward*

GRAND APPLAUSE (IRE) 6 gr.g. Mazaad 106 – Standing Ovation (Gods- – walk (USA) 130) [1995 51: a12g 10m 16.2g 13.1h⁴ 12d³ 14g 12s⁴ 1996 11.6d Aug 12] leggy, angular gelding: poor mover: modest maiden handicapper at best; never-dangerous seventh of 14 for amateur only outing in 1996: joined M. Salaman: stays 1¾m: acts on fibresand and on hard ground, very best form with some give: tried blinkered: held up. *M. D. I. Usher*

GRAND CHAPEAU (IRE) 4 b.g. Ballad Rock 122 – All Hat (Double Form 63 130) [1995 61: 6m 6g 6m⁴ 5.1m² 5.1f² 5m* 7g 5.1d 5.1m 1996 6d⁶ 6m 7m 6f 6g* 6m 5m 5g 6m Oct 23] good-topped gelding: impresses in appearance: modest handicapper: shaped well several times prior to making all at Pontefract in September: effective at 5f and 6f: acts on firm ground: often a front runner. *D. Nicholls*

GRAND DU LAC (USA) 4 ch.c. Lac Ouimet (USA) – Vast Domain (CAN) 90 (Vice Regent (CAN)) [1995 83p: 8f² 8.1g* 1996 8m⁵ 9s 8.1d May 27] big, well-made colt: fairly useful performer: improved form when fifth of 8 in well-contested minor event at Ascot in May: didn't repeat it on softer going in 2 subsequent outings: should be suited by further than 1m. *D. R. Loder*

GRANDES OREILLES (IRE) 4 b.f. Nordico (USA) – Top Knot (High Top 37 131) [1995 54: 10g 13.1f⁵ 12m a12g⁴ 1996 11.9f² 12m 11.9g 10m 12.1g Aug 26] sturdy filly: modest maiden handicapper: below form in 1996: stays 13f: acts on firm ground, yet to race on a soft surface: tried visored/blinkered, no improvement. *N. J. H. Walker*

GRAND LAD (IRE) 2 ch.c. (Mar 26) Mujtahid (USA) 118 – Supportive (IRE) 104 (Nashamaa 113) [1996 5m³ 5g* 5m⁵ 6m² 5d³ Oct 12] IR 37,000Y: lengthy colt: has a quick action: first foal: dam fairly useful Irish 5f performer: useful sprinter: made virtually all to win maiden at Ripon in May: off course 3 months after third start: ran well both starts on return, particularly when third to Easycall in Cornwallis Stakes at Ascot: speedy, but stays 6f: acts on good to firm and good to soft going. *R. W. Armstrong*

GRAND MUSICA 3 b.g. Puissance 110 – Vera Musica (USA) (Stop The Music 97 (USA)) [1995 NR 1996 8.3m² 8.3d² 7g* 7g² 7.9g⁴ Sep 3] 27,000Y: leggy, un-furnished gelding: fifth foal: half-brother to winners in Sweden and Hungary: dam 7.5f winner in Italy: useful form: 6/5 on, won maiden at Epsom in August, idling: better form when in frame in rated stakes won by Star of Zilzal at Goodwood and Kala Sunrise at York: stays 8.3f: acts on good to firm and dead ground, yet to race on extremes. *I. A. Balding*

William Hill Cup (Handicap), Goodwood—
the grey Silver Groom makes a bold bid to follow up his 1995 win, but cannot hold Grand Selection

GRANDPA LEX (IRE) 2 gr.c. (Apr 7) Kalaglow 132 – Bustling Nelly 94 – (Bustino 136) [1996 8g Sep 14] 50,000Y: tall, lengthy, unfurnished colt: brother to a winner in Germany and half-brother to several winners, including smart 3-y-o Busy Flight (up to 1½m, by Pharly): dam middle-distance winning half-sister to Further Flight: very slowly away and always behind in maiden at Goodwood: dead. *I. A. Balding*

GRAND POPO 3 b.c. Salse (USA) 128 – Rose Cordial (USA) (Blushing Groom – (FR) 131) [1995 NR 1996 8m 10.4g 7g Oct 25] third foal: half-brother to useful Irish 4-y-o 7f (at 2 yrs) and 1m winner Nayil (by Unfuwain): dam unraced: well beaten in maidens and a claimer. *S. E. Kettlewell*

GRAND SELECTION (IRE) 4 b.g. Cricket Ball (USA) 124 – Sine Labe 92 (USA) (Vaguely Noble 140) [1995 84: a8.5g* a8g² a8g* a10g* a8.5g* a9.4g³ 10m* 10g² 10.1m² 10.1m* 12f³ 10m² 12m³ 10.1g 1996 a9.4g⁴ 10.3g⁶ 10m 10m⁶ 10m* 10m* 10.4m⁶ 11.9f Sep 7] useful-looking gelding: has a round action: fairly useful handicapper: won at Kempton and Goodwood (William Hill Cup) in July, finishing strongly: sold 30,000 gns Newmarket Autumn Sales: stays 1½m: acts on all-weather surfaces and on firm ground: genuine: sent to USA. *M. Bell*

GRAND SPLENDOUR 3 b.f. Shirley Heights 130 – Mayaasa (FR) 82 (Green 79 p Desert (USA) 127) [1995 NR 1996 12.1g⁴ 10m⁵ 10.5d² 10.4g² Oct 10] lengthy, quite attractive filly: has a quick action: first foal: dam, 2-y-o 5f winner who stayed 6f, daughter of Fitnah: fair maiden: runner-up to Naazeq at Haydock and Multicoloured at York 13 days later: sold 30,000 gns Newmarket Autumn Sales: will be very well suited by return to 1½m+: taken down last and quietly final 2 starts: may well do better. *Lady Herries*

GRAND TIME 7 ch.g. Clantime 101 – Panay 77 (Arch Sculptor 123) [1995 37, – a–: a5g 5d⁶ 5m² 5.3m⁶ 5.7f⁶ 5g a5g 5m 1996 5.1f Jul 8] neat gelding: carries condition: poor handicapper: well beaten only outing in 1996: stays 6f: acts on the all-weather and any turf going: often wears blinkers/visor, but has run creditably without: often slowly away: has re-joined C. J. Hill. *R. J. Baker*

GRANNY'S PET 2 ch.c. (Feb 9) Selkirk (USA) 129 – Patsy Western 81 (Pre- 99 cocious 126) [1996 5.2d² 5g² 5m* 5m 5m⁴ 7m³ 7d⁴ Oct 12] 46,000Y: angular, close-coupled colt: has a quick action: third foal: half-brother to 4-y-o 1¼m and 1½m winner Western Sal (by Salse) and fairly useful 1m winner Western General (by Cadeaux Genereux): dam, twice-raced 6f winner, is half-sister to Mr Fluorocarbon and Western Jewel: useful form: won £9,200 event at Epsom in June: narrowly-beaten third of 23 to Papua in falsely-run race for valuable sales race at Newmarket on sixth start: probably stays 7f: acts on good to firm and good to soft going: held up. *P. F. I. Cole*

GRAPESHOT (USA) 2 b.c. Hermitage (USA) – Ardy Arnie (USA) (Hold Your 108 p Peace (USA)) [1996 6m³ 6m* 7m² 7m* Oct 4] $13,500F, IR 22,000Y: tall, rangy, rather unfurnished colt: half-brother to several winners in USA, one placed in minor stakes: dam won 4 times at up to 9f in USA: sire (by Storm Bird) unraced close

Somerville Tattersall Stakes, Newmarket—5/4 favourite Grapeshot draws clear

relative of Sadler's Wells: made most when beating Bahamian Bounty in maiden at Newmarket in summer: progressed again when third, promoted, to Putra in Lanson Champagne Stakes at Goodwood then had only to repeat that form when winning 8-runner Somerville Tattersall Stakes at Newmarket (looked extremely well) by 1¾ lengths from Musical Dancer: likely to be suited by 1m+: can improve further. *L. M. Cumani*

GRAPE TREE ROAD 3 b.c. Caerleon (USA) 132 – One Way Street 119 122 (Habitat 134) [1995 6.5g* 7g⁵ 1996 10.5g⁴ 10.5m* 12m 10m* 10.4m⁴ 12m⁴ Sep 15] IR 250,000Y: close-coupled French-trained colt: has a short, unimpressive action: eighth foal: brother to Usk The Way (stayer, rated 72), closely related to Road To The Isle (rated 98 at 2 yrs, shaped like a stayer, by Lomond) and half-brother to several winners, including Red Route (up to 14.8f, rated 117, by Polish Precedent): dam won Princess Royal Stakes: very smart performer: won newcomers event at Deauville at 2 yrs, listed race at Longchamp in April and (after only seventh in Prix du Jockey-Club) Grand Prix de Paris at Longchamp (beat Glory of Dancer a short head) in June: fourth afterwards to Halling in International Stakes at York (beaten 5¼ lengths) and to Helissio in Prix Niel at Longchamp (beaten 3½ lengths): seems to stay 1½m: acts on good to firm ground, yet to race on a soft surface: to join J. Noseda in USA. *A. Fabre, France*

GRAPEVINE (IRE) 2 b.f. (Apr 24) Sadler's Wells (USA) 132 – Gossiping 71 p (USA) (Chati (USA)) [1996 8.2g⁶ Oct 9] sixth reported foal: sister to 3-y-o Wild Rumour, 7f winner at 2 yrs, closely related to useful 1991 2-y-o Musicale (by The Minstrel), who should have been well suited by 1m, and half-sister to 1989 2-y-o 8.2f winner Idle Chat (by Assert): dam, 6f winner in USA, is half-sister to Committed: 6/1 from 3/1, 6 lengths sixth of 13 to Fascinating Rhythm in steadily-run maiden at Nottingham, in need of experience and unable to challenge after starting slowly: sure to improve. *P. W. Chapple-Hyam*

GRASSHOPPER 3 b.g. Petoski 135 – Mistral's Dancer (Shareef Dancer (USA) – 135) [1995 NR 1996 a8g Dec 11] second foal: half-brother to 4-y-o 1¼m to 1½m winner Kristal Breeze (by Risk Me): dam, maiden, best at 7f: blinkered, well beaten in Lingfield claimer. *J. L. Spearing*

GRATE TIMES 2 b.g. (Mar 14) Timeless Times (USA) 99 – Judys Girl (IRE) 75 (Simply Great (FR) 122) [1996 5d⁴ 5g⁵ 5m³ 7m³ 7s* 7.5m² 7g 7m³ 7.5f³ 7d 7.9g⁴ 7g² 7d 7g Oct 19] 7,000Y, 11,000 2-y-o: useful-looking gelding: second foal: dam of little account: fair form: won median auction maiden at Catterick in July: well beaten last 2 starts: stays 1m: acts on any going. *E. Weymes*

GREAT BEAR 4 ch.g. Dominion 123 – Bay Bay 101 (Bay Express 132) [1995 51 d 92d: 6g⁶ 7g⁴ 7f⁵ 8f 6d a5g a6g a6g 1996 a8g⁶ a8g⁶ a8g a8g 7s 10g 8.1g 7m 8f² 8m* 7g⁴ 8m 8.3g 8f 8m 8m a9.4g a10g a10g Dec 31] compact gelding: only modest form at best nowadays, narrow winner of amateurs handicap at Newcastle in July: well

Grand Prix de Paris, Longchamp—
it's on the nod as Grape Tree Road catches Glory of Dancer

beaten last 7 starts: stays 1m: probably acts on any going: no improvement tried in blinkers. *D. W. Chapman*

GREAT CHIEF   3 ch.c. Be My Chief (USA) 122 – Padelia (Thatching 131) [1995   –
NR 1996 8m 8.2m 8m 7g Oct 25] tall, quite attractive colt: fifth known foal: half-brother to useful miler Polar Boy (by Northern Baby) and 1995 3-y-o 2m winner Shining High (by Shirley Heights): dam never ran: no worthwhile form in maidens and a claimer: sold 3,000 gns Newmarket Autumn Sales. *H. R. A. Cecil*

GREAT CHILD   2 b.c. (Mar 16) Danehill (USA) 126 – Charmina (FR) (Nono-   72 +
alco (USA) 131) [1996 7d⁵ 7g⁴ 8.1s³ Nov 7] 25,000Y: strong, deep-girthed colt: half-brother to fairly useful 6f winner Floral Charms (by Shecky Greene) and several winners abroad: dam, French 8.2f winner, from family of Dahlia: shaped well when fifth of 19 in maiden at Salisbury on debut: didn't get best of runs when staying-on fourth in similar event at Doncaster later in October then looked rather one paced in slowly-run event on soft ground at Musselburgh: stays 1m. *M. R. Stoute*

GREAT EASEBY (IRE)   6 ch.g. Caerleon (USA) 132 – Kasala (USA) (Blush-   66
ing Groom (FR) 131) [1995 58: 14d 12.3f³ 14.1f³ 14s 1996 16g² 16g² 16.1g³ 20f 16.1g² 16f² 16.1m 16g* Sep 14] sturdy, good-bodied gelding: fair handicapper: gained deserved first success at Goodwood in September: should be well suited to a thorough test of stamina: acts on firm ground but races mainly on easy surface (acts on heavy) over hurdles. *W. Storey*

GREATEST   5 b.g. Superlative 118 – Pillowing 69 (Good Times (ITY)) [1995 73:   63
a7g⁵ a7g⁶ a7g³ a7g* 6.9d 7m² 8m* 7g² 8f² 10.3d 8.5s 8g 8.2m 1996 8s 8.5m 8m² 8f⁵   a78
8m a8g² a8g⁶ a8g⁶ a7g* a7g Dec 20] leggy gelding: poor mover: fair handicapper: below best on turf in 1996 (trained first 4 starts by R. Akehurst): blinkered first time since 3 yrs, back to best to win at Lingfield in December: stays 1m: acts on all-weather surfaces and firm ground, no form on a soft surface: blinkered twice as 3-y-o and last 2 starts: races prominently. *Miss Gay Kelleway*

Mr M. Tabor's "Grape Tree Road

GREAT HALL 7 gr.g. Hallgate 127 – Lily of France 81 (Monsanto (FR) 121) 50 d
[1995 65: a8g 6.9d⁵ 7s² 6g⁴ 6m 6f⁶ 7f 6m 7g⁶ 7m⁵ 6m⁴ 7m³ 6g* 5g 6.1m 6m 6m* 7f²
6m 7m 7.1d⁶ 6d 6d 7.1d 1996 7s 6m⁶ 6m 7m 6d⁵ 6m 8m a6g a7g 7m⁶ 6m 8f a7g
Sep 7] compact gelding: carries condition: unimpressive mover: poor handicapper
nowadays (trained by J. A. Harris eighth and ninth starts only): effective at 6f and 7f:
acts on firm and soft going and the all-weather: best 6-y-o form in blinkers, visored
once at 2 yrs: often bandaged behind: usually gets behind early on. *P. D. Cundell*

GREAT ORATION (IRE) 7 b. or br.g. Simply Great (FR) 122 – Spun Gold 106 58
(Thatch (USA) 136) [1995 46: 14.1m⁶ 15.8m³ 15.1f² 17.1m* 16m⁴ 15.1s a16g⁶ 1996
16.2m 17.1g⁴ 21.6m³ 16.2g 16.5g³ 18m* 15.8s³ 15.9m* 16.2m⁵ 16.2f³ 17.5m³
17.1m³ Oct 7] rather leggy gelding: has a round action: modest handicapper: won at
Pontefract in June and Chester in July: creditable efforts all subsequent starts: stays
extreme distances: probably acts on any turf going, and on fibresand: effective
visored or not (not tried in 1996): usually held up. *F. Watson*

GREAT OVATION (IRE) 2 b.c. (Feb 15) High Estate 127 – Wild Applause 103
(IRE) 71 (Sadler's Wells (USA) 132) [1996 7g* 7g* 7.1g⁶ 7g* Oct 10] 27,000Y:
quite attractive colt: first foal: dam 12.2f winner, closely related to good miler The
Noble Player: useful form: won maiden at Yarmouth in July (3 ran) and minor events
at Kempton in August and York in October (slowly-run 6-runner contest by 1¼
lengths from Bolero Boy): weak in market, something clearly amiss in Solario Stakes
at Sandown on third outing: will stay 1m. *L. M. Cumani*

GREAT SIMPLICITY 9 ch.g. Simply Great (FR) 122 – Affaire d'Amour –
(Tudor Music 131) [1995 –: 11.5s 1996 12m 17.2d Sep 30] no show for a long time:
blinkered in 1996: has joined Michael Appleby. *R. Curtis*

GREAT TERN 4 b.f. Simply Great (FR) 122 – La Neva (FR) (Arctic Tern (USA) 59 p
126) [1995 –: 8m⁶ 8m⁴ 12f⁶ 1996 a8.5g 11.7g⁶ 10d a14.8g⁴ 14m⁴ 14d* 14.6g* Oct
25] lengthy, workmanlike filly: modest handicapper: ridden by 7-lb claimer when
improved form final 2 starts, leading early in straight to win at Haydock (maiden)
in September and Doncaster (by 4 lengths) following month: effective at 1¾m and
will stay 2m+: possibly best with give in the ground: capable of better still.
N. M. Babbage

GRECIAN GARDEN 5 b.m. Sharrood (USA) 124 – Greek Goddess 82 (Young –
Generation 129) [1995 –: 6m a5g 1996 5.1g Oct 24] small, sparely-made mare: no
worthwhile form since 2 yrs. *Mrs L. Stubbs*

GREEK GOLD (IRE) 7 b.g. Rainbow Quest (USA) 134 – Gay Hellene 111 48 d
(Ela-Mana-Mou 132) [1995 61d: a11g* a11g a11g³ a10g² a10g² a9.4g a12g⁵ a8g
9.9m 8m 8.5m 8m⁴ 10m 10g 12f⁶ 10.3m a11g a8g⁶ a10g 1996 a11g a11g² 11.1g⁵
10m⁵ 11.1f⁵ 10m⁵ 12s 11.1m a9.4g Nov 11] leggy gelding: has quick action: poor
form at best since early at 6 yrs: stays 1½m: acts on firm ground and all-weather
surfaces: visored (out of form) twice as 5-y-o: has had tongue tied down: often a front
runner. *D. W. Barker*

GREEK ICON 3 b.f. Thatching 131 – Rosie Potts 83 (Shareef Dancer (USA) –
135) [1995 87: 5g³ 6m* 6m* 7g⁴ 6m³ 6g⁴ 1996 6g 6d⁵ Jul 5] smallish, well-made
filly: fairly useful performer at 2 yrs for J. Dunlop: behind in listed race at
Baden-Baden and tailed off in minor event at Haydock, only outings in 1996: stays
7f: acts on good to firm ground: sold 17,000 gns Newmarket December Sales.
M. R. Channon

GREEK NIGHT OUT (IRE) 5 b.m. Ela-Mana-Mou 132 – Ce Soir (Northern 48
Baby (CAN) 127) [1995 41: a11g² a11g a10g⁶ 8.2g 8m 12m⁵ a12g 8g 10g⁶ a8.5g a54
a12g³ 15.8g*dis 17.1m³ 18f³ a14g³ a14.8g³ 1996 a12g* a16g² a12g³ a12g⁴ 13.8s⁴
a14g* 17.1g² 14.1m 16.5g* 18m⁵ a16.2g³ a14g a14g⁶ a16g Dec 11] leggy mare:
modest handicapper: won at Southwell in January (amateurs) and April (apprentices)
and Doncaster in June: below form last 3 starts: effective at 1½m, and stays well: acts
on firm and soft ground and on fibresand: often blinkered at 4 yrs, rarely blinkered/
visored since: tends to carry head high. *J. L. Eyre*

GREEN APACHE 4 b.g. Green Desert (USA) 127 – Can Can Girl 69 (Gay –
Fandango 132) [1995 26: 8.3m 5g 6g 7f² 1996 a8g Jan 8] lengthy gelding: bad
maiden: tailed off only start in 1996: worthwhile form only at 7f on firm ground: has
shown signs of temperament. *K. G. Wingrove*

GREEN BARRIES   3 b.c. Green Desert (USA) 127 – Barari (USA) (Blushing   97
Groom (FR) 131) [1995 84: 5d 5f² 6m² 1996 6s* 6g 5d⁵ 6m² 6m⁵ 6f² 7.1m* 7.5m*
7m* 7m 7m⁶ Sep 28] good-topped, close-coupled colt: useful handicapper: won maiden at Doncaster in March and completed summer hat-trick at Sandown, Beverley
and Goodwood (£21,700 contest, raced against favoured far rail): creditable sixth of
26 to Decorated Hero in £50,100 event at Ascot final start: stays 7.5f: acts on firm
and soft ground: usually races keenly: sometimes taken early to post: sent to UAE.
M. Johnston

GREEN BENTLEY (IRE)   3 b.f. Green Desert (USA) 127 – Lady Bentley 109   –
(Bellypha 130) [1995 76+: 5m 6g³ 5.1f⁴ 7m² 7.3m² 6g⁶ 1996 7.1m 8.3m 8.3d
Aug 24] angular filly: fair maiden at 2 yrs: well below form in 1996: sold 3,500 gns
Newmarket Autumn Sales, resold 10,000 Fairyhouse December: will prove best at
7f+: acts on going to firm going. *R. Hannon*

GREEN BOPPER (USA)   3 b.c. Green Dancer (USA) 132 – Wayage (USA) (Mr   81 d
Prospector (USA)) [1995 71p: 7g 1996 8s³ 8g* 8m 7f 8.3d 7m⁴ 7s Oct 24] close-
coupled, well-made colt: fairly useful form when winning maiden at Newcastle
(under 7-lb claimer) in April: disappointing afterwards, and tried in a visor final start:
sold (M. Bell to C. Morlock) 5,600 gns Newmarket Autumn Sales: will be suited by
further than 1m: acts on soft ground. *M. Bell*

GREEN BOULEVARD (USA)   2 ch.f. (Mar 6) Green Forest (USA) 134 –   52 +
Assez Cuite (USA) 114 (Graustark) [1996 5m a6g⁵ a5g³ Dec 31] half-sister to several
winners, including Prix Royal-Oak winner El Cuite (by Vaguely Noble) and dam of
Michelozzo and Micheletti: dam smart French 2-y-o, winner at 6.5f: modest form in
maiden events: sold out of I. Balding's stable 16,500 gns Newmarket Autumn Sales
after debut: should stay beyond 5f: flashed tail early on debut. *J. Berry*

GREEN CARD (USA)   2 b.c. (Mar 30) Green Dancer (USA) 132 – Dunkellin   78 p
(USA) (Irish River (FR)) [1996 7m Oct 3] quite attractive colt: fifth foal: closely
related to a winner in USA by Seattle Dancer and half-brother to a winner in USA by
Herat: dam, winner in USA, half-sister to Criterium des Pouliches winner Oak Hill:
33/1 and green, around 5½ lengths seventh of 16 to Mashhaer in maiden at
Newmarket, fading late on: will improve. *S. P. C. Woods*

GREEN GEM (BEL)   3 b.f. Pharly (FR) 130 – Batalya (BEL) (Boulou) [1995   91
62?: 7f⁶ a6g⁴ a7g⁶ 1996 a8g² a7g³ a8.5g⁴ 6.9s* 7d⁴ 8.3s² 7.3d 8g⁴ 8f 8g² 8d³ 6.5m*
6s 7g 8s 8v Dec 6] smallish, lengthy filly: fair performer here (rated 66), trained
by S. C. Williams until after ninth start: won maiden at Folkestone in March: much
improved in France, winning handicap at Evry in September and far from disgraced
in listed race in Provinces penultimate start: stays 8.3f: acts on good to firm and soft
ground and on the all-weather: none too consistent. *P. H. Demercastel, France*

GREEN GOLIGHTLY (USA)   5 b.g. Green Dancer (USA) 132 – Polly Daniels   –
(USA) 110 (Clever Trick (USA)) [1995 –: 6g 6f 5f⁵ 5m 5g 6m 6m 6m 5m⁵ 6g 7d 6d
8g 7g a10g a10g a8g 1996 6m a6g a6g Dec 3] useful-looking gelding: fair
sprint handicapper in 1994 for M. Jarvis: no form since: tried blinkered, no
improvement. *R. M. Flower*

GREEN GREEN DESERT (FR)   5 b.g. Green Desert (USA) 127 – Green Leaf   107 §
(USA) 97 (Alydar (USA)) [1995 109d: 8.1m⁴ 10g⁴ 10.2m² 8g³ 10m² 11.6m³ 10.1s³
1996 8m³ 7.9m² 8m 8.1g³ 8m² 8m⁴ Aug 1] rangy, attractive gelding: superb mover
with a fluent, light action: useful performer: made frame on 5 of his 6 outings in 1996
(poorly drawn on the other) but again failed to add to sole (2-y-o) success: good
fourth of 18 in Schweppes Golden Mile at Goodwood final start: effective at 1m, and
probably stays 11.6f: acts on firm and soft ground: sometimes wears a net muzzle:
has run well when sweating: held up at 5 yrs: consistent, but irresolute and one to
treat with caution: won first of 2 starts over hurdles for O. Sherwood. *Lady Herries*

GREEN JEWEL   2 gr.f. (Feb 8) Environment Friend 128 – Emeraude 84 (Kris   80
135) [1996 6d³ 6g* 7m⁶ 6g² 7d² Aug 31] 4,000Y: tall, rather leggy filly: fourth foal:
dam 1m winner, half-sister to Irish St Leger winner Opale: won maiden auction at
Salisbury in June: progressive form afterwards, second in nursery at Chester final
start: will stay middle distances. *R. Hannon*

GREEN LAND   4 b.f. Hero's Honor (USA) – Heavy Land (FR) (Reci-   65
tation (USA) 124) [1995 72: 10d 8.3g² 12m* 11.8g* 12d³ 11.4d 13.6f⁴ 14.6m 12.1s³
1996 12m 14g 12.1d 14.1m⁴ 12.1f³ 12f⁵ 12m³ 11.8m 14g⁵ 10.5d 12.5d⁴ 12.5g² 10.5s

Nov 26] close-coupled filly: fair handicapper: trained by S. C. Williams until after eighth start: creditable efforts in 1996 only when placed: should stay beyond 13.6f: acts on firm and soft ground: often bandaged. *P. H. Demercastel, France*

GREEN PERFUME (USA) 4 b.c. Naevus (USA) – Pretty Is (USA) (Doonesbury (USA)) [1995 101§: 8m 7f² 7m⁶ 7.3m⁶ 6g 7g 6d⁴ 1996 7.9m 8g² 7.6f* 6f⁴ 7.9g* 7.3f* 7.3m 6m³ 8m Oct 3] strong, lengthy, good-looking colt: impresses in appearance: disappointing at 3 yrs, smart performer at 4 yrs: successful in the summer in minor event at Lingfield, £9,100 contest at York and minor event at Newbury: ran poorly in net muzzle in listed race at Newmarket final start: effective at 6f to 1m: acts on firm ground: often early/steadily to post: headstrong, and wore dropped noseband (until final start) in 1996: usually races prominently/makes running. *P. F. I. Cole* — 109

GREEN POWER 2 b.c. (Mar 13) Green Desert (USA) 127 – Shaft of Sunlight 58 (Sparkler 130) [1996 6m⁵ 6g³ Aug 14] good-topped colt: has scope: half-brother to winning stayer Winter Lightning (by Dominion) and a middle-distance winner in France by Nishapour: dam, maiden, suited by 1½m: backward and moved poorly to post on debut: well-backed favourite, third of 14 to Mukaddar at Salisbury: sold only 8,500 gns Newmarket Autumn Sales: will be suited by further than 6f. *J. R. Fanshawe* — 78

GREEN'S BID 6 gr.g. Siberian Express (USA) 125 – Arianna Aldini (Habitat 134) [1995 62d: a6g⁶ a6g⁶ a6g a6g a6g³ a8g* a8g⁶ 8m a8g 6m a5g a6g² 6m 7m² 6.9f* 7f a7g a7g a8g 6g⁴ a5g a7g 1996 a5g* a8g a6g⁴ a7g⁴ a7g⁵ a8g a6g Apr 9] lengthy gelding: modest handicapper: broke down at Southwell on final start: effective at 5f to 1m: acted on firm and good to soft ground and the all-weather: tried in blinkers/visor, no improvement: dead. *D. W. Chapman* — 50 d

GREENSPAN (IRE) 4 b.g. Be My Guest (USA) 126 – Prima Ballerina (FR) 81 (Nonoalco (USA) 131) [1995 74: 10.4m⁶ 10g 12g 13.3d 10.5g 10.5s⁵ 1996 a12g* a12g⁴ a12g* 11.9d⁵ a14.8g a11g² a12g* a12g⁴ a9.4g* Dec 28] useful-looking gelding: bad mover: fairly useful performer: won handicap in February and claimer in April, both at Southwell, then seller and claimer at Wolverhampton late on: stays 1½m: acts on soft going and fibresand: blinkered (fell) third 3-y-o start. *W. R. Muir*

GREENSTEAD (USA) 3 b.c. Green Dancer (USA) 132 – Evening Air (USA) 99 + (J O Tobin (USA) 130) [1995 NR 1996 10.3g⁵ 10g* 8m 10m* 11.9f Sep 7] good-bodied, attractive colt: sixth foal: brother to May Hill winner Midnight Air and half-brother to Irish 1¼m winner All At Night (by Al Nasr) and a jumps winner in Italy: dam unraced daughter of half-sister to Belmont Stakes and Kentucky Derby winner Bold Forbes, same family as Dunbeath and Saratoga Six: won maiden at Newmarket in July and handicap at Newbury (by 3½ lengths from Brandon Magic, travelled really strongly and readily asserted) in August: 7/4 favourite, very disappointing in rated stakes at Haydock final start (jockey reported to stewards the colt didn't act on the ground): should stay beyond 1¼m: acts on good to firm ground: has sweated twice, including when successful: stays in training. *J. H. M. Gosden*

GREENWICH AGAIN 4 b.g. Exodal (USA) – What A Challenge 70 (Sallust 65 134) [1995 72d, a75d: a7g³ a8g* 9m 7.6m* 7g⁵ 8m 7.6m³ 8f⁶ 8g a8g a8g⁴ 1996 a10g a10g⁴ a12g* a12g⁴ a10g² 11.8d 12d a12g² 10f⁶ 11.9f* 11.9m⁶ 12m² 14.4g 14m Sep 19] leggy gelding: poor walker: fair performer: won handicap at Southwell in February and minor event at Brighton in July: well beaten last 2 starts: sold 7,000 gns Newmarket Autumn Sales: stays 1½m: acts on firm and soft ground and the all-weather: inconsistent. *T. G. Mills*

GREENWICH FORE 2 b.c. (Mar 24) Formidable (USA) 125 – What A 68 Challenge 70 (Sallust 134) [1996 6m 7.6d⁴ 8g 7.6m 7m⁴ 7.3s a8.5g³ a10g⁴ a8g³ Dec 11] small, compact colt: fourth foal: half-brother to 3 winners, including 4-y-o 7f (at 2 yrs) to 1½m winner Greenwich Again (by Exodal): dam 2-y-o 6f winner: fair form: stays 8.5f: acts on good to firm and dead ground and on fibresand. *T. G. Mills*

GRESATRE 2 gr.c. (Feb 15) Absalom 128 – Mild Deception (IRE) (Glow (USA)) 58 + [1996 5s⁶ 5.1d 5m 6d³ 6m³ a7g⁴ 7.9g⁴ 7.6m⁶ 8m⁶ 8m 7m 8f⁵ Nov 5] 6,200Y: angular, good-bodied colt: first foal: dam (unraced) from the family of Dark Lomond and Gold And Ivory: modest maiden on balance of form: lacks pace, and will stay 1¼m: acts on good to firm and soft going. *C. A. Dwyer*

GRESHAM FLYER 3 b.g. Clantime 101 – Eleanor Cross (Kala Shikari 125) — [1995 –: 5m 6.1m 6m 6.1m a5g 1996 a7g a6g 8.2d⁶ 12m Apr 29] small gelding: no worthwhile form. *B. Richmond*

GRETEL 2 ch.f. (Feb 21) Hansel (USA) – Russian Royal (USA) 108 (Nureyev 100
(USA) 131) [1996 7.1g* 7.1m⁶ 8m³ 8g Sep 29] big, strong, lengthy filly: has plenty
of scope: has a powerful, rounded action: third foal: half-sister to a winner in UAE by
Bering: dam 6f (at 2 yrs) and 7f winner out of Hollywood Oaks winner Princess
Karenda: won maiden at Sandown in July by ¾ length from Medaaly: ran in listed
race and pattern events after, clearly best effort when 2¼ lengths third of 11, running
on well after encountering trouble, to Reams of Verse in May Hill at Doncaster: stays
1m: headstrong, and looks a very difficult ride. *M. R. Stoute*

GRETNA GREEN (USA) 3 b.f. Hansel (USA) – Greenland Park 124 (Red God –
128§) [1995 NR 1996 6m Jun 4] stocky filly: half-sister to good French 9.5f and
1¼m winner Fitnah (by Kris) and a winner by Touching Wood: dam sprinter: 12/1,
burly and green, slowly away and always behind in maiden at Pontefract: sent to
Australia. *Lady Herries*

GREY AGAIN 4 gr.f. Unfuwain (USA) 131 – Grey Goddess 117 (Godswalk –
(USA) 130) [1995 54: a8.5g³ a7g² 8g 7.5m³ 9.9m⁶ a7g⁴ 7g² 7m² 8f⁵ 8m a7g 7m 1996 a62
a7g⁵ a11g* a9.4g⁶ a12g² a8g⁵ a11g 7.5m 9.9m Apr 25] leggy filly: modest handicapper: won at Southwell in January: well below form last 3 starts: stays 1½m: acts
on good to firm ground and fibresand: blinkered: held up. *S. R. Bowring*

GREY CHARMER (IRE) 7 gr.h. Alzao (USA) 117 – Sashi Woo (Rusticaro –
(FR) 124) [1995 57: 5d² 5m⁴ 6m 6g⁶ 6m⁶ 6m a6g⁴ a6g² a7g a6g 1996 a6g a6g a6g
8.3m 8m 6m Aug 22] close-coupled horse: unimpressive mover: modest sprint
handicapper in 1995: trained by C. James until after third start: no worthwhile form
in 1996. *R. H. Buckler*

GREYCOAT BOY 4 gr.g. Pragmatic 115 – Sirdar Girl 69 (Milford 119) [1995 63
74: 10m 10.2m 14.6m⁴ 14.1m² 14.1m 16.2m³ 14.4m³ 15g 17.2m* 16.2s² 16d⁶
1996 16s 16d⁴ 16.5g⁴ 20f Jun 18] tall, angular gelding: fair handicapper: should
stay extreme distances: acts on good to firm and soft ground: normally blinkered.
B. J. Meehan

GREY GALAVA 3 gr.f. Generous (IRE) 139 – Galava (CAN) (Graustark) [1995 62
64: 7g⁴ 7g⁵ 1996 8d a6g² a8g³ 10f³ 12f² 13.8s* Jul 4] small filly: modest performer:
very easy winner of poor rating related maiden at Catterick in July: sold 20,000 gns
Newmarket July Sales: should stay well: acts on firm and soft ground and fibresand:
carried head high third 3-y-o start: front runner last 3 outings. *B. W. Hills*

GREY KINGDOM 5 gr.g. Grey Desire 115 – Miss Realm 86 (Realm 129) [1995 49
–: a7g 7.5g 1996 a11g 8.5m⁶ 10m 9m 7.5m² 7.5f* 8.1f³ 8.1g 7m* 8.3m⁴ 7.5g⁵ 8m⁵
a7g Nov 29] angular, leggy gelding: poor handicapper: won at Beverley (first win) in
June and Doncaster in August: stays 1m: has raced only on a sound surface on turf,
well beaten on fibresand: front runner: game. *M. Brittain*

GREY LEGEND 3 gr.c. Touch of Grey 90 – Northwold Star (USA) 71 –
(Monteverdi 129) [1995 63: 5m⁵ 6f³ 6m³ 5m 6d 1996 6f 7m May 18] compact colt:
modest form at 2 yrs: tailed off in 1996: will probably stay beyond 6f: reportedly
finished lame when blinkered fourth 2-y-o start: often sweating and edgy.
R. M. Flower

GREY RISK (FR) 3 gr.c. Kendor (FR) 122 – Swiss Risk (FR) (Last Tycoon 131) 117
[1995 8g⁵ 6.5s⁴ 7d⁵ 7d⁴ 1996 8s³ 10g⁵ 8g² 8g* 8g* 8m* 8g* 8d⁵ 8m 8v Nov 11]
second foal: brother to useful French 4-y-o 1¼m handicapper Ken Risk: dam
half-sister to Risk Me (stayed 1¼m, rated 127): smart French colt: won handicap at
Longchamp in May, minor event at Evry and listed race at Longchamp in June and
Prix Messidor at Maisons-Laffitte (rec 6 lb more than weight-for-age, beat Nec Plus
Ultra a head) in July: best form when staying-on fifth of 9 to Spinning World in Prix
Jacques Le Marois at Deauville then seventh of 9 to Ashkalani in Prix du Moulin de
Longchamp: should stay beyond 1m: acts on good to firm and dead ground, tailed off
on heavy. *P. H. Demercastel, France*

GREY SHOT 4 gr.g. Sharrood (USA) 124 – Optaria 83 (Song 132) [1995 111: 9d⁴ 115
11g⁶ 12g³ 14g² 14m² 16.2m⁶ 14.8g* 13.9m² 14.6m* 15s* 1996 16.2m² 13.9f⁴ 16g⁵
16f* 15.9m⁴ 16m Nov 5] leggy, unfurnished gelding: fine, easy mover: good walker:
smart stayer: won 7-runner Garrard Goodwood Cup in August by head from Lear
White, battling on splendidly: also ran very well when head second to Double Trigger
in Sagaro Stakes at Ascot on reappearance: seventh behind Saintly in Melbourne Cup
at Flemington on final start: reportedly suffering from back problems when below

Garrard Goodwood Cup—the utmost tenacity is required of Grey Shot (noseband) and Lear White

form second and third outings: will stay beyond 2m: acts on firm and soft ground: front runner: most game and genuine. *I. A. Balding*

GREY SONATA 9 gr.m. Horage 124 – The Grey (GER) (Pentathlon) [1995 NR – 1996 16.2f⁴ 16.2g Aug 24] poor performer nowadays: off course 5 years before reappearance: stays 2m: tried blinkered at 3 yrs. *T. J. Etherington*

GREYSTYLE 6 b.g. Grey Desire 115 – Riverstyle 63 (River Knight (FR) 118) 35 [1995 NR 1996 16.2g 13m² 11.8d⁴ 14.1m 15.8g⁵ 16s Aug 27] tall, plain gelding: poor maiden handicapper: sold 1,800 gns Doncaster October Sales: stays 13f: acts on good to firm ground: normally visored nowadays. *M. Brittain*

Mr J. C. Smith's "Grey Shot"

GREY WAY (USA)   3 gr.f. Cozzene (USA) – Northern Naiad (FR) (Nureyev   105
(USA) 131) [1995 NR 1996 10g* 9m² 10d² 11d⁵ 11g* 10d* 10.5s Nov 2] half-sister
to 5 winners in Italy, including Northern Trojan (7f at 2 yrs to 15f, by Trojan Fen) and
4-y-o Water Elf (1¼m and 11f, by Alleged): dam in frame at up to 1m in France:
useful Italian filly: won maiden at Milan in March by 8½ lengths: ½-length second of
8 to Robereva in listed race then 1¾ lengths fifth of 10 to Germignaga in Oaks
d'Italia, both at Milan in May: won minor event there (by 7 lengths) and Premio
Lydia Tesio at Rome (beat Karpacka 2 lengths), both in September: will stay 1½m:
acts on good to firm and dead ground: stays in training. *G. Botti, Italy*

GRIFFIN'S GIRL   4 ch.f. Bairn (USA) 126 – All That Crack (Stanford 121§)   –
[1995 32: a7g⁶ a6g⁶ 10g⁴ 1996 10m 10.1m Sep 18] lengthy filly: poor maiden: stays
1¼m. *P. Mooney*

GROOMS GOLD (IRE)   4 ch.g. Groom Dancer (USA) 128 – Gortynia (FR)   –
(My Swallow 134) [1995 66: 8d 10g 10f* 12.1m 10m 11.8g 1996 10.3d Mar 21]
lengthy gelding: fair winner as 3-y-o for P. Harris: well beaten on reappearance:
should stay beyond 1¼m: acts on firm ground. *P. J. Hobbs*

GROOM'S GORDON (FR)   2 b.c. (Jan 31) Groom Dancer (USA) 128 – Son-   96
oma (FR) 121 (Habitat) [1996 6d⁴ 6.1m* 7.1g* 8g⁴ 7m Oct 1] 290,000Y: well-made
colt: eighth foal: half-brother to several winners abroad, including smart French 7f
and (at 2 yrs) 1m winner Funambule and useful 1993 French 2-y-o 6f and 7f winner
Sarmaite (both by Lyphard): dam, sister to top-class Sigy, very smart sprinter:
dead-heated for maiden at Nottingham in June then won minor event at Sandown in
July: useful form when 3 lengths fourth of 7 to Equal Rights in Futurity Stakes at the
Curragh, making most: gone in coat, seemingly unbalanced over 1f out then eased
when mid-division in valuable sales race at Newmarket final outing: stays 1m: yet to
race on extremes of going: lazy sort. *J. L. Dunlop*

GROUND GAME   3 b.f. Gildoran 123 – Running Game 81 (Run The Gantlet   95
(USA)) [1995 67p: 7m³ a8g* 1996 10.3m* 10g² 12m³ 10s* 10m⁴ 10s² Oct 19] rangy,
workmanlike filly: has a long, round action: useful performer: won minor event at
Doncaster (easily) in May and handicap at Ripon (made all, found plenty under
pressure despite carrying head rather high) in August: best effort when head second
of 11 to First Smile in listed race at Gelsenkirchen (headed near finish) final start:
effective at 1¼m and bred to stay very well: acts on good to firm and soft ground and
fibresand: makes running/races prominently: has been bandaged behind. *D. R. Loder*

GROVEFAIR DANCER (IRE)   2 ch.f. (Feb 19) Soviet Lad (USA) 94 – Naval   55
Artiste (Captain's Gig (USA)) [1996 6g⁵ 6f² a7g* a7g² 6f a8.5g⁵ a8.5g Nov 2]
3,000Y: half-sister to several winners, including sprinters Naval Fan (by Taufan) and
Karla's Star (by Kampala): dam Irish 2-y-o 5f winner: trained by B. Meehan, won
seller at Wolverhampton in June, making most: stays 7f: acts on firm ground and
fibresand: visored fifth (raced freely, very stiff task) and sixth starts: sold 500 gns
Ascot December Sales. *Miss S. J. Wilton*

GROVEFAIR FLYER (IRE)   2 b.c. (Apr 13) Astronef 116 – Hitness (Hittite   62 d
Glory 125) [1996 5.2d a5g² 5m* 5m³ 6m 7g 7f⁵ 6g⁴ 5.3f⁵ Aug 6] IR 5,000Y: angular,
good-quartered colt: fifth reported foal: dam unraced: modest form: made most to
win seller at Doncaster in May: disappointing last 5 starts: will prove best at up to 6f:
acts on good to firm ground: blinkered last 3 starts: sent to UAE. *B. J. Meehan*

GROVEFAIR LAD (IRE)   2 b.g. (Apr 14) Silver Kite (USA) 111 – Cienaga   49
(Tarboosh (USA)) [1996 5m 6g 7f⁵ 6f³ 7g a7g² 6.9m⁴ 7.1m 10f⁴ 10g Oct 24] 8,000Y:
close-coupled gelding: has quick action: half-brother to several winners, including
8.3f winner Roses Have Thorns (by Ela-Mana-Mou): dam useful Irish middle-
distance filly out of half-sister to smart 1m to 1½m performer Gift Wrapped: modest
plater: sold to join Martyn Wane 3,800 gns Newmarket Autumn Sales: stays 1¼m:
acts on fibresand and firm ground: blinkered (below form) fourth and fifth starts.
B. J. Meehan

GROVEFAIR MAIDEN (IRE)   2 ch.f. (Mar 29) Red Sunset 120 – Coffee Bean   48
(Doulab (USA) 115) [1996 6d 6g² 6m* 7g 7m² Jul 29] IR 5,800Y: lengthy, sparsely-
made filly: third foal: sister to 1m seller winner Java Red and 1995 2-y-o 5.3f
and 6f winner Satellite Star: dam poor Irish maiden: ran in sellers last 4 starts,
winning at Lingfield in July: stays 7f: blinkered except on debut: sent to UAE.
B. J. Meehan

GROVEFAIR VENTURE 2 ch.c. (Apr 26) Presidium 124 – Miramede – (Norwick (USA) 125) [1996 6m 6g 5g 7f Sep 4] smallish, lengthy colt: first reported foal: dam, no worthwhile form, half-sister to one-time useful sprinter Ashtina: behind in median auction maidens and a seller: sold 2,100 gns Doncaster September Sales: tail swisher. *B. J. Meehan*

GRYADA 3 b.f. Shirley Heights 130 – Grimpola (GER) (Windwurf (GER)) [1995 – 93: 6.1m² 6.9g* 7m² 8g⁶ 8.3g* 8d³ 1996 11.4g 10g 10.1m Aug 26] good-topped filly: fairly useful performer at 2 yrs: no form in listed races in 1996: should prove suited by 1½m+: acts on good to firm ground and dead. *W. Jarvis*

GUARDS BRIGADE 5 b.g. Bustino 136 – Light Duty 113 (Queen's Hussar 124) – § [1995 49§: a11g 18g 16.2m⁵ 14m 13g⁶ 13g³ 13g⁶ 10g⁶ 1996 10.9d 13m⁵ May 18] lengthy gelding: poor and none too genuine handicapper: well beaten in 1996 (off course nearly a year before reappearance): sold (J. Hetherton to K. Frost) 900 gns Doncaster September Sales. *J. Hetherton*

GUESSTIMATION (USA) 7 b.g. Known Fact (USA) 135 – Best Guess (USA) 65 (Apalachee (USA) 137) [1995 71, a52: 7.1g³ 8m⁵ 9.7m* 8.3m³ 8f* 8g⁴ a10g⁴ 9m* a– 8.9g³ 7g² 8.5s⁴ 10d* 8.9g⁵ 8m 10f⁴ 10f³ 1996 8g 9.7m 10m⁵ 10m² 9.7m² 10m* 10.1g⁵ 10f⁵ 10.8m* 10g⁴ 10m Sep 18] good-topped gelding: fair performer: won at Sandown (apprentices) in July and Warwick (seller) in August: effective at 7f to 1¼m: acts on firm and soft ground, modest form at best on the all-weather: below form most tries in blinkers: not an easy ride nowadays. *J. Pearce*

GUEST ALLIANCE (IRE) 4 ch.g. Zaffaran (USA) 117 – Alhargah (Be My 47 Guest (USA) 126) [1995 59: 10f⁵ 6.9g a8g⁵ 10f³ 11.9f² 10f 11.9d⁶ 10g³ a12g a16g* a66 a16g 1996 a16g² a16g a12g² 11.9f⁶ 11.9f⁴ 14m a16g* a13g⁶ a16g⁵ a16g² Dec 26] modest handicapper on the all-weather: won at Lingfield in November: better suited by 2m than shorter: probably acts on any going, though goes well on equitrack. *A. Moore*

GULF OF SIAM 3 ch.g. Prince Sabo 123 – Jussoli (Don 128) [1995 62+: 6m⁴ 64 § 6g³ 6m⁵ 1996 8g 8d 11m 9f² 8.5m² 9.2m³ 11.1m³ 8.5m Sep 18] strong, lengthy gelding: modest maiden handicapper: will prove best at up to 9f: acts on firm going: edgy sort: carries head high and has looked less than keen: sold 5,000 gns Doncaster November Sales: not one to trust. *Miss S. E. Hall*

GULF SHAADI 4 b.g. Shaadi (USA) 126 – Ela Meem (USA) (Kris 135) [1995 – 78d, a85d: a7g* a7g* a8g³ a10g³ a8g* a7g* 7m⁶ 8.3m⁶ a8g² a8.5g* 10.1m 8m⁴ a59 a8.5g⁴ 7.1g 7f 8f a8g 1996 a9.4g a8g a7g a8g 8g a9.4g a7s³ a7g⁴ Dec 28] lengthy, attractive gelding: has a quick action: one-time fairly useful performer on the all-weather: only modest form at best in 1996: effective at 7f to 1¼m: acts on all-weather surfaces, and probably any turf ground: often slowly away: visored (out of form) second 4-y-o start. *E. J. Alston*

GULLIVER 3 b.g. Rainbow Quest (USA) 134 – Minskip (USA) 64 (The Minstrel 79 (CAN) 135) [1995 NR 1996 8m 10m 10m³ 10.4g⁴ 13.4g⁶ Sep 25] attractive, good-topped gelding: has a fluent action: first foal: dam, 5f winner, closely related to Ballet de France (the dam of Muhtarram) and St Hilarion: fair maiden: finished very tired when tried over 13.4f final start: sold to join N. Walker 35,000 gns Newmarket Autumn Sales and gelded: takes keen hold, and is unlikely to get much further than 1¼m. *B. W. Hills*

GUMAIR (USA) 3 ch.c. Summer Squall (USA) – Finisterre (AUS) (Biscay 74 (AUS)) [1995 76: 7g 7m⁵ 8m⁵ 8m⁶ 1996 11.4d 12m⁴ 12.1m⁴ 14f⁶ 12m⁶ Sep 24] good-bodied colt: good mover: fair maiden handicapper: tailed off final start: very much an out-and-out stayer: acts on good to firm ground. *R. Hannon*

GUNBOAT DIPLOMACY (FR) 5 b.h. Dominion 123 – Singapore Girl (FR) 120 117 (Lyphard (USA) 132) [1995 120: 10d* 12d 1996 10g* 10f⁶ 9.3s² 10d⁴ Aug 17] medium-sized, rather light-bodied horse: reportedly suffers from arthritic joints: very smart performer: won Prix Exbury at Saint-Cloud in March by 1½ lengths from Red Roses Story: ran well when 1½ lengths second of 4 to Halling in Prix d'Ispahan at Longchamp in May: bit below form when 4 lengths fourth of 10 to Carling in Prix Gontaut-Biron at Deauville 2½ months later: effective at around 1¼m and should stay 1½m: needs give in the ground (finished last on firm second 5-y-o start), and goes well in the mud: held up. *E. Lellouche, France*

GUNMAKER 7 ch.g. Gunner B 126 – Lucky Starkist 57 (Lucky Wednesday 124) 27
[1995 –, a32: a16g a12g a16.2g² a16g⁴ 12.5m a14.8g⁵ 1996 a16g⁶ a16g² 18m³ 18m a45
Jul 6] smallish gelding: poor stayer: tried blinkered, no improvement: inconsistent.
B. J. Llewellyn

GUNNER B SPECIAL 3 ch.g. Gunner B 126 – Sola Mia 78 (Tolomeo 127) 37
[1995 –: 8.1g 8.2d a7g a8g 1996 10d⁵ 14s 17.9g Oct 9] plain, good-topped gelding:
poor performer: stays 1¾m (failed to stay 17.9f): acts on soft going, yet to race on
top-of-the-ground: blinkered as 3-y-o: has been bandaged. *S. R. Bowring*

GUNNERS GLORY 2 b.c. (May 4) Aragon 118 – Massive Powder (Caerleon 69
(USA) 132) [1996 5m* 5f³ 6d² 5.3f Sep 4] fourth foal: half-brother to fairly useful
4-y-o 7f/1m handicapper Zelda Zonk (by Law Society): dam daughter of half-sister
to Alydar's Best: fair form: won median auction maiden at Windsor in July: seems to
find 5f (on firm ground at least) on sharp side. *B. J. Meehan*

GUY'S GAMBLE 3 ch.g. Mazilier (USA) 107 – Deep Blue Sea (Gulf Pearl 117) –
[1995 –: a6g 1996 a7g* a8g³ a11g⁴ 8m 8.2s a7g Nov 22] lengthy, workmanlike a56
gelding: modest performer: 33/1, won seller at Southwell in January: off course 5½
months, behind last 2 starts: stays 11f: acts on fibresand. *J. Wharton*

GWESPYR 3 ch.g. Sharpo 132 – Boozy 111 (Absalom 128) [1995 72: 5g⁵ 5m* 69
5m⁴ 5f⁵ 5g³ 1996 6.1d⁶ 6.1d 5s⁵ 5g 5g⁴ 5f³ 5m 5d* 5.1m³ 5.1m⁴ 5.1m* 5m⁶ 5g Oct
9] leggy, close-coupled gelding: fair handicapper: won at Haydock and Nottingham
(minor event) in July: lost chance with slow start final outing: sold (Jack Berry to
K. Ottesen) 8,500 gns Newmarket Autumn Sales: speedy, and may prove ideally
suited by 5f: acts on good to firm and dead ground: no improvement in visor. *J. Berry*

GYMCRAK FLYER 5 b.m. Aragon 118 – Intellect (Frimley Park 109) [1995 71
65: 8m 8g 8f 7f⁵ 7h* 7m² 8m⁴ 8.1d* 7.1d² 8d 1996 8m³ 8.5g⁴ 7g 6.9g 8f* 7m* 7f*
7m 7.1s 8f 7m Oct 29] small mare: fair handicapper: in fine form in summer, winning
at Carlisle (minor event), Redcar and Yarmouth: below form last 4 starts: stays 1m:
acts on hard ground and dead, below form only run on fibresand: usually bandaged
behind. *G. Holmes*

GYMCRAK GEM (IRE) 3 b.f. Don't Forget Me 127 – Santa Patricia (IRE) 62
(Taufan (USA) 119) [1995 57p: 6m 5d² 1996 5g⁶ 5m³ 5g⁴ 6.1m Sep 24] quite
attractive filly: modest sprint maiden: seems suited by 5f: acts on good to firm and
dead ground: blinkered last 3 starts. *G. Holmes*

GYMCRAK GORJOS 2 b. or br.f. (Apr 1) Rock Hopper 124 – Bit O' May 71 –
(Mummy's Pet 125) [1996 7.9g Sep 4] 7,400Y: close-coupled, quite good-topped
filly: half-sister to 1992 2-y-o 6f winner Summer Express (by Bay Express) and a
winner in Germany by Petong: dam poor daughter of half-sister to Oaks runner-up
Mabel: 25/1 and backward, slowly away from wide draw and never a factor in
23-runner maiden auction at York. *G. Holmes*

GYMCRAK HERO (IRE) 4 b.g. Taufan (USA) 119 – Jamie's Girl (Captain –
James 123) [1995 –: 10m 8.2d⁵ 9f a8g 1996 12.3g 8m 15.8g Jun 1] workmanlike,
close-coupled gelding: has won tubed: has failed to beat a horse in last 5 races:
blinkered/visored first 2 starts in 1996. *G. Holmes*

GYMCRAK JAREER (IRE) 4 b.g. Jareer (USA) 115 – Katzarah (IRE) –
(Pharly (FR) 130) [1995 –: 7.5m³ 8.5m⁴ 7f⁴ 8g 1996 6m Aug 14] no worthwhile
form. *D. A. Nolan*

GYMCRAK JESTER 2 b.g. (Mar 18) Derrylin 115 – Emerin 85 (King Emperor –
(USA)) [1996 6g a8g Nov 29] 2,600Y: workmanlike gelding: brother to 2 poor
maidens and half-brother to several winners on flat and over hurdles: dam 6f winner:
soundly beaten: bandaged behind and wore near-side pricker. *G. Holmes*

GYMCRAK PREMIERE 8 ch.g. Primo Dominie 121 – Oraston 115 (Morston 93 d
(FR) 125) [1995 95: 7m⁵ 7m 8.1g⁶ 8m 7.1m⁴ 7m³ 7m⁶ 7.3m* 7g 7d⁵ 7g³ 1996 7m
8.5m³ 8m 7.9m 7.6d 8m 7.9g⁵ 7g 10.5g⁶ Oct 26] lengthy, workmanlike gelding:
fairly useful handicapper at best: disappointing in 1996, easily best effort on second
start: effective at 7f to 9f: probably acts on any going: tried blinkered/visored: sometimes swerves markedly: usually bandaged behind: normally held up. *G. Holmes*

GYMCRAK WATERMILL (IRE) 2 b. or br.f. (Mar 31) River Falls 113 – –
Victorian Pageant 95 (Welsh Pageant 132) [1996 5f⁶ a5g Nov 29] IR 5,000F, 1,400Y:

good-topped filly: has scope: half-sister to several winners, including Merchant's Dream (1¾m, by Hard Fought): dam lightly-raced 1¼m winner: behind in maidens. *G. Holmes*

H

HABETA (USA)   10 ch.h. Habitat 134 – Prise (Busted 134) [1995 45§: 8m 9.2g⁴   53 d
11.1g⁵ 8.3f* 8.1m 9f² 8.3f² 1996 8g 8.5m⁵ 9m³ 8m* 8f* 8m⁴ 8.3m⁵ 8.2d 8.3g 8f
8.9g 10.1m Oct 23] quite good-topped horse: carries plenty of condition: modest
handicapper: best efforts for some time when narrow winner at Pontefract and
Carlisle in June: effective at 1m to 1¼m: acts on any going: effective blinkered or
not: held up and suited by strongly-run race: has looked temperamental in the past.
J. W. Watts

HACHIYAH (IRE)   2 b. or br.f. (Feb 24) Generous (IRE) 139 – Himmah (USA)   69 p
85 (Habitat 134) [1996 7m Aug 26] rather leggy, lengthy filly: third foal: half-sister
to useful 6f to 1m winner Hiwaya (by Doyoun): dam 6f and 7f winner from good
family: 7/1, prominent 5f when around 9 lengths seventh of 13 to Redwing in maiden
at Newcastle: joined D. Morley: will probably do better. *H. Thomson Jones*

HADADABBLE   3 ch.f. Hadeer 118 – Magnifica (Sandy Creek 123) [1995 –: 6m   43
6f 6m a7g 1996 12s 8m a8g² 8.2m a8g⁴ a8g⁵ a8g⁵ 7.6m⁶ a7g⁶ 7.6m 9.7m⁵ 8m⁵ 9g⁵
7.1m 9.7g⁶ 8f 9g a8g Nov 18] angular filly: good mover: poor maiden: probably
needs at least 1m: acts on fibresand and firm ground. *Pat Mitchell*

HADAWAH (USA)   2 ch.f. (Feb 10) Riverman (USA) 131 – Sajjaya (USA) 97   68
(Blushing Groom (FR) 131) [1996 6f 6g⁶ 6.9m⁵ 7f Sep 3] small filly: second
live foal: half-sister to 1¼m winner Raased (by Unfuwain): dam, 7f and 1m winner,
half-sister to Lahib (by Riverman): modest form: looked ill at ease on track at
Brighton final start: should have been suited by 1m+: fractious stalls second outing:
stud. *J. L. Dunlop*

HADDIT   3 b.g. Thowra (FR) – Ocean Hound 53 (Main Reef 126) [1995 NR 1996   –
11.7m 10.2d 11.8f a16g Nov 12] second foal: dam stayed 1¾m: seems of no account.
A. G. Newcombe

HADIDI   2 b.c. (Apr 25) Alzao (USA) 117 – Sesame 117 (Derrylin 115) [1996 7m   – p
7.9g⁶ 8g Oct 30] 62,000Y: good-topped colt with scope: second foal: half-brother to
3-y-o Calendula (by Be My Guest): dam, middle-distance stayer, half-sister to stayer
Celeric: has shown signs of ability without threatening in maidens: will stay well:
type to do better in time. *D. Morley*

HAGWAH (USA)   4 b.f. Dancing Brave (USA) 140 – Saraa Ree (USA) (Caro   109
133) [1995 104: 10m² 7.3g² 9g² 12f* 12m* 12d⁶ 12d 1996 12d 12m⁶ᵈⁱˢ 10m 8.5m²
10m⁵ 8g* 10.1m* 8g² 10m* 9.3d⁶ 9g⁶ Oct 18] strong, lengthy filly: unimpressive
walker: useful performer: won listed events at Leopardstown and Newcastle (held
Flame Valley a short head) in August and at Goodwood (beat Overbury 2½ lengths)
in September: gained 1½m wins setting pace in falsely-run races, and better form at
1m to 1¼m: acts on firm ground, possibly not at best on a soft surface: usually front-
runner: game and consistent. *B. Hanbury*

HAIDO'HART   4 b.g. Pharly (FR) 130 – Try Vickers (USA) 72 (Fuzzbuster   49 d
(USA) [1995 70: 7s 5g⁵ 7.8f³ 8.5g⁴ 7m 11d 1996 12m 10g 7.5m 8f⁴ 8.1f⁴ 10m 8m
10.3g Oct 26] leggy gelding: generally poor form in Britain: sold 500 gns Doncaster
November Sales: stays 8.5f: acts on firm and soft ground. *B. S. Rothwell*

HAJAT   2 ch.f. (Jan 31) Mujtahid (USA) 118 – Nur (USA) 74 (Diesis 133) [1996   64
5m⁴ 5g³ Oct 19] first foal: dam 5f and 6f winner at 2 yrs, sister to useful sprinter Ra'a:
modest form when in frame in maidens won by Heart Throb at Lingfield and La
Dolce Vita at Catterick: will stay 6f: joined N. Graham. *H. Thomson Jones*

HAKKANIYAH   2 b.f. (Mar 9) Machiavellian (USA) 123 – Mousaiha (USA)   84 +
(Shadeed (USA) 135) [1996 6.1m² 6m* 6f⁴ Jul 20] tall filly: excellent walker: has a
quick action: first live foal: dam (unraced) from the family of Forty Niner and Swale:
progressive form: won maiden at Newmarket in June: good fifth of 6 to Crystal

Crossing in listed race at Newbury following month: raced only at 6f on top-of-the-ground. *D. Morley*

HALBERT 7 b.g. Song 132 – Stoneydale 83 (Tickled Pink 114) [1995 70, a43: a7g⁶ a8g a6g 5.3m 6m 6f 5g⁵ 5m⁵ 5d³ 5f* 5f² 5f³ 5m* 5m³ 5m⁵ 5g 5.3f* 5m⁵ 5g² 5d 5g² 5g 5.3g a6g⁶ a5g⁵ 1996 a6g² a6g⁴ a6g⁴ a5g³ 5s 6f 5g 5m⁶ 5d a5g⁵ 5m 5.2m 5.1f 5f a7g⁵ 6m a6g a6g* Dec 5] sturdy, lengthy gelding: well below form on turf in 1996: more consistent on all-weather (though not so good) and won poor handicap at Lingfield in December: best form at up to 6f: acts on firm and dead going, and the all-weather: blinkered (ran creditably) in 1993, usually visored nowadays: often claimer ridden. *P. Burgoyne*   59 d a48

HALEAKALA (IRE) 3 ch.f. Kris 135 – Haiati (USA) 113 (Alydar (USA)) [1995 NR 1996 13.4m* 14f² 12f 16m³ Sep 26] leggy filly: third foal: dam won at 6f (at 2 yrs) and 7f, including in USA, and probably stayed 1¼m: useful form: won maiden at Chester in June by 6 lengths, soon off bit and running in snatches: still looked particularly green when ½-length second of 4 to Samraan in minor event at Salisbury in September, best effort: sold 60,000 gns Newmarket December Sales: should stay 2m: has raced only on top-of-the-ground. *M. Johnston*   99

HALEBID 3 b.c. Dowsing (USA) 124 – Pink Robber (USA) 85 (No Robbery) [1995 69p: 8g⁶ 8f⁶ 1996 8g⁵ a9.4g* a9.4g* a9.4g² 9m³ 10g* Aug 21] big, angular colt: fair handicapper: successful at Wolverhampton (maiden event) in June and July and at Kempton (apprentices) in August: will stay 1½m: acts on fibresand, has raced only on a sound surface on turf: sent to Hong Kong. *S. P. C. Woods*   80

HALFABOB (IRE) 4 ch.g. Broken Hearted 124 – Hasten (Northfields (USA)) [1995 –: a8g⁵ a8g⁶ 7f³ a8.5g a8.5g a10g⁶ 1996 a8g⁵ 11.8g² 9.5g⁶ 11.5g May 18] no form here, trained by D. H. Jones: second in amateur riders race on first of 3 races in French Provinces: stays 11.8f. *S. Wattel, France*   49

HALF AN INCH (IRE) 3 gr.g. Petoski 135 – Inch (English Prince 129) [1995 71: 6m 6f⁴ 7f² 7f³ 6d⁵ 7d² 7s 1996 8.1g 7f 10m⁴ 11.6m⁶ 10s⁶ 8g³ 8.5g* a10g 8f⁵ 10g 8f a12g⁶ Dec 30] sturdy gelding: modest form at best in second half of 1996: made all in claimer at Epsom in July: trained by B. Meehan until after ninth start: probably better at 1¼m than shorter: acts on firm ground, best form on dead: tried blinkered/visored: no improvement. *T. M. Jones*   69 d

HALF TONE 4 gr.c. Touch of Grey 90 – Demilinga (Nishapour (FR) 125) [1995 46, a69: a5g* 6m⁴ a5g² 6m³ 5m⁵ 5.7f² 5m³ 6g³ 6m⁵ 6f 6f⁵ 6f⁵ 5m 5g³ a5g* a5g* a6g⁶ 1996 a5g³ a5g⁴ a5g* 5m 5m³ 5m⁴ 6m 6m³ 5f³ 5g⁴ 5m² 5m² 5m* Aug 14] leggy colt: fair handicapper on the all-weather: won at Lingfield in February: not quite so good on turf, but gained a deserved success at Sandown in August: effective at 5f and 6f: acts on firm ground and the all-weather: blinkered: consistent. *R. M. Flower*   64 a74

HAL HOO YAROOM 3 b.c. Belmez (USA) 131 – Princess Nawaal (USA) 86 (Seattle Slew (USA)) [1995 71: 7m 7g 8f 1996 12.3m 14.1f* 15.4g² 15.9m 16.1m³ Aug 9] angular colt: good mover: fairly useful performer: won 4-runner maiden at Yarmouth in June and handicap at Folkestone in July: good third to Canon Can at Newmarket final start: sold 14,000 gns Newmarket Autumn Sales: stays 2m: acts on firm ground: front runner. *Major W. R. Hern*   84

HALLELUJA TIME 4 b.g. Risk Me (FR) 127 – Warm Wind 84 (Tumble Wind (USA)) [1995 –: 6m 5g 1996 a7g Jan 23] strong gelding: no worthwhile form, including in sellers. *P. C. Ritchens*   –

HALLIARD 5 b.g. Hallgate 127 – Princess Blanco 81 (Prince Regent (FR) 129) [1995 65d: a5g a5g* 5d 5m⁵ 5m* 5.3m³ 5g⁵ 5g 6m 5m⁴ 5m⁵ 5.1d⁵ a5g a5g⁴ a5g 1996 a8g⁶ 6.9s⁵ 8f 8m 6f⁵ 5m* 5g* a5g 5f 5f⁶ 6m Aug 3] tall, workmanlike gelding: modest handicapper: won twice at Lingfield in May, first in a seller: sold out of T. M. Jones's stable 6,800 gns Newmarket July Sales after penultimate start: best form at 5f: acted on equitrack and on good to firm and heavy ground, well beaten only try on fibresand: well beaten in blinkers/visor: often raced prominently: dead. *R. M. McKellar*   65

HALLIKELD 3 ch.f. Bustino 136 – Spring Sparkle 95 (Lord Gayle (USA) 124) [1995 –: 9g 7m 1996 10g 16m⁶ 16g 11.1g⁵ 15.1m 16.1m a13g Oct 28] leggy filly: poor form: blinkered final start. *T. J. Etherington*   36

HALLING (USA)   5 ch.h. Diesis 133 – Dance Machine 111 (Green Dancer   133
(USA) 132) [1995 131: a8g* a10g* 10m* 10.4m* a10s 1996 a10g* a10g 9.3s*
10g* 10.4m* 10g² Oct 19]

For a few days in November, it seemed a possibility that Halling
might remain in training. The prospect of another season from this top-notch
racehorse was something to cheer every member of the racing public, but he
didn't have much left to prove, now, did he? Twelve wins from eighteen starts,
eight of those wins on the trot and another eight in a row on turf, a surface on
which he was unbeaten for over two years; five Group 1 wins and improvement
in each of his three seasons; the top older horse over middle distances trained in
Britain in each of the last two—it is a fine record that Halling takes to Dalham
Hall, where he will be standing at a fee of £12,000, October 1st.

If he had gone back into training, some big-race records would have
been under serious threat. No horse has won the Eclipse Stakes three times, and
no six-year-old has won it since Bendigo took the inaugural running in 1886.
Both of those statistics owe a great deal to the fact that for much of its history
the Eclipse was confined to three- and four-year-olds, but Halling would not
have been unworthy. He is the best horse to have won it in the 'nineties, and to
join Orme (1892 and 1893), Buchan (1919 and 1920), Polyphontes (1924 and
1925) and Mtoto (1987 and 1988) as dual winners of the race demanded a
performance that was far superior to any other seen in winning the Eclipse this
decade. Halling started second favourite, having demonstrated his well-being
just over five weeks earlier with a clear-cut dismissal of Gunboat Diplomacy
and two others in the Prix d'Ispahan at Longchamp. Eclipse favourite Pentire
had not had a race since the Dubai World Cup but had a slight edge on 1995
form, French challenger Valanour was bidding for a 1996 hat-trick and,
although Derby winner Shaamit was withdrawn earlier in the week, the three-
year-olds still had a bang-in-form representative in Bijou d'Inde. It was the
close attentions of Bijou d'Inde and Pentire that brought out further improvement from Halling. As in 1995, he made all and got home by a neck. They did
not allow him so much rope this time, but Halling's gameness was enough in a
three-cornered battle over the last two furlongs.

The Juddmonte International at York in August has an eighty-six-year
shorter history than the Eclipse and, not surprisingly, no horse has won it three
times. It had had two dual winners—Dahlia in 1974 and 1975, and Ezzoud in
1993 and 1994—before Halling took his second bow. As in 1995, this was such
a one-horse show it could have been a lap of honour. When Dettori asked him
to quicken just after the three-furlong pole, Halling immediately changed his
legs and quite visibly lengthened his stride. None of his five rivals could live
with him for long and Halling was out on his own over the last furlong, passing
the post three lengths clear of the Sussex Stakes winner First Island without

Prix d'Ispahan, Longchamp—
Halling, Gunboat Diplomacy, Vetheuil and Montjoy in a four-runner race

Coral-Eclipse Stakes, Sandown—Bijou d'Inde and Halling (right) match strides in front of Pentire

feeling the whip; Bijou d'Inde was another length and a half back in third. Twelve months previously, held up instead of making all, Halling had beaten Bahri three and a half lengths with another length and three quarters to Annus Mirabilis. They were two breathtaking displays, the 1996 version marginally the best of Halling's career. His winning run on turf now extended to eight races, the first of those wins (off a BHB mark of 75 in a handicap at Ripon) having come two years earlier to the day. Halling's last defeat on turf had come at the hands of Grecian Slipper and four others in a maiden race at Windsor. He was to have just the one more race before retirement—without the distraction this time around of a major target on the other side of the Atlantic, Halling could line up in the Champion Stakes. An even-money favourite against four other Group 1 winners and another who had been short-headed in a Group 1, this would have been a glorious swansong, but Bosra Sham outpaced him after he'd quickened to lead briefly three furlongs out. Our interpretation of the form is that Halling was a little below his best, but in the context of his three years on the track it really does not matter—Halling's was a career to savour.

We have sung Halling's praises loudly here, but there was a down side. Although he won four times on the sand in Dubai, the only two top races that he contested that were not on turf—the Breeders' Cup Classic and Dubai World Cup—both saw Halling perform lamentably. His reputation in Dubai rests on an eight-length win over Torrential in a five-runner race at Nad Al Sheba in March. Off the sand and dirt, he could hardly have been more consistent,

Juddmonte International Stakes, York—Halling at his imperious best

Godolphin's "Halling"

Halling (USA) (ch.h. 1991)	Diesis (ch 1980)	Sharpen Up (ch 1969)	Atan
			Rocchetta
		Doubly Sure (b 1971)	Reliance II
			Soft Angels
	Dance Machine (b 1982)	Green Dancer (b 1972)	Nijinsky
			Green Valley
		Never A Lady (ch 1974)	Pontifex
			Camogie

winning on soft ground in the Prix d'Ispahan though his best efforts were on a sound surface. A preference for turf would not be a great surprise seeing as sire Diesis has had only one graded winner on dirt, the Demoiselle Stakes winner Rootentootenwooten, despite being based in Kentucky. As illustrated in the *Timeform Statistical Review*, Diesis is not far off the leading stallions today when it comes to his performers on turf. Halling is now the best of Diesis' progeny. Less remarkably, he is also the best out of his dam Dance Machine although all of her previous three foals won races, the Bering fillies Brise de Mer and Bal de Mer both over a mile in France and Allez Wijins (by Alleged) over hurdles in France (where he showed useful form) and Britain. Halling's close relation Torreglia (by Elmaamul) was a fair staying maiden in 1995. Dance Machine and her dam Never A Lady were both smart fillies. Their achievements and those of the family (Halling's fourth dam is the celebrated Mesopotamia) were detailed in *Racehorses of 1995*, so for now, to rub it in for those who missed the opportunity, we'll just repeat that Dance Machine was bought back for as little as 15,000 guineas when sent to Tattersalls in December

1993 in foal to Kris, and add that Never A Lady was purchased for 560 guineas as a yearling. The leggy, attractive Halling was a most exciting racehorse who would sometimes edge to his right in the closing stages but was otherwise an excellent ride in his races on turf, effective setting the pace or held up and always going with plenty of zest. On form, he put up the best performances seen on a British racecourse over a mile and a quarter in both 1995 and 1996. *Saeed bin Suroor*

HALLMARK (IRE)   2 b.c. (May 10) Shalford (IRE) 124§ – Cryptic Gold (Glint   65
of Gold 128) [1996 6m⁶ 6m⁶ 6.1d³ 6m³ 8g 8g² a10g⁶ a7g a7g³ Dec 13] IR 8,000Y: a55
close-coupled colt: third foal: half-brother to 3-y-o Parrot's Hill (by Nashamaa): dam
Irish middle-distance maiden: modest maiden: stays 1m well: acts on equitrack: best
form with give in the ground: blinkered (too keen) fifth start. *R. Hannon*

HALLSTAR   4 b.f. Hallgate 127 – Star Route 57 (Owen Dudley 121) [1995 NR   –
1996 a7g a12g Feb 9] close-coupled filly: no sign of ability: has joined J. C. Poulton.
K. A. Morgan

HALMANERROR   6 gr.g. Lochnager 132 – Counter Coup (Busted 134) [1995   71
74: 7s 8m 8g 6m² 6m 6m* 7m⁵ 6m* 7g³ 7g 7g 7m 1996 7g⁶ 6m 7g⁶ 6m 6m² 6.9f³ 6g⁴
6g⁵ 6m* 6m⁵ 7m⁵ 6f 6f 7g 6m 6f Nov 5] leggy, lengthy gelding: fair handicapper:
won minor event at Doncaster in August: never a threat in big fields last 5 starts:
effective at 6f to 1m: acts on firm and soft ground: sometimes gives trouble at stalls:
well suited by being held up in truly-run race. *Mrs J. R. Ramsden*

HALOWING (USA)   2 b.f. (Feb 19) Danzatore (CAN) 120 – Halo Ho (USA)   86
(Halo (USA)) [1996 5g⁵ 6f² 6g⁵ 6f* 6m 6.5m⁴ 7m² 7m⁶ Oct 5] $28,000Y: good-
topped filly: has scope: seventh foal: half-sister to winners in USA by Blade
(including minor stakes) and Premiership: dam winner at up to 9f in USA: fairly
useful performer: won nursery at Lingfield in July: very good staying-on fourth in
nursery at Doncaster on sixth start: should be suited by further than 6f: had blanket
for stalls entry on debut. *P. A. Kelleway*

HAL'S PAL   3 br.g. Caerleon (USA) 132 – Refinancing (USA) (Forli (ARG))   101
[1995 89p: 7m⁴ 7g² 1996 8.2s² 8m a9.4g* a9.4g* 8m⁶ 8g² 7.9g² 8d Oct 31] rangy
gelding: useful form: won maiden and handicap at Wolverhampton in August: good
efforts on form when runner-up in handicap at Ascot and rated stakes at York on sixth
and seventh starts, but on neither occasion seemed to go through with his effort fully:
effective at 1m and stays 9.4f: acts on fibresand and probably any turf going (yet to
race on firm): blinkered since fourth 3-y-o start, except when below form final
outing: a hard ride, well suited by waiting tactics: gelded. *D. R. Loder*

HALTARRA (USA)   2 ch.c. (Feb 5) Zilzal (USA) 137 – Snow Bride (USA) 121   92 +
(Blushing Groom (FR) 131) [1996 7g² 8m³ Sep 20] smallish, rather leggy colt: fourth
foal: brother to useful 3-y-o 1m winner Kammtarra and half-brother to Derby, King
George and Arc winner Lammtarra (by Nijinsky), also 7f winner at 2 yrs: dam,
awarded Oaks, and Yorkshire Oaks winner and Arc third Awaasif: similar form
placed in maiden at York and minor event (behind King Sound) at Newbury: seems
likely to stay well: sure to win a race. *Saeed bin Suroor*

HAMILTON GOLD   3 ch.f. Safawan 118 – Golden Della (Glint of Gold 128)   49
[1995 –: 5f⁵ 1996 6m a8g 5m 5m³ 5.1m 6d Sep 30] shallow-girthed filly: only
worthwhile form when third in handicap at Catterick in August. *M. G. Meagher*

HAMILTON SILK   4 b.g. K-Battery 108 – Silver's Girl 58 (Sweet Monday 122)   45
[1995 52: 8.3v⁴ 8.3s* 9.9m 9.2g 12.1g⁴ 10.5s 1996 11.6m⁵ 11.5f⁴ Jun 22] close-
coupled, angular gelding: modest handicapper: probably stays 12.1f: acts on soft
ground and good to firm: races prominently: fairly useful hurdler. *M. C. Pipe*

HAMLET (IRE)   3 b.c. Danehill (USA) 126 – Blasted Heath 105 (Thatching 131)   83
[1995 78p: 7m 7g 7d 1996 a8g² 10m 11m* 12m⁴ 10.1m* 10g Jul 10] big, angular
colt: has plenty of scope: unimpressive mover: fairly useful handicapper: won
steadily-run races at Redcar in May and Newcastle in June, on each occasion having
had plenty to do: reportedly bled from nose second 3-y-o start: stays 11f: acts on good
to firm ground. *M. Bell*

HAMMERSTEIN   3 b.c. Kris 135 – Musical Bliss (USA) 117 (The Minstrel   110
(CAN) 135) [1995 95: 7g⁴ 7m² 8d⁴ 1996 7g* 8m² 8.1d 8m* 8m* 7.3m⁵ 8g⁴ 8m⁵ Oct

3] sturdy, good-topped, attractive colt: smart performer: won maiden at Thirsk in May, £7,400 ladies race at Ascot in July and £14,000 event at Goodwood (beat Russian Music 1½ lengths) in August: respectable efforts in listed races last 2 starts: stays 1m well: acts on good to firm and dead going: edgy sort: joined Godolphin. *M. R. Stoute*

HAM N'EGGS 5 b.g. Robellino (USA) 127 – Rose And The Ring (Welsh 72 Pageant 132) [1995 90: 9m² 8m 8g⁶ 7.3m 8.1m⁶ 1996 8s 12.4m³ 12f⁵ Aug 3] good-topped, attractive gelding: impresses in appearance: has a quick action: fairly useful handicapper on his day at 4 yrs for R. Hannon: easily best effort in 1996 when third at Newcastle (only fair form): probably stays 1½m: easily best efforts on top-of-the-ground, appeared to act on dead at 2 yrs. *M. D. Hammond*

HANAN (USA) 2 b.f. (Jan 29) Twilight Agenda (USA) 126 – Maikai (USA) 83 p (Never Bend) [1996 6f⁵ 5.5g⁵ Jul 27] $30,000Y: lengthy, good-topped filly: has scope: half-sister to several winners in USA, including one in minor stakes: dam won 6f minor stakes at 2 yrs: sire (by Devil's Bag) useful 7f/1m winner in Ireland, later Grade 1 9f winner in USA and second in Breeders' Cup Classic: green, around 6 lengths fifth of 9 to Khassah in maiden at Ascot on debut, leading 4f: beaten around 9 lengths when fifth of 6 to Ocean Ridge in Prix Robert Papin at Maisons-Laffitte following month: wore bandages at Ascot: should stay beyond 6f: likely to improve further. *P. A. Kelleway*

HANBITOOH (USA) 3 b.g. Hansel (USA) – Bitooh 117 (Seattle Slew (USA)) 64 [1995 –: 7f 1996 10s³ 12m⁴ 12m 9.9g³ 10g⁶ 17.2g May 31] tall, useful-looking gelding: has round action: modest maiden: sold to join Mrs A. J. Perrett 22,000 gns Newmarket July Sales and gelded: stays 1½m: blinkered (pulled hard first occasion) and below form last 2 starts: not one to trust implicitly. *E. A. L. Dunlop*

HANCOCK 4 b.g. Jester 119 – Fresh Line 60 (High Line 125) [1995 –: 13.8g – 1996 a14g Dec 3] lightly raced and no form. *J. Hetherton*

HAND CRAFT (IRE) 4 b.g. Dancing Dissident (USA) 119 – Fair Flutter 79 (Beldale Flutter (USA) 130) [1995 85p: a7g* 7.1m³ 8.2m* 9m* 1996 8g 7.6g 8s 10m⁵ 10m 10.4g Oct 9] tall, good sort: progressive and fairly useful handicapper at 3 yrs: disappointing in 1996, best effort on fourth start: stays 1¼m: acts on fibresand and good to firm ground. *W. J. Haggas*

HAND OF STRAW (IRE) 4 b.g. Thatching 131 – Call Me Miss (Hello 60 d Gorgeous (USA) 128) [1995 62: 7.1g⁵ 7.5d⁶ 8f⁴ 7.5g² 8.1d 8g 7f 1996 a8.5g* a8g³ a72 d a10g a8g⁵ a9.4g² a9.4g 10.8g* 10.8f³ 10.8g⁴ 10.8f 10.8f⁴ 10.2g 10.2f 13.1m⁵ a12g 11.8f a12g a9.4g⁵ a9.4g⁶ Nov 25] dipped-backed, lengthy gelding: has a round action: fair handicapper: won at Wolverhampton (seller) in January and Warwick in April: lost his form: stays 10.8f: acts on firm and dead ground and the all-weather: tried blinkered and visored in 1996: tends to run in snatches: none too reliable. *P. G. Murphy*

HANDSOME RIDGE 2 ch.c. (Apr 1) Indian Ridge 123 – Red Rose Garden 87 87 p (Electric 126) [1996 7d* Nov 8] 42,000Y: workmanlike colt: fifth foal: half-brother to 3-y-o Petinga (by Petong) and fairly useful 8.3f (at 2 yrs) and 1¾m winner Red Bustaan (by Aragon): dam, Irish 1½m winner, daughter of half-sister to Jacinth: game winner of 20-runner maiden at Doncaster in November: likely to stay at least 1m: sure to improve. *J. H. M. Gosden*

HANG A RIGHT 9 b.g. Enchantment 115 – Martina's Magic (Martinmas 128) 39 [1995 NR 1996 10f³ 10m 7f⁶ 8m 7f a6g 8f³ Aug 5] ex-Irish gelding: poor form at best in 1996, reportedly finishing lame final start: winner at 1¾m in Ireland, but best form at 6f to 8.5f: best efforts on a sound surface. *C. A. Dwyer*

HANGONINTHERE 5 b.g. Rakaposhi King 119 – Dusky Nancy 65 (Red – Sunset 120) [1995 NR 1996 a8.5g 12m⁶ 10.8m 8.1f Sep 12] small gelding: second reported foal: dam won 1m seller: of little account. *N. M. Babbage*

HANGOVER SQUARE (IRE) 2 ch.c. (Feb 13) Jareer (USA) 115 – Dancing 86 ? Line (High Line 125) [1996 5.2d⁵ 5m⁴ 5m² 5g⁵ 5.2f 5m⁵ 5f² 5m² 5d⁵ Oct 21] IR 12,000Y: leggy, close-coupled, unfurnished colt: has a quick action: second foal: half-brother to a winner in India: dam, ran twice at 2 yrs in Ireland, out of half-sister to Scottish Reel: fairly useful maiden: sold 15,000 gns Newmarket Autumn Sales: will stay 6f: acts on firm ground: sent to Sweden. *R. Hannon*

HANG TEN 7 b.h. Kris 135 – Broken Wave 103 (Bustino 136) [1995 NR 1996 –
14.9g May 25] split a pastern at 2 yrs: has been at stud and tried over jumps:
blinkered, no sign of retaining ability. *S. Gollings*

HANK-A-CHIEF 3 b.c. Inca Chief (USA) – Be Sharp 85 (Sharpen Up 127) –
[1995 –: 6m⁶ 7d 7g 1996 a7g 7f 10m 10f Jul 6] neat colt: unimpressive mover: no
worthwhile form: blinkered final start. *B. Smart*

HANNAHS BAY 3 b.f. Buzzards Bay 128§ – Hi-Hannah 59 (Red Sunset 120) –
[1995 40: 6g 7f a7g a8g³ 1996 a11g 12s Jul 3] smallish filly: plater: tried blinkered,
no improvement: dead. *M. G. Meagher*

HANNAH'S USHER 4 b.g. Marching On 101 – La Pepper 63 (Workboy 123) 59
[1995 62, a83: a5g² a6g² a5g* 5g 6f⁶ 5m³ 5.1d a5g⁵ 1996 a6g⁶ a6g⁴ a6g a5g⁵ a5g³ a76
a5g³ a6g* a5g² 5m⁶ 6.1m 5g a6g⁶ 7.5m 7.1g Jul 22] leggy gelding: fair performer on
the all-weather, modest on turf: won claimer at Wolverhampton in March: well
below form final 5 starts: best at sprint distances: acts on any going: tried blinkered.
C. Murray

HANNALOU (FR) 3 b.f. Shareef Dancer (USA) 135 – Litani River (USA) (Irish 70
River (FR) 131) [1995 NR 1996 7m 7.5m² 7.5f² 7.6m³ 6m⁶ 7g² 7m⁶ 7f² 7f⁶ a7g Oct
28] 25,000Y: small, leggy filly: second foal: half-sister to modest 1994 2-y-o Raise
A Warning (by Warning): dam, French maiden, is sister to useful French 5.5f and 7f
winner Or Vision: fair maiden: bred to stay further than 7.5f: acts on firm going:
seems best with forcing tactics: has joined K. Ottesen. *S. P. C. Woods*

HAPPY 2 b.c. (Mar 24) Rock City 120 – Joyful Thought 51 (Green Desert (USA) –
127) [1996 6m Oct 4] 27,000Y: first foal: dam, maiden bred at sprint distances,
half-sister to Middle Park Stakes winner Creag-An-Sgor: well beaten in maiden at
Lingfield: sold 3,000 gns Newmarket Autumn Sales. *P. T. Walwyn*

HAPPY DANCER (USA) 2 b.f. (Apr 19) Seattle Dancer (USA) 119 – Happy 95
Result (USA) (Diesis 133) [1996 5.5d⁵ 7d⁴ 8m* 8g³ 8s* Oct 13] IR 20,000Y: second
foal: dam, lightly raced, half-sister to Pater Noster (miler, rated 111): French filly:
won minor event at Evry in September and Premio Dormello at Milan in October:
likely to stay beyond 1m: acts on good to firm and soft ground. *R. Collet, France*

HAPPY GO LUCKY (USA) 2 ch.f. (Apr 14) Teamster 114 – Meritsu (IRE) 54 81 p
(Lyphard's Special (USA) 122) [1996 5.7f 7m³ 8.1d* 8g Oct 18] angular filly: third
foal: half-sister to 3-y-o Redskin Lady and fairly useful 1994 Italian 2-y-o 6f and
7f winner Spaghetti House (both by Indian Ridge): dam (maiden) best at 1m/1¼m:
progressive form first 3 starts, winning maiden at Sandown in August: sweating, very
well backed but well beaten on final start: will stay beyond 1m: acts on dead ground
and good to firm: probably capable of better. *R. J. O'Sullivan*

HAPPY MINSTRAL (USA) 2 b.c. (May 13) Alleged (USA) 138 – Minstrelete 81 p
(USA) (Round Table) [1996 7m² 8.2m* Sep 16] IR 44,000Y: good-bodied colt:
fluent mover: half-brother to numerous winners here and abroad, including 1992
2-y-o 7f winner Double Bass (by The Minstrel), smart Irish 7f and 9f winner
Punctilio (by Forli) and dam of Always Fair: dam, 1m winner, half-sister to top-class
Gay Fandango: made all in 9-runner maiden at Nottingham in September: will
improve further, particularly given more of a test of stamina. *M. Johnston*

HAPPY PARTNER (IRE) 3 b.c. Nabeel Dancer (USA) 120 – Dublah (USA) 66
(Private Account (USA)) [1995 66: 5f³ 5m² 1996 a5g* Jan 9] modest performer:
trained at 2 yrs by P. Haslam: had clear chance when winning 6-runner median
auction maiden at Lingfield: should stay 6f: sent to Macau. *C. Murray*

HAPPY TAIPAN (IRE) 3 b.g. Keen 116 – Eastern View (IRE) (Persian Bold –
123) [1995 58p: 8f⁶ 1996 11.9m³ Jun 14] tailed off in 5-runner median auction
maiden at York nearly 10 months after debut, rearing at stalls opening: sold 600 gns
Newmarket Autumn Sales. *C. Murray*

HAPPY TRAVELLER (IRE) 3 b.c. Treasure Kay 114 – Elegant Owl (Tumble –
Wind (USA)) [1995 54p: a7g⁵ 1996 6m 5g 6.9m⁶ Aug 28] big, strong, lengthy colt:
shaped quite well on debut but well beaten all starts in 1996: sold 800 gns Newmarket
Autumn Sales: sent to Spain. *C. Murray*

HAPPY TYCOON (IRE) 3 br.g. Polish Patriot (USA) 128 – Art Age (Artaius –
(USA) 129) [1995 67: 5g* 5f 5.2g 1996 5g a9.4g Aug 31] close-coupled gelding: fair
winner in 1995, but found to have fractured a sesamoid after final start: tailed-off in

handicap on reappearance: stumbled at start and unseated rider in similar event 3 months later: not bred to stay much beyond 1m: visored final 2-y-o start, blinkered on reappearance. *C. Murray*

HAPPY VALENTINE 2 b.c. (Mar 17) Rainbow Quest (USA) 134 – 103 p
Nearctic Flame 111 (Sadler's Wells (USA) 132) [1996 7g* Oct 30]
The Godolphin operation considerably increased its involvement in two-year-old racing in the latest season. In 1995 Arazi's half-sister Phantom Creek was their only two-year-old runner, and she ran just twice. A year on, the bin Suroor stable signalled its intentions right from the start by running the newcomers Kumait in the Coventry Stakes and Rihan in the Queen Mary. Neither proved up to pattern company, and there were some more disappointments along the way but by the end of the season Medaaly had won the Racing Post Trophy, new acquisition Moonlight Paradise had emerged as a leading One Thousand Guineas candidate and Happy Valentine was looking a really good middle-distance prospect. Happy Valentine was an impressive winner of his only start, a seven-furlong maiden at Yarmouth at the end of October. The 7/4 favourite in a field of seventeen, he was one of a group of six who stuck to the stand side, soon prominent there and drawing right away inside the last without needing to be at all hard ridden to beat Silverani five lengths, newcomers filling the first six places. Despite the venue, this was a sufficiently convincing performance to have Happy Valentine vying for favouritism in ante-post lists for the Derby.

Happy Valentine (b.c. Mar 17, 1994)	Rainbow Quest (USA) (b 1981)	Blushing Groom (ch 1974)	Red God
			Runaway Bride
		I Will Follow (b 1975)	Herbager
			Where You Lead
	Nearctic Flame (b 1986)	Sadler's Wells (b 1981)	Northern Dancer
			Fairy Bridge
		Flame of Tara (b 1980)	Artaius
			Welsh Flame

Also towards the top of the Derby betting is the Sadler's Wells colt Entrepreneur. Both have other things in common, being the highest-priced yearlings sold at auction in Europe, joint-third in the world, in 1995 (fetching 600,000 guineas at the Houghton Sales) and bred by Cheveley Park Stud. Happy Valentine has an excellent middle-distance pedigree. He is closely related to the smart middle-distance stayer Blushing Flame (by Blushing Groom) who put up his best effort to win the Curragh Cup in the latest season. Nearctic Flame's next foal, a gelding by Kris, died at two before he saw a racecourse; she has a yearling filly by Machiavellian named Candescent and a colt foal by Rainbow Quest again in 1995. Nearctic Flame was a smart filly, winning twice at around a mile and a quarter before finishing third in a steadily-run Ribblesdale. Her sister Salsabil and half-brother Marju (runner-up in the Derby) are the names that stand out among Flame of Tara's offspring; others out of the mare include Nearctic Flame's brother Song of Tara, a smart middle-distance colt. Flame of Tara, winner of the Coronation Stakes and Pretty Polly Stakes, is a half-sister to Fruition, the dam of good stayers Kneller and Great Marquess and the Breeders' Cup Turf winner Northern Spur. While a Yarmouth maiden win is light years removed from Derby winning form this very well bred colt looks bound to go on and do well in good middle-distance company in 1997. *Saeed bin Suroor*

HAPPY VENTURER (IRE) 3 br.g. Petorius 117 – Primacara 58 (Rusticaro –
(FR) 124) [1995 NR 1996 8g⁶ a8g 10.1f⁶ 7f Aug 7] IR 13,000Y: half-brother to 2 winners, including Atherton Green (6f at 2 yrs, to 1¼m by Shy Groom): dam, half-sister to smart 7f to 1¼m performer Trucidator, stayed 1¼m: no worthwhile form: sold 600 gns Newmarket Autumn Sales. *C. Murray*

HARBET HOUSE (FR) 3 b.g. Bikala 134 – Light of Hope (USA) 101 (Lyphard 62
(USA) 132) [1995 NR 1996 10g a8g 12g 14.1m a14.8g³ a12g* a12g² a12g⁶ a16g a14g³ a14.8g 12s⁵ Oct 26] 90,000 francs F, 9,200Y: big, plain gelding: has a round

action: half-brother to 1¼m winner Savoy Truffle (by Law Society): dam, 1¼m winner, sister to Alzao from family of Tom Rolfe and Chieftain: modest form: won handicap at Southwell in June: sold 12,000 gns Newmarket Autumn Sales: shapes like a stayer: acts on soft ground and on Southwell fibresand (below form on other all-weather surfaces). *C. A. Cyzer*

HARBOUR DUES   3 b.c. Slip Anchor 136 – Quillotern (USA) (Arctic Tern (USA) 126) [1995 65p: 7.1d⁴ 7f⁴ 1996 10d* 12m* 12m³ 13.9m⁴ 11.8m² Oct 28] tall, good-topped colt: good walker: useful form: won maiden at Newbury in May and handicap at Goodwood in June: in frame in King George V Handicap at Royal Ascot (unlucky) and Ebor Handicap (joint favourite) at York: good 3 lengths second to Masehaab in minor event at Leicester final start: stays 13.9f: acts on good to firm ground and dead: held up. *Lady Herries*   103

HARBOUR ISLAND   4 b.g. Rainbow Quest (USA) 134 – Quay Line 117 (High Line 125) [1995 89p: 10g 14s* 16.5m² 1996 12f⁶ 13.9m⁶ 16.1m³ 16.2d⁴ 18g Oct 19] rather leggy gelding: has a roundish action: fairly useful handicapper: generally ran creditably in 1996: sold (M. Stoute to M. Pipe) 20,000 gns Newmarket Autumn Sales: suited by thorough test of stamina: acts on good to firm ground, but shapes as if a slog through the mud will suit him ideally: blinkered/visored since second 3-y-o start: tends to run in snatches, and isn't the easiest of rides. *M. R. Stoute*   84

HARDING   5 b.g. Dowsing (USA) 124 – Orange Hill 75 (High Top 131) [1995 –: 10f 1996 12d Oct 11] good-bodied gelding: easy mover: fair maiden handicapper as 3-y-o: bit backward only starts last 2 seasons: raced mainly at up to 1¼m, but should stay further: acts on good to firm ground and heavy. *S. Mellor*   –

HARDIPRINCESS   2 b.f. (Feb 5) Keen 116 – Hardiheroine 76 (Sandhurst Prince 128) [1996 6g 6v Nov 11] second foal: half-sister to 3-y-o 6f winner Shining Cloud (by Indian Ridge): dam should have stayed beyond 1m: well beaten in maidens. *M. Bell*   –

HARD LOVE   4 b.f. Rambo Dancer (CAN) 107 – Djimbaran Bay (Le Levanstell 122) [1995 67: 7d 7g⁴ 10.2m* 10.1m⁴ 10.1m² a12g³ 12h⁴ 10.1g² a9.4g⁴ a10g⁵ 1996 a13g a11g³ a11g⁴ a16g² 18s⁶ Mar 22] leggy filly: good walker: modest handicapper: best effort in 1996 when runner-up at Southwell in March: didn't get home under testing conditions final start: acts on good to firm ground and fibresand, saddle appeared to slip when tried on dead: takes good hold. *J. L. Eyre*   – a55

HARD TO FIGURE   10 gr.g. Telsmoss 91 – Count On Me 77 (No Mercy 126) [1995 113: 6g⁴ 6m⁵ 7m 6m 6g* 6m 6m⁵ 5.6m 6g⁶ 1996 6s⁴ 6g* 5.1g 6g³ 6f 6f 7.3f³ 6m 7g⁵ 6g 6m 6s a7g Dec 7] rather leggy, workmanlike gelding: smart performer: as good as ever when winning minor event at Kempton in April by head from Easy Dollar: well below form last 9 starts: effective at 6f and 7f: acts on any going: usually held up: genuine: pulled up when highly tried on hurdling debut. *R. J. Hodges*   113 d

HARDY DANCER   4 ch.g. Pharly (FR) 130 – Handy Dancer 87 (Green God 128) [1995 90: 8m* 9m* 12g⁵ 10.1m³ 8m 8.1f² 8.1m⁴ 8g⁵ 9d 1996 a10g 10g³ 10m² 10.3g³ 10.1m⁶ 12m 10g 10m 10.1m 10m 8m⁶ 8g Oct 29] quite attractive, close-coupled gelding: fairly useful handicapper: in very good form in first half of 1996, placed in 3 quite valuable events: below form last 7 starts: stays 1¼m well: acts on firm going: has run well when sweating: has joined T. Powell. *G. L. Moore*   92

HAREB (USA)   3 b.c. Diesis 133 – All At Once (USA) (Dixieland Band (USA)) [1995 NR 1996 8m⁵ 8m 8.3m⁴ 8m⁶ a10g* 9m⁵ 10.3d² 10m⁴ Sep 26] $50,000Y: strong, lengthy colt: third foal: dam, placed in USA, half-sister to Diminuendo and Pricket (both by Diesis): fair performer: won apprentice maiden handicap at Lingfield in July: stays 1¼m: acts on good to firm ground, dead and equitrack: has carried head awkwardly: inconsistent: sent to UAE. *J. W. Hills*   82 d a77

HARIK   2 ch.c. (Apr 16) Persian Bold 123 – Yaqut (USA) 77 (Northern Dancer) [1996 8m Oct 1] strong, workmanlike colt: sixth foal: brother to fair 7f winner Anam and half-brother to 3-y-o Alajyal (by Kris), useful 10.2f and 1½m winner Estimraar (by Bustino) and 7.5f and 8.2f winner Tahdid (by Mtoto): dam 2-y-o 7f winner from family of Alydar: 33/1, burly and green, weakened quickly final 2f when around 15 lengths tenth of 12 to Asas in maiden at Newmarket: may well do better. *B. Hanbury*   66 p

HARLEQUIN WALK (IRE)   5 ch.m. Pennine Walk 120 – Taniokey (Grundy 137) [1995 –, a54: a12g* a12g* 15.4m 1996 a12g* a16g⁴ 11.9g⁶ 9.7g* 10.2m² 10f⁴   42 a54

a8g³ a10g⁶ a10g⁵ Dec 31] sturdy mare: modest performer on all-weather: awarded claimer at Lingfield in February: only poor on turf: won selling handicap at Folke-stone (by 8 lengths) in July: best at up to 1½m: acts on all-weather surfaces, and good to firm ground: goes well in blinkers: front runner. *R. J. O'Sullivan*

HARLESTONE HEATH   3 gr.f. Aragon 118 – Harlestone Lake 78 (Riboboy –
(USA) 124) [1995 NR 1996 10m⁶ Sep 26] fourth foal: half-sister to fairly useful out-and-out stayer Harlestone Brook (by Jalmood): dam out-and-out stayer: 25/1, soundly beaten in maiden at Goodwood: sold (J. Dunlop to M. Dods) 2,000 gns Newmarket Autumn Sales. *J. L. Dunlop*

HARMONY HALL   2 ch.g. (Apr 9) Music Boy 124 – Fleeting Affair 98 (Hotfoot   70
126) [1996 6m 7m⁶ 7m⁶ 7s Nov 9] 22,000Y: big, lengthy gelding: sixth foal: brother to 3-y-o Infatuation and half-brother to 6f (at 2 yrs) to 1m winner First Crush (by Primo Dominie) and 1¼m and 1½m winner Trump (by Last Tycoon): dam 1¼m and 1½m winner who stayed 2m: fair form: will probably stay 1m: had stiffish task on soft ground: usually bandaged. *J. R. Fanshawe*

HARMONY IN RED   2 ch.c. (Apr 30) Rock Hopper 124 – Lucky Song 91   59
(Lucky Wednesday 124) [1996 5f⁴ 6m⁶ 6g⁵ a6g⁵ Nov 2] 9,500Y, 30,000 2-y-o: compact colt: sixth foal: half-brother to 2-y-o winners X My Heart (at 6f and 7f in 1991, by Aragon) and Level Xing (at 5f and 6f in 1990, by Stanford): dam 5f and 7f winner: modest maiden: stays 6f. *J. Berry*

HARRIET'S BEAU   3 b.g. Superpower 113 – Pour Moi 73 (Bay Express 132)   36
[1995 58d: 5m⁵ 5m⁵ 5g⁴ 6h⁵ 5m 5g 1996 6.1d 5g 6g 9f 6m⁵ 5.3m³ 5.3f⁵ 5g 5g Sep 7] leggy gelding: modest form first 3 2-y-o starts: seems poor at best now-adays: sold 600 gns Newmarket Autumn Sales: a sprinter: often blinkered/visored. *M. W. Easterby*

HARRY   6 ch.g. Risk Me (FR) 127 – Relko's Pride (Relko 136) [1995 NR 1996   50
a12g³ a11g a13g 12s Nov 11] lengthy gelding: modest maiden: first outing since 1994 when third in selling handicap at Lingfield in January: soundly beaten in similar company subsequently, leaving A. J. Wilson after third outing: probably needs further than 9f, and stays 1½m: acts on all-weather surfaces and heavy ground: usually races prominently: won 3 selling hurdles late in year, sold to join P. Hobbs final start: inconsistent. *D. Burchell*

HARRY'S COMING   12 b.g. Marching On 101 – Elegant Star 86 (Star Moss –
122) [1995 60d: 5d² 5m³ 5.1g* 5.1m⁵ 5g² 6g 6g* 5m⁵ 6.1m⁴ 5.1h⁶ 6f 5f 1996 5.1g Apr 22] leggy, good-topped gelding: veteran handicapper: below form last 5 11-y-o starts, and always behind sole outing in 1996: effective at 5f, and stays 7f: acts on equitrack and on firm and dead ground, unsuited by soft: tried blinkered and visored at 3 yrs. *R. J. Hodges*

HARRY'S TREAT   4 b.f. Lochnager 132 – Megara (USA) (Thatching 131)   56 ?
[1995 56: 7g³ 6g 7.5d 7.1f³ 1996 a8g 7.1g 7m³ 8m 8g⁴ 10m Jun 10] lengthy filly: modest maiden: stumbled and unseated rider after 1f final start: likely to prove suited by further than 1m: acts on firm ground. *J. L. Eyre*

HARRY WOLTON   2 b.c. (Apr 21) Distant Relative 128 – Tashinsky (USA)   86 p
(Nijinsky (CAN) 138) [1996 6g² 7m* Sep 18] 32,000Y: angular colt: fifth foal: half-brother to fairly useful 1¼m/11f winner Sovereign Page (by Caro) and 7.1f winner Ten Past Six (by Kris): dam, showed some ability in France, is half-sister to very smart miler Mukaddamah: won maiden at Yarmouth in September, first two clear: will be well suited by 1m+: should improve again. *H. R. A. Cecil*

HARSH TIMES   3 ch.f. Efisio 120 – Larnem 43 (Meldrum 112) [1995 53: 5g⁶ 5m   45
6m⁶ 7m a7g² a6g* 7g⁴ 7f⁶ a6g 1996 a7g 7.5m⁶ 10m 7m 8s³ a8.5g 8.3g Sep 29] leggy filly: poor performer: sold 1,000 gns Newmarket Autumn Sales: may prove suited by 7f: acts on fibresand, best turf effort on soft going: tried blinkered, including last 6 starts: has carried head high: one to be wary of: sent to South Korea. *T. D. Easterby*

HARTFIELDS BOY   3 b.g. Shavian 125 – Fallen Angel 88 (Quiet Fling (USA) –
124) [1995 –: 6m 5m⁵ 6m 1996 10f May 9] small gelding: showed nothing only 3-y-o start: dead. *B. J. Meehan*

HARTSHORN   2 br.c. (May 18) Warning 136 – Roxy Hart (High Top 131) [1996   57
7f 8d 7m Oct 28] 10,000Y: leggy, light-bodied colt: has a round action: half-brother to several winners, including 6f (at 2 yrs) and 1m winner Don't Presume (by Pharly)

and 4-y-o 1½m winner Chahaya Timor (by Slip Anchor): dam unraced half-sister to good sprinter Music Maestro and smart 1985 2-y-o Outer Circle: similar level of form in maidens: looked sort to do better in time, but sold 5,800 gns Newmarket Autumn Sales: sent to Sweden. *J. L. Dunlop*

HARVEST REAPER 4 gr.g. Bairn (USA) 126 – Real Silver 85 (Silly Season 127) [1995 54, a43: 7g 8g 6.9g³ a6g⁴ a7g a9.4g 1996 8.2m 6m 7d 8m³ 8.1s a9.4g Nov 25] leggy gelding: poor maiden: acts on good to firm ground and dead: tried visored, no improvement: takes keen hold: inconsistent. *J. L. Harris*   45
a–

HARVEY'S FUTURE 2 b.c. (Apr 10) Never So Bold 135 – Orba Gold (USA) 67 (Gold Crest (USA) 120) [1996 a5g⁶ Nov 29] 3,100Y: first foal: dam 7f winner: showed promise in late-season maiden auction at Southwell: will improve. *T. T. Clement*   56 p

HARVEY WHITE (IRE) 4 b. or br.g. Petorius 117 – Walkyria (Lord Gayle (USA) 124) [1995 57: 8m⁵ 10m⁶ 10m⁵ 12.1m³ 9.7f² 10.1m* 9.7s 9m⁶ a12g 1996 9.7s⁴ 10s⁵ 10m² 10.8f* 10.8f³ 10.8f⁵ 10.1f³ 10m⁴ 9f³ 10d⁴ 10g 10m* 10m³ 8.9g 10f 10.1m³ 10g 12v Nov 11] rather leggy gelding: fair handicapper: beat large fields at Warwick in May and Kempton (apprentices) in September: stays 1½m: acts on firm going and soft: usually held up: consistent. *J. Pearce*   69

HASTA LA VISTA 6 b.g. Superlative 118 – Falcon Berry (FR) (Bustino 136) [1995 53: a14g⁵ a12g a12g 12.3m³ 12.3m* 12g 12g³ 11.9m⁵ 12m³ a14g 1996 12.3g⁴ 12d* 12.4d⁴ 13.9m⁶ 15.8g⁵ 15.8s⁴ 12.3m a14g 11.9g Oct 10] compact gelding: has a round action: modest handicapper: won at Catterick in April: effective at 1½m to 2m: acts on good to firm ground, soft and fibresand: blinkered nowadays: front runner/races prominently: game. *M. W. Easterby*   54
a–

HATS OF TO HILDA 4 b.f. Aragon 118 – Incarnadine 67 (Hot Spark 126) [1995 NR 1996 8g 7m 8m 12.1m 14.1f Jul 20] leggy, sparely-made filly: of little account nowadays. *Mrs M. Reveley*   –

HATTAAFEH (IRE) 5 b.m. Mtoto 134 – Monongelia 98 (Welsh Pageant 132) [1995 60: a13g* a13g² a16g a11g³ 11.9m³ a12g³ 10g 12m a12g 1996 15.4m² 16.4g⁵ 12m² 12m² 12m³ 16.2m⁴ Jul 26] workmanlike, angular mare: modest handicapper: ran consistently well in 1996: barely stays 2m: acts on good to firm ground and the all-weather. *Miss B. Sanders*   63

HATTAB (IRE) 2 b.c. (Feb 21) Marju (IRE) 127 – Funun (USA) 84 (Fappiano (USA)) [1996 6m⁵ 6g⁴ 5m* 5m² 5d Oct 28] lengthy, attractive colt: has scope: third foal: half-brother to 3-y-o Marjaana, 5.2f winner at 2 yrs, and 4-y-o 6f winner Intiaash (both by Shaadi): dam, winner from 5f to 7f, out of half-sister to Tasso: fairly useful maiden: won maiden at Haydock in September: much better form at 5f than 6f: acts on good to firm ground, possibly not on dead. *P. T. Walwyn*   91

HATTA RIVER (USA) 6 b.g. Irish River (FR) 131 – Fallacieuse (Habitat 134) [1995 58: a12g⁴ 11.8m⁶ 11m⁴ 11m⁵ 12d a14.8g 11.8g⁵ 10.3m 1996 12d 14.9g 14.9m 12.1m Jul 25] good-topped gelding: has a long stride: no worthwhile form in 1996, trained until after reappearance by J. A. Harris: tried blinkered, including when successful: sold 800 gns Ascot December Sales. *P. T. Dalton*   –

HATTA SUNSHINE (USA) 6 b.g. Dixieland Band (USA) – Mountain Sunshine (USA) (Vaguely Noble 140) [1995 46, a55: a8g² a8g⁴ a8g* 9g⁶ a8g³ 8.3g⁵ 9m⁴ 10g⁵ 9f⁴ a10g 8f⁵ 19m a8g* a8g⁴ a8g³ a10g 9m⁶ 12d a10s⁶ a10g a10g⁴ Dec 26] lengthy gelding: modest handicapper on the all-weather: tends to go well fresh, as when winning at Lingfield (apprentices) in February: only poor on turf: stays 1¼m: acts on equitrack and firm ground, yet to race on fibresand: has run well for amateur: inconsistent. *A. Moore*   a57

HAUTE CUISINE 3 b.g. Petong 126 – Nevis 61 (Connaught 130) [1995 –: 5.1m⁵ 5m⁶ 1996 7.1g a7g 7g⁵ 10f² 11.8f 11.5m Oct 23] strong, close-coupled gelding: poor maiden: trained until after third 3-y-o start by Jack Berry: should stay 1½m: acts on firm ground. *R. J. R. Williams*   44

HAVAGO 2 b.c. (Apr 26) Risk Me (FR) 127 – Sporting Lass 37 (Blakeney 126) [1996 6.1m⁶ 6s 6.9d* 6.9v⁴ Nov 11] 6,200Y: third foal: brother to a winner in Hungary: dam staying maiden: first run for over 7 weeks, improved form to win maiden auction at Folkestone in October despite hanging badly left: stays 7f: well below best on heavy ground. *R. Hannon*   70 +

HAVANA HEIGHTS (IRE)   3 ch.f. Persian Heights 129 – Havana Blade (USA)   52
(Blade (USA)) [1995 –: a5g 5g⁶ a7g⁵ 1996 a8g⁶ a5g a11g⁶ a12g³ a14g 16.2g⁴ 13.8g*   a–
14s 15.1s a14.8g⁵ a16g Dec 11] small, sparely-made filly: improved effort to win
seller at Catterick in September: no comparable form: probably stays 2m. *J. L. Eyre*

HAVANA MISS   4 b.f. Cigar 68 – Miss Patdonna 62 (Starch Reduced 112) [1995   39
46, a38: a8g a6g⁴ a6g⁶ a6g a7g⁶ a5g 5.7f 6g⁴ 5.1h 6d 6m 6.9g⁴ 8f 1996 6m 6f
a6g a8g a8g Nov 22] leggy, sparely-made filly: poor performer: probably stays 7f:
acts on firm and soft ground and on fibresand: tried visored and blinkered:
inconsistent. *B. Palling*

HAVANA RESERVE   2 ch.g. (Mar 29) Cigar 68 – Shy Hiker (Netherkelly 112)   –
[1996 6v⁶ Nov 11] second reported foal: dam 2½m winner over hurdles: 5/1, showed
nothing in median auction maiden at Folkestone. *R. Hannon*

HAVE A NIGHTCAP   7 ch.g. Night Shift (USA) – Final Orders (USA) (Prince   37
John) [1995 –: a16g a14g 1996 a7g² 7.1g⁶ a7g³ 7f 7f³ a7g a8g⁵ Nov 18] close-
coupled gelding: poor performer: probably finds 7f a minimum nowadays: acts on
fibresand and on firm and dead ground: effective blinkered/visored. *N. P. Littmoden*

HAWA AL NASAMAAT (USA)   4 b.g. Houston (USA) – Barrera Miss (USA)   84
(Barrera (USA)) [1995 84: 7g³ 7.1m² 7m 7f* 7.1m⁴ 7f⁶ 7g 7d⁴ 1996 7s 6.1m³ 6m*
7f³ 6m Sep 21] well-made gelding: fairly useful performer: justified favouritism in
apprentice minor event at Goodwood in August, racing virtually alone against
favoured stand rail: soundly beaten in Ayr Gold Cup final start: effective at 6f and 7f:
acts on firm and dead ground, possibly not on soft. *E. A. L. Dunlop*

HAWAII STORM (FR)   8 b.g. Plugged Nickle (USA) – Slewvindaloo (USA)   –
(Seattle Slew (USA)) [1995 –, a70: a8g⁴ a8g⁴ a8g² a8g³ a8.5g a8g a8g² a10g a8g³   a71 d
a8g⁶ a7g* 1996 a7g⁶ a7g² a7g² a7g⁶ a7g⁶ 8d 7m a8g 8g a8g a7g³ a7g⁵ a8g⁵ 8g
a8.5g⁶ a7s³ a8g⁴ a7g³ Dec 11] leggy gelding: fair form at best in 1996, again
campaigned mainly on all-weather: effective at 7f and 1m (should stay further): best
form on the all-weather: blinkered (below form) 3 times in 1994: usually held up:
sometimes slowly away. *D. J. S. ffrench Davis*

HAWAIT (IRE)   2 gr.c. (Mar 19) Green Desert (USA) 127 – Hayati 94 (Hotfoot   81
126) [1996 5m⁴ 6f³ 6m* 7m 6m⁴ Sep 21] $100,000Y: well-made, quite attractive
colt: good walker: has a quick action: sixth foal: half-brother to 3 winners, notably
very smart mare at around 1¼m Ruby Tiger (by Ahonoora): dam 7f and 1¼m winner:
fairly useful performer: won 11-runner maiden at Lingfield in August readily: never
seriously threatened in nurseries last 2 starts: stays 6f: raced only on top-of-the-
ground. *B. W. Hills*

HAWANAFA   3 b.f. Tirol 127 – Woodland View (Precipice Wood 123) [1995 60+:   48
6f⁶ 7m 1996 8g 7f⁶ 7g 6m 8.3g 10m³ 12g 8m Sep 9] tall, rather unfurnished filly: has
a short action: poor maiden: sold to join J. S. Moore 3,000 gns Newmarket Autumn
Sales: appears to stay 1¼m. *R. Hannon*

HAWKISH (USA)   7 b.g. Silver Hawk (USA) 123 – Dive Royal (USA)   52
(Inverness Drive (USA)) [1995 58: 9.9m⁴ 10g² 10.1g³ 10m* 9f⁴ 10f² 1996 10g³ 10d
10.3g² 11f⁴ 12.3m⁵ 10f² Sep 10] sturdy gelding: poor mover: modest handicapper:
stays 1½m: acts on firm ground and dead: normally held up: consistent. *D. Morley*

HAWKSLEY HILL (IRE)   3 ch.g. Rahy (USA) 115 – Gaijin 97 (Caerleon   93
(USA) 132) [1995 –p: 7m 6m a5g 1996 a7g* 11.1g* 10m* 10g² 8.2f* 8m* 8f² 8m²
8m⁶ 8m² 9m⁵ 8g* 8g Nov 2] big, workmanlike gelding: has plenty of scope: progressed extremely well in handicaps, winning at Southwell, Musselburgh, Redcar,

Rothmans Royals North South Challenge Series Final (Handicap), Newmarket—
Hawksley Hill's sixth handicap win of the year comes off a mark of 83; the first was off 45

Nottingham and Newmarket (twice): gained final success in £29,700 Rothmans Royals North South Final at Newmarket in October, beating High Premium by 1½ lengths in 27-runner race: best form at 1m/9f: acts on fibresand and firm ground, yet to race on a soft surface: held up (tends to edge left and idle in front) and well suited by strong handling: tough and consistent: a credit to his trainer. *Mrs J. R. Ramsden*

HAWWAM 10 b.g. Glenstal (USA) 118 – Hone 79 (Sharpen Up 127) [1995 55, 55 a73: a7g³ a8g* a8g* a8g² a8.5g⁵ a8g* a8g⁴ 8.3v³ 8g² 8m 8g⁶ a7g⁴ 8.1m³ 8g a8g² a8g a65 a9.4g 1996 a8g² a8g⁴ a11g a11g⁴ a12g³ a12g⁵ 8g 9.2s 11.1m⁶ 10d³ 9.2g a12g 8f 8.1m³ 10m* 8f* 8m 8m³ 8.1m⁶ 9g 8m 10f 8g 10.1m Oct 23] good-topped, quite attractive gelding: fair performer on fibresand, modest on turf: won seller at Ayr and apprentice handicap at Redcar in July: well held all starts subsequently: effective at 1m to 1½m: goes well on fibresand, and probably acts on any ground on turf: best with waiting tactics: sometimes swishes tail. *E. J. Alston*

HAYAAIN 3 b.c. Shirley Heights 130 – Littlefield 100 (Bay Express 132) [1995 84 76: 7g 8m⁵ 8f 1996 12g³ 11.7m* 11.6g 13.3f Jul 20] sturdy, deep-bodied colt: carries plenty of condition: fairly useful performer: won maiden at Bath in June: disappointing in minor event and handicap afterwards: sold 8,000 gns Newmarket Autumn Sales: better suited by middle distances than shorter: front runner/races prominently. *Major W. R. Hern*

HAYA YA KEFAAH 4 b.g. Kefaah (USA) 124 – Hayat (IRE) (Sadler's Wells 70 (USA) 132) [1995 –: a9.4g a7g a8.5g a11g 1996 a12g² 12g* 11.8d 12m* 12g² 12m 11.9d* Sep 27] angular gelding: fair handicapper: won at Doncaster (apprentices) in March and May and at Haydock (beat Sugar Mill a neck in tight-finish) in September: stays 1½m: acts on good to firm and dead ground. *N. M. Babbage*

HAYDN JAMES (USA) 2 ch.c. (Mar 16) Danzig Connection (USA) – Royal Fi 78 Fi (USA) 94 (Conquistador Cielo (USA)) [1996 7m⁴ 7.1m Sep 18] $45,000Y: second foal: dam 5f and 6f winner: 33/1 and in need of run, 2¾ lengths fourth of 17 to Monza in maiden at Newbury, tracking leaders and staying on: bit below that form until subsequent start: likely to stay at least 1m. *P. W. Harris*

HAYDOWN (IRE) 4 b. or br.g. Petorius 117 – Hay Knot (Main Reef 126) [1995 32 NR 1996 12m 7.6f⁴ 11.6d⁵ 10m Aug 31] poor maiden handicapper: probably stays 11.6f: inconsistent: has joined C. P. Morlock. *C. T. Nash*

HAYES WAY (IRE) 2 b.c. (Mar 19) Lahib (USA) 129 – Edgeaway 70 (Ajdal 79 p (USA) 130) [1996 a8g* Nov 14] IR 13,000Y: first foal: dam, 7f winner who stayed 1m, out of half-sister to top 1979 2-y-o Monteverdi: won maiden at Lingfield in November: will stay at least 1¼m: should improve. *T. G. Mills*

HAYLING-BILLY 3 ch.c. Captain Webster 69 – Mistress Royal 74 (Royalty – 130) [1995 NR 1996 14m 10g Oct 9] half-brother to a poor jumper: dam winning stayer: has shown little in maidens. *P. R. Hedger*

HAYSONG (IRE) 3 ch.f. Ballad Rock 122 – Hay Knot (Main Reef 126) [1995 –: – 5g⁵ 1996 7.1d 8m 6f Jul 17] neat filly: no sign of ability. *J. P. Leigh*

HAZARD A GUESS (IRE) 6 ch.g. Digamist (USA) 110 – Guess Who 76 (Be 88 My Guest (USA) 126) [1995 80: 10.3g 10.8d⁴ 10f* 9.9m* 12g 12d³ 12m 10m⁵ 10m³ 9.9m⁶ 11.9g⁵ 11.9s 1996 10.3d² 10g* 9.9m³ 10g³ 10.1m 8.9m 10f² 10.3g⁶ 10g 10.4m⁵ 10.1f* 9.9f 10.4m 10.4g* Oct 10] tall, leggy gelding: has improved every season and is now a fairly useful handicapper: won at Kempton in April and Newcastle in August: not right in coat, below best when scrambling home in claimer at York in October: suited by middle distances: acts on any ground: has run well for lady: usually held up: consistent. *D. Nicholls*

HAZEL 4 ro.f. Risk Me (FR) 127 – Sir Tangs Gift (Runnett 125) [1995 57: 8m 7g 57 1996 7m⁵ 6.9g a8.5g Dec 28] good-topped filly: modest maiden: below from after reappearance: should stay 1m. *Miss Gay Kelleway*

HAZY DAYZ 2 gr.f. (Mar 30) Today And Tomorrow 78 – Mossaka (FR) – (Targowice (USA) 130) [1996 a6g⁶ Jun 6] 3,600Y: sixth living foal: dam French maiden: slowly away when tailed off in seller at Southwell. *D. C. O'Brien*

HEAD GARDENER (IRE) 2 b. or br.c. (Apr 5) Be My Chief (USA) 122 – Silk 73 Petal 105 (Petorius 117) [1996 7.1m 7m⁴ 7f Jul 13] good-bodied colt: third foal: half-brother to 3-y-o 7f winner Satin Bell (by Midyan) and useful 6f winner (including at 2 yrs) Star Tulip (by Night Shift): dam 7f winner out of half-sister to

Irish St Leger winner M-Lolshan: given considerate ride all starts, showing fair form: will be suited by further than 7f: looked capable of better, but sold 6,500 gns New-market Autumn Sales. *J. L. Dunlop*

HEAD GIRL (IRE)   2 ch.f. (Feb 21) Masterclass (USA) 116 – Rebecca's Girl (IRE) (Nashamaa 113) [1996 6m³ 6g² 6m⁴ 7g⁵ 6g⁵ a7g² a8g⁶ Dec 3] IR 4,000F, 2,800Y: leggy filly: second foal: dam unraced: ridden differently when winning seller at Southwell in December, making most: stays 1m: acts on fibresand: flashes tail: looked none too keen when held up on all-weather. *C. W. Thornton*   63 d a48

HEAD OVER HEELS (IRE)   2 b.f. (Jan 19) Pursuit of Love 124 – Proudfoot (IRE) (Shareef Dancer (USA) 135) [1996 5m⁵ 5.1m* 5.2f³ 5.2g* 5.2m* 5g² 5m⁴ 6m² 5d Oct 12] 8,200Y: smallish, sturdy filly: second foal: half-sister to 3-y-o 7.5f winner (in Italy) Second Barrage (by Royal Academy): dam Irish 1¾m winner: useful form: successful in maiden at Chepstow, minor event at Yarmouth and Swettenham Stud St Hugh's Stakes (pipped Olympic Spirit in final strides) at Newbury: second in listed races at Deauville and Ayr (beaten 2 lengths by Queen Sceptre) afterwards: stays 6f: acts on firm ground, ran poorly on dead: has been bandaged behind: sold 70,000 gns Newmarket December Sales. *J. H. M. Gosden*   96

HEART   3 ch.f. Cadeaux Genereux 131 – Recipe 66 (Bustino 136) [1995 NR 1996 10.1g⁴ 10m⁵ 12.3d² 13.4g² 14m⁴ 12s a12g⁵ Nov 30] sparely-made filly: second foal: half-sister to 4-y-o Signal (by Warning), successful at up to 1¾m in Scandinavia: dam stoutly-bred maiden but form only at up to 1¼m: fairly useful maiden handicapper: stays 13.4f: acts on fibresand: possibly needs give in the ground on turf: sold (M. Stoute to Miss H. Knight) 17,000 gns Newmarket December Sales. *M. R. Stoute*   82

HEART FULL OF SOUL   2 ch.g. (Feb 14) Primo Dominie 121 – Scales of Justice 85 (Final Straw 127) [1996 5m 5m 6m 7g² 8f* 8g 7.3s³ Oct 26] 4,600F: plain, good-topped gelding: first foal: dam untrustworthy 1m/9f winner, stayed 1¼m: made all in 20-runner nursery at Warwick in October: stays 1m: acts on firm and soft going: effective blinkered or not: strong-running sort, suited by forcing tactics. *P. F. I. Cole*   74 +

HEART LAKE   5 ch.h. Nureyev (USA) 131 – My Darling One (USA) (Exclusive Native (USA)) [1995 117: a8g* 7f⁵ 8f* 6g 1996 7g² 7m² a8g⁴ 7f* 8f 8m Jul 31] good-topped, attractive horse: smart performer: ran creditably in Dubai first 3 starts in 1996 before winning an extremely valuable international event (as he had in 1995) at Tokyo in May on first of 2 runs in Japan: 40/1, looked extremely well but raced too freely when soundly beaten in Sussex Stakes at Goodwood final start: stayed 1m: acted on firm and soft ground, and on sand: genuine: sold to stand at stud in Japan. *Saeed bin Suroor*   117

HEART OF ARMOR   2 b.c. (Apr 2) Tirol 127 – Hemline 77 (Sharpo 132) [1996 7g³ 8f³ 7m⁴ Sep 11] 25,000Y: fourth foal: half-brother to 6f winner (probably stays 1¼m) Pirates Gold (by Vaigly Great): dam, 7f winner who stayed 1m, is out of useful 1½m winner Ma Femme, a half-sister to Acclimatise: similar form when third in maidens at Kempton and Brighton first 2 starts: modest effort at Epsom final outing: stays 1m. *P. F. I. Cole*   78

HEART OF GOLD (IRE)   2 ch.c. (Apr 22) Broken Hearted 124 – Originality (Godswalk (USA) 130) [1996 8.1m⁶ 7.9g Oct 9] IR 15,000F, 9,400Y: leggy, sparely-made colt: sixth foal: brother to smart 6-y-o 1¼m to 1¾m performer Key To My Heart and half-brother to 7f and 1m winner Secundus (by Neshad): dam lightly raced: stayed on steadily from rear, not knocked about, in median auction maidens: will do better in due course over middle distances. *Miss S. E. Hall*   64 p

HEART THROB   2 b.f. (Feb 28) Statoblest 120 – Lets Fall In Love (USA) (Northern Baby (CAN) 127) [1996 5f² 5m* 6m⁶ 7g Oct 26] 5,000F, 12,500Y: close-coupled filly: half-sister to 3-y-o Heights of Love (by Persian Heights) and a winner in Italy by Tank's Prospect: dam minor winner in USA: fairly useful form: won maiden at Lingfield in October: sold 11,500 gns Newmarket Autumn Sales: should stay 7f: sent to Holland. *W. J. Haggas*   79

HEATHYARDS JADE   3 b.f. Damister (USA) 123 – French Cooking 70 (Royal And Regal (USA)) [1995 NR 1996 a6g a8.5g⁵ Feb 21] half-sister to 1992 2-y-o 7f and 8.1f winner Heathyards Boy (by Sayf El Arab) and 1m winner Parc des Princes (by Anfield): dam 2m winner: no promise in median auction maiden and seller. *R. Hollinshead*   –

HEATHYARDS LADY (USA) 5 b.m. Mining (USA) – Dubiously (USA) 59
(Jolie Jo (USA)) [1995 61, a74: a7g⁴ a6g³ a6g³ a6g a6g³ a6g² a7g⁴ a7g* a8.5g² 7m³ a72
7g* a9.4g³ 8g a8.5g* a7g* a8.5g⁵ a7g⁶ 1996 8m⁶ a7g⁵ a9.4g³ 7.5m⁵ 7.1m⁴ 8.2m
a9.4g a9.4g³ a9.4g⁴ a9.4g⁴ Oct 5] leggy mare: fair handicapper on all-weather, only
modest on turf: effective at 6f to 9.4f: acts on any turf ground, goes well on fibresand.
R. Hollinshead

HEATHYARDS MAGIC (IRE) 4 b.g. Magical Strike (USA) 114 – Idle 62 d
Gossip (Runnett 125) [1995 68d: a6g* 7.6m 8f² 7g³ a8.5g⁴ 8f³ 10m 8f 1996 7s 9.2d²
6.9d⁵ 8.3s 10.2g⁶ 9.2g⁵ 12.3m 12s⁶ 10m a8.5g Jul 26] tall gelding: showed little in
1996 after second outing: sold 950 gns Ascot August Sales: looked reluctant in
blinkers third start, tried visored ninth. *M. Dods*

HEATHYARDS PEARL (USA) 2 gr. or ro.f. (Mar 12) Mining (USA) – Dance 65
Dance Dance (IRE) (Dance of Life (USA)) [1996 6m⁴ 6d⁴ 6m⁶ 7g a6g⁶ Dec 7] IR
14,000Y: leggy, close-coupled filly: first foal: dam, French 9.5f winner, half-sister to
top-class American colt (won 1¼m Travers Stakes) General Assembly: modest form:
well below best last 2 starts: below form afterwards: stays 6f: acts on good to firm
and dead ground: reluctant at stalls third start. *R. Hollinshead*

HEATHYARDS ROCK 4 br.g. Rock City 120 – Prudence 68 (Grundy 137) 82
[1995 96d: a8.5g* 9g² 9d² 9m⁶ 10.3m⁵ a9.4g² 10.5g 10.3m³ a9.4g⁵ 10m⁶ 10.3g⁴
12d 10g 11.9d⁵ a12g⁶ 1996 a12g* a12g* a12g* a12g² a16g² Apr 9] tall, unfurnished
gelding: won 3 claimers at Southwell early in 1996: not discredited at 2m, very best
form at 1½m: acts on good to firm and dead ground and on fibresand: tried blinkered/
visored, no improvement: has refused to race over hurdles. *R. Hollinshead*

HEATHYARDS ROSE (IRE) 3 b.f. Conquering Hero (USA) 116 – Another –
Gayle (Tumble Wind (USA)) [1995 NR 1996 a6g a7g a8g Apr 29] first foal: dam ran
twice in Ireland: well beaten in maidens on the all-weather. *R. Hollinshead*

HEAVENLY DANCER 2 b.f. (Feb 11) Warrshan (USA) 117 – High Halo 64 52 ?
(High Top 131) [1996 7g 6.9m² a7g⁶ 10f Oct 14] sixth foal: half-sister to fairly useful
7f/1m performer High Premium (by Forzando) and a winner abroad by Formidable:
dam thrice-raced 1m winner, would have stayed further: modest form in maiden and
seller first 2 starts: subsequently left Mark Prescott's yard: well held for new stable:
should be suited by further than 7f. *Mrs N. Macauley*

HEAVENLY HAND 2 ch.f. (Mar 29) Out of Hand 84 – My Home 61 (Homing –
130) [1996 a7g a8g Dec 20] 525Y: fourth foal, all by Out of Hand: dam stayed 1m:
behind in seller and maiden. *A. Moore*

HEAVENLY MISS (IRE) 2 b.f. (Apr 21) Anita's Prince 126 – Heavenly 71
Blessed (Monseigneur (USA) 127) [1996 5g 6.1d² 6m⁶ a6g² 6m* 6m 6.1m* 6d⁴ 6s³ a68
6.1s⁵ a6g a5g* a6g² a6g⁴ Dec 31] 2,700Y: unfurnished filly: third foal: dam unraced:
fair form: won seller at Leicester in August (sold out of B. Palling's stable 9,000 gns),
and nurseries at Nottingham (penultimate outing for D. Burchell) in September and
Lingfield in December: stays 6.1f: acts on good to firm and soft ground, and on
equitrack: none too consistent. *J. J. Bridger*

HEAVENLY RAY (USA) 2 ch.f. (May 28) Rahy (USA) 115 – Highest Truth –
(USA) (Alydar (USA)) [1996 6m Aug 4] $52,000Y: second foal: dam, won at up to
9f in USA, sister to Grade 2 13f winner Buckley Boy out of very smart performer
at up to 1¼m Plankton: ran green and mostly towards rear in maiden at Lingfield.
J. R. Fanshawe

HEAVEN SENT (IRE) 3 b.f. Fayruz 116 – Folle Remont (Prince Tenderfoot –
(USA) 126) [1995 52+: 5m 5m⁴ 6m 5m 5m⁶ 1996 a7g⁶ Feb 8] modest maiden: best
form at 5f: dead. *P. Mitchell*

HEE'S A DANCER 4 b.g. Rambo Dancer (CAN) 107 – Heemee 81 (On Your 36
Mark 125) [1995 41: 8m⁵ 10m 8g 1996 9.9g⁶ Aug 24] small, leggy gelding: poor
maiden: stays 1¼m: acts on good to firm ground: sold 7,000 gns Doncaster October
Sales. *M. J. Camacho*

HEGGIES (IRE) 2 b.c. (Jan 29) High Estate 127 – Princess Pavlova (IRE) 60 +
(Sadler's Wells (USA) 132) [1996 5d 6g⁵ a6g 8g 8g³ a8.5g Nov 11] 7,500F, 5,800Y:
smallish, lengthy colt: has a round action: first foal: dam unraced sister to smart
middle-distance stayer Parthian Springs out of Irish Oaks winner Princess Pati: third

of 21 to Aficionado in seller at Newmarket: better suited by 1m than shorter and will stay further: no form on fibresand: blinkered final start. *C. R. Egerton*

HEIGHTH OF FAME   5 b.g. Shirley Heights 130 – Land of Ivory (USA) 109   –
(The Minstrel (CAN) 135) [1995 47: 8g³ 10.8m⁶ a12g² 1996 a12g⁶ a12g⁴   a76
a13g* a16g² a12g² a16g a12g³ a14.8g² a16.2g⁶ a12g* a12g² a13g* Nov 26] fair
handicapper: won seller at Lingfield in February: trained until after tenth start by
A. J. Wilson: second spell with current trainer: won at Wolverhampton (seller) in
September and Lingfield in November: stays 2m: acts on the all-weather: races up
with pace: game. *D. Burchell*

HEIGHTS OF LOVE   3 b.f. Persian Heights 129 – Lets Fall In Love (USA)   –
(Northern Baby (CAN) 127) [1995 51?: 5m 5m⁵ 5.1m⁴ 5.7m 5s 1996 5m 5.1g 7m 7f
6.1m Sep 24] neat filly: little worthwhile form in 1996: left M. Saunders' stable after
second start: often looks headstrong. *J. W. Hills*

HELEN OF SPAIN   4 b.f. Sadler's Wells (USA) 132 – Port Helene 107 (Troy   116
137) [1995 12d³ 1996 12g⁶ 10.5d* 15m³ 15d* 13.5g* 12.5g⁴ 15.5d³ Oct 27] second
living foal: half-sister to French 9.5f winner Sea of Clouds (by Soviet Star): dam, 1m
(at 2 yrs) and 1½m winner, out of half-sister to Night Off (rated 124, 1000 Guineas
winner): smart French middle-distance stayer: won minor event at Evry in March:
2½ lengths third of 12 to Double Eclipse in Prix de Barbeville at Longchamp: won
listed event at Maisons-Laffitte in July and 6-runner Prix de Pomone (beat
Camporese short neck) at Deauville in August: improved again when 1¼ lengths
fourth of 9 to Strategic Choice in Grand Prix de Deauville and 1¼ lengths third of 5
to Red Roses Story in slowly-run Prix Royal-Oak at Longchamp: stayed at least
15.5f: never raced on extremes of going: retired. *A. Fabre, France*

HELIOS   8 br.g. Blazing Saddles (AUS) – Mary Sunley 62 (Known Fact (USA)   68
135) [1995 79d: 7f 7m³ 8g³ 7m⁵ 7g 8.1m⁵ 7.1d 8s 1996 a8g 7d 8f 8f 8g 8f* 8m*
8.2m⁴ 7.6m 8f* 8f³ 8.1f⁶ 8.5m 8d⁴ Oct 2] leggy, angular gelding: unimpressive
mover: fair handicapper: won at Brighton (goes well on switchback tracks), Newbury and Salisbury (apprentices, awarded race) in the summer: ran well final start:
best form at 7f to 1m: acts on firm and dead going: blinkered (ran creditably) once as
5-y-o: often apprentice ridden: none too consistent. *N. J. H. Walker*

HELISSIO (FR)   3 b.c. Fairy King (USA) – Helice (USA) (Slewpy (USA))   136
[1995 NR 1996 10d* 11f* 10.5g* 12m⁵ 12m* 12m* 12d* 12f³ Nov 24]
'Made all, unchallenged' is not the way many racing fans would expect
to see a Prix de l'Arc de Triomphe won in their lifetime. The race has long been
too strongly contested for there to be more than the slimmest chance of that. Yet
in 1996 the French three-year-old Helissio made all, was never challenged, and
won by five lengths with the jockey having time to look round for his lost cap a
hundred yards from the finish, then standing up in the irons, waving. The
winning margin would have been greater had Helissio been ridden out. As it
was, on examination the actual margin could be seen to be a length over the
judge's five. Ribot in 1956 and Sea Bird II in 1965 had won the Arc by six
lengths; they are widely acknowledged as two of the best middle-distance
horses of modern times, regarded by some as the best two, rated by *Racehorses*
at 142 and 145 respectively.
Naturally, Helissio's victory invited comparisons. Those most closely
connected with him tended to take a very positive view of his merit. Winning
jockey Olivier Peslier, who explained his arm-waving as imitating a helicopter
(helice is rotor blade in French), claimed he could probably have won by
eight to ten lengths had he tried. Winning trainer Elie Lellouche reportedly
commented: 'I think this was probably as good as Sea Bird when he won a long
way.' Then on reflection he added: 'Maybe he is not a Sea Bird but he is
certainly the second-best horse that I have seen.' Others, on the whole, tended
to be more restrained. Our considered view is that the winner's performance in
the race was marginally the best since Dancing Brave's length-and-a-half
defeat of the previously-unbeaten Prix du Jockey-Club winner Bering in 1986,
but not so good as that one, nor those of Vaguely Noble, Mill Reef, Rheingold
and Alleged, which rank with Dancing Brave's as outstanding since Sea Bird's

Prix Lupin, Longchamp—Helissio wins, but Loup Solitaire gets to within three quarters of a length

day. At present we would rate Helissio a very good Arc winner rather than a great one, and in doing so would argue these points—one, that the runner-up Pilsudski was not yet in his Breeders' Cup form; two, that the Arc line-up was just average in strength; and three, that on the day several of its better members either did not get the run of the race or failed signally to do themselves justice.

While just average by Arc standards, the field was thoroughly representative of top European form. Down the card it read: the four-year-old colts Swain, Tamure, Classic Cliche, Oscar Schindler, Pilsudski, Leeds and Pentire; the three-year-old colts Shaamit, Radevore, Darazari, Polaris Flight, Le Destin, Zagreb and Helissio; and the three-year-old fillies Luna Wells and Leonila. Both fillies and some of the colts seemed to have plenty to find, and Tamure was having his first race since finishing fourth in the Breeders' Cup Turf in 1995, but in the current season Swain had won the Coronation Cup, Classic Cliche the Gold Cup before finishing second to Pentire in the King George VI And Queen Elizabeth Diamond Stakes, Oscar Schindler the Irish St Leger, Pilsudski the Grosser Preis von Baden, Shaamit the Derby and Zagreb the Irish Derby. Then there was Helissio.

Helissio started a hot favourite, a single reverse in a six-race career put well behind him by now. That reverse had come in the Prix du Jockey-Club at Chantilly in June in which, at even money, he had dead-heated for fifth place behind Ragmar, Polaris Flight, Le Destin and Don Micheletto, having had little left after pulling extremely hard, seeming to have resented being restrained for well over a mile. The build-up to the Jockey-Club couldn't have gone better for Helissio. A ten-length winner of a newcomers' race at Evry in March, he progressed to an easy four-length win in a five-runner Prix Noailles and again to a three-quarter-length win from the strong-finishing 1995 Grand Criterium winner Loup Solitaire in a five-runner Prix Lupin. The Noailles and the Lupin are classic trials staged at Longchamp, the Lupin most years having an important bearing on the outcome of the Jockey-Club.

Helissio soon redeemed his reputation. Before June was out he came through his stiffest test up to that point in the Grand Prix de Saint-Cloud. No horse was a better yardstick at this level in France than Swain, who started at

Grand Prix de Saint-Cloud—a first meeting with his elders sees Helissio outpoint Swain and Poliglote

Forte Meridien Prix de l'Arc de Triomphe, Longchamp—Helissio with staggering ease;
Pilsudski holds on for second from Oscar Schindler and Swain

odds on in a field of nine following his recent victory at Epsom. Having settled in behind the leader, another good French four-year-old Poliglote, Helissio began to challenge early in the straight, mastered him over two furlongs out and then proved too strong for Swain, the pair drawing clear of Poliglote on the run to the line where Helissio was comfortably a length to the good, five ahead of Poliglote who held on to third from some smart opponents. Ragmar finished a disappointing seventh, never to be seen out again. Helissio himself was not seen out again until September, when taking a well-trodden route to the Arc in the Prix Niel at Longchamp. The disappointment in the Jockey-Club had led to Dominic Boeuf's replacement by new French idol Peslier as Helissio's jockey at Saint-Cloud. With Peslier in the saddle again in the Niel, Helissio gave a glimpse of what was soon to follow, pulling off a smooth front-running success, setting a sensible pace to eight opponents, responding well when shaken up and never being in danger. Darazari and Radevore chased him home at one length and a further one and a half lengths, Darazari looking slightly unlucky in running and the winner attracting the bulk of post-race support for the Arc at quotes of around 7/2.

Helissio had been backed down to 18/10 by the time the Arc got underway. Stunningly, by the time he turned into the straight he looked 100/1-on, the contest as good as decided barring accidents. Although not taken on for the lead, he had set a sound gallop and had had most of the field on the stretch coming down the hill into the final turn. He turned two lengths up on Pilsudski, who had tracked him throughout, and when asked to quicken he soon drew right away. Pilsudski battled on to preserve second; harried by Zagreb, Leonila, Radevore and a whole pack of horses into the straight, he got no respite in the closing stages as Oscar Schindler, weaving a way through from well back, and Swain finished strongly. Luna Wells in fifth, Le Destin in sixth, Leeds (just behind Shaamit) in eighth, and Leonila in ninth, appeared to excel themselves, while Pentire in tenth, Zagreb in thirteenth, Tamure in fourteenth and Classic Cliche in fifteenth and last (Polaris Flight having broken a leg) were those who signally failed to do themselves justice.

Offers came in thick and fast for the winner afterwards, rising quickly from eight million dollars to twenty-five million. All were rejected. One week on, owner Enrique Sarasola's racing manager was reported as saying: 'The owner has refused a firm offer for one hundred per cent of Helissio, and it is now virtually a pre-condition of sale that the horse stays in training next year and that Mr Sarasola keeps fifty per cent of him. This is because Mr Sarasola believes it's a good thing for racing and for the public to see the horse race for another year.' Would that more owners of top horses were so philanthropic. Even Helissio's current season was not yet over. Although he missed the Breeders' Cup, and plans for a ten-million-dollar match with Cigar in Japan fell through, he went on show in Tokyo in the Japan Cup in late-November. No Arc winner had succeeded in fifteen previous runnings of the Japan Cup. Tony Bin had come fifth in 1988, Carroll House fourteenth in 1989 and Urban Sea eighth in 1993. Not even Helissio could buck the trend, but while he could not reproduce his Arc form and did not dominate—he raced prominently and was going easily in second-of-fifteen position at the head of the straight—he was by no means disgraced in dead-heating for third with Strategic Choice on firm

420

Mr E. Sarasola's "Helissio"

ground, a little over a length behind the winner Singspiel. Helissio was returned to France, and at the time of writing is set to race on. Whatever his fate in the Dubai World Cup, should he take up his engagement, it will take a very good three-year-old to beat him on turf at his best.

			Northern Dancer	Nearctic
Helissio (FR) (b.c. 1993)	Fairy King (USA) (b 1982)		(b 1961)	Natalma
		Fairy Bridge	Bold Reason
		(b 1975)	Special
	Helice (USA) (b 1988)	Slewpy	Seattle Slew
		(b or br 1980)	Rare Bouquet
		Hirondelle	Val de L'Orne
		(b 1981)	Hermanville

There was a poignant footnote to Sea Bird's Arc when research unearthed that his dam had ended up being sold as butcher's meat for £100. Helissio's victory sparked off a hunt for the latest winner's dam, the young mare Helice, who had last been sighted in France in 1993 when she and the eleven-month-old Helissio had passed through the Deauville December Sales, Helice, in foal to Cricket Ball, fetching 71,000 francs and her son, her first foal, 350,000 francs, sums equivalent in sterling of approximately £8,000 and £39,700 respectively. The trail led to Saudi Arabia and ended there when the Equestrian Club in Riyadh revealed that Helice had died of colic in 1996 leaving behind a two-year-old colt by Cricket Ball and a yearling colt by Power Lunch. Helice had gone one better than Sea Bird's dam on the racecourse by winning, over a mile as a two-year-old in a newcomers event at Longchamp. She was quite highly tried afterwards, lightly raced, and did not live up to expectations, but her record was one of her better selling points in the Deauville catalogue. Her family is an American one, not particularly distinguished though her grandam Hermanville was rated within 8 lb of the top two-year-old fillies in the Experimental Free Handicap of 1978. Hermanville's daughter, the once-raced Hirondelle, was exported from France to Argentina in 1992 having produced six winners, none significantly better than Helice who is by Slewpy, the American Grade 1 winner well beaten in the Derby in 1983.

Slewpy has made his mark as a sire of sprinters—Mr Nickerson among them—and with him for a grandsire and Fairy King as his sire Helissio was regarded as a doubtful stayer until he won the Grand Prix de Saint-Cloud. That win came on good to firm ground as did the win in the Niel, while both the Lupin and the Japan Cup were run on firm. The Arc was run on good to soft. At this stage of his career, then, there are no hard and fast conclusions to be drawn about Helissio's ground requirements; thus far, he has shown high-class form on firm, exceptional form on good to soft. Helissio is a tall colt, notably well balanced for one of his size and virtually guaranteed to act at Epsom should he be sent over for the Coronation Cup. British racegoers live in hope that they will see him there and at Ascot in the King George. *E. Lellouche, France*

HELLO DOLLY (IRE) 2 b.f. (Apr 14) Mujadil (USA) 119 – Great Leighs 87 (Vaigly Great 127) [1996 5s² 5g³ 5g⁶ 5f² a5g⁴ 6g* 6m⁴ 7f⁴ 7.1m² 8f³ 8g 8g⁶ a8.5g* a8.5g* a8g⁴ Dec 11] 4,100Y: leggy, sparely-made filly: fifth foal: half-sister to 3-y-o Poly Static (by Statoblest), 1993 2-y-o 7f winner Rose Ciel (by Red Sunset) and 6-y-o miler Embankment (by Tate Gallery): dam 1m winner: trained by K. Ivory first 4 starts: fair performer: successful in claimer at Newcastle in May and 2 nurseries at Wolverhampton in November: stays 8.5f: acts on any going, including all-weather: often claimer ridden. *K. R. Burke* 61 a69

HELLO (IRE) 2 b.c. (Mar 23) Lycius (USA) 124 – Itqan (IRE) 92 (Sadler's Wells (USA) 132) [1996 6g* 6f⁵ 7f² 7.1g⁴ 8g² 8d* 8s* 8f* Nov 30] IR 19,000F, 33,000Y: rather leggy, unfurnished colt: first foal: dam, 11.9f to 14.8f winner, stayed 2m: won maiden at Doncaster in May and listed race at Goodwood: ran away with listed race (beat White Gulch 9¼ lengths) and 10-runner Gran Criterium (by 3½ lengths from Panama City) at Milan in October: sold privately out of J. Dunlop's stable and narrowly won Grade 3 event at Hollywood Park in November: will stay beyond 1m: acts on any going. *R. McAnally, USA* 112 +

HELLO MISTER 5 b.h. Efisio 120 – Ginnies Petong (Petong 126) [1995 106: 7m 5g 6g 5g 6f 5.1m³ 5m 5m⁴ 6m 6g³ 5.6m* 6d 7d 5s⁴ 6m² 1996 5.1g⁶ 6m 6m⁵ 6g⁶ 6f Jun 1] sturdy, good-quartered horse: useful performer: effective at 5f and 6f: acts on good to firm and soft ground: often sweating and edgy: suited by waiting tactics, and usually ridden by P. McCabe: side-lined with split hoof, but reportedly remains in training. *T. E. Powell* 101

HELLO PETER (IRE) 4 b.g. Taufan (USA) 119 – Apple Rings 97 (Godswalk (USA) 130) [1995 49: 8d 8.5m⁴ 11.5g⁵ 1996 a11g⁶ Jan 5] unfurnished gelding: poor maiden: will probably prove best at up to 1¼m. *M. H. Tompkins* –

HELLO THERE 2 b.g. (Mar 18) Picea 99 – Estonia (Kings Lake (USA) 133) [1996 7g 6m 6m⁵ Oct 2] 3,000Y: second foal: half-brother to 3-y-o 10.8f winner Cry Baby (by Bairn): dam Irish 11f winner: always behind in maidens. *N. Tinkler* –

HELSINGOR (IRE) 3 b.g. Danehill (USA) 126 – Assya (Double Form 130) [1995 6d² 1996 8g 7d² 7m 6m³ 7g² 8d* 8.5m² 10d 9g Oct 5] medium-sized, good-topped gelding: sixth foal: half-brother to 1992 2-y-o 7f winner Prevene (by Alzao): dam unraced granddaughter of Never Too Late: useful form: 66/1 and wrong in coat, 6¾ lengths seventh of 16 to Lucayan Prince in Jersey Stakes at Royal Ascot: won maiden at Tralee in August: stays 9f: acts on good to firm and dead ground: probably effective blinkered or not. *T. Stack, Ireland* 96

HENCARLAM (IRE) 3 b.g. Astronef 116 – War Ballad (FR) (Green Dancer (USA) 132) [1995 –: 9m 8.1d 1996 10g 12g Aug 6] tall, angular gelding: little sign of ability: left M. Channon after reappearance. *V. T. O'Brien, Ireland* –

HEN HARRIER 2 ch.f. (Feb 8) Polar Falcon (USA) 126 – Circus Feathers 99 (Kris 135) [1996 6m² 6.9g* 7f² 7m³ 8m⁵ 7m Oct 1] 24,000F, 30,000Y: lengthy, unfurnished filly: has a quick action: second foal: closely related to Italian 3-y-o 6f 78 winner Time And Time (by Soviet Star): dam 1m and 9f winner, daughter of Oaks winner Circus Plume: fairly useful form: won maiden at Folkestone in July: placed afterwards in minor event at Thirsk and nursery at Newmarket: stays 1m: hung left second start, right on third. *J. L. Dunlop*

HENLEY (USA) 2 b.c. (Feb 8) Salem Drive (USA) – Leap of The Heart (USA) 83 p (Nijinsky (CAN) 138) [1996 a6g a7s* Nov 19] ninth foal: half-brother to several minor winners in North America: dam, won at up to 1¼m in North America, half-sister to Gold And Ivory: jockey reported his left foot was out of the stirrup iron as race began on debut: made all in maiden at Lingfield later in November: will stay middle distances: can do better still. *D. R. Loder*

HENRY ISLAND (IRE) 3 ch.c. Sharp Victor (USA) 114 – Monterana 99 97 (Sallust 134) [1995 –p: a8.5g⁴ 1996 8.2d³ 8g² 8d* 8f 10g⁵ 10m 10d² 10m⁴ 12g* Oct 26] workmanlike colt: good mover: useful performer: won median auction event at Leicester in May: ridden by 7-lb claimer, improved form upped in trip final start, winning 19-runner £12,200 event at Doncaster, quickening clear 2f out and holding on by short head from Wild Rita: unlikely to stay beyond 1½m: best efforts with give in the ground: tends to sweat (has run well when doing so). *G. Wragg*

HENRY OTIS 3 ch.g. Savahra Sound 111 – Seenachance 69 (King of Clubs 124) – [1995 5g⁶ 5g⁵ 7.8f³ 7.8f⁶ 1996 8f 7m 8m 10f⁴ 12g Jul 31] 5,000Y: ex-Irish gelding: first foal: dam, maiden who should have stayed 1¼m, daughter of half-sister to Champion Stakes winner Giacometti: trained at 2 yrs (rated 65) by G. Lyons: well beaten in handicaps in Britain: has raced only on a sound surface. *R. Akehurst*

HENRY THE FIFTH 3 b.c. Village Star (FR) 131 – Microcosme 100 (Golden 102 Fleece (USA) 133) [1995 92: 7m⁴ 7g 7.6d² 7s² 8d* 8m⁴ 6d⁵ 1996 8g⁴ 7d⁴ 10g³ 8f 12.5d 10s a8g Dec 5] leggy, workmanlike colt: poor mover: useful performer: in frame in listed race at Kempton, Greenham Stakes at Newbury and Prix La Force at Deauville first 3 outings: soundly beaten last 4 starts: stays 1¼m: acts on good to firm and soft ground: blinkered (out of form) final 3-y-o start: has had rope halter for stalls entry. *C. E. Brittain*

HENRY THE HAWK 5 b.g. Doulab (USA) 115 – Plum Blossom (USA) 53 (Gallant Romeo (USA)) [1995 51: a6g a5g a6g 5d⁵ 5m 6g 6m³ 5g³ 5d* 5f³ 6m² 5f⁴ 5g 6m³ 5h 6g 1996 5.9d* 5s* 5m⁵ 6g⁶ 6g⁴ 5g⁵ 7m 6g⁴ 6m 5g² 6d a6g Nov 4] small gelding: modest handicapper: successful at Carlisle (25/1 and claimer ridden) in April and Hamilton (made all from favourable draw in amateurs race) in May: stays 6f: acts on all-weather surfaces and on firm and soft ground: effective visored or not, blinkered final start: usually bandaged. *M. Dods*

HENRY WESTON 4 b.c. Statoblest 120 – Young Tearaway 90 (Young Gene- – ration 129) [1995 –: 6g 6m a6g a7g 1996 a7g Jan 19] strong colt: poor mover: no sign of ability. *P. Howling*

HERBSHAN DANCER 2 b.c. (Apr 12) Warrshan (USA) 117 – Herbary (USA) 59 ? (Herbager 136) [1996 6m 7m⁶ 7f⁵ 7f⁶ 7m Aug 26] 500Y: half-brother to fair 1¼m winner Slix (by High Top): dam never ran: seemed to show modest form second and third starts but is probably just a plater: will be better suited by test of stamina. *B. R. Millman*

HERE COMES A STAR 8 b.g. Night Shift (USA) – Rapidus (Sharpen Up 127) 80 d [1995 78: 5m 5m³ 6d 6m⁵ 6f⁴ 6m 6m 6m⁴ 5m* 6m³ 5m⁴ 5h* 6m 5g 5d 5d² 5m³ 5f 1996 5m³ 5g 5g³ 5m⁶ 6d³ 5m⁴ 5g⁶ 5m⁴ 6m 6f 6f⁴ 5g³ 5m 5g 5m³ 6m Oct 23] sturdy, lengthy gelding: has a round action: fair handicapper: better form in first half of 1996 than in second: effective at 5f and 6f: acts on hard and dead ground: blinkered (well below form) earlier in career: best with waiting tactics. *J. M. Carr*

HERE COMES HERBIE 4 ch.g. Golden Lahab (USA) – Megan's Move 36 42 (Move Off 112) [1995 –: 8m 12f 11f 1996 8g 7d⁶ 11.1g⁵ 11.1g² 12g* 11.9m⁴ 12f² 12.3m⁴ 12.1f⁶ Aug 19] poor handicapper: won at Catterick in June: will stay further than 1½m: acts on firm ground: usually apprentice ridden. *W. Storey*

HERECOMESTHEKNIGHT 2 b.g. (Mar 15) Thatching 131 – Storm Riding 74 (USA) (Storm Bird (CAN) 134) [1996 5g* 5m² 5m² 5m Jun 7] leggy, useful-looking gelding: good mover: third reported foal: dam (ran once in USA) daughter of half-sister to Kentucky Derby and Belmont winner Bold Forbes: won maiden at Kempton in April despite very slow start: broke leg at Epsom in June. *Martyn Meade*

HERE'S HONOUR (IRE) 4 ch.g. King of Clubs 124 – Coronea (High Line – 125) [1995 NR 1996 a7g Jan 12] fourth reported foal: half-brother to 1992 2-y-o 5f winner Jarena (by Jareer): dam, maiden who stayed 2m, is half-sister to smart middle-distance performer Sabre Dance: 16/1, always behind in seller at Southwell. *R. Bastiman*

HERE'S TO HOWIE (USA) 2 b.c. (Apr 26) Hermitage (USA) – Choice 76 Comment (USA) (Rich Cream (USA)) [1996 7f³ 7.6m⁴ 8s⁶ Nov 9] $15,000Y resold 9,800Y, 24,000 2-y-o: tall, leggy colt: first foal: dam won at up to 9f in USA: sire (by Storm Bird) unraced close relative of Sadler's Wells: fair maiden: should stay 1m. *R. Hannon*

HERETICAL MISS 6 br.m. Sayf El Arab (USA) 127 – Silent Prayer 58 – (Queen's Hussar 124) [1995 NR 1996 10f 12f 13.1f Jul 8] poor maiden plater: sometimes blinkered at 3 yrs, but no improvement. *J. Ffitch-Heyes*

HERITAGE 2 b.c. (Mar 19) Danehill (USA) 126 – Misty Halo 93 (High Top 131) 76 p [1996 8m⁴ Sep 25] 58,000Y: seventh foal: half-brother to 4 winners, including fairly useful 11f to 2m winner Finlaggan (by Be My Chief) and 1¼m to 1¾m winner Shifting Mist (by Night Shift): dam prolific winner from 1m to 2¼m: keeping-on fourth to Voyagers Quest in maiden at Goodwood: will improve given more of a test of stamina. *J. H. M. Gosden*

HERMANUS 2 b.g. (Mar 25) Lugana Beach 116 – Hitravelscene (Mansingh – (USA) 120) [1996 6g³ Oct 29] 7,200Y: brother to winning 3-y-o sprinter Tropical Beach, and half-brother to winning sprinter B Grade (by Lucky Wednesday): dam poor plater: remote fifth in median auction maiden at Leicester. *M. A. Jarvis*

HERODIAN (USA) 3 b. or br.c. Housebuster (USA) – Try Something New 91 (USA) (Hail The Pirates (USA) 126) [1995 81p: 6d² 1996 7.1g* 8m⁴ 9m⁴ 7.1f³ 8.5m 8.1v Oct 6] leggy, good-topped colt: shows a quick action: fairly useful performer at his best: won maiden at Haydock in April: creditable efforts in frame in handicaps third and fourth outings: sold 12,000 gns Newmarket Autumn Sales: stays 9f: acts on firm ground, well beaten on heavy final start: visored/blinkered since third 3-y-o start. *J. H. M. Gosden*

HERON ISLAND (IRE) 3 b.c. Shirley Heights 130 – Dalawara (IRE) (Top 114 Ville 129) [1995 99p: 8g* 7g⁴ 1996 9m⁶ 10m* 11.5f² 12m 12m* 14.6m 12m⁴ 14v* Nov 30] leggy colt: smart performer: won minor event at Salisbury in May: easily best efforts to win minor event at Newbury in August and listed event (by 2½ lengths from below-form Always Earnest) at Saint-Cloud in November: towards rear in St Leger: stays 1¾m, will probably get further: acts on any going: not especially reliable. *P. W. Chapple-Hyam*

HERONWATER (IRE) 3 b.f. Ela-Mana-Mou 132 – Water Girl (FR) 60 73 (Faraway Son (USA) 130) [1995 NR 1996 11.9d⁴ 14d³ Jun 7] quite attractive filly: seventh foal: half-sister to several winners, including smart French/US miler Girl of France (by Legend of France) and fairly useful Irish 10f winner Swift Tern (by Storm Bird); dam, French 3-y-o 7.5f winner on first of only 2 starts, is half-sister to Prix Vermeille winner Walensee: fair form when fourth in maiden at Haydock in May: favourite, appeared not to stay (cruised up to leader 3f out) in similar event there 2 weeks later: will prove best short of 1¾m. *M. Johnston*

HERR TRIGGER 5 gr.g. Sharrood (USA) 124 – Four-Legged Friend 101 82 (Aragon 118) [1995 77+: a10g⁴ a10g² a10g² 10m* 10f* 10m* 10m⁴ 1996 a10g² Mar 23] good-bodied gelding: has a markedly round action: fair handicapper: career best effort when second at Lingfield: stays 1¼m well: acts on firm ground and on equitrack: blinkered nowadays: carries head high: has won when sweating and edgy: consistent. *Dr J. D. Scargill*

HE'S A KING (USA) 6 b.g. Key To The Kingdom (USA) – She's A Jay – (USA) (Honey Jay (USA)) [1995 NR 1996 14m May 5] rated 76 at best in 1994 for J. Dunlop: well beaten only start in 1996: dead. *C. L. Popham*

HE'S GOT WINGS (IRE) 3 b.g. In The Wings 128 – Mariella 123 (Sir 62 Gaylord) [1995 –: 8.1s 8f 1996 8.2d 11.6m 14.1m a9.4g⁵ 10.8m² 10f⁵ 12.4m* 10.9m⁵ 16.1m* 17.1m Oct 7] smallish gelding: modest handicapper: trained until after reappearance by C. Broad: won at Newcastle in August (apprentice seller, sold out of M. Bell's stable for 6,800 gns) and October (improved form): suited by test of stamina: acts on good to firm ground, well beaten over inadequate trip on fibresand: visored/blinkered second to seventh 3-y-o starts: has been bandaged near-hind. *Mrs J. R. Ramsden*

HE'S MY LOVE (IRE)   3 ch.g. Be My Guest (USA) 126 – Taken By Force   62
(Persian Bold 123) [1995 NR 1996 10m 7m⁵ 7.5m⁶ 7.9g Sep 4] IR 9,000Y, 32,000
2-y-o: close-coupled, useful-looking gelding: seventh foal: brother to fairly useful
Irish 7f to 1½m winner Be My Hostage and half-brother to 2 winners, including 7f (at
2 yrs) to 1½m winner Hunter Valley (by Valiyar): dam Irish middle-distance winner:
modest maiden: off course 3½ months before final start: gives impression he'll be
suited by 1m+: sent to Kuwait. *J. E. Banks*

HEVER GOLF CHARGER (IRE)   2 b.g. (Feb 21) Silver Kite (USA) 111 –   60
Peace Carrier (IRE) (Doulab (USA) 115) [1996 5g 6m 6g³ 7f⁵ 6m² 6m a5g⁶ Nov
26] 12,000Y: close-coupled gelding: first foal: dam, placed over 1½m in Ireland,
half-sister to useful Irish sprinter Sandhurst Goddess: modest maiden: stays 6f: has
raced only on a sound surface on turf, acts on equitrack: refused to enter stalls once.
T. J. Naughton

HEVER GOLF CLASSIC   3 b. or br.g. Bustino 136 – Explosiva (USA) 88§   –
(Explodent (USA)) [1995 NR 1996 8d 10m⁵ 14g a12g Dec 27] 10,000Y: big, strong
gelding: bad mover: brother to 2 winners, including useful 1992 2-y-o 1m winner
Brockette, later third in Oaks d'Italia, and half-brother to several winners, including
fairly useful 1994 2-y-o 5f winner Quiz Time (by Efisio): dam 2-y-o 5f winner, bad
at start: well beaten in maidens: gelded. *T. J. Naughton*

HEVER GOLF DANCER   2 b.g. (Apr 29) Distant Relative 128 – Blue Rag 70   64
(Ragusa 137) [1996 6m 6.1m⁴ 6m⁵ a6g⁴ Dec 7] 11,000Y: half-brother to several
winners, including fair sprinter Blubella (by Balidar) and the dam of useful sprinters
Almost Blue and Golden Garter: dam won over 9f: modest maiden: best effort when
fourth of 10, hanging left, in auction race at Nottingham on second start: has been
gelded. *T. J. Naughton*

HEVER GOLF DIAMOND   3 b.g. Nomination 125 – Cadi Ha 109 (Welsh   52
Pageant 132) [1995 –: a7g 1996 a8g⁵ a7g 10g a12g² 10f a16g 10.1g³ 11m a12g a14g⁵
11.9f⁶ Sep 3] modest form at best: well beaten last 4 starts: sold to join J. Best 7,400
gns Doncaster November Sales: stays 1½m: acts on fibresand: none too reliable:
winning novice hurdler. *T. J. Naughton*

HEVER GOLF EAGLE   3 b.g. Aragon 118 – Elkie Brooks 82 (Relkino 131)   –
[1995 –: 7m 7m 1996 a6g a8g⁵ a7g³ a8g³ a10g² a8g⁶ 8.3s⁵ 8m 10g 10.1m a8g a8g³   a54
Dec 26] good-bodied gelding: modest maiden: barely stays 1¼m: best efforts on the
all-weather: blinkered (ran poorly) eighth 3-y-o start. *T. J. Naughton*

HEVER GOLF EXPRESS   3 b.g. Primo Dominie 121 – Everdene (Bustino   70
136) [1995 72: 5m 5m⁴ 5m* 6f⁵ 5m⁶ 1996 a6g² a5g⁵ 7m⁴ 7.1g³ 6g 5.7m* 5.3f³ 5m⁶   a75
Aug 26] lengthy gelding: fair performer: won claimer at Bath in August: best form at
up to 6f: acts on fibresand, has raced only on a sound surface on turf: front runner:
sent to Macau. *T. J. Naughton*

HEVER GOLF LADY   4 b.f. Dominion 123 – High Run (HOL) (Runnymede   62
123) [1995 59, a50: a9.4g³ a11g² a11g⁶ a12g³ a10g* a12g⁵ 12.5m⁵ a16g* 16d*   a50
15.4g² 16.1h² 11.8m³ a16g⁶ a16g⁴ a16g 1996 a5g³ 10.1m² 20f 14.9m⁵ 12g²
Jul 10] lengthy filly: modest handicapper: stays 2m well: acts on hard ground, dead
and the all-weather: has run creditably for lady. *T. J. Naughton*

HEVER GOLF LILY   2 ch.f. (Mar 24) Efisio 120 – Teresa Deevey 50 (Runnett   60
125) [1996 5.1d⁶ 6g⁴ 6m³ Jun 17] 7,000Y: strong, lengthy filly: has plenty of scope:
fourth foal: half-sister to 3-y-o Euro Express (by Domynsky), 1994 2-y-o 6f winner
Euro Rebel (by Roi Danzig) and 1992 2-y-o 7f winner Yeveed (by Wassl): dam
twice-raced 6f winner: stayed on when in frame in maiden auctions in summer: will
stay 7f: looked type to do better. *T. J. Naughton*

HEVER GOLF LOVER (IRE)   2 b.f. (Apr 27) Taufan (USA) 119 – Anagall   61
(USA) 81 (Irish River (FR) 131) [1996 5f 6f a6g a7g² a5g* Dec 31] IR 4,200Y:
angular filly: first foal: dam, placed at up to 7f in Ireland, half-sister to US stakes
winner at up to 9f and Grade 1-placed filly Here Comes The Bride: improving
steadily: won weak maiden event at Lingfield in December: will prove best up to 7f:
acts on equitrack: races prominently: may do better. *T. J. Naughton*

HEVER GOLF MAGIC (IRE) 2 ch.f. (Feb 12) Ballad Rock 122 – Track – Twenty Nine (IRE) (Standaan (FR) 118) [1996 7d a7s Nov 19] IR 11,000Y: tall, leggy filly: first foal: dam Irish 7f winner at 2 and 3 yrs: tailed off in maidens. *M. Johnston*

HEVER GOLF MOVER 2 ch.f. (May 5) Efisio 120 – Joyce's Best 58 (Tolomeo 66 127) [1996 5m⁴ 6m 5g a6g a8g³ a7g⁴ Dec 26] fourth foal: sister to 1993 2-y-o 6f winner Sixpees and half-sister to 3-y-o sprint winner Pharaoh's Joy (by Robellino): dam half-sister to Ormonde Stakes winner Zimbalon and Yorkshire Cup winner Band: modest form in maidens: stays 1m. *T. J. Naughton*

HEVER GOLF QUEEN 3 b.f. Efisio 120 – Blue Jane 81 (Blue Cashmere 129) – [1995 ?: 6m 6v 7.5g* 7.5d a7g⁵ 1996 a8g⁶ 9.2s⁵ 10.1m Oct 23] lengthy, good-quartered filly: won minor event in Sweden at 2 yrs: no worthwhile form in 6 races here and in France: stays 7.5f. *T. J. Naughton*

HEVER GOLF ROSE 5 b.m. Efisio 120 – Sweet Rosina 61 (Sweet Revenge 118 129) [1995 123: 7m³ 6s* 6d⁴ 6g³ 6s* 6m* 5f* 5m³ 6g* 6d* 6d* 5d* a6s 1996 5m 6g² 6g² 5f⁴ 6v² 6m³ 5m² 5m³ 6g² 6f⁴ 5.2m² 5d³ 5s³ Oct 13] small, strong, good-topped mare: has a quick action: smart performer: in frame last 12 starts, third to Pivotal in Nunthorpe Stakes at York and fourth to Iktamal in Haydock Park Sprint Cup on seventh and ninth: best of last 3 starts when 2¼ lengths third to Kistena in Prix de l'Abbaye de Longchamp: effective at 5f and 6f: acts on any going: often bandaged behind: effective from front or held up (has raced prominently of late): tough and game. *T. J. Naughton*

HEVER GOLF STAR 4 b.g. Efisio 120 – Truly Bold 76 (Bold Lad (IRE) 133) 78 [1995 78: 7g 5.3f* 6f⁵ 5m² 5m⁴ a5g² 1996 a5g* a5g³ Mar 14] sturdy, workmanlike gelding: fairly useful handicapper: won at Lingfield in January, making all: below-form when favourite there next time: speedy, and best at around 5f: acts on firm ground, yet to race on a soft surface, goes well on the all-weather. *T. J. Naughton*

HEVER GOLF STORMER (IRE) 2 b.c. (Apr 28) Mujadil (USA) 119 – 52 Clogher Head (Sandford Lad 133) [1996 6m 5.1m 5g 5m² 5f⁵ 5.1m³ 5m³ 6m³ a5g⁶ a42 a6g⁵ a7g⁴ Dec 27] IR 7,500F, 13,000Y: half-brother to three 2-y-o winners, including Irish Safari (by Kampala), 5f winner here and successful in 7.5f Group 3 event in Italy: dam twice-raced daughter of smart 1967 Irish 2-y-o Windy Gay: modest form in varied races on turf: looks poor at best on all-weather: stays 7f: acts on firm ground. *T. J. Naughton*

HEY UP DOLLY (IRE) 4 b.f. Puissance 110 – I Don't Mind 97 (Swing Easy – (USA) 126) [1995 68d: 6g 7m⁴ 7g* 7m 7.6m⁴ 7g 7.1g 8.1s 1996 8.3d 8m 11.1s⁵ May 3] compact filly: fair performer for Jack Berry in 1995: has lost her form: no improvement tried in blinkers. *J. J. O'Neill*

HIBERNATE (IRE) 2 ch.c. (Mar 7) Lahib (USA) 129 – Ministra (USA) (Deputy 75 p Minister (CAN)) [1996 8g³ Sep 14] rangy, slightly unfurnished colt: has scope: second foal: half-brother to 3-y-o 7f and 1m winner Strazo (by Alzao): dam French 12.5f winner, daughter of Irish 1000 Guineas and Irish Oaks winner Godetia: green, 1½ lengths third of 9 to Home Alone in maiden at Goodwood: will stay beyond 1m: will improve. *R. Charlton*

HIBERNICA (IRE) 2 b. or br.f. (Mar 13) Law Society (USA) 130 – Brave Ivy – 68 (Decoy Boy 129) [1996 6s Oct 24] 4,000F, 3,200Y leggy, unfurnished filly: seventh foal: half-sister to two 2-y-o winners, including 1991 6f winner International Star (by Astronef), and a winner in Belgium by Bairn: dam, placed here at 5f at 2 yrs, later winner at up to 7.5f in Italy: in need of run, soundly beaten in 23-runner maiden at Newbury. *G. B. Balding*

HICKLETON MISS 3 ch.f. Timeless Times (USA) 99 – Honest Opinion 68 58 ? (Free State 125) [1995 58: 5m⁶ 5f² 5f* 5g³ 5g² 5g 5m 6f 1996 5g a5g 6g⁵ 6g 5f⁵ 5m⁶ 6s⁶ 6g 6.1m a6g Nov 18] small, sparely-made filly: difficult to assess in 1996, appearing to run well (modest form) on third and sixth starts: stays 6f: sometimes slowly away: inconsistent. *Mrs V. A. Aconley*

HICKORY BLUE 6 ch.g. Clantime 101 – Blueit (FR) 101 (Bold Lad (IRE) 133) – [1995 72, a–: 5m* 5m 5g 5m⁶ 5m⁵ 5g⁵ 5m 5.1m³ 7f² a6g 1996 6.1m 5g 7g Oct 30] leggy gelding: fair handicapper at best: well beaten in 1996: effective at 5f, and stays

7f: acts on firm and dead going (probably on soft), has only modest form on fibre-sand: usually blinkered/visored: wears net muzzle. *K. A. Morgan*

HIDDEN MEADOW   2 b.c. (Apr 20) Selkirk (USA) 129 – Spurned (USA) 91   103 p
(Robellino (USA) 127) [1996 7m⁵ 7.9g* 7.3s³ Oct 24] lengthy, rather angular colt with a long stride: third foal: closely related to 3-y-o Jona Holley (by Sharpo) and half-brother to fairly useful sprinter Overbrook (by Storm Cat): dam stayed 1¼m: progressive form: dictated pace in steadily-run maiden at York in October, holding Teofilio (who raced on opposite side of track) by a length, pair clear: useful effort when around a length third of 8 to Desert Story in Horris Hill Stakes at Newbury 12 days later, leading after 2f out until inside last: stays 1m: likely to improve again. *I. A. Balding*

HIDDEN OASIS   3 b.c. Green Desert (USA) 127 – Secret Seeker (USA) (Mr   101
Prospector (USA)) [1995 96p: 6g⁴ 7m² 7d* 1996 7m² 8d⁶ 8f⁴ 8m Jul 20] quite attractive, rather unfurnished colt: useful performer: trained at 2 yrs by M. Stoute: best effort when fourth of 31 to North Song in Britannia Handicap at Royal Ascot: visored, pulled hard when last in £17,150 rated stakes at Newmarket month later: stays 1m: acts on firm and dead ground: tends to carry head high. *Saeed bin Suroor*

HIGH ATLAS   3 b.f. Shirley Heights 130 – Balliasta (USA) (Lyphard (USA) 132)   65
[1995 NR 1996 14m³ Aug 22] first foal: dam twice-raced daughter of Ribblesdale winner Ballinderry, dam also of Sanglamore: twice had to be withdrawn after giving trouble at stalls: no stalls, third of 6 to Generosa in slowly-run maiden at Salisbury on debut, flashing tail when hit with whip. *B. W. Hills*

HIGH BAROQUE (IRE)   3 b.g. High Estate 127 – Alpine Symphony (Northern   110
Dancer) [1995 NR 1996 8.2d⁵ 11d* 12.3g* 12m 12.5g Aug 25] 13,000F, 52,000Y: well-made gelding: has a quick action: sixth foal: brother to 1¼m winner Dancing Heights: dam unraced half-sister to smart miler Captain James: won maiden at Nottingham, £7,700 event at Newbury and Chester Vase (pushed along before halfway and idled in front when beating St Mawes 1¼ lengths), all in the spring: ran well when just over 4 lengths ninth to Ragmar in Prix du Jockey-Club at Chantilly in June, not discredited when eighth of 9 in Grand Prix de Deauville nearly 3 months later: should stay further than 12.3f: acts on good to firm and dead ground: has been gelded. *P. W. Chapple-Hyam*

HIGHBORN (IRE)   7 b. or br.g. Double Schwartz 128 – High State 72 (Free   97
State 125) [1995 88: a7g a7g⁵ 6g 6m³ 7.6m⁴ 6m⁵ 6.1m 6m⁵ 7m 6g 7d³ 6g² 6f* 1996

Chester Vase—High Baroque comes from last to first then seems to idle

HIG

6s 6g³ 7.6g* 7m⁴ 6.1m⁴ 7m² 6g 7d 7.1f 7m* 7g⁵ Oct 10] sturdy gelding: fairly useful handicapper: won at Chester in May and at Newmarket (rated stakes) in October: effective at 6f to 7.6f: acts on fibresand (yet to race on equitrack) and on firm and dead ground: sometimes slowly away: has run well when sweating: genuine and consistent. *P. S. Felgate*

HIGH COMMOTION (IRE) 4 b.f. Taufan (USA) 119 – Bumble-Bee (High 56 + Line 125) [1995 70: 8g 12m⁵ 1996 8d⁵ Apr 13] lengthy, rather sparely-made filly: has shaped quite well all 3 starts, not given hard race when fifth in claimer at Warwick on reappearance: looked open to improvement. *D. R. C. Elsworth*

HIGH CUT 3 b.f. Dashing Blade 117 – High Habit 79 (Slip Anchor 136) [1995 71 84p: 5m² 1996 7.1d² 7m⁴ 8.1m Aug 31] leggy, unfurnished filly: has a quick action: off course 12 months after only start at 2 yrs: fair form in frame in maidens: blinkered, well below form final start: should stay beyond 7.1f: sweating and edgy second start at 3 yrs. *I. A. Balding*

HIGH DESIRE (IRE) 3 b.f. High Estate 127 – Sweet Adelaide (USA) 98 (The 59 Minstrel (USA) 135) [1995 –: 7g 7f 8.1m a8g 1996 12m³ 14.1m⁴ 11.8d 12g² 11.6m² 11.6g⁴ 12m Aug 7] neat filly: modest maiden handicapper: mostly ran well in 1996 until last on final start: likely to stay well: acts on good to firm ground, possibly not on dead. *J. R. Arnold*

HIGH DOMAIN (IRE) 5 b.h. Dominion Royale 112 – Recline 70 (Wollow 132) 77 [1995 68: 5m 5m 5g⁶ 5f⁵ 5m⁵ 6m 5m³ 6m² 6m 5m⁶ 5.1d 5g 5.1m 1996 6f 5d* a6g 6d* 6g³ 6f 5m⁴ 6m 6f 6v 6.1s 5s* Nov 8] sturdy, strong-quartered horse: good mover: fair handicapper: won at Salisbury in May and Haydock in June, and 22-runner contest at Doncaster in November: stays 6f: acts on good to firm and dead ground, below form on the all-weather: effective blinkered, not tried in 1996: edgy sort: usually races prominently. *J. L. Spearing*

HIGH EXTREME (IRE) 2 b.c. (May 11) Danehill (USA) 126 – Rustic Lawn 67 (Rusticaro (FR) 124) [1996 6m⁶ 7g⁴ 8.5m³ 8f Oct 8] IR 32,000Y: sturdy, good-bodied colt: poor mover: fifth foal: brother to 3-y-o Scandator and half-brother to fairly useful winner 1m and 1¼m winner Silver Groom (by Shy Groom): dam (unraced) from family of Royal Palace: fair maiden: sold 12,500 gns Newmarket Autumn Sales: should stay beyond 7f: didn't look particularly at ease on track at Epsom third start. *P. W. Chapple-Hyam*

HIGHFIELD FIZZ 4 b.f. Efisio 120 – Jendor 82 (Condorcet (FR)) [1995 60: 7g 50 7m⁶ 10f³ 10m 10f³ 11.1f⁴ 11f⁴ 10.4g 11d* 10.5s² 14.1f⁶ 12.1s 1996 10.5d a11g 11m a– 10.5m⁵ 10s 10g⁶ 15.8g 14.1m* 16g 15.1s⁶ a14.8g Nov 16] good-topped filly: has a round action: modest performer on her day: 100/1, easily best effort in 1996 when winning handicap at Redcar in October: stays 1¾m: acts on firm and soft ground: has been bandaged off-hind: inconsistent. *C. W. Fairhurst*

HIGHFIELD PET 3 b.g. Efisio 120 – Jendor 82 (Condorcet (FR)) [1995 –: 7m – 6m 1996 8g⁶ 10m May 28] lengthy gelding: trained by M. Johnston at 2 yrs: no worthwhile form in maidens. *C. W. Fairhurst*

HIGH FLOWN (USA) 4 b.g. Lear Fan (USA) 130 – Isticanna (USA) 96 (Far – North (CAN) 120) [1995 53d, a63d: a7g* a8g⁴ a8g 12f² 9.9m⁵ 12m⁴ 16m⁶ 12m² 11f⁶ 12g³ 12m² 12.4h³ 10m⁵ a12g 1996 12.3g 14.1f 12m 11.9f Aug 6] sturdy gelding: no recent form: effective visored or not: sold 2,400 gns Doncaster October Sales. *Ronald Thompson*

HIGHFLYING 10 br.g. Shirley Heights 130 – Nomadic Pleasure 91 (Habitat 84 134) [1995 92: 16m⁶ 16.1g² 16m* 11.9m² 16.1m⁶ 15g* 16.2g* 16.1m³ 11.9m⁵ 16.1g 1996 13.9m 16.5g⁵ 14d 11.9m 16.1m 12.3m* 14m⁶ 14.1m* 14.6m⁵ 14.1f³ 13.9g Oct 12] strong, good-bodied gelding: usually impresses in appearance: poor mover: still a fairly useful handicapper: took time to come to himself in 1996, but won at Ripon in July and Redcar in August: ran as if something amiss final start: effective at 1½m to 2m: acts on firm and dead going (unsuited by very soft): sometimes bandaged: has gone well with forcing tactics. *G. M. Moore*

HIGH HOPE HENRY (USA) 3 b.g. Known Fact (USA) 135 – Parquill (USA) 88 d (One For All (USA)) [1995 80: 5g* 8.1d 1996 8s 7.8s* 8d 7m 7m 8.5m⁵ 7.6m² 7m Oct 5] close-coupled colt: trained at 2 yrs by P. Cole: fairly useful form at best in summer for C. Collins in Ireland, winning at Dundalk in May: below form both

428

outings back in Britain: sold to join M. Hammond 7,500 gns Newmarket Autumn Sales: stays 7.8f: best effort on soft ground. *R. Akehurst*

HIGH INTRIGUE (IRE) 2 b. or br.c. (Mar 7) Shirley Heights 130 – Mild 68 p
Intrigue (USA) 91 (Sir Ivor 135) [1996 8f⁶ Oct 15] IR 40,000Y: fourth foal: half-brother to Mild Dancer (by Fairy King), winner in Italy at up to 1½m: dam, 1¼m winner, is out of half-sister to Arkadina, Blood Royal and Gregorian: 5/1 from 2/1, slowly away and never dangerous when sixth of 12 in maiden at Leicester: should do better over middle distances. *H. R. A. Cecil*

HIGHLAND FAWN 3 ch.f. Safawan 118 – Highland Rowena 59 (Royben 125) –
[1995 NR 1996 a7g a6g a7g a6g a5g* 5g a5g a5g 5f⁶ 5f a5g 5f Jul 18] 11,000Y: a56 d
leggy, plain filly: second foal: half-sister to useful 4-y-o 5f performer Crofters Ceilidh (by Scottish Reel): dam sprinter: landed gamble in seller at Wolverhampton in February: no other form: sold 520 gns Doncaster August Sales: will prove best at sprint distances: acts on fibresand. *B. A. McMahon*

HIGHLAND GIFT (IRE) 3 b.f. Generous (IRE) 139 – Scots Lass 79 (Shirley 95 +
Heights 130) [1995 NR 1996 12m⁵ 10s* 10.3d³ Nov 8] big, rangy, angular filly: has scope: fifth foal: closely related to 1¼m winner Dragon's Teeth (by Caerleon) and half-sister to 2 winners, including smart middle-distance stayer Bonny Scot (by Commanche Run): dam 13f winner: reportedly jarred knees in maiden at Newmarket in April: extremely easy winner of similar event at Newbury in October: joint favourite, 9½ lengths third of 9 to Russian Snows in useful minor event at Doncaster, one pace from 3f out: will prove at least as effective over 1½m as 1¼m. *R. Charlton*

HIGHLAND PASS (IRE) 2 b.g. (Feb 24) Petorius 117 – Whatawoman (Tumble 61
Wind (USA)) [1996 5s 5g⁵ 5m⁶ 6.1s 8s Nov 9] IR 9,500F, 9,000Y: smallish, sturdy gelding: second foal: dam unraced: well backed first 2 starts but showed only modest form: left M. McCormack after third start: tailed off on soft ground after 6-month absence both starts for new trainer. *P. Burgoyne*

HIGHLAND RHAPSODY (IRE) 3 ch.f. Kris 135 – Farewell Song (USA) 80 78
(The Minstrel (CAN) 135) [1995 NR 1996 7d⁵ 7m² 7.1m 6g* 6m⁴ 7f Sep 5] strong, lengthy filly: fluent mover: fourth foal: half-sister to 4-y-o Yesterday's Song (by Shirley Heights) and a winner in Austria by King of Clubs: dam 1m winner: fair performer: taken down early (free to post and ran poorly previous outing) when winning maiden at Salisbury in August, not needing to be near her best: sold 27,000 gns Newmarket December Sales: should stay 1m: tends to hang under pressure. *I. A. Balding*

HIGHLAND SPIN 5 ch.g. Dunbeath (USA) 127 – In A Spin 59 (Windjammer –
(USA)) [1995 NR 1996 a9.4g⁶ Mar 6] second foal: dam 1½m winner: in frame in NH Flat races: ridden by 7-lb claimer, beaten long way in seller on flat debut: sold to join W. G. Mann 2,600 gns Doncaster March Sales. *Mrs M. Reveley*

HIGHLIGHTS 3 ch.f. Phountzi (USA) 104 – Idella's Gold (FR) (Glint of Gold 56
128) [1995 NR 1996 a10g⁴ a8g⁴ a9.4g³ 12s Mar 25] third foal: half-sister to a winner in Germany by Precocious: dam won over 1½m in France: poor maiden: sold 2,000 gns Newmarket July Sales, covered by Superlative: should prove effective beyond 9.4f. *D. Morris*

HIGHLY PRIZED 2 b.c. (Apr 18) Shirley Heights 130 – On The Tiles (Thatch – p
(USA) 136) [1996 8m Oct 17] deep-girthed colt: sixth foal: brother to 3-y-o Regal Eagle, closely related to Prix Saint-Alary winner Air de Rien (by Elegant Air) and half-brother to 2 winners, including smart but temperamental 7f (at 2 yrs) and 1¼m (in USA) winner Stiletto Blade (by Dashing Blade): dam, from family of Blushing Groom, won 1¼m maiden in Ireland: gone in coat, around 13 lengths ninth of 17 to Royal Crusade in maiden at Newmarket, weakening and eased: moved poorly to post: will do better. *I. A. Balding*

HIGHLY SPIRITED 3 b.c. Lochnager 132 – Soudley Lady (Glenstal (USA) –
118) [1995 NR 1996 8.3g 7m Aug 15] 800F: lengthy colt: first foal: dam unraced: burly, well beaten in claimer and a maiden. *N. M. Lampard*

HIGH NOTE 3 b.f. Shirley Heights 130 – Soprano 112 (Kris 135) [1995 70p: 7m 82
7m⁶ 7g⁴ 1996 8.2m² 8f⁶ Jun 22] lengthy, rather unfurnished filly: fluent mover: fair maiden: found less than seemed likely in handicap at Nottingham and minor event at Ascot: bred to be suited by further than 1m but seems a keen type. *R. Charlton*

HIGH ON LIFE   2 b.c. (May 24) Mazilier (USA) 107 – Tina Rosa (Bustino 136)   64
[1996 8f 10g² Oct 24] 8,000Y, 13,000 2-y-o: half-brother to a winner in USA by
Never So Bold: dam poor half-sister to very smart 7f to 1½m winner Saros: modest
form in maidens at Leicester (never dangerous) and Nottingham (steadily-run
median auction event, head second of 8 finishers to Indifferent Guy) in October: stays
1¼m. *A. C. Stewart*

HIGH PATRIARCH (IRE)   4 b.g. Alzao (USA) 117 – Freesia 78 (Shirley   94
Heights 130) [1995 79: 10m⁶ 10m 10m⁴ 12g³ 10.5g³ 14.1f³ 14g* 1996 a14.8g² Jan 3]
strong, stocky gelding: fairly useful handicapper: ran a fine first race for new stable
when head second to Lear Dancer at Wolverhampton: stays 14.8f: acts on fibresand
and firm ground, yet to race on a soft surface: blinkered/visored at 3 yrs after fifth
start. *N. J. H. Walker*

HIGH PREMIUM   8 b.g. Forzando 122 – High Halo 64 (High Top 131) [1995   85
76: a6g³ a7g³ 8g* 10d⁶ 10.4m⁴ 8.2m³ 1996 a7g² a9.4g⁶ a9.4g⁴ a8g³ a8g* a7g* 7g⁴
8g⁴ 8.1d⁴ a7g* 7.6d 8m⁵ 8m² 8.1d* 8d* 8g² 8g a9.4g³ Dec 14] sturdy, good-topped
gelding: fairly useful handicapper: won at Southwell and Wolverhampton in March
and at Wolverhampton (claimer) in June: also enjoyed a good season on turf, winning
at Haydock in September and Ascot in October: finds 7f a bare minimum, and stays
1¼m: acts on firm and dead ground and on fibresand: blinkered (ran creditably) ninth
8-y-o start: often bandaged: has idled in front. *R. A. Fahey*

HIGH PRIORITY (IRE)   3 b.c. Marju (IRE) 127 – Blinding (IRE) (High Top   –
131) [1995 92+: 6g⁴ 5.1m* 6g 5.5g 6m² 5m³ 6m² 1996 6g⁵ 6d 5d 5.6m Sep 11]
strong, lengthy colt: fairly useful form as 2-y-o, but disappointing in 1996: bred to
stay beyond 6f, but is headstrong: very edgy and reared leaving stalls fifth 2-y-o start:
tends to carry head high: has joined J. Sheehan. *M. R. Channon*

HIGH PYRENEES   4 b.g. Shirley Heights 130 – Twyla 101 (Habitat 134)   –
[1995 72p: 10.1g³ 13.1g* 1996 16.5g 11.9m Jun 15] sturdy gelding: fair form when
winning maiden at Ayr in 1995: bandaged, well held in handicap and lady amateurs
event in 1996: should stay beyond 13f. *R. Allan*

HIGH ROLLER (IRE)   2 b.c. (Mar 2) Generous (IRE) 139 – Helpless Haze   102 p
(USA) (Vaguely Noble 140) [1996 8m* 8d* Oct 12] 170,000Y: tall, angular, close-
coupled colt: eighth foal: half-brother to 3-y-o Solitaire (by Sadler's Wells) and 3
winners, including useful Irish middle-distance performer Lone Runner (by Chief
Singer): dam, 11f winner, half-sister to very smart French performer at around 9f
Baillamont: odds on both starts, winning maiden at Yarmouth (impressively) in
September and listed race at Ascot (steadily wore down Barnum Sands to lead on
post after being niggled along on home turn) in October: will be suited by a thorough
test of stamina: game: still green at Ascot, and sure to improve again. *H. R. A. Cecil*

HIGH ROMANCE   6 b. or br.m. Today And Tomorrow 78 – Nahawand 51 (High   –
Top 131) [1995 NR 1996 a6g Feb 26] lengthy, angular mare: poor sprinter at 3 yrs:
pulled up lame only start since: dead. *J. S. Wainwright*

HIGH SHOT   6 b.g. Darshaan 133 – Nollet (High Top 131) [1995 12m 8g² 10d*   –
1996 7g⁶ 11.7f³ May 11] big, good-topped ex-French gelding: half-brother to 2-y-o
6f winner Cricket Fan (by Gorytus): dam winner in Italy: successful on final start in
1995 for M. Rolland in amateurs event at Evry in November: raced freely when last
in 6-runner listed race at Leicester and 3-runner minor event at Bath: stays 1¼m: acts
on heavy ground. *G. Lewis*

HIGHSPEED (IRE)   4 ch.g. Double Schwartz 128 – High State 72 (Free State   63
125) [1995 53: 7.1m⁵ 8g 7f* 7g 1996 a7g 7d* 8d* 8m² 10f⁶ 8d⁴ 8.3f Aug 19] small,
leggy, lightly-made gelding: modest handicapper: won twice at Ayr in May: good
efforts afterwards when in frame: stays 1m: acts on firm and dead ground: held up.
S. E. Kettlewell

HIGH SPIRITS (IRE)   2 b.g. (Apr 26) Great Commotion (USA) 123 – Spoilt   63 +
Again 91 (Mummy's Pet 125) [1996 5d⁶ 5d³ 5d May 24] IR 15,000F, IR 6,200Y:
close-coupled gelding: fifth foal: half-brother to 3-y-o Larghetto (by Lycius), 6f
winner at 2 yrs, and 1¼m and 1¾m winner Teen Jay (by Teenoso): dam, 9f and 1¼m
winner, is out of Park Hill winner Reload, a half-sister to 1000 Guineas winner Full
Dress II: modest form early in season: will be suited by further than 5f. *T. D. Easterby*

HIGH SUMMER   6 b.g. Green Desert (USA) 127 – Beacon Hill 81 (Bustino 136)   –
[1995 NR 1996 13.3m 16.2d Oct 11] tall, workmanlike gelding: fair stayer at 4 yrs:
no worthwhile form in 1996. *T. Thomson Jones*

HIGH SUMMER (USA) 3 ch.f. Nureyev (USA) 131 – Miss Summer (Luthier 107 126) [1995 NR 1996 7m³ 7m* 7m 7f* 7m² 7m Sep 28] very tall, leggy, rather unfurnished filly: sister to smart French 1987 2-y-o Most Precious and half-sister to several winners, including useful 1995 3-y-o 1m winner Private Line (by Private Account) and French 10.5f winner Summer Groom (by Blushing Groom): dam French 1m winner: won maiden at Warwick in July and handicap at Salisbury (very easily) in September: useful form when second to My Branch in listed race at Doncaster, but disappointed when short-priced favourite and seemingly very well treated in £50,100 handicap at Ascot 16 days later: acts on firm ground, yet to race on an easy surface: reportedly suffers breathing difficulties, and wore tongue strap last 3 starts. *R. Charlton*

HIGHTIDE 4 b.f. Lugana Beach 116 – Moon Charter 45 (Runnymede 123) – [1995 NR 1996 a7g Dec 31] fifth foal: half-sister to 6f seller winner Kathanna (by Bold Owl): dam, plater, best run at 7f as 2-y-o: behind in bad maiden at Lingfield. *J. R. Arnold*

HIGHTOWN-PRINCESS (IRE) 8 gr.m. King Persian 107 – Ambient 68 – (Amber Rama (USA) 133) [1995 NR 1996 12.1g⁶ Aug 26] tall, sparely-made mare: poor performer: well beaten in claimer on first outing since 1994: better at 1¼m than shorter: often visored earlier in career. *P. C. Ritchens*

HIGHWAY 2 gr.c. (Apr 7) Salse (USA) 128 – Ivory Lane (USA) (Sir Ivor 135) 71 [1996 7.1f⁴ 7m⁶ Sep 20] 29,000Y: third foal: dam, lightly raced in USA, sister to Cherry Hinton winner Turkish Treasure: fair form when staying-on fourth of 7 to Apprehension in maiden at Haydock: very slowly away and always behind in minor event at Ayr 13 days later: likely to stay beyond 1m. *B. W. Hills*

HIGHWAY ROBBER (IRE) 2 b.c. (Apr 2) Robellino (USA) 127 – High Habit 57 79 (Slip Anchor 136) [1996 6g⁴ 6m a7g⁵ 7.9g Oct 10] close-coupled, quite attractive colt: second foal: half-brother to 3-y-o High Cut (by Dashing Blade): dam, second over 11.5f, half-sister to smart sprinter Blue Siren: modest form in maidens at Doncaster and Wolverhampton first and third starts: below form on good to firm ground in between: sold 6,200 gns Newmarket Autumn Sales. *J. M. P. Eustace*

HILAALA (USA) 3 ch.f. Elmaamul (USA) 125 – Halholah (USA) 65 (Secreto 88 (USA) 128) [1995 78: 6f⁴ 7m³ 7g² 7m* 1996 8.1d* 9m* 10m⁴ 8.3d² 9g 7.9g Oct 9] workmanlike filly: fairly useful performer: won minor events at Chepstow in May and Goodwood (gamely) in June: best effort when second in rated stakes at Windsor: below form final 2 starts, visored final one: stayed 9f: acted on good to firm ground, particularly well on dead: took keen hold: visits Green Desert. *P. T. Walwyn*

HILL FARM BLUES 3 b.f. Mon Tresor 113 – Loadplan Lass 63 (Nicholas – Bill 125) [1995 NR 1996 a14.8g⁴ 12m⁴ 8.6g³] third foal: half-sister to 4-y-o 9.4f winner Dannistar (by Puissance) and 5-y-o 1½m winner Hill Farm Dancer (by Gunner B): dam, poor maiden, bred to stay middle distances: only form when fourth in claimer at Catterick on second outing: seemed reluctant final start: has joined J. P. Smith. *J. L. Eyre*

HILL FARM DANCER 5 ch.m. Gunner B 126 – Loadplan Lass 63 (Nicholas 51 Bill 125) [1995 55: a12g a11g⁶ a12g³ a12g² 10.8m² 11.7m* 12m⁴ 10.8g⁴ 13f 12f⁶ a72 11.9m³ a12g³ a12g⁴ 1996 a12g² a13g a12g* a12g* a12g² 12d 11.7g⁴ 12.3m³ 17.2m³ 11.9m⁵ 15.9d a14g 10.8f a12g⁴ a12g* a12g⁵ Dec 14] sparely-made mare: fluent mover: modest handicapper on turf, fair on all-weather: won at Wolverhampton in February, March (claimer) and November (apprentices and a minor event): stays 14.8f: acts on firm ground (possibly not on a soft surface) and the all-weather: normally held up: often ridden by apprentice. *W. M. Brisbourne*

HILL FARM KATIE 5 b.m. Derrylin 115 – Kate Brook (Nicholas Bill 125) – [1995 38: a9.4g⁴ a8g a6g 7g 8m a12g⁵ 1996 a14.8g a10g a12g³ 10.8g a9.4g⁶ 7.1d a7g Jul 6] lengthy mare: no worthwhile form at 5 yrs: sold 450 gns Malvern October Sales: tried blinkered/visored, no improvement. *W. M. Brisbourne*

HILL HOUSE TEACHER 4 b.f. Komaite (USA) – Shakira Grove (Hot Grove – 128) [1995 NR 1996 6g Sep 7] first reported foal: dam winning selling hurdler: 66/1, showed nothing in maiden at Thirsk. *M. P. Bielby*

HILLSWICK 5 ch.g. Norwick (USA) 125 – Quite Lucky 69 (Precipice Wood 27 123) [1995 –: 11.9m 12.5g 14.9g 1996 11.9g⁵ 12.5f Jun 24] leggy, angular gelding: bad performer nowadays. *J. S. King*

431

HILLZAH (USA) 8 ch.g. Blushing Groom (FR) 131 – Glamour Girl (ARG) 80 (Mysolo 120) [1995 79, a82: a11g a12g* a12g⁴ a12g⁵ 11.1s² 10m³ 10f 14.1m* a74 14.1m² 10.5m* 16.2g⁵ 1996 a9.4g a12g⁶ a12g 13.8s² 14.1g 16g⁵ a14.8g² May 11] workmanlike gelding: poor mover: fair handicapper: stays 16.2f: acts on any turf going, and fibresand (unraced on equitrack): sometimes hangs markedly, but goes well for apprentice: occasionally slowly away: genuine. *R. Bastiman*

HIL RHAPSODY 2 ch.f. (Feb 24) Anshan 119 – Heavenly Note 82 (Chief 74 d Singer 131) [1996 5g* 6s⁴ 6m³ 6g³ 6m⁵ 6d 8m 6m⁶ 6m Oct 7] 3,500F, 7,000Y: unfurnished filly: fourth foal: half-sister to 3-y-o Dibley (by Statoblest): dam 2-y-o 7.5f winner, probably stayed 1½m: won median auction maiden at Leicester in April: deteriorating form in nurseries last 5 starts: stays 6f: sweating freely last 2 starts. *B. Palling*

HILTONS EXECUTIVE (IRE) 2 b.f. (Apr 30) Petorius 117 – Theatral – (Orchestra 118) [1996 5g 5s⁶ 7g 5m⁴ a5g⁵ 6g Oct 21] IR 1,000F: IR 3,600Y: leggy filly: third foal: half-sister to 3-y-o Spirit Dancer (by Carmelite House) and 8.1f and 1¼m winner Mill Dancer (by Broken Hearted): dam winning hurdler: poor form in varied events: pulled hard and hung left over 7f on first outing for 4 months. *E. J. Alston*

HINDSIGHT (IRE) 2 br.c. (Feb 14) Don't Forget Me 127 – Vian (USA) (Far 78 Out East (USA)) [1996 7.1m² 7m² 8.3d* Sep 30] 20,000Y: unfurnished colt: sixth foal: half-brother to 3-y-o Flaxen (by Thatching), useful sprinter Wavian (by Warning) and 1992 2-y-o 1m winner Ansillo (by Rousillon), later successful in France: dam unraced half-sister to Optimistic Lass, herself dam of Golden Opinion: fair form: heavily-backed odds-on favourite, made hard work of winning 6-runner median auction maiden at Hamilton in September by ¾ length, clear, from Lightning Rebel: sold 26,000 gns Newmarket Autumn Sales: stays 8.3f: acts on good to firm and dead ground: raced too freely second start. *W. J. Haggas*

HI NOD 6 b.h. Valiyar 129 – Vikris (Viking (USA)) [1995 99: 7m 7g⁴ 7f* 8m² 7m² 106 7m* 7m² 7.9m 7m* 1996 7g* 7m² 7.9g² 7m 7.9m 8m² 7m 7m⁴ 7g⁵ Oct 26] strong horse: impresses good deal in appearance: useful handicapper: better than ever to win at Doncaster in May: good second to Decorated Hero in £13,600 rated stakes at Doncaster sixth start: ran as though something amiss next outing: effective at 7f and 1m: acts on any going: has run well when sweating: usually tracks leaders: genuine. *M. J. Camacho*

HINT 2 b.c. (Mar 12) Warning 136 – Throw Away Line (USA) (Assert 134) [1996 78 p 8m⁶ Sep 20] 52,000Y: small colt: fifth foal: half-brother to 3-y-o 7.5f (at 2 yrs) and 1¼m winner Wavey (by Kris) and French 11f winner Hesperia (by Slip Anchor): dam, minor winner in USA, half-sister to 3 graded winners in USA, including Champion filly Go For Wand: 20/1, around 7 lengths sixth of 9 to King Sound in steadily-run minor event at Newbury, soon niggled along towards rear, no danger when short of room inside last: will improve: sent to USA. *P. F. I. Cole*

HINTON ROCK (IRE) 4 ch.g. Ballad Rock 122 – May Hinton 82 (Main Reef 78 126) [1995 86: 5m⁴ 5m² 6g 5g⁵ 5g⁵ 6g 5m⁵ 5m 5f² 1996 5.1g 5d 5.1m⁴ a6g 6.1m⁶ 6m³ 5m Aug 26] strong, compact gelding: fair handicapper: reportedly finished lame final start: sold 2,200 gns Doncaster October Sales: seems to stay 6f: acts on good to firm and dead ground: often blinkered/visored: often sweats: inconsistent: sent to Belgium. *A. Bailey*

HIO NOD 2 b.g. (May 6) Precocious 126 – Vikris (Viking (USA)) [1996 a6g Nov – 18] fifth foal: half-brother to useful 6-y-o Hi Nod (stays 1m, by Valiyar) and fair sprinter Nordan Raider (by Domynsky): dam lightly raced: refused to enter stalls on intended debut: well beaten in maiden at Southwell. *M. J. Camacho*

HIPPIOS 2 b. or br.g. (Mar 31) Formidable (USA) 125 – Miss Doody 63 (Gorytus – (USA) 132) [1996 6g 7d Oct 28] 21,000Y: first foal: dam 6f (at 2 yrs) and 1¼m (seller) winner: no sign of ability. *S. Dow*

HIPPY 3 b.f. Damister (USA) 123 – Breakaway 98 (Song 132) [1995 68p: 7m⁴ 80 1996 7m 10d 7g³ 8f* 7g² 7g 8m⁵ 8.1m³ 10.1m⁴ Oct 23] leggy, angular filly: unimpressive mover: fairly useful handicapper: won maiden at Yarmouth in June: good efforts last 2 starts: stays 1¼m: acts on firm ground: sent to Saudi Arabia. *C. E. Brittain*

HIPPY CHICK   2 b.f. (Mar 5) Ron's Victory (USA) 129 – Enchanted Tale   – p
(USA) 59 (Told (USA)) [1996 6m⁶ Aug 16] 1,000F, IR 3,800Y: second foal: dam
(maiden) stayed 7f: gambled on when sixth of 11 in seller at Folkestone: reportedly
returned with badly swollen head and neck: evidently thought capable of better.
D. J. S. Cosgrove

HIRASAH (IRE)   2 b.f. (Feb 5) Lahib (USA) 129 – Mayaasa (USA) 70 (Lyphard   76 p
(USA) 132) [1996 6f⁶ Jul 26] first foal: dam 1¼m winner, half-sister to very smart
miler Maroof: 9/2, won 6-runner maiden at Newmarket by short head from Literary,
making much of running, rallying when headed: bred to stay at least 1m: looked
likely to improve. *R. W. Armstrong*

HI ROCK   4 ch.f. Hard Fought 125 – Miss Racine (Dom Racine (FR) 121) [1995   49
55: a6g⁴ 7.1g² 6.1m* 6m 6.1d 6m³ 6m⁵ a6g⁶ 1996 a7g³ a7g² a7g a7g⁶ 5.9m 8g² a7g
8m 8.5f⁴ 10g⁵ 10m 10f⁵ Sep 28] neat filly: poor performer: sold out of M. Camacho's
stable 2,700 gns Doncaster March Sales after fourth start: probably stays 1¼m: acts
on firm ground and fibresand: visored (ran respectably) final start. *J. Norton*

HISMAGICMOMENT (USA)   3 b.c. Proud Birdie (USA) – Affirmed   85
Ambience (USA) (Affirmed (USA)) [1995 NR 1996 8m⁴ 10.2g⁵ 8g³ 7f² 8m³ a8f³ 9f⁵
a6.5f* 6.5f a6.5f Nov 27] $50,000 2-y-o: big colt: has scope: second foal: dam
winner at up to 6f (including at 2 yrs) in USA: sire best at 1¼m: fairly useful maiden
for P. Chapple-Hyam first 5 starts: won maiden at Santa Anita in October: well beaten
last 2 starts, claimed by J. Devereux $40,000 final one: should stay beyond 1m: raced
only on a sound surface on turf, acts on dirt: front runner. *T. Runa, jnr, USA*

HIT OR MISS   2 ch.f. (Mar 21) Be My Chief (USA) 122 – Jennies' Gem   61 d
(Sayf El Arab (USA) 127) [1996 5s* 5m³ 5d⁵ 6m⁵ 5m* 6m 6.1m³ 5m⁴ a6g Oct 19]   a?
8,800Y: small, strong filly: second foal: dam won 3 times over 5f at 2 yrs: modest
performer: won sellers at Doncaster in March and Hamilton (sold out of M. Channon's stable 5,400 gns) in August: well below form last 2 starts, and sold 3,100 gns
Doncaster October Sales: stays 6f: acts on good to firm and soft ground: inconsistent.
P. C. Haslam

HIT THE CANVAS (USA)   5 ch.g. At The Threshold (USA) – Also Royal   62
(USA) (Native Royalty (USA)) [1995 68: 12g 14.1m³ 13.1g³ 15f* 15.1m² 16.5f⁵
16.1h³ 1996 21.6m 16.2m⁴ Jul 6] leggy gelding: fluent mover: fair handicapper: will
stay extreme distances: acts on hard ground, dead and fibresand: effective blinkered/
visored or not: fairly useful hurdler. *Mrs M. Reveley*

HIT THE FLAG (IRE)   2 b.c. (May 1) Jurado (USA) – Janeswood (IRE)   –
(Henbit (USA) 130) [1996 7.1v 7f Nov 5] small colt: first reported foal: dam seemed
of little account: beaten long way in maidens. *A. B. Mulholland*

HOBBS CHOICE   3 b.f. Superpower 113 – Excavator Lady 65 (Most Secret 119)   51
[1995 –: 5d a7g 7.5m⁶ 6g⁵ 7.5d 1996 6s⁶ 6d* 6.1d⁵ 7d 6g 7f⁵ 8.3g² 10s Aug 31]
workmanlike filly: modest handicapper: won at Hamilton in April: below form last 5
starts: should stay 7f: acts on dead ground: winning hurdler. *G. M. Moore*

HOH DANCER   2 ch.f. (May 5) Indian Ridge 123 – Alteza Real 84 (Mansingh   66
(USA) 120) [1996 5m² 5m⁴ 6d Aug 24] 15,000Y: leggy, lightly-made filly: half-sister
to several winners, including useful 1987 2-y-o sprinter Infanta Real (by Formidable): dam, 5f winner, is half-sister to Forzando: beaten favourite in maiden auctions
at Sandown (keen to halfway, best effort), Haydock (off bridle by halfway) and
Windsor (seemed to lose her action): should stay 6f: tends to carry head high.
I. A. Balding

HOH DOWN (IRE)   2 b.f. (Apr 30) Fairy King (USA) – Tintomara (IRE)   –
(Niniski (USA) 125) [1996 7m a8.5g⁵ a7g⁵ Dec 13] IR 5,000Y: second foal: dam
twice-raced close relative of smart middle-distance winner Hajade: well beaten in
maidens. *K. McAuliffe*

HOH EXPRESS   4 b.g. Waajib 121 – Tissue Paper 95 (Touch Paper 113) [1995   99
101: 10.3m 8g* 8g² 8m 8m³ 10.4m⁴ 8g* 8d³ 9g 10v³ 1996 8s 8d 9s⁵ 8.1d⁶ 10.1m³ 10f
10m² 10.4m 10g³ 9g 10d⁴ Oct 12] useful handicapper: generally ran well in
competitive races, third in listed event at Baden-Baden in August: met plenty of
trouble in running last 2 starts: stays 10.4f: acts on good to firm and heavy ground:
consistent. *I. A. Balding*

HOH FLYER (USA)   2 b.f. (Apr 20) Northern Flagship (USA) 96 – Beautiful   66 +
Bedouin (USA) (His Majesty (USA)) [1996 6f 6g* 6.5m Sep 11] $27,000Y: good-
topped, quite attractive filly: fifth foal: half-sister to smart 3-y-o 1m and 1¼m winner
Wandering Star (by Red Ransom) and 1½m winner Badawi (by Script Ohio): dam
unraced half-sister to Silver Hawk: won 17-runner median auction maiden at
Kempton in August by neck from Test The Water: never-dangerous tenth of 22 to
Nightbird in nursery at Doncaster only subsequent outing: likely to be suited by 7f+.
M. Bell

HOH MAGIC   4 ch.f. Cadeaux Genereux 131 – Gunner's Belle 69 (Gunner B   –
126) [1995 108: 7.3m² 8m⁴ 8d 5f 6g³ 6.5g⁵ 6d 7g⁵ 1996 7g⁵ Apr 8] rangy filly: smart
performer as 2-y-o, winner of Prix Morny: fourth in 1000 Guineas and third in July
Cup in 1995: well below form in minor event at Warwick in April: retired shortly
afterwards and tested in foal to Lammtarra, but had to be put down after bout of colic
in May: stayed 1m: acted on firm and dead ground: was normally held up in touch.
M. Bell

HOH MAJESTIC (IRE)   3 b.g. Soviet Lad (USA) 94 – Sevens Are Wild 40   69 d
(Petorius 117) [1995 69: 5m* 5g 5.1m* 5m⁴ 6f 5.1m² 5m² 5.3f² 5g* 8m 6g 1996 5d⁶
6.1g⁶ 6g 6g⁶ 8m⁶ 6f⁵ 6m⁵ 6g³ᵈⁱˢ a5g³ 6f² 5g 6d 6m a5g³ Nov 30] quite attractive
gelding: fair handicapper in the spring: modest form at best last 8 starts: sold out of
M. Wane's stable 2,300 gns Doncaster October Sales after penultimate start: stays
6f, not discredited over 1m: acts on firm ground and on fibresand: usually visored
nowadays. *Ronald Thompson*

HOH RETURNS (IRE)   3 b.g. Fairy King (USA) – Cipriani 102 (Habitat 134)   94
[1995 80: 5.2m 6m⁵ 6g³ 6d² 6m 1996 6m⁶ 6m* 6m³ 6m 5f³ Jun 22] good-topped
gelding: has scope: unimpressive mover: fairly useful performer: won minor event
at Doncaster in May by 5 lengths: creditable third in quite valuable handicaps at
Newmarket and Ascot: very badly hampered in between: stays 6f: acts on firm
ground. *M. Bell*

HOH SURPRISE (IRE)   2 b.f. (Jan 23) Mac's Imp (USA) 116 – Musical Gem   50
(USA) (The Minstrel (CAN) 135) [1996 5g² 5m⁵ 5f² 6m³ 6d* 7f⁶ 6m⁶ 6s⁵ Oct 5]
IR 2,500Y, 10,500 2-y-o: leggy filly: first foal: dam Irish 2-y-o 7f winner: modest
performer: won seller at Windsor in August: sold 3,000 gns Newmarket Autumn
Sales: probably stays 7f: acts on firm ground but seems ideally suited by an easy
surface: has had tongue tied. *M. Bell*

HOLDERS HILL (IRE)   4 b.g. Tirol 127 – Delightful Time (Manado 130)   62
[1995 7v⁶ 6s 8m 8s³ 8m 7s 7m⁵ 7m 6d⁴ 7g 10d³ 6d 1996 a8.5g² Dec 28] IR 30,000Y:
ex-Irish gelding: half-brother to 1995 2-y-o 5f winner Beautiful Ballad (by Ballad
Rock): dam maiden half-sister to Sassafras: modest maiden: sold out of M. O'Toole's
stable only 2,400 gns Doncaster May Sales: creditable second at Wolverhampton on
debut here: stays 1¼m: acts on fibresand, best efforts on a soft surface: effective
blinkered or not: fairly useful winning hurdler in 1995/6. *M. G. Meagher*

HOLIDAY ISLAND   7 ch.g. Good Times (ITY) – Green Island 89 (St Paddy   –
133) [1995 –: a13g 11.9m 1996 a8g Feb 1] workmanlike gelding: of little account
nowadays. *P. Butler*

HOLLOWAY MELODY   3 ch.f. Cree Song 99 – Holloway Wonder 93 (Swing   55
Easy (USA) 126) [1995 38: 5m⁵ 6.1d 8.2m a7g⁶ a8g⁴ 1996 a7g⁴ a6g³ 6.9m 7g³ 8.1m⁶
8.2m⁵ 8f 8.2g* a8g a7g⁴ a7s a8g Dec 27] workmanlike filly: modest handicapper:
won claimer at Nottingham in October, finishing really strongly: stays 8.3f: acts on
firm ground and fibresand. *B. A. McMahon*

HOLLYWOOD DREAM (GER)   5 ch.m. Master Willie 129 – Holly (GER)   119
(Cortez (GER)) [1995 115: 10.5s* 10m² 12f 1996 10d* 11d⁵ 11d⁴ 12m* 12g²
12g³ 12s⁴ 10m² 10f Dec 1]
    Already the winner of the Prix Fille de l'Air at Saint-Cloud at three and
the Prix Corrida at Evry before being kept off the course for over six months at
four, Hollywood Dream was one of the top older females in Europe in 1996.
She won two Group 1 events at the chief expense of British opposition and
finished placed in the highest class on a further three occasions. A flashy
chestnut, she made quite a sight on her best days, finishing fast and late, and her
reappearance in Italy had to be seen to be believed.

Horses have won big races after seeming to have had little chance at some stage in running—few have done so when the stage in question was little over a hundred yards out. In the Premio Presidente della Repubblica at Rome in May, Hollywood Dream found a remarkable burst of speed to pull back over three lengths and head Needle Gun on the post. Two rather tame defeats on her return to Germany saw her start sixth choice in the betting in a field of seven for the Deutschland Preis at Dusseldorf in July. A fair field included British challengers Phantom Gold and Posidonas, the latter fresh from his win in the Princess of Wales's Stakes at Newmarket. In another last-gasp finish, Hollywood Dream snatched victory from Posidonas by a short head, the pair nearly two lengths clear of the veteran Protektor. A third Group 1 success eluded her, but she performed creditably in the attempt, under two lengths behind pace-dictating Luso in the Aral-Pokal at Gelsenkirchen, just over four lengths behind Lavirco in the Europa Preis at Cologne, then, on the better of two successive runs in Italy, going down by a neck to Flemensfirth in the Premio Roma.

Hollywood Dream (GER) (ch.m. 1991)	Master Willie (ch 1977)	High Line (ch 1966)	High Hat
			Time Call
		Fair Winter (ch 1964)	Set Fair
			Winter Gleam
	Holly (GER) (b 1984)	Cortez (b 1965)	Orsini
			Costa Brava
		Moss Hall (ch 1964)	Ballymoss
			Fresco

Hollywood Dream is the second foal out of Holly, following the winning miler Harper (by Anatas). Holly was successful twice at around a mile in Germany at three and is one of twelve winners out of Moss Hall. Best of these was Harris (by Arjon), a Group 3 winner over an extended nine furlongs in 1975. Fresco, who won six races, achieved greater success as a grandam than as a dam, producing Port Merion who was second in the 1965 July Cup, Palmural who was second in the 1959 Lowther Stakes before producing 1967 Prix de l'Abbaye winner Pentathlon, and Parthenon, the 1970 Queen Alexandra Stakes and Goodwood Cup winner. Fresco's dam Cornice finished third in the Coronation Stakes and is best remembered as the dam of 1952 Oaks winner Frieze.

Hollywood Dream was third in the 1994 German St Leger but raced between a mile and a quarter and a mile and a half afterwards. She was below her best on firm ground on her final outing in each of the last two seasons. However, both those races took place at Hollywood Park, a tight track which was probably not ideal for her, and it's likely she acted on any going. Her best asset was her turn of foot, something her prospective first mate, the Japan Cup winner Lando, had in abundance. *U. Ostmann, Germany*

HOME ALONE 2 b.c. (Feb 18) Groom Dancer (USA) 128 – Quiet Week-End 99 (Town And Country 124) [1996 6m 8g* 7m 8d Oct 25] 31,000Y: lengthy, quite attractive colt: third foal: half-brother to useful 3-y-o 7.5f (at 2 yrs) and 10.5f winner Pleasant Surprise (by Cadeaux Genereux) and 1m winner Tranquillity (by Night Shift): dam, 2-y-o 6f and 7f winner later successful in USA, half-sister to Lemon Souffle: made all in maiden at Goodwood in September: best effort when about 3 lengths seventh of 23 to Papua in valuable sales race at Newmarket 17 days later, disputing lead long way in falsely-run race: well held in listed race at Saint-Cloud final start: stays 1m: acts on good to firm ground: quietly to post first 3 starts, bandaged behind first and third: has worn crossed noseband: sold 25,000 gns Newmarket Autumn Sales: sent to USA. *J. H. M. Gosden*   91 ?

HOME COOKIN' 3 b.f. Salse (USA) 128 – Home Fire 99 (Firestreak 125) [1995 64?: 8m 7d 8m 1996 a8.5g 8m² 8f 8.1f³ 8m 8g³ 9g³ Aug 30] sturdy, lengthy filly: modest maiden: claimed out of Dr J. Scargill's stable £8,000 after second 3-y-o start: stays 1m: acts on good to firm ground. *M. C. Pipe*   58

HOME COUNTIES (IRE) 7 ch.g. Ela-Mana-Mou 132 – Safe Home 94 (Home Guard (USA) 129) [1995 74: 10.5g³ 10m⁶ 1996 10d⁶ 13.1s⁶ 10.5m⁵ 11.9m⁶ 11.9g   –

Oct 10] lengthy gelding: poor mover: fair handicapper at his best: failed to find his form in 1996: should stay beyond 10.5f: acts on good to firm and dead ground: sometimes visored: useful hurdler. *D. Moffatt*

HO MEI SURPRISE 4 ch.c. Hadeer 118 – By Surprise 68 (Young Generation 129) [1995 41: a7g a6g a5g⁶ a5g a6g³ a6g⁴ a5g a6g⁵ 1996 a7g a6g⁵ a6g a5g⁵ a6g 5m Aug 5] plain colt: poor walker: poor maiden handicapper: stays 6f: acts on fibresand: tried blinkered. *B. Preece*   37

HOMESTEAD 2 ch.c. (Apr 3) Indian Ridge 123 – Bertrade 75 (Homeboy 114) [1996 6m 7m 8.1g⁵ 7.3m 6m 7.3s Oct 26] 19,000Y: close-coupled colt: good walker: unimpressive mover: fifth foal: half-brother to 3-y-o Astra Martin (by Doc Marten) and 5-y-o 5f (at 2 yrs) to 7f winner Winsome Wooster (by Primo Dominie): dam, stayed 1¼m, sister to sprinter Bertie Wooster: modest maiden: well below form on soft ground final start: probably requires further than 6f. *R. Hannon*   63 ?

HONEST GUEST (IRE) 3 b.f. Be My Guest (USA) 126 – Good Policy (IRE) 80 (Thatching 131) [1995 91: 6.1m² 7.1m* 7m⁴ 7d³ 1996 7m³ 8m⁵ 12m 8g 10g⁴ 10m³ 12g Sep 29] leggy, workmanlike filly: useful performer: third in Nell Gwyn Stakes at Newmarket and 4 lengths fifth to Bosra Sham in 1000 Guineas first 2 starts: creditable efforts in France on fifth and sixth starts: stays 1¼m, not 1½m: acts on good to firm ground and dead, yet to race on extremes: visored (pulled too hard) fourth 3-y-o start: sent to USA. *M. H. Tompkins*   105

HONESTLY 3 ch.f. Weldnaas (USA) 112 – Shadha 57 (Shirley Heights 130) [1995 –, a73: 6m 7f⁶ 7d a6g³ a7g³ a8.5g⁴ a7g* 1996 a7g⁴ a7g⁶ 7f 8f a12g⁶ a9.4g* a9.4g³ Dec 28] fair form on the all-weather: returned to form after 4 poor efforts when lucky winner of claimer at Wolverhampton in November: stays 9.4f: best form on fibresand (at Wolverhampton), has shown little on turf. *B. Smart*   – a71

HONEYHALL 3 b.f. Crofthall 110 – Attila The Honey 54 (Connaught 130) [1995 NR 1996 5g 6g 7f 6m 6m a6g⁴ a6g* a6g Dec 3] sturdy filly: first reported foal: dam fair plater at up to 1m: poor performer: won handicap at Southwell in November: stays 6f: acts on fibresand, no form on turf. *N. Bycroft*   – a41

HONEY MOUNT 5 b.g. Shirley Heights 130 – Honeybeta 105 (Habitat 134) [1995 –: 16g 17.2m 1996 a14.8g Jan 3] leggy, angular gelding: fairly useful handicapper (rated 80) at 3 yrs: well beaten since: stays 1¾m: tried blinkered: winning novice hurdler (over 3m) in November. *N. J. H. Walker*   –

HONEYSHAN 4 b.f. Warrshan (USA) 117 – Divissima 62 (Music Boy 124) [1995 NR 1996 8.1m 10m Aug 14] robust, good-topped filly: fourth foal: half-sister to 1992 6f winner Nut Bush (by Aragon): dam, 6f winner, half-sister to smart 1978 2-y-o sprinter Eyelet: soundly beaten in maidens at Sandown: bandaged in front. *D. J. S. ffrench Davis*   –

HONEY TRADER 4 b.g. Beveled (USA) – Lizzie Bee (Kind of Hush 118) [1995 65d: 5d³ 5.1g 5g⁶ 5g 5f⁵ 1996 a5g⁶ a6g Apr 13] leggy, angular gelding: has a round action: modest sprint maiden at best: no promise 2 starts in 1996: probably acts on any ground: has joined M. Hourigan, Ireland. *J. Berry*   –

HONG KONG DESIGNER 4 br.g. Dunbeath (USA) 127 – Pokey's Pet 56 (Uncle Pokey 116) [1995 54: 10d 12m 14.1m 14m³ 16.2g⁴ 13.8m³ 16d 15.1g⁴ 1996 a14.8g 12g 8m 14.1f Jun 22] smallish gelding: has a round action: soundly beaten in 1996, on reappearance for A. P. James: looks a thorough stayer: acts on good to firm ground, probably on dead: visored (geed up, well beaten) third 3-y-o start. *Miss J. F. Craze*   –

HONG KONG DOLLAR 4 b.g. Superpower 113 – Daleside Ladybird 66 (Tolomeo 127) [1995 54d: 5d 7g 8m⁴ a8.5g² 7g a6g² 5.3f⁴ 6f⁴ a5g a8g a7g 1996 a8g 6m 6f 5m a8g a6g Dec 3] lengthy gelding: has shown nothing for some time: has been tried in blinkers/visor. *B. A. Pearce*   –

HONG KONG EXPRESS (IRE) 2 b.f. (Mar 9) Distinctly North (USA) 115 – North Kildare (USA) (Northjet 136) [1996 5g 7s⁴ 6m³ 6m 6f⁴ 6s Aug 31] 10,000Y: close-coupled filly: second foal: sister to 3-y-o Flying North, 5.9f winner at 2 yrs: dam unraced half-sister to high-class Fanmore out of speedy Irish filly Lady Blackfoot: modest maiden: stays 7f: acts on firm and soft going: tended to carry head high on third outing. *J. Berry*   55

HONORABLE ESTATE (IRE) 3 b.f. High Estate 127 – Holy Devotion 72
(Commanche Run 133) [1995 72p: 5m⁶ 5.1m³ 6g³ 6m* 1996 8m² 9.9m 10s⁵ 7m*
8.3m⁶ 8g 8m⁵ 8.3g³ 7g* 7g 8f² 7m 7m 8f Oct 14] quite attractive filly: fair performer:
won claimers at Goodwood in June and Leicester (very easily) in August: sold 4,200
gns Newmarket Autumn Sales: effective at 7f and 1m: acts on firm ground: found
little sixth 3-y-o start: inconsistent: sent to Saudi Arabia. *R. Hannon*

HONOURABLE FELIX 2 b.c. (May 7) Wace (USA) 82 – Lady Gilly (Re- –
mainder Man 126§) [1996 5g 7g 6g Oct 29] close-coupled colt: not a good walker:
second reported foal: dam unraced: behind in maidens, rearing stalls final start. *E. J.
Alston*

HOOFPRINTS (IRE) 3 b.c. Distinctly North (USA) 115 – Sweet Reprieve 64
(Shirley Heights 130) [1995 61p: 8m 1996 10m 10m 13.1m⁶ 14m⁵ 15.4g⁵ 14.1m a75
13.6m⁴ a13g* a12g* a12s³ Nov 19] big, strong, rangy colt: has scope: fair performer:
won maiden (idled) in October and handicap following month, both at Lingfield:
stays 15.4f: has raced only on a sound surface on turf, goes well on equitrack: usually
races prominently. *Mrs A. J. Perrett*

HOPE CHEST 2 ch.f. (May 1) Kris 135 – Hopeful Search (USA) 71 (Vaguely 70 p
Noble 140) [1996 7m³ Sep 10] fourth living foal: half-sister to 4-y-o 7f and 1m
winner Mezzoramio (by Cadeaux Genereux): dam, disappointing maiden possibly
best at 1¼m, half-sister to Treizieme and Eastern Mystic: 7/1 from 3/1, just under 2 lengths third of 14 to Corsini in maiden at
Lingfield, leading 2f, wandering through greenness 2f out: will improve. *D. R. Loder*

HOPESAY 2 b.f. (Mar 4) Warning 136 – Tatouma (USA) 79 (The Minstrel (USA) 84
135) [1996 6g³ 6m³ 6m² Sep 21] close-coupled filly: fourth foal: half-sister to 3-y-o
Atlantic Storm (by Dowsing) and 1994 2-y-o 7f winner Trimming (by Thatching):
dam 2-y-o 5f and 6f winner, from family of Law Society and Legal Bid: progressive
form in maidens: neck second of 24 to Speedball at Newbury final start: will stay 1m:
swished tail throughout on debut. *J. H. M. Gosden*

HOPPERETTA 2 b.f. (Mar 15) Rock Hopper 124 – Can Can Girl 69 (Gay 45
Fandango (USA) 132) [1996 a7g³ a7g³ 6d⁵ 8f a7g 10f 10g a7g a7g⁴ a8g³ Dec 3] a43
1,000Y: workmanlike filly: half-sister to unreliable 6f to 1m performer Languedoc
(by Rousillon): dam lightly-raced daughter of speedy Noiritza, dam of smart sprinter
Al Sylah: poor maiden: probably stays 1¼m: acts on firm and dead ground and on
fibresand: well beaten only try in blinkers: tail flasher: doesn't look the easiest of
rides. *B. Palling*

HORESTI 4 b.c. Nijinsky (CAN) 138 – Sushila (Petingo 135) [1995 78: 8m⁵ 10m² 70 d
10m⁶ 1996 12m³ 12.3g 10m 12m 13.3f 11.5m³ Aug 22] lengthy, good-topped colt:
fair maiden: easily best effort in 1996 when third at Folkestone on reappearance:
sold 10,000 gns Newmarket Autumn Sales: stays 1½m: yet to race on a soft surface:
blinkered fourth 3-y-o start: sent to Czech Republic. *C. E. Brittain*

HORNBEAM 2 b.c. (Mar 17) Rich Charlie 117 – Thinkluckybelucky (Maystreak 94 ?
118) [1996 5f⁴ 6m⁵ Aug 1] strong, workmanlike colt: fifth reported foal: half-brother
to German 4-y-o winner (at up to 8.5f) Red Astair (by Risk Me): dam sprint placer:
backward, held up and always last of 4 in maiden at Sandown in July: around 4½
lengths fifth of 7 to Easycall in Richmond Stakes at Goodwood 2 weeks later, well
behind until late headway: possibly flattered at Goodwood, but almost certainly good
enough to win a maiden. *J. R. Jenkins*

HORNPIPE 4 b.g. Handsome Sailor 125 – Snake Song 94 (Mansingh (USA) 120) 60
[1995 –: a8.5g 1996 a8g a7g³ a9.4g² a8g a11g⁵ a8g a11g⁶ a12g³ Dec 27] quite
good-topped, workmanlike gelding: modest maiden handicapper: below form last 5
starts: stays 9.4f: has raced only on fibresand. *J. Wharton*

HOSTILE NATIVE 3 b.g. Formidable (USA) 125 – Balatina 85 (Balidar 133) –
[1995 NR 1996 6m 8d 6.1s Oct 31] 18,000Y: strong, lengthy gelding: half-brother to
several winners, including 1m and 1¼m winner Latin Leep (by Castle Keep): dam
sprinter: no form. *R. Guest*

HOTCAKE 3 b.g. Sizzling Melody 117 – Bold Cookie 75 (Never So Bold 135) –
[1995 NR 1996 6f 6g Sep 7] 800Y: first foal: dam placed over 5f and 6f: never placed
to challenge in claimer at Redcar and maiden at Thirsk: may do better. *Miss S. E. Hall*

HOT DOGGING 3 b.f. Petoski 135 – Mehtab 68§ (Touching Wood (USA) 127) 34
[1995 –: 8.2d 1996 9.9m⁴ 10g a8g² 8g⁴ 7m⁶ Aug 6] big, lengthy filly: poor performer: a47
bred to stay beyond 1m but is a free-running sort: best effort on equitrack. *Mrs P. Sly*

HOTLIPS HOULIHAN 3 b.f. Risk Me (FR) 127 – Lana's Pet 70 (Tina's Pet 56 d
121) [1995 63: 5g* 5.1m³ 5d⁶ 5m 7m* 7m 7.6m a7g 1996 a8g³ a10g⁴ a10g a8g⁶ 7f
7m 7d Aug 23] rangy, unfurnished filly: modest performer at 2 yrs: no worthwhile
form in 1996 after reappearance, off course 5 months after fourth start: sold 2,800
gns Newmarket Autumn Sales: stays 1m: acts on good to firm ground and equitrack:
blinkered final start: races prominently: sent to South Korea. *R. J. R. Williams*

HOT SHOT 2 gr.g. (May 22) Chilibang 120 – Free Rein (Sagaro 133) [1996 7f Jul –
16] half-brother to 3-y-o Crabbie's Pride and several winners (all by Red Sunset),
including 1994 2-y-o 7f winner Chance Bid and 1¼m winner Ice Magic: dam
unraced from family of Troy: tailed off in claimer at Brighton. *G. L. Moore*

HOTSPUR STREET 4 b.g. Cadeaux Genereux 131 – Excellent Alibi (USA) 62 d
(Exceller (USA) 129) [1995 67: 7g⁶ a9.4g⁵ 10m⁴ 11.5m⁵ 8m³ a11g⁶ 15g³ 14g 1996
16.1s³ 16.2m 16.2g⁶ 12g 12m⁶ Jun 18] tall, workmanlike gelding: has a round
action: modest maiden handicapper: disappointing after reappearance: stays 2m: acts
on good to firm and soft ground. *M. W. Easterby*

HOTSTEPPER 3 ch.f. Never So Bold 135 – Brilliant Timing (USA) (The –
Minstrel (CAN) 135) [1995 NR 1996 8m 7f Oct 14] 6,500F: plain filly: third foal:
sister to untrustworthy 1993 2-y-o 6f winner Bold Timing and half-sister to 4-y-o
Watch The Clock (by Mtoto), fairly useful winner at 2 yrs: dam once-raced half-sister
to Grade 1 performers Timely Assertion and Timely Writer: tailed-off last in maidens.
R. J. Price

HOUGHTON VENTURE (USA) 4 ch.g. Groom Dancer (USA) 128 – Perle 73 d
Fine (USA) (Devil's Bag (USA)) [1995 73: 7.1m⁴ 7.1m³ 8g³ 8m 1996 a9.4g³ 10g
8.3s a8.5g a8g⁵ a7g⁵ 8m⁵ 10g Sep 3] quite attractive gelding: good mover: fair
maiden handicapper at his best, but little worthwhile form since 4-y-o reappearance: sold 4,200 gns Newmarket September Sales: stays 9.4f: acts on fibresand
and good to firm ground: tried blinkered, no improvement: gelded: sent to Kuwait.
S. P. C. Woods

HOUSAMIX (FR) 4 gr.c. Linamix (FR) 127 – Housatonic (USA) 59 (Riverman 117
(USA) 131) [1995 122: 9.3m² 12d* 1996 10f³ Apr 7] smart French colt: lightly raced:
won 1995 Prix Niel: not discredited when staying-on 1¾ lengths third of 6 to Valanour in Prix d'Harcourt at Longchamp on only start in 1996: stays 1½m, at least in
slowly-run race: acts on good to firm and soft ground: held up: genuine. *A. Fabre,
France*

HOUSE OF DREAMS 4 b.g. Darshaan 133 – Helens Dreamgirl 95 (Caerleon 61
(USA) 132) [1995 64: 10g⁶ 10.5g 12m³ 11.8f⁵ 1996 13.8s⁶ 12.1d⁶ 12d² Apr 24] small
gelding: shows traces of stringhalt: very poor mover: modest maiden handicapper on
flat: easily best effort in 1996 on final start (bandaged and took strong hold): stays
1½m: acts on firm and dead ground: fair winning novice hurdler. *G. M. Moore*

HOUSE OF RICHES 3 b.g. Shirley Heights 130 – Pelf (USA) 79 (Al Nasr (FR) 88 §
126) [1995 80p: 6m² 7m² 9g* 1996 10.5g² 12d⁴ 10d⁶ 11.9d⁵ 11.9v Oct 6] lengthy
gelding: has a powerful, round action: fairly useful form at best: gelded after virtually
pulling himself up second start: stays 1½m: acts on dead going, well beaten on heavy:
often edgy: has looked reluctant: sent to UAE. *L. M. Cumani*

HOWARD THE DUCK 6 ch.g. Baron Blakeney 83 – One More Try (Kemal –
(FR) 120) [1995 NR 1996 10g Apr 27] first foal: dam poor novice hurdler: tailed-off
last in seller. *R. Bastiman*

HOW COULD-I (IRE) 3 br.f. Don't Forget Me 127 – Shikari Rose (Kala 48
Shikari 125) [1995 43: 6m 6g⁴ 7m⁴ 8m⁶ 7.5d 1996 9.9g³ 14.1m a8g 8m² 8f³ 8.2m* a–
8.2f² 8g⁵ 8f 8.2f³ 8f⁵ a10g⁵ Dec 26] sparely-made filly: poor handicapper: won
seller (sold out of T. D. Easterby's stable 5,000 gns) at Nottingham in June: best
efforts at around 1m: acts on firm going: blinkered fifth to penultimate 3-y-o starts:
forces pace. *Mrs N. Macauley*

HOW LONG 3 b.c. Alzao (USA) 117 – Fresh (High Top 131) [1995 NR 1996 8s⁴ 98
8.1d² 7.1m⁴ 8m³ 7m⁵ 8m⁴ 8m 7m 7.5s² 6g² Nov 2] good-bodied, attractive colt: has
scope: sixth foal: half-brother to useful sprinter Be Fresh (by Be My Guest) and 11f

winner Dr Robert (by Commanche Run): dam, good middle-distance performer in Italy, is half-sister to high-class middle-distance filly Free Guest: useful form: won maiden at Sandown in June: creditable second in valuable event at Milan (tended to hang in behind winner) and minor race at Newmarket last 2 starts: effective at 6f and stays 1m: acts on good to firm and soft ground. *L. M. Cumani*

HOWQUA RIVER 4 b.g. Petong 126 – Deep Blue Sea (Gulf Pearl 117) [1995   **51** 53d: a8.5g³ a9.4g⁵ 10.8m 7g⁵ 8m 8m 1996 a16g⁵ 11.8d³ 14.1m⁵ 12m* 12d⁶ a13g Nov 26] quite good-topped gelding: easy mover: poor handicapper nowadays: off course 3½ months, gained first win in apprentice race at Pontefract in October: stays 1½m: blinkered (sweating, ran poorly) once. *P. W. Chapple-Hyam*

HOW'S YER FATHER 10 b.g. Daring March 116 – Dawn Ditty 100 (Song   **82 d** 132) [1995 88: 6m 6m 5.1m 6m⁶ 6g² 6m⁶ 6f⁴ 6m³ 6m 6m² 6m 6g 7g 6g 6.1s 1996 5.2d 6m⁴ 6f² 6d 6d 6f² 6.1m³ 6.1m 5.7m⁵ 6g 6g 7m* 7f 6.1s a6g² a7g⁴ a6g² a6g⁶ a7s Dec 19] leggy gelding: fairly useful performer at best in 1996: nowhere near that form last 12 starts, including when winning 20-runner seller at Yarmouth in September: stays 7f: acts on any going: tried blinkered, but not for long time: has run creditably when sweating and edgy: held up. *R. J. Hodges*

HUGWITY 4 ch.g. Cadeaux Genereux 131 – Nuit d'Ete (USA) 90 (Super   **88** Concorde (USA) 128) [1995 73p: 7.3m 8g⁴ 6m 1996 10g⁴ 10g* 10.3g* 8g* 10.1m Jun 8] big, good-bodied gelding: fairly useful handicapper: won maiden at Leicester in April, £11,000 event at Chester and £9,000 event at Goodwood (gamely, caught Green Perfume on post), both in May: sweating, ran badly in £31,800 contest at Epsom final start: finds 1m a bare minimum, and stays 10.3f: has raced only on a sound surface: wears bandages. *B. Hanbury*

HULAL 2 b.c. (Mar 13) Arazi (USA) 135 – Almarai (USA) 73 (Vaguely Noble   **– p** 140) [1996 7g Oct 30] third foal: half-brother to 3-y-o Manaya (by Marju) and 4-y-o 7f and (in Italy) 7.5f winner Mutabassim (by Green Desert): dam placed at 1m and 1¼m, half-sister to Washington D C International winner Buckhar: 25/1, outpaced from halfway when down the field in 17-runner Yarmouth maiden won by Happy Valentine: should improve. *A. C. Stewart*

HULA PRINCE (IRE) 2 b.c. (May 9) Lead On Time (USA) 123 – Hud Hud   **92** (USA) (Alydar (USA)) [1996 5m* 5g* 6f⁴ 6g 6m Aug 21] big, lengthy, good-topped colt: has plenty of scope: second foal: closely related to 3-y-o Ubetwepull (7f winner in Malaysia, by Great Commotion): dam thrice-raced daughter of close relative to leading American sprinter Mr Nickerson: fairly useful form: successful in median auction maiden at Redcar and minor event at Newcastle in May: best effort in pattern races fourth to Verglas in Coventry Stakes at Royal Ascot on third start: better suited by 6f than 5f: took strong hold to post at Ascot: sent to UAE. *M. Johnston*

HULLBANK 6 b.g. Uncle Pokey 116 – Dubavarna 72 (Dubassoff (USA)) [1995   **65** 67: 16.2m³ 14.1f* 14.6g 12m² 12d⁶ 1996 a12g⁴ 13.8s 16.2m³ 14.1m 16.2g³ 14.1g² 14.1f⁵ 16.2m² 16.2m* 15.8g² 17.1m Oct 7] tall gelding: shows knee action: fair handicapper: won at Beverley in July: rare poor effort final start: stays 2m: acts on firm going: often bandaged: blinkered (ran well) fifth 6-y-o start: held up: genuine. *W. W. Haigh*

HULM (IRE) 3 ch.f. Mujtahid (USA) 118 – Sunley Princess 69 (Ballad Rock 122)   **79** [1995 71: 6f² 7g³ 1996 7g³ 8g² 8f³ 8m² 7f* Aug 9] strong, lengthy filly: fairly useful performer: blinkered, gained a deserved success in maiden at Redcar final start, making all: effective at 7f and 1m: acts on firm going, yet to race on a soft surface: races prominently: consistent. *H. Thomson Jones*

HUMOURLESS 3 ch.c. Nashwan (USA) 135 – Sans Blague (USA) 108 (The   **95** Minstrel (CAN) 135) [1995 77p: 7m 8g⁶ 8g⁴ 1996 10g* 10.4m² May 14] good-topped, close-coupled colt: good walker and mover: won minor event at Pontefract by 5 lengths: useful form when head second to Dombey in handicap at York following month: will stay beyond 1¼m: has raced only on a sound surface: remains in training. *L. M. Cumani*

HUNTERS OF BRORA (IRE) 6 b.m. Sharpo 132 – Nihad 76 (Alleged (USA)   **–** 138) [1995 97: 8m² 8.5m* 8m 10f² 10.4m 10.1g 9g³ 9d⁵ 1996 7.9m 10.1m Aug 26] sturdy, lengthy mare: useful handicapper: not seen in 1996 until August, never dangerous in rated stakes at York and Newcastle: stays 1¼m: probably acts on any going: held up: slowly away both starts at 6 yrs. *J. D. Bethell*

HUNZA STORY 4 b.f. Rakaposhi King 119 – Sense of Occasion (Artaius (USA) 29
129) [1995 45, a33: a8g a9.4g² a12g a8g 8.2m 10m² 8m 10.8m⁶ a12g 8m⁵ 10m* 10m
10m 8.1d 8.2m⁶ 11f² 10f a9.4g⁶ a12g a13g 1996 a13g a10g⁶ 8g 10g 10m 8m 10m⁶
10.8f 10g⁵ 8g 10.8m³ 12.5f⁵ 10f 10.8m 10g 10m Sep 24] small filly: bad form
nowadays: unlikely to stay beyond 11f: acts on firm ground: no improvement in
visor, bandages, tongue tie and various nosebands. *N. P. Littmoden*

HURGILL DANCER 2 b.c. (Mar 15) Rambo Dancer (CAN) 107 – Try Vickers 66
(USA) 72 (Fuzzbuster (USA)) [1996 6g a7g² 7m³ 8m⁶ 7.9g 8g³ Oct 21] 2,500Y:
fourth foal: closely related to fair sprinter Nordico Princess (by Nordico) and half-
brother to Norwegian 3-y-o 5.5f winner Pippa Passes (by Primo Dominie): dam,
maiden, stayed 1¼m: fair maiden: ran best race given his stiffest test of stamina when
third of 19 to Double Espresso in nursery at Pontefract on final start: sold 9,500 gns
Newmarket Autumn Sales: will stay beyond 1m: sweating and edgy penultimate
start, running respectably. *J. W. Watts*

HURGILL KING (IRE) 2 gr.c. (Feb 28) Ajraas (USA) 88 – Winter Lady –
(Bonne Noel 115) [1996 a7g 8.1m 7m Oct 8] IR 3,700F, 4,000Y: half-brother to 1992
2-y-o 5f winner Wintering (by Sharpo) and 3 winners abroad: dam unraced sister
to Noelino and Little Bonny: little sign of ability: tried blinkered: sold 1,400 gns
Newmarket Autumn Sales. *J. W. Watts*

HURGILL LADY 2 ch.f. (Mar 15) Emarati (USA) 74 – Gitee (FR) (Carwhite 62
127) [1996 6s² 6m⁶ 5g² 5g Oct 18] 7,000Y: well-grown, rather unfurnished filly:
sixth foal: half-sister to Irish 7f winner Woody (by Insan) and winners in Italy at
around 1m/9f by Emarati and Handsome Sailor: dam unraced: length second of 15,
looking winner 2f out, then not staying on quite so strongly as anticipated, in maiden
auction at Ripon on debut: failed to progress: sold 5,000 gns Newmarket Autumn
Sales: gives impression really needs further than 5f: pulled too hard second start.
J. W. Watts

HURGILL MINSTREL 2 gr.c. (Apr 13) Absalom 128 – Sabonis (USA) 68 –
(The Minstrel (CAN) 135) [1996 6g May 23] 4,100F, 8,200Y: third foal: third
foal: half-brother to 3-y-o Portuguese Lil (by Master Willie): dam 2-y-o 6f winner:
visored, hopelessly tailed off in claimer at Newcastle: sold 820 gns Doncaster July
Sales. *J. W. Watts*

HURGILL TIMES 2 b.g. (Apr 8) Timeless Times (USA) 99 – Crimson Dawn 64 d
(Manado 130) [1996 6m⁴ 6m³ 7d 6g⁶ 8.3d⁵ 8m⁴ Oct 17] 860F, 7,500Y: tall gelding:
fifth foal: brother to 3-y-o Red Time: dam, maiden, probably stayed 6f: never-nearer
fourth of 8 to Rich Ground in maiden at Newcastle on debut: failed to progress: sold
8,000 gns Newmarket Autumn Sales and gelded: seems to stay 1m: tried blinkered
and visored: has joined D. Shaw. *J. W. Watts*

HURRICANE STATE (USA) 2 ch.c. (Feb 19) Miswaki (USA) 124 – Regal 109
State (USA) 122 (Affirmed (USA)) [1996 7m² 6m* 6m 6.5g* 6.5d³ Nov 9]
$130,000: good-bodied colt: keen walker: fifth foal: half-brother to 3-y-o 7.1f and
1m winner Eben Naas (by Dayjur): dam, 6f and 7f winner at 2 yrs in France, half-
sister to Prix Morny winner Seven Springs, dam of Distant View: progressive form:
won maiden at Goodwood (by 5 lengths, making all) in September and (after seventh
of 11 to Bahamian Bounty in Middle Park Stakes at Newmarket) 6-runner Prix
Eclipse at Deauville (by neck from Heaven's Command) in October: good third of 8
to Deadly Dudley in Criterium des Deux Ans at Evry on final start: stays 7f: yet to
race on extremes of going: very useful. *P. W. Chapple-Hyam*

HURTLEBERRY (IRE) 3 b.f. Tirol 127 – Allberry (Alzao (USA) 117) [1995 74
68p: 5m 5m* 1996 7m 7s a8g² Nov 12] unfurnished filly: won maiden auction at
Salisbury in summer at 2 yrs: first form since (all-weather debut) when narrowly
beaten in handicap at Lingfield: stays 1m: acts on firm ground and on equitrack.
Lord Huntingdon

HUSUN (USA) 2 b.f. (Jan 19) Sheikh Albadou 128 – Tadwin 109 (Never So Bold 60 p
135) [1996 5m⁶ Aug 19] third foal: half-sister to fairly useful sprint winners Tarf (by
Diesis) and Iltimas (by Dayjur): dam sprinting half-sister to Reesh: 6/1, over 6
lengths sixth of 13 to Joza in maiden at Windsor, green and never going pace: should
do better. *P. T. Walwyn*

HUTCHIES LADY 4 b.f. Efisio 120 – Keep Mum 63 (Mummy's Pet 125) [1995 42
–: 8d 9.2s 7g 8m 7.1m⁵ 10.9g⁶ 6f 11.1g 1996 8.3s* 8.3s⁴ 7.1g⁴ 8.1g² 9.2g⁴ 9.2g⁶

8.1f a8.5g 9.2m⁴ 8d 10.9m 12.1s a11g Nov 18] small, sparely-made filly: poor handicapper: 33/1, first worthwhile form when winning at Hamilton in May: stays 9f: goes well on soft ground: tried blinkered: inconsistent. *R. M. McKellar*

HYDE PARK (IRE) 2 b.c. (Apr 27) Alzao (USA) 117 – Park Elect (Ahonoora 122) [1996 5s⁵ 5g² a5g* Nov 12] 155,000Y: robust, good-bodied colt: has scope: second foal: half-brother to fairly useful sprinter Katya (by Dancing Dissident): dam Irish 7f and 9f winner: progressive form: confirmed previous promise when winning 10-runner maiden at Lingfield by neck from Lady Shirl: will stay at least 6f: a good sort physically who should keep improving and win more races. *Sir Mark Prescott*   75 p

HYPE ENERGY 2 b.f. (Apr 9) Tina's Pet 121 – Stoneydale 83 (Tickled Pink 114) [1996 6d 5.1m² 5f⁵ Sep 17] 13,500Y: first live foal: closely related to 5-y-o 5f and 6f winner Delrob (by Reprimand) and half-sister to winning sprinters Runs In The Family (4-y-o, by Distant Relative) and Halbert (7-y-o, by Song): dam sprinter: 33/1, best effort in maiden auctions when ½-length second of 12 to Loving And Giving at Bath: will probably stay 6f. *G. Lewis*   65

I

IAMUS 3 ch.g. Most Welcome 131 – Icefern 88 (Moorestyle 137) [1995 105?: 7.1d 7d² 7.9m² 8m⁴ 1996 8.2d² 8g⁴ 7f⁶ 7g⁴ 7m 8.2m* 8m⁶ 10m 8d⁶ Sep 30] tall, leggy gelding: unimpressive walker: fairly useful but largely disappointing performer: won maiden at Nottingham in June, hanging right and jockey never going for the whip: below form afterwards, facing very stiff task final start: sold to join T. D. Barron 21,000 gns Newmarket Autumn Sales and gelded: stays 8.2f: acts on firm ground: visored (well beaten) fifth 3-y-o start: a hard ride, and temperament under suspicion. *P. T. Walwyn*   87

IBERIAN DANCER (CAN) 3 b.f. El Gran Senor (USA) – Cutty (USA) (Smart) [1995 70p: 6f⁵ 7m³ 1996 7g⁵ 9m² 9m* 11.6g⁵ 9m² 9d 10.3m 8f⁴ Oct 15] angular filly: fairly useful performer: won maiden at Goodwood in June: well below form last 3 starts, stiff task in minor event on final outing: should prove best at up to 1¼m: acts on good to firm ground: took very keen hold second 3-y-o start. *J. W. Hills*   82

IBIN ST JAMES 2 b.c. (Mar 11) Salse (USA) 128 – St James's Antigua (IRE) 79 (Law Society (USA) 130) [1996 6m 7.5f⁴ 8f 8g Oct 18] good-topped colt: has a quick action: first foal: dam 8.3f winner: seemingly best form when 10 lengths fourth of 8, staying on, to Further Outlook in maiden at Beverley on second start: never a threat in similar race at Doncaster following month or when last of 17 in Newmarket nursery on last outing. *J. D. Bethell*   70

IBLIS (IRE) 4 b.g. Danehill (USA) 126 – In Unison (Bellypha 130) [1995 95d: 7m* 8g 7g⁶ 7m⁵ 10m 8d⁶ Aug 26] close-coupled, good-quartered gelding: won handicap at Newmarket on 3-y-o reappearance in tremendous style: well beaten afterwards, and again in handicap at Ripon on belated return: retained by trainer only 600 gns Newmarket Autumn Sales: should prove effective at 1m: acts on good to firm and dead ground, probably on soft: has been gelded. *G. Wragg*   –

IBN MASIRAH 2 b.c. (May 24) Crowning Honors (CAN) – Masirah 62 (Dunphy 124) [1996 8g 8.1m³ 7m 8f Nov 5] workmanlike colt: third foal: half-brother to 6f winner Rosa Bonheur (by Absalom): dam (maiden) stayed 6f: stayed on from rear when third in strongly-run claimer at Musselburgh on second start, best effort: will probably stay beyond 1m. *Mrs M. Reveley*   51

ICANSPELL 5 b.g. Petoski 135 – Bewitched 63 (African Sky 124) [1995 –: 8m 11.1g 1996 16.5g Jun 8] leggy gelding: has completely lost his form: sold 1,050 gns Doncaster November Sales: tried visored/blinkered. *W. Storey*   –

I CAN'T REMEMBER 2 br. or gr.g. (Mar 25) Petong 126 – Glenfield Portion 86 (Mummy's Pet 125) [1996 5.1g⁵ 5d 5s* 5m² 5g² 6m⁴ 6.1m* 5.7m⁶ 6m⁴ 7.1m⁵ 7d* 6m 8m⁴ 8m² 8f⁵ 7d 8g* 7s⁴ Nov 9] small gelding: eighth live foal: brother to 3 winners at up to 7f, including 3-y-o Don't Tell Anyone, 5f winner at 2 yrs, and 5-y-o Best Kept Secret, and half-brother to 6f and 7.5f winner Glenfield Greta (by Gabitat): dam 2-y-o 5f winner: won seller at Catterick in July, 2 nurseries at Chester in August and nursery at Doncaster in October: stays 1m: probably acts on any going: 78 didn't handle home bend well at Musselburgh: trained by Jack Berry first 2 starts: tremendously tough. *P. D. Evans*

ICE AGE 2 gr.c. (Apr 2) Chilibang 120 – Mazarine Blue 65 (Bellypha 130) 82 [1996 5m* 5f⁶ Jun 6] 2,000F, 5,800Y: rather leggy colt: second foal: half-brother to 3-y-o Orange And Blue (by Prince Sabo), 5.1f winner at 2 yrs: dam sprinting half-sister to smart sprinter Rich Charlie: made all in 8-runner maiden auction at Doncaster in May: ran as if something amiss in £7,500 event at Beverley month later. *R. J. R. Williams*

ICE MAGIC 9 ch.g. Red Sunset 120 – Free Rein (Sagaro 133) [1995 26: 10.5d – 12.3f⁵ 11.1f⁵ 12.1m⁴ 16.5f⁶ 14.1m⁵ 16.2m 1996 10.5d 12.3m 10g Jul 9] sparely-made gelding: seemingly of little account nowadays: usually visored nowadays, tried in blinkers. *F. J. Yardley*

ICENI (IRE) 3 b. or br.f. Distinctly North (USA) 115 – Princess Galicia 82 (Welsh 62 Pageant 132) [1995 –p: 6.1m⁴ 1996 7m* 7m 7g 8.2g Oct 24] won maiden at Lingfield in May: well beaten in handicaps afterwards, off course nearly 4 months prior to final start: stays 7f. *H. Candy*

ICY GUEST (USA) 2 b. or br.f. (Apr 20) Clever Trick (USA) – Minstrel Guest 68 91 (Be My Guest (USA) 126) [1996 6.1f⁶ Jul 20] third foal: half-sister to fairly useful Italian 1994 2-y-o 7.5f to 1¼m winner Portiere di Notte (by Green Forest): dam 7f to 1m winner: 9/2, around 10 lengths sixth of 7 behind easy winner Ikdam in maiden at Nottingham, held up, green and not at all knocked about, never placed to challenge: subsequently lame P. Makin: looked sure to improve. *R. Charlton*

IDENTIFY (IRE) 3 b.f. Persian Bold 123 – Nordic Pride (Horage 124) [1995 7g² 105 7f* 7g⁵ 1996 7d² 9s* 10d* 12m 12g³ 9.6g³ 8g Oct 13] rangy Irish filly: fourth foal: closely related to winning 2m hurdler Dignified (by Pennine Walk): dam Irish 2-y-o 6f winner: useful performer: won maiden at Tipperary at 2 yrs, then handicap at Leopardstown and listed race at the Curragh (beat Harghar by 5½ lengths) in the spring for J. Bolger: well beaten in the Oaks at Epsom: creditable third in Austrian Derby and (3 months later) minor event at Gowran Park: tailed off final start: stays 1½m: won only start on firm ground, best form with give and acts on soft: blinkered (no improvement) last 2 starts: sent to Canada. *D. K. Weld, Ireland*

IDLE FANCY 3 b.f. Mujtahid (USA) 118 – Pizziri (Artaius (USA) 129) [1995 79 –p: 7f 1996 8g 8.3m² 8g⁴ 8g* 8g 9s Oct 23] leggy filly: fair form: sold out of Lord Huntingdon's stable 17,000 gns Newmarket July Sales after second 3-y-o start: won maiden at Navan in October: will stay beyond 8.3f: acts on good to firm ground, well beaten on soft. *C. Collins, Ireland*

IDRICA 2 b.f. Rainbow Quest (USA) 134 – Idraak (Kris 135) [1996 8f* 80 7m 8g Oct 25] quite good-topped filly: has a quick action: first foal: dam, French middle-distance maiden, is out of half-sister to Oaks winner Snow Bride (by Blushing Groom, and now dam of Lammtarra) out of top-class middle-distance filly Awaasif: odds on, won 5-runner maiden at Leicester in September: soon tailed off and appeared to take little interest in listed race at Newmarket next outing then again slowly into stride when staying-on seventh of 15, soon scrubbed along, when in mid-field nursery at Doncaster: bred to stay middle distances: has had rope halter for stalls entry all starts. *J. H. M. Gosden*

IDRIS (IRE) 6 b.h. Ahonoora 122 – Idara 109 (Top Ville 129) [1995 111: 118 9m* 8f² 9d² 11d³ 10d* 1996 8s⁴ 8s³ 7s* 8m* 6d⁵ 9g* 7g* 8m⁴ 10m* 8m* 10g⁵ 7g³ 7d⁴ Nov 10]

Idris ran more times in 1996 than he had in 1992, 1993, 1994 and 1995 put together, and reaped the reward. He won more pattern races than any other Irish-trained horse in the latest season, his total of four being one less than Helissio and the same as Anabaa and Lavirco. Unlike that trio, Idris is no champion—all of those four wins were at Group 3 level—but he is certainly genuine and consistent. Before 1996 his record in pattern races comprised a third in both the 1994 Gladness Stakes and 1995 Blandford Stakes. After taking his only race at two years impressively, there had been wins in a minor event and listed race from five starts as a three-year-old, just the one appearance at four years and another five, including wins in a valuable handicap and a minor

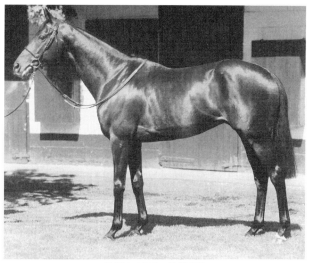

Mr Michael K. Keogh's "Idris"

		Lorenzaccio	Klairon
	Ahonoora	(ch 1965)	Phoenissa
	(ch 1975)	Helen Nichols	Martial
Idris (IRE)		(ch 1966)	Quaker Girl
(b.h. 1990)		Top Ville	High Top
	Idara	(b 1976)	Sega Ville
	(b 1981)	Enperia	Sir Ivor
		(ch 1971)	Ormara

event, at five years. After the abortive 1994 campaign, Idris was bought by Michael Keogh from the Aga Khan and transferred from John Oxx's yard to that of Jim Bolger. It was reported that Keogh purchased him as a potential stallion.

How Idris fares in that role remains to be seen, but Keogh has certainly had his money's worth out of him as a racehorse. In 1996, the six-year-old ran thirteen times, Bolger reporting that he needed frequent outings to avoid getting gross. Idris showed his form time after time, fifth in the Greenlands Stakes being easily forgiven because of the experiment at six furlongs, and the only real disappointments were his final start and his non-appearance (due to a high temperature) after travelling all the way to Hong Kong in December. The six victories—two in listed races in addition to the pattern events—all came with waiting tactics and contributed to Kevin Manning's strong challenge for the Irish jockeys' championship. For the record, the pattern races were the Gladness Stakes in April, the Horizons Ballycorus Stakes in June, Meld Stakes in July and Ridgewood Pearl Desmond Stakes in August, the second of which was at Leopardstown and the rest at the Curragh. Four lengths in the Desmond was easily his greatest winning margin, the other three all being under a length and that in the Ballycorus a head. Predappio, Song of Tara and Prince of Andros filled the frame in the Meld Stakes and were as good as any that Idris beat all year. Fourth of six was the result when Idris made a foray into Group 2 company for the Sea World International, fifth of six when he tried his luck in the Group 1 Irish Champion.

A long list of achievement such as that owned by Idris can sometimes seem rather dull, but just one race would have been an achievement for any of Idara's previous four foals. Apparently, only two of them were named. Idris was her last foal for the Aga Khan and she has since had the poor maiden Bianca Cappello (by Glenstal) and fillies in 1994 and 1996 by Dancing Dissident and Dolphin Street. Idara was a useful three-year-old, winning over eleven furlongs and a mile and a half in France. Her dam Enperia won twice there over the latter distance and was one of the mares purchased by the Aga Khan from Marcel Boussac. Out of a sister to the brilliant Coronation V, she was a half-sister to his high-class horse Locris who appeared in a host of the top one-mile to mile-and-a-quarter races in the 'sixties, racing on until he was a six-year-old like Idris but then being sent to Brazil. Idris is closer to home, at the Irish National Stud where he will be available at IR £4,000. He is surely the last good horse to represent Ahonoora, who died in 1989, and must benefit from the success of Indian Ridge, another son of that sire who is at the Irish National Stud. Ahonoora's Derby winner Dr Devious has been brought back from Japan. Idris, a sturdy horse, was just as good at seven furlongs as a mile and a quarter, and his form over eleven furlongs in the 1995 Blandford Stakes was not much worse. He acted on any going. *J. S. Bolger, Ireland*

IECHYD-DA (IRE)   2 b.g. (Apr 28) Sharp Victor (USA) 114 – Key Partner (Law   82
Society (USA) 130) [1996 5s* 5d* 6g⁴ 7m² 7m Sep 25] 6,500Y: lengthy, workman-like gelding: has scope: second foal: dam Irish 6f (at 2 yrs) to 12.5f winner, also successful over hurdles: won median auction maiden at Leicester and 3-runner minor event at Lingfield early in season: good second in minor event at Redcar in July: stays 7f: acts on soft ground and good to firm. *M. Bell*

IHTIMAAM (FR)   4 b.g. Polish Precedent (USA) 131 – Haebeh (USA) 88   –
(Alydar (USA)) [1995 69d: 8g⁵ 8m³ 8g³ 9.2f 8m 8f 1996 11.1g 7m 10.2g 8f 11.1g   a65
a11g* a12g 10.1m a11g³ a11g* a11g³ Dec 3] compact gelding: modest performer: won claimer at Southwell in July (despite jinking right) and seller on same course in November: should stay 1½m: acts on fibresand: usually gives trouble at stalls: well beaten in blinkers/visor: inconsistent. *Mrs A. Swinbank*

IHTIYATI (USA)   2 ch.c. (Apr 7) Chief's Crown (USA) – Native Twine 114 (Be   86 p
My Native (USA) 122) [1996 6m⁶ 7f 7f* Oct 8] IR 130,000Y: sturdy, lengthy colt: has scope: second foal: dam 6f (at 2 yrs) to 1¼m winner, half-sister to Alderbrook: tailed off in minor events first 2 starts: travelled smoothly and showed good turn of foot when winning steadily-run 11-runner maiden at Warwick on first run for nearly 3 months readily by 1½ lengths from Farhan: bred to stay 1¼m: should improve. *J. L. Dunlop*

IJAB (CAN)   6 b.g. Ascot Knight (CAN) 130 – Renounce (USA) (Buckpasser)   –
[1995 28, a54: a11g a11g² 12.1d a11g* a12g² a12g² 14.1f³ 10m a14g* a16g² 15.8g   a56
13.6f⁵ a14g² a14g² a14g² 1996 a16g* a14.8g⁴ Mar 16] good-topped gelding: modest handicapper on the all-weather, poor on turf: won at Southwell in March: stays 2m: acts on good to firm going and goes well on fibresand: usually blinkered nowadays. *J. Parkes*

IJTINAB   2 b.c. (Feb 28) Green Desert (USA) 127 – Nahilah 78 (Habitat 134)   –
[1996 6g Oct 9] angular, deep-girthed colt: fourth foal: half-brother to 1¼m winner Mnaafa (by Darshaan): dam lightly-raced 7f winner: 9/1, burly and green, slowly away and never a threat in maiden at York: sold 2,500 gns Newmarket Autumn Sales. *P. T. Walwyn*

IKATANIA   2 b.c. (Feb 8) Highest Honor (FR) 124 – Lady Liska (USA) (Diesis   74
133) [1996 6s⁴ 7.1g⁴ 7m⁶ 8m³ 8g Oct 18] 40,000Y: medium-sized, close-coupled colt: first foal: dam, French 7.5f winner, half-sister to dam of Breeders' Cup Sprint winner Cardmania out of half-sister to Irish River: fair form: sweating freely when

well down the field in nursery at Newmarket last start: will probably stay beyond 1m. *J. L. Dunlop*

IKDAM (USA) 2 b. or br.f. (Feb 4) Dayjur (USA) 137 – Orca (ARG) (Southern 92 p
Halo (USA)) [1996 6m³ 6.1f* 6d* Aug 12] useful-looking filly: first foal: dam, won
Argentinian 1000 Guineas, from good South American family: landed odds, not at
all hard ridden, in maiden at Nottingham in July: evens, again made all in 5-runner
minor event at Windsor 23 days later, running on well to beat Caviar Royale 1¾
lengths: sure to improve again, and should make a useful sprinter. *Major W. R. Hern*

IKE'S PET 2 ch.f. (Apr 24) Tina's Pet 121 – Cold Blow 67 (Posse (USA) 130) –
[1996 8g Nov 2] 5,400Y: first foal: dam, placed over 7f at 2 yrs, from family of
Yorkshire Oaks winners Sally Brown and Untold: 20/1 and blinkered, weakened
from 2f out when down the field in 21-runner seller at Newmarket. *M. A. Jarvis*

IKHTIRAA (USA) 6 b.g. Imperial Falcon (CAN) – True Native (USA) (Raise A 37
Native) [1995 43, a64: a16g⁴ a12g² a12g³ a12g 12m³ 11.5m 12g⁴ 10m⁴ 10f³ a12g³ a64
a16g² 1996 a16g³ a16g* a13g³ a16g² a16g⁶ 11.9f 15.4f³ 17.2f May 11] lengthy,
angular gelding: modest handicapper on the all-weather: won at Lingfield in
January: poor at best on turf, tailed off final start: stays 2m: acts on any turf ground,
goes well on all-weather surfaces: effective blinkered/visored or not: normally races
prominently: none too hearty. *R. J. O'Sullivan*

IKHTISAR (USA) 2 b. or br.f. (Mar 22) Slew O' Gold (USA) – Halholah (USA) –
65 (Secreto (USA) 128) [1996 7m⁶ Oct 17] fourth foal: half-sister to 3 winners,
including fairly useful 3-y-o 7f (at 2 yrs) to 9f winner Hilaala (by Elmaamul) and
smart 4-y-o 6f (at 2 yrs) to 10.5f winner Murajja (by Silver Hawk): dam daughter of
half-sister to Alydar: 14/1, very green and soon trailing when well-held sixth of 7 to
Meshhed in maiden at Redcar. *P. T. Walwyn*

IKTAMAL (USA) 4 ch.c. Danzig Connection (USA) – Crystal Cup (USA) 124
(Nijinsky (CAN) 138) [1995 104: 8m² 7.1m⁶ 7m² 7f* 6m⁴ 6m* 6g* 6g* 6m⁴
1996 6s⁶ 6m² 6m* 6f² 6m⁵ 6m*ᵈⁱˢ 6m⁴ 7m* 6.5d⁴ 6f* a6f⁶ Oct 26]
    Very few horses improve by as much as Iktamal. A big, strong colt, he
has always looked like a good horse in the paddock but took quite some time
before giving the same impression on the racecourse. Ninth of thirteen in a
maiden at Yarmouth in October was his only attempt at two years. He was still
battling it out in maidens on his first four starts the following season, though
battling it out is not a description that everyone would have used and it was
only by a short head that he landed odds of 5/6 in a four-runner race at Redcar.
The runner-up that day, Golden Envoy, ended 1995 rated just 68. Iktamal ended
it 104, having won another three races, including the twenty-six-runner
£16,150 William Hill Sprint Cup Handicap at Goodwood. The giant strides he
put in were due to a step down to six furlongs and a greater maturity, but 1996
was to show that the three-year-old Iktamal had been nowhere near his peak.
    It was not long before that became apparent. Second in the listed
Abernant Stakes at Newmarket in April was proof of a marked improvement
and, having travelled strongly in rear before making smooth headway at the
distance, it was evidence of even better to come. It took Iktamal a while to fulfil
that promise, however. Justifying favouritism in a minor event at Salisbury in
May was no huge feather in his cap and when he did get his head in front again
three outings later, in a listed race at Newcastle, the stewards placed him last
for the jockey having caused interference; Iktamal had been the form pick that
day, the 6/4 favourite and the winner on merit. Appearances in listed races had
not brought much luck or much reward. So his next outing was in the July Cup.
It was this step into the top grade that finally confirmed that our eyes had not
been deceiving us back in April, Iktamal staying on well at the death and failing
by just a short head to snatch third of ten behind Anabaa. He was still entered in
the Stewards' Cup at that stage, and was backed down to clear favourite for it,
but for Iktamal handicaps were now a thing of the past. He went to Newcastle
instead in Goodwood week and a dismissive last-to-first drubbing of Dance
Sequence, Branston Abby, Kahir Almaydan and the rest in the Saab Brecken-

Haydock Park Sprint Cup—
Iktamal bursts through to account for Blue Duster (noseband) and nine others

borough Beeswing Stakes suggested that there would not be many more Group 3 races in store for him either. He had three more outings in 1996, all against the best six-furlong horses around. Fourth on dead going in the Prix Maurice de Gheest was clearly not Iktamal at his best and sixth of thirteen was probably as good as could have been expected in the Breeders' Cup Sprint—he had been driven along in a vain attempt to go the early pace, and then had winner Lit de Justice sail past him from even further back—but in between those two races had come the perfect opportunity for Iktamal to register a Group 1 win. Most importantly, the line-up for the Haydock Park Sprint Cup could boast nothing in the same class as Anabaa. The Maurice de Gheest second Miesque's Son and third Danehill Dancer were there in a field of eleven, along with July Cup second and third Lucayan Prince and Hever Golf Rose, but a combination of factors, including firm ground and a strong gallop, saw 10/1-shot Iktamal turn the tables spectacularly on them all; drawn high and slowly away, he had a charmed run through before bursting into the lead fifty yards out and beating Blue Duster by a length in track-record time.

		Danzig	Northern Dancer
Iktamal (USA) (ch.c. 1992)	Danzig Connection (USA) (b 1983)	(b 1977)	Pas de Nom
		Gdynia (ch 1978)	Sir Ivor
			Classicist
	Crystal Cup (USA) (ch 1981)	Nijinsky (b 1967)	Northern Dancer
			Flaming Page
		Rose Bowl (b 1972)	Habitat
			Roseliere

A suspensory ligament injury on the day before the race ruled Iktamal out of the Hong Kong International Bowl in December when conditions should have suited him, but he is due to remain in training (after wintering in Dubai) and was the joint-best British-trained sprinter with now-retired Pivotal in 1996. He goes very well on firm going, and a strong pace helps the jockey deal with his markedly headstrong tendencies. Willie Ryan has been that jockey on Iktamal's last four starts and he holds him up in the rear before, hopefully, unleashing that good turn of foot late on. Don't be put off by Iktamal carrying his head high; in his case, it is not a habit that indicates he cannot be trusted. An implacable belief that it was will have proved expensive. That is not the only theory that Iktamal has proved the exception to, as he will also have con-

Maktoum Al Maktoum's "Iktamal"

founded a few breeding pundits. Sire Danzig Connection won the Belmont Stakes. He has sired plenty who stayed at least middle distances as well, including Star of Gdansk and Riszard, and Iktamal's dam Crystal Cup is a close relation to Ile de Bourbon no less (he is by Nijinsky out of her grandam Roseliere). Crystal Cup's dam Rose Bowl, of course, won the Champion Stakes and Queen Elizabeth II Stakes, the latter twice. Crystal Cup herself ran just twice and the only one of her first three foals to make the racecourse was the fairly useful middle-distance stayer Crystal Cross (by Roberto). Next came the Grade 2 nine-furlong Arkansas Derby winner Rockamundo (by Key To The Mint) and a winner in Japan by Woodman before Crystal Cup was sold for 58,000 dollars carrying Iktamal. A 75,000-guinea yearling, Iktamal is followed by Speed Fine (by Lear Fan), who has only been placed so far in France but looked fairly useful, and a 1995 colt who is by Danzig Connection's brother Roi Danzig. *E. A. L. Dunlop*

ILANDRA (IRE) 4 b.f. Roi Danzig (USA) – Island Goddess (Godswalk (USA) –
130) [1995 9d 12m 10f³ 10m² 12g 1996 a13g a10g a10g⁵ a12g a10g 10.8g 12d a8g² a49
a8g⁵ a10g⁴ Dec 20] ex-Irish filly: fourth foal: half-sister to 1992 2-y-o 7f winner Lyford Cay (by Waajib): dam, from family of Juliette Marny and Julio Mariner, ran once: modest maiden handicapper: trained at 3 yrs by J. G. Burns and first 5 starts in 1996 (no worthwhile form) by S. Dow: effective at 1m, and should stay 1½m: acts on firm ground and the all-weather: tried blinkered: inconsistent. *R. Akehurst*

IL DORIA (IRE) 3 ch.f. Mac's Imp (USA) 116 – Pasadena Lady (Captain James –
123) [1995 66: 5.1m² 5f 1996 6m³ 5m a5g a7g Nov 7] leggy, light-bodied, angular
filly: little wortwhile form in 1996: almost certainly a sprinter. *A. Hide*

ILE DISTINCT (IRE) 2 b.g. (Apr 25) Dancing Dissident (USA) 119 – Golden 59
Sunlight (Ile de Bourbon (USA) 133) [1996 6m 5.9f³ 7.9g Oct 9] IR 6,200F, IR
8,000Y: sixth foal: half-brother to several winners here and abroad, including 3-y-o
1¼m winner Posen Gold (by Posen) and 5-y-o 5f (at 2 yrs) to 8.5f winner Broctune
Gold (by Superpower): dam unraced: best effort in maiden events when 4½ lengths
third of 8, staying on, to Red Camellia at Carlisle in June: off course over 3 months,
well beaten at York in October: should be suited by further than 6f: slowly away first
2 starts. *Mrs A. Swinbank*

I'LL BE BOUND 5 b.g. Beveled (USA) – Treasurebound 63 (Beldale Flutter –
(USA) 130) [1995 NR 1996 a12g⁵ a12g⁴ a16g Feb 9] of little account. *W. J. Musson*

ILLEGALLY YOURS 3 br.f. Be My Chief (USA) 122 – Legal Precedent (Star 44
Appeal 133) [1995 –: 5g⁶ 6m 7m 10g a7g 1996 a8g⁴ a10g⁶ 17.2g³ a16g² 16f⁵ a16g⁶
Aug 29] leggy filly: poor maiden: seems to stay 17f: acts on equitrack: blinkered (no
improvement) first 2 3-y-o starts. *L. Montague Hall*

ILLUMINATE 3 b.c. Marju (IRE) 127 – Light Bee (USA) 86 (Majestic Light 76
(USA)) [1995 70p: 7m⁴ 1996 10.2g³ 10m⁵ 12m 10.2m⁴ 9m⁵ Aug 25] leggy, quite
attractive colt: fair maiden at best, becoming disappointing: trained until after third
start at 3 yrs by J. Toller: sold 5,000 gns Newmarket Autumn Sales: should be suited
by further than 1¼m: blinkered (took strong hold) final start. *Miss Gay Kelleway*

IL PRINCIPE (IRE) 2 b.g. (May 12) Ela-Mana-Mou 132 – Seattle Siren (USA) –
101 (Seattle Slew (USA)) [1996 5m 6g a8g Nov 14] IR 10,000F, 13,000Y: brother
to 1991 2-y-o 7f winner Sea Clover and 5-y-o middle-distance handicapper and
winning hurdler Ismeno, and half-brother to 3 winners here and abroad, including
Irish 1¼m and 1¾m winner Distant Beat (by Touching Wood): dam 6f winner at 2
yrs, is half-sister to very smart middle-distance winner Pole Position: well beaten in
maidens: moved unimpressively to post on debut. *John Berry*

IL TRASTEVERE (FR) 4 b.g. L'Emigrant (USA) 129 – Ideas At Work –
(Persepolis (FR) 127) [1995 87?: 10g⁶ 10d 8d* 8m 8g 7g⁴ 9d 7f⁴ 1996 8.1g 8m 10g
8m a9.4g Dec 28] rather leggy ex-French gelding: seemingly fairly useful form at
best in minor events at 3 yrs for J. Dunlop: well held in 1996, including in claimer:
stays 1m: acts on dead ground. *Miss Gay Kelleway*

ILUSTRE (IRE) 4 ch.g. Al Hareb (USA) 123 – Time For Pleasure (Tower Walk –
130) [1995 50: 6m⁵ 7f 6f 7m 1996 a8g a8g Feb 23] strong gelding: trained until
after final 3-y-o start by L. J. Holt: tailed off in 1996: seems to stay 7f: acts on firm
and dead ground. *G. Fierro*

IMAD (USA) 6 b. or br.g. Al Nasr (FR) 126 – Blue Grass Field 81 (Top Ville 129) – §
[1995 69: 20m 20f* 16.4m 18m 1996 17.1g 20f Jun 18] close-coupled gelding: won
Country Club Hotels Goodwood Stakes in 1995: below form since, blinkered first
time and looking reluctant final start: thorough stayer: acts on firm ground: wears a
tongue strap: fair staying hurdler. *J. White*

IMAGE MAKER (IRE) 3 gr.f. Nordico (USA) – Dream Trader (Auction Ring –
(USA) 123) [1995 44, a58: 6m⁵ 6m³ 7f⁴ a6g² 6.1d a6g a8.5g* a8.5g⁴ a8.5g⁴ a8.5g⁴
a8g⁴ a6g 1996 a7g a12g⁵ a9.4g⁵ a14.8g Jul 11] sturdy filly: lost her form: tried
blinkered, no improvement. *B. Preece*

I'M A NUT MAN 5 b.h. Shardari 134 – Zahiah 90 (So Blessed 130) [1995 NR 41
1996 12.3g 10g³ 10.3m 11.1m² 10d² 10.2m⁵ Jun 15] sparely-made horse: poor
maiden: stays 11.1f: acts on good to firm and dead ground. *C. A. Smith*

IMLAK (IRE) 4 ch.g. Ela-Mana-Mou 132 – Mashteen (USA) (Majestic Prince – §
(USA)) [1995 66§: 10g⁴ 9.9m⁴ 12s 10g 10f 1996 11.8d 14.1s⁶ 15.4f 11.8d May 27]
big, good-topped gelding: has been troublesome: fair performer at best: broke a blood
vessel (for second time) and collapsed final 3-y-o outing: below form in 1996: will
probably stay further than 1¼m: not one to rely on. *J. L. Harris*

IMPALA 2 ch.g. (May 14) Interrex (CAN) – Raleigh Gazelle (Absalom 128) 46
[1996 6.1d⁴ a6g² 7.5m⁵ 6d Oct 21] second foal: dam modest staying chaser: in frame
in sellers at Chepstow and Southwell (tended to hang right) early in season: first run

for 3½ months, soundly beaten in rating-related maiden at Folkestone on final start: probably stays 7.5f. *W. G. M. Turner*

IMPENDING DANGER 3 ch.g. Fearless Action (USA) 116 – Crimson Sol – (Crimson Beau 124) [1995 –: 7m⁴ a7g a7g⁵ 6f 1996 8m Aug 13] workmanlike gelding: little sign of ability. *K. S. Bridgwater*

IMPERIAL BID (FR) 8 b.g. No Pass No Sale 120 – Tzaritsa (USA) 113 (Young 57 Emperor 133) [1995 59: a11g a11g³ a11g³ 10.9m⁴ 11.1g* 10g⁵ 10g 11.1f³ 11.1m⁴ 11.1f⁴ 10.1m* 11.1f⁴ 10f⁵ 10f 10.1f³ 10.9g⁵ 12m 1996 a11g³ Feb 12] leggy, close-coupled gelding: modest handicapper: fit from hurdling, creditable third at Southwell only outing at 8 yrs: sold to join F. Murphy 1,900 gns Doncaster March Sales: stays 1½m: acts on hard and dead ground and on fibresand: visored (below form) final 7-y-o start: none too consistent. *Denys Smith*

IMPERIAL GARDEN (IRE) 2 ch.g. (Apr 26) Imperial Frontier (USA) 112 – 52 + Spindle Berry 92 (Dance In Time (CAN)) [1996 a5g 5f a5g* 6m 5f⁶ a6g 5s² Nov 7] a58 5,800F, IR 5,800Y, 8,000 2-y-o: lengthy, plain gelding: half-brother to several winners, including Irish 3-y-o 9f and 1¼m winner Pegwood (by High Estate) and Tiffany's Case (by Thatching), winner at around 1m: dam, 5f winner at 2 yrs, is daughter of sister to smart 1½m filly Cranberry Sauce: won 7-runner maiden auction at Wolverhampton in August by a short head: inconsistent afterwards: should stay beyond 5f: acts on fibresand and soft ground. *P. C. Haslam*

IMPERIAL OR METRIC (IRE) 2 b.g. (Apr 20) Prince Rupert (FR) 121 – 65 Caroline's Mark (On Your Mark 125) [1996 5.9g 7m⁶ 7s⁶ 7.1g² 7g³ 6m 6g 8.1m* 7.9g 8g⁶ 8g Nov 2] IR 1,500F, IR 6,000Y, 10,000 2-y-o: strong gelding: unimpressive mover: half-brother to Irish 1¼m winner Bothsidesnow (by Exhibitioner) and 2 winners in Belgium: dam Irish 2-y-o 5f winner: fair form: won claimer at Mussel-burgh in September: below form afterwards: best at 7f/1m: acts on good to firm ground. *J. Berry*

IMPERIAL PRESIDENT 2 br.c. (May 8) Known Fact (USA) 135 – House- 99 proud (USA) 115 (Riverman (USA) 131) [1996 6.1g³ 7.5m* 7f* 7m⁵ 8.1g² 7m Oct 4] leggy, close-coupled colt: has a quick action: third foal: half-brother to 1994 2-y-o 6f winner Homely (by Mr Prospector): dam won Poule d'Essai des Pouliches and is daughter of Grade 1 1m winner Proud Lou: useful colt: successful in summer in 4-runner minor event at Beverley and 5-runner Mtoto Donnington Castle Stakes (by short head from Hello) at Newbury: creditable efforts behind Putra in Lanson Champagne Stakes at Goodwood and (conceding 7 lb) Medaaly in minor event at Sandown: below form in listed race at Newmarket on final outing: stays 1m: acts on firm ground: sent to R. Frankel in USA. *H. R. A. Cecil*

IMPERIAL PROSPECT (USA) 4 b.f. Imperial Falcon (CAN) – One Tough – Lady (USA) (Mr Prospector (USA)) [1995 NR 1996 10d May 28] $11,000F: $8,000Y: tall, sparely-made filly: fourth foal: half-sister to several winners, best of them 1995 American 2-y-o Bet Twice Princess (minor sprint stakes, by Bet Twice): dam, winning sprinter, is half-sister to very useful middle-distance performer Azzaam (later Grade 1 winner in Australia) out of half-sister to top American filly Althea: well beaten in NH Flat race and Sandown maiden. *J. J. Sheehan*

IMPERIAL RED (IRE) 3 ch.g. Mac's Imp (USA) 116 – Bluemore (Morston – (FR) 125) [1995 NR 1996 5m 7.6m 6g 6m Oct 28] IR 10,500F, IR 9,000Y: compact gelding: half-brother to 5 winners, including a useful performer in Hong Kong by Montekin and fairly useful Irish 7f/1m handicapper He's A Flyer (by Whistling Deer): dam never ran: no form. *H. J. Collingridge*

IMPERIAL SCHOLAR (IRE) 2 b.f. (Apr 2) Royal Academy (USA) 130 – 75 p Last Ball (IRE) (Last Tycoon 131) [1996 6d² Aug 24] 16,000F: tall, lengthy filly: third foal: dam unraced half-sister to smart French colts Splendid Moment (at 1m/ 1¼m) and Grand Chelem (1986 2-y-o 1m winner) out of Irish Oaks third Racquette: 25/1, 1¼ lengths second of 6, not knocked about, to Desert Story in maiden at Newmarket, leaving impression would have run winner close with a trouble-free passage: will stay 1m: will improve, and should be able to win a race. *J. M. P. Eustace*

IMPETUOUS AIR 2 b.f. (Feb 16) Warning 136 – Hardihostess 104 (Be My 83 Guest (USA) 126) [1996 6m⁵ 5m² 7m* 7.1m⁴ 7m⁵ Aug 10] 15,500Y: good-bodied filly: has a quick action: half-sister to 1994 2-y-o 6f winner (stays 11f) Divina Mia (by Dowsing): dam 7f winner at 2 yrs (stayed 1½m), half-sister to Shirley Heights:

readily won maiden at Ayr in June: best form when fourth of 7 to Red Camellia in listed race at Sandown: raced only on a firm surface here: sent to Scandinavia and won over 1m in Sweden. *E. Weymes*

IMPETUOUS LADY (USA)   3 b.f. Imp Society (USA) – Urakawa (USA)   44
(Roberto (USA) 131) [1995 55d: 6.1f⁵ 6s 6g 7f 1996 6.1m⁴ 7.1m 8d Sep 30] leggy, good-topped filly: has a round action: trained by W. Musson at 2 yrs: fourth in handicap at Chepstow on reappearance: ran poorly in similar events subsequently: should stay 7f. *N. E. Berry*

IMP EXPRESS (IRE)   3 b.g. Mac's Imp (USA) 116 – Fair Chance (Young   50
Emperor 133) [1995 77: 5m⁶ 5m⁵ 5f² 5g* 5m⁶ 5m 5m³ 6g 5m⁴ 1996 5d 5g 5d 6d
5g 5g 5g³ 5f⁵ 5m⁶ 5g 5m Aug 5] good-topped gelding: only poor form in handicaps at 3 yrs, well held in seller final start: speedy, and likely to prove best at 5f: seemed suited by an easy surface at 2 yrs: blinkered/visored last 5 starts: sometimes gives trouble at stalls. *G. M. Moore*

IMPINGTON (IRE)   3 b.f. Mac's Imp (USA) 116 – Ultra (Stanford 121§) [1995   48
52+: 5.1f⁴ 6.1m³ 5g a6g a5g⁴ a5g³ 1996 a5g⁴ a5g⁶ a5g a5g⁴ a6g⁵ a5g³ Mar 18]
angular filly: poor maiden: sold 2,200 gns Doncaster March Sales: stays 6f: acts on good to firm ground and all-weather surfaces: tried visored: inconsistent: sent to Sweden and won twice over 6f there. *W. R. Muir*

IMPISH (IRE)   2 ch.g. (Apr 25) Imp Society (USA) – Halimah 56 (Be My Guest   –
(USA) 126) [1996 5m a5g 5m 6s 6g a8g Nov 4] 2,000Y: stocky gelding: second foal: dam Irish 4-y-o 9f winner out of sister to speedy Bitty Girl and Hot Spark: well beaten, including in selling nursery: unruly stalls, reared start and took no part on second start: tried blinkered. *T. J. Etherington*

IMPOSING TIME   5 b.g. Music Boy 124 – Jandell (NZ) (Shifnal) [1995 5s⁴ 6m⁴   68
5g³ 5g* 5m* 5m³ 5m 5g⁵ 1996 5s 5g³ 5g⁶ 5m² 5.3m² 5f 5.1f³ a6g² a6g* a6g² a6g Nov   a77
26] ex-Irish gelding: half-brother to 3 winners at up to 11f: dam top-rated filly in New Zealand in 1973/4, winner at up to 13f: fair handicapper: won at Wolverhampton in October: stays 6f: acts on good to firm and soft ground and goes well on fibresand: blinkered/visored since fourth 5-y-o start: withdrawn after bolting to post fourth intended 5-y-o start. *Miss Gay Kelleway*

IMPROMPTU MELODY (IRE)   3 b.f. Mac's Imp (USA) 116 – Greek Music   –
(Tachypous 128) [1995 –: 6m⁶ 5g 5f 1996 7d 6.1m Apr 30] leggy filly: no worthwhile form: blinkered final start: covered by Suluk. *B. S. Rothwell*

IMPULSIF (USA)   2 ch.c. (Jan 14) Diesis 133 – High Sevens 90 (Master Willie   73
129) [1996 5m² 6m⁴ 6.1m³ 5.7f⁵ 7g* 7g Oct 19] 16,000Y: leggy, fair sort: first foal: dam, 6f winner at 2 yrs who stayed 7f, half-sister to smart middle-distance performers Hateel (also effective at up to 2m) and Munwar: fair form: won 16-runner nursery at Brighton in October by a head, edging right and ridden out after leading almost on bridle 2f out: stays 7f: keen sort, tended to hang third outing: inconsistent. *D. J. S. ffrench Davis*

IMPULSION (IRE)   2 b.c. (Apr 18) Imp Society (USA) – Verthumna (Indian   57
King (USA) 128) [1996 5d⁵ 6m² 5.1m⁵ 5.1m⁶ 5m Sep 19] close-coupled colt: half-brother to sprint winners in Sweden (by Petorius) and Hong Kong (by Try My Best): dam maiden, ran only at 2 yrs in Ireland: modest form, including in selling company: sold 3,500 gns Newmarket Autumn Sales: stays 6f: has bolted to post: sent to Sweden. *R. Hannon*

IMPULSIVE AIR (IRE)   4 b.g. Try My Best (USA) 130 – Tracy's Sundown   69
(Red Sunset 120) [1995 88d: 8g⁵ 7m⁶ 7g 8.1g 7g 8.5d 7.1g 6s 8f 1996 6.1m⁵ 7g
6.9f* 8.3m⁵ 8f* 8.3f³ 8m² 8.9g 8g⁴ 7g Nov 2] strong, useful-looking gelding: carries condition: unimpressive mover: fair handicapper at best nowadays: won at Carlisle in June and Newcastle in August: best of last 5 starts when neck second of 25 to Gladys Althorpe in £20,000 event at Doncaster: stays 1m: acts on firm ground, probably on dead: tried visored: inconsistent, and has looked reluctant. *E. Weymes*

IMPY FOX (IRE)   2 ch.f. (Apr 10) Imp Society (USA) – Rusty Goddess (Hard   50
Fought 125) [1996 6m⁴ a6g* 6.1m⁴ 7g Oct 2] IR 1,000Y: close-coupled filly: third   a53
foal: dam Irish 4-y-o 1¼m winner: ridden by 7-lb claimer, won seller at Wolverhampton in August: should stay 7f. *C. A. Dwyer*

IMROZ (USA) 2 b.f. (Feb 14) Nureyev (USA) 131 – All At Sea (USA) 124 96
(Riverman (USA) 131) [1996 6g* 6m⁵ 7f* Sep 23] smallish, leggy, unfurnished filly:
has a quick action: first foal: dam won Prix du Moulin and Musidora and second in
Oaks: won 17-runner maiden at Newmarket in July impressively by 2½ lengths from
Rihan: heavily-backed favourite again, in trouble before halfway when fifth to
Seebe in Princess Margaret Stakes at Ascot later in month: 4/1 on, unconvincing
when winning steadily-run 3-runner minor event at Leicester after 2-month break by
a head from Musical Dancer: will stay 1m: possibly suited by an easy surface: had 2
handlers in paddock at Ascot. *H. R. A. Cecil*

I'M STILL HERE 2 gr.g. (Apr 9) Skyliner 117 – Miss Colenca (Petong 126) 61 d
[1996 5s² 5d² 5s⁴ a5g⁶ 6f² 7.1m 6g⁶ 7.1s³ Nov 7] 1,550Y resold 4,400Y: good-topped
gelding: fourth foal: half-brother to 3-y-o 7f (at 2 yrs) and 1m winner Napoleon's
Return (by Daring March): dam well beaten: modest maiden: stays 7f: acts on any
going. *J. Berry*

I'M YOUR LADY 5 ch.m. Risk Me (FR) 127 – Impala Lass 81 (Kampala 120) 75
[1995 75: 5g³ 6g 6.1m⁶ 6m 6m 5g 5m³ a5g 1996 6g 6g⁵ 7g* 7m a7g³ 6m⁴ 6.1m⁴ 6m
a7g⁵ a7g² Sep 7] plain mare: fair handicapper: won at Thirsk in May: creditable
efforts most subsequent outings: effective at 5f to 7f: acts on fibresand and any turf
going: races prominently. *B. A. McMahon*

INAMINIT 3 gr.g. Timeless Times (USA) 99 – Dolly Bevan 53 (Another Realm 60 d
118) [1995 –: 5s 6m 1996 7m 6.9m³ 6m 7m 7g 10.8f a8.5g a6g Nov 14] small
gelding: easily best effort when third in maiden at Folkestone in May: stays 7f: tried
blinkered, no improvement: refused to race final start: inconsistent and not one to
trust. *H. J. Collingridge*

IN A MOMENT (USA) 5 ch.g. Moment of Hope (USA) – Teenage Fling (USA) –
(Laomedonte (USA) 116) [1995 –, a58: a11g⁴ a11g 16.2m 14.1g 1996 a16g 13.8s
Mar 27] good-topped gelding: modest performer at best nowadays: below form over
staying trips last 4 starts: stays 11.9f: acts on fibresand, probably on good to firm
ground and heavy: tried visored/blinkered, no improvement: has joined C. Grant.
T. D. Barron

IN A TIZZY 3 b.f. Sizzling Melody 117 – Tizzy 79 (Formidable (USA) 125) 29
[1995 42, a–: 5d⁴ a6g a7g⁵ 7.1g⁴ 8.3g⁴ 1996 11.1m⁴ 9.9g 5g Sep 7] poor maiden a–
handicapper: stays 1¼m: visored (soundly beaten in seller) third 2-y-o start: winning
selling hurdler. *P. C. Haslam*

INCA BIRD 3 b.f. Inca Chief (USA) – Polly Oligant (Prince Tenderfoot (USA) –
126) [1995 –: 7g 7.1s 1996 a6g 6.1g a9.4g 8.2m 7.5m 8g Jul 24] smallish,
close-coupled filly: no worthwhile form: left B. McMahon after third start: blinkered
final outing. *T. Wall*

IN CAHOOTS 3 gr.c. Kalaglow 132 – Royal Celerity (USA) (Riverman (USA) 46
131) [1995 NR 1996 5.1g 9.9g a8.5g⁶ 10.2m 10d 11.9f 10f* 10.8f Oct 8] leggy colt:
sixth foal: half-brother to winners in Italy and Germany: dam, Irish 1m winner: poor
performer: won seller at Leicester in September: better form at 1¼m than shorter:
acts on firm ground: pulled too hard when blinkered. *A. G. Newcombe*

INCANDESCENT 2 b.f. (Mar 1) Inca Chief (USA) – Heavenly State 49 ?
(Enchantment 115) [1996 5.7g⁶ 6m a7g Jul 27] second reported foal: dam unraced:
only worthwhile form in maidens when sixth of 10 at Bath, soon tailed off after slow
start then staying on past beaten horses. *A. P. Jones*

INCAPOL 3 b.c. Inca Chief (USA) – Miss Poll Flinders (Swing Easy (USA) 126) –
[1995 62: 5m 6g 5.1m* 5m³ 5g 6d 6m⁶ a6g 1996 5d Apr 13] strong colt: modest
performer: pulled up and dismounted on reappearance: stayed 6f: acted on good to
firm ground: dead. *M. J. Ryan*

INCATIME 2 b.c. (May 5) Inca Chief (USA) – Parrot Fashion 86 (Pieces of Eight 63
128) [1996 5m³ 5m⁴ a6g a5g⁵ Dec 31] half-brother to 3-y-o 7.6f winner Designer a?
Lines (by Beveled) and several poor animals: dam best at 1¼m: similar form in
median auction maidens at Windsor and Sandown in the summer: well held on the
all-weather last 2 outings. *C. James*

INCATINKA 3 gr.f. Inca Chief (USA) – Encore L'Amour (USA) § (Monteverdi –
129) [1995 63: 5.7m³ 6f⁴ 1996 6m 5f⁶ a6g a8g Nov 12] sparely-made filly: modest

Tote Cesarewitch (Handicap), Newmarket—Inchcailloch (dark sleeves) takes a break from his chasing career; the gap comes just in time for him to beat En Vacances (right) and Canon Can

form as 2-y-o: long way below best in 1996, including in blinkers: should stay 7f. *J. L. Spearing*

INCHCAILLOCH (IRE) 7 b.g. Lomond (USA) 128 – Glowing With Pride 81 114 (Ile de Bourbon (USA) 133) [1995 68: 16.4m² 17.2m* 16m 17.2m* 17.1m 18m⁴ 16.5m 1996 16g 17.2d² 16.1f* 18g* Oct 19] big, strong, lengthy gelding: fairly useful handicapper in 1996, best form since 3 yrs: won apprentice event at Warwick and 26-runner £48,800 Tote Cesarewitch at Newmarket (under 7-lb claimer, overcame scrimmaging to head En Vacances near line), both in October: stays extreme distances: probably acts on any going: held up: progressive chaser, winner in November and December. *J. S. King*

INCHELLA 3 b.f. Inca Chief (USA) – Sandy Cap 62 (Sandy Creek 123) [1995 – NR 1996 8.3g Sep 29] first reported foal: dam 2-y-o 5f winner: tailed-off last in claimer at Hamilton. *Miss L. A. Perratt*

INCHYRE 3 b.f. Shirley Heights 130 – Inchmurrin 114 (Lomond (USA) 128) 102 [1995 81: 7m⁶ 8.1d² 1996 8m* 10.1m⁴ 12g⁴ Sep 29] leggy, sparely-made filly: useful form: 15/8 on after almost year's absence, won maiden at Warwick in August: fourth in listed races at Yarmouth (behind Flame Valley) and Ascot (behind Altamura) in September: stays 1½m: yet to race on extremes of going: has been equipped with rope halter: sold 62,000 gns Newmarket December Sales. *R. Charlton*

INCLINATION 2 b.f. (May 10) Beveled (USA) – Pallomere 85 (Blue Cashmere 64 129) [1996 7g² 7.6d² 6m⁶ Sep 21] tall, lengthy filly: half-sister to 3 winners abroad: dam best at 2 yrs, later 3-y-o 1m winner: similar form all starts in maidens: stays 7.6f: front runner/races prominently. *M. Blanshard*

INCLUDE ME OUT 2 ch.g. (Apr 14) Old Vic 136 – Tafila 101 (Adonijah 126) 69 p [1996 8m⁶ 8m 8.2g⁴ Oct 24] heavy-bodied gelding: third foal: half-brother to French 3-y-o 11f winner Udina (by Unfuwain): dam 1m and 1¼m winner: progressive form: around 4 lengths fourth of 15 to Over To You in maiden at Nottingham: will be suited by middle distances: gelded at end of year. *J. R. Fanshawe*

IN COMMAND (IRE) 2 b.c. (Feb 28) Sadler's Wells (USA) 132 – Flying 114 Melody (Auction Ring (USA) 123) [1996 6m* 7m³ 7f² 6m³ 7g* Oct 18] While the field for the latest running of the Dewhurst Stakes was back to strength numerically after only four had turned out in 1995, it still lacked the quality of most of the renewals in the 'nineties, and at this stage it is hard to imagine a Generous, a Dr Devious, a Zafonic or a Pennekamp emerging from among the eight contestants. Some of the top colts were absent from the race, for a variety of reasons: Bahhare had been put away for the year after winning the Laurent-Perrier Champagne Stakes at Doncaster, Revoque contested the Grand Criterium at Longchamp instead and Putra coughed his way out. And none of the French came over. In the circumstances In Command started at longish odds at 10/1. He had been placed behind some of the best since making a winning debut at Goodwood in July. Starting at 11/8-on to follow up in the Deploy Acomb Stakes at York the following month he spoiled his chance by pulling hard in rear in a steadily-run race and finished only third to Revoque. Racing prominently throughout next time in the Laurent-Perrier Champagne Stakes, for which he started the outsider of the quartet, In Command showed much improved form and came three and a half lengths second to Bahhare. That was over seven furlongs. He again ran well back at six in the Middle Park Stakes at Newmarket in October, performing as though he found the trip on the sharp side: unable to quicken over a furlong out, he stayed on strongly for third place, about a length down on Bahamian Bounty and Muchea.

Bahamian Bounty looked the one they had to beat in the Dewhurst fifteen days later, and In Command ran in the second colours of Maktoum Al Maktoum. Bahamian Bounty shared joint-favouritism with the Ascot conditions-race winner Kahal, ahead of the National Stakes winner Desert King, the Salamandre runner-up The West and the Newmarket maiden winner Musical Pursuit, while only Wind Cheetah, the winner of a maiden at Lingfield, and Air Express, beaten four times already in pattern races, started longer than In Command. In Command settled well, close up behind the pace set by Musical Pursuit and Kahal, was ridden along to move upsides two out and took a narrow advantage inside the last. Musical Pursuit rallied up the hill where Air Express threw down a challenge but In Command held on gamely, with just a head and a neck to spare at the line. Bahamian Bounty, just under two lengths back in fourth, was checked slightly in the Dip but it was the extra furlong rather than that incident which accounted for the reversal of the Middle Park form. Kahal, Desert King and The West all finished close up, with Wind Cheetah bringing up the rear, beaten little more than four lengths. Above all, the result served to strengthen Bahhare's position as Two Thousand Guineas favourite.

In Command may have won a substandard Dewhurst but that was still a Group 1 contest, and his dam has now achieved the feat of producing three foals who have gone on to succeed at the top level as two-year-olds, following the Nunthorpe winner Lyric Fantasy (by Sadler's Wells's brother Tate Gallery) and the Middle Park winner Royal Applause (by Waajib). Flying Melody was useful on the track in France where she won over six furlongs on her only start at two and over six and a half furlongs from eight attempts at three. She has also produced a trio of winners at a more modest level, the sprinters Mere Melody

Dewhurst Stakes, Newmarket—well-related In Command (blaze) gains a hard-fought victory; Musical Pursuit (noseband) is second and Air Express (second left) third

Maktoum Al Maktoum's "In Command"

(by Dunphy) and Flying Monarch (by Tender King), and Lucayan Cay (by Al Hareb) who won over an extended mile and was also awarded a race over hurdles early in the year. More details of the family, which is essentially one of sprinters, can be found under Royal Applause in *Racehorses of 1995* and Lyric Fantasy in *Racehorses of 1992*.

In Command (IRE) (b.c. Feb 28, 1994)	Sadler's Wells (USA) (b 1981)	Northern Dancer (b 1961)	Nearctic Natalma
		Fairy Bridge (b 1975)	Bold Reason Special
	Flying Melody (b 1979)	Auction Ring (b 1972)	Bold Bidder Hooplah
		Whispering Star (ch 1963)	Sound Track Peggy West

By Sadler's Wells out of a mare who has proved largely an influence for speed, the all-important question is how far will In Command stay? Judged on his efforts in the Middle Park and then the Dewhurst he is better suited by seven furlongs than six and, given his sire, is well worth at least one try at a mile. A second important question is will he train on? Although both Lyric Fantasy and Royal Applause managed to win as three-year-olds (both over six furlongs) their second seasons were disappointing compared to their first. The sturdy, deep-girthed In Command, a quick-actioned colt who has done all his racing on a sound surface, must have better prospects of training on, though he will need to make plenty of improvement over the winter to have a major chance in the Guineas. *B. W. Hills*

INDIAHRA 5 b.m. Indian Ridge 123 – Mavahra 93 (Mummy's Pet 125) [1995 52: 7.6m 6f⁵ 6m 6m a7g⁴ a7g³ a8.5g 7f 6m 6d 6.1d 5.1d² 5f 6f a6g² a6g 1996 a6g⁴ a6g⁶   58 a53 a7g³ a8g³ a8g³ a7g⁵ a8g⁶ a7g 5m⁴ 5m 6m³ 7g² a8g* a7g a8g² Dec 27] leggy mare: modest handicapper: left R. Hollinshead after eighth start and off course 5½ months: won minor event at Southwell in November: stays 1m: acts on fibresand, best turf efforts with some give in the ground: effective visored or not: usually held up. *J. L. Eyre*

INDIANA PRINCESS   3 b.f. Warrshan (USA) 117 – Lovely Greek Lady 63 (Ela-Mana-Mou 132) [1995 NR 1996 10m⁵ 8m⁶ 9m⁶ 12m⁶ 14d⁵ 13.6m² Oct 17] leggy, workmanlike filly: third living foal: half-sister to a winner abroad by Alleging: dam never ran: best effort when second of 15 to Broughtons Formula in handicap at Redcar final start: shapes like a stayer: acts on good to firm going. *Mrs M. Reveley*

INDIAN BLAZE   2 ch.g. (May 15) Indian Ridge 123 – Odile (Green Dancer 77 (USA) 132) [1996 7m 6g² 6m⁴ 7.1v⁵ Oct 6] 25,000Y: workmanlike gelding: eighth foal: half-brother to 3-y-o 7f winner Welcome Lu and a winner (at up to 1¼m) in Italy (both by Most Welcome) and 2 winners by Mummy's Pet, including fair 1m winner Odilex: dam once-raced granddaughter of 1000 Guineas winner Waterloo: fair maiden: stays 7f: acts on good to firm and heavy ground. *P. W. Harris*

INDIAN BRAVE   2 b.c. (Jan 26) Indian Ridge 123 – Supreme Kingdom 85 (Take 82 A Reef 127) [1996 6m² 6g³ Oct 9] lengthy colt: fifth foal: half-brother to 6f and 7f winner Sakharov (by Bay Express) and fairly useful 5-y-o 1m and 8.5f winner Equerry (by Midyan): dam 2-y-o 7.2f winner who became temperamental as 4-y-o: 1½ lengths second of 5 to Danetime in maiden at Newcastle, disputing lead much of way then running very green off bridle: started slowly, pulled hard and never reached principals when third to Wolf Mountain in maiden at York later in month. *M. Johnston*

INDIAN JOCKEY   4 b.g. Indian Ridge 123 – Number Eleven 69 (Local Suitor 68 (USA) 128) [1995 69: 10m* 10.3g* 10.2m⁴ 10.5m³ 10f 7.1g 1996 9m⁶ 8m* 8.3g 9.7m Jul 15] smallish, leggy gelding: fair handicapper: won claiming contest at Bath in June: effective at 1m to 1¼m: acts on good to firm ground: tends to pull hard: fairly useful though unreliable hurdler. *M. C. Pipe*

INDIAN NECTAR   3 b.f. Indian Ridge 123 – Sheer Nectar 72 (Piaffer (USA) 62 113) [1995 –p: 7d⁶ 1996 8f⁴ 9m 10m⁴ 10g a11g 10d Oct 2] sparely-made filly: best effort when fourth on handicap debut at Windsor in July: well beaten afterwards: stays 1¼m. *G. B. Balding*

INDIAN RAPTURE   2 ch.f. (Jan 27) Be My Chief (USA) 122 – Moments Joy 68 56 (Adonijah 126) [1996 8.1g⁶ 8.1m⁶ 8.2m⁶ 7.3s Oct 26] lengthy filly: fourth foal: half-sister to 1993 Irish 2-y-o 7f winner Oranedin (by Squill): dam (maiden) probably stayed 1½m: beaten around 9 lengths at most in maidens first 3 starts: sold to join Ronald Thompson only 500 gns Doncaster November Sales: will stay beyond 1m: well beaten on soft ground. *R. Hannon*

INDIAN RELATIVE   3 b.f. Distant Relative 128 – Elegant Tern (USA) 102 (Sea 83 Bird II 145) [1995 77: 6g⁵ 7m² a6g² 1996 8.2m 7.9f 7g³ 6f* 5.7m* 6m 6g² 6d⁵ 6m² 6m 5g Oct 21] smallish, good-quartered filly: fairly useful performer: won maiden at Redcar and minor event at Bath within 7 days in June: 25/1 and ridden by 5-lb claimer, best effort when neck second of 21 to Clan Chief in £15,000 handicap at Goodwood on ninth start: far from discredited when seventh of 28 in Ayr Silver Cup 7 days later, and met trouble in running on final outing: best at up to 7f: acts on firm going. *R. Guest*

INDIAN RHAPSODY   4 b.f. Rock City 120 – Indian Love Song 68 (Be My 56 Guest (USA) 126) [1995 56: 7g 6s 8.1g⁴ 8f* 8g² 8.1d⁴ 8d* 8f⁵ 9.9m⁶ 8f⁵ 10m³ 7m* 7g 1996 7m a7g 10m 8.1g⁴ 8m⁵ 8m* 7m 8m⁶ Sep 20] unfurnished filly: modest handicapper: won seller at Newmarket in August: sold 2,000 gns Doncaster October Sales: effective at 7f to 1¼m: acts on firm and dead ground: visored (won) once at 3 yrs: tried blinkered: sent to South Korea. *A. Bailey*

INDIAN ROCKET   2 b.c. (Mar 20) Indian Ridge 123 – Selvi (Mummy's Pet 113 + 125) [1996 6g² 6.1g* 6.1m² 6m* 6d* 6m* 6m Oct 3]
   The Bonusprint Mill Reef Stakes winner Indian Rocket has much in common with his immediate predecessor Kahir Almaydan. For a start they are stable companions. The Dunlop-trained pair showed a similar level of form at two and were given similar campaigns, raced exclusively at around six furlongs

Bonusprint Mill Reef Stakes, Newbury—the decisive winner Indian Rocket (R. Hills)

and showing steady improvement from their respective debuts in late-May up to the Mill Reef. Both won the Champion Two Yrs Old Trophy at Ripon prior to Newbury and both ran below form in the Middle Park Stakes afterwards.

Indian Rocket made his debut at Lingfield and, like Kahir Almaydan, was beaten a short head. He soon made amends in a maiden at Chepstow in June with his rivals strung out, and after being beaten in a minor event at Chester where the lack of an end-to-end gallop seemed to find him out, he won a competitive conditions race comfortably at Haydock in August and followed up in the Champion Two Yrs Old Trophy at Ripon later in the month, running out an emphatic three-length winner of the listed contest from Omaha City.

Indian Rocket's Mill Reef was a more competitive affair than that twelve months earlier, and for only the second time in twenty-five runnings attracted a double-figure field. Indian Rocket started third favourite at 100/30 behind the fillies Seebe, winner of the Princess Margaret Stakes and third in the Lowther, and Sambac who had completed a hat-trick in lesser company. Among those starting at 10/1 or longer were Omaha City, reopposing from Ripon, Maserati Monk who had beaten Indian Rocket at Lingfield but had not made the same progress in the meantime, and Proud Native who had finished last in the Gimcrack on his previous outing. Indian Rocket was always travelling strongly, and after seeing off the short-lived challenge of Proud Native he came clear inside the last, eased slightly near the line, to beat Proud Native two and a half lengths. Seebe was nearest at the finish, staying on a neck behind the runner-up. Kahir Almaydan's Mill Reef win saw him odds on for the Middle Park, Indian Rocket's saw him second favourite in what was again a larger field than that of twelve months before. Indian Rocket looked very well beforehand but he failed by a long way to give his running, swerving right from his outside draw as the stalls opened and dropping out after showing prominently early on.

A 36,000 guineas buy at the Tattersalls October Yearling Sales, Indian Rocket is much his family's best recent performer. His dam Selvi gained her only placing from six starts as a three-year-old when third in a six-furlong maiden at Folkestone but she has a better record at stud, her two other runners having won—Skerries Bell, a filly by Taufan, in Belgium; and Capodinegro, a three-year-old colt by Cyrano de Bergerac, twice over a mile in France in the latest season. Selvi is a sister to four winners, best of them the useful filly Hindi who won over five furlongs at two and a mile at three, and half-sister to three more winners, the latest the 1996 two-year-old six-furlong winner Samsung Spirit. Selvi's dam Sarong showed quite useful form when winning over a mile and she was one of five winners out of the fair winning sprinter Sharondor.

		Ahonoora	Lorenzaccio
Indian Ridge	(ch 1975)	Helen Nichols
Indian Rocket	(ch 1985)	Hillbrow	Swing Easy
(b.c. Mar 20, 1994)		(ch 1975)	Golden City
		Mummy's Pet	Sing Sing
	Selvi	(b 1968)	Money For Nothing
	(b 1985)	Sarong	Taj Dewan
		(b 1972)	Sharondor

Indian Rocket is an attractive, good-bodied colt and it was presumably his looks rather than his pedigree which contributed to his sale price, which was about twice the median for an Indian Ridge colt that year. He will almost certainly prove best as a sprinter and has shown that he acts on both good to firm and dead ground. He was sent to spend the winter in the UAE. *J. L. Dunlop*

INDIAN SERENADE 5 ch.g. Mansingh (USA) 120 – La Melodie 77 (Silly Season 127) [1995 52, a60: a7g³ a6g⁴ a7g² a7g² a8g* a8g a7g² a8g a8g² 8g 8.2m² 1996 8g 8.1g a8g 6.9g Jul 3] tall gelding: modest handicapper: trained at 4 yrs by P. Harris: off course nearly a year, well beaten on return: stays 8.2f: acts on good to firm ground and goes well on all-weather surfaces. *T. Hind* —

INDIAN SPARK 2 ch.c. (Apr 26) Indian Ridge 123 – Annes Gift (Ballymoss 136) [1996 5d⁴ 6m² May 15] 16,500Y: close-coupled colt: poor mover: half-brother to several winners here and abroad, including 7f to 10.6f winner Express Gift (also useful hurdler, by Bay Express): dam of no account: won 7-runner Brocklesby Stakes at Doncaster in March by 4 lengths from Joint Venture, making all: better form when beaten a neck by Proud Native in 7-runner minor event at York nearly 2 months later: stays 6f. *W. G. M. Turner* 94

INDIAN SUNSET 3 ch.c. Indian Ridge 123 – Alanood 85 (Northfields (USA)) [1995 –: 7m 6d 1996 7m 10.2m³ a12g Aug 17] compact, good-bodied colt: only worthwhile form when third of 7 in apprentice maiden handicap at Bath in August: better suited by 1¼m than shorter. *C. R. Egerton* 47

INDIAN WOLF 3 ch.c. Indian Ridge 123 – Red Riding Hood (FR) 62 (Mummy's Pet 125) [1995 NR 1996 10.2g 8.3m 8.1d⁵ 7.1g 10m 8m 7g a7g Nov 29] 14,000F, 15,000Y: fourth foal: half-brother to French 7f (at 2 yrs) and 1¼m winner Sizzling Rage (by Sizzling Melody): dam ran several times at 2 yrs: no sign of ability: trained by P. Murphy first 4 starts: tried blinkered. *B. J. Llewellyn* —

INDIFFERENT GUY 2 b.c. (Feb 17) Environment Friend 128 – Sarah's Love (Caerleon (USA) 132) [1996 7m 6g⁶ 8.1g⁵ 8m³ 7.9g 10g* Oct 24] strong, close-coupled colt: fourth foal: half-brother to a 1m/8.5f winner in Spain by Keen: dam, ran once at 2 yrs, closely related to smart stayer Sudden Victory out of Princess Royal winner Shebeen: fair form: well below best when winning steadily-run median auction maiden at Nottingham in October by head from High On Life, making much of running: retained by trainer 19,500 gns Newmarket Autumn Sales: should stay 1½m. *C. E. Brittain* 74

INDIHASH (USA) 2 b. or br.f. (May 17) Gulch (USA) – Linda's Magic (USA) 114 (Far North (CAN) 120) [1996 6g⁴ 7d⁵ 7m* Sep 10] tall, quite good-topped filly: fifth living foal: half-sister to useful 7f and 1m winner Mur Taasha (by Riverman) and fairly useful middle-distance stayer Shujan (by Diesis): dam 6f and 7f winner: made all when winning 12-runner maiden at Lingfield by 1¾ lengths from Woodsia: stays 7f: below best on dead ground: to winter in Dubai. *R. W. Armstrong* 81

INDIPHAR 3 ch.f. Weld 122 – Spring Drill (Blushing Scribe (USA) 107) [1995 49
NR 1996 8g 8m 9g⁴ 12f⁴ 13.1m a12g⁴ 12g Oct 18] unfurnished filly: first reported
foal: dam well beaten: poor performer: best effort when fourth in handicap at Carlisle
fourth start: soundly beaten afterwards: stays 1½m: yet to race on a soft surface.
F. H. Lee

INDIRA 3 b.f. Indian Ridge 123 – Princess Rosananti (IRE) (Shareef Dancer 63
(USA) 135) [1995 49: 5.7h⁵ 6m 6s 7.3d 1996 8.2m⁵ 8.3g 10m 12.1g* a12g 11.5m
Sep 17] smallish filly: modest form: upped in trip and dropped in class, won claimer
at Chepstow in August on final start for H. Candy: well below form afterwards (tailed
off on all-weather debut): better at around 1½m than shorter: acts on good to firm
ground: joined C. Popham and won selling hurdle in November: sold 3,000 gns Ascot
December Sales. *P. G. Murphy*

INDISCREET (CAN) 2 b.c. (May 24) St Jovite (USA) 135 – Imprudent 105 p
Love (USA) (Foolish Pleasure (USA)) [1996 6m* Aug 22]
     York's Moorestyle Convivial Maiden, run on the last day of the Ebor
meeting, has rarely failed to throw up a good-class performer in recent seasons.
High-class sprinter Danehill won it in 1988 followed by the multiple Group
1-winning filly In The Groove in 1989. The 1990 third Bog Trotter won the
following season's Greenham and Kiveton Park Stakes, and the 1991 and 1992
winners Great Palm and Revelation won Group 2 events in France as three-
year-olds. They were followed by another good sprinter in Owington in 1993,
while in 1994 Charnwood Forest finished second to Green Perfume. Only the
Saint-Cloud stewards spoiled the sequence of future pattern winners when
disqualifying the 1995 winner Desert Boy from the Prix Eugene Adam.
     The latest Moorestyle Convivial winner Indiscreet has every chance of
making his mark, too. We like him a lot, and he looks every inch a pattern-race
performer. One of six on their debut in the field of eight, he was sent off 4/1
third favourite (having opened at 5/2) behind the highly-regarded Danzig colt
Elnadim, trained by John Dunlop, and Wasp Ranger from the Paul Cole stable.
Indiscreet took the preliminaries more calmly than some of his rivals; the
favourite was coltish, while there were anxious moments when Musalsal got
loose in the paddock before being caught. It was an impressive debut, Indiscreet stretching clear in style after being pushed along from two furlongs out
and not needing to be at all hard ridden to beat one of the outsiders Swiss Law
by three lengths, with Wasp Ranger a neck away third and Elnadim, who had
run green and tired inside the last, another three lengths back in third.
Indiscreet's win came at a time when his stable's two-year-olds were enjoying
a purple patch: Bahamian Bounty had won the Prix Morny at Deauville the
Sunday before, while Abou Zouz and Bianca Nera took the Gimcrack and
Lowther at the Ebor meeting. Indiscreet held big-race engagements in the
Dewhurst and Racing Post Trophy in the autumn but it was decided to put him
away without another run.
     It bodes well for Indiscreet that he could win so readily over six
furlongs (lowering the juvenile course record and returning a good debut
timefigure of 102). He is bred to be very well suited by further, by middle
distances in fact. He was a 40,000-dollar yearling purchased by Mrs Virginia

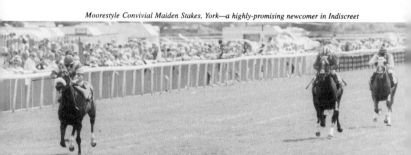

Moorestyle Convivial Maiden Stakes, York—a highly-promising newcomer in Indiscreet

Kraft Payson at the Keeneland September Sales from the first crop of her Irish Derby and King George VI and Queen Elizabeth Diamond Stakes winner St Jovite. Though ultimately well suited by a test of stamina as a two-year-old St Jovite, himself managed to win the Anglesey Stakes at around six furlongs, and it is interesting to note that St Jovite's other two winners (from a total of seven runners in Britain and Ireland), Catechism and St Lucinda, have both been successful over six furlongs. Indiscreet is Imprudent Love's sixth foal. He is closely related to a minor winner at around one mile in North America called Pleasant Interlude (by St Jovite's sire Pleasant Colony) and is half-brother to two winners by Carr de Naskra, called Carra Mia and Carressed, both of whom started out with St Jovite's trainer Jim Bolger in Ireland (where Carressed was a fairly useful six-furlong and seven-furlong winner) but ended up winning nine races on the dirt between them in America, Carra Mia at up to nine furlongs and Carressed in sprints. Imprudent Love did all her winning in the States on turf, at up to a mile and a half. Her dam's best runners were campaigned in Europe, two of note being Topsider Man, a useful middle-distance performer in Britain and later a prolific winner in Italy, and Muir Station, another Bolger-stable inmate who was a useful stayer and hurdler. Their dam Donna Inez, a winner four times at up to nine furlongs and placed in the Del Mar Oaks, was one of several stakes winners out of Banja Luka who was named broodmare of the year in 1987 for the exploits of her Breeders' Cup Classic-winning son Ferdinand.

Indiscreet (CAN) (b.c. May 24, 1994)	St Jovite (USA) (b 1989)	Pleasant Colony (b 1978)	His Majesty
			Sun Colony
		Northern Sunset (ch 1977)	Northfields
			Moss Greine
	Imprudent Love (USA) (b 1983)	Foolish Pleasure (b 1972)	What A Pleasure
			Fool-Me-Not
		Donna Inez (b 1975)	Herbager
			Banja Luka

A fluent mover, Indiscreet was still rather unfurnished in August. The 25/1 on offer about him for the Two Thousand Guineas soon disappeared and he was backed down to 10/1 third favourite behind Bahhare and Revoque, but the Guineas may come a little too quickly for him given his comparative lack of experience. He could well be more of a Derby contender. *D. R. Loder*

INDIUM   2 b.c. (Apr 17) Groom Dancer (USA) 128 – Gold Bracelet § (Golden   80
Fleece (USA) 133) [1996 7.6m 8d³ 7m³ Oct 23] 30,000Y: fifth reported foal: half-brother to useful Irish 1m (at 2 yrs) and 1½m winner Lake Kariba (by Persian Bold) and 1992 2-y-o 7f winner Mukhamedov (by Robellino), later 8.5f and 1¼m winner in Germany: dam ungenuine half-sister to top-class sprinter Thatching out of very smart sprinter Abella: fair in maidens at Lingfield, Salisbury and Yarmouth: stays 1m. *J. H. M. Gosden*

INDONESIAN (IRE)   4 b. or br.g. Alzao (USA) 117 – Miss Garuda 94 (Persian   –
Bold 123) [1995 87d: 10m* 10g 10f 12m⁴ 10g⁵ 12g 10g 10.4m 1996 8d 10m 10g⁶ 12.3m Jul 20] sturdy gelding: unimpressive mover: fairly useful handicapper at his best in 1995 for M. Bell: left C. Brooks after 4-y-o reappearance: lost his form, pulling much too hard on final start: stays 1½m: acts on good to firm going: tried visored/blinkered, no improvement. *P. Calver*

INDRAPURA (IRE)   4 b.g. Gallic League 119 – Stella Ann (Ahonoora 122)   60
[1995 64, a67: a8g* 7f³ 7g 7g a7g 1996 8f 8.3m 7m 7.1m* 7m⁵ 7f⁶ Jul 25] tall, rather leggy gelding: good mover: capable of fair form: won seller (sold out of P. Cole's stable 3,000 gns) at Chepstow in June: probably set too strong a pace both subsequent starts: stays 1m: acts on firm ground and on equitrack: best form in blinkers, visored final outing: races prominently: won first 6 starts over hurdles. *M. C. Pipe*

INDUNA MKUBWA   3 ch.c. Be My Chief (USA) 122 – Hyatti 74 (Habitat 134)   51
[1995 NR 1996 a8g 12g 8.3m 10m 12m a12g³ 11.9m² 10.9m Sep 19] 8,600Y: good-bodied colt: shows plenty of knee action: fifth foal: half-brother to sprint winners Miss Uppitty (by Absalom) and Memsahb (by Prince Sabo) and to Irish 1000

Guineas second Goodnight Kiss (by Night Shift): dam, maiden, form only at 9f: best effort when second in amateurs handicap at Haydock: stays 11.9f. *C. F. Wall*

INFAMOUS (USA)   3 ch.g. Diesis 133 – Name And Fame (USA) (Arts And   86
Letters) [1995 68p: 7g⁶ 1996 11.8s* 12d² 14d 12m 8f 11.6g² 10.8f² 14f 10d 10.3m³
Sep 11] angular gelding: shows knee action: fairly useful form: won 15-runner maiden
at Leicester in March: sold (P. Cole to R. O'Sullivan) 24,000 gns Newmarket
Autumn Sales: stays 1½m: acts on firm going and soft: blinkered penultimate start:
has had tongue tied. *P. F. I. Cole*

INFANTRY DANCER   3 ch.f. Infantry 122 – Electropet (Remainder Man 126§)   54
[1995 55: 7g⁵ 7g⁵ 7f⁵ 1996 10f a12g 8.2m⁴ 7m 8m Sep 9] modest maiden handicapper: should be suited by middle distances: acts on good to firm ground: sent to
South Korea. *G. C. Bravery*

INFATUATION   3 b.g. Music Boy 124 – Fleeting Affair 98 (Hotfoot 126) [1995   79
NR 1996 8.1m⁶ 10g⁴ 10.5d³ Sep 27] 13,500Y: tall, lengthy, unfurnished gelding: fifth
foal: half-brother to 6f (at 2 yrs) to 1m winner First Crush (by Primo Dominie) and
middle-distance stayer Trump (by Last Tycoon): dam 1¼m and 1½m winner who
stayed 2m: fractious in preliminaries and very green on debut: beaten narrowly when
fourth at Goodwood (wandered and flashed tail) and 4 lengths when third of 15 at
Haydock (shade edgy, kept on well) 13 days later: will stay 1½m. *Lady Herries*

INFIRAAJ (USA)   4 b.g. Dayjur (USA) 137 – Capricorn Belle 115 (Nonoalco   –
(USA) 131) [1995 NR 1996 a8g⁴ a7g⁶ a6g⁶ 6.1m Jun 24] related to 4 winners,
including formerly untrustworthy brother Yazaly (reformed sprinter in Dubai), useful
Desert Dirham (7f, by Blushing Groom) and fair Mr Diamond (9f and 1¼m, by Mr
Prospector): dam won from 6f (at 2 yrs) to 9f (in USA): little worthwhile form,
including in blinkers: has joined I. R. Brown. *Mrs D. Haine*

INFLATION   2 b.f. (Mar 3) Primo Dominie 121 – Fluctuate 87 (Sharpen   68
Up 127) [1996 6g³ 5f² Aug 10] half-sister to 4 winners, including useful 3-y-o Rio
Duvida (by Salse), 6f and 7f winner at 2 yrs, and fairly useful middle-distance
handicapper Prince Hannibal (by High Top): dam, 5f winner at 2 yrs, out of close
relative of Wassl: third to Dancing Drop in maiden at Windsor in July: similar form,
though seemed unsuited by step down in trip, when second to Big Ben in minor event
at Lingfield following month: really needs further than 5f. *R. F. Johnson Houghton*

INFLUENCE PEDLER   3 b.g. Keen 116 – La Vie En Primrose 104 (Henbit   64
(USA) 130) [1995 53: 7.1g 7g⁶ 10m 8.2m 1996 a11g 12s 14.1g³ 14.6m*
14.1m⁴ 16.4m² 14.1f* 15.4g² 16f² 16.4m⁴ 16m² 14.1g⁵ Oct 30] sturdy gelding:
poor mover: modest handicapper: won at Doncaster in May and Yarmouth in June:
effective at 1¾m and 2m: acts on firm ground, tailed off on fibresand: sometimes
sweats, including at Doncaster: has joined J. Old. *C. E. Brittain*

IN GOOD FAITH   4 b.g. Beveled (USA) – Dulcidene 71 (Behistoun 131) [1995   66
–: 8m 7.9g 8.1g 11.9g 11.9s 1996 8d 10g 8.1s a8g³ Dec 27] neat gelding: shows knee
action: fair handicapper nowadays: barely stays 1¼m: best turf efforts on an easy
surface, acts on fibresand. *J. J. Quinn*

IN GOOD NICK   2 b.f. (Apr 8) Nicholas (USA) 111 – Better Still (IRE) (Glenstal   61
(USA) 118) [1996 5m 5f³ 5f³ 6m 6g⁴ 6m³ 7m⁵ Oct 2] small, strong filly: first foal:
dam little worthwhile form: modest form: should stay beyond 6f+: sometimes slowly
away: on toes and swished tail on fifth outing: blinkered last 2. *M. W. Easterby*

INGRINA   3 b.f. Warning 136 – Naswara (USA) 88 (Al Nasr (FR) 126) [1995 NR   –
1996 10f⁶ 10g May 29] lengthy, good-bodied filly: first foal: dam winner at around
1½m: weak 11/4 favourite, showed signs of ability in maiden at Lingfield on debut:
only ninth of 17 in similar event at Ripon 18 days later: sold 5,000 gns Newmarket
December Sales. *H. R. A. Cecil*

INHERENT MAGIC (IRE)   7 ch.m. Magical Wonder (USA) 125 – Flo Kelly   76
(Florescence 120) [1995 95: 5m⁶ 5.6m 5g 5s* 5s a6g⁵ a5g² 1996 a5g³ a6g² a5g⁴ Feb
3] smallish, angular mare: fairly useful performer on her day: below form in claimers
at Lingfield early in 1996: stayed 6f: acted on any going, including all-weather
surfaces: bandaged: suited by strongly-run race: in foal to Reprimand. *W. R. Muir*

INIMITABLE   2 b.f. (Mar 27) Polish Precedent (USA) 131 – Saveur (Ardross   66 p
134) [1996 7f⁶ 8g Oct 25] big, lengthy filly: first reported foal: dam unraced
half-sister to smart middle-distance performers Beneficial and Jeune, latter also

460

successful in Melbourne Cup: running-on sixth in maiden at Leicester: still in need of race, never dangerous and not knocked about when tenth of 15 to Calypso Grant in similar event at Doncaster 11 days later: will be suited by further than 1m: will do better. *J. L. Dunlop*

INISHMANN (IRE) 5 ch.g. Soughaan (USA) 111 – Danova (FR) (Dan Cupid – 132) [1995 NR 1996 a13g Jan 9] 2,200F: 3,000Y: ex-Irish gelding: half-brother to several winners, including useful sprint handicapper Doublova (by M Double M): dam French middle-distance winner: modest form at best as 2-y-o: tailed off in bad Lingfield seller. *J. S. Moore*

INJAZAAT (USA) 2 b. or br.f. (Jan 30) Dayjur (USA) 137 – Basma (USA) 104   70 (Grey Dawn II 132) [1996 6m⁶ 6m 6m² Oct 4] quite attractive filly: first foal: dam, bred to stay beyond 6f, third in Cheveley Park Stakes: blinkered first time, 2½ lengths second of 12, making most, to Wind Cheetah in maiden at Lingfield, best effort: something probably amiss time before: raced only at 6f. *Major W. R. Hern*

INK POT (USA) 2 ch.f. (Mar 15) Green Dancer (USA) 132 – Refill 88 (Mill Reef   73 (USA) 141) [1996 7m 8g³ 8m⁴ 8m Oct 23] half-sister to 4 winners, including useful 1995 2-y-o 7f winner Winter Quarters and useful 1¼m performer Jumilla, 6f winner at 2 yrs (both by El Gran Senor): dam (placed over 6f here) won at up to 11f in USA: fair form: made running when placed in maidens at Thirsk and Newcastle: not ridden so forcefully when well below form in nursery at Yarmouth final start: will stay beyond 1m: visored except debut: one paced. *M. R. Stoute*

INKWELL 2 b.c. (Feb 15) Relief Pitcher 120 – Fragrant Hackette 32 (Simply Great (FR) 122) [1996 6f 6.9d Oct 21] 1,500Y: lengthy colt: first foal: dam poor maiden: behind in maiden auctions. *A. Hide*

INN AT THE TOP 4 b.g. Top Ville 129 – Woolpack (Golden Fleece (USA) 133)   59 [1995 63: a8g² a8g⁶ a10g² 12g⁵ 14.1m² a14g 16m² 16d⁶ 14g⁵ 1996 16m a14g³ 14.1d³ a14g Sep 9] tall gelding: has a round action: modest maiden handicapper: not seen until August at 4 yrs, creditable efforts when third: stays 2m: acts on good to firm and dead ground and the all-weather: visored (never going well) sixth 3-y-o start: winning novice hurdler. *J. Norton*

INNER CIRCLE (USA) 3 ch.f. El Gran Senor (USA) 136 – Conquistress   102 (USA) (Conquistador Cielo (USA)) [1995 76p: 6f³ 1996 7d* 8g 7.1d⁴ 7m⁶ 8g* 8.5g³ 8.5s² 8.5d⁴ Nov 30] rather leggy, quite attractive filly: fairly useful performer: made all in maiden at Leicester in April: 4½ lengths ninth of 14 to Beauty To Petriolo in Premio Regina Elena at Rome but then disappointing last 2 races for P. Chapple-Hyam: won allowance race at Del Mar in August (trained by J. Noseda) and ran very well when placed in valuable events at Belmont and Keeneland in October: stays 8.5f: probably acts on any going: bandaged final start. *P. B. Byrne, USA*

INOVAR 6 b.g. Midyan (USA) 124 – Princess Cinders 61 (King of Spain 121) – [1995 26: a7g 10.1d³ 1996 a12g a12g⁵ a12g* a11g 12.1g a12g Jul 1] big, workman-   a35 like gelding: poor mover: poor handicapper: very well ridden by F. Lynch to win at Southwell in March: stays 1½m: acts on dead ground, best recent form on fibresand. *C. B. B. Booth*

IN QUESTION 2 br. or b.c. (Feb 7) Deploy 131 – Questionable (Rainbow Quest   79 p (USA) 134) [1996 7m² 8.1m⁴ Sep 6] big, workmanlike colt: has plenty of scope: first foal: dam unraced sister to useful French stayer Ecologist and half-sister to dam of St Leger winner Toulon: 12/1, shaped well when second of 5 to stable-companion State Fair in listed race at Newbury, soon behind after missing break then staying on strongly: early to post, disappointing fourth in median auction maiden at Haydock following month, off bridle early in straight: needs thorough test of stamina. *B. W. Hills*

INQUISITOR (USA) 4 b.c. Alleged (USA) 138 – Imperturbable Lady (CAN)   110 (Northern Dancer) [1995 109: 10.3g* 12f 10g⁶ 11.9d* 12d⁵ 1996 10g⁶ 10m³ 10m² 10d* Oct 15] strong, good sort: impresses in appearance: has a powerful, round action: smart performer: off course 4½ months after reappearance: returned to form when second in valuable handicap (to Game Ploy) at Newbury then won listed race at Fontainebleau following month by 2½ lengths from Mister Alleged: effective at 1¼m to 1½m: acts on good to firm and good to soft going, probably unsuited by firm: has been bandaged: effective from front or held up: game: sold 135,000 gns Newmarket Autumn Sales, to Saudi Arabia. *J. H. M. Gosden*

INSATIABLE (IRE) 3 b.c. Don't Forget Me 127 – Petit Eclair 94 (Major Portion 93
129) [1995 93p: 7g⁵ 7d* 1996 8m³ 8f² Jun 18] workmanlike colt: fairly useful form:
head second of 31 to North Song in Britannia Handicap at Royal Ascot, first home on
stand side: stays 1m well: acts on good to firm and dead ground: looked likely to
progress again. *M. R. Stoute*

INSIDEOUT 3 b.g. Macmillion 110 – Parijoun (Manado 130) [1995 –: 6m 1996 –
7.5m 6.9f⁴ 5g Aug 16] good-bodied gelding: no sign of ability. *F. Watson*

INSIDER TRADER 5 b.g. Dowsing (USA) 124 – Careless Whisper 94 (Homing 82
130) [1995 82: 5.1m 5g 5g 5f⁵ 6m 5.1m 5m² 5m⁶ 5d 5m⁶ 5f* 5m a5g 1996 5g 5m
5g⁶ 5m 5g⁴ 5m³ 5f² 5m* 5g 5g 5m² 5m 5.1d³ 5m⁵ 5m 5m² 5g 5g 5m 5f⁵ Nov 5]
lengthy, workmanlike gelding: poor walker and mover: fairly useful 5f handicapper:
won at Ripon in June: acts on firm and soft going and on fibresand: effective
blinkered/visored or not, not tried 12 starts: often bandaged off-fore: has run well
for apprentice: usually races prominently. *Mrs J. R. Ramsden*

INSIYABI (USA) 3 b.c. Mr Prospector (USA) – Ashayer (USA) 118 (Lomond 98 ?
(USA) 128) [1995 81p: 6s³ 7m⁵ 1996 8d* 8m 8.1m Aug 14] tall, good sort: has plenty
of scope: won maiden at Doncaster in March in very good style, despite looking
green and carrying head high: not seen out again until last of 9 (hampered after 3f) to
Hammerstein in £14,000 event at Goodwood in August: stiff task, possibly flattered
when just over 7 lengths seventh of 8 to Centre Stalls in minor event at Sandown 11
days later, leading into straight but soon beaten 2f out: stays 1m: refused to enter
stalls on intended debut: sent to Dubai. *J. L. Dunlop*

INSTANTANEOUS 4 b.f. Rock City 120 – Mainmast 63 (Bustino 136) [1995 –
52, a60: 9.9m 10m⁵ 12m³ 14.1f³ 12m² 12m* a12g* 14.1m³ 12g⁶ a12g⁵ 12m⁴ 10.5d
a11g² a12g 1996 a12g⁶ a11g 12m 12m³ 12m⁵ 12m⁵ 11f Aug 9] sparely-made
filly: good mover: modest handicapper as 3-y-o: well held in 1996, finding little
last 2 starts (dropped out very tamely when blinkered final one): sold 3,000 gns
Newmarket Autumn Sales: effective at 11f to 1¾m: acts on firm ground, best form
on fibresand. *T. D. Easterby*

INTEABADUN 4 ch.g. Hubbly Bubbly (USA) – Madam Taylor 81 (Free State –
125) [1995 NR 1996 a16g a12g Mar 30] smallish gelding: seems of little account:
has joined B. P. J. Baugh. *A. Bailey*

INTENDANT 4 b.g. Distant Relative 128 – Bunduq 67 (Scottish Rifle 127) [1995 61
59, a–: 8.3g⁶ 8m³ 8m* 8g⁴ 8.5g 10d 9f a7g⁶ 1996 8m³ 8.3s² 8g² 8f² 8.5m 7.1g⁴ 8.1m a–
Aug 16] sturdy, lengthy gelding: modest handicapper: stays 1m: acts on firm ground,
soft and fibresand. *J. G. FitzGerald*

INTENTION (USA) 6 b.g. Shahrastani (USA) 135 – Mimi Baker (USA) (What –
Luck (USA)) [1995 –, a53: a13g* a16g³ a16g⁴ a13g 1996 a16g⁴ a16g Jan 18] big, a46
good-topped gelding: modest maiden at 5 yrs when trained by I. Campbell: below
form in handicaps at Lingfield in 1996: stays 2m: acts on heavy ground and all-
weather surfaces: tried visored. *P. R. Hedger*

INTERDREAM 2 b.g. (Apr 17) Interrex (CAN) – Dreamtime Quest (Blakeney 66 +
126) [1996 7m 7f* 7.3m 8f 7m Oct 28] 500Y: close-coupled gelding: first foal:
dam, no worthwhile form on flat or over hurdles, daughter of Fred Darling winner
Rotisserie: best form when winning steadily-run maiden auction at Brighton in
September: well beaten in nurseries afterwards: should stay beyond 7f. *R. Hannon*

INTERREGNUM 2 ch.f. (Feb 23) Interrex (CAN) – Lillicara (FR) (Caracolero –
(USA) 131) [1996 7m Jul 19] half-sister to several winners, including fairly useful
3-y-o 6f (at 2 yrs) to 1m winner Lilli Claire (by Beveled) and 7f and 1m winner
Rowlandsons Gems (by Enchantment): dam never ran: tailed off in 11-runner maiden
at Newmarket. *A. G. Foster*

IN THE BAND 3 b.f. Sharrood (USA) 124 – Upper Caen (High Top 131) 64 d
[1995 64p: 8m 1996 a10g² a8g³ a12g 11.9f⁵ 12m 10m⁴ 10m Sep 18] modest form in
maidens first 3 starts: showed little last 5 outings, visored final one: stays 1¼m: acts
on equitrack, fibresand, and probably on good to firm ground. *Lord Huntingdon*

IN THE HIGHLANDS 3 gr.f. Petong 126 – Thevetia 65 (Mummy's Pet 125) –
[1995 NR 1996 8m 6g 6f⁵ 8.2f 7g Oct 30] 8,800F, 6,200Y: fourth foal: sister to
6f winner Cool Tactician and half-sister to useful 1993 2-y-o 7f and 7.9f winner In
Like Flynn (by Handsome Sailor) and 6f (at 2 yrs) and 8.2f winner Mac Kelty (by

Wattlefield): dam should have stayed 7f: well held in maidens and handicaps.
D. J. S. Cosgrove

IN THE MONEY (IRE)   7 b.h. Top Ville 129 – Rensaler (USA) (Stop The Music   62
(USA)) [1995 62§: a12g² a13g³ a12g² a12g⁴ a12g³ a12g* a12g⁴ 12g 11.8d 12g a12g
12.3m a12g 1996 a12g⁶ a12g² a12g* a12g* 12m a12g⁴ 11.8m* a12g⁵ a12g³ 12.3m³
11.8g³ 12m⁶ 11.8m 12m³ a12g 12m a11g⁴ a12g⁵ a12g⁴ a12g² Dec 28] leggy horse:
modest handicapper: won at Wolverhampton in April (promoted) and May and at
Leicester (best effort on turf for long time) in June: stays 1½m: acts on the all-
weather and on good to firm and soft ground. *R. Hollinshead*

INTIAASH (IRE)   4 br.f. Shaadi (USA) 126 – Funun (USA) 84 (Fappiano   70
(USA)) [1995 73: 6m² 6m⁵ 6g³ 6g⁴ 5m⁴ 6d⁴ 5.2g² 6f* 6.1s 1996 a7g⁶ 6g a5g² a6g*   a79
6d³ 6.1d⁴ a7g⁴ 6.1m⁵ Jul 11] tall, lengthy, angular filly: fair performer: gambled on
when winning claimer at Wolverhampton in May: probably stays 7f: acts on fibresand and on firm and soft ground: occasionally visored: often apprentice ridden:
tends to hang left. *D. Haydn Jones*

INTIDAB (USA)   3 b.c. Phone Trick (USA) – Alqwani (USA) 83 (Mr Prospector   96
(USA)) [1995 90p: 6m⁴ 7g³ 1996 7f* 8.1m² 7.9m a6f⁵ Dec 27] well-made colt: has a
roundish action: useful performer: long odds on, won maiden at Thirsk in July: game
short-head second to Elmi Elmak in rated stakes at Haydock in August, having hard
race, then ran poorly in similar event at York 12 days later: close fifth in handicap in
Dubai in December: stays 1m well: raced only on a sound surface. *J. H. M. Gosden*

INTIKHAB (USA)   2 b.c. (May 8) Red Ransom (USA) – Crafty Example   101 p
(USA) (Crafty Prospector (USA)) [1996 6m² 6m* 6m* Oct 23] $300,000Y: sturdy
colt: second foal: dam once-raced daughter of sister to top-class miler Polish Precedent: won 12-runner maiden at Pontefract in September readily by 2½ lengths from
Polar Flight, travelling strongly before quickening clear: long odds on, hacked up in
3-runner minor event at Yarmouth in October: will improve again, and looks like
making at least a very useful sprinter. *D. Morley*

INTIMATION   3 b.f. Warning 136 – It's Terrific (Vaguely Noble 140) [1995 NR   66
1996 7m³ 7g⁵ 8.2m Sep 24] 17,500Y: close-coupled filly: half-sister to several
winners, including useful 7f and 1m winner Model Village (by Habitat) and fair 4-y-o
6f and 7f winner It's Academic (by Royal Academy): dam won from 1¼m to 13f in
Ireland: modest form in maidens: stays 1m. *J. A. R. Toller*

INTO DEBT   3 b.f. Cigar 68 – Serious Affair (Valiyar 129) [1995 NR 1996 a7g 6m   38
7.1g 5.3f⁵ 6m² 6m 5m a6g a7g Nov 15] second foal: dam never ran: only worthwhile
form when second of 18 in claiming handicap at Salisbury in August: stays 6f: acts
on good to firm ground: tends to be slowly away. *Jamie Poulton*

INTREPID FORT   7 br.g. Belfort (FR) 89 – Dauntless Flight (Golden Mallard   –
103) [1995 29: a8g⁴ a8g 8f⁶ 10m 1996 7g 8m 8f 10.3g⁶ 9.9m⁶ 10g 9f⁵ Aug 9]
workmanlike gelding: bad handicapper: stays 1¼m: acts on good to firm ground and
on fibresand: usually blinkered/visored. *B. W. Murray*

IN TUNE   3 b.c. Prince Sabo 123 – Singing Nelly 56 (Pharly (FR) 130) [1995 NR   68
1996 7g⁶ 7m Apr 29] 6,000Y: 6,200 2-y-o: workmanlike, good-quartered colt: first
foal: dam lightly raced: fair form in maidens at Kempton: dead. *P. Howling*

INVERMARK   2 b.c. (Feb 20) Machiavellian (USA) 123 – Applecross 117 (Glint   87
of Gold 128) [1996 7m 8g⁵ 8g³ Oct 30] workmanlike colt: half-brother to
3-y-o Inchrory (by Midyan), useful 7.5f and 8.1f winner at 2 yrs and Norsk 2000
Guineas and Derby winner in 1996, and to 1m winner Pennycairn (by Last Tycoon):
dam, 1¼m to 13.3f winner, second in Park Hill: 20/1, improved effort when 2½
lengths third of 13 to Mandilak in steadily-run maiden at Yarmouth, leading 2f out
and keeping on, flashing tail: very green and slowly away on debut, possibly not right
when disappointing second start: will stay beyond 1m. *J. R. Fanshawe*

INVEST WISELY   4 ch.g. Dashing Blade 117 – Saniette (Crystal Palace (FR)   85
132) [1995 89: 8d 10m³ 9.9m⁵ 13.3g⁵ 13.3f⁴ 14.1g* 14.1m* 14.1m* 18.2g* 1996
11.9m 16.5g 13.9m⁴ 16.1m 16.1g⁴ 16f⁶ 20m 16.1m Aug 26] tall, narrow gelding:
easy mover: fairly useful handicapper: well beaten last 2 starts: sold (J. Eustace
to M. Hammond) 17,500 gns Newmarket Autumn Sales: effective at 1¾m and
stays 2¼m: acts on firm ground: game and genuine: won over hurdles in December.
J. M. P. Eustace

INVIGILATE 7 ch.g. Viking (USA) – Maria Da Gloria (St Chad 120) [1995 58: 58 d 6m 6m 6f 6f⁵ 5m² 5h 5f² 6g 5.1d 6.1d 1996 6d 5g 5f⁵ 6m* 6m 5f⁵ 5m 6g⁶ 6f⁶ 6f 6d 5.1g Oct 9] workmanlike gelding: unimpressive mover: modest sprint handicapper: back to form when winning at Redcar in June: failed to repeat it: sold 1,800 gns Doncaster October Sales: acts on firm and soft ground and the all-weather: effective visored (not tried since 1994) or not: inconsistent. *Martyn Wane*

INVOCATION 9 ch.g. Kris 135 – Royal Saint (USA) (Crimson Satan) [1995 69, 55 a71: a7g³ a7g a7g⁶ a6g⁴ a6g* a6g⁵ 6g² 6m 6m 6f⁶ 6m 5.3g⁶ 6g a8g a7g⁴ a7g⁴ a7g⁴ a71 a7g 1996 a7g² a7g a6g² a7g⁶ a7g² a6g⁶ a6g⁴ a6g² 6f⁶ 6d 6m⁴ 6m³ 6m 5m⁴ 6f a7g⁴ a7g³ a5g⁵ a7s⁵ a6g Dec 5] big, strong gelding: bad mover: fair handicapper on the all-weather, modest on turf nowadays: finds 5f a bare minimum, and stays 1m: acts on equitrack and on good to firm and soft ground: often bandaged: blinkered/visored once each: usually races prominently: missed break several times in 1996: tough and game. *A. Moore*

IN YOUR DREAMS (IRE) 2 b.f. (Apr 29) Suave Dancer (USA) 136 – By – p Charter 104 (Shirley Heights 130) [1996 6.1m Sep 16] smallish, workmanlike filly: third foal: half-sister to 2-y-o 7f winners Green Charter (in 1995, by Green Desert) and Magna Carta (in 1994, by Royal Academy): dam, seemed to stay 1¼m, daughter of Time Charter: 12/1, bit backward, slowly away and always behind in 15-runner Nottingham maiden: moved poorly to post: should do better. *H. Candy*

INZAR (USA) 4 b.c. Warning 136 – Czar's Bride (USA) 78 (Northern Dancer) 112 [1995 112: 7m⁵ 7.3m* 7.1g⁴ 7m⁴ 6m² 6g² 6m 6m² 7m* 7g* 7d* 7m³ 1996 8.1g 6f³ 7.1d* 7g² 6f 7m⁶ 7d⁶ 7d² Nov 10] quite attractive colt: smart performer: won listed race at Haydock in June, holding Branston Abby by a head: good second to Wizard King in similar event at Leopardstown final start: effective at 6f, and should stay 1m: acts on firm and soft ground: blinkered (ran creditably) seventh 3-y-o start: front runner/races prominently: tough and consistent. *P. F. I. Cole*

IONIO (USA) 5 ch.g. Silver Hawk (USA) 123 – Private View (USA) 113 (Mr 92 Prospector (USA)) [1995 113: a10g* 11d⁶ 10m³ 10m² 12f⁶ 10m⁶ 10g³ 12f² 12g 12g⁴ 12d 12d 1996 12s⁴ 8m 11.5m⁴ 12m 11.9g⁴ 12m 10d 11.9f 12m³ 12g Oct 26] close-coupled gelding: good mover: seems only fairly useful at best nowadays: sold to join Mrs V. Ward 26,000 gns Newmarket Autumn Sales, and won over hurdles in November: stays 1½m: acts on firm ground, possibly not on a soft surface: below form blinkered/visored: normally tracks leaders, occasionally makes the running: inconsistent. *C. E. Brittain*

IOTA 7 b. or br.m. Niniski (USA) 125 – Iosifa 108 (Top Ville 129) [1995 –, a69: 61 d a14.8g² a14.8g² a14.8g³ a12g 1996 a14.8g a12g⁵ a14.8g a16.2g* 14.1g 14.1m a14.8g⁴ 14.1m⁵ 14.1f⁶ 15.8s* 14.9m a16.2g⁵ 16m³ a14.8g 16.1f 13.8g 14.1g³ 15.1s a16g³ a14.8g⁵ Nov 25] smallish, sparely-made mare: modest handicapper: successful at Wolverhampton in April and Catterick in July: long way below form last 7 starts: suited by test of stamina: has form on any turf ground (possibly not at best on very firm nowadays) and on firesand. *J. L. Harris*

IOULIOS 2 ch.c. (Apr 3) Shavian 125 – Touch of White 77 (Song 132) [1996 6g – Nov 1] first reported foal: dam 5f performer: soon outpaced when last of 11 in maiden at Newmarket. *J. E. Banks*

IRCHESTER LASS 4 ch.f. Presidium 124 – Fool's Errand (Milford 119) [1995 49 d 49: a8.5g⁶ a7g 5m 8.2m⁵ 7.5m 7m 6f³ 6m³ 6m* 6.1d⁶ a6g a6g² a7g² 1996 a6g⁵ a8g⁵ a8g* a7g⁴ a7g⁴ a8.5g⁶ 7g 7.5m 6f Jun 13] leggy, unfurnished filly: poor handicapper: won at Southwell in January: below form afterwards: sold 2,100 gns Doncaster September Sales: stays 1m: acts on firm ground and firesand, probably on dead: often blinkered, visored for win: usually comes from behind: sent to South Korea. *S. R. Bowring*

I RECALL (IRE) 5 b.g. Don't Forget Me 127 – Sable Lake (Thatching 131) 57 [1995 –: 10g 10m a10g⁴ 1996 10g 9m³ 10g 7.3s⁵ a8g Jun 22] workmanlike gelding: modest maiden handicapper nowadays: stays 9f: acts on good to firm and soft ground (below form both starts on equitrack): visored last 4 starts. *P. Hayward*

IRIE MON (IRE) 4 b.g. Waajib 121 – Achafalaya (USA) (Apalachee (USA) 54 137) [1995 59: a8g² a8g² a7g* 7f 7g 8.1m³ 8m³ 8.1m² 8g⁴ 1996 a7g⁶ a8g 7.5m 10m³ 10m 10g 8m Jul 20] good-bodied gelding: modest performer on his day: stays 1¼m, at least in slowly-run race: acts on equitrack and on firm ground: has had tongue tied down: inconsistent: modest winning hurdler. *M. P. Bielby*

IRISH ACCORD (USA)   2 b. or br.c. (Mar 26) Cahill Road (USA) – Dimples   90
(USA) (Smile (USA)) [1996 6m* 6g⁴ Sep 3] $50,000Y: tall, useful-looking colt:
has scope: has a fluent action: second foal: dam won at up to 7f at 2 yrs in USA:
sire, brother to champion 3-y-o colt Unbridled, Grade 1 9f winner: won 13-runner
maiden at Pontefract in August by 2 lengths from Amid Albadou, held up then
coming through strongly to lead inside last: only fourth to Lima in Timeform Futurity
there following month, as on debut hanging markedly right close home: will be
suited by further than 6f: clearly no easy ride: looked a useful prospect on debut.
Mrs J. R. Ramsden

IRISH FICTION (IRE)   2 b.g. (Feb 18) Classic Music (USA) – Wasmette (IRE)   66 d
(Wassl 125) [1996 5s² 5d² 5d³ 5.1m⁴ 5m² 7f* 7m² 7f 7m⁴ 6m² 6g 7f* 7g³ 8m⁶ a8g
Nov 15] IR 7,800F, IR 15,000Y: useful-looking, unfurnished gelding: first foal: dam
unraced half-sister to very smart middle-distance colt Nisnas: fair plater: won at
Yarmouth (sold out of M. Channon's stable 8,000 gns) in June and Brighton in
September: probably better suited by 7f than 6f, should stay 1m: probably acts on any
going. *D. J. S. Cosgrove*

IRISH GROOM   9 b.g. Shy Groom (USA) – Romany Pageant (Welsh Pageant   –
132) [1995 40: 10.8f³ 1996 10.8f May 6] angular gelding: poor handicapper: probably stays 1½m: acts on firm ground and fibresand, probably on heavy: often
blinkered in the past: lightly raced nowadays. *A. Streeter*

IRISH KINSMAN   3 b.g. Distant Relative 128 – Inesdela (Wolver Hollow 126)   –
[1995 –: 7m a6g 1996 7g⁶ 7.1m⁵ 10d 8m 12m Oct 7] rangy gelding: little worthwhile
form: left P. Walwyn after fourth start: bred to stay 1m. *G. H. Yardley*

IRISH OASIS (IRE)   3 b.g. Mazaad 106 – Alpenwind (Tumble Wind (USA))   49
[1995 –: a7g a7g 9g 1996 9.9g² 11m⁶ 13.8g 12g³ 10m² 7.5g 10g 11f Sep 27] big
gelding: poor maiden: stays 11f: visored fourth 3-y-o start. *B. S. Rothwell*

IRISH PET   2 br.f. (Mar 22) Petong 126 – Crystal's Solo (USA) (Crystal Water   63
(USA)) [1996 8.2g Oct 9] seventh foal: half-sister to 13.4f winner Crystal Blade
(by Dashing Blade), ungenuine 1988 2-y-o 7f winner Crystal Heights (by Wolver
Heights) and a winner in Macau by Robellino: dam second once from 12 starts in
USA: 40/1, slowly away and always behind in maiden at Nottingham: sold 2,000 gns
Newmarket Autumn Sales: sent to Holland. *J. M. P. Eustace*

IRISH SEA (USA)   3 b.g. Zilzal (USA) 137 – Dunkellin (USA) (Irish River (FR)   78 d
131) [1995 NR 1996 10g² 10m⁶ 11.7m³ 10m⁴ 8.5f⁵ 9g 11.5m⁵ 10.1m⁵ 12m a8g Dec
27] IR 50,000Y: leggy, close-coupled gelding: fourth foal: half-brother to 2 winners
in USA, by Herat and Seattle Dancer: dam, winner in USA, half-sister to Criterium
des Pouliches winner Oak Hill: fair form in maidens first 3 starts, then sold out of
M. Stoute's stable 7,200 gns Newmarket July Sales: well below form afterwards,
and sold out of D. Nicholls' stable only 500 gns Doncaster November Sales after
penultimate start: should stay 1½m: raced only on a sound surface on turf: tailed off
only try in blinkers. *R. F. Marvin*

IRISH STAMP (IRE)   7 b.g. Niniski (USA) 125 – Bayazida (Bustino 136) [1995   –
NR 1996 16f Jul 18] fair staying handicapper in 1993: soundly beaten all 3 starts
since: fairly useful staying chaser. *F. Murphy*

IRISH WILDCARD (NZ)   8 b.g. Lyphard's Trick (USA) 110 – Courageous   –
Mahoney (NZ) (Rocky Mountain (FR)) [1995 NR 1996 8d Apr 13] robust New
Zealand-bred gelding: 25/1, just over 8 lengths tenth of 14 in claimer at Warwick on
debut: poor hurdler. *H. Oliver*

IRON AND STEEL   3 ch.g. Dominion 123 – Fairy Fortune 78 (Rainbow Quest   –
(USA) 134) [1995 –: 5g a6g⁵ 6f⁶ 6m 6.9g 1996 a6g Mar 14] seems of little account:
tried visored. *A. Moore*

IRON GENT (USA)   5 b.g. Greinton 119 – Carrot Top 112 (High Hat 131) [1995   44 +
–: 14m 15.1m³ 1996 16m⁵ Jun 11] good-bodied gelding: fair handicapper at 3 yrs:
lightly raced and poor form since: only poor form after near 10-month absence when
fifth in claimer at Redcar: should stay beyond 1¾m: acts on good to firm and dead
ground. *S. E. Kettlewell*

IRONHEART 3 b.c. Lycius (USA) 124 – Inshirah (USA) 90 (Caro 133) [1995 83: –
7g⁴ 7g 1996 7m⁵ Apr 29] close-coupled colt: fourth of 16 in maiden at Newmarket on
debut: gave impression something amiss 2 months later, and (very easy to back)
didn't find much off bridle only outing in 1996: should stay 1m. *J. H. M. Gosden*

IRON N GOLD 4 b.g. Heights of Gold – Southern Dynasty 81 (Gunner B 126) 53
[1995 53: 12d* 11.6m⁵ a16g 15.4m⁴ 14d a13g² 1996 a16g⁶ a13g* a13g⁴ a12g Mar
14] tall, angular gelding: has a round action: modest handicapper: won at Lingfield
in January: joined T. Casey after final outing: stays 15.4f: acts on good to firm and
dead ground and on equitrack: won maiden hurdle in October. *A. Moore*

IRREPRESSIBLE (IRE) 5 b.g. Don't Forget Me 127 – Lady of Shalott 61 50
(Kings Lake (USA) 133) [1995 –: 10.8g 12.1d 1996 10m 8m* 8.3m³ 8.1m⁴ 10.2m⁶
7.1m⁴ 7.1m³ 7.6m 7m⁴ Sep 18] strong, lengthy gelding: modest handicapper: made
all in seller at Yarmouth in June: best form at up to 1m: acts on good to firm and dead
ground: visored once in 1994: races prominently. *R. J. Hodges*

IRSAL 2 ch.c. (Feb 19) Nashwan (USA) 135 – Amwag (USA) 106 (El Gran 70 p
Senor (USA) 136) [1996 7m⁵ Oct 23] first foal: dam 7f and 1m winner: 10/1, 5½
lengths fifth of 11 to Sekari in maiden at Yarmouth, travelling comfortably off pace
then not given at all a hard time after being short of room inside last: will improve.
A. C. Stewart

IRTIFA 2 ch.f. (Mar 28) Lahib (USA) 129 – Thaidah (CAN) 105 (Vice 68
Regent (CAN)) [1996 5.7f² 6m* 6d⁵ 7.9g Sep 5] fourth foal: half-sister to 3-y-o 7f
winner Tawaaded (by Nashwan) and a middle-distance winner in France by Blushing
Groom: dam, 5f (at 2 yrs) to 7f winner, half-sister to top-class American filly
Glorious Song and champion 1983 2-y-o Devil's Bag: short-headed on debut before
winning 4-runner minor event at Windsor later in July by a neck from Colombia, hard
ridden to get up close home: failed to go on as anticipated in nurseries, racing too
keenly final outing: bred to stay beyond 7f. *P. T. Walwyn*

I SAY DANCER (IRE) 3 b.f. Distinctly North (USA) 115 – Lady Marigot (Lord –
Gayle (USA) 124) [1995 NR 1996 10.5d Sep 27] IR 3,200Y: half-sister to 3 winners,
including 1988 2-y-o 6f seller winner Jay Gee (by Coquelin) and Irish 1½m winner
Saygot Lady (by Sayyaf): dam Irish 1¼m winner: tailed off in maiden at Haydock.
L. J. Barratt

ISCA MAIDEN 2 b.f. (May 13) Full Extent (USA) 113 – Sharp N' Easy 62 –
(Swing Easy (USA) 126) [1996 6m 6f 7.1s Oct 22] 500Y: lengthy, unfurnished
filly: second foal: dam, inconsistent plater, stayed 1m: no sign of ability in maidens.
P. Hayward

ISIT IZZY 4 b.f. Crofthall 110 – Angie's Girl (Dubassoff (USA)) [1995 NR 1996 58
8.5m⁴ 8m Aug 8] plain filly: second foal: dam unraced: ridden by 7-lb claimer, no
chance with winner when second of 6 to 16/1-on shot Papaha in maiden at Beverley,
demoted for bumping over 2f out: again 25/1, soundly beaten in similar event at
Pontefract month later. *B. A. McMahon*

ISITOFF 3 b.g. Vague Shot 108 – Plum Blossom (USA) (Gallant Romeo (USA)) 72
[1995 –: 7m 1996 a7g⁵ 10f³ a8g⁴ 11.6m* 11m² 14d⁵ 13.3m⁶ 11.5m³ 9.9f² 10m Sep 7]
lengthy gelding: fair handicapper: won at Windsor in May: gelded after final start:
may prove best at 1¼m to 1½m: acts on firm ground. *S. C. Williams*

ISLA DEL REY (USA) 4 ch.f. Nureyev (USA) 131 – Priceless Pearl (USA) 101 103
(Alydar (USA)) [1995 7g* 8g 1996 a7g² a6g* a6f* a6g³ 7f* 6m⁶ 7m Jul 30] tall,
lengthy, sparely-made filly: second foal: dam, 7f winner at 2 yrs, sister to Saratoga
Six and half-sister to Alydar: useful performer: trained in 1995 in Ireland by J. Oxx,
winning maiden at Tralee: ran 4 times in Dubai, winning 2 handicaps at Nad Al
Sheba in February: won listed race at Lingfield by ½ length from Carranita:
creditable sixth to Atraf in Cork and Orrery Stakes at Royal Ascot next start, but
last of 14 (boiled over in preliminaries) in listed race at Goodwood final outing:
stays 7f: acts on firm ground and sand: early to post: front runner: sent to USA.
Saeed bin Suroor

ISLA GLEN 3 b.f. Be My Chief (USA) 122 – Serration (Kris 135) [1995 –: –
5g 1996 8g 8.3m 10f 10.2g Aug 26] quite attractive filly: no form: has joined
G. Thorner. *M. McCormack*

ISLAND CASCADE   4 b.f. Hadeer 118 – Island Mill 79 (Mill Reef (USA) 141)   –
[1995 39: 8g⁶ 10m 10m² 10m 10g⁴ 10m 14.1m⁶ 15g 11d⁵ 13.6f 1996 12m 12g 12f⁵
a12g 12f³ 16.2m Jul 16] close-coupled filly: no form at 4 yrs: should stay beyond
1¼m: sent to South Korea. *Don Enrico Incisa*

ISLAND PRINCE   2 ch.g. (Feb 16) Prince Sabo 123 – Island Mead 86 (Pharly   47
(FR) 130) [1996 6m 7m 7m 8f a6g* a7g⁴ Dec 30] 12,000Y: good-topped gelding: has
scope: fourth foal: half-brother to 4-y-o Jobber's Fiddle (by Sizzling Melody), 7f
winner at 2 yrs: dam 7f winner: poor form: won nursery at Lingfield (by short head)
in December: best form at sprint distances: acts on equitrack. *N. A. Callaghan*

ISLAY BROWN (IRE)   3 b.f. Petorius 117 – Speedy Action (Horage 124) [1995   47
67?: 5g 7g⁵ 7g³ 7.1g 1996 7s 8d 8g 11.1g² 10m 10f 11f 8f Sep 27] workmanlike filly:
poor maiden on most form: sold 2,400 gns Doncaster October Sales: probably stays
11f: blinkered last 6 starts, looking none too keen on occasions. *C. W. C. Elsey*

ISLE OF CORREGIDOR (USA)   2 b.g. (Apr 5) Manila (USA) – Comtesse de   88 d
Loir (FR) 131 (Val de Loir 133) [1996 6f* 6f⁴ 7m⁵ 6d⁶ Oct 2] good-topped gelding:
has a round action: brother to middle-distance maiden Bataan and half-brother to
several winners, including disappointing 12.3f winner Fassfern (by Alleged) and
Grade 2 1½mile winner Heron Cove (by Bold Bidder): dam top-class French middle-
distance filly: odds on, won 5-runner median auction maiden at Yarmouth in June:
reportedly suffered from sore shins afterwards, and disappointing in minor events
subsequently: gelded: should be suited by further than 6f: had rope halter for stalls
entry third outing. *Mrs J. Cecil*

ISLE OF MAN (USA)   2 b.c. (Mar 19) Manila (USA) – Princess of Man 104   94 p
(Green God 128) [1996 6m² 7.1m* Jul 17] tall, good-topped colt: half-brother to
several winners, including 4-y-o 11.7f to 13.4f winner Royal Scimitar and 6f (at 2
yrs) to 11.5f winner Ausherra, both useful performers by Diesis: dam won Musidora
Stakes: won median auction maiden at Sandown in July readily by 2 lengths, clear,
from Hindsight, galloping on with plenty of enthusiasm: likely to need middle
distances at least at 3 yrs: a useful prospect if all is well with him. *P. F. I. Cole*

ISM   4 b.g. Petong 126 – Brigado 87 (Brigadier Gerard 144) [1995 56, a73: 7g a11g   –
a8g* 8.3g⁶ a7g a7g* a6g³ 6d⁵ 7s 1996 8.3m 6g a7g Jul 27] good-topped gelding: fair
handicapper on the all-weather and modest on turf at 3 yrs: no worthwhile form in
1996: effective at 6f to 1m: acts on fibresand and dead ground: effective blinkered or
not. *Major W. R. Hern*

ISTABRAQ (IRE)   4 b.g. Sadler's Wells (USA) 132 – Betty's Secret (USA)   91
(Secretariat (USA)) [1995 90: 10g 10.3m 12m² 14f* 13.9g² 15g* 16.2d 16d² 16.5m
1996 14d² Jun 8] useful-looking gelding: has a markedly round action: fairly useful
handicapper: very good second at Haydock: sold 38,000 gns Newmarket July Sales
and gelded: suited by good test of stamina: successful on firm ground, but probably
ideally suited by an easy surface: bandaged last 5 starts: front runner: very promising
hurdler. *J. H. M. Gosden*

ITALIAN SYMPHONY (IRE)   2 b.g. (May 13) Royal Academy (USA) 130 –   70
Terracotta Hut 99 (Habitat 134) [1996 7f⁵ 6m⁴ 6m⁵ 7.1m⁶ 7g⁶ 7m³ Oct 8] IR
20,000Y: close-coupled gelding: third reported foal: half-brother to 1992 2-y-o US
graded sprint winner Distinct Habit (by Distinctive Pro): dam ran once at 2 yrs, is out
of sister to Noalcoholic: fair form, running well in blinkers in claimer at Redcar final
start: stays 7f: front runner/races prominently: tends to hang left. *M. Johnston*

ITATINGA (USA)   2 b.f. (Jan 23) Riverman (USA) 131 – Ivrea 109 (Sadler's   65 ?
Wells (USA) 132) [1996 7.1v⁴ 7g Oct 30] angular filly: second foal: half-sister
to 1994 2-y-o 7f winner Hedera (by Woodman): dam, 2-y-o 7f winner, second in
Ribblesdale: very much in need of experience when fourth in maiden at Haydock on
debut: down the field in 17-runner similar event won by Happy Valentine at
Yarmouth later in month: should stay middle distances. *M. R. Stoute*

ITKAN (IRE)   3 b.f. Marju (IRE) 127 – Boldabsa 96 (Persian Bold 123) [1995   –
NR 1996 7.1m⁴ 8m⁴ 10g 9.7d Oct 21] 25,000Y: sturdy, deep-girthed filly: third foal:
half-sister to 1993 Irish 2-y-o 1m winner Oliver Messel and useful 1994 2-y-o 5f and
6f winner Painted Madam (both by Common Grounds): dam Irish 9f and 1¼m
winner: backward, signs of ability in maidens, but tailed off in handicap at Folkestone final start: sold 10,500 gns Newmarket December Sales. *C. J. Benstead*

IT'S ACADEMIC 4 b.f. Royal Academy (USA) 130 – It's Terrific (Vaguely 65 Noble 140) [1995 73: 6m⁵ 7.1m 9.9m⁴ 9g⁶ 7g* 7.5m⁵ 6m 7f³ 7m² 7f* 7m² 6.1d* 7.1g² 6s⁴ 7m⁶ 1996 8s² 8d 7g 6g 7g⁴ 7g 6g⁶ 6g⁴ 7g² 7s² Jul 4] strong filly: reportedly in foal to Muhtarram: fair handicapper: rather unlucky when second in minor event at Catterick final start, just failing after not getting clear run: effective at 6f (under testing conditions) to 1m: acted on firm and soft going: held up. *Mrs J. R. Ramsden*

ITSINTHEPOST 3 b.f. Risk Me (FR) 127 – Where's The Money 87 (Lochnager – 132) [1995 64, a77: 5s³ 5m 6m⁴ a6g* 7g 6.1s² a6g* a6g³ a7g 1996 6.1d 6g a7g a6g³ a66 a6g³ a6g 6d Oct 21] leggy filly: has a very round action: fair performer: no form on turf in 1996: stays 6f: seems ideally suited by all-weather surfaces. *V. Soane*

IT'S SO EASY 5 b.m. Shaadi (USA) 126 – Carmelina 98 (Habitat 134) [1995 –, a37: a7g a7g⁶ a7g 7m 7f a7g⁶ 7m 6f a7g a7g³ 1996 a8g a7g Jan 18] unfurnished mare: poor mover: poor performer nowadays: likely to prove best at distances short of 1m: probably acts on any ground: inconsistent: covered by Lugana Beach. *A. P. James*

IT'STHEBUSINESS 4 b.g. Most Welcome 131 – Douceur (USA) (Shadeed 64 (USA) 135) [1995 58: 6m 7f 10f⁴ 10.2m² 8.5s 10d² 9.7g 1996 8f⁵ 10g 10m 10m* 9.7m³ 11.9f⁶ 10f⁴ 10g 10f⁶ 10d⁴ 10.8f⁵ Oct 8] workmanlike gelding: modest handicapper: improved form to win at Lingfield (first win, made virtually all) in May: sold (S. Dow to M. Sheppard) 6,400 gns Newmarket Autumn Sales: stays 1¼m (looked a non-stayer over 11.9f): acts on good to firm going and dead, probably on soft: effective in a visor: rather headstrong, and tends to carry head high: none too consistent. *S. Dow*

IVAN LUIS (FR) 2 b.c. (May 11) Lycius (USA) 124 – Zivania (IRE) 101 102 (Shernazar 131) [1996 7m⁵ 7f⁶ 8.5g² 8g* 8.3g³ 8s³ Oct 20] IR 42,000Y: second foal: half-brother to German 3-y-o 8.5f to (listed race) 1¼m winner Zero Problemo (by Priolo): dam, won from 1m to 9.5f at 2 yrs in Ireland and should have stayed 1½m, from good French family: won maiden at Thirsk in September: visored, easily best effort when third in 10-runner Gran Criterium (3¾ lengths behind Hello) at Milan final outing: looks very much a stayer: acts on soft going. *M. Bell*

IVAN THE TERRIBLE (IRE) 8 ch.g. Siberian Express (USA) 125 – – Chrisanthy 81 (So Blessed 130) [1995 62, a53: a8g⁶ a8.5g² a8g³ a8.5g 9.2s* 9.2g* a8g⁶ a9.4g 8.9g 1996 a7g 10g Aug 12] lengthy, workmanlike gelding: below form last 3 starts in 1995 and both outings on return from 11-month absence: effective at 1m, stays 1½m: acts on fibresand and on good to firm and soft ground: blinkered once at 2 yrs: often a front runner. *B. Ellison*

IVOR'S DEED 3 b.c. Shadeed (USA) 135 – Gena Ivor (USA) (Sir Ivor 135) 56 [1995 54: a8g a7g⁵ 1996 10g 7.5g² 6g⁵ 7g* 7f² 7.1f³ 7f⁴ 7m 8m a7g³ Nov 15] sturdy colt: impresses in appearance: modest performer: won apprentice maiden at Catterick in June: will stay 1m: acts on firm ground and on equitrack. *C. F. Wall*

IVOR'S FLUTTER 7 b.g. Beldale Flutter (USA) 130 – Rich Line (High Line 86 125) [1995 –: 14g 16.1m 1996 16d⁶ 16m³ 22.2f⁶ 14m* 16g³ 16.2m⁴ 18g Oct 19] leggy, workmanlike gelding: fairly useful handicapper: won at Sandown in August, weaving his way through from rear then idling: woolly in coat, always in rear in Cesarewitch final start: suited by good test of stamina (needs a strong gallop): acts on firm and soft ground: needs driving, and not an easy ride. *D. R. C. Elsworth*

IVORY DAWN 2 b.f. (May 11) Batshoof 122 – Cradle of Love (USA) 87 59 (Roberto (USA) 131) [1996 6m 7f³ 7g⁶ Aug 1] 4,500Y: second foal: dam 9f winner: modest form in maiden auctions: stays 7f. *K. T. Ivory*

IVORY'S GRAB HIRE 3 b.g. Shavian 125 – Knees Up (USA) (Dancing 61 § Champ (USA)) [1995 55+: 5.1m 6.1m² 5g⁵ 5g⁶ 6g² 5.2f³ 6m⁵ 6m² 6g⁴ 6.9f³ 8.1m⁶ 1996 6.9s⁵ a7g⁴ 10.8g⁴ 9.7f⁶ a8g 8g³ 8.3m 7m³ 7f* 6m⁴ 6g⁵ 7f³ 7g 7m³ 7f² 7g⁶ 7d 7.1f³ 7m 6.1m³ 7m⁵ a7g Dec 11] lengthy, shallow-girthed gelding: modest handicapper: won at Lingfield in June: effective at 6f, and shapes as if stays 10.8f: acts on firm ground and equitrack: nearly always blinkered: has won for apprentice: has run well when sweating profusely: sometimes slowly away: inconsistent and of dubious temperament. *K. T. Ivory*

IVY LILIAN (IRE) 4 b.f. Cyrano de Bergerac 120 – Catherine Clare 58 (Sallust 31 134) [1995 41: a5g⁵ a6g⁶ a5g² a6g⁶ a5g³ 5d⁴ a5g⁴ a5g 5.1m 5f a5g 5.3m 8.1m 5.9f 1996 a5g 5g a5g 5g⁵ a5g 5d 5.1f⁶ Jul 8] small filly: unimpressive mover: poor maiden handicapper: stays 6f: acts on fibresand and good to firm and dead ground: tried visored and blinkered. *W. M. Brisbourne*

IZZA 5 b.m. Unfuwain (USA) 131 – Wantage Park 104 (Pas de Seul 133) [1995 41: 63 11.1s 8m 7g 8f 5g 8g 8f 15.8g² 16f⁶ 15.8m* 16.1h⁶ 16m 15.8g 1996 21.6m* 16.2g² 18m⁴ 16.2m⁵ 16f* 15.8g* 16m² 15.9d* 15.9g³ 16.2d 16.5s Nov 9] leggy, quite attractive mare: good mover: modest handicapper: won at Pontefract in April, at Redcar and Catterick in July and at Chester in August: suited by test of stamina: acts on firm ground and dead (faced stiff task latest start on soft): effective visored in 1995, but not tried in 1996: sometimes takes strong hold: seems best with waiting tactics nowadays. *W. Storey*

J

JAAZIM 6 ch.g. Night Shift (USA) – Mesmerize (Mill Reef (USA) 141) [1995 56 72d: a7g³ a7g* a7g a6g* a7g⁶ 7f 6m 8g 1996 a6g⁵ a7g⁴ a6g a5g a8g⁶ 8f 7m² 7m² a60 8g⁵ 7g² 7m² 6m⁵ 6m⁴ 8.3d⁵ 8f² 8f⁴ 8m 7s a7g Dec 11] strong gelding: modest handicapper: effective at 6f to 8.3f: acts on the sand and on firm and dead going: blinkered 3 times (ran creditably first occasion) as 3-y-o. *M. Madgwick*

JABAROOT (IRE) 5 b.g. Sadler's Wells (USA) 132 – Arctic Heroine (USA) – (Arctic Tern (USA) 126) [1995 –: 12d 1996 9.2d 14.1m 11.1g 12.1g 9.2g 11.1g 11.1m⁶ 13.1g 15d 12g⁵ 12.1f 16s 12.1m⁵ 10.1m 15.1m⁵ Sep 23] sparely-made gelding: has a quick action: little form in 1996, leaving D. Nolan after fifth start: tried blinkered (no improvement). *R. M. McKellar*

JACKATACK (IRE) 4 b.g. Astronef 116 – Redwood Hut (Habitat 134) [1995 ? 46, a63: a8.5g⁶ a8g* a8.5g 9.7m 8.3g⁵ 12g 8.3g² 8.1d⁵ 8f a8g a7g 1996 a8g Jan 2] useful-looking gelding: modest performer here, well beaten in handicap at Lingfield on reappearance: won 2 handicaps (over 6f and 1m) in Germany in September: stays 8.3f: acts on good to firm and soft ground and goes well on equitrack: tried visored: inconsistent. *M. R. Channon*

JACK BROWN 2 gr.c. (May 21) Robellino (USA) 127 – Crispahan (Critique 66 ? (USA) 126) [1996 6d a8.5g⁶ 10m Oct 17] 10,000Y: smallish colt: fluent mover: second foal: dam French 1½m winner, granddaughter of Irish 1000 Guineas winner Royal Danseuse: progressive form, though never on terms in steadily-run maiden won by Silver Patriarch at Pontefract on final outing (possibly flattered). *T. T. Clement*

JACK FLUSH (IRE) 2 b.g. (May 8) Broken Hearted 124 – Clubhouse Turn 64 (IRE) (King of Clubs 124) [1996 6g⁶ 7m⁴ 6.1m³ 6.1m³ 6f² 6g 7f⁵ 8g Oct 21] IR 1,300F, IR 3,600Y: leggy, unfurnished gelding: second foal: dam unraced: fair form: best form at 6f, though has given impression should be suited by further: raced only on a sound surface. *B. S. Rothwell*

JACK JENNINGS 3 ch.c. Deploy 131 – Lareyna 98 (Welsh Pageant 132) 115 [1995 94: a7g² 7f* 7m⁶ 8.1d⁴ 8d³ 1996 9m³ 10.4m³ 12m Jun 8] strong, good-bodied colt: has scope: smart performer: third to Storm Trooper in listed race at Newmarket and to Glory of Dancer (set slow pace) in Dante Stakes at York: 25/1 and patchy in coat, very good 5¾ lengths seventh of 20 to Shaamit in the Derby at Epsom on final start, leading over 1m: stays at least 1½m: acts on firm ground and dead: front runner: reportedly suffered badly bruised foreleg when cast in box in August. *B. A. McMahon*

JACK SAYS 2 b.g. (May 27) Rambo Dancer (CAN) 107 – Madam Cody (Hot 53 ? Spark 126) [1996 5m⁴ a5g³ a5g² 7s 7.9g 8m 7m Oct 8] 2,500Y: well-made gelding: a59 closely related to 2 winners by Night Shift, including 15.4f winner Mara Askari, and one by Warrshan, and half-brother to fair 1993 2-y-o 5f winner Resonant (by Forzando): dam scored over 7f to 2 yrs in Ireland: modest form in frame in maiden auction events: sold 4,000 gns Doncaster October Sales: seems to stay 1m: acts on fibresand, finished lame when tailed off on soft ground: blinkered final outing. *T. D. Easterby*

JACKSON FALLS 2 gr.g. (Mar 25) Dunbeath (USA) 127 – Hysteria (Prince Bee 64 128) [1996 6m² 7m⁴ 8m³ Sep 21] tall, quite good-topped gelding: fifth foal:

half-brother to 3-y-o 1½m winner Jackson Park (by Domynsky): dam unraced daughter of German 7f to 9f winner Kallista, dam of German 1000 Guineas winner Kazoo and daughter of good German mare Kandia: suffered sore shins after beaten a head by Pun in median auction maiden at York in June: similar form in maiden at Ayr, but poor third of 4 (on toes) at same course 2 days later: should stay beyond 7f. *T. D. Easterby*

JACKSON HILL 3 b.g. Priolo (USA) 127 – Orange Hill 75 (High Top 131) 100 [1995 85p: 7g⁶ 7m* 1996 10.3d* 10m⁵ 10m* May 5] heavy-topped gelding: type to carry condition: impresses in appearance: has a fluent, rounded action: useful form: won handicaps at Doncaster in March and Salisbury (led over 1f out and powered clear to win by 5 lengths) in May: set too strong a pace second 3-y-o start: will prove at least as effective over 1½m as 1¼m: yet to race on extremes of going: split a pastern on gallops after final start: has been gelded. *R. Charlton*

JACKSON PARK 3 gr.g. Domynsky 110 – Hysteria (Prince Bee 128) [1995 51: 67 5m 7m 7f⁴ 7.9g³ 10d² 1996 12s* 12.3m² 12d 12.3g⁶ 12.3m 12s 16s Aug 27] good-bodied gelding: fair handicapper: much improved form when winning at Catterick in March: well beaten last 5 starts: should stay further than 1½m: acts on soft ground and good to firm: blinkered penultimate start: normally a front runner: won juvenile hurdle in November. *T. D. Easterby*

JACK THE LAD (IRE) 2 b.c. (Apr 22) Shalford (IRE) 124§ – Indian Honey 64 (Indian King (USA) 128) [1996 6m³ 6f 7f 6f³ 6d⁴ 7g⁴ a8.5g Dec 14] IR 7,000F, IR 6,500Y: close-coupled colt: fifth foal: half-brother to Irish 3-y-o 7.8f winner Honeyschoice (by Distinctly North) and 2 winners abroad: dam unraced: modest maiden: sold out of C. Murray's stable 3,500 gns Newmarket Autumn Sales after sixth start: stays 7f: acts on firm and dead ground. *J. Hetherton*

JADE'S GEM 2 b.f. (Apr 24) Sulaafah (USA) 119 – Jadebelle 66 (Beldale Flutter – (USA) 130) [1996 6m 6.1m 7m Sep 25] smallish, workmanlike filly: first reported foal: dam 2-y-o 6f winner who stayed 1½m: behind in maidens at Kempton and Nottingham (free to post) and seller at Goodwood: backward and slowly away first 2 starts. *G. B. Balding*

JADES SHADOW 3 gr.c. General Wade 93 – Gellifawr 80 (Saulingo 122) [1995 – NR 1996 7m 6g 8.3d 5g Aug 30] tall, angular colt: brother to winning sprinter Shades of Jade and half-brother to 8.3f seller winner Singing Gold (by Gold Claim): dam best at 5f: tailed off all 4 starts. *J. J. Bridger*

JADE VENTURE 5 b.m. Never So Bold 135 – Our Shirley 84 (Shirley Heights 49 + 130) [1995 NR 1996 a10g² Jan 18] angular mare: rated 67 when beaten neck only start in 1994: 13/8 on and first outing since, length second of 9 in maiden at Lingfield in January: should stay 1½m: covered by Owington. *S. P. C. Woods*

JADY'S DREAM (IRE) 5 b.m. Dreams To Reality (USA) 113 – Lemon Balm – (High Top 131) [1995 NR 1996 a12g a11g Feb 5] good-topped mare: no worthwhile form: has twice refused to race over hurdles: covered by Arzanni. *B. Palling*

JAGELLON (USA) 5 b.h. Danzig Connection (USA) – Heavenlyspun (USA) 81 (His Majesty (USA)) [1995 99: 10g 10.1s⁴ 12s² 12.1d* 10d* 10m² 10d 1996 10m 10m 10d⁵ 12m Sep 13] good-topped horse: has had interrupted career: in great heart in autumn '95, showing useful form: reportedly operated on for soft palate over winter: not seen until late-July at 5 yrs, and showed little except when fifth of 13 to Ball Gown in rated stakes at Newmarket penultimate start: effective at 1¼m and may stay beyond 1½m: acts on good to firm and soft ground: has had tongue tied down. *W. R. Muir*

JALB (IRE) 2 b.g. (Mar 30) Robellino (USA) 127 – Adjacent (IRE) 82 (Doulab 69 p (USA) 115) [1996 6m⁶ 6d⁵ 7f Sep 10] 60,000Y: strong, well-made gelding: fluent mover: first foal: dam 1¼m and 1½m winner from good family: fair form in maidens at Newmarket first 2 starts: steadied stalls, held up and never placed to challenge in similar event won by Sunbeam Dance at Leicester on final outing: should stay beyond 6f: remains open to improvement. *A. C. Stewart*

JALCANTO 6 ch.g. Jalmood (USA) 126 – Bella Canto 82 (Crooner 119) [1995 57 62: 14.1f² 16.2m³ 16m⁴ 16d 1996 a16g⁵ 16m⁴ 16g³ 16m³ 16f⁵ 16.5m⁵ 16.2g* 16m a– Sep 16] tall, workmanlike gelding: easy mover: modest handicapper: dropped into seller, unimpressive winner at Beverley in August: stays 2m: acts on good to firm and

470

dead going, no form on the all-weather: often bandaged: sometimes unruly at stalls: fairly useful hurdler: sold to join R. Juckes 3,000 gns Doncaster November Sales. *Mrs M. Reveley*

JALMAID 4 ch.f. Jalmood (USA) 126 – Misowni (Niniski (USA) 125) [1995 45, a60: a7g³ a6g² a6g⁴ a6g⁵ a8g 10m⁵ 10m⁵ a7g* 10.8g a8.5g a6g a8g* a9.4g³ 1996 a8g⁴ a8g a8g² a9.4g 8.2d a8g a11g³ 10m a11g a12g a8.5g⁵ 8.2m⁶ Aug 7] good-bodied filly: modest handicapper on all-weather, only poor form on turf last 2 seasons: subsequently sold 2,700 gns Doncaster August Sales and resold 1,500 gns Doncaster September Sales: stays 11f: easily best recent form on fibresand: none too consistent: has joined H. Alexander. *B. A. McMahon* — a58

JALORE 7 gr.g. Jalmood (USA) 126 – Lorelene (FR) 97 (Lorenzaccio 130) [1995 36: a14.8g 16.2m 12.1s 12.5g 21.6f 15.8g³ 15.1f⁴ 1996 12f⁴ Jun 26] lengthy, angular gelding: has a round action: soon tailed off in amateurs minor event at Carlisle after 12-month absence: stays 2m: used to go well with give in the ground, though has won on good to firm and acts on fibresand. *S. Coathup* — –

JAMAICAN FLIGHT (USA) 3 b.c. Sunshine Forever (USA) – Kalamona (USA) (Hawaii) [1995 66: 8g² 8g 1996 7m⁴ 10.1m 11f⁵ 16.2f* 16.1m³ 16.4m² Aug 20] leggy colt: modest handicapper: made all in maiden at Beverley in July, showing more resolution than runner-up: creditable efforts in handicaps afterwards: stays 2m: has raced only on a sound surface: front runner. *J. W. Hills* — 66

JAMBO 3 b.f. Rambo Dancer (CAN) 107 – Nicholess (Nicholas Bill 125) [1995 54: 5m⁴ 6g² 6g⁶ 6m⁴ 6f² 7.1m* 1996 6d 5.9f 8.1m* 7m² 8.2m* Aug 7] leggy filly: fair handicapper: won at Musselburgh in July and Nottingham in August: effective at 7f, stays 8.2f: acts on firm ground, poorly drawn only start on a soft surface: blinkered second 3-y-o start. *J. L. Eyre* — 68

JAMES IS SPECIAL (IRE) 8 b.g. Lyphard's Special (USA) 122 – High Explosive (Mount Hagen (FR) 127) [1995 NR 1996 11.8d Apr 4] tall, leggy gelding: carries condition: poor mover: form in 1994 for H. Collingridge (rated 41) only once from 5 starts: no promise on return: probably stays 15f: acts on heavy ground: visored (soundly beaten) penultimate 6-y-o start. *R. M. Stronge* — –

JAMRAT JUMAIRAH (IRE) 3 b.f. Polar Falcon (USA) 126 – Coryana 104 (Sassafras (FR) 135) [1995 77p: 7f² 1996 8m* Aug 8] strong, lengthy filly: carries condition: 5/4 favourite, heavily bandaged and poorly to post when winning maiden event at Pontefract by 5 lengths from Glen Parker, held up, leading over 1f out, edging left and soon clear: stays 1m: looked a useful filly in the making, but is evidently difficult to train: remains in training. *E. A. L. Dunlop* — 88 p

JAMRAT SAMYA (IRE) 2 b.f. (Feb 13) Sadler's Wells (USA) 132 – Samya's Flame 97 (Artaius (USA) 129) [1996 6m⁵ Oct 5] fifth foal: sister to fairly useful 1½m winner Raneen Alwatar: dam, 9f and 1¼m winner, sister to Flame of Tara (dam of Salsabil, herself by Sadler's Wells) and half-sister to dam of Northern Spur (also by Sadler's Wells): 33/1, in need of race and ridden by 7-lb claimer, around 4½ lengths fifth of 13 to Elegant Warning in maiden at Newmarket: will stay middle distances: sure to improve, and should be able to win a race. *L. M. Cumani* — 79 p

JANGLYNYVE 2 ch.f. (Apr 27) Sharpo 132 – Wollow Maid 73 (Wollow 132) [1996 5s⁴ 6m 7g⁴ 7f³ 7.6m Sep 10] 8,000Y: half-sister to 3 winners at up to 1m, including fair 7f to 9f handicapper Reverand Thickness (by Prince Sabo): dam 1¼m winner who refused to race once: flattered when fourth in moderately-run maiden auction at Yarmouth on third outing: only poor form otherwise: stays 7f. *S. P. C. Woods* — 48

JANIB (USA) 2 ch.c. (Feb 11) Diesis 133 – Shicklah (USA) 106 (The Minstrel (CAN) 135) [1996 5d⁴ 5f* 5m* 5m⁵ Sep 14] robust, compact colt: eighth foal: brother to 3 winners, including useful sprinter Ra'a and 6f (at 2 yrs) and 7f winner Nizaal: dam 5f and 6f winner at 2 yrs, from family of Habitat: first run for 3 months when winning maiden at Thirsk in August: useful form when winning 5-runner Roses Stakes at York 2½ weeks later, going on inside last to beat Tipsy Creek 1¼ lengths: fair fifth to Easycall in Flying Childers Stakes at Doncaster on final outing: likely to stay 6f: sent to Dubai. *H. Thomson Jones* — 98

JANIE'S BOY 2 b.c. (Feb 20) Persian Bold 123 – Cornelian 78 (Great Nephew 126) [1996 5m⁵ 6m 6g³ 6m a6g Nov 2] 45,000Y: leggy colt: fifth foal: closely related — 69 ?

to fairly useful 1990 2-y-o 6f winner Bold Nephew (by Never So Bold) and half-brother to 1991 Irish 2-y-o 7f winner Donna Roseanna (by Chief Singer): dam 1½m winner: trained by M. Tompkins then John Berry first 2 starts, off course 5 months in between: raced alone when third in maiden at Catterick, apparently best effort: well beaten afterwards, blinkered final start: should stay at least 7f. *R. Guest*

JANIES GIRL (IRE) 3 ch.f. Persian Heights 129 – Lovat Spring (USA) (Storm –
Bird (CAN) 134) [1995 51: 6m³ 6f⁵ 7g 1996 7.1d 7f Oct 15] smallish filly: soundly beaten since debut. *K. R. Burke*

JARAAB 5 b.g. Sure Blade (USA) 130 – Ostora (USA) 83 (Blushing Groom (FR) –
131) [1995 51, a78: a12g* a16g* 15.4g 14.1g a14.8g* a14.8g* a16g² 15.8g⁵ 16.4g³   a90
14g a16g⁵ a14.8g a16g a14.8g a12g³ a16g* a16g* a13g⁵ 1996 a12g⁴ a16g* 16.1s a16g* a14.8g* 16.1g a16g* May 27] stocky gelding: fairly useful performer on all-weather, winning handicap at Lingfield in February, claimer at Southwell (by 20 lengths, claimed out of G. Lewis' stable £6,000) and handicap at Wolverhampton (best effort) in April and claimer at Southwell (did not have to be near best) in May: stays 2m: acts well on the all-weather, only poor form on turf during last 2 seasons: visored since fifth 4-y-o start: blinkered (gave temperamental display) third 3-y-o start. *Miss S. J. Wilton*

JARAH (USA) 3 b.c. Forty Niner (USA) – Umniyatee 104 (Green Desert   103
(USA) 127) [1995 98p: 7g* 7m³ 1996 8.2m⁵ 8g* 10m 8m³ 8d⁵ 7.9g⁶ Oct 9] strong, compact colt: good mover: useful performer: awarded minor event at Doncaster in June: best effort when ¾-length third to Decorated Hero in rated stakes at Doncaster in September: never a threat in minor event at Bath (possibly unsuited by softish surface) and rated stakes at York afterwards: seems suited by 1m: acts on good to firm ground. *Saeed bin Suroor*

JAREER DO (IRE) 4 b.f. Jareer (USA) 115 – Shining Bright (USA) (Bold   54
Bidder) [1995 69d: 8.3m⁶ 7.1m³ 7.1m⁵ 7s a6g 1996 7f⁴ 7.1m² 6m a7g⁶ a7g a7g⁵ Dec   a–
31] lengthy filly: only modest form in 1996, short-headed in seller at Chepstow on second outing: should prove at least as effective at 1m as 7f: acts on good to firm ground, no form on the all-weather. *B. Palling*

JARI (USA) 5 b.g. Dixieland Band (USA) – Dusty Heart (USA) (Run Dusty Run   §§
(USA)) [1995 73§: a9g⁵ a7g* a7g a7g a12g a8g 1996 a9.4g Jan 3] good-topped gelding: won handicap in Dubai at 4 yrs: refused to race both subsequent starts there: looked one to leave well alone back in Britain and was banned from flat racing in February. *M. J. Polglase*

JARROW 5 ch.g. Jalmood (USA) 126 – Invite 79 (Be My Guest (USA) 126) –
[1995 40d: 11.8d 13g⁴ 13g a14.8g⁶ 15.8g a14.8g⁶ a12g 1996 a11g a11g⁶ Apr 9] lengthy gelding: poor maiden: should stay beyond 13f: best effort on dead ground: tried visored, no improvement. *Mrs A. M. Naughton*

JARVEY (IRE) 4 ch.g. Jareer (USA) 115 – Blue Czarina (Sandhurst Prince 128) –
[1995 6g 8m 8g⁴ 13g⁵ 9m³ 10m⁴ 12m³ 12m 1996 a10g 10f May 9] IR 7,500Y: second foal: dam unraced half-sister to smart Italian sprinter Ginny Binny: modest maiden handicapper (rated 62) in 1995 for K. Prendergast, sold 5,600 gns Doncaster November Sales: tailed off both starts in Britain: stays 1½m: acts on good to firm ground. *P. Eccles*

JASEUR (USA) 3 b.g. Lear Fan (USA) 130 – Spur Wing (USA) (Storm Bird   79 p
(CAN) 134) [1995 NR 1996 10.5d⁴ May 25] fourth foal: closely related to useful 1993 2-y-o 7.9f winner Pearl Kite (by Silver Hawk), better at 1½m/1¾m, became disappointing: dam won 6 races, including Grade 3 9f event: 3½ lengths fourth to Mount Row in maiden at Haydock: looked sure to improve, particularly over 1½m+: stays in training. *J. H. M. Gosden*

JATO 7 b.g. Pharly (FR) 130 – Minsden's Image (Dancer's Image (USA)) [1995 –
78: 6f³ 7m² 7g 7m⁶ 6m⁶ 7g 6g 7g 1996 7g 6.9g Sep 27] small, sturdy gelding: good mover with a long stride: fair handicapper: little worthwhile form in 1996, not seen out until September: effective at 6f and 7f: acts on firm ground and dead: blinkered twice in 1992, running well first occasion. *S. C. Williams*

JAUNTY JACK 2 b.c. (Mar 23) Midyan (USA) 124 – Juliette Marny 123   90
(Blakeney 126) [1996 6g² 8m² 8.2s² Oct 31] 16,000Y: rangy, quite attractive colt: half-brother to several winners, including useful 1¼m winner Jolly Bay (by Mill

Reef) and useful French 1½m to 2½m winner Lac Ladoga (by Sharpo): dam won Oaks and Irish Oaks and is sister to Julio Mariner and half-sister to Scintillate: fairly useful form when runner-up in maidens and a minor event, beaten ½ length by Desert Horizon (pair clear) at Nottingham final start: will stay middle distances: sure to win a race. *L. M. Cumani*

JAVA BAY 2 b.f. (Mar 8) Statoblest 120 – Flopsy (Welsh Pageant 132) [1996 6d – 5.1m 6.9d⁵ Oct 21] 12,500Y: half-sister to lightly raced 3-y-o Prime Light (by Primo Dominie), useful 7f performer Captain Holly (by Absalom), 1993 2-y-o 7f winner (later stayed 1¾m) Crazy For You (by Blakeney) and a prolific minor winner in Germany (including at 1¼m) by Sharrood: dam unraced daughter of 1000 Guineas third Mrs Tiggywinkle, dam also of smart Gordian: weakened closing stages in 3 maiden auctions, achieving little in the way of form. *M. Blanshard*

JAVA RED (IRE) 4 b.g. Red Sunset 120 – Coffee Bean (Doulab (USA) 115) 55 [1995 56: 10m⁵ a8g³ 8m* 10m 1996 10m 8m⁵ a8g 8.3g⁴ Sep 2] leggy gelding: modest handicapper: should stay 1¼m: acts on fibresand and good to firm ground (yet to race on a soft surface). *J. G. FitzGerald*

JAWAAL 6 ch.g. Soviet Star (USA) 128 – Pencil Sharpener (USA) 93 (Sharpen 86 Up 127) [1995 103: 8g² 7m* 7.9g* 7.1g 8m 1996 8d 7m 7.9m 8.1g 7g⁶ 7.3m⁵ 7m 7.9g 8f³ Dec 6] strong gelding: usually impresses in appearance: has a quick action: unimpressive walker: useful handicapper in 1995: not so good at 6 yrs: sold out of Lady Herries' stable 7,400 gns Newmarket Autumn Sales after penultimate start, third in claimer at Hollywood Park afterwards: effective at 7f and 1m: acts on firm going: has tongue tied nowadays. *Frank J. Monteleone, USA*

JAWHARI 2 b.c. (Mar 18) Lahib (USA) 129 – Lady of The Land 75 (Wollow 132) 76 [1996 6f² 6d⁴ Aug 24] 50,000F: small, sturdy colt: sixth foal: half-brother to 1m winner La Fille de Cirque (by Cadeaux Genereux), 1¼m winner Sharquin (by Indian King) and a winner in Italy: dam 1m winner: odds on, 2½ lengths second to Cinema Paradiso in maiden at Newbury, running green 1f out: similar form when fourth of 6 to Desert Story in similar event at Newmarket following month, leading or disputing lead 5f: bred to be suited by further than 6f. *J. L. Dunlop*

JAYANNPEE 5 ch.g. Doulab (USA) 115 – Amina 80 (Brigadier Gerard 144) 109 [1995 100: 5.1m³ 5.1m² 5f⁶ 6m⁵ 5g³ 6m³ 5m⁶ 6g⁴ 5.6m 5d 5s 1996 5.2d 6m* 6m* 5m 6f 6f* 6m 6d⁴ 6m* 6m Sep 28] good-topped gelding: smart performer: better than ever in 1996, winning £24,900 handicap at Newmarket and rated stakes at York in

Ladbrokes Handicap, Newmarket—
Jayannpee's neck advantage over Sir Joey (near side), with Perryston View in third

May, 16-runner listed event at Newbury in July and 12-runner listed race at Taby (neck third to Humbert's Landing and Hakiki, awarded race) in September: stays 6f: acts on firm and dead ground, no form on soft: successful for apprentice: wears tongue strap. *I. A. Balding*

JAY-GEE-EM 2 b.f. (Feb 23) Aragon 118 – Mana (GER) (Windwurf (GER)) 66 p [1996 7m* 6m* 7g Aug 30] seventh reported live foal: sister to 1993 2-y-o 6f winner Maragon and half-sister to 3 winners, including 1¼m winner Spray of Orchids (by Pennine Walk): dam listed winner at 2 yrs in Germany: won 6-runner seller at Brighton (bandaged) and 6-runner claimer (claimed out of R. Guest's stable £7,500): mid-division in 17-runner claimer at Evry final start: should be suited by further than 6f. *J. Parkes*

JAY-OWE-TWO (IRE) 2 b.g. (May 17) Distinctly North (USA) 115 – Fiery 78 Song (Ballad Rock 122) [1996 6d a6g a6g² a6g* Dec 27] 12,000Y, 10,000 2-y-o: strong, lengthy gelding: fourth foal: half-brother to 4-y-o winner Contrafire (up to 1½m, also over hurdles, by Contract Law): dam lightly-raced half-sister to smart 7f and 1m winner Fiery Celt out of very smart 1972 2-y-o Fiery Diplomat: fair form: won maiden at Southwell in December: should be suited by further than 6f. *R. M. Whitaker*

JAY TEE EF (IRE) 2 br.c. (Mar 22) Mac's Imp (USA) 116 – Arachosia (Persian – Bold 123) [1996 a5g a5g⁶ a6g 5s Nov 7] 5,000 2-y-o: fifth foal: half-brother to 1992 2-y-o 6f and 7f winner Times Arrow (by Wolverlife), later successful in Hong Kong: dam ran once at 3 yrs in Ireland: well beaten in sellers and maidens: blinkered last start: sold 500 gns Doncaster November Sales: sent to Denmark. *B. A. McMahon*

JAZZ KING 3 br.g. Kalaglow 132 – Sabrine (Mount Hagen (FR) 127) [1995 NR 83 1996 11.9f* 11.6g³ 14f⁴ 13.9m Aug 20] tall, workmanlike gelding: has a long, round stride: seventh foal: half-brother to Irish 2-y-o 6f winner Solany (by Encino) and 5f to 1m winner Tyrian Purple (by Wassl): dam Irish middle-distance performer from family of Slip Anchor: fairly useful form: 11/4 on, won median auction maiden at Brighton in June: in frame in minor event at Windsor and rated stakes (behind Benatom, flashing tail) at Goodwood: ran poorly final start: should stay beyond 1¾m: has only raced on a sound surface. *Miss Gay Kelleway*

JEAN DE FLORETTE (USA) 5 b.g. Our Native (USA) – The Branks (USA) 31 (Hold Your Peace (USA)) [1995 41: a14.8g a12g 11.8g⁵ 12.1m 11.5m⁴ 12m² 11.6m³ 12m³ a14g⁶ 12f³ 12m 13.1h⁶ 11.5g 12.1d 1996 a11g⁴ 12f³ a12g² 11.8d 11.4m 14.1f a14g a14g Nov 4] lengthy gelding: has a long stride: poor maiden handicapper: stays 13.1f: acts on hard ground and fibresand, below form on a soft surface: no improvement visored or blinkered. *R. C. Spicer*

JEANNE CUTRONA 3 b.f. Risk Me (FR) 127 – Veuve Perrin (Legend of – France (USA) 124) [1995 NR 1996 7m⁶ Jun 5] 3,000Y: second foal: dam unraced: tailed off in maiden at Yarmouth: joined K. Wingrove. *N. A. Callaghan*

JEAN PIERRE 3 b.c. Anshan 119 – Astolat (Rusticaro (FR) 124) [1995 –: 6m⁴ 56 7g 8f 1996 10m 12.3m 10.8m² 10.2m² 9.7m 10.4g 9g Nov 1] useful-looking colt: worthwhile form only when second in maiden handicaps at Warwick and Bath (hung fire when brought to challenge, beaten short head, in summer: should stay further than 10.8f: has raced only on a sound surface: not the easiest of rides. *J. Pearce*

JEBI (USA) 6 b.g. Phone Trick (USA) – Smokey Legend (USA) (Hawaii) [1995 43 a8g² a8g a7g a5g³ 1996 a7g⁶ a10g³ a10g 6g⁵ 7.1m⁴ 5g⁵ Jul 22] tenth foal: brother to a minor 7f winner in North America and half-brother to several minor winners (one, by Stage Door Johnny, at up to 11f) in North America and France: dam, minor US 2-y-o 5f winner, is half-sister to top-class U.S. filly Gay Matelda: modest maiden in Dubai for S. Seemar: sold 6,000 gns Newmarket July (1995) Sales: poor at best for new stable: stays 1¼m: often blinkered/visored: has seemed reluctant. *C. Murray*

JEDI KNIGHT 2 b.c. (May 12) Emarati (USA) 74 – Hannie Caulder (Workboy 66 p 123) [1996 6m⁴ 5f³ 5g⁴ Aug 12] 9,400Y: good-topped colt: has scope: half-brother to 1¾m winner Trecauldah (by Treboro) and 5f winner Sister Hannah (by Monseigneur): dam unraced half-sister to 1000 Guineas winner Mrs McArdy: fair form in northern maidens, best effort when 3¾ lengths third of 9 to Janib at Thirsk: likely to do better at 3 yrs. *M. W. Easterby*

JEFFREY ANOTHERRED 2 b.g. (Apr 4) Emarati (USA) 74 – First Pleasure 93
73 (Dominion 123) [1996 5.1m³ 5m* 6g³ 6g* 7.3m² 7s* a7g Nov 18] 5,000Y, 8,600
2-y-o: small gelding: fifth live foal: dam, suited by 1m, half-sister to useful 9f
to 1½m winner Celtic Pleasure: made into a fairly useful performer, winning maiden
auction at Hamilton in August and nurseries at Kempton in September and Doncaster
(by short head) in November: reported to have choked when beaten favourite
(on fibresand) final outing: stays 7.3f: acts on good to firm and soft ground.
K. McAuliffe

JELALI (IRE) 3 b.g. Last Tycoon 131 – Lautreamont (Auction Ring (USA) 123) 65
[1995 68p: 7d 7g⁴ 1996 8m 10m 12.5f⁴ a1g 17.2d³ 16g Oct 24] big, leggy gelding:
showed little in 1996, except when third in handicap at Bath (trailed long way,
plugged on late) penultimate start: seems suited by a test of stamina. *D. J. G. Murray
Smith*

JELLABY ASKHIR 4 b.c. Salse (USA) 128 – Circus Act (Shirley Heights 130) –
[1995 105: 12m⁴ 12m* 14m* 14.6d 12g⁴ 12m 1996 16.2m May 1] strong, lengthy
colt: easy mover: useful performer: tailed off in Sagaro Stakes at Ascot only
start at 4 yrs, dropping himself out 4f from home: should be suited by a thorough
test of stamina: reluctant at stalls, and wears rope halter: one to treat with caution.
R. Akehurst

JEMIMA PUDDLEDUCK 5 ch.m. Tate Gallery (USA) 117 – Tittlemouse 86 –
(Castle Keep 121) [1995 59: a12g⁴ 9.7d² 11.8d³ 12m⁵ 10.8g 9.7g⁵ 10.8g 12g 12m
a11g* 1996 a11g Nov 4] close-coupled mare: modest handicapper: blinkered, won
seller at Southwell in November, 1995, on final start for D. Arbuthnot: first run of
any type for over 7 months and visored, always behind in minor event at Southwell:
stays 1½m: acts on heavy ground and fibresand, respectable effort on good to firm:
usually races prominently. *A. Streeter*

JEMSILVERTHORN (IRE) 3 b.g. Maelstrom Lake 118 – Fairy Don (Don 56 d
128) [1995 46+: 5.3f⁶ 5g 5g 5g 6m⁶ 5f⁵ 6g 7g⁶ a8.5g a6g⁶ a10g a7g⁶ a7g a8g 1996
a5g² a6g⁵ a6g 6s a5g a6g 5g Sep 2] workmanlike gelding: modest form at Lingfield
first 2 3-y-o starts: well below form afterwards, leaving J. Bridger after third outing:
effective at 5f, and stays 7f: acts on equitrack: tried blinkered/visored, no improvement. *R. C. Spicer*

JENDALI PRINCESS 3 ro.f. Jendali (USA) 111 – Hyperion Princess –
(Dragonara Palace (USA) 115) [1995 NR 1996 a7g a11g Nov 18] fifth reported live
foal: dam well beaten in 3 starts: no sign of ability. *M. J. Polglase*

JENNELLE 2 b.f. (Mar 7) Nomination 125 – Its A Romp (Hotfoot 126) [1996 5s* 97
5m* 5m 5m* 5m² 5g³ 5.5m⁴ 5v² 5d* Oct 28] 1,600Y: smallish, good-quartered filly:
sixth living foal: half-sister to 3 winners, including a fair stayer by Monteverdi and a
middle-distance filly by Bustino: dam, half-sister to high-class middle-distance
performer Whitstead, won sprint claimer in USA: useful form: won maiden auction
at Folkestone in March, minor event at Thirsk in April, nursery at Folkestone in July,
and minor event at Lingfield in October (short head from Darb Alola): unlucky
penultimate outing: speedy: acts on good to firm and heavy ground: edgy eighth start:
ridden by 7-lb claimer Jo Hunnam since fourth outing. *C. A. Dwyer*

JENNY'S CHARMER 3 ch.c. Charmer 123 – Jenny Wyllie 66 (Nishapour (FR) –
125) [1995 –: 5m 5m³ 6g 6s 5m 1996 6g 5g 7m 6f Aug 3] workmanlike colt:
signs of ability but no worthwhile form: should stay beyond 5f: tried blinkered.
S. E. Kettlewell

JEOPARDIZE 3 b.f. Polish Patriot (USA) 128 – Extra Cost (USA) (Vaguely –
Noble 140) [1995 NR 1996 8m⁵ 8.1m 10.4g 8m Sep 19] big, leggy, angular filly: has
had shins fired: fourth reported living foal: half-sister to a winner in Germany: dam
never ran: appeared to show promise in maiden on debut: well beaten all subsequent
starts: sold 800 gns (Newmarket Autumn) and 700 gns (Ascot September) Sales and
joined Miss K. George: yet to race on a soft surface. *C. E. Brittain*

JERMYN STREET (USA) 5 b.h. Alleged (USA) 138 – My Mother Mary 75
(USA) (Boldnesian) [1995 –: 12m 1996 12m 12g² 13.3f⁶ 16.2m Jul 26] medium-
sized, quite attractive horse: poor mover: fair handicapper: sweating, seemed not to
get home over 2m final start: sold 3,500 gns Newmarket Autumn Sales: stays 13f:
acts on firm ground, yet to race on a soft surface. *Mrs J. Cecil*

JERRY CUTRONA (IRE) 3 br.g. Distinctly North (USA) 115 – Foulkesmills 88
(Tanfirion 110) [1995 73: 6m 7f⁴ 7m 10d 8f³ 8f² 6.9m* a8g³ 1996 7m⁵ 6.9f⁵ 8m 6m*
6m³ 7.5m⁴ 6f⁴ 7m* 8g* 7d³ 8g 10m³ Oct 4] big, strong gelding: poor mover: fairly
useful handicapper: won at Yarmouth in June and at Lingfield and Thirsk (edged
right and swished tail) in August: good running-on third at Newmarket final start:
sold 31,000 gns Newmarket Autumn Sales: stays 1¼m: acts on firm and dead ground
and on equitrack: usually held up: sent to USA. *N. A. Callaghan*

JERSEY BELLE 4 b.f. Distant Relative 128 – Hong Kong Girl 94 (Petong 126) –
[1995 –, a47: a6g² a7g⁶ 6s a6g⁶ a6g² 6g 8.1m a6g* a6g³ a7g⁴ a7g a7g⁴ 1996 a7g a6g a52
a6g² a6g* Feb 15] modest handicapper: won at Lingfield in February: probably stays
7f: acts on fibresand and equitrack: blinkered at 3 yrs: covered by Alhijaz. *P. J. Makin*

JESSICA'S SONG 3 b.f. Colmore Row 111 – Sideloader Special 66 (Song 132) 51
[1995 55: a5g⁵ a6g⁵ 6f³ 5.1h* 6s 1996 6f⁶ 5.1g 5m⁵ 5.1g⁴ 6m a5g Jul 12] sturdy filly:
poor performer: best at 5f: acts on hard ground. *W. G. M. Turner*

JEZYAH (USA) 3 ch.f. Chief's Crown (USA) – Empress Jackie (USA) (Mount 80
Hagen (FR) 127) [1995 78: 6g 7m² 6g³ 7g* 1996 7g⁶ 10.1m Sep 18] stocky filly:
fluent mover: fair form: good sixth in rated stakes at Newmarket on reappearance:
did not appear to be beaten by trip alone when tried over 1¼m 2½ months later:
should stay beyond 7f: gives trouble in stalls, and had to be withdrawn from
intended start at 3 yrs: sold 65,000 gns Newmarket December Sales. *R. W. Armstrong*

JHAZI 2 b.c. (Apr 13) Arazi (USA) 135 – Shoot Clear 111 (Bay Express 132) 99 p
[1996 5m* 6m 6g⁴ Oct 26] 82,000F, 88,000Y: good-bodied colt: fluent mover:
closely related to 1¼m winner Elmaftun (by Rainbow Quest) and half-brother to
several winners, including useful middle-distance performer Shoot Ahead (by
Shirley Heights): dam, 5f to 7f winner at 2 yrs and fourth in 1000 Guineas, half-sister
to Yorkshire Oaks winners Sally Brown and Untold: won 15-runner maiden at
Beverley in September: came out nearly best horse at weights when tenth of 25 to
Proud Native in Redcar Two-Year-Old Trophy following month despite being drawn
well away from principals: rather lack-lustre effort when fourth of 7 to Elegant
Warning in listed race at Doncaster 9 days later: may well still be capable of better.
D. R. Loder

JIBEREEN 4 b.g. Lugana Beach 116 – Fashion Lover 70 (Shiny Tenth 120) [1995 75
78: 6m 7m 7.1g 8m 8.1m 7g 7.1d* 1996 7d⁶ 7g a6g* a6s⁴ Dec 19] strong gelding:
fair handicapper: left G. Lewis after reappearance: won at Southwell (all-weather
debut) in December, leading final strides: effective at 6f, and probably stays 1m: acts
on fibresand: best turf efforts on an easy surface. *P. Howling*

JIB JAB 2 br.g. (May 1) Jendali (USA) 111 – No Rejection (Mummy's Pet 125) 59 p
[1996 5m² 5d⁵ 7f⁶ 7m 6g Sep 3] tall gelding: fourth foal: half-brother to 5-y-o 17.2f
seller winner Wadada (by Adbass): dam unraced half-sister to smart sprinter Dream
Talk out of half-sister to Cajun: modest form: gelded after second outing: considerately handled in claimer and nursery last 2 starts: will stay beyond 7f: almost
certainly capable of better. *D. Nicholls*

JIGSAW BOY 7 ch.g. Homeboy 114 – Chiparia 82 (Song 132) [1995 65, a68: 6g⁴ 60
6g⁵ 6m⁶ 6g⁶ 6m³ 6d² 7m a6g⁵ 6g a6g⁴ a6g² a6g a7g² a6g* a6g⁴ a7g⁶ 1996 a6g⁶ a7g⁴ a71
a7g* a7g³ 5.9d⁶ 6m⁵ 6f 7d a7g* a6g⁵ a6g a7g a7g* a6g a7s⁵ a7g Dec 28] good-topped
gelding: fair handicapper: won at Wolverhampton in February (claimer), May and
November: well below form there final 3 starts: stays 7f: best recent form on
fibresand, acts on any turf going: tried visored, no improvement: usually held up.
P. G. Murphy

JILLY BEVELED 4 b.f. Beveled (USA) – Karens Valentine (Daring March 116) 45
[1995 –: 7f 8.1m 10d 8.2m 1996 8m⁵ 7d⁵ 8m⁴ 8d² a14.8g⁶ Nov 30] leggy filly: poor
maiden handicapper: sold out of P. Webber's stable 2,400 gns Doncaster October
Sales after penultimate start: stays 1m: acts on good to firm and dead ground. *Ronald
Thompson*

JILLY WOO 2 gr.f. (Mar 5) Environment Friend 128 – William's Bird (USA) 104 60 d
(Master Willie 129) [1996 5.7g³ 6g⁵ 6d⁵ 5f 6m 7m 6d³ a6g⁵ a7g Nov 25] 4,800Y: a?
rather leggy filly: third foal: dam 5f and 7f winner at 2 yrs, ran only once at 3 yrs:
modest maiden: seems to stay 7f: blinkered last 4 starts: none too consistent.
D. R. C. Elsworth

JIMBO 5 b.h. Salse (USA) 128 – Darnelle 83 (Shirley Heights 130) [1995 –: 10s – 7m 7f a8g a13g Feb 1] angular, plain horse: no worthwhile form. *J. R. Jenkins*

JIMJAREER (IRE) 3 br.c. Jareer (USA) 115 – Onthecomet (Chief Singer 131) 51 [1995 61: a5g* 6f² 6m⁴ 7g⁵ 8g 8f 1996 6d 8m⁵ a8g a8g⁴ 8f³ 8f 8.2m 11m a8g Dec 3] good-bodied colt: blind in off eye: modest handicapper: none too consistent at 3 yrs, running as if something amiss seventh start: stays 1m: acts on fibresand and firm ground, ran poorly only start on a soft surface. *Capt. J. Wilson*

JIMMY-S (IRE) 3 b.g. Marju (IRE) 127 – Amber Fizz (USA) (Effervescing – (USA)) [1995 NR 1996 10d 11.1m Aug 29] eighth foal: half-brother to 4 winners, including 4-y-o 11f winner Ambidextrous (by Shareef Dancer) and smart 5f to 7f performer Cool Jazz (by Lead On Time): dam ran once: tailed-off last in maiden and a claimer. *R. M. McKellar*

JIMMY THE SKUNK (IRE) 5 b.g. Fayruz 116 – Very Seldom (Rarity 129) 66 [1995 NR 1996 7.1s* a7g a7g Nov 29] fair performer: winner for Jack Berry at 3 yrs: subsequently successful in Jersey: having first outing on mainland for 2 years when winning jockeys challenge handicap at Chepstow in October: well held both subsequent starts: stays 7f: acts on firm and soft ground and on fibresand: effective visored or not: game. *P. D. Evans*

JINGOIST (IRE) 2 b.f. (Feb 27) Polish Patriot (USA) 128 – Hot Curry (USA) 52 (Sharpen Up 127) [1996 a5g⁶ 5m a5g⁶ 5.2f² 5m⁵ a6g² 6g* 6f⁵ 8f² 7.5m² 6s a8.5g⁵ Nov 2] IR 5,500Y: leggy filly: fourth foal: half-sister to 3-y-o Verulam (by Marju) and 4-y-o 11.5f winner Marchant Ming (also useful hurdler, by Persian Bold): dam 1m winner in USA: modest form: won selling nursery at Leicester in August: stays 8.5f: acts on firm ground and fibresand, below form on soft: blinkered last 8 starts: swishes tail, and has looked less than keen on occasions. *J. L. Harris*

JIVE BOOGIE 2 b. or br.c. (Apr 27) Nomination 125 – Jive Music 32 (Music – Boy 124) [1996 5m Sep 19] 500Y: second foal: dam 5f winner: 100/1 and blinkered, showed nothing in seller at Ayr. *N. Bycroft*

JIYUSH 3 b.c. Generous (IRE) 139 – Urjwan (USA) 98 (Seattle Slew (USA)) 107 [1995 83+: 8g² 8f⁴ 1996 10m³ 12.1d² 12m² 14m² 13.9g* 18.2m* 18g 16g Nov 1] big, good-topped colt: useful form: won handicaps at York and Yarmouth (amenable to restraint, impressive in beating Flocheck 5 lengths) in September: disappointing in Cesarewitch and listed rated stakes at Newmarket last 2 starts: stays 2¼m: probably acts on firm and dead ground, yet to race on anything softer: tends to sweat (didn't last 2 starts): has joined E. Dunlop. *H. Thomson Jones*

JOBBER'S FIDDLE 4 b.f. Sizzling Melody 117 – Island Mead 86 (Pharly (FR) 45 130) [1995 49: 8m a7g 8.3g 10m 8m⁴ 8.3m⁶ 8f⁴ 10d⁶ 1996 a12g² a10g a12g Jan 18] strong, workmanlike filly: poor performer nowadays: unlikely to stay beyond 1½m: acts on firm ground and equitrack: often visored/blinkered: usually races prominently: none too consistent. *D. L. Williams*

JOBIE 6 b.g. Precocious 126 – Lingering 96 (Kind of Hush 118) [1995 70: 5m⁵ 6m 63 d 6g⁵ 7.3g 5.7f³ 5m 5m² 6g⁴ 6g 1996 6m³ 6m 5m 6f 6.9m Aug 16] sturdy gelding: fair sprint handicapper on his day at 5 yrs: lost his form: acts on firm and dead ground: has joined R. Phillips. *B. W. Hills*

JO COLEMAN 2 b.f. (Mar 28) Puissance 110 – Miss Echo 85 (Chief Singer 131) – [1996 6m Oct 4] 2,100Y: second foal: dam (best at 2 yrs, refused to race final start at 3 yrs) was ungenuine maiden: should stayed 1¼m: 20/1, showed nothing in claimer at Lingfield. *D. Morris*

JOE JAGGER (IRE) 5 b.g. Petorius 117 – Seapoint (Major Point) [1995 –: – a16.2g 1996 13.6m Oct 17] sparely-made gelding: tailed off only start in 1995 for Miss M. K. Milligan: first run for 20 months, well beaten only outing in 1996: acts on soft ground, probably on good to firm. *M. D. Hammond*

JOHAN CRUYFF 2 b.c. (Mar 27) Danehill (USA) 126 – Teslemi (USA) 73 104 p (Ogygian (USA)) [1996 7m* 7g⁵ 8s* Oct 19] 20,000F, 30,000Y: first foal: dam 1m winner (should have stayed further) out of sister to champion grass mare De La Rose and Grade 1 1¼m winner Upper Nile: won maiden at Leopardstown in July: just over 2 lengths fifth of 10 to Desert King in National Stakes at the Curragh 2 months later, held up then staying on, never reaching leaders: 2/1 on, didn't need to repeat that

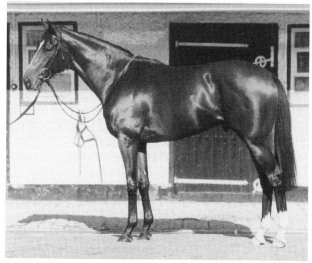

Mrs John Magnier's "Johan Cruyff"

form when winning 5-runner Juddmonte Beresford Stakes at the Curragh in October by 2 lengths from Cambodian: stays 1m: acts on soft ground: remains capable of better. *A. P. O'Brien, Ireland*

JOHAYRO 3 ch.g. Clantime 101 – Arroganza 62 (Crofthall 110) [1995 84: 5g² 5m² 5m² 5g 5g 5.7m⁵ 5f* 1996 a5g² a5g 5d 5d 5.1m 5.1f 5.1m⁵ 5m² 5m 5.1g⁶ 5g 5s Nov 8] close-coupled gelding: has a quick action: fair form at best, but largely disappointing at 3 yrs, and left W. G. M. Turner after seventh start: best at 5f: acts on firm ground: usually blinkered/visored: often apprentice ridden: front runner. *J. S. Goldie*   67 d

JOHN EMMS (IRE) 2 ch.c. (Mar 26) Shalford (IRE) 124§ – Miss Lee Ann (Tumble Wind (USA)) [1996 5m⁵ 6g Sep 5] IR 8,500Y, 36,000 2-y-o: good-topped colt: half-brother to Irish 3-y-o Errazuriz (by Classic Music), fairly useful winner at around 1m at 2 yrs, and Irish 1992 2-y-o 6f winner Cookawara (by Fairy King): dam, unraced, from family of Horage and Snurge: much better effort in maidens when around 8 lengths eighth of 16 to Tycoon Todd at York, never dangerous: will do better. *M. Bell*   68 p

JOHNNIE THE JOKER 5 gr.g. Absalom 128 – Magic Tower 76 (Tower Walk 130) [1995 52, a78: 7g 8f⁶ 7g⁴ 7g⁴ 9.9m⁴ 7m 8d 7f 10f a7g⁶ a7g⁵ a8g 1996 a6g a8g⁵ 7s⁵ a8g² 7g* 7.5m a6g⁵ a7g* a9.4g² a9.4g a8.5g⁵ a9.4g 7m³ 8f 8m a8.5g Nov 16] good-topped gelding: has a round action: fairly useful handicapper on the all-weather, only modest on turf: won at Doncaster (apprentice race) in May and at Wolverhampton in June: finds 7f a minimum and probably stays 1¼m: acts on fibresand, firm and dead ground: usually blinkered, has been visored: usually races prominently. *J. P. Leigh*   51 a79

JOHNNY STACCATO 2 b.g. (Jan 24) Statoblest 120 – Frasquita (Song 132) [1996 6d* 6m⁴ 7m⁶ 6g⁶ Oct 26] 15,000Y: useful-looking, rather unfurnished gelding: 91

keen walker: has a quick action: fifth foal: half-brother to a winner in Scandinavia by Never So Bold: dam unraced sister to smart sprinter Jester: fairly useful form: won 18-runner maiden auction at Windsor in August: close fourth to Arethusa in listed race at Kempton and sixth to Grapeshot in similar event at Newmarket next 2 starts: probably stays 7f. *J. M. P. Eustace.*

JOHN O'DREAMS 11 b.g. Indian King (USA) 128 – Mississipi Shuffle 78   54
(Steel Heart 128) [1995 52: 5m 5.1m 5.1m 5m⁶ 5.2g⁵ 5.1m⁶ 5m 5f⁵ 5.7h⁴ 5g³ 5d⁴ 5.1m 1996 5g 5m³ 5.1g⁵ 5m⁵ 6f 5.2m* 5g 5f⁶ 5.1m³ 5m⁶ 5g⁶ 5.7m³ 5m³ Sep 25] good-topped gelding: poor walker: unimpressive mover: modest handicapper: well ridden by M. Roberts when winning at Newbury in June: ran consistently well afterwards: stays 6f: acts on any going: tried blinkered (below form) and visored (has run creditably) earlier in career: often bandaged: sometimes slowly away (lost all chance by rearing fifth 11-y-o start) and is held up. *Mrs A. L. M. King*

JOHNS ACT (USA) 6 b.g. Late Act (USA) – Deluxe Type (USA) (Singh (USA))   74 d
[1995 74: a12g⁴ a12g³ a12g³ a12g* 12g 13.3g* 14g⁵ 11.9d⁵ 13.3d 12m⁶ 1996 a14.8g⁶ a12g⁵ a12g² a12g 14.9d 16d⁵ 13.3s 11.9v 14.1s a12s⁶ a12g Dec 28] good-topped gelding: good mover: fair handicapper at best: mostly well below form in 1996: stays 1¾m: acts on good to firm and soft ground and on fibresand: effective visored or not: unreliable. *D. Haydn Jones*

JOHNS JOY 11 b.g. Martin John – Saybya (Sallust 134) [1995 –: 10.8g 1996   39
12m⁶ 9m 10m⁵ 10g Jul 8] angular gelding: modest form at 9 yrs: only sign of retaining a little ability when fifth of 23 in selling handicap at Windsor penultimate start: probably suited by further than 1m: probably acts on any ground. *J. J. Bridger*

JOHN'S LAW (IRE) 3 b.g. Contract Law (USA) 108 – Vieux Carre (Pas de Seul   49
133) [1995 –: a7g 1996 8.2d 5g⁴ 5m 6s 6m⁵ 6d Sep 27] rather leggy, sparely-made gelding: modest maiden handicapper: sold 4,200 gns Newmarket Autumn Sales: stays 6f: acts on good to firm ground: visored/blinkered last 2 starts: sent to Germany. *M. J. Heaton-Ellis*

JOHN-T 3 b.c. Thatching 131 – Ower (IRE) 71 (Lomond (USA) 128) [1995 –: 7f   80 d
1996 8d 8g 9m⁶ a9.4g 10g 7g 10.5s Oct 5] smallish, sturdy colt: unimpressive mover: 33/1, best effort in maidens when seventh of 20 at Newbury, second 3-y-o start, running on from rear under considerate handling: disappointing afterwards, leaving J. Dunlop after fifth 3-y-o outing: stays 1m: seems unsuited by top-of-the-ground. *J. Berry*

JOHN TUFTY 5 ch.g. Vin St Benet 109 – Raffles Virginia 73 (Whistling Deer   –
117) [1995 NR 1996 10m 14.1f Jul 6] seems of little account on flat, but is a modest winning hurdler. *J. Pearce*

JOINT VENTURE (IRE) 2 b.c. (Apr 5) Common Grounds 118 – Renata's Ring   90
(IRE) (Auction Ring (USA) 123) [1996 5d² 5.1d⁴ 5m² 5.3f² 5d* 5m³ 5g 5m 5d³ Oct 28] 9,600Y: strong, sturdy colt: first foal: dam placed at 7f in Ireland: made all in maiden auction at Haydock in May: off course nearly 3 months, best effort when 2½ lengths fifth to Jennelle in minor event at Lingfield, final start: sold 8,500 gns Newmarket Autumn Sales: speedy: acts on firm and dead ground: blinkered and equipped with dropped noseband fifth to eighth starts. *B. J. Meehan*

JOLIS ABSENT 6 b.m. Primo Dominie 121 – Jolimo 92 (Fortissimo 111) [1995   –
–: a16g 16d 1996 14d Oct 2] robust mare: modest middle-distance staying handicapper early in 1994: lightly raced on flat and no form since: winning novice hurdler. *M. J. Ryan*

JOLI'S GREAT 8 ch.m. Vaigly Great 127 – Jolimo 92 (Fortissimo 111) [1995   –
NR 1996 9.9d 10m Jun 24] small mare: poor handicapper (rated 44) at 6 yrs: soundly beaten in 1996: stays 11f: acts on good to firm and heavy ground: visored (below form) once at 4 yrs, usually blinkered: winning hurdler. *M. J. Ryan*

JOLIS PRESENT 3 b.c. Prince Sabo 123 – Jolimo 92 (Fortissimo 111) [1995   –
70d: 5m 5m* 6f⁶ 6f⁶ 6m⁵ 5g⁴ 5m 1996 6m 5m a8g Jun 6] good-topped colt: won maiden at Windsor at 2 yrs: failed to repeat that form: form only at 5f: blinkered last 5 outings: broke down final one: dead. *M. J. Ryan*

JOLI'S PRINCE 2 b.g. (Mar 29) Superlative 118 – Joli's Girl 79 (Mansingh   –
(USA) 120) [1996 8m 8m Oct 17] 8,000Y: tall gelding: fifth foal: half-brother to useful 6f (at 2 yrs) and 1m winner Joli's Princess (by Prince Sabo) and 13f and 1¾m

winner Side Bar (by Mummy's Game): dam 9f winner who stayed 1½m: well beaten in maidens at Yarmouth and Newmarket (free to post, took keen hold in race). *C. Murray*

JOLLY HOKEY 4 b.g. Dominion 123 – Judy's Dowry 80 (Dragonara Palace – (USA) 115) [1995 –: 7g 6m 1996 a6g³ a7g Apr 24] workmanlike gelding: poor maiden: should stay 7f: acts on fibresand: has joined P. Felgate. *J. Wharton*

JOLLY JACKSON 2 br.c. (Mar 7) Primo Dominie 121 – Pounelta 91 (Tachy- 64 pous 128) [1996 7d a8g⁴ Dec 20] seventh foal: closely related to 4-y-o Anistop (by Nomination), modest performer at up to 1½m, and half-sister to 5f (at 2 yrs) to 7f winner Top Pet (by Petong) and untrustworthy 6f (at 2 yrs) and 7f winner Durneltor (by Hard Fought): dam, 2-y-o 7f winner who probably stayed 1½m, half-sister to Dead Certain: easily better effort in maidens at Lingfield when 1¾ lengths fourth of 10 to Feather Bed: stays 1m: may improve further. *R. Akehurst*

JOLTO 7 b.g. Noalto 120 – Joytime (John de Coombe 122) [1995 79: 7m⁴ 7.6m⁶ 7m³ 7m* 7m 6m⁶ 7f* 7m 7g³ 7d 7m 1996 8.1m 6.1m⁵ 7.6f⁵ a7g a7g a7g 12d Oct 21] leggy gelding: has a round action: genuine handicapper in 1995 for K. Cunningham-Brown: showed little at 7 yrs: best at up to 7.6f: acts on any turf going: visored (ran creditably) on equitrack once at 3 yrs: blinkered fifth 7-y-o start: goes well with forcing tactics: has run well when sweating. *K. McAuliffe*

JO MAXIMUS 4 b.g. Prince Sabo 123 – Final Call 79 (Town Crier 119) [1995 78 79: 5s⁶ 5.1g³ 6m² 6m 6m* 6m³ 6m² 5g³ 6m⁵ 6m 5m 7g* 7g⁴ 1996 7f³ 7f² 7m 6m⁵ a– 7g 7f 7f* a8g⁶ a6g Dec 20] workmanlike, leggy gelding: fair handicapper: usually runs well at Brighton and back to form when gamely winning there in September: stays 7f: acts on firm and soft ground, long way below form on all-weather: races prominently. *S. Dow*

JO MELL 3 b.g. Efisio 120 – Militia Girl (Rarity 129) [1995 83+: 6f⁴ 7g⁴ 7g* 89 7.9m³ 1996 8m 7g 7f 8.1d² 8g⁴ 7m³ 7m⁵ 7m³ 7.6d² 8.1v⁴ 7g³ Oct 12] leggy, lengthy gelding: has a round action: fairly useful handicapper: in frame 7 of last 8 starts, third of 27 to Persian Fayre in £11,000 event at York on final one: stays 1m, but may prove suited by shorter when conditions are testing: acts on good to firm and heavy ground: takes keen hold: usually races up with pace. *T. D. Easterby*

JONA HOLLEY 3 b.g. Sharpo 132 – Spurned (USA) 91 (Robellino (USA) 127) 41 [1995 54: 7d 6d 1996 6.9m 7m 8.2m 10m⁵ 10m Jun 24] leggy gelding: poor maiden on balance of form: should stay 1m: unruly stalls second 3-y-o start. *I. A. Balding*

JONFY (IRE) 2 b.g. (May 5) Waajib 121 – Hyland Rose (Steel Heart 128) [1996 – 5.1m⁶ 6f 5m 7g 8f Nov 5] IR 7,000F, 14,000Y: medium-sized, sturdy gelding: brother to 3-y-o Norwegian 1m winner Miss Swing King and half-brother to a winner in Macau: dam Irish maiden: poor form in maidens and nurseries. *B. W. Hills*

JONNY'S JOKER 2 b.g. (Feb 26) Precocious 126 – Mardessa 74 (Ardross 134) – [1996 5m Sep 18] quite good-topped gelding: has a quick action: first foal: dam effective from 1¼m to 1½m: 25/1, missed break completely and soon tailed off in 15-runner maiden at Beverley. *F. H. Lee*

JON'S CHOICE 8 b.g. Andy Rew 103 – Whangarei 59 (Gold Rod 129) [1995 –, 41 d a55d: a5g a5g⁵ a7g a6g⁵ a6g a6g a5g a5g⁴ a7g a6g⁶ 6m a9.4g⁴ 7m a7g a7g 1996 a8g⁴ a8g a8g a7g a9.4g a6g³ a6g⁵ 6f⁴ a6g² a7g⁴ a6g⁴ 7g a7g a7g a7g 6f a12g Nov 2] compact gelding: seems poor handicapper at best nowadays, no form last 8 starts: stays 9.4f: acts on firm ground and equitrack, best efforts on fibresand: no improvement in blinkers or visor: none too consistent. *B. Preece*

JOSEPH'S WINE (IRE) 7 b.g. Smile (USA) – Femme Gendarme (USA) – (Policeman (FR) 124) [1995 67+, a80: a11g* a12g⁵ 10.3g² 1996 a8g Nov 22] lengthy a57 + gelding: fairly useful handicapper at best: off course 20 months and without headgear, behind in 1m claimer at Southwell: should stay 1½m: goes well on the all-weather and probably acts on any turf going: best in blinkers: has run well when sweating: held up, and has good turn of foot. *D. Nicholls*

JOVIAN 2 gr.f. (Mar 1) Petong 126 – What A Pet (Mummy's Pet 125) [1996 6m – Oct 5] 29,000F: good-topped filly: sixth foal: sister to Irish 3-y-o winner Park Petard, smart performer at up to 1m Petardia, and French 11f winner Pappa's Pet, and half-sister to a winner in France at up to 13f by What A Guest: dam French 1m winner, is sister to useful filly Teacher's Pet: 25/1, burly and very green, well held in 13-runner maiden at Newmarket. *R. Guest*

JOVIE KING (IRE) 4 ch.g. Salt Dome (USA) – Jovial Josie (USA) (Sea Bird II 145) [1995 57d: 6.9g 7g 7m³ 8f 10f 10m 12s 11.9d 1996 12m a16g 10d 8m a8g 7m a7g Nov 15] leggy, workmanlike gelding: modest maiden in 1995: well held at 4 yrs, leaving P. Mitchell after sixth start: best efforts at 7f: acts on good to firm ground: blinkered/visored last 5 starts: inconsistent. *K. McAuliffe*

JOYEUSE ENTREE 2 ch.f. (Mar 1) Kendor (FR) 122 – Cape of Good Hope (FR) (Crystal Glitters (USA) 127) [1996 5.5g* 5.5d* 5.5m² 7g* 8m* Sep 15] tall, lengthy filly: has scope: first reported foal: dam 7f to 1¼m winner in France, including at 7.5f at 2 yrs: progressive French performer: successful in minor events at Evry and Deauville in May, listed contest at Saint-Cloud (beat Fine Fellow 1½ lengths) in July and 11-runner Prix d'Aumale at Longchamp (confidently ridden, brought with smooth run up rails, quickening to lead 1f out and merely nudged along to beat Dissertation 2 lengths) in September: will stay 1¼m: acts on good to firm and dead ground: rated a 3-length winner at Longchamp: one to look out for at 3 yrs, sure to win good races. *A. de Royer-Dupre, France* — 108 p

JOYFUL JOY 2 b.f. (Mar 27) River God (USA) 121 – Joyfulness (FR) 78 (Cure The Blues (USA)) [1996 6m 6d 5m a6s Dec 19] 1,000Y: leggy, plain filly: first foal: dam winning hurdler, probably stayed 1¼m: no sign of ability. *B. P. J. Baugh* — –

JOYFUL TIMES 4 br.f. Doc Marten 104 – Time For Joy 42 (Good Times (ITY)) [1995 –, a47: a7g³ a8g⁶ a7g a6g* a6g⁴ a7g⁴ a7g⁴ 8g⁶ a7g 7g 1996 a7g a8g⁶ a6g Feb 26] compact filly: poor performer: tailed off in sellers in 1996: finds 6f a bare minimum, and stays 1m: acts on fibresand: best form without blinkers/visor: usually gets behind. *Mrs N. Macauley* — –

JOZA 2 b.f. (Feb 18) Marju (IRE) 127 – Gold Runner 62 (Runnett 125) [1996 5m* 5m⁴ 5d⁴ Oct 28] 11,000Y: big, lengthy filly, freeze-fired on forelegs: fourth live foal: half-sister to 6f winner (including at 2 yrs) Golden Lady and 7.6f winner Gleam of Light (both by Danehill) and a winner in France by Ahonoora: dam, placed over 6f at 2 yrs, is half-sister to Don't Forget Me: fairly useful form: won maiden at Windsor in August: excitable to post, ran better than distance beaten suggests when 4 lengths fourth to Conspiracy in listed race at Ayr, travelling very strongly up with good pace until over 1f out: again travelled well in minor event at Lingfield last time, but unable to reach leaders: very much a sprinter: best form on top-of-the-ground: may do better. *H. Candy* — 90

JUBA 4 b.f. Dowsing (USA) 124 – Try The Duchess 99 (Try My Best (USA) 130) [1995 59p: a7g⁵ 1996 a6g⁴ 8.3m a8g a8.5g a8g a6g³ a7g a6g⁵ a6g Dec 27] poor form in varied company: should stay at least 1m. *Dr J. D. Scargill* — 38

JUBILEE PLACE (IRE) 3 br.f. Prince Sabo 123 – Labelon Lady 87 (Touching Wood (USA) 127) [1995 76: 5.1m² 5m³ 6.1m* 6m* 1996 8m 7.3d 6m⁶ 7g 7.1m 7g 6.9m⁶ Aug 16] unfurnished filly: showed little in handicaps at 3 yrs: stays 6f: sometimes bandaged. *T. Thomson Jones* — –

JUBILEE SCHOLAR (IRE) 3 b.c. Royal Academy (USA) 130 – Jaljuli 107 (Jalmood (USA) 126) [1995 7m⁴ 8g 7m⁴ 7g³ 7s⁶ 9g 1996 8d 7m 7d⁶ a8g Dec 13] ex-Irish colt: second foal: half-brother to 4-y-o Honey I Miss You (by Persian Bold): dam, best at 2 yrs when 5f and 6f winner, out of half-sister to 2000 Guineas winner Roland Gardens: fair maiden: best 3-y-o effort when sixth of 10 to Julmat John in handicap at Gowran Park on final start for J. Bolger: soon beaten in similar event at Lingfield 5½ months later: stays 7f: best efforts on an easy surface: no improvement in blinkers. *K. McAuliffe* — 67

JUCEA 7 b.m. Bluebird (USA) 125 – Appleby Park 98 (Bay Express 132) [1995 69: 5.1m* 5m⁴ 5g⁵ 5g⁴ 5.7m⁶ 5m 5m 5.1d 5g³ 5m 5f⁶ 5.1m⁵ 5m² 1996 5g 5.1g² 5.1f⁴ 5.7g* 5m* 6m 5.1f⁶ 5m³ 5m³ 5m 5f⁵ 5g³ 5.7m⁴ 5d 5g⁵ 5g 5m⁵ Oct 23] sturdy mare: poor mover: fair handicapper: better than ever in 1996, winning at Bath and Redcar in May: stays 5.7f: acts on firm ground and equitrack, seemingly not on a soft surface: no improvement in blinkers/visor: tough. *J. L. Spearing* — 77

JUCINDA 2 gr.f. (Feb 19) Midyan (USA) 124 – Catch The Sun (Kalaglow 132) [1996 7f 7g 8s Nov 9] 12,500Y: leggy filly: fifth foal: sister to smart stayer Tioman — –

Island and half-sister to fairly useful 4-y-o 1¼m and 1½m winner Remaadi Sun (by Cadeaux Genereux) and winners in Spain and Italy: behind in maidens. *J. Pearce*

JUDGEMENT CALL   9 b.g. Alzao (USA) 117 – Syllabub (Silly Season 127)   55 d
[1995 52: 5m⁶ 6m 5m⁶ 5g⁵ 6m 5.2m⁵ 5g⁴ 5.2m* 5m³ 5m³ 5m 6g⁵ 1996 6m 5m*
5g⁵ 5m 5f⁵ 6g 5f 7m 6m 6m Sep 19] close-coupled, good-quartered gelding: modest
handicapper: won at Lingfield in May: effective at 5f (best recent form) to 7f: acts on
any going: blinkered (well beaten) once earlier in career: usually bandaged:
inconsistent. *P. Howling*

JUDICIAL FIELD (IRE)   7 b.g. Law Society (USA) 130 – Bold Meadows 80   –
(Persian Bold 123) [1995 NR 1996 16.2m 17.1g 13s May 9] winner 3 times in Ireland
for D. Weld and rated 100 at 4 yrs: has shown little on flat since: stays 1¾m: used to
act on good to firm ground and soft: normally blinkered: modest chaser. *N. Tinkler*

JUDICIAL SUPREMACY   2 b.c. (Apr 23) Warning 136 – Song Test (USA)   82 p
(The Minstrel (CAN) 135) [1996 7m² Oct 23] brother to Queenbird, fairly useful
2-y-o 5f to 7f winner in 1993, and half-brother to 3 winners in USA and Italy: dam
winner at around 1m in USA: 16/1, short-head second of 9 to Courtship in slowly-run
maiden at Yarmouth, travelling comfortably in rear after slow start, weaving away
through over 1f out then finishing strongly: will stay 1m: will improve, and should be
able to win a race or two. *J. R. Fanshawe*

JUICY TING   2 ch.g. (Mar 26) Hatim (USA) 121 – Floating Note 61 (Music Boy   58
124) [1996 5m 6m 6d³ 7g² 8.3d⁶ Sep 30] 2,800Y: workmanlike gelding: unimpressive mover: second foal: dam unreliable sprint maiden: modest form, including in
selling company: ran poorly in nursery final outing: stays 7f: acts on dead ground. *P.
C. Haslam*

JUKEBOX JIVE   2 ch.f. (Mar 27) Scottish Reel 123 – My Sweet Melody 62   48
(Music Boy 124) [1996 7m 7.9g Sep 4] 2,000Y, 3,600 2-y-o: leggy, lightly-made
filly: third reported foal: dam poor maiden best at 5f: seventh of 17 to Scarlet
Crescent at Warwick in August, coming wide into straight then a little late headway,
better effort in maiden auctions. *C. Murray*

JULIASDARKINVADER   6 br.g. Lidhame 109 – Una Donna (GER) (Wind-   41
wurf (GER)) [1995 NR 1996 a16g* a16g⁶ a16g³ 15.4m⁴ a16g³ 12m⁵ a16g Aug 17]
lengthy gelding: won selling handicap at Lingfield in February: stayed 2m: acted on
equitrack and any turf going: dead. *A. Moore*

JULIA'S RELATIVE   2 b.f. (Apr 6) Distant Relative 128 – Alkion (Fordham   –
(USA) 117) [1996 6g Oct 18] 4,600Y: eighth foal: half-sister to a winner in Germany
by Stanford: dam once-raced half-sister to very useful sprinter Oscilight: 50/1,
always behind after slow start in 22-runner maiden at Newmarket: wore bandages. *R.
Guest*

JULIETTA MIA (USA)   2 ch.f. (Mar 30) Woodman (USA) 126 – Just Juliet   72
(USA) (What A Pleasure (USA)) [1996 6g 6g⁴ 7g 7.6m² 7m* 8g² 8g² Oct 21]
30,000Y: leggy, close-coupled, unfurnished filly: closely related to a winner in USA
by Mogambo and half-sister to several winners abroad: dam, 2-y-o sprint winner in
USA, half-sister to 2 Grade 1 winners out of Grade 2 7f to 8.5f winner My Juliet:
progressive form: won rating-related maiden at Newcastle in October then good
second in nurseries at Newmarket and Pontefract later in month: effective at 7f/1m:
slowly away first 2 starts: free to post second and third outings: carries head
awkwardly but seems genuine enough. *B. W. Hills*

JUMAIRAH SUNSET   3 ch.f. Be My Guest (USA) 126 – Catalonda (African   67
Sky 124) [1995 NR 1996 7.1m³ 7.1m³ 7m* 8.1d Sep 27] 45,000Y: workmanlike
filly: fifth foal: half-sister to 1991 Irish 2-y-o 6.5f winner Aladina and Windsor
Castle Stakes and (after being renamed Che Sara Sara) Hong Kong Derby winner
Brave Music (both by Persian Bold), and to useful French 1m winner Alamtara (by
Cadeaux Genereux): dam Irish 2-y-o 5f winner: fair performer: won maiden at
Lingfield by neck: unable to challenge when towards rear on dead ground in
handicap at Haydock 17 days later: sold 50,000 gns Newmarket December Sales:
stays 7f: acts on good to firm ground. *A. C. Stewart*

JUMP THE LIGHTS   3 b.g. Siberian Express (USA) 125 – Turtle Dove (Gyr   58
(USA) 131) [1995 53: a7g 10m⁶ 8.2m 1996 12s⁶ a12g* 14.6m⁶ 12m⁴ May 21] neat   a66
gelding: modest form: won maiden at Wolverhampton in April: not discredited in

handicaps afterwards: should be suited by test of stamina: reluctant at stalls final outing. *S. P. C. Woods*

JUNCTION TWENTYTWO 6 ch.g. Local Suitor (USA) 128 – Pollinella 108 – (Charlottown 127) [1995 NR 1996 a12g Jan 26] big, workmanlike gelding: modest handicapper in 1994: having first flat outing since when tailed off in amateurs race at Southwell: stays 12.5f: tried visored. *C. D. Broad*

JUNDI (IRE) 5 b.g. Sadler's Wells (USA) 132 – Royal Sister II (Claude) [1995 NR 1996 14.1m 16.5g 22.2f a14g⁵ 16s⁵ 15.8g Sep 21] smallish, strong gelding: rated 62 in 1994 for M. Stoute: no worthwhile form at 5 yrs: sold 650 gns Doncaster September Sales: stays 1¾m well: usually visored/blinkered: carries head high. *J. D. Bethell*

JUNGLE FRESH 3 b.g. Rambo Dancer (CAN) 107 – Report 'em (USA) 51 – (Staff Writer (USA)) [1995 NR 1996 10g⁴ 7g⁶ 10.5d Sep 27] close-coupled gelding: fifth foal: half-brother to 4-y-o 13f winner Victor Laszlo (by Ilium) and winning (7f) plater Chance Report (by Beldale Flutter): dam, maiden, had form only at 6f: soundly beaten in maidens. *J. D. Bethell*

JUNGLE PATROL (IRE) 4 ch.g. Night Shift (USA) – Jungle Rose 90 (Shirley 56 Heights 130) [1995 10g⁴ 1996 a9.4g a12g² a12g³ a9.4g² 8g 7m 8g⁵ 9.9f⁵ 8f⁶ a7g⁶ 5.9f Jun 26] sturdy gelding: modest handicapper at best nowadays: sold out of C. Murray's stable 5,200 gns Doncaster March Sales after fourth 4-y-o start: ran badly last 4 starts, sold only 1,000 gns Doncaster July Sales and gelded after final one: effective at 1m, and stays 1½m: acts on firm and dead ground and on fibresand: has been bandaged in front. *M. Brittain*

JUNIE (IRE) 2 ch.f. (Apr 3) Astronef 116 – Numidia (Sallust 134) [1996 6m 6m⁶ 66 6g Oct 18] IR 2,000F, IR 7,000Y: unfurnished filly: has a quick action: sister to 4-y-o Astral Invader, 5f and 6f winner at 2 yrs, and half-sister to 3-y-o 1½m winner Another Quarter (by Distinctly North) and 7f winner Premier Choice (by Petorius): dam, should have been suited by 1¼m+, half-sister to smart French middle-distance winner Dieter: modest form in maidens: will probably be suited by further than 6f. *T. G. Mills*

JUNIOR BEN (IRE) 4 b.g. Tirol 127 – Piney Pass (Persian Bold 123) [1995 68d: 51 d 10m⁴ 13.1g³ 14.1f⁴ 11.6m⁵ a11g 11.9d 1996 12g⁴ 11.6m⁴ 12.5f 11.4g⁶ 14.1f⁴ 12g⁶ 12m 10.1m 14d 11.5m⁶ 14.1g Oct 30] quite attractive gelding: modest form at best in 1996, well beaten last 6 starts: stays 1¾m: yet to race on soft going, acts on any other: tried blinkered, no improvement. *P. Howling*

JUPITER (IRE) 2 b.c. (Apr 1) Astronef 116 – Native Flower (Tumble Wind 68 (USA)) [1996 a5g* 6g 5f⁵ 5g⁶ Aug 30] IR 1,200F, IR 3,200Y, 11,000 2-y-o: tall colt: seventh foal: half-brother to a winner in Italy by Kampala: dam behind all 3 starts at 3 yrs in Ireland: won maiden auction at Southwell in June: will probably be suited by return to 6f (helped sent strong pace when tailed off in July Stakes): slowly away last 2 outings. *G. C. Bravery*

JURAL 4 ch.f. Kris 135 – Just Cause (Law Society (USA) 130) [1995 108: 11g² 102 14.6d 1996 a10g⁴ 10m² 10m² 12m⁵ Jul 20] leggy filly, rather raw boned: useful performer: runner-up in minor event (to Florid) at Newmarket and 3-runner listed race (to Bal Harbour) at Kempton: stays 11f: acts on good to firm ground and dead: often takes keen hold, and sometimes sweating and edgy earlier in career: usually front runner. *Saeed bin Suroor*

JUST A GUESS (IRE) 5 ch.g. Classic Secret (USA) 91 – Wild Justice 76 (Sweet – Revenge 129 [1995 NR 1996 14.1m⁶ Jul 11] half-brother to several winners, including Irish 7f winner Boa Restrictor (by Balbao) and Irish sprinter Gentle Rain (by Tower Walk): dam placed at up to 1m at 2 yrs: poor form in NH Flat races: showed nil in poor seller on flat debut. *J. J. O'Neill*

JUST BOB 7 b.g. Alleging (USA) 120 – Diami 81 (Swing Easy (USA) 126) [1995 75 71: 6d 5g 6m 5m 5m 5m 5f⁴ 5m² 5m5 5f² 5m⁵ 5g³ 5g⁵ 5m 1996 5s⁶ 5g 5g³ 5g 5s* 5d* a– 5m* 5g² May 17] smallish, leggy gelding: unimpressive mover: fair handicapper: won at Hamilton (minor event), Ayr and Carlisle (minor event, comfortably) within a week in May: good head second at Thirsk on final start, finishing very strongly having been last 1f out: successful over 6f but seems suited by 5f nowadays: acts on any turf ground, no form in 4 tries on the all-weather: often blinkered at 3 yrs, rarely nowadays: often slowly away and comes from behind: has won for apprentice/amateur: tough. *S. E. Kettlewell*

JUST DISSIDENT (IRE)   4 b.g. Dancing Dissident (USA) 119 – Betty Bun (St   65
Chad 120) [1995 67: 6g 5m 5m^3 5g^2 5g^2 6m^4 6f* 5.1m 6m 5g 5g 6g 7g 5.1m 1996 6g
5m 6m^5 5g^5 6.9g 6m 6.1m 10g 5m^2 5m^3 5m* 5m 5m^5 5f^3 5m^4 5m* 5m 5m 5m^5 Sep
26] leggy, good-topped gelding: usually impresses in appearance: has reportedly had
back problems: fair handicapper: made all at Pontefract in July and Carlisle in
August: barely stays 6f: has raced only on a sound surface: visored (ran well) fourth
4-y-o start: usually races prominently. *R. M. Whitaker*

JUST FLAMENCO   5 ch.g. Scorpio (FR) 127 – Suzannah's Song (Song 132)   –
[1995 56, a47: 7.1g 8g a7g^5 7f^5 10m* 10m^6 10m* 10m 10.1g 10.8g 10g a11g a8g^5
a9.4g^5 a10g 1996 a12g 8g 9.2s May 2] strong, lengthy gelding: good mover: has
shown little since winning twice at Windsor in July, 1995: stays 1¼m: acts on good
to firm, soft ground and fibresand: tried visored. *M. J. Ryan*

JUST GRAND (IRE)   2 b.c. (Mar 24) Green Desert (USA) 127 – Aljood 111   70
(Kris 135) [1996 7m^4 7d Nov 8] rather leggy, useful-looking colt: fourth foal:
half-brother to 6f winner Prolific Lady (by Nabeel Dancer) and 5-y-o 6f to 1m winner
Desert Invader (by Lead On Time): dam, maiden who stayed 1m, fourth in Prix
Marcel Boussac: staying-on fourth of 10 in steadily-run maiden at Leicester on
debut: not discredited in midfield in similar event only subsequent start: should stay
1m. *M. Johnston*

JUST HARRY   5 ch.h. High Kicker (USA) – Dorame 55 (Music Boy 124) [1995   64
71, a86: a8g* a7g* a7g a9.4g^6 6.9d^2 8m^2 8g^3 8g^2 8g^2 8.2m^2 8.5m^5 8f^2 7.6m^6 8.3m   a80
10d 8.5d^5 8d 8d^4 8s 8.2m 1996 8.3g 7m^2 8.2m^5 8.3d 7.6m^6 8f a9.4g 8f^5 8f^5 8m a8.5g^2
a9.4g^3 Nov 25] good-topped horse: fairly useful handicapper on the all-weather, fair
on turf: claimed £10,000 final start: effective at 7f and 1m: goes well on all-weather
surfaces, acts on firm and dead ground: blinkered (below form) once as 3-y-o:
usually held up. *M. J. Ryan*

JUSTINIANUS (IRE)   4 ch.c. Try My Best (USA) 130 – Justitia (Dunbeath   51 d
(USA) 127) [1995 8d 6d^3 6s 8d^4 8m 7g* 8g 7g 6m 7d^6 a6g^6 8g 1996 a7g a6g a7g^3
a8g^3 a8g^4 a8g a6g a6g a7g 6.9m^3 7f 6m 8.3g 7.1m 6g^6 7.6m^6 5m a7g 7g a7g a6s a10g
Dec 26] ex-Belgian colt: first foal: dam won 6 races at 3 yrs in Belgium: won 2 races
(at 5f and 6f) in Belgium in 1994, and claimer at Compiegne in July 1995: left Andre
Hermans after second 4-y-o start: modest form at best in Britain, well beaten in
second half of season: will prove best at up to 1m: acts on the all-weather: tried
blinkered, no improvement. *J. J. Bridger*

JUST LADY   3 b.f. Emarati (USA) 74 – Just Run (IRE) 45 (Runnett 125) [1995   57
72: 5d^6 5g* 5.1m 5m^2 5m^2 5m^4 5m 1996 5f 5f 5g^5 5g^4 a5g 5m Sep 25] leggy, lengthy
filly: modest form at best in 1996, finishing last in 4 of her 6 races: raced only at 5f:
best form on good to firm ground: active type: tends to hang and is none too easy a
ride. *W. G. M. Turner*

JUST LEX   3 b.g. Ballacashtal (CAN) – Mio Mementa 61 (Streak 119) [1995 NR   –
1996 10m Aug 7] 4,800Y, 13,000 2-y-o: sixth foal: brother to 1¾m seller winner
Chantelys and half-brother to several winners, including smart 7f/1m performer Just
Three (by Tina's Pet): dam sprint maiden: 33/1, tailed off in maiden at Kempton.
Mrs A. L. M. King

JUST LOUI   2 gr.g. (Mar 11) Lugana Beach 116 – Absaloui 64 (Absalom 128)   58
[1996 a5g a5g* 6d^6 5f^3 a5g a5g^2 5.1g^5 5f^6 a6g^2 a6g* a5g^2 a7g* a6g* Dec 31] 4,200Y: a83
first live foal: dam 2-y-o 5f winner: fairly useful performer on the all-weather: won
median auction maiden at Wolverhampton in May, claimer at Lingfield in November,
and minor event at Wolverhampton and nursery at Lingfield in December: only
modest on turf: effective at 5f to 7f: acts on firm ground, but much better suited to
all-weather: front runner/races prominently. *W. G. M. Turner*

JUST LUCKY (IRE)   4 b.g. Fools Holme (USA) – Miss Victoria (Auction Ring   –
(USA) 123) [1995 41: a8g^6 a10g^5 8m a6g 8g 7.6d^5 6.9f 8f a8g a12g^4 1996 a13g a11g
a12g^4 a16.2g Apr 13] sparely-made gelding: poor performer: left Mrs N. Macauley
after second 4-y-o start: seems to stay 1½m: acts on fibresand. *Mrs P. Sly*

JUST MILLIE (USA)   3 ch.f. Elmaamul (USA) 125 – La Plus Belle (USA)   64
(Robellino (USA) 127) [1995 67: 7f* 6g^5 7g^3 1996 10s 7m 7f^5 8f 8m^3 8g^3 8f^3 8.1m^3

10.8m 7f* 7m 8g³ 7g 7g² Oct 30] leggy, sparely-made filly: fair performer: ridden by 7-lb claimer, won minor event at Brighton in September: sold 5,200 gns Newmarket Autumn Sales: best form at 7f and 1m: acts on firm ground, well beaten only start on soft: blinkered/visored 5 of last 8 starts, including when winning: usually held up: sent to Italy. *J. E. Banks*

JUST NICK 2 b.c. (Mar 30) Nicholas (USA) 111 – Just Never Know (USA) 73
(Riverman (USA) 131) [1996 5.1g³ 5.1m⁴ 5.7d³ 6s² 6v* Nov 11] 8,200Y: angular colt: third foal: dam unraced: showed ability for M. McCormack first 2 starts: won median auction maiden at Folkestone in November: should stay beyond 6f: acts on heavy ground, also on good to firm: hung badly right on debut. *W. R. Muir*

JUST RACHEL 2 ch.f. (May 8) Primitive Rising (USA) 113 – Glendyne 58 –
(Precipice Wood 123) [1996 a8.5g Dec 14] third reported foal: dam best at 1½m on flat, won over hurdles and fences: tailed off in maiden at Wolverhampton. *S. E. Kettlewell*

JUST TYPICAL 2 ch.f. (Mar 20) Timeless Times (USA) 99 – Mayor 86 (Laxton –
105) [1996 5g Apr 27] 650Y: third reported foal: half-sister to 5f winner Nineacres (by Sayf El Arab): dam suited by 6f: 25/1, always behind in maiden auction at Ripon. *N. Tinkler*

JUST VISITING 2 b.f. (Apr 6) Superlative 118 – Just Julia (Natroun (FR) 128) 85
[1996 a5g* 6m² 5g³ 6f² 6g* 6d³ 6.5m Sep 11] 2,900Y: rather leggy, workmanlike filly: has a round action: first foal: dam no worthwhile form: fairly useful performer: won maiden at Southwell in May and minor event at Ripon in August: creditable third to Indian Rocket in listed race at Ripon penultimate outing: edgy and well below best in 22-runner nursery at Doncaster final start: stays 6f: acts on firm and dead ground. *Capt. J. Wilson*

JUWWI 2 ch.c. (Apr 1) Mujtahid (USA) 118 – Nouvelle Star (AUS) (Luskin Star 96
(AUS)) [1996 6.1m² 6m* 6g² Jul 10] smallish, lengthy robust colt: type to carry condition: has a quick action: eighth foal: half-brother to 7f winner Sariah (by Kris): dam won from 5f to 8.2f in Australia and was champion older filly at 4 yrs: won 7-runner maiden at Newbury by 5 lengths from Flaming West: useful form when beaten a head by Rich Ground in strongly-run July Stakes at Newmarket following month, soon behind after being squeezed stalls then finishing well: will be suited by further than 6f: looked sure to improve again. *Major W. R. Hern*

JUYUSH (USA) 4 b.c. Silver Hawk (USA) 123 – Silken Doll (USA) (Chieftain 109
II) [1995 104: 8g* 10.4g⁵ 8g³ 12f* 14.8g² 16f 1996 12s* 12m 12.3m³ 22.2f Jun 21] compact colt: impresses in appearance: good walker and very good mover: useful performer: won minor event at Doncaster in March by 3½ lengths from Daraydan: appeared to run well facing stiffish task when third of 5 to Kalabo in useful minor event at Chester in June: on toes, did not stay in Queen Alexandra Stakes: sold (B. Hills to J. Old) 70,000 gns Newmarket Autumn Sales: probably stays 14.8f: acts on firm and soft ground: sometimes hangs, including on reappearance: sweating (below form) third 3-y-o start: often a front runner. *B. W. Hills*

K

KAAFIH HOMM (IRE) 5 b.g. Kefaah (USA) 124 – Shereeka 76 (Shergar 140) 77
[1995 65, a77: a10g² a10g* a10g* a9.4g* a10g⁴ 12m 10m 10.8g³ 8.5d² 8.3m³ 8m* 7f³ 12m* 10d* 11.9g⁵ a8g² a10g² 1996 a10g³ 8m 12m⁴ 9.7m² 10m⁴ 11.5f* 10.1g² 9.9f⁵ 12d* 10m² Aug 31] good-topped gelding: fair handicapper: won at Yarmouth in July and Goodwood (amateurs, by 8 lengths) in August: needs further than 7f, and stays 1½m: acts on firm and dead ground and goes well on all-weather surfaces: often bandaged behind: suited by waiting tactics: withdrawn at start on veterinary advice Oct 3: sold 23,000 gns Newmarket Autumn Sales: sent to USA. *N. A. Callaghan*

KABALEVSKY (USA) 3 b.c. Nureyev (USA) 131 – Beautiful Aly (USA) (Aly- –
dar (USA)) [1995 NR 1996 7.1d Jul 4] $600,000Y: sturdy, lengthy colt: fourth foal: closely related to 2 winners by Nijinsky, including fair 11.5f winner Tegwen: dam unraced half-sister to Breeders' Cup Juvenile Fillies and Kentucky Oaks runner-

up Jeanne Jones: 4/1 (attended by two handlers and poorly to post), slowly away and never a factor (hanging right in straight) in maiden at Haydock: sent to UAE. *J. H. M. Gosden*

KABCAST 11 b.g. Kabour 80 – Final Cast 50 (Saulingo 122) [1995 51: 5g a5g 5f 48 5m 5m⁵ 5f 5m³ 5m 5h⁴ 5f 5.1d 1996 5s⁵ 5m⁶ 5m 5m* 5m⁶ 5m 5m 5g⁵ 5g Sep 29] good-bodied gelding: poor handicapper: made all in seller at Ripon in August: best at 5f: needs a sound surface on turf, no form on the all-weather: wears blinkers: often sweats: races prominently. *D. W. Chapman*

KADAMANN (IRE) 4 b.c. Doyoun 124 – Kadissya (USA) 107 (Blushing – Groom (FR) 131) [1995 10m³ 12g* 11f* 14m 11m 1996 9s 12m Jun 7] sixth foal, easily best of previous 5 being dual-Derby winner Kahyasi (by Ile de Bourbon): ex-Irish colt: unraced at 2 yrs then won maiden at Fairyhouse and minor event at the Curragh (rated 102) at 3 yrs for J. Oxx: reportedly ran as if something amiss (respiratory distress first occasion) in valuable handicaps last 2 starts in Ireland: tailed off in rated stakes at Newbury and Epsom: stays 1½m: acts on firm ground. *R. Akehurst*

KADARI 7 b.m. Commanche Run 133 – Thoughtful 86 (Northfields (USA)) – [1995 NR 1996 12.3g 16g 10m Jun 10] workmanlike mare: one-time fair stayer, no encouragement in 1996: no improvement when visored: tail swisher: modest hurdler (effective from 2m to 3m). *W. Clay*

KADASTROF (FR) 6 ch.h. Port Etienne (FR) – Kadastra (FR) (Stradavinsky 81 121) [1995 NR 1996 14.9d² 16d* 18.7g 16s 13.9m 13.9g Oct 12] good-topped horse: fairly useful handicapper: dominated when winning at Newbury in April, but well beaten afterwards: effective at 1¾m to 2m: best form with give in the ground (acts on heavy): front runner. *R. Dickin*

KADEENA 2 b.f. (May 6) Never So Bold 135 – Alencon (Northfields (USA)) 76 [1996 7g* 7m³ Oct 29] half-sister to several winners abroad, including German 4-y-o 9f/1¼m winner Alboretto (by Pennine Walk): dam, winner twice in USA at up to 9f, sister to Oats: weak 10/1, won 11-runner median auction maiden at Catterick in October, always well there: improved when 3¾ lengths third of 4 to Squeak in minor event at Redcar 11 days later: should stay 1m. *M. Johnston*

KADIRI (IRE) 5 b.g. Darshaan 133 – Kadissya (USA) 107 (Blushing Groom – (FR) 131) [1995 63, a68: a13g³ a16g* 16.2m 17.1m³ 21.6f² 14.9g⁴ 16.5g⁴ 20m a14g⁴ a16g a14g⁴ 1996 12d a14g Nov 4] lengthy gelding: modest performer: not seen at 5 yrs until October, well beaten in amateurs handicaps: a stayer: acts on firm ground and the all-weather: blinkered last 3 starts 1994. *J. R. Bosley*

KAFAF (USA) 2 b. or br.f. (Apr 30) Zilzal (USA) 137 – Alqwani (USA) 83 (Mr 76 Prospector (USA)) [1996 7g 7g⁴ 8m² Oct 2] unfurnished filly: second foal: half-sister to useful 3-y-o 7f winner Intidab (by Phone Trick): dam, 2-y-o 6f winner, out of half-sister to Bellotto: fair form: 4 lengths second to Stowaway in maiden at Newcastle final start: stays 1m: has had tongue tied down. *J. H. M. Gosden*

KAFIL (USA) 2 b. or br.c. (Apr 4) Housebuster (USA) – Alchaasibiyeh (USA) 85 75 (Seattle Slew (USA)) [1996 7d 6g Oct 18] useful-looking colt: fourth foal: half-brother to 3 winners, including useful 1993 2-y-o 6f winner Alami (by Danzig), later 1m winner in Dubai, and 1990 2-y-o 6f and 1m winner Fraar (by Topsider), later Group 1 1½m winner in Australia: dam placed from 6f to 1m is out of a smart sprinter: bandaged, better effort in maidens when around 5 lengths eighth of 22 to Baked Alaska at Newmarket on second start, never a serious threat: joined R. Hern: may do better. *H. Thomson Jones*

KAHAL 2 b.c. (Feb 16) Machiavellian (USA) 123 – Just A Mirage 76 (Green 108 p Desert (USA) 127) [1996 7f² 7g* 7g⁵ Oct 18] strong, good-topped colt: type to carry condition: good mover: first foal: dam maiden (stayed 1m) sister to smart 3-y-o miler Distant Oasis and half-sister to very smart colts Reprimand and Wiorno: won minor event at Ascot in September by 3½ lengths from Ricky Ticky Tavie, running on very strongly: led or disputed lead around 6f when 2 lengths or so fifth of 8 to In Command in Dewhurst Stakes at Newmarket: to winter in Dubai: a grand sort who's likely to develop into a smart miler. *E. A. L. Dunlop*

KAHIR ALMAYDAN (IRE) 3 b.c. Distinctly North (USA) 115 – Kilfenora 113 (Tribal Chief 125) [1995 112: 6m² 6m* 6g² 6m³ 6m* 6d* 6g³ 1996 7d² 8g⁵ 7g⁵ 7m⁴

6m[5] Aug 15] tall, angular colt: impresses in appearance: good walker and fine mover: smart performer: second of 8 to Danehill Dancer in Greenham Stakes at Newbury and fifth of 10 to Ashkalani in Poule d'Essai des Poulains at Longchamp in the spring: below form in Beeswing Stakes at Newcastle in July and minor event at Yarmouth (back over 6f, soon off bridle) 2½ weeks later: has form at 1m, may prove best at up to 7f: acts on good to firm ground and dead: races prominently: sent to Dubai. *J. L. Dunlop*

KAIRINE (IRE) 3 b.f. Kahyasi 130 – Reamur 68 (Top Ville 129) [1995 NR 1996 –
10.2g 10m 11.9f[4] Jun 17] first foal: dam maiden who stayed 1½m: has looked of little account in maidens. *M. R. Channon*

KAISER KACHE (IRE) 2 b.c. (Mar 3) Treasure Kay 114 – Poka Poka (FR) 83
(King of Macedon 126) [1996 6f 5.7m[5] 7f[2] 6m[2] 6m* 6g 8m 6m 7.3s* 8d[3] a8g[3] Nov 15] IR 1,800F, IR 5,200Y: rather leggy, close-coupled colt: fourth foal: brother to a winner in Macau: dam won from 5f to 9.2f in France, from family of Stanera: fairly useful form: best efforts when winning nurseries at Windsor in August and Newbury by ¾ length from Petite Danseuse, drifting left) in October: stays 1m: acts on equitrack and good to firm ground, goes well on soft: visored (poor effort) eighth outing. *K. McAuliffe*

KAI'S LADY (IRE) 3 b.f. Jareer (USA) 115 – Rathnaleen (Scorpio (FR) 127) –
[1995 –: 6g[6] 1996 a11g[5] a11g 10d 8m Jun 4] no sign of ability: sold 600 gns Ascot December Sales. *S. W. Campion*

KAITAK (IRE) 5 ch.g. Broken Hearted 124 – Klairelle (Klairon 131) [1995 –: 8g 69
a8.5g 1996 11.9g[5] 11.9m Aug 22] leggy, workmanlike gelding: fair handicapper: good fifth of 8 (10 lb out of handicap) in Old Newton Cup at Haydock in July: stiff task, no show in £17,300 event at York over 6 weeks later: stays 1½m: acts on good to firm and heavy ground: fairly useful hurdler. *J. M. Carr*

KAJOSTAR 6 ch.m. Country Classic – Rasimareem (Golden Mallard 103) [1995 –
–: 6m 7f 7f 6m 1996 a6g a8g Dec 11] no worthwhile form on flat. *S. W. Campion*

KALABO (USA) 4 b.c. Trempolino (USA) 135 – Kalikala (Darshaan 133) [1995 113
113: 12f[3] 12f[5] 14.6d 1996 a9.9g[2] 12.3m* 12m* 16f[6] 12f[2] 12m[5] 12s 12s[3] Nov 9] strong, compact colt: smart performer: won small-field minor events at Chester and Newmarket in mid-summer: good 1¼ lengths second of 9 to Busy Flight in listed race at Doncaster: below best afterwards: effective at 1½m, may well get 1¾m (did not stay 2m in Goodwood Cup): acts on firm ground and on sand: won on soft at 2 yrs but best form on a sound surface: usually held up. *Saeed bin Suroor*

KALAMATA 4 ch.c. Kalaglow 132 – Good Try 92 (Good Bond 122) [1995 67, –
a81: 8m[5] 10.2m[2] 12m[2] 11f[6] a12g* 1996 a12g[6] a12g Dec 28] lengthy colt: won minor event at Wolverhampton on final 3-y-o start: well beaten in 1996, off course 11 months between outings: should stay 1¾m: acts on fibresand. *J. A. Glover*

KALA NOIRE 3 gr.c. Kalaglow 132 – Noire Small (USA) (Elocutionist (USA)) 87 p
[1995 NR 1996 12f[4] Jul 26] fourth reported foal: half-brother to 2 modest winners by Aragon, including middle-distance performer Bandar Perak: dam won 3 races in Italy and ran over hurdles here: 5¾ lengths fourth of 7 to My Emma in maiden at Newmarket in July, niggled along 5f out, keeping on: should stay beyond 1½m: looked likely to improve. *G. Harwood*

KALAO TUA (IRE) 3 b.f. Shaadi (USA) 126 – Lisa's Favourite (Gorytus (USA)) –
132) [1995 66: 6m[3] 7d 1996 8m 8.3m 8g Jul 3] tall, angular filly: short-head second of 5 in maiden at Yarmouth on debut: well beaten in varied company afterwards: bred to stay 1m. *J. R. Fanshawe*

KALAR 7 b.g. Kabour 80 – Wind And Reign 55 (Tumble Wind (USA)) [1995 57, 57
a74: a5g[2] a5g[2] a5g a5g[3] a5g* a5g 5d[3] 6v[2] 5m[4] 6g[4] 5m[6] 5g[3] 5g[5] 5g[4] a6g 5m 5m[2] 5m* a79
5m 5f* 5m[5] 5g[4] 5g a5g[5] a5g[2] a5g a5g[2] a5g[3] a5g 1996 a5g a5g[6] a5g[3] a5g[5] a5g[5] 5g 5g 5g[3] 5g 5g[5] a5g 5m[2] 5g[2] 5m[6] 5g[2] 6f[2] 5m* 5g[2] 5m[3] 5m 5g[4] 5.1g a5g[5] a5g* a5g a5g[2] a5g[4] a6g* Dec 27] good-bodied gelding: fair handicapper on the all-weather, modest on turf: won at Catterick in August, Lingfield in November and Southwell in December: effective at 5f and 6f: acts on the all-weather and any turf going: usually blinkered, has been tried visored: front runner: suitable mount for 7-lb claimer: tough. *D. W. Chapman*

KALA SUNRISE 3 ch.c. Kalaglow 132 – Belle of The Dawn (Bellypha 130) 91
[1995 83?: 5.1g⁴ 5m* 6m 6d 7d 8f⁴ 1996 7.5m⁶ 8.1d⁴ 10.5d 8f 8m⁶ 10m 11.9m 8.9g⁶
8f⁴ 8m 7.9g* Oct 9] tall, workmanlike colt: fairly useful handicapper: won rated
stakes (by ¾ length from Hal's Pal) at York: also ran well in face of stiff tasks outside
handicap company eighth and ninth outings: best efforts at up to 9f: acts on firm and
dead ground. *C. Smith*

KALIMAT 2 b.f. (Mar 31) Be My Guest (USA) 126 – Kantado 93 (Saulingo 122) 74
[1996 6g 6g² 7g² Oct 18] sister to Irish 3-y-o 9f winner Exceedingly and half-sister to
several winners, notably In Excess (by Siberian Express), 6f and 7f winner here and
later top class in USA at 1m/1¼m: dam raced mainly at 5f: fair form when second in
maidens at Ayr (carried head on one side) in August and Catterick (beaten 1¼ lengths
by Kadeena) in October: should stay 1m: raced only on good ground. *W. Jarvis*

KALININI (USA) 2 ch.c. (May 20) Seattle Dancer (USA) 119 – Kaiserfahrt 71 p
(GER) (Frontal 122) [1996 7g 8m³ 7.9g⁴ Oct 9] big, strong colt: has plenty of scope:
sixth foal: half-brother to 3 winners abroad, notably smart German performer at up to
1½m Komtur (by Magesterial): dam from good German family: very backward in
York maiden on debut: in frame afterwards, showing progressive form, in steadily-
run maidens won by Panama City at Pontefract and Cybertechnology at York: will
improve further given greater test of stamina. *L. M. Cumani*

KALINKA (IRE) 2 b.f. (May 23) Soviet Star (USA) 128 – Tralthee (USA) 111 83 +
(Tromos 134) [1996 6f³ 7m* 7m² Sep 25] IR 3,700:, 23,000 2-y-o: leggy, unfurnished filly: seventh foal: half-sister to 1½m winner Dancing Tralthee (by Dancing
Brave): dam won Rockfel and Lupe Stakes: third (hung right) to Khassah in maiden
at Ascot: long odds on, simple task in maiden auction at Warwick in July: first run for
2½ months and bandaged off-hind, short-head second of 15 to White Hot in auction
event at Goodwood, tending to carry head high, edging right and failing to impress
with attitude: will stay 1m: awkward ride. *P. F. I. Cole*

KALISKO (FR) 6 b.g. Cadoudal (FR) 124 – Mista (FR) (Misti IV 132) [1995 NR –
1996 a12g Feb 7] fourth reported foal: half-brother to a 2-y-o 1m winner in France
by Gairloch: dam French winning jumper: won NH Flat race in 1993/4: poor form in
novice hurdles in 1994/5 for O. Sherwood: no promise in bad Southwell maiden on
flat debut: has joined R. Allan. *G. Fierro*

KALKO 7 b.g. Kalaglow 132 – Salchow 116 (Niniski (USA) 125) [1995 –: 9.9m –
15m⁵ 12.1g 1996 11.1m 12.1g 11.1m 13.1g Jul 20] close-coupled gelding: seems of
little account nowadays. *J. S. Goldie*

KALOU 5 b.m. K-Battery 108 – Louise Moulton 90 (Moulton 128) [1995 71: 70
9.9m⁵ 10m² 10.3m 10m² 10g³ 10.1m 10.1f⁴ 12g* 13.1g² 11.9s² 12s 12.1s³ 1996 12g³
12m 11.9g 10m² 12v Nov 11] small, lightly-made mare: fair handicapper: covered in
spring and not seen until September at 5 yrs, and performed inconsistently: effective
at 1¼m and shaped as if would stay beyond 1½m as 4-y-o: acts on firm and soft
ground: visored most 3-y-o starts and first 7 as 4-y-o. *C. W. C. Elsey*

KALOUSION 2 b.g. (May 20) K-Battery 108 – Louise Moulton 90 (Moulton –
128) [1996 6m⁴ 7.1v Oct 6] small, leggy, close-coupled gelding: brother to 5-y-o
1½m winner Kalou and half-brother to several winners here and abroad, including
useful 1985 2-y-o 7f winner Kolgong Heights (by Shirley Heights): dam 9f winner:
backward, behind in maidens at Newcastle (very slowly away) and Haydock.
C. W. C. Elsey

KAMARI (USA) 3 ch.c. Woodman (USA) 126 – Karri Valley (USA) (Storm Bird 92
(CAN) 134) [1995 71p: 7.1s⁵ 1996 8f² 9m² 8f* 7.9g⁵ 9m² 10.3d 8.5m⁶ a8f³ Dec 27]
well-made colt: fairly useful form: should have won maiden at Lingfield (allowed to
coast, short-headed) second start before easily winning one at Redcar in June: ran no
sort of race at Chester (pulled hard) sixth start: stays 9f: acts on firm ground, possibly
not on a soft surface: tends to carry head high: trained until after seventh outing by
A. Stewart. *S. Seemar, UAE*

KAMA SIMBA 4 b.g. Lear Fan (USA) 130 – Dance It (USA) (Believe It (USA)) –
[1995 59: a6g⁴ 7g⁴ 8.2m* 10m² 10f⁶ 8m² 8f⁴ 1996 10g 8.3m 8.3g 11.7m⁵ 10m Jul 26]
compact gelding: modest performer: stayed 1¼m: acted
on good to firm ground: blinkered last 2 starts: not one to trust: dead. *J. White*

KAMIKAZE 6 gr.g. Kris 135 – Infamy 123 (Shirley Heights 130) [1995 NR 1996 65
16d² 21.6m⁴ 16s May 19] strong, lengthy gelding: has a splayed action: fairly useful

hurdler: fair form on return to flat: will prove suited by an out-and-out test of stamina: has joined K. C. Bailey. *J. White*

KAMIN (USA) 2 b.c. (Mar 12) Red Ransom (USA) – Sweet Rhapsody (USA) 67 p (Sea Bird II 145) [1996 7m 7m Oct 23] $40,000F: strong, close-coupled colt: closely related to a winner in USA by Lear Fan and half-brother to several winners, including smart French 1982 2-y-o 6f winner (stayed 1m) Rhapsodien (by Habitat) and useful 1½m winner Natski (by Ela-Mana-Mou), latter second in Melbourne Cup: dam very smart French middle-distance filly: modest form in late-season maidens: likely to stay 1¼m: probably capable of better. *R. W. Armstrong*

KAMMTARRA (USA) 3 ch.c. Zilzal (USA) 137 – Snow Bride (USA) 121 109 + (Blushing Groom (FR) 131) [1995 NR 1996 8m² 10.3g³ 8.3m* 8m³ 8f* 9m Oct 5] lengthy attractive colt, progressed well physically: third foal: half-brother to Derby, King George and Arc winner Lammtarra (by Nijinsky): smart form: won 19-runner maiden at Windsor in June and conditions event at Doncaster (by 1½ lengths from Ali-Royal) in September: mid-division in Cambridgeshire (well backed) on final start, reportedly returning with a bruised foot: effective at 1m to 1¼m: acts on firm going (yet to race on a soft surface): goes well with forcing tactics: type to do well at 4 yrs. *Saeed bin Suroor*

KANAT LEE (IRE) 5 b.m. Salse (USA) 128 – Badiya (USA) (Sir Ivor 135) – [1995 43d: 10.3m 10g⁴ 9.9d⁶ 10m³ 11.9m⁵ 9.9g 10f⁶ 14.1m⁴ 16d 12.1g 1996 10m a8g Nov 18] close-coupled mare: probably of little account nowadays. *Mrs V. A. Aconley*

KANAWA 2 b.f. (May 29) Beveled (USA) – Kiri Te (Liboi (USA) 76) [1996 6.1m – Sep 16] angular, unfurnished filly: first live foal: dam unraced half-sister to smart French middle-distance winner Tonito Pitti: 33/1, slowly away and always behind in maiden at Nottingham. *A. P. Jones*

KARAWAN 2 ch.f. (Feb 26) Kris 135 – Sweetly (FR) 88 (Lyphard (USA) 132) 55 [1996 6m 6g⁴ Oct 18] IR 270,000Y: rather unfurnished filly: sister to useful 1m/ 9f performer Lightning Fire and smart French 1987 2-y-o 6f and 7f winner Common Grounds, and half-sister to several winners in France, including smart 4-y-o 1m and 1¼m winner Angel In My Heart (by Rainbow Quest): dam won 3 races at up to 9f in USA: modest form in maidens at Newbury and Catterick: should stay 1m. *J. H. M. Gosden*

KARAYLAR (IRE) 4 b.g. Kahyasi 130 – Karamana (Habitat 134) [1995 –: 7g 49 1996 10g 8f⁶ 10m 12g⁶ 16.1m⁵ 15.8g⁶ 17.2m² Aug 28] small, good-topped gelding: has a fluent round action: first worthwhile form on flat when second in maiden handicap at Carlisle final start: suited by good test of stamina: acts on good to firm ground: winning selling hurdler. *W. Storey*

KAREN'S HAT (USA) 2 ch.f. (Apr 28) Theatrical 128 – Miss Carlotita (ARG) – (Masqued Dancer (USA)) [1996 5m 6s Oct 24] $17,000Y: half-sister to several winners abroad, including smart American 1m/1¼m performer Dowty (by Irish River): dam Argentinian Grade 1 winner: slowly into stride and unable to get into contention in maidens at Windsor and Doncaster: bred to require further than sprint distances: sold 6,200 gns Newmarket Autumn Sales: sent to Norway. *I. A. Balding*

KARINSKA 6 b.m. Master Willie 129 – Kaiserchronik (GER) (Cortez (GER)) 63 [1995 71, a–: a8g⁶ a8g⁵ 7.5m 8g* 8m 8.5m⁶ 7g* 8.3g* 8m³ 8m³ 6g⁴ 8m 7g 8d³ 8.1g 7.1s³ 8m 1996 a8g³ a8g⁶ a8g² a8g⁴ a8g a7g³ 7.5d 8g 8.5g⁵ 10m⁴ 8g⁵ 8g⁶ 10m Aug 10] angular, workmanlike mare: has a quick action: modest handicapper: mostly ran creditably in 1996: stays 1¼m, at least in slowly-run race: acts on fibresand and firm ground, probably on soft: sometimes reluctant to post and slowly away: carries head awkwardly and often flashes tail: usually claimer ridden and held up. *M. C. Chapman*

KARISMA (IRE) 3 b.g. Tirol 127 – Avra (FR) 65 (Mendez (FR) 128) [1995 73: 70 7g⁴ 7.9g³ 7f³ 1996 10g⁵ 12.4g⁶ 12.3m 12.3m⁴ 11.9g³ 14.6g³ 16.5s Nov 9] sturdy, angular gelding: fair maiden: out of depth final start: stays 14.6f: best efforts with give in the ground: raced too freely and swished tail third start at 3 yrs, edgy on fourth. *Denys Smith*

KASHANA (IRE) 4 b.f. Shahrastani (USA) 135 – Kashna (USA) (Blushing 44 Groom (FR) 131) [1995 8m⁵ 12m⁴ 1996 8s 10g 6.9d⁶ 8g 15.8s 16f 13.8m 16g 12g⁴ 11m Oct 29] lengthy, rather sparely-made ex-Irish filly: second foal: dam once-raced half-sister to useful 1¼m performer Karaferya: fair form (rated 67) in 2 maidens as

3-y-o for J. Oxx: only form in 1996 when fourth in apprentice claimer at Catterick penultimate start: stays 1½m: has worn tongue strap: visored last 2 outings. *W. Storey*

KASS ALHAWA   3 b.g. Shirley Heights 130 – Silver Braid (USA) 101 (Miswaki   76 d
(USA) 124) [1995 76p: 7m⁴ 1996 10g² 12g⁵ a9.4g a9.4g a8.5g 7g 7f⁵ 12g Oct 18]
good-topped gelding: second in maiden at Pontefract on reappearance: sold out of
M. Stoute's stable 7,000 gns Newmarket July Sales after next outing: showed little
for new stable, tailed off and finishing lame behind final start: may prove best at up
to 1½m: yet to race on a soft surface, no form on the all-weather: tried blinkered, no
improvement. *D. W. Chapman*

KASSANI (IRE)   4 b.c. Alleged (USA) 138 – Kassiyda 98 (Mill Reef (USA) 141)   119
[1995 12.5g² 15.5d* 15.5m* 12d* 12d² 1996 15.5g⁶ 12s⁴ 15g* 15d² 15g* 15.5m²
20d Oct 5] second foal: half-brother to a hurdles winner by Shahrastani: dam, won 2
of 5 races at around 1¼m, is half-sister to Kahyasi (rated 130): smart French colt:
won 3 times at 3 yrs, notably listed race at Evry: won listed race at Chantilly in June
by 1½ lengths from Tot Ou Tard and 5-runner Prix Kergorlay at Deauville in August
by a length from Nononito: ¾-length second of 6 to Always Aloof (rec 4 lb) in Prix
Gladiateur at Longchamp: soundly beaten in Prix du Cadran at Longchamp, held up
and never competitive: stays 15.5f: acts on good to firm and soft ground: has joined
Bruce Wallis in New Zealand. *A. de Royer-Dupre, France*

KASSBAAN (USA)   6 b.g. Alydar (USA) – Ma Biche (USA) 125 (Key To The   99
Kingdom (USA)) [1995 104: a6g* a6g* a6g* 6m³ 1996 a6g* a6g* a6g* 6g⁵ a6f*   a109
Dec 29] big, lengthy gelding: impresses in appearance: sent to Dubai after 4-y-o turf
season, and improved into a useful performer, winning 7 races: not up to his Dubai
form on return to Britain, fading when fifth in £17,000 rated stakes at York in September: dead-heated in handicap back in Dubai in December: best form at 6f: suited
by a sound surface (acts on firm going) on turf and goes well on sand: blinkered
(below form) twice at 4 yrs: sometimes bandaged off-hind. *Saeed bin Suroor*

KATATONIC (IRE)   3 b.c. Waajib 121 – Miss Kate (FR) (Nonoalco (USA) 131)   43
[1995 NR 1996 a8g⁵ a7g³ Dec 30] IR 25,000Y: closely related to a winner in Italy by
Try My Best and half-brother to several winners, including useful 6f and 7f winner
here Glen Kate (by Glenstal), subsequently smart in USA: dam, 1¼m winner in
France, half-sister to very smart stayer Midshipman: poor form in minor event and
maiden at Lingfield in December: should stay middle distances. *J. A. R. Toller*

KATHERINE   2 ch.f. (May 6) Chilibang 120 – Kaasiha (Kings Lake (USA) 133)   –
[1996 a7g Nov 22] third reported foal: dam won NH Flat race: soundly beaten in
seller at Southwell. *J. Ringer*

KATHRYN'S PET   3 b.f. Blakeney 126 – Starky's Pet (Mummy's Pet 125) [1995   66
NR 1996 11.8s⁴ 10g⁶ 10g³ 12.1s⁵ 10.5v 12g⁵ 12.1s Nov 7] sturdy, workmanlike filly:
half-sister to 7f (at 2 yrs) and 1¼m winner Liability Order (by Norwick) and fairly
useful 7f winner Southern Sky (by Comedy Star): dam well beaten: fair maiden
handicapper: should prove suited by 1½m+: has raced only on an easy surface.
Mrs M. Reveley

KATIE IS MY LOVE (USA)   3 ch.f. Talinum (USA) – Familiar (USA) 96   –
(Diesis 133) [1995 NR 1996 a9.4g Aug 9] $7,000Y: second foal: half-sister to a 2-y-o
sprint winner in USA by Clever Trick: dam, 1m winner, half-sister to very smart 1m/
1¼m winner All At Sea, also second in Oaks: 66/1, slowly away and always behind
in maiden at Wolverhampton: sold 3,000 gns Newmarket Autumn Sales. *R. Harris*

KATIE KOMAITE   3 b.f. Komaite (USA) – City To City 55 (Windjammer   48
(USA)) [1995 54+: 5g⁵ 5g⁴ a6g 5m³ 5f 5f 6f⁶ 7.1s³ 1996 a7g⁶ 8.2g 8.2m 7.5g 7g⁴ 5.9f
7g⁵ 8.1m 8.1m³ 7.1m 8m Oct 29] leggy, angular filly: poor maiden handicapper:
probably stays 1m: acts on good to firm and soft ground: tried blinkered: has been
difficult at stalls: inconsistent: blinkered final start (ran poorly). *Capt. J. Wilson*

KATIE OLIVER   4 b.f. Squill (USA) 122 – Shih Ching (USA) (Secreto (USA)   58
128) [1995 67: 14g⁵ 14s⁵ 14.1m 1996 a12g² Jan 22] good-topped, workmanlike filly:
modest maiden: modest on, runner-up in bad median auction event at Southwell: stays
1¾m: acts on soft ground and fibresand: modest hurdler. *B. Smart*

KATY-Q (IRE)   3 b.f. Taufan (USA) 119 – Swift Chorus (Music Boy 124) [1995   52 d
58: 5g 5f³ 5f² 6f³ 6m⁶ 5g* 1996 6g 6f⁴ 5f³ 6s 5.9f 5m 5m a6g Nov 4] poor handi-

capper: best form at 5f: acts on firm ground: blinkered nowadays: races prominently. *P. Calver*

KATY'S LAD 9 b.g. Camden Town 125 – Cathryn's Song (Prince Tenderfoot (USA) 126) [1995 63: a9.4g² 10.3m* 10.4m⁵ a12g 1996 a11g Dec 27] leggy gelding: unimpressive mover: moderate performer nowadays: won claimer at Chester in June, 1995: below form all outings since: stays 12.3f: acts on good to firm ground and soft: effective with or without blinkers: often bandaged. *B. A. McMahon* –

KAWA-IB (IRE) 2 b.f. (Apr 10) Nashwan (USA) 135 – Awayed (USA) 108 (Sir Ivor 135) [1996 7.1s³ Oct 22] third foal: sister to fair 3-y-o maiden Raed: dam Irish 1m to 9.2f winner from good family: weak 11/1, shaped well when very close third of 16, clear, to Technicolour in maiden at Chepstow: bred to stay 1¼m: sure to improve. *P. T. Walwyn* 78 p

KAWANIN 3 ch.f. Generous (IRE) 139 – Nahilah 78 (Habitat 134) [1995 NR 1996 7d 9m 12.1g² 13.4m³ Jun 26] leggy filly: third foal: half-sister to 4-y-o Irshad (by Soviet Star) and 1¼m winner Mnaafa (by Darshaan): dam lightly-raced 7f winner: best effort in maidens when second at Chepstow, pushed along by halfway: sold 32,000 gns Newmarket July Sales: looks a stayer. *P. T. Walwyn* 81

KAYARTIS 7 b.m. Kaytu 112 – Polyartis 78 (Artaius (USA) 129) [1995 NR 1996 15.4m 11.7g Apr 30] rated 50+ at 5 yrs: well beaten both starts in 1996: suited by a thorough test of stamina. *C. A. Dwyer* –

KAYE'S SECRET 3 b.f. Failiq (FR) 90 – Another-Kaye (Jimmy The Singer 113) [1995 NR 1996 16.2g⁶ 10f 12g Oct 19] first reported foal: dam never ran: has shown nothing in maidens (for C. Smith) and apprentice claimer. *J. L. Harris* –

KAYF 3 ch.f. Nashwan (USA) 135 – Northshiel 85 (Northfields (USA)) [1995 NR 1996 10g May 29] 90,000F, IR 100,000Y: leggy, close-coupled filly: closely related to useful 4-y-o middle-distance performer Asterita (by Rainbow Quest) and half-sister to 3 winners, including Boloardo (by Persian Bold), successful at 1m and 9f and effective at 1½m: dam, 2-y-o 7f winner, closely related to Waajib out of useful middle-distance filly Coryana: 7/1, lame when virtually pulled up in maiden at Ripon. *L. M. Cumani* –

KAYVEE 7 gr.g. Kaldoun (FR) 122 – Secret Life (USA) (Elocutionist (USA)) [1995 107: 7m⁵ 7.9g² 8m⁵ 8f⁴ 8g* 7m 7d 9g 8m 1996 8s 7m 7m 7.9m 8m 8.1g⁴ 8m 7m² 7.3m⁴ 8.2d* 9g 7m² 9m 8g³ Nov 2] big, close-coupled gelding: impresses in appearance: useful handicapper: won minor event at Nottingham in August: good efforts afterwards when second of 26 to Decorated Hero in £50,100 race at Ascot (has good record there) and third of 26 to Saifan in £22,900 event at Newmarket: effective at 7f to 9f: acts on firm and dead ground: blinkered twice at 3 yrs: sometimes wears severe noseband: usually held up: genuine. *G. Harwood* 101

KAYZEE (IRE) 2 b.f. (Apr 25) River Falls 113 – Northern Amber (Shack (USA) 118) [1996 6f 6g⁶ Aug 26] 6,600Y: seventh foal: half-sister to winning sprinters Minizen Music (by Anita's Prince) and Karseam (by Mon Tresor): dam ran several times: showed little in maiden events at Lingfield and Epsom. *S. Dow* –

KAZIMIERA (IRE) 3 b.f. Polish Patriot (USA) 128 – Cartier Bijoux 96 (Ahonoora 122) [1995 77?: 5g³ 5g⁶ 5s³ a5g⁶ 1996 7.1g⁶ 8m² 7.6g⁵ 8m³ 8m⁴ 8.5m⁴ 7.5m³ 8m 8g⁴ 8m⁵ 7.1d 8f³ 8.2g 8.1s⁶ a8s³ a7g Nov 29] plain, leggy filly: fair maiden handicapper at best: stays 1m: acts on soft ground but best form on a sound surface: has been reluctant at stalls: sometimes doesn't find so much as expected. *C. W. C. Elsey* 74 d

KEALBRA LADY 3 b.f. Petong 126 – Greensward Blaze 50 (Sagaro 133) [1995 –: 5.7f⁶ 1996 10.2f 8.2f 5m 7f 5m Sep 25] seems of little account. *M. S. Saunders* –

KEDWICK (IRE) 7 b.g. Be My Guest (USA) 126 – Lady Pavlova 111 (Ballymore 123) [1995 60: a10g² a10g³ a12g⁵ a8g² a8g² 1996 a10g a8g⁵ a10g* a10g Dec 30] modest handicapper: not seen until late on in 1996, and won at Lingfield in December: appeared to stay 1½m in Ireland, but best efforts in Britain over shorter: raced only on equitrack in Britain: blinkered/visored at 6 yrs and last 2 starts at 7 yrs. *P. R. Hedger* 61

KEEN COMPANION 3 b.f. Keen 116 – Constant Companion 84 (Pas de Seul 133) [1995 NR 1996 a10g³ Nov 15] 6,200F: fourth foal: half-sister to 1993 2-y-o 7f winner Hobart (by Reprimand) and 7f to 8.3f winner Comanche Companion (by 48

Commanche Run): dam 1m winner who stayed 1¼m: third of 9 in maiden at Lingfield on debut: may improve. *T. J. Naughton*

KEEN DANCER 2 ch.g. (Feb 26) Keen 116 – Royal Shoe (Hotfoot 126) [1996 8f – 8.2g Oct 24] fourth reported foal: half-brother to 11.7f and 1½m winner Princess Moodyshoe (by Jalmood): dam winning jumper: well beaten in maidens at Leicester and Nottingham. *M. Bell*

KEEN SALLY 3 ch.f. Keen 116 – Super Sally 108 (Superlative 118) [1995 NR – 1996 7f Sep 28] first foal: dam, effective at 1m to 1¼m, half-sister to smart Unanimous Vote: tailed-off last in maiden at Redcar on debut. *John Berry*

KEEN TO PLEASE 2 ch.f. (Mar 9) Keen 116 – Tasseled (USA) (Tate Gallery 60 (USA) 117) [1996 7.1g³ 5m³ 5m* 6m 5f³ 5g⁴ 5g² Oct 19] 5,600Y, 9,200 2-y-o: close-coupled filly: second foal: half-sister to Fenna (by Dowsing), 6f winner at 2 yrs: dam, ran 3 times in North America, out of half-sister to Riverman: modest form: won claimer at Newcastle in August: gives impression will prove best at 5f: races prominently. *Denys Smith*

KEEN TO THE LAST (FR) 4 ch.g. Keen 116 – Derniere Danse (Gay Mecene – (USA) 128) [1995 78d: 8.1g³ 10m 10m³ 10m 12s 12g 1996 13d 12g 17.5m 17.1m Oct 7] strong gelding: fair form in maidens first 3 starts at 3 yrs (for G. Harwood): well beaten since: stays 1¼m: visored (out of form) final 3-y-o start: won maiden hurdle in October. *M. D. Hammond*

KEEN WATERS 2 b.f. (Apr 8) Keen 116 – Miss Oasis 54 (Green Desert (USA) 60 127) [1996 6m 5m³ 5.1m⁴ 6f⁶ 5m² 5g Oct 18] 3,800Y: leggy, workmanlike filly: first foal: dam twice-raced half-sister to smart sprinter Sizzling Melody: modest form, staying on, in frame in maiden events: should be suited by further than 5f. *J. R. Arnold*

KEEP BATTLING 6 b.g. Hard Fought 125 – Keep Mum 63 (Mummy's Pet 125) 56 [1995 44: 10.9m* 10g* 8.3f³ 12.1m2 10f³ 10.9g⁴ 10.1m⁵ 6m 10f⁶ 7g 12.1g⁵ 12.1g⁶ 8.9g 1996 12.1g³ 12.3g³ 10.9d² 11.1g³ 12.1f* 10m² Jun 22] unfurnished gelding: modest handicapper: in good form in 1996, winning at Musselburgh in June: stays 1½m: acts on firm and dead ground (and soft over hurdles): visored (no form) twice at 3 yrs: sometimes sweats: held up: sometimes finishes weakly. *J. S. Goldie*

KEEPERS DAWN (IRE) 3 b.f. Alzao (USA) 117 – Keepers Lock (USA) 103 d (Sunny's Halo (CAN)) [1995 85: 6m⁶ 6m 6.1d* 6g 1996 7.3d² 8m 8d 6m 6s Nov 9] robust, good-quartered filly: much improved form when 6 lengths second to Bosra Sham in Fred Darling Stakes at Newbury on reappearance, racing freely and in touch long way: ran poorly afterwards in 1000 Guineas (worked up beforehand) at Newmarket, listed event at Kempton and Cork and Orrery Stakes at Royal Ascot, and reportedly found to have been suffering from trapped nerve in back: no promise after 4½-month absence on final start: should prove at least as effective at 6f as 7f: acts on dead ground: edgy sort. *R. F. Johnson Houghton*

KEEP QUIET 4 b.f. Reprimand 122 – Silent Pool 68 (Relkino 131) [1995 –: 8m – 8.3m 16.4m a12g 12m Jun 8] neat filly: seems of no account nowadays: tried blinkered: covered by Komaite. *W. J. Musson*

KEEPSAKE (IRE) 2 b.f. (May 1) Distinctly North (USA) 115 – Souveniers – (Relko 136) [1996 5.7d 7.9g 7g Oct 18] IR 3,800Y: IR 4,500Y: tall filly with scope: half-sister to several winners, including 1994 2-y-o 5f winner Nazute (by Cyrano de Bergerac) and 7-y-o 7f/1m performer Whatever's Right (by Doulab): dam, showed ability at 3 yrs in Ireland, out of Princess Royal winner Aloft: signs of a little ability in maidens: may do better. *M. D. I. Usher*

KELLAIRE GIRL (IRE) 4 b.f. Gallic League 119 – Frensham Manor (Le – Johnston 123) [1995 43, a53: 6d⁵ 5.1g 6f⁶ 6m⁴ 8m a8g² 8m⁶ 8.5m⁴ 8f 9m a8g² a8g a43 a7g 1996 a8g⁴ a12g a10g³ a10g⁴ 8f a10g a6g Nov 14] tall, lengthy filly: poor maiden: tailed off final start, after 4½-month absence: should stay 1¼m: acts on firm and dead ground and on equitrack: blinkered (below form) once at 3 yrs, visored third and fourth starts as 4-y-o. *A. Moore*

KELLY MAC 6 b.g. Precocious 126 – Ridalia 56 (Ridan (USA)) [1995 –: 7.1d 48 1996 9.7s⁵ 12m 7.3s May 29] sturdy, good-quartered gelding: tough and game handicapper (rated 70) at 4 yrs for M. Channon: below form since: stays 1¼m: probably acts on any going. *D. C. O'Brien*

KELTOI 3 b.c. Soviet Star (USA) 128 – Celtic Assembly (USA) 95 (Secretariat 88
(USA)) [1995 NR 1996 7.1d² 8g* 8.2m 10m Aug 3] good-bodied, attractive colt: unimpressive mover in his slower paces: half-brother to several winners, notably very
smart French performer at 6f to 7f Cherokee Rose (by Dancing Brave): dam 10.6f
winner of top 1975 Irish 2-y-o filly Welsh Garden: won 20-runner maiden at
Newbury in May by head from Gold Spats: seventh of 8 in useful minor event at
Nottingham next start and disappointing in handicap at Newmarket on final one, both
steadily-run races on top-of-the-ground: should be suited by further than 1m: may
well prove suited by an easy surface: sent to UAE. *L. M. Cumani*

KEMO SABO 4 b.g. Prince Sabo 123 – Canoodle 66 (Warpath 113) [1995 83: 8d –
10.5m 9.9m 8.5m² 8g 7g⁵ 8m⁴ 8g* 7f 7.5m² 10f³ 8g⁴ 8d 1996 8d⁴ Apr 26] lengthy
gelding: good mover: fairly useful handicapper for Mrs J. Ramsden as 3-y-o: well
below form only owing in 1996: stays 8.5f: acts on any going: has run well for
amateur: improved hurdler, successful in December. *C. Parker*

KENESHA (IRE) 6 br.m. Don't Forget Me 127 – Calvino (Relkino 131) [1995 46
54d: 7.1d 6s 6.9m⁵ 5g³ 5g 5f² 5g 5m³ 5f⁶ 5g 5m² 5f² 6f⁵ 5f 5m⁴ 5g 5g 5f 1996 5g⁵ 5m⁶
May 18] workmanlike mare: poor maiden handicapper: often runs well at Musselburgh, and creditable effort there on reappearance: reportedly bled from nose when
well below form next time: best efforts at 5f: acts on firm and dead ground: often
blinkered: races prominently. *D. A. Nolan*

KENILWORTH DANCER 3 br.g. Shareef Dancer (USA) 135 – Reltop 72 –
(High Top 131) [1995 –: 6g⁶ 6d 7m 8f 1996 a12g⁵ a8g Mar 18] sturdy gelding:
trained at 2 yrs by Mrs M. Reveley: no sign of ability, in blinkers final start: has
joined B. R. Cambidge. *R. D. E. Woodhouse*

KENNEMARA STAR (IRE) 2 ch.g. (Apr 21) Kenmare (FR) 125 – Dawn Star 66 p
94 (High Line 125) [1996 7m 7.6d⁵ 7.1v⁶ Oct 6] tall gelding with scope: half-brother
to several winners, including useful pair Dawning Street (at up to 1m, by Thatching)
and 6-y-o Special Dawn (at up to 1¼m, by Be My Guest): dam 1¼m and 11f winner:
modest form in maidens: travelled smoothly until tiring last 1f or so at Salisbury and
Lingfield first 2 starts: unable to quicken 2f out and eased once beaten on heavy
ground at Haydock on final one: likely to do better. *J. L. Dunlop*

KENTAVRUS WAY (IRE) 5 b.g. Thatching 131 – Phantom Row 37 (Adonijah 41
126) [1995 –: a12g a8g a10g a16g a10g 1996 a12g a13g a10g a10g⁴ Mar 29] good-
bodied gelding: poor form at best since 1994: effective at 7f to 1¼m: acts on firm
ground, best effort on equitrack: tried visored: refused to race once over hurdles in
December. *A. Moore*

KENTFORD CONQUISTA 3 b.f. El Conquistador 109 – Notinhand (Nearly A –
Hand 115) [1995 –: 7.1s 1996 7.1m 14m⁶ Aug 22] soundly beaten in maidens.
J. W. Mullins

KENTUCKY FALL (FR) 3 b.f. Lead On Time (USA) 123 – Autumn Tint 69
(USA) (Roberto (USA) 131) [1995 NR 1996 8g⁴ 8.1m⁴ 9.7g² 10.3g Oct 25] 10,000
2-y-o: fourth foal: half-sister to 1¼m winner Minatina (by Ela-Mana-Mou): dam
French 1½m winner: fair form in maidens: tailed off in handicap at Doncaster final
start: stays 9.7f: seems one paced. *Lady Herries*

KENWOOD MELODY 2 ch.g. (Apr 9) Lead On Time (USA) 123 – Baddi 72
Baddi (USA) (Sharpen Up 127) [1996 6g² 6f⁵ 6m⁵ 6f² Jul 13] 30,000Y: fourth foal:
half-brother to French winners by Storm Bird (2-y-o sprinter, then at 1m) and Shareef
Dancer (up to 9.5f): dam, 2-y-o 1m winner in France, out of half-sister to Enstone
Spark: fair form: will stay 7f: gelded: sent to Hong Kong. *M. Bell*

KENYATTA (USA) 7 b.g. Mogambo (USA) – Caranga (USA) (Caro 133) [1995 –
–, a37: a13g⁴ 12m a10g⁵ a13g⁶ a12g³ 1996 11.9g 11.5f a13g Jun 29] leggy
gelding: poor performer: stayed 13f: acted on equitrack, no form on turf since 1992:
tried visored and blinkered, not since 1992: dead. *A. Moore*

KERNOF (IRE) 3 b.g. Rambo Dancer (CAN) 107 – Empress Wu 62 (High 55
Line 125) [1995 60+: 6m 7m⁴ 6f⁴ 7g⁵ 8g 10m⁶ 9g 10m 11.1f² 10g* 9.9m⁵ 12m*
5] leggy gelding: modest performer: won apprentice handicap at Pontefract in July,
sent on over 4f out and soon clear: stays 11f: acts on firm ground, yet to race
on a soft surface: visored then blinkered last 2 starts: winning juvenile hurdler.
M. D. Hammond

KERRIER (IRE) 4 ch.c. Nashwan (USA) 135 – Kerrera 115 (Diesis 133) [1995 –
10g² 9.5g³ 11.5g 10g* 8g* 8.8g 1996 8.3m a9.4g 8.3g 8.1m Jul 19] second foal:
dam, headstrong half-sister to Rock City out of Musidora winner Rimosa's Pet, was
runner-up in 1000 Guineas but just as effective at sprinting: won minor event in
French Provinces when trained by H. Pantall and Czech equivalent of 2000 Guineas
in 1995, then tenth of 12 in listed race at Grosseto (in Italy) for T. Satra: has shown
little in Britain, including in selling company: sold to join H. J. Manners 1,750 gns
Ascot August Sales. *R. Harris*

KERRY JANE 6 gr.m. Nestor 97 – Quaife Sport (Quayside 124) [1995 NR 1996 –
a12g Jan 17] half-sister to fairly useful hurdler Celtic Bob (by Celtic Cone): dam
never ran: poor jumper: tailed off in claimer at Wolverhampton on flat debut.
N. M. Babbage

KERRY RING 3 b.f. Sadler's Wells (USA) 132 – Kerrera 115 (Diesis 133) [1995 79
82P: 7m² 1996 7m⁴ 7.1d* 7m⁶ 7m Oct 5] strong, well-made filly: fluent mover:
favourite, gamely won maiden at Sandown in August: not discredited in handicap
next start: raced only at 7f, will be much better suited by 1m+: yet to race on extremes
of going: sent to UAE. *J. H. M. Gosden*

KESANTA 6 b.m. The Dissident 85 – Nicaline 50 (High Line 125) [1995 NR 1996 37
16.2g² 16m Sep 16] only worthwhile form when second in selling handicap at
Beverley: modest hurdler. *W. G. M. Turner*

KESTON POND (IRE) 6 b.g. Taufan (USA) 119 – Maria Renata (Jaazeiro 80
(USA) 127) [1995 77: 7f* 8m⁵ 7m 7m 7m* 6g* 7g 7f 1996 6m 7g 6m² a6g² 8g 7m*
7g² 7m² 7m⁴ 6m 7m² 7g 7m⁵ 6f Nov 5] tall, good-topped gelding: fair handicapper: won at York in July: creditable efforts most starts afterwards: effective at 6f
to 8.2f: acts on fibresand and firm ground: blinkered (tailed off) final 4-y-o start.
Mrs V. A. Aconley

KETABI (USA) 5 ch.g. Alydar (USA) – Ivory Fields (USA) 110 (Sir Ivor 135) 58
[1995 –: 10.8d 12m 1996 a12g 9.7s 10.8d 9f a10g⁴ 8m⁴ 10g 10m* 8f⁵ 8.1f 10.8f Oct
8] quite attractive gelding: easily best effort since 1994 when winning claimer at
Brighton in August: sold 2,000 gns Newmarket Autumn Sales: stays 1¼m: has won
on dead ground, better form on a sound surface: blinkered (below form) twice at 5
yrs: sent to Italy. *R. Akehurst*

KEVASINGO 4 b.g. Superpower 113 – Katharina 105 (Frankincense 120) [1995 57
65: a8g* 8.2g³ 8.2m 8g³ 10m⁴ 10g 9m³ 8f* 8m² 8f⁵ 8f⁶ 8m 8g 1996 9.7m 7d⁶ 8f³ 7.1g
9.7f 10f⁵ 10m⁴ 10f³ 10.8f⁴ 8m Oct 23] workmanlike gelding: modest handicapper:
sold out of B. Hills's stable 5,500 gns Newmarket Autumn Sales: stays 1¼m: acts
on equitrack and firm ground (shaped encouragingly on dead): blinkered last 2 starts.
B. W. Hills

KEWARRA 2 b.g. (Apr 12) Distant Relative 128 – Shalati (FR) (High Line 125) 71
[1996 5m 6.1g⁵ 6m⁴ 5.1g⁴ Aug 26] angular gelding: fifth reported foal: half-brother
to 3-y-o 10.2f winner Shalateeno (by Teenoso), 10.8f winner Shalholme (by Fools
Holme) and a winner in Norway by Northern State: dam French 1m winner: generally progressive form: likely to prove ideally suited by at least 7f. *B. R. Millman*

KEY CHANGE (IRE) 3 b.f. Darshaan 133 – Kashka (USA) (The Minstrel 117
(CAN) 135) [1995 8g⁴ 8g* 1996 10s* 12g* 12m² 12m³ 11.9m* 14m² Sep 21]
　　　John Murtagh will not have many better rides at York than his first. The
pace in the Aston Upthorpe Yorkshire Oaks was not a strong one and the Irish
champion jockey (he narrowly retained the title in 1996, in front of Kevin
Manning) seized the initiative after they had gone about four furlongs, sending
his mount up to dispute the lead on the inside. In Key Change, Murtagh had a
willing partner. They had a definite lead entering the straight and were about a
length and three quarters clear one and a half furlongs out, a margin maintained
all the way to the line. For the record, Papering finished second and Russian
Snows third, but nothing was galloping on more strongly than the winner.
　　　Key Change has an impressive record. The second of two runs the
previous October brought victory in a Leopardstown maiden courtesy of the
stewards after she had been beaten a short head, hampered twice before the
final furlong, in a good battle with the inappropriately-named Clear Blue Water.

Aston Upthorpe Yorkshire Oaks, York—
a first Irish victory in the race for fifteen years as Key Change sees off Papering (right) and Russian Snows

There was no need for photograph or stewards when Key Change came home six lengths clear in a listed race at the same course in April, and fifteen days later she made all in a four-runner minor event at Gowran Park (in which, incidentally, Clear Blue Water finished tailed off). That minor event carries the title 'Classic Trial', hugely ambitiously in most runnings, but, lo and behold, in 1996 both Key Change and the one and a half lengths second His Excellence went on to be placed in classics. His Excellence was twelve lengths adrift of Zagreb when third in the Irish Derby; Key Change proved a much tougher nut to crack in her two classics. Ridden to the fore in both, she was beaten two lengths when third to Dance Design in the Irish Oaks and three and a half lengths when second to Oscar Schindler in the Irish St Leger. It was a touch disappointing that Key Change did not actually show improved form in the Irish St Leger, given the style of racing she had exhibited over shorter distances, although, of course, it would have required an awful lot of improvement to have overturned Oscar Schindler. Key Change had never looked more of a stayer than on her first visit to Britain, back in June, for the Ribblesdale Stakes at Royal Ascot. On that occasion, she had been sluggish leaving the stalls and looked pretty sluggish through much of what followed, but still managed to get to within a neck of the winner Tulipa.

Key Change's pedigree is swiftly recognisable as her dam Kashka is a half-sister to Kadissya, the dam of Derby and Irish Derby winner Kahyasi. The link with this family and Key Change's sire Darshaan has naturally been tried before, two other noteworthy results being the St Simon Stakes winner Kithanga (who is out of another of Kashka's half-sisters, Kalata) and Kalikala (out of Kashka's dam Kalkeen) who is the dam of two smart middle-distance performers in Kalajana and Kalabo and a useful 1996 two-year-old in Mount Kamet. Of those aforementioned dams, the Aga Khan retains only Kadissya.

Lady Clague's "Key Change"

Key Change (IRE) (b.f. 1993)	Darshaan (br 1981)	Shirley Heights (b 1975)	Mill Reef
			Hardiemma
		Delsy (br 1972)	Abdos
			Kelty
	Kashka (USA) (ch 1983)	The Minstrel (ch 1974)	Northern Dancer
			Fleur
		Kalkeen (b 1974)	Sheshoon
			Gioia

Kashka went to the 1989 December Sales and fetched 80,000 guineas in foal to Shardari, and the seventeen-year-old Kalkeen made 38,000 at the same venue two years later in foal to Caerleon. Kashka carried the Aga Khan's colours only three times, winning a mile-and-a-half maiden at the central French venue of Mont Lucon-Neris-Les-Bains. She had five foals prior to Key Change and all were winners, though none of them in the same league; two were also by Darshaan and raced in Ireland, the mile-and-a-quarter winner Kazkar and middle-distance stayer Kakashda. Key Change herself is certainly more the middle-distance stayer—a mile and a half will prove a minimum if conditions are not really testing. Interestingly, she has not encountered a soft surface since her reappearance. It *might* bring about some more improvement as she has not always looked completely at ease on top-of-the-ground, notably at Royal Ascot. A rangy, angular filly, Key Change impressed in condition on both her visits to Britain. She remains in training. *J. Oxx, Ireland*

496

Stakis Casinos Doonside Cup, Ayr—no dangers to Key To My Heart

KEY LARGO (IRE) 2 b.c. (Mar 15) Priolo (USA) 127 – Pamiers (Hunter- 77
combe 133) [1996 6g* 6.1s⁶ 5v³ Nov 11] 6,000 2-y-o: angular, good-bodied colt:
second reported foal: dam Italian 7.5f and 9.5f winner: won maiden auction at
Pontefract in October: ran well though never a serious threat, edging left inside last,
when sixth behind Restless Spirit in falsely-run minor event at Nottingham 10 days
later: needs further than 5f, even when conditions are testing, and will stay beyond
6f. *M. H. Tompkins*

KEY OF LUCK (USA) 5 b.h. Chief's Crown (USA) – Balbonella (FR) 120 –
(Gay Mecene (USA) 128) [1995 5g 5m⁵ 6g⁴ 8m⁶ 8g* 8g⁴ 1996 a8g* a10g* a10g* a126
a9.5d² May 11] most progressive ex-French horse, closely related to Anabaa: useful
sprinting 2-y-o, unraced at 3 yrs then useful sprinter-miler (won an amateurs event)
as 4-y-o for Mme C. Head: won minor event (awarded race), handicap (by 12
lengths) and extremely valuable race (by 20 lengths, Cezanne, Valley of Gold and
Jural following him home) in March, all at Nad Al Sheba, making all on each
occasion: ¾-length second of 4 to Star Standard in Pimlico Special last time, always
chasing winner: very well suited by 1¼m: best on an easy surface on turf, but easily
best form on sand/dirt: underwent surgery on fractured near-fore cannon bone:
returned to Dubai. *K. P. McLaughlin, UAE*

KEY TO MY HEART (IRE) 6 b.h. Broken Hearted 124 – Originality (Gods- 113
walk (USA) 130) [1995 6s 1996 10.4f* 12.3m² 11.9g* 10.5m⁵ 13.3m⁵ 10.9m*
12m² a9.4g Dec 7] good-topped horse: unimpressive mover: smart performer: off
course 19 months, showed himself as good as ever in 1996, winning rated stakes at
York in May, Old Newton Cup at Haydock in July and falsely-run listed event at Ayr
(looking very well, beat Desert Shot easily by 3 lengths) in September: 4 lengths
second to Busy Flight in listed race at Newmarket in October: effective at 10.4f and
stays 1¾m: acts on any going: tough and game: effective from front or held up:
bandaged (except fifth start) at 6 yrs. *Miss S. E. Hall*

KHABAR 3 b.g. Forzando 122 – Ella Mon Amour 65 (Ela-Mana-Mou 132) [1995 63
76: 6.1m 7m⁶ 7f⁴ 7d⁵ 1996 8.2s 6g 7.5g 8g 10f² 11.1g 9m Oct 8] quite attractive
gelding: fair performer: stepped up in trip and gambled on, only worthwhile form at
3 yrs when second in weak handicap at Brighton in July: stays 1¼m: similar form on firm and dead ground at 2 yrs. *R. Bastiman*

KHAFAAQ 2 b.c. (Mar 19) Green Desert (USA) 127 – Ghanimah 98 (Caerleon –
(USA) 132) [1996 6s Oct 24] neat colt: fifth foal: half-brother to fairly useful 3-y-o
maiden at up to 1¼m No-Aman (by Nashwan) and 1992 2-y-o 7f winner Faez (by
Mtoto): dam, ran only at 2 yrs, winning at 6f, half-sister to Marwell: 10/1, never a
factor on unfavoured far side in 23-runner Newbury maiden. *Major W. R. Hern*

KHAIRUN NISAA 2 b.f. (Feb 9) Never So Bold 135 – Sea Clover (IRE) 77 64
(Ela-Mana-Mou 132) [1996 6v² a7g a6g² Dec 30] 1,000Y: first foal: dam 2-y-o 7f a?
winner: 33/1, beaten a neck in median auction maiden at Folkestone: long way below
that form on the all-weather. *M. J. Polglase*

KHALISA (IRE)   3 b.f. Persian Bold 123 – Khaiyla (Mill Reef (USA) 141) [1995   113
NR 1996 10g* 10.5g* 10.5g⁶ 9m* 9.5f⁴ 9.3d⁴ 10.5s Nov 2] rangy filly: fifth foal:
half-sister to 3 winners at 1¼m+, notably Khalyani (rated 100, at up to 1½m, by
Akarad) and Khayrawani (rated 103, at up to 1¾m, by Caerleon): dam once-raced
half-sister to middle-distance stayer Khairpour (rated 122) out of sister to Kalamoun
(rated 129): won newcomers event at Evry and Prix Cleopatre at Saint-Cloud (beat
Amiarma ¾ length) in the spring and (after 5½ lengths sixth of 12 to Sil Sila in
strongly-run Prix de Diane at Chantilly) Prix Chloe at Evry (beat Ecoute by a length)
in July: good fourth of 10 to Timarida in Beverly D Stakes at Arlington then to Donna
Viola in Prix de l'Opera at Longchamp: effective at 9f and should stay beyond 10.5f:
acts on firm and dead ground, below form on soft. *A. de Royer Dupre, France*

KHARIR (IRE)   2 b.c. (Feb 20) Machiavellian (USA) 123 – Alkaffeyeh (IRE)   92
(Sadler's Wells (USA) 132) [1996 6m* 6g³ 7.6g² Sep 25] quite attractive colt:
good mover: first foal: dam unraced sister to smart middle-distance filly Larrocha
and half-sister to Ardross: fairly useful form: won 6-runner maiden at Yarmouth in
August: placed in Timeform Futurity at Pontefract and minor event at Chester in
September: stays 7f: races keenly: sent to Dubai. *H. Thomson Jones*

KHARIZMI (FR)   3 ro. or gr.c. Lashkari 128 – Khariyda (FR) 118 (Shakapour   115
125) [1995 NR 1996 10.5d⁶ 12.5g³ 12g* 12d² 12d* 15g² 12.5d² 15d² Oct 5] fourth
foal: half-brother to a French 12.5f winner by Kahyasi: dam won 3 pattern races at
around 1¼m (including E P Taylor Stakes) and stayed 1½m: won minor event at
Saint-Cloud in April and handicap at Maisons-Laffitte in July: narrowly beaten by
Eurynome in Prix Berteux at Maisons-Laffitte (caught close home), by Grenadier in
minor event at Deauville and by Tarator in Prix de Lutece at Longchamp (staying on
well under sustained drive) last 3 starts: will stay beyond 15f: acts on dead ground.
A. de Royer-Dupre, France

KHASSAH   2 b.f. (Mar 14) Green Desert (USA) 127 – Kadwah (USA) 80 (Mr   105
Prospector (USA)) [1996 6f* 6g⁶ 8m* 8g² Sep 29] rangy filly: has scope: has a

Hamdan Al Maktoum's "Khassah"

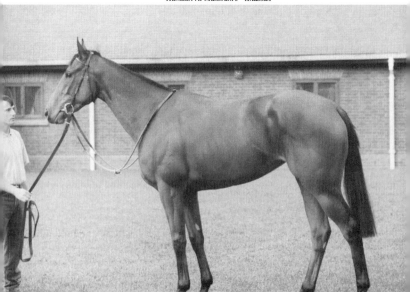

powerful, round action: third foal: sister to useful 3-y-o 7f (at 2 yrs) and 1m winner Awaamir: dam lightly-raced 1m and 1¼m winner out of high-class American turf performer Castilla: won maiden at Ascot in June readily by 2 lengths from Well Warned and 2-runner minor event at Bath in September (finished lame in Cherry Hinton Stakes in between) easily by 1¼ lengths from Ovation: in superb shape, good effort when 1¼ lengths second to Reams of Verse in Fillies' Mile at Ascot: stays 1m: acts on firm ground: sent to winter in Dubai. *J. H. M. Gosden*

KHATTAT (USA)   6 ch.g. El Gran Senor (USA) 136 – Don't Joke (USA)   72 d
(Shecky Greene (USA)) [1995 a7g³ a7g* a7g a9.9f³ a8d⁵ 1996 8m⁴ 7m⁶ a8g⁴ a5f 8m 7m 8.2g Oct 24] rated 79 in 1994 when trained by J. Dunlop, and won a handicap at Jebel Ali early in 1995: raced in Dubai early at 6 yrs but deteriorated badly: sold 3,000 gns Newmarket July Sales, and gelded: well beaten afterwards: stays 1m: acts on sand and soft going, probably on firm: tried blinkered: often gives trouble at stalls. *J. A. Harris*

KHAYRAPOUR (IRE)   6 b.g. Kahyasi 130 – Khayra (FR) (Zeddaan 130) [1995   –
92: 8m 8m 8g² 8g* 10f⁶ 8.1m² 8f* 1996 8m Aug 1] good-bodied gelding: shows knee action: fairly useful handicapper in 1995, winning Schweppes Golden Mile at Goodwood: reportedly had operation on both knees afterwards: 25/1 and backward, well beaten in same event on belated reappearance: best at around 1m: acts on firm going: blinkered last 5 starts: sometimes pulls hard, and is held up. *B. J. Meehan*

KI CHI SAGA (USA)   4 ch.g. Miswaki (USA) 124 – Cedilla (USA) 111 (Caro   85 d
133) [1995 7s* a6g* 8g 1996 7g 8m⁶ 10s⁶ 8m⁶ 8m 10v 9g 9.2g Sep 29] smallish, strong, stocky gelding: half-brother to 3 winners, including French middle-distance filly Formentera (by L'Emigrant): dam French 1m winner: won minor races in Denmark and Sweden in spring at 3 yrs: fairly useful form at best in Britain: well beaten in handicaps last 4 starts, tailed off in first-time blinkers at Hamilton on final one: sold 4,000 gns Newmarket Autumn Sales and gelded: stays 1m: acts on good to firm ground, won on soft in Denmark. *J. L. Dunlop*

KICKONSUN (IRE)   2 b.g. (Apr 24) High Estate 127 – Damezao (Alzao (USA)   –
117) [1996 7f 7d⁶ Aug 23] fourth foal: half-brother to Nose No Bounds (by Cyrano de Bergerac), 8.5f winner at 2 yrs who stayed 11f, and 1993 2-y-o 6f winner Salvezza (by Superpower): dam unraced: well beaten in maiden and seller. *R. A. Fahey*

KID ORY   5 ch.g. Rich Charlie 117 – Woomargama 69 (Creetown 123) [1995 71,   65 d
a–: a6g a8g 6m 7m⁴ 6m³ 6m⁴ 7f² 7f² 7m² 7m² 7m⁴ 7f 7f 7f 1996 7s 7.5m 7m³ 7g³ 7g   a–
7m³ 7s³ 8m³ 8.2m 7g⁶ 7m 7f⁶ a6g⁵ a7g⁶ Dec 28] close-coupled gelding: fair handicapper: sold privately out of P. Calver's stable for 5,000 gns Doncaster October Sales after twelfth start: stays 1m: acts on firm and dead ground (respectable effort on soft), no form in 6 outings on fibresand. *D. W. Chapman*

KIDSTON LASS (IRE)   3 b.f. Alzao (USA) 117 – Anthis (IRE) (Ela-Mana-Mou   80
132) [1995 NR 1996 10m⁴ 10.2f³ 10m³ Jul 26] IR 13,000Y: close-coupled filly: has a round action: first foal: dam Irish maiden half-sister to dam of Waajib: in frame in maidens at Salisbury, Bath and Ascot, keeping on willingly final start: may well prove better at 1½m than 1¼m: tail swisher. *J. A. R. Toller*

KIERCHEM (IRE)   5 b.g. Mazaad 106 – Smashing Gale (Lord Gayle (USA)   45
124) [1995 60: a12g⁴ a14.8g 1996 12.3g 9.2s³ 8.3s May 9] useful-looking gelding: little form (poor in 1996) last 3 seasons: raced too freely in blinkers final start: stays 1½m: acts on soft going and fibresand. *R. F. Fisher*

KILCORAN BAY   4 b.g. Robellino (USA) 127 – Catkin (USA) (Sir Ivor 135)   – §
[1995 79d: 8m³ 8m² 10d* 10m 10g 10m 12d 1996 14m⁴ 16s May 19] good-topped gelding: one-time fair performer: sold to join J. W. Mullins 6,800 gns Ascot June (1996) Sales: stays 1¼m: acts on good to firm and dead going: blinkered at 4 yrs: looks unco-operative and one to steer clear of. *I. A. Balding*

KILCULLEN LAD (IRE)   2 b.c. (Apr 24) Fayruz 116 – Royal Home 69   74
(Royal Palace 131) [1996 5m 6f* 6g 6f² 5f* 5g 5g² a5g² a5g* a6g* a6g⁵ Dec 31] IR 6,000Y, 10,000 2-y-o: smallish, workmanlike colt: half-brother to 3 winners, including 1989 2-y-o 5f winner Nazakat (by Known Fact) and middle-distance stayer Sweet N'Twenty (by High Top): dam 9f winner: fair performer: won seller at Lingfield in June, and nurseries at Redcar in September and Lingfield in November and December: effective at 5f and 6f: acts on firm ground and equitrack: takes a good

hold: suited by strong pace: tends to hang/drift right: blinkered/visored final 5 outings. *P. Mooney*

KILDEE LAD 6 b.g. Presidium 124 – National Time (USA) (Lord Avie (USA)) 85 [1995 73: 6g 6m⁶ 5m³ 5.1m⁶ 5m 6g 5.7m⁴ 1996 5.7g 5g² 5m 5.7m⁴ 5.7m⁴ 6m* 5.7f* 5.1m⁴ 6.1d² 6m Sep 14] leggy, close-coupled gelding: fairly useful handicapper: ran consistently well in 1996, winning at Leicester and Bath in July: effective at 5f and 6f: acts on fibresand and any turf going: visored (well below form) once at 3 yrs: usually held up: tough and genuine. *A. P. Jones*

KILERNAN 5 ch.g. K-Battery 108 – Lekuti (Le Coq d'Or 101) [1995 51: 6m 12d⁵ 51 12.3f² 15.8g* 15.8m² 16.5f² 16.1h⁴ 16d⁴ 15.8g³ 1996 12.1g* Apr 4] leggy gelding: unimpressive mover: modest handicapper: won at Musselburgh on only outing in 1996: effective at 1½m, and stays 16.5f: acts on firm and soft ground: races prominently/front runner: has run well when sweating: consistent. *T. D. Barron*

KILLATTY LARK (IRE) 3 ch.f. Noalto 120 – Killatty Sky (IRE) (Drumalis – 125) [1995 44: 6m⁴ 5g 6s 1996 a8g 7g 8.2m Jun 24] good-topped filly: unimpressive mover: no form in handicaps at 3 yrs: sold 1,600 gns Newmarket July Sales: should stay beyond 6f: possibly unsuited by good ground. *W. J. Musson*

KILL THE CRAB (IRE) 4 b.f. Petorius 117 – Final Decision (Tap On Wood 106 130) [1995 106: 8.5s³ 8g⁵ 8g* 8g* 8m* 10g* 12g² 9.3d 1996 10g⁶ 9.8g⁴ 11s⁴ 8g⁶ 9d* 12m* 10g Oct 3] leggy, quite attractive filly: useful performer: took time to come to herself in 1996, but won valuable event at Ovrevoll (beat Philidor 3½ lengths) and 14-runner Stockholm Cup at Taby (beat Dulford Lad a length): below form in Group 3 race at Hoppegarten last time: stays 1½m: acts on soft ground and good to firm: pulled hard (well beaten) final 3-y-o start: still looking very well, led out unsold at 150,000 gns Newmarket December Sales. *W. Neuroth, Norway*

KILMEENA LADY 2 b.f. (Mar 31) Inca Chief (USA) – Kilmeena Glen – (Beveled (USA)) [1996 7.1s Oct 22] first known foal: dam unraced: 66/1, well beaten in maiden at Chepstow. *J. C. Fox*

KILNAMARTYRA GIRL 6 b.m. Arkan 78 – Star Cove 58 (Porto Bello 118) – [1995 55: a7g 7.5m 8g 9.9m⁴ 9.2g 7g³ 6.9m² 7.5m² 7g 8.1m 7.5g* 7m³ 8f³ 7.5m* 7.9g 7m 8.5d 8g 1996 8.5m 8f Sep 27] lengthy mare: modest handicapper: not seen at 6 yrs until September, and well held on both outings: effective at 7f, and probably stays 1¼m: acts on firm ground: tried blinkered/visored: tends to edge left: winning hurdler. *J. Parkes*

KILSHANNY 2 b.f. (Mar 24) Groom Dancer (USA) 128 – Kiliniski 119 (Niniski 70 p (USA) 125) [1996 6m 7d² Oct 28] rangy, unfurnished filly: sixth living foal: half-sister to a winner in Belgium by Green Desert: dam 1½m winner, out of half-sister to Nureyev and the dam of Sadler's Wells: still looked inexperienced when 3 lengths second of 11 to Miss Sancerre in maiden at Lingfield in October: will be suited by 1m+: sure to improve again. *L. M. Cumani*

KILVINE 3 b.g. Shaadi (USA) 126 – Kilavea (USA) 92 (Hawaii) [1995 90: 6m⁴ 86 6m* 7g⁴ 7f⁴ 7m⁵ 1996 9g⁶ 8.1g⁶ 7g 7m⁴ 8m³ 7.5m² 7m⁶ Aug 2] well-made, attractive gelding: fairly useful handicapper: best effort at 3 yrs when second to Green Barries at Beverley: ran poorly next time: subsequently joined W. Haggas and gelded: stays 1m: has raced only on a sound surface: hung right fifth 3-y-o start. *L. M. Cumani*

KINDAKOOLA 5 b. or br.g. Kind of Hush 118 – Nikoola Eve 69 (Roscoe Blake – 120) [1995 –: 11.5g 8g 14g 1996 a11g Jan 5] good-topped gelding: no worthwhile form: dead. *M. C. Chapman*

KIND OF LIGHT 3 b.f. Primo Dominie 121 – Kind Thoughts 71 (Kashmir II 83 125) [1995 68: a7g* a7g³ 1996 a5g a6g³ a6g³ 6g 6m* 6g* 6m³ 6.1d 6m⁴ 6m a7g a68 Nov 7] fairly useful handicapper: won at Newmarket and Windsor in July: effective at 6f and 7f: acts on fibresand (below form on equitrack) and on good to firm ground, seemingly not on a soft surface: usually waited with. *R. Guest*

KINDRED GREETING 4 b.g. Most Welcome 131 – Red Berry 115 (Great 38 Nephew 126) [1995 41: a10g a11g⁶ a11g 10g 9.9m⁵ 12.1g⁵ 10g⁴ 10m⁵ 10.1m² 10.1m⁴ 10m 1996 a12g⁶ a16g 14.1f 16m 14.1m⁵ 14.1f² 14.1f² 12.3m 16m 17.1m⁵ Aug 18] stocky gelding: poor maiden: left D. Morris after reappearance: well beaten at 4 yrs except when second in handicaps at Redcar and Nottingham (seller) in July:

stays 1¾m: has raced only on a sound surface on turf (acts on firm): usually wears blinkers but has run creditably without: inconsistent. *J. A. Harris*

KING ALEX 3 b.c. Rainbow Quest (USA) 134 – Alexandrie (USA) 114 111
(Val de L'Orne (FR) 133) [1995 NR 1996 10g* 10.4f² May 16] IR 300,000Y: tall, rather unfurnished colt: has a round action: half-brother to several winners, notably Oaks third Animatrice (by Alleged) and very smart French 4-y-o middle-distance performer Poliglote (by Sadler's Wells), 1m to 1¼m winner at 2 yrs: dam won Prix Cleopatre and best at up to 1¼m: 11/10 on, most impressive when winning 16-runner maiden at Leicester in April: 3½ lengths second of 6 to Dr Massini in minor event at York 19 days later, setting sound pace until faltering last 100 yds: will be well suited by 1½m: gives impression will prove well suited by some give in the ground: reportedly lame near-hind in mid-June: looked sure to progress again. *R. Charlton*

KING ATHELSTAN (USA) 8 b.g. Sovereign Dancer (USA) – Wimbledon Star 84 d
(USA) (Hoist The Flag (USA)) [1995 NR 1996 10m 10m⁴ 9.9f 10d 10m 10.3g 8s Nov 9] lengthy gelding: fair hurdler for K. Morgan in 1995/6: sold 6,200 gns Doncaster May Sales: easily best effort at 8 yrs when fourth in falsely-run rated stakes at Ascot: stays 10.4f well: acts on good to firm ground. *B. A. McMahon*

KINGCHIP BOY 7 b.g. Petong 126 – Silk St James (Pas de Seul 133) [1995 78d, 66
a–: a7g a8g 8m 8m* 8.5m a8g⁶ 8f⁴ 8.5m⁶ 8f 8f 8.1m⁶ 8f³ 8.1m 7g 8d 8s 8.2m² a10g a72
1996 a8g a8g* a8g* a8g* a8g² a8g² a8g² 8d² 9.7m² a8g* 10m⁶ 7d 8g³ a8.5g 8f⁵ 7g 8.2g³ 8.1s⁵ a8g² a7g a8g² Dec 27] compact gelding: unimpressive mover: fair handicapper: in fine form in first half of year, winning 3 races at Southwell in January and amateurs contest there in April: effective at 7f to 9.7f: acts on the all-weather and any turf going: usually visored, blinkered on reappearance: sometimes wanders under pressure: usually ridden up with pace of late: tough. *M. J. Ryan*

KING CURAN (USA) 5 b.g. Lear Fan (USA) 130 – Runaway Lady (USA) 73
(Caucasus (USA) 127) [1995 66: 10m 8.3g³ 9.2g³ 8.3g* 10g 8g* 8.3f 10f* a9.4g 8.3m⁴ 7.6m 8.3f 1996 10.3d 12.1d 10g 8.3g 8.3m⁶ 7m* 8f⁶ 8.3m 8.3f² 8.3g* 8m 7m⁴ 9.2g³ 8.9g 8.2g Oct 24] sturdy, good-bodied gelding: fair handicapper on his day: left A. Bailey after third 5-y-o start: won at Ayr in July and Hamilton in September: stays 1¼m: acts on firm and dead ground (ran badly only start on the all-weather): usually blinkered/visored: none too consistent: sold to join P. Bowen 6,500 gns Doncaster November Sales. *D. Haydn Jones*

KINGDOM EMPEROR 2 b.g. (Apr 8) Forzando 122 – Wrangbrook (Shirley 37
Heights 130) [1996 6m 6m 7.5m Jul 6] leggy, good-topped gelding: fifth live foal: brother to useful 1990 2-y-o 6f and 7f winner Punch N'Run, later winner at up to 1m in Italy, and half-brother to 3-y-o Wight (by Sharrood), 7f winner in Italy at 2 yrs: dam little form: behind in varied events, including a seller: gave trouble stalls on debut. *M. J. Camacho*

KINGDOM PEARL 2 ch.f. (Mar 24) Statoblest 120 – Sunfleet 59 (Red Sunset –
120) [1996 a6g Dec 27] 8,200F: fifth foal: half-sister to useful 3-y-o 7f winner Russian Music (by Forzando), fairly useful 4-y-o 6f (at 2 yrs) to 11.5f winner No Pattern (by Rock City) and 1993 2-y-o 5f winner Nera (by Robellino): dam (maiden) seemed suited by 1¼m: very slowly away and always behind in median auction maiden at Southwell. *M. J. Camacho*

KINGDOM PRINCESS 3 br.f. Forzando 122 – Song of Hope 103 (Chief Singer 69
131) [1995 –p: a5g⁵ 1996 a7g⁶ a8g* a7g* a8.5g⁶ 8.5d³ a8g Dec 27] lengthy filly: poor mover: fair performer: won median auction maiden in January and handicap in February, both at Southwell: not unduly knocked about final outing, first since March: stays 8.5f well: has raced only on fibresand and dead ground. *M. J. Camacho*

KINGFISHER BRAVE 3 b.g. Rock City 120 – Lambada Style (IRE) 81 –
(Dancing Brave (USA) 140) [1995 69: 6m⁵ a7g* 7m 8m³ 8g⁶ 1996 8g 10m 10.5g⁴ a9.4g 10.3d 11.9m Sep 6] leggy gelding: fair form when trained by S. Norton in 1995: well held in handicaps at 3 yrs: out-and-out galloper who should be suited by further than 10.5f: has worn tongue strap. *M. G. Meagher*

KINGFISHER MILL (USA) 2 ch.c. (Mar 4) Riverman (USA) 131 – Charming 70 p
Life (USA) [1996 7m Aug 7] second foal: half-brother to useful 3-y-o 11.5f and 1½m winner Dear Life (by Lear Fan): dam, Australian 7f winner, half-sister to Australian Grade 1 1m winner Zabeel: 5/1, over 7 lengths seventh of 12

to Bareeq in maiden at Kempton, held up after slowish start then keeping on: should improve. *Mrs J. Cecil*

KING KATO 3 b.g. Unfuwain (USA) 131 – Sharmood (USA) (Sharpen Up 93 p 127) [1995 NR 1996 10f³ 10.2d² Sep 30] 26,000Y: big, leggy gelding: has a long stride: fifth foal: half-brother to 9.4f winner Mr Mactavish (by Salse) and a winner in USA: dam lightly-raced American maiden: burly and green (tending to carry head a bit awkwardly when let down) on debut: 10 lengths clear of remainder when short-head second to Pasternak in maiden at Bath, travelling comfortably long way: will stay 1½m: has further improvement in him, and should win a race or 2 at 4 yrs. *G. Harwood*

KING OF BABYLON (IRE) 4 b.g. Persian Heights 129 – My My Marie – (Artaius (USA) 129) [1995 –: 10m⁶ 10d 10g 1996 a10g Apr 4] useful-looking gelding: little worthwhile form on flat: has joined F. Jordan: poor winning hurdler (has refused to race). *Lady Herries*

KING OF MUNSTER (AUS) 4 gr.g. Kenmare (FR) 125 – Artistic Princess – (AUS) (Luskin Star (AUS)) [1995 NR 1996 6m 5g a7g Jun 6] lengthy gelding: had 2 starts at 2 yrs, fair form (rated 76) placed in both: well beaten in 1996: sold 600 gns Newmarket July Sales: should stay 6f: sent to Sweden. *Mrs J. Cecil*

KING OF PEACE (IRE) 3 b.g. Persian Bold 123 – Pickety Place 83 (Prince 77 Tenderfoot (USA) 126) [1995 5s 5m 5f³ 8g 7d 1996 a8g a6g 12m 8.5g² 8.5g 9f* 9d² 7m⁶ 10g² 10d⁶ Sep 27] Irish gelding: third foal: half-brother to Irish 7f winner Monopoly Money (by Taufan) and roguish 5-y-o Wicklow Boy (by Roi Danzig): dam 1m/1¼m performer: trained at 2 yrs by D. Weld: only 2 starts for M. W. Easterby, well held at Southwell first 2 outings in 1996: fair form in handicaps back in Ireland, winning at Dundalk in August: stays 1¼m: acts on firm and dead ground: blinkered last 2 outings at 2 yrs and second 3-y-o start. *D. G. McArdle, Ireland*

KING OF PERU 3 br.c. Inca Chief (USA) – Julie's Star (IRE) 45 (Thatching 105 d 131) [1995 94+: 6f² 6m* 6f⁴ 6m 6g* 6g* 7.3d 1996 6g⁶ 6m³ 7f 7g* 7m 8m 6m 7g⁵ 6d² 7m⁵ Oct 8] tall, close-coupled colt: has a quick action: useful performer: won £10,900 handicap at Goodwood in May: below that form in minor events afterwards: stays 7f: acts on firm and dead ground. *A. P. Jarvis*

KING OF SHOW (IRE) 5 b.g. Green Desert (USA) 127 – Don't Rush (USA) 62 93 (Alleged (USA) 138) [1995 65d: a12g a7g 8g 8m⁵ 8.3g 9g 12.1m 9.2f⁴ 7.1f² 7f 7m 1996 7.1m⁵ 5m* 5m* 6m² 5m 6m 6m Oct 23] leggy gelding: modest performer: stepped back to 5f, won handicaps at Ayr and Musselburgh in July: very good second in minor event at Hamilton next start but towards rear in handicaps subsequently: best 4-y-o form over 1m, but clearly effective at sprint distances: acts on firm and soft ground: effective visored (was last 6 starts) or blinkered. *R. Allan*

KING OF SPARTA 3 b.c. Kefaah (USA) 124 – Khaizaraan (CAN) 97 (Sham 85 (USA)) [1995 NR 1996 10m⁶ 10m² 11.9m² 10.2f² 9m² 9f 10f* 10.3m Sep 11] good-topped colt: has scope: half-brother to several winners abroad: dam won Blue Seal Stakes: fairly useful performer: very easy task when winning 3-runner median auction maiden at Brighton in August: sold to join O. Sherwood 34,000 gns Newmarket Autumn Sales: stays 1½m: has raced only on top-of-the-ground: reportedly choked when faltering in lead third start. *L. M. Cumani*

KING OF THE EAST (IRE) 3 b.c. Fairy King (USA) – Rising Tide 101 (Red 101 Alert 127) [1995 88: 6m⁴ 5g⁵ 6d* 6d⁵ 1996 6g⁴ 6g* 7m 5m 6f 6d⁶ 5d⁵ 6d³ Sep 30] smallish, sturdy, attractive colt: has a quick action: useful performer: won minor event at Leicester in May: sold 28,000 gns Newmarket Autumn Sales: may prove best at 6f: acts on good to firm ground and good to soft ground: sent to Sweden. *M. R. Stoute*

KING OF TUNES (FR) 4 b.c. Chief Singer 131 – Marcotte (Nebos (GER) 129) 79 [1995 72+: 8s* 8.1s⁵ 1996 a10g* a10g² 8m⁴ 10m² Jun 21] fair handicapper, lightly raced: won at Lingfield in January: rather unlucky at Goodwood (after 3½-month absence) penultimate start: neck second there final outing: should stay 1½m: acts on equitrack and good to firm and soft ground. *J. J. Sheehan*

KING PARROT (IRE) 8 br.g. King of Spain 121 – Red Lory 87 (Bay Express 59 132) [1995 –, a54: a8g* a8g⁵ a8g³ a8g⁶ 7m 8g 7m 1996 a7g* a8g³ 7m* 7f* 7.1m* 8m⁴ Sep 25] leggy, workmanlike gelding: modest handicapper: successful at Lingfield in January and Salisbury in May (both apprentices), Lingfield again in June (seller) and Chepstow in July: creditable fourth in claimer after 2-month break on final start: stays 1m: acts on all-weather surfaces and firm ground: tried visored, no improvement: goes well fresh. *Lord Huntingdon*

KING RAMBO 5 b.g. Rambo Dancer (CAN) 107 – Infanta Maria 82 (King of –
Spain 121) [1995 66, a71: a5g⁴ a6g³ a5g⁶ 5g 5m² a5g* 5g 5.1g 5m⁴ 5m⁴ a5g² 5m⁴ a71
5m⁴ 6m* 5.1m a5g² 5g 6d⁴ a6g² a6g³ 1996 a5g² a5g² a5g⁴ a5g Apr 27] sturdy,
workmanlike gelding: fair handicapper: effective at 5f and 6f: acts on fibresand, best
turf form on a sound surface: sometimes carries head awkwardly: usually held up.
R. Hollinshead

KING RAT (IRE) 5 ch.g. King of Clubs 124 – Mrs Tittlemouse (Nonoalco 83
(USA) 131) [1995 88: 6f 6g 7g 6m 5m⁶ 5m⁴ 5m⁵ 5m* 5m² 7m* 7d 6s 7g 7f² 6f⁵
a9.4g⁶ 1996 7m 6.1m 6m 7m² 7.6d 7m 8m 7f a7g* Oct 5] tall, close-coupled gelding:
poor walker: easy mover: fairly useful handicapper: mostly below form at 5 yrs but
justified favouritism in claimer at Wolverhampton (claimed to join J. G. M. O'Shea's
stable £9,000) in October: effective at 5f to 7.5f: acts on the all-weather and firm
ground: best efforts in blinkers/visor: often wears crossed noseband: usually races
prominently. *T. J. Etherington*

KING RUFUS 3 ch.c. No Evil 98 – Djanila 45 (Fabulous Dancer (USA) 124) 68
[1995 NR 1996 10g⁴ 10f 10d 10m⁶ a10g Jul 12] close-coupled colt: third foal:
half-brother to successful 4-y-o Italian sprinter Lynette Joyce (by Emarati): dam
2-y-o 7f winner: fair form: stays 1¼m: acts on dead ground, much too free to post
when well beaten on firm, and finished tailed off on all-weather debut: has joined
J. L. Eyre. *J. R. Arnold*

KING'S ACADEMY (IRE) 3 b.c. Royal Academy (USA) 130 – Regal Beauty 89
(USA) (Princely Native (USA)) [1995 NR 1996 10d 10m³ 10m⁵ 8m* 8m* 10.1m
Sep 18] leggy colt: sixth foal: half-brother to several winners, notably top-class
middle-distance performer King's Theatre (by Sadler's Wells) and high-class 1988
2-y-o 6f to 1m winner High Estate (by Shirley Heights): dam ran twice: fairly useful
performer: won maiden at Ripon in July and handicap at Redcar in August: disappointing favourite on final start: sold 11,000 gns Newmarket Autumn Sales: best
form over 1m: acts on good to firm ground: sent to Saudi Arabia. *H. R. A. Cecil*

KINGS ASSEMBLY 4 b.c. Presidium 124 – To The Point 96 (Sharpen Up 127) 81
[1995 78: 8m⁴ 8m 8m⁶ 10g* 10d² 1996 10g⁵ 10m* 10d³ 10m⁴ 10d 10.3m 10.4g Oct
9] tall, leggy colt: fairly useful handicapper: won at Nottingham in April: similar
form when in frame afterwards: stays 1¼m: acts on good to firm and soft ground:
races prominently: has yet to run well when sweating and/or edgy. *P. W. Harris*

KINGS CAY (IRE) 5 b.g. Taufan (USA) 119 – Provocation 66 (Kings Lake 64
(USA) 133) [1995 –: 10.3g⁶ 12m⁶ 12.3f³ 12.3m 10.3g⁵ 14.6m 14.1m 14d⁶ 12f⁶
12m⁴ 9.9f 11.1f² 12.3m* 12f* 12f² 11.1g* 14.1f³ 12.3m⁵ 12m⁶ Aug 3] useful-looking
gelding: fair handicapper: won ladies events at Ripon and Hamilton and minor event
at Carlisle (in between) in summer: should stay further than 1¾m: acts on firm and
dead ground: tough. *T. H. Caldwell*

KINGSDOWN TRIX (IRE) 2 b.g. (May 5) Contract Law (USA) 108 – Three 50
of Trumps 129) [1996 6g 7f⁶ 5f 7g a8g⁵ Dec 20] IR 6,200F, IR 5,500Y,
3,000 2-y-o: third reported foal: half-brother to 7f winner Wild Ace (by Dancing Dissident): dam lightly-raced daughter of sister to Derby winner Charlottown: modest
form in varied maiden events. *A. Moore*

KINGS HARMONY (IRE) 3 b.g. Nordico (USA) – Kingston Rose (Tudor 71
Music 131) [1995 a72: a7g² 6.9s⁶ 6m⁴ a06g* 1996 6.1d⁶ 6f* 6.1m² 5.1m 6g² 7.1m³ a79
7f* 7f⁶ a7g² a6g² a6g Dec 20] lengthy gelding: fair performer: made virtually all to
win minor event at Brighton in April and handicap there in August: off course 2½
months, improved from when placed at Lingfield in November: met trouble in
running final start: stays 7f: acts on firm ground, goes well on the all-weather: seems
suited by forcing tactics. *P. J. Makin*

KINGSINGER (IRE) 2 b.c. (Mar 6) Fairy King (USA) – Silly Tune (IRE) 94 d
(Coquelin (USA) 121) [1996 5s* 5d² 5m³ 5m* 5d² 6g* 5m 8d³ 8s 7d 7.5d³ Dec
14] 20,000F, 11,000Y: lengthy, rather dipped-backed colt: second foal: dam unraced
half-sister to dam of Racing Post Trophy winner Seattle Rhyme: won maiden auction
at Doncaster and minor event at Salisbury in spring and Premio Primi Passi (by 2
lengths from listed winner Doctor Leckter) at Milan in July: subsequently left M.

Channon: fair form at best afterwards, mostly in listed/pattern events: seems to stay 7.5f: probably acts on any going. *P. Ceriotti, Italy*

KINGS NIGHTCLUB 3 b.f. Shareef Dancer (USA) 135 – Troy Moon (Troy – 137) [1995 –: 7g 1996 10.2g 11.7m⁵ 16m 11.9f⁵ Sep 3] no worthwhile form. *J. White*

KING SOUND 2 br.c. (Mar 23) Caerleon (USA) 132 – Flood (USA) (Riverman 108 p (USA) 131) [1996 7g⁴ 8m* 8g³ Oct 13] 550,000Y: close-coupled colt: fifth foal: closely related to a winner in Japan by Shadeed, and half-brother to 1½m winner Mr Flood (by Al Nasr): dam 6f winner in USA from family of Generous (by Caerleon) and Triptych: heavily-backed favourite, showed good turn of foot to win steadily-run minor event at Newbury in September by ½ length from Solo Mio, idling close home: improved good deal again when 6 lengths third to Revoque in Grand Criterium at Longchamp following month: will be suited by middle distances: open to further improvement. *J. H. M. Gosden*

KING'S THEATRE (IRE) 5 b.h. Sadler's Wells (USA) 132 – Regal Beauty 109 (USA) (Princely Native (USA)) [1995 8.5g³ 9.5s 12f³ 13f⁵ 11f 1996 10s² 12m³ Jun 16] angular, quite good-topped horse: top-class performer (rated 128) in 1994 for H. Cecil, second in the Derby and winning King George VI and Queen Elizabeth Diamond Stakes: trained by W. Mott in USA at 4 yrs, well below his 3-y-o form: favourite and tongue tied, again long way below best when head second to Murajja in minor event at Newbury, cruising up over 2f out but carrying head high and unable to get past: 6¼ lengths third of 4 to Strategic Choice in Gran Premio di Milano the following month: stayed 1½m well: best form on good to firm and dead ground: retired to Ballylinch Stud, Co. Kilkenny, at IR 6,000 gns (Oct 1st). *Saeed bin Suroor*

KINGS WITNESS (USA) 3 b.g. Lear Fan (USA) 130 – Allison's Deeds 98 (Sassafras (FR) 135) [1995 98p: 7.1m² 7g³ 7.1d* 7g⁵ 1996 10m⁴ 11.9g⁵ 10f⁶ 8d³ Oct 11] quite attractive gelding: best effort at 3 yrs when fourth to Musetta in minor event at Windsor on reappearance: disappointing afterwards: sold (W. Haggas to P. Nicholls) 22,000 gns Newmarket Autumn Sales: should prove as effective at 1m as 1¼m: tailed off only start on firm going (when edgy as well): bandaged off-fore second and third starts as 3-y-o: gelded. *W. J. Haggas*

KING UBAD (USA) 7 ch.g. Trempolino (USA) 135 – Glitter (FR) 70 (Reliance 28 II 137) [1995 –: 14f⁴ 14g 12.5g⁶ 14.4m 19m 12d 14d 17.2m⁴ 17.2f⁶ Jul 24] leggy gelding: bad form at best on flat in Britain: tried blinkered. *K. O. Cunningham-Brown*

KING UNO 2 b.g. (Apr 28) Be My Chief (USA) 122 – The Kings Daughter 79 54 + (Indian King (USA) 128) [1996 5m a7g 6g⁵ 6m 7g 7m Oct 28] 7,800F, 8,200Y: strong, good-topped gelding: has plenty of scope: good mover: third foal: half-brother to 5f and 6f winner The Kings Ransom (by Cadeaux Genereux): dam sprinter: first worthwhile form in maidens on third start: never dangerous and not knocked about in nurseries on last 3: better than he's shown so far and looks sort to win races at 3 yrs. *Mrs J. R. Ramsden*

KING WILLIAM 11 b.g. Dara Monarch 128 – Norman Delight (USA) (Val de – L'Orne (FR) 133) [1995 –: a16g a16g 1996 16d 17.9g Oct 9] robust gelding: staying handicapper: no worthwhile form last 2 seasons. *N. E. Berry*

KINLOCHEWE 3 b.f. Old Vic 136 – Reuval 102 (Sharpen Up 127) [1995 NR 102 1996 10g* 10.4m² 10m 10m² 12m³ Sep 7] close-coupled filly: seventh foal: half-sister to 1¼m winner Pitcroy (by Unfuwain), smart 6f and 7f winner Ardkinglass (by Green Desert) and useful 1¼m winner Jura (by Rousillon): dam suited by 1m: useful performer: won maiden at Ripon in April: placed in minor events won by Bathilde at York, Maralinga at Windsor (beaten neck) and Poppy Carew at Kempton: stays 1½m: raced only on a sound surface: sold 62,000 gns Newmarket December Sales. *H. R. A. Cecil*

KINNESCASH (IRE) 3 ch.g. Persian Heights 129 – Gayla Orchestra (Lord 56 Gayle (USA) 124) [1995 66: 6m³ 6m³ a6g⁵ 5.7h* 5.1m⁵ 8h 7g⁶ 10d* 8d 10g 1996 a8.5g 12d 10.2g 10.8g⁶ 8.3m 8.1g a12g² a12s Dec 19] leggy, unfurnished gelding: showed little first 6 starts at 3 yrs, then sold out of M. Saunders' stable 1,500 gns Doncaster September Sales: first run for 5 months, second in seller at Wolverhampton in November, easily best effort for new stable: seems to stay 1½m: acts on hard and dead ground, and on fibresand. *P. Bowen*

KINSHIP (IRE) 2 ch.c. (Feb 17) In The Wings 128 – Happy Kin (USA) (Bold – Hitter (USA)) [1996 7f⁵ 8d Oct 2] lengthy colt: half-brother to several winners, including William Hill Futurity winner Emmson (by Ela-Mana-Mou), who later stayed 1½m, and useful middle-distance stayer League Leader (by Shirley Heights): dam 6f to 8.5f winner in USA: well beaten in £8,600 event at Newbury (very green) and maiden at Salisbury 2½ months apart: sold 5,600 gns Doncaster October Sales. *P. W. Chapple-Hyam*

KINTWYN 6 b.g. Doulab (USA) 115 – Harriet Emma (USA) (Secretariat (USA)) 41 [1995 47, a77: a8g* a9.4g* a10g³ 8m⁴ a7g 8g⁵ 10f a10g a8g⁶ 1996 a9.4g³ a9.4g³ a75 a10g* a9.4g³ a10g⁴ 10.8f⁵ 10d a9.4g 11.6g a10s a9.4g Dec 7] compact gelding: has a quick action: fair handicapper on the all-weather, generally disappointing on turf: won at Lingfield in February: trained by C. C. Elsey until after fifth start: stays 1¼m: acts on fibresand and equitrack: tried visored/blinkered, no improvement. *W. R. Muir*

KIPPILAW 2 ch.f. (Mar 31) Selkirk (USA) 129 – Contralto 100 (Busted 134) 63 [1996 7m 7m² 6d Nov 8] leggy, sparely-made filly: closely related to 3 winners, including smart performers at around 1m Soprano (by Kris) and Enharmonic (by Diesis), and half-sister to several winners, including useful 1¼m winner Top Register (by Dixieland Band): dam 2-y-o 6f and 7f winner: best effort in maidens when 4 lengths second of 8 to Society Rose in steadily-run race at Newcastle: should stay 1m. *M. Johnston*

KIRA 6 b.m. Starry Night (USA) – Irish Limerick 89 (Try My Best (USA) 130) 75 [1995 56: 6g⁵ 7g³ 7f² 6f³ 6m⁶ a6g a6g² 1996 a6g² a6g* a5g* a6g² a6g⁴ a5g* a6g⁶ 5g* 5g⁵ 6.1m 6f² 5f* 5m* 5g³ 6g² 5m⁴ 5d 5g Oct 9] leggy mare: fair handicapper: enjoyed a fine season, winning at Southwell in January (minor event) and February, Wolverhampton in March, Newcastle in April and Redcar and Pontefract in August: best form at sprint distances: acts on firm going (probably on dead) and the all-weather: effective from front or held up: usually bandaged behind: tough and genuine. *J. L. Eyre*

KIRKADIAN 6 b.m. Norwick (USA) 125 – Pushkar (Northfields (USA)) [1995 – NR 1996 a16g a14g Jun 14] angular mare: sixth foal: sister to fairly useful stayer/ smart staying hurdler Hebridean, and half-sister to several winners, including smart 6f to 10.5f winner Eradicate (by Tender King) and high-class Bijou d'Inde (by Cadeaux Genereux): dam never ran: no sign of ability: sold 15,000 gns Doncaster July Sales. *N. Bycroft*

KIRKIE CROSS 4 b.f. Efisio 120 – Balgownie 43 (Prince Tenderfoot (USA) – 126) [1995 –: 8g⁶ 9.2f³ 13.1f³ 12.1f⁴ 10.9g 1996 a14g Nov 29] no sign of ability. *K. G. Wingrove*

KIROV LADY (IRE) 3 b.f. Soviet Lad (USA) 94 – Cestrefeld 94 (Capistrano 78 120) [1995 77?: 5.1h² 6m* 7m² 6.1m⁵ 8m⁵ 1996 a10g⁴ 8.1g 8m⁶ 8f⁵ 8.1g⁶ 8.1m Sep 17] leggy filly: fair handicapper: seems to stay 1¼m: has raced only on a sound surface on turf: sent to Barbados. *R. Hannon*

KIROV PROTEGE (IRE) 4 b.g. Dancing Dissident (USA) 119 – Still River (Kings Lake (USA) 133) [1995 44, a57: a8g² a8g⁵ a8g* a8.5g² a9.4g² a8g a8.5g 10m⁴ 10.3m⁶ 9.7m² 10m 9.7g⁵ 10f³ 10m⁴ 9m a11g 1996 10.8f 10d 12f⁴ 9.7g³ 7.6m 10d 10m a10g⁵ a10s⁶ a6g a8g a10g Dec 13] smallish, leggy gelding: little show in 1996, leaving H. Collinridge after fourth start and Mrs. L. Siddall after seventh: stays 1¼m: acts on fibresand and good to firm ground: tried in blinkers and visor. *Mrs L. C. Jewell*

KIROV ROYALE 5 b.m. Rambo Dancer (CAN) 107 – Gay Princess (Lord Gayle (USA) 124) [1995 NR 1996 8d Oct 2] modest maiden as 3-y-o: tailed off only outing on flat since: should stay beyond 1m. *Mark Campion*

KISMETIM 6 b.g. Dowsing (USA) 124 – Naufrage (Main Reef 126) [1995 47: 55 d a16g a12g 12.5g a12g⁴ 12g⁶ 11.8g a12g² a11g⁵ a11g² a12g⁵ a12g⁶ a8g 12.1g 13s 11.8d 11.1g a7g a7g a11g a13g 12.3m a12g Nov 25] lengthy, workmanlike gelding: best effort for some time when second in seller at Southwell in February, first of 2 starts for W. Haigh: well beaten afterwards, blinkered/visored 4 of last 6 starts: stays 1¾m: acts on fibresand and on good to firm and dead going: carries head high: has joined G. Kelly. *D. W. Chapman*

KISSAVOS 10 ch.g. Cure The Blues (USA) – Hairbrush (USA) (Sir Gaylord) [1995 46d: a8g⁴ a8g a8g a8.5g 9.2g 8g 7.1m⁵ 7f 8m 8.1d 1996 a10g a10g Dec 13] small, angular gelding: poor handicapper: well beaten in minor events at Lingfield in 1996: stays 1m: acts on any going, including all-weather surfaces: sometimes bandaged behind: no improvement in blinkers (not tried for long time) or visor: inconsistent. *B. J. Meehan*

KISSEL 4 b.f. Warning 136 – Ice Chocolate (USA) 77 (Icecapade (USA)) [1995 – 8v² 8s⁵ 8m² 8g* 1996 7.1d⁵ 9.2g⁵ 6m 10m⁶ 8g Sep 3] leggy ex-French filly: third foal: half-sister to modest middle-distance winner Ice Rebel (by Robellino): dam, 1m and 8.5f winner at 4 yrs, is out of half-sister to dam of Oh So Sharp: trained at 3 yrs by A. Fabre, showing fairly useful form before winning minor event at La Teste: sold 16,000 gns Newmarket December (1995) Sales: well beaten in Britain, leaving A. Harrison after fourth start: stays 1m: acts on good to firm and heavy ground. *S. E. Kettlewell*

KISSING GATE (USA) 3 ch.f. Easy Goer (USA) – Love's Reward (Nonoalco – (USA) 131) [1995 62: 8.1s⁵ a8g⁴ a8.5g* 1996 a10g 12s Mar 25] progressive form in 2-y-o maidens, winning weak event at Wolverhampton in December: ran badly in handicaps at Lingfield early in 1996: should stay beyond 8.5f: acts on fibresand: covered by Salse. *R. Charlton*

KISS ME AGAIN (IRE) 3 b.f. Cyrano de Bergerac 120 – Now Serving (Super 70 Concorde (USA) 128) [1995 80: 6.1m⁴ 5g³ 6m* 6m* 6.5m 1996 6s⁵ 6m³ 8f⁴ 7.1s 6.1s Oct 22] rather sparely-made filly: has a quick action: fair form: sold 7,600 gns Newmarket Autumn Sales: probably stays 1m: acts on firm ground, well beaten on soft: sometimes hangs left: sent to Holland. *R. Hannon*

KISTENA (FR) 3 gr.f. Miswaki (USA) 124 – Mabrova 108 (Prince Mab (FR) 123 124) [1995 5g* 5.5g³ 5m³ 6g² 5g³ 6d⁶ 1996 6.5g⁵ 5.5m* 5.5g² 5m* 6m² 6g* 6g* 5d* Oct 6]

In most other years Kistena would have stood out among French sprinters, but this was stable-companion Anabaa's year, not just in France but in Europe. However, Kistena managed to upstage him in the Prix de l'Abbaye de Longchamp, and provided she recovers satisfactorily from an injury sustained there she should have a good chance of the limelight in 1997 with Anabaa retired. The Abbaye had a typical look to it in that the overseas challenge was numerically strong, outweighing the French by seven to three, but the July Cup and Maurice de Gheest winner Anabaa started a red-hot favourite. Progressive Kistena was a 146/10 chance, with the third French-trained runner Don't Worry Me a rank outsider having finished behind Kistena in four previous meetings. Chief hopes of a British victory rested with the fillies who had contested the Abbaye the year before—winner Hever Golf Rose, the third Eveningperformance and fourth Easy Option. They were accompanied by Struggler, Rambling Bear (who became upset in the stalls), the Molecomb winner Carmine Lake (the only two-year-old in the line-up), with Ailleacht a lone forlorn hope for Ireland. Notable absentees were the two colts who had dominated the top five-furlong races in England, Pivotal and Mind Games, both already retired, the former just days before the Abbaye. Looking in good shape, Kistena was held up in the early stages, with her stable companion struggling to cope with Eveningperformance's speed. When Anabaa improved under pressure to lead a furlong out, Kistena was pulled out to cover his move, and, responding to strong driving, she got up near the finish to win by a neck. Hever Golf Rose was two lengths away in third ahead of Easy Option and Carmine Lake, neither of whom had had the best of runs. Kistena thus ended the eighteen-year domination of the Abbaye by British and Irish stables, during which time French horses had filled second place five times and third place six. The Head stable had been responsible for the last home-trained winner, the two-year-old Sigy; the French haven't had the first three in their top sprint since Lianga prevailed in a finish of short heads with Primo Rico and Mendip Man in 1975.

Only those closest to Kistena would have had much of an inkling that she was a high-class sprinter in the making as a two-year-old. She had made a winning debut over the Abbaye course and distance but had consistently shown just fairly useful form during the rest of her first season, gaining places in the

Prix de l'Abbaye de Longchamp—
champion sprinter Anabaa (dark cap) is turned over by stable-companion Kistena

Prix du Bois and Prix de Cabourg. She was one of three fillies from her stable who made their reappearance in the Prix Imprudence at Evry, usually a Guineas trial; Kistena came off worst of the three in fifth place, was kept to sprinting for the rest of the season and did not look back, finishing first or second in her remaining seven starts. Her next three outings, which included wins at Evry in a minor event and a listed race (short-heading Croft Pool in the latter) earned her another crack at a pattern race in the Prix de Ris-Orangis at the same course in July. This time the photo went against her as she was caught on the line by Miesque's Son, but she gained compensation with a clear-cut victory over Titus Livius in the Prix de Meautry at Deauville in August and earned her place in the Abbaye field with another two-and-a-half-length win, this time from Don't Worry Me, in the Prix de Seine-et-Oise at Maisons-Laffitte in September. After the Abbaye, Kistena was being considered for the Breeders' Cup Sprint until it was found that she, like Anabaa, had chipped her left knee at Longchamp. Her trainer was hopeful that Kistena would recover sufficiently to race again at four.

There was just a head between Kistena's sire and maternal grandsire, Miswaki and Prince Mab, in the 1980 Prix de la Salamandre but their careers went in different directions afterwards, Miswaki commanding a stud fee in Kentucky of 35,000 dollars in 1996, Prince Mab ending up as a stallion in Denmark. Miswaki gets winners over a variety of distances, and Kistena does not have an obvious sprinting pedigree. Her half-sister Spend A Rubble (by Spend A Buck) won four mile-and-a-quarter claimers in France at three. Their dam Mabrova won over seven furlongs on her debut at two and she showed useful form when fourth in the Prix des Reservoirs, then failed to progress at three. The other winners out of grandam Makarova have all been successful over middle distances, two of them also over jumps. Makarova was a middle distance winner too; the third dam Midou a miler, and a goodish one at that judged on her fourth place in Allez France's Poule d'Essai des Pouliches. There is plenty of speed further back in the family however. Midou is out of the Cheveley Park winner Midget, dam and grandam respectively of two more

Wertheimer et Frere's "Kistena"

winners of that race, Mige and Ma Biche. Midou is the grandam of smart sprinter Mujadil, winner of the Cornwallis Stakes. Mabrova's third foal, the two-year-old Goldnaya (by Goldneyev), has yet to race. She has a filly foal by Sillery and is in foal to Last Tycoon.

Kistena (FR) (gr.f. 1993)	Miswaki (USA) (ch 1978)	Mr Prospector (b 1970)	Raise A Native Gold Digger
		Hopespringseternal (ch 1971)	Buckpasser Rose Bower
	Mabrova (gr 1987)	Prince Mab (ch 1978)	Targowice Princess Mab
		Makarova (ro 1975)	Nijinsky Midou

Kistena, a sturdy filly, seems equally effective at five and six furlongs; she is yet to race on extremes of going. If fully recovered, she should enjoy a good season in the top sprints and may be open to further progress. *Mme C. Head, France*

KITTY GALORE (IRE) 2 b.f. (Feb 18) Silver Kite (USA) 111 – Sudbury (IRE) 44
69 (Auction Ring (USA) 123) [1996 6m⁵ 5.9f³ 6m 7m 7m Oct 8] 3,000Y: close-coupled filly: first foal: dam 6f and 1m winner, ran only at 2 yrs: plater, best effort when third in maiden auction event at Carlisle in July: sold 500 gns Doncaster November Sales. *M. Dods*

KITTY KITTY CANCAN 3 b.f. Warrshan (USA) 117 – Kittycatoo Katango 73
(USA) (Verbatim (USA)) [1995 –p: 7g 1996 10m² 12m 9m 11.6m⁵ 12m 11.8g⁴ a10g³
Dec 31] rather unfurnished filly: fair maiden handicapper: should stay at least

1½m: acts on equitrack, raced only on a sound surface on turf: blinkered last 2 starts. *Lady Herries*

KIWUD   3 ch.f. Superlative 118 – Mimining 83 (Tower Walk 130) [1995 –: 5m 5m   44
5g 6.1d 1996 5d 5g 6.1m a5g 5g² 5f 5g 5g Jul 2] strong, stocky sprint type: unimpressive mover: poor maiden sprint handicapper: blinkered last 4 starts. *T. W. Donnelly*

KLIPSPINGER   3 ch.f. Formidable (USA) 125 – Distant Relation (Great   a68 d
Nephew 126) [1995 –: 5m⁶ 6g⁵ 5m 1996 a6g* a8g a6g² a6g² a6g³ 5m a5g⁵ a6g a6g
a6g Dec 3] strong, lengthy filly: bad mover: fair performer at best on the all-weather: won seller at Southwell in May: little form on turf: stays 6f: acts on fibresand: visored/blinkered fourth to seventh 3-y-o starts. *B. S. Rothwell*

KLONDIKE CHARGER (USA)   2 b.c. (May 15) Crafty Prospector (USA) –   68
Forever Waving (USA) (Hoist The Flag (USA)) [1996 7m 6m 7d Oct 28] $150,000Y: neat colt: ninth foal: brother to a winner in USA, closely related to a Grade 1-placed winner in USA by Miswaki and half-brother to 3 winners here and abroad, including 10.1f winner Jesters Farewell (by The Minstrel): dam, winner at up to 9f, is half-sister to top 1976 American 3-y-o filly Revidere: sire stakes-placed winner at up to 8.5f: signs of ability in maidens won by Bareeq at Kempton and Speedball at Newbury: will stay 1m: showed nothing on dead ground. *B. W. Hills*

KLOSTERS   4 ch.f. Royal Match 117 – Snowy Autumn (Deep Run 119) [1995   –
NR 1996 a8g Dec 11] first foal: dam winning hurdler: showed little in NH Flat race, novice hurdle and Lingfield claimer. *R. J. Hodges*

KNAVE   3 b.g. Prince Sabo 123 – Royal Agnes 71 (Royal Palace 131) [1995 66:   57 d
7m⁶ 8.2d 7g 7f⁴ 6.9m⁶ a7g³ 1996 7s⁵ 8.2g 8.1g 11.1g 9.2g⁴ Jun 12] quite attractive gelding: left R. Hannon's stable after second 3-y-o start: seemingly modest at best nowadays: dropped in class and visored, easily best effort for new stable when fourth in seller at Hamilton on final outing (still long way below best): should prove effective beyond 7f: acts on firm ground and fibresand: also visored (best effort) final 2-y-o start. *P. Monteith*

KNOBBLEENEEZE   6 ch.g. Aragon 118 – Proud Miss (USA) (Semi-Pro) [1995   80
78: 7s⁵ 7m⁴ 8g⁴ 8m 7f 8.1g² 7g 6m 7g⁴ 7g* 7g* 7.6d² 8d⁴ 7g 7g 8m 1996 8s 7s 7g 7s⁶
7.3s² 7m* 8m⁴ 8f⁵ 8d³ 7.3m⁵ 7.6d 7.1f 7.3m⁴ 7m 7g 7g 7s 7g Nov 2] sturdy gelding: fairly useful handicapper: won at Chester in June: well held last 5 starts: stays 8.3f: acts on firm and heavy ground and on equitrack: visored: successful for apprentice. *M. R. Channon*

KNOTTY HILL   4 b.g. Green Ruby (USA) 104 – Esilam 62 (Frimley Park 109)   77
[1995 NR 1996 8g⁵ 8f² 8s⁶ 7m³ 8f 8d 7m³ 8s Nov 9] tall, workmanlike gelding: third foal: dam, 2-y-o 5f winner here, won 6 races (5f to 1m) in Italy: fair form: clipped heels and fell final start: stays 1m: acts on firm ground, seems unsuited by a soft surface: often slowly away: inconsistent. *R. Craggs*

KNOWN SECRET (USA)   3 ch.g. Known Fact (USA) 135 – Loa (USA)   –
(Hawaii) [1995 –p: 6.1d 7.1s 1996 8s⁵ 8.2m Apr 30] workmanlike gelding: no form in maidens (backward) and a handicap. *Mrs J. R. Ramsden*

KOATHARY (USA)   5 b.g. Capote (USA) – Jeffo (USA) (Ridan (USA)) [1995   86
68d: 10g 10m³ 10d 10d 12.1d 10d 1996 10g⁴ 10.8f⁴ 10d³ 11.4m 10g 9f* 8.1d* 9m*
Sep 26] big, lengthy gelding: improved into a fairly useful handicapper: successful last 3 starts at Goodwood and Sandown in August and Goodwood again (apprentices, by 5 lengths) in September: best form at 1m/9f: acts on firm and dead ground: held up. *L. G. Cottrell*

KOLI   3 b.f. Sayf El Arab (USA) 127 – Miss Willow 60 (Horage 124) [1995 NR   –
1996 10s Aug 31] close-coupled filly: first foal: dam stayed 1¼m: 33/1, well beaten in maiden at Ripon, soon tailed off before some late progress: moved poorly to post. *H. J. Collingridge*

KOMASTA   2 b.c. (Mar 27) Komaite (USA) – Sky Fighter 43 (Hard Fought 125)   64
[1996 a5g³ 5.9g 5m⁴ a5g a6g a6g a7g* Dec 28] 400Y: rather leggy colt: second foal: dam, poor maiden, stayed 1½m: modest performer: won maiden auction at Wolverhampton by 7 lengths, making all: will stay beyond 7f: acts on good to firm ground and fibresand: sometimes sweating. *Capt. J. Wilson*

KOMIAMAITE   4 b.g. Komaite (USA) – Mia Scintilla 54 (Blazing Saddles   58 d
(AUS)) [1995 58: a6g a8g² a8g⁵ a9.4g² 12g a7g a7g³ 6m 8g a8g a9.4g⁵ 1996 a8g*

a8g³ a8g⁵ a11g⁶ a8g a7g³ a9.4g a9.4g Nov 25] modest handicapper: gained first success in amateurs event at Southwell in January: sold out of S. R. Bowring's stable 2,700 gns Doncaster March Sales after seventh start: finds 7f a bare minimum, and stays 9.4f: acts on fibresand, no form on turf: effective blinkered or not, visored (below form) once: usually held up. *D. Burchell*

KOMLUCKY   4 b.f. Komaite (USA) – Sweet And Lucky (Lucky Wednesday   53
124) [1995 52d: a6g⁴ a6g⁶ a6g a5g⁶ 8m 5.9f⁴ 7g 1996 a7g³ a8g 7.1g 6g⁵ a7g² 6m² 6m
a6g 8m a7g² 6.9f⁴ 7f² 7d² 7g* 7g a7g⁴ a7g⁶ Nov 30] leggy filly: modest handicapper:
won 18-runner race at Catterick in September: stays 7f: acts on fibresand and on firm
and dead ground: blinkered/visored: takes keen hold. *A. B. Mulholland*

KOMODO (USA)   4 ch.g. Ferdinand (USA) – Platonic Interest (USA) (Drone)   42
[1995 63d: a10g² 8d⁶ 10m 8.3m² 8.1g² 7g⁴ a7g⁶ a8g a7g a8g 1996 a10g 8m 10m
8.3m 6.9m⁵ 8.1g a10g³ a8g a10g a10g Dec 30] sparely-made gelding: one-time
modest maiden who has deteriorated: sold out of K. Cunningham-Brown's stable 500
gns Ascot August Sales after sixth start: effective at 7f to 1¼m: acts on good to firm
and heavy going and on equitrack: no improvement in blinkers. *J. E. Long*

KOMREYEV DANCER   4 b.g. Komaite (USA) – L'Ancressaan 67 (Dalsaan   80
125) [1995 72, a84: a8.5g² a8.5g* a8.5g⁴ a10g⁶ a9.4g² 10.3g⁴ 8d⁴ 9.9m² 12.3m   a84
12.3m a9.4g 10.3m 10m³ 10.5g⁴ 10g⁵ 1996 a9.4g⁴ a9.4g a9.4g² a8g⁵ a10g⁴ 9.9m*
10.3g 10g* 9.9f³ 10f 10m³ 10g⁶ 10m² 10.1m⁶ Jul 27] leggy gelding: has a round
action: fairly useful handicapper: won at Beverley in April and Ripon in May: ran
creditably most starts afterwards: stays 10.3f, probably not 1½m: acts on firm
ground, dead and goes well on all-weather surfaces: blinkered (well below form)
fourth 4-y-o start. *A. Bailey*

KOORDINAITE   2 b.f. (May 13) Komaite (USA) – Fair Dino 48 (Thatch (USA)   –
136) [1996 6g 6d 6m Sep 6] 500Y: workmanlike filly: half-sister to fairly useful 1½m
to 2m winner Peggy Carolyn (by Alias Smith): dam stayed 1m: well beaten in seller
and claimers. *W. J. Musson*

KORALOONA (IRE)   3 b.g. Archway (IRE) 115 – Polynesian Charm (USA)   –
(What A Pleasure (USA)) [1995 NR 1996 8m 8.3g⁶ 8.3m 10m 9.7d Oct 21] 14,000F,
9,500Y: half-brother to several winners, including Lake of Loughrea (up to 1¾m,
also fair chaser, by Kings Lake) and Tiger Trap (6f, by Al Hattab): dam half-sister to
smart 1969 American 2-y-o Clover Lane: seems of little account. *G. B. Balding*

KORAMBI   4 ch.g. Kris 135 – Green Lucia 116 (Green Dancer (USA) 132)   98
[1995 93: 10m⁶ 12m⁴ 12g* 12f 12m⁴ 10v⁶ 12m 1996 10m 12m³ 12g Sep 29] quite
attractive, unfurnished gelding: useful performer: 20/1, best effort when third to
Backgammon in rated stakes at Epsom in June, making most and caught near line: in
need of race, tailed off in £44,700 handicap at Ascot nearly 4 months later: stays
1½m: acts on good to firm ground: usually ridden up with pace. *C. E. Brittain*

KOSEVO (IRE)   2 b.g. (Apr 5) Shareef Dancer (USA) 135 – Kallista (Zeddaan   –
130) [1996 9f⁵ Sep 28] brother to 2 winners, notably German 1000 Guineas winner
Kazoo, and half-brother to winners in Germany (by King of Clubs) and Ireland (NH
Flat race, by Top Ville): dam won from 7f (at 2 yrs) to 9f in Germany: 2/1 and visored,
distant last of 5 in maiden at Redcar, reluctant to race early and eased right up
from 2f out: sold to join S. Mellor 4,000 gns Newmarket Autumn Sales and gelded.
M. R. Stoute

KOSSOLIAN   3 b.f. Emarati (USA) 74 – Cwm Deri (IRE) (Alzao (USA) 117)   –
[1995 72: 5m² 5.1m 6.1m* 6g 6.5m 7g 1996 6m 5.7g May 20] lengthy filly: fair
winner at 2 yrs, ran poorly in handicaps at 3 yrs: sold 1,800 gns Newmarket July
Sales: stays 6.5f: far from tractable, and has twice hung badly right: blinkered final
start: sent to Macau. *B. Palling*

KOWTOW   3 b.f. Forzando 122 – Aim To Please 102 (Gunner B 126) [1995 NR   –
1996 7d 7m 8f⁵ 7.1m 10.2m 6g a8.5g 10.2d 8m⁶ 8m Oct 28] deep-bodied filly:
third foal: half-sister to 1m and 1¼m winner William Tell (by Chief Singer): dam
middle-distance performer: bought out of R. Charlton's stable 1,600 gns Newmarket
Autumn (1995) Sales: poor maiden: will stay 1¼m: sold 1,050 gns Ascot December
Sales. *M. D. I. Usher*

KRALINGEN   4 ch.f. Move Off 112 – Elitist 72 (Keren 100) [1995 –: 10m 7m   –
8.1d 12.3f 8f 10m a12g 1996 15d Aug 10] sturdy filly: no worthwhile form on flat.
N. Chamberlain

KRASNIK (IRE) 3 br.g. Roi Danzig (USA) – Kermesse (IRE) (Reference Point – 139) [1995 NR 1996 12m 14.1g Oct 24] first foal: dam never ran: well beaten in maidens. *Mrs D. Haine*

KRATZ (IRE) 3 b.g. Prince Rupert (FR) 121 – Some Spice (Horage 124) [1995 – 50d: 6g⁵ 7m² 7f 7.5m³ a7g⁴ 7.9g 7.5d⁵ 7d 7f a8g 1996 a8g⁵ a7g Jan 26] leggy, unfurnished gelding: poor performer: stays 1m: acts on fibresand: usually blinkered/visored. *B. S. Rothwell*

KRISCLIFFE 3 ch.c. Kris 135 – Lady Norcliffe (USA) (Norcliffe (CAN)) [1995 83 78: 6f* 6g³ 1996 9m² 8.1d⁶ a7g 10m⁴ 12m 10m 10.5s Oct 5] good-topped colt: poor mover: fairly useful handicapper: probably stays 1½m: acts on firm ground, reportedly finished lame on dead, tailed off on fibresand and soft: has joined G. Lewis. *Miss Gay Kelleway*

KRISTAL BREEZE 4 ch.f. Risk Me (FR) 127 – Mistral's Dancer (Shareef 62 Dancer (USA) 135) [1995 –: 8.2g 9.7m 10.3m 10.2m⁵ a12g a12g a8g 10d⁴ 1996 10.1s 10g⁴ 12d² 10d* 11.1m⁶ 11.6m* 12.3m⁵ 12g* 10g* 11.9g 10g⁴ 12g Nov 1] lengthy, rather sparely-made filly: modest handicapper: successful 4 times in 1996 (2 sellers), at Leicester in May, Windsor in July, Salisbury in August and Brighton in October: effective at 1¼m and 1½m: acts on good to firm and dead ground: visored (no form) twice on fibresand: genuine. *W. R. Muir*

KRISTAL'S PARADISE (IRE) 4 b.f. Bluebird (USA) 125 – Kristal's Pride 100 (Kris 135) [1995 99: 10g³ 12g³ 14m* 16g* 16.2d⁵ 16d* 16m² 14g³ 1996 16.2g⁴ 16g 13.9m² 18g² 15d² Oct 6] rather leggy, attractive filly: poor mover: useful handicapper: runner-up in small fields last 3 starts, to Celeric in listed rated stakes at York, to Canon Can in minor event at Pontefract, and to Snow Princess in listed race at Milan: stayed 2¼m: acted on good to firm and soft ground: front runner/raced prominently: game and reliable: stud. *J. L. Dunlop*

KRISTOPHER 2 ch.c. (Mar 23) Kris 135 – Derniere Danse (Gay Mecene (USA) – 128) [1996 7g³ 8.2s Oct 31] strong, workmanlike colt: third foal: dam half-sister to smart French sprinter Divine Danse and very smart 6f to 1m performer Pursuit of Love: burly, no form in Newmarket Challenge Cup or maiden at Nottingham. *J. W. Hills*

KRYSTAL DAVEY (IRE) 2 b.g. (Jan 30) Classic Music (USA) – Robin Red 57 Breast 74 (Red Alert 127) [1996 5m⁶ a5g a6g Dec 27] 8,200Y: sixth reported foal: half-brother to 5f winners Pious Bird (by Tender King) and Rosey Nosey (at 2 yrs in 1994, by Cyrano de Bergerac): dam 2-y-o 5f winner, is granddaughter of Irish 1000 Guineas winner Princess Trudy: modest form in maiden events at Ripon (June) and Southwell (2): almost certainly a sprinter. *T. D. Barron*

KRYSTAL MAX (IRE) 3 b.g. Classic Music (USA) – Lake Isle (IRE) 72 (Caerleon (USA) 132) [1995 75, a85: 5f* 5m⁴ 5m³ 5m⁴ 5m⁶ 5g⁶ a5g* a6g* 1996 a88 a5g* a7g* 5d⁶ 6.1g 6m⁵ 7s a6g a7g Dec 7] smallish, good-topped gelding: carries condition: fairly useful performer on the all-weather, successful in handicap at Lingfield in January and claimer there in February: well below form after 5-month absence last 2 starts: fair on turf: stays 7f: acts on firm and dead ground (below form only outing on soft) and goes well on all-weather surfaces: usually apprentice ridden. *T. D. Barron*

KUALA LIPIS (USA) 3 b.c. Lear Fan (USA) 130 – Caerna (USA) (Caerleon 91 (USA) 132) [1995 NR 1996 8d⁵ 10m⁴ 7.9m* 10m⁶ Aug 2] $16,000F: strong, angular colt: fourth foal: half-brother to minor winners in USA by Mt Livermore and Buddy: dam never ran: fairly useful form: won 6-runner maiden at York in June, off bridle 3f out before forging ahead inside last: respectable sixth to Fahim in £34,000 handicap at Goodwood final start: stays 1¼m: yet to race on extremes of going. *P. F. I. Cole*

KUANTAN (USA) 3 b.g. Gone West (USA) – Cuddly Doll (USA) (Bold Hour) 101 ? [1995 101: 5f* 6m⁶ 6d² 7g 1996 6g⁴ 7g³ 8.2m 8m⁶ Jun 27] good-topped gelding: has a long stride: freeze-fired after second 2-y-o start: mostly disappointing since winning Windsor Castle Stakes on debut: best effort at 3 yrs when fourth in minor event at Goodwood on reappearance: sold 5,000 gns Newmarket Autumn Sales: stays 7f: takes a keen hold: usually difficult at stalls at 2 yrs: has worn net muzzle, and was taken early/steadily to post in 1996: fitted with severe bridle and mounted on track final start: not a betting proposition. *P. F. I. Cole*

KUD

KUDA 2 b.f. (Jan 15) Classic Secret (USA) 91 – Deverells Walk (IRE) (Godswalk – (USA) 130) [1996 5d 6g May 23] 1,700F, 1,000Y: workmanlike filly: first foal: dam well beaten all 3 starts in Ireland at 2 yrs: no form in seller and claimer: sold 620 gns Doncaster July Sales. *J. Norton*

KUDOS BLUE 3 b.f. Elmaamul (USA) 125 – Don't Be Shy (IRE) (Kafu 120) – [1995 –: a7g 7f 1996 8g 9.9g 7m 8.5m Jul 16], small, light-framed filly: no worthwhile form. *J. D. Bethell*

KULEPOPSIE (IRE) 3 b.f. Contract Law (USA) 108 – Flight Fantasy (USA) 54 – (Air Forbes Won (USA)) [1995 NR 1996 a9.4g6 Nov 25] first foal: dam 1½m winner: well beaten in claimer at Wolverhampton on debut. *A. B. Mulholland*

KULSHI MOMKEN 3 ch.g. In The Wings 128 – Gesedeh 117 (Ela-Mana-Mou – 132) [1995 NR 1996 10.5d 8m 12m Aug 18] fifth foal: dam, suited by 1¼m, half-sister to Ardross and smart middle-distance filly Larrocha: sold out of R. Phillips' stable 2,600 gns Newmarket July Sales: no sign of ability: blinkered second start: sold 500 gns Doncaster November Sales. *J. Norton*

KUMAIT (USA) 2 b. or br.c. (Apr 10) Danzig (USA) – Colour Chart (USA) 122 86 (Mr Prospector (USA)) [1996 6f 6m3 7d6 6m2 6m3 6g3 6g* Nov 1] strong-quartered, attractive colt: fluent mover: second foal: brother to 3-y-o 7f winner Chirico: dam won 1m (at 2 yrs) to 1¼m in France and is daughter of champion Canadian filly Rainbow Connection: fairly useful form: made all in steadily-run maiden at Newmarket in November to win by 1¾ lengths from Elnadim, quickening 2f out and responding well (has sometimes looked weak finisher): best form at up to 6f (set strong pace over 7f on dead): wears tongue strap nowadays. *Saeed bin Suroor*

KUMMEL KING 8 b.g. Absalom 128 – Louise 71 (Royal Palace 131) [1995 61: – 7m 6m2 7.6m 8.1d5 1996 7d 6.9d 8f 8m 6.9f Jul 6] compact gelding: modest performer in 1995: tailed off all starts at 8 yrs. *E. J. Alston*

KUNG FRODE 4 ch.c. Interrex (CAN) – Harmony Heights 67 (Music Boy 124) 66 [1995 63: 5g 5d5 5.1m 1996 a5g4 a5g5 a6g a6g Sep 21] strong colt: fair handicapper: shaped well when fourth at Southwell on reappearance: below form afterwards: best efforts at 5f: acts on fibresand and dead ground, well beaten on good to firm. *B. A. McMahon*

KUNUCU (IRE) 3 ch.f. Bluebird (USA) 125 – Kunuz (Ela-Mana-Mou 132) 94 [1995 93: 5g3 5m* 5m* 6g2 5d4 5.2g4 5.2m* 5.2m4 5g2 5s4 1996 5g3 6m 5m* 5f 5m 5m 5.2m5 6d4 5s6 5g Oct 19] good-quartered filly: good mover: fairly useful handicapper: won at Thirsk in May: best subsequent effort, in face of stiff task, when fifth of 9 to Struggler in minor event at Newbury: stays 6f but best form at 5f: acts on good to firm and dead ground. *T. D. Barron*

KURY GIRL 3 b.f. Superlative 118 – Azubah 67 (Castle Keep 121) [1995 NR – 1996 a5g5 a6g Feb 5] 6,000Y: first foal: dam 7f to 1½m winner: well held in median auction maidens at Lingfield (signs of ability) and Southwell: covered by Contract Law. *J. A. Harris*

KUSTOM KIT (IRE) 3 ch.c. Timeless Times (USA) 99 – Friendly Song 48 – (Song 132) [1995 68: 5g* 5m3 5m 6g6 5.2g 1996 5d a5g 5m a6g a5g Jul 26] small colt: well beaten in handicaps at 3 yrs: likely to prove best at 5f: has joined S. R. Bowring. *B. A. McMahon*

KUSTOM KIT KLASSIC 2 b.c. (Mar 28) Chilibang 120 – Norvi (Viking – (USA)) [1996 a6g a8.5g4 Nov 30] 3,000F, 11,500Y: first foal: dam unraced: soundly beaten in maidens at Southwell and Wolverhampton. *S. R. Bowring*

KUSTOM KIT XPRES 2 gr.f. (Mar 3) Absalom 128 – Miss Serlby 65 (Runnett 69 125) [1996 5m2 5f4 6m5 a6g a5g Dec 3] 3,000F, 8,400Y: angular filly: half-sister to a? 2-y-o sprint winners Risk Me's Girl (by Risk Me) and Left Stranded (by Governor General): dam maiden, best at 5f: modest form in maidens for M. McCormack in first half of year: never a threat at Southwell for new trainer last 2 starts, blinkered on final one: stays 6f. *S. R. Bowring*

KUTAN (IRE) 6 ch.g. Mansooj 118 – Lady Fandet (Gay Fandango (USA) 132) – [1995 NR 1996 a12g May 2] narrow gelding: no worthwhile form on flat, tried blinkered: winning plater over hurdles. *Mrs Barbara Waring*

KUTMAN (USA) 3 b.c. Seattle Slew (USA) – Ouro Verde (USA) (Cool Moon 76 (CAN)) [1995 NR 1996 8d 8.2m2 10.2d4 Sep 30] lengthy, good sort: half-brother to

Tote Bookmakers Autumn Cup (Handicap), Newbury—
Kutta (left) and Ballynakelly deservedly share the spoils

several winners in France at middle distances, including very smart Ode (by Lord Avie): dam French 7.5f winner who later won in USA: off course 5 months, best effort in maidens when second of 15 at Nottingham, staying on strongly from midfield: rather disappointing at Bath only 6 days later: will eventually prove suited by further than 1m: sold (M. Stoute to G. Balding) 30,000 gns Newmarket Autumn Sales. *M. R. Stoute*

KUTTA 4 b.c. Old Vic 136 – Ardassine (Ahonoora 122) [1995 101p: 8m 10g³ 10.4g⁴ 10g* 12m 10.3d⁶ 10d* 1996 10.4m 13.3m* 12s² 12s² Nov 9] quite attractive colt: good mover: off course 10 months prior to reappearance: developed into a smart performer in autumn: dead-heated with Ballynakelly in Tote Bookmakers Autumn Cup at Newbury in September: better form when ¾-length second to Salmon Ladder in St Simon Stakes at Newbury then neck second of 22 to Clifton Fox in November Handicap at Doncaster (quickened clear 2½f out, caught post) last 2 starts: almost certainly suited by testing conditions at 1½m and will stay beyond 13.3f: acts on good to firm and soft ground: travels well in his races: stays in training. *R. W. Armstrong*   115

KUWAM (IRE) 3 b.g. Last Tycoon 131 – Inshad 81 (Indian King (USA) 128) [1995 –: 6g⁶ 5.9f⁵ 1996 12.1m³ 11.8d 8.5g 10.1f³ 8m 8m⁴ Aug 8] well-made gelding: poor form: seems better at 1¼m than shorter. *B. Hanbury*   39

KWEILO 2 b.g. (Feb 28) Mtoto 134 – Hug Me 96 (Shareef Dancer (USA) 135) [1996 6.1m⁶ 6g 8g Oct 30] 75,000Y: workmanlike gelding: fifth foal: half-brother to 3-y-o Villeggiatura (stays 1¾m, by Machiavellian), 7f winner at 2 yrs, and winning middle-distance stayers Embracing (fairly useful) and General Yaasi (in France), both by Reference Point: dam 7f and 12.2f winner out of half-sister to Clever Trick: off course 4 months after debut (lost action 1f out): caught eye of stewards in   – p

22-runner maiden (sweating) at Newmarket, never placed to challenge under tender handling (rider and trainer both fined): eased once left behind after dictating steady pace in maiden at Yarmouth on final outing: bred to stay middle distances at least: remains capable of better. *J. W. Payne*

KYLE RHEA 2 b.f. (Mar 19) In The Wings 128 – Rynechra 102 (Blakeney 126) [1996 8g² Oct 29] sixth foal: half-sister to 3 winners, including 1m (at 2 yrs) to 14.6f winner Coigach (by Niniski) and 1¼m to 13.3f winner Applecross (by Glint of Gold), both smart fillies: dam 1½m winner who stayed 1¾m well: weak 7/2, shaped well when 2½ lengths second of 16 to Musalsal in maiden at Leicester, soon prominent and keeping on, though seeming rather green: will be suited by 1½m+: sure to improve and win races. *H. R. A. Cecil*   76 p

KYMIN (IRE) 4 b.f. Kahyasi 130 – Akila (FR) (Top Ville 129) [1995 78: 12m² 11.9f² 12s⁴ 10.2g⁶ 1996 a13g² a16g⁵ a14.8g² a16g a14.8g 14.9g⁶ 16.1f⁵ 16m 18m⁶ 17.2f⁵ Jul 24] leggy filly: disappointing maiden: probably stays 2m: tried visored/ blinkered, no improvement. *D. J. G. Murray Smith*   66 d

L

LAAFEE 3 gr.g. Machiavellian (USA) 123 – Al Sylah 118 (Nureyev (USA) 131) [1995 93: 6m² 6m* 6m² 6m² 1996 5g 5m³ 6m⁴ 7f² 7.3m 7.6d a5g² a6f* Dec 27] leggy, close-coupled gelding: useful performer: sweating, fourth of 18 in £34,200 handicap at York in June: below that form over longer trips here afterwards: trained until after sixth start by H. T. Jones: won handicap in Dubai in December: best at up to 6f: acts on good to firm ground and sand. *K. P. McLaughlin, UAE*   102

LAAL (USA) 4 b.g. Shirley Heights 130 – Afaff (USA) (Nijinsky (CAN) 138) [1995 –: 10m 10g 10.1d⁶ 1996 a12g⁵ Apr 1] strong, lengthy gelding: no worthwhile form: sent to Sweden. *M. F. Barraclough*   –

LAAZIM AFOOZ 3 b.c. Mtoto 134 – Balwa (USA) 101 (Danzig (USA)) [1995 –: 7f 1996 11.5m⁶ 12m³ 12g* 11.8g Oct 29] small colt: modest performer: won weak maiden at Catterick in October, making all: tailed off in minor event at Leicester 11 days later: retained by trainer 6,000 gns Newmarket Autumn Sales: stays 1½m well: has raced only on a sound surface. *R. T. Phillips*   63

LABEED (USA) 3 b.c. Riverman (USA) 131 – Gracious Beauty (USA) 67 (Nijinsky (CAN) 138) [1995 68: 7.1m⁶ 7.1g² 7f 8m 7d⁶ 8f² 1996 10.2g 10.3m 11.7m* 14.9m² 16g Sep 14] close-coupled, quite good-topped colt: fair performer: won minor event at Bath in June: sold out of R. Hern's stable 26,000 gns Newmarket July Sales after fourth start: broke leg at Goodwood: stayed 14.9f: raced mainly on a sound surface: dead. *R. Akehurst*   72

LA BELLE AFFAIR (USA) 2 gr.f. (May 2) Black Tie Affair – Away's Halo (USA) (Sunny's Halo (CAN)) [1996 7f Sep 5] 30,000F: fifth foal: half-sister to 4 minor winners in USA: dam sprint winner in USA, including at 2 yrs: slowly into stride and well behind from halfway in 15-runner maiden at Salisbury. *P. Mitchell*   –

LA BELLE DOMINIQUE 4 b.f. Dominion 123 – Love Street 62 (Mummy's Pet 125) [1995 59, a52: a5g 5.1g 5.1m 5.1m 5.1f 5g³ 5m 5.1m³ a5g³ 5.3f² 1996 5s 6f 5m⁴ 5.1g⁶ 5.1f 5g 5f 5g² 5.3m* 5m⁶ 5m a5g a5g Dec 5] smallish, strong filly: modest handicapper: best form since 2-y-o to gain her first win at Brighton in August: best form at around 5f: acts on firm and soft ground and on fibresand: none too consistent. *S. G. Knight*   59 a–

LA BELLE SHYANNE 5 ch.m. Shy Groom (USA) – Defy Me 75 (Bustino 136) [1995 33: a8g a12g 8.2g 11.7m⁶ 12g 13.1f 10m 8h² 8h 1996 10.2m 8m 13.1f⁴ 14.1f 10d Aug 25] plain mare: usually dull in coat: bad maiden handicapper: gambled-on fourth in seller at Bath: trained by R. Baker until after penultimate start: stays 13.1f: acts on hard and dead going: inconsistent. *C. J. Hill*   31

LABEQ (IRE) 2 b.c. (Feb 25) Lycius (USA) 124 – Ahbab (IRE) 81 (Ajdal (USA) 130) [1996 6d 7g² Oct 25] first foal: dam 7f winner out of half-sister to Fairy Footsteps and Light Cavalry: stepped up good deal on debut form when ¾-length second   81

514

of 12 to Sophomore in maiden at Doncaster, leading halfway, headed inside last: should stay 1m: may improve further. *P. T. Walwyn*

LA BLUE (GER) 3 b.f. Bluebird (USA) 125 – La Luganese (Surumu (GER)) 119 [1995 6s* 6m³ 6d⁵ 1996 8g* 8s* 11v⁴ 8s* 10d³ 8g* 9.3d² Oct 6] medium-sized, leggy filly: third foal: dam, granddaughter of top 1976 German 2-y-o filly La Dorada, dam of La Colorada (Group 3 10.5f) and grandam of Lomitas (rated 129, up to 1½m): smart performer: won maiden at Dortmund at 2 yrs then listed race and 16-runner Arag Preis at Dusseldorf (beat Dapprima by 3 lengths) in the spring: won valuable event at Hamburg and (after very good ¾-length third of 8 to Timarida in Group 1 event at Munich) Group 3 race at Baden-Baden (beat Sinyar by ½ length) in the summer: ½-length second of 10 to Donna Viola in Prix de l'Opera at Longchamp final start, leading around 1f out but collared near finish: stays 1¼m (well below best in Preis der Diana over 11f): goes well on soft ground: consistent: stays in training. *B. Schutz, Germany*

LA BOSSETTE (IRE) 4 b.f. Cyrano de Bergerac 120 – Bosquet 59 (Queen's – Hussar 124) [1995 42, a–: 6.1g 6m⁶ 6g 6g 8m⁵ 7m⁵ 6f a5g a6g a10g 1996 a12g Jan 6] small filly: appears to retain little ability: has raced only on a sound surface when on turf: no improvement in blinkers/visor: covered by Tower of Magic. *R. Ingram*

LA BRIEF 4 b.f. Law Society (USA) 130 – Lady Warninglid (Ela-Mana-Mou 132) [1995 73: 12s 12m 12.1s* a16g² a14g* a16g* 1996 14s Oct 5] compact, work-manlike filly: has a round action: progressed into a fair handicapper in the autumn at 3 yrs: in need of race, eighth of 20 at Haydock on belated return, plugging on: will prove suited by a test of stamina: acts on soft ground and the all-weather. *M. J. Ryan*

LAB TEST (IRE) 4 ch.g. Doulab (USA) 115 – Princess Reema (USA) (Affirmed (USA)) [1995 8f 8.5f⁶ 8f⁵ 1996 5.5f 5.5f a7.5f 7g Oct 25] useful performer here at 2 yrs for C. Williams: unplaced for 3 trainers in 7 races in USA, first 4 stakes events but last of them (June, tailed off) poor claimer: 10/1, poorly drawn when midfield in 21-runner claimer at Doncaster on return to Britain: stays 7.3f: best 2-y-o form on a soft surface. *J. Pearce*

LABUDD (USA) 6 ch.h. Deputy Minister (CAN) – Delightful Vie (USA) (Barbs 49 Delight) [1995 61: a7g⁶ a12g³ a12g⁶ 8g⁴ 8g 7f a10g³ 1996 a8g* a8g³ a10g⁶ a8g a7g⁴ a59 a8g a8g 10g 10.8f 8.3m 8g⁶ 9f 11.6g² 10g 12g⁵ a16g⁶ Dec 5] good-topped horse: modest and inconsistent (reportedly suffers from fibrillating heart) handicapper last 2 seasons: made most to win at Lingfield in January: seems to stay 1½m (beaten long way out over 2m): best recent form on equitrack: blinkered fifth (ran respectably) and sixth 6-y-o starts. *R. Ingram*

LACANDONA (USA) 3 b.f. Septieme Ciel (USA) 123 – Grand Luxe (USA) (Sir 71 Ivor 135) [1995 NR 1996 7m⁴ 10s⁴ a8s Nov 19] $55,000F, $210,000Y: angular filly: half-sister to numerous winners in USA, including one by Mr Prospector placed in Grade 2 9f event: dam Canadian Stakes winner out of Canadian Horse of the Year Fanfreluche: easily best effort in maidens when fourth at Newbury second start: tailed off at Lingfield last time: stays 1¼m. *P. W. Chapple-Hyam*

LA CHATELAINE 2 b.f. (Mar 18) Then Again 126 – La Domaine 89 (Dominion – p 123) [1996 7d Oct 28] first live foal: dam 1m winner: 20/1, 15½ lengths seventh of 11 to Miss Sancerre in maiden at Lingfield, slowly away and not knocked about: should do better. *G. Lewis*

LACHESIS 3 ch.f. Lycius (USA) 124 – Chance All (FR) 88 (Glenstal (USA) 118) 64 d [1995 55p: 6m³ 1996 8g³ 7.5f⁴ 6g 7.6m³ 8.2m⁵ 7g 7f⁶ a6g a8g Dec 3] compact filly: modest maiden at best: sold (R. Hollinshead to B. Richmond) 3,000 gns Newmarket Autumn Sales after seventh start: stays 1m: acts on firm going, yet to race on a soft surface. *B. Richmond*

LACRYMA CRISTI (IRE) 3 b.c. Green Desert (USA) 127 – L'Anno d'Oro 88 (Habitat 134) [1995 95+: 6m* 6g³ 1996 6d³ Jul 5] strong, good sort: good mover: fairly useful form for Mrs J. Cecil as 2-y-o: 4/1 after nearly a year off, creditable third of 6 to Averti in minor event at Haydock: has raced only at 6f: sold 11,000 gns Newmarket December Sales. *R. Charlton*

LA CURAMALAL (IRE) 2 b.f. (Mar 15) Rainbow Quest (USA) 134 – North – p Telstar 104 (Sallust 134) [1996 7g Nov 2] 47,000F, 72,000Y: sixth foal: half-sister to 3-y-o 1m winner Royal Canaska (by Royal Academy) and 7f winner Canaska Star (by Doyoun): dam Irish 6f (at 2 yrs) and 9f winner: 50/1, never a threat when seventh of 23 to Palisade in maiden at Newmarket: sold 56,000 gns Newmarket December Sales, probably to Germany: should do better. *G. Wragg*

LA DAMA (USA) 4 ch.f. Known Fact (USA) 135 – Cypria Sacra (USA) 103 35 § (Sharpen Up 127) [1995 –§: 6.1g 8.2m 7m 1996 a6g³ a6g⁶ a7g⁵ 7d 7.1g⁴ a7g 8.1g a45 § May 30] tall filly: poor maiden: stays 7f: has worn off-side pricker: wayward (pulls hard and hangs) and one to avoid. *A. B. Mulholland*

LA DOLCE VITA 2 b.f. (May 8) Mazilier (USA) 107 – Actress 73 (Known Fact 70 (USA) 135) [1996 5m 5m 5g* Oct 19] approx 24,000Y: unfurnished filly: third foal: half-sister to 3-y-o Ebony Boy (by Sayf El Arab), 7f winner at 2 yrs, and 5f (at 2 yrs) and 7f winner Russian Heroine (by Domynsky): dam 7f winner, stayed 1m: 33/1, won 14-runner maiden at Catterick in October by 1¼ lengths from Hyde Park, held up in race run at strong pace then staying on strongly: retained by trainer 7,800 gns Newmarket Autumn Sales: will prove at least as effective at 6f as 5f. *T. D. Barron*

LA DOYENNE (IRE) 2 ch.f. (Apr 20) Masterclass (USA) 116 – Sainthill (St – Alphage 119) [1996 5m 5m Oct 29] half-sister to 3 winners here and abroad, including 6f and 9f winner Knockglas (by Hardgreen): dam twice-raced sister to top-class sprinter Sandford Lad: signs of a little ability in median auction maiden at Redcar. *C. B. B. Booth*

LADY BANKES (IRE) 3 b.f. Alzao (USA) 117 – Never So Fair 65 (Never So 69 Bold 135) [1995 67: 6g 6f² 7.1s⁶ 1996 6.9f⁴ 8f³ 8.5m² 10g* 9.9f⁴ 12g 10m⁵ Sep 16] small filly: fair performer: ridden by 7-lb claimer, won minor event at Pontefract in July, dictating slow pace until sent for home early in straight: seemed not to stay sixth start: stays 1¼m, at least in slowly-run race: acts on firm ground. *W. G. M. Turner*

LADY BENSON (IRE) 3 b.f. Pennine Walk 120 – Sit Elnaas (USA) 82 (Sir Ivor – 135) [1995 NR 1996 10g 8.3g 8.2m⁴ 8.2m Aug 7] small, leggy filly: fourth foal: half-sister to a winner in Germany by Doulab and to out-and-out stayer and winning hurdler Sujud (by Shaadi): dam, winning stayer and second in Cesarewitch, granddaughter of Juliette Marny: no worthwhile form in maiden events (for W. Brisbourne on debut) and handicap. *D. J. S. Cosgrove*

LADYBIRD 2 b.f. (Feb 17) Polar Falcon (USA) 126 – Classic Heights – (Shirley Heights 130) [1996 7d⁶ 8s Nov 9] third foal: half-sister to 3-y-o Brother Roy (by Prince Sabo): dam unraced sister to Head For Heights: well held in maiden events at Lingfield and Doncaster: sold 3,300 gns Newmarket December Sales. *J. H. M. Gosden*

LADYBOWER (IRE) 4 b.f. Pennine Walk 120 – Eimkar (Junius (USA) 124) – [1995 36: a6g⁶ a6g 5.1m 8f 1996 a8g* a8g² a8g² 8f a7g 8.3g Jul 15] small filly: a49 stepped up considerably on previous form when winning weak apprentice handicap at Southwell in January: stays 1m: acts on all-weather, no worthwhile form on turf. *Lord Huntingdon*

LADY CARLA 3 b.f. Caerleon (USA) 132 – Shirley Superstar 94 (Shirley 122 Heights 130) [1995 90p: 8f* 1996 11.5f* 12m* 12m⁴ Jul 14]

It is perverse to think that Lady Carla could be remembered chiefly for anything other than her runaway triumph in the Vodafone Oaks. She remains in training and has her stud career to follow that, but will have to do something truly exceptional for racing historians not to talk first about her performance on June 7th, 1996. Lady Carla lined up for the Oaks with two starts under her belt and two easy wins, in a maiden at Leicester the previous October and the listed Champagne Ruinart Oaks Trial at Lingfield in May. Flame Valley had been the best of her three rivals at Lingfield. On the face of it, this record was not a great deal to be taking into a classic but it bore a close resemblance to that of the favourite, her former stable-companion Pricket, whose listed race at Newmarket had been more strongly-contested. The two of them dominated the Oaks betting, followed by the once-raced maiden winner Camporese, the Lupe winner Whitewater Affair and the One Thousand Guineas seventh and fifth, Bint Salsabil and Honest Guest. A hefty proportion of the eleven runners were there just for their moments in the spotlight but there weren't many of those on offer once the stalls opened, and rounding Tattenham Corner it was pretty clear

Vodafone Oaks, Epsom—a rout; Lady Carla wins and the rest wave a white flag

that only Lady Carla or Pricket could win. They were tracking leader Moody's Cat, but Pricket only flattered to deceive; when Lady Carla was pushed into the lead about three furlongs out she lengthened in fine style and the rest were going nowhere. She drew further and further clear until, eased in the last fifty yards, she passed the post nine lengths in front, Pricket second. Sun Princess' twelve lengths in 1983 is the Oaks record. Formosa (1868), Noblesse (1963) and Jet Ski Lady (1991) all won by ten. Lady Carla could have threatened that trio's achievement had her jockey, Pat Eddery, so wished, but there would surely be plenty of other opportunities for her to improve her standing.

There was nothing very controversial about Lady Carla at this stage—except perhaps whether she was better than the colts—but a right furore developed on the eve of the Irish Oaks five weeks later when, on Channel 4's *The Morning Line*, John McCririck stated that there were 'rumours at Newmarket, that she has got serious wind problems' and that he doubted whether she would run again after the Irish Oaks. Henry Cecil and the owner's racing manager immediately denied that Lady Carla had any such problem, and McCririck retracted. Chastised in many quarters—'he has devalued her offspring by hundreds of thousands of pounds', wrote National Trainers Federation president Peter Cundell—McCririck was praised in some others after 1/2-shot Lady Carla had managed only fourth of six at the Curragh. Making the running, she held on until the furlong-marker but the writing had been on the wall a lot earlier. The reason for her poor showing was unknown; she had kept changing her legs. Amid so much that is uncertain, racing is a prodigious rumour factory and the search for what is factual has always been part and parcel of it, necessarily so in the case of journalists. They cannot sacrifice objective analysis. Its traditional secrecy may lend the sport some mystical allure, but ultimately it is not in the interests of the punter who pays the bills. It was ironic therefore that the connections of Lady Carla should become embroiled in such a controversy when their behaviour over Bosra Sham's set-backs, in particular, was so exemplary.

Unfortunately, the remainder of Lady Carla's season was a triumph only for the cynics. She did not race again. Encouraging sounds were initially made about the Yorkshire Oaks and St Leger, but 'a muscle spasm in her back' ruled her out of the former after she had been declared at the five-day stage, and confirmation that she was out for the season came in September: 'she has a little inflammation on parts of her vertebrae in her back but it is nothing serious.' It is excellent news that both Lady Carla and Bosra Sham remain in training. Lady Carla has something to prove because as the season went on it became clear that although her Oaks form was markedly better than that of the previous three winners, it was nothing like so impressive as the style of her victory. Who is to

517

say, though, that she could not have done better had any of her rivals been good enough to test her? A sturdy filly, Lady Carla stays a mile and a half really well. The Irish Oaks was her fourth race on top-of-the-ground from as many starts, and it is not inconceivable that that may have played a part in her disappointing performance.

Lady Carla (b.f. 1993)	Caerleon (USA) (b 1980)	Nijinsky (b 1967)	Northern Dancer Flaming Page
		Foreseer (b or br 1969)	Round Table Regal Gleam
	Shirley Superstar (b 1985)	Shirley Heights (b 1975)	Mill Reef Hardiemma
		Odeon (b 1976)	Royal And Regal Cammina

Lady Carla was bought by Tim Bulwer-Long for Wafic Said for 220,000 guineas at the 1994 Houghton Yearling Sales, one day before they purchased the sale-topper Bosra Sham. To buy both the same year's One Thousand Guineas and Oaks winners is unprecedented. It was also an excellent year for Lady Carla's sire Caerleon, clearly his best in the British Isles since Generous' Derby year and enhanced by big winners trained abroad such as Shake The Yoke, Grape Tree Road, Auriette (the Grade 1 Gamely Handicap) and Fusaichi Concorde (Japanese Derby). Apparently, at least fifteen of Lady Carla's contemporaries by Caerleon were racing in Japan. That makes less difference than it would have done in another era seeing that Caerleon now covers over a hundred mares each year, one hundred and thirty-nine in 1996. On the dam's side, Lady Carla traces back to a famous broodmare and to

Mr Wafic Said's "Lady Carla"

another famous series of transactions at the yearling sales. That broodmare is Zanzara, Lady Carla's fourth dam, who had fourteen winners (by eleven different stallions) from seventeen foals, several of them pattern class and two of them, the sprinter Matatina and miler Showdown, top class. Lady Carla's third dam Cammina, though, was not one of those winners; she was placed in Ireland. The famous series of transactions involved one of her daughters, Odeon, who was purchased along with fellow yearlings One In A Million and Reprocolor for a total of 81,500 guineas in 1977 as a prospective foundation mare for the Meon Valley Stud. A half-sister to Princess Bonita, who made the frame in four pattern races, Odeon herself made the frame in eight and won the Galtres Stakes, but until Lady Carla came along her legacy could not have been mentioned in the same breath as those of One In A Million and Reprocolor. She had just five foals: Si Signor and Moviegoer were useful and Shirley Superstar also won a race, albeit only a two-year-old maiden at Salisbury in a career that stretched to just four starts. Shirley Superstar had two named foals prior to Lady Carla, the modest maidens Nymph Errant (by Be My Guest) and Chita Rivera (by Chief Singer). Since Lady Carla she has had the Paul Cole-trained 1996 two-year-old Azores (by Polish Precedent), a yearling filly by Night Shift who made 160,000 guineas at the Houghton, and a filly foal by Unfuwain. *H. R. A. Cecil*

LADY CAROLINE LAMB (IRE)   3 b.f. Contract Law (USA) 108 – Tuft Hill   68
92 (Grundy 137) [1995 64: 5m⁴ 5h* 5m² 5g⁴ 5.2d⁶ 5g⁶ 6m 5m² a5g⁶ 1996 5d² 5s* 5d³ 5m* 5.2m⁶ 5m 5m Aug 29] leggy, lengthy, unfurnished filly: fair performer: won minor event at Catterick in March and claimer (easily, claimed out of M. Channon's stable £9,000) at Folkestone in April: kicked in stalls and withdrawn in June: had excuses in handicaps afterwards, twice missing the break: speedy, and best form at 5f: acts on hard and soft ground: races prominently. *R. Bastiman*

LADY DIESIS (USA)   2 b.f. (Apr 20) Diesis 133 – Sedulous 107 (Tap On Wood   83
130) [1996 6m⁶ 6g* 5d⁵ Oct 28] quite attractive filly: fourth foal: half-sister to 2-y-o 6f winners Adamant (by Lyphard) and Hindaawee (by Zilzal) and useful 1m winner So Sedulous (by The Minstrel): dam winner from 5f to 1m at 2 yrs in Ireland and later won in USA: odds on, very easy winner of maiden at Catterick in October: probably better form when 3¼ lengths fifth of 9 to Jennelle in minor event at Lingfield 10 days later, no extra inside last, swishing tail when given tap with whip: bred to stay 1m. *B. W. Hills*

LADY DIGNITY (IRE)   3 b.f. Nordico (USA) – Royal Respect 82 (Kings Lake   71
(USA) 133) [1995 66: 5g⁵ 6m⁴ a7g² a7g⁴ 1996 a7g⁶ a8.5g³ a8.5g* a8g* a8g⁶ 8g⁶ 8.2f⁶ a9.4g Oct 5] angular filly: fair performer: won minor event at Wolverhampton and handicap at Lingfield in March: should stay 1¼m: acts on the all-weather, possibly unsuited by top-of-the-ground: sent to South Korea. *P. J. Makin*

LADY ECLAT   3 b.f. Nomination 125 – Romantic Saga 69 (Prince Tenderfoot   –
(USA) 126) [1995 54: 5m⁶ 6.1m⁶ 5m⁴ 7g 5g 5f⁶ a6g* a6g³ a5g² 1996 a6g a5g a6g a6g a9.4g Nov 25] good-topped filly: modest performer at 2 yrs: no form in 1996: keen sort, best at sprint distances: acts well on the all-weather: visored/blinkered nowadays: races prominently: sold (J. Glover to K. Wingrove) 500 gns Ascot December Sales. *J. A. Glover*

LADY ELIZABETH (FR)   4 b.f. Bold Arrangement 127 – Top Fille (FR) (Top   –
Ville 129) [1995 10.5d 11g⁶ 10g³ 10g 10d⁶ 10d 1996 a13g a12g⁶ a10g a7g a12g a9.4g 10d Apr 4] leggy, plain ex-French filly: third foal: sister to French 12.5f winner Range Rider and half-sister to German 8.5f to 11f winner Top Lake (by Kings Lake): dam French 9f winner: third in minor event trained by J. Hammond in 1995: well beaten in Britain: tried blinkered: returned to France. *K. O. Cunningham-Brown*

LADY GODIVA   2 b.f. (Mar 16) Keen 116 – Festival Fanfare (Ile de Bourbon   69
(USA) 133) [1996 7.1m 7m² 7g³ 8d² 7.9g* 7m⁴ Oct 1] 6,200Y: tall, unfurnished filly: fourth living foal: closely related to 3-y-o Fusco (by Sharpo): dam, maiden who stayed 1½m, sister to smart 1984 staying 2-y-o Bourbonel: fair performer: won 23-runner maiden auction at York in September: stays 1m: acts on good to firm and dead ground: consistent. *M. J. Polglase*

LADY GROVEFAIR (IRE)   2 ch.f. (May 10) Shalford (IRE) 124§ – Zinovia   38
(USA) 80 (Ziggy's Boy (USA)) [1996 6m⁶ 6d⁵ Aug 24] IR 2,600Y: first foal: dam
(ran only at 2 yrs) Irish 5f winner: poor form in sellers: sold 800 gns Doncaster
September Sales: sent to Denmark. *B. J. Meehan*

LADY ISABELL   3 b.f. Rambo Dancer (CAN) 107 – Warning Bell 88 (Bustino   62
136) [1995 58p: 7.6d⁶ 1996 7f⁴ 8m⁵ 7g Aug 21] modest maiden: well beaten last 2
starts, taking strong hold on first occasion: should be suited by 1m+. *S. Dow*

LADY JOSHUA (IRE)   3 ch.f. Royal Academy (USA) 130 – Claretta (USA) 82   82
(Roberto (USA) 131) [1995 88p: 7m⁶ 7d² 1996 10g² 12m³ 11.9g⁶ 10s⁵ 8.1s⁴ Nov
7] tall, leggy filly: fairly useful maiden: placed at Newmarket first 2 starts: rather
disappointing subsequently: stayed 1½m: has carried head high: blinkered last 2
starts: sold 18,000 gns Newmarket December Sales: has been retired. *J. L. Dunlop*

LADYKIRK   3 b.f. Slip Anchor 136 – Lady Day (FR) (Lightning (FR) 129) [1995   71
78p: 8g* 1996 10g² 12.4g⁵ 11.9d 10.1f⁵ 8.1f Sep 7] lengthy, sparely-made filly: fair
form at best: ran poorly last 3 starts: suited by middle distances. *J. W. Watts*

LADY LACEY   9 b.m. Kampala 120 – Cecily (Prince Regent (FR) 129) [1995 50:   –
8d⁶ 9g 8g 8g³ 10g⁵ 10m⁶ 10m³ 10m³ 10m⁶ 10d³ 10d⁵ 9d 1996 a12g Feb 14] rather
lightly-made mare: poor handicapper nowadays: effective at 1m to 11f: seems to act
on any going: has won with and without a visor: usually set plenty to do: covered by
Lugana Beach. *G. B. Balding*

LADY LOUISE (IRE)   2 b.f. (May 3) Lord Americo – Louisa Anne 73   –
(Mummy's Pet 125) [1996 6m⁶ Aug 8] 1,200Y: half-sister to 1988 2-y-o 5f and 7f
winner Nite Nite Louisa (by Night Shift) and a winner in Belgium: dam sprint
maiden: tailed off in 6-runner claimer at Hamilton. *M. D. Hammond*

LADY LUCRE (IRE)   3 b.f. Last Tycoon 131 – Queen Helen 112 (Troy 137)   73
[1995 NR 1996 10m⁴ Jun 8] third live foal: half-sister to 11.1f winner Helen's Bower
(by Bellypha) and a winner in Denmark: dam 7f (at 2 yrs) and 14.6f winner: 33/1,
shaped well on debut, running-on fourth of 11 to Akhla in maiden at Newmarket
in June: seemed sure to improve: sold 16,000 gns Newmarket December Sales.
M. R. Stoute

LADY MAGNUM (IRE)   3 b.f. Eve's Error 113 – Illiney Girl 66 (Lochnager   –
132) [1995 NR 1996 12.1g⁶ 10.2f 10.2f 8g 8m 8f 8m Sep 9] half-sister to 6f and
7f winner Quick Steel (by Alleging): dam winning sprinter: no form on flat: won
claiming hurdle. *J. Neville*

LADY MAIL (IRE)   2 b.f. (Feb 8) Pursuit of Love 124 – Wizardry 83 (Shirley   90 p
Heights 130) [1996 7.1g⁶ 7f* 7m⁴ 8g⁴ Sep 13] big, good-topped filly: has plenty of
scope: unimpressive mover: third reported foal: half-sister to fair 6f winner Asking
For Aces (by Thatching) and a 1¼m winner in Germany by Be My Chief: dam
maiden who stayed 1½m, is daughter of Jersey Stakes winner Merlins Charm: fairly
useful form: 33/1-winner of maiden at Redcar in July: easily best efforts when fourth
in listed events won by Catwalk at Newmarket and Falkenham at Goodwood last
2 starts: stays 1m: slowly away penultimate outing: could well improve further.
J. M. P. Eustace

LADY NASH   4 b.f. Nashwan (USA) 135 – Je Comprend (USA) (Caerleon (USA)   46
132) [1995 50: 7m 7g 8f⁶ 8m a8g² 1996 a7g³ Jan 31] sturdy, plain filly: poor
handicapper: pulls hard, and may prove best at up to 1m: acts on fibresand: covered
by Sabrehill. *C. E. Brittain*

LADY OF LEISURE (USA)   4 b.f. Diesis 133 – Lyrebird (USA) (Storm Bird   76
(CAN) 134) [1995 NR 1996 8g 10g⁴ 8m⁶ 10m² 11.5f⁴ 11m⁵ 10m* 10m* 8.9g 10.1m⁶
Oct 23] $37,000Y: lengthy filly: unimpressive mover: first foal: dam unraced sister
to Cornwallis winner Mujadil: fair performer: won minor events at Nottingham and
Pontefract in September: should stay 1½m: has raced only on a sound surface: sold
47,000 gns Newmarket December Sales. *Mrs J. Cecil*

LADY OF THE LAKE   2 b.f. (Apr 9) Caerleon (USA) 132 – Llyn Gwynant 115   68 +
(Persian Bold 123) [1996 7f³ 8.2m⁴ 7f Oct 14] tall, quite attractive filly: fourth foal:
closely related to 3-y-o Llyswen (by Generous) and half-sister to fairly useful
middle-distance performer Llia (by Shirley Heights), 7f winner at 2 yrs in 1994, and
a winner in Italy by Rousillon: dam stayed 9f: fair form in maidens: odds on but edgy,

tended to edge left when around fourth of 9 to Attitre at Nottingham on second start: bred to stay 1¼m. *J. L. Dunlop*

LADY PLOY   4 b.f. Deploy 131 – Quisissanno 76 (Be My Guest (USA) 126) – [1995 –: 7g 1996 7g 10f 7m 8g 10g Sep 3] close-coupled, sparely-made filly: shows knee action: little form. *Miss L. C. Siddall*

LADY POLY   8 b.m. Dunbeath (USA) 127 – First Temptation (USA) 67 (Mr Leader (USA)) [1995 NR 1996 a16g a13g 12m Jul 13] small, leggy mare: of little account nowadays: tried blinkered. *Jamie Poulton*

LADY RAMBO   3 b.f. Rambo Dancer (CAN) 107 – Albaciyna 74 (Hotfoot 126) [1995 NR 1996 7.1g a8.5g Jun 22] fifth foal: half-sister to a 9f winner in Germany by Glint of Gold and a winner in Sweden by Primo Dominie: dam, maiden, suited to middle distances: well beaten in claimers. *L. J. Barratt*

LADY RISK ME   7 gr.m. Risk Me (FR) 127 – Donrae 106 (Don (ITY) 123) [1995 – NR 1996 a16g May 13] of little account. *D. T. Thom*

LADY SABINA   6 ch.m. Bairn (USA) 126 – Calibina 101 (Caliban 123) [1995   43 d
52, a33: a10g a10g 8.3g⁴ 10m³ 10f³ 12f 10m² 10g* 10d⁵ 9d² 1996 a10g 10.3d 9.9m⁶   a–
8g⁴ 10.1m⁴ 10f 10g 10f⁵ 10g⁴ 10g⁴ 10m⁶ Sep 18] workmanlike mare: poor handicapper, better on turf than the all-weather: stays 1¼m, and should get further: acts on firm ground, heavy and on equitrack: covered by Komaite. *W. J. Musson*

LADY SADIE (IRE)   2 b.f. (Apr 30) Red Sunset 120 – Eimkar (Junius (USA) – 124) [1996 5.1f May 11] IR 1,200Y: fifth foal: half-sister to 4-y-o 1m winner Ladybower (by Pennine Walk): dam unraced half-sister to high-class French miler Daring Display: 33/1, tailed off in maiden auction at Bath. *J. S. Moore*

LADY SALOME   2 gr.f. (Apr 18) Absalom 128 – Lady River (FR) (Sir Gaylord) – [1996 5m 6m 7g Sep 7] 7,700Y: compact filly: has a roundish action: half-sister to numerous winners here and abroad, including 1995 2-y-o 7f and 1m winner Vanishing Point (by Rock City) and 4-y-o 1½m winner Campaspe (by Dominion): dam showed a little ability in France: poor form in maiden auctions: burly first 2 starts, slowly away second one. *J. G. FitzGerald*

LADY SEREN (IRE)   4 gr.f. Doulab (USA) 115 – Princess Pamela 70 (Dragon- – ara Palace (USA) 115) [1995 NR 1996 8f 8m⁴ 5m 7g 6m a8g Nov 4] lengthy filly: third foal: half-sister to 2 winners by Double Schwartz at up to 7f, notably useful 6-y-o sprint handicapper Double Splendour: dam, 2-y-o 5f winner who stayed 7f, failed to train on: seems of no account. *S. E. Kettlewell*

LADY SHERIFF   5 b.m. Taufan (USA) 119 – Midaan (Sallust 134) [1995 85,   90 d
a60+: 5m³ 5m* 5g* 5g² 5m 5m* 5m* 5m² 5f² 5.1m⁵ 5g² 5d⁴ 5s⁵ 5f² 5m⁴ 5m⁴ a5g⁵   a68
1996 a6g² 5m³ a5g* 5.1g⁴ 5m⁵ 5m⁶ 5.1m² 5m 6.1m⁶ 5g⁴ 6m 5m a6g⁶ a6g 5.6m 5d 5g 5f⁴ 5s Nov 8] workmanlike mare: has a markedly round action: fairly useful handicapper on turf: in good form in first half of 1996: none too consistent afterwards: only fair on the all-weather, successful at Wolverhampton in May: seems best at 5f: acts on firm and soft ground and on fibresand: usually blinkered in 1995, tried only once (well beaten) at 5 yrs: successful for owner: tough. *R. Hollinshead*

LADY SHIRL (IRE)   2 b.f. (Apr 17) Fayruz 116 – Christmas Show (Petorius   52
117) [1996 6f⁶ 6g³ a5g² Nov 12] IR 4,200F, 5,200Y, 10,000 2-y-o: angular filly: sec-   a69
ond foal: half-sister to 3-y-o 11f Belgian winner Ringing Native (by By My Native): dam Irish 1½m winner: easily best effort in maiden events when neck second to Hyde Park at Lingfield, running on well: should stay 7f: sent to Malaysia. *P. Mitchell*

LADY SILK   5 ch.m. Prince Sabo 123 – Adduce (USA) (Alleged (USA) 138)   46 §
[1995 52: 6.1m a7g a7g a6g a6g a8g³ a8g³ a7g⁶ 1996 a8g 7.5d 8.1g⁶ 9.2g⁶ a8g a6g*   a52 §
a6g³ a7g⁶ 7g a7g 6.1m 7g⁵ 8f 7g a8g³ a8g Nov 18] leggy mare: poor handicapper: won seller at Southwell in July: effective at 6f to 1m: acts on good to firm ground, soft and fibresand: tried visored but seems better without: has given trouble in preliminaries, and often early to post: has unsatisfactory temperament. *Miss J. F. Craze*

LADY SWIFT   5 ch.m. Jalmood (USA) 126 – Appealing 49 (Star Appeal 133) – [1995 NR 1996 8g 14.1g Oct 24] sparely-made mare: seems of little account. *K. W. Hogg, Isle of Man*

LADY WOODSTOCK   4 b.f. Chilibang 120 – Vent du Soir (Main Reef 126) – § [1995 –§: 12.1m 1996 a12g a16g a7g 11.9f⁶ Apr 22] lengthy filly: of little account: sold 675 gns Ascot July Sales. *Miss A. E. Embiricos*

LA FANDANGO (IRE) 3 b.f. Taufan (USA) 119 – Cursory Look (USA) –
(Nijinsky (CAN) 138) [1995 51: 7m 7m³ 7.5m⁵ 7g⁵ 8.3g 8f 8f 1996 a7g 9.9m 8f⁶
12f 10g 7d Aug 23] angular filly: has a round action: poor maiden at best at 3 yrs:
sold 3,400 gns Newmarket Autumn Sales: stays 1m: acts on firm ground: blinkered
penultimate start. *M. W. Easterby*

LA FILLE DE CIRQUE 4 ch.f. Cadeaux Genereux 131 – Lady of The Land 75   44
(Wollow 132) [1995 49: a8g⁵ a8g⁴ a6g⁶ 8g³ 8.2m 8m* 8f² 8m 10f² 10m⁴ 1996 8m⁴ 8f
10m 8f 8.2g² Oct 24] smallish filly: poor handicapper: stays 1¼m: has raced only on
a sound surface on turf: sometimes bandaged: sweating freely (ran poorly) fifth 3-y-o
start: blinkered (ran creditably) final outing: none too consistent. *R. J. R. Williams*

LA FINALE 3 ch.f. Dunbeath (USA) 127 – Jamarj 113 (Tyrnavos 129) [1995 60,   49
a45: 6m⁴ 5m³ 6m⁶ 6d 7d² 8f⁵ a7g³ a8g³ 1996 6f⁵ 6.9f³ 5g⁶ 6.1m 7g⁴ 8.3g⁵ 7g Oct 25]
smallish, close-coupled filly: has a quick action: poor form at best at 3 yrs: stays 1m:
best form on an easy surface (below form on fibresand): blinkered 4 of last 5 starts:
sent to South Korea. *D. Nicholls*

LAGAN 3 b.g. Shareef Dancer (USA) 135 – Lagta 75 (Kris 135) [1995 55+: 6.1g⁵   –
8g³ 7g⁶ a7g 1996 a8g 8.5m 7g 9f 10.8m 14.1m 16m 16m 10g a16g Aug 29] good-
bodied gelding: poor maiden handicapper on flat: probably stays 1¾m: tried blinkered, no improvement: tail swisher: winning hurdler for K. Morgan. *P. S. Felgate*

LAGO DI VARANO 4 b.g. Clantime 101 – On The Record 72 (Record Token   92
128) [1995 97d: 6g² 5m³ 6m⁵ 5m 5m 6g⁴ 5s 5f⁴ 1996 7g 5m* 5.1g² 5m 6m 6f⁴ 5g*
5g⁵ 5m² 6m 5m⁵ 5.2m⁴ 5m⁴ 6g⁴ 5.6m³ 6m 5d 5g² 5g³ Oct 26] strong, useful-looking
gelding: good walker: fairly useful handicapper: won claimer at Ripon (claimed out
of Jack Berry's stable £10,000) in April and handicap at Doncaster in June: creditable
efforts in competitive handicaps most outings afterwards: retained by trainer 22,000
gns Newmarket Autumn Sales: effective at 5f and 6f: acts on firm and soft ground:
nearly always blinkered/visored: tough and consistent. *R. M. Whitaker*

LAGUNA BAY (IRE) 2 b.f. (May 3) Arcane (USA) – Meg Daughter (IRE)   65 ?
(Doulab (USA) 115) [1996 7m 7m⁴ 7g Sep 6] close-coupled filly: second foal: dam
unraced half-sister to useful 1985 2-y-o 5f and 6f winner Barrack Street: sire, won
from 1¼m to 2m and over hurdles, brother to Rainbow Quest: modest form: may
well have been flattered second start. *A. P. Jarvis*

LAHAB NASHWAN 2 ch.c. (Mar 18) Nashwan (USA) 135 – Shadha (USA) 77   67 p
(Devil's Bag (USA)) [1996 8.2g⁵ Oct 24] first foal: dam 2-y-o 6f winner here and at
1m/9f in USA at 4 yrs, daughter of very smart French 1m to 1½m filly Treizieme, a
good family: 14/1, over 5 lengths fifth of 15 to Over To You in maiden at Nottingham,
leading over 3f out, looking green in front then given easy time when beaten: will
improve. *M. R. Channon*

LA HAYE SAINTE 3 ch.f. Rock City 120 – Billante (USA) (Graustark) [1995 –,   –
a49: a7g² a7g⁶ a7g⁶ 7g 10g 1996 10d a9.4g 8f May 6] leggy filly: narrowly beaten in
seller at Wolverhampton on debut: failed to repeat that form, in visor final start: sold
800 gns Ascot November Sales: sent to South Korea. *D. J. S. Cosgrove*

LAHIK (IRE) 3 b.g. Lycius (USA) 124 – Sangala (FR) (Jim French (USA)) [1995   –
–: 6.1m 7.5m 1996 8.2d 9.7f 12.5f 8.3m 8g 12m 16f⁵ a13g⁵ 9.7g 7g 8f a8s⁴ a10g a8g
a10g Dec 20] of little account: tried blinkered and visored. *K. T. Ivory*

LAJATTA 2 ch.c. (Apr 7) Superlative 118 – Lady Keyser 68 (Le Johnstan 123)   ?
[1996 8g⁶ 7m 6m 7.5s⁴ Dec 17] 15,500Y: fourth foal: half-brother to 6f winner
Lady-Bo-K (by Komaite): dam sprinter: signs of ability both starts in Italy: well
beaten in maidens here in between: stays 7.5f: trained first 3 starts by L. Cumani.
M. Pasquale, Italy

LAKELINE LEGEND (IRE) 3 ch.g. Caerleon (USA) 132 – Bottom Line 90   95
(Double Jump 131) [1995 77p: 8g³ 1996 12m 10m² 10m* 10.4m 12m³ 13.9m 12g
Sep 29] close-coupled, workmanlike gelding: fairly useful form: won maiden at
Newmarket in June: contested valuable handicaps afterwards, finishing third (to
Freequent) in Tote Gold Trophy at Goodwood and seventh of 20 (to Better Offer) in
£44,700 event at Ascot (sweating and edgy) final start: should prove effective over
1¾m: gelded: sent to Malaysia. *M. A. Jarvis*

LAKE SPRING (IRE) 2 b.g. (Apr 18) Shalford (IRE) 124§ – Isla Bonita (Kings   –
Lake (USA) 133) [1996 6g 5.1m⁵ a6g Sep 19] 12,000Y: fifth foal: half-brother

to Italian 3-y-o winner (at up to 11f) Ercole Il Grande (by Persian Heights): dam unraced half-sister to Norfolk Stakes winner Magic Mirror out of Cherry Hinton winner Turkish Treasure: well beaten in sellers: slowly away first 2 starts: sold 900 gns Ascot November Sales. *R. J. Hodges*

LALINDI (IRE) 5 b.m. Cadeaux Genereux 131 – Soemba 86 (General Assembly   79 (USA)) [1995 76: 14.9d* 16m⁵ 16.4m³ 14m⁵ 16m³ 16m² 16.1g* 20m 1996 18s 16g 14.9d⁶ 14m² 17.2f² 13.1g² 12g⁴ 11.5f* 11.9d* 16.1g 13.33f 13.3m 14m² 12s 16.5s Nov 9] big, strong, lengthy mare: fair handicapper: won at Lingfield (amateurs) and Haydock in the summer: lost her way towards the end of the season and sold out of D. Elsworth's stable 18,500 gns Newmarket Autumn Sales after penultimate start: stays at least 17.2f: acts on firm and dead ground and on fibresand: blinkered nowadays (wasn't final start): lazy sort who takes plenty of driving: probably unsuited by steadily-run race. *R. Champion*

LALLANS (IRE) 3 b.c. Old Vic 136 – Laluche (USA) 100 (Alleged (USA) 138)   104 [1995 NR 1996 12d* 12m² 13.9m³ 16.2m Jun 19] good-topped colt: good walker and mover: fifth foal: half-brother to smart middle-distance stayer Landowner and 1¾m winner Lala Musa (both by Kris): dam, from excellent family, won from 6f to 1m at 2 yrs: 15-length winner of maiden at Carlisle in April: placed in small-field minor events at Newmarket (to Dushyantor) and York (sweating, off bridle early in straight, stayed on very strongly at death, ¾ length behind Athenry): weakened 3f out in Queen's Vase at Royal Ascot final start: should ultimately prove well suited by 2m: yet to race on extremes of going. *M. Johnston*

LA MAFARR (USA) 3 b.c. Mr Prospector (USA) – Sense of Unity (USA)   76 (Northern Dancer) [1995 NR 1996 6m⁶ 7f⁴ Sep 28] $525,000Y: robust, close-coupled colt: third foal: brother to a stakes-placed sprint winner in USA: dam, winner in USA, half-sister to Grade 1 winner Linkage: around 3 lengths sixth of 14 to Disputed in maiden at Newmarket, looking an unlucky loser after meeting trouble in running: 11/10 on, disappointing fourth in similar event at Redcar 7 weeks later: yet to race on a soft surface: sent to UAE. *J. H. M. Gosden*

LAMARITA 2 b.f. (Feb 8) Emarati (USA) 74 – Bentinck Hotel 74 (Red God   71 128§) [1996 5f⁴ 6m² 6d⁶ Jul 5] 9,200F, 7,000Y: lengthy filly: has a quick action: half-sister to numerous winners here and abroad, including fair 7-y-o 7f to 1¼m performer Bentico (by Nordico) and useful 1989 2-y-o sprinter Shamshoon (by Shareef Dancer): dam 2-y-o 5f winner: fair form in maidens: stays 6f: disappointing on a soft surface. *J. M. P. Eustace*

LA MENORQUINA (USA) 6 b.m. Woodman (USA) 126 – Hail The Lady   31 (USA) (Hail The Pirates (USA) 126) [1995 30, a53: a12g⁵ a16g* a14g² 14.1m   a– a16g* 16.4g⁴ a14.8g⁴ a16g⁶ 1996 a16g 14.9m 16m⁴ Aug 7] quite good-topped mare: modest handicapper on the all-weather: poor on turf: suited by test of stamina: acts on the all-weather and on good to firm and soft going: often comes from long way off pace. *D. Marks*

L'AMI LOUIS (USA) 3 ch.c. Easy Goer (USA) – Jadana (Pharly (FR) 130)   111 [1995 93p: 5m² 5f* 6m* 1996 6d⁴ 8m* 8.5d a8f Nov 14] quite attractive colt: good walker and mover: smart performer: off course over 10 months prior to reappearance: visored, relished step up in trip when winning 5-runner minor event at Thirsk in May by short head from Hammerstein, getting the better of a ding-dong battle after bumping runner-up twice: left J. Gosden: off course nearly 6 months, below form in allowance races in USA: better at 1m than shorter, and should stay further: acts on firm and dead ground: blanketed for stalls entry (rather mulish) at Thirsk. *H. Tesher, USA*

LA MODISTE 3 b.f. Most Welcome 131 – Dismiss 95 (Daring March 116) [1995   – 81: 5m 6m² 6m⁴ 7m⁴ 6f* 8h* 7g⁶ 8v⁵ 1996 7g 10.1m 8m³ 7f 8f⁶ Jul 25] angular filly: fair performer: stiff tasks in fairly valuable handicaps and Kempton minor event first 3 starts: towards rear in lesser handicaps final 2: stays 1m: acts on hard ground. *S. Dow*

LAMORNA 2 ch.f. (Apr 1) Shavian 125 – Malibasta 83 (Auction Ring (USA)   73 123) [1996 6f⁶ 5f 7m³ 7f⁵ 5.7m 6m* 7d⁵ 5.2m³ 6m 6m 7.3s Oct 26] 3,000Y: quite attractive filly: has scope: has a quick action: second foal: dam 6f (at 2 yrs) and 1m winner: fair performer: won maiden auction at Warwick in June and valuable 20-runner seller (bought in 20,500 gns after beating Swiss Coast 1¾ lengths) at York in August: well below form in nurseries last 3 starts: needs further than 5f and stays 7f: acts on firm ground. *M. R. Channon*

LANCASHIRE KNIGHT 2 b.c. (Feb 25) High Estate 127 – Just A Treat (IRE) 47 (Glenstal (USA) 118) [1996 6g 6g Jun 15] 25,000Y: smallish colt: second foal: half-brother to 3-y-o Jack's Treat (by Thatching): dam 2-y-o 5f winner from family of Golden Fleece and Be My Guest: behind in maidens: reluctant stalls on debut. *S. Dow*

LANCASHIRE LEGEND 3 gr.g. Belfort (FR) 89 – Peters Pet Girl (Norwick – (USA) 125) [1995 66: 6m⁴ 6m⁴ 6d 1996 a8g² a8g³ a8g³ 6s 8f⁵ 7f 8g 8.3m a7g* a7g⁴ a70 a8g Nov 26] disappointing on turf, fair form on all-weather: off course 5 months and easy to back, well made at Lingfield in November: not sure to stay beyond 1m: acts on equitrack: visored (pulled hard, well beaten) eighth 3-y-o start. *S. Dow*

LANCASHIRE LIFE (IRE) 5 b.g. Petorius 117 – Parlais 101 (Pardao 120) – [1995 55: a7g 8m 10m 8m* 7.5m⁴ 8.1m² 8m⁶ 7.6m⁵ 8m 7.5m⁴ 10m 8.5d 8d 1996 8.3d 6.9m 7g May 17] strong gelding: modest handicapper at best: well beaten last 6 starts: should stay beyond 1m (raced too freely when tried): acts on good to firm and dead ground: often a front runner: sold 500 gns Doncaster July (1996) Sales. *E. J. Alston*

LANDFALL 3 b.g. Most Welcome 131 – Sextant 98 (Star Appeal 133) [1995 NR – 1996 10m a11g Jul 1] 8,000Y: tenth foal: half-brother to several winners, including 1995 3-y-o 12.3f winner Astrolabe (by Rainbow Quest) and Musidora Stakes runner-up Pilot (by Kris): dam, won twice at around 1¼m, out of smart Fluke, a half-sister to Bireme and Buoy: behind in maiden and a claimer. *J. G. FitzGerald*

LANDLORD 4 b.g. Be My Chief (USA) 122 – Pubby 73 (Doctor Wall 107) – [1995 71, a61: 6g 7f⁶ 7m⁴ 8m 7m 7m³ 8g a9.4g⁵ a8.5g² a12g a10g* 1996 a10g a10g a16g 11.7f⁶ Jul 24] rather unfurnished gelding: modest performer at 3 yrs: little encouragement in 1996: sold (J. Toller to Mrs J. Hawkins) 800 gns Ascot October Sales: stays 1¼m: acts on good to firm going and the all-weather: often blinkered: inconsistent. *J. A. R. Toller*

LANGTONIAN 7 br.g. Primo Dominie 121 – Yankee Special 60 (Bold Lad (IRE) 35 § 133) [1995 –§, a48§: a6g³ 7m 7.1m 8g⁶ 8.1f 8.3f⁵ a8g 7d a7g⁶ a8g 1996 a7g a6g a6g 8g³ 5.9d 8m 8.1g² 8m 7.1g 7.5m⁵ 9.2m³ 6f 10m⁴ 10d 8m⁵ Oct 2] sturdy gelding: carries condition: poor handicapper who has won once since 1991: stays 9f: acts on fibresand, probably on any turf going: usually visored/blinkered: has worn near-side pricker: usually finds little under pressure: inconsistent: sold to join G. Edwards 1,000 gns Doncaster November Sales. *J. L. Eyre*

L'ANNEE FOLLE (FR) 3 b.f. Double Bed (FR) 121 – Gai Lizza (FR) (Gairloch 108 122) [1995 NR 1996 10g* 10d⁵ 10g⁴ 10m² 12m* Jul 16] third foal: dam 1¼m (at 3 yrs) to 16.5f winner in France, also listed placed: French filly: won minor event at Saint-Cloud in April on debut and (after tailed off in Prix Saint-Alary and in frame in listed races at Evry and Saint-Cloud) 9-runner Prix Minerve at Evry (beat Leonila by a length) in July: will probably prove better suited by 1½m than shorter: yet to race extremes of going. *F. Doumen, France*

LA PELLEGRINA (IRE) 3 b.f. Be My Guest (USA) 126 – Spanish Habit 73 d (Habitat 134) [1995 NR 1996 7m 10m³ 10d 8m 8.3m⁵ 11.7m⁶ 10.3d a12g Oct 19] IR 150,000Y: angular filly: closely related to 2 winners, notably 1000 Guineas winner Las Meninas (by Glenstal), and half-sister to 2 winners abroad: dam, unraced, out of smart Irish 7f to 1¼m winner: best effort in maidens when third at Salisbury: lost her way: stays 1¼m: acts on good to firm ground (stiff task on dead): takes keen hold: disappointing. *P. W. Chapple-Hyam*

LA PERRUCHE (IRE) 3 b.f. Cyrano de Bergerac 120 – Red Lory 87 (Bay 49 Express 132) [1995 55: a6g a6g 1996 a7g³ a7g⁴ a7g⁵ Apr 29] poor maiden: probably stays 7f: has raced only on the all-weather. *Lord Huntingdon*

LA PETITE FUSEE 5 br.m. Cigar 68 – Little Missile (Ile de Bourbon (USA) 84 133) [1995 75, a81: 6m 6m² 6f⁵ 6g* 6m³ 7f 6m⁵ 6m 6g² 7f 6.1s a6g* a7g* a5g 1996 6m³ 6d³ 5m² 6m³ 6.1m* 6m* 6g 6m³ 6.1s Oct 22] rangy, workmanlike mare: fairly useful handicapper: won minor event at Chepstow in July, and 16-runner race at Salisbury in August: very good third of 28 to Cretan Gift in Silver Cup at Ayr penultimate outing: bled from the nose when down the field final one: effective at 5f to 7f: acts on firm and dead ground and goes well on fibresand: usually bandaged behind: front runner: often mounted on course and early to post: game and consistent. *R. J. O'Sullivan*

LAP OF LUXURY 7 gr.m. Sharrood (USA) 124 – Lap of Honour 100 (Final 102 Straw 127) [1995 107: 8.1m 8m 8.1m* 7f 7.9m 8m³ 8g² 8g⁶ 9m² 1996 8.1g 7.9m 7.6f³ 8m 8.1m⁴ 8.1m⁵ 8m³ Sep 14] sparely-made mare: unimpressive mover: useful performer at 6 yrs: not quite so good in 1996, sound efforts final 3 starts, narrowly-beaten third to Cadeaux Tryst in Turkey final one: stays 9f: acts on good to firm ground and dead: held up. *W. Jarvis*

LAPU-LAPU 3 b.f. Prince Sabo 123 – Seleter (Hotfoot 126) [1995 –: 6m 6m 1996 62 5m⁵ a6g⁴ 6d 6g 6m 8m* 8m⁴ 8g⁵ 8.9g⁴ 10.1m* a11g Nov 4] lengthy filly: modest handicapper: won at Pontefract in August and at Newcastle (confidently ridden) in October: favourite, tailed off in minor event at Southwell final start (jockey reported horse was probably over the top): stays 10.1f: acts on fibresand and good to firm ground, poor effort only start on a soft surface: consistent. *M. J. Camacho*

LARA (GER) 4 b.f. Sharpo 132 – La Salina (GER) (Kronzeuge) [1995 8.5v³ 9.5s⁴ 103 7g² 8d* 9s³ 9m² 9.5g² 9g* 8g² 10d⁵ 8g² 1996 8g⁶ 8m² 8g 8g⁶ 8m* 8s* Oct 20] half-sister to winners in Germany by Surumu and Caerwent: dam minor winner in Germany: useful German filly: won maiden and quite valuable race at Baden-Baden at 3 yrs: 1¼ lengths second of 10 to Bemont Park in Group 3 event at Milan in June: won conditions race at Baden-Baden in September and Group 3 event at Milan (beat Bemont Park a short neck) in October: stays 9.5f: acts on good to firm ground and soft: visits Indian Ridge. *B. Schutz, Germany*

LARGESSE 2 b.c. (Apr 17) Cadeaux Genereux 131 – Vilanika (FR) 81 (Top Ville 80 129) [1995 6m² 5g* 6.1m⁶ 5f⁴ 7.3m Sep 22] 17,000F: tall, useful-looking colt: has a long, round action: second foal: half-brother to 3-y-o Bashtheboards (by Dancing Dissident): dam stayed 1m: fairly useful form: won maiden auction at Pontefract in July: slightly better form in minor event at Chester (wandered, probably not ideally suited by track) and nursery at Beverley next 2 outings: stays 6f: edged left first 2 starts. *John Berry*

LARISSA (IRE) 3 b.f. Soviet Star (USA) 128 – Pipitina 91 (Bustino 136) [1995 67 NR 1996 7d 8m⁴ 8f⁴ 10f⁴ a12g Aug 16] quite attractive filly: has a round action: first foal: dam stayer: fair maiden: soundly beaten in handicap on all-weather debut at Southwell final start: should be suited by further than 1m: sold 3,000 gns Newmarket December Sales. *G. Wragg*

LARN FORT 6 gr.g. Belfort (FR) 89 – Larnem 43 (Meldrum 112) [1995 58: a8g³ – a8g* 10.3g⁴ 9.9m* 10g 10.3m* 10g² 10.8g⁴ 10m⁴ 9.9m² 10f⁴ 11.5m⁶ 10d a9.4g 10f⁴ a11g² a12g⁶ 1996 a11g⁵ 9.9d 8m 8m 9.2f Aug 19] tall, leggy gelding: modest handicapper at 5 yrs: disappointing in 1996, reportedly finishing lame final start: stays 11f: acts on firm ground, soft and fibresand: has won for amateur: normally visored/blinkered: usually held up. *C. W. Fairhurst*

LAROCHE (GER) 5 b.h. Nebos (GER) 129 – Laurea (GER) (Sharpman (FR) 123 124) [1995 118: 12s⁵ 12m* 11m³ 12m² 12.5g⁴ 12g 1996 12g* May 12] very smart German horse: won Group 2 Gerling Preis at Cologne in May by 1¼ lengths from Protektor: stays 1½m: acts on soft going and good to firm: blinkered since third 3-y-o start: front runner: best when able to dominate, and not the most consistent. *H. Jentzsch, Germany*

LARROCHA (IRE) 4 b.f. Sadler's Wells (USA) 132 – Le Melody 102 (Levmoss 110 + 133) [1995 116: 12m* 10m* 12g⁵ 11.9m* 12d³ 1996 a12f* a10g Mar 27] tall, rather leggy filly: fluent mover: smart performer: wide-margin winner of listed events at Newbury and York in 1995: best effort when little over a length third of 10 to Carling in Prix Vermeille at Longchamp on final start for L. Cumani: won at Dubai in February by 8 lengths: out of depth behind Cigar in Dubai World Cup next time, always in rear: smart form at 1½m and will be suited by further: acts on good to firm ground and dead (not tried on extremes), and on sand: races prominently: sent to USA. *Saeed bin Suroor*

LARRY LAMBRUSCO 3 b.g. Executive Man 119 – Freudenau (Wassl 125) – [1995 54: 6m 8.1g a8.5g⁴ 1996 a8g Jun 14] leggy gelding: best effort in maiden events at 2 yrs for M. Jarvis when fourth in falsely-run race at Wolverhampton: tailed off in median auction event at Southwell after 9-month absence: stays 8.5f: sent to Italy. *R. Champion*

LARRYLUKEATHUGH 3 b.g. Prince Sabo 123 – Hidden Asset (Hello 51 ? Gorgeous (USA) 128) [1995 56?: 6g⁴ 6m 6f⁵ 6g 7.5d 1996 7s³ 6d 7.1g 6m a8g Nov 18] lengthy, unfurnished gelding: modest maiden at best: probably flattered when third in steadily-run seller at Catterick on reappearance: sold privately 500 gns Doncaster November Sales: probably stays 7f: tried blinkered. *J. J. O'Neill*

LASER LIGHT LADY 4 b.f. Tragic Role (USA) – Raina Perera 71 (Tyrnavos – 129) [1995 NR 1996 a10g a12g May 31] half-sister to several poor animals: dam maiden (stayed 7f) here at 2 yrs later who won in Italy: tailed off in claimer and seller. *N. P. Littmoden*

LAST AMBITION (IRE) 4 b.f. Cadeaux Genereux 131 – Fabulous Rina (FR) 29 (Fabulous Dancer (USA) 124) [1995 –: 7g 9f 7.6m 6m 1996 12m⁵ 11.6m 5.1m⁴ Aug 7] trained in Ireland by T. Stack for 4-y-o reappearance only: 50/1 and dropped markedly in trip, first worthwhile form when fourth in handicap at Nottingham final start: evidently a sprinter. *R. Champion*

LAST BUT NOT LEAST 3 b.f. Dominion 123 – Almadaniyah (Dunbeath 63 (USA) 127) [1995 63: 6d 6m³ a5g⁴ 1996 a5g* a5g⁵ a5g⁵ 5m³ Apr 16] sturdy filly: modest performer: made all in minor event at Lingfield in January: acts on good to firm ground and the all-weather: has joined M. C. Pipe. *R. F. Johnson Houghton*

LAST CHANCE 2 b.c. (Apr 29) River Falls 113 – Little Red Hut (Habitat 134) 73 d [1996 6m⁴ 5.1m* 6f² 6g² 5f⁵ 5m 5g a6g Nov 14] 11,000F, 9,400Y: seventh live foal: half-brother to fairly useful 5-y-o 7f winner Orange Place (by Nordance): dam lightly-raced half-sister to Red Regent: fair form: trained by G. Lewis first 4 starts: won maiden auction at Bath in June: disappointing afterwards: stays 6f: has had tongue tied down. *C. N. Allen*

LAST ROUNDUP 4 b.g. Good Times (ITY) – Washita (Valiyar 129) [1995 –: 8d – 8g 7m 7m 10.3d 11.8g 1996 a8.5g⁴ a8.5g a12g a11g Nov 4] disappointing since 2 yrs and one to treat with caution. *C. W. Thornton*

LAST SECOND (IRE) 3 gr.f. Alzao (USA) 117 – Alruccaba 83 (Crystal 121 p Palace (FR) 132) [1995 97P: 6g* 7d* 1996 8m² 10m* 10m* Oct 5]

As a racehorse, this filly is most individual in character. The thoroughbred is a notoriously fragile animal, and Last Second seems to be considered fragile even by normal standards for a horse in training. Her 'delicate constitution' meant that when connections sat down to plan her campaign as a three-year-old they decided that it could extend to only four races—and she failed to make one of those. The interest her appearances provoked, however, was not just down to their rarity value. They revealed an abundance of talent. That makes Last Second rare enough—only some 0.4% of the horses that raced here in 1996 were rated 120 or higher—but then there was the manner in which she demonstrated that ability. In the words of her trainer, 'she can quicken but only for a very short spell.' In the words of her jockey, 'she either makes you look brilliant or gets you crucified.' Last Second and waiting tactics are a most exciting combination and we are very glad that more will be seen of them in 1997, even if it will not be very much.

It would have been frustrating if Last Second had not been kept in training, not just because she can clearly add a great deal to good races judged on the form she has shown already, but also because there is more than a lingering suspicion that the best has not been seen of her, even though she has been beaten. That ability to quicken may be a short-lived one, but we have not yet seen on the racecourse just how short-lived that is. At the finishing line, Last Second has always been running on strongly. In 1996 that brought two sparkling victories to add to those in a maiden at Redcar and the C L Weld Park Stakes at the Curragh on her only two starts as a two-year-old. First, though, was the race she could not be made ready for, the One Thousand Guineas, and the one in which she was beaten, the Coronation Stakes at Royal Ascot. The saga of Sir Mark Prescott's quest for a Group 1 victory had Pivotal cast as hero,

Vodafone Nassau Stakes, Goodwood—Sheikh Mohammed's pair Annaba (rails) and Papering try their hardest, but Last Second is about to leave them for dead

but at the Royal meeting he was very nearly upstaged by Last Second. George Duffield, Prescott's jockey for twenty-four years, described their tactics for the Coronation again in November: 'We knew she was good, but deep down didn't think she was quite that class. So the plan was to get her placed in a Group 1. Sir Mark asked my opinion and I said if I rode her to be placed she probably would be, and might even nick it. He said that was the way he read it too, and the owner agreed. We nearly pulled it off.' They certainly did, surging past the Pouliches winner Ta Rib and Irish Guineas second Dance Design, but failing to catch Shake The Yoke (whose jockey was able to take things cosily) by a neck. The nerves for these tactics had required 'four valium for Prince Faisal and three for George Duffield', according to Sir Mark afterwards. For those who had gambled Last Second from 33/1 to 12/1, the prescription might well have been an anti-depressant.

Requirements after the Nassau Stakes at Goodwood and Sun Chariot Stakes at Newmarket would have been of a purely celebratory nature. These were both Group 2 races and Last Second started favourite. What few worrying moments there were all came at Goodwood where she was being pushed along vigorously and changed her legs approaching the final furlong, but she powered past the Sheikh Mohammed pair Papering and Annaba a hundred yards out and won by two lengths, looking very strong at the finish. It was a stronger field in the Sun Chariot two months later, but the winning margin was two lengths again and Last Second was even more impressive; closing up still swinging on the bridle two furlongs out, she stormed clear when Duffield lifted his whip at

Sun Chariot Stakes, Newmarket—the 'fragile' Last Second administers another drubbing, this time to Spout

Mr Faisal Salman's "Last Second"

the distance and Spout was the only one of her opponents who could mount more than a token effort to stay in touch.

Last Second (IRE) (gr.f. 1993)	Alzao (USA) (b 1980)	Lyphard (b 1969)	Northern Dancer
			Goofed
		Lady Rebecca (b 1971)	Sir Ivor
			Pocahontas II
	Alruccaba (gr 1983)	Crystal Palace (gr 1974)	Caro
			Hermieres
		Allara (gr 1973)	Zeddaan
			Nucciolina

Last Second is the best middle-distance horse Sir Mark Prescott has trained and we expect her to show even better form as a four-year-old, when a first target is reportedly the Coronation Cup. That represents a step up in trip, as well as class, and for all that she has shown absolutely no sign of stopping at the end of a mile and a quarter, Last Second cannot be described as a certain stayer. That doubt combined with the tactics already in place should make for interesting viewing. All five of her dam Alruccaba's previous five foals were by much stronger stamina influences than Last Second's sire Alzao, but all stayed at least a mile and a half. The Darshaan fillies Arrikala and Alouette were both good enough to contest the Irish Oaks, and Arrikala looked unlucky not to win it. She also won a listed race at a mile and a quarter. The Niniski fillies Allegra and Ballymac Girl were less distinguished, the former winning an all-weather maiden and the latter three modest races at around a mile and three quarters and two novice hurdles. An established producing record is generally more important than her racing record when assessing what a dam might pass on, and Alruccaba raced only as a two-year-old anyway, winning a six-furlong maiden at Brighton. Her dam Allara, another who was lightly raced, won over seven furlongs in the French Provinces and is a half-sister to the dams of Aliysa and Nishapour. Last Second is clearly worth a try at a mile and a half. A good-topped filly, she acts on good to firm and good to soft ground but has not raced on anything more extreme. The name Last Second comes not from some early divination of her riding tactics, but apparently from her owner's finely-timed appearance to bid for her at the 1994 Irish National Yearling Sale. His final bid was IR 120,000 guineas, the top price paid for an Alzao yearling that year. *Sir Mark Prescott*

LAST SPIN 4 b.f. Unfuwain (USA) 131 – Spin (High Top 131) [1995 –: 10m 11.5f⁵ 12m 16.2g⁵ a11g 1996 9.9m 10.8f 7g 12g Jul 10] rangy, unfurnished filly: winning hurdler: disappointing maiden on flat: tried visored and blinkered. *J. R. Jenkins* —

LA SUQUET 4 b.f. Puissance 110 – Persian Case (Upper Case (USA)) [1995 72: a5g⁴ 6d² 5.1g² 5.1g² 5m⁵ 5g* 5.1m 1996 5s 5g³ 5m² 5m 5m 5d 5g³ 5f³ 5g*ᵈⁱˢ 5g Jul 12] small, good quartered filly: fair handicapper: first past post in weak 3-finisher seller at Hamilton in July, but disqualified for causing early interference: best form at 5f: acts on good to firm and soft ground, well below form on equitrack: usually races prominently: blinkered (below form) fifth 4-y-o start: covered by Presidium. *N. Tinkler* 72

LATAHAAB (USA) 5 b.h. Lyphard (USA) 132 – Eye Drop (USA) 96 (Irish River (FR) 131) [1995 92: a10g³ 12g 16.2m⁶ 16m* 16.1m 15.9m² 14.8m* 16d⁶ 16m⁶ 1996 16.5g² 20m⁵ 13.9m³ 15.9m 14f⁴ Sep 5] sturdy, quite attractive horse: fairly useful handicapper: grossly flattered in Gold Cup at Royal Ascot (beaten only 6¾ lengths by Classic Cliche) and rated on placed efforts in steadily-run rated stakes at Doncaster in May and listed rated stakes at York in July: distant last in listed race at York and minor event at Salisbury last 2 starts: effective at 16.5f, stays 2½m (at least in a steadily-run race): acts on dead ground and good to firm: tried blinkered, not when successful: races prominently: has joined J. Gifford. *R. Akehurst* 92

LA TANSANI (IRE) 3 b.c. High Estate 127 – Hana Marie 101§ (Formidable (USA) 125) [1995 60+: 6m 5m⁶ 6.1m 6f⁶ 1996 8f⁶ 6m a8g² a7g² 7.1m 6g a8g² a7g² Jul 27] good-bodied colt: modest maiden: best at 7f/1m: goes well on the all-weather, has raced only on a sound surface on turf. *R. Hannon* 60 a68

LATCHING (IRE) 4 ch.f. Thatching 131 – Keepers Lock (USA) (Sunny's Halo (CAN)) [1995 76: 8g⁶ 9g⁴ 6m³ 6m⁴ 5g³ 6g 6m³ 1996 6g* 5m 6m* 6d 6f 6g 6.1m² 7.3m 6g Oct 19] tall, lengthy filly: fairly useful handicapper: won twice at Kempton in April: best efforts at 6f, and has form over as far as 9f: acts on firm and soft ground: blinkered (below best) fourth 3-y-o start. *R. F. Johnson Houghton* 88

LATCH KEY LADY (USA) 4 b.f. Tejano (USA) – Key To The Heart (USA) (Arts And Letters) [1995 –: a12g 1996 9.9d Mar 30] leggy filly: soundly beaten since debut: covered by Foxhound. *R. D. E. Woodhouse* —

LA THUILE 4 b.f. Statoblest 120 – Mild Wind (Porto Bello 118) [1995 –: 5.1m 7g 6m 6m 8g a10g 5m 1996 8.2m 8m 11.5m Oct 23] leggy, narrow filly: no worthwhile form, hampered and brought down final start: tried blinkered. *T. J. Etherington* —

LATIN LOVER (GER) 3 br.g. Roi Danzig (USA) – Lago Real (Kings Lake (USA) 133) [1995 NR 1996 8g 10g Jul 1] DM 18,000F, IR 6,000Y, 6,600 2-y-o: robust gelding: fourth foal: half-brother to 4-y-o Tirollac (by Tirol): dam, French 1m winner, half-sister to smart French stayer El Badr: well beaten in maidens: sold 500 gns Doncaster August Sales. *M. J. Camacho* —

LATIN QUARTER (USA) 3 b.c. Zilzal (USA) 137 – Artiste 95 (Artaius (USA) 129) [1995 NR 1996 8d 10g⁶ 8g⁵ Oct 2] quite attractive colt: good mover: fifth living foal: half-brother to useful winner at up to 16.5f Allegan (by Alleged) and French 12.2f winner Sedova (by Nijinsky): dam, 1m winner who stayed 1¼m, out of Oaks second Val's Girl: fair maiden: seemed not to stay penultimate start: ran better than finishing position suggests final outing, helping set too strong a pace and losing about 72

5 lengths when hampered inside final furlong: sold 15,000 gns Newmarket Autumn Sales: should prove best at 1m: sent to Sweden. *R. Charlton*

L A TOUCH   3 b.f. Tina's Pet 121 – Silvers Era 72 (Balidar 133) [1995 53: a5g   58
a5g 5.1g⁴ 6.1m⁶ 6g² 6m* 6m 6m⁴ a6g⁵ 5.3d⁵ 6s 1996 5f² 5m² 6m⁴ 6m² 6.1m Sep 16]
strong, lengthy filly: modest handicapper: ridden by 7-lb claimer, equal second
at Yarmouth penultimate start, denied a run then finishing well: subsequently left
C. Dwyer's stable and ran poorly final outing: effective at 5f and 6f: acts on firm
ground, below form both starts on a soft surface. *J. J. Quinn*

LATVIAN   9 gr.g. Rousillon (USA) 133 – Lorelele (FR) 97 (Lorenzaccio 130)   70 §
[1995 76: 12.4g³ 11.1g² 13.1g² 13f⁶ 12m* 12.4m³ 12m* 12m⁵ 13.1g 11.1g² 12f⁶
15.1s 1996 12.4d* 12g 12.1g³ 12.1f 12f⁶ 11.1m² 15.8g² 16.1m 13.1g² 12m* 15.1m
11.1d⁵ 15.1s Nov 7] lengthy gelding: fair handicapper: won at Newcastle in May and
Carlisle (claimer) in August: effective at 11f to 15f: acts on hard ground and dead:
blinkered 3 times (won on first occasion), but not since 6 yrs: visored 3 times in 1996,
winning at Carlisle on first occasion: inconsistent at 9 yrs, and looked none too keen
on occasions, particularly when tailed off final start (also unenthusiastic when
successful over hurdles in October). *R. Allan*

LATZIO   3 b.f. Arrasas (USA) 100 – Remould 83 (Reform 132) [1995 –: 6m 6f   –
6m⁴ 5m³ a6g 7g a6g a6g a5g 1996 a6g a12g³ a12g 6.9f Apr 23] no worthwhile form:
tried blinkered. *B. A. Pearce*

LAUGHING BUCCANEER   3 ch.g. Weldnaas (USA) 112 – Atlantic Line   47
(Capricorn Line 111) [1995 62+, a57: 5g⁶ 6m³ 7f 7.3m 6f⁶ 7m² 8.5s⁵ 7m 7.3d⁵
a8g⁴ a5g a6g⁴ 1996 8.2g 10.2g 8m 10m 10g³ 10m a12g Sep 21] tall gelding: poor
maiden: sold out of A. G. Foster's stable 1,000 gns Ascot July Sales after fourth
3-y-o start: respectable third in apprentice race at Kempton easily best of remaining
3 outings: stays 1¼m: effective blinkered/visored or not: has joined D. N. Carey.
M. J. Heaton-Ellis

LAUREL DELIGHT   6 ch.m. Presidium 124 – Foudroyer (Artaius (USA) 129)   90
[1995 NR 1996 5m 5.1g⁵ 5m 5m 5g³ 5g³ 5m* 5m Aug 10] lengthy mare: good
mover: rated 104 in summer of 1994: produced a foal (to Selkirk) in spring of 1995:
fairly useful form in handicaps on return, gaining a deserved success at Newcastle:
best at 5f: acts on firm and dead ground: has run well when sweating: often a front
runner: bandaged at 6 yrs: game. *J. Berry*

LAVENDER DELLA (IRE)   3 gr.f. Shernazar 131 – All In White (FR) (Car-   66
white 127) [1995 47: 7m⁵ 7f⁶ 6g 1996 10.2g² 10m 10f² 10s a10g⁴ a12g Dec 14] neat   a–
filly: fair maiden: best effort when second to Frog in handicap at Newbury third start,
running on strongly: off course over 3 months, well held on return: will stay at least
1½m: acts on firm ground, no form on soft or all-weather. *M. J. Fetherston-Godley*

LAVIRCO (GER)   3 bl. or br.c. Konigsstuhl (GER) – La Virginia (GER) (Sur-   125
umu (GER)) [1995 107p: 8s* 8s* 1996 8.5g² 8s* 11g* 12v* 12g² 12g* Sep 22]
There's little doubt who was Germany's Horse of The Year. Lavirco
came into 1996 looking to beat in the colts' classics and left it still the
leader of his generation. He won the equivalents of the Two Thousand Guineas
and the Derby, and in beating his elders in the EMS Kurierpost Europa-Preis at
Cologne demonstrated that he will be a major contender for the top prizes in
Europe in 1997. It was not all plain sailing, however.
    A few eyebrows were raised when, on his reappearance at Krefeld, he
was beaten by Surako who had finished four lengths behind him in Germany's
most important race for two-year-olds the previous autumn. Gestut Fahrhof
owns both colts, and, in the absence of Surako, punters sent Lavirco off at odds
on for the first classic, the fourteen-runner Mehl-Mulhens-Rennen at Cologne.
In a poor-quality renewal (Brandon Magic was the only foreign challenger) he
beat Accento comfortably, the remainder strung out six lengths and more
behind. With seven weeks until the Deutsches Derby there was time for Lavirco
to pick up the Group 2 Union-Rennen over eleven furlongs back at Cologne,
settling the score with Surako by two and a half lengths, quickening decisively
over two furlongs out. As in the Mehl-Mulhens-Rennen, only one British raider
contested the German Derby at Hamburg; this was King Edward VII Stakes-

fourth Germano and he failed to give his running, finishing last. Sixteen home-based runners took Lavirco on, but his superiority over them was even greater than before, and he sauntered home four lengths clear of his old rival Surako. With the German St Leger still on the cards, Lavirco was given a preparatory race in an extremely valuable Group 2 event at Hoppegarten in August, for which he started 10/1-on in a field of six. He lost. Rank outsider Bad Bertrich Again, over twenty lengths behind in the Derby, caused the upset of the German season. Apparently this was the first occasion Lavirco had spent a night away from home, though it is to be hoped with 1997 in mind that this was not a valid excuse. Lavirco was denied his chance of Germany's triple crown in favour of a meeting with his elders in the Europa Preis at Cologne. Protektor, Hollywood Dream and Luso may not be the very best mile-and-a-half horses in Europe, but they had all won Group 1 events in the current season, and all went on to run good races afterwards. Lavirco beat them decisively, quickening smartly over two furlongs out in a race run at a good pace and three and a half lengths clear of Protektor at the line; Hollywood Dream and Luso were close up for the minor honours, the four principals finishing well clear. That was it for the season but, as with Gestut Fahrhof's recent German Derby winners Lando and Laroche, Lavirco will be back as a four-year-old. Likely to prove best ridden for a turn of foot at around a mile and a half (he would probably stay a mile and three quarters but seems most unlikely to be given the chance now), he acts well on heavy going and has yet to encounter top-of-the-ground.

Lavirco (GER) (bl. or br.c. 1993)	Konigsstuhl (GER) (br 1976)	Dschingis Khan (br 1961)	Tamerlane
			Donna Diana
		Konigskronung (br 1965)	Tiepoletto
			Kronung
	La Virginia (GER) (b 1988)	Surumu (ch 1974)	Literat
			Surama
		La Dorada (b 1974)	Kronzeuge
			Love In

Lavirco is probably the best son of his recently-deceased sire, the 1979 German triple crown winner Konigsstuhl. He is clearly the best of the six classic winners (Pik Konig, Majoritat, Alkade, Mandelbaum and Caballo are the others), and at this stage of his career is a little better than Monsun, who was retired to stud in 1996 and along with Group 1 winners Pik Konig, Caballo and Twen is also the product of a mating between Konigsstuhl and a Surumu mare. Lavirco is the first foal of La Virginia, who won twice at a mile and a quarter in Germany at three. Grandam La Dorada was the champion two-year-old filly in Germany in 1976 and did well at stud. One daughter, La Colorada, won the Preis der Winterkonigin (the top race for juvenile fillies), was second in the Arag Preis (One Thousand Guineas) and won a Group 3 contest over an extended mile and a quarter before achieving greater fame in 1991 as the dam of top-class middle-distance colt Lomitas. Another two of La Dorada's daughters were listed placed, notably La Calera who is the grandam of 1996 Arag Preis winner La Blue. The third dam, Love In, also bred both Lorena, who was the grandam of Preis der Diana winner Longa, and Liranga who was listed placed before producing 1984 German Derby winner Lagunas and the high-class miler Lirung. Love In's sister Love For Sale is the ancestress through Bessie Wallis and Alys to 1992 Arag Preis winner Princess Nana, and through Bessie Wallis and Book of Love to 1996 three-year-old Bon Jovi, the Konigsstuhl colt who finished third to Lavirco in the Union-Rennen. Lavirco certainly has the pedigree to make a fine stallion, though it's good that he's to be given a chance to fulfil his racing potential first. *P. Rau, Germany*

LA VOLTA 3 b.f. Komaite (USA) – Khadino (Relkino 131) [1995 86: 5g* 6d⁶ 6f – 7f* 8m² 1996 9s 8m⁶ 8.1m Aug 10] strong, lengthy filly: fairly useful form at 2 yrs: tailed off all starts in 1996: stays 1m: acts on firm ground. *J. G. FitzGerald*

LAW COMMISSION 6 ch.g. Ela-Mana-Mou 132 – Adjala 89 (Northfields 98 (USA)) [1995 83: 7m 6g 6g 8f³ 6f⁶ 6f* 7.3d 1996 5.1f 7.3s⁴ 6m* 6f 6m* 6f⁴ 7m* 7g²

7m⁵ 7g Oct 19] small, sturdy gelding: useful handicapper: formerly inconsistent, but in fine form in 1996: won at Folkestone, Kempton (claimer) and Ascot (7-runner rated stakes) in the summer: effective at 6f to 1m: acts on any going: sometimes hangs under pressure: held up: has broken out of stalls and been withdrawn twice, including on ninth intended 6-y-o start. *D. R. C. Elsworth*

LAW DANCER (IRE)   3 b.g. Alzao (USA) 117 – Judicial (USA) (Law Society (USA) 130) [1995 76+: 7.1d⁵ 7g⁶ 1996 a8.5g⁴ a9.4g* 10g⁶ a9.4g* 10g⁶ 8.1d a8.5g² a9.4g⁴ 8f³ 10m⁴ 10g⁶ 10v 10m Sep 19] small gelding: fair handicapper: won at Wolverhampton in March and April: stays 1¼m: acts on firm ground, well beaten on heavy penultimate start: goes well on fibresand. *T. G. Mills*   74 a78

LAWFUL FIND (IRE)   2 gr.c. (May 21) Contract Law (USA) 108 – Mrs Mutton 89 (Dancer's Image (USA)) [1996 a5g* 5.1g a5g* 5m³ 5m² 6d* 5f² 5g 6g⁶ 8g⁶ 7g⁵ 9s Oct 17] IR 4,000Y: leggy, workmanlike colt: half-brother to several winners, including fair sprinter Useful (by Thatching) and Irish 8.5f winner Steel Head (by Salmon Leap): dam, placed at 1½m, was disappointing: fair performer: successful in 2 sellers at Wolverhampton in April and in claimer at Leicester in May: claimed £7,000 out of R. Hollinshead's stable at Beverley on seventh outing: trained first 4 starts in France by G. E. Mikhalides: best form at sprint distances: acts on firm and dead ground: blinkered final start. *J. Pfersdorff, France*   60 +

LAWFUL LOVE (IRE)   6 b.g. Law Society (USA) 130 – Amata (USA) (No-double (USA)) [1995 –: 10m 12m⁶ 12d 11.9d 1996 11.8m 12.1g² Jul 1] leggy gelding: shows knee action: bad performer. *T. W. Donnelly*   28

LAWN LOTHARIO   2 ch.g. (May 17) Pursuit of Love 124 – Blade of Grass 78 (Kris 135) [1996 8g 8m² 8.2g 7.1s⁴ Nov 7] 13,000Y: strong, angular gelding: fourth foal: half-brother to useful French 3-y-o 1m winner Brindle (by Polar Falcon) and useful 4-y-o sprinter Warning Star (by Warning): dam, 7f winner, is out of Princess Elizabeth winner Clare Island: second of 4 to stable-companion Double Flight in maiden at Ayr in September: no comparable form, tending to carry head awkwardly on final outing: stays 1m: best form on top-of-the-ground. *M. Johnston*   64

LAWN ORDER   3 b.f. Efisio 120 – Zebra Grass 85 (Run The Gantlet (USA)) [1995 51p: 5f 6m 5m 6.1d 1996 6g a7g⁶ 8g 10m⁶ 12f 10g³ 12.1m* 13.1g⁵ 13m⁴ 10d Aug 26] angular, good-quartered filly: poor handicapper: won maiden event at Hamilton in July, hanging left: well beaten last 2 starts: sold 2,800 gns Newmarket Autumn Sales: stays at least 13f: acts on good to firm ground: usually held up. *Mrs J. R. Ramsden*   48

LAWNSWOOD CAPTAIN (IRE)   3 ro.c. Maelstrom Lake 118 – Morgiana 42 (Godswalk (USA) 130) [1995 50: a5g 5.1g 6m³ 5m⁶ 7.5d 6s 8f⁵ 8f 1996 7g⁴ 8m Jun 4] angular colt: poor form: stays 1m: none too consistent: sent to Lebanon. *R. Hollinshead*   42

LAWNSWOOD JUNIOR   9 gr.g. Bairn (USA) 126 – Easymede 85 (Run-nymede 123) [1995 –: 8.2g 7g 8.3g 8.1g 8.1f 10.5m 1996 a11g⁵ 10m Jun 19] workmanlike gelding: of little account on flat nowadays: blinkered once and has run well in visor, much earlier in career: modest but ungenuine hurdler. *J. L. Spearing*   –

LAWSIMINA   3 b.f. Silly Prices 110 – Star of The Sea (Absalom 128) [1995 NR 1996 a5g⁶ 6m 7g a6g⁵ a6g⁶ a5g⁵ a6g⁵ a6g⁵ a6g Dec 3] 800Y: first foal: dam of little account: poor sprinter: sometimes slowly away. *Miss J. F. Craze*   47

LAY THE BLAME   3 b.c. Reprimand 122 – Rose And The Ring (Welsh Pageant 132) [1995 90p: 7.1m⁶ 6.1d⁶ 6g* 6.1m* 1996 8.1d 8f 7m⁵ 7d Aug 30] good-bodied colt: progressive form at 2 yrs: disappointing in 1996, best effort when fifth in handicap at Kempton: sold 17,000 gns Newmarket Autumn Sales: should prove effective over further than 6f: acts on good to firm ground. *W. Jarvis*   77

LAZALI (USA)   3 ch.c. Zilzal (USA) 137 – Leyali 104 (Habitat 134) [1995 NR 1996 8d 8g³ 8m 10m 7s⁴ Jul 4] angular colt: fourth foal: half-brother to a winner in USA by Shadeed: dam, 7f winner who stayed 1m, closely related to very useful sprinters Hanu and Sanu: fair maiden: sold 3,800 gns Ascot August Sales: will prove best at up to 1m: best efforts on an easy surface: sent to Italy. *E. A. L. Dunlop*   67

LEAD HIM ON (USA)   3 b.c. Cahill Road (USA) – Wicked Ways (USA) (Devil's Bag (USA)) [1995 NR 1996 10g⁵ 10g⁶ 10f⁴ 8.1d a8g Jul 22] $70,000Y: big, good-bodied colt: has plenty of scope: first foal: dam, ran twice in USA, half-sister to   67

Grade 3 1½m winner Jaded Dancer (by Nijinsky): sire, brother to Unbridled, Grade 1 9f winner: got very upset in stalls and was withdrawn on intended debut: fair form in maidens: trailed throughout in minor event at Southwell after getting upset in stalls and missing break: bred to be suited by middle distances. *P. W. Harris*

LEADING NOTE (USA)   2 ch.f. (Apr 18) Blushing John (USA) 120 – Beat   74 p
(USA) (Nijinsky (CAN) 138) [1996 8g³ 8s³ Nov 9] big, workmanlike filly:
has plenty of scope: fourth foal: half-sister to 3-y-o Woodspell (by Woodman) and 1¼m
to 11f winner (including in UAE in 1996) Merry Festival (by Private Account): dam
1m to 9f winner in USA, half-sister to very smart US filly Too Chic and smart miler
Lord Florey (both by Blushing Groom): fair form in maidens at Leicester (reluctant
stalls) and Doncaster (median auction event, 5½ lengths third of 16 to Polar Flight)
in the autumn: will stay at least 1¼m: sort to do better. *L. M. Cumani*

LEADING PRINCESS (IRE)   5 gr.m. Double Schwartz 128 – Jenny Diver   54
(USA) (Hatchet Man (USA)) [1995 55: 5m³ 5g 5m 5f 5f³ 5f 5g 5g 5f⁵ 5m⁵ 6m 5f 6g*
5m* a6g⁴ 1996 5g 6d 5g 6s 5d⁶ 5s 5m 5f* 5m² 6m 5m 5m² 5g 6m* 6f³ 5m⁶ 5m 6d⁵
6m* a6g Nov 18] leggy mare: modest handicapper: won at Carlisle (apprentices) in
June, at Hamilton (minor event) in August and at Newcastle (made all in 20-runner
race) in October: effective at 5f and 6f: acts on firm and soft ground (below form on
fibresand): visored or blinkered since second 3-y-o start: sometimes carries head
high: unseated rider in stalls eleventh 5-y-o intended start: usually races prominently.
Miss L. A. Perratt

LEADING SPIRIT (IRE)   4 b.g. Fairy King (USA) – Shopping (FR) (Sheshoon   88
132) [1995 77: 7g⁶ 8.2m⁴ 11.6m⁵ 14.1g² a14g 11.4d* 12.1g* 11.8g⁶ 12.1s 1996 10s
12.3g² 12m* 12.3m⁴ 12m³ 12g³ 12m* Sep 7] well-made gelding: fairly useful
handicapper: improved again at 4 yrs, and won at Kempton in June and September:
stays 1¾m: acts on good to firm ground and dead, below form on soft ground and
only try on fibresand: best ridden prominently/when able to dominate. *C. F. Wall*

LEAD STORY (IRE)   3 br.g. Lead On Time (USA) 123 – Mashmoon (USA)   –
80 (Habitat 134) [1995 NR 1996 10d 10g⁶ 10m 13g Jul 5] strong, workmanlike
gelding: fourth foal: closely related to 4-y-o 1m winner Talathath (by Soviet Star)
and half-brother to Irish 6f winner Gold Braisim (by Jareer): dam, 6f (at 2 yrs) and
1m winner, half-sister to very smart French middle-distance filly Galla Placidia:
no worthwhile form: sold to join M. C. Banks 12,000 gns Newmarket July Sales.
E. A. L. Dunlop

LEAP FOR JOY   4 ch.f. Sharpo 132 – Humble Pie 92 (Known Fact (USA) 135)   110
[1995 109: 5g 5d² 5d* 6m 1996 5d² 5g⁴ 5m 6g³ 6g⁴ 6m³ 5s* 5d⁴ 6s⁵ Nov 17] compact
filly: smart performer: third in Diadem Stakes at Ascot (led 1f out in falsely-run race
and beaten only 2 short heads by Diffident and Lucayan Prince) in September: won
7-runner Group 3 race at Milan in October by 1¼ lengths from Brave Edge: stays 6f:
acts on good to firm and soft ground: consistent. *J. H. M. Gosden*

LEAP IN THE DARK (IRE)   7 br.h. Shadeed (USA) 135 – Star Guide (FR)   –
(Targowice (USA) 130) [1995 34: 16.1g⁶ 14.1m 14.1f⁴ 14.1f² 14.1f 12m 16m 14.1m²
15.8g 1996 14.1m 10g 14.1f 11.6m 12m 12g Sep 3] big, lengthy, sparely-made horse:
poor performer: well beaten last 4 starts: stays 1¾m: probably acts on firm ground:
blinkered (well beaten) once in 1993. *Miss L. C. Siddall*

LEAR DANCER (USA)   5 b. or br.g. Lear Fan (USA) 130 – Green Gown (Green   –
Dancer (USA) 132) [1995 72: 12m 11.5m² 12m⁶ 16g* 16.2d⁶ 11.9g a16g³ a16g⁴   a76
1996 a14.8g* a14.8g* a14.8g 16.4g 16g⁵ May 17] leggy, workmanlike gelding: fair
handicapper: won twice at Wolverhampton in January: ran poorly afterwards: sold to
join Miss M. E. Rowland 7,800 gns Newmarket July Sales: stays well: acts on the
all-weather and on any turf going: usually visored/blinkered: usually held up: needs
treating with caution: maiden hurdler (downed twice). *P. Mitchell*

LEAR EXPRESS (USA)   3 b.c. Lear Fan (USA) 130 – Sheer Enchantment   87
(USA) (Siberian Express (USA) 125) [1995 NR 1996 10m⁴ 11.5g² 11.5f* 12m³ Aug
8] $80,000Y: leggy, quite attractive colt: second foal: dam lightly-raced half-sister to
2 useful Italian performers: fairly useful form: all out to land the odds in steadily-run
maiden at Yarmouth in July: again odds on, third of 4 to Time For Action in £7,900
handicap at Pontefract 16 days later, looking one paced: will prove suited by 1½m+:
has raced only on a sound surface: sent to Saudi Arabia. *H. R. A. Cecil*

LEAR JET (USA) 3 b.c. Lear Fan (USA) 130 – Lajna 88 (Be My Guest (USA) 90 d
126) [1995 90: 8d⁴ 8d 1996 10.2g* 12m² 10.5d 10m⁵ 10m³ Aug 7] strong,
rangy, good sort: has plenty of scope: fairly useful performer at best: narrowly won
maiden at Bath in April and ran well in handicap at Lingfield third start: disappointing afterwards, blinkered final start: sold 9,000 gns Newmarket September
Sales: stays 1¼m (last of 3 in minor event over 1½m): acts on good to firm ground:
front-runner and a strong-galloping type: one to treat with caution on flat, but won
juvenile hurdle in November for Bob Jones. *P. F. I. Cole*

LEARNING CURVE (IRE) 3 gr.f. Archway (IRE) 115 – Children's Hour 32
(Mummy's Pet 125) [1995 43: 6m a5g³ a5g 1996 a6g⁵ a6g⁶ a6g Mar 2] poor form:
last in handicaps final 2 starts: sold 2,300 gns Doncaster March Sales: has raced only
at sprint distances: best effort on fibresand: sent to Sweden. *Sir Mark Prescott*

LEAR WHITE (USA) 5 b.h. Lear Fan (USA) 130 – White Water (FR) (Pharly 114
(FR) 130) [1995 111: 8.5g⁵ 10g² 8d* 8d* 8m* 8s* 10s⁴ 8s⁵ 8m⁴ 8m³ 8.5g² 8d 10g
1996 10g 9m 10g⁵ 10s³ 12f⁴ 12m⁴ 12g⁴ 16f² 12g³ 18m³ 12g⁵ 14.5g² 14s² Nov 24]
neat ex-Italian horse: unimpressive mover: smart and most versatile performer: in
frame in 7 pattern events in 1996, including Hardwicke Stakes, Grand Prix de Saint-
Cloud, Aral-Pokal and Doncaster Cup: came closest to winning one when beaten a
head by Grey Shot in Goodwood Cup eighth start: effective at 1¼m to 2¼m: acts on
any going: tough and consistent. *P. A. Kelleway*

LE BAL 4 b.f. Rambo Dancer (CAN) 107 – Skarberg (FR) (Noir Et Or 125) [1995 33
41: 8d 8m⁶ 6.1m² 6g 6m⁶ 6m 6.1m 8.2f 1996 a8g a8g a6g⁴ a6g⁴ Mar 2] angular
filly: poor performer: effective at 6f, probably at 1m: acts on good to firm ground
and fibresand: often blinkered/visored, wasn't last 2 starts: inconsistent: covered by
Timeless Times. *Miss J. F. Craze*

LE BAM BAM 4 ch.c. Emarati (USA) 74 – Lady Lustre 70 (On Your Mark 125) –
[1995 NR 1996 5m 7m⁶ 8.3m a7g a8g⁶ 7m Jul 10] smallish, lengthy colt: unimpressive mover: first live foal: dam 1m winner: modest form at best: stiff task and
hampered in handicap final start: will probably prove best at up to 1m. *H. Akbary*

LEBEDINSKI (IRE) 3 ch.f. Soviet Lad (USA) 94 – Excavate (Nishapour (FR) 38
125) [1995 NR 1996 9.9g⁴ 10.8g 10m⁵ 10m 10g Aug 17] IR 1,000Y: workmanlike
filly: second foal: dam fair 1¼m winner in Ireland: showed a little ability in sellers
first and third starts: soundly beaten otherwise. *Mrs P. Sly*

LE DESTIN (FR) 3 b.c. Zayyani 119 – My Darling (Ela-Mana-Mou 132) [1995 117
7d² 8g⁴ 8g² 8.5g⁴ 8g⁶ 8g⁴ 1996 8s⁵ 10g* 10.5g² 12g³ 10.5m⁴ 12m³ 12.5g⁶ 10d⁵ 12m
12d⁶ 12.5d Oct 22] leggy, angular, French colt: fourth foal: dam unplaced daughter
of Cistus (stayed 1¼m well, rated 123): smart performer: won minor event at Saint-
Cloud in March: close third of 15 to Ragmar in Prix du Jockey-Club at Chantilly,
held up in rear then staying on strongly: rather disappointing next 2 starts but ran well
when 8½ lengths sixth of 16 to Helissio in Prix de l'Arc de Triomphe at Longchamp,
slowly away, soon niggled along in rear, no chance turning in then staying on: ran
poorly in listed race at Deauville final start: stays 1½m: acts on good to firm and dead
ground. *P. H. Demercastel, France*

LEDGENDRY LINE 3 b.g. Mtoto 134 – Eider 80 (Niniski (USA) 125) [1995 73 p
NR 1996 10.3s³ 10g 10.1d⁴ 12.4g⁴ 14d⁴ 10.5s Oct 5] 6,400F, 12,000Y: leggy, good-
topped gelding: sixth foal: brother to fairly useful middle-distance stayer Foundry
Lane: dam 2-y-o 9f winner: fair maiden handicapper: off course 4 months (set plenty
to do and not knocked about) when midfield in handicap at Haydock final start:
should prove suited by 1½m/1¾m: can improve at 4 yrs. *Mrs M. Reveley*

LEEDONS PARK 4 br.g. Precocious 126 – Scottish Rose 69 (Warpath 113) [1995 –
–: 10g 14.1h⁵ 1996 a8g a8g Jan 26] lengthy gelding: no sign of ability. *M. W. Easterby*

LEGAL BRIEF 4 b.g. Law Society (USA) 130 – Ahonita 90 (Ahonoora 122) –
[1995 –: 10.1g 8m 8g 10d 1996 8.5m⁶ 8.5m 8g 10m 8f Jul 18] good-topped gelding:
seems of little account: tried blinkered/visored. *J. S. Wainwright*

LEGAL DRAMA (USA) 4 ch.f. Turkoman (USA) – Sworn Statement (USA) –
(Believe It (USA)) [1995 8m 7g 6g 8m⁶ 7.5g 10d 1996 a10g a12g a6g 9.7m 8g 9m
11.5f 9.7f 10m Aug 31] ex-Irish filly: sixth foal: half-brother to 4 winners in USA:
dam winning American sprinter: rated 60 after first two 3-y-o starts: sold out of John
Muldoon's stable 800 gns Newmarket December (1995) Sales: trained by P. McBride

first 3 starts in 1996: no worthwhile form in Britain and sold 575 gns Ascot October Sales: stays 1m: tried blinkered, no improvement. *John Berry*

LEGAL ISSUE (IRE) 4 b.c. Contract Law (USA) 108 – Natuschka (Authi 123) 71
[1995 71: 8.1g^5 7g^3 7g^2 7.1m* 8f^2 7g^2 7g^2 8h^2 8m^4 7.1m* 7g 1996 a7g^4 a8g^2 a8g a66
7.5d^4 8m 8.5g 7g^3 7g* 7s* 7m 7g 7g a6g^5 a8g^5 a7g^4 a7g^5 Nov 29] sturdy colt: usually looks well: poor mover: fair handicapper: won at Doncaster in June and minor event (best form of season) at Catterick in July: stays 1m well: acts on fibresand and any going on turf. *W. W. Haigh*

LEGAL RIGHT (USA) 3 b.c. Alleged (USA) 138 – Rose Red (USA) 92 101
(Northern Dancer) [1995 91p: 7g^2 1996 10.3g* 10g^4 12f 12.5g^5 12m Jul 31] angular, useful-looking colt: fluent mover: useful performer: won maiden at Chester in May: best form when 4¾ lengths fourth to Don Micheletto in listed race at Goodwood later that month: slightly disappointing afterwards, running respectably when fifth of 6 to Water Poet in listed race at Saint-Cloud: stays at least 12.5f: possibly not at best on top-of-the-ground. *P. W. Chapple-Hyam*

LEGATEE 5 ch.m. Risk Me (FR) 127 – Legal Sound 85 (Legal Eagle 126) [1995 –
64d: a6g^3 6.9d^6 a8.5g 6.9g^6 a8.5g^3 a7g^2 a7g* a7g^3 a8.5g 7g 6f a6g a7g a6g 1996 a7g^6 a6g a6g^4 a7g^5 Feb 2] lengthy mare: fair performer at 4 yrs: claimed out of B. Meehan's stable £4,000 eighth 4-y-o start: bandaged, well below form for new stable: effective at 6f to 8.5f: acts on fibresand and good to firm ground, very best form on soft: tried blinkered and visored: usually races prominently. *A. Streeter*

LEG BEFORUM (IRE) 2 b.g. (Jun 4) Distinctly North (USA) 115 – Paulines –
Girl (Hello Gorgeous (USA) 128) [1996 5g Jul 1] IR 1,300F, IR 4,400Y, 3,800 2-y-o: third foal: dam lightly raced on flat/over hurdles in Ireland: 33/1, soon well behind in maiden auction at Windsor: joined L. Montague Hall and gelded. *G. L. Moore*

LEGENDARY LEAP 6 b.m. Legend of France (USA) 124 – Leap In Time –
(Dance In Time (CAN)) [1995 80: 8f 8m* 10f* 10f^6 10d 9g 1996 7f Sep 5] lengthy mare: fairly useful handicapper: ran poorly last 2 starts as 5-y-o: never placed to challenge over inadequate trip at Salisbury after almost year's absence: stays 1¼m: acts on firm and dead ground, probably on soft: held up in touch at 5 yrs. *Lord Huntingdon*

LEGEND OF ARAGON 2 b.f. (Mar 3) Aragon 118 – Legendary Dancer 90 67
(Shareef Dancer (USA) 135) [1996 5.1d^4 5g^4 5d* 5g^5 May 23] 5,000Y: smallish, plain filly: second foal: half-sister to 3-y-o Illegally Yours (by Be My Chief): dam unraced sister to smart miler Star Way: modest form: made all on favoured far side when winning maiden auction at Newcastle in May: out of her depth in minor event there later in month: will be suited by further than 5f. *J. A. Glover*

LE GRAND GOUSIER (USA) 2 ch.c. (Mar 20) Strawberry Road (AUS) 128 60
– Sandy Baby (USA) (Al Hattab (USA)) [1996 a7g 7.6d 10g^4 Oct 24] 450,000 francs Y: eighth foal: half-brother to numerous winners abroad, including useful French 2-y-o winners La Grande Cascade (at 1m in 1993 by Beaudelaire) and Grand Monarque (at 6.5f in 1994 by Fortunate Prospect): dam minor stakes sprint winner in USA: first form in maidens when fourth of 8 to very easy winner Supreme Sound in median auction event at Nottingham: stays 1¼m. *R. J. R. Williams*

LEGUARD EXPRESS (IRE) 8 b.g. Double Schwartz 128 – All Moss 66 39
(Prince Tenderfoot (USA) 126) [1995 –: 7g 5.7f a7g 7g 1996 8f^3 8g* 8m^2 8f Jun 5] good-topped gelding: carries condition: poor handicapper: game winner of 18-runner event at Bath in May: effective at around 1m and stays 10.8f: acts on any going: blinkered: sometimes sweating: front runner. *O. O'Neill*

LEIF THE LUCKY (USA) 7 ch.g. Lemhi Gold (USA) 123 – Corvine (USA) 64
(Crow (FR) 134) [1995 86: 8g^4 8m 8.1g 8m 1996 a9.4g a8g 8.5m 8.9m 10.5g^3 10.1m^5 12.3s 10.4g^3 10f^6 a9.4g^3 Dec 7] rather leggy, short-backed gelding: only fair handicapper in 1996: effective at 1m and 1¼m: acts on any ground, but has gained all 5 successes on an easy surface: usually held up: sometimes finds less than expected nowadays. *Miss S. E. Hall*

LEIGH CROFTER 7 ch.g. Son of Shaka 119 – Ganadora (Good Times (ITY)) 58
[1995 73, a82: a5g^4 a5g* a5g^3 a6g^5 a5g^2 a6g^2 a5g^6 5m 6g 6d a6g 7.3d 5d^2 5.1d^4 6g^6 a78 d
7d a6g^4 a6g^2 a5g^6 1996 a6g a6g a6g^3 a5g^3 a5g a6g^6 7d 6d^3 6s^4 a6g a6g a6g 7s a8g a7g* a7g* a6g^4 a7s* a7g^4 Dec 28] workmanlike gelding: fair handicapper at best: won at Wolverhampton (minor event) and Southwell in November,

and back at Wolverhampton in December: effective at 5f to 7f: acts on good to firm and heavy ground and goes well on fibresand: usually blinkered/visored: effective from front or held up. *P. D. Cundell*

LEITH ACADEMY (USA)   3 b.f. Academy Award (USA) – Uvula (USA) (His   –
Majesty (USA)) [1995 73: 6g⁵ 6f* 7.5m² 7m³ 1996 11.6g 10m 7m⁵ a10g⁵ Aug 17]
tall, unfurnished filly: fair form at 2 yrs: well held in varied company in 1996,
blinkered final start: sold 4,000 gns Newmarket Autumn Sales, resold 1,600 Fairyhouse December: bred to stay further than 7.5f. *B. W. Hills*

LEITRIM LODGE (IRE)   2 b.f. (Feb 22) Classic Music (USA) – Gentle Free-   64
dom (Wolver Hollow 126) [1996 6m³ 5m 5g* 7g⁵ Jul 10] IR 5,000Y: leggy, unfurnished filly: poor mover: closely related to 3 winners, including 1991 2-y-o 7f winner
Fairy Fable (by Fairy King) and 6f (at 2 yrs) and 7f winner Amoret (by Jareer): dam
unraced: modest form: easy 5-length winner of seller at Folkestone in July: finished
lame only subsequent outing: sold 2,500 gns Newmarket Autumn Sales: bred to stay
7f: ran as though something amiss on second outing. *N. A. Callaghan*

LE KHOUMF (FR)   5 ch.g. Son of Silver 123 – Bentry (FR) (Ben Trovato (FR)   72
128) [1995 NR 1996 8g⁴ 10g⁵ 8f 10g 10m⁵ 10m Jun 20] workmanlike gelding:
second foal: dam minor 11f winner in France: fairly useful winning hurdler: fair form
in maidens in April and May, but failed to progress: will stay beyond 1¼m: has raced
only on a sound surface: has joined J. Neville. *J. M. Bradley*

LENNOX LEWIS   4 b.g. Superpower 113 – Song's Best (Never So Bold 135)   88 d
[1995 100: 6m⁵ 6g² 6g 5m⁴ 6g 7m 6m⁶ 6m² 6g⁵ 5.2d⁴ 6d 1996 6g 5.2d 5g 6d⁵ 6m 6f
6m 6g 6g 6m 5f⁴ a7g⁵ Nov 15] good-quartered gelding: has a quick action: useful
handicapper at 3 yrs: well below that form in 1996, best of last 5 starts when visored
in claimer at Sandown penultimate one: stays 6f: acts on dead ground, best efforts on
good to firm: has been gelded. *A. P. Jarvis*

LEONATO (FR)   4 b.g. Law Society (USA) 130 – Gala Parade 78 (Alydar   103
(USA)) [1995 8g* 10m² 1996 8.2m⁶ 10m⁵ 10m⁶ 13.4d² 11.9f 12g 16g² Nov 1] tall,
leggy gelding: has knee action: third foal: half-brother to a winning French miler by
Caerleon: dam, sent to France to win over 9.5f, probably stayed 1½m, and is half-
sister to Irish St Leger winner Authaal: unraced at 2 yrs and trained by J. R. Lyon at 3
yrs, winning minor event at Chantilly: best efforts when second in listed rated stakes
at Chester (to Royal Scimitar) and Newmarket (to eased Orchestra Stall): suited by
test of stamina: acts on dead ground. *P. D. Evans*

LEONINE (IRE)   3 gr.c. Danehill (USA) 126 – Inanna 105 (Persian Bold 123)   102
[1995 99p: 6m² 6g* 1996 8m 7m Jun 19] tall colt: easy mover: good walker: useful
form in maidens at York in 1995: always rear in 2000 Guineas (under 12 lengths
ninth of 13) and last of 16 in Jersey Stakes at Royal Ascot: should stay 1m: sold
10,000 gns Newmarket December Sales: sent to France. *P. F. I. Cole*

LEPIKHA (USA)   3 ch.f. El Gran Senor (USA) 136 – Hortensia (FR) 119   72
(Luthier 126) [1995 NR 1996 8m 10m 12.3m⁵ 11.9m 13.1m³ 12m² 14d⁴ 18g* 14.1s
16.5s Nov 9] angular filly: half-sister to several winners, including Derby second and
French 15.5f winner Glacial Storm (by Arctic Tern): dam smart at around 1¼m in
France: fair handicapper: won 20-runner race at Pontefract in October, leading well
inside final 1f: sold 19,000 gns Newmarket December Sales: suited by thorough test
of stamina: acts on good to firm and soft ground. *B. W. Hills*

LE SHUTTLE   2 b.f. (May 10) Presidium 124 – Petitesse 55 (Petong 126) [1996   49
5f 5f⁴ 6m 6g³ 6m² 5d⁴ 5m³ 5.3g² 6d 5s⁶ a5g⁶ Nov 16] 6,000Y: second foal: dam, 5f
and 6f winner (including at 2 yrs), is sister to Paris House: modest form: stays 6f:
seems ideally suited by a sound surface. *M. H. Tompkins*

LE SPORT   3 b.g. Dowsing (USA) 124 – Tendency 77 (Ballad Rock 122) [1995   –
52+, a76: 5.1m⁵ 6d 8m a7g* 1996 a8.5g a10g⁵ a6g* a8.5g* a8.5g² 7s 7.6g⁶ 7m a8.5g⁶   a90 d
a9.4g⁶ 7.6m a8.5g a9.4g a9.4g 7g 10g 10.3g Oct 25] sturdy gelding: improved form
when easy winner of 2 handicaps at Wolverhampton in March: lost his way, and left
A. Bailey after fourteenth 3-y-o start: acts on fibresand. *D. Nicholls*

LE TEMERAIRE   10 b.g. Top Ville 129 – La Mirande (FR) (Le Fabuleux 133)   –
[1995 –: 12.3f 12m 12f⁵ 10.3m a14g 1996 a16g a12g Apr 29] sturdy gelding:
probably of little account nowadays. *Don Enrico Incisa*

LE TETEU (FR)   3 b.c. Saint Andrews (FR) 128§ – Nouvelle Star (USA) (Star de   69
Naskra (USA)) [1995 –p: 6.1d 1996 12m 10g 11.6m 8.1d* 10m 8g 8.1v³ Oct 6]

Prix Jean Prat, Chantilly—it's comfortable for Le Triton and Freddie Head

rather leggy, close-coupled colt: fair handicapper: won at Haydock (in good style) in June: well held on a sound surface next 2 starts, but good third on heavy ground back at Haydock on final one: best at around 1m: suited by a soft surface: won juvenile hurdle in December. *Bob Jones*

LETLUCE 3 b.f. Aragon 118 – Childish Prank (Teenoso (USA) 135) [1995 73: 7g* 7m⁶ 1996 8g⁵ 7.1d²ᵈⁱˢ 7f⁵ 8f⁶ 8.5f⁴ Jul 25] smallish, well-made filly: fairly useful performer: similar form all 3 starts as 3-y-o in Britain for R. Arnold, disqualified for causing interference when beaten 1½ lengths by Cool Edge in rated stakes at Haydock on second outing: respectable efforts in allowance company in USA: stays 1m: acts on firm and dead ground. *D. Vienna, USA*   92

LE TRITON (USA) 3 b.c. El Gran Senor (USA) 136 – La Tritona (Touching Wood (USA) 127) [1995 111: 8g* 8s⁴ 8s* 8m⁴ 1996 10.5g⁴ 9m* 10m⁴ 8d 8m 9g*   116

Maktoum Al Maktoum's "Le Triton"

9f Dec 1] rather leggy, quite attractive colt: smart performer: won 6-runner Prix Jean Prat at Chantilly in June by 2 lengths from Martiniquais, stretching away early in straight and clear when spooking near the end: creditable fifth (promoted) to Grape Tree Road in Grand Prix de Paris later in month, below form in Prix Jacques Le Marois at Deauville and Prix du Moulin de Longchamp before leaving Mme C. Head: made all in allowance event at Churchill Downs in November: behind in Hollywood Derby in December: quite stoutly bred (dam won at up to 12.5f) but not tried beyond 10.5f: acts on good to firm ground and soft: front runner/races prominently: had 2 handlers and on toes in preliminaries, then decidedly mulish at start, at Chantilly. *W. Mott, USA*

LET'S GET LOST 7 ch.g. Chief Singer 131 – Lost In France 80 (Northfields – (USA)) [1995 –, a59: a11g⁶ a11g⁴ a11g⁸ a12g⁵ 9.9m 12.5g a11g⁴ 1996 a12g Feb 1] lengthy gelding: formerly a fair handicapper: tailed off at Lingfield on reappearance: stayed 13f: acted on equitrack and on good to firm and dead ground (never going well on soft): tried blinkered: fell fatally over hurdles in March. *J. A. Harris*

LETTERLUNA 4 ch.f. Shavian 125 – Alteza Real 84 (Mansingh (USA) 120) – [1995 53: 8.3m⁵ 1996 a9.4g⁵ Mar 16] modest form when fifth in maiden at Windsor as 3-y-o: soundly beaten in similar event at Wolverhampton on only flat outing since: sold 5,000 gns Newmarket December Sales, covered by Formidable. *D. R. Gandolfo*

LEVELLED 2 b.c. (Feb 23) Beveled (USA) – Baino Charm (USA) (Diesis 133) 72 [1996 5g³ 5m* 6g 6s Oct 26] 6,000F, 9,000Y: fourth living foal: dam French 7f winner: won 5-runner median auction maiden at Carlisle in August: well held in nurseries afterwards: bred to stay 6f, but headstrong. *M. R. Channon*

LEVITICUS (IRE) 2 b.g. (Apr 3) Law Society (USA) 130 – Rubbiera (IRE) 72 ? (Pitskelly 122) [1996 7g⁴ 7m⁵ 7d⁴ 7.9g 8.3d³ 8g Oct 25] IR 7,700Y: leggy, un- furnished gelding: second foal: half-brother to Italian 3-y-o 7f winner Ettorello (by Classic Music): dam Irish maiden from family of Ma Biche: fair form without posing a threat in maidens at York, Doncaster and at Ayr first 3 starts: rather disappointing afterwards: stays 8.2f: possibly none too hearty. *T. P. Tate*

LEXUS (IRE) 8 b.g. Gorytus (USA) 132 – Pepi Image (USA) 111 (National) – [1995 31, a39: a10g³ a10g⁵ a8g⁴ a10g a11g 10.8g³ 10f⁴ 12g 1996 12.3g Apr 10] good-bodied gelding: poor handicapper nowadays: stays 11f: acts on firm ground, soft and all-weather surfaces: seems effective blinkered or not. *R. J. R. Williams*

LIA FAIL (IRE) 3 b.f. Soviet Lad (USA) 94 – Sympathy 77 (Precocious 126) 53 [1995 56+: 5m² 6.1m⁶ 6m 6f 6f⁵ 1996 a6g⁴ a6g² a6g* a9.4g 8f a6g a7g a7s⁴ a9.4g⁵ Dec 28] leggy, angular filly: modest performer: claimer ridden, justified favouritism in maiden handicap at Wolverhampton in April, getting up near finish: mostly dis- appointing afterwards: stays 7f: acts on fibresand, raced only on top-of-the-ground on turf. *R. Hollinshead*

LIBERATRICE (FR) 3 b.f. Assert 134 – Liberale (FR) (Fabulous Dancer – (USA) 124) [1995 –p: 7g 1996 10g 10f 13.1m Sep 9] small, sturdy filly: fluent mover: no worthwhile form: bred to be suited by test of stamina. *E. A. L. Dunlop*

LIDANNA 3 b.f. Nicholas (USA) 111 – Shapely Test (USA) (Elocutionist (USA)) 113 [1995 103p: 6g³ 5m* 6.3m² 1996 5m* 6d* 5f Jun 21] 13,000Y: workmanlike filly: sixth foal: half-sister to 4 winners, including fair Birchwood Sun (up to 7f, by Bluebird) and a Czech 1000 Guineas winner by Rusticaro: dam, Irish 1m winner, granddaughter of sprint-winning close relative of Godswalk (sprinter, rated 130): smart performer: won maiden at Tipperary at 2 yrs: successful in 6-runner listed race at Tipperary (by short head from Ailleacht) and 9-runner Weatherbys Ireland Green lands Stakes at the Curragh (by 3 lengths from Catch The Blues) in May: soon off bridle (first outing on very firm ground) and far from disgraced when eighth of 17 to Pivotal in King's Stand Stakes at Royal Ascot last time: effective at 5f and bred to stay at least 7f: acts on good to firm and dead ground. *D. Hanley, Ireland*

LIDHAMA (USA) 4 b.f. Sword Dance – Running Melody 86 (Rheingold 137) 66 [1995 66: 7m 8.3m 7f 7.1d 9.7g³ 12m² 12m 1996 a12g² 12g Jul 3] big, strong, good- topped filly: had a round action: fair handicapper: fell at Epsom final start: stayed 1½m: acted on good to firm ground and fibresand: dead. *G. Lewis*

LIEFLING (USA) 3 b.f. Alleged (USA) 138 – Mata Cara 98 (Storm Bird (CAN) 80 134) [1995 –p: 7m 1996 10g⁵ 12m* 13.9m⁵ 12g Oct 11] angular filly: fair form: won

4-runner maiden at Ascot in August, pushed along from turn: stayed on steadily and ran creditably in rated stakes at York in August: behind in handicap at Ascot over 7 weeks later: should stay 2m: acts on good to firm ground, yet to race on a soft surface: sold 50,000 gns Newmarket December Sales. *J. H. M. Gosden*

LIFE IS PRECIOUS (IRE)   4 b.f. Shernazar 131 – Neelam (USA) (Arctic Tern –
(USA) 126) [1995 7s⁵ 7s 6m 6g⁶ 6g⁶ 5g⁵ 6d 7d 1996 a9.4g a7g a7g⁴ a7g⁵ a6g⁶ a7g
6.1m Apr 30] angular ex-Irish filly: second foal: half-sister to 5-y-o Neykari (by
Kahyasi): dam unraced: fair handicapper (rated 65) at best for J. J. McLoughlin: little
worthwhile form in Britain: suffered heart attack at Nottingham final start: stayed 7f:
acted on heavy going: dead. *R. Hollinshead*

LIFE ON THE STREET   2 b.f. (Jan 18) Statoblest 120 – Brave Advance (USA)   62
98 (Bold Laddie (USA)) [1996 5.2d⁵ 5s³ 5f³ 5g 6g 5.1g³ 7f³ Sep 3] 19,000Y: sturdy
filly: unimpressive mover: sister to 3-y-o Cross the Border, fairly useful 5f winner at
2 yrs, and half-sister to smart sprinter Venture Capitalist (by Never So Bold): dam, 5f
winner, raced only at 2 yrs: modest maiden: stays 7f: acts on firm ground, soundly
beaten on soft. *R. Hannon*

LIFE'S A ROAR (IRE)   2 b.g. (Apr 7) Roaring Riva 103 – Wolviston (Wolver- –
life 115) [1996 6d a6g 6m Oct 4] IR 2,000F, IR 2,200Y: half-brother to 7f (at 2 yrs)
and 1m winner Adala (by Soughaan) and a winner in Germany by Homo Sapien:
dam Irish 2-y-o 5f winner: no form: twice visored. *C. A. Dwyer*

LIFFRE (IRE)   2 b.f. (Feb 13) Sadler's Wells (USA) 132 – Liffey Lass (USA) 95   74 p
(Irish River (FR) 131) [1996 8.2g⁴ Oct 9] eighth foal: sister to French winner at
around 1m Colleen, closely related to 3-y-o On The Bank (by In The Wings), and
half-sister to several winners, including Irish 1990 2-y-o 6f and 7f winner Isle of
Glass (by Affirmed): dam, 2-y-o 7f winner, out of half-sister to high-class colts Home
Guard and Boone's Cabin: 13/2 from 4/1, 5½ lengths fourth of 13 to Fascinating
Rhythm in steadily-run maiden at Nottingham: will stay middle distances: will im-
prove. *J. H. M. Gosden*

LIFT BOY (USA)   7 b.g. Fighting Fit (USA) – Pressure Seat (USA) (Ginistrelli   52
(USA) 117) [1995 48, a66: a6g* a5g³ a6g² a6g⁴ 5.3m 7f 5g* 5m⁶ a5g a5g⁶ a6g⁵ 1m   a69
a5g* a6g⁶ a6g³ a5g* a5g⁵ a6g* a5g⁶ 5m⁶ 5m² 5m⁴ 5m* 7f 5.3m⁴ 5f a5g⁴ a6g Dec 20]
small, sturdy gelding: fair performer on the all-weather: won claimers at Lingfield in
January and February and amateurs handicap at Wolverhampton in March: modest
on turf, winning seller at Folkestone in June: effective at 5f to 7f: acts on all-weather
surfaces and good to firm and soft ground: visored (no improvement) twice at 2 yrs:
consistent. *A. Moore*

LIGHTNING BOLT (IRE)   2 b.f. (May 20) Magical Strike (USA) 114 –   58
Killyhevlin (Green God 128) [1996 6g 7m 5g⁵ 5g a6g² a5g⁴ a6g² a7g* a6s Dec 19]
IR 3,800Y: ex-Irish filly: half-sister to several winners here and abroad, including
sprinter Dawes of Nelson (by Krayyan): dam ran twice in Ireland: modest form: ran
in maidens in Ireland for W. Roper first 2 starts: won 11-runner event at Wolverhampton in December: favourite, tailed off in similar event there final outing: stays
7f: acts on all-weather. *M. Johnston*

LIGHTNING REBEL   2 b.g. (Apr 30) Rambo Dancer (CAN) 107 – Ozra 63   67
(Red Alert 127) [1996 6.1d⁵ 8.3d² 8.1s⁵ Nov 7] 4,600Y: unfurnished gelding: seventh
foal: brother to a poor plater and half-brother to 6f (at 2 yrs) to 8.1f winner Jimlil (by
Nicholas Bill) who stayed 1¼m: dam 6f and 7f winner: fair maiden: best effort
second start: stays 8.2f: raced only on a soft surface. *C. W. Thornton*

LIGHTS OF HOME   2 b.c. (Jan 15) Deploy 131 – Dream Chaser 92 (Record   –
Token 128) [1996 6v⁶ a7s Nov 19] seventh foal: brother to fairly useful 7f and
(including at 2 yrs) 1m winner Catch The Lights and half-brother to winning sprinters
Cradle Days (by Dance Of Life) and Sister Susan (by Tate Gallery): dam suited by
6f: little promise in maidens at Folkestone and Lingfield in November: has joined
Miss C. Johnsey. *R. Hannon*

LILAC RAIN   4 b.f. Petong 126 – Dame Corley (L'Enjoleur (CAN)) [1995 38:   –
10g a7g³ 10m a8g a12g 1996 a8g² a8g² a8g a8g* a8.5g⁵ a8g a8g³ 8m a8g 8m 12.1m   a51
8.3m a10g Aug 10] angular filly: poor performer on the all-weather: won (for first
time) selling handicap at Lingfield in February: left R. Arnold after tenth 4-y-o start:
would probably have shown first worthwhile form on turf penultimate start but for
running very wide entering straight in apprentice selling handicap at Windsor: should

stay 1¼m: acts on all-weather surfaces: effective blinkered or not: inconsistent, and has looked reluctant. *R. M. Stronge*

LILA PEDIGO (IRE) 3 b.f. Classic Secret (USA) 91 – Miss Goldie Locks (Dara Monarch 128) [1995 56+: a5g³ a5g³ a6g* 6g* 5m⁴ 6.1d a6g⁵ 1996 a6g a6g 6d 8g⁵ 8.2m² 8m⁵ 8f² 10m⁵ 10g* 10d³ 10m⁶ 10m Sep 24] leggy filly: unimpressive mover: modest handicapper: won 18-runner seller at Ripon in August: effective at 1m to 1¼m: acts on firm and dead ground and on fibresand. *Miss J. F. Craze* 62

LILILO (IRE) 4 b.g. Vision (USA) – Persian Royale 94 (Persian Bold 123) [1995 12m 12m³ 12m³ 14g² 12.5g 12d 1996 11.9g⁵ 12m Aug 7] IR 26,000Y: ex-Irish gelding: brother to fairly useful Irish 7f/1m handicapper Elizabeth's Pet and half-brother to a 7f winner in Ireland by Ahonoora: dam won Irish Cambridgeshire: fair form at best (rated 73) in maidens for N. Meade and D. McArdle in 1995: weak in market, always behind after slow start in apprentice handicap at Kempton final 4-y-o start and first outing here: stays 1¾m: yet to race on extremes of going. *R. Lee* –

LILLIBELLA 3 b.f. Reprimand 122 – Clarandal 80 (Young Generation 129) [1995 62: 5m⁶ 6g 1996 5d⁵ 5f³ 7f³ 6m⁴ 6.1m² 5.3f⁵ 6m⁶ 6.1m Sep 16] tall, leggy filly: good walker: modest maiden handicapper: below form last 3 starts, blinkered final one: likely to prove best at up to 7f: acts on firm ground: has given trouble at stalls. *I. A. Balding* 64

LILLI CLAIRE 3 ch.f. Beveled (USA) – Lillicara (FR) (Caracolero (USA) 131) [1995 70: 7f³ 6.9f⁴ 6m* 6.1d 7g* 1996 8g 8m* 8s 8.5m 8m² 7g* 7m 8m 7g⁶ Sep 13] leggy, sparely-made filly: fairly useful handicapper: won at Salisbury in May and Newmarket (rated stakes) in July: ran poorly penultimate start: faced stiff task on final one: effective at 7f and 1m: acts on firm ground, no form on a soft surface: held up. *A. G. Foster* 91

LILY JAQUES 2 b.f. (Feb 9) Petong 126 – Scossa (USA) 52 (Shadeed (USA) 135) [1996 6d⁵ 6.1m⁶ 6g⁶ a6s a7g² Dec 26] first foal: dam, maiden who stayed 1½m, out of Grade 3 1½m winner Scythe: poor performer: sold out of P. Cole's stable 600 gns Newmarket Autumn Sales after third start: stays 7f. *R. Guest* 50

LIMA 2 b.f. (Feb 26) Distant Relative 128 – Lady Kris (IRE) (Kris 135) [1996 6m* 6g* Sep 3] 34,000Y: unfurnished, useful-looking filly: poor mover: second foal: half-sister to fairly useful 3-y-o 1½m winner Al's Alibi (by Alzao): dam, Irish 1¼m winner, half-sister to Gimcrack winner Bel Bolide, later Grade 2 winner in USA: won maiden at Folkestone in July: followed up in 6-runner Timeform Futurity at Pontefract over 6 weeks later, losing action slightly 2f out but ridden to lead inside last, beating Nigrasine a length: will be well suited by 7f+: sure to improve again, and looks a useful filly in the making. *L. M. Cumani* 95 p

LIMERICK PRINCESS (IRE) 3 ch.f. Polish Patriot (USA) 128 – Princess of Nashua (Crowned Prince (USA) 128) [1995 68: 5m 5f³ 5m² 5g* 5f 5m⁵ 6.1m⁴ 5m 68

Timeform Futurity, Pontefract—Oscar Urbina pushes out Lima to win from Nigrasine and Kharir

5m 1996 5d⁴ a6g* 5m⁴ 6d* 6g* 7m 6m⁶ 6m⁶ Jul 8] workmanlike filly: fair handicapper: won at Wolverhampton, Haydock (apprentices) and Catterick in May: stays 6f: acts on fibresand and on firm and dead ground. *J. Berry*

LIMYSKI   3 b.g. Petoski 135 – Hachimitsu 39 (Vaigly Great 127) [1995 –: 7g 8.1g 1996 13.8g⁵ Jul 24] soundly beaten in maidens. *Mrs A. Swinbank*   –

LINCON TWENTY ONE   3 ch.f. Sharpo 132 – Angels Are Blue 73 (Stanford 121§) [1995 39: 5d³ 5m 1996 a5g 5m⁴ 7m 7m 5f Jun 29] close-coupled filly: poor sprint maiden: blinkered, tailed off final 3 outings. *M. J. Haynes*   –

LINDA'S JOY (IRE)   3 b.f. Classic Secret (USA) 91 – Enaam 65§ (Shirley Heights 130) [1995 NR 1996 10m⁵ 11.1g³ 8m* 9f 11.8m² 11.9f Jul 25] IR 1,500Y: second foal: dam ungenerous maiden who should have stayed beyond 1¼m, out of half-sister to Give Thanks, family of Teenoso: bought out of R. Guest's stable 6,700 gns after winning seller at Newmarket in June: lost all chance with very slow start next start, threw race away one after that and refused to race final start: should stay further than 1¼m: tongue tied last outing: blinkered/visored all starts: tail flasher who finds little: sent to South Korea. *M. C. Pipe*   59 §

LINDEN'S LAD (IRE)   2 b.c. (Apr 21) Distinctly North (USA) 115 – Make Or Mar 84 (Daring March 116) [1996 6m 6m⁵ 6m⁶ 8m Oct 23] workmanlike colt: second reported foal: dam 5f performer: signs of a little ability second and third outings: sprint bred. *J. R. Jenkins*   –

LINDISFARNE LADY   4 b.f. Jupiter Island 126 – Harifa (Local Suitor (USA) 128) [1995 45: 10m 12m 11f* 14.1m⁵ 12.4h² 12m⁴ 12.4g³ 11.5g 13.6f⁴ 1996 12.4d 14.1m 14.1f 12.3m Aug 5] leggy, angular filly: poor performer: no promise in 1996: stays 13.6f: acts on hard ground. *Mrs M. Reveley*   –

LINE DANCER   3 b.g. Shareef Dancer (USA) 135 – Note Book 94 (Mummy's Pet 125) [1995 101p: 6.1m* 6m² 7m³ 8g² 1996 8g⁶ 10g⁵ 8m 8d⁶ Aug 28] angular gelding: has a fluent round action: useful performer at best: left M. Jarvis after second 3-y-o start: last of 7 in Group 3 event at the Curragh (best 3-y-o form) on penultimate outing: stays 1m: yet to race on extremes of going: blinkered (not disgraced) final 3-y-o start. *G. A. Cusack, Ireland*   101

LINPAC WEST   10 b.h. Posse (USA) 130 – North Page (FR) 81 (Northfields (USA)) [1995 100: 12g⁶ 14.1g² 11.9d 13.3d 1996 12s⁶ 18.7g May 8] lengthy, angular horse: poor mover: smart performer at his peak, trained by C. W. C. Elsey prior to 1996: collapsed and died after Chester Cup: effective at 1¼m when conditions were testing and stayed 1¾m: best on an easy surface and went well in the mud: held up: game and consistent in his prime. *D. Nicholls*   –

LIONEL EDWARDS (IRE)   3 b.g. Polish Patriot (USA) 128 – Western Heights (GB) (Shirley Heights 130) [1995 73: 6g⁵ 6.1m³ 6.1m³ 7.5m³ a7g³ 1996 8d 8g⁵ 6s² 6g³ 7m* 7g* Jun 15] quite attractive gelding: fair performer: won median auction event at Goodwood, despite swishing tail and wandering: followed up in handicap at Leicester 9 days later: subsequently sold 21,000 gns Newmarket July Sales: probably suited by 7f+: acts on good to firm and soft ground: sent to Macau. *P. F. I. Cole*   79

LIONIZE (USA)   3 ch.c. Storm Cat (USA) – Pedestal (High Line 125) [1995 NR 1996 7m* 9g 8g Nov 2] 40,000Y: quite attractive colt: second foal: half-brother to 1¼m winner Plinth (by Dowsing): dam once-raced half-sister to Precocious and Jupiter Island: won slowly-run 5-runner maiden at Newmarket in April: off course 6 months, stiff tasks when last in listed races there on return. *P. W. Chapple-Hyam*   83 +

LISTED ACCOUNT (USA)   2 b.f. (May 3) Private Account (USA) – Sypharina (FR) (Lyphard (USA) 132) [1996 8.1m³ 8.1s Oct 5] 420,000 francs Y: close-coupled, workmanlike filly: second foal: half-sister to French 3-y-o 8.5f winner Sannine (by Trempolino): dam French 1m winner: shaped well when staying-on 3 lengths third of 7 to Fiji in maiden at Sandown: odds on, weakened tamely on soft ground in similar event at Haydock (bandaged near-hind) 18 days later: will stay 1¼m: worth another chance on a sound surface. *L. M. Cumani*   77 p

LITERARY   2 b.f. (Apr 26) Woodman (USA) 126 – Book Collector (USA) 80 (Irish River (FR) 131) [1996 6g⁶ 6f² 7m Aug 10] leggy, unfurnished filly: third foal: sister to 1m winner Bibliotheque: dam 6f winner here at 2 yrs, later successful at up to 1m in USA: fair maiden: favourite on second and third starts, beaten a short head when odds on for 6-runner maiden then seventh of 10 (finding little) in listed event,   76 both at Newmarket: should stay 1m: raced only on a sound surface: quietly to post final start. *J. H. M. Gosden*

LITERARY SOCIETY (USA) 3 ch.c. Runaway Groom (CAN) – Dancing 73 Gull (USA) (Northern Dancer) [1995 60: 5g⁶ 5d³ 1996 6m 5.2m³ 5.3f* 5m² 5g* 5m 5m 5m² 5g⁴ Oct 9] small, sturdy colt: has a quick action: fair handicapper: won at Brighton (maiden) in July and Thirsk in August: good efforts last 2 starts: raced mainly at 5f: acts on firm going, probably on dead: reliable. *J. A. R. Toller*

LITHE SPIRIT (IRE) 4 b.f. Dancing Dissident (USA) 119 – Afternoon Nap – (USA) (Key To Content (USA)) [1995 8s 7g⁵ 7.8f² 9m 10m 7g³ 6g⁵ 1996 a6g⁶ a6g⁶ a6g 7g a6g a7g Nov 22] ex-Irish filly: first foal: dam (fair sprint claimer in USA) won 8 races and is half-sister to smart 7f performer Bog Trotter and very promising 2-y-o Poteen: fair maiden (rated 74) at 3 yrs, sold cheaply out of J. Oxx's stable after final start: well beaten in Britain: stays 7.8f: acts on firm ground: tried blinkered: sold 5,800 gns Newmarket December Sales. *J. A. Harris*

LITTLE ACORN 2 b.g. (Feb 27) Unfuwain (USA) 131 – Plaything 69 (High 53 Top 131) [1996 8.2g a7g⁵ Nov 16] 16,000Y: third foal: dam lightly-raced 1m winner: poor form in maidens at Nottingham and Wolverhampton. *S. C. Williams*

LITTLE BLACK DRESS (USA) 3 b.f. Black Tie Affair – Seattle Kat (USA) 71 (Seattle Song (USA) 130) [1995 71: 7.6d⁵ 7g⁴ 1996 7d 8m⁵ 8m 10.2f⁶ Jul 2] smallish, quite attractive filly: fair form when fifth at Salisbury on handicap debut: well held in similar events afterwards: stays 1m: acts on good to firm ground. *R. Charlton*

LITTLE BLUE (IRE) 2 b.f. (May 16) Bluebird (USA) 125 – Winter Tern (USA) 60 (Arctic Tern (USA) 126) [1996 5g⁵ a5g⁴ a5g⁴ 5m⁴ 5m 6m* 6m⁵ 5m* 5f⁵ Sep 28] IR a46 3,000Y: smallish filly: third foal: half-sister to Irish 3-y-o 7f winner Orange Grouse (by Taufan) and 4-y-o Farmer's Tern (by Sharrood): dam unraced: modest performer: made all in sellers at Redcar in August and Ayr in September: sold 5,000 gns Doncaster October Sales: effective at 5f (best form) and 6f: acts on firm ground: well suited by forcing tactics. *T. D. Easterby*

LITTLE GENT (IRE) 5 b.g. Jareer (USA) 115 – Arfjah (Taufan (USA) 119) – [1995 NR 1996 5m 7f 7f 6f Jul 25] poor maiden: tried blinkered. *J. E. Long*

LITTLE IBNR 5 b.g. Formidable (USA) 125 – Zalatia 97 (Music Boy 124) [1995 62 64, a91: a7g² a7g* a6g* a7g* a6g a7g 6g 7g 5.1d⁴ 6s² 6d 5.1m* 5m a6g³ a7g a6g* a77 1996 a7g a6g a7g a5g a5g a6g⁵ a6g* 6.1g a6g⁵ 7.6g 5.1m a6g 6m⁶ 6m⁵ 7.6m 5g⁶ a6s Dec 19] workmanlike gelding: fairly useful performer on the all-weather in 1995, fair on turf: below best at 5 yrs, even when winning handicap at Wolverhampton in April: effective at 5f to 7f: acts on firm and soft ground and goes well on all-weather surfaces: has won in blinkers and run respectably in a visor, rarely tried nowadays: often a front runner. *P. D. Evans*

LITTLE KENNY 3 b.f. Warning 136 – Tarvie 101 (Swing Easy (USA) 126) 46 [1995 50: 6m⁶ 6.1m 6.1d⁵ 7d 1996 8f 7m³ 8g⁵ a8.5g⁴ 8.1m⁴ 8.3m³ 8m⁶ 10m³ Aug 19] leggy filly: poor maiden handicapper: effective at 1m, probably at 1¼m: acts on good to firm and dead ground, below form only start on all-weather: blinkered (not discredited) second 3-y-o start, visored last 5 outings: has joined T. Wall. *M. J. Fetherston-Godley*

LITTLE LUKE (IRE) 5 b.h. Somethingfabulous (USA) – Yours Sincerely – (USA) (Stalwart (USA)) [1995 –: a12g 1996 8g 11.6m 10.8m 11.6d Aug 12] angular, sparely-made horse: no worthwhile form in 5 races since 3 yrs. *P. Butler*

LITTLE MILLIE 3 b.f. Colmore Row 111 – Little Kraker 69 (Godswalk (USA) – 130) [1995 –: 6m 6.1d⁵ 6d 1996 8d 7m a8g 6.9g 8f Oct 14] leggy filly: little worthwhile form: left P. Hayward after third 3-y-o start, but returned to him after final one. *J. W. Mullins*

LITTLEMISSMISCHIEF (IRE) 5 b.m. Nashamaa 113 – Swan Upping 74 31 (Lord Gayle (USA) 124) [1995 a8g⁶ a8g 8.5g³ 8f² a9.8g³ 8h² 11g 10f 1996 a10g 9.3g* 9.5f⁴ a9.3g⁵ 8g 9.5g 9f* 9s 9.5g a9.3g Oct 12] poor performer: won minor event at Groenendaal in March and handicap at Ostend in July: soundly beaten afterwards: stays 9.8f: acts on hard ground and all-weather: blinkered (no improvement) final 5-y-o start. *Paul Smith, Belgium*

LITTLE MISS ROCKER 2 b.f. (Apr 13) Rock Hopper 124 – Drama School 72 59 (Young Generation 129) [1996 7m 8m⁵ Sep 26] 10,500Y: eighth foal: half-sister to several winners, including 3-y-o 1¼m winner Dramatic Moment (by Belmez) and 1989 Irish 1m winner Annie Laurie (by Aragon): dam maiden (stayed 1m) out of half-sister to Final Straw and Achieved: midfield throughout in maidens at Lingfield and Pontefract: will stay beyond 1m. *I. A. Balding*

LITTLE MURRAY 3 b.g. Mon Tresor 113 – Highland Daisy (He Loves Me 120) [1995 NR 1996 8.3m 8m Jun 1] 700F, 2,500Y: fifth living foal: half-brother to fair winning hurdler Highbank (by Puissance) and a winner in Italy by Rambo Dancer: dam ran once: behind in maidens at Windsor and Newmarket: sold 1,700 gns Newmarket Autumn Sales: joined F. Murphy and gelded. *Mrs J. Cecil* —

LITTLE NOGGINS (IRE) 3 b.f. Salt Dome (USA) – Calash (Indian King (USA) 128) [1995 78: 5m* 6m* 5m 5g³ 6m⁵ 5.2f⁴ 1996 5d* 6g 5d 6.1m a6g 6m⁶ 6m⁴ 6d Oct 21] leggy filly: fair handicapper at best: won at Doncaster in March: disappointing afterwards: sold 9,000 gns Newmarket Autumn Sales: stays 6f: acts on good to firm and dead ground, carried head high when below form on firm: tried blinkered, no improvement: tends to sweat: sent to Saudi Arabia. *C. A. Dwyer* 78 d

LITTLE PILGRIM 3 b.g. Precocious 126 – Bonny Bright Eyes 58 (Rarity 129) [1995 62?: 6s⁶ 6f 6m 1996 8.2d 6m 5m a8g a8g⁶ Dec 26] tall, lengthy gelding: well beaten since debut. *T. M. Jones* —

LITTLE PROGRESS 2 b.g. (Jun 2) Rock City 120 – Petite Hester 85 (Wollow 132) [1996 6g 6g 6m 5d a6g Dec 13] 4,400Y: half-brother to several winners here and abroad, including fairly useful middle-distance stayer Siesta Key (by Glint of Gold): dam 7f winner: no worthwhile form in maiden events and a nursery. *T. M. Jones* —

LITTLE RED 5 b.g. Dreams To Reality (USA) 113 – Qualitairess 49 (Kampala 120) [1995 NR 1996 12g 10.2g 10f 8f Jul 6] third foal: half-brother to 1m and 11.7f winner Swynford Flyer (by Valiyar): dam 1m winner: tailed off in varied company: blinkered final start. *R. Craggs* —

LITTLE REDWING 4 ch.f. Be My Chief (USA) 122 – Forward Rally 84 (Formidable (USA) 125) [1995 –: 10m 1996 13.1d⁵ 9.2g 15.1f⁵ 15.8s⁵ 15.1m⁴ 15.8g³ Jul 25] poor staying maiden: seems to act on soft going. *M. D. Hammond* 37

LITTLE SABOTEUR 7 ch.m. Prince Sabo 123 – Shoot To Win (FR) (Rabdan 129) [1995 59, a75: a5g³ a5g* a5g⁴ a5g² 5m a5g⁴ 5m⁴ a6g³ a7g a5g⁵ a5g a6g 1996 a6g a5g³ a5g⁵ a5g⁴ a5g⁴ 5m⁴ a5g Jul 12] useful-looking mare: only modest in 1996: effective at 5f and 6f: acts on good to firm and soft going and goes well on the all-weather: effective blinkered or not: has run poorly when sweating: usually bandaged near-hind. *P. J. Makin* — a62

LITTLE SCARLETT 4 b.f. Mazilier (USA) 107 – Scarlett Holly 81 (Red Sunset 120) [1995 53: a8g⁶ a8g² a8.5g* a9.4g a10g⁵ a8.5g* 1996 a8.5g⁴ a8g a8g³ a8g Mar 29] small filly: poor performer: stays 8.5f: acts on all-weather surfaces (once-raced on turf): covered by Lugana Beach. *P. J. Makin* 47

LITTLESTONE ROCKET 2 ch.c. (Mar 17) Safawan 118 – Miss Hocroft (Dominion 123) [1996 6m a6g 5m Oct 4] 10,000F, 5,000Y resold 5,600Y: first foal: dam tailed off only start, daughter of useful 2-y-o 5f winner As Blessed: little show in maidens. *W. R. Muir* —

LITTLE WOBBLY 6 ch.m. Cruise Missile – Jameena 65 (Absalom 128) [1995 NR 1996 6.9m 11.6m 7f 8f 14m a12g Oct 28] first foal: dam, best form at 2 yrs at up to 1m, possibly stayed 1¼m: tailed off all starts: tried blinkered. *P. C. Clarke* —

LITUUS (USA) 3 gr. or ro.g. El Gran Senor (USA) 136 – Liturgism (USA) (Native Charger) [1995 –p: 7m 1996 8m⁵ 9g 10.1m 9m⁵ 8m⁴ 10m⁴ Sep 26] good-topped gelding: has a round action: fairly useful maiden: off course 3 months, ran well in handicap penultimate start: will prove best short of 1¼m: yet to race on a soft surface: tried visored, no improvement: sent to UAE. *J. H. M. Gosden* 80

LIVE PROJECT (IRE) 4 b.g. Project Manager 111 – Saturday Live (Junius (USA) 124) [1995 77d: 7v* 7s 7g 7m² 7s 5g 8g a7g² a7g a8g⁴ a7g a7g 1996 a8.5g² a7g Jan 20] sparely-made gelding: fair performer, seemingly on the downgrade: stays 8.5f: acts on good to firm and heavy ground and best efforts in Britain on the all-weather. *M. Johnston* 67

LIVIO (USA) 5 b.g. Lyphard (USA) 132 – Make Change (USA) (Roberto (USA) 131) [1995 –: 11.9d 1996 17.1g Apr 23] good-topped gelding: no promise on flat in —

Blue Seal Stakes, Ascot—Lochangel (right) is always holding Corsini

recent seasons: blinkered (signs of temperament) second 3-y-o start: fairly useful hurdler at best, winner (for P. Monteith) in December. *L. Lungo*

LIZAPET (IRE) 4 b.f. Petorius 117 – Sybaris 91 (Crowned Prince (USA) 128) [1995 NR 1996 7d 8d Apr 13] plain filly: looks of no account nowadays: visored last start. *P. A. Pritchard* –

LIZIUM 4 b.f. Ilium 121 – Lizaway (Casino Boy 114) [1995 NR 1996 10m 7m 10m 12g 10g Aug 24] close-coupled, workmanlike filly: first foal: dam, non-thoroughbred, of little account over hurdles: well beaten in varied company. *J. C. Fox* –

LLOC 4 b.f. Absalom 128 – Nosey 96 (Nebbiolo 125) [1995 52: 5d 5g a5g⁴ 5g⁵ a5g 5m⁵ 5g⁴ a5g² 5m³ 5g 5.1d a5g 6f 1996 5s* 5g 5m³ 5m a5g³ 5m⁵ a5g² 5.2m² 5d 5.1m 5m 5.1g⁶ 5.1g⁵ a5g⁶ a5g a5g⁶ Nov 30] neat, good-quartered filly: modest handicapper: made winning reappearance in 16-runner race at Folkestone in March, racing alone on far side: sold 14,500 gns Newmarket December Sales: speedy, and best at 5f: acts on fibresand and any turf going: no improvement in visor or blinkers: usually races prominently. *C. A. Dwyer* 58

LLYSWEN 3 ch.c. Generous (IRE) 139 – Llyn Gwynant 115 (Persian Bold 123) [1995 NR 1996 8.3m 10g³ 10m⁵ 10d⁶ 11.6m Aug 19] robust, lengthy colt: has a fluent, round action: third foal: half-brother to fairly useful middle-distance performer Llia (by Shirley Heights), 7f winner at 2 yrs in 1994, and a prolific 5f winner in Italy by Rousillon: dam stayed 9f: best effort in maidens when third at Windsor on second start: visored, well beaten last start: stays 1¼m but is a free-going sort who should prove effective over shorter. *J. H. M. Gosden* 75

LOCHANGEL 2 ch.f. (Apr 5) Night Shift (USA) – Peckitts Well 96 (Lochnager 132) [1996 6m² 6m* Sep 28] rangy, rather unfurnished filly: has plenty of scope: has a quick action: fifth living foal: half-sister to 3 winners, including 10.2f winner Lochbelle (by Robellino) and top-class sprinter Lochsong (by Song): dam sprinter: heavily-backed favourite after eye-catching debut (when very slowly away), made all in 5-runner Blue Seal Stakes at Ascot, quickening after halfway and always holding runner-up Corsini, winning by ¾ length: will improve again and should turn out to be very useful. *I. A. Balding* 94 p

LOCH BERING (USA) 4 ch.c. Bering 136 – Passerine (USA) (Dr Fager) [1995 10g* 8s* 8g⁴ 11m* 10g² 12g³ 14s³ 12s 1996 9g⁵ a12g² 12d⁵ 14g⁵ a10g² 9d³ a8g³ 8g² a10g* a9.4g⁶ Dec 7] useful performer at 2 yrs for P. Kelleway: contested some of the better races in Scandinavia in 1996, third in listed race at Ovrevoll in August: won handicap at Taby in November: good 3½ lengths sixth of 13 to Prince of Andros in listed race at Wolverhampton final start: effective at 9f to 1¾m: effective on turf and dirt: effective in blinkers. *A. Lund, Norway* 103

LOCHBUIE 4 ch.g. Forzando 122 – Nigel's Dream (Pyjama Hunt 126) [1995 NR 1996 a7g a8g Feb 3] good-topped gelding: well beaten in maiden events: dead. *J. M. P. Eustace* –

LOCH DIBIDALE 2 b.f. (Feb 26) Robellino (USA) 127 – Carn Maire 83 (Northern Prospect (USA)) [1996 5g 5m⁴ 6f⁶ a5g² 7m 6m a6g Aug 31] 5,000F: leggy, 48

544

quite attractive filly: second foal: half-sister to 3-y-o 6f winner Maple Burl (by Dominion): dam 2-y-o 5f winner: modest maiden: well beaten last 3 starts: sold 1,450 gns Doncaster September Sales: best form at 5f: acts on fibresand: tried blinkered: sent to Holland. *J. E. Banks*

LOCH-HURN LADY 2 b.f. (Apr 17) Lochnager 132 – Knocksharry 58   62
(Palm Track 122) [1996 5g 5d 6m⁵ 6m 5m⁴ 5m² 7g 6g⁴ 8g Oct 25] 2,000Y: small, sturdy filly: unimpressive mover: fifth foal: sister to 3-y-o 1m winner Lucky Bea: dam sprinter: modest maiden: best effort when neck second of 9 in auction race at Haydock on sixth start: best form at 5f: front runner. *K. W. Hogg, Isle of Man*

LOCHINVAR 2 b.c. (Apr 21) Lochnager 132 – Starchy Cove 61 (Starch Reduced   –
112) [1996 5m 6m 5d a6g 6v Nov 11] 1,000F, 1,800Y, 2,000 2-y-o: first foal: dam 5f (at 2 yrs) and 6f winner: little worthwhile form. *J. S. Moore*

LOCHLASS (IRE) 2 b.f. (May 12) Distinctly North (USA) 115 – Littleton Song   59
73 (Song 132) [1996 a6g⁶ 6m a8g³ a10g⁵ a8g³ Dec 20] 13,000Y: angular, quite attractive filly: half-sister to 3 winners, all by Elegant Air, including 13f winner Headless Heights and 1990 2-y-o 6f seller winner Shepherd's Song: dam 2-y-o 6f winner: modest form in maiden events: probably stays 1¼m: acts on equitrack. *S. P. C. Woods*

LOCHLORE 2 b.f. (Apr 29) Lochnager 132 – Severals Princess 44 (Formidable   –
(USA) 125) [1996 5.7m a6g Jul 26] second foal: half-sister to 3-y-o Golden Silver (by Precious Metal): dam placed over 5f at 2 yrs: of no account. *Miss K. Whitehouse*

LOCHON 5 br.g. Lochnager 132 – Sky Mariner 59 (Julio Mariner 127) [1995 61:   –
6g 5f 5m 5m* 5m⁵ 6m⁵ 6m 5g 5f⁶ 5f a5g³ 1996 a5g a6g* a6g³ a6g⁴ a6g⁴ 6d⁶ 5g 6g 5g   a60
a5g Jul 15] compact, workmanlike gelding: modest handicapper: won at Lingfield in January: well held last 5 starts: effective at 5f and 6f: acts on equitrack and on any turf going: tried visored/blinkered once each: has run well when sweating. *J. L. Eyre*

LOCH PATRICK 6 b.g. Beveled (USA) – Daisy Loch (Lochnager 132) [1995   106
107: 5g⁶ 5g* 5m 5f 5g 1996 6m³ 6g* 6f⁵ 5f 5m⁴ 6m 7m³ 6m⁵ 5g Sep 29] well-made, really imposing gelding: useful performer: formerly trained by L. J. Holt: won minor event at Goodwood in May by neck from Montendre: mostly ran creditably afterwards, including when third to Wizard King at Salisbury: effective at 5f to 7f: acts on firm and dead going: usually waited with. *M. Madgwick*

LOCH STYLE 3 b.g. Lochnager 132 – Simply Style (Bairn (USA) 126) [1995   57
54: a6g⁵ a8.5g⁴ a6g⁴ 1996 a12g a7g⁵ a7g⁵ a8.5g⁶ a9.4g³ a7g³ 10.3g 8m* 9g a7g⁵ a8g⁶   a62
Nov 18] plain gelding: unimpressive mover: modest performer: well backed, won 18-runner seller at Pontefract in June: stiffish task, best effort when fifth in minor event at Wolverhampton penultimate start: effective at 7f, and probably stays 9.4f: acts on equitrack and good to firm ground: none too consistent. *R. Hollinshead*

LOCHWOOD 3 b.f. Lochnager 132 – Soltago 56 (Touching Wood (USA) 127)   –
[1995 NR 1996 a12g Nov 2] 1,000F: sister to poor 4-y-o 1m winner Percy Parrot: dam fourth in 7f seller at 2 yrs: tailed off in claimer at Wolverhampton. *A. Bailey*

LOCKET 3 b.f. Precocious 126 – Bracelet 72 (Balidar 133) [1995 NR 1996 10m   –
10m 10g Sep 14] strong, good-bodied filly: second foal: dam stayed 1½m: beaten a distance each time in maiden events. *J. A. Bennett*

LOCOROTONDO (IRE) 5 b.m. Broken Hearted 124 – Rahwah 73   67
(Northern Baby (CAN) 127) [1995 71, a66: 10m 10m 10m 10.1g² 10m a12g² a12g⁴   a63
a10g* 11m* 10g² 10d⁶ 10g 1996 a9.4g a10g⁶ 10.8g³ 10g³ a12g² a12g⁶ 10.5g Jul 6]
long-backed mare: has a short, round action: fair performer: easily best efforts at 5 yrs when placed: stays 1½m: acts on good to firm and dead ground and the all-weather: often bandaged: successful for 7-lb claimer: sold 5,000 gns Newmarket December Sales. *M. Bell*

LOFTY DEED (USA) 6 b.g. Shadeed (USA) 135 – Soar Aloft (USA) (Avatar   –
(USA)) [1995 NR 1996 12m Jun 8] well-made gelding: no form on flat since poor 2-y-o: sold 2,000 gns Ascot November Sales: tried blinkered. *W. J. Musson*

LOGANLEA (IRE) 2 br.f. (Apr 14) Petong 126 – White's Pet (Mummy's Pet   – p
125) [1996 5v⁶ Nov 11] 7,200Y: leggy, close-coupled filly: sixth foal: sister to 1990 2-y-o 1m winner Encore Au Bon, later successful in Italy, and half-sister to Italian 3-y-o 7.5f to 8.5f winner Jalmood The Best (by Mazilier): dam unraced: refused to

enter stalls on intended debut: well backed, signs of ability though well held when sixth of 8 in minor event at Folkestone. *W. J. Musson*

LOGIC 2 b.f. (Feb 18) Slip Anchor 136 – Docklands 91 (On Your Mark 125) [1996 94 ? 7m⁴ 6m 7.6m² 8g⁵ Sep 29] close-coupled filly: has a quick action: sister to a modest maiden and half-sister to useful 1½m winner Port Helene (by Troy), 4-y-o 7f and 1m winner Darcey Bussell (by Green Desert) and a winner in Germany: dam, best at up to 1m, is half-sister to 1000 Guineas winner Night Off: fair form, staying on, in frame in maidens: appeared to show good deal of improvement when around 5 lengths fifth of 8 to Reams of Verse in Fillies' Mile at Ascot on final outing: seems suited by a test of stamina: has raced only on a sound surface. *C. E. Brittain*

LOGICA (IRE) 2 b.f. (Apr 7) Priolo (USA) 127 – Salangangai (Sallust 134) [1996 81 ? 6f 7f² 7m 7.6d⁶ 8.1m⁴ 8s Oct 13] IR 16,500F, 200,000 francs Y: strong, close-coupled filly: fifth foal: half-sister to Irish 1m winner Head Home and useful Irish 7f/1m winner Millie's Choice (both by Taufan): dam unraced: fair form in maidens and minor event: appeared to show some improvement, though towards rear, in Group 3 event at Milan on final start: likely to stay beyond 1m: sent to France. *P. A. Kelleway*

LOGIE 4 ch.g. Prince Sabo 123 – Ashdown (Pharly (FR) 130) [1995 –, a56: a7g⁵ a6g a7g² 8.2g a8g⁵ 1996 6.9m⁶ May 29] lengthy gelding: modest maiden: trained at 3 yrs by M. Jarvis: fit from hurdling, well held in claimer only outing in 1996: sold to join N. M. Babbage 1,850 gns Ascot June Sales: stays 7f: acts on the all-weather, no form on turf: blinkered (stumbled) second 3-y-o start, visored at Folkestone. *D. R. Gandolfo*

LOGIE PERT LAD 4 b.g. Green Ruby (USA) 104 – Rhazya (Rousillon (USA) 29 133) [1995 –: a6g 5m 6m 6m 5g 5.1m 5f 5d 7g 6.9g 1996 5m 5.3m 5.1f a6g a10g a6g⁴ a7g a6s a7g Dec 31] leggy gelding: bad maiden. *J. J. Bridger*

LOKI (IRE) 8 ch.g. Thatching 131 – Sigym (Lord Gayle (USA) 124) [1995 87, 69 d a75: a8.5g⁶ a10g 11.4m* 12g 12g* 10d 12s a12g² a12g* a12g* 1996 8m² 10d 12g⁶ 12g 12m⁴ 12m⁴ 11.8f² 11m² a12g² Nov 7] strong gelding: sometimes dull in coat: fluent mover: not seen until August at 8 yrs and failed to recapture best form: in frame in claimers last 4 starts: seems suited by around 1½m nowadays: acts on good to firm ground and equitrack, very best form on an easy surface: occasionally blinkered/ visored (not since 1994): usually bandaged: held up. *G. Lewis*

LOMBARDIC (USA) 5 b.h. Private Account (USA) – If Winter Comes (USA) 95 (Dancing Champ (USA)) [1995 95: 13.9m⁴ 11.9m* 11.9m* 13.9m 12g 12d⁶ 1996 11.9g* 12m 12s 12m 11.9m 11.9f⁴ Sep 7] good-topped horse: has a round action: useful handicapper: dead-heated at Haydock in April, gamely making most: well beaten next 3 starts, but respectable efforts last 2 outings: best form at 1½m, but stays 13.9f: acts on firm and dead ground: normally races prominently. *Mrs J. Cecil*

LOMBERTO 3 b.c. Robellino (USA) 127 – Lamees (USA) (Lomond (USA) 128) [1995 100p: 6m⁴ 7m² 7.1d* 7.3d⁵ 1996 7d 10m⁴ 10m⁵ 11.1m 10d Oct 12] good-topped colt: failed by a long way to recapture juvenile form in 1996: should be well suited by 1m+: acts on dead ground: blinkered last 2 outings. *R. Hannon*

LOMOND LASSIE (USA) 3 b.f. Lomond (USA) 128 – Herbivorous (USA) – (Northern Jove (CAN)) [1995 NR 1996 12.3m 10.3g 12g 15.8g 8m 10m 11f 8.2s Oct 31] quite attractive filly: eighth foal: half-sister to 2 minor winners in North America: dam won 4 sprint races in USA and placed in minor stakes: left T. Kersey after third start: seems of little account. *Miss J. F. Craze*

LONELY HEART 2 b.f. (May 8) Midyan (USA) 124 – Take Heart 84 (Electric 67 126) [1996 6m 7f⁶ 7.1s⁴ Oct 22] smallish filly: second foal: dam 7f to 1¼m winner: fair form in maidens: sweating, didn't handle home bend well at Warwick on second start: 33/1, good fourth of 16 to My Valentina at Chepstow 2 weeks later, staying on: will stay middle distances. *Major D. N. Chappell*

LONELY LEADER (IRE) 3 ch.c. Royal Academy (USA) 130 – Queen To 100 Conquer (USA) 112 (King's Bishop (USA)) [1995 86p: 8g³ 1996 7.1m* 7m⁴ 7g⁴ 9m⁶ Sep 21] useful-looking colt: easy mover: useful performer: won maiden at Chepstow in June: fourth in minor events next 2 starts, and appeared to run creditably (stiff task, set steady pace) in similar event won by Phantom Quest at Newbury on final one: probably stays 9f. *R. Hannon*

LONELY VIGIL (FR) 4 b.f. Noblequest (FR) 124 – Castaway (FR) (Filiberto –
(USA) 123) [1995 9g 9g 8.3g 7g 7g⁵ 8d 1996 a6g a6g a7g Feb 28] ex-French
filly: fourth foal: dam, poor maiden, half-sister to very speedy Standaan: no worthwhile form in France for Y. Belsoeur (at 2 yrs) and P. Bourgoin: tailed off in Britain:
returned to France. *K. O. Cunningham-Brown*

LONGANO BAY (IRE) 3 b.c. Contract Law (USA) 108 – Mettle (USA) 107 –
(Pretendre) [1995 NR 1996 8.2m⁶ 11.6d Aug 12] 525 2-y-o: half-brother to several
winners, notably smart 1982 2-y-o 7f and 1m winner Polished Silver (by Try My
Best) and useful Irish filly Melody (by Lord Gayle), latter dam of smart 7f winner
Guest Performer: dam 2-y-o 5f winner who stayed 1¼m: looks of no account.
J. Pearce

LONGCROFT 4 ch.f. Weldnaas (USA) 112 – Najariya (Northfields (USA)) 42
[1995 40: 7g a7g 8.2m 10m 10m⁴ 13.1g* 12m 14.1f⁶ 11f⁵ 11.1m⁴ 12g⁴ 1996 12m
16.5g⁶ 16m⁴ 16.2m⁴ 15.8g Sep 21] leggy, sparely-made filly: poor performer: trained
until after penultimate outing by K. Hogg: won maiden hurdle for new stable before
soundly beaten in Catterick handicap on return to flat: probably stays 1¾m: acts on
firm going: unseated rider and bolted before reappearance: none too consistent.
S. E. Kettlewell

LONGHILL BOY 3 b.g. Statoblest 120 – Summer Eve 63 (Hotfoot 126) [1995 –
55?: 5m 6f 5g⁵ 6g 1996 6.9s 6.1d 6.1g 8.3g Jul 1] leggy gelding: seems of little
account: sold 1,600 gns Newmarket July Sales: tried blinkered: sent to Germany.
B. J. Meehan

LONGWICK LAD 3 ro.c. Chilibang 120 – Bells of St Martin 89 (Martinmas 80 p
128) [1995 NR 1996 5g² 6g⁵ 6m 5m² 5g 5g⁴ 5.7m* 5.2m² 5m⁶ Oct 3] workmanlike
colt: brother to winning sprinter Bellsabanging and half-brother to several winners,
including sprinter Bells of Longwick (by Myjinski): dam 2-y-o 5f winner: quickly
made into a fairly useful handicapper: won at Bath in September: ran very well
(particularly considering drawn away from front runners) penultimate start: effective
at 5f and 6f: has raced only on a sound surface: can improve again, and should make
a useful sprint handicapper at 4 yrs. *W. R. Muir*

LOOKINGFORARAINBOW (IRE) 8 ch.g. Godswalk (USA) 130 – Bridget 78
Folly (Crofter (USA) 124) [1995 80: 14.9d 12m 12.3m⁴ 12g⁵ 12g* 12m³ 12m² 12m³
11.9f⁴ 12g⁵ 6m⁶ 10m 14.8m⁶ 1996 10d² 10s⁴ 8g⁵ 10m⁵ 11.9m 12m² 12m² 10.4m 9f⁶
13.9g Oct 12] close-coupled gelding: fair handicapper: good second twice at Newmarket in June: effective at 1¼m and probably stays 2m: acts on the all-weather (not
tried since early 1994), firm and dead ground, not at his best on very soft: takes good
hold, and usually held up: has hung and found little: needs strong handling, and well
ridden by M. Wigham: tough. *Bob Jones*

LOOKOUT 2 b.f. (May 9) Salse (USA) 128 – Sea Pageant (Welsh Pageant 132) 70 p
[1996 8f⁵ Sep 13] sturdy, compact filly: half-sister to 5-y-o 11f winner Sea God (by
Rainbow Quest) and 2 other middle-distance winners, including useful Ocean Ballad
(by Grundy): dam unraced half-sister to high-class Sea Anchor: well-backed 6/1-
shot, 7 lengths fifth of 10 to Cape Cross in maiden at Doncaster, soon rear after slow
start and never placed to challenge under considerate handling: looked on the burly
side: likely to require middle distances: sure to improve. *B. W. Hills*

LOOK WHO'S CALLING (IRE) 3 b.c. Al Hareb (USA) 123 – House Call 79
(Artaius (USA) 129) [1995 NR 1996 8.2s⁶ 7d⁶ 7.1d⁵ 6g³ May 24] big, good-topped
colt: has plenty of scope: third foal: half-brother to fairly useful 4-y-o 5f and 6f
winner Munguy (by Midyan) and useful 6f winner Look Who's Here (by Heraldiste):
dam Irish maiden sister to very useful Day Is Done: fair maiden: failed to handle turn
when well beaten at Catterick second start: should have won at Pontefract final
outing, but cocked his jaw and hung violently right after leading over 1f out, beaten
less than a length by Mutadarra: best form at 6f: has raced only on an easy surface:
clearly a difficult ride. *B. A. McMahon*

LOOSE TALK 3 ch.f. Thatching 131 – Brazen Faced 84 (Bold And Free 118) 68
[1995 NR 1996 6s⁶ 5.1d² 5m⁴ 6.1d May 27] angular filly: shows a quick action:
half-sister to several winners, including smart 4-y-o sprinter Easy Option (by Prince
Sabo) and useful 7f and 1m winner Sheer Cliff (by Shirley Heights): dam 2-y-o 5f
winner: favourite, fair form when second in maiden at Nottingham: beaten at odds on

in similar event (hung right on top-of-the-ground) at Beverley 10 days later, and well held when again favourite for handicap on final outing: looks a sprinter. *W. Jarvis*

LORCANJO 5 b.m. Hallgate 127 – Perfect Double 43 (Double Form 130) – [1995 NR 1996 12.5f 18m Jul 6] little form on flat: unreliable hurdler: has joined D. N. Carey. *A. J. Chamberlain*

LORD ADVOCATE 8 br.g. Law Society (USA) 130 – Kereolle (Riverman 54 (USA) 131) [1995 42§: 14.1f³ 11.1g* 14.1m² 13f* 13f 11.1m² 12.1m⁶ 11.1m³ 11.1f⁶ 15.1f⁵ 12f⁴ 13f³ 13f⁴ 12.1f³ 12.1m* 12.1g 12.1g 1996 12.1d 12.1g⁶ 13d⁵ 13s* 14.1m⁶ 13m³ 11.1g* 13g* 12.1f² 11.1g⁵ 13.1s³ 11.1g⁵ 11.1m⁴ 12.4m² 11.1m³ 12f³ 13m⁶ 12.1f² 12.1m 8.3g 13.1m 12.1d⁵ 10.1m 15.1s⁵ Nov 7] workmanlike gelding: bad mover: modest handicapper: won at Hamilton and Musselburgh in May and at Hamilton in June: stays 2m: acts on firm ground, soft and the all-weather: visored earlier in career, blinkered nowadays: has run creditably for amateur: sometimes forces pace. *D. A. Nolan*

LORD BARNARD (IRE) 6 gr.g. Toca Madera 111 – Avital (Pitskelly 122) – [1995 38: 7g 6d⁵ a6g 1996 a8g⁶ a13g Jan 13] ex-Irish gelding: lightly raced and poor form for J. Mulhern: soundly beaten in Britain. *C. Murray*

LORD CORNELIOUS 3 b.c. Lochnager 132 – Title (Brigadier Gerard 144) – [1995 –: 5f⁴ 1996 12.1s⁶ 12.1m⁶ 5g 5f 5m⁵ 5m 5.9f 5m Aug 8] of little account. *D. A. Nolan*

LORD DISCORD 2 b.g. (Mar 23) Primo Dominie 121 – Busted Harmony 58 (Busted 134) [1996 5f⁶ 7.5m⁴ 7g 7g³ 8.3d⁴ Sep 30] 9,200Y, 10,500 2-y-o: lengthy, angular gelding: third living foal: dam, maiden, stayed 1½m: modest maiden: ran well in nurseries last 2 starts: stays 1m: acts on good to soft ground. *T. D. Easterby*

LORD ELLANGOWAN (IRE) 3 ch.c. Astronef 116 – Gossip (Sharp Edge – 123) [1995 –: 5s 6.9g a8g 1996 a8g a10g² a10g a10g⁴ a12g² a10g 12f 12m 10m 9g a47 Aug 30] small colt: poor maiden at best: probably stays 1½m: acts on equitrack, no worthwhile form on turf: blinkered 5 of last 6 starts. *R. Ingram*

LORD HASTIE (USA) 8 b.g. Affirmed (USA) – Sheika (USA) (Minnesota 70 Mac) [1995 63: 9.9m 13g a16g 14g⁴ 16.5g 14.6g³ 12.4m* 12.3f* 13f² 11.9m⁴ 12d 12.1g² 11.9s* 12m⁶ 12m⁴ 1996 9.9d⁵ 13d* 13s² 11.9m⁴ 12g⁶ 13g⁵ 11.9m⁶ 12g 11.9d⁶ 13.9g Oct 12] tall, rather leggy gelding: fair handicapper: won at Hamilton in April: effective at 1½m to 2m: acts on any turf going and on fibresand: blinkered (winner) once in 1992: tends to hang left (seemed unsuited by Epsom) and sometimes wears near-side pricker: game. *C. W. Thornton*

LORD HIGH ADMIRAL (CAN) 8 b.g. Bering 136 – Baltic Sea (CAN) 95 (Danzig (USA)) [1995 95d: 5.2m 5m³ 5g 5g* 5m* 5.6m 5g⁶ 5s 1996 6s 5.2d 5d 5f* 5m³ 5m* 5m 5m 5.2m 5f² 5d* Sep 28] tall, leggy gelding: impresses in appearance: useful handicapper: won at Sandown in June (claimer, for second year running) and July and at Haydock (fourth course success) in September: best at 5f: acts on good to firm and soft ground: often visored/blinkered: has run creditably sweating: taken down early/alone: goes particularly well for M. Roberts: usually a front runner. *M. J. Heaton-Ellis*

LORD JIM (IRE) 4 b.g. Kahyasi 130 – Sarah Georgina 79 (Persian Bold 123) 107 [1995 96: 11.8s* 12m⁴ 13.9m⁴ 14m³ 16.2m 14.6m² 15g⁶ 13.3d a12g⁴ 1996 13.9m⁵ 14m* 14g* 16g² 14.5d² 20s³ Nov 3] good-bodied gelding: useful performer: better than ever at 4 yrs to win 5-runner minor event at Salisbury in June and listed event at Leopardstown (by a length from I'm Supposin) in July: good efforts in listed events at Baden-Baden, Cologne and Mulheim last 3 starts: stays 2½m: acts on good to firm and soft ground, probably on fibresand: visored since second 4-y-o start. *Lord Huntingdon*

LORD OF THE MANOR 3 b.c. Simply Great (FR) 122 – Wharton Manor 86 65 (Galivanter 131) [1995 NR 1996 10m³ 11.1g* 12m 12.3m Jul 8] workmanlike colt: brother to French 10.5f winner Old Man Mose and half-brother to several winners: dam stayed 1m: 9/4 on, easily made all in poor median auction maiden at Musselburgh in May: stiff tasks afterwards when last in handicaps at Pontefract and Ripon: stays 11.1f. *M. Johnston*

LORD OLIVIER (IRE) 6 b.g. The Noble Player (USA) 126 – Burkina (African 82 Sky 124) [1995 98: 6g⁶ 6m 6m 6f⁴ 6m² 6m 5.6m 6g 6g 1996 5.2d 6m 6d 6.1m 6g*

6m* 6m⁵ 6m³ 6g Oct 12] strong gelding: usually looks well: bad mover: just fairly useful form at 6 yrs, taking advantage of drop in class when winning claimers at Epsom in July and Haydock (made all) in August: didn't have the best of luck in handicaps last 3 starts: stays 6f: very best efforts on a sound surface: no improvement in blinkers. *W. Jarvis*

LORD PALMERSTON (USA)   4 b.g. Hawkster (USA) – First Minister (USA) (Deputy Minister (CAN)) [1995 –: 10m 8.3g 12m 8h⁶ 1996 a8g Jan 22] tall, close-coupled gelding: has shown little since fair form as 2-y-o: stays 1m: headstrong, and has worn dropped noseband. *K. A. Morgan* —

LORD SKY   5 b.g. Emarati (USA) 74 – Summer Sky 75 (Skyliner 117) [1995 61d, a84d: a5g* a6g² a5g 5g 5m 5.1m 5g 5.1g a6g⁴ 5g 5.1d a5g⁴ a5g⁶ 1996 a5g⁶ a5g a7g a7g³ a5g⁴ a6g² a6g² a5g⁴ 5d 5.7g a5g 6g⁵ a6g a6g⁴ a6g Dec 14] leggy gelding: fair handicapper on the all-weather, modest on turf (though showed little in 3 attempts in 1996): will prove best at up to 7f: acts on good to firm and soft ground and the all-weather: no improvement in blinkers/visor: usually races prominently. *A. Bailey* — a72

LORINS GOLD   6 ch.g. Rich Charlie 117 – Woolcana 71 (Some Hand 119) [1995 36: 5m 5.7f⁵ 6f⁵ 6m 6m⁵ 7.1m 6f 8m³ 1996 6m 6f* 6g² 7.1g⁴ 6m² 6m⁵ 6f⁵ 5m⁶ 8m⁵ Aug 28] well-made gelding: tends to look dull in coat: poor handicapper: won maiden event at Brighton in May: mostly ran creditably afterwards: effective at 6f to 1m: acts on firm and dead going, below form on very soft: effective blinkered or not: usually races prominently. *Andrew Turnell* 43

LOS ALAMOS   3 b.f. Keen 116 – Washita (Valiyar 129) [1995 67: 5g³ 7.9m 8.1s⁴ a8g³ a8.5g³ 1996 a12g² a11g³ 12.1s² a11g² a14.8g* 12m² 11.8g⁶ 16s⁴ 13.8g* 15.1s Nov 7] neat filly: has a round action: fair performer: won weak claimer at Wolverhampton in July and minor event (made all, by 6 lengths) at Catterick in October: probably stays 2m: acts on good to firm and soft ground and on fibresand. *C. W. Thornton* 65 a73

LOST DREAM   7 gr.m. Niniski (USA) 125 – Rocketina 57 (Roan Rocket 128) [1995 NR 1996 12g 14.1g Oct 24] half-sister to very useful 1983 sprinter Rocket Alert (by Red Alert), later 7f winner in USA: dam won 1m seller: well beaten in apprentice claimer and maiden. *C. A. Dwyer* —

LOST LAGOON (USA)   4 ch.c. Riverman (USA) 131 – Lost Virtue (USA) (Cloudy Dawn (USA)) [1995 83p: 10m⁴ 1996 8g² 8.2m³ Sep 24] leggy, close-coupled colt: unimpressive mover: fairly useful form in frame in maidens, odds on when second of 16 to Polinesso at Ripon and third of 15 to Dawawin at Nottingham 5½ months later, on both occasions taking strong hold and finding less than might have been expected: similar form at 1m and 1¼m: stays in training. *H. R. A. Cecil* 83

LOST REALM   4 b.g. Reprimand 122 – Clarandal 80 (Young Generation 129) [1995 –: 14g 1996 11.7m 14m³ Aug 4] no worthwhile form: sold 2,200 gns New-market September Sales: sent to Germany. *Martyn Meade* —

LOSTRIS (IRE)   5 b.m. Pennine Walk 120 – Herila (FR) (Bold Lad (USA)) [1995 NR 1996 12.3g⁶ 13s⁶ 14.1m² 14.1m⁶ 18m² 18m³ 17.1m² 18g Oct 21] big, good-bodied mare: poor maiden handicapper: off course 3 months, best effort at 5 yrs when second at Pontefract penultimate start: ran poorly at same course 2 weeks later: thorough stayer: acts on good to firm ground. *M. Dods* 40

LOTHLORIEN (USA)   3 ch.f. Woodman (USA) 126 – Fairy Dancer (USA) 94 (Nijinsky (CAN) 138) [1995 76p: 7.1s² 1996 10g⁶ 10.5d² 12.1g³ 8m* 12d Sep 27] small, angular filly: fairly useful form: set steady pace and rallied when winning 4-runner maiden at Newcastle in August: flattered when last of 7 in slowly-run listed race at Saint-Cloud final start: stays 1½m: yet to race on firm going, acts on any other: sent to USA. *P. W. Chapple-Hyam* 80

LOTTIES BID   4 b.f. Ring Bidder 88 – Gleneagle 91 (Swing Easy (USA) 126) [1995 –, a45: a7g⁶ a7g⁵ a6g⁴ 6s 5d 1996 a7g May 25] big, workmanlike filly: poor maiden: should have stayed 1m: acted on fibresand, no form on turf: blinkered final start: dead. *J. A. Glover* —

LOUGH ERNE   4 b.f. Never So Bold 135 – Laugharne (Known Fact (USA) 135) [1995 73: 6g 6m⁴ 6m³ 6m⁵ 6g² 6m 6g 7s 1996 6d 6g² 6f* 6.1d* 7m³ 6v³ 7g Oct 19] tall, useful-looking filly: improved into a fairly useful handicapper at 4 yrs: won at Lingfield and Nottingham in August: good third at Doncaster (tended to edge left and 83 did not get going until late on) and Haydock fifth and sixth starts: stays 7f: acts on any ground: usually held up. *C. F. Wall*

LOUISIANA PURCHASE   3 b.g. Macmillion 110 – My Charade 79 (Caw- –
ston's Clown 113) [1995 –: 7m 7.1g 10.2m 1996 8.2d 17.2g May 31] tall, unfurnished gelding: well beaten: headstrong, and probably temperamental. *Mrs Barbara Waring*

LOUIS' QUEEN (IRE)   4 b.f. Tragic Role (USA) – Bourbon Queen 77 (Ile de   96
Bourbon (USA) 133) [1995 102: 8.1m² 8g⁶ 8s⁵ 8m⁶ 8g³ 1996 8.5m⁵ 8m* 7.6f Jul 13]
tall, quite attractive filly: reportedly in foal to Efisio: useful performer: won minor
event at Newbury in June, getting on top last 50 yds: badly hampered in listed rated
stakes at Lingfield 16 days later: stayed 1m: acted on good to firm ground and heavy.
J. L. Dunlop

LOUISVILLE BELLE (IRE)   7 ch.m. Ahonoora 122 – Lomond Fairy   47
(Lomond (USA) 128) [1995 59: 8m⁵ 7f 6.1g² 5.7m⁵ 6m* 6m⁴ 6m³ 6m 7.1m³ 6d 5g⁴
5g 7m 1996 6g 5.1f 6d⁵ 6.1d 5.7m⁶ 6m³ 6g⁶ Jul 1] small, sturdy mare: poor handicapper: effective at 5f to 1m: acts on good to firm and soft ground: often claimer
ridden: inconsistent. *M. D. I. Usher*

LOUP SOLITAIRE (USA)   3 b.c. Lear Fan (USA) 130 – Louveterie (USA) 123   117
(Nureyev (USA) 131) [1995 113p: 8m² 8g³ 8m* 1996 8m⁵ 10.5g² May 12] smart
French colt: narrowly won Grand Criterium at Longchamp at 2 yrs: much his
better effort at 3 yrs when ¾-length second of 5 to Helissio in Prix Lupin there,
tracking winner and running on well: seemed likely to be suited by 1½m: unraced on
a soft surface: looked capable of further improvement, but side-lined in May with a
back problem: to stand at Haras du Mezeray, Normandy for 25,000 francs (Oct 1).
A. Fabre, France

LOVE AND KISSES   3 ch.f. Salse (USA) 128 – Soba 127 (Most Secret 119)   65
[1995 NR 1996 7d 9m 10g 12m a14g* 15.9d⁶ Aug 30] 17,000Y: big, workmanlike   a70
filly: half-sister to several winners, including sprinter Sobering Thoughts (by Be
My Guest) and fair middle-distance handicapper Soba Up (by Persian Heights): dam
sprinter: fair handicapper: won amateur riders maiden handicap at Southwell in
August: lesser form in handicap at Chester 2 weeks later: will eventually prove
effective beyond 1¾m: may prove capable of better. *C. A. Cyzer*

LOVE BATETA (IRE)   3 b. or br.f. Caerleon (USA) 132 – Marie Noelle (FR)   71
114 (Brigadier Gerard 144) [1995 60p: 7g⁶ 19m 7m⁶ 10m 8.3m 10.1g⁶ 11.6m³ 11.9f
10.5s⁴ a12g⁶ Oct 19] rather unfurnished filly: fair maiden: trained by R. Hannon first
4 starts in 1996: stays 11.6f: acts on good to firm going. *J. E. Banks*

LOVE BIRD (IRE)   3 b.g. Bluebird (USA) 125 – Top Glad (USA) (I'm Glad   72
(ARG)) [1995 73: 6f⁴ 6m⁵ 6m 8g⁵ a8g⁴ 1996 a8g³ a10g Jan 30] good-topped gelding:
fair maiden: reportedly finished lame final start: should have stayed 1¼m: acted on
firm ground and equitrack: dead. *M. Johnston*

LOVE HAS NO PRIDE (USA)   2 gr.c. (Apr 19) El Prado (IRE) 119 – Chili Lee   83
(USA) (Belted Earl (USA) 122) [1996 7.1g⁶ 7m⁶ 6f* 6g 8m² 7.9g* 8g Oct 18]
$3,500F, IR 17,000Y: tall, angular colt: has a fluent, round action: first foal: dam won
8 times in North America at up to 9f: fairly useful performer: won maiden at Brighton
in August and nursery at York in October: edgy, below form in nursery at Newmarket
on final outing: stays 1m well. *R. Hannon*

LOVE LEGEND   11 ch.g. Glint of Gold 128 – Sweet Emma 108 (Welsh Saint   50
126) [1995 59d: a8.5g⁴ 6f 7f⁴ 8m 8.3g 7.1m* 8m⁶ 7g 7.1m 8.3m⁴ 7.5m⁴ 7m² 7m 8d⁴   a45
7g 8.2m⁴ 7f³ a9.4g a8g⁴ a8g⁵ 1996 a8g a8g⁴ a8g a7g² a8g³ a8g 7f⁶ 8g 7.1g 8f a10g
Nov 7] smallish, sparely-made gelding: often dull in coat: has a quick action: poor
handicapper nowadays: effective at 6f to 8.5f: acts on firm and dead ground and the
all-weather: tried visored/blinkered, no improvement. *D. W. P. Arbuthnot*

LOVELY MORNING   3 b.f. Thowra (FR) – Sweet Pleasure 88 (Sweet Revenge   –
129) [1995 –p: 8d 1996 a9.4g 8m³ 10f⁶ 8d Sep 30] workmanlike filly: trained by
R. Hannon at 2 yrs: little worthwhile form. *D. J. G. Murray Smith*

LOVELY PROSPECT   3 b.f. Lycius (USA) 124 – Lovely Lagoon 68 (Mill   –
Reef (USA) 141) [1995 74: 7m 7.5d² 6.9s* 8m 1996 8g⁴ 7m 10m 10m⁵ 8f Oct 14]
tall filly: well below 2-y-o form (on a sound surface) in 1996: sold 8,000 gns

Newmarket Autumn Sales: stays 7.5f: best efforts in 1996 on a soft surface: tried blinkered. *R. Guest*

LOVELY SMILE (BEL) 3 ch.f. River Smile (USA) – Love Ballad 78 (Song 28 132) [1995 5v⁶ 6d³ 8d* 8.5g³ 1996 a8g 8f³ a7.5g³ a8.5g 7g 7f⁶ 6f⁴ 7d 6d a7g Oct 12] Belgian-trained filly: first reported foal: dam 5f winner here at 2 yrs: won minor event at Ostend in September, 1995: tailed off in minor event at Lingfield on first start in 1996: in frame 3 times in Belgium after: stays 8.5f: acts on firm and good to soft ground. *Paul Smith, Belgium*

LOVE ME DO (USA) 2 b.g. (May 20) Minshaanshu Amad (USA) 91§ – I 69 Assume (USA) (Young Emperor 133) [1996 7g³ 8m⁴ 7.9g 8g Oct 21] 2,000F, 7,400Y, 21,000 2-y-o: sturdy, useful-looking gelding: half-brother to unreliable 8.3f (at 2 yrs) and 1½m winner Mr Ziegfeld (by Fred Astaire), fairly useful 6f (at 2 yrs) to 1¼m winner Nile Empress (by Upper Nile), later minor stakes winner in USA, and several winners abroad: dam maiden sister of Cheveley Park winner Sookera: fair maiden: well below form last 2 starts: stays 1m: slowly away on debut. *M. Johnston*

LOVESCAPE 5 b.m. Precocious 126 – Alpine Damsel 46 (Mountain Call 125) – [1995 NR 1996 a8.5g a12g Feb 28] small mare: probably no longer of any account. *B. J. Llewellyn*

LOVE THE BLUES 4 ch.f. Bluebird (USA) 125 – Love Match (USA) 73 69 (Affiliate (USA)) [1995 69: 8g 10d³ 10g⁶ 11.8g 1996 14.1s² 15.9g Sep 25] strong, lengthy filly: fair maiden: better effort at 4 yrs on reappearance: probably in need of race when next seen out 5½ months later: will be suited by good test of stamina, and probably by forcing tactics: acts on soft going, yet to race on top-of-the-ground. *D. Nicholson*

LOVEYOUMILLIONS (IRE) 4 b.g. Law Society (USA) 130 – Warning 88 d Sound (Red Alert 127) [1995 95d: 6m⁴ 6g⁴ 7m 6m 6g 7m³ a6g⁶ a7g⁴ 1996 a6g² a7g 7s⁶ 12d⁵ 9.2s⁴ 12g² 8.1d² 8m⁴ a9.4g Dec 14] workmanlike gelding: one-time fairly useful handicapper: well below form last 4 starts, claimed out of M. Johnston's stable £10,000 first occasion: seems to stay 1½m: acts on good to firm and soft ground and the all-weather: blinkered last 6 3-y-o starts: usually races prominently. *N. Tinkler*

LOVING AND GIVING 2 b.f. (Feb 18) Sharpo 132 – Pretty Poppy 67 (Song 84 p 132) [1996 5.1m* 5v⁴ Oct 6] lengthy filly: second foal: sister to useful 3-y-o 5f winner Speed On: dam 2-y-o 5f winner, stayed 7.6f: justified favouritism in maiden auction at Bath in September by ½ length from Hype Energy, leading inside last: 5/1, 5 lengths fourth of 6 to Superior Premium in minor event on heavy ground at Haydock 4 weeks later, travelling strongly up with pace 4f and shaping better than final point suggests: type to improve again as 3-y-o, and should win more races. *H. Candy*

LOWER EGYPT (USA) 6 br.h. Silver Hawk (USA) 123 – Naughty Nile (USA) 101 + (Upper Nile (USA)) [1995 a8g² a10g a7g⁶ a8g⁶ 8.5f² 8.5f² 8.5f⁴ 8.5f³ 8.5g³ 9f⁴ 1996 8.2m² Jun 10] good-bodied, attractive horse: smart, genuine and consistent performer (rated 111) at 4 yrs for J. Gosden, winner in listed company: ran 4 times in Dubai when in frame all 6 starts in allowance company in USA in 1995: 8/1, wearing tongue strap and crossed noseband, creditable second of 8 to Restructure in minor event at Nottingham, running on: sold only 6,000 gns Newmarket December Sales: effective at 1m and 1¼m: acts on firm ground and dead, and on sand, lack-lustre effort on soft: tends to be reluctant at stalls: held up in Britain. *Major W. R. Hern*

LOXLEY'S GIRL (IRE) 2 b.f. (Mar 10) Lahib (USA) 129 – Samnaun (USA) – (Stop The Music (USA)) [1996 5m 5g 6f Jun 3] IR 6,000Y: sturdy, lengthy filly: first foal: dam unraced half-sister to useful German performer (probably stayed 11f) Quebrada and useful 1988 2-y-o 6f winner Court out of smart 1m to 11f winner Queen To Conquer, later Grade 1 1¼m winner in USA: behind throughout in varied company: blinkered final start, and subsequently joined H. Akbary: very slowly away first 2 outings. *M. W. Easterby*

LUBABA (USA) 3 b. or br.f. Woodman (USA) 126 – Minifah (USA) 69 (Nureyev 72 (USA) 131) [1995 NR 1996 8.2m³ 7d 8f* 8.3m 8.2m Aug 7] strong filly: third foal: closely related to 7f and 1m winner Atlaal (by Machiavellian) and half-sister to useful 1m winner Bintalshaati (by Kris): dam maiden (stayed 1½m) out of half-sister to champion filly Chris Evert: made all in 5-runner maiden at Yarmouth in June: well below form subsequently, setting strong pace in blinkers on second occasion: best up to 1m: well beaten on dead ground: carried head high first 2 starts, hung left on third: visits Green Desert. *H. Thomson Jones*

LUCAYAN BEACH 2 gr.g. (Jan 31) Cyrano de Bergerac 120 – Mrs Gray 61 **68** (Red Sunset 120) [1996 5.2d⁴ 5g² 6f⁵ May 16] 7,200Y: angular gelding: second foal: half-brother to a fairly useful 4-y-o 6f to 1m winner in Sweden by Rambo Dancer: dam 2-y-o 5f winner: slowly away when in frame in maidens at Newbury and Leicester, travelling strongly much of way on second occasion: last of 5 in maiden at York in May on final outing, rider looking down as if something amiss. *B. Gubby*

LUCAYAN PRINCE (USA) 3 br.c. Fast Play (USA) – Now That's Funny **123** (USA) (Saratoga Six (USA)) [1995 94: 5m* 6g² 1996 7d⁶ 8m³ 7g² 7m* 6m² 6f⁵ 6m² 7m⁵ Oct 17]

Nobody will be forgetting Lucayan Prince's one win of 1996 in a hurry. At 50/1, it was one of the shocks of the season; coming from last to first in the final two furlongs, it was one of the rides of the season; and, on the bridle virtually the whole way, it was one of the most impressive wins at the latest Royal Ascot—Lucayan Prince won the Jersey Stakes by a length and a half from Ramooz. In a sixteen-strong race with only two of the runners at longer odds, Richard Hughes got Lucayan Prince to miss a beat at the start and immediately switched him to the centre. Very little separated the entire field two furlongs from home, with nine of them stretched out battling for the lead, but Hughes steered his mount through the eye of a needle at the furlong pole and in the last hundred yards Lucayan Prince settled the issue with a sparkling turn of foot.

'We knew that Lucayan Prince was very well and that he could win here if he did what he does at home', reported trainer David Loder. As the 50/1 indicated, his charge had not done it on three earlier visits to the racecourse as a three-year-old. Loder's string had largely been out of sorts, and the tactics on Lucayan Prince had not yet been fine-tuned. That they would need some attention had been apparent for over twelve months, since, on his second start, the colt had carried his head high and thrown away an odds-on chance by swerving left inside the final furlong. He had rewarded odds-on support in a

Jersey Stakes, Royal Ascot—50/1-shot Lucayan Prince (blinkers) surprises Ramooz (right)

maiden at Newmarket on his debut, but lost the opportunity to test the nerves of jockeys and punters any further that season by sustaining a knee injury. For all his talent—and he did not have to call on all of it by any means at Royal Ascot—and the fact that his connections know how to use it, Lucayan Prince will not find that everything can go right for him very regularly. Every horse requires some luck in running, but he needs a lot more than most. A strong enough pace, horses behind which to cover him up, a clear passage through in the closing stages—these are not things over which his connections have that much control. By our reckoning, all these ideal conditions were met on just two of Lucayan Prince's eight starts in 1996, in the Jersey Stakes and in the July Cup at Newmarket on his next appearance. A 9/1 chance, he threw down the only serious challenge to Anabaa in the July Cup, but was decisively held in the last hundred yards and went down by a length and three quarters. In the Haydock Park Sprint Cup, Lucayan Prince saw plenty of daylight after being drawn one, and finished fifth. Getting him covered up was the least of his problems in the Diadem at Ascot where just a fraction more luck in finding a way out would have resulted in Diffident's jockey Frankie Dettori settling for a 'Magnificent Six'. A slow early pace and then being checked when the tempo quickened both spoilt things in the Challenge Stakes at Newmarket. No, Lucayan Prince is not always going to have it his own way.

Lucayan Prince (USA) (br.c. 1993)	Fast Play (USA) (b or br 1986)	Seattle Slew (b or br 1974)	Bold Reasoning My Charmer
		Con Game (b or br 1974)	Buckpasser Broadway
	Now That's Funny (USA) (b 1986)	Saratoga Six (b 1982)	Alydar Priceless Fame
		Tropical Cream (b 1971)	Creme de La Creme Tropic Star

Lucayan Prince is one of just three runners in Britain so far for the stallion Fast Play, joining Star of The Dance, who won a maiden at Redcar in 1994 but was sent back to the United States after breaking blood vessels, and the modest maiden Crystal Fast. Fast Play, a half-brother to Seeking The Gold, gained four of his five wins at two years, one in the Grade 1 nine-furlong Remsen Stakes, but also showed smart form at three. He stood at 15,000 dollars in the year Lucayan Prince was conceived, but has had problems on the fertility front and was available at just 3,500 in 1996. Lucayan Prince made 45,000 dollars as a foal and 55,000 as a yearling, and he looks very much like Fast Play's best offspring so far. His dam's one previous foal, Akiba (by Tejano), won a minor 8.5-furlong stakes race in 1995. That dam, Now That's Funny, also ran in the United States, winning two minor races as a four-year-old, but some of the family are more familiar as she is a half-sister to the 1980 Prix Marcel Boussac winner Tropicaro, daughter of the 1974 Prix Cleopatre winner Tropical Cream and granddaughter of the 1962 Cheshire Oaks winner Tropic Star. The last-named is also grandam of the 1977 US turf champion Johnny D and third dam of Urgent Request and Sanmartino. Lucayan Prince is a leggy, close-coupled colt. Effective at six and seven furlongs, he raced on top-of-the-ground almost throughout the latest season, the only exception being his reappearance. He did not wear blinkers that day, but has done on all his starts since. *D. R. Loder*

LUCITINO 3 ch.f. Bustino 136 – Lucky Fingers 81 (Hotfoot 126) [1995 NR 1996 a8.5g a7g⁵ 10g a11g a8g Jun 6] angular filly: half-sister to winners abroad by Posse and (in Italy at up to 1¼m) Glint of Gold: dam maiden suited by 1½m: well beaten in maidens and handicaps: bred to need further than 1¼m: blinkered last start. *S. C. Williams* –

LUCKY ARCHER 3 b.g. North Briton 67 – Preobrajenska 93 (Double Form 130) [1995 NR 1996 8d⁶ 8d⁵ 7m³ 7m⁵ 7.1m⁶ 6g 7m 6m³ 7d⁵ 8.5m² 7.1m³ 8.5m 7m 7f² Oct 14] smallish, well-made colt: half-brother to a winner in Italy by Blakeney: dam won at 5f and 6f at 2 yrs then seemed to go wrong way temperamentally: fairly 85 useful maiden: sold 14,000 gns Newmarket Autumn Sales: probably better at 8.5f than shorter: acts on good to firm (almost certainly on firm) and dead ground: blinkered final start (bit below best). *C. E. Brittain*

LUCKY BEA 3 b.g. Lochnager 132 – Knocksharry 58 (Palm Track 122) [1995 61 50: 5d 5m 5m 5m² 5f³ 5f² 7m 6m 6f 6m⁵ 10d 7f⁵ 8f 1996 6s³ 6d³ 8g⁵ 8d* 10m⁵ 12.3g 8g² 8m³ 10m 8m³ 8.5m 8g a8g 8f 8m Oct 23] robust, close-coupled gelding: has a round action: modest handicapper: won at Newcastle in May despite carrying head rather high: stays 1m: acts on firm and soft going: often gives trouble at start and sometimes starts slowly: has been early to post: effective blinkered or not (tried only once in 1996): would probably have won novice hurdle in November but for falling last. *M. W. Easterby*

LUCKY BEGONIA (IRE) 3 br.f. Simply Great (FR) 122 – Hostess 81 (Be My 65 Guest (USA) 126) [1995 NR 1996 8m 8d⁵ 8m⁶ 10g Jul 1] IR 7,000F, 5,000Y: sturdy, workmanlike filly: sister to 1992 2-y-o 1m winner Lady Ounavarra, closely related to a winner in France and USA and half-sister to 2 winners: dam 7f and 1m winner: apparently best effort in maiden events when sixth in steadily-run race at Yarmouth penultimate start. *C. N. Allen*

LUCKY COIN 4 b.f. Hadeer 118 – Lucky Omen 99 (Queen's Hussar 60 124) [1995 73: 7m 10.2m³ 10.4g⁴ 12m 10.1g³ 14.1f³ 11.9m* 11.5m² 12m 12s 1996 12m 14.1m² 14m 14.1g² 14f 14.1m⁵ 12d 11.9f⁴ 16m Sep 16] quite attractive filly: modest handicapper: inconsistent at 4 yrs, running creditably only on her 3 trips to Yarmouth: sold 5,400 gns Newmarket Autumn Sales: effective at 1¾m, may stay 2m: acts on firm ground: has run creditably for lady: makes running/races prominently. *P. Howling*

LUCKY DIP 2 b.f. (Apr 30) Tirol 127 – Miss Loving 89 (Northfields (USA)) 65 [1996 6d 7m⁴ 7m Aug 1] unfurnished filly: closely related to 5f winner Allyana and Irish 6f winner Missing Love (both by Thatching) and half-sister to 3-y-o Pearls of Thought (by Persian Bold) and fairly useful sprinter Love Returned (by Taufan): dam 2-y-o 5f and 7f winner: clearly best effort in maidens when over 9 lengths fourth of 15 to Sandstone at Salisbury, stumbling start, no extra final 1f: again faded final outing: may do better back at 6f. *Major D. N. Chappell*

LUCKY DI (USA) 4 b.c. Diesis 133 – Lucky Song (USA) 117 (Seattle Song 118 (USA) 130) [1995 103p: 8d* 11g² 1996 10g* 10d² 10f Jun 18] tall, good sort: only third start when winning listed race at Kempton in April by 3 lengths from Star Selection, quickening impressively: reportedly had a setback afterwards: good ½-length second to Pilsudski in Brigadier Gerard Stakes at Sandown, staying on strongly: bandaged off-fore, never in hunt in very strongly-run Prince of Wales's Stakes at Royal Ascot, seeming ill-at-ease on bend into straight, hanging and carrying head awkwardly: jarred up there and not seen out again, but remains in training: should stay 1½m: acts on dead ground (yet to race on soft), possibly not on firm: held up at 4 yrs: sweating last 2 starts. *L. M. Cumani*

LUCKY HOOF 3 b.f. Batshoof 122 – Lucky Omen 99 (Queen's Hussar 124) 69 [1995 NR 1996 10.1g 11.5m² 11.5m 14d Sep 28] half-sister to several winners, including modest 4-y-o 1½m winner Lucky Coin (by Hadeer), smart 6f and 9.2f winner Lapierre (by Lafontaine) and very useful sprinter Lucky Hunter (by Huntercombe): dam 2-y-o 5f and 6f winner: only form when second of 4 in maiden at Yarmouth: sold (C. Brittain to K. Morgan) 2,200 gns Ascot December Sales. *C. E. Brittain*

LUCKY LIONEL (USA) 3 ch.c. Mt Livermore (USA) – Crafty Nan (USA) 112 (Crafty Prospector (USA)) [1995 109: 5m* 6f⁴ 5m* 6g⁶ 5.5g* 6g 5d³ 6g⁴ 1996 7m 5m² 6f⁴ 5f 6m 5m 7.3m⁶ 6m⁵ 6g⁴ 7d² Nov 2] small, quite attractive colt: easy mover: smart performer: came from off strong pace when second in Palace House Stakes (¾ length behind Cool Jazz) at Newmarket, fourth in Duke of York Stakes (to Venture Capitalist) and fourth in listed race at Newmarket (to Russian Revival): good second to Macanal in Group 3 event at Milan final start: stays 7f: acts on firm and dead ground: often gets behind: seemed unsuited by Epsom second 2-y-o start. *R. Hannon*

LUCKY OAKWOOD (USA) 2 ch.f. (Feb 4) Elmaamul (USA) 125 – Fair 73 Sousanne 75 (Busted 134) [1996 5m⁴ a5g a7g* 7m² 7m 6g³ 7m³ 6m Oct 5] 20,000Y: workmanlike filly: poor mover: closely related to 1¼m winners Obelos and Gisarne (both by Diesis), latter useful, and half-sister to several winners here and abroad, including (at 1½m) Admiral's Inn (by Shirley Heights): dam, in frame over 6f and 1¼m, out of very smart French filly Army Court: fair performer: won median auction maiden at Southwell in July by 7 lengths: creditable efforts in nurseries last 3 starts: sold 9,800 gns Newmarket Autumn Sales: needs further than 5f, stays 7f: acts on good to firm ground and fibresand: has shown her form for 7-lb claimer. *M. Bell*

LUCKY PARKES   6 b.m. Full Extent (USA) 113 – Summerhill Spruce 70   104
(Windjammer (USA)) [1995 100: 5m⁵ 5.1m* 5.1m* 5f³ 5g² 5.1g² 5f² 5m³ 5m² 5.2d⁵
5d² 1996 5d⁶ 5m 5m² 5m⁴ 5m² 5.1m* 5m 5d* 5m 5g³ 5d Sep 28] strong, lengthy,
good-quartered mare: good walker: useful performer: prolific winner of minor
events, and narrowly successful in such races at 6 yrs at Chester and Lingfield in the
summer: particularly good efforts when short-headed by To The Roof in £25,000
rated stakes at Epsom fifth start, and when third to Matula in listed race at Cologne
on penultimate one: races at around 5f: acts on firm and dead ground: tends to edge
left: forces pace: unbeaten in 4 runs at Bath: genuine and consistent. *J. Berry*

LUCKY REVENGE   3 b.f. Komaite (USA) – Sweet And Lucky (Lucky   66
Wednesday 124) [1995 62: 5.1m³ 5.1m³ a7g 6.1m 6f² 6.1m² 6m² 6.5m 1996 7m²
7m 6m⁴ 6m² 6f⁴ 7m* 6m⁴ 6d⁶ 8g² 7m³ 7m 8f Oct 14] leggy, angular filly: fair
handicapper: won apprentice maiden event at Thirsk in August: below form all
subsequent starts, and sold 4,500 gns Newmarket Autumn Sales: probably stays 1m:
acts on firm going, poor efforts on fibresand and dead ground. *Martyn Meade*

LUCKY TUCKY   5 b.g. Alleging (USA) 120 – Romana 72 (Roman Warrior 132)   39
[1995 57: 9.7d 8m 8g 7f⁴ 8m⁶ a8g⁴ a8g 1996 a8g³ a10g⁴ Jan 25] leggy, close-coupled
gelding: poor form both outings at 5 yrs: should stay 1¼m: acts on fibresand and
good to firm ground, probably on dead: ran poorly only try in a visor. *J. R. Jenkins*

LUCYBOD   2 ch.f. (Feb 22) Night Shift (USA) – Splintering 80 (Sharpo 132)   –
[1996 5s 5g 6m 5m 6d 6s Oct 5] 12,000Y: small, strong filly: unimpressive mover:
fourth foal: sister to 5f and 6f winner Midnight Break and half-sister to 3-y-o 7f
winner Smithereens (by Primo Dominie): dam sprinter: well beaten in varied
company, including selling: sold 800 gns Newmarket Autumn Sales. *N. Tinkler*

LUCY OF ARABIA (IRE)   2 b.f. (Feb 4) Mujadil (USA) 119 – Fleur-De-Luce   48
(Tumble Wind (USA)) [1996 5m 6m 6g Aug 3] 6,000Y: sixth living foal: half-sister
to 1991 5f winner Lucid (by Nashamaa), later successful in Italy, and Irish 6f winner
Lady Be Magic (by Burslem): dam Irish 9.5f winner: never a significant factor in
maiden events. *J. J. Sheehan*

LUCY'S GOLD   5 b.m. Efisio 120 – Hinton Rose (Frimley Park 109) [1995 –:
5.1g a5g a5g 5g 6g 10m 1996 a8.5g 8.2m a8.5g 14.1f a12g a7g Aug 16] compact
mare: no worthwhile form for long time: tried blinkered and visored: covered by
Keen. *M. J. Ryan*

LUCY TUFTY   5 b.m. Vin St Benet 109 – Manor Farm Toots 70 (Royalty 130)   42
[1995 NR 1996 10m⁴ 11.9g 14.1g⁴ 12s* a14.8g Nov 25] poor handicapper: 5/1 from
13/2, having first outing on a soft surface when winning 18-runner seller at Folkestone in November: stays 1¾m. *J. Pearce*

LUDO   2 br. or gr.c. (Jan 25) Petong 126 – Teacher's Game 64 (Mummy's Game   69 ?
120) [1996 6f 6f⁴ 7g Aug 14] 19,000F, 35,000Y: useful-looking colt: fifth foal: half-
brother to 1994 2-y-o 7f winner Pleasure Beach (by Pharly): dam (sprint maiden)
close relative of smart miler Teacher's Pet and half-sister to dam of Petardia (by
Petong): best effort in maidens when over 3 lengths fourth of 6 to Hirasah in steadily-
run contest at Newmarket: unimpressive to post, still didn't look fully wound up on
final outing. *R. Hannon*

LULU   2 b.f. (Apr 27) Polar Falcon (USA) 126 – Cap Camarat (CAN) 59 (Miswaki   – p
(USA) 124) [1996 6m Oct 4] second foal: dam 1m winner, half-sister to smart French
sprinter Breath Taking (by Nureyev) out of a leading sprinter in Australia: 15/2, tenth
of 12 in maiden at Lingfield, close up to halfway: should do better. *Sir Mark Prescott*

LUNA MAREZA   4 b.f. Saumarez 132 – Luna Maya (Gay Mecene (USA) 128)   113
[1995 12v* 10d* 1996 10.5g² 11s* 12g² Jun 8] third foal: half-sister to French 11f
and 1½m winner Lunar Lead (by Lead On Time): dam, 12.5f winner in France, is
half-sister to Linamix (stayed 1¼m, rated 127): won minor events at Saint-Cloud and
Evry at 3 yrs and 10-runner Group 3 event at Lyon Parilly (beat Fay Wray a length)

Prix Saint-Alary, Longchamp—Luna Wells and Miss Tahiti give Fabre the first two

in May: short-head second of 5 to Poliglote in Grand Prix d'Evry in June: stays 1½m: acts on heavy going, yet to race on top-of-the-ground. *A. Fabre, France*

LUNAR GRIS 3 gr.f. Absalom 128 – Sliprail (USA) 86 (Our Native (USA)) – [1995 –: 6m a5g⁶ 6m 6f a8g 1996 10f Sep 23] leggy filly: poor mover: no worthwhile form: sold 1,000 gns (R. Stronge to A. Chamberlain) Ascot December Sales. *R. M. Stronge*

LUNAR MIST 3 b.f. Komaite (USA) – Sugar Token 66 (Record Token 128) – [1995 93+: 5g* 6m 6.1d⁴ 5g* 6g* 5g* 6m* 6d* 1996 5g⁶ 5m 7d Aug 30] smallish filly: progressed really well at 2 yrs, successful in seller and 5 autumn nurseries: well held in 1996: stays 6f: acts on good to firm and dead ground. *Martyn Meade*

LUNAR MUSIC 2 b.f. (May 22) Komaite (USA) – Lucky Candy 61 (Lucky   67 Wednesday 124) [1996 5d 5m³ 5f* 6m⁴ 5m⁵ 6m⁵ 5m* 6m 5f Sep 28] angular filly: seventh foal: sister to 3-y-o Born A Lady, 5f winner at 2 yrs, and half-sister to 1m winner Ace Girl (by Stanford) and 4-y-o 11f winner Noble Canonire (by Gunner B): fair performer: easy winner of sellers at Lingfield in July and Musselburgh in August: well below that form in 4 non-selling nurseries: stays 6f: acts on firm ground. *Martyn Meade*

LUNAR PRINCE 6 b.g. Mansingh (USA) 120 – Lunate (Faraway Times (USA) – 123) [1995 –: a5g a7g a8g 5.2m 1996 a10g Feb 27] lengthy gelding: no sign of ability. *T. T. Clement*

LUNAR RISK 6 b.g. Risk Me (FR) 127 – Moonlight Princess 49 (Alias Smith – (USA)) [1995 44: 15.4g 16m⁶ 12f 11.4g² 12f 12.1m⁶ 12m 1996 a13g 11.9f Apr 12] good-bodied gelding: usually impresses in appearance: well beaten at 5 yrs: effective at 1½m and probably stays 2m: acts on any going: tried visored, no improvement: tricky ride: inconsistent. *Miss B. Sanders*

LUNA WELLS (IRE) 3 b.f. Sadler's Wells (USA) 132 – Lunadix (FR) (Breton   119 130) [1995 103p: 10g* 9d* 9s² 1996 9.3m* 10d* 10.5g 10g* 12m⁶ 12d⁵ 12g Oct 26] compact filly: smart performer: successful for new stable in the spring in 5-runner Prix Vanteaux at Longchamp in April by ¾ length from Ecoute and 6-runner Prix Saint-Alary at Longchamp in May by 1½ lengths from Miss Tahiti: never able to challenge in Prix de Diane but awarded Group 3 Prix de la Nonette at Deauville in August (finished neck and length behind Bint Salsabil and Bint Shadayid), after being hampered in between rivals 1f: got poor run in straight next start: 7¾ lengths fifth of 16 to Helissio in Prix de l'Arc de Triomphe (best effort, held up in midfield, stayed on steadily) in October: 10 lengths tenth of 14 to Pilsudski in Breeders' Cup Turf at Woodbine, every chance but unable to quicken: stays 1½m: acts on good to firm and soft ground: held up: sold for a record 1,700,000 gns Newmarket December Sales to join R. Mandella in USA. *A. Fabre, France*

LUNCH PARTY 4 b.g. Beveled (USA) – Crystal Sprite 74 (Crystal Glitters   59 (USA) 127) [1995 NR 1996 7g* 7g² 9g 7g 6d Sep 30] first reported foal: dam sprint winner: won once as 2-y-o and twice in 1995 (over 7f and 1m), all in Czech Republic: well backed, won seller at Thirsk in May: failed to progress, but didn't have things go his way and not discredited last 2 starts: keen sort, likely to prove best at up to 1m: has raced only on good or dead ground in Britain. *D. Nicholls*

556

J-L. Lagardère's "Luna Wells"

LUNDA (IRE)   3 b.f. Soviet Star (USA) 128 – Lucayan Princess 111 (High Line   60
125) [1995 NR 1996 7d 11.4g 8m Jun 5] close-coupled filly: sixth foal: half-sister
to very smart 4-y-o 1m to 1½m winner Luso (by Salse), smart 1¼m winner Needle
Gun (by Sure Blade) and useful 6f winner Luana (by Shaadi): dam, 2-y-o 7f winner,
stayed 1½m: modest form when eighth in newcomers event at Newbury and maiden
at Yarmouth: trailed throughout in Cheshire Oaks in between: stays in training.
C. E. Brittain

LUSO   4 b.c. Salse (USA) 128 – Lucayan Princess 111 (High Line 125) [1995   124
120: 8g 10m² 10m⁴ 12.3m* 12m* 12d² 11.9m³ 14.6d 12d 1996 9m* 10.5m²
12m* 12m² 12m⁶ 12g* 12g⁴ 12m* Dec 8]
      Travelling widely can have its rewards and its drawbacks. Luso experi-
enced both in the latest season, though fortunately for him and his connections
the former far outweighed the latter, and he ended up with wins in four different
countries which earned more than £400,000. Luso was better than ever as a
four-year-old and even more consistent. The only race in which he failed to
make any impression came at home in the King George VI and Queen
Elizabeth Diamond Stakes at Ascot, where, highly tried, he was already beaten
when losing his footing on the home turn. Luso had had no travelling to speak
of to make his reappearance in the Earl of Sefton Stakes at Newmarket, where
he looked up against it burdened with a Group 1 penalty for his win in the
Derby Italiano and running over a seemingly-inadequate nine furlongs. But
Luso had done really well from three to four, making into a big, strong colt, and
he put up a very smart performance which set the tone for the rest of his season,
rallying splendidly to pip the favourite Smart Alec. Luso was one of six Group
1 winners in a high-class field of ten for the Prix Ganay at Longchamp only

557

Aral-Pokal, Gelsenkirchen-Horst—seasoned traveller Luso dictates to Hollywood Dream and Lear White

eleven days later and he very nearly came out best of them, just unable to withstand the strong finish of favourite Valanour. A 27/1-shot that day, Luso was 10/1-on in the Group 2 Premio Ellington-Memorial Carlo d'Alessio in Rome next time; as his odds suggest it was a Group 2 in name only, and, against four locals, he made all. Italy again, and the Gran Premio di Milano, saw him meet with a common scourge of the tourist—mosquito bites. In retrospect, he hardly needed an excuse for a length-and-a-half defeat by Strategic Choice. Ascot's reverse suggested that it was time to be on the road again, well away from the likes of Pentire, and in August he popped up at Gelsenkirchen to make all in the Group 1 Aral-Pokal, beating the German mare Hollywood Dream one and three-quarter lengths, thus avenging the narrow defeat of his elder half-brother Needle Gun by the same rival in Rome earlier in the year. Luso was very well used to air travel by now but that didn't help him avoid injury on the plane to the Grosser Preis Von Baden—a minor injury which cost him only a run. He was soon back for the Europa-Preis at Cologne in September, in which he proved no match for the top German three-year-old Lavirco, being left to fight for minor honours with Protektor and Hollywood Dream.

Luso's season was not over yet, nor was his travelling. In December at Sha Tin he started favourite for the fourteen-runner Hong Kong International

Hong Kong International Vase, Sha Tin—Luso is a comfortable winner much further from home

Vase, a race open to Group 1 winners for the first time. International was the right word—he faced rivals from France (the Lutece winner Tarator), Germany (Protektor), Dubai, the United States, Australia (including the Melbourne Cup runner-up Count Chivas), New Zealand and Hong Kong, and was accompanied by Sacrament from Newmarket. Report had it that Clive Brittain had been far happier with Needle Gun, the stable's representative in the International Cup, since their arrival in Hong Kong, but it was the younger half-brother who went home with a valuable prize. Always going well behind the leader under Dettori, Luso improved on the home turn to lead over a furlong out and run out the comfortable length-and-a-half winner from the Australian veteran Royal Snack who had been third in the race the year before.

Luso (b.c. 1992)	Salse (USA) (b 1985)	Topsider (b 1974)	Northern Dancer Drumtop
		Carnival Princess (ch 1974)	Prince John Carnival Queen
	Lucayan Princess (b 1983)	High Line (ch 1966)	High Hat Time Call
		Gay France (b 1976)	Sir Gaylord Sweet And Lovely II

Both Luso and Needle Gun (winner of the Gallinule Stakes in the latest season, by Sure Blade) have been a fine advertisement for their dam, the Sweet Solera winner Lucayan Princess. Further details of Luso's family were given in *Racehorses of 1995*. Since then, his three-year-old half-sister Lunda (by Soviet Star) has shown modest form in two of her three starts, highly tried in the Cheshire Oaks, a race in which Lucayan Princess finished third on her only outing at three. There is a yearling filly by In The Wings coming along. Luso

Saeed Manana's "Luso"

has been entered for the Dubai World Cup—Needle Gun was seventh in the inaugural running in Nad al Sheba, incidentally. Luso is effective from nine furlongs to a mile and a half; he has yet to race on extremes of ground. It is unlikely he will be seen again in the blinkers he wore as Lammtarra's surprise pacemaker in the Arc at three. Luso, who usually races prominently, is a grand sort, both in appearance and attitude. *C. E. Brittain*

LYCILITY (IRE) 2 b.f. (Apr 24) Lycius (USA) 124 – She's The Tops 83 86 (Shernazar 131) [1996 6m* 5m 6g 7.1m^3 8m 7m Oct 1] 31,000Y: smallish, quite attractive filly: second foal: half-sister to 3-y-o Queen's Wake (by Old Vic): dam 1½m winner out of half-sister to Most Welcome, also the family of Teenoso: fairly useful form: won maiden at Pontefract in June: stiff tasks afterwards, best effort 8½ lengths third of 7 to Red Camellia in listed race at Sandown in August: will stay beyond 1m. *C. E. Brittain*

LYCIUS TOUCH 2 b.f. (Feb 12) Lycius (USA) 124 – Homely Touch 84 50 (Touching Wood (USA) 127) [1996 5g^6 5s* 5m^6 5f a6g^4 6f^3 7.1m 7.5m^5 8.1m^5 a8.5g^3 Nov 2] 6,000Y: smallish, leggy filly: fourth foal: half-sister to 4-y-o 5f (at 2 yrs) and 6f winner Shashi and 1995 2-y-o 6f winner Shaniko (both by Shaadi): dam, disappointing maiden who should have stayed 1¼m, granddaughter of Full Dress II: modest performer: won maiden auction at Hamilton in May: stays 8.5f: acts on firm and soft going and on fibresand: inconsistent: joined A. Newcombe. *M. Johnston*

LYNTON LAD 4 b.g. Superpower 113 – House Maid 95 (Habitat 134) [1995 88d: 79 d 6m^5 6f 7.1m 6g 6s 6g 7d^2 8.2m^5 1996 8s^2 10.8d 8m 7.3s May 29] good-topped gelding: fair handicapper: good second of 21 to Cool Edge in Spring Mile at Doncaster in March: well beaten afterwards: stays 1m, not sure to stay much further: acts on good to firm and soft ground: effective blinkered or not (usually wears them): raced up with pace in 1996. *C. P. E. Brooks*

LYRICAL BID (USA) 2 b. or br.f. (Feb 11) Lyphard (USA) 132 – Doctor Bid 77 p (USA) (Spectacular Bid (USA)) [1996 7.5m* Sep 18] small, lightly-made filly: third foal: half-sister to fairly useful 5.2f (at 2 yrs) and 6f winner Doctor's Glory (by Elmaamul): dam unraced half-sister to smart 1986 2-y-o 7f and 7.5f winner Glory Forever, later third in French 2000 Guineas: 3/1 from 7/4, won steadily-run 5-runner maiden at Beverley by short head from Flourishing Way, chasing leaders then responding well to get up final stride: should improve. *D. R. Loder*

LYZIA (IRE) 3 ch.f. Lycius (USA) 124 – Zia (USA) 88 (Shareef Dancer (USA) – 135) [1995 77: 6f^3 6g^5 7m 7d 7m^3 1996 7m 8d^4 10g^4 10g 8d Sep 25] leggy, close-coupled filly: disappointing maiden: sold out of C. Brittain's stable 9,000 gns Newmarket July Sales after reappearance: bred to stay 1m: similar form at 2 yrs on firm and dead ground: blinkered (no form) final 3-y-o start. *W. P. Browne, Ireland*

M

MA BELLE POULE 3 b.f. Slip Anchor 136 – The Kings Daughter 79 (Indian – King (USA) 128) [1995 73p: 6.1d^3 7d 1996 8.1m Aug 31] compact filly: fair form at 2 yrs: pulled hard when well beaten in maiden at Sandown only outing at 3 yrs. *P. F. I. Cole*

MACANAL (USA) 4 b.c. Northern Flagship (USA) 96 – Magnala (ARG) 114 (Mount Athos 118) [1995 113: 6v* 6g* 8m^5 6.5g* 6.5g^2 6.5d* 1996 6.5s* 6d^2 6g^4 6v^3 6.5g* 8g^4 6g^6 6.5s^2 7d* Nov 2] smart German colt: had another good year, winning listed race (by length from Takaddum) at Munich in April, and Group 3 events at Hoppegarten (Grosser Preis von Berlin, beat Waky Nao a short head) in August and Milan (Premio Chiusura, by ½ length from Lucky Lionel) in November: not discredited at 1m, may prove best at up to 7f: acts on good to firm ground and heavy: consistent. *H. Jentzsch, Germany*

MACARI 2 gr.g. (Mar 20) Arzanni 115 – View Halloa (Al Sirat (USA)) [1996 8.2g – a8g^5 a8g^5 Nov 29] 620F: fourth reported foal: dam unraced: soundly beaten in sellers and a median auction maiden. *B. P. J. Baugh*

MACARONI BEACH   2 ch.f. (Apr 12) Jupiter Island 126 – Real Princess 78   –
(Aragon 118) [1996 7m a8g a8.5g Dec 14] fourth foal: dam 7f winner out of very
speedy 2-y-o Mange Toute: well beaten in maidens at Yarmouth, Lingfield (very
slowly away) and Wolverhampton. *C. E. Brittain*

MACAROON LADY   5 b.m. Prince Sabo 123 – Cookie Time (Posse (USA) 130)   –
[1995 –: 6.1d 5d 1996 a7g a8g 8m Jun 11] workmanlike mare: no form since 1993.
N. Bycroft

MACFARLANE   8 br.g. Kala Shikari 125 – Tarvie 101 (Swing Easy (USA) 126)   67
[1995 72: 5m 5g⁴ 5g 6g² 5.1g³ 6m 5.2g³ 6g 5.1d* 5m 5s 6.1s 5m 1996 6g 5.1m⁶ 5m
Jun 14] stocky, lengthy gelding: poor mover: fair handicapper: shaped well when
sixth at Chester (has a good record there) penultimate start, but broke blood vessel
and tailed off at York 8 days later: effective at 5f and 6f: has form on firm going, but
is ideally suited for an easy surface: has worn tongue strap: broke out of stalls and
withdrawn second intended 8-y-o start. *M. J. Fetherston-Godley*

MACMORRIS (USA)   3 b.c. Silver Hawk (USA) 123 – Andover Cottage (USA)   77
(Affiliate (USA)) [1995 –: 7f 1996 10g 12m⁵ 12m² 14.1m² 14d⁴ 16.2m² 11.5m⁴ Sep
10] good-bodied colt: shows knee action: fair maiden handicapper: sold 25,000 gns
Newmarket Autumn Sales: lacks pace, and will be suited by thorough test of stamina:
acts on good to firm ground, well below form on dead. *P. F. I. Cole*

MAC OATES   3 b.g. Bairn (USA) 126 – Bit of A Lass 59 (Wassl 125) [1995 61:   51
6g 6d⁵ 6f 1996 8.3m 10m 7.1m 5.3f² 7m⁶ 5f Sep 5] lengthy, unfurnished gelding:
modest maiden handicapper: mostly well beaten at 3 yrs: bred to be suited by at least
1m: acts on firm going. *D. W. P. Arbuthnot*

MACS CLAN   3 ch.f. Clantime 101 – Kabella (Kabour 80) [1995 –: 5m 1996 5m   –
7f Oct 14] sparely-made filly: no sign of ability: gave temperamental display on
reappearance. *Miss J. Bower*

MAC'S DELIGHT   2 b.g. (Mar 4) Machiavellian (USA) 123 – Bashoosh (USA)   62 ?
(Danzig (USA)) [1996 6g 7g³ Jul 3] compact colt: second foal: half-brother to 3-y-o
5f winner Total Aloof (by Groom Dancer): dam, ran 4 times over middle distances,
daughter of Yorkshire Oaks winner Condessa: well beaten in Doncaster maiden on
debut and remote last of 3 behind Great Ovation in similar event at Yarmouth 6 weeks
later: sold 1,600 gns Newmarket Autumn Sales. *E. A. L. Dunlop*

MAC'S TAXI   4 b.g. Komaite (USA) – Orange Silk 68 (Moulton 128) [1995 70,   –
a60: a7g² a7g² a7g* a7g⁵ 7g* 8.2m² a7g 6f⁴ 7m⁴ 7g⁶ a6g 7m⁴ 1996 a7g a7g⁴ a7g   a56
a10g⁴ a8g⁴ Feb 3] compact gelding: fair handicapper as 3-y-o, better on turf than the
all-weather: below form early in 1996: seems to stay 1¼m: acts on equitrack and firm
ground: tailed off in visor: has run well when sweating: often forces pace: sold only
1,050 gns Doncaster July Sales. *P. C. Haslam*

MAD ABOUT THE GIRL (IRE)   4 b.f. Cyrano de Bergerac 120 – Makalu 79   –
(Godswalk (USA) 130) [1995 –: 7.1m⁶ 7m 7g 7f 7m 1996 6f 8m Aug 8] angular filly:
no worthwhile form. *D. J. S. Cosgrove*

MAD ALEX   3 b.g. Risk Me (FR) 127 – Princess Mona 56 (Prince Regent (FR)   –
129) [1995 NR 1996 a10g a8g Dec 11] fourth foal: dam won over 1m at 5 yrs: no
show. *M. J. Haynes*

MADAME CHINNERY   2 b.f. (Feb 16) Weldnaas (USA) 112 – Bel Esprit   76
(Sagaro 133) [1996 5m⁵ 6g² 7f² 7m* 7m⁵ 8g⁴ Oct 18] 5,800Y: lengthy, unfurnished
filly: eighth foal: sister to 3-y-o 1¼m winner Double Up and half-sister to several
winners, including 6f and 7.3f winner Fille d'Esprit (by Cragador) and fairly useful
1¾m winner Wings Cove (by Elegant Air): dam showed no form on flat or over
jumps: improved form when winning nursery at Yarmouth in September: ran well in
Newmarket nurseries afterwards, on both occasions staying on in good style: will
stay beyond 1m: failed to handle home turn then carried head high (on firm ground)
third outing: sweating and edgy final start. *J. M. P. Eustace*

MADAME STEINLEN   3 b.f. Steinlen 127 – Equadif (FR) (Abdos 134) [1995   76
78: 6d⁶ 7g⁵ 7m² 1996 10g³ 12g³ 13.4m⁴ 11.7m² 12g 10s³ a13g Nov 26] close-
coupled, good-topped filly: carries condition: fair maiden: probably stays 1½m: yet
to race on firm going, probably acts on any other: sold 20,000 gns Newmarket December Sales. *B. W. Hills*

MADAM LUCY 2 ch.f. (Mar 23) Efisio 120 – Our Aisling 82 (Blakeney 126) – [1996 5f 7f 7.5m[6] Jul 6] first foal: dam suited by test of stamina: poor form: will stay beyond 7.5f. *W. W. Haigh*

MADAM MARASH (IRE) 3 b.f. Astronef 116 – Ballybannon 76 (Ballymore – 123) [1995 51: 6g 6m 7.1s[5] 7.3d 1996 9.7f 12.1g Aug 26] leggy filly: modest maiden: no worthwhile form at 3 yrs: should be suited by further than 1m: acts on soft going, possibly not on top-of-the-ground. *A. G. Foster*

MADAM POPPY 2 b.f. (Apr 28) Risk Me (FR) 127 – Egnoussa 76 (Swing Easy – (USA) 126) [1996 5g 7f[6] Jun 13] 2,700Y: sister to 3 winning sprinters, including 3-y-o 6f winner Spotted Eagle, and half-sister to 2 winners by Formidable, including 6f winner Fiorini: dam 7f winner, half-sister to very smart Devon Ditty: well beaten in maiden auction and seller (visored). *C. A. Dwyer*

MADAM ZANDO 3 ch.f. Forzando 122 – Madam Trilby (Grundy 137) [1995 51 d 47: 5.2g[3] 6m[2] 5g 5g[6] 1996 a6g[5] a6g a7g[5] 6d[2] 6d 6g[2] 5g[5] 5.9f[5] 6m[4] 6f[4] 6m 6d[6] 7g a37 6.1m Sep 24] rather unfurnished filly: poor maiden handicapper: effective at 6f and 7f: acts on firm ground, probably on dead: tried blinkered at 2 yrs: effective for 7-lb claimer. *J. Balding*

MADE BOLD 2 b.f. (Apr 30) Never So Bold 135 – Classical Vintage 80 80 p (Stradavinsky 121) [1996 6.1m[3] Sep 24] 6,200Y: smallish, well-made filly: seventh foal: half-sister to fair sprinter Simply Sooty and irresolute 6f and 7f winner Abso (both by Absalom) and a winner in Belgium: dam 2-y-o 5f winner: 14/1, over 3 lengths third of 9 to Much Commended in maiden at Nottingham, chasing leaders then staying on well despite looking green: will improve. *H. Candy*

MADISON'S TOUCH 3 b.f. Touch of Grey 90 – Cabinet Shuffle (Thatching – 131) [1995 NR 1996 6.9d a7g a7g[5] a10g Nov 26] 480Y: fourth foal: dam never ran: little promise. *R. M. Flower*

MADISON WELCOME (IRE) 2 b.g. (Apr 7) Be My Guest (USA) 126 – 56 Subtle Change (IRE) 102 (Law Society (USA) 130) [1996 6d 6m[4] 6g 6g[5] 7g[5] Sep 21] 23,000F, 22,000Y: robust, good-bodied gelding: has scope: second foal: dam 8.5f winner at 2 yrs, later successful at 1¾m and 2m in Ireland: modest form in maidens and nurseries: will be suited by further than 7f: flashed tail fourth start. *Mrs J. R. Ramsden*

MADLY SHARP 5 ch.g. Sharpo 132 – Madison Girl 68 (Last Fandango 125) 106 [1995 97: 6m 7m* 8m 7g[4] 6m 1996 6m* 6m[2] 6f 6m 6f 7m[2] 6s[6] Oct 24] big, workmanlike gelding: has a round action: useful handicapper: won rated stakes at Newmarket (has a good record there) in May: good effort after 2½-month absence when second to Highborn there penultimate start: effective at 6f and 7f: acts on good to firm ground, not at best on soft: sometimes sweating/on toes: flashes tail under pressure: normally races just off pace. *J. W. Watts*

MAD MILITANT (IRE) 7 b.g. Vision (USA) – Ullapool (Dominion 123) [1995 55 76d: a12g* a12g[2] a12g* a12g[3] a12g[2] a12g[2] a12g* 12.5g[4] 12.3m[5] a11g* a12g 10g[5] a71 12m 1996 12g[4] 11.9g[4] 12g[6] a12g[2] a12g[3] a12g[3] Dec 28] compact gelding: unimpressive mover: fair performer nowadays: stays 1½m, probably not 2m: below form on firm ground, acts on any other turf going and on fibresand (has had only one run on equitrack): sometimes looks less than keen. *A. Streeter*

MADONNA DA ROSSI 3 b.f. Mtoto 134 – Granny's Bank 88 (Music Boy 124) 43 [1995 53: 7f[4] 6g[5] 6m[5] 7.1g[2] a8.5g[4] 1996 a7g 8.2d[4] 8m 7.1g 6f 7g[3] 7d[2] 7.1m Aug 29] lengthy, angular filly: seems poor at best nowadays: unlikely to stay beyond 8.5f: acts on firm and dead ground and fibresand: headstrong. *M. Dods*

MADRINA 3 b.f. Waajib 121 – Mainly Sunset (Red Sunset 120) [1995 NR 1996 67 5.1d[6] 5m 5g[5] 5f[5] 7m[3] 8.1g[5] 8.1g[4] 6m[3] a6g[3] a6g* a6g[4] a6g a5g Dec 28] 18,000Y: a70 lengthy, workmanlike filly: third foal: half-sister to Daily Starshine, 5f winner at 2 yrs, and Irish 5f and 6f winner Musical Sunset (by Music Boy): dam once-raced half-sister to useful sprinter Great Chaddington: fair performer: won maiden at Lingfield in November by 5 lengths: best form at 6f, will prove at least as effective over 5f: acts on firm ground and all-weather: has been early to post: ran as if something amiss final start. *J. Berry*

MAFTOOL 2 ch.c. (Mar 2) Machiavellian (USA) 123 – Majmu (USA) 105 (Al 78 Nasr (FR) 126) [1996 6m 7m[5] 7g[4] Sep 25] close-coupled colt: has scope: first foal:

dam won May Hill Stakes and stayed 1¼m: very green and coltish on debut: fair form later in maidens at Newmarket in August and Chester: will be suited by further than 7f. *J. H. M. Gosden*

MAFTUN (USA) 4 ch.c. Elmaamul (USA) 125 – Allesheny 85 (Be My Guest 60 (USA) 126) [1995 70: 10g² 10m⁶ 10d 12g⁵ 1996 12d 9.9g⁶ 10m 10m⁵ 13g² 12.4m* 12f⁵ 12.3s 13.6m Oct 17] quite attractive colt: unimpressive mover: modest handicapper nowadays: won at Newcastle in July: stays 13f: acts on good to firm going, ran poorly all 3 starts on a soft surface: has had tongue tied. *G. M. Moore*

MAFUTA (IRE) 4 b.f. Mtoto 134 – Chrism (Baptism 119) [1995 –: 9f⁵ 8d 10.2m⁴ 31 12m a13g a13g 1996 a12g a13g⁵ a12g 11.7g Apr 30] leggy, lengthy filly: poor maiden: looks a stayer: acts on equitrack: sold 1,500 gns Ascot July Sales and 2,800 gns Newmarket December Sales. *C. L. Popham*

MAGAZINE GAP 3 ch.c. Weldnaas (USA) 112 – Divissima 62 (Music Boy 124) 51 p [1995 NR 1996 a7g³ Dec 31] 6,400F, IR 10,500Y: fifth live foal: half-brother to 1992 2-y-o 6f winner Nut Bush (by Aragon): dam, 6f winner, half-sister to very useful 1978 2-y-o sprinter Eyelet: changed hands 600 gns Newmarket Autumn (1995) Sales: 1¾ lengths third of 10 in maiden at Lingfield, leading briefly in straight: should improve. *Mrs J. Cecil*

MAGELLAN (USA) 3 b. or br.c. Hansel (USA) – Dabaweyaa 118 (Shareef 111 Dancer (USA) 135) [1995 NR 1996 a9g² a8g* a7f² 10f³ 10m² 7.3m³ 10.1m* 10m⁶ Oct 17] leggy, good-topped colt: fourth foal: half-brother to very useful 1994 2-y-o 6f winner Bin Nashwan (by Nashwan), useful 6f winner Alanees (by Cadeaux Genereux) and 1m winner Aneesati (by Kris): dam 7f/1m winner second in 1000 Guineas: smart performer: had first 3 races in Dubai when trained by P. Rudkin, winning maiden at Nad Al Sheba: much better form here: easily made all in 4-runner minor event at Epsom in September: 2 lengths third to Bin Rosie in Hungerford Stakes at Newbury previous start: has shown his form over 1¼m but likely to prove best over shorter: acts on firm going: early/quietly to post and wore net muzzle first 2 starts: possibly suited by turning track: returned to UAE. *C. E. Brittain*

MAGICAL MIDNIGHT 3 ch.f. Timeless Times (USA) 99 – Mayor 86 (Laxton – 105) [1995 42: 5g 5g a5g⁵ 6.1d 6s⁵ 1996 6.1d a7g 6.1m⁶ 8m 5.9f 10f 11.1g⁴ 11f Sep 27] good-bodied filly: poor maiden: left N. Tinkler after sixth 3-y-o start: stays 6f: acts on soft ground: blinkered 3 of last 4 starts: inconsistent: sent to South Korea. *Don Enrico Incisa*

MAGICAL TIMES 2 ch.c. (Apr 20) Timeless Times (USA) 99 – Meadmore 101 Magic 68 (Mansingh (USA) 120) [1996 5s² 5m² 5f* 6m² 5m² 5.2f⁴ 6d* 6m* 6d³ 6m Oct 17] 7,000Y: smallish, good-bodied colt: poor mover: first foal: dam 5f winner at 2 yrs: useful form: won maiden auction at Lingfield in June, nursery gamely at Newmarket in August and minor event (beat Tomba 2½ lengths) at Doncaster in September: disappointing last 2 starts: stays 6f: acts on firm and soft ground: sometimes edges left: sold 32,000 gns Newmarket December Sales. *R. Boss*

MAGICATION 6 b.m. Nomination 125 – Gundreda 93 (Gunner B 126) [1995 – 40: 8g 8g 7f 7m 7m⁴ 10.2h⁴ 8m 8g⁶ 7g 10.1g 9.7s⁶ 8.2m a11g³ a12g 1996 a11g Jan 5] small, sturdy mare: carries plenty of condition: poor handicapper: stays 11f: acts on any going: tried blinkered: sometimes bandaged: has had tongue tied down: tends to get behind: none too consistent: has joined K. Wingrove. *B. Richmond*

MAGIC BLUE (IRE) 2 b.c. (Mar 24) Bluebird (USA) 125 – Sallymiss 72 (Tanfirion 110) [1996 5s 5d 5d⁶ 5d³ 5d³ 6g* 6g 6m Aug 9] 15,000Y: strong, lengthy colt: has a quick action: fifth foal: half-brother to 3-y-o Second Time Lucky (by Digamist), 6f winner at 2 yrs, and Irish 1m winner Scene One (by Scenic): dam Irish 5f winner: progressive form first 6 starts, best effort to win median auction maiden at Leicester in June: stiff tasks and sweating, soundly beaten in minor events last 2 starts: sold 5,000 gns Newmarket Autumn Sales: better suited by 6f than 5f: hung badly left second start. *R. Hollinshead*

MAGIC CAROUSEL 3 b.f. Mtoto 134 – Lap of Honour 100 (Final Straw 127) 81 [1995 NR 1996 8g* May 30] 5,000F, 12,500Y: sixth foal: half-sister to several winners, including useful miler Lap of Luxury (by Sharrood): dam won over 6f and 7f: won 4-runner maiden at Carlisle in May: dead. *M. Johnston*

MAGIC FIZZ 2 gr.c. (Mar 22) Efisio 120 – Strawberry Pink 87 (Absalom 128) 55 [1996 a6g a5g⁵ a6g³ Dec 27] 7,400Y: first foal: dam, won twice over 5f from 4 starts at 2 yrs, out of very smart sprinter Polly Peachum: modest form in maidens at Southwell: stays 6f. *T. J. Etherington*

MAGIC HEIGHTS   3 gr.c. Deploy 131 – Lady Regent (Wolver Hollow 126)   46
[1995 57p: 8.2m⁶ 1996 8f⁵ a8g⁴ a11g⁵ Sep 9] good-bodied colt: modest form at best in maidens: sold 3,600 gns Newmarket Autumn Sales: bred to be suited by further than 1m: sent to Germany. *J. E. Banks*

MAGIC JUNCTION (USA)   5 b.h. Danzig Connection (USA) – Sleeping   91
Beauty 87 (Mill Reef (USA) 141) [1995 69: 10.4m 12d² a10g⁴ 1996 a12g* Jan 17] lengthy, sturdy horse: fairly useful handicapper: visored, better than ever when winning at Wolverhampton in January: stays 1½m: acts on fibresand and heavy ground, ran creditably over hurdles (modest form) on firm: sent to Russia. *Lord Huntingdon*

MAGIC LAKE   3 b.f. Primo Dominie 121 – Magic Kingdom 76 (Kings Lake   47
(USA) 133) [1995 68?: 5m⁶ 5.1g⁶ a6g³ 7m³ 7.1m² 6d⁴ 8.3g³ 7g² 8m² 7m 1996 8m 7g 7.1d a6g⁴ 7m* 7m 7g² 7.1m⁶ 7g 6d³ 8g Oct 19] lengthy, good-topped filly: modest handicapper: won at Ayr in July: stays 1m: acts on firm and dead ground: visored last 2 starts, running well on first occasion and long way out of handicap on second. *E. J. Alston*

MAGIC LEADER (IRE)   4 b. or br.g. Architect (USA) – Magic Rotation (USA)   –
(His Majesty (USA)) [1995 –: a5g⁵ a8g 5g 8m⁶ 10m 8m⁶ 10m 7f 1996 a8g a7g⁴ a8g a8g Apr 29] small gelding: bad maiden: tried visored. *T. T. Clement*

MAGIC MAIL   3 b.c. Aragon 118 – Blue Rhythm 72 (Blue Cashmere 129) [1995   72
71p: 5m³ 1996 6s 5m⁵ 6m 5.2m 5m⁵ 5f* 5m⁶ 5g Aug 30] good-quartered colt: fair handicapper: well drawn, won at Sandown in July: well held there both starts afterwards, reported by trainer to have been struck into on first occasion: sold 4,400 gns Newmarket Autumn Sales: raced only at sprint distances: acts on firm ground, well held on soft: sent to Sweden. *J. M. P. Eustace*

MAGIC MELODY   3 b.f. Petong 126 – Miss Rossi (Artaius (USA) 129) [1995   –
62: 6.1d 6g³ 6d a6g 1996 10.2m 10m⁶ 6m 6m Oct 28] leggy filly: modest form in maidens at 2 yrs for J. Spearing: well beaten all 4 starts in 1996, first 2 for P. Cole: sprint bred: well beaten on fibresand. *J. L. Spearing*

MAGIC PEARL   6 gr.m. Belfort (FR) 89 – Oyster Gray 61 (Tanfirion 110) [1995   –
79d: 5g 5.1m³ 5g 5m 5m 6g⁶ 5f 1996 a5g⁵ Jan 31] leggy, angular mare: fairly useful handicapper at best for E. Alston: well held in claimer at Wolverhampton only outing in 1996: stays an easy 6f: acts on good to firm ground and dead: has bolted to post (stumbled going down in February, and withdrawn lame) and often taken down alone: none too consistent. *R. F. Marvin*

MAGIC ROLE   3 b.g. Tragic Role (USA) – Athens By Night (USA) 60 (London   60
Bells (CAN) 109) [1995 NR 1996 10f⁶ 10.5d 10g⁵ 14.1g a13g⁵ Oct 28] workmanlike gelding: second foal: dam, middle-distance maiden, half-sister to Oaks third Poquito Queen out of very useful staying filly Senorita Poquito: fair maiden: sold (M. Jarvis to J. Jenkins), 5,800 gns Newmarket Autumn Sales: stays 13f. *M. A. Jarvis*

MAGIC SOLUTION (IRE)   3 b.f. Magical Wonder (USA) 125 – Brook's   41
Dilemma 80 (Known Fact (USA) 135) [1995 NR 1996 7.1d 5g⁶ Jul 24] IR 1,900F, IR 3,200Y: close-coupled filly: not a good walker: fifth foal: half-sister to fairly useful sprint handicapper Royal Dome (by Salt Dome) and poor 1m winner Kay's Dilemma (by Ya Zaman): dam, 6f winner, half-sister to very useful 1987 2-y-o Obeah: poor form in maidens: bandaged behind on debut. *H. Candy*

MAGIC TIMES   5 b.g. Good Times (ITY) – Young Wilkie (Callernish) [1995 –:   –
a12g 12.1v 1996 14.1m 13m⁶ a12g⁶ May 31] big gelding: tailed off since last win in 1994: sold to join C. Grant 2,100 gns Doncaster July Sales. *M. Johnston*

MAGNIFICIENT STYLE (USA)   3 b.f. Silver Hawk (USA) 123 – Mia Karina   107
(USA) (Icecapade (USA)) [1995 NR 1996 10g* 10m³ 10.4m* 12m⁶ Jun 20] rangy, rather unfurnished filly: powerful, free mover, with a pronounced knee action: fourth live foal: half-sister to 2 winners in North America, including Grade 3 9f second Siberian Summer (by Siberian Express): dam 8.5f winner in France: impressive winner of maiden at Kempton in April: best effort and useful form when making all in Tattersalls Musidora Stakes at York in May (by 1¾ lengths from Sil Sila): 13/8 favourite and bandaged, kept changing her legs when well below form in Ribblesdale

564

Tattersalls Musidora Stakes, York—Magnificient Style lives up to her reputation; Sil Sila (rails) is second

Stakes at Royal Ascot 5 weeks later: should be suited by further than 10.4f: a strong galloper, probably suited by forcing tactics: to be trained by M. Moubarak in USA. *H. R. A. Cecil*

MAGNOLIA   2 gr.f. (Apr 22) Petong 126 – Daffodil Fields (Try My Best (USA) 130) [1996 5g⁴ 5f⁶ May 6] 32,000Y: leggy, lightly-made filly: fourth foal: sister to useful sprinter Petula and half-sister to fairly useful Italian 3-y-o 5f (at 2 yrs) to 1m winner Pappa Reale (by Indian Ridge): dam Irish maiden granddaughter of Waterloo, also grandam of Environment Friend: fourth in median auction maiden at Sandown in April: tailed off in 6-runner maiden at Warwick (free to post) following month: has joined P. Makin. *P. F. I. Cole*   52

MAGYAR TITOK (IRE)   2 br.c. (Mar 3) Treasure Kay 114 – Aliyna (FR) (Vayrann 133) [1996 5.2f⁴ 7d 5s a5g³ 6g a6g⁶ Nov 14] IR 2,500Y, 6,200 2-y-o: leggy colt: second foal: dam placed in France at up to 10.5f, from family of Aliysa: poor form: stays 6f: tends to sweat and get on edge. *Bob Jones*   47 a42

MAHOOL (USA)   7 b.g. Alydar (USA) – Tax Dodge (USA) (Seattle Slew (USA)) [1995 –, a94: a7g* 8g 7.5m 1996 7m 7.9g Sep 4] tall gelding: impresses in appearance: fairly useful handicapper at best in 1995: well below form in 1996: effective at 7f and 1m: goes well on fibresand: acts on firm and dead ground, well below form on soft: often wears crossed noseband: effective from front or held up. *J. L. Eyre*   –

MAID BY THE FIRE (USA)   2 gr.f. El Gran Senor (USA) 136 – Mist A Risin (USA) (Raise A Native) [1996 6d² 6d² 6m⁵ 5.1m² 5m² 5.7m* a6.5s⁵ Nov 17] $125,000Y: rather leggy filly; half-sister to 3 winners in USA, including one in minor 2-y-o stakes by El Baba: dam half-sister to smart French middle-distance colt Premier Role: fairly useful form: narrowly won nursery at Bath in August on final start for P. Cole: bred to stay beyond sprint distances, not certain to do so: blinkered (ran bit free) third outing: very stirred up in stalls and on way down time before. *N. J. Howard, USA*   86

565

MAIDEN CASTLE 3 b.g. Darshaan 133 – Noble Destiny 89 (Dancing Brave 94 (USA) 140) [1995 NR 1996 10s* 11d⁵ 10.3f⁵ 12m⁵ Oct 1] 36,000Y: angular, quite good-topped gelding: has a quick action: first foal: dam, 2-y-o 7f winner but disappointing at 3 yrs, out of useful mare Tender Loving Care: 11/8 on, won maiden at Leicester in March by 10 lengths: failed to cut much ice in better company subsequently, though far from discredited when fifth in steadily-run minor event at Doncaster penultimate outing: should stay 1½m: acts on soft ground: wears bandages: gelded and stays in training. *J. H. M. Gosden*

MAID FOR BAILEYS (IRE) 3 b.f. Marju (IRE) 127 – Island Time (USA) 83 (Bold Hour) [1995 77: 6g⁴ 7g² 7g 7f² 8.5m² 8g² 8g² 1996 9.9f² 10.1m 10.5m² 9.9f³ 9d² 10.3m⁵ 8.5m* 8m⁶ Oct 7] smallish, leggy filly: fairly useful handicapper: runner-up on 8 occasions prior to gaining her first win at Epsom in September: stays 10.5f: acts on firm and dead ground: consistent: sold 46,000 gns Newmarket December Sales. *M. Johnston*

MAID FOR THE HILLS 3 b.f. Indian Ridge 123 – Stinging Nettle 90 (Sharpen 99 d Up 127) [1995 101p: 6g* 6m* 1996 7m⁵ 8m 6d⁴ 6m⁵ 5.1m⁶ 5f³ 6m³ 7m 7m 5g⁶ 6f Nov 5] leggy, unfurnished filly: has a quick action: useful at best: ran well when fifth to Thrilling Day in Nell Gwyn Stakes at Newmarket on reappearance: didn't go on: stays 7f: acts on good to firm ground: tried blinkered (pulled too hard in 1000 Guineas) and visored: sold 86,000 gns Newmarket December Sales. *D. R. Loder*

MAIDMENT 5 b.m. Insan (USA) 119 – Lady Gerardina 82 (Levmoss 133) [1995 – NR 1996 10d May 28] big, lengthy mare: smart form (rated 112) at best at 3 yrs: 66/1 and in need of race, tailed off in Brigadier Gerard Stakes at Sandown on reappearance: should stay beyond 1¼m: easily best effort on soft going. *Lady Herries*

MAID O'CANNIE 5 b.m. Efisio 120 – Ichnusa 83 (Bay Express 132) [1995 62: 62 6d 5m⁴ 5m⁶ 6m 6m 6m⁶ 6d* 6.1d³ 6d 1996 7s 6g 5g⁵ 6.1m² 7m⁶ 5m 6d* 6m³ 6g 6s Aug 31] strong, workmanlike mare: fair handicapper: best effort at 5 yrs when narrowly winning at Haydock in July, well ridden by T. Quinn to lead close home: best form at 6f: acts on firm and dead ground: best efforts visored/blinkered: often taken early to post, though wasn't at Haydock: sometimes slowly away: covered by Noble Patriarch. *M. W. Easterby*

MAID OF CADIZ 6 b.m. King of Spain 121 – Maureen Mhor 70 (Taj Dewan – 128) [1995 NR 1996 8f 8f May 6] behind in a maiden at 3 yrs and 2 more in 1996. *J. W. Payne*

MAID TO LAST 3 b.f. Groom Dancer (USA) 128 – Derniere Danse (Gay – Mecene (USA) 128) [1995 NR 1996 9m⁶ 10.5d 8.1d Jun 8] lengthy, unfurnished filly: has a roundish action: first foal: dam, French maiden, half-sister to smart French sprinter Divine Danse and good 6f to 1m performer Pursuit of Love (by Groom Dancer): well beaten in maidens at Milan and Haydock (2): edgy final start. *J. W. Hills*

MAID WELCOME 9 br.m. Mummy's Pet 125 – Carolynchristensen 58 (Sweet – Revenge 129) [1995 –, a64: a7g⁴ a7g* a7g² a7g⁵ a7g⁴ a7g³ a7g* 6m a8g a7g³ a7g a58 a7g a7g² 1996 a7g a8g a7g³ a7g⁶ Feb 24] sturdy mare: has a round action: modest handicapper: races mainly at 7f nowadays: acts on any turf going, and goes well on all-weather surfaces: normally blinkered or visored: usually ridden by Amanda Sanders: front runner/races prominently: covered by Rock City. *Mrs N. Macauley*

MAITEAMIA 3 ch.g. Komaite (USA) – Mia Scintilla 54 (Blazing Saddles 76 (AUS)) [1995 45p: a7g 6.1d 6g 8g 1996 a6g* a7g² 6.1d a6g* 5s* 6d² 5g* 5.1m² 6m² 6m Aug 20] robust gelding: progressive handicapper: won at Southwell in March and April and at Hamilton and Catterick in May: good second next 2 starts: not well drawn on final one: suited by sprint distances: acts on good to firm and soft ground and on fibresand: blinkered/visored: races prominently: often apprentice ridden: game and consistent. *S. R. Bowring*

MAJAL (IRE) 7 b.g. Caerleon (USA) 132 – Park Special (Relkino 131) [1995 55: – a12g* a12g 1996 12d 12m May 7] good-bodied gelding: unimpressive mover: showed little in 1996: may well stay beyond 1½m: none too consistent. *J. S. Wainwright*

MAJARO 2 b.g. (Mar 6) Merdon Melody 98 – Bri-Ette 53 (Brittany) [1996 5s – Mar 23] 6,000Y: tall, lengthy, unfurnished gelding: brother to fair sprinting 3-y-o Craignairn and half-brother to sprint winners Mom Sally and Miss Ellie Pea (both by

Bold Owl): dam sister to useful sprinter Tinjar: 10/1 and green, well beaten in maiden auction at Doncaster: sent to Denmark. *J. Berry*

MAJBOOR YAFOOZ (USA) 6 b.g. Silver Hawk (USA) 123 – Forced To Fly – (USA) (Accipiter (USA)) [1995 65: 10m⁴ 1996 a12g Feb 10] lengthy gelding: has a round action: fair maiden at best: tailed off in handicap at Southwell only 6-y-o start: fair but unreliable maiden hurdler. *J. R. Bosley*

MAJDAK JEREEB (IRE) 3 b.g. Alzao (USA) 117 – Aunty (FR) 114 (River- 73 man (USA) 131) [1995 75: 7m⁵ 7.1d 7.1d⁴ 7d 1996 10d⁴ 10.8f³ 14m⁴ 14.1f⁴ 11.9f⁶ 14m² 16.4g Aug 30] good-bodied gelding: has an easy action: fair maiden: gelded after final start: stays 1¾m: acts on firm and dead ground: blinkered/visored last 3 starts: lacks turn of foot, and goes well with forcing tactics: sent to UAE. *Major W. R. Hern*

MAJOR CHANGE 4 gr.c. Sharrood (USA) 124 – May The Fourteenth 53 95 (Thatching 131) [1995 88: 8g⁵ 8m* 9g⁴ 10g³ 10f³ 12m³ 10g 10d⁵ 1996 10m³ 9s² 10m* 12m 10g 10d 10.1m⁶ Sep 11] close-coupled colt: fairly useful handicapper: won at Sandown in June: sold (R. Hannon to Miss Gay Kelleway) 38,000 gns Newmarket Autumn Sales: effective at 1¼m and stays 1½m: acts on firm ground and soft: sometimes front runner: genuine. *R. Hannon*

MAJOR DUNDEE (IRE) 3 b.g. Distinctly North (USA) 115 – Indigo Blue 77 (IRE) 56 (Bluebird (USA) 125) [1995 74p: 7m⁴ 1996 10g 8f² 7m³ 9m* 10m⁶ 10.2m⁵ 11.9m² 14d³ 12m³ Sep 25] useful-looking gelding: impresses in appearance: good mover: fair form: got up on line (catching rider of coasting Kamari napping) in maiden at Lingfield in May: consistent in handicaps afterwards: sold (R. Hannon to M. Pipe) 32,000 gns Newmarket Autumn Sales and gelded: stays 1¾m: acts on firm and dead ground. *R. Hannon*

MAJORIEN 2 ch.c. (Mar 24) Machiavellian (USA) 123 – Green Rosy (USA) 116 (Green Dancer (USA) 132) [1996 7g* 7g⁴ 8m² 8g² Oct 13]

Majorien is a son of Machiavellian—is it possible that his name might in some way have been inspired by that of our own esteemed Prime Minister? Perhaps not, but, by coincidence, at the time of writing it seems highly likely that John Major's day of reckoning will come on May 1st and Majorien's will be on May 11th. Which is the better bet, the Conservatives at the General Election or Majorien in his classic race target the Poule d'Essai des Poulains? It may be overdoing things to eke out any further parallels between John Major and a headstrong but notably progressive French colt, but the former is a beleaguered leader of a minority government and the latter holds a disputed claim to precedence in a crop of French two-year-olds whose talents appear so far to be distinctly unexceptional. In fact, we have found it impossible to choose between the form shown by Majorien, Varxi and Zamindar. We are sure, however, that none of that trio was in the same class as the British-trained Bahhare and Revoque. Majorien came face to face with Revoque in the Grand Criterium at Longchamp in October, showed markedly improved form, but still came off very much second best. He broke well, a little too well maybe as Freddie Head had problems settling him, trying to rein him back initially and then letting him stride along in second, Revoque on the rails in third. That looked awkward for Revoque early in the straight but Majorien's much earlier bid for the lead was all in vain as the favourite stormed clear on his outside in the final furlong. Majorien, beaten two lengths, had however drawn four clear of the rest.

Amazingly, the Grand Criterium's nine runners included two from the Bulgarian stable of P. Bogoev and none from that of A. Fabre. That Bulgarian challenge came to nothing, but British-trained horses won nine of the nineteen French pattern events for two-year-olds in 1996 and lost a tenth in the stewards room. On his previous start, Majorien had had his chances of a pattern victory boosted by the absence of any British challenger in the Prix des Chenes at Longchamp, but could not take full advantage, coming from off the pace and going down to Nombre Premier by three quarters of a length. As we said, waiting tactics had probably also been the plan in the Grand Criterium. For his first two starts, though, Majorien had made the running, to some effect when he scooted in by eight lengths in a nine-runner newcomers race at Saint-Cloud in July at odds of 11/10, but running out of steam to finish only fourth of eight in a valuable auction race at Deauville the following month when sent off at 2/1 on.

		Mr Prospector (b 1970)	Raise A Native / Gold Digger
	Machiavellian (USA) (b 1987)	Coup de Folie (b 1982)	Halo / Raise The Standard
Majorien (ch.c. Mar 24, 1994)		Green Dancer (b 1972)	Nijinsky / Green Valley
	Green Rosy (USA) (b or br 1984)	Round The Rosie (b 1973)	Cornish Prince / Rosayya

After the Grand Criterium, Majorien's trainer Mme Head stated that he would be targeted at the Prix de Fontainebleau and Poule d'Essai des Poulains. He looks to have as good a chance as any in the French Guineas—if Bahhare and Revoque stay away that is—and on breeding, if not demeanour, it is quite possible that he might appear in the Prix du Jockey-Club as well. Sire Machiavellian had a Poulains winner in his very first crop with Vettori, and will be standing at £40,000 in 1997 compared to a fee of £20,000 when he went to stud in 1991. He was also a miler himself, but in the latest season plenty of evidence emerged that his progeny can stay middle distances: nine of his eleven three-year-olds to run in Britain stayed at least a mile and a quarter, five of them at least a mile and a half. Majorien's dam Green Rosy gained her one victory (from six starts) at the latter distance, in a minor event at Evry. She also came third in a listed race and is a sister to Big Sink Hope who won a listed event over fifteen furlongs. They are two winners out of the American two-year-old six-furlong winner Round The Rosie, the other eight of which included the smart seven-furlong/one-mile performer Shmaireekh, the Gordon Richards Stakes runner-up Stapleford Manor and U.S. Grade 3 8.5 furlong winner Rose Bouquet. Green Rosy herself had previously produced the useful six- and seven-furlong performer Rose Indien (by Crystal Glitters), the French provincial 7.5 furlong and 10.5 furlong winner Green Field Park (by Akarad) and the modest novice-hurdle winner Genseric (by Groom Dancer). The last-named made 900 guineas and 700 guineas at Doncaster in the last two seasons. Fifth foal Majorien was bought for Sheikh Maktoum Al Maktoum for 1,200,000 francs at Deauville as a yearling. *Mme C. Head, France*

MAJOR QUALITY 3 b.c. Sizzling Melody 117 – Bonne de Berry (Habitat 134) 99 [1995 75p: 6m³ 1996 5m* 5d² 6m Jun 15] sturdy, workmanlike colt: impresses in appearance: has a quick action: useful performer: won maiden at Beverley in April, and ran well when second in minor event at Haydock next time, finishing clear of remainder: sweating, seemed unsuited by longer trip when eleventh of 18 in £34,200 handicap at York 6 weeks later, travelling strongly but tiring markedly closing stages: may prove best at 5f: acts on good to firm and dead ground. *J. R. Fanshawe*

MAJOR SNUGFIT 4 b.g. Tina's Pet 121 – Sequoia 87 (Sassafras (FR) 135) 41 [1995 –: 8d 1996 a8g a12g⁴ a12g⁵ Jan 26] workmanlike gelding: poor maiden handicapper, lightly raced nowadays: stays 1½m: acts on soft ground and fibresand: blinkered final start and last 4 as 2-y-o: inconsistent. *M. W. Easterby*

MAJOR TWIST (IRE) 2 b.c. (Mar 26) Dancing Dissident (USA) 119 – Kafsa – (IRE) (Vayrann 133) [1996 6d 6m Sep 27] IR 4,400F, 6,400Y, resold 15,500Y: first foal: dam Irish 2-y-o 1m winner out of half-sister to dam of Kahyasi: well beaten in maiden auction at Windsor and claimer at Folkestone. *R. Hannon*

MAKE A NOTE (USA) 5 b.g. Northern Flagship (USA) 96 – Deep Powder 82 (USA) (Researching (USA)) [1995 NR 1996 a9.4g a12g² a9.4g⁵ a14.8g⁵ Feb 14] tall, good-topped gelding: fairly useful performer in 1994 for R. Hannon: appeared to run creditably when second in claimer at Wolverhampton: well below form in handicap and claimer there afterwards: should stay beyond 1½m: acts on soft ground and all-weather, and appeared to act on firm as 2-y-o. *P. D. Evans*

MAKE A STAND 5 ch.g. Master Willie 129 – Make A Signal 76 (Royal Gunner 76 (USA)) [1995 72: 8m 10g 12f 10m 11.6m 11.8m* 14g⁶ 1996 12m² 11.9m* 12m²

13.3f Jul 20] tall, angular gelding: fair handicapper: won ladies race at York in June: well beaten on firm ground final start: should stay beyond 1½m: acts on good to firm and dead ground: blinkered (well beaten) fourth and fifth 4-y-o starts: most progressive hurdler, winner of valuable event in December. *M. C. Pipe*

MAKE READY 2 b.f. (Apr 15) Beveled (USA) – Prepare (IRE) 58 (Millfontaine 114) [1996 a5g² a5g⁶ a5g* a5g³ a5g* Sep 9] 4,400Y: first foal: dam, 7f winner who seemed to stay 9f, half-sister to high-class sprinter Anita's Prince: fair form: successful in sellers at Southwell in July and September: raced only at 5f on fibresand: races prominently. *J. Neville*   61

MAKHBAR 2 ch.c. (Apr 4) Rudimentary (USA) 118 – Primulette 82 (Mummy's Pet 125) [1996 6m* 7m⁵ 6m 5f³ Aug 22] 36,000Y: strong, lengthy colt: has scope: has a roundish action: fifth foal: half-brother to 4 winners (all successful at 2 yrs), including 3-y-o Diminuet (by Dominion), 6f winner in 1995, and fairly useful 4-y-o Bring On The Choir (by Chief Singer), 5f winner in 1994 and stays 1m: dam 5f (at 2 yrs) and 1m winner: won maiden at Newmarket in June by 5 lengths from Pun: failed to progress: sold 15,000 gns Newmarket Autumn Sales: sent to USA. *R. W. Armstrong*   83 d

MALADERIE (IRE) 2 b.g. (Feb 14) Thatching 131 – Native Melody (Tudor Music 131) [1996 6m⁴ 6m² 6m* 7.1g³ 7m⁴ 8.1g⁴ Aug 30] IR 16,000Y: close-coupled, quite good-topped gelding: half-brother to 1989 2-y-o 7f and 1m winner Asian Pete (by Persian Bold), 5f and 1m winner Formatune (by Double Form) and 2 winners abroad: dam Irish 7f winner: fairly useful form: won median auction maiden at Windsor in June: consistent form afterwards, in frame in minor events at Sandown and listed race (in between) at Baden-Baden: stays 1m: raced only on a sound surface. *M. R. Channon*   83

MALE-ANA-MOU (IRE) 3 ch.g. Ela-Mana-Mou 132 – Glasson Lady (GER) 108 (Priamos (GER) 123) [1995 NR 1996 8m³ 8.3m³ 10m* 12m 10g 12m 13.9m Aug 21] IR 15,000Y: rather leggy, unfurnished gelding: half-brother to 2 winners, including Glassblower (at 1¼m, by Shareef Dancer): dam useful Irish 7f winner: won maiden at Goodwood in June: somewhat flattered when eighth of 12 to St Mawes in Gordon Stakes at Goodwood penultimate start, never a threat: didn't have things go his way in 3 valuable handicaps, on final start 9 lb out of handicap and racing close to very strong pace long way when eleventh of 21 in the Ebor at York: should prove suited by 1½m+: yet to race on a soft surface: on toes last 2 starts. *D. R. C. Elsworth*   90 +

MALIBU MAN 4 ch.c. Ballacashtal (CAN) – National Time (USA) (Lord Avie (USA)) [1995 63, a75: 6m 6m a5g⁴ a6g* a5g³ a5g* a6g⁵ 6.1d⁵ 5g² 5.1d⁶ 5.1m 1996   72

5s² 5g 5.1g 6s⁶ 5m² a6g 5d³ 5f³ 5.1m² 5.1f* 5m 5g Oct 9] quite good-topped colt: has a round action: fair handicapper: left S. Mellor after third 4-y-o start: made all in 16-runner race at Chepstow in September, 5 lengths clear at halfway: failed to reproduce that form: stays 6f: acts on firm and dead ground and goes well on fibresand (not tried in blinkers): usually races prominently: has run well when sweating. *E. A. Wheeler*

MALIK (IRE)   2 b.c. (Mar 15) Sadler's Wells (USA) 132 – Radiant (USA)   62
(Foolish Pleasure (USA)) [1996 8m⁴ 8.1s Oct 22] 550,000Y: seventh foal: closely related to Poolesta, useful sprinter here and winner of Grade 3 8.5f event in USA, and US Grade 3 6f to 9f winner Home of The Free (both by Hero's Honor) and half-brother to a winner in Germany by Green Forest: dam, minor winner at around 6f, is half-sister to good middle-distance colt Gold And Ivory: around 11 lengths fourth of 15 to High Roller in maiden at Yarmouth on debut: blinkered and bit slowly away, slipped in rear early when always behind in 20-runner maiden at Chepstow month later. *Saeed bin Suroor*

MALLIA   3 b.g. Statoblest 120 – Pronetta (USA) (Mr Prospector (USA)) [1995 76:   86
5d⁴ 5m² 5g* 1996 6g⁵ 6g² 6m* 6m Jun 29] lengthy, dipped-backed gelding: fairly useful handicapper: 14/1 and 3 lb out of weights, best effort when winning 18-runner £34,200 William Hill Trophy at York in June by short head from Pleading, always up with strong pace: stays 6f well: yet to race on extremes of going. *T. D. Barron*

MALLOOH   3 gr.c. Niniski (USA) 125 – Kalisha (Rainbow Quest (USA) 134)   70
[1995 NR 1996 10m 10m³ 10.3g⁴ 10m⁵ Jul 20] IR 19,000Y: good-topped colt: second foal: half-brother to 4-y-o Kanika (by Be My Chief), who all but refused to race only start: dam unraced half-sister to Kala Dancer (by Niniski): fair maiden handicapper: lacks pace, and will be well suited by further than 1¼m: sent to UAE. *J. H. M. Gosden*

MALZOOM   4 b.g. Statoblest 120 – Plum Bold 83 (Be My Guest (USA) 126)   27 §
[1995 33: a8.5g⁵ a9.4g⁶ 6.1g 6s 7g 7m 7.5m⁶ 7g 8.1m² 8f³ 7.1m 8m³ 8g 11.1g 1996 a7g a7g 7d⁴ 9m 7f Jun 15] close-coupled gelding: poor maiden handicapper: stays 1m: acts on good to firm ground, probably on dead: tends to get upset in stalls, and unseated rider when he reared leaving them once at 3 yrs and 4 yrs: sold 1,000 gns Doncaster August Sales: inconsistent. *S. E. Kettlewell*

MAMLOUK   4 gr.g. Distant Relative 128 – Nelly Do Da 78 (Derring-Do 131)   –
[1995 –: 10g 1996 10f 12.1m Jul 12] rangy gelding: towards rear in varied company. *J. W. Payne*

MAMNOON (USA)   5 b.g. Nijinsky (CAN) 138 – Continual (USA) (Damascus   –
(USA)) [1995 –: 12.3m 10.5g 14.1m 1996 a7g 10m May 24] sturdy gelding: tailed off all starts on flat last 2 seasons: tried blinkered/visored: sold (W. Clay to Rob Woods) 1,050 gns Doncaster July Sales. *W. Clay*

MAM'SELLE BERGERAC (IRE)   3 b.f. Cyrano de Bergerac 120 – Miss   –
Merryweather (Sexton Blake 126) [1995 64: 6m⁶ 6m 7.6d 6.9g⁶ 7g⁴ 1996 6.9f 7f

William Hill Trophy (Handicap), York—
Mallia (second right) has a hard-gained win from Pleading (left) and Wildwood Flower (right)

8.3m 8m Sep 25] modest maiden at best in 1995: well below form at 3 yrs: stays 7f: sent to South Korea. *P. Mitchell*

MANABAR 4 b.g. Reprimand 122 – Ring of Pearl (Auction Ring (USA) 123) [1995 79d: 8f³ 8g* 9g 8g 9d 1996 a10g a8g a9.4g a7g⁴ a8g³ a8g² a7g 7d³ 9.7m³ 10g 10m⁴ 7g⁶ 9g⁵ 13g 10m 11.6d 7.9g 8.1f a8g² a10g⁶ a10g³ Dec 20] lengthy gelding: fair performer at best: stays 1¼m: acts on firm and dead ground and the all-weather: tried visored, no improvement: sometimes slowly away/reluctant: one to treat with caution. *M. J. Polglase*

66 §
a69 §

MANALOJ (USA) 3 ch.c. Gone West (USA) – Deviltante (USA) (Devil's Bag (USA)) [1995 NR 1996 8m 8m* 10.3g 8f 8.1v Oct 6] $160,000F: angular, good-topped colt: has a round action: third foal: closely related to a winner in USA at up to 7f by Fappiano and half-brother to another by Sovereign Dancer: dam, winner at up to 7f from 5 starts in USA, out of half-sister to Northern Dancer: won maiden at Salisbury in May: last in £8,100 event at Doncaster and Britannia Handicap at Royal Ascot next 2 starts, and again well below form in Haydock handicap (on heavy ground) nearly 4 months later: sold (P. Walwyn to K. Ottesen) 19,000 gns Newmarket Autumn Sales: takes keen hold, and likely to prove best at around 1m: acts on good to firm ground. *P. T. Walwyn*

87

MANCINI 3 b. or br.g. Nomination 125 – Roman Blue (Charlottown 127) [1995 80+: 6g⁴ 7f² 7f* 1996 10.4m 10.1m 8f 8m 11.6g⁶ 14m⁴ Aug 15] workmanlike gelding: fair form at 2 yrs: disappointing in 1996: stays 1¾m, at least in steadily-run race: no improvement in visor third 3-y-o start. *M. Bell*

66

MANDERELLA 3 b.f. Clantime 101 – Ascot Lass (Touching Wood (USA) 127) [1995 65: 6.1f⁶ 6m² 6g 7d² 6f 1996 6s 6m⁶ 6m a7g Jul 11] workmanlike filly: poor mover: modest maiden handicapper: stayed 7f: acted on good to firm and dead ground: dead. *J. Akehurst*

–

MANDILAK (USA) 2 b.c. (Mar 28) El Gran Senor (USA) 136 – Madiriya 119 (Diesis 133) [1996 7g 8g* Oct 30]

96 P

Mandilak's win in the Ranworth Maiden Stakes at Yarmouth on October 30th was his owner's first winner in Britain for nearly six years. The Aga Khan had had very few runners since the disqualification of Aliysa in the Oaks, and the handful of his high-class French- and Irish-trained horses who competed in 1996 had enjoyed very little luck—Timarida broke a blood vessel in the Queen Anne Stakes, Ashkalani was beaten a head when favourite for the St James's Palace Stakes, the ground was against Valanour in the Eclipse, Shamadara was not ridden to best advantage in the Yorkshire Oaks and Ashkalani reportedly pinched a nerve in his back on a return visit to Ascot for the Queen Elizabeth II Stakes. Mandilak's succeeding where the overseas runners failed has more than historical significance, for he won in the style of a very promising colt. He was a 5/1 chance having beaten only one home in an 11-runner £12,500 event at Ascot a month earlier when, according to his trainer, he never took any interest after jumping a path. Despite still seeming green in what was a rather steadily-run race at Yarmouth, Mandilak was niggled along behind the leaders from three furlongs out but quickened smartly inside the last to win going away by a length from Street General with another length and a half back to Invermark, both of whom had enjoyed first run on the winner. The three finished well clear.

			Northern Dancer	Nearctic
		El Gran Senor (USA)	(b 1961)	Natalma
		(b 1981)	Sex Appeal	Buckpasser
Mandilak (USA)			(ch 1970)	Best In Show
(b.c. Mar 28, 1994)			Diesis	Sharpen Up
		Madiriya	(ch 1980)	Doubly Sure
		(ch 1987)	Majanada	Tap On Wood
			(ch 1982)	Mounayn

Mandilak's dam Madiriya had been one of the Aga Khan's last winners for Cumani before he withdrew his horses from Britain. A mile winner at Brighton at two, she made rapid progress at three, graduating from handicaps to take the Galtres Stakes at York (the first of six consecutive winners for the stable in that event) and run her best race when sixth to Salsabil, beaten about two lengths, in the Prix Vermeille. Mandilak is Madiriya's third foal; her other runner Mandalika (by Arctic Tern) was placed at around a mile and a half in the French Provinces in the latest season. Madiriya has a colt foal by Doyoun and was covered by Lahib in 1996. The next two dams won in minor company in France, Majanada over a mile (she was also placed in listed company) and Mounayn over a mile and a quarter. The latter was a half-sister to the Grand Prix d'Evry winner Karoon, to another good French colt The Expatriate (third in the Prix Jean Prat), and to the dam of a third, Turkish Ruler. The green and red colours are due to be seen more often again on British racecourses in 1997. Mandilak and a dozen or so as-yet unraced three-year-olds are to be joined by fourteen two-year-olds at Cumani's, while five more two-year-olds are to be trained by Michael Stoute. If the well-made Mandilak takes after his dam, and the signs are that he will, he looks sure to go on to better things over middle distances, and is one to watch out for. *L. M. Cumani*

MANDY'S BET (USA)   4 b.f. Elmaamul (USA) 125 – Dols Jaminque (USA) – (Kennedy Road (CAN)) [1995 8g⁶ 8d 10m⁵ 10g 8d 8g 8.3g 1996 a10g⁵ Jan 27] ex-French filly: half-sister to several winners in France, including 1m and 9f winner Gazelia (by Icecapade) and middle-distance filly Sihame (by Crystal Palace): dam lightly raced: little worthwhile form for J. Fellows: well-held fifth in claimer at Lingfield: covered by Dolphin Street. *N. A. Callaghan*

MANFUL   4 b.g. Efisio 120 – Mandrian 103 (Mandamus 120) [1995 82d: 9d⁶   76 10.5m 12g⁵ 12g⁴ 12d⁴ 12m 12.4m⁵ 12.3m⁵ 13.8m⁴ 10.9g⁶ 13.1g 10f⁶ 11f⁵ a10g² a12g³ a12g⁴ a12g² a12g² 1996 a11g a12g⁵ a11g⁵ 10.3d* 11.1d³ 10g 10.9d* 11.1g⁴ 12.1f 10.1m² 10.1m 12.3s 12m 11.1d* 10.4g⁴ a12g* a11g* a12g² Dec 14] useful-looking gelding: fair handicapper nowadays: left J. Hetherton's stable after third 4-y-o start: won at Doncaster (ladies) in March, Ayr in May, Hamilton (claimer, made all) in September, Lingfield in October and Southwell in December: stays 1½m: acts on any going: tried visored, blinkered since third 4-y-o start: tough: rejoined J. Hetherton. *C. W. C. Elsey*

MANGUS (IRE)   2 b.c. (Mar 16) Mac's Imp (USA) 116 – Holly Bird (Runnett   62 125) [1996 5m⁵ 5f⁵ a6g⁴ 5m⁴ 5m³ Aug 16] 6,500Y: third live foal: dam Irish 7f and 1¼m winner: modest form when in frame in maidens: stays 6f: acts on good to firm ground and fibresand. *K. O. Cunningham-Brown*

MANHATTAN DIAMOND   2 ch.f. (Mar 13) Primo Dominie 121 – June Fayre   54 d (Sagaro 133) [1996 5.1g⁶ 5d² 5.1m⁵ 6d 5.2g 7s a6g a7g Nov 29] 13,500Y: good-topped filly: has a quick action: sister to 1991 2-y-o 5f winner Hay Yuen (later winning sprinter in Italy) and half-sister to several winners, including 5-y-o Absolutely Fayre (by Absalom), 6f winner at 2 yrs who stays 10.8f: dam twice-raced daughter of Pasty, top 2-y-o filly of 1975: poor form: should stay beyond 5f: tried blinkered. *A. Bailey*

MAN HOWA (IRE)   2 ch.c. (Mar 3) Lycius (USA) 124 – Almuhtarama (IRE) 84   94 p (Rainbow Quest (USA) 134) [1996 6m² 6m* Jul 20] first foal: dam 1¼m winner (should have stayed 1½m), half-sister to smart 1984 French staying 2-y-o Hello Bill: second of 6 to Yashmak in maiden at Newmarket on debut: long odds on, won 8-runner maiden there following month by a length from Undercover Agent, making all and tending to idle: will stay at least 7f: remains open to improvement. *L. M. Cumani*

MANIKATO (USA)   2 b.c. (Feb 18) Clever Trick (USA) – Pasampsi (USA)   68 (Crow (FR) 134) [1996 5g⁴ 6m 5.3f⁴ 6m⁴ 6m² 5f⁴ 7m 7d² 7g Oct 26] $40,000F, 20,000Y: leggy, close-coupled colt: fifth foal: half-brother to useful 6f/7f performer Patto (by Dixieland Band) and a winner in USA by Al Nasr: dam won at up to 9f in USA: fair maiden on balance of form: 100/1, almost certainly flattered (could be rated 81) in steadily-run race when twelfth of 23 to Papua in valuable sales event at Newmarket on seventh outing: better at 7f than shorter: has form on firm and good to soft ground: visored last 2 starts. *D. J. S. Cosgrove*

MANILA BAY (USA)   6 b.g. Manila (USA) – Betty Money (USA) (Our Native   – (USA)) [1995 –: 10m 11.7h⁴ 12.1m⁶ 14d 1996 a8g⁶ Jan 19] rangy gelding: no worthwhile form since 3 yrs. *J. S. King*

MANILENO 2 ch.g. (May 17) K-Battery 108 – Andalucia 57 (Rheingold 137) –
[1996 8m⁴ 8.3d⁵ Sep 30] small, light-framed gelding: brother to 9f to 1¾m winner
Philgun and half-brother to several winners (all at 7f+), including 4-y-o 11f and 1½m
winner Philmist (by Hard Fought): dam won 1¼m seller: little promise in maiden
events in Scotland, blinkered on final start. *J. Hetherton*

MANNAGAR (IRE) 4 ch.g. Irish River (FR) 131 – Meadow Glen Lady (USA) –
(Believe It (USA)) [1995 10m⁴ 12m 1996 10f 10s 8.3m a8.5g 7.6m Aug 17] heavy-
topped gelding: fifth foal: half-brother to 3 winners, notably useful Madaniyya (at up
to 1¼m, by Shahrastani): dam won at 6f in USA, from family of Slip Anchor: much
better effort (rated 68) for J. Oxx in Ireland in 1995 when fourth in maiden at
Leopardstown: tailed off in Britain, including over hurdles: no improvement when
blinkered: has joined W. Storey. *Jamie Poulton*

MAN OF MAY 4 b.c. High Kicker (USA) – Faldwyn 61 (Mr Fluorocarbon 126) –
[1995 NR 1996 a5g⁶ a6g a7g Jan 19] good-bodied colt: little worthwhile form.
N. P. Littmoden

MAN OF WIT (IRE) 3 b.g. Fayruz 116 – Laughing Matter 56 (Lochnager 132) 60
[1995 74: 5.2m⁶ 6m⁴ 5g 5s 1996 5d⁶ 6f⁴ 5m 5m⁴ 6.1m 7f³ a7g Aug 17] leggy, quite
good-topped gelding: modest maiden on most form: seems to stay 7f: no improvement in visor: has run well when sweating. *A. P. Jarvis*

MANOLO (FR) 3 b.g. Cricket Ball (USA) 124 – Malouna (FR) (General Holme 66
(USA) 128) [1995 66: 5m³ 1996 5m 6d 5m⁴ 5m 5g² 5m* 5m⁴ Oct 17] smallish,
lengthy gelding: modest sprinter: won maiden at Beverley in September, making
virtually all: acts on good to firm ground: blinkered last 2 starts (best form). *J. Berry*

MAN ON A MISSION 3 ch.g. Hatim (USA) 121 – Colly Cone 52 (Celtic Cone –
116) [1995 NR 1996 7g Sep 21] 480F: fifth foal: dam middle-distance stayer: 50/1,
tailed off in Catterick maiden. *A. Streeter*

MANOY 3 b.g. Precocious 126 – Redcross Miss 64 (Tower Walk 130) [1995 –: 54
6m⁶ 7m 6m 1996 8g⁵ 8m 8d⁵ 12.3g³ 14.1m⁴ 11.1g* 12f 11.6m³ 14d⁴ 14.1m 12.4m⁶
11.1m 8d 10.9m Sep 19] workmanlike gelding: modest performer: won very weak
4-runner median auction maiden at Hamilton in June: shapes as though he'll stay
further than 1¾m: acts on good to firm ground: mostly blinkered nowadays: tends to
hang. *J. Hetherton*

MANSAB (USA) 3 b.g. Housebuster (USA) – Epitome (USA) (Summing (USA)) 76 d
[1995 66: 6d⁴ 6m³ 1996 7s² 6.9f³ 8.1d 7g 6.1m⁵ 5.1g 6m³ Oct 28] neat gelding:
unimpressive mover: fair maiden: sold out of J. Dunlop's stable 13,500 gns Newmarket July Sales, gelded and off course 4 months after second 3-y-o start: only
modest form for new connections, but looked unlucky not to land gamble in
21-runner handicap at Leicester final start, faring clearly best of those drawn low:
stays 7f: acts on firm and soft going: unseated rider before start third 3-y-o start.
P. G. Murphy

MANSUR (IRE) 4 b.g. Be My Chief (USA) 122 – Moorish Idol 90 (Aragon 118) 68
[1995 75?: 12g³ 10f 14.1f² 13.8m³ 11.9m⁴ 10d⁵ 11.9d⁵ 1996 12f⁵ a12g³ 14.1f⁶ 8m a75
a11g* a9.4g* 10g² Oct 21] compact, good-topped gelding: good walker and mover:
fair handicapper on his day: had become disappointing but back to best to win at
Southwell (maiden contest, under enterprising ride) in September and Wolverhampton in October: tongue tied, creditable effort on turf final start: sold (D. Loder
to N. Henderson) 24,000 gns Newmarket Autumn Sales: stays 1¾m: visored (took
good hold, folded tamely) first 2 starts at 3 yrs. *D. R. Loder*

MANTLES PRINCE 2 ch.g. (Mar 8) Emarati (USA) 74 – Miami Mouse (Miami 79 p
Springs 121) [1996 5m³ 6g² 6m⁵ 6m⁶ 6m² Sep 24] 19,000Y: tall, good-topped
gelding: third reported foal: half-brother to 1m to 11f winner My Minnie (by Kind of
Hush): dam unraced daughter of half-sister to smart 1¼m and 2m winner Capricorn
Line: progressive form: staying-on second to Balladoole Bajan in nursery at Epsom:
will stay 7f: has been edgy and on toes: capable of better yet. *G. Lewis*

MANTOVANI (IRE) 2 b.c. (Feb 1) Treasure Kay 114 – Dream of Spring 112 p
(Hello Gorgeous (USA) 128) [1996 6g² 6g* 6g* Aug 11]

   The Irish kept the Heinz 57 Phoenix Stakes at home for only the third
time in the last twelve years through 20/1-shot Mantovani, who left his earlier
form well behind. Mantovani's previous outings had also been over Leopards-

Heinz 57 Phoenix Stakes, Leopardstown—Mantovani, at 20/1

town's six furlongs and had resulted in a short-head defeat in a £9,200 event and a narrow win at odds on in a second maiden. He had apparently been troubled by sore shins before the Phoenix Stakes and been back in work three weeks, and was the Bolger stable's second string to the filly Azra, a winner of two listed races over course and distance and mount of Kevin Manning who had ridden Mantovani on his first two starts. An Irish victory was widely anticipated, even though its provider was not. The impressive Coventry Stakes winner Verglas, running in the sponsor's colours, started 11/8 favourite, backed up by the Curragh maiden winner Star Profile, the Norfolk Stakes and Richmond Stakes runner-up Raphane, Check The Band, who had looked the best horse in the race when contesting the July Stakes, and Azra. The British challenge consisted of the Prix Robert Papin winner Ocean Ridge and Muchea, third in the Norfolk Stakes.

Mantovani still looked an unlikely winner for much of the contest, too. As Azra and Ocean Ridge took the field along against the far rail Mantovani soon began to struggle to hold position, lost his place after two furlongs and had to be ridden along the rest of the way. Two furlongs out he was back on the heels of the leaders but tight against the rail with Muchea on his outside, and it was not until approaching the last, when Azra edged left, that he got room to manoeuvre. Once through the narrow gap and in the clear Mantovani ran on well for a two-length win over Muchea. Verglas and Ocean Ridge were close behind, the draw seeming to favour the high numbers. Azra's drift left provoked a stewards inquiry, but the result was allowed to stand. Mantovani's win, the biggest in the career of his jockey Conor Everard and only his third all season, was Bolger's second in the Phoenix Stakes in three years after Eva Luna in 1994. Victory in the Phoenix Stakes led to Mantovani's sights being raised from the Anglesey Stakes to the National Stakes, but a temperature prevented him from running, and he wasn't seen out again. The intention was to prepare him for the Irish Two Thousand Guineas. However, Mantovani will be wintering in Dubai rather than County Carlow; it was announced in November that he had been purchased by Godolphin.

By Treasure Kay out of a Hello Gorgeous mare, Mantovani will be among the least fashionably-bred members of the Godolphin string in 1997.

Mantovani is the best representative yet from six crops of the Temple Stakes winner Treasure Kay; Bolger trained the sire's only other pattern-winning offspring to date, the Premio Regina Elena winner Treasure Hope. The dam Dream of Spring is from a successful family, though she did not share in that success herself; she finished unplaced in a Clonmel maiden on her only start. Mantovani is her first winner from six foals of racing age, only one other of which has raced; she has a yearling colt by Project Manager. Dream of Spring was bred to stay middle distances, and is a half-sister to the smart stayer Dam Busters. Their dam Bold Sands was an unraced half-sister to the Prix de l'Opera winner Sea Sands and the Prix Maurice de Nieuil winner Riboboy. Mantovani shares his great-grandam Slapton Sands (a minor winner in the United States) with two colts, Ganges and Lucky Lindy, who were placed in consecutive Two Thousand Guineas in the early-'nineties. Slapton Sands herself was a half-sister to Hasty Doll, Rich Tradition and Sky Clipper, all stakes winners as two-year-olds in the late-'fifties, as well as Mrs Peterkin, the grandam of Irish Derby winner Shareef Dancer and the very smart four-year-old Tamayaz.

		Mummy's Pet	Sing Sing
	Treasure Kay	(b 1968)	Money For Nothing
	(b 1983)	Welsh Blossom	Welsh Saint
Mantovani (IRE)		(b 1975)	Riding High
(b.c. Feb 1, 1994)		Hello Gorgeous	Mr Prospector
	Dream of Spring	(ch 1977)	Bonny Jet
	(ch 1983)	Bold Sands	Wajima
		(ch 1977)	Slapton Sands

Mantovani looked ready for a step up from six furlongs in the Phoenix Stakes, but how far he will stay as a three-year-old is not easy to assess. Treasure Kay was best at five furlongs and the average winning distance of his

Mrs J. S. Bolger's "Mantovani"

progeny is less than seven. Mantovani had the best form of any two-year-old in Ireland and although that does not compare with the best in Britain, he looked capable of further progress even without the perceived benefit of a winter in Dubai. *J. S. Bolger, Ireland*

MANUETTI (IRE) 2 b.f. (Feb 9) Sadler's Wells (USA) 132 – Rosefinch (USA) 68 p
117 (Blushing Groom (FR) 131) [1996 7m Jul 19] first foal: dam, won Prix Saint-Alary, is daughter of Oh So Sharp: around 7½ lengths seventh of 11 to Ovation in maiden at Newmarket, racing keenly until fading from over 1f out: bred to be well suited by middle distances: will do better. *Saeed bin Suroor*

MANWAL (IRE) 2 b.g. (Mar 14) Bluebird (USA) 125 – My My Marie (Artaius 73 ?
(USA) 129) [1996 7m 6m⁵ 7f Oct 8] 27,000F, 72,000Y: robust, good-bodied gelding: half-brother to 1993 2-y-o 6f winner Connect (by Waajib), 1¼m winner Don't Forget Marie (by Don't Forget Me) and 2 winners abroad: dam (lightly raced) out of sister to Cheveley Park winner Pasty: only form in maidens when fifth of 6 to Kharir at Yarmouth in August: tailed off at Warwick in October: sold 11,000 gns Newmarket Autumn Sales and gelded. *B. Hanbury*

MANZONI (GER) 4 b.c. Solarstern (FR) – Manege (Neckar) [1995 112: 8.5s 116
8g* 11s⁴ 12m² 12m⁴ 10g* 10g³ 1996 10g⁵ 10d⁵ 8g² 8g* 8g 9.8d⁵ Oct 5] smart German colt: won Group 2 event at Hoppegarten (beat Devil River Peek 1½ lengths) in July on penultimate start for A. Wohler: below his best afterwards: effective at 1m and stays 1½m: acts on dead ground and good to firm: blinkered second to penultimate 4-y-o starts. *J. E. Hammond, France*

MAPENGO 5 b.g. Salse (USA) 128 – Premiere Cuvee 109 (Formidable (USA) –
125) [1995 NR 1996 8f a14.8g 10d a10g a7g a14.8g² a16g⁶ Dec 26] bought 1,500 gns Doncaster March (1996) Sales: has shown little on return to flat. *J. Cullinan*

MA PETITE ANGLAISE 4 b.f. Reprimand 122 – Astolat (Rusticaro (FR) 124) 74
[1995 81: 6.9m* 8.3g* 8.1g⁵ 9g 8.3m* 7.6m 8d⁵ 8m 8m 1996 8m 10m³ 12.1d³ 12m 8.3m⁴ 10.1g 10f³ 10m Sep 7] good-bodied filly: fair handicapper: last of 18 (apprentices, ridden more prominently than usual) on final start: stays 1½m: acts on firm and dead ground: held up: covered by Superlative. *W. Jarvis*

MAPLE BAY (IRE) 7 b.g. Bold Arrangement 127 – Cannon Boy (USA) 84
(Canonero II (USA)) [1995 54+, a67: 8.1m a7g⁵ a8.5g⁵ 6g³ a7g² a6g³ a7g³ a10g a87
a9.4g⁴ a7g² 1996 a9.4g* a8.5g* a8g* a12g² a9.4g² a8g² a9.4g* a8g⁶ 8.2d* 8.3d 12.3g⁶ 8g* a8.5g 8.1g* 8.1m⁴ 8f³ 8m⁴ 8f⁵ 8m⁴ a9.4g⁵ 8m³ 8.2d* 7.6d⁴ 8g* 7.1f 8m 8.1d⁶ 8d⁶ 8g 8s a8.5g Nov 16] tall, workmanlike gelding: fairly useful handicapper who had an excellent 1996: won 3 times at Wolverhampton (second race a seller) and once at Southwell early in year: also in very good form on turf, winning at Nottingham (twice), Newcastle, Musselburgh and Pontefract: no form last 3 starts: sold (A. Bailey to B. Ellison) only 8,000 gns Doncaster November Sales: effective at 7.6f to 1½m: acts on firm and dead ground, goes very well on fibresand: tried blinkered, not when successful: usually claimer ridden: tough, genuine and versatile. *A. Bailey*

MAPLE BURL 3 b.g. Dominion 123 – Carn Maire 83 (Northern Prospect (USA)) –
[1995 68: 6g 7g 6d 6m 1996 a7g⁶ a6g³ a6g² a6g a6g* 6s⁵ a6g³ 6f⁵ 5.1g 8f Jul 24] a65
compact gelding: modest handicapper: got up close home to win at Lingfield in February: well below form all 4 turf outings at 3 yrs: sold out of S. Dow's stable 3,800 gns Ascot June Sales after ninth start: should stay 7f: acts on good to soft ground and equitrack: none too consistent. *M. C. Pipe*

MARADATA (IRE) 4 ch.f. Shardari 134 – Maridana (USA) 86 (Nijinsky (CAN) 68
138) [1995 9g³ 11g* 1996 a12g a12g⁶ a12g³ a9.4g a9.4g⁶ 10.1s⁴ 10d⁴ 9.9m³ 10.3m² 10g* 9m 10.3m* 8.9m 10.3m 10g⁶ 10.2f 8.5m² 8f 10.4g 10g* a10s² a9.4g³ a10g Dec 30] rather sparely-made ex-French filly: second foal: half-sister to French 11.3f winner Marabadan (by Chief Singer): dam lightly-raced 1m winner: trained by A. de Royer Dupre when winning maiden at Le Touquet in 1995: fair handicapper on her day in Britain: successful at Pontefract in October: effective at 8.5f, and stays 1½m: acts on good to firm and soft ground, and all-weather: not the easiest of rides. *R. Hollinshead*

MARADI (IRE) 2 b.g. (Apr 1) Marju (IRE) 127 – Tigora (Ahonoora 122) [1996 73
7g 7g⁶ 7.5f³ 7.5f³ 7.9g³ 8m³ 7.9g Oct 10] IR 25,000Y: rangy, rather unfurnished

gelding: third reported foal: half-sister to a winner abroad and to a winning hurdler: fair maiden: last of 17 in nursery at York final start: sold 17,000 gns Newmarket Autumn Sales: stays 1m well: joined M. Bell and was gelded. *D. Morley*

MARALINGA (IRE)   4 ch.g. Simply Great (FR) 122 – Bellinzona (Northfields   106 (USA)) [1995 106: a10g* 12.3m³ 10.4m² 12f 12g⁵ 9g 11s² a9.4g⁴ 1996 10g 10.1m 9m³ 10g 10g 10m* 8.9g⁴ 8m 8d⁴ a9.4g Dec 7] workmanlike gelding: useful performer: won minor event at Windsor in August, setting steady pace and responding gamely to beat Kinlochewe a neck: also ran well when third in Group 3 race at Dortmund and when fourth in listed race at York: well held last 3 starts: effective at 9f to 1½m: acts on firm and soft ground and on all-weather: front runner: has tongue tied nowadays (reportedly swallowed tongue fourth 4-y-o start). *Lady Herries*

MARA RIVER   2 b.f. (Feb 26) Efisio 120 – Island Mill 79 (Mill Reef (USA) 141)   62 p [1996 6m⁴ 7.1f⁵ Sep 12] sixth foal: half-sister to 1¾m winner Arrastra (by Bustino) and 2 middle-distance winners abroad, including one by Petong: dam suited by test of stamina: beaten 7½ lengths in maiden events at Kempton and Chepstow, over 2 months apart: will be suited by 1m+. *I. A. Balding*

MARASCHINO   3 ch.f. Lycius (USA) 124 – Mystery Ship 105 (Decoy Boy 129)   53 [1995 50: 5m 5f⁵ 6.1m 6d 1996 8f 7m a5g³ a6g 7d 5.1f⁶ 6.1m² 5.1g⁴ 6m⁵ a6g   a38 Nov 14] close-coupled filly: modest performer: seems suited by sprint distances: acts on firm ground, poor form on fibresand, soundly beaten only start on equitrack. *B. J. Meehan*

MARATHON MAID   2 gr.f. (Mar 14) Kalaglow 132 – El Rabab (USA) 70   82 (Roberto (USA) 131) [1996 5g* 6m³ 6g* 7m 6m⁶ 6m Oct 17] IR 7,000Y: leggy filly: fluent mover: first foal: dam, 2-y-o 8.1f winner who stayed 11.6f, out of Breeders' Cup Juvenile Fillies winner Brave Raj: fairly useful form: won maiden at Newcastle in April and minor event (gamely) at Pontefract in May: respectable efforts in Chesham Stakes and Princess Margaret Stakes fourth and fifth starts then creditable eleventh of 25 (never dangerous in stand-side group, principals on far side) to Proud Native in Two-Year-Old Trophy at Redcar: bred to stay middle distances. *R. A. Fahey*

MARAUD   2 ch.c. (Feb 14) Midyan (USA) 124 – Peak Squaw (USA) (Icecapade   69 (USA)) [1996 5m⁶ 6m³ 7.1m 7m³ 7d² 7.1m² 8f 7m* Oct 28] leggy, sparely-made colt: fourth reported foal: dam Irish 2-y-o 6f winner: fair performer: trained first 6 starts by R. Armstrong: won 17-runner nursery at Leicester in October by ¾ length from Swan Island, making virtually all: stays 7f: keen type, who hasn't always looked the easiest of rides: blinkered sixth start: has sweated. *J. L. Spearing*

MARCHANT MING (IRE)   4 br.g. Persian Bold 123 – Hot Curry (USA)   – (Sharpen Up 127) [1995 64, a46+: a10g⁴ a9.4g³ 11.6m 12g³ 11.7m² 10.8m 11.5m* 11.5m⁵ 11.4d⁵ 1996 12.3s 13.1m 13.9g Oct 12] sparely-made gelding: modest performer: useful juvenile hurdler in 1995/6, but well beaten back on flat: stays 1½m: acts on good to firm ground, goes well on soft surface over hurdles: blinkered fourth to final 3-y-o starts: has looked none too keen. *M. D. Hammond*

MARCHMAN   11 b.g. Daring March 116 – Saltation 111 (Sallust 134) [1995 49:   53 10m⁴ 12g 9m² 8f³ 10m 1996 10m* 10m⁵ 12g⁵ 12.5f² 10d Aug 25] big, strong, good-topped gelding: modest handicapper nowadays: won 22-runner selling race at Nottingham (usually runs well there) in May: effective at 1m and stays 1¾m: best form on a sound surface (acts on firm going): goes well fresh: usually held up and travels well. *J. S. King*

MARCH STAR (IRE)   2 b.f. (Mar 16) Mac's Imp (USA) 116 – Grade A Star   89 + (IRE) (Alzao (USA) 117) [1996 5.2d³ 5m³ 6d* 5g⁴ 5m⁵ Jun 19] IR 12,000Y: quite good-topped filly: easy mover: first foal: dam, Irish 2-y-o 1m winner who stayed 11f, out of unraced half-sister to smart stayer Saronicos: won maiden at Newbury in May: very good fifth of 13 to Dance Parade in Queen Mary Stakes at Ascot, beaten around 4 lengths: stays 6f: acts on firm and dead ground. *J. A. R. Toller*

MARCO MAGNIFICO (USA)   6 b. or br.g. Bering 136 – Viscosity (USA) (Sir   – Ivor 135) [1995 –: a16g⁴ 17.5g 12m 1996 13.8s Mar 27] leggy gelding: tailed off last 3 starts on flat: stays 1¾m well: acts on equitrack and dead ground, probably on firm: modest hurdler (sometimes tubed): has joined Miss Lucinda Russell. *T. Dyer*

MARDI GRAS (IRE)   2 b.c. (May 17) Danehill (USA) 126 – Gracieuse Majeste   77 + (FR) (Saint Cyrien (FR) 128) [1996 7m⁵ 8g² 8d⁵ Oct 2] 54,000Y: rather leggy colt:

fluent mover: fourth foal: half-brother to smart 3-y-o 1m and 10.3f winner Farasan (by Fairy King) and useful 4-y-o Suranom (by Alzao), 1m to 1½m winner in Italy: dam won at 6.5f at 2 yrs in France, from good French family: shaped well in maiden (behind Monza) at Newbury in August on debut, staying on strongly after meeting trouble in running: disappointing in similar events at Goodwood and Salisbury: likely to stay well. *J. L. Dunlop*

MAREMMA 2 b.f. (Feb 17) Robellino (USA) 127 – Maiden Way (Shareef Dancer (USA) 135) [1996 7m⁵ 7f 7g 7m⁶ 7m 8m Oct 17] 500F: first foal: dam unraced: little form including in sellers. *Don Enrico Incisa*

MARENGO 2 b.c. (Mar 12) Never So Bold 135 – Born To Dance 76 (Dancing Brave (USA) 140) [1996 6m³ 6g 6m Sep 11] 8,400F, 20,000Y: small, well-made colt: first foal: dam 8.1f winner out of half-sister to Law Society: visored, 5 lengths third to The West in newcomers race at Goodwood on debut: hung and showed good deal of temperament in both subsequent races: visored on debut and last start: needs treating with a good deal caution. *J. Akehurst*   77 d

MARGARETROSE ANNA 4 b.f. Handsome Sailor 125 – Be Bold (Bustino 136) [1995 –: 6f⁶ 1996 a5g a5g a7g² a7g a7g⁶ 5g a5g 5.1g a6g⁶ a6g⁴ Nov 18] good-topped, workmanlike filly: modest form at best since 2 yrs: left E. Alston's stable after sixth start, sold out of P. D. Evans' stable 1,250 gns Doncaster August Sales after seventh: stays 7f: acts on good to firm and soft ground and on fibresand: blinkered (no form) seventh 4-y-o start. *B. P. J. Baugh*   –
a58 d

MARGI BOO 3 ch.f. Risk Me (FR) 127 – Louisianalightning (Music Boy 124) [1995 –: 5d 5s⁴ a5g 6g 7f 1996 a9.4g⁵ a8.5g⁶ a11g a12g⁶ Mar 23] close-coupled filly: of little account. *R. T. Juckes*

MARIA DI CASTIGLIA 2 b.f. (Jan 12) Danehill (USA) 126 – Macrina Pompea (Don Roberto (USA)) [1996 6d 7m² 6.1m²] Jul 6] fourth foal: dam won 8 races in Italy from 6f (at 2 yrs) to 1½m and was second in Group 3 11.2f event: modest form when runner-up in claimers at Salisbury (bandaged, wandered and flashed tail) and Nottingham: stays 7f: sent to Australia. *R. Hannon*   57

MARIGLIANO (USA) 3 b.c. Riverman (USA) 131 – Mount Holyoke 93 (Golden Fleece (USA) 133) [1995 75p: 7m³ 1996 8m³ 7.5m* 8g³ Jun 8] tall, rather leggy colt: has a round action: fairly useful form: unimpressive in landing the odds in maiden at Beverley in May: favourite, ran well in face of stiff task on handicap debut: sold (M. Stoute to K. Morgan) 6,000 gns Newmarket Autumn Sales: will be suited by further than 1m: bandaged. *M. R. Stoute*   90

MARINO CASINO (USA) 3 b.f. Alleged (USA) 138 – In Hot Pursuit (USA) – (Bold Ruler) [1995 NR 1996 11.9d⁶ May 24] $160,000F: rangy, attractive filly: thirteenth foal: half-sister to numerous winners, notably top-class miler Posse and smart miler Hot Rodder (both by Forli): dam, sister to 2 stakes winners, was one of the best 2-y-o fillies in USA in 1973: green and in need of race when beaten around 34 lengths in 7-runner maiden at Haydock: covered by Caerleon. *H. R. A. Cecil*   –

MARINO STREET 3 b.f. Totem (USA) 118 – Demerger 61 (Dominion 123) [1995 63: 7f⁵ 6m⁴ 5f³ a6g⁵ a6g² a6g⁵ 1996 a6g² a7g³ a5g² a6g⁵ a7g² a5g² a6g⁵ a6g³ a8.5g⁵ a7g 5.9f³ 7s⁵ 5.1m³ 5g* 6f⁶ 5.9f⁵ 5m⁴ 5.1f 6.1m⁵ 7g a6g⁶ a6g a6g Nov 29] small, leggy filly: modest performer: won maiden at Leicester in July: effective at 5f to 7f: acts on firm and dead ground and the all-weather: usually visored/blinkered, seems effective without: none too consistent. *P. D. Evans*   60
a55

MARISTAX 3 b.f. Reprimand 122 – Marista (Mansingh (USA) 120) [1995 74p: 5m⁴ 6.1d⁴ 6g² 6.9g* 1996 7g 7m⁴ 7m⁵ 6d 7g Nov 2] leggy, sparely-made filly: fair performer: worth trying at 1m. *P. J. Makin*   73

MARJAANA (IRE) 3 b.f. Shaadi (USA) 118 – Funun (USA) 84 (Fappiano (USA)) [1995 76: 6f³ 5.2g* 6f² 7g⁴ 7d 1996 7.5m⁵ 7g⁵ 7f⁴ 7m² 7g 8.1m 8m 7g Oct 25] lengthy filly: fair handicapper: best efforts at up to 7f: acts on firm ground: visored last 2 starts. *P. T. Walwyn*   71

MARJORIE ROSE (IRE) 3 b.f. Magical Strike (USA) 114 – Arrapata (Thatching 131) [1995 64: 5g³ 5g² 5g⁵ 6m⁴ 1996 5d 5.1d⁴ 7g 6d 5f 5g⁴ 6f⁵ 5m a5g* a5g⁴ 5g* a6g⁴ a6g a6s* a7g² Dec 28] workmanlike filly: fair handicapper: won at Wolverhampton in July, at Hamilton (seller) in September and at Wolverhampton (claimer) in December: stays 7f: acts on good to firm and dead ground and on   64
a67 fibresand: twice slowly away in 1996: blinkered 3 times (no improvement): sometimes looks none too keen. *A. Bailey*

MARK OF ESTEEM (IRE)   3 b.c. Darshaan 133 – Homage (Ajdal (USA)   137
130) [1995 105p: 7g² 7f* 1996 8m* 8f 8g* 8m* 8g Oct 26]
      Records, as they say, are made to be broken. Some, however, prove more enduring than others. Lester Piggott's thirty British classic victories and Gordon Richards' twenty-six jockeys' championships, for example, both look certain to survive well into the next millenium. So too does Frankie Dettori's feat of riding all seven winners on a British card. Before his 'Magnificent Seven' at Ascot on Saturday September 28th, 1996, only Richards, at Chepstow in 1933, and Alec Russell, at Bogside in 1957, had gone through the card in Britain, both on a six-race programme. Richards, incidentally, had won on his last mount at Nottingham the day before his six-timer at Chepstow and went on to ride the first five the following day at Chepstow, the only authenticated instance of a jockey riding twelve consecutive winners in Britain. Dettori's day at Ascot began with three pattern-race winners for Godolphin: 2/1 favourite Wall Street in the Cumberland Lodge Stakes, 12/1-shot Diffident in the Racal Diadem Stakes and the 100/30 joint-second favourite Mark of Esteem in the Queen Elizabeth II Stakes. Mark of Esteem's striking victory over Bosra Sham and five other top milers in the Queen Elizabeth established him as the leading horse over the distance in Europe and would have dominated the racing headlines the next day, but for being eclipsed by the 'hold the front page' story that developed over the rest of the afternoon.
      By the time Dettori went to post on Decorated Hero in the fourth race, the twenty-six-runner Tote Festival Handicap, the alarm bells were ringing for the major off-course bookmakers over the scale of the liabilities on multiple bets involving Dettori's mounts from 'mug punters' up and down the country. Put in at 12/1 on course, Decorated Hero dropped to 6/1, before easing a point, supported to take out £90,000. After his victory, the offices plunged on Dettori's next mount Fatefully, 11/2 in the morning in the eighteen-runner Rosemary Rated Stakes, from 5/2 to 7/4 to get back something 'to the tune of well over £250,000', according to the *The Sporting Life's* betting reporter Doug Newton who wrote that another £200,000 or so was taken out of the racecourse bookmakers' satchels as off-course interests forced Dettori's sixth winner Lochangel from 7/4 to 5/4. The ring hadn't seen anything like it for years and the exchanges before the last race had to be seen to be believed. Dettori's seventh mount, top-weight Fujiyama Crest in the eighteen-runner Gordon Carter Handicap, had been around a 10/1 chance in the morning but 'known substantial bets' logged by Newton produced liabilities of nearly £600,000 and a starting price of 2/1. Fujiyama Crest repeated his victory of the previous year with a battling display to make all, holding the strong challenge of Northern Fleet by a neck. The 'Big Three' off-course bookmakers became the 'Slightly

Queen Elizabeth II Stakes, Ascot—
Mark of Esteem provides the centrepiece of a remarkable seven-timer for Frankie Dettori;
Bosra Sham enhances her own reputation in second

Smaller Three' as estimates put the industry-wide loss at around £30m, far and away the worst single day for bookmaking since betting shops were legalised. While Ladbrokes, a publicly-quoted company, were circumspect about their losses, Hills reported an £8m drubbing, taking £7m in bets on the day but having to pay out £15m, and Coral reportedly lost £4m. With the betting shops open for Sunday racing the next day, the big bookmakers were able to collect and develop the filmed records of all the biggest winning bets and collate the cash requirements shop by shop. Contacting the banks early on Monday, the major chains had arranged to pay all winners by close of business that day, an organisational achievement in itself. As for some of the on-course bookies at Ascot, particularly those who stood the biggest hedging bets, the wounds were, relatively, even deeper. One independent rails bookmaker, Gary Wiltshire, reportedly lost 'well into six figures' on Fujiyama Crest as he and others took on the ring (Wiltshire actually went 9/4 Fujiyama Crest—'and 9/4 me for the job centre'—just before the off). Another senior layer in Tattersalls, Barry Dennis, also had his biggest losing day. 'For me to be able to lay 2/1 about a 10/1 shot is massive value that we don't get the chance to exploit very often . . . I didn't bother squaring the books. I stood the bets and lost heavily.' The actions of the likes of Wiltshire, Dennis and others didn't please the chairman of the British Betting Offices' Association, Warwick Bartlett, who claimed that the 'system where bookmakers send money back to the course needs to be scrutinised.' Bartlett asked how Fujiyama Crest, a £10m loser for the book-making industry, could have started at 2/1, after shortening to 7/4 (at which odds Hills and Ladbrokes were among those to back him) and then drifting to 9/4. 'The system failed,' said Bartlett. 'Fujiyama Crest should have been 4/1-on, but off course we had to rely on the poor judgement of those rails bookmakers who took an opinion and laid one horse . . . we have enough problems without having to put up with this racecourse nonsense.' One obvious question for Mr Bartlett, of course, was why—if £10m was riding on Fujiyama Crest—only a reported £300,000 or so (£100,000 of it known to be from one of the Big Three) was sent back to the course. Did the starting-price bookmakers in general, many of them accountant-dominated, really do enough to protect themselves? Or were some of them simply caught on the hop, leaving it too late? After all, there are untold numbers of occasions each year that bear ample testament to the ability of the off-course offices to contract the starting prices to so-called 'realistic' levels. Far from the system failing, the events at Ascot seemed to demonstrate its worth, highlighting the strength of the market on racing's big days and proving that the major off-course operations are not always able to dictate the starting prices. And one final point. Perhaps those among Mr Bartlett's members who claimed they were 'denied the facility to hedge as the market closed down' now appreciate how their own customers feel sometimes when they can't get on!

The Dettori clean sweep—accumulative odds 25,095-1—was a public relations godsend for racing, the bookmakers themselves being the quickest to exploit it by promoting some of the big winners. Self-employed joiner Darren Yates, who won over £550,000 from Hills (taking advantage, like all the biggest winners, of the longer morning prices) on Dettori's seven winners, had the sort of newspaper and television publicity normally reserved for record-breaking pools and lottery winners. Ladbrokes had a £500,000 winner, while a Coral punter won over £235,000 for a total stake of just over £14. The admirable Dettori played his part, making a surprise appearance to congratulate Yates on GMTV's breakfast show, giving interview after interview and posing for endless photographs, including a memorable shot flanked by Mike Dillon of Ladbrokes and Mike Burton of Hills with their hands round his neck. Dillon put Dettori's feat in perspective, pointing out that, however costly it was in the short term, 'it's great for the business as a whole . . . he has introduced betting to thousands and thousands.' Ladbrokes adopted the slogan 'Follow Frankie at Ladbrokes today and everyday.' If Dettori was popular before his epic day, he became a superstar after it. The recent rise and rise of the former champion apprentice has been a remarkable racing story. A broken elbow, received in a parade-ring fall at Newbury in June, kept Dettori out of action for the best part of two months, which effectively scuppered his chances of a third successive jockeys' title. He topped the two-hundred-winner mark in each of the two previous seasons after securing a retainer in 1994 with Sheikh Mohammed's principal trainer John Gosden. Dettori had overcome a difficult period since severing his long partnership with the Cumani stable which included losing the chance of riding in Hong Kong when news of his being cautioned for a drugs-related matter became public. Dettori's recent career couldn't have been stage-managed better. His thousandth winner, for example, came in the 1995 St Leger on Classic Cliche and he couldn't have had a much bigger stage than Ascot's Festival of Racing for his seven-timer. Dettori has well and truly captured the imagination of the sporting public, helped considerably by his natural, youthful exuberance and sense of showmanship which makes him terrific on camera. His appearance on the front page of almost every Sunday and Monday newspaper after Ascot was followed by a string of televison appearances which included hosting *Top of The Pops*. In December, he came third, an unprecedented position for a racing personality, in the BBC Sports Personality of the Year poll. Racing is a minority sport and rarely figures in annual sporting awards. Not even Lester Piggott was a major challenger for the main BBC award during his long and distinguished career, though he was given a special trophy during the BBC Sports Review of the Year programme in 1995; Bob Champion and Aldaniti received the team award, presented by the BBC, after their 1981 Grand National victory.

Mark of Esteem's performance in the Queen Elizabeth II Stakes and, for that matter, his trainer's feat of saddling four winners on the card were reduced almost to a footnote in the context of the next-day coverage of a tremendous day's racing. But the victory of Mark of Esteem in particular reflected great credit on the horse himself and on those who handled him after his transfer from Henry Cecil's care, in acrimonious circumstances, at the end of his two-year-old career. Mark of Esteem ran only twice for the Cecil stable, both in maiden races, beaten a neck by Alhaarth on their debuts at Newmarket before winning in good style at Goodwood. Mark of Esteem looked up to pattern company but missed his intended autumn target, the Royal Lodge Stakes, because of a knee injury. Transferred to Dubai for the winter, Mark of Esteem made a good recovery—'We have had to watch out for the knee

Pertemps Two Thousand Guineas Stakes, Newmarket—all three jockeys have high hopes of victory as Mark of Esteem (right), Even Top (left) and Bijou d'Inde provide a grandstand finish

problem but he has been fine', Sheikh Mohammed reported—and was among thirty or so horses in the powerful Godolphin team flown back to Britain on the Monday of Guineas week. Mark of Esteem came in for strong support in the ante-post market on the Pertemps Two Thousand Guineas but, truth to tell, his odds on the day (8/1 fifth favourite) looked plenty short enough for what he had accomplished on the racecourse. The thirteen-strong field contained not a single French or Irish challenger and looked no better than average in terms of quality for a Guineas. Favourite was the previous season's top two-year-old Alhaarth who had lost his unbeaten record narrowly to the Racing Post Trophy winner Beauchamp King (second favourite for the Guineas) in the Craven Stakes over the course and distance a fortnight before. The Cecil-trained Storm Trooper, winner of the Feilden Stakes at the Craven meeting, and the unbeaten Middle Park winner Royal Applause were the others to start at odds shorter than Mark of Esteem. Mark of Esteem and Royal Applause were among six of the runners (including Alhaarth's intended pacemaker Masehaab) making their seasonal reappearance. Among the others doing so were the Racing Post Trophy runner-up Even Top, a 40/1 chance, and the northern-trained Bijou d'Inde, who had looked like making up into a good-class two-year-old until training difficulties ruined his preparation for the Royal Lodge, from which he came back lame. Mark of Esteem, Even Top and Bijou d'Inde produced a thrilling finish, Mark of Esteem hanging on by a short head and a head under strong pressure after going the best part of a length up soon after he'd taken the lead a furlong and a half out. The winner, a delicate-looking type who was trained to the minute, had a particularly hard race (the riders of the first three all received suspensions for misuse of the whip, Mark of Esteem's rider Dettori getting eight days). It remained to be seen whether he would go on after the Guineas. Though the first three pulled six lengths clear of the remainder, there were also grounds for thinking at the time that their superiority was possibly exaggerated. The Guineas field raced in two groups—the first three kept near the stand rail—and those who stayed towards the centre, including fourth-placed Alhaarth and the non-staying Royal Applause who came back to the field three out after bowling along in a clear lead, seemed at a disadvantage. The trainers of Alhaarth and Royal Applause were among those to react angrily about what they regarded as the effects of uneven watering, while Angus Gold, racing manager to Alhaarth's owner Sheikh Hamdan, was adamant that 'the ground in the middle of the course was definitely slower.' Newmarket's clerk of the course Nick Lees rejected the criticism, but it did seem that watering after racing the previous day might have been uneven. Though Alhaarth's perform-ance was a disappointment for Sheikh Hamdan, the Two Thousand Guineas represented another triumph for the Al Maktoum family. It was the family's ninth consecutive British classic victory and the fourth in a row for Sheikh Mohammed's Godolphin operation and trainer Saeed bin Suroor.

The Derby was announced as the next target for Mark of Esteem whose variable ante-post odds after the Guineas (4/1 Ladbrokes, 5/1 Hills and 8/1 Coral) reflected differing views about both the likelihood of his training on and about his stamina. Sire Darshaan had won the Prix du Jockey-Club but the dam was an unraced half-sister to two smart performers, Local Suitor and Local Talent, who showed more speed than stamina. As things happened, discussions about the possible limit of Mark of Esteem's stamina became purely academic. A temperature, coming on ten days or so before the Derby, forced him to miss Epsom and he was raced at a mile for the remainder of his career. Mark of Esteem took his chance in the St James's Palace Stakes at Royal Ascot but beat only one home, shaping either like a horse that had not recovered from that set-back or one whose hard race in the Guineas had left a permanent mark. Mark of Esteem returned after a break to show clearly that those who had thought he lacked the scope to go on were well wide of the mark. He put up a cracking performance to defy a 6 lb Group 1 penalty in the Tripleprint Cele-bration Mile at Goodwood towards the end of August, showing a fine turn of foot after having to be switched to get a clear run and trouncing Bishop of

Cashel by three and a half lengths, with Alhaarth three quarters of a length back in third. In our book, this represented the best performance of the season up to that time by a three-year-old miler and Mark of Esteem looked the one they all had to beat in the Queen Elizabeth II Stakes at Ascot, a race rightly billed as 'the milers' championship of Europe', all seven of the runners having won good races at the trip during the season. The opposing three-year-olds Bosra Sham (One Thousand Guineas), Ashkalani (Poule d'Essai des Poulains) and Bijou d'Inde (St James's Palace Stakes) had all won Group 1 events, while the challenge from the older horses comprised First Island (Sussex Stakes), Charnwood Forest (Queen Anne Stakes) and Soviet Line (Lockinge Stakes). Mark of Esteem was always travelling strongly and quickened magnificently to surge past Bosra Sham in the home straight and win going away by a length and a quarter. The others weren't in it, First Island finishing four lengths further back in third, just ahead of Charnwood Forest and the favourite Ashkalani. Dettori described the performance graphically: 'I couldn't believe it when I came to the furlong pole. It was as good a mile field as I'd ridden in and yet Mark of Esteem was still on the bridle, and when I asked him the response was electric.' Mark of Esteem's performances at Goodwood and Ascot were right out of the top drawer—there hasn't been a better winner of the Queen Elizabeth since it was raised to Group 1 status—and showed him clearly to be a much better horse than he had been in the spring. He was, however, unable to to live up to the expectations held for him in the Breeders' Cup Mile at Woodbine in late-October, struggling turning for home and never looking like getting in a challenge.

There may not be much of Mark of Esteem but he is an attractive individual all the same, with a quick, fluent action. He became the first official classic winner sired by Darshaan, though the latter was responsible for the disqualified Oaks winner Aliysa. Though he was a top-class racehorse (and a very well bred one too), Darshaan hasn't been able to match the outstanding achievements at stud of the two colts who followed him home in the Prix du Jockey-Club, Sadler's Wells and Rainbow Quest. Darshaan's best horse before Mark of Esteem was Kotashaan who, after a respectable career in Europe, went on to be Horse of the Year in America after a splendid campaign on grass as a five-year-old which reached its climax with a win in the Breeders' Cup Turf. On the distaff side, neither Mark of Esteem's dam Homage (whose first foal he is) nor his grandam Home Love saw a racecourse. Homage's half-brothers Local Suitor and Local Talent both won in good pattern company, the former winning the Mill Reef Stakes and the latter the Prix Jean Prat. Judged on the performances of these relatives, and bearing in mind that she had the crack sprinter Ajdal as her sire, Homage wouldn't have been likely to stay middle distances, though, since Mark of Esteem is the result of a covering as a three-year-old, it seems likely she was never a racing proposition. Mark of Esteem's

Godolphin's "Mark of Esteem"

Mark of Esteem (IRE) (b.c. 1993)	Darshaan (br 1981)	Shirley Heights (b 1975)	Mill Reef Hardiemma
		Delsy (br 1972)	Abdos Kelty
	Homage (b 1989)	Ajdal (b 1984)	Northern Dancer Native Partner
		Home Love (b 1976)	Vaguely Noble Homespun

grandam Home Love could have been expected to stay much better, being by Vaguely Noble, a strong influence for stamina, as well as a half-sister to the Irish St Leger winner Mashaallah. Home Love's dam Homespun was placed at up to eleven furlongs. Mark of Esteem sometimes carried his head awkwardly and was decidedly on his toes and sweating before the Queen Elizabeth II Stakes. He stayed a mile well and possessed a first-rate turn of foot (Dettori, with the benefit of hindsight, says he should have held him up much longer in the Guineas). He acted on good to firm going and never encountered a soft surface. A stud career now beckons for Mark of Esteem who has been retired to the Dalham Hall Stud at a fee of £20,000. He was our top-rated racehorse in Europe in 1996 and our Horse Of The Year. *Saeed bin Suroor*

MARL 3 ch.f. Lycius (USA) 124 – Pamela Peach 81 (Habitat 134) [1995 92: 5m^2 5.2g* 5m^6 5.2g 1996 6d^2 7m 6g^5 5m^4 5m^6 5m 6m^3 6m^2 8m^6 8d^6 Oct 11] sparely-made filly: fluent mover: fairly useful performer: best effort at 3 yrs when third of 21 in £14,800 handicap at York: best form at 6f: yet to race on extremes of going: bandaged off-hind most starts in 1996: often on toes/edgy. *R. Akehurst* 94

MARONETTA   4 ch.f. Kristian – Suzannah's Song (Song 132) [1995 43, a–: a7g   –
a10g 10.1m⁵ 11d² 11.9d² 16.4m³ a14g a13g 1996 a13g 15.4m Apr 16] angular filly:
poor maiden: stays 16.4f: acts on good to firm and dead ground, no form on
all-weather: sent to Holland. *M. J. Ryan*

MAROULLA (IRE)   2 ch.f. (Mar 24) Caerleon (USA) 132 – Mamaluna (USA)   67 p
114 (Roberto (USA) 131) [1996 7g Nov 2] third foal: dam won Nassau Stakes: 20/1,
never a threat after slow start when thirteenth of 23 in maiden at Newmarket won by
Palisade: bred to be suited by middle distances: will improve. *M. R. Stoute*

MAROUSSIE (FR)   3 br.f. Saumarez 132 – Madiyma (FR) (Top Ville 129) [1995   115
NR 1996 8g⁶ 10g³ 10g² 10g³ 10d* 10g* 10.5s* Nov 18] sixth foal: half-sister to 3
winners, notably Fialka (up to 12.5f, by Vayrann): dam won in France: smart French
filly: progressed very well in the autumn, winning minor event at Maisons-Laffitte,
quite valuable race at Deauville and Prix Fille de l'Air (comfortably best effort, beat
Dance Treat 2½ lengths) at Evry: raced only at around 1¼m, quite likely to stay 1½m:
unraced on top-of-the-ground, acts well on soft. *N. Clement, France*

MAROWINS   7 ch.g. Sweet Monday 122 – Top Cover (High Top 131) [1995 49,   –
a70: a8g a8g⁴ a9.4g a9.4g a8.5g* a8.5g* 8.3g⁴ 8.3g⁶ 8g* 8.1m a8.5g⁶ 8.1m 8g 8d
1996 a9.4g Jan 3] robust gelding: has a quick action: fair handicapper on the all-
weather, poor on turf nowadays: below form only start at 7 yrs: stays 1¼m: probably
acts on any going, goes well on fibresand: below form when visored at 2 yrs:
sometimes sweats: held up, and suited by strongly-run race: tough. *E. J. Alston*

MAROZIA (USA)   2 ch.f. (Apr 15) Storm Bird (CAN) 134 – Make Change   – p
(USA) (Roberto (USA) 131) [1996 7g Nov 2] fourth foal: half-sister to 1994 Irish
2-y-o 1m winner Vitus (by Bering): dam, 6f (at 2 yrs) to 8.5f winner (also placed in
Grade 1 events at up to 1½m), out of half-sister to Eclipse winner Solford: 9/1,
prominent around 5f when sixteenth of 23 in Newmarket maiden won by Palisade:
should do better. *J. H. M. Gosden*

MARSAD (IRE)   2 ch.c. (Mar 29) Fayruz 116 – Broad Haven (IRE) (Be My Guest   76
(USA) 126) [1996 6m⁶ 6m³ 6m³ 6g² 6g⁴ 6m 5d² Oct 21] IR 13,500Y, IR 26,000Y:
good-topped colt: has scope: third foal: dam Irish maiden (ran only at 2 yrs) out of
Gallinule Stakes winner Welsh Fantasy: fair maiden: struck into and eased right up
when in process of running well in nursery at Newmarket penultimate start: better
suited by 6f than 5f: sold 26,000 gns Newmarket Autumn Sales. *C. J. Benstead*

MARSAYAS (IRE)   3 ch.g. Classic Music (USA) – Babiana (CAN) 90 (Sharpen   59
Up 127) [1995 –: 7.5d 7f a8g⁶ 1996 10g 12d 12f² 15.1f⁴ 14.1m⁴ 16f² 16m² 15.8g*
15.8g⁴ 15.8g⁵ Oct 18] workmanlike gelding: modest handicapper: won maiden
contest at Catterick in August: stays 2m: acts on firm going, has run poorly both starts
on a soft surface. *M. J. Camacho*

MARSHALL PINDARI   6 b.h. Son of Shaka 119 – Off The Pill (Marshal Pil   –
108) [1995 NR 1996 a8.5g Jun 22] novice selling hurdler in 1993/4: well beaten in
seller and claimers on flat. *T. T. Bill*

MARSH MARIGOLD   2 br.f. (Mar 19) Tina's Pet 121 – Pulga (Blakeney 126)   58 +
[1996 5g³ 6m³ 6g⁵ 5m⁴ 7g² 7.1m⁵ 7.5m⁶ 7m² 6s* 7m⁶ 7.3s Oct 26] 2,100Y: sparely-
made filly: second foal: dam unraced: won 23-runner selling nursery at Haydock in
October by 3½ lengths: only modest form otherwise: will stay 1m: easily best form
on soft ground: often claimer ridden: tends to hang. *Martyn Meade*

MARSH'S LAW   9 br.g. Kala Shikari 125 – My Music 68 (Sole Mio (USA))   –
[1995 NR 1996 8f Sep 27] first flat outing for a long time when tailed off in amateurs
handicap at Redcar: modest hurdler at best. *G. P. Kelly*

MARSUL (USA)   2 b. or br.c. (Mar 22) Cozzene (USA) – Beside (USA) (Sportin'   – p
Life (USA)) [1996 8m Sep 19] $58,000F, $285,000Y: fourth foal: half-brother to 2
winners in USA, including Warside (by Lord At War), placed in Grade 3 9f event:
dam unraced sister to a minor stakes winner: 16/1, not given hard time in rear in
15-runner Yarmouth maiden won by High Roller: will do better: to winter in Dubai.
J. H. M. Gosden

MARTINDALE (IRE)   3 b.g. Fairy King (USA) – Whist Awhile (Caerleon   –
(USA) 132) [1995 NR 1996 7g 7f Oct 14] 30,000Y: fifth foal: half-brother to Irish 7f
winner Corleonie (by Bluebird) and a winner over hurdles by Don't Forget Me: dam

unraced half-sister to very useful 1983 2-y-o Mahogany: has shown little in maidens. *B. W. Hills*

MARTINE 2 ch.f. (Feb 23) Clantime 101 – Marcroft 91 (Crofthall 110) [1996 5m³ 68 ? 5g 5m³ 6.1d⁴ 6m Sep 21] small, sparely-made filly: unimpressive mover: second foal: half-sister to 1995 2-y-o 5f winner Safio (by Efisio): dam best at 7f to 1m: modest on balance of form: probably flattered behind Sambac in minor event at Chester on fourth outing: stays 6f. *A. Bailey*

MARTINIQUAIS (IRE) 3 ch.c. Simply Great (FR) 122 – Majolique (USA) 112 (Irish River (FR) 131) [1995 100p: 7g* 7g* 8s³ 1996 9m* 9.3g* 9m² 10m 9.8d⁶ Oct 5] leggy colt: has a quick action: half-brother to useful French 1¼m winner Marble Falls (by Tirol): smart French colt: won listed race at Evry and 6-runner Prix de Guiche at Longchamp (5/2 on, beat Kalmoss a short neck) in the spring: 2 lengths second of 6 to Le Triton in Prix Jean Prat at Chantilly: held up, off bridle early in straight then staying on under pressure: stiffish task, ran poorly in Grand Prix de Paris at Longchamp: off course 3½ months, respectable effort, always in mid-division, when sixth of 11 to Flemensfirth in Prix Dollar at Longchamp last time: should be suited by further than 9f: acts on good to firm and soft ground. *A. Fabre, France*

MARTINOSKY 10 b.g. Martinmas 128 – Bewitched 63 (African Sky 124) [1995 57 57, a47: a6g⁵ a6g 6.9d⁴ a6g 7g 1996 6f 6f 6.9m* 6f⁶ 6.1m³ 7g 6m 6.9m Aug 16] big a– gelding: good walker: modest at best nowadays: easily best effort at 10 yrs when winning claimer at Folkestone in May: suited by 6f/7f: acts on any turf going (below form all 3 all-weather starts): effective blinkered or not: none too consistent. *G. C. Bravery*

MARTINS FOLLY 3 ch.f. Beveled (USA) – Millingdale 65 (Tumble Wind – (USA) [1995 –: 5.1h⁶ 7m a8.5g 1996 12m Apr 29] no sign of ability. *J. White*

MARY CULI 2 gr.f. (Feb 15) Liboi (USA) 76 – Copper Trader 53 (Faustus (USA) – 118) [1996 7m 7.1s⁶ Oct 22] first foal: dam placed at 1¼m: probably better effort in maidens when around 11 lengths sixth of 16 to Technicolour at Chepstow, one paced from 3f out: will stay middle distances. *H. Candy*

MARYLEBONE (IRE) 2 ch.c. (Apr 28) River Falls 113 – Pasadena Lady 67 (Captain James 123) [1996 5m² 6g⁴ 5m² 5g Oct 18] IR 20,000F, 30,000Y: half-brother to several winners, including useful sprinters Another Episode, Palacegate Episode (both by Drumalis) and Palacegate Jack (by Neshad): dam never ran: in frame in maidens: stays 6f: raced only on a sound surface. *J. Berry*

MARY MACBLAIN 7 b.m. Damister (USA) 123 – Tzarina (USA) (Gallant – Romeo (USA)) [1995 40: 8.5m⁵ 8g 8g² 8f⁶ 8.1f 10.1m a7g a10g⁴ a10g 1996 8.5m 9m 8m 8.1g⁶ Jul 1] plain, shallow-girthed mare: has a round action: bad handicapper nowadays: stays 1¼m: probably acts on any ground: blinkered (ran poorly) once at 4 yrs: has worn near-side pricker: none too consistent. *J. L. Harris*

MARY MAGDALENE 2 b.f. (May 19) Night Shift (USA) – Indian Jubilee 81 – p (Indian King (USA) 128) [1996 6s Oct 24] good-bodied filly: fifth foal: half-sister to useful sprinter Roger The Butler (by Ahonoora) and a winner abroad (including at 11f) by Alzao: dam sprinter: 16/1 and not fully wound up, around 11 lengths eleventh of 23 to Za-Im in maiden at Newbury, late headway from rear: will do better. *M. Bell*

MARYTAVY 2 b.f. (Mar 10) Lycius (USA) 124 – Rose Parade (Thatching 131) – p [1996 6g 6g⁶ 6m Sep 7] 16,000F: good-topped filly: has scope: shows knee action: fourth foal: half-sister to NH Flat race winner Badger's Lane (by Don't Forget Me) and a winner in Hungary by Pharly: dam unraced granddaughter of Rose Dubarry: well beaten in maidens at Salisbury, Thirsk and at Kempton (not given hard time): sort to do better at 3 yrs over further than 6f. *Sir Mark Prescott*

MASAFAH (USA) 4 ch.f. Cadeaux Genereux 131 – Tatwij (USA) 94 (Topsider 52 (USA)) [1995 81: 6.1m 6g* 1996 5.9f³ 7m 6m Jul 12] unfurnished filly: just modest form in claimer at Carlisle on reappearance and soundly beaten both subsequent outings, final one a seller: should stay 7f. *Mrs M. Reveley*

MASAI MAN (USA) 5 ch.g. Riverman (USA) 131 – Green Oasis (FR) 108 – (Green Dancer (USA) 132) [1995 –: a14g 1996 16m 6g 7m 7g Oct 25] big, lengthy gelding: little sign of ability since 3 yrs: tried blinkered. *Miss J. Bower*

MASBRO BIRD 3 b.f. Midyan (USA) 124 – Grinning (IRE) (Bellypha 130) – [1995 –: 5g 5.1m 7f 6m 1996 7g Sep 14] leggy filly: no worthwhile form: sold 725 gns Ascot October Sales. *T. M. Jones*

MASEHAAB (IRE)　3 b.c. Mujtahid (USA) 118 – Firefly Night (Salmon Leap　105
(USA) 131) [1995 91p: 6m³ 7.1d* 7g* 1996 8m 10g 12f³ 12m² 14g² 11.8m* Oct 28]
strong, lengthy, good-looking colt: useful performer: gained deserved win in 6-
runner minor event at Leicester in October, staying on strongly to beat Harbour Dues
3 lengths: sold 100,000 gns Newmarket Autumn Sales: stays 1¾m: acts on firm and
dead ground: front runner last 3 starts: game and consistent. *J. L. Dunlop*

MASERATI MONK　2 b.c. (Apr 3) Emarati (USA) 74 – Abbotswood (Ahonoora　95
122) [1996 5m² 6g* 6f 5.7m² 6d 6m² 6m Sep 21] 15,000F, 37,000Y: tall, lengthy,
good-topped colt: has plenty of scope: has a round action: fourth foal: brother to a
winner in Malaysia and half-brother to 3-y-o 7f and 1m winner Barrack Yard (by
Forzando) and 1½m winner Mr Abbot (by Midyan): dam French maiden: won
maiden at Lingfield in May: beaten a neck by Arethusa in listed race at Kempton
penultimate outing: below form on very firm ground and good to soft: takes
keen hold: sent to Hong Kong. *B. J. Meehan*

MASHHAER (USA)　2 b. or br.c. (Apr 16) Nureyev (USA) 131 – Life's Magic　94 p
(USA) (Cox's Ridge (USA)) [1996 7m* Oct 3] angular colt: eighth foal: closely
related to a winner in USA by Danzig and half-brother to another by Mr Prospector:
dam champion filly in USA, winning from 6f to 1¼m: 6/1, won 16-runner maiden at
Newmarket by 1¼ lengths from Courtship, green when shaken up then picking up
well: showed a quick action: will stay 1m: should improve. *Saeed bin Suroor*

MASHKORAH (USA)　2 ch.f. (Jan 20) Miswaki (USA) 124 – Tom's Lassie　–
(USA) (Tom Rolfe) [1996 7.1s Oct 22] $50,000F, 720,000 francs Y: first foal: dam,
won at up to 7f in USA, half-sister to USA sprinter Claim (by Mr Prospector), placed
in graded stakes: 25/1, no promise in 16-runner maiden at Chepstow. *R. Hannon*

MASHMOUM　3 ch.f. Lycius (USA) 124 – Flaming Rose (USA) (Upper Nile　85
(USA)) [1995 NR 1996 7m 7f⁴ 7m* a8.5g Nov 16] 32,000Y: good-topped filly:
fourth foal: half-sister to modest 1m winner Crimson Shower (by Dowsing) and 6f
and 1m winner Chipaya (by Northern Prospect), smart at 2 yrs: dam, half-sister to
smart sprinter Gwydion, showed some ability in USA: moved badly to post before
winning slowly-run minor event at Leicester in October, hanging left into whip from
out and ending up alone against stand rail: sold 45,000 gns Newmarket December
Sales: should stay beyond 7f. *J. H. M. Gosden*

MASIMARA MUSIC　5 ch.m. Almushmmir 98 – Native Chant (Gone Native)　–
[1995 NR 1996 7.1m Jun 30] third known foal: dam seemed of little account: very
reluctant to race in seller at Chepstow on flat debut. *J. M. Bradley*

MASK FLOWER (USA)　3 b.f. Dayjur (USA) 137 – Nom de Plume (USA) 116　69
(Nodouble (USA)) [1995 72: 5g⁴ 5g² 5m² a5g² a6g* 1996 a7g² a6g* 6g May 22] fair
performer: favourite, won handicap at Southwell in April, making most: ran poorly
in similar event at Newcastle following month: should stay beyond 6f: acts on good
to firm ground and all-weather surfaces: races prominently: sold 13,000 gns
Newmarket December Sales. *M. Johnston*

MASNUN (USA)　11 gr.g. Nureyev (USA) 131 – Careless Kitten (USA) (Caro　73
133) [1995 71: a7g a8g* a8g² a10g* a10g* 8f⁴ a7g 7g a7g⁶ a10g³ a7g* a8g³ 1996
a10g² a8g* a10g* a10g² a10g³ a7g* a12g* Mar 29] sturdy gelding: ran 100 times and
won 15 races (was rated 97 at his peak), last 3 of them claimers at Lingfield (nine
course wins there in all) early in 1996: formerly a sprinter, but stayed 1¼m on the
all-weather at end of career: acted on equitrack and probably on any turf going: often
on toes: held up: tough: suffered fatal injuries when cast in his box in September: a
grand character. *R. J. O'Sullivan*

MASRUF (IRE)　4 b.g. Taufan (USA) 119 – Queen's Share (Main Reef 126)　–
[1995 –: 7f 7m 8m 6m⁴ 7f 7.1d 1996 7m 6m 7m 6m 6m Sep 19] good-bodied gelding:
fairly useful performer at 2 yrs: disappointing since: stays 7f: blinkered final start:
has joined K. Bailey. *T. Thomson Jones*

MASTER BEVELED　6 b.g. Beveled (USA) – Miss Anniversary §§ (Tachypous　77
128) [1995 86d: a7g a9.4g a10g 8g 8g 8.1m 10m 8.1g 8.1g 8m 7.9g⁵ 8d⁵ 8g⁶ 8d⁶ 9g　a71
8m 1996 a8g² a8g⁶ 10.8d⁴ 9m³ 10m 8d⁶ 7.9g 10.3m 8g 10.5v* 8f* 8.9g 8g a10g⁵
Dec 30] lengthy gelding: fairly useful handicapper: back to form in October to win
minor events at Haydock and Warwick 2 days later: stays 10.8f: acts on any going,
including the all-weather: tried visored/blinkered at 3 yrs: useful hurdler. *P. D. Evans*

MASTER BOBBY 2 b.g. (Feb 16) Touch of Grey 90 – Young Lady (Young –
Generation 129) [1996 a6g Dec 5] third reported foal: brother to 3-y-o 1m winner
Billaddie: dam never ran: never dangerous in maiden at Lingfield. *R. Boss*

MASTER BOOTS 3 br.c. Warning 136 – Arpero 107 (Persian Bold 123) [1995 105
NR 1996 8m 7d* 7.1d* 7.1d 8d⁶ Oct 10] 34,000Y: good-topped, quite attractive colt:
poor mover: first foal: dam won at 7f and 1m: useful performer: won maiden at
Catterick in April and minor event at Haydock (by length from Fire Dome) in May:
in rear in listed races at Haydock and Longchamp last 2 starts: should stay 1m: acts
on dead ground. *D. R. Loder*

MASTER CHARTER 4 ch.g. Master Willie 129 – Irene's Charter 72 (Persian 87
Bold 123) [1995 61: 5m 11.1g² 12m⁶ 7f 7m* 8.2m⁶ 1996 7g* 8g* 7m² 8m² 10m⁵
10m* 8m² 8m⁵ 8m 9m Oct 5] lengthy, workmanlike gelding: poor mover: fairly
useful handicapper: successful at Newcastle and Pontefract in April and at Newmarket in June: mostly good efforts afterwards, though little show in Cambridgeshire
final start: has shown his form at 7f and stays 1¼m: acts on good to firm ground, yet
to race on a soft surface: held up. *Mrs J. R. Ramsden*

MASTER FOLEY 2 ch.c. (May 31) Cigar 68 – Sultans Gift 47 (Homing 130) 61
[1996 a5g 5g a6g a5g⁴ a5g⁵ a6s* Dec 19] third known foal: dam sprint maiden: much
improved form to win seller at Wolverhampton in December, making all: probably
better at 6f than 5f. *N. P. Littmoden*

MASTER FOODBROKER (IRE) 8 br.g. Simply Great (FR) 122 – Silver –
Mantle 70 (Bustino 136) [1995 NR 1996 10.3g 16.4v Nov 11] heavy-topped gelding:
fairly useful stayer at his best, but seems to retain little ability on flat and is one to
leave alone over hurdles. *W. J. Musson*

MASTER HYDE (USA) 7 gr.g. Trempolino (USA) 135 – Sandspur (USA) (Al 60
Hattab (USA)) [1995 62: 12f* 11.9m 16.1g⁵ 12.1g 1996 15.1m³ 12f² 12.3g 12g⁵ 12g
11.9g Oct 10] leggy, workmanlike gelding: modest handicapper: clearly best effort at
7 yrs when second of 5 at Carlisle in August, carrying head awkwardly: behind when
brought down over 2f out at York final start: stays 1½m: acts on firm and soft ground
and on equitrack (below form on fibresand): has worn blinkers and visor: none too
consistent. *W. Storey*

MASTER M-E-N (IRE) 4 ch.g. My Generation 111 – Secret Lightning (USA) 61
78 (Secretariat (USA)) [1995 54: 7m 5.1f 8.1m⁴ 8f³ 8.1m 8g² 7m⁶ 8h³ 1996 10.3m³
10m² 10.2g⁵ 10m 10m 8f* 8f⁶ Sep 23] close-coupled, quite attractive gelding:
modest handicapper: best effort since 1994 when winning at Salisbury in September:
effective at 1m and stays 1¼m: acts on firm and dead ground (well beaten on soft and
fibresand): normally visored nowadays (has run well without), has been blinkered.
N. M. Babbage

MASTER MILLFIELD (IRE) 4 b.g. Prince Rupert (FR) 121 – Calash (Indian 72
King (USA) 128) [1995 68, a75: a7g³ a6g⁴ a7g³ a7g* a7g⁴ 6.1g 8f⁴ 8m² 7m⁵ 7m³
5.1h⁴ 6m³ 7f³ 5.7h* 8g⁴ 6g a7g a6g a8.5g³ a7g 1996 a6g a7g⁵ a7g⁵ a8g 5.7m 5.7m³
8.1m 8m⁵ 6m 5.7m 10m³ 8.1s³ a9.4g² a12s² Nov 19] tall gelding: fair handicapper:
trained first 4 starts at 4 yrs by C. J. Hill, next 5 by R. J. Baker and tenth by C. J. Hill
again before running well all 4 outings for current stable: similar form in 1996 at 5.7f
and 1½m: acts on any ground on turf and all-weather surfaces: below form only start
in visor: versatile. *P. D. Evans*

MASTER OF PASSION 7 b.g. Primo Dominie 121 – Crime of Passion 115 89 d
(Dragonara Palace (USA) 115) [1995 89: 6m 6g⁴ 6m⁴ 6f⁵ 5m² 6m 5.2m* 5.6m⁵ 6g⁴
5d 6g 1996 5g⁴ 6m 5m 6f 5m 5g 6m 5m 5s a5g⁴ a5g* Dec 13] lengthy, angular
gelding: has a quick action: fairly useful handicapper at 6 yrs: ran creditably first 2
starts at 7 yrs: disappointing afterwards until (still below form) winning at Lingfield
in December: effective at 5f to 7f: acts on firm and dead ground: tried blinkered/
visored, not for some time: usually races prominently. *J. M. P. Eustace*

MASTER OFTHE HOUSE 10 b.g. Kind of Hush 118 – Miss Racine (Dom 61 d
Racine (FR) 121) [1995 66: 10g 7g⁵ 8.9m 8f* 10.3g 10m⁴ 8.3f³ 8m³ 8m³ 9.2g⁶ 9f⁶
1996 a11g 12g 8g⁶ 8.3d³ 10g 10g³ 8g⁵ 12.3m 12f⁵ 10m Aug 8] sturdy gelding: poor
mover: fair handicapper: below form last 5 starts, tailed off final one: effective at 7f
to 11f: acts on any going: has been tried in blinkers and visor, but not for some time:
held up: effective for amateur/apprentice. *M. D. Hammond*

MASTER PLANNER 7 b.g. Night Shift (USA) – Shaky Puddin (Ragstone 128) –
[1995 102: 6m* 6m³ 6g⁵ 6m³ 6f 5m⁵ 5m⁴ 6m 6m 6g 1996 6m⁶ May 14] strong, close-
coupled gelding: impresses in appearance: useful handicapper: well below form
under optimum conditions last 3 starts in 1995, and again on only outing at 7 yrs:
suited by 6f and a sound surface (acts on firm ground): usually races prominently:
successful for claimer: reportedly injured a leg in June. *C. A. Cyzer*

MASTERSTROKE 2 b.g. (Feb 23) Timeless Times (USA) 99 – Fauve 71 65
(Dominion 123) [1996 5g³ 5.3f* 5d⁶ 6m* 7m⁴ 6m 6m⁵ 6m⁴ a6g a6g³ a8g⁵ Dec 11]
9,200Y: leggy, unfurnished gelding: fourth foal: dam stayed 6f, best at 2 yrs: fair
form: won median auction maiden at Brighton in April and nursery at Leicester in
July: broke out of stalls, bolted on sixth intended outing: stays 1m: acts on firm
ground and equitrack, poor effort on dead. *B. J. Meehan*

MATAM 3 b.f. Cyrano de Bergerac 120 – Tasmim 63 (Be My Guest (USA) 126) 56
[1995 NR 1996 8.2m 5m⁴ 5g³ 8.5m⁶ 10s Aug 31] tall, lengthy, unfurnished filly: first
foal: dam 11f winner at 4 yrs: modest maiden: off course nearly 3 months and stiff
task, didn't look fully wound up when in rear throughout in handicap final start: has
shaped as though she'll stay 1m. *M. W. Easterby*

MATAMOROS 4 gr.c. Kalaglow 132 – Palama (USA) (Blushing Groom (FR) –
131) [1995 77: 10.8m² 12.5f 10d⁶ 11.9d³ 13.6f² 16m 1996 10m Aug 31] sparely-
made colt: fair maiden handicapper as 3-y-o for J. Dunlop: ran over inadequate trip
only flat outing in 1996: should be suited by thorough test of stamina: acts on firm
and dead ground, well beaten on soft: visored (raced too freely) final 3-y-o start: poor
hurdler. *G. Harwood*

MATHON 3 b.g. High Estate 127 – Sunley Saint 79 (Artaius (USA) 129) 51
[1995 NR 1996 10g 12m 10d 17.2g 13.8g² 16f² 17.2f⁴ Jun 26] 31,000Y: strong,
lengthy gelding: has a short, round action: fifth foal: half-brother to 4-y-o Toaff (by
Nordico), winner in Italy at 6f to 10.5f, and Irish 6f (at 2 yrs) and 1m winner Guided
Tour (by Doubletour): dam, maiden, suited by 1½m: poor staying maiden: visored
last 3 starts: has joined I. P. Williams. *M. R. Channon*

MATIYA (IRE) 3 b.f. Alzao (USA) 117 – Purchasepaperchase 104 (Young 116
Generation 129) [1995 98: 7m* 6m³ 8.1d² 8d³ 1996 8m² 8d* 10.5g³ 8m 9.3d
Oct 6]

Matiya improved dramatically from two to three and ran well in three
classics before she lost her form. She was sent off at 25/1 in the first of them,
when making her seasonal reappearance in the One Thousand Guineas.
Considering how she turned out, the strong, well-made Matiya was bought for
a song at IR 38,000 guineas at auction; even as a two-year-old she
looked great value for money, developing into a useful filly. On her final start
in 1995 she came third in the Fillies' Mile at Ascot, three and a half lengths and
the same behind Bosra Sham and Bint Shadayid after forcing a strong pace.
These three were also the principals in the Guineas, Matiya turning the tables
on Bint Shadayid and finishing one and a half lengths second to Bosra Sham.
Matiya held a handy position from the start and responded gamely once put
under pressure two furlongs out.

The Airlie/Coolmore Irish One Thousand Guineas came next on the
agenda. With Bosra Sham absent and no French challenge, Matiya was entitled
to be favourite in the field of twelve on her Newmarket running. In fact, Bosra

Airlie/Coolmore Irish One Thousand Guineas, the Curragh—
long-striding Matiya gallops on strongly ahead of Dance Design (rails) and My Branch

Hamdan Al Maktoum's "Matiya"

Sham's inexperienced stable-companion Distant Oasis had the call at 5/2; Bint Shadayid started second favourite at 4/1, a point shorter than Matiya and the Irish-trained Dance Design, fourth in the Prix Marcel Boussac when last seen out the previous autumn. Matiya won the Irish One Thousand in fine style, by three lengths from Dance Design, taking the lead at around halfway in a well-run contest and never looking like relinquishing it, striding out with great purpose. Newmarket fourth My Branch took third place ahead of Distant Oasis, while Bint Shadayid dropped out tamely to finish last.

It was unfortunate that this fine performance of Matiya's had to share headlines with the news that the Curragh stewards had seized on the fact that her jockey Willie Carson had been wearing an unapproved helmet. In the end, Carson escaped censure and was able to team up with Matiya again in the Prix de Diane Hermes at Chantilly a fortnight later. Chantilly rather than Epsom seemed the right choice, since on breeding Matiya was far from certain to stay the mile and a half of the Oaks. Supplementing her into the Diane cost 140,000 francs, the equivalent of £18,500. Matiya finished third of twelve behind Sil Sila and Miss Tahiti in a strongly-run affair in which the first five all came from the rear. She didn't see the race out so well as Sil Sila or Miss Tahiti and was beaten a length and two and a half lengths after leading a furlong and a half out. Matiya finished last of ten in two starts over a mile afterwards, in the Sussex Stakes (bandaged behind) and the Prix de l'Opera. She has now been retired and visits Nureyev.

Matiya's dam Purchasepaperchase stayed the mile and a quarter of the Prix Saint-Alary in 1985, running second to Fitnah; her great-grandam Daphne, a half-sister to the One Thousand Guineas second Gwen, reached the frame in the Cheshire Oaks and Lingfield Oaks Trial. Of Purchasepaperchase's three earlier foals to have run, Never Explain (by Fairy King) and German-based Sandanista (by Pharly) won at a mile and a quarter and Al Naayy (by Tate Gallery) at a mile. There have also been some speedy animals in the family in fairly recent times, notably Blue Siren and Prince Spy, granddaughter and grandson respectively of Daphne. The second dam Tin Goddess was placed over nine and a half furlongs in Ireland.

Matiya (IRE) (b.f. 1993)	Alzao (USA) (b 1980)	Lyphard (b 1969)	Northern Dancer Goofed
		Lady Rebecca (b 1971)	Sir Ivor Pochahontas II
	Purchasepaperchase (b 1982)	Young Generation (b 1976)	Balidar Brig O'Doon
		Tin Goddess (ch 1973)	Petingo Daphne

Purchasepaperchase showed a round action and so did Matiya. Matiya's connections were of the opinion that some give in the ground suited her: she was said to be doubtful for the Sussex Stakes when firm ground threatened, and she bypassed the Moulin and the Queen Elizabeth II Stakes because of a lack of rain. The form-book supports them inasmuch as her run on dead in Ireland was her best, about 7 lb in advance of those at Newmarket and Chantilly. *B. Hanbury*

MATOAKA 2 b.f. (Apr 11) Be My Chief (USA) 122 – Echoing 93 (Formidable 66 (USA) 125) [1996 6m⁴ May 29] 6,200Y: sixth foal: half-sister to 1½m winner Sommersby (by Vision) and 6f winner Buckski Echo (by Petoski): dam 2-y-o 5f winner from family of Time Charter: fourth of 14, keeping-on in maiden auction at Folkestone: reportedly finished lame. *R. J. R. Williams*

MATTAWAN 3 ch.c. Nashwan (USA) 135 – Sweet Mover (USA) 95 (Nijinsky 92 (CAN) 138) [1995 NR 1996 12.1m* 11.8g² 14.8m⁵ 11.9f³ 12.3g* Sep 22] tall, good-topped colt: has scope: shows markedly round action: fifth foal: closely related to very useful French sprinter Wedding of The Sea (by Blushing Groom): dam 10.4f winner: won maiden at Hamilton in May: third to Dacha in rated stakes at Haydock then won valuable event in Zurich: should be suited by further than 12.5f: yet to race on a soft surface: stays in training. *M. Johnston*

MATTHEW DAVID 6 ch.h. Indian Forest (USA) 117 – Mazurkanova 63 (Song – 132) [1995 27+, a50: a6g² a6g⁵ a6g⁴ a6g a8g³ a7g³ a6g⁵ a6g⁶ a6g 5d⁵ a5g a6g* a6g⁴ a5g² a6g⁶ 1996 a6g⁶ Jan 12] small, sparely-made horse: has a roundish action: poor handicapper: well below form at Southwell only outing at 6 yrs (has gained all his 4 wins there): stays 6f: best form on fibresand, also acts on soft ground (has had only one run on top-of-the-ground, at 2 yrs): usually bandaged: effective blinkered or not. *S. R. Bowring*

MATTHIAS MYSTIQUE 3 gr.f. Warning (USA) 124 – Sheznice (IRE) 58 59 (Try My Best (USA) 130) [1995 –: 6m 6.9s a7g 1996 10m 12m² 11.9g⁶ a13g² a16g³ a66 a16g* a16g³ a13g⁶ Dec 31] leggy filly: fair performer: won minor event at Lingfield in December: probably better at 2m than 13f: acts on good to firm ground and equitrack. *Miss B. Sanders*

MATTIMEO (IRE) 3 b.g. Prince Rupert (FR) 121 – Herila (FR) (Bold Lad 74 (USA)) [1995 66p: 7m⁵ 1996 a10g² a8g² 10m* 11.9m 12m 12m⁴ Sep 25] stocky gelding: fair handicapper: first run for over 4 months, narrowly won 15-runner contest at Nottingham in August, leading close home: stays 1½m: acts on equitrack, has raced only on good to firm ground on turf. *A. P. Jarvis*

MAURANGI 5 b.g. Warning 136 – Spin Dry (High Top 131) [1995 58: 8.2g 8.5m – 8g⁵ 8g⁶ 8.9m⁴ 10.1m 10.1m⁴ 1996 7.1d 8f 10.1f⁶ 10.5m 8f 8m Oct 23] tall, leggy gelding: modest handicapper: showed little in 1996: stays 9f: acts on good to firm and dead ground: usually held up: effective blinkered (not tried last 2 seasons) or not. *B. W. Murray*

MA VIELLE POUQUE (IRE) 2 ch.f. (Mar 25) Fayruz 116 – Aussie Aisle 52 p
(IRE) (Godswalk (USA) 130) [1996 5.1m⁵ Sep 9] 5,600 2-y-o: first foal: dam Irish
1¼m winner, half-sister to useful sprinter Barry's Gamble: 16/1, 4 lengths fifth of 12
to Loving And Giving in maiden auction at Bath, chasing leaders 4f: should improve.
W. G. M. Turner

MAWARED (IRE) 3 ch.c. Nashwan (USA) 135 – Harmless Albatross 115 (Pas 75
de Seul 133) [1995 NR 1996 8d 8m 9g³ 11.8f³ 12.1s Oct 22] good-topped colt: fourth
foal: half-brother to 1½m winner Haniya (by Caerleon) and very smart French 6f
(at 2 yrs) to 1¼m winner Volochine (by Soviet Star): dam, French miler, out of
Ribblesdale runner-up North Forland: fair maiden: off course 5 months, improved
effort on handicap debut when third at Leicester, staying on well: tailed off on soft
ground 8 days later: sold to join J. Neville 20,000 gns Newmarket Autumn Sales:
better suited by 1½m than shorter, and will stay further. *J. L. Dunlop*

MAWHIBA (USA) 2 b. or br.f. (May 9) Dayjur (USA) 137 – Histoire (FR) 63 p
(Riverman (USA) 131) [1996 6m Aug 16] close-coupled filly: ninth foal: half-sister
to several winners, including 3-y-o Samim, 7f winner at 2 yrs, and smart 7f (at 2 yrs)
to 1¼m winner Oumaldaaya (both by Nureyev), and Derby winner Erhaab (by
Chief's Crown): dam French 10.5f winner: 20/1 and bit backward, over 5 lengths
ninth of 19 to Catechism in maiden at Newbury, slowly away and soon behind then
staying on, short of room inside last: sure to improve. *J. L. Dunlop*

MAWINGO (IRE) 3 b.c. Taufan (USA) 119 – Tappen Zee (Sandhurst Prince 84
128) [1995 63: 7m⁶ a7g⁵ 1996 6.9m⁶ 7f* 7.9f⁵ 8m* 8g* 10m⁵ 10m⁶ Oct 4] leggy colt:
fairly useful handicapper: ridden by 7-lb claimer, won at Warwick in May and twice
at Newmarket in June: ran well when staying-on fifth to Fahim in £34,000 event at
Goodwood penultimate start: below best when next seen out at Newmarket 2 months
later: stays 1¼m: has raced only on a sound surface on turf. *G. Wragg*

MAWJUD 3 b.c. Mujtahid (USA) 118 – Elfaslah (IRE) 107 (Green Desert (USA) 96
127) [1995 84p: 7f* 1996 8.2d³ 8g a7f⁶ Dec 26] lengthy, good-topped colt: not seen
at 3 yrs until August, third of 5 to Kayvee in steadily-run minor event at Nottingham,
then well beaten facing stiff task in listed race at Kempton 12 days later: takes keen
hold, and unlikely to stay further than 1m. *H. Thomson Jones*

MAWWAL (USA) 3 ch.c. Elmaamul (USA) 125 – Dish Dash 118 (Bustino 136) 98
[1995 105: 6g⁵ 6g⁴ 7.1m* 7m* 7g* 8d 1996 9m 7g³ Jul 4] tall colt: fluent mover:
useful performer: creditable third of 6 to Branston Abby in minor event at Yarmouth,
but broke leg near finish: took keen hold and best form at up to 7f: acted on good to
firm ground: dead. *R. W. Armstrong*

MAYBANK (IRE) 4 gr.g. Contract Law (USA) 108 – Katysue 98 (King's Leap –
111) [1995 –: 6g 5d 1996 a7g⁵ a7g⁴ a6g* a6g² 6.1g a7g⁴ 6d a7g⁶ a6g 6d 6m a8g a11g a66 d
Nov 18] big, good-topped gelding: fair performer on the all-weather: won maiden at
Southwell in February: led on bridle 2f out but found nil in handicap there in May,
sixth outing: below form afterwards, leaving B. McMahon after ninth start: stays 7f:
acts on fibresand, no form on turf: often races prominently, but probably needs
holding up as long as possible. *A. Streeter*

MAYFAIR 2 b.f. (Mar 2) Green Desert (USA) 127 – Emaline (FR) 105 (Empery 82
(USA) 128) [1996 6m* 7d⁵ 7g⁴ Oct 10] sturdy, angular filly: easy mover: eighth foal:
sister to smart 1991 2-y-o sprinter Magic Ring and half-sister to 3 winners, including
11f winner Wisdom (by Insan) and middle-distance stayer Monarda (by Pharly): dam
French 2-y-o 7f winner: odds on, won 5-runner maiden at Ascot in July, making all
despite edging right: failed to progress in Prestige Stakes at Goodwood and very
steadily-run minor event at York (keen to post): should stay beyond 7f. *P. F. I. Cole*

MAYFLOWER 2 b.f. (Feb 2) Midyan (USA) 124 – Chesnut Tree (USA) 97 73
(Shadeed (USA) 135) [1996 5.2f² 6g⁵ 6.1m³ 7f⁵ Oct 8] leggy, useful-looking filly:
second foal: dam, 1½m winner, daughter of Ribblesdale winner Expansive: fair
form: placed in maidens won by Song of Skye at Newbury and Telemania at
Nottingham: unfavoured by draw in between: should stay 7f: tail flasher: carried
head awkwardly penultimate outing. *I. A. Balding*

MAY KING MAYHEM 3 ch.g. Great Commotion (USA) 123 – Queen Rana- 45
valona (Sure Blade (USA) 130) [1995 –: 7m⁵ 7m 1996 7f 8g⁴ 9f 10d 12m⁶ 13.8g Oct
19] close-coupled gelding: has a round action: only worthwhile form when fourth in
claimer at Leicester in May: best effort at 1m. *Mrs A. L. M. King*

MAYLANE 2 b.c. (May 8) Mtoto 134 – Possessive Dancer 118 (Shareef Dancer 85 p
(USA) 135) [1996 7.1d⁵ 7f² 7d* Oct 28] useful-looking colt: second foal: dam, 6f
winner at 2 yrs, won Italian and Irish Oaks: progressive form: won 18-runner maiden
at Lingfield in October by 7 lengths from Stamp, leading stand-side group, clear
overall 1f out: bred to be suited by middle distances, but races keenly and may prove
best over shorter: open to further improvement. *A. C. Stewart*

MAYPOLE (IRE) 2 ch.g. (Mar 21) Mujtahid (USA) 118 – Dance Festival 101 66 p
(Nureyev (USA) 131) [1996 6s Oct 24] dipped-backed gelding: fourth foal: half-
brother to Irish 3-y-o Matsuri (by Darshaan), 9f winner at 2 yrs, and useful 7.3f and
8.5f winner Allemande (by Nashwan): dam lightly-raced maiden out of half-sister to
Boldboy: 10/1, around 11 lengths ninth of 23 to Za-Im in maiden at Newbury, rear
long way after missing break then late progress under hands and heels: should do
better. *D. R. Loder*

MAY QUEEN MEGAN 3 gr.f. Petorius 117 – Siva (FR) (Bellypha 130) [1995 56
63: 5g³ 6f⁶ 6m³ 1996 6.9s⁶ 6.1d 6g⁴ 6f⁶ 6.1d 7f⁶ 6f² 6m* 6m 6m⁴ Aug 4] leggy filly:
modest handicapper: won at Lingfield in July: stays 6f: acts on firm ground:
blinkered (no improvement) sixth 3-y-o start: has proved wayward and inconsistent.
Mrs A. L. M. King

MAYSIMP (IRE) 3 ch.f. Mac's Imp (USA) 116 – Splendid Yankee (Yankee Gold –
115) [1995 –: 6d 5f⁴ 5.1g⁵ 5f 5g 6s 1996 6.1m 6d³ 6m 5d 6f 6m⁶ 8.1m Aug 16] leggy
filly: unimpressive mover: little form: should stay beyond 6f. *B. P. J. Baugh*

MAZARA (IRE) 2 b.f. (Mar 14) High Estate 127 – Shy Jinks (Shy Groom –
(USA)) [1996 8.1d Sep 28] IR 4,400F, 7,600Y: third foal: dam Irish maiden: 66/1,
slowly away and soon tailed off in maiden at Haydock. *A. G. Foster*

MAZCOBAR 3 ch.c. Mazilier (USA) 107 – Barbary Court (Grundy 137) [1995 84
58: 6d 8g 7g⁴ 1996 8.2m³ 8.1g* 10m 8.2m* 8m* 8.2m⁴ 8.1m² 8.5g² 8m Sep 21]
good-bodied colt: fairly useful handicapper: won at Musselburgh in May and Nottingham and Goodwood in June: mostly good efforts afterwards: stays 8.5f well: acts
on good to firm ground: usually held up (ridden more prominently than usual when
well beaten final start): sent to Hong Kong. *P. J. Makin*

MAZEED (IRE) 3 ch.c. Lycius (USA) 124 – Maraatib (IRE) 93 (Green Desert –
(USA) 127) [1995 95: 6m* 6m* 6.1m² 6g⁶ 1996 6m 7g⁴ 6f³ 7d Aug 24] neat colt: not
a good walker: unable to match his 2-y-o form in 4 races in 1996, finishing last of
16 in handicap final start: stays 6f: acts on good to firm ground: sent to Dubai.
H. Thomson Jones

MAZIL 2 b.g. (Mar 24) Mazilier (USA) 107 – Gymcrak Lovebird 84 (Taufan 56
(USA) 119) [1996 5m⁵ 6m 5m² 6f⁶ 5g⁶ 6g 6s 5g Oct 18] sturdy gelding: has a round
action: third foal: half-brother to 4-y-o 5f and 6f winner Dominelle (by Domynsky):
dam 5f (at 2 yrs) to 1¼m winner: modest maiden: probably better suited by
6f than 5f: effective blinkered or not: sold 3,600 gns Doncaster October Sales.
T. D. Easterby

MAZILLA 4 b.f. Mazilier (USA) 107 – Mo Ceri 63 (Kampala 120) [1995 59d: 59
a8g² a8g* a7g* a7g⁴ a8g² a7g³ 8.2m 8g a12g a8g a9.4g² a9.4g a8.5g 1996 a8g a8g
a11g a11g* a11g* a12g a12g⁶ 10.8f a11g 10m 10d⁵ 8m⁵ 10.8f 10m* 10g⁴ 10.8m*
10f* 10.1g* 10m³ 8.5m⁵ 10m 10d Oct 2] leggy filly: modest performer: well placed
to win 6 races in 1996: won seller and handicap at Southwell in February then selling
handicaps at Nottingham and Warwick and handicaps at Nottingham and Yarmouth
in the summer: disappointing 3 of last 4 starts: stays 11f, probably finds 8.5f on the
sharp side nowadays: acts on fibresand, good to firm and soft ground: often used to
be visored, but tried only on last of final 9 outings at 4 yrs: likely to prove best with
waiting tactics. *A. Streeter*

MAZIRAH 5 b.g. Mazilier (USA) 107 – Barbary Court (Grundy 137) [1995 51: –
a9.4g³ 10m 1996 7d 7.1g 10m a12g 8g Sep 13] tall, useful-looking gelding: poor
form at best since 3 yrs: should stay beyond 1¼m: acts on any turf ground and on
fibresand: blinkered (ran respectably) once as 3-y-o: has joined R. Curtis. *P. J. Makin*

MAZUREK 3 b.c. Sadler's Wells (USA) 132 – Maria Waleska (Filiberto (USA) 74
123) [1995 NR 1996 10m 10s a7g² a8g* Nov 26] IR 100,000Y: workmanlike colt:
closely related to 3 winners by Danzig, notably high-class sprinter Polish Patriot, and

half-brother to 3 winners abroad: dam won Oaks d'Italia and Gran Premio d'Italia: fair form: won handicap at Lingfield in November: should be suited by further than 1m: sold (P. Chapple-Hyam to M. Meagher) 13,000 gns Newmarket December Sales. *P. W. Chapple-Hyam*

MAZZARELLO (IRE) 6 ch.g. Hatim (USA) 121 – Royal Demon (Tarboosh (USA)) [1995 45, a–: 5m a6g 5m* 5g* 6f⁴ 5f 5g a5g 1996 5s 5g 6m³ 5.1g 5m² 5m 5m 6m 5m Aug 7] lengthy, sparely-made gelding: modest handicapper: best effort at 6 yrs when second at Lingfield: finished last in 5 of his other 9 races: effective at 5f and 6f: acts on good to firm ground: best visored: inconsistent. *R. Curtis*   49 d a–

MBULWA 10 ch.g. Be My Guest (USA) 126 – Bundu (FR) 88 (Habitat 134) [1995 60, a–: 7g² 8g 7g 8.3f 11.1m⁵ 10.4m³ 8f* 8f³ 7m² a9.4g 1996 8m 7m³ 8.5m* 10f 8g² 7.9g⁴ 7.9g 8m Sep 14] smallish, sturdy gelding: fair handicapper, who showed his best form at 10 yrs since 1989: 25/1, won 16-runner £14,300 contest at Epsom in June: effective at 7f to 1¼m: has gained all his 8 successes on a sound surface (acts on firm ground), below form all 3 outings on the all-weather: effective blinkered (not tried for some time) or not: often early to post and mulish at stalls: usually races prominently. *R. A. Fahey*   66 a–

MCGILLYCUDDY REEKS (IRE) 5 b.m. Kefaah (USA) 124 – Kilvarnet 78 (Furry Glen 121) [1995 NR 1996 11.1m 11.1g⁶ 12m 8g⁶ 10.1m⁴ 10f⁶ 11.8f³ 11.5m³ 11m³ a12g⁴ Nov 25] poor form nowadays: stays 1½m: probably acts on any going, and on fibresand: often slowly away. *N. Tinkler*   46

MCKELLAR (IRE) 7 b.h. Lomond (USA) 128 – Local Belle (Ballymore 123) [1995 –: 8g⁶ a6g 1996 a6g a7g* a7g³ Mar 9] ex-Irish horse, lightly raced: fair form in handicaps last 2 starts, winning maiden event at Wolverhampton (by 9 lengths) and not beaten far at Southwell 7 days later: sold 650 gns Ascot October Sales and has joined R. T. Juckes: stays 8.5f, clearly effective at 7f: acts on fibresand. *T. D. Barron*   66

MD THOMPSON 4 ch.f. Siberian Express (USA) 125 – Zipperti Do 70 (Precocious 126) [1995 50: 8m 6.9m³ 7m³ a7g³ 9f⁵ 8g⁴ a8.5g³ a7g³ 1996 a13g 7d May 8] sturdy, plain filly: modest maiden handicapper as 3-y-o for S. Williams: tailed off in handicaps at Lingfield (unsuitable trip, for T. Clement) and Ayr in 1996: stays 9f: acts on firm ground and fibresand. *H. Akbary*   –

MDUDU 5 b.h. Mtoto 134 – Golden Pampas 80 (Golden Fleece (USA) 133) [1996 11g* 15g* 12g* 11.5g* 15g* 15g⁵ 11g² 12g* 14s⁶ 12m Nov 10] 3,700Y: third foal: half-brother to winners in Germany (by Precocious) and over hurdles: dam grand-daughter of champion US filly Bayou, same family as Slew o'Gold and Coastal: useful Spanish horse: unraced at 2 yrs, and won only 3 of 13 starts in Spain and France at 3-4 yrs: had a very good season in 1996, winning 6 races, last of them Group 3 event at San Sebastian in August by 1½ lengths from El Ceremonioso: below form afterwards: effective at 11f and stays 15f. *J. Campos, Spain*   108

MEADOW BLUE 3 b.f. Northern State (USA) 91 – Cornflower (USA) (Damascus (USA)) [1995 NR 1996 10g⁶ 10m 8f⁶ 8.1m 12.1m⁶ Sep 23] plain, workmanlike filly: half-sister to a winning pointer: dam won 2 races in USA: no worthwhile form. *Miss L. C. Siddall*   –

MEADOW FOODS 4 ch.g. Handsome Sailor 125 – Stern Lass 79 (Bold Lad (IRE) 133) [1995 NR 1996 a12g Feb 26] second reported foal: half-brother to a winning chaser by Scorpio: dam, 1m winner, stayed 1¼m: pulled up lame only start on flat: dead. *M. W. Easterby*   –

MEANT TO BE 6 b.m. Morston (FR) 125 – Lady Gerardina 82 (Levmoss 133) [1995 84: a14.8g⁴ 11.8g 12m³ 12m³ 16.2d⁴ 16.2s* 1996 18s 16g 16.2m 13.9g 14.6g Oct 25] lengthy mare: fairly useful and consistent handicapper at 5 yrs: long way below form in 1996: effective at 1½m, stays 16.2f: acts on fibresand, and on good to firm and heavy going: blinkered (below form) fourth 4-y-o start. *Lady Herries*   –

ME CHEROKEE 4 br.f. Persian Bold 123 – Siouan 78 (So Blessed 130) [1995 –p: 6g 7.5d 7.5m⁴ 1996 a8g a11g a12g⁴ 12.1d² 13d⁶ 11.1s⁴ 13g³ a12g 13g⁶ Jul 5] leggy filly: poor maiden handicapper: stays 1½m: acts on fibresand and soft ground: races prominently. *C. W. Thornton*   48

MECHILIE 2 b.f. (Apr 24) Belmez (USA) 131 – Tundra Goose 101 (Habitat 134) [1996 6g 8g a7g Nov 22] 2,400Y: stocky filly: seventh foal: closely related to Irish 6f to 1m winner Polar Wind (by El Gran Senor), later successful in UAE, and   –

half-sister to 3 winners, including French 1¼m winner Canadian Shield (by Slip Anchor): dam 6f (at 2 yrs) and 1m winner: soundly beaten in maiden auction and sellers. *J. W. Payne*

MEDAALY 2 gr.c. (Mar 25) Highest Honor (FR) 124 – Dance of Leaves 114 (Sadler's Wells (USA) 132) [1996 7.1g² 7m* 8.1g* 8g⁵ 8g* Oct 26]

'It is seldom indeed that one parts on good terms,' wrote Marcel Proust, 'because if one were on good terms one would not part.' With not much pretence in the parting of ways between Henry Cecil and Sheikh Mohammed in October 1995, the scene was set for a gripping trainers' championship in the latest season, a resurgent Cecil battling it out with Sheikh Mohammed's man Saeed bin Suroor. The trainers' championship is not one that normally generates much excitement, the racing public tending to be distinctly underwhelmed by the question of which man has won the most hundreds of thousands, but the 1996 running was definitely an exception. Nowadays, the championship, sanctioned by the BHB, is based on win and place prize money, and although provocative Cecil-versus-Sheikh headlines had been appearing almost as soon as the turf season got underway, the race did not really gain a full head of steam until Ascot on September 28th when Dettori donned the royal blue of Godolphin for four of his seven-out-of-seven. Having begun the day some £107,000 ahead of bin Suroor, Cecil ended it £125,000 behind, the main contributor to this dramatic turnaround being Mark of Esteem who beat Cecil's Bosra Sham into second in the Queen Elizabeth II Stakes. It was nip and tuck again over the next two days before bin Suroor settled into a clear lead for the following eighteen, but Bosra Sham took Cecil about £50,000 up when overturning Halling in the Champion Stakes, both trainers passing the £1,800,000 mark in the process. Neither camp tried to disguise how much they wanted to win the title.

It turned out, however, that the most decisive move in the trainers' championship made on October 19th was not after all Bosra Sham's win at Newmarket. Less spectacularly, that day also saw the £15,000 supplementary entry stage to Britain's final pattern race, the £75,000-added Racing Post Trophy at Doncaster one week later. Six original entries were thus joined by three extra names, the Luca Cumani-trained Poteen and the Saeed bin Suroor pair Medaaly and Asas. Henry Cecil had won the race no fewer than ten times before and he relied on Besiege, a brother to the 1992 winner Armiger. The Newmarket maiden winner Asas was out of a half-sister to Erhaab, and Medaaly was a half-brother to Charnwood Forest. Medaaly had a lot more experience than his stable-companion, having easily won a maiden at Doncaster and a minor event at Sandown (from Cecil's Imperial President) on two of his four starts, but had also seemingly had his limitations exposed when fifth of eight in the Royal Lodge at Ascot; he had finished about three and three quarter lengths behind winner Benny The Dip that day and one and three quarters lengths behind third-placed Besiege. In the Racing Post, therefore, Medaaly was sent off a 14/1-chance with Benny The Dip heavily backed at 11/10 and Besiege at 5/1, 13/2-shot Asas being preferred as well. The protagonists in the trainers' championship all had their ears pinned to commentaries from the other side of the Atlantic, where they were saddling runners for the Breeders' Cup, and they listened to the championship take its final twist. In complete contrast to the Royal Lodge, Medaaly had the edge over Benny The Dip and Besiege as soon as he made his move halfway up the straight. Asas was tailing off, but, from among the backmarkers, Poteen was making impressive headway on the outside. That looked very much like the winning move when Poteen took the lead a furlong out, but in the last seventy yards it was suddenly Medaaly who was going on the stronger and the Godolphin colt got home in front by half a length. With Henry Cecil unable to bridge the gap in what remained of the turf season and neither trainer deciding to spice up our winter fare on the all-weather, Saeed bin Suroor had won the trainers' championship. He ended the year with win and place earnings in Britain of £1,962,598, Henry Cecil

Racing Post Trophy, Doncaster—the grey Medaaly leaves his Royal Lodge running behind;
Poteen (left) is a good second ahead of Benny The Dip and Besiege

with £1,935,507, the figures those provided by the *Racing Post* which were
recognised by the BHB.

Saeed bin Suroor will have a numerically stronger team in 1997—in
the latest season he had forty-nine runners compared to Henry Cecil's one
hundred and sixteen—and must be short odds to repeat his championship
win. 1996 demonstrated, however, that an increased number of choicely-bred
two-year-olds is, of course, less a guarantee of success than the promising
three-year-olds: not counting their acquisition Moonlight Paradise, eight of bin
Suroor's fourteen two-year-old runners ran more than once but only Medaaly
and the twice-raced maiden Siyadah made any significant improvement. A
good-bodied, useful-looking colt, Medaaly should train on and, at the time of
writing, is the shortest-priced Godolphin representative in the Two Thousand
Guineas. He has 8 lb to find on Bahhare and Revoque by our reckoning. The
Godolphin team have wrought a great deal more improvement than that in
previous charges, of course, but, from the Racing Post field, we were frankly
more impressed with the prospects of Poteen.

		Kenmare	Kalamoun
	Highest Honor (FR)	(gr 1975)	Belle of Ireland
	(gr 1983)	High River	Riverman
Medaaly		(b 1978)	Hairbrush
(gr.c. Mar 25, 1994)		Sadler's Wells	Northern Dancer
	Dance of Leaves	(b 1981)	Fairy Bridge
	(b 1987)	Fall Aspen	Pretense
		(ch 1976)	Change Water

Medaaly's races so far leave no doubt that he will stay at least a mile
and a quarter. The Derby trip, though, is not clear cut, as his sire Highest Honor
was never tried beyond ten and a half furlongs, dam Dance of Leaves did not
race at all and her only previous foal, Charnwood Forest, never raced beyond a
mile. Highest Honor's best achievement on the racecourse came when winning
the nine-furlong Prix d'Ispahan but he is a stronger stamina influence than
Charnwood Forest's sire Warning. The top sire in France in 1995 by individual
winners, races won and money won, and again in 1996 in the first two of those
categories, Highest Honor had his best representative to date there in 1996 in
the Group 3 mile-and-a-quarter winner Baroud d'Honneur and a second smart
colt in Britain in the middle-distance performer Medaille Militaire. He stood at
100,000 francs in 1996. Medaaly is from an incredibly successful family on the
dam's side because Dance of Leaves is a daughter of Fall Aspen. That means

596

that Dance of Leaves is a sister to the Grand Prix de Paris winner Fort Wood; a close relation to July Cup winner Hamas, Grade 1 winner Northern Aspen and Group 2 winner Colorado Dancer; and a half-sister to triple Grade 1 winner Timber Country, Prix d'Astarte winner Elle Seule, Goodwood Cup winner Mazzacano and the ill-fated 1996 Kentucky Derby third Prince of Thieves. Dance of Leaves is the only one of Fall Aspen's first eleven foals who is not a winner, and then comes a 1995 colt by Danzig. The worst of Fall Aspen's winners is Sheroog, dam of Shareef Kabeer who won the March Stakes for Godolphin in 1996. This family is bound to be mentioned many more times in *Racehorses* annuals; the next one of Dance of Leaves's foals to bid for honours will be a 1995 filly by Rainbow Quest. *Saeed bin Suroor*

MEDAILLE MILITAIRE 4 gr.c. Highest Honor (FR) 124 – Lovely Noor (USA) (Fappiano (USA)) [1995 103: 8g* 8m* 7.6m6 10.4m* 12d5 1996 10g 10g 10.4f2 10d 10.1g* 12s* Nov 9] tall, leggy colt: smart performer: off course 5 months in the summer after disappointing on 2 of first 3 starts: won minor event at Yarmouth and 9-runner listed race at Doncaster (by ¾ length from Eva Luna, cruised up 3f out, needed riding out inside last) late in year: stays 1½m: acts on firm ground and soft: equipped with rope halter: normally held up: stays in training. *J. L. Dunlop* — 112

MEDFEE 3 b.f. Alzao (USA) 117 – Liaison (USA) (Blushing Groom (FR) 131) [1995 NR 1996 8m4 10.2d3 8m* Oct 23] neat, attractive filly: third foal: half-sister to winning 4-y-o middle-distance stayer Cross Talk (by Darshaan): dam, French 1¼m winner, sister to Two Timing, family of Chief's Crown and Winning Colors: best effort to win maiden at Yarmouth in October, quickening on over 1f out: possibly better at 1m than 1¼m: sold 19,000 gns Newmarket December Sales. *R. Charlton* — 79

MEDIA EXPRESS 4 b.g. Sayf El Arab (USA) 127 – Far Claim (USA) 35 (Far North (CAN) 120) [1995 71: 6.9d 6.1g3 6.1g* 6g 6d 6m6 7m a6g 8.1d* 1996 a8g4 a8g 10g 10g 7d 7f 8f 11.5m Oct 23] small, leggy gelding: modest performer at best: well below form after reappearance at 4 yrs, leaving M. Brittain after fifth start: subsequently gelded and off course 4 months, tailed off all 3 starts on return: stays 1m (not discredited at 1¼m): acts on any ground. *P. S. Felgate* — 57 d

MEDIA MESSENGER 7 b.g. Hadeer 118 – Willow Court (USA) (Little Current (USA)) [1995 –: a8g a12g a12g 1996 a8g a11g a12g Jan 25] close-coupled gelding: no form since 1994. *N. P. Littmoden* — –

MEDIATE (IRE) 4 b.g. Thatching 131 – Unheard Melody (Lomond (USA) 128) [1995 70§: a7g4 a7g3 8.3m a7g* 8.5m5 7g2 6f6 8m a7g3 a8.5g 1996 a8g a8g5 8f 8m — § / a64 §

Co-Operative Bank Serlby Stakes, Doncaster—
Medaille Militaire (grey) impresses against the tenacious Eva Luna

8.3m 10g 8m⁴ 7m a8g⁴ a10g² Dec 26] compact gelding: has a quick action: only modest at 4 yrs, better on all-weather: seems to stay 1¼m: acts on equitrack and good to firm ground, possibly unsuited by a soft surface: effective blinkered or not: inconsistent, and not one to rely on. *A. Hide*

MEDIEVAL LADY   3 ch.f. Efisio 120 – Ritsurin 79 (Mount Hagen (FR) 127)   89
[1995 78p: 7g⁵ 7f² 1996 7m* 8f³ 8d Oct 12] sturdy filly: carries condition: fairly useful performer: won 17-runner maiden at Newbury in June: best effort when under a length third to Dawna in listed rated stakes at Ascot 9 days later (final start for Lady Herries): stays 1m: acts on firm ground, not discredited on dead: keenly to post in 1996. *I. A. Balding*

MEDLAND (IRE)   6 ch.g. Imperial Frontier (USA) 112 – Miami Dancer 55   –
(Miami Springs 121) [1995 –, a54: a11g⁶ a10g* a10g³ a7g a9.4g⁵ a9.4g³ a8g⁴ a8.5g   a49
1996 a8.5g² a10g a8g a8g⁴ a8g a10g Dec 20] stocky gelding: poor mover: poor performer: stays 1¼m: acts on firm ground (no form on a soft surface), better on all-weather: inconsistent. *B. J. McMath*

MEGAN CAREW   2 ch.f. (Mar 30) Gunner B 126 – Molly Carew (Jimmy   –
Reppin 131) [1996 5.9f 8.1m 7f Sep 27] unfurnished filly: second reported foal: dam strong-pulling jumper: well beaten in maiden events. *D. Moffatt*

MEGA TID   4 b.g. Old Vic 136 – Dunoof 92 (Shirley Heights 130) [1995 45,   –
a50: a10g* 8g 11.9m 11.6m 10m 10g a9.4g⁴ a10g³ 9m a8.5g⁵ 10m³ a16g 1996 a12g a11g 12m 11.5f a10g Dec 20] leggy gelding: modest performer at 3 yrs, no form in handicaps in 1996: should stay beyond 1¼m: acts on good to firm ground and all-weather surfaces: occasionally bandaged: one to treat with caution. *B. A. Pearce*

MEGHDOOT   4 b.f. Celestial Storm (USA) 132 – Greenhills Joy 90 (Radetzky   69
123) [1995 75: 10m⁴ 10m² 10m² 10d⁴ 12g* 12.1s 1996 12m 10g 12g³ May 25] compact, workmanlike filly: unimpressive mover: fair handicapper: best effort at 4 yrs when third at Doncaster, setting false pace: stays 1½m well: acts on good to firm and soft ground, below form only run on equitrack. *H. J. Collingridge*

MEG'S MEMORY (IRE)   3 b.f. Superlative 118 – Meanz Beanz (High Top   59
131) [1995 53: 5.7h² 5.1h² 6g 6g 6.9g 1996 10.2g* 11.6m 10.1f⁵ 8m 10.2f⁵ 10.2m⁶ 17.2m³ 16.4m a16g Aug 29] rather leggy filly: modest handicapper: 40/1, won at Bath in April: sold (John Berry to A. Streeter) 2,500 gns Doncaster September Sales: stays 17.2f: has raced only on a sound surface on turf: blinkered (below form) last 2 starts as 2-y-o: inconsistent. *John Berry*

MELBOURNE PRINCESS   2 ch.f. (Feb 2) Primo Dominie 121 – Lurking 69   56
(Formidable (USA) 125) [1996 5g 5g³ 5m 5f⁶ 5m⁴ 5m² 5m a5g³ a5g a5g² Dec 20]   a52
11,000Y: smallish filly: third foal: half-sister to 3-y-o 5f (at 2 yrs) to 7f winner Whittle Rock (by Rock City): dam 6f winner who stayed 7f: modest form: retained by trainer 500 gns Doncaster November Sales: raced only at 5f: acts on equitrack, yet to race on a soft surface: visored (creditable effort) final start. *R. M. Whitaker*

MELDORF   3 ch.c. Lycius (USA) 124 – Melanoura (Imperial Fling (USA) 116)   76 +
[1995 93p: 6d* 6f 1996 a8g³ 8.1g Apr 27] sturdy colt: fairly useful form at 2 yrs: below form both outings in 1996, beaten at 3/1 on in Lingfield minor event and not knocked about in £12,700 handicap at Sandown nearly 3 months later: may prove best short of 1m. *D. R. Loder*

MELIKSAH (IRE)   2 ch.c. (Jan 19) Thatching 131 – Lady of Shalott 61 (Kings   97
Lake (USA) 133) [1996 5m* 5f 6g⁵ 5s⁵ 5.2m* 5m* 5d Oct 12] 11,500F, 6,500Y: robust, lengthy colt: unimpressive mover: fifth foal: half-brother to 7f winner Knight of Shalot and 5-y-o 1m seller winner Irrepressible (both by Don't Forget Me): dam maiden who stayed 1m, half-sister to Head For Heights: useful performer: won maiden auction at Redcar in May and nurseries at Newbury and Newmarket (beat Hattab by 1½ lengths, pair clear) in the autumn: well below form on softish going in Cornwallis Stakes at Ascot on final start: ideally suited by 5f and a sound surface: races prominently. *M. Bell*

MELLABY (USA)   8 ch.g. Nureyev (USA) 131 – Hitting Irish (USA) (Irish Ruler   76 +
(USA)) [1995 NR 1996 11.9m⁵ Jun 15] rangy, quite attractive gelding: lightly raced since his 4-y-o days (now used as a lead horse and acted as a pacemaker in 1992 and

1993): fifth of 14 in lady amateurs event at York on return, showing only fair form: stays 1½m: acts on firm ground and has won on soft. *M. R. Stoute*

MELLORS (IRE)   3 b.c. Common Grounds 118 – Simply Beautiful (IRE) 67
(Simply Great (FR) 122) [1995 64: 5.1m⁵ 5m³ 6m 8g⁴ 1996 8.2g 7m⁴ 7.5g³ 6g* 6f a6g 6f² 6f² 5.3f² 7.1s⁶ Oct 22] well-made colt: has a round action: fair performer: favourite, won maiden at Catterick later in June: easily best efforts afterwards when second at Brighton 3 times: sold to join M. J. Heaton-Ellis 7,000 gns Newmarket Autumn Sales: best form at sprint distances: acts on firm ground (ran poorly only outing on soft): blinkered (ran creditably) final 2-y-o start: takes keen hold, and often makes running. *J. A. R. Toller*

MELLOTTIE   11 b. or br.g. Meldrum 112 – Lottie Lehmann 69 (Goldhill 125) 91
[1995 98: 8g 8g⁶ 7.9g 9.2f² 8m 8m⁵ 8f* 9.9m* 10m* 9g 10.4m* 1996 10.3g⁴ 10m 8.3g² 10.5m³ 8s² 8.9g² 10m* Sep 26] round-barrelled gelding: carries plenty of condition: gained his most valuable win in 1991 Cambridgeshire (ran well in 5 consecutive runnings of that race), and was a smart performer (rated 115) at his best at 8 yrs: still capable of fairly useful form in 1996 and won his 16th race on flat when beating Skillington a neck in rated stakes at Pontefract in September, improving from rear to lead near post in typical fashion: effective at 1m to 1¼m: fair efforts on dead ground, but went particularly well on a sound surface: was normally held up (had a fine turn of foot at his best): needed an end-to-end gallop in recent years: tough: a great credit to his stable: has reportedly been retired. *Mrs M. Reveley*

MELLOW MASTER   3 b.g. Royal Academy (USA) 130 – Upward Trend 112 62
(Salmon Leap (USA) 131) [1995 NR 1996 6m³ 6m 7g 8.1d Jun 7] leggy, rather unfurnished gelding: second foal: dam Irish 1m/1¼m performer: modest maiden: probably stays 1m: acts on good to firm and dead ground: sweating final start: refused to enter stalls in June: has been gelded. *N. J. H. Walker*

MELLWOOD (IRE)   2 b.c. (Mar 29) Maledetto (IRE) 103 – Traminer (Status –
Seeker) [1996 6g 6m a7g 8g Nov 2] IR 4,500Y: good-bodied colt: closely related to 3 winners by Double Schwartz, including Irish 3-y-o Double Seeker, 7.8f winner at 2 yrs, and half-brother to several winners here and abroad, including Irish 1½m winner True Vintage (by Horage): dam Italian 5f to 7.5f winner: behind in varied events, including sellers. *M. H. Tompkins*

MELODICA   2 b.f. (Feb 20) Machiavellian (USA) 123 – Melodist (USA) 118 67 p
(The Minstrel (CAN) 135) [1996 7d³ Oct 28] fifth foal: half-sister to useful Irish 3-y-o 1½m winner Song of The Sword (by Kris): dam Italian Oaks winner and Irish Oaks dead-heater: 10/1 (from 6/1), 5¾ lengths third of 10 to Apache Star in maiden at Lingfield, green and soon pushed along then keeping on: likely to stay beyond 1m: looks sure to improve. *M. R. Stoute*

MELODY WHEEL   4 b.f. Merdon Melody 98 – Spare Wheel 67 (Track Spare –
125) [1995 60p: 7m⁵ 1996 a6g⁴ 8d Apr 13] angular filly: well held in claimers at 3 yrs. *A. Hide*

MELOMANIA (USA)   4 b.c. Shadeed (USA) 135 – Medley of Song (USA) –
(Secretariat (USA)) [1995 NR 1996 8.1d⁴ 10m 14g 10m a8.5g Sep 7] $35,000Y: fourth reported foal: half-brother to minor winner in USA by Saratoga Six: dam unraced half-sister to Grade 3 1m winner Tell Me All: in training with J. Dunlop at 2 yrs and 3 yrs, but never ran: sold 28,000 gns Ascot May (1996) Sales: no worthwhile form, sold to join S. R. Bowring 500 gns Doncaster October Sales: has had tongue tied. *T. J. Naughton*

MELOS   3 b.f. Emarati (USA) 74 – Double Stretch (Double-U-Jay 120) [1995 –: –
5m a6g⁶ 5m⁵ a5g 1996 8.2g Apr 8] unfurnished filly: no worthwhile form. *Ronald Thompson*

MELS BABY (IRE)   3 br.g. Contract Law (USA) 108 – Launch The Raft (Home 73
Guard (USA) 129) [1995 53: 5m 5m 6g⁴ 7m⁶ 7f⁵ 6m 7.5d 7f 6f⁶ 1996 a7g² 8.1g⁶ a54
6.1g⁴ a7g 7g² 7g² 5.9f⁶ 8f² 7s² 8.5m² 9f³ 10.4g⁵ 8f* 8m* 8s* a9.4g⁶ Dec 7] tall, leggy, light-bodied gelding: fair handicapper: in fine form at end of turf season, winning at Redcar (amateurs, first success), Pontefract, and Doncaster (ladies): needs at least 7f nowadays and stays 10.4f: acts on firm and soft ground and fibresand: tried blinkered/visored, at least as effective without: consistent. *J. L. Eyre*

MELTEMISON 3 b.g. Charmer 123 – Salchow 116 (Niniski (USA) 125) [1995 72
NR 1996 a10g² a12g³ a11g⁵ 10g 10m³ 11m 11.5f* 11.8f Oct 14] neat gelding: fifth
foal: half-brother to 7.5f winner Kalko (by Kalaglow) and 1m winner Carousella (by
Rousillon): dam won at 7f (at 2 yrs) and stayed 14.6f: fair performer: won apprentice
handicap at Lingfield in June: sold out of C. Brittain's stable 15,000 gns Newmarket
July Sales and gelded: off course 3½ months before running poorly in handicap at
Leicester: stays 1½m: acts on all-weather and firm ground: flashed tail fifth outing:
sweating (below form) sixth start. *M. D. Hammond*

MELT THE CLOUDS (CAN) 3 ch.g. Diesis 133 – Population (General 78
Assembly (USA)) [1995 73p: 7m 1996 8.5m² 8f⁴ 7.5m⁴ 7m⁵ 8m² 7f² 8.3d⁴ 10.4g⁵
10m⁵ 10.5s² 10.1m Oct 23] quite attractive gelding: fair maiden: sold 25,000 gns
Newmarket Autumn Sales: stays 1¼m: acts on firm ground and soft: usually races
prominently/leads: consistent. *P. W. Harris*

MEMBERS WELCOME (IRE) 3 b.g. Eve's Error 113 – Manuale Del Utente 54
(Montekin 125) [1995 54+: 5.1m 5.1f⁶ 5.1m³ 6.1m⁶ 5g 6g 6.1s 1996 6.1g² 5.1g⁴ 6g⁴
7.1g⁴ 6g 5f⁵ 5m 5.7m⁴ 6f 6m 6m 6m Oct 23] lengthy, angular gelding: modest
maiden: best form at up to 6f: acts on firm ground: visored nowadays. *J. M. Bradley*

MEMORISE (USA) 2 b.c. (Feb 8) Lyphard (USA) 132 – Shirley Valentine 104 64 p
(Shirley Heights 130) [1996 7m⁶ Oct 28] rather leggy, angular colt: first foal: dam,
1½m winner, sister to Deploy and half-sister to Warning, Commander In Chief and
Dushyantor: 6/4 on, around 5 lengths sixth of 10 to Ortelius in steadily-run maiden at
Leicester, chasing pace but pushed along 2f out then wandering and eased slightly
inside last: very green in preliminaries: will do better in time. *H. R. A. Cecil*

MEMORY'S MUSIC 4 b.c. Dance of Life (USA) – Sheer Luck 72 (Shergar –
140) [1995 50: 10m 7f⁶ a10g⁴ 10m⁶ a8.5g 7.1g 1996 12s 12s Nov 11] sturdy colt:
poor maiden handicapper: no promise in 1996: may well prove suited by further than
1¼m: visored (well below form) final 3-y-o start. *M. Madgwick*

MEMPHIS BEAU (IRE) 3 ch.g. Ballad Rock 122 – Texly (FR) (Lyphard 64
(USA) 132) [1995 NR 1996 7m 7.9m⁶ 8m⁶ 6f³ 5.3f* 6m 8g⁴ 7.1s Oct 22] IR 15,500Y:
workmanlike gelding: has a quick action: half-brother to several winners here and
abroad, including useful 1984 2-y-o sprinter Cameroun (by African Sky): dam,
granddaugher of brilliantly speedy Texana, showed no form in France: modest
performer: back in trip, made all to win 5-runner maiden handicap at Brighton in
August: sold 5,000 gns Newmarket Autumn Sales: probably suited by sprint
distances: acts on firm ground, finished last only outing on soft: blinkered since third
3-y-o start. *J. A. R. Toller*

MENAS GOLD 4 b.f. Heights of Gold – Tolomena 61 (Tolomeo 127) [1995 88: 85 d
8m 8m 8.5m⁴ 8f⁵ 9f 1996 10g⁶ 10d⁶ 10m 8d 9g 10m Oct 1] small filly: fairly
useful handicapper at best: not so good as at 3 yrs, best effort at Kempton on
reappearance: stays 1¼m: acts on firm and dead ground: held up nowadays:
inconsistent. *S. Dow*

MENDOZA 2 b.g. (Apr 16) Rambo Dancer (CAN) 107 – Red Poppy (IRE) 58 –
(Coquelin (USA) 121) [1996 6m 7f 8.5m⁵ 8f Oct 8] 7,000Y, 13,000 2-y-o: medium-
sized, useful-looking gelding: first foal: dam, maiden, stayed 7f: behind in varied
maiden events and a nursery. *D. J. G. Murray Smith*

MENGAAB (USA) 2 b.c. (Apr 24) Silver Hawk (USA) 123 – Cherie's Hope 90 p
(USA) (Flying Paster (USA)) [1996 7g³ Sep 4] $250,000Y: smallish, good-bodied
colt: seventh foal: brother to smart 1992 2-y-o 5f and 6f winner Silver Wizard, since
Grade 2 winner over 9f in USA, closely related to 3-y-o Dashing Invader (by Pirate
Army) and half-brother to 2 winners in USA: dam unraced: 12/1, slow-starting
length third of 11, finishing to good effect having been in rear much of way, to
Fantastic Fellow in maiden at York: wore bandages behind: had rope halter and
blanket for stalls entry: sure to improve, and win a race. *J. H. M. Gosden*

MENOO HAL BATAL (USA) 3 b.c. Gone West (USA) – Bank On Love 86
(USA) (Gallant Romeo (USA)) [1995 75p: 7f⁵ 1996 7g⁴ 7d³ 7.6g 7.1d³ 7m³ 8m²
a9.4g² 9m* Aug 25] leggy colt: fairly useful colt: odds on, readily won slowly-run
6-runner maiden at Redcar in August: placed several times previously, including in
handicaps: stays 9.4f: acts on good to firm and dead ground and on fibresand: hung
right and carried head awkwardly first 3-y-o start: has worn net muzzle to start:

withdrawn after rearing and going down in stalls seventh intended start at 3 yrs: consistent: sent to UAE. *M. R. Stoute*

MENOO WHO (IRE) 4 ch.g. Keen 116 – Flying Anna (Roan Rocket 128) [1995 8s 9g⁶ 10m³ 10m² 10f⁴ 12f² 10m⁵ 12m⁶ 1996 14d Sep 28] big gelding: half-brother to several winners, most at middle distances: dam Irish 5f winner: fair Irish maiden (rated 72) at 3 yrs for C. Collins: ran twice for D. Nicholson over hurdles before sold 8,400 gns Doncaster May Sales: no promise on return to flat: stays 1½m: acts on firm ground. *S. Gollings* —

MENTALASANYTHIN 7 b.g. Ballacashtal (CAN) – Lafrowda 71 (Crimson Beau 124) [1995 72: a9.4g a16.2g a8g* a8g⁴ a12g² a12g⁶ a12g³ 12g⁵ 10.3g 13g² 11.1g³ 13g² 13g² 10g² 10.5d* 13f* 11.1m⁴ 11.1f² 10.9g³ 11.9m² 10.9g³ 12.1g⁵ 1996 a12g² a11g⁶ a12g* a12g² a12g 12g 13.8s 12.1d² 10m 13m² 13m² 12.1f* 10.3m⁴ 10.9m 13.1m⁴ 12.1d 11.9v 10m⁴ 10f Nov 5] sturdy gelding: fair handicapper, trained in 1996 until after eighth start by A. Bailey: won at Southwell in February and Hamilton in August: stays 13f (soundly beaten over 2m): acts on the all-weather and any turf going: has run well for claimer. *D. Haydn Jones* 73 a81

MENTAL PRESSURE 3 ch.g. Polar Falcon (USA) 126 – Hysterical 68 (High Top 131) [1995 75p: 7g 8g³ 1996 12g⁶ 12.3g² 12f³ 14.1f² 12.3m² 14f² 13.9m³ Aug 20] useful-looking gelding: fairly useful maiden handicapper: best form when placed in rated stakes at Goodwood and York last 2 starts: better at 1¾m than shorter: acts on firm going, yet to race on a soft surface: often pulls hard: usually races prominently nowadays: sure to win a race. *Mrs M. Reveley* 91

MERANTI 3 b.g. Puissance 110 – Sorrowful (Moorestyle 137) [1995 67: 5g 5g⁶ 5m⁴ 5m 6m⁴ 6g⁴ 6s⁵ a8g 1996 6.1d⁵ 6m² 6m⁴ 7m 6f⁴ 6g 7g 6f Sep 23] leggy gelding: modest handicapper: trained by S. Dow until after penultimate outing: stays 6f: very best efforts on a sound surface. *J. M. Bradley* 59

MERCILESS COP 2 ch.c. (Apr 18) Efisio 120 – Naturally Bold (Bold Lad (IRE) 133) [1996 6s 5g³ 6g 7f 7.3m⁵ 8m⁴ 7m* 7d³ 7.3s⁴ a7g⁴ a6g⁵ Dec 13] 12,000Y: heavy-topped colt: carries condition: sixth foal: half-brother to a winner abroad by Prince Sabo: dam unraced: fair performer: won nursery at Lingfield in October: creditable efforts most starts afterwards: seems best at around 7f: acts on good to firm and soft ground and the all-weather: blinkered last 7 starts. *B. J. Meehan* 68

MERCURY (IRE) 3 b.g. Contract Law (USA) 108 – Monrovia (FR) (Dancer's Image (USA)) [1995 NR 1996 7g a8g* 8.5m a9.4g Jul 15] IR 3,500F, 3,200Y: strong, lengthy gelding: eighth foal: half-brother to Italian 1m winner Secret Immage (both by Classic Secret) and 1988 Irish 2-y-o 6f winner God's Country (by Burslem): dam placed in 1m claimer in France: won median auction maiden at Southwell in June by 12 lengths: failed by long way to reproduce that form in handicaps: stays 1m: acts on fibresand. *J. A. Glover* — a72

MERIBEL (IRE) 3 b.f. Nashwan (USA) 135 – Dark Lomond 122 (Lomond (USA) 128) [1995 65p: 7.1s³ 1996 11.5f⁴ 11.9d⁵ May 24] lengthy, angular filly: good mover: burly and green, 9¼ lengths last of 4 to Lady Carla in listed race at Lingfield on reappearance, outpaced 5f out: tailed off in maiden at Haydock 13 days later, never on bridle: should stay 1½m+. *P. W. Chapple-Hyam* —

MERIT (IRE) 4 b.c. Rainbow Quest (USA) 134 – Fur Hat (Habitat 134) [1995 74p: 8g 8m⁶ 11.8g 9.7g a12g* 15.1s* 16.5m* 1996 18.7g* 20f⁶ Jun 18] rangy colt: 88

Tote Chester Cup—Merit is a wide-margin winner, receiving 28 lb from Daraydan (left)

progressive handicapper: won Tote Chester Cup in May by 6 lengths from Daraydan, forging away in straight: outstanding in appearance and best form when 2¾ lengths sixth of 26 to Southern Power in Ascot Stakes at Royal Ascot, tracking pace, cruising turning for home then hanging left and unable to quicken: suited by a test of stamina: acts on firm and soft ground, and equitrack: consistent. *P. F. I. Cole*

MERLIN'S HONOUR 3 ch.f. Crowning Honors (CAN) – Miss Merlin 79 – (Manacle 123) [1995 32: 5m 5g a6g² 7.1g 7f 1996 a7g a10g Jan 20] leggy filly: poor maiden: should stay 7f: best efforts on the all-weather: sometimes slowly away: sent to Bahrain. *John Berry*

MERRIE LE BOW 4 b.f. Merdon Melody 98 – Arch Sculptress 85 (Arch 62 Sculptor 123) [1995 44, a55: a5g² a6g³ a6g³ a6g³ a5g 7g⁶ 8m 7m³ 6m⁴ 5.2g 7g⁴ 7m⁵ a– 7f 1996 7g a7g 6.1m³ a5g 6.1m⁶ 6f* 6m⁵ 6f³ 6m⁶ 7g 6m 6f⁴ 6m² 5g 6.1m* 6m² 6.1m 6d Oct 21] lengthy filly: modest handicapper: won at Lingfield in June and Nottingham in September: pulled up final start: stayed 7f: acted on firm ground and all-weather: tried visored: often apprentice ridden: dead. *Pat Mitchell*

MERRILY 3 gr.f. Sharrood (USA) 124 – Babycham Sparkle 80 (So Blessed 130) 73 d [1995 48: 6m⁵ 1996 6m⁵ 6m³ 6f³ 6m 5g² 6d 6m Oct 8] leggy, sparely-made filly: fluent mover: fair maiden at best: keen sort, and probably a sprinter: tends to be sweating and edgy: inconsistent. *Miss S. E. Hall*

MERRYHILL MARINER 2 ch.g. (Apr 7) Superlative 118 – Merryhill Maid – (IRE) 71 (M Double M (USA)) [1996 5m 6d a7g Sep 9] plain gelding: shows knee action: first foal: dam sprinter: little form. *J. L. Harris*

MERSEY BEAT 2 ch.c. (Apr 21) Rock Hopper 124 – Handy Dancer 87 (Green 76 p God 128) [1996 a10g* Nov 26] half-brother to several winners, including fairly useful 4-y-o 6f (at 2 yrs) to 9f winner Hardy Dancer (by Pharly), smart middle-distance performer Karinga Bay (by Ardross) and useful middle-distance stayer Roll A Dollar (by Spin of A Coin): dam 1¼m winner: 9/1, won 10-runner median auction maiden at Lingfield, soon ridden after slow start and running wide first turn but keeping on well to lead inside last 1f: will stay 1½m: should win more races. *G. L. Moore*

MESHHED (USA) 2 ch.f. (Mar 15) Gulch (USA) – Umniyatee 104 (Green 96 p Desert (USA) 127) [1996 6m² 7m* Oct 17] big, good-topped filly: has plenty of scope: second foal: closely related to useful 3-y-o 7f (at 2 yrs) and 1m winner Jarah (by Forty Niner): dam (winner at 7f and 1m) daughter of 1000 Guineas and Oaks winner Midway Lady: withdrawn from minor event at Newbury in September after kicking out and injuring jockey: 1½ lengths second of 13 to Elegant Warning in maiden at Newmarket following month: odds on, easy winner of 7-runner maiden at Redcar 12 days later by 3½ lengths from Nawasib, leading 3f out: will stay further than 7f: mounted in saddling boxes both starts having got upset again in paddock at Newmarket: should improve again: wintering in Dubai. *B. Hanbury*

MESSALINA (IRE) 3 b.f. Un Desperado (FR) 125 – Seven Hills (FR) 72 – (Reform 132) [1995 NR 1996 7m⁶ 8m Jun 29] fourth foal: half-sister to a winner abroad by Satco: dam 13.8f and 1¾m winner who stayed 2¼m: has shown little in maidens: refused to enter stalls for seller final intended outing. *B. Mactaggart*

METAL BADGE (IRE) 3 b.g. Doyoun 124 – Sharaya (USA) 123 (Youth (USA) – 135) [1995 NR 1996 a11g a9.4g Mar 16] IR 12,500Y: half-brother to 2 winners in Ireland, including fairly useful Sharadiya (9.6f, by Akarad): dam, French 1m to 1½m winner, half-sister to very useful French middle-distance filly Sharaniya: tailed off in maidens on all-weather, virtually pulled up on second occasion: has been gelded. *M. Johnston*

METAL BOYS 9 b.g. Krayyan 117 – Idle Gossip (Runnett 125) [1995 67: 5m 5g 58 5g 5m³ 5m 5g 5g 5m 5m³ 5m 5m 1996 5m 5g 5g² 5f⁴ 5f 5m 5m⁶ 5g Aug 30] sturdy gelding: poor mover: only modest handicapper at 9 yrs: best at 5f: acts on any ground: has won for apprentice: usually races prominently: inconsistent. *Miss L. C. Siddall*

MEZAAN (IRE) 4 ch.c. Royal Academy (USA) 130 – Arctic Heroine (USA) 99 (Arctic Tern (USA) 126) [1995 98: 10m⁵ 8m* 8.1g⁴ 10.4m⁵ 11.9g* 12d 1996 12m⁴ May 5] rangy colt: good mover: useful handicapper: encouraging fourth at Newmarket on reappearance: sold 10,000 gns Newmarket Autumn Sales: suited by at least 1½m: acts on good to firm ground and dead: sent to Saudi Arabia. *M. R. Stoute*

MEZNH (IRE) 3 ch.f. Mujtahid (USA) 118 – Johara (USA) 92 (Exclusive Native (USA)) [1995 NR 1996 7f^5 7.1d^2 7.9g 7.1d Sep 28] tall, sparely-made filly: half-sister to 3 winners, including Gold Cup winner Ashal (by Touching Wood): dam won over 6f on debut at 2 yrs: fair maiden: easily best effort when neck second to Kerry Ring at Sandown: behind afterwards: bred to stay further than 7f but would have needed to have settled to have done so: visits Salse. *H. Thomson Jones* 78

MEZZANOTTE (IRE) 3 b.c. Midyan (USA) 124 – Late Evening (USA) (Riverman (USA)) 131) [1995 NR 1996 7m 8.3m^6 10g^3 7g^2 7.1d^4 7g* Oct 19] 26,000Y: 8,200 2-y-o: sturdy colt: fifth foal: half-brother to 7f (at 2 yrs) and 1m winner Joie de Soir (by Caerleon), 6f and 6.9f winner Deeply Vale (by Pennine Walk) and a winner in Italy: dam French maiden: fairly useful form: won 22-runner handicap at Newmarket, quickening well to get on top close home: sold 33,000 gns Newmarket Autumn Sales: best form at 7f, should stay 1m: acts on dead ground: sent to Saudi Arabia. *L. M. Cumani* 82

MEZZOGIORNO 3 b.f. Unfuwain (USA) 131 – Aigue 96 (High Top 131) [1995 96p: 7m^4 7m* 7d^2 1996 7m 10g* 12m^3 12m^5 10m^5 11.9m^3 12.5d Oct 5] tall, raw-boned filly: useful performer: won listed race at Newbury in May: 9½ lengths third of 11 to Lady Carla in the Oaks at Epsom next start: best of last 4 outings when 5 lengths fourth (subsequently promoted) of 9 to Key Change in Yorkshire Oaks at York in August: seems better at 1½m than shorter: yet to race on extremes of going: takes keen hold: early to post first 2 starts at 3 yrs. *G. Wragg* 108

MEZZORAMIO 4 ch.g. Cadeaux Genereux 131 – Hopeful Search (USA) 71 (Vaguely Noble 140) [1995 44: a7g^4 a9.4g^3 a8g a8.5g^6 a7g^5 a11g 1996 a8g^3 a7g^4 a8g* a8g a8g^6 8f 10m^5 a8g 7m* 8m^2 8m* 9g 10m Sep 24] workmanlike gelding: modest handicapper: won apprentice maiden event at Southwell in February, amateurs race at Leicester in July and ladies handicap at Newmarket in August: best form at up to 1m: acts on good to firm ground and goes well on fibresand: visored/blinkered since third 3-y-o start: sometimes bandaged: usually a front runner. *K. A. Morgan* 54

MHEMEANLES 6 br.g. Jalmood (USA) 126 – Folle Idee (USA) (Foolish Pleasure (USA)) [1995 46: a11g 14m 11.1g 10g* 11.1f^4 12f^4 a14g 10.3m^4 10.2m 10.8g^6 11.8g 1996 8f May 6] compact gelding: has a round action: poor performer nowadays: well beaten only outing at 6 yrs: probably stays 1½m: used to act on any turf ground (no form either start on all-weather): tried blinkered, no improvement: inconsistent. *Capt. J. Wilson* –

MIAMI BANKER 10 ch.g. Miami Springs 121 – Banking Coyne 76 (Deep Diver 134) [1995 60: a5g^5 a5g 5g^3 5f^2 5m^2 5.1m^2 5m* 5f* 5m^5 5m^4 5m^2 5d 5.3g 1996 5.1g 5m 5m 5m^6 5f 5.2m^6 a5g^4 Jul 6] strong, lengthy gelding: unimpressive mover: poor handicapper in 1996: best at 5f: acts on any going: usually blinkered: races prominently. *W. R. Muir* 44

MIAMI MOON 2 ch.f. (Feb 25) Keen 116 – Two Moons (Bold Lad (IRE) 133) [1996 a6g a6g^3 Dec 7] second reported foal: dam no sign of ability: better effort in maidens when 4¾ lengths third of 9 to Fit For The Job at Wolverhampton: may improve again. *C. W. Thornton* 46

MICHAEL VENTURE 2 b.c. (Mar 9) Shirley Heights 130 – Ski Michaela (USA) (Devil's Bag (USA)) [1996 8m 8f^2 8g Oct 30] strong, good-bodied colt: third foal: closely related to 3-y-o Anchor Venture (by Slip Anchor) and half-brother to 4-y-o 11f to 12.5f winner Canton Venture (by Arctic Tern): dam twice-raced daughter of half-sister to Cannonade: ¾-length second of 12 to Our People in maiden at Leicester in October, always well there: seemed unsuited by steady pace in similar event at Yarmouth later in month: will be suited by middle distances. *S. P. C. Woods* 84

MICHELLE'S ELLA (IRE) 4 b.f. Ela-Mana-Mou 132 – Bustina (FR) (Busted 134) [1995 –: 10.3g^6 1996 12g 8.3m May 13] angular filly: no sign of ability. *C. D. Broad* –

MICK'S LOVE (IRE) 3 b.c. Law Society (USA) 130 – Flute (FR) (Luthier 126) [1995 102p: 8.1g* 8d* 1996 10m* May 3] sturdy, good-topped colt: has scope: wintered in Dubai: maintained his unbeaten record in 5-runner listed race at 111

603

Sunley Newmarket Stakes, Newmarket—Mick's Love (right) is Godolphin's first winner of the British season; he has a short head to spare over Bahamian Knight

Newmarket on reappearance, edging ahead 3f out and battling on gamely to beat Bahamian Knight a short head: will be well suited by 1½m+: looked a smart performer in the making, but reportedly damaged off-fore in late-May and returned to Dubai. *Saeed bin Suroor*

MIDAS MAN 5 ch.g. Gold Claim 90 – Golden Starfish (Porto Bello 118) [1995 – NR 1996 8s 10m 11.1d Sep 30] first foal: dam once-raced in points: looks of no account. *D. A. Nolan*

MIDATLANTIC 2 b.c. (Apr 21) Midyan (USA) 124 – Secret Waters 100 (Pharly 57 (FR) 130) [1996 5m 6m⁴ 7m 7m⁶ 8m 7m Oct 4] 17,500Y: small, leggy colt: first live foal: dam 12.5f to 1¾m winner, half-sister to smart 1986 2-y-o Shining Water (dam of Tenby) out of Park Hill winner Idle Waters: modest maiden at best: well held in nurseries last 3 starts, visored (wandered under pressure) on final one: sold 1,700 gns Newmarket Autumn Sales: should stay beyond 6f. *P. T. Walwyn*

MIDDAY COWBOY (USA) 3 b.g. Houston (USA) – Perfect Isn't Easy (USA) 75 (Saratoga Six (USA)) [1995 NR 1996 7m³ 8m 7m² 9m⁴ 8m⁶ 7m 8g Oct 2] $32,000Y: good-topped gelding: second foal: half-brother to 1996 US winner Sailor Smolski (by Polish Navy): dam unraced half-sister to Malinowski and the dam of El Gran Senor and Try My Best: fair form: sold to join M. Hammond 11,000 gns Newmarket Autumn Sales, and gelded: probably stays 9f: yet to race on a soft surface: has swished tail under pressure and may be of unsatisfactory temperament (ran poorly when blinkered final start): has run creditably when sweating. *G. Harwood*

MIDDLE EAST 3 b.g. Beveled (USA) – Godara (Bustino 136) [1995 66+: 5f* 74 7m⁴ 6m³ 6d 6m 1996 5d 6m² 6f* 6m⁶ 6d³ 6m 6m³ 5m⁶ Oct 23] tall, leggy gelding: fair handicapper: won at Redcar in July: keen sort who'll prove best at sprint distances: acts on firm and dead ground. *T. D. Barron*

MIDNIGHT BLUE 3 br.f. Be My Chief (USA) 122 – Guyum (Rousillon (USA) 95 133) [1995 83p: 6s* 1996 6d* 7d Oct 21] leggy, lengthy filly: off course a year, showed plenty of improvement to win minor contest at Hamilton, leading soon after halfway: 10 lengths last of 10 in listed race at Deauville 3 weeks later: sold 24,000 gns Newmarket December Sales: should stay 7f: has raced only on a soft surface. *W. Jarvis*

MIDNIGHT COOKIE 3 b.c. Midyan (USA) 124 – Midnight's Reward 84 54 d (Night Shift (USA)) [1995 54: 5.1m 5.2g 6m 5s 6.1s 5g 6m⁶ 5m a5g² 1996 5d 5.3f⁶ 5.1g 5g 5.3f⁵ a5g⁶ a5g a5g Nov 15] sturdy, good-quartered colt: modest performer on his day at 2 yrs: well beaten in handicaps last 7 starts: stays 6f: acts on good to firm and soft ground and on equitrack: races prominently. *B. A. Pearce*

MIDNIGHT ESCAPE 3 b.g. Aragon 118 – Executive Lady 59 (Night Shift 99 (USA)) [1995 80: 5g⁴ 5m* 6m⁴ 5g³ 1996 5m* 5f* 5m 5.6m 5g 5g* Oct 19] close-coupled gelding: improved into a useful handicapper at 3 yrs, winning at Windsor in May, Ascot (£14,300 contest, bravely) in June and Newmarket (22-runner rated stakes) in October: best form at 5f: yet to race on a soft surface. *C. F. Wall*

604

MIDNIGHT LEGEND   5 b.h. Night Shift (USA) – Myth 89 (Troy 137) [1995   116
118: 10d 12f² 12g 12f* 13.3m² 11.1g 1996 12m⁴ 11.5m² 11.8g* 12g⁴ 12g 12m²
13.9m Aug 21] robust, round-barrelled horse: carries condition and impresses in
appearance: good mover: smart performer: made all in listed race at Leicester in June
by ¾ length from Taufan's Melody: easily best of 4 subsequent starts (finished last in
the others) when second to Salmon Ladder in £30,600 rated stakes at Goodwood (has
good record there): reported by trainer to have been struck into during the Ebor at
York on final one: stays 1¾m: very well suited by top-of-the-ground: usually makes
running/races prominently: joined D. Nicholson. *L. M. Cumani*

MIDNIGHT ROMANCE   2 b.f. (Apr 15) Inca Chief (USA) – Run Amber Run   –
(Run The Gantlet (USA)) [1996 7m Oct 17] half-sister to several winners, including
useful 5f (at 2 yrs) and 7f winner Moon Over Miami (by Beveled) and smart
middle-distance stayer Quick Ransom (by Hostage): dam, minor winner in USA, is
half-sister to Irish Guineas second Mr John: last of 7 in maiden at Redcar. *A. P. Jarvis*

MIDNIGHT SHIFT (IRE)   2 b.f. (Apr 30) Night Shift (USA) – Old Domesday   69
Book 93 (High Top 131) [1996 7m 6g 6m⁴ Oct 28] 40,000Y: good-topped filly: sixth
foal: half-sister to 3 winners, including very smart sprinter Owington (by Green
Desert) and 7f (at 2 yrs) to 1½m winner Common Council (by Siberian Express):
dam 10.4f winner better at 1½m: last of 23 in valuable sales race at Newmarket on
debut: fair form afterwards in maidens at Newmarket and Leicester: should stay
beyond 7f: took keen hold second start. *R. Guest*

MIDNIGHT SPELL   4 ch.f. Night Shift (USA) – Bundled Up (USA) (Sharpen   72
Up 127) [1995 74: 6.9g² 6m a6g 6g³ 5.2g⁶ 5d 1996 7g 8.5f⁵ 6g 5.3f² 5.3m* 5.2m⁴
5.1m* 5g³ 5m⁴ 5m² 5s Nov 8] sturdy filly: fair handicapper: most consistent after
being dropped to 5f, winning at Brighton in July and Bath (minor event) in August:
best at 5f: acts on firm ground, probably on soft: blinkered (finished last) final 3-y-o
start. *J. W. Hills*

MIDNIGHT TIMES   2 b.f. (Mar 27) Timeless Times (USA) 99 – Midnight Lass   –
59 (Today And Tomorrow 78) [1996 a5g 5f 5.1f⁵ 5.3f Aug 5] 500Y: first foal: dam
2-y-o 5f winner: poor form in varied events, including a seller: flashed tail second
start. *D. C. O'Brien*

MIDNIGHT WATCH (USA)   2 b.c. (Mar 18) Capote (USA) – Midnight Air   77 p
(USA) 111 (Green Dancer (USA) 132) [1996 8.2g² Oct 24] first foal: dam won May
Hill Stakes and placed at up to 1¼m at 3 yrs: odds on, beaten a head by Over To You
in 15-runner maiden at Nottingham, pushed along early, progress to lead briefly over
1f out: likely to stay 1¼m: should improve, and win a race. *H. R. A. Cecil*

MIDYAN BLUE (IRE)   6 ch.g. Midyan (USA) 124 – Jarretiere 78 (Star Appeal   81
133) [1995 86: 11.8m² 13.9g* 16.5g⁴ 14m³ 14g* 14.8m⁵ 13.9m² 13.9g⁵ 13.3d
13.9g⁴ 1996 11.8g³ 13.9m⁴ 14d⁶ 14m³ 14d⁴ 15m⁶ 13.9g² 13.3m⁶ 13.9g² 14.6g 12s
Nov 9] sparely-made gelding: shows plenty of knee action: fairly useful handicapper:
inconsistent at 6 yrs, running poorly at Doncaster last 2 outings: stays 1¾m, seemingly not 16.5f: acts on good to firm ground and soft: has run well when sweating:
makes running/chases leaders: usually runs well at York. *J. M. P. Eustace*

MIDYAN QUEEN   2 b.f. (May 6) Midyan (USA) 124 – Queen of Aragon 76   60 +
(Aragon 118) [1996 6d 5.1m³ 5s³ 5g⁶ Oct 19] unfurnished filly: fourth foal: sister to
a winner in Spain and half-sister to 3-y-o Taragona (by Handsome Sailor): dam 5f
winner, stayed 6f: modest maiden: bled from the nose final outing: should stay 6f:
flashed tail third start. *R. Hollinshead*

MIDYANS SONG   2 ch.f. (Feb 19) Midyan (USA) 124 – Diva Madonna 85   46
(Chief Singer 131) [1996 5g 5g³ 6g 7.5m Sep 18] 4,000Y: unfurnished filly: third
foal: dam 1½m winner: poor maiden: should be suited by further than 5f. *J. J. O'Neill*

MIESQUE'S SON (USA)   4 b. or br.c. Mr Prospector (USA) – Miesque   117
(USA) 133 (Nureyev (USA) 131) [1995 8d⁴ 7g² 8d⁶ 1996 5m⁶ 6m* 6.5d² 6f 7d²
Oct 20]

A recent advert that caught the eye was the one for a service that advised
breeders on the right stallions for their mares. 'Using advanced computer
technology, combined with the traditional skills, we have already achieved a
remarkable degree of success,' it said. Thirteen of those successes were named
and at the top of the list was Kingmambo, followed closely by Miesque's Son.

Niarchos Family's "Miesque's Son"

How powerful a computer was needed to reveal that Mr Prospector—Miesque was a promising combination? It was dead right, though. The brilliant French miler's first foal, Kingmambo, won the Poule d'Essai des Poulains, St James's Palace Stakes and Prix du Moulin, and her second visit to the world's most successful living stallion resulted in a Group 1 performer in Miesque's Son. Group 1 performer but not quite a Group 1 winner. Miesque's Son was not so good as Kingmambo, but he was good enough to run in three Group 1 events and finish runner-up in two of them. There was never any question of more than second best against Anabaa in the Prix Maurice de Gheest at Deauville in August; Miesque's Son was, however, reeling in A Magicman fast when beaten a head in the Prix de la Foret at Longchamp in October on the final start of his career. In between those two races, Miesque's Son did less well when coming over for the Haydock Park Sprint Cup and finishing seventh of eleven, starting favourite. The reason was probably the firm ground.

For most of his career, seventh in the Haydock Park Sprint Cup would have seemed like a major triumph. He had run only in four minor events over the previous two seasons, reportedly having joint problems at two years when trained by Francois Boutin and not being seen out until the end of July as a three-year-old after twisting an ankle. Miesque's Son is also reportedly a somewhat nervous sort. A drop down to five furlongs at Evry on his first start in 1996 did nothing to alter his maiden status but a return to the same course one month later for the Prix de Ris-Orangis saw the beginning of Miesque's Son's reappraisal when he got up on the post to win from Kistena and Don't Worry Me.

		Raise A Native (ch 1961)	Native Dancer
Miesque's Son (USA) (b. or br.c. 1992)	Mr Prospector (USA) (b 1970)		Raise You
		Gold Digger (ch 1961)	Nashua
			Sequence
	Miesque (USA) (b 1984)	Nureyev (b 1977)	Northern Dancer
			Special
		Pasadoble (b 1979)	Prove Out
			Santa Quilla

There won't be many horses that retire to stud with just one Group 3 win and a valuation thought to be between eight and ten million dollars, but, as we hinted earlier, Miesque's Son is incredibly well bred. He is only the third foal of Miesque, but Kingmambo is not her only Group 1 winner—one year later along came the Poule d'Essai de Pouliches, Prix de Diane and Prix Jacques le Marois winner East of The Moon (by Private Account; incidentally, not one of the matings taken credit for in that aforementioned advert). After Miesque's Son there is his close relation the 1996 French listed winner Moon Is Up (by Woodman) and a sister in Monevassia who was runner-up in a newcomers race at Deauville on her only start so far. Another in John Hammond's stable in 1996 was Byzantium, the first foal out of Miesque's unraced sister Bravemie. He is by the Mr Prospector stallion Gulch and nearly as good as Miesque's Son, with two listed wins from three starts as a three-year-old. Miesque's Son has been syndicated to stand at the Three Chimneys Farm, Kentucky, at a reported 20,000 dollars. A close-coupled colt, effective at six and seven furlongs, he won on good to firm ground but showed better form on a soft surface. Sadler's Wells, Fairy King, Tate Gallery and Classic Music have provided a lot of stimulating opportunities to compare and contrast the influence of full brothers at stud in recent years, now let's see how Kingmambo, Miesque's Son and other members of the Miesque dynasty get on. Kingmambo will have his first runners in 1997, but it already looks as though he will be something of a hard act to follow as that first crop were very well received at the yearling sales, a colt from the family of Sadler's Wells making the top lot (at 880,000 guineas) at the Houghton. *J. E. Hammond, France*

MIGHTY FLYER (IRE) 2 ch.f. (May 6) Mujtahid (USA) 118 – Brentsville – (USA) (Arctic Tern (USA) 126) [1996 6m Oct 4] 27,000Y: second foal: half-sister to useful 3-y-o 6f winner (including at 2 yrs) Sylva Paradise (by Dancing Dissident): dam Irish 2-y-o 6f winner: joint favourite, never a factor when eleventh of 12 in maiden at Lingfield: sold 5,600 gns Newmarket Autumn Sales. *D. R. Loder*

MIGHTY KEEN 3 ch.c. Keen 116 – Mary Martin (Be My Guest (USA) 126) 73 [1995 NR 1996 7f³ 8m² 7g a8.5g* Nov 11] seventh foal: half-brother to 6 winners, all at up to 7.5f when in Europe, notably very useful Marina Park (by Local Suitor): dam unraced half-sister to 2 very smart sprinters: fair form in maidens: won median auction event at Wolverhampton, always prominent: subsequently sold (M. Johnston to M. Banks) 12,000 gns Doncaster November Sales: stays 8.5f. *M. Johnston*

MIGHTY PHANTOM (USA) 3 b.f. Lear Fan (USA) 130 – Migiyas 87 (Kings 78 Lake (USA) 133) [1995 60: 6g⁵ 7.5d 1996 6.9f⁶ 10m⁵ a16g* 15.4g³ 12m* 14f⁵ a16g² 13.9g⁴ 14.1f² Sep 28] quite attractive filly: fairly useful performer: won maiden at Lingfield in June and handicap at Doncaster in July: good efforts in handicaps afterwards: effective at 1½m, and stays 2m: acts on firm ground and equitrack, well below best on dead: reluctant at stalls penultimate start: consistent. *J. W. Hills*

MIGWAR 3 b.c. Unfuwain (USA) 131 – Pick of The Pops 109 (High Top 131) 99 [1995 68: 7g 7m⁵ 1996 10g² 12d² 10.3m* 10m* 12m Jun 20] deep-girthed, attractive colt: carries condition: useful performer: successful in May in handicap at Doncaster and £14,700 Zetland Gold Cup Handicap at Redcar, in latter (well-backed favourite) forced to wait for gaps before quickening to beat Billy Bushwacker 1½ lengths: yet to be asked for his effort when badly hampered 3f out (and eased right down) in King

*Zetland Gold Cup (Handicap), Redcar—Migwar has found a way through
and beats Billy Bushwacker (second right) a length and a half*

George V Handicap at Royal Ascot final start: should stay beyond 10.3f: acts on good to firm ground: tends to sweat, get on edge, and be coltish: injured at Royal Ascot: remains in training. *L. M. Cumani*

MIHRIZ (IRE)   4 b.g. Machiavellian (USA) 123 – Ghzaalh (USA) 87 (Northern – Dancer) [1995 84: 8m⁴ 9m² 10g⁵ 10g⁶ 1996 8s 8.3m⁶ 6.9f⁴ 8m 6f 8d 8g Sep 29] sturdy, useful-looking gelding: fluent mover: fairly useful handicapper at 3 yrs but Major W. R. Hern: well below best in 1996, though had excuses on occasions: stays 9f: acts on good to firm ground, possibly not on a soft surface. *R. Akehurst*

MIJAS   3 ch.f. Risk Me (FR) 127 – Out of Harmony 79 (Song 132) [1995 NR 1996   80
6m* 6m⁶ a6g 7f 5m⁵ 6m⁵ 5m a5g⁶ a6g a5g* a6g Dec 20] 3,600Y: fourth foal: sister to 1992 6f 2-y-o winner Risky Number and half-sister to 5.9f winner Rich Harmony (by Rich Charlie): dam 2-y-o 5f winner who stayed 6f: 33/1-winner of maiden at Lingfield in May: well held next 8 starts, but (well backed) bounced back to form to make all in handicap there in December: looks a sprinter: acts on equitrack: edgy type. *L. Montague Hall*

MIKE'S DOUBLE (IRE)   2 br.g. (Mar 6) Cyrano de Bergerac 120 – Glass   47
Minnow (IRE) 59 (Alzao (USA) 117) [1996 5g⁶ 5.3f⁴ 6d 5f 6.1s³ 6m² Oct 29] IR 9,000Y: sturdy gelding: first foal: dam, maiden, placed at up to 9f in Ireland, out of sister to high-class sprinter Abergwaun: modest maiden: needs further than 5f, and will stay 7f: acts on good to firm and soft ground: blinkered (best efforts) last 2 starts: tends to be slowly away. *G. Lewis*

MILE HIGH   2 b.c. (Mar 18) Puissance 110 – Jobiska (Dunbeath (USA) 127)   88
[1996 6.1m⁴ 6m² Jul 31] 10,000F, IR 11,500Y: quite good-topped colt: third foal: half-brother to a winner in Czech Republic by Squill: dam lightly raced: ½-length second of 8, clear, to In Command in maiden at Goodwood, making much of running: looked sure to improve again. *M. R. Channon*

MILETRIAN CITY   3 gr.g. Petong 126 – Blueit (FR) 101 (Bold Lad (IRE) 133)   60
[1995 53+: a6g 6f 5d⁵ 6g⁴ 1996 7s 7d 8m 10d⁴ 8.1f⁶ 8.1f⁴ 8m⁴ 7g² 6.9f* 7d⁴ 8.3m³ 7.1m² 7.1m⁶ Sep 17] smallish, strong gelding: has a quick action: modest performer: won claimer at Carlisle in August: stays 1m: acts on firm and dead ground: blinkered since sixth 3-y-o start. *J. Berry*

MILETRIAN FIT-OUT   3 b.g. Most Welcome 131 – White Domino 67 –
(Sharpen Up 127) [1995 NR 1996 10g 9.9m⁶ 11.8m Jun 3] 7,800Y: leggy gelding: bad mover: half-brother to useful 1993 2-y-o 6f winner Pinkerton's Pal (both by

Dominion) and 2 other winners, including useful sprinter Macrobian (by Bay Express): dam won at 1m: tailed off in maidens, blinkered final start: sold 700 gns Newmarket July Sales: tail swisher: sent to Spain. *C. E. Brittain*

MILETRIAN REFURB (IRE)   3 b. or br.g. Anita's Prince 126 – Lady of Man   63
85 (So Blessed 130) [1995 59: 5g⁵ 5.1g⁵ 5m² 7f 6.1m⁵ 6m² 5.3d* 5m⁵ 1996 6s*
6.1d⁴ 5.1g² 6d 5.1g² a5g Dec 28] compact gelding: unimpressive mover: modest performer: won seller at Newcastle in March: kicked in stalls (and withdrawn) in June, and not seen out again (when well beaten) for nearly 7 months: stays 6f: acts on good to firm and soft ground: usually races prominently. *M. R. Channon*

MILFORD SOUND   3 b.g. Batshoof 122 – Nafis (USA) (Nodouble (USA))   84
[1995 –p: 7m 1996 8m⁴ 8.3g³ 8.2m* 8m 10m 10.5s³ Oct 5] close-coupled gelding: fairly useful form: won maiden at Nottingham in July (unimpressive and not at best): below form in handicaps afterwards: sold (J. Fanshawe to P. Hobbs) 28,000 gns Newmarket Autumn Sales, and gelded: should stay 1¼m: best effort with give in the ground. *J. R. Fanshawe*

MILL DANCER (IRE)   4 b.f. Broken Hearted 124 – Theatral (Orchestra 118)   –
[1995 49: 8g 8m³ 8g³ 8.1m* 8f 10d* 10.5s⁶ 10.5d⁶ 1996 a11g⁵ a11g a8g⁴ 8.3d 9.9m 8g⁶ 8.1g⁵ 10m 7f⁵ 8.1m 9.2f 8g a11g Nov 18] leggy filly: poor performer: stays 1¼m: acts on good to firm ground (ran poorly on firm), goes well on a soft surface: sometimes takes keen hold, and below form when sweating and edgy: usually races prominently: has joined J. O'Shea. *E. J. Alston*

MILLEMAY   6 br.m. Respect 95 – Ravenscraig (Impecunious) [1995 36?: 6s⁵ 6g⁵   –
7m⁶ 1996 6s⁴ 7d⁶ 5m 6g⁶ Jun 3] good-topped mare: bad sprint maiden. *P. Monteith*

MILL END BOY   2 ch.g. (Apr 7) Clantime 101 – Annaceramic 83 (Horage 124)   60
[1996 5d 5g³ 5m 7s⁴ 7g 6f⁵ 6g⁴ 6m Oct 7] 2,700f: small, lengthy gelding: second foal: dam best at up to 7.5f: modest maiden: not bred to stay beyond 6f, but races as though he needs at least 7f: acts on firm and soft going. *M. W. Easterby*

MILL END GIRL   2 ch.f. (May 9) Superpower 113 – Estefan 58 (Taufan (USA)   55
119) [1996 5d⁴ 5m⁵ 5m* 5d* 6m Aug 21] lengthy filly: third foal: dam stayed 6f: modest performer: won claimer at Thirsk and seller at Catterick within 5 days in April: first run for 4 months when last of 20 in valuable seller at York (moved poorly to post) on final outing: should stay 6f: acts on firm and dead ground: sold 3,000 gns Newmarket Autumn Sales. *M. W. Easterby*

MILL END LADY   3 b.f. Tina's Pet 121 – Azelly 77 (Pitskelly 122) [1995 49:   44
5m⁶ 5g 7.5d 7d⁵ 5m 1996 7.1g 8g 7.5m 8f 6f* 6m 6s a5g Sep 9] tall filly: has knee action: poor handicapper: won at Thirsk in August: stays 7f: acts on firm and soft ground (stiff task and well held only outing on all-weather): blinkered last 5 starts. *M. W. Easterby*

MILLESIME (IRE)   4 ch.g. Glow (USA) – Persian Myth (Persian Bold 123)   –
[1995 71: 5m⁴ 6g 6.9m⁴ 6g⁵ 6f⁴ 6g³ 5.1m* 5.1f* 5f⁶ 5.2m² 5m 5m³ 5.1d 1996 5m 5g 5.1m⁵ 5f Sep 5] unfurnished gelding: fair performer at 3 yrs: well beaten in 1996: sold to join Martyn Wane 3,400 gns Newmarket Autumn Sales: effective at 5f (best form) and 6f: acts on firm ground, soundly beaten on dead: tongue tied last 2 3-y-o starts: races prominently. *B. Hanbury*

MILL FORCE   5 b.g. Forzando 122 – Milinetta (Milford 119) [1995 NR 1996 8m   –
10.1m Jul 27] leggy, short-backed gelding: fair performer at 2 yrs: very slowly away when midfield in handicap at Pontefract on return: held up pulling hard, stumbled and rider unseated over 3f out in similar event at Newcastle 8 days later: stays 1m: used to act on firm ground. *D. Nicholls*

MILL HOUSE BOY (IRE)   3 b.g. Astronef 116 – Avantage Service (IRE)   –
(Exactly Sharp (USA) 121) [1995 –: 7m 6m 7m 1996 12g 10f 12m Aug 6] leggy gelding: no sign of ability: tried visored. *B. S. Rothwell*

MILLROY (USA)   2 ch.g. (Feb 26) Carnivalay (USA) – Royal Millinery (USA)   82
(Regal And Royal (USA)) [1996 6m³ 7m⁶ 5m³ 6m⁶ 8m 6m a7s² a7g* a7s³ a7g² Dec 30] $26,000Y: strong, lengthy gelding: ninth foal: half-brother to several winners in USA: dam won at up to 1m in USA: sire (by Northern Dancer) 6f winner: fairly useful form: gelded after sixth start: won maiden at Lingfield in December: should prove suited by further than 7f (soon off bridle last 3 starts): acts on all-weather, raced only on good to firm on turf: has run well when blinkered. *P. A. Kelleway*

MILLTOWN CLASSIC (IRE)   4 b.f. Classic Secret (USA) 91 – Houwara   38
(IRE) (Darshaan 133) [1995 33: 7m⁴ 8g⁶ 8f 8m⁶ 9.9m⁶ 13.8g 1996 a12g⁶ a11g³ a12g⁵
a11g a11g⁵ 10g 11.1m* 10f³ 9.9m² 11f⁴ 10d 10f 11.8f Oct 15] leggy, workmanlike
filly: poor handicapper: 40/1, won seller at Musselburgh in July, leading post: stays
11.1f: acts on firm going, probably on dead: effective from front or held up: none too
consistent: sent to South Korea. *J. Parkes*

MILLYANT   6 ch.m. Primo Dominie 121 – Jubilee Song 71 (Song 132) [1995 114:   108
5g⁴ 5g* 5f 5m⁵ 5m³ 5d⁶ 5f* 1996 5g⁴ 5g⁵ 5d Oct 27] strong, long-backed mare:
carried condition: tended to be unimpressive in coat: smart performer at 6 yrs: best
effort of 1996 when 2 lengths fifth of 6 in Ballyogan Stakes at Leopardstown: off
course nearly 5 months, attempting third successive Prix du Petit Couvert at Longchamp, but beaten over 7 lengths: speedy, and raced only at 5f in Europe: acted on
firm ground and soft, below best (in America) on dirt: was usually bandaged near-
hind: retired to stud. *R. Guest*

MILNGAVIE (IRE)   6 ch.g. Pharly (FR) 130 – Wig And Gown (Mandamus 120)   –
[1995 36, a60d: a14.8g⁵ a12g³ a14.8g⁵ a12g a12g a16g 13v 12.1s³ 21.6f 15.1f²   a53
15.1m³ 15.1f⁶ 13.8m² 13f² 17.1m⁵ 12.1m⁴ 15.8g 16.4m* a13g⁵ a16g 1996 a16g*   a74
a16.2g² a16g a13g² a13g³ a16g³ a16g² a16.2g* Jul 26] close-coupled gelding: has a
round action: modest handicapper: won at Lingfield in January: trained until after
sixth 6-y-o start by M. Johnston: gamely won at Wolverhampton (amateurs) in July:
effective at 1½m, and stays 16.2f: acts on firm and soft ground, best form on all-
weather surfaces: effective blinkered or not. *B. Smart*

MILOS   5 b.g. Efisio 120 – Elkie Brooks 82 (Relkino 131) [1995 –, a79d: a7g³ a7g³   64
5m 7.1m 7.1d a7g a7g² a7g² a7g 1996 a6g⁶ a7g⁵ a6g* a6g³ a7g* a7g a7g³ a7g⁵ a7g²   a74
a6g⁴ 6f³ 6.9m⁴ 6f 8.1m 8.1d² 8f 7.1f 6d 7.1s³ a7g⁵ a7g Dec 20] big, strong gelding:
shows knee action: fair performer on the all-weather, modest on turf: won claimers at
Lingfield in January and Southwell (apprentices) in February: effective at 6f to 1m:
acts on all-weather surfaces, firm and soft ground: effective from front or held up.
T. J. Naughton

MILTAK   4 b.f. Risk Me (FR) 127 – Tralee Maiden (IRE) 63 (Persian Bold 123)   43
[1995 41: 5.1m 8.1m⁵ 8.1m³ 8m a9.4g 11.9f⁴ 12m⁴ a11g⁵ 1996 a13g² a12g² a13g²
a13g⁴ Feb 10] small, light-framed filly: poor maiden: in frame in selling handicaps at
Lingfield: stays 13f: acts on equitrack and firm ground, below form both starts on
fibresand: blinkered twice in 1994: covered by Factual. *P. J. Makin*

MILTON   3 ch.g. Groom Dancer (USA) 128 – Gold Flair 93 (Tap On Wood 130)   75
[1995 75: a8g² a8g³ 1996 10.2f⁴ Jul 2] fair maiden: sold 10,500 gns Newmarket
Autumn (1996) Sales: bred to be suited by middle distances. *P. F. I. Cole*

MIM-LOU-AND   4 b.g. Glacial Storm (USA) 127 – Tina's Melody 80 (Tina's Pet   48
121) [1995 51: 12d⁴ 14.1g⁴ 12m 9.7m³ a9.4g⁶ 9.7g 9.7m² 9.7f³ 10.2m⁴ 1996 14.1m⁴
14.9m Jul 13] close-coupled gelding: fair hurdler: modest maiden handicapper on
flat: stays 1¾m: acts on firm ground and dead: used to pull hard. *Miss H. C. Knight*

MIMOSA   3 ch.f. Midyan (USA) 124 – Figini 74 (Glint of Gold 128) [1995 66: 5m   67
5m⁵ 5m 5g 6d² 7g 1996 7d 10g 7d 8m 8f 9m 8m* 8m 9f⁵ 10g⁵ 8m 8d⁴ 9.7d² 10g a8g⁶   a63
a10s⁴ a10g Dec 11] strong filly: fair handicapper: won amateurs event at Salisbury in
June: stays 1¼m: acts on firm and good to soft ground and on equitrack: visored (no
improvement) fourth and fifth 3-y-o starts: none too consistent. *S. Dow*

MIN ALHAWA (USA)   3 b.f. Riverman (USA) 131 – Saffaanh (USA) 87 (Sha-   108
reef Dancer (USA) 135) [1995 87p: 6f² 7m* 1996 10m² 11.9g⁶ 10.2m⁴ 10g² 10.2f*
8m Sep 28] tall, rather unfurnished filly: easy mover: useful performer: runner-up in
listed races at Newbury in June and Salisbury in August: improved form to win
4-runner minor event at Chepstow in September by 3½ lengths from Miss Universal,
leading over 3f out: should have stayed 1½m (didn't get best of runs in Lancashire
Oaks when tried): acted on firm going: visits Nureyev. *Major W. R. Hern*

MIND GAMES   4 b.c. Puissance 110 – Aryaf (CAN) (Vice Regent (CAN))   121
[1995 118: 5m* 5m* 5m* 5f³ 5m⁶ 6d⁵ 5d 1996 5g* 5f² 6m 5m⁴ 6f⁶ Sep 7]
    Trainer Jack Berry is still looking for that first Group 1 victory after
Mind Games was beaten the only time an inmate of Moss Side
Racing Stables held a clear-cut chance in such company in 1996. But, in truth,
any training operation so dependent on early sorts and sprint-breds picked up at

public auction as his has been can be proud to have been knocking at the door for so long; if you have only sprinters to go into battle with, opportunities are extremely limited. There were only five Group 1 races in the entire European sprint pattern in 1996 open to three-year-olds and upwards. Mind Games ran in three of them, and, as had seemed very likely unless his stamina improved with age, he found the other two over six furlongs too far to show his best.

Mind Games looked very much the same horse at the start of his four-year-old career as he had been before—a trail-blazing, five-furlong speed merchant. He won his second Tripleprint Temple Stakes at Sandown in May by three quarters of a length from Struggler before going on for a second attempt at the King's Stand Stakes at Royal Ascot. Third place in the previous year's race had not been one of his better efforts, but on this occasion he excelled himself, running everything with him on the far side into the ground only to be deprived of victory in the Group 2 event by half a length by stand-side runner Pivotal. The pair were clear. Despite continuing doubts about his stamina Mind Games was given another chance at six furlongs next—the fifth of his career—in the Darley July Cup at Newmarket, on his way to his season's main object-ive, the Nunthorpe over five at York in August. He finished a respectable

				Thatch
		Thatching		Abella
	Puissance	(b 1975)		Balidar
	(b 1986)	Girton		Miss Dorothy
Mind Games		(b 1976)		Northern Dancer
(b.c. 1992)		Vice Regent		Victoria Regina
	Aryaf (CAN)	(ch 1967)		Habitat
	(b 1986)	Fashion Front		Front Row
		(b 1980)		

Mr Rob Hughes's "Mind Games"

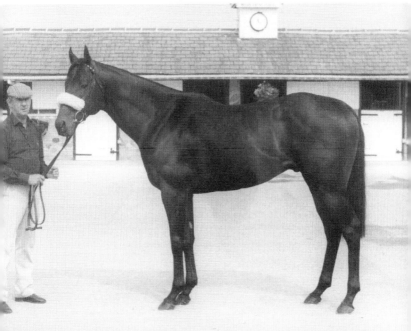

seventh of ten to Anabaa at Newmarket but again didn't look so effective being restrained, and was a spent force approaching the distance. When it came to the Nunthorpe, Mind Games appeared to have everything going for him. But that was reckoning without the spectacular show of speed from the mare Evening-performance, who managed to prevent him dominating. Driven along from two out, he just kept on without threatening into fourth behind Pivotal. Mind Games's final attempt at six furlongs, and his farewell appearance, came in the Haydock Park Sprint Cup in September, Richard Hughes replacing stable-jockey John Carroll, reportedly because the latter (hardly surprisingly if true) lacked confidence in Mind Games's ability to get the trip. While running much better in the race than he'd done in testing conditions the previous season, Mind Games finished just sixth of eleven, nearly five lengths behind Iktamal.

Mind Games has been retired to the Bearstone Stud in Shropshire at a fee of £3,500 with the October 1st concession. His trainer bought him for 18,000 guineas at the Newmarket October Yearling Sales, one of the sprinter Puissance's first crop, the result of a mating with a lightly-raced granddaughter of the Irish One Thousand Guineas winner and excellent broodmare Front Row. The dam Aryaf (a 200,000-dollar yearling in her day) has also produced the one-mile winner Able Fun to the sprinter Double Schwartz, while the second dam Fashion Front is the dam of four winners, including the quite useful 1996 two-year-old Peartree House.

The lengthy Mind Games acted on firm and dead ground, never being raced on anything softer; one reason given for his being sent to Haydock instead of having a second shot at the five-furlong Prix de l'Abbaye was that conditions might well come up too testing at Longchamp. He was a very speedy individual, little or nothing behind the stable's Paris House who came close to providing Jack Berry with that Group 1 win when twice runner-up in the Nunthorpe. *J. Berry*

MINDRACE 3 b.g. Tina's Pet 121 – High Velocity 53 (Frimley Park 109) [1995 70
73: 6m a7g 5g⁶ 6f³ 1996 6s 5g⁶ 6m 6m 7f⁴ 5m⁴ 5g⁴ 5.1m⁴* 5m² 5.1m⁴ 5m 5m 5m⁴
Oct 3] plain, leggy gelding: fair handicapper: won at Bath in July: in-and-out form subsequently: will prove best at sprint distances: acts on firm ground. *K. T. Ivory*

MINDS MUSIC (USA) 4 ch.c. Silver Hawk (USA) 123 – Misinskie (USA) 84 113
(Nijinsky (CAN) 138) [1995 115: 10m* 10.4g² 10.3g² 14.6d² 12g* 1996 13.4g³
13.3d² 12m² 12f³ Sep 13] strong, lengthy colt: poor mover: smart performer: second
in St Leger in 1995: creditable placed efforts all starts at 4 yrs, including in Ormonde
Stakes (1½ lengths third to Oscar Shindler) at Chester and listed race (2¾ lengths
third to Busy Flight) at Doncaster: stays 14.6f well: acts on firm and dead ground, yet
to race on soft: lacks turn of foot: rather lazy: consistent: reportedly sold to France.
H. R. A. Cecil

MINERAL WATER 3 ch.g. Weldnaas (USA) 112 – Joud 93 (Dancing Brave –
(USA) 140) [1995 NR 1996 12g Jul 9] first foal: dam, 6f winner at 2 yrs, bred to stay
at least 1m: 50/1, last of 9 in maiden at Pontefract: has joined Mrs D. Thomson.
J. D. Bethell

MINERSVILLE (USA) 2 b.c. (Mar 30) Forty Niner (USA) – Angel Fever 83 P
(USA) (Danzig (USA)) [1996 7g³ Oct 25] $330,000Y: big, strong, deep-girthed colt:
has plenty of scope: has had shins freeze fired: first foal: dam sprint winner and
placed in minor stakes from 2 starts at 2 yrs, sister to Preakness Stakes winner Pine
Bluff and half-sister to Grade 1 9f winner Demons Begone: 9/1, eye-catching 1¾
lengths third of 12 to Sophomore in maiden at Doncaster, held up travelling smoothly
behind leaders then running on in good style under sympathetic handling after first
two had gone clear: taken last and quietly to post: trainer subsequently fined and rider
suspended under "non triers" rule: bred to stay 1m: showed more than enough to
suggest he can win a race or two. *J. H. M. Gosden*

MINNEOLA 4 ch.f. Midyan (USA) 124 – High Halo 64 (High Top 131) [1995 –: –
10m 10m 1996 11.7m Sep 9] well beaten in maidens. *A. Barrow*

MINNIE THE MINX 5 b.m. Then Again 126 – Sahara Shadow 70 (Formidable –
(USA) 125) [1995 NR 1996 a12g a8.5g Jun 22] second foal: dam 7f and 1m winner:
seems of no account. *W. G. M. Turner*

MINNISAM 3 ch.c. Niniski (USA) 125 – Wise Speculation (USA) (Mr 71
Prospector (USA)) [1995 –p: 7f 8.1s⁴ 8.2m 1996 12s² 14.1g⁴ 12.5f³ 11.7m⁶ 12g*
11.5f⁵ 14m Aug 15] angular colt: fair handicapper: blinkered, improved form to win
at Folkestone in July, kicked clear over 3f out: blinkered again, looked one-paced in
similar events afterwards: effective at 1½m and will stay 2m: acts on firm and soft
ground: sold (J. Dunlop to A. Hobbs) 2,200 gns Ascot December Sales. *J. L. Dunlop*

MINOLETTI 3 b.g. Emarati (USA) 74 – French Plait (Thatching 131) [1995 70p: 70
6g⁵ 1996 6g² 7g³ 6m⁴ 7s⁶ Oct 24] good-bodied gelding: fair maiden: sold 9,000 gns
Newmarket Autumn Sales: stays 7f: acts on good to firm and soft ground: has been
bandaged near hind: consistent. *E. A. L. Dunlop*

MINSTER GLORY 5 b.g. Minster Son 130 – Rapid Glory 75 (Hittite Glory 125) 54
[1995 43: a12g a7g a6g 9.9m² 1996 10.5m³ 9.9g² 10.3d* 10.4g² Sep 5] strong, close-
coupled gelding: modest handicapper: won apprentice contest at Chester in August:
ran very well when second of 19 in similar event at York 6 days later: stays 10.5f:
acts on good to firm and dead ground (showed little on fibresand): blinkered last 2
starts: keen sort, races prominently. *M. W. Easterby*

MINT CONDITION 2 ch.g. (Apr 8) Superlative 118 – Penny Mint 79 (Mum- –
my's Game 120) [1996 5f 5.1m⁴ 7g Sep 7] 5,200 2-y-o: leggy, workmanlike gelding:
second foal: half-brother to 3-y-o Present Generation (by Cadeaux Genereux): dam
2-y-o 6f winner out of sister to smart miler Saher: well beaten in claimers and a
maiden auction. *Mrs L. Stubbs*

MIRACLE KID (USA) 2 b.c. (Mar 16) Red Ransom (USA) – Fan Mail (USA) 75 p
(Zen (USA)) [1996 8g a8g* Nov 14] $30,000F, 85,000Y: sixth foal: closely related
to a winner in USA by Royal Roberto and half-brother to winners in USA by
Proudest Roman and Buckfinder: dam won at up to 7f in USA: stepped up
considerably on debut form to win maiden at Lingfield in November by neck from
Protocol, making all: will stay 1¼m: should improve further. *J. H. M. Gosden*

MIRADOR 5 b.m. Town And Country 124 – Wild Jewel (Great Heron (USA) 61
127) [1995 –: 11.9m 1996 20f² 18f* 20m⁶ 16s Oct 24] close-coupled mare: modest
handicapper: won at Chepstow in July: had earlier excelled herself when 100/1 and
runner-up to Southern Power in 26-runner Ascot Stakes at Royal Ascot: never a
threat at Goodwood and (3 months later) Newbury afterwards: suited by long
distances: acts on firm ground, no form on a soft surface. *R. Curtis*

MIRANI (IRE) 3 b.f. Danehill (USA) 126 – Alriyaah 73 (Shareef Dancer (USA) 55
135) [1995 NR 1996 a7g* a8.5g Jul 26] IR 12,000Y: second foal: half-sister to poor
sprint handicapper Rotherfield Park (by High Estate): dam 2-y-o 5f winner: narrowly
won claimer at Wolverhampton in July: finished lame in similar event there later in
month: may well stay 1m. *D. J. G. Murray Smith*

MIRONOV 3 b.c. Marju (IRE) 127 – Marquina (FR) (Posse (USA) 130) [1995 98
79p: 7.5d⁴ 1996 8s² 8d 10.4f⁶ May 16] tall, leggy colt: easily best form when about 3
lengths (relegated to eighth after causing interference) of 14 to Dancer Mitral in
Premio Parioli at Rome second 3-y-o start: over 20 lengths last to Dr Massini in
minor event at York (seemed uncomfortable on firm ground) 18 days later: should be
suited by middle distances. *M. R. Channon*

MIROSWAKI (USA) 6 br.g. Miswaki (USA) 124 – Miroswava (FR) 115 (In 67
Fijar (USA) 121) [1995 71: 12g⁵ 14.1m⁶ 14.9m 16.1m 14.6m a16g² 1996 a13g* 16g
16.2m³ Sep 28] good-bodied gelding: fair performer: easily landed the odds in weak
maiden at Lingfield in January: returned to flat in September and ran well when third
of 18 to Fujiyama Crest at Ascot, running on strongly: effective at 13f to 2m: acts
on good to firm and soft ground and equitrack: has worn tongue strap and dropped
noseband. *R. Akehurst*

MIRROR FOUR LIFE (IRE) 2 b.f. (Apr 8) Treasure Kay 114 – Gazettalong 73
80 (Taufan (USA) 119) [1996 5.1m* 5.1m⁴ 6g⁴ 5m⁵ 7g* 7g 7m Oct 28] IR 3,000Y:
leggy, sparely-made filly: third foal: half-sister to Swedish 6f winner Herald Angel
(by Double Schwartz): dam 2-y-o 7f winner, later won at 1m: fair performer: won
median auction maiden at Nottingham in April and nursery at Catterick in July:
off course 3 months, well beaten last 2 starts: needs further than 5f, stays 7f.
M. H. Tompkins

MIRROR FOUR SPORT 2 ch.f. (Apr 29) Risk Me (FR) 127 – Madison Girl 68 50 ?
(Last Fandango 125) [1996 5g⁴ a6g⁵ a7g⁶ 6.1m 6m a7g Nov 29] 1,000Y: unfurnished

filly: fifth foal: closely related to useful 6f/7f performer Madly Sharp (by Sharpo): dam 12.3f and 13.8f winner and also over hurdles: poor maiden: bred to stay beyond 6f, but pulled hard when tried at 7f. *M. Johnston*

MIRUS   3 ch.g. Tina's Pet 121 – Water Stock (Roscoe Blake 120) [1995 NR 1996 –
8f³ 8g Jul 24] first foal: dam remote third in bumper: tailed off in maiden and seller.
Ronald Thompson

MISCHIEF STAR   3 b.f. Be My Chief (USA) 122 – Star Face (African Sky 124)   65
[1995 57: 7m 7m⁴ 8.1d 1996 12g 10m 14m 16.2f³ 17.2m⁵ a16g* 14m* 16.1f Oct 8]
big, good-topped filly: has a long stride: fair handicapper: won at Lingfield in August
(by 5 lengths) and September (staying on strongly, despite wandering, to lead post):
found little final outing: sold (D. Elsworth to N. Henderson) 18,000 gns Newmarket
Autumn Sales: effective at 1¾m, and will prove suited by 2m+: acts on firm ground
and equitrack, yet to race on anything softer than dead. *D. R. C. Elsworth*

MISELLINA (FR)   2 b.f. (Feb 7) Polish Precedent (USA) 131 – Misallah (IRE)   57 p
(Shirley Heights 130) [1996 8.1s⁵ Oct 5] 220,000 francsY: smallish, rather unfurnished filly: first foal: dam, well beaten here at 2 yrs then fourth over 1m and 12.5f in
France, closely related to smart Irish 7f to 13f winner The Miller out of Cherry
Hinton winner Turkish Treasure: 5/1, around 11½ lengths fifth of 8 to Noble Dane in
steadily-run maiden at Haydock, staying on at one pace: moved poorly to post: sold
4,700 gns Newmarket Autumn Sales. *D. R. Loder*

MISHAWEER   3 b.f. Primo Dominie 121 – Ideal Home 104 (Home Guard (USA)   58
129) [1995 –: 6g 1996 6g⁵ 7m⁵ 6.1m⁶ 8.2m Jul 26] best effort (modest form) when
fifth in maiden at Pontefract on reappearance: very stiff task next start, then below
form (visored) in 2 handicaps, pulling too hard on final occasion: sold 11,500 gns
Goff's November Sales: should stay further than 6f: sent to Italy. *J. R. Fanshawe*

MISH MISH   2 ch.f. (Jan 29) Groom Dancer (USA) 128 – Kirsten 77 (Kris 135)   –
[1996 7m Sep 10] first foal: dam, 12.2f winner, half-sister to Petoski: always behind
in maiden at Lingfield: sold 1,700 gns Newmarket Autumn Sales. *W. Jarvis*

MISKIN HEIGHTS (IRE)   2 ch.f. (Mar 14) Sharp Victor (USA) 114 – Nurse Jo   –
(USA) (J O Tobin (USA) 130) [1996 5g 6m a7g Nov 22] IR 600F, IR 3,000Y:
half-sister to minor winners in USA by Skywalker and Tantoul: dam twice-raced
half-sister to Irish Oaks dead-heater Melodist and US Grade 1 winner Love Sign: no
promise. *K. R. Burke*

MISKY BAY   3 b.c. Shareef Dancer (USA) 135 – Rain Date (Rainbow Quest   71 §
(USA) 134) [1995 61p: 8m 1996 8g 8.5m³ 12.3g 10.5d 8.5m 10g⁴ 10.1g a7g⁴ a7g   a60 §
Dec 11] small, stocky colt: unimpressive mover: fair maiden handicapper at best:
reportedly choked seventh 3-y-o start: sold out of J. Gosden's stable 8,000 gns
Newmarket Autumn Sales afterwards: virtually refused to race final start: needs
further than 7f and stays 1¼m: tried visored: unreliable. *D. J. S. Cosgrove*

MISLEMANI (IRE)   6 b.g. Kris 135 – Meis El-Reem 124 (Auction Ring (USA)   53
123) [1995 64: 6m 7g 8m³ a7g² a9.4g⁵ 7.1m³ 7m* 8m⁶ 7.3d 7g² 7g a8g³ a7g³ 1996
a8g² a8g a8g³ a9.4g³ 8m 8.5m 7.1m³ 7f 7g Jul 31] sturdy gelding: modest
handicapper: effective at 7f to 9.4f: acts on firm and dead going and on fibresand,
well beaten on equitrack. *A. G. Newcombe*

MISRULE (USA)   3 b.f. Miswaki (USA) 124 – Crowning Ambition (USA) 65   73
(Chief's Crown (USA)) [1995 NR 1996 7m⁶ 7f⁵ 7.6m² 7g 7m⁵ 8g* 7g Oct 19] second
foal: dam 7f winner out of top-class 6f to 8.5f winner Fabulous Notion: fair form:
won minor event at Brighton in October by 4 lengths: not sure to stay beyond 1m: yet
to race on a soft surface: often early to post: looked most awkward under pressure
third start (at Chester): sold 17,000 gns Newmarket December Sales. *J. H. M. Gosden*

MISS ALICE   2 b.f. (May 25) Komaite (USA) – Needle Sharp 64 (Kris 135) [1996   –
5f⁶ a7g⁴ 6.1d 7.5m 6s Oct 5] 400Y: leggy, sparely-made filly: first reported foal: dam,
maiden who stayed 1m, half-sister to useful middle-distance performer Telephone
Man: poor maiden: fell in selling nursery at Beverley penultimate start. *J. Norton*

MISS ARAGON   8 b.m. Aragon 118 – Lavenham Blue (Streetfighter 120) [1995   42
59: 5g² 5m 6g 6m 6m³ 6m* 6g* 6d⁵ 6.1d 6.1d 6g 5m 1996 5.9m 6g 6g⁵ 6f 6.1m 6f
6d⁶ 6m 6m a6g⁴ a6g⁶ a6g³ a6g⁵ a5g³ Dec 13] rangy mare: good mover: just a poor
handicapper in 1996: effective at 5f and 6f: possibly unsuited by very firm ground,
acts on any other. *Miss L. C. Siddall*

MISS BARCELONA (IRE)   2 b.f. (Mar 6) Mac's Imp (USA) 116 – National   53
Ballet (Shareef Dancer (USA) 135) [1996 5m 6g² 6m 6g⁵ a5g⁵ 5f² 6m³ 5.7m² 5m⁴
7m⁴ 6g⁴ 6g 5m⁴ 7m Oct 4] 5,000Y: small, workmanlike filly: not a good walker: has
a quick action: first foal: dam unraced close relative of useful middle-distance stayer
Saxon Maid out of Oaks third Britannia's Rule: modest maiden: stays 6f: yet to race
on a soft surface. *M. J. Polglase*

MISS BIGWIG   3 b.f. Distinctly North (USA) 115 – Jacqui Joy 63 (Music Boy   72
124) [1995 84: 5d* 5g⁴ 5m⁵ 5f* 5m⁶ 5m² 5d* 5s⁴ 1996 5d 5.1g⁶ 5m⁴ 5g⁵ 5g⁵ 5.7m
5m⁴ 5d 5m⁶ Oct 17] small, leggy, close-coupled filly: fair handicapper at 3 yrs: sold
4,200 gns Doncaster October Sales: raced only at around 5f: acts on firm and dead
ground (below form on soft final 2-y-o start). *J. Berry*

MISS CAROTTENE   3 b.f. Siberian Express (USA) 125 – Silk St James (Pas de   49 d
Seul 133) [1995 56: 6m 6g 5m 5g 6f² 6m 6f² 5m³ 6.1d 7d 7f a6g 1996 a7g⁴ a6g* a6g
8f 6.9d a7g a6g Nov 18] good-topped filly: modest handicapper: won at Lingfield in
January, getting up near finish: off course 8½ months, tailed off all 4 starts on return:
stays 6f: acts on equitrack and firm ground: tried blinkered/visored. *M. J. Ryan*

MISS CASHTAL (IRE)   5 b.m. Ballacashtal (CAN) – Midnight Mistress (Mid-   –
summer Night II 117) [1995 NR 1996 a13g⁵ a12g⁴ a11g Feb 2] sister to winning
hurdler Penhill and to 6f and 7f winner Secret Liaison, also successful over hurdles:
dam never ran: produced a foal in 1994: modest winning hurdler: well held in varied
company on flat. *D. T. Thom*

MISS CHARLIE   6 ch.m. Pharly (FR) 130 – Close To You 44 (Nebbiolo 125)   46
[1995 42: a8.5g² a8.5g a9.4g a10g 7m² 1996 a7g 6.9m* 8m⁵ 8f⁴ 8f a6s Dec 19] leggy,
angular mare: poor performer: won (first time) claimer at Carlisle in May: flattered
in falsely-run minor event there on fourth outing, final start for T. Wall: stays 8.5f:
acts on firm ground and fibresand: headstrong: sometimes early to post. *A. Bailey*

MISS CLONTEEN (IRE)   2 br.f. (Mar 29) Tirol 127 – Kottna (USA) (Lyphard   –
(USA) 132) [1996 5g⁵ 5.7g 7m 6m 7s Oct 17] IR 1,200Y: half-sister to 1990 Irish
2-y-o 7f winner Koti (by Shardari), later successful at 2m and in Germany: dam Irish
2-y-o 7f winner, granddaughter of Cheveley Park winner Mige: little form: left
M. Madgwick after second start: blinkered last 2 outings. *J. J. Walsh, Ireland*

MISS DARLING   2 b.f. (Feb 25) Clantime 101 – Slipperose 72 (Persepolis (FR)   –
127) [1996 5f⁶ a5g a5g Nov 16] 3,500Y: third foal: half-sister to 3-y-o Galway Blade
(by Faustus): dam 11.5f winner: little form: unseated rider to post, bolted and
withdrawn second intended outing. *J. Akehurst*

MISSED THE BOAT (IRE)   6 b.g. Cyrano de Bergerac 120 – Lady Portobello   42
(Porto Bello 118) [1995 46: 10f 13.1h* 12d a13g 1996 a12g a16g 12.1m⁶ 12g⁴ Jul
31] rather leggy gelding: poor handicapper: only form at 6 yrs when fourth at Epsom:
stays 13.1f: acts on hard going, dead and fibresand: tried blinkered/visored, not since
1993. *A. G. Newcombe*

MISSEL   4 b.c. Storm Bird (CAN) 134 – Miss Demure 106 (Shy Groom (USA))   93
[1995 92+: 8m⁵ 1996 10m 10m⁶ Aug 10] quite attractive colt: has a quick action:
rated 102 at 2 yrs but ran only once in 1995 (last start for P. Chapple-Hyam): ran in 2
handicaps at Newmarket in 1996, on both occasions keeping on and showing he
retains plenty of ability: probably stays 1¼m: sent to UAE. *M. Johnston*

MISS ELECTRA   4 b.f. Superpower 113 – Apocalypse (Auction Ring (USA)   –
123) [1995 –: 7m 6g 1996 8.3m May 20] sturdy filly: of little account. *M. Blanshard*

MISS EXPRESS (BEL)   3 gr.f. Siberian Express (USA) 125 – Landing Power   –
(Hill's Forecast 91) [1995 7g 7f 6v 1996 8m 10.8f 14.1m⁴ 16.2g Aug 24] ex-Belgian
filly: second known foal: dam won twice in Belgium: well beaten in 2 races in Belgium and one in Germany in 1995: no promise in sellers in Britain. *Mrs S. J. Smith*

MISSFORTUNA   2 b.f. (Feb 11) Priolo (USA) 127 – Lucky Round 82 (Auction   66 p
Ring (USA) 123) [1996 6m 6.1m 7d Oct 28] sturdy filly: has scope: third reported
foal: half-sister to French 3-y-o 11f winner Harmonie du Soir (by Top Ville): dam,
1¼m winner, sister to very smart 7f and 1m winner Lucky Ring: very slowly away
on debut: fair form in maiden at Nottingham on second start: held up and always
behind in similar event at Lingfield final one: will probably do better over 1m+.
Sir Mark Prescott

MISS FUGIT PENANCE 2 br.f. (Apr 16) Puissance 110 – Figment 75 (Posse – (USA) 130) [1996 5m6 5m 5m Sep 19] 5,400Y: small, leggy filly: second foal: sister to 3-y-o Quinta Boy: dam sprinting half-sister to Windsor Castle winner Prince Reymo: no form: very troublesome at start and refused to enter stalls for intended debut. *P. D. Evans*

MISS GOLDEN SANDS 2 ch.f. (Feb 3) Kris 135 – Miss Kuta Beach 91 (Bold 71 Lad (IRE) 133) [1996 6g 6m6 Oct 28] strong, quite attractive filly: fluent mover: half-sister to 3-y-o Radiant Star (by Rainbow Quest) and several winners, including 1993 2-y-o 7f winner Miss Rinjani (by Shirley Heights): dam, 6f and 1¼m winner, half-sister to smart 1m and 9f winner Bali Dancer: never-dangerous sixth of 22 to Baked Alaska in maiden at Newmarket: evens, disappointing in similar event at Leicester 10 days later, off bridle whole way: seems likely to need much further than 6f. *G. Wragg*

MISS HAVERSHAM 4 b.f. Salse (USA) 128 – Rustic Stile (Rusticaro (FR) 124) – [1995 81: 7m 8m 8.1m2 10.2d3 1996 10m6 7.9g a10g6 a8.5g a10g3 11.9m a7g 11.9f a64 Sep 4] sturdy filly: fairly useful maiden at 3 yrs: worthwhile form in 1996 only on equitrack, best effort when third in handicap wearing first-time blinkers: stays 1¼m: acts on good to firm ground and equitrack, probably on dead: also blinkered sixth and seventh 4-y-o starts: covered by Bin Ajwaad. *C. A. Cyzer*

MISSILE 3 b.g. Rock City 120 – Fast Chick 93 (Henbit (USA) 130) [1995 83p: 7g 114 6.9s2 6f* 1996 7.9f* 10g 8m* 8m2 8.9g3 9m2 Oct 5] good-topped gelding: made great strides as 3-y-o, progressing into a smart handicapper: won competitive event at York in May and rated stakes at Newmarket (showed fine turn of foot) in July: hot favourite, unlucky short-head second to Moscow Mist in Schweppes Golden Mile at

Mr J. W. Bogie's "Missile"

Goodwood (finishing strongly having met trouble in running): best effort when 2½ lengths second of 38 to Clifton Fox in Cambridgeshire at Newmarket (clear of remainder): stays 9f: acts on firm ground (best 2-y-o effort on soft): reportedly a nervous individual, and usually held up: genuine: sold for a reported £175,000 and sent to Hong Kong. *W. J. Haggas*

MISSILE TOE (IRE) 3 b.c. Exactly Sharp (USA) 121 – Debach Dust 64 (Indian 68 King (USA) 128) [1995 71: 5.1m² a5g² 6g⁵ 6m⁶ 6m* 5m⁵ 6m⁵ 6g³ 1996 6g 7m 6m⁶ 6f⁵ 6f 5m 7m⁵ 8m⁴ 8m² 8f² 8m 8g³ Oct 29] good-topped colt: poor walker: fair handicapper: stays 1m: acts on firm ground and fibresand: below form in blinkers and visor: best recent efforts when ridden prominently. *J. E. Banks*

MISS IMPULSE 3 b.f. Precocious 126 – Dingle Belle 72 (Dominion 123) [1995 43 43: 6.1m³ 6g³ a5g 6.1m⁶ 1996 7.5m² 7g a7g 10f Sep 23] compact filly: unimpressive mover: first run for nearly a year, second in claimer at Beverley: no form afterwards, including in selling company: may prove best short of 7.5f. *Miss J. Bower*

MISS IRON HEART (USA) 4 b.f. Minshaanshu Amad (USA) 91§ – Iron – Franco (USA) (Barrera (USA)) [1995 –: 7g 7.1f⁶ a7g 7g 10.3m 1996 7.1g 8m⁵ 10.8f 9.7m⁶ 8f⁶ 8.1m⁵ Jun 30] well-made, quite attractive filly: little worthwhile form since 2 yrs: stays 1m: blinkered, tongue tied and edgy final 3-y-o start: covered by Risk Me. *D. J. S. Cosgrove*

MISS KALAGLOW 2 b.f. (Mar 6) Kalaglow 132 – Dame du Moulin 81 (Shiny – Tenth 120) [1996 8.2m 7.9g Oct 9] 3,000Y: quite good-topped filly: seventh foal: half-sister to German 3-y-o Karliczek (by Superlative), 1m winner at 2 yrs: dam, 2-y-o 7f winner, is half-sister to useful middle-distance fillies Rollrights and Rollfast: well held in maidens. *C. F. Wall*

MISS KIVE 10 b.m. Kabour 80 – Final Cast 50 (Saulingo 122) [1995 NR 1996 – a6g Mar 6] leggy, rather angular mare: poor sprint handicapper (rated 30) in 1991: tailed off only outing since. *A. J. Chamberlain*

MISS LAUGHTER 4 b.f. Sulaafah (USA) 119 – Miss Comedy 56 (Comedy Star 53 (USA) 121) [1995 49: 5.1g 8f⁴ 8m 7f 7.1m⁶ 8f* 6.9h³ 8g 1996 8m 8g 8.1g* 8m 8m⁶ 10g 8.1f Sep 12] lengthy, angular filly: modest performer: best effort when making all in 18-runner selling handicap at Chepstow in June: seems suited by forcing tactics at 1m: acts on hard ground: mounted on track and early to post penultimate start: none too consistent. *J. W. Hills*

MISS MEZZANINE 2 b.f. (Apr 7) Norton Challenger 111 – Forest Fawn (FR) – 51 (Top Ville 129) [1996 8.1s Oct 22] first reported foal: dam, plating-class maiden who stayed 1¼m, successful over hurdles: slowly away and always outpaced in maiden at Chepstow. *E. A. Wheeler*

MISS MICHELLE 6 ch.m. Jalmood (USA) 126 – Southern Dynasty 81 (Gunner – B 126) [1995 NR 1996 a12g Jul 27] poor form at best at 3 yrs for S. Mellor: no promise on return to flat: bred to be suited by 1½m+: best effort on top-of-the-ground. *E. A. Wheeler*

MISS OFFSET 3 ch.f. Timeless Times (USA) 99 – Farinara (Dragonara Palace 40 (USA) 115) [1995 61: 5v² 5.3m³ 5g⁶ a5g² 6g a6g* 7d* 7f 8f⁵ 8g 1996 a8g a10g⁵ a73 a6g* a6g⁵ a6g⁴ a7g* a7g⁴ 7.1g³ a7g² a7g* a6g³ 7.5g 8.1g 6d⁵ 7.1f a7g a6g* a7s⁶ Nov 19] leggy filly: has a quick action: fair handicapper on the all-weather, poor on turf: won selling race at Southwell in February and non-sellers at Wolverhampton in March and Southwell in April and (after several poor efforts) November: effective at 6f and 7f: best form on fibresand or an easy surface on turf: blinkered since sixth 2-y-o outing: often forces pace, came from behind for final success. *M. Johnston*

MISS PICKPOCKET (IRE) 3 b.f. Petorius 117 – Fingers (Lord Gayle (USA) 58 d 124) [1995 64: 5g³ 6d⁵ 6g⁶ a7g³ a5g* 1996 a6g³ a5g² a6g⁵ 7.1m a7g Nov 11] leggy filly: modest performer: left P. Kelleway after third 3-y-o start: first outings for 6 months, well beaten in minor events at Sandown (stiff task) and Wolverhampton: stays 7f: acts on dead ground and the all-weather. *Miss Gay Kelleway*

MISS PIGALLE 5 b.m. Good Times (ITY) – Panayr (Faraway Times (USA) 44 123) [1995 40: 6g 7m³ 6m⁶ 8g⁵ 8.3f 8.1m³ 6.9f⁶ 7.1m* 8.1f⁶ 6g 6f³ 7m 7m 7f⁵ 7g⁴ 7d 1996 7f³ 7.1g³ 6.9g 8.1f² 7.1g 8.1m⁴ 7m³ 7g³ 6m 7m 8m 8.1s Nov 7] leggy mare: poor handicapper: effective at 7f to 1m: acts on firm and dead ground: blinkered. *Miss L. A. Perratt*

MISS PRAVDA 3 ch.f. Soviet Star (USA) 128 – Miss Paige (AUS) (Luskin Star 52 d
(AUS)) [1995 62: 6g 7m³ 1996 8g 8m* 8f 9.7m⁴ 10f⁵ 10f⁶ 12.1m 14.1m⁴ a12g⁴ a11g
a14.8g⁵ a12g a14.8g Nov 25] plain filly: beat sole opponent by 20 lengths in
Newmarket Challenge Whip in May: modest form at best otherwise: sold out of
P. Walwyn's stable 4,000 gns Newmarket July Sales after sixth start: ran badly last 4
starts: probably stays 1½m: yet to race on a soft surface. *B. J. Llewellyn*

MISS PRISM 3 b.f. Niniski (USA) 125 – Reflected Glory (SWE) (Relko 136) 60
[1995 –: 7m⁵ 7g 1996 8g 12m 12.5f⁴ 16m³ 16m a16g² 13.1m² 15.4g² 17.9g 13.8g²
12.1s a14.8g² a16g² Dec 5] angular filly: modest maiden handicapper: stays 2m: acts
on all-weather surfaces and on firm ground. *J. L. Dunlop*

MISS RIVIERA 3 b.f. Kris 135 – Miss Beaulieu 106 (Northfields (USA)) [1995 103
84P: 6m* 1996 9.9m² 8m⁴ 10.4m⁶ 8f² 7g² 7m³ 8g³ 8g³ 8f² Oct 15] compact filly:
useful form: ran consistently well in 1996, best efforts when placed in listed races at
Deauville and Saint-Cloud and minor event (head second to Questonia) at Leicester
last 3 starts: doesn't stay 1¼m: acts on firm going, yet to race on a soft surface.
G. Wragg

MISS RIVIERA ROSE 2 ch.f. (May 14) Niniski (USA) 125 – Miss Beaulieu 61
106 (Northfields (USA)) [1996 6m⁵ 6m Sep 7] dipped-backed filly: sister to 1¼m
and 12.5f winner Riviera Magic and half-sister to several winners, including 3-y-o
Miss Riviera (by Kris), 6f winner at 2 yrs, and unreliable 1¼m winner Riviera
Rainbow (by Rainbow Quest): dam 6f and 1¼m winner: never a factor in maidens
won by The West at Goodwood and Calypso Lady at Kempton: swished tail both
starts, and went freely to post at Kempton. *G. Wragg*

MISS ROMANCE (IRE) 3 b.f. Cyrano de Bergerac 120 – Trysting Place (He 61 d
Loves Me 120) [1995 NR 1996 8.3g 10m 10m³ 9g⁶ Aug 30] IR 2,800Y: workmanlike
filly: sister to fairly useful 1995 German 1m winner Cosy Corner and half-sister to
1m winner Grondola (by Indian King): dam unraced half-sister to dam of Madam
Gay: seventh in slowly-run maiden on debut: no comparable form. *Miss Gay
Kelleway*

MISS SANCERRE 2 b.f. (Feb 19) Last Tycoon 131 – Miss Bergerac (Bold Lad 86 p
(IRE) 133) [1996 6g² 7d* Oct 28] leggy, lengthy filly: fourth foal: half-sister to 5-y-o
7f winner (stays 1m) Allez Cyrano (by Alzao): dam sister to Cyrano de Bergerac:
length second of 22 to Baked Alaska in maiden at Newmarket: 11/10 on, won similar
event at Lingfield 10 days later by 3 lengths from Kilshanny, needing to be only
pushed along to go clear: will stay 1m: capable of better. *G. Wragg*

MISS STAMPER (IRE) 2 b.f. (Apr 27) Distinctly North (USA) 115 – June 99 +
Goddess (Junius) (USA) 124) [1996 6m 5.1m* 5.2f* 6m* 6g* 6m³ Sep 20] IR 7,500Y,
resold 10,000Y: sixth foal: half-sister to 4 winners abroad, including German 1994
2-y-o 6f winner Negria (by Al Hareb): dam Irish 7f winner: useful performer:
successful in median auction maiden at Chepstow in June, Weatherbys Super Sprint

Weatherbys Super Sprint, Newbury—Miss Stamper (right) proves a bargain buy

Tattersalls Breeders Stakes, the Curragh—
even more auction money for Miss Stamper, as she beats Paddy Lad

at Newbury in July, and £18,500 nursery (beat Demolition Man in good style by 2½ lengths) at Newmarket and 30-runner Tattersalls Breeders Stakes (beat Paddy Lad 3 lengths) at the Curragh in August: reportedly came into season just before finishing only third of 6 to Queen Sceptre in listed race at Ayr on final outing: stays 6f: sometimes swishes tail: to be trained by Jenine Sahadi in USA. *R. Hannon*

MISS ST KITTS   2 ch.f. (Feb 8) Risk Me (FR) 127 – So Beguiling (USA) 49   – §
(Woodman (USA) 126) [1996 5f⁶ 5f⁶ 5f Jul 27] first reported foal: dam 7f seller winner at 2 yrs: no form: pulled hard and looked difficult ride final outing, subsequently joining J. Pearce: visored second appearance: unseated rider to post on debut. *J. R. Jenkins*

MISS TAHITI (IRE)   3 b.f. Tirol 127 – Mini Luthe (FR) (Luthier 126) [1995   114
114p: 8g* 8d² 8d* 1996 8m³ 10d² 10.5g² 12m³ 10m Oct 5] rangy, unfurnished filly: smart performer: won Prix Marcel Boussac at 2 yrs: in the frame in three top races in France in 1996, 1½ lengths second of 6 to Luna Wells in Prix Saint-Alary, length second of 12 to Sil Sila in strongly-run Prix de Diane and around ½-length fourth of 10 (promoted) to My Emma in Prix Vermeille: ran poorly in Sun Chariot Stakes at Newmarket in October: stays 1½m: has form on good to firm ground, possibly ideally suited by give: reportedly bled on 3-y-o reappearance. *A. Fabre, France*

MISS TOFFEE NOSE (IRE)   4 b.f. Cyrano de Bergerac 120 – Sweet Reprieve   –
(Shirley Heights 130) [1995 –: a8g⁶ a8g⁵ 1996 8.2m May 24] sparely-made filly: no worthwhile form. *D. J. S. Cosgrove*

MISS TRI COLOUR   4 b.f. Shavian 125 – Bourgeonette 81 (Mummy's Pet 125)   37
[1995 –: 8.1g⁶ 10f 7g a6g 1996 a7g⁴ a6g⁵ May 9] lengthy filly: poor maiden: sold 780 gns Doncaster July Sales: headstrong, and will prove best at sprint distances: visored last 2 starts at 3 yrs. *F. H. Lee*

MISS UNIVERSAL (IRE)   3 ch.f. Lycius (USA) 124 – Madame Nureyev   107
(USA) (Nureyev (USA) 131) [1995 79?: 6d 7d 1996 8g³ 7.3d⁴ 8m 10g³ 7m² 8m⁵ 10g² 10m 8.1m² 10.2f² 10m⁶ 10.1g² 10.3d Nov 8] leggy, lengthy filly: useful performer, still a maiden: best efforts when 4 lengths fifth of 7 to Shake The Yoke in Coronation Stakes at Royal Ascot, short-head second of 28 to Sheer Danzig in £51,700 handicap at Sandown next time, and length second to Wandering Star in listed race at Sandown tenth start, all in midsummer: stays 1¼m: acts on dead ground and good to firm: blinkered fourth (ran creditably) and fifth 3-y-o starts: sometimes a front runner: tends to hang left and carry head awkwardly: to be trained by B. Cecil in USA. *C. E. Brittain*

MISS WALSH   3 b.f. Distant Relative 128 – Andbell (Trojan Fen 118) [1995 NR   –
1996 8m⁴ 7m 6m Oct 7] 3,000F, 5,800Y: third foal: dam, half-sister to useful 6f and
7f winner Bell Tower, was of little account: no worthwhile form. *C. B. B. Booth*

MISS WATERLINE   3 br.f. Rock City 120 – Final Shot 91 (Dalsaan 125) [1995   77
72: 5d⁵ 5m³ 5m 6d* 5m⁴ 7.1g³ 6d 1996 6g 6m 6m² 7m⁶ 6g 5m 6m⁶ 7.1s 6g 6f Nov 5]
neat filly: fair handicapper: none too consistent at 3 yrs, best effort when sixth of 28
to Cretan Gift in Silver Cup at Ayr, soon off bridle and keeping on well: stays 6f: acts
on good to firm and dead ground. *P. D. Evans*

MISS ZANZIBAR   4 b.f. Kefaah (USA) 124 – Circe 73 (Main Reef 126) [1995   55
60: 6m 8m* a8.5g² 9.9m³ 7.5g⁴ 10g⁴ a9.4g³ 8h³ 7m 1996 a8.5g³ a8g a8g³ a8g⁶ a9.4g³   a48
10.9d 10.2g⁴ 8m⁴ a8.5g 8f² 7f⁴ 8g⁶ Aug 12] sparely-made filly: modest handicapper:
stays 1¼m: acts on firm ground and fibresand (ran poorly only start on a soft surface):
none too consistent: covered by Noble Patriarch. *R. A. Fahey*

MISTER   4 ch.g. Risk Me (FR) 127 – Beauvoir (Artaius (USA) 129) [1995 5m 7d   –
6g 1996 a10g⁶ a12g a6g a5g⁶ a5g May 27] 4,000Y: 2,500 2-y-o: ex-Irish gelding:
half-brother to 6f (at 2 yrs) and 8.3f winner Beau Dada (by Pine Circle): dam, French
1m winner, half-sister to Sangue: modest form at best in maidens and handicaps for
R. Kelly: well held in Britain: should stay 1m: tried blinkered. *K. McAuliffe*

MISTER ASPECTO (IRE)   3 b.g. Caerleon (USA) 132 – Gironde (USA)   78
(Raise A Native) [1995 64: 7g 7g⁶ 9g 7.1s 1996 a8.5g⁴ a12g² a12g* a10g* a11g* 9g
9.9m⁵ 12.5f⁵ 12m⁵ 12f³ 15.1f² 15.1g³ 12m* 13m* 14.1m⁴ 12m 16.1m³ 15.8g⁶ Oct
18] quite good-topped gelding: fair handicapper: won at Lingfield in February
(maiden) and March, Southwell in April, Beverley in July and Hamilton in August:
stays 16.1f: acts on firm ground and the all-weather, yet to race on a soft surface:
usually blinkered/visored in 1996, including when successful: frequently looks a
difficult ride: usually makes running/races prominently. *M. Johnston*

MISTER FIRE EYES (IRE)   4 b.g. Petorius 117 – Surfing 71 (Grundy 137)   76
[1995 86, a99: a9.4g* 7g* 8d² 7.5m⁵ 7m 7g 7g 8m 8m⁴ 7m⁵ 9f² 10m⁴ 8.1d 7g 8.2m²   a99
7m a6g² a6g* 1996 a9.4g² 8s 7m 7f² 7.3s⁶ 6g 7m 7f⁵ Jul 19] strong gelding: shows a
powerful action: useful handicapper on the all-weather, fair on turf: effective at 6f to
1¼m: acts on firm and soft ground, goes well on the all-weather: effective blinkered/
visored or not: usually races up with pace: sent to USA. *C. E. Brittain*

MISTER JAY   2 b.g. (Mar 13) Batshoof 122 – Portvasco 90 (Sharpo 132) [1996   47
6m 7.6d⁶ 8d Oct 2] dipped-backed, good-quartered gelding: fifth foal: half-brother to
3-y-o Oare Budgie and fairly useful 5.3f (at 2 yrs) and 6f winner (stays 1m) Midwich
Cuckoo (both by Midyan) and 6f to 7.1f winner Oare Sparrow (by Night Shift): dam
6f winner: well held in southern maidens. *P. T. Walwyn*

MISTER JOEL   3 ch.g. Risk Me (FR) 127 – Net Call 108 (Song 132) [1995 62: 7f   62 d
6m 6g 6s² 7f² 8f 5f* 5m 1996 6g⁵ 6g 5g* 5m⁵ 6s⁵ 7g³ 5g⁶ 6d 7g 5m 5g 6m Oct 23]
lengthy, good-topped gelding: modest handicapper: made all at Catterick in June:
sold only 1,200 gns Newmarket Autumn Sales: has form at 7f, but probably suited by
sprint distances: acts on firm and soft going: best in blinkers: tail swisher: often a
front runner: sent to Italy. *M. W. Easterby*

MISTER JOLSON   7 br.g. Latest Model 115 – Impromptu 88 (My Swanee 122)   81
[1995 90d: 6g 5.2m³ 6m 6m³ 6f 6f 5g⁵ 6m 6g 5.3g⁴ 6d 6.1s 1996 6s 6g⁴ 5g* 6m 5.1f
6m² 6g 5m* 6f³ 5m 6m 6.1d Aug 25] tall, lengthy gelding: impresses in appearance:
fairly useful handicapper: won at Sandown in April (well drawn, 17-runner race) and
Salisbury in June: effective at 5f and 6f: acts on good to firm and soft ground and on
equitrack: held up: blinkered final start: none too consistent. *R. J. Hodges*

MISTER LAWSON   10 ch.g. Blushing Scribe (USA) 107 – Nonpareil (FR) 92   –
(Pharly (FR) 130) [1995 –: a14g 1996 a16g a13g⁶ a12g Feb 22] close-coupled
gelding: no longer of any account. *B. Smart*

MISTER O'GRADY (IRE)   5 b.g. Mister Majestic 122 – Judy O'Grady 60
(Whistler 129) [1995 51: 10.8f⁶ 9.7m⁵ 10.2m⁵ 9m* 10m 10f* 11.5m⁴ 1996 10.2m⁴
10m* 10g 10f² 10.2f a10g Nov 7] robust, workmanlike gelding: modest handicapper:
won at Sandown in July: suited by around 1¼m: acted on firm ground and equitrack,
well beaten with give: effective blinkered/visored: usually raced prominently: broke
leg final start: dead. *R. Akehurst*

MISTER PINK   2 gr.g. (Mar 24) Absalom 128 – Blush Rambler (IRE) (Blushing   84
Groom (FR) 131) [1996 6s⁵ 6m³ 6f² 7m³ 7m³ 7m* 7.3m³ 8m 10f³ 10g⁶ Nov 2]
9,500Y: leggy, lengthy gelding: has scope: has a markedly round action: second foal:
half-brother to 3-y-o Forest Robin (by Formidable): dam, Irish 1½m winner, half-
sister to useful Irish stayer Excellenza: fairly useful performer: won strongly-run
nursery at Newmarket in August: stays 1¼m: raced almost exclusively on
top-of-the-ground (shaped quite well on soft on debut): visored third start, blinkered
last 2: gelded. *R. F. Johnson Houghton*

MISTER RAIDER   4 ch.g. Ballacashtal (CAN) – Martian Melody 62 (En-   52
chantment 115) [1995 49: a6g 5d⁴ 6m² 5.1g⁴ 5.1m 6f 5g⁴ 6g⁵ 5m 6f⁴ 6f⁴ a5g a5g 1996   a58
a6g a7g a6g* a7g⁵ a7g 5.1m⁵ 5m³ 6f a5g* a5g a5g a5g* Dec 31] slightly
dipped-backed gelding: modest sprinter: gained first success in minor event at
Lingfield in February: left S. Mellor after fifth 4-y-o outing: won handicaps back at
Lingfield in November and December: acts on firm and dead ground and on
equitrack: effective blinkered or not. *E. A. Wheeler*

MISTER RM   4 b.g. Dominion 123 – La Cabrilla 89 (Carwhite 127) [1995 79: 6m   70
8.3m 7g* 7.3d² 7d 8s 1996 10m 10g 7.3s 7.1g 7m a8.5g* a7g* Jul 6] good-topped
gelding: fair handicapper: well beaten at 4 yrs until winning at Wolverhampton in
June, making most: followed up in minor event there following month, leading inside
final 1f and not needing to be at best: subsequently sold to join N. Twiston-Davies
11,000 gns Newmarket July Sales: effective at 7f and may stay 1¼m: acts on
fibresand, best turf efforts on an easy surface: blinkered third 4-y-o start (when out of
form): fairly useful winning novice hurdler. *R. Guest*

MISTER SEAN (IRE)   3 b.g. Mac's Imp (USA) 116 – Maid of Mourne (Fairy   –
King (USA)) [1995 65: 5g⁵ 6g 5f² 5.1m² 5m² 5m⁵ 5d⁶ 5.3d 1996 5m 5m 5g 5.1g Oct
24] compact, good-bodied gelding: poor mover: modest maiden at best as a 2-y-o:
has lost his form: speedy: acts on firm ground: tried blinkered. *J. W. Payne*

MISTER WESTSOUND   4 b.g. Cyrano de Bergerac 120 – Captivate 79   73 d
(Mansingh (USA) 120) [1995 66: 5g⁴ 5g 5g 6f⁵ 5m² 5f² 5f² 5m³ 5g³ 5f 6m* 6f* 7f²
7.1m⁶ 7g 7d⁴ 6g² 7f² 7f⁶ 6m 1996 6d² 6m³ 5.9m⁵ 6d³ 6g⁴ 6m³ 7m⁵ 7m⁶ 6m 6d⁵ 6m⁶
6f 6m 6f 7g 6m⁴ 8.1s Nov 7] workmanlike gelding: fair handicapper: ran consistently
well in first half of 1996, only for his form to deteriorate from July onwards: stays 7f:
acts on firm and dead ground: has been visored, blinkered nowadays: frequently
spoils his chance by starting slowly. *Miss L. A. Perratt*

MISTER WOODSTICK (IRE)   3 b.g. Distinctly North (USA) 115 – Crannog   60
(Habitat 134) [1995 –: 5g 8g 1996 6s 8.3d 8m* 7m³ 8m* 8m⁶ 8f 8g³ 7f⁶ 8.1d Sep 27]
robust, close-coupled gelding: modest handicapper: won at Carlisle in May and
Redcar in June: seems suited by around 1m: acts on firm ground, seemingly not on a
soft surface. *M. A. Jarvis*

MISTLE CAT (USA)   5 gr.h. Storm Cat (USA) – Mistle Toe (USA) (Maribeau)   116
[1995 111: 7m² 7.1g* 7g² 7m⁴ 7m² 6.5m 7m⁴ 6m⁶ 8m⁴ 1996 8.1g³ 7d* 8f³ 8m⁶ 7.3m²

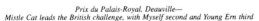

Prix du Palais-Royal, Deauville—
Mistle Cat leads the British challenge, with Myself second and Young Ern third

8d* Oct 6] angular horse: smart performer, in excellent form in 1996: won Prix du Palais Royal at Deauville in May by 2 lengths from Myself and (after finishing second to Bin Rosie in Hungerford Stakes at Newbury) 6-runner Premio Vittorio di Capua at Milan in October by 2 lengths from Gothenberg: refused to enter stalls for Prix de la Foret at Longchamp later in month: effective at 7f, and stayed 9.8f: acted on firm and soft ground: blinkered (ran respectably) final 4-y-o start: was usually a front runner: game and consistent: died in his box in late-October. *S. P. C. Woods*

MISTROY 6 gr.m. Damister (USA) 123 – Troja (Troy 137) [1995 NR 1996 15.8g –
Aug 16] modest maiden (stayed 1½m) in 1994 for M. Hammond, visored last 2 outings: well beaten on return: dead. *Miss M. K. Milligan*

MISTY CAY (IRE) 2 b.f. (Mar 18) Mujadil (USA) 119 – Quai Des Brumes 65 d
(USA) (Little Current (USA)) [1996 5.3f³ 6g⁴ 6f* 6m² 7m³ 7g* 7g⁵ 8m⁶ 7m⁵ 7g a6g⁴ Nov 14] IR 2,500F, 2,600Y, resold 1,150Y: leggy filly: eighth foal: half-sister to 3 winners in France/Italy by Be My Guest: dam French maiden half-sister to very smart 1979 French 2-y-o Nice Havrais: fair performer: won seller at Brighton and claimer (hung right) at Salisbury in the summer: probably stays 1m: acts on firm ground: twice slowly away, badly so on first occasion. *S. Dow*

MISTY RAIN 2 br.f. (Feb 16) Polar Falcon (USA) 126 – Ballerine (USA) – p
(Lyphard's Wish (FR) 124) [1996 6m Sep 21] 12,000Y: fifth foal: half-sister to Rambrino (by Robellino), useful 1994 2-y-o 6f winner who had form at 10.3f, and 3 winners abroad: dam French 8.7f and 1¼m winner from family of Bigstone: 50/1, some late progress when eleventh of 24 to Speedball in maiden at Newbury: should do better, probably over further than 6f. *B. W. Hills*

MISTY VIEW 7 gr.m. Absalom 128 – Long View 68 (Persian Bold 123) [1995 –
NR 1996 11.6d 10m Sep 18] modest performer (best form at 1¼m) in 1994: never a threat on first runs for 2 years: covered by Thowra. *J. White*

MISWAKI DANCER (USA) 6 ch.g. Miswaki (USA) 124 – Simply Divine 54
(USA) (Danzig (USA)) [1995 NR 1996 10.3m 10d⁶ 12m³ 14.1f⁵ 12d³ Aug 25] modest maiden: stays 1½m (never able to land a blow over 1¾m): acts on good to firm ground, but best 3-y-o form with some give (acted on soft): has carried head high under pressure. *Lady Herries*

MITHAK (USA) 2 b.c. Silver Hawk (USA) 123 – Kapalua Butterfly (USA) 81 p
(Stage Door Johnny) [1996 7g³ 7m³ Aug 17] $160,000Y: rather unfurnished colt: has a rather short action: fourth foal: half-brother to 3 winners in USA, including Grade 3 9f winner Polish Holiday (by Danzig): dam Grade 3 9.5f winner, sister to Grade 1 1¾m winner One On The Aisle: stayed on well when third in maidens won by Benny The Dip at Newmarket and Monza at Newbury, bit short of room on second occasion: will stay middle distances: probably capable of further improvement. *B. W. Hills*

MITHRAIC (IRE) 4 b.g. Kefaah (USA) 124 – Persian's Glory (Prince 63
Tenderfoot (USA) 126) [1995 59: 8g² 8.5m 8.1g⁶ 8g 10f³ 1996 10.2g⁵ 10f² 12s² 11.1m² 11.1m* 11.1m* 10m 12m⁵ Aug 6] big, lengthy gelding: reportedly tubed after reappearance: modest performer: made all in claimer at Hamilton and minor event at Musselburgh (set up unassailable lead in back straight then only one to come to stand side) in July: unable to dictate and well beaten last 2 starts: stays 1½m: acts on firm and soft ground: fair winning hurdler. *W. S. Cunningham*

MIXED MOOD 4 br.f. Jalmood (USA) 126 – Cool Combination 76 (Indian King –
(USA) 128) [1995 40, a65: a7g⁵ a6g* a7g⁴ 6g⁵ 7g a6g* a7g a6g 6.1d a7g 8.1d 1996 a7g a11g a7g Oct 5] lengthy, angular filly: modest performer at best: no worthwhile form for some time: sold 1,000 gns Ascot November Sales: stays 7f: acts on fibresand and soft going: tried blinkered: headstrong: sent to South Korea. *B. J. Llewellyn*

MIZYAN (IRE) 8 b.g. Melyno 130 – Maid of Erin (USA) (Irish River (FR) 131) 60
[1995 64, a71: a16g² a12g⁴ a14g* 14.1g² 14.1m* 15.8g⁶ 1996 a14.8g⁵ a16g⁴ a16g³ a65
15.4f⁵ 14.1m³ 14.9f⁵ 14.9m² 16m⁶ 17.1m 18g Oct 21] tall, leggy gelding: has a round action: fair handicapper, better form on all-weather than turf in 1996: finds 1½m a minimum and stays well: acts on good to firm ground, dead and on all-weather surfaces, probably unsuited by very firm: blinkered (no improvement) twice at 5 yrs: normally held up/tracks leaders. *J. E. Banks*

MO-ADDAB (IRE) 6 b.g. Waajib 121 – Tissue Paper 95 (Touch Paper 113) 82
[1995 84: 8m³ 8m 10.1f³ 8g⁴ 8m² 8m* 8d 8d* 8m² 8m 1996 8m 8s⁴ 8m 8m 8g 8m

8m² 8g Sep 29] leggy, useful-looking gelding: keen walker: fairly useful handicapper: back to form when second of 16 to Artful Dane in £17,800 event at Newbury in September: hampered early in £29,700 event at Ascot final start: best efforts at 1m: acts on firm and soft going: sometimes flashes tail: has run well when sweating: tough. *A. C. Stewart*

MOBILE KING   3 ch.g. Colmore Row 111 – Donosa (Posse (USA) 130) [1995 –:   –
5.1f a5g 6m 1996 6.1g Apr 22] no worthwhile form. *K. R. Burke*

MOCCASIN (IRE)   2 b.f. (Apr 15) Lahib (USA) 129 – Karine (Habitat 134)   –
[1996 6.1m 7.1s Oct 22] 10,500Y: half-sister to 3-y-o Star of Ring (by Taufan), Irish 1m winner Uptothehilt (by Kris), later winner in USA, and 2 winners abroad: dam lightly-raced half-sister to Earl of Sefton winner Heaven Knows: behind in maidens at Nottingham (auction event) and Chepstow (had worst of draw) 3½ months apart: sold 2,700 gns Newmarket Autumn Sales. *P. R. Webber*

MOCK TRIAL (IRE)   3 b.g. Old Vic 136 – Test Case 90 (Busted 134) [1995 NR   67
1996 7s 7g 8.5m 8m⁶ 10d² 12m* 12m² 17.1m 12g² 15m⁵ 10.3g Oct 25] tall, strong gelding: fourth foal: dam lightly-raced 1m winner who probably stayed 1½m: fair handicapper: got up close home at Beverley in June: good efforts afterwards when second at Pontefract: better at 1½m than shorter, and should stay further: acts on good to firm ground: usually sweating and edgy. *Mrs J. R. Ramsden*

MODEST HOPE (USA)   9 b.g. Blushing Groom (FR) 131 – Key Dancer (USA)   57
(Nijinsky (CAN) 138) [1995 51: a12g³ a11g³ a12g⁶ a11g⁵ a11g a12g² a11g* a12g² 9.9m a12g 10.3m a12g⁴ 10m 14.1m⁴ 16m 11.5g⁶ a12g 12m a14g³ a12g³ 1996 a11g* a12g⁶ a12g² a12g² a11g a14g Sep 9] big, rather angular gelding: poor mover: modest handicapper: won at Southwell (amateurs) in January: off course 7 months before final start (finished last of 17): stays 1¾m: has won only on a sound surface (acts on good to firm ground) or the all-weather: sometimes bandaged. *B. Richmond*

MOFASA   3 b.g. Shardari 134 – Round Midnight 64 (Star Appeal 133) [1995 NR   –
1996 a8g Jan 26] third foal: brother to fair 1m and 1¼m winner Midnight Jazz and half-brother to French 12.5f winner Welcome Sir (by Most Welcome): dam, out of a 1½m winner, ran only at up to 6f at 2 yrs: last of 7 in median auction maiden at Southwell: sold 3,200 gns Newmarket July Sales. *W. A. O'Gorman*

MOGIN   3 ch.f. Komaite (USA) – Misdevious (USA) (Alleged (USA) 138) [1995   56
–: 6m 7g 1996 a6g a8g⁶ a6g⁴ a7g⁴ a6g a6g³ 8.3g⁴ 7g 7m* a8g 8g a8g a8g² Dec 11]   a46
big, plain filly: modest performer: left J. Ffitch-Heyes after sixth 3-y-o start: won median auction maiden at Brighton in August: stays 1m: acts on good to firm ground and all-weather surfaces: has given trouble at stalls. *T. J. Naughton*

MOGUL   2 b.g. (Apr 9) Formidable (USA) 125 – Madiyla 73 (Darshaan 133)   – p
[1996 8s a7g⁵ Dec 11] third foal: brother to 3-y-o Formidable Flame: dam, 1½m winner, half-sister to smart Irish 1993 2-y-o Manntari: signs of ability in median auction maidens. *N. A. Graham*

MOHANNAD (IRE)   3 b.c. Royal Academy (USA) 130 – Pudibunda (Bold Lad   77
(IRE) 133) [1995 68p: 8m 1996 10m 10m⁶ 8f² Jun 13] big, rangy colt: fair form in maidens, carrying head high final start: may prove best at around 1m. *J. W. Hills*

MOHAWK RIVER (IRE)   3 b.c. Polish Precedent (USA) 131 – High Hawk 124   92
(Shirley Heights 130) [1995 NR 1996 11d⁴ 10.4g* 11.8m⁴ Oct 28] lengthy, good sort: ninth foal: half-brother to several winners, notably Breeders' Cup Turf winner In The Wings and smart French middle-distance performer Hunting Hawk (both by Sadler's Wells): dam middle-distance stayer: carrying plenty of condition for first run in over 4 months, won maiden at York in September: somewhat disappointing 9 lengths fourth of 6 to Masehaab in minor event at Leicester 8 weeks later, soon beaten in straight: should be suited by 1½m: looked useful prospect at York: stays in training. *M. R. Stoute*

MOI CANARD   3 ch.c. Bold Owl 101 – Royal Scots Greys 38 (Blazing Saddles   61
(AUS)) [1995 61, a66: a5g* a6g² a6g* 6m³ 6.1m² 6m 6m² 6f* 6f² 6m⁵ 6m⁴ 6s⁵ a6g*   a73
a6g⁴ a6g² a6g⁵ 1996 a7g⁶ a6g² a7g* a7g² a7g³ a7g* 6f⁵ 7m 7f⁴ 7m a8.5g 6.9g 7m a7g Nov 7] compact colt: fair handicapper on the all-weather: won at Lingfield in February and March: modest on turf: well beaten final 5 starts, finishing last on 3 occasions: should stay 1m: acts on firm ground and all-weather surfaces, below form on soft: held up. *B. A. Pearce*

MOK

MOKUTI 4 b.c. Green Desert (USA) 127 – Marie d'Argonne (FR) 104 (Jefferson 76
129) [1995 73: 7g⁴ 8m³ 8g³ 1996 7d⁵ 8d* 10d 10.1f³ Jun 25] small colt: fair performer: won handicap at Carlisle in April by short head, off bridle virtually
throughout and leading post: blinkered both subsequent outings, running well final
start despite again needing to be ridden some way out: stays 1¼m: acts on firm and
dead ground: a difficult ride: sent to Germany. *G. Wragg*

MOLLILY 2 ch.f. (Apr 25) Ballacashtal (CAN) – Foligno (Crofter (USA) 124) –
[1996 5.3f 5f Apr 23] 1,250Y: fourth foal: half-sister to 3-y-o February and winning
sprinters Giggleswick Gossip and Giggleswick Girl (all by Full Extent): dam won at
1½m in Ireland: always behind in median auction maiden and seller (reared stalls).
M. R. Channon

MOLLY DRUMMOND 2 b.f. (Feb 10) Sizzling Melody 117 – Miss Drummond 54
59 (The Brianstan 128) [1996 5g⁵ 5g 5d* 6m⁵ 5m 5f 5g 5d Nov 8] leggy filly: third
live foal: dam 2-y-o 5f and 6f winner, out of sister to Petong: won weak maiden at
Haydock in May: well beaten in nurseries last 4 starts, blinkered on last 2: stays 6f:
acts on good to firm and dead ground: sold 700 gns Doncaster November Sales: sent
to Denmark. *C. W. C. Elsey*

MOLLY MUSIC 2 b.f. (Feb 22) Music Boy 124 – Carlton Glory (Blakeney 126) 48
[1996 5s⁴ 5d³ 5d³ 5.1g⁶ a5g⁴ 6d⁶ 5m² a5g⁴ a5g Dec 3] 3,200F, 3,100Y: sturdy filly:
fifth foal: sister to Norwegian 1m winner Glorious Sound and half-sister to winning
stayer Reach For Glory (by Reach): dam poor half-sister to smart French miler
Gosport: poor form in varied 5f maiden events: had stiff task when tried at 6f:
blinkered/visored last 3 starts. *G. G. Margarson*

MOMENTS OF FORTUNE (USA) 4 b.g. Timeless Moment (USA) – How 101
Fortunate (USA) (What Luck (USA)) [1995 98: 8g³ 8g* 10f* 9m⁵ 12m 1996 8.1g³
7.1d⁵ 10.4f⁴ 8m 8.1g 7.9m³ 7.3m 10m 9m 8.1s Oct 22] close-coupled, good-bodied
gelding: good mover: useful performer: third in rated stakes at Sandown in April and
York (£25,300 event won by Concer Un) in August: mostly well below form
otherwise: suited by further than 7f nowadays, and stays 1¼m: acts on firm ground:
has run well blinkered or not: tends to sweat: usually races prominently: sent to UAE.
B. Hanbury

MONAASSIB 5 ch.g. Cadeaux Genereux 131 – Pluvial 90 (Habat 127) [1995 106
101: 6g⁴ 6m 7f² 7m 7f² 7m* 1996 7m² 7.9m⁵ 7.6f⁶ 6f 7g² 7m 6m* 6.5d² 7m² Oct 8]
stocky, sprint type: unimpressive mover: useful performer: better than ever at 5 yrs:
gained deserved success in minor event at Yarmouth in August: good second
afterwards in listed race at Munich and minor event at Redcar (beaten ½ length by
Desert Flame): effective at 6f to 1m: acts on firm and dead ground, yet to race on soft:
usually races prominently. *E. A. L. Dunlop*

MONACO GOLD (IRE) 4 b.g. Durgam (USA) – Monaco Ville (Rheingold 46
137) [1995 –: 15g 12.1g 1996 14.1m⁵ 13.1m* 14.1f⁴ 13m* 12.1m 15.8g⁶ Sep 21]
sparely-made gelding: poor handicapper: won at Ayr (maiden contest) in June and
Hamilton in August: should stay 2m: modest novice hurdler. *Mrs M. Reveley*

MONARCH 4 b.c. Sadler's Wells (USA) 132 – Bint Pasha (USA) 126 (Affirmed 89
(USA)) [1995 92p: a11g³ 12m* 12.3m² 12m* 12m³ 11.8g³ 1996 11.9d³ 10m⁶ 13.9m
Aug 21] strong, good-topped colt: progressive handicapper in 1995: disappointing at
4 yrs, running as if something amiss in the Ebor at York on final outing: sold only
6,000 gns Newmarket Autumn Sales: should be suited by 1¾m+: acts on good to
firm ground: bandaged first 2 starts at 4 yrs: tongue tied on reappearance: usually
held up. *P. F. I. Cole*

MONARCH'S PURSUIT 2 b.g. (Mar 12) Pursuit of Love 124 – Last Detail 73 52
(Dara Monarch 128) [1996 6d⁵ 6m⁶ Jul 27] 3,600Y: well-grown, good-topped
gelding: has plenty of scope: fourth foal: dam, maiden suited by test of stamina and
who showed signs of temperament, is sister to very smart 1m and 1¼m performer
Broken Hearted: modest form in northern maidens: slowly away on debut: gelded
after final start. *T. D. Easterby*

MON BRUCE 2 ch.c. (Mar 16) Beveled (USA) – Pendona 72 (Blue Cashmere 67
129) [1996 6g⁶ 6m⁵ a6g² 6.1s a6g² a7s⁵ Nov 19] unfurnished, workmanlike colt: a74
fourth living foal: dam, maiden best at 5f, is daughter of useful sprinter Calibina: fair
maiden: looks a sprinter: acts on equitrack, well beaten on soft ground. *W. R. Muir*

MONDRAGON   6 b.g. Niniski (USA) 125 – La Lutine 95 (My Swallow 134)   70
[1995 76: 18g 16m³ 18.7m 16.1m 16f³ 16.1m⁴ 1996 18s 16.2m⁴ 16g⁶ 16m³ 16.1g⁴
15.8g⁴ 17.1m⁴ Aug 18] smallish, leggy gelding: good mover: fair handicapper: suited
by thorough test of stamina: probably acts on any ground: tends to edge right: held
up. *Mrs M. Reveley*

MONEGHETTI   5 ch.g. Faustus (USA) 118 – The Victor Girls (Crofthall 110)   –
[1995 48: 10m³ a11g a16.2g a7g* a8g³ a8.5g³ a8g* a7g 1996 a7g³ a8g⁵ a8.5g 7m   a43
Aug 6] good-topped gelding: poor handicapper on the all-weather: showed no
worthwhile form in 3 outings over hurdles for M. Pipe then returned to former trainer
and ran respectably at Southwell first 2 starts in 1996: slowly away both subsequent
outings: stays 8.5f: acts on fibresand, no worthwhile form on turf (lightly raced): has
run creditably for amateur. *R. Hollinshead*

MONGOL WARRIOR (USA)   3 b.c. Deputy Minister (CAN) – Surely   114
Georgie's (USA) (Alleged (USA) 138) [1995 79p: 6g³ 1996 8s* 10s² 10g² 11s* 12g*
12g⁶ 12v² 12m* Nov 10] good-quartered colt: smart performer, campaigned solely
overseas since debut: won minor event at Cagnes in January, Group 2 event at
Munich in May, Swiss Derby at Frauenfeld (by 5½ lengths, nowhere near best) in
June, and Group 3 race at Madrid in November: best effort in defeat when runner-up
to Protektor (pair clear) in Group 3 event at Dusseldorf penultimate outing: stays
1½m: acts on heavy going and good to firm. *Lord Huntingdon*

MONIS (IRE)   5 ch.g. Waajib 121 – Gratify 65 (Grundy 137) [1995 53: a6g a6g⁴   49
a7g a7g⁴ a6g 7.6m 5g 6d a6g a6g⁴ 1996 a7g³ a6g² a7g³ a6g⁵ 7m 7m⁶ a7g³ a6g⁴   a59
a5g³ a6g⁴ 7m a6g⁶ a6g³ a7s² a8g⁵ Dec 27] neat gelding: modest handicapper on
all-weather at 5 yrs, not quite so good on turf: effective at 5f, and stays 8.5f: acts on
firm and dead ground and goes well on fibresand: usually blinkered/visored: takes
keen hold, and usually races prominently: usually apprentice ridden. *J. Balding*

MONKEY FACE   5 gr.m. Clantime 101 – Charming View 62 (Workboy 123)   32
[1995 42d: 7m 6g 7.5m⁴ 6m 8m 8g⁵ 1996 6m⁶ 7g⁴ May 17] leggy, lengthy mare: poor
maiden: trained at 4 yrs by J. Hetherton: probably stays 1m: yet to race on a soft
surface: ran creditably only try in blinkers. *W. W. Haigh*

MONKEY'S WEDDING   5 b.g. Skyliner 117 – Munequita (Marching On 101)   –
[1995 8.3g a8g 8s⁵ a5g 5g a6g⁶ 3.5s a6g 1996 a7g a6g Jan 22] ran in Scandinavia at 3
yrs (won 2 races at 7.5f and one at 5f) and 4 yrs: soundly beaten on return to Britain:
stayed 7.5f: had form on good to firm ground, but seemed better on an easy surface
and fibresand: usually blinkered/visored: dead. *J. Berry*

MONKEY ZANTY (IRE)   3 b.f. Distinctly North (USA) 115 – Achafalaya   –
(USA) (Apalachee (USA) 137) [1995 54: a5g² 5f² 6m 5f⁴ 5g a5g⁴ a6g⁶ a6g* a6g⁶   a49
1996 a5g a5g*dis a5g⁶ 6.1d a6g⁴ 7g⁵ 6m⁶ Jul 18] smallish filly: poor performer:
passed the post first in claimer at Lingfield (disqualified for causing interference
before halfway) in January: below form last 5 starts: stays 6f: acts on the all-weather,
best turf form on firm ground: sent to South Korea. *J. L. Harris*

MONO LADY (IRE)   3 b.f. Polish Patriot (USA) 128 – Phylella (Persian Bold   59
123) [1995 61?: 5g 5.2m⁴ 5m⁶ 5.7m⁴ 6.1s 1996 8.3m 10m⁴ 8m 11.1g⁶ 9.7d* 8.2s⁶
a8g⁴ a8.5s⁶ Dec 19] leggy, unfurnished filly: modest handicapper: won 15-runner
event at Folkestone in October, despite hanging left and swishing tail: barely stays
11f: acts on good to firm and dead ground. *D. Haydn Jones*

MON PERE   3 b.g. Belfort (FR) 89 – Lady Ever-So-Sure 80 (Malicious) [1995 –:   –
7.5m 7.1m 8.5s 7f 1996 8.3s 6g Jun 1] leggy, quite attractive gelding: tailed off in
claimer and maiden (blinkered) at 3 yrs. *K. McAuliffe*

MON PERFORMER   2 ch.g. (Apr 17) Mon Tresor 113 – Hot Performer   –
(Hotfoot 126) [1996 6m 7f 7.9g 6g⁵ Oct 18] leggy, good-topped gelding: has been
freeze fired on shins: second foal: dam 7f (at 2 yrs) and 1½m winner: no worthwhile
form in maiden events. *M. J. Camacho*

MONS   3 b.c. Deploy 131 – Morina (USA) (Lyphard (USA) 132) [1995 110: 6m*   119
7g² 7m* 8d* 8m³ 1996 10g³ 12m⁴ 11.9m² 14.6m⁴ 12s⁵ Oct 26] neat colt: unimpressive walker: fluent mover: won Royal Lodge Stakes at 2 yrs: reportedly suffered from
sore shins after reappearance in April: off course 3 months: beaten under a length in
Gordon Stakes at Goodwood (finishing best) and when second of 6 to Dushyantor
in Great Voltigeur Stakes (set just steady pace, rallied) at York: below best when

Mrs E. H. Vestey's "Mons"

beaten 7¾ lengths into fourth in St Leger at Doncaster: should be well suited by further than 1½m: acts on good to firm ground and dead (held up and below form only outing on soft): resolute galloper, who goes well with forcing tactics: sweating last 3 starts (edgy first 2 occasions) and has been fractious at stalls: stays in training. *L. M. Cumani*

MONSIEUR CULSYTH 3 b.g. Mon Tresor 113 – Regal Salute 68 (Dara – Monarch 128) [1995 59d: 5s⁵ 5g* 5m* 6g⁴ 5m⁶ a6g 5g 1996 6d a6g 6f Jun 1] leggy gelding: modest form as 2-y-o: lost his way: best form at 5f: sold 1,300 gns Doncaster July Sales. *J. Berry*

MONTAGUE DAWSON (IRE) 4 ch.g. Doulab (USA) 115 – Annacloy – (Majority Blue 126) [1995 –, a66d: a6g* a6g* a7g⁴ a6g³ 6m a8.5g⁵ a6g⁴ a7g³ 6m a6g⁶ a6g a6g a5g⁴ a6g⁴ a6g⁶ 1996 a6g a6g a6g 6.1g a6g May 9] angular gelding: modest performer at best on the all-weather: no worthwhile form for some time: tried blinkered and visored. *Mrs N. Macauley*

MONTE CAVO 5 b.g. Bustino 136 – Dance Festival 101 (Nureyev (USA) 131) 34 [1995 –: a11g 7g 1996 7.1g 8.3s 8m 8.1m 12.3m 10.5m² 9.9g³ 14s Oct 5] leggy gelding: poor maiden handicapper: stays 1½m: acts on good to firm ground: no improvement in visor or blinkers. *M. Brittain*

MONTECRISTO 3 br.g. Warning 136 – Sutosky 78 (Great Nephew 126) [1995 79 69: 8.1m⁵ 7g 7g 6.9m 1996 a10g⁴ a10g* a10g² a12g* a12g⁶ 12s³ 10g³ 9.9m* 12.3g*ᵈⁱˢ 12m⁶ Jun 20] leggy, sparely made gelding: fairly useful handicapper: first past post at Lingfield (twice, including in claimer) in February, Beverley (claimer, unimpressive) in April and Chester (barged through over 1f out and disqualified) in May: good sixth of 20 to Samraan in King George V Stakes at Royal Ascot final start and would have been in shake up but for being hampered 3f out: better at 1½m than shorter: acts on good to firm ground (probably on soft) and equitrack. *R. Guest*

MONTE FELICE (IRE) 3 ch.g. Be My Guest (USA) 126 – Elabella –
(Ela-Mana-Mou 132) [1995 NR 1996 10m 8.3d 11.7m⁶ 10.8f Oct 8] 35,000Y: third
foal: half-brother to useful sprinter Espartero (by Ballad Rock) and 1½m winner
Typographer (by Never So Bold): dam never ran: well beaten: retained 600 gns
Newmarket Autumn Sales. *G. Harwood*

MONTENDRE 9 b.g. Longleat (USA) 109 – La Lutine 95 (My Swallow 134) 102
[1995 112: 6g* 6m³ 6m⁴ 6g⁴ 6d⁶ 6d 6m 1996 6s⁵ 6m 6g² 6m 6d² 6f 7.1g³ 6d 6s⁴
6.1s³ Oct 31] leggy gelding: shows traces of stringhalt: fluent mover: seems on the
downgrade, and only useful form at best in 1996: left M. McCormack after seventh
start: best efforts when second in minor events at Goodwood and Haydock and fourth
to The Puzzler in rated stakes at Newbury: needs at least 6f nowadays, and stays 7f:
acts on good to firm and heavy ground: often has tongue tied down: held up: tough.
R. J. Hodges

MONTFORT (USA) 2 b.g. (Feb 11) Manila (USA) – Sable Coated (Caerleon 60 p
(USA) 132) $35,000Y: second foal: dam unraced daughter of
Coronation Stakes winner Sutton Place: 9/1, beaten just over 10 lengths ninth of 20
to Sausalito Bay in maiden at Chepstow gelded: should do better. *P. F. I. Cole*

MONTJOY (USA) 4 b.c. Manila (USA) – Wendy's Ten (USA) (Tentam (USA)) 120
[1995 122: 8m² 8g² 7m 10.2m* 10g² 10g* 10m³ 10m³ 1996 10d³ 9.3s⁴ 10f² 10m*
10d⁴ 11g⁴ 12f Oct 5] strong, rangy, good sort: impresses in appearance: very smart
performer: won Group 3 event at Ayr (odds on, quickened well to beat Musetta by a
neck with something to spare) in July: in frame previously in Group 1 race at Rome
(½ length behind Hollywood Dream), 4-runner Prix d'Ispahan at Longchamp (below
best, behind Halling) and Prince of Wales's Stakes at Royal Ascot (on toes, began to
sweat, 1¼ lengths behind First Island), and subsequently in Group 1 event at Munich
(just over 1½ lengths fourth to Timarida) and Man O'War Stakes at Belmont (3½
lengths behind Diplomatic Jet) on final start for P. Cole: always towards rear in Turf
Classic at Belmont last time: better at 1¼m than shorter: acts on firm and dead
ground: tough and consistent. *J. Kimmel, USA*

MONTONE (IRE) 6 b.g. Pennine Walk 120 – Aztec Princess (Indian King 69
(USA) 128) [1995 60: 8d³ 9.7g² 9g² 10m² 10m² 7g 9m 9.7f² 8.5m 11.6m³ 10m 10f⁶ a67
a10g⁴ a7g³ a10g⁵ a12g⁵ a10g 1996 a12g⁴ a8g⁴ᵈⁱˢ a8g⁵ a13g a10g³ a8g⁵ a8g² 9.7m⁴

Tennent Caledonian Breweries Scottish Classic, Ayr—Montjoy (this side) and Musetta

a8g² 10m² 8g* 8f* a7g* a8g² 9.7f* 11m³ 10g 10m⁴ 9g⁶ a8g⁴ 10m 8m* 12d a10g⁴ a8g* a10g² Dec 11] good-topped gelding: fair handicapper: usually runs in amateur riders events: successful in May/June at Warwick (twice), Southwell and Folkestone, and also at Newcastle in October and Lingfield (professionally ridden, by short head) in November: effective at 7f to 1½m: acts on the all-weather, probably on any turf going: effective held up or from front: tried blinkered, visored nowadays: has been early to post: tough, game and versatile. *J. R. Jenkins*

MONTRESTAR 3 ch.g. Mon Tresor 113 – Wing of Freedom (Troy 137) [1995   68
63: 5m* 6g⁴ 5m³ 5m 5.3f³ 6d 6g 1996 a5g⁶ 5s² 5d² 5m⁴ 6g² 5g 6.1g 6d 6f
Sep 28] strong gelding: fair handicapper: best effort when second of 16 at Ripon on fifth start: stays 6f: acts on firm and soft ground: effective blinkered/visored or not. *P. D. Evans*

MONTSERRAT 4 b.f. Aragon 118 – Follow The Stars 86 (Sparkler 130) [1995   81
78d: 5m 6g⁵ 7g 7f 6g⁵ 6g 6s⁶ 6.1s⁵ 6m⁴ 1996 6s³ 6g⁵ 6m 6m⁶ 6d* 6m⁴ 6m 6v² 6.1s 6s Nov 9] small, close-coupled filly: fairly useful handicapper: ran consistently well in 1996 until last 2 starts, gaining a deserved success at Goodwood in May: stays 6f: acts on good to firm and goes particularly well on an easy surface (acts on heavy ground): usually races prominently: visored. *L. G. Cottrell*

MONTY 4 ch.g. Colmore Row 111 – Sussarando (Music Boy 124) [1995 53: 6.1d⁴
6m⁵ a7g a7g 1996 a7g 10.8f 13.3s 11.6g³ 10.2g Aug 26] leggy gelding: modest maiden handicapper at 3 yrs: well beaten in 1996: from J. Chappell's stable 1,650 gns Ascot August Sales after fourth start: stays 7f. *G. H. Yardley*

MONTY ROYALE (IRE) 7 b.g. Montelimar (USA) 122 – Atlanta Royale   –
(Prince Tenderfoot (USA) 126) [1995 NR 1996 12.1m 14.1f Jul 20] first foal: dam ran 3 times on flat, finishing second over 1m: modest maiden (not tried beyond 1m) at 3 yrs in Ireland: never dangerous in handicaps (including a seller) in Britain: fairly useful handicap hurdler, not seen out since June 1995. *Noel T. Chance*

MONUMENT 4 ch.g. Cadeaux Genereux 131 – In Perpetuity 90 (Great Nephew   71
126) [1995 78: 8.1g⁴ 8.1g 8m* 8.1m 10.3d 1996 8.1d⁴ 8m* 10.2m 10m* 11.6m⁵ 10g 10.2f⁶ 12.1d Sep 30] quite good-topped gelding: fair performer: always prominent when successful in claimer at Salisbury in June and handicap at Windsor in July: poor efforts at 4 yrs when held up: seems to stay 11.6f: acts on good to firm and dead ground. *J. S. King*

MONZA (USA) 2 b.c. (Apr 12) Woodman (USA) 126 – Star Pastures 124   107 p
(Northfields (USA)) [1996 7m³ 7m* 9d² Oct 5] smallish, quite attractive colt: ninth foal: half-brother to several winners, including useful Irish 7f (at 2 yrs) to 13f winner Esprit d'Etoile (by Spectacular Bid) and middle-distance stayer Lord Justice (by Alleged): dam won from 6f to 1m and stayed 1¼m: progressive form: first past post in maiden at Newbury (travelled comfortably, shaken up to lead 2f out) in August and steadily-run Prix de Conde at Longchamp (quickened to lead 1½f out, but hung right and hampered short-head second New Frontier, demoted) in October: will stay 1¼m: acts on good to firm and dead ground: carries head rather high, but seems genuine: may well improve further. *P. W. Chapple-Hyam*

MOODY 4 ch.f. Risk Me (FR) 127 – Bocas Rose 106 (Jalmood (USA) 126) [1995   46
62: 7.3g 7.1m 6.1m³ 5g 1996 a7g a7g⁴ a8g³ a8g a7g a8g Mar 18] sparely-made, plain filly: poor handicapper: left Gay Kelleway's after penultimate start: sold 1,700 gns Doncaster March Sales: stays 7.3f: best turf efforts on an easy surface, and acts on soft ground: blinkered/visored (well beaten) final 3 outings. *J. A. Glover*

MOODY'S CAT (IRE) 3 b.f. Alzao (USA) 117 – Zamayem (Sadler's Wells   97
(USA) 132) [1995 93p: 7m² 8m* 8d 1996 9m⁴ 11.5f³ 12m⁵ 8.5f³ 9f⁴ 10f* Nov 4] close-coupled filly: useful form: in frame in listed races at Milan and Lingfield (never landed a blow behind Lady Carla) before 17 lengths fifth of 11 in the Oaks at Epsom: left B. Hills: won stakes race at Santa Anita in November by a head from Vena: stays 1½m: acts on firm ground. *E. Gregson, USA*

MOOFAJI 5 b.g. Night Shift (USA) – Three Piece (Jaazeiro (USA) 127) [1995   41
52d: 8.3g 10.9m 8.1f 8m⁴ 8.5m 12f 7m 1996 8g 9.2f³ 12.1m 11.1d⁶ 8m Oct 23] strong gelding: has had soft palate operation, been hobdayed and tubed: only form at 5 yrs when third in seller at Hamilton in August: stays 9f: acts on firm ground: has worn tongue strap. *F. Watson*

MOONAX (IRE) 5 ch.h. Caerleon (USA) 132 – Moonsilk (Solinus 130) 120 §
[1995 122: 13.9g* 20m² 14g² 20s² 1996 12d³ 14d* 20d² 15.5d² Oct 27]
Moonax caught the eye again in the Prix du Cadran, again not for all the right reasons. In 1995 he'd attempted to bite Always Earnest in a desperately close finish. In 1996 he was chasing the eventual winner Nononito—not looking certain to catch him—when he ducked sharply left under right-handed driving over a furlong out, losing momentum and ground. However, after it seemed that he would finish only fourth, he rallied strongly to get back into second place, a length down, and if continuing at that rate would have caught Nononito in another fifty yards. Moonax hadn't obviously shirked a finish before and connections might be right in suggesting he was making for the exit, but it looked as if he resented being hit with the whip. Either way, it would be advisable for punters not to put complete trust in him, even though he clearly retains just about all his considerable ability. He has always had his quirks; nowadays he usually gives trouble in the preliminaries, he is a tail swisher and is equipped with a rope halter.
Moonax's season got off to something of a false start as, after reappearing in the John Porter Stakes in April, a leg problem followed by a wait for the ground to ease meant his having to miss all the Cup races. Looking less forward than he had done before winning the Yorkshire Cup on his reappearance the previous season (when he had wintered in Dubai), Moonax ran respectably at Newbury over a trip shorter than ideal to be beaten less than a length in third behind Spout. It was five months before Moonax was out again, but he looked really well when he did reappear and, facing an easier task than usual, accounted for Court of Honour by a length in a four-runner minor event at Haydock, going in snatches. Three weeks after the Cadran, Moonax was back at Longchamp for the Prix Royal-Oak, a race he had won as a three-year-old; on this occasion there was no horse of that age in a disappointing field of five. Old rivals Always Earnest and Nononito were there, as was the Prix de Pomone winner Helen of Spain, but in a slowly-run race all the established stayers were outspeeded by the outsider Red Roses Story. Moonax ran to his best and behaved himself this time, keeping a straight course past the paddock exit and refraining from having a bite at Red Roses Story—something her trainer had feared—when she squeezed through on his inner.

		Nijinsky	Northern Dancer
	Caerleon (USA)	(b 1967)	Flaming Page
	(b 1980)	Foreseer	Round Table
Moonax (IRE)		(b or br 1969)	Regal Gleam
(ch.h. 1991)		Solinus	Comedy Star
	Moonsilk	(b 1975)	Cawston's Pride
	(b 1980)	Night Attire	Shantung
		(ch 1966)	Twilight Hour

The only detail to add with regard to Moonax's pedigree is that his dam Moonsilk has recorded her fifth winner, and the best other than Moonax, when her two-year-old Moon River (by Mujtahid) was a very easy winner for the Dunlop stable of a mile maiden at the Doncaster November meeting. After the Cadran it was announced that Moonax would have a light campaign over hurdles with the Cheltenham Festival as his main objective, and he was immediately quoted in the Champion Hurdle betting. However, he found the two miles at Huntingdon an inadequate test of stamina on his hurdling debut in early-December, and was beaten by a speedier recruit from the flat in Sharpical. All being well, Moonax will be back for the top staying events on the flat in 1997, and given that a soft surface suits him best, more trips to France seem likely. We look forward to seeing him again in the Cadran in particular. *B. W. Hills*

MOON BLAST 2 gr.g. (Mar 24) Reprimand 122 – Castle Moon 79 (Kalamoun 67 p
129) [1996 7.1m³ 7g⁵ Aug 14] useful-looking colt: fluent mover: half-brother to 3-y-o Moon Mischief (by Be My Chief) and several winners, notably St Leger

winner Moon Madness (by Vitiges) and Coronation Cup winner Sheriff's Star (by Posse): dam, 1m to 13f winner, sister to Castle Keep and half-sister to Ragstone: heavily-backed favourite, took good hold on way down and ran too freely in 11-runner maiden won by Gonzaga at Salisbury, weakening into fifth inside final 1f: withdrawn on veterinary advice in between: capable of better but needs to settle to show it. *Lady Herries*

MOONCUSSER 3 b.g. Forzando 122 – Ragged Moon 72 (Raga Navarro (ITY) 119) [1995 57: 5m⁵ 5m a6g 5.9f⁴ 6f⁵ 7d⁴ 1996 a7g⁴ a7g² a8g³ a11g⁶ Feb 26] smallish, sturdy gelding: has a round action: modest maiden here: sold 4,800 gns Doncaster March Sales, and won over 6f in Sweden: acts on firm and dead ground and on fibresand: effective blinkered or not. *J. G. FitzGerald*   57

MOONLIGHT AIR 5 b.m. Bold Owl 101 – Havon Air (Celtic Cone 116) [1995 –: 7.5d 7.5m 10.8f 11.9d 1996 a12g⁶ Feb 7] placed in novice hurdles, but seems of little account on flat. *J. L. Spearing*   –

MOONLIGHT CALYPSO 5 ch.m. Jupiter Island 126 – Moonlight Bay 53 (Palm Track 122) [1995 49: a12g⁵ 11.1g* 12.4g⁵ 1996 13g⁶ a12g³ 12.1s³ a16g Nov 18] lengthy mare: poor handicapper: trained first 2 starts at 5 yrs by M. Meagher: stayed 12.4f: acted on soft ground: dead. *Martyn Wane*   46 a–

MOONLIGHT INVADER (IRE) 2 br.c. (May 22) Darshaan 133 – Mashmoon (USA) 80 (Habitat 134) [1996 8m⁶ 7.1v Oct 16] big, good-bodied colt: fifth foal: half-brother to 3-y-o Lead Story (by Lead On Time), 4-y-o 1m winner Talathath (by Soviet Star), and Irish 6f winner Gold Braisim (by Jareer): dam 6f (at 2 yrs) and 1m winner, half-sister to very smart French middle-distance filly Galla Placidia: sixth of 10 to Panama City in steadily-run maiden at Pontefract, slowly into stride, some late headway: tailed off in similar event at Haydock on heavy ground following month. *E. A. L. Dunlop*   63 +

MOONLIGHT PARADISE (USA) 2 b.f. (Feb 13) Irish River (FR) 131 – Ottomwa (USA) (Strawberry Road (AUS) 128) [1996 6m* 6g* 6m² 6m² 7g* Oct 18]   111 p

Buying promising two-year-olds is not a new policy for Godolphin but most are acquired towards the end of the campaign—Heinz 57 Phoenix Stakes winner Mantovani and Prix Robert Papin winner Ocean Ridge are among several from the latest season. However, Moonlight Paradise was a mid-season purchase bought to run in the important races in the autumn. Just weeks before her sale to Godolphin, Moonlight Paradise's then owner Sir Eric Parker gave an interview in the *Racing Post* in which he talked about how he came to buy her. 'I wanted an Irish River filly as a potential broodmare and bought her cheaply [200,000 francs] at Deauville. On the basis that she doesn't have a fantastic bottom-line, I had to race her. If she did it on the racecourse, I'd have a brood-mare; if she didn't I'd have to sell her and start again.' Moonlight Paradise had indeed 'done it' on the racecourse by then, but her owner hinted at the temptation to sell when he continued 'The dilemma with fillies is that when you keep them as broodmares, it dents your cash flow.' Moonlight Paradise had caught Sheikh Mohammed's eye on her third outing at the latest, when she finished a short-head second to Seebe in the Princess Margaret Stakes at Ascot in July for John Dunlop's stable. That was her first defeat. Earlier she had overcome trouble in running in a maiden at Goodwood and landed the odds in a listed race at Newmarket. A strong, rangy, attractive filly with plenty of scope, she had stood out in the paddock at Newmarket, dwarfing her rivals; she had also impressed considerably on her way to post at Ascot; she is a good walker and a powerful mover.

Moonlight Paradise made her debut for Godolphin in the Shadwell Stud Cheveley Park Stakes as 11/2 second favourite to the Cherry Hinton winner Dazzle, and ran well in what was a muddling contest, tracking the eventual winner Pas de Reponse and staying on well up the hill to be second, beaten a length. While excuses were made for Dazzle, Moonlight Paradise was favourite to beat her when the pair met for a second time in the six-runner Rockfel Stakes over a furlong further at Newmarket later in October, and she did so in some

style, taking it up from the headstrong More Silver under two furlongs out and then running on too strongly for Dazzle up the hill to beat her two and a half lengths. It was a smart performance, better than is usually sufficient to win the Rockfel.

Moonlight Paradise (USA) (b.f. Feb 13, 1994)	Irish River (FR) (ch 1976)	Riverman (b 1969)	Never Bend / River Lady
		Irish Star (b 1960)	Klairon / Botany Bay
	Ottomwa (USA) (b 1988)	Strawberry Road (b 1979)	Whiskey Road / Giftisa
		Gulfstream Flyer (b 1984)	Well Decorated / Nervous Flyer

Deauville was the second time Moonlight Paradise had been through the ring; she had made 21,000 dollars at Keeneland back in January as part of a reduction in Allen Paulson's string. Her dam Ottomwa, the preceding lot, fetched just 14,000 dollars. Moonlight Paradise is Ottomwa's second foal; the first, Mitch (by Jade Hunter, who stayed a mile and a quarter), has shown fairly useful form in Ireland, winning over seven furlongs as a two-year-old but seeming best as a sprinter at three. Ottomwa, by the globe-trotting Strawberry Road, won twice in minor company at up to seven furlongs in the United States. Her dam Gulfstream Flyer failed to win from five starts, but overall this family has made up in quantity of winners what it lacks in quality. Moonlight Paradise's great grandam Nervous Flyer, a stakes-placed winning sprinter, foaled eight winners (they included Hatta, placed in the Ascot One Thousand Guineas Trial) and was one of twelve (who between them won 101 races) out of a mare called Wee Nip.

Irish River has already sired a One Thousand Guineas winner in Hatoof. Moonlight Paradise, who has plenty of scope to train on and will almost certainly find further improvement over a mile, will be hard to keep out of the frame when she returns from Dubai to Newmarket in the spring. She is due to run in the Guineas without a preparatory outing. *Saeed bin Suroor*

MOONLIGHT QUEST 8 gr.g. Nishapour (FR) 125 – Arabian Rose (USA) 84 (Lyphard (USA) 132) [1995 79: 16.2m* 16m² 18.7m 16m² 17.2m* 16.2f⁶ 16.2m³ 18.7g² 15.9m* 16.2m⁴ 15.9m⁵ 16d³ 1996 14.1g* 16f* Jul 19] close-coupled, work-manlike gelding: carries condition: fairly useful handicapper: has reportedly had training problems but won both his starts at 8 yrs, 4-runner race at Yarmouth and 6-runner race at Newbury, both in July: stays well: best form on ground no softer than dead: sometimes pulls hard: effective in blinkers, hasn't worn them since 1994: has wandered, but is genuine. *B. Hanbury*

MOON MISCHIEF 3 b.c. Be My Chief (USA) 122 – Castle Moon 79 (Kala- 78
moun 129) [1995 NR 1996 8m⁵ 10g⁶ 12m² Aug 2] rather leggy colt: has a quick,
fluent action: half-brother to several winners, including Sheriff's Star (by Posse) and
Moon Madness (by Vitiges): dam, 1m to 13f winner, sister to Castle Keep and
half-sister to Ragstone: fair form in maidens: stayed at least 1½m: swished tail
persistently in paddock and hung badly left off bridle second start: wasn't one to have
complete faith in: dead. *Lady Herries*

MOONRAKER (IRE) 2 b.g. (Jan 19) Classic Secret (USA) 91 – Moona (USA) –
73 (Lear Fan (USA) 130) [1996 a5g Aug 16] 9,200Y: first foal: dam 7f winner:
slowly away and soon outpaced in seller at Southwell: sold 1,350 gns Doncaster
September Sales: sent to Denmark. *J. G. FitzGerald*

MOONRAKING 3 gr.g. Rusticaro (FR) 124 – Lunaire (Try My Best (USA) 130) 54
[1995 NR 1996 7g a8g² 7.1d a12g² a12g⁶ Aug 17] 3,500Y: leggy, close-coupled
gelding: first foal: dam unraced half-sister to Premio Parioli winner Lucratif: modest
form in maidens when second at Southwell (carrying head high and wandering) and
Wolverhampton (well backed): ran creditably in maiden handicap at Wolverhampton
final start: will stay beyond 1½m: acts on fibresand. *T. J. Etherington*

MOON RIVER (IRE) 2 ch.c. (May 6) Mujtahid (USA) 118 – Moonsilk (Solinus 95 p
130) [1996 8s* Nov 9] IR 30,000Y: big, lengthy, plain colt: has plenty of scope:
eighth foal: half-brother to several winners, including Irish 3-y-o Night Spell (by
Fairy King), 1m winner at 2 yrs, and very smart 5-y-o stayer Moonax (by Caerleon):
dam, placed over 9f in France, half-sister to 1000 Guineas winner Nocturnal Spree:
8/1, very easy winner of 14-runner median auction maiden at Doncaster, improving
on bit to lead over 1f out and soon clear, eased to beat Tyrolean Dream 2½ lengths
(rated value 6): looks an interesting prospect. *J. L. Dunlop*

MOONSHELL (IRE) 4 b.f. Sadler's Wells (USA) 132 – Moon Cactus 118 (Kris –
135) [1995 117: 8m³ 12m* 1996 a8f³ 12m May 3] lengthy, angular filly: has a quick,
unimpressive action: won 1995 Vodafone Oaks at Epsom: subsequently had a training set-back: well below form in 4-runner minor event in Dubai in February, and
tailed off in Jockey Club Stakes at Newmarket: stayed 1½m: didn't race on extremes
of going on turf: genuine: has been retired, and is to visit Rainbow Quest. *Saeed bin
Suroor*

MOONSHINE DANCER 6 b.g. Northern State (USA) 91 – Double Birthday –
(Cavo Doro 124) [1995 42: a16g a16g 15.8g⁴ 17.1m⁶ 18f⁵ 1996 a16g⁵ Feb 5] sturdy,
workmanlike gelding: poor maiden staying handicapper: tailed off only outing on flat
at 6 yrs: sold to join D. W. Barker 2,200 gns Doncaster August Sales: stays 2½m: acts
on any going, including fibresand. *Mrs M. Reveley*

MOONSHINE GIRL (USA) 2 ch.f. (Mar 18) Shadeed (USA) 135 – Fly To 97 +
The Moon (USA) 90 (Blushing Groom (FR) 131) [1996 5g⁴ 5m³ 6m⁵ 6m⁵ Sep 7]
close-coupled filly: easy mover: first reported foal: dam, 1m winner here later sprint
winner on dirt in USA, sister to very useful 1987 2-y-o 5f and 6f winner Digamist:
useful performer: won maiden at Sandown in May: third of 13 to Dance Parade in
Queen Mary Stakes at Ascot and when fifth of 9 to Bianca Nera in Lowther Stakes at
York: below-form fifth of 7 to Arethusa in listed race at Kempton (edgy) on final
start: very best form at 5f: twice attended by 2 handlers in paddock. *M. R. Stoute*

MOONSHINER (USA) 2 b.c. (Feb 21) Irish River (FR) 131 – Marling (IRE) 83
124 (Lomond (USA) 128) [1996 6m 6m² 6g² Oct 9] small, sturdy colt: first foal: dam
won 7 of her 10 starts, including Cheveley Park Stakes and Sussex Stakes: very burly
and green on debut: runner-up afterwards in maidens won by Bachelors Pad at
Goodwood and Wolf Mountain at York: will stay 7f. *G. Wragg*

MOONSPELL 2 b.f. (Feb 13) Batshoof 122 – Shimmer 55 (Bustino 136) [1996 64
7.1m 8.1g³ 8d Oct 2] strong, lengthy filly: has scope: has a fluent, round action: first
foal: dam maiden daughter of smart middle-distance performer Light Duty, herself
sister to Highclere: clearly best effort when third of 8 to Ajayib in maiden at
Chepstow, pulling hard early on then keeping on well: didn't handle bend at Sandown
on debut: will stay middle distances: well held on softish ground. *R. Charlton*

MOON STRIKE (FR) 6 b. or br.g. Strike Gold (USA) – Lady Lamia (USA) 85
(Secreto (USA) 128) [1995 78, a83: a7g* a8g⁵ 7f* 7g 1996 7f⁵ 6.9m* 7g 7.1f² 5d*
5f⁶ 6m⁵ Sep 14] lengthy gelding: usually looks very well: fairly useful handicapper:
odds on, never off bridle to win claimer at Folkestone in May: left S. Williams after

fourth 6-y-o outing and made winning debut for new yard in ladies race at Newmarket in August: ran well when fifth of 21 to Clan Chief in £15,000 contest at Goodwood final start: effective at 5f, and has form over as far as 1m: acts on equitrack, firm and dead ground (tailed off on heavy): no improvement in blinkers: idles in front and best held up: bandaged last outing. *H. Akbary*

MOORBIRD (IRE) 2 b.g. (May 29) Law Society (USA) 130 – Heather Lark 53 (Red Alert 127) [1996 7.5m 8.3d³ 8g Oct 29] IR 7,000Y: good-bodied gelding: half-brother to several winners, including 1988 Irish 2-y-o sprinter Heather Seeker and Wolf Power (both by Taufan), latter winner here and in Italy at up to 1m: dam Irish 2-y-o 5f winner: modest form in maidens: stays 8.3f: acts on dead ground. *M. Johnston*

MOOR HALL PRINCESS 2 gr.f. (Feb 25) Chilibang 120 – Forgiving (Jellaby – 124) [1996 6g⁵ a6g⁶ 7m⁶ 6m a6g Aug 31] 1,500Y: small filly: fourth reported foal: dam middle-distance maiden on flat, successful over hurdles: poor plater: has flashed tail: has joined N. Babbage. *K. R. Burke*

MORE BILLS (IRE) 4 b.g. Gallic League 119 – Lady Portobello (Porto Bello – 118) [1995 39d: a5g a7g⁴ a10g 7f a12g a12g 1996 a13g Jan 13] leggy gelding: seems of little account nowadays: tried blinkered/visored. *A. Moore*

MORE SILVER (USA) 2 b.f. (Apr 9) Silver Hawk (USA) 123 – Dancing Lt 90 (USA) (San Feliou (FR)) [1996 5.2g* 5m 7g⁵ 7.3s Oct 26] $180,000Y: good-quartered filly: sister to 2 winners in USA, including a minor stakes winner at up to 1¼m, and half-sister to several winners in USA: dam unraced: odds on, impressive winner of 4-runner minor event at Newbury in May: weak in market when seventh of 14 to stable-companion Dance Parade in Queen Mary Stakes at Royal Ascot: off course 4 months, then disappointing in Rockfel Stakes at Newmarket (much too headstrong) and listed race at Newbury. *P. F. I. Cole*

MORE THAN YOU KNOW (IRE) 3 ch.f. Kefaah (USA) 124 – Foston 84 d Bridge 68 (Relkino 131) [1995 88: 7m* 8d² 1996 8m⁶ 7f⁵ 7m⁵ 10.4m 12g a12g³ a9.4g a13g³ Dec 31] leggy, angular filly: fairly useful form at 2 yrs: inconsistent in 1996: sold out of R. Hannon's stable 7,000 gns Newmarket Autumn Sales after fifth start: stays 13f: acts on good to firm and dead ground and on equitrack. *K. R. Burke*

MORNING LINE (IRE) 2 b.f. (Feb 17) Mac's Imp (USA) 116 – Sally Fay 43 (IRE) 66 (Fayruz 116) [1996 a6g⁶ a6g Nov 11] 4,000Y: first foal: dam 6f winner, seemed to stay 9f: never-dangerous sixth in median auction maiden at Wolver-hampton: well beaten in seller three month later. *R. J. R. Williams*

MORNING SIR 3 b.g. Southern Music 104 – Morning Miss 59 (Golden Dipper – 119) [1995 –: 8.1s⁶ 1996 8m⁶ 10m 10d 10.2g 10.8m 8g Aug 1] no worthwhile form. *C. R. Barwell*

MORNING STAR 2 b.f. (Apr 11) Statoblest 120 – Moushka (Song 132) [1996 58 6m 5m* Oct 29] 2,400Y: second live foal: half-sister to useful 4-y-o 5f winner Mr Oscar (by Belfort): dam unraced: favourite, made all in 9-runner median auction maiden at Redcar, given reminders early on: sprint bred: has joined W. McKeown. *M. Johnston*

MORNING SURPRISE 3 b. or br.f. Tragic Role (USA) – Fleur de Foret (USA) 58 d 61§ (Green Forest (USA) 134) [1995 58: 5g⁴ a5g a5g* a6g² 6m⁶ 6f³ 6.1d³ 7s 1996 a7g⁶ 7d 6.1m⁵ 7f² 7g² 7m 7g 7g 7m⁵ 7m 6.9d⁵ a7g⁴ a8g Dec 27] small, leggy filly: has a quick action: modest handicapper: below form after June at 3 yrs: stays 7f: acts on firm and dead ground (no chance from poor draw on soft) and fibresand: often apprentice ridden: sometimes slowly away: edgy, and sometimes gives trouble in preliminaries. *A. P. Jarvis*

MOROCCO (IRE) 7 b.g. Cyrano de Bergerac 120 – Lightning Laser 68 63 (Monseigneur (USA) 127) [1995 73?: 8.3m 8.3g 8.3f 8.1m* 8f⁵ 8.3m 8f³ 7m 8h² 6.9h* 7m⁴ 7.1m 7d³ 7g 7g² 7f 7f⁵ 7f⁶ 1996 7d 7m* 7d⁵ 7g 7m 8m⁵ 7g⁵ 6.9m⁵ 7f 7m* 6.9g³ 8.2g⁴ 7f³ 8m Oct 27] small, workmanlike gelding: unimpressive mover: modest handicapper at 7 yrs: won at Salisbury in May and at Lingfield (18-runner race, coolly ridden by 7-lb claimer A. Eddery) in September: stays 8.2f: acts on any going: blinkered/visored 4 times earlier in career: usually held up: sometimes carries head high and finds little. *M. R. Channon*

Schweppes Golden Mile (Handicap), Goodwood—one for the bookmakers;
outsider-of-eighteen Moscow Mist pips the favourite Missile (No. 10) and Prince Babar (rails)

MORRITT MAGIC 2 ch.f. (Apr 10) Absalom 128 – Vernair (USA) 73 (Super – Concorde (USA) 128) [1996 5d⁶ 5g⁵ 6f 6g a8.5g Nov 2] 1,500F, 2,600Y resold 2,500Y: small filly: sixth living foal: half-sister to 7f winner Gavin Allen (by Heraldiste): dam 6f winner here and in Italy: no worthwhile form. *C. W. Thornton*

MOSCOW DYNAMO 9 br.g. Siberian Express (USA) 125 – County Line 75 – (High Line 125) [1995 NR 1996 a8.5g Mar 15] modest form in handicaps at Southwell in 1993: tailed off in seller on first flat outing since. *N. M. Babbage*

MOSCOW MIST (IRE) 5 b.g. Soviet Star (USA) 128 – Ivory Dawn (USA) 83 (Sir Ivor 135) [1995 83: 10g⁶ 9g² 8f² 1996 8s 8.1d 8g⁴ 8m* 8m 8g Sep 29] lengthy, good-topped gelding: fairly useful handicapper, lightly raced: 66/1, best effort when beating Missile a short head in 18-runner £48,250 Schweppes Golden Mile at Goodwood in August, quickening on inside final 1f: ran poorly afterwards: should stay beyond 1m: best efforts on a sound surface: has run well when sweating. *Lady Herries*

MOST UPPITTY 4 gr.f. Absalom 128 – Hyatti 74 (Habitat 134) [1995 –, a58: 5d 50 6.1g a6g⁵ a5g³ a5g a5g² a6g⁶ a5g⁴ 5f a5g³ 5g a6g* a6g⁵ 1996 a6g a6g a6g a5g 6g 5f 6m³ a6g² 6g² 6m Jul 12] lengthy, good-topped filly: modest handicapper nowadays: stays 6f: acts on fibresand and firm ground, possibly unsuited by soft: usually races prominently: covered by Puissance. *J. Berry*

MOST WANTED (IRE) 3 ch.f. Priolo (USA) 127 – Dewan's Niece (USA) 38 (Dewan (USA)) [1995 NR 1996 10.5d 10m 8g⁶ 7f⁴ 10.4g 7g 12.1g Sep 29] 3,200Y: tall, lengthy, unfurnished filly: fifth foal: half-sister to a winning jumper in Ireland by Vision: dam, minor winner in USA, closely related to dam of William Hill Futurity winner Emmson: poor form: left P. Cole after fourth start (looked a tricky ride): soundly beaten in handicaps last 3 starts: should stay 1m. *J. J. O'Neill*

MOST WELCOME NEWS 4 b.g. Most Welcome 131 – In The Papers 87 – (Aragon 118) [1995 43: 10.8m 8.2m⁵ 8m 8g a8g⁶ 11.9f⁶ 1996 a8g a8g 6m Apr 16] well-made gelding: no form at 4 yrs: tried blinkered. *J. R. Jenkins*

MOTCOMBS CLUB 2 ch.c. (Mar 1) Deploy 131 – Unique Treasure (Young 58 Generation 129) [1996 7.1m 6g 8.1m 8g⁵ a8g⁶ a8g Dec 11] small, sturdy, lengthy colt: has a round action: third live foal: brother to modest maiden (stays 2m) Euro Forum and half-brother to 5-y-o 6f and 7f winner Don Pepe (by Dowsing): dam ran once as 2-y-o: modest maiden: should stay beyond 1m: best efforts on good ground. *N. A. Callaghan*

MOTET 2 b.c. (May 19) Mtoto 134 – Guest Artiste 110 (Be My Guest (USA) 126) 74 p [1996 7m³ Oct 23] fourth foal: half-brother to 3-y-o Questing Star (by Rainbow Quest): dam miler: 20/1, 3¾ lengths third of 11 to Sekari in maiden at Yarmouth, looking green in rear long way then finishing well: will stay beyond 7f: will improve. *G. Wragg*

MOTRIB (USA) 3 b.g. Thorn Dance (USA) 107 – Disco Singer (CAN) (Lord –
Durham (CAN)) [1995 NR 1996 8m 7m 8m Jun 3] 40,000Y: good-quartered gelding:
closely related to a winner abroad by Far North and half-brother to 2 winners abroad:
dam unraced sister to leading 1981 Canadian 2-y-o filly Choral Group: tailed off in
maidens and (visored) claimer. *M. Madgwick*

MOUJEEB (USA) 6 b.h. Riverman (USA) 131 – Capricorn Belle 115 (Nonoalco 62
(USA) 131) [1995 62: 6g⁴ 6m 6f² 7m⁴ 5m² 5g³ a5g⁵ 6g 5g 6m 5m⁵ 5m 6m⁵ 5m⁴ 5.1d
6.1d 6d 7m 5.1m² 6f² a6g a6g 1996 5m² 6m 6f 6.1m 5m May 29] lengthy, workmanlike horse: unimpressive mover: modest handicapper: ran well in minor event at
Folkestone on reappearance, below form afterwards: stays 6f: acts on firm and soft
ground and all-weather surfaces: best visored: none too consistent. *Pat Mitchell*

MOUNTAIN DREAM 3 b.c. Batshoof 122 – Echoing 93 (Formidable (USA) 70
125) [1995 65?, a–: 7m⁵ 7g a8g⁵ a10g 1996 8f⁶ 10m³ 11.6m Aug 19] fair maiden: a–
trained at 2 yrs by P. Cole: sold (L. Cumani to R. Allan) 7,000 gns Newmarket
Autumn Sales: stays 1¼m: acts on firm ground, below best on equitrack: carried head
high second 3-y-o start. *L. M. Cumani*

MOUNTAIN HOLLY 3 b.f. Shirley Heights 130 – Ela Romara 124 (Ela- 69
Mana-Mou 132) [1995 69p: 7m 1996 10.2f⁵ 12.3d⁴ Aug 26] quite attractive filly:
similar form in maidens at Newmarket and Chepstow 8 months apart: well beaten in
similar event at Ripon only subsequent outing: sold 46,000 gns Newmarket
December Sales: should be suited by middle distances. *D. R. Loder*

MOUNTGATE 4 b.g. Merdon Melody 98 – Young Whip (Bold Owl 101) [1995 79 §
78§: 9m⁶ 7g 7.5g* 8m 8g 7.1g 8m³ 7m 7m* 1996 8.5g 8g⁵ 8m⁶ 7m² 7m 8f* 7m⁴ 8d
7.9g 8m 7m 7m⁶ 7g Nov 2] robust, good-quartered gelding: fairly useful handicapper: won at Thirsk in August: will prove best at up to 1m: acts on firm and dead
ground: has given trouble in preliminaries: sometimes mounted on track and taken
early to post: sometimes slowly away: not one to rely on. *M. P. Bielby*

MOUNT HOLLY (USA) 2 b.c. (Jan 25) Woodman (USA) 126 – Mount Helena 69 p
82 (Danzig (USA)) [1996 7m⁵ Aug 26] first foal: dam, 6f winner at 2 yrs, daughter of
Irish Oaks winner Helen Street: 6/1 and very green, over 6 lengths fifth of 13 to
Redwing in maiden at Newcastle, held up after slow start then running on well: will
be suited by further than 7f: sure to improve. *J. H. M. Gosden*

MOUNT KAMET 2 b.c. (Mar 31) Seattle Dancer (USA) 119 – Kalikala 101
(Darshaan 133) [1996 7g² 7.5f* 7.1g⁵ Aug 30] tall, quite attractive colt: fourth foal:
closely related to smart French 1¼m and 10.5f winner Kalajana (by Green Dancer)
and half-brother to smart 4-y-o 1½m winner Kalabo (by Trempolino), 7f and 1m
winner at 2 yrs: dam French 1½m winner, half-sister to dam of Kahyasi: odds on,
very easily won 8-runner maiden at Beverley in July by 5 lengths: well-backed
favourite, improved again when over 3 lengths fifth of 7 to Brave Act in Solario
Stakes at Sandown: will stay 1m: almost certainly be capable of better. *D. R. Loder*

MOUNT PLEASANT (IRE) 3 b.c. Danehill (USA) 126 – Remoosh (Glint of 92
Gold 128) [1995 NR 1996 10m³ 12.3d³ 7.9g² 12m* 14g² 16g Nov 1] lengthy, rather
unfurnished colt: fifth foal: half-brother to 3 winners, including fairly useful, 7f and
1m winner Moorish (also smart hurdler, by Dominion): dam poor half-sister to
high-class 1985 2-y-o 5f and 6f winner Nomination: fairly useful form: odds on, easy
winner of maiden at Epsom in September: edgy, best effort when neck second in
handicap at Newmarket, leading on bridle 2f out and headed inside last: stays 1¾m:
flashes tail under pressure, carried head awkwardly at Epsom. *P. F. I. Cole*

MOUNT ROW 3 b.f. Alzao (USA) 117 – Temple Row (Ardross 134) [1995 NR 94
1996 10.5d⁴ 10.5d* 10g⁵ 11.9m* 13.4d⁴ Aug 31] rangy filly: third foal: half-sister to
8.5f and 9f winner (in USA) Rotten Row (by Salse): dam unraced half-sister to very
useful sprinter Colmore Row out of Irish 1000 Guineas winner Front Row: fairly
useful performer: won maiden at Haydock in May and handicap at same course (by 9
lengths, making all) in August: respectable 10 lengths fourth of 9 to Royal Scimitar
in listed rated stakes at Chester final start: suited by middle distances: acted on good
to firm and dead ground: stud. *L. M. Cumani*

MOURNE MOUNTAINS 3 b.c. Scenic 128 – Orlaith 68 (Final Straw 127) 75
[1995 –p: 7m 1996 10g 10m Aug 19] rangy colt: burly, coltish and still green, best
effort when seventh of 13 to Greenstead in maiden at Newmarket, keeping on
steadily from rear: failed to confirm that promise in similar event at Windsor (gave

lot of trouble at start) nearly 6 weeks later, folding rather tamely closing stages. *H. Candy*

MOUSEHOLE 4 b.g. Statoblest 120 – Alo Ez 100 (Alzao (USA) 117) [1995 71: 6m 6m 5g³ 6g² 6m* 5m² 6g⁴ 6g 6g 1996 6.1g 6g 5.7g⁵ 5m² 5m* 6f² 6m³ 6m⁶ 5m 5d⁵ 5f² Sep 5] strong gelding: fair handicapper: won minor event at Windsor in June: unlucky short-head second of 17 to Squire Corrie at Salisbury final start, finishing strongly after meeting trouble in running: effective at 5f and 6f: has raced almost solely on a sound surface: best recent form in blinkers. *R. Guest*   78

MOUSSE GLACEE (FR) 2 b.f. (Apr 3) Mtoto 134 – Madame Est Sortie (FR) (Longleat (USA) 109) [1996 8d* 8d* Oct 22] 100,000 francs F: third reported foal: half-sister to a winner in Switzerland by Shareef Dancer: dam 9f (at 2 yrs) to 10.5f winner, placed in Prix Penelope: French filly: won 5-runner newcomers event at Longchamp in September and 9-runner Prix des Reservoirs (by 2½ lengths from Queen Maud) at Deauville in October: will stay 1¼m+: looks a smart filly in the making. *J. Lesbordes, France*   112 p

MOVE SMARTLY (IRE) 6 b.h. Smarten (USA) – Key Maneuver (USA) (Key To Content (USA)) [1995 60: 8m 10.3m 8g⁵ 8m⁶ 8.1m² 7m 7f* 8.1m² 7m 7.1d 8d 8g 7m 1996 8g 7g⁶ 7m² 8m⁵ Jun 20] sturdy, workmanlike horse: unimpressive mover: modest performer: best effort at 6 yrs when second in seller at Redcar penultimate start: effective at 7f to 9f: acts on firm and dead ground: blinkered 3 starts at 4 yrs, visored last 9 starts in 1995, but wore neither in 1996. *F. H. Lee*   58

MOVE THE CLOUDS 2 gr.f. (Mar 11) Environment Friend 128 – Che Gambe (USA) (Lyphard (USA) 132) [1996 8g a8.5g³ Nov 30] big, strong, lengthy filly: fifth foal: half-sister to 1991 2-y-o 5f winner Walk That Walk and a winner in Spain (both by Hadeer): dam 6f winner in USA: burly and green on debut: withdrawn after getting loose second intended start: third of 9, swishing tail and hanging right, in maiden at Wolverhampton in November. *J. R. Fanshawe*   63 +

MOVE WITH EDES 4 b.g. Tragic Role (USA) – Good Time Girl 65 (Good Times (ITY)) [1995 65: 8.3g⁶ 8.3m⁵ 8m⁴ 7m* 7f 1996 8.3m² 7d 7g⁶ 6.9f* 8f⁴ a7g* Aug 17] leggy gelding: fair performer: won claimer at Carlisle in July (by 9 lengths) and handicap at Wolverhampton (by short head) in August: stays 8.3f: acts on firm ground and fibresand, below form only outing on a soft surface. *W. G. M. Turner*   71

MOVING ARROW 5 ch.g. Indian Ridge 123 – Another Move 69 (Farm Walk 111) [1995 96: 8g² 8.1m⁴ 8.5m³ 8g 8m⁶ 8g 8.1f* 7.9m⁶ 8m 7g 7.9m* 1996 8s 8.1d² 8m 8.1g 10m* 10.4m 8d⁵ Aug 26] lengthy gelding: useful handicapper: won at Newmarket in July: effective at 1m to 1¼m: probably acts on any ground: visored fifth (ran well) and sixth 4-y-o starts: sometimes early to post: races freely, but is effective from front/held up: none too consistent. *Miss S. E. Hall*   99

MOVING UP (IRE) 3 ch.f. Don't Forget Me 127 – Our Pet 64 (Mummy's Pet 125) [1995 61d: 5g³ 5.1m² 6g 6m 7g⁶ 1996 a8g a8g 10g³ 8.1g 10m 9.7g 11.9f⁴ 11.9f 10g 12s a13g Nov 26] sparely-made filly: poor plater nowadays: left G. L. Moore after eighth 3-y-o start: seems to stay 1½m: acts on good to firm ground: visored (ran poorly) eighth 3-y-o start. *T. E. Powell*   51 d

Prix des Reservoirs, Deauville—
Mousse Glacee looks a good middle-distance prospect in beating Queen Maud

MOWJOOD (USA) 2 b.c. (Mar 23) Mr Prospector (USA) – Bineyah (IRE) 109   – p
(Sadler's Wells (USA) 132) [1996 6m 7m Aug 26] tall, attractive colt: first foal: dam
11.5f winner and second in Yorkshire Oaks, sister to Royal Lodge winner Desert
Secret and St Leger fourth In Camera, out of half-sister to Seattle Slew and Lomond:
short in betting but showed little in maidens: tongue tied down second start: evidently
thought capable of better. *M. R. Stoute*

MOWLAIE 5 ch.g. Nashwan (USA) 135 – Durrah (USA) 93 (Nijinsky (CAN)   –
138) [1995 74d: 12m⁶ 10m 10f⁴ 15.8g⁶ 10m³ 10.3d 8.5d³ 8.2m a10g a14.8g a14g⁵   a55
a12g 1996 a11g⁴ Feb 12] good-topped gelding: good mover: fair handicapper at 4
yrs: 3¾ lengths fourth of 10 to Sea God at Southwell only outing in 1996: stays 1½m:
acts on good to firm and dead ground, probably on fibresand. *D. W. Chapman*

MOYLOUGH REBEL 3 ch.g. Hotfoot 126 – Stellajoe 39 (Le Dauphin 73)   –
[1995 –: 7.1g 6f⁵ 10g 1996 7m 8m⁶ 7.1m 8.3g 7.6m Aug 17] workmanlike gelding:
seems of little account. *J. E. Long*

MR BEAN 6 b.g. Salse (USA) 128 – Goody Blake 103 (Blakeney 126) [1995 67:   –
a12g⁴ a12g² a12g* a12g³ a11g* a11g² a11g* a12g³ 12f³ a12g⁵ 1996 a12g⁵ a12g⁶
a14g Dec 3] formerly a fair handicapper: off course almost a year, well below best all
starts in 1996: stays 13f: acts on fibresand, probably on firm ground: visored (below
form) 3 times earlier in career. *K. R. Burke*

MR BERGERAC (IRE) 5 b.g. Cyrano de Bergerac 120 – Makalu 79 (Godswalk   92
(USA) 130) [1995 88, a94: 5g* 5.2m³ 5m* 5.6m 5g³ 6s 5m a6g* a7g³ 1996 6g 6f
5.1f⁵ 6f² 6f* 6m² 6m² 6g 5g 6f a7g Dec 7] leggy, sparely-made gelding: fairly useful
handicapper: narrowly won at Newmarket in July: well drawn, very good second of
28 to Coastal Bluff in Ayr Gold Cup seventh start: effective at 5f to 7f: acts on firm
and soft going and goes well on the all-weather: successful when sweating. *B. Palling*

MR BLUE 4 b.g. Sylvan Express 117 – Footstool 61 (Artaius (USA) 129) [1995   –
NR 1996 7m 8m 6g⁵ a5g 6f Sep 23] third foal: dam won 3 races at 1¼m: no form.
G. P. Kelly

MR BOMBASTIQUE (IRE) 2 b.c. (May 12) Classic Music (USA) – Duende   83
75 (High Top 131) [1996 6m⁵ 6.1m* 7m⁴ 7.9g⁵ 8g² Oct 25] sturdy colt: unimpressive
mover: third living foal: half-brother to useful 1993 2-y-o 1m winner The Deep (by
Shernazar), suspiciously disappointing, and 1994 2-y-o 7f winner Zingibar (by
Caerleon): dam 2-y-o 6f winner who stayed 1m: fairly useful form: won maiden at
Chepstow in July: good second in nursery at Doncaster final outing: will stay beyond
1m: sweating and moved badly to post (tailed off) third outing. *B. W. Hills*

MR BROWNING (USA) 5 br.g. Al Nasr (FR) 126 – Crinoline 72 (Blakeney   73
126) [1995 78: a8g⁴ a10g⁵ a8g 11.9m² 12m³ 12m² 12g² 12f* 11.6m 12m* 12s 12m
1996 11.4g 12m² 11.5d 12m 12g⁴ 16.2d 16g Oct 24] well-made gelding: fair handicapper: second at Goodwood, leading until post: seems to stay 2m: acts on firm and
dead ground: usually blinkered, not last 2 starts, best forcing pace (has seemed to
throw tongue in when unable to dominate): inconsistent. *R. Akehurst*

MR CHRISTIE 4 b.g. Doulab (USA) 115 – Hi There 89 (High Top 131) [1995   –
59d: 8.5m⁶ 8m³ 10.1g⁶ 8.5d⁴ 10m 8m⁶ 7.9g 10.5g 11.9m 1996 12.4d⁶ 14g May 17]
workmanlike gelding: modest maiden at 2 yrs, disappointing since: stays 1¼m: acts
on good to firm ground and dead. *Miss L. C. Siddall*

MR COPYFORCE 6 gr.g. Sharrood (USA) 124 – Cappuccilli 111 (Lorenzaccio   48
130) [1995 –: a12g⁵ a16g⁶ 14.4m a16g 1996 a13g⁵ a16g³ 16.4m* 17.2m* 14.9f⁴ 18f³
14f² 14g⁴ 15.4g⁴ Sep 27] lengthy gelding: poor handicapper nowadays: off course
over 3 months, won poor events at Folkestone and Bath in June: mostly creditable
efforts afterwards: finds 1¾m a minimum, stays 2¼m: acts on firm and dead
ground, and on equitrack: tried visored/blinkered, no improvement. *Miss B. Sanders*

MR CUBE (IRE) 6 ch.h. Tate Gallery (USA) 117 – Truly Thankful (CAN)   61
(Graustark) [1995 63, a–: 8m² 8f³ 8f 8m 8g³ 8.2m⁵ 7g* 8m 8f⁵ 7f* 7m* 7.6m³ 7m⁴   a–
7m 7g 1996 7m 7f⁴ 7f 7g 7.1g 8.3m² 8f³ 6.9g⁵ 7f⁵ 8f⁵ 7.6m⁵ 8.2d 8f³ 7m 6.9g* 8d a7g
Nov 14] sturdy horse: modest handicapper: won strongly-run 16-runner apprentice
race at Folkestone in September: effective at 7f and 1m: acts on all-weather surfaces,
firm and soft ground: tends to wander and carry head awkwardly but has run well for
an apprentice: visored/blinkered. *J. M. Bradley*

MR FORTYWINKS (IRE) 2 ch.c. (Feb 22) Fools Holme (USA) – Dream On 58
54 (Absalom 128) [1996 5d⁵ 5m 5m³ 5m Sep 19] sparely-made colt: first foal: dam
(maiden) stayed 1¼m: modest maiden, easily best effort on third start: will be suited
by further 5f. *J. L. Eyre*

MR FROSTY 4 b.g. Absalom 128 – Chadenshe 94 (Taufan (USA) 119) [1995 62, –
a70: a7g* a7g² 7g³ 10d 8m⁴ a7g a7g³ a8g³ 1996 a8g⁵ a7g 8s a6g* a6g* a6s* Dec 19] a86
lengthy gelding: fairly useful handicapper: in good form in December, winning at
Southwell and twice at Wolverhampton: effective at 6f to 1m: goes well on the
all-weather: best turf effort on good ground. *W. Jarvis*

MR GOLD (IRE) 3 b.g. Toledo (USA) 80 – Liangold (Rheingold 137) [1995 NR –
1996 10m 8f² Jun 22] tall, leggy, unfurnished gelding: ninth foal: half-brother to
several minor winners: dam ran once: 100/1, bit reportedly slipped when tailed off in
maiden at Pontefract: remote second in 3-runner maiden won by Kamari at Redcar
18 days later: sold 3,800 gns Doncaster October Sales. *Ronald Thompson*

MR HACKER 3 b.g. Shannon Cottage (USA) 86 – Aosta (Shack (USA) 118) –
[1995 NR 1996 7d 7.1m 10g 8.3d 8m Aug 26] first foal: dam unraced: well beaten in
maidens and handicaps. *G. Thorner*

MR MAJICA 2 b.c. (Feb 18) Rudimentary (USA) 118 – Pellinora (USA) (King – p
Pellinore (USA) 127) [1996 6m Sep 21] robust colt: 17,000F, IR 30,000Y: half-
brother to 3 winners, including useful 1m (at 2 yrs) and 1¼m winner Prince Russanor
(by Rousillon) and 1½m winner Peleus (by Irish River): dam French maiden
half-sister to Park Hill winner I Want To Be, from an excellent family: 12/1 and
green, never better than midfield in 24-runner maiden at Newbury: looks capable of
better. *B. J. Meehan*

MR MARTINI (IRE) 6 b.h. Pennine Walk 120 – Arab Art (Artaius (USA) 129) 103
[1995 116: a7g⁶ 8g³ 7m 8.1m* 8m³ 8.5m* 7m 8m³ 8f* 8g³ 8d⁵ 8m a9.4g 1996 8.5m³
8f⁶ Jun 18] smallish horse: smart and much improved performer in 1995: below form
in Diomed Stakes at Epsom and Queen Anne Stakes at Royal Ascot only outings at
6 yrs: sold only 8,400 gns Newmarket Autumn Sales: best form at around 1m:
acts on any going: tried blinkered and visored, better form without: sent to Italy.
C. E. Brittain

MR MORIARTY (IRE) 5 ch.g. Tate Gallery (USA) 117 – Bernica (FR) 114 –
(Caro 133) [1995 41: a12g⁵ a12g² a12g³ a8g⁵ a11g⁵ a11g⁵ 14.1g 8.2m a8.5g⁵ a8g a46
a8g⁶ a9.4g⁴ 10.8m 6f⁴ 6m 5d 1996 a12g* a11g² a12g² a12g* a16g⁶ a12g² a12g⁵
a12g⁵ 9.2s a11g a7g⁶ 8.2d a9.4g⁵ 18g a14g Nov 4] neat gelding: poor handicapper: in
good form early in 1996, gaining first wins on flat at Southwell in January (maiden)
and February: disappointing from March onwards: should stay 1¾m: acts on
fibresand and firm and dead going: tried blinkered, no improvement: often bandaged:
usually a front runner. *S. R. Bowring*

MR MUSIC 2 ch.g. (May 22) La Grange Music 111 – Golden 69 (Don 128) [1996 –
7d 8s Nov 9] fair sort: second foal: half-brother to 3-y-o Righteous Gent (by
Superpower): dam stayed 2m: well beaten in maidens. *K. McAuliffe*

MR NEVERMIND (IRE) 6 b.g. The Noble Player (USA) 126 – Salacia 93 67
(Seaepic (USA) 100) [1995 67, a78: a7g⁵ a8g³ a8g⁴ a7g² 6.9d 7g² 6.9g² 6.9f³ 7.6m² a82
8.1m 7d a7g² a8g* a8g² a8g³ a8g³ a7g² a7g* a10g⁶ 8f⁴ 8f⁵ 8.3m 7g² 7.1g
8m 8f* 8.5m³ a7g* a8g* Dec 11] useful-looking gelding: has a quick action: quite
useful all-weather performer: won 2 claimers and handicap at Lingfield: only fair on
turf, winning claimer at Brighton in September: stays 8.5f: acts on equitrack,
probably acts on any turf ground: effective with blinkers at 2 and 3 yrs, not tried
since. *G. L. Moore*

MR OSCAR 4 b.g. Belfort (FR) 89 – Moushka (Song 132) [1995 95p: 5m* 5m* 96
1996 5.1g 5m 5m 5m Jun 28] smallish, good-quartered gelding: useful performer,
lightly raced: made encouraging reappearance in rated stakes at Chester, but failed to
go on: very speedy, and will prove best at 5f: has raced only on a sound surface:
usually leads/races prominently: has joined W. McKeown. *M. Johnston*

MR PARADISE (IRE) 2 b.g. (Mar 14) Salt Dome (USA) – Glowlamp (IRE) 93 71 +
(Glow (USA)) [1996 6m 6.9d⁶ 6g² 6v² 7v² Nov 25] IR 2,400F, IR 2,800Y resold IR
8,000Y: first foal: dam 2-y-o 9f winner: fair maiden: runner-up last 3 starts, in minor
event at Saint-Cloud on final one: stays 7f: acts on heavy ground. *T. J. Naughton*

M R POLY 2 b.c. (May 20) Green Desert (USA) 127 – Report 'em (USA) 51 (Staff 57
Writer (USA)) [1996 6m 6d 7f 6m 5f 7g 6.9d⁶ Oct 21] 11,000Y: quite good-topped
colt: sixth foal: half-brother to 7f winner Chance Report (by Beldale Flutter): dam,
maiden, form only at 6f: modest maiden at best: sold 2,200 gns Newmarket Autumn
Sales: may prove best at up to 6f: active type who takes keen hold: sent to Holland.
M. R. Channon

MR ROUGH 5 b.g. Fayruz 116 – Rheinbloom 66 (Rheingold 137) [1995 68: 8m* 64
8.3g³ 8g² 8.3g 8.3m² 7.6m⁶ 8g² 8.9g a8g 1996 8f⁶ 10.3m 10m⁶ 10.3m⁴ 8m 8m³ 8g²
8m³ 9f 8.3d 8m³ 8g⁶ a8g⁵ a8g⁶ Dec 13] sturdy gelding: modest handicapper: effective
at 7.6f, and stays 1¼m: acts on firm and dead ground (below form on soft), and on
equitrack: blinkered (ran respectably) eleventh start at 5 yrs. *D. Morris*

MRS DRUMMOND (IRE) 3 br.f. Dromod Hill – Dear France (USA) –
(Affirmed (USA)) [1995 NR 1996 10m⁶ a9.4g⁴ 10.1m 11f Sep 27] sixth reported
foal: dam never ran: no worthwhile form in claimers and sellers. *A. P. Jarvis*

MRS JAWLEYFORD (USA) 8 b.m. Dixieland Band (USA) – Did She Agree –
(USA) (Restless Native) [1995 –: a16.2g⁵ a16g a16g a14g a14g 1996 a14.8g⁵ a16g
a16g Feb 9] angular mare: has round action: modest staying handicapper at her best:
has shown nothing for some time: acts on fibresand: often bandaged. *C. Smith*

MRS KEEN 3 b.f. Beveled (USA) – Haiti Mill 68 (Free State 125) [1995 –: 6f 6m –
1996 8.1f⁵ 11.9f⁶ 8f Aug 5] workmanlike filly: no worthwhile form. *R. Simpson*

MR SLICK 4 ch.g. Sharpo 132 – Taj Victory 68 (Final Straw 127) [1995 45: 8.3s⁴ –
6g² 6g 1996 10.1s Mar 26] leggy gelding: poor maiden: stiff task and well beaten
only outing in 1996: stays 7f: tried blinkered. *W. Storey*

MRS MCBADGER 3 ch.f. Weldnaas (USA) 112 – Scottish Lady (Dunbeath –
(USA) 127) [1995 67: 5m⁴ 5g⁴ 6m 5m⁶ 6s³ 6.1s³ 6m⁶ 1996 6s⁵ 6.1d⁵ 6m a6g⁶ 7m a6g
Nov 4] rather unfurnished filly: fair maiden as 2-y-o: little form at 3 yrs: stays 6f: has
form on good to firm ground but seemed suited by soft as 2-y-o: tried blinkered:
flashed tail on reappearance. *B. Smart*

MRS MINIVER (USA) 2 b.f. (Feb 13) Septieme Ciel (USA) 123 – Becomes A 92
Rose (CAN) (Deputy Minister (CAN)) [1996 7g⁴ 7m³ 8m 8g⁶ Sep 29] $32,000Y:
leggy, angular filly: second foal: dam unraced half-sister to Canadian 8.5f/1¼m
stakes winner Strong And Steady: in frame in 2 good maidens: tailed off in May Hill
Stakes at Doncaster, something probably amiss: appeared to show plenty of
improvement when never-dangerous 6 lengths sixth of 8 to Reams of Verse in Fillies'
Mile at Ascot: stays 1m: good enough to win a race. *P. A. Kelleway*

MR SPEAKER (IRE) 3 ch.g. Statoblest 120 – Casting Vote (USA) 54 62
(Monteverdi 129) [1995 62: 5m a7g 6.1m 6d³ 6d⁶ 1996 8g 8m 8.3m 6.1m* 6m 7m⁴
7d Aug 24] close-coupled, workmanlike gelding: modest handicapper: won maiden
event at Chepstow in July: sold 8,800 gns Newmarket Autumn Sales: effective at 6f
to 1m: acts on good to firm and dead ground. *C. F. Wall*

MR SPECULATOR 3 ch.g. Kefaah (USA) 124 – Humanity (Ahonoora 122) 63
[1995 –: 8d 1996 8m 9m 10.1m 12.5f⁵ 14.9m* 14.9m a12g⁶ 16g 15.1s a14g³ a12g* a56
Dec 14] strong, lengthy gelding: won handicap at Warwick in July (third-last start
for P. Kelleway), soon off bridle: form afterwards only when winning handicap at
Wolverhampton in December: suited by test of stamina: visored since fifth 3-y-o
start: has given trouble at stalls: not one to trust implicitly. *J. E. Banks*

MR STREAKY 5 gr.g. Sizzling Melody 117 – Cawstons Prejudice 53 (Cawston's –
Clown 113) [1995 NR 1996 a7g a7g Feb 29] tall gelding: no worthwhile form.
L. Montague Hall

MR TEIGH 4 b.g. Komaite (USA) – Khadino (Relkino 131) [1995 71d: 6g⁴ 5g 72
5.1m⁵ a8g⁴ 7m⁶ 1996 a8g* a8g⁶ 8.1d³ a9.4g* a9.4g* 10.3m³ 8.1f⁴ 8m² 10f Nov 5] a81
sturdy gelding: fair handicapper: won at Lingfield (minor event) in February then at
Wolverhampton in June and (made all) July: sold out of B. Smart's stable 18,000 gns
Newmarket Autumn Sales after eighth start: took fierce hold and eased when beaten
final one: stays 10.3f: acts on good to firm ground and equitrack: blinkered second
3-y-o start, visored (set strong pace) final one. *Mrs J. R. Ramsden*

MR TITCH 3 b.g. Totem (USA) 118 – Empress Nicki (Nicholas Bill 125) [1995 –
NR 1996 8.1g 13.8g⁶ 8m 8f Jul 6] second foal: dam poor maiden: well beaten in
varied company, including selling: has joined W. McKeown. *Denys Smith*

MR TOWSER 5 b.g. Faustus (USA) 118 – Saltina (Bustino 136) [1995 62, a78: a11g² a11g⁴ a12g* 12g⁴ 12m⁵ 1996 a11g⁶ a12g a12g Feb 10] close-coupled gelding: fair handicapper: below form at 5 yrs: stays 1½m well: acts on firm and dead ground and on fibresand: has had tongue tied down and often wears a crossed noseband: usually races prominently: game. *W. W. Haigh*

MR WILD (USA) 3 b.g. Wild Again (USA) – Minstress (USA) (The Minstrel (CAN) 135) [1995 NR 1996 10m⁴ 10g⁴ 14.1g⁶ Oct 24] $60,000Y: sixth foal: half-brother to minor winners in USA by Private Account, Fappiano and Gulch: dam minor stakes winner at up to 9f, including at 2 yrs: fair form in maidens: sold to join R. Akehurst 13,000 gns Newmarket Autumn Sales: stays 1¼m (well beaten over 1¾m): yet to race on a soft surface. *B. Hanbury* 73

MS ZIMAN 2 b.f. (Feb 3) Mystiko (USA) 124 – Leave Her Be (USA) (Known Fact (USA) 135) [1996 6g 7g 6.9m⁶ Aug 20] 12,000Y: strong, lengthy filly: has scope: first foal: dam unraced from good French family: behind in maidens and seller: sold 1,300 gns Newmarket Autumn Sales. *M. Bell*

M T VESSEL 2 b.g. (Mar 10) Risk Me (FR) 127 – Brown Taw 66 (Whistlefield 118) [1996 5d 5m³ 5.1m 5m⁶ 5f 5f Jul 27] useful-looking gelding: poor mover: third reported foal: half-brother to 5f winner Stormy Heights (by Golden Heights): dam won 5f seller: poor sprint maiden: inconsistent. *J. R. Jenkins*

MUARA BAY 2 gr.c. (May 3) Absalom 128 – Inca Girl (Tribal Chief 125) [1996 6v Nov 11] 6,000Y: half-brother to 1986 2-y-o 5f and 6f seller winner Good Time Girl (by Good Times) and winners abroad by Coquelin and (sprinter) Rich Charlie: dam placed over 5f and 7f in Ireland: hampered at stalls and never a factor in median auction maiden at Folkestone: joined G. Lewis. *Miss Gay Kelleway*

MU-ARRIK 8 b. or br.h. Aragon 118 – Maravilla 73 (Mandrake Major 122) [1995 58d, a–: 6d 6.1g 5.9m 5g⁶ 6f⁶ a6g 6f 6g 6g⁵ 7f 7f 1996 6d 5.9d² 6s 5.9m⁴ 7g 6m 6.1m 5m 6m 5m 6m a8g a7g⁶ a6g Dec 3] sparely-made horse: modest handicapper: little form at 8 yrs: effective at 6f and 7f: acts on all-weather surfaces and probably any turf going: blinkered/visored: has won for amateur: inconsistent. *G. R. Oldroyd* 46 d a–

MUA-TAB 3 ch.f. Polish Precedent (USA) 131 – Alsabiha 99 (Lord Gayle (USA) 124) [1995 76p: 6g⁴ 1996 8g⁵ 8g³ 10.2f⁴ 10f 11.7m 11.9f 12.1s⁵ Oct 22] lengthy, unfurnished filly: fluent mover: fair form first 3 starts at 3 yrs, disappointing subsequently: sold (P. Walwyn to M. Hammond) 19,000 gns Newmarket Autumn Sales: should stay further than 1¼m: acts on firm ground. *P. T. Walwyn* 71

MUBARHIN (USA) 3 br.c. Silver Hawk (USA) 123 – Upper Dancer (USA) (Upper Nile (USA)) [1995 NR 1996 8m Apr 17] $300,000Y: ninth foal: brother to Grade 2 9f winner Dansil, fourth in Preakness Stakes and Kentucky Derby, and half-brother to 4 other winners in USA: dam unraced: joint favourite and poorly to post, twelfth of 20 to Farasan in newcomers event at Newmarket, held up and not at all knocked about from halfway: reportedly returned lame: sold 11,500 gns Newmarket July Sales. *J. L. Dunlop*

MUBARIZ (IRE) 4 b.g. Royal Academy (USA) 130 – Ringtail 102 (Auction Ring (USA) 123) [1995 75p: 7f² 1996 7.5m² 8.2m² 8s⁴ 8m 7f⁴ 8d⁶ 8.1f 8m Oct 28] well-made, attractive gelding: has been hobdayed: fairly useful maiden at his best, trained by E. Dunlop until after third 3-y-o start: lost his form: stays 8.2f. *C. Smith* 84 d

MUBHIJ (IRE) 3 ch.c. Mujtahid (USA) 118 – Abhaaj 91 (Kris 135) [1995 108: 5m* 5m³ 5m³ 6m² 5m* 5d² 5s* 1996 6f 5f 5m⁵ 5f Jul 26] robust, lengthy, good-quartered colt: good walker: useful performer: below form first 3 starts in 1996, but apparently had 6-runner minor event at Newmarket in safe keeping when breaking leg near finish: stayed 6f: acted on any going: strong-running sort who sometimes didn't find great deal off bridle: dead. *B. W. Hills* 100

MUCH COMMENDED 2 b.f. (Apr 7) Most Welcome 131 – Glowing With Pride 114 (Ile de Bourbon (USA) 133) [1996 6.1m* 6m³ Oct 17] tall, lengthy, rather angular filly: eighth foal: sister to smart 3-y-o 7f (at 2 yrs) and 1¼m winner Prize Giving and half-sister to several winners, including Cesarewitch winner Inchcailloch (by Lomond) and useful 6f to 7.3f winner Everglades (by Green Desert): dam 7f and 10.5f winner: won maiden at Nottingham in September: favourite, good effort 90 p

considering her lack of experience when over a length third of 25 to Proud Native in Redcar Two-Year-Old Trophy at Redcar, soon pushed along after slow start then finishing well: will improve over 7f+, and remains a useful prospect. *G. Wragg*

MUCHEA   2 ch.c. (Apr 16) Shalford (IRE) 124§ – Bargouzine 67 (Hotfoot 115
126) [1996 5d³ 5s* 5m* 5m³ 6g² 6g* 6m² Oct 3]

Bargain-buy Muchea did not stop improving all year. His campaign began with a third place in the Brocklesby on the first day of the turf season and ended with a narrow defeat in the Middle Park Stakes over six months later, bringing in more than ten times the 10,500 guineas he cost as a yearling. It did not take long for Muchea to put his experience in the Brocklesby to use: he ran out a very easy winner of minor events at Catterick and Newmarket in the next three weeks, completing a hat-trick of wins for his trainer in the latter race and looking well worth his place at Royal Ascot two months later. Muchea appeared in the Norfolk Stakes and ran well, leading the stand-side group for a long way and battling on despite hanging right into the centre of the course to be beaten less than three lengths in third by Tipsy Creek who had raced on the far side. Muchea apparently returned sore from Royal Ascot but he went on to prove himself more than just a useful early-season performer when stepped up to six furlongs for the rest of the year.

At Leopardstown in August, Muchea showed a good deal of improvement when two lengths second to Mantovani in the Heinz 57 Phoenix Stakes, having trouble getting a clear run. According to his jockey Richard Hughes, Muchea had been 'squeezed like a sardine' when the winner's stable-companion Azra had come off a true line in front allowing Mantovani first run. Compensation awaited in Germany later in the month, when he landed the odds in the Group 2 Moet & Chandon-Rennen at Baden-Baden by one and a half lengths from another British-trained colt Omaha City. A 16/1-chance in a larger-than-usual field for the Middle Park on his only subsequent outing, Muchea belied his starting price with another excellent effort. Last on the rails and tracking Bahamian Bounty behind a strong pace early on, he weaved through the pack to hit the front inside the final furlong only to be collared by Bahamian Bounty who had found a gap on the rails.

		Thatching (b 1975)	Thatch
	Shalford (IRE)		Abella
	(ch 1988)	Enigma (b 1983)	Ahonoora
Muchea			Princess Ru
(ch.c. Apr 16, 1994)		Hotfoot (br 1966)	Firestreak
	Bargouzine		Pitter Patter
	(ch 1981)	Right As Rain (b 1965)	King's Bench
			Pelting

Muchea's Catterick win was the first for his first-season sire, the very smart but unreliable sprinter Shalford. His dam Bargouzine was not the most consistent of animals either, showing fair form at up to a mile without managing to win. She has had three winning foals from seven prior to Muchea, none of them anywhere near so good as him. La Punt (by Precocious) won at up to a mile in Italy while her two fillies by Petong, Rain Splash and Alshazam, are both winning sprinters, the latter in France as a three-year-old in the latest season. Best of Bargouzine's six winning siblings was the sprinter As Friendly who showed smart form as a two-year-old; their dam Right As Rain was a sprinter too, and so was great-grandam Pelting, the pair of them five-furlong winners. Bassenthwaite (Middle Park Stakes), Keen Hunter (Prix de l'Abbaye), Ghariba (Nell Gwyn Stakes) and Braashee (Prix Royal-Oak) are just some of the pattern winners from this family in recent years.

The sparely-made Muchea looked a very speedy individual early on but the Middle Park showed he stays a strongly-run six furlongs and prompted hopes that he may get a mile. On breeding though it is most likely that sprinting will be his game. He is a game and genuine colt who probably acts on both good to firm and soft ground. *M. R. Channon*

MUCH SOUGHT AFTER 7 b.g. Adonijah 126 – Lady Clementine 68 (He –
Loves Me 120) [1995 NR 1996 a12g 12g Mar 21] close-coupled gelding: fairly
useful handicapper in 1994: no show either start in 1996: probably stays 2m: has
form on any going, all 6 wins on good or softer: tried visored. *K. R. Burke*

MUCH TOO HIGH 4 b.g. Salse (USA) 128 – Hi-Li (High Top 131) [1995 57:
10.8m⁵ 11.6m 16.4g² 14.1g³ 14.1f⁴ 14d⁵ 16.1g 1996 a12g Jan 15] angular gelding:
modest maiden handicapper: well beaten last 4 starts on flat: seems suited by test of
stamina: best form on good ground (soon off bridle only start on all-weather).
T. J. Naughton

MUDFLAP 2 b.f. (Apr 17) Slip Anchor 136 – River's Rising (FR) 88 (Mendez   82
(FR) 128) [1996 6.9g⁵ a6g² a7g* 8m⁵ 7.9g Sep 5] angular filly: unimpressive mover:
fourth foal: half-sister to winners abroad by Sharpo and Entitled: dam 1m winner:
won maiden at Wolverhampton in August: best of far side front runners in valuable
nursery at Newcastle next start: ran poorly when favourite for nursery at York final
one: stays 1m: very progressive prior to final outing. *Sir Mark Prescott*

MUDLARK 4 b.g. Salse (USA) 128 – Mortal Sin (USA) (Green Forest (USA) –
134) [1995 45: 8.3g³ 10g³ a8g⁵ 1996 a12g a16g⁵ a14g⁵ Nov 4] good-bodied gelding:
poor maiden: no form at 4 yrs: probably stays 1¼m: usually blinkered, visored last
outing. *J. Norton*

MUHANDAM (IRE) 3 b.g. Common Grounds 118 – Unbidden Melody (USA)   – §
(Chieftain II) [1995 70: 6m 6g⁵ 6g³ 1996 7m a5g⁶ Jun 28] compact gelding: trained
at 2 yrs by M. Stoute: only worthwhile form final 2-y-o start: looked none too keen
final 3-y-o start: sold (B. Hanbury to Mrs. D. Haine) 3,200 gns Newmarket July
Sales: should stay 7f: tends to carry head awkwardly. *B. Hanbury*

MUHANDIS 3 b.c. Persian Bold 123 – Night At Sea 107 (Night Shift (USA))   82
[1995 67p: 6d³ 6m 1996 7f* 7.1d⁵ Sep 28] good-bodied colt: won 9-runner maiden at
Yarmouth, moving easily long way before quickening to lead approaching final 1f:
creditable fifth of 15 in handicap at Haydock over 2 months later: should stay 1m:
seems to act on firm and dead ground: sent to Dubai. *J. H. M. Gosden*

MUHASSIL (IRE) 3 ch.g. Persian Bold 123 – Nouvelle Star (AUS) (Luskin Star   69
(AUS)) [1995 NR 1996 8m⁴ May 7] seventh foal: half-brother to fairly useful 7f
winner Sariah (by Kris): dam won from 5f to 8.2f in Australia and was champion
older filly at 4 yrs: 8/1, 6 lengths fourth of 13 in maiden at Doncaster, slowly away,
unable to quicken over 1f out and eased. *Major W. R. Hern*

MUHTADI (IRE) 3 br.g. Marju (IRE) 127 – Moon Parade 73 (Welsh Pageant   76 d
132) [1995 76: 7m 8m⁴ 8g 8m 1996 10g* 12d 14.1m 12m 10.2m⁵ Jun 30] big,
good-topped gelding: fair handicapper at best: won narrowly at Ripon in April,
moving easily to lead under 2f out then seeming to down tools: disappointing after,
looking untrustworthy and tried in blinkers on third start: sold 10,500 gns
Newmarket July Sales and gelded: should stay beyond 1¼m: one to treat with
caution. *J. L. Dunlop*

MUJADIL EXPRESS (IRE) 2 b.f. (Apr 18) Mujadil (USA) 119 – Peace   34
Mission (Dunbeath (USA) 127) [1996 7m 5.1m³ 6m⁵ a6g³ a7g³ 10f a8.5g 6.9v Nov a49
11] IR 3,200F, IR 3,000Y: third foal: half-sister to 1994 2-y-o 7f winner Tara Colleen
(by Petorius): dam Irish 1¼m winner: poor performer: well beaten after fifth start:
stays 7f: easily best form on fibresand, all at sea on heavy: has flashed tail.
J. S. Moore

MUJAZI (IRE) 2 ch.c. (Mar 31) Mujtahid (USA) 118 – Leaping Salmon (Salmon –
Leap (USA) 131) [1996 6m⁶ 7m Sep 18] 30,000F, 51,000Y: fourth foal: dam, well
beaten, half-sister to useful Irish 1977 2-y-o Do The Hustle: well beaten in maidens:
blinkered (pulled hard) second outing: sold 2,500 gns Newmarket Autumn Sales:
sent to Sweden. *R. W. Armstrong*

MUJOVA (IRE) 2 b.c. (Mar 22) Mujadil (USA) 119 – Kirsova (Absalom 128)   80
[1996 5d⁶ 5.1d³ 5.1g³ 5.1m³ 5g² 5.1m⁵ 5m⁴ 6m* 6g² 6g⁶ 7m⁵ 7.6g⁴ 6m 6.1s Oct
31] 10,500F, IR 7,400Y: lengthy colt: has scope: poor walker: has a quick action:
half-brother to several winners, including La Ballerine (up to 14.8f, by Lafontaine):
dam lightly raced: won auction event at Newcastle in July: best of last 4 starts when
midfield, never dangerous, in 25-runner Redcar Two-Year-Old Trophy on

penultimate outing: better suited by 6f than 5f, below form in steadily-run races over 7f+: best form on a sound surface. *R. Hollinshead*

MUJTAHIDA (IRE) 3 b.f. Mujtahid (USA) 118 – Domino's Nurse 104 (Dom Racine (FR) 121) [1995 NR 1996 7m 9m a6g a10g⁴ a10g⁴ a13g* Dec 13] lengthy filly: fifth foal: half-sister to untrustworthy 5f (at 2 yrs) to 10.5f winner Romios (by Common Grounds) and 2 other winners, including Irish 1¼m winner Domino's Ring (by Auction Ring): dam Irish 7f (at 2 yrs) and 1¼m winner, later successful in USA: upped in trip, improved form to win handicap at Lingfield in December, detached early then smooth headway to go clear approaching straight: suited by 13f: acts on equitrack: looked ungenuine fifth start, and shouldn't be relied on. *R. W. Armstrong*   63

MUKADDAR (USA) 2 ch.c. (Apr 18) Elmaamul (USA) 125 – Both Sides Now (USA) (Topsider (USA)) [1996 6g* 7g³ 7m² Oct 1] $10,000F, 30,000Y: leggy colt: brother to fairly useful 7f (at 2 yrs) and 1½m winner Seckar Vale and half-brother to 2 winners in USA: dam showed a little ability in USA: useful performer: 20/1, won maiden at Salisbury in August: close up throughout when narrowly beaten in minor event at Kempton and when head second of 23 (leading 3f out until final strides) to Papua in Tattersalls Houghton Sales Stakes at Newmarket: will stay 1m. *C. J. Benstead*   99

MUKEED 3 b.c. Be My Chief (USA) 122 – Rimosa's Pet 109 (Petingo 135) [1995 NR 1996 10.1g 10m 12.3m⁴ 12.3m 12m* Aug 2] 68,000F, 150,000Y: big, lengthy colt: has plenty of scope: half-brother to several winners, notably Kerrera (by Diesis) and Rock City (by Ballad Rock): dam 6f to 10.5f winner: visored and tongue tied, won ladies handicap at Newmarket in August, making all and staying on well: will prove suited by test of stamina: has raced only on a sound surface: sent to UAE. *J. H. M. Gosden*   74

MUKHLLES (USA) 3 b.c. Diesis 133 – Serenely (USA) (Alydar (USA)) [1995 69p: 6g⁵ 1996 8d³ Apr 20] small, attractive colt: fifth of 13 in maiden at Newbury only outing at 2 yrs: tongue tied, again supported in betting when third to Nash Terrace in similar event there over 9 months later: sold 1,800 gns Newmarket Autumn Sales: not certain to stay beyond 1m. *Major W. R. Hern*   82

MULHOLLANDE LAD (IRE) 3 ch.g. Mulhollande (USA) 107 – La Kumbha (FR) (Critique (USA) 126) [1995 –: 5m 7g 7g⁴ a7g a8g 1996 a8g Jan 8] small gelding: well beaten all starts. *M. C. Chapman*   –

MULIERE 2 b.f. (Mar 22) Mujtahid (USA) 118 – Shojoon (USA) (Danzig (USA)) [1996 6g 5m⁵ 6f⁴ 6.1s a8.5g⁵ Nov 11] tall, lengthy, unfurnished filly: has scope: second foal: dam, French 11f winner, closely related to Assatis and Warrshan: modest maiden: never able to land a blow in nurseries last 2 outings: should stay beyond 6f: acts on firm ground: sold 12,000 gns Ascot December Sales. *M. Johnston*   54

MULLAGH HILL LAD (IRE) 3 b.c. Cyrano de Bergerac 120 – Fantasie (FR) (General Assembly (USA)) [1995 56, a73: a5g⁶ 6f a6g 5m³ 6.1m⁴ a5g* a5g² 1996 6.1d 6.1d 7.5g 6g⁴ 5.9f⁶ 6g⁶ 6s 6.1m 6m⁶ Oct 7] dipped-backed colt: fair performer on the all-weather at 2 yrs, only poor on turf at 3 yrs: stays 6f: acts on good to firm and soft ground, goes particularly well on fibresand: blinkered (looked none too keen) sixth 3-y-o start: tends to hang. *B. A. McMahon*   48 a–

MULL HOUSE 9 b.g. Local Suitor (USA) 128 – Foudre 76 (Petingo 135) [1995 NR 1996 14g 16.2d 16s a16g a16g⁵ Dec 5] workmanlike gelding: fair staying handicapper at 7 yrs: no promise in 1996: often sweating: blinkered (below form) once at 4 yrs, visored last 2 starts: none too consistent. *G. P. Enright*   –

MULLITOVER 6 ch.g. Interrex (CAN) – Atlantic Air (Air Trooper 115) [1995 88: a8g⁴ a7g a7g² 7f⁶ 7g⁴ 8.3m* 7m* 8.1m⁴ 7m* 7g⁵ 7m* 1996 7m³ 8m⁶ 7.3m 7m Sep 28] close-coupled, workmanlike gelding: fairly useful handicapper: good efforts first 2 starts in 1996 when third of 16 in Bunbury Cup at Newmarket and sixth of 18 in Schweppes Golden Mile at Goodwood: ran poorly last 2 outings: effective at 7f to 8.3f: acts on firm and soft going and the all-weather: usually races prominently: tough. *M. J. Heaton-Ellis*   92

MULTAN 4 b.g. Indian Ridge 123 – Patchinia 77 (Patch 129) [1995 NR 1996 7g 5g 6d 7.1m⁴ 7g 10g Oct 2] tall gelding: good mover: modest maiden nowadays: retained by trainer 1,000 gns Newmarket Autumn Sales: stays 7f: acts on good to   52

firm ground (had excuses only start on a soft surface): headstrong, and virtually
bolted to post 4-y-o reappearance. *G. L. Moore*

MULTICOLOURED (IRE) 3 b.c. Rainbow Quest (USA) 134 – Greektown 111 p
(Ela-Mana-Mou 132) [1995 NR 1996 10m² 12.3d² 10.4g* 10g² Nov 1] good-bodied,
attractive colt: fluent mover: third foal: closely related to useful 7f (at 2 yrs) and
1½m winner Athens Belle (by Groom Dancer): dam, French 1¼m and 1½m winner,
half-sister to smart French stayer Sought Out (by Rainbow Quest): not seen out until
August: won maiden at York in October, setting pace and quickening clear 3f out:
much improved (and smart) form when neck second of 8 to Proper Blue in listed race
at Newmarket, staying on strongly: suited by middle distances: very much the type to
progress further at 4 yrs. *M. R. Stoute*

MULTI FRANCHISE 3 ch.g. Gabitat 119 – Gabibti (IRE) 82 (Dara Monarch 56
128) [1995 59d: 5m 6m 6f³ a7g* 8m a6g a7g 1996 a8g⁴ a8g² a10g* 10f² 10.2m⁴ 9.7g a60
8f* 8f a10g Sep 10] leggy gelding: modest performer: won claimers at Lingfield in
February and Brighton (not at best) in August: probably better at 1¼m than 1m: acts
on firm ground and the all-weather: no improvement in visor/blinkers. *B. Gubby*

MUMKIN 2 b.c. (Mar 17) Reprimand 122 – Soon To Be 84 (Hot Spark 126) [1996 76 +
6g* 6g³ 6m Sep 14] 35,000Y: tall, leggy colt: fourth reported foal: dam (6f and 7f
winner) from family of Oaks-placed Suni and Media Luna: fair form: won maiden at
Windsor in August: ran just respectably in minor events at Ripon and Doncaster
(tending to hang) afterwards: reportedly injured pelvis. *T. Thomson Jones*

MUNAADEE (USA) 4 b.c. Green Dancer (USA) 132 – Aliysa 126 (Darshaan 75
133) [1995 75: 10.1g² 1996 a11g* Mar 9] tall, good-topped colt: twice raced prior to
1996: sold out of E. Dunlop's stable 18,000 gns Doncaster October Sales: favourite,
won maiden at Southwell in March, travelling well and leading inside last: will stay
beyond 11f: finished lame (found to be suffering from an over-reach) at Southwell.
Bob Jones

MUNGO PARK 2 b.g. (Mar 9) Selkirk (USA) 129 – River Dove (USA) 86 68 p
(Riverman (USA) 131) [1996 6.1m 5s 5g⁴ 5d Nov 8] 16,500Y: big, strong, most
imposing gelding: has a roundish action: has plenty of scope: fourth foal: closely
related to 5-y-o 7f winner Square Deal (by Sharpo): dam, 2-y-o 6f winner, out of
Poule d'Essai des Pouliches second Fruhlingstag: best form in maidens when fourth
at Catterick, steadied start and well behind after 2f then running on not knocked
about, nearest finish: not well drawn, given similar ride when equal seventh of 13 to
Myrmidon in nursery at Doncaster following month: gelded afterwards: will be
suited by further than 5f: capable of better than he's shown to date, and the type to do
well in handicaps in 1997. *Mrs J. R. Ramsden*

MUNICIPAL GIRL (IRE) 2 b.f. (Feb 17) Mac's Imp (USA) 116 – Morning 40
Welcome (IRE) (Be My Guest (USA) 126) [1996 5.1m⁵ a5g⁶ 6d⁴ 7m 6g a6g a5g a8g⁵
Nov 29] IR 5,800F, IR 3,000Y: angular filly: first foal: dam, Irish maiden, probably
stayed 1½m: worthwhile form only when fourth in seller at Ripon in August.
B. Palling

MUNTAFI 5 b.g. Unfuwain (USA) 131 – Princess Sucree (USA) (Roberto (USA) –
131) [1995 –: 16m 1996 14m Aug 31] lengthy, angular gelding: lost his way at 3 yrs
when trained by J. Dunlop, and well beaten on return to flat: fair handicap hurdler:
needs treating with caution: retained 1,600 gns Ascot December Sales. *G. Harwood*

MUPPET 2 b.f. (Apr 29) Law Society (USA) 130 – Shaadin (USA) 80 (Sharpen 39
Up 127) [1996 5d⁴ 5f 5s⁵ May 9] 4,200Y: lengthy filly: third foal: dam maiden sister
to Pebbles: poor form: form only on a soft surface: sold 600 gns Newmarket July
Sales: sent to Holland. *Miss Gay Kelleway*

MURAJJA (USA) 4 ch.c. Silver Hawk (USA) 123 – Halholah (USA) 65 (Secreto 110
(USA) 128) [1995 104: 10.5m* 10m* 10.3m³ 12.6m 12d 10s* 10m⁴ 12s Oct 26]
rangy, good-topped colt: smart performer: off course 10 months prior to reappearance: improved form to win good-quality minor event at Newbury in May by head
(pair 15 lengths clear) from King's Theatre, gamely making most: off course further
2½ months before below form in 2 Group 3 events: sold 45,000 gns Newmarket
Autumn Sales: should stay 1½m: best effort on soft going, gave impression he was
unsuited by firm: looked ill-at-ease at Chester: effective from front or held up: sent to
Malaysia. *P. T. Walwyn*

MURHEB 3 b.g. Mtoto 134 – Masarrah 91 (Formidable (USA) 125) [1995 87p: 94
7m 7m² 1996 8d⁴ 10m* 8g 8.1g⁶ 10m² 10m⁵ Aug 16] rather unfurnished gelding:
fluent mover: fairly useful performer: won maiden at Kempton in April: best form
when second of 14 to Fahim in £34,000 handicap at Goodwood and when sixth of 15
to Greenstead in £9,800 handicap at Newbury: unlikely to stay beyond 1¼m: acts on
good to firm going: somewhat headstrong: sent to UAE. *R. W. Armstrong*

MURPHY'S GOLD (IRE) 5 ch.g. Salt Dome (USA) – Winter Harvest (Grundy 58
137) [1995 63: a8g 8m⁴ 8.5m² 10m⁶ 8g⁴ 7.5m* 8m³ 8.5m* 7.9m² 8.5m 7m 8.5d 1996
7.5d 8m⁶ 8m 8.5m 7.5m⁴ 7.5f² 7.5m⁴ 8.5m 8.5m⁴ 8m Oct 2] tall gelding: modest
handicapper: ran at Beverley all bar 3 starts at 5 yrs, running well when narrowly-
beaten fourth of 19 there penultimate start: stays 8.5f well, not 1¼m: acts on firm
ground, below form on soft: blinkered (well beaten) twice as 3-y-o: successful for a
lady. *R. A. Fahey*

MURRAY GREY 2 gr.f. (Feb 2) Be My Chief (USA) 122 – Couleur de Rose –
(Kalaglow 132) [1996 7.5m 7.1v 7m⁶ Oct 23] 6,800F, 11,000Y: strong, lengthy filly:
fifth foal: half-sister to 1992 2-y-o 6f winner Exclusively Yours (by Shareef Dancer):
dam unraced daughter of very smart 1980 2-y-o Exclusively Raised: signs of ability
but no worthwhile form: wears bandages. *E. Weymes*

MURRAY'S MAZDA (IRE) 7 ch.g. M Double M (USA) – Lamya 73 (Hittite 56
Glory 125) [1995 48: 5g⁴ 6f 5f 5m⁵ 5g⁶ 6m² 6f³ 6m⁴ 5f 5g 7d² 6m a7g⁵ 1996 7.1g*
7.5m⁵ 7m* 7m³ 6g² 6m 7m 7f⁴ 8m a7g* Dec 28] leggy gelding: modest handicapper:
in good form first 5 starts at 7 yrs, winning at Musselburgh in May and Thirsk (ladies)
in June: returned to best to win at Wolverhampton in December: stays 7f: seems to
act on any going, including fibresand: well beaten in blinkers/visor: sometimes
bandaged. *J. L. Eyre*

MURRON WALLACE 2 gr.f. (Feb 19) Reprimand 122 – Fair Eleanor 53
(Saritamer (USA) 130) [1996 5g⁶ 6m⁵ 7m⁵ 8g⁵ Oct 21] 6,700Y: sixth foal: half-sister
to 3 winners, none better than fair, including 1989 2-y-o Ardelle Grey (7f, by
Ardross): dam, poor plater, stayed 1m: modest form: stays 1m: swerved left stalls
second start. *R. M. Whitaker*

MUSALSAL (IRE) 2 b.c. (Mar 17) Sadler's Wells (USA) 132 – Ozone Friendly 89 p
(USA) 107 (Green Forest (USA) 134) [1996 6m⁵ 8g* Oct 29] quite good-topped colt:
third foal: dam Prix Robert Papin winner out of a 1¼m winner: won 16-runner
maiden at Leicester by 2½ lengths from Kyle Rhea, improving smoothly from 2f out
and ridden clear: will stay at least 1¼m: got loose in paddock prior to debut: should
make a useful 3-y-o. *B. W. Hills*

MUSCATANA 2 b.f. (Apr 7) Distant Relative 128 – Sauhatz (GER) (Alpenkonig 47 +
(GER)) [1996 5.7f 5.1m 6g⁶ 7.5m Sep 18] small, angular filly: half-sister to several
winners in Germany: dam won 3 times at 3 yrs in Germany: modest maiden: will
prove suited by further than 6f, poorly drawn and badly hampered when tried.
B. W. Hills

MUSE 9 ch.g. High Line 125 – Thoughtful 86 (Northfields (USA)) [1995 NR 1996 –
16s 16.2d 16s Oct 24] has a rather round action: rated 94 in 1994 but suffered tendon
injury final start that year and soundly beaten on flat at 9 yrs, blinkered final start:
stays 2m well (soundly beaten in 2½m Ascot Stakes): probably acts on any going:
has run well when sweating: suited by forcing tactics: still retains plenty of ability
over hurdles, winner in November. *D. R. C. Elsworth*

MUSETTA (IRE) 4 b.f. Cadeaux Genereux 131 – Monaiya (Shareef Dancer 107
(USA) 135) [1995 107: 8m 10m* 10.4m³ 12m⁴ 12m³ 12g⁴ 10.5f 12d 10g 1996 10g
8.5m⁶ 10m* 10m² 10m³ 10s⁴ Sep 21] lengthy filly: useful performer: won minor
event at Windsor in June by ½ length from Valley of Gold: again allowed to set steady
pace when neck second to confidently-ridden Montjoy in Group 3 event at Ayr:
found to be in season penultimate start and below best final one: stays 1½m: acts on
soft and good to firm: tends to sweat and be rather edgy: often front runner.
C. E. Brittain

MUSEUM (IRE) 5 b.g. Tate Gallery (USA) 117 – Go Anywhere (Grundy 137) –
[1995 –: 12m⁶ 10.8g 10m 12g 9f 10f 1996 a12g a11g² a11g² a11g 10f 10f Jun 21] sparely-made a68
gelding: fair performer at best nowadays: easily best effort for some time when
second in handicap at Southwell in February: first run on flat for 4 months when short

of room and not given hard race in Redcar claimer final start: stays 1¾m: acts on soft ground and good to firm and fibresand: has joined P. Winkworth. *D. Nicholls*

MUSHAHID (USA)   3 b.c. Wild Again (USA) – Playful Queen (USA) (Majestic   102
Prince (USA)) [1995 99: 6g* 6m² 7m* 7f⁴ 8.1m² 8g² 8f³ 1996 8s³ 8.1g⁴ 8g* 8f 8m*
10m 7.9m a7f² Dec 26] big, well-made colt: good mover: useful handicapper: won at
Doncaster in June (awarded race) and July (minor event by a head from Phantom
Quest): below form in valuable events next 2 starts (trained until then by J. Dunlop)
but beaten only a short head in Dubai final outing: stays 1m: acts on firm going,
probably not on soft. *K. P. McLaughlin, UAE*

MUSHARAK   2 b.c. (Jan 19) Mujtahid (USA) 118 – Mahasin (USA) 90 (Danzig   69 p
(USA)) [1996 6d⁴ 6s Oct 24] strong, lengthy, good sort: has scope: first foal: dam 7f
and 1m winner, closely related to William Hill Futurity winner Al Hareb and smart
French 9f to 1¼m winner Dr Somerville: fair form in maidens at Ascot and Newbury
(seemed to carry head bit high) in October: probably capable of better. *J. L. Dunlop*

MUSHEER (USA)   2 b.c. (May 5) Known Fact (USA) 135 – Summer Trip (USA)   110 p
117 (L'Emigrant (USA) 129) [1996 7s² 7m* 7f³ Sep 13] 40,000 2-y-o: big, close-
coupled, rather leggy colt: easy mover with a long stride: third foal: dam won Prix de
Royallieu and stayed 13.5f: stepped up good deal on debut form (very green, held up
on soft ground) when making all in 5-runner maiden at Ascot (beat Monza) in July:
looking in superb shape, 5¼ lengths third of 4 to Bahhare in Laurent-Perrier
Champagne Stakes at Doncaster, setting strong pace 5f then sticking on: will be
suited by 1m+: acts on firm ground: has plenty of scope, and remains a very useful
prospect. *Miss Gay Kelleway*

MUSICAL DANCER (USA)   2 ch.c. Dixieland Band (USA) – Parrish Empress   102
(USA) (His Majesty (USA)) [1996 7g⁵ 7.5m* 7g² 6g⁶ 7f² 7m² Oct 4] $120,000Y:
close-coupled colt: good walker: fluent mover: third foal: half-brother to a winner in
USA by Ferdinand: dam, won twice in USA, half-sister to champion older mare
Princess Rooney: won slowly-run 3-runner maiden at Beverley in July: progressed
well, 1¾ lengths second of 8 to Grapeshot in listed race at Newmarket final outing,
hanging right going into Dip then staying on well: will be suited by further than 7f:
acts on firm ground. *E. A. L. Dunlop*

MUSICAL HEIGHTS (IRE)   3 b.f. Roaring Riva 103 – Littleton Song 73   –
(Song 132) [1995 –: 5g 1996 a5g Mar 18] well held in median auction maiden and
seller. *C. A. Dwyer*

MUSICAL PURSUIT   2 b.c. (Apr 18) Pursuit of Love 124 – Gay Music (FR)   113 p
(Gay Mecene (USA) 128) [1996 6m⁵ 6m* 7g² Oct 18]
　　　　Five months after having the photo-finish verdict go against them when
Even Top was short-headed in the Two Thousand Guineas, connections had to
endure a similar fate in another big race at the track when Musical Pursuit was
beaten a head in the Dewhurst. There will be other opportunities for both
horses, and the first task for the thrice-raced Musical Pursuit will be an attempt
to go one better than Even Top in the Guineas. Stepping up from maiden
company, Musical Pursuit was fifth choice at 13/2 in an open-looking and
substandard field of eight for the Dewhurst. A leggy, good-topped colt with
scope, he looked really well in the paddock beforehand, impressing as a good
walker. Pat Eddery soon had him disputing the lead with one of the joint-
favourites Kahal and kept him in contention after inexperience had seemed
likely to tell against him running into the Dip. The horse rallied well up the hill
and in a driving finish failed by only a head to peg back In Command; he had a
neck to spare over third-placed outsider Air Express, looking as though another
furlong would have suited him better. Musical Pursuit's run was all the more
praiseworthy for that lack of experience—coughing had kept him off the track
for two and a half months after his second start. He had made his debut as a
33/1-shot at the Newmarket July meeting in what turned out to be a high-
quality maiden, staying on steadily in fifth behind Grapeshot and Bahamian
Bounty, the future winners of the Somerville Tattersall Stakes and the Prix
Morny and Middle Park Stakes respectively. A well-backed favourite for
another maiden over course and distance in early-August, Musical Pursuit was

a different proposition, enthusiastically making all for an easy four-length victory over another son of Pursuit of Love, Bachelors Pad.

Musical Pursuit's second place in the Dewhurst helped make Pursuit of Love the leading first-season sire by money won, though the St Hugh's Stakes winner Head Over Heels was actually his leading earner. Like Musical Pursuit, the game, genuine and consistent Pursuit of Love was only a twice-raced maiden winner going into the Dewhurst, in which he finished fourth to Dr Devious. At three he developed into a smart performer at six furlongs to a mile, winning the European Free Handicap, the Prix Maurice de Gheest and the Kiveton Park Stakes and reaching a place in the Two Thousand Guineas and July Cup.

Musical Pursuit (b.c. Apr 18, 1994)	Pursuit of Love (b 1989)	Groom Dancer (b 1984)	Blushing Groom Featherhill
		Dance Quest (b 1981)	Green Dancer Polyponder
	Gay Music (FR) (b 1986)	Gay Mecene (b 1975)	Vaguely Noble Gay Missile
		Moika (gr 1975)	Zeddaan Moqueuse

Musical Pursuit, who was sold for just 8,800 guineas as a foal but made 35,000 guineas as a yearling, is the third foal out of Gay Music, the first two by Dancing Dissident both having won abroad—Special Dissident over sprint distances in Italy and Dance Music over nine furlongs as a two-year-old in France. The dam has no recorded yearling but she has a foal by Night Shift. Gay Music, who was placed over a mile and ten furlongs in France for Criquette Head, is from a family that has produced numerous black-type

Mr B. Schmidt-Bodner's "Musical Pursuit"

earners there for the Wertheimers, among them Gay Music's half-brother the smart Don Mario who made the frame in the Prix Jean Prat and the Grand Prix de Paris in 1987. The third dam, the Prix de Flore runner-up Moqueuse, a winner at up to eleven furlongs, bred seven winners, all successful over middle distances. Gay Music's dam Moika, placed in listed company, was among them. Another daughter, the 1976 Prix de Pomone dead-heater Moquerie, bred four individual listed scorers while a third, Rivermaid (herself a listed winner), is the dam of Only Star, winner of the 1986 Prix de Sandringham, and Movieland who won the 1987 Prix des Reservoirs. Musical Pursuit must have a good chance of a pattern-race win himself. He certainly looks the type to do well at three and will be well suited by further than seven furlongs. From what we have seen of him he is a thoroughly genuine type. *M. H. Tompkins*

MUSICAL SEASON   4 b.g. Merdon Melody 98 – Earles-Field (Wolverlife 115)   96
[1995 92: 5m⁶ 6m⁵ 5m 6m² 5.2m 1996 6g 5d 6m⁵ 5.6m* 6m 5d 6s² Oct 24] lengthy, quite attractive gelding: keen walker: unimpressive mover: useful handicapper: 33/1 after 3-month absence, made all in 21-runner £17,300 Tote-Portland Handicap at Doncaster in September, racing against stand rail: creditable efforts all subsequent starts: stays 6f: acts on good to firm and soft ground. *T. D. Barron*

MUSICAL VOCATION (IRE)   5 ch.m. Orchestra 118 – Kentucky Calling   –
(Pry) [1995 NR 1996 a14.8g Jan 24] second foal: dam winning hurdler: tailed off in seller on flat debut. *B. Preece*

MUSIC EXPRESS (IRE)   2 b.f. (Apr 24) Classic Music (USA) – Hetty Green   56
(Bay Express 132) [1996 6m⁵ 7.1g⁴ a6g Nov 18] IR 4,800Y: half-sister to 1989 2-y-o 6f winner Cohete (by Sallust), later quite useful winner in Hong Kong: dam Irish middle-distance winner: modest form on debut only: trained first 2 starts by A. Harrison. *J. L. Eyre*

MUSIC GOLD (IRE)   3 b. or br.g. Taufan (USA) 119 – Nonnita 71 (Welsh Saint   91
126) [1995 91: 5g² 5s² 5m* 5m² 1996 5g⁴ 5m⁴ 5m⁵ Oct 3] leggy, close-coupled gelding: fairly useful performer: very stiff task, far from disgraced in listed race at Newmarket final start, first for 4½ months: will probably stay 6f: acts on good to firm and soft ground: blinkered last 2 starts. *W. A. O'Gorman*

MUSIC IN MOTION   3 b.f. Batshoof 122 – Falaka 83 (Sparkler 130) [1995 –:   –
6.9s 1996 10.1f Jul 21] showed nothing in maiden auction and seller 10 months later: sold 1,200 gns Newmarket September Sales. *P. Howling*

MUSICK HOUSE (IRE)   3 b.c. Sadler's Wells (USA) 132 – Hot Princess 101   92
(Hot Spark 126) [1995 96p: 6g² 1996 8d³ 7.1d* 8d 7m 10m Oct 17] smallish, angular colt: fairly useful form: won maiden at Haydock in May: stiff tasks, well beaten in Irish 2000 Guineas and Jersey Stakes at Royal Ascot (probably ran creditably, tenth

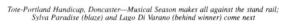

Tote-Portland Handicap, Doncaster—Musical Season makes all against the stand rail;
Sylva Paradise (blaze) and Lago Di Varano (behind winner) come next

of 16): tailed off in smart conditions event at Newmarket 4 months later: should stay further than 1m: yet to race on extremes of going: bandaged behind first 3 starts in 1996. *P. W. Chapple-Hyam*

MUSIC MISTRESS (IRE) 3 ch.f. Classic Music (USA) – Blue Scholar 60 48 ? (Hotfoot 126) [1995 55: 5f⁵ 5g² 6m³ 5m* 5.7h² 7.1m⁴ 6m³ 7d 6.1m 1996 a7g⁵ a6g a7g⁵ 8.2d 6.1m⁴ 5m 5m 7d Aug 23] smallish filly: poor performer: form at 3 yrs only when fourth of 16 (raced on favoured part of track) in seller in April: stays 7f: acts on hard ground, possibly unsuited to a soft surface: blinkered (well beaten) penultimate start. *J. S. Moore*

MUSTAHIL (IRE) 7 gr.g. Sure Blade (USA) 130 – Zumurrudah (USA) 82 – (Spectacular Bid (USA)) [1995 NR 1996 8.3m 8.1g 17.2m Jun 29] seems of little account nowadays. *R. J. Hodges*

MUSTANG 3 ch.g. Thatching 131 – Lassoo 87 (Caerleon (USA) 132) [1995 62p: – 7g 7d⁴ 1996 7.1g a8.5g⁶ Sep 21] strong, lengthy, good-topped gelding: has plenty of scope: modest form in maidens at 2 yrs: disappointing in similar events 5½ months apart in 1996: should stay further than 7f. *C. W. Thornton*

MUSTANG SCALLY 2 b.f. (May 21) Makbul – Another Scally (Scallywag – 127) [1996 8.2g a7g a7g Nov 22] first reported foal: dam poor plater over hurdles: well beaten in sellers. *J. Mackie*

MUSTARD 3 ch.f. Keen 116 – Tommys Dream (Le Bavard (FR) 125) [1995 NR – 1996 8.2m 8m 8m Jul 8] angular filly: second foal: dam winning 2m to 3m hurdler: well beaten in maidens. *A. B. Mulholland*

MUSTN'T GRUMBLE (IRE) 6 b.g. Orchestra 118 – Gentle Heiress (Prince 64 Tenderfoot (USA) 126) [1995 64, a–: a7g 6m⁵ a7g 7g⁶ 6g⁶ a7g 1996 7s² a6g² 6.1g⁴ 6.1g⁴ a6g⁴ a7g⁶ 7.1g⁶ a6g a7g² a8.5g⁶ 8.1f² 8f* 8.2g 8f³ 8g⁵ a8g⁶ a9.4g⁵ a12g Dec 28] sturdy gelding: modest performer: claimed out of D. Nicholls' stable £5,000 second 6-y-o start: won 15-runner minor event at Leicester in September: stays 1m: acts on all-weather, best turf efforts on a sound surface: often used to be blinkered, but is at least as effective when not: often visored of late: has had tongue tied down: tends to carry head high. *Miss S. J. Wilton*

MUTABARI (USA) 2 ch.c. (Feb 23) Seeking The Gold (USA) – Cagey 70 Exuberance (USA) (Exuberant (USA)) [1996 6.1m⁵ 7.1v³ 8.2g Oct 24] $100,000F, $175,000Y: rangy, unfurnished colt: fluent mover: fourth foal: closely related to 7f winner Asdaf (by Forty Niner) and half-brother to a winner in USA by Deputy Minister: dam Graded 6f and 7f winner: fair form when third in maiden at Haydock in October on first run for 4 months, moving easily to lead 2f out: possibly doesn't stay 8.2f. *D. Morley*

MUTADARRA (IRE) 3 ch.g. Mujtahid (USA) 118 – Silver Echo (Caerleon 81 § (USA) 132) [1995 89p: 6m² 1996 7m² 7g³ 6g* 7.1m 6.1m Jul 29] tall, angular gelding: fairly useful performer: odds on, narrowly won maiden at Pontefract in May: well held in handicaps afterwards, looking temperamental in first-time blinkers final start: sold (R. Armstrong to W. Musson) 2,500 gns Newmarket Autumn Sales and gelded: stays 7f: has raced only on a sound surface: tends to hang: not one to trust. *R. W. Armstrong*

MU-TADIL 4 gr.g. Be My Chief (USA) 122 – Inveraven 53 (Alias Smith (USA)) – [1995 73: 10g⁵ 13.4d 1996 11.7m⁵ 17.2d Sep 30] smallish, good-bodied gelding: no worthwhile form at 4 yrs. *R. J. Baker*

MUTAHADETH 2 ch.g. (Mar 9) Rudimentary (USA) 118 – Music In My Life 56 (IRE) 59 (Law Society (USA) 130) [1996 7m 7.5f 8f⁵ 8m⁶ Sep 26] 38,000Y: first foal: dam (maiden) stayed 1m: modest maiden: sold 4,400 gns Newmarket Autumn Sales. *N. A. Graham*

MUTAMANNI (USA) 3 b.g. Caerleon (USA) 132 – Mathkurh (USA) 97 78 (Riverman (USA) 131) [1995 84p: 6s² 6.1m² 1996 6m⁴ 7f⁴ 8.1d⁴ Jun 8] rather leggy gelding: fair handicapper: should prove suited by further than 6f: acts on firm and soft ground: sent to UAE. *H. Thomson Jones*

MUTANASSIB (IRE) 3 b.g. Mtoto 134 – Lightning Legacy (USA) 78 (Super 75 Concorde (USA) 126) [1995 NR 1996 10.1m⁶ 10f² 10.2d⁶ 14.1g⁴ Oct 24] 19,000F, 56,000Y: tall, rather leggy gelding: half-brother to 3 winners, including Sudden Spin (6f to 2m, by Doulab) and useful 1¼m to 11f winner Black Monday (by Busted): dam (maiden) stayed 1m: fair maiden: sold (A. Stewart to M. Pipe) 20,000 gns New-market Autumn Sales and gelded: stays 1¾m: acts on firm ground, quickly beaten on dead: awkward at stalls and very slowly away on debut. *A. C. Stewart*

MUTASARRIF (IRE) 3 b.c. Polish Patriot (USA) 128 – Bouffant (High Top ?
131) [1995 NR 1996 6m 7s 9.5g⁶ a7.5g⁴ 8.3d* 8.5v 7g² 8s² 9v⁵ Nov 10] third foal:
half-brother to 1995 3-y-o 1¼m winner Sahil and 1992 2-y-o 6.9f winner Fanfan
(both by Taufan): dam thrice-raced daughter of smart 1m to 1½m winner Lucent,
herself daughter of good sprinter Lucasland: ran once for H. Thomson Jones in May:
competed in Germany in the autumn, winning a minor event at Neuss then second in
similar contests at Hanover and Mulheim: stays 8.3f: acts on soft ground, probably
on sand. *Miss J. Verkerk, Belgium*

MUTASAWWAR 2 ch.c. (Apr 24) Clantime 101 – Keen Melody (USA) 60 –
(Sharpen Up 127) [1996 6m 6g Oct 29] 28,000Y: third foal: half-brother to 1995
2-y-o 7f winner Rock Sharp (by Rock City): dam stayed 1m: poor form in maidens:
bandaged front, green and coltish on debut. *E. A. L. Dunlop*

MUTAZZ (USA) 4 b.c. Woodman (USA) 126 – Ghashtah (USA) (Nijinsky –
(CAN) 138) [1995 69: 10g⁴ 12m³ 11.6m² 14d² 1996 14.1g Apr 22] neat colt: has a
round action: poor walker: fair maiden on flat: well beaten sole outing in 1996: stays
1¾m: acts on dead and good to firm ground, well beaten on soft: front runner: fair
hurdler. *Major W. R. Hern*

MUTEE (IRE) 3 b.f. Mujtahid (USA) 118 – Cum Laude 102 (Shareef Dancer –
(USA) 135) [1995 –: a6g 1996 a8g Jan 15] tailed off in maiden and seller on
all-weather: covered by Pelder. *M. Johnston*

MUTRIBAH (USA) 2 b.f. (Jan 13) Silver Hawk (USA) 123 – Pattimech (USA) 77 p
(Nureyev (USA) 131) [1996 6.9m² 8f² Sep 10] IR 120,000Y: stocky filly: has a
markedly round action: first foal: dam, won at up to 7f in USA, sister to Grade 1 9f
winner Annoconnor and half-sister to Grand Prix de Paris and Melbourne Cup
winner At Talaq (by Roberto): beaten a neck in maidens at Folkestone and Leicester,
better effort on second occasion when battling on well: looks a stayer: sent to Dubai:
may well improve again. *H. Thomson Jones*

MUZRAK (CAN) 5 ch.g. Forty Niner (USA) – Linda North (USA) (Northern –
Dancer) [1995 55: 9.9m 10m 8.5m 12g³ 13f³ 10f⁵ 12.1m² 1996 13.8s Mar 27]
angular ex-Irish gelding: modest maiden handicapper in Britain: off course over 8
months, well beaten on reappearance: stays 13f: acts on firm ground: visored (carried
head high) sixth 4-y-o start: modest winning hurdler. *M. D. Hammond*

MY ARCHIE 3 b.c. Silver Arch – My Alma (IRE) 72 (Reasonable (FR) 119) –
[1995 –: 7d 8.1d⁴ 1996 a12g⁶ a8g Mar 18] rather unfurnished colt: well behind all
starts. *R. D. E. Woodhouse*

MYASHA (USA) 7 b.g. Imp Society (USA) – Mauna Loa (USA) (Hawaii) [1995 44
74: a5g* 5m 6g⁵ 6g 5f⁵ 5g³ a7.5g⁶ a5g* 5v² a5g 1996 a7.5g⁴ 7s 5m² 5f 5f⁶ 5h³ 5f 6g⁵
5d³ 6s Nov 29] neat gelding: second in seller at Folkestone on only British outing in
1996, carrying head awkwardly: effective at 5f to 7f: acts on hard ground, dead and
equitrack: tried blinkered: often bandaged behind. *Alex Vanderhaeghen, Belgium*

MY BEAUTIFUL DREAM 3 gr.f. Kalaglow 132 – Cinderella Derek 61 –
(Hittite Glory 125) [1995 NR 1996 10f⁴ 10f May 9] 1,000Y: second foal: dam
winning sprinter, also successful over hurdles: flattered when fourth of 6 in median
auction maiden at Brighton, setting steady pace: soundly beaten in seller there 4
weeks later: has joined A. D. Smith. *A. G. Newcombe*

MY BELOVED (IRE) 2 b.f. (May 1) Polish Patriot (USA) 128 – Arbour (USA) 69
76 (Graustark) [1996 5m⁵ 6d⁴ 5.7m* 7f³ Jul 26] 1,000F, 7,200Y: fourth foal:
half-sister to 3-y-o 7f winner Alpine Hideaway (by Tirol) and a winner in Norway by
Lomond: dam twice-raced 11.7f winner, is out of half-sister to dam of Irish St Leger
winner Protection Racket: won maiden auction at Bath: good third of 12, running on
strongly, in nursery at Newmarket following month: will be well suited by further
than 7f: acts on firm and dead ground. *R. Hannon*

MY BEST VALENTINE 6 b.h. Try My Best (USA) 130 – Pas de Calais (Pas de 96
Seul 133) [1995 85: a8g 7m 6m⁴ 6f⁵ 6f 6m 7m 6m³ 6g 1996 7f* 6m 7s⁵ 6m² 7g² 6m⁶
6g 7d² 7g⁵ 8.5m 7m⁵ 7g Oct 19] compact horse: carries condition: useful handicapper, better than ever in 1996: won at Brighton in April and would have won rated

stakes at Chester in August but for being eased: good fifth of 26 to Decorated Hero in £50,100 event at Ascot penultimate start: stays 7.5f, finds even steadily-run 8.5f stretching his stamina: acts on firm and soft ground, ran poorly on equitrack on 5-y-o reappearance: effective blinkered (not tried at 6 yrs) or not. *J. White*

MY BETSY 2 gr.f. (Feb 28) Absalom 128 – Formidable Task 61 (Formidable (USA) 125) [1996 6m⁵ 6d Aug 26] strong, lengthy filly: has a round action: third foal: dam, should have stayed further than 6f, out of sister to Highclere: fifth of 12 to Mujova in maiden auction at Newcastle, staying on: well-backed 11/4-shot, always behind after sluggish start in seller at Ripon following month (subsequently reported filly had become upset in stalls): possibly capable of better. *Miss S. E. Hall* 54

MY BONUS 6 b.m. Cyrano de Bergerac 120 – Dress In Spring 63 (Northfields (USA)) [1995 –: a5g 1996 a7g Jan 6] leggy filly: fair sprint handicapper at 3 yrs: no form since. *D. J. S. Cosgrove* –

MYBOTYE 3 br.c. Rambo Dancer (CAN) 107 – Sigh 75 (Highland Melody 112) [1995 69p: 6g 5g* 6m* 1996 6.1d³ 7.5m³ 7.9f 6m⁵ 7f* 7.5m⁶ 7.1d 7m 8s Nov 9] sturdy, workmanlike colt: has a round action: fair handicapper: justified favouritism at Redcar in June, hanging left: below form afterwards: likely to prove best at up to 1m: acts on firm and dead ground: wears near-side pricker. *G. R. Oldroyd* 79

MY BRANCH 3 b.f. Distant Relative 128 – Pay The Bank 81 (High Top 131) [1995 106: 5.2g² 5m* 6m³ 6m² 6.5m* 6g* 6d² 7m³ 1996 8m⁴ 8d³ 7m 7m 7m* 7m⁴ 7m³ 8g⁵ Nov 2] leggy, attractive filly: has quick action: smart performer: around 3 lengths fourth to Bosra Sham in 1000 Guineas at Newmarket and 3½ lengths third to Matiya in Irish 1000 Guineas at the Curragh first 2 starts: ran badly next 2, sweating and not striding out to post second occasion: back to form to win 7-runner listed race at Doncaster in September by 1¼ lengths from High Summer: creditable third to 111

Mr Wafic Said's "My Branch"

Charnwood Forest in Challenge Stakes at Newmarket following month: stays 1m well: acts on good to firm and dead going, yet to race on extremes: held up. *B. W. Hills*

MY BRAVE GIRL   4 b.f. Never So Bold 135 – Souadah (USA) (General Holme (USA) 128) [1995 –: 7g⁵ 8.3m 8.3m 9.7s 1996 8g a12g Apr 29] tall, unfurnished filly: no worthwhile form. *B. Richmond*   —

MY CADEAUX   4 ch.f. Cadeaux Genereux 131 – Jubilee Song 71 (Song 132) [1995 75: 6m² 6m* 6g 1996 6m* 6g 6f 6s² Nov 22] angular filly: poor mover: fairly useful sprinter, lightly raced: won minor event at Windsor (despite edging right) in June: finished last both starts in July: best effort when neck second to Branston Abby in listed race at Cologne 3 months later: stays 6f: acts on good to firm ground, best run on soft. *R. Guest*   93

MY CHERRYWELL   6 br.m. Kirchner 110 – Cherrywood Blessin (Good Times (ITY)) [1995 54, a60: a5g 5d* 5g 5g² a5g² a5g⁵ 5m⁵ 5m³ 5m a5g 5.1d a6g* a7g 1996 a6g³ a6g³ a6g³ 5g³ 5s² a5g² a5g⁵ a5g 5g³ a6g Nov 18] lengthy mare: modest handicapper: stays 6f: acts on good to firm and dead ground and goes well on the all-weather: often bandaged behind: blinkered/visored nowadays: consistent. *L. R. Lloyd-James*   57 a61

MY DEAR WATSON   2 b.f. (Mar 24) Chilibang 120 – Mrs Bacon 82 (Balliol 125) [1996 6m 6d⁶ Jul 6] 6,000Y: sturdy, lengthy filly: half-sister to smart sprinter Sizzling Melody (by Song) and 5f winner (probably stayed 1m) Presently (by Cadeaux Genereux): dam 2-y-o 5f winner who didn't train on: behind in maiden events. *J. Berry*   —

MY DUTCH GIRL   4 b.f. Midyan (USA) 124 – Double Dutch 100 (Nicholas Bill 125) [1995 –: 12s 12s 1996 a13g Jan 13] small filly: no form since 2 yrs. *Miss B. Sanders*   —

MY EMMA   3 b.f. Marju (IRE) 127 – Pato 90 (High Top 131) [1995 63p: 7g 1996 11.9g⁵ 12f* 10g³ 12m* Sep 15]   115

In all honesty, it must have seemed an odds-on chance to most people that My Emma would end the latest season best known still for being Classic Cliche's half-sister. It was 29.1/1 according to the Pari-Mutuel against her winning the Prix Vermeille, but win it she did, and that definitely qualifies her for equine fame in her own right and not just for celebrity by association.

Connections, though, were clearly never in any danger of underestimating her, and, with just one seventh-of-eighteen in a Leicester maiden under

Prix Vermeille, Longchamp—
My Emma holds on bravely from Zafzala, Papering (rails), Miss Tahiti, Leonila (No. 9) and Luna Wells

her belt, My Emma made her 1996 reappearance in the Lancashire Oaks at Haydock. Racegoers that day took an even more lowly view than those at Longchamp two months later, sending her off at 50/1. They must have sported a few distrait expressions when she made smooth progress to move into the lead after two furlongs out, looking the likely winner, but when some of the better fancied fillies had sorted themselves out in this messy race My Emma was reeled in again and passed the post fifth of ten, beaten just under four lengths. One possible interpretation of the race was that My Emma had been flattered; trainer Rae Guest's was that she had hit the front much too soon and had been unlucky. She would be given every chance to prove it after Flamands and Ginger Fox from the Cumani and Cecil stables had first been easily despatched in a Newmarket maiden three weeks later.

My Emma's first venture back into pattern company was in the Prix de Psyche at Deauville in which she finished third to Sangria, all five runners close up in a slowly-run race. The jockey that day was Cash Asmussen—what better man to have when you want your horse holding up as long as possible—and he was in the plate again when My Emma lined up as outsider of ten in the Vermeille. As we have said so often before, too many French races are so slowly-run they end up testing the judge's skills, let alone those of the race-

My Emma (b.f. 1993)	Marju (IRE) (br 1988)	Last Tycoon (b 1983)	Try My Best Mill Princess
		Flame of Tara (b 1980)	Artaius Welsh Flame
	Pato (b 1982)	High Top (br 1969)	Derring-Do Camenae
		Patosky (b 1969)	Skymaster Los Patos

Matthews Breeding and Racing's "My Emma"

reader, and the 1996 Vermeille was yet another one. On the other hand, it made for a most thrilling spectacle. My Emma was on the rails in mid-division, pulling hard for her head in the early stages but well positioned just behind leader Papering when the contest finally got underway in the straight. Still on the bridle two furlongs out, she wore down Papering fifty yards from home and just held on as Zafzala, Miss Tahiti, Leonila and Luna Wells launched their challenges as well. The official distances were a head, a short neck, neck, short neck and half a length. It is, of course, impossible to give My Emma the rating of a really good horse on form such as this; we are, nevertheless, inclined to believe connections made the correct decision in not making expensive supplementary entries for her into the Arc and Breeders' Cup Turf. Seven of her rivals ran again, Zafzala's below-best third in the Prix de Royallieu being the highest placing in eleven attempts. My Emma will be entered for a lot more Group 1 contests in 1997 and although considerable progress is probably required from her to figure in the shake-up we are certainly not prepared to say she cannot make it. A workmanlike filly whose reappearance was delayed reportedly because of an operation to remove a nasal cyst, My Emma stays a mile and a half, acts on firm going and has yet to race on a soft surface.

1996 was a red-letter year for small British stables in top French races, the most notable addition to My Emma's Prix Vermeille being the Bryan Smart-trained Sil Sila's win at 30/1 (with Asmussen again in the saddle) in the Prix de Diane, and Marju is the stallion responsible for both of them. Another of his first crop, Toto Le Moko, won the Gran Premio d'Italia (no longer a pattern race as it has become restricted-entry) and Marju's fluctuating stud fee is now its highest to date, at IR 10,000 guineas. Fairly useful on the racecourse, where she won three times for Jocelyn Reavey and was suited by around a mile and a quarter, My Emma's dam Pato is clearly top-class at stud to have had a classic winner with her fourth foal and another Group 1 winner with her fifth. Classic Cliche was not actually her first classic runner as one of two previous winners, Threatening (by Warning), was twelfth of fifteen in the 1994 One Thousand Guineas. Pato went back to Classic Cliche's sire Salse for a filly in 1996 and was then covered by Lammtarra. She went to Pursuit of Love, however, in 1993, so the next one of her representatives to cheer on is a filly called Lust. That should be interesting. *R. Guest*

MYFANWY BETHESDA 3 b.f. Relief Pitcher 120 – Take A Break 58 (Take A – Reef 127) [1995 NR 1996 8.2m 10.2f 10.2f Jul 8] first reported foal: dam won 1m seller: last in maidens. *B. J. Llewellyn*

MYFONTAINE 9 b.h. Persepolis (FR) 127 – Mortefontaine (FR) (Polic 126) 74 [1995 68: 10.8d 10m 9.2g⁵ 10.8g* 10.8g* 10.8g* 10g⁴ 12.3m⁵ 11.6m⁶ 10g² 10.1g² a58 10d 1996 10.8d³ 10g 10.8f 10.8g* 10.8f⁵ 10m⁴ 10g 10m 10g⁵ 10g 8.9g⁵ 10.1m 8.2g² 10g a10s⁴ a13g Dec 13] leggy horse: fair handicapper: gained eighth course success at Warwick in May: effective at 1m to 10.8f: used to act on any going, but probably not at his best on top-of-the-ground nowadays: has hung left: bandaged at 9 yrs. *K. T. Ivory*

MY GALLERY (IRE) 5 ch.m. Tate Gallery (USA) 117 – Sententious (Kauto- 92 keino (FR)) [1995 57d, a68d: 9g a8.5g³ a7g⁵ a6g³ 8f² a7g* a7g* 6m 7.6m a7g⁵ a6g a75 7g⁵ a7g a6g⁶ 1996 a7g⁵ a7g² a7g* a7g* a7g* 6d* 7.1g² 7d² a8.5g³ 7.5m⁶ 8.2m³ 7.1g* 8m³ 7m⁶ 6.9f² 7.1d³ 7.6m² 7g* 8f⁴ 7.6m* 8d* 8d⁴ 7.6d* a9.4g 8m⁵ 7m⁶ 7m 7m⁵ 7g a7g⁶ Nov 7] angular mare: poor mover: fairly useful handicapper on turf, probably just fair on the all-weather: completed 4-timer at Southwell (2 wins), Wolverhampton (minor event) and Hamilton early on: better than ever in the summer, winning at Chepstow and twice each at Ayr and Chester: sold 30,000 gns Newmarket December Sales: effective at 6f to 8.5f: acts on firm and soft ground and on the all-weather: effective in blinkers, but has not worn them since fourth 4-y-o start: edgy sort: has run well when sweating: usually ridden by claimer: tremendously tough and consistent. *A. Bailey*

MY GIRL 2 b.f. (Jan 28) Mon Tresor 113 – Lady of Itatiba (BEL) (King of Mace- 33 don 126) [1996 5f³ 5m 5f⁶ 5m⁵ 6m a5g³ a5g 6s Oct 5] leggy, close-coupled filly: a39 second foal here: half-sister to 5f winner Had A Girl (by Hadeer): dam won 5 races in Belgium: poor maiden: blinkered last 3 starts. *J. Berry*

MY GIRL LUCY 2 b.f. (Mar 22) Picea 99 – English Mint 66 (Jalmood (USA) 126) [1996 6.9g⁶ Jul 3] fifth foal: dam (disappointing maiden) stayed 1m: well-beaten sixth of 11, slowly away, to Hen Harrier in maiden at Folkestone. *P. Mitchell* – –

MY GODSON 6 br.g. Valiyar 129 – Blessit 79 (So Blessed 130) [1995 45, a–: 7.1g 6g⁶ 6.9f⁴ 7m 8g⁵ 7m 8m 8g² 7d a8g 1996 a7g⁶ 5g 6s 7d* 7g² 7m 7.5m* 6g³ 6f⁴ 7m* 7.5g³ 7.9g 8.5m 7g Oct 19] sturdy gelding: has a round action: modest performer: trained by A. Mulholland on reappearance: won claimer at Newcastle in May and handicaps at Beverley (seller) in July and Catterick in August: missed break when well held last 3 starts: effective at 6f to 1m: acts on firm and soft ground, below form all 4 outings on fibresand: tried visored, usually blinkered nowadays (ran well only start without headgear at 6 yrs): held up. *J. L. Eyre* 60 a–

MY HANDSOME PRINCE 4 b.g. Handsome Sailor 125 – My Serenade (USA) 45 (Sensitive Prince (USA)) [1995 40: 8m³ 8m² 8f 8.5g 8m⁵ 1996 8g² 8f⁵ 10m 8.1g a8.5g⁵ a8.5g 8m⁵ 8.1m 10d a8.5g a9.4g⁴ Nov 25] useful-looking gelding: poor maiden handicapper: stays 1m: acts on firm ground: tried blinkered/visored, no improvement: inconsistent. *P. J. Bevan* 43

MY HANDY MAN 5 ch.g. Out of Hand 84 – My Home 61 (Homing 130) [1995 56: a11g² a12g 8m 9.2g² 8g 8g 8.3f 8.3f² 8.1f⁵ 12m 8f 1996 a7g 10.1s 8.1g 8.3d⁵ Apr 11] lengthy gelding: poor mover: poor maiden handicapper: stays 11f: acts on firm ground, dead and fibresand: has joined D. Barker. *R. Allan* 46

MY HERO (IRE) 2 b.f. (Mar 15) Bluebird (USA) 125 – Risacca (ITY) (Sir Gaylord) [1996 6m⁵ 7m⁴ 8d Oct 2] IR 10,000F, 18,000Y: well-made filly: half-sister to several winners in Italy: dam Italian 1m and 1¼m winner: fair form: should stay beyond 7f: ran poorly on dead ground. *T. G. Mills* 71

MYJINKA 6 gr.m. Myjinski (USA) – Royal Bat 69 (Crowned Prince (USA) 128) [1995 23, a56: a6g* a8g a7g⁴ a6g³ a8g² a6g* a8g 8f 8m 7m⁴ 6m 7.6m⁴ 10g a7g a6g* a7g² 1996 a6g* a6g⁴ a8g⁴ a8g a8g Mar 14] modest handicapper on the all-weather, poor on turf: won at Lingfield on reappearance (fourth course success, final outing for J. O'Donoghue): effective at 6f, and probably stays 1m: acts on firm and dead ground and goes very well on equitrack: blinkered: suitable mount for apprentice: occasionally slowly away, and usually held up: covered by Casteddu. *T. E. Powell* – a53

MY KIND 3 ch.f. Mon Tresor 113 – Kind of Shy 61 (Kind of Hush 118) [1995 59: 6g* 6m² 6m⁵ 6m² 6f⁵ 6d 7d⁴ 8f a8.5g 1996 6.1g 8.3s⁴ 9.9g 8g 8m⁴ 8.2m 8g 10m 10m⁴ Aug 19] small filly: poor performer nowadays: stays 1m: acts on good to firm and dead ground: tried visored/blinkered, no improvement: has been bandaged: sold 650 gns Doncaster September Sales. *N. Tinkler* 47 ?

MY LEARNED FRIEND 5 b. or br.g. Broken Hearted 124 – Circe 73 (Main Reef 126) [1995 88: 10m³ 10.5g* 10f* 10m³ 12m* 12g⁶ 12m 1996 10m 12g 12m² 11.9g³ 13.9m 12m⁶ 12g 12g Oct 11] workmanlike gelding: fairly useful handicapper: best efforts at 5 yrs when third in Bessborough Stakes at Royal Ascot and rated stakes at York: stays 13.9f: has raced only on a sound surface: held up. *A. Hide* 86

MY LEWICIA (IRE) 3 b.f. Taufan (USA) 119 – Christine Daae 74 (Sadler's Wells (USA) 132) [1995 –p: 7g 1996 8m² 8d* 8m² 8m⁶ Aug 3] angular, workmanlike filly: impressive winner of maiden at Kempton in May: 9/1, useful and much improved form when second to Missile (clear of remainder) in £17,150 rated stakes at Newmarket: ran no sort of race in conditions event at Goodwood 2 weeks later: will stay beyond 1m. *P. W. Harris* 100

MYLORDMAYOR 9 ch.g. Move Off 112 – Sharenka (Sharpen Up 127) [1995 NR 1996 12.1m Jun 30] modest and inconsistent maiden (best efforts on all-weather, stayed 7f) in 1990: tailed off on return to flat: appeared to break down over hurdles in October. *P. Bowen* –

MY MARIAM 3 ch.f. Salse (USA) 128 – Birch Creek (Carwhite 127) [1995 79: 6m* 6g⁴ 7d 6d 1996 7m 7.1m⁶ 7m 10.3g Oct 25] small, sturdy filly: fair form at 2 yrs, none in handicaps in 1996: should be suited by further than 7f: sold 25,000 gns Newmarket December Sales. *C. R. Egerton* –

MY MELODY PARKES 3 b.f. Teenoso (USA) 135 – Summerhill Spruce 70 (Windjammer (USA)) [1995 102: 5g* 5m⁶ 5m³ 6m² 7g³ 6g⁴ 1996 7m⁴ 8m 6m² 6m 102

6d⁴ 5g³ Aug 14] lengthy, good-looking filly: useful performer: best efforts at 3 yrs when fourth in Nell Gwyn Stakes and runner-up in listed event (beaten head by Branston Abby) at Newmarket: effective at sprint distances and finds 1m stretching her stamina: acts on good to firm going: races prominently. *J. Berry*

MY MILLIE 3 ch.f. Midyan (USA) 124 – Madam Millie 99 (Milford 119) [1995 55: 5m⁴ 5g 7g 1996 8m 7f 6g 6g 7g 11f² 12m 10.1m Oct 23] tall, lengthy, lightly-made filly: modest maiden: left R. Boss after fourth 3-y-o start: stays 11f: acts on firm going: tail flasher: visored fourth 3-y-o start (well beaten): inconsistent. *D. W. Barker*   52

MY MOTHER'S LOCAL (USA) 3 b.f. Local Talent (USA) 122 – My Mother's Eyes (FR) (Saint Cyrien (FR) 128) [1995 –: 7m a7g a7g 1996 a8g a8g 10.8g 6.9m 5.1g 5m 7f Jun 10] leggy filly: of little account: blinkered last 4 starts, virtually bolting first time: sold 800 gns Newmarket December Sales. *K. O. Cunningham-Brown*   –

MYOSOTIS 2 ch.g. (Mar 16) Don't Forget Me 127 – Ella Mon Amour 65 (Ela-Mana-Mou 132) [1996 6g 7m 7f⁶ 6g⁶ a7s Nov 19] 9,200F, 16,000Y: angular gelding: fifth foal: half-brother to 3-y-o Khabar (by Forzando) and winning 5-y-o sprinter Thatcherella (by Thatching): dam stayed 9f: apparently best effort in maidens on only occasion blinkered third start: should stay beyond 7f. *P. J. Makin*   60 ?

MY PRECIOUS 2 ch.f. (Feb 23) Mon Tresor 113 – Nipotina 51 (Simply Great (FR) 122) [1996 6d 6g 7f⁵ 7f 6f⁵ Aug 7] 4,400Y: first foal: dam 11f and 1½m winner, half-sister to smart sprinter Roman Prose: poor maiden. *M. McCormack*   ?

MYRMIDON 2 b.g. (Feb 25) Midyan (USA) 124 – Moorish Idol 90 (Aragon 118) [1996 6s² 6m⁶ 6d² 5g⁴ 5m 5d* Nov 8] 23,000Y: neat gelding: good walker: third foal: half-brother to 4-y-o 9.4f and 11f winner Mansur (by Be My Chief) and 1993 2-y-o 7.3f and 1m winner Duty Time (by Night Shift), later successful in Norsk Derby: dam 2-y-o 6f winner who probably stayed 1m: fairly useful performer: improved effort to win nursery at Doncaster in November, leading on bit under 2f out then running on strongly: sold to join Mrs L. Stubbs 11,000 gns Doncaster November Sales, and gelded: best effort at 5f, though stays 6f: needs some give in the ground: edgy, and taken last and very quietly to post final start: withdrawn after bolting to post previous intended outing. *J. L. Dunlop*   88

MY ROSSINI 7 b.g. Ardross 134 – My Tootsie 88 (Tap On Wood 130) [1995 52: 14s³ 1996 14.1m Apr 30] workmanlike gelding: modest handicapper: ran creditably only 6-y-o start, showed little only 7-y-o outing: stays 2m: used to act on good to firm and soft going: often makes the running: wears sliding bar bit: fairly useful hurdler (seemingly needs to dominate). *P. J. Bevan*   –

MYRTLE 3 b.f. Batshoof 122 – Greek Goddess 82 (Young Generation 129) [1995 96: 6g 6.9g² 6g³ 7m³ 7.5m* 8g⁵ 1996 8g Apr 6] strong, compact filly: has a fluent, round action: much improved effort when fifth in May Hill Stakes at Doncaster final 2-y-o start: 10/1 and very wintry in appearance, tenth of 13 in falsely-run listed race at Kempton: may prove suited by further than 1m: sent to USA. *R. Hannon*   –

MYRTLEBANK 2 ch.f. (Feb 2) Salse (USA) 128 – Magical Veil 73 (Majestic Light (USA)) [1996 8.1d* 8s⁶ Oct 26] close-coupled filly: second foal: dam 11.6f winner: won maiden at Haydock in September, making virtually all and finding plenty under pressure: gone in coat and weak in market, well beaten in minor event at Newbury 4 weeks later: likely to stay well. *H. R. A. Cecil*   81

MY SALTARELLO (IRE) 2 b.c. (Apr 26) Salt Dome (USA) – Daidis 66 (Welsh Pageant 132) [1996 5m⁴ 6m 7f Nov 5] IR 2,500F: useful-looking colt: half-brother to several winners, including stayers Alpha Helix (by Double Form) and Emir Sultan (by Posse): dam, placed over 1½m, is daughter of high-class filly Attica Meli: modest form: will stay beyond 7f. *A. B. Mulholland*   48

MYSELF 4 ch.f. Nashwan (USA) 135 – Pushy 112 (Sharpen Up 127) [1995 110: 7m* 8m 8m 7g⁴ 7d³ 7m 1996 8.1g⁶ 7d² 8g⁵ 7m⁴ Aug 22] smallish, angular, good-quartered filly: good walker: easy mover: smart performer: best efforts at 4 yrs when second to Mistle Cat in Prix du Palais Royal at Deauville and fifth to Sensation in Falmouth Stakes at Newmarket: very best efforts at 7f (barely stays 1m): acts on good to firm ground and dead: flashes tail: often wears bandages: normally held up. *P. W. Chapple-Hyam*   108

MYSTERIUM 2 gr.c. (May 22) Mystiko (USA) 124 – Way To Go 69 (Troy 137) –
[1996 6m a7g⁶ Aug 17] 7,200Y, 9,200 2-y-o: leggy colt: fifth foal: half-brother to
useful Irish 3-y-o 7f (including at 2 yrs) and 9f winner Troysend (by Dowsing) and
winners abroad by Hadeer and Chief Singer: dam 1¾m winner: no form in maidens.
N. P. Littmoden

MYSTERY 2 b.f. (Apr 11) Mystiko (USA) 124 – Dismiss 95 (Daring March 116) 68 d
[1996 5g⁴ 6m² 6m 6m 7d 6d a6g a7s a6g⁴ Dec 26] strong, sturdy filly: third foal:
half-sister to 3-y-o La Modiste (by Most Welcome), 6f and 1m winner at 2 yrs: dam
suited by 1¼m: second in maiden at Folkestone: no comparable form. *S. Dow*

MYSTERY MATTHIAS 3 b.f. Nicholas (USA) 111 – Devils Dirge 68 (Song 54
132) [1995 56, a51+: 5m⁶ 5m⁶ 5g⁴ 6f⁵ 5g 7d⁶ a8g a8g⁵ 1996 a7g⁶ a8g³ a7g⁴ 6m³ 6m⁴
5m⁶ 6m² 6m⁶ 7g⁶ 7f 6.9g⁵ a5g a6g⁴ a6g² Dec 5] workmanlike filly: modest maiden
handicapper: stays 7f: acts on firm ground and equitrack: blinkered/visored since
final 2-y-o start: usually races prominently. *Miss B. Sanders*

MYSTICAL ISLAND 2 b.f. (Jan 26) Deploy 131 – Do Run Run 75 (Com- –
manche Run 133) [1996 6g Jun 11] 3,200Y: first foal: dam 1m winner: 20/1, always
behind in maiden auction at Salisbury. *C. A. Cyzer*

MYSTICAL MAID 3 b.f. Aragon 118 – Persistent Girl 41 (Superlative 118) 54
[1995 NR 1996 7m² 7m a7g² a8.5g³ 7m 7f 6.9d a7g⁵ Oct 28] small filly: unimpressive mover: first foal: dam ran twice: modest form on all-weather: has shown little on
turf since debut: sold 4,700 gns Newmarket Autumn Sales: stays 8.5f: blinkered last
2 outings: sent to Italy. *H. Thomson Jones*

MYSTICAL MIND 3 gr.g. Emarati (USA) 74 – Spanish Chestnut (Philip of –
Spain 126) [1995 NR 1996 7f⁵ 8f Aug 2] 2,500F, 9,500Y: leggy, lengthy gelding:
half-brother to 1982 2-y-o 5f winner Loddon Music (by Music Boy) and 3 winners
abroad: dam poor plater: sold 6,800 gns Doncaster August (1995) Sales and gelded:
never a threat in maidens at Thirsk. *D. Nicholls*

MYSTIC CIRCLE (IRE) 2 ch.f. (May 2) Magical Wonder (USA) 125 – Rozala 69
(USA) (Roberto (USA) 131) [1996 6m⁵ 7s² 6g* 6m³ 6.5m 6m Oct 5] close-coupled,
useful-looking filly: third foal: half-sister to a winning sprinter in USA by Siberian
Express, also placed in Grade 3 events: dam ran once: won maiden at Newcastle
in August: well beaten afterwards, blinkered final start: sold 4,200 gns Newmarket
Autumn Sales: stays 7f: sometimes tail swisher: sent to Germany. *J. W. Watts*

MYSTIC DAWN 3 b.f. Aragon 118 – Ahonita 90 (Ahonoora 122) [1995 47: 5m 72
5g⁶ 6m 6d 8f 1996 8m⁴ 8m⁵ 8.3m⁶ 8f³ 8m³ 8f 8m⁴ 8g² 8f⁴ 8f* 8g Oct 29] close-
coupled filly: fair handicapper: first past post at Goodwood (edged right, demoted)
and Leicester in autumn: stays 8.3f: acts on firm ground: found little ninth 3-y-o start.
S. Dow

MYSTIC HILL 5 b.g. Shirley Heights 130 – Nuryana 107 (Nureyev (USA) 131) 92
[1995 91: 10.1f³ 12m 12f³ 12m* 12d 10v 1996 10d 12m⁵ 12m³ 13.3f* 14.8d 11.9f⁶
12m 12g Oct 26] smallish, rather leggy, useful-looking gelding: good walker and
mover: useful handicapper: won strongly-run race at Newbury in July: well below
form afterwards: sold to join R. G. Frost 14,000 gns Newmarket Autumn Sales: stays
13.3f: acts on firm and soft ground: wears crossed noseband: held up and often set
plenty to do. *G. Harwood*

MYSTIC KNIGHT 3 b.c. Caerleon (USA) 132 – Nuryana 107 (Nureyev (USA) 117
131) [1995 93p: 7f⁶ 7.6d³ 8d* 8m* 1996 11d³ 11.5f* 12m⁶ 9.5g⁶ 9f³ 12f⁵ 9f Dec 1]
angular, quite attractive colt: fluent mover: smart performer: won Tripleprint Derby
Trial at Lingfield in May by 1¼ lengths from Heron Island, making all: 14/1 and
sweating, improved markedly again when 4¾ lengths sixth of 20 to Shaamit in the
Derby at Epsom on final start for R. Charlton, always close up: respectable third of 8
in Grade 3 handicap at Bay Meadows in October: stays 1½m: good effort at the time
on dead ground but looks well suited by a sound surface: blinkered (seventh in
Hollywood Derby) final start. *J. Noseda, USA*

MYSTIC LEGEND (IRE) 4 gr.g. Standaan (FR) 118 – Mandy Girl (Manado 30
130) [1995 NR 1996 a7g a7g a12g⁵ 9.7m 8.3m 11.6m 12m 11.6m 8.2g a7g a10g
Nov 26] half-brother to 1988 2-y-o 5f winner Incendiary Blonde (by Glenstal) and 2
winners abroad: dam lightly raced in Ireland: poor maiden, trained by T. J. Naughton
first 6 starts. *J. J. Sheehan*

MYSTIC MAID (IRE) 3 b.f. Mujtahid (USA) 118 – Dandizette (Danzig (USA)) 62
[1995 NR 1996 6g 5m³ May 10] first foal: dam, third over 1m in France, daughter of
Coronation Stakes winner Chalon, dam also of high-class 1¼m performer Creator:
better effort in maidens when third at Beverley, making much of running: probably a
sprinter: sold to join J. L. Harris 1,000 gns Newmarket December Sales. *J. W. Watts*

MYSTIC QUEST (IRE) 2 b.c. (Mar 27) Arcane (USA) – Tales of Wisdom 70 65
(Rousillon (USA) 133) [1996 a6g³ 7s 6.9m⁴ 7f² 7m⁴ 7.6m a8.5g* 7g 7.3s Oct 26] IR a69
800F, IR 5,600Y: quite attractive colt: first foal: dam 12.3f winner: sire, Irish 1¼m
and 2m winner, brother to Rainbow Quest: visored first time, improved effort when
winning maiden at Wolverhampton in September: visored again, well beaten in
nurseries afterwards: stays 8.5f well: acts on firm ground (showed little on soft) and
fibresand: retained 8,200 gns Ascot December Sales. *K. McAuliffe*

MYSTIC RIDGE 2 ch.c. (Mar 31) Mystiko (USA) 124 – Vallauris 94 (Faustus –
(USA) 118) [1996 5.2s⁶ May 29] 20,000Y: good-bodied colt: second foal:
half-brother to German 3-y-o 1m winner Indian Devotion (by Indian Ridge): dam
stayed 1¼m: in need of race, always behind after slow start in maiden at Newbury:
bred to need further than 5f. *D. R. C. Elsworth*

MYSTIC TEMPO (USA) 3 ch.f. El Gran Senor (USA) 136 – Doubling Time 61
(USA) 117 (Timeless Moment (USA)) [1995 76: 5f² 6g* 6g³ 6f 6.1s⁵ a5g 1996 a6g*
a6g* a6g² a6g³ a6g² Mar 16] small filly: modest performer nowadays: left P.
Chapple-Hyam's stable after final 2-y-o start: won 2 sellers at Wolverhampton in
January, and showed consistent form afterwards: better suited by 6f than 5f: acts on
fibresand, possibly unsuited by very firm ground. *Dr J. D. Scargill*

MYSTIC TIMES 3 b.f. Timeless Times (USA) 99 – Chikala 81 (Pitskelly 122) 40
[1995 53: 5m⁴ 5g 6m⁵ 6f² 6m 6m* 6.1d 1996 6.1m 6g 5g 6.1m 7.5m 7d 9.2f* 8m⁵
11.1g⁴ 8.3g Sep 29] small, sparely-made filly: poor performer: trained by Miss J.
Craze first 5 starts at 3 yrs: won seller at Hamilton in August: may prove best at
around 1¼m: acts on firm ground: tried visored and blinkered, no improvement.
B. Mactaggart

MYSTIQUE AIR (IRE) 2 b.f. (Feb 20) Mujadil (USA) 119 – Romany Pageant 66 ?
(Welsh Pageant 132) [1996 7m³ 7.9g⁵ Oct 12] IR 3,800F, 6,600Y: tall, sparely-made
filly: half-sister to several winners, including useful Laurie's Warrior (up to 8.5f, by
Viking): dam unraced: third of 7 in steadily-run maiden at Ayr: raced too keenly in
York maiden last time: not certain to stay 1m. *E. Weymes*

MYSTIQUE SMILE 3 ch.f. Music Boy 124 – Jay Gee Ell 78 (Vaigly Great 127) 45
[1995 78d: 5m³ 5m⁴ 5.1m* 5.5m 5.2g 5g⁴ 5g 5m 1996 5d 6g 5.3f³ 5f⁶ 5f Jun 27]
leggy, useful-looking filly: good mover: fair performer at best for Jack Berry as
2-y-o: poor form in handicaps in 1996, well beaten in blinkers final outing: raced
only at sprint distances: best form on good to firm ground. *S. C. Williams*

MYTHICAL 2 gr.f. (Apr 18) Mystiko (USA) 124 – Geryea (USA) (Desert Wine 55 p
(USA)) [1996 6m a6g⁴ Nov 2] second foal: dam unraced from the family of Sure
Blade: better effort in maidens when seventh of 12 at Wolverhampton: bred to stay 1m:
should do better again. *Sir Mark Prescott*

MYTTONS MISTAKE 3 b.g. Rambo Dancer (CAN) 107 – Hi-Hunsley 82 74
(Swing Easy (USA) 126) [1995 79: 7f* 5m* 6.1g⁴ 6m 6g 6g a7g³ 1996 a7g³ a6g³ a71
a7g² a5g³ a7g³ 6.1g² 5.1m 6m 7m⁵ 5.1m⁴ 6m³ 5g 5d 5.1d 5m 6d 7g³ a6g a7g³ Dec
28] leggy, workmanlike gelding: fair handicapper: in good form first half of season,
in and out afterwards: effective at 5f to 7f: acts on the all-weather and on good to firm
ground (below best all 3 outings on a soft surface): twice below form in blinkers.
A. Bailey

MY VALENTINA 2 b.f. (Feb 14) Royal Academy (USA) 130 – Imperial Jade 84 p
105 (Lochnager 132) [1996 7m² 7.1s* 10g Nov 2] seventh foal: sister to useful 7.1f
winner Hawaash, closely related to a winner in Germany by Kings Lake, and
half-sister to 4 winners, including 3-y-o 7f winner Royal Jade (by Last Tycoon) and
useful 5-y-o sprinter Averti (by Warning): dam sprinting sister to smart sprinter
Reesh: justified favouritism in 16-runner maiden at Chepstow in October: didn't stay
1¼m in listed race at Newmarket final outing: acts on good to firm and soft ground.
B. W. Hills

MY WEST END GIRL 3 b.f. Dunbeath (USA) 127 – Carnfield 42 (Anfield 117) –
[1995 –: a6g 1996 a5g Jan 17] first reported foal: dam, maiden, effective at up to 1m:
well beaten in maiden and seller. *A. Streeter*

N

NAAMAN (IRE) 3 b. or br.f. Marju (IRE) 127 – Shaiybaniyda 74 (He Loves Me 61 120) [1995 NR 1996 8.3m 8m Jun 5] £1,000F, 9,500Y: half-sister to Irish 1¼m winner Hopesville (by Top Ville) and a winner in Hong Kong: dam 1m winner: tenderly handled in maidens, better effort when seventh of 13 at Yarmouth second start: sold only 2,500 gns Newmarket December Sales. *M. A. Jarvis*

NAAZEQ 3 ch.f. Nashwan (USA) 135 – Gharam (USA) 108 (Green Dancer 80 (USA) 132) [1995 NR 1996 10.5d* 12d Oct 12] quite attractive filly: second foal: dam, 6f winner at 2 yrs who stayed 1½m, half-sister to Grade 1 9f winner Talinum, from good family: won 15-runner maiden at Haydock in September in good style, coming stand side and leading 2f out: 14/1 and on toes, tailed-off last in Princess Royal Stakes at Ascot 15 days later: should have stayed 1½m: spooked after finish and fell on debut: visits Kingmambo. *A. C. Stewart*

NABHAAN (IRE) 3 b.c. In The Wings 128 – Miss Gris (USA) 120 (Hail The 102 Pirates (USA) 126) [1995 74+: 7f⁶ 7.5m⁴ 8g⁴ 8g 8f 1996 10g² 12.3m* 12d³ 12m⁶ 11.9g³ 14.8d⁴ 10s³ 12s³ Nov 9] big, strong, close-coupled colt: useful handicapper: won at Ripon in April and very unlucky next start: best effort when 2 lengths third to Clifton Fox in November Handicap at Doncaster final start, rallying strongly despite hanging right: effective at 1¼m under testing conditions, and should stay 1¾m: acts on good to firm ground, goes particularly well on a soft surface: has gone in snatches, and hangs off bridle: stays in training. *D. Morley*

NABJELSEDR 6 b.g. Never So Bold 135 – Klewraye (Lord Gayle (USA) 124) 43 [1995 43: 7d 7g 7g 8g 1996 7m 10d 8.1m³ 8.1m 8f⁴ Aug 22] leggy gelding: un-impressive mover: only recent worthwhile form when in frame in handicaps at Chepstow (ladies) and Salisbury (apprentices, first past post, demoted): stays 1m: acts on firm ground. *A. G. Newcombe*

NADOR 3 ch.c. Rainbow Quest (USA) 134 – Nadma (USA) 82 (Northern Dancer 95 [1995 83: 7d* 7.3d 10g⁶ 10m⁴ 12d² 12m⁵ 12.1m* 12m Jul 31] leggy, quite attractive colt: good walker: fluent mover: useful handicapper: confidently ridden to win 5-runner rated stakes at Chepstow in July: stays 1½m: acts on good to firm and dead going, yet to race on extremes: held up: sent to UAE. *D. R. Loder*

NADWATY (IRE) 4 b.f. Prince Sabo 123 – Faisalah (Gay Mecene (USA) 128) 43 [1995 59d: a6g³ a6g³ a6g a5g* 5g³ a5g 5g³ a5g 6g⁵ 6m a5g⁵ 5g 5f a6g 1996 a6g⁶ a52 5.1g⁵ 5m a5g⁶ 6m Jun 3] workmanlike filly: modest performer on her day: sold 1,500 gns Newmarket July Sales: barely stays 6f: acts on fibresand, best turf form on a sound surface: no improvement in blinkers: usually a front runner. *M. C. Chapman*

NAGNAGNAG (IRE) 4 b.f. Red Sunset 120 – Rubina Park 64 (Ashmore (FR) 100 125) [1995 103: 7m 6m⁵ 6g 7m* 8d² 8g⁶ 8g³ 7d 10d 8g⁵ 1996 7.9m 8.1d 8.5m³ 8g⁵ 7.9m⁵ 8m 8.5m² 9m 8d⁶ 9s⁶ Oct 26] leggy, workmanlike filly: useful performer: placed at Epsom in listed race (to Donna Viola) in June and rated stakes (to Star of Zilzal) in September: sold 14,500 gns Doncaster November Sales: stays 8.5f: acts on any going: successful for apprentice: held up. *S. Dow*

NAHRAWALI (IRE) 5 b.g. Kahyasi 130 – Nashkara (Shirley Heights 130) – [1995 a11g³ 10d* 10.8s a13.5g³ 13.5g² 12f 12.5g 12d 1996 a12g Jan 6] former French and Belgian-trained gelding: third foal: half-brother to French 1m winner Nabagha (by Fabulous Dancer): dam French 1¼m winner: trained at 3 yrs in France by A. de Royer Dupre and J. Gallorini: poor form in 1995, winning minor event at Groenendaal in April: blinkered, tailed off on British debut: effective at 1¼m to 13.5f: acts on dead ground and dirt: joined A. Moore and won over hurdles in September and November. *Andre Hermans, Belgium*

NAILS TAILS 3 b.g. Efisio 120 – Northern Dynasty 65 (Breeders Dream 116) – [1995 NR 1996 10m Jun 17] half-brother to several winners, including middle-distance performers Southern Dynasty (by Gunner B) and Western Dynasty (by Hot-foot): dam 1m winner: 40/1, very slowly away and always behind in maiden at Windsor. *S. Dow*

NAISSANT 3 b.f. Shaadi (USA) 126 – Nophe (USA) 95 (Super Concorde (USA) 71 128) [1995 78: 6m⁴ 5d⁴ 6m⁶ 6f² 6m⁵ 6.1d⁴ 1996 7.6g 7.5m⁵ 10m 6m³ 6d 6m⁵ 6f² 6d* 6.9m* 7g 6m 7.1d 6d⁵ 6g 6g⁶ a6g Nov 16] sparely-made filly: has a roundish action:

fair performer: sold out of C. Brittain's stable 5,500 gns Newmarket July Sales after third 3-y-o start: won handicap at Ripon (had favoured far rail, by 6 lengths) and minor event at Carlisle within 3 days in August: stays 7f: acts on firm and dead ground, yet to race on anything softer: well beaten on fibresand. *R. M. McKellar*

NAIVASHA   2 gr.f. (May 5) Petong 126 – Nevis 61 (Connaught 130) [1996 5f⁴ 6f³   62
5f⁵ 6d* 6m Sep 21] lengthy filly: second foal: dam lightly-raced half-sister to Paris House (by Petong): made all against favoured stand rail when winning seller at Ripon in August: seems to require further than 5f: acts on firm and dead ground. *J. Berry*

NAJIYA   3 b.f. Nashwan (USA) 135 – The Perfect Life (IRE) 106 (Try My Best   102
(USA) 130) [1995 100p: 6g³ 6f* 6m* 6d³ 1996 7.3d 7m⁴ 7m⁴ 8.1m 8m Sep 28] well-made, attractive filly: fine mover: useful performer: looked better than previously in 1996 and back to form when fourth to Thrilling Day in listed race at Goodwood third start, involved in bumping 2f out and finishing best of all: well beaten afterwards: stayed 7f: did not race on soft going, acted on any other: headstrong first 2 starts at 3 yrs: visits Gone West. *J. L. Dunlop*

NAJM MUBEEN (IRE)   3 b.c. Last Tycoon 131 – Ah Ya Zein (Artaius (USA)   96
129) [1995 79p: 7.6d* 7g 1996 10m* 9s² Oct 26] leggy, good-topped colt: off course over a year with hairline fracture of hind cannon bone: 16/1, returned to win handicap at Newmarket in October: second to Wilcuma in rated stakes at Newbury 3 weeks later, leading briefly 1f out: stays 1¼m: acts on good to firm and soft ground: stays in training and may improve further. *A. C. Stewart*

NAKAMI   4 b.g. Dashing Blade 117 – Dara's Bird 57 (Dara Monarch 128) [1995   51
NR 1996 6g⁴ 5g 6d Sep 27] modest form in 2 maidens in summer of 1994: only form on return when fourth of 16 in similar event at Salisbury (one of 6 to race on favoured near side): sold (P. Makin to A. Chamberlain) 500 gns Ascot December Sales. *P. J. Makin*

NAKED EMPEROR   3 b.g. Dominion Royale 112 – Torville Gold (Aragon   –
118) [1995 –: 6d a7g 1996 a8g a8g Jan 29] no worthwhile form: tried visored. *M. J. Fetherston-Godley*

NAKED POSER (IRE)   2 b.f. (Apr 3) Night Shift (USA) – Art Age (Artaius   83
(USA) 129) [1996 6s* 6g⁶ 6.5m² 7m 6g Oct 26] IR 15,000Y: good-quartered, quite attractive filly: fifth reported foal: half-sister to 3-y-o Happy Tycoon (by Polish Patriot), 5f winner at 2 yrs, and 4-y-o 1m winner Artful Dane (by Danehill): dam unraced: won 5-runner minor event at Goodwood in May: easily best subsequent effort when short-head second of 22 to Nightbird in nursery at Doncaster in September: well below that form afterwards: stays 6.5f. *R. Hannon*

NAKED WELCOME   4 ch.c. Most Welcome 131 – Stripanoora (Ahonoora 122)   110
[1995 107: 8m⁴ 10.4m* 10f 8.9g³ 9g 12m* 12m⁴ 1996 10g³ 12m 12m⁴ 12m 10f⁵
13.9m Aug 21] good-bodied colt: carries condition: usually impresses in appearance: smart performer: in frame in Gordon Richards Stakes at Sandown (3½ lengths third to Singspiel) and rated stakes at Epsom (to Backgammon): not discredited when ninth of 21 (staying on from rear) in Ebor Handicap at York on final start: seems to stay 13.9f: acts on good to firm and dead ground, probably on soft: best 2-y-o efforts in blinkers, but has worn them only once since: held up (sometimes takes little interest early and tends to get detached) and has sharp turn of foot on his day: not one to trust implicitly. *M. J. Fetherston-Godley*

NAKHAL   3 b.g. Puissance 110 – Rambadale 68 (Vaigly Great 127) [1995 66: 6m⁶   57
7.1d⁴ 7g 1996 6.9s³ 7m⁵ 7m 9.7g 8m⁴ a10g³ 8g⁴ 8g a8.5g Sep 7] workmanlike gelding: unimpressive mover: modest maiden handicapper: retained by trainer 4,500 gns Newmarket Autumn Sales: stays 1¼m: acts on firm and soft ground and equitrack: usually blinkered/visored at 3 yrs. *D. J. G. Murray Smith*

NAMASTE   8 b.g. Petoski 135 – View 88 (Shirley Heights 130) [1995 NR 1996   44
a16g³ a14g⁶ Mar 1] lengthy, workmanlike gelding: unimpressive mover: very lightly raced on flat since 3 yrs: joined P. Mooney: stays 2m: fair hurdler. *R. P. C. Hoad*

NAMELESS   3 ch.f. Doc Marten 104 – Opuntia (Rousillon (USA) 133) [1995 57,   –
a62: a5g² a5g³ a5g* a6g⁶ a6g² 6m³ 5.2f² a5g* 5.1f³ 5.3f⁵ 5g a5g 1996 a5g Feb 28] workmanlike filly: modest performer at best as a 2-y-o: last in seller at Wolver-hampton only outing in 1996: sold 3,500 gns Doncaster March Sales: speedy, and

easily best form at 5f: acts on fibresand, best turf form on firm going: blinkered final 2-y-o outing: sent to Sweden. *D. J. S. Cosgrove*

NAME OF OUR FATHER (USA) 3 b.g. Northern Baby (CAN) 127 – Ten 74 Hail Marys (USA) (Halo (USA)) [1995 75: 7d⁴ 7.1d² 7f 1996 10g 10g 10g a8.5g⁵ Nov 2] leggy, close-coupled gelding: has a markedly round action: sold out of M. Fetherston-Godley's stable 2,700 gns Ascot August Sales after reappearance: worthwhile form at 3 yrs only when tenth of 19 (beaten around 4 lengths) in handicap at Pontefract next start: seems to stay 1¼m: poor effort (sweating) on firm ground final 2-y-o start: won juvenile hurdle in December. *P. Bowen*

NAMOODAJ 3 b.g. Polish Precedent (USA) 131 – Leipzig 107 (Relkino 131) 82 [1995 NR 1996 10m 10m 11.7m³ 10.5d* 12d³ Oct 11] lengthy, heavy-bodied gelding: half-brother to useful 1m winner Pfalz and 1988 2-y-o 6f winner Zaitech (both by Pharly): dam 6f and 1m winner: progressed into a fairly useful handicapper: won at Haydock in September, leading over 2f out: not discredited, but looked an un-suitable ride for an inexperienced rider, in amateurs event at Ascot final start, duck-ing left to stall rail: subsequently joined D. Nicholson: stays 1½m. *A. C. Stewart*

NAMOUNA (IRE) 3 b.f. Sadler's Wells (USA) 132 – Amaranda (USA) 115 70 (Bold Lad (IRE) 133) [1995 NR 1996 9m⁶ 10m⁴ Jul 26] 60,000Y: leggy, close-coupled filly: sister to very useful 1m to 10.3f winner Imperial Ballet, closely related to 9f winner Town Square (by The Minstrel) and half-sister to 4 other winners, including very useful 6f (at 2 yrs) and 7f winner Bold Citadel (by Caerleon): dam, smart sprinter who stayed 7f, daughter of Favoletta: better effort in maidens when fourth at Ascot: sent to Australia. *P. W. Chapple-Hyam*

NAMPARA BAY 2 b.f. (Apr 21) Emarati (USA) 74 – Dewberry 68 (Bay Express – 132) [1996 a5g⁶ 6m May 29] 3,800Y: half-sister to several winners, including 2-y-o 5f winners Monstrosa (by Monsanto), Renta Kid (by Swing Easy) and Loganberry (by Lugana Beach): dam 6f winner: no form in maiden auctions at Southwell and Folkestone in May. *G. C. Bravery*

NANDA 3 ch.f. Nashwan (USA) 135 – Pushy 112 (Sharpen Up 127) [1995 NR 83 1996 10.5d⁶ 9g² 10.1g* Jul 3] rather leggy filly: sister to smart 4-y-o Myself, 6f (at 2 yrs) and 7f winner, and half-sister to several winners, including smart 6f and 7.3f winner Bluebook (by Secretariat) and useful miler Phountzi (by Raise a Cup): dam, Queen Mary winner, out of outstanding broodmare Mrs Moss: fairly useful form in maidens, winning at Epsom in July: should stay beyond 1¼m: stays in training. *D. R. Loder*

NANNY-B 3 br.f. Chilibang 120 – Carly-B (IRE) 42 (Commanche Run 133) [1995 – NR 1996 10.1f⁴ 10m 8g 7m Sep 17] first foal: dam, plater, stayed 1¾m: of little account. *P. Howling*

NANSHAN (IRE) 3 b.f. Nashwan (USA) 135 – Pass The Peace 116 (Alzao 92 ? (USA) 117) [1995 NR 1996 a9.4g² 7f³ Jul 21] third foal: half-sister to winners Puck's Castle (fairly useful, 1m as 2-y-o by Shirley Heights) and Take A Pew (Belgium, 11f, by Reference Point): dam won Cheveley Park Stakes and second in Poule d'Essai des Pouliches: 3/1 on, second in maiden at Wolverhampton, looking green when ridden: apparently much better effort when 2 lengths third of 5 to stable-companion Blue Duster in minor event at Yarmouth 5 months later, running on strongly over inadequate trip: will be suited by further than 9.4f: stays in training. *D. R. Loder*

NANTGARW 3 b.f. Teamster 114 – Dikay (IRE) 44 (Anita's Prince 126) [1995 – NR 1996 10.3g Oct 26] small filly: first foal: dam lightly-raced maiden: 33/1, soundly beaten in claimer at Doncaster: has joined D. Burchell. *D. R. C. Elsworth*

NANTON POINT (USA) 4 b.g. Darshaan 133 – Migiyas 87 (Kings Lake (USA) 75 + 133) [1995 83p: 9g 11.6m 12d 14.1f* 15.4g* 14.1f* 16f* 14m² 18.2g⁴ 13.9g 18m² 1996 16s⁶ May 19] lengthy, robust gelding: progressed into a fairly useful handi-capper in 1995, second in Cesarewitch final start: shaped encouragingly at Newbury on reappearance, but not seen out again: suited by good test of stamina: acts on firm ground, probably on soft: effective from front or held up: genuine. *Lady Herries*

NANT Y GAMER (FR) 2 b.c. (Feb 4) Warning 136 – Norfolk Lily 63 (Blakeney 77 126) [1996 5.9f⁵ a6g 6m* 6g² 6m³ 8m Sep 20] 39,000Y: fourth foal: half-brother tosmart French/US 1m/9f winner Guide (by Local Suitor) and French 10.5f and 11.5f winner Cromer (by Zino): dam staying maiden from family of Mystiko: fair performer: made all in 4-runner maiden at Hamilton in August: creditable efforts in nurseries afterwards when placed: should stay further than 6f. *J. Berry*

NAPHTALI 3 b.f. Nicholas Bill 125 – My Concordia 58 (Belfort (FR) 89) [1995 NR 1996 a8g Dec 5] first foal: dam 1m winner: tailed off in minor event at Lingfield. *J. R. Arnold* –

NAPIER STAR 3 b.f. Inca Chief (USA) – America Star (Norwick (USA) 125) [1995 –: 6.1d a6g⁵ a8g 1996 a7g a7g⁴ a8g⁵ a6g 5.1d a6g* a6g⁵ a5g³ a5g⁶ a6g a5g* a5g⁵ a5g² a5g² a6g⁴ a6g² a6g a6g⁴ a5g⁴ a5g³ a5g² a5g* a5g³ a5g² Dec 13] leggy, unfurnished filly: fair performer: won minor auction maiden at Southwell in April and handicaps at Wolverhampton in July and November: stays 6f: raced mainly on the all-weather: often claimer ridden: visored nowadays: races prominently: consistent. *Mrs N. Macauley* a68

NAPOLEON'S RETURN 3 gr.g. Daring March 116 – Miss Colenca (Petong 126) [1995 58: 5m⁵ 5g⁴ 6m⁵ 5f² 7m⁵ 6m⁵ 6d 5.3d⁴ 7f* 7f a8.5g⁶ 1996 8g 6d 6m 8.1g³ 6g 8.1f 8m* 8f² 7s² 7m 7g a6g 7g a8g⁴ a7g⁵ Nov 22] close-coupled gelding: modest handicapper: made all in apprentice race at Ayr in June: left A. Harrison after eleventh start at 3 yrs: stays 1m: acts on firm and soft ground, and on fibresand: probably effective visored or not: usually apprentice ridden: often forces pace. *J. L. Eyre* 49

NAPOLEON STAR (IRE) 5 ch.g. Mulhollande (USA) 107 – Lady Portobello (Porto Bello 118) [1995 74: 6g³ 6m 5.1m⁵ 6g 6g⁴ 6m² 5.7f⁵ 6m 7g⁴ 7.1d 7g 7g 1996 a6g a8.5g 7f 8g 8g 7g Jun 11] sparely-made gelding: fair handicapper at best: below form for some time: sold to join S. R. Bowring only 580 gns Doncaster September Sales: stays 7f: acts on firm ground and the all-weather, below form on a soft surface: blinkered (creditable effort at the time) once as 3-y-o. *M. S. Saunders* –

NARBONNE 5 b.m. Rousillon (USA) 133 – Historical Fact 78 (Reform 132) [1995 60: 7m³ 8m 10g⁶ 8m² 8m⁴ 1996 8.3d 8g Sep 13] workmanlike mare: fluent mover: modest performer: absent 14 months, showed nothing in handicaps on return: best form at up to 1m: acts on good to firm and dead ground: usually races prominently: consistent at 4 yrs: sold 2,000 gns Ascot December Sales. *B. J. McMath* –

NARISKIN (IRE) 2 b.c. (Apr 23) Danehill (USA) 126 – Nurah (USA) (Riverman (USA) 131) [1996 6d³ 6m³ 6d⁴ Nov 8] quite attractive colt: first foal: dam ran twice in France, half-sister to smart French 5f (at 2 yrs) to 1m winner L'Orangerie out of smart French miler Liska, herself half-sister to top-class Irish River: fair form in maidens: will probably be suited by further than 6f: on toes last 2 starts, decidedly so on first occasion: sent to race in France. *J. L. Dunlop* 75

NASEEM ALSAHAR 3 ch.f. Nashwan (USA) 135 – El Fabulous (FR) 111 (Fabulous Dancer (USA) 124) [1995 79p: 8m² 1996 10m 10m³ 8f⁵ 10.2f² 11.5m³ 10d 10m Sep 26] good-topped filly: fair form at best: lost her way: sold 7,000 gns Newmarket December Sales: should stay 1½m: acts on good to firm ground, seems unsuited by a soft surface: blinkered last 5 starts: has looked none too resolute: sent to France. *Major W. R. Hern* 75 d

NASEER (USA) 7 b.g. Hero's Honor (USA) – Sweet Delilah (USA) (Super Concorde (USA) 128) [1995 NR 1996 10m 13.1f⁶ 11.9f³ Jul 25] poor plater nowadays: sold to K. Wingrove 900 gns Ascot October Sales: stays 1¾m: acts on firm ground and on equitrack: blinkered last 3 starts in 1992: not one to trust. *K. Bishop* 36

NASHAAT (USA) 8 b.g. El Gran Senor (USA) 136 – Absentia (USA) 108 (Raise A Cup (USA)) [1995 74+, a78: 7.6m² 8m⁴ 8g⁵ 8g 8.5m 8d 7g* 7f* a7g* a8g⁶ 1996 a11g a6g a8g⁴ a7g³ a7g* a8g 7s⁶ 7m³ 7g 8.5g⁶ 8m 7g² 7m² 7f* 7g* 7m 7m² Aug 22] stocky, good-topped gelding: fairly useful handicapper: won at Southwell in February and at Yarmouth (twice) and Catterick in summer: effective at 7f to 8.5f: acts on the all-weather, firm and soft going: blinkered (ran creditably) at 5 yrs: sometimes gives trouble at stalls: has run well when sweating: has joined K. Burke. *M. C. Chapman* 80

NASHCASH (IRE) 3 ch.g. Nashamaa 113 – Six Penny Express (Bay Express 132) [1995 5s 5d³ 5g* 5g* 7f² 6m 6g³ 6d⁴ 1996 7s⁵ 7d⁴ 6d³ 5f⁶ Jun 22] IR 11,000Y: good-topped, attractive gelding: fifth living foal: half-brother to Irish 1¼m winner Copper And Steel and 2-y-o 5f winners Miss Amy Lou (by Gallic League) and Tannerun (by Runnett): dam Irish maiden: useful performer: dead-heated in minor 108 event at Tipperary before winning listed race at the Curragh in May at 2 yrs: much-improved form when 3¼ lengths third of 9 to Lidanna in Greenlands Stakes at the Curragh in May at 3 yrs: favourite, failed by 10 lb to repeat it (nonetheless second best form of career) in £14,300 handicap at Ascot month later, never travelling smoothly: since gelded: stays 7f: best effort on dead ground. *C. Collins, Ireland*

NASH HOUSE (IRE) 3 b.c. Nashwan (USA) 135 – River Dancer 118 (Irish   109
River (FR) 131) [1995 NR 1996 8d* 10.4m⁴ 10.5m Aug 10] leggy, quite attractive, unfurnished colt: fine mover with a long stride: sixth foal: closely related to 1995 Irish 2000 Guineas and Champion Stakes winner Spectrum (by Rainbow Quest) and half-brother to 2 winners, including 1¼m winner Snow Plough (by Niniski): dam French 5f (at 2 yrs) and 1m winner from family of Sun Princess and Saddlers' Hall: 9/4 on, made a most striking impression when winning maiden at Newbury on debut by 5 lengths: said to have bled internally when 2½ lengths fourth to Glory of Dancer in Dante Stakes at York and when seventh of 8 to Tamayaz in Rose of Lancaster Stakes at Haydock: should stay 1¼m+. *P. W. Chapple-Hyam*

NASH POINT 2 b.c. (Apr 17) Robellino (USA) 127 – Embroideress 80 (Stanford   79 p
121§) [1996 7d⁵ Nov 8] 7,000Y: angular, unfurnished colt: seventh foal: half-brother to 3 winners, including fairly useful sprinter Sacque (by Elegant Air) and 1m and 1¼m seller winner Tom Clapton (by Daring March): dam 5f to 7f winner: over 6 lengths fifth of 20 to Handsome Ridge in maiden at Doncaster, keeping on steadily: should improve. *I. A. Balding*

NASRUDIN (USA) 3 b.c. Nureyev (USA) 131 – Sunshine O'My Life (USA)   81
(Graustark) [1995 81p: 7d⁶ 7f² 1996 8m* 8m 8m 8.1m⁴ 8.1v Oct 6] rather leggy, quite attractive colt: fairly useful performer: won maiden at Ripon in June: failed to repeat that form in handicaps, tongue tied down last 2 starts but reportedly choking throughout when tailed off on final one: stays 1m: acts on firm ground: carries head high under pressure. *D. R. Loder*

NATALIA BAY (IRE) 2 b.f. (Feb 17) Dancing Dissident (USA) 119 – Bayazida   83
(Bustino 136) [1996 5m* 6s² 6g⁴ Jun 29] IR 16,000Y: rather unfurnished filly: seventh foal: half-sister to several winners, including useful stayer Irish Stamp (by Niniski) and Triumph Hurdle winner Paddy's Return (by Kahyasi): dam, placed in France, from family of Vaguely Noble: won 5-runner minor event at Windsor in May: head second to Naked Poser in minor event at Goodwood 10 days later, leading 2f out until last strides, then respectable fourth of 6 to Moonlight Paradise in listed race at Newmarket on final outing: will stay 1m. *P. F. I. Cole*

NATAL RIDGE 3 b.g. Indian Ridge 123 – Song Grove 61 (Song 132) [1995 55:   54
7f⁵ 6m 1996 5d 7m 6.1m 6.1m Jul 6] quite attractive gelding: modest form, not knocked about, in 4 maidens: stiffish tasks when well beaten in handicaps at Chepstow last 2 starts, blinkered when last of 15 on final one: likely to prove best at sprint distances. *D. Haydn Jones*

NATATARL (IRE) 3 ch.f. Roi Danzig (USA) – Little Me (Connaught 130) [1995   –
49: 6.1g² 6g 7.1s 1996 a7g 11.6m 7.1g⁶ 8.2m 8.3g Jul 1] good-bodied filly: poor maiden: blinkered final start: sent to South Korea. *B. Palling*

NATIONAL TREASURE 3 b.f. Shirley Heights 130 – Brocade 121 (Habitat   72
134) [1995 NR 1996 12m 12m⁵ 10s⁴ Aug 31] 390,000Y: unfurnished filly: sister to smart mare Free At Last, best over middle distances, and half-sister to 3 winners, notably Barathea (by Sadler's Wells) and smart French 1m/1¼m performer Zabar (by Dancing Brave): dam 7f and 1m winner: only fair form at best in maidens. *M. R. Stoute*

NATIVE LASS (IRE) 7 ch.m. Be My Native (USA) 122 – Fun Frolic (Sexton   –
Blake 126) [1995 NR 1996 8f Sep 23] seems of little account. *J. Balding*

NATIVE PRINCESS (IRE) 2 ch.f. (Apr 28) Shalford (IRE) 124§ – Jealous   62 ?
One (USA) (Raise A Native) [1996 6m⁶ 7.5m⁵ 7g Oct 18] IR 10,000Y: plain filly: has scope: seventh reported foal: half-sister to 3 winners, including a miler in Italy by Never So Bold: dam won at up to 9f in USA: modest form at best in maidens at Kempton, Beverley and Catterick. *B. W. Hills*

NATIVE RHYTHM (IRE) 2 ch.f. (Mar 2) Lycius (USA) 124 – Perfect Time   71
(IRE) (Dance of Life (USA)) [1996 6m² Jun 4] 47,000F: quite attractive filly: first foal: dam, French 1m winner, half-sister to Prix Marcel Boussac winner Play It Safe

and Washington International winner Providential: heavily-backed odds-on chance, 2 lengths second of 10 to Lycility in maiden at Pontefract, headed 1f out and eased close home: bandaged near-hind: had 2 attendants in paddock: should stay 1m: looked sure to improve. *P. W. Chapple-Hyam*

NATIVE SONG 3 b.f. Hatim (USA) 121 – Ivors Melody 47 (Music Maestro 119) 42 [1995 –: a8g⁶ 1996 a8g⁶ a10g 12s 9m 8.3m 10m⁶ 10m³ 12g 14d Oct 2] smallish filly: poor mover: poor performer: stays 1¼m: tried blinkered, no improvement. *M. J. Haynes*

NATTIE 2 b.g. (May 5) Almoojid 69 – Defy Me 75 (Bustino 136) [1996 5s 5.1g⁴ 47 5m⁵ 6.1d³ May 27] 500Y: leggy gelding: seventh foal: dam 2-y-o 5f winner: sire (by Sadler's Wells), disappointing maiden, closely related to Assert and half-brother to Eurobird and Bikala: plater: will stay beyond 6f. *A. G. Newcombe*

NATTIER 3 b.f. Prince Sabo 123 – Naturally Fresh 91 (Thatching 131) [1995 NR 58 1996 5m⁶ 5g 7g⁵ 5.9f² 5.9f² 6f⁴ a6g 6.9m Aug 28] good-topped filly: sixth foal: half-sister to winners abroad by Valiyar and Petoski: dam 2-y-o 5f winner: modest maiden: ran poorly last 2 starts, and sold 2,800 gns Newmarket Autumn Sales: stays 6f: acts on firm ground, ran poorly on fibresand: sent to South Korea. *Sir Mark Prescott*

NATURAL EIGHT (IRE) 2 b.c. (Apr 30) In The Wings 128 – Fenny Rough 81 p 114 (Home Guard (USA) 129) [1996 8m³ Oct 17] 32,000Y: half-brother to useful 3-y-o 6f winner Watch Me (by Green Desert) and winners abroad by Icecapade and Sharpen Up: dam 5f to 7f winner later successful in USA: 50/1 and green, 4 lengths third of 17 to Royal Crusade in maiden at Newmarket, held up, pushed along 3f out and staying on well: sure to improve. *B. W. Hills*

NATURAL KEY 3 ch.f. Safawan 118 – No Sharps Or Flats (USA) 67 (Sharpen 74 Up 127) [1995 69: 6g⁴ 5f* 6.1m* 5m² 6g² 5m 5g 6g 1996 6d 6.1g 5g 5m³ 5g 6m* 6m* 5m⁴ 6m³ 6g* 5m⁵ 7m 5g* Sep 29] smallish filly: fair performer: had 9 of her 13 races at Hamilton in 1996, winning seller in July (bought in 3,100 gns) and handicaps in August and September (2): stays 6f: acts on firm ground: tried blinkered at 2 yrs. *D. Haydn Jones*

NATURAL PATH 5 b.m. Governor General 116 – Cuba Libre (Rum (USA)) – [1995 –: 7m 1996 a7g 8f Sep 27] quite attractive mare: no form for long time: tried visored. *Mrs V. A. Aconley*

NAUGHTY PISTOL (USA) 4 ch.f. Big Pistol (USA) – Naughty Nile (USA) 57 (Upper Nile (USA)) [1995 a5.5f* a6f a6f⁵ a6s² a5.5f⁶ 5.5f* 5d² 5g² 5f⁶ 5.5f³ 5g² 6s⁴ a66 6f⁵ 1996 6m 8g⁵ 6f⁶ 6.9f⁶ a5g⁴ a6g 6m⁵ 6m 6f* 6d 7g⁴ a6g* a6g* Nov 25] $31,000Y: leggy filly: poor mover: third foal: half-sister to 2 winners, notably smart 7f (at 2 yrs) to 9f winner Lower Egypt (by Silver Hawk): dam minor winner in North America: trained at 2 and 3 yrs by B. Jackson in USA, winning 3 of 15 starts: modest form on turf in Britain, fair on the all-weather: won 17-runner claimer at Leicester in September (despite swerving and nearly unseating rider leaving stalls) and handicaps at Southwell (made virtually all) and Wolverhampton (led close home) in November: best form at sprint distances: acts on firm and dead ground and the all-weather: visored last 6 starts. *P. D. Evans*

NAUTICAL JEWEL 4 b.g. Handsome Sailor 125 – Kopjes (Bay Express 132) – § [1995 51§, a58§: a7g² 7m⁶ 8g a8g² 8m⁵ 8m³ 8.5g⁶ a12g² a11g 12s⁵ a14.8g 1996 a8g² a58 d a12g⁶ a9.4g⁴ a11g⁵ 10m 12s⁵ a8g a12s Dec 19] plain, good-topped gelding: modest maiden handicapper: stays 1½m: acts on good to firm and soft ground and on fibresand: visored (pulled hard) final 2-y-o start: sometimes sweats: held up: hangs right, and not an easy ride. *M. D. I. Usher*

NAVAL DISPATCH 2 b.f. (May 21) Slip Anchor 136 – Speed Writing (USA) – (Secretariat (USA)) [1996 8g Oct 29] third foal: half-sister to 1994 2-y-o 7f winner Lady Writer (by Warning): dam French 1m winner: 14/1, eighth of 16 in maiden at Leicester: sold 3,500 gns Newmarket December Sales. *J. H. M. Gosden*

NAVAL GAZER (IRE) 3 b.f. Sadler's Wells (USA) 132 – Naval Light (USA) 75 (Majestic Light (USA)) [1995 75p: 8g* 1996 10g⁴ 11.9d³ 9.9f 10.1m⁵ 11.9f* 11.9v Oct 6] tall, quite attractive filly: fair performer: best effort to win handicap at Brighton in September under well-judged ride: stays 1½m: acts on firm going, possibly not heavy: blinkered third 3-y-o start (took strong hold, tailed off): has carried head high and found little: probably suited by waiting tactics: sold 54,000 gns Newmarket December Sales. *D. R. Loder*

NAVAL HUNTER (USA) 3 ch.c. Jade Hunter (USA) – Navy Light (USA) 78 (Polish Navy (USA)) [1995 51: 7g 7g 1996 a8g* 9g 8g a8f a6f⁶ a8.5f Nov 11] quite attractive colt: fair form to win maiden at Southwell in March: tailed off afterwards, leaving P. Harris after third start: should stay beyond 1m: easily best effort on fibresand: blinkered last 2 starts. *Eric Guillot, USA*

NAVIGATE (USA) 3 ch.c. Diesis 133 – Libras Shiningstar (USA) 72 (Gleaming 82 (USA)) [1995 79: 5m 5m⁵ 6g² 7.1g⁴ 1996 10g 7m⁴ 8m² 7.1m 6m* 6m Sep 6] quite attractive colt: fairly useful handicapper: won maiden at Newmarket in July, travelling comfortably long way then swishing tail: sweating, ran poorly (and as if something amiss, losing his action) final start: sold only 4,500 gns Newmarket Autumn Sales: effective at 6f to 1m: raced only on a sound surface. *R. Hannon*

NAWAJI (USA) 3 b.f. Trempolino (USA) 135 – Nobile Decretum (USA) (Noble 45 Decree (USA) 127) [1995 NR 1996 10g 8g 8.3d 10d 9.7d⁴ a11g a10g Dec 13] IR 15,000Y: smallish, plain filly: sister to French 4-y-o 1m winner Layal and smart 9f and 1¼m winner Triarius, closely related to fairly useful middle-distance winner Sharp Noble (by Sharpen Up) and half-sister to 2 other winners abroad: dam unplaced in 5 races: poor maiden handicapper: stays 1¼m: blinkered (finished last) fourth 3-y-o start: inconsistent. *W. R. Muir*

NAWAR (FR) 6 b.g. Kahyasi 130 – Nabita (FR) (Akarad (FR) 130) [1995 74: – 14.4m⁶ 13.3g⁶ 11.5g⁵ 20m 16.4m 20f⁵ 1996 18.7g May 8] well-made gelding: fair form at best here over hurdles (difficult ride and not one to trust) and on flat: off course over 9 months (but looking fit), weakened quickly 5f out in Chester Cup on reappearance: sold only 850 gns Ascot July Sales: stays 2½m. *J. R. Jenkins*

NAWASIB (IRE) 2 b.f. (Feb 6) Warning 136 – Tanouma (USA) 114 (Miswaki 82 (USA) 124) [1996 6m⁵ 7g⁶ 7m² Oct 17] smallish, leggy filly: sixth foal: half-sister to several winners, including 3-y-o Tamnia (by Green Desert), useful 6f and 7f winner at 2 yrs, smart stayer Khamaseen (by Slip Anchor) and smart middle-distance stayer Azzilfi (by Ardross): dam, 6f (at 2 yrs) and 7f winner who stayed 1m, out of very speedy French 2-y-o Diffusion: tenderly handled in maidens at Goodwood first 2 starts: improved when 3½ lengths second of 7 to easy winner Meshhed in similar event at Redcar final outing, keeping on well: will stay further than 7f. *J. L. Dunlop*

NAYIB 3 b.c. Bustino 136 – Nicholas Grey 100 (Track Spare 125) [1995 NR 1996 70 12m² 10.1g 14d Jun 7] 96,000Y: rangy colt: poor mover: brother to very smart 9f to 1½m performer Terimon, closely related to middle-distance winners by Busted and Mtoto, and half-brother to several winners, none better than fairly useful: dam 2-y-o 5f to 7f winner, second in Oaks d'Italia: showed ability in maidens first 2 starts: still bit backward, dropped away rapidly over 3f out on final one: sold 4,200 gns Doncaster August Sales. *D. Morley*

NEBRANGUS (IRE) 4 ch.g. Nashamaa 113 – Choral Park (Music Boy 124) – [1995 –: 8.3g⁶ 6.9m a8g 8m 7m⁶ 10m 10d 1996 a12g a12g a12g Jan 26] small gelding: of little account: tried blinkered. *N. Bycroft*

NEC PLUS ULTRA (FR) 5 b.h. Kendor (FR) 122 – Quintefolle (FR) (Luthier 116 126) [1995 115: 8g⁵ 7m² 7g⁴ 8.5d² 8m* 8d* 6.5g 7s³ 8d³ 8g* 8g* 1996 8d³ 8g² 8g² 8g* 7g⁴ 8g² Jul 17] good-topped horse: smart French performer: won Prix du Chemin de Fer du Nord at Chantilly in June by ½ length from Manzoni: head second of 8 to Grey Risk in Prix Messidor at Maisons-Laffitte last time: effective at 7f and 1¼m, very best form at 1m: acts on heavy ground and good to firm: consistent. *A. de Royer-Dupre, France*

NED'S BONANZA 7 b.g. Green Ruby (USA) 104 – Miss Display 47 (Touch 66 Paper 113) [1995 74: 5g³ 5m⁴ 6m³ 5m 6g⁴ 5g³ 5f 5m* 5g⁶ 5g 6m* 6m⁶ 6m 6m⁶ 5g 5d 1996 5g 6g 5g 5f⁶ 6m 5m 6m⁴ 5f³ 5m* 5f 6f 5m² 5f⁶ 5m³ 5m⁵ 5f³ 5.7m² 5m³ 5m⁵ 5g Oct 21] workmanlike, good-topped gelding: fair sprint handicapper: won 20-runner race at Beverley (overcame slow start, led close home) in July: creditable efforts most starts afterwards: acts on firm ground, probably unsuited by a soft surface: visored (ran well) once as 5-y-o: usually held up. *M. Dods*

NED'S CONTESSA (IRE) 3 ch.f. Persian Heights 129 – Beechwood (USA) 46 (Blushing Groom (FR) 131) [1995 48: 5s⁵ 5g 7m a7g 7.5m 7m⁵ 7.1f² 7f³ 8m 7g³

1996 7d 8.1g 8.2m 7.1f* 7s 7m⁴ 7g⁴ 7d Aug 10] small filly: poor handicapper: won at Musselburgh in June: should stay at least 1m: acts on firm ground: blinkered (out of form) third 3-y-o start: often gets behind: sold 16,000 gns Newmarket December Sales. *M. Dods*

NEEDLE GUN (IRE)   6 b. or br.h. Sure Blade (USA) 130 – Lucayan Princess   119
111 (High Line 125) [1995 119: 10m³ 12g⁶ 10m* 10.4m⁴ 10m⁵ 12f² 1996 a10g 10d²
10g* 10f 10d 10f 10g 10m³ 9m Dec 8] tall, leggy horse: shows knee action: smart performer: won Gallinule Stakes at the Curragh in June by 2½ lengths from Prince of Andros, making all: also ran well when placed in Group 1 races at Rome in May (head second to Hollywood Dream) and November (over a length third to Flemensfirth): stays 1½m: acts on any going on turf, out of depth (behind Cigar) when tried on sand: genuine: stays in training. *C. E. Brittain*

NEEDLE MATCH   3 ch.c. Royal Academy (USA) 130 – Miss Tatting (USA) 89   59
(Miswaki (USA) 124) [1995 –p: 6m 1996 8.2d⁵ 10g 8m 7m⁵ 8.2m 6m 6m Sep 6] big, good-topped colt: modest maiden at best, disappointing after reappearance: best efforts over 7f and 1m, but rather headstrong and could prove a sprinter: has joined J. J. O'Neill. *C. F. Wall*

NEEDWOOD EPIC   3 b.f. Midyan (USA) 124 – Epure (Bellypha 130) [1995 53:   –
6f⁵ 8.1m 8.2d⁶ 1996 10m 10.8m a12g 13.6m 12g Nov 1] big, good-topped filly: modest form in maidens at 2 yrs for B. McMahon: well beaten in handicaps in 1996: visored last 2 starts: should stay beyond 1m: takes keen hold. *B. C. Morgan*

NEEDWOOD FANTASY   3 b.f. Rolfe (USA) 77 – Needwood Nymph 45 (Bold   –
Owl 101) [1995 –: 5m⁵ 7.5d 1996 a9.4g 8.2m 12g⁵ 10g 10f Sep 23] leggy filly: of little account: tried visored. *B. C. Morgan*

NEEDWOOD LEGEND   3 b. or br.c. Rolfe (USA) 77 – Enchanting Kate   –
(Enchantment 115) [1995 NR 1996 10g Oct 9] second reported foal: dam of little account: showed little in maiden at Nottingham. *B. C. Morgan*

NEEDWOOD LIMELIGHT   3 b.g. Rolfe (USA) 77 – Lime Brook 56 (Rapid   –
River 127) [1995 –: 6g 1996 6f⁵ Sep 23] broke leg after passing post in claimer at Leicester on first start for new stable: dead. *B. C. Morgan*

NEEDWOOD MUPPET   9 b.g. Rolfe (USA) 77 – Sea Dart 55 (Air Trooper   –
115) [1995 NR 1996 15.9g 17.9g Oct 9] rated 58 on flat at 5 yrs: fair hurdler, but well beaten in handicaps on return: suited by a thorough test of stamina: acts on soft ground. *A. J. Wilson*

NEEDWOOD NATIVE   8 b.g. Rolfe (USA) 77 – The Doe 82 (Alcide 136)   –
[1995 NR 1996 12m Oct 3] eighth reported foal: half-brother to a winner in Brazil and to temperamental Conigree (by Connaught): dam stayed at least 1¼m: poor 2m novice hurdler: distant last in claimer on flat debut: sold 600 gns Ascot November Sales. *A. J. Wilson*

Gallinule Stakes, the Curragh—the favourite Needle Gun makes all

NEEDWOOD NUTKIN   3 b.f. Rolfe (USA) 77 – Needwood Nut 70 (Royben   –
125) [1995 NR 1996 10g Oct 9] 400Y: third foal: sister to 2 poor maidens: dam 6f
winner: 50/1, well beaten in maiden at Nottingham. *B. C. Morgan*

NEED YOU BADLY   3 b.f. Robellino (USA) 127 – Persian Tapestry 70 (Tap On   59
Wood 130) [1995 59: 5s⁴ 5f⁴ 6f 1996 7g 5f³ 5m⁵ 5m⁶ a5g* a5g² a5g³ a6g 6s a5g Oct
19] compact filly: modest performer: all-weather debut when winning minor event at
Wolverhampton in July: sold 6,500 gns Newmarket Autumn Sales: effective at 5f
and 6f, bred to stay further: acts on fibresand and on good to firm and soft ground.
S. P. C. Woods

NEFERTITI   2 b.f. (Mar 7) Superpower 113 – Vico Equense (Absalom 128) [1996   –
a5g⁶ a5g 5.2f⁴ Jun 25] fourth foal: dam poor on flat and over hurdles: seems of little
account. *R. F. Marvin*

NELLIE NORTH   3 b.f. Northern State (USA) 91 – Kimble Princess (Kala   68 d
Shikari 125) [1995 68: 5g⁵ 5g² 5m³ 5.1m³ 5m* 5m⁶ 6m 6g⁴ 6d 1996 6m³ 5.1g⁴ 6m
5f⁵ 8.3g 6g³ 6.1d⁵ 5f 6.1m Sep 24] lengthy filly: fair handicapper: effective at 5f and
6f: acts on good to firm and dead ground: visored last 3 starts, running respectably on
first occasion: inconsistent. *G. M. McCourt*

NELLY'S COUSIN   3 b.f. Distant Relative 128 – Glint of Victory 96 (Glint of   65
Gold 128) [1995 NR 1996 a9.4g⁴ a10g⁵ 9m 10.1f² 10m⁵ 10.8m 9.7m* 10f⁴ 10f*
10.1m³ 11.6m⁴ 10.1g² Aug 26] fourth foal: dam 1¼m winner who stayed 1½m: fair
performer: won claimer at Folkestone in July and 5-runner handicap (got up on line)
at Brighton in August: spoiled chance by wandering in front last 2 starts: stays 11.6f:
acts on firm ground: sent to Saudi Arabia. *N. A. Callaghan*

NEMISTO   2 b.c. (Jan 24) Mystiko (USA) 124 – Nemesia 111 (Mill Reef (USA)   56
141) [1996 7.1f 7g⁶ Oct 25] stocky colt: third foal: dam suited by 1½m+, sister to
useful 5f and 7f winner Fairy Tern and closely related to smart 1¼m performer
Elegant Air: better effort in maidens when 10¾ lengths sixth of 12 to Sophomore
at Doncaster: will stay beyond 7f: sold 12,000 gns Newmarket Autumn Sales.
C. E. Brittain

NEON DEION (IRE)   2 b.g. (Jan 28) Alzao (USA) 117 – Sharnazad (IRE) (Track   38
Barron (USA)) [1996 5g⁴ 5m a6g 8d 7f⁶ a8.5g a8g Dec 11] 5,800Y: good-topped
gelding: first reported foal: dam (winner in Italy), half-sister to smart 1m and 1¼m
winner Feminine Wiles, out of a half-sister to Law Society: poor maiden: stays 7f:
blinkered/visored last 2 starts. *S. C. Williams*

NEREUS   3 b.c. Shareef Dancer (USA) 135 – Lady of The Sea 86 (Mill Reef   81
(USA) 141) [1995 67p: 7m 1996 10g 10.2f⁶ 10g* 14f 12m 12g⁵ Sep 21] good sort:
fairly useful form when easy winner of 5-runner maiden at Ayr in July: made little
impression in 3 handicaps, though creditable fifth at Catterick final start: should
prove suited by further than 1½m: best efforts on good ground (unimpressive to post,
swished tail in race second start on firm): sent to UAE. *B. W. Hills*

NERVOUS REX   2 b.g. (Feb 14) Reprimand 122 – Spinner 59 (Blue Cashmere   69 d
129) [1996 5m⁶ 5.1d² 5g⁴ 5m⁴ 5m 5.1d] 16,000Y: useful-looking
gelding: closely related to winning sprinters Thorner Lane and Another Lane (both
by Tina's Pet) and half-brother to several winners, including 3-y-o Supreme Power
(by Superpower), 5f winner at 2 yrs: dam sprinter: off course nearly 3 months after
third start and became disappointing: best form at 5f: blinkered, got loose on way
to stalls and bolted fifth intended outing: fractious in paddock then ran badly when
blinkered fifth actual outing: temperamental: gelded. *W. R. Muir*

NESBET   2 b.c. (May 13) Nicholas (USA) 111 – Brera (IRE) 45 (Tate Gallery   –
(USA) 117) [1996 7d⁶ a6g Sep 7] 2,200Y, 4,000 2-y-o: workmanlike colt: second
foal: dam, poor maiden, should have stayed 7f: well beaten in maidens at Chester and
Wolverhampton. *B. R. Cambidge*

NEUWEST (USA)   4 b.c. Gone West (USA) – White Mischief 103 (Dance In   86
Time (CAN)) [1995 80: 7g³ 8f* a8g² 1996 a7g⁶ a8g⁴ 8s 7f⁴ 8m 7f* 6m³ 7.1m² 6.9f*
7m 7m² 7f* 7.3m Aug 17] robust colt: poor walker: has a round action: fairly useful
handicapper: won at Lingfield in May, Folkestone in June and Lingfield (minor
event) in August: effective at 6f to 1m: acts on firm and soft going and on equitrack:
consistent. *N. J. H. Walker*

NEVADA (IRE) 2 gr.c. (Apr 6) Marju (IRE) 127 – Silver Singing (USA) 96   93
(Topsider (USA)) [1996 5m* 5m² 6m³ 5m⁶ Sep 14] IR 9,000Y: lengthy, good-topped
colt: second foal: half-brother to 4-y-o 11f and 1½m winner Troubador Song (by
King of Clubs): dam sprinter: won maiden at Tipperary in May: fairly useful form
when second of 6 to Raphane in Curragh Stakes and when sixth of 7 to Easycall in
Flying Childers Stakes at Doncaster: stays 6f: has raced only on good to firm ground:
visored final outing (sweating and edgy). *A. P. O'Brien, Ireland*

NEVER SAY SO 4 ch.f. Prince Sabo 123 – So Rewarding (Never So Bold 135)   –
[1995 48: 5m³ 5g⁴ 5d⁵ 6g 5d⁶ 6g 1996 a7g 5m 5g Sep 29] small filly: tailed off in
handicaps at 4 yrs: should stay 6f: acts on good to firm ground, well below form on
fibresand: tried visored: has joined Mrs S. Lamyman. *C. Smith*

NEVER SO BRAVE 6 ch.g. Never So Bold 135 – Another Move 69 (Farm Walk   35
111) [1995 NR 1996 12.3m 10g³ Jul 9] bad performer: stays 1¼m. *J. D. Bethell*

NEVER SO RITE (IRE) 4 b.f. Nordico (USA) – Nephrite 106 (Godswalk   –
(USA) 130) [1995 62, a52: a8g² a10g³ a8g⁵ 6.9g³ 8d² 8m* 8f² 7m³ 7f³ 8h² 8.3m³ 8g   a53
a10g³ a10g a10g⁵ 1996 a12g² a12g⁵ a12g² a12g² Feb 6] leggy filly: modest handi
capper: will prove best at up to 1½m: acts on hard and soft ground and on equitrack:
blinkered/visored once each. *D. W. P. Arbuthnot*

NEVER SO TRUE 5 b.m. Never So Bold 135 – Cottage Pie 106 (Kalamoun 129)   39
[1995 45: 7.1g 8g 8.3g 10m³ 7g⁶ 11.1f² 12.1m⁵ 13f⁴ 12.1m³ 11.1f* 9.2f² 14.1m⁴
12.4g⁴ 1996 12s 12f⁴ 11f 8f⁵ 9.2f² 8m Aug 28] lengthy, rather sparely-made mare:
poor handicapper: only worthwhile form at 5 yrs when second in seller at Hamilton:
stays 13f: acts on firm ground, dead and fibresand: tried visored/blinkered, no
improvement: races prominently: has carried head awkwardly. *Martyn Wane*

NEVER THINK TWICE 3 b.g. Never So Bold 135 – Hope And Glory (USA)   70
87 (Well Decorated (USA)) [1995 64: 5m⁴ 5m³ 6m⁵ 5g⁶ 5m 6m² 6m² 1996 5d 6f⁶ 8g   a59
6m 7g³ 6m⁴ 6m* 6g³ 6m⁵ 6m* 6d² 6f 7m 6m a6g a7s a6g a6g² a7g² Dec 20] quite
attractive gelding: fair handicapper: won at Windsor in July and Folkestone in
August: stays 7f: acts on good to firm and dead ground, modest form to date on
all-weather surfaces: usually visored or blinkered: has shown signs of unsatisfactory
temperament. *K. T. Ivory*

NEVER TIME (IRE) 4 b.g. Simply Great (FR) 122 – Islet Time (Burslem 123)   47 ?
[1995 43: a6g⁶ a8g 7g 6m 10.3m 10m 10g³ 8m 12m³ 11.9g⁴ 13.8g⁶ 11d 13.8f³ a14g
1996 a12g a16g⁶ 12d² 12m 12g 12m a14g 15.8s 12.1m⁴ 10m⁵ 12g³ 10m 12m Oct 7]
sturdy, angular gelding: poor performer: sold 2,400 gns Doncaster October Sales
since final start: stays 13.8f: acts on firm and soft ground (well below form all starts
on fibresand): tried in visor and blinkers: sometimes early to post: inconsistent, and
not one to rely on. *Mrs V. A. Aconley*

NEW ALBION (USA) 5 b. or br.g. Pleasant Colony (USA) – Grand Bonheur   61
(USA) (Blushing Groom (FR) 131) [1995 –: 12m 10g 1996 a8g² 10d 8f 9.2m² 8.1m⁶   a74
10.1m³ 10.1f³ 10g Aug 21] big, good-topped gelding: fair handicapper: sold out of
N. Henderson's stable 4,400 gns Ascot June Sales after second 5-y-o start: stays
10.2f: acts on firm ground (tailed off on dead) and equitrack. *Miss Z. A. Green*

NEWBRIDGE BOY 3 b.g. Bustino 136 – Martyrdom (USA) (Exceller (USA)   58
129) [1995 NR 1996 8m 10.5d a8g² 12.1m² a12g* a12g⁴ a12g 10.5s⁵ 10.1m⁴ 10.3g⁵
Oct 25] 3,200F: tall gelding: fourth foal: dam (unraced) from family of Magical
Wonder and Mt Livermore: modest handicapper: won maiden event at Wolverhampton (gamely made most) in July: will stay beyond 1½m: acts on good to firm
ground and fibresand: usually races prominently. *M. G. Meagher*

NEW CENTURY (USA) 4 gr.g. Manila (USA) – Casessa (USA) (Caro 133)   95
[1995 86: 10.5m⁵ 10m 7g 7.9m⁶ 7f 1996 8s⁶ 8g 8g* 7m² 8m 8g* 8m 7.9m Aug 22]
big, good-bodied gelding: useful handicapper: won at Thirsk (Hunt Cup) in May and
Doncaster in June: retained by trainer 16,000 gns Newmarket Autumn Sales: likely
to prove best at up to 1m: acts on firm going, probably on soft: tends to sweat and get
on toes (raced too freely second 4-y-o start), and is reportedly a poor traveller: seems
suited by waiting tactics. *D. Nicholls*

NEW FRONTIER (IRE) 2 b.c. (Feb 21) Sadler's Wells (USA) 132 – Diamond   107
Field (USA) 71 (Mr Prospector (USA)) [1996 8g² 8m² 9d* 10s⁴ Nov 2] IR 210,000Y:
fifth foal: brother to 3-y-o Diamond Dance, closely related to useful 6f winner Storm

Canyon (by Storm Bird), 11f winner in UAE in 1996, and half-brother to Wafayt (stays 10.8f, rated 108, by Danehill): dam, placed over 5f at 2 yrs from 2 starts, out of sister to the dam of Topsider: showed improvement when short head behind demoted Monza at the end of steadily-run Prix de Conde at Longchamp in October, leant on throughout final 1f and struck in face by whip: 5¼ lengths fourth of 10 to Shaka in Criterium de Saint-Cloud 4 weeks later: stays 1¼m: acts on good to firm and soft ground. *A. Fabre, France*

NEWGATE HUSH 4 ch.f. Kind of Hush 118 – Mummys Colleen 75 (Mummy's – Pet 125) [1995 –: 13.8g 11d 11f a11g a14g⁶ 1996 a12g 8.5m 10g 8f Jul 18] angular filly: of little account: blinkered final start. *B. W. Murray*

NEWINGTON BUTTS (IRE) 6 br.m. Dowsing (USA) 124 – Cloud Nine 97 – (Skymaster 126) [1995 48: a7g a6g a7g³ a7g⁴ 6.9d a7g a6g³ a5g³ a5g 1996 a5g⁴ a6g³ a58 a6g⁵ a6g* a6g⁶ a6g 5g a6g* a6g Jun 8] small, close-coupled mare: modest handicapper: gained first success at Lingfield in February, and put up best effort for some time when winning at Wolverhampton in May: effective at 5f to 7f: acts on good to firm and dead ground (very rarely raced on turf nowadays) and the all-weather: effective blinkered or not: often a front runner: inconsistent. *K. McAuliffe*

NEW INN 5 b.g. Petoski 135 – Pitroyal 74 (Pitskelly 122) [1995 62: a12g a12g 56 16.2m 14.1g* 14.1m⁴ 12g³ 15.8g⁵ 12.3m 11.5g 18f 1996 a12g a12g a12g⁴ Feb 12] workmanlike gelding: modest handicapper: stays 14.8f: acts on good to firm ground, dead and fibresand: visored (well beaten) third 4-y-o start: races prominently: fairly useful hurdler, winner in December. *S. Gollings*

NEWLANDS CORNER 3 b.f. Forzando 122 – Nice Lady 65 (Connaught 130) 63 [1995 –: 6d 7g 7g 1996 8f 6m 8.3m 6m 6m 6m² 6f² 5.9f* 6m* 6m* Aug 28] improved into a fair handicapper when fitted with blinkers: gained hat-trick at Carlisle, Salisbury and Brighton in space of 23 days in August, coming with late run on each occasion: best form at 6f, should prove effective over further: acts on firm ground: blinkered last 5 starts. *J. Akehurst*

NEWPORT KNIGHT 5 ch.g. Bairn (USA) 126 – Clara Barton (Youth (USA) 77 135) [1995 69: 10.2m³ 10.1m⁶ 11.5m* 12m⁵ 11.5s³ 1996 10d 11.4m 11.6g* 11.6g* 11.7m² 12d Oct 11] lengthy, dipped-backed gelding: fair handicapper: won 2 steadily-run events at Windsor in July, and short-headed at Bath in August: off course 2 months and heavily bandaged off-hind, well beaten in amateurs event final start: stays 11.7f: acts on firm ground and soft: has carried head high. *R. Akehurst*

NEW REGIME (IRE) 3 b.f. Glenstal (USA) 118 – Gay Refrain (Furry Glen – 121) [1995 NR 1996 7.5m 8g 14.1g Oct 30] IR 5,200Y, 3,200 2-y-o: quite goodtopped filly: closely related to a winner abroad by Try My Best: dam ran once at 2 yrs in Ireland: no sign of ability. *P. T. Dalton*

NEW SPAIN (USA) 4 br.c. Seeking The Gold (USA) – Trunk (USA) (Danzig – (USA)) [1995 NR 1996 7.1m³ Jun 30] $125,000Y: sixth foal: closely related to 2 winners by Forty Niner, including Golden Braids (placed in Grade 2 event at 9f), and half-brother to an allowance winner (at up to around 9f) by Caveat: dam, listed sprint winner, third in Grade 2 event over 7f at 2 yrs: weak 10/1, third in maiden at Chepstow, soon pushed along after slow start and never a threat. *J. H. M. Gosden*

NEW TECHNIQUE (FR) 3 br.f. Formidable (USA) 125 – Dolly Bea Sweet – (USA) (Super Concorde (USA) 128) [1995 –: 6m 1996 a8g⁶ a7g a7g a5g 7f 10.3g Oct 26] small filly: no form: tried visored. *K. McAuliffe*

NEXSIS STAR 3 ch.g. Absalom 128 – The High Dancer (High Line 125) [1995 – NR 1996 7.1d 10m 8m⁵ 8g 12m 12g 8.2s Oct 31] 6,200F, 10,000Y, 1,100 2-y-o: leggy gelding: brother to very useful 5f performer Boozy and 7f winner Sozzled, and half-brother to 5f and 6f winner High Principles (by Risk Me): dam poor maiden: well beaten over a variety of trips in varied company, including seller. *Mrs S. J. Smith*

NEZOOL ALMATAR (IRE) 3 b.f. Last Tycoon 131 – Rowa 83 (Great – Nephew 126) [1995 NR 1996 8.3g a9.4g⁶ Aug 9] sixth foal: sister to disappointing 4-y-o Viyapari and half-sister to 9f to 1½m winner (probably stays 1¾m) Laila Alawi (by Mtoto) and middle-distance stayer Barrish (by Wassl): dam, best form at 1¼m, disappointing half-sister to Oh So Sharp and Roussalka: slowly away when midfield in maiden at Windsor: soundly beaten in similar event at Wolverhampton month later: sold 9,000 gns Newmarket December Sales. *M. A. Jarvis*

Coldstream Guards Rockingham Stakes, York—Nightbird steps up in grade and impresses

NICHOL FIFTY 2 b.g. (Feb 21) Old Vic 136 – Jawaher (IRE) 60 (Dancing Brave 52 p (USA) 140) [1996 6.9d Oct 21] 7,800Y: first foal: dam (maiden, stayed 1½m) out of staying half-sister to high-class middle-distance stayer High Hawk, dam of In The Wings: 14/1, 8¼ lengths eighth of 13 to Havago in maiden auction at Folkestone, never a threat: stoutly bred: should do better in time. *M. H. Tompkins*

NICK OF TIME 2 b.f. (Feb 15) Mtoto 134 – Nikitina 106 (Nijinsky (CAN) 138) – p [1996 7m 7.1s Oct 22] 25,000Y: quite attractive filly: half-sister to several winners, including useful Irish middle-distance stayer Excellenza (by Exceller) and 1¾m winner Polo Kit (by Trempolino): dam, Irish 1¼m winner, out of high-class 1969 French 2-y-o Vela: signs of ability in minor event at Newbury and 16-runner maiden at Chepstow: likely to prove suited by test of stamina. *J. L. Dunlop*

NICK THE BISCUIT 5 b.g. Nicholas Bill 125 – Maryland Cookie (USA) 101 – (Bold Hour) [1995 61+: a9.4g a12g² 1996 a12g³ a12g⁴ a16.2g⁶ Apr 13] useful-looking gelding: fair maiden as 3-y-o: no worthwhile form in 1996: stays 1½m: acts on fibresand: visored (ran creditably) once, blinkered (tailed off) final start: sold 1,600 gns Ascot August Sales. *R. T. Phillips*

NICOLA'S PRINCESS 3 b.f. Handsome Sailor 125 – Barachois Princess 56 (USA) 62 (Barachois (CAN)) [1995 NR 1996 5.1d⁵ 6g⁶ 7g 7f a6g a8.5g⁵ a8.5g² a9.4g⁶ a8.5g* 8f a8g Nov 4] big, lengthy filly: has scope: first foal: dam stayed 1¼m: modest form: won maiden handicap at Wolverhampton in September: saddle slipped sixth and eighth 3-y-o outings: stays 8.5f: acts on fibresand. *B. A. McMahon*

NIFTY NORMAN 2 b.g. (Apr 26) Rock City 120 – Nifty Fifty (IRE) 97 (Runnett 62 125) [1996 5m 5m² 5m² 5m 5s³ Aug 27] 4,200Y: leggy, angular gelding: first foal: dam 5f winner at 2 yrs, probably stayed 7f: modest sprint maiden: acts on good to firm and soft ground: reared stalls second start. *J. Berry*

NIGELS CHOICE 4 gr.g. Teenoso (USA) 135 – Warm Winter 65 (Kalaglow 53 132) [1995 NR 1996 11.9f³ Apr 22] first foal: dam won over hurdles: staying-on third in claimer at Brighton: subsequently joined A. D. Smith. *A. G. Newcombe*

NIGEL'S LAD (IRE) 4 b.g. Dominion Royale 112 – Back To Earth (FR) 81 (Vayrann 133) [1995 95: a8.5g³ a10g* a8.5g² a10g* a10g⁴ 10d 10.5m² 10g* 9.9m³ a– 9.2g* a9.4g⁶ 8g* 10g 8m 10m⁵ 9m⁴ 8m² 10.5g⁶ 9.2g² 10g* 1996 a9.4g a10g 8s 9.9m⁵ 9.2s⁶ 8.5m⁶ 10f 12.4m³ 12.3s² 12g 10.3m 9m a12g Oct 19] sturdy gelding: fairly useful handicapper, not so good as at 3 yrs: best effort when second at Ripon on ninth start (after 2-month break): stays 1½m: acts on soft ground, good to firm and all-weather surfaces. *P. C. Haslam*

NIGHTBIRD (IRE)   2 b.f. (Feb 11) Night Shift (USA) – Pippas Song 75 (Refer-   95 p
ence Point 139) [1996 5f* 5.2g⁴ 6.5m* 7m* 6g* Oct 12] lengthy, good-quartered
filly: has a quick action: first foal: dam 1½m winner, daughter of Nassau Stakes
winner Dancing Rocks: won maiden at Warwick in May: off course 4 months after
next start but progressed really well afterwards, winning valuable nurseries at
Doncaster and Newmarket and listed Rockingham Stakes (quickened impressively
to beat Victory Dancer 3½ lengths) at York: bred to stay 1m+ but has plenty of speed:
raced only on a sound surface: joined Godolphin and sent to UAE. *B. W. Hills*

NIGHT CHORUS   2 b.c. (May 10) Most Welcome 131 – Choral Sundown 81   62 ?
(Night Shift (USA)) [1996 6g 5m 6g² 6g² a7g Nov 4] strong, lengthy colt: first foal: dam   a?
effective from 1m to 1½m: burly first 2 starts: 25/1 and still in need of race, only
worthwhile form when head second to Parijazz in maiden auction at Pontefract,
finishing strongly: soon rear in seller following month: really needs further than 6f:
possibly unsuited by fibresand. *B. S. Rothwell*

NIGHT CITY   5 b.g. Kris 135 – Night Secret 86 (Nijinsky (CAN) 138) [1995 103:   107
9m⁴ 8m 7g 8f 10.1m² 10.3g² 9g 8.1s* 1996 9s* 10s 8m⁴ 9m 8.1s⁴ Oct 22] useful-
looking gelding: useful performer: won rated stakes at Newbury (leading 2f out,
hanging over to stand rail, beat Major Change by 3 lengths) in May: stiffish tasks in
competitive minor events there next 3 starts: below best final one: stays 9f: acts on
good to firm ground and goes well with plenty of give: edgy sort, sometimes attended
by 2 handlers and early to post. *Lady Herries*

NIGHT DANCE   4 ch.c. Weldnaas (USA) 112 – Shift Over (USA) 62 (Night Shift   –
(USA)) [1995 99: 9m 8.1m 8g² 8m 7.1m* 8g³ 8f 7m² 7d* 8s* 8m a9.4g 1996 8s 8d
8m 8g 8d Oct 12] good-topped colt: useful handicapper at 3 yrs: disappointing in
1996, not best of runs first 2 starts but behind last 3: sold (G. Lewis to K. Morgan)
only 8,000 gns Newmarket Autumn Sales: effective at 7f and 1m: acts on good to
firm and soft ground, possibly not on firm: usually ridden for late challenge:
reportedly sometimes swallows his tongue (has worn tongue strap). *G. Lewis*

NIGHT EDITION   6 b.g. Night Shift (USA) – New Chant (CAN) (New   –
Providence) [1995 –, a38: a10g² a10g⁴ a10g⁴ a12g 12m a12g 1996 a16g Jan 2] robust
gelding: good mover: no form since early-95. *S. Dow*

NIGHT FLIGHT   2 gr.c. (Apr 16) Night Shift (USA) – Ancestry (Persepolis (FR)   70
127) [1996 5g² 5m³ 7f⁵ 5g² 6m Sep 21] 45,000Y: fifth foal: brother to fair 7f
winner Mistress Gwyn and half-brother to 3-y-o 7f winner Really A Dream (by Last
Tycoon), fairly useful 5f and 6f winner Christmas Kiss (by Taufan) and 6f to 1¼m
winner Devilry (by Faustus): dam never ran: fair form: second at Newcastle and
Hamilton: keen type, best form at 5f. *J. J. O'Neill*

NIGHT HARMONY (IRE)   3 ch.c. Digamist (USA) 110 – Quaver 86 (Song   57
132) [1995 53: 6g 6d 5g⁴ 1996 6.1d³ 5f⁶ 6.1m 6d 5.1g⁴ a5g² a6g⁵ a7g³ a6g⁴ Nov 29]   a61
leggy colt: modest handicapper: sold out of R. Hannon's stable 5,000 gns Newmarket
Autumn Sales after sixth start: stays 7f: acts on firm and dead ground and on
fibresand. *Miss S. J. Wilton*

NIGHT IN A MILLION   5 br.g. Night Shift (USA) – Ridalia 56 (Ridan (USA))   –
[1995 66: a7g² 8m 1996 8s May 22] heavy-topped gelding: one-time fair handicapper: poor efforts last 2 starts: should stay 1m: acts on fibresand, best turf efforts
on a sound surface: inconsistent. *S. Woodman*

NIGHTINGALE SONG   2 b.f. (Feb 22) Tina's Pet 121 – Songlines 78 (Night   64
Shift (USA)) [1996 5.3f³ 5m⁵ 5d 5.1m² 5.7m⁴ 5m⁴ 6g* 6m³ 5m³ Sep 19] 7,400Y:
sparely-made filly: first foal: dam (best at 5f) out of half-sister to Town And Country:
fair form: made all in seller at Windsor in July: better form at 6f than 5f: acts on good
to firm ground. *Martyn Meade*

NIGHTLARK (IRE)   2 b.f. (Feb 1) Night Shift (USA) – Overcall (Bustino 136)   77 p
[1996 8.2m² Sep 24] leggy, quite attractive filly: sixth foal: closely related to Irish
1½m winner Call My Guest (by Be My Guest) and half-sister to fairly useful 3-y-o
1m (at 2 yrs) and 10.2f winner Overruled (by Last Tycoon) and smart 5-y-o 7f (at 2
yrs) to 11f winner Overbury (by Caerleon): dam Irish middle-distance stayer: 7/2
from 2/1, 1½ lengths second of 9 to Attitre in maiden at Nottingham, tracking leaders
and keeping on: likely to stay middle distances: should improve. *D. R. Loder*

NIGHT MIRAGE (USA)   2 b.f. (Mar 29) Silver Hawk (USA) 123 – Colony   70 p
Club (USA) (Tom Rolfe) [1996 8.1s 8d⁵ Nov 8] $57,000Y: strong, workmanlike

filly: half-sister to several winners here and abroad, including useful Irish 1986 2-y-o 7f winner Queen's Bridge (by Spectacular Bid), later suited by 1½m: dam won 6 times at up to 9f in North America: had worst of draw in maiden on debut: stayed on when around 7 lengths fifth of 6 behind Catienus in minor event at Doncaster following month: will stay middle distances: likely to do better. *M. Johnston*

NIGHT OF GLASS   3 b.g. Mazilier (USA) 107 – Donna Elvira 80 (Chief Singer   64
131) [1995 –: 6m 6m 7g 1996 8.2m 8m 7f⁵ a8g 8g² 7g³ 8m* 8f 9g Nov 1] small, angular gelding: modest handicapper: won 18-runner race at Yarmouth in September: probably stays 9f: acts on good to firm going, yet to race on a soft surface: visored (best form) last 5 starts. *D. Morris*

NIGHT PARADE (USA)   3 b.c. Rory's Jester (AUS) – Nocturnal Song (USA)   91
(Northern Dancer) [1995 87: 5m² 5.1m* 5m 6g 5m 1996 6m 5.1g² a8.5f a6.5s⁴ a5.5f Nov 15] strong, deep-girthed colt: fine mover: fairly useful performer: left P. Chapple-Hyam after second 3-y-o start, P. Byrne after fifth: best form at 5f: has raced only on a sound surface on turf: blinkered (ran badly) final start. *Carlos A. Garcia, USA*

NIGHT PETTICOAT (GER)   3 b.f. Petoski 135 – Nightrockette (Rocket 122)   116
[1995 8s* 1996 11v* 11v* 11s⁶ 12m⁶ 12m³ 14d² Sep 29] half-sister to minor winners in Germany by Scenic (middle distances), Jareer (around 7f) and Lidhame (7.5f): dam German 7f and 1m winner: smart German filly: won maiden at Dusseldorf at 2 yrs and listed race (by 5 lengths) then 15-runner Preis der Diana (beat subsequent Ribblesdale winner Tulipa 2½ lengths, pair clear) at Mulheim in May: found to be in season after next start: below best afterwards, 11 lengths second of 8 to Wurftaube in Deutches St Leger last time, leading early in straight and (though maintaining clear advantage over remainder) soon comprehensively outpaced: probably stays 1¾m: goes well on soft/heavy ground. *B. Schutz, Germany*

NIGHT SCEPTRE (IRE)   2 b.f. (Mar 23) Night Shift (USA) – Spire 75 (Shirley   69
Heights 130) [1996 7g a8g² Dec 20] 25,000F, 30,000Y: third reported foal: half-sister to a winner in Hong Kong by Last Tycoon: dam, maiden who stayed 1¾m, from the family of Highclere: fair form in maidens at Newmarket (slowly away then keeping on without threatening) and Lingfield (beaten a head) 7 weeks later. *R. W. Armstrong*

NIGHTSWIMMING (IRE)   3 b.g. Mac's Imp (USA) 116 – Kilnahard (Steel   –
Heart 128) [1995 NR 1996 6m 5m 6f Jun 28] 8,000 2-y-o: half-brother to several winners, including 1990 Irish 2-y-o 5f winner Neversayneveragain (by Runnett): dam Irish 6f winner: no sign of ability. *S. Dow*

NIGHT TIME   4 b.g. Night Shift (USA) – Gathering Place (USA) (Hawaii) [1995   50 d
63: 7g² 12.1g 10m 10g³ 12m⁴ 10m⁴ 11.4d 1996 a8.5g⁴ a11g³ a12g⁶ a12g⁵ 8g a9.4g a12g May 9] strong gelding: modest maiden: worthwhile form on flat in 1996 only when third in seller at Southwell: should stay 1½m: acts on fibresand and good to firm ground, well beaten on heavy: modest winning hurdler, joined F. Jordan. *A. Streeter*

NIGHT WINK (USA)   4 ch.g. Rahy (USA) 115 – Lady In White 94 (Shareef   90
Dancer (USA) 135) [1995 84: 8m 10g 9m⁴ 8m² 8.5d 8g 7g* 7f³ 8f* 7m 1996 8s 7g⁵ 8d⁵ 8.5m⁴ 7g 7g 8f* 8m 8m⁵ 9g* 9g² 8.5m⁵ 8d 9s a10s² a8g² Dec 5] sturdy, lengthy gelding: carries condition: good mover: fairly useful handicapper: left D. Nicholls after fifth 4-y-o start: won at Brighton in July and at Goodwood (amateurs, held up over longer trip) in August: stays 1¼m: acts on firm and dead ground and equitrack: well beaten only try in visor: tricky ride, tending to pull hard and wander: often has tongue tied down, though has won without: none too consistent. *G. L. Moore*

NIGRASINE   2 b.c. (Apr 8) Mon Tresor 113 – Early Gales (Precocious 126) [1996   100
6m* 6g* 6m⁵ 6g² 6m⁴ 6m² Oct 17] 3,100Y, 12,000 2-y-o: leggy, close-coupled colt: has a quick, fluent action: first foal: dam showed nothing in 2 flat races and a hurdle: useful performer: won median auction maiden at Redcar in June and minor event at Pontefract (gamely despite hanging right) in July: best form last 3 starts in frame in Timeform Futurity at Pontefract, minor event at Doncaster and Two-Year-Old Trophy (beaten a head by Proud Native) at Redcar: will stay 7f: raced only on a sound surface: game and consistent. *J. L. Eyre*

NIJMEGEN   8 b.g. Niniski (USA) 125 – Petty Purse 115 (Petingo 135) [1995 NR   57
1996 a12g⁴ 16s 16g⁵ May 29] good-bodied gelding: rated 78 on flat at 4 yrs: fairly

useful 2m hurdler: very lightly raced on flat nowadays, and seems capable of only modest form: stays 17.1f: blinkered and bandaged last 2 starts. *J. G. FitzGerald*

NIJO 5 b.g. Top Ville 129 – Nibabu (FR) 101§ (Nishapour (FR) 125) [1995 112: 111 7g⁴ 8m² 7m⁵ 7.3m² 8g² 1996 8.1g 8m 8d² 9g² 8g² a9.4g Dec 7] tall, lengthy gelding: shows knee action: smart performer: took time to find his form in 1996, running well behind Tarawa and Ali-Royal in listed events at Newmarket final 2 outings on turf: stays 9f: acts on good to firm and dead ground, below best on fibresand: blinkered (ran poorly) once as 3-y-o, visored (set far too strong a pace) third 5-y-o start: sometimes sweating and edgy: sometimes flashes tail, carries head awkwardly and hangs markedly: often front runner in 1996. *D. R. Loder*

NIKITA'S STAR (IRE) 3 ch.g. Soviet Lad (USA) 94 – Sally Chase 101 (Sallust 69 134) [1995 68: 5m 7f⁴ 6f 7.6m⁵ 7.3d 8f³ 7.3d a8g 1996 a9.4g* a9.4g² a12g* 12s a80 11.6m 12m a11g* 12m* 14m⁵ 12m² 11.9f⁵ 11.4m⁴ 11.5m a12g* Nov 30] sturdy gelding: unimpressive mover: fair performer: won maiden and handicap at Wolverhampton early in 1996, claimer at Southwell and weak handicap at Folkestone in July, and handicap at Wolverhampton (particularly good effort) in November: stays 1½m: acts on firm ground (long way below form all 3 starts on a soft surface) and has a good record on fibresand (showed nothing on equitrack): tried visored/blinkered, no improvement: none too consistent. *D. J. G. Murray Smith*

NIKNAKS NEPHEW 4 br.g. Tragic Role (USA) – Bubulina 63 (Dunphy 124) 77 [1995 70: 12m 10g⁴ 10m 12f⁴ 12m 11.9g 1996 10g* May 17] leggy, angular gelding: fair handicapper: trained at 3 yrs by Miss A. J. Whitfield and D. Ffrench Davis: 50/1, showed improvement to win 20-runner race at Newbury by 2 lengths, edging ahead inside final 1f despite flashing tail: effective at 1¼m to 1½m: has raced only on a sound surface: blinkered final 3-y-o start. *B. J. Meehan*

NILE VALLEY (IRE) 2 b.f. (May 1) Royal Academy (USA) 130 – Sphinx 68 (GER) (Alpenkonig (GER)) [1996 8.1g² 8.1d⁴ 7f Oct 8] angular filly: half-sister to several winners here and abroad, including smart middle-distance stayers Cairo Prince and Hieroglyphic (both by Darshaan) and 5-y-o 7.5f (at 2 yrs) to 12.3f winner Suplizi (by Alzao): dam won 5 times at around 1m in Germany: similar form in frame in maidens won by Ajayib at Chepstow and Myrtle Bank at Haydock: unsuited by drop down in distance and faster conditions on final outing: will be suited by thorough test of stamina. *P. W. Chapple-Hyam*

NILGIRI HILLS (IRE) 3 ch.c. Indian Ridge 123 – Our Resolution (Caerleon 84 (USA) 132) [1995 84p: 6m³ 5.9f² 6m³ 6m² 1996 7s⁶ 8d⁵ 6d² 6m² 6m 6m³ 6.1s Oct 22] leggy, sparely-made colt: fairly useful (if luckless) maiden: below form last 3 starts, but not well drawn on final one: sold 12,000 gns Newmarket Autumn Sales: likely to prove best at up to 7f: acts on good to firm and dead ground: blinkered last outing. *J. L. Dunlop*

NIMBLE (IRE) 3 b.f. Danehill (USA) 126 – Sierra Leone (ITY) (Weimar 125) 93 [1995 NR 1996 7.5g² 8g* 10g⁴ 9f 8f 13f⁴ 9g a10s² Sep 22] IR 16,000Y: leggy filly: half-sister to several minor winners in Italy, including a 1¼m winner by High Estate and an 11f winner by Ercolano: dam unraced: beaten a nose in maiden at Pisa in March prior to winning similar event at Rome in April: left J. Hills after fourth of 5 to Mezzogiorno in listed event at Newbury: ran once for J. Servis: best effort in USA when second in allowance race at Belmont on first run on dirt: stays 1¼m: acts on firm ground and dirt. *N. Zito, USA*

NINEACRES 5 b.g. Sayf El Arab (USA) 127 – Mayor 86 (Laxton 105) [1995 51, 69 a61: a6g a6g⁶ a5g³ a5g* a5g⁵ a6g 5g⁵ 5m 5m 5m³ a5g⁶ 1996 5m 5.1f 6.1m⁶ 8f 7g² 5s³ Nov 8] angular, workmanlike gelding: fair handicapper: stays 7f: acts on firm and soft ground and the all-weather: has run well in blinkers, visored nowadays: effective from front or held up: suitable mount for claimer. *N. M. Babbage*

NINETY-FIVE 4 ch.f. Superpower 113 – Vanishing Trick 83 (Silly Season 127) 70 [1995 67: 5g² 5m⁶ 5g² 5g² a5g⁴ 5g⁶ 5m 1996 a5g³ 5g⁴ 5g* 5m 5s* 5m⁶ 5m² 5m* Aug 29] good-topped filly: fair performer: won maiden at Musselburgh (odds on) in May and handicaps at Catterick in July and Musselburgh (best effort in apprentice race) in August: suited by 5f: acts on fibresand and firm and soft ground: ran creditably only try in blinkers: consistent: covered by Timeless Times. *J. G. FitzGerald*

NINIA (USA) 4 ch.f. Affirmed (USA) – Lajna 88 (Be My Guest (USA) 126) 102 [1995 73: a8g³ 8f* 8m² 8m* 9f⁴ 8f* 7.5m* 8g* 8d 8.1s³ 8m 1996 7.1g 8g* 7m 8g⁴ 8g

8m 8m⁶ 9g* 10m* 10.1m* 10.3m 8m⁴ 8m 10d⁶ 10g⁶ Nov 1] leggy, close-coupled filly: prolific winner, who improved into a useful handicapper at 4 yrs: won at Ripon in May and August, at Sandown in August and Epsom (best effort, by 6 lengths from Clan Ben) in September: better form at 1¼m than shorter: acts on firm ground, seemingly not on a soft surface: blinkered (below form) once at 2 yrs: effective from front or held up. *M. Johnston*

NINOTCHKA (USA) 3 b.f. Nijinsky (CAN) 138 – Puget Sound 95 (High Top 131) [1995 66p: 7g⁵ 1996 10g³ 11.9d* 12m 11.9g³ 11.9m 12d³ 12d* Nov 2] strong, lengthy filly: won maiden at Haydock in May by 8 lengths: placed in Lancashire Oaks (behind Spout) in July and Princess Royal Stakes at Ascot (bandaged and sweating, behind Time Allowed) in October: smart form to win listed race at Milan in November by 3½ lengths from Truly Generous: should have been suited by further than 1½m: seemed to need give in the ground: edgy sort: to stud. *J. L. Dunlop* 110

NINTH CHORD 2 gr.c. (Mar 6) Alzao (USA) 117 – Jazz 76 (Sharrood (USA) 124) [1996 7d² Nov 8] 52,000Y: strong colt: first foal: dam (maiden) stayed 1¼m: burly and green, length second of 20 to Handsome Ridge in maiden at Doncaster, held up and finishing strongly: will prove suited by further than 7f: sure to improve. *J. H. M. Gosden* 85 p

NINTH SYMPHONY 2 ch.g. (Feb 4) Midyan (USA) 124 – Good As Gold (IRE) 50 (Glint of Gold 128) [1996 6g 6g⁶ 6d² 6g⁵ 7f* 7m⁵ 7m³ 8m 8m 7m a7g⁶ a7s⁶ Dec 19] 21,000Y: good-bodied gelding: first foal: dam (maiden) effective from 1m to 1¼m: won nursery at Newmarket in July: good third in nursery at York in August: below best afterwards: should stay 1m: acts on firm and dead ground: has run well when sweating. *P. C. Haslam* 73

NIRVANA PRINCE 7 ch.g. Celestial Storm (USA) 132 – Princess Sunshine (Busted 134) [1995 53: a12g² 1996 10m⁶ 16.2g⁴ Aug 24] rangy gelding: fairly useful hurdler (stays 3m): second in median auction maiden at Wolverhampton on flat debut: well beaten in maidens in 1996: should stay beyond 1½m. *B. Preece* –

NITA'S CHOICE 6 b.m. Valiyar 129 – What's The Matter 57 (High Top 131) [1995 23: 10g 8g⁴ a8.5g 8m 10g⁶ 1996 10f 10d Aug 25] lengthy, rather sparely-made mare: bad form. *A. G. Newcombe* –

NITEOWL RAIDER (IRE) 3 ch.g. Standaan (FR) 118 – Havana Moon (Ela-Mana-Mou 132) [1995 49: 5m 5m³ 5f⁵ a8.5g 1996 2m a7g a6g³ a6g* 5s a6g* a5g a6g 6m a6g 6.1m 5m 5.1m 6m a6g 7g a6g Nov 25] angular gelding: fair performer on the all-weather: made all in maiden at Wolverhampton in March and seller (gamely) at Southwell in April: lost his way in second half of year: little form on turf: best form at 6f: acts on fibresand: often front runner: blinkered once (out of form). *J. A. Harris* – a64 d

NITWITTY 2 b.g. (Apr 3) Nomination 125 – Dawn Ditty 100 (Song 132) [1996 7d Oct 2] seventh reported foal: half-brother to sprinter How's Yer Father and 7f/1m winner The Can Can Man (both by Daring March), and a winner abroad by Tremblant: dam sprinter: 33/1, showed nothing in maiden at Salisbury. *P. D. Cundell* –

NIVASHA 4 b.f. Shavian 125 – Rheinza 66 (Rheingold 137) [1995 39: 12f³ 14.1m⁶ 11.1f⁵ a9.4g³ 12s 12m a10g a7g⁴ a7g 1996 a6g³ a6g a6g³ a6g⁵ a8g² a8g a10g⁵ a8g⁶ a8g³ 9.7g⁵ a10g Jul 27] lengthy, workmanlike filly: poor mover: poor maiden handicapper: left R. Hoad after seventh 4-y-o start, P. Mooney 2 starts later: effective at 6f, and has form over as far as 1½m: acts on firm and dead ground and the all-weather: inconsistent. *J. Ffitch-Heyes* a44

NIZAAL (USA) 5 ch.h. Diesis 133 – Shicklah (USA) 106 (The Minstrel (CAN) 135) [1995 70d: a8g⁵ a12g³ a10g⁵ a10g 8.9g 8.2m 7m 1996 7.5d 6g 8m 8.3s 8.3m 10g⁶ 8.3g 8m⁴ Oct 2] good-topped horse: poor handicapper: left D. Nicholls' stable after fourth 5-y-o start: well backed, first form for some time when fourth in amateurs race at Newcastle on final start: stays 1m well: acts on good to firm and soft ground: tried blinkered. *R. Allan* 33

NKAPEN ROCKS (SPA) 3 b.g. Risk Me (FR) 127 – Debutina Park 87 (Averof 123) [1995 62: 5g⁵ a6g⁴ 6g 1996 7.1g³ 7d 8g a7g⁵ 7.1f² 8.1g² 7m 7.1f 8.1d a7g a6g Dec 3] tall, leggy, useful-looking gelding: modest maiden at best: stays 1m: acts on firm ground, possibly not on a soft surface: races keenly. *Capt. J. Wilson* 63 d a–

NO-AMAN 3 b.c. Nashwan (USA) 135 – Ghanimah 98 (Caerleon (USA) 132) [1995 NR 1996 8g 8m 8g² 10m² 10m⁴ Jun 17] big, good-topped colt: has plenty of 84

scope: fourth foal: half-brother to 1992 2-y-o 7f winner Faez (by Mtoto): dam, ran only at 2 yrs, winning at 6f, half-sister to Marwell: fairly useful performer: below-form favourite in maiden at Windsor final start: sold only 2,000 gns Newmarket Autumn Sales: should stay further than 1¼m. *Major W. R. Hern*

NOBBY BARNES 7 b.g. Nordance (USA) – Loving Doll 72 (Godswalk (USA) 45 130) [1995 47: 8f 8.3g⁴ 8f⁴ 8g 8g⁶ 8g³ 8.2m⁶ 10.1m⁴ 8.1m⁶ 9f³ 8.5m² 8.1m³ 9m⁶ 8.2m³ 7.9g⁴ 8.9g⁴ 8f a8g 1996 a8g 8g² 9.2s² 8.3s⁶ 8g 9.2g a8g 8f⁴ 8.2m⁶ 10m⁶ 9g 8.3g 7.9g⁶ 10.4g⁶ Oct 10] neat gelding: has a round action: poor handicapper: sometimes makes the frame, but hasn't won since June 1994: stays 1¼m: acts on firm ground, soft and all-weather surfaces: sometimes bandaged: usually held up under Kim Tinkler. *Don Enrico Incisa*

NOBLEATA 4 ch.f. Dunbeath (USA) 127 – Lobela 77 (Lorenzaccio 130) [1995 – NR 1996 10g Apr 27] smallish, plain filly: seventh reported foal: half-sister to several winners, all at up to 7.6f, including Ernestan (by Stanford) and Bold Angel (by Lochnager): dam won at 1m and 1¼m: 50/1, beat only one in 17-runner maiden at Leicester on debut. *S. R. Bowring*

NOBLE CANONIRE 4 b.f. Gunner B 126 – Lucky Candy 61 (Lucky Wed- 44 nesday 124) [1995 –: a7g a12g 10m 10d⁶ 1996 a12g⁵ a11g* a11g² a12g⁴ 9.9d⁴ 12.3g a58 a9.4g² a8g⁵ a11g⁴ May 27] sturdy, plain filly: bad walker: modest handicapper on the all-weather: won seller (easily) at Southwell in February: only poor form on turf: stays 11f well: joined D. Shaw. *S. R. Bowring*

NOBLE COLOURS 3 b.g. Distinctly North (USA) 115 – Kentucky Tears (USA) – § (Cougar (CHI)) [1995 –: 6m a6g 1996 7f 8g 11f Sep 27] little sign of ability: sold out of Jack Berry's stable 750 gns Doncaster July Sales before 3-y-o reappearance: refused to race final start: sold to join S. G. Griffiths 1,300 gns Ascot October Sales. *J. J. Quinn*

NOBLE DANCER (IRE) 2 b.c. (Apr 27) Imperial Frontier (USA) 112 – Que 65 Sera 91 (Music Boy 124) [1996 5m⁴ May 18] IR 5,000F, 1,500Y: angular, work-manlike colt: fourth foal: half-brother to winners Robsera (fairly useful, up to 9f, by Robellion) and Rancho Mirage (fair, 5f by Superlative): dam 2-y-o 5f winner: 15/2, fourth to Double Action in maiden at Thirsk: dead. *M. D. Hammond*

NOBLE DANE (IRE) 2 b.f. (Mar 10) Danehill (USA) 126 – Noble Dust (USA) 79 p (Dust Commander (USA)) [1996 7g³ 8.1s* Oct 5] IR 9,000Y: rangy, angular filly: sister to smart 4-y-o 7f to 10.5f winner Amrak Ajeeb, closely related to fairly useful 5-y-o 7f winner Czarna (by Polish Precedent) and half-sister to several winners here and abroad: dam, unraced, from good family: promising third in minor event at Kempton: similar form when winning steadily-run maiden at Haydock month later by ½ length from Almi Ad, cruising to front well over 1f out, flicking tail under pressure inside last: will stay 1¼m: can improve again and win more races. *P. W. Harris*

NOBLE HERO 2 b.c. (Mar 2) Houston (USA) – Noble Devorcee (USA) 60 (Vaguely Noble 140) [1996 7m⁵ 6m⁴ 8m 8f a8g² a10g³ Nov 26] 13,000F, 8,000Y: tall a70 colt: third foal: dam unraced half-sister to 3 stakes winners, including Grade 2 6f winner Rocky Marriage: best form when placed in a nursery and median auction maiden at Lingfield in November: stays 1¼m: acts on equitrack, raced only on a sound surface on turf. *J. J. Sheehan*

NOBLE INVESTMENT 2 b.g. (Feb 6) Shirley Heights 130 – Noble Destiny 89 70 + (Dancing Brave (USA) 140) [1996 7m 7m⁴ 7m⁵ 7m Oct 1] 5,000Y: heavy-topped, quite attractive gelding: carries condition: second foal: closely related to 3-y-o 7f winner Maiden Castle (by Darshaan): dam, 2-y-o 7f winner but disappointing at 3 yrs, out of useful mare Tender Loving Care: fair form: 66/1, tracked leaders 5f in falsely-run race when about 9¼ lengths fourteenth of 23 to Papua in valuable sales event at Newmarket final start: gelded after: bred to be well suited by middle distances. *J. M. P. Eustace*

NOBLE LORD 3 ch.g. Lord Bud 121 – Chasers' Bar (Oats 126) [1995 NR 1996 70 12m³ 10m 8.3m 11.6m 10d Aug 12] workmanlike gelding: first foal: dam NH Flat race winner and fair winning hurdler who probably stayed 3m: claimed out of Mrs J. Ramsden's stable £6,000 after finishing third in seller at Pontefract: best effort when never-dangerous eighth of 19, beaten just over 13 lengths, in maiden at Windsor third start: best form at 8.3f, should be effective over further: won first 3 starts over hurdles, showing fairly useful form. *R. H. Buckler*

NOBLE NEPTUNE 4 b.g. Governor General 116 – Calibina 101 (Caliban 123) – [1995 65: a7g⁴ 8m 8.3m⁵ 8m* 8.5m⁶ 8.1g 8m 10f⁶ 1996 a10g a10g⁶ 8m 8s 9.7m 8.3g Jul 8] smallish gelding: modest handicapper at 3 yrs: well held in 1996: sold 5,800 gns Newmarket July Sales: probably stays 1¼m: acts on good to firm (probably on firm) and dead ground: sent to Macau. *W. J. Musson*

NOBLE SOCIETY 8 b.g. Law Society (USA) 130 – Be Noble (Vaguely Noble – § 140) [1995 –§: 16d⁴ 1996 14.1m⁶ Jun 5] angular gelding: poor and inconsistent staying maiden. *K. G. Wingrove*

NOBLE SPRINTER (IRE) 4 b.c. The Noble Player (USA) 126 – Daybreaker 78 (Thatching 131) [1995 85: 8m 8.1d² 8.1g³ 8.9g³ 8m⁶ 1996 10g 10g² 8m 10g⁴ 10d⁵ 10m⁴ 10.5g* 10m 12g⁴ a12f Dec 26] good-topped colt: fair handicapper: began to disappoint and left R. Hannon after sixth 4-y-o start: won apprentice contest at Haydock in July on first run for new stable, coming from rear in very strongly-run race: stays 10.5f: acts on good to firm and dead ground: blinkered final 3-y-o start and first 6 at 4 yrs. *W. Haggas*

NOBLE STORY 2 br.f. (Jan 25) Last Tycoon 131 – Certain Story (Known Fact 61 p (USA) 135) [1996 5m⁴ Aug 19] half-sister to several winners, including 7f winner Fairy Story (by Persian Bold) and useful middle-distance winner Pharly Story (by Pharly): dam unraced daughter of useful 5f/6f winner Epithet (later stayed 1½m): 10/1, 5¾ lengths fourth of 13 (slowly into stride, stayed on) to Joza in maiden at Windsor: will be suited by further than 5f: should improve. *R. Akehurst*

NO CLASS 2 ch.f. (Mar 19) Keen 116 – Plie 75 (Superlative 118) [1996 6m 5.1m 48 6f⁵ 7m a6g Sep 7] 3,100Y: third foal: half-sister to 3-y-o Red Simba (by Absalom), 7f winner here at 2 yrs and successful in Sweden in 1996, and a winner abroad by Sayf El Arab: dam, 2-y-o 5.8f winner, stayed 1m: poor maiden: seems to stay 7f: made running/disputed lead last 3 starts: joined I. Campbell. *R. Harris*

NO CLICHES 3 ch.g. Risk Me (FR) 127 – Always On A Sunday 101 (Star 78 Appeal 133) [1995 83p: 6m⁵ 6m 6g⁶ 6m⁶ 8m* 1996 10g 8.1g 8s 10.1m⁶ 8.1m² 10m² 8m² 8m Oct 17] lengthy, workmanlike gelding: unimpressive mover: fair handicapper: close second fifth to seventh starts: sold (G. Lewis to D. Nicholls) 13,000 gns Newmarket Autumn Sales and gelded: stays 1¼m: blinkered last 5 outings: flashes tail: races prominently. *G. Lewis*

NO COMMENT 2 b.c. (Apr 6) Puissance 110 – Safidar 83 (Roan Rocket 128) – [1996 6m 5m⁵ 6g 7m Oct 4] 10,000F, IR 25,000Y: brother to useful 7f winner Anniversarypresent and half-brother to 3 winners here and abroad, including (at around 1m) Quick Silver Boy (by Kalaglow): dam 1m winner: no worthwhile form: sold 1,800 gns Newmarket Autumn Sales and sent to Spain. *M. Bell*

NOEPROB (USA) 6 b.m. Majestic Shore (USA) – Heat Haze (USA) (Jungle 57 Savage (USA)) [1995 45: 6.9d 12.3d 8f⁶ 8m⁴ 8.2m⁴ 10m⁴ 8f* 1996 9.7s 7d² 8g 8g³ 8.3m* 7.1g³ 8.3g³ 8.3g 8.1m Jul 24] leggy, rather shallow-girthed mare: modest performer: won seller at Windsor in June: best form at around 1m: acts on firm and dead ground: often sweating: suitable mount for apprentice. *R. J. Hodges*

NOETIC 2 ch.f. (Apr 19) Nomadic Way (USA) 104 – Pretty Soon 75 (Tina's Pet – 121) [1996 a8g Dec 3] fifth foal: half-sister to 4-y-o NH Flat race winner (no form on flat) Petit Flora (by Lord Bud): dam, 7f winner, possibly became ungenuine: 20/1, slowly away and soundly beaten in seller at Southwell in December. *G. Holmes*

NO EXTRADITION 2 b.g. (Mar 13) Midyan (USA) 124 – Honey Pot 111 57 (Hotfoot 126) [1996 5m⁴ 5m⁶ 5f⁵ 5m 6g Sep 3] 24,000Y: compact gelding: half-brother to several winners here and abroad, including useful 1987 2-y-o Ship of Fools (by Windjammer), useful 7.1f (at 2 yrs) and 8.1f winner (stayed 10.5f) Girl From Ipanema (by Salse) and 3-y-o Norwegian 1m and 1¼m winner Swish (by Primo Dominie): dam sprinting 2-y-o: modest form: sold 8,500 gns Newmarket Autumn Sales: should be suited by further than 5f: sent to Norway. *Mrs J. R. Ramsden*

NO EXTRAS (IRE) 6 b.g. Efisio 120 – Parkland Rose (Sweet Candy (VEN)) – [1995 106: 7m 6m² 6f 6f 5m 6m⁶ 7.3m⁵ 6m* 6g⁴ 6g² 7d 5s³ 6d 1996 6f 6g 5.2m 6g 6m 7g Nov 2] leggy, quite good-topped gelding: better than ever and useful handicapper in 1995, but sustained leg injury during winter: long way below form at

6 yrs: effective at 5f to 7.6f: acts on good to firm and soft ground, ran poorly on fibresand: often hangs: has run creditably when sweating: held up. *G. L. Moore*

NO HIDING PLACE   3 ch.c. Nabeel Dancer (USA) 120 – Blushing Pink (USA)   56
(Blushing Groom (FR) 131) [1995 –p: 7m 1996 a6g[6] 6m 8d[3] 6m 6.1m Jul 6] only form when third in median auction event at Leicester in May, clear at halfway then tiring and edging left closing stages: sold 1,200 gns Newmarket July Sales: best effort at 1m, but probably a sprinter: acts on dead ground: blinkered second 3-y-o start: sent to Italy. *B. Hanbury*

NOIR ESPRIT   3 br.c. Prince Daniel (USA) – Danse d'Esprit 54 (Lidhame 109)   –
[1995 47+: 7.5m 7.5m[5] 8.1g 8g 7d[6] 1996 10g 12m 12.1m 12m 12g[5] a11g Nov 4] rather leggy, workmanlike colt: poor maiden: stays 1½m: visored/blinkered since fourth 3-y-o start. *J. M. Carr*

NOIRIE   2 br.c. (Feb 12) Warning 136 – Callipoli (USA) 81 (Green Dancer (USA)   67 p
132) [1996 7.1d[6] 7.9g[4] Oct 12] 23,000Y: first foal: dam 1m and 9f winner, half-sister to smart Irish 7f and 9f winner Punctilio: 66/1 and green on debut: beaten 11 lengths (recovering from slow start) when fourth of 11 to Hidden Meadow in York maiden following month: likely to improve further. *M. Brittain*

NOISETTE   2 ch.f. (Mar 21) Nashwan (USA) 135 – Nadma (USA) 82 (Northern   66 p
Dancer) [1996 8.1d Sep 28] smallish filly: second foal: closely related to useful 3-y-o 7f (at 2 yrs) and 1½m winner Nador (by Rainbow Quest): dam, 1¼m winner here and in Italy, closely related to top-class American filly Sabin and half-sister to Fatah Flare: 12/1, ran good deal better than distance beaten suggests when around 18 lengths seventh of 10 to Myrtlebank in maiden at Haydock, making smooth headway over 3f out then not given hard time when tiring approaching last: bred to stay middle distances: sure to improve. *J. H. M. Gosden*

NOMADIC DANCER (IRE)   4 b.f. Nabeel Dancer (USA) 120 – Loveshine   –
(USA) (Gallant Romeo (USA)) [1995 51d: a6g[4] a6g a6g[5] 5.1m[2] 7g 5.1m 6m 6f[5] 5.1h[6] 1996 a6g[5] 5s a6g a5g 6f 6g Jul 1] poor maiden handicapper nowadays: well below form most starts at 4 yrs: tried visored: stays 6f: acts on firm and dead ground and equitrack: sold 1,550 gns (Ascot July) and 2,000 gns (Newmarket December). *M. S. Saunders*

NOMBRE PREMIER   2 gr.c. (Mar 12) Kendor (FR) 122 – Sabiola (The Wonder   108
(FR) 129) [1996 5m* 5.5d[2] 5.5m[3] 5d[2] 5.5g[2] 8m* 8g[6] Oct 13] third foal: half-brother to French winners Oversman (1¼m, by Akarad) and Shootist (7f, including at 2 yrs, by Solicitor): dam French 9.5f to 11f winner: useful French colt: won minor event at Evry in April: second of 6 to Deep Finesse in Prix du Bois at Longchamp and to Ocean Ridge in Prix Robert Papin at Maisons-Laffitte fourth and fifth starts: improved again to win 7-runner Prix des Chenes at Longchamp in September by ¾ length from Majorien: respectable 8½ lengths sixth of 9 to Revoque in Grand Criterium there month later: stays 1m: yet to race on extremes of going. *A. de Royer-Dupre, France*

NOMINATOR LAD   2 b.c. (Feb 25) Nomination 125 – Ankara's Princess (USA)   72
81 (Ankara (USA) 106) [1996 6.1m 7d[2] 6m 8.2g[3] 8.2s Oct 31] sturdy colt: second live foal: dam, 2-y-o 5f winner, stayed 6f: fair maiden: stiff task in Redcar Two-Year-Old Trophy on third outing: stays 1m: possibly unsuited by soft ground. *B. A. McMahon*

NO MONKEY NUTS   3 ch.g. Clantime 101 – Portvally (Import 127) [1995 80:   84
5f* 5g[4] 5m* 6m* 6m 6m[4] 6.1d[2] 5m[6] 1996 6m[6] 6m[3] 6m[3] 6.1m[6] a6g 6s[2] 6f* 6m[2] 5m[2]   a63
6m a6g[4] 6m* 6m a6g a7g[4] a7g[3] a7g Nov 14] strong, close-coupled gelding: fairly useful performer on turf: won claimer at Redcar in July and minor event at Haydock (made all) in September: modest form (lightly raced) on the all-weather: stays 7f: acts on firm and dead ground and the all-weather: races prominently. *J. Berry*

NO MORE HASSLE (IRE)   3 ch.g. Magical Wonder (USA) 125 – Friendly   42
Ann (Artaius (USA) 129) [1995 –: 7.5m 9g 10m 7m 8f 1996 8f 11.1m 14.1m[2] 16.2f[5] 17.2m[3] 16.4v* a16g[4] Nov 18] big, leggy gelding: poor performer: best effort when winning claiming handicap at Folkestone in November: stays very well: acts on any going, clearly goes well in mud: headstrong, and usually held up: won juvenile hurdle in December. *Mrs M. Reveley*

NOMORE MR NICEGUY   2 b.c. (Feb 19) Rambo Dancer (CAN) 107 –   87
Lariston Gale 81 (Pas de Seul 133) [1996 5.1g 5m[2] 5.1m[4] 5g* 6.1m[4] 6m 5m[6] 7g 5d[5]

a7g³ a7g³ a7s* Dec 19] 2,500F, 4,800Y: sturdy, good-bodied colt: has scope: fourth foal: half-brother to 3-y-o Cyrillic (by Rock City), 6f winner at 2 yrs: dam 2-y-o 6f winner, should have been suited by 1½m+: won median auction maiden at Hamilton in July and nursery at Wolverhampton in December, showing fairly useful form in latter: stays 7f: acts on good to firm ground, best effort on fibresand. *E. J. Alston*

NO MORE PRESSURE (IRE) 2 ch.c. (Feb 27) Thatching 131 – High Pressure   86 p
105 (Kings Lake (USA) 133) [1996 a8.5g* Dec 14] first foal: dam 1m (including at 2 yrs) to 9f winner in Ireland who stayed 1½m, out of sister to high-class middle-distance filly Give Thanks: 33/1, made all in 12-runner maiden at Wolverhampton, holding on by head from Enlisted: should improve. *N. J. H. Walker*

NONONITO (FR) 5 b.h. Nikos 124 – Feuille d'Automne (FR) (Crystal   121
Palace (FR) 132) [1995 119: 10v⁵ 10s⁶ 15.5v* 15.5d² 12.5d⁵ 15g² 15.5g⁴ 20s³
12s 1996 15s⁴ 15.5g⁴ 15m 15.5d² 20m³ 15g² 15.5m⁴ 20d* 15.5d⁴ Oct 27]
     Whatever the French is for 'standing dish', Nononito is it in the top French staying races. He has contested fourteen pattern events there in the last two seasons. Victories have been hard to come by, it's true, but Nononito made the frame in ten of those races and there was one success in both 1995 and 1996. The first of those wins came with a big step up in trip (six of his previous seven starts had been at around a mile and a quarter) in the Prix de Barbeville at Saint-Cloud where he beat The Little Thief by a length and a half with Always Earnest the same distance back in third. It was seventeen months before Nononito was in the winner's enclosure again. Thirteen starts went by in the interim but Nononito had continued to show smart form in most of them, including when third to Always Earnest and Moonax in the 1995 Prix du Cadran and when filling the same position behind Classic Cliche and Double Trigger in the 1996 Gold Cup at Royal Ascot.
     On those performances, Nononito had two and a half lengths to make up on Always Earnest and Moonax, three lengths on Double Trigger, when the four of them joined six others in the line-up for the latest Prix du Cadran at Longchamp in October. Also there were Always Aloof and Kassani, two more who had already had Nononito behind them in 1996. Nononito was an 18.7/1-chance on the Pari-Mutuel and he turned the tables on the lot of them. It was an exemplary display, moving up smoothly to lead entering the straight and never headed thereafter, but Nononito did not actually have to improve much to win, given the disappointing showings of Double Trigger and Kassani and the disaffected one from Moonax. 'Never appear with children or animals,' actors are told. A horseracing version of that maxim would have to incorporate Moonax because his performances in finishing runner-up in successive runnings of the Cadran have both been flagrant scene-stealers; in the latest revival, he deflected attention from Nononito by swerving dramatically left approaching the final furlong. Without those theatricals, Moonax would surely have gone close, because Nononito ended up beating him by only a length.
     Nononito's sire Nikos twice finished runner-up in the seven-furlong Prix de la Foret and was only once tried beyond a mile in twenty starts, but followers of British racing should not be too surprised that he could sire a stayer because in 1996 he had the Grand National runner-up Encore Un Peu. He is

Prix du Cadran, Longchamp—Nononito holds on from the rallying Moonax and Always Earnest

also sire of the Arkle Trophy winner Nakir. Available at 20,000 francs in 1996, Nikos' best representative on the flat before Nononito was the 1992 Prix de l'Opera runner-up La Favorita. Nononito's dam Feuille d'Automne had four foals before him and two winners, one of a jumps race in France and the other a middle-distance stayer in France and Belgium. Two after Nononito have won over jumps as well, one of them also on the flat. There is rather more flat form further back in this pedigree as Feuille d'Automne herself won over a mile and a quarter in the Provinces and carried the colours of Baron Guy de Rothschild, being a daughter of his 1977 Prix du Jockey-Club winner Crystal Palace and a half-sister to his 1983 Prix du Jockey-Club fourth Jeu de Paille. Second dam Serbie was a useful winner (from nine furlongs to a mile and a half) and she is a half-sister to the 1987 Prix du Cadran fourth Sir Brink.

		Nonoalco	Nearctic
	Nikos	(b 1971)	Seximee
	(br 1981)	No No Nanette	Sovereign Path
Nononito (FR)		(ro 1973)	Nuclea
(b.h. 1991)		Crystal Palace	Caro
	Feuille d'Automne (FR)	(gr 1974)	Hermieres
	(b 1979)	Serbie	Breton
		(b 1972)	Sertanie

The good-topped Nononito is a really good walker and acts on good to firm and heavy going. He is at his best with a good test of stamina, the slowly-run Prix Royal-Oak that wrapped up his 1996 season, for instance, being no use to him. In addition to his Prix de Barbeville and Cadran, we must also mention Nononito's three-year-old wins in a minor event at Evry and a listed race at Saint-Cloud. Longevity and frequent appearances on the racecourse was not

Mr Patrick Sebagh's "Nononito"

the most likely scenario when Nononito fractured a cannon bone and was off the track for six months after the first of those successes, his debut. *J. Lesbordes, France*

NON VINTAGE (IRE) 5 ch.g. Shy Groom (USA) – Great Alexandra (Runnett 54 125) [1995 62: a12g⁵ a11g³ a11g 12.3f⁵ 11.6m⁴ 13.9m 18m² 13.9g 10.1g 10d³ 14.6m² 16.5m⁴ 1996 a12g 14.6g 12m 16.1m² 16s 13.9g 18.2m 18g Oct 21] lengthy, sparely-made gelding: fairly useful hurdler: modest at best on flat last 2 seasons: seems to stay 2¼m: probably acts on any ground on turf, below best on fibresand: often blinkered in 1994, rarely since: has an awkward head carriage and often hangs left. *M. C. Chapman*

NOPALEA 2 b.f. (Feb 16) Warrshan (USA) 117 – Nophe (USA) 95 (Super Con- 75 corde (USA) 128) [1996 6g⁴ 6m² 6m³ 6.1m⁴ 5m³ 5.2g³ Oct 30] lengthy, good-quartered filly: sixth foal: half-sister to 3-y-o 6f and 7f winner Naissant (by Shaadi) and a middle-distance winner in Sweden by Zalazl: dam, 5f winner at 2 yrs who didn't train on, out of half-sister to dam of Lianga: fair form: sold 7,000 gns Ascot November Sales: really needs strong gallop and forcing tactics when at 5f, and will stay 7f: joined T. J. Naughton. *C. E. Brittain*

NO PATTERN 4 ch.g. Rock City 120 – Sunfleet 59 (Red Sunset 120) [1995 80, 78 d a86: a8g* a8g² a8g² 9m⁴ 10.2m⁴ 8m⁵ 11.5m* 11.6m⁴ 10g³ 12g⁴ 1996 a10g⁶ a12g 12d³ 12m 12m 13.3m 12g³ 11.5m⁵ 10g a12g⁴ a10g⁴ Dec 30] leggy colt: fair handicapper: stays 1½m: acts on good to firm and dead ground and equitrack: seems effective visored or not: inconsistent of late. *G. L. Moore*

NORBRECK HOUSE 2 b.g. (Apr 30) Rambo Dancer (CAN) 107 – Close The 58 d Deal 51 (Nicholas Bill 125) [1996 7f⁴ 5f⁴ 7g² 7d⁵ 7m 6g Oct 21] 2,200Y: neat gelding: third foal: dam, ran only at 2 yrs, stayed 1¼m: deteriorated sharply after debut: sold 2,000 gns Doncaster November Sales and gelded: blinkered penultimate start, sweating on final one: stays 7f. *J. Berry*

NORDAN RAIDER 8 ch.m. Domynsky 110 – Vikris (Viking (USA)) [1995 61, – a81: a6g* 6g⁶ a6g³ 7g³ 7g a6g 1996 a6g a6g⁴ a7g a6g³ 6g Apr 10] strong, lengthy a75 mare: impresses in appearance: fair handicapper on the all-weather, only modest on turf nowadays: should stay 7f: best form on turf with plenty of give in the ground, goes well on fibresand: successful for claimer: held up: covered by Efisio. *M. J. Camacho*

NORDANSK 7 ch.g. Nordance (USA) – Free On Board 73 (Free State 125) [1995 55 –: 10d 1996 12m² 11.8m⁴ 12m* 16d 14.4g⁴ Sep 6] workmanlike gelding: modest handicapper on flat: first past post at Kempton in May (hanging right, demoted) and June: stays 14.4f: acts on any going: tends to hang: fair hurdler, and has shaped well in novice chases. *M. Madgwick*

NORDIC BREEZE (IRE) 4 b. or br.g. Nordico (USA) – Baby Clair 79 (Gulf 72 Pearl 117) [1995 80: 7g 7.1m 7g* 8f² 7m² 7.1g³ 8m² 8m² 8.1g 1996 10.3g 9.9g⁴ 8m 8.5m² 8.1d⁶ 9g 8.3f Aug 19] leggy gelding: fair handicapper: stays 1¼m: acts on firm ground: blinkered first 3 4-y-o starts, visored twice: has run creditably when sweating: won novice hurdle for M. Pipe in October. *A. Bailey*

NORDIC COLOURS (IRE) 5 b.m. Nordico (USA) – Gorm (Majority Blue 25 126) [1995 9.3g a7g* a7.5g⁶ 7f³ 6v* 7v* 7h⁶ a8g⁵ 7g 8v⁶ 1996 a7g a7g³ a6g 7g⁶ Jun 22] Belgian-trained mare: third foal: dam, fair maiden, placed at up to around 1½m at 3 yrs in Ireland: ran for J. Bolger at 2 yrs in Ireland: won 3 handicaps in 1995: tailed off in seller at Lingfield in January, only start in Britain: poor form back in Belgium: signs of retaining ability back in Belgium: may be best at up to 7f: seems to act on any going: blinkered since fourth 4-y-o start. *C. Dondi, Belgium*

NORDIC CREST (IRE) 2 b.c. (Jun 6) Danehill (USA) 126 – Feather Glen 76 (Glenstal (USA) 118) [1996 8d² 8.2g⁶ Oct 24] 22,000Y: fifth foal: dam ran twice in Ireland: 7 lengths second of 12 to Yorkshire in maiden at Salisbury, staying on well having been soon off bridle: never able to challenge, not knocked about when beaten, when sixth in similar event at Nottingham later in month: will stay beyond 1m: may do better. *P. W. Harris*

NORDIC FLASH 9 b.g. Nordico (USA) – Rosemore (Ashmore (FR) 125) [1995 – NR 1996 8.3m May 20] rated 72 at best, but very lightly raced: little sign of retaining ability in claimer: sold 600 gns Malvern October Sales. *T. J. Naughton*

NORDIC GIFT (DEN) 3 ch.g. Bold Arrangement 127 – Nordic Rose (DEN) –
(Drumhead 122) [1995 NR 1996 8g 7g 7m⁴ 8s 8.1m Jul 19] half-brother to 3 foals
reported in this country: dam behind all 3 starts at 2 yrs: no worthwhile form.
Mrs D. Thomson

NORDIC HERO (IRE) 3 b.g. Nordico (USA) – Postscript (Final Straw 127) 48
[1995 NR 1996 a12g³ 12d⁶ a12g⁴ a12g a11g a12g⁵ Dec 27] sturdy gelding: fourth
reported foal: dam, well beaten only outing, from family of Kris: best effort when
fourth in seller at Wolverhampton: well beaten afterwards. *A. P. Jarvis*

NORDICO MELODY (IRE) 2 b.g. (Apr 7) Nordico (USA) – Musical Essence –
65 (Song 132) [1996 7m Jun 18] IR 4,000Y: seventh reported foal: half-brother to
1993 Irish 2-y-o 6f winner Mulmus (by Mulhollande) and middle-distance winners
in France (by Busted) and Italy (by Teenoso): dam placed over 1m from 3 starts,
half-sister to smart French middle-distance colt El Famoso: 50/1, last of 11 in median
auction maiden at Thirsk. *Mrs L. Stubbs*

NORDIC SPREE (IRE) 4 b.g. Nordico (USA) – Moonsilk (Solinus 130) [1995 –
13g 13f⁴ 16g 1996 a12g Nov 7] IR 10,000Y: ex-Irish gelding: sixth foal: half-brother
to 4 winners, notably St Leger winner Moonax (stays 2½m, by Caerleon): dam
placed over 9f: no worthwhile form. *A. Moore*

NORDIC SUN (IRE) 8 gr.g. Nordico (USA) – Cielsoleil (USA) (Conquistador 70
Cielo (USA)) [1995 61: a12g⁶ 1996 a16g a12g² 17.1g Apr 23] ex-Irish gelding: fair
handicapper on flat nowadays: second in apprentice race at Wolverhampton in
February: set too strong a pace next time: stays 17f: yet to race on firm going, acts on
any other, including fibresand: fairly useful hurdler/chaser. *L. R. Lloyd-James*

NORDINEX (IRE) 4 b.g. Nordico (USA) – Debbie's Next (USA) 82 (Arctic 79
Tern (USA) 126) [1995 81: a8g* a8g³ 8m* 8m³ 8g* 8g⁵ 7m³ 8g³ 8m a8g a7g 1996 a75
a10g a8g* a8g 8m 8g⁵ 8m⁴ 8m 8.1d³ a9.4g 9m Oct 5] well-made gelding: good
walker: fair handicapper: won at Lingfield in February: sold to join D. Elsworth
10,000 gns Newmarket Autumn Sales: should stay beyond 1m: acts on good to firm
and dead ground and on equitrack (below form both outings on fibresand): blinkered
(worst effort) second 2-y-o start: has run well for claimer: usually races prominently.
R. W. Armstrong

NORDISK LEGEND 4 b.g. Colmore Row 111 – Nordic Rose (DEN) (Drum- –
head 122) [1995 –: 6g⁶ 1996 8g 10g 7.1g 5g 5d 5m Jul 19] tall, leggy, shallow-girthed
gelding: of no account. *Mrs D. Thomson*

NORD LYS (IRE) 5 b.g. Nordico (USA) – Beach Light 89 (Bustino 136) [1995 –
–: a12g a12g 7.1g 10m a12g 1996 a8.5g 10.5d⁶ 10.2m 9.9m 8f 7m Aug 6] small
gelding: no worthwhile form on flat: tried blinkered: won weak selling hurdle in
August. *B. J. Llewellyn*

NOR-DO-I 2 ch.g. (Jan 29) Primo Dominie 121 – True Nora 99 (Ahonoora 122) 79 +
[1996 6g 6d² a5g* Nov 29] 6,500Y: lengthy gelding: sixth foal: closely related to 3
winners by Dominion, including 1m winner Dominora, and half-brother to a winner
in Germany by Rousillon: dam 5f performer best at 2 yrs, is half-sister to smart (at up
to 1½m) Mac's Reef: 3 lengths second of 17, pulling hard on unfavoured side, to
Soviet State in maiden at Doncaster in November: didn't run to that form when ready
winner of maiden auction at Southwell later in month: stays 6f: blinkered last 2 starts.
J. M. P. Eustace

NORFOLK GLORY 4 ch.g. Weldnaas (USA) 112 – Caviar Blini 80 (What A –
Guest 119) [1995 –: a8g a7g 8f⁶ 8m 10f 8.5m⁵ 1996 a8g Nov 12] rather leggy gelding: no worthwhile form: tried in blinkers and tongue strap: sold to join D. Bassett
600 gns Doncaster November Sales: looks temperamental. *D. J. G. Murray Smith*

NORLING (IRE) 6 ch.g. Nashamaa 113 – Now Then (Sandford Lad 133) [1995 –
56: 6m 6m 6g 6m⁶ 6f³ 6f⁶ 6f* 6d 6g 6f 1996 6m 5.7m 6m⁶ 6m Aug 22] sturdy
gelding: modest handicapper at best: well beaten since last win: best form at 6f to 7f:
best on a sound surface (acts on firm ground). *K. O. Cunningham-Brown*

NORMAN CONQUEST (USA) 2 ch.c. (Apr 1) Miswaki (USA) 124 – Grand 71 p
Luxe (USA) (Sir Ivor 135) [1996 7m⁵ 7g 8d⁴ Oct 2] $155,000F: strong, heavy-bodied
colt: closely related to 2 winners in USA by Mr Prospector (one a minor stakes
winner, other placed in Grade 2 9f event) and half-brother to 4 winners abroad: dam
Canadian stakes winner out of Canadian Horse of the Year Fanfreluche: backward

and green first 2 starts: clearly best effort when around 10 lengths fourth of 12 to Yorkshire in maiden at Salisbury: will stay 1¼m: likely to do better. *I. A. Balding*

NORMANTON   2 gr.c. (Mar 13) Petong 126 – Mehtab 68§ (Touching Wood   –
(USA) 127) [1996 6m Aug 5] good-topped colt: third foal: dam, 1m winner who also won over hurdles, daughter of half-sister to Zeddaan: 66/1, burly and green, slowly away and always behind in maiden at Ripon. *Mrs P. Sly*

NORSONG   4 b.g. Northern State (USA) 91 – Winsong Melody (Music Maestro   56
119) [1995 55: 7.3m 6m 6.9g⁵ 7.6m* 8.2m⁴ 8g 8.1d 7s 1996 7f 9.7m⁴ 10.1m 9.7f⁵ 11.9f³ 12g² 14m* 14m 14.4g 14m Sep 19] rangy gelding: modest handicapper: narrowly won at Salisbury in August: poor efforts afterwards: stays 1¾m: acts on good to firm and soft ground. *R. Akehurst*

NORTH ARDAR   6 b.g. Ardar 87 – Langwaite (Seaepic (USA) 100) [1995 65:   65 d
10.3g 9.9m⁵ 9m⁵ 9.9m² 12m* 11.1m* 12m² 12.3f² 11.9m 12.1g⁴ a12g 1996 10.2g*
10m* 10f* 10m* 10m² 8.3m* 12f³ 8.9g⁶ a8g* 8m⁴ 11.1d⁴ a8.5g 10g a8g⁶ a8g⁶ a12s
Dec 19] close-coupled, angular gelding: fair performer: won sellers at Catterick and Pontefract, claimer at Redcar, and seller at Ripon prior to being claimed out of Mrs M. Reveley's stable £6,000 fifth start: won seller at Hamilton in August start before claimed out of J. J. O'Neill's stable £6,000 seventh start: cosily won amateurs handicap at Southwell in September: claimed out of D. Nicholls stable £7,000 eleventh start, below form afterwards: successful at 1m and stays 12.3f: acts on all-weather surfaces, best turf form on a sound surface: has run well when sweating: held up. *T. Wall*

NORTH BEAR   4 b.g. North Briton 67 – Sarah Bear (Mansingh (USA) 120)   61
[1995 a11g⁵ 11f³ 9f³ 12g² 12g 11d 10.5g 8s 1996 11.1m³ 12f² 12m³ 12f* 13.8g
Oct 19] sturdy ex-Belgian gelding: second reported foal: dam won in Belgium at 2, 4 and 5 yrs: modest performer: set steady pace when winning seller at Beverley in August, apparently best form: stays 1½m: acts on firm going: tends to hang left. *Mrs S. J. Smith*

NORTHERN ANGEL (IRE)   2 b.c. (Mar 28) Waajib 121 – Angel Divine   –
(Ahonoora 122) [1996 7g Oct 30] IR 55,000Y: third foal: half-brother to 3-y-o 6f to 1m winner Corniche Quest (by Salt Dome): dam unraced twin: 33/1, never a threat when beating one in 17-runner maiden at Yarmouth. *Mrs J. Cecil*

NORTHERN BALLET (IRE)   3 b.f. Sadler's Wells (USA) 132 – Miranisa   64
(Habitat 134) [1995 –p: 6f 1996 10.2g 8g May 21] strong, lengthy filly: good walker: modest form at best in maidens: should stay beyond 1m. *R. Hannon*

NORTHERN CELADON (IRE)   5 b.h. Classic Secret (USA) 91 – Exemplary   62
106 (Sovereign Lord 120) [1995 74: a9.4g³ a9.4g a8g⁴ a9.4g 8d* a8.5g⁶ a8g² a7g   a60
a8.5g⁵ a8.5g³ a8.5g² a8g³ a8.5g 8g* 1996 8d* a9.4g⁵ 8.3m 8.1d⁶ a8.5g⁶ a8.5g² a8.5g
a8g 8d⁶ 8.2g³ 8.1s Nov 7] angular horse: has a quick action: modest performer in 1996: game winner of Warwick claimer (for second year running) in April: inconsistent afterwards: sold 5,600 gns Doncaster November Sales: stays 1¼m: acts on fibresand, best with give in the ground (acts on heavy) on turf: visored twice, running creditably on first occasion: successful for apprentice: usually races prominently. *M. J. Heaton-Ellis*

NORTHERN CHIEF   6 b.g. Chief Singer 131 – Pacific Gull (USA) 67 (Storm   –
Bird (CAN) 134) [1995 32: a9.4g a8.5g 10.8d 8m 8.2m 8m 7.5g 8.1f⁴ 8.1d 1996 8f
a9.4g 14.9g a8g a10g⁶ a10g Dec 30] leggy gelding: poor mover: poor handicapper: well beaten in 1996: effective at 7f and 1m: acts on any going: inconsistent: *J. Cullinan*

NORTHERN CLAN   3 b.g. Clantime 101 – Northern Line 92 (Camden Town   39 d
125) [1995 57d: 5m⁴ 5g⁴ 5m⁵ 7m 6f⁵ 7.5m 6d 1996 6.1d 9.9m⁵ 12m⁶ 8g 6m⁴ 12.1m
a12g 11.6m 7f 6m a9.4g Nov 11] sturdy gelding: has a round action: poor maiden handicapper: left M. W. Easterby's stable after fifth 3-y-o start and no form afterwards: may prove best at up to 7f: tried blinkered/visored. *A. J. Chamberlain*

NORTHERN FALCON   3 gr.f. Polar Falcon (USA) 126 – Bishah (USA) 86   34
(Balzac (USA)) [1995 48: 5m 7.5m⁴ 7g 7g 7.9m 1996 a7g 10m 10m⁵ 12s⁴ 10f Jul
17] well-grown, leggy filly: poor maiden handicapper: should be suited by middle distances: blinkered last 3 starts. *M. W. Easterby*

NORTHERN FAN (IRE)   4 b.g. Lear Fan (USA) 130 – Easy Romance (USA)   –
(Northern Jove (CAN)) [1995 73: 6.9g⁵ 8.3g² 8.2d² 8m 1996 a8.5g* a8.5g* 7m   a90
10.4g 8s Nov 9] good-topped gelding: fairly useful performer on all-weather: won
handicaps (second one an amateurs race) at Wolverhampton in May: sold out of
A. Stewart's stable 19,500 gns Newmarket July Sales: in rear in handicaps and
claimer afterwards: stays 8.5f: acts on dead going, best form on fibresand: sometimes
bandaged. *N. Tinkler*

NORTHERN FLEET   3 b.c. Slip Anchor 136 – Kamkova (USA) 62 (Northern   87
Dancer) [1995 86p: 8m⁴ 1996 12m² 12m³ 11.6g⁴ 16.2g* 16.2m² 16.2d⁵ Oct 11] quite
good-topped colt: fairly useful performer: won maiden at Beverley in August:
improved form when neck second of 18 to Fujiyama Crest in quite valuable handicap
at Ascot (had hard race) in September, responding gamely: on toes, rather disappointing there 2 weeks later (first outing on a soft surface): very much a stayer:
acts on good to firm going. *G. Harwood*

NORTHERN GIRL (IRE)   2 b.f. (Apr 25) Distinctly North (USA) 115 –   57
Auction Maid (IRE) (Auction Ring (USA) 123) [1996 5g 7g³ 6m² 6d³ 5.1m³ 5f⁴   a?
5.3g⁴ a6g⁴ Oct 19] 4,000Y: lengthy filly: first foal: dam unraced half-sister to smart
sprinter Polykratis out of smart 5f performer Blue Portion: modest form: blinkered,
below par last 2 starts: sold 6,200 gns Newmarket Autumn Sales: really needs further
than 5f and stays 7f: sent to Czech Republic. *B. J. Meehan*

NORTHERN GREY   4 gr.g. Puissance 110 – Sharp Anne 74§ (Belfort (FR) 89)   52
[1995 52: 5d a5g⁶ a6g⁶ 5.9f³ 5f³ 5.9h² 5g² 5d 6g a6g⁴ a8g⁴ a7g⁴ 1996 a8.5g⁶ a7g   a48
a7g² a6g a6g⁵ 8s 8m² 7f⁶ 8m 8m 8m³ 8f a8g Dec 27] leggy, close-coupled gelding:
modest maiden handicapper: sold out of Jack Berry's stable 2,100 gns Doncaster
March Sales after fifth 4-y-o start: stays 1m: acts on hard ground and the all-
weather: effective blinkered/visored or not: usually races prominently: inconsistent.
Dr J. D. Scargill

NORTHERN JUDGE   3 ch.g. Highest Honor (FR) 124 – Nordica 99   65 d
(Northfields (USA)) [1995 72: 6s 7f⁴ 1996 7.1d 10m 7f² 6.9f 8m 10m⁶ 7m² a7g⁶
7d* 7m 8.2g 8m Oct 28] strong, sturdy gelding: modest performer: narrowly won
claimer at Newmarket in August: well beaten afterwards: sold 4,000 gns Newmarket
Autumn Sales, and 6,200 gns Doncaster November Sales: stays 7f: acts on firm and
dead ground, below form only start on all-weather: often blinkered: inconsistent.
B. Hanbury

NORTHERN LAW   4 gr.c. Law Society (USA) 130 – Pharland (FR) (Bellypha   –
130) [1995 82: 8g 12.3m 14g 14m⁴ 13.8m² 15.8m* 16f* 16.1f 15.9d⁶ 1996 10m
10f⁶ 16.1m⁶ Aug 9] tall, rather leggy colt: fairly useful form at 3 yrs for B. Hills: no
encouragement in Newmarket handicaps (heavily bandaged in front last start) in
1996: stays 2m: acts on firm and dead ground: poor form over hurdles. *John Berry*

NORTHERN MIRACLE (IRE)   3 b.f. Distinctly North (USA) 115 – Danny's   –
Miracle (Superlative 118) [1995 –: 7m 1996 a7g⁴ a6g⁶ Feb 6] no worthwhile form,
including in seller. *C. F. Wall*

NORTHERN MOTTO   3 b.g. Mtoto 134 – Soulful (FR) (Zino 127) [1995 57:   60
7.1g 7.1s 7f 1996 10.3d 10g⁴ 10g 11.1g 12m 10m⁴ 13.1s² 11.1m 16.1m 15.1s* a12g⁴
Nov 30] leggy gelding: modest handicapper: claimed £6,000 out of Mrs J. Ramsden's
stable sixth 3-y-o start: trained by W. Storey next 3: successful on first start for
current stable at Musselburgh in November, well on top inside last: needs a test of
stamina: best efforts with give in the ground (acts well on soft). *J. S. Goldie*

NORTHERN PASS (USA)   2 ch.f. (Feb 11) Crowning (USA) – North To Pine   64 ?
Pass (USA) (Holy War (USA)) [1996 7.6d³ 7g 7d Oct 2] leggy, unfurnished filly:
third foal: dam, 2-y-o sprint winner in USA: sire, 1m and 9f winner in allowance
company, closely related to champion US 2-y-o filly Outstandingly: third in
steadily-run maiden at Lingfield on debut: well held in minor event at Kempton and
maiden at Salisbury. *R. Akehurst*

NORTHERN PRINCESS   2 b.f. (Mar 7) Nomination 125 – Glenstal Princess   –
71 (Glenstal (USA) 118) [1996 6m⁵ 7m⁶ 6m⁴ Aug 10] angular filly: first reported
foal: dam 6f winner (including at 2 yrs): little worthwhile form in maidens: sold 500
gns Doncaster November Sales. *R. Hollinshead*

NORTHERN SAGA (IRE)   3 b.g. Distinctly North (USA) 115 – Saga's   43
Humour 61 (Bustino 136) [1995 40: 5m⁵ 5m 6m⁵ a6g⁵ 6d 7d 1996 8.3g 10.8m

8m³ 10g 8d 11.8f Oct 15] robust gelding: poor maiden: stays 1¼m: inconsistent. *C. J. Drewe*

NORTHERN SAL 2 ch.f. (Jan 30) Aragon 118 – Sister Sal 74 (Bairn (USA) 126) 59 [1996 5d* 5m⁴ 5.1g 5f 5f Sep 28] unfurnished filly: second reported foal: half-sister to 1994 2-y-o 5f seller winner Exposal (by Exodal): dam 2-y-o 6f winner who later stayed 1¼m: modest form: won median auction maiden at Hamilton in April: off course nearly 4 months after second start: bred to stay beyond 5f: twice slowly away. *J. Berry*

NORTHERN SINGER 6 ch.g. Norwick (USA) 125 – Be Lyrical 95 (Song 132) – [1995 NR 1996 a10g Jan 13] second foal: dam useful sprinter, best at 2 yrs: poor winning hurdler/novice chaser: well beaten in Lingfield claimer on flat debut. *R. J. Hodges*

NORTHERN SPARK 8 b.g. Trojan Fen 118 – Heavenly Spark (Habitat 134) 50 [1995 52: 5.9m 5.9f² 6.9m* 8m 7.5g³ 7f 7m 6g⁴ 7m* 8.1s⁴ a6g⁴ a7g² 1996 7s 8.1g³ 7.1g 5.9d 7d 6.9g 9.2g* 8m⁶ 10.1m⁵ 9.2g³ 11.1m⁴ 8.1s a8g Nov 18] robust gelding: has a round action: modest performer: won seller at Hamilton in June: best at around 7f to 9f: acts on firm and soft going and on fibresand: blinkered (below form) once at 4 yrs. *Miss L. A. Perratt*

NORTHERN SPRUCE (IRE) 4 ch.g. Astronef 116 – Perle's Fashion (Sallust – 134) [1995 –: 8.3m 8g 11.6g 10m 8.3g a12g 1996 8d 12f 10s⁶ a9.4g Dec 28] workmanlike gelding: seems of little account. *A. G. Foster*

NORTHERN SUN 2 b.c. (Apr 29) Charmer 123 – Princess Dancer (Alzao (USA) 82 117) [1996 7f* 6m⁵ 7f* 7g³ 7d⁶ 8m³ 7.9g 8g Oct 18] 8,800 2-y-o: small, close-coupled colt: second foal: dam ran once at 2 yrs: fairly useful performer: successful twice at Brighton, in median auction maiden on debut in July then when well backed in nursery following month: retained by trainer 11,000 gns Newmarket Autumn Sales: stays 1m: acts on firm ground, probably on dead. *T. G. Mills*

NORTHERN TOUCH 2 b.f. (May 2) Warrshan (USA) 117 – Shirley's Touch – (Touching Wood (USA) 127) [1996 8g Nov 2] 540Y: first foal: dam unraced: 40/1, never a threat when mid-division in 21-runner seller at Newmarket. *S. C. Williams*

NORTHERN TRIAL (USA) 8 b.g. Far North (CAN) 120 – Make An Attempt 46 (USA) (Nashua) [1995 –: a9.4g⁵ a12g⁶ 1996 a10g⁵ a12g² a13g³ a13g⁶ a12g*ᵈⁱˢ a12g² a53 a12g⁵ a10g² 11.5f³ 12s⁵ Jul 3] sturdy gelding: modest performer: best effort since 3 yrs when winning claimer at Lingfield in February, but subsequently disqualified for wearing undeclared visor to post: stays 1½m: acts on all-weather: seems effective blinkered/visored or not: apprentice ridden last 6 starts. *K. R. Burke*

NORTHERN TROVE (USA) 4 b.c. Northern Jove (CAN) – Herbivorous – (USA) (Northern Jove (CAN)) [1995 75d: 8m³ 8.1g⁵ 8f³ 7f² 7m² 7m³ 10f a8.5g 7m 10f a8g 1996 a10g Jan 4] robust, sturdy colt: carries condition: fair maiden at best: has become very disappointing: one to be wary of. *Ronald Thompson*

NORTHERN UNION (CAN) 5 b.g. Alwasmi (USA) 115 – Loving Cup (USA) 97 (Big Spruce (USA)) [1995 89p: 12m 10g* 12g 1996 a12g* a12g² Mar 6] tall, close-coupled gelding: has reportedly twice suffered leg fractures: useful handicapper: won at Wolverhampton in February: good second there 2 weeks later: subsequently joined C. Parker's stable: better at 1½m than shorter, and will be well suited by further: acts on heavy going and fibresand. *M. A. Jarvis*

NORTH ESK (USA) 7 ch.g. Apalachee (USA) 137 – Six Dozen (USA) (What A 47 Pleasure (USA)) [1995 55: 8m 7g 8.2m a8g a8g a7g a10g 1996 a8g³ Feb 24] good-topped gelding: modest handicapper: respectable third in seller at Lingfield only outing on flat at 7 yrs: effective at 7f to 1¼m: acts on firm ground, dead and equitrack, possibly not on very soft: often on edge: held up: has had tongue tied. *C. A. Dwyer*

NORTHGATE CHIEF 4 ch.g. Indian Forest (USA) 117 – Warthill Lady 60 – (Hittite Glory 125) [1995 NR 1996 7.1d 5g 7g 7.5m Jul 5] rated 44p only outing as 2-y-o: off course over 2 years, no form on return. *M. Brittain*

NORTH REEF (IRE) 5 b.h. Danehill (USA) 126 – Loreef (Main Reef 126) 79 [1995 82: a8g* a10g* 10f 1996 10m² 10.5m³ 10v 8.5m⁵ 8f⁶ 10g³ 12v a8.5g⁶ a9.4g² Dec 14] tall, lengthy, good-topped horse: fair handicapper: sold out of Sir Mark Prescott's stable 10,000 gns Newmarket Autumn Sales after sixth outing: ran well

Britannia Stakes (Handicap), Royal Ascot—
second and third are out of shot to the right as North Song leads his side home

last 2 starts: stays 1¼m well: acts on good to firm ground, dead and the all-weather, but is unsuited by heavy: mulish to post once at 5 yrs: usually races prominently. *J. Pearce*

NORTH SONG 3 b.c. Anshan 119 – Norfolk Serenade 83 (Blakeney 126) [1995 NR 1996 8d² 9.9m² 9s* 8f* 8g² 8m³ 7.9m² 9g³ 9m Oct 5] 25,000F: 16,000Y: strong, rangy colt: has plenty of scope: has a round action: sixth foal: half-brother to one-time fairly useful sprinter Samsolom (by Absalom) and 6f (at 2 yrs) and 2m winner Secret Serenade (by Classic Secret): dam 11.7f winner: useful performer: won maiden at Goodwood in May and Britannia Handicap at Royal Ascot in June: best form when placed in £25,300 rated stakes at York and £14,700 handicap at Goodwood, seventh and eighth starts: creditable thirteenth in the Cambridgeshire final outing: sold 80,000 gns Newmarket Autumn Sales: effective at 1m/9f: acts on firm and soft ground: early to post last 2 starts: strong-running type, probably best suited to racing prominently/forcing tactics: genuine: sent to Saudi Arabia. *J. H. M. Gosden* 99

NORTH TO GLORY 5 b.m. Northern State (USA) 91 – Mummy's Glory 82 (Mummy's Pet 125) [1995 NR 1996 8f 11.9f May 9] small, compact mare: looks of little account. *R. M. Flower* –

NO RUSH 2 b.g. (Mar 16) Puissance 110 – Practical 95 (Ballymore 123) [1996 5m⁵ 5g² a6g⁴ 5f³ 5g⁴ Jul 2] leggy, short-backed gelding: poor mover: half-brother to several winners, including 1m (at 2 yrs) and 10.1f winner Shrewd Partner (by Ahonoora): dam Irish 9f and 1¼m winner from useful family: sprint plater: went much too fast in blinkers final outing: sold 700 gns Doncaster September Sales: showed nothing on fibresand, little on firm ground. *J. Berry* 43 a?

NORWEGIAN BLUE (IRE) 3 b.c. Mac's Imp (USA) 116 – Opening Day (Day Is Done 115) [1995 84+: 6f⁴ 5m⁵ 6m⁵ 5g² 5g⁴ 6s* 1996 6g² 5g⁴ 6g⁶ 6m 6m 5m 6v 6.1s Oct 22] big, long-backed colt: unimpressive mover: fairly useful handicapper: in frame at Kempton and Sandown in April: failed to repeat that form, soundly beaten last 2 starts: visored fifth to seventh 3-y-o starts: has run well when sweating. *A. P. Jarvis* 91 d

NOSE NO BOUNDS (IRE) 3 b.g. Cyrano de Bergerac 120 – Damezao (Alzao (USA) 117) [1995 69, a75: 6m³ 6f³ a7g² a8.5g* 7.9m⁵ a8g⁶ 1996 10g² 12.3m⁶ 12m a8g 9.9f² 10m³ 10.1m² 11.1g⁴ a10g² a9.4g⁶ a9.4g⁵ 9.2m² 9m⁶ 10g Aug 21] tall, leggy gelding: fair handicapper: stayed 11f: acted on firm ground and equitrack: usually blinkered or visored: dead. *M. Johnston* 77 a68

NOSEY NATIVE 3 b.g. Cyrano de Bergerac 120 – Native Flair 87 (Be My Native (USA) 122) [1995 80: 6m⁵ 7m² 8.5s³ 8f* 1996 12d⁵ 12d 12m⁵ 10m 10.8f⁶ 12s³ 12m 12.1m⁶ 16.5m⁶ 15d² 14.1m⁴ 12m 10.5s* 10f 8.2g⁵ Oct 24] leggy gelding: fair handicapper: clearly best effort at 3 yrs when running away with 19-runner handicap at Haydock in October, great deal to do early in straight yet winning by 8 73 lengths: tenderly handled on firm ground next start, then caught the eye finishing really well last one: stays 15f: has won on firm ground, but revels in the mud: tried visored, no improvement. *J. Pearce*

NO SPEECHES (IRE)   5 b.g. Last Tycoon 131 – Wood Violet (USA) (Riverman (USA) 131) [1995 61, a67: 10m 10m 10.8g 11.4g⁵ 12f 8m³ 10m⁵ 14m⁶ 10.8g 12s 8f² a10g* a10g² a12g² a10g³ 1996 a10g a12g* a10g³ Mar 27] leggy gelding: modest handicapper: won at Lingfield in January: off course 2½ months before final start: stays 1½m: acts on firm ground, dead and equitrack. *S. Dow* –, a67

NOSTALGIC AIR (USA)   2 gr.f. (Jan 19) El Prado (IRE) 119 – Jane Scott (USA) (Copelan (USA)) [1996 5g 5d⁵ a6g² 6m* 6g⁴ 7f³ 6f³ 8m 6g 6g⁴ 6s Oct 26] 5,700Y: lengthy, good-topped filly: has scope: has a roundish action: first foal: dam won at up to 7f in USA: fair form: won maiden auction at Pontefract in June: none too consistent in nurseries last 5 outings: sold 10,000 gns Newmarket Autumn Sales: stays 7f: acts on firm ground: sent to Saudi Arabia. *E. Weymes* 66

NO SUBMISSION (USA)   10 b.h. Melyno 130 – Creeping Kate (USA) (Stop The Music (USA)) [1995 –, a73: a8g² a8g a8g² a7g* a7g² a8g* a7g* a8g* a9.4g* a8.5g² 8.3v⁵ 10g a8g³ a7g* 10m a11g⁵ a8.5g² a7g³ a8.5g* a8.5g⁵ a11g⁴ a8.5g 10g a8g⁴ a11g 1996 a8g³ a8.5g a8g² a11g* a8g⁵ a12g³ a12g a8g² a9.4g* a8.5g² 10.1s a10g 8.1g⁶ 8g² a8g⁶ a8g 11.1m 10m 10d a8g a8g a8g a11g* a10g a8g a12g a11g Dec 27] tall, leggy horse: poor mover: has 23 wins lifetime, 15 of them at Southwell: modest performer nowadays: formerly a front runner, but came from behind when winning sellers at Southwell and Wolverhampton early in year and when landing minor event at Southwell in November: stays 1½m: has form on any turf going, goes well on fibresand: effective in blinkers/visor or not. *D. W. Chapman* 40, a62

NO SYMPATHY   3 ch.f. Ron's Victory 129 – Ackcontent (USA) (Key To Content (USA)) [1995 49: 5g⁵ 6m⁵ 5f⁴ 5g⁴ a5g 6f² 5.3f* 5m a5g⁶ a6g⁴ 1996 a6g a7g³ 7f* 6g 7f⁵ 8m 6m Aug 28] modest performer: won claimer at Brighton in May: well below form in handicaps afterwards: sold 2,000 gns Doncaster September Sales: stays 7f: acts on firm ground and equitrack: visored (below form) third 2-y-o start. *G. L. Moore* 49

NOTAIRE (IRE)   3 b.g. Law Society (USA) 130 – La Toulzanie (FR) (Sanctus II 132) [1995 NR 1996 10m 11.7m⁴ 12m 10g Aug 24] 10,500F: smallish gelding: eighth foal: half-brother to 3 winners, including useful Tamourad (up to 1¼m, by Blushing Groom): dam won at around 1½m in France: no form: dead. *I. A. Balding* –

NOT A LOT   2 ch.g. (Apr 15) Emarati (USA) 74 – Spanish Chestnut (Philip of Spain 126) [1996 6m 5g² 6m 7g 5f⁴ 5m⁴ 7.5m 8m⁶ 8g Oct 21] 2,600Y: leggy, close-coupled gelding: half-brother to 1982 2-y-o 5f winner Loddon Music (by Music Boy) and 3 winners abroad: dam poor plater: modest performer: set lot to do then not knocked about after meeting trouble in running in nursery final outing: stays 1m: has tended to hang: races keenly. *M. W. Easterby* 50

NOTE OF CAUTION (USA)   3 b.f. Diesis 133 – Silver Dollar 106 (Shirley Heights 130) [1995 58p: a8g³ 1996 a7g⁴ a8g 11.9f 9.7d a9.4g Nov 11] odds on, fourth in maiden at Wolverhampton on reappearance, carrying head rather awkwardly: sold out of Lord Huntingdon's stable 7,000 gns Newmarket July Sales after next start: soundly beaten for new stable: stays 1m, not certain to stay 1½m: one to treat with caution. *N. A. Graham* 57 d

NOT FORGOTTEN (USA)   2 b.c. (May 21) St Jovite (USA) 135 – Past Remembered (USA) (Solford (USA) 127) [1996 8.5v⁵ 10v Nov 30] first owned foal: dam won at up to 1¼m: well beaten in minor event and maiden within 4 days at Rome in November. *P. A. Kelleway* –

NOTHING DOING (IRE)   7 b.g. Sarab 123 – Spoons (Orchestra 118) [1995 41: a12g⁴ a12g⁶ a13g a16g² a16g⁵ a16.2g³ a14.8g a12g** 12m⁶ a12g 11.6m* 12m 12g 12m² 1996 12g a12g⁶ 11.6m² 11.6g³ 12.1f⁵ 14d* 12d 12s² a13g³ a16g⁴ Dec 26] sturdy gelding: has a round action: poor handicapper: won 20-runner claiming event at Salisbury in October, making all: generally creditable efforts afterwards: stays 2m: probably acts on any going: blinkered (tailed off) second 6-y-o start: rather temperamental and not one to trust implicitly. *W. J. Musson* 43

NOT OUT LAD   2 b.c. (Apr 13) Governor General 116 – Sorcha (IRE) (Shernazar 131) [1996 6g Jun 12] 3,300 2-y-o: small, stocky colt: second foal: brother to 3-y-o

6f winner Castle Governor: dam tailed off in 2 NH Flat races: 66/1 and burly, tailed off in 14-runner maiden auction at Kempton, jockey looking down as if something amiss. *P. Butler*

NOT QUITE GREY 3 gr.g. Absalom 128 – Strawberry Song 87 (Final Straw – 127) [1995 70: 7.1m 7m⁶ 10m³ 8.1s⁵ 1996 10g 12g 12g Oct 18] workmanlike gelding: best 2-y-o effort when third in median auction maiden at Nottingham: disappointing in 1996, giving impression something amiss when visored final outing: suited by a test of stamina at 2 yrs: well below form on soft ground. *K. McAuliffe*

NOUFARI (FR) 5 b.g. Kahyasi 130 – Noufiyla 68 (Top Ville 129) [1995 80, a84: 82 a14.8g* a12g* a12g* a12g⁴ 18g² 14.9d 17.1m² 18.7m 16.5g³ 20m⁶ 16.1m⁴ 16.1g² 15.9m³ 1996 16.2g³ a14.8g³ 18.7g 16.5g³ 20f 16.1m⁵ 16.1g 16.1m⁴ 15.9g 16.5s a12g⁵ Dec 7] quite good-topped gelding: fairly useful staying handicapper: acts on good to firm ground and fibresand (never going well on soft): comes from behind: takes plenty of driving, and not an easy ride: consistent, but has yet to win on turf. *R. Hollinshead*

NOYAN 6 ch.g. Northern Baby (CAN) 127 – Istiska (FR) (Irish River (FR) 131) 55 [1995 53: 13g* 13g* 16.1g⁴ 1996 a14.8g⁴ 18s² 17.1g⁵ 21.6m Apr 29] big, rangy gelding: modest handicapper: best effort at 6 yrs when second of 20 at Doncaster in March: blinkered for first time in 3 seasons, raced too freely when tailed off final outing: subsequently joined R. Fahey, and won over fences in December: stays 2¼m: acts on firm and soft ground, below form on dead ground: also blinkered/visored at 3 yrs: sweating last 2 starts: normally held up. *D. Nicholls*

NUBILE 2 b.f. (Mar 24) Pursuit of Love 124 – Trojan Lady (USA) (Irish River 71 p (FR) 131) [1996 7g Nov 2] 7,400Y: second living foal: half-sister to 4-y-o Zain Dancer (by Nabeel Dancer), 7f winner in Czech Republic in 1995: dam, placed twice from 5 starts in France, is out of half-sister to Sun Princess and Saddlers' Hall: 33/1, slowly away and never a threat when around 7 lengths eleventh of 23 to Palisade in maiden at Newmarket: should do better, probably over further. *B. W. Hills*

NUKUD (USA) 4 b.g. Topsider (USA) – Summer Silence (USA) (Stop The Music – (USA)) [1995 –: 7.1m 1996 7s 8m⁶ 7m 10g Sep 3] small, robust gelding: trained reappearance by D. Nicholls: little form: tried blinkered. *G. R. Oldroyd*

NULLAHS PET 4 b. or br.f. Tina's Pet 121 – Nullah 71 (Riverman (USA) 131) – [1995 NR 1996 7g 6m Jun 4] small, lengthy filly: half-sister to fairly useful middle-distance colt Chief's Babu (by Chief Singer) and several bad animals: dam third over 1¼m on only start: well beaten in maidens. *A. Streeter*

NUNSHARPA 3 b.f. Sharpo 132 – Missed Blessing 115 (So Blessed 130) [1995 87 65p: 6m 1996 7m⁵ 7m⁴ 7m⁵ 7.1m² 7g³ 6m 7m⁵ 7.1d* 7g Oct 12] tall, lengthy filly: fairly useful handicapper: improved form when making all at Haydock in September: better than result suggests when midfield in 27-runner contest at York 2 weeks later: probably suited by 7.1f: best effort on a soft surface: flashes tail. *J. R. Fanshawe*

NUSHKA BABUSHKA 4 b.f. Nishapour (FR) 125 – Jessamine (Jalmood – (USA) 126) [1995 –: 10.1m⁶ 8.2m⁶ 11.8g 1996 a13g Jun 29] angular, unfurnished filly: no worthwhile form. *Bob Jones*

NUTCRACKER SUITE (IRE) 4 b.f. Dancing Dissident (USA) 119 – Carlyle – Suite (USA) (Icecapade (USA)) [1995 NR 1996 6m 7g⁴ 5.9f⁵ 6m 7g Sep 23] rated 50 over 5f at 2 yrs for R. Hollinshead: showed nothing in 1996. *J. L. Eyre*

NUTHATCH (IRE) 4 b.f. Thatching 131 – New Edition 72 (Great Nephew 126) 34 [1995 36: a6g³ a7g² a7g⁵ a7g a7g³ a8g a7g 6f⁴ 7.1m 6.9g 7d⁶ 1996 a7g³ a8g⁵ a8g Feb 24] poor maiden handicapper: should stay 1m: acts on all-weather surfaces and dead ground: visored (below form) first 2 starts on turf: usually ridden by apprentice. *M. D. I. Usher*

NUZU (IRE) 3 b.c. Belmez (USA) 131 – Nutria (GER) (Tratteggio 123) [1995 94 NR 1996 8m 10m⁵ 12m² 14.1f* 16.1g 12m³ 13.9g 17.2d* Sep 30] useful-looking colt: has a quick action: half-brother to numerous winners in Germany, including good 1988 2-y-o Nuas (by Aspros): dam won 2 races in Germany: fairly useful form: won maiden at Redcar (edging left and taking nearly whole trip to get in front) in June and handicap at Bath (blinkered, travelled much better than usual and improved form) in September: suited by good test of stamina: won on firm ground, clearly acts very well on a soft surface: sent to UAE. *B. W. Hills*

NWAAMIS (USA)   4 b.c. Dayjur (USA) 137 – Lady Cutlass (USA) (Cutlass   114
(USA)) [1995 117: 8m³ 8m⁵ 8m 1996 8d³ 8.1g⁴ 8d⁶ May 18] tall, rangy, good sort:
shows a powerful, rather round action: smart performer: fifth in 2000 Guineas second
start at 3 yrs, then reportedly injured pelvis and not seen out after May: 1¼ lengths
fourth (sweating and on toes, stayed on unable to challenge, edging right) to Gabr in
Sandown Mile in April, easily best effort in 1996: tailed off in Lockinge Stakes at
Newbury final outing: likely to prove best at up to 1m: acts on good to firm ground,
impressive winner on debut on first of 3 runs on a soft surface: held up at 4 yrs: stays
in training. *J. L. Dunlop*

O

OAKBROOK ROSE   2 b.f. (Apr 3) Forzando 122 – Oakbrook Tern (USA)   52
(Arctic Tern (USA) 126) [1996 6.1m⁴ 6g 6.9d Oct 21] 6,000Y: third foal: half-sister
to French 1m winner Highest Oak (by Highest Honor): dam French 2-y-o 1m winner:
modest form in auction maidens: should stay 1m. *B. Smart*

OAKBURY (IRE)   4 ch.g. Common Grounds 118 – Doon Belle (Ardoon 124)   40
[1995 71: 10.8m 8.3m 10f 10f² 10m² 11.8m³ 10.3m³ 1996 12g 12.3g 10g 14.1m
10.3m 8m 10m 10.5m⁶ 10d² 11.8f 10.1m Oct 23] angular, leggy gelding: has a round
action: poor performer nowadays: stays 1½m: yet to race on soft ground, probably
acts on any other: blinkered once (last of 18). *Miss L. C. Siddall*

OAKEN WOOD (IRE)   2 ch.c. (Feb 25) Lycius (USA) 124 – Little Red Rose   –
(Precocious 126) [1996 7.1m 8m a8g a6g⁶ Dec 26] IR 16,000Y: close-coupled,
deep-girthed colt: second living foal: dam unraced granddaughter of Ribblesdale
winner Relfo: well beaten in maidens and nursery, visored final start. *N. A. Callaghan*

OAKLEY FOLLY   3 b.f. Puissance 110 – Brown's Cay 71 (Formidable (USA)   –
125) [1995 NR 1996 a6g a8g Feb 12] related to several winners, including 4-y-o
Samana Cay (6.9f at 2 yrs, by Pharly) and Barbary Reef (1¼m, by Sarab): dam placed
over 1m at 2 yrs, half-sister to smart stayer Antler: well beaten in maiden and seller
on all-weather. *R. Hollinshead*

OARE BUDGIE   3 ch.f. Midyan (USA) 124 – Portvasco 90 (Sharpo 132) [1995   –
51: 5g⁵ 6.9g 6.1m⁵ 5m³ 6.1m 1996 8g 10m a11g⁶ 6m 6f 7g Aug 12] close-coupled
filly: sold cheaply after showing modest form for P. Walwyn at 2 yrs: soundly beaten
in 1996: stays 7f: tried visored. *Don Enrico Incisa*

OATEY   3 ch.f. Master Willie 129 – Oatfield 69 (Great Nephew 126) [1995 61p: 68
5m 6f 6m 1996 a7g⁵ 6d 8g 5m* 5.9f³ 5g³ 5m² 5g* 5m 6m Sep 21] workmanlike filly:
fluent mover: fair handicapper: improved dropped back in trip in summer, winning at
Doncaster and Thirsk: a sprinter: acts on firm ground: held up and comes with a late
run. *Mrs J. R. Ramsden*

OBELOS (USA)   5 ch.g. Diesis 133 – Fair Sousanne 75 (Busted 134) [1995 70:   77
10m* 10f 1996 10s³ 10m⁴ 10.3m 10.5d² 10.4g² a9.4g³ a12g⁶ a12g⁶ a9.4g² Dec 28]   a71
workmanlike gelding: has a round action: fair handicapper: sold out of Mrs J. Cecil's
stable 9,000 gns Newmarket Autumn Sales after fifth start in 1996: visored, nearly
back to best when second in claimer at Wolverhampton final start: effective at 9.4f,
and stays 1½m: acts on good to firm and soft ground and on fibresand: lacks a change
of pace: races prominently. *Miss S. J. Wilton*

OBERONS BOY (IRE)   3 b.g. Fairy King (USA) – Bold Starlet (Precocious   71 §
126) [1995 85: 5m⁶ 5m² 6m² 6m 6f³ 7f⁶ 6d³ 7d* 7s³ 8d⁴ 1996 8f 8.1g 7.5m⁴ 10m³
10m⁴ 11.6m⁶ a9.4g a7g⁶ Dec 11] useful-looking gelding: only fair form at best in
1996, tending to hang and look ungenuine when in frame in 3 claimers: sold out of
B. Meehan's stable 4,400 gns Newmarket Autumn Sales after penultimate start: stays
1¼m: seemed to act on any going at 2 yrs: often blinkered nowadays: untrustworthy.
S. Dow

OBERON'S DART (IRE)   3 b.g. Fairy King (USA) – Key Maneuver (USA)   77
(Key To Content (USA)) [1995 62+: 7d³ 7g a6g⁴ 1996 7.1d⁶ a7g* a7g² 6g⁵ a6g³ 7.1d²
7g Nov 2] workmanlike, rather angular gelding: fair handicapper: won maiden event
at Wolverhampton in June: best turf effort when second at Haydock, staying on well:
stays 7f: acts on fibresand, has raced only on an easy surface on turf. *P. J. Makin*

OBSESSIVE (USA)   3 b. or br.f. Seeking The Gold (USA) – Secret Obsession   102
(USA) 89 (Secretariat (USA)) [1995 95p: 6g² 6g* 7g² 1996 7m⁴ 10.4m³ 10m 8.1m
10.2f³ Sep 12] leggy, quite attractive filly: useful performer: best efforts when third
of 5 to Magnificent Style in Musidora Stakes at York and when third of 4 to Min
Alhawa in minor event at Chepstow final start: stays 10.4f: has raced only on a sound
surface: has run well when sweating. *M. R. Stoute*

OCCAM (IRE)   2 ch.c. (May 24) Sharp Victor (USA) 114 – Monterana 99 (Sallust   58 p
134) [1996 6g⁴ Oct 29] fifth foal: brother to fairly useful 3-y-o 1m and 1½m winner
Henry Island and half-brother to 1992 2-y-o 7f winner Ginger Flower (by Niniski):
dam, 6f and 7f winner at 2 yrs, out of half-sister to Italian Derby winner Ruysdael II:
10/1, 6 lengths fourth of 12 to Refuse To Lose in maiden at Leicester, slowly away,
held up going well then running on not knocked about: sure to improve, particularly
over further than 7f. *G. Wragg*

OCEAN BREEZE   2 ch.g. (May 21) Most Welcome 131 – Sea Power 88 (Welsh   –
Pageant 132) [1996 6m 9f⁴ Sep 28] 5,500 2-y-o: big, good-topped gelding: seventh
foal: dam, fair staying maiden, is half-sister to smart 1¼m filly Upper Deck: slowly
away and showed nothing in seller and 5-runner maiden. *J. S. Wainwright*

OCEAN GROVE (IRE)   3 b.f. Fairy King (USA) – Leyete Gulf (IRE) (Slip   79
Anchor 136) [1996 84: 6g⁶ 7m⁴ 6.1d* 6d⁴ 1996 7m 5d³ 7m⁵ 7g 8d⁵ 7d 7.1d 6.1s Oct
22] sparely-made filly: fairly useful handicapper: ran poorly last 3 starts: stays 1m:
acts on good to firm and dead ground (once out of form): sold 22,000 gns
Newmarket December Sales. *P. W. Chapple-Hyam*

OCEAN LIGHT   2 ch.f. (Feb 24) Anshan 119 – Waveguide 76 (Double Form   –
130) [1996 7.1d 6m Oct 28] 3,300F, 10,500Y: rather leggy, close-coupled filly:
seventh foal: half-sister to 3-y-o Surf City (by Rock City), 1991 2-y-o 5f winner
Waveband (by Thatching) and 4-y-o 1m winner Oneoftheoldones (by Deploy): dam,
placed at 5f at 2 yrs, from family of Nicholas Bill and Time Charter: never a factor in
maidens at Haydock and Leicester (slowly away, soon pushed along) month later.
A. Bailey

OCEAN PARK   5 b.g. Dominion 123 – Chiming Melody 71 (Cure The Blues   78
(USA)) [1995 75: a8g*ᵈⁱˢ 8.5s 8.2m³ 10f³ a9.4g² 1996 a8.5g* a9.4g⁵ a10g* a10g*   a91
10d* 8m 10m 12g* 10.4g Oct 9] good-bodied gelding: good mover: fairly useful
handicapper on the all-weather: won at Wolverhampton (maiden) in January and
Lingfield in February and March: not so good on turf, but won at Leicester in April
and Folkestone (minor event) in September: stays 1½m: acts on firm and dead
ground (shaped well on soft), goes well on all-weather: blinkered (raced too freely)
once as 3-y-o, bandaged front final outing: suited by waiting tactics. *Lady Herries*

OCEAN RIDGE (USA)   2 b.f. (Mar 18) Storm Bird (CAN) 134 – Polar Bird   108
111 (Thatching 131) [1996 6m* 6g² 5.5g* 6g⁴ 6m³ Oct 1]
        The first of four French pattern races won by two-year-olds from the
Chapple-Hyam stable during the year, the Prix Robert Papin, fell to a British-
trained horse for the third year running. It was also the second victory in
the Maisons-Laffitte event for Ocean Ridge's connections during that time

Prix Robert Papin, Maisons-Laffitte—Ocean Ridge gives her stable a second win in the race in three years

following that of General Monash in 1994. Ocean Ridge made virtually all to land the odds in a field of six and the form looks sound. Runner-up Nombre Premier, the only colt in the field, finished two and a half lengths behind Ocean Ridge and later took the Prix des Chenes; the third Sheer Reason finished a close second to Deadly Dudley in the Criterium des Deux Ans at the end of the season, and the fourth Shigeru Summit won the Prix du Calvados next time.

Ocean Ridge ran consistently in defeat in good company before and after the Papin. A win over twelve other newcomers at Newbury in June earned her a run in the Cherry Hinton Stakes at Newmarket, where after taking a good hold behind the leaders she kept on strongly to finish clear of the third horse Well Warned but was left behind by Dazzle in the last quarter-mile and beaten five lengths. After the Papin, Ocean Ridge was sent to Leopardstown for the Heinz 57 Phoenix Stakes where she finished fourth, after disputing the lead for a long way, just over two lengths behind the winner Mantovani and narrowly losing out in a tight finish for the places. Back against her own sex in the Cheveley Park Stakes at Newmarket in October, Ocean Ridge set a muddling pace until being outrun up the hill, finishing a creditable third, a length and the same behind Pas de Reponse and Moonlight Paradise.

Storm Bird has had relatively few representatives in Britain in recent seasons; two of his best, Stonehatch and Balanchine, also raced for Robert Sangster as two-year-olds. As Balanchine was, so Ocean Ridge has been sold to Goldolphin. Ocean Ridge's dam Polar Bird was a smart sprinter, winning the St Hugh's Stakes at Newbury and the Group 3 Debutante Stakes at Phoenix Park at two, a handicap at Newmarket at three and another handicap in the

Mr R. E. Sangster's "Ocean Ridge"

United States at four. Ocean Ridge is her second foal, following Alpine Twist (by Seattle Dancer) who won a five-furlong maiden at Warwick in April. Polar Bird is a half-sister to two winners by Law Society, the fair six-furlong and one-mile winner Polar Storm and the fairly useful middle-distance stayer Torch Vert. Their dam, Arctic Winter, was a winner as a two-year-old in Germany and is one of eleven winners out of Tabola, herself successful at up to seven furlongs.

Ocean Ridge (USA) (b.f. Mar 18, 1994)	Storm Bird (CAN) (b 1978)	Northern Dancer (b 1961)	Nearctic Natalma
		South Ocean (b 1967)	New Providence Shining Sun
	Polar Bird (b 1987)	Thatching (b 1975)	Thatch Abella
		Arctic Winter (b 1982)	Briartic Tabola

The medium-sized, quite attractive Ocean Ridge, a sharp-actioned filly, is bred to be a sprinter and races like one; she is inclined to be rather headstrong and has made all or raced prominently in all her races to date. She has raced only on good or good to firm ground. *P. W. Chapple-Hyam*

OCEAN STREAM (IRE)   3 b.g. Waajib 121 – Kilboy Concorde (African Sky   –
124) [1995 74: 6m⁴ 6g⁴ 6.1d⁵ 6g² 6m⁴ 6m² a7g⁵ 1996 a6g⁴ 7s 8g Apr 8] compact, quite attractive colt: has a quick action: fair maiden at 2 yrs: disappointing in 1996: stays 6f: acts on good to firm and dead ground, modest form at best on the all-weather: tried blinkered. *J. L. Eyre*

OCHOS RIOS (IRE)   5 br.g. Horage 124 – Morgiana (Godswalk (USA) 130)   64
[1995 65, a61: 7.5m⁶ 8.3g 7.5g² 7.5m 7g³ 8.5d 7d⁵ 7g⁵ a7g³ a8g 1996 7.5d 7.5m⁶ 7m²   a–
7g² 7g 6m 8m³ 7m³ 7m⁴ 8m 9g 7g* 7m 7g 7g⁶ Oct 25] small gelding: good mover: modest handicapper: back to form to win 27-runner race at York in September, quickening on over 2f out and holding on despite drifting markedly right: stays 1m: acts on good to firm and heavy going and fibresand: blinkered (below form) 4 times at 3 yrs: bandaged off-hind at 5 yrs: inconsistent. *B. S. Rothwell*

OCKER (IRE)   2 br.c. (Mar 20) Astronef 116 – Violet Somers (Will Somers 114§)   77 +
[1996 5m 5.9g 6g² 6m 6d² Aug 24] IR 8,000Y: leggy colt: eighth foal: closely related to French 9f to 10.5f winner Best Dancer (by What A Guest): dam unraced sister to high-class sprinters Balidar and Balliol: second in maiden at Catterick and nursery (pipped having led inside final 1f) at Newmarket: ridden much more prominently when below best in between: stays 6f: best form on an easy surface. *M. H. Tompkins*

OCTAVIA HILL   3 ch.f. Prince Sabo 123 – Clara Barton (Youth (USA) 135)   60
[1995 NR 1996 6m 6m 7g⁶ 7m Oct 4] useful-looking filly: fourth foal: half-sister to fairly useful 4-y-o 7f handicapper Primo Lara (by Primo Dominie) and fair 5-y-o middle-distance winner Newport Knight (by Bairn): dam unraced: modest form in maidens: stiffish task, well held in handicap final start. *P. W. Harris*

ODDFELLOWS GIRL   2 b.f. (Feb 23) Nomination 125 – Kaleidophone 73   –
(Kalaglow 132) [1996 6m⁶ a7g⁴ a6g⁵ 7g⁴ 7d 7.9g 6.1m⁶ 7m 6g Oct 21] 1,800Y: angular filly: fourth foal: half-sister to a winner in Norway: dam 1m winner: poor form, fourth in 2 sellers: sold 3,000 gns Doncaster October Sales: requires further than 6f. *N. Bycroft*

OFFICE HOURS   4 b.g. Danehill (USA) 126 – Charmina (FR) (Nonoalco (USA)   68 d
131) [1995 75: 8g⁴ 7m 7f³ 7m³ 10m⁴ 8m² 10.4g 1996 a10g a7g⁶ a6g a9.4g 6.9f³ 7f   a–
7g⁵ 7g 10f 7f² 6m 8f⁴ 8m 8m Sep 25] workmanlike gelding: modest maiden now-adays: well below form last 2 starts, and sold (C. Cyzer to W. G. M. Turner) 4,200 gns Newmarket Autumn Sales: stays 1m: raced only on a sound surface on turf, seems unsuited by the all-weather: blinkered (failed to stay 1¼m) ninth 4-y-o start: inconsistent. *C. A. Cyzer*

OFF THE AIR (IRE)   5 b.m. Taufan (USA) 119 – Milly Daydream (Hard Fought   –
125) [1995 51d: a11g² a8.5g* a11g⁴ a9.4g⁴ a8.5g* a9.4g⁵ a9.4g a8g 10d 8.1d 1996 a8.5g⁶ a12g⁶ a8g⁵ a11g Feb 10] leggy mare: modest performer: won 2 sellers at Wolverhampton early at 4 yrs for I. Campbell: well beaten since: effective at 8.5f,

and stays 11f: acts on fibresand, good to firm ground and heavy: usually blinkered/
visored: covered by Contract Law. *B. J. Llewellyn*

OFF THE RAILS 2 b.f. (Feb 18) Saddlers' Hall (IRE) 126 – Sliprail (USA) 86 – p
(Our Native (USA)) [1996 7f⁶ Sep 5] second foal: half-sister to 3-y-o Lunar Gris
(by Absalom): dam 10.2f winner: 33/1, 12 lengths sixth of 15 to Sarayir in maiden at
Salisbury, keeping on never a threat: should do better over middle distances.
H. Candy

OGGI 5 gr.g. Efisio 120 – Dolly Bevan 53 (Another Realm 118) [1995 71: 6g 5m 78
6g² 5.7f³ 6g* 6m a6g⁴ 6g⁵ 6s 6g 1996 6.1g 6m 6d 6m 6f* 6m³ 7m 6m* Oct 28]
angular gelding: has reportedly had muscle problems: fairly useful handicapper: well
held at 5 yrs until winning 22-runner race at Haydock (first outing for 3 months)
in September, flashing tail under pressure: showed further improvement to justify
favouritism in 21-runner race at Leicester on final outing, travelling well up with
pace: stays 6f: acts on firm and dead ground and on fibresand: effective blinkered or
not (didn't wear them last 4 starts): used to have tongue tied down. *P. J. Makin*

OHIO ROYALE 2 ch.g. (Apr 10) Shalford (IRE) 124§ – Jupiter's Message –
(Jupiter Island 126) [1996 6m 5f a8.5g Sep 21] workmanlike gelding: second foal:
half-brother to 3-y-o 1¾m winner Bellator (by Simply Great): dam unraced: soundly
beaten in maidens and claimer. *P. C. Haslam*

OHNONOTAGAIN 4 b.f. Kind of Hush 118 – Dear Glenda 66 (Gold Song 112) –
[1995 NR 1996 a7g 5m 6.9d⁴ 7g a7g 8f 8g⁵ Aug 12] small filly: in frame in 5f and 6f
sellers (rated 45) at 2 yrs: no sign of retaining ability: tried blinkered. *B. W. Murray*

OH SO HANDY 8 b.g. Nearly A Hand 115 – Geordie Lass 58 (Bleep-Bleep 134) –
[1995 38: 16d³ 17.2f³ 18.2m⁵ 1996 a16g⁵ a16g a16g⁶ Feb 13] leggy gelding: fair
handicap chaser at up to 25f, but only poor staying maiden handicapper on flat: tried
blinkered (no improvement). *R. Curtis*

OH SUSANNAH 5 b.m. Rousillon (USA) 133 – Sue Grundy 104 (Grundy 137) 48 d
[1995 a7g* a8g a6g⁴ a6g² a7g³ a6g⁴ 7m* 1996 a7g⁴ 7m² a8g⁴ 7f 7g⁴ 7m 8.2d 6.1m 8f
7g Oct 25] rangy, unfurnished mare: has a quick action: has done much of her racing
in Dubai, winning 2 handicaps in last 2 seasons: sold out of K. McLaughlin's stable
4,000 gns Newmarket July (1996) Sales after fifth outing: well beaten in varied
company on return to Britain: best form at up to 7f: acts on good to firm ground and
sand: tried visored final start and in Dubai: has looked less than enthusiastic under
pressure. *J. A. Harris*

OH WHATAKNIGHT 3 b.f. Primo Dominie 121 – Carolside 108 (Music –
Maestro 119) [1995 85: 5f⁴ 5g⁴ 5g* 5s⁶ 1996 6m 8.3d 7.1d 6m Oct 7] workmanlike
filly: won minor event at Ayr as 2-y-o when with R. Whitaker: showed nothing in
1996: should stay 6f: seems unsuited by very soft ground: one to treat with caution.
J. W. Hills

OKAY BABY (IRE) 4 b.f. Treasure Kay 114 – Miss Tuko (Good Times (ITY)) –
[1995 51: a7g 12d 10g 8.3g³ 7m² 8m 8g² 8f² 8.1f* 7m⁴ 7g 8f a7g 1996 8m 8m Oct
23] sparely-made filly: modest form at best at 3 yrs (trained all bar final start by
M. Tompkins): has gone to the pack. *J. M. Bradley*

OK PAL 2 b.c. (Mar 25) Interrex (CAN) – Rockery 91 (Track Spare 125) [1996 6g –
Oct 29] brother to 6f and 7f winner Ok Bertie: dam 1m and 1¼m winner: 8/1, slowly
away and soon behind in 10-runner median auction maiden at Leicester. *J. Akehurst*

OLD COLONY 2 b.f. (Feb 24) Pleasant Colony (USA) – Annoconnor (USA) –
(Nureyev (USA) 131) [1996 8.1d⁵ 8.2g a8g⁴ Nov 14] big, leggy filly: has scope:
fourth foal: dam, Grade 1 9f winner from 4 to 6 yrs, half-sister to Grand Prix de Paris
and Melbourne Cup winner At Talaq: signs of ability in maidens: may do better.
P. F. I. Cole

OLD GOLD N TAN 3 ch.g. Ballacashtal (CAN) – Raleigh Gazelle (Absalom –
128) [1995 NR 1996 a8g⁶ 6s a10g 6f 5m⁵ 7f 7.6m Aug 4] first foal: dam modest
staying chaser: little sign of ability: tried blinkered. *Jamie Poulton*

OLD HOOK (IRE) 5 b. or br.h. Digamist (USA) 110 – Day Dress (Ashmore 56
(FR) 125) [1995 79: a6g a7.5g* 9g³ 9g 6g 6.5f³ 6f² 6f² 7f a7g* a7g⁴ a8g* 1996 a7g
a8g a8g* 8g⁵ 8g⁵ 7f³ 8f⁴ 7d Aug 10] neat Belgian-trained horse: fair handicapper:
twice well beaten at Lingfield in February: won at Sterrebeek in April: acts
on good to firm going and equitrack: unreliable. *Paul Smith, Belgium*

OLD HUSH WING (IRE) 3 b.g. Tirol 127 – Saneena 80 (Kris 135) [1995 NR 52
1996 5m 5m 8.3s³ 8g a8.5g⁶ a12g³ Oct 5] 12,000Y: good-topped gelding: fourth
foal: half-brother to a 13f winner in Germany by High Estate: dam 12.2f winner
out of close relative of Green Dancer: modest maiden handicapper: stays 1½m.
P. C. Haslam

OLD IRISH 3 gr.g. Old Vic 136 – Dunoof 92 (Shirley Heights 130) [1995 –p: 85
8.2m 1996 10g⁶ 10g⁴ 12m* 13.3s² 14g² 16.1g⁵ Jul 10] rather leggy gelding: good
mover: fairly useful handicapper: won at Salisbury in May, nearly throwing race
away: good efforts all starts afterwards: sold (L. Cumani to O. O'Neill) 16,000 gns
Newmarket Autumn Sales and gelded: stays at least 2m: one paced, and may prove
best with forcing tactics: worth a try in blinkers or visor: ducked both ways when
shown whip third 3-y-o start, and is no easy ride. *L. M. Cumani*

OLD PROVENCE 6 b.h. Rainbow Quest (USA) 134 – Orange Hill 75 (High Top 79
131) [1995 55: a12g* 12g⁵ a12g* a9.4g 1996 a12g* a14.8g* 18s 12m a14.8g⁴ a16g
Jun 6] big, good-topped horse: had a high knee action: fair form when winning 2
claimers at Wolverhampton early in 1996: broke leg at Southwell in June: stayed
14.8f: acted on fibresand: wore bandages: dead. *R. Harris*

OLD ROMA (IRE) 3 b.f. Old Vic 136 – Romantic Past (USA) 82 (Miswaki 76 d
(USA) 124) [1995 NR 1996 6g² 8.1d 8m⁶ 10g Jul 1] workmanlike filly: third
foal: half-sister to a middle-distance winner in Japan by Darshaan and 1995 3-y-o
French 9f winner Orlando Express (by Unfuwain): dam 1m winner: bought out of
L. Cumani's stable 3,000 gns Newmarket Autumn (1995) Sales: head second in
maiden at Pontefract in May, finishing strongly having been detached: showed little
in 2 similar events and handicap afterwards: should be suited by further than 6f.
John Berry

OLD ROUVEL (USA) 5 b.g. Riverman (USA) 131 – Marie de Russy (FR) 104
(Sassafras (FR) 135) [1995 107: a12g* 16.2m² 16.2m⁴ 16.4m² 20m⁵ 15.9m⁵ 18g³
16g⁴ 16.5m* 16m³ 1996 16.2g² 16.2m⁵ 16g⁴ 22.2f³ 16g⁶ 18m⁵ 16m⁵ 16g⁵ Nov 1] tall
gelding: shows knee action: useful stayer: kept good company as usual in 1996, and
ran well most starts, best effort when 8 lengths fifth to Celeric in Jockey Club Cup at
Newmarket penultimate outing: suited by a thorough test of stamina: acts on firm
ground: visored third to fifth 5-y-o starts: sometimes hangs right under pressure.
D. J. G. Murray Smith

OLD SCHOOL HOUSE 3 ch.c. Polar Falcon (USA) 126 – Farewell Letter 84 p
(USA) (Arts And Letters) [1995 –: 6m 8g 10m 8f 1996 12f⁴ 11.1s³ a14.8g* a12g²
11.5f² a16.2g² 16.5m* 17.2m* 14m⁴ a16g* Aug 17] quite attractive colt: much
improved handicapper since stepped up in trip: successful at Wolverhampton in June
and at Doncaster (amateurs) and Bath (evens, easily) in August: easily best effort to
win 5-finisher minor event at Lingfield on last outing, just getting better of good
battle with runner-up: suited by test of stamina: acts on firm going and both
all-weather surfaces: probably open to further progress. *T. J. Naughton*

OLEANA (IRE) 3 b.f. Alzao (USA) 117 – Buraida 64 (Balidar 133) [1995 86p: 88 +
7g* 7.3d⁵ 1996 7m² 6.5f³ 6.5f² 9f* Nov 28] angular, unfurnished filly: left P. Cole
after second to Strazo in minor event at Salisbury on reappearance, keeping on
despite carrying head rather high: won allowance event at Hollywood Park in
November: stays 9f: tends to take keen hold. *N. Drysdale, USA*

OLIFANTSFONTEIN 8 b.g. Thatching 131 – Taplow (Tap On Wood 130) –
[1995 46: a6g 5m 5m⁵ 6f⁶ 5m 1996 6f 6f 6.9f Aug 5] lengthy, good-bodied gelding:
very much on the downgrade nowadays: retained by trainer 500 gns Doncaster
September Sales: acts at 5f: probably acts on any going: occasionally blinkered/
visored. *D. Nicholls*

OLIVER (IRE) 2 b.c. (Mar 11) Priolo (USA) 127 – Daniella Drive (USA) –
(Shelter Half (USA)) [1996 7m 7d a8g Nov 14] IR 43,000Y: third reported foal:
half-brother to useful 4-y-o 7f to 8.5f winner Blomberg (by Indian Ridge): dam
won numerous minor races in USA: slowly away and always behind in 3 maidens.
R. W. Armstrong

OLIVER ROCK 3 b.g. Shareef Dancer (USA) 135 – Short Rations (Lorenzaccio –
130) [1995 79: 7m 8m 8g 1996 12d 11.6m 14m⁶ Jul 13] compact gelding: well beaten
after debut: sold 2,400 gns Newmarket September Sales: bred to be suited by middle
distances: sent to Sweden. *Major D. N. Chappell*

OLIVO (IRE) 2 ch.g. (Mar 1) Priolo (USA) 127 – Honourable Sheba (USA) 79
(Roberto (USA) 131) [1996 6f³ 6m³ 7d⁶ Oct 28] 54,000Y: strong, close-coupled
gelding: good walker: third foal: half-brother to 1995 2-y-o 1m winner Crystal Falls
(by Alzao): dam (unraced) from family of Lear Fan: fair form when third in maidens
at Newbury and Newmarket in the summer: off course nearly 3 months, well held in
similar event at Lingfield: best form at 6f on top-of-the-ground: virtually bolted to
post second start and looks headstrong: sold to join C. Horgan 22,000 gns Doncaster
November Sales, and gelded. *P. F. I. Cole*

OLYMPIC SPIRIT 2 b.f. (May 18) Puissance 110 – Stripanoora (Ahonoora 122) 94
[1996 5f³ 5f* 5f³ 6.1m* 5m⁵ 5.2m² 6.1d² 6m⁴ 5v⁶ Oct 6] 10,000Y: leggy, quite
attractive filly: fourth foal: half-sister to 3-y-o miler She's My Love and smart
middle-distance 4-y-o Naked Welcome (both by Most Welcome and also successful
at 2 yrs): dam (maiden) stayed 1m: won maiden at Warwick in June and minor event
at Chester in July: pipped on post by Head Over Heels in listed race at Newbury sixth
start: effective at 5f and 6f: best form on top-of-the-ground (well beaten on heavy):
races prominently: wears bandages behind: very slowly away seventh start: sent to
USA. *J. Berry*

OMAHA CITY (IRE) 2 b.g. (May 11) Night Shift (USA) – Be Discreet (Junius 99
(USA) 124) [1996 5.1m* 6f² 5m⁴ 6d² 6g² 6m⁶ 5d⁴ 6g³ Oct 26] 13,000F, IR 3,500Y:
strong, useful-looking gelding: half-brother to smart 3-y-o 5f (at 2 yrs) to 1m winner
Gothenberg (by Polish Patriot), 4-y-o 7f winner Don't Get Caught (by Danehill) and
1¼m winner Sarabah (by Ela-Mana-Mou): dam won at up to 7f in France: won
maiden at Chester in June on debut: ran in listed/pattern races all starts afterwards, in
frame in all but one, in Cornwallis Stakes at Ascot and listed race at Doncaster (made
running when third of 7 to Elegant Warning) last 2 outings: stays 6f: acts on firm and
dead ground: edgy sort. *B. Gubby*

OMARA (USA) 3 b.f. Storm Cat (USA) – Alamosa (Alydar (USA)) [1995 77+: 87
6m² 5g⁵ 1996 6m³ 5m⁵ 7f³ 8f⁴ 10.1g³ 9m 10.1m² 10s⁵ 9.7g* 10.1m* 10.3d Nov 8]
smallish filly: good mover: fairly useful form: placed numerous times before winning maiden at Folkestone and handicap at Yarmouth in the autumn: stiff task, tailed
off final start: stayed 1¼m: acted on firm ground: travelled strongly, but tended to
find little and needed to be held up as long as possible: retired. *H. R. A. Cecil*

OMIDJOY (IRE) 6 ch.m. Nishapour (FR) 125 – Fancy Finish 67 (Final Straw –
127) [1995 NR 1996 a16g Feb 15] smallish, sparely-made mare: seems of little
account nowadays: has joined Nigel Wrighton. *J. R. Jenkins*

ONCE MORE FOR LUCK (IRE) 5 b.g. Petorius 117 – Mrs Lucky (Royal 70
Match 117) [1995 67: 6.9m⁴ 8g² 8g 10f⁴ 10f⁴ 10.3f² 10m² 10.5m² 12g² 12g³
11.9g 10.4m³ 12f* 10f 1996 10f³ 12g⁴ 12g⁶ 12m² 11m* Oct 29] sturdy gelding:
fair handicapper: won claimer at Redcar in October: stays 1½m: acts on firm and
dead ground: fair hurdler: held up: sometimes finds little (hung right and faltered
after looking sure to win fourth start at 5 yrs) and isn't one to trust implicitly.
Mrs M. Reveley

ONE DREAM 3 b.g. Weldnaas (USA) 112 – Superb Lady 106 (Marcus Superbus –
100) [1995 –: 7m 1996 6g 6m⁴ a7g⁴ Dec 30] close-coupled gelding: no worthwhile
form. *B. Smart*

ONE FOR BAILEYS 2 b.c. (Feb 17) Unfuwain (USA) 131 – Three Stars 93 66 p
(Star Appeal 133) [1996 8.1s⁴ Nov 7] 40,000F, 45,000Y: sixth live foal: brother to
Irish Oaks winner Bolas, closely related to French 1½m winner Star of Dance (by
Sadler's Wells) and half-brother to 3-y-o 10.3f winner Three Hills (by Danehill): dam
1½m winner from staying family: 12/1 and green, 6½ lengths fourth of 7 to Wellaki
in maiden at Musselburgh, held up in steadily-run race, not able to get on terms:
stoutly bred: will improve. *M. Johnston*

ONE FOR JEANNIE 4 b.f. Clantime 101 – Miss Henry 78 (Blue Cashmere 129) 55
[1995 68: a5g² a7g² a6g* a6g a5g* a6g⁴ 5.1m⁶ 5m 5g 6.1g² 6f⁶ 1996 a5g⁴ 5.1g 5.1g
Oct 9] fair performer: off course 15 months, best effort at 4 yrs when fourth in claimer
at Southwell, making most: effective at 5f and 6f: acts on all-weather, has raced only
on a sound surface on turf: usually visored/blinkered (not last time), has won without:
bandaged in 1996. *A. Bailey*

ONEFORTHEDITCH (USA) 3 gr.f. With Approval (CAN) – Wee Dram 69
(USA) (Nostrum (USA)) [1995 79p: 6g² 1996 6m⁵ 7g³ 7m⁶ 9m⁴ 8f⁵ Oct 14] leggy

filly: fair maiden handicapper: sold (J. Gosden to J. Fanshawe) 14,500 gns New-market Autumn Sales: stays 9f: raced only on a sound surface. *J. H. M. Gosden*

ONEFOURSEVEN 3 b.g. Jumbo Hirt (USA) 90§ – Dominance (Dominion 123) 59 [1995 –: 7g 7m a7g 1996 a8g a11g⁶ a11g⁵ a9.4g³ 10d⁶ 17.2m⁴ 15.8g* 16.1m⁵ 18g² a14g* a16g* Nov 18] leggy, unfurnished gelding: shows knee action: trained until after fifth start at 3 yrs by S. R. Bowring: improved in handicaps when upped in distance, winning at Catterick in September and twice at Southwell in November: a stayer: acts on fibresand, promises to go well with testing conditions: usually blinkered for former trainer. *J. L. Eyre*

ONE IN THE EYE 3 br.c. Arrasas (USA) 100 – Mingalles 65 (Prince de Galles 62 d 125) [1995 NR 1996 7m³ 7m 10m 10m⁶ a10g⁵ 8d⁴ 9g a10g Nov 14] leggy colt: eighth reported living foal: dam 1½m winner: third in maiden at Lingfield in May: failed by a long way to repeat that form, virtually refusing to race when blinkered fourth start: stays 1m: acts on good to firm and dead ground: inconsistent. *Jamie Poulton*

ONEKNIGHT WITH YOU 2 gr.f. (Feb 12) Rudimentary (USA) 118 – 73 Inshirah (USA) 90 (Caro 133) [1996 5m⁴ 6m 5.7f³ 5m⁵ 5.1m⁴ 6.5m³ 7d 7.3s Oct 26] 11,000F: workmanlike filly: sixth foal: half-sister to 3-y-o Ironheart (by Lycius), French middle-distance winner Inchbracken (by Mtoto) and a winner in Belgium: dam 2-y-o 5f and 7f winner out of Grand Criterium winner Femme Elite: fair maiden: improved form when close third of 22 in nursery at Doncaster: well beaten on soft surface afterwards, blinkered first occasion: should stay 7f: sometimes tended to hang. *M. J. Fetherston-Godley*

ONE LADY 2 gr.f. (Apr 27) Mazilier (USA) 107 – Ashbocking 55 (Dragonara 50 p Palace (USA) 115) [1996 a6g 6.1m⁵ 5m Sep 18] 1,500F, 2,000Y, 5,000 2-y-o: leggy, angular filly: sister to a winner in Sweden and half-sister to a winner in Italy by Taufan: dam 1¼m seller winner: poor form in maidens and seller: ran well long way final start, and is almost certainly capable of better. *J. L. Eyre*

ONE LIFE TO LIVE (IRE) 3 gr.c. Classic Music (USA) – Fine Flame (Le 50 Prince 98) [1995 –, a54?: a7g⁵ 6m 6g a7g a7g 1996 10g⁴ 8g⁶ 10m Jun 11] close-coupled colt: poor maiden handicapper: had run of race when fourth in falsely-run contest at Ripon on reappearance: stays 1¼m: has joined S. Kettlewell. *A. Harrison*

ONEMORETIME 2 b.f. (Mar 12) Timeless Times (USA) 99 – Dear Glenda 66 – (Gold Song 112) [1996 6g 5m 5g⁴ Oct 19] small, leggy filly: fourth living foal: sister to 3-y-o 5f (at 2 yrs) and 6f winner Tymeera and half-sister to 5f winner Jade City (by Belfort), later successful over 1m in Belgium: dam sprinter: well beaten in maidens and minor event. *B. W. Murray*

ONE OFF THE RAIL (USA) 6 b.h. Rampage (USA) – Catty Queen (USA) – (Tom Cat) [1995 44, a77: a9.4g a12g a12g² a12g a12g³ a12g* 10g 11.9m* 12m⁴ 12f⁴ a76 14m 12m⁴ 11.9g a10g⁵ a13g 1996 a6g² a12g* a12g³ a12g* 10f Aug 18] good-bodied horse: has a round action: fair handicapper on all-weather: won 2 races at Lingfield in February, second one an apprentice event: only poor on turf: off course 6 months, well beaten on return: stays 1½m: unproven on extremes of ground on turf: goes well on equitrack, below form 3 times on fibresand at Wolverhampton: races prominently. *A. Moore*

ONEOFTHEOLDONES 4 b.g. Deploy 131 – Waveguide 76 (Double Form – 130) [1995 67: 10m⁵ a8g* 11.9m 8.1g 1996 10d 8m a8g 12.3s Aug 31] good-topped gelding: has a round action: easily best effort at 3 yrs (trained by S. Norton) when making all in median auction maiden at Southwell: no show in handicaps in 1996, gelded and off course 4 months after second outing: should stay at least 1¼m: possibly unsuited by top-of-the-ground (best form, at 2 yrs, on a soft surface), acts on fibresand: wore net muzzle last start. *J. Norton*

ONE POUND 3 b.g. Shareef Dancer (USA) 135 – Beloved Visitor (USA) 83 72 (Miswaki (USA) 124) [1995 59: 7m 7m 7.1d⁶ 1996 10.2g 12.5f* 12.3m² 12.3m 16.4m⁵ 12d Aug 25] good-topped gelding: fair performer: won 5-runner apprentices rating related maiden at Warwick in June: poor efforts last 3 starts: sold 7,000 gns Newmarket Autumn Sales: should stay further than 12.5f: acts on firm ground: sent to Italy. *B. W. Hills*

ONE SHOT (IRE) 3 b.g. Fayruz 116 – La Gravotte (FR) (Habitat 134) [1995 55: 39 6.1m 6m⁵ 6m³ 6g 1996 8.2g 7m⁵ 8g⁶ 7m⁵ 7.1g Jun 13] lengthy gelding: modest maiden at 2 yrs, disappointing in 1996: has raced only on good/good to firm ground: blinkered last 3 starts: headstrong. *W. R. Muir*

ONE SO WONDERFUL 2 b.f. (May 4) Nashwan (USA) 135 – Someone Special 105 (Habitat 134) [1996 7g* Sep 6] quite good-topped filly: has scope: half-sister to 3 winners, including smart 7f (at 2 yrs) to 10.4f winner Alnasr Alwasheek (by Sadler's Wells) and smart 2-y-o 6f and 7f winner (best form at 1¼m) Relatively Special (by Alzao): dam 7f winner who stayed 1m, half-sister to top-class Milligram out of 1000 Guineas winner One In A Million: 5/1 but not fully wound up, won 11-runner minor event at Kempton by 3½ lengths from Alphabet, leading approaching last and quickly drawing away under hands and heels: will stay 1¼m: looks a good prospect. *L. M. Cumani* — 93 p

ONE VOICE (USA) 6 ch.h. Affirmed (USA) – Elk's Ellie (USA) (Vaguely Noble 140) [1995 –: 14m^3 1996 14m Jul 24] angular horse: has a round action: fairly useful handicapper, best short of 2m at 4 yrs: no promise since. *K. Bishop* — –

ONLY (USA) 3 ch.c. Rahy (USA) 115 – Stay With Bruce (USA) (Grey Dawn II 132) [1995 48p: a8g^6 1996 7s 8d 8m^5 8m 8m^6 8m 8.1m^6 8m^5 6m Aug 22] lengthy, good-bodied colt: poor maiden on balance of form: sold 800 gns Newmarket Autumn Sales: not sure to stay beyond 1m: sent to Spain. *R. Hannon* — 46

ON THE GREEN 3 br.f. Pharly (FR) 130 – Regal Wonder 74 (Stupendous) [1995 NR 1996 10g^6 Oct 9] half-sister to useful middle-distance performer Staten Island (by Town And Country) and 1985 2-y-o 7f winner Something Casual (by Good Times): dam didn't race until 4 yrs, when 1½m and 15.5f winner: 50/1, well-beaten sixth in maiden at Nottingham, though travelled well long way: may do better. *A. Hide* — –

ON THE HOME RUN 3 b.f. Governor General 116 – In The Papers 87 (Aragon 118) [1995 –: 6g 1996 8f 7d 10.1f^6 7g 6m 7m Aug 3] no worthwhile form: tried blinkered. *J. R. Jenkins* — –

ON THE NOSE 3 ch.f. Sharpo 132 – Wollow Maid 73 (Wollow 132) [1995 NR 1996 7g Apr 8] good-topped filly: half-sister to fair 7f to 9f handicapper Reverand Thickness (by Prince Sabo) and winners at up to 1m by Superlative and Lochnager: dam, 1¼m winner, refused to race once: 66/1, burly and very green, trailed through-out in maiden at Kempton. *S. C. Williams* — –

ON THE PISTE 3 gr.f. Shirley Heights 130 – Snowing (USA) (Icecapade (USA)) [1995 NR 1996 12.1g^5 Jun 13] second foal: dam, won 4 races in USA, half-sister to very useful sprinter Two Punch: shaped like a stayer when fifth of 7 to Alessandra in maiden at Chepstow: sold 19,000 gns Newmarket December Sales. *R. Charlton* — 68

ON THE WILDSIDE 3 ch.f. Charmer 123 – No Control 82 (Bustino 136) [1995 –: 7m 8m 1996 8.3m 8.1f^2 10f Jul 25] leggy, unfurnished filly: easily best effort when second in seller at Chepstow: very keen and ran wide on turn when well beaten in handicap at Brighton final outing: should stay beyond 1m. *M. R. Channon* — 57

OOD DANCER (USA) 3 b.c. Night Shift (USA) – Homemade Cookie (USA) (Our Native (USA)) [1995 NR 1996 6.9m 7m 8f^3 10g^2 7.5m* 8m^3 7f* 7m 7.1f Sep 7] $150,000Y: well-made colt: sixth foal: half-brother to 3 minor winners in USA: dam, stakes winner at up to 7f at 2 yrs in USA (her only season to race), half-sister to Royal Lodge winner Digression: fairly useful performer: won maiden at Beverley (sweating) in June and handicap at Lingfield in July: shaped much better than position suggests when down the field in handicap at Haydock (short to post) last outing, staying on from well back when squeezed over 1f out and eased: effective at 7f and 1m (found nothing when tried over 1¼m): has raced only on a sound surface: sent to Dubai. *L. M. Cumani* — 89

OOPS PETTIE 3 ch.f. Machiavellian (USA) 123 – Miquette (FR) (Fabulous Dancer (USA) 124) [1995 NR 1996 10d^5 12g 10.2f* 10m^5 10m^5 10.3m* 10m^2 Oct 4] tall, lengthy filly: has a quick action: half-sister to 1993 2-y-o 5f and 6f winner Floating Trial (by Dowsing), later wayward and inconsistent, and a middle-distance winner in France by Shernazar: dam French 1½m and 13.5f winner: fairly useful performer: won maiden at Chepstow in July and minor event at Doncaster in September: good effort in handicap at Newmarket final start: will probably prove best at around 1¼m: acts well on top-of-the-ground: sweating fourth and fifth starts, slightly on final one. *Mrs J. Cecil* — 89

OOZLEM (IRE) 7 b.g. Burslem 123 – Fingers (Lord Gayle (USA) 124) [1995 43
44, a33: a8g³ 8m 8m 8g⁵ 9m⁶ 8.2m 9m 8f* 8g 8g⁶ 9d 8f a8g⁴ 1996 a10g⁵ a8g a8g* a47
a8g a8g⁵ 8m a10g 8.3m² 8.1m a10g a10g⁴ Dec 30] workmanlike gelding: poor
handicapper: won apprentice race at Lingfield in February: left J. Poulton after ninth
outing: effective at 1m and 1¼m: acts on equitrack and any turf going: blinkered/
visored nowadays: sometimes slowly away, and usually comes from behind: suited
by strongly-run race. *L. Montague Hall*

OPALETTE 3 b.f. Sharrood (USA) 124 – Height of Folly 81 (Shirley Heights 74
130) [1995 61p: 7g⁶ 1996 10m⁴ 10g² 10.5s Oct 5] unfurnished, workmanlike filly:
absent around 10 months after debut: fair form when head second in maiden at
Goodwood, headed near finish: well beaten at Haydock (held up) 3 weeks later: stays
1¼m. *Lady Herries*

OPAL JEWEL 3 b.f. Sadler's Wells (USA) 132 – Optimistic Lass (USA) 117 (Mr 82 p
Prospector (USA)) [1995 NR 1996 10.1m² 10d* Aug 10] ninth foal: half-sister to
1995 3-y-o 7f winner Joyful (by Green Desert) and high-class sprinter/miler Golden
Opinion (by Slew O'Gold): dam won Musidora and Nassau Stakes: 5/2, won maiden
at Ayr in August by 2 lengths from Triple Leap, held up and running on to lead over
1f out: will stay further than 1¼m: looked sure to improve further. *M. R. Stoute*

OPAQUE 4 b.g. Shirley Heights 130 – Opale 117 (Busted 134) [1995 –: 12m 14g⁶ 73
1996 12m 14.1m² 14g* 16g⁶ 14.1m Jun 19] tall, lengthy gelding: has a quick
action: fair form when winning handicap at Newmarket in May by short head: well
beaten subsequently: sold (L. Cumani to W. Storey) 18,500 gns Newmarket Autumn
Sales: should be suited by thorough test of stamina: raced only on a sound surface.
L. M. Cumani

OPEN AFFAIR 3 ch.f. Bold Arrangement 127 – Key To Enchantment (Key To 55
Content (USA)) [1995 NR 1996 8m³ 10m⁴ 8m³ 10g 10.4g 8m Sep 25] tall,
sparely-made filly: fourth foal: dam, twice raced at 2 yrs, out of half-sister to Park
Hill winner I Want To Be: modest form in claimers first 3 starts: well beaten in
handicaps afterwards: sold 1,650 gns Doncaster November Sales: should stay further
than 1¼m. *A. P. Jarvis*

OPEN CREDIT 2 ch.f. (Feb 11) Magical Wonder (USA) 125 – Forest Treasure 96 +
(USA) (Green Forest (USA) 134) [1996 5f² 6g* 6g² Oct 26] deep-girthed filly: third
foal: half-sister to a 2-y-o winner in USA at up to 9f by Siberian Express: dam
unraced daughter of very smart French filly at up to 1m Mysterious Etoile, herself
half-sister to Yorkshire Oaks winner Magnificent Star: easily won 4-runner maiden
at Newmarket in May: 5/2, 5 lengths second of 7 to Elegant Warning in listed race at
Doncaster over 5 months later, leading briefly 2f out: will stay 7f+: may be capable
of better. *H. R. A. Cecil*

OPENING CHORUS 3 ch.g. Music Boy 124 – One Sharper (Dublin Taxi) [1995 54
66: 5.1m⁵ 5f⁶ 5g* 5g 6m 1996 5d 6d 6m⁴ 5.9f⁶ 6g⁵ 6.9d⁴ Oct 21] compact gelding:
modest performer: left Mrs M. Reveley's stable after second 3-y-o start: off course
3½ months before final outing: sold 2,000 gns Newmarket Autumn Sales: stays 7f:
probably acts on firm and dead ground: sent to Italy. *D. Nicholls*

OPENING RANGE 5 b.m. Nordico (USA) – Waveguide 76 (Double Form 130) –
[1995 NR 1996 a8g a8g a8g 10m 8.2m 7f Jun 4] workmanlike mare: poor maiden at
best: tried blinkered, no improvement. *N. E. Berry*

OPERA BUFF (IRE) 5 br.g. Rousillon (USA) 133 – Obertura (USA) 100 74
(Roberto (USA) 131) [1995 65+, a85+: a12g⁶ a12g³ 12g 14.1g 14.1f³ 13.1f⁶ 14d* a98
14.1m* 15.1s⁴ a12g* a12g* a13g* 1996 a12g² a12g³ 12m³ 18.7g 12s⁴ 13.3s³ 14m
a12g⁵ a10s a12g³ Dec 7] big, good-topped gelding: useful handicapper on
all-weather, best efforts at Lingfield and Wolverhampton in January: only fair on turf:
effective at 1½m to 15f: acts on good to firm and soft ground, and very well on the
the all-weather: visored/blinkered fifth (reluctant) and sixth 4-y-o starts: tends to
hang left. *Miss Gay Kelleway*

OPTIONS OPEN 4 b.c. Then Again 126 – Zahiah 90 (So Blessed 130) [1995 106
102: 7m⁵ 7m⁵ 1996 9g* 8.2m⁴ 7m⁵ 8.1g 8m 8.1m³ 6g² 6m* 6g* Sep 4] strong, sturdy
colt: carries plenty of condition and usually takes the eye: useful performer: easily
won claimer at Pontefract in May on first run for nearly 11 months: best efforts at 4
yrs in competitive handicaps at York last 2 starts, winning £14,800 contest in August
and £17,000 rated stakes (idled, by ½ length from Cyrano's Lad) in September: sold

Lawrence Batley Rated Stakes (Handicap), York—
Options Open (right) again beats Cyrano's Lad (centre)
and Double Splendour over course and distance

96,000 gns Newmarket Autumn Sales, reportedly to join A. Hyldmo in Norway: effective at 6f, and stays 1m: acts on firm ground, yet to race on a soft surface. *Mrs J. R. Ramsden*

OPULENT 5 b.g. Robellino (USA) 127 – One Half Silver (CAN) (Plugged Nickle (USA)) [1995 8g 8g⁴ 1996 8d 10.1m³ 10m Oct 1] sturdy ex-Irish gelding: half-brother to 7f winner Silver Standard (by Jupiter Island): fairly useful form on flat: won 7f minor event at Tipperary at 3 yrs for C. Collins: 33/1 and ridden by 7-lb claimer, eye-catching third in handicap at Yarmouth on first run in Britain, finishing strongly: never going well in apprentice race at Newmarket 13 days later: stays 1¼m: acts on good to firm ground and heavy: modest 2m hurdler. *C. A. Dwyer*   77

ORANGE AND BLUE 3 br.f. Prince Sabo 123 – Mazarine Blue 65 (Bellypha 130) [1995 50: 5.1g* 5m⁵ 6g⁵ 6m 6m a7g⁴ a6g a6g 1996 8.1g a7g⁵ a6g³ 5f⁴ a5g 5m⁶ 5g 5g 6m Oct 7] leggy filly: poor mover: has only one eye, and wears an eyecover: poor handicapper: stays 7f: acts on fibresand, best turf form (at 2 yrs) on an easy surface. *Miss J. F. Craze*   39

ORANGE ORDER (IRE) 3 ch.g. Generous (IRE) 139 – Fleur d'Oranger 110 (Northfields (USA)) [1995 NR 1996 9f⁵ 10m* Aug 7] half-brother to French 7f winner Chagrin d'Amour (by Last Tycoon) and French 2-y-o 9f winners Amour Toujours (by Law Society) and Wedding Ring (by Never So Bold), latter 1m (listed race) to 1¼m winner at 3 yrs: dam 6f (at 2 yrs) and 1¼m winner who stayed 1½m: justified favouritism in claimer at Kempton in August: subsequently claimed to join J. White's stable £12,000: will stay further than 1¼m. *G. Harwood*   75

ORANGE PLACE (IRE) 5 ch.g. Nordance (USA) – Little Red Hut (Habitat 134) [1995 –: 7m⁶ 6d a7g 1996 a10g⁶ a7g⁴ 7s³ 7f⁶ 7f⁵ 8.3m³ 7s* 7m 7.1m Jun 14] lengthy gelding: has reportedly been hobdayed: fair handicapper nowadays: well ridden by T. Quinn when winning at Goodwood in May, dictating pace: stays 1m: used to act on any going, best recent efforts with give: often a front runner. *T. J. Naughton*   78

ORCHARD GOLD 5 b.g. Glint of Gold 128 – On The Top (High Top 131) [1995 –: 6.9f 7g 1996 10m 8m* 7.1m² 8.2m² 8m³ a12g Oct 5] workmanlike gelding: modest handicapper: won seller at Warwick in July: tailed off final start, first for 2 months: finds 7f a minimum, and has form over 12.1f: acts on good to firm and soft ground: takes strong hold, and is held up. *J. Pearce*   55

ORCHESTRAL DESIGNS (IRE) 5 b.g. Fappiano (USA) – Elegance In Design 105 (Habitat 134) [1995 NR 1996 a9.4g 13.1f Jul 8] ex-Irish gelding: first   –

foal: dam, useful 6f winner, sister to high-class 7f/1m filly Chalon, from good family: fair maiden at 3 yrs for D. Weld, but became disappointing: tailed off in handicaps (second one a seller) at 5 yrs: sold 800 gns Ascot August Sales. *G. A. Ham*

ORCHESTRA STALL 4 b.g. Old Vic 136 – Blue Brocade 91 (Reform 132) 107 p [1995 68p: 10s³ 1996 10s² 10g* 16f* 16s⁴ 16.1m* 18g 16g* 16.5s² Nov 9] good-topped gelding: has a splayed, rounded action: useful stayer: won quite valuable handicaps at Ripon in April and Newcastle (after 3-month break, impressively) in August: did not have things go his way in the Cesarewitch then won steadily-run listed rated stakes at Newmarket in October (readily): best effort (under 10-3) when second of 17 to Sweetness Herself at Doncaster final start: may prove best at around 2m: acts on good to firm and soft going: bandaged last 4 starts: likely to hold his own outside handicap company at 5 yrs. *J. L. Dunlop*

ORCHIDARMA 4 b.g. Reprimand 122 – My Fair Orchid 71 (Roan Rocket 128) – [1995 61d: 9m 10m⁶ 14g 10g⁴ 10m⁵ 8m⁴ 10m 10g 1996 a8g⁶ a11g Feb 19] leggy gelding: sold 7,000 gns Doncaster May Sales, to Belgium: stays 1¼m: acts on good to firm ground, well beaten only outing on soft: tried blinkered/visored, no improvement. *J. J. Quinn*

ORDAINED 3 b.f. Mtoto 134 – In The Habit (USA) 88 (Lyphard (USA) 132) 61 [1995 –: a7g 1996 a8g³ 10g³ 10g⁶ 12d 8.3s 10m² 10m⁵ 10m* 9f³ 10.1m 10f³ 12m⁶ 11f* 12.3g⁶ 10g² 11.1g 10f 10.5s Oct 5] dipped-backed filly: modest handicapper: claimed out of T. Clement's stable £4,000 second start: won at Redcar in June and August: seems to stay 1½m: best efforts on a sound surface. *E. J. Alston*

ORFIJAR (FR) 6 b.h. In Fijar (USA) 121 – Ordiana (GER) (Athenagoras (GER)) 113 [1995 8s² 8s* 8d 8s* 8m² 8m⁴ 8g⁴ 8.5v 1996 8g⁴ 8g* 8g⁴ 8s 9m⁴ 8s³ 8g* 7g 8g⁵ 8.5s⁵ Oct 6] fifth foal: half-brother to winners in Germany at up to 1½m, including 3-y-o Oleandro (by Turfkonig): dam minor winner in Germany: smart German horse: won minor event and listed race at 5 yrs, and another listed (beating Devil River Peek) in April, all at Cologne: improved form to win Group 3 event at Cologne in August by length from Royal Abjar and repeated it when fifth of 12 to Accento in Group 2 race there: well below form last time: stays 9f: acts on good to firm and soft ground. *P. Lautner, Germany*

ORIEL LAD 3 b.g. Colmore Row 111 – Consistent Queen 55 (Queen's Hussar 69 d 124) [1995 75: 5g 5m⁴ 5.2g⁴ 5.7f² 5.9f* 5m⁴ 6m² 7m 7m⁴ 6m 6g² 8g 7d* 7d⁵ 6m 1996 a9.4g⁶ a8g a7g 6.1g 7f² 7s 6m 7f⁴ 6f 7m⁴ 6f 6m⁵ 7g a8g Nov 22] sparely-made gelding: fair performer at best, disappointing at 3 yrs: sold out of P. D. Evans' stable 1,400 gns Doncaster September Sales after eleventh start: stays 7f: acts on firm and dead ground: best in visor or blinkers (didn't wear either last 3 starts): sometimes starts slowly: inconsistent and not to be trusted. *Don Enrico Incisa*

ORINOCO RIVER (USA) 3 ch.c. El Gran Senor (USA) 136 – Miss Lilian 98 91 (Sandford Lad 133) [1995 75p: 8d 8m⁶ 1996 10g 9.9m 12.3g* 12g⁶ 12m* 12m 15m² 14f Aug 1] lengthy colt: fairly useful handicapper: won at Chester in May and Pontefract in June: showed little interest when tailed off final start: sold 7,000 gns Newmarket Autumn Sales: stays 15f: acts on good to firm ground: visored since third 3-y-o start: a hard ride, usually soon off bridle. *P. W. Chapple-Hyam*

ORIOLE 3 b.g. Mazilier (USA) 107 – Odilese 82 (Mummy's Pet 125) [1995 56: 48 d 5d 5m 5g⁶ 5g² 6g⁴ 7m 5.9f² 5g 6m* 6f⁴ 7.9g⁶ 7d 6f a7g 1996 7s 6d 8g 6g 8m³ 7f⁴ 7s* 7m⁶ 7m 8g 7f 7m 8.2s Oct 31] leggy, unfurnished gelding: poor handicapper: won at Ayr in July: well beaten afterwards: stays 1m: acts on firm and soft ground: no improvement in blinkers: usually ridden by Kim Tinkler. *N. Tinkler*

ORONTES (USA) 2 b.g. (May 6) Lomond (USA) 128 – Chateau Princess (USA) 80 ? (Majestic Prince (USA)) [1996 6m³ 7g* 8.1g⁶ 7d Oct 11] $21,000Y: useful-looking gelding: has scope: fluent mover: sixth foal: half-brother to 1¼m winner Hawaiian Romance (by Hawaii) and 2 winners abroad: dam, Irish 1¼m winner, is half-sister to Henbit: won maiden at Salisbury in August: never a factor when last of 6 behind Medaaly in minor event at Sandown or when ninth of 13 in nursery at Ascot: should stay 1¼m. *R. Hannon*

ORSAY 4 gr.c. Royal Academy (USA) 130 – Bellifontaine (FR) (Bellypha 130) 81 [1995 76p: 8d* 1996 8m² 8.3d³ 9f* 7m Sep 28] big, lengthy, good-topped colt: reportedly suffered a leg injury after winning maiden on only start at 3 yrs: fairly useful handicapper: soon pushed along when tenth of 26 in £50,100 event at Ascot final start: needs further than 7f (bred to stay further than 9f): usually races prominently. *W. R. Muir*

ORTELIUS 2 b.c. (Apr 6) Rudimentary (USA) 118 – Third Movement 75 (Music   71 p
Boy 124) [1996 7.1m 8.1s 7m* Oct 28] 16,000F, 20,000Y: strong, useful-looking colt: has plenty of scope: half-brother to several winners, including 1995 2-y-o 6f winner Apple Musashi (by Never So Bold) and Italian 5f (at 2 yrs) to 7.5f winner Bruttina (by Primo Dominie), both useful: dam (maiden) stayed 7f: 40/1, won 10-runner steadily-run maiden at Leicester by neck from Prince of Denial, making virtually all: stays 7f: very slowly away on debut: will improve further. *R. Hannon*

ORTHORHOMBUS 7 b.g. Aragon 118 – Honeybeta 105 (Habitat 134) [1995   – §
67d: a8g² a8g⁵ a8g² a8.5g⁵ a8g⁵ a7g⁶ a7g² a6g 6.9d* a7g² 7.1g⁴ 7g 6m⁶ 8.5m 7m 6.9g 8.1f a7g 1996 6.9s 8.1g 7m Apr 17] strong, workmanlike gelding: showed nothing in 1996, reluctant to race on second outing: stays 1m: acts on firm ground, soft and fibresand: has run creditably visored but usually blinkered: usually comes from behind: one to avoid. *D. J. S. Cosgrove*

ORTOLAN 3 gr.c. Prince Sabo 123 – Kala Rosa 79 (Kalaglow 132) [1995 95p: 86
5g² 5m* 5.2g³ 1996 6g⁶ 6s* 6m 6g* 7m* 7m* 7f² 6m 7m 6m* Oct 7] tall, lengthy colt: useful form at 2 yrs: not so good in 1996, yet still won 5 claimers, at Goodwood in May, at Salisbury and Newmarket (2) within 10 days in August and at Pontefract in October (claimed to join J. L. Eyre's stable £14,000): effective at 6f and 7f: acts on firm ground, successful on soft. *R. Hannon*

OSCAR ROSE 3 b.g. Aragon 118 – Mossy Rose 78 (King of Spain 121) [1995   53 d
62?: 5m⁵ 7m⁴ 6m 7.3m 1996 8.2m⁴ 10m 8f 8m 10g Aug 21] small, lightly-made gelding: modest maiden handicapper: well beaten after reappearance at 3 yrs: stays 8.3f well: raced only on a sound surface: visored (well beaten) final 3-y-o start: probably not one to trust implicitly: has joined Mrs L. Richards. *Lord Huntingdon*

OSCAR SCHINDLER (IRE) 4 ch.c. Royal Academy (USA) 130 – Saraday   127
(Northfields (USA)) [1995 119: 8g² 8m⁶ 12m⁴ 10f⁴ 14g³ 1996 12s² 13.4g* 12f* 12m⁴ 14m* 12d³ 16m Nov 5]

    When the giant Oscar Schindler ended his two-year-old days the four-length winner of his only race, he did so with a reputation almost as big as himself. He was positively luminous in lists of the following season's dark horses and duly lined up in all three colt's classics at the Curragh. Classic success, though, did not come his way. Sixth in the Irish Two Thousand Guineas was followed by fourth in the Derby and third in the St Leger, and two appearances in lesser races as a three-year-old failed to see him in the winner's enclosure either. It would be a grave injustice to describe the three-year-old Oscar Schindler as a failure, but what can be said safely now is that the four-year-old Oscar Schindler was markedly better.

    It seemed that connections lowered their sights a little to start with in 1996, but Oscar Schindler could not be kept out of the top races for long and by the end of the season he was a worthy opponent for any. Starting prices of 16/1, 33/1 and 10/1 in his three classic appearances help indicate that the same could not have been said of him twelve months earlier. Being beaten six lengths when

Hardwicke Stakes, Royal Ascot—a good finish between Oscar Schindler (noseband) and Annus Mirabilis

odds-on for a minor event at Leopardstown, though, was a downbeat start to Oscar Schindler's third season; he had reportedly had a nail in his foot and missed three weeks work. The purely temporary nature of this set-back was emphasised nineteen days later, when he ran out a smooth winner over Election Day and Minds Music in the Ormonde Stakes at Chester, and again six weeks after that when he had to battle rather harder to get past Annus Mirabilis in the Hardwicke Stakes at Royal Ascot. Reportedly, owner Oliver Lehane turned down an offer at £600,000 for Oscar Schindler a week before the Hardwicke. In four races after it, his horse would bid to win more than two and a half times that amount in prize money.

First there was Britain's top middle-distance race, the King George VI and Queen Elizabeth Diamond Stakes back at Ascot. Trailing in some twelve lengths adrift of Pentire, albeit in fourth place, on the face of it demonstrated that Oscar Schindler would find things just as tough in the top grade as he had done as a three-year-old, but he had travelled well until getting boxed in early in the straight. It would have taken some prodigious bad luck in running to have seen him beaten against lesser opponents in the Jefferson Smurfit Memorial Irish St Leger nearly two months later. Oscar Schindler put right his previous classic shortcomings. This had looked a competitive renewal, with little to choose between Oscar Schindler, Posidonas, Sacrament and Key Change in a nine-runner field, but nothing could have been further from the truth once they turned into the straight, the four market leaders up front. Oscar Schindler was on the bridle, the other three being rowed along, and when given the office approaching the furlong marker he went three and a half lengths clear of Key Change while she put another two lengths between herself and the two challengers from Britain. Now Oscar Schindler's connections would have been

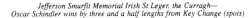

Jefferson Smurfit Memorial Irish St Leger, the Curragh—
Oscar Schindler wins by three and a half lengths from Key Change (spots)

criticised for *not* going for the top races; they did not shirk the challenge and the two chosen for him were the Prix de l'Arc de Triomphe at Longchamp and the Melbourne Cup at Flemington. To go for the latter meant that Oscar Schindler would have to go into quarantine immediately after the Arc. Lehane apparently had misgivings (expressed loudly enough in the aftermath) but they were put in the shade by an eye-catching performance in the Arc. The winning rider in the Irish St Leger, gaining his first classic success, had been Stephen Craine, but he was jocked off in favour of Asmussen at Longchamp. 'When in Rome . . .', they said. Indeed, but connections were shocked by the imperturbable American's attempt to come from last to first. Oscar Schindler had been squeezed for room after a couple of furlongs and never saw much of it thereafter, bursting into third a hundred and fifty yards out by which time Helissio's jockey was already about to commence his arm-revolving celebrations. Beaten a short neck by Pilsudski for second, it was an excellent effort from Oscar Schindler nevertheless, one that made him look decidedly well handicapped for the Melbourne Cup, the weights for which had been published before even the Irish St Leger. Mick Kinane now took over the riding duties. Ten days after Pilsudski won the Breeders' Cup Turf, however, 4/1-favourite

		Nijinsky	Northern Dancer
	Royal	(b 1967)	Flaming Page
	Academy (USA)	Crimson Saint	Crimson Satan
Oscar Schindler (IRE)	(b 1987)	(ch 1969)	Bolero Rose
(ch.c. 1992)		Northfields	Northern Dancer
	Saraday	(ch 1968)	Little Hut
	(ch 1980)	Etoile Grise	Sea Hawk II
		(gr 1972)	Place d'Etoile

Mr Oliver Lehane's "Oscar Schindler"

Oscar Schindler came in fifteenth of twenty-two in Australia, set plenty to do but looking unable to quicken anyway. Able to exercise only on grass in the build-up, something he reportedly never does at home, Oscar Schindler finished jarred up in the race. 'He will come home and be prepared for a similar campaign next year', reported the owner, 'but without the Melbourne Cup'.

The big, rangy colt Oscar Schindler stands 17.2 hands. Who's to say he has filled his frame even now? Effective at a mile and a half and a mile and three quarters, he acts on any going and is genuine and consistent. Oscar Schindler was bred by Mr Lehane and is the sixth foal out of Saraday, following a winning hurdler, the continental winners Sassicaia (by Commanche Run) and Fanny Blankers (by Persian Heights), and the useful Irish seven-furlong to a mile-and-three-quarters winner Roger Ramjet (by Law Society). The namesake theme is continued by the 1993 and 1994 colts Johann Strauss (by Royal Academy) and Babe Ruth (by Thatching). Saraday had thirty races in Ireland, from two to five years, failed to win one but was runner-up seven times, on the final occasion beaten a neck over two miles in a maiden at Wexford. She is attractively bred, though, because although her dam Etoile Grise was a maiden as well, she was also a half-sister to the 1976 Irish Two Thousand Guineas winner Northern Treasure (who was trained, like Oscar Schindler, by Kevin Prendergast), the Oaks d'Italia winner Paris Royal and Etoile de Paris, the dam of dual Yorkshire Oaks winner Only Royale. Like Iktamal and Desert King, Oscar Schindler is a 1996 Group 1 winner in-bred to Northern Dancer inside three generations. Sire Royal Academy stood in Japan in 1996, but will be back at Coolmore in 1997 at IR 15,000 guineas. He can get winners over a wide variety of distances, being represented in 1996 by the likes of Ali-Royal, Bolshoi, Carmine Lake, Equal Rights, Sea Spray, Sleepytime and Truth or Dare. Oscar Schindler, however, is Royal Academy's best to date. *K. Prendergast, Ireland*

OSCILIGHTS GIFT   4 b.f. Chauve Souris 108 – Oscilight 112 (Swing Easy (USA) 126) [1995 –: 8d 7g 8f 1996 7f 8f 6m 5g³ 5.1m³ 5m⁵ 5f a5g Dec 31] light-framed filly: poor maiden handicapper: stumbled and unseated rider leaving stalls final start (first after leaving P. Burgoyne): evidently a sprinter: acts on good to firm ground. *Mark Campion*   41 ?

OSOMENTAL   2 gr.g. (Feb 22) Petong 126 – Proper Madam 93 (Mummy's Pet 125) [1996 5d⁴ 5d⁴ 5m⁵ 6g² 5m* 5g* 6d 6.1d⁴ 6m⁶ 5m 6m Oct 17] 11,000Y, 28,000 2-y-o: strong gelding: has a fluent, round action: brother to 3-y-o Pride of Kashmir and half-brother to several winners, most at sprint distances, including 2 by Milford: dam sprinter: gelded after fourth run and won nurseries at Ayr and Leicester in July: stays 6f: usually blinkered/visored: sometimes on toes: usually slowly into stride: tends to hang, flash tail and look unco-operative. *D. Haydn Jones*   88 +

OSTIA   3 b.f. Slip Anchor 136 – Sarsina 72 (Forli (ARG)) [1995 –: 6g 1996 8m Oct 7] unfurnished filly: well beaten in maidens 13 months apart: sold 1,000 gns Newmarket Autumn Sales: sent to Germany. *Mrs J. Cecil*   –

OTARU (IRE)   4 b.f. Indian Ridge 123 – Radiant (USA) (Foolish Pleasure (USA)) [1995 NR 1996 a8.5g Jan 17] 30,000Y: sixth foal: half-sister to 3 winners here and abroad, including useful sprinter Poolesta and American Grade 3 6f to 9f winner Home of The Free (both by Hero's Honor): dam, minor winner at around 6f, is half-sister to good middle-distance colt Gold and Ivory: weak 11/1-shot, tailed off in maiden at Wolverhampton: covered by Shareef Dancer. *Sir Mark Prescott*   –

OTHER CLUB   2 ch.c. (Mar 3) Kris 135 – Tura (Northfields (USA)) [1996 8d⁶ 7g⁶ Oct 19] 50,000F, 64,000Y: lengthy, good-bodied colt: fluent mover: closely related to 1989 2-y-o 5f winner Jagged Edge (by Sharpo) and half-brother to 3-y-o Turia (by Slip Anchor) and several winners, including useful German 4-y-o 6f (at 2 yrs) and 7.7f winner Tristano (by Colmore Row): dam 7f winner in Ireland: well-backed, had worst of draw and shaped well when sixth of 13 to Bold Words in maiden at Salisbury, travelling well 6f: gone in coat, never-dangerous last of 6 in Houghton Stakes at Newmarket later in month: should stay beyond 1m: will do better. *J. A. R. Toller*   74 p

OTTAVIO FARNESE 4 ch.g. Scottish Reel 123 – Sense of Pride (Welsh 58
Pageant 132) [1995 77: 10m⁶ 8.5m² 10g* 12m 1996 10g 10m 10g 10.1m⁶ a11g Nov
4] leggy gelding: has a round action: modest form at best in 1996: stays 1¼m well:
probably acts on good to firm going. *A. Hide*

OTTO E MEZZO 4 b.g. Persian Bold 123 – Carolside 108 (Music Maestro 119) –
[1995 NR 1996 10s⁶ 9.2g³ 10m 10m 8m⁵ 7m 12f 11.9d 12g⁶ Oct 11] compact
gelding: rated 94 at 2 yrs for J. Dunlop: sold before reappearance 13,200 gns Ascot
May (1996) Sales: stiff tasks when well held first 4 starts in 1996 and no worthwhile
form in varied company (including claiming) afterwards: should stay beyond 1m:
used to act on any going. *M. J. Polglase*

OUR ADVENTURE 3 ch.f. Green Adventure (USA) 119 – Honey Dipper –
(Golden Dipper 119) [1995 NR 1996 10.2f Jul 2] sixth reported living foal:
half-sister to a fairly useful winning jumper: dam placed once from 4 starts over
hurdles: 100/1, gave trouble before start and tailed off in maiden at Chepstow.
M. P. Muggeridge

OUR ALBERT (IRE) 3 b.g. Durgam (USA) – Power Girl 77 (Tyrant (USA)) –
[1995 –: 6m 6.1m⁵ 7.5d 1996 10m 7m 6m Oct 23] stocky gelding: no worthwhile
form over a variety of trips: visored final outing. *J. A. Glover*

OUR EDDIE 7 ch.g. Gabitat 119 – Ragusa Girl (Morston (FR) 125) [1995 –, a63: –
a10g³ a10g a12g⁴ a10g⁶ 1996 a10g⁶ a10g⁴ a10g* 9g a12g a12g⁴ a10g⁶ a10g⁴ Nov a65 d
26] leggy, sparely-made gelding: shows knee action: modest handicapper: won seller
at Lingfield in August: disappointing afterwards: probably stays 1½m: easily best
efforts on equitrack: visored nowadays, tried blinkered at 3 yrs: none too consistent.
B. Gubby

OUR FUTURE (IRE) 2 b.g. (Feb 13) Imp Society (USA) – Petite Realm 95 64
(Realm 129) [1996 5d⁴ 5g 6d 6g³ 7g² 8g Aug 21] IR 7,200Y: big, good-topped
gelding: has plenty of scope: half-brother to 3 winners, including Irish 1991 2-y-o 5f
winner Selma (by Don't Forget Me) and Irish 7f and 9f winner Park Elect (by
Ahonoora): dam speedy 2-y-o: modest maiden: placed in 2 nurseries: ran badly final
outing: stays 7f: sold (M. Johnston to Ronald Thompson) 2,200 gns Doncaster
November Sales. *M. Johnston*

OUR HOME LAND (USA) 2 b.c. (Mar 23) Red Ransom (USA) – What Not 78
To Do (USA) (What Luck (USA)) [1996 5g 6g* Jul 25] $19,000Y resold 20,000Y:
smallish, sturdy colt: second foal: dam, won at up to 1m at 4 yrs in USA, half-sister
to Canadian 7f and 8.5f graded stakes winner Little To Do: won 8-runner maiden at
Catterick, making all: will stay beyond 6f: sent to Hong Kong. *M. Johnston*

OUR KEVIN 2 gr.g. (Apr 7) Chilibang 120 – Anse Chastanet (Cavo Doro 124) 63
[1996 5.3f⁴ 5s³ a5g⁴ 6g⁴ 6g* 7f² a6g² 6.1f⁶ 7g² a7g* 7f 7m⁶ 6m a6g⁶ a8.5g⁶ a7g
Nov 18] 3,600Y: strong, lengthy gelding: fifth reported foal: half-brother to 4-y-o 7f
winner Euphylia (by Superpower): dam ran 3 times: modest performer: won sellers
at Catterick in June and Wolverhampton in July: virtually no comparable form
afterwards: stays 7f: acts on firm ground and fibresand: has hung left: nearly always
blinkered/visored. *K. McAuliffe*

OUR KRIS 4 b.g. Kris 135 – Our Reverie (USA) (J O Tobin (USA) 130) [1995 73: 63
8m⁵ 11.4m 10m⁶ 14g 17.1m 14m* 1996 20f 14.9m⁴ 14g² Aug 1] strong, workmanlike gelding: has pronounced knee action: fair handicapper at best on flat:
blinkered, best effort at 4 yrs when third at Salisbury final outing, making most:
should stay 2m: has raced only on a sound surface: useful hurdler in 1995/6 but sold
to join M. Sowersby 24,000 gns Doncaster October Sales and disappointing: none
too consistent. *N. J. Henderson*

OUR LITTLE LADY 4 b.f. Queen's Soldier (USA) – Charlotte's Pearl (Mon- –
santo (FR) 121) [1995 –: 8.3m⁶ 10.1m⁶ 11.5m⁴ a8.5g 1996 9.7m 8.3g 8f⁶ Jul 17]
lengthy filly of little account. *Jamie Poulton*

OUR MAIN MAN 6 ch.g. Superlative 118 – Ophrys 90 (Nonoalco (USA) 131) –
[1995 61, a53: 12m 8g⁵ 13.1g⁴ 12m 11.1f* 10f³ 12.3m⁵ 11.9m 12.1g 8.9g 10f* a11g³ a53
a12g⁴ a11g⁶ 1996 10g 8.9g 10g a10g⁵ a12g³ a14g² a14g² a13g⁶ Dec 13] good-topped
gelding: modest handicapper: stays 13f: acts on all-weather and firm going: visored
(well beaten) once at 5 yrs: best with waiting tactics. *R. M. Whitaker*

OUR PEOPLE   2 ch.c. (Apr 23) Indian Ridge 123 – Fair And Wise 75 (High Line   90
125) [1996 8m³ 8f* 8g³ Nov 1] 16,000Y: sixth foal: brother to a winner in Denmark
and half-brother to 3 winners, including fairly useful 7f (at 2 yrs) and 1m winner
Venus Observed (by Sharpo): dam suited by 1¾m: won maiden at Leicester in
October, idling closing stages: around 3 lengths third of 4 to River Usk in steadily-run
minor event at Newmarket following month, again setting pace, carrying head
awkwardly running into the Dip then tending to edge right: likely to stay beyond 1m.
M. Johnston

OUR ROBERT   4 b.g. Faustus (USA) 118 – Duck Soup 55 (Decoy Boy 129)   59
[1995 59: 7g⁴ 8.3g³ 7.9g³ 8g 8.1g 8g 1996 a7g³ a8g⁴ a11g Feb 12] sturdy, heavy-
topped gelding: has a markedly round action: modest maiden: should stay 1¼m: acts
on fibresand and any turf going: winning novice hurdler. *J. G. FitzGerald*

OUR SHADEE (USA)   6 b.g. Shadeed (USA) 135 – Nuppence 79 (Reform 132)   54 d
[1995 50, a61: a7g² a6g* a6g² a6g* a6g² a6g 6m 6m³ 7g⁵ 6m⁵ 6f 6f³ a7g 7g 6g² a7g⁴   a73 d
7f⁶ a7g⁴ a6g³ a7g³ a6g⁵ 1996 a8g a7g a6g⁵ a6g² a6g³ a6g* a6g² a6g* a6g³ a6g* 5g⁶
6.1g 5g a6g³ 5.7g⁴ 6f³ 6f⁴ 6f⁶ 7m⁴ 7g 7.6m* 8.3d⁶ 7.6m⁶ a7g 7g⁵ 7f 7m⁵ 8m a7g 7g
a7s a10g³ a8g⁵ a7g Dec 20] lengthy gelding: fair performer at best on the all-weather:
in good form at Lingfield early at 6 yrs, winning 2 handicaps and a claimer: modest
on turf: narrowly won apprentice handicap at Lingfield in August: best at 6f/7f,
probably stays 1¼m: acts on firm and soft ground and goes well on the all-weather:
nearly always visored nowadays: usually held up. *K. T. Ivory*

OUR TOM   4 br.g. Petong 126 – Boa (Mandrake Major 122) [1995 57, a66: a7g*
a7g² a6g a8.5g² a8.5g* a7g 10d² 10g 8g 9m a9.4g a9.4g⁴ 1996 a11g* a12g a11g⁵   a72 d
a9.4g⁶ 9.7s 10m 8.2m a9.4g a9.4g Nov 11] good-topped gelding: fair handicapper on
all-weather, winner of well-contested event at Southwell in January: generally well
below form afterwards: stays 11f well: acts on good ground but much better form on
fibresand: tried blinkered, no improvement. *J. Wharton*

OUR WAY   2 ch.f. (May 8) Forzando 122 – Hanglands (Bustino 136) [1996 6f² 6m   70 ?
6m² 7m Oct 1] 16,000Y: lengthy, good-quartered filly: half-sister to 3-y-o 6.9f
winner Arterxerxes (by Anshan) and fairly useful 1992 5f and 6.1f winner Zuno
Warrior (by Dominion): dam lightly raced: much improved when 2 lengths second of
12 to The Faraway Tree in maiden at Yarmouth, making most: tailed off in nursery at
Newmarket 13 days later: should stay further than 6f. *C. E. Brittain*

OUR WORLEY (IRE)   3 b.f. Mac's Imp (USA) 116 – Castleforbes (Thatching   –
131) [1995 51: 5f⁴ 1996 6.1g⁶ 6.1m Apr 30] quite good-topped filly, rather unfurnished: only form when fourth of 6 in maiden at Warwick on debut: ran in sellers
at 3 yrs. *A. P. Jarvis*

OUTFLANKER (USA)   2 b. or br.c. (Apr 19) Danzig (USA) – Lassie's Lady   76 p
(USA) (Alydar (USA)) [1996 7.1v² 8.2s⁶ Oct 31] $375,000Y: well-made colt: eighth
foal: half-brother to very smart 7f (at 2 yrs) to 1¼m winner Shuailaan (by Roberto),
stayed 14.6f, and US 1989 2-y-o Grade 2 6f winner Bite The Bullet (by Spectacular
Bid): dam, won at up to 7f in USA, half-sister to Wolfhound from a very good family:
beaten 8 lengths in maidens won by Catienus at Haydock and Desert Horizon at
Nottingham: will do better. *P. W. Chapple-Hyam*

OUT LINE   4 gr.f. Beveled (USA) – Free Range 78 (Birdbrook 110) [1995 NR   72
1996 6m 8.3m 6m³ 7.1d³ 7g 5m⁶ Sep 25] leggy filly: fourth reported foal:
sister to 5-y-o 1m and 9f winner Thames Side and half-sister to 5f winner Rays Mead
(by Tremblant): dam 5f to 7f winner: fair maiden: best efforts when placed in the
summer: needs further than 5f, and stays 7f: acts on good to firm and dead ground.
M. Madgwick

OUT OF SIGHT (IRE)   2 ch.c. (Jan 31) Salse (USA) 128 – Starr Danias (USA)   81
(Sensitive Prince (USA)) [1996 5d⁵ 6m⁵ 7m⁵ 6g⁶ 6m 7s Nov 9] 16,000Y: deep-
girthed colt: fourth foal: half-brother to 7f winner Yaa Wale (by Persian Bold) and 6f
(at 2 yrs) and 11.8f winner Potsclose (by Miswaki): dam lightly raced in USA,
half-sister to smart 7f winner Zahdam: fairly useful maiden: stays 7f: well below
form both starts on a soft surface. *B. A. McMahon*

OUT ON A PROMISE (IRE)   4 b.g. Night Shift (USA) – Lovers' Parlour 83   –
(Beldale Flutter (USA) 130) [1995 86: 8d 8.1m⁶ 7.9g⁶ 8m³ 8g³ 7.1m 10m² 10m²
10.3m* 10m 10d³ 1996 11.9g 12m 10m 10.8g May 25] compact, quite attractive
gelding: fairly useful performer at 3 yrs for G. Wragg: disappointing in 1996: stays

1¼m: acts on good to firm and soft ground: blinkered (pulled too hard) sixth 3-y-o start: takes keen hold: won over hurdles in December. *N. J. H. Walker*

OUTSET (IRE)　6 ch.g. Persian Bold 123 – It's Now Or Never 78 (High Line 125)　– [1995 57: 14.6m⁴ 1996 16.5s Nov 9] leggy gelding: best known as a fairly useful hurdler nowadays: showed only modest form only start on flat in 1995, and well down the field at Doncaster on return (first outing of any kind for 7 months): stays 14.6f: makes running/races prominently. *M. D. Hammond*

OUTSTAYED WELCOME　4 b.g. Be My Guest (USA) 126 – Between Time　65 d 75 (Elegant Air 119) [1995 56: 7g 8.2g 8m 10g 12.3f* 11.9m² 12.1m³ 12.3f³ 14.1m* 14.1m⁴ 12d a12g⁵ a13g² a13g⁴ 1996 a16g 12g² 12.3g² 12m² 12.5f⁵ 12.3m³ 14.9m 12.1m³ 12.3m 14.4g 12m⁶ 11.5m⁶ Oct 4] leggy gelding: fair handicapper, inconsistent in 1996: should stay beyond 1¾m: acts on any going: blinkered (no improvement) twice at 2 yrs: usually bandaged behind: has won for lady: front runner. *M. J. Haynes*

OUT WEST (USA)　2 br.f. (Feb 8) Gone West (USA) – Chellingoua (USA)　90 p (Sharpen Up 127) [1996 7.5g* 7m⁴ Sep 1] good-topped filly: half-sister to 4-y-o Zamalek (by Northern Baby), 7f winner at 2 yrs, and a winner in USA by Hilal: dam lightly-raced French maiden, placed over 1m: long odds on, won 3-runner maiden at Beverley by 10 lengths from Ghayyur (who broke blood vessel): heavily-backed favourite though still bit green, around 5 lengths fourth of 5 to Benny The Dip in minor event at Doncaster following month, giving impression will be well suited by 1m+: will improve further. *H. R. A. Cecil*

OVATION　2 ch.f. (Apr 19) Generous (IRE) 139 – Bint Pasha (USA) 126　95 (Affirmed (USA)) [1996 7m* 8m² 8g Sep 29] useful-looking filly: fluent mover: fifth foal: half-sister to smart 1m (at 2 yrs) to 11f winner Revere (by Dancing Brave) and 1½m winner Monarch (by Sadler's Wells): dam won Yorkshire Oaks and Prix Vermeille: gamely made virtually all when winning maiden at Newmarket in July: readily beaten 1¼ lengths by sole rival Khassah in minor event at Bath nearly 2 months later (handled track none too well): below-form seventh of 8, free to post and in race, in Fillies' Mile at Ascot: bred to stay beyond 1m: takes keen hold. *P. F. I. Cole*

OVERBURY (IRE)　5 br.h. Caerleon (USA) 132 – Overcall (Bustino 136) [1995　116 114: 9m² 1996 a8g a12f⁵ 11g* 10g 12m⁴ 10m² 10m⁴ 12s Nov 9] strong, close-　a– coupled horse: smart performer: reportedly had operation to remove a bladder stone after only 4-y-o start for D. Loder: ran twice in Dubai before winning 14-runner Queen Elizabeth II Cup at Sha Tin in April: far from disgraced next time, and creditable 2½ lengths second to Hagwah in listed race at Goodwood in September: effective at 9f and stays 1½m: acts on firm ground, possibly unsuited by soft and sand: genuine. *Saeed bin Suroor*

OVERPOWER　12 b.g. Try My Best (USA) 130 – Just A Shadow (Laser Light　– 118) [1995 54: 10m 8g* 10m² 1996 8m Jun 5] workmanlike gelding: carries condition: veteran handicapper: off course a year: seventh of 18 in seller only outing at 12 yrs: effective at 1m and 1¼m: best form on a sound surface (acts on firm going): blinkered and visored (below form) earlier in career: has found little in front, and suited by good gallop and waiting tactics. *M. H. Tompkins*

OVERRULED (IRE)　3 b.f. Last Tycoon 131 – Overcall (Bustino 136) [1995　84 91p: 7m 8m* 1996 12.3g 14d⁵ 10.2f* 10.3m Jul 31] leggy, lengthy filly: good walker: fairly useful performer: won 6-runner handicap at Chepstow in July: visored, tailed-off last at Doncaster 4 weeks later: ran creditably at 1¾m, but probably suited by 1¼m/1½m: acts on firm and dead ground. *D. R. Loder*

OVERSMAN　3 b.g. Keen 116 – Jamaican Punch (IRE) (Shareef Dancer (USA)　80 135) [1995 –, a71: 6m a7g³ 7f 7.9m a7g 1996 a11g* a12g² 12.3g³ May 8] robust gelding: has scope: fair form: easily won maiden event at Southwell in February: sweating and better for race, creditable fourth of 13 in handicap at Chester: should stay beyond 12f: acts on fibresand. *J. G. FitzGerald*

OVER THE MOON　2 ch.f. (Feb 24) Beveled (USA) – Beyond The Moon (IRE)　– 58 (Ballad Rock 122) [1996 a7s⁶ Nov 9] first foal: dam, fourth over 6f on sole 2-y-o start, didn't train on: over 15 lengths sixth of 13 to Henley in maiden at Lingfield, not a danger in straight: may do better. *M. J. Fetherston-Godley*

OVER TO YOU (USA) 2 ch.c. (Mar 4) Rubiano (USA) – Overnight (USA) (Mr   77 p
Leader (USA)) [1996 8.2m³ 8.2g* Oct 24] $52,000Y: leggy, close-coupled colt: sixth
foal: half-brother to French 1991 2-y-o 1m winner Kritso (by Dixieland Band), later
successful at up to 9f in USA: dam, won at up to 9f in USA, half-sister to grandam of
Suave Dancer out of half-sister to Habitat: sire champion US sprinter: won 15-runner
maiden at Nottingham by a head from Midnight Watch: gives impression will stay
beyond 1m: will improve again. *E. A. L. Dunlop*

OWDBETTS (IRE) 4 b.f. High Estate 127 – Nora Yo Ya (Ahonoora 122) [1995   60
60: a8.5g⁶ 8.3m⁴ 9.7m⁵ 8.1m 7g* 7.6d 10f* 10.1m⁶ 7g 9.7s a9.4g⁵ a10g³ 1996
a8g⁶ a8g 10d 10.2m* 9.7f³ 12g 10m⁶ a10g⁶ Aug 10] workmanlike filly: has a round
action: modest handicapper: won selling event at Bath (slowly away, came from last
to first, swerving left in front) in June: sold 2,600 gns Doncaster September Sales:
stays 1¼m: acts on firm ground and fibresand, possibly not on a soft surface, poor
effort on equitrack: takes keen hold and has carried head awkwardly, but has run
creditably for amateur: inconsistent. *G. L. Moore*

OXALAGU (GER) 4 gr.c. Lagunas – Oxalis 64 (Ashmore (FR) 125) [1995 10g*   118
10.5v* 10.5m* 12g² 12m⁶ 12m² 12s⁶ 14s⁴ 1996 10g* 12g⁴ 11d² 11d⁵ 10g* 10m⁴
Nov 10] half-brother to German 10.5f to 11.5f winner Oxalit (by Windwurf): dam
middle-distance maiden: smart German colt: won maiden, minor event and listed
race at 3 yrs, when also fourth in St Leger at Dortmund: better in 1996, winning
Group 3 event at Gelsenkirchen in April by 2 lengths from Sir King and Group 3
race at Hoppegarten (by head from Galtee) in October: good 2 lengths fourth of 8 to
Flemensfirth in Premio Roma in November: stays 1¾m: acts on good to firm ground
and heavy. *B. Schutz, Germany*

OXBANE 2 b.f. (Mar 3) Soviet Star (USA) 128 – Oxslip 106 (Owen Dudley 121) –
[1996 6m Oct 28] strong, good-bodied filly: half-sister to several winners, including
useful sprinter Top Banana (by Pharly) and 1¼m and 1¾m winner Sixslip (by
Diesis): dam, 7f to 13f winner, is half-sister to smart stayer Kambalda: very green
when eleventh of 13 in maiden at Leicester: likely to do better. *H. Candy*

OXGANG (IRE) 3 b.g. Taufan (USA) 119 – Casla (Lomond (USA) 128) [1995   –
61: 7.5m a8g³ 1996 a7g a12g² 12s⁶ 8g⁵ 10m 10.3g a11g 8.3m Aug 14] good-bodied
gelding: little worthwhile form since final 2-y-o start, blinkered last 2 outings: sold
1,100 gns Doncaster November Sales: should stay beyond 1m: acts on fibresand.
J. G. FitzGerald

OZZIE JONES 5 b.g. Formidable (USA) 125 – Distant Relation (Great Nephew   –
126) [1995 –, a45: a11g³ a12g⁴ a12g² a12g⁵ a16g 12m 1996 16m Aug 7] good-
topped gelding: poor handicapper: well below form last three 4-y-o starts, for
M. Chapman: visored, set strong pace when well beaten only outing at 5 yrs: should
stay beyond 1½m: acts on fibresand and good to firm ground, probably on soft:
blinkered (well beaten) fifth 4-y-o start: sold 2,700 gns Malvern October Sales.
N. M. Babbage

P

PAB'S CHOICE 5 ch.m. Telsmoss 91 – Dido 70 (Full of Hope 125) [1995 59:   57
a6g 6.1m 7.6m² 7m 8.5m⁶ a7g a7g 1996 a6g 8f⁴ 8m 7g Jul 31] sparely-made mare:
modest handicapper: first run for 5½ months, easily best effort at 5 yrs when fourth at
Warwick: stays 8.5f: acts on equitrack, dead ground (poorly drawn on soft) and firm:
visored final start in 1995 and first in 1996: inconsistent: covered by Lugana Beach.
M. McCormack

PACIFIC GIRL (IRE) 4 b.f. Emmson 125 – Power Girl 77 (Tyrant (USA))   45
[1995 51d: 7.1m 6m a7g 5.7h³ 5m 5.1h⁵ 10.8f⁴ 10d 8m a7g⁶ a8g a7g⁶ 1996 a8g a7g⁵
Jan 2] sparely-made filly: poor maiden: should stay beyond 7f: acts on hard and
dead ground and on fibresand: below form in blinkers: inconsistent: covered by
Arzanni. *B. Palling*

PACIFIC GROVE 3 b.f. Persian Bold 123 – Dazzling Heights 99 (Shirley   –
Heights 130) [1995 89: 6m⁶ 5g³ 6m⁴ 7m² 7.3m* 7f⁴ 8h* 7d* 7.3d² 8g 1996 10.2m⁶
Jul 25] sparely-made filly: fairly useful at 2 yrs, winning 3 nurseries: stiff task and

707

never dangerous in listed race at Chepstow only outing as 3-y-o: should prove effective beyond 1m: acts on hard and dead ground: has run well for 7-lb claimer: genuine: sold 38,000 gns Newmarket December Sales. *P. F. I. Cole*

PACKITIN 3 b.g. Rich Charlie 117 – Sound Type 92 (Upper Case (USA)) [1995 – NR 1996 6f Jul 17] 580F: half-brother to 9f and 1¼m seller winner Final Sound (by Final Straw) and a winner in Belgium: dam 7f and 1¼m winner: 100/1, slowly away and tailed off in claimer at Redcar. *F. Watson*

PADAUK 2 b.c. (Apr 30) Warrshan (USA) 117 – Free On Board 73 (Free State 76 125) [1996 7g 7g⁶ 8m⁵ 7d⁵ Oct 12] strong, lengthy colt with a round action: sixth foal: brother to fair but temperamental 4-y-o 1¼m and 11.9f winner Courbaril and half-brother to 3 winners here and abroad, including 1½m winner Nordansk (by Nordance): dam stayed 1¼m: never dangerous first 2 starts but held good position almost throughout when fifth of 11 in maiden at Goodwood on third: very stiff task at Ascot final outing: probably stays 1m: difficult to weigh up. *M. J. Haynes*

PADDY HURRY 2 b.c. (Apr 1) Silver Kite (USA) 111 – Little Preston (IRE) 53 – (Pennine Walk 120) [1996 6m 8g 6g 7.8f⁴ 7m Oct 17] first reported foal: dam (maiden) stayed 1¼m: ex-Irish colt: poor form in maidens for K. Prendergast: gambled on, tailed off in 27-runner seller at Newmarket on English debut: sold 3,000 gns Newmarket Autumn Sales. *N. A. Callaghan*

PADDY LAD (IRE) 2 b. or br.c. (Apr 22) Anita's Prince 126 – Lady of Man 85 91 (So Blessed 130) [1996 a6g⁶ 6m⁵ 5m⁴ 6g² 6m³ Sep 19] IR 4,000F, IR 5,600Y: sturdy colt: brother to 3-y-o sprint winner Miletrian Refurb and 3 winners in Ireland at up to 1m: dam 5f and 7f winner: won median auction maiden at Sandown in August: much better form when both 3 lengths second of 30 to Miss Stamper in Tattersalls Breeders Stakes at the Curragh and third of 5 to Air Express in minor event at Yarmouth: stays 6f. *R. Guest*

PADDY'S RICE 5 ch.g. Hadeer 118 – Requiem (Song 132) [1995 61: 6m³ 6g 6f* 65 6g⁵ 6f² 6m³ 7m 7.6m² 7m⁶ 7d 1996 7f* 7g 7m 7m⁵ 7f³ 7.6m⁴ 7g² 7.1f 7m Sep 19] sparely-made gelding: modest handicapper: won minor event at Warwick in June: left M. McCormack after seventh 5-y-o outing, below form both runs for new stable: may stay beyond 7.6f: acts on firm ground, raced on seemingly disadvantaged side only try in last 2 seasons on a soft surface: usually held up. *M. Blanshard*

PAGEBOY 7 b.g. Tina's Pet 121 – Edwins' Princess 75 (Owen Dudley 121) [1995 72 67, a70: a6g* a6g² a6g⁵ a5g a6g⁶ a6g 5m 6m 5f 5g³ 6m⁴ 6m³ 6m⁴ 6f a6g 5g 6g⁴ 1996 a75 a6g* a6g² a6g⁶ a6g⁵ 5g⁵ 5m 6f 6m* 6m² 6d⁴ 6g a6g* 5m² 5m 5g⁶ Sep 29] small, sturdy gelding: unimpressive mover: fair handicapper: won at Lingfield in January, Hamilton in August and Wolverhampton in September: best form at sprint distances: acts on all-weather surfaces and firm ground: often a front runner: effective with or without blinkers/visor. *P. C. Haslam*

PAGEL (IRE) 2 b.g. (Mar 24) Polish Patriot (USA) 128 – Fanfan (IRE) 47 – (Taufan (USA) 119) [1996 8.2g Oct 24] IR 3,000Y: first foal: dam 7f winner at 2 yrs, her only season to race: tailed off in maiden at Nottingham: sold 600 gns Newmarket Autumn Sales. *R. Hollinshead*

PAINTED HALL (USA) 4 br.g. Imperial Falcon (CAN) – Moon O'Gold (USA) – (Slew O' Gold (USA)) [1995 73: 10m 10m* 10g⁶ 11.9m⁴ 1996 12m 10g⁶ 10d May 27] robust gelding: fair handicapper: disappointing at 4 yrs: should stay 1½m: acts on good to firm ground. *J. A. R. Toller*

PAINT IT BLACK 3 ch.g. Double Schwartz 128 – Tableaux (FR) (Welsh 78 § Pageant 132) [1995 75+: 7f 7f³ 7m* 6d⁶ 1996 7m 7f 8f 8g 8.1m² 8f⁵ 6m 7d⁴ 8f 8.2g⁶ Oct 24] sturdy gelding: fair handicapper: mostly well below form in 1996: sold (R. Hannon to D. Nicholls) 5,000 gns Newmarket Autumn Sales, and gelded: stays 1m: acts on firm ground, probably on dead: tried blinkered (ran well in them first time): hung both starts at Brighton: not one to rely on. *R. Hannon*

PAIR OF JACKS (IRE) 6 ch.g. Music Boy 124 – Lobbino 72 (Bustino 136) 28 [1995 37: a8g a8g a10g⁶ a7g⁵ a8g a8g a8g² a8g² a8g⁴ a8g³ 6m⁶ 7m 7f 7g a7g 1996 a7g a8g 6m 6.9g⁴ Jul 3] strong, lengthy gelding: poor handicapper: trained on reappearance by D. Wilson: stays 1m: best efforts on a sound surface or equitrack: tried blinkered and visored: has joined G. L. Moore: modest hurdler. *T. J. Naughton*

PALACEGATE CHIEF   3 b.g. Inca Chief (USA) – Sports Post Lady (IRE) 72   –
(M Double M (USA)) [1995 –: 5f⁵ 1996 6.1m a8.5g Jun 22] first foal: dam best at 5f:
last all outings: sold out of Jack Berry's stable 3,200 gns Doncaster March (1996)
Sales before reappearance. *N. P. Littmoden*

PALACEGATE GOLD (IRE)   7 b.g. Sarab 123 – Habilite 94 (Habitat 134)   34
[1995 –: a7g a10g 1996 a8g³ a6g³ a8g 6.9s 7d⁶ Apr 4] sturdy gelding: seems poor
nowadays: sold 500 gns Ascot November Sales: effective at 5f to 7f: probably acts
on any going: tried blinkered, no improvement. *R. J. Hodges*

PALACEGATE JACK (IRE)   5 gr.g. Neshad (USA) 108 – Pasadena Lady   82
(Captain James 123) [1995 94d: 6g 5g 5g* 5f² 5s⁵ 5m 1996 5.1g 5.1g 5.1m³ 5m³ 5m   a85
a5g* 5f³ 5f² 6v 5g 5f* a5g² a6s⁶ Dec 19] lengthy, workmanlike gelding: fairly useful
performer: justified favouritism in claimer at Southwell (claimed out of Jack Berry's
stable £10,000) in September by 5 lengths: not at best to win minor event at Redcar in
November: very best efforts over 5f: acts on any going, including fibresand: effective
blinkered or not, visored (well beaten) 4-y-o reappearance: often hangs left: has been
bandaged off-fore: usually races prominently. *C. A. Dwyer*

PALACEGATE JO (IRE)   5 b.m. Drumalis 125 – Welsh Rhyme (Welsh Term   36
126) [1995 67d: a9.4g a11g⁴ a11g² a11g* a12g* a11g⁵ a12g² a11g⁴ a11g³ a14g⁶
a12g⁴ a12g* a12g a11g a12g³ a12g* a12g a12g⁵ a9.4g⁵ a9.4g a12g a7g 1996
a8g⁶ a8g⁶ a9.4g a11g a11g² 11.5f⁵ a12g Aug 16] leggy mare: fair handicapper at best
in 1995: poor form in 1996: needs further than 1m, and stays 1½m: acts on all-
weather surfaces and goes well on very soft ground on turf: effective from front or
held up: none too consistent. *D. W. Chapman*

PALACEGATE TOUCH   6 gr.g. Petong 126 – Dancing Chimes (London Bells   85
(CAN) 109) [1995 94d: 6d* 7m⁵ 6m 6m a6g² 6.1m⁶ 6m 6f⁵ 6m⁵ 6g 5d⁴ 6f 1996
6g 6.9d* a6g² 6.9m⁵ a7g⁴ a7g³ a6g 6d⁴ a5g* 5f* 6g³ 5g* 5m² a5g³ 5f* 5m 5d⁶
5g* 5g Oct 26] tall, good-topped gelding: fairly useful handicapper: successful in
claimer at Carlisle in April, claimer at Lingfield and minor event at Warwick in July,
claimers at Catterick in August and Sandown in September and handicap at Catterick
in October: successful at 5f to 7f: acts on fibresand and equitrack, and has won on
going ranging from dead to firm on turf: blinkered/visored nowadays: often makes
running: tends to hang left (did so markedly fourth 6-y-o start) and race with head
high. *J. Berry*

PALACE OF GOLD   6 b.g. Slip Anchor 136 – Salacious (Sallust 134) [1995   42
NR 1996 16.1s⁶ 12.1d³ 13d³ 13s⁴ 13s⁴ 17.5m⁵ Sep 20] close-coupled gelding: poor
handicapper: should be suited by further than 13f: acts on soft ground: found little
and wandered second 6-y-o start. *L. Lungo*

PALAEMON   2 b.g. (Feb 1) Slip Anchor 136 – Palace Street (USA) 103 (Secreto   64
(USA) 128) [1996 6d⁵ 7m 7g 7.6m³ 8m⁵ 7.3s⁶ Oct 26] sturdy gelding: second foal:
half-brother to 3-y-o 1m winner Ca'D'Oro (by Cadeaux Genereux): dam won at 6f
and 7.2f: fair maiden: will be suited by middle distances: acts on good to firm and
soft ground. *G. B. Balding*

PALAMON (USA)   3 ch.c. Sanglamore (USA) 126 – Gantlette (Run The Gantlet   82
(USA)) [1995 76p: 8d⁶ 1996 10d³ 10m² 12m⁵ 10m* Jul 18] strong, lengthy colt:
fairly useful performer: 15/8 on and dropped in class, won median auction maiden at
Leicester in July by 6 lengths: sold 28,000 gns Newmarket Autumn Sales: stays
1½m: acts on good to firm going and dead: flashed tail and hung left on reappearance.
R. Charlton

PALDOST   2 b.c. (Apr 25) Efisio 120 – Fishki 36 (Niniski (USA) 125) [1996 7s⁵   –
6m 6g Aug 23] workmanlike colt: has a round action: first foal: dam 11.5f to 15f
winner: not successful over jumps: well beaten in maidens. *M. D. Hammond*

PALEY PRINCE (USA)   10 b.h. Tilt Up (USA) – Apalachee Princess (USA)   52
(Apalachee (USA) 137) [1995 67: 5.1m 5.1m 5g 5m⁴ 5f⁶ 5.7f⁶ 5.1h* 5g³ 5.1h³ 5.1h⁶
5.1h³ 5m* 5m⁵ 1996 5g 5m 5m 5m 5.1f⁵ Sep 25] strong-quartered, lengthy
horse: fair handicapper in 1995: only sign of retaining ability at 10 yrs when fifth at
Chepstow in September: stays 6f: acts on hard ground, dead and equitrack: effective
in visor, not tried for long time: sometimes bandaged: inconsistent. *M. D. I. Usher*

PALIO SKY   2 b.c. (Apr 26) Niniski (USA) 125 – Live Ammo 94 (Home Guard   87 p
(USA) 129) [1996 7d³ 8.1m* Sep 6] leggy, good-topped, quite attractive colt: brother

to a modest maiden and half-brother to 3 winners, including smart sprinter Powder Keg (by Tap On Wood): dam 2-y-o 6f winner: led over 2f out to win maiden at Haydock by 2 lengths from Supreme Sound: will stay beyond 1m: will improve again. *J. L. Dunlop*

PALISADE (USA) 2 b.f. (Apr 2) Gone West (USA) – Peplum (USA) 108 85 p (Nijinsky (CAN) 138) [1996 7g* Nov 2] second foal: half-sister to 3-y-o Pep Talk (by Lyphard): dam, won Cheshire Oaks, half-sister to Al Bahathri: 12/1, won 23-runner maiden at Newmarket by 1¼ lengths from Rebecca Sharp, soon prominent and running on strongly: should make useful performer at 1m+. *H. R. A. Cecil*

PALISANDER (IRE) 2 ch.g. (Feb 26) Conquering Hero (USA) 116 – Classic 62 Choice (Patch 129) [1996 6d⁶ 6m 6m⁵ 7m a8g Nov 14] IR 6,200Y, resold 31,000Y: a? eighth foal: half-brother to 1990 2-y-o 7f seller winner Classic Ring (by Auction Ring) and 2 winners abroad: dam never ran: modest maiden: poor efforts last 2 starts: should be suited by further than 6f: gelded. *S. Dow*

PALLIUM (IRE) 8 b.g. Try My Best (USA) 130 – Jungle Gardenia (Nonoalco 58 d (USA) 131) [1995 63: 5g 6g⁵ 7.5m 5m² 5m* 5f 5m 5f* 5m⁶ 5m⁴ 5h⁵ 5g 1996 5g 5f⁵ 6m 5g 5f⁴ 5m 5m³ 6f² 5m 5g 5m 6f Sep 28] good-bodied gelding: unimpressive mover: modest handicapper: best effort at 8 yrs when short-headed in seller at Newcastle in August: stays 6f: acts on firm and dead ground and the all-weather: tried in visor/blinkers, not in 1996: has hung: sometimes has tongue tied down: inconsistent. *Mrs A. M. Naughton*

PALO BLANCO 5 b.m. Precocious 126 – Linpac Mapleleaf 69 (Dominion 123) 82 [1995 78: 5m⁴ 6g⁵ 5d⁶ 6g³ 6d³ 1996 5g 5g* 6d* 6g² 6g³ 6m 6m 6g⁵ 6f⁶ Nov 5] rangy, workmanlike mare: fairly useful handicapper: won at Ayr in May: stays 6f: acts on dead going, probably on firm: usually edgy: consistent. *T. D. Barron*

PALOMA BAY (IRE) 3 b.f. Alzao (USA) 117 – Adventurine (Thatching 131) 92 [1995 92: 6m* 6m² 6g 1996 8g⁴ 7.3d⁵ 10.1m 8m Sep 28] smallish filly: good walker: has a quick action: fairly useful performer: good efforts in falsely-run listed race at Kempton and Fred Darling Stakes at Newbury: off course 5 months, well beaten in listed races at Yarmouth (pulled hard) and Ascot (virtually refused to race in rated stakes) on return: stays 1m: acts on good to firm and dead ground: sold 12,000 gns Newmarket December Sales. *M. Bell*

PAMELA'S BOY 2 ch.c. (Apr 9) Clantime 101 – Allez-Oops 65 (Moulin 103) – [1996 7g Oct 25] small, compact colt: first reported foal: dam 1m and 10.2f winner: tailed off in maiden at Doncaster. *A. Smith*

PAMPASA (FR) 2 br.f. (Mar 30) Pampabird 124 – Dounasa (FR) (Kaldoun (FR) – 122) [1996 6g Jul 15] 30,000 francs Y: first foal: dam unraced: around 10 lengths seventh of 10 in maiden at Windsor. *C. James*

PANAMA CITY (USA) 2 b.c. (May 16) El Gran Senor (USA) 136 – Obeah 112 102 p (Cure The Blues (USA)) [1996 8.1g² 8m* 8s² Oct 20] fourth foal: brother to 1994 2-y-o 7f winner Bedivere and 8.5f to 10.8f winner Morgana, latter smart in USA in 1995: dam (from successful family) smart staying 2-y-o and successful in USA: won maiden at Pontefract in September: 3½ lengths second of 10 to Hello in Gran Criterium at Milan 24 days later, keeping on: will be suited by middle distances. *P. W. Chapple-Hyam*

PANAMA JIVE (IRE) 3 ch.f. Cricket Ball (USA) – Straw Beret (USA) 80 52 § (Chief's Crown (USA)) [1995 NR 1996 a8g* a8.5g⁶ 11.1g⁴ 12d 9.9g a8f Dec 26] 2,200 2-y-o: sparely-made filly: first foal: dam, placed at up to 1m from 4 starts, half-sister to Kentucky Derby winner Sunny's Halo: poor performer: awarded seller at Southwell in January: failed to repeat that form, including in Dubai: should stay beyond 1m: very troublesome before start fourth outing: has unsatisfactory temperament, and one to steer clear of. *M. Johnston*

PANATA (IRE) 3 b.f. Tirol 127 – Rince Deas (IRE) 53 (Alzao (USA) 117) [1995 87 + NR 1996 7g⁵ 7m* 8.1m* 9m* 9g⁴ 8m Sep 28] IR 23,000Y: plain filly: tends not to impress in appearance: unimpressive walker: first foal: dam, placed at 5f at 2 yrs, sister to smart miler Mirror Black: won maiden at Yarmouth, 4-runner handicap at Chepstow (made all) and £8,300 handicap at Goodwood in the summer: ran well when fourth of 17 in £14,700 handicap at Goodwood penultimate start, switched and staying on strongly: sold 58,000 gns Newmarket December Sales: has raced only on a sound surface: may be capable of better returned to 9f+. *L. M. Cumani*

PANDICULATION   2 ch.c. (Feb 20) Statoblest 120 – Golden Panda 77 (Music   68
Boy 124) [1996 5g 5.1m⁶ 5m⁴ 5.9g³ 6d* 6m⁶ 7m Jul 11] 4,800Y, 6,200 2-y-o: strong,
lengthy, scopey colt: third foal: half-brother to 2 winners, including 1992 French
2-y-o Star of China (1m, by Celestial Storm): dam 8.2f winner: won maiden at
Haydock in June: broke leg at Redcar: dead. *E. Weymes*

PANDORA'S GIFT   3 b.f. Zalazl (USA) 120 – Lady Clementine 68 (He Loves   –
Me 120) [1995 NR 1996 a12g a12g May 31] seventh foal: half-sister to middle-
distance winners Much Too Clever and Darling Clover (both by Minster Son) and
fairly useful middle-distance stayer Much Sought After (by Adonijah): dam 5f
winner: no form in sellers at Wolverhampton. *K. R. Burke*

PANGERAN (USA)   4 b.g. Forty Niner (USA) – Smart Heiress (USA) (Vaguely   –
Noble 140) [1995 12s⁶ 1996 a7g Feb 9] ex-French gelding: closely related to smart
Homebuilder (by Mr Prospector), best at around 9f, and half-brother to several
winners: dam stakes-winning half-sister to champion 2-y-o filly Smart Angle: ran
twice in France for A. Fabre: sold twice in 1995, 26,000 gns Newmarket July Sales
and 3,000 gns Doncaster November Sales: soundly beaten in Southwell maiden on
British debut: modest hurdler. *Mrs A. Swinbank*

PANOORAS LORD (IRE)   2 b.c. (May 14) Topanoora 118 – Ladyship 76   –
(Windjammer (USA)) [1996 7f a7g Nov 15] stocky colt: seventh foal: half-brother to
winners abroad by Gorytus and Touching Wood: dam 1m winner, half-sister to very
smart sprinter Miami Springs: well held in maiden at Redcar and seller at Lingfield.
J. S. Wainwright

PANTHER (IRE)   6 ch.g. Primo Dominie 121 – High Profile (High Top 131)   75
[1995 60, a58: a6g* a6g³ a6g⁵ 6s* a7g³ 6g 7g 6m 6f² 6m⁵ 6g 7g⁶ 6g⁵ 7f⁵ a6g a8g a7g⁵   a50
1996 a6g a7g⁶ a7g 6d⁴ 6d* 6s² 6m* a7g³ 6g³ 6f* 6m⁶ 6m² a7g⁴ 5.1d* 5m⁶ 5m 5.1g
Sep 25] leggy gelding: fair performer on turf, modest on all-weather: won apprentice
race at Catterick in April, claimers at Redcar in May and Warwick (claimed out of J.
Hetherton's stable) in June and handicap at Chester (only third race over 5f, also first
run in visor for long time) in August: races mainly at sprint distances nowadays, best
form at 5f: acts on firm ground, soft and fibresand: occasionally blinkered/visored,
including last 4 starts: tends to hang. *P. D. Evans*

PANTO QUEEN   5 b.m. Lepanto (GER) – Tyqueen (Tycoon II) [1995 NR 1996   –
11.6m 10m 10.8f Jun 24] first foal: dam ran twice in points: no sign of ability in 2 NH
Flat races for Graham Richards: well beaten in varied company on flat. *C. R. Barwell*

PAOJIUNIC (IRE)   3 ch.c. Mac's Imp (USA) 116 – Audenhove (GER) (Marduk   70
(GER)) [1995 –p: 5g 1996 6m⁴ 6m⁴ 5m 7g⁴ 8m 7m 8.2g Oct 24] good-bodied colt:
fair maiden handicapper: sold 8,500 gns Newmarket Autumn Sales: probably needs
further than 5f, and stays 7f: sent to Italy. *L. M. Cumani*

PAPAHA (FR)   3 b.f. Green Desert (USA) 127 – Turban 80 (Glint of Gold 128)   103
[1995 91: 6.1d³ 7d⁴ 7m⁵ 1996 7d² 8.5m* 10.2m² 10.3d⁶ Nov 8] small, compact filly:
unimpressive mover: 16/1 on, easily made all in maiden at Beverley in July: useful
form when 1½ lengths second to Papering in listed race at Chepstow, headed inside
last: edgy, held up and never on terms in useful minor event at Doncaster 3½ months
later: will prove best at up to 1¼m: yet to race on extremes of going: has been
bandaged: sent to USA. *H. R. A. Cecil*

PAPER CLOUD   4 b.f. Lugana Beach 116 – Sweet Enough 79 (Caerleon (USA)   –
132) [1995 66: 10.3g⁴ 9m 11.6m 11.4g⁵ 10f³ 11.5g³ 11.9g⁶ 1996 12m⁶ 12.1m 12m
Sep 20] leggy filly: fair maiden handicapper in 1995 for C. Brittain: contested
amateurs and ladies events at 4 yrs, and showed no worthwhile form: stays 11.5f: acts
on good to firm ground and dead. *R. T. Phillips*

PAPERING (IRE)   3 b.f. Shaadi (USA) 126 – Wrapping 108§ (Kris 135) [1995   114
94p: 6g⁵ 7f* 7m² 1996 8m 10s³ 10.2m* 10m² 11.9m² 12m² 12d⁴ Oct 12] quite good-
topped filly, slightly unfurnished: smart performer: won listed race at Chepstow in
July by 1½ lengths from Papaha: second in Nassau Stakes (to Last Second) at Goodwood, Yorkshire Oaks (to Key Change) and in Prix Vermeille at Longchamp (very
much on toes, set pace, kept on really well, neck behind My Emma) next 3 starts:

Sheikh Mohammed's "Papering"

stays 1½m: has form on a soft surface, seems ideally suited by top-of-the-ground: stays in training. *L. M. Cumani*

PAPER MAZE 3 b.f. Mazilier (USA) 107 – Westonepaperchase (USA) 71 (Acci- –
piter (USA)) [1995 51: a5g³ 5m⁴ 5f⁴ a6g 6s⁶ 1996 7.1d 10g 9m 8m 8.1m 5m Sep 18]
close-coupled filly: modest form first 2 starts at 2 yrs, none since. *E. H. Owen jun*

PAPITA (IRE) 2 b.f. (Mar 20) Law Society (USA) 130 – Fantasise (FR) (General 77 ?
Assembly (USA)) [1996 6g⁵ 6m* 7m 6m 7m⁶ 7d Oct 11] 8,400Y: small, sturdy filly:
fourth foal: half-sister to 3-y-o sprinter Mullagh Hill Lad (by Cyrano de Bergerac)
and winners abroad by Pennine Walk (a German miler) and Nordance (in Sweden,
stays 1½m): dam second over 7f at 2 yrs in Ireland: won maiden at Goodwood in July
by 5 lengths, soon in clear lead: no comparable form and soundly beaten in Ascot
nursery final start: should stay beyond 6f. *S. Dow*

PAPUA 2 ch.c. (Mar 21) Green Dancer (USA) 132 – Fairy Tern 109 (Mill Reef 104
(USA) 141) [1996 6m⁴ 7f* 7m* 7g² 7m* 8g⁵ Oct 26] 62,000Y: tall, leggy colt:
closely related to minor US stakes winner Way of The World (by Dance of Life) and
half-brother to numerous winners here and in USA, including smart performer at up
to 9f Hoy (by Habitat): dam, winner at 5f and 7f, is closely related to smart 1¼m
performer Elegant Air: won minor events at Lingfield and Doncaster (making all) in
the summer and 23-runner Tattersalls Houghton Sales Stakes at Newmarket (by head
from Mukaddar, chasing leaders in falsely-run race and looking held 1f out) in
October: 4½ lengths fifth of 9 to Medaaly in Racing Post Trophy at Doncaster, held
up, outpaced 2½f out before running on strongly: will be suited by further than 1m:
game. *I. A. Balding*

PARADISE NAVY 7 b.g. Slip Anchor 136 – Ivory Waltz (USA) (Sir Ivor 135) 75 §
[1995 76: 16m 14m² 14m 17.2m³ 20m⁵ 16.2f³ 16.4m² 18.7g⁵ 16.2m⁵ 17.2m² 17.1m⁴

Tattersalls Houghton Sales Conditions Stakes, Newmarket—Papua (noseband, centre) leads on the line; with him are Mukaddar (striped cap), Granny's Pet (blaze) and hot favourite Abou Zouz (left)

16d[5] 16.5m[2] a16g[4] 1996 16.4g 16d 16.1f[3] 20f 16.2f[4] 16.4g 14m[4] 17.2f* 20m[4] a16g* a16g[3] 16d[6] 18.2m 15.4g[3] 16.1f[4] 18g 16g[3] 14.1s[3] 16.5s[4] a14g[4] Nov 29] close-coupled, quite attractive gelding: poor walker: fair handicapper: won at Bath and Lingfield in the summer: stays 2½m: acts on any turf going and equitrack: blinkered nowadays: usually waited with: tends not to find much off the bridle and can't be relied on. *C. R. Egerton*

Robert & Elizabeth Hitchens' "Papua"

PARADISE WATERS 4 gr.f. Celestial Storm (USA) 132 – Gleaming Water 81   73
(Kalaglow 132) [1995 62: 10.2m⁵ 10f³ 11.8g² 12m² 12f⁵ 11.6m* 11.8g² 11.4d⁴ 14g⁴
11.8g 1996 11.9f⁴ 11.7g* 12g² 13.1g* 12g* 12m⁴ Jun 21] unfurnished filly: fair
handicapper: won at Bath in April and May, and at Kempton in June: probably stays
1¾m: acts on firm ground, below best on dead: tends to race prominently and has
made all for last 3 wins: game and reliable. *R. F. Johnson Houghton*

PARELLIE 3 b.f. Inca Chief (USA) – Parklands Belle 73 (Stanford 121§) [1995   –
–: a6g 1996 a9.4g Nov 25] well beaten in seller and claimer at Wolverhampton.
P. D. Evans

PARIJAZZ (IRE) 2 b.f. (Apr 30) Astronef 116 – Brandywell (Skyliner 117)   68
[1996 6.1m⁵ 6d² 5.1m 6m² 6g* Oct 21] 1,500Y: leggy, sparely-made filly: fifth foal:
dam poor Irish maiden: fair performer: hung markedly left penultimate start: justified
favouritism in 14-runner maiden auction at Pontefract 5 weeks later, making all:
stays 6f: acts on good to firm and dead ground. *Martyn Meade*

PARIS BABE 4 b.f. Teenoso (USA) 135 – Kala's Image 55 (Kala Shikari 125)   –
[1995 94: 6d² 7m 6m⁴ 6g* 6g³ 6g* 6m⁴ 6m⁵ 6g* 6m 6g 6g 1996 7f⁶ 6s Nov 9]
smallish, workmanlike filly: fairly useful performer at 3 yrs: behind in 2 listed races
at 4 yrs, off course 6 months in between: will prove best at sprint distances: acts on
good to firm and dead ground: usually held up. *D. Morris*

PARKLIFE (IRE) 4 ch.g. Double Schwartz 128 – Silk Trade (Auction Ring   44
(USA) 123) [1995 37: a9.4g⁵ 9m 6m⁵ 6.9f⁵ 1996 a12g⁴ a12g² a12g a8g³ a11g 16.1f²
Oct 8] compact gelding: poor maiden handicapper: stays 2m: acts on fibresand and
firm ground: visored (well beaten) fifth 4-y-o start. *P. C. Haslam*

PARK RIDGE 4 b.g. Indian Ridge 123 – Aspark (Sparkler 130) [1995 62d: 9g⁶   –
8m 8.3m 10.2m 1996 12d⁶ a14g 11.9f⁴ 11.6m 8m 8m 10g Oct 2] tall gelding: poor
maiden: sold 1,200 gns Newmarket Autumn Sales: has looked a none too easy ride,
and was tried in hood and blinkers penultimate start. *T. G. Mills*

PARLIAMENT PIECE 10 ch.g. Burslem 123 – Sallywell (Manado 130) [1995   66 d
77: 8g 8f* 7f⁶ 8m⁵ 7m* 8m³ 8.1g⁶ 7g 7f 1996 7g 7.6g 8m⁴ 7g 8m² 8m⁵ 8.5f⁶ 8m 8.2g
7g 10g Oct 29] big, lengthy gelding: poor mover: modest performer nowadays:
left D. Nicholls after eighth 10-y-o start: below form for new stable: suited by 7f/1m:
acts on firm ground and dead: effective blinkered/visored or not: usually held up.
Capt. J. Wilson

PARONOMASIA 4 b.g. Precocious 126 – The Crying Game 55 (Manor Farm   –
Boy 114) [1995 –: a6g a6g⁴ a6g 7.6m 8g⁶ 1996 a8g³ a6g a7g a8g⁵ a8g 8.2d a11g   a37
10.3m⁶ 11.1g 10m 14.1m 14.1f 15.1g⁵ 14.9m 10f 8m a10g² a10s² a8g a10g Dec 20]
workmanlike gelding: poor maiden handicapper: left M. Bell's stable after fourth
4-y-o outing: stays 1¼m: acts on equitrack: often visored/blinkered, no improvement: inconsistent. *J. L. Harris*

PARQUET 2 ch.f. (Mar 1) Lead On Time (USA) 123 – Tocaronte (FR) (Kris 135)   –
[1996 a6g 5.3g Oct 2] 1,300Y: first foal: dam unraced half-sister to smart French
performer at up to 10.5f Astair: well beaten in sellers. *J. J. Sheehan*

PARROT JUNGLE (IRE) 3 b.f. High Estate 127 – Palm Dove (USA) (Storm   102
Bird (CAN) 134) [1995 99: 7m³ 7f* 8h² 7.1g² 7m² 7v² 1996 8g² 8g 10m 10g⁵ 8d³ 9d⁵
10.3d⁴ Nov 8] useful-looking filly: useful performer: unlucky neck second in listed
race at Kempton on reappearance: best effort when running-on third to Fatefully in
listed race at Ascot in October: best form at 1m, should be effective over further:
winner on firm ground at 2 yrs, bit below best on heavy: sent to race in France.
J. L. Dunlop

PARROT'S HILL (IRE) 3 b.g. Nashamaa 113 – Cryptic Gold (Glint of Gold   55
128) [1995 NR 1996 10g 8f 10m 13.8s² 11.6m⁴ 12m 11.5m⁵ 12m Oct 7] IR 4,000Y:
compact gelding: second foal: dam Irish maiden: modest maiden: probably needs at least 1½m:
seems to act on soft and good to firm ground. *M. H. Tompkins*

PARSA (USA) 3 b.f. Risen Star (USA) – Pallanza (USA) (Lyphard (USA) 132)   66
[1995 –p: 7.1s 7m 1996 10m 10m* 10.1f² 9.9m² 10.1g³ 11.8g⁵ 10d⁶ 8f⁴ 8.2s³ Oct 31]
big, good-topped filly: fair handicapper: comfortably won at Leicester in June: stays
1¼m: acts on firm and soft ground. *J. L. Dunlop*

PARSIS (USA) 3 b.c. Diesis 133 – Par Excellence (CAN) (L'Enjoleur (CAN)) 68
[1995 68: 6m⁴ 7m 7g³ 1996 8g 8.1d³ Jun 8] smallish, robust colt: fair maiden:
hooded, better effort as 3-y-o when third at Haydock, making most: sold 6,200 gns
Newmarket September Sales: stays 1m: seems to act on dead going: sent to Kuwait.
Lady Herries

PARTITA 3 b.f. Polish Precedent (USA) 131 – Pharian (USA) 114 (Diesis 133) –
[1995 NR 1996 7.1m 11.5f⁵ 10g Oct 9] second foal: dam won Cheshire Oaks and
Lancashire Oaks: well beaten in maidens: sold 3,400 gns Newmarket December
Sales. *C. E. Brittain*

PARTY POSER 3 b.f. Presidium 124 – Pooka 65 (Dominion 123) [1995 NR 1996 –
7s Mar 27] 800Y: second foal: dam best at 5f: 100/1, soon tailed off in seller at
Catterick. *B. W. Murray*

PARTY ROMANCE (USA) 2 gr.c. (May 15) Black Tie Affair – Tia Juanita 87
(USA) (My Gallant (USA)) [1996 7m⁴ 7g⁴ 7.1m³ 7.9g² 7.1v⁴ Oct 6] $22,000F,
$155,000Y: close-coupled, good-bodied colt: has scope: second foal: dam won
several minor stakes and placed in Grade 2 1¼m event: fairly useful maiden: fourth
of 10 in Chesham Stakes at Ascot on debut: failed to improve on that, but looked
unlucky not to have finished closer when second in nursery at York: stays 1m:
probably unsuited by heavy ground: strong-running sort. *B. Hanbury*

PAS DE REPONSE (USA) 2 b.f. (Apr 17) Danzig (USA) – Soundings 113 p
(USA) (Mr Prospector (USA)) [1996 6g* 6g* 5.5m* 6m* Oct 1]
        Criquette Head has joined her father Alec Head in winning three
Cheveley Park Stakes, Pas de Reponse's win in the latest running following
those of Ma Biche in 1982 and Ravinella in 1987, and, further back, those of
Alec's Midget II (1955), Opaline II (1960) and Mige (1968). A 7/1 chance
having drifted from 9/2, Pas de Reponse started third favourite to the highly
impressive Cherry Hinton winner Dazzle, who was backed down to 9/4 on.
Godolphin's recent purchase, Moonlight Paradise, second in the Princess
Margaret Stakes on her previous outing, started second favourite, with the Prix
Robert Papin winner Ocean Ridge at 12/1 and the remaining quartet at 16/1 or
longer. Pas de Reponse's rider Freddie Head has not always enjoyed a
favourable press in Britain, but on this occasion he could not be faulted; all the
criticism was for Kieran Fallon on Dazzle. Whilst Pas de Response was well
placed throughout, never far off the muddling pace set by Ocean Ridge, Dazzle
was held up. Head made his move over a furlong out and Pas de Reponse belied
her name by quickening into the lead, and then she held on well up the hill to
beat the staying-on Moonlight Paradise a length, the same distance back to
Ocean Ridge in third and Dazzle, a long way below her Cherry Hinton form, a
further half length away in fourth. Although there were grounds for doubting
the reliability of the form, Moonlight Paradise confirmed her superiority over

*Shadwell Stud Cheveley Park Stakes, Newmarket—French challenger Pas de Reponse (second left)
comes into the classic reckoning with this defeat of Moonlight Paradise,
Ocean Ridge (spotted cap) and Dazzle (extreme right)*

Dazzle in the Rockfel Stakes later in the month on the only occasion any of the principals turned out again.

Like many a good horse before her, Pas de Reponse had begun her career in the Prix Yacowlef at Deauville, starting second favourite and beating five rivals in the listed event for newcomers. Seventeen days later over the same course and distance, she was the only filly in the line-up for the five-runner Prix Morny and lost nothing in defeat behind Bahamian Bounty and Zamindar, especially considering her inexperience; she ran on without being able to land a blow and was beaten just over three lengths. Pas de Reponse had a much simpler task, and easily landed the odds, in another field of five for the Prix d'Arenberg over an extended five furlongs at Evry three weeks before being sent over to Newmarket, beating Heaven's Command a length and a half.

	Danzig (USA) (b 1977)	Northern Dancer (b 1961)	Nearctic Natalma
Pas de Reponse (USA) (b.f. Apr 17, 1994)		Pas de Nom (b or br 1968)	Admiral's Voyage Petitioner
	Soundings (USA) (b 1983)	Mr Prospector (b 1970)	Raise A Native Gold Digger
		Ocean's Answer (b 1976)	Northern Answer South Ocean

Pas de Reponse is an extremely well-bred filly, by Danzig out of a Mr Prospector mare who had previously produced the Prix Robert Papin winner Didyme and the Poule d'Essai des Poulains winner Green Tune when mated to other Northern Dancer stallions, Dixieland Band and Green Dancer respect-

Wertheimer et Frere's "Pas de Reponse"

ively. The mare Soundings was further represented on the track in the latest season by the useful three-year-old filly Ecoute (by Manila), successful over a mile (in a listed race) and a mile and a quarter and placed three times in pattern company, including in the Prix Saint-Alary. Her yearling Sound Prospector (a full brother to Didyme) will be one to look out for in 1997. Soundings, who won at up to a mile in the United States, is a sister to the smart sprinter Al Zawbaah and they are just two out of eight winners to date foaled by Ocean's Answer. Ocean's Answer, who won the Natalma Stakes in Canada as a two-year-old over an extended mile, is out of a Canadian Oaks winner and is a close relative of both Storm Bird and the Champion Canadian filly Northernette.

Both Ma Biche and Ravinella were returned to Newmarket to win the One Thousand Guineas. It would seem likely that Pas de Reponse will return, too, although immediately after the Cheveley Park trainer and jockey were no more than cautiously optimistic about Pas de Reponse staying the trip. In the opinion of Mme Head, 'You can win a Guineas with a filly that doesn't stay the mile properly. I did it with Ma Biche. I am not saying this filly will win it but I think we will be back for it.' According to her brother, 'Pas de Reponse could get the mile next year. The way she won, she was so relaxed. She has got class and speed. I am not saying she is a Ma Biche, a Ravinella or a Miesque but we'll see next year.' Pas de Reponse is bred to stay a mile. While her form doesn't measure up to that which Ma Biche and Ravinella showed at the same stage it compares well with that of her contemporaries and she is likely to continue to improve. Angular in appearance as a two-year-old, she has a quick action and a very good turn of foot. So far she has raced only on a sound surface. *Mme C. Head, France*

PASH 4 b.f. Hallgate 127 – Pashmina 68 (Blue Cashmere 129) [1995 41: a8g 8.1d* 44 7g 8f⁵ 8.1g 8g 8.1f⁶ 8m 7m 8g 8.3g³ 8.1d⁴ a10g 1996 8.1g 8g 8g 9.2g⁶ 8.3s* 8g 10d 9.2g Jun 3] small filly: poor form: won handicap at Hamilton in May: below form afterwards: sold 625 gns Ascot July Sales: should stay beyond 1m: acts on soft ground: often visored, including when successful. *C. W. Fairhurst*

PASSAGE CREEPING (IRE) 3 b.f. Persian Bold 123 – Tiptoe (Dance In Time 75 (CAN)) [1995 66p: 7m 1996 7m 8d⁵ 7g² 8g⁶ 8f² 10.1g⁴ 8.3d a8s² a8g² Dec 26] lengthy filly: fair maiden handicapper, trained until last 2 starts by L. Cumani: stays 1¼m: acts on firm ground and equitrack, seems unsuited by soft surface. *S. Dow*

PASSI D'ORLANDO (IRE) 2 ch.c. Persian Bold 123 – When Lit 91 + (Northfields (USA)) [1996 7d⁵ 7f³ 8s* 9s² 8g³ Nov 3] half-brother to several winners in Italy, notably smart middle-distance horse Guado d'Annibale (by Glint of Gold): dam won twice in Italy at 3 yrs: won minor event at Milan in September: second in minor event on same course following month and 3 lengths third of 13 to Golden Aventura in quite valuable event at Rome last time: stays at least 9f. *J. L. Dunlop*

PASSIFLORA 2 ch.f. (Jan 23) Night Shift (USA) – Pineapple 77 (Superlative 75 118) [1996 6m* 6g² 7s Nov 9] first reported foal: dam 1½m winner, half-sister to In The Groove (by Night Shift): won maiden at Folkestone in June, and second of 5 to Fanny's Choice in minor event at Windsor in July: off course over 4 months afterwards, soundly beaten on return: should be suited by further than 6f. *J. L. Dunlop*

PASSING STRANGERS (USA) 3 b.g. Lyphard (USA) 132 – The Way We 60 Were (USA) (Avatar (USA)) [1995 68: 7g 7d 1996 7m 10m 11.5m³ Aug 17] fair performer: not seen out at 3 yrs until July, never placed to challenge in maiden and handicap before third (joint favourite) in handicap at Lingfield: will prove better at 1½m than shorter. *P. W. Harris*

PASSION 2 ch.f. (Apr 27) Risk Me (FR) 127 – Gotcher 74 (Jalmood (USA) 126) 61 p [1996 6m⁵ Oct 28] fair sort: first reported foal: dam irresolute 2-y-o 6f winner who stayed 7f: 20/1 and short to post, 6½ lengths fifth of 13 to Arapi in maiden at Leicester, outpaced and green early on, staying on well: should improve. *T. G. Mills*

PASSION FOR LIFE 3 br.g. Charmer 123 – Party Game 70 (Red Alert 127) 116 [1995 82: 5s³ 5m* 5g* 5m² 5f⁴ 1996 5d³ 6g* 6m* 6f⁶ 6g² 6v 6g² Oct 19] leggy, good-topped gelding: unimpressive mover: vastly improved at 3 yrs, winning handicap at Kempton (by 8 lengths) and listed race at Newmarket (readily from Iktamal) in April and 13-runner Benazet-Rennen at Baden-Baden (made all, beat Hever Golf Rose ¾ length) in June: off course 3½ months, returned to form when second of 15 to Russian Revival in listed race at Newmarket: stays 6f: acts on good to firm ground (emerged best of front runners in strongly-run Duke of York Stakes on firm) and soft: usually early to post. *G. Lewis*

PASTERNAK 3 b.c. Soviet Star (USA) 128 – Princess Pati 124 (Top Ville 129) 93 p
[1995 77p: 7f⁵ 7g 7m³ 1996 8.3s⁵ 8.2f² 9f 10g³ 10.2d* 10.4g* Oct 9] good-topped colt: has plenty of scope: settled better than previously when winning maiden at Bath in September: well backed and looking in fine shape, followed up in 20-runner handicap at York 9 days later, denied run several times before finally getting clear approaching final 1f and storming through to win by ¾ length going away): will stay further than 10.4f: seems well suited by some give: sure to improve further at 4 yrs, and will win more races. *Sir Mark Prescott*

PASTICHE 2 b.f. (Mar 4) Kylian (USA) – Titian Beauty (Auction Ring (USA) 61 p
123) [1996 a8g⁴ Dec 20] third reported foal: half-sister to 1992 2-y-o 5f seller winner Petite Lass (by Lidhame): dam Irish maiden: sire (unraced) by Sadler's Wells out of half-sister to Storm Bird: weak 10/1, over 4 lengths fourth of 10 to Zimiri in maiden at Lingfield, always well there: should improve. *T. G. Mills*

PATER NOSTER (USA) 7 b.h. Stately Don (USA) 122 – Sainera (USA) 89 94
(Stop The Music (USA)) [1995 106: 8g⁴ 8g³ 1996 10g 8.2d⁴ Aug 25] leggy, quite attractive horse: has a round action: one-time smart performer, though has been diffi-cult to train and lightly raced: last in Prix Exbury at Saint-Cloud on reappearance: steadily to post, below-form fourth of 5 to Kayvee in minor event at Nottingham over 5 months later: stays 1m: successful on good to firm ground at 3 yrs, but best efforts on a soft surface and acts on heavy: front runner: sold to join J. A. Harris only 5,000 gns Newmarket December Sales. *Mrs J. Cecil*

PATHAZE 3 b.f. Totem (USA) 118 – Stilvella (Camden Town 125) [1995 61: 5g³ 51
5g³ 5f* 5m 5m⁵ 5g 5g 1996 6.1g 6d³ 6d 6m³ 5m² 5.9f² 6m⁴ 6f⁶ 7m³ 6m² 5m³ 6m² 7g
6g⁵ Sep 2] workmanlike filly: modest handicapper: generally creditable efforts at 3 yrs: stays 6f: acts on firm and dead ground. *N. Bycroft*

PATIALA (IRE) 3 b.f. Nashwan (USA) 135 – Catherine Parr (USA) 109 –
(Riverman (USA) 131) [1995 NR 1996 10s 14.6d⁵ a12g a14.8g⁶ Nov 25] 18,500 2-y-o: lengthy filly: first foal: dam, French maiden, who stayed 1¼m, is closely related to good-class middle-distance stayer Orban and daughter of Irish Oaks winner Regal Exception: no sign of ability. *R. W. Armstrong*

PATINA 2 ch.f. (May 20) Rudimentary (USA) 118 – Appledorn 99 (Doulab (USA) 51
115) [1996 7m a7g³ a6g³ Dec 7] workmanlike filly: first foal: dam 6f and 7f winner: tailed off in maiden at Leicester: modest form when third in similar events at Wolverhampton. *R. Hollinshead*

PATRIO (IRE) 3 b.f. Polish Patriot (USA) 128 – Fleetwood Fancy (Taufan –
(USA) 119) [1995 59: 6f 7f⁵ a7g⁵ 1996 a8g 6g⁶ 7f a7g⁶ 7g 8f 7d Aug 23] unfurnished filly: modest form in maidens at 2 yrs for M. Johnston: no worthwhile form as 3-y-o: sold 1,050 gns Newmarket September Sales: stays 7f. *S. C. Williams*

PATRITA PARK 2 br.f. (Feb 19) Flying Tyke 90 – Bellinote (FR) 71 (Noir Et Or 42
125) [1996 5m 5s 7m⁵ a7g a7g⁵ Dec 7] smallish, workmanlike filly: seventh foal: dam maiden half-sister to smart 1981 French 2-y-o stayer Beau Pretender: poor form, including in nursery and seller: stays 7f. *W. W. Haigh*

PAT SAID NO (IRE) 2 b.f. (Apr 4) Last Tycoon 131 – Fiddle-Faddle (Silly Sea- 59
son 127) [1996 5f² 6.1m⁵ Jul 6] 13,500Y, 11,500 2-y-o: half-sister to several winners, including 1m winner (better form at middle distances) Fife (by Lomond) and useful stayer El Conquistador (by Shirley Heights): dam, 1½m and 2m winner, is half-sister to Irish St Leger winner Mountain Lodge: modest form in 2 maiden auctions in the summer, well backed second start: should stay at least 1m. *D. J. S. Cosgrove*

PATSCILLA 5 b. or br.m. Squill (USA) 122 – Fortune Teller (Troy 137) [1995 NR –
1996 14.1f a12g Jul 27] compact filly: no worthwhile form: tried blinkered. *R. Dickin*

PATS DELIGHT 4 ch.f. Crofthall 110 – Petroc Concert § (Tina's Pet 121) [1995 –
44d: a5g⁶ a5g⁴ a6g⁴ a5g a5g a5g⁵ 10m⁵ 1996 a6g a7g a12g a5g 8.2d 6f May 6] leggy filly: poor maiden: best efforts over 5f: tried blinkered. *S. Coathup*

PATS FOLLY 5 bl.m. Macmillion 110 – Cavo Varka 81 (Cavo Doro 124) [1995 –
–: 10.2m a8.5g 10.8m 8h 10.8f 1996 8m 13.4g Sep 25] leggy mare: of little account.
F. J. Yardley

PAT'S SPLENDOUR 5 b.m. Primitive Rising (USA) 113 – Northern Venture 80   48
(St Alphage 119) [1995 49: 10m 8.3m⁴ 8g 9d⁴ 12m² 12m a12g a13g³ 1996 a16g a–
10f 10.1g⁵ 11.6d⁵ 10g² 10m 10.8f³ 11.5m 12s a13g Nov 26] angular mare: poor
handicapper nowadays: stays 1½m: acts on firm ground and dead: inconsistent.
H. J. Collingridge

PATSY GRIMES 6 b.m. Beveled (USA) – Blue Angel (Lord Gayle (USA) 124)   94
[1995 71: 5d 6g 5g³ 6m* 6m³ 6m² 6m 5m² 6m 6.1d⁵ a6g⁶ a6g³ 1996 a7g³ a7g a6g²
a7g⁴ a6g⁴ 6m* 6m 6.1d* 6g⁵ 7g* 7m 7m 6m* 6m 7m Sep 28] leggy mare: fairly
useful handicapper, better than ever at 6 yrs: won at Salisbury and Chepstow in May,
at Yarmouth in July and Newbury (apprentices) in August: effective at 5f to 7f (had
form over 1m in 1993): acts on any turf going and all-weather surfaces: effective
blinkered/visored, though rarely tried nowadays: often apprentice ridden: usually
comes from behind: tough. *J. S. Moore*

PAY HOMAGE 8 ch.g. Primo Dominie 121 – Embraceable Slew (USA) (Seattle   81
Slew (USA)) [1995 85: 8g 8m 9m* 8.5m 8f² 8m 9m⁵ 9g 8.5s² 7.9m 9d⁵ 8m 1996 8m
8g⁴ 8.5m⁶ 8.9m 8m⁵ 10.2m³ 9f 9g² 10.2f⁵ 9m³ Sep 26] angular, workmanlike
gelding: still fairly useful handicapper: stays 1¼m, at least when conditions aren't
testing: best form on a sound surface, but comparable efforts at 7 yrs on firm and soft
going: blinkered once at 2 yrs, visored once at 4 yrs: held up: none too consistent.
I. A. Balding

PC'S CRUISER (IRE) 4 b.g. Homo Sapien 121 – Ivy Holme (Silly Season 127)   51
[1995 53d, a57d: a8g³ a7g³ a8g* a8g³ a6g* a7g a6g⁴ 7g 7g³ 7.5m⁵ 8m² 7g a7g 8.2f
6g 7f 8.2m a11g 1996 a8g³ a8g a8g⁵ a10g a8g⁴ 7.1g² 8m² 6.9g 7g⁵ a7g⁴ a8g³ 8m a7g
a8g* 8.3g a8g⁶ 8m⁴ a8g⁴ a8g Dec 3] sturdy gelding: modest handicapper: won at
Southwell in August: stays 1m: acts on fibresand (below form only run on equitrack)
and good to firm ground: effective blinkered/visored or not: has run creditably for
lady: none too consistent. *J. L. Eyre*

PEACEFULL REPLY (USA) 6 b.h. Hold Your Peace (USA) – Drone Answer   54 d
(USA) (Drone) [1995 44: 7.1g 7g⁶ 7m 7g a7g 7d 7m a8g³ a9.4g 1996 a8.5g a11g a7g²
a8g a7g 7g 8m a7g 7.1g 8f 8m a8g a6s⁶ a6g⁵ Dec 27] close-coupled, good-topped
horse: poor mover: only worthwhile form at 6 yrs when head second in minor event
at Southwell in April: stays 1m: acts on firm ground and fibresand: tried blinkered,
no improvement: inconsistent, and not to be trusted. *F. H. Lee*

PEACE HOUSE (IRE) 3 ch.f. Magical Strike (USA) 114 – Theda 61 (Mum-   –
my's Pet 125) [1995 NR 1996 6s 5d 8.5m 6m May 28] small, sturdy filly: seventh
foal: sister to fairly useful 1994 2-y-o 6f winner I Should Cocoa, and half-sister to
sprint winners by Digamist and Kafu: dam stayed 7f: well beaten in maidens and
(blinkered) amateurs maiden handicap. *J. L. Spearing*

PEARL ANNIVERSARY (IRE) 3 ch.g. Priolo (USA) 127 – Tony Award   –
(USA) (Kirtling 129) [1995 –p: 8.2m 1996 10g⁶ a12g* 11.1m a16g⁴ a12g* a14.8g² a59
14.1f⁵ a14g⁴ 14.1m⁵ a12g² a16g³ a12g² a14.8g⁵ Sep 21] leggy, lengthy gelding: poor
walker: modest performer: won 2 sellers at Wolverhampton in May: claimed out of
M. Johnston's stable £6,000 penultimate start: soundly beaten final outing: should
prove a stayer: best efforts on fibresand. *Miss S. J. Wilton*

PEARL DAWN (IRE) 6 b.m. Jareer (USA) 115 – Spy Girl (Tanfirion 110) [1995   73 d
74, a–: a6g a6g⁴ a8.5g 5.1h⁴ 6m⁴ 6f² 5.7h* 5.1h* 5f³ 5m³ 5g 5.3g³ 5m a5g⁵ 1996 a–
a6g a6g 6f 5m³ 6g⁴ 7f⁵ 8f* 7f⁵ 7g 6f⁴ 6.9g 8f⁴ 7f 7.1s Oct 22] sparely-made
mare: fair form early in 1996, but generally disappointing from July onwards, and
some way below best when winning seller at Brighton in July on second start in 2
days: stays 1m: acts on hard and dead ground, well below form on the all-weather:
none too consistent. *G. L. Moore*

PEARL D'AZUR (USA) 3 b.g. Dayjur (USA) 137 – Priceless Pearl (USA) 101   90
(Alydar (USA)) [1995 NR 1996 7.9m³ a6g* 6m* 5m⁵ 6g Oct 12] tall, leggy gelding:
looked rather weak: third foal: half-brother to useful 4-y-o 6f and 7f winner Isla Del
Rey (by Nureyev): dam, 7f winner at 2 yrs, sister to Saratoga Six and half-sister to
Dunbeath: won maiden at Wolverhampton in July: again idled in front having led on
bridle over 2f out when winning 6-runner handicap at Newmarket 2 weeks later:

below form in similar events at Sandown and York (raced freely) afterwards: will prove as effective over 5f as 6f: likely to prove suited by waiting tactics: gelded and stays in training. *D. R. Loder*

PEARLS OF THOUGHT (IRE)   3 b.f. Persian Bold 123 – Miss Loving 89 – (Northfields (USA)) [1995 55: 5m 6m⁵ 6.1m⁵ 7s 7f 1996 6s 6d 8.3s⁶ 6.9m May 10] leggy filly: shows knee action: modest maiden at 2 yrs for P. Walwyn: scant promise in 1996. *J. S. Haldane*

PEARL VENTURE   4 b.f. Salse (USA) 128 – Our Shirley 84 (Shirley Heights 80 130) [1995 92: 7m⁵ 10g³ 10.8g* 10m 10.2m³ 10g⁴ 10.1g⁶ 10.1g 8s 1996 8s 8.1g 10.3m⁶ 8.5m 14.4g² 14.9f² 16.4g* 18.7m 14m⁵ 18.2m⁴ 16.2m 16s 16g Nov 1] lengthy, angular filly: good walker: fairly useful handicapper: very confidently ridden to lead near line when winning at Sandown in July: below form all subsequent outings: stays well: probably acts on any going: blinkered/visored (ran poorly) once each: best with waiting tactics. *S. P. C. Woods*

PEARTREE HOUSE (IRE)   2 b.c. (Apr 24) Simply Majestic (USA) – Fashion 87 Front (Habitat 134) [1996 6m⁴ 6m* 6g⁴ 7m* 8m⁶ Sep 12] IR 16,500F, 35,000Y: rangy, workmanlike colt: half-brother to winners in North America by Far North and The Minstrel and to the dam of very smart sprinter Mind Games: dam unraced daughter of Irish 1000 Guineas winner and excellent broodmare Front Row: successful in small fields for median auction maiden at Ayr and minor event at Catterick in the summer: staying-on sixth of 17 in valuable nursery at Doncaster: sold 50,000 gns Newmarket Autumn Sales: stays 1m: sometimes carries head bit high. *B. W. Hills*

PEATSVILLE (IRE)   4 b.g. Ela-Mana-Mou 132 – Windy Cheyenne (USA) – (Tumble Wind (USA)) [1995 –: 11m 8g 10.2f a14.8g 1996 a16g Dec 5] big, useful-looking gelding: no sign of ability. *M. R. Channon*

PEDALTOTHEMETAL (IRE)   4 b.f. Nordico (USA) – Full Choke 77 (Shirley 50 Heights 130) [1995 46: 10g 11.6m 8f⁴ 8.3m⁴ 8.3g⁵ 10m⁶ 10.1m⁶ 10f 7.6m 8.1d⁶ 10g⁴ 9m³ 1996 a12g² a11g⁶ 12m 16.4m 17.2m⁴ 17.2f² 15.1m⁵ 14m Jul 24] angular filly: modest maiden handicapper: brought down fourth start: stays 17.2f: acts on firm and dead ground and on fibresand: tried blinkered, not in 1996: held up. *P. Mitchell*

PEEP O DAY   5 b.m. Domynsky 110 – Betrothed (Aglojo 119) [1995 –: 10.4m 45 13.8f⁵ 15.1s 10m a16g 15.1m⁴ 10.1m 12.1s* a14g Nov 22] poor handicapper: dictated steady gallop when winning at Musselburgh in November: best efforts at around 1½m on an easy surface: modest winning (over 3m) hurdler. *J. L. Eyre*

PEETSIE (IRE)   4 b.f. Fairy King (USA) – Burning Ambition (Troy 137) [1995 – NR 1996 10m 12.1d⁶ a8g a12g Dec 14] big filly: half-sister to 5f (at 2 yrs) to 1m winner Dance On Sixpence (by Lidhame) and fairly useful 1¼m and 1½m winner Her Honour (by Teenoso), latter also very useful hurdler: dam lightly-raced half-sister to 1000 Guineas winner One In A Million: fair form in 3 NH Flat races for N. Twiston-Davies: well beaten in maidens and handicap on flat, for Lord Huntingdon first 2 starts. *N. A. Twiston-Davies*

PEGGY ESS   3 b.f. Seymour Hicks (FR) 125 – Daffodil 58 (Welsh Pageant 132) – [1995 –: 7f 8.2d 1996 8.1f 14.1f 16.4v Nov 11] neat filly: poor mover: seemingly of no account. *A. P. James*

PEGGY SPENCER   4 ch.f. Formidable (USA) 125 – Careful Dancer (Gorytus 63 (USA) 132) [1995 68: 6g 5.1g⁶ 6m³ 7.1m 6g a6g³ a6g* a7g* a6g² 1996 a7g² a8g a77 a7g* a7g⁴ 7s⁴ 7d May 8] smallish, lengthy filly: fair handicapper on the all-weather, successful at Wolverhampton in February: only modest on turf: stays 7f (never going well when tried at 1m): acts on good to firm and soft ground, and goes well on the all-weather. *C. W. Thornton*

PEGRAM (IRE)   3 b.c. Cadeaux Genereux 131 – Pertinent (Persepolis (FR) 127) 69 [1995 NR 1996 7m⁴ 8m⁵ May 5] IR 36,000Y: good-topped colt: has scope: third foal: dam, Irish 1¼m winner, half-sister to good sprinter Sayyaf: similar form in maidens at Newmarket: not certain to stay 1m: sold only 600 gns Newmarket Autumn Sales: sent to Germany. *L. M. Cumani*

PELHAM (IRE)   2 b.c. (Apr 19) Archway (IRE) 115 – Yavarro 44 (Raga Navarro 92 (ITY) 119) [1996 5.2d 5.1g* 5.1g² 6m⁴ 6f* 6f⁵ 6m² 6g³ 7m³ 6m Oct 17] IR 10,000Y: useful-looking colt: fifth foal: dam poor daughter of Cheshire Oaks winner Yelda:

won maiden auction at Bath in April and minor event at Yarmouth in June: third to Miss Stamper in Tattersalls Breeders Stakes at the Curragh: seems ideally suited by 6f: acts on firm ground: didn't handle bend at Epsom fourth start. *R. Hannon*

PENBOLA (IRE) 4 b.g. Pennine Walk 120 – Sciambola (Great Nephew 126) – [1995 –: 9.9m 14d⁶ 1996 16.2m Apr 12] tall, lengthy, rather unfurnished gelding: unimpressive mover: no worthwhile form on flat last 2 seasons: should stay at least 1m: sold 1,000 gns Doncaster August Sales. *T. D. Easterby*

PENDLEY ROSE 3 ch.f. Prince Sabo 123 – Rose Bouquet 78 (General 48 Assembly (USA)) [1995 62+: 6m⁴ 6m⁵ a7g⁵ 7g⁶ 7s⁴ 1996 8m⁶ 8.3g 8g 6m⁵ 6m⁴ 5g 6m Sep 19] modest form at 2 yrs, only poor in 1996: sold 3,100 gns Newmarket Autumn Sales: may well prove suited by further than 6f: acts on good to firm and soft ground. *P. W. Harris*

PENDOLINO (IRE) 5 b.g. Thatching 131 – Pendulina 102 (Prince Tenderfoot 43 (USA) 126) [1995 50: 7.5m 8m 8.3g 10g⁵ 12.1m 12.1g 10.4m⁶ 1996 11.9m 10m⁴ 10m⁶ 11.1g⁴ 12m⁴ Jul 30] leggy, lengthy gelding: poor handicapper: seems to stay 1½m: winner on dead ground in Ireland at 3 yrs, but has raced only on a sound surface in Britain: blinkered twice at 4 yrs and all starts in 1996. *M. Brittain*

PENGAMON 4 b.c. Efisio 120 – Dolly Bevan 53 (Another Realm 118) [1995 88 88d: 7.5m³ 7g 8f⁴ 6g a8.5g a8g⁴ a7g 1996 a7g³ a7g a8g* 8s 7g² 8.1g⁵ 7.6g⁶ 7g² 8m Jun 19] smallish, strong, well-made colt: carries condition: fairly useful handicapper: won competitive event at Lingfield in March: followed 4 creditable efforts with poor one (sweating) in Hunt Cup at Royal Ascot final start: effective at 7f and 1m: acts on firm going and all-weather surfaces. *H. J. Collingridge*

PENLOP 2 b.c. (Mar 15) Mac's Imp (USA) 116 – Marton Maid 74 (Silly Season 64 127) [1996 7g 6g⁵ 7.6m Sep 19] IR 15,000F, IR 13,500Y: leggy colt: half-brother to 3-y-o Cindy Kate and winning sprinters Florac and Megan Blaze (all by Sayf El Arab), 6f to 1½m winner Mr Devious (by Superpower) and a winner in Italy: dam, inconsistent maiden, is half-sister to good sprinter Haveroid: fifth of 21 in median auction maiden at Windsor, poorly drawn: said by rider to have lost action crossing path when last of 11 in maiden at Lingfield following month (trainer also reported horse had been hard to keep sound in summer): will probably stay 1m. *B. J. Meehan*

PENMAR 4 b.g. Reprimand 122 – Latakia 80 (Morston (FR) 125) [1995 60: a7g³ 62 a8.5g² a7g² 10.5s a8.5g³ 8.1s² a7g 1996 a8.5g⁵ a9.4g* a9.4g⁵ a12g a12g⁴ a14.8g⁵ a8g a9.4g⁵ Oct 5] good-topped gelding: modest handicapper: won maiden at Wolverhampton in May: sold 850 gns Doncaster October Sales: stays 1½m: acts on firm and soft ground and on fibresand: tried blinkered, no improvement: inconsistent. *T. J. Etherington*

PENNINE WIND (IRE) 4 b.g. Pennine Walk 120 – Wintina (Tumble Wind – (USA)) [1995 57: a10g⁵ a10g² 1996 11.8d 11.8m 10m 9.7f 12m 9.7m⁶ Aug 16] good-topped gelding: carries condition: one-time fair maiden: trained at 3 yrs by M. Johnston: no form in handicaps in 1996. *S. Dow*

PENNY A DAY (IRE) 6 b.g. Supreme Leader 123 – Mursuma (Rarity 129) 93 [1995 102: 10m* 12m⁶ 10.4m 12d⁵ 11.9d⁴ 1996 12s³ 11.9g⁴ 12g 12s Nov 9] tall, good-topped gelding: carries condition: poor mover: useful handicapper: best effort at 6 yrs when third of 6 to Juyush in conditions event at Doncaster in March: effective at 1¼m to 1½m: acts on good to firm ground and heavy: normally tracks leaders: game: promising hurdler, winner in December. *Mrs M. Reveley*

PENNY DROPS 7 b.m. Sharpo 132 – Darine 114 (Nonoalco (USA) 131) [1995 101 108: 8g⁶ 10d* 8g* 8g* 1996 8d⁴ 10d⁴ 10m⁶ Aug 23] leggy mare: in foal to Barathea: useful performer: fourth in listed races at Doncaster and Milan and sixth in Group 3 event at Baden-Baden in 1996: effective at 1m to 1¼m: has very round action, easily best efforts with give in the ground and acts on heavy: held up: tough and genuine: has been retired. *Lord Huntingdon*

PENNY PARKES 3 ch.f. Clantime 101 – Bonne Baiser 88 (Most Secret 119) 53 [1995 57: 5g* 5m² a5g³ 5m² 1996 6d⁵ 6d 6g³ 5f 5g* 5g* 5f a5g⁵ 5g Sep 2] sparely-made filly: modest performer: won sellers at Musselburgh and Hamilton (awarded 3-finisher contest) within 5 days in July: below form in handicaps afterwards, looking none too keen in seller last outing: best form at 5f on a sound surface, below form both starts on fibresand: blinkered 4 of last 5 starts, including when successful: withdrawn after bolting to post final intended outing. *J. Berry*

PENNY PEPPERMINT   4 b. or br.f. Move Off 112 – Cheeky Pigeon (Brave   –
Invader (USA)) [1995 NR 1996 12f⁶ 12m 12m⁶ 15.8g Sep 21] leggy filly: third foal:
dam poor sister to 2 winning hurdlers: behind, including in seller. *R. E. Barr*

PENNYS FROM HEAVEN   2 gr.c. (May 24) Generous (IRE) 139 – Heavenly   84 p
Cause (USA) (Grey Dawn II 132) [1996 7m 7g⁴ 8m³ Sep 25] 48,000Y: tall, rather
leggy colt: looked weak: half-brother to fairly useful 1m winner Ziska (by Danzig)
and several winners in USA, including a minor stakes winner by Mr Prospector: dam
1980 champion 2-y-o filly in USA: progressive form in frame in maidens at Kempton
and Goodwood (third of 11 to Voyagers Quest) 5 weeks later: will be well suited by
middle distances, and likely to continue improving. *H. Candy*

PENNY'S WISHING   4 b.f. Clantime 101 – Lady Pennington 51 (Blue Cash-   47 d
mere 129) [1995 60d: a7g 6g⁴ 6m 6g 7.5m⁴ 6g* a7g 7m 6d 6m 7f 7f 1996 7s 6.1g
5g³ 6.1m 5d³ 5g 6g 5f 6.1m a7g a6g Nov 18] small, lengthy filly: poor handicapper
nowadays: well beaten last 6 starts, including in blinkers: left N. Bycroft's stable
after ninth outing: stays 6f: acts on fibresand, probably on good to firm ground: none
too consistent. *C. Smith*

PENPRIO (IRE)   2 b.c. (Apr 16) Priolo (USA) 127 – Pennine Mist (IRE)   52 p
(Pennine Walk 120) [1996 6s⁴ Aug 31] 4,200Y: rather leggy colt: first foal: dam Irish
6.5f winner, closely related to useful Irish filly Diamond Seal (dam of smart French
performers Diamond Dance and Diamond Mix): 3¾ lengths fourth of 15, travelling
smoothly then staying on well having had trouble getting a run, to Certain Magic in
maiden auction at Ripon: bred to stay 1m: will improve. *B. A. McMahon*

PENSION FUND   2 b.g. (Apr 27) Emperor Fountain 112 – Navarino Bay 102   78
(Averof 123) [1996 5m 5g⁵ 5m 5m* 5f³ 7m* 8m⁶ Aug 26] 2,100Y: tall, leggy
gelding: half-brother to 7f winner Patience Please (by King of Spain) and a winner
abroad: dam won over 5f at 2 yrs and stayed 1½m: won maiden auction at Redcar in
July and £11,600 nursery (led on post) at York in August: fine sixth of 20 to The Fly
in valuable nursery at Newcastle final start: will stay beyond 1m: acts on firm
ground: usually off bridle early, and doesn't look an easy ride. *M. W. Easterby*

PENTIRE   4 b.c. Be My Guest (USA) 126 – Gull Nook 120 (Mill Reef (USA)   132
141) [1995 132: 10m* 10.3m* 10m* 12f* 12g² 11.9m* 10m* 1996 a10g⁴ 10g³
12m* 12m² 12d 12f Nov 24]

The 'sold' signs have been in short supply outside British houses in
recent years, but you will find plenty of them on the doors of British stallion
boxes. The most prominent read 'Sold To Japan'. The most prominent of the
lot reads 'Lammtarra—Sold To Japan For Thirty Million Dollars'. Previously
owned by the Al Maktoums, who are not exactly renowned for their account-
ability to commerical considerations, Lammtarra is the fifth consecutive Derby
winner to succumb to the yen, although, unlike the previous three, he at least
will go out there having sired one European crop. A report in *The Sporting Life*
on the stallion exodus refreshed the memory with a seventy-eight-strong list
of leading European horses that had made the trip, including Dancing Brave,
Rodrigo de Triano, Opera House, White Muzzle, Carnegie and Polish Patriot.
American champions to have gone Japanese include Forty Niner, Rhythm,
Timber Country, Sunshine Forever, Kotashaan, Criminal Type, Sunday Silence
and Ferdinand. On the other side of the coin, however, Dr Devious has been
brought back by Coolmore (some of whose sires maximise returns by covering
large books and often being sent to the southern hemisphere) and Carroll House
arrived back from Japan in October to stand as a dual-purpose stallion in
County Wexford. It is a long time now since the Japanese could be regarded
simply as taking delivery of our stallion rejects. The purchase of Warning for a
reported eight million dollars in September showed that they are also now
prepared to move in for stallions with established reputations, not just for
stallion prospects. The turnaround is easy enough to explain, if not to remedy—
according to figures given in *Pacemaker and Thoroughbred Breeder*, Japanese
average prize money per race is nearly twelve times that in Britain, and so is

their average earnings per individual runner. A *Racing Post* inquest contrasted the 1995 earnings of sires in Japan with those in Britain and Ireland: their top sire, Sunday Silence, and the top sire in Britain and Ireland, Sadler's Wells, both had eighty-nine runners, those of Sunday Silence bringing in £16,024,132 and those of Sadler's Wells £1,069,912. Those who have reaped the benefits by selling to Japan might well, of course, reinvest in the European bloodstock industry, and most stallion prospects will eventually end up described as stallion failures, but the chances now are that among that lengthy list of exports to Japan several names will be a significant loss to European bloodstock.

The Japanese have been particularly voracious in acquiring middle-distance talent, and at the end of July they bought Pentire. Second only to Lammtarra among the three-year-olds of 1995, he was the top-rated mile-and-a-half performer trained in Britain in 1996. Pentire was every bit as good a four-year-old as he was a three-year-old, but whereas in 1995 the King George VI and Queen Elizabeth Diamond Stakes had been his only defeat, in 1996 it was his only victory. Lammtarra was the one who narrowly defeated him in 1995, and with Shaamit taking the field twelve months later the King George runners included the Derby winner for the fifth time in the 'nineties. As Generous, Commander In Chief, Erhaab and Lammtarra had done, Shaamit started favourite. He was a 2/1 chance, followed by Pentire (100/30), the St Leger and Gold Cup winner Classic Cliche (5/1), 1995 King George third Strategic Choice (7/1), Ormonde and Hardwicke Stakes winner Oscar Schindler (10/1), the upped-in-class three-year-old Farasan (11/1), four-time pattern winner Luso (14/1) and Classic Cliche's stable-companion Annus Mirabilis (33/1). Pentire was very slowly into his stride from the stalls and reluctant to take hold of his bridle, but it was not a great disadvantage the way the race was run, Annus Mirabilis blazing the trail and the field well strung out, Pentire bringing up the rear until the final turn, just behind Shaamit. The Godolphin first string Classic Cliche had a start on them but Pentire was at his shoulder two furlongs out without any undue effort, and, sent for home at the distance, there was never any doubt that he would win. He beat Classic Cliche by one and three quarter lengths, Shaamit challenging for second and Oscar Schindler ten lengths further back in fourth after trouble in running.

Two days after the King George it was announced that Pentire would henceforth be carrying the colours of Mr Teruya Yoshida, the switch from Mollers Racing following a deal some said was worth at least £5 million. The policy of both owners with Pentire was to contest the top races. First off in 1996 had been the Dubai World Cup on sand, in which the first three places were filled by horses trained in the United States and Pentire finished best of the rest,

King George VI And Queen Elizabeth Diamond Stakes, Ascot—
Pentire's turn of foot seals victory over Classic Cliche (right) and Shaamit

nine and a quarter lengths behind Cigar. Over three months later, he made his European reappearance, over a mile and a quarter again, in the Eclipse Stakes and was a respectable third to Halling, indicating a big run at Ascot. None of the first three in the King George repeated that form. It was hard to know quite what to make of Pentire's second to Swain in his Arc trial, the Prix Foy at Longchamp in September, because he had taken a keen hold and been forced to make the running in a small field. Most, us included, thought it had little bearing on his chance on Arc day, and it turned out that if anything should be held against him from his performances earlier in the season it was something he had shown in victory at Ascot—another slow start in the Arc immediately put Pentire in a poor position and he never managed better than midfield. The dead ground—it was his first run on a soft surface—also probably had a bearing on his disappointing performance. Firm going did not result in very much better in the Japan Cup at Tokyo seven weeks later, but excuses in that particular event are seldom needed.

			Northern Dancer (b 1961)	Nearctic Natalma
Pentire (b.c. 1992)	Be My Guest (USA) (ch 1974)		What A Treat (b 1962)	Tudor Minstrel Rare Treat
	Gull Nook (b 1983)		Mill Reef (b 1968)	Never Bend Milan Mill
			Bempton (b 1976)	Blakeney Hardiemma

Mr Teruya Yoshida's "Pentire"

Pentire is a sturdy, attractive colt—markedly smaller than most of his rivals in the King George—and one who impressed in condition whenever we saw him in the latest season. His turn of foot helped make him well suited to waiting tactics and he had top-class performances at both a mile and a quarter (when getting up in the dying strides in the 1995 Irish Champion Stakes) and a mile and a half. Mollers Racing have done phenomenally well with their relatively small string; First Trump, Petardia, Nicolotte and First Island are other yearling purchases. At 54,000 guineas, Pentire cost less than any of them. Even without hindsight that did not look much seeing as his dam had had three winners from her previous four foals, including the Premio Roma winner Spring (by Sadler's Wells); as that dam was the Ribblesdale winner Gull Nook; as her dam Bempton had produced two more pattern winners in Mr Pintips and Banket; and Bempton was a half-sister to Shirley Heights who, like Gull Nook, was by Mill Reef. Pentire's sire Be My Guest had shown what he could do with his very first crop, which included Assert and On The House, but he had not had a Group 1 winner in Britain since then until Pentire took the King George. Gull Nook would be a highly-prized consort for any stallion and since visiting Be My Guest she has been barren to Salse, had colts by Suave Dancer and Kris and a filly by Barathea. The Suave Dancer colt was sent to the Doncaster breeze-up sales and made only 10,000 guineas; called Speculative, he is in training with Gay Kelleway but did not run as a two-year-old. Gull Nook is now reportedly in foal to Zilzal. *G. Wragg*

PENYGARN GUV'NOR 3 b.g. Governor General 116 – Alumia (Great Nephew 126) [1995 NR 1996 8g 9.9m⁵ a8.5g⁴ May 25] 1,300Y: close-coupled gelding: half-brother to a number of poor animals: dam unplaced 3 times at 2 yrs: no worthwhile form in maidens: 3/1 from 5/1, well-beaten fourth in claimer at Wolverhampton final start: sold 900 gns Ascot December Sales. *J. A. Glover* –

PEOPLE DIRECT 3 ch.f. Ron's Victory (USA) 129 – Ayr Classic (Local Suitor (USA) 128) [1995 54+, a60?: 5.7m 6f⁵ a6g⁶ a7g⁴ a8g* a8g⁶ 1996 a8g* a8g³ a8g* a8g² a8g* a8.5g⁶ a7g* a7g³ a8g² a8g⁶ a8g 8.5g⁶ a8.5g* a7g³ a8.5g⁴ a8g Nov 4] sparely-made filly: modest performer, campaigned almost exclusively on the all-weather: won claimer in January and sellers in February, March and April, all at Southwell: back to form to win claimer at Wolverhampton (by 5 lengths, making all) in August: stays 8.5f: best form on fibresand (well beaten at Lingfield). *K. McAuliffe* a63

PEPITIST 5 b.g. Bold Owl 101 – Misoptimist 111 (Blakeney 126) [1995 –: 13.6f 1996 11.9m 12m⁴ 11m⁴ 13.1g² 15d⁵ Aug 10] sturdy gelding: poor maiden handicapper: stays 13f: acts on firm ground: modest winning hurdler. *M. D. Hammond* 46

PEPPERS (IRE) 3 b.f. Bluebird (USA) 125 – Pepilin (Coquelin (USA) 121) [1995 68p: 7g 7g³ 6f 1996 10d 10.3g 9g² a9.4g⁶ Nov 11] angular filly: fair form in maidens for L. Cumani at 2 yrs: not seen in 1996 until October, putting up best effort when fast-finishing neck second of 21 in apprentice handicap at Newmarket: well held on all-weather debut 10 days later: stays 9f. *K. R. Burke* 71

PEP TALK (USA) 3 ch.c. Lyphard (USA) 132 – Peplum (USA) 108 (Nijinsky (CAN) 138) [1995 NR 1996 8m⁵ 9m³ 9m² 10s³ 10.4g⁴ Oct 10] angular, sparely-made colt: first foal: dam, Cheshire Oaks winner, is half-sister to Al Bahathri: fairly useful maiden: sold 15,500 gns Newmarket Autumn Sales: will stay further than 1¼m: acts on good to firm and soft ground. *H. R. A. Cecil* 82

PERANG POLLY 4 br.f. Green Ruby (USA) 104 – Perang Peggy (Bay Express 132) [1995 NR 1996 7g⁴ a8g Dec 5] second foal: dam never ran: fourth of 21 in claimer at Doncaster, staying on well: broke blood vessel next time. *Lord Huntingdon* 60

PERCHANCE TO DREAM (IRE) 2 b.f. (Feb 15) Bluebird (USA) 125 – Foliage (Thatching 131) [1996 6f 6m 5.7d Sep 30] 8,000F: well-grown, heavy-topped filly: sixth foal: half-sister to 4-y-o 5f winner Awasha (by Fairy King) and 2 winners abroad, including French 9f winner Tra Fiori (by Law Society): dam unraced sister to smart French/US 1m/9f performer Fitzwilliam Place: midfield at best in maidens, burly first 2 starts and best effort at Bath on third. *B. R. Millman* 54

PERCUSSION BIRD 4 b.f. Bold Owl 101 – Cymbal 80 (Ribero 126) [1995 NR 1996 a8g a13g Feb 1] smallish, angular filly: of little account. *Jamie Poulton* –

PERCUTANT (FR) 5 b. or br.h. Perrault 130 – Estada (FR) (Luthier 126) [1995 10.5g⁴ 10g* 10d 1996 12g⁴ 12f* 12m* 12.5g³ 12g⁴ 10d³ 12.5g³ 9.8d² 12d⁴ Oct 20] smart performer: reportedly nearly died at 4 yrs from a hock infection, but returned better than ever: won listed race and Prix d'Hedouville (by 2 lengths from Rainbow Dancer) at Longchamp in April: in frame in pattern company all starts afterwards, best efforts when 2½ lengths third of 10 to Carling in Prix Gontaut-Biron, neck third of 9 to Strategic Choice in Grand Prix (both at Deauville in August) then 2 lengths second of 11 to Flemensfirth in Prix Dollar at Longchamp (held up behind strong pace then running on in good style) in October: should stay beyond 12.5f: acts on firm and soft ground: consistent. *D. Smaga, France* 116

PERCY BRAITHWAITE (IRE) 4 b.g. Kahyasi 130 – Nasseem (FR) 118 (Zeddaan 130) [1995 85: 10.5m 8.1m 10g⁴ 8.9m² 8f⁵ 10.4m⁶ 8f 1996 10g 8d² 8.5g 8.9m⁴ 10f⁵ 8.5m⁵ 10m* 12m Jul 27] leggy gelding: shows knee action: fairly useful handicapper: won at Ripon in July, more patiently ridden than usual: sold to join Miss P. Whittle 6,000 gns Newmarket Autumn Sales: stays 1¼m: acts on firm and dead ground: blinkered from fourth 3-y-o to first 4-y-o starts: often forces pace: has run well when sweating: inconsistent. *M. Johnston* 85

PERCY ISLE (IRE) 2 br.c. (May 6) Doyoun 124 – Percy's Girl (IRE) 103 (Blakeney 126) [1996 8m 8.1s³ 8s³ Nov 9] rather sparely-made colt: first foal: dam, 1¼m and 10.3f winner probably ideally suited by 1½m, sister to smart but untrustworthy 6f to 11f winner Percy's Lass from an excellent family: fair form all 3 starts in maidens, third to Sausalito Bay at Chepstow and Moon River at Doncaster (off bit throughout): very much a stayer: looks rather a difficult ride. *M. R. Stoute* 79

PERCY PARK (USA) 3 br.g. Rajab (USA) – Clayton's Miss (USA) (Distinctive 39 (USA)) [1995 69d: 6m³ 6m⁵ 5.1m⁶ 8g 6f 7m 1996 6.1d 7d 8g 6m⁵ 8m⁴ 9f⁴ 7m Aug 1] close-coupled, workmanlike gelding: poor maiden handicapper on most form: stays 1m: blinkered 3 of last 5 starts. *M. W. Easterby*

PERCY PARROT 4 b.g. Lochnager 132 – Soltago 56 (Touching Wood (USA) 42 § 127) [1995 37: 8m 8.1d 7.1g a8.5g a8g 1996 12m 9.2s 10.9d 8m* 8m³ 8m 7.1d⁶ 8.1m⁵ 8m² 8.5m 8m 8g² Aug 12] workmanlike gelding: poor performer: 33/1, won apprentice selling handicap at Pontefract in June by 5 lengths, making most: sold to join A. C. Williams 3,200 gns Doncaster August Sales: stays 1m: acts on good to firm ground: tried visored, no improvement: usually bandaged behind: usually forces pace: inconsistent, and not one to trust. *R. M. Whitaker*

PERFECT ANGEL (IRE) 2 b.f. (Apr 5) Maledetto (IRE) 103 – Blue Infanta – (Chief Singer 131) [1996 7m 7m 6m 8f Nov 5] 20,000F: leggy, quite good-topped filly: has an unimpressive action: second foal: dam thrice-raced half-sister to smart middle-distance filly Reprocolor, dam of Cezanne and Colorspin: little form in maidens and a nursery. *M. H. Tompkins*

PERFECT BEAR 2 b.g. (May 4) Wing Park 104 – Sarah Bear (Mansingh (USA) – 120) [1996 6g⁵ Jul 1] angular, good-quartered gelding: fourth reported foal: half-brother to 3-y-o Boy Blakeney (by Blakeney) and 4-y-o 1½m seller winner North Bear (by North Briton): dam won in Belgium at 2, 4 and 5 yrs: well beaten in minor event at Pontefract. *Mrs S. J. Smith*

PERFECT BLISS 2 ch.f. (Feb 20) Superlative 118 – Nikatino 63 (Bustino 136) 73 [1996 5s³ 5d⁶ a6g³ a7g⁴ 6m* 6f* 6d² 6m* 6g* 6g* 6g⁵ 6.5m Sep 11] 2,500Y: sparely-made filly: has knee action: first foal: dam 11.7f and 13f winner, stayed well: successful in the summer in seller at Newcastle and nurseries at Newcastle, Yarmouth, Catterick (despite setting off very fast and not handling turns well) and Thirsk: sold 15,000 gns Newmarket Autumn Sales: best form at 6f: acts on firm and dead going, probably on soft: tough and genuine: ridden by 7-lb claimer for last 2 wins: sent to Saudi Arabia. *P. D. Evans*

PERFECT BRAVE 5 b.g. Indian Ridge 123 – Perfect Timing 107 (Comedy Star 59 (USA) 121) [1995 64: 6m 5g² 6m* 6m a5g³ a7g 1996 a6g a6g² a5g² 5g⁶ a5g² 5g 5s a75 a5g Nov 22] leggy, workmanlike gelding: fair handicapper on the all-weather, modest on turf: effective at 5f and 6f: acts on good to firm and heavy ground, goes well on fibresand: often claimer ridden: usually races prominently: sometimes gives trouble in stalls. *J. Balding*

PERFECT GIFT 3 ch.f. Generous (IRE) 139 – Knight's Baroness 116 (Rainbow 60
Quest (USA) 134) [1995 –: 7g 8.1m 1996 8f⁶ 12g² 13.8s⁵ 11.9f³ 17.2m⁴ 16.4m³
13.1m 11.9g Oct 2] good-topped filly: unimpressive walker: modest maiden handicapper: probably a thorough stayer: acts on firm ground, ran badly on soft: likely to
be suited by galloping track: blinkered (last) final start: sold 36,000 gns Newmarket
December Sales. *P. F. I. Cole*

PERFECT PARADIGM (IRE) 2 b.c. (Feb 21) Alzao (USA) 117 – Brilleaux 79
73 (Manado 130) [1996 8m 10m² 8.1s² Oct 22] IR 65,000Y: angular colt: has a round
action: sixth foal: brother to very smart middle-distance horse Bobzao and half-
brother to 1m (at 2 yrs) and 1¼m winner Ragsat Al Omor (by Dance of Life): dam
half-sister to useful miler Welsh Flame, herself grandam of Marju and Salsabil:
second in maidens won by Silver Patriarch at Pontefract and Sausalito Bay at
Chepstow (beaten neck), making most both times: likely to stay beyond 1¼m: acts
on good to firm and soft ground. *J. H. M. Gosden*

PERFECT POPPY 2 b.f. (Jan 25) Shareef Dancer (USA) 135 – Benazir 91 73
(High Top 131) [1996 7.5m³ 8s⁴ Nov 9] sturdy, lengthy filly: third foal: sister to a
poor maiden and half-sister to 3-y-o 7f winner With Care (by Warning): dam 7f and
1m winner: similar form in maiden events won by Lyrical Bid at Beverley (very
green) and Polar Flight at Doncaster: unseated rider on way to post on debut: likely
to stay beyond 1m. *J. R. Fanshawe*

PERICLES 2 b.g. (Feb 16) Primo Dominie 121 – Egalite (FR) (Luthier 126) [1996 71
6m² 6f³ 7m² a6g* 7g⁶ 7m⁴ Oct 28] 3,000F, 4,800Y: sturdy, good-bodied gelding:
half-brother to several winners abroad: dam French listed middle-distance winner:
fair performer: won maiden auction at Wolverhampton in September: fourth of 17 in
nursery at Leicester final start: stays 7f: acts on firm ground and fibresand: front
runner/races prominently: tail swisher: consistent. *M. Johnston*

PERILOUS PLIGHT 5 ch.g. Siberian Express (USA) 125 – Loveskate (USA) 66
78 (Overskate (CAN)) [1995 71, a76: a7g a8.5g² a8g⁴ a8g* a8g* a8g² a8g* a7g* a71
a8g⁵ a7g⁵ 8g 7m⁵ a8g⁴ 8m⁵ 7.1m 8f² 8.3g⁶ a7g⁵ a8g⁴ 1996 a7g² a8g⁴ a7g³ a10g⁶ a8g*
a7g⁴ 7f* 8g 7g⁴ 8f⁴ a8g² 8.1f* 8g³ 7f 8m² 7f* 7m³ 6.9m³ 7f⁵ 8.2g a7g³ a7g⁶ a7g
Dec 11] lengthy, angular gelding: fair performer: won seller at Lingfield in February,
handicap at Brighton in May, claimer at Musselburgh in June and seller at Redcar
(sold out of W. Muir's stable 8,200 gns) in August: good efforts most subsequent
outings: stays 1m: acts on equitrack (probably on fibresand), best efforts on turf on a
sound surface and acts on firm: patiently ridden. *Mrs L. Stubbs*

PERMISSION 2 b.f. (Apr 18) Rudimentary (USA) 118 – Ask Mama 83 (Mum- 63 d
my's Pet 125) [1996 6d⁴ 8.1g⁴ 7f 6d 8.1s⁴ 10f⁵ Oct 14] quite good-topped filly: shows
plenty of knee action: sixth foal: half-sister to 3-y-o 6f winner Pleading (by Never So
Bold) and 1992 2-y-o 7f winner Girl At The Gate (by Formidable): dam 1¼m winner:
modest maiden: failed to repeat form of first 2 starts, tailed off (soon beaten when
ridden, swishing tail) last time: sold 3,800 gns Newmarket Autumn Sales: stays 1m:
well beaten on firm ground. *R. Hannon*

PERPETUAL 2 ch.f. (May 13) Prince Sabo 123 – Brilliant Timing (USA) (The 78 +
Minstrel (CAN) 135) [1996 5m 5.1m⁴ 5g³ 6g⁶ a6g* 5f² 5.1g* 5g² 5.3f* 5m⁶ 5m³ Sep
27] fourth foal: half-sister to untrustworthy 1993 2-y-o 6f winner Bold Timing (by
Never So Bold) and fairly useful 1994 2-y-o 6.1f and 7.5f winner Watch The Clock
(by Mtoto): dam once-raced half-sister to Grade 1 performers Timely Assertion and
Timely Writer: won claimer at Southwell in July and nurseries at Chepstow in August
and Brighton in September: good sixth of 9 in listed race at Ayr penultimate start:
sold 18,000 gns Newmarket Autumn Sales: winner at 6f, but best efforts at around
5f: acts on fibresand and firm ground: often front runner. *Sir Mark Prescott*

PERPETUAL HOPE 3 b.f. Dowsing (USA) 124 – Woodfold 80 (Saritamer –
(USA) 130) [1995 NR 1996 7m 9.7g 7f Oct 14] fifth reported living foal: half-sister
to 1¼m and 10.8f winner Call Me Blue (by Kalaglow): dam sprinter: no worthwhile
form. *P. Mitchell*

PERPETUAL LIGHT 3 b.f. Petoski 135 – Butosky 71 (Busted 134) [1995 –p: 56
7.5d⁵ 1996 8g⁶ a8g* a11g a8g* 9.9m 10d 8g 9g Nov 1] quite good-topped filly: has a a67
round action: fair form: won median auction in April and handicap in June, both at
Southwell: well beaten there in between and in 4 handicaps back on turf: bred to be
suited by middle distances: best form on fibresand. *J. J. Quinn*

PERRYSTON VIEW 4 b.c. Primo Dominie 121 – Eastern Ember 85 (Indian 90
King (USA) 128) [1995 90: 5g* 5g* 6g* 6m 6g* 6f³ 6m⁶ 6g 6g 1996 6m³ 6m 5g 6m⁴
6g 5.6m 5m Oct 2] lengthy, angular colt: fairly useful handicapper: third of 24 to
Jayannpee in £24,900 contest at Newmarket on reappearance: generally disappointing afterwards: effective at 5f and 6f: probably acts on any going: visored third
2-y-o to sixth 4-y-o start: tends to hang under pressure: usually races prominently.
P. Calver

PERSEPHONE 3 ch.f. Lycius (USA) 124 – Elarrih (USA) (Sharpen Up 127) 44 ?
[1995 –: 7g 1996 8.2m 9m 10.1m 8f 8m² 7g a7g 8.5g⁶ 8g Aug 12] unfurnished filly:
poor maiden handicapper: probably flattered when second in apprentice race at
Newmarket: stays 1m: tried blinkered and (last 5 starts) visored: has pulled hard.
I. Campbell

PERSIAN AFFAIR (IRE) 5 b.g. Persian Heights 129 – Lady Chesterfield 63 §
(USA) (In Reality) [1995 72: a7g a6g 8g 7m 6g⁴ 7f* 7m 8m⁴ 5f 7f 6f 7.1m 8.1m⁵ 7m³
7m⁵ 7.1d 7g 1996 9m 7m⁶ 7f 8g 9m* 10m 8.3g Jul 8] tall, good-bodied gelding:
only modest handicapper at 5 yrs: won at Goodwood (amateurs) in June: trained by
T. J. Naughton until after penultimate start: stays 9f: acts on all-weather surfaces and
firm ground, probably on dead: inconsistent. *M. R. Channon*

PERSIAN BLUE 2 b.f. (May 19) Persian Bold 123 – Swift Pursuit 57 (Posse –
(USA) 130) [1996 7m Sep 10] fourth foal: closely related to 1994 2-y-o 5f winner
Singing Rock (by Ballad Rock) and half-sister to a winner in Austria by Danehill:
dam second over 1m at 4 yrs: no promise in maiden at Lingfield. *R. Hannon*

PERSIAN BUD (IRE) 8 b. or br.g. Persian Bold 123 – Awakening Rose (Le –
Levanstell 122) [1995 40, a–: a13g⁶ a11g⁶ a13g 12.3d⁵ 12.5g² 9.7f 14.1m⁵ 1996 12s
Nov 11] well-made gelding: poor handicapper: soundly beaten only outing at 8 yrs:
stays 12.5f: acts on good to firm and soft ground: tried visored, no improvement:
inconsistent. *J. R. Bosley*

PERSIAN BUTTERFLY 4 b.f. Dancing Dissident (USA) 119 – Butterfly Kiss 67 d
69 (Beldale Flutter (USA) 130) [1995 72: 7m⁶ 7m⁵ 1996 5d⁴ 6d 6m⁵ 6g 7.1m 6g
6g 10.2g 8g Sep 13] strong, good-bodied filly: unimpressive mover: fair maiden
handicapper: below form after third start at 4 yrs, leaving I. Campbell after seventh
(visored): should stay 7f: yet to race on extremes of going. *R. M. Stronge*

PERSIAN CONQUEST (IRE) 4 b.g. Don't Forget Me 127 – Alaroos (IRE) –
(Persian Bold 123) [1995 63, a74: a10g² a8g² a10g* a10g³ a10g⁵ a8g⁵ a10g² 12.5m a67
a10g* 8m⁴ 11.6m² a12g* 10g⁴ 11.6m 1996 10m 12m 10d 10g 12d a12g* a12g⁶
a10g* a13g a12g³ Dec 30] smallish, quite attractive gelding: poor mover: fair
performer, best on all-weather: returned to form when winning claimer and seller at
Lingfield in November: stays 1½m: acts on all-weather surfaces, good to firm ground
and probably on soft: blinkered since third 3-y-o start: normally front runner/races
prominently: none too reliable. *R. Ingram*

PERSIAN DAWN 3 br.f. Anshan 119 – Visible Form 99 (Formidable (USA) –
125) [1995 –: 7m 1996 8g 10m 8g 6f 8d Oct 11] tall, leggy filly: no worthwhile
form: sold to join R. T. Phillips 2,500 gns Newmarket Autumn Sales. *Major
D. N. Chappell*

PERSIAN ELITE (IRE) 5 ch.g. Persian Heights 129 – Late Sally 101 (Sallust –
134) [1995 88: 12g 10.8g⁵ 10m⁴ 10.5m³ 10g* 10m⁵ 12g* 12d⁴ 13.9g 1996 12g 12g
Sep 21] strong, lengthy gelding: fairly useful handicapper for P. Cole at 4 yrs: well
beaten both outings in 1996 (not seen out until August): stays 1½m: acts on good to
firm and dead ground: blinkered once (successful): front runner. *C. R. Egerton*

PERSIAN FAYRE 4 b.g. Persian Heights 129 – Dominion Fayre 49 (Dominion 90
123) [1995 69: 7g⁴ 8m* 8.3f 7f⁵ 8.1m³ 7g² 9.2f 7f⁶ 7.1m⁵ 7m 1996 8g⁶ 7.6g² 7.1g²
8d² 7m 8f³ 7m* 7.1f⁵ 7m 7g* 7g* Nov 2] sturdy gelding: fairly useful handicapper:
much improved in 1996, winning at Newcastle in August, York (27-runner £11,000
event) in October and Newmarket (28-runner race) in November: stays 1m: acts on
firm and good to soft ground: races prominently: genuine and reliable. *J. Berry*

PERSIAN GUSHER (IRE) 6 gr.g. King Persian 107 – Magnanimous 65 (Run- –
nymede 123) [1995 NR 1996 a7g a7g a6g Feb 15] leggy gelding: fair performer at 3
yrs for S. Dow: no form since: blinkered final start. *N. A. Smith*

PERSIAN HAZE (IRE) 7 ch.g. Bold Arrangement 127 – Crufty Wood (Sweet – Revenge 129) [1995 –: a11g 1996 a13g a16g a12g⁵ Mar 27] smallish gelding: no longer of much account. *B. J. McMath*

PERSIAN PUNCH (IRE) 3 ch.g. Persian Heights 129 – Rum Cay (USA) 75   112 p
(Our Native (USA)) [1995 NR 1996 10m* 14g* 16.2m³ 14.8m* 16f³ l6m³ Oct 5]
14,000Y: tall, useful-looking gelding: progressed physically: shows plenty of knee action: half-brother to 1993 Solario Stakes winner Island Magic (by Indian Ridge), also 6.3f winner in Italy at 3 yrs, and a winner in Italy by Rousillon: dam 14.6f winner out of very useful 1¼m Premio Lydia Tesio winner Oraston: smart form: won median auction maiden at Windsor in May, minor event at Salisbury in June and 6-runner listed race at Newmarket (by 1¼ lengths from Athenry) in July: third in Goodwood Cup (to Grey Shot) and Jockey Club Cup (to Celeric, beaten 2½ lengths) since: a thoroughly genuine stayer: has raced only on a sound surface: should make further improvement at 4 yrs. *D. R. C. Elsworth*

PERSIAN SECRET (FR) 3 b.f. Persian Heights 129 – Rahaam (USA) 91   101
(Secreto (USA) 128) [1995 92: 6g* 6g* 6m² 7.1g⁴ 6m³ 7.3d 1996 8m⁵ 8s³ 8g* 8g² 8g 8d 8v Dec 1] quite attractive filly: left J. W. Watts after reappearance: useful performer: won listed race at La Teste in August by a neck: blinkered, better form when ninth of 13 in similar event at Evry (around 3 lengths behind Contare) penultimate start: stays 1m: acts on good to firm and dead ground. *H. Pantall, France*

PERSIAN SMOKE 5 b.m. Persian Bold 123 – Gauloise 93 (Welsh Pageant 132)   45
[1995 45: 12g 12g 14m* 14g³ 14.1m 16.4m⁵ 14d 12m 1996 14.1m* 14g⁵ 14.1m 14.9m Jul 5] leggy mare: poor maiden handicapper: ridden by 7-lb claimer, won at Carlisle (comfortably) in May: below form afterwards: probably stays 2m: acts on good to firm ground: inconsistent. *A. Hide*

PERSIAN SYMPHONY (IRE) 5 ch.m. Persian Heights 129 – River Serenade – (USA) 80 (Riverman (USA) 131) [1995 NR 1996 12.1m⁵ a14g Jul 22] second foal: half-sister to Irish 13f winner Veritable Gallery (by Tate Gallery): dam fair but ungenuine middle-distance maiden: modest performer (rated 58) at 3 yrs for N. Meade, winning 2 claimers (over 9f, and 1½m) in Ireland: showed little in 2 races in Britain in 1996: stays 1½m: acts on good to firm ground. *Mrs A. M. Naughton*

PERSONAL LOVE (USA) 3 b.f. Diesis 133 – Personal Glory (USA) (Danzig   103
(USA)) [1995 7m⁴ 7m* 7g² 7s 8v 1996 8g⁴ 8s 6v* 7g* 6m 7g* 7m⁵ Sep 26]
$120,000Y: third foal: half-sister to smart American colt Supremo (by Gone West), Grade 2 8.5f winner at 2 yrs but ran only once at 3 yrs: dam unraced half-sister to Grade 2 9f winner Dynaformer, also second in Grade 2 13f event: won maiden at Dusseldorf at 2 yrs: creditable seventh of 16 in Arag Preis at Dusseldorf in May: won minor event at Mulheim in May and listed races at Dusseldorf in June and Gelsenkirchen (best effort, by 2½ lengths from My King) in August: stiffish task, below form in Group 3 event at Goodwood in September: has won at 6f and bred to stay beyond 1m: acts on good to firm and heavy ground. *H. Steinmetz, Germany*

PERSONIMUS 6 b.g. Ballacashtal (CAN) – Sea Charm 70 (Julio Mariner 127)   40
[1995 38: a11g a8g 8f 11.1g 9m⁴ a8g³ a9.4g² 8.1m 1996 a8g² 8.3s² a11g³ 10g 9.2g³
11.1f⁵ Jun 24] big, good-topped gelding: poor maiden handicapper: stays 11f: acts on fibresand and good to firm and soft ground: blinkered (hampered) final 3-y-o start. *Capt. J. Wilson*

PERSUASION 3 b.f. Batshoof 122 – Primetta (Precocious 126) [1995 –p: 8g   72 p
1996 10s a10g* Nov 15] unfurnished filly: second live foal: half-sister to 1m winner Positivo (by Robellino): dam unraced daughter of half-sister to Molecomb winner Hatta: promise in maidens at Leicester and Newbury 12 months apart then won similar event at Lingfield in November by 6 lengths, driven clear approaching straight: may well improve further. *Lord Huntingdon*

PERTEMPS MISSION 2 b.c. (Mar 29) Safawan 118 – Heresheis 69 (Free State   69 ?
125) [1996 7.9g 8f⁶ 10m Oct 7] 3,000Y: workmanlike colt: has a very round action: third foal: half-brother to useful 3-y-o 12.4f and 13.9f winner Athenry (by Siberian Express), better at 2m: dam stayed 2m: seemed to show fair form when sixth and seventh of 10 in maidens at Doncaster and Pontefract last 2 starts: will stay 1½m. *J. Pearce*

PETARINA 3 gr.f. Petong 126 – Katharina 105 (Frankincense 120) [1995 NR – 1996 6g⁶ 5g⁵ 8m a5g 5.1m 5g 5g a8.5g Nov 11] neat filly: half-sister to several winners here and abroad, including 4-y-o Kevasingo (at 1m, by Superpower): dam useful at up to 1m: signs of ability but no worthwhile form: probably a sprinter: tried visored: trained by Miss J. Craze first 7 starts. *T. J. Etherington*

PETER MONAMY   4 ch.g. Prince Sabo 123 – Revisit 86 (Busted 134) [1995 63: a12g³ 12.5m* 12.1m 11.8g 1996 12m⁴ Jun 7] good-bodied gelding: modest performer: creditable fourth in Goodwood claimer only outing at 4 yrs: will probably stay beyond 12.5f: acts on good to firm ground: fair hurdler. *M. C. Pipe*   59

PETER PERFECT   2 gr.c. (Apr 6) Chilibang 120 – Misdevious (USA) (Alleged (USA) 138) [1996 7.1m 7g 5d a6g³ Nov 12] eighth reported foal: half-brother to 3-y-o 7f winner Mogin (by Komaite) and 3 winners abroad: dam, unraced, from family of Cheveley Park winner Sookera: modest form: blinkered, third of 11 in nursery at Lingfield: should stay beyond 6f. *G. Lewis*   54

PETER QUINCE   6 b.h. Kris 135 – Our Reverie (USA) (J O Tobin (USA) 130) [1995 NR 1996 12m 12.1m 11.9g Jul 12] poor mover: useful middle-distance performer at 4 yrs for H. Cecil: tailed-off last of 9 in handicaps at Newmarket and York (rated stakes) on return. *M. Brittain*   –

PETERREX   3 b.g. Interrex (CAN) – Standard Rose 52 (Ile de Bourbon (USA) 133) [1995 48d: 7f³ 5g 6m a7g 1996 a8g a10g⁵ Jan 6] sturdy gelding: poor maiden here: winner over 9f in Germany. *M. R. Channon*   –

PETERS FOLLY   3 b.f. King Among Kings 60 – Santo Star 55 (Monsanto (FR) 121) [1995 41+: 5f⁴ 5g a5g⁵ 6.1d 5g⁶ 1996 a6g Jan 3] small, lightly-made filly: poor sprint maiden. *J. L. Eyre*   –

PET EXPRESS   2 b.g. (Mar 22) Petoski 135 – Hush It Up (Tina's Pet 121) [1996 a5g a6g a6s Dec 19] 1,600Y, 6,800 2-y-o: fourth live foal: half-brother to 3-y-o sprinter Subfusk (by Lugana Beach), and fairly useful middle-distance stayer Shadow Leader (by Tragic Role): dam poor maiden: signs of ability, but no form. *P. C. Haslam*   –

PETITE ANNIE   3 b.f. Statoblest 120 – Kuwait Night 67 (Morston (FR) 125) [1995 64: 5m⁶ 5m³ 5m⁶ 5g² a7g 1996 a6g a8g 7m 6.9m May 29] smallish filly: no form in 1996: sold 650 gns Newmarket September Sales: sent to South Korea. *T. G. Mills*   –

PETITE DANSEUSE   2 b.f. (Feb 16) Aragon 118 – Let Her Dance (USA) (Sovereign Dancer (USA)) [1996 5g⁵ 5.1f* 5m* 5m⁴ 5m 5g⁶ 5m 6m³ 6m³ 6m² 6m³ 6m² 6m⁴ 7.3s² 6.1s a6g Nov 22] 3,900F, 9,200Y: small, leggy filly: first foal: dam won 6 times at up to 1m in USA, including at 2 yrs: won maiden auction at Bath and minor event at Windsor in May: in frame on 7 consecutive starts, on last occasion set plenty to do, travelling well and finishing strongly when ¾-length second of 19 in nursery at Newbury: likely to prove better at 7f than shorter: acts on good to firm and soft ground (never placed to challenge only start on all-weather): claimed out of S. Dow's stable £10,000 twelfth start. *C. A. Dwyer*   79

PETITE HERITIERE   3 b.f. Last Tycoon 131 – Arianna Aldini (Habitat 134) [1995 –: 7f 5m⁶ 6g 7g 1996 8.2g 8.3s a8g 6m 7.1m 8g 8.2s⁵ a11g⁵ Nov 18] unfurnished filly: poor form when fifth in handicap at Nottingham and seller at Southwell last 2 starts: should stay 1½m: acts on soft ground and fibresand: tried blinkered and visored. *M. J. Ryan*   43

PETITE RISK   2 ch.f. (Apr 28) Risk Me (FR) 127 – Technology (FR) 82 (Top Ville 129) [1996 5f 5f 6m Jul 27] 1,000Y, resold 400Y: leggy, sparely-made filly: fourth foal: sister to a bad maiden: dam 1¼m winner: no form, in seller last time. *K. W. Hogg, Isle of Man*   –

PETIT FLORA   4 b.f. Lord Bud 121 – Pretty Soon 75 (Tina's Pet 121) [1995 NR 1996 8.5m⁶ 8m 10m 15.8g Aug 16] sturdy filly: third foal: dam, 7f winner, possibly became ungenuine: poor form in NH Flat races, winning at Market Rasen in June: well beaten in maidens and a maiden handicap on flat. *G. Holmes*   –

PETIT POINT (IRE)   3 b.f. Petorius 117 – Minnie Tudor (Tudor Melody 129) [1995 66: 6g⁴ 6.1d 196m 7m 6m² 7.3d⁴ 6m* 6g 7f 6g⁵ Jul 29] sturdy, close-coupled filly: fair handicapper: looked well suited by return to sprinting at Windsor in June, putting up best effort to win 16-runner race: below form afterwards: stays 6f: acts on good to firm ground. *R. Hannon*   78

PETOSKIN   4 b.g. Petoski 135 – Farcical (Pharly (FR) 130) [1995 10g* 11v³ 8g⁵   57
11d* 10g⁶ 12g⁴ 14s 1996 a8g 8s 10.8d 12m 12m 11.5f⁴ 12m⁵ 12g 11.5m* 12s a11g   a71
a14.8g* a14.8g* Dec 14] close-coupled gelding: rated 95? at 2 yrs for R. Hannon:
successful in Norway in 1995 on 2 occasions and also finished fourth in Norwegian
Derby: sold 18,000 gns Newmarket Autumn (1995) Sales: won selling handicap at
Yarmouth in October, claimer at Wolverhampton in November and seller (by 18
lengths) at Wolverhampton in December: stays 14.8f: probably acts on any going,
including the all-weather: tried visored and blinkered. *J. Pearce*

PETRACO (IRE)   8 b.g. Petorius 117 – Merrie Moira (Bold Lad (IRE) 133)   68
[1995 68: 5d 5m⁵ 6f³ 5m² 6g* 6m² 6g⁵ 6m 6.1m 6f² 5m* 6m 6m⁶ 6g 5g⁴ 6d² 5f 6f⁶
6m 1996 5g³ 5m³ 5g⁴ 5.9d 5.7g 6.1m 5m⁴ 5m 6m⁵ 5g⁶ 6m 6m³ 5m⁵ 6m* 5f 6.1m
6m Oct 28] workmanlike gelding: has a quick action: modest sprint handicapper:
dead-heated with Superbit in 22-runner seller at Haydock (last and steadily to post)
in September: effective at 5f and 6f: acts on the all-weather and on any turf going:
tried blinkered (not since 5 yrs), no improvement: usually races prominently: sometimes hangs: often apprentice ridden. *N. A. Smith*

PETREL   2 gr.f. (Feb 11) Petong 126 – Brise de Mer (USA) (Bering 136) [1996 6m   62
7g⁶ 7.6d⁵ 7g⁵ 7m Oct 28] 7,000F, 25,000Y: tall filly: has a quick action: first foal:
dam French 1m winner, half-sister to Halling: modest maiden: visored in nurseries
last 2 starts, never travelling particularly fluently on first occasion and well below
form on second: sold 9,000 gns Newmarket Autumn Sales: will be suited by further
than 7f. *Lord Huntingdon*

PETRINE GRAY   2 gr.f. (Apr 17) St Ninian 104 – Nellie Bly 80 (Dragonara   42
Palace (USA) 115) [1996 5m⁵ 7.5m⁴ 6d⁵ a5g 6s 7m Oct 8] useful-looking filly:
has scope: half-sister to 1994 2-y-o 5f seller winner Domybly (by Dominsky): dam,
sprinter, successful at 2 yrs: poor form in selling events and claimers: needs further
than 5f, stays 7.5f: sold 1,200 gns Doncaster October Sales. *T. D. Easterby*

PETROS PRIDE   3 b.f. Safawan 118 – Hala 57 (Persian Bold 123) [1995 59: 6g   –
8d 7g 1996 10.2g 8.5m 12m⁵ 10.8f 16.4v⁵ Nov 11] compact filly: no longer of any
account. *M. J. Bolton*

PETSONG   2 b. or br.c. (Jan 18) Petong 126 – Petriece 64 (Mummy's Pet 125)   –
[1996 7d Oct 2] 92,000Y: third foal: brother to 1993 2-y-o 5f winner Smart Pet and
half-brother to useful 3-y-o sprinter Amazing Bay (by Mazilier): dam, 7f winner who
stayed 1m, is half-sister to dam of Lochsong: behind in 18-runner maiden at
Salisbury, dictating pace 5f: may improve. *R. Hannon*

PETULA BOY   2 gr.g. (Mar 20) Nicholas (USA) 111 – Tulapet (GB) 42 (Man-   –
singh (USA) 120) [1996 5.2d⁶ 5m a6g a7g 7g Jul 24] 8,500F, 12,500Y: first foal:
dam, poor maiden (stayed 7f), sister to Petong: signs of ability in maidens first 2
starts: well beaten afterwards, twice at Southwell: no show blinkered or visored. *M.
McCormack*

PEUTETRE   4 ch.c. Niniski (USA) 125 – Marchinella 72 (Daring March 116)   –
[1995 87: a8g* 8.1m⁵ 8f³ 10g 8.5m 10g⁶ 1996 10g 11.8m a8.5g 10m Sep 24]
close-coupled colt: fairly useful form at best for C. Brittain in 1995: only poor form
over hurdles for new stable and no promise on return to flat: sold 940 gns Ascot
October Sales: should stay beyond 1m. *F. Jordan*

P GRAYCO CHOICE   3 b.f. Bold Fox 109 – Unjha (Grey Desire 115) [1995 NR   –
1996 a8g a7g a10g 11.9f Apr 12] first foal: dam tailed off both starts: no promise.
P. C. Clarke

P G TIPS (IRE)   5 ch.g. Don't Forget Me 127 – Amenaide 79 (Known Fact (USA)   –
135) [1995 NR 1996 a9.4g a11g Jun 20] fair performer at 3 yrs: tailed off on
reappearance and pulled up lame 5 months later. *Mrs N. Macauley*

PHANAN   10 ch.g. Pharly (FR) 130 – L'Ecossaise (Dancer's Image (USA)) [1995   –
–: 11.5m⁶ 11.5s a14g a14g⁶ a12g a12g a10g 1996 a11g⁵ a12g a13g 16.5m 10m a12g
a12g Dec 20] leggy, workmanlike gelding: modest middle-distance handicapper at 4
yrs: no worthwhile form since: tried blinkered. *R. E. Peacock*

PHANTOM DANCER (IRE)   3 b.g. Distinctly North (USA) 115 – Angel of   49
Music (Burslem 123) [1995 46: 5m 5g⁴ 7m³ 7f⁴ 6s⁶ 1996 8.3d 8g 9.9m² a9.4g 13.8g³
11.1f Jun 17] robust gelding: poor middle-distance maiden: only form in 1995 when
second of 8 in claimer at Beverley in April: stays 1¼m: acts on good to firm ground:

carries head awkwardly: often slowly away: blinkered (ran creditably) second 2-y-o start: sold to join M. Sowersby 4,200 gns Doncaster July Sales. *J. Berry*

PHANTOM GOLD   4 b.f. Machiavellian (USA) 123 – Trying For Gold   119
(USA) 103 (Northern Baby (CAN) 127) [1995 110: 8m³ 10g⁶ 12m* 11.9m
12d* 1996 10d 12f⁵ 11.9g² 12m⁵ 13.3m* Aug 17]

We do not know whether there was much betting on the outcome, but it took a stewards inquiry and the announcement that 'the placings remain unaltered' before the Queen was confirmed as having registered her 600th winner in the Whatcombe Conditions Stakes at Newbury on October 26th. The two-year-old responsible was Tempting Prospect and she is a half-sister to another filly who has done the Queen proud in recent years, Phantom Gold. Better horses have carried the Royal colours since Monaveen provided win number-one at Fontwell in October 1949, but Phantom Gold ended her race-course career the winner of three pattern races. The Ribblesdale and St Simon Stakes had gone her way as a three-year-old, and further improvement as a four-year-old got its reward on her final start, the Tripleprint Geoffrey Freer Stakes at Newbury in August. Phantom Gold started at 6/1 following a below-par showing in a steadily-run Group 1 in Germany three weeks earlier in which Posidonas had finished three places in front of her, beaten a short head. He was sent off at 10/11 in the Geoffrey Freer, but a sound pace set by Phantom Gold's stable-companion Whitechapel and trouble in running for Posidonas both contributed to a turnaround. Phantom Gold quickened clear in such good style while Posidonas was getting out in the open, however, that we doubt whether the result should have been any different. As it was, Phantom Gold beat him three and a half lengths. The closest she had come to winning earlier in the season was when runner-up in the Lancashire Oaks, leading inside the final furlong but cut down by Spout in the final strides.

Phantom Gold (b.f. 1992)	Machiavellian (USA) (b 1987)	Mr Prospector (b 1970)	Raise A Native / Gold Digger
		Coup de Folie (b 1982)	Halo / Raise The Standard
	Trying For Gold (USA) (b 1986)	Northern Baby (b 1976)	Northern Dancer / Two Rings
		Expansive (ch 1976)	Exbury / Amicable

The Geoffrey Freer showed that Phantom Gold had lost none of her character: she hung markedly and swished her tail after moving into the lead with apparent ease, and Tempting Prospect's deviations from a straight line at Newbury indicate that she may well have inherited some of the same traits. The

Tripleprint Geoffrey Freer Stakes, Newbury—in-foal Phantom Gold retires with a win

two of them are certainly similar to look at, both leggy and light-bodied, and the promising Tempting Prospect (by Shirley Heights) may well now embark on a similar three-year-old campaign to that of her half-sister. A tall individual, Phantom Gold acted on firm and dead ground. She never raced on soft, or beyond the 13.3 furlongs of the Geoffrey Freer. That race brought her career to an end because she was in foal, to Cadeaux Genereux. Her dam Trying For Gold had had two other foals before Tempting Prospect, one unraced and the other once-raced, and she produced to Salse in 1995 and to Machiavellian again in 1996. All of her foals have been fillies. That should give the Queen plenty of opportunities to continue her association with this family which began when she bought the third dam Amicable for 4,500 guineas as a yearling in 1961. Amicable went on to win the Nell Gwyn and Lingfield Oaks Trial on her first two races and was runner-up in the Yorkshire Oaks. Her daughter Expansive won the Ribblesdale, Trying For Gold a mile-and-a-half maiden at Salisbury and minor event at Wolverhampton. *Lord Huntingdon*

PHANTOM HAZE 3 gr.g. Absalom 128 – Caroline Lamb 74 (Hotfoot 126) 65 [1995 60: 6f⁵ 7m 6m 8m⁴ 8f⁶ 1996 10g³ 10m 10m² 12s³ 10f³ 8.3m Aug 14] workmanlike gelding: has a round action: fair maiden: suited by 1¼m+: acts on firm and soft ground: sold to join C. Parker 15,500 gns Doncaster November Sales. *Miss S. E. Hall*

PHANTOM QUEST 3 b.c. Rainbow Quest (USA) 134 – Illusory 81 (Kings 110 Lake (USA) 133) [1995 NR 1996 8d⁴ 8m* 8d⁶ 8m² 8m³ 8.1m² 9m* 8m⁴ Oct 3] well-made, good sort: unimpressive mover: reportedly split a pastern as 2-y-o: second foal: half-brother to 1994 2-y-o 5.7f winner Painted Desert (by Green Desert): dam, 6f winner, daughter of Irish 1000 Guineas second Bold Fantasy and half-sister to Lowther winner Kingscote (dam of Poule d'Essai des Poulains runner-up Rainbow Corner, also by Rainbow Quest): smart performer: won maiden (made most) at Newmarket in May and minor event (got home by only short head from Tamhid) at Newbury in September: creditable fourth of 9 to Yeast in listed race at Newmarket final start: stays 9f: acts on good to firm ground: has found less than seemed likely on several occasions and may well prove best with waiting tactics: consistent: to be trained by R. Frankel in USA. *H. R. A. Cecil*

PHARAOH'S DANCER 9 b.g. Fairy King (USA) – Marie Louise 86 (King – Emperor (USA)) [1995 70, a60: a6g a6g 7d² 7g⁵ 5.1d a7g⁶ a6g 1996 a6g Jan 22] good-topped gelding: fair handicapper in 1995: soundly beaten only 9-y-o start. *P. Burgoyne*

PHARAOH'S JOY 3 b.f. Robellino (USA) 127 – Joyce's Best 58 (Tolomeo 127) 65 [1995 65: 6m⁶ 6.1f³ 6.1m* 7m⁵ 6d 1996 6.1d 6g 6m 5f* 6m⁵ 5m³ 5.2m* 5f⁴ 5m 5.1g Oct 9] lengthy filly: fair handicapper: won at Carlisle and Yarmouth in the summer: winner at 6f in 1995, but now looks ideally suited by 5f: best efforts on top-of-the-ground: usually races prominently. *J. W. Payne*

PHAR CLOSER 3 br.f. Phardante (FR) 123 – Forever Together (Hawaiian 51 d Return (USA)) [1995 –: 8g 1996 12.4g³ 12m 8.3s 10.1g 14.1m² 11.1g 11.1g³ 12.1g⁵ 15.1m 12.1g³ 16.2g⁶ Aug 24] leggy filly: disappointing staying maiden: tried blinkered. *W. T. Kemp*

PHARLY DANCER 7 b.g. Pharly (FR) 130 – Martin-Lavell Mail (Dominion 65 123) [1995 57, a82: a12g* a12g* a12g* 12g 12g* 13.9g 12.1g a12g² a16g 1996 a77 a12g³ a12g³ a12g² a12g³ 12.1g² 12g³ a14g* 12s* 11.9d* 12m³ 12.1d 14.1m⁵ 12g⁶ a12g* a14.8g³ a14g* Dec 3] leggy, angular gelding: has suffered intermittently from knee problems: has a round action: fair performer: won claimers at Southwell, Catterick and Haydock in the summer and at Wolverhampton in November, and Southwell again in December: effective at 1½m and 1¾m: goes well on fibresand, has raced mainly on an easy surface on turf (acts on soft ground): often wears crossed noseband and has tongue tied down: tended to carry head awkwardly in 1996. *W. W. Haigh*

PHARLY REEF 4 b.g. Pharly (FR) 130 – Hay Reef 72 (Mill Reef (USA) 141) – [1995 62d: 8g 9g⁵ 8m a8g 7g⁶ a12g a8.5g 1996 a9.4g⁵ a12g⁵ Dec 28] modest maiden at best in 1995: little worthwhile form on flat for some time, but won over hurdles (selling handicap) in December. *D. Burchell*

PHARMACY 3 b.f. Mtoto 134 – Anodyne 100 (Dominion 123) [1995 80: 6m² 78 5m⁴ 6m² 6f* 6m 6m³ 1996 7.6g³ 7m 8m⁴ 6m 6m 7g⁴ 7m* Oct 29] leggy, quite attractive filly: good mover: fair handicapper: travelled smoothly and led close home when winning 18-runner race at Redcar in October: probably stays 1m: yet to race on a soft surface: none too consistent. *J. W. Watts*

PHASE ONE (IRE) 6 b.m. Horage 124 – Fayes Ben (Don 128) [1995 56, a–: a8g 51 7g⁶ 8.2m 6.9f² 6f 14.1m⁵ 8g* 8g⁴ 8d 8g 1996 9.9d 7g⁵ 10.5d⁴ 6.9f⁴ 8g Jul 9] a– good-bodied mare: poor mover: modest handicapper: has shown her form at 10.5f but probably better suited by shorter: acts on firm and dead ground, possibly not on soft: no form on fibresand: has had tongue tied down: inconsistent. *J. L. Eyre*

PHILGEM 3 b.f. Precocious 126 – Andalucia 57 (Rheingold 137) [1995 NR 1996 25 10g 10d⁶ 8.1g⁵ 7.5m⁵ 7d 10g⁵ 11.1m⁶ 10.9m 13.8g⁶ 12.1g 12g a13g Oct 28] small filly: half-sister to several winners, all at 7f+, including 4-y-o 11f and 1½m winner Philmist (by Hard Fought): dam won 1¼m seller: trained by J. Hetherton first 4 starts: bad form, mostly in claiming/selling company: probably stays 13.8f: yet to race on extremes of going. *C. W. Fairhurst*

PHILGUN 7 b.g. K-Battery 108 – Andalucia 57 (Rheingold 137) [1995 –, a59: – a12g³ a12g a12g⁶ a12g³ 1996 11.9m 11.1g⁶ 12.1m Jul 25] leggy, close-coupled gelding: one-time fair handicapper (rated 69), the winner of 8 races: long way below best in 1996, and fell fatally final start: stayed 2m: acted on any going: visored since mid-1993. *C. W. C. Elsey*

PHILISTAR 3 ch.c. Bairn (USA) 126 – Philgwyn 66 (Milford 119) [1995 60+: 72 6m⁵ 6d 6d⁶ 1996 7m 8g⁵ 10m a8g⁵ a10g* a9.4g³ a9.4g a10g³ a12g⁶ a10g⁴ Dec 31] rather leggy colt: fair handicapper: won at Lingfield in July, finishing strongly: stays 1¼m: acts on good to firm ground and the all-weather. *J. M. P. Eustace*

PHILMIST 4 b.f. Hard Fought 125 – Andalucia 57 (Rheingold 137) [1995 58: 50 12m⁶ 12.1g⁴ 12.1g⁴ 13.1g 11.1m⁵ 15.1f a12g* a14g² a16g⁵ a16g⁵ 15g 13.6f a14g a55 a14g³ 1996 a12g³ a12g² a14.8g 12.1d⁵ 13d⁴ 13s² a11g* 13g² 12.3m⁵ 12.1m² 13.1g⁴ 17.5m a13g⁵ Dec 13] leggy filly: modest handicapper: won at Southwell in May, and ran well next 4 starts: probably finds 11f a bare minimum and should stay 2m+: acts on good to firm and soft ground and on fibresand, probably on equitrack: blinkered since penultimate 3-y-o start. *C. W. C. Elsey*

PHILOSOPHER (IRE) 3 b.c. Royal Academy (USA) 130 – Flyaway Bride 79 (USA) 104 (Blushing Groom (FR) 131) [1995 –p: 7m 1996 7.1g³ 8m⁴ 8g⁴ 8.5m 7.6m⁴ 8.5m⁵ Sep 11] lengthy colt: fair maiden: soon ridden along but ran creditably final start: sold 4,000 gns Newmarket Autumn Sales: should stay beyond 8.5f: raced only on a sound surface: swished tail second 3-y-o start: may be temperamental: sent to Germany. *R. Hannon*

PHILOSOPHIC 2 b.g. (Mar 23) Be My Chief (USA) 122 – Metaphysique (FR) 52 p (Law Society (USA) 130) [1996 6.1m⁵ 6f⁵ 7m 7.6m Sep 10] 20,000Y: big, work-manlike gelding: has plenty of scope: second foal: dam French 1¼m winner out of sister to Try My Best and El Gran Senor: well beaten in maidens first 3 starts: improved effort in nursery final start and left impression can do better still: will be suited by middle distances. *Sir Mark Prescott*

PHONETIC 3 b.g. Shavian 125 – So True 116 (So Blessed 130) [1995 NR 1996 78 8m 8d³ 10.2f⁵ 8m⁴ 8m 10s⁵ Oct 24] tall, workmanlike gelding: fifth foal: half-brother to fair 1m/9f performer Keep Your Word (by Castle Keep): dam won at 5f at 2 yrs and 1m at 3, but was suited by 1½m: fair maiden: well below form last 2 starts: should prove suited by further than 1m: acts on good to firm and dead ground. *G. B. Balding*

PHYLIDA 2 b.f. (Mar 9) Mazilier (USA) 107 – May The Fourteenth 53 (That- 64 + ching 131) [1996 5m 6m⁴ 7d⁶ 6g² a7g⁶ a7g³ Dec 27] 5,000Y: small, angular filly: has a? a round action: third foal: half-sister to fairly useful 4-y-o 1m and 1¼m winner Major Change (by Sharrood): dam, stayed 1m, is half-sister to good 1977 2-y-o Aythorpe: fair maiden: sweating, wintry and ·· impressive in appearance when second of 13 in auction event at Pontefract: poor runs on fibresand: stays 7f. *P. J. Makin*

PICKENS (USA) 4 b.g. Theatrical 128 – Alchi (USA) 112 (Alleged (USA) 138) 59 [1995 9v⁴ 12s⁵ 10m² 12g² 8g² 8.5m⁴ 12m* 10m² 12m* 12d 1996 12m 16g 12m 14d⁴ 12f* 12m⁵ a16g Nov 18] stocky ex-Irish gelding: first foal: dam 1m winner and third in Marcel Boussac: fairly useful performer (rated 89) for D. Weld in 1995, winning at Roscommon (maiden) and Fairyhouse (handicap) before sold 13,000 gns: modest at best here, winning weak seller at Beverley (sweating) in July: stays 1½m: acts on firm ground, possibly not on a soft surface: blinkered twice, no improvement: has had tongue tied: won selling hurdle in October. *N. Tinkler*

PIETRO BEMBO (IRE) 2 b.g. (Mar 17) Midyan (USA) 124 – Cut No Ice 97 71 p (Great Nephew 126) [1996 7.6m⁶ 6m⁵ 6m 8m* Oct 17] 26,000Y: fourth foal: half-brother to 3-y-o Polar Refrain (by Polar Falcon) and useful sprinter Subzero (by Thatching): dam, stayed 1¼m, half-sister to useful middle-distance performer Gillson: stepped up in trip, justified favouritism in 8-runner maiden at Redcar by ¾ length from Rake Hey, getting up well inside final 1f: will be suited by further than 1m: may well prove capable of better. *Sir Mark Prescott*

PIGALLE WONDER 8 br.g. Chief Singer 131 – Hi-Tech Girl 98 (Homeboy – § 114) [1995 –§: a8g⁵ a7g⁵ a8g⁶ a8g a12g⁴ 12m a12g⁵ 1996 a8.5g Jan 10] chunky gelding: poor handicapper: effective at 1m and (at least on equitrack) 1¼m: suited by a sound surface: often blinkered: inconsistent. *N. M. Babbage*

PIGEON HOLE 3 b.f. Green Desert (USA) 127 – Cubby Hole (Town And – Country 124) [1995 –p: 5.2g 1996 6g 5m 7g May 30] leggy, lengthy filly: signs of ability but no worthwhile form: well beaten final start. *R. Hannon*

PIKE CREEK (USA) 3 b.f. Alwasmi (USA) 115 – Regal Heights (USA) (Forli 86 (ARG)) [1995 68p: 8m⁴ 1996 11.9f* 11.9m 12m⁴ 16.2m 16.2d Oct 11] lengthy filly: won 5-runner median auction maiden at Brighton in August by 15 lengths, making all: well held in handicaps at Ascot last 2 starts, sweating and having first run on a soft surface on second occasion: should stay beyond 1½m: acts on firm ground. *I. A. Balding*

PILLOW TALK (IRE) 5 b.m. Taufan (USA) 119 – Concave (Connaught 130) – [1995 60d: a9.4g² a8g a8g⁵ a9.4g⁶ 8.3m 9.7m² 10m 12m⁶ 12f³ 16.2m⁴ 1996 10m 12.1g⁵ Jul 1] leggy, angular mare: modest performer at best: soundly beaten in 1996: tried visored and blinkered. *S. W. Campion*

PILSUDSKI (IRE) 4 b.c. Polish Precedent (USA) 131 – Cocotte 111 (Troy 129 137) [1995 104p: 9m² 12m 10g* 12f* 12d³ 1996 10g² 10d* 10f 10m* 12m* 12d² 12g* Oct 26]

To the lengthy list of 'late-developers' that trainer Michael Stoute has taken to the top can now be added the name of Pilsudski. Like such as Opera House, Saddlers' Hall, Rock Hopper and Ezzoud, Pilsudski needed time to mature and was given that time. Raced only twice at two (unplaced on both occasions), Pilsudski progressed steadily in five races as a three-year-old, the last four of them in handicap company including victories over a mile and a quarter in the Duke of Cambridge Handicap at Newmarket and over a mile and a half in the Tote Gold Trophy at Goodwood. He progressed physically through that season too and *Racehorses of 1995* concluded its comments on him with 'capable of better still and looks a good prospect for 1996.' Pilsudski's graduation into pattern company as a four-year-old started promisingly when he was runner-up to his short-priced stable-companion Singspiel in the Gordon Richards Stakes at Sandown; Pilsudski had clearly made further physical development over the winter and looked as though the race would bring him on. After winning a good-quality renewal of the Spillers Brigadier Gerard Stakes at Sandown at the end of May in a close finish with Lucky Di, Pilsudski's blossoming career suffered something of a set-back at Royal Ascot. He got very much above himself beforehand and raced too keenly for his own good when only eighth of twelve behind First Island in the Prince of Wales's Stakes. Connections seemed to think that the firm ground had contributed to Pilsudski's disappointing performance (he started 4/1 favourite), though his victory in the Tote Gold Trophy the previous year had been gained under similar conditions. Whatever the reason, Pilsudski wasn't seen out for two months and was then dropped back to Group 3 company in the five-runner Royal Whip Stakes at the Curragh. He didn't have to improve on the form he'd shown in the spring to win decisively from I'm Supposin, the going on the firm side of good.

Mercedes-Benz Grosser Preis von Baden, Baden-Baden—
Pilsudski beats the 1995 winner Germany (right) and Sunshack

It was in the autumn that Pilsudski finally fulfilled the expectations of his astute trainer who had always regarded him as an individual with plenty of potential. 'If you have a decent colt or filly, they're hardly ever a surprise,' said Stoute when asked later in the season whether he'd been 'surprised' by Pilsudski's emergence. 'You tend to get disappointments in this game, rather than surprises!' Pilsudski was on his travels again a fortnight after his victory at the Curragh, this time to Germany for the very valuable Mercedes-Benz Grosser Preis von Baden, in which, with Luso withdrawn after hurting himself on the plane, he was the sole British challenger in a high-class field of seven. Starting at 11/1, he booked his ticket for the Prix de l' Arc de Triomphe with a three-quarter-length victory over the previous year's home-trained winner Germany, with French-trained Sunshack and Irish-trained Definite Article third and fourth. The return to a mile and a half—his earlier races as a four-year-old were all at around a mile and a quarter—suited Pilsudski down to the ground and with the Arc likely to provide an even stiffer test of stamina he appeared as the sort who could run well at Longchamp at rewarding odds. Those 'rewarding odds' were just over 22/1 on the French tote and Pilsudski duly ran a cracking race, tracking the leader from the start and battling on in doughty fashion for second after the front-running Helissio had impressively quickened clear of him early in the straight. Though the five-length winner was clearly in a different league from the rest, Pilsudski's performance confirmed him as a high-class performer and, along with the Arc fourth and fifth Swain and Luna Wells, he was sent next to Woodbine for the Breeders' Cup Turf.

The Prix de l'Arc de Triomphe field is usually the strongest and most representative assembled for a middle-distance race in Europe. However, the record of the first three home in the Arc in the Breeders' Cup Turf isn't outstanding. The four Arc winners to attempt the double, Dancing Brave, Trempolino, Saumarez and Subotica, were all beaten, as were Arc runners-up Behera, Hernando and Freedom Cry, and Arc thirds All Along, Pistolet Bleu and Opera House. Pilsudski surpassed the achievements of the three horses in that list which did best, All Along, Trempolino and Freedom Cry, who all finished second, respectively beaten a neck, half a length and a neck. Overseas runners dominated the latest Breeders' Cup Turf, filling the first five places. Pilsudski was again always close up and quickened in good style to get the better of his stable-companion Singspiel who had gone on leaving the back straight. Swain ran creditably as usual to finish third, with the St Leger winner

Breeders' Cup Turf, Woodbine—Pilsudski crowns his magnificent season with another overseas victory; Singspiel (rails), Swain (behind winner) and Shantou (left) also make the frame for Europe

Shantou fourth; of the other European-based challengers, Dushyantor and Wall Street came seventh and eighth, with Luna Wells tenth in a field of fourteen in which the presence of tail-ender Ricks Natural Star, an outclassed seven-year-old who had last been seen running in claimers in the middle of the previous year, provided the Breeders' Cup with the most bizarre runner in its history. Pilsudski's victory provided the sixth European success in the thirteen runnings of the Breeders' Cup Turf, following Lashkari, Pebbles (the only other British-trained winner), In The Wings, Miss Alleged and Tikkanen. The Europeans have enjoyed the same success rate in the other turf race on the programme, the Breeders' Cup Mile. Pilsudski's triumph was the first at the Breeders' Cup for his trainer who has suffered his fair share of disappointments at the meeting, including with Shadeed, Sonic Lady and Zilzal in the Mile. Sonic Lady twice started favourite and Zilzal was the shortest-priced favourite in the history of the race until Lure was sent off at odds on in 1994. The latest Breeders' Cup Turf, tinged with sadness for connections because Pilsudski's co-owner had died earlier in the year, crowned Walter Swinburn's comeback after spending a good part of the year recovering from multiple injuries suffered in a fall at Sha Tin in February. One final point about the Breeders' Cup. It was run outside the United States for the first time and, at first glance, the Woodbine turf track, a mile and a half round with sweeping turns and a home straight of just over two furlongs, looked tailor-made for the European style of racing. By contrast, at most American courses, including at 1997 venue Hollywood Park, Churchill Downs and Santa Anita, the turf course is inside the dirt track and the turns are sharper and the straights shorter. In the circumstances, it was odd that the European challenge should have fallen numerically for the second year in a row. Twelve were sent over, nine from Britain (two more than the previous year) but only three from France which has traditionally done best with its challengers.

The good-topped, quite attractive Pilsudski, who is often bandaged behind, is by the top-class miler Polish Precedent who, somewhat against expectations, has had his most important successes as a stallion so far with offspring who have registered pattern-race victories at a mile and a half or more. The Geoffrey Freer Stakes winner Red Route was followed by Pure Grain (Irish Oaks and Yorkshire Oaks) and Riyadian (Cumberland Lodge Stakes and Jockey Club Stakes) before Pilsudski made his mark. All four came from middle-distance or staying families on the distaff side. Pilsudski's dam Cocotte gained her only victory over a mile and a quarter in a maiden at Bath and was placed over the same distance in the Nassau Stakes and the Prix de Psyche. She is by the Derby winner Troy, a strong influence for stamina in his

Lord Weinstock/Exors of the late S. Weinstock's "Pilsudski"

Pilsudski (IRE) (b.c. 1992)	Polish Precedent (USA) (b 1986)	Danzig (b 1977)	Northern Dancer Pas de Nom
		Past Example (ch 1976)	Buckpasser Bold Example
	Cocotte (b 1983)	Troy (b 1976)	Petingo La Milo
		Gay Milly (b 1977)	Mill Reef Gaily

short career at stud, out of the fair winning miler Gay Milly, a daughter of the Irish One Thousand Guineas winner Gaily. Pilsudski is the fifth foal of Cocotte who was sold out of the Ballymacoll Stud, fetching 120,000 guineas (covered by Polish Precedent) at the 1992 December Sales. Pilsudski was the last of the foals produced by Cocotte at Ballymacoll, two of the earlier ones, the fairly useful Glowing Ardour (by Dancing Brave) and Red Cotton (by Soviet Star) also having been successful, both at up to a mile. The Polish Precedent foal Cocotte was carrying at the time of her sale turned out to be a filly, named Purbeck but so far unraced, and Cocotte has since had three offspring by Sadler's Wells, Conon Falls, who showed fairly useful form on the second of two starts as a two-year-old, a yearling filly who was withdrawn from the latest Houghton Sales and a foal. Pilsudski remains in training as a five-year-old and may yet be able to progress again. He looks sure to be one of the top contenders for the important, open-aged middle-distance races. Despite having a round action, which the theorists might deduce would put him at a disadvantage in top-of-the-ground conditions, Pilsudski acts on firm and dead going. He is genuine and consistent, and, as has been widely acknowledged, a thorough credit to his trainer. *M. R. Stoute*

PIMSBOY 9 b.g. Tender King 123 – Hitopah (Bustino 136) [1995 NR 1996 12f⁵ Aug 14] poor handicapper in 1993, lightly raced and little form since. *G. R. Oldroyd* –

PINCHINCHA (FR) 2 b.g. (Mar 3) Priolo (USA) 127 – Western Heights (Shirley Heights 130) [1996 8s a8g* Nov 29] workmanlike gelding: second foal: half-brother to 3-y-o 7f winner Lionel Edwards (by Polish Patriot): dam unraced half-sister to smart middle-distance filly Startino: burly on debut: 6/1 from 12/1, won seller at Southwell in November by 2 lengths from Bonne Ville: will stay 1¼m: may well do better still. *D. Morris* 62 p

PINE ESSENCE (USA) 5 ch.m. Green Forest (USA) 134 – Paradise Coffee 81 (Sharpo 132) [1995 57d: 8m⁴ 8.3f 10f* 10m* 12.1g 10.8g⁵ 10f 10f⁶ a10g⁵ a10g⁶ 1996 a10g⁴ a8g* a8g⁶ a8g* 8.2d³ 8g Apr 17] lengthy mare: modest handicapper: won at Southwell in February and (apprentices) March: effective at 1m, probably stays 1½m: acts on fibresand, possibly needs a sound surface on turf: sweating and edgy for second 4-y-o win. *J. L. Eyre* 52

PINE NEEDLE 3 ch.f. Kris 135 – Fanny's Cove 89 (Mill Reef (USA) 141) [1995 79: 8m⁵ 8.2d* 8m⁵ 1996 9.9m³ 12.4g* 12m⁵ 16.4g⁵ 14m* Jul 25] unfurnished filly: fairly useful handicapper: won at Newcastle in May and at Sandown (edgy) in July: much better suited by 1½m than shorter and probably stays 2m: acts on dead and good to firm ground. *D. Morley* 89

PINE RIDGE LAD (IRE) 6 gr.g. Taufan (USA) 119 – Rosserk (Roan Rocket 128) [1995 58, a75: a6g* a7g* a7g 6v 6d⁶ 7m² 8.5m 7m 6g³ 6m 6.9f* 7f³ 7m⁵ a7g³ a8.5g⁴ 7g 8d⁶ 9f 8m 8f² 8.1s⁵ a8g* a9.4g² 1996 a9.4g³ a7g² a8g* a7g² a7g* 7.5d* 8m 7.6m* 7g² 8f⁵ 8m³ 7g 7g 10g Oct 21] good-topped gelding: fairly useful handicapper on the all-weather: better than ever to win at Southwell and Wolverhampton in February: took advantage of much lower mark on turf to win at Beverley in March and (after 3-month absence with lung infection) at Chester (apprentices) in July: poor efforts last 3 starts: effective at 6f to 9.4f: acts on any going on turf, ideally suited by all-weather surfaces: tried visored/blinkered earlier in career: races prominently: game. *J. L. Eyre* 69 a89

PING-PONG BALL 3 b.f. Statoblest 120 – Desert Ditty 67 (Green Desert (USA) 127) [1995 –: 5m 1996 a5g a5g 5g Jun 7] small filly: no sign of ability: sold 725 gns Ascot July Sales. *T. R. Watson* –

PININFARINA 2 b.f. (Mar 11) Fairy King (USA) – Kaiserlinde (GER) (Frontal 122) [1996 5g Jul 29] 8,000F, 5,000Y: closely related to a winner in Germany by Unfuwain and half-sister to 2 winners there: dam unraced from good German family: slowly away and always behind in maiden at Windsor. *Martyn Meade* –

PINKERTON POLKA 4 b.f. Shareef Dancer (USA) 135 – Holy Day 82 (Sallust 134) [1995 –: 8g 7m 10d 8d 8m 8g 11.8f⁴ 12.1s 1996 a7g⁶ a11g a8g 8f³ 9.9m 13s 8m 10.1f 9.7f 7.5m⁴ a10g⁵ 9f 10f 12g Oct 19] strong filly: poor maiden at best: sold out of C. Brittain's stable 2,000 gns Newmarket July Sales after tenth start: probably stays 1¼m: best form on firm ground: blinkered (finished last) third 4-y-o start: inconsistent: sent to South Korea. *J. Parkes* 51 d

PINKERTON'S PAL 5 ch.g. Dominion 123 – White Domino 67 (Sharpen Up 127) [1995 97: 6m 7.9g³ 8.5m⁵ 7.1m³ 7.6m 8f 1996 7m 7.6g 8g 10m 10.1m 12.3m⁶ Jul 12] smallish, close-coupled gelding: useful handicapper in 1995: soundly beaten as 5-y-o: sold (C. Brittain to M. Pipe) 9,000 gns Newmarket Autumn Sales: stays 9f: acts on firm ground, yet to race on a soft surface: blinkered (ran badly) once as 3-y-o: usually held up: inconsistent. *C. E. Brittain* –

PINK PETAL 4 gr.f. Northern Game – Gratclo 65 (Belfort (FR) 89) [1995 –: a8g a6g 10g⁶ 10.8m 8.1m a12g 1996 10m 10.8m Jul 13] leggy filly: little worthwhile form: headstrong. *R. J. Baker* –

PIONEERHIFIDELITY 3 gr.f. Handsome Sailor 125 – Vico Equense (Absalom 128) [1995 NR 1996 10m⁴ 8m² Aug 26] 650F: third foal: dam poor on flat and over hurdles: better effort in maidens when 1¾ lengths second of 6 to Inchyre in steadily-run race at Warwick, staying on well: stays in training. *H. R. A. Cecil* 54

PIPERS GLEN 4 ch.g. Domynsky 110 – Linanhot 46 (Hot Spark 126) [1995 –: 8g⁵ 8.1m 6.9f 1996 10.9m Sep 19] workmanlike gelding: disappointing maiden: sold 550 gns Ascot November Sales. *C. Parker* –

PIP'S DREAM 5 b.m. Glint of Gold 128 – Arabian Rose (USA) (Lyphard (USA) 52
132) [1995 42: a16g 12m 11.8m² 9.7g⁴ 10f* 12m³ a10g 1996 a12g⁵ a13g 11.8d* a–
12.3g* 12f⁶ 11.7g 12m³ 11.8m³ 12g 12g 12.1s Nov 7] good-topped mare: modest
handicapper: won at Leicester and Ripon in April: carried head high after looking
probable winner eighth start: ran poorly afterwards: should stay further than 1½m:
acts on firm and dead going, seemingly not on equitrack: none too consistent.
M. J. Ryan

PIRATE'S GIRL 2 b.f. (Feb 2) Mtoto 134 – Maritime Lady (USA) 61 (Polish 57
Navy (USA)) [1996 7m³ Aug 2] first foal: dam (maiden) better suited by 1m than
shorter, from good family: ¾-length third of 10 in claimer at Thirsk: will stay at least
1m: looked likely to improve. *Sir Mark Prescott*

PIRONGIA 2 b.f. (Apr 24) Wing Park 104 – Gangawayhame 91 (Lochnager 132) –
[1996 7m 7f 7m Oct 23] sturdy filly: half-sister to 3 winning sprinters, including
Awa'wi'ye (by Daring March) and ungenuine 1992 2-y-o Whisperdales (by
Chilibang): dam 2-y-o 6f winner who stayed 7f: poor maiden. *P. Howling*

PISTOL (IRE) 6 ch.g. Glenstal (USA) 118 – First Wind (Windjammer (USA)) 80
[1995 65: 8m 10.8m 8m² 8m⁴ 10g 9.7m* 11.9m⁵ 10f 1996 9.7s 8m 12m⁶ 8s 10f²
9.7g* 9.7m* 11.7f* 10m² 11.7m* 12m⁵ Sep 7] workmanlike gelding: fairly useful
performer: successful in the summer in handicap and minor event at both Folkestone
and Bath: stays 11.7f: acts on firm and dead ground: blinkered (ran poorly on
equitrack) once as 2-y-o: held up (has found little on occasions in the past), and suited
by strongly-run race. *C. A. Horgan*

PISTOLS AT DAWN (USA) 6 b.g. Al Nasr (FR) 126 – Cannon Run (USA) 61
(Cannonade (USA)) [1995 65: a12g* a12g³ a16g⁶ a12g* a12g⁴ a12g⁴ a12g² a12g*
1996 a13g a11g a12g⁴ a12g⁴ Mar 16] lengthy gelding: poor mover: modest handicapper: not seen out after March: suited by middle distances: acts on good to firm and
soft ground and on fibresand: blinkered (below form) twice. *B. J. Meehan*

PIVOTAL 3 ch.c. Polar Falcon (USA) 126 – Fearless Revival 102 (Cozzene 124
(USA)) [1995 100P: 6d 6m* 5m* 1996 5f* 6m⁶ 5m* Aug 22]
Sir Mark Prescott's training career reached new heights in 1996. He has
long been regarded as a master of his trade, one of the best at placing his horses
to win the most races, but that trade has been plied largely at venues such as
Leicester, Lingfield and Folkestone and in races that do not live long in the
memory. There was a Prix du Palais-Royal with Harlow in 1984, the Solario
Stakes with Chicmond (two weeks after the horse had won on the all-weather)
in 1991, and the C.L. Weld Park Stakes with Last Second in 1995, along with
listed races and some big handicaps like the Cambridgeshire and Ebor; nothing,
however, to compare with the run of success that began at the latest Royal
Ascot. Brave Act, Red Camellia and Wizard King made their pattern-race
contributions, but the horses that thrust Sir Mark into the limelight were the
three-year-olds Pivotal and Last Second, rated by us respectively the joint-best
sprinter and third-best filly trained in Britain. Both won two pattern races, their
forays to Royal Ascot being described memorably by the trainer as 'an
outbreak of indiscipline among my owners'.
'If Pivotal had been owned by the boys', Prescott reflected later, 'they
would have missed Ascot with him, waited for a handicap at York, had their
brains on him, and given the bookies a hiding.' The bookies were still given a
hiding, but in the King's Stand Stakes. The decision to skip a handicap campaign had partly been made by another party, because having assessed his two
impressive wins—at Newcastle and Folkestone—and allotted a BHB handicap
mark of 86 at the end of 1995, the official handicapper then had another look
and upgraded Pivotal to 104. 'It is every trainer's nightmare', said Pivotal's
handler. Not every trainer's, perhaps, but certainly Sir Mark's. So with owners
the Cheveley Park Stud also looking for a publicity for their stallion Polar
Falcon, Pivotal made his reappearance in the King's Stand. Once 12/1 in the
morning, he opened at 5/1 on the course and went off at 13/2. With seventeen
runners, the field was the biggest for the race since Mickey The Greek beat his
twenty opponents in 1939, but it was a two-horse race over the final furlong.

King's Stand Stakes, Royal Ascot—
George Duffield on Pivotal looks anxiously across at Mind Games and John Carroll on this side

Favourite Mind Games had soon been in a clear lead in his group on the far side, and Pivotal had come through to lead his on the stand side one and a half furlongs out. He had a bit of ground to make up at that stage, but Pivotal passed the post half a length in front.

The game performances of these two sprinters, thoroughly dominant over the rest, led to speculation centring on which of their trainers could win his first Group 1: 'Two men, one goal'. The July Cup, though, went to one woman, Criquette Head gaining her umpteenth success at the top level, thanks to Anabaa, with vanquished British colts Pivotal (sixth) and Mind Games (seventh) now on their way to York for another attempt in the Nunthorpe: 'Two men with the one wish'. Mercifully, this round of headlines was brought to an end thanks to the last-ditch efforts of Pivotal. The 1996 Nunthorpe was what sprint racing is all about, Eveningperformance and Mind Games throwing down their cards as soon as the stalls opened. Missing the beat slightly at the start, it looked hard work the whole way for Pivotal. He had begun to reduce the deficit when Mind Games cracked entering the final furlong, but Eveningperformance kept going and was joined by Pivotal only on the line. It was the photograph that revealed she had not just been joined, but passed. Hever Golf Rose was a length and a

Nunthorpe Stakes, York—Pivotal pulls back Eveningperformance in the last stride;
Mind Games is fourth this time, held by Hever Golf Rose

quarter back in third. Pivotal's triumph was a popular one for the respected partnership between Prescott and his perennial stable jockey, the fifteen months-older George Duffield. Unfortunately, it also turned out to be the last we saw of Pivotal on the racecourse. After just three starts as a three-year-old and six in all, he was retired to stud when the likelihood of soft ground ruled him out of the Abbaye. A strong, angular, good sort, Pivotal impressed in condition before all his starts in 1996. He acted on firm ground and should have been capable of showing his form over six furlongs. Perhaps the July Cup came a bit too soon after Royal Ascot.

		Polar Falcon (USA) (b or br 1987)	Nureyev (b 1977)	Northern Dancer Special
Pivotal (ch.c. 1993)			Marie d' Argonne (ch 1981)	Jefferson Mohair
		Fearless Revival (ch 1987)	Cozzene (gr 1980)	Caro Ride The Trails
			Stufida (b 1981)	Bustino Zerbinetta

As mentioned earlier, the Cheveley Park Stud also stands Pivotal's sire Polar Falcon. He will be available at £10,000 (October 1st) in 1997, Pivotal at £6,000. Pivotal is the first home-bred Group 1 winner for the Cheveley Park, who usually sell their colts. Polar Falcon won a Group 1 (the Haydock Sprint Cup) in the colours of the stud's owner Mr Thompson, one of three victories for Polar Falcon after an inspired purchase at the end of his three-year-old season, the others coming over a mile in the Prix Edmond Blanc and the Lockinge.

Cheveley Park Stud's "Pivotal"

Pivotal heads his first crop, Red Camellia and Falkenham his second. You have to go back to the third and fourth dams before coming across much five-furlong form on the bottom line of Pivotal's pedigree: Zerbinetta won twice over the distance when showing fairly useful form as a two-year-old in 1972, and her dam Yucatan was a five-time five-furlong winner, smart at two years. Second dam Stufida's greatest triumph (she won eight times in Italy) came over twice that distance in the Premio Lydia Tesio and Pivotal's dam Fearless Revival showed useful mile-and-a-quarter form when third in a listed race on the second of her only two starts as a three-year-old; she had already won over six and seven furlongs as a juvenile. Pivotal's year-older half-sister Brave Revival (by Dancing Brave) was a fairly useful performer effective at a mile and a quarter and a mile, a winner over the latter distance at both two and three. One family member who will be hard pushed to win as a two-year-old is Fearless Revival's third foal, Fearless Arrival (by Generous), who was born the same year as Pivotal, on December 25th. He was sent to New Zealand and was reported to have finished in the frame on his first two starts, at Matamata and Te Awanutu. *Sir Mark Prescott*

PLACE DE L'OPERA 3 b.f. Sadler's Wells (USA) 132 – Madame Dubois 121 98 (Legend of France (USA) 124) [1995 NR 1996 10.5d² 12m* 11.8g* 12m³ 12g Sep 29] big, lengthy filly: has plenty of scope: second foal: half-sister to 1995 3-y-o 11.9f winner Richelieu (by Kris): dam won Park Hill Stakes: fractured a sesamoid and unraced at 2 yrs: landed odds in maiden at Thirsk in May and looked good prospect when winning 4-runner minor event at Leicester (by 7 lengths) in June: 5½ lengths third to Shemozzle in listed race at Newmarket the following month, easily better subsequent start: may have proved best over further than 1½m: has been retired. *H. R. A. Cecil*

PLAISIR D'AMOUR (IRE) 2 b.f. (Jan 30) Danehill (USA) 126 – Mira 65 Adonde (USA) (Sharpen Up 127) [1996 6m⁴ 6m² 6g⁴ Oct 18] IR 130,000Y: sturdy filly: fourth foal: sister to smart 3-y-o 6f (at 2 yrs) and 7f winner Danehill Dancer and half-sister to Irish 1994 2-y-o 5f winner Fakhira (by Jareer): dam once-raced granddaughter of top-class 4.5f to 1m winner Lianga: modest form: 2½ lengths second of 7 to Tycoon Girl in maiden at Redcar: uneasy joint-favourite, well below form in maiden at Catterick last time: will stay 7f. *N. A. Callaghan*

PLAN FOR PROFIT (IRE) 2 b.g. (Jan 30) Polish Patriot (USA) 128 – Wild 74 Sable (IRE) (Kris 135) [1996 5m⁵ 5d⁴ 5.9g 5m² 5m* 5m³ 5m⁶ 6d⁵ 6m⁴ 7f² Sep 27] IR 8,000Y: tall, good-topped gelding: has plenty of scope: first foal: dam, 1¼m winner from 3 starts, out of half-sister to Teenoso: made virtually all to win nursery at Hamilton in July: ran well in nurseries last 5 starts: gelded afterwards: stays 7f: best run on firm ground, shaped well on dead: has flashed tail: has edged left. *M. Johnston*

PLATINUM PLUS 4 ch.c. Hadeer 118 – Verchinina 99 (Star Appeal 133) [1995 60 NR 1996 8.3g 11.7m⁵ a14.8g a12g⁵ 10f a12g⁶ 15.1s a16g⁵ Nov 12] trained in Czech a46 Republic in 1995, winning 5 times from 1m to 13f: modest form when fifth of 8 in steadily-run handicap at Bath on second start in 1996: failed by long way to repeat it: should be suited by 1½m+. *C. A. Dwyer*

PLAYFUL JULIET (CAN) 8 b.m. Assert 134 – Running Around (USA) (What – A Pleasure (USA)) [1995 NR 1996 18m Jul 6] no longer of much account on flat: unreliable hurdler, winner in August. *A. Bailey*

PLAYMAKER 3 b.g. Primo Dominie 121 – Salacious (Sallust 134) [1995 78: 5d* 74 d 5d⁵ 6f² 6g³ 5m⁶ 1996 7.1d⁶ 6m⁵ 5m 6f⁶ 6f 6s 7g 5m 5m a5g⁵ a6g Nov 2] workmanlike gelding: fair handicapper: shaped quite well on reappearance, tiring, but well held next 2 starts, and sold out of M. Jarvis's stable 10,500 gns Newmarket July Sales: regressive form for new yard, well held last 2 outings: likely to prove best at up to 7f: acts on dead going, probably on firm: blinkered 4 of last 5 starts. *D. Nicholls*

PLAY THE TUNE 3 b.c. Music Boy 124 – Stepping Gaily 79 (Gay Fandango – (USA) 132) [1995 NR 1996 5d 7m 7m 6s Jul 4] 9,400F, 17,000Y: ninth foal: brother to 5f winner Rhythmic Dancer, 6f and 7f winner Music Dancer and a winner in

Belgium, and half-brother to useful sprinters Dominuet (by Dominion) and The Auction Bidder (by Auction Ring): dam sprinter: no worthwhile form. *K. R. Burke*

PLEADING 3 b.g. Never So Bold 135 – Ask Mama 83 (Mummy's Pet 125) [1995 94 + 77p: 6d 6d⁴ 1996 6m* 6d* 6m² 6g Jul 9] smallish, good-topped gelding: fairly useful performer: won maiden at Salisbury and handicap at Leicester in May: showed plenty of improvement when short-head second of 13 to Mallia in £34,200 handicap at York, finishing strongly: lost all chance by starting very slowly 3½ weeks later: gelded and not seen out afterwards: raced only at 6f, will prove at least as effective over further: acts on good to firm and dead ground: held up: may still have improvement in him. *H. Candy*

PLEASANT SURPRISE 3 b.g. Cadeaux Genereux 131 – Quiet Week-End 99 98 (Town And Country 124) [1995 84p: 6g⁶ 7.5g² 7.5m² 7.5m* 7d 1996 12.3g² 10.4m⁴ 10.5d* 12m⁴ 10g 11.9g 12m Sep 13] leggy, quite attractive gelding: useful handicapper: won at Haydock (blinkered and tongue tied) in June: very good fourth of 20 in King George V Stakes at Royal Ascot 12 days later: disappointing all 3 subsequent starts: sold 28,000 gns Newmarket Autumn Sales: effective at around 1¼m with testing conditions, and stays 12.3f: yet to race on extremes of going: goes well with forcing tactics. *M. Johnston*

PLEASE SUZANNE 3 b.f. Cadeaux Genereux 131 – Aquaglow 84 (Caerleon 97 (USA) 132) [1995 93: 7m* 7d² 6d³ 1996 7.3d 6m* 7m 6g⁵ 6f⁵ 7m⁶ 7g³ Sep 14] angular filly: good mover: useful performer: won minor event at Kempton in May: moved poorly to post but ran well in rated stakes at Goodwood on final start: effective at 6f and 7f: acts on firm and dead ground. *R. Hannon*

PLEASURELAND (IRE) 3 ch.g. Don't Forget Me 127 – Elminya (IRE) (Sure 61 Blade (USA) 130) [1995 61: a7g⁵ 7d 6.9g 1996 8.2g 10m a12g³ a16g³ a16g⁵ 14d Sep 28] sturdy gelding: modest maiden: stays 2m: acts on equitrack and dead ground: tried blinkered: sold to join R. Curtis 3,000 gns Newmarket Autumn Sales. *P. J. Makin*

PLEASURE TIME 3 ch.g. Clantime 101 – First Experience 58 (Le Johnstan 66 123) [1995 72: 5g⁴ 5d⁵ 5m³ 5f* 5g⁵ 5g 5m⁵ 5m* 5m 5g 1996 5d³ 5.1g 5m⁵ 6g⁵ 5g⁴ 5.1m³ 5m⁵ 5m 5.1m⁵ 5m Jul 31] leggy, good-topped gelding: fair 5f handicapper: well below form last 3 starts: acts on firm and dead ground: often blinkered/visored: has twice given trouble in stalls: hung markedly left ninth 3-y-o start. *C. Smith*

PLEASURE TRICK (USA) 5 br.g. Clever Trick (USA) – Pleasure Garden 46 (USA) (Foolish Pleasure (USA)) [1995 62: 8m 9f 8m* 8.5m⁵ 8g⁴ 1996 7.5f 8m 8m⁶ 8.5m 7g 8g⁵ 8m a8g⁴ a8g a7g* a8g Dec 27] good-quartered gelding: poor performer in 1996, winning handicap at Southwell in November: stays 1m: acts on fibresand and firm ground, may be unsuited by a soft surface: visored (ran creditably) once as 3-y-o, blinkered last 2 starts. *Don Enrico Incisa*

PLEIN GAZ (FR) 3 b.c. Lesotho (USA) 118 – Gazzara (USA) (Irish River (FR) 72 131) [1995 82?, a72: 5g* 5d⁶ 5.5g* 6g* 6d² 6d 6g* 7g³ 6g⁵ 7.5m 6s* 6g⁶ 6d² 6d a7g² 1996 a5g⁵ a7g⁴ 6s 6g 8d⁵ 8d 6m⁶ 6d² 7g⁵ 7g² 7g⁵ 7g 7d⁵ 6s 7d 6g² Nov 3] Belgian-trained colt: fair form in 2 Lingfield claimers in January: second in 3 similar races in France afterwards: stays 7f: acts on soft ground and equitrack: front runner. *Andre Hermans, Belgium*

PLINTH 5 b.g. Dowsing (USA) 124 – Pedestal (High Line 125) [1995 60: 10m⁵ – 10g* 10m² 10m² 10.2h³ 10.3g⁴ 10f² 1996 10g Jul 8] workmanlike gelding: modest middle-distance handicapper: well beaten only 5-y-o outing: won over hurdles in August. *N. A. Graham*

PLUM FIRST 6 b.g. Nomination 125 – Plum Bold 83 (Be My Guest (USA) 126) 68 [1995 64, a47: a6g⁴ 6g⁵ 6d 6g⁵ 5m* 6g 6f* 7g 5f³ 5m 5.9f 6m³ 6m⁶ 6m⁶ 6m⁴ 5m² 6m a52 6m 6.1d 1996 5d² 5g² 5g⁴ 6m 6g³ 5g 6g³ 6m⁴ 6m 6m 5m 6.1m 5m a6g⁶ a6g a6g³ Dec 3] lengthy, workmanlike gelding: has a round action: modest sprint handicapper: trained first 11 starts in 1996 by L. Lloyd-James, twelfth by D. Chapman: acts on any ground: often bandaged: effective visored/blinkered or not: tends to hang left. *J. L. Eyre*

PLUTARCH ANGEL 2 b.c. (Mar 20) King Among Kings 60 – Heavenly Pet – (Petong 126) [1996 6d 6g⁶ 8.5g⁵ 7.5m⁶ 8.1m Sep 23] 500Y: sparely-made colt: first foal: dam unraced: poor maiden: sold 650 gns Doncaster October Sales: sent to Denmark. *W. T. Kemp*

PODDINGTON   5 b.g. Crofthall 110 – Bold Gift 61 (Persian Bold 123) [1995   105
78p: 9m³ 1996 9f* 10.1g⁴ Oct 30] has had only 3 races: showed best turn of foot to win falsely-run 7-runner maiden at Lingfield in July by 2 lengths (with more in hand) from Blatant Outburst: stiff task, showed a good deal more improvement when around 5½ lengths fourth of 7 to Medaille Militaire in minor event at Yarmouth 3½ months later, though never a threat: stays 1¼m. *R. Akehurst*

POETIC DANCE (USA)   3 ch.c. Seattle Dancer (USA) 119 – French Poem   67
(USA) (Sharpen Up 127) [1995 –p: 7f 7d 1996 8d⁶ 10.5m⁶ 12.1g Sep 29] sturdy, lengthy colt: fair maiden at best: ran as if something amiss final start: sold 3,400 gns Newmarket Autumn Sales: stays 10.5f. *J. L. Dunlop*

POETRY (IRE)   3 gr.f. Treasure Kay 114 – Silver Heart (Yankee Gold 115) [1995   84
66p: 6.9g³ 1996 11.1g⁴ 6.9m² 7d* 7m* 7f* 7g⁵ 7m 7d Aug 24] tall, lengthy, sparely-made filly: fairly useful performer: won maiden at Goodwood and minor event at Redcar in May and another minor event at Lingfield in June: should stay 1m: acts on firm and dead going: front runner. *M. H. Tompkins*

POIGNANT (IRE)   2 b.g. (Apr 13) Priolo (USA) 127 – Ah Ya Zein (Artaius   –
(USA) 129) [1996 7m 7.5f 7m Aug 12] 32,000Y: tall, rather leggy gelding: sixth foal: half-brother to 3-y-o 7.6f (at 2 yrs) and 1¼m winner Najm Mubeen (by Last Tycoon) and 2 winners in France by Shahrastani: dam French 1¼m winner: behind in maidens and a claimer: sold 1,200 gns Newmarket September Sales: twice slowly away: sent to Germany. *M. R. Channon*

POINTE FINE (FR)   2 b.f. (Apr 20) Homme de Loi (IRE) 120 – Pointe Argentee   58
(Pas de Seul 133) [1996 7f 7d⁵ Oct 28] 80,000 francs Y: fourth foal: half-sister to 3 winners in France, including 3-y-o 1m winner (including at 2 yrs) Stella Marix (by Linamix): dam French 1½m winner from the family of Moon Cactus and Moonshell: 10 lengths fifth of 10 to Apache Star in maiden at Lingfield: will stay 1½m. *J. W. Hills*

POINTELLE   2 b.f. (May 10) Sharpo 132 – Clymene 86 (Vitiges (FR) 132) [1996   –
7g Nov 2] seventh foal: half-sister to fairly useful 1993 2-y-o 7.9f winner Clyde Goddess (by Scottish Reel): dam, 7f winner at 2 yrs on only start, is half-sister to useful 6f and 7f winner Saluzzo and daughter of staying half-sister to smart Harmony Hall: 33/1, soundly beaten in 23-runner maiden at Newmarket. *A. Hide*

POINTER   4 b.g. Reference Point 139 – Greenhill Lass (Upper Case (USA)) [1995   61
–: 10d 1996 a8.5g⁵ 9.9d 6m⁴ 6m⁶ 7d* 7f 7g³ 6m* 6m* 5.7f⁴ 6m² 7g⁶ 7g Sep 5] tall gelding: modest handicapper: ran well most starts in 1996, and won at Salisbury (amateurs) in May, Windsor in June and Salisbury (battled on well despite edging left) in July: effective at 6f, and should stay 1m: acts on firm and dead ground. *Mrs P. N. Dutfield*

POKER PRINCESS   2 br.f. (Feb 23) Waajib 121 – Mory Kante (USA) (Ice-   47 +
capade (USA)) [1996 5.7m⁶ 6g 5m 5f Sep 28] 24,000Y: first foal: dam won twice in Germany from 7f to 1m at 3 yrs: showed little here as 4-y-o: poor form in maidens and nursery: will prove suited by at least 6f. *M. Bell*

POLAR CHAMP   3 b.g. Polar Falcon (USA) 126 – Ceramic (USA) (Raja Baba   77
(USA)) [1995 –: 7m 1996 8m⁵ 8f² 10f⁴ 10g a9.4g² 10.1m² 10f* 12m a12g² Nov   a80
14] leggy gelding: has a round action: fair performer: won maiden at Leicester in September, idling: stays 1¼m: acts on all-weather surfaces, raced only on a sound surface on turf: blinkered final outing, visored previous 3: often soon off bridle. *S. P. C. Woods*

POLAR ECLIPSE   3 ch.g. Polar Falcon (USA) 126 – Princess Zepoli 61   95 d
(Persepolis (FR) 127) [1995 90p: 7.1d* 10m³ 1996 7g⁴ 10d⁵ 8g² 8m 8m 10m⁶ 7.9g 10s⁶ Oct 24] rangy, unfurnished gelding: fairly useful performer: best effort when length third of 4 to disqualified Aunty Jane in minor event at Doncaster on third start: well held most outings afterwards: probably stays 1¼m: acts on good to firm and dead ground: visored/blinkered last 2 starts: has had tongue tied down. *M. Johnston*

POLAR FLIGHT   2 br.c. (Feb 21) Polar Falcon (USA) 126 – Fine Honey (USA)   92 p
90 (Drone) [1996 8.2m 6m² 7f⁴ 8m² 8s* Nov 9] 22,000F: tall, angular colt: has scope:

has a round action: half-brother to several winners, including fairly useful 1986 2-y-o 7f winner Pollenate (by High Line), later successful in USA, and useful 1991 2-y-o 5f and 6f winner Gold Desert (by Green Desert): dam lightly-raced 2-y-o 5f winner: progressive colt: won 16-runner median auction at Doncaster by ½ length from Silverani, responding really well as first two came clear: will stay 1¼m: acts on soft ground, probably on firm: tends to edge/hang left: likely to continue improving. *M. Johnston*

POLARIS FLIGHT (USA) 3 b.c. Northern Flagship (USA) 96 – Any- 117
timeatall (USA) (It's Freezing (USA) 122) [1995 112: 5m* 5f³ 6g* 6m* 7g²
10g* 8g³ 1996 8m³ 8d 12m² 12m² 12m 12d Oct 6]
Although the ill-fated Polaris Flight did not win in 1996, his fine second places in the Prix du Jockey-Club and Irish Derby ensured that he added handsomely to the prize money earned during a successful two-year-old campaign. His short-head defeat by Ragmar in the Prix du Jockey-Club was a reversal of their running in the Criterium de Saint-Cloud as two-year-olds, in which Polaris Flight had gamely held off the French colt by the same margin. At Chantilly, Polaris Flight was unable to quicken as well as the winner early in the straight but stayed on very strongly and just failed to get up. Polaris Flight had gone into the race as the 43/1-outsider of Peter Chapple-Hyam's three runners and his performance capped an eventful afternoon for the Manton trainer, who had to watch the race from a sickbed behind the weighing room after being taken ill beforehand, and then endure a long wait for the decisions to both the photofinish and an objection by Polaris Flight's jockey to the winner for interference. There was no such doubt about the outcome of the Irish Derby, as Polaris Flight was beaten six lengths by Zagreb. Nevertheless it was another praiseworthy effort from Polaris Flight, bought by Prince Mitab Abdullah prior to the race, and a very much better one than in his first classic, the Premio Parioli in Rome, where he started 2/1-on following a pleasing reappearance in the Craven Stakes but was well beaten, reportedly returning home a sick horse. After the Curragh it was announced that Polaris Flight would be given a mid-season break and be brought back for the Prix de l'Arc de Triomphe, taking in the Prix Niel at Longchamp as his preparatory race. That programme was indeed followed but, sadly, nothing went to plan. He ran little better in the Niel than he had done in the Parioli, and was towards the rear of the field when he broke a leg early in the straight in the Arc. It was not possible to save him for stud.

		Northern Dancer	Nearctic
	Northern	(b 1961)	Natalma
	Flagship (USA)	Native Partner	Raise A Native
Polaris Flight (USA)	(b 1986)	(b 1966)	Dinner Partner
(b.c. 1993)		It's Freezing	TV Commercial
	Anytimeatall (USA)	(ch 1972)	Articana
	(b 1983)	Vitesse	Bold Ruler
		(b 1969)	Vit Reina

As we said in *Racehorses of 1995,* Polaris Flight's looks more than pedigree probably influenced his sale price of 70,000 dollars as a foal: at any rate, he was a grand-looking individual in training. He and the smart German colt Macanal (a dual pattern race winner at around seven furlongs in 1996) are the best runners so far for the American-based stallion Northern Flagship, a lightly-raced brother to the top sprinter-miler Ajdal. The dam Anytimeatall, like the second dam, was unraced. Since Polaris Flight (her second reported foal) she has produced two colts by Nabeel Dancer—the once-raced two-year-old Let Live who, after making 110,000 dollars as a yearling, was sold out of Aidan O'Brien's stable for just 1,200 guineas at the 1996 Newmarket Autumn Sales; and an unnamed yearling who fetched 45,000 dollars as a foal at the 1995 Keeneland November Sale. Polaris Flight stayed a mile and a half well. He was usually held up, acted on good to firm ground and, despite the odd poor run, was genuine. *P. W. Chapple-Hyam*

New Zealand Handicap, Newmarket—close between Polar Prince (rails) and Prince Babar

POLARIZE 2 ch.g. (Feb 28) Polar Falcon (USA) 126 – Comhail (USA) (No-double (USA)) [1996 7.9g 7f Nov 5] 2,800F: unfurnished gelding: second reported foal: dam ran twice, daughter of half-sister to top-class 1½m filly Comtesse de Loir: in need of run, well behind in maidens at York and Redcar. *T. D. Barron* –

POLAR PRINCE (IRE) 3 b.c. Distinctly North (USA) 115 – Staff Approved 94 (Teenoso (USA) 135) [1995 91p: 7g⁵ 7m⁵ 7.1m² 7.1g* 8m 1996 8d² 8m³ 8.1d⁵ 7m* 7m 7m* 7m⁶ 7g* 7m 7m⁶ Oct 17] robust, lengthy colt: impresses in appearance: good mover: made into a useful performer, winning valuable handicaps at Epsom in June and Newmarket in August and strongly-run minor event at Goodwood (by 1¼ lengths from Russian Music) in September: best efforts at 7f: yet to race on extremes of going: held up and has a good turn of foot: tough and consistent. *M. A. Jarvis* 108

POLAR PROSPECT 3 b.g. Polar Falcon (USA) 126 – Littlemisstrouble (USA) (My Gallant (USA)) [1995 NR 1996 7.3s² 8d 7.5f* 7.1m⁴ 8m 10m⁴ 8.5g 7.9g 8.1v⁶ Oct 6] good-topped gelding: has scope: third foal: dam won at up to 9f: fair performer: won maiden at Beverley in June: contested handicaps afterwards, running creditably only when in frame: stays 1¼m: acts on firm ground, possibly not on heavy: has been bandaged in front. *B. Hanbury* 76

POLAR REFRAIN 3 ch.f. Polar Falcon (USA) 126 – Cut No Ice 97 (Great Nephew 126) [1995 54: 5d³ 5s 5f 1996 6s² 5m 7m 6m³ 6m³ 7m 7g⁴ a6g a6g⁶ a8g⁶ a7g⁶ Dec 11] workmanlike filly: modest maiden handicapper: claimed out of Mrs J. Ramsden's stable £6,000 on reappearance: stays 7f: acts on good to firm and soft ground, well held all starts on all-weather. *C. A. Dwyer* 59 a–

POLIGLOTE 4 b.c. Sadler's Wells (USA) 132 – Alexandrie (USA) 114 (Val de L'Orne (FR) 133) [1995 121: 11m³ 12m² 12g² 10m⁵ 12d² 12g 1996 12f⁴ 12s* 12g* 12m³ 12m 12d² Oct 20] medium-sized, rather sparely made colt: very smart performer: won listed event at Longchamp (by 1½ lengths from Rainbow Dancer) in May and 5-runner Grand Prix d'Évry (by short head from Luna Mareza) in June: ran creditably when 5 lengths third of 9 to Helissio in Grand Prix de Saint-Cloud (headed over 2f out) and 2 lengths second of 7 to Annaba in Prix du Conseil de Paris 119

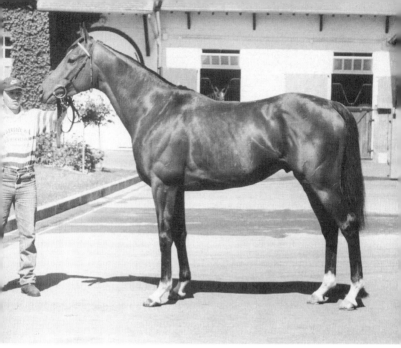

Wertheimer et Frere's "Poliglote"

at Longchamp: effective at 1½m and will be suited by further: acts on good to firm ground and soft: races prominently: game and genuine. *Mme C. Head, France*

POLINESSO   3 b.c. Polish Precedent (USA) 131 – Lypharita (FR) 125 (Lightning   100
(FR) 129) [1995 NR 1996 8d² 8g* 8.2m³ 8m² 8m⁴ 10m⁶ Aug 16] rangy, good-
bodied, attractive colt: has scope: takes eye in appearance: unimpressive mover: fifth
foal: half-brother to 7.6f and 1m winner Swordstick (by Sure Blade): dam, from good
family, won Prix de Diane: won maiden at Ripon in April: useful form in varied
events all 4 starts afterwards: keen type but stays 1¼m: yet to race on extremes of
going: effective from front or held up: coltish fourth start: flashes tail. *B. W. Hills*

POLISH LADY (IRE)   3 b.f. Posen (USA) – Dame Ross 85 (Raga Navarro   43
(ITY) 119) [1995 –: 7m 7.1s 1996 8d 8.1g 10f 8g 7g³ 7m 7.1m Sep 23] sparely-made
filly: trained until after second 3-y-o start by W. Barker: only worthwhile form when
close third of 11 in handicap at Catterick: may prove best at up to 7f. *C. Murray*

POLISH RHYTHM (IRE)   3 b.f. Polish Patriot (USA) 128 – Clanjingle   69
(Tumble Wind (USA)) [1995 NR 1996 8.3m⁶ 6m 8.1m⁵ 7m 10.1m Oct 23] 30,000Y:
leggy, workmanlike filly: half-sister to Cheveley Park winner Capricciosa and 1994
Irish 2-y-o 1m winner Delightful Chime (both by Alzao): dam placed over 5f at 2 yrs
in Ireland: fair maiden: may prove best at up to 1m: has raced only on good to firm
ground: has joined G. Hubbard. *M. H. Tompkins*

POLISH ROMANCE (USA)   2 b.f. (Apr 12) Danzig (USA) – Some Romance   83
(USA) (Fappiano (USA)) [1996 6m⁴ 6g⁵ Oct 18] $450,000Y: lengthy, quite attractive
filly: fluent mover: third foal: half-sister to a winner in USA by Alysheba: dam,
Grade 1 7f and 1m winner at 2 yrs and placed in Grade 1 events at up to 9f at 3 yrs,

half-sister to Grade 1 1½m winner Vilzak: well-backed favourite, around 3 lengths fourth of 13 to Elegant Warning in maiden at Newmarket, starting slowly and very green, no extra after getting into contention over 1f out: bandaged near-hind, raced freely when only fifth of 22 in another maiden at Newmarket 13 days later: bred to stay 1m. *M. R. Stoute*

POLISH SAGA 3 ch.f. Polish Patriot (USA) 128 – Sagar 74 (Habitat 134) [1995 59: 6f⁵ 5d 6g⁴ 6m 6f 1996 6.1d² 6d 6m a7g 7s 8f⁵ 8.1m 11.1m Aug 29] lengthy filly: poor mover: poor handicapper: disappointing after reappearance: sold 5,300 gns Doncaster October Sales: should prove effective beyond 6f: best efforts on an easy surface. *M. Dods*   54 d

POLISH SPRING (IRE) 3 ch.f. Polish Precedent (USA) 131 – Diavolina (USA) (Lear Fan (USA) 130) [1995 82+: 6g* 6.1d⁴ 6m⁵ 1996 7m 7f* 8f 8.5f* 8.5f² 8.5g² Oct 4] good-topped ex-English filly: fluent mover: useful performer: best effort in Britain to win £19,100 handicap at York in May (weaving through to lead well inside final 1f) on penultimate outing for B. Hills: won allowance race at Saratoga in August and good second in valuable handicap at Belmont Park final start: stays 8.5f: acts on firm ground, may be unsuited by a soft surface. *N. Howard, USA*   104

POLISH WARRIOR (IRE) 2 ch.g. (Apr 29) Polish Patriot (USA) 128 – Opuntia (Rousillon (USA) 133) [1996 6g⁴ 6g² 6g³ 5f* Sep 18] IR 5,700F, IR 26,000Y: stocky gelding: second foal: half-brother to 1995 2-y-o 5f winner Nameless (by Doc Marten): dam unraced: well-backed favourite, won 12-runner nursery at Sandown by a head, travelling smoothly behind leaders until going on 1f out, idling close home: will probably prove ideally suited by 5f: looked ill at ease on track at Epsom third outing: has an awkward head carriage: sold 21,000 gns Newmarket Autumn Sales and gelded: joined T. D. Barron. *P. W. Chapple-Hyam*   88

POLISH WIDOW 3 b.f. Polish Precedent (USA) 131 – Widows Walk (Habitat 134) [1995 71p: 6m⁵ 1996 8d 7m 8g³ 10f Jul 19] rangy filly: fair maiden, lightly raced: well-backed favourite but unimpressive in appearance and short to post, well-beaten last of 9 in handicap on final start: should stay at least 1¼m: possibly unsuited by very firm ground: sold 3,000 gns Newmarket December Sales. *W. Wragg*   74

POLLI PUI 4 b.f. Puissance 110 – Wing of Freedom (Troy 137) [1995 59d, a–: a6g 5d⁴ a6g⁶ 6g 8.2m a6g 7m a6g 1996 a6g 8f⁶ 6.9m 5.7g² 6m 6m 8.1g 6s 5.1g 6m Oct 28] leggy filly: poor maiden handicapper nowadays: will probably prove best at 6f/7f: acts on soft ground, well beaten on fibresand: often slowly away: thoroughly mulish in preliminaries final start: inconsistent. *W. M. Brisbourne*   41 § a– §

POLLY GOLIGHTLY 3 ch.f. Weldnaas (USA) 112 – Polly's Teahouse 68 (Shack (USA) 118) [1995 84: 5.1m* 5.1f⁴ 6m⁵ 6m³ 7f⁵ 6f⁴ 6.5m 6d³ 5m* 1996 5d 5.1g⁴ 5.1f 6m⁵ 5.1m 7m⁴ 7m³ 6g⁴ 5m 5m³ 6m³ 6f 5.1m 8f Oct 8] smallish, leggy filly: fair handicapper: best 3-y-o efforts on first 2 starts: well held last 3 outings: best form at 5f: acts on firm and dead ground: effective blinkered/visored or not: has swished tail: usually races prominently. *M. Blanshard*   77 d

POLLY PECULIAR 5 b.m. Squill (USA) 122 – Pretty Pollyanna (General Assembly (USA)) [1995 62, a–: a11g a10g⁴ 8g* 8.1m³ 8g⁶ 7g² 8g³ 9.7s* 10g⁵ a9.4g 1996 a10g³ 10g 8m⁶ 7.5f* 7g* 8f⁶ 8.2g* 8s³ a8g⁴ Nov 26] leggy mare: fair performer on turf, poor on the all-weather: won amateurs races at Beverley (handicap) in August and Goodwood (by 5 lengths) in September and handicap at Nottingham in October: effective at 7f to 1¼m: acts on firm ground, soft and equitrack: consistent. *B. Smart*   69 a49

POLO KIT (IRE) 5 b.g. Trempolino (USA) 135 – Nikitina 106 (Nijinsky (CAN) 138) [1995 82: 14.9d 14m⁴ 16.4m⁵ 16m⁴ 1996 14m 16g Sep 14] quite attractive gelding: fairly useful stayer in 1995 for J. Fanshawe: no promise in 1996: acts on soft going and good to firm: visored (ran creditably) final 4-y-o start: held up: sometimes sweating and rather edgy. *R. J. O'Sullivan*   –

POLONAISE PRINCE (USA) 3 b.c. Alleged (USA) 138 – La Polonaise (USA) (Danzig (USA)) [1995 NR 1996 10g 10s Aug 31] $55,000F, 280,000 francs Y: strong colt: fifth foal: brother to smart middle-distance stayer Poltarf and half-brother to winners in Germany and USA: dam, 6f stakes winner at 4 yrs, is half-sister to Grade 1 winner Prismatical: last in maidens at Kempton (only start for R. Akehurst) and Ripon 5 months apart. *V. Soane*   –

POLSKA (USA) 3 b.f. Danzig (USA) – Aquaba (USA) (Damascus (USA)) [1995   103
84P: 6d* 1996 7m⁵ 7m⁴ 8m Sep 28] leggy, close-coupled filly: won Blue Seal Stakes
at Ascot only 2-y-o start: didn't reappear until mid-August, easily best effort when
2¾ lengths fourth of 7 to My Branch in listed race at Doncaster: stayed 7f: retired.
D. R. Loder.

POLTARF (USA) 5 b.h. Alleged (USA) 138 – La Polonaise (USA) (Danzig   107
(USA)) [1995 111: 14.1g³ 16.2m² 1996 12m⁶ 13.4d 14d⁴³ 16m⁶ 14.6d² 14v Nov 30]
big, strong, good-bodied horse: carries condition: shows knee action: smart performer at his best: not seen out for new stable until mid-August, and didn't reproduce
his very best form, best effort when 2¼ lengths third of 4 to Moonax in minor event
at Haydock on third start: stays well: acts on firm and dead ground: sweating first 2
starts at 5 yrs: effective from front or held up: stays in training. *J. H. M. Gosden.*

POLYDAMAS 4 b.c. Last Tycoon 131 – Graecia Magna (USA) 109 (Private   91
Account (USA)) [1995 88: 10g 11.4g² 10.1m 10g² 10m* 12m 1996 10m⁴ 11.9m² 12g
12g² 12m Oct 17] tall, rangy colt: fairly useful handicapper: runner-up in 1996 at
York and Ascot: visored, tailed off in rated stakes at Newmarket final start, trainer
stating race possibly came too soon (6 days) after Ascot: sold 41,000 gns Newmarket
Autumn (1996) Sales: stays 1½m: acts on good to firm ground, shaped well on soft:
sometimes sweats and gets on edge: usually races prominently. *M. R. Stoute.*

POLY DANCER 2 b.f. (May 21) Suave Dancer (USA) 136 – Blink Naskra   –
(USA) (Naskra (USA)) [1996 6m 7m 7.1m⁵ 7m⁵ 10f Oct 14] 8,300Y: eighth foal:
half-sister to several winners abroad, including Italian 3-y-o 6f (at 2 yrs) to 1m
winner Naskramar (by Marju): dam won at up to 7f in USA and is out of half-sister to
dam of Bakharoff: no form, including in sellers: sold 3,000 gns Newmarket Autumn
Sales. *M. R. Channon.*

POLY MOON 2 b.f. (Mar 28) Mujtahid (USA) 118 – Ragged Moon 72 (Raga   52 d
Navarro (ITY) 119) [1996 5.2d⁴ 5g³ 5m² 7f⁴ 7g* 7.5f 6d² 7.1m 8f a6g⁶ 7g 6s a8.5g
Oct 19] 14,000F, IR 9,000Y, 13,000 2-y-o: smallish, well-made filly: eighth foal:
half-sister to 4 winners, including useful 1991 2-y-o 6f winner Misterioso (also by
Forzando): dam won 1m sellers: modest performer: made all in seller at Catterick in
July: lost her form last 6 starts: sold 3,500 gns Newmarket Autumn Sales: stays 7f:
best form on an easy surface (well beaten on both all-weather surfaces): sent to
Sweden. *M. R. Channon.*

POLY MY SON (IRE) 3 ch.c. Be My Guest (USA) 126 – Green Memory (USA)   53
86 (Forli (ARG)) [1995 NR 1996 10.3s 12.5g⁴ 12m⁵ 9.9g* 12m² 11.6m 10m Jul
24] IR 20,000Y: good-bodied colt: unimpressive mover: half-brother to a winner in
Belgium: dam, 12.2f winner, out of sister to Mill Reef: modest performer: made all
in seller at Beverley in May: tailed off penultimate start and pulled up after losing
action on final one: sold 2,000 gns Newmarket September Sales, resold 1,500 gns
Newmarket Autumn Sales: stays 1½m well. *M. R. Channon.*

POMMARD (IRE) 3 b.g. Darshaan 133 – Pont-Aven 113 (Try My Best (USA)   88
130) [1995 90p: 7.1g* 1996 8m⁴ 8f⁶ Sep 13] tall, lengthy gelding: has a quick action:
won maiden at Sandown only 2-y-o start: still green, well-held fourth of 5 to
Beauchamp King in steadily-run Craven Stakes at Newmarket on reappearance,
racing alone stand side for much of way: free to post, never a threat in minor event at
Doncaster 5 months later: subsequently gelded: should stay at least 1¼m+: sent to
UAE. *J. H. M. Gosden.*

POMONA 3 b.f. Puissance 110 – Plum Bold 83 (Be My Guest (USA) 126) [1995   89
NR 1996 7d 8f 7d² 7g 8.3d² 8.1d³ 8g* Oct 29] 6,400Y: leggy filly: half-sister to
several winners here and in Ireland, all at up to 1m: dam 6f winner: fairly useful
handicapper: improved efforts last 3 starts, beating Duello a short head in 19-runner
race at Leicester on final one: stays 8.3f: acts on dead ground. *P. J. Makin.*

POMPIER 3 ch.g. Be My Chief (USA) 122 – Fire Risk (Thatch (USA) 136) [1995   –
NR 1996 10g 12g⁴ May 17] 9,000F, 18,000Y: tall, useful-looking gelding: half-
brother to 1993 2-y-o 7f winner Pavaka (by Glenstal): dam unraced half-sister to
high-class milers Final Straw and Achieved: no promise in maidens at Leicester and
Newmarket in the spring: sold 4,000 gns Newmarket July Sales and gelded.
J. L. Dunlop.

PONTYNYSWEN 8 b.g. Ballacashtal (CAN) – Tropingay (Cawston's Clown   –
113) [1995 48: a12g* a12g 1996 a12g a12g⁴ a12g⁶ Nov 11] neat gelding: fairly useful

jumper: lightly raced on flat, little worthwhile form in 1996: tried visored and blinkered. *D. Burchell*

POPPY CAREW (IRE)   4 b.f. Danehill (USA) 126 – Why So Silent (Mill Reef   110
(USA) 141) [1995 107: 8m² 10m² 10f⁵ 10m* 10.1g* 10g³ 1996 10g⁵ 10g 13.4g⁴ 10d⁵
11.8g⁵ 10m*ᵈⁱˢ 11.9m⁶ 12m* 10g 12d 12s⁵ Nov 9] angular filly: has a fluent action:
useful performer: first past post in minor events at Newmarket in August (best effort,
beat Bint Salsabil a neck, but disqualified for jockey's irresponsible riding) and
Kempton in September: effective at 1¼m, stays 13.4f: acts on firm ground, below
best on a soft surface: often mulish at start. *P. W. Harris*

POPPY DANCER   2 b.f. (Mar 30) Nalchik (USA) – Zoomar 30 (Legend of   –
France (USA) 124) [1996 a5g Jul 1] 500Y: second foal: dam poor plater bred to stay
at least 1m: always towards rear in seller at Southwell. *B. Palling*

POPPY MY LOVE   3 ch.f. Clantime 101 – Yankeedoodledancer (Mashhor Dan-   41
cer (USA)) [1995 –: 5m 5g 5f⁵ 6m⁵ a6g⁵ 5m⁵ 5g a5g⁶ a8g 1996 5g⁵ Jul 24] workmanlike filly: poor sprint maiden. *R. Harris*

PORLOCK CASTLE   3 b.g. Thowra (FR) – Miss Melmore (Nishapour (FR)   –
125) [1995 NR 1996 10m 10g 10s Oct 24] unfurnished, angular gelding: brother to a
poor maiden and half-brother to 1m winner Imhotep (by Claude Monet) and
middle-distance maiden Morstock (by Beveled), both winning hurdlers: dam placed
over 6f in Ireland: towards rear in maidens at Sandown (signs of ability), Goodwood
and Newbury. *K. R. Burke*

PORTELET   4 b.f. Night Shift (USA) – Noirmant (Dominion 123) [1995 81: a8g³   91
a7g² 6.1g² a5g⁴ 5.1f 5.3f³ 5.3m² 5m⁶ 6f² 5g* 5g* 5g 5f³ 5m² 1996 5m 5.2m 5g* 5m³
5.2m³ 5m* 5d 5g⁴ 5g Oct 26] leggy filly: fairly useful handicapper: won at Epsom in
August and at Newcastle (under 5-lb claimer) in October: best at sprint distances:
acts on firm ground (finished last only run on soft surface) and equitrack: blinkered
(finished last) fifth 3-y-o start: has hung under pressure: often makes running:
game. *R. Guest*

PORTEND   4 b.g. Komaite (USA) – Token of Truth (Record Token 128) [1995 84:   94
a6g* a6g* a6g* a7g³ a6g* a6g³ a6g³ 5g* 5s* 5m⁵ 1996 6s 6g 5m⁴ 6m 5g* 5m² 5m²   a86
a6g⁶ 5m⁶ 5g 6g³ 7.6d 6m 6g a6g⁴ a5g* Nov 22] sturdy, lengthy gelding: fairly useful
handicapper, won at Ripon in May and Southwell (fifth course win) in November:
effective at 5f to 7f: acts on good to firm and soft ground and on fibresand: usually
blinkered/visored nowadays: usually claimer ridden: often taken quietly to post:
effective from front or held up: game: reportedly sold to race in Switzerland.
S. R. Bowring

PORTITE SOPHIE   5 b.m. Doulab (USA) 115 – Impropriety (Law Society   31
(USA) 130) [1995 42, a–: 8.1d 11.1m³ 11.1f² 11.1f² 9.2f⁴ 10m⁶ a12g 1996 12.3g⁶   a37
11.1m 11.1f 11.1m⁴ a8.5g* a7g Jul 22] small, wiry mare: poor handicapper: won
maiden contest at Wolverhampton in July: never going pace back at 7f next time:
effective at 8.5f, stays 11.1f: acts on firm and dead going and on fibresand: blinkered
(well below form) twice in 1994. *M. Brittain*

PORTOLANO (FR)   5 b.g. Reference Point 139 – Kottna (USA) (Lyphard   –
(USA) 132) [1995 –: a12g 14.1m 10m 10.8f 1996 14.1f Jul 20] smallish, well-made
gelding: no form for a long time: tried visored. *B. P. J. Baugh*

PORTUGUESE LIL   3 ch.f. Master Willie 129 – Sabonis (USA) 68 (The   69
Minstrel (CAN) 135) [1995 61: 7g⁵ 8m 8.1s⁶ 1996 8m 9.9m⁵ 12m 7f³ 8m 8.5g Aug
26] sturdy filly: fair maiden: outclassed in 1000 Guineas and Derby on first and third
starts: should be suited by 1m+: acts on firm going: edgy type. *D. Nicholls*

POSEIDON   2 b.c. (Apr 16) Polar Falcon (USA) 126 – Nastassia (FR) (Noble   ?
Decree (USA) 127) [1996 6g* Sep 17] 30,000F, 36,000Y: sixth foal: half-brother to
4-y-o 1¼m winner Fasih (by Rock City), Irish 9f/bumpers winner Gilt Dimension
(by Dara Monarch) and fairly useful 1987 2-y-o 7f and 1m winner Jalmoon (by
Jalmood), later successful at up to around 11f in Italy: dam, placed at up to 9.5f in
France from family of Habibti: won 8-runner maiden at Milan in September, making
all: likely to stay 1m. *M. R. Channon*

POSEN GOLD (IRE)   3 b.f. Posen (USA) – Golden Sunlight (Ile de Bourbon   65
(USA) 133) [1995 60: 6m⁵ 7m³ a7g⁴ 1996 a8g² a10g* Jan 6] angular filly: modest

performer: narrowly won median auction maiden at Lingfield in January: stays 1¼m: acts on equitrack and good to firm ground. *P. A. Kelleway*

POSIDONAS 4 b.c. Slip Anchor 136 – Tamassos 67 (Dance In Time (CAN)) 123 [1995 119: 11g* 11s 12g* 12d* 12m⁵ 1996 13.3d³ 12f³ 12g* 12m² 13.3m² 14m⁴ 12f Oct 5]

Trainer Paul Cole went into the latest season with a high-class trio of middle-distance four-year-olds. Riyadian, who would probably have turned out the best of them, was alas not seen out again after his reappearance win in the Jockey Club Stakes, but Strategic Choice and Posidonas both put in a series of good efforts. Strategic Choice's were hugely the more successful financially, but Posidonas was only marginally inferior in terms of form. This he showed on a number of occasions. That it brought only the one victory would not have mattered too much to those who backed him, because, when Posidonas gamely gave weight all round in the Princess of Wales's Stakes at Newmarket in July, it was at the rewarding odds of 20/1. He had his 5-lb penalty thanks to the previous September's weak Group 1, the Gran Premio d'Italia at Milan, a race that dropped out of the pattern in 1996 when the Italian authorities greatly restricted its terms of entry. Set beside Singspiel's series of narrow defeats in top-class company, this appeared to give Posidonas something of a stiff task in the Princess of Wales. The pair of them looked in excellent condition and treated racegoers to a gripping battle once the gauntlets were thrown down by jockeys Richard Quinn and Michael Kinane over a furlong out. Quinn on Posidonas got the better response and went on to win by a length and a quarter, well on top at the finish. Nineteen days later, Posidonas went in search of a second Group 1 on the Continent, ran to his best but was short-headed by Hollywood Dream in a steadily-run race at Dusseldorf.

Everything about Posidonas at this stage suggested that he would stay at least a mile and three quarters. He was duly stepped up in trip on his next two starts, but with unsatisfactory results. First, at odds of 10/11, he was poised to challenge over three furlongs out in the Geoffrey Freer Stakes at Newbury, but then got boxed in and carried back to last; Phantom Gold had well and truly flown by the time he managed to get out. Five weeks later Posidonas was at the Curragh for the Irish St Leger. This time he got involved in bumping with Sacrament entering the straight, but not sufficiently to have affected his position and it was disappointing to see his effort peter out in the last half furlong, resulting in his being caught on the post for third. A minor position in the frame was Posidonas' lot on five occasions in all in 1996, the races we have not already mentioned being a listed event at Newbury and the Hardwicke at Royal Ascot on his first two starts. The only time he failed to make the frame was when last of ten in the Turf Classic at Belmont in October.

Princess of Wales's Stakes, Newmarket—Posidonas and Richard Quinn (left) knuckle down to repel Singspiel

		Shirley Heights	Mill Reef
	Slip Anchor	(b 1975)	Hardiemma
	(b 1982)	Sayonara	Birkhahn
Posidonas		(b 1965)	Suleika
(b.c. 1992)		Dance In Time	Northern Dancer
	Tamassos	(b 1974)	Allegro
	(ch 1984)	Salamina	Welsh Pageant
		(ch 1978)	Femme Elite

A good-topped colt who usually impresses in appearance, Posidonas moves with plenty of knee action. He has run creditably on one of his two starts on firm going, but goes very well with some give as he showed at Newmarket. That race also left no doubts that Posidonas is genuine, for all that he tends to carry his head a little high. One horse with a high head carriage about whom less flattering things were said is Ile de Chypre, a half-brother to Posidonas' dam Tamassos. This family was detailed in *Racehorses of 1995*; an update is that Posidonas' three-year-old half-brother Rescue Time (by Mtoto) has now shown fairly useful form to win twice at around a mile and a half in Ireland. *P. F. I. Cole*

POSSESSIVE ARTISTE   3 b.f. Shareef Dancer (USA) 135 – Possessive (Posse   73
(USA) 130) [1995 71: 6m⁵ 7m 1996 8d⁴ 9m⁴ 9f⁴ 8f⁴ 10.1m³ 11.5m* Sep 10] lengthy filly: fair form: won maiden at Lingfield in September, travelling well much of way, driven out as she idled: suited by middle distances: acts on firm and dead ground: visored (no improvement) fourth 3-y-o start. *M. R. Stoute*

POTEEN (USA)   2 b.c. (Jun 8) Irish River (FR) 131 – Chaleur (CAN) (Rouge   113 p
Sang (USA)) [1996 7.1v* 8g² Oct 26]
Poteen would have needed to have overcome both inexperience and immaturity to win the Racing Post Trophy, so his narrow failure was a very fine effort which held the promise of even better to come. Poteen's previous experience amounted to just one outing three weeks before, when he won a seven-furlong maiden at Haydock comfortably by a neck from another new-comer, Ghataas. The first two pulled six lengths clear of the remainder that day. Foaled on June 8th, Poteen was much the youngest in the nine-runner field for the Racing Post Trophy, for which he started 13/2 joint-third favourite (having been well backed during the preceding week) with the Newmarket maiden winner Asas (a February foal) and behind the Royal Lodge winner Benny The Dip (March) and Armiger's brother Besiege (January). After racing quite freely in the rear early on, Poteen began to improve in fine style over two furlongs out, quickened to get his head in front at the furlong pole but then was unable to contain the rally of Medaaly on his inner inside the last. Poteen went down by half a length, Benny The Dip a length and a quarter back in third. Poteen looks the best Guineas prospect from the Racing Post field, and he looks sure to win a good race at up to one mile.

		Riverman	Never Bend
	Irish River (FR)	(b 1969)	River Lady
	(ch 1976)	Irish Star	Klairon
Poteen (USA)		(b 1960)	Botany Bay
(b.c. Jun 8, 1994)		Rouge Sang	Bold Bidder
	Chaleur (CAN)	(b 1972)	Red Damask
	(b 1979)	Brief Attire	Menetrier
		(b 1962)	Chorus Beauty

The good-bodied Poteen cost 65,000 dollars as a yearling at the Keeneland September Sale. It was not too surprising that he found a British buyer, as he is a brother to Bog Trotter who did so well for the Haggas stable not so long ago. Free-running Bog Trotter was a seven-furlong performer who at two won the Laurent-Perrier Champagne Stakes before finishing second in the Dewhurst, and at three won both the Greenham and the Kiveton Park Stakes. Poteen is the ninth foal out of Chaleur, a fairly useful winner at up to a mile in North America; details of her family can be found in the entries on Bog

Trotter in *Racehorses of 1990* and *Racehorses of 1991*. Chaleur has produced two more winners in North America since, a minor winner by Green Forest and another by Sovereign Dancer who was placed in a Grade 3 one-mile handicap. *L. M. Cumani*

POWDER RIVER 2 b.c. (Jan 24) Alzao (USA) 117 – Nest 65 (Sharpo 132) 78
[1996 5m³ 6s⁴ 7.1m³ 6g* 6f⁵ 7m⁵ Aug 16] 16,500Y: smallish, good-quartered colt: first foal: dam, placed at up to 1m, half-sister to Sheikh Albadou: made all in 5-runner maiden at Epsom in July: stays 7f: blinkered last 4 starts: races prominently: sent to Czech Republic. *R. Hannon*

POWER DON 3 ch.g. Superpower 113 – Donalee (Don 128) [1995 56: 5g³ 5f² –
a7g⁵ 6m³ 5g⁵ 5.3d³ 1996 a7g Aug 16] lengthy gelding: modest maiden: blinkered, well beaten only 3-y-o start: sold 500 gns Doncaster October Sales: stays 6f: visored last 2 2-y-o outings. *W. G. M. Turner*

POWER GAME 3 b.g. Puissance 110 – Play The Game 70 (Mummy's Game 69
120) [1995 67: 5g³ 6f² 6f⁵ 5m⁵ 6m³ 6g 6g³ 6m³ 1996 6m 6g² 8.1d³ 6m 6.9f² 8.1m⁴
8m 8.1m* 7d³ a8.5g 8g* 8m 8.3g* 7m³ 8.2g 8g* Oct 29] tall gelding: fair performer: won sellers at Haydock in August and Thirsk in September, and claimers at Hamilton in September and Leicester in October: stays 8.3f: acts on firm and dead ground, ran poorly on only all-weather outing: usually blinkered/visored nowadays. *J. Berry*

POWER PRINCESS 3 b.f. Superpower 113 – Hyde Princess 75 (Touch Paper 37
113) [1995 43: 6m 5m⁶ 5d 5g 6s 1996 6g 6g 8.2m 6g⁴ 7g⁵ Aug 12] angular, deep-bodied filly: poor maiden: probably stays 7f: usually bandaged. *J. A. Pickering*

POW WOW 2 b.c. (Mar 31) Efisio 120 – Mill Hill (USA) (Riva Ridge (USA)) 60 ?
[1996 5.1m⁴ 5g 5m Aug 18] 6,200 2-y-o: half-brother to several winners here and abroad, including 6f and 1m winner Jamaica Bridge (by Doulab) and fair miler Farm Street (by Henbit): dam, placed at up to 9f in France, is half-sister to smart sprinter Peterhof out of half-sister to Mill Reef: fourth of 7 in maiden at Chepstow on debut: well below that form later in summer and joined J. J. O'Neill. *M. R. Channon*

PRAEDITUS 2 b.c. (May 19) Cadeaux Genereux 131 – Round Midnight 64 (Star 75 p
Appeal 133) [1996 6d⁶ 6s⁴ Oct 24] 5,000Y, 33,000 2-y-o: big, strong colt: has plenty of scope: fourth foal: half-brother to 1m and 1¼m winner Midnight Jazz (by Shardari) and French 12.5f winner Welcome Sir (by Most Welcome): dam, out of a 1½m winner, ran only at up to 6f at 2 yrs: 8 lengths fourth of 23 to Za-Im in maiden at Newbury, setting pace on favoured rail then keeping on: will probably stay 1m: a nice type who looks sure to continue improving. *R. Hannon*

PRAGUE SPRING 4 b.f. Salse (USA) 128 – Wassl's Sister (Troy 137) [1995 66: 65
10g⁵ 10m* 11.7h³ 1996 10m 11.6g⁶ 16.2m³ 16m⁵ 16d⁵ 16m Sep 16] sturdy filly: fair handicapper: stays 2m: acts on hard ground: blinkered (not disgraced) final start: sometimes bandaged: tends to run in snatches and may not have the ideal attitude. *Lady Herries*

PRAIRIE FALCON (IRE) 2 b.c. (Feb 27) Alzao (USA) 117 – Sea Harrier 69 p
(Grundy 137) [1996 7m³ 7g⁵ Aug 21] 72,000Y: quite good-topped, attractive colt: good mover: brother to 3-y-o Classic Flyer, 7f winner at 2 yrs, and half-brother to useful 6f and 7f winner Hill Hopper (by Danehill) and middle-distance winners Water Boatman (by Main Reef) and Glendera (by Glenstal): dam twice-raced half-sister to high-class stayer Sea Anchor: fair form, weakening closing stages, in maidens at Goodwood and Kempton (fifth of 15 to Entrepreneur) in August: bred to stay middle distances: will improve again. *B. W. Hills*

PRAIRIE MINSTREL (USA) 2 b.c. (Apr 20) Regal Intention (CAN) – Prairie 55 ?
Sky (USA) (Gone West (USA)) [1996 6s⁶ 7m⁶ 6.1d⁶ 10m Sep 24] 9,400Y: sturdy, deep-girthed colt: first foal: dam won at up to 7f in USA, out of an unraced sister to The Minstrel: sire (by Vice Regent) won 14 times in Canada from 6f (at 2 yrs) to 1¼m: showed signs of ability first 3 starts: very stiff task on nursery debut and well beaten: stays 7f: has had tongue tied down. *R. Dickin*

PRANCING 3 br.f. Prince Sabo 123 – Valika 75 (Valiyar 129) [1995 97: 6f² 5m* 98
6g² 6f⁵ 1996 6m³ 6g³ 7m⁵ 8m³ 8d Oct 11] smallish, quite attractive filly: useful performer: best 3-y-o effort when 2 lengths third of 18 to Fatefully in listed rated stakes at Ascot penultimate start: stays 1m: acts on firm ground, below form on dead. *D. R. Loder*

PRECEDENCY 4 b.g. Polish Precedent (USA) 131 – Allegedly Blue (USA) 106 – (Alleged (USA) 138) [1995 NR 1996 14.1f⁶ 11.9d⁶ 9.7m a11g² a14g² a14.8g⁶ a11g 12m Oct 3] leggy, lengthy gelding: closely related to useful stayer Hawait Al Barr (by Green Desert) and half-brother to fairly useful stayer Owen Falls (by Mill Reef) and a winner in Germany: dam 1½m winner suited by 1¾m: only form when runner-up in claimer and amateurs handicap at Southwell in the summer: should be suited by good test of stamina: no sign of ability on turf: visored second start, saddle slipped on third. *K. McAuliffe* — a67

PRECIOUS CAROLINE (IRE) 8 b.m. The Noble Player (USA) 126 – What A Breeze (Whistling Wind 123) [1995 NR 1996 a11g Jan 12] workmanlike mare: poor handicapper: 33/1 on first run since 1993, tailed off in amateurs race at Southwell. *P. D. Cundell* —

PRECIOUS GIRL 3 ch.f. Precious Metal 106 – Oh My Oh My (Ballacashtal (CAN)) [1995 71: 5v⁴ 5m⁵ 5g 6m³ 6g* 7d 5d² 6.1m⁶ 7m⁶ 1996 5d⁴ 6g⁶ 5m* 5f⁵ 6m 5g 5m Oct 23] workmanlike filly: fair handicapper: won at Ayr in June by 5 lengths, possibly flattered in coming from off very strong pace: mostly well below that form otherwise in 1996: stays 6f: acts on good to firm and heavy ground: visored second to sixth 3-y-o starts: sometimes sweats. *D. Moffatt* — 76

PRECIOUS ISLAND 3 b.f. Jupiter Island 126 – Burmese Ruby (Good Times (ITY)) [1995 NR 1996 11.8m 8.1f⁶ 11.8f 11.8g⁵ Oct 29] plain filly: first foal: dam bumpers winner: signs of ability but little worthwhile form: has worn tongue strap. *P. T. Dalton* —

PREDAPPIO 3 b.c. Polish Precedent (USA) 131 – Khalafiya 104 (Darshaan 133) [1995 7m* 1996 8g* 10m² 10m³ 12m* 11s* Oct 19] second foal: half-brother to fairly useful 7f winner Khamseh (by Thatching): dam Irish 1m and 1½m winner: smart and generally progressive Irish colt: odds on, won 22-runner maiden at Fairyhouse at 2 yrs and minor event at Gowran Park in July: ¾-length second of 6 to Idris in Meld Stakes and just over 1½ lengths third of 5 to Pilsudski in Royal Whip Stakes, both at the Curragh: won 5-runner listed race at Galway (by ½ length from I'm Supposin) and 7-runner Blandford Stakes at the Curragh (by length from Sanoosea), both in autumn: stays 1½m: acts on good to firm ground and soft: blinkered (ran creditably) third 3-y-o start: joined Godolphin. *J. Oxx, Ireland* — 117

PREMAZING 4 ch.g. Precocious 126 – Amazing Journey (USA) (Spectacular Bid (USA)) [1995 –: 12g⁶ 12f⁶ a16g 12g 1996 11.9f Apr 22] sturdy gelding: no worthwhile form: tried visored. *R. M. Stronge* —

PREMIER 2 b.c. (Apr 24) Rainbow Quest (USA) 134 – Formosanta (USA) (Believe It (USA)) [1996 10m⁵ a8g² a8.5g* Nov 30] 36,000F: smallish, leggy colt: brother to 7f to 8.5f winner Farnham and half-brother to 3 winners, including 1988 2-y-o Little Guest (6f, by Be My Guest): dam, from good family, showed some ability in USA: fair form: made most when winning narrowly at Wolverhampton in November: gives impression will relish stiff test of stamina. *M. Johnston* — 76

PREMIER BAY 2 b.c. (Apr 16) Primo Dominie 121 – Lydia Maria 70 (Dancing Brave (USA) 140) [1996 6s* 6m² 6g² Jul 1] well-made colt: second foal: half-brother to 3-y-o Taufan Boy (by Taufan), 7f winner at 2 yrs: dam (placed at 1m and 10.2f) daughter of high-class middle-distance performer Connaught Bridge: won maiden at Newbury in May: runner-up to Proud Native in Woodcote Stakes at Epsom (lost several lengths at start then looked ill at ease down hill) and to Nigrasine in minor event at Pontefract: will be suited by further than 6f. *P. W. Harris* — 95

PREMIER CENSURE 3 b.f. Reprimand 122 – Mrs Thatcher (Law Society (USA) 130) [1995 NR 1996 7d⁴ 10m 10m Jun 21] quite good-topped filly: first foal: dam never ran: bandaged, keeping-on fourth of 17 to Inner Circle in maiden at Leicester (showed a quick action) on debut: well held in similar events afterwards: sold 3,100 gns Newmarket Autumn Sales: sent to South Korea. *J. R. Fanshawe* — 58

PREMIER DANCE 9 ch.g. Bairn (USA) 126 – Gigiolina (King Emperor (USA)) [1995 44, a64: a14.8g* a12g³ a12g³ a12g² a14.8g a12g⁶ a14.8g³ a14.8g³ 14.9g⁵ 13f⁵ a14.8g² a14.8g² a12g⁶ a14.8g a14g⁵ a13g⁶ a12g* 1996 a12g⁶ a12g* a12g* 12g 13g a14.8g⁵ a12g* 12.1m³ 11.6g a12g Dec 7] compact gelding: has quick action: fair handicapper on the all-weather, poor on turf: won at Southwell in January and at Wolverhampton in February (apprentices, hung left) and May: stays 15f: — 49 a75 successful on equitrack, best form on fibresand: effective with blinkers/visor, but hasn't worn either since 1993: sometimes carries head high. *D. Haydn Jones*

PREMIER GENERATION (IRE)   3 b.g. Cadeaux Genereux 131 – Bristle 96   65
(Thatch (USA) 136) [1995 –: 8g 8.2m 1996 8m 8m⁶ 8m 10g 10.5m⁵ 8d⁵ Oct 2] leggy, quite good-topped gelding: has a long stride: modest maiden handicapper: finished first on unfavoured stand side when fifth of 18 at Salisbury on final start: effective at 1m, and stays 10.5f: acts on good to firm and dead ground. *D. W. P. Arbuthnot*

PREMIER LEAGUE (IRE)   6 gr.g. Don't Forget Me 127 – Kilmara (USA) 78   63 d
(Caro 133) [1995 –: 7m 1996 a10g 9.7m 10m⁶ 11.6m³ 10f 10g² 10g⁴ 10m 10g⁵ 10m⁵ 8m a10g⁶ a8g a10g⁵ Dec 20] strong, round-barrelled gelding: fair performer nowadays: best efforts in 1996 at Windsor: stays 11.6f: acts on firm and soft ground, poor form on equitrack: often a front runner, not of late. *J. E. Long*

PREMIER NIGHT   3 b.f. Old Vic 136 – Warm Welcome 89 (General Assembly   74
(USA)) [1995 NR 1996 8m⁴ 9s⁵ 8g² 9f³ 12.1s Oct 22] fifth foal: half-sister to 2-y-o sprint winners Clarinda (by Lomond) and Bonjour (by Primo Dominie) and 1995 3-y-o 1¼m winner Bunting (by Shaadi), 1m winner at 2 yrs: dam, 1¼m winner, granddaughter of 1000 Guineas winner Full Dress II: fair maiden: should prove suited by 1¼m+: well beaten on soft going. *S. Dow*

PREMIER STAR   6 ch.g. Precocious 126 – Grove Star (Upper Case (USA))   –
[1995 –: a7g 1996 a10g Dec 20] no longer of account. *K. G. Wingrove*

PREMIUM GIFT   4 ch.f. Most Welcome 131 – Emerald Eagle 78 (Sandy Creek   63
123) [1995 63: 5m⁶ 5g² 5g* 5m 1996 6.1m 6m 6g³ 5g² 5g 5.1m⁶ 5f⁴ 5.2m⁴ 5.1g Oct 24] good-topped filly: modest handicapper: unlucky loser at Doncaster on fourth start: best form at 5f: has raced only on a sound surface: may prove best with waiting tactics. *C. B. B. Booth*

PRENDS CA (IRE)   3 b.f. Reprimand 122 – Cri de Coeur (USA) 82 (Lyphard   95
(USA) 132) [1995 85: 6m* 6m 7s* 7.3d⁴ 1996 8d 7.6g* 7.1d³ 7m⁴ 8f⁵ 7g⁴ 7m 7d⁶ 6m⁶ 6m* Oct 4] smallish filly: fairly useful handicapper: won £18,000 event at Chester in May, weaving through to lead inside last: always close up when winning at Newmarket in October: sold 34,000 gns Newmarket Autumn Sales: stays 7.6f: acts on good to firm and soft ground: no improvement in blinkers. *R. Hannon*

PREROGATIVE   6 ch.g. Dominion 123 – Nettle 106 (Kris 135) [1995 NR 1996   58 d
11.9f⁴ 12m 16m 17.2f 11.9f Aug 6] 33/1, about 3 lengths fourth of 11 in handicap at Brighton on reappearance: well beaten afterwards: probably stays 1½m: tried visored, no improvement: joined H. S. Howe, and won novice chase in October. *R. Simpson*

PRESENT ARMS (USA)   3 b.c. Affirmed (USA) – Au Printemps (USA)   89
(Dancing Champ (USA)) [1995 73+: 7d 8g³ 8.1s³ 1996 10.8f² 12m² 10.1m* 11.6m* 11.8f* 12s Nov 9] workmanlike colt: unimpressive mover: fairly useful handicapper: won at Newcastle (maiden, made all) in July, Windsor (blinkered) in August and Leicester in October: led 9f in November Handicap at Doncaster on final start, fading back into mid-division: better suited by 1½m than shorter: acts on firm and soft ground: tended to wander second 3-y-o start. *P. F. I. Cole*

PRESENT CHANCE   2 ch.c. (Feb 8) Cadeaux Genereux 131 – Chance All (FR)   61
88 (Glenstal (USA) 118) [1996 7f⁴ 7g Oct 25] strong, good-bodied colt: has scope: second foal: half-brother to 3-y-o Lachesis (by Lycius): dam 2-y-o 5f winner (should have stayed 7f) out of half-sister to Young Generation: around 6½ lengths fourth of 10 to easy winner Crystal Hearted in maiden at Warwick: well beaten in more strongly-contested maiden at Doncaster later in month. *B. A. McMahon*

PRESENT GENERATION   3 ch.c. Cadeaux Genereux 131 – Penny Mint 79   81
(Mummy's Game 120) [1995 NR 1996 8g 8d² 7.1m² 6m² Jul 19] 13,000F, 25,000Y: good-topped colt: has scope: first foal: dam 2-y-o 6f winner out of sister to smart miler Saher: fairly useful form when second in maidens at Kempton, Chepstow and Newmarket: as effective at 6f as 1m: acts on good to firm and dead ground. *R. Guest*

PRESENTIMENT   2 b.g. (Feb 20) Puissance 110 – Octavia (Sallust 134) [1996   54
a6g 6d 6m⁶ 8.1m 7.5m 8.3d² 8g Oct 21] 19,000Y: leggy gelding: half-brother to numerous winners here and abroad, including 1992 2-y-o 7.5f winner Costa Verde (by King of Spain) and 1¼m to 1¾m winner Kinoko (by Bairn): dam showed a little

ability: modest maiden: second of 7 in nursery at Hamilton: sold (Jack Berry to M. Wane) 2,200 gns Newmarket Autumn Sales and gelded: stays 8.2f. *J. Berry*

PRESENT IMPERFECT   3 ch.f. Cadeaux Genereux 131 – Scarcely Blessed   61
116 (So Blessed 130) [1995 NR 1996 6m 5m⁴ Sep 18] sturdy, lengthy, rather hollow-backed filly: half-sister to several winners, including very smart sprinter/7f performer College Chapel (by Sharpo): dam sprinting half-sister to Mummy's Pet: 14/1, green and short to post, kept on steadily (wandered) when under 7 lengths ninth of 14 to Disputed in maiden at Newmarket: favourite, only fourth of 14 in weaker contest at Beverley 6 weeks later. *I. A. Balding*

PRESENT 'N CORRECT   3 ch.g. Cadeaux Genereux 131 – Emerald Eagle 78   57
(Sandy Creek 123) [1995 –: 7.1d 1996 6g 8m 6g³ a6g 5g* 6m a7g a6s Dec 19] leggy,   a–
workmanlike gelding: 14/1, easily best effort when narrowly winning 24-runner maiden handicap at Thirsk in September, leading inside final 1f: well beaten all subsequent starts: best at sprint distances: yet to race on extremes of going, soundly beaten all 3 all-weather outings. *C. B. B. Booth*

PRESENT SITUATION   5 ch.g. Cadeaux Genereux 131 – Storm Warning 117   66
(Tumble Wind (USA)) [1995 57, a74: a7g⁴ 7d⁴ 7d⁵ a8g2 7g² a7g   a74
a7g³ 1996 a7g* a7g² a7g⁴ 7m* 8m⁵ 8d² 8g 8f* a8g Nov 26] sparely-made gelding: unimpressive mover: fair handicapper, best on the all-weather: won at Lingfield (minor event) in January, Goodwood (apprentices) in June and Leicester (another minor event) in October: stays 8.5f: acts on all-weather (has won on fibresand, but better form on equitrack), firm ground and dead: consistent. *Lord Huntingdon*

PRESKIDUL (IRE)   2 b.f. (Feb 2) Silver Kite (USA) 111 – Dul Dul (USA)   55 d
(Shadeed (USA) 135) [1996 5g⁵ 5.1f⁴ 6g 6d 6g 6m 7m⁶ Sep 25] 8,000Y: well-grown, useful-looking filly: first foal: dam unraced half-sister to high-class sprinter Double Schwartz: poor maiden: deteriorated after second start: sold 1,200 gns Doncaster October Sales: should stay beyond 6f: wears bandages. *D. W. P. Arbuthnot*

PRESS AGAIN   4 ch.f. Then Again 126 – Silver Empress 63 (Octavo (USA) 115)   –
[1995 –: 8m 8.3m 1996 8.3d 8.3d 10m a6g a8g Dec 13] unfurnished filly: signs of some ability but no worthwhile form: refused to enter stalls on intended reappearance: not bred to stay much further than 1m. *P. Hayward*

PRESS ON NICKY   3 b.f. Nicholas (USA) 111 – Northern Empress 80 (North-   75
fields (USA)) [1995 NR 1996 7d³ 8g 7m* 7d⁶ 8m 7.3m² 7m 7s Oct 24] sturdy filly: half-sister to several winners, including (at 6f and 7f) Nevada Mix (by Alias Smith), sprinter Press The Bell (by Belfort) and useful jumper Easy Buck (by Swing Easy): dam ran 3 times: fair performer: won maiden at Salisbury in August: inconsistent in handicaps afterwards: should stay 1m: acts on good to firm and dead ground. *W. R. Muir*

PRESTIGE LAD   4 ch.g. Weldnaas (USA) 112 – Chic Antique 60 (Rarity 129)   –
[1995 NR 1996 a8g a10g Jan 18] first foal: dam best at sprint distances: no sign of ability. *B. Smart*

PRESTIGE LASS   3 ch.f. Weldnaas (USA) 112 – Monalda (FR) (Claude) [1995   –
NR 1996 10m 10m 9m 12d Oct 21] 1,000Y: half-sister to 4 winners here and abroad, including middle-distance winners Twenty One Red (by Dunphy) and Euphonic (by Elegant Air): dam won in Italy at 2 yrs and is half-sister to Italian Derby winner Marracci: little worthwhile form: considerately handled first 2 starts: off course 4 months before amateurs handicap final one: should be suited by middle distances. *B. Smart*

PRETTY SALLY (IRE)   2 b.f. (Mar 30) Polish Patriot (USA) 128 – Sally Chase   –
101 (Sallust 134) [1996 6g a6g⁶ a6g⁶ 6d a6g Nov 11] sturdy filly: closely related to   a47
1994 2-y-o 7f and 1m winner Unanimous Vote (by Roi Danzig), later smart 8.5f winner in USA in 1995, and half-sister to several winners, including 3-y-o 9.4f to 1½m winner Nikita's Star (by Soviet Lad): dam, sprinter, ran only at 2 yrs: poor maiden: best efforts at Wolverhampton but tailed off in seller there last time. *D. J. G. Murray Smith*

PRETTY SCARCE   5 ch.m. Handsome Sailor 125 – Not Enough (Balinger 116)   –
[1995 –: a8.5g a7g a9.4g 1996 a12g Jan 26] placed in Jersey: little sign of ability on mainland: covered by Never So Bold. *B. Preece*

PRETTY SHARP 2 ch.f. (Apr 21) Interrex (CAN) – To The Point 96 (Sharpen 64 ?
Up 127) [1996 8.1d⁵ 7m⁴ 7f² 8g Oct 25] half-sister to 4-y-o 6f (at 2 yrs) to 1¼m
winner Kings Assembly (by Presidium), and several winners in USA: dam 2-y-o 5f
winner, later ran in North America: in frame in maiden events at Yarmouth and
Redcar: well beaten in steadily-run nursery at Doncaster: better form at 7f than
1m: refused to enter stalls on intended debut: slowly away first 2 starts: joined
N. Babbage. *A. P. Jarvis*

PRICKET (USA) 3 ch.f. Diesis 133 – Cacti (USA) (Tom Rolfe) [1995 85P: 111
8.1m* 1996 10m* 12m² Jun 7]
Pricket has been retired after an all-too-brief career. Her third race, the
Oaks, turned out to be her last when she failed to meet engagements in the
Yorkshire Oaks and then the St Leger, both times on account of coming back
from preparatory work not quite a hundred per cent. She was almost certainly a
better filly than she showed at Epsom, so more's the pity she was denied one
chance at least to prove it. The lengthy filly Pricket had a big reputation from
the outset, and started 7/4 favourite at Epsom following a smooth win in a
Sandown maiden as a two-year-old for Henry Cecil and an impressive one in
the R. L. Davison Pretty Polly Stakes at Newmarket in the Godolphin colours
on returning from Dubai in the spring. She won a seven-runner race for the
Pretty Polly by five lengths, looking a high-class filly in the making as she
stretched away from Faraway Waters and Magnificient Style over the last two
furlongs. However, Pricket herself was beaten almost twice as far by Lady
Carla in the Oaks four weeks later. Oddly, for a sister to the 1988 winner Diminuendo, she ran as if not getting the trip. Cruising in behind the leaders turning
for home, she was unable to stay on anything like so strongly as the winner and
was all out in the end to hang on to second place in front of Mezzogiorno and
Camporese. That connections had evidently had every intention to run Pricket
in the Leger suggests that they thought she wasn't seen at her best at Epsom, for
reasons other than a lack of stamina.

		⎧ Sharpen Up	⎧ Atan
	⎧ Diesis	⎨ (ch 1969)	⎨ Rocchetta
	⎪ (ch 1980)	⎩ Doubly Sure	⎩ Reliance II
Pricket (USA)	⎨	(b 1971)	⎧ Soft Angels
(ch.f. 1993)	⎪	⎧ Tom Rolfe	⎨ Ribot
	⎩ Cacti (USA)	⎪ (b 1962)	⎩ Pocahontas II
	(ch 1977)	⎨	⎧ Amerigo
		⎩ Desert Love	⎨ Desert Vision
		(b 1962)	

Diminuendo, of course, went on to finish a creditable second in the
Leger having won the Oaks by a long-looking four lengths. There is also a colt
bred the same way, the quite useful Bayaireg, who seemed not to stay so well as

R. L. Davison Pretty Polly Stakes, Newmarket—Pricket shortens to 6/4 for the Oaks

Diminuendo did. He won two handicaps at around a mile and a quarter for Alex Scott's stable in 1992, ridden from behind. Thus far the dam Cacti has produced six winners from seven runners. One of her winning offspring in the USA, Sister Sophie, is the dam of the good-class one-mile to mile-and-a-quarter performer Port Lucaya. *Saeed bin Suroor*

PRIDDY FAIR   3 b.f. North Briton 67 – Rainbow Ring (Rainbow Quest (USA)   –
134) [1995 54d: 5g⁶ 6m⁴ a6g 8m 7.5d 10g 1996 8m Oct 23] good-topped filly: poor maiden for R. Boss at 2 yrs: showed little in claiming handicap at Newcastle on belated reappearance: won over hurdles in December. *D. W. Barker*

PRIDE OF BRIXTON   3 b.c. Dominion 123 – Caviar Blini 80 (What A Guest   91
119) [1995 83p: 6g³ 6s² 1996 6s³ 5.1g² 5m 5.1g* 5m 5m 5m⁵ 5m 5.1g 5g² Oct 19] lengthy, useful-looking colt: fairly useful handicapper: won at Chester in May: good second of 20 at Catterick on final start: sold 30,000 gns Newmarket Autumn Sales: likely to prove best at 5f: acts on good to firm and soft going: usually early to post: usually races prominently. *G. Lewis*

PRIDE OF HAYLING (IRE)   5 ch.m. Bold Arrangement 127 – Malham Tarn   67
(Riverman (USA) 131) [1995 64d: 6f 5g⁶ 6f* 6f* 7m⁴ 6f 6d 6d a7g 1996 5g⁶ 5m³ 6m³ 6m* 6f³ 5.3f* 7f⁶ 6m 5m² 5.1g 6d Oct 21] compact mare: modest handicapper: won at Folkestone and Brighton in the summer: best form at up to 6f: acts on firm ground: sometimes slowly away. *P. R. Hedger*

PRIDE OF KASHMIR   3 gr.g. Petong 126 – Proper Madam 93 (Mummy's Pet   56
125) [1995 58: 5m 5m 7.1g⁴ 8g 7f 6.9m⁴ 1996 6.9s² 7.1g 8.2m 8m 8g⁴ 7f 9.7g⁵ 10f³ 10f³ 10d⁶ 8g 10g⁶ Oct 2] good-topped gelding: unimpressive mover: modest maiden handicapper: stays 1¼m: acts on firm and soft ground: blinkered (below form) fourth 3-y-o start: not easiest of rides: inconsistent. *P. W. Harris*

PRIDE OF MAY (IRE)   5 b.g. Law Society (USA) 130 – Aztec Princess (Indian   –
King (USA) 128) [1995 67d: a14.8g³ a16g² 18g 12m⁴ 14m² 14m⁴ 11.8m⁶ 12g⁶ 14m⁵ 12.3m² 12.3m⁴ 16.1h⁵ a16g 1996 a16g 17.1m⁶ Aug 18] workmanlike gelding: front-running handicapper: on the downgrade, well beaten in 1996. *C. W. Fairhurst*

PRIDE OF PENDLE   7 gr.m. Grey Desire 115 – Pendle's Secret 73 (Le Johnstan   74
123) [1995 80: 8g 8g 8m* 7.6m 7m⁵ 10m⁶ 8.5m⁵ 8.9m* 10f 7.9m⁵ 8f² 8f² 8m² 7.6m* 8m⁶ 8d 9g 8.9g 8m 1996 7g⁵ 8.5g 8g⁶ 7g 8.5m 7g⁵ 9f 8f⁵ 7.9g 8g² 8m³ 8m* 8g 8.9g 8g Oct 19] leggy, angular mare: fair handicapper: won £22,000 contest at Ayr in September: stays 9f well: acts on any going: held up, and ideally suited by strongly-run race: returned lame fifth 7-y-o start: splendidly tough and genuine. *D. Nicholls*

PRIDE OF WHALLEY (IRE)   3 b.f. Fayruz 116 – Wilderness 88 (Martinmas   55
128) [1995 61: 5g⁶ a5g⁴ 5m² 1996 6.1g³ 6.1m² 5m⁶ 6m May 28] workmanlike filly: modest maiden: best form at up to 6f: acts on good to firm ground. *R. A. Fahey*

PRIENA (IRE)   2 ch.f. (May 29) Priolo (USA) 127 – Isabena (Star Appeal 133)   86 p
[1996 7f* Sep 27] third foal: dam, won 5 times in Spain from 2 to 4 yrs, half-sister to useful Irish 7f/1m performer Irish Memory: odds on, won 8-runner maiden at Redcar easily by 7 lengths from Pretty Sharp, drawing right away under hands and heels from over 1f out: likely to stay beyond 1m: seems sure to improve. *D. R. Loder*

PRIMA COMINNA   4 ch.f. Unfuwain (USA) 131 – Cominna (Dominion 123)   –
[1995 84: 6m² 6m³ 7m⁴ 6g³ 5m 7m² 7m⁶ 1996 7m 7f 7g⁵ a8.5g⁴ a8g Jun 25] rather leggy, workmanlike filly: fairly useful handicapper at 3 yrs for M. Bell: well below form in 1996, including in blinkers: stays 7f: has raced only on a sound surface when on turf. *S. P. C. Woods*

PRIMA SILK   5 b.m. Primo Dominie 121 – Silk St James (Pas de Seul 133) [1995   74
80: a7g⁴ a7g a7g² 7m⁵ 6.1g⁶ 6g* 5m* 6f³ᵈⁱˢ 6m 6m 6m 5.7h 6.1d 6g 5.1d 6g⁴ 6f⁴ 5m   a80
a7g* 1996 a7g⁶ a8g 6f 6.1m⁶ 6f* 5.7g⁶ 6f² 6m⁴ 6g 5.7m² 6g 6g 5.7m² a7g² 6.1d 7f⁵ 7m 6d² 6d⁶ 6f a6g* a6g a6g⁵ Dec 20] angular mare: seldom impresses in appearance: fair handicapper: won at Lingfield in May and Wolverhampton in November: effective at 5f, and stays 7f: acts on the all-weather and on firm and dead ground: no improvement in blinkers or visor: sometimes wanders markedly: none too consistent. *M. J. Ryan*

PRIMA VERDE   3 b.f. Leading Counsel (USA) 122 – Bold Green (FR) (Green   – p
Dancer (USA) 132) [1995 NR 1996 8.1m Aug 31] 7,700Y: half-sister to several

winners abroad, including French 7.5f and 8.5f winner Going Crazy (by Persepolis): dam won over 5f and 1m in France: 20/1, 10 lengths ninth of 14 to Ruwy in slowly-run maiden at Sandown, very slowly away, staying on not knocked about: should do better. *L. M. Cumani*

PRIMA VOLTA 3 b.f. Primo Dominie 121 – Femme Formidable (Formidable 73 (USA) 125) [1995 80: 5m⁴ 6g* 7d 6m 1996 6m⁶ 7.1d⁵ 8m⁶ 8.3d 9g* 8m 8g⁶ Oct 2] angular filly: fairly useful form at 2 yrs: not so good in 1996, dropped to claimer when winning at Sandown in August: sold 5,500 gns Newmarket Autumn Sales: stays 9f: acts on good to firm and dead ground: blinkered (ran poorly) third and fourth 3-y-o starts. *R. Hannon*

PRIME LIGHT 3 ch.g. Primo Dominie 121 – Flopsy (Welsh Pageant 132) [1995 75 NR 1996 7m³ 7d³ 7m⁵ Jun 1] 56,000Y: strong, lengthy gelding: half-brother to 1993 2-y-o 7f winner Crazy For You (by Blakeney), who later stayed 14.4f, useful 7f performer Captain Holly (by Absalom) and a prolific minor winner in Germany by Sharrood: dam unraced daughter of 1000 Guineas third Mrs Tiggywinkle, dam also of smart Gordian: fair form in 3 maidens: gelded. *G. Wragg*

PRIMELTA 3 b.f. Primo Dominie 121 – Pounelta 91 (Tachypous 128) [1995 55: – 6g⁶ 6f 6.1d 1996 6g 6f 7s Oct 24] good-topped filly: always behind in handicaps in 1996: bred to be best at up to 1m. *R. Akehurst*

PRIME PARTNER 3 b.g. Formidable (USA) 125 – Baileys By Name 66 – (Nomination 125) [1995 63: 6g 5g⁶ 6m² 6f⁵ 6f 6.1s 6d 1996 6m 6g a8g a7g³ 7.1m a49 a6g⁶ Oct 5] strong gelding: poor maiden: stays 7f: acts on good to firm ground and on equitrack: blinkered (tailed off) final 2-y-o start. *W. R. Muir*

PRIME PROPERTY (IRE) 4 b.f. Tirol 127 – Busker (Bustino 136) [1995 40: – a6g 7.5m 7g 6g 10m 12m a12g 7m 6m² 6m* 7d⁶ 7f 1996 a6g 6m 6.1m 7d 6m 8f 6m 5f 5d 5m 6f Aug 3] lengthy, angular filly: poor sprint handicapper: didn't find her form at all in 1996: covered by Noble Patriarch. *M. W. Easterby*

PRIM LASS 5 b.m. Reprimand 122 – Vague Lass 85 (Vaigly Great 127) [1995 49: – 8.2m 7g³ 7m a8g 1996 a7g 7g 10m May 24] tall mare: poor maiden plater: may prove best at sprint distances: may be temperamental. *Miss J. Bower*

PRIMO LAD 3 b.g. Primo Dominie 121 – Zinzi (Song 132) [1995 –: 5f⁶ 1996 5m² 49 d 6g a8.5g a7g 5f Jun 24] leggy gelding: sprint-bred maiden: second of 5 in claimer at Folkestone on reappearance: soundly beaten all other starts: tried blinkered. *W. G. M. Turner*

PRIMO LARA 4 ch.c. Primo Dominie 121 – Clara Barton (Youth (USA) 135) 89 [1995 70: 8m² 8m⁴ 8d⁶ 8.5m⁵ 8m³ 7g³ 7f⁴ 1996 7.5d³ 7.5m* 7m* 8g 7m⁴ 7m² 6m 7.1f* 7m 7g³ 6f Nov 5] strong, lengthy colt: poor mover: improved handicapper in 1996, winner at Beverley and Thirsk in April and at Haydock (well-contested event) in September: best at 7f/easy 1m: acts on firm ground and dead: makes running/races up with pace. *P. W. Harris*

PRIMROSE PATH 3 b.f. Shaadi (USA) 126 – Crimson Conquest (USA) 85 – (Diesis 133) [1995 65: 6g 6.9f³ 8.2d⁶ 1996 9.9m May 21] quite attractive filly: fair maiden: stiff task, last of 10 in handicap at Beverley (badly hampered) only 3-y-o start: sold 5,000 gns Newmarket July Sales: should stay 1m. *C. E. Brittain*

PRIMULA BAIRN 6 b.m. Bairn (USA) 126 – Miss Primula 81 (Dominion 123) – [1995 64: a5g⁵ a5g* a5g* a6g³ a5g³ a5g* 5g a5g a6g a5g⁵ 5g 5.1d 5g 1996 a5g a6g a68 a6g⁵ a5g* a5g⁵ a5g* a5g³ a5g² 5.2m a5g a6g² a6s⁴ Dec 19] workmanlike mare: not a fluent mover: modest performer: won claimer in January and seller in March, both at Wolverhampton: stays 6f: acts on fibresand, ideally suited by give in the ground on turf (acts on heavy): usually visored or blinkered: inconsistent. *D. Nicholls*

PRINCE ARTHUR (IRE) 4 b.c. Fairy King (USA) – Daniela Samuel (USA) 107 (No Robbery) [1995 116: 7m² 8g* 8m⁵ 8g⁶ 8d² 1996 10g 10s⁵ 8f⁴ 8.5g² Nov 24] well-made colt: smart performer, winner of Premio Parioli at 3 yrs: bit below best in 1996, leaving P. Chapple-Hyam after second start and best effort probably when runner-up in allowance race at Hollywood Park in November. stays 8.5f: probably acts on firm and dead ground. *J. Noseda, USA*

PRINCE ASLIA 3 b.c. Aragon 118 – Aslia 74 (Henbit (USA) 130) [1995 98: 5m³ – 5m* 5f* 5m 5m² 5g² 5d 6f 1996 5g⁶ 7f 8d Aug 17] tall, close-coupled colt: useful form at 2 yrs: soundly beaten in listed race at Haydock (sweating freely) and £19,100 handicap at York (has no prospects of staying 7f) final start for M. Johnston before sold 27,000 gns Newmarket July Sales: suited by 5f: seems to need a sound surface: excitable sort: one to treat with caution. *G. Mikhalides, France*

PRINCE BABAR 5 b.g. Fairy King (USA) – Bell Toll 87 (High Line 125) [1995 103 NR 1996 7g⁶ 7m³ 6f² 8m³ 7m² 6m³ 7m 8d* 8g² Nov 2] sparely-made gelding: has a round action: useful performer: ran really well in competitive handicaps in 1996, finishing third in Victoria Cup and second in Wokingham at Ascot, third in Schweppes Golden Mile at Goodwood, second in New Zealand Handicap at Newmarket, third in Gold Cup at Ayr and second of 26 in £22,900 event at Newmarket: gained well-deserved success in apprentice minor event at Ascot in October: effective at 6f to 1m: below form on heavy ground at 3 yrs, acts on firm and dead: often apprentice ridden: game and consistent. *J. E. Banks*

PRINCE DANZIG (IRE) 5 ch.g. Roi Danzig (USA) – Veldt (High Top 131) 67 [1995 67, a83: a12g* a10g² a10g³ a12g⁶ a12g* a10g³ 11.9f³ 10g⁴ 11.9m² 17.2m⁴ a88 11.9f* 11.9f² 11.7h² 11.5m⁵ 11.9g² 11.9g⁴ 1996 a12g³ a12g⁴ a12g* a10g⁴ a12g a12g⁵ 11.9f* 11.9f³ 14m⁵ 12g 11.9f⁴ 11.9m² 11.9f⁴ 11.5d⁴ a12g* Dec 7] close-coupled gelding: good mover: fair handicapper on turf, fairly useful on all-weather surfaces: won at Lingfield in February, Brighton in May and Wolverhampton in December: stays 1½m: acts on any going: has worn blinkers and visor (not since 1994), better form without: usually held up. *D. J. G. Murray Smith*

PRINCE DE BERRY 5 ch.g. Ballacashtal (CAN) – Hoonah (FR) (Luthier 126) 41 [1995 NR 1996 11.6m 9m 11.5f³ 18m 12m³ Aug 2] poor maiden handicapper: stays 1½m: acts on good to firm ground: blinkered (well beaten) final 3-y-o start: sold to join G. Ham 4,800 gns Newmarket Autumn Sales: inconsistent. *B. J. Meehan*

PRINCE DE LOIR 2 b.c. (Apr 28) Be My Chief (USA) 122 – Princesse Vali (FR) (Val de L'Orne (FR) 133) [1996 7m Aug 9] 180,000 francs Y: big, strong colt: half-brother to several winners in France, including 1m and 1½m winner Prince Valry (by Pharly) and middle-distance performer Linora (by Esprit du Nord): dam French 1½m winner: last of 13 in maiden at Newmarket. *D. J. S. Cosgrove*

PRINCE DOME (IRE) 2 ch.c. (Jan 27) Salt Dome (USA) – Blazing Glory 69 (IRE) (Glow (USA)) [1996 5f 6g⁶ 5g² Aug 12] IR 5,200F, 8,600Y: unfurnished colt: has a round action: first foal: dam Irish 5f winner, including at 2 yrs: 33/1 but well drawn, clearly best effort in summer maidens when staying-on second of 12 at Thirsk: will stay 6f. *Martyn Wane*

PRINCE EQUINAME 4 gr.g. Dominion 123 – Moments Peace (Adonijah 126) – [1995 64d: 10m 12g³ 10.5g⁴ 12g a11g⁶ 12g 11.1g 19m a11g 16.2m Apr 12] smallish gelding: modest middle-distance maiden: should stay 1½m: headstrong: inconsistent: has joined T. Hind. *D. Eddy*

PRINCE JORDAN 2 ch.g. (Mar 22) Keen 116 – Diami 81 (Swing Easy (USA) – 126) [1996 7f 7m 8g Nov 2] 12,000Y: big, strong gelding: half-brother to winning sprinter Just Bob (by Alleging) and a winner abroad: dam, 2-y-o 5f winner, stayed 7f: well beaten in maiden and sellers. *I. Campbell*

PRINCE KINSKY 3 ch.c. Master Willie 129 – Princess Lieven (Royal Palace 79 131) [1995 73p: 7m 8m 1996 a10g* 10.5d⁶ 12.1m³ 14g⁶ 14.1s a12g⁴ Nov 14] angular colt: odds on, won median auction maiden at Lingfield in April by 5 lengths, carrying head high: upped in trip, best effort when close third of 5 in handicap at Chepstow in July: stays 1½m: acts on equitrack and good to firm ground, below form on a soft surface. *Lord Huntingdon*

PRINCELY AFFAIR 3 b.g. Prince Sabo 123 – Shillay (Lomond (USA) 128) 54 [1995 –: 6.1d 5s 5f 1996 10.8g 12m a8g³ 10.1m* 10m² a12g³ 11.5f² 10.1g⁶ 10m 10g 10.1m Oct 23] good-bodied gelding: poor mover: modest handicapper: won apprentice race at Yarmouth in June: well below form last 3 starts: sold (M. Bell to J. M. Bradley) 6,000 gns Newmarket Autumn Sales: stays 1½m: acts on firm ground: usually held up. *M. Bell*

PRINCELY GAIT 5 b.g. Darshaan 133 – Roussalka 123 (Habitat 134) [1995 76: 67 a13g³ a12g* a16g* a16g⁴ 1996 a12g² 16.1g a12g³ a12g Nov 7] big, good-topped gelding: fair performer: sold out of C. Cyzer's stable 3,200 gns Ascot May Sales before reappearance: placed in 2 claimers at Wolverhampton: broke leg at Lingfield: effective at 1½m to 2m: best on the all-weather: dead. *M. J. Polglase*

Bass Wulfrun Stakes, Wolverhampton—a rousing finish to the all-weather showpiece; left to right are Prince of Andros, Decorated Hero and Royal Philosopher

PRINCELY HUSH (IRE) 4 b.c. Prince Sabo 123 – So Kind 90 (Kind of Hush –
118) [1995 –: 6g 1996 5d 6d Sep 30] strong, good-topped colt: has a round action:
useful form (rated 109) at 2 yrs but has reportedly had joint problems, and soundly
beaten all 3 subsequent starts: sold 9,800 gns Newmarket December Sales: stays 6f:
best form on an easy surface. *M. Bell*

PRINCELY SOUND 3 b.g. Prince Sabo 123 – Sound of The Sea 91 (Wind- 69 §
jammer (USA)) [1995 69: 5m⁴ 5m² 6m 1996 a6g* a6g⁴ a5g* 5d 6m⁶ 6.1g* 5m 6g⁵ a75 §
5.1m⁵ 6f⁴ 6d 5.7m 5m Sep 26] good-topped gelding: fair handicapper: won at
Lingfield in January (median auction maiden) and February and at Chester in May:
unable to dominate and below form last 5 starts: sold 7,800 gns Newmarket Autumn
Sales: effective at 5f and 6f: acts on good to firm ground and on equitrack, probably
on fibresand: no improvement in visor: not one to trust: gelded. *M. Bell*

PRINCE OF ANDROS (USA) 6 b.h. Al Nasr (FR) 126 – Her Radiance (USA) 114
(Halo (USA)) [1995 116: 10m* 10m* 10m² 10m 10f 12d 10m⁴ a9.4g* 1996 10g⁶
10d 10g² 10m⁴ 10.3m* 10m⁴ 10f a9.4g* Dec 7] tall, lengthy horse: smart performer:
ran as if something amiss second 6-y-o start: won well-contested minor event at
Chester in July by 1½ lengths from Don Vito: left D. Loder after tailed off in
Arlington Million penultimate start: won listed race at Wolverhampton (second year
running) in December, heading Decorated Hero on post: effective at 1¼m and 1½m:
acts on good to firm and soft ground and on fibresand: effective blinkered/visored or
not: held up/tracks leaders. *C. F. Wall*

PRINCE OF DENIAL 2 b.c. (Apr 23) Soviet Star (USA) 128 – Gleaming Water 70
81 (Kalaglow 132) [1996 7d 7f⁴ 7m² Oct 28] 20,000Y: rather leggy colt: third foal:
half-brother to 3-y-o Faraway Waters (by Pharly), 6f winner at 2 yrs, and 4-y-o 7f (at
2 yrs) to 13f winner Paradise Waters (by Celestial Storm): dam, 2-y-o 6f winner,
sister to smart stayer Shining Water, dam of Tenby: in frame in 10-runner maidens at
Leicester, 4 lengths fourth to Attitude then neck second to Ortelius in steadily-run
contest 13 days later: will stay at least 1m: bandaged behind: wore crossed noseband
final start. *D. W. P. Arbuthnot*

PRINCE OF FORTUNE   2 b.g. (Apr 8) Prince Sabo 123 – Beautiful Orchid   –
(Hays 120) [1996 6m Jun 13] 6,000Y: rather unfurnished gelding: third foal: dam
lightly-raced half-sister to useful 7f and 1m winner Just Class, later graded winner
in USA: twelfth of 13 in Newbury maiden: gelded and joined M. Blanshard.
M. McCormack

PRINCE OF INDIA   4 b.c. Night Shift (USA) – Indian Queen 115 (Electric 126)   102
[1995 109: 10m 7.3m³ 8.5m⁵ 7m² 9g⁶ 7m³ 7d⁵ 8d 1996 8f 7g 8f⁵ Aug 18] deep-
bodied colt: good mover: useful performer: below form in 1996, best effort when
seventh of 9 in Queen Anne Stakes at Royal Ascot on reappearance: stays 1m: acts
on good to firm and dead ground: inconsistent. *Lord Huntingdon*

PRINCE OF MY HEART   3 ch.c. Prince Daniel (USA) – Blue Room 70   104
(Gorytus (USA) 132) [1995 87: 6m 7m 8.1m³ 7.1g³ 7.9m* 8f⁶ 1996 10g² 12d* 12.3g³
12m 10d⁴ 10.3f³ 9m 10m⁵ Oct 17] tall, quite attractive colt: good mover, though did
not stride out so well as usual on final start: useful performer: won minor event at
Catterick in April: creditable efforts last 3 starts, including when ninth in the
Cambridgeshire at Newmarket: effective at 9f and stays 12.3f: acts on firm and dead
ground. *B. W. Hills*

PRINCE OF PARKES   2 b.g. (Jan 30) Full Extent (USA) 113 – Summerhill   –
Spruce 70 (Windjammer (USA)) [1996 5g 6d May 31] sturdy, lengthy gelding: fifth
living foal: brother to useful sprinter Lucky Parkes and half-brother to 3 winners,
notably useful supprinting 3-y-o My Melody Parkes (by Teenoso): dam 6f winner:
behind in 2 early-season maiden events. *J. Berry*

PRINCE OF SPADES   4 ch.g. Shavian 125 – Diamond Princess 69 (Horage 124)   –
[1995 63: 8m⁵ 10m* 10g 10f* 8f 8d⁶ 10f 1996 11.6m 10.2m Jul 6] workmanlike,
good-quartered gelding: unimpressive mover: modest performer in 1995: well
beaten in 1996: stays 1¼m: acts on firm going: has joined A. Hobbs. *F. Jordan*

PRINCE ROONEY (IRE)   8 b.h. Dayeem (USA) – Fourth Degree (Oats 126)   –
[1995 NR 1996 a6g 8g 6.9m Jun 5] close-coupled horse: probably no longer of any
account. *P. Butler*

PRINCE RUDOLF (IRE)   4 b.g. Cyrano de Bergerac 120 – Princess Raisa   39
(Indian King (USA) 128) [1995 53d: a5g³ a6g² a6g⁴ a7g³ a7g³ a6g⁵ a5g⁴ 6s a6g 6g
5.3m² 6.1m 5m 7m³ 8f⁴ 8m³ 1996 a6g a6g⁶ a6g⁶ a8g 8g 7.1f⁵ 8m 8m 8f⁴ 10m⁴ 8m
a10g Dec 20] workmanlike gelding: poor performer: trained until after fifth start by
Mrs N. Macauley: stays 1m: acts on the all-weather and on firm ground, probably on
soft: often blinkered/visored: pulls hard: inconsistent. *W. G. M. Turner*

PRINCESS BELFORT   3 b.f. Belfort (FR) 89 – Domino Rose 67 (Dominion   –
123) [1995 NR 1996 5.1g 6g May 9] 1,350Y: second reported foal: dam 6f winner:
slowly away and always behind in claimer at Nottingham and seller at Southwell.
G. Fierro

PRINCESS DANIELLE   4 b.f. Prince Daniel (USA) – Bells of St Martin 89   63
(Martinmas 128) [1995 58: 7.3g 7g³ 8.2m* 8m⁵ 8.2m³ 10d* 9m 1996 10.3d³ 10s² 8m
10m 10g⁵ 10m³ 10g² 10d³ 10s² 10.1m 10d³ 10g Oct 29] leggy filly: easy mover:
modest handicapper: left C. C. Elsey after second 4-y-o start: stays 1¼m: acts on
good to firm ground and soft: consistent. *W. R. Muir*

PRINCESS EFISIO   3 b.f. Efisio 120 – Cutlass Princess (USA) 41 (Cutlass   67
(USA)) [1995 –: 5.1m⁵ 6m⁶ 1996 5.1g⁶ 5m a5g⁵ 6.1m 5f⁴ a5g* a6g* a7g² a8.5g 7.1s²
a7g⁵ Nov 2] smallish, rather dipped-backed filly: fair handicapper: won at Wolverhampton in June and July: stays 7f: acts on fibresand, easily best turf effort on soft
ground: blinkered (creditable effort at the time) fifth 3-y-o start. *B. A. McMahon*

PRINCESSE LYPHARD   3 gr.f. Keen 116 – Bercheba (Bellypha 130) [1995   36
NR 1996 8m 10m 7f 8f⁶ 7f³ a10g Dec 30] lengthy, plain filly: fifth foal: half-sister to
11.9f winner Shirl (by Shirley Heights): dam from good family: signs of only a little
ability: best efforts at 7f. *M. J. Polglase*

PRINCESS FERDINAND (IRE)   2 b.f. (Mar 2) Roi Danzig (USA) – Silvera   –
73 (Ribero 126) [1996 6d 6f⁶ 5m⁶ a6g 5.1m 6m⁴ Aug 17] 7,200Y: half-sister to fair
6f and 8.5f winner Pontevecchio Due (by Welsh Pageant) and 3 winners abroad, one
a useful winner, mostly in Belgium: dam won over 1m: poor form at best, including
in sellers: visored, pulled up fifth outing (fly jumped leaving stalls, rider lost irons).
M. McCormack

PRINCESS OF HEARTS 2 b.f. (Mar 26) Prince Sabo 123 – Constant Delight 61
80 (Never So Bold 135) [1996 6m 5.1m 6g⁴ 6.9m* 8m⁴ 8.1m³ 10m 8f 7m² a8.5g² 7m
8g⁴ a6g³ Nov 11] lengthy filly: second foal: half-sister to 1994 2-y-o 6f winner Corio
(by Sharpo): dam 9f winner out of half-sister to Forzando: modest performer: won
seller at Folkestone (sold out of W. Haggas's stable 6,200 gns) in August: consistent
afterwards: needs further than 6f and stays 8.5f: often starts slowly: blinkered 4 of
last 5 starts (below form on the other). *B. J. Meehan*

PRINCESS PAMGADDY 3 gr.f. Petong 126 – Edwins' Princess 75 (Owen 52
Dudley 121) [1995 58d: 5m³ 5g⁵ 5g 5g⁶ 7.1g* 8.3g⁶ 7f⁴ 7m 1996 a8g⁵ a8g³ 11.1m⁵
a11g a8g* 8f² 8m⁶ 8g* 8.3g 8f³ 10g⁵ 8g⁶ 8.5f Dec 31] leggy filly: poor handicapper:
won at Southwell and Newmarket (claimer, claimed £6,000 out of C. Allen's stable)
in June: left P. Cole after penultimate start: stays 1¼m: acts on fibresand and firm
ground (has raced only on a sound surface on turf): held up, and suited by sound pace:
successful for apprentice. *B. Kessinger, jnr, USA*

PRINCESS PARROT (IRE) 5 br.m. Roi Danzig (USA) – Red Lory 87 (Bay –
Express 132) [1995 NR 1996 a10g a8g⁶ Feb 3] sturdy mare: no worthwhile form:
tried visored. *Lord Huntingdon*

PRINCESS RENATA (IRE) 3 ch.f. Maelstrom Lake 118 – Sajanjal (Dance In –
Time (CAN)) [1995 –: a5g 5m⁶ 5g⁶ 6m⁶ 1996 a6g May 2] little worthwhile form.
R. Harris

PRINCESS SARARA (USA) 2 ch.f. (May 13) Trempolino (USA) 135 – Name –
And Fame (USA) (Arts And Letters) [1996 a8.5g a8g Dec 20] 24,000Y: closely
related to 3-y-o 11.8f winner Infamous (by Diesis) and half-sister to several winners
in USA: dam, winner of 3 races in USA, half-sister of Oh So Sharp and Roussalka:
soundly beaten in all-weather maidens. *Sir Mark Prescott*

PRINCESS TALLULAH 5 b.m. Chief Singer 131 – Nuts And Brazen (Bold –
Lad (IRE) 133) [1995 NR 1996 a16g 12.1g Apr 4] lengthy mare: poor maiden (rated
43) at 3 yrs for P. Murphy: well beaten in handicaps in 1996. *W. G. M. Turner*

PRINCESS TOPAZ 2 b.f. (Feb 15) Midyan (USA) 124 – Diamond Princess 69 70
(Horage 124) [1996 6g² 6f² 6g 8m³ 7.9g⁴ Oct 10] leggy, angular filly: third foal:
half-sister to 1¼m winner Prince of Spades (by Shavian): dam, 1½m winner, is
half-sister to smart Irish sprinter Princess Seal: fair maiden: stayed on well when in
frame in nurseries at Doncaster (on toes) and York (didn't take eye in appearance)
last 2 starts: likely to stay beyond 1m. *C. A. Cyzer*

PRINCE ZIZIM 3 b.c. Shareef Dancer (USA) 135 – Possessive Lady 62 (Dara –
Monarch 128) [1995 60p: 6m 8g⁴ 1996 8m 8.2m 8.3m 10f 12m 8g⁶ 9.9g 10f Sep 10]
smallish, quite attractive colt: trained by C. Dwyer until after fourth 3-y-o start: signs
of ability at 2 yrs but no worthwhile form in 1996: tried blinkered. *R. C. Spicer*

PRINCIPAL BOY (IRE) 3 br.g. Cyrano de Bergerac 120 – Shenley Lass –
(Prince Tenderfoot (USA) 126) [1995 42⁴: 6m⁵ 7m⁴ 8.1g 6g⁵ 7d 5m 5s⁶ a5g 1996 a55
a6g² a7g* a9.4g⁵ a6g² a7g a6g⁵ a6g³ a7g* a8g a7g⁴ 6m a8g⁴ a7g a8g⁴ Dec 27]
compact gelding: has a round action: modest handicapper: won at Southwell in
February and May: suited by 7f or strongly-run 6f: acts on fibresand, well beaten
only turf outing in 1996: no improvement in blinkers. *T. J. Etherington*

PRINCIPAL PLAYER (USA) 6 br.g. Chief Singer 131 – Harp Strings (FR) –
109 (Luthier 126) [1995 NR 1996 13s⁶ May 9] leggy, rather angular gelding: modest
handicapper: fair winning hurdler: well held on return to flat. *P. Monteith*

PRINTERS QUILL 4 b.g. Squill (USA) 122 – On Impulse 63 (Jellaby 124) 56
[1995 –: 10d 10.2m³ 10d 1996 10m 12m 17.2f 10.2m* 10.2g 10m³ 10m 13.6m Oct
17] leggy gelding: modest handicapper: narrowly won apprentice maiden race at
Bath in August, making all: should be suited by further than 1¼m: acts on good to
firm ground. *Major D. N. Chappell*

PRIOLINA (IRE) 3 b.f. Priolo (USA) 127 – Salustrina (Sallust 134) [1995 7m 107
8g⁶ 8g⁶ 9g² 1996 9s 10d 10g 11m² 9d² 7.8d² 12g* 12m² 12g² 14g³ 11.9m³ 12m³ 12d
Oct 12] IR 12,500Y: leggy, angular filly: sixth foal: half-sister to 3 winners, notably
Ringmaster (stayed 1½m, rated 92, by Taufan): dam Irish 7f winner: progressed very
well and is a useful performer: won maiden at Tramore in June: placed on 8 of her
other 12 starts in 1996, third to Eva Luna in Galtres Stakes at York (beaten 2 lengths)
and to Wall Street in Cumberland Lodge Stakes at Ascot (beaten 4½ lengths)

eleventh and twelfth outings: sold 50,000 gns Newmarket December Sales: stays 1¾m: best form on a sound surface, and acts on good to firm: nearly always blinkered. *J. C. Hayden, Ireland*

PRIORY BELLE (IRE) 3 ch.f. Priolo (USA) 127 – Ingabelle 108 (Taufan (USA) 119) [1995 103p: 6f* 7m² 7g* 1996 7d⁵ 8d⁵ 8m Jun 19] good-topped filly: useful performer: won Moyglare Stud Stakes in 1995: best effort, though did not look an easy ride, when 6½ lengths fifth of 12 to Matiya in Irish 1000 Guineas at the Curragh: got very upset in stalls and never going well when last of 7 in Coronation Stakes at Royal Ascot over 3 weeks later: stays 1m: winner on firm ground at 2 yrs, but best efforts with some give: usually flashes tail, and did so repeatedly at Royal Ascot. *J. S. Bolger, Ireland*   104

PRIORY GARDENS (IRE) 2 b.g. (Apr 28) Broken Hearted 124 – Rosy O'Leary (Majetta 115) [1996 6.1m 6.1d 7m 6.1s Oct 22] IR 2,750Y, 4,200 2-y-o: half-brother to several winners, including 1995 2-y-o 7f winner Magic Mill (by Simply Great) and 9f to 1½m winner Gillies Prince (by Furry Glen): dam never ran: well beaten in varied events. *J. M. Bradley*   –

PRIVATE AUDIENCE (USA) 3 b.c. Private Account (USA) – Monroe (USA) 102 (Sir Ivor 135) [1995 –p: 7.9g⁶ 1996 12g⁵ May 17] close-coupled, good-topped colt: has a quick action: well beaten in maidens: sold 16,000 gns Newmarket Autumn Sales and sent to France. *H. R. A. Cecil*   –

PRIVATE FIXTURE (IRE) 5 ch.g. The Noble Player (USA) 126 – Pennyala (Skyliner 117) [1995 –: a8g⁴ 8m 8g⁶ a8.5g a7g 1996 8d a7g a8g Nov 12] quite good-topped gelding: fair miler at best at 3 yrs: no worthwhile form since. *D. Marks*   –

PRIVATE PERCIVAL 3 b.c. Arrasas (USA) 100 – Romacina (Roman Warrior 132) [1995 NR 1996 8.3g 11.4m⁵ 14m 12d a12g 16.4v Nov 11] second reported foal: dam of little account: no worthwhile form. *Jamie Poulton*   –

PRIVATE SONG (USA) 3 b.c. Private Account (USA) – Queen of Song (USA) (His Majesty (USA)) [1995 78p: 7m² 1996 10g 10.2g² 10.2g* 12m² 12m 13.9m 10m   97

Timeform Silver Tankard Maiden Stakes, Bath—Private Song (right) from Qasida

Sep 26] lengthy colt: useful performer: won maiden at Bath in May: worn down only close home when second of 20 to Samraan in King George V Handicap at Royal Ascot: acted as pacemaker and probably flattered when 16 lengths eighth of 13 to Zagreb in Irish Derby at the Curragh: well held both outings in handicaps afterwards: stays 1½m well: yet to race on extremes of going: strong-running type, suited by forcing tactics: sent to USA. *R. Charlton*

PRIX DE CLERMONT (IRE)   2 b.g. (Mar 31) Petorius 117 – Sandra's Choice –
57 (Sandy Creek 123) [1996 7f 6v a5g Nov 29] IR 7,000F, 7,500Y: sturdy gelding: brother to 1992 2-y-o 7f and 1m winner Excess Baggage: dam placed over long distances in Ireland: little sign of ability in maiden events. *G. Lewis*

PRIZEFIGHTER   5 b.g. Rambo Dancer (CAN) 107 – Jaisalmer 97 (Castle   70
Keep 121) [1995 70: 7m 8f 8.1m⁶ 8.5m⁶ 8.1m* 8m 8.9g a8g* 1996 a8g⁶ a8g* 7g 8f* 8.1m⁵ Aug 14] neat gelding: fair handicapper: won at Southwell in February and at Carlisle (apprentices) in August: stays 8.2f: acts on the all-weather, best turf efforts on a sound surface: seems best nowadays making running/racing prominently: fairly useful hurdler, winner in September and October. *J. L. Eyre*

PRIZE GIVING   3 ch.c. Most Welcome 131 – Glowing With Pride 114 (Ile de   112
Bourbon (USA) 133) [1995 82: 6g⁶ 7f² 7m³ 7f* 1996 10m* 10.3g* 10g² 12f⁵ 10g⁴ 10g⁴ Sep 14] robust colt: impresses in appearance: carries condition: has a quick action: smart performer: won handicap at Newmarket and listed race at Chester (by ¾ length from Desert Boy) and good 1½ lengths second to Don Micheletto in listed race at Goodwood: below best in pattern events last 3 starts, whinnying in paddock on 2 of them: stays 10.3f: yet to race on a soft surface: carries head high: sent to USA. *G. Wragg*

PRIZE PUPIL (IRE)   4 b.c. Royal Academy (USA) 130 – Bestow 76 (Shirley   74
Heights 130) [1995 76: 8m² 8.3m⁵ 10g* 10m³ 11.9g 10g 1996 10m³ 11.9m 10d⁴ 10f⁴ 8m 8.1d Aug 23] strong, lengthy colt: fluent mover: fair handicapper: best 4-y-o effort on reappearance: should stay 1½m: acts on firm ground: has run well when sweating: sent to USA. *C. F. Wall*

BNFL International Dee Stakes, Chester—
Prize Giving (right) takes this listed race from Desert Boy

PROGRESSION 5 b.h. Reprimand 122 – Mainmast 63 (Bustino 136) [1995 77: 82
9g³ 12m 10m 10.1g⁴ 12g³ a12g⁵ 12f* 11.9m* 12m² 14.6m⁶ 12d 1996 a10g⁶ a12g² a76
a12g⁴ a12g³ 12m* 12m⁵ 11.9m³ 12s May 23] rather leggy horse: had a round action:
fairly useful handicapper: came from off strong pace when winning at Newmarket in
April: best form at up to 13f: acted on firm ground and equitrack: blinkered (except
reappearance) since seventh 4-y-o start: held up: dead. *C. Murray*

PROJECTION (USA) 3 b.c. Topsider (USA) – Image of Reality (USA) (In 102
Reality) [1995 89p: 6m* 1996 8s⁵ 7m² 7m* 7g⁶ 7g³ Jun 12] good-topped, attractive
colt: has a short, unimpressive action: useful performer: 1¾ lengths second of 8 to
Cayman Kai in European Free Handicap at Newmarket: made all in minor event
there in May: best effort when around 3 lengths third of 4 to Idris in Ballycorus
Stakes at Leopardstown: sold only 10,000 gns Newmarket Autumn Sales: stays 7f:
acts on good to firm ground, well beaten on soft. *B. W. Hills*

PROMISE FULFILLED (USA) 5 b.m. Bet Twice (USA) – Kind Prospect –
(USA) (Mr Prospector (USA)) [1995 76d: a9.4g 8g 7.6m 8.5m⁴ 7g⁴ 8m 10g 7.1s
1996 a6g⁵ a7g⁵ Jan 24] sturdy mare: unimpressive mover: fairly useful handicapper
at best: showed little in claimers at Wolverhampton in January: probably stays 8.5f:
best efforts on a sound surface: tried blinkered/visored: covered by Timeless Times.
A. Bailey

PROMISSORY 3 b.f. Caerleon (USA) 132 – Tricky Note 97 (Song 132) [1995 –
NR 1996 7g 10m 10s 8.3m 10f Jul 19] 51,000F, 620,000 francs Y: well-made filly:
fourth foal: sister to a winner in Japan and half-sister to Irish 9f and 1¼m winner Ros
Castle (by Reference Point): dam sprinting sister to smart sprinter Jester: signs of
ability but little worthwhile form: highly tried (in listed races) second and third starts.
C. E. Brittain

PROMPT 3 b.f. Old Vic 136 – In Perpetuity 90 (Great Nephew 126) [1995 NR –
1996 a10g⁴ Apr 4] sixth foal: half-sister to 4 winners, best of them being smart
middle-distance performer Baron Ferdinand (by Ferdinand): dam, 1¼m and 10.8f
winner, half-sister to Shirley Heights: slowly away and went in snatches when 12¾
lengths fourth of 7 to Prince Kinsky in median auction maiden at Lingfield: sold
12,000 gns Newmarket December Sales. *R. Charlton*

PROMPTLY (IRE) 3 b.f. Lead On Time (USA) 123 – Ghariba 112 (Final Straw 88
127) [1995 80p: 6m² 1996 6g* 7.9f 6m⁶ 7m Jun 29] good-topped filly: fluent mover:
fairly useful performer: won maiden at Pontefract in April: easily best effort in
handicaps when sixth of 18 to Mallia in £34,200 contest at York: ran badly only
subsequent outing: best efforts at 6f, should be suited by further: has raced only on a
sound surface: sent to USA. *M. R. Stoute*

PROPELLANT 2 b.g. (May 8) Formidable (USA) 125 – Kirsheda 73 (Busted –
134) [1996 6m 7.1v 6m Oct 23] 5,400Y: smallish, sturdy gelding: third foal:
half-brother to 3-y-o Chipalata (by Derrylin): dam staying maiden on flat, winner
over hurdles: never dangerous in claimer and maidens, burly first 2 starts.
C. W. Thornton

PROPER BLUE (USA) 3 b.c. Proper Reality (USA) – Blinking (USA) (Tom 112 p
Rolfe) [1995 88p: 6m⁴ 6m³ 7m³ 7f² 7f* 1996 9m⁵ 10d* 10g* Nov 1] small, stocky
colt: progressive form: not seen out until September: showed good turn of foot to win
rated stakes at Ascot in October and listed race at Newmarket (squeezed through gap
and ran on strongly to beat Multicoloured a neck) in November: will probably stay
1½m: acts on firm and dead going: has worn crossed noseband: smart already, and
may well have further improvement in him. *T. G. Mills*

PROPOSING (IRE) 4 b.g. Rainbow Quest (USA) 134 – La Romance (USA) 93 +
(Lyphard (USA) 132) [1995 98p: a10g* a10g² 1996 14.4m* 13.3d May 18] good-
topped gelding: useful performer, very lightly raced: reportedly fractured a knee after
final 3-y-o start: won minor event at Kempton in May, dictating slow pace: tailed-off
last of 8 in listed race at Newbury 12 days later: should prove best at 1½m+.
J. H. M. Gosden

PROSPECTOR'S COVE 3 b.g. Dowsing (USA) 124 – Pearl Cove 63 (Town 96
And Country 124) [1995 77p: 7.1s* 1996 10g* 9m 10.3g Jun 30] angular,
workmanlike gelding: useful form when winning minor event at Kempton (beat
Prince of My Heart ½ length) in April: soundly beaten in listed race at Newmarket
and handicap at Doncaster afterwards: stays 1¼m: acts on soft ground. *J. Pearce*

PROSPERO 3 b.g. Petong 126 – Pennies To Pounds 80 (Ile de Bourbon (USA) 77 p
133) [1995 –p: 8m 1996 10m⁶ 10g⁵ 12g² 11.8g* Oct 29] strong, lengthy gelding:
improved steadily, and won minor event at Leicester in October by 5 lengths from
Full Throttle despite carrying head high: stays 1½m well: probably capable of further
improvement. *G. Harwood*

PROTARAS BAY 2 b.c. (May 14) Superpower 113 – Vivid Impression (Cure –
The Blues (USA)) [1996 5m 6g 6m Jul 10] rather leggy, angular colt: fifth foal:
brother to 3-y-o 5f winner Step On Degas and half-brother to Irish 1m winner
Puppet Theatre (by Theatrical) and Irish 11.9f winner White Claret (by Alzao):
dam Irish 6f (at 2 yrs) and 1¼m winner: poor form in varied maiden races.
T. T. Clement

PROTEKTOR (GER) 7 b.h. Acatenango (GER) 127 – Prioritat (GER) 120
(Frontal 122) [1995 116: 12s² 16v⁶ 11m⁵ 12m⁵ 12g⁶ 12g³ 12s⁴ 1996 12g² 11d*
12m³ 12m⁶ 12g² 12v* 12m⁴ Dec 8]

Old man Protektor was better than ever in 1996. Winning two minor
races in the spring of 1992 and finishing a close third in the German St Leger
that autumn preceded two wins in pattern company as a four-year-old, including when giving weight to Captain Horatius in a Group 3 contest at Dusseldorf.
The next two seasons were a little disappointing, similar to each other in that
not only did they fail to yield a single win, but that, on form, easily his best
efforts came when finishing third in the Europa Preis at Cologne in September.
In 1996 he disappointed only once.

The highlights were victories in the Group 2 Idee Hansa Preis at
Hamburg in June and a second success in the Group 3 Preis der Spielbanken
des Landes Nordrhein-Westfalen at Dusseldorf in October. At Hamburg he was
only the sixth choice of eight in the betting and, receiving 7 lb, upset the odds-
on Germany by a length and a half, the pair clear of Artan, Hollywood Dream
and Oxalagu. At Dusseldorf, however, he was favourite having meanwhile put
up two very good placed efforts from three starts in Group 1 company—under
two lengths behind Hollywood Dream and Posidonas at Dusseldorf, and three
and a half lengths behind Lavirco (but narrowly ahead of Hollywood Dream
and Luso) when placed again in the Europa Preis at Cologne. He justified his
favouritism in good style too, quickening past British front-running challenger
Mongol Warrior early in the straight and in no danger thereafter. A trip to Hong
Kong for the Vase was by no means optimistic, but he was set a great deal to do
and met trouble in running before finishing fourth to old rival Luso.

		Surumu	Literat
	Acatenango (GER)	(ch 1974)	Surama
	(ch 1982)	Aggravate	Aggressor
Protektor (GER)		(b 1966)	Raven Locks
(b.h. 1989)		Frontal	Le Haar
	Prioritat (GER)	(b 1964)	Favreale
	(b 1974)	Poesie	Chief
		(br 1966)	Prestige

Protektor is the best offspring out of his unraced dam Prioritat, though
several of the others have won races. Grandam Poesie won five races (and was
third in the Preis der Winterkonigin) and produced five winners, best of which
was Partitur, whose five wins featured a Group 3 event over a mile and a half,
and whose best foal was the useful colt Praktikant. The third dam Prestige was
another to win five races, while fourth dam Prompt Payment features in some
noteworthy international pedigrees. She is the grandam of the 1967 Oaks
winner Pia, who herself is the grandam of the top-class miler of 1984, Chief
Singer. Another of Prompt Payment's granddaughters is Polana, the third dam
of 1995 Irish Derby winner Winged Love.

Protektor is effective on good to firm and heavy ground, and while his
best form is at a mile and a half, he's also been placed twice in listed company
over a mile further. A very popular horse in his native country, he looks

assured of a place at stud one day. However, connections did not find anything suitable this time around, and on the very eve of the new year, German paper *Sport-Welt* announced that Protektor's racing days are by no means over.
A. Lowe, Germany

PROTOCOL (IRE)   2 ch.c. (Apr 23) Taufan (USA) 119 – Ukraine's Affair   72
(USA) (The Minstrel (CAN) 135) [1996 8f 8g⁴ a8g² Nov 14] IR 14,000F, 14,500Y: third foal: half-brother to German 3-y-o 7f winner Umbertino (by Common Grounds) and Irish 1994 2-y-o 5f winner Aliuska (by Fijar Tango): dam unraced: in frame in maidens at Leicester and Lingfield (staying on, beaten a neck) in the autumn: retained by trainer 2,800 gns Newmarket Autumn Sales in between.
J. W. Hills

PROTON   6 b.g. Sure Blade (USA) 130 – Banket 120 (Glint of Gold 128) [1995   73 d
85: 10m 12m⁵ 12m³ 12m 12f² 12m² 12m* 13.3d 12m 1996 16g 12m 10d 12m⁵ 12g 12m 12g Oct 26] strong, quite attractive gelding: fairly useful handicapper at 5 yrs: long way below form most starts in 1996: should stay beyond 1½m: acts on any going: visored (well beaten) once at 3 yrs: races prominently: winning hurdler.
R. Akehurst

PRO TRADER (USA)   3 b. or br.c. Lyphard (USA) 132 – Fuerza (USA)   120
(Distinctive Pro (USA)) [1995 6g* 1996 7s³ 7d⁴ 8s² 7g² 8d³ 9.6m* 12.3m² 8.5g* 10f⁵ 8f³ 9g⁵ Oct 19] first foal: dam Grade 3 6f winner in USA: won maiden at Punchestown at 2 yrs: progressed into a smart performer: won handicap at Gowran Park in June and put up easily best effort to win valuable 17-runner handicap at Galway by 7 lengths from Meglio Che Posso in July: below form in 3 races in USA, including Grade 1 Secretariat Stakes at Arlington (trained until after then by D. Weld) and Grade 3 Hawthorne Derby on final outing: smart form at 12.3f but best run at 8.5f: acts on good to firm and soft ground: blinkered since third 3-y-o start.
B. Kessinger, jnr, USA

PROUD BRIGADIER (IRE)   8 b.g. Auction Ring (USA) 123 – Naughty One   55 d
Gerard (Brigadier Gerard 144) [1995 –: 8g 1996 8.3g⁵ 8.3d⁴ 8m 8d 8m Oct 28] lengthy, sparely-made gelding: fair handicapper at 6 yrs: lightly raced and modest at best since: formerly effective at 7f to 9.4f, and probably on any going. *P. Burgoyne*

PROUD IMAGE   4 b.g. Zalazl (USA) 120 – Fleur de Foret (USA) 61§ (Green   66
Forest (USA) 134) [1995 70: 8g 8f² 10m 8m⁵ 8g 8f⁴ 7.1m⁴ 8.5g⁵ 8m* 7.6d* 7m³ 7m   a58
1996 7d² 8d 6.9d* 6.9m⁴ 7s⁶ 9.7m⁵ 7g a8.5g⁴ 10.8f² a12g⁵ a12g³ a12g Nov 25] small gelding: modest performer: won claimer at Carlisle in April on penultimate start for A. Jarvis: below form all 4 starts for K. Burke: placed in claimers, including a handicap, for present stable: stays 10.8f: acts on firm and dead ground: usually visored, not for present stable: often used to be front runner. *G. M. McCourt*

PROUD LOOK   3 b.c. Dayjur (USA) 137 – Very Charming (USA) (Vaguely   70
Noble 140) [1995 NR 1996 6s² 6.9m³ 7m 7g Sep 21] sturdy, attractive colt: half-brother to several winners, most at middle distances, including smart 1¼m winner Theatrical Charmer and useful Irish middle-distance stayer Mohaajir (both by Sadler's Wells): dam, French 10.5f winner, sister to Dahlia: fair form first 2 starts: disappointing afterwards: should stay further than 7f: sent to UAE. *B. W. Hills*

PROUD MONK   3 gr.g. Aragon 118 – Silent Sister 78 (Kind of Hush 118) [1995   78
77: 6m⁴ 6.1m⁶ 5.7h³ 6f⁵ 5g⁶ 7d³ 7g³ 7.3d* 7m³ a7g 1996 7d² 8d² 7.6g 8.5m⁴ 8f 9d³ 8m 7.1m⁵ 7s⁴ 8s Nov 9] strong, lengthy gelding: fair handicapper: stays 9f: acts on good to firm and soft ground: showed little only run on fibresand: visored last 2 starts. *G. L. Moore*

PROUD NATIVE (IRE)   2 b.c. (Apr 11) Imp Society (USA) – Karamana   106
(Habitat 134) [1996 5g* 6m* 6m* 6m⁴ 6m 6m² 6m* 6.5d⁵ Nov 9] IR 6,000Y: sturdy, quite attractive colt: did well physically: poor walker and mover: fourth foal: half-brother to German 3-y-o 8.5f winner Sun Moon Stars (by Shahrastani) and useful Irish middle-distance performer Karikata (by Doyoun): dam unraced: won maiden at Ripon, minor event at York and listed race at Epsom early in season: 2½ lengths second to Indian Rocket in Mill Reef Stakes at Newbury: won 25-runner Two-Year-Old Trophy (quickened clear 1f out, held Nigrasine by a head) at Redcar in October: creditable 4¼ lengths fifth of 8 to Deadly Dudley in Group 2 at Evry:

Redcar Two-Year-Old Trophy—a £57,418 first prize for IR 6,000-guinea purchase Proud Native; he holds on well from Nigrasine

probably stays 6.5f: acts on good to firm ground, probably on dead: edgy before running poorly fifth start. *A. P. Jarvis*

PROVE THE POINT (IRE)   3 b.f. Maelstrom Lake 118 – In Review (Ela-Mana-Mou 132) [1995 7m 7s 1996 7g 8.5m Sep 11] second foal: dam 9f winner out of Lancashire Oaks winner Istiea: modest form in 2-y-o maidens for D. Weld before sold IR 6,000 gns Goffs October Sales: well beaten here. *Mrs P. N. Dutfield* —

PROVINCE   3 b.g. Dominion 123 – Shih Ching (USA) (Secreto (USA) 128) [1995 NR 1996 8d* 10.1m³ Sep 24] 16,500F, IR 23,000Y: rangy gelding: has scope: third foal: half-brother to German 7.5f and 9f winner Story Of Love (by Taufan) and winning hurdler Katie Oliver (by Squill): dam unraced half-sister to dual Grade 1 winner Dontstop Themusic: 25/1 from 6/1, won maiden at Newmarket in August by ½ length from Van Gurp, staying on strongly to lead well inside final 1f: faced extremely stiff task when well beaten in 4-runner minor event at Epsom month later: sold to join C. Mann 24,000 gns Newmarket Autumn Sales: should eventually be suited by further than 1m. *G. Lewis*   82

PRUDENT PET   4 b.f. Distant Relative 128 – Philgwyn 66 (Milford 119) [1995 65: 7.5m a7g⁵ 8.3f 9f² 8m* a8g* 10g 10.5d 8.2m a9.4g 1996 7.5m 8g 7m⁴ 9m 8m⁵ 8g⁶ 10.2m⁵ 8m² a8g 8m a8g 7g 8f 8.1s a8g Dec 3] leggy, useful-looking filly: good walker: just a modest handicapper in 1996: probably best at up to 1m: acts on soft ground, firm and fibresand: tried blinkered/visored, no improvement: inconsistent and not to be trusted. *C. W. Fairhurst*   53 d

PRUDENT PRINCESS   4 b.f. Puissance 110 – Princess Story 64 (Prince de Galles 125) [1995 63: 7m⁴ 6m⁵ 6f³ a7g⁴ 7g³ a8.5g⁶ 1996 a7g a8g⁴ 8g a8g a7g 6s a6g⁵ 6m a6g Nov 29] angular filly: modest maiden handicapper: below form last 7 starts: best at up to 1m: acts on fibresand and on good to firm ground, probably on soft: no improvement in blinkers/visor. *A. Hide*   57 d

PRUSSIA   5 b.g. Roi Danzig (USA) – Vagrant Maid (USA) 85 (Honest Pleasure (USA)) [1995 –: 10d 14s 14.1m 1996 14.1m⁴ 12m May 7] heavy-bodied gelding: poor handicapper: will stay beyond 1¾m: acts on good to firm ground: won novice hurdle in July: gelded. *W. Clay*   48

PRUSSIAN BLUE (USA)   4 b.c. Polish Navy (USA) – Lit'l Rose (USA) (Mr Prospector (USA)) [1995 91: 10m³ 12m* 12m 1996 12.3g² 14s* 14.6g² 13.9m 13.4d 14.6d* 12v* Dec 1] leggy colt: useful performer: gamely won rated stakes at Goodwood in May and (after jockey thought he swallowed his tongue fifth start) minor event at Doncaster (just got up to pip Poltarf) in November (trained by H. Cecil): won listed race at Toulouse by head from Rainbow Dancer (gave 11 lb) final   108 outing: will probably stay 2m: acts on good to firm and heavy ground: usually races prominently. *C. Laffon-Parias, France*

PSICOSSIS 3 b.c. Slip Anchor 136 – Precious Jade 72 (Northfields (USA)) [1995 NR 1996 12g⁶ Jun 12] well-made colt: brother to smart 4-y-o Italian middle-distance performer Slicious and half-brother to several winners, including smart miler Just A Flutter (by Beldale Flutter): dam stayed 1m: in need of race and 25/1, 14¼ lengths sixth of 11 to Sharaf Kabeer in maiden at Kempton, making ground from mid-division until tiring last 2f: stays in training. *H. R. A. Cecil* — 64 p

PSP LADY 3 b.f. Ballacashtal (CAN) – Sunshine Gal 68 (Alto Volante 109) [1995 NR 1996 10m 14m⁵ 12.1g Aug 26] fourth foal: dam 1¼m to 2m winner, also successful over hurdles: looks of little account. *A. P. Jones* — –

PUBLIC WAY (IRE) 6 b.g. Common Grounds 118 – Kilpeacon (Florescence 120) [1995 NR 1996 9.2s 11.1g 12g⁴ a7g 9.9m⁴ 10g 8d 8s⁵ Aug 27] small, leggy gelding: unimpressive mover: poor handicapper: stays 1½m: acts on good to firm and heavy going. *N. Chamberlain* — 43

PUCE 3 b.f. Darshaan 133 – Souk (IRE) 98 (Ahonoora 122) [1995 NR 1996 8g 9m² 10g* 12m³ 11.9g* Oct 9] small, sparely-made filly: first foal: dam, 7f winner better at 1m, out of half-sister to Dumka, dam of Doyoun and Dafayna: progressive form: ridden by 7-lb claimer, won maiden at Pontefract in July: struck into on handicap debut next start, but found expected improvement at the trip when winning minor event at York in October by 2 lengths from Step Aloft: better at 1½m than 1¼m, and will stay further: yet to race on a soft surface: stays in training and can improve again. *L. M. Cumani* — 88 p

PULGA CIRCO 3 b.f. Tina's Pet 121 – Pulga (Blakeney 126) [1995 40, a50: a6g a6g³ a7g⁵ a7g² 8m a7g⁴ 10g a8.5g a8.5g 1996 8g a8g 8.2m a12g Jul 6] good-bodied filly: poor maiden: no form in 1996. *B. A. McMahon* — –

PUMPKIN PIE (IRE) 4 b.f. Jareer (USA) 115 – Sauntry (Ballad Rock 122) [1995 NR 1996 a11g Jan 19] of no account. *A. Harrison* — –

PUN 2 b.f. (Mar 29) Batshoof 122 – Keen Wit (Kenmare (FR) 125) [1996 6m² 6m* 7.5f⁴ 8m 8f⁶ a8s⁶ Dec 28] close-coupled, useful-looking filly: has a quick action: second foal: dam poor maiden (appeared to stay 1½m) out of useful 2-y-o 6f and 7.3f winner Nettle: trained by D. Morley first 4 starts, winning maiden at York in July: seemed to show much improved form (worth rating of 73 here) when beaten 4 lengths in Grade 3 event at Hollywood Park in November on first of 2 starts in USA: needs further than 6f and probably stays 1m: acts on firm ground, tailed off only start on dirt. *Kathy Walsh, USA* — 92 ?

PUNCH 4 b.g. Reprimand 122 – Cartooness (USA) 60 (Achieved 125) [1995 57: 10m⁵ 11.1f³ 14.1f³ 12.3m⁴ 14.1h* 14.1m⁴ 15g 12.1g 1996 17.1g 14.1m 12m 11.1f⁶ 13.8m³ 16.2g⁵ Aug 24] tall, strong gelding: just a poor performer in 1996: stays 1¾m: acts on hard ground: blinkered (except reappearance) since fifth 3-y-o start: tends to find little and is not one to trust implicitly. *N. Tinkler* — 38

PUNISHMENT 5 b.h. Midyan (USA) 124 – In The Shade 89 (Bustino 136) [1995 10s 10d² 10g* 12g* 10g⁵ 1996 10g⁴ 12.5g² 12m² 12f 12g⁶ 10.4m⁶ 8.9g 9.8d 12d 12s a9.4g⁴ Dec 7] workmanlike ex-French horse: smart performer: won 3 handicaps and a listed race at 3 and 4 yrs for J. Hammond: in frame in Gordon Richards Stakes at Sandown, Prix Jean de Chaudenay at Deauville (½-length second to Sacrament) and Coronation Cup at Epsom first 3 starts in 1996: generally well below form afterwards until respectable fourth (to Prince of Andros) in listed race at Wolverhampton final start: stays 12.5f: acts on good to firm ground and soft, and on fibresand. *C. E. Brittain* — 113

PUNKAH (USA) 3 b.g. Lear Fan (USA) 130 – Gentle Persuasion 95 (Bustino 136) [1995 70: 7d⁵ 6d 1996 a10g* 12d⁴ 10m⁵ 10m* Jun 17] well-made gelding: carries condition: fair performer: won maiden at Lingfield in February and handicap at Windsor in June: sold 38,000 gns Newmarket July Sales, resold 19,000 gns Newmarket Autumn Sales: stays 1¼m. *Lord Huntingdon* — 78

PUPIL MASTER (IRE) 2 b.g. (Apr 14) Masterclass (USA) 116 – Lamya 73 (Hittite Glory 125) [1996 5m 7m a8g⁶ Nov 4] IR 7,000Y, 10,000 2-y-o: half-brother to 3-y-o South Pagoda (by Distinctly North), winning sprinter Murray's Mazda (by — –

M Double M) and a winner in Belgium: dam won 3 races in Sweden: never dangerous in large fields for seller, claimer and median auction maiden. *Denys Smith*

PURCHASING POWER (IRE)   2 b.c. (Apr 3) Danehill (USA) 126 – Pur-   –
chasepaperchase 104 (Young Generation 129) [1996 7g 6s a8g⁶ Nov 14] 48,000F,
190,000Y: half-brother to several winners, notably 1996 Irish 1000 Guineas winner
Matiya (by Alzao): dam 1m/1¼m performer: no worthwhile form in minor event and
maidens. *N. A. Callaghan*

PURIST   2 b.c. (Apr 27) Polish Precedent (USA) 131 – Mill Line 71 (Mill Reef   71 p
(USA) 141) [1996 7d Nov 8] medium-sized colt: third living foal: brother to 7f (at 2
yrs) to 1½m winner (including Irish and Yorkshire Oaks) Pure Grain and half-brother
to 3-y-o 1½m winner Serious Trust (by Alzao): dam 14.6f winner out of Park Hill
winner Quay Line: around 10 lengths ninth of 20 to Handsome Ridge in maiden at
Doncaster:unlikely-looking sort, likely to do better over middle distances. *M. R. Stoute*

PURPLE FLING   5 ch.g. Music Boy 124 – Divine Fling (Imperial Fling (USA)   76
116) [1995 76: a5g⁵ 6g⁵ 5g² 5m² a6g* 5.7f² 5g 6f* 6.9f* a6g 7g 1996 6d² 6g⁶ 6.1m³
6m⁴ 5g⁵ 5f⁵ 6v 6d* a6g⁴ Nov 26] strong gelding: fair performer: justified favouritism
in minor event at Folkestone in October: stays 7f: acts on firm and soft ground and on
all-weather surfaces: consistent. *L. G. Cottrell*

PURPLE MEMORIES   3 b.g. Don't Forget Me 127 – Tyrian Belle 77 (En-   –
chantment 115) [1995 65: 5g* 6f³ 1996 5g⁶ 7m⁶ 6d 8f Oct 14] strong, angular
gelding: fair form as 2-y-o: none in 1996. *M. Johnston*

PURPLE SPLASH   6 b.g. Ahonoora 122 – Quay Line 117 (High Line 125) [1995   95
85: 14.9d³ 14g* 16g 16g³ 13.3d⁶ 16d³ 1996 14.9d* 14d* 14s³ 16g 14.6d⁴ Nov 8]
smallish, good-topped gelding: has a scratchy action: fairly useful handicapper: won
at Warwick and Haydock (steadily-run race, easily) in the spring: stays 2m: has run
respectably on good to firm ground, but goes particularly well on an easy surface
(acts on heavy): visored/blinkered since final 4-y-o outing. *P. J. Makin*

PURSUANCE (IRE)   4 b.c. Glenstal (USA) 118 – Pocket (Tumble Wind (USA))   –
[1995 –, a66: a5g³ a6g⁴ a6g⁵ a5g* a5g⁴ 5f 5.1d a6g* a6g³ a5g 7m 1996 a5g⁵ a6g⁶ Jan   a62
12] sturdy, good-bodied colt: modest sprint handicapper: acted on good to firm and
soft ground, best form on fibresand: usually visored/blinkered: dead. *J. Balding*

PUSEY STREET BOY   9 ch.g. Vaigly Great 127 – Pusey Street 96 (Native   –
Bazaar 122) [1995 57d, a–: 7g⁴ 7f⁵ 8g 7.1m 8m² 7m 7g⁵ 8d 7g 8f⁵ 1996 8g 8m 7.1m
7g Oct 30] lengthy, plain-backed gelding: tubed: modest 7f/1m handicapper: well
beaten in 1996: acts on any going: tried visored. *J. R. Bosley*

PUSEY STREET GIRL   3 ch.f. Gildoran 123 – Pusey Street 96 (Native Bazaar   87
122) [1995 NR 1996 7m 8f 7g* 6m 7g³ Jun 20] fourth live foal: half-sister to fairly
useful 1m and 1¼m winner Windrush Lady (by Risk Me) and 7f/1m winner Pusey
Street Boy (by Vaigly Great): dam sprinter: 50/1, won maiden at Warwick in May by
short head, nosing ahead near line: unlucky third of 9 in handicap at Ripon 4 weeks
later: not seen out afterwards: effective at 6f but should stay beyond 7f. *J. R. Bosley*

PUSH A VENTURE   2 b.f. (Mar 9) Shirley Heights 130 – Push A Button (Bold   58
Lad (IRE) 133) [1996 6m 8.1m 7d⁴ Oct 28] angular filly: half-sister to 3 winners,
including Irish 1¼m winner Outside Pressure (by Shernazar): dam, Irish 2-y-o 6f
winner, half-sister to Riverman: first form in maidens when 9¾ lengths fourth of 10
to Apache Star at Lingfield: will stay beyond 7f. *S. P. C. Woods*

PUSHKA FAIR   5 b.g. Salse (USA) 128 – Orient 106 (Bay Express 132) [1995 –:   –
a7g 1996 a7g a8g 6f Aug 3] no sign of ability. *T. R. Watson*

PUTRA (USA)   2 ch.c. (Apr 10) Dixie Brass (USA) – Olatha (USA) (Miswaki   113 p
(USA) 124) [1996 7.1m* 7m* Jul 31]
     A bout of coughing in early-October ruled Putra out of the Dewhurst
Stakes, a race for which he had been trained since winning the Lanson
Champagne Vintage Stakes at Goodwood in July. But even after just two starts,
both of which he won, Putra had shown smart form, and a repetition or two slightly
better would probably have seen him go close in a below-average Dewhurst.
     Putra made his debut at Sandown in June in the first seven-furlong
maiden of the year for two-year-olds and was sent off a weak second favourite
in a field of nine. After travelling comfortably behind a very strong pace, Putra

Lanson Champagne Vintage Stakes, Goodwood—
Putra (light colours) and Sahm move ahead from Grapeshot (dark cap) and Equal Rights

looked green when asked for his effort but quickened clear in fine style in the final furlong and ran on very strongly to the finish, with another newcomer, the future Royal Lodge winner Benny The Dip, chasing him three and a half lengths behind.

Putra's inexperience (all his seven rivals had had at least two starts) showed in the preliminaries to the Lanson Champagne Stakes at Goodwood seven weeks later, but he was made second favourite to the well-regarded Sahm, the winner of both his starts at York. Next in the betting came Imperial President, winner of his last two outings, another unbeaten colt in Fun Galore, the maiden winners Grapeshot and Equal Rights, the July Stakes third Air Express and Putra's blinkered stable-companion Belgravia. Once again Putra was settled behind the pace, which was considerably steadier than at Sandown. The field was still tightly grouped with under two furlongs to go and, momentarily, Putra looked unlikely to get a run; but a gap opened and he quickened to lead inside the last from Sahm who had met trouble in running himself. Sahm finished half a length back but was placed last for bumping Air Express, Grapeshot and Equal Rights promoted to second and third. The form of the race worked out well. The placed horses went on to win the Somerville Tattersall Stakes at Newmarket and the Futurity Stakes at the Curragh respectively, while Air Express finished a close third in the Dewhurst.

A good proportion of the Cole stable's success with two-year-olds has been achieved with American-bred animals whose sires were not exactly household names in Europe. Putra's sire Dixie Brass, a son of Gold Cup winner Drum Taps's sire Dixieland Band, gained his most valuable win in the Grade 1 Metropolitan Handicap over a mile at Belmont Park. He was also successful three times over six furlongs as a two-year-old. More familiar will be Dixie

Brass's half-brother Colway Rock who won the 1993 Thirsk Classic Trial for Bill Watts. Putra was a 190,000-dollar purchase at the Keeneland September Yearling Sale from Dixie Brass's first crop which averaged around 50,000 dollars. He is the best of his dam's first five foals, all of whom are winners. Three—Tell'em Some Lies (by Runaway Groom), Mitigate (by Lost Code) and Spirit of Racing (by Garthorn)—have won in minor company in the States, the last-named also coming second in a minor stakes event over an extended mile. The fourth winner is Amber Valley (by Bering) who won a six-furlong maiden for Jack Hanson as a two-year-old in 1993 and was also successful over hurdles early in 1996. Olatha's yearling, a colt by Marquetry, made 250,000 dollars at Keeneland. Olatha won a couple of sprints in the USA but hails from a French middle-distance family. Her dam Pagaie, who won twice in modest company as a four-year-old, is a sister to the Prix de Diane and Grand Prix de Saint-Cloud winner Dunette, dam of the Rothmans International winner French Glory. Putra's great grandam was a nine-furlong winner at Longchamp, and also produced the smart French middle-distance fillies Paddle and Norland.

		Dixieland Band	Northern Dancer
	Dixie Brass (USA)	(b 1980)	Mississippi Mud
	(b 1989)	Petite Diable	Sham
Putra (USA)		(b 1981)	Taste of Life
(ch.c. Apr 10, 1994)		Miswaki	Mr Prospector
	Olatha (USA)	(ch 1978)	Hopespringseternal
	(b 1985)	Pagaie	Hard To Beat
		(b 1977)	Pram

Putra, a tall, leggy, long-striding colt, gave the impression that he was still immature at Sandown and Goodwood; that being so, it is to his credit that he has done so well as he has. He was going on strongly at the finish in both his races, suggesting that he will eventually stay beyond a mile. Provided all is well with him, Putra should win more good races. *P. F. I. Cole*

PUZZLEMENT 2 gr.c. (Apr 19) Mystiko (USA) 124 – Abuzz 101 (Absalom 60 128) [1996 5m⁶ 6s⁵ 7m 8m 8m⁵ 6m 6.1s Oct 31] big, good-bodied colt: has scope: fourth foal: half-brother to 3-y-o World Premier (by Shareef Dancer), useful 5f and 6f winner at 2 yrs: dam won at 5f (at 2 yrs) and 7.3f and is half-sister to dam of Revoque: modest maiden: finds 6f too sharp, stays 1m: acts on good to firm ground, shaped well first start on soft: sweating (below form, poorly drawn) final start. *C. E. Brittain*

PYTCHLEY DAWN 6 b.m. Welsh Captain 113 – Cawston's Arms (Cawston's – Clown 113) [1995 NR 1996 7.1m 7.1m a6g Aug 9] poor maiden (stayed 7f) in 1993: well held in 1996. *O. O'Neill*

Q

QASIDA (IRE) 3 b.c. Lycius (USA) 124 – Arab Heritage (Great Nephew 126) 88 [1995 NR 1996 12m 10m⁵ 10.2g² 16.2m 11.5g* 10.4m 11.9g Sep 5] rather leggy, quite attractive colt: fifth foal: dam twice-raced daughter of 1000 Guineas second Our Home, sister to Roussalka and half-sister to Oh So Sharp: fairly useful form: narrowly won maiden at Yarmouth in July, making all: ran badly on final outing: stays 1½m: flashed tail third start: sent to UAE. *C. E. Brittain*

Q FACTOR 4 br.f. Tragic Role (USA) – Dominiana (Dominion 123) [1995 73: 84 6.1m³ 7m 6m⁴ 6f⁴ 7f 6g 6.1s⁶ 7m a8.5g a7g 1996 a6g a8g⁴ a8g⁵ a8g³ a8g⁴ 8d³ 8.1d a69 8.2m* 8.1m⁵ 8.3m* 8.3d 8.3d* 7.1s* 6.1s⁶ Oct 22] leggy filly: has a quick action: fairly useful handicapper: narrow winner at Nottingham in June, Windsor in July and August and at Haydock (best effort, short-headed Princess Efisio) in October: may have been unsuited by shorter trip final start: stays 8.3f: acts on fibresand and any turf ground: visored (ran well) fifth 2-y-o start: often bandaged behind. *D. Haydn Jones*

QUADRANT 7 b.g. Shirley Heights 130 – Sextant 98 (Star Appeal 133) [1995 –: 44 a13g a12g⁶ a16g 1996 a12g a13g a13g⁵ Feb 10] good-bodied gelding: poor form at best nowadays: stays 2m: best on equitrack: blinkered (ran well) final 3-y-o start. *A. Moore*

QUAKERS FIELD 3 br.c. Anshan 119 – Nosey 96 (Nebbiolo 125) [1995 96: 5g 111 6m* 7d² 7g* 7.3d⁶ 1996 8d⁵ 9m 10.3m⁵ 12m⁵ 11.9g² 12m 12s Oct 26] tall, rather leggy, useful-looking colt: has a round action: smart performer: best efforts when fifth of 12 to St Mawes in Gordon Stakes at Goodwood and second of 11 to Arabian Story in rated stakes at York: in rear in pattern events at Ascot and Newbury afterwards: stays 1½m: acts on good to firm and dead ground. *G. L. Moore*

QUALITAIR BEAUTY 3 b.f. Damister (USA) 123 – Mac's Princess (USA) 67 – (Sovereign Dancer (USA)) [1995 NR 1996 8g Jun 14] first foal: dam, maiden, seemed suited by 1m: very slowly away and always behind in median auction maiden at Southwell: sold 1,000 gns Newmarket December Sales. *W. A. O'Gorman*

QUALITY (IRE) 3 b.c. Rock City 120 – Queens Welcome 60 (Northfields 80 (USA)) [1995 82, a87: 6m⁴ a7g⁴ 6.1d² 6g⁶ 6.9s⁵ 8f* 8f 7m* 7m a8g* a8g² a8g⁴ 1996 a95 a10g² a10g* 10.3d 10.5g³ 8d³ 10.2f⁴ 8f⁵ 8g⁵ 8m³ 7m* 7f⁴ 8m 7m³ Sep 26] quite attractive colt: useful performer on all-weather, successful in minor event at Lingfield in March: fairly useful handicapper on turf: won at Yarmouth in August: sold (W. O'Gorman to P. Hobbs) 25,000 gns Newmarket Autumn Sales: effective at 7f, stays 1¼m: acts on firm and good to soft ground and goes well on all-weather surfaces: effective blinkered/visored or not: takes good hold. *W. A. O'Gorman*

QUANGO 4 b.g. Charmer 123 – Quaranta 83 (Hotfoot 126) [1995 95: a8g* 8m⁴ – 7m² 10.4m* 10.4m 1996 10m 11.9m 10.5d Sep 28] tall, lengthy gelding: useful performer at his best: well beaten in handicaps in 1996, blinkered on final start: stays 10.4f well: acts on good to firm ground and on fibresand. *J. G. FitzGerald*

QUARTERSTAFF 2 b.c. (Apr 16) Charmer 123 – Quaranta 83 (Hotfoot 126) – p [1996 8s Nov 9] 9,500Y: brother to 3-y-o 7f winner Quinze and useful 1m and 10.4f winner Quango and half-brother to several winners, including Cambridgeshire winner Quinlan Terry (by Welsh Pageant), also successful at 1½m: dam 2-y-o 5f winner: backward, stumbled after 2f but no real promise in 16-runner median auction maiden at Doncaster: looks sort to do better. *C. F. Wall*

QUEEN BEE 3 ch.f. Royal Academy (USA) 130 – Honey Bridge 99 (Crepello 71 136) [1995 NR 1996 10d⁴ 10m 12m 11.9f² 11.5m⁶ Aug 22] closely related to 3 winners, notably St Leger winner Minster Son, and half-sister to a winner in Italy: dam 6f winner at 2 yrs: fair maiden at best: failed to confirm debut promise: looked likely to prove best at short of 11.5f: has been retired. *J. L. Dunlop*

QUEENFISHER 4 b. or br.f. Scottish Reel 123 – Mavahra 93 (Mummy's Pet – 125) [1995 91: 8m 7f⁴ 8f⁴ 7.3g⁵ 7f 7.1m* 7g 1996 6m 7.6f⁶ 7m 8g a6g Nov 26] leggy, useful-looking filly: fairly useful at best in 1995 for R. Hannon: disappointing at 4 yrs: takes keen hold, and likely to prove best at up to around 7f: acts on firm and dead ground: blinkered (ran poorly) fifth 3-y-o start. *G. L. Moore*

QUEEN OF ALL BIRDS (IRE) 5 b.m. Bluebird (USA) 125 – Blue Bouquet 75 (Cure The Blues (USA)) [1995 NR 1996 a8g⁵ a8g* a8g² a8g² 8s⁶ 7.6m³ 8m⁵ 8.2m⁶ a86 9m 7.1s a8g* Dec 5] workmanlike ex-Irish mare: second foal: half-sister to winning 2-y-o Thorntoun Jewel (by Durgam): dam Irish maiden: won maiden at the Curragh and minor event at Galway at 3 yrs for M. Halford: fairly useful all-weather handicapper in 1996: won at Lingfield in January and December: none too consistent on turf: best form at 1m but had looked likely to be suited by further: acts on heavy and good to firm going, best form here on the all-weather: visored (below form) penultimate 5-y-o start. *R. Boss*

QUEEN OF SHANNON (IRE) 8 b.m. Nordico (USA) – Raj Kumari (Vitiges 53 (FR) 132) [1995 –: a10g a11g 1996 8.1g² 8.1m 10.8m a8.5g 8.3m* 8f³ 8m 7f 8m⁶ Oct 28] quite good-topped, angular mare: has reportedly had 3 wind operations: modest handicapper nowadays: won apprentice seller at Windsor in August: failed to repeat the form: seems suited by around 1m: acts on any going: tried blinkered earlier in career: visored 7 times, including last 5 starts. *A. W. Carroll*

QUEEN SCEPTRE (IRE) 2 b.f. (Mar 21) Fairy King (USA) – Happy Smile 97 (IRE) 95 (Royal Match 117) [1996 5m* 6g² 6m³ 5.2m³ 7d⁴ 6m* 6m⁶ Oct 1] IR 36,000Y: good-topped, attractive filly: has a quick action: first foal: dam effective from 9f to 1½m in Ireland, half-sister to smart Irish middle-distance colt Topanoora:

useful performer: won minor event at Windsor in June and listed race at Ayr (beat Head Over Heels 2 lengths) in September: respectable sixth of 8 to Pas de Reponse in steadily-run Cheveley Park Stakes at Newmarket: best form at 6f: acts on good to firm ground, probably on dead: tends to get on toes: sweated profusely and took keen hold third outing: sold 135,000 gns Newmarket December Sales. *B. W. Hills*

QUEENS CHECK 3 b.f. Komaite (USA) – Ski Baby (Petoski 135) [1995 60?: 5d 6g⁵ 5f⁶ 5s* 1996 5s⁶ a5g* 5m a5g* 5g a6g a5g³ a6g² a6g Dec 14] first foal: dam never ran: fair sprint handicapper on the all-weather, modest at best on turf: successful at Southwell in May and July: acts on soft ground (well beaten on top-of-the-ground), goes well on fibresand: successful with or without blinkers. *Miss J. F. Craze* – a69

QUEENS CONSUL (IRE) 6 gr.m. Kalaglow 132 – Queens Connection (Bay Express 132) [1995 84, a63: a8g⁵ a8g⁶ a8g⁵ 8g 9.9m⁶ 8g² 8m² a8g 8m² 7m 10m 8.5m 8m* 8m³ 8.5m² 8f 1996 8s⁵ 7.5m⁵ 8m² 8.5m⁵ 7g* 8.1d³ 8.9m⁶ 8g 8.5m 7.9g² 7.6m 8.1m 8d* 7d 8m 8m 10.4g 8g 8s Nov 9] tall, leggy mare: fairly useful handicapper on turf, modest (lightly raced nowadays) on the all-weather: won at Catterick and Thirsk (minor event) in the summer: well held in big fields last 3 starts: best at up to 8.5f: acts on firm and soft ground and on fibresand: usually races prominently: game. *B. S. Rothwell* 87 a–

QUEENS FANCY 3 ch.f. Infantry 122 – Sagareina (Sagaro 133) [1995 –: a7g 1996 10m 10m 10g 9.7g a10g a13g Dec 31] of no account. *S. Dow* –

QUEEN'S INSIGNIA (USA) 3 b.f. Gold Crest (USA) 120 – Years (USA) (Secretariat (USA)) [1995 68: 5m⁵ 6m⁴ 6m* 8d* 8f 1996 7.3d 8.2s a8g⁵ a10s Nov 19] tall, leggy filly: fair performer at 2 yrs: well held in 1996: stays 1m: may be unsuited by very firm ground. *P. F. I. Cole* –

QUEEN'S PAGEANT 2 ch.f. (Apr 1) Risk Me (FR) 127 – Mistral's Dancer (Shareef Dancer (USA) 135) [1996 5g³ 6g⁵ 5s* 6m Oct 17] workmanlike filly: third foal: sister to 4-y-o 1¼m to 1½m winner Kristal Breeze : dam, maiden, best at 7f: didn't run near previous form when winning 12-runner maiden at Haydock in October, hanging left near finish: never a threat on stand side (principals came far side) in Redcar Two-Year-Old Trophy: stays 6f. *J. L. Spearing* 78

QUEENS STROLLER (IRE) 5 b.m. Pennine Walk 120 – Mount Isa (Miami Springs 121) [1995 59, a70: a9.4g* 9.7d* 10d 10g⁶ 9.2g 8g 8.1g⁴ 10f² 10.2m 10.1g 12d 12m a9.4g⁴ 1996 a10g a11g a12g 10m a8.5g a12g a9.4g⁴ a10g⁶ Dec 11] leggy, lightly-made mare: fair performer for C. C. Elsey in 1995: poor at best in 1996 (left T. Wall after sixth start): stays 1¼m: acts on any turf going and on fibresand: blinkered (tailed off) once at 5 yrs. *R. E. Peacock* –

QUERTIER (IRE) 2 ch.c. (Mar 14) Bluebird (USA) 125 – Ganna (ITY) (Molvedo 137) [1996 7m⁴ 7f 7f Sep 4] IR 4,200F, IR 16,000Y: good-topped colt: has scope: seventh foal: brother to 1½m winner Blue Grotto and half-brother to Irish 7f winner Slash And Burn (by Thatching) and Italian 3-y-o 1¼m winner Raffa Thermidor (by Classic Music): dam unraced sister to Italian St Leger winner Gallio and John Porter winner Salado: well beaten in maidens and a seller: sold 5,000 gns Newmarket Autumn Sales: sent to Italy. *M. R. Channon* –

QUEST AGAIN 5 ch.g. Then Again 126 – Eagle's Quest 62 (Legal Eagle 126) [1995 70: 10m 11.9m² 11.6m* 12m⁴ 14.4m 14d 12d 14.1m³ 12m⁴ 1996 14.1m⁶ 11.5f 14m Sep 19] leggy, angular, plain gelding: not a good walker: easy mover: modest handicapper: pulled up and dismounted final start: stays 14.1f: acts on dead going and good to firm: inconsistent. *D. W. P. Arbuthnot* 62

QUEST EXPRESS 2 ch.c. (Apr 30) Rudimentary (USA) 118 – Swordlestown Miss (USA) (Apalachee (USA) 137) [1996 6m* 6g⁶ 7m³ 8g⁵ 10d⁴ 7d 9s Nov 17] IR 29,000Y: tall, quite good-topped colt: has plenty of scope: has a fluent, rounded action: half-brother to several winners, including useful 1994 2-y-o Traikey (1m, by Scenic) and Sword Master (up to 17.2f, by Sayf El Arab): dam Irish 2-y-o 7f winner: won maiden at Yarmouth in June: ran in pattern events 5 of 6 starts after, sixth of 9 in July Stakes at Newmarket and about 5¾ lengths fifth of 7 to Equal Rights in Futurity Stakes at the Curragh (final start for M. Bell): below form both starts in Italy: stays 1m: yet to race on extremes of going. *A. Pellegrini, Italy* 91

QUEST FOR BEST (USA) 2 b. or br.f. (Mar 13) Quest For Fame 127 – Chic Monique (USA) (Halo (USA)) [1996 7.6d³ Aug 29] $50,000Y: third foal: half-sister 64 p to a sprint winner in USA by Skywalker: dam unraced half-sister to very smart Prima Voce (suited by 1¼m+) and granddaughter of Oaks winner Monade: 6/1 from 3/1, just over a length third of 9 to Sad Mad Bad in maiden at Lingfield, starting slowly, challenging from 2f out then staying on despite looking green: will improve, particularly over further than 1m. *J. H. M. Gosden*

QUESTING STAR   3 ch.f. Rainbow Quest (USA) 134 – Guest Artiste 110 (Be   66
My Guest (USA) 126) [1995 NR 1996 10m 10.4g 8m⁶ a7g⁴ a8s³ Nov 19] lengthy filly: third foal: dam, best at 1m, from good family: fair maiden, not seen until September: sold 32,000 gns Newmarket December Sales: will stay 1¼m: acts on good to firm ground and on equitrack. *G. Wragg*

QUESTONIA   3 b.f. Rainbow Quest (USA) 134 – Danthonia (USA) 80 (Northern   107
Dancer) [1995 NR 1996 10.1g² 11.8m² 8.3g* 10d 8m⁴ 8f* 9s⁴ 10.3d² a8.5s⁴ Dec 26] leggy, quite attractive filly: third foal: dam 2-y-o 5f winner out of useful Irish sprinter Monroe, same family as Try My Best and El Gran Senor: useful performer: won maiden at Windsor in July and minor event at Leicester (beat Miss Riviera a head, rallying well) in October: best effort when second of 9 to Russian Snows in useful minor event at Doncaster on final start for H. Cecil: stays 10.3f: acts on firm and soft ground, far from disgraced on first run on dirt: usually races prominently. *R. Frankel, USA*

QUEZON CITY   2 ch.c. (Apr 23) Keen 116 – Calachuchi 74 (Martinmas 128)   –
[1996 6m Oct 23] workmanlike colt: first foal: dam 7.5f to 12.4f winner: 50/1, burly and green, soon rear in 12-runner maiden at Newcastle. *M. J. Camacho*

QUIBBLING   2 b.f. (Apr 19) Salse (USA) 128 – Great Exception 84 (Grundy 137)   63 p
[1996 5m 7.1s⁶ Oct 22] fifth live foal: half-sister to 10.2f winner Exemption and 8.1f and 12.1f winner Exclusion (both by Ballad Rock) and a winner in Italy by Midyan: dam won at 12.2f and 14.7f: 25/1, sixth of 16 to My Valentina in maiden at Chepstow nearly 4 months after debut, staying on under hands and heels: will stay 1¼m: likely to progress. *H. Candy*

QUICK MILLION   5 b.m. Thowra (FR) – Miss Quick (Longleat (USA) 109)   –
[1995 40: a12g³ a8g a8g⁵ 14d a12g 1996 a13g a12g Jan 18] workmanlike mare: poor maiden: will probably stay 1¼m: acts on equitrack: tried visored: sold 850 gns Ascot July Sales, then 1,500 gns Ascot October Sales. *J. W. Mullins*

QUICK SILVER BOY   6 gr.g. Kalaglow 132 – Safidar 83 (Roan Rocket 128)   –
[1995 NR 1996 10g Apr 22] tall, close-coupled gelding: modest performer (rated 64) in 1993: lightly raced and little form since. *D. Burchell*

QUIET ARCH (IRE)   3 b.g. Archway (IRE) 115 – My Natalie 64 (Rheingold   69
137) [1995 NR 1996 8d 6m 10.2g a8g⁴ a8g* a8g³ a10g⁵ a8g 9g⁴ 12m⁵ 12m³ 10.4g²   a66
9.7d³ a11g⁵ Dec 27] IR 11,500F, 11,000Y: good-topped gelding: has a round action: half-brother to several winners, including fair Ned's Aura (stays 9f, by Dalsaan): dam 1m winner: fair performer: won minor event at Lingfield in June: creditable efforts 4 of last 5 starts: sold out of C. Cyzer's stable 15,000 gns Newmarket Autumn Sales after penultimate start: stays 1½m: acts on good to firm and dead ground and equitrack. *W. R. Muir*

QUIET MOMENTS (IRE)   3 b.g. Ron's Victory (USA) 129 – Saint Cynthia   –
(Welsh Saint 126) [1995 –: 6m 6m 6.1d 6.1s 1996 10.8g 12d 11.8d 11.9m Sep 6] tall, leggy gelding: no worthwhile form. *P. G. Murphy*

QUILLING   4 ch.g. Thatching 131 – Quillotern (USA) (Arctic Tern (USA) 126)   77
[1995 84: 10f⁴ 6g⁵ 7m⁵ 6m⁴ 7.5g⁵ 6m² 6f⁴ 5d³ 7f* 6d 7f* 7m² 7m 1996 8g 7g 7m⁵ 7g⁶ 7m² 7m³ 7m 7g³ 8.5m³ 7g⁴ 9g⁵ 8m⁴ 7.9g³ 7m* 8m 7f* 7g 8m 7m³ 7g Nov 2] rangy gelding: fair handicapper: won at Doncaster and Redcar in September: ducked and unseated rider as stalls opened (still wearing blindfold) eighteenth start: stays 9f: acts on firm ground, possibly not on dead: visored 4 times, running well first 2 occasions: sometimes gives trouble in preliminaries and taken early to post: genuine and consistent. *M. Dods*

QUILLWORK (USA)   4 b.f. Val de L'Orne (FR) 133 – Quaff (USA) 115 (Raise   –
A Cup (USA)) [1995 65: 14.1f a12g³ 10g⁴ 10d³ 1996 10d 10g 10.1m 12m 11.5m a16g a14g⁶ Dec 3] lengthy filly: good walker: fair maiden handicapper at best: little worthwhile form in 1996, sold out of Mrs J. Cecil's stable 4,200 gns Ascot June Sales

after second start: stays 1¼m: acts on good to firm and good to soft ground: early to post nowadays. *J. Pearce*

QUINELLA 3 b.f. Generous (IRE) 139 – Bempton 57 (Blakeney 126) [1995 NR – 1996 10g⁵ 12f Jul 26] angular filly: half-sister to 1995 3-y-o 1½m winner Shawahin (by Nashwan) and several winners, including very smart middle-distance stayer Banket (by Glint of Gold) and smart 1½m and 13.4f winner Mr Pintips (by Kris): dam, second over 1m and 9f, half-sister to Shirley Heights: no worthwhile form in maidens at Pontefract and Newmarket, looking short of pace. *Lord Huntingdon*

QUINNTESSA 3 ch.f. Risk Me (FR) 127 – Nannie Annie 60 (Persian Bold 123) 51 d [1995 51: 6g a5g a6g² a6g 1996 a6g a8g a6g⁴ a8g⁴ a7g⁶ 6s³ 7m 6m 6f Sep 23] small filly: poor and inconsistent maiden: probably stays 1m: acts on soft ground and fibresand: sent to South Korea. *B. Palling*

QUINTA BOY 3 b.g. Puissance 110 – Figment 75 (Posse (USA) 130) [1995 –: – 5g⁶ 5f 1996 5.1g 5g 5.1m Aug 7] good-quartered gelding: no worthwhile form: trained until after reappearance by Jack Berry: looks a short-runner. *J. L. Eyre*

QUINTELLINA 2 b.f. (Apr 2) Robellino (USA) 127 – High Quinta 51 (High 83 + Line 125) [1996 6g³ 7m* 8m 8.3g⁵ Sep 29] 13,000Y: good-bodied filly: third foal: dam placed at 1m, sister to useful performer at up to 1¾m Jaffa Line: heavily-backed favourite, won 15-runner maiden at Goodwood in August by 2½ lengths from Saabga, having to wait long time for gap then quickening well: failed to fulfil that promise in May Hill Stakes at Doncaster and minor event at Hamilton: should stay beyond 7f: looked a useful prospect at Goodwood. *L. M. Cumani*

QUINTUS DECIMUS 4 b.g. Nordico (USA) – Lemon Balm (High Top 131) – [1995 80: 6m 8.1m⁵ 7.9g³ 8.1m⁵ 7d 8s⁴ 10d 1996 7m 8.1d⁵ 6m 7m 8d Oct 2] smallish, useful-looking gelding: fairly useful handicapper at 3 yrs when trained by Lord Huntingdon: travelled strongly 5f when mid-division in Victoria Cup at Ascot on reappearance: well beaten afterwards, blinkered third start (final outing for R. Akehurst): sold 3,800 gns Newmarket Autumn Sales: stays 1m: acts on good to firm ground and soft: takes keen hold: sent to Spain. *B. J. Meehan*

QUINZE 3 b.g. Charmer 123 – Quaranta 83 (Hotfoot 126) [1995 NR 1996 7f* 8m* 75 8f⁶ 8.1f⁶ 10d Oct 2] leggy, close-coupled gelding: brother to useful 1m and 10.4f winner Quango and half-brother to several winners, including Cambridgeshire winner Quinlan Terry (by Welsh Pageant), also successful at 1½m: dam 2-y-o 5f winner: won median auction maiden at Brighton in July: seventh of 13 to Hammerstein in £7,400 ladies race at Ascot next start: well below that form in 2 handicaps and a minor event afterwards: sold 16,000 gns Newmarket Autumn Sales: stays 1m: acts on firm ground. *Sir Mark Prescott*

QUINZII MARTIN 8 b.g. Song 132 – Quaranta 83 (Hotfoot 126) [1995 –, a61d: – a7g a7g* a8g a7g² a7g* a7g³ a7g a8.5g a7g a9.4g³ a8g 7m⁶ a7g⁶ a7g a7g a7g a7g a59 a9.4g a7g² 1996 a7g a7g a7g³ a7g³ a7g³ a8.5g² a7g³ a8.5g a7g² a7g⁴ a7g⁵ a8g³ a8.5g⁶ a7g⁴ a7g a8.5g³ a7s* a7g Dec 28] strong, good-bodied gelding: has a quick action: modest handicapper: yet to win on turf, but successful 9 times on the all-weather: off course 3½ months, won at Wolverhampton in December: effective from 6f to 11f in 1994, races mainly at 7f nowadays: acts on all-weather surfaces: sometimes blinkered/visored. *D. Haydn Jones*

QUIVIRA 5 ch.m. Rainbow Quest (USA) 134 – Nobly Born (USA) (The Minstrel 73 (CAN) 135) [1995 81: 12g⁶ 11.6m² 10f* 10f³ 10g* 9f³ 10f 12.3m² 12g² 10.1g 8.9g 10.3m³ 1996 a9.4g 12m 12g 12m³ 12.3m Jul 20] leggy, lengthy mare: fair handicapper: trained until after 5-y-o reappearance by T. Clement: clearly best effort in 1996 when third at Newmarket on fourth start, but had run of steadily-run race: stays 1½m: acts on firm ground: visored (always behind) second 4-y-o start: tends to sweat and get on edge. *H. Akbary*

QUI VIVRA VERRA 2 b.g. (Feb 12) Saddlers' Hall (IRE) 126 – Warning Light 86 (High Top 131) [1996 6m 7.1g⁵ 7f* Aug 4] IR 12,500F, 26,000Y: lengthy, rather unfurnished gelding: third foal: half-brother to fairly useful 6f (at 2 yrs) to 1m winner Twilight Patrol (by Robellino): dam unraced daughter of sister to Highclere: made all and stayed on strongly when winning 6-runner maiden at Newcastle by 2½ lengths: will be suited by middle distances: sent to Hong Kong. *J. M. P. Eustace*

QUOTA 3 b.f. Rainbow Quest (USA) 134 – Armeria (USA) 79 (Northern Dancer) 102 [1995 NR 1996 10g* 10g² 11.9m Aug 21] leggy, sparely-made filly: has a markedly round action: second living foal: sister to top-class 1992 2-y-o 1m winner Armiger, also winner of Chester Vase and second in St Leger: dam, suited by 1¼m, half-sister to Park Hill winner I Want To Be, from good family: won maiden at Sandown in April: best effort when 3 lengths second of 5 to Mezzogiorno in steadily-run listed race at Newbury following month: well-held eighth of 9 to Key Change in steadily-run Yorkshire Oaks at York after 3-month break on final start: should have been suited by further than 1¼m: tended to get on edge: stud. *H. R. A. Cecil*

R

RAAHA 2 b.f. (Apr 16) Polar Falcon (USA) 126 – Ostora (USA) 83 (Blushing   76 p
Groom (FR) 131) [1996 6m Oct 5] lengthy, unfurnished filly: fourth foal: half-sister to 3-y-o 1¾m winner Alwarqa (by Old Vic) and fairly useful 5-y-o 1½m to 2m winner Jaraab (by Sure Blade): dam maiden (stayed 1m) out of Grade 1 winner My Darling One: 14/1 and backward, around 6 lengths seventh of 13 to Elegant Warrior in maiden at Newmarket, showing up 4f: will stay at least 1m: should do better. *R. W. Armstrong*

RAASED 4 b.g. Unfuwain (USA) 131 – Sajjaya (USA) 97 (Blushing Groom (FR)   43
131) [1995 85: 10m* 12g³ 10.1m 1996 8g 9.2g³ 8.3m 8.3f⁶ Aug 19] tall gelding: has been hobdayed: fairly useful form for J. Dunlop at 3 yrs: poor at best in 1996, reportedly finishing lame on final outing: stays 1¼m: has raced only on a sound surface: headstrong and somewhat temperamental. *F. Watson*

RABICAN (IRE) 3 b.g. Distinctly North (USA) 115 – Kaysama (FR) (Kenmare   104
(FR) 125) [1995 95+: 6m² 6m* 6m 6m* 6.5g* 6m⁴ 6.5g 1996 7g² 7m² Jul 11] leggy, lengthy gelding: useful performer: good efforts at Newmarket both starts in 1996, leading briefly entering final 1f when ½-length second of 16 to Crumpton Hill in Bunbury Cup on second one: stays 7f: acts on good to firm ground, yet to race on a soft surface: sent to Hong Kong. *M. H. Tompkins*

RACING BRENDA 5 b.m. Faustus (USA) 118 – Icecapped 91 (Caerleon (USA)   49
132) [1995 60, a–: 10.3m 8m⁵ 7.5g³ 6m⁶ 7g6 8.2m* 9m 8.5d² 8g 1996 8.2m 8g 8.2m⁴   a–
8.2m³ 8.2d⁵ 8.3g² 10.8f a9.4g Dec 14] sturdy mare: poor handicapper: stays 1¼m: acts on fibresand and on good to firm and soft ground. *B. C. Morgan*

RACING CARR 2 ch.f. (Apr 7) Anshan 119 – Bamian (USA) (Topsider (USA))   –
[1996 6m 6g 7m a7g⁴ a7g a8g⁴ Dec 3] 2,100Y, resold 4,000Y: close-coupled filly: third foal: dam French 10.5f winner, closely related to Breeders' Cup Juvenile third Slavic: little form: retained 500 gns Ascot November Sales. *T. J. Naughton*

RACING HAWK (USA) 4 ch.g. Silver Hawk (USA) 123 – Lorn Lady   55
(Lorenzaccio 130) [1995 58: 11.5m⁵ a12g² 14s 1996 a12g 11.9f 12d 8.3m⁴ 10m³ 10f* 10f⁶ 10g 8f Sep 5] rather leggy gelding: modest handicapper: won maiden event at Nottingham in July, dictating steady pace: suited by middle distances: acts on firm ground, well beaten on soft. *M. S. Saunders*

RACING HEART 2 b.f. (Feb 28) Pursuit of Love 124 – Hearten (Hittite Glory   –
125) [1996 6m 7f 7.1m 7m Oct 4] tall filly: has scope: ninth foal: half-sister to five winners, including 1¼m winner Heart of Spain (by Aragon) and smart sprinter Northern Goddess (by Night Shift): dam unraced daughter of smart middle-distance stayer Nortia: midfield at best in maidens and nursery. *P. J. Makin*

RACING TELEGRAPH 6 b.g. Claude Monet (USA) 121 – Near Enough   43
(English Prince 129) [1995 45: 7.1m 8.1g 7m³ 7g³ 7d⁴ 7m a7g⁶ 1996 a8g⁴ a8g   a32
7g⁴ 7g³ 8g⁵ 7m 10g³ a10g⁵ a8g a12g Dec 30] tall, angular gelding: has had wind operation: poor handicapper: left J. W. Payne after second 6-y-o start: probably stays 1¼m: acts on good to firm and dead ground and on equitrack. *C. N. Allen*

RADAR O'REILLY 2 b.g. (Feb 26) Almoojid 69 – Travel Bye 62 (Miller's Mate   –
116) [1996 5.1d Apr 12] 3,500F: leggy, good-topped gelding: second foal: dam should have stayed 1¼m: sire (by Sadler's Wells) disappointing maiden, closely related to Assert and half-brother to Bikala and Eurobird: ninth of 10 in maiden auction at Nottingham. *R. J. R. Williams*

RADEVORE 3 ch.c. Generous (IRE) 139 – Bloudan (USA) (Damascus (USA))   120
[1995 102: 8m⁵ 8s³ 9s³ 1996 10.5m³ 10g* 12m 10g* 12m³ 12d Oct 6] leggy colt: has

a fluent action: very smart performer: won Prix La Force at Deauville in May by ¾ length from Top Glory and Prix Eugene Adam (½ length behind Desert Boy, awarded race) at Saint-Cloud in July: ran very well when 2½ lengths third of 10 to Helissio in Prix Niel at Longchamp, tracking winner turning in: only twelfth of 16 in Prix de l'Arc de Triomphe there 3 weeks later, not clear run and eased 1½f out: stays 1½m: acts on good to firm ground and soft: has joined R. Frankel. *A. Fabre, France*

RADIANT STAR 3 b.c. Rainbow Quest (USA) 134 – Miss Kuta Beach 91 (Bold   86
Lad (IRE) 133) [1995 62p: 7m 1996 10m 10.4f⁵ 10m³ 10g³ 10.4g⁶ Sep 4] big, lengthy colt: poor mover: fairly useful maiden: placed at Newmarket in June and July: found little off bridle when favourite at York on final start: likely to prove best at up to 1¼m: yet to race on a soft surface: carried head awkwardly third 3-y-o start: not one to trust implicitly. *G. Wragg*

RADICAL EXCEPTION (IRE) 6 b.g. Radical 104 – A Stoir (Camden Town   –
125) [1995 NR 1996 8.3g 8.3d 10m Aug 28] first known foal: dam unraced: behind in claimers and maiden. *D. L. Williams*

RADMORE BRANDY 3 b.f. Derrylin 115 – Emerin 85 (King Emperor (USA))   35
[1995 –: 7m 1996 a7g a6g a9.4g⁶ a8g⁶ 10d³ a12g⁴ 12m 10.8g² 10m a9.4g 11m⁶ Oct 29] smallish, angular filly: poor maiden: gambled on on several occasions in 1996: left N. Littmoden after tenth start: stays 10.8f: best efforts on turf with give in the ground, no worthwhile form on fibresand: well beaten in visor: has joined G. Richards. *P. D. Evans*

RAED 3 b.c. Nashwan (USA) 135 – Awayed (USA) 108 (Sir Ivor 135) [1995 79+:   74
6m² 6d 1996 10m⁴ 10.8f⁴ 9m 7.9g⁴ 10m 8f² 8m⁵ Oct 17] sturdy, well-made colt: fair maiden handicapper: sold to join Mrs A. Swinbank 11,000 gns Newmarket Autumn Sales: middle distance bred, but seems best at around 1m: acts on firm ground: has twice hung badly. *P. T. Walwyn*

RAFFLES ROOSTER 4 ch.g. Galetto (FR) 118 – Singapore Girl (FR) 117   64
(Lyphard (USA) 132) [1995 77: 9.8g 10g³ 13.5s³ 12g² 13.5d² 10.5d⁶ 12.5g 12d 15g⁴ 12g² a7g³ 1996 a10g⁶ 7g 10g 12g⁴ 14d³ 16.2d Oct 11] workmanlike gelding: fair maiden: stays 15f: acts on soft ground: blinkered (well beaten) once in France: looked none too keen fifth 4-y-o start. *A. G. Newcombe*

RAFTER-J 5 b. or br.g. Petoski 135 – Coming Out (Fair Season 120) [1995 57:   –
a8g 7m 8.3m⁵ 8g* 8m 8f 10f 1996 a11g a8g a7g a7g⁶ Feb 21] lengthy gelding: modest miler: well beaten in 1996. *J. A. Harris*

RAFTERS 7 b.g. Celestial Storm (USA) 132 – Echoing 93 (Formidable (USA)   –
125) [1995 –: 10.5g 1996 8.9g 10.1m Oct 23] tall gelding: poor mover: fair maiden, lightly raced: no form last 2 seasons. *J. M. Bradley*

RAGAZZO (IRE) 6 b.g. Runnett 125 – Redecorate (USA) (Hatchet Man (USA))   28
[1995 39, a51: a5g⁵ a7g* a7g⁵ a7g² a7g a8g 6.9d 8.3m 7m 7f 5.9f⁴ 7.1m 8.3m⁶ 6g 7f⁴   a51 ?
9.2f⁶ 6g 1996 5.9d 7m 11.1g 8f 6m⁶ 5m⁵ 5g³ 6f a6g a7g 7g³] angular gelding: has a round action: poor handicapper: best form at up to 8.5f: acts on firm ground and all-weather surfaces: effective blinkered or not: inconsistent. *J. S. Wainwright*

RAGMAR (FR) 3 ch.c. Tropular – Reggae (FR) (New Chapter 106) [1995   117
112p: 8g² 10g² 1996 10.5m* 12m* 12m Jun 30]
  The story of Ragmar's season is enough to make your eyes water. He began it one of the most promising maidens in Europe and won a Group 2 and a classic on his first two starts. So far so good, but Ragmar's rapid rise was stopped in its tracks on his next outing and in July it was announced that surgeons had been operating on a twisted testicle, the delicate details being all that were heard of him in the second half of the year until the news came through in December that he had been retired. Ragmar's racing career had lasted less than eleven months. Still, he should be in good enough shape to enjoy a longer run in his next career as a stallion.
  Ragmar found one too good for him on both his starts as a two-year-old, Le Triton by a length and a half in a newcomers race at Deauville and Polaris Flight by a short head in the Criterium de Saint-Cloud. In between those two races he had been bought by Jean-Louis Bouchard from his breeder Georges

United Arab Emirates Prix du Jockey-Club, Chantilly—it's desperately close as Ragmar (No. 4) holds on from outsiders Polaris Flight (No. 8) and Le Destin (No. 6)

Sandor and transferred from Vanheeghe's stable to that of Pascal Bary who had trained Bouchard's 1994 Prix du Jockey-Club winner Celtic Arms. Ragmar began his French Derby campaign, as Celtic Arms had done, in the Prix Greffulhe at Longchamp in April but managed three places better than Celtic Arms by winning it; a 2/1-shot, he beat Egeo three lengths with Radevore another two lengths back in third. It was an impressive way to get off the mark but Ragmar was not seen out again until the Prix du Jockey-Club in June. The owner's reasons for missing the Prix Lupin were described thus in *Courses & Elevage*: 'One is rational: to avoid a hard race against Helissio, the other is more emotional: to be able to dream longer.' Helissio had acquired a mighty reputation even then and was sent off an even-money chance for the Prix du Jockey-Club on the Pari-Mutuel, unbeaten in three starts. In a total of fifteen runners, Fabre, Mme Head and Chapple-Hyam all had three runners each, the British-trained trio being High Baroque (5/1 coupled), Astor Place (33/1) and Polaris Flight (43/1). Strange to relate, Helissio managed only joint-fifth and the Head/Fabre sextet ended up filling five of the last six places; Polaris Flight and the other rank outsider Le Destin came within an ace of winning. Pacemakers set a cracking gallop in the first half mile—despite which Helissio still completely failed to settle—and the last three at halfway were the first three at the finish. A few centimetres either way and the outcome between this trio could have been very different, but the result that counted was Le Destin third, Polaris Flight second and Ragmar the winner. Eighth into the straight, Ragmar had quickened to the front towards the outside about a furlong and a half from home, gone a length clear, but then jinked left when hit with the whip and might possibly have idled a touch as well before he passed the post with the other two closing fast. After that and the judge's examination of the photo, a stewards inquiry into possible interference had to be seen out as well before Ragmar was confirmed the winner. Hopefully, these drawn-out dealings just gave his connections an extra chance to savour the moment, because there was nothing to enjoy in what followed. Ragmar trailed in seventh of nine behind Helissio in the Grand Prix de Saint-Cloud at the end of the month, the physical problem diagnosed, and surgeons ushered in shortly afterwards.

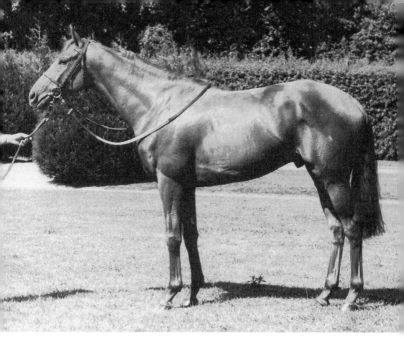

J. L. Bouchard's "Ragmar"

Ragmar (FR) (ch.c. 1993)	Tropular (br 1981)	Troy (b 1976)	Petingo La Milo
		Popular Win (ch 1975)	Lorenzaccio Jakomima
	Reggae (FR) (ch 1980)	New Chapter (ch 1966)	Crepello Matatina
		Moon Dancer (ch 1974)	Tarbes Missy

M. Bouchard apparently buys mostly horses in training, and he had already acquired both the smart filly Guislaine and the recent Marcel Boussac/Vermeille winner Sierra Madre in this manner from M. Sandor before Ragmar came along. One would call Ragmar's breeding remarkable if this sort of thing didn't seem to crop up so regularly with winners of top French races. The sire in this upwardly-mobile pedigree is Tropular whose racing career first appeared to have ended, like Ragmar's, on June 30th as a three-year-old, in his case after he had won two races (a maiden at two years and a good 9.2 furlong handicap) and been fourth in the Derby Italiano. He had a total of nine outings carrying the colours of Stavros Niarchos, but then reappeared to little effect for six more at five years in the ownership of Mme Sandor. A half-brother to Right Win, Tropular had a slow start at stud, an indication of just how slow being that one of the two registered foals in his first crop was named Sire Tropular, a ploy that failed to gain him much extra publicity when that horse fell over jumps on his only start. Things did pick up, however, and Ragmar was one of thirty-five

782

named foals born in 1993. The aforementioned Guislaine did most to spread the word at that stage, but Ragmar's dam Reggae also played her part, visiting Tropular for all five of her previous coverings and producing three winners. One of them, Robur, ran in two pattern races as a two-year-old in 1993, but finished a remote last in both. Reggae is by the 1970 Lincoln winner New Chapter and ran fifteen times on the flat, winning one ten-and-a-half-furlong handicap at Longchamp as a four-year-old. She did better over jumps, with three victories and, at 565,000 francs, four and a half times the flat prize money, and among her dam's other six winners is the high-class French jumper Collins. Grandam Moon Dancer and great-grandam Missy were both minor French winners. Fourth dam Ma won the 1965 Prix Cleopatre and was half-sister to Mister Sic Top who ran in four consecutive Arc de Triomphes in the early-'seventies. It is obviously a shame that Ragmar could not appear in even the one. A strong, close-coupled colt who ran only on good or good to firm ground, he will be standing at the Haras de Saint Gatien in Normandy, fee 25,000 francs. The 1996 fee reported for Ragmar's sire Tropular, incidentally, was 8,000 francs. *P. Bary, France*

RAGSAK JAMEEL (USA) 3 b.g. Northern Baby (CAN) 127 – Dream Play   82
(USA) (Blushing Groom (FR) 131) [1995 59p: 7m 1996 10.2g⁴ 14d 11f² 10g⁴ 10f²
11.9m* 10m² 11.8m* Aug 19] sturdy gelding: has a fluent, round action: fairly useful
handicapper: improved gradually, winning at Brighton in July and Leicester in
August: needs forcing tactics at 1¼m and should stay beyond 1½m: acts on firm
going: blinkered/visored last 6 starts: sent to UAE. *Major W. R. Hern*

RAGTIME COWGIRL 3 ch.f. Aragon 118 – Echo Chamber 89 (Music Boy   44
124) [1995 NR 1996 6s a6g 6.1g a9.4g³ 12g* 12.1m³ 12m³ 12.4m³ 10g³
10d³ 11.1m³ 10.9m 12.1g 12.1s Nov 7] 4,400Y: leggy, light-framed filly: third foal:
closely related to winner Cazanove's Pet (by Tina's Pet) and half-sister to 4-y-o
Just Jesting (by Jester): dam, sprinter, won as 2-y-o: poor performer: won selling
handicap at Pontefract in July and claimer at Musselburgh (final start for C. Thornton) in August: stays 1½m: acts on good to firm and dead ground and on fibresand.
D. A. Nolan

RAHEEFA (USA) 3 b. or br.f. Riverman (USA) 131 – Oogie Poogie (USA) 76   75
(Storm Bird (CAN) 134) [1995 NR 1996 10m 10g* Sep 14] first foal: dam, probably
stayed 1¼m here then won in USA, daughter of champion 1977 older mare
Cascapedia: still rather green, narrowly won maiden at Goodwood in September,
responding well to lead close home: would probably have stayed 1½m: should have
improved further: visits Machiavellian. *J. H. M. Gosden*

RAHEEN (USA) 3 b.c. Danzig (USA) – Belle de Jour (USA) (Speak John) [1995   79 +
93: 6g² 6f³ 6m⁴ 1996 8g⁴ a8.5g* Dec 28] rather leggy, useful-looking colt: found
less than expected on reappearance and stood out of M. Stoute's stable 13,000 gns
Newmarket Autumn Sales: blinkered, hacked up in maiden at Wolverhampton
in December, never off bridle: stays 8.5f: acts on firm ground and fibresand.
W. G. M. Turner

RAHONA (IRE) 2 b.f. (May 6) Sharp Victor (USA) 114 – Hail To You (USA)   36
(Kirtling 129) [1996 5s³ 5d 5m⁶ a5g⁴ a6g³ 6f⁵ a5g 7.5m Sep 18] IR 1,400F, IR   a44
4,800Y: rather leggy, close-coupled filly: half-sister to fair 10.8f and 1½m winner Un
Parfum de Femme (by Mill Native) and winners in USA by Thirty Eight Paces and
Caveat: dam minor winner in USA: poor maiden, in frame in sellers: stays 6f:
possibly not ideally suited by top-of-the-ground: best form when blinkered/visored.
B. S. Rothwell

RAINBOW BLUES (IRE) 3 b.c. Bluebird (USA) 125 – Tudor Loom (Sallust   117
134) [1995 5v* 5g 7f³ 7.5m³ 6m³ 6m 6d* 1996 7s³ 7d² 8d² 12m⁵ 8m³ 9f* 9f³
9f² Dec 1] IR 4,200F, IR 11,500Y: compact, workmanlike ex-Irish colt: second foal:
dam Irish maiden: won maiden at Leopardstown and listed race at the Curragh at 2
yrs: vastly improved form when 2 lengths second of 10 to Spinning World in Irish
2000 Guineas at the Curragh on third start, close up throughout and running on
really well: beaten under ½ length when creditable third of 7 to Restructure in
Group 3 event on same course in July, final outing for A. O'Brien: narrowly won

Grade 2 Del Mar Derby in September: remained in fine form, second to Marlin in Hollywood Derby last time: stays 9f well, not disgraced (15¼ lengths fifth of 13 in Irish Derby) over 1½m: acts on any going: blinkered (no improvement) fourth to sixth 2-y-o starts: genuine sort, sure to win more good races in USA. *C. Whittingham, USA*

RAINBOW RAIN (USA) 2 b.c. (Apr 11) Capote (USA) – Grana (USA) 78 (Miswaki (USA) 124) [1996 5.1g⁴ 6g³ 7g 6m⁵ 6m² Oct 17] $100,000Y: well-made colt: has plenty of scope: has a long, rather round action: fourth foal: half-brother to a winner in USA by Deputy Minister: dam, won at up to 7f in USA, half-sister to high-class French staying 2-y-o French Friend: fair maiden: good second of 18 in nursery (keen to post) at Newmarket final outing: will prove well suited by further than 6f. *M. Johnston*

RAINBOW ROAD 5 b.g. Shareef Dancer (USA) 135 – Chalkey Road 100 – (Relko 136) [1995 NR 1996 a11g⁴ Feb 10] smallish, quite attractive gelding: modest maiden handicapper (rated 60) in 1994 for G. Wragg: well held in selling handicap at Southwell on only flat outing since. *M. C. Pipe*

RAINBOWS RHAPSODY 5 b.m. Handsome Sailor 125 – Rainbow Trout 76 37 (Comedy Star (USA) 121) [1995 –, a44: a7g⁵ a8g³ 7.1d⁶ a7g 7g 1996 a7g a7g a8g 7.1g⁴ 8.1m² 8.3g⁴ 8.1m⁵ a7g 8g³ 8m⁶ 8g 7.1m⁴ 8f Sep 27] tall, lengthy mare: unimpressive mover: poor maiden handicapper: trained until after reappearance by M. Camacho: stays 1¼m: acts on good to firm ground, soft and fibresand: sent to South Korea. *D. W. Chapman*

RAINBOW TOP 4 b.c. Rainbow Quest (USA) 134 – Aigue 96 (High Top 131) 96 d [1995 NR 1996 a10g* a10g* 12.3m⁴ 13.9m⁵ 10.5m* 8s⁶ 8.9g Sep 4] 35,000Y: lengthy colt: first foal: dam, stayed 1m, is sister to very useful middle-distance performer Torchon from family of Mystiko: has reportedly suffered from sore shins and been freeze fired: easily won maiden and minor event early in year at Lingfield before off course nearly 4 months: dropped considerably in class, ready winner of claimer at Haydock in August: poor efforts in similar events afterwards, and sold only 7,800 gns Newmarket Autumn Sales: effective at 1¼m and should stay 1½m: acts on good to firm ground and on equitrack: has his problems and is unreliable as a result. *W. J. Haggas*

RAINBOW WALK (IRE) 6 ch.g. Rainbow Quest (USA) 134 – Widows Walk – (Habitat 134) [1995 –: a9.4g a9.4g⁶ a12g 8g 1996 a9.4g a11g Feb 2] lengthy gelding: fairly useful performer at best: little worthwhile form for some time. *J. G. M. O'Shea*

RAINDANCING (IRE) 2 b.f. (Mar 30) Tirol 127 – Persian Song 45 (Persian 94 Bold 123) [1996 6d⁴ 6m² 6m* 6m³ 8m⁵ 7m Oct 1] 50,000Y: leggy filly: has a quick action: first foal: dam three-raced sister to high-class performer at up to 1¼m Bold Arrangement: won median auction maiden at Kempton in July: third of 8 to Seebe in Princess Margaret Stakes at Ascot and fifth 11 to Reams of Verse in May Hill Stakes at Doncaster: bandaged, well below form in valuable sales race at Newmarket final start: stays 1m. *R. Hannon*

RAINDEER QUEST 4 ch.f. Hadeer 118 – Rainbow Ring (Rainbow Quest 48 (USA) 134) [1995 –: 11.1g⁶ 6d 1996 8.1g⁴ 8g* 8g³ 9.2s⁴ 8.1g 8m⁴ 10g² 10m³ 10.5m⁴ 10f 8.1s a8g⁵ a10g⁴ a11g* Dec 27] sturdy, angular filly: has knee action: poor handicapper: won at Pontefract (seller) in April and Wolverhampton (by 12 lengths) in December: stays 11f: acts on good to firm ground and fibresand. *J. L. Eyre*

RAINELLE 4 ch.f. Rainbow Quest (USA) 134 – Dame Ashfield 90 (Grundy 137) – [1995 –: 10m 12m³ 11.9g⁶ 11.4m 11.4d 1996 17.1m 13.6m a11g Nov 4] lengthy filly: no worthwhile form: tried blinkered/visored. *J. W. Watts*

RAINWATCH 2 b.c. (Apr 24) Rainbow Quest (USA) 134 – Third Watch 114 83 p (Slip Anchor 136) [1996 8m⁵ Sep 20] leggy, close-coupled colt: second foal: half-brother to 3-y-o Tria Kemata (by Kris), 7f winner at 2 yrs: dam, winner at 7f at 2 yrs and of Ribblesdale Stakes, half-sister to Oaks-placed Three Tails and Maysoon, and very smart middle-distance performer Richard of York (by Rainbow Quest): 33/1, about 4 lengths fifth of 9 to King Sound in steadily-run minor event at Newbury, in rear then keeping on without threatening: will be well suited by middle distances: will improve. *J. L. Dunlop*

RAINY DAY SONG 3 br.f. Persian Bold 123 – Sawaki 71 (Song 132) [1995 61p: – 6f 1996 7m 8g a10s a6g Dec 5] some promise in maiden for Gay Kelleway on only 2-y-o start: off course 10½ months, soundly beaten in 1996. *Lord Huntingdon*

RAISA POINT 5 ch.m. Raised Socially (USA) – To The Point 96 (Sharpen Up 33 127) [1995 55d: 5.1m⁴ 5m 5g⁵ 5.1h³ 6m 6f 1996 5.1g a5g² 5f³ 5g Jul 15] leggy mare: a51 poor handicapper: clearly best 5-y-o effort (on only all-weather outing) when second at Southwell: should stay 6f: acts on hard ground and goes well on fibresand: blinkered (well beaten) once at 3 yrs: races prominently. *W. R. Muir*

RAISE A PRINCE (FR) 3 b.g. Machiavellian (USA) 123 – Enfant d'Amour 76 (USA) (Lyphard (USA) 132) [1995 85p: 7g⁵ 1996 8d⁴ 8m 10m² 10.3d⁵ 10.5d⁴ 10g² 10.3g⁴ Oct 25] rather leggy gelding: fair maiden: trained until after second 3-y-o start by R. Armstrong: ran creditably despite meeting trouble in running last 2 starts: stays 10.5f: acts on good to firm and dead going: has tongue tied down. *J. W. Hills*

RAISE A RIPPLE 3 b.c. Primitive Rising (USA) 113 – Bonnybrook (Tanfirion – 110) [1995 NR 1996 8g 7g 12.1m⁵ 8.3m 11.1m Jul 19] lengthy, workmanlike colt: first reported foal: dam looked poor under all codes: little worthwhile form. *Mrs D. Thomson*

RAIVUE 2 ch.g. (Mar 16) Beveled (USA) – Halka (Daring March 116) [1996 7.1v – Oct 16] 6,800Y resold 9,000Y: sixth live foal: half-brother to winning sprinters Nuclear Express and Rose of High Legh (both by Martinmas): dam unraced: 16/1, backward and green, pulled hard when well beaten in maiden at Haydock. *E. Weymes*

RAIYOUN (IRE) 3 b.c. Doyoun 124 – Raymouna (IRE) (High Top 131) [1995 115 8g* 1996 10m⁵ 8m² 8m⁵ 8m² 8g* 7g⁶ Sep 21] first foal: dam, Irish 1m winner, half-sister to Irish St Leger second Rayseka: Irish colt: won maiden at Gowran Park at 2 yrs: useful form when 2½ lengths fifth of 7 to Restructure in Minstrel Stakes in July and 4 lengths second of 6 to Idris in Desmond Stakes in August, both at the Curragh: improved effort when winning valuable handicap at the Curragh in September: 6/4 favourite, never able to land a blow in falsely-run listed race there last time: stays 1m: has raced only on a sound surface. *J. Oxx, Ireland*

RAJAH 3 b. or br.g. Be My Chief (USA) 122 – Pretty Thing 83 (Star Appeal 133) 53 [1995 NR 1996 a7g⁶ a7g a6g⁴ a8.5g* 11.1g³ a8g May 27] 7,600Y, 4,200 2-y-o: third foal: half-brother to German 1¼m winner Loncherina (by Formidable): dam, suited by 1½m, out of half-sister to Oaks second Maina: modest form: won handicap at Wolverhampton in March: stays best at around 1¼m. *C. W. Thornton*

RAKE HEY 2 gr.c. (Mar 24) Petong 126 – Dancing Daughter 79 (Dance In Time 64 (CAN)) [1996 5.2d 5g⁵ 5.1g 7.1f 8m² 6.9v⁶ Nov 11] leggy, quite good-topped colt, unfurnished at 2 yrs: seventh live foal: brother to fair 6f winner Gone To Pot and half-brother to 3 winners, including fairly useful 1m winner Take Two (by Jupiter Island): dam 13.4f winner: modest maiden: blinkered first time, improved effort when second at Redcar: stays 1m: may well be unsuited by very soft ground: blinkered last 2 starts. *R. F. Johnson Houghton*

RAKIS (IRE) 6 b. or br.g. Alzao (USA) 117 – Bristle 96 (Thatch (USA) 136) 80 [1995 70+: 7.1m a7g⁵ 7g a7g* 1996 a7g* a7g* a7g* 7f⁵ 7g⁶ 8s 8m³ 7.1m* 7m a92 7g⁴ 7m 7m³ 7.1m* 8.1d⁵ 7g a7g⁴ Dec 7] good-topped gelding: fairly useful handicapper: better than ever and unbeaten for M. Brittain early in year, winning 4 times (including £9,600 event) at Lingfield: not so good on turf, but still won at Sandown in June and September: best at up to 1m: acts on firm ground, soft and the all-weather: effective blinkered in 1993: usually held up. *Mrs L. Stubbs*

RALITSA (IRE) 4 b.g. Nordico (USA) – Bold-E-Be (Persian Bold 123) [1995 – 7g⁵ 7d⁶ 12m² 11f 11d* 10m 1996 14.1m Oct 8] ex-Irish gelding: fourth foal: half-brother to useful Irish pair Rondelli (5f and 9f winner, by Ahonoora) and Razida (7f winner at 2 yrs, by Last Tycoon): dam Irish middle-distance winner: fair form (rated 75) at 3 yrs for J. Bolger, winning handicap at Killarney in July: fair hurdler here: first beaten in handicap at Redcar on return to flat: stays 1½m: acts on good to firm ground, best effort on dead: blinkered last 4 starts at 3 yrs. *M. D. Hammond*

RAMADOUR (IRE) 2 b.c. (Mar 18) Rambo Dancer (CAN) 107 – Minwah 58 (USA) (Diesis 133) [1996 8m 10g³ Oct 24] first living foal: dam unraced daughter of smart middle-distance stayer Ivory Fields: third of 8 to Indifferent Guy in steadily-run median auction maiden at Nottingham: stays 1¼m. *J. R. Fanshawe*

King George Stakes, Goodwood—Hever Golf Rose came from last to first in 1995; twelve months on, she can't hold the late run of Rambling Bear (white face)

RAMBLING BEAR 3 ch.c. Sharrood (USA) 124 – Supreme Rose 95 (Frimley 112 Park 109) [1995 101: 5.2g² 5m* 5m2 6g* 5d⁴ 1996 6m⁶ 6g* 6f* 6m 6f⁵ 5m* 6d³ 6f 5d Oct 6] leggy, workmanlike colt: smart performer: won minor event at Newbury in May, listed race at Lingfield in June and King George Stakes at Goodwood (beat Hever Golf Rose a length, running on strongly to lead well inside final 1f) in July: sweating and on toes, far from disgraced in Haydock Park Sprint Cup and Prix de l'Abbaye de Longchamp last 2 starts: effective at 5f and 6f: acts on firm and dead ground: takes keen hold, and is held up: often alone to post: broke out of stalls at Longchamp: genuine. *M. Blanshard*

RAMBOLD 5 b.m. Rambo Dancer (CAN) 107 – Boldie 81 (Bold Lad (IRE) 133) 66 [1995 67d: a6g⁵ 6g 6m 6m² 6m 6m 6.1d a6g 6f 1996 6.1d³ 6g* 6g 6.1m² 6m 5.7f³ 6g* 6f³ 6m³ 6m⁴ 5.7m 6.1m 6m⁵ Oct 28] angular mare: fair handicapper: consistent in 1996, winning at Hamilton (minor event) in June and Yarmouth in August: stays 6f: acts on firm and dead ground: sometimes sweats: usually races prominently. *N. E. Berry*

RAMBO'S HALL 11 b.g. Crofthall 110 – Murton Crags 81 (No Argument 107) 87 [1995 87: 7g⁶ 7m 10m⁵ 8d⁵ 9g 10d a8g⁵ 1996 a11g² Jan 8] workmanlike gelding: smart performer (rated 112) at 8 yrs, but missed 1994 with leg injury: just fairly useful at end of career, reportedly retired after second in handicap on only 11-y-o outing: effective at 1m to 11f: best efforts on an easy surface: often gave trouble at stalls: held up: game and genuine. *J. A. Glover*

RAMBO'S RUMTIME 4 b.f. Rambo Dancer (CAN) 107 – Errol Emerald 60 – (Dom Racine (FR) 121) [1995 –: 5.9f 7f 7f⁵ 1996 6.9f 11.1m⁶ Aug 14] of little account. *F. Watson*

RAMBO TANGO 2 b.g. (Feb 13) Rambo Dancer (CAN) 107 – Jumra (Thatch – (USA) 136) [1996 a7g Aug 17] 4,800Y, 5,000 2-y-o: fifth foal: half-brother to 3-y-o Cortes (by Roi Danzig) and 1990 2-y-o 1m seller winner Sharp Glow (by Reach): dam unraced: 66/1, tailed off in 7-runner seller at Wolverhampton. *B. R. Cambidge*

RAMBO WALTZER 4 b.g. Rambo Dancer (CAN) 107 – Vindictive Lady 69 (USA) (Foolish Pleasure (USA)) [1995 51, a80: 10.3g 7.5m⁵ 10g⁵ 9f⁶ 8m⁴ a7g a8.5g³ a85 a8.5g⁴ 1996 a8g* a9.4g⁵ a8g⁶ a7g* a8g⁶ 7.5d² 8.3d* 8m* 8g* 8g 8.5g 9g 7.6d 8g 8m 8.1d 8.9g 8g a9.4g Dec 28] smallish, sturdy gelding: fairly useful all-weather performer: won claimers at Southwell and Wolverhampton in January: just fair on turf, but won handicaps at Hamilton (apprentices), Thirsk and Ripon (ladies event) in April: absent 3 months, then below form last 8 starts: retained 3,000 gns Newmarket Autumn Sales: effective at 7f, and stays 1¼m: acts on fibresand and on good to firm and dead ground (no form either start on very soft): visored (below form) once as 3-y-o: game. *D. Nicholls*

RAMIKE (IRE) 2 b.c. (May 1) Caerleon (USA) 132 – Marie Noelle (FR) 114 – (Brigadier Gerard 144) [1996 8.1s 8.2s Oct 31] 40,000Y: sturdy, angular colt: brother

786

to 3-y-o Love Bateta, closely related to useful 9f winner (best at 1½m) Triquetti (by Royal Academy) and half-brother to several winners, including Prix Marcel Boussac winner Mary Linoa (by L'Emigrant) and smart French 5-y-o middle-distance stayer Ming Dynasty (by Sadler's Wells): dam French 2-y-o 7.5f winner, later won at up to 1¼m in USA: 25/1, towards rear in maidens. *M. Johnston*

RAMOOZ (USA)   3 b.c. Rambo Dancer (CAN) 107 – My Shafy 92 (Rousillon   109
(USA) 133) [1995 102: 6m2 6.1m2 7m2 7.9g4* 7.3d* 8v4 1996 8m* 10m3 7m*
7m2 7g5 8g6 7g2 7m4 7g4 Oct 26] rangy, useful-looking colt: useful performer:
won fairly valuable minor events at Thirsk in April and Epsom in June: 1½ lengths
second of 16 to Lucayan Prince in Jersey Stakes at Royal Ascot: back to form
last 3 starts in listed race at the Curragh, £50,100 handicap at Ascot and steadily-run
minor event (fourth of 6 to Diffident) at Doncaster: best at up to 1m: acts on good to
firm and dead ground, ran respectably on heavy at 2 yrs: blinkered (best effort at the
time) third outing at 2 yrs: suited by waiting tactics and has a good turn of foot.
B. Hanbury

RAMSEY HOPE   3 b.c. Timeless Times (USA) 99 – Marfen (Lochnager 132)   78
[1995 80: 5g 5d2 5m4 5m4 5m4 6g2 6f* 6m4 6m4 5g2 7m3 5m3 6m* 6d 6g 6m
1996 5d 5g 6g 6g 6g2 6m 6m 5f2 6s 6f5 5m 5m 5m5 a6g5 5m 6.1m a5g* a5g*
a5g2 Nov 15] compact colt: tough and genuine at 2 yrs: inconsistent for much of
1996, but back almost to best towards end of year, winning handicaps at Wolverhampton in October and Lingfield in November: stays 6f: acts on firm and dead
ground and the all-weather: usually blinkered/visored: normally races prominently.
C. W. Fairhurst

RAMSEY PRIDE   2 b.f. (Feb 18) Timeless Times (USA) 99 – Lindrake's Pride   –
(Mandrake Major 122) [1996 3d5 5g 5g a5g6 7m 7g Oct 18] 5,200Y: well-grown
filly: unimpressive mover: seventh foal: half-sister to 4-y-o 6f (at 2 yrs) and 7f
winner Superpride (by Superpower) and 1990 2-y-o 7.5f winner Darika Lad (by
Belfort): dam never ran: poor form, including in sellers: trained first 5 outings by
C. Fairhurst: tail flasher. *J. Hetherton*

RANDOM   5 ch.m. Beveled (USA) – Martian Melody 62 (Enchantment 115)   54
[1995 56, a60: a5g5 a5g4 5.1g5 5.1m 5g5 5m a5g3 6m2 6f4 5.7h5 6g a7g6 a6g5 1996   a59
a6g a6g* a6g6 a6g3 a6g6 6g3 6m6 6m6 6m5 6m4 Aug 2] sparely-made mare: modest
handicapper: won at Lingfield in January: sold 3,200 gns Newmarket Autumn Sales:
effective at 5f and 6f, should stay 7f: acts on firm ground, dead and equitrack: held
up: sent to Saudi Arabia. *C. James*

RANDOM KINDNESS   3 b.g. Alzao (USA) 117 – Lady Tippins (USA) 83 (Star   76
de Naskra (USA)) [1995 NR 1996 10.2g 10.2g3 10m3 12.3m2 12m Jul 10] quite
attractive gelding: sixth foal: half-brother to 2 winners, including untrustworthy
sprinter Access Travel (by Auction Ring), useful at 2 yrs: dam 6f and 7f winner: fair
form when placed in maidens at Bath, Pontefract and Ripon before running as though
something amiss in similar event at Kempton: sold 5,000 gns Newmarket Autumn
Sales: stays 12.3f. *P. W. Harris*

RANGER SLOANE   4 ch.g. Gunner B 126 – Lucky Amy (Lucky Wednesday   –
124) [1995 43: a12g2 a12g 11.9g 10g 1996 a16.2g a14.8g 8f 10m Jun 10] leggy
gelding: poor maiden, well beaten since 3-y-o reappearance: tried blinkered: has
joined A. Streeter. *G. Fierro*

RANKAIDADE   5 b.m. Governor General 116 – Keep Cool (FR) 42 (Northern   21
Treat (USA)) [1995 –: 6d 5m 5m6 6g 6m 5g 7m 1996 a6g 5m 5.1g 6s 6m 5g 5g 6m
a6g 5m5 a5g 5m5 5g Aug 16] strong mare: bad handicapper: stays 6f: acts on good to
firm and soft going: tried blinkered. *Don Enrico Incisa*

RAPHANE (USA)   2 b.c. (Mar 11) Rahy (USA) 115 – Fast Nellie (USA) (Ack   102
Ack (USA)) [1996 5s6 5d2 5d* 5m2 5m* 6m2 6g Aug 11] $110,000Y: strong colt:
fourth foal: brother to a minor juvenile sprint winner in USA and half-brother to a
winner in Panama by Topsider: dam unraced sister to Grade 1 8.5f winner Caline:
useful form: won listed race at the Curragh in May: length second of 10 to Tipsy
Creek in Norfolk Stakes at Royal Ascot: blinkered/visored, won 6-runner Curragh
Stakes (by 1½ lengths from Nevada) then creditable 3 lengths second of 7 to Easycall
in Richmond Stakes at Goodwood, both in July: no headgear, well below form in
Heinz 57 Phoenix Stakes at Leopardstown final start: stays 6f: acts on good to firm

RAP

Mr P. D. Savill's "Raphane"

and dead ground: usually a front runner: sometimes wears tongue strap: tends to swish tail: sent to USA. *C. Collins, Ireland*

RAPID LINER 3 b.g. Skyliner 117 – Stellaris (Star Appeal 133) [1995 60+: 5m⁵ 6m⁶ 5m 7m⁴ 6m 1996 6.1d a6g 7f 8g May 20] tall, lengthy gelding: has a round action: modest performer at best for A. Harrison at 2 yrs: well below form in 1996: should stay beyond 7f: visored second 3-y-o start: sold to join R. Baker 500 gns Malvern October Sales. *H. Oliver*

RAPID MOVER 9 ch.g. Final Straw 127 – Larive 80 (Blakeney 126) [1995 –: 11.1s⁶ 1996 11.1d 12.1g 8.3d⁶ 8.3s³ 11.1g⁶ 8.1g 9.2g 8.3g 8.1f 11.1g⁶ 11.1m⁴ 11.1m 8.3f⁵ 12.1m Aug 29] workmanlike gelding: poor handicapper: stays 1½m: acts on good to firm and soft ground: wears blinkers: inconsistent. *D. A. Nolan*

RAPID RETREAT (FR) 3 ch.f. Polish Precedent (USA) 131 – Rapide Pied (USA) 117 (Raise A Native) [1995 NR 1996 8.3m 7m Aug 15] leggy filly: unimpressive mover: sixth live foal: half-sister to 1990 2-y-o 6f winner Joud (by Dancing Brave): dam French 7f and 1m winner: well beaten in maidens at Windsor and (bandaged) Salisbury: sold 2,000 gns Doncaster September Sales. *E. A. L. Dunlop*

RAPIER 2 b.c. (Apr 22) Sharpo 132 – Sahara Breeze 85 (Ela-Mana-Mou 132) [1996 6d³ 8f* 7.6g³ Sep 25] 15,500Y: leggy, unfurnished colt: third foal: dam, should have stayed 1¼m, half-sister to Fillies' Mile winner Ivanka: 11/8, won 7-runner maiden at Brighton by ¾ length, leading 1f out: creditable third but never a threat in steadily-run minor event at Chester 22 days later: sold 32,000 gns Newmarket Autumn Sales. *R. Hannon*

RAPIER POINT (IRE) 5 gr.g. Cyrano de Bergerac 120 – Renzola (Dragonara Palace (USA) 115) [1995 63d, a51d: a6g a6g⁶ a6g 6g 8g 7m⁴ 6g⁶ a5g 6.1d 1996 6m 6m 7g a7g Nov 22] strong, compact gelding: modest performer in 1995 for P. Haslam: well held as 5-y-o: needs further than 5f and should stay 7f: acts on good to firm and heavy ground and on fibresand: below form in visor/blinkers. *C. Murray*

RAQIB   5 b.g. Slip Anchor 136 – Reine Maid (USA) (Mr Prospector (USA)) [1995 – NR 1996 17.2f May 11] rangy gelding: fair staying hurdler: no worthwhile form on flat. *P. C. Ritchens*

RASAYEL (USA)   6 b.m. Bering 136 – Reham 67 (Mill Reef (USA) 141) [1995 56: a16.2g a12g⁶ 10m³ 10.8f² 13.1f* 12g⁶ 13f⁶ 11.1m² 10m⁶ 12.3m³ 10.3m³ 10.4g* 10g⁶ 10.5g 1996 a9.4g 10.3m* 13.1g³ a11g⁶ 10.5d³ 10.3g⁴ 10.2m³ 12.3m* 12g² 10.3d⁵ 10.4g 15.9g 12g³ 12g 12.1s² a14.8g³ a11g⁴ a10g a12s* a12g⁶ a13g* Dec 31] big, leggy mare: has a round action: fair handicapper on turf, modest on all-weather: won at Doncaster in May, Chester in August and at Wolverhampton (amateurs) and Lingfield (apprentices) in December: effective at 1¼m to 1¾m, but appears not to stay 2m: acts on firm and soft ground and on the all-weather: blinkered (out of form) final 4-y-o start: sometimes pulls hard: probably best held up. *P. D. Evans*
68
a55

RASH GIFT   3 ch.f. Cadeaux Genereux 131 – Nettle 106 (Kris 135) [1995 78p: 7g² 1996 7f³ 8m Oct 23] fair maiden, very lightly raced: weak in market after 14½-month absence, creditable third of 13 in apprentice race at Leicester, staying on under considerable handling: well beaten at Yarmouth 9 days later: should stay 1m. *Lord Huntingdon*
73

RASIN CHARGE   5 b.g. Governor General 116 – Airlanka (Corvaro (USA) 124) [1995 NR 1996 8f⁵ 7f⁵ Aug 9] fourth foal: dam poor half-sister to Poule d'Essai des Pouliches third Speedy Girl: always behind in maidens at Thirsk and Redcar, upset in stalls and very slowly away on debut. *R. Craggs*
–

RASMI (CAN)   5 ch.h. Riverman (USA) 131 – Snow Blossom (CAN) (The Minstrel (CAN) 135) [1995 71d: 7m⁵ 6.9m⁵ 8g⁶ 10.2m⁵ 7m 7g a13g 1996 14.1m 10m 8g a7g 8m 7g Aug 1] good-topped horse: fair maiden for A. Stewart first 4 starts in 1995: soundly beaten for new connections. *P. Howling*
–

RASMUSSEN (IRE)   2 b.c. (Apr 8) Sadler's Wells (USA) 132 – Arctic Heroine (USA) (Arctic Tern (USA) 126) [1996 7g⁵ 8.1g⁴ 8.2m⁵ 8g Oct 18] good-quartered, attractive colt: has a roundish action: fourth foal: brother to 3-y-o 11.5f winner Arktikos and 12.3f winner Jabaroot and half-brother to useful 1m and 1½m winner Mezaan (by Royal Academy): dam twice-raced half-sister to smart middle-distance filly Ghaiya out of half-sister to dam of Nonoalco: fair maiden: creditable eighth of 17 when bandaged and tongue tied in nursery at Newmarket final outing: will be suited by further than 1m: sent to UAE. *J. H. M. Gosden*
67

RATTLE   3 b.g. Mazilier (USA) 107 – Snake Song 94 (Mansingh (USA) 120) [1995 52: 5f³ 5g⁴ 6g a7g⁵ 6s⁴ 8f 1996 6s⁵ 8.3d³ 8.3d⁵ 12m 10d² 11.1m⁴ 10d³ a14.8g 13g⁵ 11.1m⁵ Jul 19] small gelding: modest maiden: well below form last 3 starts: stays 1¼m: acts on firm and soft ground, showed little on fibresand: seems effective blinkered or not. *J. J. O'Neill*
52

RAVEN MASTER (USA)   2 b.c. (May 1) Shalford (IRE) 124§ – Face The Facts (Lomond (USA) 128) [1996 5.1g² 5.2s* 5m 6g⁵ 7.3m⁵ 8m 8g Oct 25] small, well-made colt: has a roundish action: second foal: dam, ran twice at 2 yrs in Ireland, closely related to smart sprinter Acushla and Oaks winner Intrepidity: gamely won maiden at Newbury in May: ran in pattern company next 2 starts and in nurseries on last 3, mostly respectably: stays 7.3f: acts on good to firm and soft ground: visored (ran respectably) last 2 starts: sent to Czech Republic. *P. W. Chapple-Hyam*
83

RAVEN'S ROOST (IRE)   5 b.g. Taufan (USA) 119 – Al Zumurrud 80 (Be My Guest (USA) 126) [1995 §§: 10m 8.3g 8f 1996 8f² 8.1g Jun 13] leggy, lengthy gelding: refused to race final 4-y-o start: good second in amateurs handicap at War-wick on flat reappearance but refused to race again in selling handicap at Chepstow 8 days later: effective at 1m to 1¼m: acts on firm ground: sold to join G. Jones 1,600 gns Ascot July Sales, and won 2 handicap hurdles in August: one to leave alone. *A. J. Chamberlain*
53 §

RAW DEAL   3 ch.f. Domynsky 110 – Close The Deal 51 (Nicholas Bill 125) [1995 NR 1996 a8g May 9] 1,000Y: second foal: sister to modest maiden Borrowby: dam, ran only at 2 yrs, stayed 1¼m: slowly away and soundly beaten in Southwell claimer: has joined G. Barnett. *G. Fierro*
–

RAWI   3 ch.g. Forzando 122 – Finally (Final Straw 127) [1995 64: 5g 6m 6m 6g⁶ 6g⁶ 8g a7g⁴ a7g a6g a7g 1996 a8g² a7g² a7g³ a8g³ a7g² 6m⁵ a8g⁶ 7.1m 5.3f⁴ 6m⁶ 7f³ a8.5g a6g³ a7g* Dec 30] workmanlike gelding: modest maiden: claimed out of W.
64

Muir's stable £3,000 fifth 3-y-o start: won weak maiden at Lingfield in December: best efforts over 7f/1m: acts on firm ground and the all-weather: effective blinkered/visored or not: races prominently. *Miss Gay Kelleway*

REACT 3 b.f. Reprimand 122 – Shehana (USA) 86 (The Minstrel (CAN) 135) 101
[1995 86+: 6m² 6g* 6m³ 7m⁵ 7d 1996 7.6g² 6m³ 6m Jun 15] rangy, good-quartered, useful-looking filly: useful performer: best effort when close third of 8 to Branston Abby in listed race at Newmarket in June: ran poorly when favourite for £34,200 handicap at York (short to post) 2 weeks later: stays 7.6f: yet to race on extremes of going: to be trained by N. Drysdale in USA. *W. Jarvis*

READ YOUR CONTRACT (IRE) 2 ch.g. (May 13) Imp Society (USA) – –
Princess of Nashua (Crowned Prince (USA) 128) [1996 5m 7m a7g⁶ a7g⁵ 6m Sep 6] 9,500Y: quite good-topped gelding: half-brother to several winners, including 3-y-o sprinter Limerick Princess (by Polish Patriot) and useful 1994 2-y-o sprinter Limerick Belle (by Roi Danzig): dam unraced: no worthwhile form, including in sellers: visored last 3 starts: joined P. D. Evans. *J. Berry*

READY TEDDY (IRE) 3 b.f. Fayruz 116 – Racey Naskra (USA) 75 (Star de 51
Naskra (USA)) [1995 –: 5f⁵ 5g 6g 1996 6d 5s⁶ 5g² 5f 5f² 5g³ 5m³ 5f Jul 18] modest maiden handicapper: best 2 efforts at Musselburgh: best form at 5f: acts on firm ground. *Miss L. A. Perratt*

READY TO DRAW (IRE) 7 ch.g. On Your Mark 125 – Mitsubishi Art (Cure –
The Blues (USA)) [1995 NR 1996 a12g² 15.4m a16g³ a14g² a14.8g³ Jul 11] sparely- a44
made, angular gelding: bad mover: modest hurdler: poor handicapper nowadays on flat: best at up to 1¾m: acts on the all-weather, best turf efforts on an easy surface. *R. J. O'Sullivan*

REAGANESQUE (USA) 4 b.g. Nijinsky (CAN) 138 – Basoof (USA) 83 57
(Believe It (USA)) [1995 –: 10g 10m⁵ 10m⁵ 10d 13.6f 1996 14.1s 16.4g 12m⁴ 12.5f⁴ 12.5f* 12.1m* 14m 12m² 11.9m* Aug 16] tall, lengthy gelding: has a round action: modest handicapper: won at Warwick, Chepstow and Haydock in the summer: should stay 1¾m: acts on firm going, no form either run on a soft surface: often a front runner: fair hurdler, winner in December. *P. G. Murphy*

REAL ESTATE 2 b.c. (Mar 25) High Estate 127 – Haitienne (FR) (Green Dancer 68
(USA) 132) [1996 6m⁶ 8m Oct 17] 18,000Y: strong, sturdy colt: sixth foal: half-brother to several winners in Ireland and Germany, including useful Irish 1m and 1¼m winner Park Charger (by Tirol): dam, French 1m winner, is sister to smart French 2-y-o Harifa out of smart filly at up to 1m Hamada: off course nearly 4 months, much better effort in Newmarket maidens when keeping-on seventh to Royal Crusade: will stay middle distances: may do better again. *C. F. Wall*

REAL FIRE (IRE) 2 b.g. (Apr 25) Astronef 116 – Golden Arum 67 (Home 47
Guard (USA) 129) [1996 5m⁶ 5m a6g 8.1m 8m 6s 6g a8.5g Nov 25] IR 4,000Y: a?
leggy gelding: unimpressive mover: half-brother to 1991 Irish 2-y-o 5f winner Astro d'Argento (by Fayruz): dam, maiden who ran only at 2 yrs, should have stayed at least 6f: poor maiden: stays 6f: blinkered (stiff task) fifth start: soundly beaten on fibresand and soft ground. *M. G. Meagher*

REAL GEM 3 b.f. Formidable (USA) 125 – Emerald Ring 74 (Auction Ring 55 d
(USA) 123) [1995 62d: 6.1m³ a6g⁶ 7g⁵ 7g 1996 6.1m³ a5g⁶ 6g 6m 8m Sep 25] sparely-made filly: modest maiden: showed little after reappearance: sold 700 gns Ascot October Sales: best efforts at 6f: sent to South Korea. *P. J. Makin*

REALLY A DREAM (IRE) 3 br.f. Last Tycoon 131 – Ancestry (Persepolis 81
(FR) 127) [1995 74p: 7m⁴ 1996 7m² 8m⁵ 8m 8m³ 7.1d⁴ 7m⁶ 8g³ 7g* Oct 25] rangy filly: good walker and mover: capable of fairly useful form: won 22-runner apprentice handicap at Doncaster in October by 3 lengths from Waypoint, always well there: stays 1m: visored (looked reluctant) sixth 3-y-o start: tends to take good hold: sold 9,000 gns Newmarket December Sales. *M. R. Stoute*

REAL MADRID 5 b.g. Dreams To Reality (USA) 113 – Spanish Princess (King –
of Spain 121) [1995 34: 8.3m 8g 7.6m⁵ 7.6d 8g 7d a9.3g⁴ 9.3v* a10g³ 1996 a10g² a50
a8g a10g* a10g a12g⁵ a12g⁵ a10g 10.1f⁶ 10f Jun 25] good-bodied gelding: modest handicapper on the all-weather: won at Lingfield in January: stays 1½m: acts on equitrack (well beaten only outing on fibresand), little worthwhile turf form in Britain (successful on heavy ground in Belgium): blinkered/visored. *G. P. Enright*

REALMS OF GLORY (IRE) 3 b.c. Reprimand 122 – Wasaif (IRE) 79 –
(Lomond (USA) 128) [1995 56p: 5.7m⁶ 7g 1996 6s 8m a8g⁵ a8g 10f 8m 10.4g Oct a51
10] lengthy colt: no form at 3 yrs except (only time visored) when fifth of 16 in
handicap at Southwell in June: not bred to be suited by much further than 1m:
blinkered (set strong pace, tailed off) penultimate outing. *P. Mitchell*

REAMS OF VERSE (USA) 2 ch.f. (Apr 23) Nureyev (USA) 131 – Modena 108 p
(USA) (Roberto (USA) 131) [1996 7m² 7d* 8m* 8g* Sep 29]
   The Cecil stable's grip on the top staying events for two-year-old fillies
remains as tight as ever. Reams of Verse was her trainer's tenth winner of the
May Hill Stakes and sixth of the Fillies' Mile, and she became his third to
win both events after Formulate in 1978 and Tessla in 1988. To underline the
stable's strength in that department, Reams of Verse was less-fancied at Ascot
than Sleepytime, and a third Warren Place filly, Yashmak, came within inches
of winning the Prix Marcel Boussac a week later.
   Reams of Verse went to Ascot as the winner of two of her three starts.
After a narrow defeat at Newmarket when a well-backed favourite, she made
amends in another maiden at the same course in August with a neck defeat of
Bint Baladee, the pair fourteen lengths clear. The two renewed rivalry in the
May Hill Stakes at Doncaster nearly three weeks later, Reams of Verse the 2/1
favourite in a field of eleven and Bint Baladee second favourite. This time
Reams of Verse came out much the better, moving easily into the lead under
three furlongs out and shaking off the challenge of the Queen Mary runner-up
Dame Laura inside the last to win by two lengths, with a none-too-enthusiastic
Bint Baladee over five lengths away in fourth.
   Reams of Verse had won well, but at Ascot she started just third
favourite behind two fillies who had scored in most impressive fashion last
time out, 6/4-chance Sleepytime and 2/1-chance Red Camellia. Pat Eddery,
who had ridden both Cecil fillies on their previous outings, opted for Sleepytime, leaving Michael Kinane to take the ride on Reams of Verse. Also in the
field of eight were the May Hill third Gretel and Mrs Miniver, who had been
tailed off at Doncaster, and two fillies Reams of Verse had already met on her
debut—Ovation, who had won the race and the maiden Logic who had failed to
progress. Completing the field was Khassah who had won two of her starts.
What promised to be an informative contest turned into a muddling race. With
Red Camellia setting just a steady early pace, the field was still tightly grouped
entering the short straight, Reams of Verse better placed than most. As Ovation
dropped away two out Reams of Verse became the main challenger to Red
Camellia on the rails and stayed on strongly to head her inside the last but
edging right as she did so, tightening up Sleepytime as the favourite looked for
room. Idling once in front, Reams of Verse held on by a length and a quarter
from Khassah, who had got a clear run towards the outside, with the unlucky

May Hill Stakes, Doncaster—Henry Cecil wins it yet again, thanks to Reams of Verse

Fillies' Mile, Ascot—Reams of Verse goes past Red Camellia (rails)
but Sleepytime (black cap) is boxed in as Khassah challenges

Sleepytime and Red Camellia a neck and a short head away in third and fourth. Outsiders Logic and Mrs Miniver were not beaten far in fifth and sixth, appearing to show plenty of improvement. Although the post-race attention focussed on Sleepytime's misfortune, that should not detract from Reams of Verse who had improved with each of her runs and has the makings of a good-class three-year-old. Cecil commented afterwards, 'I don't want to say at this stage that one's better than the other. The winner will never win hard on the bridle as she's a lazy filly.'

	Nureyev (USA)	Northern Dancer	Nearctic
	(b 1977)	(b 1961)	Natalma
		Special	Forli
Reams of Verse (USA)		(b 1969)	Thong
(ch.f. Apr 23, 1994)		Roberto	Hail To Reason
	Modena (USA)	(b 1969)	Bramalea
	(b 1983)	Mofida	Right Tack
		(ch 1974)	Wold Lass

Bought in for 270 guineas after winning an apprentice seller at Ayr as a four-year-old, Reams of Verse's great grandam, the sprinter Wold Lass, proved hugely more valuable at stud. She produced the smart and tough filly (at up to seven furlongs) Mofida, herself the dam not only of Reams of Verse's dam Modena but also of one of Khalid Abdulla's most successful broodmares Zaizafon. The unraced Modena, sold in foal to Diesis for 85,000 dollars at Keeneland in 1986, had four winners from five foals prior to Reams of Verse, none better than that first one, the Eclipse winner Elmaamul, who also came third in the Derby. Modena's subsequent winners have all been successful for Mr Abdulla. Modesto (by Al Nasr) had fair form at up to a mile and a half, Modernise (by Known Fact) was a useful performer, winning over seven furlongs at two and in Grade 3 company over nine furlongs in the United

Mr K. Abdulla's "Reams of Verse"

Stakes, and Modern Day (by Dayjur) was successful over seven and a half furlongs as a two-year-old for the Cecil stable in 1995. Modena's half-sister Zaizafon was a smart performer in her own right, best at a mile, and is the dam of Zafonic; further details can be found in Zamindar's commentary.

Reams of Verse, a tall, rather leggy, quite attractive filly and a fluent mover, has the scope to continue improving at three. If, as their trainer intends, Reams of Verse and Sleepytime meet again in the Guineas our preference would, at this juncture, be for the latter. Reams of Verse will have other opportunities, particularly beyond a mile, though whether she will have enough stamina for the Oaks trip is another matter. *H. R. A. Cecil*

REBECCA SHARP 2 b.f. (Apr 10) Machiavellian (USA) 123 – Nuryana 107 (Nureyev (USA) 131) [1996 7g^2 Nov 2] fifth foal: half-sister to 4 winners, including smart 3-y-o 1m (at 2 yrs) and 11.5f winner Mystic Knight (by Caerleon) and fairly useful 5-y-o middle-distance stayer Mystic Hill (by Shirley Heights): dam 1m winner out of half-sister to 1000 Guineas winner On The House: 7/2 favourite, slow-starting 1¼ lengths second of 23 to Palisade in maiden at Newmarket, challenging in the Dip, travelling smoothly then not quite so hard ridden as winner, no extra late on: sure to improve, and win a race or two. *G. Wragg*   82 p

REBEL COUNTY (IRE) 3 b.f. Maelstrom Lake 118 – Haven Bridge 88 (Connaught 130) [1995 68: 5m^5 6.1m^4 5m^2 5m^2 6m* 6s^2 7f 1996 7s 7m^6 7m^5 8g* 8g* 8f^3 10m^2 10.3m* 10.5g^6 10.3m 10.3m 8.1m^4 8f^2 8.5g* 7.6d^3 7f^3 8m 10m* 8g^5 8.1v* 8g 9s a9.4g Dec 7] good-topped filly: made into a useful performer: won claimers at Newmarket, Leicester (claimed out of D. Cosgrove's stable £12,500) and Chester (claimed out of M. Pipe's stable £12,000) in May/June: successful for current stable   97 in handicaps at Epsom in August, Ayr in September and Haydock in October: seems suited by 1m to 1¼m: acts on any ground: has carried head awkwardly: has had tongue tied: tough. *A. Bailey*

REBOUNDER 3 b.g. Reprimand 122 – So Bold (Never So Bold 135) [1995 8g 1996 a6g 8.1g 8.1f Jul 2] 2,500F: ex-French gelding: second foal: half-brother to 4-y-o 5f to 7f winner Stoppes Brow (by Primo Dominie): dam ran 4 times: trained only 2-y-o start by P. Paquet: no form here in sellers: tried blinkered and visored: has joined D. ffrench Davis. *K. McAuliffe* –

REBUKE 2 b.g. (Feb 24) Reprimand 122 – Lyra (Blakeney 126) [1996 5g 5g 5f⁴ 7m⁵ 7m⁶ 8g a7g* Nov 15] 3,800Y: workmanlike gelding: fifth foal: half-brother to winners in Germany (including at 11f) by Dowsing and to 1m winner Ever So Lyrical (by Never So Bold): dam won 3 races in Belgium: blinkered, unseated rider and bolted before start but still won seller at Lingfield in November: subsequently sold 3,000 gns Doncaster November Sales: stays 7f: acts on equitrack, raced only on a sound surface on turf: also blinkered third outing. *R. F. Johnson Houghton* 52 a61

RECALL TO MIND 3 b.g. Don't Forget Me 127 – Northern Notion (USA) (Northern Baby (CAN) 127) [1995 66?: 6m 7.5m 8.5m⁴ 8f 1996 10m 12m 10f Jun 21] close-coupled, leggy gelding: clearly best effort on third 2-y-o outing: no form in handicaps and claimer (blinkered) in 1996: should stay beyond 8.5f: has joined M. Sowersby. *T. D. Easterby* –

RECESSIONS OVER 5 b.g. Komaite (USA) – Lucky Councillor (Lucky Wednesday 124) [1995 –: a6g 1996 a8g Jan 5] signs of ability but no worthwhile form in fibresand claimers. *N. P. Littmoden* –

RECHULLIN 2 ch.f. (Mar 27) Niniski (USA) 125 – Rechanit (IRE) (Local Suitor (USA) 128) [1996 6.9d³ a7g* Nov 25] 7,500Y: second foal: half-sister to 3-y-o 1¼m winner Simply Katie (by Most Welcome): dam, ran once here then won 4 times in Italy from 5f to 7f, half-sister to very smart middle-distance stayer Sapience: some promise on debut, and won 12-runner fillies maiden auction at Wolverhampton month later: will stay 1¼m+: should continue to progress. *D. R. Loder* 82 p

RECLUSE 5 b.g. Last Tycoon 131 – Nomadic Pleasure 91 (Habitat 134) [1995 –§: 14m 12g 1996 13d 11.1m 15.1f Jun 24] well-made gelding: disappointing performer for several stables, and is one to leave alone. *Miss L. A. Perratt* – §

RECONDITE (IRE) 2 b.c. (Mar 9) Polish Patriot (USA) 128 – Recherchee (Rainbow Quest (USA) 134) [1996 5d² 5m* 6g³ 7m* 8g² 8g Sep 29] 30,000F, IR 52,000Y: useful-looking colt, rather unfurnished: has scope: has a short, round action: second foal: dam unraced daughter of half-sister to Oaks winner Fair Salinia: won maiden at Carlisle in May and 6-runner listed race at Newmarket (by 1¼ lengths from Boojum) in July: 1½ lengths second of 7 to Equal Rights in Futurity Stakes at the Curragh: wrong in coat, tailed off in Royal Lodge Stakes at Ascot in September: stays 1m: yet to race on extremes of going. *M. R. Channon* 99

RECORD LOVER (IRE) 6 b.g. Alzao (USA) 117 – Spun Gold 106 (Thatch (USA) 136) [1995 45d: 10.5d 18m⁴ 16.2f 14.1m 10m⁶ 12m 18m⁴ 16m 14s 18f⁴ 1996 a12g³ a12g³ a16g* a16g a14g⁴ a12g a16g⁴ 18m⁶ 12m² 12g⁶ 11.5m⁵ a14g Nov 4] leggy, close-coupled gelding: poor handicapper at best nowadays: won at Southwell (amateurs) in February: stays 2m: acts on firm ground and all-weather surfaces, probably on soft going. *M. C. Chapman* 33 a43

RECOURSE (USA) 2 b.c. (Feb 4) Alleged (USA) – Queens Only (USA) (Marshua's Dancer (USA)) [1996 8f⁴ 8m⁵ Oct 2] tall, close-coupled, good-topped colt: brother to smart 1991 2-y-o French 1m winner Contested Bid, later third in Prix du Jockey-Club and Irish Derby, and half-brother to several winners here and abroad: dam, 6f or 1m winner in USA, closely related to Native Royalty, smart at around 9f: very green, promising fourth of 10 to Cape Cross in maiden at Doncaster: odds on, only fifth of 6 behind Stowaway at Newcastle following month, carrying head high off bridle and seemingly not letting himself down: should stay at least 1½m: may do better on an easier surface. *H. R. A. Cecil* 78

RED ACUISLE (IRE) 3 br.c. Soviet Lad (USA) 94 – Scottish Gaelic (USA) (Highland Park (USA)) [1995 61: 5m³ 5f² 5m 6m⁵ 5m⁶ 6d⁵ 6s a8.5g² a6g² a7g² a6g⁶ a7g 1996 a6g⁵ a6g a5g³ a5g³ a6g⁶ a5g⁵ Feb 28] modest maiden here: sold 1,800 gns Doncaster March Sales: seems effective from 5f to 8.5f: acts on firm and dead ground 56 and all-weather surfaces: blinkered last 4 starts, visored (well beaten) once: winner over 6f in Sweden. *J. Berry*

RED ADAIR (IRE)   4 ch.g. Waajib 121 – Little Red Hut (Habitat 134) [1995 8m⁵ 7g 7g⁵ 6m 10m 1996 a12g 8m Jun 5] 9,200 2-y-o: ex-Irish gelding: sixth live foal: half-brother to fairly useful 7f winner Orange Place (by Nordance): dam lightly-raced half-sister to Red Regent: fair form (rated 66) at best in 7f/1m maidens for G. Cusack: no form here: tried blinkered. *Bob Jones*   –

RED ADMIRAL   6 ch.g. Formidable (USA) 125 – Dancing Meg (USA) 113 (Marshua's Dancer (USA)) [1995 64, a69: a6g³ a5g 6g 5m 6g* 6m⁵ 6f³ 6f² 5.2m⁵ 6m⁴ 6f* 5m⁵ 1996 6f⁴ 5f⁴ 6g² 7f³ 6m² 6g⁶ 6f⁶ a6g⁶ a6g* a6g Oct 5] heavy-topped, workmanlike gelding: fair handicapper: won at Wolverhampton in September: effective at 5f and 6f: acts on firm ground and the all-weather: has run creditably when sweating: successful for 7-lb claimer: usually bandaged behind: races prominently: refused to enter stalls final intended outing. *C. Murray*   64 a69

REDBROOK LADY   3 ch.f. Clantime 101 – Silently Yours (USA) 53 (Silent Screen (USA)) [1995 43: 5f 5m⁵ 6.1d 5g a5g 1996 6m May 13] sturdy filly: poor sprint maiden: tailed off only 3-y-o outing. *J. M. Jefferson*   –

RED CAMELLIA   2 b.f. (Mar 22) Polar Falcon (USA) 126 – Cerise Bouquet 75 (Mummy's Pet 125) [1996 5.9f* 7.1m* 7d* 8g⁴ Sep 29]   116

'I don't feel that I'm on the same planet. I normally manage one of these every two years or so and now I've had two in less than a week.' Sir Mark Prescott was referring to winning pattern races after saddling Red Camellia in the Crowson Prestige Stakes just days after Pivotal had taken the Nunthorpe for the same owners Cheveley Park Stud. There can have been few easier winners of a pattern race all season than Red Camellia at Goodwood. Admittedly, none her four rivals had shown the same level of form but Fernanda and Queen Sceptre had been placed in listed races and Velour and Mayfair had looked likely to do better. Red Camellia started odds on. In front from the start, she had her opponents off the bridle over two furlongs out, but George Duffield kept her up to her work until inside the final furlong, where, on looking around, he found they had put some ten lengths between themselves and their struggling rivals; after another peek, he eased her right down in the last hundred yards but still had six lengths to spare over Fernanda at the post. It was a smart performance, and sufficiently convincing for her to be quoted 7/1 second favourite for the One Thousand Guineas afterwards behind Cheveley Park Stud's other leading two-year-old filly Dazzle.

Few classic hopes can have made their debut as Red Camellia did, at Carlisle, where she won a six-furlong maiden in June. A month later she took the step up from Carlisle to Sandown and to listed company in her stride, in the Milcars Star Stakes. It was also a step up in distance but connections clearly had no worries where stamina was concerned. Duffield set a searching pace and his mount stayed on strongly to hold the hot favourite Yashmak by two and a half lengths, breaking the two-year-old course record in the process. Prescott summed up the tactics as: 'I told George to go out in front and rattle every bone in the opposition's bodies.'

Unfortunately, some of the bones rattling on her final outing of the season were Red Camellia's. The Goodwood win made her the form pick in the Fillies' Mile at Ascot at the end of September but the highly-regarded Sandown maiden winner Sleepytime was preferred in the betting. Trying the trip for the first time, Red Camellia took a position at the head of the field, setting just a steady pace early on. Turning for home, she soon looked in trouble but kept on gamely until edging left off the rail in the closing stages, hampering Sleepytime before being overtaken by Reams of Verse, Khassah and the favourite, and finishing about one and a half lengths down in fourth. It was subsequently found that Red Camellia had sustained a fracture to her off-fore knee, which probably accounts for her hanging. She was due to be operated on in early-October and was then to go to the Cheveley Park Stud after a period of box rest before being put back into training in January. With Pivotal in his first crop and

Cheveley Park Stud's "Red Camellia"

Red Camellia in his second, Polar Falcon has made an excellent start at the Cheveley Park Stud. He was retired there after enjoying his best season on the track as a four-year-old, successful in the Lockinge Stakes and the Ladbroke Sprint Cup.

Red Camellia (b.f. Mar 22, 1994)	Polar Falcon (USA) (b or br 1987)	Nureyev (b 1977)	Northern Dancer, Special
		Marie d' Argonne (ch 1981)	Jefferson, Mohair
	Cerise Bouquet (b 1982)	Mummy's Pet (b 1968)	Sing Sing, Money For Nothing
		Rosia Bay (b 1977)	High Top, Ouija

Red Camellia's dam, Cerise Bouquet, was sold by Cheveley Park at Tattersalls December Sales in 1995 for 20,000 guineas in foal to Shirley Heights. By then she had produced three winners on the flat—the Irish seven-furlong winner Bourree (by Nordance), the German middle-distance stayer Red Bouquet (by Reference Point) and the fairly useful seven-furlong and mile-and-a-quarter winner Red Azalea (by Shirley Heights). Cerise Bouquet had been through the December Sales ring before, on that occasion fetching 45,000 guineas at the end of her racing career as a two-year-old during which she won a five-furlong maiden at Newbury for Major Hern. She has still some way to go to match the producing records of her dam Rosia Bay and grandam Ouija, who were both useful at around a mile on the track. The former is the dam of Irish St Leger winner Ibn Bey and Yorkshire Oaks winner Roseate Tern while the latter bred Teleprompter and Chatoyant. This is also the family of July Cup winner

Owington who sadly had to be put down at the end of the year after covering just one book of mares.

The lengthy, quite attractive Red Camellia, a short-actioned filly, has shown some of the best form among those of her age and sex and deserves a place in the One Thousand Guineas field, though her future, of course, depends on how she comes out of the operation (it was reported in January that she had made a complete recovery). Before her injury she showed that she could act on firm ground and good to soft. *Sir Mark Prescott*

RED CARNIVAL (USA) 4 b.f. Mr Prospector (USA) – Seaside Attraction 94 (USA) (Seattle Slew (USA)) [1995 109: 7m³ 8g² 7m³ 1996 9m⁴ 8d Oct 11] strong, lengthy filly: useful performer at best: not seen out until late-September in 1996, when below form (found little) in minor event at Newbury and listed race at Ascot: stays 1m: yet to race on extremes of going: bandaged behind final start: carries head awkwardly under pressure. *M. R. Stoute*

RED CHANNEL (IRE) 6 b.g. Import 127 – Winscarlet North (Garland Knight – 92) [1995 –: a7g⁶ 1996 a10g Jan 18] no sign of ability: sold 3,000 gns Ascot June Sales. *T. Casey*

RED EMBERS 2 gr.f. (Mar 27) Saddlers' Hall (IRE) 126 – Kala Rosa 79 (Kala- 64 glow 132) [1996 5.7g⁴ 6g⁵ Jul 1] fourth foal: half-sister to 3-y-o 5f (at 2 yrs) to 7f winner Ortolan (by Prince Sabo) and 1993 2-y-o 6.1f winner Daily Star (by Music Boy): dam lightly-raced maiden, placed over 6f at 2 yrs: won maiden at Bath in May, finishing strongly: gave impression something amiss in minor event at Windsor over a month later. *R. Hannon*

RED FIVE 5 b.g. Clantime 101 – Miami Dolphin 85 (Derrylin 115) [1995 –: a6g 52 6s⁶ 6s 7m a7g 1996 5m² May 18] sturdy, plain gelding: modest maiden, lightly raced: 33/1, almost back to best when second of 14 in apprentice handicap at Hamilton, coming home strongly: not seen out afterwards: stays 6f: acts on soft ground. *J. Berry*

RED GARTER (IRE) 2 b.f. (Feb 4) Common Grounds 118 – Red Magic (Red 52 God 128§) [1996 5s² 5g² 5m⁵ 5m⁵ 5m 5.7m 6g⁶ 7g⁶ a6g⁵ 5f Sep 18] 10,000Y: useful-looking filly: sister to 2 maidens and half-sister to 1985 2-y-o 6f winner D'Artigny (by Dalsaan) and 2m winner As Always (by Hatim): dam lightly-raced sister to smart 1970 Irish 2-y-o Supernatural: modest sprint maiden: below best only start on fibresand: blinkered fifth start (got very stirred up), visored final one: sold 3,000 gns Newmarket Autumn Sales. *K. McAuliffe*

RED GUARD 2 ch.c. (Feb 14) Soviet Star (USA) 128 – Zinzara (USA) 119 (Stage 86 Door Johnny) [1996 7m 7m³ 8g⁴ Oct 30] big, useful-looking colt: has plenty of scope: half-brother to useful 1½m winner Zinsky and smart stayer Romany Rye (both by Nijinsky): dam 6f and 1¼m winner: third to Mashhaer in 16-runner maiden at Newmarket, making most: stumbled at halfway when well beaten in maiden at Yarmouth later in month: should be suited by further than 7f. *G. Wragg*

RED HOT RISK 4 b.g. Risk Me (FR) 127 – Hot Sunday Sport 42 (Star Appeal – § 133) [1995 –§: 5m 7g 7m 10m 8m 1996 a8g Jan 12] compact gelding: no form for some time: temperamental and best left alone. *S. W. Campion*

RED INDIAN 10 ch.g. Be My Native (USA) 122 – Martialette (Welsh Saint 126) – [1995 36, a52: a12g* a11g⁵ a12g⁴ a12g³ 10m 9.9d⁵ a11g⁴ 1996 a12g a12g⁶ a12g May 9] tall, lengthy gelding: poor middle-distance performer: showed little in 1996. *B. Richmond*

RED LEO (USA) 3 b.g. Crafty Prospector (USA) – Lucky Brook (USA) (What – Luck (USA)) [1995 NR 1996 5d Apr 13] $87,000Y: strong gelding: half-brother to Spot Prize (by Seattle Dancer), 5f winner at 2 yrs and fourth in Oaks, and to 2 minor winners in USA: dam won 4 races in USA at up to 7f: burly and green, showed little in maiden at Warwick: sold 750 gns Ascot July Sales. *P. F. I. Cole*

RED LIGHT 4 b.g. Reprimand 122 – Trull (Lomond (USA) 128) [1995 71: 8.1m⁶ – 10g⁶ 8s⁵ 12d⁶ 1996 14.1m⁵ Jun 5] sparely-made gelding: fair handicapper at best in 1995 for Lord Huntingdon: no promise on return: should be suited by further than 1m (shapes as if stays 1½m): acts on soft ground: tried visored: unreliable hurdler. *J. R. Jenkins*

RED MARCH HARE 5 b.m. Daring March 116 – Happy Harriet (Red Sunset 35
120) [1995 –: a8g 1996 6m 8.1m 7.1m² Sep 23] angular mare: poor and lightly-raced
maiden: seems effective from 7f to 1¼m: acts on good to firm and dead ground.
D. Moffatt

RED NYMPH 3 b.f. Sharpo 132 – Red Gloves 83 (Red God 128§) [1995 91?: 6m³ 95
6m* 6m⁴ 7d 1996 6g² 6m 6m⁴ 6g⁴ 6g⁶ 6v Oct 6] tall filly: fairly useful handicapper:
best effort when always-prominent fourth of 16 to Wildwood Flower in £14,500
event at Goodwood: flashed tail under pressure next time, ran poorly on heavy
ground on final start: sold 28,000 gns Newmarket Autumn Sales: stays 6f: acts on
good to firm ground: sent to Saudi Arabia. *W. Jarvis*

RED O'REILLY 4 ch.g. Hubbly Bubbly (USA) – Name The Game 66 (Fair Sea- –
son 120) [1995 47: 6g a6g 6.1g 6.1m⁵ 8g a8g 1996 a12g Mar 9] workmanlike
gelding: poor maiden plater: tried visored/blinkered: sold 1,000 gns Doncaster
November Sales. *J. L. Eyre*

RED PHANTOM (IRE) 4 ch.g. Kefaah (USA) 124 – Highland Culture (Lom- 66
ond (USA) 128) [1995 71: a7g⁴ a12g³ a12g* a9.4g* 1996 a12g a12g³ a14g³ a11g³
a12g⁵ 12d a12g³ Nov 16] fair performer: stays 1½m: acts on fibresand, no show only
turf outing. *S. Mellor*

RED RAINBOW 8 b.h. Rainbow Quest (USA) 134 – Red Berry 115 (Great –
Nephew 126) [1995 NR 1996 10s 8g Nov 2] tall horse: rated 95 here at 3 yrs and
showed useful form to win 3 of 6 races in Dubai in 1993/4: not seen until late-October
in 1996, when well beaten in large fields of handicappers. *B. Hanbury*

RED RAJA 3 b.g. Persian Heights 129 – Jenny Splendid 101 (John Splendid 116) –
[1995 –: 7f 7g 6m 7.3d 1996 12m 16.1f⁶ 12.1s Oct 22] workmanlike gelding: signs of
ability but no worthwhile form on flat: probably a stayer: fairly useful winner over
hurdles. *P. Mitchell*

RED ROBBO (CAN) 3 b.c. Red Ransom (USA) – Aunt Jobiska (USA) (What 93
Luck (USA)) [1995 92: 7g* 8d⁵ 1996 8.1g³ 10.3g May 9] good-topped colt: carries
condition: fairly useful form: 3 lengths third of 7 to Regal Archive in minor event at
Sandown on reappearance: upset in stalls, last of 7 in listed race at Chester 2 weeks
later: stays 1m. *H. R. A. Cecil*

RED ROMANCE 2 b.g. (Mar 12) Prince Daniel (USA) – Rio Piedras 86 (Kala 60 d
Shikari 125) [1996 5m³ 5g² 6g 5m² 5g³ 5f² 5m⁴ 7.1s⁶ Nov 7] 750F, 850Y: first living
foal: dam ideally suited by around 1¼m: modest maiden: best form at 5f on top-of-
the-ground: broke out of stalls intended seventh start. *Denys Smith*

RED ROSES STORY (FR) 4 ch.f. Pink (FR) 123 – Roses For The Star (USA) 118
114 (Stage Door Johnny) [1995 12s* 12g* 12d² 1996 10.5s* 10g² 12f² 15.5d* Oct

*Prix Royal-Oak, Longchamp—a first try at staying distances for Red Roses Story
results in a Group 1 victory over Moonax and Helen of Spain*

27] eighth foal: half-sister to 2 winners, notably Centenary (allowance at around 1m in USA, by Alydar): dam 7f (at 2 yrs) and 1¾m winner, second in Oaks and Park Hill: smart French filly: unraced at 2 yrs: won minor events at Chantilly and Saint-Cloud at 3 yrs: ridden by 5-lb claimer, won well-contested minor event at Evry in February: second to Gunboat Diplomacy in Prix Exbury at Saint-Cloud and to Percutant in listed race at Longchamp in the spring: off course 6½ months, best effort to win slowly-run 5-runner Prix Royal-Oak at Longchamp by ½ length from Moonax: sold 320,000 gns Newmarket December Sales: stays 15.5f: acts on soft going and firm: consistent. *Mme Pat Barbe, France*

RED RUSTY (USA)   3 ch.g. The Carpenter (USA) – Super Sisters (AUS) (Call –
Report (USA)) [1995 69: a8g a8.5g² a8g* 1996 7m a9.4g a8g³ 8.2f⁵ a10g⁶ a8g⁶   a56 d
11.4m a8.5g 8g a10g Dec 30] strong, workmanlike gelding: modest maiden at best: out of form at end of 1996, leaving D. Morris after penultimate start: should stay beyond 8.5f: acts on equitrack and fibresand, no form on turf: tried blinkered. *P. R. Hedger*

REDSKIN LADY   3 ch.f. Indian Ridge 123 – Meritsu (IRE) 54 (Lyphard's   55
Special (USA) 122) [1995 NR 1996 7m 8g 7.1d⁵ 6f⁴ 6m³ 6g² 7m 7g 6m a6g Nov 18] compact filly: has a short action: second foal: sister to fairly useful 1994 2-y-o 6f and 7f winner (in Italy) Spaghetti House: dam, maiden, best form at 1m/1¼m: modest maiden: behind last 4 starts, leaving D. Elsworth after second of them: stays 7f: acts on firm and dead ground. *R. J. O'Sullivan*

RED SKY DELIGHT (IRE)   3 b.f. Skyliner 117 – Blazing Sunset 55 (Blazing   –
Saddles (AUS)) [1995 –: 5d 5m 6f⁶ 5g 6f 6g 1996 10f 6.9m 9.7f Jun 28] leggy filly: seems of little account. *P. Butler*

RED SPECTACLE (IRE)   4 b.g. Red Sunset 120 – Buz Kashi 123 (Bold Lad   53
(IRE) 133) [1995 62: a8g⁶ a9.4g* a8g a9.4g⁶ 10g 10m 12.1m³ 9.2m² 11.1f² 11.1f⁴   a56
12m 12h* 14.1m* 1996 a16g³ a13g⁴ a16g a12g³ a12g⁴ 14.1m 13g⁵ 14.1f 12.1g³ 15.1m 13m³ 13m⁴ Aug 14] quite good-topped gelding: modest handicapper: effective at 1¾m, and probably stays 2m: acts on the all-weather and on hard going, possibly unsuited by soft: well beaten only try in blinkers: usually a front runner: winning hurdler. *P. C. Haslam*

REDSPET   2 ch.f. (Apr 10) Tina's Pet 121 – Manabel 73 (Manado 130) [1996 5m
Oct 29] third living foal: dam effective from 5f to 9f: 25/1, showed nothing in median auction maiden at Redcar. *S. R. Bowring*

REDSTELLA (USA)   7 ch.h. Theatrical 128 – Orange Squash 78 (Red God   –
128§) [1995 68: 10.5g⁵ 11.9m⁴ 1996 12g 11.9m⁵ 13.1s⁴ a14g⁶ Jul 22] big, good-topped horse: fairly useful performer (rated 87) at 4 yrs: very much on the downgrade: finished lame final start: stays 1½m: acts on good to firm and heavy going: tried visored: held up. *R. M. Whitaker*

RED TEST (USA)   2 b.g. (Feb 17) Glitterman (USA) – Cut Test (USA) (Relaunch   63 +
(USA)) [1996 a6g⁵ a5g² 5m³ 5f⁴ a5g Aug 16] $14,000Y: second foal: dam won at up to 9f in USA: sire very smart sprinter at 5 yrs: modest maiden: gelded after third start: blinkered, raced freely and alone when running poorly in seller on final one: sold 3,500 gns Newmarket Autumn Sales: best form at 5f: acts on firm ground and fibresand: races prominently. *W. A. O'Gorman*

RED TIE AFFAIR (USA)   3 b.c. Miswaki (USA) 124 – Quiet Rendezvous   54
(USA) (Nureyev (USA) 131) [1995 –: 8g 1996 a8g⁴ 7f 7m 7m⁵ 10.8m⁶ a12g 10m³ 12m 10m⁶ 12.1g⁶ Sep 29] good-bodied colt: modest maiden handicapper: ran twice in Dubai early in year: sold (M. Bell to J. M. Bradley) 4,500 gns Newmarket Autumn Sales: stays 1¼m, possibly not 1½m: has raced only on a sound surface: visored sixth to eighth 3-y-o starts: often bandaged near fore. *M. Bell*

RED TIME   3 br.g. Timeless Times (USA) 99 – Crimson Dawn (Manado 130)   56
[1995 39: 6.1g⁵ 5g⁵ 1996 a8.5g 5.1g⁵ 7f³ 6s³ 8g 6g 5.1m⁶ 6m⁶ 7m⁵ 5f 5m Sep 25] rather leggy gelding: modest maiden handicapper: stays 7f: acts on firm and soft ground, well beaten only all-weather outing: usually races prominently. *M. S. Saunders*

RED VALERIAN   5 b.g. Robellino (USA) 127 – Fleur Rouge 71 (Pharly (FR)   77
130) [1995 76, a89: a7g* a8g² a8g² a8g⁶ 8g 10.8d² 10m 10f⁴ 10.3m² 10.3g³ 8.3m³   a–
1996 8f 10g⁴ 10m* 10v² Aug 27] close-coupled gelding: fairly useful handicapper

on the all-weather, fair on turf: won at Redcar in August: stayed 10.8f: acted on equitrack and on any turf going: visored (below form) once at 2 yrs, usually blinkered: sometimes bandaged off-hind: fairly useful hurdler, winner twice in 1996/7 but broke down in October: dead. *G. M. Moore*

RED VIPER 4 b.g. Posen (USA) – Within A Whisper (Welsh Pageant 132) [1995 – NR 1996 11.9f³ 10m 8m 8m 11.6d 8f Aug 22] close-coupled, workmanlike gelding: fifth foal: dam unraced: behind in 3 NH Flat races in the spring: well beaten afterwards on flat. *N. M. Lampard*

REDWING 2 b.g. (Apr 2) Reprimand 122 – Bronzewing 103 (Beldale Flutter 83 + (USA) 130) [1996 7m³ 7m* 8.3g⁶ Sep 29] big, leggy, workmanlike gelding: fifth foal: half-brother to 2m winner Sun Grebe (by Arctic Tern): dam 6f and 1m winner: won 13-runner maiden at Newcastle in August by a head from Hurricane State: only sixth of 7 on easier ground in minor event at Hamilton: should stay 1m. *J. L. Dunlop*

REED MY LIPS (IRE) 5 br.g. Thatching 131 – Taunsa 85 (Nishapour (FR) 125) – [1995 38: 10.3g 8m 8f 6.9f⁶ 8.1g³ 8g 7g² 8f 7.1m³ 7.5g⁵ 7f 8.1d 7.1g⁵ 10.5s 1996 7s 8d 8m 8m 10.3m⁴ Jun 26] angular gelding: poor performer: little worthwhile form in 1996. *B. P. J. Baugh*

REEFA'S MILL (IRE) 4 b.g. Astronef 116 – Pharly's Myth (Pharly (FR) 130) – [1995 71: 8.3m² 8.5m² 7m⁵ 9m² 10g⁵ 1996 10g 10.8f 9.9f⁴ 10.8f 8m Aug 8] lengthy gelding: fair maiden in 1995 for J. Hills, but seems to have deteriorated badly: likely to prove suited by middle distances: has raced only on a sound surface: visored/blinkered last 3 starts. *J. Neville*

REEF RAIDER 3 gr.g. Siberian Express (USA) 125 – Superior Quality 67 (Star – Appeal 133) [1995 –: 6g 6m 6m 8.3g 10m 8.2m 1996 10d 14.1g Apr 8] leggy gelding: no form, including in seller: tried blinkered. *N. Tinkler*

REEM FEVER (IRE) 3 b.f. Fairy King (USA) – Jungle Jezebel 107 (Thatching 68 d 131) [1995 5g 6m³ 1996 5s⁴ 7s⁵ 6g⁶ 7d⁵ 7m⁶ 7g 7g 6.1m 9.7d a7g a10g Dec 20] 66,000Y: workmanlike ex-Irish filly: third reported foal: half-sister to a winner over jumps in France by Ti King: dam, 2-y-o 7f winner who stayed 1m, granddaughter of Irish 1000 Guineas winner Lady Capulet: disappointing maiden, rated 79 on final 2-y-o start: sold out of D. Weld's stable 11,000 gns Newmarket July Sales after fifth 3-y-o start: well held in Britain: probably stays 7f: tried blinkered. *D. W. P. Arbuthnot*

REFERENDUM (IRE) 2 b.c. (Feb 21) Common Grounds 118 – Final Decision 107 (Tap On Wood 130) [1996 5.2d³ 6f² 6g* 7g² 8g⁴ Oct 13] 48,000Y, IR 35,000Y: good-topped colt: has scope: fourth foal: fourth foal: half-brother to 1993 2-y-o 5f winner Sweet Decision and half-brother to 2 winners abroad, notably useful 4-y-o 7f (at 2 yrs) to 1½m winner Kill The Crab (by Petorius): dam Irish middle-distance winner: first run for over 3 months, won 19-runner median auction maiden at Goodwood in August by 7 lengths: useful form last 2 starts, ½-length second of 10 to Desert King in National Stakes at the Curragh (caught close home) and 6¼ lengths fourth of 9 to Revoque in Grand Criterium at Longchamp: stays 1m: front runner. *G. Lewis*

REFUSE TO LOSE 2 ch.c. (Feb 24) Emarati (USA) 74 – Petrol 73 (Troy 137) 74 p [1996 6m⁵ 6g* Oct 29] 10,000F, 40,000Y: big, good-topped colt with plenty of scope: seventh foal: brother to 4-y-o 1¼m winner Westcourt Princess and half-brother to several winners, including Dhakrah (2m, by Touching Wood): dam won at 1m and stayed 1¼m: 11/10 favourite, won 12-runner maiden at Leicester by 1¼ lengths from Mr Paradise, leading over 3f out, clear inside last and eased: will stay 1m: likeable type, sure to do better. *J. M. P. Eustace*

REGAIT 2 b.c. (May 13) In The Wings 128 – Rowa 83 (Great Nephew 126) [1996 – p 8m 8.2s Oct 31] quite attractive colt: has a rounded action: seventh foal: half-brother to fairly useful 11f and 1¾m winner Barrish (by Wassl) and middle-distance winner (useful in Norway in 1996) Laila Alawi (by Mtoto): dam best at 1¼m but a disappointing maiden, half-sister to Oh So Sharp and Roussalka: never on terms in maidens at Newmarket and Nottingham: looked a long-term prospect. *M. A. Jarvis*

REGAL ACADEMY (IRE) 2 b.f. (Jan 9) Royal Academy (USA) 130 – 66 p Polistatic 53 (Free State 125) [1996 7m⁶ Sep 10] first foal: dam, 11f and 1½m winner, sister to smart middle-distance winner Mango Express and Ebor winner Western Dancer: 50/1, about 6 lengths sixth of 12 to Indihash in maiden at Lingfield, green and losing place at halfway then staying on well not knocked about: sure to improve. *C. A. Horgan*

REGAL ARCHIVE (IRE)   3 b.c. Fairy King (USA) – Marseillaise (Artaius   109
(USA) 129) [1995 NR 1996 7g* 8.1g* 8d* 9m⁵ 9g* 10f Aug 25] 30,000Y: strong,
lengthy colt: has a quick action: fifth foal: half-brother to fairly useful 1m winner
Leonova (by Alzao) and 6-y-o German winner (at up to 1¼m) Field of Stars (by
Salse): dam unraced half-sister to Irish 2000 Guineas winner Northern Treasure:
useful performer: won maiden at Kempton, minor event at Sandown and listed race
at Kempton (narrowly beat Sorbie Tower and Wixim) in the spring: decidedly
lethargic in preliminaries, moved poorly to post and did not go with usual zest in Prix
Jean Prat at Chantilly in June: won 4-runner Prix Daphnis at Maisons-Laffitte in July
by 1½ lengths from Brindle: stiff task, towards rear in Secretariat Stakes at Arlington
on final start: stays 9f well and should get 1¼m: best efforts on an easy surface:
bandaged behind. *P. W. Chapple-Hyam*

REGAL EAGLE   3 b.c. Shirley Heights 130 – On The Tiles (Thatch (USA) 136)   72
[1995 –: 7m 1996 10d 10.5d 12m⁵ 13.3m 11.6d Aug 12] angular, good-bodied colt:
fair maiden: well beaten last 2 starts: sold 8,000 gns Newmarket Autumn Sales: stays
1½m well. *I. A. Balding*

REGAL EQUITY   2 b.c. (Apr 30) Keen 116 – Nazmiah 73 (Free State 125) [1996   64
6f 7f⁶ 5m³ 6g 5f 5.2g⁴ 5d Nov 8] strong, sturdy colt: has a round action: second foal:
dam stayed 1½m: fair form: well held from unfavourable draw in nursery at Doncaster on final start: should prove effective at 6f: poor effort in blinkers fifth start.
B. J. Meehan

REGAL FANFARE (IRE)   4 b.f. Taufan (USA) 119 – Tender Time (Tender   57
King 123) [1995 69: 8m 7f⁵ 8f 7m² 7f⁵ 10m⁶ 11.9g 1996 5.3f⁵ 6.9m 6m 5.9f³ 6g 7g⁴
7g² 7g a7g Nov 15] smallish filly: modest performer at best in 1996: should stay
beyond 7f: acts on good to firm ground: often blinkered: wandered under pressure
sixth and seventh starts. *Mrs L. Stubbs*

REGAL PATROL   2 b.g. (Mar 19) Red Ransom (USA) – River Patrol 96   72
(Rousillon (USA) 133) [1996 6m⁴ 7.1m⁴ Jun 14] 26,000F, 170,000Y: well-made
gelding: has a quick action: first foal: dam 10.2f winner who should have been better
at 1½m, half-sister to smart middle-distance stayer Dry Dock from the family of
Bireme and Buoy: heavily-backed favourite when fourth in maiden at Yarmouth on
debut, losing action and position 2f out then running on again close up after rider had
almost given up: hung left when over 10 lengths fourth of 9 to Putra in similar event
at Sandown 9 days later: will stay at least 1m: gelded: looked sort to do better.
M. R. Stoute

REGAL REPRIMAND   2 b.c. (Mar 17) Reprimand 122 – Queen Caroline   – p
(USA) 67 (Chief's Crown (USA)) [1996 7f 8.1s Oct 22] 16,000Y: strong, close-
coupled colt: first foal: dam maiden (stayed 10.5f) half-sister to smart 1986 2-y-o
Glory Forever, later third in Poule d'Essai des Poulains: backward and bandaged
behind, soon off bridle then modest late progress in maiden at Warwick on debut:
again better than distance beaten suggests in maiden at Chepstow (eased): should do
better. *G. Lewis*

REGAL SPLENDOUR (CAN)   3 ch.g. Vice Regent (CAN) – Seattle Princess   71
(USA) (Seattle Slew (USA)) [1995 NR 1996 8d 7m² 8.2m 7f² 7s Oct 24] $140,000Y:
good-topped gelding: first foal: dam never ran: easily best effort in maidens when
neck second of 15 to Jumairah Sunset at Lingfield on second start, pair racing alone
on far side: sold (P. Cole to R. O'Sullivan) 11,000 gns Newmarket Autumn Sales:
should prove effective over 1m: acts on firm ground, may be unsuited by soft.
P. F. I. Cole

REGAL THUNDER (USA)   2 b.c. (Feb 15) Chief's Crown (USA) – Summer-   76 p
time Showers (USA) (Raise A Native) [1996 7m⁵ Oct 3] $15,000Y: first foal: dam,
won at up to 7f at 2 yrs in USA, sister to very useful sprinter Wonder Dancer and
half-sister to useful middle-distance performer Lindon Lime: 7/1, around 6 lengths
fifth of 16 to Mashhaer in maiden at Newmarket, running green after slow start then
good late progress: will improve. *M. R. Stoute*

REGIMENT (IRE)   3 gr.c. Shaadi (USA) 126 – Rossaldene 79 (Mummy's Pet   107
125) [1995 87: 6g* 7.1m² 1996 8g* 8m a9.5s⁵ 8.5g⁵ 9f a7s⁵ a8.5f Oct 3] tall, rather
unfurnished colt: has a fluent action: sweating and edgy (quietly to post), useful form

when winning falsely-run listed race at Kempton on reappearance by length from Centre Stalls, idling and wandering after leading over 1f out: last of 13 in 2000 Guineas (jockey glanced down a couple of times as if something possibly amiss) final outing for R. Hannon: disappointing in USA, well beaten in $50,000 claimer at Belmont last time: should prove best at up to 1m. *N. Zito, USA*

REHAAB 3 b.f. Mtoto 134 – Top Treat (USA) 101 (Topsider (USA)) [1995 NR 72 1996 8m² 10m* 10.1m 11.9f⁵ Sep 4] fourth foal: sister to 13f and 1¾m winner Ela Man Howa: dam, 6f winner, stayed 1m: fair form when winning maiden at Nottingham in July by 2 lengths from Agdistis (pair clear): disappointing in handicaps both subsequent outings: sold only 2,800 gns Newmarket December Sales: stays 1¼m, possibly not 1½m: takes keen hold. *A. C. Stewart*

REHEARSAL (IRE) 2 b.g. (May 2) Royal Academy (USA) 130 – Yashville 73 (Top Ville 129) [1996 6m³ 7g 7g³ Jul 12] 24,000Y: useful-looking gelding: fifth foal: half-brother to 7f to 8.3f winner Boldville Bash (by Bold Arrangement) and a winner in Belgium by Persian Heights: dam unraced: best effort in maidens when visored in 5-runner race at York on final start, finishing 4½ lengths third of 5 to Flaming West: should stay beyond 7f. *C. A. Cyzer*

REIMEI 7 b.g. Top Ville 129 – Brilliant Reay 74 (Ribero 126) [1995 71: 12s³ 12m 74 1996 12g⁵ 12m* 13.3f 16.2m 12g Oct 11] tall, angular gelding: fair handicapper: easily best effort in 1996 when winning steadily-run event at Newmarket in June: should be suited by further than 1½m: acts on good to firm ground and soft: none too consistent. *R. Akehurst*

REINHARDT (IRE) 3 b.g. Bluebird (USA) 125 – Rhein Bridge 107 (Rheingold 81 d 137) [1995 84+: 7f³ 7m² 6m 7g² 10.2m³ 1996 8d³ 12d³ 8f⁵ 8m⁴ 8g 12f⁴ 10.1f 8.3m 9.9g 11f⁶ Sep 27] angular gelding: good mover: fairly useful maiden at best, but deteriorated with virtually every outing in 1996, sold out of P. Chapple-Hyam's stable 7,600 gns Newmarket July Sales after fifth one: should stay 1½m: blinkered final start: a hard ride: has looked reluctant, and one to treat with caution. *J. S. Wainwright*

REITERATE 3 b.f. Then Again 126 – Indubitable 87 (Sharpo 132) [1995 –p: 7d⁵ 1996 10g 10m 12g 11.6g 12g Aug 14] good-bodied filly: no worthwhile form. *G. B. Balding*

REJOICING (IRE) 2 b.f. (Feb 28) Damister (USA) 123 – Rocket Alert 110 (Red 75 Alert 127) [1996 6m⁴ 7m² 6m³ Aug 22] heavy-topped filly: sister to 6f/7f winners Miss Gorgeous and Rejoice and half-sister to French 3-y-o 8.5f winner Winning Pearl (by Great Commotion) and useful 1¼m and 10.6f winner Ardlui (by Lomond): dam 6f and 7f winner: fair form in maidens and in 2-runner Yarmouth minor event: stays 7f. *W. A. O'Gorman*

RELATIVELY HIGH 5 b.m. Persian Heights 129 – Kissin' Cousin 74 (Be – Friendly 130) [1995 NR 1996 8.1m Jun 30] no worthwhile form. *P. Bowen*

RELIQUARY (USA) 2 b.g. (May 6) Zilzal (USA) 137 – Reloy (USA) 119 99 (Liloy (FR) 124) [1996 6m* 7f⁴ 6g³ Oct 12] strong, close-coupled gelding: has plenty of scope: fifth foal: closely related to useful 1994 2-y-o 5f and 6f winner Loyalize (by Nureyev) and half-brother to a winner in North America by Secreto: dam won 10.5f Prix de Royaumont and Grade 1 events at 9f and 1¼m in USA: odds-on chance, won maiden at Haydock in July, always travelling well: looked sure to improve a good deal, but rather disappointing in Champagne Stakes (got upset in stalls) at Doncaster and listed event at York (found little off bridle when third to Nightbird): subsequently gelded: bred to stay 1m: will have to settle to fulfil his potential. *D. R. Loder*

REMAADI SUN 4 gr.g. Cadeaux Genereux 131 – Catch The Sun (Kalaglow 132) 89 [1995 –: 10m 10g 10m⁴ 9m a8g a8g³ a9.4g 1996 6s 10d³ 10s⁶ 10m* 11.9m* 12g⁵ 12m⁶ 16.1m 11.9g⁴ 18.7m 13.9m⁵ 11.9f⁵ 13.3m⁴ 12g Sep 29] lengthy gelding: carries condition: has a round action: fairly useful handicapper: won at Pontefract and York (idled) in the spring: very good staying-on fifth of 21 to Clerkenwell in the Ebor at York: stays 1¾m well: acts on good to firm and dead ground: edgy (ran creditably) sixth 4-y-o start: usually set plenty to do: usually ridden by R. Street. *M. D. I. Usher*

REMEMBER STAR 3 ch.f. Don't Forget Me 127 – Star Girl Gay (Lord Gayle – (USA) 124) [1995 NR 1996 7d 11d 7f 12d May 22] unfurnished filly: half-sister to winners in Germany at up to 9f by Salt Dome and Be My Native: dam Irish middle-distance maiden: bandaged, in rear in maidens and claimers: has joined A. Smith. *A. G. Newcombe*

REMONTANT (IRE)   4 ch.f. Al Hareb (USA) 123 – Red Red Rose (USA) 90 [Blushing Groom (FR) 131] [1995 40: a7g³ 14.1m⁵ a14.8g a12g⁵ 14.1f 12g² 12m³ 12m³ 14.1h⁴ 11d³ 14.1m⁶ a12g 1996 12.3g a9.4g 12f⁶ 10m² 18m 12.5f Jun 24] close-coupled filly: poor mover: poor maiden plater: sold 1,450 gns Doncaster October Sales: stays 1¾m: acts on good to firm and dead ground and on fibresand: has looked unenthusiastic. *R. Hollinshead*   **34**

REMSKI   2 b.c. (Apr 6) Risk Me (FR) 127 – Dona Krista 84 (King of Spain 121) [1996 5g Apr 27] 10,000F, 30,000Y resold 20,000Y: good-topped colt: has scope: fourth foal (all by Risk Me): brother to sprinter Risky, smart at 2 yrs: dam 2-y-o 6f winner with best run at 7f: co-favourite, tailed off in 10-runner median auction maiden at Leicester: sold 1,200 gns Newmarket Autumn Sales. *M. A. Jarvis*   **–**

RENATA'S PRINCE (IRE)   3 b.g. Prince Rupert (FR) 121 – Maria Renata (Jaazeiro (USA) 127) [1995 5d 5m 6m⁵ 1996 12.5d⁶ 9m⁵ 9m* 10g⁴ 9g 8d 10f a10g a9.4g Dec 7] ex-Irish gelding: half-brother to several winners, including 6-y-o 6f to 1m performer Keston Pond (by Taufan) and Irish 1½m winner Christmas Snow (by Petorius): dam, placed twice at 1m in Ireland, half-sister to dam of Middle Park winner Balla Cove: fair handicapper at best: won at Tipperary in May third last outing for Mrs. J. Harrington: soundly beaten afterwards: stays 1¼m: acts on good to firm ground: blinkered (out of form) seventh 3-y-o start. *K. R. Burke*   **77 d**

RENNYHOLME   5 ch.g. Rich Charlie 117 – Jacqui Joy 63 (Music Boy 124) [1995 –: 5m 7g 10g a6g a5g⁶ 1996 a5g⁴ a6g a5g² a5g² a5g³ a5g* 5g a5g a5g³ a5g³ a5g a7g a5g a5g Dec 28] leggy, close-coupled gelding: modest 5f performer at best: gained first success in seller at Wolverhampton in March: acts on the all-weather, lightly raced and no form on turf: normally blinkered. *J. Hetherton*   **a60 d**

RENO'S TREASURE (USA)   3 ch.f. Beau Genius (CAN) – Ligia M (USA) (Noholme Jr (USA)) [1995 NR 1996 7g 8.2f⁵ 10m⁵ 10.1m⁵ 10d Aug 25] 10,500 2-y-o: tall, rather sparely-made filly: half-sister to numerous minor winners in USA: dam won 3 times at 3 yrs in USA: little sign of ability. *J. A. Harris*   **–**

RENOWN   4 b.g. Soviet Star (USA) 128 – Starlet 119 (Teenoso (USA) 135) [1995 72: a8g⁴ a7g* a8.5g² a8g⁵ a10g* 1996 a10g a10g* 10m 11.9f* 9g 10g² a12g Dec 7] small, angular gelding: fair handicapper: won at Lingfield (under 5-lb claimer) in March and Brighton (slowly-run race) in June: stays 11.9f: acts on firm ground, goes well on the all-weather: races prominently: inconsistent. *Lord Huntingdon*   **75
a80**

RENZO (IRE)   3 b.g. Alzao (USA) 117 – Watership (USA) (Foolish Pleasure (USA)) [1995 NR 1996 10g⁴ 10.2f² 10m² 14m³ 11f* Nov 5] strong gelding: sixth foal: half-brother to useful 10.2f to 2¼m (Cesarewitch) winner Captain's Guest (by Be My Guest): dam poor in USA: fairly useful performer: awarded handicap at Redcar in November after being beaten neck by Blurred: effective at 11f but gives impression he'll be suited by return to 1½m+ (stays 1¾m): yet to race on a soft surface (acts on firm ground): slowly away first 3 starts: tends to wander and carry head high: probably ungenuine: gelded. *G. Harwood*   **84 §**

REPERTORY   3 b.g. Anshan 119 – Susie's Baby (Balidar 133) [1995 84: 5m² 5.1m² 5g* 1996 5g² 5g 6m 5g 6s Oct 24] tall, angular gelding: fairly useful form early at 2 yrs (subsequently said by trainer to have had a muscle problem): good second of 6 to Westcourt Magic in listed race at Haydock on reappearance: stiffish tasks in rated stakes afterwards, well beaten last 2 starts: sold to join M. Saunders 8,500 gns Newmarket Autumn Sales: should stay 6f. *M. R. Channon*   **89**

REPLOY   3 gr.f. Deploy 131 – Nelly Do Da 78 (Derring-Do 131) [1995 66: 7.1s⁴ a8g⁶ 1996 a8.5g² a11g³ 13.8g Oct 19] modest maiden: beaten long way out (after 8-month absence) on final outing: should be suited by at least 1½m: acts on soft ground and fibresand, well beaten on equitrack. *Lord Huntingdon*   **60**

REQUESTED   9 b.g. Rainbow Quest (USA) 134 – Melody Hour 105 (Sing Sing 134) [1995 60d: 11.8d 16m 14.1m³ 14m* 14s² 14g² 16.4m⁵ 14d 16.2s 16m 14.1m⁶ 16.4m 1996 14d⁵ 16.2f² 16.2m 14.1d⁴ 14.4g 16m² Sep 16] leggy, sparely-made gelding: poor mover: modest handicapper: ran well despite very slow start final outing: stays 2½m: acts on any going: sometimes blinkered in the past, rarely nowadays: not one to place maximum faith in. *P. Burgoyne*   **55**

REQUIN BLEU (IRE)　3 b.c. Thatching 131 – Robertet (USA) 118 (Roberto　105 (USA) 131) [1995 NR 1996 7s* 7g* 8d² 7m Jun 19] tall colt: second foal: half-brother to useful French 1995 3-y-o 7f and 1¼m winner Redwood Falls (by Dancing Brave): dam won Grand Prix de Deauville and stayed 15.5f: useful performer: won 22-runner maiden at the Curragh in March and minor event at Naas in May: never going well (showed quick action, first race on top-of-the-ground) in Jersey Stakes at Royal Ascot: stays 1m: acts on soft ground: blinkered/visored last 2 starts. *A. P. O'Brien, Ireland*

RESOUNDER (USA)　3 b.g. Explodent (USA) – Rub Al Khali (USA) (Mr　– Prospector (USA)) [1995 102: 6g 6m* 6f² 6d⁴ 6g⁵ 6g* 6m² 1996 6m⁴ 6m⁶ 7.1g⁴ 7g 7m Oct 4] useful-looking gelding: useful performer at 2 yrs: well held in 1996, visored final start. *J. H. M. Gosden*

RESPECTABLE JONES　10 ch.g. Tina's Pet 121 – Jonesee 64 (Dublin Taxi)　– [1995 42, a52: a7g² a6g a6g⁴ a7g³ a8g 8.2g⁶ 6m 7m⁵ 8m⁵ 7g 5.9f* 7g a7g⁴ a7g 1996　a54 d a7g⁴ a6g³ a6g³ a6g 5f 5.9f 6d⁶ 7f a7g Nov 2] leggy, lengthy gelding: poor performer on turf nowadays, modest on the all-weather: soundly beaten last 5 starts: effective at 6f to 1m: used to act on any turf going: effective visored/blinkered or not: usually held up. *R. Hollinshead*

RESPECT A SECRET　4 ch.f. Respect 95 – Pendle's Secret 73 (Le Johnstan　48 123) [1995 –: 7.1m 5m⁴ 8f⁴ 6g 6g 1996 7m 6m* 5f³ 7m Jun 18] strong, angular filly: 16/1, first worthwhile form when winning 18-runner amateurs maiden handicap at Redcar in May: destroyed after finishing lame at Thirsk following month: best efforts at sprint distances: raced only on a sound surface. *S. E. Kettlewell*

RESPECTING　3 b.g. Respect 95 – Pricey (Silly Prices 110) [1995 NR 1996 12d⁵　62 10m 8s³ 7m Jul 29] good-topped gelding: first reported foal: dam never ran: only sign of ability in maidens when 13 lengths third of 9 to Sabrak at Ayr. *Denys Smith*

RESTATE (IRE)　5 b.m. Soviet Star (USA) 128 – Busca (USA) 49 (Mr Pros-　52 pector (USA)) [1995 NR 1996 a8.5g³ a8g⁵ Feb 3] 2,800 4-y-o: angular mare: fourth living foal: half-sister to several winners, including useful 8.5f winner Blisland (by Danehill): dam (stayed 9.4f) out of Kentucky Oaks winner Bag of Tunes: unraced on flat (injured after rearing in stalls in 1994) until 5 yrs, better effort when 10 lengths third of 8 to Ocean Park in maiden at Wolverhampton on debut: sold 575 gns Ascot December Sales. *F. Murphy*

RESTLESS SPIRIT (USA)　2 b.c. (May 9) Sheikh Albadou 128 – Wayward　83 p Lass (USA) (Hail The Pirates (USA) 126) [1996 6.1m⁴ 6m² 6.1s* Oct 31] robust, good-bodied colt: has scope: closely related to a winner in Italy (including at 12.5f) by Green Desert and half-brother to several winners, including fair 4-y-o Errant (at up to 1¼m, by Last Tycoon) and useful Syrtos (1¾m, by Shareef Dancer): dam champion 3-y-o filly in USA in 1981: made all in minor event at Nottingham, quickening steady pace 2f out and wandering in front: no match for Intikhab at Yarmouth previous outing: will stay 7f: type to keep progressing. *M. Johnston*

RESTRUCTURE (IRE)　4 b.c. Danehill (USA) 126 – Twine (Thatching 131)　118 [1995 112p: 8.3m 8g² 8m* 8m 8m* 10.4m³ 9m* 1996 9m⁵ 8.2m* 8f² 8m* 8m⁵ 8g⁴ 8m³ 8g 8m² Oct 3] big, deep-bodied, attractive colt: impresses in appearance, rarely on way to post: smart performer: won minor event at Nottingham (sweating) in June and Ragusa Stud Minstrel Stakes at the Curragh (by head from Bin Rosie) in July: subsequently fifth of 10 in Sussex Stakes and fourth of 7 in Celebration Mile, both at Goodwood, third in Park Stakes at Doncaster and second of 9 to Yeast in listed race at Newmarket: best efforts at 1m/9f: has raced almost exclusively on top-of-the-ground: game and consistent. *Mrs J. Cecil*

RETENDER (USA)　7 br.g. Storm Bird (CAN) 134 – Dandy Bury (FR) (Exbury　– 138) [1995 68, a60: 9.9m³ 12m 12m a12g³ a10g⁵ 1996 a16g a12g Feb 20] useful-looking gelding: fair middle-distance staying handicapper at 6 yrs: well beaten in 1996: needs a sound surface on turf, acts on equitrack. *J. Pearce*

RET FREM (IRE)　3 b.g. Posen (USA) – New Light 78 (Reform 132) [1995 54p:　70 7m 7f 6m 1996 8.2g 11.6m³ 8.3m* 8g² 8f⁴ 8m* 8m Sep 20] well-made gelding: fair handicapper: won at Windsor in June and at Doncaster (dictated steady pace) in July: subsequently left M. Jarvis' stable: well held only flat outing for new yard: effective at 1m and stays 11.6f: has raced only on a sound surface: effective from front or held up. *C. Parker*

RETICENT 3 b.c. Sadler's Wells (USA) 132 – Shy Princess (USA) 117 (Irish 72
River (FR) 131) [1995 NR 1996 8f⁵ 10m⁵ 10.4g 10.2d Sep 30] fourth foal: closely
related to very smart 4-y-o 6f/7f winner Diffident (by Nureyev), and half-brother to 2
French 1m winners by Groom Dancer: dam, French 6f to 7f winner, half-sister to
Opening Verse: form only when fifth of 15 in maiden at Sandown: stays 1¼m:
bandaged: sent to UAE. *J. H. M. Gosden*

RETOTO 2 ch.f. (May 16) Totem (USA) 118 – Responder 70 (Vitiges (FR) 132) 49 ?
[1996 6m² 6g* 7f 6m Aug 16] fifth reported foal: half-sister to 1m winner Genuine
Lady (by Lidhame): dam maiden, stayed 1¼m: trained by C. Fairhurst on debut:
favourite, won 6-runner seller at Yarmouth in July: poor efforts afterwards: should
stay 7f. *B. J. McMath*

RETURN OF AMIN 2 ch.c. (Mar 23) Salse (USA) 128 – Ghassanah 73 (Pas de 82
Seul 133) [1996 5g⁶ 6m a7g³ 6m 7m³ 6.9v* a7g* Nov 29] angular, good-bodied colt:
has a quick action: fourth foal: half-brother to 3 winners, including fairly useful 1994
2-y-o 7f and 7.6f winner Amin (by Last Tycoon) and useful sprinter Alzianah (by
Alzao): dam, lightly-raced 7f winner, half-sister to Derby Italiano winner Don
Orazio: improved form when winning nurseries at Folkestone (by 3 lengths) and
Southwell (by 4 lengths) in November: will be suited by further than 7f: acts on
heavy ground and fibresand. *J. D. Bethell*

RETURN TO BRIGHTON 4 b.f. Then Again 126 – Regency Brighton (Royal 51
Palace 131) [1995 –: 8m 8m 8.1g 1996 8m² 8m* 8m⁴ 8f⁵ 8.1m 8.3m⁵ 9.2f a8g a10s a–
Nov 19] rather leggy filly: modest handicapper: won apprentice seller at Ripon in
June: well beaten last 3 starts: should stay beyond 1m: acts on good to firm ground,
yet to race on a soft surface. *J. M. Bradley*

REUNION (IRE) 2 br.f. (Feb 25) Be My Guest (USA) 126 – Phylella (Persian 88 ?
Bold 123) [1996 6m* 7f³ Sep 23] IR 15,000Y: fourth foal: half-sister to 3-y-o 9.7f
winner Mono Lady (by Polish Patriot) and 1994 Irish 2-y-o 6f winner Foravella (by
Cadeaux Genereux): dam won in France (at 1¼m) and USA: favourite, won 6-runner
median auction maiden at Redcar by a neck, hanging left from halfway then running
on when straightened: over 2 lengths third of 3 to Imroz in steadily-run minor event
at Leicester 4 months later: will stay 1m: not easy to assess. *J. W. Hills*

REVERAND THICKNESS 5 b.g. Prince Sabo 123 – Wollow Maid 73 78
(Wollow 132) [1995 78: a6g³ 7.1d* a7g* 7g³ 7g⁴ 6m 8m³ 7.9g⁶ 9g⁴ 10d 9g 8m⁵ 1996
a7g⁶ a9.4g 6.9s 8d* 8.1d³ 10.3m Jun 6] lengthy, angular gelding: fair handicapper:
won claimer at Warwick in April (carried head high) on final outing for S. Williams:
broke leg at Chester on second outing for new yard: stayed 9f: acted on good to firm
and dead ground and on fibresand: tried blinkered: sometimes wandered under
pressure, and was suited by strong handling: dead. *A. Bailey*

REVEUSE DE JOUR (IRE) 3 b.f. Sadler's Wells (USA) 132 – Magic of Life 79
(USA) 118 (Seattle Slew (USA)) [1995 –p: 7g 1996 7g⁴ 7m² Apr 29] smallish,
attractive filly: good mover: progressive form in maidens, 4 lengths second of 13 to
West Humble at Kempton on final start: will be well suited by further than 7f: looked
sure to improve again. *R. Charlton*

REVOQUE (IRE) 2 b.c. (Jan 21) Fairy King (USA) – La Bella Fontana 122 p
(Lafontaine (USA) 117) [1996 6m* 7m* 7m* 8g* Oct 13]

Revoque's winning debut in the European Breeders Fund Maiden
Stakes, the race before the King George VI and Queen Elizabeth Diamond
Stakes at Ascot in July, attracted less attention than it would have done had
many racegoers not been keeping half an eye on the giant TV screen for
coverage of Steve Redgrave's progress towards his record-breaking fourth
successive Olympic rowing gold medal. The race in question—the one at Ascot
not Atlanta—was for newcomers and Bint Shadayid's half-brother Shawaf
started an uneasy favourite. Two horses pulled clear in the closing stages, the
powerful-looking Revoque and the quick-starting Shii-Take who made most
of the running. There was a lot to like about Revoque's effort—he tracked
Shii-Take before quickening under pressure to take the lead inside the final
furlong—and he looked just the type to improve. Coral produced a quote of
33/1 for the Two Thousand Guineas immediately afterwards.

Prix de la Salamandre, Longchamp—Revoque forges ahead as The West (dark colours) and Zamindar tire

The Deploy Acomb Stakes, the first race on the opening day of York's big August meeting, produced more widespread acknowledgement of Revoque's potential. The race is often won by a good-class colt in the making and punters latched on to the choicely-bred In Command who had made a pleasing first appearance at Goodwood. In Command, Revoque and the other winner in the line-up, Shadow Lead, conceded 4 lb all round and were the only ones shorter than 20/1 in the betting. Revoque looked in superb condition and, handy in a race that wasn't run at a true gallop, was always in control after taking over in front approaching the final furlong. In Command, disadvantaged by being held up last, managed only third, beaten also by 20/1-shot Symonds Inn. The next intended target for Revoque was the Laurent-Perrier Champagne Stakes at Doncaster but he was an eleventh-hour withdrawal on account of firm ground. Revoque's absence from the Champagne Stakes—in which In Command finished second to the Guineas ante-post favourite Bahhare—seemed a much more significant loss for the race after Revoque's next two outings than it did at the time. Odds-on Bahhare would still have been a hot favourite at Doncaster with Revoque in the line-up, but by the end of the season there looked, in all honesty, nothing to choose between them on form.

British racegoers had no further opportunity to see Revoque who maintained his unbeaten record, and enhanced his reputation significantly, in two Group 1 races at Longchamp, the Prix de la Salamandre two days after the Champagne Stakes, and the Grand Criterium in mid-October. The Salamandre was a strangely-run affair, the second British challenger The West and odds-on favourite Zamindar paying the penalty for setting far too strong an early pace as

Grand Criterium, Longchamp—now he improves again to beat Majorien

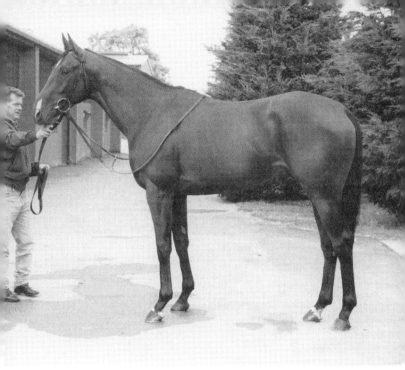

Mr R. E. Sangster's "Revoque"

Revoque (IRE) (b.c. Jan 21, 1994)	Fairy King (USA) (b 1982)	Northern Dancer (b 1961)	Nearctic Natalma
		Fairy Bridge (b 1975)	Bold Reason Special
	La Bella Fontana (b 1985)	Lafontaine (b 1977)	Sham Valya
		Sorebelle (b 1974)	Prince Tenderfoot La Belle

Revoque, sticking to his task after being markedly outpaced, forged ahead inside the final furlong to win by three lengths. Though there were other doubts about the precise value of the form (the filly Dame d'Havard, beaten in her three previous races, was alongside The West and Zamindar at the finish), the Salamandre demonstrated two things about Revoque: he was a smart performer at the very least and he looked sure to be suited by an extra furlong in the Grand Criterium. Revoque was odds on for the Criterium in the largest field for the race since the last British success with Tenby in 1992. The field of nine did, however, include two runners from Bulgaria, both out of their depth it soon transpired, as well as the National Stakes runner-up Referendum and the promising King Sound from Britain. The British-trained challengers filled three of the first four places in a contest that was much more satisfactory than the Salamandre. Referendum set a sound pace until Majorien, one of only three

807

home-trained colts in the field, took over with a little more than a furlong left. Switched off the rails to make his run towards the outside, Revoque quickened in excellent style to beat Majorien by two lengths, with King Sound four lengths further away in third, a neck ahead of Referendum. The form of the Grand Criterium is as good—the way we read it—as that of any other two-year-old race run in Europe in 1996. That said, Revoque will almost certainly need to improve a little further to win a classic, though he has the scope to do so. He should give a good account of himself in the Two Thousand Guineas, though there is some talk that he could go for the Poule d'Essai des Poulains instead.

The lengthy, good-topped Revoque, who went through the sale-ring for 36,000 guineas as a foal, is by Sadler's Wells's brother Fairy King who has done well at stud, notably in producing the Prix de l'Arc de Triomphe winner Helissio and the Irish Two Thousand Guineas winner Turtle Island. Fairy King, who was raced only once (last of eleven in a listed race), is a very different sire from Sadler's Wells, being an influence for speed rather than for stamina and a noted sire of two-year-olds. Revoque's dam La Bella Fontana also ran only once, fourth of five in a mile maiden at Newcastle as a three-year-old, and was sold for 12,000 guineas in foal to Absalom at the 1989 December Sales. She has bred two other winners, the foal she was carrying at the time of her sale, Barsal, who gained his only victory in a selling hurdle, and Revoque's brother Swinging Sixties, a fair handicapper successful at up to 9.7 furlongs. La Bella Fontana went through the ring again at the 1995 Goff's November Sales, making a paltry IR 1,200 guineas in foal to Scenic; her filly foal by Distinctly North fetched even less, IR 1,000 guineas, at the same sales, though twelve months on she realised IR 54,000 guineas. La Bella Fontana, a half-sister to the useful five-to-seven-furlong winner Abuzz and the fairly useful six- and seven-furlong performer Local Lass, is out of the useful Sorebelle who was best at up to a mile. The third dam La Belle won the Diadem Stakes and, on pedigree at least, there have to be considerable doubts about Revoque's ability to stay the Derby trip. It's no surprise to see him available at 33/1 in winter ante-post lists for the Epsom classic. Revoque acts on good to firm ground and has yet to race on soft. He's got a good turn of foot. *P. W. Chapple-Hyam*

REX MUNDI 4 b.g. Gunner B 126 – Rose Standish 71 (Gulf Pearl 117) [1995 NR 1996 10g 10m 10f² 10m³ 15.8g⁴ 10.9m* 11.9d⁴ 12d⁵ 10g³ 10f³ a13g³ Nov 26] angular gelding: fair handicapper: won at Ayr (amateurs) in September: good efforts afterwards in frame (went rather in snatches from an eighth start): stays 13f: acts on firm and dead ground, and equitrack. *P. D. Evans*   68

RHAPSODY IN WHITE (IRE) 2 b.g. (Apr 20) Contract Law (USA) 108 – Lux Aeterna (Sandhurst Prince 128) [1996 6m 7f² a8g⁴ Nov 4] IR 8,000F, 17,500Y: smallish, useful-looking gelding: second foal: brother to Italian 3-y-o 7.5f (at 2 yrs) and 1m winner Nick Raider: dam ran twice in Ireland: 50/1, set steady gallop when equal-second of 11 to Ihtiyati in maiden at Warwick, quite probably flattered: soon ridden along remote fourth in median auction maiden at Southwell following month. *M. A. Jarvis*   70 ? a?

RHEINBOLD 2 br.g. (Apr 22) Never So Bold 135 – Rheinbloom 66 (Rheingold 137) [1996 7g Oct 25] 9,000Y: strong gelding: half-brother to several winners here and abroad, including 5-y-o 1m winner Mr Rough (by Fayruz) and fairly useful middle-distance stayer Rhusted (by Busted): dam 1½m winner, half-sister to high-class Gold Rod: 50/1, burly and green, around 13 lengths seventh of 12 to Sophomore in maiden at Doncaster, niggled along early then not knocked about closing stages: should do better. *T. J. Etherington*   – p

RHYTHMIC BALL 3 ch.f. Classic Music (USA) – Chrisanthy 81 (So Blessed 130) [1995 56: a6g⁶ 6g⁵ 6g 1996 6.1d 6d 6d 7m⁵ 8.2m⁶ 8.5m Jul 16] sparely-made filly: modest maiden at best: stays 1m: tends to carry head high: inconsistent. *T. R. Watson*   49

RICASSO 2 b.g. (Apr 18) Kris 135 – Chicarica (USA) 112 (The Minstrel (CAN) 135) [1996 a6g² 6g³ 5.3f³ 6d 6m⁴ Oct 5] close-coupled gelding: has a round action: first foal: dam won Cherry Hinton Stakes: fair form in frame in maidens and a   69

nursery: will be suited by 7f+: edgy and pulled too hard in blinkers penultimate start: sent to UAE. *D. R. Loder*

RICCARTON 3 b.g. Nomination 125 – Legendary Dancer 90 (Shareef Dancer 52 (USA) 135) [1995 NR 1996 8g 8g 8g 8.1d⁵ 7s³ 8.1m³ 6.9f² 8.3g³ 8m⁶ Sep 19] 11,000Y: big, quite attractive gelding: third foal: dam 1½m winner from family of Wassl: modest maiden handicapper: stays 8.3f, should prove effective over 6f: acts on firm and soft ground: hung left eighth start. *P. Calver*

RICHARD HOUSE LAD 3 b.c. Warrshan (USA) 117 – Sirenivo (USA) 113 49 (Sir Ivor 135) [1995 59, a48: 5.1g 5m 7g⁶ a7g⁶ 8.2m⁶ a8.5g a7g a8g 1996 8.2d a12g⁶ a– 8g⁴ 8m 8.2m⁴ 8.2m⁵ 8m⁶ 8m 10g⁶ 8m* 8.2g a8g a9.4g Nov 25] smallish, quite attractive colt: poor handicapper: made all in seller at Bath in September: stays 1m: acts on good to firm ground. *R. Hollinshead*

RICH GLOW 5 b.g. Rich Charlie 117 – Mayglow (Sparkling Boy 110) [1995 70: 67 5d 5m 5.9m² 5m* 5g³ 5g* 6m 5f* 5m⁵ 6m 5m² 5g² 5m⁴ 5f⁵ 6m 6m² 6g 6g 5d 5m 1996 5s 6g 5.9d 6m 6m 6d 6m 5m³ 5d* 5g⁶ 5g 6m⁴ 5m⁵ 5m* 5f 5m⁶ 6f 5m⁶ 5.1g 5m Oct 2] leggy, angular gelding: fair sprint handicapper: won at Ayr (fourth course win) and Pontefract in the summer: acts on firm and soft ground: effective blinkered, not tried since 4-y-o reappearance: has worn tongue strap: usually held up, and suited by strongly-run race. *N. Bycroft*

RICH GROUND 2 gr.c. (Mar 19) Common Grounds 118 – Gratclo 65 (Belfort 96 (FR) 89) [1996 6g 6m* 6g* 6g⁴ 6m Oct 3] 8,400Y: close-coupled colt: has a fluent action: third foal: dam seemed suited by 7f: made great strides to win maiden at Newcastle then TNT International Aviation July Stakes (came from off strong pace to beat Juwwi a head) at Newmarket: respectable effort when fourth of 5 to Bahamian Bounty in Prix Morny at Deauville, reportedly finishing lame after losing shoe: not discredited when ninth of 11 to same horse in Middle Park Stakes at Newmarket: should stay further than 6f. *J. D. Bethell*

RICH IN LOVE (IRE) 2 b.f. (Apr 12) Alzao (USA) 117 – Chief's Quest (USA) 95 (Chief's Crown (USA)) [1996 6g² 6m* 6g⁵ 7.1m⁵ 7m² 8m⁴ 7m Oct 1] 20,000Y: rangy, rather unfurnished filly, shade unfurnished: third foal: dam, French 8.5f winner, half-sister to Prix de la Salamandre winner Noblequest and the dam of Divine Danse and Pursuit of Love: won minor event at Ripon in June: useful form when fourth of 20 to The Fly in valuable nursery at Newcastle penultimate outing: gone in coat, well below form in valuable sales race at Newmarket 5 weeks later: stays 1m well. *C. A. Cyzer*

RICKY TICKY TAVIE (USA) 2 b.c. (Apr 20) Dixieland Band (USA) – Save 97 p The Doe (USA) (Spend A Buck (USA)) [1996 7g² Sep 29] smallish, rather leggy colt: first foal: dam, minor stakes winner at up to 9f in USA, out of half-sister to high-class performer at up to 7f Beaudelaire: well-backed favourite, 3½ lengths second of 11 to Kahal in minor event at Ascot, taking keen hold early: moved keenly to post: sure to improve and win races: joined Godolphin. *D. R. Loder*

RIDE SALLY RIDE (IRE) 2 ch.c. (May 7) Shalford (IRE) 124§ – Sally St Clair 87 (Sallust 134) [1996 5g⁴ 5m* 5g⁶ 5.1m² 6g³ 6g³ 5g² 7s⁵ 6g⁶ 6g 7d Sep 25] IR 14,000Y:

TNT International Aviation July Stakes, Newmarket—victory goes to the 40/1-outsider of nine as the grey Rich Ground tackles Air Express (No. 2), Juwwi (obscured) and Check The Band (rails)

good-topped colt, quite attractive: has a roundish action: half-brother to several winners, including fairly useful Irish 3-y-o 5f to 7f winner Lancaster House (by Mac's Imp): dam, winner in Canada, half-sister to Superlative: trained by Jack Berry first 5 starts, winning maiden auction at Hamilton in May and placed in minor events at Bath and Pontefract: below best last 3 starts in France: best form at 5f/6f. *G. E. Mikhalides, France*

RIFIFI 3 ch.c. Aragon 118 – Bundled Up (USA) (Sharpen Up 127) [1995 66: 7g[5] 6.9g 1996 6.9f 6m[5] 6g[4] 6m Jun 5] small, sturdy colt: modest maiden: stays 7f: has raced only on a sound surface: withdrawn after giving trouble stalls third intended 3-y-o start. *R. Ingram* 60

RIGHTEOUS GENT 3 b.g. Superpower 113 – Golden 69 (Don 128) [1995 43, a59?: 7.1m[6] 6.1d 8m[6] a7g a8g[3] a7g[4] 1996 a8g[3] a10g a10g[4] a14.8g a7g a12g[5] Aug 9] rangy, unfurnished gelding: modest maiden: well beaten after reappearance: sold 800 gns Newmarket Autumn Sales: stays 1m: acts on equitrack: often blinkered. *K. McAuliffe* – a57 d

RIGHT MAN 2 gr.c. (Mar 23) Robellino (USA) 127 – High Matinee (Shirley Heights 130) [1996 6g[5] 6m 6m Sep 26] 10,000F, 13,000Y: brother to a winner in Hong Kong and half-brother to several winners abroad: dam French 7.5f and 1m winner, half-sister to dam of Caramba and Lemon Souffle: behind throughout in maidens at Epsom (2) and Goodwood (not given hard time): slowly away first 2 starts: almost certainly needs further than 6f: will do better. *B. Hanbury* – p

RIGHT TUNE 2 b.f. (Jan 29) Green Desert (USA) 127 – Triste Oeil (USA) 103 (Raise A Cup (USA)) [1996 6g 7m* 8d[4] 7g[2] Sep 13] big, good-bodied filly: type to carry condition: has a fluent, round action: fourth foal: half-sister to fairly useful Irish 7f and 11f winner Desert Wish (by Shirley Heights) and a 6f to 1m winner in UAE by Soviet Star: dam 7f (at 2 yrs) and 1¼m winner: won maiden at Newmarket in August, making all and holding on gamely despite hanging left: good second in nursery at Goodwood on final start: best form at 7f: strong galloper who goes well with forcing tactics: may well improve further. *B. Hanbury* 81 p

RIGHT WING (IRE) 2 b.c. (Apr 4) In The Wings 128 – Nekhbet 74 (Artaius (USA) 129) [1996 7.1v[3] Oct 16] 35,000F, 36,000Y: rather leggy, useful-looking colt: seventh foal: half-brother to 4 winners, including useful 6/7f performer Cim Bom Bom (by Dowsing) and French listed 10.5f winner Tarquina (by Niniski): dam, in frame from 5f to 7f, is half-sister to Irish St Leger winner M-Lolshan and useful sprinter Chemin: 6/1, 11½ lengths third of 10 to Catienus in maiden at Haydock, slowly away, green and last into straight then staying on: will do better. *Major W. R. Hern* 67 p

RIGHT WIN (IRE) 6 br.h. Law Society (USA) 130 – Popular Win 103 (Lorenzaccio 130) [1995 112: 12g[4] 10.5v 12g 13.3m[5] 12s[3] 12d 1996 12s[5] Mar 23] lengthy, workmanlike horse: smart middle-distance stayer in 1995: had been hurdling, ran as if something amiss in minor event at Doncaster in March. *R. Hannon* –

RIGHTY HO 2 b.g. (Mar 25) Reprimand 122 – Challanging 95 (Mill Reef (USA) 141) [1996 6d 7.9g 7.5m[4] 8f Oct 8] 4,000Y: tall, leggy gelding: sixth foal: half-brother to 4-y-o 11f and 15f winner Sarasota Storm (by Petoski) and 3 winners in France/USA: dam 2-y-o 7f winner, is daughter of useful miler Vital Match: modest form in maiden auctions and a nursery: will prove suited by test of stamina. *P. T. Walwyn* 60

RIHAN (USA) 2 b. or br.f. (May 12) Dayjur (USA) 137 – Sweet Roberta (USA) (Roberto (USA) 131) [1996 5m 6g[2] 6m* 7s[5] Nov 9] rangy, rather unfurnished filly: has scope: third foal: sister to useful 3-y-o Elshabiba, 6f winner at 2 yrs, and half-sister to a winner in USA by Relaunch: dam 1m (at 2 yrs) to 9f winner in USA and second in Breeders' Cup Juvenile Fillies: around 5 lengths eighth of 13 to Dance Parade in Queen Mary Stakes at Ascot on debut: gone in coat and first run for 3½ months, below that form when winning maiden at Newcastle in October: tongue tied, beaten long way in nursery final start: should stay further than 6f: probably unsuited by soft ground. *Saeed bin Suroor* 84 ?

RINCA 2 b.f. (Apr 24) Unfuwain (USA) 131 – Branitska (Mummy's Pet 125) [1996 8m 8g Nov 2] leggy, lengthy filly: sixth foal: sister to 1¼m winner Superluminal and half-sister to smart 1989 2-y-o 6f and 7.5f winner Call To Arms (by North Briton) and 1½m winner War Beat (by Wolver Heights): dam poor maiden –

from family of Dominion: in rear in large fields for maiden and seller at Newmarket. *J. Pearce*

RING OF VISION (IRE) 4 br.g. Scenic 128 – Circus Lady (High Top 131) 60 [1995 52: 8g 10m* 10m⁵ 1996 12m 10m²ᵈⁱˢ 12.3m 11m* 10m² 10.4g 10.9m⁶ 11.9g Oct 10] sturdy gelding: good walker: modest handicapper: successful in amateurs race at Redcar in July: sold (Mrs. M. Reveley to C. Mann) 11,000 gns Newmarket Autumn Sales: should stay further than 11f: acts on good to firm and dead ground: none too consistent. *Mrs M. Reveley*

RING THE CHIEF 4 b.g. Chief Singer 131 – Lomond Ring (Lomond (USA) 43 128) [1995 57: 8f a6g² 6.1m a6g² a5g³ a6g a7g⁶ a6g 1996 a7g a8.5g⁵ a8.5g a7g⁶ a7g² a7g⁵ a8.5g³ 10g³ Jul 8] leggy, workmanlike gelding: has a round action: just a poor maiden handicapper in 1996: stays 1¼m: acts on fibresand, has raced only on a sound surface on turf. *M. D. I. Usher*

RINUS MANOR (IRE) 5 b.g. Ballad Rock 122 – Never Never Land (Habitat 48 134) [1995 48?: a6g 6g⁶ 7g⁵ 8g 6d⁶ 1996 6d 5.9d 5s³ 5m⁵ 5g⁴ 5g⁴ 6.9f 5m⁶ 5m⁵ 6m 6m Oct 23] sturdy gelding: poor maiden handicapper: effective at 5f, and stays 7f: acts on fibresand and dead ground: tried visored: inconsistent. *E. J. Alston*

RIO DUVIDA 3 ch.c. Salse (USA) 128 – Fluctuate 87 (Sharpen Up 127) [1995 98 107: 6g* 6f* 6g⁴ 7g² 7d* 1996 8m⁵ 10g⁵ 8.5m⁵ 8g³ 8.5f 7.5f⁶ Nov 29] leggy, useful-looking colt: has a quick action: useful performer: failed to find his top form in 1996, best effort when fifth of 9 to Don Micheletto in listed race at Goodwood second start: left D. Loder after penultimate outing: probably stays 1¼m: acts on firm and dead ground: carries head high under pressure. *N. Drysdale, USA*

RIPARIUS (USA) 5 b.g. Riverman (USA) 131 – Sweet Simone (FR) (Green 81 § Dancer (USA) 132) [1995 81: 12m⁵ 12d* 12m 11.8g⁵ 12m³ 11.9g 16.2s 1996 11.8g* 12g⁵ 14d³ 12g 12.3m⁶ 10g⁶ 11.8m Aug 19] rangy, workmanlike gelding: fairly useful handicapper: won at Leicester in April, leading near finish: well below form last 4 starts, showing little enthusiasm on occasions: stays 1¾m, apparently not 16.2f: acts on soft going and good to firm: effective blinkered or not: often looks none too keen and is one to treat with caution: has joined P. Webber. *H. Candy*

RIPSNORTER (IRE) 7 ch.g. Rousillon (USA) 133 – Formulate 119 (Reform – 132) [1995 –, a47: 10g 8g a8g⁶ a8g a8g a10g 1996 8g 8.3m⁵ a8g 10g Aug 14] big, strong gelding: little worthwhile form in 1996. *K. Bishop*

RISCATTO (USA) 2 b.c. (Feb 9) Red Ransom (USA) – Ultima Cena (USA) – (Leonardo Da Vinci (FR)) [1996 6g⁶ a7g² a7g⁴ 7.3m 7.1m Aug 31] $25,000F, IR a54 ? 10,500Y, resold 675Y: tall, plain colt: brother to a minor winner on turf in USA and half-brother to 3 winners: dam ran once: second in seller at Wolverhampton: well beaten in nurseries last 2 starts: stays 7f: acts on fibresand. *W. R. Muir*

RISE 'N SHINE 2 ch.f. (May 11) Night Shift (USA) – Clunk Click 72 (Star 67 Appeal 133) [1996 6m⁶ 5f² 5m³ 6g² 5m² 5f³ 5m Sep 27] 16,000Y: closely related to 3-y-o Cisco Wells (by Sadler's Wells), winner over 7.8f in Germany at 2 yrs, and half-sister to several winners, including fairly useful 6f (at 2 yrs) and 7f winner Crazy Paving (by Danehill) and useful French sprinter Touch And Love (by Green Desert): dam middle-distance maiden: modest form: should stay 6f. *C. A. Cyzer*

RISE UP SINGING 8 ch.g. Noalto 120 – Incarnadine 67 (Hot Spark 126) [1995 49 62: 7m² 8g 6m³ 7g 1996 6m 7g 8g 7g² 8m 7.6f³ 7.6m Aug 17] strong, lengthy gelding: unimpressive mover: poor handicapper at best nowadays: has gained 7 of his 8 victories at Newmarket: ideally suited by 7f to 1m: acts on any going, except apparently heavy: best in blinkers: often sweats: usually races up with pace: inconsistent. *W. J. Musson*

RISING COLOURS 3 gr.c. Rusticaro (FR) 124 – Galina (Bon Sang (FR) 126) 112 [1995 6.5d⁵ 7d³ 8d 8s 1996 8d* 8g⁴ 8g⁴ 5.5m⁵ 6d⁴ 8d² 8g* 8d* 8g* 10s⁵ 7d 8v Nov 11] fourth foal: half-brother to French 10.5f winner Big Basile (by Mont Basile): dam, placed in France, half-sister to a useful middle-distance stayer in Spain out of La Hougue (rated 111, stayed 1½m well): smart performer: won handicap at Evry in March, then 2 handicaps (including a valuable listed contest) and 7-runner Prix Quincey (beat Trojan Sea by a neck), all at Deauville in August: below best last 3 starts: stays 1m: acts on dead ground. *P. H. Demercastel, France*

RISING DOUGH (IRE) 4 br.g. Dowsing (USA) 124 – Shortning Bread 83   74
(Blakeney 126) [1995 76: 10m² 8m² 9m* 7.6m⁵ 8f* 8.5m⁴ 1996 9.7m 12m 10.1m*
12g⁴ 11.9f² 10.1g³ 10m⁴ 12m Sep 11] good-bodied, workmanlike gelding: fair
handicapper: won ladies event at Epsom in June: probably stays 1½m: acts on firm
ground, seems unsuited by heavy: visored (below form) final 2-y-o outing: tends to
edge left under pressure. *G. L. Moore*

RISING GLORY 2 b.g. (Apr 23) Absalom 128 – Glow Again 78 (The Brianstan
128) [1996 6s a6g 8.1m⁶ 8.2g 8m a7g 5s Nov 7] 12,000Y: small, good-topped
gelding: fifth foal: half-brother to 3-y-o 1¼m and 1½m winner General Glow and
4-y-o Double Glow (both by Presidium), latter 5f winner at 2 yrs: dam 2-y-o 5f and
6f winner: bad maiden: blinkered final outing: sold 600 gns Doncaster November
Sales. *Miss J. F. Craze*

RISING SPRAY 5 ch.g. Waajib 121 – Rose Bouquet 78 (General Assembly   66
(USA)) [1995 55§: 12m 12m 12g 10g⁶ 8.3g³ 7f 8g 7d 8m³ 9d³ 10g 1996 11.4m⁵
10.8m 14f³ 16.2m 12m⁶ 12m* 12m* 10.2g² 12m² Sep 20] quite good-topped
gelding: has a quick action: fair handicapper: comfortable winner twice in 5 days at
Folkestone in August: good second both subsequent outings: stays 1½m, not 2m: acts
on good to firm ground and dead: has run well for amateur: held up, quite often
slowly away. *C. A. Horgan*

RISKIE THINGS 5 ch.m. Risk Me (FR) 127 – Foolish Things (Song 132) [1995   –
49: 10m² 6f 6.9g 5m⁶ 6m 5m a5g 1996 a6g a7g Jan 23] close-coupled mare: poor
sprinter: well held in 1996: acts on any turf going and on equitrack: tried visored
earlier in career. *J. S. Moore*

RISKING 3 b.f. Risk Me (FR) 127 – Dark Kristal (IRE) 66 (Gorytus (USA) 132)   48
[1995 –: a6g 1996 7d 6f³ 5f a5g a5g a7s Nov 19] good-topped filly: poor maiden:
stays 7f: sold 800 gns Newmarket December Sales. *G. Lewis*

RISKY BABY 4 ch.f. Risk Me (FR) 127 – Gemma Kaye 91 (Cure The Blues   –
(USA)) [1995 NR 1996 8f 6m 7g Jun 12] rated 62 when second in maiden at Wolverhampton on only outing in October at 2 yrs: well beaten in 1996. *T. Hind*

RISKY FLIGHT 2 ch.g. (Apr 17) Risk Me (FR) 127 – Stairway To Heaven (IRE)   –
74 (Godswalk (USA) 130) [1996 5s 5m⁶ 5f a5g 5m Sep 18] 3,600Y: tall, plain,
angular gelding: first foal: dam 6f (at 2 yrs) to 1m winner: no worthwhile form in
maiden events or selling nursery: edgy in blinkers final start. *A. Smith*

RISKY MISSILE 2 b.f. (Mar 3) Risk Me (FR) 127 – Veuve Perrin (Legend of   64 +
France (USA) 124) [1996 6f⁴ 5d³ Oct 21] 2,400Y: lengthy filly: third foal: dam
unraced: better effort in maiden events when third of 13 to Unshaken at Folkestone,
first home of those drawn high: should stay beyond 5f. *J. E. Banks*

RISKY ROMEO 4 b.g. Charmer 123 – Chances Are (He Loves Me 120) [1995   68 §
68: 7g⁴ 8d 8.2g 7.6m⁴ 8m 10m 7.1g⁴ 10g⁵ 8.3m 8f* 8d 7f 8.2m a8.5g a8g⁵ a8g⁶ 1996
8f* 7f 8g 8m 14m Jul 13] leggy, workmanlike gelding: fair handicapper on his day:
won 21-runner apprentice contest at Warwick in May: stays 1m: acts on equitrack, on
firm going and probably on dead: tends to sweat: takes keen hold, and usually held
up: sometimes slowly away: virtually refused to race third 4-y-o start, and is one to
treat with caution. *G. C. Bravery*

RISKY ROSE 4 b.f. Risk Me (FR) 127 – Moharabuiee 60 (Pas de Seul 133) [1995   49
44: a8g⁶ a8g⁴ a8g⁵ 10g⁵ 12f* 9.9m⁴ 13.8g* 12m⁵ 13.1f 12m³ 12h⁴ 1996 10m 10m
10.8f² 14.1f* 14.1f⁴ 12.1m 15.8m³ 10f Sep 28] neat filly: poor handicapper: won
seller at Nottingham in July: well below form last 3 starts: stays 1¾m: acts on firm
ground and the all-weather, yet to race on a soft surface. *R. Hollinshead*

RISKY TU 5 ch.m. Risk Me (FR) 127 – Sarah Gillian (USA) (Zen (USA)) [1995   46
54d, a61d: a11g a16g² a16g³ a16g³ 12g³ a12g⁵ 12g a14g a12g a14g³ a11g² a12g⁴
1996 a10g⁴ a10g⁵ 11.9f⁵ 9.9m⁵ 11.9f³ 14.1g⁴ 12m 10f⁵ 11.9f⁶ a11g³ Dec 27] tall,
leggy mare: poor handicapper: stays 2m: acts on the all-weather and any turf going:
normally tracks leaders: none too consistent. *P. A. Kelleway*

RISSAGA 2 ch.f. (Mar 8) Meqdaam (USA) – Crosby Place 60 (Crooner 119)   –
[1996 a7g Nov 16] first reported foal: dam won from 9.7f to 1½m: 50/1, well beaten
in 9-runner maiden at Wolverhampton. *C. W. Fairhurst*

RIVA LA BELLE 2 b.f. (Feb 23) Riva's Victory (USA) 129 – Haunting 79 (Lord   – §
Gayle (USA) 124) [1996 5m 6g⁶ 7f⁴ 8f 10m 10f Oct 14] 6,000Y: leggy filly: half-
sister to numerous winners here and abroad, including useful 1986 2-y-o 5f and 6f

winner Amigo Sucio (by Stanford): dam stayed 1m: poor maiden: tried blinkered: very on toes, edgy and mulish to post fourth start: flashes tail, and is of doubtful temperament. *J. Wharton*

RIVAL BID (USA) 8 b.g. Cannonade (USA) – Love Triangle (USA) (Nodouble 74 (USA)) [1995 71, a55: 10m 10g⁶ 10m⁴ 9m⁵ 10.3f⁵ 9m² 12m a8g⁵ 10.1g³ 10d² 10.8g* a62 10g⁴ 10f* a11g⁶ a10g⁴ 1996 a10g* a10g³ a12g⁵ a12g⁶ 10d 9m 10.8f* 10m a12g⁵ a10g 10m 10g⁴ 8.2d 10f³ 10m⁴ 12g⁵ 10f* 10g⁵ Oct 21] workmanlike, close-coupled gelding: modest on the all-weather, successful in minor event at Lingfield in January: fair handicapper on turf, winning at Warwick (looked rather reluctant early on) in June and Leicester in October: effective at 9f to 1½m: acts on firm and dead ground and the all-weather: often has tongue tied down nowadays: often sweating: often slowly away: usually held up, and suited by strongly-run race: tough. *Mrs N. Macauley*

RIVAL QUEEN (IRE) 4 ch.f. Royal Academy (USA) 130 – Maria Stuarda – (Royal And Regal (USA)) [1995 –: 8f⁵ 10d⁴ 1996 a12g⁶ 10.3d a12g³ 12m May 10] angular filly: fair form only 2-y-o start, but well held since: sold 11,000 gns Newmarket December Sales. *M. D. Hammond*

RIVA ROCK 6 b.g. Roaring Riva 103 – Kivulini (Hotfoot 126) [1995 31: 9.7m⁶ – a8g 9.7g⁶ 11.9f² 1996 12f⁶ Jun 28] sturdy, lengthy gelding: poor maiden handicapper: showed little only start in 1996. *T. P. McGovern*

RIVA'S BOOK (USA) 5 b.g. Mari's Book (USA) – Riva's Revenge (USA) (Riva – Ridge (USA)) [1995 –: a12g 1996 11.1m May 18] compact gelding: no form last 2 seasons. *M. G. Meagher*

RIVER BAY (USA) 3 ch.c. Irish River (FR) 131 – Buckeye Gal (USA) (Good 121 Counsel 89) [1995 8g* 9s³ 1996 10.5m³ 8s* 8d⁵ 10d* 8v* Nov 11] $80,000Y: good-topped colt: third foal: half-brother to French 1993 2-y-o 5.5f winner Filha Do Ar (by Trempolino): dam stakes winner at up to 9f in USA: won minor event at Evry late on at 2 yrs: off course nearly 5 months after reappearance: won minor event and 6 lengths fifth of 10 to Alhaarth in Prix du Rond-Point at Longchamp, then won sales event at Deauville: best effort when winning 10-runner Prix Perth at Saint-Cloud in November by 1½ lengths from Decorated Hero: stays 10.5f, but clearly fully effective at testing 1m: acts on good to firm ground, goes well on soft/heavy: may yet do better back over further than 1m. *J. E. Hammond, France*

RIVERBOURNE (USA) 3 b.c. Riverman (USA) 131 – Umaimah (USA) 94 55 (Halo (USA)) [1995 NR 1996 6s⁵ 7m Aug 15] $7,000Y resold 15,000Y: quite good-topped colt: third foal: half-brother to French 4-y-o Fol Espoir (by Storm Bird): dam, 2-y-o 7f winner, half-sister to high-class 1m and 1¼m performer Lahib (by Riverman): fifth of 15 in maiden at Doncaster in March, hanging left: reported following month to have fractured pelvis: showed little only subsequent outing, and sold 2,200 gns Newmarket Autumn Sales: sent to Italy. *M. R. Channon*

RIVER CAPTAIN (USA) 3 ch.g. Riverman (USA) 131 – Katsura (USA) – (Northern Dancer) [1995 NR 1996 10g Apr 8] close-coupled gelding: brother to French 11f winner Rustaka, and half-brother to several winners, including 1990 2-y-o 7f winner Arokat (by Caro) and useful middle-distance performer Katzina (by Cox's Ridge): dam Irish 7f and 1¼m winner: favourite, well beaten in maiden at Kempton, slowly away, weakening over 3f out: sold (J. Gosden to D. Murray Smith) 8,000 gns Newmarket Autumn Sales and gelded. *J. H. M. Gosden*

RIVERCARE (IRE) 3 b.c. Alzao (USA) 117 – Still River (Kings Lake (USA) 62 d 133) [1995 8d 8g 7d 1996 a9.4g⁶ 12s 14.1g⁵ 12d³ 14.6m⁴ 13.9m⁴ 11.4d² 11.6m a16g⁶ 14g⁴ 12.3m 14d⁶ 16.4g 15.9g 14d 17.9g Oct 9] IR 5,000Y: smallish, robust ex-Irish colt: fourth foal: half-brother to 4-y-o 1m winner Kirov Protege (by Dancing Dissident): dam French maiden half-sister to dam of Sure Blade: trained by K. Prendergast at 2 yrs: modest form at best here: stays 14.6f: acts on good to firm and dead ground: usually front runner: sold 4,000 gns Newmarket Autumn Sales: ungenuine: sent to Spain. *M. J. Polglase*

RIVER FOYLE (USA) 2 ch.c. (Apr 29) Irish River (FR) 131 – Katsura (USA) 77 p (Northern Dancer) [1996 8g⁴ Sep 7] closely related to French 8.5f to 1½m winner Rustaka (by Riverman) and half-brother to several winners, including smart 7f (at 2 yrs) and 10.2f winner Rambushka (by Roberto): dam, Irish 7f and 1½m winner, is from family of Trillionaire: 14/1, 3 lengths fourth of 15, slowly away before staying on without being given too hard a time, to Ivan Luis in maiden at Thirsk: looked sure to improve: sold 36,000 gns Newmarket Autumn Sales. *J. H. M. Gosden*

RIVER GARNOCK   4 br.g. Dowsing (USA) 124 – Duboff 120 (So Blessed 130)   46
[1995 –: 6g 5f 1996 5g 6d 8d⁴ a7g 8.1f⁵ 5d⁶ Jul 4] big, good-bodied gelding: lightly raced: fairly useful form (rated 82) at 2 yrs: poor form at best since: seems effective at 1m but may prove best over shorter: acts on firm ground: tried blinkered: swished tail third 4-y-o start. *D. Nicholls*

RIVERINE   2 ch.f. (Feb 16) Risk Me (FR) 127 – Celtic River (IRE) (Caerleon   –
(USA) 132) [1996 5d 6v⁵ Nov 11] 500Y: first foal: dam French 1m winner, half-sister to Yorkshire Oaks winner and St Leger second Hellenic: no form in minor event and weak median auction maiden. *G. Lewis*

RIVER KEEN (IRE)   4 ch.c. Keen 116 – Immediate Impact (Caerleon (USA)   84 +
132) [1995 82, a102: 8d⁴ 7m 9g⁶ 10g* 9f 10.1g 12s⁵ 12.1s a10g* a12g* 1996 a12g*   a102
16g 12g⁵ 12g⁶ Oct 26] tall, leggy, sparely-made colt: useful handicapper on the all-weather, fairly useful on turf: won at Wolverhampton in March, leading close home: stays 1½m: possibly unsuited by top-of-the-ground, acts on soft and goes well on the all-weather: effective blinkered (not tried in 1996) or not. *R. W. Armstrong*

RIVER KING   2 b.c. (Feb 27) River Falls 113 – Sialia (IRE) (Bluebird (USA)   50 +
125) [1996 7.1m 7m 7g 8m 10m⁶ Sep 24] IR 35,000Y: sturdy colt: first foal: dam unraced half-sister to smart 7f/1m performer Rasa Penang: modest form: harshly assessed in nurseries last 2 outings: sold 3,500 gns Newmarket Autumn Sales: probably stays 1¼m. *R. Hannon*

RIVER NORTH (IRE)   6 ch.g. Lomond (USA) 128 – Petillante (USA) (River-   109
man (USA) 131) [1995 105+: 12g 1996 10d⁵ 11d³ 10m³ 12m 12m⁵ Aug 16] sturdy gelding: impresses in appearance: has a quick action: rated 122 in 1994, but only useful form since, best 6-y-o efforts when third of 8 to Germany in Group 2 contest at Baden-Baden and minor event at Windsor: stays 1½m well (yet to be tried over further): best with give in the ground: held up: reportedly suffers from leg problems, and wears bandages: tongue tied final start: sometimes hangs under pressure. *Lady Herries*

RIVER OF FORTUNE (IRE)   2 b.f. (Mar 30) Lahib (USA) 129 – Debach   68
Delight 97 (Great Nephew 126) [1996 6g⁶ 7f³ 6m² 7g² 7g² 7g² 7.5m² 7g 7m² 7m* 7.3s⁵ Oct 26] IR 7,000Y: leggy, lengthy filly: fourth foal: half-sister to 9.7f winner Joy of Freedom (by Damister) and a winner over hurdles in Italy by Dominion: dam 11f and 1½m winner: fair performer: short-head winner of 27-runner seller at Newmarket in October: sold 8,500 gns Newmarket Autumn Sales: stays 7f: acts on good to firm and soft ground: looked awkward on track at Epsom fifth outing. *M. H. Tompkins*

RIVER RUN (IRE)   4 b.c. Nordico (USA) – Irish Call (USA) (Irish River (FR)   64 d
131) [1995 8v 9g 10f³ 12f 12m⁴ 12.5f⁶ 12g 8.5g 10m 13m 10m² 10m6 10m* 7.8d⁴ 10d* 12g 10g⁶ 9g⁵ a9.4g a11g a9.4g Dec 7] ex-Irish colt: first foal: dam unraced: modest handicapper: won twice at Clonmel in May: left J. Bolger after sixth start: well beaten for new yard: stays 1½m, best form at 1¼m: acts on firm and dead ground: usually blinkered. *R. Hollinshead*

RIVER SEINE (FR)   4 b.f. Shining Steel – River Sans Retour (FR) (Vacarme   50
(USA) 121) [1995 NR 1996 a7g a6g³ a8g⁴ a7g* Dec 31] modest performer: won weak maiden at Lingfield in December: should stay 1m: has had tongue tied down, and worn bandages. *S. G. Knight*

RIVERSIDE GIRL (IRE)   2 b.f. (Apr 15) River Falls 113 – Ballywhat (IRE)   –
(Be My Native (USA) 122) [1996 8.2g⁶ 7m Oct 17] first reported foal: dam fourth in Irish NH Flat race only start at 4 yrs, placed in similar event in 1996: well held in sellers at Nottingham and Newmarket. *J. S. Moore*

RIVERS MAGIC   3 b.g. Dominion 123 – Rivers Maid 83 (Rarity 129) [1995 NR   78
1996 7m 7.1d* 8d 6.1s Oct 22] 15,000Y: sturdy gelding: brother to Richmond Stakes winner Nomination and half-brother to modest 1¼m winner Desert Power (by Green Desert): dam, 2-y-o 7f winner, sister to very useful middle-distance performer and high-class hurdler Decent Fellow: won maiden at Haydock in July, gamely making all: stiff task when eighth of 14 in apprentice race at Ascot over 3 months later: soundly beaten in handicap at Chepstow only subsequent outing: sold (Major

D. N. Chappell to J. White) 7,500 gns Newmarket Autumn Sales: stays 1m. *Major D. N. Chappell*

RIVER'S SOURCE (USA) 2 b.c. (Apr 30) Irish River (FR) 131 – Singing 81 (USA) 91 (The Minstrel (CAN) 135) [1996 7d⁴ 7f² Oct 15] second foal: half-brother to fairly useful if unreliable 3-y-o 7f (at 2 yrs) to 10.3f winner Gold Disc (by Slew O'Gold): dam, 7f winner, half-sister to very smart 1¼m winner Two Timing out of half-sister to champion American mare Chris Evert: fourth of 18 to Dacoit in maiden at Salisbury: 9/4 on, failed to improve as anticipated (on much firmer ground) when 2 lengths second of 10 to Attitude in similar event at Leicester 2 weeks later: will stay at least 1m: may still do better. *B. W. Hills*

RIVER TERN 3 b.g. Puissance 110 – Millaine 69 (Formidable (USA) 125) [1995 71 § 58p: 6m 5f³ 6d⁴ 1996 a7g⁵ 6f² 5m 6m³ 5g³ 6g* 6f 6m 5m Oct 23] tall, leggy gelding: has a high knee action: clearly best effort when winning maiden at Thirsk in September, flashing tail: well beaten afterwards: sold 500 gns Doncaster November Sales: stays 6f: acts on firm and dead ground: has pulled hard and carried head high: visored/blinkered last 5 starts: tongue tied final start, when also very slowly away: not one to rely on. *J. Berry*

RIVER USK 2 b.c. (Feb 20) Caerleon (USA) 132 – Shining Water 111 (Kalaglow 98 p 132) [1996 7.1d⁴* 7f⁴ 8g* Nov 1] smallish, well-made colt: sixth foal: brother to Grand Criterium and Dante winner Tenby and 3-y-o 1m (at 2 yrs) and 1¼m winner Bright Water, and half-brother to 2 winners, including 9f/1½m performer Reflecting (by Ahonoora): dam, won Solario Stakes at 2 yrs and stayed well as 3-y-o, is daughter of Park Hill winner Idle Waters: 11/8 on and green, won maiden at Haydock in September by a neck: possibly unsuited by firm ground next time: useful form when winning 4-runner minor event at Newmarket in November by a head from Barnum Sands, held up, hampered and outpaced slightly going into Dip then running on strongly to lead post: will be suited by middle distances: likely to improve further. *H. R. A. Cecil*

RIVER WYE (IRE) 4 b.g. Jareer (USA) 115 – Sun Gift (Guillaume Tell (USA) – 121) [1995 49: 8g⁵ 10m 8m⁵ 8m 10d a7g a8g⁵ 1996 8d Sep 30] tall gelding: poor maiden: bred to stay 1¼m, but looks headstrong. *G. H. Yardley*

RIVONIA (USA) 2 ch.f. (Feb 18) Irish River (FR) 131 – Princess Ivy (USA) 60 (Lyphard's Wish (FR) 124) [1996 6g⁴ 5f³ 5.1m⁵ 6f⁴ 7.5f 5m⁵ 7m⁴ 8g⁴ Oct 21] $35,000Y: small filly: first reported foal: dam won at up to 9f at 4 yrs in USA: modest form: sold 5,000 gns Newmarket Autumn Sales: stays 1m well: sent to Czech Republic. *Mrs J. R. Ramsden*

RIYADIAN 4 ch.c. Polish Precedent (USA) 131 – Knight's Baroness 116 (Rain- 120 bow Quest (USA) 134) [1995 122: 10m³ 10g* 11.5f² 12f 10.3g* 12d* 10m² 1996

Pertemps Jockey Club Stakes, Newmarket—
the future looks bright for Riyadian (right) as he beats Burooj (rails) and Sacrament

12m* May 3] medium-sized, lengthy colt: has a short action: very smart form: won Cumberland Lodge Stakes at Ascot and second of 8 to Spectrum in Champion Stakes at Newmarket at 3 yrs: 11/10 on, made a winning reappearance in 9-runner Pertemps Jockey Club Stakes at Newmarket, taking strong hold early on, cruising through to join issue 3f out and not coming under maximum pressure to beat Burooj a neck: stays 1½m well: acts on good to firm and dead ground: on toes and keen to post at Ascot: looked capable of better still and was being trained for the Arc when reportedly returned stiff and sore from a gallop in September. *P. F. I. Cole*

RIZAL (USA) 4 ch.g. Zilzal (USA) 137 – Sigy (FR) 132 (Habitat 134) [1995 NR – 1996 a6g a8g a8g Feb 24] closely related to several winners by Nureyev, including smart sprinter King's Signet, and half-brother to high-class Sicyos (sprinter, by Lyphard) and smart Radjhasi (sprinter-miler, by Raja Baba): dam won Prix de l'Abbaye as 2-y-o: behind in maidens at Wolverhampton and Lingfield: temperamental hurdler for R. Eckley. *D. J. G. Murray Smith*

ROAD RACER (IRE) 3 br.g. Scenic 128 – Rally 88 (Relko 136) [1995 NR 1996 56 8.2m 8m 8f⁴ 8g⁴ 10.4g 12m³ 12.1g⁴ 12m Oct 7] IR 10,000Y: tall, leggy gelding: easy mover: half-brother to several winners, including very useful juveniles Picatrix (by Thatch) and Times Domain (by Good Times), successful at 7f/1m: dam won over 1½m: modest maiden handicapper: better suited by 1½m than shorter: yet to race on a soft surface. *Mrs J. R. Ramsden*

ROAR ON TOUR 7 b.g. Dunbeath (USA) 127 – Tickled Trout 70 (Red Alert – § 127) [1995 –, a69: a8g* a8g* a8g⁴ a8g* a8g* a8g³ a8g 8.3v 1996 a8g a8g a8g 8.2d a62 § 8.3s⁶ 8m 8m a8g* a8g a8g a8g Dec 3] good-bodied gelding: modest handicapper on the all-weather: only worthwhile form in 1996 when winning at Southwell in July: stays 1m: acts on fibresand: used to act on good to firm ground and soft: effective blinkered/visored or not: unreliable, and not one to trust. *Mrs M. Reveley*

ROBAMASET (IRE) 3 b.g. Caerleon (USA) 132 – Smageta (High Top 131) 92 [1995 77p: 7m⁵ 7.5s 8m⁴ 1996 10m⁵ 11g⁵ 7f² 7f* Oct 14] robust, lengthy gelding: fairly useful form: justified favouritism in apprentice maiden at Leicester in October by 5 lengths: sold 30,000 gns Newmarket Autumn Sales: effective at 7f and stays 11f: acts on firm ground. *L. M. Cumani*

ROBEC GIRL (IRE) 2 ch.f. (Mar 2) Masterclass (USA) 116 – Resiusa (ITY) 66 (Niniski (USA) 125) [1996 5s³ 5g* 5m² 5m³ 5g⁴ 5m 5m³ 5m⁴ a5g* a6g³ a6g* Nov a69 11] IR 2,000Y: fifth reported foal: half-sister to 2 winners, including sprinter Tirols Result (by Tirol): dam Italian 7f (at 2 yrs) to 11.2f winner: fair form: won maiden auction at Catterick in May (by 4 lengths) and 11-runner sellers at Wolverhampton in October (nursery) and November (made all): better suited by 6f than 5f: acts on good to firm ground and fibresand. *J. Berry*

ROBELLION 5 b.g. Robellino (USA) 127 – Tickled Trout 70 (Red Alert 127) 74 [1995 74: 7m 7f⁴ 6g³ 5.7m² 5.7f⁴ 5m⁵ 5.2g² 5.1m* 5m 5.2m⁴ 5m 5m² 5.1d 5g 5m 6.1s 6f a5g a6g a7g⁴ 1996 a8g⁴ a8g* a7g³ a10g* a10g³ a10g a10g³ a10g⁵ 8g 6.9f 6m² 5.1m* 6m* 5m⁴ 6g 6.1d 6g⁴ 5.7m⁶ 6m⁵ 7f⁵ 5.1g Oct 24] sturdy, workmanlike gelding: fair handicapper: won at Lingfield in January and February, at Chepstow (for second year running) in July and at Newmarket in August: effective at 5f, and stays 1¼m: acts on equitrack and firm ground, below form all 5 outings on a soft surface: usually wears visor: usually bandaged behind nowadays: usually held up: versatile. *D. W. P. Arbuthnot*

ROBERTO RIVA 3 b.c. Shirley Heights 130 – Rustle of Silk 67 (General – Assembly (USA)) [1995 NR 1996 10.5d Sep 27] rangy, workmanlike colt: has scope: closely related to 1¾m winner Opus One (by Slip Anchor) and half-brother to several winners, including middle-distance stayer Royal York (by Bustino), 6f winners Craven (by Thatching) and Royal Diva (by Chief Singer) and very smart hurdler Squire Silk (by Natroun): dam lightly-raced half-sister to very smart middle-distance horse Kirtling and daughter of Irish 1000 Guineas second Silky: in need of race, 20 lengths eighth of 15 to Naazeq in maiden at Haydock: may do better. *J. L. Dunlop*

ROBINGO (IRE) 7 b.g. Bob Back (USA) 124 – Mill's Girl (Le Levanstell 122) 77 [1995 –: 14g 16.4m 1996 14d² May 6] close-coupled gelding: useful stayer (rated 102) for M. Pipe as 4-y-o: just fair form when second of 8 in steadily-run handicap at Haydock on only outing in 1996: blinkered and bandaged nowadays. *J. Neville*

ROBIN ISLAND   4 b.g. Robellino (USA) 127 – Irish Isle 67 (Realm 129) [1995 –
–: 7.6m⁴ 8.2m 10.1g⁶ 8m 1996 a10s a10g Nov 26] seems of little account these days.
P. R. Hedger

ROBO MAGIC (USA)   4 b.g. Tejano (USA) – Bubble Magic (USA) (Clever   52
Trick (USA)) [1995 58, a75: a7g³ a7g a6g* a7g⁵ 7g 7g⁴ 6m⁴ 6.1m 6m 6m* 6m 7d   a86
a7g⁴ a6g a5g² a6g* 1996 a6g³ a7g⁴ a6g* a6g* a6g⁵ 5d 6f 6m 6m⁶ 6m⁴ 5m 6f a6g
Dec 20] neat gelding: improved into a fairly useful handicapper on the all-weather at
Lingfield, winning twice in February: form on turf remains modest at best: effective
at 5f and probably at 7f: acts on good to firm and dead ground (below form on soft)
and goes well on equitrack: effective blinkered (rarely tried) or not. *L. Montague
Hall*

ROBSERA (IRE)   5 b.g. Robellino (USA) 127 – Que Sera 91 (Music Boy 124)   –
[1995 72: 8g 7m 8m 8.5m 8m a8.5g⁴ 8f⁵ 8.3m 8g 8.2m⁴ 1996 7.9g Sep 4] strong
gelding: fair handicapper in 1995 for G. Lewis: soundly beaten only flat outing for
new connections, but won over hurdles in December. *J. J. Quinn*

ROBUSTA (IRE)   3 b.f. Batshoof 122 – Loucoum (FR) 93 (Iron Duke (FR) 122)   69
[1995 NR 1996 8m 10m May 13] good-bodied filly: fourth foal: half-sister to 3
winners, including 4-y-o Iktasab (1m, by Cadeaux Genereux): dam pattern-placed at
2 yrs in France before winning 7 races in USA, most at around 1m: burly and very
green, ninth of 20 in newcomers event at Newmarket: broke leg at Windsor following
month: would have been suited by further than 1m: dead. *A. C. Stewart*

ROCHEA   2 br.f. (May 12) Rock City 120 – Pervenche (Latest Model 115) [1996   67
6m⁶ 6m⁴ a6g⁴ Oct 5] fifth foal: dam (unplaced here and USA) half-sister to 2000   a?
Guineas fourth Cut Throat: modest form in maidens at Yarmouth and Pontefract:
rather disappointing at Wolverhampton following month: not certain to stay beyond
7f. *W. J. Haggas*

ROCK AND REIGN   2 b.f. (Apr 22) Rock City 120 – Reina 24 (Homeboy 114)   –
[1996 7.1f Sep 12] first foal: dam, poor maiden, stayed 7f: 33/1, slowly away and
always behind in 18-runner maiden at Chepstow. *P. G. Murphy*

ROCKAROUNDTHECLOCK   2 b.g. (Mar 20) Rock City 120 – Times 55   65 d
(Junius (USA) 124) [1996 5d³ 5m 6d⁵ 6f³ a6g 6.1s Oct 22] 13,000Y: close-coupled   a?
gelding: fifth reported foal: half-brother to 1993 2-y-o 7f and 1m winner Times
Zando (by Forzando) and 1991 2-y-o 7f winner Military Expert (by Superlative):
dam disappointing maiden: easily best efforts when running-on third in maiden at
Haydock and nursery at Leicester: stays 6f: slowly away penultimate outing.
P. D. Evans

ROCKCRACKER (IRE)   4 ch.g. Ballad Rock 122 – Forest Blaze (USA) 82   67
(Green Forest (USA) 134) [1995 64, a56: a6g⁴ a7g 6.1g⁵ 6m 5.1m a7g 1996 a6g³ a6g   a56
a6g 5s⁵ 6f⁴ 5.1g 6f* 5m² 5.7g 6f 7f⁵ 6m* 6g⁵ 5m 6.1d 5.7m 6.1m 6m Oct 28] strong,
neat gelding: fair handicapper: won twice at Warwick, in May (minor event, gambled
on) and July: effective at 5f and 6f: acts on firm and soft ground and the all-weather:
usually blinkered/visored: none too consistent. *G. G. Margarson*

ROCK DAISY   3 b. or br.f. Rock City 120 – New Pastures (Formidable (USA)   –
125) [1995 –: 6d 1996 7m 8m Jun 14] no sign of ability. *M. Madgwick*

ROCK FANTASY   2 b.f. (Mar 1) Keen 116 – Runelia (Runnett 125) [1996 6m⁵   57 d
6m⁴ 7m 7m 6g 8m Sep 19] leggy, angular filly: has a round action: fourth reported
foal: half-sister to 3-y-o Sporting Fantasy (by Primo Dominie), 5f seller winner at 2
yrs, and 7f (at 2 yrs) and 8.3f winner Rock Foundation (by Rock City): dam half-
sister to smarter sprinter Touch Paper: appeared to show modest form first 2 starts:
never a factor in nurseries last 3 outings: stays 6f: blinkered last 2 starts (very keen to
post on first occasion): sweating profusely fourth outing. *C. Murray*

ROCK GROUP   4 b.g. Rock City 120 – Norska 67 (Northfields (USA)) [1995 61:   58
11.8g 12m³ 1996 12g 11.8d³ 15.4m⁶ 13s 14g³ 14d³ 16.4m⁴ Jun 5] tall gelding:
modest maiden handicapper: sold 800 gns Newmarket Autumn Sales: stays 1¾m:
acts on good to firm and dead going, poor efforts both outings on soft: tends to hang
right, and has looked a difficult ride. *J. Pearce*

ROCK OYSTER   4 b.g. Ballad Rock 122 – Bombshell 76 (Le Levanstell 122)   –
[1995 53: 8g 8.2m 8.3m 10m³ 11.6m 10f 8m⁶ 8f a9.4g 1996 a16g Jan 13] rangy
gelding: modest maiden at best: soundly beaten only 4-y-o outing. *B. J. Meehan*

ROCK SYMPHONY 6 ch.g. Ballad Rock 122 – Shamasiya (FR) (Vayrann 133) 88 d
[1995 93: 6m 6f⁴ 6f 6m⁶ 6f* 6m 6m 5m 1996 5g⁶ 6m 6m 6m⁴ 6.1m 6g 6m⁴ 6m 6g
Aug 24] strong gelding: fairly useful handicapper: not at best in 1996, going in
snatches fifth start and finding little on sixth: effective at stiff 5f to 7f: acts on firm
and dead ground: tried visored and blinkered, no improvement: held up. *W. J. Haggas*

ROCK THE BARNEY (IRE) 7 ch.h. Coquelin (USA) 121 – Lady Loire 94 53 d
(Wolverlife 115) [1995 59: 10d 10m³ 10g⁵ 11.4g* 12f* 11.4m 12f³ 11.9m 12g 12m⁵
1996 11.8d⁵ 11.6m⁶ 11.4m 12m 10m² 14d 11.9g 11.5m² a2g4 a13g Nov 26]
smallish horse: unimpressive mover: modest handicapper: short-headed at Sandown
(apprentices) in September, cruising up to lead 2f out but caught post: stays 1½m:
acts on any going: tried blinkered/visored (looked none too keen), no improvement:
best held up. *P. Burgoyne*

ROCK THE CASBAH 2 ch.g. (Feb 21) Rock City 120 – Romantic Saga 69 59 d
(Prince Tenderfoot (USA) 126) [1996 6m⁴ 6m 7d a5g a7g a8g⁶ Dec 11] 4,000Y,
10,500 2-y-o: leggy, close-coupled gelding: has a short action: third foal: half-brother
to 3-y-o Lady Eclat (by Nomination), 6f seller winner at 2 yrs: dam placed over 5f
and 6f at 2 yrs: keeping-on fourth in median auction maiden at York on debut: well
beaten afterwards. *J. Hetherton*

ROCK TO THE TOP (IRE) 2 b.c. (May 2) Rudimentary (USA) 118 – Well 66
Bought (IRE) 35 (Auction Ring (USA) 123) [1996 6m 7g 6.9d a5g⁴ a5g a6g² Dec 31]
12,000Y: first foal: dam, poor maiden half-sister to smart middle-distance winner
Open Day and smart 1977 French 2-y-o River Knight, from very good family: fair
maiden: should stay beyond 6f. *J. J. Sheehan*

ROCKUSA 4 b.f. Rock City 120 – Miss Derby (USA) (Master Derby (USA)) –
[1995 41: 9g 10g a8.5g⁴ 8d³ 7g⁵ 9m 1996 7.6m 11.9g 11.8f Oct 15] neat filly: poor
maiden: tried visored, no improvement: sold 1,200 gns Ascot November Sales: sent
to South Korea. *P. R. Hedger*

ROCKVILLE PIKE (IRE) 4 b.g. Glenstal (USA) 118 – Sound Pet (Runnett 53 §
125) [1995 83: 6m 6g⁴ 6f⁴ a6g 1996 a6g 6s a10g 7d* 6f 8m 8.3m⁵ 8.3m⁵ 6.9m³ 7f 8m
Jul 5] compact gelding: modest performer at best nowadays: made all in seller at
Leicester in April: sold out of S. Dow's stable 4,100 gns Ascot June Sales after ninth
4-y-o start: stays 8.3f: acts on good to firm and dead ground: usually visored:
unreliable. *John Berry*

ROCKY FORUM 4 ch.f. Deploy 131 – Beau's Delight (USA) (Lypheor 118) 78
[1995 64: a10g⁵ a8g⁴ a10g⁶ 12d² 11.6m⁶ 11.4g⁴ 14d* 13.3f⁶ a12g² a16g* 1996
16.4g² 16s* 16d* 14d² 20f Jun 18] fair handicapper: won at Newbury and Kempton
in May: ran well in Ascot Stakes final start: stayed very well: acted on any going:
bandaged at 4 yrs: tough and consistent: dead. *G. L. Moore*

ROCKY OASIS (USA) 3 b.c. Gulch (USA) – Knoosh (USA) 113 (Storm Bird 93
(CAN) 134) [1995 84p: 7g³ 1996 10d² May 28] rangy colt: good mover: improved
on only 2-y-o effort when ¾-length second of 16 to Shantou in maiden at Sandown,
travelling smoothly to lead 2f out and running on strongly once headed: stays 1¼m:
looked sure to win a race. *M. R. Stoute*

ROCKY'S METEOR 3 b.c. Emarati (USA) 74 – Hoop La (Final Straw 127) –
[1995 61: 6m² a6g 1996 7.1d⁶ 8.1d Jun 7] rather leggy colt: modest maiden: stiff task
at Haydock on reappearance: tongue tied, well beaten there only subsequent outing:
sold 500 gns Doncaster November Sales: probably stays 7f. *R. A. Fahey*

ROCKY STREAM 3 b.f. Reprimand 122 – Pebble Creek (IRE) (Reference Point 43
139) [1995 NR 1996 6g 7g 6g 5f⁵ 8.2m 7s³ a7g 7d⁶ 9.9g 6f⁶ Sep 23] 5,200Y:
sparely-made filly: first foal: dam unraced daughter of Pebbles: poor maiden
handicapper: sold 1,500 gns Doncaster September Sales: should stay 1m (well below
form at 1¼m): acts on firm and soft ground, tailed off only start on the all-weather:
hung left from halfway fourth start: sent to South Korea. *R. M. Whitaker*

ROCKY TWO 5 b.g. Cree Song 99 – Holloway Wonder 93 (Swing Easy (USA) –
126) [1995 60: a5g² 5d⁶ a5g⁵ a5g a6g 5m 6m⁵ 6g 5m³ 5f⁵ 5m⁶ 5.1d 5.3g a5g³ a5g⁵
a5g 1996 a5g a6g⁵ a7g a7g⁵ 6.9s 6g⁶ 7m 5m⁶ 5.1m 8m Aug 13] leggy gelding: has a
quick action: poor handicapper at best nowadays: sold out of P. Howling's stable
1,000 gns Ascot June (1996) Sales: well beaten both starts for new yard: stays 6f,

very best form at 5f: acts on the all-weather and any turf ground: often wears blinkers/visor: usually races prominently. *N. R. Mitchell*

ROCKY WATERS (USA) 7 b. or br.g. Rocky Marriage (USA) 95 – Running 59 Melody 86 (Rheingold 137) [1995 64, a75: a6g³ a7g² a7g³ a6g² a6g⁵ 7m a7g⁴ 7g 6m 6m 7.1m 5g 1996 6g 6.1g 7f² 8g² 8g a8.5g⁴ 8f² 8.1m⁵ 7f⁴ a7g³ 8g 8m Sep 25] leggy, lightly-made gelding: has a roundish action: modest handicapper: stays 8.5f: acts on all-weather surfaces and on firm ground, probably on soft: tends to sweat: sometimes takes strong hold: bandaged behind in 1996: visored last 3 starts. *P. Burgoyne*

ROCQUAINE BAY 9 b.m. Morston (FR) 125 – Queen's Royale 80 (Tobrouk 42 (FR)) [1995 46: 12m⁴ 12g 12m⁴ 12f⁵ 14m⁵ 12m* 12f* 11.9f³ 1996 12g⁵ 12g⁴ 12g 12g⁴ 12m⁴ 11.9f 14m⁶ 17.2d Sep 30] good-topped mare: poor handicapper: probably stays 1¾m: best on a sound surface: held up: unseated rider and bolted (reportedly upset by patriotic racegoers celebrating Shearer's goal) before second intended 9-y-o start. *M. J. Bolton*

RODEO STAR (USA) 10 ch.g. Nodouble (USA) – Roundup Rose (USA) – (Minnesota Mac) [1995 NR 1996 16.1g May 22] workmanlike, plain gelding: formerly a fairly useful staying handicapper: fair chaser nowadays: showed nil on return to flat. *N. Tinkler*

RODERICK HUDSON 4 b.g. Elmaamul (USA) 125 – Moviegoer 104 (Pharly – (FR) 130) [1995 86: 7m⁶ 7f² 7m² 7m* 7.1m⁵ 7f 1996 7m 7.3m 5g Aug 26] angular gelding: fairly useful performer at 3 yrs: tongue tied and well beaten in 1996: raced mainly at 7f (bred to stay further but takes keen hold and may not do so): has raced only on a sound surface: has worn crossed noseband. *J. A. R. Toller*

ROFFEY SPINNEY (IRE) 2 ch.c. (Apr 27) Masterclass (USA) 116 – Crossed 65 Line (Thatching 131) [1996 6v³ a8g Dec 20] IR 6,000F, IR 21,000Y: resold: dam unplaced all 4 starts in Ireland, half-sister to useful Irish sprinter Aberuschka out of half-sister to high-class sprinter Abergwaun: much better effort in maidens when never-nearer third at Folkestone on debut: not certain to stay 1m. *R. Hannon*

ROGUE TRADER (IRE) 3 b.g. Mazaad 106 – Ruby Relic (Monseigneur – (USA) 127) [1995 NR 1996 8g May 17] IR 3,200Y: workmanlike gelding: seventh reported foal: half-brother to 7f winner Jolly Fisherman (by Montekin): dam never ran: moved poorly to post and always in rear in Newmarket claimer. *Dr J. D. Scargill*

ROI DE LA MER (IRE) 5 b.h. Fairy King (USA) – Sea Mistress (Habitat 134) 63 [1995 70: 8g 10d 10m 10.8f⁴ 8g 9m 8.3g³ 8.1g* 10m 8g⁶ 8d⁵ 8.2m⁵ 1996 8d⁴ 10g 10m 8.2m³ 8.1m 8m* 10m 8f 8f 10.1m² 8m 7f⁵ Oct 15] leggy, angular horse: fair performer: unlucky third and fourth starts but generally disappointing afterwards, not needing to be at best to win seller at Ripon in July: sold 7,000 gns Newmarket Autumn Sales: very best form at 1m/9f: acts on firm ground and dead: visored (below form) twice in 1995: has carried head awkwardly: takes good hold (suited by a good gallop) and best waited with: sent to Italy. *J. Akehurst*

ROI DU NORD (FR) 4 b.g. Top Ville 129 – Ridja (FR) (Djakao (FR) 124) [1995 72 d 13g⁴ 1996 8m⁶ 10.1m³ 10s 10.1m 10m⁶ Sep 26] 400,000 francs Y: workmanlike ex-French gelding: half-brother to several winners in France and Spain, including useful 9f to 10.5f winner Carridge (by Carwhite): dam French 1m winner from good family: close fourth of 9 in maiden at Saint-Malo at 3 yrs for J. Hammond: winner over hurdles here before showing fair form at best on flat: stays 1¼m: none too consistent. *S. W. Campion*

ROISIN CLOVER 5 ch.m. Faustus (USA) 118 – Valiyen (Valiyar 129) [1995 69: 73 d 12g* 12m³ 12f² 12m 12m⁴ 10d 1996 12m* 12m 12m 12m⁵ 12g 12m 14m³ 11.5m² 12g Nov 1] leggy, lengthy mare: fair handicapper: won at Kempton in April for second successive year: below form afterwards, leaving S. Dow's stable after eighth start: probably stays 1¾m: acts on firm and dead going: normally held up. *R. Rowe*

ROKA 4 br.f. Rock City 120 – Kalandariya 78 (Kris 135) [1995 58: 7m 6g 7g 1996 – 6g 7m 8g 6f Jun 1] close-coupled filly: modest maiden, lightly raced: well beaten in handicaps in 1996: tried blinkered. *R. Hannon*

ROKEBY BOWL 4 b.g. Salse (USA) 128 – Rose Bowl (USA) 131 (Habitat 134) 95 [1995 101: 6g⁴ 6.9g 7.5m² 7.9g 10g* 9g* 10.3m² 10.4m⁴ 12f² 11.9g² 12d 10v⁵ 1996 10g³ 10m⁴ 12m⁵ Aug 2] small, quite attractive gelding: useful handicapper: not seen until July, fourth and fifth in valuable events at Goodwood on last 2 starts: stays

1½m well: acts on firm ground, below form on a soft surface: held up: genuine and consistent. *I. A. Balding*

ROMALITO 6 b.g. Robellino (USA) 127 – Princess Zita 90 (Manado 130) [1995 –
43: a16g³ 16m 14.9g 16.5g 14.1f* 14g⁵ 14g⁵ 16m⁶ 16m⁵ 16d 17.2m⁵ 16.1g 1996
a16g 17.2f May 11] good-topped gelding: has a markedly round action: below form
in 1996: stays 17.2f: acts on good to firm ground and dead: blinkered/visored (below
form) once each. *M. Blanshard*

ROMAN GOLD (IRE) 3 b.c. Petorius 117 – Saffron (FR) (Fabulous Dancer 83
(USA) 124) [1995 94: 7f⁵ 6g 7f⁴ 6f⁶ 7m⁴ 8m³ 8.5s² a8g* a8g* 1996 10.5g* 12d 9g
8.1v a8.5g⁵ Dec 13] close-coupled colt: fairly useful handicapper: won rated stakes
at Haydock in April: showed little afterwards: sold out of R. Hannon's stable 15,500
gns Newmarket Autumn Sales after penultimate outing: should stay further than
10.5f: acts on firm and soft going, best 2-y-o form on the all-weather. *M. Machowsky,
USA*

ROMAN IMP (IRE) 2 ch.g. (Mar 9) Imp Society (USA) – Luvi Ullmann 97
(Thatching 131) [1996 5m² 5g* 5g² 5m⁴ 6m³ Aug 1] IR 14,000Y: angular, useful-
looking gelding: not a good walker or mover: fifth foal: half-brother to several
winners in Italy, including (at up to 1¼m) Lavezzola (by Salmon Leap): dam won 7
times in Italy at 5f/6f: sire Grade 2/3 winner in USA from 8.5f to 1¼m: won maiden
at Sandown in April: good efforts in listed/pattern events afterwards, on last 2 outings
fourth to Tipsy Creek in Norfolk Stakes at Ascot and third to Easycall in Richmond
Stakes at Goodwood: stays 6f: acts on good to firm ground: swished tail first 2 starts:
gelded: sent to Hong Kong. *A. P. Jarvis*

ROMAN REEL (USA) 5 ch.g. Sword Dance – Our Mimi (USA) (Believe It 69
(USA)) [1995 71, a62: a8g⁶ a9.4g a10g* a10g a10g⁴ 9.7g³ 8m 10m⁴ 8.1m* 10.1m⁵ a60
8f² a10g 9f³ 8f a10g 1996 a8g² a8g² a8g² a8g⁴ 8g 10f* 10f* 8.1m² 10.1g 10f⁶ 10m²
10f³ 10f Oct 15] lengthy, good-quartered gelding: good mover: fair handicapper:
confidently ridden to win seller in May and claimer in June, both at Brighton:
effective at 1m and 1¼m: acts very well on firm going, below form all 5 starts on
dead ground: also effective on the all-weather: suitable mount for an inexperienced
rider: effective from front or held up. *G. L. Moore*

ROMANTIC WARRIOR 3 b.g. Welsh Captain 113 – Romantic Melody 56 –
(Battle Hymn 103) [1995 NR 1996 8.2m 10g⁶ Oct 9] tall, workmanlike gelding: first
foal: dam, maiden, stayed 1m: little form in maidens at Nottingham. *K. S. Bridgwater*

ROMIOS (IRE) 4 ch.c. Common Grounds 118 – Domino's Nurse 104 (Dom 90 §
Racine (FR) 121) [1995 91: 10.4m³ 10m 10.5g* 10g 10v² 1996 10g 8d 10.3g 10d
11.9m³ 11.9g² 10m³ 12g⁶ 11.9f² 12g 12m³ 12s Nov 9] sturdy, workmanlike colt:
fairly useful handicapper: stays 1½m: acts on any going: effective blinkered at 2 yrs,
has not worn them since: tends to pull hard: sweating (respectable eighth in very
valuable event) tenth 4-y-o start: has looked reluctant, appearing to throw race away
sixth 4-y-o start. *P. F. I. Cole*

RONQUISTA D'OR 2 b.c. (Feb 14) Ron's Victory (USA) 129 – Gild The Lily –
83 (Ile de Bourbon (USA) 133) [1996 a7g 8.1s Oct 22] second reported foal: dam 9f
winner who seemed to stay 2m: showed nothing in maidens at Wolverhampton and
Chepstow over 2 months apart. *G. A. Ham*

RONS REVENGE 2 b. or br.g. (Apr 2) Midyan (USA) 124 – Nip (Bay Express 50 d
132) [1996 a5g 6.1d⁵ a6g³ 7.5m* 7f⁶ 7f⁵ 7.5f 7.1m 7.6m Sep 10] 1,200 2-y-o: first
foal: dam no worthwhile form: made all in 11-runner seller at Beverley in July:
soundly beaten afterwards, including in similar company: sold to join G. L. Moore
2,600 gns Doncaster November Sales: stays 7.5f: acts on good to firm ground, has
shown nothing on fibresand: blinkered final start. *M. J. Ryan*

RON'S ROUND 2 ch.c. (Mar 28) Ron's Victory (USA) 129 – Magical Spirit 70 –
(Top Ville 129) [1996 6m Aug 15] 7,800F, 5,000Y: rather leggy colt: third foal: half-
brother to fairly useful 4-y-o 9f and 1¼m winner Sharpical (also winning hurdler, by
Sharpo): dam, placed over middle distances, half-sister to good 7f to 1½m winner
John French: 33/1 and very green, slowly away and always behind in maiden auction
at Salisbury. *K. O. Cunningham-Brown*

RON'S SECRET 4 br.f. Efisio 120 – Primrose Bank 91 (Charlottown 127) [1995 74
92: 7m⁵ 8m³ 8f* 8m⁴ 9f* 10m³ 10m 8.1d⁴ 8.1s* 8g³ 8m 1996 8.1g 8s 8m 10m 10m

$9m^5 9g^4 9g^5 8m^6 10.5v^4 8.2g$ Oct 24] neat filly: has a round action: fairly useful handicapper at 3 yrs: not so good in 1996: stays $1\frac{1}{4}$m: acts on firm and soft going: creditable efforts both starts in blinkers: sold 5,000 gns Newmarket December Sales. *J. W. Payne*

ROOD MUSIC   5 ro.g. Sharrood (USA) 124 – Rose Music 86 (Luthier 126) [1995 – 60, a78: 8g 8.1m* 10.1f 7m 8.1g 9f 8.1s^6 a8g* a9.4g^2 a8g* 1996 8.3m 8.1m^5 10.1m a9.4g Dec 14] lengthy, workmanlike gelding: fair handicapper on the all-weather: modest on turf: well beaten in 1996: stays 9.4f: acts on good to firm ground and on fibresand. *M. G. Meagher*

ROOKERY GIRL   4 b.f. Pharly (FR) 130 – Persian Grey (Persepolis (FR) 127) – [1995 55: a8g 7d 7g 7.3g 7m 1996 10g 9.7m Jul 15] angular filly: modest maiden: well beaten in 1996: should prove suited by 1m+. *H. J. Collingridge*

RORY   5 b.g. Dowsing (USA) 124 – Crymlyn 68 (Welsh Pageant 132) [1995 82: 80 $9.9m^4 10m 9m^5 8g 8g^5 8.9g^6 8f^6$ 1996 8g 8g 10m* 10m 10.3m^3 10.1m^2 9m^5 Sep 26] leggy gelding: fairly useful handicapper: won at Ripon in June: effective at 1m to $1\frac{1}{4}$m: acts on firm and dead ground: held up. *Mrs J. Cecil*

ROSEATE LODGE   10 b.g. Habitat 134 – Elegant Tern (USA) 102 (Sea Bird II 47 145) [1995 62d: a8g^5 7d* 6m^4 8.3m^2 8m^2 8g^4 8m^5 8.9m 8m^5 8.1d 7g 8g^3 7d 8g 1996 10.3d 8g 8.5g 8g 7.1g 8m 8.1m^6 6m* 7m^2 8m^3 6f^6 8.3g^6 8g^3 8m Sep 20] compact, workmanlike gelding: poor handicapper nowadays: won contest for amateurs and trainers at Hamilton in August: effective at 6f, and stays $1\frac{1}{4}$m: acts on any going: tried blinkered, not in 1996: usually held up. *S. E. Kettlewell*

ROSEBERRY AVENUE (IRE)   3 b.c. Sadler's Wells (USA) 132 – Lady's 79 Bridge (USA) 81 (Sir Ivor 135) [1995 76p: 7g 10g^6 8f^5 1996 12m^5 14d* 16.4g^3 15m^2 Sep 19] good-topped colt: has scope: fairly useful handicapper: won at Sandown in August by 5 lengths, stretching clear from over 2f out despite wandering: stays 2m: acts on good to firm and dead ground: won over hurdles for R. Akehurst in December. *Lady Herries*

ROSEBERRY TOPPING   7 gr.g. Nicholas Bill 125 – Habitab (Sovereign Path – 125) [1995 59: a11g^3 1996 a12g Jan 5] big, workmanlike gelding: modest maiden handicapper, lightly raced: below form only 7-y-o start: stays 11f: acts on fibresand: usually edgy: rather headstrong, and sometimes finds little. *Mrs M. Reveley*

ROSE CARNIVAL   2 b.f. (Apr 13) Salse (USA) 128 – Jungle Rose 90 (Shirley 74 Heights 130) [1996 6m 7g* 7m Oct 1] rangy, unfurnished filly: looked weak: fourth foal: half-sister to 1994 2-y-o 5.9f winner Jungle Patrol (by Night Shift) and 1m to 10.5f winner Desert Fighter (by Green Desert): dam lightly-raced $1\frac{1}{4}$m winner out of Lowther winner Prickle: odds on, won maiden auction at Thirsk in September by 2 lengths from River of Fortune: keen to post, fair ninth of 14 to Nightbird in nursery at Newmarket following month: likely to stay beyond 7f: tends to carry head high: may be capable of better. *D. R. Loder*

ROSE CHIME (IRE)   4 b. or br.f. Tirol 127 – Repicado Rose (USA) (Repicado – (CHI)) [1995 45, a37: a8.5g^5 a7g^5 a8g^4 9.2g^6 8g 7f^5 a12g^4 11.1f^6 a8g 1996 a11g a12g^6 a11g 9.9m 12g^5 11.8d 14.1f a12g 8m Aug 8] leggy, lengthy filly: poor performer: well held in 1996: probably stays 1m: acts on good to firm and soft ground: tried blinkered, no improvement. *J. L. Harris*

ROSENKAVALIER (IRE)   2 b.g. (Mar 19) Classic Music (USA) – Top Bloom – (Thatch (USA) 136) [1996 5.1f 6g 6m 8f Oct 8] 12,000Y: smallish gelding: third reported foal: half-brother to 2-y-o sprint winners Thorny Flat (by Precocious) and Serious Option (by Reprimand): dam (ran twice in Ireland) is half-sister to smart Irish 5f to 7f winner Hegemony, later successful at 1m in USA: well beaten in varied company. *L. G. Cottrell*

ROSE OF GLENN   5 b.m. Crofthall 110 – May Kells (Artaius (USA) 129) [1995 45 55, a51: a16g^3 a12g^4 a16g^3 a14g a14g^4 17.2f* 17.2f^6 16m 11.7h^2 16d^3 14d a12g^6 16.4m a14g a14g* a13g^6 1996 a16g^4 a16g a13g a16g 14.1d a14g 15.4g 14d^2 11.8f^5 a12g a14.8g^2 a14.8g a14.8g^5 Dec 14] leggy, sparely-made mare: poor handicapper: stays 17.2f: acts on hard ground, soft and all-weather surfaces: visored (below form) once at 2 yrs: races prominently: none too consistent. *B. Palling*

ROSE OF SIBERIA (USA)   3 gr.f. Siberian Express (USA) 125 – Exuberine – (FR) 82 (Be My Guest (USA) 126) [1995 68: 5g^4 7m^5 6.1m^2 6m^6 10d^4 10m* 1996

10.3d 14.6m May 6] workmanlike filly: fair form at 2 yrs: well below form in handicaps in 1996: sold 20,000 gns Newmarket December Sales: should stay 1½m: acts on good to firm and dead ground. *M. Bell*

ROSE SHARP   2 b.f. (Apr 13) Forzando 122 – Katie Scarlett 70 (Lochnager 132)   –
[1996 8.2m Sep 24] close-coupled filly: second foal: half-sister to 3-y-o 8.3f winner Antarctic Storm (by Emarati): dam 1¼m winner, also won over hurdles: 66/1, green and in need of race, tailed off in maiden at Nottingham: sold 650 gns Doncaster October Sales. *C. Smith*

ROSES IN THE SNOW (IRE)   3 gr.f. Be My Guest (USA) 126 – Desert   101
Bluebell 83 (Kalaglow 132) [1995 82: 5m² 5m⁴ 6m² 6g⁶ 5m² 6m² 7d 7f² 1996 8f* 8f⁶ 7g 10m 10.1m² 12d 10g⁵ Nov 1] leggy, close-coupled filly: fluent mover: useful performer: won maiden at Bath in May: sweating, very stiff task and 40/1, best effort when around 6½ lengths seventh of 11 to Time Allowed in Princess Royal Stakes at Ascot on penultimate start, pushed along some way out and never nearer: may be better at 1½m than shorter: acts on firm and dead ground. *J. W. Hills*

ROSE TINT (IRE)   3 b.f. Salse (USA) 128 – Sally Rose 92 (Sallust 134) [1995   –
–p: 5.2g⁶ 1996 7m 8.1m 8d a10g⁴ a9.4g⁵ Nov 25] small filly: has a quick action: poor maiden: sold 1,200 gns Newmarket December Sales. *Lord Huntingdon*

ROSSEL (USA)   3 b.g. Blushing John (USA) 120 – Northern Aspen (USA) 120   67
(Northern Dancer) [1995 65p: 7g 8f⁵ 1996 6.9m 8.2m 11f³ 12.1g* 15m⁵ 12.4f⁴ 13m 12.1f Aug 19] rangy gelding: fair form: 3/1 on, won claimer at Musselburgh (claimed out of M. Stoute's stable £8,000) in July: well below form in handicaps last 2 starts: probably stays 15f: yet to race on a soft surface: visored (wandered and looked none too keen) third 3-y-o start: won over hurdles three times up to December. *P. Monteith*

ROSTAQ   3 b.g. Keen 116 – American Beauty 74 (Mill Reef (USA) 141) [1995 68:   –
7g³ 7m² 1996 a9.4g³ a11g⁴ 10.2g a9.4g May 25] angular gelding: fair form at 2 yrs: well below form in 1996: should stay 1¼m: tried blinkered. *D. J. G. Murray Smith*

ROSY OUTLOOK (USA)   2 b. or br.f. (Jan 21) Trempolino (USA) 135 –   66
Rosyphard (USA) (Lyphard (USA) 132) [1996 6m⁶ 7g Sep 25] 30,000Y: rather leggy filly: first foal: dam once-raced sister to smart French sprinter Tenue de Soiree, closely related to smart French 7f/1m performer Neverneyev and half-sister to very smart French pair Squill and Baiser Vole: shaped promisingly in Kempton maiden on debut: gave impression something amiss only subsequent start. *I. A. Balding*

ROTHERFIELD PARK (IRE)   4 b.f. High Estate 127 – Alriyaah 73 (Shareef   40
Dancer (USA) 135) [1995 40: a6g⁵ a6g a6g⁴ 6m a5g 5m 5d 6m a6g 1996 5g 5g⁶ 6m⁵ 5f² 6.1m⁴ 5m⁴ 5m⁴ 5f Aug 14] neat filly: poor sprint handicapper: acts on firm ground and the all-weather. *C. Smith*

ROTHERFIELD QUEEN (IRE)   2 b.f. (Apr 19) Mac's Imp (USA) 116 –   –
Blazing Success (Blazing Saddles (AUS)) [1996 5g 6g 6g Aug 3] IR 9,200Y: third foal: half-sister to German 3-y-o 6f (at 2 yrs) to 1m winner Fast Indian (by Classic Secret): dam unraced half-sister to useful sprinter Rotherfield Greys: behind in varied maiden events at Windsor. *G. M. McCourt*

ROTHLEY IMP (IRE)   3 b.f. Mac's Imp (USA) 116 – Valediction 71 (Town   –
Crier 119) [1995 55: 5m 6g 7g⁵ 7m⁶ 6m² 5m² 6d 1996 a6g⁶ a7g 6.1d 6.1g 7f 6m 11f Sep 27] tall, leggy filly: modest maiden: well below form in 1996: should stay at least 7f: acts on good to firm ground. *J. Wharton*

ROTOR MAN (IRE)   2 b.c. (Apr 27) River Falls 113 – Need For Cash (USA)   67 ?
(Raise A Native) [1996 6m 6g 6g Nov 1] IR 19,000F, 30,000Y: leggy, useful-looking colt: half-brother to 3 winners abroad, including German 6.5f winner Nantesio (by Tate Gallery): dam won at up to 7f in USA: down the field in maidens late in year, not beaten far in steadily-run race second start: not easy to assess. *J. D. Bethell*

ROUFONTAINE   5 gr.m. Rousillon (USA) 133 – Bellifontaine (FR) (Bellypha   85
130) [1995 72§: 10m² 10g 10m⁵ 10.2m⁵ 12m⁵ 12f⁴ 1996 a12g* a12g 12.1d* 10.2g* 10.2m* 9f⁴ 10m⁶ 10m* 10.2f⁴ 10m⁵ 12d Oct 11] workmanlike mare: fairly useful performer: formerly unreliable but in good form for much of 1996, winning maiden at Southwell (hung right) in February and handicaps at Chepstow in May and June (2) and at Sandown (amateurs minor event) in August: unlikely to stay much beyond 1½m: acts on firm and dead ground and on fibresand: blinkered (ran creditably) final 4-y-o start: sometimes find little. *W. R. Muir*

ROUGE RANCON (USA) 3 b.f. Red Ransom (USA) – Lady O'Lyph (Lyphard 86
(USA) 132) [1995 98: 6g* 7g⁵ 8d⁴ 1996 10.4m³ 9g⁶ Dec 28] tall, good-topped filly:
failed to progress as expected at 2 yrs: headstrong in minor event at York only 3-y-o
outing in Britain, for P. Cole: should prove best at around 1m. *M. D. Wolfson, USA*

ROUSHAN 3 ch.c. Anshan 119 – Fleur Rouge 71 (Pharly (FR) 130) [1995 –p: 6g 86
1996 7m⁵ 7.1d³ 8g 8d⁴ 7g* 8m³ 7.1m* 7m Oct 4] leggy, angular colt: bolted to post
on fifth intended outing in 1996 and subsequently left J. O'Shea: won maiden at Ayr
in August (on first outing for new yard) and minor event at Sandown following
month: sold 10,000 gns Newmarket Autumn Sales: likely to prove best at up to 1m:
acts on good to firm and dead going: tends to hang under pressure, but ran on gamely
at Sandown: usually makes running: sent to Sweden. *S. C. Williams*

ROUSITTO 8 ch.g. Rousillon (USA) 133 – Helenetta 97 (Troy 137) [1995 –, a63: –
a11g* a12g³ a11g² a12g⁵ a12g⁴ a14g⁶ a12g² 1996 a12g a12g a14.8g a12g⁵ Nov 25]
modest performer: tailed off in 1996: sometimes looks none too keen. *R. Hollinshead*

ROUSSI (USA) 4 b.g. Nureyev (USA) 131 – Iva Reputation (USA) (Sir Ivor 135) –
[1995 69: 10g³ 11.9d 10d⁴ 1996 10.1s 8g 9.9g a8g a9.4g Nov 11] good-bodied
gelding: fair maiden for M. Stoute in 1995: has shown little for new stable: should
stay beyond 1¼m. *D. Nicholls*

ROVING MINSTREL 5 ch.h. Cree Song 99 – Klairove 74 (Averof 123) [1995 95
92: 8g* 8g 7m 7.9g 7m² 8g⁴ 7.6m 8d² 9g 1996 8s² 7m³ 7m 7.1d May 6] good-topped
horse: often looks very well: fairly useful handicapper: placed in the Lincoln at
Doncaster (a race he won in 1995) and rated stakes at Newmarket first 2 5-y-o starts:
well below form both subsequent outings: effective at 7f to 1m: twice below form
on very firm ground, acts on any other, including fibresand: races close up: game.
B. A. McMahon

ROWLANDSONS CHARM (IRE) 3 b.f. Fayruz 116 – Magic Gold (Sallust –
134) [1995 60, a64: 5g³ 6m 5m 5m 6m³ 5g 6.9s 6.9g a7g⁶ a7g² a7g³ 1996 a8g* a62
a7g² a8g* a10g² a10g⁴ a8g* a8g³ a7g² 8.3m 9.7d a10g² a13g⁵ a13g Dec 13] sturdy,
workmanlike filly: carries condition: modest performer: won 2 claimers and a seller
at Lingfield early in year for G. L. Moore: trained ninth start only by A. Moore:
acts on the all-weather: usually visored: usually forces pace: carries head awkwardly:
wayward, and not one to trust implicitly. *Miss B. Sanders*

ROWLANDSONS STUD (IRE) 3 b. or br.g. Distinctly North (USA) 115 – Be 52
My Million (Taufan (USA) 119) [1995 –, a64: 6m⁵ 6m a6g a5g⁴ 1996 a6g² a6g³ a63
a6g³ a5g³ a6g² a6g⁶ a6g* 6f³ 5.1g 5g 6m 5.1f a6g⁴ 7m 6m a6g Nov 25] modest
handicapper: won at Lingfield in March: left G. L. Moore after ninth start and A.
Moore after tenth: stays 6f: goes well on equitrack, and acts on firm ground:
inconsistent. *P. Burgoyne*

ROXANE (IRE) 3 b.f. Cyrano de Bergerac 120 – Janet Oliphant 49 (Red Sunset –
120) [1995 –: a7g 1996 a7g a6g a5g 5d 5g May 31] leggy filly: no sign of ability.
A. Bailey

ROYAL ACCLAIM 11 ch.g. Tender King 123 – Glimmer 58 (Hot Spark 126) – §
[1995 –§, a46§: a8.5g⁵ a8.5g⁴ a11g⁵ a8g⁵ a9.4g³ a8g⁵ 10.3g 9.7g 10g a9.4g 1996 a8g a33 §
a11g a9.4g⁵ 10g a8g³ 10.5d 9.7f⁶ 8.1f Jul 2] sturdy gelding: carries condition: poor
handicapper: sold (J. M. Bradley to R. Dickin) 600 gns Ascot October Sales: stays
11f: acts on all-weather surfaces, probably on any turf going: tried blinkered, nearly
always visored: usually ridden by apprentice/amateur: often gets behind: none too
resolute. *J. M. Bradley*

ROYAL ACTION 3 b.c. Royal Academy (USA) 130 – Ivor's Honey 91 (Sir Ivor 75
135) [1995 NR 1996 8.2s⁵ 10g 8m³ 8.3m⁵ 11.5f² 10.1m⁴ 12m 11.9g 8m³ a8s* Nov a83
19] 24,000Y: good-topped colt: good mover: half-brother to useful 1¼m winner Stif-
felio (by Be My Guest), winning middle-distance stayer Artaius Mead (by Artaius)
and a winner abroad by Nureyev: dam, Irish 1¼m winner, sister to Irish Oaks third
I've A Bee: fairly useful performer: improved effort on first run on equitrack to win
maiden at Lingfield in November by 5 lengths: effective at 1m to 11.5f: acts on firm
and soft ground, and on equitrack: blinkered (finished last) seventh start. *J. E. Banks*

ROYAL AMARETTO (IRE) 2 b.c. (May 11) Fairy King (USA) – Melbourne 103
Miss (Chaparral (FR) 128) [1996 7g³ 7.1m⁴ 7.1f* 7.3s² Oct 24] IR 36,000F, 18,000Y:
big, strong colt: has plenty of scope: closely related to winners abroad by Northfields

and Jareer and half-brother to stayer Taroudant (by Pharly) and a winner in Italy by Bob Back: dam unraced close relation to Grand Prix de Paris winner Tennyson: third to Bahhare in maiden at Newmarket on debut: won 18-runner maiden at Chepstow in September: showed himself a useful colt when battling ¾-length second to Desert Story in Horris Hill at Newbury: will probably stay 1¼m: has won on firm ground but easily best effort on soft: took keen hold third start. *B. J. Meehan*

ROYAL APPLAUSE 3 b.c. Waajib 121 – Flying Melody (Auction Ring (USA) 123) [1995 123p: 5.2g* 6m* 6m* 6g* 1996 8m 5f⁶ 6m* 6f Sep 7] medium-sized colt: good mover: unbeaten at 2 yrs, impressive winner of Middle Park Stakes at Newmarket: well below form in 1996, in 2000 Guineas at Newmarket (allowed to bowl along in clear lead) and King's Stand Stakes at Royal Ascot on first 2 starts: unimpressive in landing odds in 5-runner minor event at Doncaster in July by neck from Russian Revival, and ninth of 11 in Haydock Park Sprint Cup: may prove best at around 6f: yet to race on a soft surface. *B. W. Hills* — 109

ROYAL ATY (IRE) 2 b.c. (Feb 27) Royal Academy (USA) 130 – Atyaaf (USA) 48 (Irish River (FR) 131) [1996 8d² Nov 3] 52,000F, 56,000Y: second foal: dam thrice-raced half-sister to smart 6f and 7.2f winner Weldnaas: second to subsequent Group 2 runner-up Yavlensky in minor event at Milan in November: will probably stay beyond 1m: sure to do better. *P. A. Kelleway* — 90 p

ROYAL BLACKBIRD 2 br.f. (Feb 7) Most Welcome 131 – Thulium (Mansingh 64 (USA) 120) [1996 6m 5.3g* 5.2g² 5d³ Nov 8] 13,000Y: fifth foal: half-sister to several winners, including 3-y-o 6f winner Watch The Fire (by Statoblest), and fairly useful 5f performer Crystal Magic and 1m winner Mighty Marston (both by Mazilier): dam lightly-raced sister to Petong: first run for over 3 months, won seller at Brighton in October: improved again when beaten short head in non-selling nursery at Yarmouth later in month, and ran well considering poor draw when third of 13 (plenty to do halfway, ran on strongly despite hanging left) to Myrmidon in similar event at Doncaster final start: will stay 6f: tends to be slowly away: awkward to start at Brighton. *J. E. Banks* — 64

ROYAL BORN 2 ch.g. (Apr 4) Prince Sabo 123 – Shernborne (Kalaglow 132) 71 [1996 6m⁴ 7f³ 6.9d Oct 21] 8,500Y: lengthy, workmanlike gelding: second foal: dam out of half-sister to Blakeney and Morston: fair form in maidens at Goodwood and Warwick (sweating and looked slightly temperamental beforehand, pulled hard) first 2 starts: sold 10,500 gns Newmarket Autumn Sales. *W. Jarvis* — 71

ROYAL CANASKA 3 ch.c. Royal Academy (USA) 130 – North Telstar 104 91 (Sallust 134) [1995 81p: 7f³ 1996 8d* 8.1g⁴ 10m 8f 7m 5.5f Nov 20] rather leggy, quite attractive colt: fairly useful performer: landed the odds in maiden at Leicester in April: visored, creditable eighth of 31 to North Song in Britannia Handicap at Royal Ascot fourth start, final one for D. Loder: well beaten next start, only outing for M. Heaton-Ellis: stays 1m, seemingly not 1¼m: acts on firm and dead ground. *W. Shoemaker, USA* — 91

ROYAL CARLTON (IRE) 4 b.g. Mulhollande (USA) 107 – Saintly Angel 87 58 + (So Blessed 130) [1995 –: 6f⁶ 5.2g 5m 5d 7m 1996 6f 6m a8g³ a8g* Dec 26] modest performer: left T. J. Naughton after second 4-y-o start: won maiden at Lingfield in December readily by 4 lengths: stays 1m: acts on equitrack. *G. L. Moore* — 58 +

ROYAL CASCADE (IRE) 2 b.g. (Mar 3) River Falls 113 – Relative Stranger 56 (Cragador 110) [1996 a6s⁶ a7g² Dec 28] IR 9,500Y 6,200 2-y-o: first foal: dam tailed off only start: better effort when 7 lengths second of 6 in maiden auction at Wolverhampton: should stay 1m. *B. A. McMahon* — 56

ROYAL CASTLE (IRE) 2 b.c. (Mar 19) Caerleon (USA) 132 – Sun Princess 65 p 130 (English Prince 129) [1996 7d Nov 8] sturdy, lengthy colt: eighth foal: closely related to 1¼m winner Ruby Setting (by Gorytus) and half-brother to several winners, including high-class 7f (at 2 yrs) and 1¼m winner Prince of Dance and useful middle-distance performer Golden Ball (both by Sadler's Wells): dam won Oaks and St Leger and is half-sister to Saddlers' Hall: around 9 lengths eighth of 20 to Handsome Ridge in maiden at Doncaster, chasing pace and keeping on steadily: will do better over middle distances. *Major W. R. Hern* — 65 p

ROYAL CEILIDH (IRE) 3 b.f. Prince Rupert (FR) 121 – Isa (Dance In Time 82 (CAN)) [1995 74: 5g⁸ 5d⁶ 6m³ 7m⁵ 8g 7f* 1996 6g³ 6g⁶ 8m* 7f³ 8m⁶ 8g² 8d³ 7.9g² 8m 8g 7m 8s Nov 9] big, strong, lengthy filly: has a quick action: fairly useful — 82

handicapper: in good form for most of year, winning at Thirsk in May: stays 1m: acts on firm ground and dead: tends to get on toes: game. *Denys Smith*

ROYAL CIRCUS 7 b.g. Kris 135 – Circus Ring 122 (High Top 131) [1995 40: 42
a16g a13g* a12g² a12g⁴ a13g⁴ a13g* a12g a13g² 12g 13f² 13f 12.1m⁵ 11.1f 1996 a47
a13g⁴ a16g⁴ a12g* a12g⁵ a12g⁵ a16g 16.1f² 14.1m² 12f³ 14.9m⁶ 16.2m Jul 16]
workmanlike gelding: poor handicapper: won amateurs race at Lingfield in January:
effective at 1½m and 2m: acts on firm and dead ground and on equitrack: front
runner/races prominently. *P. R. Webber*

ROYAL COMEDIAN 7 gr.m. Jester 119 – Royal Huntress (Royal Avenue 123) 44
[1995 47d, a–: a6g 7m* a7g 7m³ 7.6m⁴ 7m 8g⁵ 7g 7.1s 8f 1996 8g 7m 7.1d² 7.6m⁵ a–
Jul 12] leggy mare: poor handicapper: stays 7.6f: acts on good to firm and soft going,
no worthwhile form on fibresand: takes good hold: none too consistent. *B. W. Murray*

ROYAL COURT (IRE) 3 b.c. Sadler's Wells (USA) 132 – Rose of Jericho 116
(USA) (Alleged (USA) 138) [1995 NR 1996 12.1d* 11.9g* 11.9m³ 12m⁴
Sep 28]
     A twenty-length winner of almost any race on the flat is bound to make
people sit up and take notice, and when that winner is making his debut and is
a Sadler's Wells half-brother to Dr Devious...The race in question was just a
six-runner maiden at Chepstow in May, steadily-run at that, but the way in
which Royal Court disposed of Jiyush led to *Timeform* giving him a rating of
111. It was no act of daring to say that this was a pattern-class performer. In
the same race twelve months earlier, trainer Peter Chapple-Hyam had sent out
another newcomer to win in similarly satisfactory style, Salsabil's brother Song
of Tara, saying afterwards that 'I honestly thought he was useless.' And Royal
Court? 'We thought nothing of him' reflected owner Robert Sangster after his
next race. Like Song of Tara, Royal Court made that second appearance in a
listed race and won it. Royal Court's was the Robert Sice Memorial July
Trophy at Haydock and he was sent off second favourite in a five-runner field,
at 15/8 just one eighth of a point longer than the Derby third Shantou. The battle
seemed to be predominantly one of Shantou versus himself when the favourite
moved up to challenge Weet-A-Minute. Royal Court, however, had no such

Robert Sice Memorial July Trophy Stakes, Haydock—
Royal Court storms past Shantou (left) and Weet-A-Minute

qualms and surged through to take the lead inside the final furlong and win by three and a half lengths.

Now on to pattern races, and the one chosen for Royal Court was the Great Voltigeur Stakes at York. Inexperience and a sore joint may have played their part at Haydock, but basically that performance looked to be one of a colt who was strong on stamina. It was not tested in the Great Voltigeur. Dushyantor showed a much better turn of foot and Royal Court could not get past Mons either. Still, it puts Royal Court in a much better light to reflect on that race rather than on his fourth of seven in the Cumberland Lodge at Ascot over five weeks later when he never looked likely to take a hand. A shade edgy in the preliminaries, Royal Court also moved short to post. He had been made an 11/4-chance at both York and Ascot. Amazingly then, Royal Court's longest starting price so far was for that maiden at Chepstow when he went off at 3/1 having opened at 6/4.

		Northern Dancer (b 1961)	Nearctic
	Sadler's Wells (USA) (b 1981)		Natalma
		Fairy Bridge (b 1975)	Bold Reason
Royal Court (IRE) (b.c. 1993)			Special
		Alleged (b 1974)	Hoist The Flag
	Rose of Jericho (USA) (b 1984)		Princess Pout
		Rose Red (ch 1979)	Northern Dancer
			Cambrienne

Dr Devious (by Ahonoora) is, of course, one of the five consecutive Derby winners who were sold to stand in Japan, but Coolmore have bought him back and he will covering in Ireland in 1997 at a fee of IR 12,500 guineas. Rose of Jericho's next foal died and was followed by a colt and filly by Fairy King, called Shinko King and Rose of Suzuka, who, as the names suggest, were also bought by the Japanese, but this time before they reached racing age. *The Statistical Record* has Shinko King down as a winner, of £556,143 no less with three wins in both 1994 and 1995, from six furlongs to a mile. Rose of Suzuka was an IR 320,000-guinea purchase as a yearling. Next comes Royal Court and his brother Royal Crown who was eighth of twelve in a Newmarket maiden in October. The unraced Rose of Jericho's only other foal is her first, the smart Irish sprinter Archway (by Thatching), and her family is packed with other significant winners, including her dam's half-brother, the smart middle-distance performer Critique, and the 1990 Queen Elizabeth II Stakes winner Markofdistinction who, like Royal Court, is a great grandson of Cambrienne. Markofdistinction died in 1996 having made a good start to his stallion career—in Japan.

The good-topped, long-striding Royal Court obviously has a place at stud waiting for him somewhere, but he may be capable of further improvement and should win more good races first. It looks as if he will be well suited by a good test of stamina when racing at a mile and a half—something he has yet to have—and is sure to stay further. He has also given the impression that he might prove best with some give in the ground. Royal Court has still to fulfil the promise of his wins at Chepstow and Haydock. *P. W. Chapple-Hyam*

ROYAL CROWN (IRE) 2 b.c. (Apr 14) Sadler's Wells (USA) 132 – Rose of 74 p Jericho (USA) (Alleged (USA) 138) [1996 8m Oct 1] seventh foal: brother to smart 3-y-o 1½m winner Royal Court and half-brother to Derby winner Dr Devious (by Ahonoora) and smart Irish sprinter Archway (by Thatching): dam (unraced) from very good family: 12/1 from 6/1, burly and green, never in contention in 12-runner maiden at Newmarket won by Asas, beaten around 14 lengths: should do better. *P. W. Chapple-Hyam*

ROYAL CRUSADE (USA) 2 b.c. (Apr 12) Diesis 133 – Sainte Croix (USA) 89 P (Nijinsky (CAN) 138) [1996 8m* Oct 17] $95,000Y: strong, lengthy, good sort: sixth foal: half-brother to 9f and 9.7f winner Waki Gold (by Miswaki) and 3 winners abroad, including useful 1991 French 2-y-o 1m winner Saintry (by Groom Dancer): dam, French maiden, is sister to smart Irish middle-distance stayer Empire Glory and half-sister to Irish 1000 Guineas winner Gaily: weak 11/2 and looking very well, won

17-runner maiden at Newmarket in good style by 3 lengths from Catchable, soon close up in steadily-run race, leading 2f out and staying on strongly: strong-running type who should be well suited by further than 1m: a most interesting prospect. *W. J. Haggas*

ROYAL DANCER   4 ch.f. Dancing Dissident (USA) 119 – Aquarula 88 (Dominion 123) [1995 –: a7g 1996 a8g a7g a6g a11g 8s Mar 28] small filly: of no account. *R. J. Weaver*   –

ROYAL DIVERSION (IRE)   3 b.f. Marju (IRE) 127 – Royal Recreation (USA) (His Majesty (USA)) [1995 73p: 6s⁶ 7g² 1996 7d³ 9m 10d³ 10m 9m⁶ 10m³ 11.4m³ 11.9g³ 12s* Oct 26] unfurnished filly: fair performer: clearly best 3-y-o effort when 14-length winner of 16-runner claimer at Newbury in October: should be suited by further than 1½m: goes very well with testing conditions: has joined M. Pipe. *J. L. Dunlop*   82

ROYAL DOME (IRE)   4 b.g. Salt Dome (USA) – Brook's Dilemma 80 (Known Fact (USA) 135) [1995 75p: 7.1g³ a6g⁵ 6g 5f² 5f⁴ 5.1m* 5h² 5g* 5g² 5m* 1996 5m² 5m 5g 5m⁴ 5g 5m² 5m* 6m² 5m* 6m 5m 5m 5d³ 5g 5d Oct 12] good-quartered gelding: fairly useful performer: won minor event at Beverley in July and competitive handicap at Haydock in August: barely stays 6f: acts on good to firm and dead ground (ran creditably) fifth 3-y-o start: game. *Martyn Wane*   78

ROYALE FIGURINE (IRE)   5 ch.m. Dominion Royale 112 – Cree's Figurine 63 (Creetown 123) [1995 106: 5.2m* 5.1m⁶ 5g³ 6f 5g⁴ 6m² 6g* 6m* 5f² 6m³ 1996 6f³ 5f⁵ 6m⁶ 6m* 5d 6g⁶ 6s Nov 9] quite attractive mare: useful performer: third of 12 to Venture Capitalist in Duke of York Stakes and fifth of 17 to Pivotal in King's Stand Stakes at Royal Ascot on first 2 starts: didn't need to be at best to justify favouritism in minor event at Newmarket in August: effective at 5f and 6f: acts on firm and soft ground: usually held up: genuine. *M. J. Fetherston-Godley*   107

ROYALE FINALE (IRE)   2 ch.c. (Jan 22) Royal Academy (USA) 130 – Final Farewell (USA) (Proud Truth (USA)) [1996 7d³ Oct 28] 200,000Y: first foal: dam once-raced half-sister to dam of Danehill out of a sprinting half-sister to Northern Dancer: favourite, shaped with promise when 10 lengths third of 18 to Maylane in maiden at Lingfield, keeping on well: sure to do better. *H. R. A. Cecil*   65 p

ROYAL EMBLEM   2 gr.f. (Mar 10) Presidium 124 – Lily of France 81 (Monsanto (FR) 121) [1996 5.3f² 5g³ 6.1m⁵ 5.3f² 6g a6g Nov 12] workmanlike filly: sixth foal: half-sister to winning sprinters Great Hall (by Hallgate) and Marwell Mitzi (by Interrex): dam sprinter: modest maiden: should be suited by further than 5f: raced only on a sound surface on turf, tailed off on all-weather debut. *A. G. Foster*   56

ROYAL EXPOSE (USA)   3 ch.c. Unzipped (USA) – Royal Tasha (USA) (Northern Prospect (USA)) [1995 –p: 8g 1996 10m 12m⁵ 10m 12.1m⁴ 11.9f⁴ 10m 11.8g Aug 12] strong, workmanlike colt: modest maiden at best: pulled up (saddle reportedly slipped) after seemingly refusing to race third 3-y-o start: appears to stay 1½m: inconsistent: has joined K. Ottesen. *R. Hannon*   59

ROYAL EXPRESSION   4 b.g. Sylvan Express 117 – Edwins' Princess 75 (Owen Dudley 121) [1995 58: 11.1g³ 12g⁴ 11.1f* 12.3m² 10.9g⁵ 1996 a12g³ 16.2g* 16.1g² 14.1g* 16.5g² Jun 8] tall, leggy gelding: has a round action: fair handicapper: in good form in first half of year, winning at Beverley and Carlisle in May: effective at 1¾m to 2m: acts on firm ground and on equitrack: blinkered (ran well) final 2-y-o start. *Mrs M. Reveley*   76

ROYAL INTRUSION   3 ch.g. Roman Warrior 132 – Image of War 70 (Warpath 113) [1995 NR 1996 10m 6g⁶ 7g 8f Sep 23] second foal: dam 2m winner: no worthwhile form. *R. J. Hodges*   –

ROYAL JADE   3 b.f. Last Tycoon 131 – Imperial Jade 105 (Lochnager 132) [1995 82p: 6f³ 1996 7m⁵ 7f² 8f 7f* 7g 8g Nov 2] sturdy, good-quartered filly: fair performer at best: won maiden (though still below form) at Redcar in September after 3-month absence: should stay 1m: has raced only on a sound surface. *B. W. Hills*   82 d

ROYAL LEGEND   4 b.g. Fairy King (USA) – Legend of Arabia (Great Nephew 126) [1995 NR 1996 a13g³ 10.1m 8g 12.1m³ a12g² Dec 27] leggy gelding: just a modest maiden nowadays: seems to stay 12.1f. *J. Pearce*   56

ROYAL MARK (IRE)   3 b.g. Fairy King (USA) – Take Your Mark (USA) (Round Table) [1995 84: 6m³ 7g* 7m* 7m² 7d 1996 8m⁵ 7f² 8f 6g³ 7m 7d 7g Oct 19]   88

Ladbrokes Spring Cup (Handicap), Newbury—Cool Edge tries in vain to reel in 25/1-shot Royal Philosopher

good-topped gelding: fairly useful handicapper on his day: ran as though something amiss at Chester on sixth start: withdrawn on veterinary advice next intended outing: changed hands 22,000 gns Newmarket Autumn Sales: blinkered, always behind only start afterwards: stays 1m: acts on firm ground. *J. W. Watts*

ROYAL ORCHID (IRE) 2 ch.f. (Apr 19) Shalford (IRE) 124§ – Indigo Blue 74 (IRE) 56 (Bluebird (USA) 125) [1996 5m2 5m6 6m4 6m5 7f4 7.1s a6g Dec 26] 32,000Y: neat filly: second foal: half-sister to 3-y-o 9f winner (stays 1¾m) Major Dundee (by Distinctly North): dam sprinting half-sister to Mistertopogigo out of sister to Hallgate: capable of fair form but has an in-and-out record: stays 7f: ran poorly on soft ground: has been bandaged near-hind: should be treated with caution. *R. Hannon*

ROYAL PHILOSOPHER 4 b.c. Faustus (USA) 118 – Princess Lucy 42 (Local 111 Suitor (USA) 128) [1995 99: 8m3 8.5m 8g2 9d 1996 8d* 7.1d 8.1d2 8g* 8g3 8g4 8m 8v4 a9.4g3 Dec 7] big, strong colt: smart performer: won Ladbrokes Spring Cup (Handicap) at Newbury in April and listed event at Evry in June: in frame in Prix Messidor at Maisons-Laffitte, Prix Quincey at Deauville, Prix Perth at Saint-Cloud and listed race at Wolverhampton (beaten a neck behind Prince of Andros) afterwards: stays 9.4f: best efforts with give in the ground (or fibresand) and acts on heavy: has run well when sweating: takes keen hold, and is well suited by front-running tactics: edgy sort: consistent. *J. W. Hills*

ROYAL PRINT (IRE) 7 ch.g. Kings Lake (USA) 133 – Reprint 99 (Kampala 35 120) [1995 –: a16.2g 1996 a13g6 a12g4 a12g4 a16g6 Feb 13] sturdy gelding: formerly fairly useful hurdler: poor staying maiden on flat: acts on the all-weather: tried blinkered. *W. R. Muir*

ROYAL RAPPORT 3 ch.g. Rich Charlie 117 – Miss Camellia 70 (Sonnen Gold 55 121) [1995 55+: 5m 5m5 6g 7.5d 6g 1996 10d 8.2d2 a8g 8g a8g5 a7g6 a6g5 Aug 9] compact gelding: modest maiden: sold to join J. O'Shea 1,250 gns Doncaster August Sales: stays 8.2f: no improvement blinkered/visored: has been bandaged: won novice hurdle in September: inconsistent. *B. A. McMahon*

ROYAL RESULT (USA) 3 b. or br.g. Gone West (USA) – Norette (Northfields 85 (USA)) [1995 NR 1996 7g 8g5 8.1m2 8f* 9g 9.2g4 8m3 Oct 17] good-bodied, attractive gelding: brother to 4-y-o Western Horizon and half-brother to several winners, including useful 1992 2-y-o 7.3f winner Redenham and useful stayer Ivory Fields (both by Sir Ivor): dam, Irish 9f winner, sister to Stewards' Cup winner Repetitious and Ribblesdale winner Nantitious: fairly useful performer: 5/1 on, won maiden at Thirsk in August: best effort in handicaps when third of 12 at Redcar on final start: sold 33,000 gns Newmarket Autumn Sales and gelded: best form at 1m: raced only on a sound surface: usually races prominently. *M. R. Stoute*

ROYAL RIGGER 3 gr.f. Reprimand 122 – Overdraft (Bustino 136) [1995 35: – 5g5 5g a5g3 10d 1996 9.9g 11.9f 8.3g Sep 29] neat filly: bad maiden. *C. Smith*

ROYAL ROULETTE 2 ch.f. (Apr 22) Risk Me (FR) 127 – Princess Lily 65 45 + (Blakeney 126) [1996 6g a8.5g5 8.2g a8.5g3 8g a7g5 a8g2 a7g Dec 13] 1,500F, IR 3,000Y: sixth foal: sister to Italian 3-y-o 1¼m winner Missionary Man (also winner over hurdles) and 1991 2-y-o 7f winner Personal Hazard: dam, maiden who stayed 1½m, sister to smart 1½m winner Believer: modest maiden: stays 8.5f: acts on all-weather: blinkered/visored last 4 starts. *S. P. C. Woods*

ROYAL SCIMITAR (USA) 4 ch.c. Diesis 133 – Princess of Man 104 (Green 100
God 128) [1995 97: 12f² 12m* 12.3m⁶ 12m 11.8m³ 11.9m⁴ 12m 12d 1996 11.7f*
12s³ 13.9m³ 11.9g² 12m 13.4d* Aug 31] close-coupled, lightly-made colt: good
walker and mover: useful performer: easy task when winning minor event at Bath in
May: best effort when winning 9-runner listed rated stakes at Chester in August by
1¾ lengths from Leonato, leading 3f out: effective at 1½m, unlikely to stay beyond
1¾m: acts on firm and soft ground: blinkered (below form) final 3-y-o start: lacks
turn of foot: game and consistent: sold to join Mrs A. Perrett 30,000 gns Newmarket
December Sales. *P. F. I. Cole*

ROYAL THIMBLE (IRE) 5 b.m. Prince Rupert (FR) 121 – Tootsie Roll 60
(Comedy Star (USA) 121) [1995 8s⁴ 10g³ 9g 8g² 9m 7.8f⁴ 10m 7m 9f⁴ 1996 8f 10f
12m 10.2m* 10f 10m⁴ 8m⁶ 10f² Sep 4] ex-Irish mare: half-sister to fair sprinter Sand
Or Stone (by Sandhurst Prince): dam unplaced: fair maiden (rated 75) at 4 yrs for
J. Kavanagh: modest handicapper here: won at Bath in July: suited by further
than 1m nowadays and stays 10.2f well: acts on firm and soft going: best recent
efforts in blinkers/visor: retained by trainer 6,400 gns Doncaster October Sales.
Noel T. Chance

ROYAL VACATION 7 b.g. King of Spain 121 – Crane Beach (High Top 131) 52
[1995 NR 1996 17.2f* 16f⁶ 17.1m³ Aug 18] winning jumper: very lightly raced on
flat, first worthwhile form when making all in poor maiden at Carlisle in June: stays
very well: acts on firm ground. *G. M. Moore*

ROY BOY 4 b.g. Emarati (USA) 74 – Starky's Pet (Mummy's Pet 125) [1995 72: –
7g⁵ 8.5m⁶ 6g² 5m³ 6m⁴ 6g 1996 10m⁶ 12g⁶ Jun 7] rangy, good-topped gelding: good
mover: fair maiden: below form over middle distances in 1996: stays 7f: acts on good
to firm and dead ground: below form only try in blinkers: sometimes carries head
awkwardly, and looks temperamental. *Mrs M. Reveley*

ROYRACE 4 b.g. Wace (USA) 82 – Royal Tycoon (Tycoon II) [1995 –: 13.4d –
11.8g 14.1m 1996 11.8d⁶ 12m 14.1m 14.9g⁵ 17.9g 18g Oct 21] tall gelding: signs of
a little ability but no worthwhile form. *W. M. Brisbourne*

ROZEL BAY 3 ch.f. Beveled (USA) 132 – Salinas 65 (Bay Express 132) [1995 49: –
5g⁵ a7g² a7g a8.5g⁵ a8.5g 1996 a8g a12s Dec 19] poor maiden at best: well beaten
last 5 starts: stays 7f: twice below form blinkered. *N. A. Twiston-Davies*

RUBADUB 5 b.m. Kalaglow 132 – Ravens Peak (High Top 131) [1995 41d: 8f –
10.2f 10m⁵ 12.5g⁵ 10.8m 11.1m⁵ 7.1m 10f 1996 a10g a11g a10g⁵ Feb 20] tall,
sparely-made mare: seems of little account nowadays: sold 500 gns Ascot December
Sales. *J. M. Bradley*

RUB AL KHALI 5 br.g. Green Ruby (USA) 104 – Nullah 71 (Riverman (USA) –
131) [1995 NR 1996 a8g Dec 3] of little account nowadays: reportedly broke blood
vessel only 5-y-o start. *A. Streeter*

RUBBIYATI 4 ch.f. Cadeaux Genereux 131 – Ibtisamm (USA) 71 (Caucasus 56
(USA) 127) [1995 NR 1996 a7g² a8.5g⁶ a10g 6.9g³ 8.3g* 8.3m³ 10m 10m Oct 29]
half-sister to 3 winners, notably useful Aljazzaf (middle distances, by Mtoto) and fair
Al Sadi (7f, by Sharpo): dam 1m winner: modest form: best effort to win handicap at
Windsor in July: below form afterwards: stays 8.3f. *C. E. Brittain*

RUBY ANGEL 3 ch.f. Superlative 118 – Queen Angel 88 (Anfield 117) [1995 47
NR 1996 7.1d⁶ a8.5g⁵ a8g³ Nov 22] compact filly: second foal: dam, 11f winner,
half-sister to Oaks third Pearl Angel: poor form in maidens: stays 1m. *H. Candy*

RUBY PLUS 5 b.m. Energy Plus 69 – Irish Grace 61 (Home Guard (USA) 129) –
[1995 NR 1996 a7g 8m 6m 8m a11g Jun 14] workmanlike mare: no worthwhile
form: visored last 3 starts. *G. R. Oldroyd*

RUBY PRINCESS (IRE) 2 b.f. (Feb 18) Mac's Imp (USA) 116 – Princess Raisa 70 +
(Indian King (USA) 128) [1996 5g² May 25] IR 7,000F, IR 3,000Y: 9,000 2-y-o:
fourth foal: half-sister to 4-y-o Prince Rudolf (by Cyrano de Bergerac), 5.3f and 6f
winner at 2 yrs, and a winner in Japan by Distinctly North: dam Irish maiden:
co-favourite, 4 lengths second of 8 to Deep Finesse in median auction maiden at
Warwick: looked speedy. *P. F. I. Cole*

RUBY TUESDAY 2 b.f. (Feb 11) Al Nasr (FR) 126 – Habibay (Habitat 134) 54 +
[1996 5.1g⁴ 5d³ 6.1d³ 5s 6m Oct 28] 10,500Y: good-topped, workmanlike filly: has
scope: unimpressive mover: fifth foal: half-sister to a French provincial 1½m winner

by Noblequest and to fairly useful French jumps winner Belle Illusion (by Dom Pasquini): dam unraced half-sister to very smart stayer Assessor: modest maiden: flattered in minor event at Chester on third outing: seems better suited by 6f than 5f. *B. A. McMahon*

RUDE AWAKENING   2 b.c. (Mar 6) Rudimentary (USA) 118 – Final Call 79   79
(Town Crier 119) [1996 5g² 5m² 5g* 6g⁶ 5m⁴ 7m Oct 4] 28,000F, 42,000Y: sturdy, good sort: takes eye in appearance: half-brother to several winners, including fairly useful 1995 5f 2-y-o winner Anotheranniversary (by Emarati) and 1985 2-y-o 7f winner Stage Hand (by Sagaro), latter winner at 8.2f and 1½m in France: dam, 5f winner who ran only at 2 yrs, half-sister to good sprinter On Stage: won maiden at Pontefract in April: below best in minor event at Pontefract, £9,200 race at Epsom (blinkered, seemed ill at ease on track) and listed race at Newmarket (first run for 4 months, gave impression something amiss) afterwards: sold 20,000 gns Newmarket Autumn Sales: should stay beyond 5f: usually lethargic in paddock. *G. Lewis*

RUDIMENTAL   2 b.g. (Jan 18) Rudimentary (USA) 118 – Full Orchestra 83   74
(Shirley Heights 130) [1996 a7g³ a6g* Jul 11] 17,500F, 17,000Y: third foal: half-brother to 3-y-o First Fiddler (by Primo Dominie), 5f winner at 2 yrs, and 1m to 1¼m winner Music Maker (by Unfuwain), 8.5f winner at 2 yrs: dam 1¼m winner: won 12-runner maiden at Wolverhampton by ½ length from Ricasso, leading close home: should stay 7f+: looked sure to improve again. *Sir Mark Prescott*

RUDI'S PET (IRE)   2 ch.c. (May 15) Don't Forget Me 127 – Pink Fondant   92
(Northfields (USA)) [1996 5m⁴ 6m⁶ 5g* 5m⁵ 5m⁴ 5m³ 5g* 5d⁶ 6.5g⁵ Oct 23] 19,500Y: strong, close-coupled colt: sixth foal: half-brother to 4 winners, including useful performer at up to 1m Face North (by Fayruz) and 4-y-o Sue Me (by Contract Law), 6f winner at 2 yrs: dam ran twice at 2 yrs: generally progressive form: won maiden auction at Windsor in July and nursery at Sandown in August: stiff tasks last 2 starts: should stay beyond 5f: raced only on a sound surface. *R. Hannon*

RUMBA RHYTHM (CAN)   3 ch.f. Thorn Dance (USA) 107 – Skoblikova   61
(USA) (Phone Trick (USA)) [1995 70: 5m⁵ 6g⁴ 5m⁴ 1996 7m 7g⁴ 6m⁶ Jul 19] unfurnished filly: good mover: only modest form in handicaps in 1996: sold 2,300 gns Newmarket September Sales: probably stays 7f. *R. W. Armstrong*

RUMBUSTIOUS   2 b.f. (Mar 24) Rambo Dancer (CAN) 107 – Persian Alexandra   65
(Persian Bold 123) [1996 6g 7m² 6m* 7f* 7.6m 7m⁵ 6.1s⁶ Oct 22] 10,500Y: leggy filly: half-sister to 2 winners in Italy, including useful 1¼m winner Taff's Acre (by Dance of Life): dam, Irish 2-y-o 7f winner, half-sister to Windsor Castle winner Sea Falcon: fair performer: won seller at Lingfield in August and non-selling nursery at Brighton in September: will stay 1m: acts on firm ground, below form on soft. *R. Hannon*

RUM LAD   2 gr.c. (May 10) Efisio 120 – She's Smart 88 (Absalom 128) [1996   65
5m³ 5g⁶ 5m⁴ 6g² 6d 6m⁶ Oct 7] strong, sturdy colt: first foal: dam sprinter: fair form: off course 2½ months and below form after fourth start: may be better suited by 7f. *J. J. Quinn*

RUMPELSTILTSKIN   4 ch.g. Sharpo 132 – Ouija 104 (Silly Season 127) [1995   –
–: 7m 8m 8.1g 1996 a7g Nov 22] no form. *H. S. Howe*

RUNAWAY PETE (USA)   6 b.g. Runaway Groom (CAN) – Pete's Damas   –
(USA) (Cutlass (USA)) [1995 NR 1996 16.1f 18g Oct 19] rated 79 at 4 yrs for P. Cole: fairly useful handicap hurdler (prolific winner): soundly beaten on return to flat: stays 17.1f: probably acts on any going. *M. C. Pipe*

RUNFORACTION (IRE)   4 b.f. Contract Law (USA) 108 – Prissy Miss 68   –
(Free State 125) [1995 –, a43: a8g⁴ a8g⁴ a8g a8g³ a11g⁶ a11g a8g 12.3f 12m 1996 a12g a7g a7g 6.9f Aug 5] small, sparely-made filly: poor performer: little form in 1996, trained until after reappearance by B. Rothwell: best form at up to 1m: acts on fibresand: tried blinkered: inconsistent: sent to South Korea. *L. R. Lloyd-James*

RUN FOR US (IRE)   2 b.f. (Feb 27) Runnett 125 – Blue Elver (Kings Lake   –
(USA) 133) [1996 5d⁴ 5.3f⁵ 5d a6g⁴ 5g 5.2f³ a5g a6g a7g⁵ a5g 7m Oct 17] IR 1,100Y: angular, unfurnished filly: fourth reported foal: sister to 1991 2-y-o 5f winner Most Surprising: dam maiden daughter of half-sister to top 1960 2-y-o colt Typhoon: little worthwhile form in auction maiden events and sellers: blinkered twice: sold 800 gns Newmarket Autumn Sales. *C. A. Dwyer*

RUNIC SYMBOL 5 b.g. Warning 136 – Pagan Deity 88 (Brigadier Gerard 144) 43 [1995 42d: 8m³ 8f⁵ 8g⁴ 8.1m 7.6d³ 8.1m⁶ 10.2m⁶ 8g 1996 8f² 8g⁴ 10d³ 10m* 10g² 10m⁵ 10g³ 10m 10g 9m a9.4g⁵ Nov 11] leggy, angular gelding: poor handicapper: gained first success at Nottingham in June: effective at 1m, and probably stays 11.6f: acts on firm and soft ground: blinkered (well beaten) final 4-y-o start: usually comes from behind. *M. Blanshard*

RUN LUCY RUN 2 b.f. (Mar 28) Risk Me (FR) 127 – Pat Or Else 72 (Alzao 55 (USA) 117) [1996 5f⁵ a5g² a5g² a6g* 7g⁴ 7g³ 8g⁴ 7.1m* a7g⁶ 7g 6.9v⁵ a7g⁵ Dec 30] sparely-made filly: first foal: dam staying maiden half-sister to St Leger winner Classic Cliche and Prix Vermeille winner My Emma: successful in seller at Wolverhampton in May and selling nursery (sold out of R. Guest's stable 5,000 gns) at Sandown in August: poor form for new stable: stays 1m: acts on good to firm ground and fibresand. *Miss Gay Kelleway*

RUNNING FLAME (FR) 4 b.c. Assert 134 – Fanning The Flame (Commanche 123 Run 133) [1995 10v 12d⁵ 12g³ 14v⁴ 12g⁴ 14g³ 14g* 1996 13s* 15g³ 12.5g³ 10s* 12d⁶ 12g* Dec 15] first foal: dam, French 1m winner, half-sister to smart middle-distance filly Premier Amour: very smart performer: unraced at 2 yrs: won quite valuable race in the Provinces at 3 yrs and in May: third of 6 in listed races at Chantilly in June and Deauville in August: best effort in Europe when winning 8-runner La Coupe de Maisons-Laffitte in September by 1½ lengths from Carling on penultimate start for J. Hammond: running on Lasix, much-improved form when winning Hollywood Turf Cup in December by 2 lengths from Marlin: stays 15f, but fully effective over much shorter: acts on any going. *M. Puype, USA*

RUNNING FREE (IRE) 2 b.g. (Apr 28) Waajib 121 – Selchis (Main Reef 126) 55 [1996 6m 7g 7g⁴ 8m 7m a8.5g⁴ Nov 2] IR 6,800F, 13,000Y: workmanlike gelding: third living foal: dam placed over 1m in Ireland: easily best efforts when fourth in claimer at Salisbury and selling nursery (beaten about a length) at Wolverhampton: stays 8.5f: blinkered/visored last 4 starts. *M. J. Fetherston-Godley*

RUNNING GREEN 5 b.g. Green Desert (USA) 127 – Smeralda (GER) 63 (Dschingis Khan) [1995 63: 9.2s³ 1996 11m a8g⁴ a8g* a7s Dec 19] lightly raced on flat, gaining first success in handicap at Southwell in December: stays 9.2f: acts on soft ground and on fibresand. *D. Moffatt*

RUNS IN THE FAMILY 4 b.f. Distant Relative 128 – Stoneydale 83 (Tickled 55 Pink 114) [1995 57, a43: 6.1g⁵ 6.1m 5.7f 6g⁶ a6g a6g⁴ a7g 5g³ 5g 5.1d 1996 5g⁵ a52 a5g³ 5m³ 5m⁴ 6g 6s⁶ 5m Sep 25] sturdy, useful-looking filly: modest handicapper: effective at 5f (best recent form) and 6f: acts on fibresand and good to firm ground, goes well on soft: often blinkered/visored: usually raced prominently in 1996. *G. M. McCourt*

RUN WITH PRIDE 3 b.f. Mandrake Major 122 – Kirkby 85 (Midsummer Night – II 117) [1995 NR 1996 8.1m 12m⁵ Aug 28] sister to 6f to 10.6f winner Majority Holding, and half-sister to several winners, including 7f winner Train of Thought (by Bay Express): dam won twice over 1¼m: behind in seller and claimer. *E. Weymes*

RUPERT MANNERS 3 b.g. Mazilier (USA) 107 – Entourage 75 (Posse (USA) – 130) [1995 NR 1996 7f⁶ 8m 6g Sep 7] 1,900F: second foal: dam, fourth over 7f at 2 yrs, out of half-sister to Forzando: tailed off in maidens. *E. J. Alston*

RUPERT'S DOUBLE (IRE) 2 ch.g. (Mar 1) Silver Kite (USA) 111 – Perfect – Guest (What A Guest 119) [1996 6m 6m Jun 24] 7,700F, 10,500Y: lengthy, rather unfurnished gelding: sixth foal: half-brother to Irish 1m winner Floral Street (by Dara Monarch) and Irish 1½m/13f winner Return Again (by Top Ville): dam unraced daughter of sister to Seymour Hicks and half-sister to Princess Pati: behind in maiden events at Newbury and Windsor: sold 775 gns Ascot August Sales. *B. J. Meehan*

RUPERT'S PRINCESS (IRE) 4 b.f. Prince Rupert (FR) 121 – Llanelli (Welsh – Saint 126) [1995 52: 6s⁶ a5g⁶ 6.1g⁴ a6g² 6g 1996 a7g a6g a6g Feb 26] lengthy filly: modest performer at 3 yrs: well beaten in sellers at Southwell in 1996: has joined H. Haynes. *M. J. Heaton-Ellis*

RUPIANA (IRE) 4 b.f. Prince Rupert (FR) 121 – Webbiana (African Sky 124) – [1995 –: 8m 7.3g 8m 1996 7m 8g 10m 12.5f⁶ 14g Aug 1] lengthy filly: of little account nowadays: sold 2,000 gns Newmarket July Sales: sent to South Korea. *C. Murray*

RURAL LAD   7 b.g. Town And Country 124 – French Plait (Thatching 131) [1995 –
NR 1996 a9.4g May 11] rather sparely-made gelding: rated 56 in 1994: fell only start
in 1996: stayed 1m: dead. *R. C. Spicer*

RUSHCUTTER BAY   3 br.c. Mon Tresor 113 – Llwy Bren (Lidhame 109) [1995   92
80: a5g⁴ 5g* 6m³ 6m⁶ 1996 5m⁶ 6m 5.1m* 5f 5m² 5.1m⁵ 6m³ 5m⁴ 5m⁴ 6g 5.6m Sep
11] neat colt: impresses in appearance: fairly useful handicapper: won at Nottingham
in June: strung together 5 creditable efforts later in the summer: stays 6f: acts on good
to firm going, yet to race on a soft surface: effective visored or not. *T. T. Clement*

RUSHEN RAIDER   4 br.g. Reprimand 122 – Travel Storm 77 (Lord Gayle   77
(USA) 124) [1995 62: 7.5m 7m* 7g⁶ 8.1d⁵ 10m⁶ 10f* 9.9m⁵ 10f⁵ 1996 10m 10.3m
9.9g⁵ 11.8m* 12m* 12m* 16.2f* 14.6m⁴ 17.5m⁴ Sep 20] leggy, shallow-girthed
gelding: fair performer: much improved in 1996, winning claimer at Leicester, seller
at Doncaster, claimer at Catterick and handicap at Beverley, all in the summer: stays
16.2f: acts on firm and dead ground: reportedly broke blood vessel over hurdles in
October. *K. W. Hogg, Isle of Man*

RUSK   3 b.c. Pharly (FR) 130 – Springwell 73 (Miami Springs 121) [1995 73p: 79
7.9g⁴ 1996 10m⁶ 10m² 11.9m 12.3s⁴ 11.9d³ 11.9v⁵ 11f⁵ Nov 5] smallish, good-
topped colt: has a round action: fair maiden handicapper: stays 12.3f: acts on firm
ground, goes well on a soft surface: sometimes takes keen hold: usually held up:
consistent. *J. Pearce*

RUSSIAN ASPECT   2 br.c. (May 27) Al Nasr (FR) 126 – Bourbon Topsy 108   –
(Ile de Bourbon (USA) 133) [1996 7.1d 7.9g Oct 12] 6,200Y: tall colt: has scope:
fourth foal: half-brother to 3-y-o Bourbonist (by Soviet Star) and 1½m and 2m
winner Anjou (by Saumarez): dam, middle-distance stayer, half-sister to top-class
middle-distance performer Most Welcome out of smart half-sister to Teenoso: long
odds, backward and green, well beaten in maidens at Haydock and York in the
autumn: will need a test of stamina. *M. W. Easterby*

RUSSIAN MUSIC   3 b.g. Forzando 122 – Sunfleet 59 (Red Sunset 120) [1995   105
91+: 6m³ 6g³ 1996 7m* 7g² 8f³ 8m³ 8m² 7m² 7.1g² 7g² 7m³ 8d² 6s Oct 24] smallish,
good-quartered gelding: impresses in appearance: useful performer: bought out of
P. Haslam's stable 35,000 gns Doncaster March Sales: won maiden at Lingfield in
May: placed next 9 starts, including in Britannia Handicap (third of 31 to North
Song) and Tote Festival Handicap (third of 26 to Decorated Hero) at Ascot: back in
trip, disadvantaged by racing widest of all on final start: stays 1m well: acts on firm
and dead ground: consistent. *Miss Gay Kelleway*

RUSSIAN OLIVE   2 b.f. (Feb 23) Primo Dominie 121 – Cottonwood 80   70 p
(Teenoso (USA) 135) [1996 7g 8s⁴ Nov 9] first foal: dam 1¼m winner: similar form
in maidens when twelfth of 23 (to Palisade) at Newmarket and fourth of 14 (to easy
winner Moon River in median auction) at Doncaster: tongue tied at Doncaster: has
joined Lord Huntingdon: may do better. *L. M. Cumani*

RUSSIAN RASCAL (IRE)   3 b.g. Soviet Lad (USA) 94 – Anglo Irish (Busted   69
134) [1995 64: 5m 6g* 6m³ 6m³ 7.5m² 8g 1996 7.9f⁶ 8g² 10m 8m⁵ 8.5m⁵ Jul 6]
good-topped gelding: fair handicapper: below form last 3 starts: should stay beyond
1m: has raced only on a sound surface. *T. D. Easterby*

RUSSIAN REQUEST (IRE)   3 b.f. Soviet Star (USA) 128 – I Want To Be   74
(USA) 116 (Roberto (USA) 131) [1995 NR 1996 8m² 10m² 10.1g⁴ 12f⁴ 10m Sep 19]
angular, quite attractive filly: fifth foal: half-sister to useful middle-distance
performer Danish Fort (by Danzig): dam, winner of Park Hill Stakes, half-sister to
dam of Armiger and Besiege: fair maiden: failed to progress: will probably prove
suited by at least 1½m: sent to Japan. *M. R. Stoute*

RUSSIAN REVIVAL (USA)   3 ch.c. Nureyev (USA) 131 – Memories (USA)   116
(Hail The Pirates (USA) 126) [1995 108p: 6m* 6m² 6g⁴ 1996 8d 7m 6m² 6d 6m* 6g*
7g² 6s³ Nov 9] angular colt: fine mover: smart performer: wintered in Dubai: well
below form in Irish 2000 Guineas and Jersey Stakes first two 3-y-o starts, racing
freely up with pace: beat sole rival in minor event at Yarmouth in September and
followed up in 15-runner listed event at Newmarket (by 1½ lengths from Passion
For Life) in October: good efforts in minor event and listed race at Doncaster (to
Astrac) last 2 starts: ran creditably over 7f, but may prove ideally suited by 6f: acts
on good to firm and soft ground: tongue tied in 1996: front runner for both 3-y-o
wins. *Saeed bin Suroor*

RUSSIAN ROSE (IRE) 3 b.f. Soviet Lad (USA) 94 – Thornbeam (Beldale 74
Flutter (USA) 130) [1995 NR 1996 10m 10d 10m* 10s Aug 31] IR 5,000F, 5,200Y:
smallish filly: half-sister to 1993 2-y-o 6f winner Bet A Plan (by Cyrano de Bergerac)
and a winner in Belgium by Phardante: dam never ran: only worthwhile form when
winning median auction maiden at Ripon in June: hung badly right (reportedly had
muscle problem) final start: should stay further than 1¼m: acts on good to firm
ground. *A. Hide*

RUSSIAN ROULETTE 3 b.f. Niniski (USA) 125 – Gaucherie (USA) (Sharpen –
Up 127) [1995 NR 1996 12g 13.8g⁶ Jul 24] IR 10,500Y: leggy, narrow filly: half-
sister to several winners, including useful sprinter Green's Canaletto (by Hagley):
dam won at up to 7f: well beaten in maiden events: sold 550 gns Doncaster August
(1996) Sales. *M. Johnston*

RUSSIAN RULER (IRE) 2 b.c. (May 17) Bering 136 – Whitecairn (Sure Blade 78 p
(USA) 130) [1996 7g⁵ 7f³ Nov 5] IR 11,000Y: quite attractive colt: first foal: dam,
ran twice in France, half-sister to smart French middle-distance stayer Whitehaven
out of US Grade 1 8.5f to 1¼m winner White Star Line: 20/1 and green, around 10
lengths fifth of 6 to Crimson Tide in Houghton Stakes at Newmarket on debut: gave
impression race was still needed when 3 lengths third of 16 to Tayseer in maiden at
Redcar following month: will be suited by further than 7f: will improve again, and
should win a race. *A. P. Jarvis*

RUSSIAN SABLE 2 b.f. (Mar 9) Statoblest 120 – Princess Zita 90 (Manado 130) 57 d
[1996 6d 6m* 5m³ 7m³ 6.1f⁵ 6g 6d³ 6m⁶ 7g 6m³ 6m Oct 4] 6,000Y: useful-looking
filly: seventh foal: half-sister to several winners here and abroad, including fairly
useful stayer Prince Mercury (by Sharrood): dam 7f winner out of half-sister to smart
stayer Karadar: won claimer at Goodwood in June: rather in and out afterwards, form
deteriorating somewhat last 6 starts: sold 4,200 gns Newmarket Autumn Sales: stays
7f: acts on good to firm and dead ground: sent to Saudi Arabia. *M. R. Channon*

RUSSIAN SNOWS (IRE) 4 b.f. Sadler's Wells (USA) 132 – Arctique Royale 113
114 (Royal And Regal (USA)) [1995 113p: 10m* 10g² 12g² 10f² 12g* 12.5s* 1996
a9.9g² 11.9m⁶ 14.6m⁴ 12g³ 12d 10.3d* Nov 8] good-topped filly: smart performer:
in frame for new stable in 1996 in minor event in Dubai, steadily-run Yorkshire Oaks
(best effort of season, finished 2 lengths third to Key Change, placed sixth), Park Hill
Stakes at Doncaster (beaten before trip became a factor) and listed race at Ascot:
didn't need to show best form when making all in minor event at Doncaster in
November: stays 12.5f well: acts on firm and soft ground (probably on sand). *Saeed
bin Suroor*

RUSTIC LEAGUE (IRE) 5 b.g. Gallic League 119 – Walnut Lass (Tap On –
Wood 130) [1995 38: a7g a7g³ a6g⁴ a6g 5d³ a6g 5.3m 1996 a7g⁶ Feb 27]
poor maiden handicapper: stays 7f: acts on fibresand and dead ground. *A. J. Wilson*

RUSTIC SONG (IRE) 3 b.f. Fayruz 116 – Red Note (Rusticaro (FR) 124) [1995 –
53: 5m 5m³ a6g 5g² 5g 6.1m 1996 6.1d 6.1d 8.2m a7g⁴ a8.5g a6g Jul 22] close-
coupled, angular filly: modest form at 2 yrs: well held in handicaps in 1996: a
sprinter. *J. Wharton*

*Bedford Lodge Hotel Bentinck Stakes, Newmarket—
Russian Revival comes good in the Godolphin second colours*

RUSTY (IRE) 2 ch.f. (Mar 20) Shalford (IRE) 124§ – Karoi (IRE) (Kafu 120) 54 [1996 5m⁶ 5f* 6g 5f a5g Oct 5] IR 2,100F, IR 3,000Y, 5,000 2-y-o: compact filly: first foal: dam Irish 9f and 9.5f winner: made all in 12-runner claimer at Beverley in August: well beaten in sellers and a claimer subsequently: sold 4,500 gns Doncaster October Sales: visored final outing. *J. Berry*

RUTH'S GAMBLE 8 b.g. Kabour 80 – Hilly's Daughter (Hillandale 125) [1995 – NR 1996 12f a8g Jul 1] rated 56 (stayed 1m, acted on any going) on flat at 4 yrs: very lightly raced and no form since. *Mrs L. C. Jewell*

RUWY 3 b.f. Soviet Star (USA) 128 – Psylla 96 (Beldale Flutter (USA) 130) [1995 77 68p: 7g³ 1996 7m² 7f⁴ 7m 8.1m* 7m 7g Nov 2] well-made filly: fair performer: won maiden at Sandown in August in game style: ran poorly in handicaps afterwards: better at 1m than 7f: raced only on a sound surface: sold 6,800 gns Newmarket December Sales. *C. J. Benstead*

RUZNAMA (USA) 3 ch.f. Forty Niner (USA) – Last Feather (USA) 120 104 (Vaguely Noble 140) [1995 105p: 6m 7m* 8g³ 7g* 1996 10m⁴ 10.4m⁴ 8m* 7m* 8m⁶ Sep 12] close-coupled, deep-girthed filly: good mover: useful performer: won well-contested and minor event at Doncaster (by head from Bishop of Cashel) and listed race at York (led halfway, held Ali-Royal, gave 10 lb, by a length), both in August: below form in Group 3 event won by Bishop of Cashel at Doncaster on final start: stayed 1¼m, at least as effective over shorter: raced only on good or good to firm ground: took good hold: visits Danzig. *B. W. Hills*

RYAFAN (USA) 2 b.f. (Mar 8) Lear Fan (USA) 130 – Carya (USA) 110 (Northern Dancer) [1996 7g² 7g² 8d* Oct 6]
Khalid Abdulla had a particularly strong band of two-year-old fillies in 1996. Nowhere was that more apparent than in the top mile events where his Reams of Verse won the Fillies' Mile at Ascot and only a week later Ryafan and Yashmak fought out a tremendous finish to France's equivalent, the Prix Marcel Boussac at Longchamp. The Marcel Boussac looked an open race beforehand, seemingly lacking an outstanding filly from either France or Britain. The majority of the home-trained fillies had already met in the Prix du Calvados at Deauville in August where Shigeru Summit had emerged best from Dame d'Harvard (second), Green Lady (third), Veiled Threat (fourth) and Spring Dance (seventh). Green Lady had gone on to finish fourth in the Prix d'Aumale behind another two Marcel Boussac runners Dissertation and Nawal. The Aumale winner Joyeuse Entree though was a notable absentee. The foreign challenge, which made up almost half the field, consisted of the French-bred Bulgarian-trained outsider Dancing Fire, and, from a more usual quarter, Family Tradition from Ireland and the British quartet of Bianca Nera, Dance Parade and the Abdulla pair Ryafan, representing John Gosden, and Yashmak from Henry Cecil's stable. Ryafan had already met both Bianca Nera and Family Tradition in the Moyglare Stud Stakes over seven furlongs at the Curragh four weeks earlier, where, running in only her second race (she had

Prix Marcel Boussac (Criterium des Pouliches), Longchamp—
Khalid Abdulla's pair have a great battle, Ryafan (No. 1) just edging Yashmak

been well backed when making all in a Doncaster maiden on her debut in June) she had gone down by half a length to Bianca Nera, losing the lead over a furlong out then rallying well near the line. Although Bianca Nera won more comfortably than the winning margin suggests after meeting trouble in running, Ryafan's jockey Pat Eddery was confident of turning the tables over a mile. However, at Longchamp Eddery took the mount on Yashmak, leaving Dettori to ride Ryafan. Yashmak had shown similar form to Ryafan prior to the Marcel Boussac, making a successful debut at Newmarket before finishing second to Red Camellia in a listed race at Sandown in July.

It looked very unlikely that either of the Abdulla fillies would be given a pacemaking role in the Boussac. As it was, Dissertation cut out the running at a sound pace, with Ryafan chasing the leaders and Yashmak racing in second. Once in the straight Yashmak took over but Ryafan had followed her through and the two battled it out to the line, Dettori just forcing Ryafan's head in front near the post. Family Tradition stayed on two and a half lengths back in third with Bianca Nera, again denied a clear run, keeping the French fillies out of the frame in fourth. Incidentally, Dettori's flying dismount apparently found greater favour with French officialdom than it did with their British counter-parts—'part of the show and good for the sport' was the reaction of France

Ryafan (USA) (b.f. Mar 8, 1994)	Lear Fan (USA) (b 1981)	Roberto (b 1969)	Hail To Reason Bramalea
		Wac (b 1969)	Lt Stevens Belthazar
	Carya (USA) (ch 1986)	Northern Dancer (b 1961)	Nearctic Natalma
		Autumn Glory (br 1978)	Graustark Golden Trail

Mr K. Abdulla's "Ryafan"

Galop's Louis Romanet. There was less tolerance of the use of the whip by both Dettori and Eddery, each being fined a thousand francs afterwards.

The Boussac's reputation as a guide to the classics has taken a knock in recent years and the early signs are that the latest running was not a vintage one. Family Tradition ran poorly in the Gran Criterium in Italy next time and the French fillies who turned out again failed to boost the form. Nonetheless, Ryafan is rated a genuine classic prospect by her trainer: 'She'll be trained for the Guineas. I think she'll stay too, and though she's a bit keen and took Frankie on early on, she'll be trained for the Oaks, with the Prix de Diane a strong possibility if we decided that a mile and a half was going to be beyond her.'

On breeding, it could well be that distances around a mile and a quarter will suit Ryafan best. Her dam Carya ran only three times for Andre Fabre, unable to better her second placing over nine and a half furlongs on her debut at three. Ryafan is her second foal after the Italian nine-furlong winner Hong Kong King (by Rousillon) and she has a foal who is a full sister to Ryafan. Carya is closely related to the smart French middle-distance stayer Glorify (by Nijinsky) and a half-sister to the 1994 Prix d'Arenberg winner Doree. Their dam Autumn Glory won from six furlongs to nine furlongs in the United States and was placed in the Grade 1 Acorn Stakes. She was one of a dozen winners out of Golden Trail, one of no fewer than eight by Graustark. This family has produced numerous stakes winners over the years, the most recent being the very smart American three-year-old filly Memories of Silver, a granddaughter of one of Autumn Glory's sisters Java Moon. The choice of Lear Fan as a mate for Carya was no doubt inspired by the fact that descendants of Golden Trail have an excellent record with Lear Fan's sire Roberto. Another of Autumn Glory's sisters Kelley's Day produced the Florida Derby winner Brian's Time to him and the same mating with yet another full sister Outward Sunshine resulted in champion turf horse Sunshine Forever. One of Autumn Glory's half-sisters, On The Trail, is the dam and grandam respectively of Grade 2 winners Darby Creek Road and Dynaformer—both by Roberto.

The well-made, attractive Ryafan may well end up racing in the States herself, as many of her owner's older horses do. Before then, connections face the task of keeping Ryafan, Yashmak, Reams of Verse, and the runaway Goodwood maiden winner Fleet River apart, as far as possible. Ryafan should stay a mile and a quarter; she is a game filly in a finish as she showed at Longchamp. *J. H. M. Gosden*

RYLES DANCER 2 ch.g. (Feb 26) Chilibang 120 – Bee Dee Dancer (Balla- – cashtal (CAN)) [1996 10g a8g Nov 4] first foal: dam well beaten only start: well beaten in median auction maidens at Nottingham and Southwell: will prove best short of 1m. *Dr J. D. Scargill*

RYMER'S RASCAL 4 b.g. Rymer 121 – City Sound 63 (On Your Mark 125) – [1995 67: 6m 6.1m⁵ 8m 6g² 6g³ 6f 5g 6s a6g 1996 7g Apr 8] sturdy gelding: fair handicapper: well beaten last 3 starts in 1995 and (burly) only one in 1996: stays 6f: acts on good to firm and soft ground, ran poorly on firm. *E. J. Alston*

S

SAABGA (USA) 2 ch.f. (Feb 3) Woodman (USA) 126 – Catopetl (USA) (North- 83 p ern Dancer) [1996 7m² Aug 1] 300,000Y: smallish, quite attractive filly: half-sister to 3 winners, including smart middle-distance performers Close Conflict (by High Estate) and Newton's Law (by Law Society): dam unraced sister to Secreto: 10/1 and in need of run, 2½ lengths second of 15 to Quintellina in maiden at Goodwood, getting very poor run from 2f out until inside last, finishing strongly: likely to stay 1¼m: sure to improve, and win a race. *J. H. M. Gosden*

SAAFEYA (IRE) 2 b.f. (Feb 12) Sadler's Wells (USA) 132 – Safa 109 (Shirley 74 p Heights 130) [1996 7.9g³ Oct 12] attractive, rather unfurnished filly: first foal: dam,

6f winner at 2 yrs and effective at 1½m, from the family of Ajdal and Arazi: shaped well, making good headway after a slow start, when 5 lengths third (not given an unduly hard time) to Hidden Meadow at York in October on debut: will be suited by middle distances: bound to improve. *J. H. M. Gosden*

SAAFI (IRE)   5 b.g. Primo Dominie 121 – Baby's Smile 68 (Shirley Heights 130)   – [1995 –: 12g 11.6m 14f 14f⁵ 1996 16.1f Oct 8] strong gelding: modest maiden: no form since 3 yrs, taking charge of his apprentice rider only start in 1996. *R. J. Baker*

SABAAH ELFULL   3 ch.f. Kris 135 – Putupon 89 (Mummy's Pet 125) [1995   62 75+: 6m 7.5d³ 1996 7m 5m* 5g 7g⁶ 5m 6m Oct 28] lengthy filly: failed to reproduce her best 2-y-o form, winning weak maiden at Newcastle in July: stays 7.5f: clearly best effort only try on a soft surface: sold 50,000 gns Newmarket December Sales. *A. C. Stewart*

SABINA   2 b.f. (Feb 14) Prince Sabo 123 – High Savannah 77 (Rousillon (USA)   87 p 133) [1996 6m³ 5.7d* 5d Oct 12] lengthy, rather unfurnished filly: first foal: dam, maiden who stayed 1½m, half-sister to useful 2-y-o sprinters Maid For Walking (by Prince Sabo) and Maid For The Hills: won maiden at Bath in September by 1¾ lengths from Tigrello, quickening 5 lengths clear 1f out then tiring late on: again showed plenty of speed before fading in Cornwallis Stakes at Ascot on final start: capable of better, and could well be a useful sprinter in the making. *I. A. Balding*

SABOT   3 b.c. Polar Falcon (USA) 126 – Power Take Off 109 (Aragon 118) [1995   86 86: 6m⁶ 6d² 6m⁴ 1996 7m² 7m* 7.9g⁴ 7m⁴ 7m Sep 28] tall, good-topped colt: fairly useful performer: 4/1 on, very easy winner of maiden at Thirsk in June: stiff tasks, creditable efforts when last of 4 in minor events at York and Chester next 2 starts: bandaged near-hind, well beaten in £50,100 handicap at Ascot final outing: sold (B. Hills to C. Thornton) 8,500 gns Newmarket Autumn Sales: stays 7f: acts on good to firm and dead ground: edgy (below form) final 2-y-o start. *B. W. Hills*

SABOTINI   2 b.f. (Feb 15) Prince Sabo 123 – Low Line 66 (High Line 125) [1996   62 + 5g* 5m⁵ 7m Aug 2] robust, lengthy filly: has scope: fourth foal: half-brother to Canons Park (by Keen), 7f winner at 2 yrs, and 6f (at 2 yrs) to 1¼m (in Jersey) winner Time Lapse (by Noble Player): dam, sister to Park Hill winner Quay Line, and Shore Line, fourth in Oaks and dam of Soviet Line: won median auction maiden at Sandown in April: last of 5 in minor event (well backed) at Windsor following month then last of 7, setting strong pace nearly 6f, in nursery at Ascot 2½ months later: sold 12,000 gns Newmarket Autumn Sales: may prove best at sprint distances. *B. W. Hills*

SABRAK (IRE)   3 b.c. Fairy King (USA) – Embryo (Busted 134) [1995 NR 1996   88 7.1d 8g⁴ 7.9m⁴ 8s* 8m 10m 8.5g⁵ Aug 26] IR 26,000Y: strong, lengthy colt: unimpressive mover: closely related to 1986 Irish 2-y-o 7f winner Strath Farrar (by Nijinsky) and half-brother to several winners, notably Oaks d'Italia and E P Taylor Stakes winner Ivor's Image (by Sir Ivor): dam, sister to smart Irish middle-distance performer Bog Road, won 3 times at around 1m in Ireland: fairly useful performer: won maiden at Ayr in July: needs good test at 1m, and stays 1¼m: acts on good to firm and soft ground: sent to UAE. *M. A. Jarvis*

SACHO (IRE)   3 b.c. Sadler's Wells (USA) 132 – Oh So Sharp 131 (Kris 135)   89 p [1995 89P: 8m² 1996 10m² Apr 16] lengthy, good sort: good walker: has a fluent, rounded action: evens favourite (just in need of race), failed to improve on form of highly promising debut when ½-length second of 16 to Dovaly in maiden at Newmarket, quickening pace 3f out, caught near line: reportedly suffered bone damage to a hock in race: will stay 1½m: looked capable of better: stays in training. *J. H. M. Gosden*

SACRAMENT   5 b.h. Shirley Heights 130 – Blessed Event 117 (Kings Lake   118 (USA) 133) [1995 116: 12m⁴ 1996 9m 12m³ 12.5g* 11.1m* 14m³ 12s² 12m Dec 8] tall horse: smart performer: reportedly cracked a knee bone after only 4-y-o start: won 4-runner Prix Jean de Chaudenay at Deauville (by ½ length from Punishment) in May and successfully conceded weight all round in 7-runner Grosvenor Casinos September Stakes at Kempton (held on in close finish from Salmon Ladder and Ela-Aristokrati) in September: in frame in Irish St Leger at the Curragh (5½ lengths third to Oscar Schindler) and Gran Premio del Jockey Club at Milan (3 lengths second to Shantou): in mid-division behind Luso in Hong Kong Inter-

national Vase at Sha Tin final start: stays 1¾m: acts on good to firm and soft ground: game. *M. R. Stoute*

SACRED LOCH (USA) 3 ch.g. Lomond (USA) 128 – Cypria Sacra (USA) 103 –
(Sharpen Up 127) [1995 NR 1996 10g 10.4g Oct 10] rangy gelding: third reported living foal: half-brother to a winner over hurdles by Riverman and to unreliable 4-y-o La Dama (by Known Fact): dam 11.7f and 1½m winner: well beaten in maidens at Goodwood (rather edgy) and York (sweating freely, pulled hard) in the autumn: sold (G. Harwood to M. Dods) 6,000 gns Newmarket Autumn Sales and gelded. *G. Harwood*

SACRED MIRROR (IRE) 5 b.m. Shaadi (USA) 126 – Heavenly Abode (FR) 57
(Habitat 134) [1995 52: a8g a8g⁵ a12g 9.7d⁵ 11.7m⁵ 1996 a12g* a13g⁶ a12g a16g 11.8m 12f* 12g² 12g⁵ 12.3m⁴ Aug 4] good-bodied mare: modest handicapper: won at Lingfield (first time) in January and at Folkestone in June: sold 1,000 gns Newmarket Autumn Sales: stays 1½m: acts on firm and soft ground and on equi-track: races prominently: inconsistent: sent to South Korea. *C. E. Brittain*

SADDLEHOME (USA) 7 b.g. Aragon 118 – Kesarini (USA) 87 (Singh (USA)) 73
[1995 83, a86: a5g* 6d² 5g⁶ 6m 5g² 6f* 6m 5.1m⁶ 1996 5s 5g 5m 6m 5m 5m 5m a82
5m 6d⁴ 5g 5g 6m* 7m 6f a6g a5g⁵ Nov 22] leggy, short-backed gelding: fair handicapper: not at best in 1996, but quickened to lead near finish in 19-runner race at Newcastle in October: stays 6f: acts on fibresand and any turf going: visored (below form) once at 3 yrs: held up. *T. D. Barron*

SADDLERS' HOPE 2 b.f. (Feb 5) Saddlers' Hall (IRE) 126 – Hope And Glory 75
(USA) 87 (Well Decorated (USA)) [1996 7m³ 8.1d⁴ Aug 23] fifth foal: half-sister

to 3-y-o 6f winner Never Think Twice (by Never So Bold) and winners in Spain and Germany: dam, 2-y-o 6f winner, only season to race, is daughter of half-sister to Legal Bid and Law Society: similar form in maidens at Kempton (to Bareeq) and Sandown (disappointing favourite) in August: likely to stay beyond 1m. *J. R. Fanshawe*

SADLER'S BLAZE (IRE)   2 b.c. (Apr 14) Alzao (USA) 117 – Christine Daae   – p 74 (Sadler's Wells (USA) 132) [1996 7.1f Sep 12] third foal: half-brother to useful 3-y-o 1m winner My Lewicia (by Taufan) and useful 4-y-o sprinter To The Roof (by Thatching): dam, stayed 1¼m, half-sister to very useful 1981 2-y-o sprinter Travel On out of sister to Red Alert: 20/1, slowly away and always behind in 18-runner maiden at Chepstow: will probably do better. *P. W. Harris*

SADLER'S REALM   3 b.g. Sadler's Wells (USA) 132 – Rensaler (USA) (Stop   72 The Music (USA)) [1995 63p: 8.2m⁶ 1996 10.2g 10f² 12.4g 10g³ Aug 21] quite attractive gelding: fair maiden: sold 13,000 gns Newmarket Autumn (1996) Sales and gelded: stays 1¼m: has raced only on a sound surface: found little penultimate start, hanging left final one: joined P. Hobbs. *M. R. Stoute*

SADLER'S WALK   5 b.g. Sadler's Wells (USA) 132 – Widows Walk (Habitat   76 134) [1995 82: 10d⁴ 10m⁵ 10.3m² 10f³ 10f* 10f⁴ 10d 10.4m² 1996 10g 10m 10m 10.1m⁵ 10.1m⁵ a10s Nov 19] good-bodied gelding: impresses in appearance: has a quick action: fair handicapper: should stay 1½m: acts on firm going, not at his best on a soft surface: no improvement in blinkers: usually held up. *G. Wragg*

SAD MAD BAD (USA)   2 b.g. (May 4) Sunny's Halo (CAN) – Quite Attractive   71 (USA) (Well Decorated (USA)) [1996 6g³ 7.6d* 8m Sep 12] $97,000Y: strong, workmanlike gelding: second foal: half-brother to A V Eight (by Wavering Monarch), Grade 3 6f winner at 2 yrs in USA in 1995: dam won at up to 1m in USA: sire won Kentucky Derby: won maiden at Lingfield in August, staying on well: sweating, went freely to post and well beaten in valuable nursery at Doncaster on final start: should stay 1m: acts on good to soft ground: gelded. *M. Johnston*

SAEKO-BEAUTY   2 b.f. (Mar 24) Warrshan (USA) 117 – Jalopy 71 (Jalmood   – (USA) 126) [1996 a7g a7g⁶ Dec 11] 10,500Y: fourth foal: sister to French provincial 8.5f winner Alenou: dam, 5f winner, is half-sister to useful sprinter Point of Light: no show in maidens at Wolverhampton (very slowly away) and Lingfield. *Sir Mark Prescott*

SAFA DANCER   3 b.f. Safawan 118 – Dalby Dancer 71 (Bustiki) [1995 NR 1996   – a8g³ 8.2m a8.5g⁶ 8g 10g 8.1f Sep 12] first foal: dam stayed well: poor maiden: best   a41 effort on debut. *B. A. McMahon*

SAFA (USA)   3 b.f. Green Dancer (USA) 132 – Romanette (USA) (Alleged (USA)   71 ? 138) [1995 NR 1996 10m 16.2g² 11.5m 17.1m Oct 7] $130,000Y: big, unfurnished filly: half-sister to smart 7f (at 2 yrs) to 1½m performer Blush Rambler (by Blushing Groom), useful German 9f winner Romanowa (by Topsider) and a sprint winner in North America by In Reality: dam useful winner at up to 11f: off course 4½ months, clearly best effort when 2½ lengths second of 6 in maiden at Beverley, plugging on: soundly beaten both subsequent outings, going with little zest: sold 84,000 gns Newmarket December Sales: one to treat with caution. *A. C. Stewart*

SAFECRACKER   3 ch.g. Sayf El Arab (USA) 127 – My Polished Corner (IRE)   67 53 (Tate Gallery (USA) 117) [1995 –: 7.1m 7.6d 1996 a8g² 9.7f* 10m 11.6m 10g Aug 21] lengthy gelding: good mover: fair handicapper: won at Folkestone in April: failed to repeat the form, blinkered final start: stays 9.7f: acts on firm going and equitrack, tailed off on a soft ground: has joined C. Morlock. *J. W. Hills*

SAFETY (USA)   9 b.g. Topsider (USA) – Flare Pass (USA) (Buckpasser) [1995   – NR 1996 9m 17.2m 11.6m 8m a10g Dec 11] compact gelding: modest handicapper (rated 52) at 5 yrs: lightly raced and little form on flat since. *J. White*

SAFEY ANA (USA)   5 b.g. Dixieland Band (USA) – Whatsoraire (USA) (Mr   63 Prospector (USA)) [1995 77: 8d⁶ 8m⁵ 10m 8m³ 7m* 6m 7g* 7.6m⁵ 7m⁶ 7g³ 7.3d 7g 1996 7m 7m 7m⁶ 6m 7m² 7m⁴ 7g⁴ 7.3m 8.2g Oct 9] good-bodied gelding: poor mover: just a modest handicapper in 1996: effective at 7f, and stays 1¼m: acts on good to firm and dead ground: effective blinkered, but not tried for long time: sometimes rears stalls: wears bandages. *B. Hanbury*

SAFFRON ROSE   2 b.f. (Apr 6) Polar Falcon (USA) 126 – Tweedling (USA)   66
(Sir Ivor 135) [1996 6m 7m⁵ 7.1f⁴ 7g 7m Oct 4] 4,200Y: tall, unfurnished filly: eighth
foal: half-sister to several winners here and abroad, including 6f to 1m winner Scots
Law (by Law Society) and 11f winner Lovely Lagoon (by Mill Reef): dam won at
around 1m in USA: fair form: best effort when fourth of 18 to Royal Amaretto in
maiden at Chepstow in September: below form in nurseries afterwards: will stay at
least 1m: flashed tail second start. *M. Blanshard*

SAFIO   3 ch.g. Efisio 120 – Marcroft 91 (Crofthall 110) [1995 79?: 5g⁸ 6g⁶ 6g³ 5f   –
5m⁵ 6m 5.2d 1996 6g 7g⁴ 7f⁶ 7.1m 7.5m⁵ 6d Aug 10] workmanlike gelding: fair form
at best as 2-y-o: well held in 1996: should stay beyond 6f. *C. Smith*

SAGEBRUSH ROLLER   8 br.g. Sharpo 132 – Sunita (Owen Dudley 121)   81 d
[1995 87: 6g 7m³ 7.6m 7g 7m⁶ 7g⁴ 7g² 7g 7g 7m 1996 7g³ 6.9d³ 7d⁴ 7m⁵ 7m⁴ 7g²
7.6m⁵ 7g⁴ 7s a6g a7g Nov 22] rangy gelding: fair form on
reappearance: effective at 6f to 1m: probably acts on any going: visored (below form)
once at 4 yrs: sometimes hangs under pressure, and best held up. *J. W. Watts*

SAHARA RIVER (USA)   2 b.f. (Feb 24) Riverman (USA) 131 – Sahara Forest   80 p
(Green Desert (USA) 127) [1996 6m⁴ Aug 16] smallish, well-made filly: first reported foal: dam unraced half-sister to Reference Point: 25/1 and not fully wound up,
1½ lengths fourth of 19 to Catechism in maiden at Newbury, stopped in run then
finishing in good style: sure to improve, particularly over 7f+. *R. Charlton*

SAHEEEL (USA)   3 b.c. Dayjur (USA) 137 – Qirmazi (USA) 113 (Riverman   99
(USA) 131) [1995 NR 1996 6m² 5.2m* 5s⁴ 5g 6g* Nov 2] compact, attractive colt:
second foal: half-brother to 1m winner Quinwood (by Woodman): dam French 6f (at
2 yrs) and 9.2f winner also third in 10.5f Prix Saint-Alary: useful form: won maiden
at Yarmouth (after 4½-month break, making all) and minor event at Newmarket
(dictated pace and beat How Long by 1¼ lengths) in the autumn: a sprinter: seemed
unsuited by soft ground. *Saeed bin Suroor*

SAHHAR   3 ch.c. Sayf El Arab (USA) 127 – Native Magic 97 (Be My Native   56
(USA) 122) [1995 65: 6m a10g³ a8g² 1996 a10g⁶ a8g⁶ a14g 11.5m⁴ a12g⁴ Sep 7]
small colt: modest maiden: below best in 1996: sold (R. Armstrong to P. Bevan) 700
gns Newmarket Autumn Sales: stays 1¼m. *R. W. Armstrong*

SAHM (USA)   2 b. or br.c. (Feb 16) Mr Prospector (USA) – Salsabil 130 (Sadler's   112
Wells (USA) 132) [1996 6m* 7m* 7m²ᵈⁱˢ 7g Sep 21] finely-made, lengthy colt: good
walker: third foal: half-brother to 3-y-o Bint Salsabil (by Nashwan), useful 6f and 7f
winner at 2 yrs: dam won 1000 Guineas, Oaks and Irish Derby and is half-sister to
Marju: successful at York in maiden in June and 2-runner minor event (by 5 lengths)
in July: still bit coltish, smart form when ½-length second of 8 to Putra in Lanson
Champagne Vintage Stakes at Goodwood, causing interference when switched left
2f out (relegated to last) then running on strongly: again favourite, below form in
National Stakes at the Curragh 7 weeks later, never looking like threatening and
around 2½ lengths seventh of 10 behind Desert King at the line: should be at least as
effective at 1m as 7f: raced only on a sound surface: sent to Dubai, where reportedly
had wind operation. *J. L. Dunlop*

SAIFAN   7 ch.g. Beveled (USA) – Superfrost 49 (Tickled Pink 114) [1995 79: 7s   89
8m² 8m 8g³ 8m* 8g⁶ 8m² 8f⁴ 7m* 8d 8m 8f 8m 1996 8.1g 8m 8s³ 8m* 8m⁴ 7m⁶ 8g

Leonard Sainer European Breeders Fund Stakes, York—Sahm shows some potential

8f* 8m² 8m 8m⁶ 8g 8g 8g* Nov 2] tall, close-coupled, angular gelding: has a round action: fairly useful handicapper: won at Newmarket and Yarmouth in the summer and 26-runner £22,900 event at Newmarket in November(33/1) by neck from Prince Babar: effective at 7f and 1m: probably acts on any going: almost always blinkered or visored: sometimes slowly away (badly so twice in 1996): held up. *D. Morris*

SAILORMAITE 5 ch.g. Komaite (USA) – Marina Plata (Julio Mariner 127) [1995 87, a96; a96: 5g² 6d⁴ 6m 6d* a6g* 5g² 5.6m 6g a6g⁴ a7g² 1996 a7g⁵ 5.2d⁴ 6g 6d 5d* 5m 5m⁶ 6g 6.1d 5d⁶ 6v⁶ 7g 5g² a7g⁶ Dec 7] tall, leggy gelding: fairly useful handicapper, best on the all-weather: well drawn, won at Haydock in May: successful at 8.5f, but best at up to 7f: acts on fibresand and soft going, not at best on top-of-the-ground: sometimes blinkered, including for 1996 success: often mounted on track and taken down early: rather a difficult ride (carries head high, tends to idle and has unseated jockey to post): refused to race sixth 5-y-o start and unseated rider leaving stalls on twelfth: not one to trust. *S. R. Bowring*   87 § a80 §

SAILS LEGEND 5 b.h. Hotfoot 126 – Miss Polly Peck (March Past 124) [1995 –: 16.4m 16m 12s 16.1g 1996 14m 12d May 22] smallish, workmanlike horse: no worthwhile form on flat since 2 yrs. *Mrs M. E. Long*   –

SAINT AMIGO 4 gr.g. Presidium 124 – Little Token (Shack (USA) 118) [1995 52?: 8f 8.2m 8f 5.9f⁶ 7m 6g 6m 8.2m 7m a11g a6g 1996 6m 5m a7g Nov 15] small gelding: modest performer, mostly disappointing and no form in 1996: sold 700 gns Doncaster November Sales. *R. M. Whitaker*   –

SAINT EXPRESS 6 ch.g. Clantime 101 – Redgrave Design 77 (Nebbiolo 125) [1995 109: 5g² 5m* 5m² 5f³ 6m⁴ 5m 5d³ 6m 1996 5m 5g 5m 5m 6m 6m 5.6m 5m³ 6g 5m 7m⁴ 6f⁴ Nov 5] lengthy, workmanlike gelding: has a quick action: fairly useful handicapper at best in 1996: stays 7f: acts on soft going, best efforts on top-of-the-ground: tried blinkered, at least as good without: usually held up. *Mrs M. Reveley*   83

SAINT WHO (USA) 2 b.g. (Mar 25) Hooched (USA) – Saint Pea (USA) (Christopher R (USA)) [1996 6m 6m² 7d 7f² 6m* 6m Oct 5] $1,600Y: strong, good-bodied gelding: fifth foal: half-brother to winners in USA by Dancing Count (2) and Brother Liam: dam won at up to 7f in USA: sire (by Danzig) half-brother to Breeders' Cup Distaff winner Life's Magic: runner-up in seller second start: progressed afterwards, winning rating related maiden at Lingfield by 6 lengths in September: wandered and never travelled with any fluency in Newmarket nursery final start: takes keen hold and best form at 6f: wears crossed noseband. *W. A. O'Gorman*   73

SAKHAROV 7 b.g. Bay Express 132 – Supreme Kingdom 85 (Take A Reef 127) [1995 59: a6g² a6g⁶ 5.9m 6f³ 8.3f² 6.9f³ 8m² 1996 7m* 8.1g 5.9f² 7.5m³ 8m⁵ Jul 8] leggy gelding: modest performer: made all in seller at Redcar in May: effective at 6f, stays 8.3f: acts on firm and dead ground and on fibresand: normally held up: most consistent: has joined B. Palling. *M. Johnston*   59

SALABATNI 2 b.f. (Apr 28) Rainbow Quest (USA) 134 – Balwa (USA) 101 (Danzig (USA)) [1996 6d⁶ 6g 7g³ 8m 8f Nov 5] leggy filly: second foal: half-sister to 3-y-o 1½m winner Laazim Afooz (by Mtoto): dam 5f (at 2 yrs) and 7f winner from very good family: modest form at best: never a factor in nurseries last 2 starts: should prove effective at 1m: tail flasher: pulled hard second outing: becoming disappointing: sold 55,000 gns Newmarket December Sales. *E. A. L. Dunlop*   61 ?

SALAMANDER KING 4 b.g. Distant Relative 128 – Spirit of The Wind (USA) (Little Current (USA)) [1995 –: 8g 1996 14d⁵ Jun 7] good-topped gelding: well held in maidens. *Lady Herries*   –

SALAMAN (FR) 4 b.g. Saumarez 132 – Merry Sharp (Sharpen Up 127) [1995 89p: 10s 12.3m³ 12m⁵ 14.9m* 16.2m* 18.7g* 20f³ 18m* 18m 1996 18s 16g 16d 16.2f 20m⁵ 16m³ 16g Sep 14] sturdy, lengthy gelding: unimpressive mover: fairly useful handicapper: sold to D. C. O'Brien only 4,000 gns Newmarket Autumn Sales: needs a good test of stamina: best form on a sound surface (acts on firm going): blinkered last 2 starts, finding little on first of them. *J. L. Dunlop*   83

SALEEMAH (USA) 3 ch.f. Storm Bird (CAN) 134 – Retire (USA) (Secretariat (USA)) [1995 NR 1996 7m⁶ 8m³ 8g⁴ 7.1d² 8m* 7.6f* 8m* 8d⁴ 8m 8f³ Oct 15] $100,000F: big, workmanlike filly: has a fluent action: fifth foal: half-sister to 2 winners in North America, both at 1m+: dam unplaced in 2 outings: useful performer: won maiden at Bath and handicaps at Lingfield and Salisbury in the summer: 96 stayed 1m: acted on firm ground, possibly unsuited by dead: visits Machiavellian. *J. L. Dunlop*

SALFORD LAD   2 b.c. (Feb 22) Don't Forget Me 127 – Adjusting (IRE) (Busted – 134) [1996 7g 8s Nov 9] 32,000Y: first foal: dam, ran once at 2 yrs, half-sister to Dee Stakes winner and Belmont Stakes runner-up My Memoirs (by Don't Forget Me): burly, tailed off in maidens at Yarmouth (hung left) and Doncaster (pulled hard). *G. Wragg*

SALLY ARMSTRONG   3 b.f. Batshoof 122 – Salinity (NZ) (Standaan (FR) – 118) [1995 NR 1996 a6s Dec 19] 2,000F: fifth reported foal: half-sister to 2 winners abroad: dam ran once in New Zealand: slowly away when seventh of 13 in claimer at Wolverhampton. *C. W. Thornton*

SALLY GREEN (IRE)   2 b.f. (Mar 30) Common Grounds 118 – Redwood Hut (Habitat 134) [1996 6g 5.1m 6d a6g* a7g⁵ Nov 29] IR 9,000F, 215,000 francs Y: angular filly: fourth foal: half-sister to 4-y-o 1m winner Jackatack (by Astronef): dam unraced half-sister to Red Regent: fair form: won maiden at Southwell in November: ran creditably over 7f, though shaping as if may prove best at 6f: acts on fibresand. *C. F. Wall*   ? a65

SALLYOREALLY (IRE)   5 b.m. Common Grounds 118 – Prosapia (USA) (Our Native (USA)) [1995 –: 10m 12g 12.4g 10g 10f 10.1m⁵ 8m 15.8m⁶ 15.1g⁶ 12f 8f 1996 10.1s 8g 6.9d 7d³ 6g⁵ 5g⁶ 6m³ 8f⁴ 8m⁵ 6m 6m 5g Sep 7] leggy, lengthy mare: poor maiden handicapper: best recent efforts at up to 1m: probably acts on any going. *W. Storey*   38

SALLY SLADE   4 b.f. Dowsing (USA) 124 – Single Gal 97 (Mansingh (USA) 120) [1995 80: a5g⁵ 6m 5m* 5.1m 6g² 5f 1996 6g 5g 5g⁵ 6.1d⁶ 5m* 5m⁵ 5m⁵ 6g 5g 5g 5.2m⁵ 5g 5g⁶ 5f a5g² Dec 13] leggy filly: fair handicapper: won at Goodwood in June: stays 6f: acts on good to firm and soft ground, and on equitrack: well beaten only try in blinkers: none too consistent. *C. A. Cyzer*   80

SALLY'S TWINS   3 b.f. Dowsing (USA) 124 – Bird of Love 82 (Ela-Mana-Mou 132) [1995 59: 7.6d 8d⁶ 10g 1996 12m⁶ 11.6g 9.7d 12s³ Oct 26] good-topped filly: modest maiden: stays 1½m: acts on soft going. *J. S. Moore*   60

SALMIS   3 b.f. Salse (USA) 128 – Misguided 106 (Homing 130) [1995 84p: 6.9s* 8.1d² 1996 9g⁴ 10.5d 8g⁴ 8.2m* 8.1g 7.1s⁶ Oct 5] smallish, angular filly: has fluent, quick action: fair handicapper: best 3-y-o effort when winning at Nottingham in July, always close up in falsely-run race: sold 12,500 gns Newmarket December Sales: should stay beyond 1m: acts on good to firm ground and soft: has had tongue tied down. *J. R. Fanshawe*   79

SALMON LADDER (USA)   4 b.c. Bering 136 – Ballerina Princess (USA) (Mr Prospector (USA)) [1995 101: 10.4g⁶ 12f 12d⁵ 1996 9.2g* 10f* 10g 10f² 12m* 10d² 11.1m² 12m² 12s* Oct 26]   117

Salmon Ladder was a very different horse in the latest season from the one who had failed by a long way to live up to expectations as a three-year-old, when he'd been touted as a possible Derby winner. An operation to correct a wind problem was deemed necessary after he had finished a well-beaten tenth in the Derby and it proved a success, although the benefits were realized in the long term rather than the short. On his only subsequent start at three years Salmon Ladder was a never-dangerous fifth in the Perpetual St Simon Stakes at Newbury, but twelve months later he crowned a most rewarding 1996 season by winning that event, a race sponsored by Salmon Ladder's owner's company.

Salmon Ladder made his first appearance of 1996 in a minor contest at Hamilton in June, and in trouncing Billy Bushwacker and four others he enabled Richard Quinn, his usual rider, to achieve the notable feat of having ridden a winner on every flat racecourse in Britain. The return to a top track wasn't long in coming. Ten days later Salmon Ladder, carrying 10-0 and conceding at least 7 lb all round, won a valuable eleven-runner handicap at Ascot gamely by a length from Ellie Ardensky. Another handicap success came at Goodwood in August, in the Schroders Glorious Rated Stakes, a strongly-run event in which Salmon Ladder, prominent throughout as usual, wore down Midnight Legend approaching the final furlong and went on to beat him a

Schroders Glorious Rated Stakes (Handicap), Goodwood—the third win in an excellent year for Salmon Ladder; Midnight Legend and Better Offer are placed

length and a quarter. Salmon Ladder's remaining four runs all came in Group 3 events, and he gained a well-deserved success in the St Simon Stakes after finishing second three times, beaten three quarters of a length by Annus Mirabilis in the Winter Hill Stakes at Windsor, a neck by Sacrament in the September Stakes at Kempton and half a length by Wall Street in the Cumberland Lodge Stakes at Ascot. Salmon Ladder, encountering very soft ground for the first time, made virtually all at Newbury, where he and Kutta pulled clear in the last two furlongs. The latter kept up a persistent challenge, but despite Quinn dropping the reins briefly at the distance, Salmon Ladder was always holding him and had three quarters of a length to spare at the line.

		Arctic Tern	Sea Bird II
	Bering	(ch 1973)	Bubbling Beauty
	(ch 1983)	Beaune	Lyphard
Salmon Ladder (USA)		(ch 1974)	Barbra
(b.c. 1992)	Ballerina	Mr Prospector	Raise A Native
	Princess (USA)	(b 1970)	Gold Digger
	(b 1986)	Aladancer	Northern Dancer
		(ch 1968)	Mock Orange

Salmon Ladder is the second foal of Ballerina Princess, who was placed twice from five starts in the USA; the first was a minor winner by Deputy Minister. The second dam Aladancer, a half-sister to the good stayer Duke of Marmalade, was a smart stakes winner at up to one and a quarter miles and went on to produce the South African Grade 1 winner Vigliotto. Aladancer is grandam of several other good horses, including the Grade 1 Californian Stakes winner Latin American. Salmon Ladder, a good-topped, attractive colt, impressed in appearance throughout the season, though he did sweat on his last three starts. He stays a mile and a half and acts on any going. Thoroughly game and genuine, Salmon Ladder will continue to do well, and he'll win races in all but the best company. *P. F. I. Cole*

SALOME 2 ch.f. (Apr 5) Risk Me (FR) 127 – Dancing Belle 80 (Dance In Time (CAN)) [1996 5d⁴ a5g⁴ Apr 29] 1,700Y: fourth foal: sister to 1993 2-y-o 5f winner Dances With Risk and useful 1994 2-y-o 6f and 7.3f winner Circa: dam sprinter: soundly beaten in maiden and seller. *N. A. Graham* –

SALSEE LAD 2 b.g. (Apr 12) Salse (USA) 128 – Jamarj 113 (Tyrnavos 129) [1996 7m Oct 3] strong, good-topped gelding: fourth foal: dam best at 1m/9f: 33/1 and burly, tailed off in 16-runner maiden at Newmarket: gelded. *J. R. Fanshawe* –

SALSIAN 3 b.f. Salse (USA) 128 – Phylae (Habitat 134) [1995 –p: 8g 8.2m 1996 8g 8.3s⁶ 12m a14.8g a9.4g 12.1g⁴ Jul 2] angular, lengthy, dipped-backed filly: no worthwhile form: tried blinkered: sold (S. Williams to P. Winkworth) 1,100 gns Newmarket July Sales. *S. C. Williams* –

843

SALSKA   5 b.m. Salse (USA) 128 – Anzeige (GER) (Soderini 123) [1995 51: a9.4g   58
10m 8.1m⁴ 10m 10m 10m² 11m³ 10m⁶ 10m 10d⁵ 14g* 16m 1996 10.5d⁵ 14.1m²
14.1f 14.6g³ 14.9m* 14.1f* Jul 17] strong, lengthy mare: modest handicapper: won
at Warwick and Redcar within 5 days in July, on both occasions travelling well,
leading over 1f out and forging clear: should stay 2m: acts on firm ground, probably
on dead: tried visored, no improvement. *A. Streeter*

SALTANDO (IRE)   5 b.g. Salt Dome (USA) – Ange de Feu (Double Form 130)   62
[1995 55: 6g 6m 8.2m⁴ 8m 7m³ 8g⁴ 10d 8g³ 8s³ 8m 10f 12m a8g* a11g⁴ 1996 12m
8m⁶ 10d² 11.8m 12m 8.1m⁶ a8g 10m 8m 10m 8d 8m* 8g Nov 2] angular gelding:
modest handicapper: easily best effort in 1996 when winning (13 lb out of handicap)
at Newmarket in October: stays 1¼m: acts on good to firm and soft going and on
fibresand. *Pat Mitchell*

SALTIMBANCO   2 ch.c. (Jan 14) Green Forest (USA) 134 – Tea And Scandals   68
(USA) (Key To The Kingdom (USA)) [1996 6m⁶ 6g 6m³ 6m Oct 17] 38,000Y:
seventh reported foal: half-brother to high-class French sprinter Ron's Victory (by
General Holme): dam French 6f winner: improved effort when 5 lengths third to
Wind Cheetah in maiden at Lingfield, keeping on to finish well clear of remainder:
never in contention in 18-runner nursery at Newmarket later in month: sold 13,000
gns Newmarket Autumn Sales: will stay beyond 6f. *I. A. Balding*

SALTIS (IRE)   4 ch.g. Salt Dome (USA) – Mrs Tittlemouse (Nonoalco (USA)   –
131) [1995 56: 8.3m a8g⁴ 7.1m⁴ 8m⁴ 7m 7m 7s⁴ 7m a7g a10g 1996 a10g 12g 10m
17.2m Jun 29] angular gelding: modest maiden handicapper: no form in 1996: sold
1,800 gns Ascot July Sales: resold 2,100 gns Ascot August Sales. *D. W. P. Arbuthnot*

SALTY BEHAVIOUR (IRE)   2 ch.c. (Apr 10) Salt Dome (USA) – Good   83
Behaviour (Artaius (USA) 129) [1996 5d³ 6m* 5d⁶ 5d 5v* Nov 11] IR 3,700F, IR
6,700Y: rangy colt: brother to German 9f winner Plinius and half-brother to a middle-
distance winner in Italy by Glow: dam unraced daughter of half-sister to Habitat:
fairly useful form: won in maiden auction at Salisbury in July and minor event (led
then rallied to beat Sous Le Nez a head) at Folkestone: stays 6f: probably acts on any
going: off course 3 months after debut and second start. *R. Hannon*

SALTY GIRL (IRE)   3 b.f. Scenic 128 – Sodium's Niece (Northfields (USA))   64
[1995 70: 6g⁵ 7f³ 8g⁴ 7.1s² 6.9g⁶ 1996 10g 10m³ 11f⁶ 12g⁵ Oct 19] sturdy filly: fair
maiden: well below form last 2 starts: stays 1¼m: acts on firm and soft ground.
B. W. Hills

SALTY JACK (IRE)   2 b.c. (Jan 23) Salt Dome (USA) – Play The Queen (IRE)   81
(King of Clubs 124) [1996 5m 6g³ 6m³ 6m* 7g³ 7.3m³ Sep 20] 8,800F, 4,000Y: small
colt: has a roundish action: second foal: dam Irish 7f winner out of Coronation Stakes
winner Orchestration: generally progressive form: won maiden auction at Salisbury
in August: never far away and kept on when third in nurseries at Goodwood and
Newbury last 2 starts: stays 7.3f: has joined V. Soane. *S. Dow*

SALUTATION (IRE)   5 b.g. Salt Dome (USA) – Salvationist (Mill Reef (USA)   –
141) [1995 –: a11g 1996 14.1f 14.1f Jul 6] no worthwhile form: tried visored.
T. Kersey

SAMAKA HARA (IRE)   4 b.g. Taufan (USA) 119 – Aunt Hester (IRE) 68   –
(Caerleon (USA) 132) [1995 54, a40: 7.1g⁶ a8g⁶ 8.3g* 9.2g⁵ 8.1g⁴ a8g² 8.5g³ 11.1f²
10.4g 10g 1996 a10g⁶ Feb 27] rather unfurnished gelding: modest performer on turf
in 1995, poor on the all-weather: well beaten only 4-y-o start: stays 11.1f: acts on
firm ground and fibresand: has joined G. Roe. *W. S. Cunningham*

SAMANA CAY   4 ch.f. Pharly (FR) 130 – Brown's Cay 71 (Formidable (USA)   –
125) [1995 40, a48: a6g⁴ a7g² a8g⁴ a8g³ a8g³ 10m⁴ 12g⁵ 6.9f⁵ 8.3f³ 8m 1996 a8g a8g
a11g a16g a12g Feb 28] small, stocky filly: poor performer: well beaten in 1996.
P. S. Felgate

SAMARA (IRE)   3 ch.f. Polish Patriot (USA) 128 – Smeralda (GER) (Dschingis   96
Khan) [1995 69p: 6d 6s 6f² 1996 8.2m* 8g* 8f⁴ Jun 22] good-topped filly: has plenty
of scope: carries condition: useful form: won handicaps at Nottingham in April and
Pontefract (quickened on 1½f out and soon clear in very strongly-run race) in May:
fourth of 9 in listed rated stakes at Ascot final start, reportedly having pulled muscles
in her back: likely to prove suited by further than 1m: acts on firm ground: stays in
training. *J. L. Dunlop*

SAMARA SONG   3 ch.g. Savahra Sound 111 – Hosting (Thatching 131) [1995 –: 61
6m 8.1m 6d 1996 a9.4g 8.3m⁶ 7f⁵ a7g⁴ 8g⁵ 6f⁵ 8m² 8d 10.8f a7g⁶ Oct 28]
lengthy, unfurnished gelding: modest maiden handicapper: stays 1m, but has looked
headstrong and unlikely to get further: acts on good to firm ground and equitrack,
probably on fibresand: seems effective blinkered or not, below form only start in
visor. *W. G. M. Turner*

SAMBAC (USA)   2 b.f. (Apr 21) Mr Prospector (USA) – Kingscote 118 (Kings 96
Lake (USA) 133) [1996 6m³ 6g* 6m* 6.1d* 6m⁵ 7g⁴ Oct 18] neat filly: has a short,
round action: half-sister to very smart French/US 1m winner Rainbow
Corner (by Rainbow Quest): dam 2-y-o 5f and 6f winner from good family: success-
ful in the summer in maiden at Yarmouth and minor events at Doncaster and
Chester: useful form behind Indian Rocket in Mill Reef Stakes at Newbury and
Moonlight Paradise in Rockfel Stakes (gone in coat) at Newmarket: stays 7f: acts on
good to firm and dead ground. *H. R. A. Cecil*

SAMBA SHARPLY   5 b.g. Rambo Dancer (CAN) 107 – Sharper Still (Sharpen 84
Up 127) [1995 84: 8m 8.1g² 8f² 8m⁵ 7m³ 8d 8.2m* 8m 1996 8g 8m² 8g 8.9m 8m³ 8g
8g Sep 3] compact gelding: fairly useful handicapper: not discredited over 7f, but
really needs further (stays 1¼m): acts on firm and soft ground: respectable efforts
both tries in blinkers: sweating (below form) final 4-y-o start: none too consistent.
A. Hide

SAMIM (USA)   3 b.c. Nureyev (USA) 131 – Histoire (FR) (Riverman (USA) 131) 78 d
[1995 84p: 7m⁶ 7g³ 8.5m³ 7d* 7.9m⁴ 1996 10.3d 10.5g⁵ 12.3m⁴ 12.3g⁴ 10.3m 10.5d⁵
10.5s⁶ 10.4g⁵ Oct 10] small, attractive colt: fairly useful performer on his day: sold
out of J. Dunlop's stable 9,000 gns Newmarket July Sales after fourth start: well
below best for new yard: stays 12.3f: acts on good to firm ground, better suited by
a soft surface: blinkered since third 3-y-o start: hung badly left fourth 3-y-o start.
S. Gollings

SAMORELLE   3 ch.f. High Kicker (USA) – Lemelasor 75 (Town Crier 119) –
[1995 NR 1996 8.3m 8.3d 7.6m³ 9.9g a8g Dec 3] half-sister to 1991 2-y-o 5f
winner Ravecino (by Ballacashtal): dam 5f (at 2 yrs) to 9f winner: no worthwhile
form. *M. J. Ryan*

SAM PEEB   2 b.g. (May 7) Keen 116 – Lutine Royal 46 (Formidable (USA) 125) –
[1996 6m 6s 7.5m Sep 18] 3,400Y: long-backed, rather unfurnished gelding: unimpressive mover: third live foal: dam (lightly raced) from family of Royal Palace:
behind in maiden auctions in the North. *R. A. Fahey*

SAMRAAN (USA)   3 br.c. Green Dancer (USA) 132 – Sedra 116 (Nebbiolo 125) 117
[1995 68p: 7m⁴ 1996 10g* 12m³ 12d* 12m* 11.9g⁴ 12m⁶ 13.3m⁴ 14f* 14.6m³ 14d⁵

King George V Stakes (Handicap), Royal Ascot—
Samraan (centre) and Private Song have missed the mayhem on the turn; Harbour Dues (right) finishes fast

Mr K. M. Al-Mudhaf's "Samraan"

Sep 29] angular, unfurnished colt: smart performer: won maiden at Kempton in April, rated stakes at Newbury in May, King George V Handicap at Royal Ascot in June and minor event at Salisbury in September: also contested 4 pattern events, running a splendid race when about 4¼ lengths third of 11 to Shantou in the St Leger at Doncaster: well below form in German equivalent final start: better at 1¾m than shorter and may improve further over 2m: acts on firm and dead going: thoroughly game and genuine: stays in training. *J. L. Dunlop*

SAM ROCKETT 3 b.g. Petong 126 – Art Deco (Artaius (USA) 129) [1995 NR 1996 7g 8d 8m 10m 10g 11.9f 14d⁴ 12d⁶ a16g a12g² Dec 30] 15,000Y: leggy gelding: half-brother to 2 winners by Ile de Bourbon, including Anatroccolo (up to 1m): dam (unraced) out of sister to 1000 Guineas winner Glad Rags: poor maiden: sold out of C. Horgan's stable 8,200 gns Ascot November Sales after eighth 3-y-o start: should stay 2m: blinkered last 2 starts: has worn crossed noseband. *P. Mooney*   43

SAMSOLOM 8 b.g. Absalom 128 – Norfolk Serenade 83 (Blakeney 126) [1995 76: 6d 6g 6m 6f⁴ 6m⁴ 6d⁶ 6f* 6m³ 6m² 6m 6m* 6f² 6m 6m⁴ 6g 7f⁶ 7f 1996 a6g⁶ a6g 6s 6g 6m⁵ 6f⁶ 6m 6.1m 6f⁵ 6f³ 6m 6m 6m³ 7m² 7g⁵ 6.9m 7m³ 7g 7m 7m 6m a7g⁶ a6g⁴ a7g Dec 11] strong, good-quartered gelding: has round action: modest handicapper: stays 7f: has won on dead ground, but easily best form on a sound surface (acts on firm) or the all-weather: tried blinkered/visored, not since 4 yrs: usually held up: often bandaged behind: usually early to post. *P. Howling*   64

SAMSPET 2 ch.g. (Apr 8) Pharly (FR) 130 – Almond Blossom 69 (Grundy 137) [1996 5m 7m⁴ 7f a7g⁵ 6m⁵ 8.1m 6s Oct 5] 5,200Y: small gelding: closely related to a winner abroad by Bellypha and half-brother to 2 others by Northern State: dam 1½m winner and daughter of Lingfield Oaks Trial winner Riboreen: poor form, mostly in sellers: bred to stay well: blinkered/visored last 3 starts. *R. A. Fahey*   43 d

SAMSUNG LOVELYLADY (IRE) 4 b.f. Petorius 117 – Kentucky Wildcat 40 d
64 (Be My Guest (USA) 126) [1995 47: 5.1g 7g 5m6 5g 5m4 a5g 6m 1996 7.1g 6d5
6.1m 5m6 6f 6s 5g Sep 7] lengthy filly: poor maiden handicapper: stays 6f: acts on
good to firm and dead ground: no improvement in visor: sold 2,000 gns Newmarket
December Sales: inconsistent and one to treat with caution. *E. Weymes*

SAMSUNG SPIRIT 2 b.f. (May 14) Statoblest 120 – Sarong 97 (Taj Dewan 128) 71
[1996 6d* 7m3 7m2 7m5 6g5 Oct 12] lengthy, quite good-topped filly: has scope: has
a quick action: half-sister to several winners here and abroad, including useful 5f
and 1m winner Hindi and fairly useful 1985 2-y-o 7f winner Illumineux (both by
Mummy's Pet): dam 1m winner: fair form: won median auction maiden at Ayr in
May: stiff tasks in minor events and a listed race (best effort) afterwards: stays 7f.
E. Weymes

SAM'S YER MAN 2 b.c. (May 31) Full Extent (USA) 113 – Falls of Lora 107 –
(Scottish Rifle 127) [1996 6m 7m 8g Nov 2] 3,100Y, 6,800 2-y-o: half-brother to
useful 1m and 1¼m winner You Know The Rules (by Castle Keep) and 2m winner
She Knew The Rules (by Jamesmead): dam won from 6f to 1½m: well beaten in
claimer and sellers. *S. C. Williams*

SAMUEL SCOTT 3 b.g. Shareef Dancer (USA) 135 – Revisit 86 (Busted 134) 62
[1995 –p: 6m 1996 8m 7m 11.8d6 14d Jun 7] quite attractive gelding: modest maiden:
best effort on third 3-y-o start: bred to stay beyond 11.8f. *M. Bell*

SAMWAR 4 b.g. Warning 136 – Samaza (USA) 90 (Arctic Tern (USA) 126) [1995 98
78+: 7m4 6m4 6g6 a7g* 1996 7m6 7.6g 6m4 6g* 6g2 5g2 5d 6s Oct 24] small gelding:
unimpressive mover: useful handicapper, generally progressive: reportedly finished
sore second 4-y-o start: won £19,600 William Hill Great St Wilfrid Handicap at
Ripon in August: good efforts in competitive events at Goodwood and Ascot (fast-
finishing second of 17 to Bolshoi) next 2 starts: reportedly finished distressed final
outing: best at 5f or 6f: has won on equitrack: best efforts on an easy surface on turf,
but may be unsuited by very soft ground: bandaged in front nowadays: usually held
up. *Miss Gay Kelleway*

SANDABAR 3 b.g. Green Desert (USA) 127 – Children's Corner (FR) 106 (Top 76 +
Ville 129) [1995 60p: 7f 1996 6.9m* Apr 16] useful-looking gelding: first run for 8
months, won maiden at Folkestone in April by ¾ length from Consort, running on
strongly to lead close home: will prove suited by further than 7f: gelded and stays in
training. *M. R. Stoute*

William Hill Great St Wilfrid Handicap, Ripon—Samwar breezes in ahead of Options Open

Cadogan Silver Salver Handicap, York—
co-favourites Sandmoor Chambray (right) and Carlito Brigante (noseband) are ahead of Seventeens Lucky

SANDBAGGEDAGAIN 2 b.c. (May 15) Prince Daniel (USA) – Paircullis 74
(Tower Walk 130) [1996 5g 7s⁵ 5f³ 7m² 7.9g³ 8m² 8m³ 7.9g³ Oct 10] 550Y: leggy,
shallow-girthed colt: fourth foal: half-brother to a winner in Hong Kong by Vaigly
Great: dam unraced: fair form: placed in nurseries last 3 starts: needs a good gallop
at 1m and will stay further: acts on good to firm ground: sometimes hangs.
M. W. Easterby

SANDBLASTER 3 ch.f. Most Welcome 131 – Honeychurch (USA) 93 (Bering 55
136) [1995 47p: 5m 5g 7m 5f 6f⁴ 1996 7d⁶ 8m² 8g³ 8g² 9f⁶ 8f⁶ 9.9f⁵ 9.9m⁵ 8.9g Sep
4] sparely-made filly: modest maiden handicapper: left Mrs J. Ramsden's stable after
sixth start: stays 1m: acts on good to firm ground: has been early to post: keen sort.
D. Nicholls

SAND CAY (USA) 2 ch.c. (Apr 12) Geiger Counter (USA) – Lily Lily Rose –
(USA) (Lypheor 118) [1996 8g 7.1v 8g Oct 29] $62,000F, 32,000Y: rangy colt: has
scope: fourth foal: closely related to a winner in USA by Mogambo: dam won at up
to 9f in USA: sire, minor sprint winner, son of Mr Prospector: no worthwhile form in
maidens: edgy, and in need of race first 2 starts, early to post second one. *R. Hannon*

SANDHILL (IRE) 3 b.f. Danehill (USA) 126 – Sand Grouse (USA) (Arctic Tern 96
(USA) 126) [1995 NR 1996 7d⁴ 7g⁶ 7.1d* 7m 7m 8.5g⁴ 8.1m² Sep 17] workmanlike
filly: powerful galloper: third foal: sister and half-sister to winners abroad: dam
French 1¼m winner: progressive form: won maiden at Haydock in May: game second
of 9 to Fatefully in handicap at Sandown on final outing: not sure to stay much
beyond 8.5f: acts on good and dead ground: front runner/races prominently: sold
to join J. J. O'Neill 55,000 gns Newmarket December Sales. *J. H. M. Gosden*

SANDICLIFFE (USA) 3 b.f. Imp Society (USA) – Sad Song (USA) (Roberto –
(USA) 131) [1995 –: 7g 1996 7s 9m 10m⁵ 10.8m 16m⁴ 16m 14.1d Aug 25] tall filly:
little worthwhile form: retained by trainer 7,000 gns Newmarket Autumn Sales.
B. W. Hills

SANDKATOON (IRE) 2 br.f. (May 11) Archway (IRE) 115 – Indian Sand –
(Indian King (USA) 128) [1996 5m 6g a6g Nov 11] IR 4,000Y: angular, workmanlike
filly: third foal: sister to 3-y-o 5f (at 2 yrs) and 6f winner Weetman's Weigh: dam

848

poor Irish maiden: no worthwhile form in maiden events 6 months apart, and seller: unseated rider to post and withdrawn second intended outing. *J. S. Moore*

SANDMOOR CHAMBRAY   5 ch.g. Most Welcome 131 – Valadon 72 (High   88
Line 125) [1995 75: 8g 7.5m* 8m 8m² 8.1g⁴ 8m⁶ 8d 7d 1996 8g² 8.5m 8g² 8.5m³ 8.9m* 8m² 8.5m² 10.1m 9g² 10v⁵ 8m 8g 8g⁶ 8g 8s² Nov 9] lengthy gelding: fairly useful handicapper: in good form for most of season, winning at York in June: stays 9f: acts on good to firm and soft ground (finished very tired on heavy): effective blinkered or not: usually front runner/races prominently: game. *T. D. Easterby*

SANDMOOR DENIM   9 b.g. Red Sunset 120 – Holernzaye 93 (Sallust 134)   –
[1995 72, a69: a8g³ a7g⁶ a8g 7s* a8.5g⁵ 8m a8g² a8.5g 8.5d 8g a8.5g³ a8g² a7g⁵ 1996   a69 d
a8g⁴ 8.3s a9.4g³ 8g a9.4g* a8.5g a8.5g³ a9.4g a11g⁶ a8g a8.5g 8g a8g a9.4g³ a8g³ a11g Dec 3] close-coupled gelding: carries condition: fair performer: won claimer at Wolverhampton in May: finished lame next start, and mostly well below form afterwards: stays 9.4f: acts on firm and soft ground and the all-weather: blinkered (below form) earlier in career: usually bandaged: usually held up: often ridden by 7-lb claimer: tough. *S. R. Bowring*

SANDMOOR ZOE   2 b.f. (Mar 18) Puissance 110 – Chiquitita 44 (Reliance II   41 +
137) [1996 6d 6m⁴ 7.9g Sep 4] 2,000F, 6,200Y: tall, angular filly: half-sister to 1992 2-y-o 6f and 7f winner Another Kingdom (by Another Realm), middle-distance winner in Germany in 1995, and 1986 2-y-o 5f winner Quite So (by Mansingh), later ungenuine: dam won 1¼m seller: appeared to shape with some promise (could be rated 49?) on debut: well held in seller and maiden auction subsequently. *T. D. Easterby*

SANDPIPER   3 b.f. Green Desert (USA) 127 – Sojourn 87 (Be My Guest (USA)   –
126) [1995 –: 7d 1996 8.3m 7m Aug 15] neat filly: well beaten in maidens: sold 5,000 gns Newmarket Autumn Sales. *K. O. Cunningham-Brown*

SANDRA DEE (IRE)   4 ch.f. Be My Guest (USA) 126 – Adventurine (Thatching   –
131) [1995 60d: a7g² a8g³ a7g⁵ a7g a7g⁵ 6.9m 5.3m⁵ 7m⁵ 7f a7g a10g 7g 1996 7.1m 6m a6g 8f Aug 22] leggy filly: modest maiden at best: soundly beaten in 1996: inconsistent. *E. A. Wheeler*

SAND STAR   4 b.f. Lugana Beach 116 – Overseas 48 (Sea Hawk II 131) [1995 75:   73 d
a7g a6g⁴ a8.5g² a7g* a8g⁶ a7g² a6g a8.5g a7g³ a7g* a7g² 1996 a8g³ 7g 7m³ 7.1d 7.1m 7m 7f 6.9g² 8.2g Oct 9] sturdy, close-coupled filly: fair handicapper: looked temperamental in apprentice race at Folkestone (swerved left under whip before finishing strongly) penultimate start: barely stays 1m: acts on good to firm ground and the all-weather: usually races prominently: very slowly away twice in 1996: not one to trust implicitly. *D. Haydn Jones*

SANDSTONE (IRE)   2 b.c. (Apr 4) Green Desert (USA) 127 – Rose de Thai   100
(USA) 99 (Lear Fan (USA) 130) [1996 7m* 7g⁵ 8.1f² 7m⁵ 8g Oct 26] 62,000F, 90,000Y: leggy, quite good-topped colt: third foal: half-brother to smart Irish 3-y-o 1m and 1¼m winner Truth Or Dare (by Royal Academy): dam, French 1m winner (including at 2 yrs), granddaughter of Poule d'Essai des Pouliches winner Riverqueen: useful performer: won maiden at Salisbury in July: head second to Besiege in minor event at Haydock (best effort) and about 1¼ lengths fifth of 23 to Papua in Tattersalls Houghton Sales Stakes at Newmarket next 2 starts: not discredited when seventh in Racing Post Trophy at Doncaster final outing: stays 1m well: raced only on a sound surface. *J. L. Dunlop*

SANDWELD   2 b.c. (Mar 13) Weldnaas (USA) 112 – Scottish Lady (Dunbeath   –
(USA) 127) [1996 5m a5g⁴ 7.1v Oct 6] 3,200Y, 6,600 2-y-o: angular colt: third foal: brother to 4-y-o 6f to 7.6f winner Sharp 'N Smart: dam won in Italy from 6f to 7.5f: signs of ability but no worthwhile form in 3 maiden events, considerately handled final outing: should be well suited by further than 5f. *C. A. Dwyer*

SANDY FLOSS (IRE)   3 b.c. Green Desert (USA) 127 – Mill On The Floss 117   80
(Mill Reef (USA) 141) [1995 –p: 7f⁴ 1996 8.2s³ 7m⁴ 10d² 10.5d³ Jun 8] good-topped, attractive colt: good walker: easy mover: fair maiden: sold 16,000 gns Newmarket Autumn Sales: should stay beyond 1¼m: similar form on soft ground and good to firm. *H. R. A. Cecil*

SANDYSTONES   2 b.f. (May 4) Selkirk (USA) 129 – Sharanella (Shareef Dancer   – p
(USA) 135) [1996 7m Aug 9] 15,000Y: leggy, close-coupled filly: fourth foal:

half-sister to useful 4-y-o 1m/1¼m performer Sonic Boy (by Celestial Storm) and 2 winners in Germany: dam (unraced) from good German family: 33/1, green and attended by two handlers in paddock, slowly away when just over 12 lengths ninth of 13 to Blue River in maiden at Newmarket, getting hang of things late on: will stay at least 1m: should improve. *N. A. Graham*

SANG D'ANTIBES (FR)   2 ch.f. (Mar 2) Sanglamore (USA) 126 – Baratoga   58
(USA) (Bering 136) [1996 6g⁴ 6g Oct 18] 180,000 francs Y: first foal: dam French maiden half-sister to smart French 6.5f (at 2 yrs) and 7f winner Borodislew out of smart French performer at up to 7f Breath Taking: fourth in maiden at Hamilton, leading 2f out then hanging right and carrying head awkwardly: tailed off as though something amiss (pulled hard) in similar event at Catterick 19 days later: bred to stay middle distances. *D. J. S. Cosgrove*

SANGRIA (USA)   3 ch.f. El Gran Senor (USA) 136 – Champagne Coctail (USA)   112
(Roberto (USA) 131) [1995 6g* 6g 8d⁵ 1996 9.3m⁵ 8m⁴ 9m⁴ 10g* 9.3d³ 10g Oct 27] strong-quartered, attractive filly: ninth foal: half-sister to minor winners by Mr Prospector (1m), Alleged (7f) and Irish River (7f): dam, French 2-y-o 1m winner, half-sister to Arctic Tern (rated 126): smart performer: won newcomers listed race at Deauville at 2 yrs: progressed gradually in 1996, and won slowly-run 5-runner Prix de Psyche by short neck from Binary at Deauville in August: ran well when third of 10 to Donna Viola in Prix de l'Opera at Longchamp: below form in Grade 2 event at Woodbine: stays 1¼m: yet to race on extremes of going. *A. Fabre, France*

SANMARTINO (IRE)   4 b.c. Salse (USA) 128 – Oscura (USA) 82 (Caro 133)   115
[1995 102: 10m⁴ 10.3m² 10.5g* 12f⁵ 13.9m⁴ 15s⁴ 1996 14m* 16.2m⁶ 12m⁵ 12m⁴ 15.9m³ 16m² Oct 5] sturdy colt: impresses in appearance: good mover: smart stayer: ready winner of 4-runner handicap at Newmarket in April: ran well when placed behind Celeric on last 2 starts, game head second in Jockey Club Cup at Newmarket on final one: needs further than 1½m and stays 2m: acts on good to firm ground and soft: has joined D. Nicholson, and won over hurdles. *B. W. Hills*

SANOOSEA (USA)   4 b.c. Storm Bird (CAN) 134 – Nobiliare (USA) (Vaguely   113
Noble 140) [1995 105: 7g³ 7.1m* 8.1m² 10.3m² 11.8f⁵ 1996 10.4f³ 10d⁴ 10m⁴ 11s² 10m Nov 10] good-topped colt: carries condition: smart performer: best efforts when staying-on fourth of 8 to Definite Article in strongly-run Group 2 event at the Curragh in May and when length second of 7 to Predappio in Blandford Stakes there in October: stays 11f: acts on firm and soft ground. *M. R. Stoute*

SANTA ROSA (IRE)   2 b.f. (Mar 12) Lahib (USA) 129 – Bequeath (USA)   64 +
(Lyphard (USA) 132) [1996 7d⁴ 6m⁴ 7m³ Oct 23] IR 26,000Y: tall, leggy, quite attractive filly: fluent mover: fourth foal: half-sister to German 3-y-o Give Warning, 6f winner at 2 yrs, smart 4-y-o 7f and 1m winner Decorated Hero (both by Warning) and 6f (at 2 yrs) and 7f winner Beneficiary (by Jalmood): dam lightly-raced 9f winner in France: in frame in maidens at Newmarket, Redcar and Newcastle: will be well suited by further than 7f. *J. L. Dunlop*

SANTELLA CAPE   3 b.c. Alzao (USA) 117 – Kijafa (USA) 65 (Chief's Crown   –
(USA)) [1995 NR 1996 11d 12m May 5] 45,000F, 40,000Y: close-coupled colt: first foal: dam, 1¾m winner, out of half-sister to good 1979 2-y-o Romeo Romani: tailed off in maidens at Newbury and (unruly in stalls) Salisbury: sold to join N. Hawke 5,000 gns Ascot June Sales. *R. Hannon*

SANTELLA KATIE   3 ch.f. Anshan 119 – Mary Bankes (USA) (Northern Baby   71
(CAN) 127) [1995 NR 1996 7m⁶ 7.1m² 8.1m⁴ 10.2m⁵ Aug 8] 4,200F, 7,500Y: leggy, lightly-made filly: has a quick, unimpressive action: third foal: half-sister to 1993 2-y-o 5f winner Mild Rebuke (by Reprimand): dam out of half-sister to high-class filly Treizieme and Gold Cup runner-up Eastern Mystic: fair form in maidens: disappointing when stepped up in trip on final start, sold to join Mrs. L. Stubbs 3,500 gns Newmarket Autumn Sales: has raced only on good to firm ground. *Major D. N. Chappell*

SANTELLA TWINKLE (IRE)   2 b.f. (Feb 25) Jareer (USA) 115 – Hellicroft   –
(High Line 125) [1996 8g a7g⁶ Nov 15] 600F, 500Y: second foal: dam unraced: well held in sellers. *D. Morris*

SANTILLANA (USA)   3 ch.c. El Gran Senor (USA) 136 – Galway (FR) (Irish   116
River (FR) 131) [1995 87p: 7g³ 8.1s* 1996 9g* 10g* Apr 27] rangy, attractive colt: progressive form: won 4-runner minor event at Ripon in April: looking very well,

Thresher Classic Trial, Sandown—
a fourth win in the last five runnings for trainer John Gosden as Santillana (right) beats Glory of Dancer

followed up by beating Glory of Dancer (gave 6 lb) a neck (clear) in 9-runner Thresher Classic Trial at Sandown 2½ weeks later, held up, leading 1½f out and running on bravely despite drifting right: reportedly damaged a hock, and not seen out afterwards: not bred to stay much beyond 1¼m: yet to race on top-of-the-ground: smart: stays in training. *J. H. M. Gosden*

SAPPHIRE SON (IRE)   4 ch.g. Maelstrom Lake 118 – Gluhwein (Ballymoss 136) [1995 60d: a7g 7f³ 7g² 7.1m³ 7g⁶ 7m 7g a7g 7g 1996 6.9m² 8m⁵ a8g⁴ 6.9g² 7m 6.9m⁴ 7d 6.9g⁴ a7g a8g a8g a10g² Dec 20] sparely-made gelding: modest handicapper: left D. Morris after seventh 4-y-o start: stays 1¼m: acts on firm ground and all-weather: effective with or without visor. *P. C. Clarke*   54 a52

SARABI   2 b.f. (Feb 12) Alzao (USA) 117 – Sure Enough (IRE) (Diesis 133) [1996 5g 5.1m⁵ 5.1m 6m 5g* 5.2g 5d Nov 8] 9,500Y: small, sturdy filly: first foal: dam (unraced) from the family of Sure Blade and Sure Sharp: 33/1, won 17-runner nursery at Catterick in October: no comparable form: bred to stay further than 5f: sometimes slowly away: reported by trainer to be highly strung. *J. Pearce*   64

SARASI   4 ch.g. Midyan (USA) 124 – Early Call 102 (Kind of Hush 118) [1995 73: a7g* a8g⁴ a9.4g⁵ a8g⁴ 7.9g a8g⁶ a7g a9.4g* 1996 a11g³ a8.5g³ a11g² a8g* a8.5g a9.4g Dec 7] angular gelding: fair handicapper: won at Southwell in February: modest form at up to 11f (which he barely stays), best efforts at up to 8.5f: acts on the all weather and on good to firm ground: below form only try in visor: races prominently, and made all for last 2 wins. *M. J. Camacho*   72

SARASOTA RYDE   3 gr.f. Komaite (USA) – Freedom Line (Absalom 128) [1995 NR 1996 6m 8g a6g Nov 29] plain filly: second reported foal: dam of little account: soundly beaten in claimers. *J. E. Banks*   –

SARASOTA STORM   4 b.g. Petoski 135 – Challanging 95 (Mill Reef (USA) 141) [1995 67d: 11.1d* 12m 14g⁴ 8m 8m⁶ 8m 10m 1996 10s 10.3m 10.8g 15.1f* 16.2m⁶ 15.1m* 16.2m 14.1m⁴ 14.4g 15.1m* Sep 23] workmanlike gelding: modest handicapper: won at Musselburgh (unbeaten in 4 runs there) in June, July and September: effective at 1m at 3 yrs, stays 15f: acts on firm and dead going: visored (raced too freely) third 4-y-o start: usually held up: inconsistent. *M. Bell*   59

SARATOGA RED (USA)   2 ch.c. (Apr 7) Saratoga Six (USA) – Wajibird (USA) (Storm Bird (CAN) 134) [1996 a6g³ 6m³ 6f 7d Aug 23] $10,200F, $23,000Y: strong, workmanlike colt: has a round action: sixth foal: half-brother to 2 minor winners abroad by Strawberry Road: dam unraced: best form when keeping-on third in Pontefract minor event won by Alpine Time: not discredited when down the field in   71

Oh So Sharp Stakes, Newmarket—
Sarayir shows some of the ability of her half-brothers Nashwan and Unfuwain

Coventry Stakes at Ascot and Newmarket maiden subsequently: should be at least as
effective at 7f as 6f. *W. A. O'Gorman*

SARAWAT   8 b.g. Slip Anchor 136 – Eljazzi 92 (Artaius (USA) 129) [1995 –: 9.9m   72
16m 13.9g 14g 1996 12g 13.8s⁵ 13d² 13s* 13.9m⁵ May 15] smallish, workmanlike
gelding: has been hobdayed: has a round action: rated 83 at 6 yrs: best effort for
some time to win handicap at Hamilton in May: reportedly finished sore at York only
subsequent outing: effective at 13f and 2m: acts on soft going, used to act on firm
D. Nicholls

SARAYIR (USA)   2 b.f. (Apr 7) Mr Prospector (USA) – Height of Fashion (FR)   100 p
124 (Bustino 136) [1996 7f* 7m* Oct 5] tall, rangy filly, still unfurnished: ninth foal:
sister to 1m winner (including at 2 yrs) Bashayer and 1m and 10.4f winner Wijdan,
both useful, and half-sister to 4 winners, notably Nashwan (by Blushing Groom) and
Unfuwain (by Northern Dancer): dam 7f to 1½m winner from very good family:
won maiden at Salisbury in great style by 5 lengths (value nearer 10): odds on again,
followed up in 7-runner Oh So Sharp Stakes at Newmarket following month by 1¼
lengths from Fernanda, leading 2f out then driven out to win in workmanlike fashion:
will stay at least 1¼m: will improve again: to winter in Dubai. *Major W. R. Hern*

SARDONIC   3 b.f. Kris 135 – Sardegna 111 (Pharly (FR) 130) [1995 NR 1996   105
10m* 10m* 8g⁶ 10m⁶ 10g 10.1m Sep 17] smallish, well-made filly: first foal: dam,
7f (at 2 yrs) and 1¼m winner who stayed 13f, out of Lancashire Oaks winner Sandy
Island, a close relative of Slip Anchor: useful performer: won maiden at Salisbury in
May and listed race at Newbury in June: good efforts when sixth in Falmouth Stakes
at Newmarket and in Nassau Stakes (edgy, raced freely) at Goodwood next 2 starts:
well below form afterwards: stayed 1¼m: raced only on a sound surface: keen sort,
sometimes early to post: front runner: stud. *H. R. A. Cecil*

SARMATIAN (USA)   5 br.g. Northern Flagship (USA) 96 – Tracy L (USA)   77
(Bold Favorite (USA)) [1995 70: 8.3v² 7m³ 7g 8.3f² 8.3m³ 8.3f* 1996 9.2s³ 10g²
10d* 10f 10.3g⁵ 8.5m Jul 30] leggy gelding: fair handicapper: won at Ayr in May:
well below form in blinkers (took good hold) final start: in good form over hurdles
afterwards: effective at 7f to 1¼m: acts on any ground. *M. D. Hammond*

SARTEANO   2 ch.f. (Apr 12) Anshan 119 – Daisy Girl 69 (Main Reef 126) [1996   –
6f⁶ 7.5g³ Aug 24] leggy, unfurnished filly: first foal: dam, 1¼m to 12.4f winner, also
successful over hurdles: well beaten in small-field maidens at Thirsk (tongue tied)
and Beverley. *J. Mackie*

SARUM   10 b.g. Tina's Pet 121 – Contessa (HUN) (Peleid 125) [1995 NR 1996   56 d
a8g⁵ a9.4g⁴ a8g* a8g⁵ a8g⁶ a10g a8g a8g 7d 6.9m 9m 9.7f a8g 7g a10g a8g⁶ a8g Dec
11] tall, rather narrow gelding: poor mover: modest handicapper: won amateurs race

852

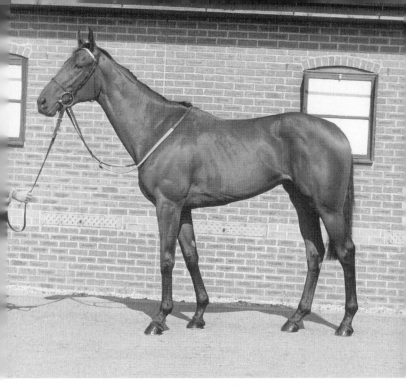

Hamdan Al Maktoum's "Sarayir"

at Lingfield in March: below form afterwards, leaving C. Wildman's stable after eighth start: stays 1m: acts particularly well on equitrack, best turf form on ground no softer than dead: held up. *J. E. Long*

SASEEDO (USA) 6 ch.g. Afleet (CAN) – Barbara's Moment (USA) (Super Moment (USA)) [1995 90, a79: 7m 6m* 7m 6m⁶ 6f 7g 6g⁶ 7.3d 5d⁵ 7g⁴ 5s⁶ 5m 6f* a7g⁴ 1996 7m 6m⁶ 7g* 6f 6g* 7.1d* 7m 7m⁵ 7g 7m³ 7g Oct 19] close-coupled gelding: unimpressive mover: useful handicapper: successful at Newmarket (rated stakes) in May and at Pontefract and Haydock (rated stakes) in July: stays 7f: acts on any ground on turf, and probably also on the all-weather: equipped with rope halter and blanket for stalls entry: tends to sweat: often slowly away: held up. *W. A. O'Gorman* 99 a–

SASSETTA (IRE) 3 ch.f. Soviet Lad (USA) 94 – Sun Gift (Guillaume Tell (USA) 121) [1995 –: 6.1m 7f⁵ 7g 7d 7f 1996 10g 9.9m⁶ Apr 25] sparely-made filly: little form, in need of race in 1996. *N. Tinkler* –

SASSIVER (USA) 6 b.g. Riverman (USA) 131 – Sassabunda 108 (Sassafras (FR) 135) [1995 45: a16.2g⁴ a16g³ a16.2g a14.8g⁴ a16.2g a16g 1996 a16g⁶ a12g³ a13g⁵ Feb 3] strong gelding: poor performer: stays 2m: acts on soft going and fibresand: blinkered in 1996. *P. A. Kelleway* 40

SASURU   3 b.c. Most Welcome 131 – Sassalya (Sassafras (FR) 135) [1995   113 p
95p: 6m² 7g² 8d³ 1996 12m² 12.3g⁴ 10.1g* 10.4m* 10d* Aug 15]

The annual Timeform Charity Day at York in June continues to be one
of the best-attended meetings in the Calendar. A total of 658,319 people have
supported the events since their inception in 1971, and have helped raise
£2,107,762 in aid of the Cancer Relief Macmillan Fund and other charities.
While the latest Charity Day raised a six-figure sum for the ninth successive
year, the crowd of 19,163 was the lowest since 1977, fifteen per cent down on
the previous year, as a result of clashing with the England-Scotland football
match in Euro '96. Racegoers were at least offered a competitive card, a direct
appeal to trainers from the organisers, who had been concerned about some of
the small fields the previous year, resulting in a twenty-four per cent increase in
the number of runners and good fields for nearly all the races.

Undoubtedly the best performance on Timeform Charity Day came
from Sasuru who confirmed himself a smart performer when giving weight all
round in the nine-runner Daniel Prenn Royal Yorkshire Rated Stakes. It was an
impressive handicap debut, following victory in a useful maiden at Newcastle.
Quickening clear approaching the final furlong, Sasuru beat Skillington by two
and a half lengths in a strongly-run race at York, winning with something in
hand. Even better followed on Sasuru's next start two months later when he
prevailed in a three-way photo for the Group 2 Prix Guillaume d'Ornano at
Deauville, getting home by a short head from the French-trained favourite
Android in a slowly-run race, in which less than four lengths covered the nine
runners at the finish.

Sasuru comes from an excellent family, one which has provided many
successes in the Oppenheimer colours for trainer Geoff Wragg over the years.
Sasuru's sire Most Welcome was a great servant while the dam Sassalya has
produced twelve winners from her thirteen foals who have raced. These include
the useful stayer Chauvre Souris (by Beldale Flutter), the smart but ill-fated
Jersey Stakes winner Sally Rous (by Rousillon) and the useful miler Little Bean

Daniel Prenn Royal Yorkshire Rated Stakes (Handicap), York—Sasuru gives weight all round

Lady Oppenheimer's "Sasuru"

(by Ajdal). Sasuru's full sister Tzu'mu showed plenty of promise when winning over six furlongs at two, but died after two unplaced outings the following season. The Faraway Tree, a two-year-old half-sister to Sasuru by Suave Dancer, maintained the dam's impressive record when winning a six-furlong maiden at Yarmouth in September, looking a useful prospect. An Inchinor yearling half-brother to Sasuru was foaled in 1996 when Sassalya was covered again by Most Welcome. Most Welcome has had a very good 61 per cent of his three-year-olds in Britain win a race, and another of those three-year-olds in 1996 was the Wragg stable's Dee Stakes winner Prize Giving.

Sasuru (b.c. 1993)	Most Welcome (ch 1984)	Be My Guest (ch 1974)	Northern Dancer
			What A Treat
		Topsy (ch 1976)	Habitat
			Furioso
	Sassalya (b 1973)	Sassafras (b 1967)	Sheshoon
			Ruta
		Valya (b 1965)	Vandale II
			Lilya

The lengthy, good-bodied Sasuru is a fluent mover. He stays a mile and a half but may well prove ideally suited by around a mile and a quarter. He acts on good to firm and dead ground and has yet to race on extremes. Sasuru, who is usually bandaged, was not seen out again after Deauville but he had been progressing well and may be open to further improvement, provided all is well with him. *G. Wragg*

SATIN BELL 3 b.f. Midyan (USA) 124 – Silk Petal 105 (Petorius 117) [1995 NR   99
1996 7d* 8m³ 7m⁶ 8g⁵ 8m 8d Oct 11] neat filly: second foal: half-sister to useful Star

Tulip (by Night Shift), 6f winner at 2 and 3 yrs: dam 7f winner out of half-sister to Irish St Leger winner M-Lolshan: impressive winner of newcomers event at Newbury in April: best effort when around 2 lengths fifth of 8 to Moon Is Up in listed race at Deauville on fourth start: stayed 1m: suited by give in the ground: stud. *J. L. Dunlop*

SATIN LOVER 8 ch.g. Tina's Pet 121 – Canoodle 66 (Warpath) [1995 NR 76 1996 18s 14d⁴ 16m² 14d* 14d⁶ 14.6g⁴ Jun 29] workmanlike gelding: rated 95 in 1992: fair form in handicaps at 8 yrs, winning at Haydock in May: stays 2m: used to act on firm and dead ground: used to idle in front. *Mrs M. Reveley*

SAUCY SOUL 3 ch.g. Ballacashtal (CAN) – Ninotchka 72 (Niniski (USA) 125) – [1995 NR 1996 6m 10.2g May 20] third reported foal: half-brother to useful jumper Dancing Paddy (by Nordance): dam, maiden who stayed 1¼m, half-sister to useful sprinter Novello out of sister to high-class Pyjama Hunt: tailed off in 2 maidens: has joined W. G. M. Turner. *Simon Earle*

SAUNDERS WREN 2 b.f. (Mar 8) Handsome Sailor 125 – Saunders Lass 68 65 d (Hillandale 125) [1996 5m* 5m 6g³ 5m 5f* 5f Aug 15] 2,100Y: long-backed filly: first foal: dam winning plater over 6f at 2 yrs and over hurdles: fair form on first 3 starts, winning maiden at Windsor in May: claimed out of M. Channon's yard £8,000 after winning claimer at Beverley (below best) in July: stays 6f: acts on firm ground: sweating fifth outing. *Mrs L. Stubbs*

SAUSALITO BAY 2 b.c. (Apr 29) Salse (USA) 128 – Cantico 58 (Green Dancer 81 p (USA) 132) [1996 8d⁵ 8.1s* Oct 22] sixth foal: half-brother to 6f winner Regal Racer (by Elegant Air), 7f winner Dauntess (by Formidable) and a winner in Norway by Primo Dominie: dam staying maiden, half-sister to very smart 1m to 1½m filly Calderina, same family as Mystiko: 11/1, won 20-runner maiden at Chepstow by ¾ length from Perfect Paradigm, always prominent and staying on dourly to lead inside final 1f: will need middle distances as 3-y-o: will improve again. *I. A. Balding*

SAVANNA BLUE 3 b.f. Moor House 84 – Lady Havana Bay VII (Damsire – Unregistered) [1995 NR 1996 a8g⁶ a8g⁶ a5g⁶ Mar 18] third reported foal: dam of unregistered pedigree: tailed off at Southwell. *J. L. Eyre*

SAVING POWER 3 b.g. Superlative 118 – Scented Goddess (IRE) 54 (Godswalk (USA) 130) [1995 NR 1996 7m 7m 6g 6m Oct 23] 3,800Y: good-quartered, workmanlike gelding: first foal: dam 7f (at 2 yrs) and 8.3f winner also successful over hurdles: signs of ability but no worthwhile form: has had tongue tied down. *P. W. Harris*

SAVONA (IRE) 2 b.f. (Mar 12) Cyrano de Bergerac 120 – Shannon Lady 67 70 (Monsanto (FR) 121) [1996 5s⁴ 6.1s³ 6d⁵ Nov 8] 26,000Y: smallish, sturdy filly: unimpressive mover: fifth foal: sister to 1993 2-y-o 5f winner Pommes Frites and half-sister to 2 winners, including 3-y-o Fervent Fan (by Soviet Lad), 6f winner at 2 yrs: dam poor maiden: fair form in maidens and a minor event: stays 6f. *P. J. Makin*

SAWA-ID 3 b. or br.c. Anshan 119 – Bermuda Lily 78 (Dunbeath (USA) 127) 82 [1995 –p: 8m 1996 9m⁴ 10m⁵ 9.7m* 10.5m* 9m² Sep 26] rangy colt: fairly useful performer, progressing steadily: won handicaps at Folkestone (maiden contest) in August and Haydock (idled and flashed tail when hit with whip) in September: stays 10.5f: has raced only on good to firm ground: gives impression will be suited by waiting tactics: sent to Dubai. *J. H. M. Gosden*

SAXON BAY 4 ch.g. Cadeaux Genereux 131 – Princess Athena 119 (Ahonoora 57 122) [1995 NR 1996 8.2m 8g⁵ Nov 22] 68,000Y: workmanlike gelding: second foal: brother to 3-y-o 7f winner Waypoint: dam beat at 5f: in rear in maiden at Nottingham: changed hands only 1,000 gns Ascot November Sales: fifth of 13 in claimer at Southwell, having been last for a long way. *K. O. Cunningham-Brown*

SAXONBURY 2 b.c. (Apr 28) Shirley Heights 130 – Dancing Vaguely (USA) – (Vaguely Noble 140) [1996 8d Oct 2] seventh foal: half-brother to 2 winners in France, including 5-y-o 1¼m and 10.5f winner Vagamo (by Nashwan): dam French 1½m winner: 7/1, soundly beaten in maiden at Salisbury: sold 5,000 gns Doncaster November Sales. *M. R. Stoute*

SAYEH (IRE) 4 b.c. Fools Holme (USA) – Piffle 87 (Shirley Heights 130) [1995 98 98: 8g³ 10.4g⁵ 10.4m³ 10.1m* 10.1m* 10d 1996 a9.9f² a10g⁴ 10.3m 9g Sep 13] big, deep-girthed colt: has a round action: useful performer at his best: ran creditably both starts in Dubai in February for E. Charpy: below form on return to Britain: sold (Major R. Hern to Mrs. D. Haine) 9,000 gns Newmarket Autumn Sales: stays 1¼m: yet to race on firm going, acts on any other, including sand: pulls hard, and wears special bridle: early to post final start. *Major W. R. Hern*

SAYITAGAIN 4 b.g. Bering 136 – Casey 119 (Caerleon (USA) 132) [1995 68: 8d⁶ 10g 1996 10s⁶ 11.8g 12m 10d 12m Jun 8] lengthy gelding: has a quick action: sold cheaply out of T. Mills's stable after final 3-y-o start and no worthwhile form since. *J. R. Jenkins* –

SCANDATOR (IRE) 3 b.c. Danehill (USA) 126 – Rustic Lawn (Rusticaro (FR) 124) [1995 NR 1996 10.3s 10g 10g Apr 27] 20,000Y: medium-sized colt: fourth foal: half-brother to fairly useful 6-y-o 1m and 1¼m winner Silver Groom (by Shy Groom): dam unraced, from family of Royal Palace: no worthwhile form. *P. W. Harris* –

SCARABEN 8 b.g. Dunbeath (USA) 127 – Varushka 74 (Sharpen Up 127) [1995 76: 8.3v* 9.2f³ 8m* 8m* 8m* 8g* 8d² 8g* 8m 1996 7g 8g 8g 8m 8g³ 8.3g³ 8m⁴ 8m² 8m* 8m³ 8f⁴ 8m 8m 8g 8.1s* Nov 7] big, strong, lengthy gelding: has a quick action: fair handicapper: won at Pontefract in July and Musselburgh in November: effective at 7f (under testing conditions) and stays 1¼m: acts on any ground: has run well for amateur: usually held up: genuine. *S. E. Kettlewell* 79

SCARLET CRESCENT 2 b.f. (Feb 1) Midyan (USA) 124 – Scarlet Veil 75 (Tyrnavos 129) [1996 6.1m³ 6m³ 7m* 7m Sep 17] 5,200Y: angular filly: second living foal: half-sister to 6f (at 2 yrs) to 8.3f winner Comeonup (by Most Welcome): dam, stayed 1¼m, is out of very useful 2-y-o 5f and 6f winner Red Velvet: won maiden auction at Warwick in August: below form in steadily-run nursery following month: will be well suited by 1m+. *P. T. Walwyn* 66 +

SCARLET LAKE 2 b.f. (Mar 8) Reprimand 122 – Stinging Nettle 90 (Sharpen Up 127) [1996 5.1m⁵ 7.1m⁵ 6g 6.1s Oct 31] leggy, quite attractive filly: sixth foal: half-sister to several winners, including useful 3-y-o Maid For The Hills (by Indian Ridge), 6f winner at 2 yrs, and 1994 2-y-o 5f and 6f winner Maid For Walking (by Prince Sabo), both useful fillies: dam, 6f winner on 2-y-o debut but no form after, half-sister to very smart 7f to 1¼m winner Gairloch: modest form: gave impression something amiss third start then poor effort final one: may prove best at 6f: gave trouble stalls on debut. *D. R. Loder* 60

SCARLET PLUME 3 b.f. Warning 136 – Circus Plume 124 (High Top 131) [1995 100p: 6m² 7m³ 8.1d* 8d* 1996 10m⁶ 10s⁴ 10.2m 10.1m 8d² 8d Nov 9] small, angular filly: has a quick action: useful performer: best efforts in 1996 in listed races at Goodwood (finished fourth) in May, Ascot (1½ lengths second to Fatefully) in October and Evry (close seventh of 13) in November: stayed 1¼m: best with give in the ground: usually front runner: stud. *J. L. Dunlop* 103

SCARPETTA (USA) 3 ch.f. Seattle Dancer (USA) 119 – Pump (USA) (Forli (ARG)) [1995 NR 1996 7m⁴ 8.1m 8m² 10g² 10s⁶ 8g Nov 2] 46,000Y: lengthy filly: has scope: closely related to 3 winners by Nijinsky, including useful middle-distance performer Classic Sport, and half-sister to 1994 Swiss Derby winner Filao Beach (by Alysheba): dam (unraced) from excellent family: fair maiden: stays 1¼m: best efforts when ridden up with pace. *J. W. Hills* 75

SCARROTS 2 b.c. (Feb 27) Mazilier (USA) 107 – Bath 76 (Runnett 125) [1996 5.1d 6.9m⁵ 7m 7g⁶ 7.5m* 8f⁴ Oct 8] 6,500Y: good-bodied colt: third foal: half-brother to 3-y-o Thai Morning (by Petong), 5f winner at 2 yrs and useful 1¼m all-weather performer: dam suited by 7f/1m: won 15-finisher selling nursery at Beverley in September: ran well when fourth of 20 in non-selling nursery at Warwick nearly 3 weeks later: stays 1m: acts on firm ground. *S. C. Williams* 59

SCATHEBURY 3 b.g. Aragon 118 – Lady Bequick 81 (Sharpen Up 127) [1995 60§, a69§: 5m² 5m⁴ a6g² a6g² 6m a7g⁶ a6g* 6m 7.9m² 8f 1996 a8.5g³ 8f⁴ a8.5g⁴ 6.9m² a7g 6g⁴ a5g 7.6m 7g² 6m⁴ 7.1m* 7g 8.1m 6.9g 6m 6.9d² a7g a7g a6g⁶ Dec 3] smallish, compact gelding: modest performer: trained by S. Woods until after fourth 3-y-o start: won handicap at Musselburgh in August under good ride from K. Fallon: stays 1m: acts on firm ground and on fibresand: effective blinkered/visored or not: carries head awkwardly, and often looks ungenuine: inconsistent. *K. R. Burke* 62 §

SCBOO 7 b.g. Full Extent (USA) 113 – Maygo 57 (Maystreak 118) [1995 –: 8f 8.3m a7g 1996 a6g a7g⁵ a12g Feb 22] tall gelding: no sign of ability. *R. E. Peacock* –

SCENE STEALER 3 b.f. Scenic 128 – Sindos 89 (Busted 134) [1995 NR 1996 – 12.5g Apr 8] leggy filly: half-sister to 1990 2-y-o 6f winner Hold Court, also successful over jumps, and a winning sprinter/miler in Germany, both by The Noble Player: dam 7.2f and 1¼m winner: tailed-off last of 7 in Warwick claimer: has joined A. Smith. *A. Barrow*

SCENIC DANCER 8 b.g. Shareef Dancer (USA) 135 – Bridestones 92 (Jan 48 § Ekels 122) [1995 50: 10g³ 11.6m³ 10.1d⁴ 11.6g³ 12.1m 12g 11.5m⁴ 16.2m 11.5g* 11.8g⁴ 12m 1996 11.9f⁵ 11.6m² 12m 11.9m 11.8m Jul 18] small, stocky gelding: modest handicapper on his day: has become very moody and refused to race last 2 starts: effective at 1¼m to 1¾m: acts on firm and dead ground, looked all at sea on soft: tried blinkered and visored, no improvement: often slowly away: one to leave well alone. *A. Hide*

SCENICRIS (IRE) 3 b.f. Scenic 128 – Princesse Smile 99 (Balidar 133) [1995 73 66, a53: 5g 5m³ 7g⁵ 7m² 7f² 7d⁵ 6g³ 7m³ 7.1s² a7g³ a7g 1996 a8.5g³ a8.5g⁶ a8g⁵ a8g a54 a7g 7m³ 9.9m 7f 7m³ 7.6m 7m 8.1m⁴ 8m³ 8m⁵ 8m³ 8.2s* a8g⁴ Dec 3] smallish, workmanlike filly: fair handicapper: won 17-runner race at Nottingham in October: stays 8.5f: goes well on soft ground: held up. *R. Hollinshead*

SCENT OF POWER 6 b.g. Fairy King (USA) – Agreloui 59 (Tower Walk 130) – [1995 38: a6g 7.1d⁴ a7g 7m 8.2m* 8g 1996 a8g⁵ a8g⁶ a10g Jan 25] good-topped gelding: unimpressive mover: poor handicapper: below form in 1996, virtually pulled up final start: stays 1m: acts on good to firm going and fibresand: blinkered (no improvement) twice at 4 yrs. *N. M. Babbage*

SCHARNHORST 4 b.g. Tacheron 52 – Stardyn (Star Appeal 133) [1995 75d: 5d 80 a7g 7m* 7.1m* 7m² 8f³ 7f 7.1d 7d 7d a8g a10g 1996 a8g 7s* 7d 6.9f* 7.6g⁵ 6d* 7.1m 7m 6m 6m⁶ Sep 19] sturdy, useful-looking gelding: fair handicapper: won at Leicester in March, Folkestone (minor event) in April and Kempton in May, making all on each occasion: below form last 4 starts: effective at 6f (possibly needs a test of stamina at the trip) and stays 7.6f: acts on firm ground and soft: often apprentice ridden: front runner/races prominently. *S. Dow*

SCHERMA 3 b.f. Green Desert (USA) 127 – Escrime (USA) 92 (Sharpen Up 127) 71 [1995 NR 1996 7.1d⁶ 8.1m³ a8s⁴ a8.5s Dec 19] second foal: dam, 1m and 1¼m a– winner, sister to Kris and Diesis: not seen until late-August, easily best effort when third of 14 (always close up in slowly-run race) in maiden at Sandown. *W. Jarvis*

SCHISANDRA 2 b.f. (Jan 26) Petong 126 – Volcalmeh 67 (Lidhame 109) [1996 – 6f 7g 6m 7m Oct 4] first reported foal: dam, 7f winner, stayed 1¼m: well held in maidens, valuable seller and a nursery: heavily bandaged penultimate start. *M. J. Fetherston-Godley*

SCHOOL BOY 3 b.c. Aragon 118 – Grovehurst (Homing 130) [1995 74: 7g 6d² 72 6f 1996 a6g² a9.4g² 8g³ 7.6g a9.4g 7g³ 7f⁶ 7.1m² 6f² 7m 5.3f³ 7m a6g a8.5g³ a6g² a69 a8g Nov 22] well-made colt: fair maiden handicapper: disappointing in second half of year: effective at 6f, barely stays 9.4f: acts on firm and dead ground and on fibresand: blinkered (well beaten) once as 3-y-o: edgy sort: has had tongue tied down: none too consistent. *T. J. Naughton*

SCHOOL OF SCIENCE 6 b.g. Then Again 126 – Girl's Brigade (Brigadier – Gerard 144) [1995 –: 11f 1996 12.1g 12.1g⁶ 13g 8.1g³ 8.3m³ 10d 11.1m⁵ Aug 14] workmanlike gelding: trained until after second start by R. McKellar: no longer of much account. *D. A. Nolan*

SCIMITAR 3 ch.c. Prince Sabo 123 – Siokra 67 (Kris 135) [1995 NR 1996 8d 7m⁶ 57 7d⁶ 8m 10g 7g 8d³ 9g Nov 1] 15,000Y: good-topped colt: second foal: dam should have been suited by 1¼m: modest maiden: sold (P. Makin to P. Hobbs) 4,700 gns Ascot November Sales: should prove effective at 1¼m: yet to race on extremes of going. *P. J. Makin*

SCISSOR RIDGE 4 ch.g. Indian Ridge 123 – Golden Scissors 76 (Kalaglow 70 132) [1995 47, a59: a7g⁶ a8g⁴ a7g⁴ 6s a8g⁶ 7g 8m 7f⁴ a6g³ 7g 6.9g⁶ 7m² a7g a10g a76 a7g⁵ a7g² a7g* 1996 a6g⁵ 6m² 7m a7g⁶ 7m 6m² 6m⁵ 6m* 7m⁴ 6m³ 6m² 6m 6f² 6m² 6m² 6m⁴ 5m* 5d 6m⁶ a5g a6g* a5g* a6g⁴ Dec 20] sparely-made gelding: fair handicapper: won at Goodwood in June and September and at Lingfield in November and December: effective at 5f and stays 7f: acts on firm and dead ground and goes well on the all-weather: occasionally blinkered, better form when not: has run well when sweating: takes keen hold, and usually races prominently: tough and consistent. *J. J. Bridger*

SCORED AGAIN 6 b.g. Music Boy 124 – Thorner Lane 86 (Tina's Pet 121) 49
[1995 62: a5g⁶ a5g* a5g* a5g⁴ a5g⁵ a5g² 1996 a5g a6g a5g⁵ 5.1m⁵ 5g³ a5g⁶ 5m⁶ 6m a57
5m Sep 25] lengthy gelding: modest handicapper: best at 5f: acts on good to firm and
soft ground and on fibresand: well beaten only try in visor: usually ridden by claimer
Amanda Sanders: inconsistent. *M. J. Heaton-Ellis*

SCORPIUS 6 b.h. Soviet Star (USA) 128 – Sally Brown 120 (Posse (USA) 130) 49 d
[1995 68d: a9g² a8g² a12g⁶ a10g a10g 7m⁵ 7m 11.5g 9.7s 1996 7.5d⁵ 8.3s⁴ 10.8f⁶
10m 8m 10.5d 7f 8m Oct 29] leggy, angular horse: poor mover: poor handicapper:
stays 1½m: acts on good to firm ground and the sand: has been bandaged in front:
tried blinkered: none too reliable. *T. T. Clement*

SCOTMAIL LASS 2 b.f. (May 22) Clantime 101 – Sapphirine 73 (Trojan Fen 44
118) [1996 5g⁵ 5m⁵ 6f⁶ Aug 19] 1,500Y: plain, lengthy filly: has a round action: first
foal: dam effective from 1½m to 15f: poor form in maiden auctions and a claimer,
running in snatches final start: should stay 6f. *G. M. Moore*

SCOTTISH BAMBI 8 ch.g. Scottish Reel 123 – Bambolona 108 (Bustino 136) 66
[1995 –: 10m 10m⁶ 10.8g⁵ 10.8g 1996 9.7m* 10g 10m⁴ 10m⁵ May 24] rangy,
workmanlike gelding: has a round action: back to fair form in 1996, winning
amateurs handicap at Folkestone in April: effective at 1m and 1¼m: acts on firm
and dead ground: normally held up: won over fences in November and December.
P. R. Webber

SCOTTISH HERO 3 b.c. North Briton 67 – Tartan Pimpernel 109 (Blakeney –
126) [1995 NR 1996 10m 10m 14.1f⁴ 12m Aug 3] compact colt: half-brother to
several winners, including 1m winner Colour Sergeant (by Green Desert) and fairly
useful 1983 2-y-o 7f winner Elusive (by Little Current): dam, half-sister to Dunferm-
line, won May Hill and Galtres Stakes: signs of ability but no worthwhile form: sold
to join Miss H. Knight 11,500 gns Newmarket Autumn Sales. *J. R. Fanshawe*

SCOTTISH PARK 7 ch.m. Scottish Reel 123 – Moss Agate (Alias Smith 47
(USA)) [1995 47d: a10g* a9.4g a10g⁶ 10d a9.4g 10g a8g⁶ a11g 8m³ 8.5d⁶ 9m 8f 8m
1996 a8.5g a10g³ a10g 7d⁴ 8g³ 10m⁶ 8m* 8.1f³ 10.8m⁴ 11.7m⁶ Jul 18] sturdy,
lengthy mare: poor performer: won claimer at Leicester (claimed out of J. L. Harris'
stable £4,000) in June: effective at 7f to 1¼m: acts on good to firm and soft ground
and the all-weather: effective visored/blinkered or not: often soon off bridle: difficult
ride. *M. C. Pipe*

SCOTT'S RISK 6 b.g. Risk Me (FR) 127 – Madam de Seul 104 (Pas de Seul 133) –
[1995 NR 1996 7g 5g 6.1m Jun 24] stocky gelding: no sign of ability. *L. J. Barratt*

SCRIPT 5 b.g. Squill (USA) 122 – Vitry 48 (Vitiges (FR) 132) [1995 17m² 16g³ –
18g 1996 a12g Feb 27] ex-Irish gelding: fourth foal: half-brother to a French 11f
winner by Exactly Sharp: dam stayed 1½m: poor maiden: stays 17f: acts on good to
firm ground, tailed off on equitrack: tried blinkered. *J. R. Jenkins*

SEA-AYR (IRE) 6 ch.m. Magical Wonder (USA) 125 – Kunuz (Ela-Mana-Mou –
132) [1995 51: 7.5m² 8m 7.5g 7g² 7.5g 1996 7.5d 7m 8.5m May 10] small mare: has
a round action: modest handicapper: showed little in 1996: stays 8.5f: acts on good to
firm and soft ground: sometimes hangs (has worn near-side pricker): bandaged:
covered by Handsome Sailor. *Mrs S. M. Austin*

SEA BUCK 10 b.g. Simply Great (FR) 122 – Heatherside 80 (Hethersett 134) –
[1995 NR 1996 16m Sep 16] modest maiden on flat at 3 yrs: fair hurdler on his day in
1993/4: no form either start since on flat. *H. Candy*

SEA DANE 3 b.c. Danehill (USA) 126 – Shimmering Sea 89 (Slip Anchor 136) 107
[1995 94+: 6m* 6m⁶ 6m* 7g⁴ 6d 1996 6m* 6f 6d 6g 5.6m 5g⁵ 6g Oct 19] sturdy,
close-coupled colt: not the best of walkers: has a powerful, round action: useful
performer on his day: awarded 10-runner listed race at Newcastle in June after being
beaten 1¼ lengths by Iktamal: not disgraced last 3 starts: stays 6f: acts on good to
firm ground, has run poorly all 3 starts on a soft surface: usually bandaged in front:
sometimes slowly away. *P. W. Harris*

SEA DANZIG 3 ch.g. Roi Danzig (USA) – Tosara 84 (Main Reef 126) [1995 64: 68
7f 6m⁴ 6m⁶ 1996 6.1d² 6m 8.2m 8g⁵ 8.1m 8.2m 6g⁶ 6g 6m² 7m⁵ 5g 7g⁵ 7m⁴ 7m 7m*
7s 7g⁶ a8g⁴ a7s³ Dec 19] big, plain gelding: fair handicapper: left P. Howling after

eighth 3-y-o start: gained first success at Lingfield in October, making all: effective at 6f to 1m: acts on good to firm and dead ground and on all-weather, well beaten on soft: races prominently: none too consistent. *J. J. Bridger*

SEA-DEER 7 ch.g. Hadeer 118 – Hi-Tech Girl 98 (Homeboy 114) [1995 90: 6g 94
6m 5m⁵ 6f 5.2g⁴ 6g 1996 a6g⁴ a5g³ a5g⁵ a6g⁴ a6g³ a6g² 5m³ 6g² 5m² 6m⁴ 5g* 5g*
6f* 6f* 6m² 5g⁶ 5m³ 5f* 6m 5m³ 5.2m² a6g* 5.6m 6m 6v 5g Oct 19] strong, deep-
girthed gelding: fairly useful performer: had a fine year, winning seller at Newcastle,
claimer (claimed out of D. Chapman's stable £5,000) at Catterick, 2 handicaps (on
consecutive days) at Yarmouth, minor event (left in front when Mubhij fell near
finish) at Newmarket and another handicap at Wolverhampton: effective at 5f and
6f: acts on fibresand, raced mainly on a sound surface on turf: held up: tough.
C. A. Dwyer

SEA DEVIL 10 gr.g. Absalom 128 – Miss Poinciana 78 (Averof 123) [1995 56, –
a71: a6g² a6g² a6g² a6g² a6g* a7g* a6g² 7d⁴ a6g² a6g* 1996 a7g a6g² a6g* a6g² a66
7s 6g a6g² a7g May 13] lengthy, heavy-topped gelding: carries plenty of condition:
unimpressive mover: grand old campaigner, still capable of fair form on the all-
weather: won seller at Southwell in February: only modest on turf in 1995, and below
form on it in 1996: stays 7f, at least when conditions aren't testing: acts on fibresand
and on any turf going: visored (well below form) third 8-y-o start: usually held up:
tough. *M. J. Camacho*

SEA FREEDOM 5 b.h. Slip Anchor 136 – Rostova 91 (Blakeney 126) [1995 73: 66 §
10g 12g 13.3g 16.1g² 16.4m⁶ 14f³ 14.4m² 16g⁴ 16.2d 16.2s⁴ 18m 14.1m⁵ 1996 18s⁵
16g 14.9d³ 14m⁶ 16d² 14d² 20f 18m⁵ 14g² 15d³ 16d² 16.4g⁶ 17.2d⁴ 16.2d² 16s⁵ Oct
24] strong, workmanlike horse: has a quick action: fair handicapper, still a maiden:
effective at 1¾m, and stays long distances: acts on firm and soft ground: visored
since second 5-y-o start: consistent, but none too enthusiastic and usually soon off
bridle. *G. B. Balding*

SEA GOD 5 ch.g. Rainbow Quest (USA) 134 – Sea Pageant (Welsh Pageant 132) 44
[1995 44: 8f a11g a6g⁵ 1996 a8g⁴ a7g⁵ a8g² a8g⁴ a11g* a11g⁶ a11g⁵ 9.9d 10.1f⁶ a52
10.3g³ 10f⁴ 12g Oct 18] tall, angular gelding: modest handicapper: won at Southwell in February: stays 11f: acts on fibresand, best turf effort on good ground.
M. C. Chapman

SEA IDOL (IRE) 3 b.f. Astronef 116 – Pharjoy (FR) 85 (Pharly (FR) 130) [1995 –
6m 1996 6m 8g 6f 7d Oct 26] IR 5,000Y: ex-Irish filly: fifth living foal: half-sister to
1993 2-y-o 7f winner Call To Mind (by Don't Forget Me) and fairly useful 7f to 1½m
winner El Volador (by Beldale Flutter): dam best at 2 yrs when 6f winner: modest
form in maiden at Naas at 2 yrs for by A. O'Brien: no form for P. Cole (2 starts,
gave impression something amiss first occasion) and present stable in 1996. *Martin
Brassil, Ireland*

SEA MIST (IRE) 2 ch.f. (Apr 22) Shalford (IRE) 124§ – Somnifere (USA) 63 53
(Nijinsky (CAN) 138) [1996 5g 5.1m 7m 7g⁶ 7g a8.5g Nov 25] good-topped filly:
first foal: dam lightly-raced maiden, closely related to smart 1989 2-y-o Line of
Thunder (dam of Thunder Gulch) and daughter of Irish Oaks winner and Gold Cup
second Shoot A Line: modest form: off course 4 months after debut: stays 7f: sold
1,600 gns Newmarket December Sales. *P. W. Chapple-Hyam*

SEAMUS 2 ch.c. (May 9) Almoojid 69 – Royal Celerity (USA) (Riverman (USA) –
131) [1996 5s Mar 23] 3,200Y: seventh foal: half-brother to 3-y-o 1¼m seller winner
In Cahoots (by Kalaglow) and winners in Italy by Kings Lake and Germany by
Gorytus: dam, Irish 1m winner, sister to Sulaafah: sire (by Sadler's Wells), disappointing maiden, closely related to Assert and half-brother to Eurobird and Bikala:
33/1 and in need of run, slow-starting eleventh of 12 in maiden auction at Doncaster
(jockey reported horse had been struck into and lost his action). *A. G. Newcombe*

SEANCHAI (IRE) 3 b.g. Treasure Kay 114 – Blue Infanta (Chief Singer 131) –
[1995 NR 1996 a6g a6s Dec 19] first foal: dam, stayed 1¼m, half-sister to very useful
middle-distance filly Reprocolor, dam of Cezanne, Colorspin and Bella Colora:
behind in claimers. *P. S. Felgate*

SEA OF STONE (USA) 3 ch.f. Sanglamore (USA) 126 – Ocean Ballad 104 71
(Grundy 137) [1995 NR 1996 8m² 10g² 14.1g² Oct 24] third foal: closely related to
5-y-o 14.1f winner Frozen Sea (by Diesis): dam 1½m winner from staying family:

fair form in maidens: reportedly finished lame final start: should prove suited by good test of stamina: yet to race on a soft surface: stays in training. *L. M. Cumani*

SEA PLANE 7 gr.h. Nishapour (FR) 125 – Pirogue 99 (Reliance II 137) [1995 10m 14.5s 12f² 15d 12g⁵ 11g 12g⁴ 14.5g² 17g* 15.5d 12s⁵ 15.5d⁶ 20d* 16.8g 1996 12d 15.5d 12m 14.5g³ 17g 17g 13d* 18g 20v⁶ 16.8s³ Nov 20] tall, leggy horse: ran here early in career, but sent to France at 4 yrs and has won 4 races there, including handicap at Maisons-Laffitte in September: prominent long way when facing stiff task in Cesarewitch eighth 7-y-o start: stays long distances: acts on firm ground and dead: often blinkered. *A. L. Bates, France* 62

SEASIDE (IRE) 2 b.f. (Mar 11) Salt Dome (USA) – Cipriani 102 (Habitat 134) [1996 5.3f² 5s* 5g³ 5.2f 6f⁵ Aug 9] IR 3,000Y: tall, rather unfurnished filly: fifth foal: half-sister to 3-y-o 6f winner Hoh Returns (by Fairy King): dam, Irish mare best at 7f/1m, daughter of champion New Zealand mare La Mer: fair form: won 5-runner maiden auction at Hamilton in May: slowly away and not pace to challenge in Super Sprint at Newbury penultimate outing: should stay 6f. *John Berry* 75

SEASONAL SPLENDOUR (IRE) 6 b.m. Prince Rupert (FR) 121 – Snoozy Time 65 (Cavo Doro 124) [1995 92: 12f* 11.9m⁴ 12m⁶ 12m 16d*⁽ᵈⁱˢ⁾ 16d 1996 16g⁶ 18.7g 16s 20f 14d⁵ Jul 5] workmanlike mare: fairly useful handicapper: below form in 1996: stays 2m (hasn't had best of runs when twice tried over further): probably acts on any going: blinkered (below form) twice as 3-y-o: best held up. *M. C. Pipe* 82

SEA SPOUSE 5 ch.g. Jalmood (USA) 126 – Bambolona 108 (Bustino 136) [1995 44: a8g a12g* a12g a12g 10g 8.3g² 8.3m 8g 8.1d 8.2m a9.4g³ 1996 a11g⁵ a8g³ a8g* a8g³ a8.5g³ 6.9s* 7m a7g a7g³ a7g* 7.1d 8.3d a7g² a7g⁵ a7s⁴ Dec 19] workmanlike gelding: fair handicapper on the all-weather: made all at Southwell in February and June: poor on turf, narrow winner at Folkestone in March: effective at 7f, and has won at 1½m: acts on fibresand and on soft ground: races prominently: none too consistent. *M. Blanshard* 46 a67

SEA SPRAY (IRE) 3 b.f. Royal Academy (USA) 130 – Sailor's Mate 114 (Shirley Heights 130) [1995 88p: 7m* 8d 1996 8g* 10.4m⁵ 12m 10d 10.5s Nov 2] lengthy, sparely-made filly: won listed race at Kempton in April by neck from unlucky Parrot Jungle on third-last start for P. Chapple-Hyam: finished last next 3 starts (not at all discredited in 1¼m listed event at Longchamp): stiffish task in Prix de Flore at Saint-Cloud final one: probably stays 1¼m. *J. E. Hammond, France* 101

SEA THUNDER 4 ro.f. Salse (USA) 128 – Money Moon (Auction Ring (USA) 123) [1995 83: 7m² 6g² 6m³ 6g* 6m⁵ 6g 7d³ 6d 1996 6m 7s 6m 6m 7m⁶ Jun 26] quite good-topped filly: poor mover: fairly useful at best at 3 yrs: long way below form in handicaps in 1996: stays 7f: acts on good to firm and dead ground: visored (poorly drawn) third 4-y-o start: has joined M. Johnston. *I. A. Balding* 67

SEATTLE ALLEY (USA) 3 b.g. Seattle Dancer (USA) 119 – Alyanaabi (USA) 74 (Roberto (USA) 131) [1995 60p: 7g 6d⁶ 7g 7f 1996 7s 8d 8g 10.3m⁴ 10m* 10m* Jun 17] good-topped gelding: easy mover: fair handicapper: won twice at Pontefract in June, taking fierce hold in slowly-run race and flashing tail under pressure on first occasion: joined P. Webber: better suited by 1¼m than shorter: acts on good to firm ground: upset in stalls fourth start. *Mrs J. R. Ramsden* 68

SEATTLE ART (USA) 2 b.c. (Mar 24) Seattle Slew (USA) – Artiste 95 (Artaius (USA) 129) [1996 8g Oct 30] sixth living foal: half-brother to useful winner at up to 16.5f Allegan (by Alleged) and French 12.2f winner Sedova (by Nijinsky): dam 1m and 8.2f winner who stayed 1¼m, is out of Oaks second Val's Girl: 4/1, well-beaten ninth of 13 in steadily-run maiden won by Mandilak at Yarmouth, eased once outpaced: should do better. *H. R. A. Cecil* – p

SEATTLE SAGA (USA) 3 b.c. Seattle Dancer (USA) 119 – Sid's Kate (USA) (Chieftain II) [1995 NR 1996 a12g* 12.3m² 16.2m³ Jul 25] $72,000F: ninth foal: half-brother to 3 winners abroad, including Flying Julia (by Flying Paster), Grade 1 9f winner in USA: dam, ran 3 times in USA, half-sister to 9f Hollywood Oaks winner Answer: won maiden at Lingfield in February: some improvement when second of 4 in steadily-run minor event at Chester 5 months later: dropped tamely away over 3f out in 4-runner handicap at Chepstow: stays 12.3f: sent to UAE. *D. R. Loder* 72

SEATTLE SWING 2 b.f. (Mar 2) Saddlers' Hall (IRE) 126 – Sweet Slew (USA) 96 (Seattle Slew (USA)) [1996 8.2m⁵ Sep 24] angular filly: half-sister to winners in 68 p

North America by Polish Navy and Nodouble: dam, placed at 6f and 1m here then won twice in USA, half-sister to high-class winners at up to 1½m On The Sly and Northern Trick: 10/1 from 7/2, around 6 lengths fifth of 9 to Attitre in maiden at Nottingham: will stay beyond 1m: wore bandages behind: should do better. *J. H. M. Gosden*

SEA VICTOR 4 b.g. Slip Anchor 136 – Victoriana (USA) (Storm Bird (CAN) 84 134) [1995 84: 10.3g* 12g⁴ 10.1m 8.1m 14g 10m⁶ 11.5g³ 15.1g³ 11.8g³ 15.8m* 18f² 16m* 16.5m³ a16g² a12g² 1996 11.8g 18.7g 16g³ 16g a16g* 14.4g* 20f⁴ 16.1m 15.9m⁴ 20m² 18.7m* 16.2f⁶ 16.1m 16.2m 14.1m⁴ 18g⁵ 16g² 16.5s a12g² Dec 7] sturdy, good-topped gelding: fairly useful performer: won claimer at Southwell and minor event at Kempton in June and (4 days after beaten neck in Goodwood Stakes) £15,200 handicap at Chester in August: fifth of 26 to Inchcailloch in Cesarewitch at Newmarket on sixteenth start: stays well: has raced mainly on a sound surface (acts on firm going) or the all-weather: soundly beaten on soft ground: seems effective visored or not: won novice hurdle in December: very tough, game and genuine. *J. L. Harris*

SEA WEDDING 3 ch.f. Groom Dancer (USA) 128 – Cruising Height 112 (Shir- 72 ley Heights 130) [1995 NR 1996 10g³ 10s⁴ Oct 24] sparely-made filly: unimpressive mover: second foal: half-sister to smart 4-y-o 11.9f to 14.6f winner Corradini (by Rainbow Quest): dam, stayed 1½m, half-sister to Park Hill winner Trampship out of half-sister to Prix Vermeille winner Paulista: much better effort in maidens when 5 lengths third of 10 to Smilin N Wishin in steadily-run race at Nottingham on debut, slowly away and not knocked about: sold 17,000 gns Newmarket December Sales: likely to prove well suited by 1½m+. *H. R. A. Cecil*

SEA YA MAITE 2 b.g. (Apr 16) Komaite (USA) – Marina Plata (Julio Mariner – 127) [1996 7g Oct 25] fourth foal: brother to 3-y-o 5f winner and 6f winner First Maite and useful but untrustworthy 5-y-o (best at up to 7f) Sailormaite, and half-brother to 9.4f winner Asmarina (by Ascendant): dam won twice at around 1m: 50/1 and burly, front rank around 3f in 12-runner maiden at Doncaster: gave trouble stalls when withdrawn from maiden at same course following month. *S. R. Bowring*

SECOND BARRAGE 3 b.c. Royal Academy (USA) 130 – Proudfoot (IRE) 83 (Shareef Dancer (USA) 135) [1995 NR 1996 7.5m* 7m⁶ Jun 26] 17,000Y: first foal: dam Irish 1¾m winner: won 12-runner maiden at Milan in May by 10 lengths: weak 9/2-shot, last of 6 in minor event at Salisbury month later: should stay middle distances. *L. M. Cumani*

SECOND COLOURS (USA) 6 b. or br.g. Timeless Moment (USA) – Ruffled 69 Silk (USA) (Our Hero (USA)) [1995 69, a81: a7g³ a8.5g* 7.5m a8.5g² a8g 7g⁵ 8.2m* a81 8.3f⁵ 10m⁵ 8f* 9.2f* 8g² 9f⁵ 8.5m* a8.5g* 8.9g* 8g⁶ a9.4g³ a8g² 1996 a9.4g a8g* a8g* a8g³ 10.3m² 8.5m³ 8m 8f 10.3d⁴ Aug 30] strong, compact gelding: carries condition: unimpressive mover: fairly useful performer: won claimers at Lingfield in January and Southwell in February: left Mrs M. Reveley after eighth outing: stays 10.3f: acts on firm and dead ground and goes well on the all-weather: visored (ran well) once at 2 yrs: successful when sweating. *M. C. Pipe*

SECONDMENT 3 b.c. Shernazar 131 – Designate (USA) 82 (Nureyev (USA) 70 131) [1995 NR 1996 12g 10m 10g⁴ 10m³ 10g Jul 1] sturdy, workmanlike colt: first foal: dam 1¾m winner, half-sister to dam of useful sprinter Millstream out of daughter of Oaks winner Monade: form only when blinkered and in frame in 2 maiden events at Ripon in May and June: no blinkers, well beaten final start: stays 1¼m: sent to UAE. *L. M. Cumani*

SECONDS AWAY 5 b.g. Hard Fought 125 – Keep Mum 63 (Mummy's Pet 125) 31 [1995 41d: 6s 8.1m⁴ 8f 7.1m⁴ 8g 8.3f⁴ 7f 6g³ 1996 a7g 5d² 5m 7.1g⁵ 5g 6g 6m⁶ 7.1g³ 8.1m² 6m⁴ 8.3m 8.3m³ 9.2f⁴ 12.1m 8m 8m⁶ Oct 2] small gelding: poor maiden handicapper: effective at 5f, and stays 9f: acts on firm and dead ground: effective blinkered/visored or not. *J. S. Goldie*

SECRET ALY (CAN) 6 b.g. Secreto (USA) 128 – Bouffant (USA) (Alydar 87 (USA)) [1995 86, a90: a7g a10g³ a10g* a10g² 10m⁴ 10m 8.1g* 10f 8g 8f* 7.6m 9g 9g 8.9g 8f* a8g⁴ 1996 a10g a8g 10g 12m⁵ 10.3g⁴ 8.9m 10m² 10.4m 10m 10.1m* 10.5d⁶ 10s Oct 24] good-bodied gelding: usually impresses in appearance: fairly useful handicapper: switched wide and stormed through from last place to win 16-runner contest at Yarmouth in September: below form on a soft surface last 2 starts: effective at 1m to 1¼m: acts on the all-weather and goes well on firm going: effective racing prominently or held up: none too consistent. *C. E. Brittain*

SECRETARY OF STATE   10 b.g. Alzao (USA) 117 – Colonial Line (USA) 75   55
(Plenty Old (USA)) [1995 NR 1996 a10g² 10.8g 10g Apr 22] strong, workmanlike gelding: carries condition: good mover: one-time useful performer, probably only modest nowadays: off course over 3½ years before reappearance: stays 1¼m: modest jumper, winner of novice chase in June. *D. W. P. Arbuthnot*

SECRET BALLOT (IRE)   2 b.c. (Mar 13) Taufan (USA) 119 – Ballet Society   55
(FR) (Sadler's Wells (USA) 132) [1996 6m 6g 8.2g Oct 24] IR 10,500Y resold 27,000Y: tall, quite attractive colt: has a round action: first foal: dam once-raced daughter of smart sprinter Gwydion: beaten 9 lengths or more in maidens: sold 3,000 gns Doncaster November Sales. *R. Hannon*

SECRET COMBE (IRE)   2 b.f. (Feb 23) Mujadil (USA) 119 – Crimbourne 83   74
(Mummy's Pet 125) [1996 5.7m² 6m* 5.2f⁶ 6d⁴ 6m 6.1s⁵ a6g⁵ Nov 22] IR 3,000Y: small filly: has a quick action: sixth foal: half-sister to Italian 3-y-o 9f winner Baggio The Best (by Taufan), 7f and (in Germany) 1m winner Storey's Gate (by Red Sunset) and fairly useful middle-distance performer Gone For A Burton (by Bustino): dam, maiden best at 7f, is daughter of smart 1m to 1½m winner Lucent, herself daughter of good sprinter Lucasland: fair form: won maiden auction at Folkestone in July by 8 lengths: 5 lengths sixth of 14 to Miss Stamper in Super Sprint at Newbury next start: generally ran creditably afterwards: will stay beyond 6.1f: acts on firm and soft ground, and on fibresand. *P. J. Makin*

SECRET GIFT   3 ch.f. Cadeaux Genereux 131 – Triste Oeil (USA) 103 (Raise A   74
Cup (USA)) [1995 NR 1996 10m⁶ 14.1f³ 10g³ Jul 1] tall, leggy, lengthy filly: third foal: half-sister to quite useful Irish 7f and 11f winner Desert Wish (by Shirley Heights) and a 6f to 1m winner in UAE by Soviet Star: dam 7f (at 2 yrs) and 1¼m winner: fair maiden: sold to join Mrs J. Pitman 6,800 gns Newmarket July Sales: probably better suited by 1¾m than shorter. *B. Hanbury*

SECRET MISS   4 ch.f. Beveled (USA) – Zamindara (Crofter (USA) 124) [1995   55
55, a–: 5d 5.1g 6.1m⁵ 6m 5g² 6g 5m⁶ 5g 6m⁶ 5.1m 6g 5d* 5g a6g⁵ a7g a6g 1996 a6g   a–
5s 5g⁴ 5m⁵ 5.1g 5m⁴ 5f⁶ 5.1f Jul 8] leggy, sparely-made filly: modest sprint handicapper: acts on good to firm and dead ground: tried blinkered/visored, no improvement: sometimes hangs: none too consistent. *A. P. Jones*

SECRET PASS (USA)   2 ch.c. (Apr 21) Diesis 133 – Mlle Lyphard (USA) (Ly-   63 ?
phard (USA) 132) [1996 6g⁵ 7.5f⁶ 6m 7g Oct 2] $17,000Y: fourth foal: half-brother to French 9f/1¼m winner Mr Peillon (by Irish River): dam won 3 races in USA at around 1m: poor form except on second start: sold 3,000 gns Newmarket Autumn Sales: probably requires further than 6f: sent to Sweden. *E. A. L. Dunlop*

SECRET PLEASURE (IRE)   3 ch.f. Classic Secret (USA) 91 – Abbessingh   62
(Mansingh (USA) 120) [1995 66: 6g⁵ 5g⁴ 7.6d³ 8d 6m 1996 6.9s 6m⁶ 7g 6.9m⁹ 7f²
7.1f⁶ 8d 8f Oct 14] smallish, workmanlike filly: modest maiden handicapper: sold 2,700 gns Newmarket Autumn Sales: will prove best short of 1m: acts on firm and dead ground: sent to South Korea. *R. Hannon*

SECRET SERVICE (IRE)   4 b.g. Classic Secret (USA) 91 – Mystery Bid   78
(Auction Ring (USA) 123) [1995 78: 10d 8g 12m* 12m³ 1996 a12g⁵ 12.4d³ 14d³
13.3s 14.4g³ 16.1m³ 15m 13.9g⁵ 11.9d 18g Oct 19] compact, attractive gelding: fair handicapper: third in Northumberland Plate at Newcastle sixth outing: sold 14,000 gns Newmarket Autumn Sales: stays 2m, probably not 2¼m: acts on good to firm and dead ground, possibly not on soft or fibresand. *C. W. Thornton*

SECRET SPRING (FR)   4 b.g. Dowsing (USA) 124 – Nordica 99 (Northfields   93
(USA)) [1995 81: a8g² 6.9g³ 8m² 10g³ 8d⁵ 10d 1996 a10g² a8g* a8g* a8g⁵ 7.3m⁶ 9m
9s Oct 26] leggy gelding: fairly useful performer: won maiden and handicap (in very good style) at Lingfield in February: below form (after 6½-month absence) last 3 starts, wearing crossed noseband: stays 1¼m, but best form at 1m: acts on good to firm ground and on equitrack: won novice hurdle in November. *P. R. Hedger*

SECRET VOUCHER   3 b.c. Vouchsafe 91 – Welsh Secret 85 (Welsh Captain   73
113) [1995 68: 5.1m⁶ 5f³ 5m⁵ 5m* 5g³ 1996 5d⁴ 5d* 5.1g 6m Jun 15] leggy, sparely-made colt: poor mover: fair handicapper: won at Warwick in April: broke shoulder in

£34,200 contest at York: raced mainly at 5f: acted on good to firm and good to soft ground: dead. *B. A. McMahon*

SEDBERGH (USA) 3 b.g. Northern Flagship (USA) 96 – Crumbaugh Pike (USA) (Within Hail (USA)) [1995 61: 6m a7g² 8.1g⁶ 7d³ 1996 10.3d 11.1g³ a12g² 12.1s⁴ 11.8d 13.8g* 16f* 14.1m⁵ Jul 11] good-topped gelding: fair performer: won claimers at Catterick (by 4 lengths) and Yarmouth (by 6 lengths) within 6 days in June: ran well in handicap at Redcar on final start despite receiving unenterprising ride and meeting trouble in running: a stayer: acts on firm and soft going: looked capable of better. *Mrs M. Reveley*   71 p

SEDVICTA 4 b.g. Primitive Rising (USA) 113 – Annes Gift (Ballymoss 136) [1995 53: 12.3d 11.1g² 14.1m 1996 14d 14s 18g Oct 21] good-topped gelding: has a quick action: modest maiden handicapper: below best in 1996: should stay long distances: won over hurdles in December. *Mrs M. Reveley*   –

SEEBE (USA) 2 b.f. (Mar 17) Danzig (USA) – Annie Edge 118 (Nebbiolo 125) [1996 5f⁶ 6m* 6m³ 6m³ Sep 21] rangy filly, shade unfurnished: has plenty of scope: good walker: has a fluent, round action: sister to 3-y-o 1¼m winner Skillington and half-sister to several winners, notably top-class miler Selkirk (by Sharpen Up): dam 5f and 7f winner here who later won at up to 11f in USA: won maiden at Sandown in July then, 10 days later, strongly-run 8-runner Princess Margaret Stakes (beat Moonlight Paradise a short head) at Ascot: looking extremely well, similar form when third in Lowther Stakes at York (less than length behind Bianca Nera) and Mill Reef Stakes at Newbury (beaten 2¾ lengths by Indian Rocket): will be well suited by 7f+: raced only on top-of-the-ground. *I. A. Balding*   103

SEEKING DESTINY (IRE) 3 b.g. Two Timing (USA) 124 – Heads We Called (IRE) (Bluebird (USA) 125) [1995 –, a47+: 5g 6m 5s 7f a8g 1996 a7g³ a6g* a6g* a6g a6g a7g⁵ a7g³ a6g³ a6g a8g² 10m⁶ a8g a7g⁴ 8m 11.5m Sep 17] modest handicapper: won at Southwell in January and February: mostly below form afterwards: stays 1m: acts on fibresand, no form on turf: tried blinkered, no improvement: usually races prominently. *M. C. Chapman*   a53

SEEKING FORTUNE (USA) 3 b.f. Seeking The Gold (USA) – Gabfest (USA) (Tom Rolfe) [1995 75p: 7g⁶ 1996 8.2m³ 10g⁴ 8m⁵ 10.1m⁴ 8.1m⁶ Sep 18] fair maiden handicapper: stays 1¼m: has raced only on a sound surface: keen to post and upset in stalls on reappearance, taken down last and quietly third start. *J. R. Fanshawe*   75

SEENTHELIGHT 4 ch.f. Rich Charlie 117 – Ackabarrow 97 (Laser Light 118) [1995 39: a6g 6s 8.3g 6g 6m⁴ 7g 5.9f 1996 a6g 9.2d Apr 3] workmanlike filly: looks of little account nowadays: sold 550 gns Doncaster August Sales. *D. Moffatt*   –

SEE YOU AGAIN 4 b.c. Then Again 126 – Down The Valley 73 (Kampala 120) [1995 54: a10g⁶ 10f⁵ 7f⁶ 8h⁵ 7f² 7g 7g a8.5g 1996 a12g Jan 25] modest maiden at best: stayed 1¼m: dead. *M. Brittain*   –

SEE YOU SOON 2 b.g. (Apr 30) Distant Relative 128 – Our Resolution (Caerleon (USA) 132) [1996 6m Sep 6] 5,500Y: unfurnished gelding: fourth foal: half-

Princess Margaret Stakes, Ascot—Seebe (right) is driven back up to short head Moonlight Paradise

brother to fairly useful 3-y-o Nilgiri Hills (by Indian Ridge): dam no sign of ability: 25/1, slowly away when tailed off in 19-runner claimer at Haydock. *C. W. Thornton*

SEGALA (IRE) 5 b.g. Petorius 117 – Cerosia (Pitskelly 122) [1995 74: a8.5g³ 9g 9.2g⁴ 1996 10g 8d 8.3s 13m May 18] quite good-topped gelding: fair handicapper at 4 yrs for Sir Mark Prescott: well beaten in 1996: stays 9.2f: acts on fibresand and any turf going: tried blinkered, no improvement. *J. J. O'Neill* —

SEIGNEURIAL 4 b.g. Primo Dominie 121 – Spinner 59 (Blue Cashmere 129) [1995 85: 5g 5s 5m 6f² 5m 1996 6g* 6m⁵ 6m 6m 5m⁶ 6m* 7m⁶ 6g 7g Oct 19] lengthy, workmanlike gelding: good mover: fairly useful handicapper: won at Kempton (dead heat) in April and Lingfield in September: sold 22,000 gns Newmarket Autumn Sales: very best form at 6f: acts on firm and soft ground: consistent: sent to USA. *G. Harwood* 93

SEIRENES 3 b.f. Formidable (USA) 125 – Seriema 72 (Petingo 135) [1995 78p: 6d⁴ 1996 7m³ 10m² 10m 9.7g³ 10.3g⁶ Oct 25] neat filly: fair maiden: off course nearly 4 months after third start and below form afterwards, reportedly lame on final start: stays 1¼m: swished tail penultimate outing. *P. T. Walwyn* 76

SEJAAL (IRE) 4 b.g. Persian Heights 129 – Cremets 94 (Mummy's Pet 125) [1995 71: 8g 8f³ 8.3m³ 8h* 7.6d 1996 8.1g 8.3d 7m 8.5m Sep 24] rangy, attractive gelding: fair form at 3 yrs for J. Dunlop: well held in handicaps in 1996: stays 1m: acts on hard ground, not on a soft surface: takes strong hold. *R. Akehurst* —

SEKARI 2 b.c. (Jan 10) Polish Precedent (USA) 131 – Secret Seeker (USA) (Mr Prospector (USA)) [1996 7m* Oct 23] second living foal: closely related to useful 3-y-o (at up to 1m) Hidden Oasis (by Green Desert), 7f winner at 2 yrs: dam, 6f winner in USA, sister to Gone West and Lion Cavern, same family as Known Fact: odds on, won 11-runner maiden at Yarmouth readily by ¾ length from Alezal, pair clear, making ground to lead on bridle over 1f out then showing good turn of foot: will stay 1m: looks a useful prospect. *D. R. Loder* 88 p

SELBERRY 2 b.g. (May 28) Selkirk (USA) 129 – Choke Cherry (Connaught 130) [1996 6g⁴ a8.5g² Nov 30] 13,000Y: good-topped gelding: has scope: half-brother to 5f winner Freckles Kelly (by Shavian) and several winners in USA, one placed in Grade 2 event: dam unraced daughter of sister to Sun Chariot winner Cranberry Sauce: fair form in maidens at York (awkward at stalls) and Wolverhampton (beaten a neck) in the autumn: stays 8.5f: will probably do better. *P. C. Haslam* 76 p

SELECT CHOICE (IRE) 2 b.g. (May 28) Waajib 121 – Stella Ann (Ahonoora 122) [1996 6g⁵ 6m 6m 6m³ 6m³ 6.9d² Oct 21] IR 4,600Y: compact gelding: has a quick action: fifth reported foal: half-brother to fair 4-y-o 7f and 1m winner Indrapura (by Gallic League): dam best at around 7f in Ireland: fair maiden: stays 7f. *A. P. Jarvis* 77

SELECT FEW 3 b.c. Alzao (USA) 117 – Elect (USA) 113 (Vaguely Noble 140) [1995 84p: 7m 8.2d⁵ 8g* 1996 10m³ 10g 8.3m* 8f 8.1g* 10m Oct 4] big, rangy colt: fairly useful performer: won minor event at Windsor (held up) in June and handicap at Sandown (first run for 2 months, gamely made all) in August: disappointed on 3 of his other 4 3-y-o starts: effective at 1m and 1¼m: acts on good to firm ground: wore a bandage last 3 starts: sent to Dubai. *L. M. Cumani* 92

SELECT LADY 2 b.f. (Apr 22) Presidium 124 – Child Star (Precocious 126) [1996 6m³ 5.1m⁴ a6g Oct 19] fourth foal: half-sister to 3-y-o Beeny (by Lugana Beach), 5f winner at 2 yrs: dam little worthwhile form: poor form: sold 500 gns Doncaster November Sales. *A. P. Jarvis* 45

SELECT STAR (IRE) 2 b.g. (Jan 15) Arcane (USA) – Chevrefeuille 87 (Ile de Bourbon (USA) 133) [1996 7m² 7g 8.1g³ 7.9g 8m² 8m 8m³ 8f Nov 5] IR 2,000Y: good-bodied colt: fourth foal: half-brother to 1992 5f winner Esthal (by Kalaglow): dam 12.2f winner out of Vielle: sire, won from 1¼m to 2m and over hurdles, brother to Rainbow Quest: fair form when placed in 3 maidens and a nursery but has also run 3 poor races: sold 3,600 gns Doncaster November Sales: stays 1m: has sometimes shown unsatisfactory temperament: unreliable. *A. P. Jarvis* 65 §

SELF EXPRESSION 8 b.g. Homing 130 – Subtlety (Grundy 137) [1995 58, a62: a8g² 8.2g 8g 8m⁶ a8g⁴ 8g 8g² 8.5d³ 8g 9.9m² 9.9m⁶ 1996 7.5d 8g 8g⁶ May 13] leggy gelding: poor mover: modest handicapper: below form in 1996, leaving Mrs J. Ramsden's after third start: effective at 1m and 1¼m: acts on firm and dead 44 a–

ground and on fibresand, below form on very soft: tried blinkered/visored at 4 yrs, no improvement: effective from front or held up: carries head high and tends to hang, but has run well for inexperienced claimer. *J. A. Harris*

SELHURSTPARK FLYER (IRE) 5 b.g. Northiam (USA) – Wisdom To 93 Know (Bay Express 132) [1995 84d: 6m 6m 7m⁴ 6m 7m 7m 6g 6d 5m 1996 7m⁴ 5.9m* 6m³ 6m* 6f 6.1m² 6m 5.2m⁵ 6m* 6m 6d Sep 30] leggy, workmanlike gelding: useful handicapper, mostly in good form in 1996: successful at Carlisle in May and at Epsom in June (£18,400 contest) and September (well-contested 9-runner minor event): stays 7f: acts on firm and dead ground, well beaten on soft and heavy: below form when tried in blinkers/visor in 1994: races prominently (well handled by 5-lb claimer P. Roberts for Epsom wins): sometimes bandaged in front. *J. Berry*

SELLETTE (IRE) 2 ch.f. (Apr 28) Selkirk (USA) 129 – Near The End (Shirley 74 Heights 130) [1996 7.1f 8.2m³ 8d³ Oct 2] IR 21,000Y: rangy filly: has scope: half-sister to several winners here and abroad, including useful Irish 6f and 7f winner Dashing Colours (by Be My Native) and a middle-distance winner by Law Society: dam unraced: fair form in maidens, 2 lengths third of 13 to Bold Words at Salisbury last outing: will stay 1¼m: acts on good to firm and dead ground. *D. Haydn Jones*

SELMESTON (IRE) 4 b.g. Double Schwartz 128 – Baracuda (FR) (Zeddaan 45 130) [1995 –: 8g a6g a6g 1996 a8g⁵ a12g a12g³ a12g⁵ a16g* 16.1s 16.2m a16g a16g May 27] leggy gelding: poor handicapper: very easy winner at Southwell in March: well below that form afterwards: stays 2m: acts on fibresand. *P. S. Felgate*

SENATE SWINGS 2 gr.c. (Jan 28) Timeless Times (USA) 99 – Heaven-Liegh- 48 Grey 90 (Grey Desire 115) [1996 5g⁶ 5m³ 6g³ a5g⁵ 6d³ a6g⁴ 6s a8g² a7g³ a7g⁵ Dec a56 27] 12,000Y: lengthy, good-quartered colt: has scope: first foal: dam best at around 5f: modest maiden: best form up to 7f: acts on good to firm and dead ground but very best efforts on fibresand. *W. R. Muir*

SENDMETOMARY 2 b.f. (May 12) Efisio 120 – Dreams To Riches (Busted – 134) [1996 7.5m Jul 6] 4,000Y: third foal: dam, should have stayed well, half-sister to smart stayer Inde Pulse and Dee Stakes winner Great Idea: 16/1, slowly away and always behind in 11-runner seller at Beverley. *T. D. Easterby*

SENORITA MATILDA (USA) 2 b.f. (Feb 6) El Gran Senor (USA) 136 – Cop- 73 p perama (AUS) (Comeram (FR) 127) [1996 6m⁶ 6g⁵ Jul 10] IR 10,000Y: smallish, sturdy filly: sister to a winner in USA and closely related to 3-y-o 1m winner Al Shadeedah and 1993 2-y-o 7.6f winner Shalbourne (both by Nureyev) and Irish 7f and 1m winner Stormy Exchange (by Storm Bird): dam leading performer in Australia, winner of VATC 1000 Guineas: over 5 lengths fifth of 17 to Imroz in maiden at Newmarket: seemed sure to improve again. *R. Hannon*

SENSATION 3 b.f. Soviet Star (USA) 128 – Outstandingly (USA) (Exclusive Na- 114 tive (USA)) [1995 NR 1996 8g* 8d* 8m* 8g* 8d 9f Oct 5] close-coupled, attractive

Falmouth Stakes, Newmarket—
Sensation (right) extends her winning sequence, against Ta Rib (centre) and Donna Viola (second left)

Sheikh Mohammed's "Sensation"

filly: fifth live foal: half-sister to 3 minor winners, including Grade 2 8.5f third
Outlasting (by Seattle Slew): dam, won Breeders' Cup Juvenile Fillies and 3 graded
stakes at 4 yrs, stayed 1¼m: smart form: won newcomers event at Evry in April,
listed race at Deauville in May, Prix de Sandringham at Chantilly (beat Patch of Blue
2½ lengths) in June and Falmouth Stakes at Newmarket (rec 6 lb from Ta Rib, won
by 1¾ lengths) in July: well below form in Prix Jacques Le Marois at Deauville
(tailed off) and Queen Elizabeth II Stakes at Keeneland last 2 starts: should stay
beyond 1m: acts on good to firm and dead ground: effective as front runner (first and
third starts) or tracking pace: joined Godolphin. *Mme C. Head, France*

SENSE OF PRIORITY   7 ch.g. Primo Dominie 121 – Sense of Pride (Welsh   66
Pageant 132) [1995 59, a68: a7g a6g³ a6g⁴ a6g³ 6f 5g⁶ 6m 5.9f⁴ 6m* a6g* 6m⁵ 7m⁵   a70
7f⁵ a7g 1996 a6g* a7g³ a7g a6g² a7g⁴ a6g* a6g* a6g⁶ 6m 5g⁵ 6m 5.9f* 6d² 5g 6m⁵
6f⁶ 6f⁶ a6g³ Aug 9] leggy, workmanlike gelding: fair performer: won claimer at
Wolverhampton in January, claimer and seller at Southwell in February and another
claimer at Carlisle in June: best at up to 7f: acts on hard and dead ground, goes well
on the all-weather: visored twice at 4 yrs. *D. Nicholls*

SENSO (IRE)   5 b.g. Persian Heights 129 – Flosshilde (Rheingold 137) [1995 –:   –
10g⁴ 1996 a12g Feb 16] fair form at best in Italy at 3 yrs for J. Dunlop: tailed off on
flat here. *J. S. Wainwright*

SERAPE   3 b.f. Primo Dominie 121 – Absaloute Service 96 (Absalom 128) [1995   59
NR 1996 7g 7m 6g⁶ 6f Aug 10] fifth foal: half-sister to 5-y-o 1m and 9.4f winner
Benjamins Law (by Mtoto) and fair 1991 2-y-o 6f winner Ring Cycle (by Auction
Ring): dam 2-y-o 5f winner: modest form in maidens, second on unfavoured far
side at Salisbury on third start: sold 800 gns Newmarket Autumn Sales: stays 7f.
H. Candy

SERENADE (IRE)   2 gr.g. (Apr 2) Classic Music (USA) – Friendly Thoughts   61 ?
(USA) (Al Hattab (USA)) [1996 7.1m 7g⁶ 8s a8g⁴ a10g Nov 26] 8,600F, 12,000Y: a49

close-coupled gelding: half-brother to 3 winners here and abroad, including fair 6f (at 2 yrs) to 11.5f winner Fancy Me (by Dunbeath): dam unraced: modest maiden: stays 1m. *M. J. Haynes*

SERENDIPITY (FR)   3 b.g. Mtoto 134 – Bint Damascus (USA) (Damascus   86
(USA)) [1995 85p: 7f⁵ 8m⁵ 1996 8g 9.9m* 10m⁴ 12m 10m 8m³ 8d 10.3m⁵ 8g 8m³
Oct 17] good-quartered gelding: fairly useful performer: won maiden at Beverley in
May: several creditable efforts in handicaps afterwards, sold to join B. R. Millman
25,000 gns Newmarket Autumn Sales after final start: best at up to 1¼m: acts on
good to firm ground, well beaten on dead: well beaten only try in blinkers: possibly
best ridden up with/close to pace: inconsistent: gelded. *J. L. Dunlop*

SERENITY   2 b.f. (Mar 14) Selkirk (USA) 129 – Mystery Ship 105 (Decoy Boy   98
129) [1996 6m⁵ 6m* 6m* 7g³ Oct 18] 15,500F, IR 31,000Y: leggy, shallow-girthed
filly: half-sister to several winners here and abroad, including 7f and 1m winner Final
Enigma (by Final Straw): dam 2-y-o 5f and 7f winner: progressive form: beat
Intikhab a head in maiden at Ripon in August and Sharp Hat readily by 1¼ lengths in
nursery at Newmarket in October: held up then stayed on when 4¼ lengths third
behind Moonlight Paradise and Dazzle in Rockfel Stakes at Newmarket on final
outing: will probably stay 1m: has a turn of foot: sweating final start. *J. R. Fanshawe*

SERENUS (USA)   3 b.c. Sunshine Forever (USA) – Curl And Set (USA)   86
(Nijinsky (CAN) 138) [1995 NR 1996 10m³ 11.5g³ 10m² 12m⁴ Sep 24] $42,000Y:
leggy colt: fifth foal: brother to a minor winner in USA and half-brother to another:
dam minor winner at up to 1¼m in USA: fairly useful maiden: placed at Goodwood,
Yarmouth and Ascot (edged left) in midsummer: should prove better at 1½m than
1¼m: winning hurdler for N. Henderson. *Lord Huntingdon*

SERETSE'S NEPHEW   2 b.c. (Mar 3) Chilibang 120 – Bunnyloch 49§   43
(Lochnager 132) [1996 7m⁵ 5.3g⁶ 7m a6g* a5g³ a6g Dec 13] third foal: dam sprinter: a55
poor form in sellers on turf: improved effort to win nursery at Lingfield in November:
stays 6f: acts on equitrack. *S. C. Williams*

SERGEYEV (IRE)   4 ch.c. Mulhollande (USA) 107 – Escape Path (Wolver   102
Hollow 126) [1995 112: 7m* 6m* 6g* 7m* 6g 7m 1996 6m 6m³ 7m⁵ 8g 6m² 7m⁶
7g⁶ Oct 26] useful-looking colt: smart performer at 3 yrs, winner of Jersey Stakes:
reportedly had a wind operation before reappearing in 1996, and mostly well below
3-y-o form: effective at 6f and 7f: acts on good to firm ground, disappointing only
start on dead: pulls hard, and is nearly always held up for a late run. *R. Hannon*

SERGIO (IRE)   4 ch.g. Doubletour (USA) – Shygate (Shy Groom (USA)) [1995   –
–: a8g a8g a8.5g⁵ a11g 12f 1996 a11g Jan 12] no worthwhile form, including in
sellers. *J. P. Leigh*

SERIOUS   6 b.g. Shadeed (USA) 135 – Azallya (FR) (Habitat 134) [1995 89: 7m   102 ?
9m⁶ 7.3g 8m 10.5g² 10v 8m² 1996 8m² 8m 8g⁴ 8m Aug 1] lengthy, good-topped
gelding: normally impresses in appearance: fairly useful handicapper: hasn't won on
flat since his 2-y-o days, but was first home on unfavoured far side in Hunt Cup at
Royal Ascot on second 6-y-o start and appeared to run very well when close fourth of
8 to Royal Philosopher in listed race at Evry later in June: sold (Lady Herries to K.
Bailey) 37,000 gns Newmarket Autumn Sales: effective at 1m, and stays 10.5f: acts
on good to firm and dead going, stiff task on heavy: visored (well beaten) once as
4-y-o: has run creditably when sweating: has tongue tied down: tends to carry head
high. *Lady Herries*

SERIOUS ACCOUNT (USA)   3 b.c. Danzig (USA) – Topicount (USA)   –
(Private Account (USA)) [1995 NR 1996 8m May 6] second foal: half-brother to
American 4-y-o Laguna Seca (by Seattle Slew), fairly useful at up to 1m: dam minor
stakes winner at up to 9f: weak 5/1-shot, shaped much better than last-of-9 position
suggests in maiden at Kempton, tiring after disputing lead briefly over 2f out: sold
6,400 gns Newmarket December Sales. *H. R. A. Cecil*

SERIOUS FACT   4 b.g. Aragon 118 – Plain Tree 71 (Wolver Hollow 126) [1995   45
41: 5m a6g⁵ 1996 a6g² a6g⁶ a7g* a7g³ a8g⁵ 6.9m⁶ a6g May 31] workmanlike
gelding: poor handicapper: gained first success in maiden event at Wolverhampton
in January: below form afterwards, sold out of Sir Mark Prescott's stable 2,200 gns
Doncaster March Sales after fifth start: stays 7f: acts on fibresand and equitrack: sold
520 gns Doncaster July Sales. *Mrs L. Stubbs*

SERIOUS HURRY 8 ch.g. Forzando 122 – Lady Bequick 81 (Sharpen Up 127) 51 d
[1995 56: 5d 5g 5g³ 5g 5g 5f 5m² 5f 5g 5f 5f* 5h⁴ 5h* 5m² 6g 5f 1996 a5g 5g 5g 5g⁵
5g² 5f⁴ 5f 5g⁴ 5m⁶ 5d 5m 5.1m Sep 16] strong, heavy-topped gelding: has a quick
action: poor handicapper: best at around 5f: acts on hard ground and equitrack, seems
unsuited by a soft surface: often blinkered: usually forces pace: none too consistent.
R. M. McKellar

SERIOUS OPTION (IRE) 5 b.g. Reprimand 122 – Top Bloom (Thatch (USA) –
136) [1995 69d: 7s 6m 7g 8.1g⁴ 7.6m 8.3m⁴ 11.5m³ 1996 a12g 7m 10g May 17]
sturdy, well-made gelding: showed little in 1996: sold (P. Cole to R. Curtis) 2,800 gns
Newmarket Autumn Sales: stays 1m: tried blinkered, no improvement. *P. F. I. Cole* ·

SERIOUS SENSATION 3 ch.g. Be My Chief (USA) 122 – Maiyaasah 75 (Kris 69
135) [1995 NR 1996 8s⁵ 8.3g a6g² a9.4g* a9.4g² 8d⁵ 7g³ 7m³ 7.1s Oct 22] 17,000F, a94
9,800Y: half-brother to 4-y-o 7f and 8.3f winner Aldaneh (by Indian Ridge) and
useful 6f (at 2 yrs) and 1m winner Lead The Dance (by Lead On Time): dam lightly-
raced maiden, ran only at 1m: fairly useful form on the all-weather at Wolverhampton, winning maiden in August: just fair form in 6 turf outings: sold 18,000 gns
Newmarket Autumn Sales: best efforts over 9.4f, but should prove as effective over
shorter: sent to Saudi Arabia. *Sir Mark Prescott*

SERIOUS TRUST 3 b.c. Alzao (USA) 117 – Mill Line 71 (Mill Reef (USA) 60
141) [1995 52: 7.5m⁵ 7.5m 7m⁵ 7g 7f 1996 12m* 11.1f⁴ 14.1m³ 16f³ a16g Aug 10]
good-topped colt: modest handicapper: landed gamble at Salisbury in May: well
below best (led to 4f out, beaten in a matter of strides) when again well backed on
all-weather debut at Lingfield final start: sold (Sir Mark Prescott to Mrs. L. Jewell)
12,500 gns Newmarket Autumn Sales: suited by a test of stamina: has raced only on
a sound surface. *Sir Mark Prescott*

SET ADRIFT 3 b.c. Slip Anchor 136 – Cephira (FR) (Abdos 134) [1995 NR 1996 86
11d² 12m⁶ 10f* Jun 25] tall, quite attractive colt: has a short, round action: brother to
disappointing maiden Seraphic and half-brother to several winners, including useful
1987 French 2-y-o 5f winner Shaindy (by American Stress), later winner at up to 7f:
dam fourth over 6f at 2 yrs: fairly useful form: justified favouritism in maiden at
Lingfield in June, dictating steady pace: should stay 1½m: acts on firm and dead
ground: has reportedly been sold. *H. R. A. Cecil*

SET THE FASHION 7 br.g. Green Desert (USA) 127 – Prelude 89 (Troy 137) 61 §
[1995 –, a76: 8m 8m 8d 7m a7g* a8g* a7g 1996 8m⁵ 11.5f⁵ 10.2m⁴ 9.9m² 8.2m* 9f
8.2d⁶ 8f 16m 14.5g* a12g Dec 14] good-topped gelding: has a round action: fair
handicapper: won at Nottingham in July: failed to repeat the form here (looking
unwilling eighth start): narrowly won Pivovar Pardubice St Leger at Pardubice in
October: seems to stay 14.5f, appeared not to stay 2m: acts on all-weather surfaces
and probably on any turf going: best in visor: blinkered (tailed off) final start: not to
be trusted. *D. L. Williams*

SEVA (IRE) 2 b.f. (Jan 17) Night Shift (USA) – Swallowcliffe 83 (Caerleon 61
(USA) 132) [1996 6.1m³ 6m³ 6.1m 8m⁵ Oct 17] IR 31,000F, 25,000Y: angular filly:
unimpressive mover: first foal: dam 2-y-o 6f winner (stayed 1m), half-sister to smart
sprinter Ya Malak out of half-sister to Cadeaux Genereux: modest form in maidens:
would have proved best short of 1m: dead. *D. R. Loder*

SEVEN CROWNS (USA) 3 b.c. Chief's Crown (USA) – Ivory Dance (USA) 61
(Sir Ivor 135) [1995 65: 6m⁶ 7.1g⁴ 8f⁵ 9m⁶ 1996 8.3m 9m³ 10m 12g³ 12.1m⁵ 11.6g
12g 13.1m Sep 9] stocky colt: unimpressive mover: modest maiden handicapper:
well beaten last 4 starts: stays 1½m: raced only on a sound surface: tried blinkered,
no improvement: tends to race prominently: has joined C. Popham. *R. Hannon*

SEVENTEENS LUCKY 4 gr.g. Touch of Grey 90 – Westminster Waltz (Dance 82
In Time (CAN)) [1995 76: 6m 7g² 7m² 8m 7.5g³ 7f² 7m⁴ 7f⁶ 8m³ 8.9g* 10d a10g⁴
1996 a12g² a12g⁵ 10.3d⁶ 10d 8m* 8.5m 8.9m³ 10.4m 8m 8.1m³ 8.3d⁵ 7.9g* 8g
8.9g 8g⁶ Oct 29] close-coupled gelding: fairly useful handicapper: won at Kempton
(apprentices) in June and York (23-runner race) in September: effective at 1m, and
has form over as far as 1½m: acts on firm going and equitrack, below form on a soft
surface: visored (ran well) once as 3-y-o. *Bob Jones*

SEVENTH EDITION 3 b.g. Classic Music (USA) – Funny-Do (Derring-Do –
131) [1995 NR 1996 10g 10f 10d⁵ 10m 14.1m 10m⁴ 12.1m a9.4g Aug 9] leggy,

sparely-made gelding: half-brother to several poor animals: dam never ran: little worthwhile form. *D. Burchell*

SEVERN MILL   5 ch.g. Librate 91 – Staryllis Girl 67 (Star Moss 122) [1995 NR   –
1996 7g 10m 8.2m⁵ 7.1m 10.2m⁶ 8f 8m Sep 19] half-brother to 2 winning jumpers: dam 5f winner also successful over hurdles: little worthwhile form. *J. M. Bradley*

SHAAMIT (IRE)   3 b.c. Mtoto 134 – Shomoose (Habitat 134) [1995 90p: 8d⁴   127
8m* 1996 12m* 12m³ 10g⁴ 12d Oct 6]

In recent years the Derby's struggle to retain its status as one of the great British sporting institutions has occupied more column inches than the battles on the track. Like the Grand National, the Derby is one of the few occasions when racing can reach outside its own boundaries, affording an opportunity for the sport to show itself off in all its glory. In an effort to restore the big-race atmosphere at Epsom on Derby Day and to make the race more widely 'accessible', it was switched from its traditional Wednesday to Saturday in 1995. 'It was impossible not to do it, there was such a will for it,' said Edward Gillespie, who had a central role in remodelling the Derby meeting. 'We assume it's better for the industry, because everyone tells us that it is. There was an inevitability about switching it that we couldn't resist,' said Gillespie when explaining the change of day. Twelve months on, the Epsom executive must have been bemused by the controversy that broke out after the second Saturday Derby. With the Derby, it seems difficult to please some people from one year to the next. Many of those who pushed for the Saturday switch, and applauded the Epsom team for its initiative, joined a campaign after the latest edition for it to be moved back to Wednesday! The attendance on course, 56,253, was up on the previous year and the Downs looked busier, but Channel 4, who have signed a new five-year deal to show the Derby, reported that viewing figures fell from 3.9 million to 2.5 million (the audience for an ordinary Saturday's racing on Channel 4 is around a million) and off-course bookmakers generally complained of disappointing turnover, down between twenty and twenty-five per cent since the move to Saturday. Both Saturday Derbys have attracted a smaller TV audience than either of the two preceding Wednesday Derbys which had around 4.3 million each. The reason isn't hard to find. Television's sporting audience has had appealing alternatives in each of the last two years, the Rugby Union World Cup in 1995 and the Euro '96 football tournament held in Britain in 1996. Those who stuck to their guns and continued to back a Saturday Derby pointed out that 1995 and 1996 were exceptional years—the race will not face such tough competition in the next two—and that racing could hardly square its newly-espoused 'customer-friendly' approach with switching its flagship flat race back to a day when over three quarters of the adult population was at work. Furthermore, there was plenty of evidence that the Derby had been 'declining' on a Wednesday for over a decade before the change was made.

In truth, the Derby has more problems than the day on which it is run and it will be an uphill task to restore it to its former pre-eminence. Racing itself, for example, does the Derby no favours by continuing to stage a full Saturday programme of race meetings, seven in all on the latest Derby Day. All compete for precious space and attention on the biggest sporting day of the week. The FA Cup Final, football's showpiece, doesn't take place on the same day as a full league programme and the racing authorities have been slow to recognise that the Derby, no longer guaranteed the wide media coverage it had on a Wednesday, probably deserves similar consideration. Apart from that, it's largely a question of marketing. The BBC, which does such a splendid job promoting the Grand National for weeks in advance, apparently made no direct approach when the new contract came up with Televised Racing Ltd (composed of six major courses including Epsom). Marketing the Derby will be more difficult than it would be if the race was on BBC 1; having the race on a minority channel, however good its coverage, imposes limitations. Reaching 'a wider audience during the build-up . . . getting the race off the racing pages and

*Vodafone Derby Stakes, Epsom—Jack Jennings leads round Tattenham Corner;
the eventual first three are close together in mid-division,
Shantou and Dushyantor (both white sleeves) just behind Shaamit (star on forehead)*

on to the news pages' is said to be the central plank of a major marketing drive in 1997. Establishing a race-day crowd of 75,000 is one of the stated long-term targets which it is hoped will be reached by raising the overall quality of racing at the Derby meeting which, in 1997, is being cut to two days, Friday and Saturday. As they say, watch this space . . .

The BHB's senior handicapper Geoffrey Gibbs made his own contribution to the Derby debate in the latest season, claiming that another cause of the race's slow loss of prestige is the trend for more of the runners to be unknown or unexposed to the public. 'From the public's point of view it isn't easy to enthuse about the race,' he said. 'It would be easier for the Epsom management if they had some stars going into the race.' Gibbs suggested that it was generally felt by professionals that the Derby comes too soon. 'Imagine if it fell two or three weeks after the Irish Derby; by then I am sure there would be a good horse to sell the race on.' While the decision to run Celtic Swing at Chantilly rather than Epsom in 1995 was a blow to the Derby's status, that year's race still looked to have a 'star' in the unbeaten Two Thousand Guineas winner Pennekamp, though he beat only four home and was afterwards found to have sustained a hairline fracture to his off-fore (the Derby turned out to be his final race). The latest Derby, however, looked one of the most open for years. During York week in May, for example, there were three different ante-post favourites in as many days, the Two Thousand Guineas runner-up Even Top, the Dante winner Glory of Dancer and the Glasgow Stakes winner Dr Massini, the last-named following up a maiden-race success at Kempton and going from unraced colt to Derby favourite in only ten days. On the big day, it was the Dante runner-up Dushyantor who started favourite at 9/2, followed by Even Top at 11/2 and Glory of Dancer at 6/1 in a field of twenty, from which Dr Massini (lameness) and the Two Thousand Guineas winner Mark of Esteem (temperature) were among those who didn't make the line-up. On the 12/1 mark was Shaamit, a late-developing two-year-old who had been well backed when winning a maiden at Doncaster impressively on the second of two starts. Like the previous year's Derby winner Lammtarra, Shaamit hadn't been seen out as a three-year-old, suffering from an abscess on his withers in the spring and then missing an intended preparatory race in either the Dante or the Glasgow Stakes because of an overreach. Shaamit had entered the Derby betting at 33/1 when supplemented at a cost of £8,000—along with seven others (including Mark of Esteem and Glory of Dancer) in April—and he increasingly came into the reckoning as a result of his impressive home work. He caught the eye of the work-watchers in the run-up to York when galloping with classic types from the Cecil string, and then, a week before the Derby, he pulled clear of Glory of Dancer (whose trainer promptly backed Shaamit for the Derby!) in a workout recorded by Channel 4's *The Morning Line*. Also in the Derby field were the winter ante-post favourite Alhaarth, who had been beaten in the Craven and the Guineas, and the beaten joint-favourite in the Dante, Storm Trooper, both on 15/2. Sheikh Mohammed, still looking for a first Derby winner to carry his colours, was represented by 25/1-shot Shantou who hadn't contested any of the recognised Derby trials after being unraced as a two-year-old and had only very recently got off the mark on his third start in a maiden at Sandown.

Shaamit—'the talking horse' of the race—lived up to his lofty home reputation in no uncertain manner, winning the Derby in a style that suggested he could go on to make an even bigger impression on the racing year. Shaamit was held up in the middle of the Derby field and, like a number of similarly-placed rivals, looked short of room running down to Tattenham Corner. Dushyantor and Shantou were also among those who had a far from smooth passage and were further adrift than Shaamit as Jack Jennings, Mystic Knight and Chief Contender led the field into the home straight where Glory of Dancer, tucked in on the heels of the leaders, was best placed of the leading contenders. Glory of Dancer led briefly before Shaamit, brought to challenge towards the outside, produced a fine turn of foot to hit the front and go clear just inside the two-furlong marker. Shaamit began to flag in the closing stages—'the longest hundred yards of my life', reported his rider Michael Hills—but always looked to have enough in hand to hold off the strong-finishing Dushyantor and Shantou. A length and a quarter and the same were the distances, with Glory of Dancer a length away fourth, just in front of Alhaarth. Approximately ten lengths covered the first thirteen home, suggesting it was, at best, only an average Derby. But the result at least reiterated that the Derby isn't the sole

Vodafone Derby Stakes, Epsom—Shaamit from Dushyantor,
and the second year running that the Derby is won by a colt making his seasonal debut

preserve of the big battalions, the multi-millionaire owners and the stables with hundred-plus strings. Shaamit's owner has only a handful of horses and trainer William Haggas, saddling his first Group 1 winner, handles around forty. Haggas had to share the limelight afterwards with his father-in-law Lester Piggott, for whom the media were keen to discover a role in Shaamit's success. Piggott, a Derby legend, did his best to ensure the credit on this occasion went where it belonged, to Haggas and his team. The Epsom stewards, by the way, deserve a mention for not tainting Derby Day with bans for over-use of the whip, though they did hold inquiries into the riding of the jockeys on the first two. The issue of the whip is dealt with in a wider context in the essay on Dushyantor.

It was Shaamit's acceleration in the straight—coupled with the fact that he was only the third horse this century to win the Derby on his seasonal debut—that marked him down as possibly a top-class horse in the making; for all the arguments about whether the runner-up, who certainly met with plenty of interference, was unlucky, there wasn't much room to doubt that Shaamit, carrying plenty of condition for his reappearance, was his superior. Plans outlined for Shaamit after the Derby included the Budweiser Irish Derby but he missed that race after twisting a shoe and returning lame from exercise the weekend before. Talk of his contesting the Coral-Eclipse came to nothing either and he was next seen out in the King George VI and Queen Elizabeth Diamond Stakes at Ascot at the end of July, starting favourite in a field of eight ahead of the four-year-olds Pentire and Classic Cliche. Shaamit was the twenty-first Epsom Derby winner to run in the King George as a three-year-old. Twelve of his predecessors, including Reference Point, Nashwan, Generous and Lammtarra in the last ten years, had landed the double. Shaamit, held up again, stayed on under pressure but was beaten fairly and squarely, a length and three quarters and a neck by Pentire and Classic Cliche in a very strongly-run race, in which fourth-placed Oscar Schindler finished a further ten lengths back. Shaamit joined Commander in Chief, third in 1993, and Erhaab, seventh in 1994, as Derby winners beaten in the King George in the past decade. The final verdict on Shaamit, who went on to be beaten also in the Irish Champion Stakes and the Prix de l'Arc de Triomphe, is that he showed himself to be of very similar merit to those two: run-of-the-mill as Derby winners go, in other words. He was below form at both Leopardstown, where he was hemmed in early in the straight and finished a place behind Glory of Dancer when fourth to Timarida, and at Longchamp, where he pulled very hard when seventh to Helissio. At one time, Shaamit's connections had planned that his three-year-old season would end with the Irish Champion and he'd be put away for a four-year-old campaign. 'He is all there in front but still has to furnish behind,' said his trainer. 'We need to give him time to develop and then he'll be a real racehorse next year.' However, after the Arc, in which Shaamit reportedly incurred a tendon injury, there was a re-think and he was retired to the National Stud at Newmarket. Shaamit will be available at a fee of £7,500 in 1997 when he will be the only one of the last seven Derby winners at stud in Britain and the first since Mill Reef to stand at the National Stud. Alongside him, incidentally, will be the 1995 Prix du Jockey-Club winner Celtic Swing (fee £6,500) who, kept in training after suffering a serious near-fore knee injury as a three-year-old, was unable to resume his racing career in the latest season.

One of the questions about most Derby contenders before the race is whether they will stay, as relatively few tackle the full distance before Epsom. Shaamit's prospects of getting a mile and a half looked good. His sire Mtoto and his paternal grandsire Busted (an 'old-fashioned' stallion whose offspring tended to need time and distance) stayed the trip well, while Shaamit also has the Derby winners Crepello and Mill Reef among his four great grandsires. Shaamit's unraced dam Shomoose, whose third foal and first winner he is, is a daughter of the useful racemare Epithet who, like her sire Mill Reef, stayed a mile and a half well. Epithet was a half-sister to another racehorse who made much more of a name for himself than most recent members of the family, the

Shaamit (IRE) (b.c. 1993)	Mtoto (b 1983)	Busted (b 1963)	Crepello Sans Le Sou
		Amazer (b 1967)	Mincio Alzara
	Shomoose (b 1985)	Habitat (b 1966)	Sir Gaylord Little Hut
		Epithet (b 1979)	Mill Reef Namecaller

Victoria Cup winner and Duke of York Stakes runner-up Columnist who was by the sprinter Swing Easy. Habitat, the sire of Shomoose, became a top broodmare sire as well as being a top sire of racehorses and is also the maternal grandsire of Reference Point, in whose pedigree, coincidentally, Mill Reef (sire) and Busted (third generation) also appear. As with Reference Point, there is no Northern Dancer influence in Shaamit's pedigree, something he also has in common with Nashwan, the most recent Derby winner before Shaamit still at stud in Britain. Shomoose has had three foals since Shaamit, the unraced two-year-old filly Wafa (by Kefaah), in training with Haggas, a colt (by Kefaah) who died as a foal, and a colt foal full brother to Shaamit. The tall, rather leggy, good-topped Shaamit had a good turn of foot. He stayed a mile and half and acted on good to firm ground, encountering a soft surface for the only time in his career in the Prix de l'Arc. He was a genuine type. *W. J. Haggas*

SHAANXI (USA) 4 ch.f. Zilzal (USA) 137 – Rich And Riotous (USA) (Empery (USA) 128) [1995 122: 8v* 8d² 8d³ 10.5m⁶ 8g² 8g³ 8m² 8d* 8s 9f 1996 7f 8f 8g* 8d³ 8m⁶ 8d² 7d³ Oct 20] compact filly: smart performer: back to form on return from

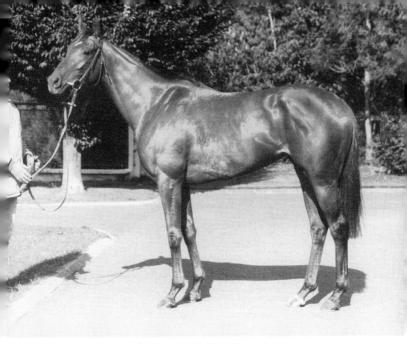

Mr Teruya Yoshida's "Shaanxi"

racing in Japan to win 5-runner Prix d'Astarte at Deauville in August by ¾ length
from Zarannda: 1¼ lengths third of 9 to Spinning World in Prix Jacques Le Marois
there and 1½ lengths second of 10 to Alhaarth in Prix du Rond-Point (soon chasing
winner, kept on well) at Longchamp: best form at 1m, stayed 10.5f: acted on good to
firm ground and heavy: wore crossed noseband: withdrawn from Hong Kong Bowl
in December due to injury: visits Rainbow Quest. *E. Lellouche, France*

SHAARID (USA)   8 b.g. El Gran Senor (USA) 136 – Summer Silence (USA)   –
(Stop The Music (USA)) [1995 68: 9.7g⁴ 10m³ 1996 a13g⁶ Jan 2] smallish gelding:
fair form in amateurs handicaps early in 1995: below form in similar contest at Lingfield on reappearance: should stay at least 13f: acts on firm ground and equitrack: fair
jumper. *I. A. Balding*

SHAA SPIN   4 b.f. Shaadi (USA) 126 – Tight Spin (High Top 131) [1995 NR 1996   –
8f 6g a7g 6m⁶ 6m⁶ 8.3m⁶ 7.1m 10f Sep 28] modest maiden (rated 63) at 2 yrs: well
held in 1996. *J. Berry*

SHABANAZ   11 b.g. Imperial Fling (USA) 116 – Claironcita 97 (Don Carlos)   69
[1995 62, a57: 12m⁴ 10m 12m² 9.7m* 10m* 11.6g² a11g² 10f 12.1m⁴ 11.6m* 9m³
10.8f* 11f* a12g⁶ a10g³ 1996 12m² 10m⁶ 11.9d³ 11.6g* 10m* 11.6d* 12.1g² 10g²
10.1m⁶ 12m 11.8f⁶ Oct 15] rangy, angular gelding: veteran who mainly contests
sellers or claimers nowadays: won poor events at Windsor (twice) and Brighton in
the summer: effective at 9.7f to 13f: acts on fibresand and probably on any turf going:
visored (well below form) once at 7 yrs: has run well in blinkers, not tried for long
time: sometimes slowly away, and is held up: suitable mount for a claimer. *W. R. Muir*

SHADDAD (USA)   2 b.c. (Apr 4) Shadeed (USA) 135 – Desirable 119 (Lord   75 p
Gayle (USA) 124) [1996 6m 6m⁵ Aug 3] big, lengthy colt: has plenty of scope: sixth

living foal: brother to 1000 Guineas winner Shadayid and half-brother to 3 winners, including smart 7f/1m performer Dumaani (by Danzig): dam, 2-y-o 6f winner placed in 1000 Guineas and at 1¼m, is from excellent family: still green, much better effort in maidens at Newmarket when around 6 lengths fifth of 11 to Musical Pursuit, chasing leaders then keeping on same pace: will improve again, particularly at 7f+. *J. L. Dunlop*

SHADED (IRE) 2 b.g. (Apr 23) Night Shift (USA) – Sarsaparilla (FR) 60 (Shirley Heights 130) [1996 7m a7g⁵ 6g Sep 21] 16,500F, 220,000 francs Y: good-topped gelding: has scope: second foal: dam ran 4 times here, successful in Germany at around 9f/1¼m at 4/5 yrs: signs of ability in maidens, particularly at Catterick on final outing, making headway under tender handling when hampered and eased inside final 1f: will stay 1m: open to further improvement. *J. W. Watts*   60 p

SHADES OF LOVE 2 b.c. (Apr 30) Pursuit of Love 124 – Shadiliya 90 (Red Alert 127) [1996 7d Nov 8] good-topped colt: half-brother to several winners, including fairly useful 4-y-o sprinter Twice As Sharp (by Sharpo) and 1989 2-y-o 7f winner Tears of Happiness (by Rousillon): dam, 7f winner at 2 yrs, is closely related to very useful 5f to 1m winner Shasavaan: 16/1, tailed off in maiden at Doncaster, pulling hard. *V. Soane*   –

SHADIRWAN (IRE) 5 b.h. Kahyasi 130 – Shademah 88 (Thatch (USA) 136) [1995 83: 16m² 16m⁴ 20m⁴ 16.1m 16g 16.2d 18m 1996 18s* 16d 16d 20f 16.4g 18.7m⁶ Aug 4] small horse: fairly useful handicapper: very easy winner at Doncaster in March: inconsistent afterwards: stays 2½m: acts on any going: blinkered (out of form) final 4-y-o start: has twice run poorly when sweating. *R. Akehurst*   82

SHADOW CASTING 3 b.f. Warning 136 – Fanciful (FR) (Gay Mecene (USA) 128) [1995 NR 1996 8g⁵ 7.1m* 7.1m⁴ 7m 8m Oct 29] fourth foal: half-sister to 7f and 1m winner Solar Flight (by Soviet Star): dam, French 1m winner, half-sister to Lowther winner Kingscote out of sprinter/miler Bold Fantasy: fair form: failed to progress after winning maiden at Chepstow in July: should stay 1m: has raced only on a sound surface: sold 7,000 gns Newmarket December Sales. *B. W. Hills*   72

SHADOW JURY 6 ch.g. Doulab (USA) 115 – Texita 65 (Young Generation 129) [1995 80, a75: a6g⁴ a6g³ a6g³ a6g* a5g⁵ a6g 6g⁶ 5m³ 5m* 5f* 5m³ 5m² 5m* 5g* a5g* 6.1m⁵ 6m² 5m² 5f 5h⁶ a6g⁶ 5m 5g 5d 5d 5m⁶ 5m⁶ a5g³ a7g a5g³ 1996 a5g* a5g⁴ 5s 5g 5m 6g 5m⁴ 5f³ 5m⁶ 5m 5g⁵ 5m² 5g* 5g 5.7f² 5m 5.1m² 5m 5d 5m 5g 5m² 5s a5g a6g⁶ Dec 20] rather leggy gelding: has a quick action: fair handicapper: won at Wolverhampton in January and at Newmarket in July: effective at 5f and 6f: acts on the all-weather and probably on any turf ground: nearly always blinkered nowadays (ran creditably in visor and without headgear earlier in career): usually races prominently: tough. *D. W. Chapman*   70 a81

SHADOW LEAD 2 b.c. (Feb 13) Midyan (USA) 124 – Shadow Bird 70 (Martinmas 128) [1996 6m⁴ 6.1m* 7m⁴ 10g³ Nov 2] 17,000Y: good-bodied colt: first foal: dam best at around 1½m: made heavy weather of winning 5-runner maiden auction at Chepstow in July: dictated steady early gallop in Acomb Stakes at York following month, finishing 4¼ lengths fourth of 7 behind Revoque: best effort when around a length third of 10 to Silver Patriarch in steadily-run listed event at Newmarket 2½ months later: stays 1¼m: should make a useful handicapper. *L. M. Cumani*   95 p

SHADOW LEADER 5 br.g. Tragic Role (USA) – Hush It Up (Tina's Pet 121) [1995 86: 12g² 12m² 12g⁵ 14m⁴ 12g 12m³ 11.9m³ 13.9m⁶ 11.9d³ 13.3d 1996 12m 13.3f 11.9d 12g* 12s Nov 9] sturdy gelding: fairly useful handicapper: clearly best 5-y-o effort when winning at Ascot in October: best at around 1½m and 1¾m: acts on any going: normally held up/tracks leaders. *C. R. Egerton*   86

SHADY GIRL (IRE) 3 b.f. Shaadi (USA) 126 – Octavia Girl 104 (Octavo (USA) 115) [1995 67: 6.1d 6d 7f⁵ 1996 6m⁴ 8g⁴ 7m a8g⁶ 10.5m⁴ 9m Sep 26] leggy, quite good-topped, attractive filly: fair maiden: didn't impress with her attitude, hanging sharply right under pressure, on third start: sold 2,800 gns Newmarket Autumn Sales: stays 10.5f: ran badly in blinkers: sent to South Korea. *B. W. Hills*   69 §

SHAFFISHAYES 4 ch.g. Clantime 101 – Mischievous Miss 73 (Niniski (USA) 125) [1995 63+: 7.1g* 8m³ 7m 7d 1996 8m* 8g³ 9m⁴ 8.9g 10g⁶ 10f² a12g² a11g Dec 3] lengthy gelding: twice suffered hairline fracture of cannon bone as 3-y-o: fair handicapper: won minor event at Pontefract in April: stays 1½m: acts on firm ground and fibresand. *Mrs M. Reveley*   70

SHAFT OF LIGHT   4 gr.g. Sharrood (USA) 124 – Reflection 111 (Mill Reef   –
(USA) 141) [1995 90: a10g² a9.4g² a11g* a10g* 12m* 13.3g² 14f² 13.9m³ 1996 12m
Oct 17] tall gelding: has scope: has a roundish action: fairly useful performer: off
course 14 months, in rear in rated stakes at Newmarket on only 4-y-o start: will be
very well suited by further than 1¾m: acts on firm ground and the all-weather:
blinkered last 2 starts on all-weather: resolute galloper, well suited by forcing tactics:
genuine. *Lord Huntingdon*

SHAHA   3 b.c. Polish Precedent (USA) 131 – Height of Passion (Shirley Heights   71
130) [1995 65+: 6g⁶ 8.1m⁶ 1996 10d 10m² 10m 10m² 11.6m* 12m⁴ 12m a10f⁶ Dec
29] useful-looking colt: unimpressive walker: fair handicapper: won at Windsor in
June: below form after, including in Dubai: stays 1½m: acts on good to firm ground:
blinkered last 4 starts: best with forcing tactics. *R. Hannon*

SHAHBOOR (USA)   2 b.c. (Jan 13) Zilzal (USA) 137 – Iva Reputation (USA)   – p
(Sir Ivor 135) [1996 7g Sep 29] tall, rather leggy colt: brother to smart 7f (at 2 yrs) to
13.4f winner Zilzal Zamaan and half-brother to several winners, including prolific
Canadian stakes winner Triple Wow (by Coastal): dam unraced: 20/1, always rear in
minor event at Ascot won by Kahal: showed a quick action: sold 50,000 gns
Newmarket Autumn Sales: almost certainly capable of better. *M. R. Stoute*

SHAHIK (USA)   6 b.g. Spectacular Bid (USA) – Sham Street (USA) (Sham   71
(USA)) [1995 a9g⁵ 1996 a12g a7g a7g³ a9.4g² 12g 10d* a12g a9.4g* a9.4g a9.4g⁴
a12g⁴ Dec 28] good-bodied gelding: carries condition: half-brother to several
winners here and in North America, including stakes winner Queen's Gray Bee (by
Drone), successful at up to 1¼m: dam won 4 races at up to 1¼m: fairly useful
performer in Ireland at 3 yrs: won minor event in Dubai in 1994: sold 9,000 gns
Newmarket July (1995) Sales: fair form in handicaps here, trained first 2 outings by
J. O'Shea: won at Salisbury in October and at Wolverhampton in November: stays
1¼m: acts on fibresand and used to on good to firm and dead ground: well beaten
only try in visor. *D. Haydn Jones*

SHAHRANI   4 b.g. Lear Fan (USA) 130 – Windmill Princess 55 (Gorytus (USA)   –
132) [1995 64?: 8m⁵ 10g 11.8f 1996 11.9f 14.1m 17.2f 16.2m Jul 26] lengthy gelding: poor and inconsistent maiden on flat: trained first 3 starts in 1996 by B. Meehan
before returning to previous trainer: probably stays 1¾m: acts on good to firm
ground: sometimes sweats, and has taken strong hold: prolific winning hurdler.
M. C. Pipe

SHAHRUR (USA)   3 b. or br.c. Riverman (USA) 131 – Give Thanks 123 (Relko   –
136) [1995 NR 1996 8m Apr 17] strong, good sort: half-brother to fair 12.2f winner
Saffaanh (by Shareef Dancer), now the dam of Harayir, and a winner in UAE: dam
won from 9f to 1½m, including Irish Oaks, and was second in Park Hill: 33/1, very
much in need of race and green, always rear in 20-runner newcomers event at
Newmarket: sold 24,000 gns Newmarket July Sales. *A. C. Stewart*

SHAKA   2 b.c. (Mar 30) Exit To Nowhere (USA) 122 – Serafica (No Pass No   113 p
Sale 120) [1996 6g² 6g* 8d* 8g* 10s* Nov 2]
  Shaka emerged from the relative obscurity of the Provinces to keep the
last Group 1 event of the year in France for two-year-olds, the Criterium de
Saint-Cloud, in French hands. British stables had won the four others—with
Bahamian Bounty, Revoque and Ryafan—plus another five of the nineteen
pattern races in the French two-year-old programme, improving on what had
been an outstanding season the year before.
  Trained by Jean-Claude Rouget, whose stable strength had grown to
198 in 1996 according to *Horses In Training,* Shaka had been compared to
Millkom, the colt largely responsible for making the stable known outside the
south-west of France. Shaka has achieved more than Millkom did as a two-
year-old—the latter was not seen in Paris until the May of his three-year-old
season. After meeting with defeat on his debut, Shaka ran up a sequence of
wins, beginning with a couple of minor events at La Teste by eight lengths and
then four. They were followed by the Grand Criterium de Bordeaux, a listed
event which Millkom himself had won three years earlier. Shaka's defeat of his
stable-companion Loma Preata looked only fairly useful form at the time but
this was clearly an above-average event for the Provinces as Shaka's win at

Criterium de Saint-Cloud—
smart form from Provincial colt Shaka who inflicts a first defeat on both Daylami and Sendoro

Saint-Cloud was preceded by the third horse, Happy Dancer, winning the Group 3 Premio Dormello at Milan.

Shaka faced nine rivals at Saint-Cloud, among them the Aga Khan's unbeaten pair Daylami and Sendoro, coupled at odds on, the Prix La Rochette winner Fine Fellow, New Frontier, who had been awarded the Prix de Conde, and two British-trained runners, the Goodwood maiden winner Voyagers Quest and Alcalali, the only filly in the field and making her debut. The Aga Khan's colts made much of the running but no sooner had Daylami taken over from Sendoro a furlong and a half out than Shaka joined issue and went on inside the last to beat Daylami three quarters of a length with two lengths back to Sendoro. The fifth home, Voyagers Quest, took on Sendoro again in the Prix Saint-Roman at Evry later in November, beating him half a length.

The Criterium de Saint-Cloud has been as good a guide as any two-year-old event to the Prix du Jockey-Club in recent years. Polaris Flight and Ragmar fought out the finish at Saint-Cloud in 1995 and were the first two again (in reverse order) in the latest Jockey-Club. The 1994 Criterium de Saint-Cloud winner Poliglote was runner-up at Chantilly in 1995. Although France has not been short of high-class middle-distance colts in the 'nineties, the likes of Hernando, Carnegie, Swain and Helissio were nowhere to be seen as two-year-olds, while Suave Dancer and Tikkanen ran just the once at two. Shaka's form puts him among the best of his age seen out in France so far—just behind Majorien, Varxi and Zamindar—but we don't rate them in the same class as the Grand Criterium winner Revoque and it would be no surprise if they are overtaken by later-developing sorts in due course.

		Irish River	Riverman
	Exit To	(ch 1976)	Irish Star
	Nowhere (USA)	Coup de Folie	Halo
Shaka	(b 1988)	(b 1982)	Raise The Standard
(b.c. Mar 30, 1994)		No Pass No Sale	Northfields
	Serafica	(b 1982)	No Disgrace
	(b 1987)	Servia	Le Marmot
		(b 1982)	Secretive

Shaka is from the first crop of Exit To Nowhere, who won the Prix Thomas Bryon at two, had a comparatively disappointing time at three, then bounced back at four to take the Prix Jacques le Marois. Although best at a mile, Exit To Nowhere finished a very creditable fourth in the Arlington Million over a mile and a quarter and could be expected to get middle-distance performers, just as his less stoutly-bred half-brother Machiavellian is doing. The dam Serafica won over seven furlongs at Compiegne on her debut at two but failed to make the first three in six further outings. Shaka is her second foal after the three-year-old stable-companion Surf City (by Groom Dancer), a winner over six furlongs (at two) and eleven furlongs in the Provinces. Serafica is a half-sister to four middle-distance winners in France, the three-year-old Creepshow showing useful form in the latest season for the Rouget stable.

Grandam Servia won twice at around a mile and a half in France; she is a half-sister (out of the once-raced Secretive) to Secret Form, winner of the Prix de l'Opera and runner-up in the Poule d'Essai des Pouliches, Prix Saint-Alary and Prix de Diane in 1986.

Shaka, who cost 150,000 francs as a foal and 290,000 francs as a yearling, remains open to improvement. A testing mile and a quarter posed him no real problem at Saint-Cloud and he seems certain to stay a mile and a half. He acts on soft going and has yet to race on top-of-the-ground, indeed his trainer is of the opinion that he needs some cut. *J-C. Rouget, France*

SHAKEN UP   2 b.c. (Feb 9) Kendor (FR) 122 – Oshawa 97 (Alzao (USA) 117)   54
[1996 6g 6m 7g 8m⁶ Oct 17] 5,000Y, 9,200 2-y-o: strong, good-topped colt: has scope: second foal: half-brother to Danish 3-y-o 7f and 8.5f winner Canadian Dream (by Marju): dam 10.2f to 16.5f winner: modest form in maiden events: off course over 2 months before final start: should stay 1¼m. *Mrs D. Haine*

SHAKE THE YOKE   3 b.f. Caerleon (USA) 132 – Bermuda Classic 98   122
(Double Form 130) [1995 110: 7g⁴ 6.5g 8d* 8d² 1996 8m* 8g² 8m* 8m³ 9f²
Oct 5]
Paris-Turf cannot have had to ponder long on their 'meilleure impression' from the Prix de la Grotte at Longchamp in April. For a start, they had just the four options: the Marcel Boussac first and second, Miss Tahiti and Shake The Yoke, and the Prix de Reservoirs first and second, Occupandiste and Raisonable. Then, although the betting had the quartet closely matched, the race saw Shake The Yoke bolt in by ten lengths. Unusually for the time of year, this was not a result exaggerated by soft ground. The Grotte is the principal trial for the Poule d'Essai des Pouliches, for which, in a nine-runner race, Shake The Yoke was sent off at 3/5. Seventeen of the twenty-four journalists polled in the *Paris-Turf* selected her as the likely winner; five of the remainder had her as their next best. Forty-eight hours later, Shake The Yoke had the 'meilleure impression' as well, but she had not won the race. Not much went right for her. The pace was a steady one with Shake The Yoke held up, pulling hard; entering the straight she was boxed in in mid-division and got a hefty bump; switched to the outside one and a half furlongs out with about three and a half lengths to make up, Shake The Yoke put in good work in pursuit of Ta Rib but was three quarters of a length too late. When the season came to a close, it was as clear as it had been at the time—Shake The Yoke was the best horse in the Poule d'Essai des Pouliches.

The rest of Shake The Yoke's season consisted of three races and she ran well in them all. In the Coronation Stakes at Royal Ascot it was to justify even-money favouritism, turning the tables on Ta Rib in the process. Last Second and Dance Design got the better of Ta Rib as well, but Shake The

Coronation Stakes, Royal Ascot—
Shake The Yoke wears down Dance Design (rails) and holds off Last Second (right)

Yoke's jockey (Peslier replacing Boeuf, as he was about to do on Helissio) could afford to take things cosily as Last Second finished strongly to go down by a neck. That Shake The Yoke was capable of better than that bare result suggested was confirmed after a break of nearly three months, in which time she had been sold by Serge Brunswick to American owner B. Wayne Hughes. This presaged a trip across the water but first came what was effectively the French milers' championship, in the Prix du Moulin de Longchamp. There was no doubt about winner Ashkalani's status, but, on the day, Shake The Yoke looked unlucky to be beaten a short head for second by Spinning World. It was a strongly-run contest this time, but up the straight Shake The Yoke's race unfolded in much the same manner as in the Pouliches; switched, bumped and unbalanced, she found her stride only in the final furlong. Finally, while European eyes were glued to events at Longchamp and Newmarket on the first weekend in October, France's top filly over a mile was making her debut in the United States. Mr B. Wayne Hughes again had to do without a win from her but Shake The Yoke's form in going down by a half length to Memories of Silver in the Queen Elizabeth II Challenge Cup at Keeneland was right up with her best.

Shake The Yoke (b.f. 1993)	Caerleon (USA) (b 1980)	Nijinsky (b 1967)	Northern Dancer
			Flaming Page
		Foreseer (b or br 1969)	Round Table
			Regal Gleam
	Bermuda Classic (b 1983)	Double Form (b 1975)	Habitat
			Fanghorn
		Minnie Tudor (b 1976)	Tudor Melody
			Tiny Toque

B. Wayne Hughes's "Shake The Yoke"

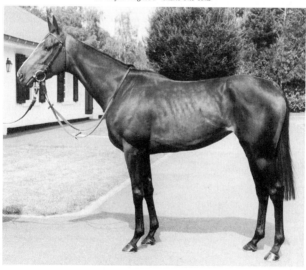

Shake The Yoke stays nine furlongs and acts on firm and dead going, not having raced on anything softer. She is a small, lightly-made filly, a keen walker in the preliminaries, and perhaps that lack of physique helps explain why she made 400,000 francs when sent to Deauville as a yearling. That was well below average for a Caerleon filly despite Shake The Yoke having a strong selling point in her half-sister the very smart sprinter Tropical (by Green Desert). Interestingly, the following year a brother to Tropical came on the market and made only 200,000 francs. Called Shadoof, he is in training with Willie Muir, but did not race in 1996. The dam Bermuda Classic has three other foals of racing age, none winners. Trained by Paddy Mullins, she was a useful sprinter/miler whose two wins both came at two years, in the Railway Stakes and Curragh Stakes. Grandam Minnie Tudor won over six furlongs and a mile in Ireland, and her dam Tiny Toque was a half-sister to Lingfield Oaks Trial winner Javata and Fred Darling winner Rotisserie. *E. Lellouche, France*

SHAKIYR (FR) 5 gr.g. Lashkari 128 – Shakamiyn (Nishapour (FR) 125) [1995 64, a69: a11g* a12g⁶ a12g* a12g* a14.8g⁴ 12.3m² 12g 11.9g 13.9g 12m a12g² 1996 a14.8g³ 14.8g² a16.2g* a12g⁶ 18s 16.2m⁶ 17.1g⁶ 14d⁵ a14.8g⁶ 15.9m³ 15.8g⁴ 15.9d⁴ 14s 14.6g⁶ 14.1s 15.1s³ a16g⁶ Nov 18] workmanlike gelding: fair handicapper on the all-weather: won at Wolverhampton in January: only modest on turf: stays 16.2f well: acts on good to firm and soft ground, best form on fibresand: held up: often soon off bridle. *R. Hollinshead* — 54 a72

SHALAAL (USA) 2 b.c. (Mar 15) Sheikh Albadou 128 – One Fine Day (USA) (Quadratic (USA)) [1996 7g⁶ 7.1m⁵ 7m Oct 1] $60,000F, 62,000Y: big, useful-looking colt with plenty of scope: has a rather round action: fifth foal: half-brother to 3 winners abroad, including French winner at up to 7.5f (including 6f listed race at 2 yrs) Clever Day (by Clever Trick): dam, won in USA, daughter of CCA Oaks winner Missile Belle: fair form in maidens at Kempton and Sandown: 50/1, again never dangerous when seventeenth of 23 in falsely-run valuable sales event at Newmarket final start: probably capable of better. *E. A. L. Dunlop* — 76 p

SHALATEENO 3 b.f. Teenoso (USA) 135 – Shalati (FR) (High Line 125) [1995 NR 1996 7d 10.2g⁴ 10m 12.1d⁶ 17.2g⁴ 12.5f² 10g⁶ 12.1m 8g⁶ 10g³ 10.2g* 10.5m² 12m Sep 25] sturdy filly: fourth reported foal: half-sister to 10.8f winner Shalholme (by Fools Holme): dam French 1m winner: fair handicapper: trained by M. Channon first 8 starts: dictated pace when winning at Chepstow in August: best efforts at around 1¼m: acts on firm and dead ground: front runner. *B. R. Millman* — 70

SHALL WE GO (IRE) 2 b.f. (Apr 1) Shalford (IRE) 124§ – Grapette (Nebbiolo 125) [1996 6g 5.7m 6m⁵ 7f 7m* 7g* 7g 7m⁶ Oct 4] IR 4,500Y: lengthy filly: closely related to a winner in Hong Kong by Thatching, and half-sister to one-time useful sprinter Gorinsky (by Gorytus) and a winner in Italy by Taufan: dam Irish 1¼m and hurdles winner: modest performer: successful in August in seller at Newmarket and nursery (by short head) at Epsom: sold 9,000 gns Newmarket Autumn Sales: stays 7f: game: sent to Saudi Arabia. *R. Hannon* — 63

SHALSTAYHOLY (IRE) 2 ch.f. (May 7) Shalford (IRE) 124§ – Saintly Guest (What A Guest 119) [1996 5.1m 6.9d⁴ 7g 6v⁴ Nov 11] 11,000Y: closely related to 3-y-o Arch Angel (by Archway), 6f and 7f winner at 2 yrs, and half-sister to fairly useful sprinter Benzoe (by Taufan) and 8.5f winner King's Guest (by Tender King): dam, lightly raced in France, from family of Stanford Lad: modest form when fourth in auction events at Folkestone: stays 7f: acts on heavy ground. *G. L. Moore* — 60

SHALTA CHIEF 4 b.g. Be My Chief (USA) 122 – Shalta (FR) (Targowice (USA) 130) [1995 NR 1996 7.5f⁶ 8.5m⁵ 10.3d⁶ 8f Oct 8] workmanlike gelding: probably of little account. *E. H. Owen jun* — –

SHAMADARA (IRE) 3 b.f. Kahyasi 130 – Shamarzana (Darshaan 133) [1995 NR 1996 11s² 10g* 12m* 12m² 11.9m⁴ 12m Sep 15] good-topped filly: second foal: half-sister to 1995 3-y-o French 13f winner (reportedly looked like winning 15f Group 2 event when going lame) Shamardar (by Green Desert): dam, twice-raced, sister to Sharamana (rated 110p, Prix Minerve) and half-sister to Shergar (rated 140) and Shernazar (rated 131): smart French filly: won minor event at Evry and Prix de Malleret at Saint-Cloud (by 3 lengths from Leonila) in June: short-head second of 6 to Dance Design in Irish Oaks at the Curragh, having led 1f out: below form in — 114

steadily-run Yorkshire Oaks (held up last and never threatening) and in Prix Vermeille at Longchamp (soon off bit when tempo increased) last 2 starts: suited by good test of stamina at 1½m, and likely to stay further: probably acts on good to firm and soft ground. *A. de Royer-Dupre, France*

SHAMAND (USA) 3 br.g. Minshaanshu Amad (USA) 91§ – Rose And Betty (USA) (Dare To Command (USA)) [1995 –: 7f 7.1g 7m 10d 1996 12s 12.5g³ 12m a12g³ 17.2g a14.8g 16f³ 14.1f Jul 6] robust gelding: best effort when third of 11 in poor seller at Wolverhampton in May on fourth start: sold 5,200 gns Newmarket July Sales: looked reluctant in blinkers fifth 3-y-o start: not one to trust: sent to Germany. *B. J. Meehan* — 50 §

SHAMANIC 4 b.c. Fairy King (USA) – Annie Albright (USA) (Verbatim (USA)) [1995 97: 6m* 6g 6m 7.3g 7f⁶ 5m 6m² 6g⁶ 6m 1996 6m 6m 6m⁴ 7g³ 6f 6m 7.3m⁶ 6m 6m Sep 21] smallish, useful-looking colt: fairly useful handicapper: not at best in 1996: stays 7f: has raced only on a sound surface: none too consistent. *R. Hannon* — 89

SHAMBO 9 b.h. Lafontaine (USA) 117 – Lucky Appeal 36 (Star Appeal 133) [1995 113: 12g³ 13.4m² 13.9g³ 1996 13.4g May 9] strong, attractive horse: unimpressive mover: smart performer who held his form remarkably well from 4 yrs to 8 yrs: ran as though in need of race in Ormonde Stakes at Chester on only 9-y-o start: effective at 1½m and stayed 2m: had useful form on soft ground, but better form on firm and dead: was held up: reportedly retired. *C. E. Brittain* — –

SHAMIKH 2 b.c. (Feb 14) Unfuwain (USA) 131 – Narjis (USA) 87 (Blushing Groom (FR) 131) [1996 7m* Jun 20] well-made colt: fifth foal: brother to 1994 May Hill Stakes winner Mamlakah and closely related to 1992 2-y-o 5f winner Tahasun (by Shareef Dancer): dam, 2-y-o 5f winner, out of smart 6f/7f stakes winner Mashteen: 8/1, won 12-runner Chesham Stakes at Ascot by a length from State Fair, held up going well, quickening ahead after 2f out then running green late on: looked a very useful colt in the making, but wasn't seen out again. *Saeed bin Suroor* — 96 +

SHAMOKIN 4 b.g. Green Desert (USA) 127 – Shajan (Kris 135) [1995 –: 8m –
1996 8m⁶ 8m⁵ 8.3m⁵ 12g 10.1m a8g Nov 4] workmanlike gelding: no worthwhile
form. *F. Watson*

SHAMROCK FAIR (IRE) 4 ch.f. Shavian 125 – Fair Country 89 (Town And 71
Country 124) [1995 65: 6g⁴ 8f⁵ 1996 8m⁵ 7.6d 8m a7g Nov 7] compact filly: good
mover: fair performer: best 4-y-o effort on reappearance: should stay at least 1m: acts
on firm ground: often early to post. *Lord Huntingdon*

SHANALADEE 3 b.c. Darshaan 133 – Sahara Baladee (USA) 79 (Shadeed 102
(USA) 135) [1995 NR 1996 10m* 10.3m⁴ 14g⁶ Aug 24] rather unfurnished colt: unimpressive mover: second foal: half-brother to a winner in Sweden by Alzao: dam
(maiden) would have stayed beyond 1m: won maiden at Sandown in June: useful
form when 4½ lengths fourth of 8 to Prince of Andros in well-contested minor event
at Chester: well beaten in listed race at Goodwood final start: sold 16,000 gns
Newmarket Autumn Sales: should stay 1½m: sent to Saudi Arabia. *M. R. Stoute*

SHANDANA 2 b.f. (Apr 25) Merdon Melody 98 – Thabeh 57 (Shareef Dancer 45
(USA) 135) [1996 5m⁴ a6g² 7f a6g⁴ 6g⁴ a6g⁵ 8f Sep 10] 3,000Y: unfurnished filly:
third foal: dam poor maiden: poor form: sold 2,800 gns Doncaster October Sales:
stays 6f: visored fifth and final starts. *P. C. Haslam*

SHANGHAI GIRL 3 b.f. Distant Relative 128 – Come On Rosi 77 (Valiyar 129) 102
[1995 NR 1996 a8g⁴ 6m* 6m² 6f⁶ 5m 7d 6m⁶ 5d⁵ 5g* 6s⁶ Nov 9] lengthy, angular
filly: second foal: sister to smart 4-y-o 7f/1m performer Bin Rosie: dam 6f winner:
last of 4 when odds on for median auction maiden at Lingfield (equitrack) on debut:
won similar event at Redcar in May: improved efforts last 2 starts, winning strongly-
run rated stakes at Doncaster in October in good style: bred to stay 1m but best at
sprint distances: visored last 6 outings: carries head high, and found nothing under
pressure on fourth start. *D. R. Loder*

SHANGHAI LIL 4 b.f. Petong 126 – Toccata (USA) 64 (Mr Leader (USA)) 32
[1995 –, a42: a6g* a6g 7m 6f 8m 8.3m 1996 a8g⁵ a6g⁶ a8.5g² 8.2m 8m⁶ 8.1f 8.2g a49
a8g* a10g³ Dec 20] smallish filly: poor performer: won handicap at Lingfield in
December: stays 1¼m: used to act on good to firm and dead ground, and all-weather:
tried blinkered, below form. *M. J. Fetherston-Godley*

SHANOORA (IRE) 3 gr.f. Don't Forget Me 127 – Shalara (Dancer's Image –
(USA)) [1995 53: 5d⁵ a5g* a6g⁵ 6.1g³ 8m 7.5d 8g a8.5g⁶ a7g⁶ a7g⁴ a7g⁵ a6g 1996
a7g a8g⁵ a12g⁵ a6g⁶ a7g a7g Jul 11] lengthy filly: plater: well beaten in 1996: stays
7f, not 1½m: acts on all-weather surfaces: often blinkered/visored. *Mrs N. Macauley*

SHANTARSKIE (IRE) 2 b.c. (Apr 10) Mujadil (USA) 119 – Bay Supreme 65 p
(Martinmas 128) [1996 6m⁴ Sep 19] IR 11,000F, IR 5,000Y, 26,000 2-y-o: half-
brother to several winners, including Pesidanamich (6f at 2 yrs and 7f, by Mummy's
Treasure) and one in Germany (including at 9f) by The Noble Player: dam unraced:
4/1, 6¼ lengths fourth of 10 to Caution in maiden auction at Ayr, chasing leaders and
keeping on: will improve: sent to UAE. *C. F. Wall*

SHANTOU (USA) 3 b.c. Alleged (USA) 138 – Shaima (USA) 110 (Shareef 124
Dancer (USA) 135) [1995 NR 1996 8m³ 10.3g² 10d* 12m³ 12f³ 11.9g² 11.6d*
14.6m* 12s* 12g⁴ Oct 26]
        'Squiggle horse wins classic'—that was one headline that could have
appeared after Shantou's triumph in the St Leger. The ever-reliable Jockey
Club whip instruction H9 came to the rescue, of course, but the squiggle issue
naturally turned more heads at *Timeform*. Just four weeks later, the squiggled
seven-year-old Set The Fashion won the Pivovar Pardubice St Leger to cause
additional anguish! Daily raceratings have been produced by *Timeform*
throughout its fifty-year history but, unfortunately, it has not been possible to
establish how many precedents, if any, there are to Shantou's, for us, decidedly
contrary achievement. Annual ratings are available, though, and research into
some celebrated/infamous squiggle horses for a chapter in a forthcoming
anniversary publication revealed that only one major classic winner ended its
classic year with the § symbol. This was the 1952 French Derby winner Auriban. A champion 'so far as innate ability goes', Auriban also had temperamental shortcomings, the most obvious of which was a tendency to act like 'a

Pertemps St Leger, Doncaster—Shantou (left) and Dushyantor dominate the finish; Samraan (rails) is third, Mons fourth and St Mawes (wide) fifth

holy terror' at the starting gate. He was an impressive winner of the Prix du Jockey-Club after being left at least ten lengths, facing the wrong way, at the start. Here, however, is how *Racehorses of 1952* described another of his characterful displays:

'If this superlative performance in the French Derby displayed the best in Auriban, the Grand Prix de Paris showed the worst in him. His behaviour both at the start and in the race was execrable. It was a sweltering hot day and the start was delayed by one thing and another, so that when finally the runners were called upon to line up Auriban was, in Quintin Gilbey's graphic words, "all of a wash and hopping mad." He jumped and bounded this way and that, did his best to knock Charlie Smirke off Indian Hemp, and generally played the very devil. Eventually, sandwiched between two other horses he came in the right way, and presto! the tapes went up and he was away. That however, was only the beginning! All the way Auriban fought for his head and refused to settle down, so that before they reached the straight Johnstone decided it would be better to let him get on with it. It didn't take Auriban long to race to the head of affairs after rounding the bend, but immediately he had done so he made a dive for the rails which put the whole field in a heap. Auriban was still galloping in headstrong fashion, and he paid the penalty. His antics had by now exhausted him, he was passed by Orfeo (who had missed the bumping at the turn) and it was all Johnstone could do to get Auriban to hang on to second place, beaten 2 lengths.

Auriban didn't run again. An ambitious programme had been mapped out for him, but, quite understandably, this was shelved. There is no doubt that he is a horse of really exceptional ability, and a grand looking individual to boot—but what an obstinate and obstreperous rascal he can be on the racecourse!'

Shantou wasn't that bad! The behaviour of racehorses nowadays in the preliminaries seems to have improved dramatically and Shantou shows no particular obstreperousness, looking edgy and a bit of a character on occasions but nothing like the character apparently seen at home, where he receives very individual treatment and his regular rider has been 'dumped on numerous occasions'. Shantou's misdemeanours came when racing, more specifically when losing two races in midsummer which on form, before and after, he clearly should have won. Lots of horses do that, but Shantou looked unwilling. In a five-runner listed race at Haydock in July, he moved up to tackle the pacesetter three furlongs out but looked reluctant to go past, doing so eventually but only when another of the runners, Royal Court, had gone clear. Suspicions had already been raised in the King Edward VII Stakes at Royal Ascot on his previous start when he had dropped to the rear half a mile out, got on terms again in the final furlong but challenged strongly enough only for third, carrying his head rather to one side. He got the benefit of the doubt on that occasion for two reasons, firm ground, and a hard race on his previous race thirteen days earlier. The latter excuse did not appear to hold much sway with Shantou's connections as they followed the thirteen-day rest with one of just fifteen.

Shantou was sent off 9/4 favourite at Royal Ascot and 7/4 favourite at Haydock. He had had four races before that and would not have started at anything like such short odds judged on what he showed in three of them. These were his first three appearances, all in maidens, a good one in the Wood Ditton at Newmarket to get things underway followed by another placed effort at Chester and then a three-quarters-of-a-length success at 5/4-on over Rocky Oasis at Sandown. Shantou had been under vigorous hands and heels to lead inside the final furlong for that victory. Hard, then, to envisage him making much of a show in the Derby eleven days later. In the run-up to the race, Sheikh Mohammed's only runner was available at 50/1. Eighteen defeats for the maroon and white in the Derby duly became nineteen, but Shantou confounded most expectations for him by becoming only the third Sheikh Mohammed representative to reach the frame. He joined King's Theatre and Tamure in that surprisingly elite club by being beaten only two and a half lengths in third, tracking Shaamit in mid-division into the straight, left for dead by that rival three furlongs out but sticking to his guns well thereafter in company with Dushyantor.

Dushyantor was one of ten opponents for Shantou in the Pertemps St Leger. He had won the Great Voltigeur at York in August and started a clear favourite at Doncaster at 2/1, the others at shorter odds than 10/1 being Volti-

Gran Premio Del Jockey-Club, Milan—Shantou goes from strength to strength; Sacrament and Strategic Choice chase him home this time; Coral Reef (rails) finished sixth

Sheikh Mohammed's "Shantou"

geur runner-up Mons, the Dermot Weld-trained Queen's Vase winner Gordi, Gordon Stakes winner St Mawes and Shantou. Shantou was an 8/1-chance. He had been in action during Ebor week as well, but at Windsor not York, and in a conditions stakes rather than a pattern event. This time, however, he had successfully dealt with inferior opposition in something approaching the style suggested by his Derby form, beating Double Leaf by three and a half lengths. In the St Leger three weeks later, Mons's attempt to make all came to nothing approaching the three-furlong marker, with Gordi dropping quickly to the rear and St Mawes making only a little headway in the opposite direction. Dushyantor looked odds on: Pat Eddery had him restrained on the heels of the leaders from three furlongs out until two furlongs out and then asked for his effort. It is misguided to state that Dushyantor did not stay: he drew four lengths clear of the rest. Shantou, though, stayed on even better. Rowed along in fifth and having to be switched when Dushyantor went by, Shantou mounted a steady challenge, looked to be getting the worse of the battle but then pulled out all the stops to get up by a neck. As we said in the essay on Dushyantor, Dettori and Eddery were excellent. Forget what the stewards had to say. The other major story of the St Leger was that it provided a first British classic victory for Sheikh Mohammed's principal trainer John Gosden. The squiggle was removed from Shantou. He had been asked to dig deep to come out on top, and did so, a key factor surely being that he had the unstoppable Dettori in the saddle. Dettori had bided his time and made up his mind for him, succeeding where Mick Kinane had failed at Royal Ascot, Pat Eddery at Haydock. Shantou takes some knowing. A close eye was obviously going to be kept on him afterwards, but anyone hoping for a return to Mr Hyde from Dr Jekyll would have been disappointed. Shantou had no problems justifying favouritism in the Gran Premio Del Jockey-Club at Milan in October. The form he showed to beat Sacrament and Strategic Choice by three lengths and two and a half was at least as good as that of the St Leger, and Shantou all but repeated it again when a five lengths fourth of fourteen to Pilsudski in the Breeders' Cup Turf at Woodbine.

		Hoist The Flag (b 1968)	Tom Rolfe
			Wavy Navy
	Alleged (USA) (b 1974)	Princess Pout (b 1966)	Prince John
			Determined Lady
Shantou (USA) (b.c. 1993)		Shareef Dancer (b 1980)	Northern Dancer
			Sweet Alliance
	Shaima (USA) (b 1988)	Oh So Sharp (ch 1982)	Kris
			Oh So Fair

A small, quite attractive colt, Shantou has a powerful, round action and tends to carry his head rather high. Effective at a mile and a half, he showed no sign of stopping when the post came in the St Leger. He acts on good to firm ground and soft. Shantou's St Leger ties in neatly with Sheikh Mohammed's first victory in the race, because his grandam is the 1985 fillies' triple crown winner Oh So Sharp. At the start of the latest season, Oh So Sharp's son Sacho looked the classic prospect for the Gosden/Sheikh Mohammed team and Shantou had not been heard of—he had been a wobbler in his early days. In the event, it was Sacho's classic hopes that were scuppered by injury, but Oh So Sharp had already had a fair measure of success at stud with the Prix Saint-Alary winner Rosefinch and two useful performers in Felitza and Shantou's dam Shaima. Winner of the Radley Stakes at Newbury as a two-year-old, Shaima took another listed race at York the following September over nine furlongs and the Grade 2 Long Island Handicap at Belmont Park over a mile and a half on her final start for Luca Cumani. Two unplaced races in the United States brought her racing career to a close, since when she has produced Shantou, the unraced Mr Prospector filly Shimna and a 1995 colt by Nashwan. She has laid out her credentials as a broodmare at the first opportunity. Those of Shantou's sire are long established. He is a strong influence for class and stamina, so it is no surprise that Alleged should sire a winner of the St Leger, the only race in which he himself was beaten. *J. H. M. Gosden*

SHARAF (IRE)   3 b.c. Sadler's Wells (USA) 132 – Marie de Flandre (FR) 109   **87 d**
(Crystal Palace (FR) 132) [1995 83p: 8g 9g⁵ 8.1s² 1996 11.8s² 12m* 14d³ 16.4g⁴ 14f 11.9m⁴ 13.3m 14m⁴ 16.2d 16s Oct 24] lengthy, unfurnished colt: unimpressive walker: fairly useful performer at best: won maiden at Folkestone in April: sold out of J. Dunlop's stable 44,000 gns Newmarket July Sales after fourth start: mostly well below form for new stable: stays 2m: acts on good to firm and soft ground: tried blinkered, no improvement: sometimes carries head high and goes in snatches: usually front runner/races prominently. *W. R. Muir*

SHARAF KABEER   3 ch.c. Machiavellian (USA) 123 – Sheroog (USA) 77   **110**
(Shareef Dancer (USA) 135) [1995 NR 1996 10d² 12g* 12m 14g* 14.6m 12m³ Oct 4] tall, rather angular colt: impresses in appearance: fluent mover: first foal: dam, 7f winner who probably stayed 1¼m, daughter of good racemare and outstanding broodmare Fall Aspen, dam of numerous pattern/graded winners: smart performer: won maiden at Kempton in June and listed race at Goodwood (by 2½ lengths from Masehaab) in August: not disgraced when seventh in St Leger at Doncaster: ran well when 5½ lengths third of 4 to Busy Flight in listed event at Newmarket final start: stays 1¾m: yet to race on extremes of going. *Saeed bin Suroor*

SHARAZAMATAZ   2 b.f. (Mar 1) Shareef Dancer (USA) 135 – Phylae (Habitat   **49 ?**
134) [1996 5.1m 6g⁵ 6.9m⁶ 7f² 6d Aug 12] 7,500Y: fourth foal: half-sister to middle-distance winner Phylian (by Glint of Gold): dam poor maiden, from family of Upper Nile and champion US grass filly De La Rose: best effort when second in seller at

Yarmouth (claimed out of W. Haggas' stable £6,000): well out of handicap and unsuited by trip in nursery final outing: will be suited by 1m+. *K. T. Ivory*

SHARE DELIGHT (IRE) 2 b.c. (Feb 19) Common Grounds 118 – Dorado   68
Llave (USA) (Well Decorated (USA)) [1996 6m 6d⁶ a6g² a6g⁶ Dec 27] 50,000Y:
neat colt: second foal: dam out of sister to dam of Sure Blade: fair form in maidens:
will stay 7f: acts on dead ground and equitrack, ran poorly on fibresand. *B. W. Hills*

SHARED RISK 4 ch.g. Risk Me (FR) 127 – Late Idea 78 (Tumble Wind (USA))   –
[1995 –, a59: a6g a7g² 8f a8g a12g⁴ a11g² a11g² a16g 10d a12g 1996 a8g Sep 9] tall,
leggy gelding: modest performer at best: showed nil on belated reappearance (for
new yard): stays 1½m: acts on fibresand: tried blinkered. *J. Norton*

SHAREEF ALLAH 2 b.f. (May 25) Shareef Dancer (USA) 135 – Elegant Rain-   73 ?
bow 99 (Formidable (USA) 125) [1996 7.5g⁴ 10v⁵ 9s² Dec 26] IR 7,000Y: third live
foal: half-sister to fairly useful 1993 Irish 2-y-o 6f winner Jedwa (by Lead On Time)
and French 3-y-o Luminous Sun (by Shaadi): dam, out of very smart Sun Chariot
winner Duboff, 5f and 6f winner and second in 1m listed race: in frame in newcomers
race at Rome and maiden at Naples: stays 9f. *K. McAuliffe*

SHAREOFTHEACTION 5 gr.g. Sharrood (USA) 124 – Action Belle (Auction   40
Ring (USA) 123) [1995 45: 13.1g² a16g 14.1m a9.4g a9.4g a8g 1996 8g⁴ a7g⁶ 7d 8g
May 19] poor handicapper nowadays, best effort on reappearance: should stay
beyond 1m: acts on all-weather surfaces and good to firm ground, no form on dead:
often blinkered/visored. *Mrs A. M. Naughton*

SHARKASHKA (IRE) 6 ch.m. Shardari 134 – Kashka (USA) (The Minstrel   56
(CAN) 135) [1995 –: 16m⁶ 12d 12.3f 9.9g 1996 12m³ 11f 12.4m⁴ Jul 29] angular
mare: fairly useful hurdler: just a modest handicapper on flat in 1996, best effort on
reappearance: will stay beyond 1½m: blinkered (looked none too keen) final start.
T. D. Easterby

SHARK (IRE) 3 b.c. Tirol 127 – Gay Appeal 76 (Star Appeal 133) [1995 NR   –
1996 8d May 25] IR 28,000F, 46,000Y: fifth foal: half-brother to a winner in Austria
by Petong: dam 1½m winner: tended to hang when down the field in maiden at
Kempton on only start: sold 8,000 gns Newmarket July Sales. *H. Thomson Jones*

SHARKIYAH (IRE) 2 ch.f. (Feb 7) Polish Precedent (USA) 131 – Peace Girl 98   75 p
(Dominion 123) [1996 7g Nov 2] fourth foal: half-sister to useful 6f/7f performer
Matila (by Persian Bold) and a winner in Germany by Cadeaux Genereux, and
closely related to fairly useful 7f winner Mokaafi (by Green Desert): dam Irish
sprinter: 14/1, around 5½ lengths eighth of 23 to Palisade in maiden at Newmarket,
soon travelling well in stand-side group (third home on that side) then not knocked
about: sure to improve. *R. W. Armstrong*

SHARMOOR 4 b.f. Shardari 134 – Linpac North Moor 69 (Moorestyle 137)   –
[1995 –: 14.1m 10g 1996 12.1d 14.1s Apr 12] lightly-made filly: of no account.
Miss L. C. Siddall

SHARP BUT FAIR 2 gr.f. (Mar 31) Sharpo 132 – Fair Minded (Shareef Dancer   48 +
(USA) 135) [1996 5f⁴ 5m⁴ a5g⁴ a5g⁵ Jul 1] lengthy filly: first foal: dam unraced   a42
half-sister to smart performer at up to 1m Radwell: poor form in varied 5f events,
including selling: sold 5,400 gns Newmarket July Sales: not the easiest of rides. *Sir
Mark Prescott*

SHARP COMMAND 3 ch.g. Sharpo 132 – Bluish (USA) (Alleged (USA) 138)   61
[1995 NR 1996 8.2d⁶ 6.9m 12g 10m a8g⁴ 10.5m a8.5g⁵ 12d⁵ a14g⁴ a12g² a14.8g*
a16g Dec 5] 54,000Y: good-topped gelding: has a quick action: first foal: dam won 3
races abroad: modest form at best: sold out of R. Armstrong's stable 8,200 gns
Doncaster July Sales after fifth start, and gelded: won handicap at Wolverhampton in
November: stays 14.8f: acts on fibresand. *P. Eccles*

SHARP CONSUL (IRE) 4 br.g. Exactly Sharp (USA) 121 – Alicia Markova 64   80
(Habat 127) [1995 73: 8g 7.1g⁶ 8.3m³ 7m 7.3d 7s* 8f 1996 9m⁶ 10g 10d* 8g³ 10.2m²
9f 10d* 10v⁶ Aug 27] rangy gelding: poor mover: fair handicapper: won at Leicester
in May and at Windsor (apprentices) in August: stays 1¼m: acts on good to firm and
soft going, below form on both extremes. *H. Candy*

SHARP DEED (IRE) 2 ch.g. (Apr 29) Sharp Victor (USA) 114 – Fabulous Deed   60
(USA) 77 (Shadeed (USA) 135) [1996 7f 6g Oct 21] IR 2,700Y: strong, close-
coupled gelding: first foal: dam placed over 1¼m both starts, half-sister to smart

middle-distance filly Knoosh: slowly away and failed to handle home turn when never dangerous in maiden at Warwick: unsuited by shorter trip in maiden auction at Pontefract 2 weeks later: has scope, and may do better at over 1m+. *P. J. Makin*

SHARPEST 2 ch.c. (Apr 6) Sharpo 132 – Anna Karietta 82 (Precocious 126) 69 [1996 6m 7d 7m⁵ Oct 28] close-coupled colt: has a rounded action: third foal: half-brother to fairly useful 3-y-o 1m winner Frezeliere (by Be My Chief): dam 6f and 7f winner from useful family: made steady improvement in maidens: 33/1, beaten about a length when fifth in steadily-run race at Leicester final start: sold 10,000 gns Newmarket Autumn Sales: stays 7f. *J. L. Dunlop*

SHARP GAZELLE 6 ch.m. Beveled (USA) – Shadha 57 (Shirley Heights 130) 46 [1995 41: a8g⁵ a8.5g³ a8g a8g 11.9m 10.2m³ 9.7f 9.7m⁵ 10f 1996 a11g⁴ a11g* a11g⁴ a49 a14g⁵ 10f⁵ 10d* 10f Sep 4] leggy mare: has a round action: modest performer: won sellers at Southwell in January and Nottingham (23-runner handicap) in August: broke blood vessel over hurdles in May: stays 11f, not 1¾m: acts on dead going and on fibresand, no form on firm ground since 3 yrs: no form on equitrack. *B. Smart*

SHARP HAT 2 ch.c. (Apr 29) Shavian 125 – Madam Trilby (Grundy 137) [1996 81 7m 7f² 6g 6m* 6m* 6m² 6m Oct 17] leggy, lengthy colt: fourth foal: half-brother to a winner in Scandinavia: dam out of half-sister to Circus Plume: fairly useful form: won nurseries at Warwick in August and Doncaster in September: good efforts last 2 runs: sold 22,000 gns Newmarket Autumn Sales: bred to stay beyond 7f, but races keenly and may not do so: free to post fourth to sixth starts, taken quietly and last on final one. *R. Hannon*

SHARP HOLLY (IRE) 4 b.f. Exactly Sharp (USA) 121 – Children's Hour – (Mummy's Pet 125) [1995 50: a7g⁴ a6g² a6g³ 6d⁴ a6g⁵ a6g⁶ 5.1m³ 6f⁴ 5m 5g⁵ 6d 7g a6g 1996 5f a5g a7g 7f⁶ 8f⁵ 8m Aug 13] shallow-girthed filly: no worthwhile form for some time. *J. A. Bennett*

SHARPICAL 4 b.g. Sharpo 132 – Magical Spirit 70 (Top Ville 129) [1995 74: 89 6.9g 8.5m³ 8m⁴ 8m 9m* 10m² 8g² 8g³ 1996 7g³ a10g* 10m³ 10g² 10m* 10g* 10m⁴ 9m Oct 5] leggy, angular gelding: fairly useful performer: won minor event at Lingfield (only all-weather outing) in May and handicaps at Ascot and Leicester (tended to idle) in August: sold 25,000 gns Newmarket Autumn Sales: likely to prove best at up to 1¼m: acts on equitrack, has raced only on a sound surface on turf: rather a headstrong sort, suited by waiting tactics: winning hurdler for N. Henderson in December. *Sir Mark Prescott*

SHARP IMP 6 b.g. Sharpo 132 – Implore 71 (Ile de Bourbon (USA) 133) [1995 62 53: a7g² a7g³ 7g 7m 7f⁶ 6f* 7m⁵ 6m³ 6.9f⁴ 6f* 7f² 7.1m⁵ a6g² a5g² a7g⁴ 1996 a6g* a7g a6g² a6g² a6g⁴ 6f 6g 6m 6f³ 6f* 6.9g 7f⁶ 6m³ 7f* 6f⁵ 5.3f⁴ a7g 7f³ 7m 7m a6g³ Dec 20] workmanlike gelding: modest handicapper: successful at Lingfield in January and at Brighton in June and (minor event) August: effective at 6f and 7f: acts on the all-weather, best turf efforts on a sound surface: nearly always blinkered: tends to hang/edge left under pressure: held up of late: tough. *R. M. Flower*

SHARP MONTY 3 b.g. Mon Tresor 113 – Sharp Anne 74§ (Belfort (FR) 89) 63 [1995 66: 5g 5g⁵ 6g⁴ 5.9f³ 7m² 6.1m 1996 6s 5s⁴ a6g 6d⁶ 6m* 5d² 6f² 5m⁵ 8m⁶ 6d 7f² Sep 10] leggy, good-topped gelding: modest handicapper: won 21-runner seller at Leicester in June: sold 4,500 gns Newmarket Autumn Sales: stays 7f (raced too freely over 1m): acts on firm and dead ground, below form both starts on soft: takes keen hold: sent to Italy. *R. Hollinshead*

SHARP MOVE 4 ch.f. Night Shift (USA) – Judeah 69 (Great Nephew 126) [1995 – NR 1996 7g 7m 5m 6m a7g Nov 29] trained by M. Tompkins at 2 yrs, unraced at 3 yrs: little form in 1996: bred to stay 1m. *Mrs J. Cecil*

SHARP 'N' SHADY 3 b.f. Sharpo 132 – Shadiliya 90 (Red Alert 127) [1995 –: 59 6f 6m a6g 1996 6.9s 7d³ 7.3d 8m 7g⁵ 7g³ Oct 30] heavy-topped filly: modest handicapper: gambled on, best effort on final start: should stay 1m. *C. F. Wall*

SHARP 'N SMART 4 ch.g. Weldnaas (USA) 112 – Scottish Lady (Dunbeath 75 d (USA) 127) [1995 77: 6.9d² a6g² 6.9m 6f* 6m 6f⁴ 7.6d* 7g 8s a8g⁴ 1996 a7g* a6g⁶ 7d 6f 7.3s 6m⁶ 7m 6d² a7g a7g³ Nov 15] workmanlike gelding: fair handicapper: won at Lingfield in January: below form afterwards: stays 7.6f: acts on firm and soft ground and the all-weather: races prominently: inconsistent. *B. Smart*

SHARP PEARL   3 ch.g. Sharpo 132 – Silent Pearl (USA) (Silent Screen (USA))   77
[1995 73: 6m 6d⁵ 6s⁴ 6d 1996 6m 5.1g² 5.3f* 5f 6g 5.1m³ 5m 5.3m⁵ 5f⁴ 5m a5g³ a6g
Nov 26] good-topped, quite attractive gelding: fair handicapper: won at Brighton in
June: best form at around 5f: acts on firm and dead ground, and equitrack: effective
blinkered or not. *J. White*

SHARP POPPET   2 ch.f. (Apr 5) Statoblest 120 – Razor Blade 65 (Sharp Edge   –
123) [1996 6m 6g 6.1m Aug 7] 5,000F, 7,000Y: half-sister to several winners,
including 3-y-o Swedish 1¼m winner By A Whisker (by Keen) and fair sprinter
Keen Edge (by Good Times): dam 2-y-o 5f and 7f winner: no sign of ability in
auction maiden events: pulled up almost immediately after leaving stalls in seller last
outing: sold 1,400 gns Newmarket September Sales. *M. Bell*

SHARP PROGRESS   3 b.c. Inca Chief (USA) – Sharp Venita 84 (Sharp Edge   –
123) [1995 NR 1996 8g 12m⁵ 10m 12m Aug 2] eighth foal: half-brother to useful 7f
and 7.6f winner Sharpalto (by Noalto), 6f and 7f winner Sharp Times (by Faraway
Times) and 4-y-o 1¼m and 11.6f winner Fern's Governor (by Governor General):
dam sprinter: signs of ability but no worthwhile form. *A. P. Jones*

SHARP PROSPECT   6 ch.h. Sharpo 132 – Sabatina (USA) 95 (Verbatim   79
(USA)) [1995 83: 8g* 8g 1996 8s 8.2d⁵ 7.1f 8m 7g Oct 12] big, strong horse: poor
mover: fairly useful handicapper, lightly raced: reportedly chipped a knee second
outing in 1995: went lame when favourite for the Lincoln at Doncaster on reappearance: subsequently left R. Akehurst's stable: best effort for new yard when
respectable seventh of 14 at Haydock third start: stays 1m: acts on firm and soft
ground: normally held up. *V. Soane*

SHARP REBUFF   5 b.h. Reprimand 122 – Kukri (Kris 135) [1995 77: 7s³ 7.1g²   84
8.3g² 7m² 8g* 7g⁵ 7.3d³ 8s a7g 1996 7m⁵ 7s⁴ 8m⁵ 7m² 8m* Jul 10] lengthy horse:
good walker: poor mover: fairly useful handicapper: in good form in 1996, gaining
deserved success at Kempton on final start: probably best at 7f/1m: acts on good to
firm and soft ground, below form on fibresand: consistent. *P. J. Makin*

SHARP RETURN   2 b.c. (Feb 6) Sharpo 132 – Langtry Lady 91 (Pas de Seul   59
133) [1996 5m⁴ 6m 6g 5m 6m⁶ 7.6m 6s³ 6d* 6.1s² a7g³ a6g⁴ Dec 13] 24,000Y:
compact colt: poor mover: first foal: dam effective at 7f and stayed 1¼m: modest
form: won rating-related maiden at Folkestone in October: stays 7f: acts on soft
ground and the all-weather: has been coltish. *M. J. Ryan*

SHARP SENSATION   6 ch.g. Crofthall 110 – Pink Sensation 69 (Sagaro 133)   42
[1995 39: a11g a14.8g⁶ a12g⁵ a11g 15.1f³ 15.1f⁴ 1996 12g 14.1m² 14.1f 15.1f³
15.1g² 15.1m² 13.8m⁵ 16g³ 16d⁴ Aug 23] leggy, workmanlike gelding: poor
handicapper: stays 15f (looked to be outstayed over 2m): acts on fibresand and firm
ground, seemingly not on a soft surface: blinkered (below form) once as 4-y-o.
D. W. Barker

SHARP SHUFFLE (IRE)   3 ch.g. Exactly Sharp (USA) 121 – Style (Homing   76
130) [1995 65: 5.3m⁵ 6m 7m² 10m⁵ 8m² 1996 8m 7.1m³ 8m² 8.5g² 8m² 8m 7g*
8m⁵ 7g³ Oct 25] smallish gelding: unimpressive mover: fair handicapper: won at
Kempton in September: effective at 7f with truly-run race, and stays 1m: has raced
only on good or good to firm ground: sweating (ran well) third 2-y-o start. *R. Hannon*

SHARP STOCK   3 b.c. Tina's Pet 121 – Mrewa (Runnymede 123) [1995 70: 5g²   –
5g⁴ 1996 6s 6m May 13] fair form as 2-y-o: well beaten in 1996. *B. J. Meehan*

SHARP THRILL   5 ch.g. Squill (USA) 122 – Brightelmstone 105 (Prince Regent   –
(FR) 129) [1995 38, a45: a12g² a11g a12g⁶ 12m⁵ a12g³ 1996 a13g⁶ a12g⁶ a12g⁶ Jan
26] close-coupled gelding: poor and inconsistent maiden: tried blinkered/visored.
B. Smart

SHARVIC (IRE)   3 b.g. Sharp Victor (USA) 114 – Binnissima (USA) (Tilt Up   –
(USA)) [1995 NR 1996 6s a6g 5g May 22] 4,000 2-y-o: brother to 1993 Irish
2-y-o 6f winner Viva Victor: dam minor winner in USA: no sign of ability.
Miss M. K. Milligan

SHASHI (IRE)   4 br.f. Shaadi (USA) 126 – Homely Touch 84 (Touching Wood   67
(USA) 127) [1995 79: 5m² 5.3f² 6g⁵ 5m³ 5m³ 5.1h 5g 1996 5m 6m 7g 6g⁴ 6f⁶
5.9f* 5.1m² 5m⁵ 6.1m 7f 7.1s 6m a6g⁶ a6g⁶ a6s² Dec 19] smallish filly: fair
handicapper: won at Carlisle (minor event) in July and Southwell in November: stays

6f: acts on firm ground and fibresand: sometimes blinkered, including when successful: saddle slipped tenth 4-y-o start: has joined Pat Mitchell. *W. W. Haigh*

SHAVINSKY 3 b.c. Shavian 125 – Alteza Real 84 (Mansingh (USA) 120) [1995 NR 1996 8m 8m⁶ 8.1d a8g 6m² 6m 6m² 6g⁶ 5.2m⁵ Sep 17] 5,200Y 2-y-o: lengthy, good-topped colt: half-brother to several winners, including useful 1987 2-y-o sprinter Infanta Real and German middle-distance 7-y-o Anziano (both by Formidable): dam, 5f winner, half-sister to Forzando: fair maiden: clearly best efforts when second at Folkestone in the summer: found little penultimate start: probably a sprinter: may not be entirely trustworthy. *P. Howling* 69

SHAWAF (USA) 2 b.c. (May 28) Mr Prospector (USA) – Shadayid (USA) 122 (Shadeed (USA) 135) [1996 6m³ Jul 27] rather leggy, quite attractive colt: second foal: half-brother to 3-y-o Bint Shadayid (by Nashwan), 6f and 7f winner at 2 yrs and third in 1000 Guineas: dam, winner of 1000 Guineas and non-staying third in Oaks, is half-sister to Irish Oaks winner Alydaress: favourite though very green, 5½ lengths third of 9 to Revoque in maiden at Ascot, chasing leaders running in snatches then keeping on without threatening, not knocked about: to winter in Dubai: will improve. *J. L. Dunlop* 80 p

SHAWANNI 3 gr.f. Shareef Dancer (USA) 135 – Negligent 118 (Ahonoora 122) [1995 95p: 7g* 8d⁵ 1996 8g⁶ May 12] well-made filly: impressive winner of maiden at Yarmouth on debut, but became very agitated before running poorly in Fillies' Mile at Ascot on final start for B. Hills: wintered in Dubai: 3¼ lengths sixth of 9 to Ta Rib in Poule d'Essai des Pouliches at Longchamp, setting steady pace: tongue tied, reared over in paddock and withdrawn (jockey injured) before Newbury listed race June 13: stayed 1¼m. *Saeed bin Suroor* 105

SHAWM 2 b.c. (Mar 28) Alzao (USA) 117 – Flute (USA) 87 (Woodman (USA) 126) [1996 7g³ Oct 30] first foal: dam 7f winner, stayed 1m: 8/1, 6½ lengths third of 17 to Happy Valentine in maiden at Yarmouth improving to chase winner on stand side 2f out, not given hard time when held: sure to do better. *D. R. Loder* 84 p

SHAYA 2 ch.c. (Jan 10) Nashwan (USA) 135 – Gharam (USA) 108 (Green Dancer (USA) 132) [1996 8f² Sep 13] big, lengthy colt: plenty of scope: third foal: brother to 3-y-o 10.5f winner Naazeq: dam, 6f winner at 2 yrs, third in Poule d'Essai des Pouliches and stayed 1½m: 11/4 from 11/10 and looking really well, 1¼ lengths second of 10 to Cape Cross in maiden at Doncaster, running green 2f out, taking time to get hang of things then running on strongly: needed experience quite considerably, and is sure to improve and win races over middle distances: to winter in Dubai. *Major W. R. Hern* 86 P

SHAYIM (USA) 4 b. or br.c. Storm Cat (USA) – Bundler (USA) (Raise A Native) [1995 82: 7.5m* 6g⁵ 8.5m² 10m 8.1g 1996 8m 8m 7.1m⁴ 7m Jun 21] compact colt: unimpressive mover: just fair form in handicaps in 1996 for new stable: needs further than 6f, but possibly does not stay 1¼m: yet to race on a soft surface: blinkered (well beaten) final 3-y-o start. *R. Hannon* 71

SHAYNES DOMAIN 5 b.g. Dominion 123 – Glen Na Smole 86 (Ballymore 123) [1995 48: a7g 9g 7m⁴ 8f 7g² 7m 7f 8f a7g 1996 a7g a8g a6g⁵ a6g 6m 10m 7d³ 6m 7g Jun 11] lengthy gelding: carries condition: poor handicapper: stays 7f: acts on fibresand and on good to firm and dead ground: often blinkered: inconsistent. *R. M. Flower* 45

SHEDANSAR (IRE) 4 b.g. In The Wings 128 – Evening Kiss (Kris 135) [1995 –: 8.3m a8g 1996 a12g a13g a13g a13g a16g⁶ 11.5m a11g a8g a8g Dec 27] workmanlike, angular gelding: no worthwhile form: left G. L. Moore after fifth 4-y-o outing: blinkered last 3 starts. *R. C. Spicer* –

SHEEBA 2 ch.f. (May 3) Meqdaam (USA) – Normanby Damsel 55 (High Line 125) [1996 a8.5g Oct 19] second reported living foal: dam poor maiden: 50/1 and ridden by 7-lb claimer, tailed off in seller at Wolverhampton. *Miss A. E. Embiricos* –

SHEEMORE (IRE) 3 b.g. Don't Forget Me 127 – Curie Abu (Crofter (USA) 124) [1995 –: 6m 7g 6g a10g 1996 a8.5g 10g⁵ Apr 10] big, lengthy gelding: has scope: has a round action: first worthwhile form when fifth of 15 in falsely-run handicap at Ripon, always close up: retained by trainer 5,800 gns Doncaster August Sales, then sold 6,100 gns Doncaster November Sales: stays 1¼m: tail swisher. *J. D. Bethell* 46

Hong Kong Jockey Club Trophy (Handicap), Sandown—
Sheer Danzig (rails) and Miss Universal slug it out in a heavy downpour

SHEER DANZIG (IRE)   4 b.c. Roi Danzig (USA) – Sheer Audacity (Troy 137)   105
[1995 91: a8g* 10m³ 7.9g 8m 7.1m 8m* 7.9g² 8g⁵ 10.4m* 10d 1996 10g 9s 10m³
10g* 10m³ 11.9m² 11.1m⁵ 12g² 12s Nov 9] tall, rangy colt: impresses in appearance:
useful handicapper: got up final strides to win £51,700 Hong Kong Jockey Club
Trophy at Sandown in July: remained in fine form, finishing fifth in September
Stakes at Kempton and 1¼ lengths second to Better Offer in £44,700 handicap at
Ascot: much better at around 1¼m than shorter, and stays 1½m well: best on a sound
surface, also acts on fibresand: held up: consistent. *R. W. Armstrong*

SHEER FACE   2 b.c. (Mar 1) Midyan (USA) 124 – Rock Face 77 (Ballad Rock   85
122) [1996 7.1m⁶ 7m⁵ 7f* 7.3m² 8m* 7m⁴ 8d³ Oct 12] 13,500Y: sturdy, close-
coupled colt: first foal: dam 1¼m to 1¾m winner: fairly useful form: won maiden
auction at Brighton in August and nursery at Bath in September: ran well last 2 starts,
8 lengths third of 5 to High Roller in listed race at Ascot on final one: will stay
beyond 1m: acts on top-of-the-ground and good to soft: reliable. *W. R. Muir*

SHEER FOLLY (USA)   2 ch.c. (Mar 25) Woodman (USA) 126 – Why So Much   88
(USA) (Northern Baby (CAN) 127) [1996 7m* Jun 26] $180,000Y: third foal:
closely related to a winner in USA by Miswaki: dam, won at up to 7f at 2 yrs in USA,
from the family of Grade 1 winner Rockhill Native: 4/1, won 13-runner maiden at
Kempton by 1¾ lengths from Eurolink Excaliber, starting slowly, staying on well to
lead inside last, tending to carry head high: looked sure to improve. *P. F. I. Cole*

SHEER REASON (USA)   2 b.f. (Feb 16) Danzig (USA) – Hiaam (USA) 110   110
(Alydar (USA)) [1996 5g³ 6g* 5.5g³ 7g⁶ 6d* 6.5d² Nov 9] fifth foal: closely related
to useful 11.5f winner Munnaya (stayed 1½m, rated 101, temperament came under
suspicion, by Nijinsky) and half-sister to 2 winners by Shadeed, including Balla
Jidaal (best as sprinter, rated 100): dam, 6f to 1m winner, half-sister to 3 North
American Grade 1 winners from the family of Swain: useful performer: won minor
event at Chantilly in June and (after beaten 3 lengths or so when third of 6 to Ocean
Ridge in Prix Robert Papin at Maisons-Laffitte and sixth of 10 to Shigeru Summit
in Prix du Calvados at Deauville) listed event at Evry (by ¾ length from Heaven's
Command) in October: ¾-length second of 8 to Deadly Dudley in Criterium des
Deux Ans at Evry in November: stays 7f: raced only on good or dead ground.
Mme C. Head, France

892

SHEFFIELD SHARK (IRE)   2 b.c. (Feb 19) Alzao (USA) 117 – Settlement   –
(USA) 75 (Irish River (FR) 131) [1996 8m 8d 7m Oct 17] 17,000Y: third foal: half-
brother to a winner in Sweden by High Estate: dam 10.2f winner: well beaten in maidens and a seller (visored): sold 2,600 gns Newmarket Autumn Sales.
D. W. P. Arbuthnot

SHEHAB (IRE)   3 b.g. Persian Bold 123 – Fenjaan 77 (Trojan Fen 118) [1995 NR   86
1996 8.5f² 10m* 10m 10s Oct 24] workmanlike gelding: third foal: half-brother to a
winner in Dubai (by Doyoun): dam miler from family of Royal Palace: off course 4
months after making all in claimer at Sandown (claimed out of W. Haggas' stable
£18,000) in June by 7 lengths: tailed off for new stable: stays 1¼m. *P. R. Hedger*

SHEILANA (IRE)   3 b.f. Bluebird (USA) 125 – Shadia (USA) 53 (Naskra   51
(USA)) [1995 69: 6m 6.1m³ 6m⁵ 6.1d² 6g 1996 7s 7m 8.3m 10f³ 9.7g 10f 10f⁵ 9.9g
Aug 24] small filly: fair form at best at 2 yrs: showed little in 1996: sold 2,400 gns
Newmarket Autumn Sales: sent to South Korea. *T. G. Mills*

SHEILAS DREAM   3 b.f. Inca Chief (USA) – Windlass (Persian Bold 123)   53
[1995 –: 7g 1996 a7g⁶ a9.4g² a7g 8.5f² Aug 14] modest maiden: second in seller at
Wolverhampton and claimer at Beverley: stays 9.4f: acts on firm going and fibresand: has joined H. S. Howe. *R. Simpson*

SHE KNEW THE RULES (IRE)   6 ch.m. Jamesmead 86 – Falls of Lora 107   –
(Scottish Rifle 127) [1995 NR 1996 a16.2g Apr 13] lightly-made mare: rated 45
when winning 2m seller in 1995: tailed off only 6-y-o start. *F. Jordan*

SHELL GINGER (IRE)   2 ch.f. (Feb 8) Woodman (USA) 126 – Truly Bound   110 p
(USA) (In Reality) [1996 8g³ 7s* 7s* Oct 28] 650,000 francs Y: half-sister to 3
winners, notably listed American sprint winner Houseband (by Pancho Villa): dam,
Grade 2 winner at 2 yrs and 3 yrs, stayed at least 9f and from very good middle-
distance family: won maiden at Gowran Park and 6-runner Bord Gais Killavullan
Stakes at Leopardstown (allowed to set up clear lead in first furlong, in no danger
afterwards, beat Lil's Boy 12 lengths) within 5 days in October: should stay middle
distances: goes well on soft going, yet to race on top-of-the-ground: interesting
prospect. *A. P. O'Brien, Ireland*

SHEMOZZLE (IRE)   3 b.f. Shirley Heights 130 – Reactress (USA) (Sharpen Up   108
127) [1995 71p: 7m* 7m* 1996 11.4g³ 10s² 12m³ 11.9g⁴ 12m* 11.9m Aug 21] leggy
filly: has quick action: useful performer: in frame in Cheshire Oaks at Chester,
Lupe Stakes at Goodwood, Ribblesdale Stakes at Royal Ascot and Lancashire Oaks
(getting poor run) at Haydock: justified favouritism in listed race at Newmarket in
July by 2 lengths from Balalaika: 6¾ lengths seventh of 9 to Key Change in Yorkshire Oaks final outing: stays 1½m: acts on good to firm going and probably on soft:
consistent: sent to USA. *J. H. M. Gosden*

SHENANGO (IRE)   3 b.g. Shernazar 131 – Pipina (USA) 81 (Sir Gaylord) [1995   73 §
65p: a8g² 1996 a9.4g⁴ 10m³ 12m 12.3m 11.9m⁶ 12m Sep 18] angular gelding: fair
maiden at best: well held last 4 starts: should stay further than 1¼m: has looked a
hard ride most starts (turned it in completely on final one) and is one to avoid: sent to
UAE. *G. Wragg*

SHEPHERDS DEAN (IRE)   3 b.f. Tirol 127 – Royal Episode (Royal Match   –
117) [1995 –: 5m a7g a7g 1996 8g 9f⁶ 10g Aug 17] leggy, sparely-made filly: no
worthwhile form. *P. C. Haslam*

SHEPHERDS REST (IRE)   4 b.g. Accordion – Mandy's Last (Krayyan 117)   27
[1995 44?: 10m 10m 10.2f 10.8g⁴ 12f 12.1m⁵ a12g⁵ 1996 a12g³ Apr 24] good-topped
gelding: poor maiden on flat: best effort only start on an easy surface: fair
winning hurdler. *S. Mellor*

SHERATON GIRL   2 b.f. (Feb 28) Mon Tresor 113 – Sara Sprint (Formidable   49 d
(USA) 125) [1996 5g⁵ 5m³ 5m 6m⁴ 5m⁵ a5g⁵ 8f⁵ 7.5m⁴ 8.1m Sep 23] 5,600Y: sturdy
filly: fourth foal: dam Italian 6f (at 2 yrs) and 7f winner, half-sister to very smart 1m/
1¼m performer Radetzky: poor maiden: sold 2,000 gns Doncaster September Sales:
probably stays 7.5f: tends to hang right: blinkered (poor efforts) fifth and sixth starts.
M. Johnston

SHERAZ (IRE)   4 b.c. Persian Bold 123 – Miss Siddons (Cure The Blues (USA))   61 d
[1995 80: 8.3m 10.1m² 10m³ 1996 8s⁶ 12m⁵⁵ 10.3g 12g 7.1d a8g⁶ 7.1d⁵ 10.5g   a68 d
a8g a7g⁶ a8g a10g⁴ a12g⁴ a11g⁶ Dec 27] strong, attractive colt: fluent mover: just a

fair handicapper in 1996: won at Southwell in June: failed to repeat the form: best at 1m to 1¼m: acts on fibresand and good to firm ground, possibly unsuited by soft: has had tongue tied. *N. Tinkler*

SHERIFF 5 b.g. Midyan (USA) 124 – Daisy Warwick (USA) 91 (Ribot 142) 60 [1995 47+: 12f 11.9m³ 1996 a16g* 14.9g² 16m⁵ a16g⁴ Aug 10] small, close-coupled gelding: bad mover: modest handicapper on flat nowadays: won at Lingfield in February: stays 2m: acts on good to firm and dead ground and on equitrack: blinkered (below form) final 4-y-o start: fairly useful hurdler. *J. W. Hills*

SHERMOOD 3 b.f. Shere Khan – Jalebird Blues (Jalmood (USA) 126) [1995 42 42+: a7g 7f 1996 a7g⁵ 10m 8m 6f⁶ 7g⁴ 8m 7g⁵ 8m³ a10g⁶ 7d³ 8m 7m 7m a6g a8g⁵ a– a7g Dec 31] leggy, lightly-made filly: poor maiden handicapper: left M. Bell's stable after second 3-y-o start: stays 1m: acts on good to firm ground and dead. *K. T. Ivory*

SHERNA (IRE) 3 ch.f. Eurobus – Zulu Hut (Shack (USA) 118) [1995 NR 1996 – 9s⁶ 12m 10m Aug 7] sixth foal: dam of no account: well beaten in maidens and claimer. *I. A. Balding*

SHEROOT 4 b.c. Cigar 68 – Act of Treason 80 (Absalom 128) [1995 –: 7g 6g 11d – 7m 7m 1996 a8.5g a7g 8.1g 9.2s 10d⁵ May 8] dipped-backed colt: of little account. *D. Moffatt*

SHERPAS (IRE) 3 b.c. Shirley Heights 130 – Ala Mahlik 116 (Ahonoora 122) 97 + [1995 NR 1996 12m* 16.2m Jun 19] good-bodied, angular, attractive colt: type to carry condition: fourth known foal: half brother to 12.5f winner Storm Crossing and French 1m winner Mali (both by Storm Bird): dam, 2-y-o 6f winner who later stayed 10.5f, sister to Negligent and out-and-out stayer Ala Hounak: won 10-runner maiden at Newmarket in April by head from Sasuru, leading 4f out and staying on strongly despite edging left: again favourite, never travelling well in Queen's Vase at Royal Ascot (got upset in stalls) on only subsequent outing: should be suited by further than 1½m: showed a quick, unimpressive action to post on debut. *H. R. A. Cecil*

SHERZETTO 2 b.f. (Apr 28) Classic Music (USA) – Lake Isle (IRE) (Caerleon 68 (USA) 132) [1996 6m 6f* 6d⁴ a6g Nov 22] smallish, sturdy filly: has a quick action: second foal: sister to 3-y-o 5f to 7f winner Krystal Max: dam, lightly-raced Irish 7f winner, from family of Sadler's Wells: fair form to win maiden at Thirsk in July: sold out of J. Fanshawe's stable 6,700 gns Newmarket Autumn Sales after next start: will stay 7f: acts on firm ground, ran badly on fibresand. *D. W. Chapman*

SHE'S A CRACKER 2 b.f. (Mar 21) Deploy 131 – Red Secret (IRE) 49 (Valiyar – 129) [1996 8m Sep 19] 8,000Y: second foal: half-sister to German 3-y-o Top Express (by Siberian Express), 5f winner at 2 yrs: dam 1½m winner: 50/1, trailed throughout in 15-runner maiden at Yarmouth won by High Roller. *C. A. Dwyer*

SHE SAID NO 4 ch.f. Beveled (USA) – She Said Yes (Local Suitor (USA) 128) – [1995 56: 6m 7g 6g⁵ a8.5g² a10g* 1996 a9.4g a10g 10d⁶ a10g 10m⁵ a10g a10g a10g Dec 30] angular filly: no form in 1996: sold out of Lord Huntingdon's stable 3,200 gns Ascot June Sales after third start: stays 1¼m: acts on all-weather. *A. Moore*

SHE'S A MADAM 5 b.m. Kabour 80 – Mrs Buzby 71 (Abwah 118) [1995 –: – a5g⁴ 1996 a5g 5m a6g a5g Dec 13] sturdy mare: of little account. *L. R. Lloyd-James*

SHE'S A WINNER (IRE) 3 ch.f. Classic Music (USA) – Eyre Square (IRE) 49 (Flash of Steel 120) [1995 NR 1996 8.3d* 8.3s⁵ 9g⁶ 9.2g 8m Jun 21] IR 4,600F: IR 1,000Y: leggy filly: first foal: dam (raced twice at around 1¾m in Ireland) half-sister to Stayers' Hurdle winner Galmoy: made winning debut in weak seller at Hamilton in April, sold out of S. Williams' stable 6,600 gns: well beaten for new yard. *P. Monteith*

SHE'S DAWAN (IRE) 2 b.f. (May 24) Taufan (USA) 119 – Bellinzona – p (Northfields (USA)) [1996 7f Oct 8] 6,500Y resold IR 4,000Y, 25,000 2-y-o: sister to fairly useful 1m/1¼m performer Bellefan and half-sister to several winners, including useful 4-y-o middle-distance performer Maralinga (by Simply Great): dam French 9.5f winner: 20/1, ninth of 13 in maiden at Warwick won by Dragonada, chasing leaders then one pace: likely to do better. *P. Mitchell*

SHE'S ELECTRIC 2 ch.f. (Feb 28) Superlative 118 – What A Looker (USA) – (Raise A Native) [1996 a6g a6g a7g a5g⁶ Dec 31] 500F, 520Y: fourth foal: dam minor winner in USA: no form. *J. J. Bridger*

894

SHE'S MY LOVE   3 ch.f. Most Welcome 131 – Stripanoora (Ahonoora 122)   80
[1995 76: 6.1f* 7m³ 8m⁴ 7g 1996 8m² 9.9m 8f 8m⁵ 8m 7d 7g Oct 19] lengthy, unfurnished filly: fair handicapper: best effort on reappearance: sold 15,000 gns Newmarket
Autumn Sales: bred to be suited by further than 1m, but rather headstrong: winner on
firm ground, well below form only start on a soft surface. *J. E. Banks*

SHE'S SIMPLY GREAT (IRE)   3 b.f. Simply Great (FR) 122 – Petrine (IRE)   54
(Petorius 117) [1995 –: 6m⁴ 6f⁴ 8.3g 1996 11.1g² 11.1g⁴ 10m 8f 8g² 8.1m 10g² 10s⁶
Aug 31] smallish filly: modest maiden handicapper: effective at 1m and probably
stays 11.1f: well beaten only start on soft ground: none too consistent. *J. J. O'Neill*

SHIFT AGAIN (IRE)   4 b.f. Siberian Express (USA) 125 – Pushkinia (FR) 95   63 +
(Pharly (FR) 130) [1995 68: 7g⁵ 7m³ 8m* 8m⁵ 9.9m 7.5m⁶ 8.5s 10.5d⁴ 12.1s³ 1996
10g 12.1d 12g⁵ Jun 12] tall, leggy filly: modest form at best on flat: stays 12.1f: acts
on good to firm and soft ground: best 4-y-o effort when tried in blinkers: won over
hurdles in December: tends to carry head high and best treated with some caution.
S. E. Sherwood

SHIFTING MOON   4 b.g. Night Shift (USA) – Moonscape 87 (Ribero 126)   –
[1995 86: 8m 7.6m⁵ 8m 7.9m³ 8.1m* 8f² 8f² 1996 10s Oct 24] stocky gelding: poor
mover: fairly useful handicapper in 1995 for I. Balding: modest winner over hurdles:
well beaten only flat outing in 1996: should stay beyond 8.1f: acts on firm and dead
ground: tried visored and blinkered. *F. Jordan*

SHIFTING TIME   2 b.f. (Mar 31) Night Shift (USA) – Timely Raise (USA)   70
(Raise A Man (USA)) [1996 6m⁴ 6m 6m² Oct 4] attractive filly: fifth known foal:
half-sister to fairly useful 3-y-o 9f and 1¼m winner Double Bluff (by Sharrood),
useful sprinter Poker Chip (by Bluebird) and 1993 2-y-o 5f winner Double Down
(by Salse): dam, miler successful 6 times in North America, sister to very useful
middle-distance stayer Primitive Rising: showed promise in maidens at Goodwood
and Newbury: well backed when head second of 12 to Bint Albaadiya in similar
event at Lingfield final start: will stay further than 6f. *I. A. Balding*

SHIGERU SUMMIT   2 b.f. (Feb 3) Be My Chief (USA) 122 – Riveryev (USA)   105
(Irish River (FR) 131) [1996 6g² 5.5d* 5.5g⁴ 7g* 8d 6.5d Nov 9] 140,000 francs Y:
close-coupled, workmanlike filly: has a quick action: second foal: half-sister to
Italian 3-y-o Giampeiro Ruocco (by Bluebird), 6f winner at 2 yrs: dam placed at
around 9f in France: won 11-runner minor event at Maisons-Laffitte in July: better
form when around 3 lengths fourth of 6 to Ocean Ride in Prix Robert Papin there
and again when winning 10-runner Prix du Calvados at Deauville in August by 1½
lengths from Dame d'Harvard: towards rear in Prix Marcel Boussac at Longchamp
(held up and never able to mount a challenge) and Criterium des Deux Ans at Evry
last 2 starts: should stay 1m: raced only on good or dead ground. *C. Boutin, France*

SHII-TAKE   2 b.c. (May 3) Deploy 131 – Super Sally 108 (Superlative 118) [1996   91
6m² 7m² 7m* 7d³ Oct 12] 6,200Y, resold 16,000Y: compact colt: has a round action:
second foal: dam, effective at 1m to 1¼m, half-sister to smart Unanimous Vote: fairly
useful form in maidens prior to winning median auction event at Epsom in
September by 3 lengths: ran well when third (kept on gamely) to Andreyev in useful
conditions event at Ascot final outing: will stay 1m: acts on good to firm and good to
soft going: front runner. *R. Akehurst*

SHIKARI'S SON   9 br.g. Kala Shikari 125 – Have Form (Haveroid 122) [1995   83
99: 6m* 7m 7.6m⁵ 7m⁴ 6f³ 6f 7m² 7g⁵ 6m* 7.3m 7m 6g 1996 6f⁶ 6m 7f 6d 6m 6f 6g⁵
6m⁵ 6m Aug 31] tall, leggy gelding: useful handicapper at best: below 8-y-o form in
1996: effective at 5f and probably stays 1m: acts on hard and dead ground: goes well
on sharp tracks, and successful 9 times at Brighton: usually held up. *J. Cullinan*

SHIMAZU (IRE)   2 b.c. (Jan 20) Darshaan 133 – Shamshir 116 (Kris 135) [1996   75
6m⁵ a7g* 7m⁴ 7.9g 7.3s Oct 26] small colt: second foal: dam, won Fillies' Mile and
second in Oaks, daughter of high-class performer at up to 1½m Free Guest: modest
form: impressive winner of weak maiden at Southwell in July: behind in large-field
nurseries at York (on toes, good hold to post) and Newbury (tongue tied) in October:
should stay 1m+: to UAE. *J. H. M. Gosden*

SHINE   3 ch.f. Sharrood (USA) 124 – Varnish 85 (Final Straw 127) [1995 NR 1996   –
7d 7m 7.1g Jun 13] second foal: dam winner at 7f at 2 yrs and fourth in May Hill:
towards rear in varied company, looking none too keen final start: sold 2,600 gns
Newmarket July Sales. *I. A. Balding*

SHINEROLLA 4 b.g. Thatching 131 – Primrolla 64 (Relko 136) [1995 88: 5g³   88
5s⁴ 7g² 8m² 8f* 7.9g² 8g* 10g² 8.3f⁴ 8g 8d 8m* 8m³ 1996 a7g³ 8s⁴ 8d 8.1d May 24]
tall, leggy gelding: fairly useful handicapper: shaped encouragingly in well-
contested event at Wolverhampton on reappearance, but failed to confirm: effective
at 7f to 1¼m: acts on firm and soft ground and on fibresand: held up. *C. Parker*

SHINING CLOUD 3 ch.f. Indian Ridge 123 – Hardiheroine 76 (Sandhurst   71
Prince 128) [1995 77: 7m³ 5m² 1996 6g 7.1d 6.1m* 5m³ Oct 3] lengthy filly: fair
performer: left L. G. Cottrell after second 3-y-o start: well backed, returned to form
in style on first run for new stable when making all (by 6 lengths) in 23-runner minor
event at Nottingham: ran well despite seeming unsuited by shorter trip in handicap at
Newmarket 9 days later: likely to prove suited by 6f+: acts on good to firm ground.
M. Bell

SHINING DANCER 4 b.f. Rainbow Quest (USA) 134 – Strike Home 82 (Be   66
My Guest (USA) 126) [1995 61d: 9g⁶ 13.8m⁵ 10g 12s a12g a16g⁶ 1996 10m⁶ 10m*
10m 12g³ 12g³ 11.5d³ 12m² 16.2m⁵ 16s Oct 24] angular filly: has a markedly round
action: fair handicapper: dead-heated with Bakheta at Windsor in June: mostly good
efforts afterwards: stays 16.2f: acts on good to firm and dead ground, well beaten
both outings on soft: takes strong hold and suited by strong handling. *S. Dow*

SHINING EXAMPLE 4 ch.g. Hadeer 118 – Kick The Habit 94 (Habitat 134)   75
[1995 75: 8m 7.1m⁵ 8.5d³ a11g² 10.5s² 9m* 1996 10m⁶ 10m* 12m⁵ 10m⁶ 8.9g⁶ 10s
Oct 24] strong, workmanlike gelding: fairly useful handicapper: won minor event at
Windsor in May despite edging right: stays 11f: acts on fibresand and good to firm
and soft ground: has run well when sweating: consistent. *P. J. Makin*

SHIP'S DANCER 3 b.f. Shareef Dancer (USA) 135 – Sunderland (Dancer's   56 d
Image (USA)) [1995 62p: 7m 8.2d 8g 1996 10.8g 12m⁴ 14.1m⁵ 14.1f³ 14.1f⁶ 16.2f⁴
12f⁶ 15.8g 11.1g 13.8g 16.1m⁶ Oct 2] quite attractive filly: modest maiden
handicapper: sold out of J. Dunlop's stable 4,600 gns Newmarket July Sales after
fifth start: well below form afterwards: stays 1¾m: acts on firm ground: tried
blinkered/visored: not one to trust implicitly. *Don Enrico Incisa*

SHIRLATY 3 b.f. Shirley Heights 130 – Jameelaty (USA) 96 (Nureyev (USA)   –
131) [1995 –: 6g 7g 1996 10.5d 8.2s Oct 31] lengthy filly: no worthwhile form.
C. W. Thornton

SHIRLEY SUE 3 b.f. Shirley Heights 130 – Dame Ashfield 90 (Grundy 137)   76
[1995 56: 7g 8m a8g⁴ 1996 8.1g 12.5f 13g* 14.1m⁶ a14g* a12g² 16.1m* 16g* 16m⁴
16s² 15.9d 16g⁶ 17.5m² 17.1m⁴ 16.5s⁵ Nov 9] sturdy filly: fair handicapper: won at
Hamilton (maiden contest), Southwell, Newcastle and Thirsk (gamely made most),
all in the summer: suited by thorough test of stamina: acts on fibresand, good to firm
and soft ground: usually races prominently: flashes tail but is genuine and consistent.
M. Johnston

SHIRLEY VENTURE 3 b.f. Be My Chief (USA) 122 – Our Shirley 84 (Shirley   74
Heights 130) [1995 NR 1996 12g² 12m³ 12m 14g⁵ 14.1m³ 16.2g³ 14m⁵ a13g⁴ Oct
28] unfurnished filly: half-sister to several winners, including Pearl Venture (up to
16.4f, by Salse) and Soviet Express (7f, by Siberian Express): dam, 1¼m winner,
half-sister to smart Miner's Lamp: fair maiden: disappointing at Lingfield last 2
starts: stays 2m. *S. P. C. Woods*

SHOCK VALUE (IRE) 2 b.c. (Mar 12) Danehill (USA) 126 – Rince Deas (IRE)   98 p
53 (Alzao (USA) 117) [1996 6m* 6f⁶ 7m⁴ Oct 4] 42,000F: sturdy, quite attractive
colt: good mover: second foal: half-brother to 3-y-o 7f and 1m winner Panata (by
Tirol): dam, ran only at 2 yrs, maiden sister to smart miler Mirror Black: won maiden
at Newmarket in June: seemed to become unbalanced crossing path and never
dangerous when sixth of 15 to Verglas in Coventry Stakes at Ascot: first run for 3½
months and useful form when staying-on 3½ lengths fourth of 8 to Grapeshot in listed
race at Newmarket: will stay 1m: will improve again. *M. R. Stoute*

SHOEMAKER LEVY 3 b.f. Bedford (USA) 109 – Little Missile (Ile de   –
Bourbon (USA) 133) [1995 NR 1996 8f 8f 10m 9f 16f⁶ Jul 27] fourth foal: half-sister
to fairly useful 6f winner La Petite Fusee (by Cigar) and 1m and 1¼m winner Little
Miss Ribot (by Lighter): dam of little account: of little account. *R. J. O'Sullivan*

SHOJA 3 ch.g. Persian Bold 123 – Dancing Berry (Sadler's Wells (USA) 132)   –
[1995 NR 1996 11f 12g Oct 19] 25,000Y: second foal: dam twice-raced close relative

of useful 7f winner Lidhame out of Cheveley Park winner Red Berry: soundly beaten in maiden seller at Redcar and apprentice claimer at Catterick. *Mrs V. A. Aconley*

SHONARA'S WAY 5 b.m. Slip Anchor 136 – Favorable Exchange (USA) (Exceller (USA) 129) [1995 96: 14.8m² 13.3d 16d² 18m 16m⁵ 1996 13.1m Sep 21] leggy mare: useful handicapper for R. Charlton at 4 yrs: modest hurdler: tailed off (in need of race) on return to flat: stays 2m: acts on good to firm and soft ground: inconsistent. *P. Monteith*

SHONTAINE 3 b.g. Pharly (FR) 130 – Hinari Televideo 97 (Caerleon (USA) 65 132) [1995 79: 6d³ 6m* 6m 6m* 7m 6m² 6g 7f 1996 a6g⁴ a7g⁶ 6g 6m 7f³ 7s⁶ 7.1g² 7g* 7m³ 7m 6d 7g⁵ a6g³ 6.9d³ 7s 8.1s a7g³ a7g* a8g⁶ a7g⁶ Dec 20] small gelding: fair handicapper: won at Catterick (apprentice seller) in July and at Southwell in November: stays 7f: acts on firm ground and on the all-weather: races prominently. *M. Johnston*

SHOODAH (IRE) 5 ch.g. Common Grounds 118 – Tunguska 76 (Busted 134) – [1995 –: 8.3m 8.1g a8g a10g 1996 a10g Jan 11] close-coupled gelding: little sign of ability: sold (P. Hayward to L. Snook) 825 gns Ascot December Sales. *P. Hayward*

SHOOFK 5 ch.g. Dunbeath (USA) 127 – River Reem (USA) (Irish River (FR) – 131) [1995 58: 9.7d 9.7g⁶ 10.8m⁴ 12.5g 1996 10g Oct 2] plain, good-topped gelding: fairly useful hurdler: lightly raced on flat nowadays, and well beaten only start in 1996. *S. Dow*

SHOOTING LIGHT (IRE) 3 b.g. Shernazar 131 – Church Light 88 (Caerleon 79 (USA) 132) [1995 –: 8m 1996 10g² 12.1s* 14.1m³ 14g³ 14d⁴ 14m 16.2m Sep 28] workmanlike gelding: fair performer: made heavy weather of winning maiden at Hamilton in May: sold out of M. Jarvis' stable 21,000 gns Newmarket July Sales after fourth start: should stay 2m: acts on good to firm and soft ground: winning juvenile hurdler. *P. G. Murphy*

SHOOT THE MINSTREL 3 ch.c. Brotherly (USA) 80 – Shoot To Win (FR) 40 (Rabdan 129) [1995 –: a8.5g 1996 a6g a5g a5g a5g⁵ a6g Feb 14] poor sprint maiden plater. *J. A. Pickering*

SHOSHONE 3 ch.f. Be My Chief (USA) 122 – Bridestones 92 (Jan Ekels 122) – [1995 NR 1996 10m 10s⁶ a13g⁶ 12v⁶ a14.8g⁴ Nov 25] half-sister to several winners, including smart 7f to 1¼m performer Lockton (by Moorestyle): dam, half-sister to high-class stayer Crash Course, won 4 times over middle distances: no worthwhile form: shapes like a stayer. *J. H. M. Gosden*

SHOTLEY AGAIN 6 b.g. Then Again 126 – Sweet Candice 71 (African Sky – 124) [1995 –: 6g 5.9m 7m⁵ a8g 7g 1996 a8g a8g² a11g⁴ a8g⁶ a12g⁵ a11g⁶ Feb 10] a34 tall, angular gelding: has a markedly round action: poor handicapper: stays 1½m: acts on fibresand and any turf going: sold 500 gns Doncaster November Sales: unpredictable. *N. Bycroft*

SHOTLEY PRINCESS 2 ch.f. (Jan 30) Risk Me (FR) 127 – Miss Camellia 70 – (Sonnen Gold 121) [1996 5d⁶ 5g⁴ a5g 6m a5g 5m 5f Sep 28] strong, lengthy filly: third foal: half-sister to 3-y-o winning novice hurdler Royal Rapport (by Rich Charlie): dam won from 1m (at 2 yrs) to 13.8f: probably of little account. *N. Bycroft*

SHOUK 2 b.f. (Mar 31) Shirley Heights 130 – Souk (IRE) 98 (Ahonoora 122) 81 p [1996 7m 7m² Aug 2] rangy filly: second foal: closely related to 3-y-o 1¼m and 1½m winner Puce (by Darshaan): dam 7f winner, had better form at 1m: stepped up good deal on debut form when neck second of 9 to Right Tune in maiden at Newmarket, pushed along after 2f out then running on well: sure to progress again. *L. M. Cumani*

SHOULDBEGREY 3 ch.g. Siberian Express (USA) 125 – Miss Magnetism 50 (Baptism 119) [1995 NR 1996 8d 6.9m 7.3s⁴ 8g 8.3m⁴ a9.4g⁴ 10f 10m⁵ 8g 8m³ 8d* 9g⁵ Nov 1] tall, leggy gelding: half-brother to poor maiden Magnetic Reel (by Scottish Reel): dam poor plater on flat, won over hurdles: poor handicapper: best efforts last 3 starts, winning 18-runner maiden event at Bath in October: stays 9f: acts on good to firm and dead ground. *W. R. Muir*

SHOUMATARA (USA) 2 ch.c. (Mar 14) Seeking The Gold (USA) – Crown 84 Quest (USA) (Chief's Crown (USA)) [1996 7g⁵ 7.1m² 7f² 7m Aug 20] $450,000F: rangy colt: has scope: third foal: half-brother to a 2-y-o sprint winner in USA by Majestic Light: dam won minor stakes and placed in Grade 3 8.5f event at 2 yrs, out of half-sister to champion 1980 US 2-y-o Heavenly Cause: ½-length second of 10 to

Tarski in maiden at Sandown, second start: rather disappointing afterwards, folding tamely when last in nursery at York on final outing: bred to stay 1m. *M. R. Stoute*

SHOWBOAT 2 b.c. (Mar 27) Warning 136 – Boathouse 116 (Habitat 134) [1996 92 p 7f* 7.3s Oct 24] useful-looking colt: half-brother to 10.2f winner River Patrol (by Rousillon) and smart middle-distance stayer Dry Dock (by High Line): dam, stayed 1¼m, is half-sister to Bireme and high-class middle-distance stayer Buoy: made winning debut in 10-runner maiden at Leicester, impressively from Maylane: 4/1, well beaten on much softer ground in 8-runner Horris Hill Stakes at Newbury 9 days later, pushed along in rear at halfway: will stay 1m+: will do better. *B. W. Hills*

SHOWCASE 2 b.f. (May 22) Shareef Dancer (USA) 135 – Perfolia (USA) 104 68 (Nodouble (USA)) [1996 7g⁵ 7g Oct 2] angular filly: first foal: dam, very useful 7f winner, half-sister to Culture Vulture from the family of Polish Precedent and Zilzal: modest form in maidens at Chester and Brighton (very slowly away, carried head high): sold 18,000 gns Newmarket Autumn Sales. *M. R. Stoute*

SHOW FAITH (IRE) 6 ch.g. Exhibitioner 111 – Keep The Faith 86 (Furry Glen – 121) [1995 90: 10d³ 10m 8.1m³ 8.1g³ 8m 8g* 10f 10m 10d³ 9g⁴ 9d 1996 8s 8g 9m 8d 8g a8g Nov 12] good-topped gelding: formerly fairly useful handicapper on his day: no form in 1996: temperamental. *R. Hannon*

SHOWGIRL 2 ch.f. (Apr 6) Handsome Sailor 125 – Early Doors (Ballad Rock 59 122) [1996 6g a6g* Nov 30] fifth foal: dam no worthwhile form: won 6-runner seller at Wolverhampton in November: will prove best at up to 6f. *Capt. J. Wilson*

SHOW OFF 2 ch.f. (Mar 6) Efisio 120 – Brazen Faced 84 (Bold And Free 118) 56 [1996 5g⁶ 6f 5m 5m⁵ Sep 27] rather leggy, useful-looking filly: unimpressive mover: half-sister to several winners, including smart sprinter Easy Option (by Prince Sabo) and useful 7f and 1m winner Sheer Cliff (by Shirley Heights): dam 2-y-o 5f winner: pulled hard early when 4½ lengths fourth of 6 to Sherzetto in maiden at Thirsk on second start: last in maiden events at Windsor and Folkestone subsequently. *W. Jarvis*

SHOWTIME BLUES (IRE) 7 b.g. Kafu 120 – Susan's Blues (Cure The Blues – (USA)) [1995 NR 1996 a8.5g⁶ a8g a8.5g a6g Mar 15] first foal: dam placed at 9f in Ireland: little sign of ability: tried blinkered. *A. Bailey*

SHU FLY (NZ) 12 ch.g. Tom's Shu (USA) – Alycone (NZ) (Philoctetes 111) – [1995 NR 1996 a7g Feb 26] workmanlike gelding: one-time useful jumper: lightly raced and little form on flat. *H. Oliver*

SHU GAA (IRE) 3 ch.g. Salse (USA) 128 – River Reem (USA) (Irish River (FR) 73 131) [1995 70p: 7.5m⁶ 8d 1996 8.2d* 10g 11m⁴ 11.4g³ 14m⁴ 10.5v Oct 6] big, sturdy, deep-bodied gelding: fair performer: failed to progress after winning maiden at Nottingham in April: stays 11f: acts on good to firm and dead ground: joined O. Sherwood and won over hurdles. *W. J. Haggas*

SHUTTLECOCK 5 ch.g. Pharly (FR) 130 – Upper Sister (Upper Case (USA)) 39 [1995 43, a66: a8g* a8g* a8.5g a8g³ a8g⁶ a8g 10m⁶ 12.4g⁵ 14.9g 10m⁴ 8.2m³ a47 7.6m a7g⁵ 1996 a8g⁶ a8g a8g⁵ a8g 10d 8m 10m³ 10m a8g⁶ 10f a8g 10d 11.8f a12g⁶ Nov 7] angular gelding: poor performer on flat nowadays: seems to stay 12.4f: acts on good to firm ground, dead and all-weather surfaces: tried visored/blinkered: usually races prominently: won over hurdles in October. *Mrs N. Macauley*

SHUWAIKH 2 b.c. (Feb 8) Puissance 110 – Femme Formidable (Formidable 66 (USA) 125) [1996 6m⁶ 6m⁴ 6g³ 6g 7g Oct 2] 25,000F, 22,000Y: rather unfurnished colt: fourth foal: half-brother to 3-y-o 6f (at 2 yrs) and 9f winner Prima Volta (by Primo Dominie), 1994 2-y-o 6f winner Femme Savante (by Glenstal) and an Irish bumper winner by Faustus: dam poor maiden, stayed 1m: fair form: disappointing in nurseries on last 2 outings: stays 6f: sent to Saudi Arabia. *R. Hannon*

SHY MYSTIC 6 ch.m. Shy Groom (USA) – Misowni (Niniski (USA) 125) [1995 – NR 1996 a13g Jan 13] first foal: closely-related to modest 1995 3-y-o 7f and 1m winner Jalmaid (by Jalmood): dam unraced half-sister to Bustomi: tailed off in bad maiden at Lingfield. *R. J. Hodges*

SHY PADDY (IRE) 4 b.g. Shy Groom (USA) – Griqualand (Connaught 130) – [1995 –: a10g a8.5g³ 14.1m a14.8g 10m 1996 11.8d 12m May 29] workmanlike gelding: well beaten since modest 2-y-o: tried blinkered. *K. O. Cunningham-Brown*

SIAN WYN 6 ch.m. Hotfoot 126 – Curzon House 73 (Green God 128) [1995 25: –
a9.4g³ 12g 1996 12g Mar 21] workmanlike mare: poor maiden: winning selling
hurdler. *K. R. Burke*

SIBERIAN HENRY 3 b.g. Siberian Express (USA) 125 – Semperflorens (Don –
128) [1995 –: 10m 1996 14.1g Oct 24] useful-looking gelding: little form in 2 races,
seventh of 17 in maiden at Nottingham only 3-y-o start. *B. Smart*

SIBERIAN MYSTIC 3 gr.f. Siberian Express (USA) 125 – Mystic Crystal (IRE) 39
85 (Caerleon (USA) 132) [1995 43+: 5g 5.1m⁶ 6g 7f 1996 9.7f 8m 9.9g* Aug 24]
lengthy filly: poor walker: poor performer: gambled on, first form since third start as
2-y-o when winning apprentice maiden handicap at Beverley, leading under pressure
over 1f out: stays 1¼m: poor winning hurdler. *P. G. Murphy*

SIBERIAN ROSE 3 b.f. Siberian Express (USA) 125 – Deanta In Eirinn (Red –
Sunset 120) [1995 NR 1996 7g 7d 6f 8g Oct 29] fourth foal: half-sister to 5.2f winner
Newbury Coat (by Chilibang) and a middle-distance winner in Germany by Scottish
Reel: dam ran once: soundly beaten in claimers. *J. Wharton*

SIBOR STAR 2 b.g. (Apr 15) Man Among Men (IRE) – My Ratbag 56 (Main 39
Reef 126) [1996 a7g⁵ Jul 6] first known foal: dam, 1¼m winner, stayed 11f: fifth of
6 in seller at Wolverhampton, slowly away and modest late progress: gelded.
D. Burchell

SICARIAN 4 b.g. Kris 135 – Sharka 97 (Shareef Dancer (USA) 135) [1995 –: 10g –
10.5g 1996 8m⁶ a14g 14d⁶ 14s Oct 5] big, leggy gelding: no worthwhile form, though
signs of a little ability: has joined Merrita Jones. *M. J. Heaton-Ellis*

SIDE NOTE 3 b.c. Warning 136 – Sarah Siddons (FR) 122 (Le Levanstell 122) 104
[1995 NR 1996 8m* 10g⁶ 11.6d³ Aug 24] small, sturdy colt: has quick action: half-
brother to numerous winners, including high-class middle-distance performers
Seymour Hicks (by Ballymore) and Princess Pati (by Top Ville): dam won Irish 1000
Guineas and Yorkshire Oaks: progressive form: won maiden at Salisbury in May:
best effort when 7 lengths third of 6 to Shantou in minor event at Windsor, keeping
on: stays 11.6f: sold 46,000 gns Newmarket Autumn Sales, to join Three Kings
Racing in USA. *H. R. A. Cecil*

SIDNEY THE KIDNEY 2 b.f. (Apr 19) Mystiko (USA) 124 – Martin-Lavell 53
Mail (Dominion 123) [1996 6.9d³ a7g a7g⁴ Dec 13] 1,100Y: half-sister to 3-y-o a?
Sonic Mail (by Keen), 5.1f winner at 2 yrs, middle-distance stayer Pharly Dancer (by
Pharly) and a winner abroad by Petorius: dam unraced: third of 13 in maiden auction
at Folkestone in October, staying on without being given hard race: well beaten on
all-weather afterwards: ridden by 7-lb claimer all starts. *M. J. Ryan*

SIEGE PERILOUS (IRE) 3 b.g. Taufan (USA) 119 – Carado 82 (Manado 130) 74
[1995 –: 8.2d 7.1g 10m 1996 12s* a11g³ 14.1g* 12d² 14.6m³ 11.9m⁶ 15.8g⁴ 14.1s²
12v³ Nov 11] rangy, unfurnished gelding: made into a fair handicapper, winning at
Folkestone in March and at Nottingham (gamely) in April: good efforts last 2 starts:
stays 1¾m well: acts on good to firm ground, goes well with plenty of give: genuine.
S. C. Williams

SIESTA TIME (USA) 6 ch.m. Cure The Blues (USA) – Villa Rose (USA) (Key 54
To The Mint (USA)) [1995 NR 1996 10.8f³ 8.3g⁵ 11.7m² 10m² 11.9f⁶ 12.1g³
a12g Sep 21] fifth foal: half-sister to 3 winners in USA, including allowance winner
at around 1m by Super Concorde: dam unraced: modest maiden: sold out of
R. O'Sullivan's stable 1,400 gns Ascot July Sales after second start: left C. Popham
after sixth: stays 12.1f: refused to race over hurdles once in October. *D. Burchell*

SIGAMA (USA) 10 ch.g. Stop The Music (USA) – Lady Speedwell (USA) –
(Secretariat (USA)) [1995 55, a64: a5g* a5g⁶ 5d⁴ a5g² 5m⁴ 5m⁶ 5m⁴ 5g⁴ 5m 5m
5m 1996 a5g 5g May 22] sturdy, dipped-backed gelding: modest sprinter at 9 yrs:
well beaten in 1996, leaving D. Nicholls after reappearance: 5f specialist: acts on
fibresand, ideally top-of-the-ground when on turf: blinkered (out of form)
last 2 starts in 1994: usually a front runner. *J. M. Carr*

SIGNS AND WONDERS 2 b.f. (Jan 31) Danehill (USA) 126 – Front Line 67
Romance 89 (Caerleon (USA) 132) [1996 6g⁴ 6m⁶ 6m⁶ 5f Aug 10] 16,000Y: angular
filly: third foal: half-sister to 3-y-o Fog City (by Damister), 6f winner at 2 yrs: dam
stayed 1¼m: best effort in maidens when ½-length second of 6 to Lima at Folkestone

in July: virtually pulled up and reportedly lame in minor event at Lingfield final start: should stay beyond 6f. *C. A. Cyzer*

SIGNS R US (IRE) 3 b.g. Al Hareb (USA) 123 – O La Bamba (IRE) (Commanche Run 133) [1995 –: 6m 5m 7m 1996 a10g Jan 30] small gelding: no worthwhile form. *Dr J. D. Scargill*

SIHAFI (USA) 3 ch.g. Elmaamul (USA) 125 – Kit's Double (USA) (Spring   72 d
Double) [1995 77p: 6m 6m² 1996 6s⁴ 6d⁵ 5m² 7g⁴ 6f² 6d 5g 7m a6g a7s a6g* a5g²
Dec 31] tall, rather leggy gelding: fair form on turf up to June: hung under pressure fourth 3-y-o start: sold out of E. Dunlop's stable 15,000 gns Newmarket July Sales and gelded after fifth: backed at long odds and showed modest form to win handicap at Lingfield in December: stays 6f: acts on firm and dead ground and on equitrack: takes keen hold. *J. M. Carr*

SILCA BLANKA (IRE) 4 b.c. Law Society (USA) 130 – Reality 88 (Known   104
Fact 125) [1995 104: 7m 8m 6g⁵ 7f* 7m 8m² 1996 7.9m 8s⁶ 8.5m⁴ 8g⁵ 10m
8g⁶ 10g Aug 30] quite attractive colt: useful performer: fourth of 8 to Blomberg in Diomed Stakes at Epsom in June, twice hampered during final 2f: good fifth to Orfijar in Group 3 event at Cologne in August: stays 8.5f: acts on firm and dead ground. *M. R. Channon*

SILCA KEY SILCA 2 ch.f. (Mar 25) Polar Falcon (USA) 126 – Night   77
Transaction 59 (Tina's Pet 121) [1996 5m³ 5g⁵ 6g* 5.2m⁵ 5m² Sep 27] 9,500Y:
lengthy filly: has scope: second foal: dam 7.6f and 1m winner at 4/5 yrs: won 4-runner maiden at Ayr in August: ran well in nursery at Folkestone on final outing: sold 12,000 gns Newmarket Autumn Sales: stays 6f. *M. R. Channon*

SILCA'S MY KEY (IRE) 2 b.c. (Apr 27) Persian Bold 123 – Cloud Peak (USA)   63
60 (Storm Bird (CAN) 134) [1996 7m 7.5m³ 7g³ 7f* 7m² 7g 7m² 8g⁵ 7f⁵ 7.6m⁵ 8m
7m* 7d 7.3s Oct 26] IR 17,000Y: neat colt: first foal: dam (maiden) stayed 1¼m,
closely related to Prix Marcel Boussac winner Ashayer: modest performer: successful in sellers at Yarmouth in July and Goodwood in September: sold 6,500 gns Newmarket Autumn Sales: should stay beyond 7f: acts on firm ground, below form both outings on a soft surface: visored last 3 outings: runs the odd poor race. *M. R. Channon*

SILENT EXPRESSION 6 gr.m. Siberian Express (USA) 125 – Silent Sun 90   88
(Blakeney 126) [1995 88: a6g* a8g 7m* 6g⁴ 5.7m* 6.1m³ 6m 6m⁵ 7m* 7g 1996 6m
6f 6m² 7m⁶ 6f⁶ 6f³ 7m³ 7m⁴ 7m⁵ Aug 10] rangy mare: unimpressive mover: fairly useful handicapper: best at up to 7f: acted on equitrack, suited by a sound surface on turf: visored (no improvement) 5 times as 4-y-o: dead. *B. J. Meehan*

SILENT GUEST (IRE) 3 b.g. Don't Forget Me 127 – Guest House (What A   –
Guest 119) [1995 57: 6g⁶ 7.1d⁵ 7m 6.9m a7g 1996 8.3s a8g 10f 10s³ Jul 4]
good-topped gelding: modest form at 2 yrs: no worthwhile form on flat in 1996,
blinkered final start: sold (Sir Mark Prescott to M. Hammond) 9,000 gns Newmarket July Sales: won novice hurdle in November. *Sir Mark Prescott*

SILENTLY 4 b.g. Slip Anchor 136 – Land of Ivory (USA) 109 (The Minstrel   83 §
(CAN) 135) [1995 83§: 10d* 10g 10m⁴ 11.4g 10m² 10m* 10.2h* 11.9f⁵ 12m⁴ 10m⁶
10g³ 10.4m⁵ 1996 10.8d⁶ 10.2f⁶ 10d² 10.8f² 10m⁶ 12g² 16f⁵ 12m 12m² 12g 16.2m
11.9g³ Oct 9] good-topped gelding: fairly useful handicapper on his day: sold 10,000 gns Newmarket Autumn Sales: effective at around 1¼m, and stays 2m: acts on dead ground and hard: blinkered (ran poorly) eighth 4-y-o start: has an awkward head carriage: tail swisher and sometimes looks none too genuine: not one to trust. *I. A. Balding*

SILENT MIRACLE (IRE) 2 b.f. (Mar 21) Night Shift (USA) – Curie Point   61 p
(USA) (Sharpen Up 127) [1996 6m Sep 7] 20,000Y: stocky filly: second foal:
half-sister to ex-Irish 3-y-o 1½m winner Desert Mountain (by Alzao): dam unraced half-sister to useful 7f performer Mazilier: 25/1 and in need of race, around 7 lengths ninth of 14 to Calypso Lady in maiden at Kempton: unimpressive to post: should stay 1m: should do better. *M. Bell*

SILENT SYSTEM (IRE) 3 gr.g. Petong 126 – Light Thatch (Thatch (USA)   –
136) [1995 –: a6g a8.5g 1996 a5g 7m Oct 8] no form: sold out of J. FitzGerald's stable 700 gns Doncaster August Sales before reappearance. *D. W. Chapman*

SILENT VALLEY 2 b.f. (May 10) Forzando 122 – Tremmin 67 (Horage 124) 47
[1996 7g a6g 7f² 6.1m 7g 7m⁶ 7g a6g⁴ a6g² a8g⁶ Dec 3] sparely-made filly: second
reported foal: dam, winning plater, stayed 1m: poor maiden plater: trained by J.
Neville first 3 starts, next 6 by B. Meehan, then sold to join present stable 3,000
gns Doncaster November Sales: stays 7f: acts on firm going: blinkered fifth to ninth
outings. *D. Nicholls*

SILENT WELLS 2 b.f. (Mar 20) Saddlers' Hall (IRE) 126 – Silent Plea 43 (Star –
Appeal 133) [1996 a7g 7f 6.1m⁴ 6f Aug 19] third reported foal: half-sister to 5f (at
2 yrs) and 11f winner Sporting Spirit (by Dunbeath): dam, plater, stayed 6f: little
worthwhile form in varied company, fourth in seller third outing: should be suited by
further than 6f. *J. J. Quinn*

SILHOUETTE (IRE) 3 gr.f. Standaan (FR) 118 – Frill (Henbit (USA) 130) 37
[1995 36: 7m 6g 5.3d⁶ 5g 1996 7m 8g⁵ 7m⁶ 6m 12g⁶ 10s⁵ 12s Nov 1] leggy filly:
poor maiden on balance of form: sold out of D. Elsworth's stable 3,300 gns Newmarket July Sales after fourth start. *G. A. Cusack, Ireland*

SILK COTTAGE 4 b.g. Superpower 113 – Flute Royale 74 (Horage 124) [1995 66
67: 5m 5f 5d 5g⁵ 5d⁵ 5m⁴ a5g² 5.1m 5m⁵ a6g 1996 5g 6g 5g³ 5m⁵ a5g² 5d² 5m* 5m³
5g⁵ 5m³ 5m² 5.1m² 5m 5m 5.1d 5.1m 5g 5g⁴ a5g a5g a5g Dec 13] sturdy, good-
quartered gelding: fair handicapper: in good form in the summer, and won (first time)
at Musselburgh in July: best form at around 5f: acts on good to firm and soft ground
and on all-weather: often blinkered/visored: sometimes hangs markedly left: usually
races prominently. *R. M. Whitaker*

SILK MASQUE (USA) 3 b.f. Woodman (USA) 126 – Silk Slippers (USA) 104 91
(Nureyev (USA) 131) [1995 85p: 6f* 1996 7.3d⁶ 10s⁶ 8m⁴ 10.2m⁵ 8f* Dec 19]
angular, unfurnished filly: good walker: ran well (though never raced) facing stiff
tasks when sixth of 9 to Bosra Sham in Fred Darling Stakes at Newbury on reappearance and when fifth of 7 to Papering in listed race at Chepstow on final start in
Britain: left P. Chapple-Hyam: off course nearly 5 months, won allowance event at
Hollywood Park in December: probably stays 10.2f. *J. Noseda, USA*

SILK ST JOHN 2 b.c. (Apr 8) Damister (USA) 123 – Silk St James (Pas de Seul 72
133) [1996 8g⁶ 7m⁵ 7m 7m² 6.9v² Nov 11] close-coupled, rather leggy colt: fifth
reported foal: half-brother to 4 winners, including 3-y-o 6f winner Miss Carottene
(by Siberian Express) and 1m winner Misty Silks (by Scottish Reel): dam unraced:
fair form when runner-up in nurseries on last 2 starts: will prove at least as effective
at 1m as 7f: acts on good to firm and heavy ground. *M. J. Ryan*

SILKTAIL (IRE) 4 b.f. Jalmood (USA) 126 – Silky (USA) 112 (Nijinsky (CAN) 70
138) [1995 74, a–: 6.9d 8.2g⁴ 11.6m³ 10m a9.4g⁶ 12g 10f² 12m* 11.9m* 11.9m 10m⁵ a54
11.9g³ 12.1s a13g⁶ 1996 a12g³ a10g² a12g⁴ 10.3d 11.9m 12f² 14m* 14m³ 14g⁵ 11.9f³
Sep 4] lengthy, attractive filly: in foal to Mtoto: fair handicapper on turf, modest on
the all-weather: didn't need to be at best to win minor event at Salisbury in July:
stayed 1¾m: best form on a sound surface. *Miss Gay Kelleway*

SILKY SMOOTH (IRE) 3 b.f. Thatching 131 – Smoo 84 (Kris 135) [1995 NR –
1996 8m 6f Jun 15] 4,000Y, 2,000Y: fourth foal: half-sister to ungenuine 6f (at 2 yrs)
and 8.2f winner Barik (by Be My Guest): dam twice-raced and placed at 1m: soundly
beaten in maidens at Yarmouth and Lingfield: sold 1,300 gns Doncaster October
Sales. *Mrs N. Macauley*

SIL SILA (IRE) 3 b.f. Marju (IRE) 127 – Porto Alegre (Habitat 134) [1995 116
97: 7g* 7.3d* 1996 8g 7.3d³ 10.4m² 10.5g* 11.9m Aug 21]
   The argument that small stables or small owners have no chance in the
classics against the massed ranks of the mega-rich who dominate flat racing in
Europe took a knock or two in the latest season, Sil Sila's success in the Prix de
Diane Hermes being a notable case in point. Her trainer, Bryan Smart, Jenny
Pitman's stable jockey in her early days as a trainer, had had just ten winners on
the Flat in 1995, but that was still more than his combined total for nine
previous seasons with a licence, while Sil Sila's owner-breeder, Luis Alvarez
Cervera, who has represented Spain at three-day eventing, had only three
horses run in his name in Britain in 1996. Sil Sila's success at Chantilly was
unexpected, by punters at least, who allowed her to start at around 30/1 on the

Prix de Diane Hermes, Chantilly—Sil Sila (No. 3) quickens well to beat Miss Tahiti and Matiya

Pari-Mutuel. It had been a similar story when she had won both her races late in the season at two, a Warwick maiden where she started at 50/1 and the listed Radley Stakes at Newbury at 25/1. She looked potentially useful, but three runs in classic trials in the spring in Britain didn't offer much encouragement for her chance at Chantilly, though in hindsight the trip in the Masaka Stakes at Kempton and the Fred Darling at Newbury was surely against her; she had run a better race when a staying-on second of five to Magnificient Style over a mile and a quarter in the Musidora Stakes at York. A strongly-run race on easier going at Chantilly suited her down to the ground and she quickened well from the rear, after initially not getting an ideal run, to lead inside the final furlong, winning by a length from the Prix Saint-Alary second Miss Tahiti with the Irish One Thousand Guineas winner Matiya third.

The latest renewal of the Prix de Diane wasn't a strong race, particularly with the short-priced favourite Luna Wells, the Saint-Alary winner, running below form, and Sil Sila is as lowly-rated a winner of the Diane as any since Timeform began. In common with other classics, it generally seems to take a lesser performance to win the Diane these days than before, possibly because of the way horses with classic pretensions have been campaigned in recent years; the latest Diane just wasn't much of a race for a classic. Though the runner-up went on to run creditably in the Prix Vermeille, only two of the twelve fillies won subsequently, the sixth Khalisa and Luna Wells scoring in Group 3 company, the latter awarded her race. Sil Sila herself ran once after Chantilly, in the Yorkshire Oaks ten weeks later. The step up to a mile and a half at York might have been expected to suit her but she ran as if something was amiss, finishing tailed-off last of nine, and it transpired she had a high white cell count. She then missed an engagement in the Sun Chariot Stakes at Newmarket in October. Her trainer expressed the unsurprising hope that she'd be kept in training at four, and entered her for the Dubai World Cup. That looked possible after she was led out unsold at 290,000 guineas at the Newmarket December Sales; however, later in the month it was announced she'd be sent to the paddocks instead, reportedly to be covered by either Lure or Fairy King.

Sil Sila (IRE) (b.f. 1993)	Marju (IRE) (br 1988)	Last Tycoon (b 1983)	Try My Best Mill Princess
		Flame of Tara (b 1980)	Artaius Welsh Flame
	Porto Alegre (b 1975)	Habitat (b 1966)	Sir Gaylord Little Hut
		Powerscourt (ch 1970)	Salvo Kew

Sil Sila's pedigree is unexceptional, and her success has had beneficial effects for those who stand her sire Marju (fee doubled to IR 10,000 guineas) and who owned her unraced two-year-old half-sister by Waajib, Kiera Marie (sold for 16,500 guineas at the December Sales having cost only IR 6,000 guineas as a yearling). Sil Sila's dam Porto Alegre, a six-furlong winner at three years in Germany, produced only one runner of any consequence in six living foals prior to Sil Sila, Frequent Flyer (by Night Shift), a useful two-year-old here at up to a mile before proving a durable performer in the States where he won eight and was placed in nineteen of his sixty-six starts. The grandam Powerscourt was a modest middle-distance stayer in Ireland, taking after her sire rather than her dam, the speedy and very useful two-year-old Kew who was herself a sister to the top-class sprinter Floribunda. Sil Sila, a leggy filly, is a good walker even though reportedly an off-set knee prevented her going to the

Turquoise Trading Ltd's "Sil Sila"

sales as a yearling. She should have stayed a mile and a half and raced on ground ranging from dead to good to firm. *B. Smart*

SILVERANI (IRE) 2 b.c. (Mar 22) High Estate 127 – Rose Society (Caerleon 91 (USA) 132) [1996 7g² 8s² Nov 9] 43,000Y: smallish, sturdy colt: first foal: dam Irish maiden (placed at up to 1½m) from family of Greenland Park and Red Sunset: runner-up in maidens won by Happy Valentine at Yarmouth (carried head and tail awkwardly) and Polar Flight at Doncaster (made most): will stay middle distances: can win a race. *L. M. Cumani*

SILVER BUTTON 2 b.g. (Mar 16) Silver Kite (USA) 111 – Klairover 50 53 + (Smackover 107) [1996 6m 6s 7d Nov 8] 10,000Y: lengthy, good-quartered, rather unfurnished gelding: first foal: dam, 5f and 6f winner who stayed 1m, half-sister to smart sprinter Bunty Boo: seventh of 20 in valuable seller at York on debut, keeping on steadily without being given hard race: possibly unsuited by the soft surface in maiden events afterwards, sweating and on toes final start. *Miss S. E. Hall*

SILVERDALE COUNT 4 b.g. Nomination 125 – Its My Turn 80 (Palm Track – 122) [1995 47: 12.3m 15.8m⁵ 13.1f⁴ 1996 15.8g Jun 1] leggy, lengthy gelding: little form apart from when winning poor seller in 1995. *K. W. Hogg, Isle of Man*

SILVERDALE KNIGHT 3 b.c. Nomination 125 – Its My Turn 80 (Palm Track 59 122) [1995 65: 5m 5.1m³ 6g³ 5f* 5d⁶ 6m⁶ 6g⁴ 7m³ 7h 7.5m⁶ 8f⁴ 7g 8.3g 6m 1996 7s³ 8.5d⁵ 8.2m² 8d² 7.5g⁶ 10m⁶ 9.9f² 10m³ 12f⁵ 11f⁵ 10m⁶ 13.8m² 11.9m⁵ 15m⁶ Sep 19] workmanlike colt: modest handicapper: stays 13.8f: acts on firm and soft ground: sometimes sweats: usually races prominently: won juvenile hurdle in September. *K. W. Hogg, Isle of Man*

SILVER DOME (USA) 3 b. or br.c. Silver Hawk (USA) 123 – Pink Topaze (FR) 103 p (Djakao (FR) 124) [1995 90P: 8m* 1996 10g⁵ Apr 27] tall, good-topped, close-coupled colt: shows plenty of knee action: won maiden at Newmarket at 2 yrs: 4/1 from 2/1, in need of race when 7¾ lengths fifth of 9 to Santillana in Classic Trial at Sandown, held up and never able to challenge: will be well suited by 1½m+: looked capable of better: reportedly joined M. Moubarak in USA. *H. R. A. Cecil*

SILVER GROOM (IRE) 6 gr.g. Shy Groom (USA) – Rustic Lawn (Rusticaro 85 (FR) 124) [1995 80: 10m 10f* 10m 10m³ 10d⁵ 9g 10d⁴ 1996 10m⁵ 10g⁴ 10m² 10d 9m Oct 5] smallish, angular gelding: fairly useful handicapper: narrowly failed in attempting repeat win in William Hill Cup at Goodwood on third start: well below form both outings afterwards: stays 1¼m well: successful on soft ground at 3 yrs (modest form) and over hurdles, goes very well on firm: has turn of foot: useful hurdler, winner in November. *R. Akehurst*

SILVER HARROW 3 gr.g. Belmez (USA) 131 – Dancing Diana 82 (Raga 63 Navarro (ITY) 119) [1995 74d: 6g² 6.1m⁴ 7g⁴ 7m³ 6f³ 6m⁶ 6g³ 1996 7d 5.1g³ 7m² a50 7m⁵ 6.1m⁴ 8m³ 8f⁴ 8.5g³ a8.5g⁵ 8.1f⁴ 7f* 7g⁵ a7g a8.5s⁵ a8g⁶ Dec 27] workmanlike gelding: modest handicapper: consistent in 1996, gaining first win in 18-runner seller at Leicester in October: stays 8.5f: acts on firm ground, below form on all-weather: tried blinkered at 2 yrs, no improvement. *A. G. Newcombe*

SILVER HUNTER (USA) 5 b.g. Silver Hawk (USA) 123 – Martha Queen 53 (USA) (Nijinsky (CAN) 138) [1995 62: 12m 10m 11.1g 12m 12m 14.4m⁵ 16d 12g 1996 a11g² 12m⁵ 11.4m³ 11.1f³ 14.1g³ a11g a12g Nov 15] big, close-coupled gelding: carries condition: modest handicapper: stays 14.4f, may stay 2m: acts on soft ground and firm and on fibresand: visored sixth to final 4-y-o starts: upset in stalls (below form) second 5-y-o start: often has tongue tied down. *G. C. Bravery*

SILVER JUBILEE 2 b.f. (May 1) Sylvan Express 117 – Addison's Jubilee 73 – (Sparkler 130) [1996 a5g⁵ Apr 29] 900F, 2,700Y: sister to 4-y-o Boundary Express, winner at around 1½m, and half-sister to several winners, including 9f winner Ci Siamo (by Formidable), and fairly useful sprinter Addison's Blade (by Pas de Seul): dam 1m and 1¼m winner: well beaten in seller at Southwell. *B. Palling*

SILVER KRISTAL 2 gr.f. (May 3) Kris 135 – Reine d'Beaute 97 (Caerleon 77 p (USA) 132) [1996 6m³ 7g⁴ Nov 2] good-bodied filly: third foal: half-sister to useful German 3-y-o 7f (at 2 yrs) to 11f winner Silver Sign (by Shirley Heights) and 4-y-o Western Playboy (by Law Society): dam, 4-y-o 1m and 9f winner, only starts, from very good family: 5 lengths third of 14 to Blane Water in maiden at Kempton, making most and keeping on: stepped up a little on that form when staying-on 3¼ lengths fourth of 23, held up and not knocked about unduly, to Palisade in similar event at Newmarket around 2 months later: will stay 1m: likely to win a race. *R. Akehurst*

SILVER LINING 2 b.g. (Mar 15) Beveled (USA) – Seymour Ann (Krayyan 117) 64 ?
[1996 5m* 6f⁵ 5d 6m Oct 4] fourth foal: half-brother to 4-y-o Captain's Day (by Ballacashtal), 7f winner at 2 yrs, and a winner in Jersey by Interrex: dam unraced: won seller at Leicester in July: well below form in selling nursery and claimer (not well drawn) last 2 starts: stays 6f: may be unsuited by a soft surface. *A. P. Jones*

SILVER MOON 2 gr.f. (Feb 3) Environment Friend 128 – High And Bright 95 –
(Shirley Heights 130) [1996 a7g⁵ 6.1m a6g⁶ 6s Oct 5] 1,800Y: leggy filly: fourth foal: dam, twice-raced 1¼m winner, closely related to high-class middle-distance horse Main Reef: little form in median auction maiden and sellers: bred to stay middle distances. *B. A. McMahon*

SILVER PATRIARCH (IRE) 2 gr.c. (May 8) Saddlers' Hall (IRE) 126 – Early 98 p
Rising (USA) (Grey Dawn II 132) [1996 7g 8.2m⁴ 10m* 10g* Nov 2] tall, leggy colt: looked weak at 2 yrs: ninth foal: half-brother to several winners, including fairly useful sprinter Silver Singing (by Topsider) and smart stayer My Patriarch (by Be My Guest): dam minor winner in USA at around 1m, is out of half-sister to top-class Key To The Mint: most progressive form: won maiden at Pontefract in October by 3 lengths from Perfect Paradigm, leading 1f out, quickly clear then eased: workmanlike winner of listed Zetland Stakes at Newmarket following month, soon prominent and staying on resolutely to beat Eldorado ¾ length: likely to develop into a very useful middle-distance stayer. *J. L. Dunlop*

SILVER PREY (USA) 3 b.c. Silver Hawk (USA) 123 – Truly My Style (USA) 97
(Mount Hagen (FR) 122) [1995 92p: 7g³ 7m* 1996 7g³ 8m⁶ Oct 3] tall, close-coupled colt: useful performer: first run for 13 months when third of 8 in minor event at Goodwood: stiff task, creditable sixth of 9 to Yeast in listed race at Newmarket 3 weeks later (reportedly returned lame): probably stays 1m: has raced only on a sound surface. *E. A. L. Dunlop*

SILVER PURSE 2 ch.f. (Apr 3) Interrex (CAN) – Money Supply (Brigadier Ger- 67
ard 144) [1996 5.7f* 6m³ 5.2m Aug 17] sturdy filly: half-sister to several winners, including 7f to 1½m winner Credit Squeeze (by Superlative): dam unraced sister to smart Irish 1m winner Senior Citizen: won maiden at Bath in July: well beaten in listed race (flashed tail) at Newbury on final outing: stays 6f. *A. P. Jones*

SILVER RAJ 2 gr.g. (Apr 16) Rope Trick – Pilar 67 (Godswalk (USA) 130) [1996 45 ?
5s⁴ 5g 6g³ 6g⁶ 7.1g⁶ 6g 7g³ 7d 7.5m 8.1m Sep 23] 600Y: leggy, sparely-made gelding: second foal: dam, 7f winner at 2 yrs, showed best form at 1m: sire (by Indian King) 2-y-o 5f winner: plater: best form in blinkers: very slowly away eighth and ninth starts: sold 1,250 gns Doncaster October Sales. *W. T. Kemp*

SILVER SAMURAI 7 b.g. Alleging (USA) 120 – Be My Lady (Be My Guest §§
(USA) 126) [1995 –: a11g 9.9m a12g 1996 10.3d 10g 12g May 17] smallish gelding: refused to race last 2 starts: one to avoid. *Mrs V. A. Aconley*

SILVER SANDS 2 gr.f. (May 10) Chilibang 120 – Sayida-Shahira (Record Run 58 ?
127) [1996 7m 7m⁵ 6m Oct 4] lengthy filly: sixth foal: dam unraced: modest form at best in maidens (possibly flattered in steadily-run race second start). *T. P. McGovern*

SILVER SECRET 2 gr.c. (Feb 27) Absalom 128 – Secret Dance (Sadler's Wells 62
(USA) 132) [1996 6g 6g 7f³ 7m⁵ Oct 28] 9,200F, 25,000Y: first foal: dam unraced half-sister to smart but temperamental 1977 2-y-o 6f winner Royal Harmony: modest form: will be suited by further than 7f: will stay 1m: raced only on a sound surface. *M. J. Heaton-Ellis*

SILVER SHOWERS (USA) 3 ch.f. Zilzal (USA) 137 – Katies First (USA) 110 73
(Kris 135) [1995 NR 1996 7m⁶ 8f² May 11] leggy, sparely-made filly: first foal: dam sprinting daughter of Irish 1000 Guineas winner Katies: still green, better effort when 2½ lengths second of 10 to Roses In The Snow in maiden at Bath: sold 31,000 gns Newmarket December Sales. *M. R. Stoute*

SILVER SLEEVE (IRE) 4 b.g. Taufan (USA) 119 – Sable Coated (Caerleon –
(USA) 132) [1995 –: 10d 1996 10m 8.5m 8.1m Jul 19] lengthy gelding: modest maiden at 2 yrs: well held last 2 seasons: tried blinkered. *M. D. Hammond*

SILVER SPELL 2 gr.f. (Apr 18) Aragon 118 – Silver Berry (Lorenzaccio 130) 54
[1996 5g⁶ 5.7m 7g 5.3f* 5m 6m 7f Sep 3] 11,000Y: close-coupled filly: sister to 2

winners, notably smart sprinter Argentum, and half-sister to several winners, including fair miler Eurodollar (by Sparkler): dam poor half-sister to very smart 1¼m filly Cranberry Sauce: didn't look keen when winning 4-runner median auction maiden at Brighton in July: soundly beaten in nurseries afterwards: should stay beyond 5f: visored second to sixth starts: has her share of temperament. *Dr J. D. Scargill*

SILVER TZAR   4 gr.g. Dominion 123 – Altaia (FR) 90 (Sicyos (USA) 126) [1995 –: 7m 7m 6m 6f⁵ 1996 6m a10g⁵ a10g Sep 10] lengthy gelding: little worthwhile form since fair 2-y-o: sold 775 gns Ascot October Sales. *R. T. Phillips*   –

SILVER WELCOME   3 ch.g. Most Welcome 131 – Silver Ore (FR) 94 (Silver Hawk (USA) 123) [1995 65d: 5.9f³ 5m⁴ 6h² 5h² 7g* 7d⁶ 8g 7f⁵ 8m 1996 7d² 6d⁴ a7g 7g 7m⁴ 6.9f³ 7s* Jul 4] sturdy gelding: modest handicapper: made all at Catterick in July: sold 9,000 gns Newmarket July Sales: stays 7f: acts on any turf ground, seemingly not on fibresand: tends to carry head high: has gone early to post: races prominently: sent to Macau. *T. D. Easterby*   62

SILVER WIDGET (USA)   2 ch.c. (Apr 3) Silver Hawk (USA) 123 – Nijit (USA) (Nijinsky (CAN) 138) [1996 6m³ 7m² 7m⁴ Jul 26] $110,000Y: close-coupled colt: eighth foal: closely related to a minor stakes winner by Roberto and half-brother to fairly useful 1½m winner Julfaar (by Arctic Tern) and several winners in USA: dam, stakes-placed sprint winner in USA, sister to high-class performer at up to 7f Beaudelaire: placed in maidens won by Shock Value at Newmarket and Sandstone at Salisbury: sweating freely and very edgy, something probably amiss final start: will stay 1m+: sent to USA. *R. Charlton*   87

SILVER WING (USA)   3 b.f. Silver Hawk (USA) 123 – Cojinx (USA) (Crafty Prospector (USA)) [1995 73: 7m⁵ 9g⁴ 7.9g² 1996 9.9m³ 12.5f⁴ 10g² 10m⁴ Jun 1] angular filly: has a fluent, round action: fair maiden: effective at 1¼m and stays 12.5f: yet to race on a soft surface: has been bandaged near-hind/behind. *M. Bell*   74

SILVIAN BLISS (USA)   4 ch.g. Green Forest (USA) 134 – Welcome Proposal (Be My Guest (USA) 126) [1995 8v 6s⁴ 9d³ 6m³ 9g* 8g* 10g 1996 8s⁴ 8g* 8d² 8m 8.5g⁴ 7m⁴ 8f⁴ 8d² Oct 26] big Irish gelding: second foal: half-brother to 1993 Irish 2-y-o 7f and 1m winner Peace Role (by Trempolino): dam, Irish 1¼m winner, is half-sister to Lyphard's Wish: useful handicapper: won at Leopardstown and the Curragh (4 days later) in summer at 3 yrs, and at Killarney in May: not ideally drawn when well held in Hunt Cup at Royal Ascot fourth start: stays 9f: acts on firm ground, probably on soft: blinkered (ran well) since fifth 4-y-o start: consistent. *D. K. Weld, Ireland*   96

SILVRETTA (IRE)   3 br.f. Tirol 127 – Lepoushka 97 (Salmon Leap (USA) 131) [1995 NR 1996 8m⁴ 8d 10g 12.1g³ 13.8g³ 12g* Nov 1] IR 23,000Y: leggy filly: has a round action: first foal: dam useful Irish 7f/1m performer: fair form: blinkered first time when winning 17-runner handicap at Newmarket in November, getting up near finish: should prove effective beyond 1½m: wrong in her coat second and third starts: sold 15,500 gns Newmarket December Sales and joined J. Gifford. *A. C. Stewart*   73

SIMAFAR (IRE)   5 b.g. Kahyasi 130 – Sidama (FR) (Top Ville 129) [1995 73?: 14m 14s⁶ 20m 16g 16.2d 1996 a16g⁵ 16.2m Apr 12] sparely-made gelding: fairly useful (rated 87) handicapper in Ireland at 3 yrs: soundly beaten in 1996, visored final start: stays 2½m: acts on good to firm ground and heavy: has joined R. Allan. *N. A. Graham*   –

SIMAND   4 b.f. Reprimand 122 – Emmylou (Arctic Tern (USA) 126) [1995 59, a–: 7g 8g⁶ 8.1g 10g² a11g 8m⁴ 8m* 6.9f* 8h⁴ 8g a7g 1996 6.9m⁶ 8g 10.2g² 9.2g 8.1f³ 12s⁴ 10m⁴ 8.5f³ Aug 14] leggy, sparely-made filly: good walker: poor performer at best in 1996: effective at 7f to 1¼m: acts on any turf going: won selling hurdle in August. *G. M. Moore*   45 a–

SIMPLE LOGIC   2 ch.f. (Mar 29) Aragon 118 – Dancing Chimes (London Bells (CAN) 109) [1996 6d³ 6g* 7m³ 7m Aug 10] tall, leggy, close-coupled filly: has scope: fifth foal: half-sister to 3 winners at up to 7f, including fairly useful 6-y-o Palacegate Touch (by Petong): dam unraced: won 14-runner maiden auction at Kempton in June: ran well when over 7 lengths third of 6 to Recondite in listed race at Newmarket next start, but well beaten in similar event there month later: stays 7f: bandaged behind third start. *A. G. Foster*   73

SIMPLY A SEQUEL (IRE) 5 ch.g. Simply Great (FR) 122 – Salique (Sallust –
134) [1995 NR 1996 8d Apr 13] useful-looking gelding: little worthwhile form since
2-y-o days. *C. F. C. Jackson*

SIMPLY BLESSED 2 gr.f. (Feb 25) Ballacashtal (CAN) – Lucky Starkist 57 –
(Lucky Wednesday 124) [1996 a6g⁵ Jul 26] 1,200Y: fourth foal: dam 5f to 7f winner:
12/1, beaten around 10 lengths in seller at Wolverhampton, struggling by halfway:
unseated rider and got loose before start. *J. Neville*

SIMPLY (IRE) 7 b.g. Simply Great (FR) 122 – Be A Dancer (Be Friendly 130) –
[1995 –: 15.4m 1996 14f⁴ᵈⁱˢ Jul 13] small gelding: fair jumper: poor performer at best
on flat nowadays. *T. P. McGovern*

SIMPLY KATIE 3 ch.f. Most Welcome 131 – Rechanit (IRE) (Local Suitor 93 +
(USA) 128) [1995 NR 1996 a10g* 9.9m* Apr 12] 4,000Y: first foal: dam, ran once
here then won 4 times in Italy from 5f to 7f, half-sister to very smart middle-distance
stayer Sapience: easy winner of 4-runner median auction maiden at Lingfield (hard
held) in February and 3-runner minor event at Beverley (made all, eased inside last,
beating Miss Riviera 8 lengths) in April: sold 19,000 gns Newmarket December
Sales: will stay further than 1¼m: looked sure to improve again. *D. R. Loder*

SIMPLY SEVEN 3 b.g. Seven Hearts 98 – Simply Spim 65 (Simply Great (FR) –
122) [1995 NR 1996 7f 8.3m Jun 3] first reported foal: dam, maiden, probably stayed
1½m: well beaten in claimer and seller. *P. Butler*

SIMPLY TIMES (USA) 2 b.f. (Feb 11) Dodge (USA) – Nesian's Burn (USA) 64 ?
(Big Burn (USA)) [1996 5m a6g Nov 18] $6,000F, $18,000Y: leggy, close-coupled
filly: half-sister to several winners in USA, including 1994 Grade 3 5.5f winner
Bucky's Baby (by Buckaroo): dam won at up to 1m in USA and placed in minor
stakes: sire (by Mr Prospector) Grade 3 6f winner: fell close home in 6-runner
maiden at Newmarket in April, fading having made good progress by halfway after
very slow start: well beaten at Southwell 7 months later. *W. A. O'Gorman*

SINCLAIR LAD (IRE) 8 ch.g. Muscatite 122 – Kitty Frisk 64 (Prince Tender- 38
foot (USA) 126) [1995 41: 10m 11.6m 10m³ 10m⁶ 10m 10.8m⁵ 1996 12d⁵ 11.9g
a14g⁴ 10m³ 9.7g³ 9.7g 9.7m Jul 10] leggy, quite good-topped gelding: poor mover:
poor performer: stays 1¾m: acts on any ground on turf and on the all-weather:
visored once at 3 yrs, usually blinkered nowadays: sold 640 gns Ascot December
Sales. *R. J. Hodges*

SINECURE (USA) 2 br.c. (Jan 27) Explodent (USA) – Caithness (USA) 77
(Roberto (USA) 131) [1996 5f³ 6g* 6m⁶ 7d³ 8m⁴ 8f⁶ Oct 8] lengthy, useful-looking
colt: shows some back action: first living foal: dam, French 11f winner, half-sister to
very smart performer at around 7f Condrillac: fairly useful form: made all in 5-runner
maiden at Doncaster in June, racing with head on one side most of way: creditable
efforts in nurseries last 3 starts: sold 16,000 gns Newmarket Autumn Sales: looks a
stayer: fractious at stalls third start: sent to France. *J. H. M. Gosden*

SING AND DANCE 3 b.f. Rambo Dancer (CAN) 107 – Musical Princess 66 50
(Cavo Doro 124) [1995 –: 7d 7m 1996 10m 8m² 9.9m* 10.5m 10m 8m 12g 12.1s⁵
Nov 7] big, workmanlike filly: modest maiden handicapper: well held last 5 starts:
stays 1¼m well: acts on good to firm ground. *E. Weymes*

SINGAPORE STING (USA) 3 br.f. Dayjur (USA) 137 – Ambassador of Luck 73
(USA) (What Luck (USA)) [1995 NR 1996 7m 8m* 8g⁶ 8g⁵ 8m⁴ 8g 8f Oct 8]
$62,000Y: strong, good-bodied filly: sister to fair maiden Golden Envoy and
half-sister to several winners, including very useful 1¼m winner Felawnah (by Mr
Prospector) and Grade 3 1m winner Alydavid (by Alydar): dam (stayed 1m)
champion mare in USA: fair performer: won maiden at Doncaster in May: mostly
disappointing afterwards: should stay beyond 1m: acts on good to firm ground, yet to
race on a soft surface: sold 30,000 gns Newmarket December Sales, reportedly to
join D. Cantillon. *H. R. A. Cecil*

SINGFORYOURSUPPER 2 ch.f. (Feb 25) Superlative 118 – Suzannah's Song 47
(Song 132) [1996 5.3f⁶ 5g⁴ 6g 6.9g 5.3f⁴ 6m⁴ 5d* 6m a5g⁴ 7m⁶ Sep 17] workmanlike
filly: half-sister to 1992 2-y-o 5f winner Meadmore Magic (by Mansingh) and 5-y-o
6f (at 2 yrs) and 1¼m winner Just Flamenco (by Scorpio): dam unraced: fair form:
won selling nursery at Sandown in August: best form at 5f on an easy surface.
G. G. Margarson

SINGSPIEL (IRE) 4 b.c. In The Wings 128 – Glorious Song (CAN) (Halo 127
(USA)) [1995 121: 10m² 12.3m⁴ 10m² 10m² 11.9m² 12g* 1996 10g* 12m²
12g² 10g* 12s* 12g² 12f* Nov 24]

British-trained horses won races in more than a dozen overseas countries during 1996 and earned a record total of £11,409,297 on foreign soil,
according to figures produced by the International Racing Bureau. France, with
forty-four victories and earnings of £3,251,425, proved the happiest hunting
ground, followed by Japan, Italy, Canada, Ireland, Germany and Hong Kong.
The high placings of Japan and Canada largely reflect the prize money picked
up by the Michael Stoute stable in the Japan Cup and in two big races in
Canada, including the Breeders' Cup Turf at Woodbine (Breeders' Cup day
was held outside the United States for the first time). More particularly, the
figures owe a good deal to the achievements of Singspiel, whose victories in
the Canadian International and the Japan Cup and second place in the Breeders'
Cup Turf yielded a staggering £1,634,745. Even without Singspiel's globe-
trotting exploits in the autumn Michael Stoute would still have been a clear-cut
winner of the International Racing Bureau's annual award to the leading
British-based trainer overseas. Stoute's earnings during the year of £2,948,136
were more than three times those of his closest pursuer Peter Chapple-Hyam
and were easily a record for a British trainer abroad. Chapple-Hyam was
followed in the table by John Gosden, Clive Brittain, Saeed bin Suroor, Geoff
Wragg and Paul Cole, all of whom topped the £500,000 mark. Cole had set the
previous record in 1990. Approximately two thirds of Singspiel's total came as
a result of his victory in the Japan Cup at Tokyo at the end of November, when,
under a very strong ride from Dettori, he rallied to beat the home-trained
three-year-old Fabulous La Fouine by a nose. European challengers Strategic
Choice and Prix de l'Arc winner Helissio dead-heated for third, just ahead of

Canadian International Stakes, Woodbine—Singspiel (Gary Stevens) wins

908

Japan Cup, Tokyo—
Singspiel (No. 14) lands the mammoth prize in a driving finish from Fabulous La Fouine (hood, right)
and dead-heaters Strategic Choice (blinkers, left) and Helissio

the consistent American horse Awad; the fourth European runner Pentire finished back in eighth, well below his best. Singspiel's victory at Tokyo took him past Snurge as the record British prize-money earner, though the exact figure for his earnings is open to question; the turf authorities and most statisticians (including those who compile the International Racing Bureau figures) use a single rate of exchange for the whole year, so Singspiel's earnings in the Japan Cup will appear in most record books as £1,093,662, whereas at the exchange rate prevailing at the time the conversion was £946,040. In itself, this is relatively unimportant since such statistics, though interesting, are of limited significance with the level of prize money rising over the years as the value of money falls. In this era of internationalism, there is also a wide variation in the prize money offered in different countries and very big prizes distort the statistics. Only a handful of British-trained horses, for example, have ever won as much in their whole careers, let alone in one race, as Singspiel earned in the Japan Cup. Singspiel may be the record-holder when it comes to earnings (£1,904,321 is the 'official' figure) but, in terms of racing merit, he cannot even be regarded as the best four-year-old in his own stable, let alone the best four-year-old trained in Britain during the year. His stable-mate the Prix de l'Arc de Triomphe runner-up Pilsudski beat him fairly and squarely by a length and a quarter in the Breeders' Cup Turf, a race in which Singspiel improved a little on the form he had shown when taking the less strongly-contested Canadian International at the same course the previous month. Singspiel started favourite for that race and ran out a decisive winner from the very smart Canadian horse Chief Bearhart.

The splendid autumn campaign—which led to Singspiel taking the Eclipse Award as champion turf horse in the United States, the first to win one without having run there—was a most welcome change of fortune for Singspiel. The line between success and failure had been agonisingly thin on so many occasions previously. The *Racehorses* essay covering Singspiel's three-year-old career began by pointing out that 'one judiciously-spread length would have won him the Thresher Classic Trial, Grand Prix de Paris, Eclipse Stakes and Great Voltigeur'. As it was, Singspiel's only victory in six starts that year came in a listed event at Doncaster. He gained his first pattern-race success on his reappearance at Sandown in April, standing out at the weights in the Group 3 T.G.I. Friday's Gordon Richards Stakes in which pattern winners were penalized. Pilsudski, 16/1 on this occasion, followed home hot favourite Singspiel at a respectful three lengths. Singspiel resumed the role of 'bridesmaid' on his next outing, in a close finish with the Arc third Swain in a disappointing turnout for the Coronation Cup at Epsom. By all accounts, Singspiel didn't have a straightforward preparation for the Coronation Cup and after a further defeat, at the hands of Posidonas in the Princess of Wales's Stakes at Newmarket the following month, he was given a break. Singspiel picked up the winning thread when favourite for another Group 3 event, the four-runner Westminster Taxi Insurance Select Stakes at Goodwood in mid-September, and the rest, as they say, is history.

Singspiel (IRE) (b.c. 1992)	In The Wings (b 1986)	Sadler's Wells (b 1981)	Northern Dancer
			Fairy Bridge
		High Hawk (b 1980)	Shirley Heights
			Sunbittern
	Glorious Song (CAN) (b 1976)	Halo (b or br 1969)	Hail To Reason
			Cosmah
		Ballade (b 1972)	Herbager
			Miss Swapsco

Singspiel is a lengthy, quite attractive individual, and a good walker. As he stays in training, with good prospects of adding significantly to his astounding prize-money earnings, there will almost certainly be another occasion in these Annuals to provide full details again about his pedigree. Both his sire and dam excelled themselves at Singspiel's age, In The Wings winning the Coronation Cup, the Grand Prix de Saint-Cloud and the Breeders' Cup Turf and Glorious Song achieving the distinction of being Canadian Horse of The Year and Champion Older Mare in both Canada and the States. Glorious Song, who also held an earnings record when becoming the first Canadian horse to top the million-dollar mark, was bought privately by Sheikh Mohammed in foal to Northern Dancer in early-1987. Her most significant foal before Singspiel was Rahy (by Blushing Groom) who showed smart form for Stoute as a two-year-old and went on to win in graded company in North America before making a name for himself as a stallion (he is the sire of the high-class American filly Serena's Song and of European pattern winners Applaud and Raphane). Glorious Song's brother Devil's Bag was the top American two-year-old of his year and stands at Claiborne. The sire of Glorious Song and Devil's Bag, Halo, will probably be familiar to most readers as the sire of American Horse of the Year Sunday Silence. Sunday Silence has become a stallion sensation in Japan and it's a fair bet that the Japanese will be keen to get their hands on Singspiel when his racing days are over. He is a most consistent racehorse—he has finished out of the first two only twice in his career—and the fact that he travelled something like 24,000 miles (including two transatlantic crossings) to contest his last three races is testament to his toughness. Singspiel stays a mile and a half and probably acts on any going (he has yet to race on heavy). Reportedly he is to be trained for the Dubai World Cup. *M. R. Stoute*

SING UP 4 b.g. Sizzling Melody 117 – Hellene (Dominion 123) [1995 47: 7.3d 64 8m⁶ 10d a8g⁶ a7g 1996 6m⁴ 6.1m² 6f⁵ 6g⁴ 6m³ Jul 10] sturdy gelding: fair maiden: stayed 7f: acted on equitrack and on firm ground: dead. *M. McCormack*

SING WITH THE BAND 5 b.m. Chief Singer 131 – Ra Ra Girl 77 (Shack 73 (USA) 118) [1995 62, a74: 5m³ a6g² 5m a5g* a5g⁶ a5g⁴ a5g* 5m⁵ a6g³ 5g² 5.1d a6g² a80 a6g³ 1996 5g 6.1g 5g² 5d² 5.1m 6g⁶ a6g³ 5f* 5d⁵ 5m⁶ 5m² a6g² 5m 5d 5m⁵ 5s Nov 8] strong, compact mare: fair handicapper: won at Warwick in June: acts on firm and dead ground and goes well on fibresand: usually races prominently. *B. A. McMahon*

SINKING SUN 3 gr.f. Danehill (USA) 126 – Oscura (USA) 82 (Caro 133) [1995 72 § 68p: 8m⁵ 1996 8g⁶ 10d⁴ 10.1m 10m³ 12.1s Oct 22] big, heavy-topped filly: fair maiden: shirked issue when brought to challenge penultimate start, veering right despite strong ride: tailed off 4 weeks later: bred to stay further than 1¼m: blinkered/visored all starts: not one to trust. *B. W. Hills*

SINYAR 4 b. or br.c. Machiavellian (USA) 123 – Place of Honour (Be My Guest 115 (USA) 126) [1995 7v* 7v* 8.5s² 8g 8m* 8g* 8d⁵ 8g⁵ 1996 8g* 8s* 8g 8g² 8g Sep 21] 70,000Y: sixth foal: half-brother to 3 winners, including German 1¼m winner Sure Winner (by Sure Blade), and to dam of smart miler Ventiquattrofogli: dam Irish middle-distance winner out of Coronation Stakes winner Sutton Place, family of Nikoli: smart German colt: won maiden and minor event at Dusseldorf, valuable listed event at Hamburg and valuable race at Cologne at 3 yrs: won minor event at Gelsenkirchen in May then Badener Meile (by ½ length from Kalatos) in June: very good second of 9 to La Blue in Group 3 event at Baden-Baden: should stay beyond 8.5f: probably acts on any going. *B. Schutz, Germany*

SIOUX 2 ch.f. (Mar 3) Kris 135 – Lassoo 87 (Caerleon (USA) 132) [1996 7g 8.2s³ 76 p Oct 31] leggy, unfurnished filly: second foal: dam, maiden placed from 7f (at 2 yrs) to 11f, half-sister to very smart middle-distance colt Apache: 4½ lengths third of 13, staying on resolutely, to Desert Horizon at Nottingham, easily better effort in maidens: will be well suited by middle distances: should improve again. *C. W. Thornton*

SIOUXROUGE 2 b.g. (Apr 23) Indian Ridge 123 – Scarlett Holly 81 (Red Sunset 73 p 120) [1996 5g 6m³ a7g³ a6g³ Nov 22] 16,000Y: leggy gelding: second foal: half-brother to 4-y-o 8.5f winner Little Scarlett (by Mazilier): dam 6f and 7f winner: fair form: may prove best at 6f: acts on good to firm ground and fibresand: probably capable of better. *P. C. Haslam*

SIPOWITZ 2 b.g. (Apr 21) Warrshan (USA) 117 – Springs Welcome 86 (Blake- – ney 126) [1996 8m Sep 19] second foal: dam stayed 2m: 50/1, slowly away and always behind in 15-runner maiden at Yarmouth. *C. A. Cyzer*

SIR ALIDAF 2 b.g. (Mar 4) Broadsword (USA) 104 – Bolton Flyer (Aragon 118) – [1996 5.1g⁴ May 20] first reported foal: dam Irish 7f winner who stayed 1¼m: 50/1, tailed off in 4-runner minor event at Bath. *O. O'Neill*

SIR ARTHUR HOBBS 9 b.g. Lyphard's Special (USA) 122 – Song Grove 61 58 (Song 132) [1995 62: 8.3f⁴ 10m⁶ 9.2f² 8.1m² 8.3f⁵ 1996 9.2g² 8m* 9.2g* 8f* 8m³ 8m⁴ Oct 23] strong gelding: unimpressive mover (has reportedly broken down twice): modest performer: narrow winner of claimers at Ayr and Hamilton before winning apprentice handicap at Thirsk, all in June/July: stays 9.2f, possibly not 1¼m: acts on firm ground, dead and fibresand: tried blinkered (refused to enter stalls) and visored, not for long time: genuine. *J. L. Eyre*

SIR JOEY (USA) 7 ch.g. Honest Pleasure (USA) – Sougoli (Realm 129) [1995 92 92: 5.2m⁶ 5m 6m³ 5g⁶ 6m³ 6f 5.1m* 6m⁵ 6m 5m⁵ 6g 5s 6.1s 1996 6s 6g 5g² 6m² 5.1f⁵ 6d 6g* 6f⁵ 5.1f³ 6m³ 6g⁵ 5.6m 6m 5d³ 5g Oct 19] lengthy, workmanlike gelding: has been hobdayed: fairly useful handicapper: has maintained a similar level of form last 4 seasons: won at Salisbury in June: ran excellent races when fifth in the Wokingham (first home on far side) at Royal Ascot and third in Stewards' Cup at Goodwood: effective at 5f and 6f: acts on any going: successful for apprentice: held up, and suited by strongly-run race: tough. *P. G. Murphy*

SIR NORMAN HOLT (IRE) 7 b.g. Ela-Mana-Mou 132 – Ploy 87 (Posse – (USA) 130) [1995 –, a63: 8m 9.7g a12g² a10g⁶ 1996 a12g⁴ a16g* Jan 18] good- a72 topped gelding: fair handicapper on the all-weather, only modest on turf: won at Lingfield in January in game style, reportedly finishing lame: stays 2m: acts on firm ground and equitrack, not on a soft surface: tried visored, usually blinkered nowadays: effective from front or held up. *R. J. O'Sullivan*

SIR OLIVER (IRE) 7 b.g. Auction Ring (USA) 123 – Eurorose (Busted 134) – [1995 –: a10g a8g a7g 1996 9f 8.3d Aug 12] good-topped gelding: poor handicapper: no promise last 2 seasons. *B. A. Pearce*

SIR RICKY (USA) 2 b.g. (Jan 20) Woodman (USA) 126 – Opera Queen (IRE) – p
(Sadler's Wells (USA) 132) [1996 7m Aug 17] 200,000Y: useful-looking gelding:
has a round action: first foal: dam, 6f winner in Japan, sister to Oaks winner Intrepidity: 12/1 and bit backward, never a factor in 17-runner Newbury maiden won by
Monza: showed a round action: looks sort to do better: gelded. *R. Charlton*

SIR SILVER SOX (USA) 4 gr.g. Corwyn Bay 115 – Sox In The Box (USA) 104 d
(Cresta Rider (USA) 124) [1995 107: 7d⁶ 7.5g⁶ 6m² 6m* 6m⁵ 6g 1996 7s 6g⁴ 6d⁶ 6f
6m 6.3m 7d⁶ 7g 6s Oct 19] leggy gelding: useful handicapper on his day: good fourth
at Leopardstown in May: upset in paddock and reluctant at stalls (was also on only
other British outing) when well held in Wokingham at Royal Ascot fourth start: well
below form afterwards: sold (T. Stack to T.D. Barron) 7,000 gns Newmarket Autumn
Sales and gelded: best efforts at 6f: acts on good to firm and dead ground: usually
blinkered/visored. *T. Stack, Ireland*

SIR TALBOT 2 b.c. (Mar 15) Ardross 134 – Bermuda Lily 78 (Dunbeath (USA) 73
127) [1996 7d⁴ 7.9g⁵ Oct 9] 6,000F: rather leggy colt: looked weak: third foal:
half-brother to fairly useful 3-y-o 9.7f and 10.5f winner Sawa-Id (by Anshan) and
4-y-o (stays 1¼m) Dee-Lady (by Deploy), 5f winner at 2 yrs: dam 2-y-o 5f winner:
similar form when fourth of 19, swishing tail, to Entice in maiden at Salisbury and
when fifth of 13 to Cybertechnology in steadily-run median auction maiden at York
later in month: will stay middle distances. *R. Hannon*

SIR TASKER 8 b.h. Lidhame 109 – Susie's Baby (Balidar 133) [1995 60, a84: 54 d
a5g* a5g a5g⁵ a6g* a6g⁵ a6g* a6g* 6.1g 5m 5m⁵ 5g 6m 5m² 5f² 5m 6f² 6m* 6d a5g⁴ a66 d
6g a7g⁶ 5f 6m a6g⁶ a5g a6g⁴ a6g 1996 a6g² a6g³ a5g⁴ a6g⁴ a6g³ a6g⁵ a6g⁴ a6g a6g³
5.1g⁴ a5g⁵ 6g 6d 6m a5g a6g a6s⁵ Dec 19] compact, quite attractive horse: just a
modest performer in 1996: effective at 5f and 6f: acts on firm and dead ground and
the all-weather: has won in visor and without: blinkered (ran creditably) on 8-y-o
reappearance. *J. L. Harris*

SIR THOMAS BEECHAM 6 b.g. Daring March 116 – Balinese 86 (Balidar) –
[1995 –, a64: a13g² 14.9d 15.4m a13g 1996 a16g a16g⁶ a16g* a16g a16g² 15.4m a61
14.1m Apr 30] leggy gelding: modest handicapper: won at Lingfield in February:
well below form on return to turf: stays 2m: acts on good to firm ground and on
equitrack: inconsistent. *S. Dow*

SIS GARDEN 3 b.f. Damister (USA) 123 – Miss Nanna 56§ (Vayrann 133) [1995 49
52: 7g 7m⁴ a8g6 1996 7m 8m 12g a11g³ a9.4g² a8g a8.5g² 8m² 8f 7m 7d* 8m a7g* a65
7g³ a7g* a8g a7g³ a7g Dec 28] unfurnished filly: modest handicapper: won seller at
Ayr in August, claimer at Wolverhampton (claimed out of T. Easterby's stable
£3,000) in September and minor event at Wolverhampton (improved form, making
all) in November: best form at 7f/1m: acts on good to firm and dead ground, goes
well on fibresand: usually blinkered: has sometimes looked reluctant. *J. Cullinan*

SISTAR ACT 3 b.f. Salse (USA) 128 – Unsuitable (Local Suitor (USA) 128) 71
[1995 –: 6g⁴ 6m 1996 7s 8.2d* 7f⁶ 8g* 8.3m 10.1f* 10m⁵ 8f⁵ 8m 10d⁴ 8m 8.1m⁴ 10d
10.5v⁵ 8f 10m 9g Nov 1] well-made filly: good walker: fair performer: won seller at
Nottingham in April and handicaps at Bath in May and Yarmouth (ridden by 7-lb
claimer) in June: better at around 1¼m than shorter: acts on any going: visored (not
disgraced) final start: sold 12,000 gns Newmarket December Sales. *M. R. Channon*

SISTER KIT (IRE) 3 b.f. Glacial Storm (USA) 127 – Good Holidays 60 (Good –
Times (ITY)) [1995 59: 8.2d 8d⁴ 8g 1996 10.3s 10.8g 11.6m⁶ 8.3g a14.8g³ Jul 15]
robust filly: showed little in 1996: should be suited by middle distances. *B. Palling*

SIX CLERKS (IRE) 3 b.g. Shadeed (USA) 135 – Skidmore Girl (USA) 58
(Vaguely Noble 140) [1995 68: 7g 6m⁴ 6m³ 7.9m a8g⁵ a8g² 1996 a8g² 10.3d⁵ 12d a69
10m 8g⁵ May 30] tall, strong gelding: fair maiden: best form at 1m, seemed not to
stay 1½m: goes well on the all-weather, yet to race on extremes of going on turf:
blinkered (raced freely but ran respectably) final start. *J. G. FitzGerald*

SIX FOR LUCK 4 b.g. Handsome Sailor 125 – Fire Sprite 83 (Mummy's Game 61 §
120) [1995 57§: 6m² 6.1m⁴ 6f 6g⁵ 5m 1996 5g 5g⁵ 5m 5g⁶ 5g 5g⁵ 5m⁵ 5m⁵ 6m³
6m³ 6d² 5m 5m 5g 5m Oct 23] leggy, lengthy gelding: good mover: modest sprint
handicapper: acts on good to firm and dead ground: tried blinkered: usually bandaged
behind: has had tongue tied down: carries head high: temperamental. *D. A. Nolan*

SIX SHOOTER 2 b.f. (Apr 24) Damister (USA) 123 – Ten To Six 66 (Night Shift –
(USA)) [1996 7f Nov 5] sturdy, lengthy filly: first foal: dam 6f winner from 3 starts
at 2 yrs: 50/1, soundly beaten in maiden at Redcar. *E. Weymes*

SIXTIES MELODY 2 b.g. (Feb 4) Merdon Melody 98 – Balidilemma 77 – (Balidar 133) [1996 7f Oct 15] half-brother to 6f winner Able Mabel (by Absalom): dam 1m winner, is half-sister to high-class 6f to 1m performer Joshua: 50/1, always behind in maiden at Leicester: gelded. *R. Boss*

SIYADAH (USA) 2 ch.f. (Jan 22) Mr Prospector (USA) – Roseate Tern 123 79 p
(Blakeney 126) [1996 7g³ 7m⁵ Sep 20] lengthy, unfurnished filly: easy mover: second foal: dam, winner of Yorkshire Oaks and third in Oaks and St Leger, half-sister to high-class middle-distance performer Ibn Bey out of half-sister to Tele-prompter and Chatoyant: very green when over 9 lengths third of 7 to Fleet River in maiden at Goodwood: favourite, some improvement when fifth to Etoile in minor event at Newbury following month: will stay further than 7f. *Saeed bin Suroor*

SIZZLING 4 b.g. Sizzling Melody 117 – Oriental Splendour 85 (Runnett 125) 64
[1995 65: 5.1g⁶ 5.1f* 5m⁵ 6m 6m⁴ 6m³ 5m⁴ 5g⁶ 6f* 1996 6.1g 6m 6f 6m² 6m⁵ 6m⁴ 5m³ Jul 24] smallish, sturdy gelding: modest handicapper: well beaten only try in blinkers: stays 6f: acts on firm ground. *R. Hannon*

SIZZLING ROMP 4 b.f. Sizzling Melody 117 – Its A Romp (Hotfoot 126) 52
[1995 –: a6g 5g 5g a5g 5.2m⁶ 1996 a5g 5.2m⁵ 7m 5g Sep 7] sturdy filly: modest maiden, rated 59 at 2 yrs: form in 1996 only on second start: should stay 6f: acts on good to firm ground: covered by Rock Hopper. *D. T. Thom*

SIZZLING SERENADE 3 gr.f. Sizzling Melody 117 – Trynova 66 (Tyrnavos –
129) [1995 –: 5d 7f a6g 1996 8.2f 8.5m 7d Aug 24] strong, close-coupled filly: no worthwhile form. *J. A. Harris*

SIZZLING SYMPHONY 3 b.g. Sizzling Melody 117 – Polly Worth 55 –
(Wolver Hollow 126) [1995 66: 5g 6m 7f* 7m⁴ 1996 7m 8.2m 10.5s 10.1m Oct 23] tall, lengthy gelding: won seller at Redcar at 2 yrs: no form in 1996. *R. A. Fahey*

SKEDADDLE 4 b.f. Formidable (USA) 125 – Norfolk Serenade 83 (Blakeney –
126) [1995 57: 7g⁴ 7m 8.5d⁴ 8m⁴ 9.9m⁴ a12g 10m 13.8g³ a14g² a13g⁵ 1996 a12g Jan 15] lengthy filly: modest maiden at best: visored, well beaten only 4-y-o outing: should stay beyond 1¼m: acts on good to firm ground and dead, yet to race on extremes: inconsistent: covered by Anshan. *Ronald Thompson*

SKELTON COUNTESS (IRE) 3 ch.f. Imperial Frontier (USA) 112 – Running 59
Brook (Run The Gantlet (USA)) [1995 54: 5m 5g 5.1m 5g⁴ 6m³ a5g⁶ 5m³ 1996 a2m⁶ a–
a8g a7g a7g Nov 30] leggy filly: modest maiden: stays 8.2f: has run poorly all 4 starts on fibresand. *R. Hollinshead*

SKELTON SOVEREIGN (IRE) 2 b.c. (May 15) Contract Law (USA) 108 – 63
Mrs Lucky (Royal Match 117) [1996 a5g⁵ a6g 5f⁶ 7f⁴ 7g⁴ 7.5f² 8m 7d 8m 8f 10f* 8g a59
a8.5g² a8.5g⁵ Nov 25] IR 3,100F, IR 4,000Y: smallish colt: seventh foal: half-brother to 5-y-o 11f and 1½m winner Once More For Luck (by Petorius), 5f and 1m winner at 2 yrs: dam Irish 6f winner: modest performer: won seller at Leicester in October: stays 1¼m: acts on firm ground and fibresand: often swishes away. *R. Hollinshead*

SKETCH PAD 2 br.f. (Jan 26) Warning 136 – Scribbling (USA) 88 (Secretariat 78
(USA)) [1996 5m³ 5g May 27] smallish, sturdy filly: first living foal: dam 1¼m and 10.6f winner: well backed in 2 maidens in May, looked up to scratch when third of 5 to Dance Parade at York, pulled up lame at Sandown. *R. Charlton*

SKI ACADEMY (IRE) 3 b.g. Royal Academy (USA) 130 – Cochineal (USA) –
52 (Vaguely Noble 140) [1995 96p: 8.1m* 8g³ 7d 1996 10.4m 12m⁵ 10.3d⁶ 12m 12.1s Oct 22] tall gelding: disappointing at 3 yrs, and sold only 3,200 gns Newmarket Autumn Sales: should be suited by 1¼m+: soundly beaten on soft surface: tried blinkered: one to treat with caution. *P. W. Chapple-Hyam*

SKI FOR GOLD 3 b.f. Shirley Heights 130 – Quest (USA) 90§ (The Minstrel 71
(CAN) 135) [1995 76p: 7m⁴ 8g⁶ 7.1s* 1996 10g⁴ 11.8d³ 16s³ 13.9g 14.1s⁵ Oct 31] quite attractive filly: good mover: fair handicapper: may have proved best at around 1¾m: best efforts on a soft surface: swished tail second 3-y-o start: stud. *J. L. Dunlop*

SKILLINGTON (USA) 3 b.g. Danzig (USA) – Annie Edge 118 (Nebbiolo 125) 94
[1995 92: 7g² 7m⁶ 8m³ 8g² 1996 10d 10m* 10.4m² 10g 12m⁵ 11.9m 10.3m 10m² Sep 26] big, good-topped, round-actioned gelding: usually takes the eye: fairly useful performer: won maiden at Pontefract in June: fifth in Tote Gold Trophy at Goodwood on fifth start: visored, back to form when neck second of 11 to Mellottie in rated stakes at Pontefract on final start: stays 1½m: acts on good to firm ground, well

beaten only start on a soft surface: often a front runner: gelded: sent to USA. *I. A. Balding*

SKIPMAN (IRE) 3 b.g. Posen (USA) – Near Miracle (Be My Guest (USA) 126) – [1995 –: a8.5g⁶ 1996 a7g a11g⁶ Feb 2] well beaten in fibresand and maidens: dead. *N. A. Smith*

SKIPPY WAS A KIWI (IRE) 2 b.f. (Apr 29) River Falls 113 – Hit For Six (Tap 47 On Wood 130) [1996 5m⁴ 6m² 6m⁵ Aug 19] IR 4,500F, IR 4,000Y: fifth foal: half-sister to 2 winners in Italy, including 3-y-o Hit Lady (7.5f, by Soviet Lad): dam, 1988 Irish 2-y-o 5f winner, granddaughter of Mesopotamia: best effort when length second of 14 in seller at Redcar: likely to be suited by further than 6f. *A. P. Jarvis*

SKRAM 3 b.g. Rambo Dancer (CAN) 107 – Skarberg (FR) (Noir Et Or 125) [1995 – –: 7.1m 6.1d 7g 1996 12m 10g Jul 8] lengthy gelding: little worthwhile form on flat: modest winning hurdler. *R. Dickin*

SKY COMMANDER (USA) 2 b. or br.c. (Mar 31) Storm Bird (CAN) 134 – 91 p Fairy Footsteps 123 (Mill Reef (USA) 141) [1996 6m² Aug 22] $160,000Y: closely related to 1½m winner Haunted Wood (by Nijinsky) and half-brother to 3 winners, including fairly useful 11.7f and 1½m winner Lovely Fairy (by Beldale Flutter): dam won 1000 Guineas and is half-sister to St Leger winner Light Cavalry: 7/2, ½-length second of 6 to Kharir in maiden at Yarmouth, held up after slow start then coming from well back without being at all hard ridden, giving impression would have won has his run begun sooner: will stay 1m+: sure to improve, and win a race. *M. R. Stoute*

SKY DOME (IRE) 3 ch.c. Bluebird (USA) 125 – God Speed Her (Pas de Seul 92 133) [1995 5m⁶ 5m* 5d⁴ 1996 7m⁶ 7m⁶ 7.9f 8m 8m* 8d* 8g 9m 8g⁵ Nov 2] lengthy, leggy colt: made into a fairly useful handicapper, winning at Newmarket in April and back there and at Goodwood in August: probably stays 9f: acts on good to firm ground and dead: front runner/races prominently. *M. H. Tompkins*

SKYERS FLYER (IRE) 2 b. or br.f. (Apr 12) Magical Wonder (USA) 125 – 77 Siwana (IRE) (Dom Racine (FR) 121) [1996 5s⁶ 5d⁴ 5m* 6g³ 5m³ 5m⁴ 6m² 5g⁴ 6f³ a? 5.3f* 5f⁵ 6.5m 6m 7f⁵ a6g Oct 19] IR 2,500F, 900Y: rangy, angular filly: has a round action: second foal: dam winning Irish sprinter: fair form: won seller at Beverley in May and nursery at Brighton in August: ran poorly on all-weather debut: best form at 5f: acts on good to firm ground: races keenly. *Ronald Thompson*

SKYERS TRYER 2 b.f. (Feb 19) Lugana Beach 116 – Saltina (Bustino 136) 54 [1996 5f 5f⁵ 6d⁶ 5m* a5g a8.5g⁶ a6g Nov 11] lengthy, unfurnished filly: fourth foal: a– half-sister to 5-y-o 1½m winner Mr Towser (by Faustus): dam little form: clearly best effort when winning rating-related maiden at Musselburgh in September: well beaten in sellers at Wolverhampton subsequently: should stay 6f: below form on dead ground, seems unsuited by fibresand. *Ronald Thompson*

SKYLIGHT 3 ch.g. Domynsky 110 – Indian Flower 87 (Mansingh (USA) 120) – [1995 NR 1996 7.5m 7g 8m Aug 18] 5,100Y: small gelding: fifth reported foal: dam 5f winner here who later won in USA: well beaten in maidens. *Miss M. K. Milligan*

SLAPY DAM 4 b.g. Deploy 131 – Key To The River (USA) (Irish River (FR) 53 131) [1995 67: a8g⁵ a8g⁵ 10g² 11.1g* 14.6m 11.6m 10m 10m³ 10.5m⁴ 10d⁴ 12s* 11.8g* 12.1s⁶ 1996 a12g⁶ 11.8g 12g 11.8m 14.6g 12m⁶ 10m⁴ 11.8m⁵ 10.4g 10f Sep 28] close-coupled gelding: modest handicapper: disappointing in 1996: sold 3,900 gns Doncaster October Sales: should stay further than 1½m (out of form when tried): acts on good to firm and soft ground: visored last 4 starts. *J. Mackie*

SLAYJAY (IRE) 3 ch.f. Mujtahid (USA) 118 – Fire Flash 74 (Bustino 136) [1995 94 6g⁵ 6g² 1996 5m* 5g⁶ 6m³ 5m³ 5m² 6g³ 5m 5g Sep 8] IR 24,000Y: lengthy, Irish-trained filly: half-sister to disappointing 4-y-o Sotoboy (by Danehill), useful 6f winner at 2 yrs, and several other winners, including Flame of Persia (1m at 2 yrs to 1¼m, by Persian Heights): dam, never tried beyond 1¼m, out of smart 7f and 1m performer Dazzling Light, a half-sister to Welsh Pageant: useful performer: won maiden at Tipperary in May: best effort when second of 8 in valuable handicap at the Curragh in July: respectable effort in similar event at York penultimate start: effective at 5f (best form) and 6f: raced only on a sound surface: sold 63,000 gns Newmarket December Sales. *J. C. Hayden, Ireland*

SLEEPLESS 2 b.f. (Apr 2) Night Shift (USA) – Late Evening (USA) (Riverman 81 (USA) 131) [1996 6m² 5f³ 7m⁴ Sep 20] 18,500Y: good-topped, quite attractive filly:

SLE

has scope: sixth foal: half-sister to several winners, including 3-y-o 7f winner Mezzanotte (by Midyan) and useful 7f (at 2 yrs) and 1m winner Joie De Soir (by Caerleon): dam French maiden: in frame in maidens at Ascot and Beverley and minor event (4½ lengths fourth of 9 to Etoile) at Newbury: will stay 1m. *N. A. Graham*

SLEEPTITE (FR) 6 gr.g. Double Bed (FR) 121 – Rajan Grey (Absalom 128) – [1995 –, a65: a13g* a12g² a16g² a14.8g³ 16.2m a12g³ a12g⁴ 1996 a16g Nov 12] modest middle-distance stayer: successful over hurdles prior to well beaten only 6-y-o start. *W. G. M. Turner*

SLEEPY BOY 3 br.g. Zero Watt (USA) 107 – Furnace Lass VII (Damsire – Unregistered) [1995 –: 7f⁴ 1996 10m 12.4m Aug 7] seems of little account. *W. Storey*

SLEEPYTIME (IRE) 2 b.f. (Feb 20) Royal Academy (USA) 130 – Alidiva 108 P 105 (Chief Singer 131) [1996 7.1m* 8g³ Sep 29]
Sleepytime went into winter quarters the shortest-priced of the ante-post favourites for the first four classics, variously quoted at 3/1 and 7/2 for the One Thousand Guineas. Those who availed themselves of the 40/1 on offer shortly before she made her racecourse debut saw her odds contract to as low as 6/1 after she made a striking impression in a Sandown maiden in mid-September. Starting at 100/30-on, Sleepytime duly proved in a completely different league to her admittedly ordinary rivals, quickening clear effortlessly over a furlong out and cruising home five lengths clear, eased right down as she reached the post and value for much more. Even at this very early stage, she looked every inch a One Thousand Guineas candidate in the making. Her trainer, who wasn't exactly given to praising two-year-old fillies, described Sleepytime afterwards as 'potentially the best I've got' and said he rated her in 'the same sort of league' as Bosra Sham.
Sleepytime was seen out only once more in her first season, in the Fillies' Mile at Ascot, a race Bosra Sham had won the previous year. She was joined in the line-up by the stable's May Hill winner Reams of Verse but there didn't seem much room to doubt which was the stable's first string: Pat Eddery, who had ridden both fillies on their previous start, was on Sleepytime who started 6/4 favourite. The 2/1 shot Red Camellia, the form pick on two recent good efforts, and Reams of Verse at 5/1 were the only others at single figures in the betting. Sleepytime had absolutely no luck, becoming sandwiched when making her effort between Reams of Verse and Red Camellia after Eddery had had her poised to challenge, full of running, from early in the straight. Neither Reams of Verse nor Red Camellia helped matters by failing to keep straight in the last furlong or so and when Sleepytime stumbled after clipping Red Camellia Eddery wisely didn't persevere seriously with her. Reams of Verse won by a length and a quarter from the 10/1-shot Khassah, who had every chance, with Sleepytime and Red Camellia a neck and a short head further away. The stewards found that Reams of Verse and Red Camellia had interfered with Sleepytime but, as they judged the interference to be accidental, the placings remained unaltered. Eddery was in no doubt Sleepytime would have won. 'I've had to squeeze her out and when I've got out it's too late,' he said. 'I definitely would have won and I've ended up not pushing.' The bookmakers shared the view, reducing Sleepytime's Guineas odds further to 9/2, behind the then-favourite Dazzle; Reams of Verse was cut from around 20/1 to 7/1. Trainer Henry Cecil, on the other hand, who had encouraged the owner of Reams of Verse to run because 'you should never be scared of one horse', said he hadn't been sure which of the pair would win and still didn't know which was the better. Did this mean Cecil now thought he had two fillies not far off the Bosra Sham class, or was there, perhaps, a touch of diplomacy about his post-race comments? A steady early pace and the relatively close proximity at the finish of rank outsiders Logic and Mrs Miniver, to say nothing of Sleepytime not getting a clear run, meant that the Fillies' Mile wasn't so informative, at least as a form guide, as it might have been. But, that said, Sleepytime is clearly capable of a good deal better than she was able to show at Ascot and it's hardly

915

surprising that the bookmakers have decided to tread carefully with her. The possibility of injury, loss of form or failure to train on are always there to haunt those connected with any leading classic candidate over the winter months, but Sleepytime clearly has the makings of a filly who should prove well up to normal Guineas-winning standard.

Sleepytime (IRE) (b.f. Feb 20, 1994)	Royal Academy (USA) (b 1987)	Nijinsky (b 1967)	Northern Dancer Flaming Page
		Crimson Saint (ch 1969)	Crimson Satan Bolero Rose
	Alidiva (b 1987)	Chief Singer (b 1981)	Ballad Rock Principia
		Alligatrix (br 1980)	Alleged Shore

Sleepytime, a tall, close-coupled filly, looks just the type to train on. She was green in the Fillies' Mile preliminaries, where she was attended by two handlers, and it was interesting that her trainer decided not to run her in the Rockfel Stakes at Newmarket's October meeting when that race attracted a strong field. 'She'll be very much better once she matures over the winter,' Cecil said. 'She would have been taking on some of the fillies that will be running in the Guineas and I didn't want her to have too hard a race so late in the year.' Sleepytime is the third foal of the useful Alidiva, who was successful at up to a mile, and both of Alidiva's previous foals have made the anticipated improvement from two to three. Her first, Taipan (by Last Tycoon), developed into a useful performer (successful at up to a mile and a half) and her second Ali-Royal, a full brother to Sleepytime, showed smart form at seven furlongs and a mile in the latest season. Sleepytime's grandam Alligatrix failed to train on, however, after winning at seven furlongs as a two-year-old and finishing third in the Fillies' Mile. Further back, Sleepytime's pedigree is American, her great grandam Shore being a very useful two-year-old and a sister to two very smart performers Cabildo and Canal. Sleepytime's sire, the July Cup and Breeders' Cup Mile winner Royal Academy, was never raced beyond a mile and it's likely that Sleepytime will make her mark at around that trip. She has a quick, fluent action and the ease with which she travelled through the race in the Fillies' Mile demonstrated that she is by no means short of speed.
H. R. A. Cecil

SLICIOUS   4 b.c. Slip Anchor 136 – Precious Jade 72 (Northfields (USA)) [1995   116
118: 8d² 10f⁵ 12s* 12g* 12d² 12m² 10m* 1996 10d* 10.5m 10d 11g* 12s⁵ 10m⁶ Nov
10] smart Italian colt: won Group 1 Premio Roma in 1995: not nearly so consistent as
at 3 yrs, running to form only when winning listed race in April and, after 4-month
break, Group 3 event (by 2¾ lengths from Concepcion) in September, both at Milan:
stayed 1½m: acted on heavy ground and good to firm: has been retired to stud.
V. Caruso, Italy

SLIEMA CREEK   2 gr.g. (Jan 21) Beveled (USA) – Sea Farer Lake 74 (Gairloch   – p
122) [1996 a6g⁵ Dec 27] 6,000Y: fifth foal: brother to a winning hurdler and half-
brother to 1989 2-y-o 6f winner Sirse (by Enchantment): dam 1m and 1¼m winner:
very easy to back, slowly away and never dangerous in maiden at Southwell: will
probably do better. *T. D. Barron*

SLIEVENAMON   3 br.c. Warning 136 – Twice A Fool (USA) (Foolish Pleasure   59 +
(USA)) [1995 NR 1996 8m 8f 8.3m a8.5g⁵ a9.4g* a8g* Dec 27] 16,000Y, 15,000
2-y-o: close-coupled colt: half-brother to 1m winners Twin Jet (by Lear Fan) and
Twin Falls (by Trempolino) and to several winners in USA, all at up to 1m: dam
unraced daughter of sister to Habitat: well beaten until winning handicaps at
Wolverhampton (making much of running to land a gamble) in November and
Southwell (by 5 lengths) in December: stays 9.4f well: acts on fibresand. *J. E. Banks*

SLIGHTLY OLIVER (IRE)   2 b.g. (Mar 1) Silver Kite (USA) 111 – Red Note   §§
(Rusticaro (FR) 124) [1996 8.5m⁶ 8.2g⁴ a7g² a7g³ a8g Nov 29] 11,000Y: fourth foal:
half-brother to 4-y-o Sound The Trumpet, 5f winner at 2 yrs (by Fayruz), and a winner in Hungary: dam unraced: modest maiden plater (rated 53) before sold out of G.
Lewis' stable 3,200 gns Doncaster November Sales after fourth outing: very slowly

away penultimate one: virtually refused to race initially on final start, then unseated rider: stays 8.2f: blinkered/visored last 4 outings: one to avoid. *Mrs N. Macauley*

SLIGHTLY SPEEDY (IRE) 3 b.g. Prince Rupert (FR) 121 – Moutalina 98 (Ela-Mana-Mou 132) [1995 7f⁶ 7m³ 8m* 8g 6m³ 7d* 9d³ 1996 7s⁶ 8s⁵ 7d⁴ 8f 6m 8.5g 7m* 7g³ 8g 8f Oct 12] IR 1,200F, IR 2,000Y: smallish, good-quartered colt: fourth foal: half-brother to Irish 1992 2-y-o 6f winner Never Told (by Classic Secret): dam Irish middle-distance maiden: useful performer: won maiden at Tralee and minor event at Gowran Park at 2 yrs and handicap at the Curragh in August: sold 26,000 gns Newmarket Autumn Sales: stays 9f: acts on good to firm ground (well held twice on firm, including in Britannia Handicap fourth 3-y-o start) and dead. *J. T. Gorman, Ireland*

SLIPARIS 3 b.f. Slip Anchor 136 – Parisian Express (FR) 48 (Siberian Express – (USA) 125) [1995 –: 8d 1996 14g 10m 12m 14d Oct 2] unfurnished filly: seems of no account. *K. O. Cunningham-Brown*

SLIP JIG (IRE) 3 b.c. Marju (IRE) 127 – Taking Steps 100 (Gay Fandango 84 (USA) 132) [1995 NR 1996 8g 7d* 7m³ 8m 10m⁶ 8.5g³ 8m 8g a7g a8g³ a10g² a10g² a71 Dec 30] IR 20,000Y: small colt: fourth foal: closely related to Last Step (by Last Tycoon) and half-brother to Strutting (by Ela-Mana Mou), both useful middle-distance performers in 1995: dam Irish 9f winner (also third in Irish 1000 Guineas) who probably stayed 11f: fairly useful form on turf, fair so far on all-weather: won maiden at Salisbury in May: will stay 1½m: acts on good to firm and dead ground, and on equitrack: has been bandaged near-fore. *R. Hannon*

SLIPPERY FIN 4 b.f. Slip Anchor 136 – Finyska (FR) (Niniski (USA) 125) 51 [1995 10.5g⁵ 10.8g 11.5g⁴ 11.5g³ 10.5s 12g⁴ 12m⁶ 12s 11.5g 11.3g⁴ 1996 a12g³ a16g a12g² Jul 27] ex-French filly: second foal: half-sister to a 2-y-o 5.5f winner in France by Baillamont: dam French 9f to 11f winner: unraced at 2 yrs: modest form in varied company, including claiming, at 3 yrs for D. Sepulchre: placed twice in sellers here: stays 1½m: often blinkered. *W. G. M. Turner*

SLIPSTREAM STAR 2 b.f. (Mar 16) Slip Anchor 136 – Alsiba 68 (Northfields – p (USA)) [1996 7d Oct 28] sixth foal: closely related to fairly useful 1¼m and 1½m winner Smart Blade (by Elegant Air): dam staying daughter of half-sister to Irish 2000 Guineas winner Northern Treasure: 16/1, behind in maiden at Lingfield, chasing leaders until dropping away over 1f out: likely to do better. *I. A. Balding*

SLIP THE NET (IRE) 2 b.c. (Feb 18) Slip Anchor 136 – Circus Ring 122 (High 87 Top 131) [1996 8m⁴ 10.2d² Sep 30] 85,000Y: small, good-topped colt: ninth live foal: brother to useful 4-y-o 9f and 1¼m winner Ellie Ardensky, closely related to smart 7f (at 2 yrs) and 1¼m winner Lady Shipley (by Shirley Heights) and half-brother to several winners: dam unbeaten at 2 yrs but ran only once afterwards: similar form when around 4 lengths fourth of 9 to King Sound in steadily-run minor event at Newbury and when 2½ lengths second of 6 to Eldorado in maiden at Bath following month: will stay 1½m. *P. F. I. Cole*

SLIVOVITZ 6 b.g. Petoski 135 – Hiding 84 (So Blessed 130) [1995 59: 6m 6g – 6m 6m 6f 6m 5f³ 6m³ a7g⁵ a6g 1996 a6g Jan 6] rangy gelding: fair sprint handicapper (rated 68 in 1994) at best: broke leg only start in 1996: acted on equitrack and good to firm ground, probably on a soft surface: usually blinkered or visored, but successful without either: usually a front runner: dead. *M. J. Heaton-Ellis*

SLMAAT 5 ch.m. Sharpo 132 – Wasslaweyeh (USA) 66 (Damascus (USA)) [1995 – 75: a11g* a11g³ a12g 11.8d² 11.8m⁴ 12.3m 12g 12m 12.1s 1996 a14.8g a11g a11g a8g a11g Mar 18] sparely-made mare: fair handicapper for Mrs M. Reveley in spring at 4 yrs: subsequently changed stables twice (left D. Nicholls after third 5-y-o start) and lost all form: stays 1½m: acts on fibresand and good to firm ground, well suited by a soft surface: tried blinkered. *R. D. E. Woodhouse*

SLOE BRANDY 6 b.m. Hotfoot 126 – Emblazon 91 (Wolver Hollow 126) [1995 35 –: a12g 1996 12m³ 12.3m Jun 19] shallow-girthed mare: poor form when third in ladies handicap at Newmarket on reappearance: soundly beaten in similar event at Ripon 11 days later: subsequently joined Mrs H. Walton. stays 1½m. *J. Wharton*

SLY LADY 4 b.f. Rambo Dancer (CAN) 107 – Countess of Honour (USA) (Troy – 137) [1995 NR 1996 12g 10g⁵ 7g⁶ Jul 24] leggy filly: first foal: dam, poor maiden, stayed 1½m: no form. *C. W. C. Elsey*

SMALL RISK 2 b.f. (Mar 5) Risk Me (FR) 127 – Small Double (IRE) 55 (Double 48
Schwartz 128) [1996 5d³ 5m² a5g Apr 27] 1,400Y: angular filly: second foal: dam
2-y-o 5f winner: well backed when placed in maiden auction and seller at Beverley
early in season: well held in seller at Wolverhampton on last outing. *C. A. Dwyer*

SMART ALEC 4 b.g. Diesis 133 – Ahead 113 (Shirley Heights 130) [1995 NR 115
1996 9m² 8d⁴ May 18] strong, rangy, good sort: has a powerful, round action:
impressed when winning both starts at 2 yrs: suffered an injury in the spring of 1995:
heavily-backed favourite though looking just in need of run, head second of 9 to Luso
(gave 8 lb) in Earl of Sefton Stakes at Newmarket in April, produced to lead in the
Dip but just run out of it up the hill: creditable fourth of 7 to Soviet Line in Lockinge
Stakes at Newbury month later: subsequently gelded: stays 9f: acts on good to firm
ground and dead: looked well able to win a pattern race. *L. M. Cumani*

SMART BOY (IRE) 2 ch.c. (Mar 22) Polish Patriot (USA) 128 – Bouffant (High 77
Top 131) [1996 5m* 6f³ 7f Jul 26] IR 85,000Y: fourth foal: brother to 3-y-o German
1m winner Mutasarrif and half-brother to 1992 2-y-o 6.9f winner Fanfan and 9.9f
winner Sahil (both by Taufan): dam thrice-raced daughter of smart 1m to 1½m
winner Lucent, herself daughter of good sprinter Lucasland: won maiden at Lingfield
in May: below that form afterwards: should stay beyond 5f: possibly unsuited by
very firm ground. *P. F. I. Cole*

SMART DOMINION 2 b.c. (Apr 9) Sharpo 132 – Anodyne 100 (Dominion 74 p
123) [1996 6s Oct 24] 46,000Y: lengthy colt: fourth foal: brother to fairly useful 1993
2-y-o 5f winner Stimulant, later successful in USA, and half-brother to 3-y-o 6f (at 2
yrs) and 7f winner Pharmacy (by Mtoto) and 6f winner Showery (by Rainbow
Quest): dam, 6f winner, sister to very useful (at up to 1½m in USA) Domynsky: 20/1,
second home on unfavoured far side when tenth of 23 behind Za-Im in maiden at
Newbury: will do better. *Lord Huntingdon*

SMARTER CHARTER 3 br.c. Master Willie 129 – Irene's Charter 72 (Persian 81
Bold 123) [1995 –p: 6.1d 5s 1996 5d 8m⁴ 7.5g* 8m² 8g² 8m⁶ 8.5m³ 10g⁶ 8m⁶ 8.5m*
8m⁵ 9m⁴ Aug 7] tall, leggy colt: has reportedly been hobdayed: fairly useful
handicapper: won at Beverley in May and July, on second occasion looking less than
keen before leading 1½f out: unsuited by falsely-run races last 2 starts: suited by
good stamina test at around 1m, and will stay 1¼m: acts on good to firm ground:
held up (often soon off bridle), and probably suited by strongly-run race and strong
handling: has joined Mrs L. Stubbs. *Mrs J. R. Ramsden*

SMART GUEST 4 ch.g. Be My Guest (USA) 126 – Konbola 91 (Superlative 60
118) [1995 90: 7m 8m* 7f⁴ 8m 7.1m 1996 a8g⁵ 8s 6g* 7.6g May 9] sturdy, lengthy
gelding: unimpressive mover: fairly useful performer at best in 1995: only 4-y-o
form when winning seller at Pontefract in April: effective at 6f, stays 1m: acts on firm
and dead ground: takes keen hold. *J. A. Harris*

SMART PLAY (USA) 3 gr.c. Sovereign Dancer (USA) – Casessa (USA) (Caro 101
133) [1995 NR 1996 11d⁵ 12g* 10.3g⁴ 12f⁶ 12m Oct 1] $110,000Y resold
$130,000Y: good-topped colt: has a quick action: second foal: half-brother to useful
4-y-o 7.5f (at 2 yrs) and 1m winner New Century (by Manila): dam maiden half-sister
to 1000 Guineas winner Musical Bliss: won maiden at Thirsk in May: ran well facing
stiffish tasks in £8,100 event (behind Farasan) in May and listed race (behind Busy
Flight) in September, both at Doncaster: soundly beaten in rated stakes at Newmarket
on final start: will stay beyond 1½m. *Mrs J. Cecil*

SMART PROSPECT 2 b.g. (Mar 31) Superpower 113 – Bustilly 65 (Busted –
134) [1996 7g 7m a7g Sep 9] 3,200F, 3,400Y: good-topped gelding: half-brother to a
winner in Austria by Relkino: dam 1¼m winner out of half-sister to smart stayer
Celtic Cone: soundly beaten in maidens. *B. J. Meehan*

SMART SPIRIT (IRE) 2 b.f. (Apr 15) Persian Bold 123 – Sharp Ego (USA) 66 p
(Sharpen Up 127) [1996 7.9g 8.1d 8.1s³ 8f Nov 5] IR 6,700F, IR 6,500Y, 13,000
2-y-o: tall, good-topped filly: has plenty of scope: sixth foal: half-sister to 1994 2-y-o
5f winner Sapiston Girl (by Nordico) and 5-y-o 1m to 1½m winner El Bailador (by
Dance of Life): dam Irish 5f winner: 33/1, best effort in maidens when third to Noble
Dane in steadily-run race at Haydock in October, running on under considerable
handling: pulled hard and seemed to hang when eighth of 18, never placed to
challenge, to Epic Stand in nursery at Redcar on last start: stays 1m: stirred up in
preliminaries second start: likely to do better. *Mrs M. Reveley*

SMILE FOREVER (USA) 3 b.f. Sunshine Forever (USA) – Awenita (Rarity –
129) [1995 69: 6.9f² 8.2d⁵ 7m 1996 a7g 8m 9.7g⁵ 11.9g a10g⁴ a12s Nov 19] sturdy
filly: modest maiden: no worthwhile form in 1996: left J. Toller's stable after second
3-y-o start: rather headstrong. *Miss Gay Kelleway*

SMILEY FACE 4 b.g. Colmore Row 111 – Count On Me 77 (No Mercy 126) –
[1995 –: 5.1m 1996 a10g Feb 1] sparely-made gelding: poor form at 2 yrs: soundly
beaten only flat outings since. *R. J. Hodges*

SMILING BESS 3 b.f. Salse (USA) 128 – Wanda 74 (Taufan (USA) 119) [1995 –
–: 6.1d 5s 1996 10m⁴ 6.1m a8.5g Nov 2] angular filly: no form. *R. Hollinshead*

SMILIN N WISHIN (USA) 3 b.f. Lyphard's Wish (FR) 124 – Smilin Michele 81
(USA) (Sharpen Up 127) [1995 79p: 8.1s² 1996 11d³ 11.4g⁵ 10m⁵ 10g* a12g Nov
14] angular, lightly-made filly: fairly useful form: off course over 4 months before
winning steadily-run maiden at Nottingham in October by 4 lengths from Scarpetta,
leading 2f out: stays 1m and at least as effective at 1¼m as 1¼m: best form with give in
the ground: sold only 4,000 gns Newmarket December Sales. *P. W. Chapple-Hyam*

SMITHEREENS 3 ch.f. Primo Dominie 121 – Splintering 80 (Sharpo 132) 65
[1995 74: 6g 5m² 1996 5d³ 6m 6.1m 5.2m³ 5m a5g 5.1g⁶ a7g* a7g* a7s² Nov 19] a75
leggy, lengthy filly: has a quick action: fair performer: disappointing until really
finding her form (on the all-weather, stepped up in trip) in November, winning
maiden and apprentice handicap at Lingfield: stays 7f: acts on good to firm ground,
goes well on the all-weather: visored once, well below form: races prominently.
P. T. Walwyn

SMOCKING 6 ch.m. Night Shift (USA) – Sue Grundy 104 (Grundy 137) [1995 –
35: 12m² 10f⁵ 11.5g⁴ 12m 12m a13g a12g a10g⁴ 1996 11.4m a8g Jun 25] angular,
plain mare: poor middle-distance maiden handicapper: tailed off in 1996: blinkered
once at 3 yrs. *Miss K. M. George*

SMOKEBUSH 2 gr.c. (Mar 28) Petong 126 – Kimberley Park 72 (Try My Best 61 ?
(USA) 130) [1996 5f⁶ 6m 7f⁵ Oct 15] 26,000Y: good-topped colt: has scope: first
foal: dam 7f winner who stayed 1m: modest form in maidens at Sandown, Goodwood
and Leicester: sold 7,500 gns Newmarket Autumn Sales: stays 7f: raced only on
top-of-the-ground: sent to Sweden. *Lord Huntingdon*

SMOKE'N'JO (IRE) 2 ch.c. (Mar 27) Masterclass (USA) 116 – Alpine Dance 44 +
(USA) 62§ (Apalachee (USA) 137) [1996 6m 5m⁶ 7.5f⁵ 7g 8.5g⁶ Aug 24] IR 5,200Y:
rather leggy, plain colt: fifth reported foal: half-brother to 7f (at 2 yrs) and 1¼m
winner Northern Bailiwick (by Nordance): dam middle-distance maiden, probably
ungenuine: poor form in maiden events: bred to stay at least 1m. *M. W. Easterby*

SMOKEY FROM CAPLAW 2 b.g. (Feb 16) Sizzling Melody 117 – Mary 63
From Dunlow (GB) 49 (Nicholas Bill 125) [1996 5g 6m* 7g 5m² 7.1m Aug 29]
strong, compact gelding: has a round action: second foal: half-brother to 3-y-o
Danish 7.5f winner Marketeer Magic (by Clantime): dam 2-y-o 5f winner, later had
form at 1m: won 4-runner claimer at Hamilton in May: good second, staying on
carrying head awkwardly, to Bold African in nursery at Haydock in August: probably
doesn't stay 7f: sold 4,600 gns Doncaster October Sales. *J. J. O'Neill*

SMOKEY PETE 2 gr.c. (Mar 7) Petong 126 – Quick Profit 78 (Formidable 88
(USA) 125) [1996 5m* 6m 6f⁶ Jul 20] 19,000F, 30,000Y: strong, compact colt: has a
quick action: third foal: half-brother to fair 4-y-o 1m/1¼m winner Battleship Bruce
(by Mazilier): dam 7f winner: well-backed favourite, won 6-runner minor event at
Ascot in May, getting unbalanced crossing path then responding well to lead line:
gave impression something amiss in minor event at York and (after 2-month break)
listed race at Newbury afterwards: has reportedly been operated on to have chip
removed from near-fore joint: looked a useful prospect on debut. *R. Hannon*

SMOOTH ASSET (IRE) 3 b.f. Fairy King (USA) – Sofala 103 (Home Guard 65
(USA) 129) [1995 NR 1996 7m⁴ 7d⁴ 8m² 8m 8g a6g⁶ Oct 19] 48,000Y: leggy,
unfurnished filly: eighth foal: half-sister to several winners including useful stayer
Bourbon Boy (by Ile De Bourbon), US 5-y-o Electric Society (Grade 2 and 3 at up to
11f, by Law Society) and useful North Queen (6f and 7f, by Northfields): dam won at
up to 8.5f: modest maiden: stays 1m: yet to race on extremes of going: sent to USA.
P. W. Chapple-Hyam

SMUGGLER'S POINT (USA) 6 b.g. Lyphard (USA) 132 – Smuggly (USA) – 121 (Caro 133) [1995 –: 14.1g 15.4m 1996 12d a12s Dec 19] fair staying handicapper (rated 67) in 1994: lightly raced and no worthwhile form on flat since. *J. J. Bridger*

SMUGURS (IRE) 2 ch.f. (Apr 10) Masterclass (USA) 116 – Blue Vista (IRE) 60 (Pennine Walk 120) [1996 6g² 6.1m² 6.9m² 7f⁶ 6g⁴ 7.9g⁶ 7g* 7.9g Oct 10] 3,700Y: leggy, unfurnished filly: second foal: dam unraced half-sister to smart sprinter Polykratis: modest form: won strongly-run nursery at Chester in September by a head from Grate Times, always up with pace and all out: sold 6,500 gns Newmarket Autumn Sales: probably stays 1m: edgy sort. *R. J. R. Williams*

SNAKE PLISSKEN (IRE) 5 ch.g. Reasonable (FR) 119 – Shalie (Windjammer 48 (USA)) [1995 46: 8.1m⁴ a8.5g⁵ 8g a7g⁵ a10g⁶ 1996 a8g⁵ a8g² a9.4g⁶ 8.3d² 7d 11.1m a55 May 18] modest maiden handicapper: stays 1m well: acts on all-weather surfaces and good to firm and dead ground: sometimes wears tongue strap. *D. Haydn Jones*

SNAKE SNAP 3 b.c. Shareef Dancer (USA) 135 – Clare Court 89 (Glint of Gold 115 128) [1995 9d⁵ 9g⁴ 9d⁴ 1996 9g* 10g* 10d* 12d³ 10g* 11g² 12s³ 10m⁵ Nov 10] 12,000Y: first foal: dam, very game and genuine filly, won at up to 1¾m and would have stayed 2m: useful performer on most form: won 4 of first 5 starts in 1996, notably listed race at Rome in May and Group 3 event at Naples (beat Scribano 3½ lengths) in July: creditable efforts placed in listed race at Rome and very valuable event at Milan next 2 starts: improved form when 5½ lengths fifth of 8 to Flemensfirth in Premio Roma last time: stays at least 1½m: acts on soft ground, seems to go well on good to firm: to be trained by B. Cecil in USA. *V. Caruso, Italy*

SNAP CRACKLE POP (IRE) 2 b.f. (Apr 26) Statoblest 120 – Spinelle 88§ 87 (Great Nephew 126) [1996 5.2f 5m² 5m* 5.2m⁴ 5m³ 6m 6m Oct 17] 6,500Y: leggy, workmanlike filly: fifth foal: half-sister to untrustworthy 7f winner Sweet Jaffa (by Never So Bold): dam, 1½m winner, disappointing daughter of Jacinth: progressive form: won maiden auction at Haydock in August: beaten around 3 lengths in listed races at Newbury and Ayr fourth and fifth starts: ran creditably when ninth of 25, travelling smoothly long way, to Proud Native in Redcar Two-Year-Old Trophy on last outing: probably stays 6f: raced only on top-of-the-ground. *R. F. Johnson Houghton*

SNAPPY GIRL (IRE) 2 b.f. (Apr 23) Caerleon (USA) 132 – Don't Rush (USA) – 93 (Alleged (USA) 138) [1996 7.1s Oct 22] fourth foal: half-sister to 5-y-o 5f winner King of Show (by Green Desert) and fairly useful 8.3f winner Reine de Neige (by Kris): dam 1½m winner, is half-sister to 1984 champion Canadian 3-y-o Key To The Moon out of champion Canadian filly Kamar: weak 10/1-shot, slowly away and well held in 16-runner maiden at Chepstow. *M. R. Stoute*

SNIPE HALL 5 b.m. Crofthall 110 – Geopelia 109 (Raffingora 130) [1995 88: 5m – 5g⁴ 6m⁶ 6m 1996 6m 5d Sep 28] leggy, good-quartered mare: fairly useful sprinter at best: reportedly returned lame final 4-y-o start: last of 21 and 15 in handicaps at York and Haydock on belated return. *T. R. Watson*

SNITCH 3 ch.g. Blow The Whistle 72 – Whispering Sea 52 (Bustino 136) [1995 36 49, a–: a5g⁶ 5m⁵ 5g 5m⁵ 5g² 5m 5m a6g a5g a5g 1996 5.1g 5g 5g⁶ 5f⁵ 5g⁶ 5f Jul 18] a– lengthy, sparely-made gelding: poor front-running maiden: sold 850 gns Doncaster September Sales: barely stays 5f: no form on fibresand: usually visored/blinkered. *C. Smith*

SNOW DOMINO (IRE) 3 ch.g. Habyom – Magic Picture (Deep Diver 134) 38 [1995 –: 7f a8g⁵ a8.5g 1996 a8g⁵ Jan 29] strong gelding: poor maiden: stays 1m: acts on fibresand. *J. M. Jefferson*

SNOW EAGLE (IRE) 2 b.f. (Mar 25) Polar Falcon (USA) 126 – Icefern 88 57 ? (Moorestyle 137) [1996 6m 7d a5g⁶ a6g⁴ a8.5g⁶ Dec 14] IR 14,000F, IR 21,000Y: tall, lengthy filly: fourth foal: half-sister to 2 winners, notably temperamentally suspect 3-y-o Iamus (at 8.2f, by Most Welcome): dam sprinter: modest form at best in maidens: likely to prove best short of 8.5f: retained 2,200 gns Newmarket Autumn Sales after third start. *R. Hannon*

SNOW FALCON 3 b.g. Polar Falcon (USA) 126 – Cameroun 106 (African Sky 71 124) [1995 76: 7m³ 7f⁶ 6m⁶ 7.3d 1996 a8.5g⁵ 8g⁶ 6m⁴ 7g⁶ 6g⁶ 10.1f* 12m* 11.6m 12g³ 12g 12m² 14.1m³ 13.6m⁵ Oct 17] good-bodied gelding: fair handicapper: led well inside final 1f to win at Yarmouth (seller) and Newmarket (by short head) in the summer: sold 17,000 gns Newmarket Autumn Sales: may prove best at up to around 1½m: acts on firm ground: tried blinkered/visored, better form without: sometimes slowly away: held up, and suited by strongly-run race. *M. Bell*

SNOW PARTRIDGE (USA)   2 ch.c. (Mar 10) Arctic Tern (USA) 126 – Lady   84 +
Sharp (FR) (Sharpman) [1996 7m² 7.9g³ Oct 9] $145,000Y: rather leggy, useful-looking colt: half-brother to several winners in France, including smart 9f to 1½m winner Lady Blessington (by Baillamont), later Grade 2 winner in USA: dam, French 1¼m winner, is half-sister to smart French 6.5f to 1m winner Prospero: staying-on second to Musheer in maiden at Ascot in July: disappointing only subsequent start, 2½ months later: looks a stayer. *P. F. I. Cole*

SNOWPOLES   3 b.f. High Estate 127 – Bronzewing 103 (Beldale Flutter (USA)   –
130) [1995 57p: 7.6d 1996 8g 7.1m 12f 10d Aug 26] tall, rather unfurnished filly: modest maiden: well beaten over middle distances last 2 starts after racing freely in lead: bred to stay beyond 1m: tongue tied final start. *Mrs J. Cecil*

SNOW PRINCESS (IRE)   4 b.f. Ela-Mana-Mou 132 – Karelia (USA) 111 (Sir   104
Ivor 135) [1995 87p: 10m 10.5g⁶ 10.5s* 12.1s* 12m* 12m* 1996 16.5g* 16.1m²
13.9m 13.4d³ 15d* 15s⁴ Nov 12] leggy filly: useful handicapper: won rated stakes at Doncaster in May and listed race at Milan (by 5¾ lengths from Kristal's Paradise) in October: second in Northumberland Plate at Newcastle in between: stays 16.5f well: acts on good to firm and soft ground: held up: genuine. *Lord Huntingdon*

SNOWY MANTLE   3 b.f. Siberian Express (USA) 125 – Mollified 67 (Lombard   –
(GER) 126) [1995 NR 1996 a8g⁴ 10m³ 10f⁵ 8f Oct 14] lengthy filly: half-sister to 3 middle-distance winners, including one by Longleat: dam stayed 1¼m: little worth-while form. *J. D. Bethell*

SOAKED   3 b.g. Dowsing (USA) 124 – Water Well 96 (Sadler's Wells (USA) 132)   66
[1995 NR 1996 7m 8d⁶ 10m 8g⁴ 8.3g Jul 8] quite good-topped gelding: has a short action: first foal: dam, stayed 1m, daughter of Soba: fair maiden: visored, tailed off after helping set strong pace in handicap at Windsor on final start, looking wayward: sold (J. Fanshawe to D. Chapman) 3,100 gns Newmarket Autumn Sales and gelded: not sure to stay 1¼m: not one to trust impicitly. *J. R. Fanshawe*

SOAKING   6 b.g. Dowsing (USA) 124 – Moaning Low 85 (Burglar 128) [1995 67:   54
a7g² 7g 7m⁵ a8g⁶ 7.1m a8g⁵ 7.1m* 7f² 7m² 8.3m 7m 7.1d⁵ 8d 1996 a7g* a7g⁴ a7g⁵   a80
6.9s 8f 7m⁵ 8g 7g 7m* 7m 7.1f 8m⁶ 7g a7g² a8g* Dec 13] strong, useful-looking gelding: fairly useful handicapper on the all-weather, modest on turf: won at Ling-field in January, Kempton in July and back at Lingfield in December: stays 1m: acts on firm and soft ground and on equitrack: sometimes swishes tail: none too consistent. *P. Burgoyne*

SO AMAZING   4 b.f. Hallgate 127 – Jussoli (Don 128) [1995 61: 10m⁶ 7g⁴ 8m⁴   55
5.9h³ 7m⁶ 10m6 a7g* a7g* a8g* a7g* 7.5m 6g 8g⁴ 7g a8.5g a7g⁵ Dec 28] strong,   a84 d
good-topped filly: good walker: fairly useful performer at best on the all-weather: won 3 handicaps at Southwell in January and claimer there (by 5 lengths, subsequently claimed out of Miss S. Hall's stable £12,000) in March: modest at best on turf (showed nil on return to all-weather late on): will prove best at up to 1m: goes well on fibresand and acts on good to firm and soft ground, not on hard: races prominently. *J. L. Eyre*

SOBA UP   6 ch.m. Persian Heights 129 – Soba 127 (Most Secret 119) [1995 74:   74
12g³ 9.2g³ 9.9m⁶ 12d 12.1m* 11.1f* 12.3m* 11.1m² 12.1f* 12.3m* 12m² 12.3m²
13.4m³ 13.9g 14.1m 12.1s⁴ 1996 12g 12g 12.1f 12.3m* 15.9m 12.4m⁵ 12.3g 12.1m²
12.1d² 11.9v Oct 6] big, lengthy, workmanlike mare: fair handicapper: won at Chester (for second year running) in June after prolonged duel: stays 13.4f well: acts on firm and soft going: blinkered (below form) once as 5-y-o: has won only at Musselburgh (3 times) and Chester (4 times): tough. *T. J. Etherington*

SOBELOVED   4 gr.g. Beveled (USA) – Miss Solo (Runnymede 123) [1995 50:   –
6.9d³ 8.3g 8g 8.3m 8.1m² 8.2m 8.1m⁵ 7.6m⁴ 7f⁴ 8h 7d 1996 8g 9f 7.1m 7.1m⁶ 7.6m
8m Aug 13] leggy, sparely-made gelding: modest maiden: no form in 1996: tried blinkered: sold 2,000 gns Ascot November Sales. *N. E. Berry*

SOCIAL PILLAR (USA)   2 b.c. (Mar 15) Gone West (USA) – Social Column   85 +
(USA) (Swoon's Son) [1996 7m⁶ 7.1f² 7m⁴ 8m* Oct 23] tall, quite attractive colt:

good mover: half-brother to several winners, notably very smart 1¼m winner Two Timing (by Blushing Groom): dam, placed at 6f, is half-sister to champion US filly Chris Evert: won 10-runner nursery at Yarmouth (well-backed favourite) by a head from Polar Flight, running on strongly: stays 1m: raced only on a firm surface: sold 75,000 gns Newmarket Autumn Sales. *J. H. M. Gosden*

SOCIETY GIRL   3 b.f. Shavian 125 – Sirene Bleu Marine (USA) (Secreto (USA)   63
128) [1995 73?: 6g 6m* 7g* 7m² 7m³ 6g³ 6.5m 7m⁶ 1996 a10g⁵ a7g⁴ a7g³ a8g² a7g⁵ a7g 8g* 8f⁴ 8f⁴ 10s* 10f⁶ 8.3m* 8m² 8g* 8.5m Sep 18] workmanlike filly: has a fluent, round action: modest performer: won claimers at Ripon in May, Ayr in July and Hamilton in August and handicap at Thirsk in September: bandaged near-hind, well below form on final start: sold 8,800 gns Newmarket Autumn Sales, resold 8,000 gns Doncaster November Sales: probably stays 1¼m: acts on firm ground and all-weather, probably on soft. *C. W. Thornton*

SOCIETY MAGIC (USA)   3 b.g. Imp Society (USA) – Lady Kirtling (USA)   63
(Kirtling 129) [1995 63: 7.9m⁵ 8.1s⁶ 1996 8m 8.2m 7f 7.1m* 7m Oct 4] big gelding: has scope: has a round action: modest performer: uneasy favourite after 3½-month absence, worthwhile form since debut only when winning maiden handicap at Musselburgh in September: sold (I. Balding to C. Mann) 16,000 gns Newmarket Autumn Sales: unlikely to stay much beyond 1m. *I. A. Balding*

SOCIETY ROSE   2 b.f. (Apr 9) Saddlers' Hall (IRE) 126 – Ruthless Rose (USA)   79 p
(Conquistador Cielo (USA)) [1996 7m* Oct 23] rather leggy, lengthy filly: fifth foal: half-sister to 1992 2-y-o 6f winner Delta Downs (by Deputy Minister) and winners abroad by Polish Precedent and Danehill: dam twice-raced half-sister to high-class miler Shaadi: 2/1 on, won steadily-run 8-runner maiden at Newcastle by 4 lengths from Kippilaw, tracking pace, leading under 2f out and soon clear: showed a quick action to post: will stay further than 7f: sure to improve. *M. R. Stoute*

SODA   2 gr.g. (Apr 18) Belfort (FR) 89 – Bella Seville 71 (King of Spain 121) [1996   58 d
5m³ 5m³ 5m 6m⁶ a6g⁴ a5g Dec 3] third foal: dam best at 5f: failed to repeat form shown on first 2 starts, off course over 3 months after third: probably a sprinter. *T. D. Barron*

SODA POP (IRE)   2 b.c. (Apr 5) River Falls 113 – Riviere Salee (FR) (Luthier   64 ?
126) [1996 6m⁵ 7.1f Sep 12] IR 12,500F, 13,500Y: leggy colt: half-brother to smart 8.5f and 1¼m winner Azayim (by Be My Guest), 16.2f winner Riviere Actor (by Theatrical) and 2 winners in France: dam lightly-raced sister to French/Italian Group 3 winners Riverton and Robertissimo: backward, never dangerous in Newbury maiden on debut: showed up only 4f in 18-runner similar event at Chepstow 2½ months later. *C. E. Brittain*

SODELK   2 ch.f. (Mar 17) Interrex (CAN) – Summoned By Bells 55 (Stanford   –
121§) [1996 7g⁶ a7g Nov 4] 1,500Y: lengthy filly: first reported foal: dam sprint-bred maiden: no sign of ability in minor event and seller. *J. Hetherton*

SODEN (IRE)   2 b.f. (Feb 15) Mujadil (USA) 119 – Elminya (IRE) (Sure Blade   68
(USA) 130) [1996 6.9g 6.1f³ 7m 7m* 7.3m 7.9g 8m Sep 19] 20,000Y: smallish, good-topped filly: second foal: half-sister to 3-y-o Pleasureland (by Don't Forget Me): dam unraced half-sister to very smart middle-distance mare Ruby Tiger: fair form: won steadily-run 4-runner maiden at Redcar in August: stays 1m: raced only on a sound surface. *T. G. Mills*

SO INTREPID (IRE)   6 ch.h. Never So Bold 135 – Double River (USA) (Irish   84
River (FR) 131) [1995 78, a–: a6g a6g⁴ 6g⁶ 6m 6g⁶ 5g* 6g² 5g* 5.7f 5g³ 5m* 6f⁴ 5.1m 6m 6g⁶ 5g 1996 a6g* a7g³ 6g 6g* 6f⁴ 5g³ 6d³ 6d⁵ 6m* 6m* 6m 5m⁶ 6m 6m⁶ 6m 6.1s⁶ 6f Nov 5] tall, close-coupled horse: fairly useful handicapper: successful at Wolverhampton in March, Leicester in April and at Windsor and Kempton in June: stays 6f: acts on firm and soft ground and on fibresand: has run well when sweating: usually held up. *J. M. Bradley*

SO KEEN   3 ch.g. Keen 116 – Diana's Bow (Great Nephew 126) [1995 NR 1996   –
10.5d 8.1d 10m⁶ 13.4m⁵ 17.2m 14d Sep 28] 6,300F, 9,400Y: rather leggy gelding: half-brother to fairly useful 9f winner Bespoken (by Danzig) and a 7f winner in Hungary by North Briton: dam unraced daughter of Oaks third Moonlight Night, a half-sister to Main Reef: no worthwhile form. *A. Bailey*

SOLAR CRYSTAL (IRE)   3 b.f. Alzao (USA) 117 – Crystal Spray 75 (Beldale   105
Flutter (USA) 130) [1995 110: 6m* 6m⁴ 7.1g² 8g* 8d³ 1996 11.4g² 10.5g 10.3m³

10m 8.1m⁶ Aug 31] neat filly: easy mover: won May Hill Stakes at 2 yrs: best efforts in 1996 in Cheshire Oaks (2 lengths second to Tout A Coup) at Chester and Prix de Diane at Chantilly first 2 starts: should have stayed 1½m: did not race on extremes of going: usually front runner. *H. R. A. Cecil*

SOLATIUM (IRE)   4 b.g. Rainbow Quest (USA) 134 – Consolation 95 (Troy   62 §
137) [1995 –: 12f 10.4m⁵ 14.1m 1996 11.8m 20f 17.2m² 18m Jul 6] lengthy, good-topped gelding: disappointing maiden: looks none too keen, and is one to treat with caution. *M. C. Pipe*

SOLDIER BLUE   3 ch.g. Infantry 122 – Greenhil Jazz Time 70 (Music Boy 124)   –
[1995 NR 1996 10m 11.7m 10.5d Sep 27] fourth foal: dam 5f winner: behind in maidens. *P. J. Hobbs*

SOLDIER COVE (USA)   6 ch.g. Manila (USA) – Secret Form 120 (Formidable   50
(USA) 125) [1995 57?: 5g⁴ 10.1s⁵ 10.4m 6f 1996 8f⁶ 8.5m 8f 14s a10g² Nov 26] sparely-made gelding: poor performer: stays 1¼m: acts on firm ground and equi-track. *Martyn Meade*

SOLDIER MAK   3 ch.g. Infantry 122 – Truly Blest 75 (So Blessed 130) [1995   66
62: 6m 7g 8f 6.9m 1996 7m² 8m 11.4d³ 11.7m³ 14.1f³ 11.5m² 11.9m⁴ 11.9g² 12g⁴ Oct 18] workmanlike gelding: modest maiden handicapper: in frame on 8 of 9 starts in 1996: stays 1¾m: yet to race on soft ground, probably acts on any other. *A. Hide*

SOLDIER'S SONG   3 b.f. Infantry 122 – Top Soprano 89 (High Top 131) [1995   –
NR 1996 8g 10f⁵ 8m Jul 5] half-sister to several winning jumpers, best of them Linton Rocks and Setter Country (both by Town And Country): dam 5f winner at 2 yrs: well beaten in maidens. *R. J. Hodges*

SOLFEGIETTO   2 b.f. (Mar 24) Music Boy 124 – Maria Isabella (FR) (Young   76
Generation 129) [1996 6g³ 5f² 5g* 6m⁶ Sep 20] 7,600F, 30,000Y: well-grown, rather leggy filly: has scope: seventh foal: half-sister to 3 winners, including useful Italian middle-distance performer Streisand (by Unfuwain) and 1¼m to 1½m winner Top Royal (by High Top): dam, ran 3 times in France, half-sister to useful 1986 French 2-y-o Microcosme: fair performer: unimpressive when winning 7-runner maiden at Hamilton in September: outclassed in listed race at Ayr final outing: likely to prove suited by further than 5f. *M. Bell*

SOLO MIO (IRE)   2 b.c. (Jan 26) Sadler's Wells (USA) 132 – Marie de Flandre   92 p
(FR) 109 (Crystal Palace (FR) 132) [1996 7g 8m² 8g Oct 26] 160,000Y: rangy, good-bodied, attractive colt: fine mover: eighth foal: brother to 3-y-o 1½m winner (stays 2m) Sharaf, closely related to French middle-distance winners by Shareef Dancer and In The Wings and half-brother to 2 winners by Green Desert: dam, French 1¼m and 10.5f winner, half-sister to Sakura Reiko: ½-length second of 9 to King Sound in steadily-run minor event at Newbury: looked sure to improve again, but slowly away and always struggling in Racing Post Trophy at Doncaster: sort to do better over middle distances. *B. W. Hills*

SOLO PRIZE   4 b.g. Chief Singer 131 – Raffle 82 (Balidar 133) [1995 62d: 5m   – §
6.1m 6g 6g 6f a6g 1996 a8g a7g Jan 18] stocky gelding: below form since fair 2-y-o: sometimes reluctant to race: tried blinkered: not one to trust. *P. Howling*

SOLO SYMPHONY (IRE)   3 ch.f. Fayruz 116 – Keen Note 69 (Sharpo 132)   67 d
[1995 67: 5d³ 1996 5.1d³ 5.1g⁴ 5m⁴ 6f⁵ a5g³ a5g Jul 26] quite attractive filly: poor mover: modest maiden: best 3-y-o effort on reappearance: may prove best at 6f: sold 1,500 gns Newmarket December Sales. *P. W. Chapple-Hyam*

SOLO VOLUMES   7 ch.g. Ballacashtal (CAN) – Miss Solo (Runnymede 123)   –
[1995 NR 1996 10m Aug 14] eighth foal: half-brother to fairly useful 7f to 9f performer Single (by Jellaby): dam poor plater: no sign of ability under NH rules: tailed off in maiden at Sandown on flat debut. *H. G. Rowsell*

SOME HORSE (IRE)   3 ch.g. Astronef 116 – Daniela Lepida (ITY) (El-Muleta)   –
[1995 93: 5g² a6g 5g* 6d* 7.6d⁴ 7m⁴ 1996 8.1d 7.1d 9f 8m Sep 20] tall gelding: fairly useful form at 2 yrs: showed little in handicaps in 1996: stays 7f: used to act on good to firm and dead ground, well beaten on fibresand. *M. G. Meagher*

SOMERTON BOY (IRE)   6 b.h. Thatching 131 – Bonnie Bess 95 (Ardoon 124)   75
[1995 83: 8m 8g* 7g⁶ 7g* 7g² 7d 7g 7m⁶ a7g 1996 7g 7g 7g 7m* 7m⁶ 7m³ 8f³ 7.6d⁶ 8m 7g⁶ Oct 12] quite attractive horse: fair handicapper: won at Ayr in June: stays 1m: acts on any going: blinkered twice (in Ireland) early in career: held up. *P. Calver*

SOMETHING BLUE   2 b.f. (May 14) Petong 126 – Blueit (FR) 101 (Bold Lad   –
(IRE) 133) [1996 5f 5s 5g Oct 19] close-coupled filly: sister to 3-y-o 6.9f winner
Miletrian City and half-sister to several winning sprinters, including useful Blues
Indigo (by Music Boy): dam 2-y-o 5f winner: well beaten in maidens. *T. R. Watson*

SOMETHING SPEEDY (IRE)   4 b.f. Sayf El Arab (USA) 127 – Fabulous Pet   –
(Somethingfabulous (USA)) [1995 42: a9.4g⁵ a11g a12g⁴ a14.8g 1996 a11g
Jan 19] sturdy filly: poor performer: tailed off only 4-y-o start: sold (P. Bevan to
M. Hammond) 850 gns Doncaster March Sales: stays 1½m: acts on fibresand: twice
blinkered. *P. J. Bevan*

SOMMERSBY (IRE)   5 b.g. Vision (USA) – Echoing 93 (Formidable (USA)   –
125) [1995 51, a71: 10m⁴ a12g² a12g* a12g² a12g³ a12g⁶ a12g³ a12g* 11.9m a12g   a50
a12g 1996 a12g a12g a12g a14.8g⁶ a9.4g⁴ a12g³ a14.8g Nov 16] sturdy gelding:
modest form at best in 1996: stays at least 1½m: acts on good to firm ground and on
fibresand: tried visored, no improvement. *Mrs N. Macauley*

SO NATURAL (IRE)   4 ch.f. Sharpo 132 – Sympathy 77 (Precocious 126) [1995   –
8.5g 7m⁵ 7g⁶ 6.5g⁶ 1996 a5g a7g⁶ a7g⁴ a7g³ a7g a6g⁶ 6s 6g a6g Jun 28] workmanlike   a49
ex-Irish filly: unimpressive mover: second foal: dam 7f winner at 3 yrs (her only
start) out of half-sister to very smart middle-distance performer John French: trained
in Ireland at 3 yrs by C. Collins: modest maiden here: stays 7f: acts on fibresand, no
form on turf in 1996: blinkered (edgy, hung markedly left) eighth 4-y-o start: usually
races prominently. *E. J. Alston*

SONDERISE   7 br.g. Mummy's Game 120 – Demderise 80 (Vaigly Great 127)   57
[1995 50: 5d² 5g⁴ 6g 5m 5m 5g 1996 5s⁴ 5g⁴ 5.9d³ 5.9m³ 5g⁵ 6g* 6m³ 6.1m⁶ 6m³
5m⁴ 5m³ᵈⁱˢ 6f Sep 7] lengthy, rather dipped-backed gelding: carries condition: modest sprint handicapper: formerly inconsistent, but held his form well in 1996, winning
at Catterick in June: stays 6f: acts on good to firm and heavy going: tried blinkered/
visored, better without: usually held up: sometimes wanders under pressure.
N. Tinkler

SONDOS   3 b.f. Dowsing (USA) 124 – Krameria 72 (Kris 135) [1995 63: 6m³ 6m⁴   67
1996 a6g* 6g⁵ 7.3d⁵ a7g Jul 22] tall filly: fair performer: won median auction maiden
at Wolverhampton in April: below form afterwards, putting head in air and again
finding little under pressure on final start: should stay beyond 6f: acts on good to firm
ground and on fibresand: sent to UAE. *J. W. Hills*

SONG FOR JESS (IRE)   3 b.f. Accordion – Ritual Girl (Ballad Rock 122) [1995   –
NR 1996 11.7m⁶ 11.8m⁵ Jul 18] first reported foal: dam Irish 11f winner: well beaten
in maiden and claimer. *F. Jordan*

SONG MIST (IRE)   2 gr.f. (Mar 23) Kenmare (FR) 125 – Farewell Song (USA)   74
80 (The Minstrel (CAN) 135) [1996 5m⁵ 6.9g² 6f* 6m⁵ 6.5m⁶ 7m⁶ Oct 1] leggy filly:
fifth foal: half-sister to 3-y-o 6f winner Highland Rhapsody (by Kris) and a winner in
Austria by King of Clubs: dam 1m winner: fair form: made all in 5-runner maiden at
Brighton in July: best subsequent effort in nurseries when sixth of 22, keeping on
well for 7-lb claimer, at Doncaster on fifth start: stays 7f: raced only on a sound
surface. *P. F. I. Cole*

SONG OF FREEDOM   2 ch.c. (Mar 8) Arazi (USA) 135 – Glorious Song   78 p
(CAN) (Halo (USA)) [1996 7f⁴ Nov 5] rangy colt: has plenty of scope: closely
related to 2 winners by Blushing Groom, notably smart 6f (at 2 yrs) and 1m winner
Rahy, and half-brother to several winners, notably high-class 4-y-o middle-distance
colt Singspiel (by In The Wings): dam top-class performer at around 9f in Canada:
25/1, burly and very green, around 3¼ lengths fourth of 16 to Tayseer in maiden
at Redcar, tracking leaders and running on: will stay 1¼m: sure to do better.
J. H. M. Gosden

SONG OF SKYE   2 b.f. (Mar 26) Warning 136 – Song of Hope 103 (Chief Singer   82
131) [1996 5.2f* 5.2g² 6m⁵ 6m 6s Oct 26] 22,000Y: leggy, close-coupled filly: fourth
foal: half-sister to 3 winners, including 3-y-o 7f and 1m winner Kingdom Princess
(by Forzando) and 1994 2-y-o 6f winner Stolen Melody (by Robellino): dam 2-y-o 5f
winner from family of Mummy's Pet: 33/1, won 5-runner maiden at Newbury in
July: quite highly tried next 3 starts, well below form in nursery at Newbury (on soft
ground) final one: stays 6f: has hung left. *T. J. Naughton*

SONG OF TARA (IRE)   4 b.c. Sadler's Wells (USA) 132 – Flame of Tara 124   115
(Artaius (USA) 129) [1995 116: 12.1g* 12d* 12d⁴ 1996 10d³ 10m³ 13.3m³ Aug 17]

well-made colt: has a short, round action: smart performer: has had only 6 races: third in 1996 in Brigadier Gerard Stakes at Sandown (2 lengths behind Pilsudski), Meld Stakes at the Curragh and Geoffrey Freer Stakes at Newbury: should prove suited by 1½m+: may well prove best on an easy surface. *P. W. Chapple-Hyam*

SONGSHEET 3 b.f. Dominion 123 – Songstead 92 (Song 132) [1995 74: 5m² 5g² 69 5m⁵ 1996 5.1g* 5m⁵ 5.7m⁵ 5.2g² a5g² 5.7m³ 5m⁵ 5m⁴ 5.1f a5g⁶ Oct 19] lengthy filly: fair performer: won seller at Bath (sold out of R. Guest's stable 10,000 gns) in April: creditable efforts most starts afterwards: sold (Martyn Meade to M. Saunders) 5,500 gns Newmarket Autumn Sales: raced mainly at 5f: acts on fibresand, has raced only on a sound surface on turf. *Martyn Meade*

SONG SONG BLUE (IRE) 3 b. or br.g. Ballad Rock 122 – Bluethroat 95 – (Ballymore 123) [1995 –: 6m 9g 1996 8.2d Apr 12] close-coupled gelding: well beaten in sellers and maiden. *N. Tinkler*

SONIC MAIL 3 b.g. Keen 116 – Martin-Lavell Mail (Dominion 123) [1995 77: 5m⁵ 5g² 5.1m* 5m³ 5f⁴ 1996 6m 6m May 7] leggy gelding: speedy as 2-y-o, not seen out after August: tailed off in 1996: sold 1,000 gns Newmarket Autumn Sales. *K. McAuliffe*

SON OF SHARP SHOT (IRE) 6 b. or br.h. Sharp Shot 82 – Gay Fantasy (Troy 105 137) [1995 105: 10.8m* 10.3m² 12m* 12m* 12f⁴ 13.9m⁴ 12d 12m⁵ 1996 12m 12m² 12m 11.9g* 12m⁶ 12f 12g 12m⁵ Oct 17] leggy, quite attractive horse: impressed in appearance: good mover: useful handicapper: none too consistent in 1996 (reportedly suffered from broken blood vessels), but won at York (by short head) in July: stays 13.9f but at least as effective over shorter: has won on soft going, best form on a sound surface: usually held up, suited by a good gallop and was a tricky ride: tail swisher, but genuine: reportedly to stand at stud in Ireland. *J. L. Dunlop*

SOOJAMA (IRE) 6 b.g. Mansooj 118 – Pyjama Game 56 (Cavo Doro 124) 54 [1995 48: 15.4g* 15.4m² 14.1m⁵ 17.2m⁵ 16.4g* 16.1g² 14.1m⁴ 16.2f 16.1g² 12g² a– a14g 1996 15.4m 12m 12m* 16.4g 16.2m 12m² a16g⁵ Aug 10] rather leggy gelding: modest handicapper: won 22-runner ladies race at Newmarket in June: needs at least 1½m and stays well: acts on good to firm and soft ground, well beaten on fibresand and equitrack: often blinkered nowadays: held up of late: inconsistent. *R. M. Flower*

SOOTY TERN 9 br.h. Wassl 125 – High Tern 93 (High Line 125) [1995 78, a56: 72 a8.5g⁴ 9g⁵ 8m⁶ 7.6m⁵ 8g 8g* 8m* a8g 8f⁵ 8.1m⁴ 8.3m* 8m⁵ 8m⁵ 7.6m² 7.6m a7g² 8g a59 8d 1996 a8.5g⁴ a8g⁴ a8.5g⁴ 9m² 8g⁶ a8g* 8g 8f⁵ 8m 8.5m⁵ 8m 8.3f* 8m² 8m 8.1d a8g⁴ a8g² a8g⁵ a7g² Dec 28] compact horse: fair handicapper at best on turf, successful at Hamilton in August: modest on the all-weather, winner at Lingfield in May: best at 7f to 9f: acts on any going: usually races prominently: often ridden by apprentice: tough. *J. M. Bradley*

SOPHIE LOCKETT 3 b.f. Mon Tresor 113 – Silverdale Rose (Nomination 125) – [1995 NR 1996 11.8m⁶ 10m⁶ 10.5m Aug 9] workmanlike filly: first foal: dam ran twice: little worthwhile form. *K. W. Hogg, Isle of Man*

SOPHIE MAY 5 b.m. Glint of Gold 128 – Rosana Park 83 (Music Boy 124) [1995 – NR 1996 a16g Jan 2] leggy mare: modest hurdler: no form on flat for a long time. *G. L. Moore*

SOPHISM (USA) 7 b.g. Al Nasr (FR) 126 – Over The Waves (Main Reef 126) 42 [1995 48?: 12g⁶ 17.2m⁵ 16m 1996 16.1f⁴ 17.2m³ 17.2f³ Jul 8] close-coupled gelding: fair performer: poor maiden on flat: stays 17.2f: acts on good to firm and dead ground: has twice refused to race over fences. *M. C. Pipe*

SOPHOMORE 2 b.c. (Mar 25) Sanglamore (USA) 126 – Livry (USA) (Lyphard 83 p (USA) 132) [1996 7g* Oct 25] rangy colt: fifth foal: half-brother to 6f winner Deliver (by Rousillon): dam, French 11f winner, half-sister to very smart middle-distance performer Defensive Play: favourite though green, won 12-runner maiden at Doncaster by ¾ lengths from Labeq, held up just off pace, leading 1f out and running on, idling a little: will be suited by middle distances: sure to improve. *B. W. Hills*

SORARA 3 ch.f. Aragon 118 – Sorebelle 95 (Prince Tenderfoot (USA) 126) [1995 – NR 1996 7g⁴ Aug 21] half-sister to 5f and 7f winner Abuzz (by Absalom) and 6f (in USA) to 7f winner Local Lass (by Local Suitor), both useful: dam best at up to 1m:

bought out of C. Brittain's stable 5,000 gns Newmarket July (1996) Sales: showed nothing in 4-runner maiden at Ayr. *D. Moffatt*

SORBIE TOWER (IRE)   3 b.c. Soviet Lad (USA) 94 – Nozet (Nishapour   120
(FR) 125) [1995 67p: 7d 6g² 1996 7s* 8d* 8.1g* 8d² 8f³ 8m⁴ 7s Sep 22]

Thirty-three-year-old trainer Gay Kelleway has made quite an impression in recent years and in 1996 none of her horses did so more than Sorbie Tower. This three-year-old progressed phenomenally in the first three months of the turf season. For eye-catching improvement through the ranks, he was perhaps rivalled by Anzio whom Miss Kelleway picked up from a claimer at Lingfield in February for £6,000 and with whom she won another five races, including a Group 3 at Leopardstown and a listed event at Doncaster. Sorbie Tower, however, is a better horse than that.

At the start of the year, Sorbie Tower had been selected for Timeform's *Horses To Follow*, but even the compilers must have been surprised by just how good he turned out to be. The second of his two runs as a two-year-old had revealed plenty of promise, but that had been in a maiden auction at Warwick and it seemed that the most likely plan for 1996 would be to exploit a lowly handicap mark. The BHB marks eventually allotted to Sorbie Tower were indeed made to look pretty lowly, but there was no question of biding time with him and keeping his light hidden under some bushel. When he made his reappearance on the second day of the turf season in a maiden at Doncaster, Sorbie Tower won it, and by three and a half lengths. Sorbie Tower's handicap debut came at Warwick three weeks later off a BHB mark of 80 and he won that too, by eight lengths. It was pretty clear now that this was not just a handicapper, but, for those not convinced, Sorbie Tower took his chance next (raised 16 lb in the weights) in a £12,718 handicap at Sandown on Whitbread day. This he won by two lengths, well in command after quickening on in the final furlong, as he had been at Warwick.

Sorbie Tower (IRE) (b.c. 1993)	Soviet Lad (USA) (b 1985)	Nureyev (b 1977)	Nothern Dancer, Special
		Green Valley (br 1967)	Val de Loir, Sly Pola
	Nozet (ch 1983)	Nishapour (gr 1975)	Zeddaan, Alama
		Sunblast (ro 1971)	Roan Rocket, Sun Palace

Gay Kelleway has increased her total of winners in every one of the five seasons that she has held a licence in Britain (she previously trained for several months in New Zealand for one winner), but Sorbie Tower's contribution to the latest tally remained at three. He must nevertheless have gained many more admirers after Sandown. His first taste of defeat was by just a neck, at the hands of Regal Archive in a listed race at Kempton when he was the last of the principals to be asked for his effort. His second was not by much more, and that was in the St James's Palace Stakes at Royal Ascot. Nine years earlier, his trainer became the first and so far only woman to ride a winner at Royal Ascot, on Sprowston Boy in the Queen Alexandra. If she has to wait much longer for her first success there as a trainer it will not be for lack of ambition. Sorbie Tower was taking on three classic winners among eight rivals and was sent off at 33/1. Bijou d'Inde beat Ashkalani by a head and Sorbie Tower was a length behind him. The Sussex Stakes at Goodwood was a similarly-bold next choice of race for Sorbie Tower and he again made the frame, beaten three and a half lengths into fourth behind First Island. These two Group 1 races demonstrated that Sorbie Tower is capable of winning pattern races. The Sussex, however, was the first time in his career that he had not shown improvement. A much greater cause for disappointment was Sorbie Tower's seventh of ten in a listed race at Longchamp in September, a race he had the form to win, and he was put away for the year to be targeted at 'all the top mile races' in 1997, with a try at a mile and a quarter apparently on the agenda as well.

Sorbie Tower is a tall, useful-looking colt who wears bandages behind. He takes a keen hold, has a good turn of foot and is held up, often hanging under pressure. It is doubtful whether any further than a mile will suit him. He probably acts on any going. His sire Soviet Lad has been something of a peripatetic individual, born in the United States, racing for two seasons in France (with two wins, one in a one-mile listed race), for a third in North America (winning once and, most notably, coming second in the Grade 1 nine-furlong Bernard Baruch Handicap), beginning his stud career in Kentucky, covering for five seasons in Ireland and now being domiciled in Australia. A stud career was almost guaranteed for Soviet Lad, and for a host of half-brothers and close relations, because his dam's first foal had been Green Dancer. A half-sister is Alhaarth's dam Irish Valley. Sorbie Tower is from Soviet Lad's first Irish crop. A 15,000-guinea foal and 13,000-guinea yearling, he is the fourth foal of racing age out of Nozet. Two of the others were winners, both at two years, Penang Star (by Jareer) over six furlongs at Southwell and Christan (by Al Hareb) over five furlongs in Belgium. Nozet herself recorded just the one minor win, over nine furlongs at Evreux in France, and was fourth of seven in a claimer on her only start here. Her dam Sunblast was considerably better, a winner at two years who showed useful form over seven furlongs and a mile at three, and third dam Sun Palace was a fairly useful winner at a mile and a half. *Miss Gay Kelleway*

SORISKY 4 ch.g. Risk Me (FR) 127 – Minabella (Dance In Time (CAN)) [1995 44 –: 11.6m 10m 8g 8.3m a12g⁶ 1996 a13g⁵ a13g* a16g a13g⁵ a13g a16g⁵ 12m Jun 26] tall gelding: poor handicapper: first form since 1994 when winning bad selling contest at Lingfield in January: failed to repeat it: stays 13f: acts on equitrack and on firm ground. *B. Gubby*

SOTOBOY (IRE) 4 b.c. Danehill (USA) 126 – Fire Flash 74 (Bustino 136) [1995 – 90: 8m 10m³ 7m 8m³ 8m 7m⁵ 7g 8.5s 8m⁶ 1996 8.1g 7.6m⁵ 10d 10m a8g Jun 25] small, well-made colt: fairly useful form at best in 1995: has become very disappointing: will prove best at up to 1¼m: acts on good to firm ground, below form on a soft surface: has twice bolted to post, and usually taken down early. *P. W. Harris*

SOTONIAN (HOL) 3 br.g. Statoblest 120 – Visage 75 (Vision (USA)) [1995 NR 36 1996 5g a7g 10m 6f 5.1m 5.1g a5g a5g³ Dec 28] 26,000Y: rather sparely-made gelding: first reported foal: dam, 1¼m and 10.6f winner, daughter of top-class (at up to 7f) Be Tuneful: trained first 3 starts by Mrs L. Stubbs: first worthwhile form when third in handicap at Wolverhampton: probably a sprinter: tried blinkered, no improvement. *P. S. Felgate*

SOUFRIERE (IRE) 3 b. or br.f. Caerleon (USA) 132 – Shelbiana (USA) – (Chieftain II) [1995 NR 1996 8g 10.3g Jun 29] IR 86,000Y: fifth known foal: half-sister to Dubai 5f and 6f winner Moonlight Acre (by Night Shift) and 1991 2-y-o 1m winner Ajib (by Woodman): dam won at up to 9f at 2 yrs: never dangerous in maidens at Salisbury and Doncaster: sent to Saudi Arabia. *L. M. Cumani*

SOUL SISTER 3 b.f. Distant Relative 128 – Lappet (Kampala 120) [1995 NR 1996 8m⁶ 6g a8.5g a8g Nov 18] 8,000Y: fourth foal: dam ran twice: well beaten. *D. Haydn Jones*

SOUND APPEAL 2 b.f. (Apr 19) Robellino (USA) 127 – Son Et Lumiere 69 (Rainbow Quest (USA) 134) [1996 7m 7.9g⁵ 7.1s 7d⁴ Oct 28] 775Y: tall, leggy, unfurnished filly: has scope: third foal: sister to Irish 4-y-o 7.8f winner Ansal Boy and half-sister to unreliable 3-y-o Uncle George (by Anshan), 6f winner at 2 yrs: dam lightly-raced maiden: blinkered first time, improved when fourth of 11 at Lingfield on final start, dictating pace: best effort at 7f: well beaten on soft ground: mulish leaving paddock second start, sweating on third. *A. G. Foster*

SOUND CHECK 3 b.f. Formidable (USA) 125 – Imperatrice (USA) (Kings Lake 60 (USA) 133) [1995 62: 5m 5m 6g⁴ 6g³ 7g² 7m* 8m 8h 1996 8g 8m* 10g⁵ 8.3m³ 8.2m³ 8m⁴ 7.1m 8m⁶ Jul 13] lengthy filly: has a round action: modest handicapper: won at Salisbury in May: stays 8.3f, probably not 1¼m: acts on good to firm ground, yet to race on soft surface: blinkered last 5 starts: wandered and found little for amateur sixth 3-y-o start: requires strong handling. *B. J. Meehan*

SOUNDS LEGAL 3 b.f. Rich Charlie 117 – Legal Sound 85 (Legal Eagle 126) 68
[1995 NR 1996 a8.5g² a8.5g⁵ Dec 28] 1,700F: sixth foal: half-sister to 5f (at 2 yrs) to
7f winner Legatee (by Risk Me) and winning sprinter Brisas (by Vaigly Great): dam
6f winner: failed to repeat form of second of 12 in maiden at Wolverhampton on
belated debut. *P. D. Evans*

SOUND THE TRUMPET (IRE) 4 b.g. Fayruz 116 – Red Note (Rusticaro 56
(FR) 124) [1995 52: 5.1m⁶ 6f⁶ 5f⁶ a5g 5g a6g 1996 a6g⁵ a5g² a6g 6.1g⁵ 6f a6g⁵ 6m²
6m⁴ 5m a6g⁶ Dec 27] rangy gelding: modest handicapper: stays 7f: acts on fibresand,
seems suited by a sound surface on turf: tried blinkered or visored, not in 1996.
R. C. Spicer

SOUPERFICIAL 5 gr.g. Petong 126 – Duck Soup 55 (Decoy Boy 129) [1995 63
69, a71: a6g⁵ a6g* a6g* a6g³ 7g² a6g a7g* 7g 6m² 6.9f⁴ 6m* 6m⁶ 6m a6g² 6d a6g 8g
1996 7.5m 7m 7g a6g 6m 5d a7g³ a8g a7g* 5.1m* 6m a5g⁵ 5.1m⁶ 5f* 5.1g 5g 6m²
a6g⁴ a6g a7s Dec 19] sturdy gelding: modest handicapper: won at Nottingham in
August and at Leicester in September: sold out of J. Glover's stable 4,000 gns Doncaster November Sales before third-last start: effective at 5f to 7f: acts on firm and
dead ground and on fibresand: usually visored/blinkered: usually held up: none too
consistent. *N. Tinkler*

SOURA (USA) 2 ch.f. (Mar 16) Beau Genius (CAN) – First Division (CHI) 49 ?
(Domineau (USA)) [1996 7m 6m a8g⁶ a7g³ Dec 26] $8,500F, $20,000Y: tall,
lengthy, unfurnished filly: fourth foal: dam won graded stakes in Chile: only worthwhile form when sixth of 10 in maiden at Lingfield in December. *P. A. Kelleway*

SOURCE OF LIGHT 7 b.g. Rainbow Quest (USA) 134 – De Stael (USA) 93 101
(Nijinsky (CAN) 138) [1995 106: 12m⁴ 12m⁶ 11.9m 12f³ 13.4m* 14m* 16g⁶ 1996
14.1g³ 14s⁴ 12m 11.9g Jul 6] leggy, good-topped gelding: good mover: useful
performer: ran poorly in Old Newton Cup at Haydock final start: effective at 1¼m to
1¾m: acts on any going: effective from front or held up. *R. Charlton*

SOUS LE NEZ 2 b.f. (Apr 28) Midyan (USA) 124 – Miss Swansong 61 (Young 83
Generation 129) [1996 5g² 5m* 5.2g³ 5m⁴ 6g³ 5f 5g⁵ 5d⁶ 5v² Nov 11] 7,500Y:
sparely-made filly: third foal: sister to Italian 3-y-o 7f and (at 2 yrs) 1m winner
D'Amore E Ombra: dam lightly-raced sister to Prince Sabo: won 4-runner maiden at
Doncaster in July: fairly useful form when head second of 8, nearly losing off-fore
shoe, to Salty Behaviour in minor event at Folkestone final outing: sold 22,000 gns
Newmarket December Sales: stays 6f: acts on good to firm and heavy ground.
R. Guest

*Ascot Stakes (Handicap), Royal Ascot—Olivier Peslier rides the winner Southern Power for Reg Akehurst;
runner-up, 100/1-shot Mirador, is next right with noseband*

SOUTH EASTERN FRED   5 b.h. Primo Dominie 121 – Soheir 74 (Track Spare   52
125) [1995 61, a87: a10g* a9.4g* 10m⁴ 8.5m⁴ 8g⁵ 10m⁴ 8.3m⁶ 7d 10f a10g² a8g   a89
1996 a9.4g² a10g⁵ a9.4g³ a12g³ a9.4g⁵ a12g⁶ a10g 9.7m⁵ 10m 9.7g² 10m a9.4g⁴
a9.4g* 8.5m a10s³ a9.4g* Dec 14] tall, workmanlike horse: poor mover: has had leg
problems: fairly useful handicapper on the all-weather, modest at best on turf: none
too consistent in 1996, winning at Wolverhampton in September and December:
probably best at around 1¼m: acts on fibresand and equitrack. *H. J. Collingridge*

SOUTHERLY WIND   2 b.c. (Apr 7) Slip Anchor 136 – Karavina (Karabas 132)   79 p
[1996 5g 6m* 8m⁵ 8m² 8m* 8g³ Oct 25] 11,000Y: big, rangy colt: has plenty of
scope: half-brother to useful 1986 Irish 2-y-o 6f winner Kalorama (by Bold Lad),
8.5f winner Villavina (by Top Ville) and 2 winners abroad: dam Irish 6f and 7f
winner: won maiden auction at Pontefract in July and nursery there in September:
looked in fine shape when creditable third of 15 in steadily-run nursery at Doncaster
on final outing, best work at finish: will be well suited by 1¼m+: will improve
further. *Mrs J. R. Ramsden*

SOUTHERN CHIEF   2 b.g. (Feb 16) Be My Chief (USA) 122 – Southern Sky   –
89 (Comedy Star (USA) 121) [1996 a8.5g 10.2d⁶ Sep 30] third live foal: half-brother
to 4-y-o 5f and 6f winner Southern Dominion (by Dominion) and 5-y-o Southern
Ridge (by Indian Ridge), fairly useful 6f winner at 2 yrs: dam 7f and 1m winner:
tailed off in maidens at Wolverhampton and Bath. *W. G. M. Turner*

SOUTHERN DOMINION   4 ch.g. Dominion 123 – Southern Sky 89 (Comedy   –
Star (USA) 121) [1995 65, a62: a5g⁵ 5.1m* 5.1f² a5g 5.1m³ 5m 5f² a5g* a5g⁴ 5f⁵   a62 d
5m⁴ 6f⁴ 7.1m⁴ 5g 6g² 5g a5g³ a6g* a6g³ a5g⁵ a6g² 1996 a5g⁴ a6g⁵ a5g² a6g a6g a6g
5g 6f 7g⁵ 6.9g 7f Oct 15] small gelding: modest handicapper: left M. Johnston after
third 4-y-o start: well below form afterwards: sold privately to join Miss J. Craze   600
gns Doncaster November Sales: effective at 5f to 7f: acts on all-weather surfaces,
ideally suited by a sound surface on turf: sometimes blinkered/visored: often a front
runner. *C. N. Allen*

SOUTHERN POWER (IRE)   5 b.g. Midyan (USA) 124 – Tap The Line (Tap   91
On Wood 130) [1995 82: 9.9m² 10.8m³ 12g⁴ 12.4g² 9.9m³ 1996 12g³ 20f* 16.1g³
20m* 16m⁴ Sep 26] leggy, good-topped gelding: good mover: fairly useful handi-

Marriott Hotels Goodwood Stakes (Handicap), Goodwood—
Southern Power (Richard Quinn this time) and the never-say-die Sea Victor

capper: won 26-runner Ascot Stakes (by ¾ length from Mirador) in June and 9-runner Marriott Hotels Goodwood Stakes (by a neck from Sea Victor) in July: reportedly finished lame near-hind final start: suited by test of stamina: acts on any going: visored (ran creditably) final 4-y-o start: usually bandaged near-hind: sometimes edges left: usually waited with: game. *R. Akehurst*

SOUTHERN RIDGE 5 b.g. Indian Ridge 123 – Southern Sky 89 (Comedy Star – (USA) 121) [1995 –: 6m 6m 8.3m 1996 a8g Feb 1] neat gelding: no worthwhile form on flat since 2 yrs: won novice hurdle in September for R. Frost. *R. J. Baker*

SOUTHERN RULE 9 b.g. Law Society (USA) 130 – Isobelline (USA) (Pronto) 41 d [1995 7.8f 5m⁵ 5g 5m 5g 5m* 5g 1996 5s 5d⁶ 5m 5m 5s⁶ a6g⁶ a6g⁶ a6s Dec 19] 36,000F: half-brother to several winners, notably Royal Lodge winner Robellino (by Roberto): dam Irish 7f winner: modest sprinter: had 56 races in Ireland over the years, winning 4 times: only poor form in 1996, trained first 5 starts by S. Donohoe, next by K. Morgan. stays 6f: acts on any going: usually blinkered. *Miss M. E. Rowland*

SOUTH PAGODA (IRE) 3 b.g. Distinctly North (USA) 115 – Lamya 73 – (Hittite Glory 125) [1995 64: 6m⁴ 6m 6.9g 1996 10g 7g 7f 9.9m Jul 5] workmanlike gelding: modest form at 2 yrs for P. Chapple-Hyam, reportedly lame after second outing: disappointing in 2 maidens and 2 handicaps for new stable: bred to be best at up to 1m: blinkered (took keen hold) final start. *D. Nicholls*

SOUTH SALEM (USA) 3 b.c. Salem Drive (USA) – Azzurrina (Knightly 104 Manner (USA)) [1995 107p: 5m* 6g* 6m³ 1996 10g 10.3g² a12f Jun 8] strong, good-bodied colt: carries condition: useful performer: well-beaten eighth of 9 in Classic Trial at Sandown on reappearance: 8 lengths second of 8 to Farasan in well-contested minor event at Doncaster month later, staying on after having to be switched: pulled up in Belmont Stakes in USA final start, leading early but reportedly disliking dirt in his face: should prove suited by 1¼m+. *D. R. Loder*

SOUTH SEA BUBBLE (IRE) 4 b.f. Bustino 136 – Night At Sea 107 (Night 75 Shift (USA)) [1995 71p: 10g⁶ 10m³ 1996 10g 10m 10m³ 12.3g³ 12m⁵ 10.5v³ 10m* Oct 29] lengthy, robust filly: fair performer: justified favouritism in minor event at Redcar in October, dictating pace: stays 1½m: acts on good to firm and heavy ground: found little fifth start, made running both subsequent ones. *L. M. Cumani*

SOUTH WIND 3 b.f. Tina's Pet 121 – Warm Wind 84 (Tumble Wind (USA)) 62 [1995 NR 1996 9m 10m⁴ 9f³ 11.5f³ 11.9f³ a12g⁴ Aug 16] 8,000Y: sister to 5f (at 2 yrs) to 7f winner Blue Bomber and half-sister to 2 winners, including 6f (at 2 yrs) to 13.3f winner Warm Spell (by Northern State): dam, 7f to 1¼m winner, half-sister to Yorkshire Oaks winners Sally Brown and Untold: modest maiden: below form last 2 starts: better suited by around 1½m: has raced only on top-of-the-ground when on turf: sold 1,200 gns Newmarket December Sales. *Mrs J. Cecil*

SOVEREIGN CREST (IRE) 3 gr.g. Priolo (USA) 127 – Abergwrle (Absalom – 128) [1995 NR 1996 8.3m 8.3d 10g 10m Sep 26] IR 32,000Y: workmanlike gelding: fifth foal: half-brother to useful Irish filly Anemone Garden, 6f winner at 2 yrs in 1994, 1993 2-y-o 5f winner Allwight Then (both by Dancing Dissident), and a winner in Italy: dam twice-raced daughter of 1000 Guineas winner Caergwrle: no worthwhile form in maidens, clipping heels and falling at Goodwood on third start: very slowly away there 2 weeks later. *C. A. Horgan*

SOVEREIGN PAGE (USA) 7 ch.g. Caro 133 – Tashinsky (USA) (Nijinsky 83 (CAN) 138) [1995 82: 10m² 10.3m⁴ 10m³ 1996 10m⁵ 10g 10.8f* 8.9m⁵ 10.1f* 10.2m Jul 6] tall, rather leggy gelding: good mover: fairly useful handicapper: off course almost a year prior to reappearance: won at Warwick (best turn of foot in falsely-run race) and Yarmouth in June: ideally suited by around 1¼m: goes very well on top-of-the-ground: blinkered (no improvement) twice at 3 yrs: usually bandaged: held up/tracks leaders: consistent. *B. Hanbury*

SOVEREIGN PRINCE (IRE) 3 b.c. Bluebird (USA) 125 – Everything Nice 54 107 (Sovereign Path 125) [1995 –: 8d a8g⁶ a8.5g a6g 1996 a7g* a8g³ a10g³ a10g⁴ 8g⁶ Jun 29] smallish, quite good-topped colt: modest handicapper: won at Lingfield in January: sold 3,700 gns Newmarket July Sales: stays 1¼m: acts on equitrack: blinkered (below form) fourth 3-y-o start: sent to Macau. *N. A. Callaghan*

SOVEREIGNS COURT   3 ch.g. Statoblest 120 – Clare Celeste 73 (Coquelin   71 p
(USA) 121) [1995 NR 1996 7m 7m 7m⁵ 7g 8d³ 7g 7s² Oct 24] 14,000Y: tall, angular
gelding: third foal: half-brother to 1992 2-y-o 6f winner Abergele (by Absalom): dam
poor maiden (best effort at 7f at 2 yrs) half-sister to very useful 6f and 7f winner
Braddells: fair handicapper: good second of 26 in apprentice race at Newbury on
final start: subsequently sold to join L. G. Cottrell 21,000 gns Newmarket Autumn
Sales: will prove best at up to 1m: acts on good to firm and soft ground: may well be
capable of better. *Major D. N. Chappell*

SOVIET BRIDE (IRE)   4 b.f. Soviet Star (USA) 128 – Nihad 76 (Alleged   77
(USA) 138) [1995 72: 8.2g⁵ 8g⁵ 10f* 10.1m* 10f² 12f² 10m⁴ 11.9g⁴ 11.8g⁴ 12.1s
1996 11.7g² 12m³ 12m 10m² 10.1g* 10m⁶ 10f⁴ 10.2f* Sep 12] lengthy filly: fair
handicapper: won at Epsom (apprentices) in July and Chepstow (from Game Ploy) in
September: stays 1½m well: acts on firm ground, well beaten only run on soft:
sometimes bandaged behind: takes keen hold: effective from front or held up. *S. Dow*

SOVIET KING (IRE)   3 b.g. Soviet Lad (USA) 94 – Finessing (Indian King   56
(USA) 128) [1995 61?: 8g³ 10.2m⁶ 10m 10m 8.3d⁴ 8m⁵ 10f³ 12m⁴ Jul 15] angular
gelding: has a round action: modest maiden: best form at up to 1¼m: acts on firm
ground. *P. Mitchell*

SOVIET LADY (IRE)   2 b.f. (Mar 13) Soviet Lad (USA) 94 – La Vosgienne   54 +
(Ashmore (FR) 125) [1996 5d 6m³ 7g⁶ a7g³ 7m⁵ 6m⁵ 7d* 7.5m³ Sep 18] 6,000Y,
2,900 2-y-o: sparely-made filly: half-sister to several winners, including 3-y-o Bum-
blefoot (by Cyrano de Bergerac), 7f winner at 2 yrs: dam, showed some ability in
France, is half-sister to Royal Lodge winner Bengal Fire: won seller at Thirsk in
August: should stay beyond 1m: acts on good to firm and dead ground and fibresand.
J. L. Eyre

SOVIET LINE (IRE)   6 b.g. Soviet Star (USA) 128 – Shore Line 107 (High   123
Line 125) [1995 121: 8m* 8m³ 8f⁵ 8d³ 7m² 8s⁶ 1996 6m 8.1g² 8d* 8f⁵ 8m 8d
Oct 6]
        Small fields have contested the two runnings of the Juddmonte Lock-
inge Stakes at Newbury since it was upgraded to Group 1 status, a fact which
emphasised the relative shortage of top-class older milers in training. However,
Michael Stoute, a trainer who has enjoyed considerable success with older
horses, has had just the right candidate in the six-year-old gelding Soviet Line
who recorded his second successive win in the race in 1996. Soviet Line put up
a performance as good as any in his career to win the latest Lockinge, racing
close up throughout and battling on tenaciously, though edging left, to hold on
by a neck from Charnwood Forest, the pair four lengths clear of the favourite
Spectrum. Soviet Line had shown himself in very good heart prior to Newbury
with a fast-finishing short-head second to Gabr in the Sandown Mile when
conceding weight all round. After Newbury, Soviet Line's season followed a
similar pattern to that of 1995, struggling under a Group 1 penalty and proving
none too consistent. He was a disappointing fifth of nine to Charnwood Forest
in the Queen Anne Stakes at Royal Ascot, wasn't disgraced when 25/1 outsider
of seven in the Queen Elizabeth II Stakes there on returning from a three and a

Juddmonte Lockinge Stakes, Newbury—
Soviet Line (rails) wins the race again, on this occasion from Charnwood Forest and Spectrum

half months absence, but then ran poorly behind Alhaarth in the Prix du Rond-Point at Longchamp. It was reported that Soviet Line had been sent to the Nad Al Sheba stables of Bill Mather for a winter campaign in Dubai. At the time of writing he has yet to run there, and there has been no announcement about whether he will be returned to race in Britain. The Lockinge is obviously the race for him should he return.

Soviet Line's pedigree has been discussed in previous editions of *Racehorses*. He remains the best offspring of the 1983 Oaks fourth Shore Line, whose only subsequent representative to reach the racecourse has been his lightly-raced brother Soviet Shore. Having missed the 1995 season after reportedly fracturing a knee, Soviet Shore finished second when 7/4-on in a maiden at Lingfield at March. The dam produced a Prince Sabo yearling half-sister to Soviet Line in 1996, and was covered by Polish Precedent later in the year. Soviet Line's half-sister Lajna (by Be My Guest) has also had some success with her offspring, who include the USA Grade 3-winning sprinter Gold Land and the useful handicapper Ninia.

		Nureyev	Northern Dancer
	Soviet Star (USA)	(b 1977)	Special
	(b 1984)	Veruschka	Venture VII
Soviet Line (IRE)		(b 1967)	Marie d'Anjou
(b.g. 1990)		High Line	High Hat
	Shore Line	(ch 1966)	Time Call
	(b 1980)	Dark Finale	Javelot
		(b 1965)	Peeky

A compact gelding who usually impresses in appearance, Soviet Line is a quirky character who has a tendency to hang left and has occasionally failed to run on. He is effective held up or setting the pace (both Lockinge wins have come with enterprising tactics) and is best at around a mile, although he was far

Maktoum Al Maktoum's "Soviet Line"

SOVEREIGNS COURT 3 ch.g. Statoblest 120 – Clare Celeste 73 (Coquelin 71 p
(USA) 121) [1995 NR 1996 7m 7m 7m 7m⁵ 7g 8d³ 7g 7s² Oct 24] 14,000Y: tall, angular
gelding: third foal: half-brother to 1992 2-y-o 6f winner Abergele (by Absalom): dam
poor maiden (best effort at 7f at 2 yrs) half-sister to very useful 6f and 7f winner
Braddells: fair handicapper: good second of 26 in apprentice race at Newbury on
final start: subsequently sold to join L. G. Cottrell 21,000 gns Newmarket Autumn
Sales: will prove best up to 1m: acts on good to firm and soft ground: may well be
capable of better. *Major D. N. Chappell*

SOVIET BRIDE (IRE) 4 b.f. Soviet Star (USA) 128 – Nihad 76 (Alleged 77
(USA) 138) [1995 72: 8.2g⁵ 8g⁵ 10f* 10.1m* 10f² 12f² 10m⁴ 11.9g⁴ 11.8g⁴ 12.1s
1996 11.7g² 12m³ 12m 10m² 10.1g* 10m⁶ 10f⁴ 10.2f* Sep 12] lengthy filly: fair
handicapper: won at Epsom (apprentices) in July and Chepstow (from Game Ploy) in
September: stays 1½m well: acts on firm ground, well beaten only run on soft:
sometimes bandaged behind: takes keen hold: effective from front or held up. *S. Dow*

SOVIET KING (IRE) 3 b.g. Soviet Lad (USA) 94 – Finessing (Indian King 56
(USA) 128) [1995 61: 8g³ 10.2m⁶ 10m 1996 8.3d⁴ 8m⁵ 10f³ 12m⁴ Jul 15] angular
gelding: has a round action: modest maiden: best form at up to 1¼m: acts on firm
ground. *P. Mitchell*

SOVIET LADY (IRE) 2 b.f. (Mar 13) Soviet Lad (USA) 94 – La Vosgienne 54 +
(Ashmore (FR) 125) [1996 5d 6m³ 7g⁶ a7g³ 7m⁵ 6m⁵ 7d⁷ 7.5m³ Sep 18] 6,000Y,
2,900 2-y-o: sparely-made filly: half-sister to several winners, including 3-y-o Bum-
blefoot (by Cyrano de Bergerac), 7f winner at 2 yrs: dam, showed some ability in
France, is half-sister to Royal Lodge winner Bengal Fire: won seller at Thirsk in
August: should stay beyond 1m: acts on good to firm and dead ground and fibresand.
J. L. Eyre

SOVIET LINE (IRE) 6 b.g. Soviet Star (USA) 128 – Shore Line 107 (High 123
Line 125) [1995 121: 8m* 8m³ 8f⁵ 8d³ 7m² 8s⁶ 1996 6m 8.1g² 8d* 8f⁵ 8m 8d
Oct 6]
Small fields have contested the two runnings of the Juddmonte Lockinge Stakes at Newbury since it was upgraded to Group 1 status, a fact which
emphasised the relative shortage of top-class older milers in training. However,
Michael Stoute, a trainer who has enjoyed considerable success with older
horses, has had just the right candidate in the six-year-old gelding Soviet Line
who recorded his second successive win in the race in 1996. Soviet Line put up
a performance as good as any in his career to win the latest Lockinge, racing
close up throughout and battling on tenaciously, though edging left, to hold on
by a neck from Charnwood Forest and four lengths clear of the favourite
Spectrum. Soviet Line had shown himself in very good heart prior to Newbury
with a fast-finishing short-head second to Gabr in the Sandown Mile when
conceding weight all round. After Newbury, Soviet Line's season followed a
similar pattern to that of 1995, struggling under a Group 1 penalty and proving
none too consistent. He was a disappointing fifth of nine to Charnwood Forest
in the Queen Anne Stakes at Royal Ascot, wasn't disgraced when 25/1 outsider
of seven in the Queen Elizabeth II Stakes there on returning from a three and a

Juddmonte Lockinge Stakes, Newbury—
Soviet Line (rails) wins the race again, on this occasion from Charnwood Forest and Spectrum

half months absence, but then ran poorly behind Alhaarth in the Prix du Rond-Point at Longchamp. It was reported that Soviet Line had been sent to the Nad Al Sheba stables of Bill Mather for a winter campaign in Dubai. At the time of writing he has yet to run there, and there has been no announcement about whether he will be returned to race in Britain. The Lockinge is obviously the race for him should he return.

Soviet Line's pedigree has been discussed in previous editions of *Racehorses*. He remains the best offspring of the 1983 Oaks fourth Shore Line, whose only subsequent representative to reach the racecourse has been his lightly-raced brother Soviet Shore. Having missed the 1995 season after reportedly fracturing a knee, Soviet Shore finished second when 7/4-on in a maiden at Lingfield at March. The dam produced a Prince Sabo yearling half-sister to Soviet Line in 1996, and was covered by Polish Precedent later in the year. Soviet Line's half-sister Lajna (by Be My Guest) has also had some success with her offspring, who include the USA Grade 3-winning sprinter Gold Land and the useful handicapper Ninia.

Soviet Line (IRE) (b.g. 1990)	Soviet Star (USA) (b 1984)	Nureyev (b 1977)	Northern Dancer, Special
		Veruschka (b 1967)	Venture VII, Marie d'Anjou
	Shore Line (b 1980)	High Line (ch 1966)	High Hat, Time Call
		Dark Finale (b 1965)	Javelot, Peeky

A compact gelding who usually impresses in appearance, Soviet Line is a quirky character who has a tendency to hang left and has occasionally failed to run on. He is effective held up or setting the pace (both Lockinge wins have come with enterprising tactics) and is best at around a mile, although he was far

Maktoum Al Maktoum's "Soviet Line"

from disgraced when tried over six furlongs on his reappearance. Soviet Line used to be regarded as a top-of-the-ground performer, but he acts on any going. *M. R. Stoute*

SOVIET SAKTI (IRE)   3 b.g. Soviet Lad (USA) 94 – Hill's Realm (USA) 68   – (Key To The Kingdom (USA)) [1995 49+: 6.1f 6.1m⁶ 7m 6m 5g 10d 8f 1996 10.8m 8.1m Jul 24] workmanlike gelding: poor form at 2 yrs: tailed off in 1996: likely to prove best short of 1¼m: blinkered/visored twice at 2 yrs. *P. Mitchell*

SOVIET SHORE   4 b.c. Soviet Star (USA) 128 – Shore Line 107 (High Line 125)   66 [1995 NR 1996 a10g² Mar 29] attractive colt: fluent mover: third of 9 in maiden at Yarmouth (rated 77p) at 2 yrs, but reportedly fractured a knee in 1995: 7/4 on, 6 lengths second of 10 to Carol's Dream in maiden at Lingfield on only 4-y-o start, never able to challenge: probably stays 1¼m. *D. R. Loder*

SOVIET STATE (USA)   2 b.c. (Mar 23) Nureyev (USA) 131 – Absentia (USA)   88 108 (Raise A Cup (USA)) [1996 6s² 6d* 6s⁵ Nov 29] $275,000Y: smallish, attractive colt: unimpressive mover: brother to smart sprinter Dancing Dissident and closely related to several winners here and in North America, including useful sprinter Nimphidia (by Nijinsky): dam, useful miler in France later smart in USA, is from family of top-class American horses Chieftain and Tom Rolfe: withdrawn at start after found to be lame on intended debut: well-backed 6/5-shot, made all in 17-runner maiden at Doncaster: beaten 8¾ lengths in listed race at Evry later in month: bred to stay beyond 6f, but looks speedy: raced only on a soft surface: may do better. *P. W. Chapple-Hyam*

SPA LANE   3 ch.g. Presidium 124 – Sleekit 78 (Blakeney 126) [1995 –: 7.1m 6g   63 8g 6f 1996 8.2m² 10m* 10f⁴ 10.8f³ 14.1d* Aug 25] leggy gelding: modest performer: won minor events at Nottingham in June (apprentice race) and August: sold (P. Makin to M. Bielby) 8,000 gns Newmarket Autumn Sales: stays 1¾m: acts on firm and dead ground. *P. J. Makin*

SPANDREL   4 ch.f. Pharly (FR) 130 – Oxslip 106 (Owen Dudley 121) [1995 –: 7f   61 1996 7m 6m 6m 6g² 7g Aug 21] smallish filly: modest maiden: looked sure to improve over longer trip, but finished last of 15 in handicap at Kempton on final start: should stay 7f+: has raced only on a sound surface. *H. Candy*

SPANIARDS CLOSE   8 b.g. King of Spain 121 – Avon Belle 75 (Balidar 133)   77 [1995 101: 5.2m a5g* 5g* 5d* 6d² 1996 5f² 6m² Jul 10] lengthy, workmanlike gelding: useful performer in 1995: well-below-par second in top-of-the-ground claimers at Sandown and Kempton in 1996: stays 6f: acts on fibresand: possibly unsuited by extremes: visored (tailed off) once at 5 yrs: held up. *P. J. Makin*

SPANIARDS INN   2 b.g. (Jan 24) Dominion 123 – Zelda (USA) (Sharpen Up   82 127) [1996 5g⁶ 6s 6m⁴ 6m* Aug 7] 16,000F, 35,000Y: sturdy, lengthy gelding: carries condition: second living foal: dam once-raced half-sister to Moorestyle: progressive form: won nursery at Kempton: will probably stay 7f: sent to Hong Kong. *B. J. Meehan*

SPANIARD'S MOUNT   2 b.c. (May 15) Distant Relative 128 – Confection   67 (Formidable (USA) 125) [1996 6f⁵ 6m 7f 8g 7g⁶ 7.1s* 6.9v³ a7g⁵ Nov 18] 35,000Y: a? small, sturdy colt: brother to useful 3-y-o Anthelia (stays 1¼m), 5f and 6f winner at 2 yrs, and half-brother to 1991 2-y-o 5f and 6f winner (winner at up to around 1m in Denmark) Titch Wizard (by Bairn): dam twice-raced daughter of useful middle-distance stayer Mint: well backed, won 6-runner rating related maiden at Musselburgh by a short head from Zorba: good effort in nursery at Folkestone 4 days later: stays 7f: best form on an easy surface and acts on heavy ground, well below form only outing on fibresand: visored last 4 starts. *M. H. Tompkins*

SPANISH FALLS   3 ch.f. Belmez (USA) 131 – Flamenco Wave (USA) 103   106 (Desert Wine (USA)) [1995 7.5d* 1996 10.5d³ 10.5g 12d* 12m³ 12.5d Oct 5] fourth foal: half-sister to 4-y-o 1½m winner Cante Chico (by Reference Point) and fairly useful Irish 1½m winner (stays 2m) Father Sky (by Dancing Brave): dam won Moyglare Stud Stakes: won minor event at Maisons-Laffitte at 2 yrs: stepped up in trip and improved form to win Prix de Royaumont at Saint-Cloud in June by nose from demoted Leonila: creditable 5½ lengths third of 6 to Shamadara in Prix de Malleret but below form in Prix de Royallieu last time, both at Longchamp: better at

1½m than shorter: acted on dead and good to firm ground: retired. *Mme C. Head, France*

SPANISH KNOT (USA) 2 b.f. (Mar 28) El Gran Senor (USA) 136 – Ingenuity 75
68 (Clever Trick (USA)) [1996 6m⁵ 7g² 8f⁵ Oct 15] first foal: dam 6f winner, bred to stay at least 1m: fair form in maidens, best effort (boxed in 2f out then too much ground to make up) when 1¼ lengths second to eased Cosmic Prince at Brighton in October: should stay 1m: below form on firm ground. *Lord Huntingdon*

SPANISH STEPS (IRE) 4 b.g. Danehill (USA) 126 – Belle Enfant 87 (Beldale 62
Flutter (USA) 130) [1995 62d: 8m³ 12m 8g⁵ 8g³ 1996 10.1s 8m 8m* 8g 6.9g² 7.1d Jul 4] tall gelding: shows knee action: modest handicapper: won at Redcar (ladies race) in May: sold 1,600 gns Newmarket Autumn Sales: likely to prove best at up to 1m: acts on good to firm ground, well beaten all 3 starts on a soft surface: blinkered 5 times, including last 4 starts. *M. W. Easterby*

SPANISH STRIPPER (USA) 5 b.g. El Gran Senor (USA) 136 – Gourmet 57
Dinner (USA) (Raise A Cup (USA)) [1995 69, a48: a7g a7g⁴ a8.5g² a7g a7g³ a8g⁵ a–
a8g a8g a11g 7g⁴ 10f 8m⁶ a8g 6m* 6.9g 5m³ 7m 7m³ 7.5m⁵ 7f 1996 a7g 7f a6g 6g 8m² 7g 7m 6m 7f 9m 11.5m a8g a11g Nov 18] good-topped gelding: fair handicapper on turf, poor on the all-weather: below best in 1996: may prove best at up to 7f: acts on good to firm ground and on fibresand: has run well when sweating: none too consistent. *M. C. Chapman*

SPANISH VERDICT 9 b.g. King of Spain 121 – Counsel's Verdict (Firestreak 72
125) [1995 74: 7.1g⁶ 8g³ 8m² 8m 8.1g 8m² 8f² 8.1f³ 8.3m⁵ 8m² 8f* 9m⁵ 8h² 8m* 8g 9f 8f 8f 1996 7s 8d 8g 8g 6.9g 8f* 8f² 8f² 8m 8f⁴ 9g 8d³ 8g 8m 10f⁶ 9m² 8m⁶ 10m 10f Nov 5] sturdy, good-quartered gelding: impresses in appearance: has a round action: fair handicapper: successful at least once every year in the 'nineties: won in 1996 at Thirsk in June: effective at 7f, probably at 1¼m: has some form on soft going, but goes particularly well (all but one of 13 wins) on top-of-the-ground: sometimes visored early in career: often claimer ridden: genuine. *Denys Smith*

SPANISH WARRIOR 2 b.g. (Mar 19) Warrshan (USA) 117 – Spanish Heart 86 –
(King of Spain 121) [1996 6g Aug 21] 8,800Y: third foal: half-brother to 1995 2-y-o 7f winner Spanish Luck (by Mazilier): dam effective from 7f to 9f: 12/1, always behind in 17-runner median auction maiden at Kempton. *J. W. Hills*

SPARGO EXPRESS 2 b.c. (Apr 12) Mystiko (USA) 124 – Noora's Rose (NZ) –
(Ahonoora 122) [1996 a7g⁶ Dec 28] 11,000Y: first foal: dam ran 3 times: weak 5/1, tailed off in maiden auction at Wolverhampton. *B. W. Hills*

SPARKLING EDGE 2 b.f. (May 27) Beveled (USA) – Sparkalot (USA) (Duel) 54
[1996 6m* 6d⁶ 5f 7d 5.2g⁵ a5g⁶ a5g* a5g Dec 3] sister to 7f winner Screwball Anaconda and half-sister to several winners in USA: dam won at 2 yrs in USA and is half-sister to dam of 3 graded or group winners: modest form: won sellers at Folkestone (sold out of A. Jones's stable 5,000 gns) in August and Wolverhampton in November: stays 6f: acts on good to firm ground and fibresand: inconsistent. *C. A. Dwyer*

SPARKLING HARRY 2 ch.c. (Mar 25) Tina's Pet 121 – Sparkling Hock (Hot 60
Spark 126) [1996 5m⁶ 5.1m 5m⁶ 5s 5m 5s⁶ 6g³ 6.1s Oct 31] 1,300Y: quite good-topped colt: fifth foal: dam ran once: modest maiden: stays 6f: acts on soft ground: blinkered last 2 starts. *Miss L. C. Siddall*

SPARKY 2 b.g. (Mar 3) Warrshan (USA) 117 – Pebble Creek (IRE) (Reference 56
Point 139) [1996 5m⁶ 6m⁴ 7f 7g 6f* 7.5f* 7.9g 8m 6m³ Oct 7] 450F: workmanlike gelding: has a round action: second foal: half-brother to 3-y-o Rocky Stream (by Reprimand): dam unraced daughter of Pebbles: modest form: won seller at Brighton and nursery at Beverley in August: stays 7.5f: acts on firm ground, yet to race on a soft surface: blinkered last 5 starts. *M. W. Easterby*

SPARTAN GIRL (IRE) 2 ch.f. (Mar 21) Ela-Mana-Mou 132 – Well Head (IRE) 62 p
(Sadler's Wells (USA) 132) [1996 7.1v⁴ Oct 16] lengthy filly: first reported foal: dam unraced half-sister to Spectrum from the family of Sun Princess and Saddlers' Hall: 5/1 and very green, around 12 lengths fourth of 10 to Catienus in maiden at Haydock, struggling from over 2f out: will do better. *Lord Huntingdon*

SPARTAN HEARTBEAT 3 b.c. Shareef Dancer (USA) 135 – Helen's Dream 106
(Troy 137) [1995 –: 8f 8m 1996 10g³ 10f³ 12.4g³ 12m 12m⁶ 16f⁵ Aug 1] good-bodied

colt: looked just fair maiden after first 3 3-y-o starts: subsequently showed useful form facing very stiff tasks when fourteenth of 20 to Shaamit in the Derby at Epsom, sixth of 13 to Zagreb in Irish Derby at the Curragh and 6 lengths fifth of 7 (sweating profusely) to Grey Shot in Goodwood Cup: stays 2m: acts on firm ground: blinkered (no improvement) third 3-y-o start: tends to sweat and be edgy/coltish: often soon pushed along. *C. E. Brittain*

SPECIAL BEAT 4 b.f. Bustino 136 – Special Guest 67 (Be My Guest (USA) 65
126) [1995 61: 10.1m⁵ 10m⁴ 8.3m⁵ 13.1h⁵ 11.4d 1996 11.9m 17.2f* 17.2f² Jul 24]
unfurnished filly: has a round action: modest form: won poor maiden handicap at Bath in July: stays 17.2f: acts on hard ground, ran badly on dead: has joined N. Henderson. *P. F. I. Cole*

SPECIAL DAWN (IRE) 6 ch.g. Be My Guest (USA) 126 – Dawn Star 94 (High 94
Line 125) [1995 96: 10m* 10m 10g* 10m* 9g 10d 10v 1996 10g² 10m⁵ 10g 10g²
10m 10g³ 10m Sep 21] lengthy gelding: good mover: useful handicapper: was reportedly difficult to train: best efforts in 1996 when in frame in Rosebery Handicap at Kempton, rated stakes at Windsor and quite valuable event at the Curragh: stayed 1½m, best form at 1¼m: acted on good to firm and heavy going: held up: usually went well fresh: has been retired. *J. L. Dunlop*

SPECIALIZE 4 b.g. Faustus (USA) 118 – Scholastika (GER) (Alpenkonig –
(GER)) [1995 48?: 10.8m 8f 10m 10f 1996 12.3g Apr 10] good-bodied gelding: little worthwhile form on flat. *K. R. Burke*

SPECIAL-K 4 br.f. Treasure Kay 114 – Lissi Gori (FR) (Bolkonski 134) [1995 65
65: 6m² 6f³ 5.9f² 7f* 7.5g* 8f⁶ 7m⁶ 7.5m³ 8m* 1996 7m⁴ 8g 7.5m 7.5f⁴ 7.9g³ 10.3m⁵
8m 9g⁶ 6.9m² 8g 8.5m 7g Sep 21] leggy filly: fair handicapper: consistent at 3 yrs, not in 1996: stays 1m: acts on firm ground: usually races prominently: visored (respectable effort) final start. *E. Weymes*

SPECIAL RISK (IRE) 6 br.g. Simply Great (FR) 122 – Ahonita 90 (Ahonoora –
122) [1995 –: 14.1g 1996 10m 16.1f Oct 8] small, leggy gelding: poor handicapper: well beaten since 4 yrs. *R. Akehurst*

SPECTACLE JIM 7 b.g. Mummy's Game 120 – Welsh Blossom 100 (Welsh 48
Saint 126) [1995 53: a6g³ 6m⁶ 6m 6m³ 8.3m 6m 6f² 8s 6g 7m a5g² a5g⁶ 1996 6g⁶ 6m
6f 8g 6.9m⁵ 6m 6g a7g Jul 27] leggy gelding: poor handicapper: little form in 1996, and sold 950 gns Ascot November Sales: effective at 5f, and stays 8.3f: acts on equitrack and on firm and soft ground: usually blinkered/visored: wears dropped noseband: inconsistent. *M. J. Haynes*

SPECTRUM (IRE) 4 b.c. Rainbow Quest (USA) 134 – River Dancer 118 122
(Irish River (FR) 131) [1995 126: 8.1m* 8m* 12f 10s² 10m* 1996 10.5m⁴ 8d³
10.4m⁵ Aug 20]
Spectrum's racing career is likely to be remembered almost as much for what might have been as for what actually was. Nine races in three seasons is a disappointing attendance record for one who was not far off top of the class at his best, and by the end there was still a feeling of untapped potential with him. An odd comment, maybe, on a horse who won two Group 1 races, the Irish Two Thousand Guineas and the Champion Stakes in 1995. But a back injury sustained in that year's Derby (for which he started second favourite) meant that it was never proven whether Spectrum was effective at a mile and a half. And recurrences of that injury limited him to just three outings in 1996, during which he failed to recapture his very best form or add to his previous successes.

His reappearance, in the Prix Ganay at Longchamp in April, was not without promise, Spectrum running as if in need of the race in finishing fourth, beaten slightly more than four lengths by Valanour. But Spectrum went backwards, being beaten a similar margin into third by Soviet Line in the Juddmonte Lockinge Stakes at Newbury the following month, and then not being seen out again until York's August meeting. His fifth of six to Halling in the Juddmonte International Stakes at York in August was still a fair bit behind what had been expected of him at the season's outset, though, on form, it was, in fact, marginally his best of the season. His probable retirement was announced in Septem-

935

ber, when it became clear that he would not be ready for an attempted repeat win in the Champion Stakes.

Spectrum (IRE) (b.c. 1992)	Rainbow Quest (USA) (b 1981)	Blushing Groom (ch 1974)	Red God
			Runaway Bride
		I Will Follow (b 1975)	Herbager
			Where You Lead
	River Dancer (b 1983)	Irish River (ch 1976)	Riverman
			Irish Star
		Dancing Shadow (b 1977)	Dancer's Image
			Sunny Valley

Coolmore in Ireland will be Spectrum's new home, the Stud having bought a half-share in him at the end of his three-year-old career and acquired more in 1996. He is to stand at a fee of IR 12,500 guineas with the October 1st concession. Whatever Spectrum's problems, he was clearly capable of high-class form at his best and is bred well enough into the bargain to be an interesting proposition as a stallion. His sire Rainbow Quest has been a resounding success at stud, establishing himself as the top sire based in Britain. Spectrum's dam River Dancer was a smart performer in her own right, third in the Poule d'Essai des Pouliches, and she has bred three other winners. Neither Snow Plough (by Niniski), a winner over a mile and a quarter, nor Ballet Shoes (by Ela-Mana-Mou), who was suited by sprint distances, was especially talented. But Spectrum's year-younger close relative Nash House (by Nashwan) showed useful form in winning a Newbury maiden and finishing fourth in the Dante Stakes at York in the latest season, and looked potentially a good deal better than that before encountering recurring problems with breaking blood vessels. Further back, Spectrum's family abounds with winners. Most notably, his grandam Dancing Shadow was smart at up to a mile and a quarter and is a half-sister to the Oaks and St Leger winner Sun Princess and the St Leger runner-up Saddlers' Hall.

Spectrum is a prepossessing individual as well, a rangy, attractive colt. He had a quick action in his slower paces and tended to flash his tail in the preliminaries and give some trouble at the stalls. He should have stayed beyond a mile and a quarter, and he showed that he acted on any going other than firm, the ground conditions on Derby Day. *P. W. Chapple-Hyam*

SPEEDBALL (IRE) 2 b.c. (Jan 26) Waajib 121 – Lady Taufan (IRE) (Taufan (USA) 119) [1996 6g³ 6m* 6d² 6m Oct 17] IR 15,500Y: useful-looking colt: first foal: dam, Irish maiden, stayed 9f: useful form: beat Hopesay ½ length in 24-runner maiden at Newbury: good second of 5 to Tomba in minor event at Salisbury in October: never threatened when down the field in Redcar Two-Year-Old Trophy on final outing: will stay beyond 6f. *I. A. Balding*   96

SPEEDBOAT (USA) 2 ch.c. (Jan 22) Diesis 133 – Ocean Ballad 104 (Grundy 137) [1996 7g³ Oct 2] $35,000Y: fourth foal: brother to 5-y-o 14.1f winner Frozen Sea and closely related to 3-y-o Sea of Stone (by Sanglamore): dam 1½m winner from staying family: 8/1, 1¼ lengths third of 15 to Cosmic Prince in maiden at Brighton, tracking leaders then staying on steadily: sold (L. Cumani to J. L. Eyre) 40,000 gns Newmarket Autumn Sales: will improve, particularly over further than 7f. *L. M. Cumani*   80 p

SPEEDFIT 2 gr.c. (May 19) Mystiko (USA) 124 – Softly Spoken 87 (Mummy's Pet 125) [1996 5m 6s May 19] 13,500Y: tall, short-backed colt: fourth foal: half-brother to three 2-y-o sprint winners, including 3-y-o Branston Danni (by Ron's Victory): dam sprinter: weakened 2f out (on unfavoured part of track) when down the field in maidens at Kempton and Newbury: reluctant stalls on debut. *G. G. Margarson*   –

SPEED ON 3 b.g. Sharpo 132 – Pretty Poppy 67 (Song 132) [1995 NR 1996 5d² 5m* 5f² 6m³ 5m⁶ 5g Sep 29] 21,000Y: compact gelding: good walker: reportedly chipped knee as 2-y-o: first foal: dam (5f winner at 2 yrs) stayed 7.6f: useful performer: confirmed considerable promise of debut by winning maiden at Beverley in May by 5 lengths: best efforts on next 3 starts, sixth of 9 to Anzio in listed race at Doncaster on last of them: best efforts at 5f: acts on firm and dead ground. *H. Candy*   103

SPEED TO LEAD (IRE)　4 b.f. Darshaan 133 – Instant Desire (USA) 86　90
(Northern Dancer) [1995 84: 11.5m² 11.8f³ 1996 12m² 16.4g³ 16m* 22.2f² 16.1m⁶
Aug 26] leggy filly: fairly useful handicapper, lightly raced: won at Goodwood in
June: game second of 10 to Admiral's Well in Queen Alexandra Stakes at Royal
Ascot next time: sold 14,000 gns Newmarket December Sales, to join Miss Gay
Kelleway: stays extreme distances: acts on firm and dead ground: front runner last 4
starts. *H. R. A. Cecil*

SPEEDY CLASSIC (USA)　7 br.g. Storm Cat (USA) – Shadows Lengthen 73　63
(Star Appeal 133) [1995 68: a6g² a6g³ a5g⁴ a6g⁴ 6m 5m⁶ a6g⁴ a5g² a5g² a6g⁴ 1996　a85
a6g⁴ a6g a7g* a6g³ 6f² 6f 5m 6g 6m⁵ 6f a7g* 7.1f* 6.1m⁴ 7m⁶ a7g⁵ a7g* Dec 20]
workmanlike gelding: has round action: fairly useful handicapper on the all-weather
at Lingfield, and won there in February (claimer), August and December (by 4
lengths, career-best effort): made all at Chepstow on turf in September: effective at
5f to 7f: acts on all-weather surfaces and on firm ground: effective blinkered (rarely
tried) or not: has given trouble at stalls and often taken down early: often makes
running. *M. J. Heaton-Ellis*

SPEEDY SNAPS IMAGE　5 ch.g. Ballacashtal (CAN) – Lillicara (FR) (Cara-　–
colero (USA) 131) [1995 NR 1996 8.1d 7f Jun 15] compact gelding: poor maiden on
flat (stayed 7f, tried blinkered) in 1994: first runs of any sort since October that year
when well beaten in claimer and selling handicap: has joined P. Rodford. *J. E. Long*

SPEEDY SNAPS PRIDE　4 gr.g. Hallgate 127 – Pineapple's Pride 60 (John de　53
Coombe 122) [1995 46, a38: a7g³ a8.5g 6s⁵ a7g³ a6g³ a7g³ 8.3g a6g⁵ 7g³ 7m² 7m　a36
8m⁴ 1996 a6g a7g⁶ a7g a8g a7g⁶ 6.9s 9.7m⁶ 10m 10d⁴ a8g³ 7m³ 8.1m 7m³ 7d* 6m 7f
8m Oct 28] plain, sparely-made gelding: modest handicapper: trained fourth outing
only by J. A. Harris: won seller at Newmarket in August, idling in front: well beaten
afterwards: effective at 7f, and probably stays 1¼m: acts on fibresand and on good to
firm and soft going: usually blinkered nowadays. *P. D. Cundell*

SPENCER'S REVENGE　7 ch.g. Bay Express 132 – Armour of Light (Hot　81 d
Spark 126) [1995 81: a7g* a7g* a7g* a7g² a7g³ a8g 7g* a7g* 7f* 7f² a8g* 1996
a8g* a7g³ a8g² a8g² a7g³ 7s⁶ 8d⁵ a8g* a9.4g⁵ a8g⁶ a8g⁴ Dec 11] sturdy gelding: poor
mover: fairly useful performer: won claimers at Southwell in January (claimed out of
M. Ryan's stable £8,000 2 starts later) and April: below form (after 6-month absence)
last 2 starts: effective at 7f and 1m: acts on all-weather surfaces, no form on turf in
1996: tried visored and blinkered, no improvement: comes from behind: often looks
a hard ride. *N. Tinkler*

SPENCER STALLONE　3 b.g. Rambo Dancer (CAN) 107 – Armour of Light　–
(Hot Spark 126) [1995 NR 1996 a8g⁵ 8d⁴ 8.3g 8g⁵ Jul 24] 1,500Y: fourth foal:
half-brother to fairly useful 7f and 1m winner Spencer's Revenge (by Bay Express):
dam poor maiden: no worthwhile form in maidens and sellers: has joined Graeme
Roe. *Lord Huntingdon*

SPENDER　7 b. or br.g. Last Tycoon 131 – Lady Hester (Native Prince) [1995 76,　80
a83: a6g³ a6g² a5g* a6g⁴ a5g³ a6g⁶ a5g* 5m³ 5m² 5g 5.1h* 5.2m 5m⁶ 5.1d 5f 1996　a91
a6g a5g² a6g a6g³ a5g* a5g⁶ 6g 5f² 5g² 5m 5.1m³ 5f 5.2m⁶ 5g³ 5s⁴ Nov 8] small,
well-made gelding: fairly useful sprint handicapper: best on the all-weather, and
better than ever when winning at Lingfield in March: effective at 5f and 6f: acts on
fibresand and equitrack and on hard and soft ground: tough and genuine. *P. W. Harris*

SPHINX LEVELV (IRE)　3 ch.g. Digamist (USA) 110 – Fantoccini (Taufan　–
(USA) 119) [1995 52, a45: 6g a6g⁴ a7g⁶ 6.1m³ 7.1m 6d a7g 1996 a8g³ 10g a8g 8.1m
Jul 24] smallish gelding: plater: well below form in 1996. *A. P. Jarvis*

SPICE AND SUGAR　6 ch.m. Chilibang 120 – Pretty Miss (So Blessed 130)　–
[1995 –: a14.8g 1996 10m 10.8f 12.5f⁴ 10f Sep 10] lengthy mare: poor performer:
lightly raced and little form since 1994: sold 500 gns Doncaster November Sales.
B. R. Cambidge

SPICETRESS　2 gr.f. (Apr 27) Chilibang 120 – Foreign Mistress (Darshaan 133)　52
[1996 6f 6g⁴ 8s Nov 9] 1,000Y: lengthy filly: second foal: dam placed several
times in Italy: 33/1, best effort in maiden events when always-prominent fourth
of 14 to Parijazz at Pontefract in October: soundly beaten over 1m on soft ground.
J. L. Spearing

SPILLO　3 b.c. Midyan (USA) 124 – Myth 89 (Troy 137) [1995 80p: 7g 8d 7.1d³　97
1996 8.5d⁴ 10f* 10m² 12g⁴ 10.4m³ 12.1m² 12m⁴ 11.9m 12m* 12m⁶ Oct 1] smallish,

well-made colt: fairly useful handicapper: won at Brighton (maiden) in April and at Doncaster (ridden off pace some way out in strongly-run race, leading final 1f) in September: suited by stamina test at 1½m, and may well do even better over further: acts on firm and dead ground: consistent: sold to Norway. *L. M. Cumani*

SPINNING MOUSE 3 b.f. Bustino 136 – Minute Waltz (Sadler's Wells (USA) 65 132) [1995 –: 8.2m 8m a7g 1996 11.6m 11.8d⁵ 11.5f² 13.8m* 14.1m² 15.8g⁵ 11.5m Oct 4] quite good-topped filly: fair handicapper: comfortable winner at Catterick in August: below form last 2 starts: stays 1¾m well: acts on firm going, shaped well on dead. *D. Morley*

SPINNING WORLD (USA) 3 ch.c. Nureyev (USA) 131 – Imperfect Circle 125 (USA) 111 (Riverman (USA) 131) [1995 106p: 8m* 9s* 1996 8m³ 8g² 8d* 8f⁶ 8d* 8m² 8g² Oct 26]

Little more than a year separated the deaths of trainer Francois Boutin and owner Stavros Niarchos. Their's was a legendary partnership in French racing in the 'eighties and 'nineties, with Nureyev, Cresta Rider, L'Emigrant, Persepolis, Seattle Song, Northern Trick, Procida, Miesque, Machiavellian, Hector Protector, Shangai, Kingmambo, Hernando and East of The Moon just a few of the horses that saw them in the winner's enclosure together. The Greek shipping tycoon Niarchos, eighty-six when he died in April, had plenty of success with other trainers too, going back as far as 1953 in Britain when Harvey Leader sent out Oleandrin to be third in the Two Thousand Guineas. Henry Cecil, Jeremy Tree and Roger Charlton all benefited from his patronage and Vincent O'Brien had charge of such as Law Society and Seattle Dancer when Niarchos briefly joined forces with the Sangster team. The last race meeting that Stavros Niarchos attended was reportedly the 1994 Breeders' Cup when East of The Moon and Hernando both finished unplaced but Johann Quatz, a horse he bred, finished second in the Mile. In 1996 the dark blue, light blue cross belts, striped sleeves and white cap represented the Niarchos Family and their leading performer was another Breeders' Cup Mile runner-up, Spinning World.

In addition to that fine effort at Woodbine, doing easily best of the European challengers behind Da Hoss, Spinning World won both the First National Building Society Irish Two Thousand Guineas and the Prix du Haras de Fresnay-le-Buffard Jacques le Marois. The Jacques le Marois sponsors, incidentally, are another testimony to the glory days of Stavros Niarchos. Performances such as those of Spinning World might be enough for recognition as France's top miler in some years, but he was a contemporary of Ashkalani. The two of them met four times in 1996 and Ashkalani finished ahead of him on all four. After the first two of those races, though, there was no difficulty in finding observers who claimed that Spinning World was the better racehorse. The Prix de Fontainebleau had seen both colts reappearing and then in the Poule d'Essai des Poulains Spinning World did not have so clear a run, coming from the rear and being beaten three quarters of a length into second. Unlucky was not an adjective we attached to Spinning World at the time, and his subsequently finishing sixth to Ashkalani's second in the St James's Palace Stakes and second (beaten a length and a half) to Ashkalani's first in the Prix du Moulin made the case for Ashkalani's overall superiority look very convincing (mind you, on the same basis Spinning World ended the season with a 2-0 victory over Mark of Esteem). The Moulin clinched the issue for us, with Spinning World a length up on his rival early in the straight but still being brushed aside.

It would have been an injustice if a racehorse of Spinning World's quality had been kept out of the winner's enclosure as a three-year-old, and, as mentioned earlier, he deservedly picked up two Group 1 victories. For that in the Irish Guineas, a first win in the race apparently for a French-trained horse, Spinning World started 7/4 favourite and was troubled most by the outsider of ten, 50/1-shot Rainbow Blues; not troubled much though, as Spinning World cruised into the lead and went on to win by two lengths, perhaps not so great a

margin as seemed likely for a long way but nevertheless a most clear-cut victory. The Irish-trained Rainbow Blues was followed in by British challengers Beauchamp King, Bijou d'Inde, Tagula, Phantom Quest, Russian Revival and Musick House, with the last two positions filled by the only other Irish runners, Deed of Love and Flame of Athens. The opposition was a good deal stronger in the Jacques le Marois at Deauville nearly three months later and Spinning World had to work hard to get his nose in front half a furlong out and keep it there ahead of Vetheuil, Shaanxi and Charnwood Forest. Spinning World edged left in front at the Curragh, and is ridden with waiting tactics of varying degree. A high-class miler, he shapes as if he will be just as good over a bit further, indeed the second of his two wins at two years was over nine furlongs. Firm ground is against him on the evidence of Royal Ascot but he has a good second on good to firm (in the Moulin) to add to his unbeaten record on a soft surface.

Niarchos Family's "Spinning World"

Spinning World (USA) (ch.c. 1993)	Nureyev (USA) (b 1977)	Northern Dancer (b 1961)	Nearctic Natalma
		Special (b 1969)	Forli Thong
	Imperfect Circle (USA) (b 1988)	Riverman (b 1969)	Never Bend River Lady
		Aviance (ch 1982)	Northfields Minnie Hauk

The rather leggy, good-topped Spinning World comes from a mating between two Niarchos performers. Nureyev was hugely famous in his day, infamous perhaps after disqualification from first place in the Two Thousand Guineas, the end of his three-race career. He had earlier hacked up in both the Prix Thomas Bryon and Prix Djebel. Purchased for 1,300,000 dollars as a yearling, Nureyev now has progeny earnings of about thirty million. Unsurprisingly, he was the first stallion to whom Niarchos sent his Cheveley Park Stakes runner-up Imperfect Circle. Winner of the listed Firth of Clyde Stakes earlier at two years, Imperfect Circle however made her reappearance not in a classic or classic trial but in a minor event at Salisbury. She won it, but eighth of fifteen in a listed contest brought her racing career to an end after just five starts. Her year-older half-sister Chimes of Freedom had a much better run, doing one place worse than Imperfect Circle in the Cheveley Park but winning six of her other eight starts including the Cherry Hinton, Moyglare Stud, Coronation and Child Stakes. Their dam Aviance won the Heinz '57' Phoenix

940

Stakes and was a creditable sixth in the One Thousand Guineas and July Cup. She is from a famous family, as Spinning World's third dam Minnie Hauk was a sister to Malinowski and Gielgud, and a half-sister to Sex Appeal who is the dam of Try My Best and El Gran Senor. Spinning World is likely to have another season on the racecourse before he takes up stud duties. *J. E. Pease, France*

SPIRAL FLYER (IRE)   3 b. or br.f. Contract Law (USA) 108 – Souveniers   41
(Relko 136) [1995 –: 6m 6g 7g 1996 a7g⁶ 9.7f 8m 8g 8m 10g⁶ 8m Sep 9] good-topped filly: poor maiden: seems better at 1¼m than shorter. *M. D. I. Usher*

SPIRIT OF SPORT   3 b.f. Forzando 122 – What's The Matter 57 (High Top 131)   –
[1995 NR 1996 a8g⁶ a8.5g Feb 28] third foal: dam maiden (stayed 1¼m) out of a stayer: little promise in claimer and maiden. *A. G. Newcombe*

SPIRITO LIBRO (USA)   3 b.f. Lear Fan (USA) 130 – Teeming Shore (USA)   89
110 (L'Emigrant (USA) 129) [1995 62: 6m⁴ 6f⁴ 7f³ 5m* 6m* 7g 7s 7m 1996 8.1g²
7.1g⁴ 8m* 7.9f³ 10.1m* 9m⁴ 10g³ 10.4m² Jul 13] smallish, sparely-made filly: made into a fairly useful handicapper, winning £14,700 contest at Newmarket in May and £17,800 event at Epsom in June: very good placed efforts in £51,700 event at Sandown (from out of handicap) and Magnet Cup at York (neck second of 17 to Wilcuma) last 2 starts, staying on well: should stay beyond 1¼m: goes well on top-of-the-ground, well beaten only start on soft: often apprentice ridden. *C. N. Allen*

SPITFIRE BRIDGE (IRE)   4 b.g. Cyrano de Bergerac 120 – Maria Renata   –
(Jaazeiro (USA) 127) [1995 50, a69: a8g³ a12g⁵ 10m³ a10g⁴ 8.3m⁶ 10.2m*10d
10.8g³ a10g* a10g* a12g⁶ a10g⁵ 1996 a10g⁵ 10g 10m 10.2m⁶ Jun 15] compact gelding: fair all-weather performer, modest on turf: below form in 1996: stays 10.2f: acts on good to firm and dead ground and on equitrack (well beaten on fibresand): blinkered twice at 2 yrs: has joined G. McCourt. *M. McCormack*

SPLASHED   2 gr.f. (May 31) Absalom 128 – Riverain 65 (Bustino 136) [1996 6g⁴   61
6m³ a5g³ Nov 12] second foal: dam 2-y-o 7f winner, also successful over hurdles: best effort in maidens when 3½ lengths third of 7 to Tycoon Girl in fillies event at Redcar in October: needs further than 5f, and will probably stay 7f. *T. D. Barron*

SPLICING   3 ch.f. Sharpo 132 – Soluce 98 (Junius (USA) 124) [1995 69: 5g² 5f⁴   82
6m³ 6.5m 1996 5.1d* 6g* a6g² 7g a6g 6d² a6g³ 6m 6v 6.1s⁴ 5f³ 5s Nov 8] lengthy filly: fairly useful performer: won maiden at Nottingham and handicap at Pontefract in April: in and out afterwards: stays 6f: acts on fibresand and soft ground. *W. J. Haggas*

SPLINTER (IRE)   3 b.c. Warning 136 – Sharpthorne (USA) 91 (Sharpen Up 127)   77
[1995 81p: 5.1f* 1996 5m⁶ 6m⁶ 5m Aug 21] fair performer, lightly raced: sold 6,000 gns Newmarket Autumn Sales: may prove best at 5f: has raced only on top-of-the-ground: presumably difficult to train. *R. Charlton*

SPONDULICKS (IRE)   2 b.g. (Mar 26) Silver Kite (USA) 111 – Greek Music   55 §
(Tachypous 128) [1996 5s³ 5g² 5m⁴ 6d⁵ 7m⁴ 7g⁶ 7f² 7g⁵ 6.9m⁵ 7.1m⁴ 8f³ 10m
a8.5g⁶ Nov 2] 5,400Y workmanlike gelding: fourth foal: half-brother to 2-y-o sprint winners Leap of Faith (by Northiam) and Angels Answer (by Stalker): dam ran twice: modest maiden: left R. Hannon after penultimate start: stays 8.5f (below form but not beaten far at 1¼m): acts on any going: very slowly away fifth outing: visored (ran creditably) final start: unreliable. *B. P. J. Baugh*

SPORTING FANTASY   3 b.g. Primo Dominie 121 – Runelia (Runnett 125)   41
[1995 61d: 5m 5g 5g³ 5f² 5m* 5g 5f⁴ a5g a6g 1996 a8g⁴ a11g a8.5g⁴ a8g⁶ 5g Jul 1] smallish, robust gelding: poor at best in 1996: probably stays 8.5f: yet to race on a soft surface: tried visored. *J. Balding*

SPORTING FELLOW   2 ch.c. (Apr 19) Groom Dancer (USA) 128 – Shameem   73 +
(USA) 65 (Nureyev (USA) 131) [1996 7f³ 7m⁴ Oct 23] first foal: dam thrice-raced half-sister to Kentucky Oaks winner Lucky Lucky Lucky: weak 11/2, 4 lengths third of 5 to Amid Albadu in steadily-run minor event at Leicester: similar form when 4½ lengths fourth of 11 to Sekari in maiden at Yarmouth 8 days later: likely to stay 1¼m: sent to Barbados. *M. R. Stoute*

SPORTING RISK   4 b.g. Risk Me (FR) 127 – Sunday Sport's Pet 58 (Mummy's   51
Pet 125) [1995 52: 7g 8g 8.3m 8f³ 8.5g 8m⁴ a8.5g⁵ 8m 8g 1996 a7g⁴ a8g⁵ a8.5g²   a45

Letheby & Christopher Lancashire Oaks, Haydock—
left to right, Spout is switched to obtain a run outside Ninotchka, My Emma and Phantom Gold

a9.4g 8m 9f* 9.9m³ 8.2m³ 7.6m a8g³ 8m Sep 25] leggy gelding: modest handicapper: trained by P. Webber on reappearance: won at Lingfield in June: sold 2,900 gns Newmarket Autumn Sales: stays 1¼m: acts on firm ground and fibresand (unraced on soft surface since 2 yrs): blinkered (below form) once at 3 yrs. *P. W. Harris*

SPOTTED EAGLE   3 ch.g. Risk Me (FR) 127 – Egnoussa 76 (Swing Easy   81 (USA) 126) [1995 60: 5.2g⁵ 1996 6s 6f* 6m 6m 6d 6.1s Oct 22] close-coupled gelding: has a quick action: fair performer: won median auction maiden at Folkestone in April: badly hampered (unseated rider) fourth start: soundly beaten afterwards: reportedly retained by trainer 1,000 gns Newmarket Autumn Sales, but has since joined Martyn Wane: will stay 7f: acts on firm going, no form on a soft surface. *R. Hannon*

SPOUT   4 b.f. Salse (USA) 128 – Arderelle (FR) 80 (Pharly (FR) 130) [1995 110:   115 8m 10g* 10m³ 12d* 12v³ 1996 12d* 14m⁶ 11.9g* 13.5g³ 10m² 12d² Oct 12] strong, lengthy filly: good walker: easy mover: smart performer: won 9-runner Lanes End John Porter Stakes at Newbury (got up on line to beat Wayne County short head) in April and 10-runner Lancashire Oaks at Haydock (overcame trouble in running to beat Phantom Gold ¾ length) in July: around 1¾ lengths third of 6 to Helen of Spain in Prix de Pomone at Deauville, 2 lengths second of 9 to Last Second in Sun Chariot Stakes at Newmarket and short-head second of 11 to Time Allowed in Princess Royal Stakes at Ascot: effective at 1¼m and should stay further than 13.5f (reportedly heavily in season in Curragh Cup when tried): acts on good to firm ground and good to soft, probably not on heavy: has good turn of foot: has won when sweating: equipped with rope halter and wears blanket for stalls entry: genuine and consistent. *R. Charlton*

SPREAD THE WORD   4 b.f. Deploy 131 – Apply 87 (Kings Lake (USA) 133)   56 [1995 69: 9g 12m 10g³ 10d 11.5s² 12g 1996 12g 14g 12.1m² 11.6d³ 12d⁶ 13.1m⁵ 14d⁵ 12d² Oct 21] lengthy filly: just a modest maiden handicapper nowadays: should stay 1¾m: acts on good to firm and soft ground: visored since third 4-y-o start: inconsistent. *L. G. Cottrell*

SPRING CAMPAIGN (IRE)   3 b.g. Sayaarr (USA) – March The Second   – (Millfontaine 114) [1995 70: 7.1m⁵ 7.9m⁴ 10m⁴ 1996 10m 10.2f⁶ 12m⁶ 8.2g 8.2s Oct 31] big, angular gelding: fair maiden at 2 yrs: little worthwhile form in 1996: should be suited by further than 1¼m: tried blinkered: gelded. *M. C. Pipe*

942

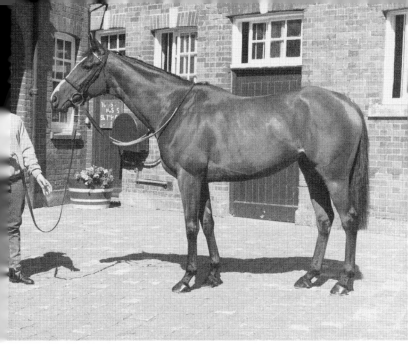

Lady Rothschild's "Spout"

SPRING SUNRISE 6 b.m. Robellino (USA) 127 – Saniette (Crystal Palace (FR) –
132) [1995 NR 1996 a11g⁶ Jan 12] tall, lengthy mare: of little account on flat.
B. De Haan

SPRING TO GLORY 9 b.g. Teenoso (USA) 135 – English Spring (USA) 116 –
(Grey Dawn II 132) [1995 NR 1996 14d Oct 2] poor staying handicapper on flat: well
held only 9-y-o start. *P. Hayward*

SPRIOLO 2 b.f. (Feb 28) Priolo (USA) 127 – Springtime Sugar (USA) (Halo –
(USA)) [1996 8g Oct 25] small filly: second reported foal: dam placed once from
5 starts in USA: 25/1 and blinkered, showed nothing in maiden at Doncaster.
R. W. Armstrong

SPUMANTE 4 ch.g. Executive Man 119 – Midler (Comedy Star (USA) 121) –
[1995 65d: 8.3m 8.2f² 8.2m⁶ 7f 8.2m a7g 1996 11.9f 16d Aug 25] rangy gelding: fair
maiden at best at 3 yrs: tailed off in 1996. *M. P. Muggeridge*

SPY KNOLL 2 b.c. (Feb 15) Shirley Heights 130 – Garden Pink (FR) (Bellypha 79 p
130) [1996 7m⁶ 8f⁴ Oct 15] very tall, rangy colt, rather unfurnished: third foal: dam,
French 8.2f and 10.5f winner, half-sister to smart French 1¼m performer Pink out of
half-sister to Green Dancer: very green and in need of race on debut: again shaped
encouragingly when 5¼ lengths fourth of 12 to Our People in maiden at Leicester
12 days later: likely to prove suited by middle distances: looks sort to make good
progress at 3 yrs. *M. R. Stoute*

SQUARED AWAY 4 b.c. Blakeney 126 – Maureen Mhor 70 (Taj Dewan 128) 55
[1995 NR 1996 8g 8.5m 8m 10m 12m 8f* 10.1g² 8m 8f 8f⁵ 9m Oct 8] good-topped
colt: fifth reported foal: dam best at 2 yrs: modest handicapper: won ladies race at

943

Redcar in June: will stay beyond 1¼m: acts on firm ground, yet to race on a soft surface: blinkered 5 of last 6 starts. *J. W. Payne*

SQUARE DEAL (FR) 5 b.g. Sharpo 132 – River Dove (USA) 86 (Riverman (USA) 131) [1995 8g³ 6m 1996 a7g² a7g* a8g² a8g a8g⁴ a7g⁵ a8.5g⁶ 6.1g a5g a6g⁵ a6g a7g a11g Dec 31] ex-Irish gelding: first foal: dam, 2-y-o 6f winner, out of Poule d'Essai des Pouliches second Fruhlingstag: fair performer, very lightly raced in Ireland for D. Hanley: landed the odds in median auction maiden at Southwell in January on second run here: below form in handicaps last 8 starts, gambled on in blinkers on fourth of them: stays 1m: acts on firm and dead ground and on fibresand: tends to hang left and look hard ride. *S. R. Bowring* 71 d

SQUARE MILE MISS (IRE) 3 b.f. Last Tycoon 131 – Call Me Miss (Hello Gorgeous (USA) 128) [1995 NR 1996 8f⁶ 10g 7f 8g 7d⁶ 7m 8m 8g a7g⁶ Dec 31] IR 17,000Y: unfurnished filly: fourth foal: sister to a winner in Spain and half-sister to 4-y-o 8.5f to 10.8f winner Hand of Straw (by Thatching): dam, Irish 1¼m winner, half-sister to Coronation Stakes winner Orchestration and Prix d'Harcourt winner Welsh Term: poor form in varied company, including selling: takes good hold, and may be worth a try at sprint distances. *P. Howling* 42

SQUEAK 2 ch.f. (Jan 19) Selkirk (USA) 129 – Santa Linda (USA) (Sir Ivor 135) [1996 7g* 7m* Oct 29] lengthy filly: seventh foal: half-sister to several winners, including 1993 2-y-o 7f winner Crackling Sike (by Salse) and fairly useful middle-distance winner Gold Pavilion (by Lemhi Gold): dam unraced half-sister to smart middle-distance colt Noble Saint out of half-sister to Tom Rolfe and Chieftain: 5/2 on, made most for easy win in 3-runner Newmarket Challenge Cup in October: still green, fairly useful form when following up in 4-runner minor event at Redcar 11 days later, coming from last to first and beating Cybertechnology by 2 lengths: will stay at least 1m: will improve further. *J. H. M. Gosden* 83 p

SQUIRE CORRIE 4 b.g. Distant Relative 128 – Fast Car (FR) (Carwhite 127) [1995 73: 6m 5m 6f³ 8m 6m² 6g 5g* 5f³ a5g⁴ 1996 a6g a6g 6.1g 5m 5m 5f 7g 7m 5f⁵ 5m* 5m⁵ 5m² 5d³ 5g* 5f* 6m 5m⁴ 5g³ a5g a6g a5g³ Dec 31] tall, workmanlike gelding: unimpressive mover: fair handicapper: won at Sandown in July and August and at Salisbury in September: sold out of G. Harwood's stable 11,000 gns Newmarket Autumn Sales after eighteenth 4-y-o start: effective at 5f (best form) and 6f: acts on equitrack (below form on fibresand) and on firm and dead ground: usually blinkered/visored: tends to sweat: often apprentice ridden: races prominently. *D. W. Chapman* 70 a64

SQUIRE'S OCCASION (CAN) 3 b.g. Black Tie Affair – Tayana (USA) (Wajima (USA)) [1995 8g⁴ 8m³ 8g 1996 12.5d 7m³ 8d⁵ 6.5m⁴ 6m 7g 7g⁵ 8m Sep 7] $100,000Y: smallish ex-Irish gelding: half-brother to several winners in North America, including Grade 2 7f winner Perfect Spy (by Stonewalk): dam won 2 of 7 races in North America: sire (half-brother to Great Palm) won Breeders' Cup Classic: fair maiden for T. Stack, best efforts on second and fourth 3-y-o starts: always behind in handicap at Kempton on only flat outing here: stays 7f: yet to race on extremes of going: won novice hurdle in November. *R. Akehurst* 72

STACKATTACK (IRE) 3 b.g. Salt Dome (USA) – Must Hurry (Kampala 120) [1995 NR 1996 8.3g a6g³ 7m⁶ 7.9g 8.1f⁵ 10d 7g² 7g 8s⁶ Nov 9] tall, useful-looking gelding: has scope: first foal: dam fair Irish 1m (Irish Cambridgeshire) to 1½m winner: fair maiden: sold out of P. Webber's stable 10,000 gns Newmarket Autumn Sales after eighth start: probably stays 1m: acts on fibresand and good to firm ground, respectable effort on soft. *Mrs J. R. Ramsden* 65 a73

ST ADELE (USA) 3 b.f. Pleasant Colony (USA) – Northern Sunset (Northfields (USA)) [1995 –p: 8f 1996 10f³ 11.5g⁶ a9f⁶ 9f² 9f Dec 30] leggy filly: fair maiden: left D. Loder after second 3-y-o start: second at Calder in December: should stay 1½m: blinkered last 2 starts. *H. J. Bond, USA* 66

STAGE FRIGHT 5 b.g. Sure Blade (USA) 130 – First Act (Sadler's Wells (USA) 132) [1995 NR 1996 14d Jun 7] big, lengthy gelding: has a round action: second foal: brother to fair 7f winner (stays 1¼m) Suntara: dam unraced novice hurdler: unable to go pace in maiden at Haydock on flat debut. *F. Murphy* –

STAHR 2 b.g. (Mar 8) Liboi (USA) 76 – Celia Brady 62 (Last Tycoon 131) [1996 8g 7d Nov 8] fair sort: first foal: dam effective from 7f to 10.8f: signs of ability in late-season maidens: likely to do better. *H. Candy* –

STAKIS CASINOS LAD (IRE) 2 ch.c. (Apr 28) Red Sunset 120 – Stradey 50
Lynn 57 (Derrylin 115) [1996 5m 6g a7g* Nov 4] IR 8,200F: IR 5000Y: brother to 2
winners, including fair 4-y-o sprinter Baileys Sunset and half-brother to 2 winners,
including Northern Printer (up to 1m, by Baptism): dam poor maiden: well beaten in
seller and median auction maiden before winning seller at Southwell by a neck from
Slightly Oliver, pair 7 lengths clear: stays 7f: acts on fibresand. *M. Johnston*

STALLED (IRE) 6 b.g. Glenstal (USA) 118 – Chauffeuse 76 (Gay Fandango 57
(USA) 132) [1995 57: 12g 16m 16.4m a16g 11.8m⁵ 12g³ 11.5m* 12m³ a16.2g⁴ a14g⁶ a61
a10g a14g* a12g⁴ a12g* 1996 a13g³ a16g⁵ 10.3d 16g⁵ 15.4m³ 14d³ 16s 12m 14.4g
12m³ 14s⁵ 12d⁴ a14g² a12g⁵ a14g⁵ a12g² Dec 20] sturdy gelding: modest handicapper: often contests ladies/amateurs events: stays 2m: acts on good to firm ground,
soft and the all-weather: visored (well below form) once at 3 yrs: sometimes hangs:
held up, and often set plenty to do. *P. T. Walwyn*

STAMP (IRE) 2 ch.c. (Apr 23) Sharpo 132 – Likeness 101 (Young Generation 71 +
129) [1996 7d² 6d Nov 8] 8,500F: fifth foal: brother to 8.5f winner Sharp Conquest,
winner in Sweden in 1996: dam maiden, third in Rockfel Stakes but disappointing
and none too genuine at 3 yrs: 14/1 from 33/1, 7 lengths second of 18 to Maylane in
maiden at Lingfield, first home on far side: pulled very hard in similar event at
Doncaster following month. *B. Smart*

STANDOWN 3 b.g. Reprimand 122 – Ashdown (Pharly (FR) 130) [1995 69: 5m* 72
5.1m³ 5g² 5m 5g* 5g⁴ 6m⁶ 6m⁴ 7m 1996 a5g* 6g 5.1g⁵ 6.1m* 6m⁶ 6f³ a6g⁵ 5m⁴ 6g⁵ a75
6d 6d 6m² 5.1g a7g⁵ a6g a6s⁵ Dec 19] compact gelding: fair performer: narrowly
won claimers at Wolverhampton in April and Chester in June: stays 6f: acts on
fibresand and on good to firm ground: often apprentice ridden. *J. Berry*

STAND TALL 4 b.g. Unfuwain (USA) 131 – Antilla 87 (Averof 123) [1995 59: 63
7g 7.1m⁶ 8m 10g 7g 6d 5g 6m⁴ a7g² a6g* 1996 a6g³ a6g* a6g² a6g* a6g* a5g² 5g⁴ a84
6m³ 6d⁴ 6g² 6d⁴ a6g⁵ 6g* 7g Sep 5] tall, quite good-topped gelding: fairly useful
handicapper on the all-weather, successful at Southwell (twice) and Lingfield early
in year: modest on turf, winner at Hamilton (idled) in July: sold to join Lady Herries
17,500 gns Newmarket Autumn Sales: effective at 5f, and stays 7f: acts on all-
weather surfaces and good to firm and dead ground. *C. W. Thornton*

STANTON HARCOURT (USA) 2 b.c. (Feb 4) Sovereign Dancer (USA) – 90
Island Style (USA) (Manila (USA)) [1996 7m³ 7g⁶ 8m² Sep 25] $57,000Y: lengthy,
useful-looking colt: has scope: first foal: dam ran 6 times in USA: placed in maidens
won by Blue River at Newmarket and Voyagers Quest at Goodwood: ran rather freely
when below form in between: stays 1m: may prove suited by exaggerated waiting
tactics: will stay 1¼m. *J. L. Dunlop*

STAR AND GARTER 3 ch.f. Soviet Star (USA) 128 – On Show 92 (Welsh 56
Pageant 132) [1995 75: 5m³ 6g³ 6.1d⁶ 7f⁴ 1996 7m 8g⁴ 10m Sep 16] leggy, close-
coupled filly: fair maiden as 2-y-o: below form in 1996, not looking keen on second
start: subsequently left G. Wragg's stable: should stay beyond 7f: acts on firm
ground, badly drawn on dead. *W. P. Mullins, Ireland*

STAR ANISE 4 ch.f. Prince Daniel (USA) – Elmajarrah (CAN) 77 (Caro 133) 44
[1995 –: 7m⁵ 8.5m 1996 10m 12g³ 12m³ Aug 2] poor maiden: may prove ideally
suited by shorter than 1½m. *Mrs D. Haine*

STARBOROUGH 2 ch.c. (May 15) Soviet Star (USA) 128 – Flamenco Wave 102
(USA) 103 (Desert Wine (USA)) [1996 6g* 6m³ 7.3s⁴ Oct 24] angular colt: fifth foal:
half-brother to useful French 3-y-o 7.5f (at 2 yrs) and 1½m winner Spanish Falls (by
Belmez), 4-y-o 1½m winner Cante Chico (by Reference Point) and fairly useful Irish
1½m winner (stays 2m) Father Sky (by Dancing Brave): dam won Moyglare Stud
Stakes: progressive and useful form: odds on, made all in maiden at Thirsk (easily) in
August: beaten neck and same by Arethusa and Maserati Monk in listed race at
Kempton following month, racing alone in centre of course much of way then
rallying: again put in best work at finish when just over a length fourth of 8 to
Desert Story in Horris Hill Stakes at Newbury: will be suited by further than 7.3f.
D. R. Loder

STAR DANCER 3 ch.f. Groom Dancer (USA) 128 – Pencarreg 87 (Caerleon –
(USA) 132) [1995 NR 1996 6.9m May 10] 2,800 2-y-o: second foal: half-sister to
4-y-o 9f winner (in Ireland) Ath Cheannaithe (by Persian Heights): dam, 2-y-o 7f

winner, out of half-sister to Irish 1000 Guineas and Yorkshire Oaks winner Sarah Siddons: tailed off in claimer: sold 1,500 gns Doncaster July Sales. *J. Norton*

STAR ENTRY 2 b.f. (Feb 17) In The Wings 128 – Top Berry 87 (High Top 131) [1996 6m⁵ a7g⁴ a8g⁵ Dec 3] 7,200F: third foal: half-sister to 1994 2-y-o 7f winner Anna Bannanna (by Prince Sabo): dam, 1m winner, granddaughter of Cheveley Park runner-up Red Berry: fifth of 12 to The Faraway Tree in maiden at Yarmouth on debut, slowly away and late headway: below that form both outings on fibresand, in seller final one: should stay at least 1m. *W. Jarvis*   50 + a45

STAR FIGHTER 4 gr.c. Siberian Express (USA) 125 – Eezepeeze 88 (Alzao (USA) 117) [1995 47, a62: a10g⁴ a10g⁴ a10g* a10g a8.5g⁵ 12.5m⁴ a8g 12g⁴ 12d⁶ 14.1g⁶ 8m a10g⁶ 1996 11.6m 12g Jun 12] quite good-topped colt: modest performer at 3 yrs for W. O'Gorman: well held in 1996: unlikely to stay beyond 1¾m: acts on firm ground and equitrack (below form on fibresand): tried blinkered and visored, no improvement: held up. *M. J. Haynes*   –

STARLIGHT FLYER 9 b.g. In Fijar (USA) 121 – Nareen (USA) (The Minstrel (CAN) 135) [1995 –: 9.7g 11.9m 10m a8.5g⁴ 10m 8m⁵ 7g a14g 1996 a13g Jan 9] good-bodied gelding: bad handicapper: virtually refused to race on reappearance, and subsequently joined Jamie Poulton: one to avoid. *J. E. Long*   – §

STARLIGHT WALTZER 3 b.g. Arzanni 115 – Marchiness Drake (Marechal Drake 101) [1995 NR 1996 10g Oct 9] half-brother to some poor animals under NH rules: dam never ran: 100/1, last of 10 in maiden at Nottingham. *K. S. Bridgwater*   –

STAR MANAGER (USA) 6 b.g. Lyphard (USA) 132 – Angel Clare (FR) (Mill Reef (USA) 141) [1995 83: 8g* 8m 7.9m⁴ 10f 10d 8s⁶ 8f³ 1996 8.1g* 8m⁴ 9s⁴ 8m⁵ 7.9m⁶ 10.1m 9m 9s³ Oct 26] close-coupled gelding: fluent mover: fairly useful handicapper, more consistent in 1996 than in the past: produced strong late burst to win rated stakes at Sandown in April: fifth of 31 in Hunt Cup at Royal Ascot on fifth start: stays 9f (not beaten by trip when tried at 1¼m): acts on any going: below form 4 times when sweating and/or edgy: takes good hold, and usually held up in rear. *P. F. I. Cole*   89

STAR OF GOLD 4 b.g. Night Shift (USA) – Sure Gold 100 (Glint of Gold 128) [1995 65: 6m 6m 7.5m⁶ 8.2m² 8.2f³ 8f⁴ 8.3m³ 7m* 7.1m⁶ 7f 7d 1996 a7g 6.9g* 7m 8f* 8m² Aug 8] small, sturdy gelding: good mover: fair handicapper: better than ever in 1996, comfortably making all at Folkestone and Bath in July: stays 1m: acts on firm ground: tends to carry tail awkwardly: usually races prominently. *C. R. Egerton*   77

STAR OF LUGANA 3 b.f. Lugana Beach 116 – Cala Galera 45 (Mummy's Pet 125) [1995 NR 1996 a12g a14.8g Dec 14] half-sister to several poor animals: dam plater: showed nothing in 2 sellers. *T. T. Clement*   –

STAR OF RING (IRE) 3 b.g. Taufan (USA) 119 – Karine (Habitat 134) [1995 71: 7.1g⁶ 7.1g⁵ 1996 8.2s Apr 12] big, good-bodied gelding: good mover: fair form on first of 2 runs at 2 yrs: led over 5f in maiden at Nottingham on reappearance, but finished well held: subsequently gelded: may prove best short of 1m. *M. J. Heaton-Ellis*   –

STAR OF THE ROAD 2 b.c. (Apr 26) Risk Me (FR) 127 – Astrid Gilberto 75 (Runnett 125) [1996 5m⁶ May 27] workmanlike colt: third foal: brother to 3-y-o 1¼m winner Esperto and a poor maiden: dam 2-y-o 5f and 6f winner: 20/1, burly and green, around 9 lengths sixth of 7 in maiden auction at Redcar, fading from 2f out having recovered quickly from swerving markedly left at stalls. *J. M. Carr*   49

STAR OF ZILZAL (USA) 4 b.g. Zilzal (USA) 137 – Tell Me Sumthing (USA) (Summing (USA)) [1995 101: 7g* 8m 7m⁶ 7m 8m⁴ 8m* 10m³ 1996 7.3f⁴ 7m³ 10.4m 7g* 8.5m* 7g Oct 10] tall, lengthy gelding: useful performer: won rated stakes at Goodwood and Epsom (saddle may have slipped, hung markedly right) in September, ridden more prominently than usual on each occasion: sold 32,000 gns Newmarket Autumn Sales: stays 8.5f: acts on good to firm ground: has run creditably when sweating: none too consistent: sent to USA. *M. R. Stoute*   108

STAR PERFORMER (IRE) 5 b.g. Petorius 117 – Whitstar 93 (Whitstead 125) [1995 49: a7g 7m⁴ 9f⁶ 7m⁵ 8g 8d 1996 8g³ a14g⁴ a14g⁴ 17.2m* a14g² 17.5m 17.1m⁵ Oct 7] sturdy, good-bodied gelding: modest form at best since 2 yrs: won maiden handicap at Carlisle in August: suited by strong pace when short of 2m, and stays

17.2f: acts on good to firm and good to soft going: sometimes unruly at stalls: tends to edge left under pressure. *Mrs M. Reveley*

STAR PRECISION 2 ch.f. (Mar 29) Shavian 125 – Accuracy 83 (Gunner B 126) [1996 7d 7.1v⁶ 7d⁵ Oct 28] third foal: half-sister to temperamental 1¼m winner Matching Green (by Green Ruby) and fair 1¾m and 2m winner Brave Tornado (by Dominion): dam suited by test of stamina: never dangerous in maidens at Salisbury, Haydock (still burly) and Lingfield: bred to stay well. *G. B. Balding* — 59

STAR RAGE (IRE) 6 b.g. Horage 124 – Star Bound (Crowned Prince (USA) 128) [1995 84: 12d⁵ 13.9m 20m 16.1m 14m⁵ 16.1h* 16.2m* 16m⁵ 13.9m 14.1m² 16.1g* 13.9g 15.9d⁴ 17.2m⁴ 14.1f⁴ 13.9g³ 18m 1996 a14.8g² Apr 27] angular gelding: fairly useful handicapper: remarkably tough and consistent at 4 and 5 yrs for M. Johnston: had a successful 1995/6 over hurdles, and ran creditably at Wolverhampton on only start on flat in 1996: stays 17.2f: acts on hard and dead ground and on fibresand (below form only start on heavy): normally held up. *J. L. Harris* — 79

STAR SELECTION 5 b.g. Rainbow Quest (USA) 134 – Selection Board 75 (Welsh Pageant 132) [1995 NR 1996 10g² 12.3g⁴ 10d 8.9g Sep 5] leggy, lengthy gelding: sixth of 23 in 1994 2000 Guineas (rated 113) but disappointing afterwards and sold cheaply out of P. Cole's stable: useful form when 3 lengths second of 12 to Lucky Di in listed race at Kempton on reappearance, but failed to repeat it: stays 1¼m: acts on firm and dead going: takes keen hold: won over hurdles in December: one to treat with caution. *J. Mackie* — 105

STAR TALENT (USA) 5 b.g. Local Talent (USA) 122 – Sedra 116 (Nebbiolo 125) [1995 105: 7m* 7m⁵ 6m 1996 a7g* a6g⁴ a7g² a6g⁵ a7g³ 8d 7f* 8d⁵ 7g² 8g³ 7s 8.5m² 8m 7m⁴ 7f⁴ a7g² a7g⁵ Dec 20] robust gelding: impresses in appearance: has had wind problems: useful performer at best in 1995 for D. Elsworth: first fairly useful form at 5 yrs, winning claimer at Lingfield in January and minor event at Brighton in April: barely stays 8.5f: acts on firm and dead ground and on equitrack: tried visored, no improvement: suited by waiting tactics. *Miss Gay Kelleway* — 87 a75

STARTINGO 3 b.c. Rustingo 94 – Spartan's Girl (Spartan General 109) [1995 NR 1996 8.3m Aug 3] half-brother to several winning jumpers: dam winning pointer: always behind in maiden at Windsor: has joined R. Brown. *B. J. Llewellyn* — –

STAR TURN (IRE) 2 ch.c. (May 16) Night Shift (USA) – Ringtail 102 (Auction Ring (USA) 123) [1996 6d 6f⁵ 6.9d Oct 21] IR 6,500Y: strong colt: half-brother to 3 winners, including 7f/1m winner Waterlord (by Bob Back) and useful 6f winner Mohawk Chief (by Ahonoora): dam 2-y-o 5f winner: still backward, best effort in maiden auctions when about 7 lengths fifth of 15 to Craigievar at Warwick in October: poorly drawn on debut: possibly unsuited by soft surface. *M. Bell* — 61

STATAJACK (IRE) 8 b.g. King of Clubs 124 – Statira 103 (Skymaster 126) [1995 90: 12m 10m³ 10m⁴ 1996 a10g³ a10g 12m⁶ 10m 10.2f 10s⁴ 12m* 11.6m² 10m* 10m 9.7m⁴ a11g² Jul 22] leggy, sparely-made gelding: fairly useful performer on his day: won claimer and handicap at Goodwood in June: effective at 1¼m and 1½m: acts on any turf ground and on equitrack: best form in blinkers: sometimes carries head high and runs in snatches: suited by strong handling and well ridden by T. Quinn: held up: one to treat with some caution. *D. R. C. Elsworth* — 83

STATE APPROVAL 3 b.g. Pharly (FR) 130 – Tabeeba (Diesis 133) [1995 61: a6g² 6m a7g² 8g 8g 8m³ 1996 12d⁵ a12g⁴ 11.6m² 11.4d 13.1m² 16m⁵ 12m* a12g* 14d⁵ 11.5m⁶ 12m⁶ a12g³ Nov 11] small gelding: fair handicapper: successful in apprentice races at Kempton and Wolverhampton (by 9 lengths) within 3 days in August: stays 13f: acts on fibresand and good to firm ground, seemingly not on a soft surface: sold to join P. Eccles 8,600 gns Doncaster November Sales. *A. P. Jarvis* — 69 a72

STATE CIRCUS 3 b.f. Soviet Star (USA) 128 – Wily Trick (USA) 83 (Clever Trick (USA)) [1995 NR 1996 a8.5g² a10g³ 11.8m⁶ 10g Jul 1] sparely-made filly: first foal: dam, very well bred, placed from 7f to 1m: failed to progress from debut in Wolverhampton maiden: broke down final start: dead. *Lord Huntingdon* — 62

STATE FAIR 2 b.c. (Feb 16) Shirley Heights 130 – Lobinda 80 (Shareef Dancer (USA) 135) [1996 6m³ 7m² 7m* 7m* 8g Sep 29] 12,000Y: compact, quite attractive colt: stable-walker: first foal: dam 1m (at 2 yrs) and 1½m winner: fairly useful colt: won 3-runner maiden at Chester (by 7 lengths) and 5-runner Washington Singer Stakes at Newbury (ridden out to beat stable-companion In Question by 1¼ lengths) — 92 +

947

in August: not discredited when seventh of 8 in Royal Lodge Stakes at Ascot in September: bred to stay middle distances. *B. W. Hills*

STATELY DANCER 3 b.f. Be My Guest (USA) 126 – Wild Pavane (Dancing 77 Brave (USA) 140) [1995 65p: 6m 6f³ 1996 10g⁵ 10g 10m* 12g 10m 10.1m* 12m 10.4g Oct 9] leggy, angular filly: fluent mover: fair performer: won maiden at Salisbury in May and handicap at Yarmouth in August: best efforts at around 1¼m: yet to race on a soft surface. *G. Wragg*

STATE OF CAUTION 3 b.g. Reprimand 122 – Hithermoor Lass 75 (Red Alert 83 127) [1995 76p: 7g 7g⁵ 1996 7g² 7.5m⁴ 7g³ 7m⁴ 8m³ 8m Oct 7] useful-looking gelding: good walker: fairly useful maiden at his best, but rather disappointing: blinkered, well below form final start: sold 13,000 gns Newmarket Autumn Sales and gelded: stays 7.5f: has raced only on a sound surface. *J. L. Dunlop*

STATE OF GOLD (IRE) 2 b.g. (May 10) High Estate 127 – Mawaal Habeebee – (Northfields (USA)) [1996 7g 7.6m 7g 47g⁶ Dec 14] fifth foal: dam unraced half-sister to smart sprinter Chapel Cottage: almost certainly flattered when around 6 lengths eighth of 11 to Bandore in steadily-run maiden at Lingfield on second start (could be rated 67?): no comparable form: sold out of W. Haggas' stable 3,800 gns Newmarket Autumn Sales after third outing. *J. Hetherton*

STATESMAN 2 b.c. (Jan 30) Doyoun 124 – Affair of State (IRE) 99 (Tate Gallery 92 (USA) 117) [1996 5m* 6d* 6f 6g³ 7.1g Aug 30] sturdy colt: first foal: dam 2-y-o 5f and 6f winner, well beaten both starts at 3 yrs: capable of useful form: successful in maiden at Ripon in April and minor event at Kempton in May: well beaten in Coventry Stakes at Ascot on third outing and Solario Stakes at Sandown (never went with any fluency) on final one: sold 23,000 gns Newmarket Autumn Sales: stays 6f: may be unsuited by very firm ground. *M. R. Channon*

STATE THEATRE (IRE) 3 b.c. Sadler's Wells (USA) 132 – Fruition 89 75 (Rheingold 137) [1995 70p: 8d 1996 11.8m 14g⁴ 13.3m⁴ 16.2m³ Jul 26] rather leggy colt: has a round action: fair maiden handicapper: progressed steadily, best effort when third of 20 at Ascot, staying on well: likely to prove suited by a thorough test of stamina. *P. W. Chapple-Hyam*

STATIC LOVE 3 b.f. Statoblest 120 – Run For Love 70 (Runnett 125) [1995 –: – 5m a5g⁶ 7f 1996 5m 8m Jun 21] good-topped filly: little sign of ability. *H. Akbary*

STATION EXPRESS (IRE) 8 b.g. Rusticaro (FR) 124 – Vallee d'O (FR) (Poly- – foto 124) [1995 NR 1996 16m Jun 24] of little account: sold 750 gns Ascot July Sales. *B. J. Llewellyn*

STATISTICIAN 4 b.g. Statoblest 120 – Sharp Lady 70 (Sharpen Up 127) [1995 64 72: 7m⁴ 8m 6m³ 6f² 6g* 1996 5.2g⁴ 5f⁴ 6m 6m⁴ 6d 8f 7f² 7g 7g⁴ a7g³ a7g a7g Dec 11] tall gelding: just a modest handicapper in 1996: stays 7f: acts on firm ground and all-weather surfaces: blinkered last 7 starts: upset in stalls and withdrawn sixth intended 4-y-o start. *John Berry*

STATOYORK 3 b.g. Statoblest 120 – Ultimate Dream 74 (Kafu 120) [1995 76p: 80 d 6f⁵ 7m⁶ 1996 6m⁵ 6f*ᵈⁱˢ 7m* 6m 7m 7m 7m Oct 5] strong, attractive gelding: fairly useful performer: first past post in maidens at Brighton (disqualified for causing interference over 1f out) and Ayr (led over 1f out) in June: in rear in 4 handicaps afterwards: stays 7f, and should prove at least as effective at sprint distances: has raced only on top-of-the-ground. *B. W. Hills*

STATUETTE 2 b.f. (Feb 8) Statoblest 120 – La Pirouette (USA) 73 (Kennedy 57 Road (CAN)) [1996 5m⁴ 5.1m* 5.3f 6.1m 5m a5g Nov 7] sturdy filly: sixth reported foal: half-sister to 1989 2-y-o 5.8f winner Plie (by Superlative): dam 7f winner: first run for nearly 3 months, made all in seller at Bath (by 5 lengths, in August): well beaten subsequently, twice dropping out soon after halfway: speedy. *B. Palling*

ST BLAINE (CAN) 2 b.f. (Apr 23) St Jovite (USA) 135 – Blaine (USA) 79 p (Lyphard's Wish (FR) 124) [1996 7g⁵ Nov 2] second foal: dam, ran 4 times in North America, half-sister to Fillies Mile third Alligatrix: 25/1, around 3½ lengths fifth of 23 to Palisade in maiden at Newmarket, waited with, travelling well, then keeping on without reaching principals who raced on far side: will stay middle distances: sure to improve, and should be able to win a race. *D. R. Loder*

STEADFAST ELITE (IRE) 5 b.m. Glenstal (USA) 118 – Etching 109 47
(Auction Ring (USA) 123) [1995 –: 8f 10.9g 1996 10.1s² 11.1d⁴ 11.1m³ 11.1g* 10m²
11.1f⁴ 11.1g⁶ 11.9d⁵ a8.5g Jul 26] workmanlike mare: poor handicapper: gamely
won at Musselburgh in May: stays 11.1f: acts on good to firm and soft ground: tried
blinkered, no improvement: modest hurdler, winner twice in October. *J. J. O'Neill*

STEADY READY GO (IRE) 4 b.g. Night Shift (USA) – Smeralda (GER) –
(Dschingis Khan) [1995 103: 10f⁴ 8m² 10m* 1996 10.1g Oct 30] tall gelding: useful
performer at 3 yrs for L. Cumani: tailed off, saddle having slipped, in minor event at
Yarmouth on belated reappearance. *Jamie Poulton*

STEAL 'EM 3 b.f. Efisio 120 – Eastern Ember 85 (Indian King (USA) 128) [1995 66
53+: 6d 6.1m⁵ 7m 7.1g⁴ 1996 a5g⁶ 7.6m* 7m 7d a6g⁶ a7g Nov 30] workmanlike
filly: fair performer: improved to win 4-runner maiden at Chester in July, dictating
pace under shrewd ride from J. Fortune: stays 7.6f: acts on good to firm ground and
fibresand, well held on dead. *A. Bailey*

STEAMROLLER STANLY 3 b.g. Shirley Heights 130 – Miss Demure 106 84
(Shy Groom (USA)) [1995 70p: 6d a8g² 1996 10g⁶ 13.3m* 15d⁴ 14m⁶ 12g³ 18.2m⁵
11.9g a12g* Nov 14] sturdy gelding: fairly useful performer: won handicap at
Newbury in June and minor event at Lingfield in November: effective at 1½m,
and seems to stay 2¼m: acts on good to firm and dead ground and on equitrack.
C. A. Cyzer

STEEL SOVEREIGN 5 gr.g. Nishapour (FR) 125 – Perioscope (Legend of –
France (USA) 124) [1995 NR 1996 7d 6m 6g 6m 5.9f 6.9f⁴ 8f 8m 7f Aug 9] poor
handicapper (rated 47) at 3 yrs: well held in 1996: tried blinkered. *M. Dods*

STELLAR LINE (USA) 3 ch.g. Zilzal (USA) 137 – Stellaria (USA) 98 72
(Roberto (USA) 131) [1995 87: 6m 7.1d⁴ 7.1g² 1996 8f⁴ 8m⁴ 7.9g⁴ 7g⁴ 10g⁵ Oct 9]
leggy, close-coupled gelding: fairly useful maiden at best as 2-y-o: disappointing in
1996, looking reluctant on reappearance: sold 9,500 gns Newmarket Autumn Sales:
best at up to 7f: tends to be mulish at stalls: one to treat with caution. *B. W. Hills*

STEP ALOFT 4 b.f. Shirley Heights 130 – Pas de Deux 80 (Nijinsky (CAN) 138) 87
[1995 83: 8.3m 12.1g⁴ 10m² 12s² 10.4m² 12m² 1996 12g² 13.3f 11.4d² 10m* 11.9g²
12g Oct 26] angular filly: has a quick action: fairly useful performer: best effort when
winning apprentice handicap at Newmarket in October: best with strongly-run race
at 1¼m, and stays 1½m: best form on good to firm ground, respectable effort on soft:
sometimes edgy and takes keen hold. *Lord Huntingdon*

STEPHENSONS ROCKET 5 ch.g. Music Boy 124 – Martian Princess 90 60
(Cure The Blues (USA)) [1995 70: 5g 5g 5m 7g 7g 1996 a6g 5s 6g 5m⁵ 5g 5.1m 5m
5g² 5g 5m a6g Nov 4] good-topped gelding: impresses in appearance: shows knee
action: modest handicapper at best in 1996: suited by 5f: acts on firm and dead
ground: effective blinkered or not. *D. Nicholls*

STEP N GO (IRE) 2 b.f. (May 15) Alzao (USA) 117 – River Jet (USA) (Lear 60 +
Fan (USA) 130) [1996 5.1m⁵ 5m² 5f⁶ 6g 6.1s⁴ Oct 31] 26,000Y: robust, good-
quartered filly: unimpressive mover: first foal: dam French 1m (at 2 yrs) and 10.5f
winner, half-sister to useful French stayer River Test: modest form: last at halfway
then stayed on under hands and heels when fourth behind impressive Craigievar in
nursery at Nottingham on last outing: will be well suited by further than 6f: may well
be capable of better. *Mrs J. R. Ramsden*

Shadwell Stud Apprentice Series Final (Handicap), Newmarket—
Step Aloft (Aimee Cook) finally breaks her duck

STEP ON DEGAS 3 b.f. Superpower 113 – Vivid Impression (Cure The Blues 67
(USA)) [1995 60+: 5m⁵ 5g 6m³ 6m² 1996 5f* 5.2m⁵ 5.1m 5m 5m a5g² 5m a5g²
a6g⁵ a6g² Dec 20] rather leggy filly: fair handicapper: dead-heated in maiden event
at Warwick in June: in-and-out form afterwards: stays 6f: acts on the all-weather,
has raced only on a sound surface on turf: ran poorly both tries in visor.
M. J. Fetherston-Godley

STERIN 3 b.f. Chauve Souris 108 – Sweet Lore (Law Society (USA) 130) [1995 –
NR 1996 10m 7m Sep 10] first foal: dam never ran: well beaten in maidens at
Windsor and Lingfield. *Mark Campion*

STERLING FELLOW 3 b.c. Pharly (FR) 130 – Favorable Exchange (USA) 66
(Exceller (USA) 129) [1995 64: 7.6d 7g⁵ a10g² 1996 a10g 12m⁶ 12d⁴ 17.2g⁵ 12.5f³
16f* 17.2m² 14m² 14.1d⁵ 15.4g 17.9g³ 18g³ Oct 21] neat colt: fair handicapper: won
at Lingfield in July: best efforts on last 2 starts: sold (R. Hannon to D. Williams)
5,000 gns Newmarket Autumn Sales: suited by test of stamina: acts on equitrack and
firm ground, below form on a soft surface: blinkered last 8 starts. *R. Hannon*

STEVIE'S WONDER (IRE) 6 ch.g. Don't Forget Me 127 – Azurai 80 (Dance –
In Time (CAN)) [1995 63, a72: a12g* a12g* a12g* a12g² 11.8m 12g⁵ 11.8g* 12m⁴ a70 d
11.6m a11g* a14.8g⁴ 12d 14d*ᵈⁱˢ a12g² a12g⁴ a11g 1996 a14.8g* a12g² a14.8g⁶
17.2f a12g 11.8m a12g a12g a11g³ a16.2g a12g Nov 25] sturdy gelding: fair performer: won seller at Wolverhampton in January: claimed out of M. Ryan's stable
£5,000 next start: long way below form for new stable: stays 1¾m: acts on the
all-weather and on any turf going: blinkered (below form) once at 2 yrs, effective
visored or not: wears a tongue strap: has won for 7-lb claimer: front runner/races
close up. *B. J. Llewellyn*

ST HONORINE (IRE) 4 b.f. Ela-Mana-Mou 132 – Taken By Force (Persian –
Bold 123) [1995 NR 1996 13.4g⁵ 12m 12g Oct 19] leggy, lengthy, angular filly: sixth
foal: half-sister to 3 winners, including fairly useful Irish 7f to 1½m winner Be My
Hostage (by Be My Guest): dam Irish middle-distance winner: well beaten in maiden
and claimers: has been bandaged: sold 1,300 gns Newmarket Autumn Sales: sent to
Saudi Arabia. *C. Murray*

STICKS AND STONES (IRE) 4 b.g. Waajib 121 – Maiacourt (Malacate –
(USA) 131) [1995 78: 7.9g 7g 10.5g⁴ 8f⁴ 1996 8m⁵ Jun 27] strong, attractive gelding:
impresses in appearance: good mover: fair handicapper: ran creditably all starts in
1995, below form only 4-y-o outing: sold only 700 gns Newmarket Autumn Sales:
stays 10.5f: acts on firm going: ran creditably only try in blinkers. *Mrs J. Cecil*

STILLET (IRE) 2 b.c. Tirol 127 – Legal Steps (Law Society (USA) 130) [1996 –
8s⁶ Nov 11] 24,000Y: first foal: dam Irish 12.5f winner: favourite, soundly beaten in
maiden at Milan: evidently though capable of better. *L. M. Cumani*

STILL HERE (IRE) 3 b.g. Astronef 116 – Covey's Quick Step (Godswalk 41
(USA) 130) [1995 55: a6g a7g⁴ a6g⁵ a7g³ 6s 1996 a7g⁶ a10g⁴ a9.4g* 10d 9.9g 10.1f⁵ a55
10m a10g 8.3m a14.8g³ Dec 14] sturdy gelding: modest performer on the all-
weather: won apprentice handicap at Wolverhampton in March: no comparable form:
sold out of M. Heaton-Ellis' stable 1,600 gns Doncaster November Sales before final
start: stays 1¼m: acts on the all-weather, has looked poor at best on turf: no
improvement visored. *P. Bowen*

STILLY NIGHT (IRE) 3 b.f. Martin John – Syndikos (USA) (Nashua) [1995 –
5m 6m⁶ 7m 6m 5d 1996 a7g⁵ a6g Jan 19] ex-Irish filly: half-sister to useful sprinter
Imperial Bailiwick (by Imperial Frontier) and several winners in France, all at 1m+:
dam second 6 times from 13 starts in USA: modest maiden (rated 65) at 2 yrs for
K. O' Sullivan: long way below form for new stable: stays 7f: acts on good to firm
and dead ground. *J. Wharton*

STINGING REPLY 4 ch.f. Belmez (USA) 131 – Nettle 106 (Kris 135) [1995 –
75: 8g⁴ 8m 9g⁵ 10.2m² 10g⁶ 8h³ 1996 a8g⁶ Feb 7] sparely-made filly: has a round
action: fair performer at 3 yrs for I. Balding: well below form only start for new yard:
may prove best at up to 1¼m: acts on good to firm ground, probably on soft: covered
by Tirol. *Lord Huntingdon*

ST LAWRENCE (CAN) 2 gr.c. (Feb 27) With Approval (CAN) – Mingan Isle 75
(USA) (Lord Avie (USA)) [1996 7g 8f² 8m² Sep 26] $40,000F, 60,000Y: first foal:
dam won 6 times at up to 7f in USA: sire high-class middle-distance performer:

similar level of form when placed in maidens won by Rapier at Brighton and Panama City at Pontefract: will be suited by middle distances. *C. E. Brittain*

ST LUCINDA (CAN)   2 b.f. (Mar 17) St Jovite (USA) 135 – Majestic Nature   71 p
(USA) (Majestic Prince (USA)) [1996 6f* Sep 28] 29,000Y: seventh foal: half-sister to several winners abroad, including 1990 French 2-y-o 1m winner Gypsy Trail (by Darby Creek Road): dam won at up to 1m in USA, sister to Grade 3 2-y-o 6.5f winner Royal Suite: 9/4, dead-heated with Thahabyah in 6-runner maiden at Redcar, keeping on strongly to lead inside final 1f, joined on line: will be suited by further than 6f: sure to improve: sent to USA. *D. R. Loder*

ST MAWES (FR)   3 ch.c. Shahrastani (USA) 135 – Exemina (USA) (Slip   115
Anchor 136) [1995 89p: 7g 7f* 1996 9m² 12.3g² 10g³ 12m 12m* 14.6m⁵ 12m⁶ Sep 28]
    The 1986 Derby winner Shahrastani had his first British classic runner during the latest season, with St Mawes contesting both the Derby and the St Leger. Although St Mawes never looked like emulating his sire at Epsom (at 20/1, he finished seventeenth and reportedly got jarred up), he still went off 8/1 joint-fourth favourite of eleven for the season's final classic. His prominence in the betting at Doncaster followed an improved performance on his previous start to win the Group 3 Westminster Taxi Insurance Gordon Stakes at Goodwood in July, when, tried in blinkers for the first time, he overcame trouble in running to get up close home from fellow Derby also-rans Chief Contender and Storm Trooper in a three-way photo finish. As St Mawes had given the strong impression that he would be suited by both a galloping track and further than a mile and a half, the St Leger should have seen him to better advantage. But in the event, blinkered again, he could not reproduce his Gordon Stakes form and managed only a respectable fifth behind Shantou, not for the first time looking a tricky ride. In truth, St Mawes had already been exposed as being below classic-winning standard when making the frame in the Feilden Stakes at Newmarket, the Chester Vase at Chester and the Predominate Stakes at Goodwood. Nevertheless he was a smart performer and a big loss to his owner Lord Swaythling (for whom he provided a first Derby runner in forty-one years of ownership) when he had to be put down in early-October, reportedly due to a twisted gut.
    St Mawes's sire and both grandsires were all Derby winners. Shahrastani, however, has yet to really make his mark as a stallion and St Mawes

Westminster Taxi Insurance Gordon Stakes, Goodwood—
right to left, blinkered-first-time St Mawes, Chief Contender and Storm Trooper

will probably be the last as well as the first of his British classic runners, as he was sent to Japan early in 1994 having already tried his hand in the USA as well as Ireland. St Mawes was up with the best of Shahrastani's progeny to have raced in Europe so far, Rifapour having won the Prix Hocquart and Dariyoun having come third in the Cadran and eleventh in the Arc. St Mawes was the first foal of Exemina, a French provincial winner over a mile and a half in 1991. Exemina's second foal, by Sanglamore, fetched 150,000 francs at the 1996 Deauville Yearling Sales in August when St Mawes had made 320,000 francs two years earlier. The second and third dams, El Fabulous and El Mina, were both smart middle-distance performers who won Group 3 races in France at around a mile and a quarter and have largely been an influence for stamina in their offspring.

		Nijinsky	Northern Dancer
St Mawes (FR)	Shahrastani (USA)	(b 1967)	Flaming Page
(ch.c. 1993)	(ch 1983)	Shademah	Thatch
		(b 1978)	Shamim
		Slip Anchor	Shirley Heights
	Exemina (USA)	(b 1982)	Sayonara
	(b 1988)	El Fabulous	Fabulous Dancer
		(ch 1983)	El Mina

Stamina always appeared to be St Mawes's strong suit too, but he did not prove it, and, after the St Leger, was put back to a mile and a half for the Cumberland Lodge Stakes at Ascot, where, without the blinkers, he finished a respectable sixth of seven after twice being hampered at crucial stages. A tall and attractive colt, St Mawes was an unimpressive mover with a quick action who tended to hang under pressure and was not the easiest of rides. *J. L. Dunlop*

STOCK HILL DANCER 2 ch.f. (Apr 8) Interrex (CAN) – Stocktina 42 (Tina's 56 Pet 121) [1996 5m⁶ 6m 5d⁴ Oct 21] first foal: dam 5f winner: modest form in median auction maidens at Sandown and Folkestone: down the field in maiden at Epsom in between: should stay 6f. *K. R. Burke*

STOLEAMARCH 3 br.g. Daring March 116 – Pennine Star (IRE) 68 (Pennine 43 Walk 120) [1995 –: 5g⁶ 6g⁶ 7m 1996 10m 12.1g² 12m⁴ a14g 12m⁴ Aug 28] rather leggy gelding: only worthwhile form when second of 5 in claimer at Musselburgh in June: stays 1½m: sold (Mrs M. Reveley to A. Forbes) 1,700 gns Doncaster September Sales. *Mrs M. Reveley*

STOLEN KISS (IRE) 4 b. or br.f. Taufan (USA) 119 – Sweet Goodbye (Petorius 79 117) [1995 76: 6m⁴ 6m⁵ 6g⁴ 5g² 6g² 5m* 5f⁵ 5m² 5.1m⁵ 5m⁵ 5g² 6g³ 5d 5s 1996 5s* 5m⁵ 5m 5m⁵ 5g 5d 5g Oct 9] big, workmanlike filly: poor mover: fair handicapper: won at Newcastle in March: in and out afterwards, reportedly choking throughout (after 2½-month absence) penultimate start: effective at 5f and 6f: acts on firm and soft ground: usually blinkered/visored. *M. W. Easterby*

STOLEN MELODY 4 b.f. Robellino (USA) 127 – Song of Hope 103 (Chief 67 Singer 131) [1995 69: 8.5s 7g 7m⁵ 7f 1996 7d 6g 7f⁴ 7g⁴ 6.9f⁶ Jun 28] sturdy, lengthy filly: poor mover: fair handicapper: stays 7f: acts on firm and dead ground. *S. Dow*

STOLEN MUSIC (IRE) 3 b.f. Taufan (USA) 119 – Causa Sua (Try My Best – (USA) 130) [1995 –p: 7g 1996 8.1m 8m Sep 20] workmanlike filly: never a threat in maidens: sold 600 gns Newmarket Autumn Sales. *Major D. N. Chappell*

STOMPIN 5 b.g. Alzao (USA) 117 – Celebrity 101 (Troy 137) [1995 NR 1996 77 12g 14.9g* 16.1f* 20f 16.5m 16.1m³ Aug 26] good-bodied gelding: useful hurdler, winner of valuable event at Aintree in April: returned better than ever on flat, winning handicaps at Warwick in May and June: stays 2m: acts on firm and dead ground, tailed off on heavy: ridden by 7-lb claimer when successful. *Miss H. C. Knight*

STONE CROSS (IRE) 4 b.g. Pennine Walk 120 – Micro Mover (Artaius (USA) – 129) [1995 60: 11.1d² 12g⁵ 1996 8g⁴ a11g⁴ 15.8g Aug 16] leggy, angular gelding: modest form early on at 3 yrs: showed little in 1996, leaving R. Fisher's stable after reappearance. *Martin Todhunter*

STONECUTTER 3 b.g. Warning 136 – South Shore 102 (Caerleon (USA) 132) – [1995 NR 1996 a8.5g Dec 28] 30,000Y: second foal: half-brother to useful 7f to 8.2f winner South Rock (by Rock City): dam (stayed 1½m) half-sister to Soviet Line, out of Oaks fourth Shore Line, a sister to Park Hill winner Quay Line: visored, beaten over 20 lengths in Wolverhampton maiden on flat debut: won selling hurdle (tongue tied) in December. *M. R. Channon*

STONE FLOWER (USA) 2 b.f. (Apr 6) Storm Bird (CAN) 134 – Lively Living   83
(USA) (Key To The Mint (USA)) [1996 6f⁶ 5g* 6d³ 6.1d⁵ 6.5m 6m³ Oct 17] well-made filly: fluent mover: sister to smart 1993 2-y-o Stonehatch, closely related to French 9f winner Sheila Dacre (by Nureyev) and half-sister to 2 winners in USA, notably Grade 1 1¼m winner Danger's Hour (by Coastal), successful at up to 1½m: dam, twice-raced half-sister to smart 1977 2-y-o 5f winner Deed of Gift, from excellent family: won minor event at Ayr in July: creditable third of 18 to Cryhavoc in nursery at Newmarket on final outing: stays 6f: best form on a sound surface. *P. W. Chapple-Hyam*

STONE ISLAND 3 b.g. Rambo Dancer (CAN) 107 – Single Gal 97 (Mansingh   60 d
(USA) 120) [1995 NR 1996 7m⁵ 8g 6.9m⁴ 6f³ 8m⁵ 8g 8f 7.6m 6m Aug 17] workmanlike gelding: half-brother to 4-y-o 5f winner Sally Slade (by Dowsing) and several other winners, including fairly useful middle-distance performer Age of Miracles (by Simply Great): apparently modest form early on: pulled up sixth start: tailed off in blinkers next time: looks one to leave alone on flat, but won selling hurdle in November for P. Hobbs: sold to join John Whyte 1,550 gns Ascot December Sales. *C. A. Cyzer*

STONE RIDGE (IRE) 4 b.c. Indian Ridge 123 – Cut In Stone (USA) 72 (Assert   95
134) [1995 91: 10m 8m* 9m⁶ 7.1m 8m⁵ 8.1m⁵ 8d 8m* 8m 1996 8s* 8d 8g⁵ 10.1m 8m 9m 9s⁵ 7d Nov 10] useful-looking colt: fairly useful handicapper: 33/1, won 24-runner William Hill Lincoln at Doncaster in March: mostly below form afterwards: barely stays 9f, at least when conditions are testing: acts on good to firm ground and soft (yet to race on firm): blinkered (below form) once as 3-y-o: often ridden by apprentice: tends to carry head high, but is game. *R. Hannon*

STONEY END (USA) 3 b.g. High Brite (USA) – Cranareen (USA) (Nice   72 d
Dancer (CAN)) [1995 –p: 6m 1996 8d 6m⁶ 6g⁵ 6f* 5f² 5m 7f⁴ 5m 5m⁴ 6m Aug 15] strong, good-topped gelding: fair performer: awarded maiden at Brighton in June:

William Hill Lincoln Handicap, Doncaster—Stone Ridge and Roving Minstrel draw away in testing conditions

Prince Fahd Salman's "Storm Trooper"

tailed off (jockey reporting him reluctant to race) sixth start: stays 6f, probably not 7f: acts on firm ground: usually races prominently: sometimes slowly away: sold 2,700 gns Newmarket Autumn Sales, and gelded: sent to Spain. *M. R. Channon*

STOPPES BROW 4 b.g. Primo Dominie 121 – So Bold (Never So Bold 135) 81 [1995 72, a89: a5g* a6g* a6g³ a6g* 6m 5m 6m⁶ 6f⁴ 7f⁴ 7m* 7g⁴ 7g³ 6g² a6g 1996 a98 a6g a5g² 6g 7m⁴ 7.6g 7s³ 6s* 6.9m³ 5.7m 6m 6.1s³ 7g⁴ a7g² Dec 7] strong, lengthy gelding: poor mover: fairly useful handicapper: won at Newbury in May: good efforts in frame last 3 starts: stays 7f: acts on firm and soft going and the all-weather: effective visored or not, blinkered (below form) once: successful for 7-lb claimer: usually held up: consistent. *G. L. Moore*

STOP PLAY (IRE) 3 b.f. Distinctly North (USA) 115 – Church Mountain 83 72 (Furry Glen 121) [1995 78: 5m⁵ 5g⁵ 5.2g* 6m 5m³ 6m² 6d⁵ 6.1m 7m⁵ 1996 7.1d 6m³ Jun 5] good-topped filly: fair performer: respectable third in handicap at Yarmouth in June: stays 6f: acts on good to firm and good to soft ground: visored (raced freely) final 2-y-o start: consistent. *M. H. Tompkins*

STORIES TO TELL (USA) 2 ch.c. (Feb 13) Shadeed (USA) 135 – Million 85 p Stories (USA) (Exclusive Native (USA)) [1996 7f² 7.5f² Aug 14] fourth foal: half-brother to 1992 2-y-o 5f winner Classic Story and a winner in USA (both by Green Forest): dam French 7.5f winner, is daughter of Perlee, dam also of Poule d'Essai des Pouliches winner Pearl Bracelet: second in maidens at Redcar and Beverley (quite useful form, staying on) in the summer: will probably stay 1¼m: should improve again, and win an ordinary maiden. *H. R. A. Cecil*

STORM BID (USA) 4 b. or br.g. Storm Cat (USA) – Slam Bid (USA) (Forli – (ARG)) [1995 89: 7g² 7g* 6g⁴ 1996 7d 7g May 4] lengthy gelding: fairly useful form at 3 yrs, not seen after June: well held in handicaps in 1996: sold 10,500 gns Newmarket July Sales: should stay 1m: races prominently. *E. A. L. Dunlop*

STORMLESS 5 b.g. Silly Prices 110 – Phyl's Pet (Aberdeen 109) [1995 40: 11.1g⁶ 12.1g 12.1g³ 11.9m⁶ 1996 10.9d 9g⁴ 10d² 10m* 11.1m² 10g* 10.9m³ 10.5v Oct 6] tall gelding: modest handicapper: won twice at Ayr in the summer, on second occasion under 7-lb claimer: has shown his form at 10.9f, but may well prove ideally suited by a bit shorter: acts on good to firm and dead ground: tends to wander under pressure. *P. Monteith* 57

STORM TROOPER (USA) 3 b.c. Diesis 133 – Stormette (USA) (Assert 134) [1995 104p: 7f⁵ 7g² 8.2d* 8v² 1996 9m* 8m 10.4m⁶ 12m 12m³ 10d³ 10.3f² Sep 13] leggy, close-coupled colt: has a fluent, round action: capable of smart form: won listed race at Newmarket (impressive when beating St Mawes by 4 lengths) in April: had excuses in 2000 Guineas (trip), Dante Stakes (held up in very slowly-run race) and Derby (bumped early stages and never travelling) next 3 starts: placed afterwards in Gordon Stakes (looked like taking plenty of catching 2f out, but collared by St Mawes and Chief Contender close home) at Goodwood, Winter Hill Stakes at Windsor (1½ lengths third to Annus Mirabilis) and minor event at Doncaster: should prove best at up to 1½m: acts on any ground: to be trained by N. Drysdale in USA. *H. R. A. Cecil* 114

STORM WIND (IRE) 3 ch.g. Digamist (USA) 110 – Hilton Gateway (Hello Gorgeous (USA) 128) [1995 –: 7.1g 7g 1996 10s 13.8g Sep 21] close-coupled gelding: well beaten in maidens, claimer and seller. *K. R. Burke* –

STORY LINE 3 ch.f. In The Wings 128 – Known Line 100 (Known Fact (USA) 135) [1995 93p: 7d* 1996 10m² 11d 8d³ 12s 10.3d⁵ Nov 8] sturdy, good-bodied filly: useful performer: easily best 3-y-o efforts on first 2 starts, around 4 lengths seventh of 10 to Germignaga in Oaks d'Italia at Milan on second of them: sold 15,000 gns Newmarket December Sales: needs at least 1¼m and should stay 1½m: has been bandaged behind. *B. W. Hills* 98

STOWAWAY 2 b.c. (Feb 26) Slip Anchor 136 – On Credit (FR) (No Pass No Sale 120) [1996 8m* Oct 2] 25,000Y: first foal: dam French 7f (at 2 yrs) to 10.5f winner and placed in Group 3 events: second favourite, won 6-runner maiden at Newcastle by 4 lengths from Kafaf, travelling well long way behind leaders then stretching clear under neats and heels: bred to stay at least 1¼m: looks a useful prospect: has joined Godolphin. *M. A. Jarvis* 94 p

STRAFFAN GOLD (USA) 2 b.c. (Apr 11) Lear Fan (USA) 130 – Oro Bianco (USA) (Lyphard's Wish (FR) 124) [1996 7g 8s Nov 9] $160,000Y: quite attractive colt: first reported foal: dam, French 10.5f winner, half-sister to very smart French middle-distance filly Ode: well beaten in maidens. *G. Wragg* –

STRAIGHT THINKING (USA) 3 ch.c. Bering 136 – Sharp Perception (USA) (Sharpen Up 127) [1995 54: 6g⁴ a8g⁵ 1996 a8.5g 8.2m⁵ 8.3m 8m 12m 8f 11.5m 7f Oct 15] strong, angular colt: modest maiden at best: sold out of P. Cole's stable 1,400 gns Doncaster July Sales after fourth 3-y-o outing: showed little afterwards, including in blinkers. *J. L. Spearing* 54 d

STRATA FLORIDA 3 b.g. Fearless Action (USA) 116 – Fair Seas 72 (General Assembly (USA)) [1995 NR 1996 10.1m⁴ Jul 29] 800Y: first foal: dam lightly-raced maiden: tailed off in maiden at Newcastle. *Mrs M. Reveley* –

STRATEGIC CHOICE (USA) 5 b.h. Alleged (USA) 138 – Danlu (USA) (Danzig (USA)) [1995 122: 12g* 12f³ 12g³ 12s 14g* 12d 1996 13.9f² 12m* 12m 12.5g* 12s³ 12f³ Nov 24]

To start where we left off, this time last year Strategic Choice had about one million pounds to go before matching, in financial terms, his owner's other standard-bearer Snurge. He's made a good fist of it so far. Expenses were defrayed to the tune of some £460,000 in 1996, but those expenses should not be underestimated because, like Snurge, Strategic Choice has accumulated a lot of air miles. Easily his longest trip away has been his final start in the latest season, to Tokyo for the Japan Cup. It also brought easily the greatest return, £216,828 officially when the yen was cashed in for Strategic Choice's third of fifteen, beaten about a length and a half. He threatened to make that calculation

Gran Premio di Milano—Strategic Choice wins a four-horse race from Luso

a seven-figure one when leading briefly early in the straight, but Singspiel and Fabulous La Fouine both outpaced him. Singspiel's massive reward, incidentally, meant that Snurge's record as top British-trained earner had lasted little more than two years.

Prior to the Japan Cup, Strategic Choice's travels had been confined to Europe, in 1996 to Milan twice and Deauville once. He paid for his fare on all three occasions, many, many times over on the first of them when shrewdly bypassing Royal Ascot for the Gran Premio di Milano. This Group 1 event saw a pathetic turnout: the home team mustered just the 1993 St Leger Italiano winner Pay Me Back; King's Theatre was making a short-lived comeback; Luso, a worthy opponent on paper, had apparently been plagued by mosquitos; and that was it, a field of four competing for a first prize of just over £110,000. Strategic Choice beat Luso a length and a half. The penalty for that win ensured that Strategic Choice would have to work a little harder against eight rivals in the Grand Prix de Deauville Lancel just over two months later—not a great price to pay, and not enough to prevent him coming out on top in a close finish with Tarator and Percutant. That added about £65,000 to the kitty and, despite Strategic Choice performing well below his best, another £50,000 or so came in for third place in the Gran Premio del Jockey-Club in October. Strategic Choice's two appearances in Britain, contrastingly, saw a return of £18,853 when he was a creditable second to Classic Cliche in the Yorkshire Cup. There was no reward for last of eight in the King George, Strategic Choice taking up second through the early stages of a very strongly-run race.

		Hoist The Flag	Tom Rolfe
	Alleged (USA)	(b 1968)	Wavy Navy
	(b 1974)	Princess Pout	Prince John
Strategic Choice (USA)		(b 1966)	Determined Lady
(b.h. 1991)		Danzig	Northern Dancer
	Danlu (USA)	(b 1977)	Pas de Nom
	(b 1985)	Lulu Mon Amour	Tom Rolfe
		(b 1980)	Sister Shu

Strategic Choice has not been seen out so frequently as Snurge so far—he had foot trouble earlier in his career—but he is due to race on in 1997. Both, of course, have won St Legers, and Strategic Choice's triumph in the Irish version is not nearly remote enough in the memory for us to regard the Yorkshire Cup as sufficient evidence that he does not stay a mile and three quarters, as some suggested. Many of his other races suggest a mile and a half is not far enough, but that is where the money is. Strategic Choice's 1994 St Simon Stakes second, however, does now look misleading—his record on a soft surface since then is a poor one. He will always find ground conditions to his liking in Japan. A big, strong horse with an easy action, he was fitted with blinkers for the first time in the Japan Cup. Details of Strategic Choice's pedigree were given in *Racehorses of 1995*, and his younger half-brothers Swift Fandango (by Lear Fan) and the once-raced Swing West (by Gone West) provided next to no material for an update. *P. F. I. Cole*

STRATEGIC PLOY 3 b.f. Deploy 131 – Wryneck 89 (Niniski (USA) 125) 71 [1995 –p: 7d⁵ 7f 7f 1996 10.3d 10g 9.9m⁴ 12m³ 12m* 12g* 11.8d* 12m 12m⁴ 14m⁴ Aug 10] strong, angular filly: unimpressive mover: fair handicapper: won at Beverley (edged right), Pontefract and Leicester in May: sold 25,000 gns Newmarket Autumn Sales: should be suited by further than 1½m: acts on good to firm and dead ground: held up. *Mrs J. R. Ramsden*

STRATHMORE CLEAR 2 b.c. (Apr 3) Batshoof 122 – Sunflower Seed 70 75 (Mummy's Pet 125) [1996 6s³ 7m Jun 20] 26,000Y: tall, close-coupled colt, quite attractive: second foal: dam, stayed 1½m, granddaughter of Highclere: running-on third of 9 to Falkenham in maiden at Goodwood: slowly away and well beaten in Chesham Stakes at Ascot following month: should stay beyond 6f: looked sort to do better. *G. Lewis*

STRATHTORE DREAM (IRE) 5 b. or br.m. Jareer (USA) 115 – Beyond – Words (Ballad Rock 122) [1995 –: 7.1d 6s 6g 8g 5g 7.1g 6g 1996 a6g 7.1g 5.9d 8.3s 8.1g 8d⁶ May 31] leggy mare: little sign of ability: sold 1,000 gns Doncaster November Sales. *Miss L. A. Perratt*

STRAT'S LEGACY 9 b.g. Chukaroo 103 – State Romance 67 (Free State 125) 46 [1995 48: a13g 11.5m⁴ 12.1m* 12g⁶ 12.1m⁵ 12d⁴ 12g a12g⁴ a12g⁴ a16g⁵ 1996 a13g a39 a16g 12.1m 12m⁴ 12d² 12m³ 12m 12m⁴ 12d a13g a16g⁴ Dec 11] small, light-framed gelding: poor handicapper: best over 1½m+ (stays 2m): acts on all-weather tracks, firm and dead ground: tried blinkered: often bandaged behind. *D. W. P. Arbuthnot*

STRAT'S QUEST 2 b.f. (Apr 16) Nicholas (USA) 111 – Eagle's Quest 62 (Legal 61 Eagle 126) [1996 5.1m⁶ 6.1m⁴ 5.7m⁵ 7m⁴ 7.6m 7.3m 6.1s* a6g Nov 22] small, quite attractive filly: has a quick action: half-sister to several winners, including 4-y-o 5f (at 2 yrs) to 1m winner David James' Girl (by Faustus) and 5-y-o 11.6f winner Quest Again (by Then Again): dam 5f winner: modest performer: won 16-runner nursery at Chepstow (led 2f out) in October: stays 7f: acts on good to firm and soft ground (disappointing on fibresand): flashed tail third start: has been bandaged. *D. W. P. Arbuthnot*

STRAVANO 2 b.f. (Mar 24) Handsome Sailor 125 – La Stravaganza 74 (Slip – Anchor 136) [1996 5m a7g 5f 5f Aug 15] 1,050Y: leggy, lengthy filly: first foal: dam, maiden, stayed 1¼m: no promise. *B. P. J. Baugh*

STRAWBERRY ROAN (IRE) 2 b.f. (Apr 15) Sadler's Wells (USA) 132 – 103 p Doff The Derby (USA) (Master Derby (USA)) [1996 7d³ 8g* 9d* Nov 10] 240,000Y: half-sister to several winners here and abroad, notably top-class middle-distance colt Generous (by Caerleon) and useful Irish performer at up to 1m, Wedding Bouquet (by Kings Lake): dam unraced half-sister to Trillion, dam of Triptych: won minor event at Navan (by 8 lengths) in October and 9-runner listed event at Leopardstown (2/1 on, by 1½ lengths from Buddy Marvel, field strung out behind) in November: will be very well suited by middle distances: has a quick, round action: hit running rail with near fore under 1f out at Leopardstown: looks a smart prospect. *A. P. O'Brien, Ireland*

STRAZO (IRE) 3 b.g. Alzao (USA) 117 – Ministra (USA) (Deputy Minister 94 (CAN)) [1995 NR 1996 8g⁵ 8.1d* 7m* 8m Jul 11] good-bodied gelding: poor walker: first foal: dam, winner at 12.5f in France, out of Irish 1000 Guineas and Oaks winner Godetia: useful form: won maiden at Chepstow (odds on, made all) in May and minor event at Salisbury in June: below form after forcing pace in handicap at Newmarket on final start: sold (J. Gosden to Lady Herries) 11,000 gns Newmarket Autumn Sales: bred to stay further than 1m: gelded. *J. H. M. Gosden*

STREAKY HAWK (USA) 4 b.g. Hawkster (USA) – Veroom Maid (USA) 51 (Distinctive (USA)) [1995 58d: 11m 10f³ a14.8g a14g² 12d 14g a12g⁵ 1996 a12g a12g³ Feb 15] strong, lengthy gelding: disappointing maiden: stays 1½m: best effort on soft ground at 2 yrs, acts on the all-weather. *J. Pearce*

STREAMLINE (IRE) 2 ch.c. (Apr 29) River Falls 113 – Kowalski (IRE) –
(Cyrano de Bergerac 120) [1996 5g 8f 7m 6.9d Oct 21] IR 10,500F, IR 9,000Y:
second foal: half-brother to 1995 2-y-o 5f to 1m winner Arctic Romancer (by
Distinctly North): dam ran twice as 2-y-o in Ireland: behind in maidens: has worn a
tongue strap: sold 1,700 gns Newmarket Autumn Sales: sent to Holland. *G. Lewis*

STREET GENERAL 2 b.c. (May 12) Generous (IRE) 139 – Hotel Street (USA) 90 p
93 (Alleged (USA) 138) [1996 8g² Oct 30] 12,000Y: seventh foal: brother to fairly
useful 3-y-o 1¾m winner Generosa and half-brother to 7f (at 2 yrs) and 11f winner
Widyan (by Fappiano) and 1991 2-y-o 7f winner Providence (by Diesis): dam,
lightly-raced 1½m winner, half-sister to Royal and Regal and Regal And Royal:
20/1, length second of 13 to Mandilak in steadily-run maiden at Yarmouth, held up
then ridden to lead briefly final 1f: will be suited by middle distances: will improve,
and should win a race. *H. R. A. Cecil*

STREET KENDRA (FR) 4 b.f. Kendor (FR) 122 – Street Opera (Sadler's Wells 92 d
(USA) 132) [1995 8f³ 8g⁴ 8g³ 8m⁴ 8g* 8s⁴ 8d 8d 1996 8d⁵ 8g 8g 10.5m 8.1s Oct
22] ex-French filly: second foal: half-sister to 2 winners in France, notably smart
middle-distance 3-y-o Stretarez (by Saumarez): dam unraced half-sister to Grape
Tree Road and Red Route: fairly useful at 3 yrs, winning handicap at Saint-Cloud:
disappointing in 1996 after reappearance: sold out of E. Donguy's stable 180,000
francs Goffs (France) July Sales after penultimate start then retained by trainer
21,000 gns Newmarket December Sales: stays 1m: probably acts on any going.
B. Smart

STRELITZA (IRE) 2 b.f. (Apr 18) Taufan (USA) 119 – Strident Note 89 (The 53
Minstrel (CAN) 135) [1996 5m 5g 5s⁶ a5g³ 7f³ Sep 27] IR 7,200Y: workmanlike
filly: has a round action: half-sister to 1991 2-y-o 1¼m winner Castillet (by
Rousillon) and a winner in UAE by Shernazar: dam, maiden best at 2 yrs, half-
sister to Topsy and Teenoso: blinkered, best efforts when staying-on third in nurseries
at Southwell (selling event) and Redcar: stays 7f: has had tongue tied down.
M. W. Easterby

STRETCHING (IRE) 3 br.g. Contract Law (USA) 108 – Mrs Mutton 89 –
(Dancer's Image (USA)) [1995 NR 1996 a8.5g a8.5g a10g Nov 15] IR 4,800Y: 2,100
2-y-o: half-brother to several winners, including fair sprinter Useful (by Thatching)
and Irish 8.5f winner Steel Head (by Salmon Leap): dam, placed at 1½m, was
disappointing: well held in maidens. *A. Bailey*

STRICTLY HARD 2 b.f. (Mar 8) Reprimand 122 – Formidable Dancer 70 58
(Formidable (USA) 125) [1996 6.9d 8g⁶ 8s Nov 9] 1,900F, 3,800Y: sixth foal: half-
sister to 5f to 7f winner Fighter Squadron and a winner in Belgium (both by Primo
Dominie): dam (maiden) stayed 1½m: best effort in maiden events when sixth of 16
at Leicester, still seeming green, nearest finish: likely to stay beyond 1m: slowly
away first 2 starts. *G. C. Bravery*

STRIDE 2 b.f. (Apr 26) Batshoof 122 – The Strid (IRE) 53 (Persian Bold 123) 72 +
[1996 6g⁴ 6m⁴ 7f* 7.1g* 7m* 7g⁶ 7m 7.3m⁶ 7.1m⁴ 7.6m* 8m Sep 20] small filly:
first foal: dam ran once at 2 yrs: fair performer: comfortable winner of sellers at
Redcar (sold out of D. Morley's stable 9,400 gns) and Musselburgh in the summer
and non-selling nurseries at Chester in July and Lingfield in September: sold 15,000
gns Newmarket Autumn Sales: stays 7.6f: acts on firm ground: successful for 7-lb
claimer. *Martyn Meade*

STRIFFOLINO 4 b.g. Robellino (USA) 127 – Tizona (Pharly (FR) 130) [1995 –
74: 9f* 10.1m⁵ 8f³ 8m⁵ 7m 8g⁴ 1996 10f 10.8f⁵ Jun 24] lengthy, lengthy, dipped-
backed gelding: good mover: fair handicapper at 3 yrs for T. D. Barron: well below
form in 1996: stays 9f: has raced only on a sound surface. *John Berry*

STRIP CARTOON (IRE) 8 ch.g. Tate Gallery (USA) 117 – Reveal (Pitskelly –
122) [1995 –: 6d 1996 a6g Jan 12] smallish, workmanlike gelding: modest
handicapper: very tough at 5 yrs (rated 62), but raced only twice since February 1994
and well beaten. *S. R. Bowring*

ST RITA 3 gr.f. Bustino 136 – Able Mabel 77 (Absalom 128) [1995 NR 1996 10g³ 74
12m⁴ 14d⁶ 11.9f⁵ Jul 17] lengthy, unfurnished filly: second foal: dam 6f mudlark: in
frame in middle-distance maidens at Leicester and Thirsk (set steady pace, clearly
best effort) first 2 starts: well held afterwards: sold 7,400 gns Newmarket Autumn
Sales. *J. L. Dunlop*

STRUGGLER 4 b.c. Night Shift (USA) – Dreamawhile 85 (Known Fact (USA) 114
135) [1995 111: 5.5g* 5g* 5g³ 5f² 5f 1996 6m³ 5m⁴ 5m* 5g² 5f 5g² 5m⁶ 5.2m* 5d 6g
Oct 19] small, strong, good-bodied ex-French colt: poor mover: smart performer:
trained in 1995 by C. Laffon-Parias: won minor events at Beverley in May and
Newbury (by a length from Hever Golf Rose) in September: good efforts when
second in Temple Stakes at Sandown (beaten ¾ length by Mind Games), sixth of 8 to
Pivotal in Nunthorpe Stakes at York (looked outstandingly well) in August and
seventh of 10 to Kistena in Prix de l'Abbaye de Longchamp in October (penultimate
start): stays 6f: acts on firm ground and dead: visored (stumbled start, run best
ignored) fifth 4-y-o start: held up. *D. R. Loder*

STUDIO THIRTY 4 gr.g. Rock City 120 – Chepstow Vale (USA) 97 (Key To 41
The Mint (USA)) [1995 –, a56: a9.4g 7.5m 10g a8.5g⁴ 8g a9.4g* a9.4g a9.4g⁶ 10.3m⁶ a–
a12g a10g⁶ a10g* a10g³ a8.5g⁶ 1996 10g 10m 10d 10.1m³ 10.1f a8g 11.5m⁵ 10.2g
14d Oct 2] leggy gelding: poor handicapper: left D. Morris after sixth 4-y-o start:
appears to stay 11.5f: tried blinkered and visored, no improvement: has re-joined
R. Dickin. *C. A. Smith*

STUFFED 4 ch.g. Clantime 101 – Puff Pastry 78 (Reform 132) [1995 64: 5g² 6m² 89 +
5m 5f² 6m² 1996 5g 5m* 6m⁴ 5g² 5m⁵ 6m⁴ 6m 6m 5g² 5g* 5m* Oct 23] workmanlike gelding: fairly useful handicapper, generally progressive: won at Thirsk in
April: gained further deserved successes in 17-runner race at Pontefract and
18-runner race at Newcastle (2 days later and bandaged) in October: effective at 5f
and 6f: acts on firm ground, hasn't raced on soft since 2 yrs: effective blinkered or
not: reliable: may well be capable of better still. *M. W. Easterby*

STURGEON 2 ch.c. (Feb 23) Caerleon (USA) 132 – Ridge The Times 84
(USA) 78 (Riva Ridge (USA)) [1996 6s 7g² 7g² Jul 12] IR 175,000Y: smallish colt:
half-brother to several winners, including smart sprinter Pharaoh's Delight (by Fairy
King) and 1½m Oslo Cup winner Kateb (by Pennine Walk): dam 2-y-o 5f winner:
second in maidens at Newmarket (behind Benny The Dip) and York (odds on though
unimpressive in appearance and to post, always held when crossed inside last) in the
summer: should stay at least 1m. *P. F. I. Cole*

STYGIAN (USA) 2 ch.f. (Jan 9) Irish River (FR) 131 – Sin Lucha (USA) 73
(Northfields (USA)) [1996 6m 5m* 6.5m 6f* 6m 5.2g Oct 30] neat filly: sixth foal:
half-sister to 3-y-o 6f winner Dark Deed (by Known Fact) and a 2-y-o winner in USA
by Tejano: dam unraced sister to top-class miler Northjet: fair form: won maiden at
Folkestone in August and nursery at Leicester (wandered under pressure) in
September: will be suited by further than 6f: acts on firm ground: inconsistent: sold
24,000 gns Newmarket December Sales. *B. W. Hills*

STYLE DANCER (IRE) 2 b.g. (Mar 11) Dancing Dissident (USA) 119 – 70
Showing Style (Pas de Seul 133) [1996 5m 5g 6g 5m⁴ 5m³ 6g² 6m 6m* Oct 29]
11,000F, 13,000Y: tall gelding: good mover: third reported foal: half-brother to Irish
6f winner Southern Review (by Magical Wonder): dam unraced: improved effort
when winning nursery at Redcar in October convincingly, held up and leading final
1f: probably better suited by 6f than 5f: has scope and may improve again.
R. M. Whitaker

STYLISH GENT 9 br.g. Vitiges (FR) 132 – Squire's Daughter (Bay Express 132) –
[1995 NR 1996 a12g a12g 12d Mar 30] strong, lengthy gelding: no longer of any
account. *G. R. Oldroyd*

STYLISH WAYS (IRE) 4 b.g. Thatching 131 – Style of Life (USA) (The 96 d
Minstrel (CAN) 135) [1995 98: 6g* 6m³ 7m³ 7m⁵ 6m 1996 6m⁴ 6m⁴ 6f 6m 6g 6g 5m
6f Nov 5] compact, quite attractive gelding: fluent mover: useful performer:
respectable efforts in rated stakes at York first 2 4-y-o starts, but well beaten in
handicaps afterwards: stays 7f: acts on good to firm and soft ground. *Miss S. E. Hall*

SUALTACH (IRE) 3 b.c. Marju (IRE) 127 – Astra Adastra (Mount Hagen (FR) 84 §
127) [1995 78: 5.1m³ 6g⁴ 6.1m² 6.1m* 6m 7g⁴ 6m 1996 a8.5g 7s* 7m 7.5m² 7.6g⁴ 7f a78 §
a7g* a8.5g⁵ 6d⁵ 8m 7m² 9m 7d 8.1v 7g Nov 2] strong, lengthy colt: has a fluent,
round action: operated on after final 2-y-o outing to free trapped testicle: fairly useful
handicapper on his day: won at Doncaster in March and Wolverhampton in May:
stays 7.6f, seemingly not 8.5f: acts on good to firm ground and fibresand, usually
goes well on a soft surface: visored (well beaten) once: has found little and wandered:
unreliable. *R. Hollinshead*

SUAVE STAR 2 ch.f. (Apr 26) Suave Dancer (USA) 136 – Princess Arabella 73   48
(Crowned Prince (USA) 128) [1996 5d² a6g⁶ 6d³ 7g⁴ 8g 7m a8.5g Nov 11] 4,100Y:
tall, leggy filly: half-sister to useful 6f and 1m winner Nordica (by Northfields), later
dam of Sueboog, Irish 1m winner Casla (by Lomond) and a winner in South Africa:
dam 7f winner, half-sister to Oaks winner Fair Salinia: poor performer: trained first 3
starts by P. D. Evans: well beaten after next outing: should stay 1m: very on toes and
awkward stalls on third outing, sweating and very worked up fifth start: sold 23,000
gns Newmarket December Sales. *C. A. Dwyer*

SUBFUSK 3 b.f. Lugana Beach 116 – Hush It Up (Tina's Pet 121) [1995 56, a60:   –
a6g* 6m⁵ 6g 5m³ a6g* 7d 6.1d a5g 1996 a5g⁴ 6d a5g a5g May 25] smallish filly: a61
poor mover: modest performer: well beaten last 3 starts: stays 6f: acts on good to firm
ground (well below form all 3 outings on dead) and fibresand: tends to hang left:
covered by Formidable. *W. G. M. Turner*

SUBTERFUGE 3 br.f. Machiavellian (USA) 123 – Sandy Island 110 (Mill Reef   86
(USA) 141) [1995 78p: 7g* 1996 12m⁶ 12g⁴ Oct 11] tall, angular filly: won 4-runner
maiden at Newmarket at 2 yrs: much her better effort on return when 3½ lengths
fourth of 15 to Shadow Leader in handicap at Ascot, staying on: should stay further
than 1½m: may do better still: has reportedly been sold. *H. R. A. Cecil*

SUBTLE ONE (IRE) 3 b.f. Polish Patriot (USA) 128 – Subtle Change (IRE) 102   –
(Law Society (USA) 130) [1995 –: 6m⁴ 7g 7g 10g 1996 a7g 6m Jun 24] close-
coupled filly: no form. *T. T. Clement*

SUCH BOLDNESS 2 b.c. (Feb 14) Persian Bold 123 – Bone China (IRE)   – p
(Sadler's Wells (USA) 132) [1996 7d Oct 28] 27,000Y: second foal: dam Irish 11f
and 1½m winner: 25/1, signs of ability in maiden at Lingfield, close up on far side
until 2f out: will do better. *R. Akehurst*

SUCH PRESENCE 2 ch.g. (May 21) Arzanni 115 – Marchiness Drake (Mare-   –
chal Drake 101) [1996 7f 10g⁶ 8s Nov 9] tall, leggy, short-backed gelding:
half-brother to some poor animals under NH rules: dam never ran: no form in
maidens. *K. S. Bridgwater*

SUDDEN SPIN 6 b.g. Doulab (USA) 115 – Lightning Legacy (USA) 78 (Super   48
Concorde (USA) 128) [1995 40+, a66: a11g* a12g³ 10g⁶ 12g⁴ a11g* a12g³ 12m⁴   a–
a9.4g² a12g⁶ 10g³ a9.4g* a9.4g³ 1996 a11g⁵ 16.1s⁵ 16.2m* 16.2g⁴ 13.8m 16g Aug
12] leggy, good-topped gelding: fair handicapper on all-weather in 1995, very poor
on turf: won at Beverley in April: soundly beaten last 2 starts: stays 16.2f well: acts
on good to firm and soft ground and goes well on fibresand: tried visored earlier in
career. *J. Norton*

SUDEST (IRE) 2 b.c. (Feb 1) Taufan (USA) 119 – Frill (Henbit (USA) 130)   67
[1996 7.1m⁶ 6g⁶ 7m⁵ 8f 8g Oct 25] 20,000F, 55,000Y: quite attractive colt: fourth
foal: half-brother to French 6f and 7f (at 2 yrs) winner Lady Frill (by Standaan):
dam, Irish 1½m winner, half-sister to high-class miler Pitcairn: modest form, never a
factor, in maidens and nurseries: should prove well suited by 1m+. *I. A. Balding*

SUEDORO 6 b.m. Hard Fought 125 – Bamdoro 54 (Cavo Doro 124) [1995 51: 8g   –
6g⁵ 9.9m 6.9m 6f* 5.9f⁶ 6f⁴ 6g 6f* 6f⁴ 6f* 7g 6g 1996 6d 6s 5s⁴ 5m 6g 6g Jul 24]
angular mare: poor handicapper: best form at 6f: acts on firm ground. *R. M. McKellar*

SUE ME (IRE) 4 b. or br.g. Contract Law (USA) 108 – Pink Fondant (Northfields   64
(USA)) [1995 75, a64: a7g² 5m 6m⁵ 6g 6d² 6g 6d 6.1s a6g 1996 5s 7d 6d a6g 7.3s⁶   a55
8.1d 6m 7.1s 6m⁴ a7g⁶ a6g Nov 29] quite attractive gelding: fair handicapper at 3 yrs,
disappointing in 1996: stays 7f: acts on good to firm and heavy ground, not at best on
fibresand: blinkered (well beaten) fourth 4-y-o start: weak finisher. *W. R. Muir*

SUE'S RETURN 4 b.f. Beveled (USA) – Return To Tara (Homing 130) [1995   83
91: 7m 8.1g² 10g⁶ 8.1m⁵ 9f² 7.9m 10m 8d 9g 7f³ 1996 8d⁶ 8g 8.5m 7.9g 7f² 8m⁵
8d³ 8m* 8g 9m Oct 5] angular filly: fairly useful handicapper: won at Yarmouth in
September: stays 9f: acts on firm and dead ground. *A. P. Jarvis*

SUFUF 3 b. or br.f. Caerleon (USA) 132 – Deira (NZ) (Sir Tristram 115) [1995 NR   65
1996 8.2m⁶ 10.4g 8m Oct 23] tall, leggy, unfurnished filly: second foal: half-sister to
1995 3-y-o 7f winner Karayb (by Last Tycoon): dam won from 5f to 7f in Australasia:
never-nearer sixth of 15 in maiden at Nottingham on debut: last in similar events at
York and Yarmouth: sold 6,500 gns Newmarket December Sales. *D. Morley*

SUGARFOOT 2 ch.c. (Jan 29) Thatching 131 – Norpella 95 (Northfields (USA)) 82
[1996 6g* Jul 20] 31,000Y: fifth live foal: half-brother to 4 winners, including 4-y-o
Carlito Brigante (1¼m by Robellino) and useful performer at around 1m Ultimo
Imperatore (by Cadeaux Genereux): dam, 1¼m and 1½m winner who stayed 14.8f,
from good family: 6/1, won 6-runner maiden at Ayr by 1¼ lengths, clear, from
Farringdon Future, held up racing keenly after slowish start then quickening well:
looked sure to improve. *N. Tinkler*

SUGAR MILL 6 b.g. Slip Anchor 136 – Great Tom 99 (Great Nephew 126) [1995 82
70: 10m³ 10m 10m 11.9m³ 14g² 14.6m* 16.5m 1996 14d⁶ 14.8m 12.3g* 12.3s*
11.9d² 11.9v* 12g³ 12s⁵ Nov 9] tall, angular gelding: has round action: fairly useful
handicapper: in good form in 1996, winning at Ripon (twice) in August and at
Haydock in October: finds 1½m a bare minimum, and stays 14.6f: acts on good to
firm and heavy ground: often soon off bridle. *Mrs M. Reveley*

SUGAR PLUM 2 br.f. (May 14) Primo Dominie 121 – Ile de Danse 76 (Ile de –
Bourbon (USA) 133) [1996 6g Jul 10] 15,000Y: unfurnished, workmanlike filly:
fourth foal: half-sister to a winner in Spain by Blakeney: dam, French 10.5f winner at
4 yrs, is from family of Bonne Ile and Ile de Nisky: 40/1, slowly away and always
towards rear in 17-runner Newmarket maiden. *R. Hannon*

SUITE ADDITION (IRE) 2 ch.f. (Apr 24) Common Grounds 118 – Mint 46
Addition 50 (Tate Gallery (USA) 117) [1996 6m 5g⁶ 7g 6d⁴ a5g Nov 7] IR 8,000Y: a?
ex-Irish filly: first foal: dam maiden bred to stay 1m+: well beaten in maidens at
Naas, Bellewstown and Galway for E. Lynam: ran twice in Britain, fourth in poor
rating-related maiden at Folkestone on first occasion: probably needs further than 5f:
sold 960 gns Ascot December Sales. *C. A. Horgan*

SUITE FACTORS 2 b.g. (Jun 7) Timeless Times (USA) 99 – Uptown Girl 65 58
(Caruso 112) [1996 5.1m⁶ 5.1m² 5g⁴ 5m² 5.1m³ 5.1m* 6g 5f⁴ 5m⁶ 5g a5g⁴
a6g a5g Dec 3] 6,000Y: rather leggy gelding: fourth foal: half-brother to 3-y-o 5f
winner Charterhouse Xpres (by Clantime) and a winner abroad by Domynsky: dam
sprinter: fair performer at best: all out to win claimer at Nottingham (claimed out of
J. Glover's stable £8,000) in August: barely stays 5f: best form on turf on
top-of-the-ground, below best all tries on fibresand: visored eleventh and twelfth
starts. *K. R. Burke*

SUITOR 3 b.c. Groom Dancer (USA) 128 – Meliora 73 (Crowned Prince (USA) 52
128) [1995 –p: 8m 8f 1996 10g 11f 10m 15.8g³ 17.2m⁵ a13g a16g⁴ a13g a10g² Dec
31] big, rangy colt: has pronounced knee action: trained until after fifth 3-y-o start by
W. Jarvis: out of handicap, stayed on well after being outpaced when runner-up at
Lingfield final start, best effort: should prove suited by return to further than 1¼m:
acts on equitrack. *S. Dow*

SUIVEZ 6 b.g. Persian Bold 123 – Butterfly Kiss 69 (Beldale Flutter (USA) 130) –
[1995 58: a14.8g⁶ a9.4g⁴ a11g³ a11g* a11g* a11g⁵ 1996 a11g⁴ 16m⁶ May 13] sturdy a47
gelding: fairly useful hurdler: modest middle-distance performer on flat: well below
form in 1996: acts on firm ground, dead and fibresand. *Mrs N. Macauley*

SUJUD (IRE) 4 b. or br.f. Shaadi (USA) 126 – Sit Elnaas (USA) 82 (Sir Ivor 135) 56
[1995 58: 7m⁶ 8m 9.7m⁵ 11.9d 14.1m² 1996 17.1g³ 21.6m⁶ 16.1g⁵ 17.2m Aug 28]
leggy, narrow filly: modest maiden handicapper: left Mrs J. Ramsden after
penultimate start: looks a dyed-in-the-wool stayer: acts on good to firm ground,
possibly not on dead: won twice over hurdles in September. *M. D. Hammond*

SULAWESI (IRE) 3 b.f. In The Wings 128 – Royal Loft 105 (Homing 130) 67
[1995 NR 1996 8.3d⁵ 10.1m⁵ 10.1m⁵ 10s Oct 24] 6,500Y: close-coupled filly: sixth foal:
closely related to fairly useful 1994 2-y-o 7f winner Wigberto (by Old Vic) and
half-sister to 3 winners, including fairly useful Irish 7f and 9f winner Sir Slaves (by
Salse): dam 6f and 7f winner who stayed 1m: fair maiden: failed to improve from
debut: sold (W. Jarvis to N. Twiston-Davies) 7,500 gns Newmarket Autumn Sales.
W. Jarvis

SULEIKA DANCER 3 b.f. Slip Anchor 136 – Starr Danias (USA) (Sensitive –
Prince (USA)) [1995 NR 1996 a14.8g⁴ a14.8g⁶ Dec 14] 26,000Y: third reported foal:
half-sister to 5f (Dubai) and 7f winner Yaa Wale (by Persian Bold), and 6f (at 2 yrs)
and 11.8f winner Potsclose (by Miswaki): dam (ran twice in USA) half-sister to
outstanding American chaser Zaccio and Acomb winner Kohaylan: sold out of J.

Gosden's stable 2,800 gns Newmarket July (1996) Sales: well beaten in claimer and seller at Wolverhampton. *P. D. Evans*

SUMMER BEAUTY 3 ch.f. Cadeaux Genereux 131 – Try The Duchess 99 (Try   69
My Best (USA) 130) [1995 NR 1996 8.1m⁵ 7m 8.1m 7.1s 7g Oct 30] 13,000F,
25,000Y: tall, useful-looking filly: fluent mover: half-sister to 5-y-o 1¼m and 1½m
winner Uncharted Waters (by Celestial Storm) and a winner in Dubai by Primo
Dominie: dam 2-y-o 6f and 7f winner: fair form when fifth of 12 in maiden at
Sandown on debut: failed to progress, and soundly beaten in handicaps last 2 starts:
should prove best short of 1m: bandaged behind. *J. H. M. Gosden*

SUMMER DANCE 2 b.f. (Apr 10) Sadler's Wells (USA) 132 – Hyabella 111   86 p
(Shirley Heights 130) [1996 8g² Oct 25] 205,000Y: tall, leggy, lengthy filly: second
foal: dam, 1m winner, half-sister to high-class 1¼m performer Stagecraft (by
Sadler's Wells) out of half-sister to Colorspin, the dam of Opera House (by Sadler's
Wells): favourite, 1¾ lengths second of 15 to Calypso Grant in maiden at Doncaster,
travelling well behind leaders but no answer to winner: short and green to post: will
stay middle distances: sure to improve, and win races. *M. R. Stoute*

SUMMERHILL SPECIAL (IRE) 5 b.m. Roi Danzig (USA) – Special Thanks   59
(Kampala 120) [1995 –: 10d 1996 12m 12s⁶ 8.5m 10m⁵ 10m⁴ 8.3g⁶ 8m 6m 10.4g
7.1f 14m 14d 12d* Oct 21] sturdy, good-bodied ex-Irish mare: fairly useful handicapper (rated 80) in 1994 for M. Kauntze: modest form at best here, winning
amateurs race at Folkestone in October: sold (Mrs P. N. Dutfield to D. Barker) 8,000
gns Newmarket Autumn Sales: stays 1½m: acts on any ground: effective blinkered
or not. *Mrs P. N. Dutfield*

SUMMEROSA (USA) 2 ch.f. (Mar 20) Woodman (USA) 126 – Rose Red   78
(USA) 92 (Northern Dancer) [1996 6m³ 5.2m⁶ 7.1s² Oct 22] attractive filly: half-
sister to useful 3-y-o 10.3f winner Legal Right (probably stays at least 12.5f, by
Alleged), useful Zind (won at 13f, by Law Society), a winner in USA by Seattle Slew
and to the dam of Derby winner Dr Devious: dam, Irish 2-y-o 6f winner unraced at 3
yrs, is half-sister to high-class 1m to 1½m winner Critique: fair form: placed in
maidens at Ascot in July and Chepstow (set steady pace until headed over 1f out,
rallied but caught again on post) in October: needs further than 5.2f and will stay at
least 1m: acts on good to firm and soft ground. *P. W. Chapple-Hyam*

SUMMER PRINCESS 3 ch.f. Prince Sabo 123 – Lafrowda 71 (Crimson Beau   –
124) [1995 NR 1996 5.1g 5m⁶ 6.1g a6g a7g Nov 22] 1,500Y: fifth live foal: half-
sister to tough 7-y-o 6f to 13f winner Mentalasanythin (by Ballacashtal): dam 6f and
7.6f winner: no worthwhile form, for G. Fierro first 3 starts: visored final outing.
A. Streeter

SUMMER QUEEN 2 b.f. (May 3) Robellino (USA) 127 – Carolside 108 (Music   62
Maestro 119) [1996 5m³ 5.7g⁵ a6g³ a7g⁵ Aug 9] sparely-made filly: half-sister to
several winners, including 3-y-o Oh Whataknight (by Primo Dominie), 5f winner at
2 yrs, and useful 1m to 9f winner Eton Lad (by Never So Bold): dam 2-y-o 5f winner
who didn't progress: modest maiden: stays 6f: acts on good to firm ground and on
fibresand. *S. P. C. Woods*

SUMMER RISOTTO 2 ch.f. (Jan 25) Forzando 122 – Indian Summer 78   50 d
(Young Generation 129) [1996 5s⁵ 5.1f 6m⁴ 6f⁴ 6.1m* 6m 6m⁵ 6d⁴ a5g 6m⁴ 6m 6.1s²
Oct 22] 4,600F, 2,000Y: sister to a winner in Hong Kong and half-sister to a 2-y-o 5f
winner in Italy by Emarati: dam, won in Belgium and placed at up to 7f here (would
have stayed further), out of half-sister to Bustino: won 3-runner claimer at Nottingham in July: failed to repeat the form, respectable second of 16 in nursery at
Chepstow last time, staying on well: sold 4,500 gns Newmarket Autumn Sales:
should stay 7f: acts on firm and soft ground: sent to Sweden. *D. J. S. ffrench Davis*

SUMMER SPELL (USA) 3 b.c. Alleged (USA) 138 – Summertime Lady   104
(USA) (No Robbery) [1995 NR 1996 10.3s* 13.9m² 12m 14g³ 12s⁶ Oct 26]
$55,000Y: leggy, unfurnished colt: has a fluent, round action: half-brother to useful
winners Darby Lady (at 7f at 2 yrs then 10.5f, by Darby Creek Road) and Santella
Sam (over 8.2f at 2 yrs, by Balzac), and 3 winners in USA: dam lightly-raced half-
sister to high-class Bohemian Grove: useful performer: won maiden at Doncaster in
March by 8 lengths: good third of 7 to Sharaf Kabeer in listed race at Goodwood in
August: creditable sixth of 12 to Salmon Ladder in St Simon Stakes at Newbury final

start: subsequently joined N. Henderson to go hurdling: should stay 2m: acts on good to firm ground and soft. *R. Charlton*

SUMMER VILLA   4 b.f. Nomination 125 – Maravilla 73 (Mandrake Major 122)   41 [1995 43, a52: a8g³ a8g* a8.5g* a10g 8f 8m² 8.1f³ 7m⁴ 8m a7g 1996 a8g a8g³ 7g⁴ 8.3g³ 8f⁵ 8f⁶ 6f 6.9f Aug 5] neat filly: poor handicapper: left P. Haslam after second 4-y-o start: stays 8.5f: acts on fibresand and firm ground: tried blinkered. *J. Hetherton*

SUMMERVILLE WOOD   2 b.c. (May 2) Nomination 125 – Four Love (Pas de   58 Seul 133) [1996 5f³ 5g 6.1m* 7f⁵ 7.1m³ 7.6m 7m³ 8.2g 7m⁴ 8g⁶ Nov 2] 7,200Y, 11,000 2-y-o: second foal: half-brother to 3-y-o Eastern Prophets (by Emarati), useful 5f winner at 2 yrs: dam Irish 1m winner: modest performer: ridden by 7-lb claimer, landed small gamble when winning seller at Nottingham in August: stays 1m: acts on good to firm ground: best form in blinkers, though successful without. *P. Mooney*

SUNBEAM DANCE (USA)   2 b.c. (May 23) Gone West (USA) – Encorelle   93 (FR) (Arctic Tern (USA) 126) [1996 7f* 7g⁴ 8g⁴ 8d² Nov 8] big, close-coupled good-topped colt: has plenty of scope: easy mover: ninth foal: brother to very smart German miler Royal Abjar and half-brother to several winners abroad, including useful French 1m (at 2 yrs) and 1¼m winner After The Sun (by Storm Bird): dam unraced sister to Prix de Diane winner Escaline: fairly useful form: narrowly won maiden at Leicester in September: creditable head second of 6, clear, to Catienus in minor event at Doncaster last time: stays 1m. *Saeed bin Suroor*

SUN CIRCUS   4 b.f. Statoblest 120 – Carmen Maria (Bold Lad (IRE) 133) [1995   – –: 8.2d 7g 10d⁶ 1996 10.8g 8f Jun 22] useful-looking filly: seems of little account: sold 500 gns Doncaster September Sales. *J. L. Spearing*

SUNDAY MAELSTROM (IRE)   3 b.f. Distinctly North (USA) 115 – Make   – Your Mark (On Your Mark 125) [1995 –: 5g 6g 5f⁵ 1996 8d⁶ May 8] unfurnished filly: no worthwhile form: bolted to post and tailed off only 3-y-o start: hung badly left on debut: seems temperamental. *T. Dyer*

SUNDAY MAIL TOO (IRE)   4 b.f. Fayruz 116 – Slick Chick 89 (Shiny Tenth   51 120) [1995 40: 5d⁶ 6s 5g 6g 5g⁶ 5g 5f 7.1m⁴ 7.1f⁵ 5m 5m⁶ 6f⁵ 6m⁶ 5g 6f⁶ 5.9f⁵ 5f⁶ 5m 6g 1996 a6g 6s⁵ 5d 5s 8.1g⁴ 8.1g⁴ 6g* 5g 8.1f⁶ 6m² 6g⁴ 5m* 6m⁵ 6d 6f 5g⁴ 5m 5g 6d 6m Oct 23] sparely-made filly: modest handicapper: won at Hamilton in June and at Ayr (selling event) in July: best recent form at 5f or 6f: acts on any ground: tried visored/blinkered: sometimes hangs. *Miss L. A. Perratt*

SUNDAY MARKET (USA)   2 b.g. (Feb 19) Lear Fan (USA) 130 – Sunday   – Bazaar (USA) (Nureyev (USA) 131) [1996 7m 7.6d Aug 29] second foal: half-brother to 3-y-o Sahara Belle (by Sanglamore), a winner in Norway: dam French 1½m winner, half-sister to high-class American 1m/1¼m performer Bates Motel and very smart colts Hatim and Super Asset: well behind from halfway in maidens at Salisbury (hampered start) and Lingfield: sold 3,200 gns Newmarket Autumn Sales and gelded. *G. Harwood*

SUNGROVE'S BEST   9 ch.g. Buzzards Bay 128§ – Judann (Some Hand 119)   – [1995 NR 1996 a8.5g a12g 10d 8.3m Jun 3] lengthy gelding: of little account. *P. Eccles*

SUNLEY SECURE   3 b.g. Warrshan (USA) 117 – Brown Velvet 68 (Mansingh   59 (USA) 120) [1995 71: 7.1d² 8.3g⁵ 1996 7s 10f² 6.9f 8.3s* 8d⁴ 8.3m 10.8g⁴ 10f³ 8m* 8m³ 8.5g³ 8m² 7m Jul 21] workmanlike gelding: modest performer: won claimers at Hamilton in May and Goodwood in June: best form at around 1m: acts on good to firm and soft ground: has hung left, and looked untrustworthy on occasions: has joined Noel Chance. *M. R. Channon*

SUN O'TIROL (IRE)   2 b.c. (Apr 20) Tirol 127 – Nous 76 (Le Johnstan 123)   65 d [1996 5.1g⁵ 6s 7m 6.9m* 7m⁴ 7.3m 8d 8m Sep 26] IR 6,600F, IR 7,000Y: work-manlike colt: half-brother to several winners, including Irish 11f winner Autumn Gorse (by Salmon Leap): dam sprinter: much improved effort when winning maiden auction at Folkestone in July: disappointing: stays 7f: has joined J. R. Arnold. *M. R. Channon*

SUNSET HARBOUR (IRE)   3 br.f. Prince Sabo 123 – City Link Pet 79 (Tina's   51 Pet 121) [1995 53: 5f⁶ 5.2g⁵ 5g⁵ 6m⁴ 5.1h³ 5.2d 1996 a6g² a5g³ a6g⁵ a6g³ a5g² a6g⁵   a60

5d 8m 7m 6m 5m³ 6g 5f* 5m⁴ 5f³ 5m Aug 29] tall filly: modest handicapper: trained first 2 starts by D. A. Wilson: sold out of T. J. Naughton's stable 1,900 gns Newmarket July Sales: first start for new yard (9 days later) when winning selling event at Redcar: effective at 5f (best turf form) and 6f: acts on hard ground and on equitrack: effective blinkered or not for former stable. *S. E. Kettlewell*

SUNSET WELLS (USA)   3 b.f. Sadler's Wells (USA) 132 – Alysunset (USA)   79
73 (Alydar (USA)) [1995 NR 1996 10g² 12m² 10g⁴ a9.4g 9f Nov 25] \$170,000Y: angular, unfurnished filly: unimpressive mover: first foal: dam, Irish 8.5f winner at 2 yrs, half-sister to several winners, among them Irish Derby winner St Jovite and very smart French middle-distance performer Norberto: fair maiden: ran poorly last 2 starts, leaving D. Loder in between: effective at 1¼m ridden for stamina and will stay beyond 1½m: carried head high and wandered second start. *H. J. Bond, USA*

SUNSHACK   5 b.h. Rainbow Quest (USA) 134 – Suntrap (USA) 112 (Roberto   121
(USA) 131) [1995 122: 12v⁴ 12g* 12f* 12d⁵ 15.5f* 1996 12.5g² 12m³ Sep 1] leggy, attractive horse: very smart performer: won Coronation Cup and Prix Royal-Oak in 1995: below form when short-head second of 6 to Water Poet in listed race at Deauville: back to best when 2½ lengths third of 7 to Pilsudski in Grosser Preis von Baden following month: effective at 1½m and stays 2m: acts on firm and soft going: normally held up: genuine: stays in training. *A. Fabre, France*

SUPAMOVA (USA)   3 b.f. Seattle Slew (USA) – Maximova (FR) 121 (Green   80
Dancer (USA) 132) [1995 88p: 7d³ 6d⁵ 1996 7m⁴ 10.1g² 12.3d³ 8.5m* 8m Sep 28] tall, lengthy filly: reportedly suffers from breathing problems: fair performer on balance of form: dominated maiden at Epsom in September, beating rather unlucky Lucky Archer by ¾ length: well beaten in listed rated stakes at Ascot 17 days later: stays 1¼m: yet to race on extremes of going. *P. F. I. Cole*

SUPAROY   3 b.g. Midyan (USA) 124 – Champ d'Avril 89 (Northfields (USA))   53 d
[1995 62d: 6m⁵ 8f³ 8g 10d a10g a8g⁴ 1996 a8g⁶ a10g⁵ a11g² a11g a12g² 12m a16g May 25] neat gelding: modest maiden: probably stays 1½m: acts on firm ground and the all-weather: inconsistent. *T. G. Mills*

SUPERBELLE   2 b.f. (Feb 9) Damister (USA) 123 – Nell of The North (USA)   78
(Canadian Gil (CAN)) [1996 7m³ 7f² a7g² a8.5g³ Dec 14] 6,000F, 8,000Y: leggy, unfurnished filly: sister to a winner in Norway and half-sister to 4-y-o 1m and 8.5f winner Super High (by Superlative) and 3 winners abroad: dam won at up to 9f in USA: fair form in maidens: should stay 1¼m: acts on fibresand. *M. A. Jarvis*

SUPER BENZ   10 ch.g. Hello Gorgeous (USA) 128 – Investiture 62 (Welsh   84
Pageant 132) [1995 65: a7g* a7g⁴ a7g³ a8g³ a6g⁶ a7g³ 7m* 7m² 7h² 6m 7g 7f³ 7m³ a7g a7g⁴ 1996 a8g* a7g⁵ a6g* a7g* 7s* 6g* 7g May 25] leggy, lengthy gelding: fairly useful performer: has won at least once every year since 1988: in excellent form in 1996, winning at Southwell (twice), Lingfield, Catterick and Ripon, particularly impressive in competitive 24-runner contest on last-named course: reportedly finished lame final start: effective at 6f to 1m: acts on hard and soft ground and on all-weather surfaces: tried blinkered and visored, no improvement: successful for apprentice: tough and game. *J. L. Eyre*

SUPERBIRD   3 b.f. Superpower 113 – Gymcrak Lovebird 84 (Taufan (USA) 119)   –
[1995 NR 1996 7m 13.8g 8m Jun 17] 2,300F: angular filly: second foal: half-sister to 4-y-o 5f and 6f winner Dominelle (by Domynsky): dam 5f (at 2 yrs) to 1¼m winner: no worthwhile form: tried blinkered. *T. D. Easterby*

SUPERBIT   4 b.g. Superpower 113 – On A Bit 66 (Mummy's Pet 125) [1995 52:   64
a5g⁵ a5g³ a6g² a6g³ a5g 5d a5g 5.1m a6g 5.1m* 5g³ 5g 5.1f⁴ 5.1m⁶ 5m 5f 6d a7g⁴   a53
a6g⁶ a5g³ 1996 a8g a5g 6m 5.1m² 5m³ 6m* 5.1m³ 6.1m 5.1g⁵ 5m 5.1g* a6g³ a5g⁵ Nov 30] small, good-bodied gelding: poor mover: modest handicapper: won 22-runner seller at Haydock (dead-heated, rallying gamely) in September and 17-runner minor event at Nottingham in October: effective at 5f, and stays 7f: acts on firm and dead ground and on fibresand: blinkered (finished last) once. *B. A. McMahon*

SUPERBOOTS   2 b.f. (May 3) Superpower 113 – Wellington Bear (Dragonara   –
Palace (USA) 115) [1996 5f⁵ a5g 5f 6m 7.5m 6s Oct 5] workmanlike filly: half-sister to 1989 2-y-o 7f winner Freddie's Star (by Tina's Pet) and 1992 2-y-o 6f winner Marchwell Lad (by Marching On): dam unraced: poor plater: blinkered (no form) final start: sold 800 gns Doncaster October Sales. *W. W. Haigh*

SUPERCAL 2 gr.f. (Jan 30) Environment Friend 128 – Sorayah 89 (Persian Bold 83
123) [1996 5m⁶ 6d⁶ 6m* 6m* 7m Jun 20] 7,200Y: tall, quite attractive filly: fifth
foal: half-sister to 3 winners, including 1995 2-y-o Ginger Glint (7f, by Hadeer): dam
sprinter here, later won at up to 11f in USA: improved form to win maiden at Folkestone and median auction event at Epsom in May/June: never reached challenging
position in Chesham Stakes at Ascot: will probably stay middle distances.
D. R. C. Elsworth

SUPERCHARMER 2 ch.g. (Feb 13) Charmer 123 – Surpassing 79 (Superlative 69
118) [1996 5g 6g³ 6f⁴ 6m⁶ 7f⁴ 7g 7g⁵ Oct 2] sturdy gelding: has scope: second foal:
dam, 7f winner at 2 yrs, stayed 9f: fair maiden: stays 7f: acts on firm ground:
blinkered (went very freely, tailed off) third start: pulled too hard sixth outing: sold
6,000 gns Newmarket Autumn Sales: joined D. Nicholls. *C. E. Brittain*

SUPERCOOL 5 ch.g. Superlative 118 – Florentynna Bay 61 (Aragon 118) [1995 –
56d: a8g a8.5g⁴ 8d a7g a9.4g 1996 a7g a11g a8g⁶ Feb 23] strong gelding: poor
maiden: stays 8.5f: acts on fibresand. *D. W. Chapman*

SUPERENSIS 6 ch.g. Sayf El Arab (USA) 127 – Superlife (USA) 64 (Super –
Concorde (USA) 128) [1995 NR 1996 10.1m Sep 18] poor miler here in 1993:
subsequently campaigned in Jersey, winning over 7f in 1995: well held in seller at
Yarmouth on return here. *John Berry*

SUPERFRILLS 3 b.f. Superpower 113 – Pod's Daughter (IRE) 43 (Tender King 50
123) [1995 48: 5f 5m 5f³ 5f⁶ 5g³ 5g a5g 5f 1996 5g⁴ 5g 5m 5m² 5g⁵ 5g 5.1g Oct 9]
small filly: poor maiden: has raced only at 5f on a sound surface: none too consistent.
Miss L. C. Siddall

SUPERGOLD (IRE) 3 ch.g. Keen 116 – Superflash (Superlative 118) [1995 –: –
a8.5g 1996 a7g Feb 9] well beaten in maidens: tried blinkered: has joined C. Murray.
W. A. O'Gorman

SUPER HERO 4 ch.g. Superlative 118 – Beaute Fatale (Hello Gorgeous (USA) 39
128) [1995 NR 1996 7d 7.1m 8.1m² Jul 24] small gelding: rated 61 at 2 yrs: only poor
form in 1996: stays 1m, will prove as effective at 7f. *A. G. Newcombe*

SUPER HIGH 4 b.g. Superlative 118 – Nell of The North (USA) (Canadian Gil 59
(CAN)) [1995 65, a75: 7g⁶ a8g* a8.5g* 8m 8g⁵ 7d 9.7s² 9.7g⁴ 8.2m³ 8.1s 1996 8m a87
10g a9.4g³ a8.5g³ 10g a8.5g* a9.4g³ a9.4g² 10m 10.1m³ a8.5g Nov 16] big, good-
topped gelding: has a round action: fairly useful handicapper on the all-weather,
winner at Wolverhampton in August: only modest on turf: stays 1¼m: acts on good
to firm and soft ground and goes well on fibresand: often blinkered: has had tongue
tied down: often early to post: usually races prominently. *P. Howling*

SUPERHOO 5 b.g. Superlative 118 – Boo Hoo 68 (Mummy's Pet 125) [1995 NR –
1996 12m 15.8s 15.8g Sep 21] poor maiden for C. Thornton at 3 yrs: won handicap
hurdles in May and June but no encouragement on flat in 1996. *R. Craggs*

SUPERIOR FORCE 3 ch.g. Superlative 118 – Gleeful 72 (Sayf El Arab (USA) 68
127) [1995 63: 6s⁴ 6.9g 1996 7g 7f³ 7.1d⁵ 8.3m 8.3m a8g* 8m² a10g³ 10.1g⁶ 8.1m⁶
a7g 8f 8.1m* 8.5m 8d Oct 12] smallish, workmanlike gelding: fair handicapper: won
at Lingfield (maiden event) in June and at Sandown (got up close home) in September: stays 1¼m: acts on firm and soft ground and on equitrack. *Miss B. Sanders*

SUPERIOR PREMIUM 2 br.c. (Apr 26) Forzando 122 – Devils Dirge 68 (Song 94
132) [1996 5.1d* 5d² 5f² 5f⁶ 5m⁶ 5m² 5v* 5d⁵ 6g⁵ Oct 26] 3,800F, 2,800Y: good-
topped colt: progressed physically: second foal: dam maiden who probably stayed
7f: fairly useful performer: won maiden auction at Nottingham in April and minor
event at Haydock in October: good fifth to Easycall in Cornwallis Stakes at Ascot on
penultimate outing: stays 6f: acts on any ground: sometimes edgy in preliminaries:
reliable. *R. A. Fahey*

SUPERLAO (BEL) 4 b.f. Bacalao (USA) – Princess of Import (Import 127) 45
[1995 57: a5g⁴ a5g² 7.5d a5g⁶ 5f 5f* 5f⁴ a5g a8g 1996 a6g⁶ a5g⁶ a6g a5g⁶ a5g a5g a49
6m 5m³ 5f³ 5f⁴ 6m 5f⁴ 5g 5m 6m⁴ 5f Sep 5] ex-Belgian filly: winner 5 times in
Belgium: poor form in handicaps here, leaving Andre Hermans after third 4-y-o start:
stays 6.5f: acts on firm ground and dirt. *J. J. Bridger*

SUPERMICK 5 ch.g. Faustus (USA) 118 – Lardana 65 (Burglar 128) [1995 –: 43
10g 7m 7m 1996 10m 13.1f³ 14.1f* 12g* 12m³ a14g 12m⁵ 14s Oct 5] angular
gelding: poor handicapper: won at Nottingham (seller) and Epsom in July: stays

1¾m: acts on firm ground (below form on soft) and all-weather surfaces: tried visored and blinkered: modest hurdler, winner in November: game. *W. R. Muir*

SUPERMISTER 3 br.g. Damister (USA) 123 – Superfina (USA) (Fluorescent – Light (USA)) [1995 51: 7m⁵ 7.5m 6m⁵ 8g⁴ 1996 7m⁶ 8m 7m 6.9f 9.9g Aug 24] workmanlike gelding: modest form at 2 yrs: well held in 1996: tried blinkered. *T. D. Easterby*

SUPERMODEL 4 gr.f. Unfuwain (USA) 131 – Well Off (Welsh Pageant 132) 55 [1995 NR 1996 a16g² 10m⁵ 11.5m⁴ a14.8g³ Sep 21] 7,000Y: half-sister to several winners, including useful 6f and 7f winner Royal Loft (by Homing) and fairly useful 9f winner Jiggery Pokery (by Final Straw), dam, of little account, half-sister to useful sprinter Doc Marten: only start for M. Johnston, second in claimer at Southwell in January: winning hurdler for new yard: respectable efforts on return to flat: stays 2m: acts on fibresand. *Mrs N. Macauley*

SUPER MONARCH 2 ch.c. (May 7) Cadeaux Genereux 131 – Miss Fancy That 71 p (USA) 99 (The Minstrel (CAN) 135) [1996 7d Aug 23] sturdy, good-bodied colt: fourth foal: half-brother to 3-y-o 1¾m winner Fancy Heights (by Shirley Heights) and 7.1f (at 2 yrs) and 10.1f winner Tajannab (by Kris): dam 2-y-o 7f winner, closely related to top-class French 1m/9f winner Thrill Show: 20/1, over 8 lengths seventh of 13 in Newmarket maiden won by Yalaietanee, keeping on not knocked about: wore bandages behind: upset at stalls: will do better. *E. A. L. Dunlop*

SUPEROO 10 b.g. Superlative 118 – Shirleen (Daring Display (USA) 129) [1995 70 75: 7m 8.5m³ 8g³ 7.5m 7m* 8.5m 8d 7f a7g a7g* a7g* a7g 1996 a7g⁶ Jan 20] big, workmanlike gelding: fair handicapper: respectable effort only 10-y-o outing: effective at 7f to 8.5f: acts on firm going and equitrack: blinkered 4 times (including when successful) at 7 yrs. *Mrs P. Sly*

SUPER PARK 4 b.g. Superpower 113 – Everingham Park 54 (Record Token 128) 61 d [1995 69: 6f⁴ 5m 6g 5.1d 5d 5f 7f 1996 a8g 6.9m⁴ 7m 6g⁴ 7f⁴ 7.5m⁶ 7.6m³ 7f 7m 7f 8m a9.4g a8g Dec 3] strong, lengthy gelding: modest at best in 1996, below even that form last 6 starts: stays 7.6f: acts on firm and dead ground: no improvement in blinkers: inconsistent. *J. Pearce*

SUPERPRIDE 4 b.g. Superpower 113 – Lindrake's Pride (Mandrake Major 122) 69 [1995 69: 5g 5m² 5g³ 6m 6d 7f 5m 1996 5.9d⁴ 7m 6.9g⁶ 6m³ 6m 5.9f⁴ 10m⁴ 9f 7g* 7m⁶ 7m² 7g 7g 7m Oct 29] good-topped gelding: fair handicapper: won at Ayr in August: well beaten last 3 starts: effective as sprinter and seems to stay 1¼m: acts on good to firm and dead ground: blinkered fourth to sixth 4-y-o starts, no improvement: usually races prominently. *Mrs M. Reveley*

SUPERQUEST 2 ch.c. (Apr 28) Superlative 118 – More Or Less 64 (Morston 64 (FR) 125) [1996 a6g⁴ 6f³ 6f⁴ 7f⁶ 7m⁵ a7g⁶ Aug 9] 10,000Y: brother to Oaks third Pearl Angel, 7f winner at 2 yrs, and half-brother to several winners: dam winning stayer: modest maiden: stays 7f: blinkered (below form) final start: sent to Malaysia. *W. A. O'Gorman*

SUPER ROCKY 7 b.g. Clantime 101 – Starproof 46 (Comedy Star (USA) 121) 71 [1995 78, a67+: a5g 5g* 5g⁶ 5.2m² 5m* 5f* 5m* 5m 5d 5f⁵ a5g* 1996 a5g* a5g⁴ a5g 5m⁵ 5.1g² 5m⁴ 5g a5g⁶ 5.2g³ 5m³ 5f² 5m⁶ 5m Aug 26] good-topped gelding: fair handicapper: won at Wolverhampton in January: best form at 5f: acts on firm going and the all-weather: effective blinkered or not: tends to hang left: wears bandages: successful for apprentice: has run well when sweating. *R. Bastiman*

SUPER SAINT 2 b.g. (Feb 5) Superpower 113 – Martyrdom (USA) (Exceller 57 (USA) 129) [1996 5g⁶ a5g⁵ 5f⁴ 6g⁴ 6g³ 7g⁴ 7f Sep 27] 5,200Y: tall, unfurnished gelding: fifth foal: half-brother to 3-y-o 1½m winner Newbridge Boy (by Bustino): dam unraced: modest maiden: sold 3,000 gns Doncaster October Sales: stays 7f: best form on good ground: failed to handle bends on both outings at Catterick: sent to Belgium. *T. D. Barron*

SUPER SCRAVELS 2 ch.f. (Mar 10) Superlative 118 – Scravels Saran (IRE) 57 37 (Indian King (USA) 128) [1996 5m 6f³ a5g 7.5m 7.1m² 7m³ 6g⁵ 7.1m 6.9d Oct 21] first foal: dam, only worthwhile form when placed over 7f at 2 yrs, became ungenuine: poor plater: sold 1,100 gns Doncaster November Sales: stays 7f: inconsistent. *Dr J. D. Scargill*

SUPER SERENADE 7 b.g. Beldale Flutter (USA) 130 – Super Melody 72 58
(Song 132) [1995 54: 6m 8.3m³ 7.1m 8.3m 8.3m⁵ 8f² 8m⁴ 1996 7.1g⁵ 9.7f⁴ 8.1f*
9.2m 8m⁵ 11.6d⁴ 12d 10f⁶ Sep 4] angular gelding: modest handicapper: ran in
amateurs races in 1996, winning at Chepstow in July: effective at 1m and probably
stays 11.6f: acts on firm ground, soft and equitrack: sometimes sweats. *G. B. Balding*

SUPER SHERIFF 2 b.c. (May 3) Superpower 113 – Spinney Hill (Dominion 39
123) [1996 5m⁵ 5m 5m May 21] workmanlike colt: fifth foal: half-brother to a winner
in Belgium by Dashing Blade: dam poor close relative of prolific winner Misty Halo:
probably just a poor plater. *M. W. Easterby*

SUPER SONATA 4 b.f. Interrex (CAN) – Super Lady (Averof 123) [1995 52, a–: –
a5g 5m⁶ 5m³ 5m a5g 1996 a5g 5m 5g 5g⁵ 5m a5g 5.1f Sep 12] small filly: modest
sprinter at best in 1995: little form at 4 yrs: tried visored/blinkered. *T. Wall*

SUPERTOP 8 b. or br.g. High Top 131 – Myth 89 (Troy 137) [1995 54: 11.1g⁶ –
12m 1996 10.9m Sep 19] leggy, workmanlike gelding: modest handicapper on flat in
1995: mid-division in amateurs race at Ayr only 8-y-o start: fairly useful hurdler,
winner 4 times before end of year. *L. Lungo*

SUPLIZI (IRE) 5 b.h. Alzao (USA) 117 – Sphinx (GER) (Alpenkonig (GER)) 101
[1995 NR 1996 12.3g* 13.3d⁴ May 18] smart performer (rated 112) in 1994: shaped
as though retaining his ability after 21-month absence when winning slowly-run
4-runner minor event at Ripon in April: well held in listed race at Newbury 3 weeks
later, and sold only 6,000 gns Newmarket Autumn Sales: stays 1½m: acts on good to
firm and dead going. *L. M. Cumani*

SUPPLY AND DEMAND 2 b.g. (Mar 29) Belmez (USA) 131 – Sipsi Fach 100 80 +
(Prince Sabo 123) [1996 7m² 7m⁵ 7g⁵ 8g 8s⁶ Nov 9] 20,000Y: second foal: dam 6f
(at 2 yrs) to 10.4f winner: fairly useful maiden: tenderly handled throughout (trainer
fined and later banned) in median auction maiden at Doncaster final start: will be
suited by middle distances: twice slowly away: capable of winning a race.
G. L. Moore

SUPREME DESIRE 8 gr.m. Grey Desire 115 – Fire Mountain 87 (Dragonara –
Palace (USA) 115) [1995 –: 5m 5g 5m 5m 6.1m 7.5m 1996 5g⁶ 5.1m 5g 5g 5.1g a8g
Nov 18] angular mare: no longer of any account. *Miss J. F. Craze*

SUPREME ILLUSION (AUS) 3 ch.f. Rory's Jester (AUS) – Counterfeit Coin –
(AUS) (Comeram (FR) 127) [1995 NR 1996 a5g a5g 6s a7g⁴ a8g 10g⁴ a8g⁶ 7f a6g
a8.5g Dec 28] third foal: half-sister to a winner in Macau by Danzatore: dam winner
3 times in Australia and third in Queensland Oaks: bought out of P. Chapple-Hyam's
stable 1,800 gns Newmarket December (1995) Sales: of little account: tried
blinkered. *John Berry*

SUPREME MAIMOON 2 b.c. (Apr 27) Jareer (USA) 115 – Princess Zena 96 70 p
(Habitat 134) [1996 6g⁶ a7g* Dec 13] 3,500Y: half-brother to several winners,
including 4-y-o 7f winner Brave Princess (by Dancing Brave) and very smart 1m to
1¼m winner Supreme Leader (by Bustino): dam, 2-y-o 5f winner, half-sister to dam
of Pebbles: confirmed debut promise when winning maiden auction at Lingfield
by 4 lengths, forging clear final 1f: will stay 1m: will probably improve again.
M. J. Polglase

SUPREME SCHOLAR 3 b.f. Superpower 113 – Double Decree 69 (Sayf El –
Arab (USA) 127) [1995 –: 5m 6g 1996 6s Mar 26] sparely-made filly: no sign of
ability: tried blinkered. *B. W. Murray*

SUPREME SOUND 2 b.c. (Apr 6) Superlative 118 – Sing Softly 112 (Luthier 83 p
126) [1996 7g 8.1m² 10g* Oct 24] strong, lengthy colt: has a round action:
half-brother to 3-y-o Whispered Melody (by Primo Dominie) and fairly useful stayer
Top Cees (by Shirley Heights): dam, 6f winner at 2 yrs, later very useful over middle
distances: odds on, very easy winner of maiden at Nottingham in October, leading
early in straight and pulling 10 lengths clear before eased to beat Tommy Tortoise 2½
lengths: will stay 1½m: remains capable of better. *P. W. Harris*

SUPREME STAR (USA) 5 b.g. Gulch (USA) – Just A Game 108 (Tarboosh 64
(USA)) [1995 75, a59: 11.6m 12.5g* 12f³ 14g* 14f² 14m* 12m² 16g² 16.2d³ 16.2s⁶ a–
16m² 16.5m a16g³ a16g³ 1996 16m 16.4g 14m² 14m⁶ 11.6m⁶ 14m⁶ 14.4g⁶ a16g³
Dec 5] lightly-made, quite attractive gelding: fair handicapper, not at best in 1996:

stays 2m well: acts on firm and dead ground, modest form on the all-weather: tried blinkered/visored: won novice hurdle in September. *P. R. Hedger*

SUPREME THOUGHT   4 b.f. Emarati (USA) 74 – Who's That Girl (Skyliner   64 +
117) [1995 66d: 7g² 6m⁵ 5.1f⁵ 5d⁵ 5g 1996 7g⁵ 5f⁵ 6.1s Oct 22] tall filly: fair maiden handicapper, lightly raced: better than result suggests (poorly drawn) last 2 starts: stays 7f: acts on firm and dead ground: may be capable of better. *L. G. Cottrell*

SUPREMISM   2 b.c. (Mar 6) Be My Chief (USA) 122 – Ever Welcome 58 (Be   77
My Guest (USA) 126) [1996 7g⁵ 6m³ Jul 20] good-topped colt: fourth living foal: half-brother to 4-y-o 6f and 1m winner Tame Deer (by Hadeer) and 1m winner Exotic Forest (by Dominion): dam 4-y-o 1¼m winner: fair form in maidens at Newmarket: will stay middle distances: looked sure to improve. *C. E. Brittain*

SURAKO (GER)   3 bl.c. Konigsstuhl (GER) – Surata (Lagunas) [1995 7m³ 7g*   114
7g⁴ 8s* 8s³ 1996 8.5g* 11g² 12v² 12m⁴ 11g³ 10g Oct 3] brother to 8.3f to 10.5f winner Subia and half-brother to 6f and 1m winner Sunita (by Abary), both in Germany: smart German colt: won maiden at Gelsenkirchen and valuable event at Dusseldorf, then 4 lengths third of 11 to Lavirco in Preis des Winterfavoriten at Cologne at 2 yrs: won Group 3 event at Krefeld in April by a length from Lavirco: 2½ lengths second of 7 to Lavirco in Group 2 event at Cologne in June then 4 lengths second of 18 to Lavirco in Deutsches Derby at Hamburg in July: 4¼ lengths fourth to Hollywood Dream in Group 1 race at Dusseldorf but below best when ¾-length second (demoted) to Wurftaube in Group 3 race at Baden-Baden in August: ran poorly in Group 3 event at Hoppegarten last time: stays 1½m: acts on heavy ground and good to firm. *H. Jentzsch, Germany*

SURANOM (IRE)   4 b.c. Alzao (USA) 117 – Gracieuse Majeste (FR) (Saint   102
Cyrien (FR) 128) [1995 99: 8v* 8m² 10d* 11d² 1996 12.3g³ 12d* 12.3m⁵ 12d* 12m³ 10d⁵ Aug 25] useful performer: raced only at Milan at 3 yrs: successful in 1996 in minor events there in May and June: best effort here when third in similar contest at Ripon on reappearance: sold (L. Cumani to Mrs. D. Haine) 19,000 gns Newmarket Autumn Sales: probably stays 12.3f: has won on heavy going, below form on top-of-the-ground. *L. M. Cumani*

SURF CITY   3 ch.g. Rock City 120 – Waveguide 76 (Double Form 130) [1995 NR   61
1996 7d⁵ 7g 7.1d⁴ 7f⁶ 7.1d⁴ 6g 8m a8.5g⁴ a7g² a7g⁴ Nov 29] 5,800F, 8,600Y: sturdy gelding: sixth foal: half-brother to 1m winner Oneoftheoldones (by Deploy) and 1991 2-y-o winner Waveband (by Thatching): dam, placed at 5f at 2 yrs, out of half-sister to dam of Centrocon (dam of Time Charter) and Nicholas Bill: fair maiden: should stay beyond 7f: acts on dead ground and on fibresand. *W. W. Haigh*

SURPRISE EVENT   2 b.g. (Mar 7) Tragic Role (USA) – Eleckydo 47 (Electric   57 d
126) [1996 6.1g 6.1f³ 7f³ 7f⁴ a7g⁴ 6d⁶ Aug 24] first reported foal: dam poor maiden on flat (stayed 1½m) and over hurdles: modest maiden at best: ran poorly last 3 starts: stays 7f: blinkered final start. *W. G. M. Turner*

SURPRISE GUEST (IRE)   5 ch.g. Be My Guest (USA) 126 – Olderfleet 59   –
(Steel Heart 128) [1995 66d: a10g⁴ a12g² a13g⁴ 12m a14.8g 12f 14.1m 14.9m⁴ a12g 1996 a12g Jan 18] good-bodied gelding: on the downgrade, and well beaten only 5-y-o start: has joined T. Clement. *C. A. Dwyer*

SURPRISE MISSION   4 ch.g. Clantime 101 – Indigo 86 (Primo Dominie 121)   79
[1995 74p: 5m 5m 5g* 5.1m* 5f³ 1996 5m 5d⁵ 5m³ 5g 5g 5m 5m* 5d⁴ 5g 5g Oct 21] leggy gelding: fairly useful handicapper: left R. Whitaker after second 4-y-o start: won 21-runner contest at Doncaster (challenged on bridle 1f out) in September: speedy (travels strongly), and best at 5f: has raced mainly on a sound surface. *Mrs J. R. Ramsden*

SURREY DANCER   8 b.g. Shareef Dancer (USA) 135 – Juliette Marny 123   –
(Blakeney 126) [1995 60+: 12g³ 10.4m 1996 10.5v 10.1m 12v⁵ Nov 11] leggy gelding: usually impresses in appearance: has been fired: poor mover: fair handicapper on flat in 1994: not given hard time in 3 races at 8 yrs: suited by middle distances: probably acts on any going, very best efforts with some give: occasionally blinkered, not since 1993: has won for amateur/apprentice: usually held up, and suited by good gallop: useful hurdler, injured when winning in December. *Mrs M. Reveley*

SUSSEX GORSE   5 ch.g. Arrasas (USA) 100 – Testarossa (Tower Walk 130)   –
[1995 NR 1996 a8g a7g a16g 12m 16.4v a10g Nov 26] third reported foal: dam of little account: no better himself. *J. E. Long*

SUVALU (USA)   4 b.g. Woodman (USA) 126 – Danlu (USA) (Danzig (USA))   76 d
[1995 75: 8m³ 10m 10m⁵ 10.1m⁴ 1996 a8g* a12g a8.5g 10m 8.5m 10g May 24] tall,
close-coupled gelding: fair performer: trained in 1995 by P. Cole: made winning
debut for new connections in maiden at Southwell in February: well held in
handicaps afterwards: stays 1¼m: acts on fibresand, has raced only on a sound
surface on turf. *M. G. Meagher*

SVELTANA   4 b.f. Soviet Star (USA) 128 – Sally Brown 120 (Posse (USA) 130)   75
[1995 82: 7m* 8g⁴ 10g 1996 8g 10m 9m 10v Aug 27] leggy, angular filly: shows
knee action: fair handicapper: only form in 1996 when seventh of 12 to Moving
Arrow at Newmarket on second start: found little both subsequent outings: probably
stays 1¼m: should be suited by further than 1m: sold 36,000 gns Newmarket
December Sales. *G. Wragg*

SWAIN (IRE)   4 b.c. Nashwan (USA) 135 – Love Smitten (CAN) (Key To   125
The Mint (USA)) [1995 128: 14v* 14g* 14m* 12.5g* 12.5g* 12d³ 1996
10.5m³ 12m* 12m² 12m* 12d⁴ 12g³ Oct 26]
　　　　There were few better and none more consistent over middle distances
in Europe in 1996 than Swain. His only undisputed superior in a French stable
was the three-year-old Helissio, who beat him a length in the Grand Prix de
Saint-Cloud on their first meeting and by around six in the Prix de l'Arc de
Triomphe on their second. Fourth in the Arc was Swain's worst finish all
season. On his four other starts he came third in the Prix Ganay and the
Breeders' Cup Turf and won the Coronation Cup and the Prix Foy. Previously
Sheikh Mohammed's, this high-class colt has now joined the Godolphin
operation—one of the first to do so from France's top string—and it's a safe bet
that Andre Fabre was very sorry to see him go.

Vodafone Coronation Cup, Epsom—
Sheikh Mohammed has the first two home, Swain (right) and Singspiel

Swain was widely tipped to do well as a four-year-old, for obvious reasons. He had had six races the previous year and had lost only one, his last, when going down by three quarters of a length and two lengths to Lammtarra and Freedom Cry in the Arc. With those two retired, he looked set for a fairly smooth run until such time as he came up against the current classic crop, probably in either the King George VI and Queen Elizabeth Stakes or the Arc; many anticipated an even better showing from him in the latter race than as an inexperienced three-year-old. His main objective in 1996 before the King George was the Coronation Cup, and he started favourite at Epsom following a creditable run in conditions on the sharp side for him in the Prix Ganay when he finished a close third to Valanour and Luso. Swain started 11/10 favourite in a disappointingly small field for the Vodafone Coronation Cup, opposed by Singspiel, who had reportedly had a set-back since winning the Gordon Richards Stakes at Sandown, Fabre's De Quest and a typically high-flying runner of Clive Brittain's, Punishment. Swain had surprised some with his pace in his first Arc—he had been raced over a mile and three quarters on his first three starts—and he likewise surprised many by showing the pace to win in a sprint finish at Epsom. The field didn't begin to race in earnest there until three furlongs from home. Swain, who had led on sufferance, responded with great resolution when tackled by Singspiel and got home by a neck, the pair of them clear.

Swain failed to turn up for the King George. Firmish ground was given as the reason, but he had in the meantime met with that reverse in the Grand Prix de Saint-Cloud in late-June; and in any case, his owner had plenty to choose from for Ascot, Godolphin eventually running two, Classic Cliche and Annus Mirabilis. Swain looked to have a great chance of following his Coronation Cup victory with another at Saint-Cloud, and started a shade of odds on in a field which included the Prix du Jockey-Club winner Ragmar. But Helissio, highly regarded until only fifth behind Ragmar at Chantilly, redeemed himself by winning on merit by a length. Swain came out easily second-best ahead of another good four-year-old Poliglote, with Ragmar only seventh and on his way into retirement.

Swain had lost nothing in defeat. The Arc was still very much on the agenda, and he eventually started second favourite to Helissio for the race, coupled with Classic Cliche and Tamure, following his win in the Prix Foy on returning at Longchamp in September. The Foy was a farce of a race, but once more it served to confirm that Swain is rather more than a stayer. The element of farce lay in what passed for 'early pace' in what is supposed to be an Arc

Prix Foy, Longchamp—Swain just on top in another sprint finish; Pentire is beaten half a length

trial. There was no early pace, just a slow crawl. The King George winner Pentire, a 'turn-of-foot horse' par-excellence also warming up for the Arc, was sent into the lead with a mile to go. Swain tracked him, proved the stronger in the final stages, and won by half a length. Pentire started slowly in the Arc and never looked likely to get beyond mid-field. Swain did much better but he, too, never looked likely to win, niggled along out wide a good way from home, hanging early in the straight, then staying on to be nearest at the finish. He was beaten five lengths, a short neck and a length into fourth place behind Helissio, Pilsudski and Oscar Schindler. In hindsight his jockey (and some of the others) would almost certainly have taken care to lie up closer. Swain was reported to be lame afterwards but if that was so it can't have amounted to anything much. Three weeks later he was at Woodbine for the Breeders' Cup Turf, and in fine form. Despite losing his position making the turn for home, he finished third of fourteen behind Pilsudski and Singspiel, recovering ground well in the straight. The distances were one and a quarter lengths twice; Shantou completed a clean sweep for European horses in fourth and a two-three-four for Sheikh Mohammed.

Swain (IRE) (b.c. 1992)	Nashwan (USA) (ch 1986)	Blushing Groom (ch 1974)	Red God / Runaway Bride
		Height of Fashion (b 1979)	Bustino / Highclere
	Love Smitten (CAN) (b 1981)	Key To The Mint (b 1969)	Graustark / Key Bridge
		Square Angel (b 1970)	Quadrangle / Nangela

Good as he was at four, Swain did not show the amount of improvement from his three-year-old days that had been widely anticipated. It will be

Sheikh Mohammed's "Swain"

interesting to see what a winter in the sunshine does for him between four and five. His joining Godolphin will presumably mean that we are going to see more of him in Britain; if so, so much the better, for he will be a welcome runner in any of the top middle-distance races here. No doubt the Coronation Cup and the King George are again on the agenda for 1997. Whatever impression might have been given to the contrary at the time of his withdrawal from the last King George, Swain acts perfectly well on good to firm ground—he encountered it in all four of his starts before the Arc in 1996. He also acts on good to soft, almost certainly on heavy. Swain is a robust, attractive colt with a fluent, rather round action. A mile and a half suits him better than a mile and a quarter, though he is capable of high-class form at the shorter distance; he also stays a mile and three quarters and may well get further, given the opportunity. He is game and, as we said, very reliable. His breeding was detailed in *Racehorses of 1995*. His dam was a Grade 1 winner as a five-year-old, which is encouraging for his prospects at the same age. In the latest season there came along another above-average colt in France out of Love Smitten, namely Water Poet (by Sadler's Wells), winner of middle-distance listed races at Saint-Cloud and Deauville for Fabre, and not disgraced behind Helissio in the Prix Niel on his final outing. *A. Fabre, France*

SWALLOW BREEZE   2 b.f. (Apr 19) Salse (USA) 128 – Pica 84 (Diesis 133)   62 + [1996 6.9g 7g⁵ 7f⁴ 8d³ 10m* 10g Nov 2] 6,000Y, 8,200 2-y-o: workmanlike filly: has a round action: first foal: dam 12.5f winner who should have stayed 2m, out of half-sister to high-class US 2-y-o filly Althea (stayed 9f) and to dam of Green Desert: progressive form: edgy, won nursery at Nottingham in September, behind 4f out then staying on strongly: out of depth in listed race at Newmarket, though ran well in eighth of 10 (could be rated 70?) behind Silver Patriarch: suited by a good test of stamina: sometimes flashes tail. *Dr J. D. Scargill*

SWALLOWS DREAM (IRE)   5 ch.g. Bluebird (USA) 125 – Gay Fantasy   80 (Troy 137) [1995 88: 11.9m² 12g² 14g⁴ 12f³ 12g³ 12g 12s 10d 1996 10.8d² 10.3m⁵ 10m Jun 21] quite attractive gelding: fairly useful handicapper: easily best 5-y-o effort when second of 15 at Warwick on reappearance: effective at 10.8f, barely stayed 1¾m: acted on firm and dead going: blinkered (when out of form) last 2 starts at 4 yrs: normally held up: inconsistent: has been retired. *J. L. Dunlop*

SWAN AT WHALLEY   4 b.g. Statoblest 120 – My Precious Daisy (Sharpo 132)   71 [1995 71d: a5g 5g⁴ 5g 5.1m⁴ 5m⁴ 5f⁴ 5g 5m 1996 a5g⁴ a5g 5.1g³ a5g 5s 5g² 5g² 5f² 5g* 5m² 5f³ 5.1g 5m 5g Oct 19] compact gelding: fair sprint handicapper: won at Musselburgh (amateurs) in July: speedy, raced only at 5f: acts on firm ground: tailed off in visor and blinkers: usually a front runner: troublesome at stalls, 3 times leading to withdrawal in 1996. *Martyn Wane*

SWANDALE FLYER   4 ch.g. Weldnaas (USA) 112 – Misfire 56 (Gunner B 126)   – [1995 –: 9m 8g 8.1m⁵ 10.5g 10.5s 1996 a8g a7g⁶ 10d⁴ 11.9m 8d⁶ 10.5m⁶ 10g⁵ 10.9m 12.1d⁶ 15.1s Nov 7] big, workmanlike gelding: poor maiden handicapper: may prove best at around 1m. *N. Bycroft*

SWAN HUNTER   3 b.c. Sharrood (USA) 124 – Cache (Bustino 136) [1995 NR   73 1996 11.1g* 12d² 11.6g⁶ 14.8d⁶ 12m Sep 7] 7,000F, 16,500Y: angular, useful-looking colt: bad mover: first foal: dam, maiden, closely related to useful middle-distance winner Black Monday, later Grade 2 winner in USA: fair form first 3 starts, winning median auction maiden at Musselburgh in April: soundly beaten in handicaps last 2 outings: stays 1½m well: acts on dead ground. *D. J. S. Cosgrove*

SWAN ISLAND   2 ch.f. (Apr 9) Hubbly Bubbly (USA) – Green's Cassatt (USA)   62 74 (Apalachee (USA) 137) [1996 7g⁶ 7f 8.1s⁶ 7m² Oct 28] tall filly: first foal: dam 6f (at 2 yrs) to 11.9f winner: improved effort on nursery debut when ¾-length second of 17 at Leicester: should stay 1m: refused to enter stalls third intended start: wears bandages. *B. Palling*

SWEDISH INVADER   5 b.g. Jareer (USA) 115 – Nihad 76 (Alleged (USA) 138)   – [1995 NR 1996 8f 8m Jun 29] fair form (rated 68, sometimes none too keen) in 1994: modest winner over hurdles in 1995: last in handicaps, first races of any sort since. *J. White*

SWEEPING STATEMENT 2 b.f. (Feb 22) Statoblest 120 – Sweep Along 43
(IRE) 67 (Persian Bold 123) [1996 6m⁴ 7.1g⁴ a7g⁶ 7.1m* 7m⁶ Aug 2] 3,600Y: first
foal: dam poor maiden on flat and over hurdles: dictated steady pace and won bad
seller at Musselburgh in July: stays 7.1f: joined John Berry. *J. Berry*

SWEET ALLEGIANCE 6 b.m. Alleging (USA) 120 – Child of Grace 100 –
(King's Leap 111) [1995 59?: 8.3m 7.1m⁴ 7m⁶ 7g 8g 7d a8g 1996 a10g⁴ 10m 7.6m a45
7.6m 8m 9.7g Sep 27] leggy mare: poor maiden: well beaten after reappearance:
stays 1¼m: acts on good to firm ground and equitrack. *Jamie Poulton*

SWEET AMORET 3 b.f. Forzando 122 – Primrose Way 59 (Young Generation 52
129) [1995 –: 6g 6m 7.5d 1996 10d⁵ a9.4g* a12g⁵ a8g a8.5g 8m⁶ 7m⁶ 8m² 10m⁵ 8g
10.1m 6.9d 8g a10g² a10g⁶ a10g⁶ Dec 30] workmanlike filly: poor mover: modest
performer: made all in seller at Wolverhampton in April: effective at 1m, probably at
1½m: acts on good to firm ground and all-weather surfaces: usually races
prominently: has found little on occasions, and possibly none too keen: inconsistent.
P. Howling

SWEET BETTSIE 2 b.f. (Apr 9) Presidium 124 – Sweet And Sure (Known Fact 72
(USA) 135) [1996 5.7d 6s⁵ Oct 24] leggy filly: second reported foal: half-sister to
4-y-o 6f winner Dark Menace (by Beveled): dam well beaten: first home on
unfavoured far side (made all there) when fifth of 23 in maiden at Newbury in
October: unseated rider at stalls before debut: may do better still. *A. G. Foster*

SWEET DISORDER (IRE) 6 br.m. Never So Bold 135 – Mists of Avalon –
(USA) 76 (Nureyev (USA) 131) [1995 –: 11.9m a9.4g a12g 1996 a12g⁶ a10g Jan 13]
leggy, sparely-made mare: modest maiden (rated 58) at 3 yrs for G. Pritchard-
Gordon: successful 5 times since in Jersey, but well beaten back on mainland: has
joined H. Manners. *B. J. Meehan*

SWEET EMMALINE 2 b.f. (Feb 14) Emarati (USA) 74 – Chapelfell (Pennine 63 d
Walk 120) [1996 5g* 5m⁴ 5m³ 5m⁶ 5m a6g⁴ Nov 30] 2,800F, 3,500Y: workmanlike
filly: first foal: dam unraced daughter of Cesarewich winner Orange Hill, a half-sister
to top Canadian filly Carotene: made virtually all to win maiden auction at
Musselburgh in April: below form last 3 starts, off course 4½ months before seller on
final one: should stay 6f: has given trouble beforehand or gone freely down before
running poorly on 2 occasions. *W. G. M. Turner*

SWEETEN UP 2 b.f. (Mar 14) Shirley Heights 130 – Honeybeta 105 (Habitat 76
134) [1996 7f³ 7d² Oct 28] smallish, sturdy filly: sister to 5-y-o Honey Mount, fairly
useful middle-distance stayer at 3 yrs, and half-sister to 6f/7f winner Orthorhumbus
(by Aragon) and a winner in Norway: dam 9f to 1½m winner, daughter of Attica
Meli: placed in maidens at Warwick (running on from some way back) and Lingfield
(made most) in October: will be suited by middle distances. *H. R. A. Cecil*

SWEET MAGIC 5 ch.g. Sweet Monday 122 – Charm Bird 60 (Daring March 87
116) [1995 87: 5m² 6m³ 5m² 5m* 5m² 1996 6m 5m⁴ 6m 5m⁵ 6m 5m 5.2m Sep 17]
lengthy, plain gelding: tends to look dull in coat: fairly useful handicapper: well
below form last 3 outings, carrying head awkwardly final start: should stay 6f: acts
on firm ground: usually races prominently. *P. Howling*

SWEET MATE 4 ch.g. Komaite (USA) – Be My Sweet 78 (Galivanter 131) –
[1995 48, a60: a7g a8g³ a8g⁶ a6g* a6g⁴ 8g⁶ a8g⁶ 7.5m 6.1m⁵ 6m² 5f 5m⁵ 6d⁵ 7f⁴ 7m a62
a6g² a6g³ a7g⁶ 1996 a6g⁴ a7g* a7g² a7g⁴ a7g⁴ a6g 7g a8g Nov 26] workmanlike
gelding: has a round action: modest handicapper: has gained both his successes at
Southwell, and came wide and late to win narrowly in February: left S. R. Bowring
and off course 6½ months after sixth start: effective at 6f to 1m: acts on firm and dead
ground and goes well on fibresand: usually wears adapted (one-eyed) blinkers: has
run well when sweating: somewhat wayward, but successful for apprentice. *Martyn Meade*

SWEET NATURE (IRE) 3 b.f. Classic Secret (USA) 91 – So Kind 90 (Kind of 71
Hush 118) [1995 70+: 5.2g² 5g a6g* 6m 1996 6.1d⁴ 6g a6g 6g⁶ 7d Oct 26] sturdy
filly: fair handicapper: sold out of W. Jarvis's stable 800 gns Newmarket July Sales
after third 3-y-o start: will stay 7f: acts on fibresand and dead ground: blinkered (stiff
task) once at 3 yrs. *M. Halford, Ireland*

SWEETNESS HERSELF 3 ch.f. Unfuwain (USA) 131 – No Sugar Baby (FR) 89 p
(Crystal Glitters (USA) 127) [1995 74: 8.2d³ 7g⁴ 1996 10g³ 8.3s⁴ 9.9m⁴ 10m 10m

11.8g* 14s* 12.1s* 14.1s* 16.5s* Nov 9] tall, rather leggy filly: improved into a fairly useful handicapper, winning at Leicester (minor event) in August and at Haydock, Chepstow and Nottingham in October: completed 5-timer in 17-runner race at Doncaster in November, leading under 3f out and holding on by ½ length from Orchestra Stall: effective at 1½m and stays 16.5f: acts on good to firm ground, goes extremely well on soft: often claimer ridden: held up: game and genuine: may well be capable of better still. *M. J. Ryan*

SWEET NOBLE (IRE) 7 ch.g. The Noble Player (USA) 126 – Penny Candy (Tamerlane 128) [1995 NR 1996 21.6m Apr 29] no worthwhile form since 2 yrs. *K. J. Drewry, Isle of Man*

SWEET PAVLOVA (USA) 4 b.f. Zilzal (USA) 137 – Meringue Pie (USA) 59 (Silent Screen (USA)) [1995 71: 6m⁶ 8f 10.2m² 11.5f² 10.2h* 12m 1996 10.2f 11.9m³ 10g Aug 14] leggy, lengthy filly: fair middle-distance handicapper at best: out of form in 1996: has raced only on a sound surface, acts on hard ground. *P. F. I. Cole*

SWEET SERANADE (IRE) 3 b.f. Ballad Rock 122 – Little Honey (Prince Bee – 128) [1995 NR 1996 a8g a9.4g Apr 13] IR 2,000Y: fourth foal: dam unraced: tailed off in maiden and seller: has joined Miss J. Bower. *N. P. Littmoden*

SWEET SEVENTEEN 3 gr.f. Touch of Grey 90 – Westminster Waltz (Dance In – Time (CAN)) [1995 NR 1996 5g 6m⁵ 5m Aug 26] angular, workmanlike filly: fourth foal: sister to 4-y-o 1m and 9f winner Seventeens Lucky and half-sister to 1991 2-y-o 7f winner Juldee (by Cragador): dam twice-raced daughter of half-sister to Busted: no form. *H. J. Collingridge*

SWEET SUPPOSIN (IRE) 5 b.h. Posen (USA) – Go Honey Go (General – Assembly (USA)) [1995 61, a90: a8g³ a11g⁵ a8g² a7g* a7g* a7g³ a6g³ 6m 6.9m³ a81 d 6.9g a8.5g* a7g* 7.6m a7g* 8g a7g a8g a9.4g* a8g² 1996 a9.4g a8g⁵ a10g² a10g* a10g* a8g⁶ a12g* 10s a9.4g* a8.5g² a9.4g⁴ a9.4g a9.4g⁶ a12g⁴ a8g⁵ a12g a9.4g Dec 7] lengthy horse: fairly useful performer on the all-weather, modest on turf: won claimers at Lingfield (3) and Wolverhampton (claimed out of C. Dwyer's stable £8,000) by May: trained tenth start only by Miss S. Wilton, next 4 by John Berry before returning to present stable: stays 1½m: best efforts on good ground (seemed unable to act on soft) or the all-weather: usually blinkered in 1995/visored in 1996: normally held up. *C. A. Dwyer*

SWEET TIMES 3 ch.f. Riverman (USA) 131 – Affection Affirmed (USA) 57 (Affirmed (USA)) [1995 60p: 7g 7g⁶ 1996 7m⁴ a7g⁶ Jul 27] unfurnished filly: modest maiden: well beaten second 3-y-o start: should stay beyond 7f: sold 66,000 gns Newmarket December Sales. *P. F. I. Cole*

SWEET WILHELMINA 3 b.f. Indian Ridge 123 – Henpot (IRE) 68 (Alzao 65 (USA) 117) [1995 83p: 7g a7g* a8g* 1996 8.5g 7m 8g² a7s Nov 19] fair performer at 2 yrs: not seen in 1996 until late-August, only form when runner-up in a minor event at Brighton in October: will stay beyond 1m: yet to race on a soft surface, acts on all-weather surfaces. *Lord Huntingdon*

SWIFT 2 ch.c. (May 16) Sharpo 132 – Three Terns (USA) (Arctic Tern (USA) 126) 61 [1996 7m 7m 5f 5m⁶ 5g* 5.2g 5g⁶ Nov 1] 9,000F, 12,000Y: strong, lengthy colt: poor mover: third living foal: half-brother to smart French 1¼m performer Thames (by Fabulous Dancer): dam, French 9f winner from 2 starts, is out of top-class racemare Three Troikas: modest form: won weakly-contested 5-runner minor event at Catterick in October: bred to stay beyond 5f. *M. J. Polglase*

SWIFT FANDANGO (USA) 3 b.g. Lear Fan (USA) 130 – Danlu (USA) (Dan- 94 ? zig (USA)) [1995 90p: 7m* 7m² 1996 10g 8m 8m⁴ 10m Aug 16] tall, good-topped gelding: fairly useful form at 2 yrs: ran as if something amiss in listed race at Goodwood on reappearance: stiff tasks next 2 starts, possibly flattered in £14,000 conditions event on second of them: last of 15 in handicap at Newbury on final outing: sold 4,000 gns Newmarket Autumn Sales and gelded: unlikely to stay 1¼m: joined Lady Herries. *P. F. I. Cole*

SWIFT MAIDEN 3 gr.f. Sharrood (USA) 124 – Gunner Girl 85 (Gunner B 126) 77 [1995 62+: 6m⁶ 8.1m³ 8d³ 7.3d 7m 1996 8.2m 10.3m 8g 10s* May 29] sturdy filly: clearly best effort when very easy winner of claimer at Newbury in May, subsequently claimed £10,000: should stay further than 1¼m: goes very well on soft ground: races prominently. *J. Neville*

SWIFT MOVE 4 ch.f. Move Off 112 – Phyl's Pet (Aberdeen 109) [1995 –: 11.1g – 1996 11.1g⁶ Sep 2] tailed off in claimer and maiden. *P. Monteith*

SWIFT REFUSAL 2 ch.f. (Apr 9) Emarati (USA) 74 – Dark Hush (Kind of Hush 64 d 118) [1996 5s² 5.1g² 5f⁴ 5f⁶ 6m 5f 5m 5d Oct 21] 2,500Y: rather unfurnished filly: first foal: dam unraced daughter of half-sister to smart middle-distance stayer Rakaposhi King: looked a modest maiden early on, poor at best from late-June onwards: should prove suited by 6f+: best form on an easy surface: blinkered (no improvement) sixth outing: sold 500 gns Ascot December Sales. *M. J. Haynes*

SWIFTWAY 2 ch.g. (Mar 16) Anshan 119 – Solemn Occasion (USA) (Secreto 62 (USA) 128) [1996 7m⁶ 9f³ 10g Oct 24] 3,100Y: third live foal: dam twice-raced (at 2 yrs) half-sister to smart miler Soprano: easily best effort when third of 5 in maiden at Redcar, keeping on steadily: pulled up after bit reportedly slipped at Nottingham month later: probably a stayer. *K. W. Hogg, Isle of Man*

SWIFTY NIFTY (IRE) 3 b.f. Runnett 125 – Swift Verdict 89 (My Swallow 43 d 134) [1995 –: 5m 5m 5g 5s⁵ 5f 1996 5s 8.1g 7g 6m 5f 5f³ 5m 6f³ 6m 5g 5m 6f 5m a6g Nov 18] sparely-made filly: poor maiden, mostly disappointing: sold 1,600 gns Doncaster November Sales: should stay 7f: acts on firm ground: hung badly left fourth 3-y-o start: sent to Denmark. *W. W. Haigh*

SWING AND BRAVE (IRE) 2 b.f. (Apr 15) Arctic Tern (USA) 126 – Sweet – Snow (USA) (Lyphard (USA) 132) [1996 10v⁶ Nov 30] half-sister to several winners, notably very useful 1994 Gimcrack winner Chilly Billy (by Master Willie): dam French 10.5f winner out of Kentucky Oaks winner Sun And Snow: well beaten in maiden at Rome in November. *Lord Huntingdon*

SWINGING SIXTIES (IRE) 5 b.g. Fairy King (USA) – La Bella Fontana 65 (Lafontaine (USA) 117) [1995 64: 7.1m 7.6m 8g* 1996 9.7s* 10d 11.1s² May 3] tall, lengthy gelding: fair handicapper: won at Folkestone in March: stays 11f, at least in slowly-run race: acts on firm ground and soft: tried in blinkers/visor, better form without: sometimes slowly away: has joined T. Powell: none too consistent. *G. L. Moore*

SWINGING THE BLUES (IRE) 2 b.c. (Mar 1) Bluebird (USA) 125 – 55 + Winsong Melody (Music Maestro 119) [1996 6m 7m Oct 28] useful-looking colt: sixth foal: half-brother to several winners, including useful 5f performer El Yasaf (by Sayf El Arab) and 4-y-o 7.6f and 1¾m winner Norsong (by Northern State): dam sprint maiden: around 11 lengths eighth of 15 in maiden at Epsom, slowly away then hampered: still in need of race, below that form in steadily-run maiden at Leicester nearly 7 weeks later. *R. Akehurst*

SWINGS'N'THINGS (USA) 4 b.f. Shernazar 131 – Quickshine (USA) (The – Minstrel (CAN) 135) [1995 8m² 14m² 10g* 1996 9s 14g 12g 16g⁶ a14g Sep 9] ex-Irish filly: first foal: dam Irish maiden placed over 7f/1m: fairly useful form at 3 yrs, winning maiden at the Curragh (rated 84), before sold out of D. Weld's stable IR 13,000 gns Goffs November Sales: no form in 1996, for S. J. Treacy in Ireland on first 4 starts: stays 1¾m: acts on good to firm ground: tried blinkered, no improvement: modest hurdler, winner in October. *B. Palling*

SWING WEST (USA) 2 b.c. (Mar 12) Gone West (USA) – Danlu (USA) – (Danzig (USA)) [1996 8.1s Oct 22] fourth reported foal: closely related to 4-y-o 1m winner Suvalu (by Woodman) and half-brother to 3-y-o Swift Fandango (by Lear Fan), 7f winner at 2 yrs, and very smart 5-y-o middle-distance stayer Strategic Choice (by Alleged): dam, probably stayed 1¼m in Ireland, is sister to smart 6f/7f performer Nicholas out of half-sister to Nordance: 25/1, twelfth of 20 to Sausalito Bay in maiden at Chepstow, weakening from 2f out after chasing leaders: may do better. *P. F. I. Cole*

SWINO 2 b.g. (Apr 14) Forzando 122 – St Helena (Monsanto (FR) 121) [1996 5s³ 77 5g² 5g² 5g² 5.1g⁶ 5d² 5g² 5m² 5f* 6d Aug 24] 5,200Y: leggy, unfurnished gelding: unimpressive mover: half-brother to several winners in Italy, including one at 7f and 7.5f in 1996 by Beveled: dam, won 7 sprints in Italy, half-sister to useful sprinter Up And At'Em (by Forzando): fair form: easily made all in 5-runner maiden auction at

Carlisle in August: should stay 6f (possibly had worst of draw when tried): acts on firm and soft going: consistent. *P. D. Evans*

SWISS COAST (IRE) 2 b.c. (Apr 18) Mujadil (USA) 119 – Rose A Village 74 (River Beauty 105) [1996 5.9g² 6m⁵ 5m³ 5f³ 6f⁴ 6m² 7f² 7.5m Sep 18] IR 4,000F, 9,400Y: leggy, useful-looking colt: looked on weak side: has quick action: fourth foal: half-brother to a winner in Norway by Cut Above: dam maiden half-sister to smart 6f to 8.5f winner Rose Above: fair form: claimed out of Mrs J. Ramsden's stable £10,000 after sixth start: should prove as good at 7f as 6f: visored (below best) last 2 starts: temperament under suspicion. *N. Tinkler*

SWISS LAW 2 b.c. (Feb 22) Machiavellian (USA) 123 – Seductress 94 (Known 88 p Fact (USA) 135) [1996 6m² 7m Oct 1] 30,000Y: smallish, quite attractive colt: second foal: half-brother to German 3-y-o winner (at up to 1½m) Juicy (by Marju): dam sprinter: 16/1 and carrying condition, 3 lengths second of 8 to impressive winner Indiscreet in valuable maiden at York, tracking leaders and keeping on strongly: in need of race, not far below that form in valuable sales event at Newmarket 6 weeks later, held up in falsely-run race, off bridle 3f out and probably still green: should stay 1m: has joined Godolphin. *J. G. FitzGerald*

SWORD ARM 2 b.g. (Jan 25) Be My Guest (USA) 126 – Gai Bulga 110 (Kris 77 135) [1996 7g⁴ 7.6d⁴ 8.2m² Sep 16] rather leggy, lengthy gelding: good mover: first foal: dam effective from 1¼m to 1½m: progressive form in maidens: will be suited by middle distances: possibly not ideally suited by a soft surface: may do better: gelded. *R. Charlton*

SWORDKING (IRE) 7 ch.g. Kris 135 – Reine Mathilde (USA) 123 (Vaguely 41 Noble 140) [1995 47: a14g⁵ a14.8g a16.2g a14g⁴ 14.1g* 14.1g 14.1m a14.8g² 14.1g⁶ 14.1m⁵ a14.8g⁴ a14.8g³ a14g 1996 a14.8g a16.8g³ a16g³ a16g³ a14.8g³ a14g² a16.2g² a16g⁵ May 13] stocky gelding: poor handicapper: reluctant to race seventh 7-y-o outing: stays 16.2f: acts on fibresand, best turf form on good/dead ground: effective visored or not: inconsistent and not one to trust implicitly. *J. L. Harris*

SWYNFORD CHARMER 2 ch.g. (Apr 8) Charmer 123 – Qualitairess 49 – (Kampala 120) [1996 7m a6g a7g Dec 7] sixth foal: half-brother to 1m and 11.7f winner Swynford Flyer (by Valiyar): dam 1m winner: well held in sellers and a maiden event. *J. F. Bottomley*

SWYNFORD DREAM 3 b.g. Statoblest 120 – Qualitair Dream 80 (Dreams To 92 Reality (USA) 113) [1995 85: 5.1m⁵ 5g* 5g² 5g² 5m* 5m 1996 5g 5m² 5m 5m 5g 5m 5m⁶ 5.1d² 5m* 5d 5g³ 5g Oct 26] workmanlike gelding: fairly useful handicapper: gained a deserved success at Newmarket (made all) in October: speedy, and raced only at 5f: acts on good to firm and dead ground: usually races prominently: consistent. *J. F. Bottomley*

SWYNFORD FLYER 7 b.m. Valiyar 129 – Qualitairess 49 (Kampala 120) – [1995 32, a43: a9.4g a9.4g² a11g⁴ a12g a9.4g a9.4g 10m a8g 8f⁴ 8m⁶ 11.6m 8.3m a31 10m⁴ 7m 8.2m a8g a10g² a10g a10g⁴ 1996 a10g⁴ a10g⁶ a12g⁵ a12g a13g a11g⁶ Feb 10] plain, good-topped mare: poor handicapper at best nowadays: stays 1½m: acts on firm ground and the all-weather: tried blinkered: inconsistent. *J. A. Harris*

SWYNFORD SUPREME 3 ch.g. Statoblest 120 – Comtec Princess 73 (Gulf – Pearl 117) [1995 NR 1996 9m⁵ 10.1m³ 10m 10g 11f a12g Nov 2] big, plain gelding: half-brother to several winners, including 6-y-o Comtec's Legend (7f at 2 yrs to 12.3f, by Legend of France) and fairly useful Qualitair Aviator (up to 2m, by Valiyar): dam 1m to 1¼m winner: no worthwhile form: tried blinkered. *J. F. Bottomley*

SYCAMORE BOY (USA) 2 ch.c. (Mar 21) Woodman (USA) 126 – Kafiyah 67 (USA) 41 (Shadeed (USA) 135) [1996 6f⁵ Jul 19] $72,000F, IR 66,000Y: good-bodied colt: second foal: dam, 6f winner from 4 starts at 2 yrs, daughter of Grade 3 1½m-winning half-sister to Alydar's Best: 8/1, 5¾ lengths fifth of 13 to Cinema Paradiso in maiden at Newbury, running green early on then keeping on in good style: will be suited by 1m+: looked sure to improve. *Lord Huntingdon*

SYCAMORE LODGE (IRE) 5 ch.g. Thatching 131 – Bell Tower 98 74 (Lyphard's Wish (FR) 124) [1995 74: 7g³ 8m⁶ 7g² 7g² 8.9m⁶ 8f² 10f² 10.1m⁴ 10m⁵ 1996 6s² 7s³ 7.5m³ 8g⁴ a8g⁴ 7m² 7g⁵ 7g³ 7.1m⁵ 8f⁶ 6g* 7m⁶ Jul 13] lengthy gelding: shows a quick action: fair handicapper: finally won a race when beating Lough Erne a neck in maiden event at Doncaster in June: finds 6f a bare minimum, and stays

976

1¼m: acts on firm and soft ground: effective blinkered when trained in Ireland, tried here only on eighth 4-y-o start: tends to hang: has flashed tail: held up: consistent on form, but sometimes finds little, and one to be wary of. *Mrs J. R. Ramsden*

SYLVAN CELEBRATION 5 b.m. Sylvan Express 117 – Footstool 61 (Artaius – (USA) 129) [1995 –: 11.1g 13g 11.1g⁶ 9.2m 8.3f⁵ 11.1f⁵ 13.1f⁴ 1996 12.1d 12.3g Apr 10] tall mare: of little account on flat. *J. S. Goldie*

SYLVAN DANCER (IRE) 2 b. or br.f. (Apr 28) Dancing Dissident (USA) 119 64
– Unspoiled (Tina's Pet 121) [1996 5g² 5g³ 6m 5g Oct 19] quite attractive filly: fifth foal: half-sister to 1991 2-y-o 6f winner Sylvan (by Taufan): dam unraced half-sister to useful middle-distance colt Riberetto: modest maiden: sweating, hung badly left (looked virtually unrideable) second start: stays 6f. *C. F. Wall*

SYLVAN HEIGHTS 3 b.c. Reprimand 122 – Shibui (Shirley Heights 130) [1995 – NR 1996 10m 8.3g 11.4m⁴ Jul 17] first foal: dam granddaughter of Park Hill winner Quay Line: probably of little account. *R. T. Phillips*

SYLVANIA LIGHTS 2 b.f. (May 9) Emarati (USA) 74 – Harmony Park 55 – §
(Music Boy 124) [1996 a5g 5m Jul 18] 6,000Y: fourth foal: half-sister to 1994 2-y-o 6f winner Vocalize (by Petong): dam, 7f winner, sister to useful sprinter Melody Park: well beaten in sellers: has twice unseated rider beforehand and been withdrawn. *W. R. Muir*

SYLVAN JUBILACION 2 b.c. (May 6) Sylvan Express 117 – This Sensation –
48 (Balidar 133) [1996 7m 7d Oct 28] 1,200F, 4,000Y, 8,000 2-y-o: fifth foal: brother to a winner abroad, and half-brother to 1¾m winner Electrolyte (by Electric) and a winner in Germany: dam maiden sprinter: no promise either start. *P. Mitchell*

SYLVAN PRINCESS 3 b.f. Sylvan Express 117 – Ela-Yianni-Mou 73 (Anfield 67
117) [1995 –: 7.1m 10m 1996 11.1g⁵ 10d 8m⁶ 8f⁴ 7g³ 7.1m* 7m* 8g* 8m⁴ 8f* 8f³ 8m* 7g⁶ 8m 8m Sep 21] leggy, unfurnished filly: fair handicapper: successful at Sandown, Newcastle, Salisbury, Brighton and Yarmouth within 5 weeks in July/August, on last 2 occasions in minor events: effective at 7f/1m: acts on firm ground, well beaten only start on soft surface: tried blinkered, better without: usually apprentice ridden: tough. *C. N. Allen*

SYLVAN SABRE (IRE) 7 b.g. Flash of Steel 120 – Flute (FR) (Luthier 126) – §
[1995 NR 1996 11m 8m 10d Aug 25] modest handicapper (rated 64) when in the mood for P. Mitchell at 5 yrs: fair hurdler, finished lame in June: bandaged, well beaten on return to flat: unreliable. *K. A. Morgan*

SYLVA PARADISE (IRE) 3 b.c. Dancing Dissident (USA) 119 – Brentsville 98 +
(USA) (Arctic Tern (USA) 126) [1995 79: 6m⁶ 5.2g⁶ 6m⁴ 6d* 1996 8d 7f² 7g⁴ 7m³ 5f² 6f* 5m² 6m 5.6m² 6m 6m⁴ Sep 28] smallish, lengthy colt: made into a useful handicapper, winning at Yarmouth in July and good second in rated stakes at Ascot and the Portland (to Musical Season) at Doncaster: pulled up, reportedly lame, in Ayr Gold Cup penultimate start: clearly over that but probably flattered nonetheless when close fourth of 12 to Diffident in Diadem Stakes at Ascot following week, leading under 2f out in falsely-run race (could be rated 111): will prove best at up to 7f: successful on dead going, very best efforts on top-of-the-ground: consistent. *C. E. Brittain*

SYLVELLA 3 b.f. Lear Fan (USA) 130 – Suprematie (FR) (Gay Mecene (USA) 51
128) [1995 –: 6g 7m 1996 10d 8f⁵ 10f⁵ 8m⁴ 10.1m² 11.5m a12g³ 11f³ 12g Oct 18] leggy filly: modest maiden: sold 4,500 gns Newmarket Autumn Sales: stays 11f: acts on firm going, well held only start on fibresand: looked none too keen third 3-y-o start. *M. A. Jarvis*

SYMMETRICAL 7 ch.g. Kris 135 – Flawless Image (USA) 109 (The Minstrel –
(CAN) 135) [1995 NR 1996 a7g Aug 29] very lightly raced and little worthwhile form. *M. Madgwick*

SYMONDS INN 2 ch.c. (Feb 3) In The Wings 128 – Shining Eyes (USA) (Mr 96
Prospector (USA)) [1996 6m³ 7m² 8g³ Oct 21] 200,000 francs Y: rangy, rather unfurnished colt: fifth foal: half-brother to Italian 3-y-o 1m winner Jareer's Eye (by Jareer) and 1¼m winner (later 9.5f to 11f winner in France) Nedaarah (by Reference Point): dam unraced daughter of high-class French miler Phydilla, a half-sister to Observation Post: progressive form: 2½ lengths second to Revoque (In Command third) in Acomb Stakes at York in August: seemed not to go through with his

effort fully when beaten neck and ½ length by Entice and Fahris in listed race at Pontefract in October: will stay middle distances: easily good enough to win a race. *J. G. FitzGerald*

T

TAAHHUB (IRE)   6 b.g. Nordico (USA) – Undiscovered (Tap On Wood 130)   – [1995 47: a12g⁴ a10g 8m⁴ 10.8g⁴ 12.3m 1996 a12g Feb 21] big gelding: fairly useful form at 2 yrs: poor at best on flat since mid-1993, but did win 3 races over hurdles: stayed 1½m: blinkered once at 3 yrs: dead. *R. J. Price*

TA AWUN (USA)   3 b.f. Housebuster (USA) – Barakat 93 (Bustino 136) [1995   99 NR 1996 9s² 10m* 10g³ 12m 12g Sep 29] big, good-topped filly: has plenty of scope: second foal: half-sister to 4-y-o 7f winner Fakih (by Zilzal): dam, stayed 1¾m, half-sister to Ibn Bey and Roseate Tern out of half-sister to Teleprompter and Chatoyant: useful performer: easily made all in maiden at Ascot in July: best effort when third of 9 to Altamura in listed race at Salisbury: finished last (blinkered and looked leery in paddock final start) afterwards: should have stayed 1½m: visits Mark of Esteem. *A. C. Stewart*

TABLETS OF STONE (IRE)   3 b.g. Contract Law (USA) 108 – Remember   46 Mulvilla (Ballad Rock 122) [1995 –: 6m 6f 8.2m 8f a10g 1996 a10g⁴ 9.7m 10.8m⁴   a41 a12g 12s⁶ a14g Nov 22] compact gelding: poor maiden: stays 1½m: acts on good to firm ground, probably on soft: tried visored, no improvement. *J. R. Bosley*

TABL (IRE)   3 b.f. Nashwan (USA) 135 – Idle Gossip (USA) (Lyphard (USA)   59 132) [1995 NR 1996 8g⁴ 10m⁵ 8m³ 7f³ 8d 12.5m Oct 10] workmanlike filly: fifth foal: sister to disappointing 1995 3-y-o Incha and half-sister to a winner abroad by Sharpen Up: dam won from 6f to 9f in USA and from good family: modest maiden: trained first 3 starts by H. Thomson Jones: probably stays 12.5f: well beaten only outing on a soft surface. *David Wachman, Ireland*

TABRIZ   3 b.f. Persian Heights 129 – Faisalah (Gay Mecene (USA) 128) [1995 74:   75 d 5m³ 7m³ 6m³ 7m² 7d⁶ 8m⁶ 7.1s⁴ 1996 8.5d* 10m 8.3s³ 8g⁵ 9.9f 8m a12g² 11.1m⁴ a14g 10.3g Oct 26] angular, leggy filly: has a round action: fair handicapper: won at Beverley in March: below form afterwards: sold (J. Bethell to Mrs P. Avison) 3,800 gns Newmarket Autumn Sales: seems to stay 1½m: best efforts on good to firm and dead ground: soundly beaten in visor/blinkers: often gives trouble in preliminaries: not one to trust. *J. D. Bethell*

TACHYCARDIA   4 ch.f. Weldnaas (USA) 112 – Gold Ducat 74 (Young Genera-   49 tion 129) [1995 50, a44: a8g⁴ a10g a8g⁵ a6g a6g a6g a7g⁵ 5m³ 5.3m* 6g 5m² 6f⁶   a43 5.3f³ 6m 5g 6m⁵ 5.3m⁴ 5f 5m a5g⁴ a6g Dec 5] rather sparely-made filly: poor handicapper: effective at 5f and stays 8.5f: acts on firm ground and all-weather surfaces (below form on a soft surface): none too consistent. *R. J. O'Sullivan*

TADELLAL (IRE)   5 ch.m. Glint of Gold 128 – Meissarah (USA) (Silver Hawk   – (USA) 123) [1995 59, a64: 12g⁵ 7f⁵ 10m 11.5m⁵ a10g 10g a10g* a10g* 10.2m³ a14.8g⁵ a12g⁴ a10g² a12g⁵ a12g⁴ 1996 a10g a10g⁵ a11g Nov 4] modest performer at 4 yrs, no form in 1996: stayed 1¼m: dead. *W. G. M. Turner*

TADEO   3 ch.g. Primo Dominie 121 – Royal Passion 78 (Ahonoora 122) [1995 92:   107 5m⁴ 5f² 5f* 5.1f² 5f² 5f⁵ 5m⁶ 6.1m³ 5g² 5m⁵ 5g³ 6g⁴ 5g* 1996 5.1g³ 5m 5f 5m⁵ 5.1m² 5m 6m 5m 5d 5s* 5d* 5g 6s⁵ Nov 9] small, strong gelding: useful performer: gelded after eighth start: improved form afterwards, making all in minor event at Haydock and £18,200 handicap at Ascot (battled on well, holding To The Roof by a length) within 8 days in October: best effort when fifth of 16 to Astrac in listed race at Doncaster: effective at 5f and 6f: acts on any ground, but does seem to go well with some give: usually races prominently. *M. Johnston*

TAEL OF SILVER   4 b.f. Today And Tomorrow 78 – Schula 81 (Kala Shikari   70 125) [1995 69, a57: a6g⁶ a7g⁵ a7g⁶ 6.1g* 6.1m 6m 6m⁶ 5m* 6g² 6g³ 6f⁶ a6g 6.1d³ 6g   a43 5.1m 1996 a6g 6g⁵ 6.1m a6g 7g* 8m² 9m⁴ 8.2m 7m 7g 7.1s⁴ 8.2g⁶ 8.1s a7g² a8g Dec 3] leggy filly: fair handicapper on turf, poor on the all-weather: trained by K. Burke until after fifth 4-y-o start: 25/1, back to best on first start for new stable when winning at Doncaster in June: stays 9f: acts on good to firm and dead ground: no improvement in blinkers or visor: none too consistent. *A. Bailey*

TAFAHHUS 4 b.g. Green Desert (USA) 127 – Mileeha (USA) 97 (Blushing Groom (FR) 131) [1995 84d: 6.1g⁴ 6m* 7f⁵ 6f* 6m³ 6g 6f* 6m* 6g⁵ 6m 5m⁶ a6g a6g a6g 1996 a8g a8g a6g⁶ a6g⁴ a5g³ a6g⁶ 6s 6f³ 5.2d 6m 6f⁴ 6g⁶ 5.1m* 5.7f⁶ 6g² 6f* 6f 5g 5f 6f³ Sep 23] attractive gelding: fairly useful handicapper at best in 1995, mainly for R. Armstrong: inconsistent for new stable: dropped in class, won claimer at Bath in July and seller at Brighton in August: stays 6f: acts on firm ground: often blinkered/visored: often a front runner: sent to Italy. *M. J. Polglase* **78 d** **a56**

TAGATAY 3 b.g. Nomination 125 – Salala 83 (Connaught 130) [1995 –: a8g a6g 1996 a7g⁶ 8m 12m* a14g Nov 22] good-bodied gelding: poor handicapper: won weak and slowly-run seller at Beverley (shade edgy and sweating) in July: soundly beaten at Southwell 4 months later. *M. J. Camacho* **44**

TAGULA (IRE) 3 b.c. Taufan (USA) 119 – Twin Island (IRE) (Standaan (FR) 118) [1995 116: 6m⁵ 6g* 6m⁴ 6g* 6g* 7m³ 1996 7d³ 8g³ 8d⁵ 7m* 7d⁵ 7m⁴ Dec 8] good-topped colt: tends to look very well: smart performer: good third in Poule d'Essai des Poulains at Longchamp (led briefly inside last, beaten 1¼ lengths by Ashkalani) in May on second start: had a set-back after Irish 2000 Guineas and off course 4 months before winning Charlton Hunt Supreme Stakes at Goodwood in September by head from Wizard King, carrying head bit high under pressure but wearing long-time leader down on post: good fourth of 13 (beaten around 1½ lengths) to Monopolize in Hong Kong International Bowl at Sha Tin: effective at 7f and stayed an easy 1m: respectable efforts on dead ground, acted well on good to firm: genuine: retired to Rathbarry Stud, Cork, fee IR 4,000 gns (Oct 1st). *I. A. Balding* **116**

TAHARQA (IRE) 3 b.c. Sadler's Wells (USA) 132 – Too Phar 101 (Pharly (FR) 130) [1995 NR 1996 10g² 10g⁶ 12f⁶ 11.9m 14d² Sep 28] smallish, well-made, attractive colt: has a round action: fourth foal: closely related to Irish 4-y-o 1½m and 1¾m winner Soaring High (by In The Wings) and half-brother to 1991 Irish 2-y-o 1m winner Mack's Smile (by Sure Blade) and Italian 5-y-o 8f to 11f winner Kenjitsu (by Thatching): dam, Irish stayer, out of Group 1 Italian winner Azzurrina: fair maiden: tongue tied down, good second of 19 in handicap at Haydock on final start: better suited by 1¾m than shorter: acts on dead ground: sent to UAE. *J. H. M. Gosden* **77**

TAHYA (USA) 3 ch.f. Elmaamul (USA) 125 – Tatwij (USA) 94 (Topsider (USA)) [1995 52: 5m 5s⁵ 5f a7g³ 1996 a8g a7g³ a7g³ a8g Mar 23] lengthy filly: unimpressive mover: poor maiden: stays 7f: acts on equitrack and on soft ground: has joined G. Bravery. *C. C. Elsey* **51**

TAILWIND 2 ch.c. (May 18) Clantime 101 – Casbar Lady 79 (Native Bazaar 122) [1996 5.1m⁶ 5g 5m 6g⁵ 5.2m² 5m³ 6g⁵ 7.3s Oct 26] 4,800Y, 15,000 2-y-o: leggy, workmanlike colt: half-brother to 3 winning sprinters, including 1988 2-y-o 5f seller winner Dublin Dragon (by Dublin Taxi): dam 5f winner: modest form: stays 6f: has pulled hard/tended to hang. *W. R. Muir* **64**

Charlton Hunt Supreme Stakes, Goodwood—Tagula (noseband) just wears down Wizard King

TAIPAN (IRE) 4 b.c. Last Tycoon 131 – Alidiva 105 (Chief Singer 131) [1995 108
91: 10m 10.4m⁴ 10.5g² 12m 1996 11.9g* 12m² 12s* 12g* Jun 24] leggy colt: good
walker: has a roundish action: useful performer, better than ever at 4 yrs: won
handicaps at Haydock (dead heat) in April and Goodwood in May, and listed contest
at Lyon Parilly (beat Leeds ¾ length) in June: stays 1½m: acts on good to firm and
soft ground: has run well when sweating: genuine: stays in training. *J. L. Dunlop*

TAJREBAH (USA) 2 b.f. (Mar 18) Dayjur (USA) 137 – Petrava (NZ) (Imposing 70
(AUS)) [1996 6m 7.1v 6m³ Oct 28] good topped filly: half-sister to several winners
at up to 1m, including fairly useful 3-y-o 7f (at 2 yrs) and 7.6f winner Alhawa (by Mt
Livermore) and 1990 2-y-o 6f winner Jallad (by Blushing Groom): dam won from
6.5f to 9f in South Africa, where champion filly at 3 yrs: staying-on third in maiden
at Leicester on final start: will stay beyond 6f: soundly beaten on heavy going.
P. T. Walwyn

TAKADOU (IRE) 5 br.h. Double Schwartz 128 – Taka (Blakeney 126) [1995 92: 94 d
5g⁴ 5m 5m 6f⁶ 5m 5.1d⁵ 5d* 5s³ 5s 5m* 5m 6m 1996 5m 5m³ 5m 5m 5m 5g 5s⁵
6g 5g 5m 6f 6s Nov 9] big, lengthy horse: impresses in appearance: fairly useful
performer: stiff tasks most starts in 1996, and failed to make frame last 11 outings:
effective at 5f to 7f: acts on good to firm and soft going: effective blinkered or not
(last tried as 3-y-o): has run well when sweating: held up, and often gets behind:
inconsistent. *Miss L. C. Siddall*

TAKE NOTE (IRE) 3 b.c. Don't Forget Me 127 – Verthumna (Indian King –
(USA) 128) [1995 50: 7f⁶ 7.1m a7g⁴ 1996 a8g 8.2d 12m May 29] good-topped colt:
modest maiden: tailed off in 1996. *N. A. Graham*

TAKE NOTICE 3 b.c. Warning 136 – Metair 118 (Laser Light 118) [1995 NR 77
1996 8.3m⁴ 8.3d 8d³ 7m 6m Oct 8] close-coupled colt: brother to 1995 3-y-o 7f winner Alarming and a winner abroad, closely related to fairly useful 1m winner Connue
(by Known Fact) and half-brother to several winners, including useful sprinters
Meteoric (by High Line) and Fine Edge (by Sharpen Up): dam game sprinter: clearly
best effort in maidens when third of 12 to Province at Newmarket, carrying head
high: disappointing afterwards, and sold 18,000 gns Newmarket Autumn Sales:
likely to prove best at up to 1m. *G. Harwood*

TAKESHI (IRE) 4 b.f. Cadeaux Genereux 131 – Taplow (Tap On Wood 130) –
[1995 65: 7g² 8m² 7m 7g² 7.1m² 6.9f⁵ 7m⁶ 7m 8g⁶ a7g² a7g⁶ a8g 1996 a7g a7g⁴
a8g Feb 23] compact filly: modest maiden handicapper: well below form in 1996:
effective at 7f and 1m: acts on good to firm and equitrack, well beaten only
outing on heavy: tried blinkered and visored: covered by Bin Ajwaad. *W. R. Muir*

TAKE TWO 8 b.g. Jupiter Island 126 – Dancing Daughter 79 (Dance In Time 45
(CAN)) [1995 –: 10m⁶ a10g 1996 11.1m² 12m⁶ 12g⁶ Aug 16] workmanlike gelding:
modest jumper: lightly raced and poor at best on flat nowadays: stays 11f: blinkered
twice in 1991. *Miss M. K. Milligan*

TAKHLID (USA) 5 b.h. Nureyev (USA) 131 – Savonnerie (USA) 108 (Irish 67
River (FR) 131) [1995 83: 7g³ 6g³ 7.1g² 8m³ 7m⁵ 7f* 8.5s* 1996 a7g⁴ a7g⁴ a9g⁶ 8g⁴
a8.5g 5m 6f 8s Nov 9] strong, compact horse: fairly useful in 1995 with H. Thomson
Jones: fourth in 3 of his 4 races in Dubai for E. Charpy, showing only modest form:
sold 13,500 gns Newmarket July (1996) Sales: well held in 4 handicaps for new yard:
stays 8.5f: acts on firm ground and soft: carried head high in 1995 but was game.
D. W. Chapman

TAKING LIBERTIES (IRE) 3 b.f. Royal Academy (USA) 130 – Lady Liberty 57
(NZ) (Noble Bijou (USA)) [1995 NR 1996 7d⁶ Apr 19] tall, angular filly: third foal:
half-sister to 2 winners in Australasia, including a graded winner at 2 yrs by Bluebird:
dam Australian Grade 1 1½m winner: joint favourite, 13 lengths sixth of 17 to Satin
Bell in newcomers event at Newbury, never dangerous: likely to prove suited by
middle distances. *P. W. Chapple-Hyam*

TAKKATAMM (USA) 4 ch.c. Forty Niner (USA) – Relasure (USA) 116 113 ?
(Relaunch (USA)) [1995 NR 1996 a8g* a8g² 7.1d³ 8.5m⁶ Jun 7] lengthy, good-
bodied colt: fluent mover: smart form at 2 yrs for M. Stoute, fourth in Dewhurst
Stakes: not seen out again until February 1996, back to best when winning minor
event in Dubai by 1½ lengths from Tereshkova: good second to that filly in listed
race next time but below form both starts back in Britain, in Diomed Stakes (tongue
tied, probably went too fast early on) at Epsom on final one: should stay beyond 1m:

acts on sand, best turf form on a sound surface: last and quietly to post at Epsom. *Saeed bin Suroor*

TALATHATH (FR) 4 b.g. Soviet Star (USA) 128 – Mashmoon (USA) 80 80
(Habitat 134) [1995 NR 1996 10s⁵ 10s 7m 8s 8m³ 7g⁵ 8g³ 8f² 8f* 8.3d* 8m³ 8m³ 8g⁶
8.9g³ Oct 12] workmanlike gelding: unimpressive mover: fair handicapper: won in
August at Brighton (apprentices) and Windsor: good third of 27 at York on final start,
and subsequently joined D. Nicholson: stays 9f: acts on firm and soft ground: usually
visored: consistent. *C. A. Dwyer*

TALENTED TING (IRE) 7 ch.g. Hatim (USA) 121 – An Tig Gaelige (Thatch 65 d
(USA) 136) [1995 74, a58: 8.2g a8.5g 8m 10.3m 10m 9.2f* 8.3f* 8.3f⁵ 8.1m⁶ 10m a–
8.3m² 8.3f³ 8.3f² a9.4g 8h⁴ 9.2g a10g⁶ a13g⁴ 1996 a12g a12g 10.3d 9.2d 8.3d 8.5m
8.3g² 10f² 9.2m⁵ 10m 10g 8.3f⁴ 8.3g Sep 2] strong, lengthy gelding: good walker:
fair handicapper: well below form last 4 starts: effective at 1m and not discredited
over 13f: acts on firm ground, seems unsuited by soft and has only modest form at
best last 2 seasons on the all-weather: effective with or without visor, blinkered
(raced too freely) once as 5-y-o: has won for apprentice: successful 7 times at
Hamilton: usually races prominently: takes time to come to hand. *P. C. Haslam*

TALIB (USA) 2 b.c. (Mar 25) Silver Hawk (USA) 123 – Dance For Lucy (USA) 59
(Dance Bid (USA) 114) [1996 8m⁵ 8m⁶ Oct 2] $110,000F, $190,000Y: second foal:
dam minor stakes winner from 7f (at 2 yrs) to 9f in USA: signs of ability in maiden
on debut: tailed off final start. *D. Morley*

TALISMAN (IRE) 2 b.g. (May 4) Silver Kite (USA) 111 – Sports Post Lady 55
(IRE) 72 (M Double M (USA)) [1996 5m⁶ 5m⁵ 6g⁵ 7.3m 8m Sep 26] 15,000Y:
useful-looking gelding: second foal: half-brother to 3-y-o Palacegate Chief (by Inca
Chief): dam best at 5f: modest form: well beaten in nurseries final 2 starts: stays 6f.
S. Dow

TALLULAH BELLE 3 b.f. Crowning Honors (CAN) – Fine A Leau (USA) 51 52
(Youth (USA) 135) [1995 37, a55: 6.1m a6g² a7g⁶ 5g a6g⁵ 6f 1996 a6g a9.4g a6g a–
6.9m² 7g⁶ 8m³ 8.2m⁴ 8m 8.2f⁴ 8.3m 8f⁵ 7.6m 8m 10f³ 10g² Oct 2] modest maiden
handicapper: best 3-y-o efforts when placed at Brighton last 2 starts: stays 1¼m: acts
on fibresand (though no form on it in 1996) and on firm ground: tried visored, no
improvement. *N. P. Littmoden*

TAL-Y-LLYN (IRE) 2 ch.c. (Apr 24) Common Grounds 118 – Welsh Fantasy 77
104 (Welsh Pageant 132) [1996 6g⁵ 6m² 6.1s⁴ Oct 31] 30,000F, IR 42,000Y: close-
coupled, quite attractive colt: has a quick, unimpressive action: sixth foal: half-
brother to fairly useful 1m winners Jetbeeah (by Lomond) and Muktabas (by Alzao),
latter also successful over 6f at 2 yrs: dam Irish 6f (at 2 yrs) and 1¼m winner: fair
form in maidens and a minor event: will stay beyond 6f: off bridle early last 2 starts.
B. W. Hills

TAMANDU 6 b.m. Petoski 135 – Gohar (USA) (Barachois (CAN)) [1995 40: –
a12g⁴ 1996 a12g⁵ a12g⁶ 12s Oct 26] sturdy mare: poor maiden. *C. James*

TAMAYAZ (CAN) 4 b.c. Gone West (USA) – Minstrelsy (USA) (The 121
Minstrel (CAN) 135) [1995 119: 8f* 8g⁴ 1996 a8g* a9.9s* a10g⁵ 10d⁴ 10f³ 8m³
10.5m* 10g⁶ a10f⁶ Oct 26]

Restricted by injury to just two runs in each of his first two seasons,
Tamayaz had plenty of opportunities to show his true worth in 1996. On the go
from February through to October, he competed in nine races and won three of
them, showing very smart form when romping home in the Rose of Lancaster
Stakes at Haydock in August.

The winner of a seven-furlong maiden at two years and of a one-mile
minor event at three, Tamayaz did most of his racing in the latest season, which
began for him in Dubai, over a mile and a quarter. Tamayaz took on Cigar and
company at that trip in the Dubai World Cup in March, two wins since the Nad
Al Sheba track already under his belt, and acquitted himself as well as could
have been expected in finishing fifth of eleven, beaten around thirteen lengths.
He faced less exacting tasks on his return to Britain, and it was in a Group 3
race that he gained his third win of the season. The Rose of Lancaster Stakes
attracted eight runners, four of them three-year-olds, including Glory of Dancer

Rose of Lancaster Stakes, Haydock—Tamayaz is a surprisingly clear-cut winner

and Nash House who headed the betting at 2/1 and 9/4 respectively, with Tamayaz next best at 11/2. The race, however, was dominated by the older horses, or to be more precise by Tamayaz who moved easily into the lead two furlongs out and quickly settled the issue when pushed along, winning by five lengths from Ela-Aristokrati. This represents Tamayaz's best form to date. His limitations were exposed when he tackled Group 1 events on his two subsequent starts. On neither occasion was he disgraced, though. Tamayaz

Godolphin's "Tamayaz"

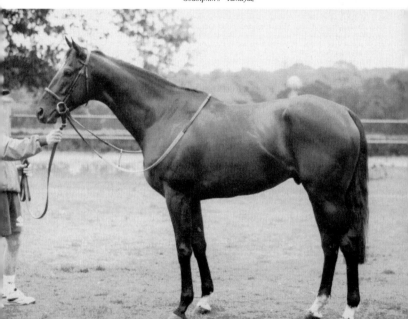

finished around four lengths behind Timarida when last of six in the Irish Champion Stakes at Leopardstown, and around four and a half lengths behind Alphabet Soup when sixth of thirteen, always in mid-division, in the Breeders' Cup Classic at Woodbine.

Tamayaz (CAN) (b.c. 1992)	Gone West (USA) (b 1984)	Mr Prospector (b 1970)	Raise A Native
			Gold Digger
		Secrettame (ch 1978)	Secretariat
			Tamerett
	Minstrelsy (USA) (b 1979)	The Minstrel (ch 1974)	Northern Dancer
			Fleur
		Mrs Peterkin (b 1965)	Tom Fool
			Legendra

Tamayaz, a tall, good-topped colt, is the eighth foal of the one-mile winner Minstrelsy, a half-sister to the Kentucky Oaks winner Sweet Alliance, dam of the Irish Derby winner Shareef Dancer. This is an excellent family. Tamayaz's grandam Mrs Peterkin, who won six races including a stakes at around a mile, is a half-sister to nine winners and has bred other good winners herself, among them Whydidju, who won six races including the California Oaks, and Dancing Champ, successful in the Massachusetts Handicap and the Woodlawn Stakes. Minstrelsy herself has produced several other winners, the best of them Star Standing (by Assert) who won a Grade 2 event over one and a half miles. Tamayaz, who normally races prominently, goes well on top-of-the-ground, and he also acts on sand and dirt. *Saeed bin Suroor*

TAME DEER 4 ch.c. Hadeer 118 – Ever Welcome 58 (Be My Guest (USA) 126) [1995 NR 1996 a7g⁴ a6g* a6g⁴ a6g a6g⁵ 7m 10.3m 8m³ 8m a7g⁴ a8g⁴ a6g⁶ a5g⁵ a7g³ 8s* 8.9g Sep 4] sturdy colt: fair performer at best: has reportedly had leg problems: won seller at Southwell (sold out of W. O'Gorman's stable 5,000 gns) in January and claimer at Ripon in August: mostly well below form in between: stays 1m well: best efforts on Southwell fibresand (yet to race on other all-weather tracks) and soft ground. *M. C. Chapman* 56 a67

TAMHID (USA) 3 b.c. Gulch (USA) – Futuh (USA) 95 (Diesis 133) [1995 94: 6g* 6m⁵ 6d² 6f* 1996 8m⁴ 8m⁴ 7m 8.1m³ 8.9g² 9m² a10f* Dec 12] strong, compact colt: useful performer: in frame on 5 of 6 starts here in 1996, 3 lengths second to Even Top in listed race at York and short-headed by Phantom Quest in minor event at Newbury on last 2 (trained by H. Thomson Jones): won handicap in Dubai in December: stays 1¼m: acts on firm and dead ground and sand: sweating (well beaten in Jersey Stakes) third 3-y-o start: consistent. *K. P. McLaughlin, UAE* 108

TAMNIA 3 br.f. Green Desert (USA) 127 – Tanouma (USA) 114 (Miswaki (USA) 124) [1995 101: 6m² 6m* 7.1g* 7g⁴ 7g² 7d⁵ 1996 8g 8s 8m² 7m³ 7m⁶ 8m³ 9g Oct 18] smallish, angular filly: useful performer: best effort when third of 9 to Yeast in listed race at Newmarket on sixth start, finishing well: ran poorly only subsequent outing: stayed 1m: acted on good to firm ground, ran respectably on dead: blinkered (not disgraced) fifth 3-y-o start: stud. *J. L. Dunlop* 106

TAMURE (IRE) 4 b.c. Sadler's Wells (USA) 132 – Three Tails 121 (Blakeney 126) [1995 125: 11m* 12m* 10.4g* 12f² 10s* 10m⁴ 12s⁴ 1996 12d Oct 6] lengthy, rather unfurnished colt: high-class performer, second in 1995 Derby: looked in smashing shape on first start for nearly a year, but ran no sort of race in Prix de l'Arc de Triomphe at Longchamp, soon off bit and eased in straight: stays 1½m well: acts on any going: sweating (soon off bridle but ran respectably in Champion Stakes) penultimate 3-y-o start: stays in training. *J. H. M. Gosden* –

TANAASA (IRE) 2 b.c. (May 18) Sadler's Wells (USA) 132 – Mesmerize (Mill Reef (USA) 141) [1996 7m³ Oct 28] rangy colt: has plenty of scope: has a powerful, rounded action: closely related to 2 winners by Night Shift, including smart 6f (at 2 yrs) to 1¼m winner Just Happy, and half-brother to 3 winners, notably very smart 1990 2-y-o Mujtahid (by Woodman): dam unraced: nervy and green, very close third in steadily-run maiden at Leicester in October: bandaged behind: will stay middle distances: sure to improve. *M. R. Stoute* 70 p

TANCRED MISCHIEF 5 b.m. Northern State (USA) 91 – Mischievous Miss 73 (Niniski (USA) 125) [1995 31: 8m 12m⁴ 12m⁴ 15.8m³ 1996 12.1g⁴ 14.1g⁵ 16m⁶ 28

17.2f⁵ Jun 26] small, lengthy mare: has a round action: poor handicapper: stays 2m: acts on good to firm ground. *D. W. Barker*

TANDRIDGE (IRE) 4 gr.f. Kefaah (USA) 124 – Roof (Thatch (USA) 136) – [1995 8v⁴ 9m⁵ 8.5m 12m 1996 a7g a10g 8g May 30] IR 1,000Y: seventh foal: half-sister to minor Irish winners Time Is Up (stayer, by Dance of Life) and Motcombs (sprinter, by Glenstal): dam Irish 2-y-o 6f winner: modest maiden: trained at 2 and 3 yrs by D. Weld: no form in Britain: stays 1m: seems to act on any going: sent to South Korea. *J. R. Jenkins*

TANGO KING 2 b.c. (Mar 11) Suave Dancer (USA) 136 – Be My Queen 84 (Be 66 p My Guest (USA) 126) [1996 7m 7g 8m Sep 26] 28,000Y: unfurnished colt: has a round action: seventh foal: half-brother to Italian winner at up to 1½m Sarasota Bay (by Petoski) and 1¼m and 11f winner Bay Queen (by Damister): dam 1m winner out of half-sister to Derby second Cavo Doro: very green on debut: never placed to challenge under tender handling after: will be suited by middle distances: will do better. *J. L. Dunlop*

TANGO TEASER 3 b. or br.f. Shareef Dancer (USA) 135 – Ever Genial 117 – (Brigadier Gerard 144) [1995 NR 1996 7.5f⁵ a6g Jul 26] leggy filly: fifth foal: half-sister to 3 winners, all at 1¼m+, including fairly useful Highly Praised (by Shirley Heights): dam, 7f to 1m winner, granddaughter of smart middle-distance stayer Guillotine: well held in maidens at Beverley (favourite, took keen hold) and Wolverhampton. *A. C. Stewart*

TANGSHAN (CAN) 2 ch.f. (Feb 16) Zilzal (USA) 137 – Manzanares (USA) 67 p (Sir Ivor) [1996 7f⁵ Oct 14] $30,000Y: half-sister to several minor winners in North

Mr Wafic Said's "Tarator"

America: dam won at up to 9f at 2 yrs in North America, from good Canadian family: fifth to Vanishing Trick in maiden at Leicester late in year: should stay at least 1m: should improve. *M. R. Stoute*

TANIYAR (FR) 4 b.g. Glenstal (USA) 118 – Taeesha (Mill Reef (USA) 141) [1995 –: a8g⁴ 1996 a13g a10g⁴ a12g a12g⁵ a7g⁴ a7g 10.8m⁵ 16.2m a11g⁵ a12g 10.4g 11.8f⁴ 10.3g³ a12g² a10g a12g⁶ Dec 27] poor maiden on balance of form: stays 1½m: ran respectably only try in visor: often claimer ridden: one to leave alone. *R. Hollinshead*   52 § a39 §

TANSEEQ 5 b.g. Green Desert (USA) 127 – Kawkeb (USA) 72 (Vaguely Noble 140) [1995 59: 8g 9g 8f⁵ 1996 a8.5g Oct 19] big, good-bodied gelding: modest at best at 4 yrs for H. Thomson Jones: well beaten only flat outing in 1996: should stay 1¼m: acts on good to firm and dead ground: blinkered (raced too freely) final 4-y-o start: won handicap hurdle in November. *M. G. Meagher*   –

TAOME (IRE) 2 b.f. (Apr 7) Roi Danzig (USA) – Blue Bell Lady 75 (Dunphy 124) [1996 6m³ 6g 5f* 6.1m³ Jul 6] 1,800Y: small filly: fourth foal: dam sprinter: won seller at Carlisle in June: well below that form only subsequent start: stays 6f: acts on firm ground. *P. D. Evans*   59 d

TAP ON TOOTSIE 4 b.f. Faustus (USA) 118 – My Tootsie 88 (Tap On Wood 130) [1995 –: 8d⁵ 8.3m 10m 12s a14.8g³ a13g 1996 a12g⁶ a12g⁴ a12g a16g Mar 9] good-topped filly: no worthwhile form on flat: won novice hurdle in May. *T. Wall*   –

TAPPETO 4 b.g. Liboi (USA) 76 – Persian Carpet (FR) (Kalamoun 129) [1995 78: 10.2m⁴ 9m⁴ 10m³ 10m* 10.5g 12.1d⁶ 1996 10.8d 10m 10.8g 12g 12.1m² 11.7m³ 12m 12m Sep 20] workmanlike gelding: fair handicapper: stays 12.1f: acts on good to firm and dead ground: blinkered (below best) second 4-y-o start: sometimes carries head awkwardly. *H. Candy*   74

TARAGONA 3 b.f. Handsome Sailor 125 – Queen of Aragon 76 (Aragon 118) [1995 NR 1996 6m Jun 4] workmanlike filly: third foal: half-sister to a winner in Spain by Midyan: dam sprinter: burly and green, well held in maiden at Pontefract. *R. Hollinshead*   –

TARATOR (USA) 3 ch.c Green Dancer (USA) 132 – Happy Gal (FR) (Habitat 134) [1995 NR 1996 10.5g³ 12.5g* 12d* 11g* 15d* 12.5g² 12m⁶ 15d* 12m⁶ Dec 8] $30,000F, 325,000 francs Y: strong, close-coupled colt: fourth foal: half-brother to a winner in Mexico by Graustark: dam, French 9.5f winner, granddaughter of Gimcrack winner Be Careful: progressed into a very smart performer: won minor event at Angers, then 2 handicaps and 5-runner Prix Hubert de Chaudenay (beat Irish Woman 10 lengths), at Longchamp: neck second of 9 to Strategic Choice in Grand Prix de Deauville: won 8-runner Prix de Lutece at Longchamp in October by a neck from Kharizmi, staying on to lead inside last: has smart form at around 1½m, but shapes very much like a stayer: yet to race on extremes of going, best form with give. *E. Lellouche, France*   120

TARAWA (IRE) 4 br.g. Caerleon (USA) 132 – Sagar 74 (Habitat 134) [1995 103: 7.3m 8d* 8s³ 8m* 8m* a9.4g³ 1996 7m* 8m* 7.9m⁴ 8m 8m⁶ 7g 9m 9g* Oct 18] tall,   112

Baring International Darley Stakes, Newmarket—
Tarawa confirms the promise of his Cambridgeshire run, beating Nijo (rails) and Forest Buck

workmanlike gelding: has a short, round action: smart performer: won well-contested events at Newmarket (rated stakes) in April and Ascot (sweating, minor event) in May: finished second on unfavoured far side when seventh of 38 to Clifton Fox in the Cambridgeshire at Newmarket, and gained fourth course success in 10-runner listed race there (led in Dip and pushed clear to beat Nijo 2½ lengths) later in October: effective at 7f, and stays 9.4f: acts on good to firm and soft ground and on fibresand: usually held up: sold 110,000 gns Newmarket Autumn Sales, and sent to Italy. *N. A. Callaghan*

TARF (USA) 3 ch.f. Diesis 133 – Tadwin 109 (Never So Bold 135) [1995 92: 5g² 5d³ 5.1m² 5f² 5f* 5g 1996 5m⁵ 5m 5f 5m 5s Oct 5] neat filly: fluent mover: fairly useful form at 2 yrs: not at best in 1996, and well held last 3 starts: sold 22,000 gns Newmarket December Sales: raced only at 5f: acts on firm and dead ground. *P. T. Walwyn* **82**

TARIAN (USA) 4 b.g. Lyphard (USA) 132 – Chain Fern (USA) (Blushing Groom (FR) 131) [1995 –: 10m 1996 10s 7g 7m 8.2m 10.8f⁶ 10m² 10.8m 10f Jul 6] smallish gelding: modest maiden handicapper: stays 1¼m. *G. B. Balding* **53**

TA RIB (USA) 3 ch.f. Mr Prospector (USA) – Madame Secretary (USA) (Secretariat (USA)) [1995 89p: 7m² 7d³ 1996 7m* 8g* 8m⁴ 8g² 7.3m⁴ Aug 16] **116**
   Never mind the gap between handicaps and pattern races, Ta Rib leapt the one between maiden race and classic. Shaamit did the same, but, in marked contrast to his achievement, the time to mature between Ta Rib's maiden and classic victories was just nine days. After showing fairly useful form when placed on both her starts as a two-year-old, Ta Rib's maiden success came in a fourteen-runner contest at Newmarket on May 3rd when she beat Fatefully by five lengths without needing to be ridden out firmly. On May 12th, she was at Longchamp for the Poule d'Essai des Pouliches. She was the first classic runner for her trainer, the twenty-seven-year-old Ed Dunlop who had taken over the reins at Oak Stables (now renamed the Gainsborough Stables) in Newmarket less than two years previously, following the murder of Alex Scott to whom he was assistant. Both the horse and her trainer, then, were uninitiated at this level, but they had the assistance of veteran Willie Carson in the saddle and victory in the Pouliches owed a good deal to him and his tactical awareness. The race got off to a steady start with the running soon taken up by Saeed bin Suroor's Shawanni, Ta Rib in second to her outside. It is less than two and a half furlongs from the end of the final turn to the winning post, but the race had still not begun in earnest when the field straightened up. Carson chose to make his effort two furlongs out, quickly had the lead and made the best of his way home while the French team were still sorting themselves out. The 3/5-favourite Shake The Yoke had about three and a half lengths to make up and managed to reduce that to three quarters of a length at the line. She had been boxed in, chiefly by Housa Dancer, ridden by Jarnet whom Shake The Yoke's trainer suggested 'should be given his 3.5 kilo allowance back so he can ride in apprentice races.' C'est la vie, as connections of Ta Rib might have observed.

Dubai Poule d'Essai des Pouliches, Longchamp—Ta Rib graduates from maiden race to classic; those on her heels are Shake The Yoke (No. 3), Sagar Pride (rails), A Votre Sante and the grey Shawanni

Hamdan Al Maktoum's "Ta Rib"

Ta Rib (USA) (ch.f. 1993)	Mr Prospector (USA) (b 1970)	Raise A Native (ch 1961)	Native Dancer
			Raise You
		Gold Digger (b 1962)	Nashua
			Sequence
	Madame Secretary (USA) (ch 1982)	Secretariat (ch 1970)	Bold Ruler
			Something Royal
		Ruby Tuesday (br 1974)	T V Lark
			Thoroly Blue

That was Ta Rib's day. The remainder of the season confirmed that Shake The Yoke had been the best filly in the race, and having found so much improvement to triumph at Longchamp, Ta Rib could not come up with a great deal more. She sweated up in the preliminaries on a few occasions and was very edgy as well before the rematch with Shake The Yoke in the Coronation Stakes at Royal Ascot, finishing only a respectable fourth. Two races after that saw her do better, running to a slightly higher level of form in fact than that required to win at Longchamp, but it was still only good enough for second to Sensation (who received 6 lb) in the Falmouth Stakes and fourth to Bin Rosie in the Hungerford. In September it was announced that she had been retired, the owner's racing manager saying that 'Her breathing was never quite right, and it was decided to retire her after she was scoped one day and we found she had bled a bit.' Dunlop reflected that 'if she hadn't been so highly-strung, she could have been a champion.' Four days earlier Willie Carson had sustained serious internal injuries when kicked by a two-year-old in the paddock at Newbury. He, however, will hopefully be back.

Ta Rib is by top stallion Mr Prospector and the sixth foal and fifth winner out of the broodmare Madame Secretary. The only maiden was the fairly useful Afaared (by Danzig) who is now a sire in Thailand. Best of the first four earlier winners was Tabdea (by Topsider) whose three wins included two in listed races, over six fulongs at Ayr as a two-year-old and a mile at Doncaster at three. She had been purchased by Sheikh Hamdan's Shadwell Estates for 160,000 dollars as a yearling in 1988 and a year later they bought Madame Secretary herself for 725,000 dollars. A half-sister to both the 1986 Stewards' Cup and Ayr Gold Cup winner Green Ruby and the 1988 Ascot Stakes winner Zero Watt, Madame Secretary won twice at around a mile in the USA as a three-year-old, including in the Dolly Val Handicap, a minor stakes race. She is out of a half-sister to Cresta Rider whose wins included the Prix Jean Prat and placed efforts the Poule d'Essai des Poulains. The latest Pouliches winner Ta Rib is a good-topped filly with a quick action. It was unlikely that she would have stayed much beyond a mile. She never raced on extremes of going, and not on a soft surface as a three-year-old. For all that she was rather highly-strung, Ta Rib was a genuine racehorse. She visits Nashwan in 1997. *E. A. L. Dunlop*

TARIFF (IRE) 2 b.f. (Feb 26) Common Grounds 118 – Tasskeen (FR) (Lyphard (USA) 132) [1996 7f 7d Oct 28] 5,500Y: sister to 1993 Irish 2-y-o 7f winner Yahthab and half-sister to 3-y-o Fijon (by Doyoun) and several winners in France: dam, ran once in France, granddaughter of French champion 2-y-o Texana: showed nothing in maidens. *N. A. Graham* –

TARNEEM (USA) 3 b.f. Zilzal (USA) 137 – Willowy Mood (USA) (Will Win (USA)) [1995 82: 6g5 6d2 7m2 1996 8m6 7f 8m2 8s2 8m* 7f2 9d4 8.1m6 Sep 17] leggy, workmanlike filly: fairly useful performer: won maiden at Brighton in July: sold 22,000 gns Newmarket Autumn Sales: likely to prove best at up to 9f: acts on firm and dead ground. *M. R. Stoute* 87

TAROUDANT 9 b.g. Pharly (FR) 130 – Melbourne Miss (Chaparral (FR) 128) [1995 67: a16.2g5 a16g4 a14.8g5 1996 16g 18.7g May 8] rangy gelding: still a fair staying handicapper at 8 yrs for Mrs M. Reveley, but well beaten in 1996, including in blinkers. *R. D. E. Woodhouse* –

TARRADALE 2 br.g. (May 12) Interrex (CAN) – Encore L'Amour (USA) § (Monteverdi 129) [1996 7d Nov 8] 1,500F, IR 5,400Y, 10,000 2-y-o: heavy-topped, plain gelding: fifth live foal: half-brother to 3-y-o Incatinka (by Inca Chief) and 5f and 6f winner Evening Falls (by Beveled): dam no form and was temperamental: tailed off in maiden at Doncaster. *C. B. B. Booth* –

TARRY 3 b.f. Salse (USA) 128 – Waitingformargaret 78 (Kris 135) [1995 62: 6m 6m 7m* 8m6 8m 7g 8f2 8f3 1996 8g 11.6m5 9.9m6 10m5 Jul 29] small filly: modest handicapper: left S. Sherwood after third 3-y-o start: better at 11.6f than 1¼m: acts on firm going: blinkered/visored last 2 starts at 2 yrs, running well: won novice hurdle in September. *A. Streeter* 60

TARSKI 2 ch.c. (Apr 25) Polish Precedent (USA) 131 – Illusory 81 (Kings Lake (USA) 133) [1996 7.1m* 7g4 Aug 21] third foal: closely related to 1994 2-y-o 5.8f winner Painted Desert (by Green Desert) and half-brother to smart 3-y-o 1m and 9f winner Phantom Quest (by Rainbow Quest): dam, 6f winner, daughter of Irish 1000 Guineas second Bold Fantasy: won maiden at Sandown in July: helped set good gallop when fourth in minor event at Kempton in August: will stay 1m. *H. R. A. Cecil* 91

TART 3 b.f. Tragic Role (USA) – Fee 111 (Mandamus 120) [1995 68+: 7m a8g2 a8.5g* 1996 10m4 11.4m* 12.1s Oct 22] workmanlike filly: off course 6 months before reappearance, 3½ months after it due to poisoned foot: fairly useful form when winning strongly-run 15-runner handicap at Sandown in September by 5 lengths: sold 13,500 gns Newmarket Autumn Sales: should be suited by further than 11f: acts on good to firm ground and the all-weather, possibly not on soft: sent to USA. *R. F. Johnson Houghton* 81

TART AND A HALF 4 b.f. Distant Relative 128 – Vaigrant Wind 75 (Vaigly Great 127) [1995 81: 5m 5.1m4 5.1m2 5.3f4 6g 5f 5m3 7m4 8g 5m4 5m3 5m3 1996 6f 5g 5.1f2 6d 5m4 5m 5m2 5m5 5m 5.1m6 5.2m 5g4 5f 5m2 6m a6g a6g Nov 26] rather leggy filly: fairly useful handicapper: creditable efforts in 1996 when in frame: effec- 83
a–

988

tive at 5f, probably at 7f: acts on firm ground, well beaten on dead and on all-weather (probably out of form): effective blinkered or not: usually races prominently. *B. J. Meehan*

TARTAN EXPRESS (IRE) 3 b.g. New Express 95 – Running Feud (Prince –
Tenderfoot (USA) 126) [1995 –: 6m⁵ a7g⁶ 6m 7f a8g 1996 a10g a10g a12g⁴ 12s 11.9f
Apr 12] sturdy gelding: of no account. *B. A. Pearce*

TARTAN GEM (IRE) 5 ch.h. Lomond (USA) 128 – Red Jade 82 (Red God 71
128§) [1995 54+: 9g 10d a9.4g² 1996 a11g* a12g* a12g³ a12g a12g³ a14g⁵ a12g³
12g Mar 21] lengthy, dipped-backed horse: unimpressive mover: fair performer: won
seller at Southwell and apprentice claimer at Lingfield on successive days in January:
left M. Brittain after fifth start: stayed 1½m: acted on the all-weather and on good to
firm ground: dead. *Miss Gay Kelleway*

TARTAN PARTY 2 gr.c. (Apr 11) Environment Friend 128 – Northern Scene 78 61
(Habitat 134) [1996 7.9g 7m 7f 10g³ Oct 24] 1,600Y, 9,400 2-y-o: close-coupled colt:
half-brother to several winners here and abroad, including fairly useful 6f (at 2 yrs)
and 7f winner Rocton North (by Ballad Rock): dam Irish 2-y-o 5f winner: staying-on
third in weak median auction event final start, only form: looks a stayer. *P. F. I. Cole*

TARTE AUX POMMES (USA) 4 br.f. Local Talent (USA) 122 – My Mother's –
Eyes (FR) (Saint Cyrien (FR) 128) [1995 8m* 10.5g⁴ 10g³ 9m⁵ 8g² 8d 1996 10.1m
8m 8.1m 10.3f⁶ 10m Oct 1] leggy, sparely-made, ex-French filly: first foal: dam
maiden from good French family: trained at 3 yrs by A. Fabre, winning minor event
at Evry in May and showing useful form in listed races afterwards: no form in
Britain: stays 10.5f: acts on good to firm and dead ground. *C. E. Brittain*

TART (FR) 3 br.f. Warning 136 – Sharp Girl (FR) 114 (Sharpman) [1995 NR 1996 76
8.2s⁴ 10m² 10m² 11.6m³ 8g³ 10s³ 11.5m* a12g² Nov 30] close-coupled, workmanlike filly: half-sister to fair middle-distance performer Gold Blade (by Rousillon) and
winners in France (at 1m+) by Rousillon and Polish Precedent: dam French 1¼m
winner who stayed 1½m, from good family: fair performer: dropped in class and
justified favouritism in claimer at Yarmouth (claimed out of J. Fanshawe's stable
£10,500) in September: stays 1½m: acts on fibresand, best turf form on top-of-the-
ground. *J. Pearce*

TASDID 3 ch.c. In The Wings 128 – Ghaadah (USA) (Linkage (USA)) [1995 7g⁴ 101
7m* 1996 8s³ 8m⁴ 12m 14m 10m* 10m⁵ 14d³ Aug 24] angular, useful-looking colt:
second foal: dam, Irish 1m winner, half-sister to dam of very smart Irish sprinter
Big Shuffle: useful performer: won minor event at Naas in July and would probably
have run creditably (badly hampered and lost all chance 1f out) in Group 3 event at
the Curragh fourth start: twelfth of 20 in Derby third outing: in frame in 3 listed races
at Leopardstown: stays 1¾m: acts on good to firm and soft ground: probably effective blinkered or not: has wandered under pressure: sent to Dubai. *K. Prendergast,
Ireland*

TASHJIR (USA) 3 ch.f. Slew O' Gold (USA) – Mashaarif (USA) (Mr Prospector –
(USA)) [1995 –: 7g 7g 8.2m 1996 10.3m 12m 12g Jun 7] lengthy filly: has been
hobdayed: poor mover: no worthwhile form: pulled up (reportedly distressed) on
reappearance: has worn tongue strap. *D. Morley*

TASHKENT 4 b.g. Thowra (FR) – Royal Bat 69 (Crowned Prince (USA) 128) –
[1995 NR 1996 8m Jul 5] half-brother to 5-y-o 6f winner Myjinka (by Myjinski),
1¼m to 1½m winner Crosby Place (by Crooner) and a winning hurdler: dam 6f
winner who stayed 1m: tailed off in 2 NH Flat races in the spring: well beaten in
Warwick maiden: subsequently joined T. Hind. *Miss K. M. George*

TASHTAIYA 3 b.f. Totem (USA) 118 – Bonita Estrella (Macmillion 110) [1995 –
NR 1996 a6g⁵ a6g a9.4g Aug 9] first reported foal: dam never ran: well beaten in
fibresand maidens: sold 550 gns Doncaster September Sales. *N. P. Littmoden*

TASIK CHINI (USA) 2 b. or br.g. (Apr 20) St Jovite (USA) 135 – Ten Hail 72 d
Marys (USA) (Halo (USA)) [1996 7f³ 7m⁶ 7m 8m Aug 26] $90,000Y: workmanlike
gelding: has a round action: third foal: half-brother to 3-y-o Name of Our Father (by
Northern Baby): dam minor 2-y-o winner at up to 9f in USA, sister to 8.5f stakes
winner: deteriorated after showing fair form on debut: well beaten in blinkers final
start than gelded: stays 7f: takes a strong hold, and looks of unsatisfactory temperament. *P. F. I. Cole*

TASLIYA (USA) 3 ch.f. Gulch (USA) – Aghani (USA) (Blushing Groom (FR)   –
131) [1995 86p: 6g 6.1m 6m 7m³ 1996 8g⁵ 7f May 6] quite attractive filly: good
mover: easily best effort on final 2-y-o start: soundly beaten in 1996: sent to New
Zealand. *J. L. Dunlop*

TASSILI (IRE) 3 b.g. Old Vic 136 – Topsy 124 (Habitat 134) [1995 NR 1996   –
10g⁶ 10s Oct 24] small, quite attractive gelding: half-brother to several winners,
notably top-class middle-distance performer Most Welcome (by Be My Guest): dam,
very smart at up to 1¼m, is half-sister to Teenoso: shaped with plenty of promise
when staying-on sixth of 15 to Magnificient Style in maiden at Kempton in April, but
sold out of G. Wragg's stable 15,000 gns Newmarket July Sales and gelded: weak in
market, remote tenth of 15 in similar event at Newbury. *Lady Herries*

TATHMIN 3 b.g. Weldnaas (USA) 112 – Alcassa (FR) (Satingo 129) [1995 NR   –
1996 10m 10.2f a9.4g⁵ 11.5m Oct 4] 10,000F, 24,000Y: half-brother to 2 winners,
including Albert The Bold (by Never So Bold) who probably stayed 1m: dam French
11f winner at 4 yrs: signs of a little ability but no worthwhile form. *J. R. Bosley*

TATIKA 6 ch.g. Tate Gallery (USA) 117 – Independentia 68 (Home Guard (USA)   77
129) [1995 75: a8.5g² 7.5m³ 6m² 7m⁴ 7g 7f 6m⁶ a8.5g a8g³ a7g⁵ 1996 a8g* a8g*   a90
10.3g 8.1d⁵ 8.3g⁶ 8g 8.1m* 7.9g 7s⁵ a8g* Dec 5] lengthy gelding: fairly useful on the
all-weather, successful in 2 handicaps at Southwell in February and in minor event
(didn't have to be at best) at Lingfield in December: fair on turf, winner of apprentice
handicap at Sandown in August: finds 6f a bare minimum, and stays 8.5f: acts on
all-weather surfaces and on good to firm and soft ground: blinkered (below form)
twice in 1995: sometimes pulls hard: often claimer ridden: usually held up. *G. Wragg*

TAUBER 12 b.g. Taufan (USA) 119 – Our Bernie (Continuation 120) [1995 NR   45
1996 5s 6g 5g³ 6f⁶ Jun 1] rather leggy gelding: has a markedly round action: just a
poor handicapper in 1996: finished lame at Lingfield (successful 11 times there) on
final start, and reportedly unlikely to race again: used to be effective at 5f to 1m:
acted on any going. *Pat Mitchell*

TAUFAN BOY 3 b.c. Taufan (USA) 119 – Lydia Maria 70 (Dancing Brave (USA)   81
140) [1995 79: 7.1m³ 7f³ a7g* 7d 7f 1996 8m³ 10m⁶ a9.4g³ 10.3m² 10m 11.7m⁴
12.3s⁶ 12m 11.9g⁴ 12.1s² 14.1s⁶ Oct 31] quite attractive colt: has a round action:
fairly useful handicapper: stays 1¾m: acts on fibresand and firm and soft ground: no
improvement in visor/blinkers: wore dropped noseband (ran respectably despite
going in snatches) final start. *P. W. Harris*

TAUFAN ROOKIE (IRE) 2 b.c. (Mar 11) Taufan (USA) 119 – Royal Wolff   92
(Prince Tenderfoot (USA) 126) [1996 5m² 5f⁴ 6f³ Jul 21] IR 7,000F, 35,000Y:
medium-sized, rather leggy colt: seventh foal: half-brother to 3 modest winners
at up to 7f: dam Irish sprinter: fairly useful form behind Abou Zouz in maiden at
Newmarket and Dazzle in Windsor Castle Stakes (tended to hang) at Ascot first 2
starts: finished lame only subsequent start: should be suited by further than 5f: sent to
Norway. *R. Hannon*

TAUFAN'S MELODY 5 b.g. Taufan (USA) 119 – Glorious Fate (Northfields   111
(USA)) [1995 111: 10m² 10.4g⁵ 12m 10g² 10.4m² 12d* 12g* 12d* 12d³ 1996
11.5m* 11.8g² 14g⁴ 12m³ 12g² 12s² Nov 3] rather leggy, good-topped gelding: smart
performer: won minor event at Lingfield (by short head from Midnight Legend) in
June: in frame in listed races at Leicester and Vichy, well-contested minor event at
Newbury and listed events at Lyon and Nantes: probably stays 1¾m: acts on good to
firm and soft ground: genuine and consistent. *Lady Herries*

TAUFELIANE 5 b.m. Taufan (USA) 119 – Sweet Eliane (Birdbrook 110) [1995   –
NR 1996 12d Mar 30] leggy, good-topped mare: no longer of much account.
J. L. Harris

TAUNT 2 b.c. (Apr 17) Robellino (USA) 127 – Minute Waltz (Sadler's Wells   82 p
(USA) 132) [1996 7m³ Aug 26] well-made colt: fourth foal: half-brother to 3-y-o
13.8f winner Spinning Mouse (by Bustino), useful 4-y-o 1m and 9f winner Daunt (by
Darshaan) and 1¼m winner Changing Partners (by Rainbow Quest): dam (unraced)
out of smart half-sister to Welsh Pageant: burly and green, close third in maiden at
Newcastle in August: should stay at least 1m: sure to improve. *D. Morley*

TAUREAN FIRE 3 ch.g. Tina's Pet 121 – Golden Decoy 73 (Decoy Boy 129)   35
[1995 41: 5m 6f⁵ 6m 5g 6f 1996 7d⁵ 6m 6g 7.1g 6f Aug 3] unfurnished gelding: poor

maiden handicapper at best: well held last 4 3-y-o starts, reported by vet to be in distressed state (after bolting to start) on first of them: sold to join D. Bassett 700 gns Doncaster August Sales: likely to prove best at up to 7f. *Mrs M. Reveley*

TAUTEN (IRE)   6 br.m. Taufan (USA) 119 – Pitaka (Pitskelly 122) [1995 –: 8f 12m 1996 8.3m² a8g 11.4m 10m 8.3g 11.6g⁵ 8m 8.3m⁶ 7g⁵ 12m Sep 20] leggy, lengthy mare: first form since 3 yrs when second of 20 in claimer at Windsor on reappearance: failed to repeat it: effective at 7f, and stays 10.8f: acts on heavy and good to firm ground: visored last 6 starts: has had tongue tied down. *P. Burgoyne*   58 d

TAWAADED (IRE)   3 ch.f. Nashwan (USA) 135 – Thaidah (CAN) 105 (Vice Regent (CAN)) [1995 –p: 6s 1996 7m⁷ 8m² 7g 8f 7f³ 7f Sep 5] big, rangy filly: fine mover with a powerful, fluent action: fairly useful form on first 2 3-y-o starts, winning maiden at Newmarket in April: well held afterwards, finding little on final start: stayed 1m: raced prominently: carried head awkwardly second 3-y-o outing: visits Machiavellian. *P. T. Walwyn*   91 d

TAWAFEK (USA)   3 br.c. Silver Hawk (USA) 123 – Tippy Tippy Toe (USA) 60 (Nureyev (USA) 131) [1995 76p: 8g 8f³ 1996 8d 8g 9m May 6] close-coupled colt: has a round action: fair maiden: failed to repeat form of second 2-y-o start, well held final outing: sold (D. Morley to S. Dow) 9,500 gns Newmarket Autumn Sales: should be very well suited by 1¼m+. *D. Morley*   71

TAWAFIJ (USA)   7 ch.g. Diesis 133 – Dancing Brownie (USA) (Nijinsky (CAN) 138) [1995 87: 7s 7m 7g² 7m* 7g⁵ 7m⁵ 7m⁵ 7.9m 7g 8g 1996 7g 7g⁶ 7g 7m⁴ 8g 8m⁶ 7m⁴ 7m Aug 10] good-topped, attractive gelding: fairly useful handicapper: below best in 1996: trained until after third start by T. Dyer: unsuited by steady pace last 3 outings: stays 1m: probably acts on any going: tried visored, no improvement: held up. *M. D. Hammond*   81

TAWKIL (USA)   3 b.c. Riverman (USA) 131 – Lyphette (FR) (Lyphard (USA) 132) [1995 99p: 7f² 7m* 1996 9m⁵ 10.3g⁶ 10.1m⁵ 10.4m 8f³ Sep 13] robust, attractive colt: has a quick action: useful performer: best efforts when fifth in listed race at Newmarket (to Storm Trooper) on reappearance and when third in useful minor event at Doncaster (4 lengths behind Kammtarra): stays 10.5f: acts on firm ground, yet to race on a soft surface: sent to Dubai. *B. W. Hills*   99

TAXI DE NUIT (USA)   4 b.c. Runaway Groom (CAN) – Mot d'Amour (FR) (Bon Mot III 132) [1995 6g 6g 7g* 8.8g 7.5d³ 6g 6g⁵ 8m* 7g* 8d* 1996 7.5s* 8d* 8g² 8g* 8d⁵ 7m* 7g* 8m* Nov 10] $22,000Y: brother to 2 winners, notably German listed winner My Power, and half-brother to 2 winners, notably Son Of Love (St Leger, rated 126, by Jefferson): dam French 10.5f winner: smart Italian colt: successful 5 times in minor company from 12 starts prior to 1996: won 6 of his 8 starts in 1996, most notably Group 2 Premio Ribot at Rome (made all, beat Golden Agos 3½ lengths) in November: successful earlier in 3 minor events and a listed race on same course: stays 1m well: acts on good to firm ground and soft. *A. Verdesi, Italy*   112

TAYLORS REVIVAL   5 b.m. Sizzling Melody 117 – Taylors Pet 57 (Tina's Pet 121) [1995 NR 1996 a5g a8g a9.4g 10m 11.9f Jul 25] first foal: dam, maiden, stayed 11.5f: no promise. *H. J. Collingridge*   –

TAYOVULLIN (IRE)   2 ch.f. (Mar 20) Shalford (IRE) 124§ – Fifth Quarter (Cure The Blues (USA)) [1996 5.1m 5.7d⁶ Sep 30] 13,000Y: half-sister to 3 winners abroad, including French 1¼m handicapper Mon Bugey (by Akarad): dam 1m and 1¼m winner in France, half-sister to Vintage Crop: signs of ability in maidens at Bath: will stay beyond 5.7f: sold to join H. Morrison 8,500 gns Newmarket Autumn Sales: may do better. *R. Charlton*   61

TAYSEER (USA)   2 ch.c. (Feb 28) Sheikh Albadou 128 – Millfit (USA) 62 (Blushing Groom (FR) 131) [1996 6m³ 6g⁴ 7f* Nov 5] leggy colt: has a quick action: first foal: dam 7f winner who should have stayed 1m, out of half-sister to Gay Fandango: shaped well first 2 starts then readily won maiden at Redcar in November: gives impression will prove suited by further than 7f: acts on firm ground: progressive. *E. A. L. Dunlop*   89 p

TAZIBARI   2 b.f. (Mar 5) Barrys Gamble 102 – Jersey Maid 82 (On Your Mark 125) [1996 5d² 5s* 5m⁵ 5g⁵ Oct 19] 720Y: workmanlike filly: has a quick action: fourth live foal: half-sister to poor miler Mai Pen Rai (by All Systems Go): dam   62

2-y-o 5f winner who stayed 7f: won median auction maiden at Hamilton in May: well beaten after: should be suited by further than 5f. *D. Moffatt*

TAZIO NUVOLARI 2 b.f. (Mar 20) Weldnaas (USA) 112 – Ty High (IRE) – (High Line 125) [1996 a5g⁶ a6g³ a8.5g a8.5g Nov 2] first foal: dam, ran 3 times, bred to stay at least 1¼m: little worthwhile form in Wolverhampton sellers: bred to stay beyond 6f. *W. G. M. Turner*

TE AMO (IRE) 4 b.c. Waajib 121 – Avebury Ring (Auction Ring (USA) 123) 65 [1995 83: 8.1m 7m⁵ 7m² 8m⁶ 8.5s³ 10g 9d 1996 10g 10.3g 8.1d 11.6m⁴ a11g 9.7m³ 11.6m² 11.8m³ 14m⁶ 11.8f* 12s⁶ 12v Nov 11] small, good-bodied colt: shows a quick action: fairly useful performer at best at 3 yrs: not nearly so good in 1996, winning 20-runner claimer at Leicester (claimed out of R. Akehurst's stable £6,000) in October: ran badly last 2 starts: stays 11.8f: acts on any ground: ran poorly in blinkers and visor: has joined M. Pipe. *M. Bell*

TEA PARTY (USA) 3 b.f. Night Shift (USA) – Meringue Pie (USA) (Silent 76 Screen (USA)) [1995 NR 1996 9m⁴ 9m⁴ 10.1g 10f⁴ 8g 8g⁴ a8.5g³ a8.5g* a9.4g² 10g³ 8s Nov 26] $40,000Y: strong filly: eighth foal: half-sister to several winners, including very useful 7f to 10.5f winner Monsagem (by Nureyev) and 4-y-o 1¼m winner Sweet Pavlova (by Zilzal): dam stakes winner at up to 9f: fair performer: won maiden handicap at Wolverhampton in September: ran in France last 2 starts, out of depth in listed race on final one: stays 1¼m: acts on fibresand, best turf efforts on good ground. *K. O. Cunningham-Brown*

TEAR WHITE (IRE) 2 b.g. (Jan 28) Mac's Imp (USA) 116 – Exemplary 106 70 § (Sovereign Lord 120) [1996 5g 5m³ 5g⁶ 6f⁵ 5m* 5m² 5.3f⁶ 5g⁵ 5f⁶ 5m⁵ a6g Dec 13] 9,400Y: sturdy gelding: half-brother to numerous winners here and abroad, including fair 7f to 8.5f winner Northern Celadon (by Classic Secret) and fairly useful sprinter Sheila's Secret (by Bluebird): dam best at 5f: fair form on his day: won maiden at Ripon in July: headstrong, and best at 5f: blinkered or visored last 10 starts: looked ill at ease on track at Brighton seventh start: temperamental (hung badly left and crashed through rail on debut). *T. G. Mills*

TECHNICOLOUR (IRE) 2 b.f. (Apr 3) Rainbow Quest (USA) 134 – Grecian 79 p Urn 123 (Ela-Mana-Mou 132) [1996 7.1s* Oct 22] third foal: half-sister to useful French 4-y-o 1¼m to 12.5f winner Grecian Dart (by Darshaan) and French 1¼m winner Dictionary (by Reference Point): dam French 6.5f to 9f winner, placed in several pattern races: won 16-runner maiden at Chepstow in October by head from Summerosa, taking keen hold in steadily-run race then finishing strongly despite looking green: will be well suited by middle distances: sure to improve. *M. R. Stoute*

TEDBURROW 4 b.g. Dowsing (USA) 124 – Gwiffina 87 (Welsh Saint 126) 96 [1995 85+: 6g³ 6m 5f* 5m* 5g* 6f⁵ 5m⁶ 7g⁶ 6g 1996 6m 5d⁴ 6m² 5m⁴ 5g² 5m* 5m³ 5m 5m 5.6m⁴ 6m 6g 5g⁵ 5g⁴ Oct 26] leggy, workmanlike gelding: useful handicapper: got up close home to win at Newmarket in July: good fourth of 21 to Musical Season in the Portland at Doncaster: better than result suggests last 3 starts, twice meeting trouble in running: effective at 5f and 6f: acts on firm and dead ground: successful when sweating: usually held up: genuine. *Mrs A. M. Naughton*

TEDDY'S BOW (IRE) 2 b. or br.f. (Feb 19) Archway (IRE) 115 – Gale Force 52 ? Seven (Strong Gale 116) [1996 5m⁵ 5m⁴ Jul 8] IR 2,500Y: plain filly: has a round action: fourth foal: half-sister to 3-y-o Escobar (by Cyrano de Bergerac): dam unraced: modest form in summer auction maiden events at Ripon: will be suited by further than 5f. *M. W. Easterby*

TEE-EMM 6 b.g. Lidhame 109 – Tower Glades 90 (Tower Walk 130) [1995 42, 40 a59: a5g⁴ a5g³ a5g³ 5m 5m⁶ 5m 5m⁶ 5m* 5m 5m 5.2m⁴ 5m⁴ 5m a5g³ a5g⁴ a5g³ a5g⁵ a56 1996 a5g⁵ a5g⁴ a5g⁴ 5f Jun 22] good-topped, plain gelding: carries condition: modest handicapper on the all-weather, poor on turf: left P. Howling after third start: stays 6f, best form at 5f: acts on all-weather surfaces and on firm and dead ground: usually front runner. *T. Hind*

TEEJAY'N'AITCH (IRE) 4 b.g. Maelstrom Lake 118 – Middle Verde (USA) 44 (Sham (USA)) [1995 52d: 8m⁶ 11.1g⁶ 8g⁴ 6f² 7f 7g³ 7m 9.2f⁶ 6f⁵ 8g 7g 7.1g⁶ 7d³ 7f 1996 7.1g⁶ 7d 8d³ 11.1f³ 13.1m⁶ 8.1g 11.1m⁶ Jul 8] lengthy gelding: good mover: poor maiden handicapper: effective at 7f, probably at 11f: acts on firm and dead ground: no improvement in visor or blinkers: inconsistent. *J. S. Goldie*

TEEN JAY 6 b.h. Teenoso (USA) 135 – Spoilt Again 91 (Mummy's Pet 125) 60 [1995 73: 10.3g³ 12g⁵ 12.3m³ 10.3f³ 11.5g 10d a12g⁴ 1996 10d 8f 11.4m 10m 15.9m² 16.2m² 16m² a16g 16d a14.8g a14g 16m 17.2d⁵ 14.1m* Oct 17] lengthy horse: shows round action: just a modest handicapper in 1996, clearly best of last 7 starts when winning slowly-run race at Redcar in October: stays 2m: acts on firm and dead going: tried visored/blinkered, no improvement: has run well when sweating. *B. J. Llewellyn*

TEE TEE TOO (IRE) 4 ch.g. Hatim (USA) 121 – Scottish Welcome (Be My – Guest (USA) 126) [1995 75d: a6g² a7g⁵ a6g⁵ 7g 6d⁴ 6m 5g² 5g 5g⁴ 6m 8.1f³ 7m⁶ 6f 6f³ 6m 1996 8m 6.9d 9.2s 7d 10f 12m 11.5m Oct 23] stocky gelding: fair handicapper at best in 1995 for P. Haslam: no form in 1996, leaving A. Harrison after fourth start: sold 2,600 gns Ascot November Sales and joined A. W. Carroll: effective at 5f, probably at 1m: best efforts on dead ground or fibresand: tried blinkered. *Miss M. K. Milligan*

TELEMANIA (IRE) 2 b.f. (Mar 2) Mujtahid (USA) 118 – African Dance (USA) 83 p (El Gran Senor (USA) 136) [1996 6.1f⁴ 6.1m* 7m³ Oct 1] tall, lengthy filly: carries condition: has scope: third foal: closely related to 4-y-o H'Ani (by Woodman) and half-sister to 3-y-o 1¼m winner Congo Man (by Rainbow Quest): dam Irish maiden daughter of Irish Oaks second Fleur Royale, a well-related broodmare: won maiden at Nottingham in September: good third in nursery final start: will be suited by further than 7f: will improve further. *W. J. Haggas*

TELEPHUS 7 b.g. Efisio 120 – Mrs Bizz (Status Seeker) [1995 –: a12g a12g 10m – a12g a12g a13g 1996 a16g⁶ a13g a12g a12g⁴ Mar 27] compact gelding: modest handicapper in 1994: no form since. *B. J. McMath*

TELLOFF 2 b.f. (Feb 28) Reprimand 122 – La Primavera (Northfields (USA)) – [1996 7m 7g Oct 18] 12,000Y: leggy, quite attractive filly: eighth foal: half-sister to several winners here and abroad, notably very smart middle-distance performer Highland Chieftain (by Kampala): dam Irish 1½m winner: well beaten in valuable sales race at Newmarket and maiden at Catterick. *M. A. Jarvis*

TEMPERING 10 b.g. Kris 135 – Mixed Applause (USA) 101 (Nijinsky (CAN) – 138) [1995 –, a58: a11g* a11g³ a11g a11g⁴ a12g a12g a11g⁵ 1996 a11g⁴ a12g³ a59 a11g* a12g⁵ a11g⁶ a12g* a16g² a11g³ a14g³ a12g² a12g² a12g³ a12g Jul 1] strong, good-bodied gelding: game and genuine front runner on the fibresand at Southwell: still capable of modest form, and won handicaps there in February and (22nd course success) March: tailed off after 2-month absence on final start: barely stays 2m, probably ideally suited by 11f to 1¾m: suited by fibresand (below form on equitrack): acts (though only poor form) on any turf going: no improvement in blinkers: often sweats. *D. W. Chapman*

TEMPTING (IRE) 4 b.f. Waajib 121 – Balela (African Sky 124) [1995 62: 10m – 8m⁵ 1996 a11g Jan 5] good-topped filly: modest maiden at 3 yrs for R. Hannon: tailed off in Southwell seller only outing for new connections: middle-distance bred: covered by Weldnaas. *J. Norton*

TEMPTING PROSPECT 2 b.f. (Feb 19) Shirley Heights 130 – Trying For 89 p Gold (USA) 103 (Northern Baby (CAN) 127) [1996 7m⁴ 8s* Oct 26] leggy, light-bodied filly: fourth foal: half-sister to smart 4-y-o 8.1f (at 2 yrs) to 13.3f winner Phantom Gold (by Machiavellian): dam 1½m winner out of Ribblesdale winner Expansive: improved good deal when winning minor event at Newbury in October by 2 lengths from Badlesmere, staying on despite wandering: will be suited by middle distances: useful filly in the making. *Lord Huntingdon*

TEMPTRESS 3 br.f. Kalaglow 132 – Circe 73 (Main Reef 126) [1995 –: 6m³ 7.5d 68 6.9s 1996 10d* 12m* 11.9d⁶ 12m³ 12m 10.1m⁶ 11.4m 10d² 10f 12g³ Nov 1] lengthy filly: fair handicapper: made all at Ayr (maiden) in May and Newbury in June: stays 1½m: acts on good to firm and dead ground: visored 4 times, including last 3 starts: usually races up with pace: sold 4,000 gns Newmarket December Sales. *P. T. Walwyn*

TENOR 5 b.g. Music Boy 124 – Songstead 92 (Song 132) [1995 69: a7g⁶ a6g⁶ a6g 60 a6g a5g* a5g* a5g³ 5g² 5g* 5m 5m⁶ 5m⁶ 5g⁴ 5g⁵ 5g 5m 5g 5g 5d 5m 1996 a5g a66 a6g a5g⁶ a5g* a5g³ a5g³ 5g³ 5g 5m 5g 5m 5m Jul 21] strong, lengthy gelding: fair 5f handicapper: took advantage of drop in weights to win at Lingfield in February: below form last 5 starts, and sold only 1,300 gns Doncaster September Sales:

acts on equitrack (below form on fibresand) and on good to firm ground: best held up for a turn of foot: genuine. *D. Nicholls*

TEN PAST SIX   4 ch.g. Kris 135 – Tashinsky (USA) (Nijinsky (CAN) 138) [1995   93 d
98: 7.1m* 10.4g 8m² 9d 1996 9.2s² 10.3g² 10.4f⁵ 9.2g⁴ 12.4m⁶ 10.4g 10s 10.3g⁵ 12s
Nov 9] lengthy, angular, good-quartered gelding: fairly useful handicapper: runner-
up on first 2 4-y-o starts: long way below form afterwards: should stay beyond 10.3f:
acts on good to firm and soft ground. *Martyn Wane*

TEOFILIO (IRE)   2 ch.c. (May 9) Night Shift (USA) – Rivoltade (USA) (Sir Ivor   87
135) [1996 8m² 7.9g² Oct 12] IR 21,000Y: attractive colt: eighth foal: closely related
to Italian 3-y-o Reine Wells (by Sadler's Wells) and half-brother to several winners,
including smart but temperamental French stayer Rachmaninov (by Brustolon): dam
unraced half-sister to Poule d'Essai des Pouliches winner Riverqueen: runner-up in
useful autumn maidens at Yarmouth and York (behind Hidden Meadow): will stay
beyond 1m: sure to win a race. *D. R. Loder*

TEOROMA   6 ch.h. Teofane – Poppy Kelly (Netherkelly 112) [1995 28: a16g³   –
16.5g a13g⁵ 18.2m⁶ 1996 14.1f⁶ 14.1f 17.2m Aug 28] close-coupled, workmanlike
horse: bad maiden handicapper: suited by 2m+: acts on equitrack: held up: looked
none too keen penultimate start. *Dr J. D. Scargill*

TERAAB   2 b.g. (Mar 14) Primo Dominie 121 – Valika 75 (Valiyar 129) [1996 6f⁶   –
Jul 26] 65,000F, 66,000Y: fifth foal: brother to Middle Park winner First Trump and
6f and 7f winner First Veil and half-brother to 2 winners by Prince Sabo, including
3-y-o Prancing, 5f winner at 2 yrs: dam, maiden placed from 1m to 1½m, half-sister
to high-class sprinter Mr Brooks: slowly away and last of 6 in maiden at Newmarket.
J. H. M. Gosden

TERDAD (USA)   3 ch.g. Lomond (USA) 128 – Istiska (FR) (Irish River (FR)   77
131) [1995 88: 7g⁵ 8d⁵ 1996 8g² Apr 8] big, rangy gelding: fairly useful maiden:
sweating, below 2-y-o form when second of 12 at Newcastle on only start at 3 yrs:
sold 16,000 gns Newmarket Autumn Sales, joined T. D. Barron and gelded: will be
suited by further than 1m. *M. R. Stoute*

TERESHKOVA (USA)   4 b.f. Mr Prospector (USA) – Lypatia (FR) (Lyphard   113 ?
(USA) 132) [1995 113: 6.5g⁴ 8d 7g* 6d² 1996 a8g* a8g² a7s* a8g* 8.5m⁴ 7g 8d Oct
11] angular, quite attractive, ex-French filly: smart performer: best effort in Europe
when neck second to Hever Golf Rose in Prix de Seine-Et-Oise at Chantilly on final
3-y-o start for A. Fabre: in fine form in Dubai early in 1996, winning a handicap,
minor event and listed race (from Takkatamm): below form in 2 listed races and a
Group 3 event on return to Europe: stays 1m: acts on good to firm and dead ground
and on sand: sent to USA. *Saeed bin Suroor*

TERMON   3 b.f. Puissance 110 – Alipura 74 (Anfield 117) [1995 58: 5g⁶ 6f³ 6m⁵   59
6g⁵ 6g⁴ 7d 6g² 7m⁴ 1996 8.1g² 8.1f² 8m⁴ 8.1g* 7g 9.2m⁴ 8.3m⁵ 7.1m 8.3g³ Sep 29]
leggy filly: modest performer: won maiden at Musselburgh in July: well below form
all subsequent starts, and sold 4,200 gns Doncaster October Sales: unlikely to stay
much beyond 1m: acts on firm ground, showed little on dead: no improvement in
visor. *Miss L. A. Perratt*

TERRY'S ROSE   2 br.f. (Mar 27) Nomination 125 – Moharabuiee 60 (Pas de   42 +
Seul 133) [1996 5d⁴ 6m⁶ a8.5g 6m a6s² Dec 19] 3,600Y: close-coupled filly: third
foal: half-sister to 3-y-o Effectual (by Efisio) and 4-y-o 1½m winner Risky
Rose (by Risk Me): dam, plater, stayed 1¼m: runner-up in late-season seller at
Wolverhampton: will stay beyond 6f. *R. Hollinshead*

TERTIUM (IRE)   4 b.g. Nordico (USA) – Nouniya (Vayrann 133) [1995 82: 8m²   93
8m* 10.3g⁶ 8m 7.3d 8f⁶ 1996 8d³ 8g 8.5g³ 8.5m* 10m⁴ 10.1m² 8m² 10.4m 8.1m⁵
9.9f⁶ 7.9m 8m 8m⁶ 9m 7.9g Oct 9] strong, good-bodied gelding: fairly useful handicapper: won rated stakes at Beverley in May: second in valuable events at Epsom and
Royal Ascot (Hunt Cup) in June: effective at 1m to 1¼m: acts on firm and dead
ground: has reportedly choked on occasions, and usually has tongue tied nowadays.
Martyn Wane

TESSAJOE   4 ch.g. Clantime 101 – Busted Love (Busted 134) [1995 74: 10d⁶   76
12.3m⁶ 12.3m⁵ 12m* 10.9g* 12.3m* 12g⁵ 10.5s⁴ 12m 1996 11.9g⁶ 12m* 11.9d⁴ 12f⁴
12.4f³ 11.9m 12g² 12g* 12g 12g Oct 26] workmanlike gelding: fair handicapper:
won at Thirsk (minor event) in April and at Catterick in September: should stay 1¾m:

acts on good to firm ground and soft: bandaged behind last 3 starts: usually travels long way on bridle: suited by waiting tactics: genuine. *M. J. Camacho*

TEST THE WATER (IRE) 2 ch.c. (Mar 13) Maelstrom Lake 118 – Baliana 89 (CAN) (Riverman (USA) 131) [1996 6m 5m² 6g² 6m² 6m³ 7d* Oct 11] IR 8,200Y: quite attractive colt: brother to Irish 1993 2-y-o 6f winner Shiowen and French winner at up to 1½m Maelstrom River: dam unraced: fairly useful performer: came from well back to win nursery at Ascot in October: needs further than 6f and will stay 1m: acts on good to firm ground and dead. *R. Hannon*

TETRIS (IRE) 2 b.f. (Feb 19) Nordico (USA) – Firefly Night (Salmon Leap ? (USA) 131) [1996 6s² 6v⁵ Nov 11] IR 10,000Y, 19,000 2-y-o: fourth foal: half-sister to 3-y-o 1½m winner Masehaab (by Mujtahid), 7f winner at 2 yrs, and 1m winner Classical Rock (by Ballad Rock): dam unraced: second in minor event at Milan in September: well beaten in weakly-contested median auction maiden at Folkestone in November: should stay 1m. *C. F. Wall*

TEUTONIC LASS (IRE) 2 b.f. (Apr 15) Night Shift (USA) – Highness Lady – (GER) (Cagliostro (GER)) [1996 6m 7f 8g Oct 25] 18,000Y: medium sized, sturdy filly: second foal: half-sister to German 3-y-o Hope The Best (by Alzao), 7f winner at 2 yrs: dam, 1m (at 2 yrs) to 1½m winner who won German Oaks, half-sister to very smart middle-distance colt Helikon: well beaten in maidens: sold 7,000 gns Newmarket Autumn Sales: sent to Germany. *P. T. Walwyn*

THAHABYAH (USA) 2 b.f. (Mar 29) Sheikh Albadou 128 – Golden Cap (USA) 71 p 76 (Hagley (USA)) [1996 6g⁴ 6m³ 6f* Sep 28] 22,000F, 22,000Y: first foal: dam 5f (at 2 yrs) and 6f winner, stayed 1m: progressive form in maidens: dead-heated at Redcar in September: stays 6f: acts on firm ground: joined D. Morley: will probably improve again. *H. Thomson Jones*

THAI MORNING 3 gr.c. Petong 126 – Bath 76 (Runnett 125) [1995 70: 5g 5.1g³ 65 + 6g⁶ 6.1f 5m* 5g⁴ 5m⁴ 1996 5s 5d⁶ 6g³ 6m⁶ 5m 6m⁵ 6g 7.1f⁴ 8d a8.5g* a8g* a10s* a108 a9.4g⁵ Dec 7] compact, sturdy colt: has a fluent action: modest handicapper on turf: improved dramatically on the all-weather late in year, winning handicap at Wolverhampton in October (by 8 lengths) and handicap and minor event at Lingfield in November: excellent fifth to Prince of Andros in listed race at Wolverhampton on final start: stays 1¼m: acts on firm ground, probably on dead, goes extremely well on the all-weather: no improvement in blinkers. *P. W. Harris*

THAKI 3 b.g. Distant Relative 128 – Highly Polished 79 (High Top 131) [1995 NR – 1996 8.5m Apr 25] 5,600F, 37,000Y: good-topped gelding: half-brother to middle-distance handicapper Star North (by Star Appeal): dam fourth at 2 yrs on only start: burly and green, tailed off in maiden at Beverley: moved poorly to post: sold 1,400 gns Newmarket July Sales. *E. A. L. Dunlop*

THALEROS 6 b.g. Green Desert (USA) 127 – Graecia Magna (USA) 109 49 § (Private Account (USA)) [1995 60, a66: a12g* a12g³ a12g³ a12g a12g 16.2m a62 § 12.4g⁶ 11.9m⁵ 14.1f² 10.1m 12m* 10m⁵ 12m³ 10m⁵ 9m² 10m* 10.1f 10m 9.2g⁵ 8.9g 1996 a18g² a8g² a8g⁵ 8m⁶ 8.5m⁵ 12f Jun 12] big, strong, lengthy gelding: modest handicapper: mulish in paddock and refused to race final start: stays 1½m: acts on fibresand (ran poorly only outing on equitrack) and firm ground, probably on soft: blinkered (mulish, tailed off) tenth 5-y-o start: often a front runner: not one to trust implicitly. *G. M. Moore*

THALJANAH (IRE) 4 ch.g. In The Wings 128 – Dawn Is Breaking (Import 86 127) [1995 92: 8d 9.9m⁵ᵈⁱˢ 12.3m* 12m* 12m⁴ 14g* 14m² 14.8m³ 1996 11.9g⁵ 14m³ 18.7g 16s³ 16m Jun 6] smallish, workmanlike gelding: fairly useful handicapper: best 3-y-o effort when third of 16 to Rocky Forum at Newbury: stays 2m: acts on good to firm ground and soft: edgy sort, sometimes sweating and on toes: has joined B. Smart. *D. L. Williams*

THAMES SIDE 5 gr.g. Beveled (USA) – Free Range 78 (Birdbrook 110) [1995 70 65: a8g⁴ a10g² 11.9m 8.3m³ 9.7m⁴ 10m³ 10m 7f² 10f² 10m² 9m⁴ 10d 8m* 10g²ᵈⁱˢ 10f⁵ 1996 8s³ 9m⁴ 8m² 9f* 9f Aug 1] tall gelding: fair handicapper: got up on line to dead-heat at Newbury in July: suited by strong pace at 1m/9f, and should have stayed beyond 1¼m: acted on equitrack, firm ground and soft: well beaten in visor at 4 yrs: held up: game and consistent: dead. *M. Madgwick*

THATCHAM ISLAND 3 ch.f. Jupiter Island 126 – Floreal 68 (Formidable – (USA) 125) [1995 NR 1996 10m 10s Oct 24] 3,200Y: big, plain filly: has a round action: third foal: sister to 8-y-o Chatham Island, prolific winner from 1m to 1¾m, and closely related to 7-y-o Essayeffsee (by Precocious), successful 6 times at 1¼m: dam ran twice at 2 yrs: in need of race, tailed off in maidens at Goodwood and Newbury. *D. L. Williams*

THATCHED (IRE)   6 b.g. Thatching 131 – Shadia (USA) 53 (Naskra (USA))   55 [1995 62: 9.9m⁶ 8g* 8m³ 8.5m⁶ 9m⁶ 8g⁵ 8f³ 8.1m* 8m⁴ 8f⁴ 8.3f⁴ 8h* 8g² 9.2g 8.9g 8f⁴ 8f⁵ 1996 8m 8.5m 7.1g⁶ 8f³ 8f⁵ 8.1g³ 8f³ 7.5m* 8f⁵ 8.3m³ 7.5g² 8g⁴ 8.5m* 8f 8m 10g 8m* 10f Nov 5] tall, leggy gelding: has a quick action: modest handicapper: won at Beverley in July and September and at Redcar in October: effective at 7.5f to 1¼m: acts on hard going: effective blinkered/visored or not: suitable mount for apprentice: tough. *R. E. Barr*

THATCHERELLA   5 br.m. Thatching 131 – Ella Mon Amour 65 (Ela-   75 Mana-Mou 132) [1995 80d: 6m* 6g³ 6.1g* 6f² 5m 6m⁵ 6m 6g 5.3g⁵ 5f 7m 1996 6m 6d* 6m 6m 6.1m⁶ 6m Aug 16] smallish, good-bodied mare: fair handicapper: won at Newbury in May: below form afterwards: effective at 5f and 6f: acts on firm and dead ground: successful when sweating: mulish in preliminaries third 5-y-o start: covered by Magic Ring. *Major D. N. Chappell*

THATCHER'S ERA (IRE)   4 ch.f. Never So Bold 135 – Prima Domina (FR)   55 89 (Dominion 123) [1995 57: 8m³ 8f² 10f 10.5s 8g⁵ 1996 a12g³ a12g a16g Jan 29] workmanlike filly: modest maiden handicapper: stays 1½m: acts on firm ground and fibresand: sold 2,600 gns Newmarket December Sales. *T. D. Barron*

THATCHMASTER (IRE)   5 b.g. Thatching 131 – Key Maneuver (USA) (Key   65 To Content (USA)) [1995 54: 10.8f 7g 8m⁴ 8g 10m 10m 8g⁴ 8g 1996 7m⁶ 8s⁶ 7f² 8m² 8.1m* 10g² 10g* 8g³ Sep 13] tall gelding: modest handicapper: won at Sandown (made all) in July and Goodwood (claiming event) in August: stays 1¼m, may well get further: acts on firm ground: headstrong: carried head awkwardly on reappearance: front runner/races prominently. *C. A. Horgan*

THAT MAN AGAIN   4 ch.g. Prince Sabo 123 – Milne's Way 83 (The Noble   101 Player (USA) 126) [1995 105: 5g⁵ a5g⁶ 5m⁴ 6m⁵ 6g⁵ 5f³ 5m* 5.1f* 5f* 5m⁴ 5d 5m³ 1996 5.1g⁴ 6g 5m 5f⁴ 5m 5d⁶ 5.6m 5g 5g Oct 19] small, compact gelding: useful handicapper: below best in 1996, leaving G. Lewis after penultimate start: best at 5f: probably acts on any going on turf, below form only run on the all-weather: usually blinkered: has won for claimer: usually races prominently. *S. C. Williams*

THAT OLD FEELING (IRE)   4 b.g. Waajib 121 – Swift Reply (He Loves Me   – 120) [1995 94: 8.1m⁴ 8m⁴ 8g⁶ 10m² 8m⁶ 10.1s² 10m 1996 8d Oct 12] quite good-topped gelding: fairly useful for R. Hannon at 3 yrs: unseated rider and bolted before tailed-off last of 24 in handicap at Ascot on belated return to flat. *J. White*

THE ATHELING (IRE)   6 b.g. Taufan (USA) 119 – Shady Glade (Sun Prince   47 128) [1995 NR 1996 6.9m 9.2g⁴ Jul 5] poor maiden, very lightly raced nowadays. *M. H. Tompkins*

THEATRE MAGIC   3 b.g. Sayf El Arab (USA) 127 – Miss Orient (Damister   64 (USA) 123) [1995 50, a66: 5f⁴ 5.1m³ 5f⁶ 5m 7.5d a7g* 1996 a7g² a8.5g² a6g⁵ 7s⁴   a68 8.5d² 8m⁵ 6d 6g a8g³ 8g a8g² a6g⁵ a9.4g³ 10g 7g a9.4g³ a7g³ a6g⁴ Dec 14] close-coupled gelding: unimpressive mover: fair handicapper: effective at 6f, and stays 9.4f: acts on fibresand and dead ground: effective blinkered/visored or not: takes keen hold, and usually forces pace/races prominently. *S. R. Bowring*

THEATRE'S DREAM (IRE)   3 b.c. Danehill (USA) 126 – Habituee (Habitat   – 134) [1995 NR 1996 8.3m 10m Aug 19] 9,500Y: half-brother to numerous winners, including 1995 French 3-y-o 7.5f winner Serviable (by Royal Academy), smart 7f and 1m winner Dabaweyaa (by Shareef Dancer) and Oaks second Acclimitise (by Shirley Heights): dam 1m winner: behind in maiden at Windsor and claimer at Leicester: sold 3,400 gns Newmarket September Sales. *J. E. Banks*

THEA (USA)   3 br.f. Marju (IRE) 127 – Switched On 84 (Known Fact (USA) 135)   95 [1995 76p: 8m⁶ 1996 7g* 8.1m 7m Sep 12] lengthy, heavy-bodied filly: useful form to win 16-runner maiden at Kempton in April by 4 lengths, showing good turn of foot to lead 1f out: off course nearly 5 months and below form afterwards, wearing crossed noseband on final start: should stay 1m. *J. R. Fanshawe*

THE BARNSLEY BELLE (IRE)   3 b.f. Distinctly North (USA) 115 – La   50 Tanque (USA) (Last Raise (USA)) [1995 –, a54: a6g 6g a6g⁶ 7m⁵ 6f a5g 1996 7.5g⁵   a59

8.1g⁶ 7g⁶ 6.9f⁵ 7.1m³ 7m² 7g a6g² a7g² a7g* a7g a8g⁵ Dec 27] leggy, angular filly: modest handicapper: won at Southwell in November: effective at 6f to 1m: acts on good to firm ground, goes well on fibresand. *J. L. Eyre*

THE BEE MAN 2 br.g. (Apr 24) Superpower 113 – Puffin Point (Ballad Rock 122) [1996 5g⁶ 5m 5m⁴ 7g⁵ 6m³ 6g Aug 16] big, plain gelding: fourth foal: dam unraced: modest maiden: stays 6f: carried head high final start: sometimes hangs left. *M. W. Easterby* — 49

THE BLACK DUBH (IRE) 3 b.g. Classic Secret (USA) 91 – Coral Cave 79 (Ashmore (FR) 125) [1995 –: 6m⁴ 7m 5h⁴ 1996 8g 10g Aug 17] rangy gelding: little worthwhile form. *J. J. Quinn* — –

THE BOOZING BRIEF (USA) 3 b.g. Turkoman (USA) – Evening Silk (USA) (Damascus (USA)) [1995 69: 8g² 7f⁵ 1996 10g 11.6m 12m⁴ 11.4g⁴ 14.1f 12m⁴ a11g⁶ 12.1g² Sep 29] tall gelding: modest maiden handicapper: should stay further than 1½m: has raced only on a sound surface on turf: blinkered (ran well) final start: has joined C. Parker's stable. *M. A. Jarvis* — 63

THE BUTTERWICK KID 3 ch.g. Interrex (CAN) – Ville Air 85 (Town Crier 119) [1995 61: 6m² 5g* 7d 6m 1996 6.1d 6g 8m 7f⁴ 6m⁵ 5.9f 13.8g³ 12.1g* 14s⁴ 18g Oct 21] workmanlike gelding: modest handicapper: won at Hamilton in September: retained by trainer 6,000 gns Doncaster November Sales: should stay 2m: acts on good to firm and soft ground: no improvement blinkered or visored: has looked a difficult ride. *R. A. Fahey* — 51

THE CAPE DOCTOR (IRE) 4 b.g. Distant Relative 128 – Yldizlar 77 (Star Appeal 133) [1995 64d: a8g³ a9.4g⁶ 6.1g 8.2m 10g 7m⁴ a9.4g 1996 a7g a11g⁴ a12g a10g 11.9f Apr 12] quite attractive gelding: poor at best nowadays: stays 11f: acts on good to firm ground and the all-weather: blinkered (no improvement) last 2 starts at 3 yrs. *A. G. Foster* — – a45

THE COMMODORE (IRE) 2 b.c. (Apr 4) Common Grounds 118 – Hinari Disk Deck 75 (Indian King (USA) 128) [1996 6d 7m 6m Oct 4] IR 7,700F, 12,000Y, 10,000 2-y-o: fourth reported foal: dam 2-y-o winner: well beaten, in claimer final start: sold 1,400 gns Newmarket Autumn Sales to go to Holland. *W. Jarvis* — –

THE COTTONWOOL KID 4 b.g. Blakeney 126 – Relatively Smart 76 (Great Nephew 126) [1995 –: 11.1f a11g a13.4m⁵ a14.8g³ a16g 1996 12g Sep 3] close-coupled gelding: sold out of T. Caldwell's stable 1,200 gns Doncaster March Sales: of no account. *T. Kersey* — –

THE DEEJAY (IRE) 2 ch.c. (Apr 14) Desse Zenny (USA) – White Jasmin 53 (Jalmood (USA) 126) [1996 5m 7m² 5.9f² 7m² 7m* 7m³ 8m 8m 7f⁶ Sep 27] IR 1,000Y, 5,400 2-y-o: smallish, workmanlike colt: third foal: dam 2m winner, also successful over hurdles: sire maiden brother to US champion 2-y-o Tasso: made all in median auction maiden at Newcastle in July: below form last 3 starts: stays 7f: visored penultimate outing: usually races prominently. *M. Brittain* — 64

THE DILETTANTI (USA) 3 br.c. Red Ransom (USA) – Rich Thought (USA) (Rich Cream (USA)) [1995 –p: 7d 1996 8d² 8m⁴ 8g* 10.4m 8m 10m⁴ 10.4m Aug 21] sturdy colt: carries condition: fluent mover: fairly useful performer: made all in maiden at Bath in May: good fourth to Fahim in £34,000 handicap at Goodwood in August: stays 1¼m: acts on good to firm and dead ground: sweating (ran respectably) fifth 3-y-o start. *J. A. R. Toller* — 90

THE DUBIOUS GOOSE 2 b.g. (May 30) Yaheeb (USA) 95§ – Dunnington (Risk Me (FR) 127) [1996 5f 6m 8.2g Oct 9] small gelding: has a round action: first foal: dam no worthwhile form: never on terms in claimer and sellers: trained by M. W. Easterby first 2 starts. *J. G. FitzGerald* — –

THE FARAWAY TREE 2 b.f. (May 12) Suave Dancer (USA) 136 – Sassalya (Sassafras (FR) 135) [1996 6m* Sep 18] half-sister to several winners, including smart 3-y-o middle-distance colt Sasuru (by Most Welcome), smart 7f performer Sally Rous (by Rousillon) and useful stayer Chauve Souris (by Beldale Flutter): dam useful Irish 7f and 1¼m winner: won maiden at Yarmouth in September by 2 lengths from Our Way, quickening well under hands and heels: will be suited by 1m+: sure to improve, and looks a useful prospect. *G. Wragg* — 85 p

THE FED 6 ch.g. Clantime 101 – Hyde Princess 75 (Touch Paper 113) [1995 59d: 5d 5m 5m 5f⁴ 5f³ 5m 5m 5f⁴ 5.1m³ 5m 5.1d⁴ 5d 5f 5.1m 6m 1996 a6g³ a6g a6g⁶ a5g — 43

5.1g 5m 6.1m Jun 24] small, strong gelding: poor handicapper at best in 1996: best form at 5f: acts on firm and dead ground: best efforts at 5 yrs in visor, wore one only once in 1996: usually races prominently: inconsistent. *J. A. Pickering*

THE FLY 2 gr.c. (May 2) Pharly (FR) 130 – Nelly Do Da 78 (Derring-Do 131) 95 p [1996 7g 7d* 8m* 8m⁴ Sep 12] 11,000Y: leggy, useful-looking colt: half-brother to 3-y-o Reploy (by Deploy) and several winners, including stayers Retouch (by Touching Wood) and Jonsalan (by Robellino): dam 2-y-o 5.8f winner, half-sister to Further Flight (by Pharly): useful performer: won median auction maiden at Ayr and valuable 20-runner nursery at Newcastle (in good style by 3 lengths from Demolition Man) in August: shade disappointing in valuable nursery final start, hanging: will prove well suited by further than 1m: likeable type, capable of better. *B. W. Hills*

THE FOUR ISLES 2 b.g. (Apr 25) Never So Bold 135 – Far Claim (USA) 35 53 (Far North (CAN) 120) [1996 5d³ 6m 5.1m⁶ 5g⁶ 5m⁴ 6f⁵ 6m⁶ 6d 7s Nov 9] 3,400Y, 2,800 2-y-o: workmanlike gelding: third foal: half-brother to 4-y-o 5f (at 2 yrs) to 1m winner Media Express (by Sayf El Arab): dam, plater, suited by 6f: modest form: bolted to start and withdrawn sixth intended outing: sold 2,000 gns Doncaster November Sales: probably stays 6f: very slowly away on soft ground. *D. Haydn Jones*

THE FRISKY FARMER 3 b.g. Emarati (USA) 74 – Farceuse (Comedy Star 63 d (USA) 121) [1995 73: 5m* 5g² 6g² 7m 6m² 6m a5g 1996 a7g⁶ a6g a6g² a6g a6g² a6g⁵ 6s* a6g² 6.1g 6.1m³ 5.1g³ 6.1m⁶ 6d⁵ 6m a6g a7g⁴ Dec 11] leggy gelding: fair performer: won 4-runner seller at Leicester in March: stays 6f: acts on good to firm and soft ground and the all-weather: races prominently: blinkered final start (out of form). *W. G. M. Turner*

THE FUGATIVE 3 b.f. Nicholas (USA) 111 – Miss Runaway 73 (Runnett 125) 58 d [1995 NR 1996 8m 7f⁵ a7g² a8s a10g Dec 20] small filly: third reported foal: dam, 6f winner, stayed 7f: modest maiden at best: inconsistent. *P. Mitchell*

THE FULLBANGLADESH 3 ch.f. Hubbly Bubbly (USA) – Oakhurst § – (Mandrake Major 122) [1995 48: 7m⁶ a7g² a8.5g 1996 a6g a8g a7g⁶ 11.1g⁵ 12g⁶ 12g⁴ Jul 1] leggy, lengthy filly: poor maiden: little worthwhile form in 1996: probably stays 8.5f. *J. L. Eyre*

THE GAY FOX 2 gr.c. (Feb 21) Never So Bold 135 – School Concert 80 (Music 80 Boy 124) [1996 5g³ 5d² 5s⁴ 6.1m² 6m⁵ 6m 6.1s Oct 31] 10,500Y: good-topped colt: has scope: third foal: half-brother to 6f winner First Play (by Primo Dominie): dam 6f winner, sister to high-class French sprinter Kind Music: fairly useful maiden: stays 6f: acts on good to firm ground, ran creditably first start on soft. *B. A. McMahon*

THE GREAT FLOOD 3 ch.g. Risk Me (FR) 127 – Yukosan 69 (Absalom 128) 55 [1995 NR 1996 8d 7.5m⁴ 10g⁶ 12.1g⁴ a7g⁵ a8.5g⁴ Sep 21] 14,500Y: plain gelding: second foal: brother to fair 1994 2-y-o 1m winner Lochbroom Commando: dam 5f and 6f winner: well beaten for N. Tinkler first 4 starts: signs of ability in claimer and maiden handicap at Wolverhampton for new yard: probably stays 8.5f: acts on fibresand: won over hurdles in November. *C. A. Dwyer*

THE GREEN GREY 2 gr.c. (Apr 9) Environment Friend 128 – Pea Green 98 59 (Try My Best (USA) 130) [1996 6m⁶ 7.1m 6g Nov 1] big, workmanlike colt: fifth foal: half-brother to fairly useful sprinter Jade Pet (by Petong) and 1994 2-y-o 6f winner Green City (by Rock City): dam raced mostly at sprint distances but probably stayed 1m: modest form on debut: raced freely second start, off course 3½ months after: should stay beyond 6f. *Lord Huntingdon*

THE GREY WEAVER 3 gr.c. Touch of Grey 90 – Foggy Dew 45 (Smoggy 115) – [1995 NR 1996 7m 7m 7d 7f 7.6m 8g a10g Nov 26] 480Y: second foal: dam 1¼m winner: of little account: tried blinkered. *R. M. Flower*

THE HAPPY FOX (IRE) 4 ch.c. Ballad Rock 122 – Amanzi 94 (African Sky 83 d 124) [1995 89: 5.1m³ 5g⁴ 5f 5m⁵ 5.1m⁶ 5f² 5m* 6m 6g⁴ 5m⁴ 1996 6s 5.1g⁵ 6m 6f 6g 5m⁵ 6m 5g² 5m⁴ 5m³ 6f 5.1g 5g 6.1s⁶ a6s³ Dec 19] strong, lengthy colt: fairly useful sprinter at best: acts on fibresand and firm ground (below form on soft): effective blinkered or not: tends to hang left: none too consistent. *B. A. McMahon*

THE IN-LAWS (IRE) 2 ch.f. (Mar 15) Be My Guest (USA) 126 – Amboselli 73 83 (Raga Navarro (ITY) 119) [1996 6.9m* 8m 8.3g 7g⁴ 7g³ Oct 26] leggy, unfurnished filly: closely related to fairly useful 7f winner Mrs Fisher and 1m winner River Chase (both by Salmon Leap) and half-sister to several winners, including 1993 2-y-o 8.3f winner Amnesia (by Don't Forget Me): dam placed over 5f at 2 yrs: fairly useful performer: won maiden at Folkestone in August: not disgraced in May Hill Stakes at Doncaster second outing: best effort final start: may stay beyond 1m: has raced only on a sound surface. *Sir Mark Prescott*

THE INSTITUTE BOY 6 b.g. Fairy King (USA) – To Oneiro 69 (Absalom 128) [1995 46, a56: a6g² a5g² a6g⁶ a5g a6g 6g 5f⁵ a5g² a5g⁴ 5m³ a5g⁶ 5m⁴ 5f⁵ 5g a5g 5m⁶ 5h 5f⁴ 5.1d 1996 a5g² a5g⁶ a5g* a6g³ a5g² a5g⁴ a6g* a6g⁴ 6d³ a5g 5g³ 6g 5m 5g² 5m⁵ 5g* 5g⁴ 5m² 5m Aug 19] smallish, strong gelding: poor mover: fair handicapper on the all-weather: won at Lingfield in February and March: modest on turf, helped by racing against favoured stand rail when winning at Catterick in July: effective at 5f and 6f: goes well on the all-weather, acts on firm and dead ground: effective in blinkers/visor (rarely tried nowadays) or not. *Miss J. F. Craze* — 53, a66

THE JOLLY BARMAID (IRE) 3 b.f. Don't Forget Me 127 – Gay Broad 78 (Gay Fandango (USA) 132) [1995 –: 6.1d 6g 1996 8.2m 10m 10m 12s⁵ 14.1m³ Jul 29] lengthy filly: poor maiden plater: probably stays 1¾m. *P. Calver* — 35

THE LAD 7 b.g. Bold Owl 101 – Solbella (Starch Reduced 112) [1995 14m⁶ 10f 8.5d 6m 6.5m⁴ 7m 8m 10d⁶ 6d 1996 a12g⁴ a16g* a16g⁵ 15.4f* 17.2f⁴ 12.1m* 16.2m a16g⁶ 14.4g Sep 6] leggy ex-Irish gelding: first foal: dam never ran: trained at 6 yrs in Ireland by M. McElhone: modest performer: won handicaps at Lingfield in February, Folkestone in April and Chepstow (apprentices) in July: below form last 3 starts: effective at 1½m, and stays 17.2f: acts on firm ground and equitrack, possibly un-suited by fibresand: usually apprentice ridden. *L. Montague Hall* — 52, a39

THE LAMBTON WORM 2 b.c. (May 13) Superpower 113 – Springwell 73 (Miami Springs 121) [1996 5m² 6m² 6m³ 6m* 6m⁴ 6d⁶ 5m Sep 19] 13,000Y: 21,000 2-y-o: strong, well-made colt: has scope: sixth foal: half-brother to 3-y-o Rusk (by Pharly), 1½m winner Marros Mill (by Glint of Gold), and a winner in Sweden by Primo Dominie: dam 10.2f winner: fair form: won maiden at Ayr in July: stays 6f: acts on good to firm ground. *Denys Smith* — 80

THE LEGIONS PRIDE 3 b.c. Rambo Dancer (CAN) 107 – Immaculate Girl 67 (Habat 127) [1995 58: 6m 6m⁴ 7g 7.3m⁵ 7m⁵ 8d 1996 10f⁶ 11.9f² 11.5m Aug 22] leggy colt: modest maiden on flat: sold 9,500 gns Newmarket Autumn Sales: prob-ably stays 1½m: acts on firm ground: sent to Sweden. *J. W. Hills* — 58

THE LITTLE FERRET 6 ch.g. Scottish Reel 123 – Third Movement 75 (Music Boy 124) [1995 63d: a8g⁵ a7g² a8g a7g² a8g 8m a8g² 7f⁶ 7f⁵ a10g⁴ a10g 7f⁶ a8g a10g² a10g⁶ a8g 1996 a10g 10f⁴ 10m 11.9g⁴ 10f Jun 17] leggy gelding: poor form at best in first season: seemed to stay 1½m: acted on soft and good to firm ground and on equitrack: none too consistent: dead. *A. Moore* — 46

THEME ARENA 3 b.f. Tragic Role (USA) – Sea Siesta (Vaigly Great 127) [1995 NR 1996 9.4g⁵ 11.5m 14m Oct 4] third foal: dam lightly-raced maiden: no form on flat: winning selling hurdler for M. Pipe. *S. Mellor* — –

THE MESTRAL 4 br.f. Formidable (USA) 125 – Lariston Gale 81 (Pas de Seul 133) [1995 48: 6.1g⁶ 6g 6m² 5f⁴ 6m 7m⁴ 8.2m⁴ 8.3m² 8m² 7f a7g a8.5g⁵ a7g⁵ 1996 a10g a8g³ a8g a8g² a7g a7g⁶ a8g Feb 19] small, compact filly: has a round action: poor handicapper: short-headed at Southwell fourth start: disappointing afterwards: best at up to 1m: acts on good to firm ground and on fibresand: tried blinkered/visored, better form without: tail swisher: front runner: sent to Holland. *M. J. Ryan* — 42

THE NOBLE OAK (IRE) 8 ch.g. The Noble Player (USA) 126 – Sea Palace (Huntercombe 133) [1995 51d, a–: 5.3m 5g 5g⁶ 5g 6m 5.1h² 5.1m 5m⁴ 5m 6f 5m⁶ 5m 1996 5m 5m 6m 5m⁴ 5g 5m 8f Sep 4] small, strong gelding: modest 5f handicapper: little form in 1996: acts on hard and dead ground and on equitrack: tried blinkered/visored, no improvement: usually races prominently: inconsistent. *M. J. Bolton* — –

THENORTHERNPLAYBOY (IRE) 3 gr.c. Distinctly North (USA) 115 – Monetary Wish (Wishing Star 117) [1995 –: 6.1m 1996 a7g a12g Apr 13] sparely-made colt: well beaten in maidens: sprint bred. *B. Preece* — –

THE ODDFELLOW 3 b.g. Efisio 120 – Agnes Jane (Sweet Monday 122) [1995 NR 1996 a8g⁶ 10s⁴ Jul 4] 12,000Y: first foal: dam unraced: well beaten in maiden and claimer. *N. Bycroft* — –

THE ORRAMAN (IRE) 2 b.g. (Mar 3) Taufan (USA) 119 – Miss Pennine (IRE) (Pennine Walk 120) [1996 5m 6d May 31] IR 10,500F, 10,000Y: first foal: dam

999

Irish maiden sister to useful and versatile Irish mare Cheviot Amble: slowly into stride and never a factor in auction maiden events. *J. J. O'Neill*

THE POLYMATH 3 ch.g. Sharpo 132 – Nisha (Nishapour (FR) 125) [1995 NR 1996 8.2m⁶ 8.3m Aug 3] first foal: dam lightly-raced out of sister to high-class sprinter New Model: seemed green when keeping-on sixth of 13 to Iamus in maiden at Nottingham: sweating, pulled very hard and well beaten in similar event at Windsor nearly 6 weeks later. *H. Candy*

THE PUZZLER (IRE) 5 br.g. Sharpo 132 – Enigma 87 (Ahonoora 122) [1995 109§: 5g⁵ 6m* 6m 5m 7g³ 6m 6m 7g⁶ 7f 6d 7d⁶ 1996 6s² 6g³ 5g 5f⁶ 6s* 6.1s⁵ 6s Nov 9] leggy, useful-looking gelding: bad mover: useful performer on his day: trained until 1996 by M. Kauntze in Ireland: second to Fire Dome in listed race at Doncaster in March: returned to best to win rated stakes at Newbury in October by ¾ length from Musical Season, leading inside final 1f: below form in minor event at Nottingham (faltered over 1f out) and listed race at Doncaster afterwards: stays 7f: acts on good to firm and heavy going: usually bandaged in front: has gone lame while racing on several occasions, and, for that reason, cannot be relied on. *B. W. Hills* 109 §

THE REAL MCCOY 2 b.g. (Mar 10) Deploy 131 – Mukhayyalah (Dancing Brave (USA) 140) [1996 6m 8g 6v Nov 11] rangy, good-topped gelding: has plenty of scope: first foal: dam unraced daughter of half-sister to Irish Oaks winner Give Thanks (grandam of Harayir): well beaten in maidens: very slowly away on debut then much too free last 2 starts. *M. R. Channon*

THE REAL WHIZZBANG (IRE) 5 b. or br.h. New Express 95 – Gail's Crystal (Crofter (USA) 124) [1995 35+, a51: a7g a6g⁵ a7g a6g³ a6g⁴ a6g a5g* a5g³ a6g 5.1g⁵ a5g³ a6g 5.1d a5g 1996 a5g³ a5g Jan 10] smallish, strong horse: poor handicapper: best at 5f on fibresand: best recent form in blinkers: often claimer ridden: usually forces pace. *P. S. Felgate* a50

THERHEA (IRE) 3 b.g. Pennine Walk 120 – Arab Art (Artaius (USA) 129) [1995 73+: 5g³ 5m³ 6f⁴ 7m⁵ 6m 7.3d⁶ 5.7m² 6f 1996 6s⁴ 8d* 7.9f 8f 8.1v 10s Oct 24] good-bodied gelding: fairly useful handicapper: well-backed, showed much improved form to win rated stakes at Newbury in April by 5 lengths: well held all 4 starts afterwards: better at 1m than shorter: best effort on dead ground: blinkered (appeared to run creditably) final 2-y-o start. *B. R. Millman* 89 d

THE ROUNDSILLS 2 ch.c. (Apr 16) Handsome Sailor 125 – Eye Sight 67 (Roscoe Blake 120) [1996 7f⁶ 8.2g a8g⁵ Nov 14] third foal: half-brother to 1993 2-y-o 7.5f seller winner Kings Vision (by Absalom): dam middle-distance maiden: little worthwhile form in maidens. *R. F. Johnson Houghton*

THE SCYTHIAN 4 ch.g. Komaite (USA) – City To City 55 (Windjammer (USA)) [1995 74: 6m* 6.1m 6m* 6f² 6m³ 5g⁴ 1996 6g 5g⁴ 6m 6d 5m² 6g⁶ 6m 6g⁴ Oct 12] stocky, deep-girthed gelding: fair handicapper: inconsistent in 1996: stayed 6f: acted on firm ground: often soon off bridle: dead. *Bob Jones* 74

THE STAGER (IRE) 4 b.c. Danehill (USA) 126 – Wedgewood Blue (USA) 87 (Sir Ivor 135) [1995 74: 7.5m* 7.5m⁴ 9m⁴ 8m 8m⁶ 8.1m⁴ 7m⁶ 12f 7f⁴ 7m² 1996 6.9f² 7g* 7m³ 10f⁶ 8g⁶ Jun 30] tall, lengthy colt: good mover, with a long stride: fair handicapper: won minor event at Newmarket in May: stays 9f, but at very best at around 7f to 1m: acts on firm ground: blinkered last 2 starts at 3 yrs: takes good hold. *J. R. Jenkins* 77

THE SUBSTITUTE 4 b.f. Colmore Row 111 – Snow Chief 90 (Tribal Chief 125) [1995 NR 1996 a8g Feb 24] half-sister to a 5f winner by Young Generation: dam miler: last of 21 in NH Flat race before tenth of 11 in Lingfield maiden. *R. Curtis*

THE SWAN 3 ch.f. Old Vic 136 – El Vino (Habitat 134) [1995 65p: 7.6d⁴ 8d 8.2m 1996 11.4d⁴ 14d* 16.2m* 16.2f 15.9d³ 15.9g⁵ 16g Oct 24] leggy filly: fairly useful handicapper: won at Haydock and Chepstow in July: very good third of 9 to Izza at Chester (hampered under 2f out, would have gone close to winning) following month: sold 24,000 gns Newmarket Autumn Sales: suited by test of stamina: winner on good to firm ground, may be ideally suited by an easy surface: often makes running: joined N. Meade in Ireland. *J. L. Dunlop* 84

THE TIG 2 b.g. (Mar 19) Tigani 120 – The Ranee (Royal Palace 131) [1996 8m 8g Oct 30] seventh reported foal: half-brother to 7f and 1m winner Alipura (by Anfield)

and a winning sprinter in Germany by Beveled: dam behind in modest company: behind in steadily-run maidens. *L. R. Lloyd-James*

THE WAD 3 b.g. Emarati (USA) 74 – Fair Melys (FR) 81 (Welsh Pageant 132) 73 [1995 56: 6m 7.5m 7m 5m 7.5d² 7.9m 7f⁶ 1996 a8.5g⁶ a7g⁴ a8g a7g⁴ a6g² a6g 6.1g* 6g³ 6g⁴ 6.1m² 6m 7s⁴ 6m* 6f⁴ 5f 6m Aug 20] good-topped, leggy gelding: unimpressive mover: fair performer: won seller at Nottingham in April and handicap at Ripon in July: well below best last 3 starts: seems ideally suited by 6f: acts on firm and dead ground (respectable effort on soft) and on fibresand: blinkered (pulled too hard) once at 2 yrs: goes well with forcing tactics: sometimes hangs under pressure. *D. Nicholls*

THE WEST (USA) 2 ch.c. (Jan 20) Gone West (USA) – Lady For Two (USA) 107 + (Storm Bird (CAN) 134) [1996 6m* 6m³ 7m² 7g Oct 18] $140,000Y: big, rangy, imposing colt: not the best of walkers: fifth foal: half-brother to My True Lady (by Seattle Slew), minor stakes winner at up to 9f in USA: dam 7f winner out of smart US filly at up to 9f Very Special Lady: comfortably won newcomers race at Goodwood in August: 1¾ lengths third of 9 to Abou Zouz in Gimcrack Stakes at York then 3 lengths second of 5 to Revoque in Prix de la Salamandre (engaged in throat-cutting battle with Zamindar and out on his feet at the line) at Longchamp: held up taking good hold when creditable seventh of 8 to In Command in Dewhurst Stakes at Newmarket on final outing, hampered late on but result not affected: will stay 1m. *P. F. I. Cole*

THEWRIGHTONE (IRE) 2 b.f. (Apr 23) Fayruz 116 – Vote Barolo (Nebbiolo – 125) [1996 5g 5m 6f 5f⁵ 5f³ 5f a5g 5m⁵ 6g 5s a7g Nov 22] IR 1,000Y: leggy filly: eighth foal: sister to modest 1995 2-y-o Shock-A-Lot and half-sister to Irish 1989 2-y-o 7f winner Manuale Del Utente (by Montekin): dam ran twice at 2 yrs: bad maiden: blinkered last 8 starts: tends to take keen hold. *G. R. Oldroyd*

THE WYANDOTTE INN 2 ch.c. (Feb 24) Ballacashtal (CAN) – Carolyn- 57 christensen 58 (Sweet Revenge 129) [1996 5g a6g⁵ a6g³ 7g a5g² a6g³ 6.1s 5m² a5g² a68 a5g³ a6g² a6g² a6g* Dec 30] 4,200Y: plain, quite good-topped colt: carries condition: poor mover: seventh foal: brother to 5.7f (at 2 yrs) and 7.6f winner Canadian Capers and half-brother to fair 7f performer Maid Welcome (by Mummy's Pet) and a winner in Germany by Nicholas Bill: dam won from 5f to 9.4f: won maiden at Lingfield in December: stays 6f: acts on good to firm ground and both all-weather surfaces. *R. Hollinshead*

THICK AS THIEVES 4 b.g. Shavian 125 – Vivienda 93 (Known Fact (USA) – 135) [1995 59d: 5m⁵ 5m⁴ 6m 6g 5g 6m a5g a6g a5g⁴ 1996 a6g⁵ a7g a6g 6.1g 6d 5g⁶ 5f 7.5m 5m a7g Nov 11] strong, workmanlike gelding: modest handicapper nowa- days: no worthwhile form in 1996: stays 6f: acts on firm and dead ground: visored (given early reminders) seventh 4-y-o start: inconsistent. *Ronald Thompson*

THIRD PARTY 2 gr.f. (Apr 17) Terimon 124 – Party Game 70 (Red Alert 127) 62 [1996 5f³ 5g⁴ 5m⁴ 6f³ Jul 13] half-sister to 3 winning sprinters, notably smart 3-y-o Passion For Life (by Charmer), and a winner in Belgium: dam 6f winner who stayed 7f: modest form in maidens and nursery (pulled hard): probably better suited by 6f than 5f. *S. Dow*

THISONESFORALICE 8 b.g. Lochnager 132 – Bamdoro 54 (Cavo Doro 124) – [1995 40: 9.2g 8.3g 11.1f² 12.1m² 9.2m 12.1m² 10.9g 1996 8.1g Apr 4] leggy gelding: poor middle-distance handicapper: well beaten only 8-y-o outing: tried visored: found little sixth 7-y-o start. *J. S. Goldie*

THOMAS CROWN (IRE) 4 ch.c. Last Tycoon 131 – Upward Trend 112 – (Salmon Leap (USA) 131) [1995 –: 8g 8g 1996 a7g a10g a9.4g⁵ a8.5g Mar 15] of little account: sold 650 gns Doncaster March Sales. *N. J. H. Walker*

THORDIS 3 b.g. Mazilier (USA) 107 – Doppio 62 (Dublin Taxi) [1995 77: 6.1d⁵ 78 a6g² 6f* 1996 6m² 6f⁵ 6.1m⁴ 7f⁵ 6m 7g* a7g Dec 20] quite good-topped gelding: fair performer: clearly best effort since reappearance when winning 21-runner claimer at Doncaster in October by 5 lengths, overcoming unfavourable draw: ran wide when well held in handicap 2 months later: stays 7f well: acts on firm and dead ground and on fibresand: visored last 2 starts. *P. J. Makin*

THORNBY PARK 2 b.f. (Apr 2) Unfuwain (USA) 131 – Wantage Park 104 (Pas 72 p de Seul 133) [1996 8.2g 8g⁶ Oct 25] sturdy, lengthy filly: third foal: sister to winning

5-y-o stayer Izza: dam stayed 7f: staying-on sixth in Doncaster maiden on final start: will probably stay middle distances: will improve further. *J. L. Dunlop*

THORNIWAMA 5 b.m. Hadeer 118 – Hidden Asset (Hello Gorgeous (USA) – 128) [1995 41?: a10g⁴ a13g⁶ a10g⁵ a8g³ a12g a8g 1996 a10g a12g a8g⁵ a7g⁴ a10g³ a10g* 9.7m 11.7g a11g 10f 11.6m Jul 22] leggy mare: poor handicapper: won at Lingfield in April: needs further than 7f and stays 1¼m: acts on equitrack (ran poorly only run on fibresand), no form on turf: usually blinkered/visored. *J. J. Bridger* — a45

THORNTON (USA) 2 b.c. (Jan 14) Woodman (USA) 126 – Dolsk (Danzig (USA)) [1996 6g 7f⁵ 6s Oct 24] small, good-bodied colt: first foal: dam French 1¼m and 11f winner, half-sister to Pebbles: no form on soft ground. *J. H. M. Gosden* — 66

THORNTOUN ESTATE (IRE) 3 b.g. Durgam (USA) – Furry Friend (USA) (Bold Bidder) [1995 64: a8.5g⁵ 8.3g⁴ 10g⁴ a8.5g³ a10g* 1996 a10g³ a10g* a11g a10g³ a12g² 12s⁴ 12.1d⁴ 12d 13s 14.6m May 6] leggy gelding: modest handicapper: narrowly won at Lingfield in January: ran poorly last 3 starts: stays 1½m: acts on the all-weather and on soft ground: blinkered (sweating, ran poorly) eighth 3-y-o start: temperament under suspicion: has joined M. Todhunter. *M. Johnston* — 59 a62

THORNTOUN HOUSE (IRE) 3 b.g. Durgam (USA) – Commanche Song 48 (Commanche Run 133) [1995 NR 1996 10g⁵ 15.8m⁴ Aug 6] first foal: dam maiden: well held in maiden and seller. *J. S. Goldie* —

THORNTOUN JEWEL (IRE) 3 b.f. Durgam (USA) – Blue Bouquet (Cure The Blues (USA)) [1995 50: 5g⁵ 5g² 6g* 6m⁶ 7m³ 7h⁵ 6.1d 7g 6s 1996 a6g 6m⁵ 7m 6m 7.1f⁵ 5.9f Jun 26] smallish filly: modest performer at best at 2 yrs: no worthwhile form in claiming/selling company in 1996, sold out of J. Balding's stable 1,050 gns Ascot June Sales after fourth start: usually blinkered. *Miss Z. A. Green* —

THORNY BISHOP 5 b.g. Belfort (FR) 89 – Hill of Fare (Brigadier Gerard 144) [1995 –: a6g⁶ a6g³ a6g⁵ 1996 a7g a8g a6g⁵ 7f 5m May 18] big, lengthy gelding: of no account. *B. A. Pearce* —

THOR'S PHANTOM 3 ch.g. Weldnaas (USA) 112 – La Carlotta (Ela-Mana-Mou 132) [1995 NR 1996 8.3d 7d 9g Aug 30] third foal: brother to 4-y-o Fastini Gold: dam unraced: well beaten in maiden and claimers. *M. D. I. Usher* —

THREADNEEDLE (USA) 3 b.g. Danzig Connection (USA) – Sleeping Beauty 87 (Mill Reef (USA) 141) [1995 NR 1996 8.2d 8m* 8d Oct 12] workmanlike gelding: fourth foal: brother to fair 8.5f to 1½m winner Magic Junction and half-brother to 4-y-o Twilight Sleep (by Shadeed), 7f winner at 2 yrs: dam, 1m winner, half-sister to 2 Galtres Stakes winners: off course 5½ months, clearly best effort when winning 12-runner maiden at Newbury in September by ½ length from Scarpetta, travelling well much of way and edging ahead entering last: co favourite, dropped right out (jockey reported horse had lost action completely) to finish in rear in 24-runner handicap at Ascot 22 days later: bred to be suited by further than 1m: worth another chance to confirm Newbury promise. *Lord Huntingdon* — 81 p

THREE ARCH BRIDGE 4 ch.f. Sayf El Arab (USA) 127 – Alanood 85 (Northfields (USA)) [1995 68: a7g² a7g² a7g a8g⁴ a7g³ a7g* 8f 8g² 9.2g³ 7.5m² 8m 7g⁴ 8d³ 7f² 8.3f* 8.5g a9.4g² 9.2f* 8.2m² 8.3f⁶ 8h³ 8m⁶ 8.5d* 8d 8m⁶ 1996 8m 8.3s³ 8.3s⁵ 6.9g³ 9.2g* 7.5m* a9.4g² 7.5f³ 8f* 8f 8.1g 8.3m 8.5m⁴ 8f a7g a9.4g a7s⁶ a8g⁴ Dec 27] quite good-topped filly: fair handicapper: successful at Hamilton, Beverley and Carlisle (sixth run in 15 days) in June: stays 9.4f: acts on the all-weather and on any turf ground: blinkered since sixth 3-y-o start: usually races prominently: tough. *M. Johnston* — 71

THREE CARD TRICK (IRE) 2 ch.f. (May 19) Shalford (IRE) 124§ – Tricky 66 (Song 132) [1996 6m 6g 7f Sep 4] 8,200f: smallish filly: fifth foal: half-sister to fair 5f winner Magic Orb (by Primo Dominie) and 1¾m winner Witches Coven (by Sharrood): dam poor sister to smart sprinter Jester: never a factor in varied events, including a seller: sold 1,000 gns Newmarket Autumn Sales. *R. Hannon* —

THREE CHEERS (IRE) 2 b. or br.g. (Feb 22) Slip Anchor 136 – Three Tails 121 (Blakeney 126) [1996 8g Oct 29] fifth foal: half-brother to 3-y-o 1¼m winner Triple Leap and very smart middle-distance 4-y-o Tamure (both by Sadler's Wells):

dam, 1½m winner, half-sister to 1000 Guineas and Oaks placed Maysoon out of smart Triple First: behind in maiden at Leicester. *J. H. M. Gosden*

THREE FOR A POUND 2 b.c. (Mar 5) Risk Me (FR) 127 – Lompoa (Lomond 58 (USA) 128) [1996 6g⁴ Jun 15] 5,800F, 6,000Y resold 3,400Y: sturdy, lengthy colt: has scope: third foal: brother to 3-y-o Credite Risque: dam ran twice: fourth in median auction maiden at Leicester in June: very coltish beforehand: seemed sure to improve. *J. A. Glover*

THREE HILLS 3 b.c. Danehill (USA) 126 – Three Stars 93 (Star Appeal 133) 87 [1995 82p: 7d⁵ 8m³ 1996 10.3s⁵ 10m² 12.3g 10m² 10.3g* 11.9g⁵ 11.9m 12m⁵ 10m 12m Oct 17] strong, deep-bodied colt: fluent mover: fairly useful performer: made all in maiden at Doncaster in June: mostly below form in handicaps afterwards, and sold 19,000 gns Newmarket Autumn Sales: should prove best at up to 1½m: acts on good to firm ground, may be unsuited by a soft surface: blinkered eighth (ran creditably) and ninth (well beaten) 3-y-o starts: not one to rely on. *B. W. Hills*

THREEPLAY (IRE) 2 b.c. (Apr 19) Mac's Imp (USA) 116 – Houwara (IRE) 64 (Darshaan 133) [1996 6m⁵ 5g⁴ 6m⁵ 5g³ 6m 6.1s a5g⁵ a5g² a6g⁶ a5g³ Dec 20] IR 7,400F, 7,000Y, resold 3,100Y: smallish, angular, round-actioned colt: third foal: half-brother to 4-y-o 11f seller winner Milltown Classic (by Classic Secret): dam unraced: modest form: best form at 5f: acts on good to firm ground (well beaten on soft) and equitrack: thrice visored (ran well only first occasion). *J. Akehurst*

THREESOCKS 3 ch.f. Weldnaas (USA) 112 – Jeethgaya (USA) 61 (Critique – (USA) 126) [1995 62?: a7g⁶ 8.1m⁵ 8.1d⁶ 1996 a8g³ a11g⁴ Feb 23] modest maiden at best: has shown distinct signs of unsatisfactory temperament, flashing tail when hit with whip and giving trouble in preliminaries: should stay beyond 1m. *B. Smart*

THREESOME (USA) 3 ch.f. Seattle Dancer (USA) 119 – Triode (USA) 105 – (Sharpen Up 127) [1995 79: 7m³ 7m⁵ 7d² 1996 8g⁶ 8.2m Jun 10] lengthy filly: good mover: fair form in maidens at 2 yrs: well beaten in 1996, giving impression something amiss on second start: sold 11,000 gns Newmarket July Sales: should be suited by 1m+. *L. M. Cumani*

THREE WEEKS 3 ch.g. Formidable (USA) 125 – Zilda (FR) 46§ (Zino 127) 67 [1995 –: 7.1d 7.1d 1996 10s a8g a8g² a8g* a8.5s* Dec 19] lengthy, rather unfurn-ished gelding: unimpressive mover: much improved late in year, winning handicaps at Southwell and Wolverhampton in December: should prove at least as effective over 1¼m as 1m: acts on fibresand, raced only on a soft surface on turf. *W. R. Muir*

THRILLING DAY 3 b.f. Groom Dancer (USA) 128 – Pushoff (USA) 78 (Sauce 112 Boat (USA)) [1995 100: 6m³ 6m² 6m* 6m⁴ 6g* 7m⁶ 6m* 1996 7m* 6f 8m⁶ 7m*

Shadwell Stud Nell Gwyn Stakes, Newmarket—
Thrilling Day (black cap) is dwarfed by Bint Salsabil on her left;
further across are My Melody Parkes and Honest Guest

Bloomsbury Stud's "Thrilling Day"

7.3m 7m³ 7m⁴ 8.5f Nov 23] small, close-coupled filly: has a quick action: smart performer: won Shadwell Stud Nell Gwyn Stakes at Newmarket in April by short head from Bint Salsabil (gave 3 lb) and 14-runner listed race at Goodwood in July by 1¾ lengths from Forest Cat: below form in Group/Graded races afterwards, including in USA final start: suited by 7f: acted on good to firm ground: held up: went well fresh: tail flasher, but game: reportedly to stay in USA and be covered in 1997. *N. A. Graham*

THROWER 5 b.g. Thowra (FR) – Atlantic Line (Capricorn Line 111) [1995 48: 11.8m⁴ 14.1m 10.8g² 12.3m⁵ 11.4m 10m 10.5m 14g³ 14d² 1996 a14.8g⁴ Jan 10] sparely-made gelding: poor maiden handicapper: stays 1¾m: acts on good to firm and dead ground and on fibresand: has joined W. Brisbourne. *B. Preece*   41

THRUSHWOOD 4 b.f. Move Off 112 – Spring Garden 54 (Silly Prices 110) [1995 –: 7g 10m 1996 6.9d a11g 7m Aug 6] robust filly: of no account. *N. Chamberlain*   –

THUNDEROUS 5 b.g. Green Desert (USA) 127 – Mixed Applause (USA) 101 (Nijinsky (CAN) 138) [1995 –: a10g 1996 a7g⁶ a10g⁵ a12g Jan 25] lengthy, well-made gelding: well bred but no worthwhile form. *J. J. Bridger*   –

THUNDER RIVER (IRE) 6 ch.g. Thatching 131 – In For More (Don 128) [1995 67: 7f 7f 7g 7g* 8d 7d 7m⁶ 1996 8g 7m 7g⁶ Aug 1] lengthy gelding: poor mover: fair handicapper: below form in 1996: stays 7f: acts on firm and dead going: usually visored: usually races prominently. *M. J. Heaton-Ellis*   55

THURSTASTON (IRE)   3 b.c. Thatching 131 – Bell Tower 98 (Lyphard's Wish   –
(FR) 124) [1995 NR 1996 8.1m 8.3m Aug 3] 35,000F, 30,000Y: strong, good-bodied
colt: fourth foal: brother to 5-y-o 6f winner Sycamore Lodge and half-brother to Irish
6f winner Markievicz (by Doyoun): dam, Irish mare, stayed 1m: well beaten in
maidens: dead. *J. H. M. Gosden*

THWAAB   4 b.g. Dominion 123 – Velvet Habit 89 (Habitat 134) [1995 43: 7.1f⁵   73
7m³ 7g⁶ 7.1g 7m⁴ a8g⁶ 1996 a7g 6.9d² 7d 6.9m⁵ 6.9g 5.9f⁵ 6m* 6g³ 6m* 6g² 6m* 6m
6m² 7m⁴ 6f Nov 5] strong, good-bodied gelding: fair handicapper: much improved
efforts since tried in headgear on seventh 4-y-o start, winning at Ayr in June and July
and at Redcar in August: short-headed by Cretan Gift in Silver Cup back at Ayr on
thirteenth start, finishing strongly: effective at 6f and 7f: acts on good to firm and
dead ground: visored or blinkered last 9 outings: usually held up. *F. Watson*

TIAMA (IRE)   3 b.f. Last Tycoon 131 – Soyata (Bustino 136) [1995 50: 7m⁵ 6s 7g   –
1996 7m 7.3d 9.7m⁵ 10f⁶ a10g 12m Aug 16] small filly: little worthwhile form in
1996. *S. Dow*

TIAPHENA   5 b.m. Derrylin 115 – Velda 74 (Thatch (USA) 136) [1995 NR 1996   49
14.1s⁵ 17.1g a16g² 15.8g* 18m Jun 17] big, workmanlike mare: poor handicapper:
won at Catterick in June: stays 2m, possibly not 2¼m. *J. Mackie*

TIBBI BLUES   9 b.m. Cure The Blues (USA) – Tiberly (FR) (Lyphard (USA)   –
132) [1995 NR 1996 6.9f² 8.3m² 5g 8m Aug 28] half-sister to minor winners in
France, including (at 11f) by Ela-Mana-Mou: dam unraced: won over 1m in France
at 2 yrs: went to stud and produced a foal in 1991: little worthwhile form in Britain,
gambled on first 2 starts. *W. Storey*

TICKA TICKA TIMING   3 b.g. Timeless Times (USA) 99 – Belltina 41   –
(Belfort (FR) 89) [1995 –, a59: 6g 7m 7f 6m⁶ a6g* 6f⁶ a6g 6s a7g³ 1996 a7g a7g a6g
Mar 9] small gelding: modest performer at 2 yrs: well beaten in 1996. *B. W. Murray*

TICKNTIMA   2 ch.c. (Mar 21) Precocious 126 – Stolon Time 80 (Good Times   63
(ITY)) [1996 5g⁴ 5f³ 5g⁵ 6g⁵ Jul 20] lengthy, workmanlike colt: third reported foal:
dam 2-y-o 6f winner bred to stay at least 1m: modest form in varied races: probably
stays 6f. *M. D. Hammond*

TIFASI (IRE)   6 b.g. Shardari 134 – Tikrara (USA) 87 (Assert 134) [1995 NR   –
1996 a16g Jan 12] ex-Irish gelding: won NH Flat race in July 1994 for D. Carroll:
little form on flat. *John Berry*

TIGER LAKE   3 ch.c. Nashwan (USA) 135 – Tiger Flower 103 (Sadler's Wells   82 +
(USA) 132) [1995 NR 1996 10.1g⁵ 12m* 16.2m Jun 19] lengthy, well-made, attractive colt: has scope: good mover: first foal: dam, 1¼m winner placed at 1½m, out of
sister to high-class American middle-distance stayer One On The Aisle: clearly best
effort when winning maiden at Goodwood in June, leading over 3f out then carrying
head high (probably green): very stiff task, tailed off in Queen's Vase at Royal Ascot
only subsequent start: better suited by 1½m than 1¼m. *Saeed bin Suroor*

TIGER SHOOT   9 b.g. Indian King (USA) 128 – Grand Occasion 63 (Great   –
Nephew 126) [1995 –, a61+: a11g⁴ a13g⁵ a12g⁶ 1996 a11g 11.8d a12g May 9] close-
coupled, workmanlike gelding: fair handicapper at best: never placed to challenge at
Southwell (trainer fined, jockey suspended and horse banned for 30 days as a result)
final 8-y-o start: well beaten in 1996. *D. T. Thom*

TIGRELLO   2 ch.c. (Mar 10) Efisio 120 – Prejudice 83 (Young Generation 129)   77 p
[1996 5f⁵ 5.7d² 6g⁶ Oct 18] 19,000Y: leggy, quite good-topped colt: fourth foal:
brother to 1995 2-y-o 6f winner Privileged and fair 7f to (in Italy) 10.5f winner Al
Moulouki and half-brother to fairly useful 6f/1m performer Hob Green (by Move
Off): dam (maiden) suited by 1m: fair form in maidens at Bath and Newmarket last 2
starts: likely to stay 1m: remains capable of improvement. *G. Lewis*

TILAAL (USA)   4 ch.c. Gulch (USA) – Eye Drop (USA) 96 (Irish River (FR)   80
131) [1995 77§: 10m³ 10g⁴ 10.3g³ 11.9m⁶ 8m³ 8m⁴ 10d 1996 8g³ 8m May 1] strong,
angular colt: fair maiden: disappointed and looked ungenuine at 3 yrs for E. Dunlop:
best effort when third of 16 at Ripon on reappearance: didn't get best of runs when
ninth of 31 in handicap at Ascot 3 weeks later: stays 1¼m: acts on good to firm
ground: visored (tailed off) final 3-y-o start. *M. D. Hammond*

TILER (IRE)   4 br.g. Ballad Rock 122 – Fair Siobahn (Petingo 135) [1995 86: 7g²   86
7m 7m⁵ 7g 8f 6m* 7m² 6m 6g 7d 6f³ 1996 6s⁵ 7d³ 6g⁴ 6m 7g 7m 6.1m³ 6d 6m²

6f* 6m² 6m² 6m 5.6m 6m 6v 7g 6f² a6g Nov 16] tall, lengthy gelding: fairly useful handicapper on his day: made all against favoured stand rail at Thirsk in July: good efforts afterwards when second: effective at 6f and 7f: acts on firm and soft ground, and fibresand: well beaten only try in blinkers: tends to wander under pressure: races prominently. *M. Johnston*

TILLYARD (IRE) 3 b.f. Caerleon (USA) 132 – Royal Heroine 121 (Lypheor 118) [1995 NR 1996 7g 8g² 8m³ Jul 29] leggy, unfurnished filly: fourth reported living foal: half-sister to 1991 2-y-o 6f winner Castilian Queen (by Diesis) and useful 6f and 7f winner (stayed 1¼m) Regal Sabre (by Sharpen Up): dam won Breeders' Cup Mile: fair form in maidens: will be well suited by further than 1m: sent to Australia. *P. W. Chapple-Hyam*   78

TILLYBOY 6 b.g. Little Wolf 127 – Redgrave Creative 67 (Swing Easy (USA) 126) [1995 NR 1996 13.1d³ May 31] first foal: dam 7f winner in NH Flat races, winning in 1994/5 season: 5 lengths third of 5 to Candle Smile in steadily-run minor event at Ayr on Flat debut, set plenty to do: should improve. *Mrs M. Reveley*   75 p

TILLY OWL 5 b.m. Formidable (USA) 125 – Tilly Tavi 74 (Welsh Pageant 132) [1995 47: a8g a8g a7g² a7g* a8.5g⁵ a12g a7g³ 1996 a8g⁶ a7g a7g³ a6g a7g Apr 27] small, angular mare: poor handicapper on her day: should stay 1m: acts on fibresand. *J. A. Harris*   47

TILSTON 5 b.g. Dunbeath (USA) 127 – Cribyn 96 (Brigadier Gerard 144) [1995 NR 1996 10s Aug 31] big, workmanlike gelding: half-brother to fairly useful 6f to 1m performer Duckington (by Bustino): dam, 7f and 1m winner on only starts, half-sister to Caergwrle: signs of a little ability in first of 2 NH Flat races in the spring: well beaten in maiden at Ripon on flat debut. *Mrs J. Cecil*   –

TIMARIDA (IRE) 4 gr.f. Kalaglow 132 – Triumphant 90 (Track Spare 125) [1995 124: 7v* 7g* 8.5s* 8m* 8f³ 8g* 9.3d* 10g* 1996 10d² 8f 8m² 10d* 9.5f* 10g* 10g³ 10f⁴ Dec 1]   125

In 1995, Timarida was Europe's highest-rated female over middle distances. In 1996, she was deprived of that distinction only by Bosra Sham's late step up in trip. Timarida was in the field that day, in the Champion Stakes at Newmarket, and was beaten three and a half lengths into third of six. Her participation had been in some doubt when she coughed after work on the Monday, but blood tests apparently showed that a slight bacterial infection had

Grosser Dallmayr Preis-Bayeriches Zuchtrennen, Munich—
the fillies Timarida and La Blue are first and third, separated by Germany (rails)

Irish Champion Stakes, Leopardstown—Timarida shows much the best turn of foot; behind, right to left, are Dance Design, Shaamit, Tamayaz and Glory of Dancer

cleared up. She was also slightly hampered running into the Dip, but, though she finished strongly, there is no way that Timarida looked capable of troubling the winner. Timarida ran to her best, only a length behind Halling.

That Champion Stakes run might not have been good enough to merit a second accolade as best of that division in Europe, but it was sufficient to win two European Group 1 races in 1996 and for a Grade 1 victory that put her into serious contention for an Eclipse award as the year's top female on turf in North America. For her first victory of the season, however, Timarida established her pre-eminence in Germany; in Germany and against Germany, for it was that five-year-old who provided the sternest opposition in the snappily-titled Grosser Dallmayr Preis-Bayeriches Zuchtrennen at Munich in August, Timarida holding him off by half a length. She had had three earlier outings, twice a creditable runner-up, but trailing in a long way behind in the Queen Anne Stakes at Royal Ascot where she broke a blood vessel. That did not stop connections embarking on a top-level European campaign with her, but it must have made races in North America doubly attractive given their permissive drugs laws, and three weeks after her German triumph Timarida was administered with lasix for the first time in the Beverly D Stakes at Arlington. She was most impressive. The ex-French filly Matiara (who had been beaten by Timarida in the E.P. Taylor at Woodbine ten months earlier) tragically sustained a fatal injury but there were half a dozen others of similar quality left in the field and only one presented Timarida with a problem. Perfect Arc had a clear lead entering the short straight but Timarida made up the three lengths on her and then added another two and a half for good measure, the pair well clear.

At this stage of her career, Irish racegoers had still not seen Timarida near her best on home soil. That was put right in the Irish Champion Stakes at Leopardstown in September. There were just the six runners, but, with the exception of the clash with Bosra Sham and Halling five weeks later, it was the stiffest test Timarida has had to face. Her opponents were, in the order they took up in the steadily-run early stages, Irish Oaks winner Dance Design, Godolphin colt Tamayaz, Derby winner Shaamit, Dante winner Glory of Dancer and four-

H. H. Aga Khan's "Timarida"

Timarida (IRE) (gr.f. 1992)	Kalaglow (gr 1978)	Kalamoun (gr 1970)	Zeddaan
			Khairunissa
		Rossiter (ch 1970)	Pall Mall
			Sonia
	Triumphant (b 1977)	Track Spare (b 1963)	Sound Track
			Rosy Myth
		Pugnacity (b 1962)	Pampered King
			Ballynulta

time pattern winner Idris, but Timarida swept past them all in the space of a furlong in the straight. She won going away by a length and a half and the rest finished in a heap, Shaamit hemmed in for part of the home straight. In December it was reported that Timarida would be in training again as a five-year-old so she should be back for the Irish Champion in 1997. Bar the Irish St Leger—she is worth a try at a mile and a half, but the St Leger would be taking things too far—that is the only Group 1 race in Ireland open to her and Timarida is very much a Group 1 performer. She is by necessity an international per-former, and has so far won in five countries. After Leopardstown in 1996, it was off to Newmarket to try to add Britain to the list, and after that Timarida was back in America. This, though, was one of her very rare disappointments. Having missed the Yellow Ribbon with a temperature, Timarida performed some way below her best in the Matriarch Stakes at Hollywood Park, a race won by Wandesta who later received the Eclipse Award for Champion Turf Female.

Supplementing Timarida for the 1996 Arc was under consideration for a while, but whether she ever gets a crack at a mile and a half remains to be seen—she looks an increasingly formidable opponent at around a mile and a quarter and sometimes takes a keen hold. A step up in trip is not usually the preferred option for horses who exhibit the excellent turn of foot that she possesses. Sometimes bandaged, the good-topped filly Timarida acts on any going and is tough, game and consistent. Her pedigree was detailed in *Racehorses of 1995*. Sire Kalaglow is a stamina influence but her dam Triumphant raced only at around seven furlongs or a mile. Triumphant is daughter of a smart performer in Pugnacity and half-sister to a top-class one in Relkino. She had four winners prior to Timarida and a 1996 three-year-old Tiyana (by Zayyani) who has made the frame a few times in the French Provinces. Triumphant was sold for IR 5,200 guineas in February 1994, since when her entries in *Return of Mares* have been two 'no returns' and a 1996 colt by Roi Danzig, the breeders of which are listed as Azienda Agricola Le Ferriere. The Aga Khan may not have received a lot for her but he is getting an awful lot out of her. *J. Oxx, Ireland*

TIME ALLOWED   3 b.f. Sadler's Wells (USA) 132 – Time Charter 131 (Saritamer (USA) 130) [1995 –p: 7m 1996 12g² 12m* 12m² 11.9m² 14.6m² 12g² 12d* Oct 12] rather unfurnished filly: smart performer: won maiden at Kempton in July: second in Tote Gold Trophy at Goodwood, listed race at York (head behind Eva Luna), Park Hill Stakes at Doncaster (1¾ lengths behind Eva Luna) and listed race at Ascot (sweating slightly, 2 lengths behind Altamura) next 4 starts: gone in coat, had front-running tactics adopted when winning Princess Royal Stakes at Ascot in October by short head from Spout (pair 4 lengths clear), battling back to get up on the nod: effective at 1½m and stays 14.6f: acts on good to firm and dead ground: bandaged last 2 starts: game. *M. R. Stoute*   113

Princess Royal Stakes, Ascot—Time Allowed (left) and Spout have a battle royal

TIME CAN TELL 2 ch.g. (Apr 23) Sylvan Express 117 – Stellaris (Star Appeal 71 133) [1996 5g 5m 7d⁴ 8f⁶ 8.1m² 8.2g* 8m⁴ 8f⁴ Nov 5] 4,000F, 5,500Y, 2,500 2-y-o: big, strong, heavy-topped gelding: has plenty of scope: half-brother to 3-y-o Rapid Liner (by Skyliner) and 3 winners, including one-time fairly useful 6f/1m performer Ashdren (by Lochnager): dam lightly raced: stayed on strongly when winning seller at Nottingham in October: good fourth in non-selling nurseries after: suited by a test of stamina: visored fourth start (below form): usually bandaged. *C. Murray*

TIME CLASH 3 b.f. Timeless Times (USA) 99 – Ash Amour 54 (Hotfoot 126) 62 d [1995 63, a67: a5g⁶ 6f⁴ 6.1m⁵ 6g* 7.3d 7g 6.1s a7g a6g* a6g² 1996 a7g³ 7d 7m⁴ 6g a7g 7f 6.1m a7g a9.4g a7g Nov 22] sparely-made filly: modest performer at best: lost her way final 7 starts: stays 7f: acts on equitrack and good to firm ground, may well be unsuited by a soft surface: none too consistent. *B. Palling*

TIME FOR ACTION (IRE) 4 b.g. Alzao (USA) 117 – Beyond Words (Ballad 91 Rock 122) [1995 90: 12.3m 12g⁴ 12m 11.9m² 10m⁴ 12m 1996 10m 12m 12m* 13.9m 11.9f 12m³ 12g 10.4g³ 10s Oct 24] small gelding: fairly useful handicapper: 9-length winner of 4-runner £7,900 event at Pontefract in August: other creditable 4-y-o efforts only when third: effective at 1¼m and should stay beyond 1½m: acts on good to firm and dead ground: goes well with forcing tactics: game. *M. H. Tompkins*

TIME FOR A GLASS 3 b.f. Timeless Times (USA) 99 – Marie Zephyr 75 (Tre- 42 boro (USA) 114) [1995 –: 5f⁵ 7g⁴ 1996 5.9f 10s² 10m⁴ 12f⁵ 10m⁵ Aug 10] poor maiden: sold 2,500 gns Doncaster August Sales: seems best at around 1¼m: acts on good to firm and soft ground. *D. Moffatt*

TIME FOR TEA (IRE) 3 ch.f. Imperial Frontier (USA) 112 – Glowing Embers 70 d 107 (Nebbiolo 125) [1995 73: 5m 6m² 6f⁴ 6f³ 5.2f³ a5g² a6g⁵ 1996 6m⁵ 6f³ 7m 6m 7g⁶ 6m 8f 10.3d³ 11.5m 6.9g a6g⁵ a8g a8g Dec 13] sturdy filly: fair maiden handi-capper at best: stays 10.3f: yet to race on soft ground, acts on any other and also on equitrack: swished tail under pressure penultimate outing. *C. A. Cyzer*

TIME GOES ON 4 b.f. Latest Model 115 – Impromptu 88 (My Swanee 122) – [1995 NR 1996 8m 6g 5.7m 6f Sep 23] sister to fairly useful sprint handicapper Mister Jolson, and half-sister to several other winners, including useful sprinter Easy Line (by Swing Easy): dam won over 7f and 1¼m: signs of ability but no worthwhile form. *R. J. Hodges*

TIME LEADER 4 ch.g. Lead On Time (USA) 123 – Green Leaf (USA) 97 – § (Alydar (USA)) [1995 67§: 7m 10m 8m⁴ 8m 1996 8.9g Oct 12] quite attractive gelding: fair maiden at best in 1995 for M. Stoute, dropping himself out final start (visored): well held only 4-y-o outing: should stay 1¼m: one to treat with caution. *R. Dickin*

TIMELESS 4 b.f. Royal Academy (USA) 130 – Glory of Hera 99 (Formidable 53 (USA) 125) [1995 58: 11.4m⁶ 10g⁵ 8f³ 1996 a8g Mar 14] long-backed, attractive filly: modest maiden: probably stays 11.4f: acts on firm ground and equitrack: covered by Night Shift. *C. A. Dwyer*

TIMELY EXAMPLE (USA) 5 ch.h. Timeless Moment (USA) – Dearest – Mongo (USA) (Mongo) [1995 –: a7g 1996 a8.5g a12g⁴ a12g⁴ a14g 8g a12g⁵ May 31] workmanlike horse: no longer of much account on flat. *B. R. Cambidge*

TIMELY TIMES 3 ch.f. Timeless Times (USA) 99 – Times 55 (Junius (USA) – 124) [1995 NR 1996 5.2m⁶ 6.9d a8.5g Nov 11] fourth reported live foal: half-sister to 2-y-o 7f/1m winners Military Expert (by Superlative) and Times Zando (by For-zando): dam disappointing maiden: no sign of ability in maidens and seller. *C. A. Dwyer*

TIMELY TOUCH 2 ch.f. (Apr 9) Timeless Times (USA) 99 – Miss Sherbrooke – (Workboy 123) [1996 5f⁴ 5s³ 5m 6m 7g Aug 16] second reported foal: sister to un-genuine 3-y-o Time Ticks On: dam poor novice hurdler of little account on flat: little form in sellers. *M. W. Ellerby*

TIME OF NIGHT (USA) 3 gr. or ro.f. Night Shift (USA) – Tihama (USA) 70 (Sassafras (FR) 135) [1995 65: 7m⁵ 8.1m⁴ 6.1d⁶ 6d³ 1996 8d 8.2m 8g² 8f³ 7.1m⁴ 7m⁶ 8.2m 8.3d³ 7g² Sep 6] leggy, unfurnished filly: has a fluent, quick action: fair maiden handicapper: stays 1m (probably finds 7f a minimum): acts on firm and dead ground: effective from front or held up. *R. Guest*

TIMES OF TIMES (IRE) 3 b.f. Distinctly North (USA) 115 – Lady Fandet 71 (Gay Fandango (USA) 132) [1995 78, a50: a5g⁶ 6m* a6g³ 6.1m* 6f* 6m³ 6f* 6m² a– 7g* 7g⁶ 6f* 5m⁶ a6g 1996 6m 5.7m 5.2g* 6g 5g 6m 6m 6m* 6f⁶ 6m⁵ a6g 7m 6.1m Sep 16] rather leggy filly: fair performer: came through late to win apprentice race at Yarmouth in July and handicap at Lingfield in August: stays 7f: acts on firm ground, below form on the all-weather: blinkered (out of form) final start: none too consistent. *M. J. Ryan*

TIME TICKS ON 3 b.g. Timeless Times (USA) 99 – Miss Sherbrooke (Workboy – § 123) [1995 NR 1996 6d 6f 6g⁴ 5m 5g Sep 7] sparely-made gelding: first reported foal: dam, poor novice hurdler, of little account on flat: well beaten in varied company, reluctant to race (blinkered) penultimate start: one to leave alone. *M. W. Ellerby*

TIME TO FLY 3 b.g. Timeless Times (USA) 99 – Dauntless Flight (Golden – Mallard 103) [1995 59: 5m⁵ 5f 6h³ 5m⁵ 5h³ 5m 6f² 1996 6g⁵ 5.9f 5m a5g⁶ 5g 7f a6g Nov 4] smallish, good-bodied gelding: modest sprint maiden: well below form in 1996: retained by trainer 500 gns Doncaster November Sales. *B. W. Murray*

TIME TO TANGO 3 b.f. Timeless Times (USA) 99 – Tangalooma 56 (Hotfoot 73 126) [1995 57p: 5f⁵ 5f² 1996 5g³ 5f* 5f* 5m⁶ 5f⁴ Aug 9] smallish filly: fair performer: won maiden at Musselburgh in June and handicap at Carlisle (clearly best effort) in July: raced only at 5f on a sound surface: pulled too hard in small field final start. *G. M. Moore*

TIMOTHY GEORGE (IRE) 2 b.g. (Apr 23) Don't Forget Me 127 – Ward of – Court (IRE) (Law Society (USA) 130) [1996 8m 6s 7d Oct 28] strong, lengthy gelding: third foal: half-brother to modest sprint maiden Cork Street Girl (by Bold Arrangement): dam never ran: behind in large fields of maidens. *G. B. Balding*

TINA KATERINA 3 ch.f. Executive Man 119 – Tria Romantica (Another Realm – 118) [1995 42: 6.1d 7g a6g a8.5g² 1996 a8g 8m a9.4g⁶ Aug 17] plain, good-topped filly: poor maiden: well beaten in 1996: needs further than 6f (stays 8.5f): acts on fibresand. *R. Champion*

TINASHAAN (IRE) 4 b.f. Darshaan 133 – Catina 102 (Nureyev (USA) 131) 94 [1995 100: 7m² 8m² 10.3g² 11.5m* 12m² 12g* 12d 1996 10m⁴ 14.6g² 11.9g⁶ Jul 12] good-topped filly: useful performer: bandaged and bit backward, best 4-y-o effort when fourth of 5 to Florid in minor event at Newmarket on reappearance: stays 1½m, possibly not 14.6f: acts on good to firm ground, possibly not on good to soft: wears rope halter and blanket for stalls entry. *J. R. Fanshawe*

TINKERBELL 2 ch.f. (Jan 31) Sharpo 132 – Chasing Moonbeams 99 (Final 74 Straw 127) [1996 5m⁵ 6.1g⁶ a7g* 7g⁵ a7g³ a7g* 6m² a7g² 7m² 8g⁵ 7m⁶ Oct 28] a61 angular filly: unimpressive mover: sixth foal: half-sister to 5f winner Desert Dagger (by Green Desert): dam 2-y-o 5f winner who deteriorated after, is half-sister to stayers Cap Del Mond and Storm Cloud: fair performer: won sellers at Wolverhampton in July and August (final start for Lord Huntingdon): creditable efforts in nurseries next 2 starts for Miss S. Wilton: ran very well when second in similar event at Newmarket on first start for present stable: stays 7f (out of depth at 1m): acts on fibresand but better form on good to firm ground: visored since third start. *W. R. Muir*

TINKER OSMASTON 5 br.m. Dunbeath (USA) 127 – Miss Primula 81 69 (Dominion 123) [1995 79: 5.1m 5m 5.7f* 6.1g⁵ 6m² 5.1m³ 6m³ 5.1m⁴ 6g 5g⁴ 5.1d* 6.1s² 5.1m 5m 1996 6g 5g 5.1f 6.1d² 5m 5.7m 6g⁴ 5.1m⁴ 5m Jul 31] workmanlike mare: fair handicapper: stays 6f: acts on firm ground, goes well on a soft surface (had such conditions only once in 1996): effective blinkered at 3 yrs, not tried since. *M. S. Saunders*

TINKER'S SURPRISE (IRE) 2 b.g. (Mar 28) Cyrano de Bergerac 120 – Lils 54 Fairy (Fairy King (USA)) [1996 5s 5m⁴ 5m* 5f⁵ 5g⁵ a5g⁴ 5d⁵ 5m² 6m a5g² a6g³ a57 5s⁴ a5g⁵ Nov 16] IR 3,000Y: second foal: dam unraced: won seller at Goodwood in June: sold out of B. Meehan's stable 2,400 gns Doncaster September Sales after penultimate outing: best at 5f: best turf form on sound surface, also acts on fibresand, probably on equitrack: effective with or without blinkers: takes keen hold: has looked none too resolute. *J. Balding*

TINKLERS FOLLY 4 ch.g. Bairn (USA) 126 – Lucky Straw 57 (Tumble Wind 68 (USA)) [1995 48: 7g 8g⁴ 8.1g 7.1m² 7.1f² 10f⁴ 8.1f* 8m³ 8.3f⁴ 7.1m³ 8d 1996 8.3d⁴ 7.1g* 7d 7.1g 8.1g 8.1f* 6.9f* 8.1g² 7m 7g* 7.5f⁶ 7m 7f Sep 27] strong, sturdy gelding: fair handicapper: won at Musselburgh in April, on same course and at Carlisle (ladies race) in June and at Newcastle in August: well held last 3 starts: sold 5,700 gns Doncaster October Sales: stays 8.3f: acts on firm and dead ground. *Denys Smith*

TINTARA (IRE) 3 b.f. Caerleon (USA) 132 – Justsayno (USA) (Dr Blum (USA)) [1995 63p: 7g 7m a8g³ 1996 10.8g³ 12.5f* a12g a14g 16.2m⁴ Jul 25] tall, leggy filly: fair form at best: well beaten after winning handicap at Warwick in May: stays 12.5f well: has raced only on a sound surface on turf: sold 15,000 gns Newmarket December Sales. *B. W. Hills*   72 d

TINY ASTRO 3 b.g. Superpower 113 – Moonwalker (Night Shift (USA)) [1995 –: 5g⁶ 1996 6s Mar 26] small, chunky gelding: lightly raced and no form. *T. D. Easterby*   –

TIP IT IN 7 gr.g. Le Solaret (FR) – Alidante 65 (Sahib 114) [1995 NR 1996 a8g a14g Jun 14] fair winning hurdler: no worthwhile form on flat. *A. Smith*   –

TIPPERARY SUNSET (IRE) 2 gr.c. (May 25) Red Sunset 120 – Chapter And Verse (Dancer's Image (USA)) [1996 5g⁶ Sep 29] IR 3,600Y: half-brother to Irish 1½m winner Spencer Bridge (by Run The Gantlet): dam unraced daughter of 1000 Guineas and Oaks winner Altesse Royale: slowly away and always behind in median auction maiden. *J. J. Quinn*   –

TIPSY CREEK (USA) 2 b.c. (Mar 16) Dayjur (USA) 137 – Copper Creek (Habitat) [1996 5m* 5m* 5m⁶ 5m² Aug 21] $90,000Y: robust, good-quartered colt: has scope: brother to headstrong 1995 2-y-o Mukabir and half-brother to 1992 2-y-o 6f and 7f winner Wathik (by Ogygian), 5f winner My Sovereign (by Sovereign Dancer) and a winner in USA: dam 6f winner from good family: won maiden at Salisbury in May in good style by 3½ lengths from Maserati Monk then Norfolk Stakes at Ascot by a length from Raphane after being held up in last place: heavily-backed favourite, sixth of 7 behind Carmine Lake in Molecomb Stakes at Goodwood (beaten in a matter of strides over 1f out) and 1¼ lengths second of 5 behind Janib in Roses Stakes at York (stumbled stalls, blazed trail, collared inside last): speedy: bandaged behind last 3 starts: changed hands after Royal Ascot: wintering in Dubai. *B. Hanbury*   104

TIP THE DOVE 7 br.m. Riberetto 107 – Nimble Dove 62 (Starch Reduced 112) [1995 –: a10g⁶ 10s 16.2m 1996 18s Mar 22] plain mare: fair NH Flat race winner in 1993/4: modest novice hurdler: tailed off on flat. *R. J. Price*   –

TIRAGE 2 ch.c. (Apr 16) Charmer 123 – Maid of Essex 66 (Bustino 136) [1996 7m 6m 7.5f⁵ 8.1m³ 7m 7m Oct 4] small, sturdy colt: second foal: half-brother to 3-y-o Uoni (by Minster Son): dam best at 1¼m to 1½m: fair form: will be well suited by further than 1m: sold 11,000 gns Newmarket Autumn Sales. *C. E. Brittain*   70

TIRLIE (IRE) 4 b.g. Tirol 127 – Lisa's Favourite (Gorytus (USA)) [1995 –: 8d 1996 10.3m a11g a12g Jul 27] big, good-topped gelding: no worthwhile form: sold 1,150 gns Newmarket September Sales: tried visored. *J. W. Payne*   –

TIROLETTE (IRE) 4 b.f. Tirol 127 – Etage (Ile de Bourbon (USA) 133) [1995 64: 10.3m 10g³ 10.1d* 11.5f⁵ 12m* 11.9g 12m 1996 12m 13.1g 12m⁴ a12g³ 14.4g⁵ 15.9g 12s Oct 26] tall, leggy filly: modest handicapper on her day: sold (R. Williams to K. Morgan) 7,800 gns Newmarket Autumn Sales: should stay 1¾m, appeared not to get 15.9f: acts on good to firm and dead ground, ran poorly on soft: blinkered nowadays: has run well for apprentice: unreliable. *R. J. R. Williams*   59 §

TIROL'S TREASURE (IRE) 2 b.f. (May 12) Tirol 127 – Lisa's Favourite (Gorytus (USA) 132) [1996 7f⁶ 6g 6d a8g Dec 20] 4,800 2-y-o: fourth foal: sister to 4-y-o Tirlie and half-sister to 3-y-o Kalao Tua (by Shaadi) and 1993 2-y-o 7f winner Majestic Heights (by High Estate): dam Irish maiden best at around 1m: no form, including in sellers: blinkered third start. *K. T. Ivory*   –

TIROLS TYRANT (IRE) 3 b.g. Tirol 127 – Justitia (Dunbeath (USA) 127) [1995 67p: 7m 1996 a8.5g 8d 8f³ 8.1m 12.1m 10m⁶ 10g⁴ 11.5m Oct 23] smallish, leggy gelding: poor form: broke leg first start after leaving Mrs A. Swinbank: stayed 1¼m: acted on firm ground. *M. Johnston*   43

TIRRA-LIRRA (IRE) 4 b.f. Tirol 127 – Run My Beauty (Runnett 125) [1995 NR 1996 a7g⁶ a8.5g³ a9.4g⁶ 7f 8.2m 12d Oct 21] IR 8,500Y: lengthy, good-topped filly: first foal: dam Irish 1m winner: only form when third of 13 in maiden at   63 d

Wolverhampton in March: off course 6 months after next start: sold 700 gns Ascot December Sales. *C. E. Brittain*

TISIMA (FR) 2 ch.f. (Apr 13) Selkirk (USA) 129 – Georgia Stephens (USA) 64 – (The Minstrel (CAN) 135) [1996 6m⁵ Jun 13] 240,000 francs Y: tall, unfurnished filly: has scope: third foal: half-sister to UAE 7f winner Heartbreak House (by Shavian): dam placed over 1m: signs of ability when fifth of 6 to Fun Galore in minor event at Newbury in June: looked sure to do better. *I. A. Balding*

TISSISAT (USA) 7 ch.g. Green Forest (USA) 134 – Expansive 111 (Exbury 138) – [1995 NR 1996 10m 10g May 17] tall, angular gelding: fair miler (rated 79) at 5 yrs for I. Balding: well beaten in handicaps (bandaged in front) in 1996. *John Berry*

TISSUE OF LIES (USA) 3 b. or br.g. Ascot Knight (CAN) 130 – Choral Group 74 (CAN) (Lord Durham (CAN)) [1995 79p: 9g⁶ 10m⁵ 8g² 1996 10m 12.4g 8.5m³ 8.2m² 8.5m⁶ 8f⁵ 11.1m² 9m² 8d 10.5v a8s* a12g³ a9.4g a8g² Dec 13] strong, rangy gelding: powerful galloper: fair handicapper: won maiden at Lingfield in November: effective at 1m, and stays 1½m: acts on good to firm ground and the all-weather, below form both starts on a soft surface on turf. *M. Johnston*

TITANIUM HONDA (IRE) 5 gr.g. Doulab (USA) 115 – Cumbrian Melody 83 – (Petong 126) [1995 –, a50: a7g⁶ a8g⁴ a8g⁴ a8g⁵ a6g² a8g⁵ a7g* a7g a7g 7g 6g a8g³ 7f a6g⁶ 8h 7g 1996 6.9s a6g⁶ a7g 7d a7g Jun 6] sturdy gelding: poor handicapper on the all-weather, no worthwhile form on turf: well below form in 1996: effective at 6f to 1m: tried blinkered, no improvement. *D. C. O'Brien*

TITCHWELL LASS 3 ch.f. Lead On Time (USA) 123 – Bodham 88 (Bustino 57 136) [1995 NR 1996 8m³ 10m* 10.1g 10g Oct 21] 4,200Y: unfurnished filly: half-sister to several winners, including fairly useful Barsham (1¼m, by Be My Guest) and Arabian Bold (1½m, by Persian Bold): dam, 1½m and 13.3f winner, out of half-sister to Blakeney and Morston: modest performer: easily won claimer at Newmarket in June: towards rear in handicaps at Yarmouth (reluctant stalls) and Pontefract (nearly 3 months later, something possibly amiss) afterwards: sold (J. Banks to W. Haigh) 3,200 gns Newmarket Autumn Sales: stays 1¼m: has raced only on a sound surface. *J. E. Banks*

TITHCAR 2 b.f. (Feb 27) Cadeaux Genereux 131 – Miznah (IRE) 102 (Sadler's – p Wells (USA) 132) [1996 6g Oct 18] workmanlike filly: first foal: dam Irish 2-y-o 6f winner, placed at 7f at 3 yrs, closely related to dam of Champion Turf Mare Flawlessly: backed at long odds, never threatened leaders or given hard time in 22-runner Newmarket maiden: should improve. *B. Hanbury*

TITTA RUFFO 2 b.c. (Mar 11) Reprimand 122 – Hithermoor Lass 75 (Red Alert 85 p 127) [1996 7d³ Oct 2] 16,500F, 13,000Y: brother to 3-y-o State of Caution and half-brother to several winners, including smart sprinter Poyle George (by Sharpo) and 1990 2-y-o 7f winner Eastern Magic (by Faustus): dam placed from 5f to 7f: shaped well when running-on third of 18, checked twice, to Dacoit in maiden at Salisbury: not bred to stay beyond 1m: sure to improve. *B. J. Meehan*

TITUS LIVIUS (FR) 3 ch.c. Machiavellian (USA) 123 – Party Doll 108 (Be My 110 Guest (USA) 126) [1995 113+: 6g³ 5.5g*⁽ᵈⁱˢ⁾ 7s⁴ 6.5g* 6.5g* 1996 6.5g³ 5d⁴ 5f 6g² 7s⁶ 5d³ 6s⁵ Nov 22] quite attractive colt: smart performer, won 2 pattern races at 2 yrs: first outing on top-of-the-ground when only ninth of 17 in King's Stand Stakes at Royal Ascot: off course 2 months afterwards: ran well when 2½ lengths second of 9 to Kistena in Prix de Meautry at Deauville and 3 lengths third of 9 to Don't Worry Me at Longchamp: will prove best at up to 7f: acts on soft ground. *J. E. Pease, France*

TIUTCHEV 3 b.g. Soviet Star (USA) 128 – Cut Ahead 85 (Kalaglow 132) [1995 71 NR 1996 10.5d⁶ 10.4g⁵ 10s³ Oct 24] big, useful-looking gelding: third foal: brother to 4-y-o 8.2f to 1½m winner Far Ahead: dam 1¼m winner out of smart 1¼m and 10.5f winner Cut Loose, a sister to St Leger winner Cut Above and half-sister to Irish 2000 Guineas winner Sharp Edge: fair form in autumn maidens: sold (R. Charlton to Miss H. Knight) 31,000 gns Newmarket Autumn Sales: will prove suited by further than 10.5f: has raced only on an easy surface. *R. Charlton*

T-N-T EXPRESS 2 b.c. (Apr 11) Sizzling Melody 117 – Lady Minstrel (Tudor – Music 131) [1996 5m 6g 8.2s a7g Dec 7] 4,200Y: leggy colt: half-brother to several winners here and abroad, including useful 7f (at 2 yrs) and 1¼m winner Mary Davies (by Tyrnavos) and 11.5f winner Horowitz (by Beldale Flutter): dam, placed over

TOB

hurdles in Ireland, is half-sister to 2000 Guineas winner Tap On Wood: no form: trained on debut by M. Meagher. *E. J. Alston*

TOBY BROWN 3 b.g. Arzanni 115 – Forest Nymph (NZ) 66 (Oak Ridge (FR) 69) [1995 NR 1996 11.5m 14m Oct 4] first reported foal: dam, modest form here, won over 1m as 3-y-o in New Zealand: showed nothing in maidens at Lingfield: has joined D. Nicholson. *Mrs A. L. M. King* —

TOCCO JEWEL 6 br.m. Reesh 117 – Blackpool Belle 70 (The Brianstan 128) [1995 22: 11.1g 10m 10m 8g 9.7m⁶ 11.6m 1996 8.3m 9.7g² 10.8m 11.6m Jul 22] smallish mare: poor plater: seems to stay 1½m: acts on soft ground and good to firm: tried blinkered. *M. J. Ryan* 22

TODD (USA) 5 b.g. Theatrical 128 – Boldara (USA) (Alydar (USA)) [1995 –: 10m 12m a10g⁶ a12g 1996 a12g⁵ a10g* a10g⁵ a9.4g⁴ 9.7s⁶ 9.7m⁵ 12m 10g⁵ 14m a12g⁴ Sep 21] modest performer: won maiden at Lingfield in January: seems to stay 1½m: acts on good to firm ground and the all-weather: no improvement in blinkers: sold (P. Mitchell to A. Harvey) 9,500 gns Newmarket Autumn Sales. *P. Mitchell* 51 a57

TOE TAPPIN MUSIC (USA) 3 b.g. Show Dancer (USA) – Miss Garrett (USA) (Speak John) [1995 –: 5m⁶ 6.1d 5g 1996 6d⁵ 7m 5.1g 7.1g Jun 13] good-topped gelding: no worthwhile form: tried blinkered. *Martyn Meade* —

TOFFEE 3 ch.f. Midyan (USA) 124 – Vaula 49 (Henbit (USA) 130) [1995 66+: 6g⁵ 7.5m² 7m 7d 1996 a8g May 13] unfurnished filly: has a quick action: fair maiden at 2 yrs: well beaten only outing in 1996: sold 2,600 gns Newmarket July Sales: should be well suited by middle distances. *J. R. Fanshawe* —

TOI TOI (IRE) 2 b.f. (Apr 1) In The Wings 128 – Walliser (Niniski (USA) 125) [1996 7.1s⁵ 7d⁴ Nov 8] IR 21,000Y: lengthy, workmanlike filly: third foal: dam, Irish 7f to 1¼m winner (including at 2 yrs), sister to very smart stayer Assessor out of sister to Pitcairn: beaten about 5 lengths in maidens at Chepstow and Doncaster: will be well suited by middle distances: will do better. *D. W. P. Arbuthnot* 71 p

TOKEN GESTURE (IRE) 2 b.f. Alzao (USA) 117 – Temporary Lull (USA) (Super Concorde (USA) 128) [1996 7m 7m* 7g* Oct 5] half-sister to several winners including US Grade 2 9f winner Wait Till Monday (by Maelstrom Lake) and useful Irish middle-distance performers Rare Holiday (by Caerleon) and Blazing Spectacle (rated 97, by Sadler's Wells): dam unraced sister to Martha Stevens (best short of 1m, rated 102) out of 1½m CCA Oaks winner Magazine: progressive form: won 10-runner maiden at Galway in September and 8-runner C L Weld Park Stakes at the Curragh (by head from Melleray) in October: bred to be suited by at least 1m: will do better still. *D. K. Weld, Ireland* 96 p

TOLEPA (IRE) 3 b.f. Contract Law (USA) 108 – Our Investment (Crofter (USA) 124) [1995 NR 1996 10m 7f⁴ a8.5g 10.9m 8.3g⁴ 10.1m Oct 23] lengthy filly: third foal: sister to French 4-y-o 11f and 13f winner Estoppel: dam Irish 7f winner who stayed 1¼m: no worthwhile form. *J. J. O'Neill* —

TOMAL 4 b.g. King Among Kings 60 – Jacinda (Thatching 131) [1995 54: 5m 6m 5m a5g⁶ 7f⁵ 6.9f² 8f³ 8g 8.5s⁶ 7f⁵ 6.9g⁵ 7f a7g 1996 a12g³ a10g a13g a8g 8m² 8f⁶ 8.1m³ 10f 8.3d² 8m⁵ 10m Sep 19] small gelding: poor handicapper: stays 8.3f, seemingly not 1¼m: acts on firm and dead ground, probably on soft: little form on the all-weather: well beaten in blinkers: sometimes bandaged behind. *R. Ingram* 49

TOMBA 2 ch.c. (Feb 13) Efisio 120 – Indian Love Song 68 (Be My Guest (USA) 126) [1996 5g⁶ 6m³ 6g* 6m² 6d* 6m⁶ 6s* Nov 29] quite well-made colt: fourth foal: half-brother to 4-y-o 7f and 1m winner Indian Rhapsody (by Rock City): dam, middle-distance maiden, granddaughter of Oaks runner-up Maina: useful colt: won maiden at Epsom in August, minor event at Salisbury in October and listed Prix Zeddaan (by ½ length from Heaven's Command, first two 5 lengths clear) at Evry in November: bred to stay beyond 6f: acts very well on soft ground. *B. J. Meehan* 106

TOM MI DAH 2 b.g. (Feb 24) Superlative 118 – Queensbury Star 76 (Wishing Star 117) [1996 6g⁵ 5m³ 5f 6m² 7g Sep 21] 4,600Y, 10,000 2-y-o: half-brother to 2 winners by Longleat, 7f winner Vuchterbacher and 1989 2-y-o 6f and 7f winner Beehive Boy: dam won over 6f at 2 yrs but no form after: modest form: stays 6f: raced only on a sound surface: stiff task third outing: gelded. *M. D. Hammond* 60 ?

TOM MORGAN 5 b.g. Faustus (USA) 118 – Pirate Maid (Auction Ring (USA) 123) [1995 83: 7.3g 7g⁵ 7.3d 7g 1996 a7g a7g Dec 20] lengthy, good-topped gelding: fairly useful handicapper at best: soundly beaten on belated return. *P. T. Walwyn* —

1014

TOMMY COOPER 5 br.h. Macmillion 110 – My Charade 79 (Cawston's Clown – 113) [1995 46: 14.1m⁶ 14.9m⁵ 18.2m² 16m² 16.4m⁶ 16d 17.2m⁶ 1996 14.1d 16g Oct 24] leggy horse: poor maiden handicapper: bandaged in front, well beaten both starts in 1996: thorough stayer. *Mrs Barbara Waring*

TOMMYKNOCKER (IRE) 4 ch.g. Woodman (USA) 126 – Repercutionist – § (USA) 111 (Beaudelaire (USA) 125) [1995 39d: 12d⁵ 14.1g⁵ 14.1m 16m⁴ 1996 11.9g May 30] leggy, angular gelding: disappointing maiden: sold (J. Jenkins to L. Saunders) 725 gns Ascot July Sales: stays at least 1¼m: acts on good to firm ground, probably on soft: tried blinkered/visored: ungenuine. *J. R. Jenkins*

TOMMY TEMPEST 7 ch.g. Northern Tempest (USA) 120 – Silently Yours 46 (USA) 53 (Silent Screen (USA)) [1995 40, a43: a5g a5g a5g a5g³ a5g⁴ a5g 5g a5g⁶ a38 a6g a5g a5g* a5g⁶ 5.1h² 5.1m 5m⁶ 5.7h a5g 1996 a5g a5g a5g 5m 5.7g 5.1m a5g 5f⁶ 5f⁵ 5.1f⁵ a5g⁵ 5.1m⁶ 5.1m a5g Aug 9] angular gelding: poor 5f handicapper: acts on firm ground and the all-weather: often blinkered/visored. *R. E. Peacock*

TOMMY TORTOISE 2 b.c. (Mar 20) Rock Hopper 124 – Wish You Well 78 70 (Sadler's Wells (USA) 132) [1996 8.5m² 10m⁶ 10g² Oct 24] 6,000Y: strong colt: has scope: third foal: half-brother to 3-y-o 1m winner Forza Figlio (by Warning): dam stoutly-bred half-sister to very smart 1983 2-y-o Creag-An-Sgor: fair form in maidens: sold to join Miss G. Kelleway 15,000 gns Newmarket Autumn Sales: will be suited by further than 1¼m. *P. F. I. Cole*

TOM PLADDEY 2 ch.c. (May 11) Clantime 101 – Croft Original § (Crofthall 55 110) [1996 a5g⁶ 6m⁴ 7g 6g⁶ 6.9v Nov 11] 15,500 2-y-o: rather leggy colt: fourth reported foal: dam, probably ungenuine, ran 4 times: modest form: stays 6f: soundly beaten on heavy ground, signs of ability on fibresand. *R. Bastiman*

TOM SWIFT (IRE) 3 b.g. Law Society (USA) 130 – Debbie's Next (USA) 82 – (Arctic Tern (USA) 126) [1995 –: 7f 7m 1996 10m 10m 10f 10.1m Sep 18] small, good-topped gelding: no worthwhile form. *R. C. Spicer*

TOM TAILOR (GER) 2 b.c. (Apr 29) Beldale Flutter (USA) 130 – Thoughtful 72 p 86 (Northfields (USA)) [1996 7m 7f⁴ 6m 8g³ Oct 18] tall colt: half-brother to fairly useful middle-distance stayer/high-class hurdler Muse (by High Line), stayer Kadari (by Commanche Run), 8.1f winner at 2 yrs, and a winner in Germany by Master Willie: dam, 1¼m winner, half-sister to Princess Royal winner Heavenly Thought: strong-finishing third to Bold Words in nursery at Newmarket on final outing: had shown promise previously: will be well suited by further than 1m: remains capable of better. *D. R. C. Elsworth*

TONDRES (USA) 5 br.g. Chief's Crown (USA) – Icing 112 (Prince Tenderfoot 60 (USA) 126) [1995 72d: a10g⁶ a13g⁴ a10g 10m⁴ 12f 11.4m 13.3g 10m 16.4m 1996 a12g² a12g Feb 27] big, good-bodied gelding: has a free, round action: modest maiden: sold 900 gns Doncaster August (1996) Sales: probably stays 13f: best form on a sound surface (acts on firm ground, also on equitrack): tried once in visor, blinkered last 6 starts at 4 yrs: none too consistent. *R. Ingram*

TONIC CHORD 3 b.f. La Grange Music 111 – Tight (Lochnager 132) [1995 NR 49 1996 6f⁴ 7m⁵ 8.2m⁵ 7m 7m² 8g⁵ 8m Sep 19] fourth foal: half-sister to winning sprinter Tongue Tied (by Petong): dam non-thoroughbred half-sister to useful sprinter Clantime: poor maiden: stays 1m: has raced only on a sound surface. *J. R. Fanshawe*

TONKA 4 b.g. Mazilier (USA) 107 – Royal Meeting 44 (Dara Monarch 128) [1995 64 71d: a8g⁵ a9.4g 12.5m³ 9.9m* 12.3m⁵ 12g⁵ 10m 10.2h⁵ 10m⁶ 10m⁵ 11.4d² 9.7s³ a33 9.7g⁶ 12m 1996 a11g³ 10g 12v* a11g Dec 27] small, close-coupled gelding: has a quick action: modest performer on turf: led over 1f out when winning handicap at Folkestone in November: poor at best on the all-weather: stays 12.3f: acts on good to firm and heavy ground: tried visored earlier in career. *P. J. Makin*

TONTO 3 b.g. Nomination 125 – Brigado 87 (Brigadier Gerard 144) [1995 –: 8.1s – 1996 a8g⁶ a8g³ 8f Jul 6] only worthwhile form in maiden events when plugging-on a49 third of 9 (beaten just over 12 lengths) at Southwell in June: should stay beyond 1m: acts on fibresand: sold to join W. Tinning 10,000 gns Doncaster November Sales. *C. W. Thornton*

TONY'S DELIGHT (IRE) 8 b.g. Krayyan 117 – Tinas Image (He Loves Me – 120) [1995 –: a9.4g 1996 10g Jul 1] lightly-raced novice hurdler: well beaten back on flat. *J. R. Jenkins*

TONYS GIFT 4 b.f. Midyan (USA) 124 – Harmonical (USA) 70 (Lyphard's Wish 73
(FR) 124) [1995 69: 6m⁴ 5g 6f² 6m³ 6g³ 7m* 7g 8g³ 8f* 1996 12g³ 14.9f* 14.9m³
14g⁶ Aug 1] sparely-made filly: fair handicapper: won steadily-run event at Warwick
in June after good tussle: stays 14.9f: has raced only on a sound surface on flat
(successful on heavy over hurdles): has run well when sweating. *M. C. Pipe*

TONY'S MIST 6 b.g. Digamist (USA) 110 – Tinas Image (He Loves Me 120) 43
[1995 55: 10.8m 10.8f 10.2m 10.8m² 9.9m⁶ 1996 a12g⁵ 10g 9m 10m 8g 8m⁴ 8.1g³
8.1m 8m 8.1m Jul 24] close-coupled gelding: poor handicapper: seems to stay 10.8f:
acts on good to firm ground, used to go well on a soft surface: blinkered (at 2 yrs) and
visored once each, below form: winning selling hurdler: inconsistent. *J. M. Bradley*

TOOELE 2 b.g. (Mar 22) Full Extent (USA) 113 – Little Madam 66 (Habat 127) –
[1996 5s⁶ 7g Jul 24] 1,100F, 400Y: half-brother to 6f winner Monsieur Petong (by
Petong) and 1988 2-y-o 5f seller winner Alo' Niko (by Mansingh): dam 5f winner:
soundly beaten in sellers: visored final outing: sold 500 gns Doncaster September
Sales. *J. Norton*

TOO HASTY 3 b.g. Dunbeath (USA) 127 – Suggia (Alzao (USA) 117) [1995 77: 63 d
6m⁴ 7m² 7m* 7m 7g⁶ 6g⁴ 7f 1996 7g 8g 6g 7.5g 8m⁵ 8f 6m 7m⁵ 7m 7m⁴ Oct 8]
smallish, sturdy gelding: just a modest handicapper at best in 1996: has form at 1m,
but may prove best at up to 7f: has raced only on a sound surface. *T. D. Easterby*

TOON FLYER 2 b.g. (Feb 10) Shirley Heights 130 – Caroline Lady (JPN) (Caro –
133) [1996 6m 7f Nov 5] IR 7,000Y: rangy gelding: has a rounded action: second
foal: half-brother to a winner in Japan by Generous: dam French 1½m winner:
backward, tailed off in maidens. *W. Storey*

TOPAGLOW (IRE) 3 ch.g. Topanoora 118 – River Glow (River Knight (FR) –
118) [1995 46: 5m 5m 6m a7g 8.1s 1996 16m⁵ Sep 24] small gelding: poor maiden:
well beaten only 3-y-o start: should stay at least 1½m. *P. T. Dalton*

TOPANGA 4 b.g. Dancing Brave (USA) 140 – Trampship 110 (High Line 125) –
[1995 71: 12m⁴ 14.1f³ 1996 12m a12g Jun 22] sturdy, compact gelding: fair form in
2 maidens for H. Cecil at 3 yrs: well beaten in 1996. *J. A. Bennett*

TOPANOORA BAY (IRE) 3 b.g. Topanoora 118 – Life's Chance (IRE) –
(Wolverlife 115) [1995 NR 1996 a8g a7g 12.4g⁵ Apr 8] 1,000Y: sparely-made gelding: first foal: dam never ran: seems of little account. *Mrs V. A. Aconley*

TOPATORI (IRE) 2 ch.f. (Mar 21) Topanoora 118 – Partygoer (General Assem- 69
bly (USA)) [1996 5g⁵ 6m² 5f² Jun 17] IR 5,500Y: angular, quite good-topped filly:
third foal: half-sister to Irish 3-y-o Fast Princess (by Al Hareb), 6.5f winner at 2 yrs,
and a winner in Germany by Common Grounds at around 1m: dam lightly-raced
daughter of useful sprinter Toast of The Town: placed in auction maiden events at the
minor tracks in the summer: really needs further than 5f. *M. H. Tompkins*

TOP BANANA 5 ch.g. Pharly (FR) 130 – Oxslip 106 (Owen Dudley 121) [1995 99
94: 7m³ 8m 6g* 5.2f* 5.2g* 6m² 6m³ 6g 1996 5.2d² 6m³ 5m* 6f 6f 5m³ 5.2m 6.1s²
Oct 31] close-coupled, workmanlike gelding: useful handicapper: got up close home
to win at Newmarket in June: ran as though something amiss at Royal Ascot fourth
start: creditable efforts last 3 outings: stays 7f, best form at sprint distances: acts on
firm and soft ground: blinkered (not disgraced) penultimate start. *H. Candy*

TOP CEES 6 b.g. Shirley Heights 130 – Sing Softly 112 (Luthier 126) [1995 86: 90
12g⁶ 14m⁵ 18.7m* 20m 14.6m⁴ 18m³ 1996 16.4g 14.8m* 18.7m 13.9m⁶ Aug 21]
close-coupled gelding: has a round action: fairly useful handicapper: as good as ever
at 6 yrs, winning at Newmarket in July: good sixth of 21 in the Ebor at York on final
start: effective at 1¾m and stays extremely well: acts on good to firm ground,
probably on dead: usually held up. *Mrs J. R. Ramsden*

TOP OF THE FORM (IRE) 2 ch.f. (May 7) Masterclass (USA) 116 – Hara- 79
abah (USA) 99 (Topsider (USA)) [1996 5g⁴ 5f* 5g³ 5m* 5m³ 6g 5m⁴ Oct 3] IR
5,800Y: sparely-made filly: fifth foal: half-sister to useful 4-y-o sprinter Double
Quick (by Superpower): dam 5f to 7f winner out of half-sister to high-class 1m to 13f
performer Dom Alaric: fair form: won median auction maiden at Musselburgh and
nursery at York in summer: creditable effort in between and most starts after: best
form at 5f on top-of-the-ground: tends to carry head rather high, but game enough.
M. Johnston

TOP OF THE GREEN (IRE)   2 b.c. (Apr 18) Common Grounds 118 – Gray- –
foot 87 (Grundy 137) [1996 7d 6s Oct 24] 9,000Y: tall colt: half-brother to a winner
in Sweden by Commanche Run: dam, maiden half-sister to Irish Oaks winner
Swiftfoot, was possibly temperamental: last in big fields of maidens. *P. J. Makin*

TOP OF THE WIND (IRE)   2 b.f. (Apr 28) Silver Kite (USA) 111 – Domino's   72
Nurse 104 (Dom Racine (FR) 121) [1996 5g² 5m⁵ 5m⁴ 6g² 7g⁶ 8m 6.5m 8g 7s⁶ Nov
9] 15,000Y: rather leggy, unfurnished filly: good mover: sixth foal: half-sister to
3-y-o 13f winner Mujtahida (by Mujtahid) and 3 other winners, including 5f (at 2
yrs) to 10.5f winner Romios (by Common Grounds) and Irish 1¼m winner Domino
Ring (by Auction Ring): dam, Irish 7f (at 2 yrs) and 1¼m winner, later successful in
USA: fair form: won nursery at Newcastle in August: below best last 3 outings:
probably stays 1m: often mulish in preliminaries but gave no trouble last 2 outings:
sold 3,000 gns Newmarket December Sales: sent to Sweden. *J. J. O'Neill*

TOP PET (IRE)   6 br.g. Petong 126 – Pounelta 91 (Tachypous 128) [1995 60d: 48
7m 7f⁶ 8.1g⁵ 6.9g⁴ 7.1m⁴ 11.5m³ 12m⁵ 10m³ 10m⁴ 7g 7g 8g 1996 a8g a9.4g³ a8.5g⁴
a8g Mar 29] leggy gelding: poor handicapper nowadays: stays 1¼m: acts on
fibresand and on firm and dead ground, well below best on heavy: often needs plenty
of driving, and worth a try in blinkers/visor: not one to trust implicitly. *R. Akehurst*

TOP PRIZE   8 b.g. High Top 131 – Raffle 82 (Balidar 133) [1995 44: a16g⁶ a14g   42 d
16.2m⁴ 14.1m* 16.2m* 15.4m 17.5g 17.1m 1996 16.1s² 16.2m 21.6m 14.1m a16g*
14.1m a12g⁵ 16.2m a14g³ 16.2g³ 17.1m Oct 7] leggy, lengthy gelding: poor
handicapper: thorough stayer: won at Southwell in May: acts on firm and soft ground
and on fibresand: visored since fourth 7-y-o start: lazy, and suited by strong handling.
M. Brittain

TOPPS TRIO   2 ch.f. (Apr 12) Risk Me (FR) 127 – Ramz (IRE) (The Minstrel   –
(CAN) 135) [1996 5.7f 6g 7m Sep 10] unfurnished filly: has a round action: second
foal: dam unraced daughter of half-sister to Poule d'Essai des Pouliches winner
Ukraine Girl: little worthwhile form in maidens: sold 600 gns Ascot December Sales.
K. O. Cunningham-Brown

TO PROVE A POINT   4 b.g. Weldnaas (USA) 112 – Run Little Lady (USA) 81   –
(J O Tobin (USA) 130) [1995 34: 5.9m 8.3g 10m⁵ 10m⁵ 10m 1996 9.2d 6.9d⁶ Apr
26] small gelding: poor maiden: well beaten in 1996: stays 1¼m: acts on good to firm
ground: tried blinkered. *J. J. O'Neill*

TOP ROYAL   7 br.g. High Top 131 – Maria Isabella (FR) (Young Generation 129)   –
[1995 –: 11.5m⁵ 14.4m 1996 14.1g 14.1m Apr 30] good-bodied gelding: tough and
consistent handicapper (rated 85) in 1992 for J. Dunlop: no form since. *J. Pearce*

TOP SHELF   2 b.f. (Apr 7) Warning 136 – Troy Moon (Troy 137) [1996 7g 7f 8g⁵   67
Oct 30] smallish filly: half-sister to 3-y-o Kings Nightclub (by Shareef Dancer), 7f
winner The Cuckoo's Nest (by Precocious) and 1991 2-y-o 7f winner Jupiter Moon
(by Jupiter Island): dam maiden (stayed 1¼m) out of half-sister to Sharpen Up: modest form in maidens: best effort final start: likely to stay beyond 1m. *C. E. Brittain*

TOP SKIPPER (IRE)   4 b.g. Nordico (USA) – Scarlet Slipper (Gay Mecene   –
(USA) 128) [1995 67d: 8g⁶ 8g⁶ 8f⁵ 8g 10d 7.1g 8f 1996 8.3g 8g Sep 7] close-coupled
gelding: disappointing maiden on flat, but successful over hurdles in November (27f)
and December, on second occasion for V. Greenway. *Martyn Wane*

TOP TITFER   2 ch.f. (May 5) Cap Diamant (USA) – Top Yard (Teekay) [1996 6d   –
7m 7g 8f Sep 10] leggy filly: third foal: dam unraced: behind in low-class events:
visored final start: has worn bandages. *A. G. Foster*

TOPUP   3 b.g. Weldnaas (USA) 112 – Daisy Topper (Top Ville 129) [1995 NR   57 ?
1996 7.1d 10g 8.2m³ 8m a10g Dec 26] third foal: half-brother to Italian 5f winner
Baby Taison (by Beveled): dam (unraced) out of half-sister to Robellino: poor
maiden: probably flattered when third of 6 to 5/1-on shot Milford Sound in steadily-
run maiden at Nottingham. *J. W. Hills*

TORCH VERT (IRE)   4 b.g. Law Society (USA) 130 – Arctic Winter (CAN)   –
(Briartic (CAN)) [1995 87: 12f⁶ 13.9m 12m* 15g² 14f⁵ 14.6m⁵ 13.1g* 18m⁶ 1996
18s 16g 16.5s Nov 9] compact, attractive gelding: fairly useful handicapper on his
day: well beaten in 1996: may prove best at up to 2m: acts on good to firm ground.
N. J. H. Walker

TORMOUNT (USA) 3 b.c. Local Talent (USA) 122 – Virginia Hills (USA) 73 d
(Tom Rolfe) [1995 NR 1996 a8g a8g* a10g 8f 10g a10g⁵ a9.4g⁵ a9.4g⁴ Dec 7]
$20,000Y, resold 15,000Y: smallish, useful-looking colt: closely related to 2 winners,
notably Niniski (by Nijinsky), and half-brother to several winners including Oak
Apple (11.5f, by Theatrical): dam 9f winner: fair form to win maiden at Lingfield in
January: failed to repeat it: stays 1m: has had tongue tied down: sold 4,200 gns Ascot
December Sales. *Lord Huntingdon*

TORONTO 2 b.c. (Mar 21) Puissance 110 – Impala Lass 81 (Kampala 120) [1996 65 d
6d⁶ 5.1m² 5g⁵ 6g 5s 7g Oct 19] dipped-backed, good-quartered colt: fourth foal:
half-brother to 3-y-o 1m to 9.4f winner Yeoman Oliver (by Precocious), a 4-y-o 7f
winner Young Benson (by Zalazl) and 5-y-o 6f and 7f winner I'm Your Lady (by Risk
Me): dam 5f performer: deteriorated after second start and ran badly last 3: best
efforts at 5f: tends to hang badly and looks a difficult ride: has flashed tail. *J. Berry*

TORREMOLINOS (USA) 3 ch.c. Trempolino (USA) 135 – Honor Guard 83 p
(USA) (Vaguely Noble 140) [1995 a6f² a6f⁴ a8f⁴ 1996 10.4g³ 10m² 10g* Oct 9]
$50,000Y: ex-American colt: eighth foal: half-brother to 3 winners, including a
stakes winner by Hold Your Peace: dam, placed at 2 yrs in USA and in modest
company at 9f and 1¼m in France, is half-sister to top-class miler Lear Fan: trained
by R. Mulhall in USA at 2 yrs, in frame in 2 maidens and a listed race: fairly useful
form in maidens here, forcing pace and quickening over 1f out to beat Raise A Prince
4 lengths at Nottingham in October: should stay 1½m: probably capable of better:
sent to Saudi Arabia. *H. R. A. Cecil*

TORREY PINES (IRE) 4 b.g. Red Sunset 120 – Yukon Baby (USA) (Northern 40
Dancer) [1995 46: a10g a8.5g³ a8g 10m 10.5m³ 12.1m⁴ 1996 a12g⁵ a12g⁶ Mar 1]
good-topped gelding: poor maiden: stays 12.1f: acts on fibresand: visored at 4 yrs.
M. Bell

TOSKANO 4 b.g. Salse (USA) 128 – Kukri (Kris 135) [1995 63: 10g⁵ 9d⁴ 10m³ –
11.5s 1996 a12g Jan 20] big, quite attractive gelding: modest middle-distance
maiden: well below form only 4-y-o start, but did win selling hurdle in April.
D. L. Williams

TOSSUP (USA) 3 br.f. Gone West (USA) – Tovalop (USA) (Northern Dancer) 103
[1995 6g² 6g³ 6f² 1996 8m* 8d 8g 8m² 8g⁶ 9.6g⁴ Sep 19] sister to 1m winner 7f and 1m
winner Torrey Canyon and half-sister to 3 winners, including Tigersong (11f, by
Seattle Song): dam won 3 races at up to 1m: off course nearly 11 months prior to
reappearance, and won 8-runner listed race at Leopardstown in May by ½ length
from Asmara, whole field covered by under 5 lengths: mostly below that form
afterwards, including in Falmouth Stakes: stays 1m: probably acts on firm ground,
out of depth (in Irish 1000 Guineas) on dead: blinkered (no improvement) final 3-y-o
start. *J. G. Burns, Ireland*

TOTAL ALOOF 3 b.f. Groom Dancer (USA) 128 – Bashoosh (USA) (Danzig 72
(USA)) [1995 60p: 6.1m 5f² 1996 5m* 6.1g 5.1g* 5f 5m³ 5.1m Jul 18] sparely-made
filly: fair sprinter: won maiden at Beverley in April and minor event at Bath in May:
raced only on a sound surface: usually races prominently: sold 6,400 gns Newmarket
December Sales. *W. J. Haggas*

TOTALLY DIFFERENT 3 b.g. Totem (USA) 118 – Bold Difference 66 (Bold –
Owl 101) [1995 –: 7f 7m 1996 7.5f 10f 8.5m 8m 10g Aug 17] small, angular gelding:
no sign of ability: tried visored. *G. R. Oldroyd*

TOTALLY YOURS (IRE) 3 b.f. Classic Music (USA) – Dominia (Derring-Do 50
131) [1995 NR 1996 8g 8.3m 7m 10m⁵ 10f³ 12g² 12g⁴ 12.1s⁶ Nov 7] IR 8,500Y:
leggy, close-coupled filly: half-sister to several winners abroad, including a 7f
winner by Bluebird: dam won at around 1m in USA: modest maiden: best effort over
1½m, should stay further: best efforts on good ground. *M. R. Channon*

TOTAL RACH (IRE) 4 b.f. Nordico (USA) – Miss Kelly (Pitskelly 122) [1995 52
59: 8.2g 9m 10f 8g⁵ 10.8g 8g⁶ 8f* a10g a10g³ a12g a10g* 1996 a10g³ a10g a10g⁴
a10g² a10g 8g 8m 11.9f 9.7m 8m⁴ 8.1g⁵ 8.3g* 8m Jul 5] close-coupled filly: modest
performer: won seller at Windsor in July: stays 1¼m: acts on firm and dead ground
and on equitrack: blinkered (except once) since sixth 3-y-o start: usually wears
bandages: has joined A. Newcombe. *R. Ingram*

TOTEM DANCER 3 b.f. Mtoto 134 – Ballad Opera (Sadler's Wells (USA) 132) 83 p
[1995 NR 1996 12g³ 13.8g³ 10m⁴ 11m² 11.1g² 12m⁴ 14.1m² 14.1m² 14.1g* Oct 24]

9,000Y: sparely-made filly: has a short action: first foal: dam, placed at 1m in France, half-sister to very smart 1m to 1½m performer Supreme Leader from the family of Pebbles: fairly useful performer, generally progressive: gained a deserved success in 17-runner maiden at Nottingham (beat Sea of Stone by 10 lengths) in October: will prove suited by test of stamina: acts on good to firm ground, yet to race on a soft surface: sure to make an even better 4-y-o. *J. L. Eyre*

TO THE ROOF (IRE)   4 b.g. Thatching 131 – Christine Daae 74 (Sadler's Wells   105 (USA) 132) [1995 70: 7m 6f² a6g³ 6m³ 6g⁶ 5.1d² 1996 6s⁵ 5g* 6g² 6g² 5.1f* 6m* 5m* 6f⁶ 5m 6m 5g 5d² 5g² Oct 26] lengthy, good-bodied gelding: carries condition: impresses in appearance: useful handicapper, much improved (after hobday operation) in 1996: won at Musselburgh in April, Bath and Thirsk in May and at Epsom (listed rated stakes) in June: very good second in competitive events at Ascot and Doncaster last 2 starts: effective at 5f and 6f: acts on firm and dead ground and on fibresand: usually races prominently: game and genuine. *P. W. Harris*

TO THE WHIRE   3 br.f. Rock City 120 – Free Dance (FR) (Green Dancer (USA)   – 132) [1995 73: 5m⁴ 5m* 6m³ 6f⁴ 5m a6g⁵ 1996 a8g⁴ 7f⁵ 7f 10m Sep 19] leggy, rather unfurnished filly: fair form first three 2-y-o starts: has deteriorated considerably: sold 2,500 gns Doncaster September Sales: should stay beyond 6f: has raced only on top-of-the-ground when on turf. *G. L. Moore*

TOT OU TARD (IRE)   6 b.h. Robellino (USA) 127 – She's My Lovely (Sharpo   116 132) [1995 116: 10g⁶ 11g³ 13s⁵ 15.5s⁵ 15.5s 12m* 12v* 12g* 12d 12d³ 12d 15.5f 12f 1996 10g³ 10f⁵ 10.5m 15g² 14g² 14v⁶ Nov 30] sturdy horse: creditable French horse: creditable efforts in Prix Exbury at Saint-Cloud (1½ lengths third to Gunboat Diplomacy) and Prix d'Harcourt and Prix Ganay at Longchamp first 3 starts at 6 yrs: below best last 3 outings, although won when second in listed races at Chantilly and Vichy: best at up to 1½m: acts on any ground: trained most of year by J. Foresi. *G. E. Mikhalides, France*

TOUCH A MILLION (USA)   4 b.c. Mr Prospector (USA) – Magic Gleam   – (USA) 122 (Danzig (USA)) [1995 78: 7.1g² 8m* 8g⁵ 1996 10d 8g 8.5g May 11] sturdy colt: fair performer at 3 yrs: well below form in handicaps in 1996: sold 11,000 gns Newmarket July Sales: should stay beyond 1m: acts on good to firm ground: visored last 2 starts: sent to Peru. *E. A. L. Dunlop*

TOUCH'N'GO   2 b.c. (May 13) Rainbow Quest (USA) 134 – Mary Martin (Be   – My Guest (USA) 126) [1996 8.1s⁶ a8.5g Nov 30] eighth foal: brother to fair 1m winner Robbies Rainbow and half-brother to 3-y-o 8.5f winner Mighty Keen (by Keen) and several other winners, notably smart 5f to 7f performer (later winner at up to 8.5f in USA) Marina Park (by Local Suitor): dam unraced half-sister to 2 very smart sprinters: behind in maidens at Musselburgh and Wolverhampton. *M. Johnston*

TOUCH OF FANTASY   3 b.f. Never So Bold 135 – Brera (IRE) 45 (Tate   – Gallery (USA) 117) [1995 43: 5m⁶ 5g³ 5.1m⁵ a5g⁴ a5g³ 5m a5g⁴ a5g⁵ a5g 1996 a5g a5g⁵ Mar 18] smallish, sparely-made filly: poor sprint maiden at best: well beaten in 1996. *C. A. Dwyer*

TOUCH OF SNOW   3 b.f. Touch of Grey 90 – Snow Huntress 80 (Shirley   – Heights 130) [1995 –: 6f⁵ a7g 6.9g 1996 a7g Jan 17] little sign of ability. *J. A. Bennett*

TOUGH ACT   2 b.c. (Mar 1) Be My Chief (USA) 122 – Forelino (USA) 62§   81 (Trempolino (USA) 135) [1996 5m⁵ 7.1m² 7d 8g⁵ Oct 18] 26,000Y: neat colt: first foal: dam 10.6f winner, should have been effective over further: fair maiden: will stay beyond 1m. *G. Harwood*

TOUGH LEADER   2 b.c. (Mar 7) Lead On Time (USA) 123 – Al Guswa 98   71 (Shernazar 131) [1996 5m² 6g⁴ 5d⁴ 7m* 7.5m³ Jul 6] quite attractive colt: keen walker: first foal: dam Irish 1m (at 2 yrs) and 1¼m winner: won median auction maiden at Thirsk in June: fair effort only subsequent start: will stay at least 1m: spoilt finishing effort by hanging left on second start. *B. Hanbury*

TOUJOURS RIVIERA   6 ch.g. Rainbow Quest (USA) 134 – Miss Beaulieu 106   81 (Northfields (USA)) [1995 91: 9m 8m* 8f 8m⁴ 8.3m⁶ 8d⁴ 8s 9m a8g³ 1996 a10g 8m 7m 7g⁶ 8g 8m² 8m 8.1m⁴ 9d⁶ 8.9g 8m 8d 8m² Oct 17] rangy gelding: fairly useful handicapper, not at best in 1996: sold 4,600 gns Newmarket Autumn Sales: needs further than 7f nowadays (stays 1¼m): acts on firm and dead going, probably on equitrack: effective held up or from front. *J. Pearce*

TOULSTON LADY (IRE) 4 b.f. Handsome Sailor 125 – Rainbow Lady 65 52
(Jaazeiro (USA) 127) [1995 NR 1996 10f⁴ 8.5m³ 8m 12g⁴ 13.8m a11g a14.8g Nov a–
25] strong, lengthy filly: third reported living foal: dam, stayer, won over hurdles:
modest maiden, trained first 5 starts by M. Camacho: showed nothing on fibresand
last 2 starts: stays 1½m: got very upset in stalls third start: won selling hurdle in
December. *J. Wharton*

TOUT A COUP (IRE) 3 b.f. Ela-Mana-Mou 132 – Coupe d'Hebe 87 (Ile de 105
Bourbon (USA) 133) [1995 7f* 8m 8g² 8g³ 1996 8s* 11.4g* 12m* 12m⁶ 14d⁵ Aug
24] tall, unfurnished filly: half-sister to 3 winners, including fair Simply-H (up to
13.1f, by Simply Great): dam won only start, over 1m at 2 yrs: useful performer:
successful in 1996 in minor event at the Curragh in April, and listed events at Chester
(by 2 lengths from Solar Crystal) in May and Gowran Park (by short head from
Ceirseach) in June: finished last on both starts afterwards, in Irish Oaks first
occasion: stays 1½m: acts on firm and soft ground. *G. A. Cusack, Ireland*

TOUT DE VAL 7 b.m. Tout Ensemble – Julie Emma (Farm Walk 111) [1995 31: 33
8f⁵ 8g 10m³ a13g 9.7m 10f⁴ 10.2h² 10.2m 1996 9f 14.1f 11.9f* 11.9f 10d Aug 25]
strong mare: poor handicapper: won bad seller at Brighton in July: should stay 1¾m:
acts on hard going: tends to hang and carry head high. *K. Bishop*

TOVARICH 5 b.g. Soviet Star (USA) 128 – Pretty Lucky 68 (Shirley Heights –
130) [1995 62, a66: a7g⁵ a8g⁶ a8g 9.9m 8m* 8f³ 8g a8g⁴ a12g² 13.3g⁶ a11g³ a12g*
a12g² a12g 1996 a12g Oct 19] strong gelding: still a fair 1m to 1½m handicapper in
1995: off course a year, tailed off only 5-y-o outing. *Ronald Thompson*

TOY PRINCESS (USA) 4 b.f. Arctic Tern (USA) 126 – Princess Toy (Prince 80
Tenderfoot (USA) 126) [1995 69: a12g² a8g³ 10d³ 12.5m* 14.6m⁵ 14.1m⁴ 14.1m² a–
1996 a12g⁵ a12g a14.8g⁶ 15.4m* 16.4g 16s⁵ 12m 14.6g² 16.2m 16m 18.2m³ Sep 19]
tall, unfurnished mover: fair handicapper: won at Folkestone in
April: best at 1¾m+ nowadays and stays 2¼m: acts on good to firm and soft going
and on all-weather surfaces: edgy (ran poorly) tenth 4-y-o start: races prominently.
C. E. Brittain

TRACEABILITY 3 b.g. Puissance 110 – Miss Petella (Dunphy 124) [1995 72: 87
5m 7m* 7m⁴ 7m 7.1f* 7f* 8m* 1996 8m 8m⁴ 10m 10.8f* 12m 11.4d* 11.9g 11.9d
14g 11f² Nov 5] tall, lengthy gelding: shows knee action: fairly useful performer:
won minor events at Warwick in June and Sandown in August: stays 1½m: acts on
firm and dead ground: has been tongue tied: often races prominently. *S. C. Williams*

TRACI'S CASTLE (IRE) 3 b.f. Ajraas (USA) 88 – Mia Gigi (Hard Fought –
125) [1995 –: 6g 1996 7g Apr 8] smallish, sturdy filly: never a factor in maidens:
covered by Never So Bold. *R. Akehurst*

TRACKS OF MY TEARS 2 gr.f. (Apr 8) Damister (USA) 123 – Carose (Caro 52 ?
133) [1996 8f⁴ 10m 10f² Oct 14] angular, plain filly: half-sister to several winners,
including 3-y-o Crimson And Clover (by Midyan), 7f seller winner at 2 yrs, and 1¼m
winner Jason's Quest (by Golden Fleece): dam half-sister to very smart French
middle-distance colt Noir Et Or: runner-up in Leicester seller final start: looks a
stayer. *W. G. M. Turner*

TRADE WIND 5 br.g. Rambo Dancer (CAN) 107 – Cadasi 68 (Persian Bold 123) 63 §
[1995 75: 12g 10m* 12g 12g⁴ 10m* 11.6m⁵ 10d 12s⁵ 1996 10.8f⁴ 11.9d² 12.3m
11.7m⁴ Jul 18] big, lengthy gelding: impresses in appearance: good mover: fair
performer at best at 4 yrs for D. Elsworth: just modest in 1996: sold (J. O'Shea to D.
Bassett) 4,400 gns Doncaster September Sales: stays 1½m: acts on firm and dead
ground: usually blinkered/visored: held up: fair hurdler, winner in July and August:
sometimes looks none too keen. *J. G. M. O'Shea*

TRADING ACES 2 b.f. (Feb 15) Be My Chief (USA) 122 – Corn Futures 78 63
(Nomination 125) [1996 5g⁴ 5f⁶ 5f⁵ 7m 7.6m 6d⁴ 7d⁵ Oct 11] 17,500Y: lengthy filly:
has scope: first foal: dam, 6f winner at 2 yrs, out of close relative to Wassl: came from
well off strong pace when winning nursery at Haydock in October: probably stays
7.6f: best form on an easy surface. *M. Bell*

TRAFALGAR LADY (USA) 3 b.f. Fairy King (USA) – Tremulous (USA) 102 84
(Gregorian (USA) 124) [1995 86p: 6d* 6.1d² 1996 6f⁶ 6m⁵ 7d² 7.1f⁶ 8.1v⁵ Oct 6]
neat filly: fairly useful handicapper: should stay 1m granted less testing conditions

than on final start: acts on firm and dead ground: equipped with rope halter and blanket last 3 starts: sold 23,000 gns Newmarket December Sales. *R. Charlton*

TRAGIC HERO 4 b.g. Tragic Role (USA) – Pink Mex (Tickled Pink 114) [1995 63: 9g⁴ 8.5d⁵ 10f 8g⁶ 8.3m² 8h* 10m* 8g 1996 a8g 14.1f³ 14m³ Jul 13] compact gelding: very useful hurdler: modest performer on flat: stays 1¾m: acts on hard ground, always behind on all-weather debut on reappearance: blinkered 3 times, including last 2 starts. *M. C. Pipe* 64

TRAILBLAZER 2 b.c. (Mar 30) Efisio 120 – Flicker Toa Flame (USA) 85 (Empery (USA) 128) [1996 5m⁶ 6g³ a6g* a7g⁴ Dec 14] 19,000F, 30,000Y: compact colt: half-brother to 3-y-o 1¼m winner Cumbrian Maestro (by Puissance), 1m and 10.4f winner Quavering (by The Minstrel) and a winner in Germany by Niniski: dam, stayed 1m, half-sister to Motovato, smart at up to 1m: won median auction maiden at Wolverhampton in November: creditable effort in minor event there on final start: stays 7f: : acts on fibresand, shaped well on good to firm on debut: tended to carry head high and wander second start. *C. W. Thornton* 81

TRAINGLOT 9 ch.g. Dominion 123 – Mary Green 81 (Sahib 114) [1995 –: 14g 1996 18.7g⁶ 13.9g 15.9g 18g Oct 19] robust gelding: rated 110 as 4-y-o but very lightly raced since on flat: well-backed favourite, best 9-y-o effort when sixth of 18 in Chester Cup in May: off course 4 months, bandaged last 3 starts: needs a thorough test of stamina: acts on any going: still smart over hurdles, winner in November. *J. G. FitzGerald* 79

TRAPPER NORMAN 4 b.g. Mazilier (USA) 107 – Free Skip 68 (Free State 125) [1995 –: a7g 1996 a8g 8f⁶ 7f 7m 7f 14m a16g a13g Nov 26] no worthwhile form. *R. Ingram* –

TRAUMA (IRE) 4 b.f. Broken Hearted 124 – Remoosh (Glint of Gold 128) [1995 –: 10.3g a7g⁶ 1996 a14g Dec 3] long-backed filly: well beaten in maidens at 3 yrs: sold out of W. Jarvis' stable 700 gns Ascot May Sales and tailed-off last of 15 in claimer at Southwell on return. *W. G. M. Turner* –

TRAVELMATE 2 b.g. (Mar 9) Persian Bold 123 – Ustka 60 (Lomond (USA) 128) [1996 7m Sep 18] 7,500Y: first foal: dam, 7f winner, closely related to useful middle-distance winner Adam Smith and smart middle-distance stayer Braashee: late headway when eighth to Harry Wolton in maiden at Yarmouth: should improve over 1m+. *J. R. Fanshawe* 62 p

TREASURED SPIRIT (IRE) 2 b.f. (May 15) Treasure Kay 114 – Thread of Gold (Huntercombe 133) [1996 a5g Aug 16] IR 1,400Y: half-sister to 3 winners in Ireland, including 1¼m winner Golden Rhythm (by Cure The Blues), 1¾m winner Ivory Thread (by Sir Ivor) and a winner in Japan by Caerleon: dam, Irish 2-y-o 7.5f winner, half-sister to smart 7f to 1¼m performer Happy Bride and smart middle-distance colt Topanoora: well beaten in seller at Southwell. *C. A. Dwyer* –

TREASURE TOUCH (IRE) 2 b.g. (Feb 24) Treasure Kay 114 – Bally Pourri (IRE) (Law Society (USA) 130) [1996 5g⁴ 6s³ 6m a7g⁶ Nov 29] IR 4,800F, IR 5,000Y: tall gelding: first foal: dam Irish 1¼m winner: gambled-on favourite, awkward at stalls and withdrawn from seller on intended debut: modest form after, trained by A. Harrison on first run: should stay 7f: acts on soft ground. *G. M. Moore* 57

TREGARON (USA) 5 b.h. Lyphard (USA) 132 – Klarifi 91 (Habitat 134) [1995 77d: 8d⁵ 8m³ 8.1g 7.9m⁶ 8g 1996 8m* 8s⁵ 8m* 8m 7.3m³ 7.9m⁴ Aug 22] useful-looking horse: has a short action: much improved handicapper for new stable in 1996, easily winning 31-runner race at Ascot in May and 5-runner race at Salisbury in June: best efforts when in frame in rated stakes at Newbury and York last 2 starts: effective at 7f and 1m: acts on good to firm ground, below form on soft: held up. *R. Akehurst* 96

TREMENDISTO 6 b.g. Petoski 135 – Misty Halo 93 (High Top 131) [1995 55, a51: 10.5d⁵ a14.8g⁶ 12.1g² a12g³ 12m⁴ 15.1s² a14.8g⁴ a14g 1996 a12g⁶ a16g⁵ a16g⁴ 17.1g 14d⁶ 14.1m³ 13.1m a12g⁴ Nov 11] strong, plain gelding: shows a round action: modest maiden handicapper: effective at 1½m to 2m: acts on good to firm and dead ground and the all-weather: usually races prominently: won over hurdles in November. *Capt. J. Wilson* 50 a41

TREMPLIN (USA) 4 gr.c. Trempolino (USA) 135 – Stresa (Mill Reef (USA) 141) [1995 104: 10s* 10m 10g³ 12g⁵ 10d³ 10.8s 1996 10m⁵ 10s 10.1m 8d 8g Nov 2] –

TRE

rather leggy, short-necked colt: useful form in France in 1995 for A. Fabre: little
worthwhile form here: stays 1¼m: acts on heavy ground. *N. A. Callaghan*

TRENDY AUCTIONEER (IRE) 8 b.g. Mazaad 106 – Trendy Princess –
(Prince Tenderfoot (USA) 126) [1995 NR 1996 12f Apr 23] selling hurdler: well
beaten only start on flat since 1992. *Mrs L. C. Jewell*

TREVOR MITCHELL 2 b.f. (Apr 13) Backchat (USA) 98 – Versaillesprincess –
(Legend of France (USA) 124) [1996 6m a5g a6g a8g Dec 20] sparely-made filly:
first reported foal: dam, ran once on flat and twice over hurdles, no form: poor form.
J. J. Bridger

TRIA KEMATA 3 b.c. Kris 135 – Third Watch 114 (Slip Anchor 136) [1995 95: –
7g³ 7f⁶ 7g² 7d* 7g³ 1996 10g⁴ 7m Aug 15] rangy colt: fairly useful at 2 yrs: bandaged
off-fore, increasingly restive in preliminaries and took fierce hold in race when below
form in minor event at Kempton on reappearance: faced stiff task only subsequent
outing, and sold only 2,200 gns Newmarket Autumn Sales: acts on good to soft
ground: sometimes sweating: early to post in 1996: headstrong (bred to stay middle
distances but needs to settle) and one to treat with some caution. *J. L. Dunlop*

TRIANNA 3 b.f. General Holme (USA) 128 – Triemma (IRE) (M Double M 39
(USA)) [1995 NR 1996 6s⁶ a9.4g⁴ 8g³ a9.4g⁶ Jun 22] second foal: sister to 4-y-o
Triple: dam poor maiden (raced only at 2 yrs) from German family: poor maiden:
will stay 1¼m: has joined R. Brotherton. *Lord Huntingdon*

TRIBAL MISCHIEF 2 br.f. (Apr 10) Be My Chief (USA) 122 – Lammastide 93 61
(Martinmas 128) [1996 5g³ 5s² 5m⁴ 7m⁶ 5f⁵ 5s* 7g⁶ 6m Oct 29] 4,400Y: tall, leggy
filly: half-sister to 4 winners at up to 1m, including 3-y-o 7f winner Amber Fort (by
Indian Ridge): dam 2-y-o 5f winner: modest form: won maiden auction at Ripon in
August: should be well suited by further than 5f: needs give in the ground and
particularly well suited by the mud: visored (hung left) fifth start. *D. Moffatt*

TRIBAL MOON (IRE) 3 b.g. Ela-Mana-Mou 132 – Silk Blend (Busted 134) –
[1995 NR 1996 11d 10m Apr 29] IR 15,000Y: brother to very smart middle-distance
stayer Almaarad and half-brother to several middle-distance animals: dam unraced
sister to Silk Buds, a very useful performer at up to 1¼m: towards rear in maidens:
sold 900 gns Ascot July Sales and gelded. *Lady Herries*

TRIBAL PEACE (IRE) 4 ch.g. Red Sunset 120 – Mirabiliary (USA) 74 (Crow 74
(FR) 134) [1995 74: a10g* a10g² 10.5m⁴ 9m 9m² 10m 10d 9d* 9.7g 9d⁶ a8g a10g²
1996 a10g a10g* a10g 10g 10m a10g⁵ Nov 14] small gelding: fair performer: won
claimer at Lingfield (originally disqualified for interference but reinstated on appeal)
in January: off course 3 months after third start, 6 after fifth: stays 1¼m: acts on good
to firm and dead ground and the all-weather. *B. Gubby*

TRIBLE PET 3 b.f. Petong 126 – Fire Sprite 83 (Mummy's Game 120) [1995 48: 49
5g⁴ 5g⁴ 5f⁶ a5g² 5m⁵ 5m a6g⁶ 1996 a7g⁴ a8g⁴ Mar 2] sparely-made filly: poor
maiden: probably stays 7f: acts on the all-weather: tried blinkered. *B. Gubby*

TRICK (IRE) 3 b.f. Shirley Heights 130 – Hocus 88 (High Top 131) [1995 NR 76
1996 10g 10m⁶ 10.1m* 10.3m 10m⁴ 11.8f² 14.1s Oct 31] rangy, quite attractive filly:
third foal: half-sister to 1993 2-y-o 5f winner Hali (by Rousillon): dam, 7f winner,
half-sister to Hittite Glory: fair performer: narrowly won maiden at Yarmouth in
August: ran creditably most starts in handicaps afterwards: should have stayed 1¾m:
acted on firm ground, seemingly not on soft: flashed tail fifth and sixth starts: stud.
L. M. Cumani

TRICKLEDOWN 3 b.f. Dowsing (USA) 124 – Pillowing 69 (Good Times –
(ITY)) [1995 58d, a46: 5m⁵ 6m⁴ 6g 6g a6g² a5g 1996 a7g Jan 8] rather leggy filly:
poor sprint maiden: tailed off only 3-y-o outing: often mulish in preliminaries:
temperamental. *Martyn Wane*

TRIENTA MIL 2 b.g. (Jun 15) Prince Sabo 123 – Burmese Ruby (Good Times –
(ITY)) [1996 8.2s Oct 31] second foal: half-brother to 3-y-o Precious Island (by
Jupiter Island): dam NH Flat race winner: no promise in maiden at Nottingham.
P. T. Dalton

TRILBY 3 b.f. In The Wings 128 – Fur Hat (Habitat 134) [1995 71p: 8m⁴ 1996 72
11.8m 8g⁵ 10m⁵ 10.2f³ 10f² 12f* a16g⁴ 11.9g 12.1s⁴ Oct 22] smallish filly: has a
round action: fair handicapper: narrowly won at Thirsk in August, battling on stoutly:
should stay 2m: acts on firm ground, probably on soft: blinkered (ran poorly on

1022

equitrack) seventh 3-y-o start: sold 19,000 gns Newmarket December Sales, reportedly to join G. Richards. *P. F. I. Cole*

TRIPLE (FR) 4 b.f. General Holme (USA) 128 – Triemma (IRE) (M Double M – (USA)) [1995 –: a8g 1996 a8g Apr 24] tailed off in claimers. *P. Eccles*

TRIPLE HAY 2 ch.c. (Mar 25) Safawan 118 – Davinia 92 (Gold Form 108) [1996 80 p 7g 6f² 6g* Oct 29] 15,500F, 12,000Y: rather leggy colt: half-brother to Irish 1994 2-y-o 5f winner Duke of Aragon (by Aragon) and winning sprinters Paparelli (by King of Spain) and Divine Pet (by Tina's Pet): dam 2-y-o 5f winner: progressive form: faced simple task when very easy winner of median auction maiden at Leicester in October: may well stay beyond 6f: should improve further. *R. Hannon*

TRIPLE LEAP 3 b.c. Sadler's Wells (USA) 132 – Three Tails 121 (Blakeney 93 p 126) [1995 NR 1996 10m 10d² 10s* Aug 31] heavy-topped, attractive colt: has an unimpressive, quick action: fourth foal: brother to very smart middle-distance performer (second in 1995 Derby) Tamure: dam, 1½m winner, half-sister to 1000 Guineas and Oaks-placed Maysoon out of smart Triple First: progressive form: justified favouritism in maiden at Ripon in August by 3 lengths (rated value 5) from Classic Parisian, smooth headway to lead 3f out, eased close home: slowly away and green first 2 starts: will stay at least 1½m: looked sure to improve further and win more races: stays in training. *J. H. M. Gosden*

TRIPLE TERM 2 br.g. (Mar 31) Terimon 124 – Triple Reef (Mill Reef (USA) 72 141) [1996 7f⁴ 7.5f 8f⁴ 10m 8g⁴ Oct 25] close-coupled gelding: closely related to smart 1¼m winner Talented (by Bustino) and half-brother to several winners, including useful 6f/7f performer Triple Joy (by Most Welcome) and fairly useful middle-distance stayer Trazl (by Zalazl): dam unraced daughter of smart middle-distance filly Triple First and half-sister to Three Tails and Maysoon: fair form: should stay 1¼m: sold to join J. Smyth-Osbourne 17,000 gns Newmarket Autumn Sales and gelded. *J. L. Dunlop*

TRIPLE TIE (USA) 5 ch.m. The Minstrel (CAN) 135 – Tea And Roses (USA) 36 (Fleet Nasrullah) [1995 54d: 16m 11.8m 10m 10f⁶ 12m⁶ 11.8m⁵ 14s 12.1d 1996 a12g 13.1g⁶ 11.8m 11.4m 8.2m⁵ Aug 7] sparely-made mare: has a very round action: just a poor handicapper in 1996: stays 1¾m: acts on dead ground: tends to sweat. *M. Blanshard*

TRISTAN'S COMET 9 br.g. Sayf El Arab (USA) 127 – Gleneagle 91 (Swing – Easy (USA) 126) [1995 –, a49: a12g⁴ 16.2m 1996 a16g Jan 12] leggy gelding: very lightly raced on flat in recent seasons: visored, tailed off in weak Southwell claimer only 9-y-o start. *J. L. Harris*

TROIA (IRE) 2 b.f. (Apr 8) Last Tycoon 131 – Dubai Lady 78 (Kris 135) [1996 54 ? 7m⁵ a8g⁵ Dec 20] 5,000Y: third living foal: half-sister to smart 4-y-o 1¼m performer Ela-Aristokrati (by Danehill): dam middle-distance maiden out of half-sister to Princess Royal winner Trillionaire: first run for over 5 months and better effort in Lingfield maiden on final outing: will stay 1¼m. *B. Smart*

TROIKA (IRE) 3 ch.f. Roi Danzig (USA) – Trojan Relation (Trojan Fen 118) – [1995 NR 1996 8g 12d 10.1g 10m Jun 11] IR 10,000Y: quite good-topped filly: third foal: half-sister to fairly useful 6f winner Darren Boy (by Ballad Rock): dam unraced: no promise in 3 maidens and a handicap: sold 650 gns Doncaster July Sales. *J. Berry*

TROJAN RISK 3 ch.g. Risk Me (FR) 127 – Troyes 81 (Troy 137) [1995 73: 7m⁴ 91 7.6d⁴ 6.9s⁴ 6.9g² a6g⁴ 1996 9g 10.2g² 9m* 10.1m² 10m³ 10.3m² 10m 8.9g² Oct 12] sturdy, good-bodied colt: made into a fairly useful handicapper: won at Kempton in May: clearly best effort when second of 27 to Dreams End at York on final start: stays 1¼m: acts on good to firm ground, may well be unsuited by very soft: tends to be slowly away and is held up. *G. Lewis*

TROON 6 gr.h. Beveled (USA) – Cestrefeld 94 (Capistrano 120) [1995 6.5s⁶ 102 a5.5g⁶ 6g³ 6g* 6m 6g³ a6g⁶ 5g³ 6g 6g* 5s³ 6s* 6g 1996 6g⁶ 6g⁴ 6d 6v 8g* 6g* 6m⁵ 7m Oct 17] quite attractive horse: useful performer in Scandinavia nowadays: won 2 minor events at Taby in the summer: set steady pace 4f when 7¾ lengths seventh of 8 to Charnwood Forest in Challenge Stakes at Newmarket last time: effective at 6f and 1m: acts on firm and dead ground: blinkered once here. *Rune Haugen, Norway*

TROOPER 2 b.g. (Mar 25) Rock Hopper 124 – Silica (USA) 66 (Mr Prospector 65 (USA)) [1996 8d 7.9g⁶ 10g⁶ Oct 24] 55,000Y: first foal: dam 6f winner out of very smart US performer at up to 9f Skillful Joy: modest form: below best at 1¼m: sold (P. Cole to R. Akehurst) 13,000 gns Newmarket Autumn Sales. *P. F. I. Cole*

TROPICAL BEACH 3 b.g. Lugana Beach 116 – Hitravelscene (Mansingh 69 (USA) 120) [1995 56: 5g* 5g* 5d⁴ 5d 6f 1996 a6g 5g⁶ 5g³ 5g* 6m 5.9f 5g³ 6m⁴ 6f* 5m* 6m⁴ 6f⁵ 5d² 5m 5m⁴ 5m 5g⁵ 5f Nov 5] leggy gelding: fair sprint handicapper: successful in amateurs race at Hamilton, ladies seller at Thirsk and apprentice race at Hamilton in summer: acts on firm and dead ground, yet to race on anything softer: blinkered fourth and fifth 3-y-o starts. *J. Berry*

TROPICAL DANCE (USA) 3 ch.f. Thorn Dance (USA) 107 – Missuma 90 (USA) (Procida (USA) 129) [1995 93: 5m 5m³ 5m* 5m⁵ 6g* 6m* 7m⁵ 6.1m* 6g⁵ 1996 7.1d 6m 6m³ 6m 6m² 6g 6m 6m⁴ Oct 4] close-coupled, workmanlike filly: fairly useful performer: best form at 6f: acts on good to firm ground. *Mrs J. Cecil*

TROUBADOUR SONG 4 b.g. King of Clubs 124 – Silver Singing (USA) 96 56 (Topsider (USA)) [1995 77: 8.3m⁶ 8m² 10m⁴ 8.5d 8m 1996 a11g² 10g⁵ 10.2g a78 a11g* a12g* a11g* 10.1f² 10.4g a12g³ 10g⁵ a12g Dec 7] close-coupled gelding: fair performer on the all-weather: won claimers at Southwell (2) and Wolverhampton in the summer: only modest on turf: should stay further than 1½m: acts on good to firm ground and on fibresand: blinkered (well beaten) once at 2 yrs: has reportedly broken blood vessels: usually held up. *W. W. Haigh*

TROUBLE'S BREWING 5 gr.m. Hubbly Bubbly (USA) – Chemin de Guerre – 78 (Warpath 113) [1995 NR 1996 a7g⁵ Jun 8] fifth foal: half-sister to 3 winning hurdlers: dam successful at up to 19f, also useful hurdler: signs of ability in NH Flat races: well held in Wolverhampton claimer on flat debut. *P. R. Webber*

TROYSEND 3 b.g. Dowsing (USA) 124 – Way To Go 69 (Troy 137) [1995 6g² 101 7g² 8m² 6f⁴ 6g³ 6m² 7g* 6m 9d⁶ 1996 10d⁴ 9g* 8m³ 8d⁶ 7d* 8f 8.5f Aug 11] 2,200F, IR 4,100Y: sturdy, good-bodied ex-Irish gelding: half-brother to winners abroad by Hadeer and Chief Singer: dam 1¾m winner: useful performer: won auction event at Listowel at 2 yrs, minor event at Gowran Park in May and handicap at Naas in June: good third in listed race at Leopardstown in between: well beaten in Britannia Handicap at Royal Ascot penultimate start, and left A. O'Brien: effective at 7f to 9f: acts on good to firm and dead ground: sometimes blinkered/visored, including 4 of last 5 starts. *Jenine Sahadi, USA*

TRUANCY 3 b.g. Polar Falcon (USA) 126 – Zalfa (Luthier 126) [1995 84+: 6g – 6.1m* 7g⁶ 6g⁵ 1996 7m 7.9f 10.5d⁴ 10.4m⁶ 8g⁵ 13.3m Sep 21] smallish, useful-looking gelding: fairly useful performer at 2 yrs: disappointing in 1996, sold out of M. Bell's stable 10,500 gns Newmarket July Sales after fifth start: probably stays 10.5f: acts on good to firm ground and dead: visored fourth and fifth 3-y-o starts: winning juvenile hurdler. *C. J. Mann*

TRUE BIRD (IRE) 4 b.f. In The Wings 128 – I Want My Say (USA) (Tilt Up 58 (USA)) [1995 63: 12g² 10.4g⁶ 13.1g⁴ᵈⁱˢ 14g 15.8m² 1996 16.2m⁵ Apr 12] close-coupled, angular filly: modest maiden: stays 16.2f: has raced only on a sound surface. *J. D. Bethell*

TRUE GLORY (IRE) 2 b.f. (Feb 13) In The Wings 128 – Truly Special 116 67 p (Caerleon (USA) 132) [1996 8g Oct 25] medium-sized, sturdy filly: fifth foal: half-sister to 2 winners in France, notably smart middle-distance filly Truly A Dream (by Darshaan): dam, won 10.5f Prix de Royaumont, half-sister to Modhish and Russian Snows (both by Sadler's Wells) out of Irish 1000 Guineas winner Arctique Royale: bandaged, promising seventh of 15 to Calypso Grant in maiden at Doncaster in October: will improve, particularly over middle distances, and should be able to win a race. *J. H. M. Gosden*

TRUE JOY (IRE) 3 ch.f. Zilzal (USA) 137 – Foreign Courier (USA) (Sir Ivor – 135) [1995 NR 1996 7f⁶ Jun 12] closely related to fairly useful 1992 Irish 2-y-o 5f winner Moumayaz (by Nureyev) and half-sister to several winners, including 4 sprint winners by Danzig, notably Green Desert: dam unraced half-sister to top-class filly Althea: weak 7/1-shot, well-held sixth of 7 to Fatefully in maiden at Yarmouth: sold 140,000 gns Newmarket December Sales. *M. R. Stoute*

TRUE PERSPECTIVE 2 b.c. (Apr 15) Presidium 124 – Madam Muffin 77 – (Sparkler 130) [1996 5f⁶ 5m 6m a5g Dec 3] fourth reported foal: brother to 5f to 7f winner True Precision: dam sprinter: poor maiden: blinkered final start. *J. D. Bethell*

TRUE VISION   2 ch.f. (May 17) Interrex (CAN) – Lysithea 63 (Imperial Fling   –
(USA) 116) [1996 a7g 6m⁵ Jul 12] third reported foal: sister to 5f (at 2 yrs) and 12.5f
winner Lying Eyes: dam 6f seller winner later placed over jumps: well beaten in
sellers. *W. G. M. Turner*

TRULY BAY   3 b.g. Reprimand 122 – Daymer Bay (Lomond (USA) 128) [1995   40
NR 1996 7m 7m³ 7.1d 7.1m a7g⁴ a8g Dec 3] 16,500Y: leggy gelding: first foal: dam,
stayed 1m, from family of Teenoso and Most Welcome: only worthwhile form in
handicap at Southwell penultimate start, never a threat in 1m. *T. D. Barron*

TRULYFAN (IRE)   2 b. or br.f. (Mar 16) Taufan (USA) 119 – Whateveryousay   45 ?
(USA) (Verbatim (USA)) [1996 5.1m⁵ 5.1m 5g 5m⁶ Sep 23] 7,200 2-y-o: fifth foal:
dam unraced half-sister to 1000 Guineas third Crystal Gazing: poor form: visored
final outing. *R. A. Fahey*

TRULY PARCHED (USA)   2 b.c. (May 4) Known Fact (USA) 135 – Drought   80 p
(IRE) 69 (Rainbow Quest (USA) 134) [1996 7g⁶ 6m Oct 17] lengthy, good-topped
colt: first foal: dam 1¾m winner, should have been suited by 2m+: never a threat in
minor event at Ascot won by Kahal and Redcar Two-Year-Old Trophy: will be suited
by 7f+: will do better. *P. W. Chapple-Hyam*

TRUMBLE   4 b.g. Tragic Role (USA) – Sideloader Special 66 (Song 132) [1995   48 §
53: 8g⁴ 7g 8m² 8.2m 8m⁴ 12m² 12h² 12.4g* 13.8g⁵ 11f⁵ 1996 a12g a11g⁵ a11g³
a9.4g⁴ a8g⁴ a11g⁵ 10m 11.6g Jul 1] small, quite attractive gelding: poor performer
nowadays: left C. Thornton after fifth 4-y-o start, hanging left and looking none
too keen on seventh one: sold 1,200 gns Doncaster October Sales, returning to
C. Thornton: should stay 1¾m: acts on fibresand and probably on any turf ground:
often a front runner: one to treat with caution. *Mrs N. Macauley*

TRUMPED (IRE)   4 b.f. Last Tycoon 131 – Sweetbird (Ela-Mana-Mou 132)   45
[1995 12f⁶ 9.6d 5m 10m 12f⁴ 12g 10f 1996 10d⁴ 11.1m 11.1g³ 12.1f⁵ 15.1f 11.1m³
11.1m⁶ 13.1g* 12m² Aug 28] IR 11,000Y: ex-Irish filly: fourth foal: half-sister to
Italian 5-y-o 9f (at 2 yrs) to 2m winner Chiupi Doll (by Alzao) and winning hurdler
Morning Blush (by Glow): dam Irish staying maiden: poor performer: trained in
1995 by N. Meade: won weak 5-runner seller at Ayr in August by 13 lengths: stays
13.1f: acts on firm ground: pulled hard seventh start. *P. Monteith*

TRUTH   3 b.f. Prince Sabo 123 – Pursuit of Truth (USA) 69 (Irish River (FR) 131)   –
[1995 66p: 6f a6g⁵ a7g* 1996 6m 7.1g⁶ 7f⁶ Aug 6] unfurnished filly: failed to
reproduce 2-y-o form, and sold 4,100 gns Newmarket September Sales: may need
further than 7f nowadays: acts on equitrack: sent to Lebanon. *Sir Mark Prescott*

TRUTH OR DARE   3 b.c. Royal Academy (USA) 130 – Rose de Thai (USA) 99   110
(Lear Fan (USA) 130) [1995 8g⁶ 1996 10s⁴ 8d* 10m* 10g⁶ 12m Jun 30] 360,000
francs Y: second foal: dam, French 1m winner, granddaughter of Riverqueen (stayed
12.5f, rated 128): smart Irish-trained colt: won maiden at the Curragh in April, and
7-runner Derrinstown Stud Derby Trial at Leopardstown in May by 6 lengths from
Touch Judge: disappointing in Gallinule Stakes at the Curragh then returned there
and tailed off in Irish Derby 3 weeks later: stays 1¼m: acts on good to firm ground,
also successful on dead: sent to France. *Charles O'Brien, Ireland*

TRYPH   4 b.f. Pharly (FR) 130 – Troja (Troy 137) [1995 –: 8.1g 1996 12.1m⁶ a12g⁶   –
Jul 27] rather leggy filly: of little account on flat nowadays: sold 1,500 gns Doncaster
November Sales. *M. D. Hammond*

TSARINA   2 b.f. (Mar 23) Rudimentary (USA) 118 – Dance A Jig (Dance In Time   –
(CAN)) [1996 5m Aug 19] fifth foal: half-sister to 5f and 7f winner Tyrone Flyer
(by Celestial Storm) and fairly useful French 4-y-o sprinter Always Dancing (by
Common Grounds): dam once-raced granddaughter of smart Fluke, a half-sister to
Bireme and Buoy: slowly into stride and never a threat in maiden at Windsor in
August. *R. Hannon*

TSARNISTA   3 b.f. Soviet Star (USA) 128 – Princess Genista 108 (Ile de Bourbon   100
(USA) 133) [1995 80: 6m⁴ 7m 6g² 7g* 8m⁶ 1996 8d⁶ 8m 7.6m² 8m³ 8.1g⁴ 8.1m⁴ 8g⁴
8d⁶ Nov 9] leggy, sparely-made filly: useful performer: best efforts in listed events at
Naas and Evry last 2 starts: stays 1m: acts on good to firm and dead going: sometimes
sweats: stays in training. *J. L. Dunlop*

TSARSKAYA   3 ch.f. Elmaamul (USA) 125 – Wyandra (So Blessed 130)   60
[1995 68p: 6g⁵ 1996 8m⁵ 8g⁵ 11.6m⁵ 10.8m Jul 5] modest maiden: should be suited
by further than 1m, but below form when tried. *Mrs J. Cecil*

TTYFRAN 6 b.g. Petong 126 – So It Goes 73 (Free State 125) [1995 –: 12m 14.1g 38
1996 10.3m³ 14.1f³ 14.1f³ 12m³ 16m 16.2g Aug 24] workmanlike gelding: poor
handicapper at best nowadays: should stay 2m: suited by a sound surface.
B. P. J. Baugh

TUDOR FALCON 3 b.g. Midyan (USA) 124 – Tudorealm (USA) (Palace Music 62
(USA) 129) [1995 NR 1996 10g a8g⁴ 8g May 28] 12,000Y: quite attractive gelding:
first foal: dam, bred to have been suited by further than 1m, granddaughter of
Princess Royal winner Trillionaire: modest maiden, lightly raced: best effort in
claimer at Southwell on second start: sold (W. Haggas to P. Bradley) 2,500 gns Newmarket July Sales. *W. J. Haggas*

TUDOR FLIGHT 5 b.m. Forzando 122 – Tudor Pilgrim 58 (Welsh Pageant 132) –
[1995 –: a10g 1996 a12g 11.9g May 30] leggy mare: one-time fair maiden
handicapper, but seems to have lost her way: sold 1,000 gns Ascot July Sales.
A. G. Newcombe

TUDOR ISLAND 7 b.g. Jupiter Island 126 – Catherine Howard 68 (Tower Walk 86
130) [1995 86: 14m* 12m 16.4m³ 14g² 13.9m 14.6m³ 13.9g* 14.6m 1996 14d 14m²
14m³ 14.8d² 14.6m³ 16.2m Sep 28] strong, close-coupled gelding: fairly useful
handicapper: creditable efforts in 1996 when placed: stays 16.4f: acts on good to firm
ground, soft and equitrack: blinkered (easily best effort at the time) once at 3 yrs:
sometimes hangs, but is genuine. *C. E. Brittain*

TUIGAMALA 5 b.g. Welsh Captain 113 – Nelliellamay (Super Splash (USA) –
106) [1995 46, a62: 9g 7m 7f* 8.1m 8f a10g a7g* a7g 1996 a7g⁴ a7g⁴ a7g⁵ a7g⁴ a8g* a62
a8g⁴ a10g⁴ 10f 10g Oct 2] good-topped gelding: poor performer on turf, modest on
the all-weather: won handicap at Lingfield in February: stays 1m: acts on firm going
and goes well on equitrack. *R. Ingram*

TUKAPA 2 b.g. (Mar 27) Risk Me (FR) 127 – Haddon Anna (Dragonara Palace –
(USA) 115) [1996 5m 5m Sep 6] rather leggy gelding: eighth foal: half-brother to
winning sprinters Followmegirls (by Sparkling Boy) and Banbury Flyer (by Mummy's Game): dam unraced granddaughter of very speedy Granville Greta: behind in
maidens: gave trouble at stalls second start. *Mrs A. L. M. King*

TULIPA (USA) 3 b.f. Alleged (USA) 138 – Black Tulip (FR) (Fabulous Dancer 111
(USA) 124) [1995 8g⁶ 8g³ 1996 10g* 10.5g* 11v² 12m* 12m Sep 15] good-bodied
filly: second foal: half-sister to smart German 1m/9f colt Devil River Peek (by Silver
Hawk): dam won 7 races at 1¼m to 1½m in France and second in 2 Grade 2 events at
1½m in USA: won minor event at Evry in March and Prix Penelope at Saint-Cloud in
April: 2½ lengths second of 15 to Night Petticoat in Preis der Diana at Mulheim in
May: decidedly on toes, won 10-runner Ribblesdale Stakes at Royal Ascot by neck
from Key Change, travelling comfortably, leading over 1f out and battling on well
despite edging right: off course nearly 3 months but looking really well, below form
in Prix Vermeille at Longchamp, held up and unable to land a blow: stays 1½m well:
acts on good to firm ground and heavy: joined Godolphin. *A. Fabre, France*

*Ribblesdale Stakes, Royal Ascot—
a hard-gained victory for Tulipa (centre) from Key Change (right) and Shemozzle*

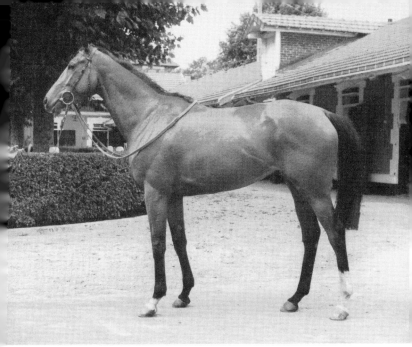

Sheikh Mohammed's "Tulipa"

TULSA (IRE)   2 b.g. (Mar 25) Priolo (USA) 127 – Lagrion (USA) (Diesis 133)   56 ?
[1996 7m 7m 6m Oct 4] IR 10,000Y: first foal: dam, Irish maiden who stayed 1½m,
sister to smart 1988 2-y-o 6f winner Pure Genius out of half-sister to smart winner at
up to 1½m Gift Wrapped: well held in varied events, including a claimer: visored last
2 starts: gelded. *B. Gubby*

TULU   5 ch.m. Nicholas Bill 125 – Falcrello 51 (Falcon 131) [1995 78: 10g* 10.5g⁶   73
1996 8s 10.8d 11.8g⁴ 12m⁶ 12g 12f* Jun 12] sturdy mare: fair handicapper: won at
Beverley in June by short head from Chatham Island, leading post: stays 1½m: acts
on any going: held up and has turn of foot: bandaged in 1996. *Mrs J. R. Ramsden*

TUMBLEWEED PEARL   2 b.f. (Apr 19) Aragon 118 – Billie Blue 63 (Ballad   90
Rock 122) [1996 6m⁴ 5.7m* 6f* 7.3s⁵ Oct 26] 2,500F, 28,000Y: well-made filly: has
scope: third foal: half-sister to useful 3-y-o Tumbleweed Ridge (by Indian Ridge), 5f
and 7.3f (Horris Hill Stakes) winner at 2 yrs, and 1993 2-y-o 7f winner Billie Grey
(by Chilibang): dam second over 7f on only start: useful form: won median auction
maiden at Bath in July and minor event at Thirsk (carrying head awkwardly) in
August: ran well in listed race at Newbury after near 3-month absence on final start,
staying on steadily: will stay 1m: acts on firm and soft ground. *B. J. Meehan*

TUMBLEWEED RIDGE   3 ch.c. Indian Ridge 123 – Billie Blue 63 (Ballad   102 d
Rock 122) [1995 106: 6g² 5f⁴ 5m* 6m² 7g² 7.3d* 1996 7m⁵ 8m 6m 6g 7m³
Oct 28] well-made colt: good walker: useful form at 2 yrs, won Horris Hill Stakes:
respectable fifth of 8 to Cayman Kai in European Free Handicap at Newmarket on
reappearance: well beaten in good company next 3 starts, and well below best when
third of 4 in slowly-run minor event at Leicester on final outing: stays 7f: acts on firm

and dead ground: blinkered (well beaten) third 3-y-o start: wore tongue strap and dropped noseband next time. *B. J. Meehan*

TUMI (USA) 3 ch.f. Diesis 133 – Carotene (CAN) (Great Nephew 126) [1995 NR 84 ? 1996 10.4g 10.1g⁶ Oct 30] quite good-topped filly: third foal: sister to useful 1m winner Teshami and half-sister to 1994 2-y-o 6f winner Ginger Tree (by Dayjur): dam multiple champion Canadian filly (winning at up to 1½m) out of Galtres winner Carrot Top: seventh of 10 to Multicoloured in maiden at York on debut, never a threat: very stiff task, possibly flattered when well-held sixth of 7 to Medaille Militaire in minor event at Yarmouth 3 weeks later, swishing tail under pressure: sold 50,000 gns Newmarket December Sales. *J. H. M. Gosden*

TURBO NORTH 3 b.g. Nordico (USA) – Turbo Rose 81 (Taufan (USA) 119) – [1995 –: 5m 6m 5d 1996 8.1g 6.1m 9.9g 8g May 29] leggy gelding: no worthwhile form, including in visor: sold 1,000 gns Doncaster July Sales. *M. Dods*

TURGENEV (IRE) 7 b.g. Sadler's Wells (USA) 132 – Tilia (ITY) (Dschingis 70 Khan) [1995 NR 1996 a12g 11.8d 12.1d⁵ 13s 13.9m³ 14d* 14d² 16.2m Jul 26] strong, deep-bodied gelding: has a fluent action: useful at 4 yrs for J. Gosden before having winless spell in Dubai: fair handicapper on return to Britain, winning at Haydock in June: stays 1¾m well: best form with give in the ground and acts on soft: tried blinkered (last 7 starts)/visored: usually held up. *R. Bastiman*

TURIA 3 b.f. Slip Anchor 136 – Tura (Northfields (USA)) [1995 –: 7g 1996 10m⁵ 66 12g⁴ 11.9d⁴ 12g Aug 14] small, sturdy filly: half-sister to 4 winners, including 1995 German 3-y-o 1m listed winner Tristano (by Colmore Row) and fairly useful 6f winner Young Turpin (by Young Generation): dam 7f winner in Ireland: modest form first 2 starts in 1996: at least as effective at 1¼m as over 1½m. *Major D. N. Chappell*

TURNING WHEEL (USA) 3 b.f. Seeking The Gold (USA) – Misinskie (USA) 99 + 84 (Nijinsky (CAN) 138) [1995 NR 1996 10m² 10m* 8d Oct 11] strong, lengthy filly: closely related to 2 winners, notably very useful miler Ajfan (by Woodman), and half-sister to smart 4-y-o middle-distance stayer Minds Music (by Silver Hawk) and 2 other winners: dam, best at 2 yrs, half-sister to high-class sprinter/miler Clever Trick: heavily-backed favourite for 2 maidens at Windsor in August, very easy winner from Multicoloured on second occasion: looked in tremendous shape but moved short to post when respectable seventh of 12 to Fatefully in listed race at Ascot 2 months later, faring best of group which kept to inside in back straight: stays in training and may still do better, particularly back over middle distances. *H. R. A. Cecil*

TURNPOLE (IRE) 5 br.g. Satco (FR) 114 – Mountain Chase (Mount Hagen 70 (FR) 127) [1995 72: 10m⁵ 10m 10.1g⁵ 12.4m² 11f* 12m² 1996 13.9g⁵ 14.6g Oct 25] strong gelding: fair handicapper: stays 1¾m: acts on firm ground, yet to race on a soft surface: has run well when sweating: useful hurdler. *Mrs M. Reveley*

TURTLE MOON 2 gr.c. (Apr 11) Absalom 128 – Port Na Blath (On Your Mark 65 125) [1996 5g⁴ 5g 6m³ Oct 23] 10,500F, 24,000Y: sixth foal: half-brother to 2-y-o 6f winners Flood's Fancy (by Then Again) and Combination (fairly useful, by Primo Dominie): dam Irish 6f winner: modest form: off course 5 months after debut: sold 7,000 gns Newmarket Autumn Sales. *M. H. Tompkins*

TUSCAN DAWN 6 ch.g. Clantime 101 – Excavator Lady 65 (Most Secret 119) 83 [1995 81d: 5.1m⁵ 5g 5f 5m 5m 5m⁶ 5.1m 1996 5g* 5d³ 5m 5m⁶ 5g⁵ 5.1d 5m* 5.1g⁴ 5g Oct 19] leggy, lengthy gelding: unimpressive mover: fairly useful handicapper: won at Thirsk in May and Epsom in September: speedy, and best at 5f: acts on any going: usually makes running: sometimes ruins chance by rearing in stalls (usually put in last). *J. Berry*

TUSCANY 2 b.c. (Feb 25) Pursuit of Love 124 – Jhansi Ki Rani (USA) 94 (Far 92 North (CAN) 120) [1996 6m* 6f 7m² 7g³ a8s⁴ Sep 29] 35,000Y: angular, useful-looking colt: has a quick action: half-brother to several winners, including useful 1991 2-y-o 6f winner Colway Bold (by Never So Bold) and 12.5f and 13.8f winner Memorable (by Don't Forget Me): dam 7f and 1m winner: fairly useful form: won maiden at Goodwood in June: kept useful company after, running creditably each time: stays 7f: trained until after penultimate start by P. Cole. *C. Clement, USA*

TUTU SIXTYSIX 5 br.m. Petong 126 – Odilese 82 (Mummy's Pet 125) [1995 36 43: 6f 5m⁵ 6m 6g 6m 5.9f⁵ 5m 5g 6f² 5m 6m 1996 6.1m 5.9m⁶ 6g 5g 5f⁴ 5f⁶ 7m 6m

5m 5.1m Sep 16] leggy, sparely-made mare: poor sprint handicapper: acts on firm ground, dead and equitrack: often blinkered/visored: generally comes from off pace and often meets trouble in running: usually ridden by Kim Tinkler. *Don Enrico Incisa*

TWICE AS SHARP   4 ch.c. Sharpo 132 – Shadiliya 90 (Red Alert 127) [1995   93
87: 6m² 6g* 6g³ 7.1m 6g 5d* 5s 1996 5g 5m³ 6d 6m⁶ 5m* 5g 5.2m 5g 5m⁵ 5d 5g
Oct 19] fairly useful handicapper: gained most important success in Northern Rock
Gosforth Park Cup at Newcastle in June: effective at 5f (best form) and 6f: acts on
good to firm and soft ground: usually races prominently. *P. W. Harris*

TWICE PURPLE (IRE)   4 b.g. Then Again 126 – Tyrian Belle 77 (Enchantment   62
115) [1995 62: 8g 7g 7m⁶ 8.1d⁴ 8g⁶ 1996 7m 6d⁴ 6f⁴ a6g 6m² 7.1m Jul 11] tall,
good-topped gelding: modest maiden handicapper: effective at 6f to 1m: acts on firm
and dead ground, below form only all-weather outing: blinkered last 4 starts.
B. J. Meehan

TWICE REMOVED   3 b.f. Distant Relative 128 – Nigel's Dream (Pyjama Hunt   –
126) [1995 –: 6m 1996 7m 6g 8m Aug 19] no sign of ability. *S. Dow*

TWICE THE GROOM (IRE)   6 b.g. Digamist (USA) 110 – Monaco Lady 83   –
(Manado 130) [1995 60: 12.3m³ 11.9s 1996 a16.2g 15.9m Jul 13] tall, rather leggy
gelding: bad mover: modest handicapper: tailed off both starts in 1996: sold 950 gns
Doncaster November Sales. *R. Lee*

TWILIGHT SLEEP (USA)   4 b.g. Shadeed (USA) 135 – Sleeping Beauty 87   –
(Mill Reef (USA) 141) [1995 83: 8g⁶ 10m 14m 1996 9s Oct 26] strong, compact
gelding: fairly useful performer: pulled up on final 3-y-o start: first outing on a soft
surface, tailed off on belated reappearance. *Lord Huntingdon*

TWIN CREEKS   5 b.g. Alzao (USA) 117 – Double River (USA) (Irish River   –
(FR) 131) [1995 56, a61: a8g⁶ a7g* a7g⁶ 7.6m 6.9m 7.5m 6.9f³ 8.1m⁵ 9.2m* 8m 7d   a75
1996 a8g a8g⁵ a8g* a9.4g 8m a8g a7g² 8m⁶ a8.5g³ a7g* a7s* Nov 19]
compact gelding: fair handicapper on the all-weather, poor at best on turf in 1996:
won at Southwell in February: left M. Hammond after sixth start: again led closing
stages when winning at Lingfield in October and November, putting up career-best
efforts: stays 9f: acts on fibresand and equitrack and on firm ground, well beaten on a
soft surface: takes keen hold: found little eighth start, and overall is none too
consistent. *V. Soane*

TWIN FALLS (IRE)   5 b.g. Trempolino (USA) 135 – Twice A Fool (USA)   –
(Foolish Pleasure (USA)) [1995 NR 1996 14.1g May 30] fair performer (rated 79) at
3 yrs for R. Hannon: well beaten on flat but winner over jumps (November and
December) since. *G. M. Moore*

TWO BILLS   2 b.g. (Feb 12) Totem (USA) 118 – Chess Mistress (USA) 59 (Run   – p
The Gantlet (USA)) [1996 6.1m 6.1d⁶ 6.1m Sep 16] 2,500Y, 2,500 2-y-o: tall
gelding: has scope: second reported foal: half-brother to 4-y-o Chesters Quest (by
Domynsky): dam 1½m winner in France at 4 yrs: poor form without being fully
wound up: has had tongue tied down: may do better. *A. Streeter*

TWO ON THE BRIDGE   2 b.g. (Apr 14) Chilibang 120 – Constant Companion   59
84 (Pas de Seul 133) [1996 5.9g* 5m³ Jul 11] 1,100F, 4,800Y: fifth foal: half-brother
to 1993 2-y-o 7f winner Hobart (by Reprimand) and fairly useful 7f/1m performer
Comanche Companion (by Commanche Run): dam 1m winner who stayed 1¼m: in
frame in maiden auctions: likely to prove suited by at least 6f: tail swisher: gelded.
Denys Smith

TWO SOCKS   3 ch.g. Phountzi (USA) 104 – Mrs Feathers 57 (Pyjama Hunt 126)   63
[1995 49, a60: 5.2m 6m 6g 6m a7g⁴ a7g³ a8.5g² 7.6d⁵ 6.9g a8g 1996 a8.5g a10g⁶ 8g⁵
10f⁴ 12.5f² 10f² 11.5f* 11.5m 10d 10f Oct 15] leggy, unfurnished gelding: modest
handicapper: won at Lingfield in July: left M. McCormack's stable after next start
and well beaten for new yard: stays 12.5f: acts on firm ground and on fibresand:
seemed to run in snatches fourth 3-y-o start: blinkered (below form) once at 2 yrs:
suited by waiting tactics. *P. Burgoyne*

TWO TO TANGO (IRE)   3 ch.f. Anshan 119 – Marie de Sologne (Lashkari 128)   74
[1995 NR 1996 8m⁵ a8.5g* a10s Nov 19] 90,000 francs Y: second foal: half-sister to
useful French 4-y-o 1¼m and 1½m winner Minervitta (by Warrshan): dam unraced
half-sister to smart 8.5f to 1½m winner Coeur de Lion: odds on, confirmed debut
promise when winning maiden at Wolverhampton in November: stiffish task, not

Bessborough Stakes (Handicap), Royal Ascot—Tykeyvor is clear

discredited in minor event at Lingfield later in month: sold 20,000 gns Newmarket December Sales: seems to stay 1¼m. *J. H. M. Gosden*

TYCOON GIRL (IRE) 2 b.f. (Mar 26) Last Tycoon 131 – Forest Berries (IRE) (Thatching 131) [1996 6.1m⁵ 6m* Oct 8] IR 17,000Y: lengthy filly: second foal; half-sister to 3-y-o Butterwick Belle (by Distinctly North): dam unraced half-sister to smart middle-distance colt Pencader: improved effort in maidens when winning at Redcar in October: will probably stay beyond 6f: should improve again. *B. J. Meehan* — 74 p

TYCOON TINA 2 b.f. (May 9) Tina's Pet 121 – Royal Tycoon (Tycoon II) [1996 a6g⁵ 8.1s a8.5g Oct 19] tall, rather sparely-made filly: third reported foal: dam winning jumper: well beaten in sellers and maiden. *W. M. Brisbourne* — –

TYCOON TODD (USA) 2 gr.c. (Mar 29) Cozzene (USA) – Thirty Below (USA) (It's Freezing (USA) 122) [1996 6g* Sep 5] $27,000F, $55,000Y: leggy, unfurnished colt: first foal: dam winning sprinter in USA (including at 2 yrs) from the family of Temperence Hill and Vanlandingham: heavily-backed favourite, won 16-runner maiden at York in September readily by 2½ lengths from Harry Wolton, tracking leaders then showing nice turn of foot inside last: should stay 1m, possibly more: has joined Godolphin: sure to improve. *D. R. Loder* — 98 p

TYKEYVOR (IRE) 6 b.g. Last Tycoon 131 – Ivoronica 89 (Targowice (USA) 130) [1995 81: 8.3m⁵ 10g* 8.9m³ 10m* 10d 9g 12m⁵ 1996 10g⁶ 11.9m³ 12f* 12m* Jun 19] lengthy, good-topped gelding: impresses in appearance: fairly useful handicapper, better than ever in 1996: won at Beverley and Royal Ascot (20-runner Bessborough Stakes, always going comfortably just off pace under claimer F. Lynch and beat My Learned Friend by 3 lengths) in June: better suited by 1½m than shorter: acts on firm ground, no form on a soft surface: visored twice in 1994, running well on first occasion: usually bandaged. *Lady Herries* — 92

TYMEERA 3 b.f. Timeless Times (USA) 99 – Dear Glenda 66 (Gold Song 112) [1995 62: a5g³ a5g⁴ 5f* 5.1m* 5g⁶ 1996 6.1d* 5d⁴ 6.1m 6.1m a6g⁴ 6m⁶ 6m² 5.1f a5g a6g Dec 3] small filly: unimpressive mover: modest handicapper: won at Nottingham in April: stays 6f: acts on firm and dead ground, only poor form on fibresand: well beaten only try in visor: tends to hang left. *B. Palling* — 60 a47

TYPHOON EIGHT (IRE) 4 b.c. High Estate 127 – Dance Date (IRE) (Sadler's Wells (USA) 132) [1995 78: 11m 10.2f⁶ 11.4m⁵ 12g⁴ 16.2d 1996 16g 12m 10.8g² — 74

12m 10g 12m 12g* 12v Nov 11] smallish, sturdy colt: poor mover: fair handicapper: gained first win at Catterick in October: needs at least 10.8f and should prove suited by further than 1¼m: best form with give in the ground, but well beaten on heavy: blinkered third to fifth 4-y-o starts: sometimes looks none too resolute. *B. W. Hills*

TYPHOON LAD 3 ch.c. Risk Me (FR) 127 – Muninga 108 (St Alphage 119)   73
[1995 6d 7m⁴ 1996 6d⁶ 7s⁶ 9s⁵ 10f² 10.2f⁴ 11.9f⁴ 8.5m Sep 24] 6,200F, 9,500Y: ex-Irish colt: half-brother to 7f winner Lizzy Cantle and 1m winner Mr Kewmill (both by Homing) and a winner abroad by Blazing Saddles: dam 5f winner: fair maiden: left M. Halford's stable after third 3-y-o start: good efforts on first 2 outings here: stays 1¼m: acts on firm and soft ground. *S. Dow*

TYRIAN PURPLE (IRE) 8 b.h. Wassl 125 – Sabrine (Mount Hagen (FR) 127)   –
[1995 61, a70: a5g⁴ a7g⁴ a6g⁴ a6g* a6g* a6g² a6g a5g³ 6m 6m 5m³ 5.3f* 6f³ a5g 6d   a47
a7g 1996 a6g a5g⁴ Jan 11] leggy, angular horse: modest performer: well below form both 8-y-o outings: effective at 5f to 1m: acts on firm and dead ground and all-weather surfaces: usually blinkered. *T. J. Naughton*

TYROLEAN DANCER (IRE) 2 b.f. (Mar 17) Tirol 127 – Waffling 68 (Lo-   49
mond (USA) 128) [1996 7f 7f⁴ 7d Oct 28] second foal: dam, maiden who probably stayed 1¼m, granddaughter of 1000 Guineas winner Night Off: poor form in maidens. *S. P. C. Woods*

TYROLEAN DREAM (IRE) 2 b.c. (Mar 3) Tirol 127 – Heavenly Hope   84 p
(Glenstal (USA) 118) [1996 7m 8s² Nov 9] 45,000Y: first foal: dam winning Irish stayer/hurdler: better effort in maidens when second to eased-down Moon River in median aution event at Doncaster in November: will stay 1¼m: may well progress again. *M. H. Tompkins*

U

ULTIMATE WARRIOR 6 b.g. Master Willie 129 – Fighting Lady 104 (Chebs   64
Lad 120) [1995 71, a62: a10g a8g* a8g 10m³ a10g³ a10g⁵ a14.8g 1996 a10g² 12m³   a60
10m 8m⁴ 10g 12.1g⁴ a10g Sep 10] lengthy, angular gelding: modest performer: sold 3,500 gns Newmarket Autumn Sales: stays 1½m: acts on heavy and good to firm ground and on equitrack. *C. A. Cyzer*

ULTRA BARLEY 3 ch.g. Beveled (USA) – Chapter One (Hello Gorgeous   –
(USA) 128) [1995 68+, a79: 6m⁵ a6g* 6f* 6m⁴ 6f³ 6g a6g* a7g* 1996 a7g* a6g   a82
Jan 31] workmanlike gelding: fairly useful performer: landed the odds in claimer at Lingfield in January: stays 7f: acts on good to firm ground, best on all-weather surfaces: sent to Macau, renamed Creative Stories and won twice there over 5f. *P. C. Haslam*

ULTRA BEET 4 b.g. Puissance 110 – Cassiar 84 (Connaught 130) [1995 75, a84:   58
a5g⁴ a5g* a5g* a5g* a5g* 5g 5g⁵ a5g² 6.1g³ 6f* 5m⁶ 5g a5g a5g 1996 a6g⁵ a5g⁵   a71
a6g² a6g³ a7g a7g 6d 5g 5m 7m⁶ 6m² 6f³ a6g* 6f⁴ a6g a6s³ Dec 19] compact gelding: fair performer on the all-weather, modest on turf: won seller at Wolverhampton in August: effective at 5f and 6f: acts on firm ground, goes well on the all-weather: usually blinkered/visored nowadays: usually races prominently. *P. C. Haslam*

ULTRA BOY 2 b.g. (Feb 15) Music Boy 124 – Golden Award 65 (Last Tycoon   73
131) [1996 5m 6d 6f³ 6m³ 6f* Aug 9] 6,800F, 8,000Y: quite good-topped gelding: third foal: dam twice-raced daughter of half-sister to Main Reef and Moonlight Night: fair form: won nursery at Redcar in August, leading well inside final 1f: will stay 7f: acts on firm ground. *P. C. Haslam*

UMBERSTON (IRE) 3 b.g. Nabeel Dancer (USA) 120 – Pivotal Walk (IRE)   53
(Pennine Walk 120) [1995 52+: 7m 8g 10m 1996 11.8d 12.3m⁵ 14.1m 12m⁵ Aug 2] useful-looking gelding: modest maiden: sold (L. Cumani to P. Hedger) 20,000 gns Newmarket Autumn Sales: shapes as though he'll stay beyond 1½m: blinkered (far from disgraced after meeting trouble in running) penultimate 3-y-o start. *L. M. Cumani*

UNALLOYED (USA) 3 b.f. Silver Hawk (USA) 123 – Copperhead (USA)   78
(Hawaii) [1995 NR 1996 10g⁵ 10m² 9.7g⁴ Sep 27] $140,000F: tall, leggy filly: fifth

reported foal: sister to 2 winners, including Silver Ending, very smart graded stakes winner at up to 1¼m, and half-sister to a minor sprint winner by Sing Sing: dam minor sprint winner: fair maiden: narrowly beaten second start: odds on, probably went too fast for own good (reportedly finishing distressed) only subsequent outing: stays 1¼m: stays in training. *D. R. Loder*

UNASSAILABLE 3 ch.f. Hadeer 118 – Penny In My Shoe (USA) (Sir Ivor 135) –
[1995 NR 1996 10m⁵ Sep 18] sister to 1992 2-y-o 5f winner Other One and half-sister to a winner in USA by Believe It: dam half-sister to Gorytus out of 1000 Guineas winner Glad Rags II: tailed-off last of 5 in Sandown maiden. *C. E. Brittain*

UNCHANGED 4 b.f. Unfuwain (USA) 131 – Favorable Exchange (USA) 79
(Exceller (USA) 129) [1995 78: 12m² 11.9f⁴ 15.4m* 15.9d* 17.1m² 1996 14m² 16g⁴ 18.7g⁴ 13.1g⁵ 20f 16f⁴ 20m³ Jul 31] good-topped filly: fair handicapper: dyed-in-the-wool stayer: acts on firm ground and dead, yet to race on soft: blinkered (unsuited by drop in trip) fourth 4-y-o start. *C. E. Brittain*

UNCHARTED WATERS 5 b.m. Celestial Storm (USA) 132 – Try The Duchess 57
99 (Try My Best (USA) 130) [1995 68: a10g a14.8g 11.7m³ 13.1f⁶ 11.9m⁶ a–
12m⁵ 11.4m⁵ 14g 12m 9.7s⁴ 12.1d 1996 a12g⁵ a12g 11.9f* 15.4m⁵ 11.7g 11.9f²
13.1g⁴ 12.1d² 11.8m⁵ 12g² 16.2f 12g⁴ 12g⁶ Jul 10] lengthy, angular mare: modest handicapper at best nowadays: won at Brighton in April: stays 1½m: acts on firm and dead ground, below form on the all-weather: blinkered (out of form) eighth 4-y-o start: sometimes looks lazy: covered by Muhtarram. *C. A. Cyzer*

UNCLE DOUG 5 b.g. Common Grounds 118 – Taqa 85 (Blakeney 126) [1995 68
57: 16m² 13.9g⁴ 16m³ 20m 15.8g 1996 14.1g 14.1m⁶ 16g* 16g 14.1f² 16.1g⁶ 16g²
16s* 17.5m²ᵈⁱˢ 14.1m⁴ 16.5s Nov 9] close-coupled, quite attractive gelding: fair handicapper: won at Thirsk in May and Ripon in August: has run well at least as effective at 1¾m/2m, but at least as effective at 1¾m/2m, but at least as effective when sweating: sometimes looks reluctant, and not an easy ride. *Mrs M. Reveley*

UNCLE GEORGE 3 ch.g. Anshan 119 – Son Et Lumiere (Rainbow Quest 61 §
(USA) 134) [1995 73: 5.1g⁵ 6m 6m* 8g⁶ 6g 1996 8m 8d⁵ 8g² 8g 7.5m³ 8m⁵
7f² 8m 7m² 8f⁴ 7d² 7.1m 7m⁶ Sep 17] lengthy gelding: fair performer on his day: sold 4,000 gns Newmarket Autumn Sales: stays 1m: acts on firm and dead ground: usually blinkered/visored: has looked an awkward ride: unreliable: sent to Germany. *M. H. Tompkins*

UNCLE OSWALD 5 ch.g. Nashwan (USA) 135 – Riviere Bleue (Riverman 64 +
(USA) 131) [1995 86: 12g 10m⁵ 8m⁵ 8m⁶ 10g² 12m 10.2m² 10m⁵ 1996 a11g³ Jul 22]
close-coupled, sturdy gelding: fairly useful handicapper in 1995: favourite after near 12-month absence, long way below best when third of 9 in poor claimer at Southwell: stays 1¼m: acts on good to firm ground. *R. Hannon*

UNCONDITIONAL LOVE (IRE) 3 b.f. Polish Patriot (USA) 128 – Thatch- 100
erite (Final Straw 127) [1995 93: 5d² 5m* 5m* 5.2g³ 5m⁴ 5m 1996 5g³ 6m² 7g³ 7f²
7m⁴ 7m Sep 28] sturdy, lengthy, good sort: good walker and powerful mover: useful performer: in frame first 5 starts in 1996, best effort when third in rated stakes at Newmarket in July: sweating, behind in £50,100 handicap at Ascot on only subsequent outing: probably better at 7f than shorter: acts on firm ground: active type who tends to swish tail. *M. Johnston*

UNDAWATERSCUBADIVA 4 ch.g. Keen 116 – Northern Scene 78 (Habitat –
134) [1995 –: 8g 7g 6.1m 5g 6d 1996 a7g⁶ a7g a9.4g⁵ 10m a11g⁶ a12g⁵ 10g a8g Nov
22] leggy, sparely-made gelding: poor maiden plater: stays 11f. *M. P. Bielby*

UNDERCOVER AGENT (IRE) 2 b.f. (Apr 27) Fairy King (USA) – Auden- 79 p
hove (GER) (Marduk (GER)) [1996 6m² 7g* 6.5m Sep 11] 5,000F, 10,000Y: sturdy, lengthy filly: closely related to 6f to 6.5f winner Rooftop Flyer (by Nordico) and half-sister to several winners abroad: dam won in Germany: fair form: odds on, won steadily-run maiden auction at Yarmouth in August in workmanlike fashion, getting on top only well inside last: never a threat in 22-runner nursery at Doncaster following month: will stay beyond 7f: probably remains capable of improvement. *J. L. Dunlop*

UNDER PRESSURE 2 ch.f. (Mar 14) Keen 116 – Cal Norma's Lady (IRE) 87 66
(Lyphard's Special (USA) 122) [1996 6m⁴ 5m⁶ 6m⁴ 5m* 5g² 5f² 6f⁶ Aug 9] 4,400Y leggy, unfurnished filly: first reported foal: dam, 6f and 7f winner at 2 yrs, stayed

1¼m: fair form: won maiden auction at Ripon in July: good second next 2 starts in nurseries at Musselburgh and Thirsk: sold only 1,800 gns Doncaster October Sales: best form at 5f: acts on firm ground. *T. D. Easterby*

UNION TOWN (IRE) 2 b.c. (Feb 21) Generous (IRE) 139 – Exclusive Life 88 (USA) (Exclusive Native (USA)) [1996 a7g 6.1m* 7f* 7m* 8.1f⁴ Sep 7] IR 9,500Y: rangy, good-topped colt: has scope: sixth foal: half-brother to 3 winners, including Life At Sea (1½m, by Slip Anchor) and useful 1991 2-y-o 6f winner Fair Cop (by Al Nasr): dam sprint winner in USA: fairly useful form: won maiden auction at Nottingham, minor event at Thirsk and nursery (by 6 lengths) at Ascot in the summer: never-dangerous fourth of 5, but ran creditably, in minor event at Haydock: will stay middle distances: raced on top-of-the-ground except debut. *Sir Mark Prescott*

UNITUS (IRE) 3 b.c. Soviet Star (USA) 128 – Unite 126 (Kris 135) [1995 NR 85 p 1996 8.1d⁵ 8m² 10g* 12m Jul 30] good-bodied colt: fifth foal: closely related to smart 1m and 1¼m winner La Confederation (by Nureyev) and half-brother to 1m to 1¼m winner United Kingdom (by Danzig) and a winner in UAE by Lyphard: dam won Oaks and Irish Oaks and is from good family: easy winner of maiden at Windsor in July: ran as if something amiss in Gordon Stakes at Goodwood 15 days later: should stay 1½m: looked to have the makings of a smart colt: stays in training. *M. R. Stoute*

UNKNOWN TERRITORY (IRE) 2 ch.g. (May 13) Imperial Frontier (USA) 60 d 112 – Lilac Lass (Virginia Boy 106) [1996 7m⁵ 6m² 6d² 6m 10f Oct 14] IR 1,650F, IR 6,400Y: lengthy, rather unfurnished gelding: unimpressive mover: half-brother to 7f (at 2 yrs) to 8.5f winner Viceroy Lad (by Miami Springs), later successful in USA: dam unraced: runner-up in sellers at Lingfield (carried head awkwardly) and Ripon for M. Channon: well beaten for new stable: should stay beyond 6f: acts on good to firm and dead ground: visored final start. *Ronald Thompson*

U-NO-HARRY (IRE) 3 b.c. Mansooj 118 – Lady Roberta (USA) (Roberto 74 (USA) 131) [1995 67: 5m a5g² a5g² a6g 6m* 7m⁴ 5f³ 5g* 6.1m² 5.7h⁴ 5m 5m³ 5m³ 6d 6g² 6m 5m⁵ 1996 5d 6.1d 6.1g 6.1m 6.1m³ 6m* 6f* 6d³ 5.1m* 6m⁴ 5g⁶ 5m 5m⁵ Oct 3] sturdy colt: poor mover: usually looks well: fair handicapper: won at Thirsk and Lingfield within a week in June and at Chester in July: stays 6f: acts on hard and dead ground and on fibresand: ran poorly in blinkers fourth 2-y-o start: sometimes sweats: tough and genuine. *R. Hollinshead*

UNREAL CITY (IRE) 3 b.c. Rock City 120 – Tolmi 122 (Great Nephew 126) 101 [1995 78p: 7f² 1996 8g* 8d⁴ May 25] sturdy, good-bodied colt: progressive form: won maiden at Ripon in April, making all: showed much improved form when 4½ lengths fourth of 9 to Regal Archive in steadily-run listed race at Kempton on only subsequent outing, readily outpaced closing stages: will stay 1¼m: sent to France. *H. R. A. Cecil*

UNSHAKEN 2 b.c. (Mar 3) Environment Friend 128 – Reel Foyle (USA) 77 84 p (Irish River (FR) 131) [1996 7m 5d* 6g⁵ Nov 2] strong, sturdy colt: second foal: dam 5f winner: won maiden at Folkestone in October: good effort in useful mixed-aged event at Newmarket final start: stays 6f: acts on dead ground: will improve further. *J. R. Fanshawe*

UNSPOKEN PRAYER 3 br.f. Inca Chief (USA) – Dancing Doll (USA) (Buck- 47 finder (USA)) [1995 –: 6.1d 6s a6g a7g⁶ 1996 8g 6m⁵ 7f 8m³ 7d a6g⁴ Dec 27] leggy filly: poor maiden handicapper: will prove best at up to 1m: acts on good to firm ground, no form on a soft surface. *J. R. Arnold*

UNSUSPICIOUS (IRE) 6 ch.g. Caerleon (USA) 132 – Lady's Bridge (USA) 81 – (Sir Ivor 135) [1995 NR 1996 a14.8g⁵ a16g May 25] trained by D. Wintle, rated 53 on one of 6 starts in 1994: no promise on return to flat. *C. D. Broad*

UONI 3 ch.f. Minster Son 130 – Maid of Essex 66 (Bustino 136) [1995 51: 5m a7g³ 57 d a8.5g³ 1996 a10g a11g³ a10g³ 10.8g² 12.5f² 12m⁶ 14.1f⁴ 14.9m 12m⁵ a12g 11.9f a10g⁵ Dec 26] lengthy filly: modest maiden handicapper: below form last 7 starts: sold out of C. Brittain's stable 2,400 gns Newmarket Autumn Sales before final start: should stay further than 12.5f: tried blinkered, no improvement. *P. Butler*

UPEX LE GOLD TOO 4 ch.g. Precocious 126 – Restless Star (Star Appeal 133) 32 [1995 38: 7g 10m⁴ 9.9m 6g 8.1m⁴ 8f 12.1m⁶ 7m* 8m⁵ 7g⁶ 1996 8m 8f⁶ 7m⁵ 6m³ 8f Sep 27] neat gelding: has a round action: poor handicapper: left L. Lloyd-James after fourth start: effective at 6f to 9f: acts on dead ground and good to firm. *D. W. Chapman*

UP IN FLAMES (IRE) 5 br.g. Nashamaa 113 – Bella Lucia (Camden Town 125) 74 [1995 85: 7.5m 8g⁵ 8.1g* 8.5m* 8m³ 10f 1996 7.5m 6g 8g 8.1d⁶ 8.5m⁵ 8.9m 8g 8.5m⁶ 8f² 8.3m 8m⁶ Aug 25] leggy gelding: fairly useful handicapper at 4 yrs: fair at best in 1996: likely to stay beyond 8.5f: acts on soft and firm going, below form on fibresand: has joined S. R. Bowring and been gelded. *M. D. Hammond*

UPLIFT 3 ch.f. Bustino 136 – Relatively Easy 70 (Relkino 131) [1995 –: 7g 7g 8m 58 1996 17.2f² 11.1g⁵ 16m* 17.2m Aug 8] angular filly: clearly best effort when winning handicap at Nottingham in July, dictating steady pace: pulled up lame only subsequent outing: thorough stayer. *Sir Mark Prescott*

UPPER CLUB (IRE) 4 b.f. Taufan (USA) 119 – Sixpenny (English Prince 129) – [1995 8v 9v³ 8s⁴ 8.5m 10d 1996 a11g 14d Oct 2] IR 9,000Y: ex-Irish filly: half-sister to 2 winners, notably useful 1m to 1¼m performer Cumbrian Challenge (by Be My Native): dam unraced: modest maiden at best in Ireland for A. Maxwell (rated 59?), well held last 2 outings in 1995, reportedly very reluctant to race on final one: soundly beaten in handicaps here, blinkered final start: stays 9f: acts on heavy ground: sold 3,200 gns Doncaster November Sales. *P. R. Webber*

UPPER GALLERY (IRE) 3 b.c. Sadler's Wells (USA) 132 – Elevate 98 (Ela- 92 Mana-Mou 132) [1995 NR 1996 10m⁴ 10m³ 10d³ 16.1m² 16.2m 15.8g² 16s² Oct 24] lengthy, heavy-topped colt: fourth foal: closely related to French 9f winner Elite Guest (by Be My Guest) and half-brother to 6f winner Hoist (by Bluebird): dam, 1½m winner, half-sister to Sun Princess and Saddlers' Hall (by Sadler's Wells): fairly useful maiden handicapper: best efforts on last 2 starts, blinkered on final one: stays 16.1f: acts on good to firm and soft ground: wandered markedly under pressure fourth outing: sold 57,000 gns Newmarket Autumn Sales, to go to France. *P. W. Chapple-Hyam*

UPPER MOUNT CLAIR 6 b.m. Ela-Mana-Mou 132 – Sun Street 73 (Ile de 71 Bourbon (USA) 133) [1995 64, a54: a14.8g a16g⁵ a13g⁴ a16g³ a16g 18g* 16m a60 17.1m 14.1g* 20m 18.7g³ 20f² 16.1f⁴ 18.2g² a16g⁵ 16m a16g² a16g* 18s⁴ 16g³ 17.1g* 16m⁵ 20m⁶ 18.7m⁵ Aug 4] smallish, leggy mare: fair handicapper: won at Southwell (twice) in February and at Pontefract in April: thorough stayer: acts on firm ground and fibresand, respectable effort on soft: blinkered (no improvement) first 3 starts at 5 yrs: tough. *C. E. Brittain*

URBAN DANCING (USA) 7 ch.g. Nureyev (USA) 131 – Afifa (USA) (Dewan 45 (USA)) [1995 14g 14s⁵ 16g 1996 14.1m³ 16.1g May 22] ex-Irish gelding: modest maiden handicapper in 1995 for A. L. T. Moore: fairly useful 2m to 2½m hurdler: poor form on return to flat: will stay 2m: acts on firm and dead ground. *B. Ellison*

URBAN LILY 6 ch.m. Town And Country 124 – Laval (Cheval 117) [1995 NR – 1996 a14g⁵ Jun 14] sixth foal: half-sister to winning jumpers Lapiaffe (by Piaffer) and Lavalight (by Lighter): dam won 19f novice hurdle: poor hurdler, winner in May and December: blinkered, showed little in claimer at Southwell on flat debut. *R. J. Hodges*

URGENT SWIFT 3 ch.g. Beveled (USA) – Good Natured § (Troy 137) [1995 73 65: 6g⁵ 7f⁴ 7.1m 7f² 7m 7.9m 6.9g⁵ 1996 9g⁵ 10g 9f² 9f² 10m³ 10f* 10.5v Oct 6] rangy, unfurnished gelding: fair handicapper: narrowly won steadily-run race at Redcar in September, leading 1f out having been very keen early on: stays 1¼m: acts on firm going, seemingly not on heavy. *A. P. Jarvis*

URSA MAJOR 2 b.c. (Apr 3) Warning 136 – Double Entendre 81 (Dominion 81 123) [1996 7g⁵ 7d⁶ 6.1s² a6g* Dec 5] small colt: first foal: dam 1m to 1¼m winner: fairly useful form in minor events prior to winning maiden at Lingfield by 6 lengths: will stay 1m: acts on equitrack, raced only on an easy surface on turf. *P. A. Kelleway*

UTAH (IRE) 2 b.c. (Apr 15) High Estate 127 – Easy Romance (USA) (Northern – Jove (CAN)) [1996 8m 7d⁵ Oct 28] IR 13,500Y: third reported foal: half-brother to 4-y-o 8.5f winner Northern Fan (by Lear Fan) and a winner in USA by Rare Performer: dam won at up to 7f in USA: beaten at least 15 lengths in maidens at Goodwood and Lingfield: stays 1m: joined B. Gubby. *L. Montague Hall*

UTMOST ZEAL (USA) 3 b.c. Cozzene (USA) – Zealous Lady (USA) (High- 68 land Blade (USA)) [1995 72p: 7f⁵ 1996 8m 8g 6m 7m 7g 6.9m* 7.5g 7m² 6.9g 7g³ a7s³ a8g Nov 26] unfurnished colt: fair handicapper: made all at Folkestone in August: should stay further than 7f: acts on equitrack, raced only on a sound surface on turf: suited by front-running tactics (held up both outings on all-weather). *P. W. Harris*

V

VAGABOND CHANTEUSE 2 ch.f. (Jan 31) Sanglamore (USA) 126 – Eclipsing (IRE) 93 (Baillamont (USA) 124) [1996 6m³ 6m⁴ 7g* 8m³ 8m⁶ Sep 12] 10,000Y: tall, lengthy filly: first foal: dam 1m winner from the family of Sanglamore: progressive form: narrowly won maiden auction at Thirsk in August: around 10 lengths sixth of 11, never dangerous, to Reams of Verse in May Hill Stakes at Doncaster final start: will stay beyond 1m: may prove best with exaggerated waiting tactics. *T. J. Etherington*   81

VAIN PRINCE 9 b.g. Sandhurst Prince 128 – Vain Deb 66 (Gay Fandango (USA) 132) [1995 58: 16.2m² 16m⁵ 14.1m* 14.1m 15.1f* 15.1m* 16.2g⁴ 13f* 16f³ 1996 16.2g 16g⁴ 14.1m⁴ 15.1f⁶ 15.1g⁴ 16.2m⁶ 15.1m³ Sep 23] rangy gelding: modest handicapper: below form last 4 starts: stays 2m: acts on any going: effective blinkered or not. *N. Tinkler*   53 d

VALAGALORE 2 b.f. (Apr 24) Generous (IRE) 139 – Victoria Cross (USA) (Spectacular Bid (USA)) [1996 8m⁴ 7d⁶ Nov 8] 30,000Y: very tall, leggy filly: looked weak: fifth foal: half-sister to England Expects (by Topsider), successful in USA, including in Grade 3 event at 2 yrs at 5.5f: dam unraced half-sister to US Grade 1 winners Hero's Honor and Sea Hero: fair form in big fields of maidens at Newmarket and Doncaster in the autumn: will prove suited by further than 1m: should do better as she strengthens. *B. W. Hills*   74 p

VALANOUR (IRE) 4 b.c. Lomond (USA) 128 – Vearia (Mill Reef (USA) 141) [1995 122: 8g* 9.3m* 9g⁶ 10m* 10m⁶ 1996 10f* 10.5m* 10g⁶ 10f Aug 25]   125

So far, only Parisian racegoers have been lucky enough to see Valanour at his best first hand. This high-class mile-and-a-quarter performer has won five out of six races at home but run poorly in all three abroad and it is beginning to look as though he's a poor traveller. Valanour began his four-year-old campaign in cracking form, winning two important races on top-of-the-ground

Prix Ganay, Longchamp—the first three in a strong renewal are Valanour, Luso (rails) and Swain

H. H. Aga Khan's "Valanour"

at Longchamp in April and promising to be one of the season's stars. First time up he took a good-quality renewal of the Prix d'Harcourt by one and a half lengths from the Diane and Vermeille winner Carling and then, three weeks later, tackled a particularly strong field in the Prix Ganay. The Ganay brought together six Group 1 winners from the previous year in a field of ten. Valanour was one of them himself, having won the Grand Prix de Paris, so was Carling, and the others were Muncie (Prix Saint-Alary), the Italian colt Slicious (Premio Roma) and the British-trained Spectrum (Irish Two Thousand Guineas and Champion Stakes) and Luso (Derby Italiano), the last-named fresh from a winning reappearance in the Earl of Sefton Stakes. The Arc third Swain was pick of the remainder which also included the 1994 Ganay winner Marildo running in the race for the fourth consecutive year. Marildo led to two out but is at the veteran stage nowadays and was soon swallowed up, with Luso, Valanour and Swain becoming the main players. Valanour had taken a very strong hold early on, but was still able to produce the speed to cut down Luso inside the final furlong and run out a half-length winner with Swain, running over a trip hitherto regarded as shorter than ideal, a neck back in third.

A month later, conditions at Longchamp had changed dramatically and the soft going led to Valanour's being withdrawn from the Prix d'Ispahan, which fell to Halling. Valanour and Halling eventually met in the Eclipse at Sandown in July, Valanour's participation even in that race having hung in the balance until the last moment after connections' misgivings about the ground, which seemed to be good. Weak in the betting at 7/1, Valanour was still in touch in the straight but failed to produce the acceleration he had shown at Longchamp and beat only one home behind Halling in sixth. He fared no better in the Arlington Million in August. On firm going he was sent off second favourite in a field of nine, the best fancied of four European runners. It was clear some way out that he was in trouble, and he had already lost touch rounding the home turn when he made hard enough contact with the running rail to bring two sections down; he eventually trailed in eighth behind the American colt Mecke. Valanour wasn't seen out again so for the second year running a season that had begun so well at home ended with a tame defeat abroad; his three-year-old campaign had fizzled out in the Irish Champion Stakes.

		Northern Dancer	Nearctic
Valanour (IRE) (b.c. 1992)	Lomond (USA) (b 1980)	(b 1961)	Natalma
		My Charmer (ch 1969)	Poker
			Fair Charmer
	Vearia (b 1985)	Mill Reef (b 1968)	Never Bend
			Milan Mill
		Val Divine (b 1971)	Val de Loir
			Pola Bella

Valanour's breeding was reviewed in *Racehorses of 1995*. Suffice to say that he is Lomond's best son to date from a family that has produced other good-class performers, including the 1981 Champion Stakes winner Vayrann (a half-brother to Valanour's dam) and the 1987 Prix du Jockey-Club winner Natroun, another grandson of Val Divine. Valanour remains the only winner so far out of the French listed mile-and-a-quarter winner Vearia. The next foal, her third, the two-year-old filly Vereva (by Kahyasi) has yet to race and she has a yearling colt by Kenmare.

Valanour has not been tried at a mile and a half, and his jockey is adamant he will not stay the trip. The next campaign will probably be along the same lines as the latest one, conditions permitting. Valanour is very well suited by top-of-the-ground. A strong, sturdy colt, he is inclined to take a good hold and carry his head awkwardly under pressure but, on his day, his turn of foot makes him a match for the best at around ten furlongs. *A. de Royer-Dupre, France*

VALEDICTORY 3 b.c. Slip Anchor 136 – Khandjar 77 (Kris 135) [1995 NR   100
1996 12m³ 14m* 16.2m⁶ 14.8m⁴ Jul 11] strong, well-made colt: has scope: un-impressive mover with a round action: sixth live foal: half-brother to 3 winners, including 12.3f winner Iridal (by Rainbow Quest) and 14.8f winner Shelegai (by Shernazar): dam, 9f winner, sister to Shavian and half-sister to Paean: useful performer: unimpressive winner of steadily-run maiden at Newmarket in June: best effort when sixth of 14 to Gordi in Queen's Vase at Royal Ascot, fading having been headed 2f out: well held in listed race at Newmarket on final start: suited by test of stamina: has raced only on good to firm ground: heavily bandaged last 3 starts: stays in training. *H. R. A. Cecil*

VALENCIA 2 b.f. (Apr 21) Kenmare (FR) 125 – De Stael (USA) 93 (Nijinsky   79 p
(CAN) 138) [1996 8.1d² Sep 28] quite good-topped filly: seventh foal: half-sister to 3-y-o 1½m winner Fine Detail (by Shirley Heights), useful middle-distance stayer Source of Light (by Rainbow Quest), and (very) smart middle-distance performers Turners Hill (by Top Ville), Wandesta (by Nashwan) and De Quest (by Rainbow Quest): dam 2-y-o 6f winner, sister to Peacetime and Quiet Fling: 8/1 and noticeably green beforehand, shaped with plenty of promise when 1¼ lengths second of 10 (pair clear) to Myrtlebank in maiden at Haydock, travelling strongly in midfield, looking dangerous approaching final 1f then no impression inside last: wore blanket for stalls entry: bred to stay at least 1m: sure to do better, and win a maiden at least. *R. Charlton*

VALENTINE FAIRY 2 b.f. (Feb 14) Access Travel 109§ – Forest Fairy 66   52
(Faustus (USA) 118) [1996 5.2f⁵ 6.1m³ 5m Aug 19] first foal: dam 5f winner, stayed 6f: modest maiden plater: stayed 6.1f: dead. *R. Boss*

VALES ALES 3 b.g. Dominion Royale 112 – Keep Mum 63 (Mummy's Pet 125)   –
[1995 –: 5v⁶ 5g⁵ 5m⁴ 5f³ 8.3g 1996 6d 7m Jul 21] leggy, sparely-made gelding: no worthwhile form. *R. M. McKellar*

VALIANT DASH 10 b.g. Valiyar 129 – Dame Ashfield 90 (Grundy 137) [1995 –
NR 1996 15d Aug 10] poor handicapper on flat for S. Kettlewell in 1991: well beaten
in amateurs race at Ayr on return: modest hurdler, winner in September. *J. S. Goldie*

VALIANT MAN 5 br.g. Valiyar 129 – Redcross Miss 64 (Tower Walk 130) [1995 37
53: a8g⁶ 1996 6.9m⁴ 7g³ 6m a7g³ a6g⁶ a7g⁵ 7.5g Aug 24] leggy, lengthy gelding: just
a poor performer nowadays: stays 1m: acts on any turf going and on fibresand: tried
blinkered/visored: none too consistent. *J. Wharton*

VALISE 3 b.f. Salse (USA) 128 – Secret Valentine 71 (Wollow 132) [1995 52: 5f⁴ –
5f³ 6g 1996 10m 13.8g⁵ 16f⁴ Jun 13] modest form in maiden auctions at 2 yrs: well
below form in 1996: bred to stay at least 1m. *Mrs M. Reveley*

VALISKY 6 gr.m. Valiyar 129 – Rocket Trip (Tyrnavos 129) [1995 NR 1996 a13g –
Jan 13] second foal: dam unraced half-sister to very useful 1983 5f and 6f winner
Rocket Alert, later successful over 7f in USA: soundly beaten in maiden at Lingfield:
fell fatally in handicap hurdle in July: dead. *R. Lee*

VALJESS 3 b.f. Today And Tomorrow 78 – Emmer Green 64 (Music Boy 124) –
[1995 –: 6s 1996 a7g a11g 6.9s a7g Apr 29] no worthwhile form. *D. C. O'Brien*

VALLEY OF GOLD (FR) 4 b.f. Shirley Heights 130 – Lustre (USA) 90 (Halo 115
(USA)) [1995 117: 10s* 10.5s* 10.5g³ 10.5g* 11d* 12g³ 12d² 1996 a9.9g* a10g³
12m⁶ 10m² Jun 24] tall, sparely-made filly: smart performer: trained at 3 yrs by
A. Fabre: narrow winner (from Russian Snows) of minor event in Dubai in February:
not at her best here (on top-of-the-ground), ½-length second of 8 to Musetta in
steadily-run minor event at Windsor: stays 1½m: acts on sand, best turf form on an
easy surface (acts on soft going). *Saeed bin Suroor*

VANADIUM ORE 3 b.c. Precious Metal 106 – Rockefillee (Tycoon II) [1995 59
NR 1996 8f² 8m⁴ 11.1g² 10.5s 9m 8m a8.5s Dec 19] leggy colt: fifth foal: half-
brother to fair chaser Really A Rascal (by Scallywag): dam lightly-raced novice
hurdler: modest maiden: stays 11f: below form on soft ground: visored last 4 starts.
J. L. Eyre

VANBOROUGH LAD 7 b.g. Precocious 126 – Lustrous 73 (Golden Act (USA)) –
[1995 56: 7m³ 8.3g⁵ 8f* 8g 8.3m² 8.1m⁴ 7.1m⁵ 8.3m⁴ 8g 1996 8m 8.1m 7s 8m 8.1s
a10s a8g⁶ Dec 11] strong, lengthy gelding: modest handicapper at 6 yrs: no worthwhile form in 1996. *M. J. Bolton*

VAN CHINO 2 b.c. (May 29) Suave Dancer (USA) 136 – Atlantic Flyer (USA) 98 – p
(Storm Bird (CAN) 134) [1996 6d Nov 8] rangy colt: second foal: half-brother to
useful 3-y-o 1m winner Van Gurp (by Generous): dam should have stayed beyond
1m: 33/1 and in need of race, never a factor in maiden at Doncaster: bandaged
off-hind: should do better. *B. A. McMahon*

VAN GURP 3 ch.c. Generous (IRE) 139 – Atlantic Flyer (USA) 98 (Storm Bird 96
(CAN) 134) [1995 81: 7.1d³ 7d 1996 8m⁵ 10.4f⁴ 8.1d 8m³ 8m 8d² 7.9g* 8f 8d⁵ Oct
11] small, close-coupled colt: fluent mover: useful performer: 3 lengths equal third
to Mushahid in minor event at Doncaster in July: not at best after fluent start, but still
won maiden at York in September, despite pulling hard in race late on and not
handling home bend well: bred to stay beyond 1m, but takes keen hold and may not
do so: seems ideally suited by sound surface. *B. A. McMahon*

VANISHING TRICK (USA) 2 ch.f. (Feb 19) Gone West (USA) – Wand (IRE) 78 p
69 (Reference Point 139) [1996 7f⁶ 7f* Oct 14] sturdy, close-coupled filly: first foal:
dam, 1¾m winner, is out of close relative of Sadler's Wells: burly, green and slowly
away on debut: won maiden at Leicester in October by ½ length from Apache Star,
making most and forging ahead again close home having been strongly pressed from
2f out: will stay at least 1m: should improve again. *H. R. A. Cecil*

VARXI (FR) 2 gr.c. (Mar 25) Kaldoun (FR) 122 – Girl of France (Legend of 116
France (USA) 124) [1996 7.5d* 8d³ 8v* Nov 11]
Conditions had become so testing at Saint-Cloud by late-autumn that
the winner of the big two-year-old race, Varxi, took 1m 53.80sec to cover the
mile of the Prix Thomas Bryon; the previous year's winner Ashkalani had done
it in 1m 42.30sec on good ground. Given the conditions, it might be that
outsider-of-six Varxi's five lengths winning margin over the Grand Criterium
fifth Aneysar flatters him. But on the book his performance puts him up with

Prix Thomas Bryon, Saint-Cloud—Varxi by five lengths

the best of his contemporaries trained in France though still significantly behind the Grand Criterium winner Revoque. Varxi raced in second place to Aneysar in the Thomas Bryon until going on two furlongs out; he was clear over a furlong out. The third home Keos, a full brother to Bosra Sham's dam Korveya, had won his only previous race; the fourth, Kaldou Star, had previously run well in the Group 3 Prix de Conde; the fifth, Film Noir, had won the listed Prix Isonomy at the track on his previous start; and last home Inkatha had shown useful form in the Provinces. However you look at it, Varxi's form was a step up on anything he had shown before. He had made a winning debut in a sixteen-runner newcomers race at Maisons-Laffitte in September, then the following month finished two and three quarter lengths third of eight to Film Noir in the Isonomy, both races being run on good to soft ground.

	Kaldoun (FR) (gr 1975)	Caro (gr 1967)	Fortino II
			Chambord
		Katana (b 1970)	Le Haar
Varxi (FR)			Embellie
(gr.c. Mar 25, 1994)	Girl of France (b 1986)	Legend of France (b 1980)	Lyphard
			Lupe
		Water Girl (b 1980)	Faraway Son
			Warsaw

Varxi's sire is very much better known inside France than outside it. Strange to relate, a runner by Kaldoun is a rare sight in Britain (Kayvee is by him) while just across the Channel he is a leading sire, and has been for a long time, although still without a classic winner. Smart at up to a mile, Kaldoun was bred to stay further and has sired a Prix du Cadran winner in Mercalle. Varxi's dam, whose second foal and first runner he is, showed very useful form at around a mile, winning in listed company at Longchamp as a three-year-old and Santa Anita at four. The next dam Water Girl was an ordinary daughter of a good-class racemare and broodmare, failing to improve on a win in a newcomers race in the mud over a mile at Saint-Cloud as a three-year-old; she raced in handicaps in Britain the following season for Olivier Douieb. That good mare Warsaw produced six winners besides Water Girl, foremost among them Walensee (Prix Vermeille) and World Citizen (champion French jumper).

It remains to be seen how effective Varxi is on a sounder surface. The chances of his appearing in Britain will probably be much reduced if it turns out that soft ground does suit him best. Varxi needs to make plenty of improvement to be challenging for a big race abroad in any case, but his trainer David Smaga has not been averse to travelling with the right horse—Lancastrian, Budweiser International winner Leariva and Marildo, for instance. Varxi will need at least a mile at three; he will stay a mile and a quarter and almost certainly a mile and a half. *D. Smaga, France*

VASARI (IRE) 2 ch.c. (Mar 3) Imperial Frontier (USA) 112 – Why Not Glow (IRE) (Glow (USA)) [1996 5g² 5.1g* 6m 5v³ 6m⁵ 6g³ Nov 2] IR 10,000F, IR 14,000Y: close-coupled, useful-looking colt: second foal: won maiden at Chester in May: off course 4½ months (reportedly with pelvic problem) afterwards: fairly useful form in minor event at Haydock, Redcar Two-Year-Old Trophy and minor event at Newmarket (always prominent, keeping on, 1½ lengths behind Saheeel) on last 3 starts: stays 6f: acts on heavy going and good to firm: much too free going down third start, early to post otherwise. *M. R. Channon* 94

VASILIEV 8 b.g. Sadler's Wells (USA) 132 – Poquito Queen (CAN) 113 (Ex- – §
plodent (USA)) [1995 –§: 14.1g 1996 a12g Feb 10] big gelding: fair hurdler (often
reluctant) at best nowadays: no worthwhile form on flat since 1993: sold 2,200 gns
Doncaster July Sales: not one to trust. *S. Gollings*

VAUGRENIER (IRE) 4 b.g. Scenic 128 – Church Mountain 83 (Furry Glen 79
121) [1995 84: 12f 10m³ 11.9f* 12m⁴ 12m² 12f⁶ 12.1s 11f³ 1996 12g 11.9g³ 12m
12m 11.9g 10s Oct 24] strong, good-bodied, attractive gelding: fair handicapper:
easily best effort in 1996 on second start: off course 5 months after next outing: sold
only 3,800 gns Doncaster November Sales: stays 1½m: acts on firm ground, well
beaten both starts on soft: quietly to post (tried to run away) fourth 4-y-o start: usually
held up. *R. Hannon*

VAX NEW WAY 3 gr.g. Siberian Express (USA) 125 – Misty Arch (Starch 62
Reduced 112) [1995 67: 5g⁶ a6g* 5g⁵ 6m⁵ 6.1s 6.1m³ 1996 5d a6g* 6g⁶ a6g² a7g a75
a6g² 5.1m⁴ a6g 6f⁴ 6m² Oct 23] sturdy, lengthy gelding: fair handicapper: best efforts
in 1996 on the all-weather, and won at Wolverhampton in May: sold 6,200 gns
Doncaster October Sales: stays 6f: goes well on fibresand, acts on firm ground:
usually blinkered. *J. L. Spearing*

VAX STAR 2 gr.f. (Feb 20) Petong 126 – Vax Lady 98 (Millfontaine 114) [1996 96
5g² 5g* 5f² 5m⁴ 5m Aug 2] smallish, sturdy, good-quartered filly: has a quick
action: second foal: dam sprinter: fairly useful form: won maiden at Catterick and
2½ lengths second of 10 to Dazzle in Windsor Castle Stakes at Royal Ascot in June:
game winner from Compton Place of listed race at Sandown in July: ran poorly in
Molecomb Stakes at Goodwood final outing: speedy: acts on firm ground.
J. L. Spearing

VEERAPONG (IRE) 2 b.f. (Feb 16) Royal Academy (USA) 130 – Persian 53
Solitare (IRE) (Persian Bold 123) [1996 5m⁶ 5g 5f⁶ 6d² 6m⁶ 6m 6d 6s² a8.5g⁴ Oct
19] IR 4,200Y: leggy angular filly: first foal: dam unraced sister to Persian Tiara,
useful 1m to 1½m winner here and later Grade 2 winner and Grade 1 placed in USA:
modest maiden plater: sold 2,000 gns Doncaster October Sales: should be effective
over further than 6f: best efforts on a soft surface: blinkered (except once) since fifth
start: has been bandaged off-hind. *M. W. Easterby*

VEESEY 3 b.f. Rock City 120 – Travel On 111 (Tachypous 128) [1995 57: 5m⁴
5.1m 5.2g 5.2d⁵ 5g 6g³ 5f 1996 6.1d 6m Apr 16] sturdy, good-quartered filly: modest
maiden at 2 yrs: well beaten in 1996: better form at 6f than 5f. *John Berry*

VEILED DANCER (IRE) 3 b.f. Shareef Dancer (USA) 135 – Fatal Distraction
(Formidable (USA) 125) [1995 69p: 7f 8.1d³ 1996 10m 13.3m 14d 13.6m Oct 17]
angular filly: fair maiden: showed promise at Newmarket on reappearance, but well
beaten in handicaps all 3 subsequent starts: sold 3,000 gns Newmarket Autumn
Sales: should be suited by 1½m+. *J. L. Dunlop*

VELMEZ 3 ch.g. Belmez (USA) 131 – Current Raiser 108 (Filiberto (USA) 123) 73
[1995 NR 1996 10g⁴ 12g⁴ 14m⁶ a9.4g Jul 26] sixth foal: half-brother to fair stayer
Doyce (by Formidable), successful earlier in career at around 1m: dam won Lupe
Stakes: fair form in maidens first 2 starts, staying on: well beaten afterwards, and
sold (R. Guest to R. Mathew) 3,200 gns Newmarket September Sales: should stay
1¾m. *R. Guest*

VELOUR 2 b.f. (Feb 7) Mtoto 134 – Silk Braid (USA) 105 (Danzig (USA)) [1996 94 p
7m² 7m* 7d³ Aug 25] third foal: half-sister to 4-y-o 1m winner in UAE Modelliste
(by Machiavellian), second in German listed race: dam 9f and 1½m (Italian listed
race) winner, half-sister to Belmont and Preakness winner Risen Star: long odds on,
won slowly-run 2-runner minor event at Yarmouth in August, needing to be ridden
vigorously to get on top: much better form when 6 lengths fifth of 5 to Red Camellia
in Prestige Stakes at Goodwood, outpaced 2f out then keeping on: will be suited
by middle distances: yet to race on extremes of going: remains capable of better.
D. R. Loder

VELVET JONES 3 b. or gr.g. Sharrood (USA) 124 – Cradle of Love (USA) 87 60
(Roberto (USA) 131) [1995 55: 6m 5m² a6g² 6m⁶ 8.1m² 8m³ 7g⁴ 7d 10g⁶ a8g 1996
6m 7f² 7f³ 7f⁴ 7m⁴ 8.5g⁵ 7f⁵ 7m³ 7f⁶ 8m³ 8f Oct 14] angular gelding: modest maiden:
in frame 4 times at Brighton in 1996: should stay beyond 1m: acts on firm ground:
below form in blinkers ninth 3-y-o start. *G. F. H. Charles-Jones*

VENDETTA 3 b.f. Belmez (USA) 131 – Storm Warning 117 (Tumble Wind 63
(USA)) [1995 –p: 6m 1996 10m 12g 10.8m 10f⁵ Jul 20] good-bodied, attractive filly:

*Duke of York Stakes, York—Venture Capitalist's one win of 1996 is his most important yet;
two heads separate him from Branston Abby (right) and Royale Figurine (left)*

modest maiden at best: failed to progress: sold 4,000 gns Newmarket September Sales: sent to Lebanon. *I. A. Balding*

VENETIAN SCENE 2 ch.f. (Feb 18) Night Shift (USA) – Revisit 86 (Busted 134) [1996 5m³ 7.1s 7d⁶ Oct 28] small filly: fifth living foal: half-sister to 12.5f winner Peter Monamy (by Prince Sabo): dam stayer: modest form: off course 4½ months after debut: bred to be suited by middle distances: acts on good to firm ground, respectable effort on dead. *P. F. I. Cole*   58

VENI VIDI VICI (IRE) 3 b.c. Fayruz 116 – Divine Apsara (Godswalk (USA) 130) [1995 68p: 7g⁵ 6f 1996 a8g⁵ a7g 8m* 8m* 7.1d 8.2g Oct 9] stocky colt: unimpressive mover: fair handicapper: led well inside final 1f to beat big fields at Warwick in August and Kempton in September: stays 1m: acts on good to firm ground, below form on a soft surface and fibresand. *M. J. Heaton-Ellis*   71

VENTURE CAPITALIST 7 ch.g. Never So Bold 135 – Brave Advance (USA) 98 (Bold Laddie (USA)) [1995 112: 6g⁶ 5m⁴ 6g* 7.1m⁴ 6m* 7.6g⁵ 6f⁴ 6m⁴ 7m⁶ 6g² 5.6m 6g 1996 5d³ 6m³ 6m² 6f* 7.1d 6m 6m² 5m² 6f³ 6m 6d Aug 23] lengthy, deep-girthed gelding: unimpressive mover: smart performer: better than ever in 1996, and won first pattern race when beating Branston Abby a head in Duke of York Stakes in May: good efforts afterwards when placed in listed races at Newcastle (1½ lengths behind demoted Iktamal), Sandown (went down by ½ length to Eveningperformance) and Newbury (length third to Jayannpee): stays 6f: may need a sound surface nowadays (acts on firm ground): effective blinkered or not, tried only once in 1996: best coming with late challenge off strong pace: tough and genuine. *D. Nicholls*   114

VENTURE CONNECT 2 ch.g. (May 12) Interrex (CAN) – Tricata (Electric 126) [1996 a6g² Sep 7] 3,000Y, 13,000 2-y-o: fourth foal: dam unraced: 6/1, 4 lengths second of 13 to Pericles in maiden auction at Wolverhampton: should improve. *C. P. E. Brooks*   61 p

VENTURE FOURTH 7 b.g. Hotfoot 126 – Four Lawns 77 (Forlorn River 124) – [1995 –: a7g⁵ a11g a8g 12.3d 6.9m⁶ 11.1g 9.2f⁴ 12m 8.3f 1996 12f 12s Jul 3] leggy gelding: seems of little account nowadays: pulled up final start. *Miss M. K. Milligan*

VENUS VICTORIOUS (IRE) 5 ch.m. Tate Gallery (USA) 117 – Persian – § Royale 94 (Persian Bold 123) [1995 NR 1996 6.9f⁵ 7f 6f 7m Sep 17] modest maiden (rated 58 at best) at 3 yrs: became disappointing: scant promise on return, refusing to race penultimate start. *R. Bastiman*

VERA'S FIRST (IRE) 3 b.f. Exodal (USA) – Shades of Vera 76 (Precocious – 126) [1995 69, a64: 5m 6g⁵ 5f² 6.9g⁶ 6f³ 6f³ 6m² 6m⁴ 6.1s⁴ 6.1m⁵ a7g* a7g² a6g 1996 a7g⁶ a7g Feb 24] leggy, workmanlike filly: fair performer at 2 yrs: tailed off in 1996: has joined Miss Gay Kelleway. *G. Lewis*

VERDE LUNA 4 b.g. Green Desert (USA) 127 – Mamaluna (USA) 114 (Roberto (USA) 131) [1995 71: 8.3m 7.5m² 8g² 10m 8m 7m⁴ 8.2m³ 8g 8g 7s 1996 a8g⁶ a12g 13.1m Sep 9] quite good-topped gelding: fair maiden handicapper at best in 1995 for M. Tompkins: well beaten in 1996. *D. W. P. Arbuthnot* —

VERGLAS (IRE) 2 gr.c. (Apr 4) Highest Honor (FR) 124 – Rahaam (USA) 91 (Secreto (USA) 128) [1996 5d³ 6g* 6f* 6g³ 7g⁶ Sep 21] IR 26,000Y: second foal: half-brother to 3-y-o 6f (at 2 yrs) to 1m (listed) winner Persian Secret (by Persian Heights): dam 7f winner who stayed 1¼m: useful Irish colt: successful in maiden (by 8 lengths) at Leopardstown in May and 15-runner Coventry Stakes (quickened well and ran on strongly to beat Daylight In Dubai by 2½ lengths) at Royal Ascot: ran creditably when keeping-on third of 9 to Mantovani in Heinz 57 Phoenix Stakes at Leopardstown, respectably when sixth of 10 to Desert King in National Stakes at the Curragh (never really looked like mounting a challenge) 6 weeks later: likely to stay 1m: acts on firm ground. *K. Prendergast, Ireland* 107

VERIDIAN 3 b.g. Green Desert (USA) 127 – Alik (FR) 113 (Targowice (USA) 130) [1995 NR 1996 8g⁴ 7.9m⁵ 8.3g 10m⁶ 9.7m² 11.5d* Aug 29] 58,000F, 52,000Y: neat gelding: half-brother to several winners abroad, notably smart French 7f to 1¼m performer Goofalik (by Lyphard): dam French 1m winner out of sister to dam of Irish River: fairly useful handicapper: seemed well suited by increased test of stamina when winning at Lingfield in August: not seen out afterwards: better suited by around 1½m than shorter: acts on good to firm ground, and goes well on dead. *P. W. Harris* 83

VERINDER'S GIFT 2 ch.g. (Mar 13) Chilibang 120 – A Nymph Too Far (IRE) 49 (Precocious 126) [1996 a6g a6g 8.2g² a8.5g Nov 2] first foal: dam 1m winner: easily best effort when 5 lengths second of 14 in seller at Nottingham in October: stays 8.2f. *Dr J. D. Scargill* 55 a45

VERONICA FRANCO 3 b.f. Darshaan 133 – Maiden Eileen (Stradavinsky 121) [1995 –: 7m 1996 10g⁵ 12m 11.4d 11.5m 15.4g 14m 9.7d a7g⁴ a10g Nov 26] leggy filly: disappointing maiden: sold out of J. Dunlop's stable 6,400 gns Newmarket July Sales after third 3-y-o start: blinkered last 2 starts: has shown signs of unsatisfactory temperament. *B. A. Pearce* 58 d

VERRO (USA) 9 ch.g. Irish River (FR) 131 – Royal Rafale (USA) (Reneged) [1995 18§: a12g a13g³ 14.1f a16.2g 1996 a12g a13g a7g 7.1g a6g⁵ a7g⁶ a6g Jul 22] robust, good-quartered gelding: bad performer: stays 13f: acts on all-weather and heavy ground: tried blinkered/visored: none too keen and not one to rely on. *K. Bishop* – §

VERZEN (IRE) 4 ch.c. Salse (USA) 128 – Virelai 72 (Kris 135) [1995 99, a106: 7m* 8m 7m* 7d 7.9m³ a9.4g² 1996 10m 8g³ 7f* 7m 8g³ 7g* 8d³ a8f* Dec 29] lengthy, workmanlike colt: useful performer: won rated stakes at Yarmouth (by 6 lengths) in July and York in October: respectable third of 6 to Decorated Hero in listed race at Evry on final start for D. Loder then won 4-runner handicap in Dubai: effective at 7f to 9.4f: acts on firm and dead ground and on fibresand and sand: visored (ran well) fifth 3-y-o start: tends to carry head awkwardly. *K. P. McLaughlin, UAE* 107

Mrs A. J. F. O'Reilly's "Verglas"

VESHCA LADY (IRE) 3 b.f. Contract Law (USA) 108 – Genzyme Gene 38 49
(Riboboy (USA) 124) [1995 54: 5m 5m³ 5m* a6g 5m⁴ 7f⁶ 7.1m² 7m³ 7h³ 7m* 7.1m³
7f 7f 1996 7d 7.5g 8m⁴ 8.2m 10m⁴ 10m³ 12f⁴ 12m² 8.3m⁴ Aug 14] leggy filly: poor
performer: stays 1½m, at least in steadily-run race: acts on hard ground, ran poorly
on dead and fibresand: tried visored, no improvement: sweating and edgy (well
below form) first two 3-y-o starts. *E. Weymes*

VETHEUIL (USA) 4 ch.c. Riverman (USA) 131 – Venise (USA) (Nureyev 124
(USA) 131) [1995 8s² 8s⁶ 8g* 8m* 9.8s 1996 8g* 9.3s³ 8g³ 8g⁵ 8d² 8m⁴ 8f Dec 26]
strong, compact colt: fourth foal: half-brother to Verveine (stayed 1½m, rated 120,
by Lear Fan) and Vanishing Prairie (won up to 1½m in Ireland, by Alysheba): dam,
unraced, out of Virunga (stayed 1½m, rated 120), dam also of Vacarme (stayed 9.7f,
rated 121) and Vin de France (best at 1m, rated 123): very smart performer: won
minor event at Deauville and listed race at Chantilly at 3 yrs: won 6-runner Prix du
Muguet at Saint-Cloud in May by ½ length from Nec Plus Ultra: improved effort
when staying-on ½-length second of 9 to Spinning World in Prix Jacques Le Marois
at Deauville and not far below that level when 3½ lengths fourth of 9 to Ashkalani in
Prix du Moulin de Longchamp last 2 starts for A. Fabre: disqualified after finishing
only third in allowance event at Santa Anita in December: effective at 1m and should
stay 1¼m: acts on firm and soft ground. *George Vogel, USA*

VIARDOT (IRE) 7 b.g. Sadler's Wells (USA) 132 – Vive La Reine (Vienna 127) 51
[1995 –: 12.3m⁵ 12g 1996 12f² 16m⁶ Jun 24] big, rangy gelding: carries condition:
has a quick action: lightly raced and only modest form in claimers last 2 seasons: ran
in snatches final 7-y-o start: stays 1¾m: acts on firm ground, very best effort on soft:
sometimes looks none too keen: sold (Mrs M. Reveley to H. Alexander) 2,300 gns
Doncaster October Sales. *Mrs M. Reveley*

VICKI ROMARA 2 ch.f. (Feb 24) Old Vic 136 – Romara 105 (Bold Lad (IRE) 75
133) [1996 10m⁴ 10f⁴ Oct 14] 25,000Y: small filly: half-sister to numerous winners,
including fairly useful So Romantic (7f at 2 yrs, to 9f, by Teenoso) and smart Ela
Romara (6f and 1½m, by Ela-Mana-Mou): dam 6f and 1m winner: fourth in steadily-
run maiden at Pontefract (burly) and 5-runner minor event at Leicester (over 4¼
lengths behind Windsor Castle, eased once held) week later: will stay 1½m.
M. Johnston

VICKYS DOUBLE 2 b.f. (Feb 4) Mazilier (USA) 107 – Mrs Waddilove 79 34
(Bustino 136) [1996 5m⁵ 6f⁴ 5m⁶ 6g 7g Aug 14] small filly: fifth living foal: half-
sister to 3-y-o 1¼m winner Get Tough (by Petong): dam, maiden, stayed 7f: poor
plater: should stay beyond 5f. *J. S. Moore*

VICTIM OF LOVE 3 b.f. Damister (USA) 123 – Tantalizing Song (CAN) (The –
Minstrel (CAN) 135) [1995 75: 7m a8g⁴ a7g* a7g² 1996 a7g³ a8.5g a9.4g⁴ a8.5g³ a73
a7g³ a7g* 6m 7.3d May 18] angular filly: fair handicapper: favourite, best effort
when winning at Wolverhampton in April: well held on return to turf: sold 7,200 gns
Newmarket July Sales: should stay 1m: acts on fibresand, probably on equitrack:
successful at 2 yrs when sweating. *R. Charlton*

VICTORIA DAY 4 b.f. Reference Point 139 – Victoress (USA) (Conquistador –
Cielo (USA)) [1995 –: 12m 13.4m⁴ 12.3m⁵ 15g 1996 16.2g 14.9m⁶ 16m 15.8g 17.2m
17.9g Oct 9] well-made filly: little sign of ability on flat. *B. A. McMahon*

VICTORIAN STYLE 3 ch.f. Nashwan (USA) 135 – Victoriana (USA) (Storm 88
Bird (CAN) 134) [1995 NR 1996 8g³ 8.1d* 8.2f* 9m 8m⁶ Aug 15] unfurnished filly:
second foal: half-sister to 4-y-o stayer Sea Victor (by Slip Anchor): dam, French 5f
winner, closely related to Grand Criterium runner-up Masterclass from family of Try
My Best and El Gran Senor: fairly useful performer: won maiden at Haydock in June
and handicap at Nottingham in July: should stay beyond 8.2f: acts on firm and dead
ground: tends to flash tail: sweating (respectable effort) final start: sent to USA.
R. Charlton

VICTORIA'S DREAM (IRE) 2 b.f. (Feb 4) Royal Academy (USA) 130 – 56
Woodland Garden (Godswalk (USA) 130) [1996 5.7g 6g 5.1m⁴ 5.7m⁶ 6d* 6m⁶
7m Oct 17] IR 11,000Y: smallish, workmanlike filly: second reported living foal:
half-sister to fairly useful 1994 Irish 2-y-o 7f winner Boscabel (by Fairy King): dam
unraced: modest performer: made all and held on gamely in seller at Haydock in July:
failed to repeat the form: sold 8,500 gns Newmarket Autumn Sales: should stay 7f:
acts on good to firm ground and (best effort) dead. *M. R. Channon*

VICTORIA SIOUX 3 ch.f. Ron's Victory (USA) 129 – Blues Indigo 103 (Music 51 d
Boy 124) [1995 54: 5m⁶ 6.1m⁴ 6m⁵ 6.1d 1996 a5g⁵ a6g a5g² a6g⁴ a7g³ a6g⁶ a6g⁶
6.1m⁵ 6f 6f Jun 5] useful-looking filly: poor maiden: left J. Wharton after second
3-y-o start: tailed off last 2 outings: stays 6f: acts on good to firm ground and fibresand: well beaten in blinkers. *J. A. Pickering*

VICTORIA'S SECRET (IRE) 4 b.f. Law Society (USA) 130 – Organdy 84 56
(Blakeney 126) [1995 65: 8m 10f 10g² 12f³ 13.1h 9.7g 1996 8s⁴ 11.8d 14.1s 12g⁶
12m⁴ 10.8m⁴ 12.1m² 11.1m 12.1g* 11.6g Jul 29] leggy filly: poor mover: just a
modest handicapper nowadays: won weak maiden event at Musselburgh in July
by 10 lengths: well beaten only subsequent outing: stays 1½m: acts on firm and
dead ground: best efforts in 1995 in blinkers: not tried in 1996: covered by Piccolo.
M. R. Channon

VICTOR LASZLO 4 b.g. Ilium 121 – Report 'em (USA) 51 (Staff Writer 43
(USA)) [1995 –: 10g³ 12.3m⁵ 13.8g a14g 1996 13m* 13g 11.1g 15.1m 11.1m 12.1d
Sep 30] workmanlike gelding: won bad handicap at Hamilton in May: tailed off
afterwards: should stay beyond 13f. *R. Allan*

VICTORY AT HART 2 ch.g. (Feb 23) Ron's Victory (USA) 129 – Ceramic –
(USA) (Raja Baba (USA)) [1996 6f⁴ 6g⁶ 6g⁶ 6g⁶ Aug 1] sixth foal: half-brother to
several winners, including 3-y-o Polar Champ (1¼m, by Polar Falcon): dam ran
once: poor plater. *I. Campbell*

VICTORY BOUND (USA) 3 ch.c. Bering 136 – Furajet (USA) 101 (The Min- 72
strel (CAN) 135) [1995 NR 1996 a7g³ 8g⁴ 8m³ 8g⁴ 10g Aug 5] leggy, useful-looking
sort: first foal: dam best at 5f, closely related to Prix Robert Papin winner General
Monash: in frame in 3 maidens and a handicap before sold out of M. Johnston's stable

7,000 gns Newmarket July Sales: below form in handicap on Irish debut: should stay beyond 1m: has had tongue tied down. *G. T. Hourigan, Ireland*

VICTORY COMMANDER 3 b.g. Efisio 120 – Gay Hostess (FR) (Direct – Flight) [1995 –: 6g 5m 7.1m 1996 a8g 6.1m 6s 7f Jun 4] sturdy gelding: poor mover: no worthwhile form. *T. J. Naughton*

VICTORY DANCER 2 b.g. (Apr 14) Ron's Victory (USA) 129 – Villajoyosa 91 (FR) (Satingo 129) [1996 5.1m³ 5f* 6g* 6f³ 6m² 7s⁴ 6.1d⁵ 6g² Oct 12] 8,000F, 6,800Y: sturdy, quite attractive gelding: has a quick action: sixth foal: half-brother to 1m winner Joyrider (by Risk Me) and a winner in Hong Kong by Buzzards Bay: dam, plater, won at up to 1m in France: generally progressive form: won maiden auction at Lingfield in June and minor event at Windsor in July: best effort (after below form at Chester) in listed race at York (3½ lengths second of 5 to Nightbird) final start: sold 28,000 gns Newmarket Autumn Sales: stays 7f: acts on firm ground and soft: blinkered since fifth start: sent to USA. *B. J. Meehan*

VICTORY TEAM (IRE) 4 b.g. Danehill (USA) 126 – Hogan's Sister (USA) 72 (Speak John) [1995 69: 7m 8.3m⁴ 8.1g 8m³ 8g 12s⁶ 1996 a8g² a8g* a8g* 8f³ 7m⁵ 7m a79 6g² 7m² 7m 7f⁵ Aug 22] strong, good-bodied gelding: good mover: fair handicapper: won twice in 3 days at Lingfield in March: effective at 6f, and stays 1m: acts on firm ground, goes well on equitrack: has tongue tied down nowadays: usually held up. *G. B. Balding*

VIENNESE DANCER 3 b.f. Prince Sabo 123 – Harmony Park 55 (Music Boy – 124) [1995 NR 1996 6f 7f 6.9d Oct 21] 6,600Y: third foal: half-sister to 1994 2-y-o 6f winner Vocalize (by Petong), 6f winner at 2 yrs: dam, 7f winner, sister to useful sprinter Melody Park: no form. *R. J. R. Williams*

VILLAGE KING (IRE) 3 b.c. Rol Danzig (USA) – Honorine (USA) (Blushing 79 Groom (FR) 131) [1995 74: 8m 8m 1996 8d 10m⁶ 10m⁶ 12m* 12.3m³ 14m³ 12m⁵ 11.9m 11.5d Aug 29] strong, sturdy colt: carries condition: has a short action: fair handicapper: won at Salisbury in June: below form last 3 starts, blinkered on final one: sold 21,000 gns Newmarket Autumn Sales: stays 1¾m: acts on good to firm ground, possibly not on dead: often soon off bridle. *R. Hannon*

VILLAGE NATIVE (FR) 3 ch.c. Village Star (FR) 131 – Zedative (FR) 74 60 (Zeddaan 130) [1995 72: 7g 5m² 5g³ 6g⁵ 7f⁵ 6m* a6g 1996 6f 7m⁶ 6m 8g⁶ 8g 8m Sep 10] lengthy, angular colt: fair performer at 2 yrs: well below form in 1996: gives impression will prove best at sprint distances: tried blinkered: highly strung: trained by K. Cunningham-Brown first 4 3-y-o starts. *S. Wattel, France*

VILLAGE OPERA 3 gr.f. Rock City 120 – Lucky Song 91 (Lucky Wednesday – 124) [1995 –: 5m 5m 8g 1996 7m 14.1m a11g Jun 20] no worthwhile form. *G. M. Moore*

VILLAGE PUB (FR) 2 ch.c. (May 7) Village Star (FR) 131 – Sloe Berry 82 67 ? (Sharpo 132) [1996 7.1f 6m 7d 6g⁵ 6v⁴ a6g a6g⁵ Dec 7] second foal: dam sprinter: fair maiden: best effort at 6f on good to firm ground: blinkered last 3 starts. *K. O. Cunningham-Brown*

VILLAGE STORM (FR) 6 ch.h. Village Star (FR) 131 – Purple Rain (FR) 112 (Zino 127) [1995 9d* 9m⁶ a8g² 9.8g* 9s 9m⁵ 9f⁶ a8g 9g 12g 8.5d⁴ 10d 8d⁵ 1996 9g 9g² 9.8g 10m* 8g* 8d⁴ 8.5s* Oct 6] first foal: dam French 2-y-o 9f winner: useful Scandinavian horse: quite heavily campaigned in 1995, winner of quite valuable event at Taby: successful in 1996 in similar contests at Dresden in June, Klampenberg in September and in Group 2 event at Dusseldorf (by 5 lengths from Tres Heureux) in October: stays 1¼m, at least as effective around 1m: acts on good to firm and soft ground. *S. Jensen, Denmark*

VILLARICA (IRE) 2 b.f. (Feb 19) Fairy King (USA) – Bolivia (GER) (Wind- 75 p wurf (GER)) [1996 6m⁴ Sep 7] leggy, unfurnished filly: seventh foal: half-sister to several winners, including fairly useful 1991 2-y-o Cochabamba (up to 7f, by Thatching) and Lake Poopo (up to 7f, by Persian Heights): dam useful winner at 2 yrs in Germany: 10/1 from 4/1, 5¾ lengths fourth of 14 to Blane Water in maiden at Kempton, every chance 2f out then staying on: moved short to post: should improve. *P. W. Chapple-Hyam*

VILLEGGIATURA 3 b.g. Machiavellian (USA) 123 – Hug Me 96 (Shareef 80 Dancer (USA) 135) [1995 84: 6m² 7g 7f* 7g⁴ 1996 10m 10.4m⁶ 10m⁵ 10.5d 10.1f⁵

10f⁵ 10.1m² 12f² 14.1m² 13.9g Sep 4] smallish, strong gelding: fair handicapper: sold out of B. Hills's stable 11,000 gns Newmarket July Sales after fifth 3-y-o start: stays 1¾m: acts on firm ground, below form on a soft surface: blinkered (soundly beaten) twice at 3 yrs. *Mrs J. R. Ramsden*

VINDALOO 4 ch.g. Indian Ridge 123 – Lovely Lagoon 68 (Mill Reef (USA) 141) [1995 91: a8g² a10g⁵ a8.5g⁴ a10g⁴ 7.1g* 7g⁵ 8g* 8.1g⁶ 8g* 10.1g* 10m* 10.8g* 10m⁴ 10f* 10.1m³ 12.4m² 12f* 11.8g* a9.4g* 14f⁴ 9.9m 11.9m³ a7g³ 10m² 11.9g⁴ 10.1g⁴ 10g² 9.2g³ 10g 1996 9.9f 10.4m 10m 10.1m Sep 18] robust, close-coupled gelding: fairly useful handicapper in 1995, winning 11 of 30 races but finishing lame final start: not seen in 1996 until August, and no worthwhile form: best form from 9f to 1¾m: acts on any going. *J. L. Harris*

VINTAGE TAITTINGER (IRE) 4 b.g. Nordico (USA) – Kalonji (Red Alert – 127) [1995 34+, a47: 5d a12g* 11.1g⁵ a14.8g³ a12g² a12g 1996 13d 11.1m May 18] small, plain gelding: poor handicapper at 3 yrs for M. Bell: well held in 1996: has joined Miss Lucinda Russell. *T. Dyer*

V I P CHARLIE 2 b.c. (Apr 4) Risk Me (FR) 127 – Important Guest 53 (Be My 56 Guest (USA) 126) [1996 5m⁵ 6g 6m 7m Oct 4] third foal: dam, ran 4 times, bred to stay middle distances: modest form in maidens and a nursery: should stay beyond 5f. *J. R. Jenkins*

VIRIDIS (USA) 3 b.f. Green Dancer (USA) 132 – Vachti (FR) 114 (Crystal 58 Palace (FR) 132) [1995 59p: 8.2m⁴ 1996 10m⁵ 10d 14.4g⁵ 12g Jul 10] leggy filly: modest maiden: should be suited by 1½m+: sent to USA. *H. R. A. Cecil*

VISCOUNTESS BRAVE (IRE) 2 br.f. Law Society (USA) 130 – Vadrouille 80 ? (USA) 111 (Foolish Pleasure (USA)) [1996 7.5d* 7v* Nov 30] sister to Italian 7f and 1¼m winner Viconago and half-sister to 11f and 13f winner Vanie (by Niniski) and 1½m seller winner (smart staying hurdler) Vagog (by Glint of Gold): dam, from good family, won over 1m and 1¼m: won maiden at Milan in October and minor event at Rome in November: will stay middle distances: acts on heavy ground. *Lord Huntingdon*

VITUS 4 b.c. Dancing Brave (USA) 140 – Sancta 106 (So Blessed 130) [1995 82p: – 11m 1996 10g Apr 27] lengthy colt: shaped quite well in maiden only 3-y-o start: upset in stalls when in rear in similar event 12 months later: likely to stay well: stays in training. *H. R. A. Cecil*

VIVA VERDI (IRE) 2 b.f. (Mar 8) Green Desert (USA) 127 – Vaison La Rom- 70 + aine 100 (Arctic Tern (USA) 126) [1996 7m⁴ 7f Nov 5] lengthy filly, unfurnished at 2 yrs: has scope: half-sister to several winners abroad, including smart German middle-distance performer Vialli (by Niniski) and 6f to 1m (listed) winner Queenemara (by King of Clubs): dam, placed over 7f here at 2 yrs, later won over 7.5f in France: eye-catching effort on debut: reportedly suffered knee injury afterwards: pulled very hard, getting involved in early scrimmaging, at Redcar 2 months later, fading from 2f out: may very well do better if she learns to settle. *J. L. Dunlop*

VIVORA 2 ch.f. (Apr 17) Risk Me (FR) 127 – Valldemosa 81 (Music Boy 124) – [1996 5d⁵ 5m 7f⁶ Jun 24] 2,300Y: leggy filly: fourth foal: sister to modest 3-y-o 5f winner Forzara: dam best at 5f: no worthwhile form: sold 2,800 gns Newmarket September Sales: sent to Germany. *Martyn Meade*

VLADIVOSTOK 6 gr.g. Siberian Express (USA) 125 – Tsungani 64 (Cure The – Blues (USA)) [1995 48: 11.6m 8f a6g³ a6g² a6g⁴ 1996 a6g a6g Jan 12] leggy gelding: poor maiden nowadays: best efforts at 6f: acts on firm ground and the all-weather. *B. De Haan*

VOCAL COMMAND 4 b.g. Chief Singer 131 – To Oneiro 69 (Absalom 128) – [1995 –: a5g a8g a8g 1996 a8.5g Jan 10] leggy gelding: lightly raced and well beaten in Britain since 1994: sent to Sweden, and won over 1m there. *W. W. Haigh*

VOICES IN THE SKY 5 b.m. Petoski 135 – Saltation 111 (Sallust 134) [1995 51 NR 1996 a12g 10g 8f a9.4g⁴ 10.2m² 10m* 10.1g⁴ 12m* 11.9f² 10.2g³ 11.9f² 12m 11.9g Oct 10] modest handicapper: led closing stages to win seller at Windsor in June and apprentice race at Ascot in August: effective at 1¼m and 1½m: acts on firm ground, yet to race on a soft surface. *A. G. Newcombe*

VOILA PREMIERE (IRE) 4 b.g. Roi Danzig (USA) – Salustrina (Sallust 134) 80 [1995 68: 6.1g 6.1g 8.3g* 9g² 10.5g⁵ 1996 10m 8m 10g³ 10.2m² 10m² 10m³ 11.9v²

11.9g* 12s Nov 9] compact gelding: impresses in appearance: fair handicapper: won 22-runner apprentice contest at York in October: effective at 1¼m to 1½m: yet to race on firm going, acts on any other: races prominently. *M. H. Tompkins*

VOLARE 3 b.f. Prince Sabo 123 – Nazmiah 73 (Free State 125) [1995 60: 5g³ –
1996 6m⁶ 8f 7.3d 5.3f⁴ 6m 6.1m 6g Jul 8] modest maiden: little form in 1996: should have stayed 1m: tried blinkered: dead. *B. J. Meehan*

VOLA VIA (USA) 3 b. or br.g. Known Fact (USA) 135 – Pinking Shears (USA) 85
(Sharpen Up 127) [1995 86: 6g 5m⁴ 6.1m⁵ 5.7h* 6g⁴ 7.3m³ 7m² 7.3d 7d 1996 8d 9s 10.1m³ 10g 9f⁵ 10m³ 10d² 10m⁶ 10s Oct 24] quite good-topped gelding: unimpressive mover: fairly useful handicapper: mostly creditable efforts in 1996: stays 1¼m: acts on hard and dead ground, probably on soft: has flashed tail. *I. A. Balding*

VOLLEY (IRE) 3 b.f. Al Hareb (USA) 123 – Highdrive (Ballymore 123) [1995 86
NR 1996 6m* 6g⁴ 8s Nov 26] fifth foal: half-sister to 2 winners, notably vastly-improved and smart 5-y-o sprinter Anzio (by Hatim), also successful at 7f: dam well beaten: convincing winner of 14-runner maiden at Redcar in October: again showed fairly useful form when 2¾ lengths fourth of 8 to Saheeel in minor event at Newmarket 25 days later, staying on having been soon ridden along after slow start: last of 11 in listed race at Evry (1m, soft ground) on final start: sold 25,000 gns Newmarket December Sales. *J. Berry*

VOLUNTEER (IRE) 4 b.g. Midyan (USA) 124 – Sistabelle (Bellypha 130) –
[1995 66: 10.2m⁴ 10m 10d 10d⁴ a13g 1996 12g Aug 21] smallish, sturdy gelding: fair maiden at best at 3 yrs: successful twice over hurdles in 1995/6: well tailed off on return to flat: should stay beyond 1¼m. *R. J. O'Sullivan*

VOODOO ROCKET 3 ch.f. Lycius (USA) 124 – Vestal Flame 45 (Habitat 134) 56
[1995 NR 1996 7g 7m 7d a8g 8g 9g a7g⁵ Nov 11] 14,000F: leggy filly: fifth foal: half-sister to 3 winners, including 4-y-o 1¼m and 1½m winner Fairy Knight (by Fairy King) and 7f and 8.3f winner Cameron Highland (by Night Shift): dam staying maiden: modest maiden: failed to progress: probably stays 9f: sold 1,000 gns Newmarket December Sales. *J. H. M. Gosden*

VOYAGERS QUEST (USA) 2 b. or br.c. (Apr 29) Dynaformer (USA) – 108 p
Orange Sickle (USA) (Rich Cream (USA)) [1996 8f³ 8m* 10s⁵ 9s* Nov 26] rather leggy, close-coupled colt: second foal: dam won at up to 9f in USA, including minor stakes at 2 yrs: sire won Grade 2 1¼m Jersey Derby: won maiden at Goodwood in September, rallying stoutly to lead near line: showed plenty of improvement on last 2 starts, following fifth of 10 to Shaka in Criterium de Saint-Cloud by winning Prix Saint-Roman at Evry (by ½ length from Sendoro) later in November: stays 1¼m: successful on good to firm ground, best efforts on soft: likely to improve further. *P. W. Chapple-Hyam*

W

WACKY (IRE) 5 b. or br.m. Petorius 117 – Zany (Junius (USA) 124) [1995 –: 7m –
1996 7g⁵ 8f 7m Aug 6] smallish, sturdy mare: tubed: most disappointing since 2 yrs: tried blinkered. *W. Storey*

WADADA 5 b. or br.g. Adbass (USA) 102 – No Rejection (Mummy's Pet 125) 45
[1995 –: 12g 7d 1996 a12g⁴ 17.2m* 17.2f³ 16m⁶ a14.8g⁵ Aug 31] small gelding: a33
poor handicapper: won selling event at Bath in June: clearly a stayer: acts on firm going: fair winning hurdler. *D. Burchell*

WADERS DREAM (IRE) 7 b.g. Doulab (USA) 115 – Sea Mistress (Habitat 51 §
134) [1995 48, a31: a7g a6g a6g a6g⁵ a6g⁵ 7f 5g⁶ 6g 7m 6f³ 6f³ 6m⁶ 6g 7f a– §
1996 6m 5.2g⁵ 6m⁶ 6f² 6m⁴ 6m* 7f⁵ 6m 6.1m 7f⁶ Oct 15] leggy gelding: modest performer: won minor event at Folkestone in August: stays 7f: acts on firm ground: has been blinkered, usually visored nowadays: inconsistent and not one to rely on. *Pat Mitchell*

WAFIR (IRE) 4 b.c. Scenic 128 – Taniokey (Grundy 137) [1995 12g² 12g* 14g 88
12g⁶ 12m³ 8.5m² 8d⁵ 1996 9.9m⁶ 10.3m⁴ 10m³ 12m 10.4m 10.1m¹ 12.3g² 10v* 12g⁶ 10.5d Sep 28] IR 10,500F, IR 55,000Y: ex-Irish colt: impresses in appearance: fifth foal: half-brother to 3 winners, namely Harlequin Walk (1½m, by Pennine Walk), My Trelawny (6f to 1m in Ireland, by Dowsing) and Do The Right Thing (1½m, by

Busted): dam, Irish 1m winner, half-sister to Kittyhawk: fairly useful handicapper: trained at 3 yrs by D. Weld, winning maiden at the Curragh: won in desperate conditions at Ripon in August: looked a hard ride final start, wandering off bridle: stays 1½m: acts on good to firm ground, goes well on heavy: effective blinkered or not at 3 yrs. *P. Calver*

WAFT (USA) 3 ch.f. Topsider (USA) – Gliding By (USA) (Tom Rolfe) [1995 –p: 67 a7g⁶ 1996 8d 8f 8.2g³ 8f⁶ 10m⁵ a8g Nov 26] robust filly: fair maiden: should prove ideally suited by middle distances: well below form both starts on firm ground. *B. W. Hills*

WAGGA MOON (IRE) 2 b.c. (Jan 18) Mac's Imp (USA) 116 – Faapette 55 (Runnett 125) [1996 5s³ 5g⁴ 6m⁵ 6g Sep 3] 20,000Y: lengthy, good-bodied colt: has a fluent, rounded action: sixth foal: half-brother to 3 winners, including Irish 11f winner Premier Leap (by Salmon Leap) and 1990 2-y-o 5f winner Bellerofonte (by Tate Gallery): dam Irish 2-y-o 1m winner: modest maiden: stays 6f: sweating (best effort) third start: bandaged (stiff task, well beaten) final outing. *J. J. O'Neill*

WAGON LOAD 11 ch.g. Bustino 136 – Noble Girl (Be Friendly 130) [1995 NR – 1996 6.9m 9m Jun 14] well behind at 4 yrs: fairly useful winning hurdler in 1990/1 for R. Akehurst: no promise in amateurs handicaps back on flat. *R. White*

WAHAB 3 b.g. Unfuwain (USA) 131 – Mileeha (USA) 97 (Blushing Groom (FR) – 131) [1995 NR 1996 7m a14g Dec 3] second foal: half-brother to fairly useful 6f winner Tafahhus (by Green Desert): dam 9f winner: no sign of ability. *R. F. Marvin*

WAHEM (IRE) 6 b.g. Lomond (USA) 128 – Pro Patria 86 (Petingo 135) [1995 43 43: a10g a10g a8.5g 10f² a10g² a10g 1996 a13g⁶ a14.8g a13g* a12g⁶ Feb 20] small, sturdy gelding: good mover: poor performer at best nowadays: 20/1, easy winner of selling handicap at Lingfield in February, making all: stays 13f: acts on equitrack, best turf efforts on a sound surface: tried blinkered, no improvement: inconsistent. *C. E. Brittain*

WAHIBA SANDS 3 b.g. Pharly (FR) 130 – Lovely Noor (USA) (Fappiano 94 p (USA)) [1995 79p: 7m* 1996 10m 11.8m³ Oct 28] big, good-topped gelding: has plenty of scope: has a rounded action: fairly useful form, lightly raced: marginally better effort at 3 yrs when seventh of 9 to Bright Water in £8,900 event at Newmarket on reappearance: not knocked about on useful minor event 11 days later: stays at least 1¼m: a good-looking type who remains capable of better. *J. L. Dunlop*

WAIKIKI BEACH (USA) 5 ch.g. Fighting Fit (USA) – Running Melody 86 70 (Rheingold 137) [1995 65: 7m 8.1m 7m 7m 7m 7.6d³ 7g a8g a8g⁵ 1996 a8g² a8.5g* a82 6.9f⁴ a8g³ a8.5g⁴ a8g* a8.5g⁴ a9.4g a8g² a10g* Dec 26] lengthy gelding: useful performer (rated 100) at 3 yrs but most disappointing in 1995, reportedly after kidney trouble: back to fairly useful form at 5 yrs, winner of minor events at Wolverhampton in April and Lingfield in June and claimer (by short head) at Lingfield in December: stays 8.5f: acts on firm ground and all-weather surfaces: tried visored at 4 yrs, no improvement. *G. L. Moore*

WAIT FOR ROSIE 2 b.f. (Apr 18) Reprimand 122 – Turbo Rose 81 (Taufan 77 (USA) 119) [1996 5g³ 5g³ 5.3f* 5m² 6s³ 6.1m⁴ 6d Aug 12] leggy filly: fifth foal: closely related to fair 2-y-o 6f winner Co Pilot (by Petorius) and half-sister to Irish 2-y-o 6f winner, also successful over 1m in Sweden in 1995, Quick Blush (by Fools Holme): dam miler: fair form: won 4-runner maiden at Brighton in May: ran creditably next 3 starts: looked poorly drawn final one: stays 6f: acts on firm and soft going: joined V. Soane. *M. R. Channon*

WAITING GAME (IRE) 2 b.c. (Feb 1) Reprimand 122 – Walesiana (GER) 94 (Star Appeal 133) [1996 a7g* 8.3g² Sep 29] second foal: half-brother to 1½m winner Warluskee (by Dancing Brave): dam German 6.3f (at 2 yrs) to 1m (Group 2) winner: odds on, decisively won maiden at Southwell in September: much better form when head second of 7 to Further Outlook in minor event at Hamilton 20 days later, making running then rallying gamely: likely to stay beyond 8.3f: may improve further. *D. R. Loder*

WAKEEL (USA) 4 b.g. Gulch (USA) – Raahia (CAN) 91 (Vice Regent (CAN)) 87 [1995 93: 10.3g⁵ 11.8m⁵ 10m⁵ 8.3m² 10.1m⁶ 10d 9g 8m 1996 8s² 8v* 8s⁴ 8m 8g⁶ 10.1m 8m³ 8d 8d Oct 12] tall, attractive gelding: fairly useful performer: won minor event at Cagnes-sur-Mer in January: mostly ran in useful handicaps afterwards: probably best at around 1m: acts on any going: visored (looked none too keen) once as 2-y-o. *S. Dow*

WAKY NAO 3 b.c. Alzao (USA) 117 – Waky Na (IRE) (Ahonoora 122) [1995 NR 110 1996 7g* 8g² 6g* 6g* 6v* 6.5g² 6g⁵ 5s⁵ Oct 13] first foal: dam, useful winning miler in Germany, out of useful (at up to 7f) half-sister to Park Express (stayed 1½m, rated 123): smart German colt: won newcomers event at Krefield in April, listed race and minor event at Hanover in June and Group 3 Holsten-Trophy at Hamburg (beat Hever Golf Rose ½ length) in July: rec 4 lb more than weight-for-age when short-head second of 10 to Macanal in Group 3 event at Hoppegarten: below best last 2 starts: effective at 5f to 1m (best effort at 6.5f): acts on heavy going. *H. Blume, Germany*

WALK IN THE WILD 4 b.f. Bold Owl 101 – Tripolitaine (FR) (Nonoalco – (USA) 131) [1995 –: 8g a8.5g 1996 a16g 11.1d Sep 30] no form: left A. Bailey's stable after reappearance. *D. A. Nolan*

WALK ON BY 2 gr.c. (May 16) Terimon 124 – Try G'S (Hotfoot 126) [1996 8d 57 10g⁴ Oct 24] 7,400Y: fifth foal: half-brother to 2 winners in Italy, including 3-y-o Mahafir (1¼m, by Efisio): dam unraced: modest form in maidens at Salisbury and (steadily-run race, close up until over 1f out) Nottingham: likely to stay 1½m. *R. Hannon*

WALK THE BEAT 6 b.g. Interrex (CAN) – Plaits 93 (Thatching 131) [1995 67: 67 a5g² a6g⁴ a7g² a6g⁶ a7g⁶ a6g* 7.6m a7g 5f³ 6f² 6m² 5f⁴ 5.1d 1996 5m⁶ 6m 5f* 5.1f* a69 5f 5m³ 5.1m 5.7m 5m⁵ a6g* a6g³ 5.1g³ 5s Nov 8] strong gelding: impresses in appearance: has a round action: fair handicapper: successful at Lingfield and Bath (apprentices) in the summer, getting up close home to win by short head both times, and at Wolverhampton (in good style) in October: stays 6f: acts on firm and dead going and on fibresand: blinkered/visored once each, and below best: sometimes bandaged. *Martyn Meade*

WALL STREET (USA) 3 ch.c. Mr Prospector (USA) – Wajd (USA) 121 118 (Northern Dancer) [1995 NR 1996 8m² 8m* 8f 10f* 10d⁴ 10g² 12m* 12g Oct 26]

At present Wall Street is remembered chiefly as the horse who sparked off Dettori's seven-timer when winning the Cumberland Lodge Stakes at Ascot in September. He may still be open to improvement—he was unraced at two and has had just eight outings to date—and while unlikely to develop into a major contender for the top prizes he should win more pattern races. Started off over a mile, at which trip he easily landed the odds in a maiden at Newmarket, Wall Street proved much better suited by middle distances, winning on his first attempt at both a mile and a quarter and a mile and a half, in the six-runner Steventon Stakes at Newbury (where he sweated and got on edge) and the seven-runner Cumberland Lodge Stakes respectively. Wall Street had come from off a very strong pace when winning by a length at Newbury, ridden by

Cumberland Lodge Stakes, Ascot—
Wall Street hangs on from Salmon Ladder for the first leg of Frankie Dettori's 'Magnificent Seven'

John Reid, but he made all for his half-length success at Ascot. Dettori, clearly harbouring no doubts about Wall Street's stamina, set a pace which had all of his rivals stretching by halfway, then gave his mount a breather before kicking on turning for home. Only Salmon Ladder was able to go with Wall Street, putting in a persistent challenge which threatened to take him to the front but never quite did. Both horses ran on most gamely, and it wasn't until the last hundred yards that Wall Street gained a decisive advantage. Tried again over a mile and a half on his only subsequent start, in the Breeders' Cup Turf at Woodbine, Wall Street ran better than his eighth-of-fourteen position suggests. Only a length or so behind the winner Pilsudski going into the home turn, he didn't handle it well and dropped to the rear. Although he ran on well once he'd straightened up, he had no chance of getting back into contention and was nine and a half lengths behind Pilsudski at the line.

Wall Street (USA) (ch.c. 1993)	Mr Prospector (USA) (b 1970)	Raise A Native (ch 1961)	Native Dancer Raise You
		Gold Digger (b 1962)	Nashua Sequence
	Wajd (USA) (ch 1987)	Northern Dancer (b 1961)	Nearctic Natalma
		Dahlia (ch 1970)	Vaguely Noble Charming Alibi

Wall Street, a tall, attractive colt who has been freeze-fired, is the first foal of Wajd, a smart middle-distance filly at three years when trained by Andre Fabre. Wajd won three races, including the Group 3 Prix Minerve, and finished in the frame in both the Yorkshire Oaks and Prix Vermeille. By Northern Dancer out of the brilliant racemare Dahlia, Wajd, bought as a yearling for 1,300,000 guineas, is closely related to the good middle-distance colt Dahar. She's also a half-sister to several other winners, notably the smart French middle-distance stayer Rivlia who later showed high-class form in the USA, and Dahlia's Dreamer (by Theatrical), winner of the Grade 1 Flower Bowl Handicap at Belmont. Wall Street, a fluent mover, acts on firm and dead ground and has yet to race on very soft going. He is genuine and consistent. *Saeed bin Suroor*

WALTZ TIME 2 b.f. (Apr 10) Rambo Dancer (CAN) 107 – Kiveton Komet 71 – (Precocious 126) [1996 5m^6 6g^6 5g 5s Nov 7] 1,000Y: second foal: dam sprinter: probably a plater. *Miss L. A. Perratt*

WALWORTH LADY 5 gr.m. Belfort (FR) 89 – Manna Green (Bustino 136) 52 [1995 NR 1996 12.3g^5 10g* 10.9d^5 11.1m May 18] big, lengthy mare: modest performer: won seller at Ripon in April, rallying: stays 12.3f: acts on fibresand and on good to firm ground, poor effort on heavy: pulls hard (bolted to start on reappearance): bandaged in front in 1996: none too consistent: covered by Clantime. *M. Dods*

WANDERING STAR (USA) 3 b.f. Red Ransom (USA) – Beautiful Bedouin 115 (USA) (His Majesty (USA)) [1995 –p: 6g 1996 9m^3 8g* 8m* 8.1m* 10m^5 10g* 12f^2 Nov 16] lengthy filly: progressed into a smart performer, winning maiden at Salis-

E. P. Taylor Stakes, Woodbine—
Wandering Star (striped sleeves) from another British-trained filly Flame Valley (rails)

bury, minor event at Kempton (edged left) and listed race at Sandown (beat Miss Universal a length) in the summer, then (after good fifth to Last Second in Sun Chariot Stakes at Newmarket) Grade 2 event at Woodbine in October by 1½ lengths from Flame Valley on final start for J. Fanshawe: length second to Ampulla in similar event at Aqueduct last time: stays 1½m: acts on firm going: genuine. *C. McGaughey, USA*

WANNAPLANTATREE 5 b.m. Niniski (USA) 125 – Cataclysmic 78 (Ela-Mana-Mou 132) [1995 62: a12g⁶ 14.9d 17.2m 14.4m² 14m⁴ 14.9m³ a14g⁵ 14.1m* 14g⁴ 1996 16g* 14m⁶ Jun 15] sparely-made mare: fair handicapper: 25/1, won 18-runner Queen's Prize at Kempton in April: reportedly broke blood vessel only subsequent outing: stayed well: acted on good to firm and dead ground: visored (below form) sixth 4-y-o start: held up: reportedly retired. *N. M. Babbage* 67

WANSTEAD (IRE) 4 ch.g. Be My Native (USA) 122 – All The Same (Cajun 120) [1995 9f⁶ 1996 12g⁶ Jul 3] IR 4,000Y: ex-Irish gelding: half-brother to 2 winners, including Italian sprinter Fellini (by Fayruz): dam unraced: lightly-raced maiden: visored, well held only outing in 1996: has broken blood vessels over hurdles. *J. R. Jenkins* –

WARBROOK 3 b.c. Warrshan (USA) 117 – Bracey Brook (Gay Fandango (USA) 132) [1995 87: 6.1m⁵ 7.1m 7.1m³ 8g² 10m* 8f² 1996 12d⁶ 12m 13.9m⁶ 11.9g⁶ 10m⁴ 13.9g 12v Nov 25] rather leggy, quite attractive colt: shows plenty of knee action: fairly useful handicapper: sold out of I. Balding's stable 24,000 gns Newmarket Autumn Sales after sixth 3-y-o start: should be suited by a test of stamina: acts on firm ground. *R. Crepon, France* 87

WARDARA 4 ch.f. Sharpo 132 – Ward One 68 (Mr Fluorocarbon 126) [1995 62: 6m 7m 7d⁵ 6g a7g 1996 5s 6.1g a6g³ a6g³ a5g a6g³ a6g* 6g* a6g* 6.1m² 6g³ 6m* 5d 6s² 7m² 6m⁴ 8s 6s Nov 17] strong, stocky filly: fair handicapper: won at Wolverhampton, Leicester and Southwell (minor event) within 2 weeks in June, and at Yarmouth (originally disqualified but later reinstated) in August: good efforts most other outings, first home on far side when fourth in Ayr Silver Cup: left C. Dwyer and out of depth in Group 3 races in Italy last 2 starts: stays 7f: acts on fibresand and on good to firm and heavy ground: usually visored/blinkered. *V. Valiani, Italy* 77

WARHURST (IRE) 5 b.g. Nordance (USA) – Pourboire 47 (Star Appeal 133) [1995 46: a8g a7g⁴ a8g a9.4g³ 1996 a8g⁴ a8g* a8.5g⁴ a11g⁶ 10.1m Oct 23] angular gelding: modest performer: has reportedly had leg problems: disappointing in 1994 and 1995, but (well backed) back almost to best to win apprentice handicap at Southwell in January: below form afterwards, off course 9 months before final start: effective at 1m, and stays 10.3f well: acts on fibresand: goes well for claimer: inconsistent. *D. Nicholls* – a63

WARM HEARTED (USA) 4 ch.g. Known Fact (USA) 135 – Lovin' Lass (USA) (Cutlass (USA)) [1995 60: 5.1m a7g a7g⁴ 1996 a6g⁵ a6g⁵ 6.1m Jun 30] sparely-made gelding: modest maiden: ran as though something amiss after 5-month absence on final start: stays 7f: acts on equitrack and fibresand. *A. G. Newcombe* 57

WARMING TRENDS 3 b.g. Warning 136 – Sunny Davis (USA) 71 (Alydar (USA)) [1995 86p: 6m 6f 6m 6d* 7d* 7s* 1996 7m³ 7.1f 8.1v² 7g² 7g² Oct 19] rather lightly-made gelding: has a quick action: reportedly hobdayed as 2-y-o: useful handicapper: best efforts when runner-up last 3 starts, faring easily best of those drawn high in 27-runner event at York (finished strongly) on penultimate one and beaten only a neck by Mezzanotte in 22-runner race at Newmarket week later: sold 20,000 gns Newmarket Autumn Sales: stays 1m: acts on good to firm and heavy ground: sent to Sweden. *Sir Mark Prescott* 96

WARM SPELL 6 b.g. Northern State (USA) 91 – Warm Wind 84 (Tumble Wind (USA)) [1995 77: a13g* 10.2m² 13.3g 12m 12m⁵ 13.3d⁵ 11.9g 1996 a12g 16g 15.4f⁶ 10m 12d⁴ Oct 11] good-quartered gelding: has a round action: fair handicapper at 5 yrs: long way below form in 1996, well beaten until final start: effective at 1¼m to 1¾m: has form on good to firm ground and equitrack, revels in the mud: normally held up in touch: game: useful hurdler. *G. L. Moore* 56 +

WARNING REEF 3 b.g. Warning 136 – Horseshoe Reef 88 (Mill Reef (USA) 141) [1995 76: 7.1g⁵ 7f² 7g 7.3m⁴ 1996 10.5g⁴ 8.1g³ 8m⁶ 10.4m³ 10.1m 12m 11.7m² 14g² Jul 5] rangy gelding: unimpressive mover: fairly useful maiden: stays 1¾m: has raced only on a sound surface: has joined C. Popham. *M. R. Channon* 86

WAR

WARNING SHOT 4 b.g. Dowsing (USA) 124 – Warning Bell 88 (Bustino 136) – [1995 79d: 7m⁶ 7g⁴ 7.1g 7f 6f a6g 8.1d 7.1d⁶ 5.1m 1996 9.7s 8.1g 8.1g Jun 13] big, workmanlike gelding: has a round action: capable of fair form in 1995 but generally most disappointing, and well beaten at 4 yrs: sold 1,500 gns Newmarket Autumn Sales: should be suited by further than 7f. *Martyn Meade*

WARNING STAR 4 b.f. Warning 136 – Blade of Grass 78 (Kris 135) [1995 104: 5m* 5g 7m 5m³ 6g² 5m⁵ 6m 1996 5.1g³ 6d 6f* 6m³ 6g⁶ 6g 6.5s⁴ 6s Nov 9] smallish, leggy filly: has a quick action: useful performer: comfortable winner of 3-runner minor event at Yarmouth in June: contested listed/pattern events afterwards, running creditably in 3 of them: sold 66,000 gns Newmarket December Sales: effective at 5f and should stay 7f: acts on firm ground and soft: has been bandaged off-hind. *B. W. Hills*   102

WARNING TIME 3 b.c. Warning 136 – Ballad Island 83 (Ballad Rock 122) [1995 96: 5m* 7g⁶ 6g* 6d³ 6g² 1996 6m 6g³ 7m² 6m 7.3f⁵ 5f⁴ Jul 26] strong, workmanlike colt: has a short action: useful performer: 1¼ lengths second to Ramooz in minor event at Epsom in June: not at best last 3 starts: will prove best at up to 7f: acts on good to firm and dead ground. *B. J. Meehan*   100

WARP DRIVE (IRE) 2 ch.c. (Mar 22) Warning 136 – Red Roman 87 – (Solinus 130) [1996 a6g a8g⁶ Dec 20] 15,500F, IR 7,500Y, 16,000 2-y-o: half-brother to 3 winners abroad: dam 2-y-o 5f winner mainly disappointing afterwards: always behind in all-weather maidens. *W. R. Muir*

WARREN KNIGHT 3 b.g. Weldnaas (USA) 112 – Trigamy 112 (Tribal Chief 125) [1995 –: 6s 1996 7g⁶ 8d 8m 7m Sep 19] good-quartered gelding: modest maiden: stays 1m: gelded after final start. *C. A. Horgan*   64

WAR REQUIEM (IRE) 6 b.g. Don't Forget Me 127 – Ladiz (Persian Bold 123) [1995 –: a10g a10g⁵ 10d 1996 10g³ 14d Oct 2] strong, good-quartered gelding: poor form at best nowadays: should stay further than 1¼m: sold 600 gns Newmarket Autumn Sales. *R. J. O'Sullivan*   39

WARRING 2 b.g. (Feb 12) Warrshan (USA) 117 – Emerald Ring 74 (Auction Ring (USA) 123) [1996 7g 7.1f 7d 7m Oct 17] 7,000F, IR 10,000Y: third foal: dam sprinter: never a threat in maidens and a seller: reportedly retained 2,800 gns Newmarket Autumn Sales: subsequently joined M. Saunders. *M. R. Channon*   48

WARRLIN 2 b.c. (Apr 12) Warrshan (USA) 117 – Lahin (Rainbow Quest (USA) 134) [1996 6g 7m⁴ 7.5f⁴ 7.9g 10m³ 10m Oct 7] 2,100F, 5,800Y: leggy colt: has a round action: first foal: dam once-raced half-sister to very smart 1985 2-y-o Nomination: modest maiden: likely to stay long distances. *C. W. Fairhurst*   59

WAR SHANTY 3 b.f. Warrshan (USA) 117 – Daring Ditty (Daring March 116) [1995 –: 8m 1996 10.2d⁵ Sep 30] fair maiden, very lightly raced (trained at 2 yrs by J. R. Arnold): kept on steadily when around 13 lengths fifth of 10 to Pasternak at Bath on only 3-y-o start: stays 10.2f: may do better. *Lady Herries*   66

WARSPITE 6 b.g. Slip Anchor 136 – Valkyrie 87 (Bold Lad (IRE) 133) [1995 NR 1996 12m 10g 12g 10g a11g⁴ 14d a10g⁵ Dec 30] poor maiden nowadays: sold out of R. O'Sullivan's stable 1,900 gns Ascot November Sales before final start: stays 1½m: best runs on good going or equitrack: has looked difficult ride. *P. Mooney*   38

WARWICK MIST (IRE) 4 ch.f. Digamist (USA) 110 – Flash Donna (USA) 70 (Well Decorated) [1995 35: a8g⁴ a8g² a7g 1996 12.1m³ 11.1m 13.1g⁴ Aug 21] leggy filly: poor maiden: appears to stay 1½m: acts on good to firm ground and fibresand (no form on dead at 2 yrs): sent to South Korea. *B. Mactaggart*   33

WASBLEST 4 b.f. Statoblest 120 – Safety First (Wassl 125) [1995 56: a5g³ a5g² a5g² a5g 5m² 5f⁴ 5m² 5m² 5f⁴ 1996 a5g³ a5g a5g⁶ 7.1f⁴ 6.9f⁵ 6.9f⁶ Jul 6] workmanlike filly: modest handicapper: tough and consistent at 3 yrs for M. Johnston, but sold very cheaply out of his stable and less reliable in 1996: seems effective at 5f to 7f: acts on the all-weather and on firm ground: blinkered (ran to form) final 3-y-o start: usually races prominently. *J. Berry*   56

WASHINGTON REEF (USA) 3 b.g. Seattle Dancer (USA) 119 – Broken Wave 103 (Bustino 136) [1995 –: 8d 8g 1996 8.2s 14.1m a16g³ 17.2f³ 18m² Jul 6] strong, attractive gelding: has a markedly round action: modest staying maiden handicapper: best effort on final start: visored/blinkered since second 3-y-o start: has been bandaged: sent to UAE. *J. H. M. Gosden*   61

WASP RANGER (USA) 2 b.c. (May 20) Red Ransom (USA) – Lady Climber 87 (USA) (Mount Hagen (FR) 127) [1996 6m³ 7g⁵ 7d² Oct 2] $13,000Y: very tall, good sort: has plenty of scope: easy mover: fourth foal: half-brother to a winner in USA by Pass The Tab and in Panama by Westheimer: dam won at up to 7f in USA: fairly useful form: will stay beyond 7f: acts on good to firm ground (best effort, despite wandering under pressure) and dead: races prominently: sure to win a race. *P. F. I. Cole*

WATCH ME GO (IRE) 7 b.g. On Your Mark 125 – Nighty Night (Sassafras 45 (FR) 135) [1995 33+, a50: 7.5m⁶ a10g* a10g² 1996 12.3g² 10.3m a11g⁴ 11.9g² a13g³ Jun 29] quite attractive gelding: poor handicapper: stays 13f: acts on firm ground, dead and all-weather surfaces: tried visored at 4 yrs, but no improvement: headstrong on occasions: none too consistent. *Bob Jones*

WATCH ME (IRE) 3 b.f. Green Desert (USA) 127 – Fenny Rough 114 (Home 106 Guard (USA) 129) [1995 78: 6g² 5g⁴ 6m 1996 6m² 6m* 6m³ 6m⁵ Aug 2] well-made filly: useful sprinter: won maiden at Salisbury in May by 12 lengths: clearly best effort when third of 17 to Atraf in Cork and Orrery Stakes at Royal Ascot over 6 weeks later, leading for over 5f: gave impression something amiss (found to be coughing) final start: stays 6f: has raced only on a sound surface. *R. Hannon*

WATCH THE FIRE 3 b.f. Statoblest 120 – Thulium (Mansingh (USA) 120) 71 [1995 NR 1996 5.1g³ 6f² 6m* 6g Jul 29] 10,500Y: fourth foal: half-sister to 4-y-o 1m winner Mighty Marston and fairly useful 5f performer Crystal Magic (both by Mazilier), and 1992 2-y-o 5f and 6f winner Iolite (by Forzando): dam lightly-raced sister to Petong: fair form: won median auction maiden at Folkestone in July, leading near finish: stays 6f: has raced only on a sound surface. *J. E. Banks*

WATER CHESTNUT 3 ch.g. Most Welcome 131 – Water Pageant 58 (Welsh – Pageant 132) [1995 –: a8g 1996 a12g May 2] well beaten in maiden and seller: sold 500 gns Doncaster November Sales. *Mrs N. Macauley*

WATERCOLOUR (IRE) 2 b.f. (Mar 31) Groom Dancer (USA) 128 – River – Nomad 99 (Gorytus (USA) 132) [1996 6d 6f 6.9g Jul 3] IR 19,000Y: second foal: closely related to 3-y-o Czech 1½m winner Autumn (by Rainbow Quest): dam 1m winner: poor form in maidens: sold 2,000 gns Newmarket Autumn Sales: may prove suited by further than 7f. *P. F. I. Cole*

WATER GARDEN 2 ch.c. (May 2) Most Welcome 131 – On Show 92 (Welsh – p Pageant 132) [1996 6g 7g Oct 30] good-topped colt: closely related to 2 winners by Be My Guest, including smart miler Guest Artiste, and half-brother to several winners, including miler Inchmurrin (by Lomond) and 1989 2-y-o 6f winner Welney (by Habitat), both smart: dam 1¼m winner out of Park Hill winner African Dancer: behind in maidens at Newmarket (burly) and Yarmouth 12 days later: looks sort to do better. *G. Wragg*

WATER HAZARD (IRE) 4 b.g. Maelstrom Lake 118 – Simply Inch (Simply – Great (FR) 122) [1995 53, a57: a7g* a8g³ a8g⁴ a7g* a7g⁵ 8m 7g 8g a8g⁵ a10g² 7g 8f³ a10g⁴ 11.9f* 10f³ 10g² a12g a12g 1996 a12g Jan 4] compact gelding: modest handicapper in 1995: well beaten only 4-y-o start: stays 1½m: acts on firm ground and equitrack: usually held up. *S. Dow*

WATERLORD (IRE) 6 b.g. Bob Back (USA) 124 – Ringtail 102 (Auction Ring 41 (USA) 123) [1995 40: a7g 7.5m 8m 8m 7m⁴ 8.3g 10g 8.2m 1996 8.3d 8g³ 8g 9.2s⁵ 8.1g³ 7.5m 8m Jun 20] small, sturdy gelding: carries condition: poor performer nowadays: sold 750 gns Doncaster September Sales and 500 gns Doncaster October Sales: stays 9.2f: probably acts on any going: blinkered (below form) once at 3 yrs: sometimes has tongue tied down. *D. Nicholls*

WATERSPOUT (USA) 2 b.c. (Mar 10) Theatrical 128 – Water Angel (USA) 75 (Halo (USA)) [1996 7.1f³ 8m⁶ Sep 25] second foal: half-brother to 1995 2-y-o 8.1f winner Waterland (by Explodent): dam unraced daughter of sister to Canadian Oaks winner Northernette and Storm Bird, an excellent family: fair form in maidens at Chepstow (slowly away, edging right late on) and Goodwood (shade mulish stalls) 13 days later: will stay beyond 1m: wears a crossed noseband. *G. Harwood*

WATERVILLE BOY (IRE) 2 ch.c. (Apr 21) Don't Forget Me 127 – East River 56 (FR) (Arctic Tern (USA) 126) [1996 6m 8.5m⁴ 6m⁴ 7m a7g⁵ Nov 15] sparely-made colt: seventh living foal: brother to disappointing 3-y-o Charlie Chang, 1m winner at

2 yrs, and 7f (at 2 yrs) to 9f (Grade 2 event in USA) winner Eastern Memories and half-brother to 2 winners: modest form in maidens then soundly beaten in sellers last 2 starts: sold 3,200 gns Doncaster November Sales. *R. Hannon*

WATHBAT NASHWAN 2 ch.c. (May 1) Nashwan (USA) 135 – Alwathba 66 p (USA) 100 (Lyphard (USA) 132) [1996 8f 7g Oct 30] third foal: half-brother to fairly useful 1¼m winner Wathbat Mtoto (by Mtoto): dam, 2-y-o 6f winner (suited by 1m), is sister to smart 7f performer Dreams To Reality from good family: never dangerous under 7-lb claimer in maidens at Leicester and Yarmouth (held up well off pace, ran on steadily not knocked about) 15 days later: will improve, particularly back at 1m+. *L. M. Cumani*

WAVERLEY STAR 11 br.g. Pitskelly 122 – Quelle Blague (Red God 128§) – [1995 42d: a6g⁴ a6g² a6g a6g⁶ a6g a6g⁶ a8g 6m³ 6m 6m 5g⁵ 6f 6f a5g 1996 5g 6m 5m 6f 5m 5g Sep 2] big, workmanlike gelding: poor sprinter, little form in 1996. *J. S. Wainwright*

WAVIAN 4 b.c. Warning 136 – Vian (USA) (Far Out East (USA)) [1995 96: 5m² 98 5m 6g 6m⁵ 5m² 6m⁴ 1996 6g⁴ 6m 5.1g² 6g⁵ 5m 5f 5.1f 5m Jul 6] neat, attractive colt: has a quick action: useful performer: 3½ lengths second to Cape Merino in minor event at Bath in April: stays 6f: has raced only on a sound surface: blinkered last 2 starts in 1995: sent to Saudi Arabia. *R. Hannon*

WAVY RUN (IRE) 5 b.h. Commanche Run 133 – Wavy Reef (Kris 135) [1995 113 8g* 8g* 5.5g⁶ 5.5s⁵ 7m⁵ 8m⁶ 8d⁴ 8s² 10d 8g² 8d* 8d⁵ 1996 8d² 8d* 8g* 8.5f² 8f² 8f³ 9f⁵ 6.5f³ 7m Dec 8] second foal: half-brother to French 7f to 9f winner General Torres (by Magical Wonder): dam, unraced, out of half-sister to Oaks-placed Maysoon (also second in 1000 Guineas) and Three Tails: smart ex-Spanish horse: successful on 6 occasions in Spain from 6f (at 2 and 3 yrs) to 1m (at 3 and 4 yrs) and once in France prior to 1996: in fine form as a 5-y-o, winning listed race in March and 5-runner Prix Edmond Blanc (held on by length from Nec Plus Ultra) in April, both at Saint-Cloud for C. Laffon-Parias: placed, including in Grade 3 event at Churchill Downs, for new connections: stays 1m: front runner. *D. Vienna, USA*

WAYNE COUNTY (IRE) 6 b.h. Sadler's Wells (USA) 132 – Detroit (FR) 131 110 (Riverman (USA) 131) [1995 110: 9.9m* 12m⁵ 12g 12m 12m⁴ 10d⁴ 11.8m⁶ 12m* 11.1g³ 10g³ 12d⁴ 1996 12d² 10d 10.1m⁶ 12g 13.3m Aug 17] good-topped horse: impresses in appearance: smart performer: ran a fine race when short-headed by Spout in John Porter Stakes at Newbury on reappearance: well below form all 4 starts afterwards: effective at 1¼m and probably stays 1¾m: won a maiden on soft ground, but has not raced on extremes of going (acts on good to firm and dead) for a long time: probably effective visored/blinkered or not: sometimes sweats: often coltish, extremely so final start: sent to USA. *R. Akehurst*

WAYPOINT 3 b.f. Cadeaux Genereux 131 – Princess Athena 119 (Ahonoora 122) 77 [1995 –p: 7.1d⁶ 1996 a7g* 7m⁴ 7m 7g² 8.2s a7g⁵ Dec 11] big, lengthy filly: fair form: a73 won maiden at Lingfield in March: off course over 5 months after next start: may prove as effective over 6f as 7f: well beaten (over unsuitable trip) on soft ground. *R. Charlton*

WEDDING MUSIC 2 b.f. (Mar 5) Music Boy 124 – Diamond Wedding (USA) 48 65 (Diamond Shoal 130) [1996 a5g a5g⁵ 6g⁴ 5m² 5d 5m⁴ a5g⁵ a6g⁶ Nov 30] 1,000Y: a35 first foal: dam (maiden) should have stayed beyond 1½m: sprint plater: beaten a neck at Hamilton in August: failed to reproduce that form: acts on good to firm ground, bad form on fibresand: visored penultimate start. *P. C. Haslam*

WEE DRAM 2 ch.f. (Apr 24) Most Welcome 131 – Scottish Legend (Legend of 67 France (USA) 124) [1996 6m 5f⁶ 5.7d⁴ Sep 30] 6,000Y: third foal: half-sister to 4-y-o Flamboro (by Handsome Sailor), 6f and 7f winner at 2 yrs: dam unraced half-sister to useful sprinter Rotherfield Greys: progressive form: fourth of 12 in maiden at Bath: bred to stay 1m. *R. Hannon*

WEEHEBY (USA) 7 ch.g. Woodman (USA) 126 – Fearless Dame (USA) 56 (Fearless Knight) [1995 a7g⁶ 1996 a12g⁵ Oct 5] modest performer: raced in Dubai at 5 and 6 yrs: stays 1½m: acts on good to firm and soft ground and on fibresand: blinkered (below form, hung under pressure) once at 3 yrs: has had tongue tied down. *M. F. Barraclough*

WEE HOPE (USA) 3 b.c. Housebuster (USA) – Tell Me Sumthing (USA) 72 (Summing (USA)) [1995 82: 6m⁶ 6.1d² 6g³ 1996 5m 6g⁴ 5g* Jun 8] leggy, quite good-topped colt: fair performer: tended to hang closing stages when placed as 2-y-o: visored, won maiden at Doncaster in June, coming with strong run to lead inside final 1f: sold 7,500 gns Newmarket July Sales: raced only at sprint distances: yet to race on extremes of going: sent to Macau. *M. R. Stoute*

WEET A BIT (IRE)   2 b.c. (May 1) Archway (IRE) 115 – Aridje 79 (Mummy's   – Pet 125) [1996 5g a7g⁵ Dec 28] IR 10,000Y: leggy colt: seventh foal: half-brother to 3 winners, including useful 1987 2-y-o 5f and 6f winner Lust of Power and 7f winner Lust of Love (both by Sallust): dam, out of half-sister to very speedy Singing Bede, won over 5f at 2 yrs: well held in maiden auctions nearly 9 months apart. *R. Hollinshead*

WEET-A-MINUTE (IRE)   3 ro.c. Nabeel Dancer (USA) 120 – Ludovica   106 (Bustino 136) [1995 95: 7f⁵ 7m³ 8.1g³ 7.5d* 7.9m* 8f* 10m² 1996 9m⁴ 10.3g³ 12f⁴ 11.9g³ 10.3m⁶ 10.5m⁶ 14g 12f 11.8m⁵ 12s⁶ a10s⁴ Nov 19] lengthy colt: fine mover: useful performer: in frame in listed events on 3 of first 4 starts in 1996, 4¼ lengths third of 5 to Royal Court at Haydock on last occasion: long way below form in smart company afterwards, and on all-weather debut: stays 1½m: acts on firm and good to soft ground. *R. Hollinshead*

WEET EES GIRL (IRE)   2 ro.f. (May 24) Common Grounds 118 – Kastiliya   75 (Kalamoun 129) [1996 5.1d* 5.1g⁴ 6.1m⁵ 6.1m³ 5f⁶ 6.1d⁶ Aug 30] IR 5,000F, 5,000Y: unfurnished filly: half-sister to 3 winners, including 7f (at 2 yrs) and 11f winner Kastamoun (by Ile de Bourbon): dam, French 2-y-o 7f winner, is half-sister to top-class 1m to 1½m filly Kozana and high-class stayer Karkour: fair form: won maiden at Nottingham in April: best efforts at Chester third and fourth starts: performed poorly afterwards, at Chester last time: should stay beyond 6.1f. *P. D. Evans*

WEE TINKERBELL   3 ch.f. Timeless Times (USA) 99 – Kiveton Komet 71   – (Precocious 126) [1995 51: 5g³ 5g⁶ 6f⁴ 1996 a8.5g May 25] modest form in frame in 2-y-o maiden for Miss L. Perratt: visored, always behind in claimer at Wolver-hampton on reappearance: stays 6f. *R. T. Juckes*

WEETMAN'S WEIGH (IRE)   3 b.c. Archway (IRE) 115 – Indian Sand   75 (Indian King (USA) 128) [1995 66: a5g³ a6g⁵ 6m² a6g² 6.1m⁴ 5f* 6m⁶ 6m² 6m 1996 a6g* a6g² a7g² a6g* 6s* 6m³ 6.1g³ May 8] useful-looking colt: fair handicapper: won at Southwell (gamely) and Wolverhampton in January and at Leicester on return to turf in March: stays 7f: acts on firm ground, soft and fibresand: sometimes hangs left: often soon off bridle: has tongue tied down: consistent. *R. Hollinshead*

WELCOME BRIEF   3 b.f. Most Welcome 131 – Lawful 76 (Law Society (USA)   – 130) [1995 NR 1996 8.3m 7.1d 7g a8.5g 8g 1.1g⁵ Aug 21] smallish, sturdy filly: bad mover: second foal: sister to once-raced Sue The Star: dam, second at around 1¼m on both starts, is half-sister to smart French middle-distance performer French Glory out of French Oaks winner Dunette: no worthwhile form: claimed out of W. Musson's stable £5,000 after debut. *E. J. Alston*

WELCOME HEIGHTS   2 b.g. (May 16) Most Welcome 131 – Mount Ida   – (USA) 79 (Conquistador Cielo (USA)) [1996 6m 6.9d 6g Oct 29] 2,000Y: good-topped, workmanlike gelding: second foal: dam 10.2f winner: no worthwhile form. *M. J. Fetherston-Godley*

WELCOME HOME   2 b.f. (May 12) Most Welcome 131 – Miss Cindy 95   – (Mansingh (USA) 120) [1996 8.1m 8.1d Sep 28] tall, good-topped filly: half-sister to several winners, including useful sprinter Gipsy Fiddler (by Bairn): dam 5f to 7f performer, is sister to Petong: no promise in maiden events. *P. T. Dalton*

WELCOME LU   3 ch.f. Most Welcome 131 – Odile (Green Dancer (USA) 132)   45 [1995 –: 6f 6f 1996 a8g a7g⁴ a11g a8g 6f 5f 7g³ 7f* 7g* 7.5g 7f Sep 10] strong-quartered filly: poor handicapper: left P. Felgate after fifth 3-y-o start: won at Brighton (maiden event, wandered markedly) and Catterick (missed break, got up near finish) in August: stays 7f (bred to be suited by further): has raced only on a sound surface: tried blinkered. *J. L. Harris*

WELCOME PARADE   3 b.c. Generous (IRE) 139 – Jubilee Trail 82 (Shareef   92 Dancer (USA) 135) [1995 NR 1996 11.5f³ 11.5m* 12g* 13.9g Sep 4] angular, quite attractive colt: shows knee action: second foal: half-brother to useful 7f/1m winner Peace Envoy (by Warning): dam, 10.4f winner, half-sister to Park Hill winner Rejuvenate: fairly useful performer: won maiden at Yarmouth and handicap at Kempton (still green in front), both in August: well-backed favourite, well below form in handicap at York on final start: sold 20,000 gns Newmarket Autumn Sales: should stay further than 1½m: joined T. Taaffe in Ireland. *H. R. A. Cecil*

WELCOME ROYALE (IRE) 3 ch.g. Be My Guest (USA) 126 – Kirsova – (Absalom 128) [1995 68: 6m⁵ 7m⁴ 7.5m 8g⁶ 8d³ 8f⁴ 1996 10.3d 7f 8.3m a8g 9.7m⁴ 12g⁴ Sep 3] strong, heavy-topped gelding: unimpressive mover: modest maiden handicapper, disappointing in 1996: probably stays 1½m: acts on firm and dead ground. *M. H. Tompkins*

WELLAKI (USA) 2 ch.c. (Jan 12) Miswaki (USA) 124 – Wellomond (FR) 80 p (Lomond (USA) 128) [1996 8.1s⁴ 8.1s* Nov 7] 580,000 francs Y: second foal: dam French 1¼m winner, half-sister to high-class miler Last Fandango: favourite, won steadily-run 7-runner maiden at Musselburgh in November, readily: will stay beyond 8.1f: will improve again. *J. H. M. Gosden*

WELL ARRANGED (IRE) 5 ch.g. Bold Arrangement 127 – Eurynome (Be – My Guest (USA) 126) [1995 –: 16m 13.9g 14g 12f 16.1g 1996 14.1g a14.8g* a12g⁶ a67 14.8m a16g 16d a14.8g³ a14g 14.1g Oct 30] lengthy gelding: fairly useful form on soft ground at 3 yrs: just a modest handicapper in 1996, successful at Wolverhampton in May: left R. Akehurst after fourth start: should stay 2m: acts on fibresand, used to go well on soft ground: blinkered 2 of last 3 starts. *M. J. Polglase*

WELLCOME INN 2 ch.c. (Feb 23) Most Welcome 131 – Mimining 83 (Tower – Walk 130) [1996 8f Sep 13] 5,400Y: big, lengthy colt: has plenty of scope: second foal: half-brother to poor sprint 3-y-o Kiwud (by Superlative): dam sprinter: 33/1, burly and very green, tailed off in maiden at Doncaster. *J. A. Harris*

WELL DONE 2 gr.f. (Feb 4) Petong 126 – Mrs Darling 70 (Mummy's Pet 125) – [1996 7m 6.1m 6m Oct 4] 16,000F: fifth foal: half-sister to fair (at best) winners by Robellino (7f), Sharrood (6f) and Deploy (1m): dam, maiden who stayed 6f, is out of Portland Handicap winner Matinee, grandam of Lemon Souffle: soundly beaten in maidens. *M. Bell*

WELL DRAWN 3 b.g. Dowsing (USA) 124 – Classic Design (Busted 134) [1995 84 + 65p: 7m a8g³ 1996 a8g* Jan 11] rangy, quite attractive gelding: progressive form: justified favouritism in well-contested maiden at Lingfield on reappearance by short head from Blue Flyer (pair clear), leading until halfway, soon under pressure but staying on well to get up again close home: subsequently gelded: will be well suited by 1¼m+: acts on equitrack: looked open to further improvement. *H. Candy*

WELLIRAN 3 ch.g. Hadeer 118 – Iranian 81 (Indian King (USA) 128) [1995 NR 65 1996 7s⁴ Mar 22] 2,800Y: lengthy, angular gelding: fourth live foal: dam, 7f winner, half-sister to smart sprinter Polykratis: 10/1 and burly, 7½ lengths fourth of 14 to Sorbie Tower in maiden at Doncaster, setting steady early pace. *A. G. Foster*

WELL SUITED 6 b.g. Elegant Air 119 – Gay Appeal 76 (Star Appeal 133) [1995 – –: a11g⁵ 1996 a16g 8f 11.9g 10.8f 12g Jul 3] lengthy gelding: soundly beaten since fair 3-y-o maiden: stays 1¼m: tried blinkered. *T. Hind*

WELL WARNED 2 b.f. (Jan 29) Warning 136 – Well Beyond (IRE) 101 (Don't 92 Forget Me 127) [1996 6f² 6g³ 6m* 6m Aug 22] quite good-topped filly: has scope: good mover: first foal: dam 5f (at 2 yrs) to 1m winner, out of sister to Zaizafon, herself dam of Zafonic: 8½ lengths third of 9 to Dazzle in Cherry Hinton Stakes at Newmarket on second start: landed the odds in 5-runner maiden at Haydock in August, readily making all: sweating and edgy, only eighth of 9 behind Bianca Nera in Lowther Stakes at York: should stay 7f: best effort on good ground. *B. W. Hills*

WELSH EMBLEM (IRE) 3 b.c. Mujtahid (USA) 118 – David's Star (Welsh 73 Saint 126) [1995 NR 1996 7d⁴ 6m⁶ 6f a9.4g³ Aug 9] 30,000F, 50,000Y: quite attractive colt: third foal: half-brother to Irish 5-y-o middle-distance maiden Zara's Birthday (by Waajib): dam daughter of useful winner from 5f to 1m Belitis, herself out of Mesopotamia: fair maiden: should prove suited by 1m+: sold 13,000 gns Newmarket Autumn Sales: sent to France. *G. Wragg*

WELSH MELODY 3 b.f. Merdon Melody 98 – Young Whip (Bold Owl 101) – [1995 –, a47: 6.1m a6g* a6g a7g⁶ 6s a8.5g a6g⁵ a7g³ 1996 a7g² a7g² a8g⁵ a7g Nov a53 22] modest performer: off course 8½ months before tailed off final outing: should stay 1m: best form on fibresand: visored/blinkered penultimate 2-y-o to penultimate 3-y-o starts. *K. R. Burke*

WELSH MILL (IRE) 7 b.g. Caerleon (USA) 132 – Gay Milly (FR) 74 (Mill 81 Reef (USA) 141) [1995 –: 11.9g 11.9m 1996 12g² 13g* 13g⁴ 14d* 15m³ 16.1m⁴ 16.1m⁵ Aug 26] close-coupled, attractive gelding: has been fired: fairly useful handicapper: won at Hamilton in June and at Haydock in July: stays 2m: probably acts on any ground. *Mrs M. Reveley*

WELSH MIST 5 b.m. Damister (USA) 123 – Welwyn 92 (Welsh Saint 126) 101 ? [1995 102: 5m 6m⁶ 6m³ 6m⁵ 5m 6m³ 5f⁵ 7m⁵ 6g 5.6m 1996 6m⁶ 6m 6f 6m⁵ 6g 5m 5m 5g⁵ Aug 14] workmanlike mare: useful performer: inconsistent in 1996, seemingly best effort (in face of stiff task) when seventh of 14 to Rambling Bear in King George Stakes at Goodwood on seventh start: stays 6f: acts on firm ground, possibly unsuited by a soft surface: well beaten both tries in blinkers: has run creditably when sweating and edgy: often races prominently. *R. Boss*

WELSH MOUNTAIN 3 b.g. Welsh Captain 113 – Miss Nelski 84 (Most Secret 68 119) [1995 74: 5m⁵ 5m² 5g³ 5m* 6m 5m² 5g³ 1996 5d 6g 6m⁵ 5.7m 5.1m 6f 6m Oct 23] smallish, good-bodied gelding: fair handicapper on his day: barely stays 6f: acts on good to firm ground: visored 4 of last 5 starts: none too consistent: gelded. *M. J. Heaton-Ellis*

WELTON ARSENAL 4 b.g. Statoblest 120 – Miller's Gait 74§ (Mill Reef 92 (USA) 141) [1995 101: 8g⁵ 6m² 5.1m⁴ 7.6m 7g⁴ 6g² 6g 6m 1996 8s 7g* 8d⁴ 7.6f⁵ 7g⁶ 7g 8.1s² 7m⁴ 8g Nov 2] sturdy gelding: fairly useful handicapper: won minor event at Warwick in April under fine ride from R. Hughes, produced to lead well inside final 1f, barely coming off bridle: joined K. Bishop after final start: effective at 6f and 7f: acts on firm and soft ground: visored (soundly beaten) final start: often travels well but finds little: a tricky ride, and not one to trust implicitly. *M. R. Channon*

WELVILLE 3 b.c. Most Welcome 131 – Miss Top Ville (FR) (Top Ville 129) 94 + [1995 87p: 5m 5m² 6g* 1996 7m² Apr 16] rangy colt: bit backward, improved when head second of 13 to Sky Dome in handicap at Newmarket, making most and looking sure to win over 1f out: not seen out afterwards: should stay 1m: looked capable of better still. *P. J. Makin*

WENTBRIDGE LAD (IRE) 6 b.g. Coquelin (USA) 121 – Cathryn's Song 72 (Prince Tenderfoot (USA) 126) [1995 68, a80: 10.8d⁵ 9.9m⁴ 8f³ a9.4g² 8f² 8g² 9.2f⁵ a– a7g* 7.1m³ a6g⁵ 8f a7g² a8.5g⁵ a8.5g* 7.6m* 10m³ 8.1m³ 8m⁵ 7.6m⁴ 8m⁵ 10.3d³ 8.1g 8d⁵ 11.9s⁶ 10.4m 8.9g 12m a8.5g 1996 a7g 8m² 8g⁴ 8m 8g 7.6g³ 8g² a9.4g⁵ 10.3m² a9.4g 7.1g² 8g 10.3m⁶ 7m⁴ 10m 7.6m² 8m³ 8d⁵ Aug 25] lengthy gelding: fair handicapper: put up a number of creditable efforts in 1996 without winning a race: effective at 7f to 1¼m: acts on soft and firm ground and on fibresand (winner 6 times at Wolverhampton though disappointing there in 1996): often wears blinkers/visor, but effective without: has run well for amateur: normally held up: carries head high: tough. *P. D. Evans*

WE'RE JOKEN 4 b.f. Statoblest 120 – Jay Gee Ell 78 (Vaigly Great 127) [1995 – 55, a50: a7g⁶ 7.1g 6g* 6.1m a6g* 6g* 6.1g⁴ 6f⁵ 6g a6g a6g 1996 a6g a6g Jan 29] leggy filly: modest sprint handicapper: well beaten in 1996: covered by Foxhound. *S. Gollings*

WESLEY'S LAD (IRE) 2 b. or br.g. (May 14) Classic Secret (USA) 91 – 55 + Galouga (FR) (Lou Piguet (FR) 126) [1996 10.2d⁴ 8.1s a8g³ Nov 4] IR 2,000Y: second foal: dam unraced: modest maiden: probably stays 10.2f. *J. Neville*

WESTCOURT MAGIC 3 b.g. Emarati (USA) 74 – Magic Milly 60 (Simply 105 Great (FR) 122) [1995 99: 5m 5f 7.5g 5m* 5m* 5m* 6f* 5g² 5g* 5s² 1996 5g* 5m³ 6f 6m 6d⁵ 5m Sep 11] sturdy gelding: useful performer: won listed event at Haydock in April, and ran well when third of 11 to Cool Jazz in Palace House Stakes at Newmarket following month: not at best afterwards: successful over 6f, best form at 5f: acts on firm going: rather an edgy type, and often taken early to post: usually a front runner. *M. W. Easterby*

WESTCOURT PRINCESS 4 b.f. Emarati (USA) 74 – Petrol 73 (Troy 137) 52 + [1995 59: a7g a6g⁴ 6m 10m 9f⁴ 9.9m* 8.5g 9.9m² 10m* 10.4g⁴ 10.5s 8.9g 1996 9.9m⁴ 9.9m 8.5m⁴ May 10] workmanlike filly: modest handicapper: stays 1¼m: acts on firm ground and fibresand, seemingly not on a soft surface: occasionally blinkered, including on final 4-y-o start (when set too strong a pace): has worn sliding bar bit: takes good hold: usually front runner. *M. W. Easterby*

WESTERN COUNTRY 4 ch.g. Beveled (USA) – Country Singer (Town And – Country 124) [1995 –: 8m 10.2f 1996 8.2m 8d 12s Oct 26] big, workmanlike gelding: of no account. *E. A. Wheeler*

WESTERN DYNASTY 10 ch.g. Hotfoot 126 – Northern Dynasty 65 (Breeders Dream 116) [1995 NR 1996 11.8d 14.1g 13.3s May 29] big, lengthy gelding: fair handicapper (rated 76) at 7 yrs for M. Ryan, winner twice: well beaten in 1996, leaving S. Mellor after second start. *E. A. Wheeler*

WESTERN GENERAL 5 ch.g. Cadeaux Genereux 131 – Patsy Western 81 78 (Precocious 126) [1995 83: 8m* 8.5m 8m 10.5g³ 8m 10.4m² 10.3m⁴ 1996 10.3d 8g⁵ 8g 8.3g* Jun 12] quite attractive gelding: fair handicapper: best 5-y-o effort when winning at Hamilton in June, leading well inside final 1f: effective at 1m to 10.5f: acts on good to firm and soft ground: tried blinkered, at least as effective without: inconsistent. *Miss M. K. Milligan*

WESTERN HORIZON (USA) 4 ch.f. Gone West (USA) – Norette (North- 36 fields (USA)) [1995 49: 6.9d⁴ a8g⁴ 9.7m⁵ 9.9m 14.1g 12.1f⁴ 10f⁵ 12f⁴ 13.1h² 13.4d 14s⁶ 13.6f³ a12g 1996 9.9m 12m 16.1g 10.1m⁶ 8m 9.7g Jul 3] smallish filly: un-impressive mover: poor maiden: mostly well beaten in handicaps in 1996: should stay beyond 1¾m (pulled very hard over 2m): acts on hard and dead ground, seemingly not on equitrack: blinkered (not discredited) eleventh 3-y-o start. *C. E. Brittain*

WESTERN HOUR (USA) 2 b.f. (Feb 27) Gone West (USA) – Out On The 77 Town (USA) (Spend A Buck (USA)) [1996 7g⁶ 7m³ Oct 17] tall, rather unfurnished filly: third foal: dam, ran 5 times in North America, sister to top Canadian 2-y-o Medaille d'Or and half-sister to dual Canadian Horse of the Year L'Enjoleur: fair form in minor event at Kempton (starting slowly then keeping on steadily without being given a hard race) and maiden at Redcar (keeping on having been ridden 3f out) in the autumn: will be suited by 1m+. *P. W. Chapple-Hyam*

WESTERN PLAYBOY 4 b.g. Law Society (USA) 130 – Reine d'Beaute 97 – (Caerleon (USA) 132) [1995 –p: 10m 1996 10f⁵ 10.2g⁶ 11.8m Jun 3] tall, lengthy gelding: poor walker: off course over 12 months and gelded before reappearance: signs of ability when not knocked about in maidens first 2 4-y-o starts: last of 16 in handicap at Leicester on final outing: sold 1,600 gns Ascot July Sales, resold 3,200 gns Malvern October Sales and joined R. J. Baker: should stay further than 1¼m. *R. Hannon*

WESTERN SAL 4 b.f. Salse (USA) 128 – Patsy Western 81 (Precocious 126) 73 [1995 75: 7g³ 7.1m² 8.3m³ 10m* 10d 1996 10d⁴ 10.3m³ 12m* 12m⁶ 12.3m⁴ 16.1m⁵ 14.8d³ 14m Aug 31] close-coupled filly: has a fluent, round action: fair handicapper: won at Newmarket in June, squeezing through to challenge final 1f: stays 14.8f: acts on good to firm ground and dead: inconsistent: covered by First Trump. *J. L. Harris*

WESTERN SONATA (IRE) 3 b.f. Alzao (USA) 117 – Musique Classique 63 (USA) 100 (Exclusive Native (USA)) [1995 NR 1996 8s⁶ 6.5v a8.5g³ Feb 28] sixth foal: half-sister to French 1m (at 2 yrs) and 1¼m winner Mutual Consent (by Reference Point) and a winner in Sweden by Shareef Dancer: dam, 7f winner better at 1¼m, closely related to Claude Monet out of Pouliches/Diane winner Madelia: sixth of 20 then seventh of 11 (disqualified after jockey failed to weigh in) in minor events at Cagnes early in year: joint favourite, modest form when 11 lengths third of 11 to Yeoman Oliver in maiden at Wolverhampton on British debut, always well there. *Lord Huntingdon*

WESTERN VENTURE (IRE) 3 ch.g. Two Timing (USA) 124 – Star Gazing 55 (IRE) (Caerleon (USA) 132) [1995 67: 6m³ 5g³ 5f* 5m 1996 7f 7.1d 7d⁶ 8f² 8.3g² 9m 8m a6g 8.1s a12g⁵ Nov 16] quite attractive gelding: has a quick action: modest performer: left J. W. Payne after fifth start: ran poorly for new yard: likely to stay further than 1m: acts on firm ground. *R. M. McKellar*

WEST-HATCH-SPIRIT 3 b.f. Forzando 122 – Fairy Ballerina (Fairy King – (USA)) [1995 NR 1996 10m Jul 29] second foal: dam Irish 2-y-o 7f winner: 66/1, showed little in maiden at Nottingham. *S. G. Knight*

WEST HUMBLE 3 ch.f. Pharly (FR) 130 – Humble Pie 92 (Known Fact (USA) 93
135) [1995 81p: 7g³ 1996 7m* 7g⁵ 7m³ Jun 3] leggy, quite attractive filly: fairly
useful form: won maiden at Kempton in April by 4 lengths, quickening to lead over
1f out: tongue tied down, much her better subsequent effort when third of 6 to
Bewitching in minor event at Leicester, improving to challenge over 2f out then
faltering noticeably closing stages: should stay beyond 7f: keen sort. *Lady Herries*

WESTMINSTER (IRE) 4 ch.g. Nashamaa 113 – Our Galadrial (Salmon Leap 70
(USA) 131) [1995 65: 12.3m² 12.1g* 12m⁴ 10g⁵ 1996 10s 11.6m* 12.1f⁴ 12m
11.8m³ 12m² Jul 31] angular gelding: fair performer: won claimer at Windsor in
June: pulled hard early on and found less than expected in seller on final start: stays
12.1f: acts on good to firm ground, no form in 3 runs on soft: often visored/blinkered:
normally held up. *M. H. Tompkins*

WEST RIVER (USA) 2 ch.f. (Feb 19) Gone West (USA) – Rixe River (USA) –
(Irish River (FR) 131) [1996 6g Jul 10] 240,000 francs Y: leggy filly: fourth foal:
closely related to useful French 1m winner River Waki (by Miswaki): dam French
10.5f and 1½m winner, also second in listed event: 40/1 and bit backward, always
towards rear in 17-runner Newmarket maiden: sent to France. *P. A. Kelleway*

WET PATCH (IRE) 4 b. or br.g. Common Grounds 118 – Disco Girl (FR) 68
(Green Dancer (USA) 132) [1995 68: 9.7m 10g² 8.3g⁴ 11.6m⁴ 10g² 10m⁴ 10m* 10m⁵
9m a10g* 1996 a12g a10g 9.7s³ a10g⁴ 10m² 9.7m 10.8f² 10f⁴ 10g 10m⁵ 10m 10m³
10g 10.3g Oct 26] sturdy, good-bodied gelding: has a round action: fair handicapper
at his best: well below form from 5 of last 6 starts, and sold 3,800 gns Newmarket Autumn
Sales: needs further than 9f (stays 11.6f): acts on firm ground (probably on soft) and
on equitrack: usually held up. *R. Hannon*

WEY RIVER MIST 3 b.f. General Wade 93 – Donroya 55 (Don 128) [1995 NR –
1996 6f 8.3m a7g Nov 12] third foal: dam won 1m seller at 2 yrs: well beaten in
maidens. *J. J. Bridger*

WHACKFORD SQUEERS 4 ch.g. Komaite (USA) – Manhunt 70 (Posse –
(USA) 130) [1995 66: a8g* a8g⁵ 8m 1996 a8g a7g a8g 8f⁶ Jun 3] most disappoint-
ing since winning median auction maiden at Lingfield early in 1995 for C. Cyzer.
D. Nicholls

WHAT A FUSS 3 b.g. Great Commotion (USA) 123 – Hafwah (Gorytus (USA) –
132) [1995 NR 1996 10g 10m a9.4g³ 8m a8.5g² a7g Oct 28] good-topped gelding: a70
third foal: half-brother to 4-y-o 6f and 7f winner Courageous Dancer (by Cadeaux
Genereux) and 9f winner Rupan (by Taufan): dam unraced half-sister to dam of Sure
Blade: fair maiden at best, form only when placed twice at Wolverhampton: retained
12,500 gns Newmarket Autumn Sales: stays 9.4f: acts on fibresand. *B. Hanbury*

WHAT A NIGHTMARE (IRE) 4 gr.g. Petorius 117 – Mysterious Lady (Mel- –
yno 130) [1995 66, a70: a9.4g⁴ a9.4g³ a7g* a6g a8g⁴ a7g⁶ a7g² a7g* a7g² a7g*
7.6m* 7m* 7m³ 7d a7g³ a7g a7g 1996 a8g⁵ a7g⁵ a8g a7g⁶ a7g⁴ a8.5g a7g Aug 17]
sparely-made gelding: shows a markedly round action: won 5 times in 1995 for
J. Glover: well below form in 1996, and sold 1,700 gns Newmarket Autumn Sales:
effective at 7f to 9.4f: acts on good to firm and soft ground and on fibresand: usually
visored/blinkered nowadays. *P. Howling*

WHATASHOWMAN (IRE) 4 b.g. Exhibitioner 111 – Whatawoman (Tumble –
Wind (USA)) [1995 NR 1996 8g 10.2g 10f Jun 21] first foal: dam unraced: poor form
in 3 NH Flat races, blinkered (looked very reluctant) final occasion: well held in
sellers and claimer on flat: sold (S. Kettlewell to S. Robinson) 1,000 gns Doncaster
August Sales. *S. E. Kettlewell*

WHATEVER'S RIGHT (IRE) 7 b.g. Doulab (USA) 115 – Souveniers 68
(Relko 136) [1995 75, a68: 8m a8g* 8m⁵ 7g* 7m³ 7f³ 7m² 7.1m³ 7m⁴ 7g a7g² a8g² a71
1996 7m 10g 8.3m 7f* a7g* 6.9m² 7g⁴ 7m Sep 19] workmanlike gelding: fair handicapper: won apprentice race at Warwick and minor event at Lingfield in July: best
form at 7f/1m: acts on equitrack, firm and dead ground: blinkered (well beaten) once
as 4-y-o: occasionally bandaged: usually makes running/races close up: genuine and
consistent. *M. D. I. Usher*

WHAT HAPPENED WAS 2 b.f. (Apr 21) Deploy 131 – Berberana 68 (Never 82 ?
So Bold 135) [1996 5.1f³ 5.2g³ 6m⁵ 6g⁴ 6m² 5f² 5m* 5.7m⁴ 7m* Sep 20] 4,000F,
1,600Y: neat filly: unimpressive mover: has a quick action: second living foal: dam,

2-y-o 6f winner, out of half-sister to very smart So Factual: modest form on most starts: stayed on strongly, getting up on line, when winning maiden auction event at Beverley in July: probably improved good deal when winning minor event at Ayr in September, in first two throughout in race run at steady pace and running on gamely: almost certainly needs further than 6f: acts on good to firm ground, unraced on a soft surface. *Martyn Meade*

WHAT JIM WANTS (IRE) 3 b.g. Magical Strike (USA) 114 – Sally Gone 39 (IRE) (Last Tycoon 131) [1995 –: a7g 5g 7f 7.1d⁶ 10m 7.1s 1996 12.1d⁶ 12m⁴ 14.1m³ 13.8s⁴ 14.1m 15.1m⁶ 12.4m² 11.9m 18g Oct 21] smallish gelding: poor mover: poor maiden: should stay further than 1¾m: acts on good to firm and dead ground. *J. J. O'Neill*

WHAT'S THAT AMY 2 b.f. (May 4) Sizzling Melody 117 – Lady Pennington – 51 (Blue Cashmere 129) [1996 6d a7g Sep 9] third foal: half-sister to modest 6f winner Penny's Wishing (by Clantime): dam, probably stayed 7f, ran only at 2 yrs: well beaten. *N. Bycroft*

WHAT'S THE VERDICT (IRE) 4 b.g. Law Society (USA) 130 – Cecina 100 73 (Welsh Saint 126) [1995 73: a10g³ 12.3m⁵ 10.8g² 10g* 1996 a12g² Jan 12] tall gelding: fair performer: probably ran creditably when 13 lengths second of 6 in minor event at Southwell on only 4-y-o start, leading for over 1m: probably stays 1½m: acts on good to firm and dead ground and the all-weather: sometimes early to post: takes keen hold, and best allowed to stride on: carried head awkwardly when winning in 1995. *M. Johnston*

WHERE'S WALLY (IRE) 2 ch.g. (Apr 7) Archway (IRE) 115 – Zanskar (Gods- 42 walk (USA) 130) [1996 6g 6m 5s² 5m⁶ Aug 14] IR 6,200Y: tall gelding: half-brother to fair 5f to 7f performer Iron King (by Tender King) and 7f to 8.3f winner White Creek (by Don't Forget Me): dam Irish 2-y-o 5f winner: poor plater: best effort on soft ground: blinkered last 2 starts, flashing tail in middle of race first occasion: sold 2,000 gns Doncaster September Sales: sent to Holland. *J. Berry*

WHICKSEY PERRY 3 b.g. Presidium 124 – Phamilla (IRE) (Bellypha 130) – [1995 83: 5d* 5m* 5m* 5d³ 5m⁶ 5g 5d 1996 5d⁶ May 6] leggy, lengthy gelding: unimpressive mover: fairly useful 5f performer as 2-y-o: stiff task, well beaten in minor event at Haydock only 3-y-o start. *J. Berry*

WHIPPERS DELIGHT (IRE) 8 ch.g. King Persian 107 – Crashing Juno – (Crash Course 128) [1995 NR 1996 a12g⁴ Dec 30] leggy gelding: mainly races over jumps nowadays: no promise on return to flat. *G. F. H. Charles-Jones*

WHIRLAWHILE (USA) 2 b.c. (Apr 29) Silver Hawk (USA) 123 – My Tur- 62 p bulent Beau (USA) (Beau's Eagle (USA)) [1996 8m Sep 26] $140,000Y: fourth foal: brother to a winner in USA and half-brother to another by Alysheba: dam minor stakes winner and placed in Grade 2 1m event, half-sister to Breeders' Cup Turf winner Prized: 12/1, left behind from 3f out when around 11 lengths eighth of 10 in Panama City in steadily-run maiden at Pontefract: should do better. *E. A. L. Dunlop*

WHIRL POOL 2 b.f. (May 11) Superpower 113 – Rainbow Trout 76 (Comedy – Star (USA) 121) [1996 7m a7g Nov 4] sparely-made filly: fourth living foal: dam maiden stayed 6f: showed little in maiden (moved poorly to post) and seller: sold 500 gns Doncaster November Sales. *M. J. Camacho*

WHISPERED MELODY 3 b.f. Primo Dominie 121 – Sing Softly 112 (Luthier 60 126) [1995 NR 1996 7d⁵ 8.2m⁵ 10.1g a9.4g⁴ 7m⁴ 6.1m⁶ 5m Sep 26] unfurnished filly: closely related to useful hurdler Dominant Serenade (by Dominion) and half-sister to Chester Cup winner Top Cees (by Shirley Heights): dam 6f winner at 2 yrs later very useful over middle distances: modest maiden handicapper: sold (P. Harris to R. Akehurst) 9,000 gns Newmarket Autumn Sales: best efforts at 6f/7f: acts on good to firm and dead ground and on fibresand. *P. W. Harris*

WHISPERING DAWN 3 b.f. Then Again 126 – Summer Sky 75 (Skyliner 117) 71 [1995 66: 5g⁴ 6g 6.1g* 6g⁴ 8m 8g* 10d 9m6 8.2g³ 8m 8d 8g⁶ 9g* 8.1s⁴ Nov 7] tall, leggy filly: has a round action: fair handicapper: off course 5½ months after second start: best effort when winning 21-runner apprentice race at Newmarket in November: creditable fourth of 14 at Musselburgh 6 days later, racing more prominently: stays 9f: acts on soft ground: usually held up. *M. R. Channon*

WHISPER LOW (IRE)   2 ch.f. (Apr 22) Shalford (IRE) 124§ – Idle Gossip   63
(Runnett 125) [1996 5m 5m 5f⁴ 5d a5g a5g⁵ a6g Dec 27] IR 3,000Y: strong, smallish   a–
filly: half-sister to winning sprinters Metal Boys (by Krayyan) and Heathyards
Magic (by Magical Strike): dam never ran: easily best effort when fourth in maiden
at Beverley, leading 3f: off course nearly 3 months, last all subsequent outings: will
probably be suited by sharp 5f: acts on firm ground. *R. Hollinshead*

WHITECHAPEL (USA)   8 b.g. Arctic Tern (USA) 126 – Christchurch (FR) 88   92
(So Blessed 130) [1995 94+: 12g⁴ 12m 13.9m 13.3d* 12d⁴ 12m³ 12d³ 12m 1996
13.3m⁶ 11.9f 13.3m³ 12g 12s⁴ Nov 17] big, lengthy gelding: useful handicapper:
creditable staying-on third of 12 to Kutta and Ballynakelly in strongly-run Tote
Autumn Cup at Newbury on third start: respectable fourth in listed race at Bordeaux
final one: effective at 1½m to 2m: acts on fibresand, good to firm ground (probably
not very firm) and soft: sometimes makes the running: game. *Lord Huntingdon*

WHITE CLARET   4 b.g. Alzao (USA) 117 – Vivid Impression (Cure The Blues   –
(USA)) [1995 8v⁵ 10s⁶ 9d 11.9g* 12g² 14f² 16s 1996 12m 15.4g 14.1s Oct 31] IR
18,000Y: ex-Irish gelding: third foal: half-brother to Irish 1m winner Puppet Theatre
(by Theatrical): dam Irish 6f (at 2 yrs) and 1¼m winner: fair handicapper (rated 69)
at 3 yrs for N. Meade, winning at Downpatrick: below form here, gambled on but
tailed off final start: stays 1¾m: best form on a sound surface, and acts on firm going:
blinkered (poor effort) second 3-y-o start. *R. Akehurst*

WHITE EMIR   3 b.g. Emarati (USA) 74 – White African (Carwhite 127) [1995   90
86: 5g 5m* 5m² 5g⁶ 6m² 5g* 5.2d 6m³ 1996 6g 5g⁵ 6m⁵ 6m⁴ 5f⁵ 6g² 5.1m² 5m³ 7d
6m² 5d Oct 12] good-quartered gelding: fairly useful handicapper: stays 6f: acts on
firm ground: blinkered since sixth 3-y-o start: twice ran poorly (finding little) when
having second race in quick succession at 2 yrs: flashes tail: sometimes wanders
under pressure: nervy sort: races prominently. *B. J. Meehan*

WHITEGATE'S SON   2 ch.g. (Feb 4) Minster Son 130 – Whitegates Lady (Le   –
Coq d'Or 101) [1996 6g 6m 7f Nov 5] close-coupled, workmanlike gelding: seventh
reported foal: dam winning 2½m hurdler: well beaten in maidens. *B. Ellison*

WHITE HARE   3 b.f. Indian Ridge 123 – Pomade 79 (Luthier 126) [1995 NR   56
1996 7.1d 8m³ 6g 7.1s Oct 5] 9,200F, 8,700Y: smallish, lengthy filly: half-sister to
several winners, including 1m winner Face Up (by Top Ville) and middle-distance
stayer Spikenard (by Slip Anchor): dam disqualified 9f winner on sole outing:
modest form when 11 lengths third of 9 to Glen Parker at Pontefract, not given hard
race: unsuited by drop to 6f next time: tailed off on handicap debut at Haydock on
final start. *Mrs M. Reveley*

WHITE HEAT   4 b.f. Last Tycoon 131 – Sweeping 104 (Indian King (USA) 128)   –
[1995 57d: 8m⁵ 8.3m 10m 8g 8g 1996 a8g⁶ a13g Feb 1] leggy filly: fair form at best
for M. Heaton-Ellis in 1994 and 1995: well beaten since 3-y-o reappearance: won't
be inconvenienced by a return to distances short of 1m: tried visored: covered by
Mistertopogigo. *W. G. M. Turner*

WHITE HOT   2 b.c. (Jan 30) Weldnaas (USA) 112 – Glowing Reference (Refer-   98
ence Point 139) [1996 6g³ 6m 7.5m* 7m* 8f⁵ Nov 11] 12,500Y: good-bodied colt:
first foal: dam unraced close relative of King Edward VII Stakes winner Private
Tender: off course 10 weeks after second start, greatly improved on return: raced
very prominently and won auction races at Beverley and Goodwood (by a short head)
within a week in September (trained by E. Dunlop): good fifth of 8 in valuable event
at Hollywood Park 7 weeks later: should be suited by 1m+: flashes tail (and has
carried head awkwardly) but is genuine. *Kathy Walsh, USA*

WHITELOCK QUEST   8 b.g. Rainbow Quest (USA) 134 – Sagar 74 (Habitat   –
134) [1995 40: a8g* a8g a8.5g* 1996 a9.4g Mar 2] poor handicapper: well beaten
only 8-y-o outing. *N. E. Berry*

WHITE NEMESIS (IRE)   2 b.f. (Apr 29) Sillery (USA) 122 – Top The Rest   –
(Top Ville 129) [1996 a5g Apr 27] 1,800Y: first foal: dam French 11f winner out of
half-sister to disqualified Irish Oaks winner Sorbus: 25/1, soon behind in seller at
Wolverhampton: sold (Martyn Meade to C. W. C. Elsey) 500 gns Ascot July Sales.
Martyn Meade

WHITE PLAINS (IRE)   3 b.g. Nordico (USA) – Flying Diva 100 (Chief Singer   77
131) [1995 72p: 7g 6m⁵ 6m* 1996 6s³ 7m³ 7d⁵ 7m⁵ 9.7m² 10m³ 10f* 9.9m⁴ 10m⁴

9m* 10m 10f* 10m* 10m Oct 1] good-bodied gelding: fair handicapper: had a good year, winning at Lingfield (apprentices) and Newcastle (minor event) in the summer, and at Leicester (apprentices) and Lingfield in September: sold (M. Bell to M. Pipe) 22,000 gns Newmarket Autumn Sales: should stay 1½m: acts on firm ground: has run well when sweating: often apprentice ridden: consistent: gelded. *M. Bell*

WHITE SEA (IRE)   3 ch.f. Soviet Lad (USA) 94 – Bilander 78 (High Line 125)   79
[1995 76: 7g² 7m⁴ 7.1m³ 8d* 7.3d 1996 12.1d⁴ 12g* 11.5f³ Jun 25] leggy, sparely-made filly: fairly useful handicapper: creditable efforts all 3 starts in 1996, winning at Salisbury in June: stays 12.1f: acts on firm and dead ground: sweating, mounted on track, mulish and early to post before refusing to enter stalls at Goodwood in August: very encouraging winning debut over hurdles for M. Pipe. *P. F. I. Cole*

WHITE SETTLER   3 b.g. Polish Patriot (USA) 128 – Oasis (Valiyar 129) [1995   73 +
62+: 7m⁵ 6m³ 6g 1996 5.1g 10m 7m³ 7.1m* 8g² 6m³ 7g Sep 5] sturdy gelding: fair   a–
handicapper: got up near finish to win at Chepstow in July after travelling smoothly: a little unlucky when never-nearer third of 16 at Salisbury penultimate start: stays 1m, but will prove best at 6f/7f: has raced only on a sound surface: may do better still in 1997. *R. J. Hodges*

WHITE SORREL   5 ro.h. Chilibang 120 – Midnight Imperial (Night Shift   61
(USA)) [1995 69, a87: a6g* a6g* 6g 6m⁵ 5.1g² 5m 6m³ a6g 6g a6g a7g 1996 a7g*   a77
a6g² a7g 5g 7m⁶ 6m 7g⁶ 6g Sep 3] small, stocky horse: fair handicapper: not at best in 1996, coaxed home when winning at Southwell in January: left A. Harrison after seventh outing: stays 7f: goes well on fibresand, has raced only on a sound surface on turf: no improvement in blinkers: tends to hang: inconsistent. *S. E. Kettlewell*

WHITEWATER AFFAIR   3 ch.f. Machiavellian (USA) 123 – Much Too   110
Risky 87 (Bustino 136) [1995 NR 1996 8m² 8m* 10s* 12m⁶ 10m⁴ 11.9m⁵ 12.5d² 12s⁴ Oct 26] tall, raw-boned filly: has a powerful, round action: half-sister to several winners, including 1990 2-y-o 5f and 6f winner Seductress (by Known Fact) and 11f and 13f winner Boy Emperor (by Precocious): dam 2-y-o 7.2f and 1m winner out of half-sister to very smart pair He Loves Me and Wattlefield: smart performer: won maiden at Kempton and listed race at Goodwood in May: sixth of 11 in the Oaks at Epsom and ran well afterwards when 3¾ lengths fourth of 8 to Last Second in Nassau Stakes at Goodwood, fifth of 9 to Key Change in Yorkshire Oaks at York and 4 lengths second of 13 to Annaba in Prix de Royallieu at Longchamp: bandaged, not discredited when fourth of 12 to Salmon Ladder in St Simon Stakes at Newbury on final start, never nearer: stays 12.5f: acts on good to firm ground and soft. *M. R. Stoute*

WHITE WILLOW   7 br.g. Touching Wood (USA) 127 – Dimant Blanche (USA)   62
77 (Gummo (USA) 117) [1995 70, a–: 16.2m³ 16m⁴ 14g 1996 16.1s⁴ Mar 26] sturdy   a–
gelding: impresses in appearance: useful hurdler, winner (landed odds in claimer) in December: fair handicapper on flat, bit below form only 7-y-o start: stays 16.2f: acts on any going: no improvement in blinkers/visor: moody and not easiest of rides: joined T. Wall. *Mrs M. Reveley*

WHITLEY GRANGE BOY   3 b.g. Hubbly Bubbly (USA) – Choir (High Top   54
131) [1995 65: 8g 7.9g⁵ a8g³ a5g 1996 8g³ a5² 8.5d 11m May 27] tall, sparely-made gelding: modest maiden: stays 1m: hung badly left penultimate start: possibly temperamental. *J. L. Eyre*

WHITTLE ROCK   3 b.f. Rock City 120 – Lurking 69 (Formidable (USA) 125)   91
[1995 74: 5g 5d³ 5m⁵ 5g² 5.1g* 5m 6.1m³ 6.1m³ 5g⁴ 5s² 1996 6d 6g² 6.1g 7f 6m* 6d⁶ 6m 6m⁶ 7d* 7.6d Aug 31] strong, lengthy filly: fairly useful handicapper: won at Ripon in June, gamely making most: left E. Alston's stable after seventh outing: better for new yard, winning at Newmarket in August despite wandering: stays 7f: acts on good to firm and soft ground: well beaten in blinkers: quietly to post final outing. *Mrs M. Reveley*

WHITTLE TIMES   2 ch.f. (Feb 12) Timeless Times (USA) 99 – La Pepper 63   –
(Workboy 123) [1996 5d⁶ 6g 5f⁵ a5g⁶ 5m³ Jul 19] 5,200Y: compact filly: half-sister to sprint winners 3-y-o Abbott of Whalley (at 2 yrs) and Hannah's Usher (both by Marching On) and ungenuine Blazing Belle (by Belfort): dam, plater, won over 1m at 2 yrs: of little account: visored last 2 starts. *E. J. Alston*

WHIZZ KID   2 b.f. (Mar 11) Puissance 110 – Panienka (POL) 70 (Dom Racine   59 ?
(FR) 121) [1996 5f⁶ a5g² 6s⁵ 5m* 5m³ 6m⁴ 6m 5.2m 5.3f a6g⁴ 7m⁴ Sep 25] 400Y: tall

filly: second foal: dam suited by test of stamina on flat, also successful over hurdles: modest performer: won seller at Windsor in June: stays 6f: acts on good to firm and soft ground and fibresand: inconsistent. *J. J. Bridger*

WHO (IRE) 2 b. or br.g. (Apr 30) Don't Forget Me 127 – Femme de Fer (USA) 80 – (Mr Leader (USA)) [1996 7g 6m 7d Aug 23] IR 3,000F, 1,300Y: sixth foal: dam, little form after 7f debut, sister to smart middle-distance performer Leadburn: well beaten in sellers: unseated rider and bolted before final start. *T. D. Easterby*

WHOTHEHELLISHARRY 3 ch.g. Rich Charlie 117 – Ballagarrow Girl 66 – (North Stoke 130) [1995 –: 5f 8.5m⁵ 8.1g a8g⁴ 1996 9f⁴ 10.1g⁶ 11f Sep 27] quite good-topped gelding: little worthwhile form. *J. Berry*

WHO TOLD VICKY (IRE) 2 b.f. (Apr 10) Anita's Prince 126 – Little Club 50 (King of Clubs 124) [1996 5f³ a5g² a5g² a5g* 6f³ 5.3f Aug 6] IR 1,000Y: fourth foal: dam unraced: modest form: won seller at Southwell in May: stays 6f: acts on firm and fibresand: sent to Czech Republic. *J. S. Moore*

WHYNOTRISKME 2 b.f. (Mar 9) Risk Me (FR) 127 – Spirit Away 54 (Dom- – inion 123) [1996 6m 7m Aug 9] 1,000Y: workmanlike filly: second foal: dam 1½m winner: tailed off in maiden auction and seller. *R. Harris*

WHY O SIX 2 b.g. (Jan 28) Efisio 120 – Scotch Imp 83 (Imperial Fling (USA) 51 116) [1996 5m 6m 6s⁶ 6d 6m⁴ Oct 29] 9,200Y: strong, good-bodied gelding: first living foal: dam suited by 6f to 7f: modest form: stays 6f: acts on good to firm and soft ground: very unruly to post (ran well) third start: gambled on (below form) on fourth: gelded and may do better. *R. A. Fahey*

WICKINS 6 b.g. Petong 126 – Bo' Babbity 75 (Strong Gale 116) [1995 NR 1996 65 8g⁶ 10m Sep 18] trained at 2 yrs by G. Lewis before being moved to Jersey: prolific winner there, and won 5 races (including Jersey Derby) in 1996 for J. Arthur: staying-on sixth of 15 in handicap at Pontefract on return here: last of 17 at Sandown (apprentices, raced too freely) 15 days later: stays 1¼m well: effective in blinkers at 2 yrs. *J. Collingridge*

WICKLOW BOY (IRE) 5 b.g. Roi Danzig (USA) – Pickety Place 83 (Prince §§ Tenderfoot (USA) 126) [1995 36: a16g⁶ a12g³ a12g a13g 1996 a16g a12g Feb 19] sturdy gelding: poor maiden: has become an arrant rogue, refusing to race final outing: sold 575 gns Ascot December Sales. *R. J. Weaver*

WIGBERTO (IRE) 4 ch.c. Old Vic 136 – Royal Loft 105 (Homing 130) [1995 – 96?: 7d 8.1s³ a7g 1996 6s Mar 22] compact colt: fairly useful at 2 yrs for D. Loder: possibly flattered when showing best 3-y-o form for Major D. Chappell: soundly beaten in handicap at Doncaster only start in 1996. *J. L. Eyre*

WIGHT 3 gr.f. Sharrood (USA) 124 – Wrangbrook (Shirley Heights 130) [1995 – 78+: 7d* 7m³ 1996 8s⁴ 10g⁵ 10g⁶ 12m Sep 13] angular filly: has a roundish action: fair form at 2 yrs: showed little worthwhile form (last of 5 in listed race at Newbury second start) in 1996: bred to stay middle distances: sold 5,400 gns Newmarket December Sales. *R. Hannon*

WIJARA (IRE) 4 b.c. Waajib 121 – Nawara 75 (Welsh Pageant 132) [1995 108: 108 9m⁵ 10m⁵ 10d⁴ 9d* 9m³ 1996 8d² 10g 8m⁴ 10s² 10s⁴ 10.3f* Sep 13] sturdy, quite attractive colt: impresses in appearance: powerful galloper with a rather round action: useful performer: best 4-y-o efforts when second to First Island and Captain Horatius in listed races at Doncaster and Goodwood (beaten 2½ lengths): effective at 1m to 1¼m: acts on good to firm and soft ground: best efforts when racing prominently/making running. *R. Hannon*

WILAWANDER 3 ch.c. Nashwan (USA) 135 – Wilayif (USA) 75 (Danzig 106 (USA)) [1995 89: 7g⁵ 7m² 7d⁴ 1996 12m⁴ 12m² 12f² 16.2m⁴ 13.8g* 13.9m² 14.6m⁶ Sep 14] tall, quite attractive colt: fluent mover: useful performer: made all in maiden at Catterick in July: much better efforts in defeat, close fourth to Gordi in Queen's Vase at Royal Ascot on fourth start and sixth of 11 to Shantou in the St Leger at Doncaster on final one: stays 16.2f: acts on firm and dead ground. *B. W. Hills*

WILCUMA 5 b.g. Most Welcome 131 – Miss Top Ville (FR) (Top Ville 129) 109 [1995 94: 8.1m⁵ 9m³ 8g⁴ 8m 9g⁶ 8.1g* 9g 9d² 1996 8d 8.1d⁵ 10g⁵ 10.4m* 10d² 9s* 10s* Dec 3] sturdy, useful-looking gelding: useful handicapper, better than ever at 5 yrs: won 17-runner £58,200 John Smith's Magnet Cup at York in July by neck from Spirito Libro, leading inside final 1f: off course 3 months afterwards: showed further

John Smith's Magnet Cup (Handicap), York—
Wilcuma (right) and Spirito Libro throw down their challenges inside the final furlong

improvement on return, winning rated stakes at Newbury in October by 2 lengths from Najm Mubeen and listed race at Evry in December: stays 10.4f: acts on good to firm and soft ground: held up: has run well when sweating: consistent. *P. J. Makin*

WILD CITY (USA) 2 b. or br.c. (Mar 7) Wild Again (USA) – Garvin's Gal –
(USA) (Seattle Slew (USA)) [1996 6g May 25] $130,000Y: robust colt: first foal: dam, won at up to 7f in USA, sister to Grade 2 8.5f winner Tokatee and half-sister to Grade 1 2-y-o 6f winner Share The Fantasy: 8/1, burly and green, last of 9 in maiden at Doncaster, slowly into stride. *B. Hanbury*

WILDFIRE (SWI) 5 br.g. Beldale Flutter (USA) 130 – Little White Star (Mill 56
Reef (USA) 141) [1995 59: 12g 12.1g³ 12m 14m a14g⁴ a11g* a13g³ 1996 a11g³ a10g⁴ 12v a11g⁵ a12s⁴ Dec 19] sturdy gelding: has a quick action: modest handicapper: off course 9½ months after second start: stays 1¾m: acts on soft ground and the all-weather: races prominently. *R. Akehurst*

WILD HADEER 2 ch.c. (Mar 24) Hadeer 118 – Wild Moon (USA) (Arctic –
Tern (USA) 126) [1996 6m⁶ 6g Oct 21] 2,100F, 4,500Y: quite good-topped colt: second reported foal: dam French 1m winner: well beaten in maidens at Lingfield. *W. J. Haggas*

WILDMOOR 2 ch.g. (Feb 11) Common Grounds 118 – Impropriety (Law 56 ?
Society (USA) 130) [1996 6m 7f⁶ 8.5g⁴ 10m 7m Oct 2] 11,500Y: good-topped gelding: third foal: half-brother to poor 5-y-o 8.5f winner Portite Sophie (by Doulab): dam unraced half-sister to Fred Darling winner Mahogany: has twice appeared to show modest form: seems to stay 8.5f: blinkered (no form) final outing. *J. D. Bethell*

WILD NETTLE 2 ch.f. (Apr 29) Beveled (USA) – Pink Pumpkin 52 (Tickled 46
Pink 114) [1996 5g 5f⁶ 5m 5.3f 6.1s⁴ 6.9v Nov 11] third foal: dam sprinter: poor maiden: stays 6f: acts on firm and soft ground, tailed off on heavy. *J. C. Fox*

WILD PALM 4 b.g. Darshaan 133 – Tarasova (USA) (Green Forest (USA) 134) 76
[1995 74p: 8.3m⁴ 10m⁵ 8.2d* 8g⁶ 1996 a10g⁵ 10.8d 8m 7g⁴ 6.1m 8m 7m⁵ 7g* 8g* 7f⁴ 7g³ a8g⁵ 7g² 7.3m 7m Oct 5] sturdy, useful-looking gelding: unimpressive mover:

fair handicapper: won at Newmarket (apprentice race, flashed tail) in June and at Yarmouth in July: effective at 7f and 1m: acts on firm ground and dead: usually blinkered/visored: has worn severe noseband/citation bridle and had tongue tied down: gelded. *W. A. O'Gorman*

WILD PROSPECT 8 b.g. Homing 130 – Cappuccilli 111 (Lorenzaccio 130) – [1995 –: 8m 8g 1996 7g a8g Nov 18] smallish, good-quartered gelding: rated 44 in 1994: tailed off in 1995 for B. Rothwell, and no promise on return. *A. Bailey*

WILD RICE 4 b.g. Green Desert (USA) 127 – On Show 92 (Welsh Pageant 132) 93 [1995 92: a7g* a10g* 7m³ 7f* 7m* 7d 1996 7m 7f³ 7m 8m 7m⁶ 7g⁴ Oct 19] strong, good-bodied gelding: fairly useful handicapper: effective at 7f and stays 1¼m: acts on firm ground and equitrack, never going well only start on a soft surface: visored (shaped quite well in Hunt Cup) fourth 4-y-o start: wears bandages: tends to carry head high. *G. Wragg*

WILD RITA 4 ch.f. Risk Me (FR) 127 – Ma Pierrette 77 (Cawston's Clown 113) 85 [1995 74: 8f² 8m³ 8m³ 10g 11.9g* 11.9g⁵ 10.5d³ 12.1s⁴ 1996 11.6m* 12m² 12g² 11.9v 12g² 12s Nov 9] leggy, lengthy filly: fairly useful handicapper: won at Windsor in August, making virtually all: clearly best effort when runner-up in competitive event at Doncaster, finishing strongly, penultimate outing: stays 1½m well: acts on firm and dead ground, probably on heavy. *W. R. Muir*

WILD RUMOUR (IRE) 3 b.f. Sadler's Wells (USA) 132 – Gossiping (USA) – (Chati (USA)) [1995 89p: 7d* 1996 7m 10.4m⁴ 13.4d⁶ Aug 31] big, rangy filly: promising winner on only 2-y-o outing: disappointing in Nell Gwyn Stakes at Newmarket (unimpressive to post), minor event at York (carried head high) and listed rated stakes at Chester (stiffish task, after 3½-month break) in 1996: should stay at least 1¼m: acts on dead ground: wrong in coat last 2 starts: sent to USA. *P. W. Chapple-Hyam*

WILD SKY (IRE) 2 br.c. (May 15) Warning 136 – Erwinna (USA) (Lyphard 75 (USA) 132) [1996 6d³ a7s⁴ Nov 19] 15,000F, IR 19,000Y: small colt: fifth foal: half-brother to 4 winners in Italy, including 3-y-o Er Prince (1¼m, by Prince Rupert): dam French maiden daughter of half-sister to Blushing Groom: staying-on third of 17 in maiden at Doncaster: failed to repeat that form in similar event on equitrack at Lingfield later in month: should stay 7f. *M. J. Heaton-Ellis*

WILD STRAWBERRY 7 ro.m. Ballacashtal (CAN) – Pts Fairway (Runnymede 69 123) [1995 64: a16g⁴ 16m 16.4m⁴ 12m⁴ 13.1f² 12f² 14.4m* 16.2f⁴ 14m² 14m⁶ 11.9g³ 18m 1996 a16g* a16g² a12g³ a16g⁴ Feb 24] tall, workmanlike mare: fair handicapper: won amateurs event at Lingfield in January: finds 1½m a bare minimum, and stays 16.4f: acts on firm ground and equitrack: out of form when tried on dead going and in visor at 3 yrs: reluctant to race over hurdles in May, but genuine and very consistent on flat. *Miss B. Sanders*

WILDWOOD FLOWER 3 b.f. Distant Relative 128 – Tolstoya (Northfields 101 (USA)) [1995 81p: 6g 5s⁶ 6.1d³ 6f* 1996 6m² 6.1g⁴ 6m* 5m² 6m³ 6g* 6m⁵ 6g* 6m⁵ 6g⁵ Oct 19] small, sturdy, lengthy filly: improved into a useful sprint handicapper, winning at Windsor in May, Newmarket (rated stakes) in July and Goodwood in August: first home on far side when very good fifth of 28 to Coastal Bluff in Ayr

Ladbroke Racing Sprint Stakes (Handicap), Goodwood—
a good little 'un, Wildwood Flower, successfully carries top weight of 9-12

Gold Cup: creditable fifth of 15 to Russian Revival in listed race at Newmarket 4 weeks later: stays 6f: acts on firm and dead going: game and reliable. *R. Hannon*

WILFULL LAD (IRE) 3 b.g. Distinctly North (USA) 115 – Lisa's Music 64 d (Abwah 118) [1995 64: 7g 5f* 5m 6m 8h⁵ 1996 7f⁵ 8m³ 7.1d 8m⁶ 6m 10g 8m⁶ Sep 9] workmanlike gelding: modest handicapper at best: sold 3,000 gns Newmarket Autumn Sales: stays 1m, unlikely to get further: acts on firm ground: withdrawn after bolting to post before ladies race seventh intended 3-y-o start: sent to Spain. *Martyn Meade*

WILL DO 3 br.g. Weldnaas (USA) 112 – Philogyny 94 (Philip of Spain 126) [1995 70 NR 1996 6s 6m³ 7f a5g⁵ Dec 5] ninth foal: half-brother to 1m winner Sporting Wednesday (by Martinmas) and 1¼m winner The Footman (by Hotfoot): dam won 5 sprints: fair maiden: off course over 5 months after second start: stays 6f: acts on good to firm ground and equitrack. *Martyn Meade*

WILLIAM'S WELL 2 ch.c. (May 8) Superpower 113 – Catherines Well 99 53 (Junius (USA) 124) [1996 6g 6m 5g 6g 8g 5f³ 5g 6m³ 5d⁴ Nov 8] useful-looking colt: fourth reported foal: half-brother to Occhiobello (by Sadler's Wells), winner abroad at up to 1m: dam sprinter: modest maiden: effective at 5f and 6f: acts on firm and dead ground: blinkered (and improved form) since sixth start: hung fire penultimate outing. *M. W. Easterby*

WILLIAM WALLACE 2 b.c. (Apr 17) Rudimentary (USA) 118 – Irish Impulse 68 (USA) 50 (Irish River (FR) 131) [1996 6g 7m⁶ 7g⁶ 6m³ Aug 3] 10,500F, IR 9,000Y resold 9,500Y, 11,000 2-y-o: quite good-topped colt: unimpressive mover: third foal: dam, poor maiden, daughter of smart staying 2-y-o Exclusively Raised: progressive form: third of 4 in maiden at Hamilton in August: joined D. Haydn Jones: should stay 1m: seemed open to further improvement. *C. Murray*

WILLIE CONQUER 4 ch.g. Master Willie 129 – Maryland Cookie (USA) 101 93 (Bold Hour) [1995 80p: 7m³ 8m⁵ 7g 1996 10m 10g 10m² 12m* 12g* 12g⁵ 12m* Oct 17] smallish, lengthy, good-bodied gelding: has a quick action: fairly useful performer: won minor events at Newbury in August and Goodwood in September and rated stakes at Newmarket (led 1f out, beat Arabian Story ¾ length) in October: stays 1½m well: acts on good to firm ground (unraced on soft surface since debut): held up. *R. Akehurst*

WILLIE MILES 3 b.g. Dancing Dissident (USA) 119 – Madam Bold (Never So 78 ? Bold 135) [1995 NR 1996 6m³ 7.1d a6g 6f Sep 7] 10,000Y: tall, rather unfurnished gelding: second foal: half-brother to 1994 2-y-o 5f winner Rigsby (by Fools Holme), 5f winner at 2 yrs: dam (unraced) from family of Sigy and Sonoma: bandaged behind and in need of race, started slowly before staying on well closing stages when third of 7 in maiden at Redcar: failed by a long way to repeat the form. *J. W. Watts*

WILLIE RUSHTON 3 ch.f. Master Willie 129 – Amberush 41 (No Rush) [1995 60 63: 5f 7g⁴ 7f³ 7.1m² 8m⁴ 10g* 1996 a8g³ a10g⁵ 10.2g 11.6m² 12m Jun 13] lengthy filly: modest handicapper: stays 11.6f: acts on equitrack and on good to firm ground, yet to race on a soft surface: often bandaged behind: takes keen hold: sometimes taken down early: has joined T. Powell. *G. L. Moore*

WILLISA 3 ch.f. Polar Falcon (USA) 126 – Ghassanah 73 (Pas de Seul 133) [1995 66 67: 5m⁶ 6m³ 6f⁴ 6g 6g 7.3d 1996 7m* 8m 6g⁶ 7m⁶ 8m⁵ 8m Sep 7] tall, unfurnished filly: fair performer: made all in maiden at Thirsk in April: stays 1m: acts on firm and dead ground: sold 9,200 gns Newmarket December Sales. *J. D. Bethell*

WILLOW DALE (IRE) 3 b.f. Danehill (USA) 126 – Miss Willow Bend (USA) 82 d (Willow Hour (USA)) [1995 80: 6g 5g⁴ 5f* 6m* 6.5m⁶ 5.2d* 6d 7m 1996 8g 6m⁵ 5m³ 6g 5f 5g 6.1s Oct 31] leggy, close-coupled filly: fairly useful handicapper: well held after third 3-y-o start: seems to stay 7f: acts on firm and dead ground, stiff task on soft: tried visored and blinkered, no improvement: sometimes flashes tail. *D. R. C. Elsworth*

WILLRACK FARRIER 4 b.f. Lugana Beach 116 – Bonny Bright Eyes 58 – (Rarity 129) [1995 NR 1996 a8g a6g a6g 5.7g May 20] sturdy, workmanlike filly: won first 2 races (over 5f) at 2 yrs for Jack Berry but subsequently lost her form: well beaten all 4 starts on belated return: covered by Timeless Times. *B. J. Meehan*

WILLSKIP (USA) 2 b.g. (Mar 6) Minshaanshu Amad (USA) 91§ – Eighty Lady (USA) (Flying Lark (USA)) [1996 6m 5m⁵ 7.5m Sep 18] 5,000F, 8,000 2-y-o:

smallish gelding: brother to Italian winner (including at 1m) Zizzi Canguro and half-brother to 3 winners in USA: dam winning sprinter in USA, including at 2 yrs: well beaten in maidens: swerved badly left stalls on debut: rather edgy last time. *J. Berry*

WILL TO WIN   2 b.f. (Mar 7) Mazilier (USA) 107 – Adana (FR) (Green Dancer 54
(USA) 132) [1996 5g⁵ 5m⁴ 6g³ 5f³ 6m 5.1m² 5d³ 6m a5g² 6.1s a5g a7g a6s³ Dec 19]
3,800Y: unfurnished filly: sister to Italian 4-y-o Mazada (5f winner at 2 yrs, 9f at
3 yrs) and half-sister to Anadax (by Mummy's Game), a fair 1m winner here later
prolifically successful in Italy: dam French 9.5f winner: modest maiden: stays 6f:
acts on fibresand, and on firm and dead ground: sometimes bandaged behind:
unseated rider then bolted to post fifth outing: none too consistent. *P. G. Murphy*

WILL YOU DANCE   2 b.f. (Feb 11) Shareef Dancer (USA) 135 – Padelia 79 p
(Thatching 131) [1996 7m⁶ 7.9g² Oct 9] strong, lengthy filly: has plenty of scope:
sixth known foal: closely related to useful miler Polar Boy (by Northern Baby) and
half-sister to fairly useful stayer Shining High (by Shirley Heights): dam never ran:
fair from both starts, ½-length second of 13, clear, to Cybertechnology in steadily-
run median auction maiden at York last time, plenty to do entering straight when
pushed along then staying on: will improve given greater test of stamina than she
faced at 2 yrs, and can win a race. *J. L. Dunlop*

WILLY STAR (BEL)   6 b.g. Minstrel Star – Landing Power (Hill's Forecast 91) 55
[1995 8.5s 7s⁶ 8g 7g⁴ 10.5g⁴ 10.5d⁶ 12s³ 10f 13.5g⁵ 9f 1996 10f³ 9.2g² 10m⁶ 11.6m⁴
8m 12m⁵ 10f 11m⁴ Oct 29] tall, leggy ex-Belgian gelding: first known foal: dam won
twice in Belgium: poor form in Germany and Belgium (last 3 starts) in 1995: modest
form at best here, including in sellers: stays 11.6f: has raced only on a sound surface
in Britain: tried blinkered in 1995: looked none too genuine (found little) sixth start:
winning selling hurdler. *Mrs S. J. Smith*

WINDBORN   2 b.f. (Mar 20) Superpower 113 – Chablisse 69 (Radetzky 123) 51
[1996 5g⁶ 5g³ 5.1f⁶ 6d⁵ 5.7g 5g² 6m a6g² a6g² 7m a7g⁴ a6g³ Dec 30] 9,500Y: small, a49
angular filly: unimpressive mover: fourth foal: half-sister to 3 winners, including 7f
(at 2 yrs) to 1¼m winner Ooh Ah Cantona (by Crofthall): dam, 1¼m to 1½m winner,
half-sister to useful sprinter Tuxford Hideaway (dam of Branston Abby): modest
maiden: trained by K. McAuliffe until after ninth start: best form at up to 6f: acts on
all-weather, may well be suited by a soft surface on turf: blinkered (stiff task) final
outing. *C. N. Allen*

WIND CHEETAH (USA)   2 b. or br.c. (Mar 14) Storm Cat (USA) – Won't She 102
Tell (USA) (Banner Sport (USA)) [1996 6g⁶ 6m* 7g Oct 18] $500,000Y: tall, leggy,
useful-looking colt: has plenty of scope: fifth foal: half-brother to useful 1992 2-y-o
6f and 7f winner White Crown (by Secreto) and 11.8f winner (useful at around 2m)
Zuboon (by The Minstrel): dam multiple winner in North America who stayed at
least 9f, closely related to Affirmed: won maiden at Lingfield in October, edging
right after leading 1f out, ridden out: sweating and edgy, beaten only 4 lengths
or so when last of 8 in Dewhurst Stakes at Newmarket 2 weeks later, looking well
held 2f out then staying on: will be suited by further than 7f: may progress again.
M. R. Stoute

WINDMACHINE (SWE)   5 b.m. River Scape (USA) 93 – Miami Flyer (Miami 106
Springs 121) [1995 106: 6m 5m 5g 5f 5m 6g* 5s* 5f⁵ 1996 a6s² a6g⁴ a5g* 6g* a6g*
a6g⁵ 5m 6m 6m⁵ Sep 17] big, lengthy mare: useful performer: successful in listed
races at Jagersro in May and Taby (beat Hever Golf Rose a nose) in June and in minor
event (by 9 lengths) at Taby in June: soon outpaced in Nunthorpe Stakes at York,
seventh start and only outing in Britain in 1996: stays 6f: acts on firm and soft ground
and on dirt: tried blinkered: bandaged in front: usually forces pace. *Bjoern T. Olsen,
Norway*

WINDRUSH BOY   6 br.g. Dowsing (USA) 124 – Bridge Street Lady 93 (Decoy 61
Boy 129) [1995 66: 5m⁶ 6f 5m⁴ 5g 5g² 5m⁵ 5m² 5.1m³ 5m⁵ 5m* 5m 5.3g a5g a5g⁵ a48
1996 5m 5f⁵ 5.1m 5.1m⁵ 5m 5m* 5f 5.1m a5g a5g a5g a5g⁵ a5g⁵ Dec 31] lengthy,
leggy gelding: modest performer: won claimer at Warwick in August: well held in
handicaps afterwards: best form at 5f: acts on good to firm going, not at best on
equitrack: successful when sweating: suitable mount for an inexperienced rider.
J. R. Bosley

WINDRUSH HOLLY   3 br.f. Gildoran 123 – Bridge Street Lady 93 (Decoy Boy 62
129) [1995 NR 1996 7.1d⁵ 10s 6g a8.5s Dec 19] lengthy filly: third live foal: half-

sister to 5f handicapper Windrush Boy (by Dowsing): dam sprinter: modest maiden: best effort when keeping-on fifth of 9 at Sandown on debut: stiff task penultimate start, poor effort on fibresand final one. *J. R. Bosley*

WINDSOR CASTLE 2 b.c. (Mar 13) Generous (IRE) 139 – One Way Street 119 (Habitat 134) [1996 9f* 10f* Oct 14] closely related to very smart French 3-y-o 6.5f (at 2 yrs) to 10.5f winner Grape Tree Road and 2m winner Usk The Way (both by Caerleon), and half-brother to several winners, notably smart Red Route (up to 14.8f, by Polish Precedent): dam won Princess Royal Stakes: won poorly-contested 5-runner maiden at Redcar (very green, soon pushed along after slow start and hard ridden 4f out before staying on strongly to lead inside last) and 5-runner minor event at Leicester (by head from Atlantic Desire, pushed along before turn, wandering and looking held, eventually getting up under sustained pressure) in the autumn: will stay 1½m+: will improve further. *P. F. I. Cole* **91 p**

WINDSWEPT (IRE) 3 b.f. Taufan (USA) 119 – Sutica 91 (Don 128) [1995 68: 5.2m³ 5f* 6m⁴ 6m⁶ 5f⁵ 6.5m⁵ 6g 1996 8.2m 8g 7g⁶ 6m⁵ 7m² 6f 8m² 7f³ 7m Sep 19] leggy filly: good mover: modest handicapper: suited by further than 6f nowadays (stays 1m): acts on firm going, yet to race on a soft surface: tried blinkered, no improvement: tried with tongue tied down at 2 yrs. *D. J. S. ffrench Davis* **59**

WINDWARD ARIOM 10 ch.g. Pas de Seul 133 – Deja Vu (FR) (Be My Guest (USA) 126) [1995 NR 1996 13.8s Mar 27] leggy, close-coupled gelding: fairly useful hurdler at best: no form on flat for a long time: has joined P. Mitchell. *K. R. Burke* **–**

WINDYEDGE (USA) 3 ch.g. Woodman (USA) 126 – Abeesh (USA) 77 (Nijinsky (CAN) 138) [1995 –p: 7m 1996 10.2g 10m⁶ 10m² 13.8m⁴ 11.5m Aug 22] tall, angular gelding: modest maiden: sold (B. Hills to Mrs A. Naughton) 5,400 gns Ascot October Sales, and gelded: should stay further than 1¼m. *B. W. Hills* **61**

WING AND A PRAYER (IRE) 2 ch.f. (Mar 3) Shalford (IRE) 124§ – God Speed Her (Pas de Seul 133) [1996 6m 7f⁴ 6m Sep 18] IR 10,500F, 25,000Y: third foal: half-sister to 3-y-o 5f (at 2 yrs) to 1m winner Sky Dome (by Bluebird): dam, Irish maiden, half-sister to smart middle-distance performer Noble Patriarch: held good position throughout in steadily-run maiden when 9½ lengths fourth of 15 at Salisbury, easily best effort and quite possibly flattered. *R. Hannon* **63 ?**

WINGED PRINCE 3 b.g. Prince Daniel (USA) – Phyl (Ballad Rock 122) [1995 –: 6.1m 7f 7m 8m 1996 10g 11.8d 16.1f Jun 10] rangy, rather unfurnished gelding: little form: sold 500 gns Ascot July Sales. *A. G. Foster* **–**

WINGNUT (IRE) 3 ch.f. Digamist (USA) 110 – Royal Cloak (Hardicanute 130) [1995 61, a43: 5m 5f⁵ a6g 5.1m³ a5g³ 5g* 5m³ 5g 6f² 5.3f⁵ 5d³ a5g a6g⁴ 1996 a8g a7g⁶ a6g⁶ a6g⁵ a7g⁶ 6.1g 5.1g 7f⁶ 10.8g³ 10f 8.5g² 10.1g⁵ a8g a10s Nov 19] unfurnished filly: poor form at best in 1996, trained by J. Bridger first 5 starts and for next 7 by M. Haynes: stays a steadily-run 10.8f: acts on the all-weather and on firm ground, probably on dead: tried blinkered/visored: none too consistent. *R. Ingram* **46 a–**

WING OF A PRAYER 2 b.c. (Apr 12) Statoblest 120 – Queen Angel 88 (Anfield 117) [1996 6f 6g Oct 29] 12,000Y: useful-looking colt: third foal: dam 11.1f and 11.7f winner, half-sister to Oaks third Pearl Angel: slowly away, swerved stalls and never a threat in maiden auction at Warwick on debut: raced too freely at Leicester 3 weeks later. *W. Jarvis* **61 ?**

WINN CALEY 3 ch.f. Beveled (USA) – Responder 70 (Vitiges (FR) 132) [1995 NR 1996 7.5m 8g⁴ a12g Aug 16] fourth reported foal: half-sister to 1m winner Genuine Lady (by Lidhame): dam, maiden who stayed 1¼m, out of fairly useful 2-y-o 7f winner Clean Canasta: no worthwhile form: has a markedly round action. *C. W. Fairhurst* **–**

WINNEBAGO 3 b.f. Kris 135 – Siouan 78 (So Blessed 130) [1995 NR 1996 7.9g⁵ 10.5d 8m 8.2s Oct 31] angular, workmanlike filly: has a round action: sister to 4-y-o Me Cherokee and half-sister to several winners, including very smart middle-distance colt Apache (by Great Nephew): dam, 1¼m winner, half-sister to Warpath: 9 lengths fifth of 7 to Van Gurp in maiden at York on debut, never on terms, not given hard race: below that form afterwards, off bit some way out last 2 starts: should stay 1½m. *C. W. Thornton* **63**

WINNING WONDER 4 b.f. Charmer 123 – Salchow 116 (Niniski (USA) 125) [1995 –: a6g⁶ 1996 8.3m Jun 3] workmanlike filly: no sign of ability. *Miss Jacqueline S. Doyle* **–**

WINSOME WOOSTER 5 ch.m. Primo Dominie 121 – Bertrade 75 (Homeboy 67
114) [1995 70: 5.1m³ 5.1m² 6g⁴ 5.7m 6f 6m⁴ 6m² 6m 5.7h⁴ 7m³ 7.1d 7m⁵ 7m⁴ 1996
6d⁶ 6g⁵ 7m⁴ 8.3g 7f⁴ 7g* 6m⁶ 7f³ 5.7m⁵ 6.1m 7s 7g Nov 2] plain, close-coupled
mare: fair handicapper: won at Salisbury in August: stays 7f: acts on hard and dead
ground: sometimes unruly at stalls: usually held up. *P. G. Murphy*

WINSTON 3 b.g. Safawan 118 – Lady Leman 74 (Pitskelly 122) [1995 –: 6m⁶ 7g 73
1996 a8g⁵ 8.2g* 8d³ 8g* 8d⁵ 10.1m³ 8m² 8f 8m 8g 8g Nov 2] sturdy gelding: fair
handicapper: won at Nottingham in April and Newcastle in May: ran respectably
despite being checked penultimate outing, poorly drawn on final one: will stay
further than 8.3f: acts on good to firm and dead ground: carries head awkwardly:
seems suited by being held up in strongly-run race. *J. D. Bethell*

WINTERED OUT 2 b.f. (Apr 17) Digamist (USA) 110 – Record Song (Indian –
King (USA) 128) [1996 6g Oct 18] 800F: good-topped filly: first foal: dam unraced:
50/1 and burly, slowly away and always behind in 22-runner maiden at Newmarket.
G. L. Moore

WINTER GARDEN 2 ch.c. (Feb 23) Old Vic 136 – Winter Queen 60 (Welsh 66 p
Pageant 132) [1996 7d Nov 8] strong, lengthy colt: ninth living foal: half-brother to
smart 1m and 1¼m winner Main Objective (by Main Reef) and smart stayer Safety
In Numbers (by Slip Anchor): dam 13f winner at 4 yrs in Ireland: burly and green,
just over 8 lengths seventh of 20 to Handsome Ridge in maiden at Doncaster,
steadied start, switched to far side, getting hang of things late on, keeping on nicely
not knocked about: has plenty of scope, and sure to do better over middle distances.
L. M. Cumani

WINTER ROMANCE 3 ch.c. Cadeaux Genereux 131 – Island Wedding (USA) 106
89 (Blushing Groom (FR) 131) [1995 93p: 7g 7d³ 7g² 1996 7.9f² 8.1d* 8f 10g 10.4m⁶
9m³ 9g⁵ Oct 18] good-topped, attractive colt: good mover: useful handicapper:
impressive winner of £21,300 contest at Haydock in May: ran creditably in listed
races at Evry and Newmarket (won by Tarawa) last 2 starts: effective at 1m to 1¼m:
acts on firm and dead ground: tends to carry head high. *E. A. L. Dunlop*

WINTER SCOUT (USA) 8 ch.g. It's Freezing (USA) 122 – His Squaw (USA) 60
(Tom Rolfe) [1995 63: 7m³ 7m⁵ 6m⁴ 6g* 7g⁵ 1996 6.1g 6m 7d 7f 5.9f* 6.9f⁴ 7.1d 7m
7g 12m Sep 20] strong, good-bodied gelding: poor mover: modest performer: won
claimer at Carlisle in June: ran poorly last 4 starts: stays 7f well: acts on firm ground
(best Irish form with some give), stiffish task on fibresand: sometimes blinkered,
including for 8-y-o success. *C. P. E. Brooks*

Tote Credit Silver Bowl (Handicap), Haydock—
Winter Romance powers clear from Jo Mell for the only win of his career so far

WIRE ACT (USA) 3 gr.g. Gate Dancer (USA) – Giovanelli (USA) (Monteverdi 62 129) [1995 63: 7f 8.1g⁴ 8g 7s a6g³ 8f 1996 7.1g 10f⁵ 12d 5.1g³ 5f² 5.9f* 7.1d 7m⁶ 8f Oct 14] tall gelding: unimpressive mover: modest performer: led close home when winning maiden at Carlisle in June: well below form all 3 subsequent starts: sold 6,000 gns Newmarket Autumn Sales: best efforts in sprints: acts on firm ground and fibresand, may be unsuited by a soft surface: tried blinkered, better without: tends to hang left: sent to Spain. *Martyn Meade*

WISAM 3 b.g. Shaadi (USA) 126 – Moon Drop 103 (Dominion 123) [1995 100p: 91 5m* 6m 6m⁴ 1996 6d³ 8m⁶ 7g 7.6f⁴ 7m 7d 7m a6f² Dec 27] tall gelding: fluent mover: fairly useful performer: below form in handicaps last 3 starts here (trained by R. Hannon): creditable second in handicap in Dubai in December: stays 7.6f: acts on firm going and sand: blinkered (no improvement) third 3-y-o start: often steadily to post. *W. D. Mather, UAE*

WITCHING HOUR (IRE) 2 b.f. (May 9) Alzao (USA) 117 – Itching (IRE) 88 (Thatching 131) [1996 6d* 6m² Jun 14] second reported foal: dam unraced daughter of smart 2-y-o 7f winner Alligatrix, dam also of three useful animals, including Sleepytime's dam Alidiva: won maiden at Salisbury in May, soon with leaders and running on strongly final 1f: always-prominent second of 5 in minor event at York following month, clear of remainder: will be at least as effective at 7f as 6f: seemed likely to do better. *Mrs J. Cecil*

WITCH OF FIFE (USA) 3 b.f. Lear Fan (USA) 130 – Fife (IRE) 95 (Lomond – (USA) 128) [1995 91: 6m* 7m³ 8g 7.1g* 1996 10m 14m⁵ Jun 27] small, lengthy filly: successful as 2-y-o in maiden at Newmarket and minor event (awarded race) at Haydock: well beaten in 1996, seventh of 10 in listed race on reappearance: bred to stay 1m+: retired. *B. W. Hills*

WITH A WILL 2 b.g. (Apr 1) Rambo Dancer (CAN) 107 – Henceforth 58 (Full – p of Hope 125) [1996 6.1d⁴ 6m 6m⁵ Oct 4] small, good-bodied gelding: half-brother to 4 winners by Nicholas Bill, including fair sprinter Willbutwhen and middle-distance performer William Four: dam 5f winner from 3 races at 2 yrs: fourth in maiden auction at Nottingham on debut, soon pushed along in rear after slow start then getting hang of things late on: not given hard race either start afterwards and though beaten long way, gives impression may well be capable of better: bandaged behind. *H. Candy*

WITH CARE 3 b.f. Warning 136 – Benazir 91 (High Top 131) [1995 NR 1996 7f⁵ 78 7f* 7d 7f 7g Oct 12] sparely-made filly: second foal: half-sister to poor maiden Asian Elegance (by Shareef Dancer): dam 7f and 1m winner: fair form: won maiden at Thirsk in August: well below form in handicaps last 2 outings, shaping as if worth a try over 1m. *W. Jarvis*

WITHERKAY 3 b.g. Safawan 118 – High Heather (Shirley Heights 130) [1995 62 NR 1996 8g 8g⁴ 8m² 10m 8m 8.1m³ 8d 10.4g⁴ Oct 10] 7,200Y, resold 6,200Y: tall, leggy gelding: second foal: half-brother to 7f winner Arawa (by Doulab): dam unraced: modest maiden handicapper: stays 1¼m: acts on good to firm ground. *R. Hannon*

WITHOUT A FLAG (USA) 6 ch.g. Stately Don (USA) 122 – Northerly Cheer – (USA) (Northjet 136) [1995 –: 12m 1996 11.6g Jul 1] smallish, sturdy gelding: modest middle-distance handicapper: lightly raced and no promise since 4 yrs. *J. White*

WITHOUT FRIENDS (IRE) 2 b.c. (Mar 6) Thatching 131 – Soha (USA) 58 77 (Dancing Brave (USA) 140) [1996 5f* 6g* 6m²ᵈⁱˢ 6.1f* 5m 7g⁴ Aug 5] leggy, narrow, hollow-backed filly: first reported foal: dam placed once from 3 starts at 1½m, daughter of Italian Oaks winner Paris Royal, herself half-sister to Irish 2000 Guineas winner Northern Treasure: fair form: won seller at Folkestone in April and claimers at Goodwood (left R. Hannon's yard £10,000) in May and Chepstow (only start for Mrs L. Stubbs) in July: fourth in a claimer at Clairefontaine: stays 7f: acts on firm ground: tends to carry head high. *G. Mikhalides, France*

WITH THE TEMPO (IRE) 3 b.f. Last Tycoon 131 – Starlust 79 (Sallust 134) 53 [1995 NR 1996 8.5m² 7f⁵ 8m 7g 12s Nov 11] IR 11,000Y: leggy filly: tenth foal: half-sister to several winners, including (at 6f to 1m) useful Bronzewing (by Beldale Flutter) and (at 1¼m) Travel Storm (by Lord Gayle): dam, 2-y-o 5f winner, is half-sister to Welsh Pearl, very useful at up to 1m, and to dam of Gay Lemur: modest form in maiden at Beverley on debut: failed to progress, well beaten in seller final start: retained 500 gns Ascot December Sales. *Dr J. D. Scargill*

WITNEY-DE-BERGERAC (IRE) 4 b.g. Cyrano de Bergerac 120 – Spy Girl (Tanfirion 110) [1995 67, a61: a8g³ a8g⁵ a10g⁴ a10g³ a10g 8f⁴ 8.3m 11.6m³ 12d* 16.2d 12d a12g 1996 10.3d⁵ 16g² 16d⁴ 14m 11.9m 16.2f⁵ 18f⁴ 12m⁵ 18g a14g⁶ Nov 4] close-coupled gelding: fair handicapper: second in Queen's Prize at Kempton second outing: below form last 4 starts: stays 2m: acts on firm and dead ground and on equitrack: visored (well beaten) once as 2-y-o: held up, and suited by strongly-run race: inconsistent. *J. S. Moore*   66 d a–

WITNEY-LA-ROCHE 2 ch.g. (May 10) Superlative 118 – Ever Reckless 52 (Crever 94) [1996 6m 7m Oct 17] 1,000F, 1050Y: first foal: dam best at 5f: signs of a little ability in claimer and seller and is probably a sprint plater. *J. S. Moore*   –

WIXIM (USA) 3 ch.c. Diesis 133 – River Lullaby (USA) (Riverman (USA) 131) [1995 NR 1996 8s² 8g* 8m* 8d³ May 25] smallish, angular colt: fourth foal: half-brother to 3 winners, including very useful middle-distance performers Berceau (by Alleged) and Run Softly (by Deputy Minister): dam Irish 2-y-o 6f winner, third in 1¼m listed race at 3 yrs: progressive form: won maiden at Ripon in April and minor event at Doncaster in May: not seen out after very good third (beaten neck and short head) to Regal Archive and Sorbie Tower in listed event at Kempton: will stay beyond 1m. *R. Charlton*   108

WIZARD KING 5 b.h. Shaadi (USA) 126 – Broomstick Cottage (Habitat 134) [1995 114: 7.6m² 8g³ 8f* 7m 7g* 7f² 8d³ 1996 7m⁵ 7m* 7m* 7.1g* 8g² 7m² 7g* 7d* Nov 10] tall, lengthy horse: poor mover: smart performer: as good as ever in 1996: landed the odds in minor events at Chester, Salisbury and Chepstow in August: game   116

Sheikh Ahmed bin Saeed Al Maktoum's "Wizard King"

efforts when second in listed race at Kempton (to Centre Stalls) and Supreme Stakes at Goodwood (caught post by Tagula) in September: finished season with wins in 5-runner Concorde Stakes at Tipperary (by 1½ lengths from Cool Edge) in October and 12-runner listed race at Leopardstown (by 2 lengths from Inzar) in November: effective at 7f and 1m: acts on firm and dead going, probably also on heavy: often front runner: genuine and consistent: stays in training: a credit to his trainer. *Sir Mark Prescott*

WOBBLE 2 ch.g. (Feb 24) Kris 135 – Horseshoe Reef 88 (Mill Reef (USA) 141) 67 [1996 6g⁵ 6m⁶ 7f 8m⁵ Oct 23] 24,000Y: quite good-topped gelding: third foal: half-brother to 3-y-o Warning Reef (by Warning) and 1m winner (probably stayed 1¾m) Pumice (by Salse): dam 1¼m winner, daughter of smart mare Miss Toshiba: fair maiden: better at 1m than shorter, and will stay further: acts on good to firm ground, saddle slipped on firm. *W. J. Haggas*

WOLF CLEUGH (IRE) 3 b.f. Last Tycoon 131 – Santa Roseanna 111 (Caracol 63 (FR)) [1995 65p: 7m 1996 8g⁶ 8m⁵ Jul 5] smallish, lengthy filly: modest form in maidens: sold 7,200 gns Newmarket September Sales: will stay beyond 1m. *A. Hide*

WOLF MOUNTAIN 2 ch.c. (Apr 16) Selkirk (USA) 129 – Cubby Hole (Town 92 And Country 124) [1996 6m² 7f³ 7m 6g* Oct 9] 40,000Y: leggy, lengthy colt: has a quick action: sixth foal: half-brother to 1000 Guineas runner-up Niche (by Risk Me) and 1m (at 2 yrs) and fairly useful 1½m winner Alcove (by Faustus): dam half-sister to Little Wolf and Smuggler, family also of Sheikh Albadou: fairly useful form: third in Donnington Castle Stakes at Newbury second start: won maiden at York in October: stays 7f, but rather headstrong and probably at least as good at 6f: acts on firm ground. *R. Hannon*

WOLLSTONECRAFT (IRE) 3 b.f. Danehill (USA) 126 – Ivory Thread 73 (USA) (Sir Ivor 135) [1995 85: 5m³ 1996 6m⁶ 6g 5.2m² 6m² 5g 5f⁶ a5g Nov 22] lengthy, quite attractive filly: fair maiden: well below form last 3 starts: should stay further than 6f: raced only on a sound surface on turf: often early/quietly to post: sold only 3,500 gns Newmarket December Sales. *J. H. M. Gosden*

WOMAN OF WIT (IRE) 2 b. or br.f. (Feb 26) Petorius 117 – Laughing Matter 49 56 (Lochnager 132) [1996 5d² Apr 13] 4,600F, 7,200Y: close-coupled, good-topped filly: half-sister to 3-y-o Man of Wit (by Fayruz) and 2 winners in France by Moulin, including middle-distance performer Winged Flight: dam maiden sprinter: well-backed favourite, second of 5 in maiden at Warwick in April, caught inside last having quickened ahead on turn. *A. P. Jarvis*

WONDERBOY (IRE) 2 ch.c. (Apr 26) Arazi (USA) 135 – Alsaaybah (USA) 73 – (Diesis 133) [1996 7m Oct 3] IR 8,000Y: leggy, close-coupled colt: second foal: dam ran twice, winning at 7f at 2 yrs: 33/1, prominent early, behind in maiden at Newmarket: may do better. *R. Akehurst*

WONDERFUL DAY 5 b.m. Niniski (USA) 125 – Zipperti Do 70 (Precocious 65 126) [1995 71: 9.9m* 12.4g³ 12d² 12.4m⁴ 10f 1996 a11g² a12g³ 10m 9.9f Jun 12] leggy, sparely-made mare: fair handicapper: left T. Clement after second 5-y-o start: long way below form for new yard: stays 1½m: acts on good to firm and dead ground and on fibresand. *H. Akbary*

WOODBOROUGH (USA) 3 ch.c. Woodman (USA) 126 – Performing Arts 112 104 (The Minstrel (CAN) 135) [1995 110: 5.2m 6f* 6m² 6.3m* 7s³ 6g² 1996 7d⁵ 6f⁵ 5g³ 6m⁴ 6g⁴ Aug 11] strong colt: smart performer: particularly good efforts when fourth of 17 to Atraf in Cork and Orrery Stakes at Royal Ascot and fourth of 8 to Daring Destiny in Phoenix Sprint Stakes at Leopardstown on last 2 starts: ideally suited by further than 5f, and stays 7f: acts on firm and soft ground: often early to post: sent to USA. *P. W. Chapple-Hyam*

WOODBURY LAD (USA) 3 ch.c. Woodman (USA) 126 – Habibti 136 (Habi- 76 tat 134) [1995 73p: 6.5g 5g 1996 6m 6f² 7m² 7.1d³ a7g² a7g³ Nov 12] strong, lengthy a63 colt: good mover: fair maiden, generally disappointing: reportedly had testicular operation after reappearance: stays 7f: acts on firm ground: sweating, edgy and free to post on reappearance, early to post fourth 3-y-o start: blinkered final outing: weak finisher. *W. R. Muir*

WOODERINE (USA) 2 ch.f. (Apr 7) Woodman (USA) 126 – Exuberine (FR) – 82 (Be My Guest (USA) 126) [1996 5m⁵ Apr 17] $90,000F, IR 40,000Y: quite attractive filly: eighth foal: half-sister to several winners, including 3-y-o Rose of Siberia,

1¼m winner at 2 yrs, and Premio Regina Elena winner Ancestral Dancer (both by Siberian Express): dam 1m winner: left behind from halfway in 6-runner maiden at Newmarket: looked capable of better: sent to Italy. *M. Bell*

WOODETTO (IRE)   2 b.g. (May 15) Maledetto (IRE) 103 – Wood Kay (IRE)   53
(Treasure Kay 114) [1996 6m 7f² 6d⁴ 5m⁵ Jul 11] IR 900F, IR 1,800Y, 6,500 2-y-o:
close-coupled, workmanlike gelding: poor mover: first foal: dam no form here at 4
yrs: held up and ran on when second of 12 in seller at Redcar, in June: well below that
form afterwards: best form at 7f. *E. Weymes*

WOODLAND DOVE   2 ch.f. (Mar 16) Weldnaas (USA) 112 – Jove's Voodoo   –
(USA) 74 (Northern Jove (CAN)) [1996 5m a6g a7g a8g Nov 29] 2,000Y: half-sister
to several winners, including 7.5f winner Brightness (by Elegant Air) and 1½m
winner Spirit Away (by Dominion): dam 6f winner: of no account. *K. G. Wingrove*

WOODLAND NYMPH   2 gr.f. (May 6) Norton Challenger 111 – Royal Meeting   –
44 (Dara Monarch 128) [1996 7d 7.1s Oct 22] fifth reported foal: half-sister to 3
winners, including modest 4-y-o 7f (at 2 yrs) to 1½m winner Tonka (by Mazilier):
dam won 1m seller: signs of ability, never a real threat, in large fields of maidens.
D. J. G. Murray Smith

WOODLANDS ELECTRIC   6 b.g. Rich Charlie 117 – Hallowed (Wolver   –
Hollow 126) [1995 –: a5g a6g 7m⁶ 7.6m⁶ 6m 5d a6g 1996 4g 5.1f 5.1m 5.3m⁵ Jul
29] neat gelding: no worthwhile form: tried visored. *P. A. Pritchard*

WOODLANDS ENERGY   5 b.m. Risk Me (FR) 127 – Hallowed (Wolver   –
Hollow 126) [1995 –: 8m⁵ 8.3m 10m 10d 10.8g 1996 13.1f 10.8m 12.5f Jul 20]
workmanlike mare: of no account. *P. A. Pritchard*

WOODLANDS LAD TOO   4 b.g. Risk Me (FR) 127 – Hallowed (Wolver   –
Hollow 126) [1995 –: 8m³ 10d 10.2m 1996 a8g Jan 8] leggy gelding: of no account.
P. A. Pritchard

WOOD MAGIC   3 b.g. Shaadi (USA) 126 – Majenica (USA) (Majestic Light   105
(USA)) [1995 96p: 7f⁴ a7g* 7.6d* 1996 8g 10.4m⁴ 9m 10.9m⁴ Sep 21] tall, rather
leggy gelding: useful performer: off course 4½ months, best effort when fourth of 16
(always prominent in steadily-run race) to Amrak Ajeeb in rated stakes at York in
August on second start: stays 10.4f: acts on good to firm ground and dead: has been
taken early to post: sent to UAE. *D. R. Loder*

WOODRISING   4 b.f. Nomination 125 – Bodham 88 (Bustino 136) [1995 64: 6d³   –
8.1g² a7g 8m² 10g³ 10.8m⁵ 10g* 12m 10.1m* 10m* 1996 11.9m Jun 14] smallish
filly: modest performer at 3 yrs: well beaten in apprentice handicap at York only flat
outing in 1996: should stay further than 1¼m: acts on good to firm going and dead:
tried blinkered. *C. R. Egerton*

WOODSIA   2 b.f. (Mar 18) Woodman (USA) 126 – Aquaba (USA) (Damascus   76
(USA)) [1996 7d³ 7m² 8.2g Oct 9] medium-sized filly: fourth foal: half-sister to
useful 3-y-o Polska (by Danzig), 6f winner at 2 yrs, and useful sprinter Millstream
(by Dayjur): dam, 7f to 9f winner in USA, including in Grade 3 event, granddaughter
of Monade, also grandam of Sadeem: placed in maidens at Newmarket and Lingfield
on first 2 outings: below form last time: stays 7f: yet to race on extremes of going.
D. R. Loder

WOOLVERSTONE HALL (IRE)   4 b.f. Roi Danzig (USA) – Silver Mantle   38
70 (Bustino 136) [1995 42: a6g a6g⁴ 6f a10g⁵ a7g⁵ a7g 1996 a7g a6g a7g² a7g a7g²
a8g a6g 6.9m⁶ May 29] compact filly: poor maiden at best nowadays: stays 7f: acts
on the all-weather: blinkered since third 4-y-o start. *D. J. G. Murray Smith*

WORDSMITH (IRE)   6 b.g. Cyrano de Bergerac 120 – Cordon 89 (Morston   –
(FR) 125) [1995 46: a12g 8.1g 8g a11g a8m⁶ 10m² 10.1g 1996 10d 10d Aug 25]
compact, good-quartered gelding: poor performer at best on flat nowadays: no form
in 1996. *J. L. Harris*

WORLD EXPRESS (IRE)   6 b.g. Jareer (USA) 115 – Eight Mile Rock 76   59 §
(Dominion 123) [1995 –: a12g 1996 11.8d 12d³ 14d* 17.2m⁵ 16.4g⁶ Jul 6] rather
leggy gelding: just a modest handicapper in 1996: got up close home to win at
Sandown in May: suited by test of stamina: ideally suited by a soft surface: blinkered
(below form) first 2 6-y-o starts: sometimes looks reluctant: fair winner over hurdles
in November: not one to trust. *B. R. Millman*

WORLD PREMIER   3 b.c. Shareef Dancer (USA) 135 – Abuzz 101 (Absalom   103
128) [1995 103: 5g* 5m² 6g⁵ 6f² 6m* 6g³ 6g⁶ 1996 7m³ 8m 7g³ 8f 7g⁴ 8f⁵ 7m 6s

Oct 24] smallish, good-topped colt: impresses in appearance: useful performer: reportedly had 2 operations for colic (and nearly died) between 2 and 3 yrs: third of 8 to Cayman Kai in European Free Handicap at Newmarket on reappearance: long way below form last 3 starts, under unsuitable conditions in rated stakes at Newbury on final one: stays 1m: acts on firm ground. *C. E. Brittain*

WORLDWIDE ELSIE (USA) 3 b.f. Java Gold (USA) – Tender Camilla 115 **73** (Prince Tenderfoot (USA) 126) [1995 76, a90: 5g⁶ 5m³ a6g* 6m 7f 7f* 6.9m² **a–** a8.5g* 1996 10.3d 7m⁴ a8.5g⁶ 7m⁶ a8.5g 7g⁵ a9.4g Dec 14] tall, useful-looking filly: fair handicapper at best in 1996, but lost her way: trained by R. Harris until after penultimate outing: should stay 1¼m: acts on firm ground, best on fibresand. *I. Campbell*

WOT NO FAX 3 ch.g. Sharrood (USA) 124 – Priors Dean 61 (Monsanto (FR) **96** 121) [1995 NR 1996 10f* 10.1m³ 10m⁶ 10m 10m 10.1m Sep 11] 2,700F: plain gelding: half-brother to winners abroad by King of Spain and (at sprint distances) Petong: dam ran only at 2 yrs, when best at 6f: 50/1, won maiden at Lingfield in May: useful form facing stiff tasks in conditions events at Epsom and Windsor next 2 starts: behind in handicaps afterwards, giving impression something amiss on final outing: should stay further than 1¼m: has raced only on top-of-the-ground. *S. Dow*

WOTTASHAMBLES 5 b. or br.g. Arrasas (USA) 100 – Manawa 81 (Manda- **41** mus 120) [1995 48, a43: a12g² a13g⁶ a16g⁶ a16g a12g⁴ 12f⁴ 12.1m* 12m 14f³ **a62** 14.4m⁴ 12m² 12m a12g 1996 a16g* a13g² a16g⁵ a13g⁴ a16g⁴ 11.8d² 12g³ 12f 12m⁶ 14m³ a16g* a16g* Dec 26] leggy gelding: has a round action: modest handicapper: won at Lingfield in January and December (twice), putting up easily best effort when trotting up final outing: stays 2m well: acts on firm and soft ground, goes well on equitrack: blinkered (below form) second 4-y-o start: sometimes bandaged: fair hurdler. *L. Montague Hall*

WRITTEN AGREEMENT 8 ch.g. Stanford 121§ – Covenant 75 (Good Bond **–** 122) [1995 –: a12g a12g a13g⁶ a16g 1996 11.5f 10g 12.1m a16.2g a14g Aug 16] sparely-made gelding: bad maiden: tried visored/blinkered. *R. E. Peacock*

WRN PRINCESS 2 ch.f. (Apr 27) Handsome Sailor 125 – Sovereign Rose 116 **–** (Sharpen Up 127) [1996 6g 6m 6g⁶ Oct 29] tall, unfurnished filly: half-sister to several winners, including 5f (at 2 yrs) and 7f winner Precious Platinum (by Gorytus) and useful 7f and 1½m winner Hauwmal (by Troy): dam won Diadem Stakes: little form in maidens. *B. J. Meehan*

WRONG BRIDE 2 b.f. (May 5) Reprimand 122 – Ivory Bride 86 (Domynsky **–** 110) [1996 6m Jul 30] angular filly: unimpressive mover: second foal: half-sister to 3-y-o Cabcharge Striker (by Rambo Dancer), 5f to 1m winner here and in Italy at 2 yrs: dam 2-y-o 6f winner who stayed 1m: in need of race, soon tailed off in maiden at Goodwood. *M. R. Channon*

WURFTAUBE (GER) 3 ch.f. Acatenango (GER) 127 – Wurfbahn (GER) **119** (Frontal 122) [1995 NR 1996 10g⁴ 10.5g* 11s* 11s* 12g* 11g* 14d* Sep 29]

Wurftaube's wide-margin win in the German St Leger on the final start of her excellent three-year-old season entitles her to be regarded as one of the year's leading staying fillies in Europe, one well worth trying outside her own parish in future. It may turn out that she needs a test of stamina to be seen at her best—that win came on her first start at a mile and three quarters, and on good to soft ground. If she proves just as effective back at a mile and a half and under faster conditions she will surely be one to look out for in 1997.

After a sighter on her debut in April, Wurftaube made steady progress in the summer, winning five in the process. A maiden at Hanover was followed by a minor contest at Baden-Baden before she caught our attention when beating Anno Luce by a length and a half in the Group 3 Deutscher Herold-Preis at Hamburg at the end of June, and by just a little further in a listed race at Krefeld the following month. Wurftaube ventured out of races confined to her own sex to land the steadily-run Group 3 Furstenberg-Rennen at Baden-Baden in Aug- ust by three quarters of a length from subsequently-demoted Surako. Back in June, Surako had finished four lengths second in the Deutsches Derby, and for most of the summer the Derby winner Lavirco was reported as being on target for the Deutsches St Leger. Come the day, Wurftaube took her place alongside old rivals Anno Luce, Narrabeth and Night Petticoat, as well as recent Doncaster St Leger third Samraan, in a field of eight; Lavirco wasn't there, having gone for the Europa-Preis at Cologne the previous weekend. He might have become the first German triple crown winner since 1979 had he run—but after what happened we cannot be sure. No sooner had Night Petticoat taken the lead in the three-furlong straight than Wurftaube loomed up on the wide outside and, merely shaken up, ran right away from her hard-ridden rivals. The winning margin was an ever-increasing eleven lengths. The Preis der Diana winner Night Petticoat kept on to finish five lengths clear in second, and nearly eight more lengths back in fifth came Samraan, completely unable to mount a challenge.

		Surumu	Literat
	Acatenango (GER)	(ch 1974)	Surama
	(ch 1982)	Aggravate	Aggressor
Wurftaube (GER)		(b 1966)	Raven Locks
(ch.f. 1993)		Frontal	Le Haar
	Wurfbahn (GER)	(b 1964)	Favreale
	(b 1987)	Wolkenpracht	Pitskelly
		(br 1980)	Wolke

Wurftaube is the second notable example in Germany of a mating between Acatenango and a Frontal mare, following Protektor. She is a first foal and has a year-younger close relative called Wurfkeil, a colt by Surumu. The distaff side of Wurftaube's family has produced only minor winners of late; Wurfbahn, successful over a mile at three, was the second and last foal produced by Wolkenpracht before she died. Further back, however, this is an excellent pedigree, tracing via the fifth dam Windstille to the Ravensberg Stud's foundation mare Waldrun. Windstille won the 1952 Deutscher Stutenpreis over a mile and a half and was placed in both fillies classics, and she proved even better at stud. She produced the 1959 Schwarzgold-Rennen winner Wiesenblute (later the grandam of top-class middle-distance stayer Windwurf who, like Wurftaube's third dam Wolke, was by Kaiseradler); she also had the 1962 Aral Pokal winner Windbruch, the 1965 German Derby and St Leger winner Waidwerk, the grandam of Bayerisches Zuchtrennen winner Wanderu, and Wurftaube's fourth dam Westfahlen who was fourth in the Preis de Diana.

Recent winners of the German St Leger have not been particularly successful in middle-distance events in subsequent seasons, though 1996 Group 1 winners Protektor and Hollywood Dream both finished third in their year. Don't bet too heavily against Wurftaube making her mark in 1997. *H. Remmert, Germany*

WYBARA 3 ch.f. Nashwan (USA) 135 – Twyla 101 (Habitat 134) [1995 NR 1996 53 10m 11.7m⁴ 13.4g⁴ 12g⁶ Oct 18] good-topped filly: fifth foal: closely related to smart 7f (at 2 yrs) to 12.3f winner Twist And Turn (by Groom Dancer) and half-sister to 4-y-o 13.1f winner High Pyrenees (by Shirley Heights): dam, 2-y-o 6f winner, sister to smart sprinter Defecting Dancer: modest form, only in maiden at Bath on second start: should stay well: sold 26,000 gns Newmarket December Sales. *J. H. M. Gosden*

WYSE FOLLY 3 ch.f. Colmore Row 111 – Water Folly (Sharpo 132) [1995 NR – 1996 5.1d 6.1g Apr 22] 400Y: leggy filly: half-sister to 5f winner Karykera (by Hallgate) and winning selling hurdler Bill And Win (by Faustus): dam never ran: no promise in maiden and seller. *R. Bastiman*

X

XENOPHON OF CUNAXA (IRE) 3 b.g. Cyrano de Bergerac 120 – Annais 78 d Nin (Dominion 123) [1995 83p: 6f⁵ 5.7h* 6m 1996 6m 7.3s* 8.1d⁴ 7f³ 7f 5.7m a7g a7g⁶ Nov 29] tall, leggy gelding: unimpressive mover: fair performer: initially demoted to second but later reinstated after beating Zygo a head in minor event at Newbury in May: well below form last 4 starts: should stay 1m: acts on hard and soft ground: has gone early to post: tends to wander. *M. J. Fetherston-Godley*

Y

YAAKUM 7 b.g. Glint of Gold 128 – Nawadder 73 (Kris 135) [1995 –: 16.5g 32
15.8g 13.1g³ 1996 15.1f 15.8s 14.1f⁶ 13.1g³ Jul 20] robust gelding: poor form at
best on flat nowadays: stays 2m: tried visored/blinkered: modest winning chaser in
August. *S. E. Kettlewell*

YABINT EL SULTAN 2 ch.f. (Apr 12) Safawan 118 – Dalby Dancer 71 –
(Bustiki) [1996 6s a6g Nov 2] 1,700Y: rather unfurnished filly: second foal: dam
stayed well: showed signs of ability in Newbury maiden on debut: bred to stay well.
B. A. McMahon

YACHT 4 b.g. Warning 136 – Bireme 127 (Grundy 137) [1995 –: 10m 10g 1996 –
14.4g⁶ Jun 12] tall gelding: modest but irresolute hurdler: not one to be interested in
on flat. *T. Hind*

YALAIETANEE 2 b.c. (Mar 19) Sadler's Wells (USA) 132 – Vaigly Star 118 96 p
(Star Appeal 133) [1996 7m⁴ 7d* Aug 23] quite attractive colt: seventh foal: half-
brother to Molecomb winner Sahara Star (by Green Desert) and a winner abroad:
dam, best at 6f, half-sister to high-class sprinter Vaigly Great: heavily-backed
favourite, stepped up good deal on debut form when winning 13-runner maiden at
Newmarket by 4 lengths from Flirting Around, held up travelling well, leading 1f out
then running on strongly: will stay 1m: took good hold to post both starts: will
improve again. *M. R. Stoute*

YALTA (IRE) 3 b.g. Soviet Star (USA) 128 – Gay Hellene 111 (Ela-Mana-Mou 88
132) [1995 NR 1996 8.3g² 8.1m* 10m³ Aug 16] strong, good-bodied gelding: has a
short action: fifth foal: half-brother to useful middle-distance performer Nash
Terrace (by Nashwan) and 3 other winners, including 1¼m to 16.2f winner Gay Glint
(by Glint of Gold): dam 1¼m and 10.5f winner: fairly useful form: won maiden at
Sandown in July, leading near finish: favourite again, good third of 15 to Greenstead
in handicap at Newbury on only subsequent outing, unable to quicken: stays 1¼m:
gelded. *R. Charlton*

YA MALAK 5 b.g. Fairy King (USA) – La Tuerta 96 (Hot Spark 126) [1995 116: 108 ?
5g³ 5f² 5g* 5m² 5.1g⁶ 5g⁴ 5m² 5m⁶ 1996 5d⁵ 5m⁵ 5m⁵ 5f⁵ 5f 5.1m³ 5f⁵ 5.2m 5m⁶ Oct
3] good-topped gelding: good mover: smart performer at best in 1995: well below
form at 5 yrs, leaving J. W. Payne after seventh outing: sold 23,000 gns Doncaster
October Sales: races at around 5f: acts on good to firm and dead ground: blinkered
(finished last in King's Stand Stakes) fifth 5-y-o start: has run well when sweating.
I. A. Balding

YA MARHABA 3 b.g. Efisio 120 – Ichnusa 83 (Bay Express 132) [1995 –: 5d 5s 35
a5g 1996 6d 7m 7m² 5.9f⁴ a8g⁵ a8g³ a8g² Dec 3] workmanlike gelding: has a round a56
action: modest maiden handicapper: stays 1m: acts on firm ground, clearly best form
on fibresand. *J. W. Payne*

YAM-SING 2 b.g. (Mar 17) Aragon 118 – Pushoff (USA) 78 (Sauce Boat (USA)) –
[1996 6g 7.1d 7.1v Oct 6] 12,500Y: close-coupled gelding: unimpressive mover:
half-brother to 2 winners, notably smart 3-y-o 6f (at 2 yrs) and 7f winner (Nell Gwyn)
Thrilling Day (by Groom Dancer): dam, 5f winner, half-sister to 1995 Nell Gwyn
winner Myself, out of Queen Mary and Cornwallis winner Pushy: well held in
maidens. *T. D. Easterby*

YAMUNA (USA) 3 b.f. Forty Niner (USA) – Nimble Feet (USA) 82 (Danzig 103
(USA)) [1995 67p: 6g⁵ 1996 7f⁴ 8.3d* 8.1m³ 10.1m Sep 17] good-quartered filly:
useful performer: off course 14 months after debut: won maiden at Windsor in
August in good style: third of 11 to Wandering Star in listed race at Sandown next
time, staying on strongly: walked out of stalls, losing all chance, in listed race at
Yarmouth on final start: should be suited by further than 1m: acts on good to firm and
dead ground: wears blanket for stalls entry: sent to USA. *H. R. A. Cecil*

YANAVANAVANO (IRE) 2 b.g. (Apr 17) Maledetto (IRE) 103 – Dublin –
Millennium (Dalsaan 125) [1996 5.2d 5.1g Apr 30] 8,400Y: sturdy gelding: poor
mover: fourth foal: half-brother to Cliburnel News (by Horage), winner at up to 15f:
dam twice-raced Irish 12.5f winner: always behind in maidens: steadied start, modest
late headway not knocked about last time: probably not a sprinter: gelded. *G. Lewis*

YANGTZE (IRE) 2 b.c. (May 1) River Falls 113 – Sister Dympna 63 (Grundy –
137) [1996 5g 7m 7.1m Jul 17] IR 8,200F, IR 15,000Y: angular colt: half-brother to

tough and smart Irish 5-y-o 5f to 9f winner Ger's Royale (by Dominion Royale) and a winner in Belgium by Burslem: dam should have been suited by 1¾m+: behind in maiden events. *B. R. Millman*

YAROB (IRE) 3 ch.c. Unfuwain (USA) 131 – Azyaa 101 (Kris 135) [1995 97: 6m* 7m² 6d 1996 7m 7.1d⁴ 10.3g⁶ 10.1m² 10.4m 10m a8f⁵ Dec 27] quite good-topped colt: useful form, after being short of room 2f out, to run Bal Harbour to 2 lengths in minor event at Epsom on fourth start: poor efforts in handicaps at York (sweating), Newbury (pulled hard) and Jebel Ali last 3 starts: stays 10.3f: acts on good to firm ground: edgy sort. *H. Thomson Jones* — 99

YASHMAK (USA) 2 b.f. (May 8) Danzig (USA) – Slightly Dangerous (USA) 122 (Roberto (USA) 131) [1996 6m* 7.1m² 8d² Oct 6] closely-coupled, quite attractive filly: closely related to 1996 Derby and St Leger second Dushyantor (by Sadler's Wells), and half-sister to several winners, notably champion miler Warning (by Known Fact), top-class middle-distance colt Deploy (by Shirley Heights) and Derby winner Commander In Chief (by Dancing Brave): dam second in Oaks: most progressive form: won maiden at Newmarket in June: 2½ lengths second of 7, clear, to Red Camellia in listed race at Sandown in July: going in coat and mulish stalls, head second of 13 to Ryafan in Prix Marcel Boussac at Longchamp, scrubbed along to lie second early on, leading in straight but just unable to withstand the winner despite battling on gamely: will prove suited by further than 1m: yet to race on extremes of going. *H. R. A. Cecil* — 110

YAVERLAND (IRE) 4 b.c. Astronef 116 – Lautreamont (Auction Ring (USA) 123) [1995 59: 8.2d 8m 1996 10m⁵ 10g 10m a11g³ Sep 9] big, strong colt: has a round action: modest maiden handicapper: stays 11f: acts on fibresand and on good to firm and dead ground: bandaged behind in 1996. *C. A. Dwyer* — 61

YAVLENSKY (IRE) 2 b.c. (Feb 23) Caerleon (USA) 132 – Schwanensee (USA) (Mr Leader (USA)) [1996 7.5d 7.6m⁵ 8d* 9s² Nov 17] fifth foal: half-brother to 3 winners, notably fairly useful 4-y-o Albinor (1m, by Danehill): dam, unraced, from good German family: progressive form: won minor event at Milan in November: good second to Golden Aventura in Group 2 at Rome 2 weeks later: will stay 1½m: acts on soft going: will improve again. *J. L. Dunlop* — 97 p

YEAST 4 b.g. Salse (USA) 128 – Orient 106 (Bay Express 132) [1995 80p: 6g⁶ 7m³ 7g² 1996 8s* 7m* 7.6m² 8m* 10g 8m* 8g 8m* 9m Oct 5] — 114

    Trainer William Haggas had a memorable 1996. There was Shaamit's Derby, of course, but there were many other highlights, among them a career-best winning total, a first Ascot winner (which meant he had been successful on

Royal Hunt Cup (Handicap), Royal Ascot—Tertium (noseband) and Crumpton Hill have no chance with Yeast

Mr B. Haggas' "Yeast"

every course in Britain) then a first Royal Ascot winner. In any previous year either of that much improved pair Missile and Yeast would have stood out in the string. It was the strapping four-year-old gelding Yeast who was responsible for ending his trainer's wait for that full house of courses in the Insulpak Victoria Cup in May. Running off a BHB mark of 80 following a recent win in a maiden at Newcastle, he made light of his inexperience against twenty-three opponents. After the stable had waited so long for that first Ascot win Yeast soon added two more, first of all emulating Face North's 1994 Victoria Cup-Hunt Cup double. Although the draw played a major part in the Hunt Cup, Yeast still scored most decisively in a strong handicap, making most to beat Tertium by two and a half lengths. The gelding put up an even better performance in a £14,135 twelve-runner handicap on King George day in July, making all to beat Master Charter by three lengths, racing off a mark 17lb higher than in the Victoria. An unsuccessful first venture into pattern company followed in a Group 3 event at Baden-Baden, where he seemed ill-at-ease on the turns, but Yeast bounced back to form and put up his best performance to date in the nine-runner listed Joel Stakes at Newmarket, where he made all again and ran on with great determination to beat Restructure by one and a quarter lengths. Unexpectedly, he was turned out in the Cambridgeshire only two days later. He could make little impact, running off a mark of 112 over a distance that is probably beyond his best.

	Salse (USA) (b 1985)	Topsider (b 1974)	Northern Dancer Drumtop
Yeast (b.g. 1992)		Carnival Princess (ch 1974)	Prince John Carnival Queen
	Orient (b 1983)	Bay Express (b 1971)	Polyfoto Pal Sinna
		Gundi (b 1976)	Mummy's Pet Little Bird

Yeast's pedigree is discussed in some detail in the entry on fellow Royal Ascot winner Atraf; both are out of grand-daughters of Little Bird. The dam Orient, a useful sprinter who finished third in the 1987 King's Stand Stakes, had produced only one winner prior to her fourth foal Yeast, and that was the modest seven-furlong performer Lamsonetti (by Never So Bold). Pushka Fair, a year-older full-brother to Yeast, has yet to reveal any ability. The dam has had other foals but no further runners since Yeast. Yeast is a big and good-bodied gelding, whom jockey Kieran Fallon likened to 'riding a chaser, but with a lot more speed and ability'. He is best at seven furlongs or a mile, and failed to stay in his one race over a mile and a quarter. He seems ideally suited to a straight, galloping track like Ascot and Newmarket, while he acts on good to firm and soft ground. With Shaamit now resident at the National Stud and Missile sold to race in Hong Kong, the trainer will be grateful that Yeast will be still around in 1997. There won't be many handicaps open to the horse, but he looks well worth other chances in minor pattern company. *W. J. Haggas*

YEATH (IRE) 4 ch.g. Exhibitioner 111 – Grain of Sand (Sandford Lad 133) – [1995 57: 7.1g 8.3m⁶ 8.3m 8.1m 10d 1996 a8g 9.7m 7g Sep 6] rather leggy gelding: modest maiden handicapper: well below form in 1996: should stay beyond 1m: looks one paced. *R. Akehurst*

YELLOW DRAGON (IRE) 3 b.g. Kefaah (USA) 124 – Veldt (High Top 131) – § [1995 55: 5g 8.5s⁶ 10g³ 1996 a12g⁶ a10g⁶ 12f⁵ 10m a10g⁵ 10m a11g* a12g a13g a51 § 9.7g 11.6m 11.5m a10g⁴ 11.5m Oct 23] unfurnished gelding: has a round action: modest handicapper at best: first run on fibresand and gambled on, won selling event at Southwell in June: well beaten afterwards: should be suited by further than 11f: well beaten all 5 starts on equitrack: tried visored: ran out fourth 3-y-o start: sometimes slowly away: inconsistent and one to treat with caution. *B. A. Pearce*

YEOMAN OLIVER 3 b.c. Precocious 126 – Impala Lass 81 (Kampala 120) 73 [1995 –p: a5g⁶ a6g⁶ 1996 a7g² a8g² a8g³ a8g a8.5g* a8.5g² 8.2g⁶ 10g⁶ 8m⁴ a8g* 8.1d² a9.4g a9.4g a9.4g* a8.5g⁵ 7.1s⁴ 8g² 8.1s a9.4g² a9.4g a8.5s³ a9.4g Dec 28] fair handicapper: won at Wolverhampton (maiden) in February, Southwell in May and Wolverhampton (claimer, blinkered first time) in August: stays 9.4f: acts on fibresand and on soft ground: effective blinkered or not: usually races prominently: none too consistent. *B. A. McMahon*

YET-AGAIN 4 ch.g. Weldnaas (USA) 112 – Brightelmstone 105 (Prince Regent 53 + (FR) 129) [1995 61: a10g⁶ 10m² 8.5d⁵ 11.9m* 12g 10.1g 8d 1996 12f 12m 10s 10d 8m³ 10m 10.8f* 9.7g 9.2g⁶ 12s a12g* Dec 30] compact, good-bodied gelding: modest performer: won seller at Warwick in June: sold out of B. Hanbury's stable 5,200 gns Newmarket July Sales after ninth 4-y-o start: won 2 novice hurdles prior to landing odds in handicap at Lingfield in December (easily): stays 1½m: acts on firm ground and equitrack, below form on a soft surface: effective blinkered or not: progressing for new stable. *Miss Gay Kelleway*

YEZZA (IRE) 3 b.f. Distinctly North (USA) 115 – Small Paradise (Habat 127) 57 [1995 61p: 6m⁵ 1996 a8.5g 7d 8m 8.2m⁵ 8m 8.2m 7m⁴ 8g 8m 9.7d⁵ Oct 21] workmanlike filly: modest maiden handicapper: should stay beyond 1m: yet to race on extremes of going on turf: visored (no improvement) twice: inconsistent: sold 8,800 gns Newmarket Autumn Sales: sent to Germany. *A. P. Jarvis*

YIPSILANTI 3 ch.c. Master Willie 129 – Reel Foyle (USA) 77 (Irish River (FR) 131) [1995 NR 1996 8.1m Jul 25] medium-sized, sturdy colt: first foal: dam 5f winner: bought 7,200 gns Newmarket Autumn (1995) Sales: 25/1 and bandaged near-hind, 14 lengths seventh of 12 to Yalta in maiden at Sandown, taking keen hold then fading. *Lady Herries*

YO KIRI-B 5 b.m. Night Shift (USA) – Briar Creek (Busted 134) [1995 58, a54: 58
a10g⁵ 9.7g³ 8m⁶ 8m⁵ 9.7m* 9m⁵ 10f a10g⁴ a8g⁶ a7g³ 1996 a7g a7g³ a7g³ a7g* a61
a8.5g² a6g² 6g³ 7g² 6f a6g⁴ Oct 19] good-quartered mare: modest handicapper:
mostly in good form in 1996, winning at Southwell in March: left J. Ffitch-Heyes
after next start: effective at 6f, and appears to stay 10.3f: acts on good to firm and soft
ground and goes well on the all-weather: blinkered (not disgraced) once at 4 yrs.
T. J. Naughton

YOM JAMEEL (IRE) 3 b.c. Caerleon (USA) 132 – Topping Girl (Sea Hawk II 107
131) [1995 NR 1996 8m 10m* 12m² 10.1m⁴ 13.9m* 13.4d Aug 31] IR 80,000Y:
sturdy, good sort: half-brother to 8 winners, 3 at least useful, notably smart Irish
middle-distance performer Topanoora (by Ahonoora): dam never ran: useful form:
won maiden at Kempton in April and rated stakes at York (looked very well on first
run for 10 weeks, beat Wilawander by ¾ length) in August: never going well in listed
rated stakes on dead going at Chester on final start, reportedly finishing distressed:
should stay 2m+: acts on good to firm ground: may be capable of better still: sent to
UAE. *M. R. Stoute*

YORKIE GEORGE 2 b.c. (Feb 13) Efisio 120 – Petonica (IRE) 77 (Petoski 87
135) [1996 6g 6g* 6s* 7s³ Nov 9] 13,500Y, 14,000 2-y-o: sturdy, lengthy colt: first
foal: dam thrice-raced half-sister to Lochonica, useful sprinter at 2 yrs: fairly useful
form: won maiden at Hamilton and nursery at Newbury (leading just inside final 1f
and staying on strongly) in the autumn: stays 7f: acts on soft ground: bandaged off-
hind final start. *L. M. Cumani*

YORKSHIRE (IRE) 2 ch.c. (Feb 26) Generous (IRE) 139 – Ausherra (USA) 90 p
106 (Diesis 133) [1996 8d* Oct 2] second foal: dam won Lingfield Oaks Trial: 2/1
second favourite, overcame greenness to win 12-runner maiden at Salisbury in good
style by 7 lengths from Nordic Crest, soon pushed along, but travelling much better
when challenging 2f out and forging clear: will be well suited by middle distances:
sure to improve and win more races. *P. F. I. Cole*

YOUDONTSAY 4 ch.f. Most Welcome 131 – Fabulous Luba (Luthier 126) [1995 85
85: 5m² 6m* 5.1f⁴ 6g⁴ 6m* 6f² 5g⁵ 7d² 5s 7m 1996 6m⁴ 6f 5m* 5m 5g² 5m 6m 5g
Oct 19] workmanlike filly: fairly useful handicapper: none too consistent in 1996,
but came late to win strongly-run race at Goodwood in July: effective at 5f to 7f: acts
on firm and dead ground. *T. J. Naughton*

YOUGO 4 b.g. Good Times (ITY) – Young Wilkie (Callernish) [1995 74: 16.2m³ 75
13.4d³ 14s 15.8m⁴ a16g⁵ a13g³ a13g 1996 a12g* a16g³ a16g² a16g³ Feb 24] big,
workmanlike gelding: had a round action: fair performer: won weak maiden at
Southwell in January by 30 lengths: stayed 2m: acted on good to firm and dead
ground and the all-weather: front runner/raced prominently: dead. *M. Johnston*

YOUNG ANNABEL (USA) 3 ch.f. Cahill Road (USA) – Only For Eve (USA) 62
87 (Barachois (CAN)) [1995 NR 1996 8.2d⁶ 7m 8m a7g* 7g⁵ a8g 7.9g Sep 4] a68
lengthy, unfurnished filly: third foal: dam 2-y-o 5f to 7f winner: no worthwhile form
in 3 maidens on turf: well backed and having first run for 11 weeks when winning at
Southwell in July on handicap debut, travelling strongly to lead 2f out: below that
form in handicaps afterwards: should prove as effective over 6f as 7f: acts on fibresand. *C. A. Dwyer*

YOUNG BEN (IRE) 4 ch.g. Fayruz 116 – Jive (Ahonoora 122) [1995 –: 6m⁶ 41
7.5m⁵ 7m 5g 6d a6g 1996 a6g⁶ a7g a6g 5f 7.5m 5g³ 5m⁶ 5m³ 5m 5g³ 5m⁵ 6m Oct 23]
smallish gelding: poor maiden handicapper: will stay 6f: visored/blinkered last 7
starts. *J. S. Wainwright*

YOUNG BENSON 4 b.g. Zalazl (USA) 120 – Impala Lass 81 (Kampala 120) 63
[1995 71d: 7.1m⁵ 7.5m³ 7.5d⁵ 7m 7.1m² 7m³ 8m⁴ 8.2m⁵ 8f³ 7g 8.2m a6g a7g 1996
a8g⁶ a8.5g⁵ a11g³ a11g 10.8g 7m* a7g* a8.5g³ a7g a7g a9.4g⁶ Dec 28] angular,
workmanlike gelding: modest performer: won maiden at Thirsk and handicap at
Wolverhampton (made all) in the spring: left B. McMahon's stable after next outing:
ran poorly (blinkered/visored) all 3 starts for new yard: probably best at up to 1m:
acts on good to firm and dead ground and fibresand: also ran poorly in blinkers
second 4-y-o start. *T. Wall*

YOUNG BIGWIG (IRE) 2 b.c. (Mar 24) Anita's Prince 126 – Humble Mission 95
(Shack (USA) 118) [1996 5m⁴ a5g* 5g² 6m² 5.2f² 6m* 6d⁵ 6m³ Sep 14] IR 3,600F,
7,800Y: strong, lengthy colt: did well physically: fourth reported foal: half-brother to

7f winner Emphatic Candidate (by Salt Dome) and a 1m winner in Czech Republic by Magical Wonder: dam placed over 7f and 1m in Ireland: fairly useful form: won maiden auction at Wolverhampton in May and nursery (by short head) at Goodwood in July: below best last 2 starts: stays 6f: modest form to win on fibresand, acts on firm ground (beaten ½ length in Super Sprint at Newbury), possibly not on a soft surface. *J. Berry*

YOUNG BUTT 3 ch.c. Bold Owl 101 – Cymbal 80 (Ribero 126) [1995 60: 5m 66 6m 7.1g 6f a7g³ a6g⁶ 7g⁴ 10g² a8.5g* 1996 a11g⁵ 8f 8s* 10g³ 10m Jun 14] leggy colt: fair handicapper: 33/1-winner at Goodwood in May: stays 1¼m: acts on soft going and on fibresand. *J. Ffitch-Heyes*

YOUNG DUKE (IRE) 8 gr.g. Double Schwartz 128 – Princess Pamela 70 80 (Dragonara Palace (USA) 115) [1995 70: 8m² 1996 7m* 7f* 7.1f³ᵈⁱˢ 7.3m³ Sep 20] leggy gelding: fluent mover: reportedly suffers from leg problems: fairly useful handicapper: lightly raced: trained by R. Baker for belated reappearance, winning at Kempton in June: returned to former trainer and followed up at Newbury just over 3 weeks later, quickening in good style: decidedly unlucky not to complete hat-trick at Haydock (subsequently disqualified for interference) penultimate start: effective at 7f and stays 1m well: acts on firm ground, soft and equitrack: effective in blinkers or visor, has worn neither since 1992: sometimes carries head awkwardly and wanders under pressure. *Mrs S. D. Williams*

YOUNG ERN 6 b.h. Efisio 120 – Stardyn (Star Appeal 133) [1995 120: 7m* 8m² 114 8.5m⁶ 8m⁴ 6.5g² 7s² 6d² 7m 7f 1996 7g*⁷ 7d³ 8f⁴ 6.5d Aug 11] good-topped horse with a round action: gained his most prestigious wins in 1994 (Palais Royal, Hungerford) but remained a smart performer: clear-cut winner (for second year running) of listed race at Leicester in April: third of 6 to Mistle Cat in Prix du Palais Royal at Deauville and fourth of 9 to Charnwood Forest in Queen Anne Stakes at Royal Ascot next 2 outings: below form in Prix Maurice de Gheest at Deauville final start: effective at 6f to 1m: acted on any going: held up: genuine and consistent: retired to Cobhambury Farm Stud, Edenbridge, Kent, fee £2,500 (Oct 1st). *S. Dow*

YOUNG FREDERICK (IRE) 3 ch.g. Polish Patriot (USA) 128 – Notre – Histoire (Habitat 134) [1995 55: 6.9g a6g a7g⁵ 1996 a7g³ a7g³ a7g⁵ 7s 8g Jul 24] a63 modest maiden handicapper: should stay 1m: acts on equitrack and fibresand, well beaten on turf. *K. R. Burke*

YOUNG MAZAAD (IRE) 3 b.g. Mazaad 106 – Lucky Charm (IRE) (Pennine 67 Walk 120) [1995 –: 6g 8g 1996 a6g² 6s⁴ a6g⁴ 6.9m⁴ a7g² a8g² 8g² 6.9m* 6.9m² 6.9f² 8m Jun 29] workmanlike gelding: fair performer: won median auction maiden at Folkestone in May: effective at 7f, stays 1m well: acts on equitrack and on soft and firm ground: usually races prominently: visored/blinkered last 5 starts: consistent. *D. C. O'Brien*

YOUNG PRECEDENT 2 b.c. (Apr 23) Polish Precedent (USA) 131 – Guyum 65 p (Rousillon (USA) 133) [1996 7d⁴ Oct 28] 21,000F: second foal: half-brother to fairly useful 3-y-o 6f winner (including at 2 yrs) Midnight Blue (by Be My Chief): dam half-sister to smart sprinter Enchantment: 13/2, 11 lengths fourth of 18 to Maylane in maiden at Lingfield, soon prominent and keeping on: will improve. *P. W. Harris*

YOUNG ROSE 4 b.f. Aragon 118 – Primrose Way 59 (Young Generation 129) – [1995 NR 1996 a6g 7.1m 8.1m 12m 14.1g Oct 24] tall, workmanlike filly: modest form (rated 51) at 2 yrs: soundly beaten in 1996. *Pat Mitchell*

YOUNG SAFFY 3 ch.g. Safawan 118 – Miss Pisces 86 (Salmon Leap (USA) – 131) [1995 –: 8.1g 8.2d 7.1d 1996 11.9m Sep 6] rather leggy gelding: has a round action: no worthwhile form. *Mrs M. Reveley*

YOUR MOST WELCOME 5 b.m. Most Welcome 131 – Blues Player 70 62 (Jaazeiro (USA) 127) [1995 –: 10m³ 11.4m 8.2d⁶ 1996 a10g⁶ a10g* a10g a8g a10g* a66 12m 9m* 10g 12g 10f⁵ a12s⁴ a10g Dec 11] good-bodied mare: modest handicapper: won in January (maiden) and February (by 15 lengths), both at Lingfield: off course 7 months afterwards: came from off strong pace to win at Redcar in October: probably stays 1½m: acts on firm ground and on equitrack: twice blinkered, running well on first occasion. *D. J. S. ffrench Davis*

YOXALL LODGE 6 b.h. Aragon 118 – Opal Fancy 83 (Kibenka 119) [1995 63: 63 7.5m 8m 9.2g 7g³ 8.1g² a8g⁴ 1996 8.2m² 7s 8g 8g Sep 13] big, lengthy horse: modest handicapper: well beaten in 1996 after reappearance: stayed 1m: acted on heavy ground and on good to firm: used to race prominently: dead. *H. J. Collingridge*

YUBRALEE (USA) 4 ch.g. Zilzal (USA) 137 – Kentucky Lill (USA) (Raise A – Native) [1995 72: 7g⁵ 7m 10.2m 8.1g* 8.2m³ 10.8g⁵ 8.1d 1996 a10g 10.1m Jun 9] lengthy, quite attractive gelding: good mover: fair performer on flat in 1995, best at around 1m: fairly useful form over hurdles, winner in October and November: well beaten on flat in 1996. *M. C. Pipe*

YUKON HOPE (USA) 3 b.f. Forty Niner (USA) – Sahara Forest (Green Desert 75 (USA) 127) [1995 NR 1996 6g³ 6m⁴ 8.1m² 8.5m⁶ 8m² 8m⁴ Oct 23] quite attractive filly: first foal: dam unraced half-sister to Reference Point: fair maiden: will stay 1¼m. *R. Charlton*

YUPPY GIRL (IRE) 3 ch.f. Salt Dome (USA) – Sloane Ranger 84 (Sharpen Up 52 127) [1995 61: 6m⁶ 6.1m² 7m⁵ 7g² 7.5d⁴ 6g⁴ 6f⁴ 1996 a7g⁴ a8.5g³ 8.1g⁵ 8m 10g 10m² 10g 10.8m⁵ a12g 10f 8m⁴ a11g⁶ Nov 18] sparely-made filly: modest maiden: stays 1¼m: acts on good to firm ground: usually comes from behind: not easiest of rides. *Capt. J. Wilson*

Z

ZAAHIR (IRE) 2 b.c. (Apr 5) Marju (IRE) 127 – Abhaaj 91 (Kris 135) [1996 6g³ 75 p Nov 1] fourth foal: half-brother to 3 winners, including useful sprinter Mubhij (by Mujtahid) and 1m winner Dalu (by Dancing Brave): dam 2-y-o 5f winner who ran once at 3 yrs, out of 5f-winning half-sister to Danzig: 4¾ lengths third of 11 to Kumait in maiden at Newmarket, chasing winner after slow start but unable to match strides from 2f out, not given a hard time: will improve. *B. W. Hills*

ZAALEFF (USA) 4 ch.c. Zilzal (USA) 137 – Continual (USA) (Damascus 54 d (USA)) [1995 63: 7.1g 8.3m 1996 7g 14.1g a12g⁴ a12g⁵ 10m³ a9.4g 10m² 8.2m 8.3g⁴ 10f 10m Jul 29] strong, lengthy colt: modest maiden handicapper: barely stays 1½m: acts on good to firm ground and on fibresand: blinkered since third 4-y-o start: inconsistent: has joined Dr J. D. Scargill. *B. Hanbury*

ZABADI (IRE) 4 b.g. Shahrastani (USA) 135 – Zerzaya 90 (Beldale Flutter – (USA) 130) [1995 7v* 10g² 7m* 1996 12d Apr 20] lengthy, good-quartered ex-Irish gelding: third foal: half-brother to fair Irish 1¼m winner Zabargar (by Riverman): dam, 1¼m winner, is half-sister to Zayyani: rated 101 in spring of 1995 for J. Oxx, winning minor events at Tipperary and Naas: one of the top juvenile hurdlers in 1995/6 for present stable: behind in John Porter Stakes at Newbury on return to flat: should stay 1½m: acts on good to firm and heavy ground. *D. Nicholson*

ZACAROON 5 b.m. Last Tycoon 131 – Samaza (USA) 90 (Arctic Tern (USA) – 126) [1995 69, a64: a10g⁵ a8g³ a8g³ a10g² 10.3m² 10g³ 10g* 10m² 10g⁵ a8.5g⁴ 10f⁵ a10g a10g 1996 a8g a10g 11.4d⁴ 8f 8.1s Oct 22] lengthy mare: fair 1¼m performer at best in 1995 for Lord Huntingdon: soundly beaten in 1996. *J. Ffitch-Heyes*

ZAFARELLI 2 gr.g. (Feb 1) Nishapour (FR) 125 – Voltigeuse (USA) (Filiberto – (USA) 123) [1996 8g Nov 2] IR 6,500Y: half-brother to several winners, including stayer Vaniski (by Niniski) and (at 1¼m) Volte Face (by Blakeney): dam (unraced) out of sister to Valoris and half-sister to Val De Loir: 25/1, always behind in 21-runner seller at Newmarket. *S. C. Williams*

ZAFORUM 3 b.c. Deploy 131 – Beau's Delight (USA) (Lypheor 118) [1995 89?: 100 9m⁵ 8.1d⁵ 10g⁵ 10m⁴ 9s 1996 12m⁶ 11.5f³ 12m 16.2m 14g⁵ 14m* 16g³ Nov 1] strong colt: has a round action: useful performer: best efforts when third of 6 to Mystic Knight in Derby Trial at Lingfield in May and third of 11 to easy winner Orchestra Stall in rated stakes at Newmarket in November, both steadily-run races: won maiden at Lingfield in October: suited by a test of stamina: acts on firm ground: blinkered (and front runner) last 2 starts: sweating (well beaten in the Derby) third 3-y-o start. *L. Montague Hall*

ZAFZALA (IRE) 3 b.f. Kahyasi 130 – Zerzaya 90 (Beldale Flutter (USA) 130) 115 [1995 6d² 6m* 1996 7d² 8d⁶ 10m² 12m* 12m⁵ 12.5d³ 11s⁴ Oct 19] leggy filly: fourth foal: half-sister to dual-purpose winners Zabadi (useful on flat, by Shahrastani) and Zabargar (stays 1½m, by Riverman): dam, 1¼m winner, is half-sister to Zayyani (stayed 1½m, rated 119): smart Irish performer: won maiden at Naas at 2 yrs: 1½ lengths second to Dance Design in Pretty Polly Stakes at the Curragh before winning listed event at Leopardstown in July by a length from Fill The Bill: very best effort when head second of 10 to My Emma in Prix Vermeille (edging left under strong drive and demoted to fifth) at Longchamp: creditable 4 lengths third of 13 to Annaba in Prix de Royallieu (ran on from rear unable to land a blow) there later in the autumn: will stay beyond 12.5f: acts on good to firm and dead ground, ran respectably on soft: blinkered (ran creditably in Irish 1000 Guineas) second 3-y-o start. *J. Oxx, Ireland*

ZAGREB (USA) 3 b.c. Theatrical 128 – Sophonisbe (Wollow 132) [1995 NR 127 1996 10s* 12g² 12m* 12d Oct 6]

Zagreb joined the exodus of classic winners to Japan quietly in November. A news item in an inside corner of *Racing Post* reported his sale for an 'undisclosed multi-million sum' and briefly outlined his career—runaway 20/1-winner of the Budweiser Irish Derby on only his third start, disappointing in the Prix de l'Arc de Triomphe on his fourth and last. Disappointing would have been altogether too mild a word to describe multi-million Zagreb's finishing out with the washing behind Helissio except for the fact that he had not put in an appearance since that runaway win in June and had passed up a firm date in the Irish Champion Stakes in September. After all, just after the Irish Derby, and just before the King George, he had been quoted 6/1 ante-post favourite for the Arc by bookmakers William Hill ahead of Helissio (7/1), Riyadian (8/1), Darazari (10/1), Shaamit (10/1), Swain (10/1) and Pentire (12/1). All that seems a long time ago now.

Shaamit had caused a minor sensation by winning the Derby as a twice-raced maiden winner who had never previously tackled pattern company. Zagreb won the Irish Derby with similar credentials, his earned as a three-year-old. Odds of 20/1 about the inexperienced Zagreb for the Irish Derby did not seem particularly generous. He had recently been beaten a head by the four-year-old Damancher on unfavourable terms in a minor event at Leopardstown, having previously decisively won a well-contested maiden race at the Curragh on his debut. While neither Shaamit nor Ragmar were among his twelve opponents, the Derby runner-up Dushyantor and the Prix du Jockey-Club runner-up Polaris Flight were, along with the one-time Derby favourite Dr Massini and the previous season's top two-year-old Alhaarth. Weld's stable-jockey Kinane stuck by Stoute's Dr Massini, leaving the ride on Zagreb to thirty-three-year-old Pat Shanahan whose biggest win had been on Princess Pati in the Irish Oaks of 1984. The two jockeys' post-race comments told much of the Irish Derby story, Kinane's 'he was never travelling' contrasting with Shanahan's 'he was always travelling well and I just couldn't believe how easily he was going coming down the hill. I kicked on two out and saw no more horses after.'

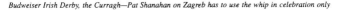

Budweiser Irish Derby, the Curragh—Pat Shanahan on Zagreb has to use the whip in celebration only

Zagreb had had his opponents well beaten two furlongs out and galloped on with great zest, looking the best middle-distance three-year-old seen out so far as he put six lengths between himself and Polaris Flight. Dr Massini came a remote seventh, Alhaarth ninth, while a below-form Dushyantor in fourth was beaten the best part of thirteen lengths, unable to hold off 50/1-shot His Excellence. This overwhelming victory brought Zagreb's trainer the full set of Irish classics after twenty-four years with a licence. It also raised hopes, widely, of even better to come from Zagreb and held out possibilities of a vintage three-year-old crop. So much more disappointing to record, therefore, that Zagreb, Shaamit and the nine-length winner of the Oaks, Lady Carla, did not muster another win between them. Zagreb's stable-companion the Irish Oaks winner Dance Design filled in admirably for him in the Irish Champion Stakes, coming second to Timarida, and the way things turned out she would not have had much difficulty in beating him in the Arc. Zagreb was soon going strongly behind Helissio at Longchamp but was quickly done with once into the straight and his jockey (Kinane) eased right up in the closing stages. The newspapers had it that Zagreb would probably run next in the Breeders' Cup Turf, the owners having turned down a big offer from Japan. He missed Woodbine because of a 'head cold'—he also reportedly had one in the spring—but report-edly remained in training for the Japan Cup. So much for that. He eventually left for the Far East with a very different assignment, and left us with little more to remember him by than one very impressive performance.

Zagreb went one better in the Irish Derby than his sire, the then Dermot Weld-trained Theatrical who improved at four and again at five in different stables in the United States and at five won the Breeders' Cup Turf from the Arc winner Trempolino. Zagreb is one of the best of a commendable number of good-class runners sired by Theatrical worldwide. The St Leger second Broadway Flyer and the Pouliches winner Madeleine's Dream have been among the sire's other representatives in Europe. Zagreb's dam Sophonisbe won a small race over eleven furlongs at Longchamp as a three-year-old for her breeder Daniel Wildenstein. That same year the family provided Wildenstein with his Arc winner Sagace, who was by Luthier out of Seneca, a daughter of the German One Thousand Guineas and Oaks winner Schonbrunn. And the previous year, 1983, Sophonisbe's dam the useful stayer Southern Seas had foaled a colt by Habitat who was to earn well over three million dollars on the track: his name was Steinlen, Breeders' Cup Mile winner and champion grass horse. Sophonisbe herself produced minor winners by Top Ville, Shareef Dancer and Blushing John from seven foals prior to Zagreb. Her next foal, a colt by Jade Hunter, made 1,380,000 francs (approximately £176,000) at the Deauville Yearling Sales in August.

	Theatrical (b 1982)	Nureyev (b 1977)	Northern Dancer Special
Zagreb (USA) (b.c. 1993)		Tree of Knowledge (b 1977)	Sassafras Sensibility
	Sophonisbe (b 1981)	Wollow (b 1973)	Wolver Hollow Wichuraiana
		Southern Seas (b or br 1975)	Jim French Schonbrunn

Zagreb is a tall colt. He looked to have lots of scope to develop further, which was all the more reason to be enthusiastic about him and his prospects. In an interview before the Arc his trainer said of him 'With Zagreb, I have always looked at the big picture; I see him as reaching his peak as a four-year-old and as a five-year-old.' Zagreb was not tested enough to reveal much about his ground requirements. He won the Curragh maiden pulling away by four and a half lengths from twenty-six opponents on soft. He got the green light to run in the Irish Derby only when connections had passed the going as not too firm shortly before forty-eight-hour declaration time; on the day it seemed to be good to firm and no firmer. The ground was good to soft for the Arc. As to his merit, he can be rated only on what he did in an average renewal of the Irish Derby. There is a distinct possibility that he was better than that, but we will never know. *D. K. Weld, Ireland*

ZAGROS (IRE) 2 b.g. (Mar 5) Persian Heights 129 – Hana Marie 101§ – (Formidable (USA) 125) [1996 5.9g May 30] 3,200Y: third foal: half-brother to 3-y-o La Tansani (by High Estate): dam 2-y-o 5f and 6f winner: never a factor, not knocked about, in maiden auction at Carlisle: gelded: seemed likely to do better. *T. D. Easterby*

ZAHID (USA) 5 ch.g. Storm Cat (USA) – Time An' Care (USA) (Twin Time – (USA)) [1995 50: 10.3g 15.4g 14m⁴ 12.5m⁵ 9.7g⁴ 9.7m³ 9m⁴ 10m⁶ 8m⁴ 1996 a10g² a64 a10g² a10g* a9.4g* a9.4g³ a10g² 9.7m a10s a10g³ a12g³ a10g⁶ Dec 30] good-topped, attractive gelding: impresses in appearance: modest handicapper on the all-weather, poor on turf: won at Lingfield (minor event) in February and Wolverhampton in March: probably stays 12.5f: acts on fibresand and equitrack, raced only on a sound surface on turf: effective blinkered/visored or not: modest hurdler, winner twice in June. *K. R. Burke*

ZAHRAN (IRE) 5 b.h. Groom Dancer (USA) 128 – Welsh Berry (USA) (Sir Ivor 46 135) [1995 60d: a8.5g⁴ a8.5g⁶ a8g a8g² a9.4g⁴ a8g⁴ a8g* a8.5g 7g a8g 8m 8g² 10.2m a49 a8.5g⁶ 8f² 8m³ 8.1g 8m⁴ 9.2f* 10m⁶ a10g⁴ 10.1g⁶ 1996 a8g³ a7g³ a8g a8g a8g³ 8f 8f⁴ 8g² 10m³ 9m⁵ 10.8f⁶ 8.2m⁶ 10m² 9.7g⁴ 10g 10f 10m⁶ a10g 9.2f⁶ 10d 10.1m⁴ a8g³ a8g* a10s a8g³ a8g Dec 13] strong, good-topped horse: unimpressive mover: poor handicapper in 1996, winner at Lingfield in November: stays 1¼m: acts on firm and soft ground and goes well on all-weather surfaces: tried visored/blinkered, no improvement. *J. M. Bradley*

ZA-IM 2 b.c. (May 3) Green Desert (USA) 127 – Al Bahathri (USA) 123 (Blushing 100 p Groom (FR) 131) [1996 5.7d⁵ 6s* Oct 24] good-bodied, attractive colt: fluent mover:

seventh foal: half-brother to 3 winners, including useful 1m winner (stayed 1¼m) Goalwah (by Sadler's Wells) and smart 7f/1m performer Hasbah (by Kris): dam won Lowther Stakes and Irish 1000 Guineas: stepped up good deal on debut form when winning 23-runner maiden at Newbury in October in good style by 2 lengths from Soviet State, always travelling really well and nudged clear over 1f out: will be suited by further than 6f: raced only on a soft surface: useful already, and will improve again. *B. W. Hills*

ZAIMA (IRE) 2 b.f. (Apr 13) Green Desert (USA) 127 – Usaylah 98 (Siberian Express (USA) 125) [1996 6.1f⁵ 6m⁴ 6m⁴ 7f* 8m³ Oct 23] third foal: closely related to 1m winner Kaf (by Polish Precedent): dam 9f to 10.6f winner and half-sister to Alhijaz: fairly useful form: won nursery at Redcar in September, leading over 1f out and always looking like holding on: stays 1m: raced only on top-of-the-ground. *J. L. Dunlop* — 82

ZAIN DANCER 4 ch.g. Nabeel Dancer (USA) 120 – Trojan Lady (USA) (Irish River (FR) 131) [1995 NR 1996 a7g⁶ 7s 7m 7g² 7.1g² 8f³ 7m⁴ 7g⁶ 7m³ 7g Sep 5] good-topped gelding: has a long, low stride: modest maiden at 2 yrs for A. Scott: raced in Czech Republic in 1995, winning over 7f: modest handicapper on return to Britain: stays 1m: acts on firm ground, has failed to handle soft conditions twice: tried blinkered, no improvement. *D. Nicholls* — 59

ZAJIRA (IRE) 6 b.m. Ela-Mana-Mou 132 – Awsaaf (USA) 94 (Naskra (USA)) [1995 NR 1996 12m⁶ 16.2m Jul 26] sturdy mare: fairly useful performer in 1993: first runs on flat since 1994 when well beaten in handicaps at Doncaster and Ascot: covered by Teenoso. *P. Eccles* — –

ZAJKO (USA) 6 b.g. Nureyev (USA) 131 – Hope For All (USA) (Secretariat (USA)) [1995 83: 8m 8m* 10f 8d 7g 8f² 1996 8m 8s 8.1m⁶ 8d 8g³ 8d Oct 12] good-topped gelding: fairly useful handicapper: clearly best 6-y-o effort when third of 25 to Amrak Ajeeb in £29,700 event (didn't have best of draw) at Ascot on penultimate start: best at 1m: acts on firm ground, possibly not on a soft surface: visored (ran poorly) once at 2 yrs: best held up behind sound pace. *Lady Herries* — 78

ZALAMENT 4 b.f. Zalazl (USA) 120 – Key To Enchantment (Key To Content (USA)) [1995 57d: 11m 10.5g⁵ 10g 12m³ 14m⁵ 12s 11.9m a12g a7g 1996 a12g Jan 8] leggy, angular filly: modest maiden: no worthwhile form last 5 starts: sold 500 gns Doncaster July Sales. *N. P. Littmoden* — –

ZALOTTI (IRE) 3 ch.f. Polish Patriot (USA) 128 – Honest Penny (USA) (Honest Pleasure (USA)) [1995 84: 5g* 1996 5m* 5m 5f Sep 17] quite attractive filly: reportedly sustained fracture of off-hind cannon bone after winning only race at 2 yrs: comfortably won claimer at Pontefract (idled, claimed out of T. Etherington's stable £15,000) on return in August: well held in handicap and claimer afterwards: raced only at 5f on a sound surface. *M. H. Tompkins* — 78

ZALOTTO (IRE) 2 b.g. (Mar 22) Polish Patriot (USA) 128 – Honest Penny (USA) (Honest Pleasure (USA)) [1996 7g Sep 4] 10,000F, IR 38,000Y: good-topped gelding: has plenty of scope: brother to 3-y-o 5f winner Zalotti and half-brother to several winners, including 7f to 12.5f winner Return To Romance (by Trojan Fen) and fair 1991 2-y-o 6f winner Penny Orchid (by Taufan): dam placed over 5f at 2 yrs in Ireland: 25/1, backward and green, tailed off in 12-runner maiden at York. *T. J. Etherington* — –

ZAMALEK (USA) 4 b.g. Northern Baby (CAN) 127 – Chellingoua (USA) (Sharpen Up 127) [1995 85: 8g⁴ 10.4m⁴ 8m⁵ 1996 7f 8g 12m 10m 10m a10g⁶ 8m Sep 25] sturdy, good sort: fairly useful for H. Cecil in 1995: well below form in handicaps in 1996: best form at up to around 1m: acts on soft ground, respectable effort at 3 yrs on good to firm: tried blinkered/visored, no improvement: temperamentally suspect: has joined R. M. Flower. *G. L. Moore* — –

ZAMHAREER (USA) 5 b.g. Lear Fan (USA) 130 – Awenita (Rarity 129) [1995 48: 12.1s⁵ 15.8g 14g⁶ 14s⁵ 1996 14.1m⁵ 16.1g* 16g* 16.2f⁶ 15.9m 16s 17.5m Sep 20] rather leggy gelding: fairly useful staying hurdler: modest form on flat: ridden by 7-lb claimer Iona Wands when winning handicaps at Newcastle and Ripon in May: below form for her, seeming to run moody races, last 2 starts: should stay further than 2m: best form on flat with some give in the ground: usually forces pace. *W. Storey* — 55

ZAMINDAR (USA)   2 b.c. (Apr 7) Gone West (USA) – Zaizafon (USA) 119   116
(The Minstrel (CAN) 135) [1996 5.5d* 6g* 6g² 7m³ Sep 15]

    In 1992 Zafonic went into winter quarters the shortest-priced favourite
for the Two Thousand Guineas for more than forty years. For a while in the
summer of 1996 his two-year-old brother Zamindar looked like being pretty
short for the race himself, until defeated in the Prix Morny and then the Prix de
la Salamandre, both races that Zafonic had won. Things got off to a bad start for
the much-touted Zamindar when he reared in the stalls and banged his head on
his intended debut at Chantilly in June and had to be withdrawn. There were no
problems at Maisons-Laffitte the following month though, when he beat four
rivals by five lengths in a newcomers race at long odds on. Nor were there any
at Deauville a month later where Zamindar easily accounted for an even
smaller field in the Group 3 Prix de Cabourg, beating Dyhim Diamond by two
and a half lengths, again making all. At Deauville later in August, Zamindar
started at 10/3-on for the Prix Morny in a field of five in which the Prix
Yacowlef winner Pas de Reponse was the only other French-trained runner.
After a steadily-run first furlong he was at the head of affairs again but, when
tackled by Bahamian Bounty approaching the last, Zamindar, who had been
travelling the better two out, was unable to respond and went down by a short
neck. While connections attributed his defeat partly to inexperience, his trainer
was apparently furious with Jarnet for not making more use of him. The same
criticism could not be levelled after the Prix de la Salamandre at Longchamp

Prix de Cabourg, Deauville—Zamindar provokes comparisons with his brother Zafonic

but again things did not go to plan. This time Zamindar was provided with a pacemaker, Sacristan, but the latter soon proved redundant after an indifferent start as Zamindar, odds on again, and The West began to fight for the lead at a suicidal pace (officially 55.1 seconds for the first one thousand metres). They had nothing left when Revoque challenged. In the end Zamindar was beaten three lengths and a short head into third behind Revoque and The West, not surprisingly failing to reproduce his Morny form. He did not run again, but the Guineas reportedly remains his target in 1997.

A stunning victory in the Guineas was the highlight of Zafonic's career which ended after he was found to have bled when flopping in the Sussex Stakes. He and Zamindar are two of five winners produced by their dam Zaizafon, the others being Botanic (by Mr Prospector) and Bold Empress (by Diesis) who have won over sprint distances in the United States and France respectively, and Press Baron (by Private Account) who won twice in France over a mile at two. Zaizafon, who has a yearling sister to Zamindar and Zafonic and a foal by Danzig, won two races over seven furlongs at two, including the Group 3 Seaton Delaval Stakes, but showed her best form on top-of-the-ground at a mile at three with smart performances in the frame in the Child Stakes and the Queen Elizabeth II Stakes. This family, which has shot to prominence in the 'nineties, is clearly one we will be hearing more of. Zaizafon is half-sister to another of Khalid Abdulla's notable broodmares, the unraced Modena, responsible for Elmaamul and the latest Fillies' Mile winner Reams of Verse. Zaizafon is also a sibling of two other animals who were useful performers at two for Khalid Abdulla, the Middle Park third Factual and close relative Dangora who was beaten a head in the Lowther Stakes. The latter's own two-year-old daughter Corsini was successful in the latest season for Khalid Abdulla, as was the Cherry Hinton third Well Warned, a granddaughter of Zaizafon's sister Mariakova. Zamindar's grandam Mofida was a tough and smart performer at up to seven furlongs but her dam Wold Lass, a half-sister to the smart miler Chebs Lad, was just a winning plater.

Zamindar (USA) (b.c. Apr 7, 1994)	Gone West (USA) (b 1984)	Mr Prospector (b 1970)	Raise A Native
			Gold Digger
		Secrettame (ch 1978)	Secretariat
			Tamerett
	Zaizafon (USA) (ch 1982)	The Minstrel (ch 1974)	Northern Dancer
			Fleur
		Mofida (ch 1974)	Right Tack
			Wold Lass

A big, good-topped individual, Zamindar is physically very much in the same mould as his brother. While clearly not in the same class as Zafonic, Zamindar is a smart colt and the subsequent wins of Bahamian Bounty in the Middle Park, Pas de Reponse in the Cheveley Park and Revoque in the Grand Criterium put his efforts in the Prix Morny and the Prix de la Salamandre in a better light. Although bred to stay a mile, there has to be a strong possibility that Zamindar will prove best as a sprinter, though it has to be said that small fields have hardly helped him settle in behind, tactics which proved best for Zafonic. Zamindar has long since lost his place at the head of the Guineas market (he is 20/1 at the time of writing) but he will be an interesting runner all the same if he takes his chance at Newmarket. *A. Fabre, France*

ZANABAY 2 b.f. (Apr 14) Unfuwain (USA) 131 – Chrisanthy 81 (So Blessed 130) 53
[1996 5.2d 7m⁴ 7f 6d⁴ 6m⁵ Sep 10] 7,200Y: closely related to 7f (at 2 yrs) to 1¼m winner Satis Dancer (by Mashhor Dancer) and half-sister to 2 winners, including 7f (at 2 yrs) to 1¼m winner Ivan The Terrible (by Siberian Express): dam 2-y-o 5f winner who failed to train on: modest maiden: seems to stay 7f: best efforts on top-of-the-ground. *Martyn Meade*

ZANZARA (IRE) 5 ch.m. Efisio 120 – Slick Chick 89 (Shiny Tenth 120) [1995 –
54: a7g³ a8g⁶ a8g 10m 8f a8g⁵ 10g 10m⁴ a12g 13.8m* 17.1m² a16g 13.8f* 15.1s 1996 a16g Feb 9] smallish, strong mare: modest performer in first half of 1995: tailed off only 5-y-o start: covered by Clantime. *Mrs V. A. Aconley*

ZARALASKA 5 ch.g. Shernazar 131 – Eskimo Spring (USA) (Riverman (USA) 90
131) [1995 98p: 8d 10f² 12g* 12m² 1996 12g 12g Oct 26] sturdy, quite attractive
gelding: has a quick action: progressive form at 4 yrs: not seen in 1996 until late-
September, shaping fairly well in £44,700 handicap at Ascot and £12,200 handicap
at Doncaster (finished very tired when eighth of 19) 4 weeks later: much better at
1½m than shorter, and should stay 1¾m: acts on good to firm ground, unraced on a
soft surface except for 1995 reappearance. *L. M. Cumani*

ZARETSKI 2 b.c. (Mar 17) Pursuit of Love 124 – Tolstoya (Northfields (USA)) 77
[1996 5m 6m³ 6m⁴ 7m² 7f⁴ 6m Oct 3] 34,000F, IR 65,000Y: strong, good-bodied
colt: carries condition: half-brother to several winners, including useful 3-y-o
sprinter (fairly useful as 2-y-o) Wildwood Flower (by Distant Relative): dam Irish
2-y-o 5f winner: fair form: stays 7f but may well prove more effective at sprint
distances (behind in Middle Park Stakes final outing): has raced only on top-of-
the-ground. *C. E. Brittain*

ZATOPEK 4 b. or br.g. Reprimand 122 – Executive Lady 59 (Night 65 d
Shift (USA)) [1995 61: 7f⁵ 9g 8g⁴ 7d 1996 6.9s³ 8d 7.3s 8m⁵ a9.4g a12g² a9.4g⁶ a12g
a8g Dec 3] sturdy gelding: has quick action: modest maiden handicapper: below
form after reappearance: stays 1½m: acts on any going: blinkered/visored once each.
J. Cullinan

ZDENKA 3 b.f. Dominion 123 – Short And Sharp 88 (Sharpen Up 127) [1995 67: 47 d
6f 7m² 7m² 7f⁵ 6.9s² 8g⁶ 1996 8m 7.1d 11.6m⁴ 10f⁵ 8.3g 7g 8g 8m 8g⁵ Oct 29] leggy
filly: unimpressive mover: just a poor maiden on balance of form in 1996: claimed to
join M. Pipe £3,000 final start: stays 1m: acts on good to firm ground, apparently best
effort on soft. *M. Blanshard*

ZELAYA (IRE) 3 b.f. Shaadi (USA) 126 – Zizania 77 (Ahonoora 122) [1995 62p: 45
6g 1996 a7g⁶ a8g³ a7g² Dec 30] good-topped filly: sold out of C. Brittain's stable
only 600 gns Newmarket July (1996) Sales: poor form at Lingfield late in 1996: stays
1m. *G. L. Moore*

ZELDA ZONK 4 b.f. Law Society (USA) 130 – Massive Powder (Caerleon 80
(USA) 132) [1995 67: 7.3m 8m⁵ 8d³ 7d 8m⁴ 7m³ 1996 8m³ 7m* 7.3s⁵ 8m 7g* 7m⁴
7g³ 7f³ 7g² Aug 1] sturdy filly: fairly useful handicapper: won at Redcar in May and
Kempton in June: effective at 7f, and stays 1m: acts on firm and dead ground,
possibly not on soft: has been bandaged behind: genuine. *B. J. Meehan*

ZELIBA 4 br.f. Doyoun 124 – Zia (USA) 88 (Shareef Dancer (USA) 135) [1995 –: 43
a7g a7g⁶ 7f 1996 a8g 11.9f 8g 9.7m³ 10m² 10g 12.5f* a12g⁵ 11.9f* 12m³ 11.9f 16m⁴ a–
15.4g 17.9g² 18g 14.1g⁶ a14.8g a16g Dec 26] smallish, leggy filly: poor
handicapper: claimed out of C. Brittain's stable £6,000 on fifth start: subsequently
won sellers at Warwick in July and Brighton in August: retained 1,200 gns Doncaster
November Sales: tailed off last 2 starts: effective at 1½m, and stays 2¼m: acts on
firm ground, little form on all-weather. *Mrs N. Macauley*

ZELZELAH (USA) 3 b.f. Timeless Moment (USA) – Allevition (USA) –
(Alleged (USA) 138) [1995 96: 7g* 7g 8d⁶ 1996 10.4m⁵ May 15] long-backed filly:
useful form on debut: failed to repeat it: short to post, thoroughly mulish and off bit
before straight in minor event at York in May: dead. *P. A. Kelleway*

ZERMATT (IRE) 6 b.h. Sadler's Wells (USA) 132 – Chamonis (USA) 101 74
(Affirmed (USA)) [1995 74: 10m 10.1f 8m* 8f² 8.1m³ 8m⁴ 8m 10m⁵ 8.3m 10.5g⁵ 9d
1996 10.8d⁵ 10g⁶ 12m⁴ 10.2f² 10d* 10.1m 11.6g 10m⁶ 9f⁶ Jul 20] tall, strong horse:
unimpressive mover: fair handicapper: won at Kempton in May, dictating pace in
falsely-run affair: barely stays 1½m and is better at shorter distances: acts on firm and
soft ground. *M. D. I. Usher*

ZESTI 4 br.g. Charmer 123 – Lutine Royal 46 (Formidable (USA) 125) [1995 43: 36
a8.5g³ a8g a8.5g 8.3g 8.2m 1996 a12g² a12g³ a16g⁵ a14g 12s³ Nov 11] poor maiden:
only 4-y-o form in selling handicap at Folkestone on final start: stays 1½m: acts on
heavy ground: won selling hurdle in December. *T. T. Clement*

ZEST (USA) 2 gr. or ro.f. (Apr 20) Zilzal (USA) 137 – Toveris 91 (Homing 130) –
[1996 6g Nov 1] $40,000Y: eighth foal: half-sister to several winners in North
America and a champion in Mexico: dam, 2-y-o 7f winner, didn't recover form:
hampered at start, soon behind (raced away from principals) in 11-runner Newmarket
maiden. *M. Bell*

ZIBETH 2 b.f. (Feb 11) Rainbow Quest (USA) 134 – Tiger Flower 103 (Sadler's – p
Wells (USA) 132) [1996 8f Oct 15] second foal: closely related to 3-y-o 1½m winner
Tiger Lake (by Nashwan): dam, 1¼m winner placed at 1½m, out of sister to high-
class American middle-distance stayer One On The Aisle: weak 10/1-shot, just over
16 lengths ninth of 12 to Our People in maiden at Leicester, outpaced from halfway:
will be suited by middle distances: should do better in time. *L. M. Cumani*

ZIDAC 4 b. or br.g. Statoblest 120 – Sule Skerry 78 (Scottish Rifle 127) [1995 75: 82
10g⁴ 10m⁵ 9m⁴ 10m⁴ 10g 12.1s 1996 a11g² 10g* 10m* 10m Oct 1] tall gelding: fair
handicapper: won at Leicester (first time) and Lingfield (amateurs) in the spring: off
course nearly 5 months before tailed off on final outing: likely to prove best at up to
11f: acts on good to firm ground: sometimes flashes tail but is genuine: races
prominently. *P. J. Makin*

ZIGGY'S DANCER (USA) 5 b.h. Ziggy's Boy (USA) – My Shy Dancer 88
(USA) (Northjet 136) [1995 97: a9.4g a7g³ a7g* a7g² a6g* 6g 5.9m* 6m² 5f* 6m 6f
6.1m² 6m⁴ 5.1g* 5g⁶ 6g 5m 5s⁶ 6g 5m⁴ 5m⁶ a5g* 1996 5d⁴ 5.2d⁶ 6g 5.1g³ 5m⁶ 5d
6.1m⁵ 5m² 5.1m⁴ 5m 5m⁴ 6m³ 6g 5.1d⁴ 5f² 6m 7m⁴ 5g 5m³ a6g Nov 16] lengthy
horse: poor mover: fairly useful handicapper: failed to win in 1996, but ran creditably
most starts: effective at 5f to 7f: acts on firm and dead ground and the all-weather:
tough and consistent. *E. J. Alston*

ZIGGY'S VIOLA (IRE) 2 b.f. (Jan 10) Roi Danzig (USA) – Olivia Jane (IRE) 56
(Ela-Mana-Mou 132) [1996 7.9g 7g⁶ a8g² a8.5g Nov 25] IR 6,000Y, 18,000 2-y-o:
smallish, angular filly: first foal: dam unraced daughter of smart Irish middle-
distance filly Green Lucia, herself half-sister to Old Vic: modest form in autumn
maidens: stiffish task in nursery final outing: will stay beyond 1m. *Mrs M. Reveley*

ZIGSE 2 b.g. (Apr 10) Emarati (USA) 74 – Primrose Way 59 (Young Generation 64
129) [1996 6m 9f² Sep 28] 4,000F, 7,000Y: sixth foal: half-brother to 3-y-o 9.4f seller
winner Sweet Amoret (by Forzando): dam middle-distance maiden: much better
effort in maiden events when 1¾ lengths second of 5 to Windsor Castle at Redcar:
will stay at least 1¼m: sold 6,000 gns Newmarket Autumn Sales: sent to Holland.
T. D. Barron

ZILCLARE (IRE) 3 ch.f. Zilzal (USA) 137 – Clara Bow (USA) (Coastal 75
(USA)) [1995 NR 1996 7d 8m³ 8g* 10.1m Oct 23] rather unfurnished filly: has a
quick action: half-sister to fairly useful 1991 Irish 2-y-o 7f to 1¼m winner Fawaayid
(by Vaguely Noble) and 1992 Irish 1m winner Europe (by Lear Fan): dam won 3
times from 6 starts at up to 9f in USA: off course 5½ months after debut: fair form in
autumn maidens next 2 starts, beating Golden Thunderbolt 1¾ lengths at Brighton:
well beaten in handicap at Yarmouth on final start: sold 23,000 gns Newmarket
Autumn Sales: should stay beyond 1m: yet to race on extremes of going.
E. A. L. Dunlop

ZIMIRI 2 ch.c. (Mar 18) Keen 116 – Annabrianna 88 (Night Shift (USA)) [1996 75 p
7g a8g* Dec 20] good-bodied colt: second foal: half-brother to fairly useful 1m and
1¼m winner Jalfrezi (by Jalmood): dam 1¼m winner who stayed 1½m: last of 10 in
minor event at Kempton on debut: well backed, led near finish to win maiden at
Lingfield: will stay 1¼m: should improve further. *J. A. R. Toller*

ZIMMY 3 ch.g. Zalazl (USA) 120 – Zealous (Hard Fought 125) [1995 NR 1996 –
10.3s Mar 22] leggy, plain gelding: first foal: dam well beaten only outing: 33/1 and
bandaged, well tailed off in maiden at Doncaster. *T. T. Clement*

ZINGARO (IRE) 2 b.c. (Mar 18) Mujtahid (USA) 118 – Zia (USA) 88 (Shareef 61
Dancer (USA) 135) [1996 8g⁵ 7g Oct 2] robust colt: fourth foal: half-brother to 4-y-o
sellers winner Zeliba (up to 12.5f, stays 2¼m, by Doyoun): dam, 12.2f winner,
closely related to smart 1m to 1¼m performer Media Starguest and from good
family: modest form in maidens at Goodwood and Brighton: may stay beyond 1m.
C. E. Brittain

ZINZARI (FR) 2 ch.c. (Mar 21) Arctic Tern (USA) 126 – Model Girl (FR) 70 p
(Lyphard (USA) 132) [1996 8s⁵ Nov 9] 750,000 Francs Y: useful-looking colt:
half-brother to useful 6f (at 2 yrs) to 1m winner Arousal (by Rousillon) and several
winners in France, including (at up to 1½m) In Focus (by Sharpman): dam, French
1¼m and 10.5f winner, half-sister to dam of Belmez: 6/1, just over 9 lengths fifth of
14 to easy winner Moon River in median auction maiden at Doncaster, with leaders

until one pace from 2f out: will be suited by middle distances: will do better. *D. R. Loder*

ZORBA 2 b.g. (Mar 30) Shareef Dancer (USA) 135 – Zabelina (USA) 57 (Diesis 133) [1996 5d a6g 7m³ 7.1m³ 7.9g 7m³ 7g³ 7.1s² a8.5g⁴ Nov 25] 14,000Y: leggy, quite good-topped gelding: second foal: dam (maiden) closely related to smart 7f/1m performer Lunar Mover: fair maiden: sweated and pulled too hard when below form fifth outing: stays 8.5f: acts on soft ground and fibresand: keen type: gelded. *C. W. Thornton*   67

ZORRO 2 gr.c. (Apr 6) Touch of Grey 90 – Snow Huntress 80 (Shirley Heights 130) [1996 7m 7d a7s Nov 19] third foal: dam 1¼m and 1½m winner: no worthwhile form, including in a seller. *R. M. Flower*   –

ZUBOON (USA) 5 ch.g. The Minstrel (CAN) 135 – Won't She Tell (USA) – (Banner Sport (USA)) [1995 NR 1996 14d May 6] useful stayer (rated 101, probably acted on any going) for J. Dunlop in 1994: modest form over hurdles 1995/6: no promise on return to flat. *J. J. O'Neill*

ZUGUDI 2 b.c. (Mar 29) Night Shift (USA) – Overdrive 99 (Shirley Heights 130) [1996 6m⁴ 7g 6f* 6g 7m 6g Oct 9] 34,000Y: strong, heavy-topped colt: has scope: second reported foal: half-brother to 1992 2-y-o 1m winner Dakar Rally (by Green Desert): dam, needed good test of stamina, from fine staying family: made virtually all to win 3-runner maiden at Yarmouth in July: stiff tasks afterwards, appearing to run well in valuable 7f sales race at Newmarket: should stay beyond 7f: has twice made running: has worn a tongue strap. *B. Hanbury*   67 +

ZUNO FLYER (USA) 4 br.g. Lyphard (USA) 132 – Triple Tipple (USA) 111 (Raise A Cup (USA)) [1995 –: 6.9g 8m⁶ 6m 10g 11.7m 7m 12s 7f a7g 1996 a8g a10g³ a10g⁴ a12g⁴ a12g⁴ a10g² a9.4g a10g⁴ a16g⁵ 11.9f⁵ 10f⁴ 14m⁶ a12g* a12g⁵ Dec 30] stocky gelding: poor performer: won amateurs race (by short head) at Lingfield in December: stays 1½m: acts on firm ground and on equitrack: tried blinkered, visored third to ninth 4-y-o starts: none too consistent. *A. Moore*   47

ZUNO PRINCESS (IRE) 3 br.f. Distinctly North (USA) 115 – Flash Donna – (USA) 70 (Well Decorated (USA)) [1995 –: 5d 5g 5.1h⁴ 5m a8.5g 1996 a5g a6g⁵ a6g Mar 27] good-bodied filly: well beaten in varied company (trained until after reappearance by J. O'Donoghue), including in blinkers. *T. E. Powell*

ZURS (IRE) 3 b.g. Tirol 127 – Needy (High Top 131) [1995 NR 1996 8g 7m³ 8m² 7.9g³ 7.6m⁴ Sep 19] IR 42,000Y: sturdy gelding: half-brother to several winners, including useful Irish middle-distance colt Sondrio (by Nebbiolo), also a good winner in USA and over hurdles, and very useful 1992 2-y-o 5f winner Time's Time (by Whistling Deer): dam fairly useful Irish 2-y-o 6f and 7f winner: fair maiden: trained debut by J. Toller: placed at Salisbury, Newcastle and York: tailed off in minor event at Lingfield on final start: stays 1m: has been bandaged behind: gelded. *Miss Gay Kelleway*   77

ZYDECHO QUEEN 2 b.f. (Mar 17) Then Again 126 – Royal Resort 57 (King – of Spain 121) [1996 5.9f⁶ 6m 7d Aug 23] 400Y: first foal: dam 7f seller winner who stayed 10.2f: no promise: sold 700 gns Doncaster October Sales. *P. Calver*

ZYGO (USA) 4 b.c. Diesis 133 – La Papagena (Habitat 134) [1995 72p: 8m⁴ 1996 7g³ 7.3s² 8.3m² 8m 7f⁴ Aug 10] lengthy, useful-looking colt: unimpressive mover: fairly useful performer, lightly raced: sold (W. Jarvis to R. Phillips) 11,000 gns Newmarket Autumn Sales: likely to prove best at up to 1m: acts on good to firm and soft ground. *W. Jarvis*   82

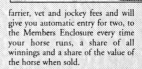

PROMISING HORSES

All the horses in *Racehorses of 1996* thought capable of noteworthy improvement are listed below under the trainers for whom they last ran.

R. AKEHURST
Noble Story 2 br.f 61p
Silver Kristal 2 gr.f 77p
Such Boldness 2 b.c —p

D. W. P. ARBUTHNOT
Brand New Dance 2 b.g 68p
Toi Toi (IRE) 2 b.f 71p

R. W. ARMSTRONG
Hirasah (IRE) 2 b.f 76p
Kamin (USA) 2 b.c 67p
Raaha 2 b.f 76p
Sharkiyah (IRE) 2 ch.f 75p

J. R. ARNOLD
Cryhavoc 2 b.c 90p
Clan Chief 3 b.g 87p

N. M. BABBAGE
Great Tern 4 b.f 59p

I. A. BALDING
Al Azhar 2 b.c 92P
Dead Aim (IRE) 2 b.g 78p
Dulcinea 2 ch.f —p
Hidden Meadow 2 b.c 103p
Highly Prized 2 b.c —p
Lochangel 2 ch.f 94p
Mara River 2 b.f 62p
Nash Point 2 b.c 79p
Norman Conquest (USA) 2 ch.c 71p
Sabina 2 b.f 87p
Sausalito Bay 2 b.c 81p
Slipstream Star 2 b.f —p
Bold Buster 3 b.g —p

T. D. BARRON
Barnburgh Boy 2 ch.c 70p
Sliema Creek 2 gr.g —p
Coastal Bluff 4 gr.g 117p

M. BELL
Arantxa 2 b.f 72p
John Emms (IRE) 2 ch.c 68p
Mary Magdalene 2 b.f —p
Silent Miracle (IRE) 2 b.f 61p

J. S. BOLGER, IRELAND
Mantovani (IRE) 2 b.c 112p

C. E. BRITTAIN
Fantastic Fellow (USA) 2 b.c 112p

M. BRITTAIN
Noirie 2 br.c 67p

C. P. E. BROOKS
Venture Connect 2 ch.g 61p

N. A. CALLAGHAN
Danetime (IRE) 2 b.c 96p
Cadeau Elegant 3 ch.f 64p

H. CANDY
Attitude 2 b.g 83p
Crystal Hearted 2 b.c 85p
For Lara (IRE) 2 ch.f —p
In Your Dreams (IRE) 2 b.f —p
Loving And Giving 2 b.f 84p
Made Bold 2 b.f 80p
Off The Rails 2 b.f —p
Pennys From Heaven 2 gr.c 84p
Quibbling 2 b.f 63p
With A Will 2 b.g —p

H. R. A. CECIL
Catchable 2 b.c 83p
Corsini 2 b.f 88p
Courtship 2 b.c 88p
Darnaway 2 b.c 82p
Fascinating Rhythm 2 b.f 85p
Fiji 2 b.f 92p
Fleet River (USA) 2 b.f 93p
Gingersnap 2 ch.f 75p
Harry Wolton 2 b.c 86p
High Intrigue (IRE) 2 b.c 68p
High Roller (IRE) 2 b.c 102p
Kyle Rhea 2 b.f 76p
Memorise (USA) 2 b.c 64p
Midnight Watch (USA) 2 b.c 77p
Out West (USA) 2 br.f 90p
Palisade (USA) 2 b.f 85p
Reams of Verse (USA) 2 ch.f 108p
River Usk 2 b.c 98p
Royale Finale (IRE) 2 ch.c 65p
Seattle Art (USA) 2 b.c —p
Sleepytime (IRE) 2 b.f 108P
Stories To Tell (USA) 2 ch.c 85p
Street General 2 b.c 90p
Vanishing Trick (USA) 2 ch.f 78p
Psicossis 3 b.c 64p
Silver Dome (USA) 3 b.c 103p
Torremolinos (USA) 3 ch.c 83p

MRS J. CECIL
Finarts Bay 2 b.f 59p
Kingfisher Mill (USA) 2 ch.c 70p
Magazine Gap 3 ch.c 51p
Adamton 4 b.g 75p

M. R. CHANNON
Lahab Nashwan 2 ch.c 67p

MAJOR D. N. CHAPPELL
Davids Revenge 2 b.c 70p
Sovereigns Court 3 ch.g 71p

P. W. CHAPPLE-HYAM
Captain Collins (IRE) 2 gr.c 99p
City Hall (IRE) 2 gr.c 66p
Comic Opera (IRE) 2 b.f —p

Dances With Dreams 2 b.f 98p
Grapevine (IRE) 2 b.f 71p
Monza (USA) 2 b.c 107p
Outflanker (USA) 2 b.c 76p
Panama City (USA) 2 b.c 102p
Revoque (IRE) 2 b.c 122p
Royal Crown (IRE) 2 b.c 74p
Truly Parched (USA) 2 b.c 80p
Villarica (IRE) 2 b.f 75p
Voyagers Quest (USA) 2 b.c 108p

R. CHARLTON
Ar Hyd Y Knos 2 b.f —p
Burning Truth (USA) 2 ch.c 57p
Hibernate (IRE) 2 ch.c 75p
Sahara River (USA) 2 b.f 80p
Sir Ricky (USA) 2 b.g —p
Valencia 2 b.f 79p
Biscay 3 b.f 67p

T. T. CLEMENT
Harvey's Future 2 b.c 56p

P. F. I. COLE
Badlesmere (USA) 2 b.c 87p
Deep Water (USA) 2 b.c 82p
Fig Tree Drive (USA) 2 b.f 94p
Hint 2 b.c 78p
Isle of Man (USA) 2 b.c 94p
Montfort (USA) 2 b.c 60p
Putra (USA) 2 ch.c 113p
Windsor Castle 2 b.c 91p
Yorkshire (IRE) 2 ch.c 90p
Filmore West 3 b.c 89p

D. J. S. COSGROVE
Hippy Chick 2 b.f —p

L. M. CUMANI
Coretta (IRE) 2 b.f 78p
Etna 2 b.f 87p
Eurolink Profile 2 b.f —p
Farnese (IRE) 2 b.c 77p
Grapeshot (USA) 2 b.c 108p
Jamrat Samya (IRE) 2 b.f 79p
Kalinini (USA) 2 ch.c 71p
Kilshanny 2 b.f 70p
Leading Note (USA) 2 ch.f 74p
Lima 2 b.f 95p
Listed Account (USA) 2 b.f 77p
Mandilak (USA) 2 b.c 96P
Man Howa (IRE) 2 ch.c 94p
One So Wonderful 2 b.f 93p
Poteen (USA) 2 b.c 113p
Russian Olive 2 b.f 70p
Shadow Lead 2 b.c 95p
Shouk 2 b.f 81p
Speedboat (USA) 2 ch.c 80p
Wathbat Nashwan 2 ch.c 66p
Winter Garden 2 ch.c 66p
Zibeth 2 b.f —p
Bourbonist (FR) 3 b.g 63p
Crown Court (USA) 3 b.c 91p
Elmi Elmak (IRE) 3 b.c 95p

Prima Verde 3 b.f —p
Puce 3 b.f 88p

E. A. L. DUNLOP
Bold Words (CAN) 2 ch.c 90p
Broad River (USA) 2 b.c —p
Fellwah (IRE) 2 b.f 66p
Flowing Fortune 2 b.c 67p
Generous Gift 2 ch.c 82p
Kahal 2 b.c 108p
Over To You (USA) 2 ch.c 77p
Shalaal (USA) 2 b.c 76p
Super Monarch 2 ch.c 71p
Tayseer (USA) 2 ch.c 89p
Whirlawhile (USA) 2 b.c 62p
Jamrat Jumairah (IRE) 3 b.f 88p

J. L. DUNLOP
Bahhare (USA) 2 b.c 122p
Beauchamp Lion 2 ch.c —p
Bubbly 2 b.c 74p
Classic Line 2 b.f —p
Conspiracy 2 b.f 98p
Dust Dancer 2 ch.f 74p
Elnadim (USA) 2 b.c 83p
Ghataas 2 b.c 94p
Ginzbourg 2 b.g 86p
Gonzaga (IRE) 2 gr.c 81p
Ihtiyati (USA) 2 ch.c 86p
Inimitable 2 b.f 66p
Kennemara Star (IRE) 2 ch.g 66p
Mawhiba (USA) 2 b.f 63p
Moon River (IRE) 2 ch.c 95p
Musharak 2 b.c 69p
Nick of Time 2 b.f —p
Palio Sky 2 b.c 87p
Rainwatch 2 b.c 83p
Shaddad (USA) 2 b.c 75p
Shawaf (USA) 2 b.c 80p
Silver Patriarch (IRE) 2 gr.c 98p
Tango King 2 b.c 66p
Thornby Park 2 b.f 72p
Undercover Agent (IRE) 2 b.f 79p
Will You Dance 2 b.f 79p
Yavlensky (IRE) 2 b.c 97p
Wahiba Sands 3 b.g 94p
Alfredo Alfredo (USA) 4 b.g 71p
Orchestra Stall 4 b.g 107p

M. W. EASTERBY
Future Perfect 2 b.g 73p
Jedi Knight 2 b.c 66p

T. D. EASTERBY
Bollin Terry 2 b.c 58p

D. R. C. ELSWORTH
Colour Key (USA) 2 b.g 60p
First Chance (IRE) 2 b.f 56p
Tom Tailor (GER) 2 b.c 72p
Persian Punch (IRE) 3 ch.g 112p

T. J. ETHERINGTON
Rheinbold 2 br.g —p

J. M. P. EUSTACE
Eastern Eagle 2 b.c 58p
Imperial Scholar (IRE) 2 b.f 75p
Lady Mail (IRE) 2 b.f 90p
Refuse To Lose 2 ch.c 74p

J. L. EYRE
Captain Carparts 2 b.c —p
One Lady 2 gr.f 50p
Totem Dancer 3 b.f 83p

J. R. FANSHAWE
Academy Star 2 b.f 65p
Craigievar 2 b.c 94p
Include Me Out 2 ch.g 69p
Judicial Supremacy 2 b.c 82p
Travelmate 2 b.g 62p
Unshaken 2 b.c 84p

J. G. FITZGERALD
Swiss Law 2 b.c 88p

G. FRATINI, ITALY
Golden Aventura (IRE) 2 b.c 100p

J. H. M. GOSDEN
Amaryllis (IRE) 2 b.f 71p
Cape Cross (IRE) 2 b.c 88p
Ceanothus (IRE) 2 ch.f —p
Conon Falls (IRE) 2 b.c 86p
Crinolette (IRE) 2 b.f —p
Crystal Hills (IRE) 2 b.c —p
Dark Mile (USA) 2 b.f 86p
Desert Horizon 2 b.c 91p
Desert Track 2 b.c 76p
Fatal Sahra (IRE) 2 ch.c 67p
Handsome Ridge 2 ch.c 87p
Heritage 2 b.c 76p
King Sound 2 br.c 108p
Liffre (IRE) 2 b.f 74p
Marozia (USA) 2 ch.f —p
Marsul (USA) 2 b.c —p
Mengaab (USA) 2 b.c 90p
Minersville (USA) 2 b.c 83P
Miracle Kid (USA) 2 b.c 75p
Mount Holly (USA) 2 b.c 69p
Ninth Chord 2 gr.c 85p
Noisette 2 ch.f 66p
Quest For Best (USA) 2 b.f 64p
River Foyle (USA) 2 ch.c 77p
Saabga (USA) 2 ch.f 83p
Saafeya (IRE) 2 b.f 74p
Seattle Swing 2 b.f 68p
Song of Freedom 2 ch.c 78p
Squeak 2 ch.f 83p
True Glory (IRE) 2 b.f 67p
Wellaki (USA) 2 ch.c 80p
Arctiid 3 b.c 93p
Canyon Creek (IRE) 3 b.c 87p
Chirico (USA) 3 b.c 79p
Elsaleet (USA) 3 b.c 96p
Galb Alasad (IRE) 3 b.c 69p
Jaseur (USA) 3 b.g 79p
Sacho (IRE) 3 b.c 89p
Triple Leap 3 b.c 93p

N. A. GRAHAM
Craven Hill (IRE) 2 gr.g —p
Mogul 2 b.g —p
Sandystones 2 b.f —p

R. GUEST
Baby Jane 2 b.f 63p

W. J. HAGGAS
Alyportent 2 b.c —p
Royal Crusade (USA) 2 b.c 89P
Telemania (IRE) 2 b.f 83p

MISS S. E. HALL
Heart of Gold (IRE) 2 ch.c 64p

B. HANBURY
Harik 2 ch.c 66p
Meshhed (USA) 2 ch.f 96p
Right Tune 2 b.f 81p
Tithcar 2 b.f —p

R. HANNON
Blushing Desert 2 b.f —p
Ellens Lad (IRE) 2 b.c 81p
Ortelius 2 b.c 71p
Praeditus 2 b.c 75p
Senorita Matilda (USA) 2 b.f 73p
Triple Hay 2 ch.c 80p

P. W. HARRIS
Calypso Grant (IRE) 2 b.f 91p
Daniel Deronda 2 b.c 70p
Flyaway Hill (FR) 2 b.f 70p
Noble Dane (IRE) 2 b.f 79p
Sadler's Blaze (IRE) 2 b.c —p
Supreme Sound 2 b.c 83p
Young Precedent 2 b.c 65p

R. HARRIS
Classic Ribbon (IRE) 3 b.f 63p

G. HARWOOD
Kala Noire 3 gr.c 87p
King Kato 3 b.g 93p
Prospero 3 b.g 77p

P. C. HASLAM
Selberry 2 b.g 76p
Siouxrouge 2 b.g 73p

MME C. HEAD, FRANCE
Always Loyal (USA) 2 b.f 98p
Pas de Reponse (USA) 2 b.f 113p

MAJOR W. R. HERN
Fallah 2 b.c 77p
Georgina (IRE) 2 b.f 67p
Ikdam (USA) 2 b.f 92p
Right Wing (IRE) 2 b.c 67p
Royal Castle (IRE) 2 b.c 65p
Sarayir (USA) 2 b.f 100p
Shaya 2 ch.c 86P

LADY HERRIES
Moon Blast 2 gr.g 67p

Bear Hug 3 b.g 72p
Grand Splendour 3 b.f 79p

B. W. HILLS
Awash 2 b.c —p
Dundel (IRE) 2 gr.f 82p
Entice (FR) 2 b.f 93p
Fife Major (USA) 2 b.c —p
Furnish 2 b.f 87p
In Question 2 br.c 79p
Lookout 2 b.f 70p
Misty Rain 2 br.f —p
Mithak (USA) 2 b.c 81p
Musalsal (IRE) 2 b.c 89p
My Valentina 2 b.f 84p
Natural Eight (IRE) 2 b.c 81p
Nightbird (IRE) 2 b.f 95p
Nubile 2 b.f 71p
Prairie Falcon (IRE) 2 b.c 69p
Showboat 2 b.c 92p
Solo Mio (IRE) 2 b.c 92p
Sophomore 2 b.c 83p
The Fly 2 gr.c 95p
Valagalore 2 b.f 74p
Zaahir (IRE) 2 b.c 75p
Za-Im 2 b.c 100p
Busy Flight 3 b.c 119p

J. W. HILLS
Arriving 2 br.f 67p
Crimson Tide (IRE) 2 b.c 95p
Fully Booked 2 b.f —p

C. A. HORGAN
Regal Academy (IRE) 2 b.f 66p

LORD HUNTINGDON
Bathe In Light (USA) 2 ch.f 66p
Dick Turpin (USA) 2 br.c 71p
Eliza 2 ch.f —p
Glacier 2 b.f —p
Smart Dominion 2 b.c 74p
Spartan Girl (IRE) 2 ch.f 62p
Tempting Prospect 2 b.f 89p
Persuasion 3 b.f 72p
Threadneedle (USA) 3 b.g 81p

A. P. JARVIS
Gee Bee Boy 2 ch.c —p
Russian Ruler (IRE) 2 b.c 78p

M. A. JARVIS
Cosmic Prince (IRE) 2 b.c 85p
Regait 2 b.c —p
Stowaway 2 b.c 94p

W. JARVIS
Alezal 2 b.c 81p
Beguine (USA) 2 br.f 77p

M. JOHNSTON
Audencia (IRE) 2 b.f 50p
Belle Bijou 2 ch.f —p
Chaluz 2 b.c 54p
Dargo 2 b.c 74p

Double Alleged (USA) 2 b.c 70p
Double Crest (IRE) 2 b.f 69p
Eldorado (IRE) 2 b.c 97p
Fly To The Stars 2 b.c 83p
Happy Minstral (USA) 2 b.c 81p
Night Mirage (USA) 2 b.f 70p
One For Baileys 2 b.c 66p
Polar Flight 2 br.c 92p
Restless Spirit (USA) 2 b.c 83p

MISS GAY KELLEWAY
Musheer (USA) 2 b.c 110p

P. A. KELLEWAY
Alcalali (USA) 2 ch.f 94p
Hanan (USA) 2 b.f 83p
Royal Aty (IRE) 2 b.c 90p

J. LESBORDES, FRANCE
Mousse Glacee (FR) 2 b.f 112p

G. LEWIS
La Chatelaine 2 b.f —p
Mantles Prince 2 ch.g 79p
Regal Reprimand 2 b.c —p
Right Man 2 gr.c —p
Tigrello 2 ch.c 77p

D. R. LODER
Apprehension 2 b.c 95p
Bandore (IRE) 2 ch.c 81p
Doyella (IRE) 2 b.f 71p
Generous Libra 2 b.c 87p
Graceful Lass 2 b.f 72p
Henley (USA) 2 b.c 83p
Hope Chest 2 ch.f 70p
Indiscreet (CAN) 2 b.c 105p
Jhazi 2 b.c 99p
Lyrical Bid (USA) 2 b.f 77p
Maypole (IRE) 2 ch.g 66p
Misellina (FR) 2 b.f 57p
Nightlark (IRE) 2 b.f 77p
Priena (IRE) 2 ch.f 86p
Rechullin 2 ch.f 82p
Ricky Ticky Tavie (USA) 2 b.c 97p
Sekari 2 b.c 88p
Shawm 2 b.c 84p
St Blaine (CAN) 2 b.f 79p
St Lucinda (CAN) 2 b.f 71p
Tycoon Todd (USA) 2 gr.c 98p
Velour 2 b.f 94p
Zinzari (FR) 2 ch.c 70p

P. J. MAKIN
Always On My Mind 2 b.f 75p

B. A. MCMAHON
Penprio (IRE) 2 b.c 52p
Van Chino 2 b.c —p

MARTYN MEADE
Ballerina's Dream 2 b.f —p

B. J. MEEHAN
Mr Majica 2 b.c —p

Titta Ruffo 2 b.c 85p
Tycoon Girl (IRE) 2 b.f 74p

T. G. MILLS
Hayes Way (IRE) 2 b.c 79p
Passion 2 ch.f 61p
Pastiche 2 b.f 61p
Proper Blue (USA) 3 b.c 112p

P. MITCHELL
She's Dawan (IRE) 2 b.f —p

G. L. MOORE
Mersey Beat 2 ch.c 76p

D. MORLEY
Hadidi 2 b.c —p
Intikhab (USA) 2 b.c 101p
Taunt 2 b.c 82p

D. MORRIS
Pinchincha (FR) 2 b.g 62p

W. R. MUIR
Longwick Lad 3 ro.c 80p

C. MURRAY
William Wallace 2 b.c 68p

W. J. MUSSON
Batsman 2 b.c 66p
Ella Lamees 2 b.f —p
Loganlea (IRE) 2 br.f —p
Formidable Flame 3 ch.g —p

T. J. NAUGHTON
Old School House 3 ch.c 84p

D. NICHOLLS
Jib Jab 2 br.g 59p

D. NICHOLSON
Circus Star 3 b.g 76p

A. P. O'BRIEN, IRELAND
Johan Cruyff 2 b.c 104p
Shell Ginger (IRE) 2 ch.f 110p
Strawberry Roan (IRE) 2 b.f 103p

R. J. O'SULLIVAN
Happy Go Lucky 2 ch.f 81p

J. A. B. OLD
Chai-Yo 6 b.h —p

J. PARKES
Jay-Gee-Em 2 b.f 66p

J. W. PAYNE
Al Masroor (USA) 2 b.c 65p
Al Muallim (USA) 2 b.c 79p
Kweilo 2 b.g —p

MISS L. A. PERRATT
Brave Montgomerie 2 ch.c 77p

R. T. PHILLIPS
Cold Lazarus 2 br.g —p

M. C. PIPE
Blush 2 b.f 50p

M. J. POLGLASE
Supreme Maimoon 2 b.c 70p

SIR MARK PRESCOTT
All Is Fair 2 b.f 79p
Cartouche 2 gr.g 66p
Drift 2 b.g 59p
Enlisted (IRE) 2 b.f 81p
Hyde Park (IRE) 2 b.c 75p
Lulu 2 b.f —p
Marytavy 2 b.f —p
Missfortuna 2 b.f 66p
Mythical 2 gr.f 55p
Philosophic 2 b.g 52p
Pietro Bembo (IRE) 2 b.g 71p
Last Second (IRE) 3 gr.f 121p
Pasternak 3 b.c 93p

MRS J. R. RAMSDEN
Bishops Court 2 ch.g 81p
Bold Gayle 2 ch.f 49p
Caution 2 b.f 78p
Fantasy Flight 2 b.f —p
Mungo Park 2 b.g 68p
Southerly Wind 2 b.c 79p

MRS M. REVELEY
Smart Spirit (IRE) 2 b.f 66p
Ledgendry Line 3 b.g 73p
Sedbergh (USA) 3 b.g 71p
Tillyboy 6 b.g 75p

J-C. ROUGET, FRANCE
Shaka 2 b.c 113p

A. DE ROYER-DUPRE, FRANCE
Astarabad (USA) 2 b.c 83P
Daylami (IRE) 2 gr.c 112p
Joyeuse Entree 2 ch.f 108p

M. J. RYAN
Sweetness Herself 3 ch.f 89p

B. SMART
Basman (IRE) 2 b.c 51p

A. C. STEWART
Alifandango (IRE) 2 b.f —p
Baked Alaska 2 b.f 90p
Epworth 2 b.f 66p
Gharib (USA) 2 b.c 80p
Hulal 2 b.c —p
Irsal 2 ch.c 70p
Jalb (IRE) 2 b.g 69p
Maylane 2 b.c 85p
Barrack Yard 3 b.c 62p

M. R. STOUTE
Aerleon Pete (IRE) 2 b.c 79p
Arabian 2 ch.c 83p
Arco Colora 2 b.f 64p
Bint Albaadiya (USA) 2 ch.f 77p
Cowtharee 2 ch.f 70p

Crown of Light 2 b.f   77p
Crystal Gold 2 ch.c   66p
Dacoit (USA) 2 b.c   92p
Dazzling Stone 2 b.g   76p
Delilah (IRE) 2 b.f   75p
Desert Beauty (IRE) 2 b.f   76p
Entrepreneur 2 b.c   106p
Fatal Baraari 2 b.c   81p
Gersey 2 ch.f   —p
Go For Salt (USA) 2 b.f   75p
Maroulla (IRE) 2 ch.f   67p
Melodica 2 b.f   67p
Mowjood (USA) 2 b.c   —p
Purist 2 b.c   71p
Regal Thunder (USA) 2 b.c   76p
Shahboor (USA) 2 b.c   —p
Shock Value (IRE) 2 b.c   98p
Sky Commander (USA) 2 b.c   91p
Society Rose 2 b.f   79p
Spy Knoll 2 b.c   79p
Summer Dance 2 b.f   86p
Tanaasa (IRE) 2 b.c   70p
Tangshan (CAN) 2 ch.f   67p
Technicolour (IRE) 2 b.f   79p
Yalaietanee 2 b.c   96p
Congo Man 3 b.c   86p
Multicoloured (IRE) 3 b.c   111p
Opal Jewel 3 b.f   82p
Unitus (IRE) 3 b.c   85p

A. STREETER
Two Bills 2 b.g   —p

SAEED BIN SUROOR
Bold Demand 2 b.c   72p
Happy Valentine 2 b.c   103p
Manuetti (IRE) 2 b.f   68p
Mashhaer (USA) 2 b.c   94p
Moonlight Paradise (USA) 2 b.f   111p
Siyadah (USA) 2 ch.f   79p

H. THOMSON JONES
Alumisiyah (USA) 2 b.f   80p
Fahris (IRE) 2 ch.c   97p
Fayik 2 ch.c   76p
Hachiyah (IRE) 2 b.f   69p
Mutribah (USA) 2 b.f   77p
Thahabyah (USA) 2 b.f   71p

C. W. THORNTON
Sioux 2 ch.f   76p
Give Me A Ring (IRE) 3 b.c   89p

J. A. R. TOLLER
Other Club 2 ch.c   74p
Zimiri 2 ch.c   75p

M. H. TOMPKINS
Musical Pursuit 2 b.c   113p
Nichol Fifty 2 b.g   52p
Tyrolean Dream (IRE) 2 b.c   84p
Blurred (IRE) 3 ch.g   85p

W. G. M. TURNER
Chief Island 2 b.f   62p
Ma Vielle Pouque (IRE) 2 ch.f   52p

N. J. H. WALKER
No More Pressure (IRE) 2 ch.c   86p

C. F. WALL
Quarterstaff 2 b.c   —p
Shantarskie (IRE) 2 b.c   65p
Atomic Shell (CAN) 3 ch.c   —p

P. T. WALWYN
Husun (USA) 2 b.f   60p
Kawa-Ib (IRE) 2 b.f   78p

J. W. WATTS
Shaded (IRE) 2 b.g   60p

D. K. WELD, IRELAND
Token Gesture (IRE) 2 b.f   96p

R. M. WHITAKER
Fairy Ring (IRE) 2 b.f   69p

S. C. WILLIAMS
Allied Academy 2 ch.c   67p

S. P. C. WOODS
Green Card (USA) 2 b.c   78p

G. WRAGG
Apache Star 2 b.f   80p
Fabled Light (IRE) 2 b.c   60p
La Curamalal (IRE) 2 b.f   —p
Miss Sancerre 2 b.f   86p
Motet 2 b.f   74p
Much Commended 2 b.f   90p
Occam (IRE) 2 ch.c   58p
Rebecca Sharp 2 b.f   82p
The Faraway Tree 2 b.f   85p
Water Garden 2 ch.c   —p
Dantesque (IRE) 3 b.c   69p
Sasuru 3 b.c   113p

YORK

Set your sights on a winner

Unparalleled new facilities for Tattersalls and County Stand racegoers, featuring the fabulous dine & view

EBOR RESTAURANT
(ENQUIRIES on 01904 638971)

We look forward to welcoming you

🌹🌹🌹 FIXTURES 🌹🌹🌹

TUESDAY 13th MAY
The Tattersalls Musidora Stakes (Group 3)
WEDNESDAY 14th MAY
The Dante Stakes (Group 2)
THURSDAY 15th MAY
The Yorkshire Cup (Group 2)

FRIDAY 13th JUNE
The Shepherd Sprint Stakes
SATURDAY 14th JUNE
The 27th Timeform Charity Day

FRIDAY 11th JULY
The Manchester - Singapore Summer Stakes
(Listed Race)
SATURDAY 12th JULY
The 38th John Smith's Magnet Cup

TUESDAY 19th AUGUST
The Juddmonte International (Group 1)
WEDNESDAY 20th AUGUST
The Tote Ebor
THURSDAY 21st AUGUST
The Nunthorpe Stakes (Group 1)

WEDNESDAY 3rd SEPTEMBER
The 10th Batley's Cash & Carry Day
THURSDAY 4th SEPTEMBER
The Sun Life of Canada Garrowby Stakes

WEDNESDAY 8th OCTOBER
The Booker Chef's Larder Stakes
THURSDAY 9th OCTOBER
The Allied Dunbar Rated Stakes
SATURDAY 11th OCTOBER
The Coral Sprint Trophy

For a full raceday information guide or
Sponsorship/Corporate Hospitality brochure contact us at:
The Racecourse, York YO2 1EX Tel: (01904) 620911 Fax: (01904) 611071

SELECTED BIG RACES 1996

Prize money for racing abroad has been converted to £ sterling at the exchange rate current at the time of the race. The figures are correct to the nearest £.

NAD AL SHEBA Wednesday, Mar 27   GOOD
1   **Dubai World Cup (4yo+) £1,568,627**   1¼m

CIGAR (USA) *WMott,USA* 6-8-12 JBailey		1
SOUL OF THE MATTER (USA) *RMandella,USA* 5-8-12 GStevens		½ 2
L'CARRIERE (USA) *HaroldJamesBond,USA* 5-8-12 (b) JChavez		8 3
Pentire *GWragg,GB* 4-8-11 MHills		¾ 4
Tamayaz (CAN) *SaeedbinSuroor,UAE* 4-8-11 CMcCarron		3½ 5
Lively Mount (JPN) *FShibata,Japan* 5-8-12 MIshibashi		6 6
Needle Gun (IRE) *CEBrittain,GB* 6-8-12 BDoyle		1 7
Torrential (USA) *SaeedbinSuroor,UAE* 4-8-11 OPeslier		¾ 8
Larrocha (IRE) *SaeedbinSuroor,UAE* 4-8-8 PatEddery		3 9
Danewin (AUS) *RThomsen,Australia* 5-8-12 DOliver		¾ 10
Halling (USA) *SaeedbinSuroor,UAE* 5-8-12 LDettori		12 11

Mr Allen E. Paulson 11ran 2m03.84

NEWMARKET Wednesday, Apr 17   GOOD to FIRM (Rowley Mile Course)
2   **Earl of Sefton Stks (A) (Gr 3) (4yo+) £19,188**   1m1f

LUSO *CEBrittain* 4-9-4 MJKinane (1)	14/1	1
SMART ALEC *LMCumani* 4-8-10 LDettori (5)	6/4f	hd 2
FIRST ISLAND (IRE) *GWragg* 4-8-10 MHills (9)	4/1	1½ 3
Gabr *RWArmstrong* 6-8-10 WCarson (3)	10/1	¾ 4
Restructure (IRE) *MrsJCecil* 4-8-10 PaulEddery (6)	7/1	2 5
Desert Shot *MRStoute* 6-8-13 PatEddery (8)	11/2	¾ 6
Sacrament *MRStoute* 5-8-10 TQuinn (2)	20/1	1¼ 7
Beauchamp Jazz *JLDunlop* 4-8-10 JReid (4)	20/1	1 8
Lear White (USA) *PAKelleway* 5-8-13 RCochrane (7)	50/1	½ 9

Mr Saeed Manana 9ran 1m47.96

SANDOWN Friday, Apr 26   GOOD
3   **Sandown Mile (A) (Gr 2) (4yo+) £36,605**   1m14y

2	GABR *RWArmstrong* 6-9-0 WCarson (2)	13/2	1
	SOVIET LINE (IRE) *MRStoute* 6-9-6 PatEddery (8)	6/1	sh 2
	MISTLE CAT (USA) *SPCWoods* 5-9-0 WWoods (11)	16/1	½ 3
	Nwaamis (USA) *JLDunlop* 4-9-0 RHills (4)	10/1	¾ 4
2	First Island (IRE) *GWragg* 4-9-0 MHills (1)	11/2	1¾ 5
	Myself *PWChapple-Hyam* 4-8-11 JReid (3)	9/2f	2½ 6
	Lap of Luxury *WJarvis* 7-8-11 BThomson (12)	33/1	6 7
	Autumn Affair *CEBrittain* 4-8-11 WRyan (6)	40/1	½ 8
	Bishop of Cashel *JRFanshawe* 4-9-0 DHarrison (10)	7/1	½ 9
	Nijo *DRLoder* 5-9-0 RHughes (4)	9/1	4 10
	Inzar (USA) *PFICole* 4-9-0 RCochrane (9)	9/1	1½ 11
	Decorated Hero *JHMGosden* 4-9-0 LDettori (7)	20/1	28 12

Mr Hamdan Al Maktoum 12ran 1m41.34

LONGCHAMP Sunday, Apr 28   GOOD
4   **Prix Ganay (Gr 1) (4yo+ c+f) £64,516**   1¼m110y

	VALANOUR (IRE) *AdeRoyer-Dupre,France* 4-9-2 GMosse	12/10f	1
2	LUSO *CEBrittain,GB* 4-9-2 MJKinane	27/1	½ 2
	SWAIN (IRE) *AFabre,France* 4-9-2 TJarnet	51/10	nk 3
	Spectrum (IRE) *PWChapple-Hyam,GB* 4-9-2 JReid	4/1	2½ 4
	Muncie (IRE) *AFabre,France* 4-8-13 OPeslier	23/1	1 5
	Diamond Mix (IRE) *AFabre,France* 4-9-2 SGuillot	27/1	sh 6
	Tot Ou Tard (IRE) *JForesi,France* 6-9-2 WMongil	51/1	1 7
	Marildo (FR) *DSmaga,France* 9-9-2 (b) FHead	31/1	2½ 8
	Carling (FR) *MmePatBarbe,France* 4-8-13 TThulliez	55/10	hd 9
	Slicious *VCaruso,Italy* 4-9-2 CAsmussen	76/10	1½ 10

H.H. Aga Khan 10ran 2m10.90

NEWMARKET Saturday, May 4   GOOD to FIRM (Rowley Mile Course)

5   Pertemps 2000 Guineas Stks (A) (Gr 1) (3yo c+f) £122,262   1m

MARK OF ESTEEM (IRE) *SaeedbinSuroor* 3-9-0 LDettori (2)	8/1		1
EVEN TOP (IRE) *MHTompkins* 3-9-0 PRobinson (5)	40/1	sh	2
BIJOU D'INDE *MJohnston* 3-9-0 JWeaver (4)	14/1	hd	3
Alhaarth (IRE) *MajorWRHern* 3-9-0 WCarson (12)	2/1f	6	4
Beauchamp King *JLDunlop* 3-9-0 JReid (6)	9/2	2	5
Danehill Dancer (IRE) *NACallaghan* 3-9-0 MJKinane (11)	10/1	1	6
Masehaab (IRE) *JLDunlop* 3-9-0 RHills (3)	200/1	1	7
World Premier *CEBrittain* 3-9-0 BDoyle (1)	66/1	1¼	8
Leonine (IRE) *PFICole* 3-9-0 TQuinn (9)	50/1	½	9
Royal Applause *BWHills* 3-9-0 MHills (8)	15/2	4	10
Storm Trooper (USA) *HRACecil* 3-9-0 PatEddery (10)	5/1	3½	11
Tumbleweed Ridge *BJMeehan* 3-9-0 RHughes (7)	66/1	¾	12
Regiment (IRE) *RHannon* 3-9-0 KDarley (13)	33/1	3½	13

Godolphin 13ran 1m37.59

NEWMARKET Sunday, May 5   GOOD to FIRM (Rowley Mile Course)

6   Pertemps 1000 Guineas Stks (A) (Gr 1) (3yo f) £100,525   1m

BOSRA SHAM (USA) *HRACecil* 3-9-0 PatEddery (11)	10/11f		1
MATIYA (IRE) *BHanbury* 3-9-0 RHills (4)	25/1	1½	2
BINT SHADAYID (USA) *SaeedbinSuroor* 3-9-0 LDettori (6)	11/2	hd	3
My Branch *BWHills* 3-9-0 MHills (1)	14/1	1½	4
Honest Guest (IRE) *MHTompkins* 3-9-0 PRobinson (3)	14/1	¾	5
Dance Sequence (USA) *MRStoute* 3-9-0 JReid (2)	12/1	1	6
Bint Salsabil (USA) *JLDunlop* 3-9-0 WCarson (5)	6/1	hd	7
My Melody Parkes *JBerry* 3-9-0 JCarroll (8)	66/1	2	8
Miss Universal (IRE) *CEBrittain* 3-9-0 BDoyle (9)	100/1	6	9
Portuguese Lil *DNicholls* 3-9-0 AlexGreaves (12)	500/1	nk	10
Papering (IRE) *LMCumani* 3-9-0 GCarter (10)	33/1	6	11
Maid For The Hills *DRLoder* 3-9-0 (b) DHarrison (7)	33/1	7	12
Keepers Dawn (IRE) *RFJohnsonHoughton* 3-9-0 KDarley (13)	50/1	2	13

Mr Wafic Said 13ran 1m37.75

LONGCHAMP Sunday, May 12   GOOD

7   Dubai Poule d'Essai Des Pouliches (Gr 1) (3yo f) £128,866   1m

TA RIB (USA) *EALDunlop,GB* 3-9-0 WCarson	141/10		1
SHAKE THE YOKE *ELellouche,France* 3-9-0 DBoeuf	3/5f	¾	2
SAGAR PRIDE (IRE) *JGBurns,Ireland* 3-9-0 OPeslier	21/1	½	3
A Votre Sante (USA) *MmeCHead,France* 3-9-0 FHead	61/10	1	4
True Flare (USA) *MmeCHead,France* 3-9-0 PatEddery	86/10	sn	5
Shawanni *SaeedbinSuroor,GB* 3-9-0 LDettori	96/10	¾	6
Raisonnable *DSepulchre,France* 3-9-0 CAsmussen	16/1	hd	7
Housa Dancer (FR) *AFabre,France* 3-9-0 TJarnet	13/2	nk	8
Parade Sauvage (FR) *CharlesO'Brien,Ireland* 3-9-0 CRoche	95/1	nk	9

Mr Hamdan Al Maktoum 9ran 1m38.70

8   Dubai Poule d'Essai Des Poulains (Gr 1) (3yo c) £128,866   1m

ASHKALANI (IRE) *AdeRoyer-Dupre,France* 3-9-2 GMosse	4/5f		1
SPINNING WORLD (USA) *JEPease,France* 3-9-2 CAsmussen	61/10	¾	2
TAGULA (IRE) *IABalding,GB* 3-9-2 KDarley	414/10	½	3
Cayman Kai (IRE) *RHannon,GB* 3-9-2 PatEddery	5/1	¾	4
Kahir Almaydan (IRE) *JLDunlop,GB* 3-9-2 WCarson	26/1	nk	5
Barricade (USA) *AFabre,France* 3-9-2 TJarnet	11/1	1½	6
Eternity Range (USA) *PBary,France* 3-9-2 FHead	10/1	1½	7
Don Micheletto *SaeedbinSuroor,GB* 3-9-2 LDettori	12/1	1½	8
5 Danehill Dancer (IRE) *NACallaghan,GB* 3-9-2 RHughes	14/1	1½	9
Gothenberg (IRE) *MJohnston,GB* 3-9-2 JWeaver	35/1	4	10

H.H. Aga Khan 10ran 1m37.60

ROME Sunday, May 12   GOOD to SOFT

9   Premio Presidente Della Repubblica (Gr 1) (4yo+ c+f) £55,807   1¼m

HOLLYWOOD DREAM (GER) *UOstmann,Germany* 5-8-13 JReid	29/10cp		1
1 NEEDLE GUN (IRE) *CEBrittain,GB* 6-9-2 BDoyle		hd	2
MONTJOY (USA) *PFICole,GB* 3-9-2 TQuinn		½	3

Concepcion (GER) *HJentzsch,Germany* 6-9-2 PSchiergen 29/10cp 1½ 4
Manzoni (GER) *AWohler,Germany* 4-9-2 (b) ABoschert................................ ½ 5
Cezanne *SaeedbinSuroor,GB* 7-9-2 MJKinane...................................... 1½ 6
4 Slicious *VCaruso,Italy* 4-9-2 MEsposito... 3 7
Tarhelm (ITY) *GColleo,Italy* 4-9-2 MLatorre... 4½ 8
Big River (ITY) *VCaruso,Italy* 4-9-2 LFicucietto.................................... dist 9

Gestut Haus Ittlingen 9ran 2m06.40

YORK Thursday, May 16   FIRM

10   East Coast Yorkshire Cup (A) (Gr 2) (4yo+) £52,482   1m5f194y

CLASSIC CLICHE (IRE) *SaeedbinSuroor* 4-9-0 MJKinane (5) 2/1   1
STRATEGIC CHOICE (USA) *PFICole* 5-9-0 TQuinn (4) 13/8f 1½ 2
COURT OF HONOUR (IRE) *PWChapple-Hyam* 4-9-0 JReid (3) 10/1   2 3
Grey Shot *IABalding* 4-8-9 KDarley (1) 10/3 3½ 4
Asterita *RHannon* 4-8-6 PatEddery (2) 16/1   9 5

Godolphin 5ran 2m52.77

NEWBURY Saturday, May 18   GOOD to SOFT

11   Juddmonte Lockinge Stks (A) (Gr 1) (4yo+) £74,731   1m

3 SOVIET LINE (IRE) *MRStoute* 6-9-0 TQuinn (1)................................ 13/2   1
CHARNWOOD FOREST (IRE) *SaeedbinSuroor* 4-9-0 MJKinane (2)... 3/1   nk 2
4 SPECTRUM (IRE) *PWChapple-Hyam* 4-9-0 JReid (5) 11/10f   4 3
2 Smart Alec *LMCumani* 4-9-0 RCochrane (7)....................................... 8/1   nk 4
3 Gabr *RWArmstrong* 6-9-0 WCarson (3).. 10/1   8 5
3 Nwaamis (USA) *JLDunlop* 4-9-0 PatEddery (4) 14/1   13 6
Brief Glimpse (IRE) *MajorDNChappell* 4-8-11 MHills (6) 50/1   4 7

Maktoum Al Maktoum 7ran 1m44.22

CURRAGH Saturday, May 25   GOOD to SOFT

12   Airlie Coolmore Irish 1,000 Guineas (Gr 1) (3yo f) £86,856   1m

6 MATIYA (IRE) *BHanbury,GB* 3-9-0 WCarson 5/1   1
DANCE DESIGN (IRE) *DKWeld,Ireland* 3-9-0 MJKinane 5/1   3 2
6 MY BRANCH (IRE) *BWHills,GB* 3-9-0 MHills.................................... 6/1   ½ 3
Distant Oasis (USA) *HRACecil,GB* 3-9-0 PatEddery 5/2f 1½ 4
Priory Belle (IRE) *JSBolger,Ireland* 3-9-0 KJManning 25/1 1½ 5
Zafzala (IRE) *JOxx,Ireland* 3-9-0 (b) JPMurtagh .... 12/1   ½ 6
Sheraka (IRE) *JOxx,Ireland* 3-9-0 GMosse....................................... 14/1   1 7
Asmara (USA) *JOxx,Ireland* 3-9-0 CRoche 25/1   1 8
Tossup (USA) *JGBurns,Ireland* 3-9-0 PShanahan 20/1 15 9
Abir *HThomsonJones,GB* 3-9-0 WJSupple 150/1 5½ 10
Princess Tycoon (IRE) *APO'Brien,Ireland* 3-9-0 SCraine................... 200/1   3 11
6 Bint Shadayid (USA) *SaeedbinSuroor,GB* 3-9-0 LDettori.................. 4/1 20 12

Mr Hamdan Al Maktoum 12ran 1m39.80

CURRAGH Sunday, May 26   GOOD to SOFT

13   First National Building Society Irish 2,000 Guineas (Gr 1) (3yo c+f)   1m
£116,186

8 SPINNING WORLD (USA) *JEPease,France* 3-9-0 CAsmussen 7/4f   1
RAINBOW BLUES (IRE) *APO'Brien,Ireland* 3-9-0 CRoche 50/1   2 2
5 BEAUCHAMP KING *JLDunlop,GB* 3-9-0 MJKinane............................ 9/2 1½ 3
5 Bijou d'Inde *MJohnston,GB* 3-9-0 JWeaver 3/1   3 4
8 Tagula (IRE) *IABalding,GB* 3-9-0 KDarley 11/1   1 5
Phantom Quest *HRACecil,GB* 3-9-0 PatEddery 10/1 2½ 6
Russian Revival (USA) *SaeedbinSuroor,GB* 3-9-0 LDettori 12/1   9 7
Musick House (IRE) *PWChapple-Hyam,GB* 3-9-0 BThomson........... 16/1 2½ 8
Deed of Love (USA) *JSBolger,Ireland* 3-9-0 KJManning .... 14/1   ½ 9
Flame of Athens (IRE) *MJGrassick,Ireland* 3-9-0 JPMurtagh 40/1   7 10

Niarchos Family 10ran 1m38.80

LONGCHAMP Monday, May 27   SOFT

14   Prix d'Ispahan (Gr 1) (4yo+ c+f) £63,371   1m1f55y

1 HALLING (USA) *SaeedbinSuroor,GB* 5-9-2 LDettori 11/10   1
GUNBOAT DIPLOMACY (FR) *ELellouche,France* 5-9-2 DBoeuf... 4/5cpf 1½ 2
VETHEUIL (USA) *AFabre,France* 4-9-2 OPeslier............................. 4/5cpf 1½ 3

9 Montjoy (USA) *PFICole,GB* 4-9-2 TQuinn... 34/10 1½ 4
Godolphin 4ran 2m02.90

CHANTILLY Sunday, Jun 2   GOOD to FIRM
15 **United Arab Emirates Prix du Jockey-Club (Gr 1) (3yo c+f)** £316,857   1½m
    RAGMAR (FR) *PBary,France* 3-9-2 GMosse.. 93/10   1
    POLARIS FLIGHT (USA) *PWChapple-Hyam,GB* 3-9-2 MJKinane..... 43/1   ns 2
    LE DESTIN (FR) *PHDemercastel,France* 3-9-2 TGillet .... 46/1   sn 3
  8 Don Micheletto *SaeedbinSuroor,GB* 3-9-2 LDettori 10/1cp 2 4
    Oliviero (FR) *AMauchamp,France* 3-9-2 (b) TThulliez .... 51/1 ¾ 5
    Helissio (FR) *ELellouche,France* 3-9-2 DBoeuf......................... 1/1f dh 5
    Grape Tree Road *AFabre,France* 3-9-2 TJarnet............................ 5/1cp nk 7
    Astor Place (IRE) *PWChapple-Hyam,GB* 3-9-2 PatEddery.................. 33/1 ¾ 8
    High Baroque (IRE) *PWChapple-Hyam,GB* 3-9-2 JReid .... 5/1cp sn 9
    Arbatax (IRE) *PBary,France* 3-9-2 CAsmussen 5/1 1½ 10
    L'Africain Bleu (FR) *MmeCHead,France* 3-9-2 GGuignard............... 13/2cp 2 11
    Water Poet (IRE) *AFabre,France* 3-9-2 SGuillot.............................. 10/1cp 3 12
    Radevore *AFabre,France* 3-9-2 OPeslier................................... 7/1cp 2 13
    Dark Nile (USA) *MmeCHead,France* 3-9-2 FHead 7/1cp 10 14
    Hoist to Heaven (USA) *MmeCHead,France* 3-9-2 NGuesdon.......... 13/2cp 15 15
  Mr J-L. Bouchard 15ran 2m27.20

EPSOM DOWNS Friday, Jun 7   GOOD to FIRM
16 **Vodafone Oaks (A) (Gr 1) (3yo f)** £201,000   1½m10y
    LADY CARLA *HRACecil* 3-9-0 PatEddery (9) 10/3   1
    PRICKET (USA) *SaeedbinSuroor* 3-9-0 LDettori (4) 7/4f 9 2
    MEZZOGIORNO *GWragg* 3-9-0 CAsmussen (8) .... 14/1 ½ 3
    Camporese (IRE) *PWChapple-Hyam* 3-9-0 JReid (2) .... 9/1 ½ 4
    Moody's Cat (IRE) *BWHills* 3-9-0 MHills (10)............................ 100/1 7 5
    Whitewater Affair *MRStoute* 3-9-0 TQuinn (3) .... 9/1 nk 6
    Faraway Waters *DWPArbuthnot* 3-9-0 KDarley (1)............................ 100/1 ½ 7
  6 Honest Guest (IRE) *MHTompkins* 3-9-0 PRobinson (7) 14/1 5 8
    Identify (IRE) *DKWeld,Ireland* 3-9-0 MJKinane (5) 16/1 2½ 9
    Shirley Venture *SPCWoods* 3-9-0 WWoods (11)................................ 200/1 22 10
  6 Bint Salsabil (USA) *JLDunlop* 3-9-0 WCarson (6) .... 10/1 dist 11
  Mr Wafic Said 11ran 2m35.55

EPSOM DOWNS Saturday, Jun 8   GOOD to FIRM
17 **Vodafone Derby Stks (A) (Gr 1) (3yo c+f)** £523,100   1½m10y
    SHAAMIT (IRE) *WJHaggas* 3-9-0 MHills (3) 12/1   1
    DUSHYANTOR (USA) *HRACecil* 3-9-0 PatEddery (4) 9/2f 1¼ 2
    SHANTOU (USA) *JHMGosden* 3-9-0 LDettori (6) 25/1 1¼ 3
    Glory of Dancer *PAKelleway* 3-9-0 OPeslier (8) 6/1 1 4
  5 Alhaarth (IRE) *MajorWRHern* 3-9-0 WCarson (14)............................ 15/2 hd 5
    Mystic Knight *RCharlton* 3-9-0 KDarley (19) 14/1 1¼ 6
    Jack Jennings *BAMcMahon* 3-9-0 JReid (7) 25/1 1 7
    Acharne *CEBrittain* 3-9-0 WJO'Connor (11).......................... 200/1 1¼ 8
    Chief Contender (IRE) *PWChapple-Hyam* 3-9-0 DHarrison (21) 15/1 1¾ 9
    Double Leaf *MRStoute* 3-9-0 JMurtagh (5).................................... 16/1 ½ 10
    Classic Eagle *RHarris* 3-9-0 AMackay (3) .... 200/1 nk 11
    Tasdid *KPrendergast,Ireland* 3-9-0 WSupple (15).......................... 200/1 sh 12
  5 Even Top (IRE) *MHTompkins* 3-9-0 PRobinson (13) .... 11/2 hd 13
    Spartan Heartbeat *CEBrittain* 3-9-0 MBirch (1) 200/1 6 14
  5 Storm Trooper (USA) *HRACecil* 3-9-0 MJKinane (17).................... 15/2 1½ 15
    Zaforum *LMontagueHall* 3-9-0 DaneO'Neill (2) 150/1 1¾ 16
    St Mawes (FR) *JLDunlop* 3-9-0 TQuinn (16)................................ 20/1 1 17
    Busy Flight *BWHills* 3-9-0 CAsmussen (20) 25/1 5 18
    Prince of My Heart *BWHills* 3-9-0 BThomson (18) 100/1 7 19
  6 Portuguese Lil *DNicholls* 3-8-9 AlexGreaves (10) 500/1 3 20
  Mr Khalifa Dasmal 20ran 2m35.05
18 **Vodafone Coronation Cup (A) (Gr 1) (4yo+)** £106,560   1½m10y
  4 SWAIN (IRE) *AFabre,France* 4-9-0 LDettori (2)............................... 11/10f   1
    SINGSPIEL (IRE) *MRStoute* 4-9-0 MJKinane (1) .... 9/4 nk 2
    DE QUEST *AFabre,France* 4-9-0 PatEddery (3) 7/2 5 3

Punishment *CEBrittain* 5-9-0 TQuinn (4) .... 14/1   sh 4
Sheikh Mohammed 4ran 2m40.36

CHANTILLY Sunday, Jun 9   GOOD
19   **Prix de Diane Hermes (Gr 1) (3yo f) £174,563**   1¼m110y
    SIL SILA (IRE) *BSmart,GB* 3-9-0 CAsmussen 30/1   1
    MISS TAHITI (IRE) *AFabre,France* 3-9-0 OPeslier............................... 5/1   1 2
  12   MATIYA (IRE) *BHanbury,GB* 3-9-0 WCarson.................................... 11/2   2½ 3
    Averring (USA) *JCunningtonjnr,France* 3-9-0 FSanchez............... 63/1   hd 4
    Wedding Gift (FR) *PHDemercastel,France* 3-9-0 TGillet................ 18/1   1½ 5
    Khalisa (IRE) *AdeRoyer-Dupre,France* 3-9-0 GMosse .... 4/1   ½ 6
    Luna Wells (IRE) *AFabre,France* 3-9-0 TJarnet................................ 1/1cpf   ½ 7
    Solar Crystal (IRE) *HRACecil,GB* 3-9-0 WRyan........................... 21/1   5 8
   7   A Votre Sante (USA) *MmeCHead,France* 3-9-0 FHead...................... 9/1cp   1 9
    Whenby (USA) *MmeCHead,France* 3-9-0 DBoeuf........................... 9/1cp   ¾ 10
    Melina Mou (IRE) *GEMikhalides,France* 3-9-0 MBoutin .... 38/1   dist 11
    Restless Mixa (IRE) *AFabre,France* 3-9-0 SGuillot........................ 1/1cpf   5 12
Mr L. Alvarez Cervera 12ran 2m07.30

MILAN Sunday, Jun 16   GOOD to FIRM
20   **Gran Premio di Milano (Gr 1) (3yo+ c+f) £114,879**   1½m
  10   STRATEGIC CHOICE (USA) *PFICole,GB* 5-9-6 TQuinn................. 11/10f   1
   4   LUSO *CEBrittain,GB* 4-9-6 MJKinane.. 21/10   1½ 2
    KING'S THEATRE (IRE) *SaeedbinSuroor,GB* 5-9-6 JReid 6/4   4¾ 3
    Pay Me Back (IRE) *GVerricelli,Italy* 6-9-6 LSorrentino 82/10   1½ 4
Mr M. Arbib 4ran 2m27.20

ASCOT Tuesday, Jun 18   FIRM
21   **Queen Anne Stks (A) (Gr 2) (3yo+) £59,890**   1m (Str.)
  11   CHARNWOOD FOREST (IRE) *SaeedbinSuroor* 4-9-2   1
      MJKinane (6).. 10/11f
   2   RESTRUCTURE (IRE) *MrsJCecil* 4-9-2 PaulEddery (8)...................... 11/1   4 2
   3   MISTLE CAT (USA) *SPCWoods* 5-9-2 WWoods (1)............................ 20/1   hd 3
    Young Ern *SDow* 5-9-2 CAsmussen (4) 20/1   1¼ 4
  11   Soviet Line (IRE) *MRStoute* 6-9-7 JReid (2) 13/2   1½ 5
    Mr Martini (USA) *CEBrittain* 6-9-2 BDoyle (5)................................ 40/1   4 6
    Prince of India *LordHuntingdon* 4-9-2 JWeaver (9) .... 50/1   ½ 7
    Timarida (IRE) *JOxx,Ireland* 4-9-2 JMurtagh (7) 6/1   15 8
  11   Gabr *RWArmstrong* 6-9-5 WCarson (3).. 12/1   hd 9
Godolphin 9ran 1m38.71

22   **Prince of Wales's Stks (A) (Gr 2) (3yo+) £63,325**   1¼m
   3   FIRST ISLAND (IRE) *GWragg* 4-9-3 MHills (3) 9/1   1
  14   MONTJOY (USA) *PFICole* 4-9-6 RHills (13) 16/1   1¼ 2
   1   TAMAYAZ (CAN) *SaeedbinSuroor* 4-9-3 OPeslier (11).................... 11/1   1¼ 3
    Dankeston (USA) *MBell* 3-8-5 MRoberts (12) 50/1   3½ 4
   9   Cezanne *SaeedbinSuroor* 7-9-3 JMurtagh (1) .... 25/1   nk 5
    Fahal (USA) *DMorley* 4-9-3 WCarson (5) .... 7/1   sh 6
   2   Desert Shot *MRStoute* 6-9-3 CAsmussen (4) 20/1   1¼ 7
    Pilsudski (IRE) *MRStoute* 4-9-3 PatEddery (9)............................ 4/1f   1¼ 8
    Lucky Di (USA) *LMCumani* 4-9-3 JWeaver (10)............................ 9/2   2½ 9
    Clever Cliche *HRACecil* 3-8-6 JReid (7) .... 16/1   ½ 10
    Cap Juluca (IRE) *RCharlton* 4-9-3 RHughes (8) .... 5/1   nk 11
   9   Needle Gun (IRE) *CEBrittain* 6-9-6 MJKinane (6) 14/1   9 12
Mollers Racing 12ran 2m02.76

23   **St James's Palace Stks (A) (Gr 1) (3yo c+f) £135,720**   1m (Rnd)
  13   BIJOU D'INDE *MJohnston* 3-9-0 JWeaver (7) 9/1   1
   8   ASHKALANI (IRE) *AdeRoyer-Dupre,France* 3-9-0 MJKinane (9) ..... 13/8f   hd 2
    SORBIE TOWER (IRE) *MissGayKelleway* 3-9-0 RHughes (6) 33/1   1 3
  13   Beauchamp King *JLDunlop* 3-9-0 JReid (8) 14/1   1¼ 4
   8   Cayman Kai (IRE) *RHannon* 3-9-0 PatEddery (3) 12/1   1¼ 5
  13   Spinning World (USA) *JEPease,France* 3-9-0 CAsmussen (5) 10/3   1¾ 6
    Wall Street (USA) *SaeedbinSuroor* 3-9-0 BThomson (2)...................... 16/1   5 7
   5   Mark of Esteem (IRE) *SaeedbinSuroor* 3-9-0 OPeslier (1) 11/2   1½ 8

    5 World Premier *CEBrittain* 3-9-0 BDoyle (4) .... 100/1   ½ 9

Mr J. S. Morrison 9ran 1m39.70

ASCOT Wednesday, Jun 19   GOOD to FIRM
24 Coronation Stks (A) (Gr 1) (3yo f) £120,726   1m (Rnd)
    7 SHAKE THE YOKE *ELellouche,France* 3-9-0 OPeslier (4) 1/1f   1
       LAST SECOND (IRE) *SirMarkPrescott* 3-9-0 GDuffield (7) .... 12/1   nk 2
   12 DANCE DESIGN (IRE) *DKWeld,Ireland* 3-9-0 MJKinane (1) .... 9/2   ½ 3
    7 Ta Rib (USA) *EALDunlop* 3-9-0 WCarson (2) 10/3   2½ 4
    6 Miss Universal (IRE) *CEBrittain* 3-9-0 BDoyle (5) .... 50/1   ¾ 5
       Thrilling Day *NAGraham* 3-9-0 DHarrison (3) 16/1   4 6
   12 Priory Belle (IRE) *JSBolger,Ireland* 3-9-0 KJManning (6) 16/1   2 7

Mr S. Brunswick 7ran 1m40.45

ASCOT Thursday, Jun 20   GOOD to FIRM
25 Gold Cup (A) (Gr 1) (4yo+) £118,872   2½m
   10 CLASSIC CLICHE (IRE) *SaeedbinSuroor* 4-9-0 MJKinane (7) 3/1   1
       DOUBLE TRIGGER (IRE) *MJohnston* 5-9-2 JWeaver (2).................... 1/2f   1½ 2
       NONONITO (FR) *JLesbordes,France* 5-9-2 SGuillot (4) 16/1   3 3
       Always Aloof (USA) *MRStoute* 5-9-2 WCarson (5).......................... 16/1   1½ 4
       Latahaab (USA) *RAkehurst* 5-9-2 TQuinn (3) .... 50/1   ¾ 5
       Upper Mount Clair *CEBrittain* 6-8-13 BDoyle (6) 66/1   13 6
       Assessor (IRE) *RHannon* 7-9-2 RHughes (1) 20/1   5 7

Godolphin 7ran 4m23.20

ASCOT Friday, Jun 21   FIRM
26 Hardwicke Stks (A) (Gr 2) (4yo+) £70,970   1½m
       OSCAR SCHINDLER (IRE) *KPrendergast,Ireland* 4-8-9
       MJKinane (8)... 7/4f   1
       ANNUS MIRABILIS (FR) *SaeedbinSuroor* 4-8-9 JCarroll (2) .... 5/1   ½ 2
       POSIDONAS *PFICole* 4-9-0 TQuinn (7) 16/1   3½ 3
    2 Lear White (USA) *PAKelleway* 5-8-9 JWeaver (5)............................. 33/1   sh 4
       Phantom Gold *LordHuntingdon* 4-8-9 MHills (1)................................ 10/1   1¼ 5
       Dance A Dream *MRStoute* 4-8-6 PatEddery (6) 8/1   1 6
   18 Punishment *CEBrittain* 5-8-9 BDoyle (3) .... 16/1   hd 7
       Election Day (IRE) *MRStoute* 4-8-9 WCarson (4)............................... 10/3 dist 8

Mr Oliver Lehane 8ran 2m27.84

27 King's Stand Stks (A) (Gr 2) (3yo+) £65,390   5f
       PIVOTAL *SirMarkPrescott* 3-8-10 GDuffield (7) 13/2   1
       MIND GAMES *JBerry* 4-9-2 JCarroll (14) .... 3/1f   ½ 2
       ALMATY (IRE) *CCollins,Ireland* 3-8-10 KDarley (10) 20/1   3½ 3
       Hever Golf Rose *TJNaughton* 5-9-2 PatEddery (11) 11/1   1¾ 4
       Royale Figurine (IRE) *MJFetherston-Godley* 5-8-13 JReid (16) .... 25/1   hd 5
    5 Royal Applause *BWHills* 3-8-13 MHills (6) .... 11/2   nk 6
       Loch Patrick *MMadgwick* 6-9-2 AMcGlone (18) .... 50/1   hd 7
       Lidanna *DHanley,Ireland* 3-8-7 MJKinane (15) .... 9/1   nk 8
       Titus Livius (FR) *JEPease,France* 3-8-10 CAsmussen (12) .... 20/1   hd 9
       Eveningperformance *HCandy* 5-8-13 WNewnes (5)........................... 14/1   ½ 10
       Mubhij (IRE) *BWHills* 3-8-10 WCarson (4) .... 25/1   nk 11
       Lucky Lionel (USA) *RHannon* 3-8-10 TQuinn (13)............................ 14/1   ½ 12
       Wavian *RHannon* 4-9-2 WJO'Connor (9) .... 100/1   nk 13
       Ailleacht (USA) *JSBolger,Ireland* 4-8-13 KJManning (3)................... 33/1   nk 14
       Double Quick (iRE) *MJohnston* 4-8-13 JWeaver (2)........................... 25/1   1¼ 15
       Struggler *DRLoder* 4-9-2 (v) RHughes (1)... 15/2   2½ 16
       Ya Malak *JWPayne* 5-9-2 (b) BThomson (8)...................................... 50/1   11 17

Cheveley Park Stud 17ran 59.49secs

LONGCHAMP Sunday, Jun 23   GOOD to FIRM
28 Grand Prix de Paris (Gr 1) (3yo c+f) £151,134   1¼m
       Order as they passed the post
   15 GRAPE TREE ROAD *AFabre,France* 3-9-2 TJarnet 10/1   1
   17 GLORY OF DANCER *PAKelleway,GB* 3-9-2 CAsmussen .... 24/10f   sh 2
       ANDROID (USA) *AFabre,France* 3-9-2 OPeslier 46/10cp   2 3

1105

```
         Farasan (IRE) HRACecil,GB 3-9-2 JReid.............................................. 26/10      sn  4
         Le Triton (USA) MmeCHead,France 3-9-2 FHead ................................ 37/10      sh  5
         Blackwater (USA) MZilber,France 3-9-2 GGuignard............................ 25/1      hd  6
    15   Oliviero (FR) PHDemercastel,France 3-9-2 (b) TThulliez ................... 30/1      nk  7
         Milford Track (IRE) HVandePoele,France 3-9-2 ODoleuze ................. 13/1      1½ 8
         Fort Nottingham (USA) JEHammond,France 3-9-2 GMosse ............... 13/1       6  9
         Martiniquais (IRE) AFabre,France 3-9-2 SGuillot............................. 49/10cp     8 10
         After a stewards' inquiry Farasan was demoted to sixth place
         Mr M. Tabor 10ran 2m02.30
```

CURRAGH Sunday, Jun 30   GOOD to FIRM

29   Budweiser Irish Derby (Gr 1) (3yo c+f) £352,423   1½m

```
         ZAGREB (USA) DKWeld,Ireland 3-9-0 PShanahan ............................. 20/1      1
    15   POLARIS FLIGHT (USA) PWChapple-Hyam,GB 3-9-0 JReid ............. 7/1      6  2
         HIS EXCELLENCE (USA) APO'Brien,Ireland 3-9-0 (b) WJSupple.... 50/1      6  3
    17   Dushyantor (USA) HRACecil,GB 3-9-0 PatEddery ............................. 5/4f     ¾  4
    13   Rainbow Blues (IRE) APO'Brien,Ireland 3-9-0 JAHeffernan.............. 33/1      2½ 5
    17   Spartan Heartbeat CEBrittain,GB 3-9-0 WJO'Connor......................... 100/1      ½  6
         Dr Massini (IRE) MRStoute,GB 3-9-0 MJKinane................................. 9/4      nk 7
         Private Song (USA) RCharlton,GB 3-9-0 WRyan................................ 66/1      sh 8
    17   Alhaarth (IRE) MajorWRHern,GB 3-9-0 (b) WCarson .................... 13/2      4½ 9
    15   Don Micheletto SaeedbinSuroor,GB 3-9-0 TQuinn............................ 14/1      ½ 10
         Sharaf Kabeer SaeedbinSuroor,GB 3-9-0 JPMurtagh......................... 10/1      2½ 11
         Truth Or Dare CharlesO'Brien,Ireland 3-9-0 CRoche......................... 33/1      dist 12
         Amfortas (IRE) CEBrittain,GB 3-9-0 DHolland ................................. 20/1      7 13
         Mr Allen E. Paulson 13ran 2m30.60
```

SAINT-CLOUD Sunday, Jun 30   GOOD to FIRM

30   Grand Prix de Saint-Cloud (Gr 1) (3yo+ c+f) £150,376   1½m

```
    15   HELISSIO (FR) ELellouche,France 3-8-8 OPeslier............................. 27/10      1
    18   SWAIN (IRE) AFabre,France 4-9-8 TJarnet ....................................... 9/10f     1  2
         POLIGLOTE MmeCHead,France 4-9-8 FHead ................................... 12/1      4  3
    26   Lear White (USA) PAKelleway,GB 5-9-8 GGuignard ....................... 49/1      ½  4
    28   Oliviero (FR) PHDemercastel,France 3-8-8 (b) ESaint-Martin ........... 18/1      ½  5
    18   De Quest AFabre,France 4-9-8 DBoeuf ............................................ 22/1      3  6
    15   Ragmar (FR) PBary,France 3-8-8 GMosse......................................... 57/10      ¾  7
         Bahamian Knight (CAN) DRLoder,GB 3-8-8 RHughes ..................... 20/1      1½ 8
     4   Carling (FR) MmePatBarbe,France 4-9-5 TThulliez............................ 12/1      2½ 9
         Mr E. Sarasola 9ran 2m27.40
```

SANDOWN Saturday, Jul 6   GOOD

31   Coral-Eclipse Stks (A) (Gr 1) (3yo+) £147,600   1¼m7y

```
    14   HALLING (USA) SaeedbinSuroor 5-9-7 JReid (1)............................... 10/3      1
    23   BIJOU D'INDE MJohnston 3-8-10 JWeaver (2) ................................ 12/1      nk 2
     1   PENTIRE GWragg 4-9-7 MHills (5)................................................... 2/1f     1¾ 3
         Ela-Aristokrati (IRE) LMCumani 4-9-7 KFallon (6) ........................ 16/1      5  4
         Definite Article DKWeld,Ireland 4-9-7 (v) MJKinane (7) ................ 7/2      nk 5
     4   Valanour (IRE) AdeRoyer-Dupre,France 4-9-7 GMosse (4) ............ 7/1      2  6
    23   Beauchamp King JLDunlop 3-8-10 TQuinn (3)................................ 16/1      6  7
         Godolphin 7ran 2m08.05
```

NEWMARKET Tuesday, Jul 9   GOOD (July Course)

32   Hillsdown Cherry Hinton Stks (A) (Gr 2) (2yo f) £22,792   6f

```
         DAZZLE MRStoute 2-8-9 KFallon (3)................................................. 2/1f     1
         OCEAN RIDGE (USA) PWChapple-Hyam 2-8-9 JReid (2)................... 4/1      5  2
         WELL WARNED BWHills 2-8-9 PatEddery (6) .................................. 9/1      3½ 3
         Eye Shadow BJMeehan 2-8-9 MJKinane (4) ...................................... 25/1      4  4
         Rich In Love (IRE) CACyzer 2-8-9 MRoberts (9)............................... 25/1      1¼ 5
         Khassah JHMGosden 2-8-9 WCarson (7) .......................................... 7/2      sh 6
         Lycility (IRE) CEBrittain 2-8-9 BDoyle (5) ..................................... 50/1      hd 7
         Dame Laura (IRE) PFICole 2-8-9 TQuinn (8) .................................. 13/2      1¾ 8
         Connemara (IRE) CADwyer 2-8-9 JWeaver (1) ................................ 12/1      1¼ 9
         Cheveley Park Stud 9ran 1m11.02
```

33   **Princess of Wales's Stks (A) (Gr 2) (3yo+) £36,504**   1½m

26	POSIDONAS *PFICole* 4-9-7 TQuinn (6)	20/1	1
18	SINGSPIEL (IRE) *MRStoute* 4-9-2 MJKinane (3)	7/4	1¼ 2
26	ANNUS MIRABILIS (FR) *SaeedbinSuroor* 4-9-2 JReid (1)	9/2	2½ 3
30	Lear White (USA) *PAKelleway* 4-9-2 KFallon (2)	25/1	2½ 4
	Bequeath *HRACecil* 4-9-2 PatEddery (5)	13/8f	2 5
26	Punishment *CEBrittain* 5-9-2 BDoyle (4)	40/1	3½ 6
	Wayne County (IRE) *RAkehurst* 6-9-2 SSanders (7)	50/1	14 7
	Midnight Legend *LMCumani* 5-9-2 JWeaver (9)	20/1	6 8

Mr Athos Christodoulou 8ran 2m28.92

NEWMARKET Thursday, Jul 11   GOOD to FIRM

34   **Darley July Cup (A) (Gr 1) (3yo+) £90,588**   6f

	ANABAA (USA) *MmeCHead,France* 4-9-5 FHead (2)	11/4	1
	LUCAYAN PRINCE (USA) *DRLoder* 3-8-13 (b) RHughes (1)	9/1	1¾ 2
27	HEVER GOLF ROSE *TJNaughton* 5-9-2 PatEddery (6)	14/1	3 3
	Iktamal (USA) *EALDunlop* 4-9-5 RHills (3)	16/1	sh 4
8	Danehill Dancer (IRE) *NACallaghan* 3-8-13 MJKinane (5)	7/1	sh 5
27	Pivotal *SirMarkPrescott* 3-8-13 GDuffield (8)	9/4f	hd 6
27	Mind Games *JBerry* 4-9-5 JCarroll (10)	15/2	hd 7
27	Lucky Lionel (USA) *RHannon* 3-8-13 OPeslier (4)	25/1	3 8
	Cool Jazz *CEBrittain* 5-9-5 KDarley (7)	40/1	nk 9
8	Gothenberg (IRE) *MJohnston* 3-8-13 JWeaver (9)	20/1	½ 10

Mme A. Head 10ran 1m10.63

CURRAGH Sunday, Jul 14   GOOD to FIRM

35   **Kildangan Stud Irish Oaks (Gr 1) (3yo f) £122,371**   1½m

24	DANCE DESIGN (IRE) *DKWeld,Ireland* 3-9-0 MJKinane	9/2	1
	SHAMADARA (IRE) *AdeRoyer-Dupre,France* 3-9-0 GMosse	6/1	sh 2
	KEY CHANGE (IRE) *JOxx,Ireland* 3-9-0 JMurtagh	8/1	2 3
16	Lady Carla *HRACecil,GB* 3-9-0 PatEddery	1/2f	2½ 4
	French Ballerina (IRE) *PJFlynn,Ireland* 3-9-0 PVGilson	100/1	1 5
	Tout A Coup (IRE) *GACusack,Ireland* 3-9-0 RHughes	14/1	13 6

Moyglare Stud Farms Ltd 6ran 2m29.70

ASCOT Saturday, Jul 27   GOOD to FIRM

36   **King George VI And Queen Elizabeth Diamond Stks (A) (Gr 1) (3yo+)**   1½m
£294,600

31	PENTIRE *GWragg* 4-9-7 MHills (7)	10/3	1
25	CLASSIC CLICHE (IRE) *SaeedbinSuroor* 4-9-7 MJKinane (5)	5/1	1¾ 2
17	SHAAMIT (IRE) *WJHaggas* 3-8-9 PatEddery (1)	2/1f	nk 3
26	Oscar Schindler (IRE) *KPrendergast,Ireland* 4-9-7 RHughes (4)	10/1	10 4
33	Annus Mirabilis (FR) *SaeedbinSuroor* 4-9-7 (v) RHills (6)	33/1	11 5
20	Luso *CEBrittain* 4-9-7 JReid (3)	14/1	1¾ 6
28	Farasan (IRE) *HRACecil* 3-8-9 RCochrane (2)	11/1	dh 6
20	Strategic Choice (USA) *PFICole* 5-9-7 TQuinn (8)	7/1	1¾ 8

Mollers Racing 8ran 2m28.11

DUSSELDORF Sunday, Jul 28   GOOD to FIRM

37   **Deutschlandpreis 50 Jahre Nordrhein-Westfalen (Gr 1) (3yo+) £78,261**   1½m

9	HOLLYWOOD DREAM (GER) *UOstmann,Germany* 5-9-2 JReid	181/10	1
33	POSIDONAS *PFICole,GB* 4-9-6 TQuinn		sh 2
	PROTEKTOR (GER) *ALowe,Germany* 7-9-6 THellier		1¾ 3
	Surako (GER) *HJentzsch,Germany* 3-8-6 PSchiergen		2½ 4
26	Phantom Gold *LordHuntingdon,GB* 4-9-2 DHarrison		2 5
	Night Petticoat (GER) *BSchutz,Germany* 3-8-3 AStarke		4 6
	Caballo (GER) *HJentzsch,Germany* 5-9-6 SEccles		24 7

Gestut Ittlingen 7ran 2m26.35

GOODWOOD Wednesday, Jul 31   GOOD to FIRM

38   **Lanson Champagne Vintage Stks (A) (Gr 3) (2yo) £23,380**   7f

	PUTRA (USA) *PFICole* 2-8-11 TQuinn (6)	10/3	1
	SAHM (USA) *JLDunlop* 2-8-11 RHills (8)	7/4f	½ 2
	GRAPESHOT (USA) *LMCumani* 2-8-11 KDarley (3)	9/1	2 3

Equal Rights (IRE) *PWChapple-Hyam* 2-8-11 JReid (7)...................... 12/1 nk 4
Air Express (IRE) *CEBrittain* 2-8-11 BDoyle (2)................................. 12/1 1¼ 5
Imperial President *HRACecil* 2-8-11 PatEddery (1)............................... 13/2 1 6
Fun Galore (USA) *BWHills* 2-8-11 MHills (5) 8/1 10 7
Belgravia *PFICole* 2-8-11 (b) MJKinane (4) 33/1 3½ 8

H.R.H. Sultan Ahmad Shah 8ran 1m27.32

39   Sussex Stks (A) (Gr 1) (3yo+) £89,770   1m

22 FIRST ISLAND (IRE) *GWragg* 4-9-7 MHills (9) 5/1 1
21 CHARNWOOD FOREST (IRE) *SaeedbinSuroor* 4-9-7 MJKinane (7).. 1/1f 1 2
29 ALHAARTH (IRE) *MajorWRHern* 3-8-13 (b) KDarley (8) 14/1 1¾ 3
23 Sorbie Tower (IRE) *MissGayKelleway* 3-8-13 RHughes (4) .... 8/1 ¾ 4
21 Restructure (IRE) *MrsJCecil* 4-9-7 PaulEddery (5)............................ 25/1 sh 5
21 Mistle Cat (USA) *SPCWoods* 5-9-7 WWoods (3) 25/1 5 6
   Ali-Royal (IRE) *HRACecil* 3-8-13 PatEddery (6)................................ 12/1 3½ 7
23 Cayman Kai (IRE) *RHannon* 3-8-13 TQuinn (3)................................. 25/1 7 8
   Heart Lake *SaeedbinSuroor* 5-9-7 JReid (1) .... 40/1 hd 9
19 Matiya (IRE) *BHanbury* 3-8-10 RHills (10) .... 8/1 sh 10

Mollers Racing 10ran 1m37.75

MUNICH Sunday, Aug 4   GOOD to SOFT

40   Grosser Dallmayr Preis-Bayerisches Zuchtrennen (Gr 1) (3yo+) £95,652   1¼m

21 TIMARIDA (IRE) *JOxx,Ireland* 4-9-2 JPMurtagh 27/10 1
   GERMANY (USA) *BSchutz,Germany* 5-9-6 RCochrane .... ½ 2
   LA BLUE (GER) *BSchutz,Germany* 3-8-9 DHolland................................ nk 3
22 Montjoy (USA) *PFICole,GB* 4-9-6 TQuinn 1 4
   Devil River Peek (USA) *BSchutz,Germany* 4-9-6 AStarke .... ¾ 5
   Artan (GER) *MRolke,Germany* 4-9-6 JTandari 2 6
22 Needle Gun (IRE) *CEBrittain,GB* 6-9-6 MJKinane 2 7
   Hondero (GER) *BoerjeOlsson,Germany* 6-9-6 PPiatkowski 1½ 8

H.H. Aga Khan 8ran 2m06.60

HAYDOCK Saturday, Aug 10   GOOD to FIRM

41   Rose of Lancaster Stks (A) (Gr 3) (3yo+) £21,760   1¼m120y

22 TAMAYAZ (CAN) *SaeedbinSuroor* 4-9-3 GCarter (7) 11/2 1
31 ELA-ARISTOKRATI (IRE) *LMCumani* 4-9-3 OUrbina (1) 13/2 5 2
   CAPTAIN HORATIUS (IRE) *JLDunlop* 7-9-3 SSanders (3)................ 20/1 1¾ 3
28 Glory of Dancer *PAKelleway* 3-9-0 PatEddery (2)................................ 2/1f nk 4
   Key To My Heart (IRE) *MissSEHall* 6-9-3 DeanMcKeown (8) .... 9/1 nk 5
   Weet-A-Minute (IRE) *RHollinshead* 3-8-7 KFallon (4) 33/1 6 6
   Nash House (IRE) *PWChapple-Hyam* 3-8-7 JReid (5)............................ 9/4 ¾ 7
17 Acharne *CEBrittain* 3-8-7 JQuinn (6) 14/1 7 8

Godolphin 8ran 2m13.15

DEAUVILLE Sunday, Aug 11   GOOD to SOFT

42   Prix Maurice de Gheest (Gr 1) (3yo+) £64,599   6f110y

34 ANABAA (USA) *MmeCHead,France* 4-9-2 FHead 1/2f 1
   MIESQUE'S SON (USA) *JEHammond,France* 4-9-2 CAsmussen 1½ 2
34 DANEHILL DANCER (IRE) *NACallaghan,GB* 3-8-12 RCochrane .... hd 3
34 Iktamal (USA) *EALDunlop,GB* 4-9-2 WRyan 5 4
   Blue Duster (USA) *DRLoder,GB* 3-8-9 PatEddery .... ¾ 5
   A Magicman (FR) *HSteguweit,Germany* 4-9-2 NGrant 2 6
21 Young Ern *SDow,GB* 6-9-2 TQuinn .... sh 7
   Easy Dollar *BGubby,GB* 4-9-2 (b) TJarnet 2 8
   Poplar Bluff (IRE) *AFabre,France* 4-9-2 OPeslier 8 9

Mme A. Head 9ran 1m19.00

LEOPARDSTOWN Sunday, Aug 11   GOOD

43   Heinz 57 Phoenix Stks (Gr 1) (2yo c+f) £88,021   6f

   MANTOVANI (IRE) *JSBolger,Ireland* 2-9-0 CEverard 20/1 1
   MUCHEA *MRChannon,GB* 2-9-0 RHughes 10/1 2 2
   VERGLAS (IRE) *KPrendergast,Ireland* 2-9-0 WJSupple .... 11/8f hd 3
32 Ocean Ridge (USA) *PWChapple-Hyam,GB* 2-8-11 JReid...................... 4/1 sh 4
   Star Profile (IRE) *DKWeld,Ireland* 2-8-11 MJKinane............................ 13/2 1½ 5
   Azra (IRE) *JSBolger,Ireland* 2-8-11 KJManning 8/1 1 6

Raphane (USA) *CCollins,Ireland* 2-9-0 SCraine 8/1   8 7
Check The Band (USA) *APO'Brien,Ireland* 2-9-0 (b) CRoche .... 8/1   ¾ 8
Scottish Mist (IRE) *GMLyons,Ireland* 2-8-11 (b) LDettori 50/1   12 9
Mrs J. S. Bolger 9ran 1m13.60

DEAUVILLE Thursday, Aug 15   GOOD to SOFT

44   **Prix du Haras de Fresnay-Le-Buffard Jacques Le Marois (Gr 1) (3yo+**   1m
    c+f) £127,714
23 SPINNING WORLD (USA) *JEPease,France* 3-8-11 CAsmussen 17/10   1
14 VETHEUIL (USA) *AFabre,France* 4-9-4 OPeslier .... 107/10   ½ 2
    SHAANXI (USA) *ELellouche,France* 4-9-1 MEbina .... 73/10   ¾ 3
39 Charnwood Forest (IRE) *SaeedbinSuroor,GB* 4-9-4 LDettori .... 13/10cpf   ¾ 4
    Grey Risk (FR) *PHDemercastel,France* 3-8-11 SGuillot 86/10   1 5
    Zarannda (IRE) *AdeRoyer-Dupre,France* 3-8-8 GMosse.................... 62/10   2½ 6
34 Gothenberg (IRE) *MJohnston,GB* 3-8-11 JWeaver 39/1   2½ 7
28 Le Triton (USA) *MmeCHead,France* 3-8-11 FHead 13/10cpf   3 8
    Sensation *MmeCHead,France* 3-8-8 MJKinane.............................. 13/10cpf   10 9
Niarchos Family 9ran 1m39.10

NEWBURY Saturday, Aug 17   GOOD to FIRM

45   **Tripleprint Geoffrey Freer Stks (A) (Gr 2) (3yo+)** £42,824   1m5f61y
37 PHANTOM GOLD *LordHuntingdon* 4-9-3 LDettori (5)........................ 6/1   1
37 POSIDONAS *PFICole* 4-9-9 TQuinn (4) 10/11f   3½ 2
    SONG OF TARA (IRE) *PWChapple-Hyam* 4-9-3 JReid (7) .... 4/1   hd 3
    Samraan (USA) *JLDunlop* 3-8-6 MHills (6)................................... 11/1   nk 4
41 Key To My Heart (IRE) *MissSEHall* 6-9-3 RHughes (3)....................... 6/1   5 5
    Whitechapel (USA) *LordHuntingdon* 8-9-3 TIves (1) 40/1   9 6
33 Wayne County (IRE) *RAkehurst* 6-9-3 SSanders (2) .... 50/1   dist 7
The Queen 7ran 2m46.18

DEAUVILLE Sunday, Aug 18   GOOD

46   **Prix Morny Piaget (Gr 1) (2yo c+f)** £102,171   6f
    BAHAMIAN BOUNTY *DRLoder,GB* 2-9-0 LDettori 56/10   1
    ZAMINDAR (USA) *AFabre,France* 2-9-0 TJarnet.............................. 3/10f   sn 2
    PAS DE REPONSE (USA) *MmeCHead,France* 2-8-11 FHead 41/10   3 3
    Rich Ground *JDBethell,GB* 2-9-0 PaulEddery 77/10   4 4
    Blue Ridge *RHannon,GB* 2-9-0 RHughes .... 20/1   sn 5
Lucayan Stud 5ran 1m11.00

GELSENKIRCHEN-HORST Sunday, Aug 18   GOOD

47   **Aral-Pokal (Gr 1) (3yo+)** £91,703   1½m
36 LUSO *CEBrittain,GB* 4-9-6 MJKinane 1/1   1
37 HOLLYWOOD DREAM (GER) *UOstmann,Germany* 5-9-2 JReid 1¾ 2
33 LEAR WHITE (USA) *PAKelleway,GB* 5-9-6 FJovine 3 3
    Lentini *BSchutz,Germany* 5-9-6 THellier 1½ 4
    Wind of Chance (GER) *BSchutz,Germany* 3-8-8 AStarke.................... nk 5
    Little Smart (GER) *PLautner,Germany* 4-9-6 WNewnes 9 6
    O'Connor (IRE) *AWohler,Germany* 4-9-6 ABoschert 5 7
37 Caballo (GER) *HJentzsch,Germany* 5-9-6 LHammer-Hansen...................... 2 8
Mr Saeed Manana 8ran 2m32.98

YORK Tuesday, Aug 20   GOOD to FIRM

48   **Juddmonte International Stks (A) (Gr 1) (3yo+)** £165,548   1¼m85y
31 HALLING (USA) *SaeedbinSuroor* 5-9-5 LDettori (1)............................. 6/4f   1
39 FIRST ISLAND (IRE) *GWragg* 4-9-5 MHills (4) 3/1   3 2
31 BIJOU D'INDE *MJohnston* 3-8-11 JWeaver (5) 4/1   1½ 3
28 Grape Tree Road *AFabre,France* 3-8-11 TJarnet (3)................................ 9/1   ¾ 4
11 Spectrum (IRE) *PWChapple-Hyam* 4-9-5 JReid (6) .... 6/1   nk 5
33 Punishment *CEBrittain* 5-9-5 BDoyle (2) 66/1   1 6
Godolphin 6ran 2m06.88

49   **Great Voltigeur Stks (A) (Gr 2) (3yo c+g)** £48,451   1m3f195y
29 DUSHYANTOR (USA) *HRACecil* 3-8-9 PatEddery (2) 3/1   1
    MONS *LMCumani* 3-8-9 LDettori (5).. 7/2   ½ 2

ROYAL COURT (IRE) *PWChapple-Hyam* 3-8-9 JReid (6)................. 11/4f 1½ 3
36 Farasan (IRE) *HRACecil* 3-8-9 KFallon (2) 9/1 1¼ 4
17 Even Top (IRE) *MHTompkins* 3-8-9 PRobinson (1) 7/2 2 5
22 Dankeston (USA) *MBell* 3-8-9 WCarson (4) 12/1 7 6

Mr K. Abdulla 6ran 2m30.64

YORK Wednesday, Aug 21   GOOD to FIRM

50   **Aston Upthorpe Yorkshire Oaks (A) (Gr 1) (3yo+ f+m)** £78,816   1m3f195y
Order as they passed the post

35 KEY CHANGE (IRE) *JOxx,Ireland* 3-8-8 JMurtagh (1) 7/1 1
6 PAPERING (IRE) *LMCumani* 3-8-8 KDarley (6)............................... 8/1 1¾ 2
RUSSIAN SNOWS (IRE) *SaeedbinSuroor* 4-9-4 LDettori (3)............... 11/2 nk 3
16 Mezzogiorno *GWragg* 3-8-8 MHills (5) 16/1 3 4
35 Shamadara (IRE) *AdeRoyer-Dupre,France* 3-8-8 GMosse (8)............... 2/1f nk 5
16 Whitewater Affair *MRStoute* 3-8-8 TQuinn (7) .... 14/1 nk 6
Shemozzle (IRE) *JHMGosden* 3-8-8 PatEddery (4) 15/2 1 7
Quota *HRACecil* 3-8-8 WRyan (2).. 16/1 4 8
19 Sil Sila (IRE) *BSmart* 3-8-8 LCochrane (9).. 9/2 24 9

After a stewards' inquiry Russian Snows was demoted to sixth place
Lady Clague 9ran 2m27.56

YORK Thursday, Aug 22   GOOD to FIRM

51   **Nunthorpe Stks (A) (Gr 1) (2yo+)** £72,465   5f

34 PIVOTAL *SirMarkPrescott* 3-9-7 GDuffield (5) 10/3 1
27 EVENINGPERFORMANCE *HCandy* 5-9-6 CRutter (1)....................... 16/1 sh 2
34 HEVER GOLF ROSE *TJNaughton* 5-9-6 JWeaver (3) 11/4 1¼ 3
34 Mind Games *JBerry* 4-9-9 JCarroll (7) .... 7/4f ¾ 4
Catch The Blues (IRE) *APO'Brien,Ireland* 4-9-6 (v) CRoche (6) .... 20/1 ½ 5
27 Struggler *DRLoder* 4-9-9 LDettori (2)... 10/1 1½ 6
34 Cool Jazz *CEBrittain* 5-9-9 TQuinn (8) 20/1 1½ 7
Windmachine (SWE) *BjoernTOlsen,Norway* 5-9-6 FDiaz (4)............... 33/1 4 8

Cheveley Park Stud 8ran 56.53secs

GOODWOOD Saturday, Aug 24   GOOD

52   **Tripleprint Celebration Mile (A) (Gr 2) (3yo+)** £35,170   1m

23 MARK OF ESTEEM (IRE) *SaeedbinSuroor* 3-9-1 LDettori (7) 11/4f 1
3 BISHOP OF CASHEL *JRFanshawe* 4-9-1 WRSwinburn (5)................. 5/1 3½ 2
39 ALHAARTH (IRE) *MajorWRHern* 3-8-9 WCarson (1)......................... 7/2 ¾ 3
39 Restructure (IRE) *MrsJCecil* 4-9-1 PaulEddery (6) .... 6/1 ¾ 4
12 Distant Oasis (USA) *HRACecil* 3-8-6 WRyan (4) .... 6/1 ¾ 5
44 Gothenberg (IRE) *MJohnston* 3-8-12 JWeaver (2) 12/1 5 6
31 Beauchamp King *JLDunlop* 3-8-9 JReid (3)....................................... 6/1 7 7

Godolphin 7ran 1m41.18

ARLINGTON Saturday, Aug 24   FIRM

53   **Beverly D Stks (Gr 1) (3yo+ f+m)** £193,548   1m1f110y

40 TIMARIDA (IRE) *JOxx,Ireland* 4-8-11 JPMurtagh 16/10cpf 1
PERFECT ARC (USA) *APennajr,USA* 4-8-11 JRVelazquez 2½ 2
ALPRIDE (IRE) *RMcAnally,USA* 5-8-11 CMcCarron.......................... 3½ 3
19 Khalisa (IRE) *AdeRoyer-Dupre,France* 3-8-5 GMosse 16/10cpf 1 4
Bail Out Becky (USA) *WMott,USA* 4-8-11 CPerret .... ns 5
Auriette (IRE) *MJones,USA* 4-8-11 KDesormeaux.............................. hd 6
Duda (USA) *WMott,USA* 5-8-11 PValenzuela................................... nk 7
Memories (IRE) *BKessinger,jnr,USA* 5-8-11 SSellers........................... 2 8
Olimpia Dukakis (ITY) *RMcAnally,USA* 4-8-11 AGryder..................... 5 9
Flagbird (USA) *JNoseda,USA* 5-8-11 EDelahoussaye............................ pu
Matiara (USA) *RMandella,USA* 4-8-11 CNakatani............................... pu

H.H. Aga Khan 11ran 1m54.06

GOODWOOD Sunday, Aug 25   GOOD to SOFT

54   **Crowson Prestige Stks (A) (Gr 3) (2yo f)** £21,180   7f

RED CAMELLIA *SirMarkPrescott* 2-8-12 GDuffield (1) 10/11f 1
FERNANDA *JLDunlop* 2-8-9 (b) TSprake (4)...................................... 10/1 6 2

VELOUR *DRLoder* 2-8-9 KDarley (5) .... 4/1   sh 3
Queen Sceptre (IRE) *BWHills* 2-8-9 MHills (2) 14/1   1½ 4
Mayfair *PFICole* 2-8-9 RHughes (3).. 9/2   7 5

Cheveley Park Stud 5ran 1m31.41

ARLINGTON Sunday, Aug 25   FIRM

55   **Arlington Million XVI (Gr 1) (3yo+) £387,097**   1¼m

     MECKE (USA) *ETortora,USA* 4-9-0 (b) RobbieDavis 155/10   1
     AWAD (USA) *DDonk,USA* 6-9-0 (b) CMcCarron 7/2   2 2
     SANDPIT (BRZ) *RMandella,USA* 7-9-0 CNakatani 14/10f   2¼ 3
41   Glory of Dancer *PAKelleway,GB* 3-8-8 MJKinane 15/1   1¼ 4
     Torch Rouge *RFrankel,USA* 5-9-0 PDay.. 62/10   2½ 5
     Diplomatic Jet (USA) *JEPicou,USA* 4-9-0 RRomero 16/1   3 6
40   Needle Gun (IRE) *CEBrittain,GB* 6-9-0 SSellers .... 32/1   nk 7
31   Valanour (IRE) *AdeRoyer-Dupre,France* 4-9-0 GMosse 33/10   15 8
     Prince of Andros (USA) *DRLoder,GB* 6-9-0 PatEddery...................... 48/1   9 9

Mr James Lewis, jnr 9ran 2m00.49

DEAUVILLE Sunday, Aug 25   GOOD

56   **Grand Prix de Deauville Lancel (Gr 2) (3yo+) £63,291**   1½m110y

36   STRATEGIC CHOICE (USA) *PFICole,GB* 5-9-1 TQuinn 7/1   1
     TARATOR (USA) *ELellouche,France* 5-8-10 OPeslier .... 11/10f   nk 2
     PERCUTANT (FR) *DSmaga,France* 5-9-4 DBoeuf.......................... 129/10   sh 3
     Helen of Spain *AFabre,France* 4-9-4 TJarnet.................................... 24/10cp   1 4
     Leeds (IRE) *HVandePoele,France* 4-9-4 SGuillot 96/10cp   1½ 5
30   Oliviero (FR) *AVergeade,France* 3-8-7 (b) MBoutin .... 20/1   hd 6
15   Water Poet (IRE) *AFabre,France* 3-8-7 LDettori .... 24/10cp   sn 7
15   High Baroque (IRE) *PWChapple-Hyam,GB* 3-8-7 JReid 52/10   3 8
     Matarun (IRE) *HVandePoele,France* 8-9-4 AJunk 96/10cp   3 9

Mr M. Arbib 9ran 2m44.30

BADEN-BADEN Sunday, Sep 1   GOOD to FIRM

57   **Mercedes-Benz Grosser Preis Von Baden (Gr 1) (3yo+) £140,692**   1½m

22   PILSUDSKI (IRE) *MRStoute,GB* 4-9-6 WRSwinburn 11/1   1
40   GERMANY (USA) *BSchutz,Germany* 5-9-6 LDettori ....   ¾ 2
     SUNSHACK *AFabre,France* 5-9-6 SGuillot..   1¾ 3
31   Definite Article *DKWeld,Ireland* 4-9-6 MJKinane 1¼ 4
     Agnelli *HJentzsch,Germany* 3-8-9 PSchiergen 2½ 5
37   Protektor (GER) *ALowe,Germany* 7-9-6 THellier..   1½ 6
30   Poliglote *MmeCHead,France* 4-9-6 FHead..   1 7

Lord Weinstock/Exors of late S.Weinstock 7ran 2m26.74

HAYDOCK Saturday, Sep 7   FIRM

58   **Haydock Park Sprint Cup (A) (Gr 1) (3yo+) £77,250**   6f

42   IKTAMAL (USA) *EALDunlop* 4-9-0 WRyan (9).................................. 10/1   1
42   BLUE DUSTER (USA) *DRLoder* 3-8-9 JReid (11) 9/1   1 2
51   CATCH THE BLUES (IRE) *APO'Brien,Ireland* 4-8-11 (v)
        CRoche (4) 20/1   1¼ 3
51   Hever Golf Rose *TJNaughton* 5-8-11 JFortune (10)............................... 7/1   ½ 4
34   Lucayan Prince (USA) *DRLoder* 3-8-12 (b) LDettori (1) .... 3/1   ½ 5
51   Mind Games *JBerry* 4-9-0 RHughes (6) 14/1   1½ 6
42   Miesque's Son (USA) *JEHammond,France* 4-9-0 CAsmussen (3)......... 5/2f   hd 7
     Rambling Bear *MBlanshard* 3-8-12 RCochrane (8)............................. 20/1   ½ 8
27   Royal Applause *BWHills* 3-8-12 KFallon (2).. 16/1   1½ 9
51   Cool Jazz *CEBrittain* 5-9-0 BDoyle (7) 33/1   1¼ 10
42   Danehill Dancer (IRE) *NACallaghan* 3-8-12 PatEddery (5)................... 7/1   6 11

Maktoum Al Maktoum 11ran 1m09.92

LONGCHAMP Sunday, Sep 8   GOOD to FIRM

59   **Emirates Prix du Moulin de Longchamp (Gr 1) (3yo+ c+f) £113,924**   1m

23   ASHKALANI (IRE) *AdeRoyer-Dupre,France* 3-8-11 GMosse 4/5f   1
44   SPINNING WORLD (USA) *JEPease,France* 3-8-11 CAsmussen ... 35/10cp   1½ 2
24   SHAKE THE YOKE *ELellouche,France* 3-8-8 SGuillot.................... 35/10   sh 3
44   Vetheuil (USA) *AFabre,France* 4-9-2 OPeslier 75/10   2 4

30	Carling (FR) *MmePatBarbe,France* 4-8-12 TThulliez	11/1cp	sn 5
44	Shaanxi (USA) *ELellouche,France* 4-8-12 MEbina	11/1cp	2½ 6
44	Grey Risk (FR) *PHDemercastel,France* 3-8-11 TJarnet	21/1	¾ 7
44	Le Triton (USA) *MmeCHead,France* 3-8-11 (b) FHead	26/1	1½ 8
	Metaphor (USA) *JEPease,France* 3-8-8 FSanchez	35/10cp	20 9

H.H. Aga Khan 9ran 1m37.20

DONCASTER Thursday, Sep 12   GOOD to FIRM

60   East Coast Doncaster Cup (A) (Gr 3) (3yo+) £19,072   2¼m

25	DOUBLE TRIGGER (IRE) *MJohnston* 5-9-7 LDettori (5)	1/1f	1
	CELERIC *DMorley* 4-9-0 WCarson (2)	13/8	2 2
47	LEAR WHITE (USA) *PAKelleway* 5-9-0 OPeslier (3)	13/2	2 3
	Admiral's Well (IRE) *RAkehurst* 6-9-0 TQuinn (1)	25/1	2 4
	Old Rouvel (USA) *DJGMurraySmith* 5-9-0 KDarley (6)	50/1	4 5
25	Assessor (IRE) *RHannon* 7-9-3 JReid (4)	25/1	7 6

Mr R. W. Huggins 6ran 3m53.00

DONCASTER Friday, Sep 13   FIRM

61   Laurent-Perrier Champagne Stks (A) (Gr 2) (2yo c+g) £45,940   7f

	BAHHARE (USA) *JLDunlop* 2-8-10 WCarson (3)	4/6f	1
	IN COMMAND (IRE) *BWHills* 2-8-10 MHills (1)	9/1	3½ 2
	MUSHEER (USA) *MissGayKelleway* 2-8-10 KFallon (5)	9/2	1¾ 3
	Reliquary (USA) *DRLoder* 2-8-10 LDettori (4)	4/1	4 4

Mr Hamdan Al Maktoum 4ran 1m23.21

DONCASTER Saturday, Sep 14   GOOD to FIRM

62   Pertemps St Leger Stks (A) (Gr 1) (3yo c+f) £174,688   1¾m132y

17	SHANTOU (USA) *JHMGosden* 3-9-0 LDettori (10)	8/1	1
49	DUSHYANTOR (USA) *HRACecil* 3-9-0 PatEddery (9)	2/1f	nk 2
45	SAMRAAN (USA) *JLDunlop* 3-9-0 JCarroll (3)	28/1	4 3
49	Mons *LMCumani* 3-9-0 OUrbina (5)	5/1	3½ 4
17	St Mawes (FR) *JLDunlop* 3-9-0 (b) KDarley (8)	8/1	1¼ 5
	Wilawander *BWHills* 3-9-0 RHills (1)	16/1	2½ 6
29	Sharaf Kabeer *SaeedbinSuroor* 3-9-0 TQuinn (6)	10/1	2 7
	Heron Island (IRE) *PWChapple-Hyam* 3-9-0 JReid (12)	10/1	1¾ 8
	Flying Legend (IRE) *HRACecil* 3-9-0 WRyan (7)	18/1	8 9
	Gordi (USA) *DKWeld,Ireland* 3-9-0 KFallon (11)	7/1	hd 10
	Desert Boy (IRE) *PWChapple-Hyam* 3-9-0 WCarson (4)	50/1	dist 11

Sheikh Mohammed 11ran 3m05.10

LEOPARDSTOWN Saturday, Sep 14   GOOD

63   Irish Champion Stks (Gr 1) (3yo+ c+f) £94,062   1¼m

53	TIMARIDA (IRE) *JOxx,Ireland* 4-9-1 JPMurtagh	3/1	1
35	DANCE DESIGN (IRE) *DKWeld,Ireland* 3-8-8 MJKinane	9/2	1½ 2
55	GLORY OF DANCER *PAKelleway,GB* 3-8-11 OPeslier	10/1	nk 3
36	Shaamit (IRE) *WJHaggas,GB* 3-8-11 MHills	5/4f	1½ 4
	Idris (IRE) *JSBolger,Ireland* 6-9-4 KManning	14/1	nk 5
41	Tamayaz (CAN) *SaeedbinSuroor,GB* 4-9-4 GCarter	6/1	nk 6

H.H. Aga Khan 6ran 2m06.20

LONGCHAMP Sunday, Sep 15   GOOD to FIRM

64   Prix Vermeille (Gr 1) (3yo f) £100,629   1½m

Order as they passed the post

	MY EMMA *RGuest,GB* 3-9-0 CAsmussen	291/10	1
12	ZAFZALA (IRE) *JOxx,Ireland* 3-9-0 JPMurtagh	35/10cp	hd 2
50	PAPERING (IRE) *LMCumani,GB* 3-9-0 LDettori	26/10cp	sn 3
19	Miss Tahiti (IRE) *AFabre,France* 3-9-0 OPeslier	24/10f	nk 4
	Leonila (IRE) *RCollet,France* 3-9-0 DBoeuf	245/10	sn 5
19	Luna Wells (IRE) *AFabre,France* 3-9-0 TJarnet	26/10	½ 6
50	Shamadara (IRE) *AdeRoyer-Dupre,France* 3-9-0 GMosse	35/10cp	3 7
	Tulipa (USA) *AFabre,France* 3-9-0 SGuillot	26/10cp	3 8
16	Bint Salsabil (USA) *JLDunlop,GB* 3-9-0 WCarson	102/10	½ 9

Camille (FR) *PHDemercastel,France* 3-9-0 AJunk 18/1   8 10
After a stewards' inquiry Zafzala was demoted to fifth place
Matthews Breeding and Racing 10ran 2m29.04

65   Prix Niel (Gr 2) (3yo c+f) £50,315   1½m
30   HELISSIO (FR) *ELellouche,France* 3-9-2 OPeslier 4/5f   1
      DARAZARI (IRE) *AdeRoyerDupre,France* 3-9-2 GMosse 41/10   1 2
15   RADEVORE *AFabre,France* 3-9-2 TJarnet 20/1   1½ 3
48   Grape Tree Road *AFabre,France* 3-9-2 SGuillot 181/10   1 4
15   Arbatax (IRE) *PBary,France* 3-9-2 CAsmussen 16/1   3 5
56   Tarator (USA) *ELellouche,France* 3-9-2 TQuinn .... 11/1   sn 6
56   Water Poet (IRE) *AFabre,France* 3-9-2 LDettori .... 21/1   nk 7
15   Le Destin (FR) *PHDemercastel,France* 3-9-2 AJunk 25/1   3 8
29   Polaris Flight (USA) *PWChapple-Hyam,GB* 3-9-2 JReid.................... 52/10   1½ 9
      Palatal (USA) *FPoulsen,Denmark* 3-9-2 FJohansson 27/1   2½ 10
      Mr E. Sarasola 10ran 2m30.40

66   Prix de La Salamandre (Gr 1) (2yo c+f) £50,315   7f
      REVOQUE (IRE) *PWChapple-Hyam,GB* 2-9-0 JReid 21/10   1
      THE WEST (USA) *PFICole,GB* 2-9-0 TQuinn 53/10   3 2
46   ZAMINDAR (USA) *AFabre,France* 2-9-0 TJarnet .... 1/2cpf   sh 3
      Dame d'Harvard (USA) *RCollet,France* 2-8-11 OPeslier .... 69/10   nk 4
      Sacristan *AFabre,France* 2-9-0 (b) SGuillot .... 1/2cp   dist 5
      Mr R. E. Sangster 5ran 1m20.90

67   Prix Foy (Gr 3) (4yo+ c+f) £27,673   1½m
30   SWAIN (IRE) *AFabre,France* 4-9-2 TJarnet 1/1   1
36   PENTIRE *GWragg,GB* 4-9-2 MHills .... 4/5f   ½ 2
56   LEEDS (IRE) *HVandePoele,France* 4-9-2 SGuillot 136/10   3 3
      Rainbow Dancer (FR) *PBary,France* 5-9-2 DBoeuf .... 128/10   ¾ 4
      Solid Illusion (USA) *PHDemercastel,France* 5-9-2 AJunk.................. 12/1   1½ 5
      Sheikh Mohammed 5ran 2m33.90

NEWBURY Saturday, Sep 21   GOOD to FIRM
68   Bonusprint Mill Reef Stks (A) (Gr 2) (2yo) £33,085   6f8y
      INDIAN ROCKET *JLDunlop* 2-8-12 RHills (1) 10/3   1
      PROUD NATIVE (IRE) *APJarvis* 2-8-12 RCochrane (7).................... 25/1   2½ 2
      SEEBE (USA) *IABalding* 2-8-10 LDettori (10)................................ 11/4f   nk 3
      Andreyev (IRE) *RHannon* 2-8-12 RHughes (9)................................ 4/1   1½ 4
      Sambac (USA) *HRACecil* 2-8-7 WRyan (5) .... 3/1   hd 5
      Omaha City (IRE) *BGubby* 2-8-12 PatEddery (6) 10/1   4 6
      General Song (USA) *KMcAuliffe* 2-8-12 GDuffield (2)........................ 14/1   ½ 7
      Maserati Monk *BJMeehan* 2-8-12 SSanders (3).......................... 16/1   nk 8
      Millroy (USA) *PAKelleway* 2-8-12 (b) MWigham (4)...................... 50/1   3½ 9
      Vasari (IRE) *MRChannon* 2-8-12 OUrbina (8) .... 14/1   dist 10
      Mr Khalil Alsayegh 10ran 1m11.52

CURRAGH Saturday, Sep 21   Straight course: GOOD
                                Round course: GOOD to FIRM
69   Jefferson Smurfit Memorial Irish St Leger (Gr 1) (3yo+) £88,454   1¾m
36   OSCAR SCHINDLER (IRE) *KPrendergast,Ireland* 4-9-8 SCraine.... 4/1   1
50   KEY CHANGE (IRE) *JOxx,Ireland* 3-9-2 JPMurtagh 11/4f   3½ 2
2   SACRAMENT *MRStoute,GB* 5-9-8 WRSwinburn 9/2   2 3
45   Posidonas *PFICole,GB* 4-9-8 TQuinn .... 9/2   sh 4
      I'm Supposin (IRE) *KPrendergast,Ireland* 4-9-8 WJSupple.................. 14/1   2 5
62   Gordi (USA) *DKWeld,Ireland* 3-8-12 MJKinane 8/1   5 6
      Blushing Flame (USA) *MRStoute,GB* 5-9-8 JReid 10/1   4½ 7
      Viaticum (IRE) *NMeade,Ireland* 4-9-5 (b) JoannaMorgan 50/1   9 8
      Fill The Bill (IRE) *APO'Brien,Ireland* 4-9-8 JAHeffernan .... 25/1   sh 9
      Mr Oliver Lehane 9ran 2m59.10

70   Aga Khan's Studs National Stks (Gr 1) (2yo c+f) £116,082   7f
      DESERT KING (IRE) *APO'Brien,Ireland* 2-9-0 WRSwinburn.............. 11/1   1
      REFERENDUM (IRE) *GLewis,GB* 2-9-0 JReid................................ 10/1   nk 2
43   AZRA (IRE) *JSBolger,Ireland* 2-8-11 (b) KJManning 10/1   1 3
      Fantastic Fellow (USA) *CEBrittain,GB* 2-9-0 MRoberts .... 7/1   sh 4
      Johan Cruyff *APO'Brien,Ireland* 2-9-0 JPMurtagh.............................. 11/1   nk 5

1113

Verglas (IRE) *KPrendergast,Ireland* 2-9-0 WJSupple .... 4/1   sh 6
38 Sahm (USA) *JLDunlop,GB* 2-9-0 TQuinn .... 6/4f   hd 7
    Daylight In Dubai (USA) *PWChapple-Hyam,GB* 2-9-0 KDarley 8/1   1½ 8
    Beautiful Fire (IRE) *DKWeld,Ireland* 2-9-0 MJKinane 11/2   3½ 9
    Stonehaven (IRE) *TStack,Ireland* 2-9-0 PJSmullen .... 25/1   hd 10
    Mr M. Tabor 10ran 1m25.70

COLOGNE Sunday, Sep 22   GOOD

71 **Ems Kurierpost Europa-Preis (Gr 1) (3yo+)** £127,659   1½m

     LAVIRCO (GER) *PRau,Germany* 3-8-10 TMundry................................. 6/5   1
57   PROTEKTOR (GER) *ALowe,Germany* 7-9-6 THellier 3½ 2
47   HOLLYWOOD DREAM (GER) *UOstmann,Germany* 5-9-2 JReid ....   ¾ 3
47   Luso *CEBrittain,GB* 4-9-6 MJKinane ....   nk 4
60   Lear White (USA) *PAKelleway,GB* 5-9-6 JWeaver..................................   7 5
     Mongol Warrior (USA) *LordHuntingdon,GB* 3-8-10 DHarrison 2½ 6
47   Caballo (GER) *HJentzsch,Germany* 5-9-6 PSchiergen 10 7
     Gestut Fahrhof 7ran 2m28.63

ASCOT Saturday, Sep 28   GOOD to FIRM

72 **Queen Elizabeth II Stks (A) (Gr 1) (3yo+)** £199,020   1m (Rnd)

52   MARK OF ESTEEM (IRE) *SaeedbinSuroor* 3-8-11 LDettori (5) 10/3   1
6   BOSRA SHAM (IRE) *HRACecil* 3-8-8 PatEddery (7) 10/3   1¼ 2
48   FIRST ISLAND (IRE) *GWragg* 4-9-1 MHills (4) 11/2   4 3
44   Charnwood Forest (IRE) *SaeedbinSuroor* 4-9-1 MJKinane (3).............. 14/1   ½ 4
59   Ashkalani (IRE) *AdeRoyer-Dupre,France* 3-8-11 GMosse (2)................ 9/4f   ¾ 5
48   Bijou d'Inde *MJohnston* 3-8-11 JWeaver (1) 10/1   1¼ 6
21   Soviet Line (IRE) *MRStoute* 6-9-1 TQuinn (6)..................................... 25/1   1 7
     Godolphin 7ran 1m40.95

ASCOT Sunday, Sep 29   GOOD

73 **Fillies' Mile (A) (Gr 1) (2yo f)** £91,840   1m (Rnd)

     REAMS OF VERSE (USA) *HRACecil* 2-8-10 MJKinane (2) 5/1   1
32   KHASSAH *JHMGosden* 2-8-10 RHills (5).. 10/1   1¼ 2
     SLEEPYTIME (IRE) *HRACecil* 2-8-10 PatEddery (8) .... 6/4f   nk 3
54   Red Camellia *SirMarkPrescott* 2-8-10 GDuffield (7) .... 2/1   sh 4
     Logic *CEBrittain* 2-8-10 LDettori (6) 50/1   3½ 5
     Mrs Miniver (USA) *PAKelleway* 2-8-10 MRoberts (3) 100/1   1¼ 6
     Ovation *PFICole* 2-8-10 TQuinn (1).. 25/1   2 7
     Gretel *MRStoute* 2-8-10 WRSwinburn (4) 20/1   1 8
     Mr K. Abdulla 8ran 1m44.32

WOODBINE Sunday, Sep 29   SOFT

74 **Canadian International Stks (Gr 1) (3yo+)** £281,690   1½m

33   SINGSPIEL (IRE) *MRStoute,GB* 4-9-0 GStevens 19/10f   1
     CHIEF BEARHART (USA) *MFrostad,Canada* 3-8-6 (b) SHawley 78/10   2 2
55   MECKE (USA) *ETortora,USA* 4-9-0 (b) RobbieDavis 5/2   3½ 3
     Windsharp (USA) *WDollase,USA* 5-8-11 CNakatani........................... 41/10   3½ 4
     Dernier Empereur (USA) *BenCecil,USA* 6-9-0 (b) PValenzuela 9/1   4 5
     Lassigny (USA) *WMott,USA* 5-9-0 PDay.. 56/10   2¾ 6
     Dancing Fred (USA) *DanielJVella,Canada* 3-8-6 TKabel.................... 24/1   2½ 7
     Sheikh Mohammed 7ran 2m33.20

NEWMARKET Tuesday, Oct 1   GOOD to FIRM (Rowley Mile Course)

75 **Shadwell Stud Cheveley Park Stks (A) (Gr 1) (2yo f)** £69,309   6f

46   PAS DE REPONSE (USA) *MmeCHead,France* 2-8-11 FHead (3) 7/1   1
     MOONLIGHT PARADISE (USA) *SaeedbinSuroor* 2-8-11   1 2
         LDettori (6)... 11/2
43   OCEAN RIDGE (USA) *PWChapple-Hyam* 2-8-11 JReid (9)................ 12/1   1 3
32   Dazzle *MRStoute* 2-8-11 KFallon (4) .... 4/9f   ½ 4
     Arethusa *RHannon* 2-8-11 DaneO'Neill (2) 16/1   2½ 5
54   Queen Sceptre (IRE) *BWHills* 2-8-11 PatEddery (7).............................. 16/1   2½ 6
     Snap Crackle Pop (IRE) *RFJohnsonHoughton* 2-8-11 AMcGlone (5)... 50/1   2 7
     Carati *RBoss* 2-8-11 GDuffield (8) .... 50/1   hd 8
     Wertheimer et Frere 8ran 1m11.16

NEWMARKET Thursday, Oct 3   GOOD to FIRM (Rowley Mile Course)

76   Middle Park Stks (A) (Gr 1) (2yo c) £81,533   6f

46	BAHAMIAN BOUNTY *DRLoder* 2-8-11 LDettori (2)	7/4f	1
43	MUCHEA *MRChannon* 2-8-11 RHughes (1)	16/1	hd 2
61	IN COMMAND (IRE) *BWHills* 2-8-11 MHills (8)	8/1	1 3
70	Fantastic Fellow (USA) *CEBrittain* 2-8-11 OPeslier (9)	10/1	sh 4
	Deep Finesse *MAJarvis* 2-8-11 PatEddery (3)	16/1	1¼ 5
	Easycall *BJMeehan* 2-8-11 MTebbutt (10)	7/1	1 6
	Hurricane State (USA) *PWChapple-Hyam* 2-8-11 JReid (7)	13/2	nk 7
68	Andreyev (IRE) *RHannon* 2-8-11 DaneO'Neill (4)	33/1	1½ 8
46	Rich Ground *JDBethell* 2-8-11 JWeaver (5)	33/1	3½ 9
68	Indian Rocket *JLDunlop* 2-8-11 RHills (11)	9/2	½ 10
	Zaretski *CEBrittain* 2-8-11 MRoberts (6)	100/1	6 11

Maktoum Al Maktoum 11ran 1m11.95

LONGCHAMP Saturday, Oct 5   GOOD to SOFT

77   Prix du Cadran (Gr 1) (4yo+) £62,035   2½m

25	NONONITO (FR) *JLesbordes,France* 5-9-2 TJarnet	187/10	1
	MOONAX (IRE) *BWHills,GB* 5-9-2 LDettori	26/10	1 2
	ALWAYS EARNEST (USA) *MmeMBollack-Badel,France* 8-9-2 (b) ABadel		2½ 3
		17/1	
	Camp David (GER) *AWohler,Germany* 6-9-2 ABoschert	11/1	1½ 4
60	Double Trigger (IRE) *MJohnston,GB* 5-9-2 JWeaver	19/10f	3 5
25	Always Aloof (USA) *MRStoute,GB* 5-9-2 OPeslier	94/10	5 6
	Separate Lives (SWE) *ASpanu,France* 5-9-2 FSanchez	18/1	10 7
	Kassani (IRE) *AdeRoyer-Dupre,France* 4-9-2 GMosse	26/10	2½ 8
	Flamingo Paradise *HBlume,Germany* 5-9-2 THellier	72/1	8 9
	Juste Ciel *LCharbonnier,France* 4-8-13 (b) JJacquet	74/1	dist 10

Mr Patrick Sebagh 10ran 4m31.50

LONGCHAMP Sunday, Oct 6   GOOD to SOFT

78   Prix de L'Abbaye de Longchamp (Gr 1) (2yo+ c+f) £62,035   5f

	KISTENA (FR) *MmeCHead,France* 3-9-8 ODoleuze	146/10	1
42	ANABAA (USA) *MmeCHead,France* 4-9-11 FHead	3/10f	nk 2
58	HEVER GOLF ROSE *TJNaughton,GB* 4-9-8 PatEddery	89/10	2 3
	Easy Option (IRE) *SaeedbinSuroor,GB* 4-9-8 LDettori	74/10	½ 4
	Carmine Lake (IRE) *PWChapple-Hyam,GB* 2-8-4 TQuinn	271/10	1 5
51	Eveningperformance *HCandy,GB* 5-9-8 CRutter	126/10	ns 6
51	Struggler *DRLoder,GB* 4-9-11 OPeslier	161/10	hd 7
	Don't Worry Me (IRE) *GHenrot,France* 4-9-8 AJunk	476/10	1 8
58	Rambling Bear *MBlanshard,GB* 3-9-11 RCochrane	57/1	3 9
27	Ailleacht (USA) *JSBolger,Ireland* 4-9-8 MJKinane	577/10	nk 10

Wertheimer et Frere 10ran 59.30secs

79   Prix Marcel Boussac (Criterium Des Pouliches) (Gr 1) (2yo f) £99,256   1m

	RYAFAN (USA) *JHMGosden,GB* 2-8-11 LDettori	2/1cf	1
	YASHMAK (USA) *HRACecil,GB* 2-8-11 PatEddery	2/1cf	hd 2
	FAMILY TRADITION (IRE) *APO'Brien,Ireland* 2-8-11 WRSwinburn	26/1	2½ 3
	Bianca Nera *DRLoder,GB* 2-8-11 KDarley	24/10	1½ 4
	Veiled Threat (IRE) *RCollet,France* 2-8-11 SGuillot	457/10	nk 5
	Dissertation (FR) *MmeCHead,France* 2-8-11 FHead	97/10	hd 6
	Green Lady (IRE) *AFabre,France* 2-8-11 TJarnet	88/10	hd 7
	Spring Dance (FR) *PBary,France* 2-8-11 GMosse	92/10cp	2 8
	Nawal (FR) *JdeRoualle,France* 2-8-11 CAsmussen	20/1	1 9
	Shigeru Summit *CBoutin,France* 2-8-11 MBoutin	72/10	1½ 10
	Dance Parade (USA) *PFICole,France* 2-8-11 TQuinn	97/10	11
66	Dame d'Harvard (USA) *RCollet,France* 2-8-11 OPeslier	92/10cp	12
	Dancing Fire (FR) *PBogoev,Bulgaria* 2-8-11 BYusmianov	624/10	13

Mr K. Abdulla 13ran 1m39.80

80   Forte Meridien Prix de L'Arc de Triomphe (Gr 1) (3yo+ c+f) £496,278   1½m

65	HELISSIO (FR) *ELellouche,France* 3-8-11 OPeslier	18/10f	1
57	PILSUDSKI (IRE) *MRStoute,GB* 4-9-5 WRSwinburn	221/10	5 2
69	OSCAR SCHINDLER (IRE) *KPrendergast,Ireland* 4-9-5		sn 3
	CAsmussen	148/10	
67	Swain (IRE) *AFabre,France* 4-9-5 TJarnet	5/2cf	1 4

1115

	64	Luna Wells (IRE) *AFabre,France* 3-8-8 TThulliez	61/1	1½ 5
	65	Le Destin (FR) *PHDemercastel,France* 3-8-11 DBoeuf	47/1	¾ 6
	63	Shaamit (IRE) *WJHaggas,GB* 3-8-11 PatEddery	22/1	½ 7
	67	Leeds (IRE) *HVandePoele,France* 4-9-5 ODoleuze	52/1	½ 8
	64	Leonila (IRE) *RCollet,France* 3-8-8 GGuignard	59/1	sh 9
	67	Pentire *GWragg,GB* 4-9-5 MHills	73/10	1 10
	65	Darazari (IRE) *AdeRoyerDupre,France* 3-8-11 GMosse	8/1	sn 11
	65	Radevore *AFabre,France* 3-8-11 SGuillot	60/1	3 12
	29	Zagreb (USA) *DKWeld,Ireland* 3-8-11 MJKinane	66/10	nk 13
		Tamure (IRE) *JHMGosden,GB* 4-9-5 FHead	5/2cf	1½ 14
	36	Classic Cliche (IRE) *SaeedbinSuroor,GB* 4-9-5 LDettori	5/2cf	15 15
	65	Polaris Flight (USA) *PWChapple-Hyam,GB* 3-8-11 JReid	47/1	f

Mr E. Sarasola 16ran 2m29.90

81 Prix du Rond-Point (Gr 2) (3yo+) £49,628   1m

	52	ALHAARTH (IRE) *MajorWRHern,GB* 3-8-12 (b) RHills	81/10	1
	59	SHAANXI (USA) *ELellouche,France* 4-9-0 OPeslier	29/10	1½ 2
		BIN ROSIE *DRLoder,GB* 4-9-1 (b) LDettori	57/10	2½ 3
	52	Bishop of Cashel *JRFanshawe,GB* 4-9-1 WRSwinburn	12/5f	2 4
		River Bay (USA) *JEHammond,France* 3-8-12 SGuillot	121/10	sh 5
	8	Barricade (USA) *AFabre,France* 3-8-12 TJarnet	95/10cp	1½ 6
	28	Blackwater (USA) *MZilber,France* 3-8-12 DBoeuf	95/10cp	1½ 7
		Centre Stalls (IRE) *RFJohnsonHoughton,GB* 3-8-12 JReid	74/10	1½ 8
	72	Soviet Line (IRE) *MRStoute,GB* 6-9-5 TQuinn	108/10	3 9
		Moon Is Up (USA) *JEHammond,France* 3-8-8 CAsmussen	123/10	15 10

Mr Hamdan Al Maktoum 10ran 1m38.60

ASCOT Saturday, Oct 12   GOOD to SOFT

82 Willmott Dixon Cornwallis Stks (A) (Gr 3) (2yo) £22,295   5f

	76	EASYCALL *BJMeehan* 2-9-4 MTebbutt	11/2	1
	43	CHECK THE BAND (USA) *APO'Brien,Ireland* 2-8-12 CRoche (1)	9/2jf	1½ 2
		GRAND LAD (IRE) *RWArmstrong* 2-8-12 RHills (8)	11/1	½ 3
	68	Omaha City (IRE) *BGubby* 2-8-12 BDoyle (10)	16/1	2 4
		Superior Premium *RAFahey* 2-8-12 ACulhane (4)	25/1	1¼ 5
		Rudi's Pet (IRE) *RHannon* 2-8-12 DaneO'Neill (5)	20/1	2 6
	46	Blue Ridge *RHannon* 2-8-12 MJKinane (3)	25/1	5 7
		Head Over Heels (IRE) *JHMGosden* 2-8-7 LDettori (11)	7/1	½ 8
		Sabina *IABalding* 2-8-7 TQuinn (2)	8/1	hd 9
	76	Deep Finesse *MAJarvis* 2-9-1 PatEddery (7)	9/2jf	8 10
		Meliksah (IRE) *MBell* 2-8-12 MFenton (9)	10/1	nk 11

Easycall Partnership 11ran 1m01.94

LONGCHAMP Sunday, Oct 13   GOOD

83 Grand Criterium (Gr 1) (2yo c+f) £123,609   1m

	66	REVOQUE (IRE) *PWChapple-Hyam,GB* 2-9-0 JReid	4/5f	1
		MAJORIEN *MmeCHead,France* 2-9-0 FHead	109/10	2 2
		KING SOUND *JHMGosden,GB* 2-9-0 TJarnet	38/10	4 3
	70	Referendum (IRE) *GLewis,GB* 2-9-0 PatEddery	107/10	nk 4
		Aneysar (IRE) *AdeRoyer-Dupre,France* 2-9-0 GMosse	101/10	nk 5
		Nombre Premier *AdeRoyer-Dupre,France* 2-9-0 PSogorb	76/10	2 6
		Olympic Majesty (FR) *CharlesO'Brien,Ireland* 2-9-0 OPeslier	12/1	8 7
		Le Topolino (USA) *PBogoev,Bulgaria* 2-9-0 MGalabov	23/1cp	2½ 8
		Wild Thyme (FR) *PBogoev,Bulgaria* 2-9-0 BYasmianov	23/1cp	2½ 9

Mr R. E. Sangster 9ran 1m37.70

MILAN Sunday, Oct 13   SOFT

84 Gran Premio Del Jockey-Club (Gr 1) (3yo+ c+f) £167,096   1½m

	62	SHANTOU (USA) *JHMGosden,GB* 3-8-11 LDettori	14/10f	1
	69	SACRAMENT *MRStoute,GB* 5-9-4 WRSwinburn	5/1	3 2
	56	STRATEGIC CHOICE (USA) *PFICole,GB* 5-9-4 TQuinn	18/10	2½ 3
	71	Hollywood Dream (GER) *UOstmann,Germany* 5-9-1 CAsmussen	47/10cp	½ 4
	9	Slicious *VCaruso,Italy* 4-9-4 MEsposito	63/10	¾ 5
		Coral Reef (ITY) *GColleo,Italy* 3-8-11 EBotti	14/1cp	1¾ 6
	9	Tarhelm (ITY) *GColleo,Italy* 4-9-4 LSorrentino	14/1cp	4½ 7
	9	Concepcion (GER) *HJentzsch,Germany* 6-9-4 SEccles	47/10cp	1¾ 8

Sheikh Mohammed 8ran 2m32.40

NEWMARKET Thursday, Oct 17   GOOD to FIRM
85 Challenge Stks (A) (Gr 2) (3yo+) £35,431   7f
 72 CHARNWOOD FOREST (IRE) *SaeedbinSuroor* 4-9-4 LDettori (8)... 15/8f   1
 81 BISHOP OF CASHEL *JRFanshawe* 4-9-0 WRSwinburn (3) 4/1   2 2
 12 MY BRANCH *BWHills* 3-8-9 MHills (7) 15/2   2 3
 24 Thrilling Day *NAGraham* 3-8-9 TQuinn (2) 12/1   1¼ 4
 58 Lucayan Prince (USA) *DRLoder* 3-8-12 (b) RHughes (1) .... 9/4   ¾ 5
     Polar Prince (IRE) *MAJarvis* 3-8-12 RCochrane (6) .... 20/1   nk 6
     Troon *RuneHaugen,Norway* 6-9-0 ManuelSantos (4) 100/1   1½ 7
     Daring Destiny *KRBurke* 5-9-1 OUrbina (5) .... 25/1   sh 8
     Godolphin 8ran 1m25.12

NEWMARKET Friday, Oct 18   GOOD (Rowley Mile Course)
86 Dewhurst Stks (A) (Gr 1) (2yo c+f) £83,535   7f
 76 IN COMMAND (IRE) *BWHills* 2-9-0 MHills (2) 10/1   1
     MUSICAL PURSUIT *MHTompkins* 2-9-0 PatEddery (7) .... 13/2   hd 2
 38 AIR EXPRESS (IRE) *CEBrittain* 2-9-0 BDoyle (6).............................. 50/1   nk 3
 76 Bahamian Bounty *DRLoder* 2-9-0 LDettori (3) 7/2jf 1¼ 4
     Kahal *EALDunlop* 2-9-0 RHills (4) .... 7/2jf nk 5
 70 Desert King (IRE) *APO'Brien,Ireland* 2-9-0 CRoche (8)...................... 4/1   nk 6
 66 The West (USA) *PFICole* 2-9-0 TQuinn (1)...................................... 9/2   ½ 7
     Wind Cheetah (USA) *MRStoute* 2-9-0 MJKinane (5)........................... 33/1   1½ 8
     Maktoum Al Maktoum 8ran 1m25.93

NEWMARKET Saturday, Oct 19   GOOD (Rowley Mile Course)
87 Dubai Champion Stks (A) (Gr 1) (3yo+) £174,126   1¼m
 72 BOSRA SHAM (USA) *HRACecil* 4-8-8 PatEddery (4) 9/4   1
 48 HALLING (USA) *SaeedbinSuroor* 5-9-2 LDettori (2) 1/1f 2½ 2
 63 TIMARIDA (IRE) *JOxx,Ireland* 4-8-13 JMurtagh (1)........................... 15/2 1 3
 49 Even Top (IRE) *MHTompkins* 3-8-11 JQuinn (3) .... 14/1 hd 4
 72 First Island (IRE) *GWragg* 4-9-2 MHills (5).................................... 14/1 2½ 5
 63 Glory of Dancer *PAKelleway* 3-8-11 OPeslier (6).............................. 40/1 hd 6
     Mr Wafic Said 6ran 2m03.71

LONGCHAMP Sunday, Oct 20   GOOD to SOFT
88 Prix de La Foret (Gr 1) (3yo+ c+f) £61,274   7f
 42 A MAGICMAN (FR) *HSteguweit,Germany* 4-9-2 ASuborics 225/10   1
 58 MIESQUE'S SON (USA) *JEHammond,France* 4-9-2 CAsmussen ..... 41/10 hd 2
 81 SHAANXI (USA) *ELellouche,France* 4-8-13 OPeslier..................... 16/10f ¾ 3
 44 Zarannda (IRE) *AdeRoyer-Dupre,France* 3-8-11 GMosse................. 34/10cp 1½ 4
 13 Tagula (IRE) *IABalding,GB* 3-9-0 KDarley 46/10 1½ 5
  3 Inzar (IRE) *PFICole,GB* 4-9-2 TQuinn .... 38/1   nk 6
 81 Blackwater (USA) *MZilber,France* 3-9-0 LDettori .... 14/1   sh 7
     General Monash (USA) *CLaffon-Parias,France* 4-9-2 ODoleuze 24/1   3 8
     Rising Colours *PHDemercastel,France* 3-9-0 AJunk 20/1   3 9
     Winning Smile (FR) *TClout,France* 6-9-2 (b) SGuillot......................... 20/1   4 10
     Hamirpour (IRE) *AdeRoyer-Dupre,France* 3-9-0 EAlloix................ 34/10cp 11
     Stall Dagobert 11ran 1m22.80

DONCASTER Saturday, Oct 26   GOOD
89 Racing Post Trophy (A) (Gr 1) (2yo c+f) £97,490   1m (Rnd)
     MEDAALY *SaeedbinSuroor* 2-9-0 GHind (6) 14/1   1
     POTEEN (USA) *LMCumani* 2-9-0 JWeaver (9) .... 13/2   ½ 2
     BENNY THE DIP (USA) *JHMGosden* 2-9-0 JReid (7) 11/10f 1¼ 3
     Besiege *HRACecil* 2-9-0 MRoberts (5).. 5/1   1¼ 4
     Papua *IABalding* 2-9-0 GCarter (1)... 14/1   1½ 5
 70 Daylight In Dubai (USA) *PWChapple-Hyam* 2-9-0 KDarley (4)........... 33/1   2½ 6
     Sandstone (IRE) *JLDunlop* 2-9-0 GDuffield (2) 12/1   2 7
     Solo Mio (IRE) *BWHills* 2-9-0 MHills (3)... 16/1   3½ 8
     Asas *SaeedbinSuroor* 2-9-0 RHills (8) 13/2   13 9
     Godolphin 9ran 1m41.12

WOODBINE Saturday, Oct 26   Turf course: GOOD
Dirt course: FAST

90 **Breeders' Cup Sprint (Gr 1) (3yo+) £330,803**   6f

LIT DE JUSTICE (USA) *JenineSahadi,USA* 6-9-0 (b) CNakatani........ 4/1f	1
PAYING DUES (USA) *CliffordSisejnr* 4-9-0 PDay............................ 31/1cp	1¼ 2
HONOUR AND GLORY (USA) *DWayneLukas,USA* 3-8-11	nk 3
GStevens.. 52/10	
Lord Carson (USA) *DWayneLukas,USA* 4-9-0 SSellers 545/100	1¼ 4
Lakota Brave (USA) *BHeadley,USA* 7-9-0 ASolis 21/1	nk 5
58 Iktamal (USA) *EALDunlop,GB* 4-9-0 WRyan 22/1	1½ 6
Capote Belle (USA) *DPeitz,USA* 3-8-8 JRVelazquez 44/10	hd 7
Langfuhr (CAN) *MKeogh,Canada* 4-9-0 JChavez................................ 68/10	½ 8
Boundless Moment (USA) *KathyWalsh,USA* 4-9-0 KDesormeaux 29/1	nk 9
Appealing Skier (USA) *BPerkinssnr,USA* 3-8-11 MSmith.................... 77/10	¾ 10
Friendly Lover (USA) *JHPiercejnr,USA* 8-9-0 (b) HMcCauley 79/1	3 11
Criollito (ARG) *RBaffert,USA* 5-9-0 CMcCarron 13/1	2½ 12
Jess C'S Whirl (USA) *JForbes,USA* 6-9-0 JulieKrone...................... 31/1cp	4½ 13

Evergreen Farm 13ran 1m08.60

91 **Breeders' Cup Mile (Gr 1) (3yo+) £330,803**   1m

DA HOSS (USA) *MWDickinson,USA* 4-9-0 GStevens 845/100	1
59 SPINNING WORLD (USA) *JEPease,France* 3-8-10 CAsmussen .. 795/100	1½ 2
SAME OLD WISH (USA) *RBarbara,USA* 6-9-0 (b) SSellers.......... 472/10	2½ 3
Kiridashi (CAN) *MrsBMinshall,Canada* 4-9-0 MWalls 109/10	½ 4
Memories of Silver (USA) *JToner,USA* 3-8-7 JBailey......................... 86/10	1½ 5
Helmsman (USA) *WDollase,USA* 4-9-0 (b) CNakatani...................... 19/1	1½ 6
72 Mark of Esteem (IRE) *SaeedbinSuroor,GB* 3-8-10 LDettori 125/100cf	1¼ 7
Volochine (IRE) *NO'Callaghan,USA* 5-9-0 PDay 23/1	ns 8
85 Charnwood Forest (IRE) *SaeedbinSuroor,GB* 4-9-0 WRSwinburn 125/100cf	nk 9
Urgent Request (IRE) *CWhittingham,USA* 6-9-0 ASolis...................... 13/1	1¼ 10
Smooth Runner (USA) *RMettee,USA* 5-9-0 CMcCarron 11/1	4 11
Dumaani (USA) *KPMcLaughlin,UAE* 5-9-0 JulieKrone 50/1	1¼ 12
Mighty Forum *MHennig,USA* 5-9-0 JRVelazquez 50/1	1½ 13
Chaposa Springs (USA) *MartinDWolfson,USA* 4-8-11 CPerret............. 22/1	9 14

Prestonwood Farm Inc 14ran 1m35.80

92 **Breeders' Cup Turf (Gr 1) (3yo+) £661,606**   1½m

80 PILSUDSKI (IRE) *MRStoute,GB* 4-9-0 WRSwinburn 137/10	1
74 SINGSPIEL (IRE) *MRStoute,GB* 4-9-0 GStevens 11/10cpf	1¼ 2
80 SWAIN (IRE) *AFabre,France* 4-9-0 OPeslier................................ 11/10cpf	1¼ 3
84 Shantou (USA) *JHMGosden,GB* 3-8-9 LDettori............................. 11/10cpf	2½ 4
74 Windsharp (USA) *WDollase,USA* 5-8-11 CNakatani...................... 337/10	¾ 5
Talloires (USA) *RMandella,USA* 6-9-0 (b) KDesormeaux 69/10	nk 6
62 Dushyantor (USA) *HRACecil,GB* 3-8-9 PatEddery 124/10	1½ 7
23 Wall Street (USA) *SaeedbinSuroor,GB* 3-8-9 JSantos 11/10cpf	2 8
55 Awad (USA) *DDonk,USA* 6-9-0 (b) CMcCarron 49/10	nk 9
80 Luna Wells (IRE) *AFabre,France* 3-8-6 TJarnet.......................... 296/10	nk 10
74 Chief Bearhart (USA) *MFrostad,Canada* 3-8-9 (b) SHawley 201/10	1 11
55 Diplomatic Jet (USA) *JEPicou,USA* 4-9-0 JChavez 695/100	3¾ 12
Marlin (USA) *DWayneLukas,USA* 3-8-9 SSellers.............................. 437/10	6 13
Ricks Natural Star (USA) *JCheeney,USA* 9-9-0 LisaMacfarland . 561/10	dist 14

Lord Weinstock/Exors of late S.Weinstock 14ran 2m30.20

93 **Breeders' Cup Classic (Gr 1) (3yo+) £1,323,210**   1¼m

ALPHABET SOUP (USA) *DHofmans,USA* 5-9-0 CMcCarron 1985/100	1
LOUIS QUATORZE (USA) *NZito,USA* 3-8-9 PDay............................ 18/1	ns 2
1 CIGAR (USA) *WMott,USA* 6-9-0 JDBailey................................. 65/100f	hd 3
Mt Sassafras (CAN) *MrsBMinshall,Canada* 4-9-0 MWalls................. 101/1	½ 4
Formal Gold (CAN) *WPerry,USA* 3-8-9 MSmith 209/10	4 5
63 Tamayaz (CAN) *SaeedbinSuroor,GB* 4-9-0 LDettori....................... 703/10	hd 6
Will's Way (USA) *HaroldJamesBond,USA* 3-8-9 JChavez 8/1	1¼ 7
Atticus (USA) *RMandella,USA* 4-9-0 (b) CNakatani 755/100	hd 8
Dramatic Gold (USA) *DHofmans,USA* 5-9-0 KDesormeaux 179/10	¾ 9
Mahogany Hall (USA) *JBaker,USA* 5-9-0 SSellers........................... 209/10	3¾ 10
Dare And Go (USA) *RMandella,USA* 5-9-0 ASolis............................ 755/100	5 11
Editor's Note (USA) *DWayneLukas,USA* 3-8-9 (b) GStevens................ 11/1	10 12
Taiki Blizzard (USA) *KFujisawa,Japan* 5-9-0 YOkabe 205/10	1¼ 13

Ridder Thoroughbred Stable 13ran 2m01.00

1118

94 Prix Royal-Oak (Gr 1) (3yo+) £48,251   1m7f110y

	RED ROSES STORY (FR) *MmePatBarbe,France* 4-9-1 VVion 59/10		1
77	MOONAX (IRE) *BWHills,GB* 5-9-4 PatEddery 7/10cpf	½	2
56	HELEN OF SPAIN *AFabre,France* 4-9-1 TJarnet............................ 7/10cpf	¾	3
77	Nononito (FR) *JLesbordes,France* 5-9-4 SGuillot.................................... 2/1	1	4
77	Always Earnest (USA) *MmeMBollack-Badel,France* 8-9-4 (b) ABadel 41/10	5	5

Mme Pat Barbe 5ran 3m38.40

95 Criterium de Saint-Cloud (Gr 1) (2yo c+f) £48,485   1¼m

	SHAKA *J-CRouget,France* 2-9-0 J-BEyquem..................................... 67/10		1
	DAYLAMI (IRE) *AdeRoyer-Dupre,France* 2-9-0 GMosse 4/5cpf	¾	2
	SENDORO (IRE) *AdeRoyer-Dupre,France* 2-9-0 CAsmussen 4/5cpf	2	3
	New Frontier (IRE) *AFabre,France* 2-9-0 OPeslier.............................. 33/10	2½	4
	Voyagers Quest (USA) *PWChapple-Hyam,GB* 2-9-0 JReid 143/10	2	5
	Fine Fellow (IRE) *MmeCHead,France* 2-9-0 FHead........................... 58/10	nk	6
	Alcalali (USA) *PAKelleway,GB* 2-8-11 ODoleuze 283/10	¾	7
	Kaldoun Choice (FR) *RCollet,France* 2-9-0 CHanotel.......................... 27/1	sn	8
	Reef d'Irlande (FR) *RMongil,France* 2-9-0 AJunk.............................. 80/1	15	9
	Keroub (FR) *PBary,France* 2-9-0 SGuillot 199/10	4	10

Mr R. Bousquet 10ran 2m15.80

96 Criterium Des Deux Ans (Gr 2) (2yo) £41,716   6f110y

	DEADLY DUDLEY (IRE) *RHannon,GB* 2-8-11 OPeslier................ 131/10		1
	SHEER REASON (USA) *MmeCHead,France* 2-8-8 FHead............ 21/10f	¾	2
76	HURRICANE STATE (USA) *PWChapple-Hyam,GB* 2-8-11 JReid 32/10	1½	3
	Heaven's Command *NClement,France* 2-8-8 GMosse 57/10	ns	4
68	Proud Native (IRE) *APJarvis,GB* 2-8-11 WRyan 38/10	2	5
	Boojum *BWHills,GB* 2-8-8 AClark 25/1	ns	6
79	Shigeru Summit *CBoutin,France* 2-8-8 MBoutin 48/10	2	7
	Luminosity *JEPease,France* 2-8-8 FSanchez....................................... 18/1	2	8

Lucayan Stud 8ran 1m20.11

97 Premio Roma (Gr 1) (3yo+ c+f) £89,368   1¼m

	FLEMENSFIRTH (USA) *JHMGosden,GB* 4-9-3 LDettori 1/2f		1
84	HOLLYWOOD DREAM (GER) *UOstmann,Germany* 5-9-0 CAsmussen... 44/10	nk	2
55	NEEDLE GUN (IRE) *CEBrittain,GB* 6-9-3 MRoberts 29/1	1	3
	Oxalagu (GER) *BSchutz,Germany* 4-9-3 AStarke................................ 12/1	¾	4
	Snake Snap *VCaruso,Italy* 3-9-1 FJovine 41/10cp	3½	5
84	Slicious *VCaruso,Italy* 4-9-3 MEsposito 41/10cp	3½	6
	Sanoosea (IRE) *MRStoute,GB* 4-9-3 JReid 74/10	5	7
	Dancer Mitral *LBrogi,Italy* 3-9-1 VMezzatesta.................................. 16/1	3	8

Sheikh Mohammed 8ran 2m00.80

98 Prix Thomas Bryon (Gr 3) (2yo) £26,253   1m

	VARXI (FR) *DSmaga,France* 2-8-9 DBoeuf...................................... 197/10		1
83	ANEYSAR (IRE) *AdeRoyer-Dupre,France* 2-8-9 GMosse.................... 27/10	5	2
	KEOS (USA) *JEHammond,France* 2-8-9 CAsmussen 27/10	2	3
	Kaldou Star (FR) *ELellouche,France* 2-8-9 OPeslier 9/2	1½	4
	Film Noir (USA) *MmeCHead,France* 2-8-9 ODoleuze...................... 17/10f	2	5
	Inkatha (FR) *FDoumen,France* 2-8-9 TJarnet...................................... 10/1	4	6

Baron T. de Zuylen de Nyevelt 6ran 1m53.80

99 Japan Cup (Gr 1) (3yo+) £946,040   1½m

92	SINGSPIEL (IRE) *MRStoute,GB* 4-9-0 LDettori................................... 66/10		1
	FABULOUS LA FOUINE (FR) *HNagahama,Japan* 3-8-5	ns	2

```
          MMatsunaga ...................................................................  16/1
84  STRATEGIC CHOICE (USA) PFICole,GB 5-9-0 TQuinn ..................  36/1    1¼ 3
80  HELISSIO (FR) ELellouche,France 3-8-10 OPeslier .........................  24/10f   dh 3
92  Awad (USA) DDonk,USA 6-9-0 CMcCarron .........................................  23/1    nk 5
    Taiki Fortune (USA) YTakahashi,Japan 3-8-10 YShibata ......................  11/1    1½ 6
    Hishi Natalie (USA) MSayama,Japan 3-8-5 KTsunoda ......................  46/1    nk 7
80  Pentire GWragg,GB 4-9-0 MHills ...............................................  58/1    hd 8
    Flag Down (CAN) CClement,USA 6-9-0 JSantos .................................  48/1    2 9
    Dance Partner (JPN) TShirai,Japan 4-8-10 HShii ..............................  126/10  5 10
    Go Go Z (JPN) HArai,Japan 5-9-0 YMuramoto ...................................  69/1    nk 11
    Yu Sensho (JPN) SMatsumoto,Japan 4-9-0 HKawachi ......................  66/1    3½ 12
    Bubble Gum Fellow (JPN) KFujisawa,Japan 3-8-10 YOkabe .............  27/10   3 13
    Kanetsu Cross (JPN) YNishizuka,Japan 5-9-0 HMatoba ......................  29/1    nk 14
    Sakura Keizan O (JPN) KSakai,Japan 3-8-10 NYokoyama .................  36/1   dist 15
    Sheikh Mohammed 15ran 2m23.80

    SHA TIN Sunday, Dec 8    GOOD to FIRM
100 Hong Kong International Vase (Gr 2) (3yo+) £267,898                    1½m
71  LUSO CEBrittain,GB 4-9-5 LDettori ................................................  21/10f    1
    ROYAL SNACK (AUS) GHanlon,Australia 8-9-2 DOliver ................  15/1    1½ 2
    PRIVILEGE (IRE) IWAllan,HongKong 5-9-0 (v) BMarcus ..................  19/1    2¾ 3
71  Protektor (GER) ALowe,Germany 7-9-2 THellier ...............................  28/1    2¼ 4
    Count Chivas (NZ) DLFreedman,Australia 5-9-5 SKing ...................  34/10   sh 5
65  Tarator (USA) ELellouche,France 3-8-7 OPeslier ..............................  9/1    sh 6
    Clear Rose (NZ) LKLaxon,NewZealand 4-9-2 (b) DBeadman ..............  34/1    ¾ 7
84  Sacrament MRStoute,GB 5-9-2 GStevens ........................................  74/10   ¾ 8
    Deauville (FR) P-LBiancone,HongKong 4-9-0 ELegrix ......................  33/1    hd 9
    Learmont (USA) ECharpy,UAE 6-9-0 WSupple ..................................  18/1    2 10
    Mazal (IRE) DOughton,HongKong 4-9-0 MJKinane ...........................  28/1    hd 11
    Time Star (USA) NDrysdale,USA 5-9-5 CAsmussen ..........................  13/2    sh 12
    Eagar To Sgor (NZ) JEagar,NewZealand 5-9-0 BCompton .............  42/1    1½ 13
    Success Partners (IRE) IWAllan,HongKong 4-9-0 (b) LDittman ..........  99/1    16 14
    Mr Saeed Manana 14ran 2m26.10
```

INDEX TO SELECTED BIG RACES

Veiled Threat (IRE) 79[5]
Velour 54[3]
Verglas (IRE) 43[3],70[6]
Vetheuil (USA) 14[3],44[2],59[4]
Viaticum (IRE) 69
Volochine (IRE) 91
Voyagers Quest (USA) 95[5]

Wall Street (USA) 23,92
Water Poet (IRE) 15,56,65
Wavian 27
Wayne County (IRE) 33,45
Wedding Gift (FR) 19[5]

Weet-A-Minute (IRE) 41[6]
Well Warned 32[3]
Whenby (USA) 19
Whitechapel (USA) 45[6]
Whitewater Affair 16[6],50[5]
Wilawander 62[6]
Wild Thyme (FR) 83
Will's Way (USA) a93
Wind Cheetah (USA) 86
Windmachine (SWE) 51
Wind of Chance (GER) 47[5]
Windsharp (USA) 74[4],92[5]
Winning Smile (FR) 88

World Premier 5,23

Ya Malak 27
Yashmak (USA) 79[2]
Young Ern 21[4],42
Yu Sensho (JPN) 99

Zaforum 17
Zafzala (IRE) 12[6],64[5]
Zagreb (USA) 29*,80
Zamindar (USA) 46[2],66[3]
Zarannda (IRE) 44[6],88[4]
Zaretski 76

ERRATA & ADDENDA
'Racehorses of 1995'

Ahjay	disqualified at Yarmouth (failed dope test)
Al Moulouki	sold *2,900 gns* Ascot June Sales
Batoutoftheblue	wasn't dead
Carnegie (Ire)	P182 did not run on lasix at Belmont
Croft Pool	disqualified at Newmarket (failed dope test)
Elburg (Ire)	disqualified at Pontefract (failed dope test)
Elshabiba (USA)	dam *out* of half-sister to Cure The Blues
Greek Night Out (Ire)	disqualified at Catterick (failed dope test)
Manolete	sold *850 gns* Ascot June Sales
Oliver Rock	wasn't dead
Pretty Average	disqualified at Thirsk (flapping)
Ragmar (Fr)	is a colt
Stevie's Wonder (Ire)	disqualified at Salisbury (failed dope test)

'Racehorses of 1996'

Volunteer (Ire)	has been renamed Volunteer

FIXTURES
1997

AYR

SCOTLAND'S PREMIER COURSE

JANUARY	Thursday 2nd	N.H.
	Saturday 25th	N.H.
FEBRUARY	Saturday 8th	N.H.
MARCH	Friday 7th	N.H.
	Saturday 8th	N.H.
APRIL	*Scottish Grand National Meeting*	
	Thursday 17th	N.H.
	Friday 18th	N.H.
	Saturday 19th	N.H.
MAY	Wednesday 21st	FLAT
	Friday 30th	FLAT
JUNE	Friday 20th	FLAT
	Saturday 21st	FLAT
JULY	Monday 14th	FLAT
	Saturday 19th (Eve)	FLAT
	Monday 21st	FLAT
AUGUST	Saturday 9th	FLAT
SEPTEMBER	*The Western Meeting*	
	Thursday 18th	FLAT
	Friday 19th	FLAT
	Saturday 20th	FLAT
OCTOBER	Monday 13th	FLAT
	Tuesday 14th	FLAT
NOVEMBER	Saturday 15th	N.H.
	Sunday 16th	N.H.
DECEMBER	Friday 26th	N.H.

How to get there

Glasgow Airport 1 Hour by Car
Prestwick Airport 10 Minutes by Car
Racecourse Landing Ground Helicopters Only
Train Service Every 30 Minutes from Glasgow

All enquiries to The Racecourse Office
2 Whitletts Road, Ayr KA8 0JE
Telephone Ayr (01292) 264179

THE TIMEFORM 'TOP HORSES ABROAD'

This review of the year covers Ireland, the major racing countries of mainland Europe and North America. It includes Timeform Ratings for the top two-year-olds, three-year-olds and older horses. Horses not rated highly enough to be included in the main lists but which finished in the first three in a European pattern race during the season are included below the cut-off line. Fillies and mares are denoted by (f); * denotes the horse was trained for only a part of the season in the country concerned. The *Timeform Statistical Review* also contains a section on overseas racing which includes noteform comments for each horse that was in the first three in a pattern race in Europe, or won a listed race. In addition, all the winners of the Grade 1 races in the USA are included, as well as twenty or so of the better ex-Europeans or top Americans which did not win one. Overseas customers wishing to keep in touch with Timeform's coverage of racing through the year can subscribe to Computer Timeform or Timeform Perspective for reports on all the pattern races (Grade 1 in USA) and many of the listed races.

IRELAND The **Irish Horseracing Authority** has produced a Five-Year Strategic Plan which includes modernising the Irish Tote as well as giving the lion's share of the IR £30m Capital Development Fund to a small number of high-profile tracks. Other proposals include beaming pictures of Irish racing into Irish betting shops on a regular basis (at present the staple diet is British!).

On the track, the Irish kept six of their nine Group 1 races at home, up from three and two in the two previous years. However, eleven of the twenty-two Group 3 races went to British-trained horses (in five of the home successes there was no overseas challenge). In only nine of the thirty-six listed races was there a foreign contender, these amounting to thirteen in all. The financial reward in these listed races is not all that tempting (roughly IR £10,000 each), but quite often these 'black type' races take place at the big meetings, often enabling transport costs to be reduced. The best handicaps in Ireland (called 'Premier') are worth, on average, around IR £13,000 to the winner, are quite competitive, and attract few overseas challengers. Interestingly, in the latest season, the level of the ratings for the three-year-olds and older handicappers was dropped 3 lb by the Irish handicapper at the beginning of September, which would give them a slight edge against British handicappers in early 1997.

. The retirement of **Vintage Crop** marked the end of a notable career, but the older horse division was well represented by **Oscar Schindler** and **Timarida**, both of whom won at home and abroad. **Zagreb**'s runaway win in the Irish Derby was easily the best performance by a three-year-old, though mention should be made of **Rainbow Blues**, doing well in the States, and **Pro Trader**, who put up a remarkable performance (yet to be repeated) in the McDonagh Handicap at Galway; **Dance Design** took the Irish Oaks, while **Key Change** won the equivalent race at York—both went on to run creditably against their elders. **Mantovani**, **Shell Ginger** and **Desert King** achieved the most, in terms of form, among the two-year-olds, while **Verglas**'s Coventry Stakes was their most notable win overseas. At least as interesting for 1997 are the progressive pair **Johan Cruyff** and **Strawberry Roan**.

The progressive three-year-olds **French Ballerina** and **Predappio** are likely to be stepped up in class in 1997. Two doughty veterans made a big impression with their consistency in 1996. The tough and useful handicapper **The Bower** had a fine season and **Idris**, still an entire, was seldom out of the news. It seemed every time there was a good race to be contested in Ireland, Idris was there, game and determined, and, whether winning his four Group 3 races, thwarted under top weight in a handicap, or unavailingly as rank outsider in a Group 1, he would give his running.

Two-Year-Olds		92	Rasin	103	Proud Titania (f)
112p	Mantovani			103	Theano (f)
110p	Shell Ginger (f)	**Three-Year-Olds**		103	Tossup (f)
110+	Desert King	127	Zagreb	102	Samakaan
107	Verglas	120	*Pro Trader	102	Sharazan
105	Check The Band	119	Dance Design (f)	101+	By Charlie Allen
105	Family Tradition (f)	117	Key Change (f)	101	Cossack Count
104p	Johan Cruyff	117	Predappio	101	Harveys Point
103p	Strawberry Roan (f)	117	*Rainbow Blues	101	Line Dancer
102+	Swift Gulliver	115	Raiyoun	101	Megascene (f)
102	Azra (f)	115	Zafzala (f)	101	Tasdid
102	Raphane	114	*Harghar	101	*Troysend
101	Buddy Marvel	113	Lidanna (f)	100	Ceirseach (f)
101?	Velvet Appeal (f)	112	Ahkaam	100	Flame of Athens
100	Star Profile (f)	111+	French Ballerina (f)	100	Force of Will
99	Beautiful Fire	111	His Excellence	100	Orange Grouse (f)
99	Churchland	110	Almaty	100	Peace Offering (f)
99	Mosconi	110	L'Opera	100	Tirol Hope (f)
99?	Mount Rushmore	110	Sunset Reigns (f)	100	Touch Judge
98p	Act of Defiance	110	Truth Or Dare		
98p	Rayouni	109+	Oriane (f)	**Older Horses**	
97p	Casey Tibbs	109	Asmara (f)	127	Oscar Schindler
97p	Nobility	109	*Dancing Fred	125	Timarida (f)
97?	Gunfire	109	Escrito	121	Definite Article
96p	Khairabar	109	Gordi	118	Idris
96p	Token Gesture (f)	109	Sagar Pride (f)	116	Humbel
96	Air of Distinction (f)	108	Charlock (f)	115	Catch The Blues (f)
96	Caiseal Ros (f)	108	Deed of Love	115	Ger's Royale
95p	Red Castle	108	Nashcash	113	Al Mohaajir
95	Cambodian	108	Sheraka (f)	113	Burden of Proof
95	Melleray (f)	107	Lacinia (f)	113	I'm Supposin
95	Quws	107	Priolina (f)	112	Mohaajir
95	Sharemono	106	Deynawari	111	Ailleacht (f)
94p	Absolute Glee (f)	106	Hamad	110	Petite Fantasy (f)
94p	Kris Green (f)	105+	Layik	110	The Bower
94+	Desert Ease (f)	105	Identify (f)	108	Viaticum (f)
94	Classic Park (f)	105	Lone Eagle	107	Munif
94	Gan Ainm (f)	105	Peace Prize	106	America's Cup
94	Gaultier Gale	105	Requin Bleu	106	Fill The Bill
93p	Mohawk Dance	105	Sheffield (f)	106	Wandering Thoughts
93	Nevada	105	Symboli Kildare	104	Free To Speak
92p	Angellino	105	Tout A Coup (f)	103	Archive Footage
92p	Klinsman	104	Priory Belle (f)	103	Damancher
92p	Zeferina (f)	104	Qualtron	101	Sharatan
92	Olympic Majesty	103	Ashbal	101	Taklif
		103	Matangi (f)		

FRANCE   Helissio's stunning victory in the Prix de l'Arc de Triomphe was probably the most memorable event of the year for racing in France; he won by five lengths (we made it six) and not since Sea Bird in 1965 had the race clearly been in safe keeping so far from home. It was an important year for French racing behind the scenes as well.

The authorities in France are trying to rekindle the public's love of racing. **France-Galop**'s Jean-Claude Halle, quoted in an article in *Paris Turf*, stressed the need to promote racing as 'a spectacle, a sport, a bet and as an economic activity' saying that, at present, in the eyes of the public, racing was about the Tierce (a popular bet, usually on a big field of handicappers, where a large amount may be won for a small stake) and little else. A TV and cinema campaign will attempt to depict racing as more than a tote ticket. Further efforts are to be made to bring 'personalities' from other walks of life to the races—'the show should also be in the grandstands'—and to woo the public back to the courses.'We don't want to present racing as a dynamic sport and then have to show empty racetracks on television.' Subsidised by the proceeds of a tote monopoly racetracks rely less on turnstile income than they do in Britain, and experiments are taking place to see if racegoers can be lured by free admission. One track they will not be going to is **Evry** which has been closed despite its being one of the most modern in France; previously, Deauville, Chantilly and Maisons-Laffitte had survived similar threats after support from their local authorities.

Horses trained in Britain had a very good year in France, winning no fewer than eight Group 1 events. They particularly dominated the two-year-old races, only **Shaka** in the Criterium de Saint-Cloud preventing a clean sweep of the five Group 1 contests. The French had their successes in Britain too, of course: **Swain** won the Coronation Cup, **Shake The Yoke** the Coronation Stakes, **Tulipa** the Ribblesdale, **Anabaa** the July Cup, **Sensation** the Falmouth and **Pas de Reponse** the Cheveley Park. However, French challengers in Britain were heavily outnumbered by British runners in France. Prize money (at pattern and listed level) cannot be the reason; maybe some of the French owners and trainers are lacking a little in initiative and adventure!

Andre Fabre maintained his stranglehold on the trainers' championship, despite an ordinary year by his lofty standards—down 10m francs from 1995 and with only Swain's Coronation Cup and Luna Wells's Prix Saint-Alary in the top flight. Criquette Head finished second again, clear of Alain de Royer-Dupre, Elie Lellouche, Jean-Claude Rouget, Pascal Bary and John Hammond, the others who were above the 10m franc mark. Among the jockeys, Olivier Peslier turned the tables on Thierry Jarnet from the year before, with Gerald Mosse again the only other rider to pass the hundred-mark. The race for the owners' championship was the closest: 80,200 francs (£9,000, give or take) was all that kept the Aga Khan ahead of Sheikh Mohammed as both approached the 11m franc mark. Fairy King was the leading sire, not surprisingly given that he had the leading earners among the two- and three-year-olds in Revoque (G.B.-trained) and Helissio. The pick of the French studs for strength in depth is the Haras du Quesnay. Three of their established sires, Highest Honor (2nd), Saumarez (12th) and Bering (17th) were in the top twenty; their Sillery was the leading first-season sire just ahead of the Haras de Fresnay-Le-Buffard's Exit To Nowhere. Anabaa has now been retired to the Haras du Quesnay as well.

Two-Year-Olds

116	Majorien
116	Varxi
116	Zamindar
113p	Pas de Reponse (f)
113p	Shaka
112p	Daylami
112p	Mousse Glacee (f)
110	Sheer Reason (f)
108p	Joyeuse Entree (f)
108	Nombre Premier
108	Sendoro
107	Aneysar
107	New Frontier
106p	Keos
106	Alpha Plus
106	Fine Fellow
106	Heaven's Comm'd (f)
106	Kaldou Star
106	Queen Maud (f)
106	Rate Cut
105p	Peintre Celebre
105p	Shigeru Summit (f)
104	Dissertation (f)
103+	Nawal (f)
103?	Dame d'Harvard (f)
102	Speedfriend
101	Gazelle Royale (f)
101	Green Lady (f)
98	Dyhim Diamond
95	Ballade Viennoise (f)
95	Happy Dancer (f)
91	Elle Est Revenue (f)
89	Alberelle (f)

Three-Year-Olds

136	Helissio
128	Ashkalani
125	Spinning World
123	Darazari
123	Kistena (f)
122	Grape Tree Road
122	Shake The Yoke (f)
121	River Bay
120	Radevore
120	Tarator
119	Luna Wells (f)
117	Baroud d'Honneur
117	Grey Risk
117	Le Destin
117	Loup Solitaire
117	Ragmar
116	Android
116	*Jaunatxo
116	Le Triton
115	Blackwater
115	Kharizmi
115	Maroussie (f)
114	Miss Tahiti (f)
114	Oliviero
114	Sensation (f)
114	Shamadara (f)
113	Arbatax
113	Fort Nottingham
113	Khalisa (f)
113	Leonila (f)
112	Martiniquais
112	Rising Colours
112	Sangria (f)

GERMANY   The quality of German racing continues to rise. Pilsudski, Timarida and Luso won three of the six Group 1 races contested there in 1996 (the three previous seasons had each seen only one foreign victory) but German horses did well to win Group 1 races in France and Italy as well as keeping thirty-one of their forty pattern races at home—a percentage higher than the Irish, French and Italians, although those countries receive significantly more foreign challengers.

Racing in Germany differs fundamentally from that in the rest of Europe in a number of respects. Most interesting is the seeming desire to bring two-year-olds along slowly—none may race more than eight times, jockeys are allowed to carry only an 'educational' whip (much shorter and wider than the real thing) and there will be only two German races for juveniles in the European pattern in 1997, including the most prestigious, the Preis der Winterfavoriten. There are only a handful of listed races in support.

Another feature of the German pattern is the lack of opportunity at the extremes of racing's distance spectrum. There are only four sprint races and two staying events (of which the St Leger is confined to three-year-olds), and indeed the six Group 1 races are all contested at a mile and a quarter (just the Bayerisches Zuchtrennen) or a mile and a half, and four of them take place in a five-week period in the summer. There is room for variety at the top level, as indicated by the fact that **A Magicman** needed to go to France to win his Group 1, the Prix de la Foret.

The leading three-year-old of 1995, **Solon**, who sadly had only one start in 1996, is to take up stud duties at Haras du Preaux in Normandy. **Lavirco** was a worthy successor, and while the purists might have liked to have seen him attempt to complete the triple crown in the autumn, his facile win in the Europa Preis showed that he could be a major contender for top honours in Europe in 1997. He represents the leading sire, Konigsstuhl (now deceased), as well as the top owners and breeders

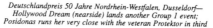

Deutschlandpreis 50 Jahre Nordrhein-Westfalen, Dusseldorf—
Hollywood Dream (nearside) lands another Group 1 event;
Posidonas runs her very close with the veteran Protektor in third

Gestut Fahrhof. Others who made notable contributions to the German racing year were **Hollywood Dream**, a Group 1 winner at home and abroad, popular veteran **Protektor**, who found a new lease of life and stays in training, and **Wurftaube**, whose demolition of the German St Leger field marks her down as a filly to look out for in the coming season. **Camp David** remained the nation's best older stayer, aforementioned A Magicman was marginally the pick of the milers (**Royal Abjar** returned after failing as a stallion, but ran only twice), and a rather vulnerable set of sprinters seemed to lack a clear leader. The strongest group was at middle distances, and of those not already mentioned, most interesting was **Germany**, another back on the track after failing at stud in the spring; he ran most consistently, though usually in defeat. The two-year-olds were led by the unbeaten colt **Eden Rock**, who looked workmanlike when coming out best of Bruno Schutz's strong hand in the Preis der Winterfavoriten, and the unbeaten filly **Oriental Flower**, who represented the champion trainer (in terms of number of winners) Uwe Stoltefuss, and won the Preis der Winterkonigin.

The coming year is the final one as a trainer for legendary **Heinz Jentzsch**, champion trainer no fewer than thirty-one times, before he hands over the reins to champion jockey Peter Schiergen.

Two-Year-Olds

106p	Eden Rock
103	Caitano
103	Oriental Flower (f)
100	Mr Finch
99	Don't Worry
99	Etmal
98	Alte Kunst (f)
98	Icemoon
97	Widar
96	Tottenham
96?	Urban Cookie (f)
95	Fan
95	I Go Bye (f)
94	Anna Thea (f)
94	Genevra (f)
94	Is Tirol
94	Panthere (f)
94	Southern Secret

Three-Year-Olds

125	Lavirco
119	La Blue (f)
119	Wurftaube (f)
116	Bad Bertrich Again
116	Night Petticoat (f)
114	Accento
114	Surako
113	Albaran
113	Sir Warren
113	Zero Problemo
112	Agnelli
110	Waky Nao
108	Mill King

108	Ocean Sea
108	Wind of Chance
107	Dapprima (f)
106	Ardilan
106	Narrabeth
106	Power Flame
106	Trudeau
105	Anno Luce (f)
105	Barlovento
105	Bon Jovi
105	Domian
105	Flamingo Garden

104	Catoki
103	Nataliana (f)
103	Salonrolle (f)
101	The Blade (f)
100	Niniska (f)

Older Horses

124	Germany
123	Laroche
120	Protektor
119	Artan
119	Hollywood Dream (f)
118	Oxalagu
117	A Magicman
116	Camp David
116	*Manzoni
115	Concepcion
115	Devil River Peek
115	Galtee
115	Sinyar
114	Macanal

114?	Munaaji
113	Orfijar
113	Royal Abjar
112	Aratikos
112	First Hello
111	Chato
111	Lentini
111	Sir King
110	Kalatos
110	Ladoni
109+	Solon
109	Flamingo Paradise
109	Lambada
109	Matula
109	Siberian Grey
109	Takin
108	No Dancer
107	Diktys
107	Prince Firebird
107	Silent Lake
107	Tres Hereux
106	Auenadler
106	Favourite Prince
106	Nautiker
106	Prairie Shadow
106	Sharp Prod
105	Bad Bertrich
105	Kornado
105	Moltaire
105	Pacajas

104	Caballo
104	Little Smart
103	Lara (f)

ITALY   Racing at the top level in Italy is truly cosmopolitan, horses arriving from all over Europe to compete. To the Italian professionals, though, this is surely a mixed blessing. The influx stems from good prize-money and realisation that, at present, the home team is vulnerable.

In 1996, seven Italian races were removed from the European pattern and restrictive conditions placed on entry in a bid to reduce the number of valuable prizes going abroad. The foreigners came for most of the twenty-five which remained—and won more than half. Thirteen–twelve was the final score, two of the 'home wins' uncontested. Italy's shortage of top-quality horses is illustrated by the fact that the home team won only one of the eight Group 1 races in 1996 and, in the last four years, only Misil (124) has been rated above 118—and he was bred in America and subsequently returned to race there.

A glance at the list of horses imported into Italy in 1996 indicates a shortage of horses with top-class pedigrees. The median price from the major yearling sales in Italy was around 9,500 guineas, among the sires represented Sikeston (around 10,000) and Luge (around 12,000 from two sales), had the best of those standing in Italy. The lack of quality among the home-based stallions probably accounts for why the majority of the pattern winners which were trained in Italy were bred abroad. Germany, in marked contrast, has a strong breeding base.

Quite a surprising number of British-trained two-year-olds make their debut in Italy nowadays. There are two advantages: firstly, the race itself is often easier to win than one in England, but, more importantly, horses which make their debut in Italy become qualified for the restricted races there, some of which, though no longer in the pattern, carry big prizes. The Gran Premio d'Italia is one such. Worth over £100,000 to the winner, it attracted Luca Cumani's Freequent (whose debut was the only one of eight previous races he had contested in Italy), though he managed only fourth of fifteen. Surprisingly, despite good prize-money in the listed races, there were not too many challengers from abroad for them.

Two-Year-Olds

108	Golden Oriental	91	White Gulch	114	Beat of Drums
101	Woodex			114	Late Parade
100p	Golden Aventura	**Three-Year-Olds**		112	Taxi de Nuit
99	Plumbird	115	Duke of Flite	111	Morigi
97	Doctor Leckter	115	Snake Snap	111	Ravier
97	Hambye (f)	111	Toto Le Moko	110	*Wings Bash
97	Miliardaire	110	Coral Reef	109	Tarhelm
97	War Declaration	107	Canarino Mannaro	108	Imprevedibile
96	Madler	107	Dancer Mitral	107	Sotabrasciet
94	She Bat (f)	107	Golden Agos	107	Steve Lucky
94	Woods of Cisterna	106	Dungeon Master	106	Dark Street
93	Special Lad	105	Germignaga (f)	106	Welsh Liberty
93	Special Star	105	Grey Way (f)	105	Tiana
92	Classem Ducere				
92	Lonely Man	104	Bella Michela (f)	104	Bemont Park (f)
92	Sopran Mariduff (f)	103	Beauty To Petriolo (f)	103	Gentle Fan
91	Counterplot (f)	103	Blu Meltemi (f)	100	Tycoon Lady (f)
91	Mister Rock	103	Bog Wild (f)	99	Karpacka (f)
91	Rose Wine (f)	98	Blu Tuama (f)	99	Scribano
91	Simil (f)			96	Speed Rahy
91	Tiffar	**Older Horses**			
		116	Slicious		

SCANDINAVIA There is one Group 3 contest (in Sweden) and twenty-one listed races (spread across Sweden, Norway and Denmark) which connections of useful horses might consider targeting. The ratings of the horses successful in the 'black-type' events in 1996 puts the quality of these races into context. We cannot list all those races here, but they take place between May and September, at between five and thirteen furlongs (five of them on dirt), and are mainly for three-year-olds and up. Some trainers have taken the hint and the latest season saw photo-finish defeats for British-trained Hever Golf Rose, Amrak Ajeeb and Jayannpee (who was awarded his race) at Taby in Sweden. Incidentally, it was confirmed by the BHB that their book *European Pattern Races 1997* would contain details of the races.

On the track, **Windmachine** and **Sharp Matt** had the best records in the sprints, though **Glenlivet** spent much of his time raiding Germany and won two listed races there. **Federico** won three listed events, between nine furlongs and a mile and a half at Klampenborg (Denmark) where he has yet to be beaten, though he was far less successful elsewhere. In contrast, **Village Storm** took a listed event over a mile there before going on to bigger things abroad, landing a Group 2 contest at Dusseldorf. **Blue Chief** won over a mile both on turf and dirt, while **Laila Alawi** was versatile in a different sense, dead-heating with Ballet Prince over a mile and a half then dropping down to win a fillies' event over a mile. Ex-British horses **Philidor, Coconut Johnny** and **Coneybury** each won listed races in Sweden, while a Swede that came to Royal Ascot, Queen Alexandra fifth **Dance D'Ore**, was also a winner there. In Norway, ex-Henry Cecil colt **Inchrory** won his first seven races in 1996, including a listed contest and the Two Thousand Guineas and Derby, and while he failed by half a length to join Sunorius (1987) and Trainers Seat (1976) as triple crown winners in the last twenty years, he should win more good races in 1997. **Kill The Crab** showed herself as good as she had been in 1995 (when she'd beaten Royal Abjar in a Group 2 at Hoppegarten), coming to herself in late-summer to win a listed race at Ovrevoll (Norway) and then the Group 3 Stockholm Cup where she had a representative Scandinavian field, as well as the likes of Overbury, behind her. She's highly prized, too, judging by the Newmarket December Sales, where she was led out unsold at 150,000 guineas.

There may be horses in Scandinavia as good or better than some mentioned here, but for this review we have concerned ourselves only with performances in races carrying 'black type'. The classics do not carry listed status, though they are open to foreign challengers and there is a desire among Scandinavian officials to attract quality European challengers.

Three-Year-Olds		Older Horses		105	Coconut Johnny
105	General Alan	112	Village Storm	105	Haikiki
		110	Glenlivet	105	Humbert's Landing
104	Inchrory	107	Federico	105	Senador
		106	Kill The Crab (f)	105	Subzero
		106	Sharp Matt		
		106	Windmachine (f)	104	Dulford Lad

SPAIN That there were two Group 3 races and ten listed events in Spain in the latest season might well be news to many. It wasn't to Lord Huntingdon, who sent Prince of India (to little effect) for a listed event and Mongol Warrior to win the Memorial Duque de Toledo, a Group 3 contest at Madrid in November. Apart from a few contenders from France, though, these races were home-based affairs and not easy to equate on an international level. The peseta lost around 15% of its value against the pound in 1996, making the first prize in some of the listed races look unappealing at around £7,000, and though the Group 3 races were more than three times as valuable, the fact they are to lose their pattern status in 1997 will not help.

A few smart horses have raced in Spain in recent years, notably Partipral who went on to win the 1995 Hong Kong International Vase, but there was nothing of that quality in 1996. The classic races were shared among these horses. The Cimera (2000 Guineas) winner **Okawango** went on to do quite well against his elders. However, the Valderas (1000 Guineas) and Oaks winner, **Sua**, and the Derby and Villamejor (St Leger) winner, **Batu**, were both rather disappointing against older horses. Batu was beaten in the two pattern races, the one at San Sebastian won by **Mdudu** from 1995 Derby two-one **El Ceremonioso** and **Madrileno**, the other won by Mongol Warrior from **Leonard Quercus**, **Wild Park** and **Toba**. There is only one listed race for two-year-olds and it went to **Kashwan** who went on to show useful form in pattern company in France.

Three-Year-Olds		Older Horses	
107	Okawango	108	Mdudu
		107	Madrileno
102	Wild Park	105	El Ceremoniso

NORTH AMERICA   The dust has settled, and a great career is over. **Cigar** has been retired to the Ashford Stud in Kentucky. His splendid year is covered in an essay in the main body of *Racehorses* which recounts his victory in the Dubai World Cup and his feat of equalling Citation's sixteen-race unbeaten sequence. Cigar was an extraordinary horse whose fame spread beyond the racing pages and brought new fans to the sport. The horse, his owner, his trainer and all who worked with them deserve immense credit.

The American two-year-old colts were not a good bunch. The phrase 'pro-tem leader' applied successively to **Kelly Kip**, **Smoke Glacken**, **Traitor** and **Ordway**. In the end **Boston Harbor**, who had sidestepped most of the traditional contests to chase (successfully) a million-dollar bonus in Kentucky, made all the running and held on to win the Breeders' Cup Juvenile. There was no doubt he would win the Eclipse Award as top juvenile male. We have serious doubts though whether he will pick up the three-year-old award as well. He benefited from a fine ride, and from ill-luck in running to two of his principal rivals, **Acceptable** and Ordway. Those two may well turn the form round in 1997, and some as-yet relatively unexposed types to come to the fore as the spring trials unfold. The fillies division was much more clear-cut. **Storm Song**'s performances in the Frizette, and particularly at the Breeders' Cup, marked her down as a high-class performer, indeed she had the best form—the way we read it—of any two-year-old in the northern hemisphere. **Sharp Cat** also had a fine year, but after beating Storm Song a length in the Matron in September came off second best in the Frizette. She was durable though, a thrashing at the Breeders' Cup preceding a defeat of stable-companion **City Band** in the Hollywood Starlet. **Oath** was precocious enough to win the Spinaway on her second and final start, while catching the eye late in the year in Grade 2 company at Aqueduct was **Ajina**; her seven-length win over nine furlongs was a smart performance and her third consecutive success from four starts—she should progress to the top grade in 1997.

There are plenty of opportunities for three-year-olds, and many have extensive campaigns. The best of the latest crop **Skip Away** had contested four Grade 1 races by the beginning of August without winning any, though he was runner-up in the Preakness and Belmont Stakes. He was better in the autumn, climaxing with a win in the Jockey Club Gold Cup when he held off Cigar by a head. Classic winners **Grindstone** (injured in the act), **Louis Quatorze** (tough and game like Skip Away) and **Editor's Note** (none too consistent) plus the later-developing **Will's Way** were among those to have success at the highest level. Another to do so was **Unbridled's Song**, whose Florida Derby win in March reads well even now, Editor's Note, Skip Away and Louis Quatorze filling the frame five and three quarter lengths and more behind. After injuring himself prior to the Kentucky Derby he never recaptured his form, and a further injury ended his career. The other two-year-olds we held particularly high hopes for in last year's review ran but twice each; **Cobra King** won a Grade 3 (beating Editor's Note) before finishing well beaten in the Florida Derby, while **Ide** won a pair of Grade 3 contests before injury intervened.

In the first part of the year, several three-year-old fillies put forward claims to be considered the best. **Antespend** picked up the Las Virgenes Stakes and Santa Anita Oaks before running into **Escena** in a Grade 2 event at Oaklawn; Escena went down narrowly to the progressive **Pike Place Dancer** in the Kentucky Oaks, while **My Flag**, who ran poorly that day (as she did on other occasions) had won the Ashland

1134

Stakes and went on to take the CCA Oaks. In July **Listening** went to the top of many lists when taking the Hollywood Oaks ahead of Antespend for her fourth win from five starts in the year. **Yanks Music** was a close second to **Star de Lady Ann** in the Acorn and second, conceding 7 lb, to **Top Secret** in the Monmouth Oaks before running out an impressive winner of the Alabama Stakes, relishing the mile and a quarter, and stretching away from Escena, My Flag and Listening. All three beaten fillies went on to run well in the highest class, but it was Yanks Music who dominated from then on. Taking on her elders and back in trip she twice beat the reliable Serena's Song, on the second occasion at weight-for-age. Her entry in the Breeders' Cup Classic looked an excellent decision, particularly as she is well suited to a mile and a quarter, but a swelling in her ankle on the day of the race ruled her out. Sadly she also missed the Top Flight Handicap later on where **Flat Fleet Feet** (second to the fine sprinter **Capote Belle** in the Test Stakes in July) gained her first Grade 1 win and she has now been retired—her first mate will be Cigar.

Cigar's trainer Bill Mott had an abundance of talent in the older-horse division, including **Wekiva Springs** and **Geri**. Both were Grade 1 winners, and while Wekiva Springs has been retired to stud, Geri should return to the track in 1997. Richard Mandella also had a pair of aces in **Siphon** and **Dare And Go**, and while Dare And Go will forever be remembered as the horse who broke Cigar's streak, Siphon had more than a little to do with it; prior to the race, Siphon's hat-trick of front-running wins, including a defeat of Geri in the Hollywood Gold Cup, convinced some that Cigar might be beaten in the Pacific Classic at Del Mar if Siphon were allowed to set a slow pace in front. After Siphon raced the first six furlongs with Cigar in 1: 09.2, the race was set up for Dare And Go. Siphon did not reappear; Dare And Go did but was rather lack-lustre. Early in the year, **Mr Purple**, **Helmsman** and **Tinners Way** (who broke down in the Pacific Classic) all won Grade 1 races in California but did not go on to have a major effect on the season, while later on **Dramatic Gold** and **Mahogany Hall** were well placed to win slightly substandard contests. Two who did not reappear after their finest moments were **Star Standard**, who took advantage

Breeders' Cup Classic, Woodbine—
The grey Alphabet Soup wins from Louis Quatorze (second right) and Cigar (left)

Breeders' Cup Mile, Woodbine—
Da Hoss gives trainer Michael Dickinson his biggest win; Spinning World is second

of a light weight to beat **Key of Luck** in the Pimlico Special, and **Soul of The Matter**, who covered himself in glory in his narrow defeat by Cigar in the Dubai World Cup, pulling over eight lengths clear of the rest of a strong field. The sprinters, and in America seven furlongs is a sprint, were quite good, without any one of them being outstanding. **Lite The Fuse** started well, winning a second successive Carter Handicap, **Prospect Bay**, off bottom weight, defeated a strong field in a Grade 2 at Saratoga, **Lord Carson** showed tremendous early pace and put up a fine effort to win a similar event at Belmont, and **Langfuhr** was particularly effective at seven furlongs, picking up the Vosburgh Stakes, but vulnerable at shorter. Ultimately the Eclipse Award went to **Lit de Justice**, after he made Jenine Sahadi the first woman to train the winner of a Breeders' Cup race on the flat. He was quite a sight that day, needing to be backed into the stalls, over ten lengths behind after two furlongs, then, in commentator Tom Durkin's memorable phrase 'a grey blur in the stretch' as he caught Paying Dues near the line. But you cannot talk about sprinters without mentioning **Alphabet Soup**. In a tremendous season, he had Lit de Justice three and a half lengths behind him in a Grade 3 event over seven furlongs at Del Mar in August, then crowned his career with a narrow defeat of Louis Quatorze and Cigar in the Breeders' Cup Classic over a mile and a quarter in October. Nothing left to prove at age five? Maybe, but racegoers in America will still be able to see this tough and genuine horse in 1997.

It seems the older female division is strong every year. Iron filly **Serena's Song** won three Grade 1 events and enough money to become the leading distaff earner of all time, but she was not so dominant as in 1995. **Twice The Vice** made a bold bid for championship honours, scoring a hat-trick of Grade 1 wins, twice beating Jewel Princess, including by three quarters of a length in the Milady Handicap in June when subsequent John A. Morris Handicap winner **Urbane** was back in third. It was unfortunate she was not seen out after her next start. **Twist Afleet** had compiled a fine record at shorter trips, but she was upstaged by **Chaposa Springs** in the Ballerina Handicap. **Exotic Wood** has only one defeat in her life, but that was narrowly to Serena's Song when in receipt of weight and her win in the Go For Wand in July on her last start does not read well enough to suggest she could have turned the tables had she been seen in the autumn. **Different** had lost only one in ten coming into the Breeders' Cup, and her win in the Spinster gave the ex-Argentinian a fine chance to follow her connections' successes with other imports Bayakoa and Paseana, but she seemed to have no excuses on the day. **Jewel Princess**, the winner, was in top form at the right time, and while it would have been ideal if she could have evened the score with Twice The Vice, her form with Serena's Song clearly shows her progression: May 3, game winner by a neck when in receipt of 5 lb; July 21, three-length winner when in receipt of 5 lb; October 26, decisive winner by a length and a half at levels at the Breeders' Cup.

With **Northern Spur** not encountering suitably extreme conditions (which had seen him win the 1995 Breeders' Cup Turf) before his retirement through injury, the middle-distance horses on turf were not particularly good, and Europeans filled the first four places in the Breeders' Cup Turf at Woodbine. Best of the Americans during the year was **Sandpit**, who won a pair of Grade 1 events and put up a fine effort in defeat behind **Talloires** when conceding the ex-French horse 9 lb. **Mecke** is not the most reliable, but he's very good on his day, as when winning the Arlington Million, while **Diplomatic Jet** is particularly at home around Belmont Park, where he won three Grade 1 events. Ex-Europeans abound in this division, Eclipse Award-winning female **Wandesta** being one, though the top three-year-old colt and filly to be trained in America in 1997, **Marlin** and **Memories of Silver**, do not fall into this category. **Da Hoss** also never raced in Europe, and, after a fine campaign for Michael Dickinson, was rated best miler. Not seen until July when unable to concede 6 lb to **Smooth Runner** and beaten three and a half lengths, he won three of his last four, culminating in a tactical triumph in the Breeders' Cup Mile. One major contender, **Fastness**, was missing at Woodbine. Undefeated since his second in the Breeders' Cup Mile of 1995, he took his second straight Eddie Read Handicap when conceding 10 lb to Smooth Runner and holding him off by half a length, the pair clear. Sadly, he was injured soon afterwards and has been retired to stud.

Eras come to an end and the racing goes on. While many were out doing their Christmas shopping a horse who had been progressing quietly since his arrival from Argentina (where he'd been champion three-year-old) suddenly burst onto the scene. The genuine and consistent Dramatic Gold was left nine lengths in the wake of **Gentlemen** in a Grade 3 event at Hollywood Park, the track record shattered by 1.4 seconds. Effective on turf and dirt, at nine furlongs to a mile and a half, he looks a horse to pay very close attention to in 1997. At time of writing he is on course for the Dubai World Cup, a race for which his trainer Richard Mandella produced Soul of The Matter in peak condition to run Cigar so close in the inaugural running.

European-trained horses who showed or reproduced their best form in North America are included in this list † commentary in *Racehorses of 1996*		

Two-Year-Olds

				DIRT	
123	Storm Song (f)	113	Haint		
122	Boston Harbor	113	Leo's Gypsy Dancer (f)		
121	Acceptable	113	Silver Charm	**Three-Year-Olds**	
120	Ajina (f)	113	Southern Playgirl (f)	128	Skip Away
120	Smoke Glacken	112	Annie Cake (f)	127	Yanks Music (f)
119	Sharp Cat (f)	112	Fabulously Fast (f)	125	Editor's Note
117	Blazing Sword	112	†Hello	125	Louis Quatorze
117	Ordway	112	Pearl City (f)	125	Unbridled's Song
117	Swiss Yodeller	111	Cash Deposit	125	Will's Way
116	City Band (f)	111	Gold Tribute	124	Cavonnier
116	Stolen Gold	110	Captain Bodgit	124	Grindstone
115	Kelly Kip	110	Carmen's Baby	123	My Flag (f)
115	Love That Jazz (f)	110	In Excessive Bull	123	Pike Place Dancer (f)
115	Traitor	110	Jules	122	Escena (f)
114	Arthur L.	110	Night In Reno	122	Honour And Glory
114	Oath (f)	110	Starry Ice (f)	121	Formal Gold
		110	The Silver Move	121	Listening (f)
		109	Concerto	120	Capote Belle (f)
		109	Cotton Carnival (f)	120	Victory Speech
		109	Critical Factor (f)	119	Antespend (f)
		109	Desert Digger (f)	119	Gold Fever
		109	Miss Huff N' Puff (f)	119	Prince of Thieves
		109	Rexy Sexy (f)	118	Halo Sunshine
				118	In Contention
				118	Star de Lady Ann (f)

118? Secreto de Estado
117 Alyrob
117 Cara Rafaela (f)
117 Hesabull
117 Top Secret (f)
116 Appealing Skier
116 Cobra King
116 King of The Heap
116 Roar
115 Flat Fleet Feet (f)
115 Golden Attraction (f)
115 Ide
115 Jamies First Punch
115 Plum Country (f)
115 Seacliff
115 Stephanotis
115 Stop Traffic (f)
115 The Barking Shark
115 Victor Cooley

Older Horses
138 †Cigar
132 Soul of The Matter
129 Jewel Princess (f)
126 Alphabet Soup
126 †Key of Luck
126 Serena's Song (f)
125 Dare And Go
125 Different (f)
125 Gentlemen
125 Lit de Justice
124 Dramatic Gold
124 Langfuhr
124 Mt Sassafras
123 Siphon
123 Wekiva Springs
122 Afternoon Deelites
122 Geri
122 L'Carriere
122 Paying Dues
122 Peaks And Valleys
122 Twice The Vice (f)
121 Helmsman
121 Lite The Fuse
121 Lord Carson
121 Meadow Monster
121 Smart Strike
121? Golden Larch
120 Chaposa Springs (f)
120 Exotic Wood (f)
120 Forest Wildcat
120 Isitingood
120 Mr Purple
120 Not Surprising
120 Pyramid Peak
119 Star Standard
119 Twist Afleet (f)
119 Urbane (f)
118 Abaginone
118 Borodislew (f)
118 Eltish
118 Lakota Brave
118 Letthebighossroll

118 Megan's Interco
118 Top Rung (f)
118 Track Gal (f)
117 Clear Mandate (f)
117 Friendly Lover
117 Mahogany Hall
117 Prospect Bay
117 Savinio
116 Atticus
116 Basquean
116 Golden Gear
116 Halo's Image
116 Sleep Easy (f)
116 Urgent Request
115 Classic Fit
115 Del Mar Dennis
115 Flying Chevron
115 Halo America (f)
115 Kingdom Found
115 Love Grows
115 Scott's Scoundrel
115 Tinners Way
115 Top Account

TURF

Three-Year-Olds
125 †Spinning World
124 †Shantou
123 Memories of Silver (f)
122 Marlin
122 †Shake The Yoke (f)
121 Chief Bearhart
121 Trail City
118 Allied Forces
118 Sir Cat
117 Defacto
117 Devil's Cup
117 †Rainbow Blues
116 †Bad Bertrich Again
116 Jaunatxo
116 More Royal
116 Odyle
115 Ambivalent
115 Mateo
115 †Wandering Star (f)

Older Horses
129 Da Hoss
129 †Pilsudski
129 Sandpit
127 Fastness
127 †Singspiel
126 Mecke
126 Northern Spur
125 Diplomatic Jet
125 †Swain
125 †Timarida (f)
124 Awad
123 †Running Flame
123 Talloires
122 Celtic Arms

121 Broadway Flyer
121 Flag Down
121 Lassigny
121 Same Old Wish
121 Signal Tap
121 Wandesta (f)
120 Auriette (f)
120 Kiridashi
120 †Montjoy
120 Perfect Arc (f)
120 Raintrap
120 Windsharp (f)
119 Angel In My Heart (f)
119 Bail Out Becky (f)
119 Labeeb
119 Matiara (f)
119 Mr Bluebird
119 The Vid
118 Dernier Empereur
118 Pharma (f)
118 Romarin
118 Tychonic
118 Vladivostock
117 Ampulla (f)
117 Class Kris (f)
117 †Donna Viola (f)
117 Gold And Steel
117 Ops Smile
117 Silver Wizard
116 Chelsey Flower (f)
116 Debutant Trick
116 Dixie Pearl (f)
116 Flagbird (f)
116 Flitch
116 Green Means Go
116 Northern Emerald (f)
116 Real Connection (f)
116 Smooth Runner
116 Special Price
116 Via Lombardia
115 Admise (f)
115 Alpride (f)
115 Comininalittlehot
115 Didina (f)
115 Kiri's Clown
115 Petit Poucet
115 Rare Reason
115 Royal Chariot
115 Tejano Run

THE FULL TIMEFORM IRISH HANDICAP

Here are listed the Timeform Ratings for every horse that ran on the flat in Ireland, plus a few who were trained there and ran abroad, during the 1996 season. † indicates that the horse appears in commentary or essay form in *Racehorses of 1996*.

Two-Year-Olds

65	Absent Beauty
94p	Absolute Glee
71	Acadelli
–	Accounts Academy
98p	Act of Defiance
61	Admiral Wings
76	Adua
96	Air of Distinction†
80p	Akdariya
73	Alma Latina
86	Almost Skint
72	Alparost
–	Althea Mist
47+	Amocachi
–	Amolene
92p	Angellino
89	Animagic
–	Another Sally
78	Arc
–	Argyle
91p	Argyle Street
66	Arts Project
–p	Ash Project
–	Aspen Gem
69?	Astronome
62?	Audrey's Pearl
–	Audriano
–	Avalon Accord
68	Axel Foley
102	Azra†
–	Back To Bavaria
65?	Ballinola Lad
56	Ballylennon Mist
74	Ballymote†
–	Bansha Hero
68	Baptismal Rock
–	Barnacranny
–	Beach Project
–	Beal Na Blath
76	Beamingallover
99	Beautiful Fire
80d	Beckenbauer
63	Belike The Wind
–p	Better Be Sure
107+	Bianca Nera†
61	Biddy Blackhurst
–	Big Boy John
70	Binneas
90	Blasket Island
74	Blind Date
73	Blue Jazz
65	Blue Stocking
85	Blushing Minstrel
–	Bobbella

62	Bob Cullen
88	Bob The Broker†
–	Bohemian Belle
80	Bold Hunter
85p	Bold Tycoon
61	Bollero†
84+	Bonnington
64	Boughtbyphone
–	Breffni Star
62	Briion
?	Broken Innate
–	Bualadh Bos Babe
101	Buddy Marvel
64	Buncrana
80?	Burnt Toast
87p	Burtown
–	Burubako
–p	Bye Bold Aileen
56	By Jay
56	Caduga
96	Caiseal Ros
67	Calamity Kate
79	Call My Bluff
–	Camassia
95	Cambodian
77p	Canadian Vista
58p	Candide
82	Cannikin
–	Capall Farraige
65	Carhue Lass
84	Carlisle Bay
97p	Casey Tibbs
–	Castletubber Lady
84	Catarata
–	Celtic Link
–	Celtic Minstrel
74	Celtic Slip
71?	Chaghaf
76p	Chania
79	Charita
105	Check The Band†
64	Chipstead Bay
71	Chu Culainn
99	Churchland
–	Cian Points
–	Cidaris
71	Cinnamon Rose
76	Ciro's Pearl†
80	Ciste
67	Clarecastle
71	Classical Risk
94	Classic Park†
69	Classic Referendum
74p	Code of Honour
–	Common Currency

–	Consuming Passions
–	Coolarne Lad
67d	Copper Faced Jacks
–	Crest of The Wave
70	Crimson Tirol
82	Crown Regent
65	Cryptic Pattern
99	Crystal Crossing†
–	Culloville North
–	Cumas
–	Daddy's Polly
76+	Daffodil Dale
–	Dama de Seda
81	Danccini
–	Dance Crazy
–	Danny's Joy
63p	Darbela
–p	Dark Kestrel
64	Davenport
47	Dawn's Folly
100+	Daylight In Dubai†
63	Deerfield Fame
–	Delray Flyer
94+	Desert Ease
110+	Desert King†
–	Dicky's Rock
67	Distant Affair
78	Distinctly West
61	Doellan
66?	Don Wattle
75	Doucette
78	Dragon Century
69	Dream Project
81p	Dreamworks
67	Driftwood
81p	Dr Johnson
55	Drumcooley
–	Early Present
72	Ein Tresor
80+	Elida
67	Elinor Dashwood
69	Emlah
–	En-Jay-Bee
77p	Epic Tale
109	Equal Rights†
65	Executive Decision
–	Extatic
64	Fabricate
93	Fairy Song
62	Falls O'Moness†
105	Family Tradition
–	Fanciful
112p	Fantastic Fellow†
78	Fantasticus
70	Far Niente

70+	Fastnet View	73p	Karatisa	–	Miss Clonteen†
71?	Feather Bed†	–	Kate Emily	80	Missigoni
–	Female Lead	78	Katydid	68	Miss Margaux
69	Feminine Heart	75	Keeping The Faith	99+	Miss Stamper†
78	Fiery Guest	?	Kenaftor	80p	Mo Chos Chle
65p	Figile	96p	Khairabar	93p	Mohawk Dance
77	Fine Project	76	Kharshani	54	Molly Coates
–	Flags Up	84p	Kilbride Lad	74	Monongahela
–	Flying Blind	79	King of Persia	84+	Moon Flower
66	Fly Your Kite	94d	Kingsinger†	60?	Moonlight Melody
80	Footlight	–	King Wah Victory	74+	More's The Pity
–	Forlorn Point	–	Kinnari	99	Mosconi
76	Freshford Jim	68	Kitty Kildare	99?	Mount Rushmore
80	Future Prospect†	92p	Klinsman	91p	Moving On Up
94	Gan Ainm	–	Know What	62	Moynoe Princess
–	Garavogue	68	Kram	75p	Mr Lightfoot
70	Gardd	94p	Kris Green	–	Mr Pundit
94	Gaultier Gale	74	Kristal Blue	80+	Mubadara
82	Geimhriuil	72p	La Charpentiere	115	Muchea†
–	Gentleman John	57	La Coeur L'Amour	80	Mujova†
–	Ginola	67	Lady Assassin	74p	Mukarrab
–	Global Diamond	–	Lady Oranswell	–	Mullawn Dancer
84	Glorious Encounter	–	Lady Rolfe	–	Multimedia
75	God Forbid	–	La Fenice	64+	My Legal Eagle
–p	Golden Saddle	76	Lake Quilty	90p	Mynador
80	Go Thunder	–	Laramie	51+	Myran
63p	Granny Kelly	71	Last Project	70d	My River
–	Greek Belle	–	Latin Project	72	Mystic Belle
–	Greenmount Lady	–	Le Ciel	77	Mystic Magic
96	Groom's Gordon†	–	Legal Project	74	Mystik Day
–	Guest Cailin	58	Leola	93	Nevada†
97?	Gunfire	–	Let Live	72	Nidaa
66	Hamamelis	58	Lightning Bolt†	82	Night Raider
71	Handaza	89	Lil's Boy	73p	Nitha
72	Harkness	–	Lisieux Lilly	97p	Nobility
58	Harrison Hill	72	Lisnatine	–	Northern Brief
83	Hartstown House	53	Little Monica	86	No Slouch
–	Hassiba	–	Load And Lock	67	Nutty Stan
–p	Hayward	63	Lord Cromby	108	Ocean Ridge†
–	Heir Apparent	79	Luisa di Camerata	–	O'Garney Park
71	High As A Kite	65	Lunasa	68	Okay
–	Honor's Stag	75p	Lymax	–p	Old Ivory
55	Honourable Chap	74	Mac Nicholas	92	Olympic Majesty
–	Hustle An Bustle	65	Magic Annemarie	–	Olympic Rock
75	Hyperico	–	Main Man Paul	83	Omy Dancer
–	Hytherm	–	Mairead	83	Onbendedknee
66	I Have To Go	–p	Malatuko	–	One To Two
65	Imperial Or Metric†	62	Mandalay	73	One Won One
71	Imprevue	112p	Mantovani†	–	On The Canvas
85	Inishargy	79	Maratana	89	Orange Jasmine
75	Iolanta	–	Marble Halls	82	Our Bart
88	Irish John	–	Marie Rambert	57	Our Risk
63	Islamorada	–	Martino	–	Over You Go
?	Islandeady	68	Maskul	–	Paddy Hurry†
70	Jackeen's	63	Master of Milltown	91	Paddy Lad†
64	Jack Flush†	56p	Media Frenzy	69	Peace Melody
–	Jawah	64	Meet And Greet	–	Peace Train
104p	Johan Cruyff†	55	Megabyte	58	Peig Sayers
–	Joyful Tidings	95	Melleray	92	Pelham†
84	Junikay	90	Menja	86	Pelmeny
65	Just Like Annie	–	Midnight Lover	62	Pennant Flame
81p	Just Try Me	–	Mielisa	–	Petite Flyer
83	Kaiser Kache†	88p	Mingling Glances	89	Petite Princess
74p	Kallavesi	68	Ministerial Model	67p	Pixie Dancer

Three-Year-Olds

94	Blending Element	97	Dathuil	–	Fast Feather
81	Blue Bit	34	Daughter In Law	–	Feelin' Looser
105	Blue Iris†	–	Davenport Guest	81p	Fern Fields
76	Bluemas	68	Debs Affair	52	Fiddes
81	Blues Project	108	Deed of Love	60	Film Buff
92	Bold And Gorgeous	69	Desert Gift	77	Fireball
–	Bonny	90	Desert Mountain	–	Fire Water
71d	Breffni Lady	106	Deynawari	100	Flame of Athens
89	Broken Rites	97	Diali	–	Flower Show
78	Bustinardo	72d	Dieci Anno†	100	Force of Will
101+	By Charlie Allen	83	Diesel Dan	87	Forsake Me Not
–	Caca Milis	66	Dillon's Taxi	–	Foulage
–	Caer Melyn	71	Disposen	68	Franziska
–	Calm Beauty	47	Dissident Lady	111+	French Ballerina
87	Canadian Patriot	91	Dissident Prince	83	Fridolin
75	Canadian Project	111	Distant Oasis†	81	Friendly Bird
83	Carransprawn	71	Distant Shore	64	Fun Fashion
69	Cascatelle Bleue	50+	Dolly Dimpler	74	Gaelic Symphony
91	Cashel Princess	113	Don Micheletto†	64	Gail Gordon
98	Catalyst	–	Doubleback	–	Gale Eight
83	Caudillo	92	Double Diamond†	–	Galici
77	Ceannanas	–	Double Indemnity	98	Gan Saru
100	Ceirseach†	–	Double Seeker	98	Gates
75	Celtic Project	92	Doyles Corner	77	Genuine John†
82	Cento	94	Draft of Vintage	–	Gisbella
108	Charlock	77	Dr Beat	52	Gleaming Heather
–	Cheerful Knight	73	Dr Bones	–	Global Walk
70	Child of Fortune	–	Dreams And Schemes†	121	Glory of Dancer†
77	Choosey's Treasure	–	Dream Tycoon	74	God Speed
–	Chuiphoga	115	Dr Massini†	–	Golden Anchor
75	Cimarosa	–	Dubai Dolly	–	Golden Reproach
–	Cinnibar	–	Duggan Duff	63	Gold Glider
–	Ckr Racing	76	Dunemer	79	Gold Wind
90	Classic Express	77	Dunrally Fort	109	Gordi†
72	Classic Mix	79	Durrah Green	57	Go Sasha
93	Class Note	123	Dushyantor†	113	Gothenberg†
70	Clear Blue Water	–	Dusky Walk	83	Greenhue
64	Cohiba	–	Earhart	54	Green Patriot
87	Cois Na Farraige†	97	Easy Definition	90	Grief
47	Comrade Chinnery	69	Eliza Orzeszkowa	78	Hakone
–	Confectioner	–	Elle L'A Atteint	106	Hamad
–	Connies Fancy	–	Emmal	67d	Hanna Dome
–	Cool Scotch	79	Emmets Lady	–	Happy Medium
77	Cooraclare	73	Enfant Prodige	–	Hard News
–	Copelands	77	Epigram	114	Harghar
84	Cordial Knight	79	Equity Silver	101	Harveys Point
81	Corn Abbey	–	Erin Oileain Acla	–	Head To Toe
101	Cossack Count	80	Erne Project	74	Health And Wealth
–	Coulthard	61	Errant Earl	–	Heather Music
95	Courier	94	Errazuriz	–	Heather's Folly
82d	Couverture	–p	Escamillo	71	Hello John
89	Cuddles	109	Escrito	96	Helsingor†
–	Curragh Council	–	Ever Bubbly	–	Hencarlam†
77	Daddy's Hat	81	Evriza	83	Henrietta Street
71	Dafwan	63	Exceedingly	88d	High Hope Henry†
–	Dame Pique	–	Extreme	84	Highly Motivated
99	Dance Clear	76	Ezanak	80	High Powered
119	Dance Design†	74	Fairly Sharp	76	Hillcrest
70	Dance Twister	88	Fairy Lake	93	Hint of Humour
79	Dancing Bluebell	75	Falcon's Fire	86	Hint-Of-Romance
109	Dancing Fred	–	Fallens	92	Hi Plains Drifter
98	Dancing Hours	89	Family Project	85	Hisar
75	Dansk	109	Farhana†	111	His Excellence
81	Dasharan	–	Fashion Scout	87	Hogans Alley

SPOT THE OWNER

To find out more about the excitement
of racehorse ownership call 01753 897211
and get a free copy of our brochure.

INTERNATIONAL CLASSIFICATIONS

The International Classifications were published on 16th January, 1997.
The leading horses are shown (* trained exclusively outside Europe).

Two-Year-Olds
123	Revoque
121	Bahhare
119	Bahamian Bounty
119	Majorien
118	Easycall
118	Zamindar
117	In Command
117	Indian Rocket
117	Muchea
116	Air Express
116	Mantovani
116	Medaaly
116	Musical Pursuit
116	Pas de Reponse
115	Fantastic Fellow
115	Poteen
115	Putra
114	Deadly Dudley
114	Reams of Verse
114	Red Camellia
114	Sahm
114	Shaka
113	Abou Zouz
113	Benny The Dip
113	Deep Finesse
113	Desert King
113	Kahal
113	King Sound
113	Moonlight Paradise
113	Ryafan
113	Varxi
113	The West
112	Aneysar
112	Compton Place
112	Daylami
112	Hello
112	Proud Native
112	Referendum
112	Yashmak
111	Besiege
111	Desert Story
111	Equal Rights
111	Khashah
111	Musheer
111	Ocean Ridge
111	Sleepytime
111	Verglas
110	Bianca Nera
110	Brave Act
110	Carmine Lake
110	Dazzle
110	Elegant Warning
110	Grapeshot
110	Hurricane State
110	Joyeuse Entree

110	Raphane
110	Seebe
110	Sendoro
110	Tipsy Creek
109	Andreyev
109	Dame d'Harvard
109	Falkenham
109	Johan Cruyff
109	Royal Amaretto
109	Sheer Reason
109	Voyagers Quest
108	Arethusa
108	Family Tradition
108	Hidden Meadow
108	Maserati Monk
108	Monza
108	Mousse Glacee
108	Nombre Premier
108	Papua
108	Recondite
108	Rich Ground
108	Shell Ginger
108	Shigeru Summit
108	Wind Cheetah
107	Azra
107	Check The Band
107	Connemara
107	Eden Rock
107	Fine Fellow
107	Juwwi
107	Mukaddar
107	New Frontier
107	Omaha City
107	Rate Cut
107	Starborough
106	Alpha Plus
106	Dame Laura
106	Dance Parade
106	Daylight In Dubai
106	Dissertation
106	Dyhim Diamond
106	Fahris
106	Golden Oriental
106	Grand Lad
106	Great Ovation
106	Heaven's Command
106	Ivan Luis
106	Kaldou Star
106	Keos
106	Panama City
106	Roman Imp
106	Tomba
106	Veiled Threat
106	Velvet Appeal

Three-Year-Olds
134	Helissio
133	Mark of Esteem
131	Bosra Sham
130	Skip Away*
127	Bijou d'Inde
126	Even Top
126	Louis Quatorze*
126	Unbridled's Song*
126	Yanks Music*
125	Ashkalani
125	Zagreb
124	Editor's Note *
124	Shaamit
123	Grindstone*
123	Lavirco
123	Will's Way*
122	Cavonnier*
122	Lady Carla
122	Lucayan Prince
122	My Flag*
122	Shantou
122	Spinning World
121	Alhaarth
121	Antespend*
121	Glory of Dancer
121	Honour And Glory*
121	Memories of Silver*
120	Capote Belle*
120	Dushyantor
120	Fabulous La Fouine*
120	Pivotal
120	Sorbie Tower
119	Dance Design
119	Escena*
119	Grape Tree Road
119	Kistena
119	Listening*
119	Marlin*
119	Pike Place Dancer*
119	Shake The Yoke
119	Taiki Fortune*
118	Appealing Skier*
118	Beauchamp King
118	Danehill Dancer
118	Formal Gold*
118	Last Second
118	Loup Solitaire
118	Matiya
118	Tagula
118	Tarator
117	Cara Rafaela*
117	Chief Bearhart*
117	Ide*
117	Luna Wells
117	Mons

1150

1151

INDEX TO PHOTOGRAPHS

PORTRAITS & SNAPSHOTS

RACE PHOTOGRAPHS

Hardwicke Stakes (Royal Ascot)	*George Selwyn*	700
Harvest Stakes (Ascot)	*John Crofts*	47
Haydock Park Sprint Cup (Haydock Park)	*Alec Russell*	446
Heath Court Hotel Fred Archer Stakes (Newmarket)	*John Crofts*	115
Heinz 57 Phoenix Stakes (Leopardstown)	*Peter Mooney*	574
Hillsdown Cherry Hinton Stakes (Newmarket)	*John Crofts*	253
Homeowners Dante Stakes (York)	*Alec Russell*	380
Hong Kong International Cup (Sha Tin)	*George Selwyn*	344
Hong Kong International Vase (Sha Tin)	*George Selwyn*	558
Hong Kong Jockey Club Trophy (Handicap) (Sandown)	*George Selwyn*	892
Insulpak Sagaro Stakes (Ascot)	*John Crofts*	287
Irish Champion Stakes (Leopardstown)	*Peter Mooney*	1007
Japan Cup (Tokyo)	*George Selwyn*	909
Jefferson Smurfit Memorial Irish St Leger (the Curragh)	*Peter Mooney*	701
Jersey Stakes (Royal Ascot)	*Alec Russell*	552
Jockey Club Cup (Newmarket)	*Alec Russell*	180
Jockey Club of Kenya Molecomb Stakes (Goodwood)	*John Crofts*	172
John Smith's Magnet Cup (Handicap) (York)	*Alec Russell*	1064
JRA Nakayama Rous Stakes (Newmarket)	*John Crofts*	230
Juddmonte International Stakes (York)	*Alec Russell*	405
Juddmonte Lockinge Stakes (Newbury)	*John Crofts*	931
Kildangan Stud Irish Oaks (the Curragh)	*Peter Mooney*	238
King Charles II Stakes (Newmarket)	*John Crofts*	41
King Edward VII Stakes (Royal Ascot)	*George Selwyn*	51
King George Stakes (Goodwood)	*John Crofts*	786
King George V Stakes (Handicap) (Royal Ascot)	*John Crofts*	845
King George VI and Queen Elizabeth Diamond Stakes (Ascot)	*John Crofts*	723
King's Stand Stakes (Royal Ascot)	*Alec Russell*	741
Ladbroke (Ayr) Gold Cup (Handicap) (Ayr)	*Alec Russell*	213
Ladbroke (Ayr) Silver Cup (Handicap) (Ayr)	*Alec Russell*	228
Ladbroke Bunbury Cup (Handicap) (Newmarket)	*George Selwyn*	231
Ladbroke Racing Sprint Stakes (Handicap) (Goodwood)	*John Crofts*	1065
Ladbrokes Handicap (Newmarket)	*John Crofts*	473
Ladbrokes Spring Cup (Handicap) (Newbury)	*John Crofts*	828
Lanson Champagne Vintage Stakes (Goodwood)	*Alec Russell*	773
Laurent-Perrier Champagne Stakes (Doncaster)	*John Crofts*	91
Lawrence Batley Rated Stakes (Handicap) (York)	*Alec Russell*	698
Leonard Sainer European Breeders Fund Stakes (York)	*Alec Russell*	840
Letheby & Christopher Lancashire Oaks (Haydock)	*Alec Russell*	942
Mail On Sunday Mile Final (Handicap) (Ascot)	*John Crofts*	53
Marriott Hotels Goodwood Stakes (Handicap)(Goodwood)	*W. Everitt*	929
May Hill Stakes (Doncaster)	*John Crofts*	791
Mercedes-Benz Grosser Preis von Baden (Baden-Baden)	*Frank Nolting*	736
Michael Seely Memorial Glasgow Conditions Stakes (York)	*George Selwyn*	292
Michael Sobell Silver Tankard Handicap (York)	*Alec Russell*	235
'Michelozzo' Conditions Stakes (Nottingham)	*Alec Russell*	366
Middle Park Stakes (Newmarket)	*John Crofts*	89
Moorestyle Convivial Maiden Stakes (York)	*Alec Russell*	458
Moyglare Stud Stakes (the Curragh)	*Peter Mooney*	119
'Newcastle Brown Ale' Northumberland Plate (Newcastle)	*Alec Russell*	179
New Zealand Handicap (Newmarket)	*W. Everitt*	747
Nunthorpe Stakes (York)	*John Crofts*	741
Oh So Sharp Stakes (Newmarket)	*Alec Russell*	852
O. & K. Troy Stakes (Doncaster)	*George Selwyn*	160
Owen Brown Houghton Conditions Stakes (Newmarket)	*Alec Russell*	229
Pertemps Jockey Club Stakes (Newmarket)	*John Crofts*	815
Pertemps One Thousand Guineas Stakes (Newmarket)	*John Crofts*	143
Pertemps St Leger (Doncaster)	*John Crofts*	884
Pertemps Two Thousand Guineas Stakes (Newmarket)	*George Selwyn*	581
Polypipe Plc Flying Childers Stakes (Doncaster)	*John Crofts*	302
Portland Place Properties Hopeful Stakes (Newmarket)	*John Crofts*	173

1155

DARLEY STUD MANAGEMENT

Standing at Dalham Hall Stud, Newmarket

HALLING
1991 by Diesis - Dance Machine
Champion 4yo and 5yo in Europe - winner of **5 Group 1 races**
Retires to stud in 1997

LION CAVERN
1989 by Mr Prospector - Secrettame
Dual **GW**, own brother to **GONE WEST**
1st 2-year-olds in 1997

MACHIAVELLIAN
1987 by Mr Prospector - Coup de Folie
Classic Sire of 12 individual Stakes Winners
from his first two crops

MARK OF ESTEEM
1993 by Darshaan - Homage
Champion Miler in Europe 1996, dual Group 1 Winner
Timeform Horse of the Year 1996
Retires to stud in 1997

POLISH PRECEDENT
1986 by Danzig - Past Example
Classic Sire of PURE GRAIN and GWs PILSUDSKI,
RED ROUTE, RIYADIAN

SHAREEF DANCER
1980 by Northern Dancer - Sweet Alliance
A Leading European Sire of 29 individual **GW/SWs** of 56 races

WOLFHOUND
1989 by Nureyev - Lassie Dear
Champion European Sprinter, dual Group 1 Winner
1st 2-year-olds in 1997

STALLIONS for 1997

Standing at Aston Upthorpe Stud, Oxfordshire

MTOTO
1983 by Busted - Amazer
Derby Sire of SHAAMIT and **PRESENTING,**
Sire of GWs ARBATAX, CELERIC, MDUDU, MOUSSE GLACEE
and **SWs BEAU TEMPS, FARU, LAILA ALAWI, LOBBYIST**
TOTOSTAR

Standing at Ragusa Stud, Co. Kildare

IN THE WINGS
1986 by Sadler's Wells - High Hawk
Classic Sire of WINGED LOVE and **Champion SINGSPIEL**
and **GWs/SWs ANNABA, CENTRE STALLS, IRISH WINGS,**
KAFHAR, STAGE MANNER, WINGS BASH etc

LYCIUS
1988 by Mr Prospector - Lypatia
Sire of G1W HELLO, and **GWs MEDIA NOX** and **AYLESBURY**

PENNEKAMP
1992 by Bering - Coral Dance
Champion 2yo in Europe - multiple **Group 1 Winner**
Retires to stud in 1997

Standing at Haras des Chartreux, France

BELMEZ
1987 by El Gran Senor - Grace Note
Sire of GWs CARAMBA and **SPANISH FALLS**

Darley Stud Management Company Ltd.,
Dalham Hall Stud, Duchess Drive, Newmarket. CB8 9HD.
Telephone: Newmarket (01638) 730070.
Fax: (01638) 730167.

LONDON THOROUGHBRED SERVICES LTD.

Purchases · Sales · Shares · Nominations
Stallion Management · Valuation · Transport · Insurance

1997 STALLION FEES

FORZANDO	£3,000	NFNF	October 1st
INCHINOR	£3,000	NFNF	October 1st
KRIS	£17,500	NFNF	October 1st
PHARLY	£2,000	NFNF	October 1st
PURSUIT OF LOVE	£7,000	NFNF	October 1st
ROBELLINO	£5,000	NFNF	October 1st
SELKIRK	£8,000	NFNF	October 1st
SLIP ANCHOR	£8,000	NFNF	October 1st
ZIETEN	IR£5,000	NFNF	October 1st

<u>APPROVED</u> <u>MARES</u> <u>ONLY</u>

All nominations subject to Availability

Enquiries to:
LONDON THOROUGHBRED SERVICES LTD.,
Biddlesgate Farm, Nr Cranborne, Dorset BH21 5RS.
Telephone: 01725 - 517711. Fax: 01725 - 517833.

Standing at Britton House Stud

FORZANDO

bay 1981 by FORMIDABLE - PRINCELY MAID by King's Troop

Multiple Group Winner
Won 12 races including: Metropolitan H'cap **Gr.1**
including 5 consecutive races as a 2-year-old

Year after year
Sire of Top Consistent - Sound 2 Year Olds
**EASYCALL, GREAT DEEDS, HIGH PREMIUM,
MISTERIOSO, PHILIDOR, PUNCH N'RUN
PURE FORMALITY, SHARPNESS IN MIND,
SUPERIOR PREMIUM, UP AND AT'EM, etc.**

Fee: £3,000 October 1st NFNF
R.A. Fowlston, Hewing Bere, Crewkerne, Somerset TA18 7TG.
Telephone: Corscombe 01935 - 891778. Fax: 01935 - 891756.

Enquiries to:
LONDON THOROUGHBRED SERVICES LTD.,
Biddlesgate Farm, Nr Cranborne, Dorset BH21 5RS.
Telephone: 01725 - 517711. Fax: 01725 - 517833.

Standing at Plantation Stud

KRIS

chesnut 1976 by SHARPEN UP - DOUBLY SURE by Reliance

CHAMPION EUROPEAN MILER
in 1979 and 1980

CHAMPION SIRE of Group 1 winners:
**OH SO SHARP, COMMON GROUNDS, UNITE, FITNAH,
FLASH OF STEEL, SUDDEN LOVE, RAFHA, SHAVIAN, SHAMSHIR**

Fee: £17,500 October 1st NFNF

Leslie Harrison, Plantation Stud, Exning, Newmarket, Suffolk CB8 7L
Telephone: 01638 - 577341. Fax: 01638 - 578474.
Enquiries to:
LONDON THOROUGHBRED SERVICES LTD.,
Biddlesgate Farm, Nr Cranborne, Dorset BH21 5RS.
Telephone: 01725 - 517711. Fax: 01725 - 517833.

Standing at Plantation Stud

PURSUIT OF LOVE

bay 1989 by GROOM DANCER - DANCE QUEST by Green Dancer

Champion European
3yo Sprinter 1992

LEADING BRITISH
FIRST SEASON SIRE
in 1996

Fee: £7,000 October 1st NFNF

Leslie Harrison, Plantation Stud, Exning, Newmarket, Suffolk CB8 7LJ.
Telephone: 01638 - 577341. Fax: 01638 - 578474.
Enquiries to:
LONDON THOROUGHBRED SERVICES LTD.,
Biddlesgate Farm, Nr Cranborne, Dorset BH21 5RS.
Telephone: 01725 - 517711. Fax: 01725 - 517833.

Standing at Littleton Stud

ROBELLINO

bay 1979 by ROBERTO - ISOBELLINE by Pronto
Dual Group Winner, broke course record at Ascot at 2

Sire of winners of 600 races and £4,680,000 including 58 individual 2yo winners

A Leading 2yo Sire in Europe as well as Sire of 1994 2000 Guineas winner
MISTER BAILEYS

Fee: £5,000 October 1st NFNF

Standing at Littleton Stud, Winchester, Hants. SO22 6QX.
Telephone: Winchester 01962 - 880210. Fax: 01962 - 882290.

Enquiries to:
LONDON THOROUGHBRED SERVICES LTD.,
Biddlesgate Farm, Nr Cranborne, Dorset BH21 5RS.
Telephone: 01725 - 517711. Fax: 01725 - 517833.

Standing at Plantation Stud

SLIP ANCHOR

bay 1982 by SHIRLEY HEIGHTS - SAYONARA by Birkhahn

Champion European 3-year-old in 1985
Sire of the winners of over £4 million
Champion British Based Sire in 1992

Sire of 17 GW/SWs including:
USER FRIENDLY - POSIDONAS
SLICIOUS - THIRD WATCH
Fertility average to date over 90%

Fee: £8,000 October 1st NFNF

Leslie Harrison, Plantation Stud, Exning, Newmarket, Suffolk CB8 7L
Telephone: 01638 - 577341. Fax: 01638 - 578474.

Enquiries to:
LONDON THOROUGHBRED SERVICES LTD.,
Biddlesgate Farm, Nr Cranborne, Dorset BH21 5RS.
Telephone: 01725 - 517711. Fax: 01725 - 517833.